3 Enoch

Eupolemus

Pseudo-Eupolemus

Apocryphon of Ezekiel

Ezekiel the Tragedian

Fourth Book of Ezra

Greek Apocalypse of Ezra

Questions of Ezra

Revelation of Ezra

Vision of Ezra

Fragments of Pseudo-Greek Poets

Pseudo-Hecataeus

Hellenistic Synagogal Prayers

Martyrdom and Ascension of Isaiah

Ladder of Jacob

Prayer of Jacob

Jannes and Jambres

Testament of Job

Joseph and Asenath

History of Joseph

Prayer of Joseph

Jubilees

3 Maccabees

4 Maccabees

Prayer of Manasseh

Syriac Menander

Testament of Moses

Orphica

Philo the Epic Poet

Pseudo-Philo

Pseudo-Phocylides

The Lives of the Prophets

History of the Rechabites

Apocalypse of Sedrach

Treatise of Shem

Sibylline Oracles

Odes of Solomon

Psalms of Solomon

Testament of Solomon

Theodotus

Testaments of the Three Patriarchs

Testaments of the Twelve Patriarchs

Apocalypse of Zephaniah

THE OLD TESTAMENT PSEUDEPIGRAPHA

THE OLD TESTAMENT
PSEUDEPIGRAPHA

VOLUME 1

Apocalyptic Literature and Testaments

EDITED BY

JAMES H. CHARLESWORTH,

DUKE UNIVERSITY

1983

DOUBLEDAY & COMPANY, INC.

GARDEN CITY, NEW YORK

The publisher gratefully acknowledges permission to use the following: An extract from Josephus' *Antiquities* from The Loeb Classical Library, Harvard University Press, publisher, in "The Testament of Solomon," translated by Dennis C. Duling. Quotation from *Hermetica*, vol. 4, translated by W. Scott and A. S. Ferguson, 1936, in "The Testament of Solomon," translated by Dennis C. Duling. Used by permission of Oxford University Press.
Quotations from *Archív orientálni* by C. H. Gordon, vol. 6, 1934, in "The Testament of Solomon," translated by Dennis C. Duling.

Library of Congress Catalog Card Number:
ISBN: 0-385-09630-5
Copyright © 1983 by James H. Charlesworth
All Rights Reserved
Printed in the United States of America
First Edition

Designed by Joseph P. Ascherl

Library of Congress Cataloging in Publication Data
Main entry under title:

Old Testament pseudepigrapha.

Bibliography: p.
Includes indexes.
1. Apocryphal books (Old Testament)—Criticism,
interpretation, etc.   I. Charlesworth, James H.
BS1830.A3   1983   229   80-2443
ISBN 0-385-09630-5 (v. 1)
ISBN 0-385-18813-7 (v. 2)

Dedicated to my family
—Jerrie, Michelle, Eve, and James—
to other families supporting our
common labors,
and to families who read these
documents.

CONTENTS

DOCUMENTS

APOCALYPTIC LITERATURE AND RELATED WORKS

TESTAMENTS (OFTEN WITH APOCALYPTIC SECTIONS)

FOREWORD

GEORGE W. MACRAE, S.J.

The ancient Jewish and Jewish-Christian documents that are here called Pseudepigrapha have in their long history been both problematic and promising in both Jewish and Christian communities. It is heartening to observe that the very publication of this new collection testifies more to their promise than to their problems. An ancient witness to both problem and promise can be found within two late books of the New Testament itself. The Epistle of Jude, in its strong antiheretical polemic, refers at least twice to the language of the book we call 1 Enoch and in a third instance quotes it in an authoritative manner as prophetic. It also refers to a legend about the body of Moses known to us in the book called the Assumption of Moses. The Second Epistle of Peter, generally regarded as the latest of the New Testament books, incorporates much of Jude into its second chapter, but it is very careful to excise all of the allusions to the Pseudepigrapha.

The problem to which this situation points is that of the canonical status of the Pseudepigrapha in early Christianity—and the consequent propriety or impropriety of citing them in public documents. Clearly the authors of Jude and 2 Peter reflect different views. This problem persisted for centuries in the Church and can further be seen in the reluctance of some churches to accept Jude into the New Testament because of its controversial sources. In the synagogue the problem did not persist so long, and the decision was clearly against the Pseudepigrapha.

The promise to which the episode of Jude and 2 Peter points is the value of studying the Pseudepigrapha for a better understanding of prerabbinic Judaism and of the religious matrix of Christianity. Whatever canonical decisions were taken by the official leadership, it is clear that in popular religious circles, especially Christian ones, this literature continued to be prominent and to influence thought and piety.

The most recent decades have seen an astonishing rebirth of scholarly interest in the Pseudepigrapha, and these volumes are an excellent guide to much of it. The renewed interest has been and continues to be stimulated in part by new manuscript discoveries. One thinks of the Dead Sea Scrolls among others. These have provided access to much more extensive knowledge of Judaism in the period immediately following the Old Testament. But perhaps even more important than such a largely accidental factor as manuscript discoveries has been the ever increasing acceptance of historical-critical method on the part of students of the Bible at all levels. To study the Bible by this method involves knowing as much as one can about the biblical world in all of its facets. And this of course includes knowing the Jewish and Christian religious literature that ultimately did not become part of the Bible. What we find, as these volumes show, is a bewildering variety of ideas, styles, and literary genres that is as diversified as the Bible itself yet often quite different from it./One of the merits of this edition, especially when compared to the few earlier ones in modern languages, is that it is inclusive rather than exclusive. It includes much more of the surviving literature than others have. Thus it affords a rich insight into the creative religious imagination from a singularly important formative period in Western religious culture.

Readers of these volumes and those who consult them for reference should include scholars and teachers, students, and any others who have an interest in the biblical world. All will be grateful to the many scholars who have contributed to the work. But more especially, they will have an enormous debt of gratitude to Professor Charlesworth and his immediate associates who boldly undertook and so competently executed the formidable task of editing this major work.

FOREWORD FOR CHRISTIANS

JAMES T. CLELAND

As one brought up in the home of a Church of Scotland minister, my father, and as one prepared for the Christian ministry in the Divinity Hall of Glasgow University, I have been trying to recall any unique impact made upon me by these related experiences, apart from family worship; the daily reading of the Word of God: Genesis to Revelation, one chapter per night, before falling asleep. The unexpected outcome is that I still find it somewhat difficult to decide if a Scots Presbyterian is an Old Testament Christian, with a stress on the Law and the Psalms, or a New Testament Jew, who attends his synagogue—as Jesus' custom was—on the sabbath day (Luke 4:16). There he hears a sermon which may be based on the Old Testament, or on the New Testament, or on both, as equally valid, equally authoritative. Why not? Is it not the same God in both testaments?

Many years later, in a Duke Divinity School morning chapel service, instead of a meditation, I just read the Prayer of Manasseh, now recognized, in its own right, as one of the Pseudepigrapha. After the service, a colleague asked me, "Where did you find that?" I told him. His surprised, almost awed, comment was: "That is the gospel outside of the Gospels." Why such a reaction? Manasseh was acknowledged to be the wickedest king of Judah, one who both majored and minored in iniquity, and yet maintained his throne in Jerusalem for fifty-five years, which was something of a record. Dr. James Moffatt sums up Manasseh, that royal rake, in a few simple words: "He did ample evil in the sight of the eternal to vex him" (2Chr 33:6). That is the emphasis of underemphasis. However, Manasseh repented; he prayed; God forgave (2Chr 33:13). The God who forgave is the same, yesterday, today, and forever, the God of Jew and Christian alike.

What I, a pulpiteer, hope from this volume, supervised by Professor Charlesworth, aided and abetted by scholars throughout the world, is that, as never before, Judaism and Christianity will be recognized as heirs of the same God, with what Jew and Christian have in common uniting us, rather than continuing a separation which may be emotionally understandable but is spiritually devitalizing. The very text of parts of the Pseudepigrapha may have been edited by later Jews *or* Christians. It would be good if one of the scholars discovered in his research that a section was prepared by Jew *and* Christian working together, not always in agreement in minor matters, but one in scholarship and editing because each had faith, academic and spiritual, in the same Father, who is at the heart of both testaments, and to be found in the Pseudepigrapha.

So, may it come to pass that what unites us as brethren will far surpass what seems to separate us, too often, even too willingly. We need each other. We are both children of the Kingdom, and the Pseudepigrapha may become a bridge between the Old and New testaments, helping us cross to and fro, back and forth, until we are equally at home in both, to our mental satisfaction, and our spiritual growth in grace.

So read the Prayer of Manasseh in the Pseudepigrapha. It is a model for a prayer, public or private: the invocation of God: "O Lord, God of our fathers, . . . unending and immeasurable are your promised mercies" (vss. 1–6); the confession of sin, verses 9–10: "O Lord, I am justly afflicted . . . because I did evil things before you"; the entreaty for forgiveness, verses 11–15, including the wonderful metaphor of complete surrender to God: "And now behold I am bending the knees of my heart" (v. 11); "Forgive me, O Lord, forgive me" (v. 13); "I shall praise you continually all the days of my life" (v. 15). It is a bonny prayer; my gratitude to the Jew who wrote it. I shall use it.

This prayer is to more than a few people the most famous instance of "the infinite compassion of God." If a Manasseh can be absolved, there is hope for anyone—including me. No wonder that I bend "the knees of my heart." It is the gospel outside the Gospels.

FOREWORD FOR JEWS

SAMUEL SANDMEL

By the strangest quirk of fate respecting literature that I know of, large numbers of writings by Jews were completely lost from the transmitted Jewish heritage. These documents stem roughly from 200 B.C. to A.D. 200. Not only the so-called Pseudepigrapha, but even such important and extensive writings as those by Philo and Josephus have not been part of the Jewish inheritance from its past; these were preserved and transmitted by Christians. It was rather only in the backwash of the Renaissance that Jews began to encounter Philo and Josephus. A sixteenth-century Italian rabbi, Azariah de Rossi, in a book called *Me-or Enayim* ("Light for the

Eyes''), inaugurated this Jewish rediscovery of the "lost" literature. He wrote with great praise of Philo, but with only reserved admiration for Josephus, whose Jewish loyalty he doubted. After de Rossi, Jews began slowly to deepen their study of Josephus and Philo, and thereafter the other literature, as legitimate parts of the Jewish heritage.

The ancient literary legacy which Jews did preserve and transmit was primarily the rabbinic literature. This huge body of writings might be divided into three categories: one, the Midrashim; two, Mishna and Gemara; and three, the Targumim. The Midrashim are commentaries on Scripture arranged according to the sequence of the biblical verses. The Mishna is a laconic statement of the secondary laws (Halacha) derived from Scripture. The Targumim allude to the Aramaic translation of Scripture; these translations have come down to us in differing styles and in somewhat differing ages. While within the rabbinic literature, especially in passages called haggadic ("narrative"), there are allusions to some of the documents found in the Apocrypha and occasionally to those in the Pseudepigrapha, it is only Ecclesiasticus (Jesus, the son of Sirach) who figures in any prominence at all in the talmudic literature. The Pseudepigrapha as such might be said with very little exaggeration to be without reflection in rabbinic literature.

As is known, the Pseudepigrapha were first gathered by Johannes Fabricius in the early part of the eighteenth century. Subsequent collectors of this material were able to add certain books that were unknown to Fabricius and certain editors, such as R. H. Charles, included in editions of the Pseudepigrapha materials the presence of which might be questioned. Charles, for example, included the talmudic tractate the Ethics of the Fathers. The point is that there is no such thing as a "canon" of the Pseudepigrapha. Rather, there is an abundance of this scattered literature, some of it preserved in entirety and some preserved in part, usually in translation rather than in the original Hebrew or Aramaic. It is in reality only in the eighteenth century that the earnest and ever increasing study of the Pseudepigrapha began. Because most of the Pseudepigrapha were not preserved in Hebrew or Aramaic, it has been only the rare Jewish scholar who has made this study a major concern. By and large it has been Christians who have done the painstaking work of gathering this material, comparing the various manuscripts, producing critical editions, and providing translations into modern languages.

I do not think it is wrong to say that much of the Christian interest in the Pseudepigrapha in the early nineteenth century was based on the light this literature was deemed to throw on early Christianity. Since the documents in the Pseudepigrapha were not being studied for their own sake, often that roundedness which one should expect from the best of scientific scholarship was absent. Even more to be deplored was the circumstance that there were Christian scholars who seemed to feel the need to choose, as it were, between the Pseudepigrapha on the one hand and the rabbinic literature on the other hand, and who, on the basis of only part of the total Jewish literary productivity, came to some occasionally quixotic or reckless or even partisan conclusions about the nature of Judaism at the time of the birth of Christianity. Such an allegation would not be unjust respecting R. H. Charles.

A complete turnaround in the approach to the Pseudepigrapha in the last decades has been most gratifying. These writings have become the object of study for their own sake, part of the wish to illuminate the totality of the Jewish creativity of that bygone age. The recent scholarship has not tried to make the literature fit into a procrustean bed for some parochial purpose. It should be said that the relevancy of the Pseudepigrapha to early Christianity is not in any way diminished by the recent admirable mode of the study of Pseudepigrapha.

The result of the work of fine scholars, such as are represented herein, has been a significant broadening and deepening of the appreciation of the Jewish literary creativity. The cooperative study enlisting the gifted minds of Christians of various denominations and Jews of varying backgrounds is surely as moving and exciting a development as any cooperative academic venture could be. Perhaps it was the abundance of this ancient literature which the author of Ecclesiastes had in mind when he spoke rather cynically in these words: "of making many books there is no end and most of them are a weariness of the flesh." Obviously the author of Ecclesiastes did not admire every bit of writing that was in his ken. I do not think that the modern student needs to admire every example of the Pseudepigrapha, any more than we today need to regard every novel as a masterpiece. But he can still be astonished, amazed, enlightened, and overwhelmed by the abundance and variety and recurrent high quality of the Jewish literary activity of that period.

Old as this literature is for most modern people, it is also in a sense something brand-new, for most American laypeople have never heard the word Pseudepigrapha, or, if they have heard it, are not sure what it means. Now through the work of Professor Charlesworth and his associates a door is being opened anew to treasures that are very old. How gratifying it is that scholars devote themselves to the recovery of that which was lost or strayed or hidden. How gratifying that cooperative study is reviving this literature. How much such study contributes to understanding the richness of the Jewish legacy, now the heritage of both Jews and Christians.

EDITOR'S PREFACE

The present work is designed for the scholar and for the interested non-specialist. The general introduction, the introductions to each subdivision and to each document, and the translations with accompanying notes are shaped to help the reader understand these ancient writings. At the outset it is wise to stress three caveats for the general reader: 1) The following collection of writings, many of which claim to preserve a message from God for his people, are not gathered here in order to replace or add to those scriptures considered canonical by Jews or the larger collections claimed to be canonical by various groups of Christians. 2) In order to understand the Bible better the Pseudepigrapha should not be read in isolation, but along with the writings collected in the Old and New testaments (terms used for convenience and without confessional bias), and in ten other collections of ancient Jewish or early Christian writings (see Introduction). 3) The expanded definition of the Pseudepigrapha, now universally recognized as necessary by scholars, represents a more extended historical period than Charles's selection of writings; hence it must not be used *prima facie* as a group of writings representative of Early Judaism. The late documents, and Christian expansions of early Jewish writings, as the contributors themselves clarify, must not be read as if they were composed by contemporaries of the early ones. Conversely, late writings must not be ignored in a search for ideas possibly characteristic of Early Judaism; these documents frequently preserve edited portions of early Jewish writings.

In the fall of 1972, an editor at Doubleday, John J. Delaney, on the advice of his consultants, invited me to prepare a new edition of the Pseudepigrapha. The present work, completed ten years later, is the product of an international team of collaborators. Because it is a widely used term today, we have decided to retain the technical term "Pseudepigrapha"; it is explained in the following Introduction.

Each contributor was asked to discuss all issues requisite for a meaningful reading of the document translated, and given some freedom in utilizing the following format:

> The contributor begins the presentation either with a synopsis of the narrative or with a discussion of the key characteristics and central ideas in a non-narrative writing.
>
> *Texts.* The scholar discusses only the most important extant texts, and clarifies the textual base or the critical edition behind the translation.
>
> *Original Language.* The translator briefly discusses the original language of the document, reviews published scholarly conclusions, and usually advocates one possibility.
>
> *Date.* The contributor assesses the debates (if any) over the date of the original composition, explains, if appropriate, the dates of any subsequent expansions or interpolations, and then presents his or her own scholarly opinion.

Provenance. The expert briefly evaluates the hypotheses regarding the place or places in which the work may have been composed, and subsequently voices his or her own judgment.

Historical Importance. The contributor discusses the importance of the document for an appreciation of the historical period in which it was composed.

Theological Importance. The specialist explains the motifs, symbols, and major theological ideas contained in the pseudepigraphon.

Relation to Canonical Books. The expert assesses the possible relationships between the pseudepigraphon and writings now customarily judged canonical.

Relation to Apocryphal Books. The scholar succinctly discusses the apocryphal books to which the document is especially close.

Cultural Importance. If appropriate, the contributor discusses the importance of the pseudepigraphon for a better understanding of the origin of our culture. Briefly mentioned are possible parallels between it and the great classics, such as Plato's *Dialogues*, Dante's *Divina Commedia*, and Milton's *Paradise Lost*.

At the end of each introduction to a document the contributor lists the most important publications on the document.

The organization of these documents follows considerable discussion with the Board of Advisors and the contributors themselves. Any system for ordering these documents has weaknesses. A listing of the documents in chronological order is impractical at the present time. We are still uncertain about the date or dates of composition for many of these writings; moreover, some are composite and represent more than one century. Merely placing them in alphabetical order is attractive in the sense that one knows where a particular document is in such a recognized sequence; hence, an alphabetical listing on the endpapers of this volume. An alphabetical listing is confusing, however, because some of the documents collected below are known by more than one title, some may be listed alphabetically according to more than one word in the title, and—most importantly— an alphabetical order is artificial and does not signal the relationships between documents that are related. We have decided to organize the documents according to broadly conceived literary types. Within these groups they are listed chronologically in terms of the earliest probable date with the exception that cycles of traditions, like the Enoch and Ezra books, are grouped together.

In the past scholars often felt free to emend a text and to aim at a loose idiomatic translation (although Charles himself was a literalist). Modern scholarship has demanded more rigorous devotion to extant readings, more thorough attempts to understand the grammar and syntax of ancient languages, and, in general, more loyalty to the manuscripts. While we have aimed whenever possible at an idiomatic rendering, we have avoided the temptation to paraphrase the meaning of a complicated passage or to conceal sometimes confusing readings behind elegant English prose. Besides trustworthiness to the transmitted text, there are other advantages in these literal renderings: The reader is introduced to the flavor of ancient expressions, phrases, and images. We have also presented literal translations of texts written in a language two or three times removed from that of the lost original. For example, Pseudo-Philo is extant in Latin but the original was composed in another language, probably Hebrew. The same situation lies behind 1 Enoch and Jubilees; both seem to derive ultimately from a Semitic language, which may be immediately behind the Ethiopic or be separated from it by an intermediary Greek version.

The preparation of this volume has been financed by generous grants and gifts from the Phillips Investment Corporation, the Phillips family, the Mary Duke Biddle Foundation, Brigham Young University's Religious Studies Center, Raymond and Hazel Mueller, Frances DeMott, the Welch family, and the Duke University Research Council. I am deeply grateful to each of them.

Finally after years of sacrificial work by so many it is difficult to articulate my deep appreciation and indebtedness to all those who have helped in the completion of the present edition of the Pseudepigrapha. I am indebted to the editors and staff at Doubleday, to my Board of Advisors, to the external readers, notably H. D. Betz, I. Gruenwald, J. Neusner, J. F. Oates, B. Schaller, J. L. Sharpe III, J. F. Strange, N. Turner, J. C. VanderKam, and F. W. Young, who have labored over many of these contributions, and to the contributors, who had to live for a long time with a frequently stern and demanding editor. I am grateful to my colleagues here at Duke, who had to live with unexpected responsibilities due to the tasks that fell my way, to the administrators, especially President Sanford, Chairman Bill Poteat, Chairman Bob Osborn, and Dean Langford, who provided space for editing and preparing the work. W. D. Davies, Moody Smith, Ray Brown, and John Strugnell helped me improve the Introduction. Many of my assistants worked long and hard hours, often during the trying summer months in Durham, and I wish to express my appreciations to all of them, notably Gary Martin, Jim Dumke, Dave Fiensy, Steve Robinson, George Zervos, and most especially to James Mueller, who served the longest, saw the task through to completion, and has proved to be a gifted and dedicated assistant. Marie Smith, my secretary, has without complaint typed and retyped much of the manuscript, and all of the voluminous correspondence. To all of these mentioned and many others I wish to express my sincere appreciation and hope that the final product is worthy of their sacrifices and support.

J. H. Charlesworth

Duke University
December 1982

CONTRIBUTORS TO VOLUME ONE

Agourides, S., Professor of Biblical Studies, Athens University, Athens, Greece
Apocalypse of Sedrach

Alexander, P., Department of Near Eastern Studies, University of Manchester, Manchester, England
3 (Hebrew Apocalypse of) Enoch

Andersen, F. I., Professor of Studies in Religion, University of Queensland, Brisbane, Australia
2 (Slavonic Apocalypse of) Enoch

Charlesworth, J. H., Associate Professor of Religion, Director of the International Center for the Study of Christian Origins, Duke University, Durham, North Carolina
Editor's Preface, Introduction for the General Reader, Introduction to Apocalyptic Literature and Related Works, *Treatise of Shem*, Introduction to Testaments

Collins, J. J., Associate Professor of Religious Studies, De Paul University, Chicago, Illinois
Sibylline Oracles

Duling, D. C., Associate Professor, Department of Religious Studies, Canisius College, Buffalo, New York
Testament of Solomon

Fiensy, D. A., Assistant Professor of Religion, Kentucky Christian College, Grayson, Kentucky
Revelation of Ezra

Gaylord, H. E., Jr., Rijksuniversiteit Groningen, Groningen, The Netherlands
3 (Greek Apocalypse of) Baruch

Isaac, E., Visiting Professor, Bard College, Annandale-on-Hudson, New York
1 (Ethiopic Apocalypse of) Enoch

Kee, H. C., Professor of New Testament and Director of Biblical-Historical Graduate Studies, Boston University School of Theology, Boston, Massachusetts
Testaments of the Twelve Patriarchs

Klijn, A. F. J., Haren (Gr.), The Netherlands
2 (Syriac Apocalypse of) Baruch

MacRae, G., Stillman Professor of Roman Catholic Studies, Harvard Divinity School, Cambridge, Massachusetts
Apocalypse of Adam

Metzger, B. M., George L. Collord Professor of New Testament Language and Literature, Princeton Theological Seminary, Princeton, New Jersey
The Fourth Book of Ezra

Mueller, J. R., Visiting Instructor of Religion, North Carolina State University, Raleigh, North Carolina
Apocryphon of Ezekiel, Vision of Ezra

Priest, J., Professor of Religion, Department of Religion, Florida State University, Tallahassee, Florida
Testament of Moses

Robbins, G. A., Assistant Professor of Religion, Wichita State University, Wichita, Kansas
Vision of Ezra

Robinson, S. E., Assistant Professor of Religion, Lycoming College, Williamsport, Pennsylvania
Apocryphon of Ezekiel, Testament of Adam

Rubinkiewicz, R., Assistant Professor, Catholic University, Lublin, Poland
Apocalypse of Abraham

Sanders, E. P., Professor of Religious Studies, Department of Religion, McMaster University, Hamilton, Ontario, Canada
Introduction to Testaments of the Three Patriarchs, *Testament of Abraham*

Spittler, R. P., Associate Professor of New Testament, Assistant Dean for Academic Programs, Fuller Theological Seminary, Pasadena, California
Testament of Job

Stinespring, W. F., Professor Emeritus of Old Testament and Semitics, Duke University Divinity School, Durham, North Carolina
Testament of Isaac, Testament of Jacob

Stone, M. E., Associate Professor of Armenian Studies, The Hebrew University of Jerusalem, Israel
Greek *Apocalypse of Ezra, Questions of Ezra*

Wintermute, O. S., Professor of Religion, Duke University, Durham, North Carolina
Apocalypse of Zephaniah, Apocalypse of Elijah

Zervos, G. T., Research Assistant, Duke University, Durham, North Carolina
Apocalypse of Daniel

INTRODUCTION FOR THE GENERAL READER

BY J. H. CHARLESWORTH

Western culture has been largely shaped by a unique collection of ancient books: the Bible. Not only our culture's language, but also its theology, philosophy, art, and law have been affected profoundly by the ideas, symbols, morality, commitments, perceptions, and dreams preserved in the biblical books. In the attempt to understand these books, scholars, especially since the time of the European Enlightenment, in the seventeenth and eighteenth centuries, have coupled an intensive study of them with a search for other ancient writings related to them.

The Search for Lost Writings

Mere perusal of the biblical books discloses that their authors depended upon sources that are no longer extant. We know so little about these sources that we cannot be certain of the extent to which they were actual documents. A list of these lost sources would be extensive; it would include at least the following: the Book of the Wars of Yahweh (Num 21:14), the Book of the Just (Josh 10:13, 2Sam 1:18), the Book of the Acts of Solomon (1Kgs 11:41), the Book of the Annals of the Kings of Israel (1Kgs 14:19, 2Chr 33:18; cf. 2Chr 20:34), the Book of the Annals of the Kings of Judah (1Kgs 14:29, 15:7), the Annals of Samuel the seer (1Chr 29:29), the History of Nathan the prophet (2Chr 9:29), the Annals of Shemaiah the prophet and of Iddo the seer (2Chr 12:15), the Annals of Jehu son of Hanani (2Chr 20:34), an unknown and untitled writing of Isaiah (2Chr 26:22), the Annals of Hozai (2Chr 33:18), and an unknown lament for Josiah by Jeremiah (2Chr 35:25). In the Apocrypha (defined below) lost books also are mentioned; in particular, 1 Maccabees 16:24 refers to the Annals of John Hyrcanus. Within the Pseudepigrapha themselves there are references to "documents" now lost (cf. e.g. TJob 40:14, 41:6, 49:3, 50:3).

Christianity and rabbinic Judaism evolved within a milieu that was distinguished by considerable and significant literary activity. Some of the documents composed during the early centuries have been transmitted by copyists; many remain lost; and others have been recovered during the last two centuries. The search for lost writings is aided by ancient lists of "extracanonical" books. One of these lists is a catalogue, perhaps from the sixth century, falsely attributed to Athanasius of Alexandria (c. 296–373). The author includes among the disputed parts of the Old Testament (*ta antilegomena tēs palaias diathēkēs*), the four Books of the Maccabees (1–4 Mac), the Psalms and Ode (*sic*) of Solomon. He defines the Apocrypha of the Old Testament (*ta de apokrupha palin tēs palaias diathēkēs tauta*') as follows:

Enoch	Elijah the Prophet
Patriarchs	Zephaniah the Prophet
Prayer of Joseph	Zechariah the Father of John
Testament of Moses	Baruch
Assumption of Moses	Habakkuk
(And the) pseudepigrapha	Ezekiel
(*pseudepigrapha*) of Abraham	Daniel
Eldad and Modad	

All of the documents judged to be disputed parts of the Old Testament or the Apocrypha (if we understand their titles correctly) are included, if only fragmentarily, in the present collection, except for 1 and 2 Maccabees (which belong in the Apocrypha), and except for the lost pseudepigrapha attributed to Habakkuk and Zechariah (which is to be placed among the New Testament Pseudepigrapha because it is related to Zechariah the father of John the Baptist).

Numerous writings not mentioned by Pseudo-Athanasius are included in this volume. Many of these are named in other canonical lists, notably the List of Sixty Books (c. sixth to seventh century?) and the list of Mechitar of Ayrivank‘ (c. 1290). Others do not appear in any early list. Some pseudepigrapha mentioned in medieval lists are not included; they are judged to be characteristically different from and too late for the present collection (see below). The search continues for documents not yet found but cited in the classical lists: an Apocryphon of Lamech (Sixty Books), the Interdiction of Solomon (Gelasian Decree), and the Book of the Daughters of Adam (Gelasian Decree; perhaps this document is another name for Jubilees). Likewise scholars are seeking to understand the origin of ancient quotations from or allusions to unnamed Jewish apocryphal documents. Many of these citations or traditions are preserved by the Church Fathers, especially Clement of Rome, Clement of Alexandria, Hippolytus, Tertullian, Origen, and the compiler of the Apostolic Constitutions, as well as by the Byzantine chroniclers (especially George Syncellus [c. 800] and George Cedrenus [c. 1057]).

The present edition of the Pseudepigrapha reflects the search for lost writings. We have included many apocryphal documents, fragmentary or complete, which may be related to those named in the canonical lists or cited by the Church Fathers; note, for example, the following: Apocalypse of Adam, Apocalypse of Abraham, Testament of Abraham, Prayer of Joseph, Eldad and Modad (still preserved in only one brief quotation), Apocalypse of Elijah, Apocryphon of Ezekiel, Apocalypse of Zephaniah, and Apocalypse of Ezra.

Many documents, recently discovered in the Near East or recognized in distinguished libraries, are translated here into English for the first time. Not including the documents placed in the Supplement, the writings now available for the first time in English are the Testament of Adam, the Testaments of Isaac and Jacob (from the Arabic), the Apocalypse of Daniel, the Revelation of Ezra, the Vision of Ezra, the History of Joseph, Syriac Menander, and the History of the Rechabites (from the Syriac). Additional writings translated for the first time in a full English translation are the Questions of Ezra, the Ladder of Jacob, Jannes and Jambres, and the Apocalypse of Sedrach.

In addition to these documents, four writings presented only in a truncated version in Charles's edition are presented here in their full extant form. From the

Martyrdom of Isaiah Charles himself included only chapters 1, 2, 3, and 5; the present edition presents all of that document along with the other traditions now preserved in the Martyrdom and Ascension of Isaiah. From 2 Enoch Forbes and Charles omitted the conclusion to the document; the present edition includes chapters 68 through 73, which contain the fascinating account of Melchisedek's miraculous birth. From the Sibylline Oracles Lanchester collected only the fragments and Books 3, 4, and 5; the present edition includes all of the Sibylline Oracles now extant. Finally, from 4 Ezra Box selected chapters 3–14; the present edition also includes the Christian additions (chapters 1 and 2, and 15 and 16).

Canon

The preceding discussion brings forward the question of the origin of the closed canons of the Old and New testaments. Impressive research is presently focused upon these issues, and it is possible to summarize only briefly my own opinions regarding this complex issue. For a long time scholars postulated that two canons of the Old Testament developed, one in Palestine and another in Egypt, and that Alexandrian Jews added the Apocrypha (see below) to the Hebrew canon. It now seems clear that there never was a rival Alexandrian canon. Philo and other Jews in Alexandria did not cite the Apocrypha, and the Alexandrian Church Fathers witness to the fact that Alexandrian Jews did not have an expanded canon.

When R. H. Charles published his edition of the Pseudepigrapha there was widespread agreement that the Hebrew canon, the Old Testament, was fixed finally at Jamnia around A.D. 90. Today there is considerable debate regarding the importance of the rabbinic school at Jamnia in the history of the codification of the Hebrew canon. On the one hand, it is becoming obvious that the process of canonization began long before the first century A.D., and that perhaps the earliest part of the Bible, the Law, had been closed and defined as authoritative well before the second century B.C., and the Prophets surely by that time. On the other hand, it is clear that after A.D. 90 there were still debates regarding the canonicity of such writings as the Song of Songs, Ecclesiastes, and Esther, but it is not clear what were the full ramifications of these debates. It seems to follow, therefore, both that the early pseudepigrapha were composed during a period in which the limits of the canon apparently remained fluid at least to some Jews, and that some Jews and Christians inherited and passed on these documents as inspired. They did not necessarily regard them as apocryphal, or outside a canon.

The writings collected into the New Testament were written during the end of this same period since they are dated from about A.D. 50 to 150. The New Testament canon was not closed in the Latin Church until much later; certainly not before the late fourth century and long after Constantine the Great established Christianity as the official religion of the Roman Empire. All the twenty-seven books of the New Testament, for example, are listed for the first time as the *only* canonical New Testament scriptures by Athanasius, bishop of Alexandria, in his Easter letter of A.D. 367. If the Latin Church finally accepted twenty-seven books as the canonical New Testament by the fifth century, the Greek Church apparently was not thoroughly convinced about the canonicity of one book, Revelation, until about the tenth century. The Syrian Church witnessed to an even more complicated debate over the canon of the New Testament; for many east Syrians today the

Peshitta is the canon and it contains only twenty-two documents, excluding 2 Peter, 2 and 3 John, Jude, and Revelation. Moreover, the assumption that all Christians have the same canon is further shattered by the recognition that the Copts and Ethiopians have added other documents to the canon.

Even in America today there are different canons among the various Christian communions: for example, Protestants exclude from the canon the Apocrypha, the additional books in the Greek Old Testament; the Roman Catholics, following the edicts of the Council of Trent in 1546, include them as deuterocanonical. The Mormons, moreover, argue that more books belong in the canon, and that it should remain open.

Most Jews throughout the world acknowledge only the Old Testament as canonical (cf. e.g. 4Ezra 14:37–48). The Falashas, Ethiopian Jews probably dependent on Ethiopian Christianity, however, have an expanded canon, including various apocrypha and pseudepigrapha, especially the Prayer of Manasseh, Jubilees, 1 Enoch, 3 and 4 Ezra.

For our present purposes it is wise to add to the above insights the recognition that many authors of pseudepigrapha believed they were recording God's infallible words. Early communities, both Jewish and Christian, apparently took some pseudepigrapha very seriously. The author of Jude, in verses 14 and 15, quoted as prophecy a portion of 1 Enoch, and this passage, 1 Enoch 1:9, has now been recovered in Aramaic from one of the caves that contained the Dead Sea Scrolls. Jude probably also was dependent, in verses 9 and 10, upon a lost Jewish apocryphon about Moses.

This brief overview of the historical development of the canons reveals that to call the Pseudepigrapha "non-canonical," or the biblical books "canonical," can be historically inaccurate prior to A.D. 100 and the period in which most of these documents were written. These terms should be used as an expression of some later "orthodoxy" with regard to a collection that is well defined regarding what belongs within and what is to be excluded from it. It is potentially misleading to use the terms "non-canonical," "canonical," "heresy," and "orthodoxy" when describing either Early Judaism or Early Christianity.

Definition of Pseudepigrapha

The technical term "pseudepigrapha" has a long and distinguished history. It was used in the late second century by Serapion when he referred to the New Testament Pseudepigrapha (*ta pseudepigrapha*, "with false superscription"; cf. Eusebius, *HE* 6.12). It was given prominence in the early years of the eighteenth century by J. A. Fabricius, who called the first volume of his massive work *Codex pseudepigraphus veteris testamenti*. The nineteenth-century collection of "pseudepigrapha" was by the Roman Catholic M. L'Abbé J.-P. Migne and titled *Dictionnaire des apocryphes, ou collection de tous les livres apocryphes relatifs à l'ancien et au nouveau testament*; this work did not use the term "pseudepigrapha" because Roman Catholics consider the Apocrypha to be deuterocanonical writings and refer to the Pseudepigrapha as "the Apocrypha." In the year 1900, E. Kautzsch edited the first German collection of the Pseudepigrapha, titled *Die Apokryphen und Pseudepigraphen des Alten Testaments*. The first, and until the present the only, English collection of the Pseudepigrapha was published in 1913 by the Clarendon Press of Oxford, England, and edited by R. H. Charles; he included in his large two-volume work both *The Apocrypha and Pseudepigrapha of the Old Testament*. The importance of the Pseudepigrapha in the international community at the present time is evidenced by the preparation of translations into Danish, Italian, French, German, modern Greek, Japanese, Dutch, and Spanish.

It is appropriate at this point to clarify the meaning of the term "pseudepigrapha." Several definitions are current. Webster's Third New International Dictionary (p. 1830) defines the term as denoting "spurious works purporting to emanate from biblical characters." That definition is misleading; ancient writings are dismissed subjectively as illegitimate. The Random House Dictionary of the English Language (the Unabridged Edition, p. 1159) offers the following: "Certain writings (other than the canonical books and the Apocrypha) professing to be Biblical in character, but not considered canonical or inspired." Three reactions appear to this definition: First, it would have been informative to clarify for whom the writings are "not considered canonical or inspired." Second, it is good to see a recognition of the claim to be "Biblical in character," which I believe is implied by some pseudepigrapha of the Old Testament. Third, it is unfortunate that neither of the two definitions presented by these authoritative volumes recognizes that this term is also employed for documents not related to the Bible. Scholars have used the term, for example, to denote some rabbinic writings, referring to the *Othijoth de Rabbi 'Akiba* and the *Pirḳê de Rabbi Eliezer* as rabbinic pseudepigrapha; moreover, "pseudepigrapha" is a technical term for some writings by the post-Platonic Pythagoreans.

Strictly speaking, the term "pseudepigrapha" has evolved from *pseudepigrapha*, a transliteration of a Greek plural noun that denotes writings "with false super-scription." *The Old Testament Pseudepigrapha*, the title of this collection, etymologically denotes writings falsely attributed to ideal figures featured in the Old Testament. Contemporary scholars employ the term "pseudepigrapha" not because it denotes something spurious about the documents collected under that title, but because the term has been inherited and is now used internationally.

In entitling the volume *The Old Testament Pseudepigrapha*, I have had to take a stance on the definition of "pseudepigrapha" as illustrated by the selection of works other than those included by Charles. Only two works from Charles's volume of seventeen documents are not included: Pirke Aboth and "The Fragments of a Zadokite Work," the former because it is rabbinic and the latter because it is now recognized to belong among the Dead Sea Scrolls. The following collection of fifty-two writings together with a long Supplement has evolved from the consensus that the Pseudepigrapha must be defined broadly so as to include all documents that conceivably belong to the Old Testament Pseudepigrapha. The present description of the Pseudepigrapha is as follows: Those writings 1) that, with the exception of Ahiqar, are Jewish or Christian; 2) that are often attributed to ideal figures in Israel's past; 3) that customarily claim to contain God's word or message; 4) that frequently build upon ideas and narratives present in the Old Testament; 5) and that almost always were composed either during the period 200 B.C. to A.D. 200 or, though late, apparently preserve, albeit in an edited form, Jewish traditions that date from that period. Obviously, the numerous qualifications (e.g. "with the exception of," "often," "customarily," "frequently," "almost always") warn that the above comments do not define the term "pseudepigrapha"; they merely describe the features of this collection.

Writings cognate to the Pseudepigrapha

Including fifty-two documents plus a Supplement in the present collection of the Pseudepigrapha meant excluding other writings, although they may have some characteristics of the Pseudepigrapha. These writings were usually omitted because they were far removed from the Old Testament in date and character. Most notable among them are the following: The Vision of Daniel, The Death of Abraham (both ed. by A. Vassiliev in *Anecdota Graeco-Byzantina*, vol. 1. Moscow, 1893), the Hebrew Apocalypse of Elijah (ed. and trans. M. Buttenwieser, *Die hebräische Elias-Apokalypse*. Leipzig, 1897), the Book of Jasher (ed. J. Ilive, *The Book of Jasher*. Bristol, 1829), the Conflict of Adam and Eve with Satan (ed. A. Dillmann, *Das christliche Adambuch des Orients*. Göttingen, 1853; ET: S. C. Malan, *The Book of Adam and Eve*. London, 1882), the Cave of Treasures (ed. C. Bezold, *Die Schatzhöhle: Syrisch und Deutsch*, 2 vols. Leipzig, 1883, 1888; ET: E. A. W. Budge, *The Book of the Cave of Treasures*. London, 1927), the Book of the Rolls (cf. M. D. Gibson, *Apocrypha Arabica*. Studia Sinaitica 8. London, 1901), the Sin of Solomon (unpublished, probably a homily, cf. Cod. Par. Gr. 1021, fols. 184v–185v in the Bibliothèque Nationale), *Pirķê de Rabbi Eliezer* (trans. G. Friedlander, *Pirķê de Rabbi Eliezer*. New York, 1981[4]), the Syriac Apocalypse of Ezra (ed. and trans. J.-B. Chabot, "L'Apocalypse d'Esdras," *Revue sémitique* 2 [1894] 242–50, 333–46), the Book of the Bee (ed. and trans. E. A. W. Budge, *The Book of the Bee*. Anecdota Oxoniensia, Sem. Ser. 1.2. Oxford, 1886), and the Questions Addressed by the Queen (of Sheba), and Answers Given by Solomon (trans. J. Issaverdens, *The Uncanonical Writings of the Old Testament*. Venice, 1901).

Later documents related to the Pseudepigrapha have been edited in important collections; most important are those from Armenian by Jacques Issaverdens, from Ethiopic by Wolf Leslau, and from rabbinic Hebrew by Adolph Jellinek (cf. the German translation by A. Wünsche). Recently Father Martin McNamara in *The Apocrypha in the Irish Church* (Dublin, 1975) drew attention to "probably the richest crop of apocrypha in any of the European vernaculars, possibly in any vernacular language" (p. 2).

While some of the documents mentioned above may prove to be ancient or preserve portions of early Jewish pseudepigrapha, the following ten collections of ancient Jewish or early Christian writings are recognized as important for understanding the period in which the Pseudepigrapha were composed. First and second are the works of the Jewish philosopher and exegete Philo of Alexandria (c. 20 B.C.–A.D. 50) and the Jewish historian Josephus (c. A.D. 37–c. 100); these are essential reading for an understanding of first-century Jewish life and thought. Third are the Dead Sea Scrolls, which are Jewish sectarian documents first found in 1947 in caves to the west of the Dead Sea; these inform us of the apocalyptic and eschatological ideas and of the surprising interpretations of the Old Testament by one sect of Jews, which flourished from the second century B.C. (c. 150 B.C.) to the first century A.D. (viz. A.D. 68). These scrolls are extremely important for an understanding of many pseudepigrapha, especially Jubilees, the Testaments of the Twelve Patriarchs, 1 Enoch, and the Odes of Solomon. Fourth are the rabbinic writings, and there can be no doubt that some of the traditions recorded in these documents predate the destruction of the Temple in A.D. 70; these early traditions are helpful in understanding the daily life of the religious Jew before the destruction of the nation and the Temple. Fifth are the targums, which are Aramaic translations and expansive interpretations of the Hebrew scriptures; these sometimes seem to preserve important evidence of an ancient understanding of the Old Testament. Since a Targum of Job, dating from the first half of the first century A.D., was found at Qumran, it is now clear that the earliest traditions in the other, but much later, targums must be included in an assessment of early Judaism. Sixth are the "Jewish" magical papyri, especially those edited by K. L. Preisendanz; these should not be ignored, as should become evident from a careful reading of some pseudepigrapha, especially the Prayer of Jacob, the Prayer of Joseph, and the History of Joseph. Seventh are the Hermetica, which are writings of the first few centuries A.D. attributed to Hermes that describe the means to personal salvation; these may contain (although I personally am not convinced) some early Jewish traditions that are important for an understanding of Early Judaism and earliest Christianity. Eighth are the Nag Hammadi codices; these Coptic codices were composed from perhaps the first to the fourth centuries A.D., but were not found until 1945 in Upper Egypt. These writings, most of which are gnostic, are intermittently influenced by early Jewish traditions. Of special importance among these codices is the Apocalypse of Adam included below. Ninth are the New Testament Apocrypha and Pseudepigrapha, which contain many early Christian writings that are usually legendary expansions of the New Testament itself; these only infrequently were shaped by early Jewish traditions.

Tenth are the Apocrypha, which are writings that like many pseudepigrapha are usually related to the Hebrew scriptures; as indicated earlier, the Apocrypha are documents preserved in the Greek, but not in the Hebrew, Old Testament. These documents are often designated by Roman Catholics as "deuterocanonical," but most scholars have now accepted the Protestant terminology and call them "Apocrypha."

Different collections of the Apocrypha are available today. In order to harmonize with the contemporary, enlarged concept of Pseudepigrapha the Apocrypha should include only the additional writings preserved in almost all Septuagint manuscripts, and not the additional documents in the Vulgate (see *PMR*, p. 19). The Apocrypha, therefore, includes thirteen documents: 2 Ezra (= 1 Esdras),* Tobit, Judith, Additions to Esther, Wisdom of Solomon, Sirach, 1 Baruch, Letter of Jeremiah, Prayer of Azariah with the Song of the Three Young Men, Susanna, Bel and the Dragon, 1 Maccabees, and 2 Maccabees. Often two pseudepigrapha, 4 Ezra (= 2 Esdras)* and the Prayer of Manasseh,* are considered part of the Apocrypha. The thirteen documents in the Apocrypha, with the exception of Tobit, which may be much earlier, date from the last two centuries before the common era. These documents may be found in Protestant ecumenical Bibles that contain the Apocrypha in a center section between the testaments, or at the end of the two testaments. All except the three marked with asterisks will be found in Roman Catholic Bibles interspersed among the Old Testament writings or even as part of them (esp. Esth and Dan).

It is important to draw attention to these other significant collections of early Jewish and Christian documents. Along with them, the Pseudepigrapha preserve ideas essential for an understanding of Early Judaism and Early Christianity.

Importance of the Pseudepigrapha

We may now assess briefly the importance of the Pseudepigrapha for a better understanding of the history and thought of Jews during the centuries that preceded and followed the beginning of the common era. Four aspects of that period are impressive. First, there is the very abundance of the literature, although we possess only part of the writings produced by Jews during the period 200 B.C. to A.D. 200. We know many works are lost since early Christians quoted from and referred to documents now lost, since some writings are available only in truncated manuscripts or in fragments, since there are references to lost volumes produced, for example, by Jason of Cyrene, Justus of Tiberias, and Nicolaus of Damascus, and since each new discovery of a manuscript reminds us that there are still more works to be recovered.

It is obvious that post-exilic Judaism was distinguished by voluminous and varied literature: from the production of epics or tragedies in hexameters or iambic trimeters (viz. PhEPoet, EzekTrag) to philosophical tractates (viz. Aristob, Philo, 4Mac), from perhaps reliable histories (viz. 1Mac, some of Josephus' publications) to imaginative recreations of the past (viz. the Chronicler, 3Mac, JosAsen), from apocalyptic dreams and visions of another world (viz. 1En, 2Bar; cf. HistRech) to humanistic wisdom (viz. Sir, Ps-Phoc), and even from charges against God in seemingly Promethean arrogance (viz. Eccl; cf. ApSedr) to hymnic and introspective submissions to God as the sole means of righteousness and salvation (viz. 1QH, PrMan; cf. OdesSol). During the post-exilic period, the Jewish genius exploded into creative new writings.

Second, the Pseudepigrapha illustrate the pervasive influence of the Old Testament books upon Early Judaism. That is seen not only in the following group of works designated "Expansions of the Old Testament," but also in many similar ones, especially in the selection of "apocalypses" and "testaments." Judaism became for all time a religion of the Book, God's eternal message.

Third, we learn from the Pseudepigrapha that the consecutive conquests of Palestinian Jews by Persians, Greeks, and Romans, and the intermittent invasions by Syrian, Egyptian, and Parthian armies did not dampen the enthusiasm of religious Jews for their ancestral traditions. The ancient Davidic Psalter was constantly expanded until some collections included 155 psalms. Other psalmbooks appeared, especially the Psalms of Solomon, the Hodayoth, the Odes of Solomon, and perhaps the Hellenistic Synagogal Hymns. Apocalypses that stressed the grandeur and transcendence of God were customarily interspersed with hymns that celebrated God's nearness, and by prayers that were perceived as heard and answered. Post-exilic Judaism was a living and devout religion. New hymns, psalms, and odes witness to the fact that persecution could not choke the blessings by the faithful.

Fourth, the Pseudepigrapha attest that post-exilic Jews often were torn within by divisions and sects, and intermittently conquered from without by foreign nations who insulted, abused, and frequently employed fatal torture. Persecutions inflamed the desire to revolt and some pseudepigrapha mirror the tensions among the Jews. Especially noteworthy are the Psalms of Solomon and the Testament of Moses, which record the idea that God alone is the source of power; it is he who will initiate action against the gentiles and purge Jerusalem of the foreigners. The apocalypses usually are pessimistic about the present: God had withdrawn from the arena of history and from the earth; he would return only to consummate the end and to inaugurate the new. Thereby the apocalyptists affirm the loyalty of God to covenant, invite the reader to live in terms of, indeed within, another world, and envisage an optimistic conclusion for Israel in God's completed story.

The Pseudepigrapha, therefore, are an important source for understanding the social dimensions of Early Judaism. The simplistic picture of Early Judaism should be recast; it certainly was neither a religion which had fallen into arduous legalism due to the crippling demands of the Law, nor was it characterized by four dominant sects. A new picture has been emerging because of ideas preserved in the documents collected below. Three examples suffice to demonstrate this insight: First, none of the present translators strives to identify a document with a particular Jewish sect. We cannot identify with certainty any author of a pseudepigraphon as being a Pharisee or an Essene or a member of another sect. Second, Palestinian Jews were influenced by Egyptian, Persian, and Greek ideas. Hence, the old distinction between "Palestinian Judaism" and "Hellenistic Judaism" must be either redefined or discarded. Third, because of the variegated, even contradictory, nature of the ideas popular in many sectors of post-exilic Judaism, it is obvious that Judaism was not monolithically structured or shaped by a central and all-powerful "orthodoxy."

When Charles published his edition of the Pseudepigrapha, it was widely held that Early Judaism was shaped and characterized by "normative Judaism" or a ruling orthodoxy centered in Jerusalem. This idea is no longer defended by most biblical scholars. Since 1947, when the first of the Dead Sea Scrolls were discovered, there has even been a tendency to emphasize unduly the diversity in Early Judaism. While it is now recognized that foreign ideas penetrated deep into many aspects of Jewish thought, and that sometimes it is difficult to decide whether an early document is essentially Jewish or Christian, it is, nevertheless, unwise to exaggerate the diversity in Early Judaism. In the first century Judaism was neither uniformly normative nor chaotically diverse.

The above discussion leads to the following observations that should be emphasized. The documents contained herein certainly demonstrate the rich vitality and diversity of Judaism during the early centuries. This is not the place to attempt to articulate further what, if anything, seems to unify them. Certainly confirmed is Charles's own statement that was controversial in his time: Without the Apocrypha and Pseudepigrapha (and we would add other documents recovered since his time, notably the Dead Sea Scrolls) "it is absolutely impossible to explain the course of religious development between 200 B.C. and A.D. 100" (*APOT*, vol. 1, p. x).

Significant theological conceptions

The general reader will find it helpful, when reading the documents collected below, to learn that at least four significant theological concerns are frequently found in the Pseudepigrapha: preoccupations with the meaning of sin, the origins of evil, and the problem of theodicy; stresses upon God's transcendence; concerns with the coming of the Messiah; and beliefs in a resurrection that are often accompanied with descriptions of Paradise. Each of these interests was developed—

at least partly—from ideas and beliefs found in the Old Testament. At the beginning it is prudent to emphasize that scholars' understanding of early Jewish theology has evolved from decades of research not only upon the Pseudepigrapha, but also upon the Old Testament, the Apocrypha, early rabbinics, Philo, Josephus, and the Dead Sea Scrolls.

Sin, Evil, and the Problem of Theodicy. The Jews who returned to Palestine following the sixth-century B.C. exile in Babylon attempted to be faithful to the covenant; they rebuilt the Temple and emphasized the study of the Torah. Dedication to purity involved not only heightened rules for worship and daily life but also racial purity and separation from the heathen. Despite renewed dedication and faithfulness, the righteous did not prosper and live in a holy land free from domination. It was the sinners and the unfaithful who seemed to be rewarded, and the land—indeed the land promised to Abraham as an inheritance—was ruled by foreign oppressors. Sin and injustice were rewarded; evil appeared to be the ruling power in a world created by God. Raised repeatedly was the question: "How could the God of Israel be holy, just, and all-powerful, and at the same time permit evil forces to oppress the righteous?" Many pseudepigrapha are shaped by this question and the problem of theodicy (see especially 4Ezra, 2Bar, ApAbr, 3Bar).

This problem evoked mutually exclusive reactions in Judaism. Qoheleth concluded, "Vanity of vanities. All is vanity!" (Eccl 1:2). Authors of some pseudepigrapha, basing their insight upon the story of Adam and Eve's first sin, described in Genesis 3, took the position that evil was dominant in the world because of Eve's sin. The author of the Life of Adam and Eve 18:1, as the author of Sirach 25:24 (in the Apocrypha), put the blame squarely upon Eve. The source of the guilt shifts completely from Eve to Adam in 4 Ezra. Evil reigns in the world certainly not because of God's actions, but because of Adam, who "transgressed" and was overcome, and not only he himself but all who descend from him (4Ezra 3:20f.; cf. 7:118). About the same time as 4 Ezra, the author of 2 Baruch argued that sin is in the world and continues to be a power because each individual chooses to sin (2Bar 54:15, 19; cf. 1En 98:4f.).

An appreciably different explanation for the origin of sin is found emphasized in numerous pseudepigrapha. Taking as their starting point the story in Genesis 6 about "the sons of God" who married "the daughters of men," the authors of some pseudepigrapha—especially the authors of 1 and 2 Enoch—claim that evil is in the world and is a powerful force because of evil angels. Four possible explanations for the fall of these angels may be discerned: 1) The angels had lusted for earth's beautiful women (1En 6:1–16:4, 40:7, 54:6; 2En 18). 2) The angels perhaps had desired to reproduce themselves (1En 6:2b, 7:1–3). 3) The Devil and his followers refused to worship Adam (*Vita* 14:3). 4) An angel and his legions desired to exalt themselves (2En 29:4f.). All these explanations, despite their significant differences, reflect the seriousness with which evil was perceived by post-exilic Jews, and all attempt to absolve God of the responsibility for evil. This balanced perspective is upset in a much later document, the Apocalypse of Sedrach (ch. 5).

Evil is a dominant force in the world, despite God's will and actions. The righteous suffer primarily because of the power evil has obtained on the earth. The land of Israel has been engulfed by nations either sent by God to punish his sinful people or by foreigners ruled by evil forces or angels; hence God can both send evil and allow it to continue. God's people suffer, and he tends to remove himself from a special portion of his creation.

Transcendence of God. The emphasis in many pseudepigrapha that God is far from Israel contrasts markedly with earlier traditions, especially two accounts: According to Genesis 18 God encountered Abraham on the earth and by the oaks of Mamre, just north of Hebron; according to Exodus 3 the Lord God calls Moses from a burning bush on Mount Horeb, and the presence of God defines the place as "holy ground." After the exile God is usually perceived as one who is above. The apocalyptists place him in the highest heaven, far removed from the earth (1En 1:4, 71:5–11; 2En 20:5), but the prayers interspersed through the apocalypses reveal that he is not inaccessible. He has withdrawn from the world and no longer acts in its history; he will, however, act again, probably through intermediaries (PssSol 17, TLevi 18, TJud 24, 4Ezra 7, 2Bar 72f.). Most pseudepigrapha, in contrast to earlier Jewish writings, are characterized by an increasing claim that God is thoroughly majestic and transcendent (2Mac 3:39; 3Mac 2:15; SibOr 3.1, 11, 81, 807; 5.298, 352; MartIs 1:6b; 1En 71:5–11; 2En 20:5). Knowledge of him is obtained almost always only through the sacred books, the descent of angels (TAb 2:15), the gift of vision (1En 1:2), or the journey of a seer through the various heavens (2En, AscenIs). The contrast of these ideas with earlier ones is demonstrated by the way the author of the Testament of Abraham rewrites Genesis 18: God does not descend to visit Abraham; he sends his angel Michael to speak with the patriarch (TAb 1; cf. 16).

The contrast between ideas or tendencies in early documents, such as Genesis, and those in the Pseudepigrapha should not be exaggerated; and the rewriting of God's encounter with Abraham should not be interpreted to mean that religious Jews came to believe that God was absolutely extramundane, remote, and exiled. As the hymns, odes, and prayers in the apocalypses themselves demonstrate, the Jew continued to affirm efficacious and personal communion with God. With these caveats it is possible to point out that early Jews tended to *emphasize* God's holiness, majesty, gloriousness, and sovereignty; he was transcendent.

Messianism. The belief in a Messiah—a term which here means an ideal person, probably a king or priest, who will bring in perfect peace—is not found in the Old Testament, in the Apocrypha, or in Philo and Josephus (except for allusions). The belief in a future messianic Davidic king, however, is recorded in the prophets (viz. Isa 9:2–7, 11:1–9; Jer 33:14–22; Ezek 37:24–28); and the belief in a future Messiah (or Anointed One) of Aaron and Israel (CD Text B 19.10f.; cf. 1QS 9.11) is recorded in the Dead Sea Scrolls. The term "Messiah" also appears in the later Targums (especially Pseudo-Jonathan [Jerusalem Targum] at Gen 49:1 and Num 24:17–24). Numerous titles were given to the expected messianic figure; but since it is difficult to be certain in which passages these are indeed titles for the Messiah, it is wise to limit this overview only to the places in the Pseudepigrapha which mention the terms "the Messiah" (the Heb. noun) or "the Christ" (the Gk. translation) or "the Anointed One" (which is the meaning of both the Heb. and the Gk.).

Significantly, most pseudepigrapha do *not* contain a reference to the coming of a Messiah; and it is impossible to derive a systematic description of the functions of the Messiah from the extant references to him. Only five pseudepigrapha contain clearly Jewish traditions about the Messiah. Late in the first century B.C. the author of the Psalms of Solomon yearned for the coming of the Messiah, who will "purge Jerusalem from gentiles." Notably he shall perform this task "with the word of his mouth," and do this not from his own initiative, but because he is God's agent and belongs to God (PssSol 17f.).

Apparently late in the first century A.D.—when many of the New Testament writings were being written, especially Matthew, Luke, and John—three authors of pseudepigrapha elaborated on traditions concerning the Messiah. The author of 2 Baruch focused upon the role of the Messiah in three separate sections (chs. 29f., 39–42, 72–74). When "all is accomplished" the Messiah will be revealed and the righteous resurrected (2Bar 29f.). In contrast to this apparently passive role, the Messiah, according to the second section (2Bar 39–42), will act decisively, convicting and putting to death the last evil leader, and protecting God's people. The Messiah is also active in the third section (2Bar 72–74): He shall summon all the nations, sparing those who have not mistreated Israel, and slaying those who have ruled over her. In both the second and third messianic sections the Messiah appears to be described as a militant warrior who slays the gentiles by the sword (72:6).

At about the same time as the author of 2 Baruch the author of 4 Ezra, in three passages (chs. 7, 11:37–12:34, 13:3–14:9), discusses the functions of the Messiah. According to the first of these (4Ezra 7), in the future age, the world to come (7:50, 8:1), the Messiah shall be revealed, bringing rejoicing for four hundred years, and eventually die (7:28f.). According to the second passage (4Ezra 11:37– 12:34), the Messiah, who is depicted as "the lion," will denounce, judge, and destroy the ungodly; but he shall deliver the faithful and make them joyful. According to the third section (4Ezra 13:3–14:9), the Messiah, who is "my son" (13:32, 37, 52; 14:9; cf. 7:28f.) and "a man" (13:26, 32), withstands a warring multitude and consumes them with "a stream of fire" that proceeds from his mouth.

Perhaps roughly contemporaneously with 2 Baruch and 4 Ezra (see the introduction to 1En), the author of 1 Enoch 37–71 recorded his ideas about the Messiah. In contrast to his vivid depictions of "the Son of Man," "the Righteous One," and "the Elect One," the author's two meager references to the Messiah (or "the Anointed One") are surprisingly brief (48:10, 52:4). No functions are attributed to the Messiah.

The fifth document in the Pseudepigrapha that contains a clearly Jewish perspective on the Messiah is the late document titled 3 Enoch. Noteworthy is the portrayal of a Messiah who is son of Joseph, and a Messiah who is son of David (45:5). It is possible that one Messiah is meant; but if two Messiahs are denoted, then the Messiahs of Israel will wage war against Gog and Magog at the end of time. This war appears to end in a draw; God himself eventually enters the war and wins the last battle. Subsequently the author of 3 Enoch describes the celebration of Israel's salvation (48:10A). The possibly early date of these traditions has been raised by the discovery of similar ones in the Dead Sea Scrolls (especially 1QS, CD, 1QM).

Obviously different from the above are the references to "the Messiah" (and derived terms) in the pseudepigrapha that appear to be Christian compositions. Observe especially the use of the term in the Odes of Solomon (9:3, 17:17, 24:1, 29:6, 39:11, 41:3, 41:15), the Apocalypse of Zephaniah (10:24–12:32), the

Apocalypse of Elijah (13:15–15:14, 25:8–19), and the Apocalypse of Sedrach (ch. 12). Lengthy Christian additions in the Vision of Isaiah (9:12–13, 30:7–15) and the Testament of Adam (Rec. 2) also contain significant references to "the Anointed One" or "the Christ."

Resurrection and Paradise. Scholars generally agree that the Old Testament writings, with the possible exception of Isaiah 26 and Daniel 12, do not contain explicit references to the resurrection of the dead. At death the individual simply is gathered to his final (or father's) place, the tomb. Sheol and the netherworld (*'ereṣ*) is described as the abode of the dead, not of people who continue to live after death (cf. Isa 38:18, Sir 17:28, 14:12–19). Only through his reputation or a son does his life continue on the earth. In contrast to this perception are the ideas developed in post-exilic Judaism. Some books in the Apocrypha contain numerous explicit references to the resurrection of the dead (see especially 2Mac 7, 14), or possibly even to the immortality of the soul (WisSol), and the Dead Sea Scrolls preserve ambiguous sections possibly referring to an afterlife (see especially 1QH 5.34, 6.29f., 11.10–14). Some pseudepigrapha, even more than these other documents, contain many passages that with pellucid clarity express the belief in a resurrection after death (viz. TJob, PssSol, 4Mac, Ps-Phoc, 2En, HistRech). The author of 2 Baruch, moreover, devotes a section, 49–52, to the description of the resurrected body.

Logically subsequent to the development of this idea is the attempt to describe the future place of rest for the righteous. Hence, picturesque images of Paradise appear in many pseudepigrapha. The various pictoral descriptions are characterized by mutually exclusive ideas. Paradise is placed sometimes in the third heaven (2En 8A, ApMos 37:5, 40:1), and sometimes on the earth (1En 32; 2En 8:1–6A, 30:1A; ApMos 38:5). It is depicted as either without inhabitants (1En 32, 2En 8f., 4Ezra 8:52) or with inhabitants (PssSol 14, 2En 42:3B, ApAb 21, OdesSol 11:16–24; cf. HistRech). It is portrayed as both an eternal inheritance (PssSol 14:3f.; 2En 65:10A; OdesSol 11:16d, 16f.; 4Ezra 8:52) and a state preceding the end (ApMos 37:5, 40:1–41:3; *Vita* 48:6f.; AscenIs 9; cf. HistRech 13–15). There are some common beliefs, notably that Paradise is full of fruitful trees (see 2En 8A, OdesSol 11:11–16, 23) and distinguished by a sweet-smelling odor (viz. see 1En 32:3, 2En 8A, OdesSol 11:15, 2En 23:18).

The contradicting ideas should not be explained away or forced into an artificial system. Such ideas in the Pseudepigrapha witness to the fact that Early Judaism was not a speculative philosophical movement or theological system, even though the Jews demonstrated impressive speculative fecundity. The Pseudepigrapha mirror a living religion in which the attempt was made to come to terms with the dynamic phenomena of history and experience.

These are only four of the theological characteristics of the Pseudepigrapha, namely the problems of sin and theodicy, emphasis upon God's transcendence, speculations about the Messiah, and the ideas concerning the afterlife. Many other theological features could also be highlighted. The choice between a lunar and a solar calendar (see Jub and 1En) produced major upheavals in Judaism in the second century B.C. Calendrical issues contained cosmic and profound theological dimensions. How exasperating to discover you were not observing the Sabbath on the correct day and with the angels and the rest of the universe. How astounding to learn that Passover was celebrated at the wrong time. Similarly, the search for authority and reliable insight into God's will is reflected in the search for the quintessence of Torah and its text. The search for God himself and the tendency toward belief in a transcendent and apparently aloof Creator spawned complex angelologies. The impossibility of obtaining satisfactory meaning in present history helped produce the theological perspectives behind apocalypticism.

Conclusion

These introductory comments are far too brief to constitute an introduction to the Pseudepigrapha, and they should not be taken to indicate that scholars have arrived at anything like a consensus on the major issues. These few comments should, however, enable the general reader to understand better the documents collected below; at least they reflect how the editor perceives them. Each of the Pseudepigrapha is preceded by an introduction (see Editor's Preface) and organized under categories which also have brief introductions. These collectively serve to help the reader appreciate the documents themselves.

EXPLANATION OF TYPOGRAPHICAL
AND REFERENCE SYSTEMS

Chapter and verse numbers

We have endeavored to present the documents below in a format similar to that of the Jerusalem Bible. Hence, chapters and verses are supplied. A new chapter is indicated by a large bold numeral. Verse numbers are placed in the margin in ordinary roman type; in the text itself, the beginning of each verse is marked by a • which precedes the first word of the verse except when the verse begins a new line or a new chapter. Because of their linguistic nature, some documents—such as the Sibylline Oracles, Letter of Aristeas, and Syriac Menander—are not divided into chapters and verses. These are presented so that the beginning of each line or section of text is noted in the margin with numbers in ordinary roman type as with verse numbers.

Italics in the text

Italic type in the text denotes full or partial quotations of the Bible. The biblical passage from which the quotation is derived is noted in the margin.

Brackets and other sigla in the translation

[ ]	Square brackets denote restorations.
⟨ ⟩	Pointed brackets signify corrections to a text.
( )	Parentheses circumscribe words added by the translator. Ancient languages are cryptic; verbs, nouns, and pronouns are often omitted. These are, of course, necessary for idiomatic English and are presented within parentheses.
| |	This siglum indicates a letter incorrectly omitted by an ancient scribe.
{ }	Braces denote unnecessary words or letters in an ancient text.

Footnotes

In each chapter, footnotes are lettered alphabetically. The footnotes are not intended to be a mini-commentary, but to supply significant information, such as important related thoughts contained in ancient writings not considered either canonical or extracanonical. Only significant variants in the manuscripts are cited. These notes assume that the reader has read the general introduction and the introduction to each document being footnoted.

Punctuation of biblical references

Chapter and verse are separated by a colon, e.g. Ex 20:7. A subsequent verse in the same chapter is separated from the preceding by a comma. Subsequent citations in other biblical or apocryphal writings are separated by semicolons: e.g. Ex 20:17, 20; Lev 9:15. Citations which are not preceded by an abbreviation refer to the respective passage in a document being footnoted.

Marginal references

Marginal references are kept to a minimum and except in rare occasions are limited to significant parallels in biblical and apocryphal writings. These marginal references should help the reader better understand the relevant passage by drawing attention to the source of a biblical quotation, and to other uses of special terms, phrases, or images. The references in the margin often occur in groups all relating to one text line; in such cases, the position of the first reference indicates the line to which the whole group applies. Marginal references not preceded by the abbreviation of a book indicate a passage elsewhere in the document before the reader.

Care has been taken to assure that each marginal reference begins on the line to which it refers. However, in some cases this is not possible because of the length of necessary marginal references. In these cases, the marginal reference is preceded by a verse reference (i.e. the letter *v* plus the number of the verse) so the reader can attach the marginal references to the correct verses.

Secondary divisions within the document

The manuscripts from which the translators have worked usually do not separate the text so that each new thought or development in the narrative is indicated. The translators have supplied the subdivisions to help the reader follow the flow of the document.

LIST OF ABBREVIATIONS

I. MODERN PUBLICATIONS

AAR	American Academy of Religion
AcOr	*Acta orientalia*
AGAJU	Arbeiten zur Geschichte des antiken Judentums und des Urchristentums
Agrapha	Resch, A., ed. *Agrapha: Aussercanonische Schriftfragmente.* TU 30.3–4; Leipzig, 1906.
ALBO	Analecta lovaniensia biblica et orientalia
ALGHJ	Arbeiten zur Literatur und Geschichte des hellenistischen Judentums
ALUOS	*Annual of the Leeds University Oriental Society*
ANET	Pritchard, J. B., ed. *Ancient Near Eastern Texts.* Princeton, 1969³.
ANF	Roberts, A., and J. Donaldson, eds. *The Ante-Nicene Fathers: Translations of the Writings of the Fathers down to A.D. 325.* 10 vols. Edinburgh, 1868–72; rev. and repr. Grand Rapids, Mich., 1950–52.
ANRW	Haase, W., and H. Temporini, eds. *Aufstieg und Niedergang der römischen Welt.* Berlin, New York, 1979– .
ANT	James, M. R. *The Apocryphal New Testament.* Oxford, 1924; corrected ed., 1955.
APAT	Kautzsch, E., ed. *Die Apokryphen und Pseudepigraphen des Alten Testaments.* 2 vols. Tübingen, 1900.
Apoc. Lit.	Torrey, C. C. *The Apocryphal Literature: A Brief Introduction.* New Haven, Conn., 1945; repr. Hamden, Conn., 1963.
Apocrifi del NT	Erbetta, M. *Gli Apocrifi del Nuovo Testamento.* 3 vols. Turin, 1966–69.
APOT	Charles, R. H., ed. *The Apocrypha and Pseudepigrapha of the Old Testament in English.* 2 vols. Oxford, 1913.
ArOr	*Archiv orientální*
ASOR	American Schools of Oriental Research
ASTI	*Annual of the Swedish Theological Institute*
ATANT	Abhandlungen zur Theologie des Alten und Neuen Testaments
ATR	*Anglican Theological Review*
AusBR	*Australian Biblical Review*
BA	*The Biblical Archeologist*
BASOR	*Bulletin of the American Schools of Oriental Research*
BDT	Harrison, E. F., *et al.*, eds. *Baker's Dictionary of Theology.* Grand Rapids, Mich., 1960.
BEvT	Beiträge zur evangelischen Theologie
BHH	Reicke, B., and L. Rost, eds. *Biblisch-historisches Handwörterbuch.* 3 vols. Göttingen, 1962–66.

BHM	Jellinek, A. *Bet ha-Midrasch*. 2 vols. Jerusalem, 1967³.
Bib	*Biblica*
Biblia Sacra	Weber, R., *et al.*, eds. *Biblia Sacra: Iuxta Vulgatam Versionem*. 2 vols. Stuttgart, 1969.
Bibliographie	Delling, G. *Bibliographie zur jüdisch-hellenistischen und intertestamentarischen Literatur 1900–1970*. TU 106²; Berlin, 1975².
BibSt	Biblische Studien
BIFAO	*Bulletin de l'institut français d'archéologie orientale*
BiKi	*Bibel und Kirche*
BIOSCS	*Bulletin of the International Organization for Septuagint and Cognate Studies*
BJRL, BJRULM	*Bulletin of the John Rylands Library, Bulletin of the John Rylands University Library of Manchester*
B-L²	Haag, H., ed. *Bibel-Lexikon*. Zurich, 1968².
BLE	*Bulletin de littérature ecclésiastique*
BO	*Bibliotheca orientalis*
BSOAS	*Bulletin of the School of Oriental and African Studies*
BZ	*Biblische Zeitschrift*
BZAW	Beihefte zur Zeitschrift für die alttestamentliche Wissenschaft
BZNW	Beihefte zur Zeitschrift für die neutestamentliche Wissenschaft und die Kunde der älteren Kirche
CB	*Cultura bíblica*
CBQ	*Catholic Biblical Quarterly*
CCSL	Corpus Christianorum. Series Latina.
CETEDOC	Centre de traitement électronique des documents
CG	Cairensis Gnosticus
Crucible	Toynbee, A., ed. *The Crucible of Christianity: Judaism, Hellenism and the Historical Background to the Christian Faith*. New York, 1969.
CSCO	Corpus scriptorum christianorum orientalium
CTM	*Concordia Theological Monthly*
DB	Vigouroux, F., ed. *Dictionnaire de la Bible*. 5 vols. Paris, 1895–1912.
DBSup	Pirot, L., *et al.*, eds. *Dictionnaire de la Bible, Suppléments*. Paris, 1928– .
DJD	Discoveries in the Judaean Desert
Dogmengeschichte⁴	Harnack, A. *Lehrbuch der Dogmengeschichte*. 3 vols. Tübingen, 1909–10⁴.
DTT	*Dansk teologisk Tidsskrift*
Enciclopedia de la Biblia	Gutiérrez-Larraya, J. A., ed. *Enciclopedia de la Biblia*. 6 vols. Barcelona, 1963.
Encyclopedia of Christianity	Palmer, E. H., *et al.*, eds. *The Encyclopedia of Christianity*. Wilmington, Del., 1964– .
EncyJud	Roth, C., *et al.*, eds. *Encyclopedia Judaica*. 16 vols. New York, 1971–72.
EOS	*Eos. Commentarii Societatis Philologae Polonorum*
ETL	*Ephemerides theologicae lovanienses*
EvT	*Evangelische Theologie*
Exégèse biblique et judaïsme	Ménard, J.-E., ed. *Exégèse biblique et judaïsme*. Strasbourg, 1973.
ExpT²	*Expository Times*

Falasha Anthology	Leslau, W. *Falasha Anthology*. Yale Judaica Series 6; New Haven, 1951.
FBBS	Facet Books, Biblical Series
FGH	Jacoby, F., ed. *Fragmente der griechischen Historiker*. 3 vols. Leiden, 1923– .
FRLANT	Forschungen zur Religion und Literatur des Alten und Neuen Testaments
GamPseud	Hammershaimb, E., *et al.*, eds. *De Gammeltestamentlige Pseudepigrapher*. 2 vols. Copenhagen, 1953–76.
GCS	Die griechischen christlichen Schriftsteller der ersten drei Jahrhunderte
GDBL	Nielsen, E., and B. Noack, eds. *Gads Danske Bibel Leksikon*. 2 vols. Copenhagen, 1965–66.
Geschichte [Baumstark]	Baumstark, A. *Geschichte der syrischen Literatur mit Ausschluss der christlichpalästinensischen Texte*. Bonn, 1922.
Geschichte [Graf]	Graf, G. "Apokryphen und Pseudepigraphen," *Geschichte der christlichen arabischen Literatur*. Studi e Testi 118; Vatican, 1944; vol. 1, pp. 196–297.
GLAJJ	Stern, M., ed. *Greek and Latin Authors on Jews and Judaism*. Vol. 1: *From Herodotus to Plutarch*. Jerusalem, 1974.
GNT	Grundrisse zum Neuen Testament
Goodenough Festschrift	Neusner, J., ed. *Religions in Antiquity: Essays in Memory of Erwin Ramsdell Goodenough*. Sup *Numen* 14; Leiden, 1968.
Gottesvolk	Janssen, E. *Das Gottesvolk und seine Geschichte: Geschichtsbild und Selbstverständnis im palästinensischen Schrifttum von Jesus Sirach bis Jehuda ha-Nasi*. Neukirchen-Vluyn, 1971.
Gunkel Festschrift	Schmidt, H., ed. *Eucharistērion: Studien zur Religion des Alten und Neuen Testaments*. H. Gunkel Festschrift. Part 2: *Zur Religion und Literatur des Neuen Testaments*. Göttingen, 1923.
Hastings' *DB*	Hastings, J., ed. *Dictionary of the Bible*, rev. ed. by F. C. Grant and H. H. Rowley. New York, 1963.
HAW	Handbuch der Altertumswissenschaft
HeyJ	*Heythrop Journal*
History [Pfeiffer]	Pfeiffer, R. H. *History of the New Testament Times with an Introduction to the Apocrypha*. New York, 1949.
History [Schürer]	Schürer, E. *A History of the Jewish People in the Time of Jesus Christ*. 5 vols., plus index, trans. J. MacPherson *et al*. Edinburgh, 1897–98.
History . . . The Time of the Apostles	Hausrath, A. *A History of New Testament Times: The Time of the Apostles*. 4 vols., trans. L. Huxley. London, 1895.
HNT	Handbuch zum Neuen Testament
HSW	Hennecke, E., W. Schneemelcher, and R. McL. Wilson, eds. *New Testament Apocrypha*. 2 vols. London, 1963–65.
HTKNT	Herders theologischer Kommentar zum Neuen Testament
HTR	*Harvard Theological Review*
HTS	Harvard Theological Studies

HUCA	*Hebrew Union College Annual*
IB	Buttrick, G. A., *et al.*, eds. *The Interpreter's Bible*. 12 vols. New York, 1952–57.
ICC	International Critical Commentary
IDB	Buttrick, G. A., *et al.*, eds. *The Interpreter's Dictionary of the Bible*. 4 vols. New York, 1962.
IDBS	Crim, K., *et al.*, eds. *The Interpreter's Dictionary of the Bible, Supplementary Volume*. Nashville, Tenn., 1976.
IEJ	*Israel Exploration Journal*
Int	*Interpretation*
Intr. to the Apoc.	Metzger, B. M. *An Introduction to the Apocrypha*. New York, 1957.
Introduction	Denis, A.-M. *Introduction aux pseudépigraphes grecs d'Ancien Testament*. SVTP 1; Leiden, 1970.
IOCB	Laymon, C. M., ed. *The Interpreter's One-Volume Commentary on the Bible*. New York, 1971.
ITQ	*Irish Theological Quarterly*
JA	*Journal asiatique*
JAAR	*Journal of the American Academy of Religion*
JAC	*Jahrbuch für Antike und Christentum*
JAL	Jewish Apocryphal Literature
JAOS	*Journal of the American Oriental Society*
JBC	Brown, R. E., J. A. Fitzmyer, and R. E. Murphy, eds. *The Jerome Biblical Commentary*. Englewood Cliffs, N.J., 1968.
JBL	*Journal of Biblical Literature*
JBLMS	Journal of Biblical Literature Monograph Series
JE	Singer, I., *et al.*, eds. *The Jewish Encyclopedia*. 12 vols. New York, London, 1901–6.
Jewish Symbols	Goodenough, E. R. *Jewish Symbols in the Greco-Roman Period*. 13 vols. New York, 1953–68.
JJS	*Journal of Jewish Studies*
JNES	*Journal of Near Eastern Studies*
JPOS	*Journal of the Palestine Oriental Society*
JQR	*Jewish Quarterly Review*
JRAS	*Journal of the Royal Asiatic Society*
JSHRZ	Kümmel, W. G., *et al. Jüdische Schriften aus hellenistisch-römischer Zeit*. Gütersloh, 1973– .
JSJ	*Journal for the Study of Judaism*
JSS	*Journal of Semitic Studies*
JThC	*Journal for Theology and the Church*
JTS	*Journal of Theological Studies*
Judaic Tradition	Glatzer, N. N. *The Judaic Tradition: Texts Edited and Introduced*. Boston, 1969.
Kommentar	Strack, H. L., and P. Billerbeck. *Kommentar zum Neuen Testament aus Talmud und Midrasch*. 5 vols. Munich, 1922–56.
KS	*Kirjath Sepher*
Kuhn Festschrift	Jeremias, G., H.-W. Kuhn, and H. Stegemann, eds. *Tradition und Glaube: Das frühe Christentum in seiner Umwelt. Festgabe für Karl Georg Kuhn zum 65. Geburtstag*. Göttingen, 1971.

Lampe	Lampe, G. W. H., ed. *A Patristic Greek Lexicon*. Oxford, 1961–68.
LAOT	James, M. R. *The Lost Apocrypha of the Old Testament*. TED; London, New York, 1920.
LCL	Loeb Classical Library
Legends	Ginzberg, L. *The Legends of the Jews*. 7 vols., trans. H. Szold. Philadelphia, 1909–38; repr. 1937–66.
Literatur und Religion des Frühjudentums	Maier, J., and J. Schreiner, eds. *Literatur und Religion des Frühjudentums*. Gütersloh, 1973.
LSJM	Liddell, H. G., and R. Scott. *A Greek-English Lexicon*, rev. by H. S. Jones and R. McKenzie. Oxford, 1940.
LTK²	Buchberger, M., J. Höfer, and K. Rahner, eds. *Lexikon für Theologie und Kirche*. 11 vols. Freiburg, 1957–67².
LUOS MS	Leeds University Oriental Society Monograph Series
MBPAR	Münchener Beiträge zur Papyrusforschung und Antiken Rechtsgeschichte
McCQ	*McCormick Quarterly*
MGWJ	*Monatsschrift für Geschichte und Wissenschaft des Judentums*
Missionsliteratur	Dalbert, P. *Die Theologie der hellenistisch-jüdischen Missionsliteratur unter Ausschluss von Philo und Josephus*. Hamburg-Volksdorf, 1954.
M. Smith Festschrift	Neusner, J., ed. *Christianity, Judaism and Other Greco-Roman Cults: Studies for Morton Smith at Sixty*. SJLA 12; Leiden, 1975.
NCCHS	Fuller, R. C., *et al.*, eds. *A New Catholic Commentary on Holy Scripture*. London, 1969.
NCE	McDonald, W. J., *et al.*, eds. *New Catholic Encyclopedia*. 15 vols. New York, 1967– .
NEB	New English Bible
NHC	Nag Hammadi Codex
NHL	Nag Hammadi Library
NHS	Nag Hammadi Studies
NovT	*Novum Testamentum*
*NovT*Sup	*Novum Testamentum*, Supplements
NTS	*New Testament Studies*
NTTS	New Testament Tools and Studies
OCA	*Orientalia Christiana Analeta*
Or	*Orientalia*
OrChr	*Orientalia Christiana*
OrSyr	*L'Orient syrien*
OTS	Oudtestamentische Studiën
Pauly-Wissowa	Wissowa, G., *et al.*, eds. *Paulys Real-Encyclopädie der classischen Altertumswissenschaft*, neue Bearbeitung. Stuttgart, Munich, 1893–1972.
PCB	Peake, A. S., M. Black, and H. H. Rowley, eds. *Peake's Commentary on the Bible*. London, New York, 1962.
PEQ	*Palestine Exploration Quarterly*
PETSE	Papers of the Estonian Theological Society in Exile
Peshitta	*The Old Testament in Syriac According to the Peshitta Version*. Leiden, 1966– .
PG	Patrologiae graecae, ed. J. Migne
PIOL	Publications de l'institut orientaliste de Louvain

PL	Patrologiae latinae, ed. J. Migne
PMR	Charlesworth, J. H. *The Pseudepigrapha and Modern Research.* SCS 7; Missoula, Mont., 1976.
Pseud I	Fritz, K. von, ed. *Pseudepigrapha 1: Pseudopythagorica, lettres de Platon, littérature pseudépigraphe juive.* Entretiens sur l'antiquité classique 18; Geneva, 1972.
Pseudépigraphes	Philonenko, M., *et al. Pseudépigraphes de l'Ancien Testament et manuscrits de la mer morte.* Cahiers de la *RHPR* 41; Paris, 1967.
PVTG	Pseudepigrapha Veteris Testamenti Graece
RAC	Klauser, T., *et al.*, eds. *Reallexikon für Antike und Christentum: Sachwörterbuch zur Auseinandersetzung des Christentums mit der antiken Welt.* Stuttgart, 1950– .
RB	*Revue biblique*
RBen	*Revue bénédictine*
RechBib	Recherches bibliques
REJ	*Revue des études juives*
RESl	*Revue des études slaves*
RevistB	*Revista bíblica*
RevSem	*Revue sémitique*
*RGG*³	Galling, K., *et al.*, eds. *Die Religion in Geschichte und Gegenwart.* 6 vols. plus index. Tübingen, 1957–65³.
RHPR	*Revue d'histoire et de philosophie religieuse*
RHR	*Revue de l'histoire des religions*
Riessler	Riessler, P. *Altjüdisches Schrifttum ausserhalb der Bibel.* Heidelberg, 1927; repr. 1966.
RivB	*Rivista biblica*
ROC	*Revue de l'orient chrétien*
RQ	*Revue de Qumran*
RSR	*Recherches de science religieuse*
RSV	Revised Standard Version
RTP	*Revue de théologie et de philosophie*
Sacramentum Mundi	Rahner, K., *et al.*, eds. *Sacramentum Mundi: An Encyclopedia of Theology.* 6 vols. New York, 1968–70.
SBFLA	*Studii biblici franciscani liber annuus*
SBLDS	Society of Biblical Literature Dissertation Series
SBLMS	Society of Biblical Literature Monograph Series
SBL 1971 Seminar Papers	*The Society of Biblical Literature One Hundred Seventh Annual Meeting Seminar Papers—28–31 October 1971, Regency Hyatt House—Atlanta, Ga.* 2 vols. Missoula, Mont., 1971.
SBL 1972 Seminar Papers	McGaughy, L. C., ed. *The Society of Biblical Literature One Hundred Eighth Annual Meeting Book of Seminar Papers: Friday–Tuesday, 1–5 September 1972, Century Plaza Hotel—Los Angeles, Ca.* 2 vols. Missoula, Mont., 1972.
SBL 1974 Seminar Papers	MacRae, G., ed. *Society of Biblical Literature 1974 Seminar Papers: One Hundred Tenth Annual Meeting, 24–27 October 1974, Washington Hilton, Washington, D.C.* 2 vols. Cambridge, Mass., 1974.
SBT	Studies in Biblical Theology

SC	Sources chrétiennes
ScEs	*Science et esprit*
SCS	Septuagint and Cognate Studies
SCS 2	Kraft, R. A., ed. *1972 Proceedings: International Organization for Septuagint and Cognate Studies and the Society of Biblical Literature Pseudepigrapha Seminar.* SCS 2; Missoula, Mont., 1972.
SCS 4	Nickelsburg, G. W. E. Jr., ed. *Studies on the Testament of Moses: Seminar Papers.* SCS 4; Cambridge, Mass., 1973.
SCS 5	Nickelsburg, G. W. E. Jr., ed. *Studies on the Testament of Joseph.* SCS 5; Missoula, Mont., 1975.
SCS 6	Nickelsburg, G. W. E. Jr., ed. *Studies on the Testament of Abraham.* SCS 6; Missoula, Mont., 1976.
SEA	*Svensk exegetisk Årsbok*
Sem	*Semitica*
Septuaginta	Rahlfs, A., ed. *Septuaginta: Id est Vetus Testamentum graece iuxta LXX interpretes.* 2 vols. Stuttgart, 1935; repr. 1965.
SJLA	Studies in Judaism in Late Antiquity
SJT	*Scottish Journal of Theology*
SNTS MS	*Studiorum Novi Testamenti Societas* Monograph Series
SPB	Studia postbiblica
ST	*Studia Theologica*
StANT	Studien zum Alten und Neuen Testament
Studien	Eltester, W., ed. *Studien zu den Testamenten der zwölf Patriarchen.* BZNW 36; Berlin, 1969.
Studies on T12P	Jonge, M. de. *Studies on the Testaments of the Twelve Patriarchs: Text and Interpretation.* SVTP 3; Leiden, 1975.
Sup *Numen*	Supplements to *Numen*
SVTP	Studia in Veteris Testamenti Pseudepigrapha
T&S	Texts and Studies
T&T	Texts and Translations
TBT	*The Bible Today*
TDNT	Kittel, G., ed. *Theological Dictionary of the New Testament.* 10 vols., trans. G. W. Bromiley. Grand Rapids, Mich., London, 1964–76.
TED	Translations of Early Documents
ThĒE	Martinos, A., ed. *Thrēskeutikē kai Ēthikē Enkuklopaideia.* 12 vols. Athens, 1962–68.
ThRu	*Theologische Rundschau*
TLZ	*Theologische Literaturzeitung*
TQ	*Theologische Quartalschrift*
TU	Texte und Untersuchungen
TWAT	Botterweck, G. J., and H. Ringgren, eds. *Theologisches Wörterbuch zum Alten Testament.* Stuttgart, 1970– .
TZ	*Theologische Zeitschrift*
USQR	*Union Seminar Quarterly Review*
VC	*Vigiliae christianae*
VT	*Vetus Testamentum*

*VT*Sup 22	Boer, P. A. H. de, ed. *Congress Volume: Uppsala 1971.* Supplements to *VT* 22; Leiden, 1972.
Widengren Festschrift	Bergman, J., *et al.*, eds. *Ex Orbe Religionum: Studia Geo Widengren.* 2 vols. Studies in the History of Religions 21, 22; Leiden, 1972.
WUNT	Wissenschaftliche Untersuchungen zum Neuen Testament
WZHalle	*Wissenschaftliche Zeitschrift der Martin-Luther-Universität, Halle-Wittenberg. Gesellschafts- und Sprachwissenschaftliche Reihe*
WZJena	*Wissenschaftliche Zeitschrift der Friedrich-Schiller-Universität, Jena. Gesellschafts- und Sprachwissenschaftliche Reihe*
WZKM	*Wiener Zeitschrift für die Kunde des Morgenlandes*
ZAW	*Zeitschrift für die alttestamentliche Wissenschaft*
ZDMG	*Zeitschrift der deutschen morgenländischen Gesellschaft*
ZKG	*Zeitschrift für Kirchengeschichte*
ZNW	*Zeitschrift für die neutestamentliche Wissenschaft und die Kunde der älteren Kirche*
ZPEB	Tenney, M. C., ed. *The Zondervan Pictorial Encyclopedia of the Bible.* 5 vols. Grand Rapids, Mich., 1975.
ZRGG	*Zeitschrift für Religions- und Geistesgeschichte*
ZTK	*Zeitschrift für Theologie und Kirche*
ZWT	*Zeitschrift für wissenschaftliche Theologie*

Additional Abbreviations

Ar.	Arabic	lit.	literally
Aram.	Aramaic	LXX	Septuagint
Arm.	Armenian	MS(S)	Manuscript(s)
BM	British Museum	MT	Masoretic Text
c.	circa	n. nn.	note(s)
cf.	compare	NAB	New American Bible
ch(s).	chapter(s)	NEB	New English Bible
col(s).	column(s)	NT	New Testament
Cop.	Coptic	OT	Old Testament
ET	English translation	pt(s).	part(s)
Eth.	Ethiopic	rec(s).	recension(s)
fol(s).	folio(s)	RSV	Revised Standard Version
Gk.	Greek	Russ.	Russian
GNMM	Good News for Modern Man	SBL	Society of Biblical Literature
Heb.	Hebrew	Slav.	Slavic
JB	Jerusalem Bible	SV	Standard Version
Kar.	Karshuni	Syr.	Syriac
KJV	King James Version	Vat.	Vatican
l. ll.	line(s)	vs(s).	verse(s)
Lat.	Latin		

II. ANCIENT DOCUMENTS

Bible and Apocrypha

Gen	Genesis	Tob	Tobit
Ex	Exodus	Jdt	Judith
Lev	Leviticus	AddEsth	Additions to Esther
Num	Numbers	WisSol	Wisdom of Solomon
Deut	Deuteronomy	Sir	Sirach
Josh	Joshua	1Bar	1 Baruch
Judg	Judges	LetJer	Letter of Jeremiah
Ruth	Ruth	PrAzar	Prayer of Azariah
1Sam	1 Samuel	Sus	Susanna
2Sam	2 Samuel	Bel	Bel and the Dragon
1Kgs	1 Kings	1Mac	1 Maccabees
2Kgs	2 Kings	2Mac	2 Maccabees
1Chr	1 Chronicles	Mt	Matthew
2Chr	2 Chronicles	Mk	Mark
Ezra	Ezra	Lk	Luke
Neh	Nehemiah	Jn	John
Esth	Esther	Acts	Acts
Job	Job	Rom	Romans
Ps(s)	Psalms	1Cor	1 Corinthians
Prov	Proverbs	2Cor	2 Corinthians
Eccl (Qoh)	Ecclesiastes	Gal	Galatians
Song	Song of Songs	Eph	Ephesians
Isa	Isaiah	Phil	Philippians
Jer	Jeremiah	Col	Colossians
Lam	Lamentations	1Thes	1 Thessalonians
Ezek	Ezekiel	2Thes	2 Thessalonians
Dan	Daniel	1Tim	1 Timothy
Hos	Hosea	2Tim	2 Timothy
Joel	Joel	Tit	Titus
Amos	Amos	Phlm	Philemon
Obad	Obadiah	Heb	Hebrews
Jonah	Jonah	Jas	James
Micah	Micah	1Pet	1 Peter
Nah	Nahum	2Pet	2 Peter
Hab	Habakkuk	1Jn	1 John
Zeph	Zephaniah	2Jn	2 John
Hag	Haggai	3Jn	3 John
Zech	Zechariah	Jude	Jude
Mal	Malachi	Rev	Revelation
2Ezra	2 Ezra		

Pseudepigrapha

ApAb	Apocalypse of Abraham
TAb	Testament of Abraham
ApAdam	Apocalypse of Adam
TAdam	Testament of Adam
LAE	Life of Adam and Eve
Ah	Ahiqar
AnonSam	An Anonymous Samaritan Text

LetAris	Letter of Aristeas
ArisEx	Aristeas the Exegete
Aristob	Aristobulus
Art	Artapanus
2Bar	2 (Syriac Apocalypse of) Baruch
3Bar	3 (Greek Apocalypse of) Baruch
4Bar	4 Baruch
CavTr	Cave of Treasures
ClMal	Cleodemus Malchus
ApDan	Apocalypse of Daniel
Dem	Demetrius
ElMod	Eldad and Modad
ApEl	Apocalypse of Elijah
HebApEl	Hebrew Apocalypse of Elijah
1En	1 (Ethiopic Apocalypse of) Enoch
2En	2 (Slavonic Apocalypse of) Enoch
3En	3 (Hebrew Apocalypse of) Enoch
Eup	Eupolemus
Ps-Eup	Pseudo-Eupolemus
ApocEzek	Apocryphon of Ezekiel
ApEzek	Apocalypse of Ezekiel
EzekTrag	Ezekiel the Tragedian
4Ezra	4 Ezra
GkApEzra	Greek Apocalypse of Ezra
QuesEzra	Questions of Ezra
RevEzra	Revelation of Ezra
VisEzra	Vision of Ezra
HecAb	Hecataeus of Abdera
Ps-Hec	Pseudo-Hecataeus
HelSynPr	Hellenistic Synagogal Prayers
THez	Testament of Hezekiah
FrgsHistWrks	Fragments of Historical Works
TIsaac	Testament of Isaac
AscenIs	Ascension of Isaiah
MartIs	Martyrdom of Isaiah
VisIs	Vision of Isaiah
LadJac	Ladder of Jacob
PrJac	Prayer of Jacob
TJac	Testament of Jacob
JanJam	Jannes and Jambres
TJob	Testament of Job
JosAsen	Joseph and Asenath
HistJos	History of Joseph
PrJos	Prayer of Joseph
Jub	Jubilees
LAB	*Liber Antiquitatum Biblicarum*
LosTr	The Lost Tribes
3Mac	3 Maccabees
4Mac	4 Maccabees
5Mac	5 Maccabees
PrMan	Prayer of Manasseh
SyrMen	Syriac Menander

ApMos	Apocalypse of Moses
AsMos	Assumption of Moses
PrMos	Prayer of Moses
TMos	Testament of Moses
BkNoah	Book of Noah
Ps-Orph	Pseudo-Orpheus
PJ	*Paraleipomena Jeremiou*
PhEPoet	Philo the Epic Poet
Ps-Philo	Pseudo-Philo
Ps-Phoc	Pseudo-Phocylides
FrgsPoetWrks	Fragments of Poetical Works
LivPro	Lives of the Prophets
HistRech	History of the Rechabites
ApSedr	Apocalypse of Sedrach
TrShem	Treatise of Shem
SibOr	Sibylline Oracles
OdesSol	Odes of Solomon
PssSol	Psalms of Solomon
TSol	Testament of Solomon
5ApocSyrPss	Five Apocryphal Syriac Psalms
Thal	Thallus
Theod	Theodotus
T12P	Testaments of the Twelve Patriarchs
TReu	Testament of Reuben
TSim	Testament of Simeon
TLevi	Testament of Levi
TJud	Testament of Judah
TIss	Testament of Issachar
TZeb	Testament of Zebulun
TDan	Testament of Dan
TNaph	Testament of Naphtali
TGad	Testament of Gad
TAsh	Testament of Asher
TJos	Testament of Joseph
TBenj	Testament of Benjamin
Vita	*Vita Adae et Evae*
ApZeph	Apocalypse of Zephaniah
ApZos	Apocalypse of Zosimus

Other Writings

Dead Sea Scrolls
All abbreviations are according to J. A. Fitzmyer, S.J. *The Dead Sea Scrolls: Major Publications and Tools for Study.* SBL Sources for Biblical Study 8; Missoula, Mont., 1975; expanded ed., 1977.

Philo
All abbreviations are according to *Studia Philonica* with the exception that titles of Philonic treatises are italicized.

Josephus

Ant	*Jewish Antiquities*
Apion	*Against Apion*
Life	*Life of Josephus*
War	*Jewish Wars*

New Testament Apocrypha and Pseudepigrapha

EBar	Epistle of Barnabas
GBart	Gospel of Bartholomew
QuesBart	Questions of Bartholomew
1Clem	1 Clement
2Clem	2 Clement
PseudClemRec	Pseudo-Clementine Recognitions
Did	Didache
GEbion	Gospel of the Ebionites
GEgyp	Gospel of the Egyptians
GHeb	Gospel of the Hebrews
ShepHerm	Shepherd of Hermes
ApIoan	*Apokalypsis tou hagiou Iōannou*
ProtJames	Protoevangelium of James
ActsJn	Acts of John
GMatthias	Gospel of Matthias
GNic	Gospel of Nicodemus
ActsPaul	Acts of Paul
ApPaul	Apocalypse of Paul
ApPet	Apocalypse of Peter
GPet	Gospel of Peter
PrPet	Preaching of Peter
ActsPhil	Acts of Philip
GPhil	Gospel of Philip
RevSteph	Revelation of Stephen
ActsThom	Acts of Thomas
ApThom	Apocalypse of Thomas
GThom	Gospel of Thomas
GTr	Gospel of Truth
ApVirg	Apocalypse of the Virgin

Early Fathers

AdvHaer	Epiphanius, *Adversus haereses*
AposCon	Apostolic Constitutions

LIST OF ABBREVIATIONS

Nidd	Niddah
NumR	Bemidbar Rabbah
OM	Ozar Midrashim
Pes	Pesaḥim
PetMos	Petiroth Moshe
PR	Pesikta Rabbati
PRE	Pirke de-Rabbi Eliezer
RH	Rosh Hashanah
RuthR	Rut Rabbah
Sanh	Sanhedrin
SER	Seder Eliyahu Rabbah
Shab	Shabbat
SifDeut	Sifre Deuteronomy
SongR	Šir Hašširim Rabbah
Soṭ	Soṭah
Sukk	Sukkah
t. (before a rabbinic text)	Tosephta
Ta'an	Ta'anit
TargOnk	Targum Onkelos
TargYer	Targum Yerushalmi
TarJon	Targum Jonathan
Ter	Terumot
y. (before a rabbinic text)	Jerusalem Talmud
Yad	Yadayim
Yeb	Yebamot
Zeb	Zebahim

Rabbinics

THE OLD TESTAMENT PSEUDEPIGRAPHA

DOCUMENTS

APOCALYPTIC LITERATURE
AND RELATED WORKS

INTRODUCTION

J. H. CHARLESWORTH

Apocalyptic—from the Greek word *apokalupsis* meaning "revelation" or "disclosure"—is an adjective that has been used to describe both a certain type of literature and a special feature of religions in late antiquity. Unfortunately there is presently no consensus regarding the precise definition of this adjective; confusion sometimes arises because it is employed frequently in contradictory ways. Some scholars have argued that "apocalyptic" denotes a specific type of revelatory literature that has a narrative structure and unique characteristics, such as pseudonymity, bizarre images, and visions of the end of time or of the numerous heavens; according to them apocalyptic literature tends to represent a well-defined literary *genre*. Other scholars—more impressed by the different features of the documents that are "apocalypses"—have claimed that "apocalyptic" does not denote a specific genre but a religious bearing that is preoccupied by the approach of the end of all normal time and history.

Some specialists have written about apocalyptic religion as if it were a *movement*. The dissimilarities and contradictions among the apocalyptic writings—especially the different attitudes toward revolution and the contrasting descriptions of the various heavens and Paradise—should caution us against perceiving late biblical religion as if it were a coherent uniform movement.

The Old Testament contains only one apocalypse: the Book of Daniel. The New Testament adds only one more: the Book of Revelation. These writings were selected from numerous apocalypses that were popular during the time when the canons of the Old Testament and New Testament were still open. Both of the canons, moreover, contain important apocalyptic sections (viz. Ezek 40–48; Isa 24–27, 34f., 56–66; Zech 9–14; Mk 13 and par., 1Thes 4; 1Cor 15). The present edition of the Pseudepigrapha includes nineteen documents that are apocalypses or related documents. In the past, the definition of "apocalyptic" was derived from a study of only some of the extant apocalypses, especially "the Apocalypse," the Book of Revelation. It will be easier now to perceive more adequately the richness of apocalyptic literature and the extent of early Jewish and Christian apocalyptic ideas and apocalyptic religion. The possible importance of apocalyptic Judaism to earliest Christianity is demonstrated by the claim by some New Testament specialists and Christian theologians that apocalyptic Judaism was the mother of all Christian theology.

In assessing the nature and importance of the apocalypses translated below, the reader should examine also other pseudepigrapha that contain apocalyptic sections, especially the Testaments of the Twelve Patriarchs, the Testament of Abraham, the

Testament of Moses, Jubilees, the Martyrdom and Ascension of Isaiah, and 4 Baruch. It is important also to consult the Dead Sea Scrolls, many of which are apocalyptic writings, and the apocalypses and apocalyptically inspired writings in the New Testament Apocrypha and Pseudepigrapha.

A final caveat seems necessary. The presence of the term "apocalypse" in the title of a document does not qualify it immediately as an apocalypse; likewise the absence of such a term does not exclude it from being an apocalypse. Sometimes these titles were added by individuals far removed chronologically and geographically from the authors, and some pseudepigrapha bear discrepant titles; for example, the History of the Rechabites in some writings is titled the Testament of Zosimus, in others the Apocalypse of Zosimus; the Life of Adam and Eve is essentially the same as the Apocalypse of Moses (an inapt title for the story of Adam and Eve). The various pseudepigrapha must not be forced into categories developed by modern analysis; the following collection is arranged primarily for convenience and to denote general literary similarities and differences.

CONTENTS

1 (Ethiopic Apocalypse of) ENOCH

(Second Century B.C. – First Century A.D.)

A NEW TRANSLATION AND INTRODUCTION
BY E. ISAAC

The Ethiopic Book of Enoch (Hēnok), also known as 1 Enoch, is the oldest of the three pseudepigrapha attributed to Enoch, the seventh descendant of Adam and Eve, the first man and woman. According to Genesis 5:24, "Enoch walked with God. Then he vanished because God took him." This tradition of Enoch's spiritual relocation gave rise to many haggadic stories, including one that Enoch, son of Jared, when he was taken away by God, saw the secrets of the mysteries of the universe, the future of the world, and the predetermined course of human history.[1]

The first part of the book contains an introduction (chs. 1–5), which portrays the eschatological era and the final judgment of the righteous and the wicked, and a narrative (chs. 6–36) which concerns the fallen angels, their intercourse with women (Gen 6:1–4), their corruption of all men, Enoch's unsuccessful intercession on their behalf, a prediction of their doom, and various visions of Enoch during a tour of the earth, Sheol, and heaven. The second part—the Similitudes, or the so-called "parables" (chs. 37–71)—deals respectively with the coming judgment of the righteous and the wicked; the Messiah, the Son of Man, the Righteous One, and the Elect One; the exposition of additional heavenly secrets; the measuring of Paradise; the resurrection of the righteous; and the punishment of the fallen angels. The third part, an astrological treatise (chs. 72–82), concerns the reckoning of time by the sun, the nature of the solar year of 364 days, and the cosmic disorders of the last days. The fourth part, the Dream Visions (chs. 83–90), consists of two visions concerning the future history (from Enoch's antediluvian perspective) of the world and Israel: the coming punishment of sinful society by the Deluge, and the history of Israel from Adam to the Maccabeans presented with bold symbolic imagery. Oxen symbolize the patriarchs; sheep, the faithful Israelites; beasts and birds of prey, the heathen oppressors of Israel; a great horned sheep, a rising Jewish leader; a white bull with great horns, the Messiah. There is also additional material on the fallen angels, the throne of judgment, and the new Jerusalem, together with Enoch's experience of his earlier visions. The fifth part (chs. 91–104), Enoch's testament, recapitulates the theme of the spiritual blessedness of the righteous and the sorrowful end of the sinners. Woes are pronounced upon the sinners, who are repeatedly identified with the exploitative wealthy and oppressive powers. This section, known particularly for its inclusion of the Apocalypse of Weeks (91:12–17 and 93:1–10), summarizes the events that would unfold upon the earth during ten (actually seven and three respectively) consecutive world weeks. An appendix (chs. 105–8) contains fragments of independent works, especially from the Book of Noah (chs. 106f.), and an editor's conclusion.

---

[1] For other synopses of the narrative, see M. Rist, "Enoch, Book of," *IDB*, vol. 2, pp. 104f.; R. H. Charles, *The Book of Enoch*, pp. 22f.; R. H. Charles, *Religious Development Between the Old and the New Testaments* (New York, 1914) pp. 223–26. [I am most thankful to Professor O. Neugebauer of the Institute for Advanced Studies, Princeton, who kindly read my translation of 1En 72–82 (the astronomical section) and made some very valuable suggestions which have helped me to improve my presentation of this difficult part of the book, which contains so many textual corruptions. I also thank Mr. E. G. Martin, who has labored so long and carefully over my translation, and Professor J. H. Charlesworth for his improvements to the Introduction.]

Texts

1 Enoch is found complete only in the Ethiopic (Ge'ez) Version, for which more than forty manuscripts are known to exist as of this writing. However, fragments of the work are also found in Aramaic, Greek, and Latin.

1. *Aramaic:* Aramaic fragments of 1 Enoch were found at Qumran and have been recently published, together with a major study of the text and history of 1 Enoch.[2]

2. *Ethiopic:* As has been indicated above, the complete version of 1 Enoch is preserved only in Ethiopic. Below are a list of five major and important manuscripts, one of which (A) has been utilized as the base text of the present English translation, and another of which (C) has been used very extensively in the same work:

    A. Kebrän 9/II (Hammerschmidt—*Ṭānāsee* 9/II); fifteenth century.[3]

    B. Princeton Ethiopic 3 (Garrett collection—Isaac 3); eighteenth or nineteenth century.[4]

    C. EMML 2080; fifteenth (possibly 14th) century.[5]

    D. Abbadianus 55; possibly fifteenth century.[6]

    E. British Museum Orient 485 (Wright 6); first half of the sixteenth century.[7]

3. *Greek:* The Greek fragments are found principally in the following:

    a. Codex Panopolitanus (two 8th-cent. or later MSS, found in 1886–87 in a Christian grave in Akhmim, Egypt), containing 1 Enoch 1:1–32:6 (designated G^a in this work).

    b. Chronographia of Georgius Syncellus (c. 800), containing 1 Enoch 6:1–10:14; 15:8–16:1 (designated G^s in this work).

    c. Chester Beatty papyrus of 1 Enoch containing 97:6–104; 106f. (published by C. Bonner, *The Last Chapters of Enoch in Greek*) (designated G^p in this work).

    d. Vatican Greek MS 1809, containing 1 Enoch 89:42–49.

4. *Latin:* a Latin fragment, containing 1 Enoch 106:1–18, found in an eighth-century manuscript.[8]

Original language

Some scholars believe that the original language of 1 Enoch is Hebrew; others, however, think it is Aramaic; still others contend that the book, like Daniel, was composed partly in Hebrew and partly in Aramaic.[9] Recently there have been attempts either to counter[10] or to substantiate entirely[11] the Aramaic origin of the Ethiopic text. Neither theory provides wholly convincing arguments which may be accepted without reservations.

Our text of A shows an additional closeness between the Ethiopic and Greek versions, but not sufficient to rule out the possibility that a major portion of the Ethiopic text of 1 Enoch was of Aramaic origin. Moreover, Halévy's argument that portions of the Ethiopic text derive ultimately from a Hebrew original has not been disproved. Consequently, the thesis that part of 1 Enoch, like the canonical Daniel, was composed partially in Aramaic and partially in Hebrew has to be considered probable.

Date

1 Enoch is clearly composite, representing numerous periods and writers. Before the

[2] J. T. Milik and M. Black, *The Books of Enoch.*

[3] For a brief description of this MS see E. Hammerschmidt, *Äthiopische Handschriften vom Ṭānāsee* (Wiesbaden, 1973) pp. 107f.

[4] For a brief description of the MS see E. Isaac, *A Catalogue of Ethiopic (Ge'ez) Manuscripts in the Princeton University Library (Garrett Collection)* (Princeton Univ. Library, 1974) p. 3.

[5] A microfilm copy of this MS is preserved at St. John's University, Collegeville, Minnesota. There are two additional important MSS of the 17th cent. (EMML 4437 and EMML 4750) in the same collection, which the present author has investigated.

[6] See A. Antoine D'Abbadie, *Catalogue raisonné de manuscrits éthiopiens* (Paris, 1859) pp. 75f.

[7] See W. Wright, *Catalogue of the Ethiopic Manuscripts in the British Museum* (London, 1877) pp. 7f.

[8] Discovered by M. R. James in 1893 in the British Museum and published in *Apocrypha Anecdota* (T&S 2.3; Cambridge, 1893; repr. 1967) pp. 146–50.

[9] See J. Halévy, "Recherches sur la langue de la rédaction primitive du livre d'Hénoch," *JA* 6.9 (1867) 352–95; R. H. Charles, *The Ethiopic Version of the Book of Enoch,* p. xxvii; N. Schmidt, "The Original Language of the Parables of Enoch," in *Old Testament and Semitic Studies in Memory of W. R. Harper* (Chicago, 1908) vol. 2, pp. 329–49.

[10] M. Black, "The Fragments of the Aramaic Enoch from Qumran" in W. C. van Unnik, ed., *La littérature juive entre Tenach et Mischna* (Leiden, 1974) pp. 15–28.

[11] E. Ullendorff, "An Aramaic 'Vorlage' of the Ethiopic Text of Enoch," *Atti del convegno internazionale di studi ~ici* (Rome, 1960) pp. 259–67.

discovery of fragments of 1 Enoch among the Dead Sea Scrolls, the following outline of sections and their dates was essentially the consensus of critical scholars:[12]

1. Apocalypse of Weeks	91:12–17; 93:1–10	early pre-Maccabean
2. Fragments of Enochic Visions	12–16	early pre-Maccabean
3. Fragments of the Book of Noah	6–11; 106f. cf. 54:7–55:2; 60; 65–69:25	late pre-Maccabean
4. Independent Fragment	105	? pre-Maccabean
5. Dream Visions	83–90	c. 165–161 B.C.
6. Book of Heavenly Luminaries	72–82	c. 110 B.C.
7. Similitudes	37–71	c. 105–64 B.C.
8. Later Additions to Dream Visions	91:1–11, 18, 19; 92; 94–104	c. 105–104 B.C
9. Introductory Chapters	1–5	late pre-Christian

The discovery of these fragments of 1 Enoch has awakened new interest in the structure and dating of 1 Enoch. Following to some extent the former views that this work is a collection of independent writings, Milik has argued for the categorization of the Ethiopic version into five primary books with the last chapter being taken as a much later addition.[13] These are:

1. The Book of the Watchers (1–36)
2. The Book of the Similitudes (37–71)
3. The Book of Astronomical Writings (72–82)
4. The Book of Dream Visions (83–90)
5. The Book of the Epistle of Enoch (91–107)

Milik argues for a pre-Christian Qumran Enochic Pentateuch which contained a much longer version of the astrological writings, and, most importantly, instead of the Similitudes, another work entitled the Book of Giants.[14] He bases his argument on the fact that fragments of only four of the five constituent parts of the Ethiopic Enoch have been discovered at Qumran. No fragment from the Similitudes has been recovered.

Milik argues that by the year A.D. 400 the Book of Giants as in the Qumran Aramaic Enoch had been replaced by the late Christian work, the Similitudes, in a new Greek Enochic Pentateuch. This hypothesis is not supported by any solid evidence and has been subjected to serious criticism, in particular by the members of the *SNTS* Pseudepigrapha Seminar which met in 1977 in Tübingen and in 1978 in Paris.[15] The consensus of the members was that the Similitudes were Jewish and dated from the first century A.D. At these meetings, it was also agreed that Milik should have worked more directly with the Ethiopic evidence. Unfortunately, he took Charles's dated text and translation at face value and incorrectly assumed that all Ethiopic manuscripts of 1 Enoch are very recent, except possibly a fifteenth-century text (Charles's u—Abbadianus 55). We now have at least three definitely fifteenth-century Ethiopic manuscripts, and it seems probable that even earlier ones may be discovered. Indeed, one of the readings in the fifteenth-century manuscript used herein as a base text casts serious doubts on one of Milik's arguments for the late date of the Similitudes. Milik has argued that the reference to angels flying "with wings" (1En 61:1) points to a post-Christian period for the composition of the Similitudes. Our manuscript does not support him; it has no reference to angels flying "with wings" (see translation and n. below). Milik is correct that his text of 61:1 is late; he failed to see, however, that the late part is a late variant. In conclusion, I am convinced that 1 Enoch already contained the Similitudes by the end of the first century A.D.

Provenance

We are not certain about the city or place in which 1 Enoch was, or its constituent parts

---

[12] Cf. R. H. Charles, "The Book of Enoch," in *APOT*, vol. 2, pp. 170f.

[13] Cf. J. T. Milik, *HTR* 64 (1971) 333–78. Also see Milik, *The Books of Enoch*, pp. 4–135.

[14] This work, believed to have been in circulation among the Manicheans, has been recovered from various fragments by W. B. Henning. See "The Book of Giants," *BSOAS* 11 (1943) 52–74.

[15] See J. H. Charlesworth, *NTS* 25 (1979) 315–23: M. A. Knibb, "The Date of the Parables of Enoch: A Critical Review," *NTS* 25 (1979) 345–59; C. L. Mearns, "Dating the Similitudes of Enoch," *NTS* 25 (1979) 360–69.

were, composed. However, it is clear that the work originated in Judea and was in use at Qumran before the beginning of the Christian period.

The evidence concerning the origin of the Ethiopic version of 1 Enoch is also lacking. We can be relatively certain that the version was produced in Ethiopia during the earliest period of Ethiopic literature (c. A.D. 350–650). However, this was a time of extensive translating and copying by Christian scribes in Ethiopia, and exact dates and cities are unknown.

Historical importance

Information regarding the usage and importance of the work in the Jewish and Christian communities, other than the Ethiopian Church, is sparse. It is difficult, therefore, to understand its exact origin. It seems clear, nonetheless, that 1 Enoch was well known to many Jews, particularly the Essenes, and early Christians, notably the author of Jude. The earliest portions of the work originated probably in a proto-Essene milieu; the latter sections perhaps in a setting quite different from Qumran Essenism.

1 Enoch reflects the historical events immediately preceding and following the Maccabean Revolt. More important, however, is the light it throws upon early Essene theology and upon earliest Christianity. It was used by the authors of Jubilees, the Testaments of the Twelve Patriarchs, the Assumption of Moses, 2 Baruch, and 4 Ezra. Some New Testament authors seem to have been acquainted with the work, and were influenced by it, including Jude, who quotes it explicitly (1:14f.). At any rate, it is clear that Enochic concepts are found in various New Testament books, including the Gospels and Revelation.

1 Enoch played a significant role in the early Church; it was used by the authors of the Epistle of Barnabas, the Apocalypse of Peter, and a number of apologetic works. Many Church Fathers, including Justin Martyr, Irenaeus, Origen, and Clement of Alexandria, either knew 1 Enoch or were inspired by it. Among those who were familiar with 1 Enoch, Tertullian had an exceptionally high regard for it. But, beginning in the fourth century, the book came to be regarded with disfavor and received negative reviews from Augustine, Hilary, and Jerome. Thereafter, with the exception of a few extracts made by Georgius Syncellus, a learned monk of the eighth century, and the Greek fragments found in a Christian grave in Egypt (c. A.D. 800), 1 Enoch ceased to be appreciated except in Ethiopia. The relegation of 1 Enoch to virtual oblivion by medieval minds should not diminish its significance for Christian origins; few other apocryphal books so indelibly marked the religious history and thought of the time of Jesus.

The interest in 1 Enoch in Ethiopia began with its initial translation and has continued thereafter. During the earliest period of Ethiopic literature many biblical, apocryphal, pseudepigraphical, and distinctly Christian works were translated into Ethiopic (Ge'ez) and copied extensively by scribes. Most of these early copies probably perished during the various periods of political upheavals that took place in Ethiopia (c. A.D. 950, c. A.D. 1270, or c. A.D. 1527–43). Thus, most scholars take for granted that no manuscripts of this early period actually exist; nevertheless, it is premature to dismiss the possibility at this time. Although research in Ethiopian studies in general is quite advanced, research into manuscripts and manuscript collections found in Ethiopian monasteries and churches is still at an elementary stage. As of now, our three oldest manuscripts of 1 Enoch date from the fifteenth century.

In the early seventeenth century, some European scholars thought that a version of 1 Enoch which was identical with the one quoted by Jude and early Church Fathers existed in Ethiopia. A learned Capuchin monk was believed to have brought to Europe a copy of the work, which passed into the possession of Nicolas Claude Fabri, the Seigneur of Peiresc (1580–1637). This manuscript, which aroused great excitement in Europe, drew the attention of the first great European Ethiopic scholar, Ludolfus Hiob, who traced it to the Bibliotheca Regia in Paris in 1683. He was disappointed to learn that the manuscript was not of 1 Enoch but that of an unknown Ethiopic work called the Book of the Mysteries of Heaven and Earth. It took another century before copies of 1 Enoch finally arrived in Europe. They were brought in 1773 by J. Bruce, the adventurous Scottish traveler to Africa. Nothing occurred until 1800, when Silvestre de Sacy, in his "Notice sur le livre d'Hénoch" (in *Magazine encyclopédique* 6/1, p. 382), first published excerpts from the book together with Latin translations of chapters 1, 2, 5–16, and 22–32. In 1821 Lawrence issued the first English version of the work. In 1853 Dillmann published a translation which aroused much interest in the work.

Theological importance

1 Enoch helps clarify the rich complexities of both intertestamental Jewish thought and
early Christian theology. In this brief introduction it is only possible to sketch a few of 1
Enoch's many ideas, motifs, symbolisms, and important theological concepts.

The God of 1 Enoch is the righteous and just God of the Old Testament; he is the Creator
of the world, the holy lawgiver, the dispenser of history, and the ultimate judge of all.

Genesis 6:1–4 alludes to the sons of God who had intercourse with the daughters of the
people. 1 Enoch transforms this idea into a theology of fallen angels, who consorted with
women and produced giants who sinned against the people. They corrupted the people
through the instructions in forbidden sciences like making arms, cosmetics, precious metals.
Enoch's intercession on behalf of the fallen angels fails; he is instructed, on the contrary,
to predict their final doom (12—16). Allusions to the legend of the fallen angels occur
elsewhere in Jewish writings (viz. Jub; Sir 16:7; CD 2.14–3.13; 4Q 180f.; and rabbinic
Midrashim).[16]

One of the extensively discussed concepts in 1 Enoch, particularly by students of New
Testament theology, is that of the heavenly Messiah (45–57). The Messiah in 1 Enoch,
called the Righteous One, and the Son of Man, is depicted as a pre-existent heavenly being
who is resplendent and majestic, possesses all dominion, and sits on his throne of glory
passing judgment upon all mortal and spiritual beings.

This description of the Messiah is placed in the Similitudes in the context of reflections
upon the last judgment, the coming destruction of the wicked, and the triumph of the
righteous ones. This eschatological concept is the most prominent and recurring theme
throughout the whole book. The very introduction (1–5) opens with an announcement of the
final, coming punishment, the destruction of the wicked ones and the resurrection of the
righteous ones to an endless and sinless eternal life. Likewise, in the Dream Visions (83–90)
the same theme is recalled. In this case, the righteous dead, including converted gentiles,
will be resurrected, the Messiah will appear, his kingdom will be founded, and the new
Jerusalem established; on the other hand, the sinners, the fallen angels, including the apostate
Jews, will be judged. The last major section of 1 Enoch (91–105) is an admonition to
righteousness, for he predicts that the wicked shall be condemned to eternal punishment in
Sheol, whereas the righteous shall have a blessed resurrection to enjoy the bliss of heaven.

One of the central emphases of 1 Enoch is that sinners are economic exploiters, the
political oppressors, and the socially unjust people of this world. Thus, while 1 Enoch will
deepen our insights into and broaden our perspectives of intertestamental Jewish and early
Christian theology, it also will help us to appreciate the revolutionary mood of Jews and
their staunch opposition not only to Greek and Roman imperialism, but also to Jewish
aristocracy itself.

There is also a social concern behind 1 Enoch's computation of time and understanding
of the calendar. Time should be reckoned only by the sun, not by the moon as in the
Pharisaic lunar calendar. The author's solar year consists of 364 days, and not 365¼, a fact
of which he is also aware. The calendrical discussion is tied to a spiritual concern; in the
last days the sun, moon, stars, and earth will be disrupted in cosmic chaos.

Relation to biblical and apocryphal books

It should be evident from what has been said above that 1 Enoch is as dependent upon
the Old Testament as it is influential upon the New Testament and later extracanonical
literature. During the exilic and post-exilic periods, apocalyptic became a major trend in
Jewish thought. It was inherited by Christianity and remains an element in it to the present.
Apocalyptic is both prophetic and revelatory; in apocalyptic literature we find, on the one
hand, moral indignation about the present world, and, on the other, the foreboding predictions
of eschatological events and the ultimate destiny of the world.

Old Testament ideas and stories such as the account of the fallen angels, the Flood, the
history of Israel, the distinction between the righteous and the wicked, and the Messiah are
interpreted, elaborated, and presented through the paradigm of apocalyptic dualism, wherein

---

[16] Cf. D. Dimant, " 'The Fallen Angels' in the Dead Sea Scrolls and in the Apocryphal and Pseudepigraphic Books
Related to Them'' (Ph.D. thesis, Hebrew Univ., 1974).

sharp distinctions are drawn between the opposing cosmic powers of good and evil and between the present and coming ages. These concepts in 1 Enoch also permeate Jubilees, the Testaments of the Twelve Patriarchs, the Assumption of Moses, the Testament and Apocalypse of Abraham, 2 Baruch, and 4 Ezra. Likewise, even though Charles may have exaggerated when he claimed that "nearly all" the writers of the New Testament were familiar with 1 Enoch, there is no doubt that the New Testament world was influenced by its language and thought. It influenced Matthew, Luke, John, Acts, Romans, 1 and 2 Corinthians, Ephesians, Colossians, 1 and 2 Thessalonians, 1 Timothy, Hebrews, 1 John, Jude (which quotes it directly), and Revelation (with numerous points of contact). There is little doubt that 1 Enoch was influential in molding New Testament doctrines concerning the nature of the Messiah, the Son of Man, the messianic kingdom, demonology, the future, resurrection, final judgment, the whole eschatological theater, and symbolism. No wonder, therefore, that the book was highly regarded by many of the earliest apostolic and Church Fathers.

Cultural importance

1 Enoch, as we have seen, made an impact on early Christian thought and left its indelible mark upon the New Testament. It also contributes *indirectly* to our understanding of Western culture; however, inasmuch as it was altogether a lost book to the Western world until the last century, 1 Enoch played no role in, and made no contributions to, the development of the intellectual history of modern Western culture. On the other hand, it is hardly possible to understand any aspect of the religious tradition and thought of Ethiopia, the country in which it survived, without an understanding of it. No wonder that the indigenous Ethiopic Book of the Mysteries of Heaven and Earth created such a sensation in seventeenth-century Europe as being the very "Book of Enoch" itself. The style, the language, the symbolisms, and the concepts of the Book of Mysteries, though different in many ways from those of 1 Enoch, clearly manifest a conscious effort to emulate 1 Enoch. For instance, the fourth part of the Book of Mysteries, called "A Discourse Concerning the Birth of Enoch," recapitulates the Apocalypse of Weeks, brings the last three weeks through to the Christian era, and ends with the Antichrist in the tenth.[17]

The Book of Mysteries is only one example of the influence of 1 Enoch on Ethiopic literature. The *Kebra Nagast*, the famous Ethiopian royal saga, is another example of a work that utilizes 1 Enoch generously. Other Ethiopic religious works contain references from, and show influences of, 1 Enoch. Ethiopic poetic literature, the *gadles* (the Ethiopic hagiographies), and some of the magical works manifest the influence of 1 Enoch in their language, imageries, angelology, and demonology.

Still more significant is the influence of Enochic ideas on Ethiopian Christian theology. What distinguishes Ethiopian Christian theology from that of either Western or Eastern Christendom may well be the Ethiopian emphases on Enochic thought. Sin does not originate from Adam's transgression alone; Satan, the demons, and evil spirits (the fallen angels) are equally responsible for its origin; they continue to lead man astray, causing moral ruin on the earth. On the other hand, there are the protective angels, with their various orders and ranks, who play an important part in both the religious and social life of the Ethiopian people; these angels—particularly Michael, Gabriel, Rufael, Uriel, as well as the cherubim (Krubel) and the seraphim (Surāfēl)—serve as personal guardians of those specially dedicated to them and who celebrate with meticulous observance the dates of their special festivals.

Introducing the following translation

My primary base text (A) for this translation of Ethiopic Enoch is a fifteenth-century Ethiopic manuscript found in a monastery in Kebran, in Lake Tana. I obtained a copy of this manuscript from a microfilm (A) now found in West Germany.[18] Though I have chosen to use as my base text a single manuscript, instead of an existing eclectic text or one created temporarily as the real basis of my translation, I have continually compared A with another

---

[17] Cf. J. Perruchon and I. Guidi, "Le Livre des Mystères du Ciel et de la Terre" in *Patrologia Orientalis* 1/1 (1907) 1–95; and S. Grébaut, "Les Trois Derniers Traites du Livre des Mystères du Ciel et de la Terre," *Patrologia Orientalis* 6/3 (1911) 361–464.

[18] E. Hammerschmidt, *Äthiopische Handschriften vom Ṭānāsee*, p. 107.

Ethiopic manuscript of the late eighteenth century (B) found in the Garrett collection of Princeton University as well as with the text of R. H. Charles (C),[19] and, in a few cases, followed them instead of A where the latter is clearly wrong or unintelligible. I have been as faithful as possible to A, following it even when B and C and all other known witnesses, attested by the variations of other manuscripts given in the apparatus of Charles (EC), disagree with it, except in clear cases where A obviously transmits grammatical, syntactical, or scribal errors. Only the most significant or relevant variations of other witnesses are shown in my notations. If B or C are clearly erroneous (scribal, typographic, grammatical), I do not always give them as variations. Wherever possible or necessary I have also been able to compare A with the texts of the existing Greek fragments as given in the Charles edition of 1 Enoch: G^a (the fragments from Akhmim—G^{a1} and G^{a2} the duplicate passages of the same if they exist), G^s (the fragments preserved by Syncellus), and G^p (the Greek papyrus as edited by Bonner). The Qumran Aramaic fragments of 1 Enoch have been consulted but have not influenced the following translation.[20]

It appears to me that in general A is superior to B and C, often giving shorter and more difficult readings (see, for instance, 71:8f.). I have been able to examine briefly microfilms of three important Enoch manuscripts—EMML 2080 (15th cent.), 4437 (17th cent.), and 4750 (17th cent.)—copies of which are presently found in the Hill Monastic Microfilm Library, St. John's University, Collegeville, Minnesota, to ascertain the importance of A. Of the manuscripts that Charles studied, A appears to be closest to his g (early 16th cent.)[21] and his u (possibly 15th cent.).[22] But in many interesting or important cases, A may agree with other manuscripts used by Charles. For instance, A agrees with not only u but also Charles's m and t in omitting "Son" from the "Son of Man" (69:26). In at least one crucial place, A agrees with q against other witnesses. Scholars have thought that the reference to Enoch's travel in a "chariot of wind" as found in a *Mani Codex* (which relied on an Apocalypse of Enoch) is missing from the Ethiopic Enoch; if we follow A and q (cf. 52:1) this may not be wholly the case. In general A agrees with the Ethiopic textual tradition against the Greek; nevertheless, there are a few cases where it agrees with the Greek against other Ethiopic traditions (e.g. 18:9; 24:5). The importance of A is unfortunately reduced by the carelessness of the scribe (e.g. 45:1; 48:10). It is also possible that the scribe of A used two manuscripts as he worked or copied one manuscript freely; that may be the reason why fols. 103r–106v (1En 78:8b–82:20) are a duplicate of fols. 96r–99r (or vice versa), showing each time several variations—perhaps two scribes with very similar hands copied parts of A, using separate texts.

It should be noted here that my translation, though very faithful to the text, is in general not always literal. Therefore, I may render a single Ethiopic word into different English expressions depending on the context or idiom. For instance, *mangest* may be rendered "kingdom" or "empire," *ḥāyl*, "power," "force," "forces," "army," or "array," *samay*, "heaven" or "sky," and so on. In this respect, I have also translated the expression *re'esa mawā'el* as the "Antecedent of Time" or the "Before-Time," instead of the literal "Head of Days"; on the other hand, it has not been easy to find a more adequate expression for the more or less literal "Son of Man." I generally bear in mind not only the context of the language but also the context of the milieu of the languages of 1 Enoch; thus, I translate *kramt* "rainy season" rather than "winter," *hagay* "dry season" rather than "summer." It should also be noted that despite the freedom in Ethiopic regarding the use of the singular and the plural, both in the case of nouns and verbs, I have tried to render all Ethiopic expressions into acceptable English; moreover, except in certain cases (e.g. the sun is generally feminine, the moon, masculine), it has not always been possible to indicate the gender of Ethiopic words in the translation. A major dilemma always arises in rendering the simple but ubiquitous Ethiopic conjunction *wa-* into English; the reader should know that I have been very generous in using whatever connective English conjunction I felt to be appropriate in many cases (e.g. "and," "or," "but," "moreover," "furthermore," "then,"

---

[19] Charles, *The Ethiopic Version of the Book of Enoch.*
[20] These are now edited by Milik, *The Books of Enoch,* pp. 139–407.
[21] W. Wright, *A Catalogue of Ethiopian Manuscripts in the British Museum* (London, 1896) no. 6.
[22] See D'Abbadie, *Catalogue,* no. 55.

"as well as," "also," and so on) and have dropped it altogether in several other cases where in English "and" would be superfluous.

In conclusion, even though I have not tried to annotate all my restorations of grammatical, scribal, and textual errors and variant readings, I have provided ample notes in order that the reader may appreciate the problems of translating this difficult work and understand better this translation. I am the last person to claim that this translation is flawless; by its nature, every translation involves a subjective dimension which may lead to errors.[23]

[23] I am thankful to Professor James Charlesworth of Duke University, who invited me to do this work, and to Professor Michael Stone, who urged me to accept the invitation. Professor Ernst Hammerschmidt of the University of Hamburg kindly and promptly sent a copy of the 15th-cent. Enoch manuscript (A) to the Widener Library; I am grateful to him as well as to the Interlibrary Loan staff at Widener for their kind assistance.

SELECT BIBLIOGRAPHY

Charlesworth, *PMR*, pp. 98–103.
Delling, *Bibliographie*, pp. 157–59.
Denis, *Introduction*, pp. 15–28.

Black, M. (ed.). *Apocalypsis Henochi Graeci in Pseudepigrapha Veteris Testamenti*. PVTG 3; Leiden, 1970.
Bonner, C. *The Last Chapters of Enoch in Greek in Studies and Documents*. London, 1937.
Charles, R. H. *The Ethiopic Version of the Book of Enoch in Anecdota Oxoniensia*. Oxford, 1906.
———. *The Book of Enoch*. Oxford, 1893.
———. "The Book of Enoch," *Apocrypha and Pseudepigrapha of the Old Testament*. Oxford, 1913; vol. 2, pp. 163–281.
Charlesworth, J. H. "The SNTS Pseudepigrapha Seminars at Tübingen and Paris on the Books of Enoch," *NTS* 25 (1979) 315–23.
Flemming, J., and L. Radermacher. *Das Buch Henoch*. Leipzig, 1901.
Greenfield, J. C., and M. Stone. "The Enochic Pentateuch and the Date of the Similitudes," *HTR* 70 (1977) 51–65.
Hindley, J. C. "Toward a Date for the Similitudes of Enoch, an Historical Approach," *NTS* 14 (1968) 551–65.
Knibb, M. A. *The Ethiopic Book of Enoch*. Oxford, 1978; 2 vols. [Knibb's book appeared long after Isaac had completed his contribution on 1 Enoch. J.H.C.]
Lewis, J. P. *A Study of the Interpretation of Noah and the Flood in Jewish Christian Literature*. Leiden, 1968.
Martin, F. *Le Livre d'Hénoch*. Paris, 1906.
Milik, J. T. "Problèmes de la littérature Hénochique à la lumière des fragments araméens de Qumrân," *HTR* 64 (1971) 333–78.
———. "Turfan et Qumran, Livre des Géants juif et manichéen"; in *Tradition und Glaube: Das frühe Christentum in seiner Umwelt*, eds.. G. Jeremias *et al.* (K. G. Kuhn Festschrift). Göttingen, 1971; pp. 117–27.
———. "Fragments grecs du livre d'Hénoch," *Chronique d'Égypte* 40 (1971) 321–43.
———, and M. Black. *The Books of Enoch*. Oxford, 1976.
Nickelsburg, G. W. E., Jr. "Enoch 97–104, a Study of the Greek and Ethiopic Texts," *Armenian and Biblical Studies*, ed. M. E. Stone. Supplementary vol. 1 to *Sion*. Jerusalem, 1976; pp. 90–156.
Sjöberg, E. *Der Menschensohn in äthiopischen Henochbuch*. Lund, 1946.
Ullendorff, E. "An Aramaic 'Vorlage' of the Ethiopic Text of Enoch," *Atti del convegno internazionale di studi ethiopici*. Rome, 1960; pp. 259–67.

THE BOOK OF ENOCH

Book I (1–36)
The Parable of Enoch

INTRODUCTORY VISIONS AND PARABLES OF ENOCH

The righteous and the wicked

1 **1** The blessing[a] of Enoch: with which he blessed the elect and the righteous who would be present on the day of tribulation at (the time of) the removal of all the 2 ungodly ones.[b] •And Enoch, the blessed and righteous[c] man of the Lord,[d] took up (his parable)[e] while his eyes[f] were open and he saw, and said, "(This is) a holy vision from the heavens which the angels showed me: and I heard from them everything and I understood. I look not for this generation but for the distant one 3 that is coming.[g] I speak about the elect ones and concerning them." •And I took up with a parable[h] (saying), "The God of the universe, the Holy Great One, will come 4 forth from his dwelling.[i] •And from there he will march upon Mount Sinai and appear in his camp emerging from heaven[j] with a mighty power.[k] And everyone shall be 5 afraid, and Watchers[l] shall quiver. •And great fear and trembling shall seize them 6 unto the ends of the earth. •Mountains and high places[m] will fall down[n] and be frightened. And high hills shall be made low; and they shall melt like a honeycomb[o] 7 before[p] the flame. •And earth shall be rent asunder;[q] and all that is upon the earth 8 shall perish. And there shall be a judgment upon all, (including) the righteous.[r] •And to all the righteous[s] he will grant peace. He will preserve the elect, and kindness shall be upon them. They shall all belong to God[t] and they shall prosper and be 9 blessed; and the light of God shall shine unto them. •Behold, he will arrive with ten

Pss Sol 4:9

Num 24:3f.

Num 24:3f.

Micah 1:3;
Isa 26:21;
AsMos 10:3

Dan
4:13,17,23

WisSol
4:15

Sir 43:26

Jude 14,15

---

1 a. The Eth. *qāla barakat* should be translated simply as "the blessing" and not lit. as "the word(s) of blessing" as Charles does.

b. B and C, following several possibly later and inflated MSS, read *'ekuyān(a) wa-rasi'ān(a)*, "the evil and ungodly ones." Note to the reader: The letters A, B, C respectively represent our basic text (*Kebrān* MS 9/II); the text of Princeton Ethiopic 3; and the printed text of Charles. EC represents the notes in Charles's edition of the Eth. Enoch. (For others see "Texts.")

c. B and C, following supposedly all Charles's MSS, read *be'si ṣādiq*, "the righteous man."

d. [The various Eth. words for God or Lord have been translated consistently through 1En as follows: 1. *'Egzi'abḥēr* represents LORD (the Eth. translation of Yahweh in the OT). 2. *'Egzi'a* represents Lord (the Eth. translation of Adonai in the OT). 3. *'Amlak* represents God (the Eth. translation of Elohim in the OT). Note that "Lord ['*Egzi'a*] of the Spirits" occurs only in chs. 37–71. —*J. H. Charlesworth and E. G. Martin*]

e. The extant Gk. text reads *analabōn tēn parabolēn*, "he took up his parable." So also 4QEn[a] 1:1 (Milik, *The Books of Enoch*, p. 182).

f. So A B C against the Gk. *orasis*, "his mouth."

g. B reads, as do some other MSS of Charles, *lazaymaṣ'u tewled reḥuqān*, "distant generations that will be coming."

h. B and C, following supposedly all of Charles's MSS, read *mesla*, which is unintelligible. *Mesla mesālē*, "with a proverb [or "parable"]," which is attested in A, is accurate, and the other MSS must have lost *mesālē*, probably because of homoeoteleu-

ton.

i. So A. B reads *yewaṣe' qeddus . . . wa-'amlāka 'alam wa-'emheyya*, creating an impossible phraseology. Charles kept the *wa-* before '*amlāka* as some of his MSS did and, contrary to all his MSS, which he claimed were wrong, dropped the *wa-* before '*emheyya*, creating an artificial text in C.

j. Lit. "and appear from heaven."

k. B reads "his mighty power."

l. Lit. "Diligent guards." [Watchers are the fallen angels.]

m. So A. B and C read "high mountains."

n. Eth. *waywadqu*, "will fall down," is not attested in B and C.

o. A B C read *ma'ara gerā*, "honeycomb," not *gerā ma'ar*, "wax." However, the two expressions are sometimes confused in usage.

p. Lit. "from."

q. B had "shall sink."

r. B: "and all the righteous." It seems to me that Charles wrongly assumed *lā'la ṣādiqān k"elomu*, "upon all the righteous," to be a dittography of words before and after.

s. B and C read respectively "as to the righteous" and "to the righteous."

t. Or "they will become God's property." So Ethiopian commentators.

u. All of Charles's MSS, except e, read *maṣ'a*, "he came." Ethiopian commentators who follow this reading argue that the perfect tense is used to emphasize that "he will certainly come." Cf. Jude 14 also. The Eth. *te'lft* designates ten thousand times a thousand. Cf. *Wa-'atah Mērb'bot Qôdesh* in Deut 33:2. LXX reads *syn myriasyn Kadēs*.

million[u] of the holy ones in order to execute judgment upon all.[v] He will destroy the wicked ones[w] and censure[x] all flesh on account of everything that they have done, that which the sinners and the wicked ones committed against him."[y]

1 **2** Examine all the activit(ies which take place) in the sky[a] and how[b] they do not alter their ways, (and examine) the luminaries of heaven, how each one of them rises and sets; each one is systematic according to its respective season; and they do not divert 2 from their appointed order.[c] •And look at the earth and turn in your mind[d] concerning the action which is taking place[e] in her[f] from the beginning to the end: how all the 3 work[g] of God as being manifested[h] does not change. •And behold[i] the summer and the winter,[j] how the whole earth is filled with water and clouds and dew;[k] and he causes rain[l] to rest upon her.

1 **3** Examine[a] and observe[b] everything—and the trees,[c] how all their leaves appear as if they wither and had fallen,[d] except fourteen[e] trees[f] whose (leaves) do not fall but[g] the old (foliage) remains for about two to three years[h] until the new (leaves) come.[i]

1 **4** And again, examine the days of the summer,[a] how (the heat of) the sun[b] is upon (the earth)[c] and dominates her.[d] And as for you, you will crave[e] shade and shelter on account of the heat of the sun; and the earth shall burn with scorching heat, and you are not able to walk on the earth or on the rock on account of the heat.[f]

1 **5** Observe how the verdant trees are covered with leaves and they bear fruit.[a] Pay attention[b] concerning all things and know in what manner he fashioned[c] them.[d] All 2 of them belong to him who lives forever. •His work proceeds and progresses[e] from

---

v. B and C read "upon them." It appears that A is in this respect the least corrupt text, since it seems to agree with the Gk., Pseudo-Cyprian, and Jude 15.

w. The Gk., Pseudo-Cyprian, Pseudo-Vigilius, and Jude 15 read "all the evil ones."

x. Or "rebuke."

y. Following Jude 15, Pseudo-Cyprian, and the Gk., Charles has suggested emending the text to read "And of all the hard things which ungodly sinners have spoken against him."

2 a. The syntax of A, *ṭayyequ kʷulo gebra za-westa samāy*, is superior to that of B and C. B and all the other MSS which Charles studied also give the wrong grammatical form: *ṭayyaqu* for *ṭayyequ*, which is found in A. Some Ethiopian commentators also read *ṭayyaqqu*, "I inquired [or "examined"]."

b. B and C read "how," not "and how."

c. B reads *'emte'zāzomu*, "their appointed commandments."

d. Lit. "understand," "take notice," "think," "be mindful of."

e. Lit. "which is being acted."

f. So A, *westētā*. B and C have "upon her," *lā'lēhā*.

g. A B: *gebru*. C: *megbāru*.

h. Eth. *'enza yāstar'i* is a somewhat dangling phrase. Cf. EC, p. 6, nn. 13, 15, regarding the clause in Gk., which is lost in Eth.

i. A: *war'ikewo*. B and C: *r'eyywā*.

j. Lit. "the dry and rainy season."

k. A (*māya, wa-dammanā wa-ṭala wa-zenāma*) has the right text over against B and C (*māya wa-dammanā wa-ṭal wazenām*). Cf. EC, p. 6, n. 22.

l. Cf. 4QEnᵃ. It is distantly possible to render A "and the cloud causes dew and rain to rest upon her [the earth]."

3 a. A C: *ṭayyequ*. B: *ṭayyaqu*, as in all of the other Charles MSS.

b. B has *re'iku*.

c. B: "Examine and observe the trees." C: "Examine and observe all the trees." Cf. 4QEnᵃ: "Observe that all the trees wither" (Milik, *The Books of Enoch*, pp. 146f.).

d. B C: "how they seem as though they had withered and all their leaves shed."

e. B: "twelve."

f. Cf. Geoponica 11:1.

g. A and B and all known Eth. MSS read *'lla*, "which."

h. Or "rainy season."

i. Lit. "they will remain from the old to the new."

4 a. Lit. "dry season."

b. Lit. "the sun."

c. Lit. "upon her."

d. Lit. "her first," "her greater one," "ahead of her." B: *ba-qedmēhā*, "in her face," "in front of her." C: *ba-qadamehā*, "against her."

e. Lit. "seek."

f. B C: "her heat."

5 a. Eth. *'eṣ ba-hamalmala yetkaddanu ba-qʷaṣel wa-yefarryu*. The reading of B and C, *'eṣaw ba-hamalmala 'aqʷuṣel yetkaddanu wa-yefarreyu*, "trees cover themselves with green leaves and bear fruit," is an easier and grammatically smoother one.

b. B C: "and pay attention."

c. Erroneously *gebromu* for *gabromu*.

d. Overall, the reading of A is closer to the Gk. *epoiēsen auta hutōs*. The reading of B, *ba-kama gabra la-kemu'la 'elontu kʷolomu zaḥeyyāw la-'alam*, and that of C, *ba-kama gabarkemu la-'eluntu kʷulomu*, are both corrupt and not very intelligible.

e. Eth. *qadama*. B C: *qedmēhu*, "before him."

year to year. And all his work prospers and obeys[f] him,[g] and it does not change; but
3 everything functions[h] in the way in which God has ordered[i] it. •And look at the seas:[j]
4 They do not part;[k] they fulfill all their duties. •But as for you, you have not been long-
suffering and you have not done the commandments of the Lord, but you have
transgressed and spoken slanderously[l] grave and harsh words with your impure mouths
5 against his greatness. Oh, you hard-hearted, may you not find peace! •Therefore, you
shall curse your days, and the years of your life shall perish and multiply in eternal
6 execration; and there will not be any mercy unto you. • In those days, you shall make
your names[m] an eternal execration unto all the righteous; and the sinners shall curse
7 you continually—you together with the sinners.[n] •But to the elect there shall be light,
joy, and peace, and they shall inherit the earth. To you, wicked ones, on the contrary,
8 there will be a curse. •And then[o] wisdom shall be given[p] to the elect. And they shall
all live and not return again to sin,[q] either by being wicked or through pride; but
9 those who have wisdom shall be humble and not return again to sin. •And they shall
not be judged all the days of their lives;[r] nor die through plague[s] or wrath,[t] but[u] they
10 shall complete the (designated) number of the days of their life. •And peace shall
increase their lives[v] and the years of their happiness shall be multiplied forever in
gladness and peace all the days of their life.

The fall of angels

1 **6** In those days, when the children of man had multiplied, it happened that there Gen. 6:1-4
2 were born unto them handsome and beautiful daughters. •And the angels, the children
of heaven, saw them and desired them; and they said to one another, "Come, let us
choose wives for ourselves from among the daughters[a] of man and beget us children."
3 And Semyaz,[b] being their leader,[c] said unto them, "I fear that perhaps you will not
consent that this deed should be done, and I alone will become (responsible)[d] for this
4 great sin." •But they all responded to him,[e] "Let us all swear an oath and bind
everyone among us by a curse not to abandon this suggestion but to do the deed."[f]
5 Then they all swore together and bound one another by (the curse).[g] •And they were
6 altogether[h] two hundred; and they descended into 'Ardos,[i] which is the summit of
Hermon.[j] And they called the mount Armon, for they swore and bound one another
7 by a curse.[k] •And their names are as follows:[l] Semyaz,[m] the leader of Arakeb,
Rame'el, Tam'el, Ram'el, Dan'el, Ezeqel, Baraqyal, As'el, Armaros, Batar'el,

f. Lit. "they obey."
g. B and C have the awkward reading *wa-mege-bāru qedmēhu . . . zayekawun wa-k^wulu megbāru yetqannay* [B: *yetqanayu*] *lotu.*
h. Lit. "it is done."
i. I.e. organized.
j. Eth. *bāhrata,* in the accusative form. B and C give the common plural form *'abḥert,* in the nominative form.
k. So A: *wa-ifalag,* lit. "it does not part." This reading of A appears to be corrupt. B and C, in agreement with the Gk., *hē thalassa kai hoi potamoi,* read *'abḥert wa-'afag ḥebura,* "the seas and the rivers together."
l. I.e. in a backbiting manner.
m. B: "your peace."
n. The Eth. is corrupt. As for the variations in the different Gk. texts, particularly in the Akhmim additions, see EC, p. 9.
o. B: *wa-'emmahi.*
p. Eth. *yetwahab.* B C: *yetwahabomu.*
q. Lit. "they shall not repeat sin." C: "they will not again sin."
r. For the variation in the Gk. fragments, cf. EC, pp. 10f.
s. I.e. divine punishment.
t. I.e. divine wrath.
u. Eth. *'ella,* wrong for *'allā.*

v. B C Gk. fragments: "and their lives shall be increased in peace."

6 a. Lit. "the children."
b. B C: Semyaza.
c. B: "who is their leader."
d. Cf. B: "I alone will become the payer." Text of A, *fadfāda,* "exceedingly," is corrupt for *fadāyi.* C, *'ekawwen . . . fadāya,* is somewhat awkward.
e. B C: "they responded to him and said."
f. Eth. *zāti gebr,* "this deed." B and C, *zāti mekr gebra* and *zāti (mekr) gebr* respectively, are redundant.
g. Lit. "by it."
h. Lit. "And all of them were . . ."
i. B C: 'Ardis.
j. B C: "Mount Hermon." Following the Gk. fragment, the correct reading may be "and they descended in the days of Jared on the summit of Mount Hermon." Cf. EC, p. 13f.
k. Regarding the paronomasia between Hermon (of Mount Hermon) and *herem,* "curse," cf. EC, p. 14.
l. Lit. "And here are [this is (the list) of] their names, it is like this . . ." C and B read "And these are the names of their leaders."
m. B: Semyaza. C: Sami'azaz.

8 Anan'el, Zaqe'el, Sasomasp^we'el, Kestar'el, Tur'el, Yamayol, and Arazyal.ⁿ • These are their chiefsᵒ of tensᵖ and of all the others with them.

1 **7** And theyᵃ took wives unto themselves, and everyone (respectively) chose one woman for himself, and they began to go unto them.ᵇ And they taught them magical
2 medicine, incantations, the cutting of roots, and taught themᶜ (about) plants. •And the women became pregnant and gave birth to great giants whose heightsᵈ were three
3 hundred cubits. • Theseᵉ (giants) consumed the produceᶠ of all the peopleᵍ until the
4 people detested feeding them.ʰ •Soⁱ the giants turned against (the people) in order to
5 eat them. •And they began to sin against birds, wild beasts, reptiles, and fish. And
6 their flesh was devoured the one by the other, and they drank blood.ʲ •And then the earth brought an accusation against the oppressors.

Right margin refs: WisSol 14:6; Tob 6:14; Sir 16:7; 1Bar 3:26; 3Mac 2:4; Jub 7:22f. Gen 9:4; 1Sam 14:32–34; Acts 15:20; Jub 7:28; 21:6

1 **8** And Azaz'el taught the people (the art of) making swords and knives, and shields, and breastplates; and he showed to their chosen onesᵃ bracelets, decorations, (shadowing of the eye) with antimony,ᵇ ornamentation, the beautifying of the eyelids, all
2 kinds of precious stones,ᶜ and all coloring tinctures and alchemy.ᵈ •And there were many wicked onesᵉ and they committed adultery and erred, and all their conduct
3 became corrupt. •Amasrasᶠ taught incantation and the cutting of roots; and Armaros the resolving of incantations; and Baraqiyalᵍ astrology,ʰ and Kokarer'elⁱ (the knowledge of) the signs,ʲ and Tam'elᵏ taught the seeing of the stars, and Asder'elˡ taught the
4 course of the moon as well as the deceptionᵐ of man.ⁿ •And (the people) cried and their voice reached unto heaven.

Dan 5:12

1 **9** Then Michael, Surafel,ᵃ and Gabriel observed carefully from the sky and they saw much blood being shed upon the earth,ᵇ and all the oppression being wrought upon
2 the earth. •And they said to one another, "The earth, (from) her empty (foundation),
3 has brought the cry of their voice unto the gates of heaven. •And now, [O] holy ones of heaven, the souls of people are putting their case before you pleading, 'Bring our

---

n. B C: "Sami'azaz [B: Semyaza], who is their leader, Arakibarame'el [B: Urakibarame'el], Kokabi'el [B: Akibe'el], Tami'el [B: Tame'el], Rami'el [B: Raw'el], Dan'el, Ezeqe'el, Baraqiyal [B: Laraquyal], Asa'el, Armaros [B: Armeses], Baṭar'el [B: Baṭra'al], Anan'el, Zaqi'el [B: Zaqebe], Samsape'el, Saṭar'el [B: Sart'el], Tur'el, Yomya'el, Arazyal.'' Cf. EC, p. 14.

o. Eth. 'abayta. B C wrongly: habayta and habaytomu respectively.

p. B adds "of the two hundred angels."

7 a. C: "they and all the others with them."

b. B and C add "and became added unto them." For variations in the Gk. fragments in this and ch. 8, see EC, pp. 17f.

c. Eth. maharewon. B C: 'amarewon.

d. Lit. "and their heights."

e. C: "who." Cf. 4QEnᵃ, which is closer to A.

f. Lit. "toil," "labor." So 4QEnᵃ.

g. A should be rendered either "All of these consumed the toil of the people" or "These consumed the toil of all the people" by transposing the correctly nominative Eth. kʷellu in the phrase 'ellu bal'u kʷellu ṣāmā sabe. Cf. 4QEnᵃ. All of Charles's MSS give the accusative kwellu. Cf. EC, p. 16, nn. 9, 10.

h. Eth. sēsyota sab'e. C: sab'e sēsyota.

i. Lit. "And."

j. Possibly "And they devoured one another's flesh, and drank the blood." B adds 'emnēhā, which is a doublet of the following word.

8 a. Eth. za-'emḥrēhomu. C and B have za-'emdḥrēhomu, "those after them," which Charles thinks is a corruption of the Gˢ ta metalla (cf. ta met'auta). Gᵃ has megala. Cf. EC, p. 16, n. 30. C and B also add "the making of them." Eth. za-'emdḥrēhomu is rendered as "their successors" or "their children" by Ethiopian commentators.

b. Lit. "antimony."

c. Lit. "and of stones all kinds of precious and chosen stones."

d. A adds tawaleṭo 'alam, "transmutation of the world." I render it as "alchemy." Cf. EC, p. 18, n. 5. Ethiopian commentators explain this phrase as "changing a man into a horse or mule or vice versa, or transferring an embryo from one womb to another."

e. B C: "and there was [great and] much wickedness."

f. B: Amezaras. C: Amizaras.

g. B: Baraq'al.

h. Lit. "the seeing of stars."

i. B C: Kokab'el.

j. I.e. miraculous signs.

k. B: Ṭem'el. C: Ṭami'el.

l. B: Asrad'el.

m. B and C read "destruction."

n. Concerning variations in the Gk. fragments see EC, p. 18f.

9 a. B: Uryan and Suryan. C: Ur'el and Rufa'el.

b. A also adds ba-tāhetu, "under it."

4 judgment before the Most High.' "[c] •And they said to the Lord of the potentates,[d]
"For[e] he is the Lord of lords, and the God of gods,[f] and the King[g] of kings, and the
seat of his glory[h] (stands) throughout all the generations of the world. Your name is
5 holy, and blessed, and glorious throughout the whole world.[i] •You have made
everything[j] and with you is the authority for everything. Everything[k] is naked and
open before your sight, and you see everything; and there is nothing which can hide
6 itself from you. •You see what Azaz'el has done; how he[l] has taught all (forms of)
oppression upon the earth. And they revealed[m] eternal secrets which are performed
7 in heaven (and which) man learned.[n] •(Moreover) Semyaz,[o] to whom you have given
power to rule over his companions, co-operating,[p] they went in unto the daughters
8 of the people on earth;[q] •and they lay together with them—with those women—and
9 defiled themselves, and revealed to them every (kind of) sin. •As for the women,
they gave birth to giants to the degree that the whole earth was filled with blood and
10 oppression. •And now behold, the Holy One will cry,[r] and those who have died will
bring their suit up to the gate of heaven. Their[s] groaning has ascended (into heaven),
but[t] they could not get out from before the face of the oppression that is being
11 wrought on earth. •And you know everything (even) before it came to existence,[u]
and you see (this thing)[v] (but) you do not tell us what is proper for us that we may
do regarding it."

1 **10** And then spoke the Most High, the Great and Holy One![a] And he sent Asuryal[b]
2 to the son of Lamech, (saying), •"Tell him[c] in my name, 'Hide yourself!' and reveal
to him the end of what is coming; for the earth and everything[d] will be destroyed.
And the Deluge is about to come upon all the earth; and all that is in it will be
3 destroyed.[e] •And now instruct him in order that he may flee, and his seed will be
4 preserved for all generations."[f] •And secondly the Lord said to Raphael,[g] "Bind
Azaz'el hand[h] and foot[i] (and) throw him into the darkness!" And he made a hole in
5 the desert which was in Duda'el and cast him there; •he threw on top of him rugged Jude 6
6 and sharp rocks. And he covered his face[j] in order that he may not see light;[k] •and
7 in order that he may be sent into the fire on the great day of judgment. •And give
life to the earth which the angels have corrupted. And he will proclaim[l] life for the
earth: that he is giving life to her.[m] And all the children of the people will not perish

c. B C: "the souls of people are making their suit, saying, 'Bring our case [lit. "judgment"] before the Most High.' "

d. Lit. "kings." One of the duplicate versions of the Syncellus Gk. fragment reads "The Lord of the ages," or "of the world," *tōn aiōnōn*.

e. Eth. *'esma*, "for," "because." In the Syncellus fragment we have *Su*, "you," instead.

f. Lit. "your God." B C: "their God."

g. Lit. "your king." B C: "their king."

h. C: "your glory."

i. B and C repeat "glorious."

j. A omits "everything," found in the other MSS.

k. A omits "Everything," found in the other MSS.

l. B and C read "who."

m. B C: "and he revealed."

n. B: *wa-'amara sablātāt*. C: *wa-'amara sabe'a*. Cf. EC, p. 22, n. 15, and p. 23.

o. B: Semyaza. C: "and of Semyaza."

p. Lit. "together with."

q. B omits "on earth" and wrongly repeats "together with."

r. This phrase is attested neither in other Eth. MSS nor in the Gk. fragments. Instead, we have "the souls of the dead." Cf. EC, pp. 22f.

s. Lit. "and their."

t. Lit. "and."

u. B omits "everything before it came to existence."

v. The Eth. text is corrupt. Cf. EC, p. 24, n. 12, and p. 25.

10 a. C: "Then spoke the Most High, the Great and Holy One said." Cf. EC, p. 24, n. 20.

b. B: Arsayalaldor. C: 'Asarya Leyur. Cf. also EC, p. 24, n. 23.

c. C, supported by G^s, adds "Go to Noah and tell him . . ." See EC, p. 24, n. 25.

d. So A. B C: "the whole earth."

e. B omits "all." C, following the Gk. fragments, reads "it will destroy all that is in it."

f. So B and C. The text of A, which reads "and his seed will kneel down [worship] for all generations," is obviously corrupt.

g. The name designates "God is a healer."

h. Lit. "by hand." Cf. TarJon Gen 6:3, in which the names Semyaza and Azaz'el appear.

i. Lit. "by foot."

j. B and C add "cover him with darkness and let him abide there forever."

k. The preceding two sentences are given in the imperative form in B and C: "And make a hole in the desert . . ."

l. Lit. "he will make you know."

m. Lit. "to the earth." The Gk. fragments read "that he may heal the plague." Cf. also EC, p. 26, n. 4.

8 through all the secrets (of the angels),[n] which they taught to their sons. •And the whole earth has been corrupted by Azaz'el's teaching of his (own) actions; and write

9 upon him all sin. •And to Gabriel the Lord said, "Proceed against the bastards and the reprobates and against the children of adultery; and destroy the children of adultery and expel the children of the Watchers from among the people.[o] And send them against one another (so that) they may be destroyed in the fight, for length of days have they not.

10 •They[p] will beg you everything—for their fathers on behalf of themselves—because they hope to live an eternal life. (They hope) that[q] each one of

11 them will live a period of five hundred years." •And to Michael God said, "Make known to Semyaza[r] and the others who are with him,[s] who fornicated[t] with the   Jub 4:22

12 women,[u] that they will die[v] together with them in all their defilement. •And when they and[w] all their children have battled with each other, and when they have seen   67:4–7; Jub 5:10 the destruction of their beloved ones, bind them for seventy[x] generations underneath the rocks of the ground until the day of their judgment and of their consummation,   Jude 6

13 until the eternal judgment is concluded. • In those days they will lead them into the   Rev 20:10, 14,15; bottom of the fire—and in torment—in the prison (where) they will be locked up   Mt 25:41

14 forever. •And at the time when[y] they will burn and die, those who collaborated with them will be bound together with them from henceforth unto the end of (all)

15 generations.[z] •And destroy all the souls of pleasure and the children of the Watchers,

16 for they have done injustice to man. •Destroy[a2] injustice from the face of the earth. And every iniquitous deed will end, and the plant of righteousness and truth will

17 appear forever and he will plant joy.[b2] •And then all the righteous ones will escape; and become the living ones until they multiply and become[c2] tens of hundreds; and all the days of their youth and the years of their retirement[d2] they will complete in

18 peace. •And in those days the whole earth will be worked in righteousness, all of

19 her[e2] planted with trees, and will find blessing.[f2] •And they shall plant pleasant trees[g2] upon her—vines.[h2] And he who plants a vine upon her will produce wine for   Isa 5:10; 2Bar 29:5 plenitude.[i2] And every seed that is sown on her, one measure will yield a thousand (measures) and one measure of olives will yield ten measures[j2] of presses of oil.

20 And you cleanse the earth from all injustice, and from all defilement, and from all oppression, and from all sin, and from all iniquity[k2] which is being done on earth;

21 remove them[l2] from the earth. •And all the children of the people will become righteous, and all nations shall worship and bless me; and they will all prostrate

n. Lit. "through all the secrets which the Watchers killed," which is obviously a corruption. Cf. EC, p. 26, n. 23. The Syncellus fragment reads "disclosed" instead of "killed."

o. B C: "and destroy . . . from among the people; and expel them."

p. Lit. "and they."

q. Lit. "and that."

r. Charles, after Radermacher, prefers "Bind Semyaza." See EC, p. 28, n. 15, and p. 29. C (and G) reads "Go, make known to Semyaza."

s. Or "his companions."

t. Lit. *gabru*, "did." 4QEn[b]: "(who) associated."

u. B C: "who united with the women."

v. Or "decay," "corrupt."

w. B and C omit "they and."

x. A and B wrongly have *la-sabe'a*.

y. Charles thinks the reading *hotan*, "when," is a corruption of *hos an*, "everyone who . . ." (EC, p. 28, n. 31). Cf. Milik, *The Books of Enoch*, p. 190.

z. This is a free translation. The text is corrupt. EC, following the Syncellus fragment, reads "whoever shall be condemned and destroyed will from henceforth be bound with them . . ." Cf. also EC, p. 29, n. 5.

a2. Lit. "and disappear."

b2. B C: "Destroy all injustice from the face of the earth and let every evil work come to an end; and let the plant of righteousness and truth appear:

and it shall become a blessing; the works of righteousness and truth shall be planted in truth and joy forevermore." A can be rendered ". . . and the plant of righteousness will appear, and plant eternal truth and joy."

c2. Lit. "they become and beget." B and C omit "they become."

d2. Or "rest," "their sabbaths," *sanbatāta zi'a-homu*. B C: *sanbata zi'ahomo*, "their sabbath," which is intelligible. Therefore Charles, following Wellhausen, *Skizzen und Vorarbeiten* 6 (Berlin, 1899) pp. 241, 260, suggested substituting *reš'anihomu* for *sanbat*, which he considered a corruption from the Heb. *sĕbuthon*, "their old age." Cf. EC, p. 30, n. 9, and p. 31, n. 1. The Eth. *sanbatāt* in plural (so also G) (cf. *sanābet*), found in A, does convey a sense of "weeks of rest" or "periods of rest or retirement." A notion equivalent to the suggested Heb. expression is given by Ethiopian commentators who render the phrase simply as "the period of old age."

e2. G reads *en autē*, "in her."

f2. B C: "will be filled with blessing."

g2. Lit. "trees of joy." C reads "trees of joy shall be planted." Cf. also G.

h2. B C: "And they shall plant vines."

i2. Lit. "for the satisfaction of the appetite."

j2. B and C omit "measures."

k2. A repeats "and from all defilement."

l2. So A. B C: "finish them."

22 themselves to me. •And the earth shall be cleansed from all pollution, and from all sin, and from all plague, and from all suffering; and it shall not happen again that I shall send (these) upon the earth[m2] from generation to generation and forever.

1 **11** "And in those days I shall open the storerooms of blessing which are in the heavens,[a] so that I shall send them down upon the earth, over the work and the toil 2 of the children of man. •And peace and truth shall become partners together[b] in all the days of the world, and in all the generations of the world."

Deut 28:12

Ps 85:10;
Isa 32:17

Dream vision of Enoch: his intercession for the fallen angels

1 **12** Before these things (happened) Enoch was hidden, and no one of the children 2 of the people knew by what he was hidden and where he was. •And his dwelling place[a] as well as his activities were with the Watchers and the holy ones; and (so 3 were) his days. •And I, Enoch, began to bless the Lord of the mighty ones[b] and the 4 King of the universe.[c] •At that moment[d] the Watchers were calling me.[e] And they[f] said to me, "Enoch, scribe of righteousness, go and make known to the Watchers of heaven who have abandoned the high heaven, the holy eternal place, and have defiled themselves with women, as their[g] deeds move the children of the world,[h] and have taken unto themselves wives: They[i] have defiled themselves with great defilement 5 upon the earth; •neither will there be peace unto them nor the forgiveness of sin. 6 For their children delight in seeing the murder of their beloved ones.[j] But they shall groan and beg forever over the destruction of their children, and there shall not be peace unto them even forever."[k]

His intercession for Azaz'el

1 **13** As for Enoch,[a] he proceeded and said to Azaz'el, "There will not be peace unto 2 you; a grave judgment has come upon you. •They will put you in bonds,[b] and you will not have (an opportunity for)[c] rest and supplication,[d] because you have taught injustice and because[e] you have shown to the people deeds of shame, injustice, and 3 sin." •Then I went and spoke to all of them together; and they were all frightened, 4 and fear and trembling seized them. •And they begged me to write for them a memorial prayer[f] in order that there may be for them a prayer[g] of forgiveness, and so that I may 5 raise their memorial prayer unto the Lord of heaven. •For, as for themselves, from henceforth they will not be able to speak, nor will they raise their eyes unto heaven 6 as a result of their sins which have been condemned. •And then I wrote down their memorial prayers and the petitions on behalf of their spirits and the deeds of each one of them, on account of the fact that they have prayed in order that[h] there may be for 7 them forgiveness (of sin) and a length (of days). •And I went and sat down upon the waters of Dan—in Dan which is on the southwest of Hermon—and I read their 8 memorial prayers until I fell asleep. •And behold a dream came to me and visions fell

---

m2. Lit. "upon her."

11 a. B C: "in heaven."
　　b. B and C omit "together."

12 a. So A. Instead of *wa-makâno*, "his dwelling place," B and C read: *wa-menta kona*, "and what he had become," or "what had become of him." Apparently this is an error due to homoeoteleuton.
　　b. B reads "great Lord." C, on the basis of the Gk. fragments, reads "Lord of Majesty." Cf. EC, p. 32, nn. 8f.
　　c. Also "King of the ages" and "the eternal King" are possible.
　　d. Lit. "And behold," "And lo."
　　e. Lit. "they were calling me Enoch." B C: "they were calling me Enoch, the scribe."

f. Lit. "he."
g. Lit. "his."
h. Lit. "of the people." In the preceding clause, *kama yegassewo*(?), the text is unclear. B C: "they have done as the children of the people do."
i. The Gk. has "you." Cf. EC, p. 33.
j. C: "they delight in their children . . ."
k. B C: "there shall not be mercy and peace unto them."

13 a. B C: "and Enoch."
b. So A.
c. Lit. "it will not be."
d. Text, "for error and supplication," corrupt.
e. Text unclear.
f. Lit. "a remembrance of prayer."
g. Omitted by B and C.
h. Text corrupt: "they have beseeched you."

upon me, and I saw a vision[i] of plagues[j] (so that) I may speak to the children of
9 heaven and reprimand them. •And upon my awakening, I came unto them (while)
they were all conferring[k] together, in Lesya'el,[l] which is (located) between Lebanon
10 and Sanser,[m] while weeping and with their faces covered. •And I recounted before
them all the visions that I had seen in sleep and began to speak those words of
righteousness and to reprimand[n] the Watchers of heaven.

Deut 3:9;
Song 4:8

1Cor 6:3

1 **14** This is the book of the words of righteousness and the chastisement of the eternal
Watchers, in accordance with how the Holy and Great One had commanded in this
2 vision. •I saw in my sleep what I now speak with my tongue of flesh and the breath
of the mouth which the Great One has given to man (so that) he (man) may speak
with it[a]—and (so that) he may have understanding with his heart as he (the Great
3 One) has created and given it to man. •Accordingly he has created me and given me
the word of understanding[b] so that I may reprimand the Watchers, the children of
4 heaven. •I wrote down your prayers—so it appeared in vision[c]—for your prayers will
not be heard[d] throughout all the days of eternity; and judgment is passed[e] upon you.
5 From now on you will not be able to ascend into heaven unto all eternity, but you
6 shall remain[f] inside the earth, imprisoned[g] all the days of eternity. •Before that you
will have seen[h] the destruction of your beloved sons and you will not have their
7 treasures,[i] which[j] will fall before your eyes by the sword. •And your petitions on
their behalf will not be heard—neither will those on your own behalf (which you
offer) weeping (and) praying—and you will not speak even a word contained in the
book which I wrote.[k]

1Cor 6:3

Enoch's vision

8 And behold I saw[l] the clouds: And they were calling me in a vision; and the fogs
were calling me; and the course of the stars and the lightnings were rushing me and
causing me to desire;[m] and in the vision, the winds were causing me to fly and
9 rushing me high up into heaven.[n] •And I kept coming (into heaven) until I approached
a wall which was built of white marble and surrounded by tongues[o] of fire; and it
10 began to frighten me. •And I came into the tongues of the fire and drew near to a
great house which was built of white marble, and the inner wall(s)[p] were like mosaics[q]
11 of white marble, the floor[r] of crystal, •the ceiling like the path of the stars and
12 lightnings between which (stood) fiery cherubim and their heaven of water;[s] •and
13 flaming fire surrounded the wall(s), and its gates were burning with fire. •And I
entered into the house, which[t] was hot like fire and cold like ice, and there was

Mt 17:5;
Pss
18:10,11;
104:3

Isa 30:30

i. C: "visions."
j. The Gk. omits "plague" and reads "and a voice came saying."
k. Or "gathered." B C: "sitting."
l. B: Abelsya'el. C: Abelsya'il.
m. B: Senser. C: Seniser.
n. Lit. "reprimand them."

14 a. B C: "and with my breath (which) the Great One has given the mouth . . ." Cf. EC, p. 34, n. 52.
b. This is a reconstruction; the text seems corrupt. Cf. B C: "As he has created man and given him the word of understanding, and likewise he has created me and given to me the (authority of) reprimanding." G omits "he has created me and given me the word of understanding."
c. B C: "my vision." 4QEn[c]: "a vision to me."
d. Lit. "it will not happen for you."
e. Lit. "fulfilled."
f. Eth. *tenabberu*, "you shall sit," "dwell," "remain." Cf. *tenagara*, "it is spoken," in B and C. See EC, p. 37, n. 6.
g. Lit. "they will imprison you."
h. Lit. "you saw."

i. Cf. EC, p. 36, n. 24: "and you shall have no pleasure in them."
j. B C: "but."
k. Charles suggests restoring the text to read "though you weep and pray and speak all the words . . ." Cf. EC, p. 37, n. 11.
l. A, "And to me, he saw lo the clouds," seems corrupt. B C: "And he showed me a vision thus . . ."
m. Some think this to be inaccurate. Cf. EC, p. 37, n. 13.
n. B and C add "lifted me up into heaven."
o. B C: "tongue."
p. Lit. "and the walls inside the house." B and C have *we'tu*, "it," "this," "he," instead of *westa*, "in," "inside."
q. Lit. "tessellated sheets."
r. Lit. "the ground."
s. So B, C, and the Gk. fragments. A has *samayomu* instead of *samāyomu*, giving the reading "he named them water" instead of "their heaven was of water."
t. Lit. "and."
u. B C: "there was no pleasure of life in it."

14 nothing inside it;[u] (so) fear covered me and trembling seized me. •And as I shook
15 and trembled, I fell upon my face and saw a vision. •And behold there was an
opening before me (and) a second house which is greater than the former[v] and
16 everything[w] was built with tongues of fire. •And in every respect it excelled (the
other)—in glory and great honor[x]—to the extent that it is impossible for me to recount
17 to you[y] concerning its glory and greatness. •As for its floor,[z] it was of fire and above
it was lightning and the path of the stars; and as for the ceiling, it was flaming fire.   Isa 6; Ezek
18 And I observed and saw inside it a lofty throne—its appearance was like crystal and   1:9; 26;
Dan 7:9,10;
19 its wheels like the shining sun; and (I heard?) the voice of the cherubim; •and from   Ps 104:2;
1Kgs 22:19;
beneath the throne[a2] were issuing streams of flaming fire. It was difficult[b2] to look at   AsMos 4:2
20 it.[c2] •And the Great Glory was sitting upon it—as for his gown, which was shining   T Levi 5:1;
Rev 4:2–3
21 more brightly than the sun, it was whiter than any snow. •None of the angels was
able to come in and see the face of the Excellent and the Glorious One;[d2] and no one
22 of the flesh can see him— •the flaming fire was round about him, and a great fire
stood before him. No one could come near unto him from among those that surrounded   Sir 42:21;
23 the tens of millions (that stood) before him. •He needed no council,[e2] but the most   2En 33:4
holy ones who are near to him neither go far away at night nor move away from
24 him. •Until then I was prostrate on my face covered[f2] and trembling. And the Lord
called me with his own mouth and said to me, "Come near to me, Enoch, and to
25 my holy[g2] Word." •And he lifted me up and brought me near to the gate, but I
(continued) to look down with my face.

1 **15** But he raised me up[a] and said to me with his voice, "Enoch."[b] I (then) heard,
"Do not fear, Enoch, righteous man, scribe of righteousness; come near to me and
2 hear my voice. •And tell[c] the Watchers of heaven on whose behalf you have been
sent[d] to intercede:[e] 'It is meet (for you) that you intercede on behalf of man, and not
3 man on your behalf. •For what reason have you abandoned the high, holy, and eternal
heaven; and slept with women and defiled yourselves with the daughters of the people,
4 taking wives, acting like the children of the earth, and begetting giant sons? •Surely
you, you [used to be] holy, spiritual, the living ones, [possessing] eternal life; but
(now) you have defiled yourselves with women, and with the blood of the flesh
begotten children, you have lusted with the blood of the people, like them[f] producing
5 blood and flesh, (which) die and perish. •On that account, I have given you[g] wives
in order that (seeds) might be sown upon them and children born by them, so that the
6 deeds that are done upon the earth will not be withheld from you.[h] •Indeed you,
formerly you were spiritual, (having) eternal life,[i] and immortal in all the generations
7 of the world. •That is why (formerly) I did not make wives for you, for the dwelling
of the spiritual beings of heaven is heaven.'

8 "But now the giants who are born from the (union of) the spirits and the flesh shall
be called evil spirits upon the earth, because[j] their dwelling shall be upon the earth[k]
9 and inside the earth. •Evil spirits[l] have come out of their bodies. Because from the
day that they were created from the holy ones they became the Watchers; their first
origin[m] is the spiritual foundation.[n] They will become evil upon the earth and shall

---

v. B C: "behold a second house . . . and the
entire portal was open before me."
w. B and C omit "everything."
x. B C: "in glory, honor, and greatness."
y. Lit. "I cannot recount to you."
z. Lit. "ground."
a2. B adds "great."
b2. Lit. "they could not."
c2. B C: "looking," "seeing."
d2. The Gk. reads "on account of the honor and
glory."
e2. Cf. EC, p. 40, n. 21.
f2. Charles suggests omitting "covered." Cf. EC,
p. 40, n. 25.
g2. Charles prefers the Gk. *akouson*, "hear,"
instead of the Eth. "holy." For this and succeeding
phrase see EC, p. 40, n. 28.

15 a. B C: "and he replied."
b. B C: "and I heard his voice."
c. B C: "And go and tell."
d. B C: "who sent you."
e. Lit. "pray."
f. B C: "you have done like them."
g. Lit. "them."
h. B C: "that nothing might be wanting to them
on earth."
i. B C: "living the eternal life."
j. B and C omit "because."
k. B and C omit "upon the earth."
l. B and C read *nafsāt*, "soul," instead of *manāfest*, as in A.
m. Lit. "their first beginning."
n. C, following the Gk.: "they are born from men
and the holy Watchers in their beginning . . ."

10 be called evil spirits. •The dwelling of the spiritual beings of heaven is heaven; but
the dwelling of the spirits of the earth, which are born upon the earth, is in the earth.°

11 The spirits of the giants oppress each other;ᵖ they�q will corrupt, fall, be excited, and
fall upon the earth, and cause sorrow.ʳ They eat no food,ˢ nor become thirsty, nor

12 find obstacles.ᵗ •And these spirits shall rise upᵘ against the children of the people and
against the women, because they have proceeded forth (from them).

1 **16** "From the days of the slaughter and destruction, and the death of the giants and
the spiritual beings of the spirit, and the flesh, from which they have proceeded forth,
which will corrupt without incurring judgment, they will corrupt until the day of the
great conclusion, until the great age is consummated, until everything is concluded

2 (upon) the Watchers and the wicked ones.ᵃ •And soᵇ to the Watchers on whose behalf

3 you have been sent to intercede—who were formerly in heaven—(say to them), •'You
were (once) in heaven, but not all the mysteries (of heaven) are open to you, and you
(only) know the rejected mysteries.ᶜ Those onesᵈ you have broadcast to the women
in the hardness of your hearts and by those mysteriesᵉ the women and men multiply
evil deeds upon the earth.' Tell them, 'Therefore, you will have no peace!' "

Jub
10:5–11;
Mt 8:29

Enoch's Tour of the Earth and Sheol
The first journey

1 **17** And they lifted me up intoᵃ one place where there were (the ones) like the flaming

2 fire. And when they (so) desire they appear like men. •And they took me into a place

3 of whirlwindᵇ in the mountain; the top of its summit was reaching into heaven. •And
I saw chambersᶜ of light and thunderᵈ in the ultimate end of the depthᵉ toward (the
place where) the bow,ᶠ the arrow, and their quiver and a fiery sword and all the

4 lightnings were. •And they lifted me up unto the waters of life,ᵍ unto the occidental

5 fire which receivesʰ every setting of the sun. •And I came to the river of fire which

6 flows like waterⁱ and empties itself into the great sea in the direction of the west. •And
I saw allʲ the great riversᵏ and reached to the great darkness and went into the place

7 where all flesh must walk cautiously.ˡ •And I saw the mountains of the dark storms

8 of the rainy season and from where the waters of all the seasᵐ flow. •And I saw the
mouths of all the rivers of the earth and the mouth of the sea.

Ps 104:4

1 **18** And I saw the storerooms of all the winds and saw how with them he has

2 embroidered all creation as well as the foundations of the earth. •I saw the cornerstone
of the earth; I saw the four winds which bear the earth as well as the firmament of

3 heaven. •I saw how the winds ride the heights of heavenᵃ and stand between heaven

2Sam
22:16; Ps
18:15
Job 38:6

---

o. Cf. vss. 7 and 8 above. The Syncellus fragment
omits vs. 10.

p. So A. I have omitted *dammanāta*, "clouds,"
which seems to be dangling in the phrase. Eth.
dammanā could also mean "mass," "enormity,"
"immensity," and one could possibly read the text
as "The spirits of the giants oppress each other
massively." On the other hand the *dammanāta* in
this verse has been regarded by some as a corruption.
The Syncellus fragment has "laying waste." Cf. EC,
p. 44, n. **3.**

q. Lit. "who."

r. Cf. EC, pp. 44f.

s. The Gk. fragments add "but nevertheless hunger."

t. So A. C, on the basis of Dillmann's emendation,
reads "cause offense" or "become obstacle." B and
other MSS have "they will not be known."

u. A: "shall not rise up."

16 a. The preceding passage is not completely intelligible and is a difficult reading. Cf. also C and
EC, pp. 44f.

b. Lit. "And now."

c. Lit. "the rejected mystery."

d. Lit. "This one."

e. Lit. "this mystery."

17 a. The Gk. adds "and brought me."

b. Gᵃ: "darkness."

c. Lit. "places."

d. Gᵃ adds "and the treasures of the stars."

e. B and C add *ḥaba*, "unto," before "depth,"
a somewhat unintelligible reading.

f. B C: "fiery bow."

g. C: "living waters." B: "water of life." A and
other MSS add a gloss: *za-yetnāgar* or *za-'iyetnāgar*.

h. Lit. "seizes."

i. C: "whose fire flows like water."

j. C omits "all."

k. Gᵃ adds "and the great river."

l. C, in agreement with the Gk. fragments, reads
"where no flesh can walk."

m. B C: "the lake."

18 a. So A. B C: *yerababewā*, "stretch out," instead
of *yerakabewā*, "ride."

4 and earth: These are the very pillars of heaven. •I saw the winds which turn the Job 26:11
5 heaven and cause the star to set—the sun as well as all the stars.[b] •I saw the souls Job 36:29;
carried by the clouds.[c] I saw the path of the angels in the ultimate end of the earth, 37:16
6 and the firmament of the heaven above.[d] •And I kept moving[e] in the direction of the
west; and it was flaming[f] day and night toward the seven mountains of precious
7 stones—three toward the east and three toward the south. •As for those toward the
east, they were of colored stones—one of pearl stone and one of healing stone;[g] and
8 as for those toward the south, they were of red stone. •The ones[h] in the middle were
pressing into heaven like the throne of God, which is of alabaster and whose summit[i] Ezek 1:26
9 is of sapphire;[j] •and I saw a flaming fire. •And I saw what was inside those[k]
10 mountains—a place,[l] beyond the great earth, where[m] the heavens[n] come together.[o]
11 And I saw a deep pit[p] with heavenly fire on its pillars; I saw inside them descending
12 pillars of fire[q] that were immeasurable (in respect to both) altitude[r] and depth.[s] •And
on top of that pit I saw a place without the heavenly firmament above it or earthly
foundation under it or water. There was nothing on it—not even birds[t]—but it was a
13 desolate and terrible place. •And I saw there the seven stars (which) were like great,
14 burning mountains.[u] •(Then) the angel said (to me), "This place is the (ultimate) end
of heaven and earth: it is the prison house[v] for the stars[w] and the powers of heaven.
15 •And the stars which roll over upon the fire, they are the ones which have transgressed
the commandments of God from the beginning of their rising because they did not
16 arrive punctually.[x] •And he was wroth with them and bound them until the time of
the completion of their sin in the year of mystery."[y]

1 **19** And Uriel said to me, "Here shall stand in many different appearances the spirits
of the angels which have united themselves with women. They[a] have defiled the
people and will lead them into error so that they[b] will offer sacrifices to the demons
as unto gods, until the great day of judgment in which they shall be judged till they
2 are finished. •And their women whom the angels have led astray will be peaceful
3 ones."[c] •(So) I, Enoch, I saw the vision of the end of everything alone; and none
among human beings will see as I have seen.

Names of archangels

1
2 **20** And these are names of the holy angels who watch: •Suru'el,[a] one of the holy
3 angels—for (he is) of eternity[b] and of trembling.[c] •Raphael, one of the holy angels, cf Next
4 for (he is) of the spirits of man. •Raguel, one of the holy angels who take vengeance page
5 for the world and for the luminaries.[d] •Michael, one of the holy angels, for (he is)

b. B C: "turn the heaven and cause the ball of
the sun and all the stars to set."

c. B C: "I saw the winds on the earth which carry
the clouds."

d. B C: "I saw the path of the angels. I saw in
the ultimate end of the earth the firmament of heaven
above."

e. B C: "And I passed."

f. C, in accordance with the Gk.: "and I saw a
place which burns . . ."

g. Charles suggests "jacinth." Cf. EC, p. 49, n.
13.

h. B C: "The one."

i. Lit. "the summit of the throne."

j. Or "stone."

k. So A and G. B and C read "all."

l. Lit. "there was a place." B and C add "and I
saw."

m. Lit. "there."

n. B: "waters."

o. G: "are completed."

p. B reads "a deep pit in the earth."

q. B: "heavenly pillars of fire."

r. Lit. "either in the direction of the heights."

s. Lit. "or in the direction of the depth."

t. B C: "There was no water on it and no birds."

u. Text adds "and like the spirit that was questioning me." Regarding this corruption see EC, p.
51, n. 5.

v. B and G add "this."

w. B: "stars of heaven."

x. Lit. "because they did not come [A wrongly:
"bring"] in their (allotted) time."

y. G: "for a myriad years."

19 a. Lit. "You."

b. "The people."

c. Charles considers the Eth. *salāmāweyān* (Gk.
hōs eirēnaioi) a corruption of *eis seirēn*, "into
sirens." Cf. EC, p. 51, n. 49.

20 a. B C: "Uriel."

b. B: "of roaring." C: "of the world."

c. G: "Tartarus." The Gk. reads: "Uriel . . .
who is over the world and Tartarus."

d. G: ". . . takes vengeance on the world of the
luminaries."

6 obedient in his benevolence over the people and the nations.ᶜ •Saraqa'el, one of the
7 holy angels who are (set) over the spirits of mankindᶠ who sin in the spirit. •Gabriel,
one of the holy angels who oversee the garden of Eden, and the serpents, and the
cherubim.ᵍ

Enoch's second journey: preliminary and final place of punishment of fallen stars

1
2 **21** And I came to an empty place.ᵃ •And I saw (there) neither a heaven above nor
3 an earth below,ᵇ but a chaoticᶜ and terrible place. •And there I saw seven stars of
4 heaven bound together in it,ᵈ like great mountains, and burning with fire. •At that
moment I said, "For which sin are they bound, and for what reason were they cast
5 in here." •Then one of the holy angels, Uriel, who was with me, guiding me,ᵉ spoke
to me and said to me, "Enoch, for what reason are you asking and for what reason
6 do you question and exhibit eagerness?ᶠ •These are among the stars of heavenᵍ which
have transgressed the commandments of the Lord and are bound in this placeʰ until
7 the completion of ten million years, (according) to the number of their sins."ⁱ •I then
proceeded from that area to another place which is even more terrible and saw a
terrible thing: a great fire that was burning and flaming; the placeʲ had a cleavage
(that extended) to the last sea, pouring outᵏ great pillars of fire; neither its extent nor
8 its magnitude could I see nor was I able to estimate.ˡ •At that moment, what a terrible
9 openingᵐ is this place and a pain to look at!ⁿ •Then Ura'el, (one) of the holy angels
who was with me, responded and said to me,ᵒ "Enoch, why are you afraid like this?"ᵖ
10 (I answered and said), q • "I am frightened because of this terrible place and the
spectacle of this painful thing."ʳ And he said unto me, "This place is the prison house
of the angels; they are detained here forever."

1 **22** Thenᵃ I went to another place, and he showed me on the west side a great and
2 high mountain ofᵇ hard rock •and inside it four beautifulᶜ corners; it had [in it] a deep,
wide, and smoothᵈ (thing) which was rolling over;ᵉ and it (the place) was deep and
3 dark to look at.ᶠ •At that moment, Rufael, one of the holy angels, who was with me,
responded to me; and he said to me, "These beautifulᵍ corners (are here) in order that   Mt 24:31
the spirits of the souls of the dead should assemble into them—they are created so
4 that the souls of the children of the peopleʰ should gather here. •They prepared these
placesⁱ in order to put them (i.e. the souls of the people) there until the day of their
5 judgment and the appointed time of the great judgment upon them."ʲ •I saw the spirits

e. G: "set over the best part of mankind and chaos."

f. G omits "mankind."

g. Gᵃ² adds "Remiel, one of the holy angels, whom God set over those who rise"; Gᵃ¹ adds "the names of the angels seven"; and Gᵃ², "the names of the angels."

21 a. Lit. "where nothing is done." G: "a chaotic place." B and C add "I saw there a terrible thing."

b. Lit. "an earth with a foundation."

c. Lit. "which is not organized," "prepared," "orderly." C: "a place which has no order." B is unintelligible: "an orderly wilderness"(?).

d. Lit. "on it."

e. G: "leading them."

f. G: "eager for the truth." Cf. EC, p. 55, n. 2.

g. B and C omit "heaven."

h. Lit. "here."

i. B C: "the number of the days of their sins."

j. B: "the border."

k. Lit. "causing to descend."

l. B and C repeat *naṣero*, "seeing," before 'ayno, "estimating."

m. Lit. "mouth."

n. B C (cf. G): "At that moment I said, 'How terrible is this place and (how) painful to look at!' "

o. Lit. "and responded to me."

p. B and C add here "and your affright."

q. Cf. EC, p. 55, n. 46.

r. Lit. "this pain."

22 a. B C: "Thence."

b. Lit. "and."

c. G has *koiloi*, "hollow," instead of *kaloi*, "beautiful."

d. Gᵃ omits "wide," and adds "three of them being dark and one bright, and there was a fountain of water in the middle of it."

e. Or "slippery," or "a place which causes one to slide, roll, or go off balance"—according to Ethiopian commentators. Charles suggests the Eth. to come from Gk. *kuklōmata*, which is a corruption of the Gk. *koilōmata*, "hollow places."

f. B, C, and Gᵃ add "how smooth."

g. Gᵃ: "hollow."

h. Eth. agrees with 4QEnᶜ against G, which omits "of the children of."

i. Cf. Charles: "these places were made." EC, p. 56, n. 31.

j. Or "the age [so A only] of the great judgment upon them." Cf. 4QEnᶜ, Milik, *The Books of Enoch*, p. 229f. B and C add "till their appointed period."

of the children of the people[k] who were dead, and their voices[l] were reaching unto
6 heaven until this very moment.[m] •I asked Rufael, the angel who was with me, and
said to him, "This spirit, the voice of which is reaching (into heaven) like this and
7 is making suit, whose (spirit) is it?" •And he answered me, saying,[n] "This is the Gen 4:10
spirit which had left Abel, whom Cain, his brother, had killed; it (continues to) sue
him until all of (Cain's) seed is exterminated from the face of the earth, and his seed
8 has disintegrated from among the seed of the people." •At that moment, I raised a
question regarding him[o] and regarding the judgment of all,[p] "For what reason is one
9 separated from the other?" •And he replied[q] and said to me, "These three have been
made in order that the spirits of the dead might be separated. And in the manner in
which the souls[r] of the righteous are separated[s] (by) this spring of water with light
10 upon it,[t] •in like manner, the sinners are set apart[u] when they die and are buried in
11 the earth and judgment has not been executed upon them in their lifetime,[v] •upon this
great pain, until the great day of judgment—and to those who curse[w] (there will be)
plague and pain forever, and the retribution of their spirits. They[x] will bind them there
12 forever—even if from the beginning of the world.[y] •And in this manner is a separation
made for the souls of those who make the suit (and) those who disclose concerning
13 destruction, as they were killed in the days of the sinners.[z] •Such has been made for
the souls of the people who are not righteous, but sinners and perfect criminals;[a2] they
shall be together with (other) criminals who are like them, (whose)[b2] souls will not
14 be killed on the day of judgment but will not rise from there." •At that moment I
blessed the Lord of Glory[c2] and I said, "Blessed[d2] be my Lord,[e2] the Lord of
righteousness who rules forever."[f2]

The fire of the luminaries of heaven

1 **23** And from there I (departed and) went[a] to another place in the direction of the west
2 until the (extreme) ends of the earth. •And I saw[b] a burning fire which was running
3 without rest;[c] and it did not diminish its speed[d] night and day.[e] •And I asked, saying,
4 "What is this (thing) which has no rest?" •At that moment, Raguel, one of the holy
angels, who was with me, answered me and said to me, "This (thing) which you saw
is the course (of the fire) and this,[f] the fire which is burning[g] in the direction of the
west, is the luminaries of heaven."

The seven mountains of the northwest and the tree of life

1 **24** From there I went to another place of the earth, and he showed me a mountain

---

k. Charles corrects the Gk. to "a dead man." Cf.
also 4QEn[c]. 4QEn[c] also adds *t'ān,* "there."

l. Charles corrects the Gk. to "his voice."

m. So A. Eth. *wa'eska we' tu gizē* may be a
corruption for *waysaki,* "was making suit," followed
by *we' tu gizē,* "and at that moment," which we
have in B and C. On the other hand, it may reflect
upon words found in 4QEn[c], "crying out unceasingly
and making accusations."

n. B C: "And he answered me and said to me
saying."

o. Or "regarding it." Hence regarding Cain or
what he saw earlier.

p. Charles suggests *koilōmatōn,* "of hollow places,"
instead of *krimatōn,* "of judgment." See EC, p. 58,
n. 19.

q. Lit. "replied to me."

r. B C: "spirits."

s. B C: "and such a division has been made."
G[a]: "this division is made."

t. G[a]: "this bright spring of water."

u. B C: "such has been created for sinners." In
A we have *tafaltu* instead of *tafatru.*

v. B and C add "their souls will be set apart."

w. G: "the accursed."

x. B C: "He."

y. Charles considers "even . . . world" an Eth.
intrusion.

z. G[a]: "his division has been made for the spirits
of those making suits . . . when they were slain in
the days of the sinners."

a2. Lit. "of perfect crime."

b2. Lit. "and."

c2. B adds "of righteousness who rules forever,"
and omits the following.

d2. A erroneously reads "be not blessed."

e2. G[a]: "are you."

f2. G[a]: "rules over the world."

23 a. 4QEn[d]: "I was transported."

b. 4QEn[d]: "I was shown."

c. Lit. "while it was not resting."

d. Lit. "decrease from its running." 4QEn[d]: "nor
halting its running," and adds "at the same time
remaining constant."

e. A adds "those like them." B and C add "but
(ran) regularly."

f. Flemming suggests *zeni* to be a corruption of
wā'ey, "burning."

f. Charles considers this a corruption for: "which
is persecuting." Cf. EC, p. 60, n. 25.

2 of fire which was flaming day and night. •And I went in its direction and saw seven dignified mountains—all different one from the other, of[a] precious and beautiful stones, and all dignified and glorious in respect to their visualization and beautiful in respect to their facade—three[b] in the direction of the east, one[c] founded on the other, and three in the direction of the north, one[d] upon the other, with[e] deep and crooked

3 ravines, each one (of which) is removed[f] from the other. •The seven mountains were (situated) in the midst of these (ravines) and (in respect to) their heights[g] all resembled

4 the seat of a throne (which is) surrounded by fragrant trees. •And among them, there was one tree such as I have never at all smelled; there was not a single one among those or other (trees) which is like it; among all the fragrances nothing could be so fragrant; its leaves, its flowers, and its wood would never wither forever; its fruit is

5 beautiful[h] and[i] resembles the clustered fruits of a palm tree. •At that moment I said, "This is a beautiful[j] tree, beautiful to view,[k] with leaves (so) handsome and blossoms[l]

6 (so) magnificant[m] in appearance." •Then Michael, one of the holy and revered[n] angels—he is their chief—who was with me, responded to me.

1 **25** And he said unto me, Enoch, "What is it that you are asking me concerning the

2 fragrance of this tree and[a] you are so inquisitive about?"[b] •At that moment, I answered, saying, "I am desirous[c] of knowing everything, but specially about this

3 thing."[d] •He answered, saying, "This tall mountain which you saw[e] whose summit resembles the throne of God is (indeed) his throne, on which the Holy and Great Lord of Glory, the Eternal King, will sit when he descends to visit the earth with

4 goodness. •And as for this fragrant tree, not a single human being has the authority to touch it until the great judgment, when he shall take vengeance on all and conclude

5 (everything) forever. •This is[f] for the righteous and the pious. And the elect will be presented with its fruit for life.[g] He will plant it in the direction of the northeast,[h] upon the holy place—in the direction of the house of the Lord, the Eternal King.

6 Then they shall be glad and rejoice in gladness,[i]
    and they shall enter into the holy (place);
    its fragrance shall (penetrate) their bones,
    long[j] life will they live[k] on earth,
    such as your fathers lived in their days."[l]

7 At that moment, I blessed the God of Glory, the Eternal King, for he has prepared such things for the righteous people, as he had created (them) and given it to them.[m]

Jerusalem and its surroundings

1 **26** And from there I went into the center of the earth and saw a blessed place,

2 shaded[a] with branches which live and bloom from a tree that was cut. •And there I saw a holy mountain; underneath the mountain, in the direction of the east, there was

Margin references: 10:17; 24:4; Gen 2:9; 3:22; 2Bar 73:2,3,6,7; 74; 4Ezra 8:52; Rev 2:7; 22:2,14

Margin references (26): Ezek 38:12; 5:5; Jub 8:12,19

24 a. Lit. "and."
b. G[a] omits "three."
c. G[a] omits "one."
d. G[a] omits "one."
e. Lit. "and."
f. Lit. "do not come near."
g. G[a]: "it excelled in height."
h. G[a] omits "is beautiful."
i. E repeats "its fruit," omitted by G[a].
j. G[a]: "How beautiful . . ."
k. G[a]: "fragrant."
l. So A. A agrees with G[a] against B and C, which read "fruit."
m. B and C add "very." A agrees with G.
n. G omits "revered."

25 a. G adds "why."
b. Lit. "you examine in order to know."
c. So A. B and C read "I want."
d. So A. B and C read "this tree."

e. Omitted by G.
f. B C: "It shall be given."
g. Charles considers this to be a corruption, comparing it to G, which reads "its fruit shall be food for the elect," and Ezek 47:12, which he claims "the writer had before him." See EC, p. 63, n. 15, and p. 62, n. 49.
h. Charles considers mas'e, "northeast" (G: eis borran), a mistake for la'kel, "for food" (G: eis boran). See EC, p. 63, n. 52.
i. B C: "be glad in gladness and rejoice."
j. Lit. "Much."
k. So B and C. A: "which they live."
l. B and C add "Sorrow, pain, torment, and plague shall not touch them."
m. Lit. "and he said, 'I gave it to them.' "

26 a. G: "in which there were trees." Cf. EC, p. 64, nn. 21f. 4QEn[d]: "in which were trees."

3 a stream which was flowing in the direction of the north. • And I saw in a second
direction, (another) mountain[b] which was higher than (the former).[c] Between them[d]
was a deep and narrow[e] valley. In the direction of the (latter) mountain ran a stream.[f]
4 In the direction of the west from this one there was (yet) another mountain, smaller
than it and not so high,[g] with a valley under it,[h] and between them besides,[i] (another)
5 valley which is[j] deep and dry.[k] • (The valleys)[l] were narrow,[m] (formed) of hard rocks
6 and no tree growing on them.[n] • And I marveled at the mountain(s)[o] and I marveled
at the valley(s): I marveled very deeply.

The accursed valley

1 **27** At that moment, I said, "For what purpose does this blessed land, entirely filled
2 with trees, (have) in its midst this accursed valley?" • Then, Uriel, one of the holy
angels, who was with me,[a] answered me and said to me, "This accursed valley is for   Mt 5:29,30
those accursed forever; here will gather together all (those) accursed ones,[b] those who
speak with their mouth unbecoming words against the Lord and utter hard words
concerning his glory. Here shall they be gathered together, and here shall be their
3 judgment,[c] in the last days. • There will be upon them the spectacle of the righteous
judgment, in the presence of the righteous forever.[d] The merciful will bless the Lord
4 of Glory, the Eternal King, all the day.[e] • In the days of the judgment of (the accursed),[f]
the (merciful)[g] shall bless him for the mercy which he had bestowed upon them."[h]
5 At that moment, I blessed the Lord of Glory and gave him the praise that befits his
glory.[i]

Journey to the east

1 **28** And from there I went in the direction of the east[a] into the center of the mountain[b]
2 of the desert; and I saw a wilderness and it was solitary, full of trees and seeds.[c] • And
3 there was a stream on top of it, and it gushed forth from above it. • It appeared like
a waterfall which cascaded greatly[d] as if toward the direction of west of the northeast;[e]
water and dew ascended from it all over.

1 **29** Then I went into another place in the desert; and I approached the easterly
2 direction of this mountain. • And there I saw the tree of judgment (which has) the
smell of rubbish; its tree looked like that of frankincense and myrrh.[a]

---

b. B and C read "toward the east a second
mountain."

c. Lit. "than this."

d. So 4QEn[d]. The Gk. reads *autou* instead of
autōn.

e. Lit. "without breadth."

f. Lit. "water." A adds erroneously *litani*, "to
me . . ." This may be a corruption from *botuni;* see
B and EC, p. 64, n. 38.

g. Lit. "having no height."

h. G[a]: "deep and dry."

i. Lit. "and."

j. Lit. "which are."

k. B and C add "at the extremities of the three."

l. B C: "All the valleys."

m. B C: "deep and narrow."

n. A erroneously: "and tree(s) will be planted on
them."

o. So also 4QEn[d]. The Eth. means "mountain,"
"hill," "hard rock." G[a] omits "mountain."

27 a. G[a] omits the preceding words.

b. B and C omit "accursed ones."

c. G[a]: "the place of their habitation."

d. G[a]: "In the last times, in the days of the true
judgment, before the righteous forever."

e. Text unclear.

f. Lit. "their judgment."

g. Lit. "they."

h. Lit. "according to how he has divided it to
them."

i. Lit. "I made a proclamation and a remembrance
that befits his glory." G: "set forth his glory and
lauded him . . ."

28 a. G omits "in the direction of the east."

b. G omits "of the mountain."

c. Lit. "and seeds from it" or "its seeds." Charles
holds "seeds from it" to be a corruption and suggests
instead "plants" as the original. Cf. EC, p. 68, n.
6.

d. Lit. "much."

e. G: "Rushing like a copious watercourse toward
the northwest . . ."

29 a. This rendition of the Eth., following A closely,
may be wrong. The text is awkward. Charles, following Beer and Praetorius, and partially in accordance with G, has suggested the emendation of the
text to read ". . . I saw aromatic trees exhaling the
fragrance of frankincense and myrrh, and the trees
also were similar [B: "not similar"] to the almond
tree." Cf. EC, p. 68, nn. 27–29, and p. 69, nn. 14–
18.

1 **30** And beyond it—beyond those above the easterly mountains—it is not far.[a] And
2 I saw a place which is a valley of water that is endless.[b] •And I saw a beautiful tree[c]
3 which resembles[d] a tree whose fragrance is like that of mastic. •And in the direction
of the sides[e] of those valleys, I saw a fragrant cinnamon tree. And over these, I
proceeded in the easterly direction.

1 **31** And I saw other mountains with trees[a] in them. There flowed from them (the
2 trees) something like nectar, called sarara[b] and galbanum. • And over these mountains,
I saw (yet) another mountain[c] and in it there were aloe trees,[d] and the whole forest[e]
3 was full of (trees) like sturdy almond trees.[f] •And when one picks[g] the fruit it gives
the most pleasant odor.[h]

1 **32** And after (experiencing) this fragrant odor,[a] while looking toward the northeast
over the mountains, I saw seven mountains full of excellent nard, fragrant trees,
2 cinnamon trees, and pepper. • From there I went over the summits of the mountains,[b]
far toward the east of the earth.[c] I (then) passed over the Erythraean Sea and went far
3 from it, and passed over the head of angel[d] Zutu'el.[e] •And I came to the garden of
righteousness[f] and saw beyond those trees many (other)[g] large (ones) growing there[h]—
their fragrance sweet, large ones,[i] with much elegance, and glorious. And the tree of
4 wisdom, of which one eats[j] and knows great wisdom, (was among them). •It looked
like[k] the colors[l] of the carob tree, its fruit like very beautiful grape clusters, and the
5 fragrance of this tree travels and reaches[m] afar.[n] •And I said,[o] "This tree is beautiful[p]
6 and its appearance beautiful[q] and pleasant!" •Then the holy angel Raphael, who was
with me, responded to me and said,[r] "This very thing is the tree of wisdom from
which your old father and aged mother, they who are your precursors,[s] ate and came
to know wisdom; and (consequently) their eyes were opened and they realized[t] that
they were naked and (so) they were expelled from the garden."

1 **33** And from there I went to the extreme ends of the earth and saw there huge beasts,
each different from the other—and different birds (also) differing from one another
in appearance, beauty, and voice. And to the east of those beasts, I saw the ultimate
2 ends of the earth which rests on the heaven. •And the gates of heaven were open, and
3 I saw how the stars of heaven come out; •and I counted the gates out of which they
exit and wrote down all their exits for each one: according to their numbers,[a] their

30 a. The Eth. seems corrupt. Cf. G: "Beyond
these, I went afar to the east."
b. G omits "that is endless."
c. Lit. "trees." G: "there was a tree."
d. G[a]: "color."
e. Lit. "wings."

31 a. G: "tree groves."
b. Meaning uncertain, perhaps "sarara" derives
from Heb. ṣ[e]rî, a type of balsam.
c. G[a] adds "to the east of the ends of the earth."
d. Charles suggests that these aloe trees were
eaglewood. G[a] omits "in it there were aloe trees."
e. Lit. "all those trees."
f. Or "hard almond trees." Charles amends this
sentence to read "all the trees were full of stacte,
being like almond-trees." Cf. EC, p. 70, nn. 37–
39.
g. Lit. "they pick."
h. Lit. "it pleases above all odors." Charles
amends this sentence to read ". . . when one burnt
it, it smelt sweeter than any fragrant odor." Cf. EC,
p. 71, nn. 15, 40.

32 a. Lit. "after this." B C: "after these odors."
G[a] omits this phrase.
b. G[a] adds "all."

c. B and C omit "of the earth." A agrees with
G.
d. G[a] omits "angel."
e. B C: Zut'el.
f. In A 1En 32:3–34:2 (i.e. A, fols. 80v[b]–81r[a])
were written by a different scribe.
g. B C: "many trees."
h. G omits "growing there," and adds "two
trees . . ."
i. All MSS add "large ones."
j. Lit. "they eat."
k. G[a]: "That tree is in height like the fir and its
leaves are . . ."
l. So A. G: to dendra, "leaves." Other Eth. MSS
do not make sense.
m. B and C omit "reaches."
n. Lit. "long way."
o. A wrongly has wâ'ey, "burning," instead of
'ebē, "I said."
p. G: "How beautiful is the tree . . ."
q. G omits "beautiful."
r. G omits "and said."
s. Lit. "those who preceded you."
t. Lit. "they knew."

33 a. So B and C. A could possibly be translated:
"according to their keepers."

names, their ranks, their seats, their periods, their months, as Uriel, the holy angel

4 who was with me, showed me. •He showed me all things and wrote them down for me[b]—also in addition he wrote down their names, their laws,[c] and their companies.

Journey to the north

1 **34** From there I went in the direction of the north, to the extreme ends of the earth, and there at the extreme end of the whole world I saw a great and glorious seat.[a]

2 There (also) I saw three open gates of heaven; when it blows cold, hail, frost, snow,[b] dew, and rain, through each one of the (gates) the winds proceed in the northwesterly

3 direction. •Through one gate they blow good things; but when they blow with force through the two (other) gates, they blow violence and sorrow upon the earth.

Journey to the west

1 **35** And from there I went in the direction of the west to the extreme ends of the earth, and saw there three open gates of heaven, (just) like the one that I saw in the east in respect to the number of its exits.[a]

Journey to the south

1 **36** And from there I went in the direction of the south to the extreme ends of the earth, and saw there three open gates of the heaven from where[a] the south wind, dew,

2 rain, and wind come forth. •From there I went in the direction of the extreme ends of the heaven[b] and saw there open gates of heaven, with small gates above them, in

3 the direction of the east. •Through one[c] of these small gates pass the stars of heaven

4 and travel westward on the path which is shown to them. •And when I saw (this) I blessed—and I shall always[d] bless—the Lord of Glory, who performed great and blessed miracles in order that he may manifest his great deeds to his angels, the winds,[e] and to the people so that they might praise the effect[f] of all his creation[g]—so that they might see the effect[h] of his power and praise him in respect to the great work of his hands and bless him forever.

Book II (37–71)

The Book of the Similitudes

Introduction

1 **37** Book two:[a] The vision which Enoch[b] saw the second time—the vision of wisdom which Enoch, son of Jared,[c] son of Mahalalel,[d] son of Kenan,[e] son of Enosh,[f] son of

2 Seth, son of Adam, saw: •This is the beginning of the words of wisdom which I commenced[g] to propound, saying to those who dwell in the earth, "Listen, you first

---

b. So B and C. A wrongly reads "for him."
c. Lit. "commandments."

34 a. B reads "miracle." C: "counsel," "device."
b. So B and C. A reads "ash," "white dust."

35 a. B and C add "and gates."

36 a. Or "from there, the south." The word *'azēb* can mean "south," "southwest." Charles suggests "moisture" instead of the word "south." Cf. EC, p. 75, n. 25.
b. B C: "in the direction of the east to the extreme ends of the heaven."
c. So B. C emended by Charles reads "through each one . . ." A is defective.
d. Lit. "all times."

e. B: "to the souls of men." C: "to the souls and to people."
f. Lit. "the action."
g. B C: "his deeds and his creation."
h. Lit. "the action."

37 a. This division, which is indicated in A by an Eth. number, is missing in B and C, and other Eth. MSS.
b. Lit. "he."
c. Or Eth. Yared.
d. A: Malkel. B C: Malal'el.
e. Or Eth. Qaynan.
f. Eth. Henos, erroneously written Ḥenok (Enoch) in A.
g. Lit. "I took up."

ones, and look, you last ones, the words of the Holy One, which I teach[h] before the
3 Lord of the Spirits. •It is good to declare these words to those of former times, but
4 one should not withhold[i] the beginning of wisdom from those of latter days.[j] •Until
now such wisdom, which I have received as I recited (it) in accordance with the will
of the Lord of the Spirits, had not been bestowed upon me before the face of the
5 Lord of the Spirits. From him, the lot of eternal life has been given to me. •Three
things[k] were imparted to me''; and I began[l] to recount them to those who dwell upon
the earth.

Coming judgment of the wicked

1 **38** The first thing:

> When the congregation of the righteous shall appear,
> sinners shall be judged for their sins,[a]
> they shall be driven from the face of the earth,
2   and when the Righteous One shall appear before the face of the righteous,
> those elect ones, their deeds are hung upon the Lord of the Spirits,
> he shall reveal light to the righteous and the elect who dwell upon the
>   earth,
> where will the dwelling of the sinners be,
> and where the resting place of those who denied the name[b] of the Lord
>   of the Spirits?
> It would have been better for them not to have been born.
3   When the secrets of the Righteous One[c] are revealed,
> he shall judge the sinners;[d]
> and the wicked ones will be driven from the presence of the righteous
>   and the elect,
4   and from that time, those who possess the earth will neither be rulers
>   nor princes,
> they shall not be able to behold the faces of the holy ones,
> for the light of the Lord of the Spirits has shined[e]
> upon the face of the holy, the righteous, and the elect.
5   At that moment, kings and rulers shall perish,
> they shall be delivered into the hands of the righteous and holy ones,
6   and from thenceforth no one shall be able to induce the Lord of the
>   Spirits to show them mercy,
> for their life is annihilated.

The home of the righteous

1 **39** And it shall come to pass in those days that the children of the elect and the
holy ones [will descend] from the high heaven and their seed will become one with
2 the children of the people. •And in those days Enoch received the books of zeal and
wrath as well as the books of haste and whirlwind.[a] The Lord of the Spirits says that
mercy shall not be upon them.

3   In those days, whirlwinds carried me off from the earth,
> and set me down into the ultimate ends of the heavens.
4   There I saw other[b] dwelling places of the holy ones[c] and their resting
>   places too.[d]

---

h. Eth. *'a'mer,* which is found in A, is generally
understood to mean "I know," "I understand," but
among Ethiopian grammarians it is also used, in its
correct grammatical form, to mean "I teach," "I
cause to understand." B and C read "I speak."
   i. Lit. "prevent."
   j. This sentence is an approximation of the Eth.,
which is unclear.
   k. So Ethiopian commentators.
   l. Lit. "I took up."
38 a. A: "and their sins."

b. B and C omit "name."
c. B C: "secrets of the righteous."
d. B C: "sinners shall be judged."
e. Lit. "is seen."

39 a. B C: "disturbance."
   b. C: "another vision."
   c. B reads "with the angels" instead of "the holy
ones."
   d. B adds "of the holy ones." C adds "of the
righteous ones."

5 So there my eyes saw their dwelling places with the holy angels,[e]
and their resting places with the holy ones,[f]
and they interceded and petitioned and prayed on behalf of the children
of the people,
and righteousness flowed before them like water,
and mercy like dew upon the earth,
and thus it is in their midst forever and ever.

6 And in those days[g] my eyes saw the Elect One of righteousness and of
faith,
and righteousness shall prevail in his days,
and the righteous and elect ones shall be without number before him
forever and ever.

7 And I saw a dwelling place[h] underneath the wings of the Lord of the
Spirits;
and all the righteous and the elect before him shall be as intense[i] as the
light of fire.
Their mouth shall be full of blessing;
and their lips will praise the name of the Lord of the Spirits,
and righteousness before him will have no end;
and uprightness before him will not cease.[j]

8 There (underneath his wings) I wanted to dwell;
and my soul desired that dwelling place.
Already[k] my portion is there;
for thus has it been reserved for me[l] before the Lord of the Spirits.

9 In those days, I praised and prayed to[m] the name of the Lord of the Spirits with
blessings and praises, for he had strengthened me by blessings and praises in
10 accordance with the will of the Lord of the Spirits. •And I gazed at that place[n] (under
his wings), and I blessed and praised, saying, "Blessed is he, and may he be blessed,
11 from the beginning and forever more. •There is no such thing as non-existence[o] before
him. (Even) before the world was created, he knows what is forever and what will
12 be from generation to generation. •Those who do not slumber but stand before your
glory, did bless[p] you. They shall bless, praise, and extol (you), saying, 'Holy, Holy,
13 Holy, Lord of the Spirits; the spirits fill the earth.' "[q] •And at that place (under his
wings) my eyes saw others who stood[r] before him sleepless[s] (and) blessed (him),
14 saying, •"Blessed are you and blessed is the name of the Lord of the Spirits[t] forever
and ever." And my face was changed on account of the fact that I could not withstand
the sight.[u]

The four angels

1 **40** And after that, I saw a hundred thousand times a hundred thousand, ten million
times ten million, an innumerable and uncountable[a] (multitude) who stand before the
2 glory[b] of the Lord of the Spirits. •I saw them standing[c]—on the four wings of the
Lord of the Spirits—and saw four other faces among those who do not slumber,[d] and
I came to know their names, which[e] the angel who came with me revealed[f] to me;

e. C: "righteous angels."
f. B omits the last two lines.
g. C: "in that place."
h. B: "their dwelling place." C: "his dwelling place."
i. B C: "shall be beautiful."
j. Lit. "will have no end."
k. "Before," "Previously," "Of old."
l. Lit. "confirmed [made firm] . . . on my behalf."
m. B C: "I extolled."
n. Lit. "my eyes kept looking," "my eyes lingered contemplating, seeing." The passage could also be translated: "I watched and watched."
o. Lit. "ending," "ceasing."
p. B C: "will bless."

q. Because case endings are not indicated, the passage could also be translated "the earth is full of the spirits." B and C read "he will fill the earth with spirits."
r. Lit. "who stand."
s. Lit. "they do not slumber."
t. B C: "Lord."
u. Lit. "on account of the fact that I hated to look."
40 a. Lit. "they have no number and count."
b. C omits "glory."
c. B C: "I saw them."
d. B: "among those who stand." C: "four faces different from those who do not slumber."
e. Lit. "which names."
f. Lit. "made known."

3 and he (also) showed me all the hidden things. •(Then) I heard the voices of those
4 four faces while they were saying praises before the Lord of Glory. •The first voice
5 was blessing the name of the Lord of the Spirits. •The second voice I heard blessing
6 the Elect One and the elect ones who are clinging onto the Lord of the Spirits. •And
the third voice I heard interceding and praying on behalf of those who dwell upon
7 the earth and supplicating in the name of the Lord of the Spirits. •And the fourth
voice I heard expelling the demons[g] and forbidding them from coming to the Lord
8 of the Spirits in order to accuse those who dwell upon the earth. •And after that, I
asked the angel of peace, who was going with me and showed me everything that
was hidden, "Who are these four faces which I have seen and whose voices I have
9 heard and written down?" •And he said to me, "The first one is the merciful and
forbearing[h] Michael; the second one, who is set over all disease and every wound of
the children of the people, is Raphael; the third, who is set over all exercise of
strength, is Gabriel; and the fourth, who is set over all actions of repentance unto the
10 hope of those who would inherit eternal life, is Phanuel by name." •(So) these are
his four angels: they[i] are of the Lord of the Spirits, and the four voices which I heard
in those days.

The Lord of the Spirits, and the four voices which I heard in those days.

1 **41** And after that, I saw all the secrets in heaven, and how a kingdom breaks up,
2 and how the actions of the people are weighed in the balance. •And there I saw the
dwelling place of the sinners[a] and the company of the holy ones;[b] and my eyes saw
the sinners[c]—those who deny the name of the Lord of the Spirits—being expelled
from there and being dragged off; and they could not stand still because of the plague
which proceeds forth from the Lord of the Spirits.

Cosmic secrets

3   And there my eyes saw the secrets of lightning and thunder, and the mysteries
of the winds, how they are distributed in order to blow upon the earth, and the secrets
of the clouds and the dew I saw there from where they proceed in that place and (how)
4 from there they satiate the dust of the earth. • At that place, I (also) saw sealed
storerooms from which the winds of the storerooms of hail and the winds of the
storerooms of mist[d] are distributed; and these clouds hover over the earth from the
5 beginning of the world. •And I saw the storerooms of the sun and the moon, from
what place they come out and to which place they return, and their glorious return—
how in their travel one festival[e] is celebrated more than the other. They do not depart
from their orbit, neither increase nor decrease it;[f] but they keep faith one with another:
6 in accordance with an oath they set[g] and they rise.[h] •From the first is the sun;[i] and it
executes its course in accordance with the commandment of the Lord of the Spirits—
7 his name shall persist forever and ever. • After that[j] is found (both) the hidden and the
visible path of the moon; and the path of its orbit it completes by day and by night
at that place. And the two[k] will gaze directly into[l] the glory of the Lord of the Spirits.[m]
They give thanks, they praise, and they do not economize (on energy), for their very
essence[n] generates new power.[o]
8   Surely the many changes of the sun have (both) a blessing and a curse,
         and the course of the moon's path is light to the
         righteous (on the one hand) and darkness to the sinners (on the other),

g. Lit. "the *Sayṭans*."
h. Lit. "of distant wrath."
i. B and C omit "they."

41 a. B: "of the righteous." C: "of the elect."
b. B C: "the dwelling place of the holy ones."
c. B C: "all the sinners."
d. B C: "the storerooms of hail and winds and the storerooms of mist and clouds."
e. B and C read instead *be'ul*, "rich," "wealthy."
f. Lit. "their orbit."
g. Lit. "stay over(night)."

h. Lit. "come out." B and C omit "they set and they rise."
i. B C: "the sun goes out first."
j. C adds: "I saw."
k. Lit. "the one with the other."
l. Lit. "before."
m. C omits "the glory of the Lord." B omits "the glory."
n. Lit. *kʷunatomu*, "their being," "nature," "condition," "creation." Cf. also 43:2 for this reading. B C: *akʷotẽtomu*, "their thanksgiving."
o. Lit. "is rest to them."

in the name of the Lord of the Spirits, who created the distinction[p]
    between light and darkness
and separated the spirits of the people,
and strengthened the spirits of the righteous in the name of his right-
    eousness.

9 Surely, neither an angel nor Satan[q] has the power to hinder;
for there is a judge to all of them,[r]
he will glance,[s] and all of them are before him,
he is the judge.[t]

The abode of Wisdom and Iniquity

1 **42** Wisdom could not find a place in which she could dwell;
but a place was found (for her) in the heavens.
2 Then Wisdom went out to dwell with the children of the people,
but she found no dwelling place.
(So) Wisdom returned to her place
and she settled permanently[a] among the angels.
3 Then Iniquity went out of her rooms,
and found whom she did not expect.
And she dwelt with them,
like rain in a desert,
like dew on a thirsty land.

More secrets of the cosmos

1 **43** And I saw other lightnings and the stars of heaven. And I saw how he called
2 them[a] each by their (respective) names, and they obeyed him. •And I saw the impartial
scales[b] for the purpose of balancing their lights at their widest areas. And their natures[c]
are as follows: Their revolutions produce lightning; and in number they[d] are (as many
3 as) the angels; they keep their faith each one according to their names.[e] •And I asked
the angel who was going with me and who had shown me the secret things, "What
4 are these things?" •And he said to me, "The Lord of the Spirits has shown you the
prototype[f] of each one of them: These are the names of the holy ones who dwell upon
the earth and believe[g] in the name[h] of the Lord of the Spirits forever and ever."

1 **44** And I saw another thing regarding lightning: how some stars arise and become
lightning and cannot dwell with the rest.[a]

Lot of unbelievers: new heaven and new earth

1 **45** This is the second parable concerning those who deny the name of the Lord of
the Spirits[a] and the congregation of the holy ones.[b]

2 Neither will they ascend into heaven,[c]
nor will they reach the ground;
such will be the lot of the sinners,
who will deny[d] the name of the Lord of the Spirits,

p. Lit. "the median."
q. B C: "no authority or power."
r. B: "For he will see a judge for them." C: "For
he will appoint a judge for them."
s. Cf. n. r.
t. Lit. "He judges."

42 a. Lit. "became firm [settled]," "established
(herself)," "stayed put." B C: "she sat."

43 a. B and C add "all of them."
b. Or "the balance of righteousness."
c. B C: "the day of their being [or "appearance"]."
d. Lit. "their revolutions."

e. B C: "they keep their faith with each other."
f. Or "the significance." Lit. "the parable,"
"example," "similitude."
g. A wrongly: "do not believe."
h. So B and C. A omits "the name."

44 a. Lit. "dwell [ḥadira] with them." B: "leave
[ḥadiga] with them." C: "leave their prototypes."

45 a. B C: "the name of the dwelling of the Lord."
b. B and C omit "the congregation of the holy
ones."
c. So B and C. A is corrupt.
d. C: "have denied."

those who in this manner will be preserved for the day of burden and
    tribulation.

3   On that day, my Elect One shall sit on the seat of glory
and make a selection[e] of their deeds,
their resting places will be without number,   Jn 14:23
their souls[f] shall be firm within them when they see my Elect One,[g]
those[h] who have appealed to my glorious[i] name.

4   On that day, I shall cause my Elect One[j] to dwell among them,
I shall transform heaven and make it[k] a blessing of light forever.

5   I shall (also) transform the earth and make it[l] a blessing,
and cause my Elect One[m] to dwell in her.
Then those who have committed sin and crime shall not set foot in her.

6   For in peace I have looked (with favor) upon my righteous ones and given
    them mercy,
and have caused them to dwell before me.
But sinners have come before me so that by judgment
I shall destroy them from before the face of the earth.

1 **46** At that place, I saw the One to whom belongs the time before time.[a] And his head
was white like wool, and there was with him another individual, whose face was like
that of a human being.[b] His countenance was full of grace like that of one among the
2 holy angels. •And I asked the one—from among the angels—who was going with me,
and who had revealed to me all the secrets regarding the One who was born of human
beings,[c] "Who is this, and from whence is he who is going as the prototype of the
3 Before-Time?"[d] •And he answered me and said to me, "This is the Son of Man,[e] to
whom belongs righteousness, and with whom righteousness dwells. And he will open[f]
all the hidden storerooms; for the Lord of the Spirits has chosen[g] him, and he is
4 destined to be victorious before the Lord of the Spirits in eternal[h] uprightness. •This
Son of Man whom you[i] have seen is the One who would remove[j] the kings and the
mighty ones from their comfortable seats[k] and the strong ones from their thrones. He
5 shall loosen the reins of the strong and crush[l] the teeth of the sinners. • He shall depose[m]
the kings from their thrones and kingdoms. For[n] they do not extol and glorify him,
6 and neither do they obey him, the source of their kingship.[o] •The faces of the strong
will be slapped and be filled with shame and gloom. Their dwelling places and their
beds will be worms.[p] They shall have no hope to rise from their beds, for they do not
7 extol the name of the Lord of the Spirits. •And they have become the judges[q] of the

---

e. Charles thinks that "he will make a selection"
is a corruption and suggests "he will try" instead.
See EC, p. 85, n. 21.
  f. B: "their spirits."
  g. Text: "ones."
  h. So B and C. A reads *la'ela*, "over," "upon,"
instead of *la'ela*.
  i. B adds "holy."
  j. Text: "ones."
  k. Lit. "her."
  l. Lit. "her."
  m. Text: "ones."

46 a. Lit. "Head of days," "Chief of days," "he
who precedes time," "the Beginning of days," "the
First of days," "he who is of primordial days," "the
Antecedent of time."
  b. Lit. "whose face was like the appearance of a
person."
  c. Eth. *zatawalda 'emsabe'*. B and C read *zeku
walda sabe'*, "that Son of Man [or "human beings"]."
  d. Following B and C, we should translate this
passage: ". . . from where could he be, and for *what*
reason does he go with him who precedes time?" A
could also be adjusted to give the same reading with

the addition of *ment*, "what"—which it omits.
However, I have here translated the passage as it
stands, with a minimum adjustment.
  e. "Man" in this context means "people" or
"human beings." Though this passage could be
rendered "Son of human beings," to avoid unnecessary confusion, I have used "Son of Man," which
has become an accepted and standard expression
among scholars for a long time.
  f. So B and C. A: "it will be open."
  g. So B and C. A: "has dwelled."
  h. So B and C. A: "above."
  i. A: "I."
  j. Lit. "lift them up" or "unseat."
  k. Lit. "beds." Cf. "couches," "reclining chairs,"
"sofas."
  l. Lit. "fell."
  m. Lit. "push off."
  n. So B and C.
  o. Lit. "from where the kingdom was bestowed
upon them."
  p. B C: "Their dwelling places will be darkness,
and their beds will be worms."
  q. Lit. "those who judge." Also cf. EC, p. 87,
n. 24.

stars of heaven; they raise their hands (to reach) the Most High[r] while walking upon the earth and dwelling in her. They manifest all their deeds in oppression; all their deeds are oppression.[s] Their power (depends) upon their wealth. And their devotion is to the gods which they have fashioned with their own hands. But they deny the

8 name of the Lord of the Spirits. •Yet they like to congregate in his houses and (with) the faithful ones who cling to the Lord of the Spirits.[t]

Prayer of the righteous

1 **47** "In those days, the prayers of the righteous ascended into heaven, and the blood
2 of the righteous from the earth before the Lord of the Spirits. •There shall be days[a] when all[b] the holy ones who dwell in the heavens above shall dwell (together).[c] And with one voice, they shall supplicate and pray—glorifying, praising, and blessing the name of the Lord of the Spirits—on behalf of the blood of the righteous ones which has been shed. Their prayers[d] shall not stop from exhaustion before the Lord of the Spirits—neither will they relax[e] forever—(until)[f] judgment is executed for them."
3 In those days, I saw him—the Antecedent of Time, while he was sitting upon the throne of his glory, and the books of the living ones were open before him. And all
4 his power in heaven above and his escorts[g] stood before him. • The hearts of the holy ones are filled with joy, because the number of the righteous has been offered, the prayers of the righteous ones have been heard, and the blood of the righteous has been admitted before the Lord of the Spirits.

The Son of Man: the Antecedent of Time: his judgment

1 **48** Furthermore, in that place I saw the fountain of righteousness, which does not become depleted and is surrounded completely by numerous fountains of wisdom. All the thirsty ones drink (of the water) and become filled with wisdom. (Then) their
2 dwelling places become with the holy, righteous, and elect ones. •At that hour, that Son[a] of Man was given a name,[b] in the presence of the Lord of the Spirits, the Before-
3 Time;[c] •even before the creation of the sun and the moon,[d] before the creation of the
4 stars, he was given a name in the presence of the Lord of the Spirits. • He will become a staff for the righteous ones in order that they may lean on him and not fall. He is the light of the gentiles and he will become the hope of those who are sick in their
5 hearts. •All those who dwell upon the earth shall fall and worship before him; they
6 shall glorify, bless, and sing the name[e] of the Lord of the Spirits. •For this purpose he became the Chosen One; he was concealed in the presence of (the Lord of the
7 Spirits)[f] prior to the creation of the world, and for eternity. •And he has revealed the wisdom of the Lord of the Spirits to the righteous and the holy ones, for he has preserved the portion of the righteous because they have hated and despised this world of oppression (together with)[g] all its ways of life[h] and its habits[i] in the name of the Lord of the Spirits; and because they will be saved in his name and it is his good
8 pleasure that they have life. •In those days,[j] the kings of the earth and the mighty

Odes Sol 6:11

Odes Sol 36:3

Lk 2:32

---

r. Lit. "into the Most High."
s. So A and B. C omits "all their deeds are oppression."
t. B and C read, possibly more correctly, "they persecute the houses of his congregations and the faithful who cling to the Lord of the Spirits."

47 a. B C: "In those days."
  b. B and C omit "all."
  c. B and C, which read "unite," "be companions," "co-operate," may be more accurate.
  d. B and C add "of the righteous ones."
  e. Lit. "there will not be patience to them."
  f. Lit. "in order that," "so that," "to the end that."
  g. Lit. "which surround him."

48 a. A erroneously: "sons."
  b. Lit. "named . . . by the name."
  c. Lit. "before the beginning [or "head"] of days."
  d. Eth. *ta'amer*, "the wondrous thing"—but to be understood in Ge'ez (Eth.) as "the moon" (cf. 2Chr 33:3; Jer 10:2; Jub 4:17).
  e. B: "they shall glorify . . . to him, to the name." C omits "the name."
  f. Lit. "he concealed (him) in his (own) presence."
  g. Lit. "and hated."
  h. Lit. "its deeds."
  i. Lit. "its ways."
  j. C reads erroneously "In vain days."

landowners[k] shall be humiliated[l] on account of the deeds of their hands. Therefore, on the day of their misery[m] and weariness, they will not be able to save themselves. 9 I shall deliver them into the hands of my elect ones like grass in the fire and like lead in the water, so they shall burn before the face of the holy ones[n] and sink before their[o] 10 sight,[p] and no place will be found for them. • On the day of their weariness, there shall be an obstacle[q] on the earth and they shall fall on their faces; and they shall not rise up (again), nor anyone (be found) who will take them with his hands and raise them up. For they have denied the Lord of the Spirits and his Messiah. Blessed be the name of the Lord of the Spirits!

Wisdom and power of the Elect One

1 **49** So[a] wisdom flows[b] like water and glory is measureless before him forever and 2 ever. • For his might is in all the mysteries of righteousness,[c] and oppression will vanish[d] like a shadow having no foundation. The Elect One[e] stands before the Lord 3 of the Spirits; his glory is forever and ever and his power is unto all generations. • In him dwells the spirit of wisdom, the spirit which gives thoughtfulness, the spirit of knowledge and strength, and the spirit of those who have fallen asleep in righteousness. 4 He shall judge the secret things.[f] And no one will be able to utter vain words[g] in his presence. For he is the Elect One before the Lord of the Spirits according to his good pleasure.

His mercy and his judgment

1 **50** In those days, there will be a change for the holy and the righteous ones and the light of days shall rest upon them; and glory and honor shall be given back to the holy 2 ones, on the day of weariness. • He heaped[a] evil upon the sinners; but the righteous ones shall be victorious in the name of the Lord of the Spirits. He will cause the 3 others to see this so that they may repent and forsake the deeds of their hands. • There shall not be honor unto them in the name of the Lord of the Spirits. But through his name they shall be saved, and the Lord of the Spirits shall have mercy upon them, 4 for his mercy is considerable. • He is righteous[b] in his judgment and in the glory that is before him.[c] Oppression cannot survive his judgment; and the unrepentant in his 5 presence shall perish. • The Lord of the Spirits has said that from henceforth he will not have mercy on them.

Resurrection of the dead

1 **51** In those days, Sheol will return all the deposits which she had received[a] and hell 2 will give back all that which it owes. • And he shall choose the righteous and the holy ones from among (the risen dead),[b] for the day when they shall be selected[c] and saved[d] 3 has arrived.[e] • In those days, (the Elect One)[f] shall sit on my throne, and from the

---

k. Lit. "the strong ones by whom the land is possessed."

l. Lit. "be humble in countenance."

m. A wrongly reads *şedqomu*, "their righteousness," instead of *sā'qomu*, "their misery."

n. B: "righteous ones."

o. Lit. "the holy ones."

p. Lit. "their face." C reads "Like grass in the fire, so they shall burn before the face of the holy ones; and like lead in the water, they shall sink before the face of the righteous ones."

q. B C: "a rest."

49 a. Lit. "because."

b. B: "it is poured out." C: "poured out."

c. B C: "For he is mighty in all the secrets of righteousness."

d. Lit. "pass."

e. Lit. "Because the Elect One."

f. So B and C. A reads "that which has the secret

things."

g. So B and C. A reads: *bakama*, "so that," "in order that," "in accordance with," "as," instead of *bak*, "vain," "useless," "stale."

50 a. B C: "which has been heaped." Cf. EC, p. 93, n. 6.

b. A wrongly: "righteousness."

c. B C: "and before his glory."

51 a. B C: ". . . the earth will bring together all her deposits and Sheol will bring together all her deposits which she has received."

b. Lit. "from among them."

c. B and C omit "they shall be selected."

d. Lit. "they shall be saved and selected."

e. Lit. "has approached." It is possible to translate the passage: "for the day when they shall be saved has arrived, they shall be elected."

f. So B and C. A omits "the Elect One."

conscience of his mouth shall come out all the secrets of wisdom, for the Lord of the
4 Spirits has given them to him and glorified him. • In those days, mountains shall dance
like rams; and the hills shall leap like kidsg satiated with milk. And the faces of all   Ps 114:4
the angels in heaven shall glow with joy, because on that day the Elect One has arisen.
5 And the earth shall rejoice; and the righteous ones shall dwell upon her and the elect
ones shall walk upon her.

The metal mountains

1 **52** After those days, in the same place where I had seen all the secret visions, having
been carried off in a wind vehiclea and taken to the west, my eyes saw there all the
2 secret things of heaven and the future things.b • There were (there) a mountain of iron,
a mountain of copper, a mountain of silver, a mountain of gold, a mountain of colored
3 metal,c and a mountain of lead. • And I asked the angel who was going with me,
4 saying, "What are these things which I have seen in secret?"d • And he said to me,
"All these things which you have seen happen bye the authority of his Messiah so that
5 he may give orders and be praisedf upon the earth." • Then this angel of peace
answered, saying to me, "Wait a little, and all secret things which encircle the Lord
6 of the Spirits will be revealed unto you. • As for these mountains which you have seen
with your own eyesg—the mountain of iron, the mountain of copper, the mountain
of silver, the mountain of gold, the mountain of colored metal, and the mountain of
lead—all of them, in the presence of the Elect One, will become like a honeycomb
(that melts) before fire, like water that gushes downh from the top of such mountains,i
7 and become helplessj byk his feet. • It shall happen in those days that no onel shall be
8 saved either by gold or by silver; and no one shall be able to escape. • There shall be
no iron for war, nor shall anyone wear a breastplate. Neither bronzem nor tinn shall
be to any avail or be of any value;o and there will be no need of lead whatsoever.
9 All these substances will be removedp and destroyed from the surface of the earth
when the Elect One shall appear before the face of the Lord of the Spirits."

The scene of judgment

1 **53** My eyes saw there a deep valley with a wide mouth.a And all those who dwell
upon the earth, the sea, and the islands shall bring to itb gifts, presents, and tributes;
2 yet this deep valley shall not become full. • They shall fulfill the criminal deeds of
their hands and eat all the produce of crime which the sinners toil for. Sinners shall
be destroyed from before the face of the Lord of the Spirits—they shall perish eternally,
3 standing before the face of his earth. • So I saw all the angels of plague co-operating
4 and preparing all the chainsc of Satan. • And I asked the angel of peace, who was
5 going with me, "For whom are they preparing these chains?"d • And he answered me,
saying,e "They are preparingf these for the kings and the potentates of this earth in
6 order that they may be destroyed thereby. • After this, the Righteousg and Elect One

---

g. Or "lambs."

52 a. Eth. *mankʷorkʷor.* So also Charles's q.
Charles's choice of the most common MSS reading,
nakʷorkʷāra nafās, "wind balls" (translated as
"whirlwind" by him), instead of that of q, has misled
some scholars to think erroneously that the expression
"chariot of wind" mentioned in *Mani Codex* is
missing from 1En, and that the Apocalypse of Enoch
to which the Codex refers is not the same work as
our 1En. (In EMML 2080 there is an Amharic
marginal note translating *mankʷorkʷor* as *saragalā,*
a nonambiguous word meaning "chariot.")
  b. Lit. "that which is to become."
  c. Or "mixed metal," "purple metal."
  d. Or "What are these secret things which I have
seen?"
  e. B C: "to."
  f. Or "be given a gift." B C: "be powerful."

g. B: "which you saw." C: "which your eyes
have seen."
  h. Lit. "descends."
  i. B and C read "from above it upon these
mountains."
  j. Lit. "tired," "weak," "powerless."
  k. Lit. "before."
  l. Lit. "they."
  m. Or "brass."
  n. Or "solder."
  o. Lit. "will not be counted."
  p. Lit. "denied," "turned away," "abandoned."
53 a. C: "a valley with a wide and deep mouth."
  b. I.e. "to the valley."
  c. A erroneously: "victuals." So C.
  d. C: "victuals."
  e. B C: "and he said to me."
  f. C omits "they are preparing."
  g. A erroneously: "righteousness."

will reveal the house of his congregation. From that time, they shall not be hindered
7 in the name of the Lord of the Spirits. •And these mountains[h] shall become (flat) like
earth in the presence of his righteousness, and the hills shall become like a fountain
of water. And the righteous ones shall have rest from the oppression of sinners.''

1 **54** Then I looked and turned to another face of the earth and saw there a valley, deep
2 and burning with fire. • And they were bringing kings and potentates and were throwing
3 them into this deep valley. • And my eyes saw there their chains while they were
4 making them into iron fetters[a] of immense[b] weight. •And I asked the angel of peace,
who was going with me, saying, ''For whom are these imprisonment chains[c] being
5 prepared?'' • And he said unto me, ''These are being prepared for the armies of
Azaz'el, in order that they may take them and cast them into the abyss of complete
condemnation, and as the Lord of the Spirits has commanded it, they shall cover their
6 jaws with rocky stones. • Then Michael, Raphael, Gabriel, and Phanuel themselves
shall seize them on that great day of judgment and cast them[d] into the furnace (of fire)
that is burning that day, so that the Lord of the Spirits may take vengeance on them
on account of their oppressive deeds which (they performed) as messengers of Satan,
leading astray those who dwell upon the earth.''

The great judgment of the Flood[e]

7   And in those days, the punishment of the Lord of the Spirits shall be carried out,[f]
and they shall open all the storerooms of water[g] in the heavens above, in addition to[h]
8 the fountains of water which are on earth.[i] •And all the waters shall be united with
(all) other waters.[j] That which is from the heavens above is masculine water,[k] (whereas)
9 that which is underneath the earth is feminine.[l] • And they shall obliterate all those that
dwell upon the earth as well as those that dwell underneath the ultimate ends of
10 heaven. •On account of the fact that they did not recognize[m] their oppressive deeds
which they carried out on the earth, they shall be destroyed by (the Flood).[n]

1 **55** And after that the Antecedent of Time repented and said, ''In vain have I destroyed
2 all those who dwell[a] in the earth.'' •And he swore by his own great name that from
thenceforth he would not do (as he had done) to all who live upon the earth. (And
he said), ''I shall put up a sign in the heavens, and it shall become a (symbol) of faith
between me and them forever, so long as heaven is above the earth, which is in
accordance with my command.

Final judgment of Azaz'el and the fallen angels

3   ''When I would give consent so that they should be seized by the hands of the
angels on the day of tribulation[b] and pain, already I would have caused my punishment
and my wrath to abide upon them[c]—my punishment and my wrath,''[d] says the Lord
4 of the Spirits. •''Kings, potentates, dwellers upon the earth: You would have to see
my Elect One, how he sits in the throne of glory and judges Azaz'el and all his
company, and his army, in the name of the Lord of the Spirits!''

h. B C: ''not these mountains.''

54 a. Lit. ''imprisonment.''
   b. Lit. ''immeasurable.''
   c. A actually reads ''heads of chains.'' But I have
assumed that *'ar'esta*, ''heads of,'' was erroneously
substituted for *ma'aserta*, which we also find in the
preceding verse. B reads only ''chains.'' C has *'esrat*.
Regarding the latter, see EC, p. 97, n. 44, and p.
98, n. 1.
   d. So B and C. A omits ''cast them.''
   e. This is believed to be part of the lost BkNoah.
   f. Lit. ''come out.''
   g. So B and C. A reads *samāyāt*, ''heavens,''
instead of *māyāt*.
   h. Lit. ''above,'' ''on top of,'' ''beyond.''

i. Lit. ''which are below.'' B C: ''which are below
the heavens.''
   j. B adds: ''of the heavens above.''
   k. B and C omit ''water.''
   l. B and C add ''water.''
   m. B: ''And because of this they recognized''; C:
''On account of the fact that they recognized.'' Cf.
EC, p. 99, n. 12.
   n. Lit. ''by it.''

55 a. B C: ''who live.''
   b. A wrongly: ''my tribulation.''
   c. Lit. ''before this, I will cause to abide upon
them . . .'' This passage is probably corrupt.
   d. This repetition is omitted by C.

1 **56** Then I saw there an army of the angels of punishment marching, holding[a] nets[b]
2 of iron and bronze. • And I asked the angel of peace, who was walking with me,
3 saying to him, "To whom are they going, these who are holding (the nets)?"[c] • And
he said to me, "(They are going) to their elect and beloved ones in order that they
4 may be cast into the crevices of the abyss of the valley. • Then the valley shall be
filled with their elect and beloved ones; and the epoch of their lives, the era of their
glory,[d] and the age of their leading (others) astray shall come to an end and shall not
henceforth be reckoned.

The struggle of Israel with its enemies

5 "In those days, the angels will assemble and thrust[e] themselves to the east at the
Parthians and Medes. They will shake up the kings (so that) a spirit of unrest shall
come upon them, and stir them up from their thrones; and they will break forth from
6 their beds like lions and like hungry hyenas among their own flocks. • And they will
go up and trample upon the land of my elect ones,[f] and the land of my[g] elect ones will
7 be before them like a threshing floor or a highway. • But the city of my righteous ones
will become an obstacle[h] to their horses. And they shall begin to fight among
themselves; and (by) their own right hands they shall prevail against themselves.[i] A
man shall not recognize his brother, nor a son his mother,[j] until there shall be a
(significant) number of corpses from among them.[k] Their punishment is (indeed) not
8 in vain. • In those days, Sheol shall open her mouth, and they shall be swallowed up
into it and perish.[l] (Thus) Sheol shall swallow up the sinners in the presence of the
elect ones."

1 **57** And it happened afterward that I had another vision of a whole array of chariots
loaded with people;[a] and they were advancing[b] upon the air from the east and from
2 the west until midday. • And the sound of their chariots (was clamorous);[c] and when
this commotion took place, the holy ones in heaven took notice of it and the pillars
of the earth were shaken from their foundations;[d] and the sound (of the noise) could
be heard from the extreme end of the sky unto the extreme end of the earth[e] in one
3 hour.[f] • Then all shall fall down and worship the Lord of the Spirits. Here ends the
second parable.[g]

The eternal light of the righteous and elect ones

1 **58** And I began to speak another[a] parable concerning the righteous and the elect:
2 Blessed are you, righteous and elect ones, for glorious is your portion. • The righteous
3 ones shall be in the light of the sun and the elect ones in the light of eternal life which
4 has no end, and the days of the life of the holy ones cannot be numbered.[b] • They shall
seek light and find righteousness with the Lord of the Spirits. Peace (be) to the
5 righteous ones in the peace of the Eternal Lord![c] • After this, it shall be told to the holy
ones in heaven that they should scrutinize the mysteries of righteousness, the gift[d] of

---

56 a. So B and C. A omits "holding."
  b. Or "traps." C reads "plagues and nets of . . ."
  c. C: "To whom are these who are holding plagues going?"
  d. B and C omit "the era of their glory."
  e. Lit. "cast down," "throw."
  f. B: "their elect ones." C: "his elect ones."
  g. B C: "his."
  h. Or "stumbling block."
  i. Lit. "their own right hand shall prevail against them." Often in Eth. the singular form (as "hand" here) stands for the plural sense in the context.
  j. B and C add "and his father."
  k. B C: "from their dying."
  l. C: "and their destruction shall be left" (?).

57 a. B adds "upon them." C adds "inside them."
  b. Lit. "causing to come." B C: "they are coming."
  c. B C: "was heard." Possibly A inadvertently omits "it was heard."
  d. Lit. "shaken from their seats."
  e. Lit. "from the extreme end of the earth unto the extreme end of heaven." C: "from the extreme end of heaven to the extreme end."
  f. B C: "in one day."
  g. Lit. "and this is the end of the second parable."

58 a. B C: "the third."
  b. Lit. "number(ing) of days they do not have," i.e. "they have countless days."
  c. B: "by that which is with the Eternal Lord." C: "in the name of the Eternal Lord."
  d. Lit. "the portion," "the lot," "the part."

6 faith. For the sun has shined upon the earth and darkness is over.ᵉ •There shall be a light that has no end, and they shall not have to count daysᶠ (anymore). For alreadyᵍ darkness has been destroyed, light shall be permanent before the Lord of the Spirits, and the light of uprightness shall stand firm forever and ever before the Lord of the Spirits.

The lightnings and the thunder

1 **59** In those days, my eyes saw the mysteries of lightnings, and of lights, and their judgments; they flash lights for a blessing or a curse, according to the will of the Lord 2 of the Spirits. •And there I (also) saw the secrets of the thunder and the secrets of (how when) it resoundsᵃ in the heights of heaven itsᵇ voice is heard (in)ᶜ the earthly dwellings.ᵈ He showed me whether the sound of the thunder is for peace and blessing 3 or for a curse, according to the word of the Lord of the Spirits. •After that, all the mysteries of the lights and lightnings were shown to me (that) they glow with light for blessing and for contentment.ᵉ

Heavenly quake, the great monsters, and mysteries of natureᵃ

1 **60** In the year five hundred, in the seventh month, on the fourteenth day of the month in the life of Enoch;ᵇ in the same parable (I saw)ᶜ that the heaven of heavens was quaking and trembling with a mighty tremulous agitation, and the forces of the Most High and the angels, ten thousand times a million and ten million times ten million, 2 were agitated with great agitation. •And the Antecedent of Time was sitting on the 3 throne of his glory surrounded by the angels and the righteous ones. •(Then) a great trembling and fear seized meᵈ and my loins and kidneys lost control.ᵉ So I fell upon 4 my face. •Then Michael sent another angel from among the holy ones and he raised me up. And when he had raised me up, my spirit returned; for (I had fainted) because I could not withstand the sight of these forcesᶠ and (because) heaven has stirred up 5 and agitated itself. •Then Michael said unto me, "What have you seen that has so disturbed you? This day of mercyᵍ has lasted until today; and he has been merciful 6 and long-sufferingʰ toward those that dwell upon the earth. •And when this day arrives—and the power, the punishment, and the judgment, which the Lord of the Spirits has prepared for those who do notⁱ worship the righteous judgment, for those who deny the righteous judgment, and for those who take his name in vain—itʲ will become a dayᵏ of covenant for the elect and inquisitionˡ for the sinners."

7 On that day, two monstersᵐ will beⁿ parted—oneᵒ monster, a female named Levi-
8 athan, in order to dwell in the abyss of the ocean over the fountains of water; •and (the other), a male called Behemoth, which holds his chest in an invisible desert whose name is Dundayin,ᵖ east of the garden of Eden, wherein the elect and the righteous ones dwell,�q wherein my grandfather was taken, the seventh from Adam, the first man

---

e. Lit. "has passed."
f. Lit. "to the number(ing) of days they do not come."
g. Lit. "first."

59 a. A: "the secrets of it is resounding," is grammatically difficult. B and C, "and when it resounds," may be more accurate.
b. Lit. "their."
c. Text reads "and."
d. The reading is difficult. Charles suggests "judgments" instead of "dwellings," which he considers to be a corrupt reading of the Gk. Cf. EC, p. 103, n. 23.
e. Lit. "satiation."

60 a. This is believed to be part of the lost BkNoah.
b. Some think that Enoch is a later substitute for Noah. Cf. EC, p. 103, n. 39.
c. So B and C. A omits "I saw."
d. B C: "a great trembling took hold of me and

fear seized me."
e. Lit. "were loosened." B C: "my loins were frightened ["were punished," "were bent"] and my kidneys were loosened."
f. Lit. "for I could not have endurance [patience] seeing this power."
g. B C: "his mercy."
h. Lit. "of distant wrath."
i. So C, possibly rightly. A omits the negation. Cf. EC, p. 104, n. 28.
j. Lit. "this day."
k. B and C omit "it will become a day . . ." A adds, and B and C read "this day is prepared."
l. So B and C. A wrongly reads *tāḥta*, "under," "underneath," instead of *ḥatatā*.
m. Or "whales." So B and C. A: "leopards."
n. C: "were."
o. B and C omit "one."
p. B: Dundayen. C: Dunudayen. Cf. "land of Nod," Gen 4:16. See also *JE*, vol. 8, p. 39.
q. A omits "dwell."

9 whom the Lord of the Spirits created.ʳ •Then I asked the second angel in order that
he may show me (how) strong these monsters are,ˢ how they were separated on this
dayᵗ and were cast, the one into the abysses of the ocean, and the other into the dry
10 desert. •And he said to me, "You, son of man, according (to the degree) to which
it will be permitted, you will know the hidden things."ᵘ
11　　Then the other angel who was going with me was showing me the hidden things:
what is first and last in heaven, above it, beneath the earth, in the depth, in the extreme
12 ends of heaven, the extent of heaven;ᵛ •the storerooms of the winds,ʷ how the winds
are divided, how they are weighed, how the winds divideˣ and dissipate,ʸ the openingsᶻ
of the winds, each according to the strength of its wind; the power of the light of the
moon and how it is the right amount,ᵃ² the divisions of the stars, each according to
13 its nomenclature, and all the subdivisions; • the thunders according to the places where
they fall, and the subdivisions of the lightningsᵇ² according to their flashing of light
14 and the velocity of the obedience of the whole array of them. •So the thunders have
their (respective) moments of rest with patience; and (each thunder) is markedᶜ² by
its (respective) sound. Neither the thunder nor the lightning becomes disjoined one
15 from the other; both go together in a single breeze and do not part. •For when the
lightning flashes light,ᵈ² the thunder uttersᵉ² its sound; also, at that moment, the wind
causes (the thunder) to come to rest and divides equally (the time) between each one
of them. For the reservoir of their moments (of thunderings) is like the sand, (so) each
one of them is restrainedᶠ² with a bridle and turned back by the power of the wind and
16 driven in this manner all over the numerous corners of the earth.ᵍ² •Now, the sea
breeze is masculine and strong and according to the power of its strength it holds back
(the air) and, in this manner, is driven and dispersed among all the mountains of the
17 world. •The frost-wind is its own guardianʰ² and the hail-wind is a kind messenger.ⁱ²
18 The snow-wind has evacuated (its reservoir); it does not existʲ² because of its strength;
there is in it only a breeze that ascends from (the reservoir) like smoke, and its name
19 is frost. •And the wind and the mist do not dwell together with them in their reservoirs.
But (the mist) has its own reservoir, for its course is glorious. It hasᵏ² light and
darkness both in the rainy season and the dry season; and its reservoir is itself an
20 angel. •The dwelling place of the dew-breeze is in the extreme ends of heaven and
is linked together with the reservoirs of the rain in (both) its courses of the rainy
season and the dry season; also the clouds of (the dew) and the clouds of the mist are
21 associated feeding each other mutually.ˡ² •When the rain-windᵐ² becomes activated
in its reservoir, the angels come and open the reservoir and let it out; and when it is
sprayed over the whole earth, it becomes united with the water which is upon the
22 earth; •and whensoever it unites with (other waters, it unites) with the water upon the
earth which is for the use of those who dwell on the earth, for it is nourishment for
the earth (sent) from the Most High in heaven. So in this manner there is a measuring
23 system for the rain given to the angels. •All these things I saw as far as the garden
24 of the righteous ones. •And the angel of peace who was with me said to me, "These

r. So B and C. A reads: "wherein man was
returned [changed], I shall bring ['ab'e, possibly a
corruption for sāb'e, "seventh"], from Adam before
[qedmē-, possibly a corruption for qadāmi-, "the
first"] the people which the Lord of the Spirits
created." This difficult reading seems to contain
errors.
　s. Lit. "the power of these monsters."
　t. B C: "in one day."
　u. Lit. "that which is hidden." B C: "by here
you want, you will know that which is hidden."
　v. B C: "the foundations of heaven."
　w. So B and C. A: "of the Lord."
　x. B and C omit "how the winds divide."
　y. Lit. "they are finished." B: "how the fountains
are counted." C: "how the portals are counted."
　z. C: "the portals."

　a2. Lit. "the right [just] power."
　b2. So B and C. A reads wrongly bamesrāq, "in
the east," instead of bamabraq.
　c2. Lit. "given."
　d2. So B and C. A reads wrongly yesarq, "it will
rise," instead of yebarq.
　e2. Lit. "gives."
　f2. Lit. "caught," "held."
　g2. Lit. "in accordance with the multiplicity of
the districts of the earth."
　h2. Lit. "its own angel."
　i2. Or "angel."
　j2. B and C omit "it does not exist."
　k2. B and C omit "It has."
　l2. Lit. "one gives to the other."
　m2. So B and C. A: "the rain-soul."

two monsters are prepared for the great day[n2] of the Lord (when) they shall turn into
25 food.[o2] • So that the punishment of the Lord of the Spirits should come down upon them
in order that the punishment of the Lord of the Spirits should not be issued in vain
but slay the children with their mothers, and the children with their fathers, when the
punishment of the Lord of the Spirits comes down upon everyone.[p2] After that there
shall be the judgment according to his mercy and his patience."

2Bar 29:4;
4Ezra
6:49–52

The measurement of the garden of Eden and the judgment and praise of the Elect One

1 **61** I saw in those days that long ropes were given to those angels; and hoisting up
their own (respective) portions[a] (of the ropes), they soared[b] going in the direction of
2 the northeast. • And I asked the angel, saying unto him, "Why have those (angels)
hoisted these ropes and gone off?" And he said unto me, "They have gone in order
3 to make measurements." • The angel who was going with me also said unto me,
"These (angels) are the ones who shall bring the measuring ropes of the righteous
ones as well as their binding cords[c] in order that they might lean upon the name of the
Lord of the Spirits forever and ever. Then the elect ones shall begin to walk[d] with the
4 elect ones. • These are the measurements which shall be given to faith and which shall
5 strengthen righteousness. • And these measurements shall reveal all the secrets of the
depths of the earth, those who have been destroyed in the desert, those who have been
devoured by the wild beasts,[e] and those who have been eaten by the fish of the sea.
So that they all[f] return and find hope in[g] the day of the Elect One. For there is no one
6 who perishes before the Lord of the Spirits, and no one who should perish.[h] • And
those who are in heaven above and all the powers received a command—one voice
7 and one light like fire. • And him, the First Word,[i] they shall bless, extol, and glorify
with wisdom. They shall be wise in utterance in the spirit of life and in the Lord of
8 the Spirits. • He placed the Elect One on the throne of glory; and he shall judge all
the works of the holy ones in heaven above, weighing in the balance their deeds.
9 And when he shall lift up his countenance in order to judge the secret ways of theirs,
by the word[j] of the name of the Lord of the Spirits, and their conduct, by the method
of the righteous judgment of the Lord of the Spirits, then they shall all speak with one
voice, blessing, glorifying, extolling, sanctifying the name of the Lord of the Spirits.
10 And he will summon all the forces of the heavens, and all the holy ones above, and
the forces of the Lord—the cherubim, seraphim, ophanim, all the angels of governance,
11 the Elect One, and the other forces on earth (and) over the water. • On that day, they
shall lift up in one voice, blessing, glorifying, and extolling in the spirit of faith, in
the spirit of wisdom and patience, in the spirit of mercy, in the spirit of justice and
peace, and in the spirit of generosity. They shall all say in one voice, 'Blessed (is he)
12 and may the name of the Lord of the Spirits be blessed forever and evermore.' • All
the vigilant ones[k] in heaven above shall bless him; all the holy ones who are in heaven
shall bless him; all the elect ones who dwell in the garden of life (shall bless him);
every spirit of light that is capable of blessing,[l] glorifying, extolling, and sanctifying
your blessed name (shall bless him); and all flesh shall glorify and bless your name

Heb 5:12

---

n2. B and C read *la'ela 'ebay*, "upon the greatness," instead of *la'elat 'abāy*.
o2. Or "they shall be eaten," "be food," or
"become food."
p2. So A. Because of the problem of dittography,
this passage is repeated and made senseless in both
B and C, and all other MSS used by Charles.

61 a. B and C read "wings."
b. Or "hovered," "flew." Cf. *kanifa*, "to fly."
c. Lit. "the binding cords of the righteous
ones . . . for the righteous ones."
d. B C: "to dwell."
e. So B and C. A reads *mazāgebt*, "storerooms,"
"reservoirs," instead of *'arāwit*.
f. B and C omit "all."

g. Lit. "lean upon, rely upon, depend on, support
oneself by."
h. Lit. "who is being destroyed."
i. Or "the First Oracle." According to A, these
are preferable renditions. However, the passage could
possibly also be translated "with the first word,"
"with the first oracle," or simply "the fundamental
(first) principles of the oracle" or "the elementary
principles of the oracle." Cf. Heb 5:12.
j. So B and C. A: "and the word."
k. Lit. "All those who do not sleep."
l. So B and C. A has *zatakala barakat*, grammatically an impossible structure that can be adjusted
to mean either "of the plant of blessing" or "that
planted a blessing."

13 with an exceedingly limitless power[m] forever and ever. •For the mercy of the Lord of the Spirits is great in quantity, and he is long-suffering. All his works and all the dimensions of his creation, he has revealed to the righteous and the elect ones in the name of the Lord of the Spirits."

some seilors pre-Maccabean

105 BC.

Condemnation of the ruling class and blessedness of the righteous ones

1 **62** Thus the Lord commanded the kings, the governors, the high officials,[a] and the landlords[b] and said, "Open your eyes and lift up your eyebrows—if you are able to 2 recognize the Elect One!" •The Lord of the Spirits has sat down[c] on the throne of his glory, and the spirit of righteousness has been poured out upon him. The word of his mouth will do the sinners[d] in; and all the oppressors shall be eliminated[e] from before 3 his face. •On the day of judgment,[f] all the kings, the governors, the high officials, and the landlords shall see and recognize him—how he sits on the throne of his glory, and righteousness is judged before him, and that no nonsensical talk shall be uttered 4 in his presence. •Then pain shall come upon them as on a woman in travail with birth pangs[g]—when she is giving birth (the child) enters the mouth of the womb and she 5 suffers from childbearing. •One half portion of them[h] shall glance at the other half; they shall be terrified and dejected;[i] and pain shall seize them when they see that Son 6 of Man sitting on the throne of his glory. • (These) kings, governors, and all the landlords shall (try to) bless, glorify, extol him who rules over everything, him who 7 has been concealed. •For the Son of Man[j] was concealed from the beginning, and the Most High One preserved him in the presence of his power; then he revealed him to 8 the holy and the elect ones.[k] •The congregation of the holy ones[l] shall be planted,[m] 9 and all the elect ones shall stand before him. • On that day, all the kings, the governors, the high officials, and those who rule the earth shall fall down before him on their faces, and worship and raise their hopes in that Son of Man; they shall beg and plead 10 for mercy at his feet.[n] •But the Lord of the Spirits himself will cause them to be frantic, so that they shall rush and depart from his presence. Their faces shall be filled 11 with shame, and their countenances shall be crowned with darkness. • So he will deliver them[o] to the angels for punishments in order that vengeance shall be executed 12 on them—oppressors of his children and his elect ones. • It shall become quite a scene for my[p] righteous and elect ones. They shall rejoice over (the kings, the governors, the high officials, and the landlords) because the wrath of the Lord of the Spirits shall

---

m. Lit. "with that which exceeds power."

62 a. Lit. "the exalted ones."

b. Or "landowners," "administrators [governors] of the land." Lit. "those who hold ["possess," "seize"] the land [the earth]." B and C, *yaḥadrwā lameder*, could be adjusted to mean "who dwell on the land."

c. Dillmann prefers *wa'anbro*, "and he has seated him," instead of *wanabara*, "and he has sat down," which is found in all the known MSS.

d. B C: "all the sinners."

e. Or "destroyed."

f. Lit. "On that day."

g. Lit. "she suffers in childbearing."

h. Lit. "One half of them."

i. Lit. "they shall cast down their faces."

j. Here the Eth. expression *walda 'egʷula-'emmaḥeyyāw* (sic) is used instead of *walda sab'e*, which we have seen above. Though both expressions, *'egʷula-'emma ḥeyyāw* and *sab'e*, designate "man," "a human being," "a living person," "a mortal being," the latter term has a collective ("people"), more abstract ("humanity"), and more universalistic ("man") connotation, whereas the former expression emphasizes the individualistic, naturalistic, and par-

ticularistic aspect of man. It (the former expression) literally means "offspring of the mother of the living." The first person to be described as "the mother of the living" in the Bible is Eve (cf. Gen 3:20), so Eth. grammarians sometimes interpret the expression as "offspring of Eve." (This expression should not be confused with *'egʷula-maḥeyyāw*, which, though having the same meaning ["man"] and more likely the same etymological origin, has come to be regarded by Eth. grammarians as of different etymology: "the offspring of the one whom the Living One has brought forth from the earth" or "offspring of the Living One and the earth," or simply "the Son of God," i.e. man as God's offspring.) If one were to be literal, one would translate the two Eth. expressions found in 1En respectively as "Son of the Offspring of the Mother of the Living" (or "Son of Eve's Offspring," "Son of Man") and "Son of People."

k. B and C omit "to the holy ones."

l. B and C add "and of the elect ones."

m. Lit. "sown."

n. Lit. "at him."

o. Lit. "he turned them," "he returned them," "he changed them."

p. B C: "his."

13 rest upon them and his sword[q] (shall obtain) from them a sacrifice.[r] •The righteous
and elect ones shall be saved on that day; and from thenceforth they shall never see
14 the faces of the sinners and the oppressors. •The Lord of the Spirits will abide over
15 them; they shall eat and rest and rise with that Son of Man forever and ever. •The
righteous and elect ones shall rise from the earth and shall cease being of downcast
16 face. They shall wear[s] the garments of glory. •These garments of yours shall become
the garments of life from the Lord of the Spirits. Neither shall your garments wear
out, nor your glory come to an end before the Lord of the Spirits.

The hopeless end of the kings, rulers, and landlords

1 **63** In those days, the governors and the kings who possess the land[a] shall plead that
he may give them a little breathing spell from the angels of his punishment to whom
they have been delivered;[b] so that they shall fall and worship before the Lord of the
2 Spirits, and confess their sins before him. •They shall bless and glorify the Lord of
the Spirits and say, "Blessed is the Lord of the Spirits—the Lord of kings, the Lord
of rulers, and the Master of the rich—the Lord of glory and the Lord of wisdom.
3 Your power exposes[c] every secret thing from generation to generation and your glory
is forever and ever. Deep are all your mysteries—and numberless; and your right-
4 eousness is beyond accounting. •Now we have come to know that we should glorify
5 and bless the Lord of kings—him who rules over all kings." •Moreover, they shall
say, "Would that someone had given us a chance so that we should glorify, praise,
6 and have faith before his glory! •This time, however, we are begging for a little rest
but find it not; we pursue (it), but procure it not. Light has vanished from before us
7 and darkness has become our habitation[d] forever and ever; • because we have formerly[e]
neither had faith nor glorified the name of the Lord of the Spirits and kings,[f] nor
glorified the Lord in all his creation.[g] We had put our hopes upon the scepters of our
8 empires.[h] •(Now) on the day of our hardship and our tribulation he is not saving us;
and we have no chance to become believers.[i] For our Lord is faithful in all his works,
his judgments, and his righteousness; and his judgments have no respect of persons.
9 (So) we will vanish away from before his face on account of our deeds; and all our
10 sins are consumed[j] by righteousness." •Furthermore, at that time, you shall say,[k]
"Our souls are satiated with exploitation[l] money which[m] could not save us[n] from being
11 cast into the oppressive[o] Sheol."[p] •After that, their faces shall be filled with shame[q]
before that Son of Man; and from before his face they shall be driven out. And the
12 sword shall abide in their midst, before his face. •Thus says the Lord of the Spirits,
"This is the ordinance and the judgment, before the Lord of the Spirits, (prepared)
for the governors, kings, high officials, and landlords."

The fallen angels

1,2 **64** Then I saw in that place other mysterious faces. •And I heard the voice of an
angel saying, "These are the angels who descended[a] upon the earth and revealed what
was hidden[b] to the children of the people, and led the children of the people astray
to commit sin."

q. B: "the sword of the Lord of the Spirits." C:
"the sword." A is unintelligible but the reading is
close to B and C.

r. Lit. "a memorial feast." B: "shall be drunk
from them." C (as emended by Charles): "shall be
drunk with their blood." If this passage is related to
Isa 34:6, then the reading of "sacrifice" is close to
it.

s. Lit. "they wore."

63 a. Or "the kings (and) the landowners."

b. So B and C. A: "by which they were idolatrous," or "through which they became idolatrous."
Perhaps A's reading is original.

c. Lit. "it lights."

d. B: "our deeds."

e. So A. B C: "before him."

f. B: "in the name of the Lord of kings."

g. So B. A and C omit "in all his creation."

h. Lit. "our kingdoms." B and C add "and our
glory."

i. Lit. "to believe."

j. Lit. "finished."

k. B C: "they shall say."

l. Or "oppression."

m. Lit. "and."

n. Lit. "prevent."

o. Lit. "weighty," "burdensome," "grave."

p. B: "flames of the burden of Sheol." C: "the
heart of the burden of Sheol."

q. B and C add "and with darkness."

64 a. So B and C. A: "will descend."

b. So B and C. A: "what was hidden is revealed."

Enoch's predictions concerning the Deluge and himself

1 **65** In those days, Noah saw the earth, that she had become deformed, and that her
2 destruction was at hand. •And (Noah) took off from there[a] and went unto the extreme
ends of the earth. And he cried out to his grandfather, Enoch, and said to him,[b] three
3 times, with a bitter voice, "Hear me! Hear me! Hear me!" •And I said unto him,
"Tell me what this thing is which is being done upon the earth, for the earth is
struggling[c] in this manner and is being shaken; perhaps I will perish with her in the
4 impact."[d] •At that moment, there took place a tremendous turbulence upon the earth;
5 and a voice from heaven was heard, and I fell upon my face. • Then Enoch, my
grandfather, came and stood by me, saying to me, "Why did you cry out so sorrowfully[e]
and with bitter tears?

6   "An order has been issued from the court[f] of the Lord against those who dwell
upon the earth, that their doom[g] has arrived because they have acquired the knowledge
of all the secrets of the angels, all the oppressive deeds of the Satans, as well as all
their most occult powers, all the powers of those who practice sorcery, all the powers
of (those who mix) many colors,[h] all the powers[i] of those who make molten images;[j]
7 how silver is produced from the dust of the earth, and how bronze[k] is made upon the
8 earth— •for lead and tin are produced[l] from the earth like silver[m]—their source is a
9 fountain inside (which) stands an angel, and he is a running angel."[n] •After that, my
grandfather, Enoch, took hold of me by my hand and raised me up and said to me,
"Go, for I have asked[o] the Lord of the Spirits regarding this turbulence (which is
10 taking place) on the earth." •He (continued to) say to me, "Because their oppression
has been carried out (on the earth), their judgment will be limitless[p] before me. On
account of the abstract things[q] which they have investigated and experienced, the earth
11 shall perish (together with) those who dwell upon her. •And those (who taught them
these things) will have no haven[r] forever, because they have revealed to them the
things which are secret—to[s] the condemned ones; but, as for you, my son, the Lord
of the Spirits knows that you are pure and kindhearted; you detest the secret things.[t]
12 He has preserved your name for[u] the holy ones; he will protect you from those who
dwell upon the earth; he has preserved your righteous seed for kingship and great
glory; and from your seed will emerge a fountain of the righteous and holy ones
without number forever."

Angels in charge of the Flood

1 **66** After this he showed me the angels of punishment[a] who are prepared to come and
release all the powers of the waters which are underground to become judgment and

---

65 a. Lit. "And he lifted his feet from there."
    b. Lit. "and Noah said."
    c. So B and C. A: "glowing."
    d. Or "pushing," "shoving." B and C, instead
of badāḥef, read badeḥera, "after . . ." which could
be placed before the succeeding phrase, "this moment."
    e. B and C add "unto me."
    f. Lit. "from the presence."
    g. Lit. "end."
    h. Eth. ḥebrāt, "(those who mix) many colors"
or "(those who make) dyes," makes sense in the
context, whereas ḥebrāt, "provinces," "regions,"
"areas," "parts," found in A B C does not seem to
do so.
    i. A: "and all of them." B C: "and the powers."
    j. Lit. "idols."
    k. Lit. "mixed metals."
    l. B C: "are not produced."
    m. Lit. "like the first."
    n. Lit. "and this angel runs."
    o. Or "you have asked him."
    p. Lit. "they will not be counted." Charles sug-
gests that 'iyetḥolaqʷu, which he equates with the

Heb. lo-yeḥāšēb, is a corruption of lo-yeḥāsēk, "will
not be restrained [withheld]." See EC, p. 118, n. 24.
    q. Or "gold." Perhaps this is an allusion to 8:1.
A has 'awrāq, which I have translated as "abstract
things." This expression, whose singular form I
assume to be warq, "gold" (see wariq, "to spit,"
"to be fine like a leaf," "to be slender," or "to be
abstract"; cf. raqiq), is not attested in known Eth.
literature. B and C have 'awrāḥ, "months," "moons."
Charles, following Halévy, suggests this expression,
which corresponds to the Heb. ḥᵃdāšîm, to be a
corruption for harashim, "sorceries."
    r. Lit. "a place to go [or "turn"] to," "a refuge,"
"resort." Charles, following Halévy, and assuming
that megbā'e means "return," suggested that this
expression is a translation of the Heb. teshubah,
meaning "repentance," "return." Cf. EC, p. 118,
n. 29.
    s. B C: "and."
    t. B C: "you are free from the blame."
    u. B C: "among."

66 a. So B and C. A: "the angels showed me the
punishment."

2 destruction unto all who live and dwell upon the earth. •But the Lord of the Spirits gave an order to the angels who were on duty[b] that they should not raise the (water) enclosures[c] but guard (them)—for they were the angels who were in charge of the waters.[d] Then I left[e] from the presence of Enoch.

God's promise to Noah: punishment of the angels and kings

1 **67** In those days, the word of God came unto me, and said unto me, "Noah, your
2 lot has come up before me—a lot without blame, a lot of true love.[a] •At this time the angels are working with wood (making an ark) and when it is completed,[b] I shall place my hands upon it[c] and protect it,[d] and the seed of life shall arise from it; and a substitute[e] (generation) will come so that the earth will not remain empty (without
3 inhabitants). •I shall strengthen your seed before me forever and ever as well as the seeds of those who dwell with you; I shall not put it to trial[f] on the face of the earth; but it shall be blessed and multiply on the earth in the name of the Lord."

4 And they shall imprison[g] those angels who revealed oppression in that burning valley which my grandfather Enoch had formerly shown me in the West among the
5 mountains of gold, silver, iron, bronze, and tin. •I also saw that valley in which there
6 took place a great turbulence and the stirring of the waters. •Now, when all this took place, there was produced from that bronze and fire a smell of sulfur (which) blended
7 with those waters. •This valley of the perversive angels shall (continue to) burn punitively[h] underneath that ground; in respect to its troughs,[i] they shall be filled with[j] rivers of water by which those angels who perverted those who dwell upon the earth shall be punished.[k]

8 Those waters shall become in those days a poisonous drug[l] of the body and a punishment[m] of the spirit unto the kings, rulers, and exalted ones, and those who dwell on the earth; lust shall fill their souls[n] so that their bodies shall be punished, for they have denied the Lord of the Spirits; they shall see their own punishment every
9 day but cannot believe in his name. •In proportion to the great degree of the burning of their bodies will be the transmutation of their spirits forever and ever and ever,[o] for there is none that can speak a nonsensical word before the Lord of the Spirits.
10 So the judgment shall come upon them, because they believe in the debauchery of
11 their bodies and deny the spirit of the Lord. •And these waters will undergo change in those days; for (on the one hand) when those angels are being punished by these waters, the temperatures of those fountains of water will be altered (and become hot), but (on the other hand) when the angels get out,[p] those waters of the fountains shall
12 be transformed and become cold.[q] •Then I heard Michael responding and saying, "This verdict by which the angels are being punished is itself a testimony to the kings
13 and the rulers who control the world." •For these waters of judgment are poison to the bodies of the angels[r] as well as sensational to their flesh; (hence) they will neither see nor believe that these waters become transformed and become a fire that burns forever.

b. Lit. "who were going out."

c. A reads 'aweda, which I have taken as 'aweda, since the former expression is nonexistent. B and C read "do not raise the hands."

d. B C: "for these angels were in charge of the powers of the waters."

e. So B and C. A: "I came."

67 a. B C: "a lot of love and uprightness."

b. All MSS add "to these angels."

c. Lit. "her."

d. Lit. "her."

e. Lit. "it was changed [substituted]."

f. So A: 'iyyāmakker. B C: 'iyymaker, "he will not counsel it." Charles emended the text to read "he will not be barren," 'iyymaken.

g. So C, and possibly A and B. A and B could give the meaning "they shall harden [petrify]" or "they shall cast lots." It seems to me that the original

translator(s), or the copyists of A and C, were attempting a play on words: The good angels were working "wood," 'eṣawa (67:2), while they will "make wood," ya'ṣwomu, "harden," "petrify," out of the evil angels.

h. B and C omit "punitively."

i. Lit. "valleys."

j. B: "shall be out." C: "shall come."

k. Lit. "condemned."

l. Eth. fawes has the meaning of (1) "a healing medicine," "a good medicine," and (2) "a killing drug," "a bad medicine."

m. Lit. "judgment."

n. B C: "their spirits."

o. So A. B C: "forever and ever."

p. Lit. "ascend."

q. So B and C. A: "shall be knotted."

r. So all MSS. Perhaps we should read "bodies of kings."

The angel Michael discusses the judgment with Raphael

1 **68** After that, he gave me instructions[a] in all the secret things (found) in the book of my grandfather, Enoch,[b] and in the parables which were given to him; and he put
2 them together for me in the words of the book which is with me.[c] •On that day, Michael addressed himself to[d] Raphael, saying to him, "The power of the spirit grabs me and causes me to go up[e] on account of the severity of the judgment concerning (the knowledge of) the secrets. Who is able to endure the severity of the judgment
3 which has been executed and before which one melts[f] away?" •Michael continued to speak further, saying to Raphael, "Who is he whose heart does not become sordid[g] in respect to this matter and whose reins do not become stirred up from the word of
4 the judgment which has been pronounced against them."[h] •Then it happened that when they stood[i] before the Lord of the Spirits, Michael said to Raphael thus, "They shall not prosper before the eye of the Lord; for they have quarreled with the Lord of the
5 Spirits because they make the image of the Lord.[j] •Therefore, all that which has been concealed shall come upon them forever and ever; for neither an angel[k] nor a man should be assigned his role;[l] (so) those (evil ones) alone have received their judgment forever and ever."

Names and misdeeds of the fallen angels

1 **69** After this judgment, they shall frighten them and make them scream because they
2 have shown this (knowledge of secret things) to those who dwell on the earth. •Now behold, I am naming[a] the names of those angels! These are their names: The first of them is Semyaz, the second Aristaqis, the third Armen, the fourth Kokba'el, the fifth Tur'el, the sixth Rumyal, the seventh Danyul, the eighth Neqa'el, the ninth Baraqel, the tenth Azaz'el, the eleventh Armaros, the twelfth Betryal, the thirteenth Basas'el, the fourteenth Hanan'el, the fifteenth Tur'el, the sixteenth Sip^{W}ese'el, (the seventeenth Yeter'el),[b] the eighteenth Tuma'el, the nineteenth Tur'el, the twentieth Rum'el, and
3 the twenty-first Azaz'el.[c] •These are the chiefs of their angels, their names, their centurions,[d] their chiefs over fifties, and their chiefs over tens.
4 The name of the first is Yeqon; he is the one who misled all the children of the angels,[e] brought them down upon the earth, and perverted them by the daughters of
5 the people. •The second was named Asb'el; he is the one who gave the children of the holy angels an evil counsel[f] and misled them so that they would defile their bodies
6 by the daughters of the people. •The third was named Gader'el; this one is he who showed the children of the people all the blows of death, who misled Eve, who showed the children of the people (how to make) the instruments of death (such as) the shield, the breastplate, and the sword for warfare, and all (the other) instruments of death to
7 the children of the people. •Through their agency (death) proceeds against the people

---

68 a. B C: "signs," "miracles."

b. B C: "my grandfather, Enoch, gave me the signs of all secret things (found) in the book."

c. B C: "in the words of the book of the parables."

d. A wrongly: "responded to me."

e. Lit. "rouses me." B C: "provokes me," "angers me."

f. Lit. "they melt."

g. So A and C. B: "does not become soft," "does not become compassionate."

h. A adds: "There were among them those who responded to them thus." B and C add: "There were among them those whom they led out thus."

i. B C: "he stood."

j. Or "because they act in the style of the Lord."

k. So B and C. A: "an image." Perhaps A is original. See following note.

l. Lit. "his portion." A possible rendition according to A may be: "for no image—and no human (image)—should be made for him." The whole

paragraph is problematic. If A is right, this passage may be a reference to Ex 20:4.

69 a. B and C omit "I am naming."

b. So B and C.

c. B C: "the first Semyaza, the second Arestiqifa [C: Artaqifa] . . . the fourth Kokaba'el [C: Kokab'el], the fifth [C: Turu'el] . . . the seventh Danyal, the eighth [B: Nuqa'el], the ninth Baraq'el . . . the eleventh [B: Armores], the twelfth Bataryal, the thirteenth Basasa'el [C: Basasa'eyal], the fourteenth [B: Anan'el] [C: Hanan'el], the fifteenth [B: Turyal], the sixteenth Simapisi'el [C: Simipesi'el] . . . the nineteenth [B: Tar'el], the twentieth Ruma'el, the twenty-first Aze'el [B: Azazel]."

d. Lit. "the chiefs of their one hundred."

e. Or "the angelic children."

f. Lit. "he counseled them with an evil counsel." B C: "he told ["taught," "showed"] them an evil counsel."

8 who dwell upon the earth,^g from that day forevermore. • The fourth is named Pinem'e;^h this one demonstrated to the children of the people the bitter and the sweet and
9 revealed to them all the secrets of their wisdom. •Furthermore he caused the people to penetrate (the secret of) writingⁱ and (the use of) ink and paper;^j on account of this matter, there are many who have erred from eternity to eternity, until this very day.
10 For human beings are not created^k for such purposes to take up^l their beliefs with pen
11 and ink. • For indeed human beings were not created but to be like angels, permanently to maintain^m pure and righteous lives. Death, which destroys everything, would have not touched them, had it not been through their knowledge by which they shall perish;
12 deathⁿ is (now) eating us^o by means of this power. •The fifth is named Kasadya;^p it is he who revealed to the children of the people (the various) flagellations of all evil— (the flagellation) of the souls and the demons, the smashing of the embryo in the womb so that it may be crushed, the flagellation of the soul, snake bites, sunstrokes,^q
13 the son of the serpent, whose name is Taba'ta.^r •And this is the number of Kasb'el,^s the chief (executor) of the oath which he revealed to the holy ones while he was (still)
14 dwelling in the highest in glory. • His name was (then) Beqa;^t and he spoke to Michael^u to disclose to him his secret name so that he would memorize this secret name of his,^v so that he would call it up in an oath in order that they shall tremble before it^w and
15 the oath. • He (then) revealed these^x to the children of the people, (and) all the hidden things and this power of this oath, for it is power and strength itself.^y The Evil One^z placed this oath in Michael's hand.
16 These are the secrets of this oath—and they are sustained by the oath:

The heaven was suspended before the creation of the world; and forever!
17   By it the earth is founded upon the water; from the hidden places of the mountains come beautiful waters, from the beginning of creation;^{a2} and forever!
18   By that oath, the sea was created; and he put down for it a foundation of sand which cannot be transgressed at a time of its anger, from the beginning of creation; and forever!
19   And by that oath the depths are made firm; they stand still and do not move from their places from the beginning (of creation); and forever!
20   By the same oath the sun and the moon complete their courses of travel, and do not deviate from the laws (made) for them, from the beginning (of creation); and forever!
21   And by the same oath the stars complete their courses of travel; if they call^{b2} their names, he causes them to respond^{c2} from the beginning (of creation); and forever!

---

g. Lit. "From their hands it proceeds against those who dwell upon the earth."
h. B C: Penemu.
i. Lit. "to comprehend book(s)."
j. B C: "to comprehend writing [books] with ink and paper."
k. Lit. "born."
l. B C: "to confirm."
m. Lit. "to live."
n. Lit. "it."
o. B C: "eating me."
p. B: Kasdyas. C: Kasdya.
q. Lit. "the flagellation that happens at noon."
r. An obscure name which, if taken as a common noun in Eth., means "male." For an attempt to restore this and the following verse, see N. Schmidt,

"The Original Language of the Parables of Enoch," *Old Testament and Semitic Studies,* vol. 2, p. 341.
s. B: Kesb'el. C: Kasb'el.
t. C: Biqa.
u. B: "holy Michael."
v. B: "that he would show him that secret name." C omits both.
w. Lit. "from it."
x. B C: "which they revealed."
y. B C: "for it is powerful and strong."
z. So A. B: 'Aka'. C: 'Aka', which may be proper names or corruptions of the 'ekuy of A, or vice versa. Cf. EC, p. 125, n. 14.
a2. Lit. "from the creation of the world."
b2. B C: "he calls."
c2. B C: "they shall respond."

22   Likewise the waters and their souls, all the winds[d2] and their paths of
travel from all the directions of winds;

23   the voice of the thunder and the light of the lightning are kept there;

24   the reservoirs of hail, the reservoirs of frost, the reservoirs of mist, the
reservoirs of rain and dew are kept there;

25   All these believe and give thanks in the presence of the Lord of the
Spirits;

they glorify with all their might, and please him[e2] in all this thanksgiving;

they shall thank, glorify, exalt the Lord of the Spirits forever and ever!

26   This oath has become dominant over them; they are preserved by it and their paths
are preserved by it (so that) their courses of travel do not perish.

27   (Then) there came to them a great joy. And they blessed, glorified, and extolled
(the Lord) on account of the fact that the name of that (Son of) Man[f2] was revealed

28 to them.[g2] He shall never pass away or perish from before the face of the earth.[h2] •But
those who have led the world astray shall be bound with chains; and their ruinous
congregation shall be imprisoned; all their deeds shall vanish from before the face of

29 the earth. •Thenceforth nothing that is corruptible shall be found;[i2] for that Son of
Man has appeared and has seated himself upon the throne of his glory; and all evil
shall disappear from before his face; he shall go and tell[j2] to that Son of Man, and he
shall be strong before the Lord of the Spirits. Here ends the third parable of Enoch.[k2]

Translation of Enoch and vision of earliest human ancestors

1 **70** And it happened after this that his living name was raised up before[a] that Son of
2 Man and to the Lord from among those who dwell upon the earth; •it was lifted up
3 in a wind[b] chariot and it[c] disappeared from among them.[d] •From that day on, I was
not counted among them. But he placed me between two winds,[e] between the northeast
and the west, where the angels took a cord to measure for me the place for the elect
4 and righteous ones. •And there I saw the first (human) ancestors[f] and the righteous
ones of old, dwelling in that place.

Vision of the fiery house and the Antecedent of Days

1 **71** (Thus) it happened after this that my spirit passed out of sight[a] and ascended into
the heavens. And I saw the sons of the holy angels walking upon the flame of fire;
their garments were white—and their overcoats—and the light of their faces was like
2 snow. •Also I saw two rivers of fire, the light of which fire was shining like hyacinth.
3 Then I fell upon my face before the Lord of the Spirits. •And the angel Michael, one
of the archangels,[b] seizing me by my right hand and lifting me up, led me out into
4 all the secrets of mercy;[c] and he showed me[d] all the secrets of righteousness.[e] •He
also showed me all the secrets of the extreme ends of heaven and all the reservoirs
of the stars and the luminaries—from where they come out (to shine) before the faces
5 of the holy ones. •He carried off[f] my spirit, and I,[g] Enoch, was in the heaven of
heavens. There I saw—in the midst of that light—a structure built of crystals; and

d2. B and C read "Likewise, the souls of the
waters, of the winds, and all the winds . . ."

e2. B C: "and their food."

f2. A reads "the name of that man."

g2. B and C interpolate at this place a passage
(omitted by A): "And he sat on the throne of his
glory; and the presidency [lit. "head"] of the (final)
judgment was given unto the Son of Man."

h2. B C: "He shall cause the sinners to pass away
and perish from before the face of the earth."

i2. Lit. "From thenceforth what perishes will not
happen."

j2. B C: "they shall tell."

k2. Lit. "This is the third parable of Enoch."

70 a. A: "before to." B C: "to."

b. Or "spirit."

c. A: "his name." B C: "the name."

d. Lit. "it went out ["disappeared," "vanished"]
among them."

e. Eth. *nafāsāt.* B: *manāfest.* C: *manfasāt,* "winds"
or "spirits."

f. Lit. "the first fathers." Cf. "the earliest fathers," "the first forefathers," "the original ancestors."

71 a. Lit. "became hidden," "became concealed,"
"disappeared," "vanished," "were extinguished."

b. Lit. "head [chief] angels."

c. C omits "of mercy."

d. B omits "and he showed me."

e. C: "of mercy."

f. Lit. "He hid," "He concealed."

g. B and C omit "and I."

6 between those crystals tongues of living fire. • And my spirit saw a ring[h] which encircled[i] this structure[j] of fire. On its four sides[k] were rivers full of living fire which
7 encircled it.[l] • Moreover, seraphim, cherubim, and ophanim—the sleepless ones[m] who
8 guard the throne of his glory—also encircled it. • And I saw countless angels—a hundred thousand times a hundred thousand, ten million times ten million—encircling that house. Michael, Raphael, Gabriel, Phanuel, and numerous (other) holy angels
9 that are in heaven above, go in and out of that house— • Michael, Raphael, Gabriel,
10 Phanuel, and numerous (other) holy angels that are countless.[n] • With them is the Antecedent of Time: His head is white and pure like wool and his garment is
11 indescribable. • I fell on my face, my whole body mollified and my spirit transformed. Then I cried with a great voice by the spirit of the power, blessing, glorifying, and
12 extolling. • And those are the blessings which went forth[o] out of my mouth, being
13 well-pleasing in the presence of that Antecedent of Time. • Then the Antecedent of Time came with Michael, Gabriel, Raphael, Phanuel, and a hundred thousand and
14 ten million times a hundred thousand[p] angels that are countless. • Then an angel[q] came to me and greeted me[r] and said to me, "You, son of man,[s] who art born in[t] righteousness and upon whom righteousness has dwelt, the righteousness of the Antecedent of Time
15 will not forsake you." • He added and said to me, "He shall proclaim peace to you in the name of the world that is to become.[u] For from here proceeds peace since the
16 creation of the world, and so it shall be unto you forever and ever and ever. • Everyone that will come to exist and walk shall (follow)[v] your path, since righteousness never forsakes you. Together with you shall be their dwelling places; and together with you shall be their portion. They shall not be separated from you forever and ever and
17 ever." • So there shall be length of days with that Son of Man, and peace to the righteous ones; his path is upright for the righteous, in the name of the Lord of the Spirits forever and ever.

Book III (72–82)
The Book of Heavenly Luminaries

The sun

1 **72** (Book) Three:[a] • The Book of the Itinerary of the Luminaries of Heaven: the position of each and every one, in respect to their ranks, in respect to their authorities, and in respect to their seasons; each one according to their names[b] and their places of origin and according to their months, which Uriel, the holy angel who was with me, and who (also) is their guide, showed me—just as he showed me all their treatises[c] and the nature[d] of the years of the world unto eternity, till the new creation which abides forever is created.

h. Or "a belt," "a circular thing."
i. Or "encompassed," "surrounded."
j. Lit. "house."
k. So B and C. A is unintelligible.
l. Lit. "that house."
m. Lit. "those who do not sleep."
n. B and C add "they go out from that house."
o. Here ends ch. 71 in A. The scribe has transposed to this place 78:8b–82:20. How this happened is difficult to imagine, because the ending of this section and the beginning of the following (i.e. the Book of the Heavenly Luminaries) are clearly delineated in most MSS; in another 15th-cent. MS—EMML 2080—which I have consulted, the ending of the preceding section is found at the top of the left-hand column, half of which is left empty; and the Book of the Heavenly Luminaries starts at the top of a new column on the right. However, there is a tendency to repeat some of the vss. (9b–12a) of the end of this ch. in some MSS; cf. EC, p. 180, n. 24. My

translation of 71:12b–17 is based on B and C.
p. C: "a hundred thousand and ten million."
q. Lit. "this angel." C: "he."
r. Lit. "greeted me with his voice."
s. This expression, "son of man," should be distinguished from the "Son of Man." As explained above, "Man" in the "Son of Man" is a translation of either *sab'e*, "people," or *'eg^wula-'emma heyyāw*, "son of the mother of the living," i.e. "human being"; in the present case, however, we have *be'esi*, "man," "a masculine person."
t. C: "unto," "to."
u. Or "in his name which exists forever."
v. Lit. "upon."

72 a. So A. Other MSS omit "Three."
b. Lit. "its name."
c. Lit. "books."
d. Lit. "how."

2 This is the first commandment of the luminaries: The sun is a luminary whose egress is an opening[e] of heaven, which is (located) in the direction of the east, and whose 3 ingress[f] is (another) opening of heaven, (located) in the west. •I saw six openings through which the sun rises and six openings through which it sets. The moon also rises and sets through the same openings, and they are guided by the stars;[g] together with those whom they lead, they are six[h] in the east and six[i] in the west heaven.[j] All of them (are arranged) one after another in a constant order.[k] There are many windows 4 (both) to the left and the right of these openings. •First there goes out the great light[l] whose name is the sun; its roundness is like the roundness of the sky; and it is totally 5 filled with light and heat. •The chariot on which it ascends is (driven by) the blowing wind. The sun sets in the sky (in the west) and returns by the northeast in order to go to the east; it is guided so that it shall reach the[m] eastern gate[n] and shine in the face 6 of the sky. • In this manner it rises in the first month[o] through the major gate; it proceeds (through this gate) which is the fourth (among) those six[p] openings which 7 are (located) in the direction of the east. •By this fourth gate through which the sun rises during the first month there are twelve open windows from which a flame flows, 8 when they are opened at the appropriate time.[q] •When (the sun) rises (in the east) in the sky, it goes out through this fourth gate for thirty mornings and descends faithfully 9 through the fourth gate in the western sky. •During those (thirty) days the day daily 10 becomes longer and the night nightly shorter, for thirty days.[r] •On that day, the day is longer than the night by one ninth;[s] so the day turns out to be exactly ten parts and 11 the night to be eight parts. •The sun rises from that fourth (eastern) gate and sets in the fourth (western) one, and then it turns and comes into[t] the fifth gate of the east 12 for thirty days,[u] through which it rises, and sets in the fifth gate. •At that time the day further becomes longer[v] and becomes[w] eleven parts and the night shortens[x] and becomes 13 seven parts on account of the sun.[y] • It then returns to the east and comes into the sixth (gate), rising and setting through that sixth gate for thirty-one[z] days,[a2] according to 14 the principle[b2] of (the gate).[c2] • On that day the day becomes longer than the night still further;[d2] so the day becomes twelve parts and the night shortens and becomes six 15 parts. •Then the sun is raised in such a way that (its duration) shortens[e2] and night occurs;[f2] the sun returns to the east and enters the sixth gate, rising and setting through 16 it[g2] for thirty days.[h2] •When thirty days[i2] are completed, the day decreases exactly by 17 one part, and becomes[j2] eleven parts, and the night seven. •Then the sun, leaving the west by that sixth gate and going to the east, rises through the fifth gate for thirty 18 mornings and sets again in the fifth gate in the west. •On that day the day decreases 19 by two parts; so (the day) becomes ten parts and the night eight parts. • Then the sun,

Isa 65:17;
66:22
2Pet 3:3,13
Rev 21:1

---

e. The word *ḥewḥew* is sometimes translated as "portal" or "gate." But it simply signifies "a hole," "a crack," "an aperture," "a slot," or "a vent."

f. Lit. "setting."

g. B C: "guides of the stars."

h. A could be read "seven," which is meaningless.

i. A could be read "seven," which is meaningless.

j. B and C read "west (of the) sun."

k. Lit. "uprightly."

l. So C. A B: "the light that excels."

m. Lit. "that."

n. Eth. *ḥwoḥet.* I have decided to translate this term as "gate." It appears in the Eth. Bible in several places as an equivalent for Heb. *delet* and *ša'ār* or Gk. *thura* and *pylē.* Cf. Job 31:32 (*delet, thura*); Isa 26:20 (*delet, thura*); Ps 24(23): 7, 9 (*ša'ār, pylē*); Ps 107(106): 16 (*delet, pylē*).

o. Ethiopian commentators begin here with the Ethiopian month Miyazya.

p. A could be read "seven," which is meaningless.

q. Lit. "in their seasons."

r. Lit. "for thirty mornings."

s. Lit. "the day is longer twice double as much as nine parts of the night."

t. B and C omit "comes into."

u. Lit. "mornings."

v. Lit. "the day becomes longer doublefold."

w. Lit. "the day becomes."

x. Lit. "decreases."

y. Lit. "on account of her sun." The word for sun used here is *ta'amer,* "wonder," "sign," "sun," "moon." The whole phrase is wrongly placed at the end of vs. 12. Cf. 48:3; Jub 4:17; 2Chr 33:3; Jer 10:2.

z. So B and C. A: "thirty."

a2. Lit. "mornings."

b2. Lit. "according to her sign." The Eth. *ta'amer,* "wonder," "sign," can also designate "sun" or "moon."

c2. Lit. "her."

d2. Lit. "the day double the night."

e2. Lit. "it shortens."

f2. B C: "it shortens the day and lengthens the night."

g2. Lit. "rising through it and setting."

h2. Lit. "mornings."

i2. Lit. "mornings."

j2. Lit. "the day becomes."

departing from that fifth gate and setting in the fifth gate, in the west, rises in the fourth gate for thirty-one days[k2] according to the principle of (the gate),[l2] and sets in

20 the west. •On that day the day is aligned with the night, so that they become equal;

21 so the night becomes nine parts and the day nine parts. •Then the sun,[m2] departing from that gate and setting in the west, returns to the east and comes out through the

22 third gate for thirty days,[n2] and sets in the third gate in the west. •On that day the night becomes longer than the day; it becomes longer than the (previous) night[o2] and the day becomes shorter than the (previous) day[p2] for thirty day;[q2] so the night turns out

23 to be exactly ten parts and the day to be eight parts. •Then the sun, departing from that third gate in the west and returning to the east, comes out through the second gate in the east for thirty days,[r2] and in the same manner it sets through the second gate

24 in the western sky. •On that day the night becomes eleven parts and the day seven

25 parts. •Then the sun, departing on that day from that second gate and setting in the west in the second gate, returns to the east and rises in the first gate for thirty-one

26 days, and sets on that day in the western sky. •On that day the night lengthens[s2] and

27 becomes twelve parts, whereas the day (shortens and becomes) six parts. •Thus the sun completes[t2] its appearances,[u2] and goes through those same cycles of appearances a second time,[v2] coming out through all the openings[w2] for thirty days[x2] and setting

28 also in the west opposite to it. •On that night the length of the night decreases by one

29 ninth;[y2] so the night becomes eleven parts and the day seven[z2] parts. •Then the sun, returning and entering the second gate which is in the east, resumes its appearances[a3]

30 for thirty mornings, rising and setting (as usual). •On that day the night[b3] becomes

31 shorter,[c3] so the night becomes ten parts and the day eight parts. •On that day the sun, departing from this second gate and setting in the west, returns to the east and rises

32 through the third gate for thirty-one days, and sets in the western sky. •On that day the night shortens and becomes nine parts and the day nine parts. Then the night becomes equal with the day, and the days (of the year)[d3] add up to exactly three

33 hundred sixty-four days. • The lengths of the day and the night as well as the shortnesses of the day and the night are (determined) by (the course of) the circuit[e3] of the sun,

34 and distinguished by it. •The circuit becomes longer or shorter day by day and night

35 by night (respectively). •Thus this is the order for[f3] the course of the movement and the settlement of the sun—that great luminary which is called the sun, for the duration

36 of the year(s) of the universe[g3]—in respect to its going in[h3] and coming out. • It is that very (luminary) which manifests itself in its appearance[i3] as God has commanded that

37 it shall come out and go in, in this manner.[j3] •And neither does it diminish (in respect to its brightness) nor take rest but continue to run day[k3] and night. As for the intensity of its light, it is sevenfold brighter than that of the moon; nevertheless, (the sun and the moon) are equal in regard to their (respective) sizes.

k2. Lit. "mornings."

l2. See n. b2.

m2. Cf. n. y to vs. 12.

n2. Lit. "mornings."

o2. Lit. "the night becomes longer than the night."

p2. Lit. "the day becomes shorter than the day."

q2. Lit. "mornings."

r2. Lit. "mornings." So B and C. A omits "mornings."

s2. B and C add "becomes double the day."

t2. Lit. "completed," "having completed."

u2. B and C read 'ar'estihu, "its beginnings," "its chiefs," "its headlines," instead of 'ar'ayātihu as in A.

v2. B C: 'ar'estihu. See n. u2.

w2. B C: "through the same openings."

x2. Lit. "mornings."

y2. Lit. "the night diminishes from her ninefold length by one part."

z2. So B and C. A: "nine."

a3. B C: 'ar'estihu. See n. u2.

b3. So B, C, and emendation in A. A reads: "the day."

c3. Lit. "diminishes from her length."

d3. B C: "and the year."

e3. Or "route," "course."

f3. Lit. "and."

g3. So A. B C: "forever and ever." Both grammatically and theologically, the reading of A seems better.

h3. B and C read "going in sixty times," which makes no sense.

i3. B and C add "that which is called the great luminary."

j3. Lit. "come out in this manner and go in."

k3. A omits "day."

The moon and the varying amounts of its illuminations

1 **73** After I saw this (set of) regulation(s for the sun) I saw another (set of) regulation(s)[a]
2 concerning the minor luminary whose name is moon. •Its[b] roundness is like the roundness of the sky,[c] and the wind drives[d] the chariot on which it rides;[e] and it is
3 given light in (varying) measure. •Its coming out and its going in change every month. Its days are like the days of the sun; and when its light becomes evenly (distributed)
4 then it amounts to one seventh of the light of the sun. •It (the moon) rises in this manner: Its head[f] faces the easterly direction, coming out on the thirtieth day,[g] on that day, (that is,) on the thirtieth day, it comes into existence,[h] and it appears with the sun in the gate through which the sun exits;[i] and you have the beginning of the month.[j]
5 (Considering) half of it to be (divisible into) seven parts,[k] the whole disk of it is without light,[l] with the exception of one-seventh part of the fourteenth part of the
6 light (of the sun), one seventh of its (half) light.[m] •On the day when it receives one-seventh part of its one half,[n] as the sun sets, it becomes (equivalent to) one-seventh
7 light of one half of it. •Then when the sun rises, the moon[o] rises together with it, taking a portion of one half of its light; that night (the moon), just beginning its monthly journey[p] on its first lunar day, sets with the sun and becomes dark, in respect to its thirteen[q] parts[r] that night. On that day it rises and shines with exactly one-seventh
8 part (of its semicircle). •Then it comes out and recedes toward the east (away from) where the sun rises, (continuing) to be bright(er) in one sixth of one seventh[s] (of one half of the light of the sun) during the remaining days.[t]

1 **74**[a] Furthermore, I saw another system of rotation[b] with its own regulation[c] whereby[d]
2 the system fulfills its monthly course of movement. •All these things—including their fixed positions—Uriel, the holy angel who is the guide of all of them, showed to me. And I wrote down their fixed positions as he showed them to me; and I wrote down their months as they were, as well as the (variable) aspects[e] of their illumination until
3 the completion of fifteen days. •The moon wanes in fifteen steps during a period of
4 fifteen days, and waxes in fourteen steps in the east and the west respectively.[f] •In (certain) designated months it alters its (westerly) settings and in (certain) designated
5 months it fulfills its unusual[g] courses of movement. •For two months it (the moon) sets with the sun, and uses[h] those two middle openings (which are) the third and the

---

73 a. Lit. "After this commandment I saw another commandment."

b. Whereas the sun is generally personified as feminine, and feminine grammatical forms (though sometimes masculine forms) are applied to it, the moon is generally personified as masculine (though sometimes as feminine), and masculine grammatical forms are most commonly used for it.

c. Some late MSS read "the sun."

d. So B and C. A: "lengthens."

e. Lit. "its chariot on which it rides."

f. According to Ethiopian commentators, the crescent-shaped head of the new moon.

g. Or "morning."

h. Lit. "it appears," "it manifests itself," etc.

i. The term *yewaṣe'* is ambiguous, since it could mean either "it came out" or "it went out." The verb *waṣi'a*, "to go out," "to come out," "to depart," "to go far," etc., is an approximate equivalent of the English "to exit." The term denotes the "rising" of the sun (or the moon) in the sense that the sun "comes out of" or "exits from" its chamber.

j. Lit. "it becomes for you the head ["the beginning"] of the month."

k. B and C add *reḥuq*, to give the reading "half of it is distant [or "moves away"] by one seventh." Flemming suggests emending the text by substituting *re'uy*, "visible," for *reḥuq*. Cf. EC, p. 138, n. 7.

l. Lit. "as though without light." B C: "empty without light."

m. The passage is in general difficult. But it seems to me to imply that "one-seventh part of the half of the moon represents one-fourteenth part of the light of the whole moon." B and C omit the last phrase: "one seventh of its (half) light."

n. B and C add "its light."

o. So B and C. A: "it."

p. Lit. "it is at the beginning [head] of its morning."

q. A B: "six and seven." C: "seven seven."

r. Lit. "six and seven parts of its hemisphere(s)."

s. Lit. "six (and) seven."

t. This section, 73:4–8, is a badly garbled description of the variations in the moon's illuminated area: on the first day one quarter, on the next one seventh, then one seventh plus one fourteenth, etc.

74 a. This ch. is primarily a variant of the preceding ch. 73.

b. Lit. "route," "course of movement."

c. Lit. "command."

d. Lit. "by which commandment."

e. Lit. "appearance."

f. Lit. "It completes its darkness in four (and) seven parts for fifteen days and completes all its lights in seven (and) seven parts in the east and the west." B and C read: "In one-seven-seven parts it completes its light in the east and in each seven-seven parts completes its darkness in the west."

g. Lit. "one-one."

h. Lit. "it has." B and C omit "it has."

6 fourth gate. •It comes out for seven days and completes a circuit as it returns again to the gate through which the sun rises. In this manner it waxes[i] and recedes from the
7 sun, entering the sixth gate through which the sun rises in eight days. •When the sun rises through the fourth gate (the moon) comes out for seven days, until it starts coming out through the fifth. It then turns back toward the fourth gate in seven days,
8 waxing as it recedes, and enters the first gate in eight days. •Then again it returns to
9 the fourth gate through which the sun rises in seven days.[j] •This is how[k] I saw their fixed positions—how the moon rises and shines when the sun sets—in those days.
10 If five years are combined the sun gains thirty extra days; consequently one of those five years gains, and when it is completed, it turns out to be three hundred sixty-four
11 days. •The gain of the sun and of the stars turns out to be six[l] days; in five years, six days every year add up to thirty days;[m] and the moon[n] falls behind the sun and the
12 stars for thirty days.[o] •They[p] bring about all the years punctiliously, so that they forever neither gain upon nor fall behind their fixed positions for a single day, but they convert
13 the year with punctilious justice into three hundred sixty-four days. •In three (years)[q] there are one thousand ninety-two days and in five years one thousand eight hundred and twenty days, so that in eight years there are two thousand nine hundred and twelve
14 days. •For the moon singly in three (years) its days add up to one thousand thirty
15 days,[r] so that it falls behind by sixty-two days in three years.[s] •In five years (they add up to) one thousand eight hundred seventy days,[t] so that it falls behind by fifty days
16 in five years. Thus it is for the moon. •In eight years the days (add up to) two thousand eight hundred thirty-two days, so that it falls behind by eight days in eight years.[u]
17 (In this way) the years are completed with precision,[v] in accordance with their fixed positions in the universe and the fixed stations of the sun which shine, the gate through which it (the sun) rises and sets for thirty days.

1 **75** The leaders of the chiefs of the thousands, which are appointed over the whole creation and upon all the stars, are counted together with the four (leaders of the seasons); they do not leave from the[a] fixed stations[b] according to the reckoning of the year; and they do render service on the four days which are not counted in the reckoning
2 of the year. •On this account, people err in them, for those luminaries scrupulously render service to the fixed positions in the cosmos—one in the first gate of heaven, one in the third,[c] one in the fourth, one in the fifth,[d] and one in the sixth. In this manner the year is completed scrupulously in three hundred sixty-four fixed stations
3 of the cosmos. •Thus the signs, the durations of time, the years, and the days were shown[e] to me (by) the angel Uriel, whom the Lord, God of eternal glory, has appointed[f] over all the luminaries of heaven—(both) in heaven and the world—in order that they—the sun, the moon, the stars, and all the created objects which circulate in all

i. Lit. "completes all her light."

j. Vss. 7–9 is a corrupt rendering of the simple rule: The moon rises (and sets) during seven or eight days in the outermost gates (i.e. gates six and one) but only one or two days in all other gates (i.e. gates two to five).

k. Lit. "in this way."

l. So B and C. A reads "eight" as emended.

m. So B and C. A: "five years gain thirty days."

n. So B and C. A: "it."

o. So B and C. A: "it falls behind the sun and the stars for thirty days"—behind the sun, the moon, and the stars." Cf. EC, p. 141, nn. 1, 2.

p. So A. B: "The moon." C: "The sun and the stars." Cf. also EC, p. 141, nn. 3, 4.

q. Text unclear.

r. B: "one thousand and sixty days." C: "one thousand and sixty-two."

s. B and C omit "it falls behind by sixty-two days in three years."

t. Lit. "there are one thousand seven hundred seventy days in five years." In B and C vss. 14f. are corrupt.

u. A, B, and C all repeat the preceding clause.

The section 74:10–12 is meaningless as it stands; while the whole section 74:10–16 seems to be a later fragmentary intrusion. The computation in this section is a rather trivial one:

(1) solar (civil) years: $364 \times 5 = 1820$
$364 \times 3 = 1092$
$364 \times 8 = 2912$
(2) lunar years: $354 \times 5 = 1770$
$354 \times 3 = 1062$
$354 \times 8 = 2832$

Thus in 8 civil years the excess over 8 lunar years is $2912 - 2832 = 80$ (or simply $364 - 354 = 10$; thus $8 \times 10 = 80$).

v. Lit. "in justice," "justly."

75 a. Lit. "its."

b. B: "they do not leave from their fixed stations." C: "they do not become separated from their deeds [actions]."

c. All MSS add "gate of heaven."

d. B and C omit "fifth."

e. Lit. "he showed."

f. C adds "forever."

the chariots of heaven—should rule in the face of the sky and be seen on the earth
4 to be guides for the day and the night.[g] •Likewise Uriel showed me twelve wide
openings in the sky, along the course of the chariots of the sun, from which[h] the rays
of the sun break out and from which heat[i] is diffused upon the earth, when they are
5 opened during the designated seasons. •Their openings (affect) the winds and the spirit
6 of the dew,[j] •(that is) when the twelve wide openings[k] are opened in the sky, in the
extreme ends[l] of the earth, through which (also) the sun, the moon, the stars, and all
7 the (other) heavenly objects come out in the west.[m] •There are many open windows
to the left and the right, but one window produces the heat[n] at its designated time in
the manner of those openings through which the stars rise in accordance with their
8 orders and set according to their numbers. •I also saw chariots in heaven running in
9 the universe above those openings[o] in which the stars that do not set[p] revolve. •One
(circuit) is larger than the rest of them all, and it circles the entire cosmos at the
extreme ends of the earth.[q]

The twelve winds and their gates

1 **76** And I saw[a] the twelve wide openings in all the directions[b] through which the
2 winds come out and blow over the earth. •Three of them are open in the forefront[c]
of the sky, three in the west, three in the right of the sky,[d] and three on the left;[e]
3 (in other words) the first three are those on the morning side (followed by) three in
the direction of the north;[f] the last three are those on the left, in the direction of the
4 south (followed by) three in the west. •Through four of the (openings)[g] blow out winds
of blessing[h] (and) through eight of them blow out winds of pestilence—when they are
sent in order to destroy the whole earth, the water upon her, all those who dwell upon
her, and all those which exist in the waters[i] and the dry land.
5 The first (group of) winds goes out from those openings called the easterly.[j] Out
of the first gate, which is in the direction of the east and inclines toward the south,
6 proceed extirpation, drought, pestilence,[k] and destruction. •Out of the second gate,
(located) directly in the center, proceed[l] rain and fruitfulness together with dew.[m] Out
of the third gate, which is in the direction of the northeast, proceed (both) cold and
drought.
7 After these winds, there go out the southerly ones through three gates. Among
these, out of the first gate, which inclines in the direction of the east, proceed the
8 winds of heat.[n] •Out of the central gate, which is next to it, proceed beautiful fragrance,
9 dew, rain, peace, and life. •And out of the third gate, in the direction of the west,
proceed dew, rain, young locusts,[o] and desolation.
10 After these, there goes (the group) of the northerly[p] winds whose name is the Sea.[q]
There proceed from the seventh gate, which is in the direction of the east, toward the

g. The section 75:1–3 is a slightly different version of the same topic in 82:4–6.

h. So B and C. A: "with which."

i. B omits the whole preceding clause and substitutes *mot*, "death," for *mwoq*, "heat."

j. Texts unclear. So A, conjecturally. B: "The winds and the spirit of the dew during the seasons when the openings in the sky are opened upon the extreme ends." C: "As for the winds and the spirit of the dew, when they are opened, open in the sky upon the extreme ends."

k. B: "I saw the twelve openings."

l. Or "end."

m. B C: "from the east and the west."

n. Lit. "heats heat."

o. B adds "and beneath them."

p. So B and C. A: "that do not watch [keep]."

q. So A.

76 a. B and C start "At the extreme ends of the world I saw."

b. Lit. "to all the winds."

c. I.e. "the east."

d. I.e. "the south."

e. I.e. "the north."

f. Lit. "northeast."

g. Lit. "For four of them."

h. B and C add "and of peace."

i. So B and C. A: "on the earth."

j. Lit. "the Orient."

k. B: "death." C: "heat."

l. B and C: "what is right goes out."

m. So A. B and C have *salām*, "peace," instead of *mesla*, "with," resulting in the reading "peace and dew."

n. B: "the wind of death." C: "the wind of heat."

o. Lit. "newly sloughed locusts," "baboons," "invaders," "spoilers."

p. Lit. "northeasterly."

q. Eth. *baḥr*.

11 south,[r] dew, rain, young locusts,[s] and desolation. •Out of the central gate proceed
life, rain, and dew directly;[t] and out of the third gate, which is in the direction of the
west, which inclines toward the northeast, proceed cloud, frost, snow, rain, dew, and
young locusts.[u]
12 After these come the fourth (group) of winds—the westerly. Out of the first gate,
which is in the northeasterly direction, proceed dew, frost, cold, snow, and hoarfrost.
13 Out of the central gate proceed dew, rain, peace, and blessing. And out of the last
gate, which is in the direction of the south, proceed drought, desolation, burning,
14 and destruction. •Thus the twelve openings of the four heavenly directions[v] are
completed; all their orders, all their evil effects,[w] and all their beneficial effects[x] have
I revealed to you, (O) my son, Methuselah!

The four directions, the seven mountains, the seven rivers

Ezek 42:20

1 **77** The first direction[a] is called the Orient, because it is the very first.[b] •The second
2 is called the South,[c] because the Most High will descend[d] there, indeed because[e] the
3 Eternally Blessed will descend there.[f] •(The third) direction[g] is the Occident, its name
(means) the diminished, (because) there all the luminaries of the sky wane and descend.
4 The fourth direction,[h] whose name is the North,[i] is divided into three parts: One of
them is the dwelling of human beings; the second the seas of water, lakes, forests,
rivers, darkness, and clouds; and the third part[j] the garden of righteousness.
5 I saw seven high mountains which were higher than all the mountains of the earth;
6 out of them proceeds frost; and days and year(s) traverse (them) in due season.[k] •I
saw seven[l] rivers upon the earth, larger than all the rivers; one of them emerges from
7 the West[m] and empties its water into the Great Sea.[n] •Two (others)[o] come from the
8 Northeast to the sea and empty their water into the Erythraean Sea, in the East. •The
four remaining ones come out of the side of the Northeast to their own (respective)
seas—(two of them) to the Erythraean Sea and two of them to the Great Sea, pouring
9 themselves therein; some say to the seventh[p] desert.[q] •I (also) saw big islands in the
sea and the land[r]—seventy-two in the Erythraean Sea.[s]

Names of the sun and the moon; waxing and waning of the moon

1 2 **78** These are the names of the sun:[a] the first, 'Oryares[b] and the second, Tomas.[c] •The

r. The text may be corrupt. B reads "After these are the winds in the direction of the northeast, its name is *baḥr* [the Sea], from the three seventh exits in the direction of the east which inclines toward the south . . ." Charles saw two interpolations here. Cf. EC, p. 145, nn. 36–40.

s. See n. o above.

t. B and C add "peace."

u. See n. o.

v. Lit. "openings."

w. Lit. "plagues."

x. Lit. "their peace."

77 a. Lit. "wind."

b. Cf. Heb. *qedem*.

c. Lit. also "Southwest."

d. Charles suggests that the Eth. *'azēb* is equivalent to the Heb. *dārōm*, from a play on *yērēd rām*, "the Most High will descend."

e. B omits "indeed because." C omits "because."

f. B omits "will descend there."

g. Lit. "wind."

h. Lit. "wind."

i. Lit. "Northeast."

j. So B and C. A: "the second, rivers."

k. B C: "and days and season and year traverse (them)." B adds "and go."

l. So B and C. A omits "seven."

m. I.e. possibly the Nile, which lies southwest of the land of Israel.

n. I.e. the Mediterranean Sea.

o. Lit. "These two," possibly referring to the Euphrates and Tigris. The references to these rivers may have been omitted due to scribal errors in this defective passage.

p. So A. Only one MS of Charles, u, reads clearly "seven." Others are corrupt.

q. So B and C. A reads *mabder* instead of *madbar*, "desert." The verb *bdr* means "to run," "race," "prefer," etc., but *mabder* does not seem to have an intelligible meaning in the present context.

r. Perhaps "in the land" is an intrusion.

s. The reading of A is difficult but better. B and C read "I saw seven big islands in the sea and the land—two in the land and five in the Great Sea." Cf. also EC, p. 148, nn. 8–10. Perhaps the non-corrupted original read "I saw seven big islands—two in the Great Sea, and five in the Red Sea."

78 a. Lit. "like this."

b. Heb. *'ōr ḥeres*, "light of the sun."

c. Heb. *šemeš*, "sun," according to Charles. Heb. *ḥamāh*, "heat," according to Halévy.

moon has four names: Its first name is Asenya;[d] its second, 'Abla;[e] the third, Banase;[f]
3 and the fourth, 'Era.[g] • These are the two great luminaries. Their roundness is like the
roundness of the sky; and the magnitude of their roundness is equivalent for both.[h]
4 There are seven (more) portions of light that move[i] in the sun's sphere than in the
moon's and it increases in measure until seventy[j] portions of the sun are completed.[k]
5 The (moon) comes in and goes out[l] by the western openings, and circles[m] via the
6 northeast and rises through the eastern openings upon the face of the earth. • When
the moon (begins its cycle),[n] it appears in the sky one half of a seventh part; it will
7 become fully illumined from the fourteenth (day); • it completes its illumination the
fifteenth,[o] becoming[p] fulfilled according to the sign of the year and becoming fifteen[q]
8 parts. Thus the moon waxes[r] in fifteen parts.[s] • In its waning, (the moon) decreases
on the first day to fourteen parts of its light; on the second day, it decreases to thirteen
parts of light; on the third, to twelve parts; on the fourth, to eleven parts; on the fifth,
to ten parts; on the sixth, to nine parts; on the seventh, to eight parts; on the eighth,
to seven parts; on the ninth, to six parts;[t] on the tenth, to five parts; on the eleventh,
to four parts; on the twelfth, to three parts; on the thirteenth, to one half (of the
preceding);[u] on the fourteenth, all its light decreases to one half of one seventh; and
9 on the fifteenth, all the remaining (light) disappears. • In certain fixed months, the
moon completes its cycle[v] every twenty-nine days, (in certain others), every twenty-
10 eight. • Then Uriel showed me another order (concerning) when light is beamed[w] into
11 the moon, from which (direction) of the bright[x] sun it is beamed. • During all the
seasons when the moon is made to run its cycle,[y] the light is being beamed into it
(the moon) facing the sun until the illumination (of the moon) is completed in the
course of fourteen days; and when it is lit completely, it radiates[z] light in the sky.
12 On the first day, it is called[a2] the new moon because on that day the illumination
13 begins to set upon it.[b2] • These[c2] (illuminations) are completed with exactitude on the
day when the sun descends[d2] into the west, and the moon (simultaneously) rises in the
east in the evening,[e2] shining during the night[f2] until the sun rises opposite it, and it[g2]
14 is over against the sun. • From the same side where light entered the moon, from there

---

d. B C: *'Asonya*. According to Halévy this word
comes from Heb. *'îshôn yāh*, "diminutive person,"
"pupil of the eye," designating the human-like figure
of the moon.
e. According to Halévy, corrupted from Heb.
l'bānāh, "moon."
f. B C: Benase. According to Halévy, corrupted
from Heb. *bēn kēsēḥ*, "full moon."
g. Cf. Heb. *yārēḥ*, "moon." For the various
names of the sun and the moon given here cf. J.
Halévy, "Recherches sur la langue de la rédaction
primitive du livre d'Hénoch," *JA* 6.9 (1867), 352–
95.
h. So B and C. A reads "the magnitude of their
roundness is like the roundness of the sky, co-
equivalent for both." "Like the roundness of the
sky" seems to be a dittography. One could possibly
translate the passage to read "the magnitude of their
circuits is like the roundness of the sky, co-equivalent
for both."
i. B C: "that is added."
j. So A, which does not seem to make sense. B
C: "seventh." The meaning of the text is that when
seven parts of the sun's light have been transferred
to the moon, the moon is fully illuminated.
k. Lit. "passes." The text is difficult.
l. B C: "they set and come in." The masculine
singular verbal form in A seems to indicate the moon.
m. B C: "they circle."
n. Lit. "when the moon comes out."
o. Lit. "three-fiveness." B and C also add: "fifteen portions of light are added into it until the
fifteenth day."
p. Lit. "its light becomes."

q. Lit. "three-fiveness."
r. Lit. "becomes."
s. Lit. "half of seventh."
t. The passage from 78:8b (fol. 103v) to 82:20
(fol. 106v) has been copied twice, first as an interpolation between the end of ch. 71 (fol. 96r) and
72:1 (fol. 99r), and here, where it normally belongs.
Both sections are of the same period and seem to be
by the same hand; nevertheless, they are not identical.
A study of their variations can contribute to an
understanding of the Ethiopian scribal philosophy.
Of course, no attempt is made here to deal with that
problem.
u. B and C read "to two parts."
v. Lit. "the moon [or "month"] becomes."
w. Lit. "thrown," "cast," "projected."
x. Lit. "morning ["day" or "east"]." B and C
omit "morning."
y. Lit. "made to go."
z. Lit. "it fulfills," "accomplishes," "executes."
a2. So B and C. A reads *wasamāy*, "and heaven,"
instead of *tesamay*. Note here also that the feminine
instead of the masculine singular is used for the
moon, as elsewhere (see below) in this passage the
masculine instead of the feminine singular is used
for the sun.
b2. Lit. "light rises upon her." Here also the
feminine form is applied to the moon.
c2. B and C drop "these."
d2. The masculine form is used for the sun.
e2. Lit. "night."
f2. B and C read "the whole night."
g2. Lit. "the moon."

also it (gradually) wanes until all the illumination disappears and the days of the moon expire, its disk empty without light.

15　(The moon) coordinates,[h2] in respect to its days and seasons, (four) three-month[i2] (divisions). In the course of its recession[j2] it makes (three months each in thirty days) and three months each in twenty-nine days; during this season[k2] it makes its recession, in the first period, (starting) in the first gate, (in) one hundred and seventy-seven days.

16 In the course (of) its progression,[12] it appears three months each in thirty days and

17 three months each in twenty-nine days. •By night it appears like a man,[m2] and by day it appears like the sky; for there is no other thing in it except its light.[n2]

Conclusion of the vision of astronomical laws

1 **79** (Thus) now, my son,[a] I have revealed to you everything; (so) the rules concerning

2 all the stars of heaven are concluded (here). •(Indeed) he showed me all their respective rules for every day, for every season,[b] and for every year; the procession of each one

3 according to the commandment, every month and every week. •(He showed me) the total[c] decrement (i.e. during a half lunar year) of the moon which it makes (from the first) through the sixth gate,[d] for (after) the light of[e] this sixth gate is disposed of (at

4 the end of the series of the six gates),[f] the beginning of the decrement •(i.e. during the other half lunar year) which it makes (in returning) in the first gate takes place in its[g] own season until one hundred and seventy-seven days are fulfilled, following

5 the rule of (counting) weeks, twenty-five (weeks) and two days. •(The moon) falls behind the sun according to the order of[h] the stars exactly five days during one period

6 (i.e. one half year), and when the place which you behold has been traversed.[i] •Such is the appearance and the picture of all the luminaries which Uriel the archangel, who is their leader, showed unto me.

1 **80** In those days, the angel Uriel responded[a] and said to me, "Behold, I have shown you everything, Enoch, and I have revealed everything to you (so that) you might see this sun, this moon, and those that guide the stars of heaven as well as all those who interchange[b] their activities and their seasons and rotate[c] their processions.

2　In respect to their days, the sinners and the winter[d] are cut short.[e] Their seed(s)[f] shall lag behind[g] in their lands and in their fertile fields,[h] and in all their activities upon the earth.[i] He will turn[j] and appear in their time,[k] and withhold rain;[l] and the sky

3 shall stand still at that time. •Then the vegetable[m] shall slacken[n] and not grow in its

4 season, and the fruit[o] shall not be born[p] in its (proper) season. •The moon shall alter

---

h2. So A. Lit. "It unites," "It combines," "It associates." Other MSS: "It makes."

i2. So A. B C: "and three months it makes thirty days in its season(s)."

j2. I.e. as it moves from gate six to one. Lit. "when it is waning," "when it is receding."

k2. Lit. "which in them."

l2. I.e. as it moves from gate one to six. Lit. "in the (due) season, its coming out."

m2. B and C add "for twenty days."

n2. In the last two sentences, the moon is again described in feminine gender.

79 a. B adds "Methuselah."

b. B and C add "of every authority."

c. Lit. "in all," or "in everything." B and C omit "in all," or "in everything."

d. Lit. "in the sixth gate" or "by the sixth gate." The passage could be translated "the total decrement of the moon which it makes by the sixth gate."

e. Lit. "her light," i.e. the light of the sixth gate.

f. Lit. "after these" or "from these."

g. Lit. "her," i.e. the first gate's season.

h. So A and B. C reads *lašer'āta*, "(for) the order of," instead of *bašer'āta*. Cf. EC, p. 152, n. 1.

i. Lit. "completed."

80 a. Lit. "answered me."

b. Lit. "turn."

c. B and C omit "and rotate [turn]."

d. Lit. "rainy season."

e. Lit. "In respect to the days of the sinners and the winter, they are cut short." B and C read "In the days of sinners the winters ["seasons," "years"] are cut short."

f. The term "seeds" has a double entendre here; it can mean "their offspring" or "the seeds they sow."

g. Lit. "it shall become the last."

h. B: "plowed fields."

i. B C: "all the activities upon the earth shall alter."

j. So A. For B and C see preceding note.

k. B: "He will not appear in his [its] time." C: "He will not appear for their times."

l. B C: "rain will be withheld."

m. Lit. "fruit of the ground."

n. Lit. "shall become the last one."

o. Lit. "fruit of the tree."

p. Lit. "shall be withheld."

5 its order, and will not be seen according to its (normal) cycles. •In those days it will appear in the sky[q] and it shall arrive in the evening[r] in the extreme ends of the great lunar path,[s] in the west. And it shall shine (more brightly), exceeding the normal 6 degree of light.[t] •Many of the chiefs of the stars shall make errors in respect to the orders given to them; they shall change their courses and functions and not appear 7 during the seasons which have been prescribed for them. •All the orders of the stars shall harden (in disposition) against the sinners and the conscience of those that dwell upon the earth. They (the stars) shall err against them (the sinners); and modify all their courses. Then they (the sinners) shall err and take them (the stars) to be gods. 8 And evil things shall be multiplied upon them; and plagues shall come upon them, so as to destroy all.

The heavenly book and Enoch's mission

1 **81** Then he said unto me, "Enoch, look at the[a] tablet(s)[b] of heaven; read what is 2 written upon them and understand (each element on them) one by one. •So I looked at the tablet(s) of heaven, read all the writing (on them), and came to understand everything. I read that[c] book and[d] all the deeds of humanity and all the children of 3 the flesh upon the earth for[e] all the generations of the world. •At that very moment, I blessed the Great Lord, the King of Glory for ever, for he has created all the phenomena in the world. I praised the Lord because of his patience; and I wept on 4 account of the children of the people upon the earth.[f] •After that, I said:

> Blessed is the man who dies righteous and upright,
> against whom no record[g] of oppression has been written,
> and who received no judgment on that day.[h]

5 Then the seven holy ones[i] brought me[j] and placed me on the ground in front of the gate of my house, and said to me, "Make everything known to your son, Methuselah, and show to all your children that no one of the flesh can be just before the Lord; for 6 they are merely his own creation.[k] •We shall let you stay with your son[l] for one year, so that you may teach your children another law[m] and write it down for them and give all of them[n] a warning;[o] and in the second year, you shall be taken away from (among) 7 all of them.[p] •Let your heart be strong! For the upright shall announce righteousness to the upright; and the righteous ones shall rejoice with the righteous ones and 8 congratulate each other.[q] •But the sinners shall die together with the sinners; and the 9 apostate shall sink together with the apostate. •But those who do right shall not die[r] on account of the (evil) deeds of the people; it[s] will gather on account of the deeds 10 of the evil ones."[t] •In those days, (those seven holy ones) concluded speaking with me; and then I returned to my people, blessing the Lord of the universe.

Job 9:2;
Ps 14:1

2Kgs 22:20;
Isa 57:1;
WisSol
4:7–14

---

q. Charles, following Halévy, suggests "the sun" instead of "the sky." See EC, p. 153, n. 1.

r. Text reads "drought," "famine." But Charles, following Halévy, has suggested perhaps correctly that the Eth. *'abār*, corresponding to the Heb. *rā'āb*, "hunger," is a corruption of the Heb. *ereb*, "evening," attributable to the Gk. translator. Cf. EC, p. 153, nn. 1, 2.

s. Lit. "chariot."

t. Lit. "the order of light."

81 a. B C: "this."

b. Lit. "slate," "polished and flat stone," "brick," "tile," "stone-table."

c. B and C omit "that."

d. B C: "of."

e. Lit. "unto."

f. Lit. "I wept upon the earth on account of the children of the people." B and C read "I blessed" instead of "I wept on account of," "upon the children of the people" instead of "upon the earth," thus giving the reading "I blessed upon the children of the people."

g. Lit. "book."

h. B: "Upon whom no guile has been found." C: "Who did not find the day of judgment."

i. All MSS add "they."

j. A omits "me."

k. Lit. "for he has created them."

l. Lit. "We shall leave you with your son."

m. B C: "until you give other commandments, that you may teach your children."

n. Lit. "all of your children."

o. Lit. "make all of your children hear [understand]."

p. Lit. "they shall take you away from all of them." B and C read "from their midst" instead of "from all of them."

q. Or "present each other with gifts."

r. B C: "shall die on account of the deeds of the people."

s. I.e. the flood water.

t. B C: "they will assemble on account of the deeds of the evil ones."

Additional astronomical-calendrical visions

1 **82** Now, Methuselah, my son, I shall recount all these things to you and write them down for you. I have revealed to you[a] and given you the book[b] concerning all these things. Preserve, my son, the book from your father's hands in order that you may
2 pass[c] it to the generations of the world. •I have given wisdom to you, to your children, and to those who shall become your children in order that they may pass it (in turn) to their own children and to the generations that are discerning.[d] All the wise ones
3 shall give praise,[e] and wisdom shall dwell upon your consciousness;[f] •they shall not slumber but be thinking;[g] they shall cause their ears to listen in order that they may learn this wisdom; and it shall please those who feast on it[h] more than good food.
4 Blessed are all the righteous ones; blessed are those who walk in the street of righteousness[i] and have no sin like the sinners in the computation of the days in which the sun goes its course in the sky. It (the sun) comes in through a door[j] and rises for thirty[k] days together with the chiefs of the thousands of the orders of the stars, together with the four which are added to determine[l] the intervals within (the year, that is, the intervals) between the four seasons[m] of the year;[n] those that lead them along[o] come
5 in on four[p] days. •On this account there are people that err; they count them (the four?) in the computation of the year:[q] for the people make error and do not recognize
6 them accurately; for they belong to the reckoning of the year. •Truly, they are recorded forever: one in the first gate, one in the third,[r] one in the fourth, and one in the sixth. The year is completed in three hundred and sixty-four days.[s]
7   True is the matter of the exact computation of that which has been recorded; for Uriel—whom the Lord of all the creation of the world has ordered for me (in order to explain)[t] the host of heaven—has revealed to me and breathed over me concerning
8 the luminaries, the months, the festivals, the years, and the days. •He has the power in the heaven both day and night so that he may cause the light to shine over the people—sun, moon, and stars, and all the principalities of the heaven which revolve
9 in their (respective) circuits. • These are the orders of the stars which set in their
10 (respective) places, seasons, festivals, and months. •And these are the names of those which lead the ones that come out and go down[u] in their (appointed) seasons, which lead them in their (respective) places, orders, times, months, authorities, and locations.
11 The four leaders[v] which distinguish the four seasons of the year enter first; after them (enter) the twelve leaders of the orders which distinguish the months; and the three hundred and sixty captains[w] which divide the days and the four epagomenal days,
12 (and) leaders which divide the four seasons of the year. • These captains over thousands are added between leader and leader, each behind a place to stand; but their leaders
13 make the division. •And these are the names of the leaders which divide the four seasons[x] of the years which are fixed: Malki'ēl, Hēla'emmemēlek, Milāy'ul, and Nārēl.[y]
14 The names of those who lead them are 'Adnār'ul, 'Iyāsus-'ēl, 'Ēlum'ēl[z]—these three

Ps 78:5f.

Pss 19:10;
119:103

follow the leaders of the orders, as well as the four[n2] which follow after the three
leaders of the orders, which follow after those leaders of the stations that divide the
15 four seasons of the year. •At the very beginning,[b2] Malkiyāl,[c2] whose name is called
Tam'ayen[d2]—and the sun—rises and rules; and all the days of his authority—during
16 which he reigns—are ninety-one days. •And these are the signs of the days which
become manifest during the period of his authority: sweat, heat, and dryness;[e2] all the
trees bear fruit (and) leaves grow on all trees; (there will be) good harvest,[f2] rose
flowers, and all the flowers which grow in the field; but the winter tree[g2] shall wither.
17 And these are the names of the leaders which are their subordinates: Berkā'ēl,
Zalebsā'ēl,[h2] and another additional one, a captain of a thousand, named Hēluyāsāf[i2]—
18 the days of the authority of this one have been completed. •The next leader after him
is Hela'emmemēlēk,[j2] whose name they call the bright sun; and all the days of his light
19 are ninety-one days. •And these are the days of signs upon signs[k2] upon the earth:
scorching heat and drought; and trees will produce their glowing fruits[l2] and impart
of their ripened ones;[m2] the sheep shall seek (one another) and become pregnant; and
all the fruits of the earth are gathered in, and all that is in the fields as well as the
20 winepress. (These things) shall take place in the days of his authority. •These are the
names, the orders, and the subordinates[n2] of those captains over thousands: Gēda'iyāl,
Hēlyā'ēl, and Ki'ēl;[o2] and the name of the one that is added together with them is a
captain over a thousand called 'Asfā'ēl[p2]—the days of the authority of this one have
been completed.

Book IV (83–90)
The Dream Visions

Vision of the Deluge

1 **83** (Book) Four.[a] •Now, my son Methuselah, I will show you all the visions[b] which
2 I saw,[c] recounting them before you. •I saw two (visions) before I got married;[d] and
neither one of them resembles the other: The first one (I saw) when I (was beginning
to) learn book(s), and the second, before I got married to[e] your mother. First,[f] I saw
3 a scary vision regarding which[g] I prayed to the Lord. •I was (then) sleeping[h] in my
grandfather Mahalalel's house, and[i] I saw in a vision the sky being hurled down and
4 snatched and falling upon the earth. •When it fell upon the earth, I saw the earth being
swallowed up[j] into the great abyss, the mountains being suspended upon mountains,
the hills sinking down upon the hills, and tall trees being uprooted[k] and thrown and
5 sinking into the deep abyss. •Thereupon a word[l] fell into my mouth; and I began
6 crying aloud, saying, "The earth is being destroyed." •Then my grandfather,
Mahalalel, woke me up while I was sleeping together with him[m] and said to me,

---

a2. B C: "one."
b2. Lit. "Before the first." B C: "Before the first
year."
c2. B C: Melkyāl.
d2. B: Tam'ana. C: Tam'ayeni.
e2. Or "sorrow." C reads *wazāḥen*, "rest,"
"calm." The word *ḥazan* in A and B could also be
a corruption of *waḥāzyān*, "springs," "fountains."
f2. B C: "harvest of wheat."
g2. Lit. "the tree of the rainy season."
h2. B C: Berke'ēl [C: Berka'el], Zēlebsā'ēl [C:
Zēlebse'ēl].
i2. B: Hēluyāsēf. C: Hēluyasef.
j2. B: Ḥelemmemēlēk. C: Helemmemēlek.
k2. B C: "the signs of the day."
l2. B: "glowing and ripe."
m2. Lit. "their ripened fruits." B: "their dried
fruits." C: "their glowing and ripened fruits."
n2. C omits "the subordinates."

o2. B C: Gedā'ēyāl [C: Gidā'iyal], Kē'ēl, and
Hē'ēl.
p2. B: 'Esfā'ēl.

83 a. So A. B reads *keft*, "part." C omits both.
b. C: "my visions."
c. So B and C. A reads "all the visions, but the
visions, which I saw."
d. Lit. "I took a wife."
e. Lit. "I took."
f. B and C omit "First."
g. B C: "regarding them."
h. Or "lying still," "lying down," "resting."
i. B and C omit "and."
j. A: "being heaped[?]."
k. Lit. "being cut from their stems."
l. Or "a speech," "a statement."
m. B C: "by [near] him."

"What happened to you that you are crying aloud like this, my son, and why are
7 you lamenting in this manner?" •And I recounted to him the whole vision which I
had seen. And he said unto me, "How terrifying a thing have you seen, my son!
You have seen in your dream[n] a powerful vision—all the sins of the whole world[o] as
8 it was sinking into the abyss and being destroyed with great destruction. •Now, my
son, rise and pray to the Lord of glory, for you are a man of faith, so that a remnant
9 shall remain upon the earth and that the whole earth shall not be blotted out."[p] •My
son, all the things upon the earth shall take place from heaven; and there will occur
10 a great destruction upon the earth. •After that, I rose and prayed, made a petition,
and begged; and I wrote down all the prayers of the generations of the world.[q] I will
11 show you everything, my son, Methuselah. •Had[r] I descended underneath and seen
the sky, the sun rising in the east, the moon descending in the west, the diminishing
of the stars, and the whole earth, I would have recognized[s] everything upon her.[t] So
I blessed the Lord of judgment and extolled him. For he has made the sun to come
out from the windows of the east; so it ascended and rose upon the face of the sky,
starting to go the way that it was shown.

1 **84** Then I raised up my hands in righteousness and blessed the Holy and Great One;
and I spoke with the breath of my mouth and the tongue of flesh which God has made
for the children of the flesh, the people, so that they should speak with it; he gave
them the breath and the mouth so that they should speak with it.

2   Blessed are you, O Great King,
       you are mighty in your greatness,
       O Lord of all the creation of heaven,
       King of kings and God of the whole world.
       Your authority[a] and kingdom[b] abide forever and ever;
       and your dominion throughout all the generations of generations;
       all the heavens are your throne forever,   Isa 66:1
       and the whole earth is your footstool forever and ever and ever.
3   For you have created (all),
       and all things you rule;
       not a single thing is hard for you—(absolutely) not a single thing[c] or
            wisdom;[d]
       Your throne has not retreated from her station[e] nor from before your
            presence.[f]
       Everything you know, you see, and you hear;
       nothing exists that can be hidden from you, for everything you expose.[g]
4   The angels of your heavens are now committing sin (upon the earth),
       and your wrath shall rest[h] upon the flesh of the people until (the arrival
            of) the great day of judgment

5   "Now, O God, and Lord and Great King, I pray and beg so that you may sustain
my prayer and[i] save for me (a generation) that will succeed me in the earth; and do
not destroy all the flesh of the people and empty the earth (so that) there shall be
6 eternal destruction. •Do now destroy, O my Lord, the flesh that has angered you
from upon the earth, but sustain the flesh of righteousness and uprightness as a plant
of eternal seed; and hide not your face from the prayer of your servant, O Lord."

n. Lit. "You have dreamed." B and C: "your
dream."
o. B C: "the secret of the sins of the whole
world."
p. C: "that he may not blot out."
q. B C: "and I wrote down my prayers for the
generations of the world."
r. A unclear. B C: "When."
s. Cf. EC, p. 161, nn. 9–12.
t. B C: "he had known it in the beginning."

84 a. Or "dominion," "divinity," "kingship."

b. B and C add "your greatness."
c. B and C omit "thing."
d. B has a meaningless word, qa'ab.
e. Lit. "condition," "state of life," "age,"
"nourishment . . ."
f. The whole clause is a difficult one. C reads:
"Wisdom does not depart from the place of your
throne, nor turn away from your presence." Concerning this emendation see EC, p. 162, nn. 12f.
g. B C: "you see."
h. Lit. "become," "happen," "take place."
i. All MSS add "so that."

Vision of various cows

85 After this, I saw another dream; and I will show you everything,[a] my son. •Then Enoch responded[b] and said to his son, Methuselah: I shall speak to you, my son, hear
3 my words and incline your ears to the dream vision of your father. •Before I married your mother, Edna, I was seeing a vision on my bed, and behold a cow[c] emerged[d] from the earth, and that bovid was snow-white;[e] and after it, there came forth one female calf together with two other calves, one of which was dark and the other[f] red.
4 The dark calf gored that red calf and pursued it over the earth; thereafter I was not
5 able to see[g] that red calf. •But the dark calf grew big, and it brought along[h] that female calf; and I saw that many bovids, which resembled it, proceeded forth from it, and
6 followed after them.[i] •That first heifer[j] departed from before the face of that first bovid,[k] and looked for that red calf, but could not find it; so she lamented over it with
7 great lamentation, in searching for it. •I kept looking until that first cow came[l] and
8 quieted her; from that moment, she stopped crying. •After that she bore two snow-
9 white cows;[m] and after it she bore many more cows as well as dark heifers. •I also saw in my sleep that snow-white bull, and he grew big likewise and became a great snow-white bull; and there proceeded forth from him many snow-white cows which
10 resembled him. •Then they began to give birth to many snow-white cows which resembled them, each one following many others.[n]

Vision of the fallen stars among the cows

1 **86** Again I saw (a vision) with my own eyes as I was sleeping, and saw the lofty heaven; and as I looked, behold, a star fell down from heaven but (managed) to rise
2 and eat and to be pastured among those cows. •Then I saw these big and dark cows, and behold they all changed their cattle-sheds, their pastures, and their calves; and
3 they began to lament[a] with each other.[b] •Once again I saw a vision, and I observed the sky and behold, I saw[c] many stars descending and casting themselves down from the sky upon that first star; and they became bovids among those calves and were
4 pastured together with them, in their midst. •I kept observing, and behold, I saw all of them extending[d] their sexual organs like horses and commencing to mount upon the heifers, the bovids;[e] and they (the latter) all became pregnant and bore elephants,
5 camels, and donkeys. •So (the cattle) became fearful and frightened of them and
6 began to bite with their teeth and swallow and to gore with their horns. •Then they began to eat those bovids. And behold, all the children of the earth began to tremble and to shake before them and to flee from them.

Vision of four heavenly beings

1 **87** Again I saw them commencing to gore and devour one another; so the earth
2 began to cry aloud. •And I lifted my eyes unto heaven and saw a vision: And behold, there came forth[a] from heaven (a being) in the form of a snow-white person—one
3 came out of that place and three (others) with him.[b] •Those ones[c] which had come out last seized me by my hand and took me[d] from the generations of the earth, lifted

---

85 a. C adds "the whole dream."

  b. B C: "took up."

  c. The Eth. *āhm* (pl. *'alhmt*, "cattle") refers to a bovine animal regardless of age or sex.

  d. Masculine singular verb.

  e. The Eth. *ṣa'ādā* refers to "snow-white, bright, pure." The word does not normally describe a person's color.

  f. Lit. "one."

  g. A reads "to see them."

  h. B C: "she came."

  i. B C: "followed after it."

  j. B C: "That female heifer that first one."

  k. The qualifying adjectives are in masculine form.

  l. A adds "to it." B and C add "to her."

m. B C: "another snow-white cow."

  n. Lit. "the other many."

86 a. C: "to live."

  b. But cf. EC, p. 165, n. 12.

  c. A repeats "I saw."

  d. Lit. "bringing out."

  e. C: "the heifers of the bovids."

87 a. A: "he came forth." B C: "they came forth."

  b. So B. A reads "four came out of that place and three with him." C reads "four came out of that place and three with them."

  c. B C: "Those three."

  d. B C: "raised me."

me up into a high place, and showed me a high tower above the earth,[e] and all the
4 hills were firm.[f] • (One of them) said to me, "Stay here until you see everything that
will happen to these elephants, camels, and donkeys, as well as to the stars and to
the bovids—all of them."

Vision of the punishment of the fallen stars

1 **88** I then saw one of those four who had come out earlier seizing that first star,
binding his hands and feet, and throwing him into an abyss—this abyss was narrow
2 and deep, empty[a] and dark. • Also one of them drew a sword and gave it to those
elephants, camels,[b] and donkeys; then they began to attack one another, and on account
3 of them the whole earth was quaking. • And as I continued to see in the vision, behold,
from that time, one of the four, among those who had come out, was stoning from
the sky, and gathering and taking away all the mighty[c] stars, whose sexual organs
were like the sexual organs of horses; then he bound all of them hand and foot, and
cast them into the pits of the earth.

The Great Flood

1 **89** Then one of those four went to those snow-white bovids[a] and taught (one of them)
a secret: he was born a bovid but became a person; and he built for himself a big boat[b]
and dwelt upon it. Three cows dwelt together with him in that boat, and that boat[c]
2 was covered (over) them. • Again I raised my eyes toward heaven, and saw a lofty
ceiling with seven cascading streams upon it; and those cascading streams[d] flowed
3 with much water into one enclosed area. • Again I saw, and behold, fountains were
opened upon the ground of that great enclosed area, and the water began to swell and
rise upon the ground; and I saw that enclosed area until the whole ground was
4 (completely) covered with water. • Water, darkness, and mist accumulated heavily
upon it; and I looked at the ascent of that water going up and up until[e] it rose above
that enclosed area, and was streaming above the enclosed area;[f] thus it was standing
5 above the ground. • And everything[g] that was in the enclosed area;[h] and (all those on
the ground) were gathered together until I saw them sinking, being swallowed up,
6 and perishing in that water. • Yet that boat was floating above the water, though all
the cattle, elephants, camels, and donkeys were sinking to the bottom; so I could (no
longer) see any one of the animals (for) they had no ability to come out but (only)
7 to perish and sink into the deep water.[i] • Again I kept seeing in the vision until those
cascading streams were dissipated from that high ceiling, the fountains of the earth
8 were normalized, and other pits[j] were opened. • Then the water began to descend into
them until the ground became visible,[k] that boat settled upon the earth, the darkness
9 vanished, and it became light. • Then the snow-white cow which became a man[l] came
out from that boat together with three cows. One of those three cows was snow-
white, similar to that (first) cow, and one of them red like blood.[m] Now that (first)
snow-white cow departed from them.

---

e. So B and C. A reads *'emdeḥera*, "after,"
instead of *'emmedera*.

f. So A. B C: "every hill was small."

88 a. B C: "serious," "difficult."

b. So B and C. A omits "camels."

c. Lit. "stern," "powerful." B C: "great." 4QEn[e]:
"many." Cf. Milik, *The Books of Enoch*, pp. 238f.
It is possible that *'azizāna* (A) is a corruption of
bezuḥāna, "many."

89 a. C: "that . . . bovid."

b. A reads wrongly *meśrāqa*, "East," instead of
masqara. Cf. 4QEn[e], *'arb ḥadah*, "a boat," "a
ship."

c. B and C omit "that boat."

d. 4QEn[e]: "[and I] was looking and, behold, seven
sluices pouring out [on the earth much water]." So
Milik, *The Books of Enoch*, p. 238.

e. B and C omit "going up and up until."

f. A has the Eth. number "nine" (or "nine
times"?) at the end of this sentence.

g. B C: "all the cows." Cf. also 4QEn[e]. See
following n.

h. Milik contends that the Eth. (vss. 4–5a) is
"much more developed" than the Aram., which he
reconstructs "[. . . And] I was looking until the earth
was covered by the waters [and by darkness and
mist, and they were] standing upon it," starting with
vs. 3. See Milik, *The Books of Enoch*, p. 238.

i. Lit. "depth," "lake."

j. Milik, *The Books of Enoch*, p. 241: "chambers."

k. Milik, *The Books of Enoch*, pp. 241f.: "until
[the waters] vanished."

l. According to Milik, this clause, "which became
a man," is not original. Cf. *The Books of Enoch*,
pp. 241f.

m. B and C add: "and one black."

From the Flood to the exodus

10   Then they began to bear the beasts of the fields and the birds. There arose out of
them all classes of population: lions, leopards, wolves,[n] snakes,[o] hyenas, wild boars,
foxes, squirrels,[p] swine, hawks, eagles,[q] kites,[r] striped crow(s),[s] and ravens. Among
11 them there was also born a snow-white cow. •Then they began to bite[t] one another
among themselves. That snow-white cow which was born in their midst begat a wild
12 ass,[u] and a snow-white cow with it; and the wild asses multiplied. •And that cow[v]
which was born from him bore a black wild boar and a snow-white sheep;[w] the former
13 then bore healthy beasts[x] and the latter[y] bore twelve sheep. •When those twelve sheep
had grown up, they gave away one of their own members[z] to the donkeys, which[a2] in
turn gave him[b2] away to the wolves;[c2] so this sheep grew up in the midst of the
14 wolves.[d2] • Then the Lord[e2] brought the eleven sheep to dwell with him, and to pasture[f2]
in the midst of the wolves; and they multiplied and became many flocks of sheep.
15 Then the wolves began to fear[g2] them; so they tortured them until their little ones were
being killed (for) they cast away their little ones into a river of great quantity of water.
So those sheep began to cry aloud on behalf of their little ones and to complain unto
16 their Lord. • Then one sheep which had been saved from the wolves fled and escaped[h2]
to the wild asses. But I saw the sheep continuing to lament and cry aloud; and they
kept praying to their Lord with all their strength until the Lord of the sheep descended
17 at their entreatment,[i2] from a lofty palace, arriving to visit[j2] them. •He called that
sheep which had escaped from the wolves and told him concerning the wolves that
18 he should warn the wolves not to touch the sheep. • The sheep then went to the wolves
in accordance with the word of the Lord, together with another sheep which he had
met,[k2] so the two of them went on and arrived together into the assembly of those
19 wolves, and spoke to them and warned them not to touch the sheep. •But thenceforth
I saw how the wolves even intensified their pressure upon the sheep.[l2] They, the sheep,
20 cried aloud—they cried aloud with all their strength. • Then their Lord came to (the
rescue of) the sheep, whereupon they began to whip those wolves. So the wolves
began to make lamentations, but the sheep thereafter became quiet and stopped crying
21 aloud. • I continued to see the sheep until they departed from (the presence) of the
wolves, and the wolves (until) their eyes were dazzled; yet the wolves went out to
22 pursue those sheep, with all their might. • But the Lord of the sheep went with them
as their leader, while all his sheep were following him; his face was glorious, adorable,
23 and marvelous to behold. • As for the wolves, they continued[m2] to pursue those sheep
24 until they found them at a certain pool of water. • Then the pool of water was rent
asunder, and the water stood apart on this and on that side before their very eyes,[n2]
25 and their Lord, their leader, stood between them and the wolves. • Those wolves were
still not able to see the sheep, and (the sheep) walked through that pool of water; then
26 the wolves followed the sheep and ran after them into that pool of water. • Then when
they saw the Lord of the sheep, they turned in order to flee from before his face. But

---

n. Or "hyenas."

o. B C: "dogs."

p. A wrongly reads *gizēyāt*, "times," instead of *gaḥayāt*.

q. B reads "vultures."

r. Or "baboons." The Eth. is ambiguous in that the term *hobāy* can mean either "kite" or "baboon."

s. Or "colobus monkey." The Eth. is ambiguous in that the term *feqens* of A (cf. *foqānes*, *fonqās*) can mean "colobus monkey" or "striped bird ["crow"]."

t. 4QEn[d]: "to bite and chase."

u. Or "zebra."

v. 4QEn[e]: "a calf." So Milik, *The Books of Enoch*, p. 241.

w. Milik suggests the reading of 4QEn[d] as "a ram] of the flock." Cf. also 4QEn[e] (*The Books of Enoch*, p. 241).

x. B C: "bore many wild boars."

y. Lit. "that sheep."

z. Lit. "one of them."

a2. Lit. "those." B C: "those donkeys."

b2. Lit. "that sheep."

c2. Or "hyenas."

d2. Or "hyenas."

e2. 4QEn[e]: "the ram." So Milik, *The Books of Enoch*, pp. 241f.

f2. C adds: "with him."

g2. 4QEn[e]: "to oppress." So Milik, *The Books of Enoch*, p. 241.

h2. Lit. "passed."

i2. Lit. "at the voice of the sheep."

j2. Verb not clear.

k2. Lit. "and he met another sheep and went with him."

l2. B and C add "with all their strength."

m2. Lit. "they began."

n2. Lit. "before their face."

that pool of water gathered itself together and immediately returned to its normal state,[o2] the water became full and rose high until it covered (completely) those wolves.
27 Thus I saw till the wolves[p2] which pursued those sheep perished and were drowned.[q2]

From the exodus to the entrance to the land of Canaan

28   So the sheep proceeded past that water and arrived in the desert, where there was no water or grass;[r2] but they began to open their eyes[s2] and see. Then I saw the Lord of the sheep bringing them to a pasture and giving them grass and water. Also that
29 sheep was leading them as they were proceeding forward.[t2] • That sheep then ascended to the summit of that lofty rock; and the Lord of the sheep sent (him)[u2] to them[v2]
30 After that, I saw the Lord of the sheep, who stood before them; his appearance was majestic, marvelous, and powerful; all those sheep beheld him and were afraid before
31 his face. • All of them feared and trembled because of him, and cried aloud to that sheep (who was) leading them and to the other sheep who was also in their midst,[w2] saying,[x2] "We are not able to stand before the presence of our Lord and to look at
32 him." • Then that sheep which was leading them turned back and (again) ascended to the summit of that rock; meanwhile the sheep began to be dim-sighted in their eyes, and went astray from the path which he had shown them; but that sheep was not aware
33 of it. • So the Lord of the sheep became angry at them with great wrath; and that sheep became aware of it, and having descended from the summit of that rock, came to the sheep and found that the majority of them had been blinded in their eyes and gone
34 astray. • And those who saw[y2] him became afraid, trembling in his presence, and
35 wanted to return to their folds. • So that sheep took some other different sheep together with them[z2] and came to those sheep which had gone astray, slaying them;[a3] and the sheep became frightened in his presence. He, that sheep, thus caused those sheep
36 which went astray to return, and brought them back[b3] into their folds. • I continued to see in that vision till that sheep was transformed[c3] into a man and built a house for
37 the Lord of the sheep, and placed the sheep in it.[d3] • I, moreover, continued to see until that sheep, which had met the sheep that was their leader, fell asleep and all the senior sheep perished, junior ones rising to take their places. Then coming into a pasture,
38 they approached a stream of water. • (There) that sheep who was leading them—the one who had become a man—departed from them, and all of them went to sleep.[e3] (Then the rest of) the sheep sought him; and there took place[f3] a great cry over him.
39 And I kept looking till they quieted down from crying for that sheep, crossed that stream of water, and all of the sheep stopped. Those who were leading them made
40 agreements with those whom they found,[g3] and they led them.[h3] • I still kept seeing the sheep till they arrived at a very pleasant place and in a land beautiful and glorious; I saw those sheep being satiated; and that house was in their midst in the beautiful land, by which their eyes become opened.

o2. Lit. "it became its own creation."

p2. B C: "all the wolves."

q2. 4QEn[c]: "the waters covered them over." So Milik, *The Books of Enoch*, pp. 243f.

r2. Milik restores 4QEn[e]: "water to drink [and grass to eat]." Cf. *The Books of Enoch*, pp. 243f.

s2. So B and C. A reads "they do not open their eyes." 4QEn[e]: "and their eyes were opened."

t2. B C: "as he was going." Cf. 4QEn[e]. Milik (*The Books of Enoch*, p. 244) contends that "the phrase 'and the sheep walked and guided them' [so Milik] was not in the Aramaic text, perhaps omitted by homoeoteleuton . . ."

u2. A possible rendition is "and the Lord of the sheep sent (his Torah) to them."

v2. On the basis of his restoration of 4QEn[e], Milik adds "and they all stood at [a distance]." See Milik, *The Books of Enoch*, p. 244.

w2. B: ". . . to that sheep which was with him, to the other sheep which was in their midst." C:

". . . to that sheep with them, which was in their midst." Cf. 4QEn[c] (Milik, *The Books of Enoch*, p. 204f.).

x2. B and C omit "saying."

y2. B C: "And when they saw."

z2. B C: "with him."

a3. B C: "began to slay them."

b3. B C: "they came back."

c3. Lit. "became."

d3. B C: "in that house."

e3. So A. B C: "and he went to sleep ["lay down"]."

f3. Lit. "came."

g3. B: "those who had slept."

h3. So B. A: *marḥewomu*, "their key," instead of *marḥewomu*. The whole sentence seems to be corrupt. Charles has emended it to read "There arose two sheep who were leading them, taking the place of those who slept and were leading them." EC, p. 173.

From Judges to the building of the Temple

41   And when their eyes become dim-sighted[i3] until another sheep arose and led them,
42 they would all return and their eyes became opened. •Now the dogs, foxes, and the
wild boars began to devour those sheep till the Lord of the sheep raised up another
43 sheep,[j3] one from among them—a ram which would lead them. •That ram began to
fight on all sides[k3] those dogs, foxes, and wild boars until he destroyed all of them.
44 Then that sheep had his eyes opened;[l3] and he saw that ram which was among the
sheep, how[m3] he abandoned his own glory and began to attack those sheep, to trample
45 upon them, and went away without dignity. •So the Lord of the sheep sent the sheep[n3]
to another sheep[o3] and promoted him to become a ram and lead the sheep in place of
46 that sheep[p3] which had abandoned his own glory. •After having gone to him, he spoke
to him privately[q3] and raised[r3] that ram, making him a judge[s3] and a leader of the
47 people—throughout (this time) the dogs were continuing to covet the sheep. • The first
ram then persecuted that second[t3] ram, so that latter ram arose and escaped from before
his (the former's) presence; and then I continued to look until those dogs toppled that
48 first sheep. •But that second ram arose and led the little sheep.[u3] That ram begat many
sheep and fell asleep before[v3] a little sheep became a ram in his place, a judge and
49 a leader of those sheep. •Those sheep grew and multiplied, but all those dogs, foxes,
and wild boars feared and fled before him. That ram attacked and killed all the wild
beasts; and all the wild beasts were no longer able to return among the sheep or to
50 rob absolutely anything from them. •Then that house became great and spacious; a
lofty building[w3] was built upon it[x3] for that sheep, as well as a tall and great tower
upon it[y3] for the Lord of the sheep; that house was low but the tower was really elevated
and lofty. Then the Lord of the sheep stood upon that tower, and they offered a full
table[z3] before him.

The two kingdoms of Israel and Judah: the destruction of Jerusalem

51   Again I saw those sheep, how they went astray, going in diverse ways and
abandoning that house of his.[a4] Then the Lord of the sheep called some from among
52 the sheep and sent them to the sheep, but the sheep began to slay them. •However,
one of them was not killed but escaped alive[b4] and fled away;[c4] he cried aloud to[d4] the
sheep, and they wanted to kill him, but the Lord of the sheep rescued him from the
53 sheep and caused him to ascend to me and settle down. •He sent many other sheep
54 to those sheep to testify to them and to lament over them. •Thereafter I saw that,
when they abandoned the house of the Lord and his tower, they went astray completely,
and their eyes became blindfolded. Then I saw the Lord of the sheep, how he executed
much slaughter upon them, in their flocks, until those sheep (began to) invoke[e4] that
55 slaughter, and he[f4] vindicated[g4] his place.[h4] •He left them in the hands of the lions,
leopards, and wolves, hyenas, as well as in the hands of the foxes and to[i4] all the wild
beasts; and these wild beasts of the wilderness began to tear those sheep into pieces.
56 I saw how he left that house of theirs and that tower of theirs and cast all of them

---

i3. Text is difficult. C: "at times their eyes were opened and at times dim-sighted."

j3. So C. Cf. the Vatican Gk. fragment. A and B read "till arose the Lord of the sheep . . ."

k3. A: "from here." B C: "from here and from here."

l3. C: "whose eyes were opened."

m3. Lit. "who."

n3. G: "lamb."

o3. G: "lamb."

p3. C: "that ram."

q3. Lit. "by themselves alone."

r3. So B and C (cf. G). A: "he replied . . ."

s3. So B and C. G: "lord." A: "place," or "location . . ."

t3. Lit. "latter."

u3. G reads "led the sheep."

v3. Lit. "and."

w3. B: "tower." C omits both.

x3. Lit. "upon that house."

y3. Lit. "built upon that house."

z3. So B and C. A: "a full tower."

a4. B C: "their house."

b4. Lit. "he was safe and was not killed."

c4. So B and C. A reads ḥanaṣa, "he built," instead of qanaṣa.

d4. B C: "over."

e4. All MSS: "call it by name," "summon."

f4. B C: "they."

g4. Or "he caused to return," "he caused to give back," "he handed over," "he righted."

h4. A wrongly reads mākano.

i4. Lit. "upon," "over."

into the hands of the lions—(even) into the hands of all the wild beasts—so that they
57 may tear them into pieces and eat them. •Then I began to cry aloud with all my
strength and to call upon the Lord of the lions[j4] and to reveal to him concerning the
58 sheep, for he had fed them to all the wild beasts.[k4] • But he remained quiet[l4] and happy[m4]
because they were being devoured, swallowed, and snatched; so he abandoned them
59 into the hands of all the wild beasts for food. •He then summoned seventy shepherds
and surrendered[n4] those sheep to them so that they might pasture them. He spoke to
the shepherds and their colleagues, "From now on, let each and every one of you
60 graze the sheep; and do everything which I command you. •I shall hand them over
to you duly counted[o4] and tell you which among them are[p4] to be destroyed; and you
61 shall destroy them!"[q4] •So he handed over those sheep to them. Then calling another
(group of shepherds), he told them, "Take notice and see everything which the
shepherds will do to those sheep; for they will destroy from among them a greater
62 number than those which I have commanded them. • You write down every excess
and destruction that will be wrought through the shepherds[r4]—how many they destroy
according to my command, and how many they will destroy of their own accord!
Write down every destruction that each and every shepherd causes, against their
63 records! • And read aloud before me each particular case[s4]—how many they destroy
and how many they give over to destruction—so that this may become a testimony
for me against them, so that I may know all the deeds of the shepherds, (and) so that
I may evaluate them[t4] and see what they do, whether[u4] they act[v4] according to my
64 command which I have commanded them or not. •If they do not know[w4] it, do not
reveal it to them, neither admonish them, but write down every destruction caused
by[x4] the shepherds—for each and every one in his appointed time[y4]—and elevate all
65 of it to me." • And I saw till those shepherds in their appointed time pastured (the
sheep) and began killing and destroying many in excess of what they had been
66 commanded; and they abandoned those sheep into the hands of the lions. •So the lions
and the leopards ate and devoured the majority of those sheep; the wild boars also ate
67 along with them. Then they burned that tower and plowed that house. •And I became
exceedingly sorrowful on account of that tower, for that house of the sheep was being
plowed; thereafter I was unable to see whether those sheep could enter that house.

From the destruction of Jerusalem to the return from exile

68 So the shepherds and their colleagues handed over those sheep to all the wild beasts
so that they might devour them. At the appointed time, each one among them (the
shepherds) receives (the sheep) in a fixed number; and each one among them (the
shepherds) hands them (the sheep) over to the other (the colleague) in a fixed number.[z4]
(Then) they shall write down for the other (the colleague) in a book[a5] how many among
69 them (the sheep) would perish. • Each and every one of them kills and destroys in
excess of their order. So I began to weep and cry aloud on account of those sheep.
70 In this manner I saw that writer[b5] in my vision—how he writes down that which was
destroyed by those shepherds, every day, and (how) he elevates, puts down, and
shows the whole book to the Lord of the sheep; everything that each one has done;
everything that each and every one of them has eliminated; and everything that they

j4. B C: "Lord of the sheep."

k4. A: "you shall devour all the wild beasts,"
which could read with the adjustment of the verb
"you have fed them to all the wild beasts." B C:
"They are eaten by the wild beasts."

l4. B and C add "while seeing."

m4. Lit. "he rejoiced."

n4. Lit. "cast [threw] away," "left."

o4. Or "particularized," "numbered." Lit. "in
number."

p4. Lit. "is."

q4. So B and C. A not intelligible.

r4. So B and C. A: "to the shepherds."

s4. Lit. "in number."

t4. I accept Charles's emendation of the Eth.
'watenomu to 'ematenomu. Cf. EC, p. 179, n. 13.

u4. So B and C. A reads instead "to those."

v4. B C: "they [abide] dwell."

w4. B C: "And they do not know."

x4. Lit. "of the."

y4. Lit. "in his [its] time."

z4. So A. B and C omit "they hand them over in
a fixed number."

a5. A has an additional "and the book," B and
C have an additional "in the book" dangling at the
opening of this sentence.

b5. B C: "the one who writes down."

71 have given over to destruction. •The book was read before the Lord of the sheep; and
he took it from his hand, read it, sealed it, and laid it down.

72   Thereafter I saw the shepherds pasturing for twelve hours: behold, three of those
sheep returning, arriving, entering, and beginning to build all (the parts) of that house
which had fallen down! The wild boars came[c5] and tried to hinder them but were
unsuccessful.

From the return of the exiles to the beginning of the hellenistic period

73   They again began to build as before; and they raised up that tower which is called
the high tower. But they started to place a table before the tower, with all the food
74 which is upon it being polluted and impure. •Regarding all these matters, the eyes
of the sheep became so dim-sighted that they could not see[d5]—and likewise in respect
to their shepherds—and they were delivered[e5] to their shepherds for an excessive
75 destruction, so that the sheep were trampled upon and eaten.[f5] •The Lord of the sheep
remained silent until all the sheep were dispersed into the woods and got mixed among
76 the wild beasts,[g5]—and could not be rescued[h5] from the hands of the beasts. •The one
who was writing a book elevated and showed it and read the grave words of the Lord
of the sheep.[i5] He then pleaded to him and begged him on account of the sheep,[j5]
while manifesting to him all the deeds of the shepherds and giving testimony before
77 him against all the shepherds. •Then taking it, he placed that very book beside him
in this manner[k5] and departed.

1 **90** Then I saw after that how[a] thirty-seven[b] shepherds were pasturing (the sheep); all
of them completed (their duties) in their own respective periods, like the former ones;
and aliens took (the sheep) into their hands in order to pasture them in their own
2 respective periods—each shepherd in his own period. •After that I saw with my own
eyes[c] all the birds of heaven—eagles, vultures, kites, and ravens—coming; the eagles
were the ones who were leading all the birds; and they began to eat those sheep, to
3 dig out their eyes, and to eat their flesh. •Then the sheep cried aloud, for their flesh
was being eaten by the birds. I, too, cried aloud and lamented in my sleep on account
4 of that shepherd who was grazing the sheep. • I kept seeing till those sheep were eaten
by the dogs, the eagles, and the kites; and they left neither flesh, nor skin, nor sinew
on them absolutely, until their bones stood there bare; then their bones fell to the
5 ground, and the sheep became few. • I kept seeing till twenty-three shepherds[d] pastured
(the sheep), and all of them completed fifty-eight seasons in their own respective
periods.

From the Maccabean revolt to the establishment of the messianic kingdom

6   Then, behold lambs were born from those snow-white sheep; and they began to
7 open their eyes and see, and cried aloud to the sheep. •But as for the sheep, they (the
lambs) cried aloud to them,[e] yet they (the sheep) did not listen to what they (the
lambs) were telling them but became exceedingly deafened, and their eyes became
8 exceedingly dim-sighted.[f] •Then I saw in a vision ravens flying above those lambs,
9 and they seized one of those lambs; and then smashing the sheep, they ate them. •I
kept seeing till those lambs grew horns; but the ravens crushed[g] their horns. Then I

---

c5. B and C omit "came."

d5. Lit. ". . . became dim-sighted and could not
see."

e5. Lit. "they delivered them."

f5. Lit. "they trampled upon the sheep and ate
them."

g5. Lit. "they were joined together with them."

h5. Lit. "they could not rescue them."

i5. So A. B: ". . . he read it in the houses of the
Lord of the sheep." C: ". . . he read it before the
Lord of the sheep."

j5. Lit. "on their account."

k5. B and C omit "in this manner."

90 a. B and C add "in this manner."

b. Charles suggests emending this to "thirty-
five." EC, p. 181, n. 37.

c. So A. B: "in a vision." C: "in my vision."

d. So B. A and C omit "shepherds." A is partially
corrupt and reads šegā, "flesh," instead of 'eśrā,
"twenty."

e. B: "But the sheep cried aloud to them." C:
"But they oppressed them." Cf. EC, p. 183, n. 2.

f. A adds "and he pondered."

g. B C: "fell."

kept seeing till one great horn sprouted on one of those sheep, and he opened their
10 eyes;[h] and they had vision in them[i] and their eyes were opened.[j] •He cried aloud to
11 the sheep, and all the rams saw him and ran unto him. •In spite of this, all those
eagles, vultures, ravens, and kites until now continue to rip the sheep, swooping
down upon them and eating them. As for the sheep, they remained silent; but the rams
12 are lamenting and crying aloud. •Those ravens gather[k] and battle with him (the horned
ram) and seek to remove his horn, but without any success.[l]

13 I saw thereafter[m] the shepherds coming; and those vultures[n] and kites cried aloud
to the ravens so that they should smash the horn of that ram. But he battled with
them,[o] and they fought each other;[p] and he cried aloud, while battling with them, so
14 that (God's) help should come. •I kept seeing till that man, who writes down the
names of the shepherds and elevates them before the Lord of the sheep, came; it is
he who helped him[q] and revealed (to him) everything; thus[r] help came down for that
15 ram.[s] •And I kept seeing till the Lord of the sheep came upon[t] them in wrath, and all
16 who saw him fled and fell all into darkness,[u] from before his face. •All the eagles,
vultures, ravens, and kites gathered, with all the sheep of the field lining up with
them;[v] and having thus come together in unity, all of them cooperated in order to
17 smash the horn[w] of the ram. •I saw that man who was writing a book by the command[x]
of the Lord, for he opened[y] that book (of) the destruction which those twelve last
shepherds caused; and he revealed before the Lord of the sheep that they had much
18 greater destruction than their predecessors. •I kept seeing till the Lord of the sheep
came unto them and took in his hand the rod of his wrath and smote the earth;[z] and
all the beasts and all the birds of the heaven fell down from the midst of those sheep
19 and were swallowed up in the earth, and it was covered upon them.[a2] •Then I saw
that[b2] a great sword was given to the sheep; and the sheep proceeded against all the
beasts of the field in order to kill them; and all the beasts and birds of heaven fled
from before their face.

20 Then I kept seeing till a throne was erected in a pleasant land;[c2] and he sat upon
it[d2] for the Lord of the sheep;[e2] and he took all[f2] the sealed books and opened those
21 very books in the presence of the Lord of the sheep. •Then the Lord called those
people, the seven first snow-white ones, and ordered them to bring before him (some)
from among the first star(s) that arose,[g2] and from among those stars[h2] whose sexual
organs were like those of the horses,[i2] as well as (that) first star which had fallen
22 down[j2] earlier. And they brought them all before him. •He spoke to the man who was
writing in his presence—that (man) being one of those seven snow-white ones—
saying, "Take those seven[k2] shepherds to whom I had handed over the sheep, but who
23 decided to kill many more than they were ordered."[l2] •Behold, I saw all of them
24 bound; and they all stood before him. •Then his judgment took place. First among
the stars, they received their judgment and were found guilty, and they went to the

h. B C: "their eyes were opened."

i. Text may be corrupt. B and C read "and he looked at [in] them."

j. Possibly a repetition due to a scribal error.

k. B C: "combat," "contest."

l. Lit. "they could not."

m. B C: "until."

n. B and C read "the eagles" before "those vultures."

o. B: "And he battled with him."

p. C: "and they battled and fought with him."

q. C adds "and saved him."

r. Lit. "and." B omits "and."

s. C has been emended to read "and he revealed to that lamb an army." Cf. EC, p. 184, n. 26.

t. B C: "to."

u. B: "into his shadow." C: "into shadow."

v. Lit. "coming together with them."

w. B and C read "that horn."

x. Lit. "word."

y. B C: "until he opened."

z. B and C add "and the earth was rent asunder."

a2. F. Martin suggests that vss. 13–15 and 16–18 are doublets. See *Le livre d'Hénoch* (Paris, 1906), p. 228.

b2. B C: "till."

c2. So B and C. A omits "in," and reads "pleasant" in the plural.

d2. So B and C. A reads "upon them."

e2. So A. B and C read "the Lord of the sheep sat upon it."

f2. Charles suggests emending the text to read "the other one took," changing "all" to "other." EC, p. 185, n. 25.

g2. So A. B and C read "from the first star that preceded."

h2. Lit. "and from those stars." B and C omit "and."

i2. Lit. "like the sexual organs of the horses."

j2. C: "that came out."

k2. B C: "seventy."

l2. B C: "many more than I commanded them."

place of condemnation; and they were thrown[m2] into an abyss, full of fire and flame[n2]
25 and full of the pillar[o2] of fire. •Then those seventy shepherds[p2] were judged and found
26 guilty; and they were cast into that fiery abyss. •In the meantime[q2] I saw how another
abyss[r2] like it, full of fire, was opened wide in the middle of the ground; and they
brought those blinded sheep, all of which were judged, found guilty, and cast into
27 this fiery abyss, and they were burned—the abyss[s2] is to the right of that house; •thus
I saw those sheep while they were burning—their bones also were burning.

28   Then I stood still, looking at that ancient house being transformed: All the pillars
and all the columns[t2] were pulled out;[u2] and the ornaments of that house were packed
and taken out together with them and abandoned[v2] in a certain[w2] place in the South
29 of the land. •I went on seeing until the Lord of the sheep brought about a new house,
greater and loftier than the first one, and set it up in the first location which had been
covered up—all its pillars were new, the columns new;[x2] and the ornaments new as
well as greater than those of the first, (that is) the old (house) which was gone.[y2] All
the sheep were within it.

30   Then I saw all the sheep that had survived as well as all the animals upon the earth
and the birds of heaven, falling down and worshiping[z2] those sheep, making petition
31 to them and obeying them in every respect.[a3] •Thereafter, those three who were
wearing snow-white (clothes), the former ones who had caused me to go up, grabbed
me by my hand—also the hand of that ram holding me—and I ascended;[b3] they set
me down in the midst of those sheep prior to the occurrence of this[c3] judgment.
32 Those sheep were all snow-white, and their wool considerable and clean. •All those
33 which have been destroyed and dispersed, and all the beasts of the field and the birds
of the sky were gathered together in that house; and the Lord of the sheep rejoiced
34 with great joy because they had all become gentle and returned to his house. •I went
on seeing until they had laid down that sword which was given to the sheep; they
returned it to the house and sealed it in the presence of the Lord. All the sheep were
35 invited to that house[d3] but it could not contain them (all). •The eyes of all of them
were opened, and they saw the beautiful things; not a single one existed among them
36 that could not see.[e3] •Also I noticed that the house was large, wide, and exceedingly
full.

37   Then I saw that a snow-white cow was born, with huge horns; all the beasts of the
field and all the birds of the sky feared him and made petition to him all the time.
38 I went on seeing until all their kindred were transformed, and became snow-white
cows; and the first among them became something,[f3] and that something became a
great beast with huge black horns on its head. The Lord of the sheep rejoiced over
39 it[g3] and over all the cows. •I myself became satiated[h3] in their midst. Then I woke up
and saw everything.

40   This is the vision which I saw while I was sleeping. Then I woke up and blessed
41 the Lord of righteousness and gave him glory. •And I wept with a great weeping, and
my tears could not stop, till I had no more endurance left, but flowed down[i3] on
account of what I had seen until[j3] everything should come and be fulfilled. The deeds

---

m2. Lit. "they threw them."
n2. B C: "it was flaming."
o2. C: "pillars."
p2. Cf. above, vs. 22, "seven shepherds."
q2. Lit. "at that time."
r2. Lit. "one abyss."
s2. Lit. "that abyss [pit]."
t2. Lit. "trees," "planted things."
u2. Lit. "they pulled out."
v2. Lit. "they took them out and abandoned
them."
w2. Lit. "one."
x2. Lit. "the planted things new," omitted by B
and C.
y2. B C: "which he had taken out."
z2. Or "kneeling down to."

a3. Lit. "in every word."
b3. B C: "they elevated me."
c3. B and C omit "this."
d3. So B and C. A omits "house."
e3. So B and C. A, apparently erroneously, reads
"that could see."
f3. Lit. "a thing," "a word," "a deed." Charles
suggests *nagar* to be a misreading of Gk. *rhēm*,
which was a transliteration of Heb. *r'ēm*. Cf. EC,
p. 188, n. 38.
g3. Lit. "over them."
h3. B C: "I slept."
i3. B and C read "when I saw," instead of "but
flowed down."
j3. So A. B C: "because."

42 of the people were also shown to me, each according to its type. •On that night I remembered the first dream and wept on its account, and I was restless because I had (just) seen that vision.

Book V (91–107)[a]

The Two Ways of the Righteous and the Sinner
Including the Apocalypse of Weeks

Enoch's admonition to his children

1 **91**[b] Now, my son Methuselah, (please) summon all your brothers on my behalf, and gather together to me all the sons of your mother; for a voice[c] calls me, and the spirit is poured over me so that I may show you everything that shall happen to you forever. 2 Then Methuselah went and summoned his brothers, and having summoned them to 3 him, gathered his family together.[d] •Then he (Enoch) spoke to all of them, children of righteousness, and said, "Hear, all you children of Enoch, the talk of your father[e] 4 and listen to my voice[f] in uprightness; • for I exhort you, (my) beloved, and say to you: Love uprightness, and it alone.[g] Do not draw near uprightness with an ambivalent attitude,[h] and neither associate with hypocrites.[i] But walk in righteousness, my children, 5 and it shall lead you in the good paths; and righteousness shall be your friend. •For I know that the state of violence will intensify upon the earth; a great plague shall be executed upon the earth; all (forms of) oppression[j] will be carried out; and everything 6 shall be uprooted;[k] and every arrow shall fly fast.[l] •Oppression shall recur once more and be carried out upon the earth; every (form of) oppression, injustice, and iniquity 7 shall infect[m] (the world) twofold. •When sin, oppression, blasphemy, and injustice increase,[n] crime,[o] iniquity, and uncleanliness shall be committed[p] and increase (likewise). Then a great plague shall take place from heaven upon all these; the holy Lord shall emerge with wrath and plague in order that he may execute judgment upon the 8 earth. • In those days, injustice shall be cut off from its (sources of succulent) fountain[q] and from its roots—(likewise) oppression together with deceit; they shall be destroyed[r] 9 from underneath heaven. • All that which is (common) with the heathen shall be surrendered; the towers[s] shall be inflamed with fire, and be removed[t] from the whole earth. They[u] shall be thrown into the judgment of fire, and perish in wrath and in the 10 force of the eternal judgment. •Then the righteous one shall arise from his sleep, and 11 the wise one shall arise;[v] and he shall be given unto them (the people), •and through

91 a. According to A the fifth Book of Enoch begins at 92:1.

b. Charles, in *APOT*, vol. 2, p. 260, suggests rearranging chs. 91–104; he takes 93:1–10 and 91:12–17 as an earlier fragment of the Apocalypse of Weeks and gives the order 92 + 91:1–10, 18f., 93:1–10, 91:12–17, 94–104. Milik (*The Books of Enoch*, p. 267) also thinks that 91:12–17 followed 93:3–10.

c. Or "word."

d. So A. B and C read "Then Methuselah went and summoned all his brothers to him and gathered his relatives together."

e. So A. B and C read "Hear, children of Enoch, all the talk of your father."

f. Eth. *'af,* lit. "mouth." It can also mean "word," "voice," "speech." B and C read "the word of my mouth."

g. So A. B and C read "Love uprightness and walk in it."

h. Lit. "with a double heart."

i. Or "two-faced persons," "indecisive persons,"

"oscillating persons," "double-dealing persons"; lit. "those who walk [B and C omit "walk"] with two heart(s)."

j. So B and C. A omits "all oppression."

k. Lit. "everything shall be cut off from its roots." So A. B and C read "all oppression shall be carried out [or "completed"] and it shall be cut off from its roots."

l. So A. B C: "every building shall pass."

m. Lit. "seize." B C: "shall be seized."

n. B and C add "in all deeds."

o. Or "apostasy."

p. So A. B and C read instead "in all deeds."

q. Or "drink." B and C omit "drink," "fountain."

r. C omits "shall be destroyed."

s. Or "palaces," "castles."

t. Lit. "they shall be taken out," "uprooted."

u. Text ambiguous: the heathen or the towers?

v. B C: "wisdom shall arise."

him the roots of oppression shall be cut off. Sinners shall be destroyed; by the sword they shall be cut off[w] (together with) the blasphemers in every place;[x] and those who design oppression and commit blasphemy shall perish by the knife.[y]

12 "Then after that there shall occur the second eighth week[z]—the week[a2] of righteousness.[b2] A sword shall be given to it[c2] in order that judgment shall be executed in righteousness[d2] on the oppressors, and sinners shall be delivered into the hands of 13 the righteous. •At its completion, they shall acquire great things[e2] through their righteousness. A house shall be built for the Great King in glory for evermore.[f2]

14 "Then after that in the ninth week[g2] the righteous judgment shall be revealed to the whole world.[h2] All the deeds of the sinners[i2] shall depart from upon the whole earth, and be written off for eternal destruction;[j2] and all people shall direct their sight to the path of uprightness.

15 "Then, after this matter,[k2] on the tenth week[l2] in[m2] the seventh part, there shall be the eternal judgment;[n2] and it shall be executed by[o2] the angels[p2] of the eternal heaven— 16 the great (judgment) which emanates from all of the angels.[q2] •The first heaven shall depart and pass away; a new heaven shall appear; and all the powers of heaven[r2] shall shine forever[s2] sevenfold.

17 "Then after that there shall be many weeks[t2] without number forever; it shall be (a time) of goodness and righteousness, and sin shall no more be heard of[u2] forever.

18 "Now I shall speak unto you, my children, and show you the ways of righteousness and the ways of wickedness. Moreover, I shall make a revelation to you so that you 19 may know that which is going to take place. •Now listen to me, my children, and walk in the way of righteousness, and do not walk in the way of wickedness, for all those who walk in the ways of injustice shall perish."

1 **92** (Book) five,[a] which is written by Enoch, the writer[b] of all the signs of[c] wisdom among all the people.[d] He is blessed and noble[e] in[f] all the earth. (It is written) for all the offspring[g] that dwell upon the earth, and for the latter generations which uphold[h] uprightness and peace.

---

w. So B and C. A reads "they shall cut off."

x. Text corrupt. "The blasphemers" added as an afterthought.

y. 4QEn[n]: "And they will have rooted out the foundations of violence and the structure of falsehood therein to execute [judgment]."

z. Or "the second eighth sabbath," "another eighth sabbath," "another eighth week," "second [another] eighth rest." Following possible influence from other Eth. languages, the phrase can also be translated: "the second week shall be a sabbath [rest]," "there shall be a sabbath the second week."

a2. Or "the sabbath," "the rest."

b2. B and C omit "the week." 4QEn[g]: "the eighth week."

c2. Or "him." 4QEn[g]: "[a sword] shall be given to all the righteous." Milik (*The Books of Enoch*, p. 266).

d2. B: "judgment and righteousness shall be executed." C: "a righteous judgment." 4QEn[g]: "to exact a righteous judgement from all the wicked." Milik (*The Books of Enoch*, p. 266f.).

e2. B and C read "houses" instead of "great things." EMML 2080: "goods." 4QEn[g]: "riches."

f2. 4QEn[g]: "a royal Temple of the Great One in his glorious splendor, for all generations, forever."

g2. Or "sabbath."

h2. 4QEn[g]: "for all the children of the whole earth."

i2. 4QEn[g]: "all the wonders (of impiety)."

j2. Or "hell." B C: "the world shall be written for destruction." 4QEn[g]: "and they will be cast into the [eternal] Pit." Milik (*The Books of Enoch*, p. 267).

k2. C: "after this."

l2. Or "sabbath."

m2. Lit. "and."

n2. 4QEn[g]: "an eternal judgment and the [fixed] time of the great judgment."

o2. Lit. "from."

p2. Lit. "Watchers."

q2. Text may be corrupt. B reads "and it shall be executed from the Watchers; and the great, eternal peace which emanates from the midst of the angels." C reads: "and it shall be executed from the Watchers of the eternal heaven; the great (judgment) in which he will execute vengeance among the angels." 4QEn[g]: "an eternal Judgement and the (fixed) time of the Great Judgement [shall be executed in vengeance . . .]." Milik (*The Books of Enoch*, p. 267).

r2. B: "the powers of the heavens." C: "the power of the heavens."

s2. C omits "forever." 4QEn[g]: "of heaven shall rise for all eternity [with sevenfold] brightness." Milik (*The Books of Enoch*, p. 267).

t2. Or "sabbaths."

u2. Lit. "spoken," "told."

92 a. See ch. 91, n. a. Other MSS omit "five." Charles's g has "book" in the opening phrase.

b. C reads "he wrote."

c. B: "the learning of."

d. 4QEn[g], following Milik, *The Books of Enoch*, p. 260: "the wisest of men."

e. Or "judge."

f. Lit. "and."

g. Lit. "children." B C: "my children."

h. Lit. "do," "perform," "accomplish," "observe."

2 Let not your spirit be troubled by the times, for the Holy and Great One has
3 designated[i] (specific) days for all things. •The Righteous One shall awaken from his
sleep; he shall arise and walk[j] in the ways of righteousness; and all the way of his
4 conduct[k] shall be in goodness and generosity forever. • He will be generous to the
Righteous One, and give him eternal uprightness; he will give authority, and judge
5 in kindness[l] and righteousness; and they[m] shall walk in eternal light. • Sin and darkness
shall perish[n] forever, and shall no more be seen from that day forevermore.

The Apocalypse of Weeks

1 **93** Then after that Enoch happened to be recounting from the books.[a] •And Enoch
2 said, "Concerning the children of righteousness, concerning the elect ones of the
world, and concerning the plant of truth,[b] I will speak these things, my children,
verily I, Enoch, myself, and let you know (about it) according to that which was
revealed to me from the heavenly vision, that which I have learned from the words
3 of the holy angels, and understood from the heavenly tablets." • He[c] then began to
recount from the books and said, "I was born the seventh during the first week,[d]
4 during which time judgment and righteousness continued to endure. •After me there
shall arise in the second week[e] great and evil things;[f] deceit should grow,[g] and therein
the first consummation will take place. But therein (also) a (certain) man shall be
saved. After it is ended, injustice shall become greater, and he shall make a law[h] for
the sinners.
5 "Then after that at the completion of the third week[i] a (certain) man shall be elected
as the plant of the righteous judgment,[j] and after him[k] one (other)[l] shall emerge[m] as
the eternal plant of righteousness.
6 "After that at the completion of the fourth week[n] visions of the old and righteous
ones shall be seen; and a law shall be made with a fence,[o] for all the generations.
7 "After that in the fifth week,[p] at the completion of glory, a house[q] and a kingdom
shall be built.
8 "After that in the sixth week[r] those who happen to be in it shall all of them be
blindfolded, and the hearts of them all shall forget wisdom. Therein, a (certain) man
shall ascend. And, at its completion, the house of the kingdom[s] shall be burnt with
fire; and therein the whole clan of the chosen root shall be dispersed.
9 "After that in the seventh week[t] an apostate generation shall arise; its deeds shall
10 be many, and all of them[u] criminal. •At its completion, there shall be elected the elect
ones of righteousness[v] from the eternal plant of righteousness, to whom[w] shall be given
sevenfold instruction[x] concerning all his flock.[y]
11 "For what kind of a human being[z] is there that is able to hear the voice of the Holy

i. Lit. "gave."
j. Lit. "pass," "traverse."
k. B C: "his way and his conduct."
l. B C: "and become in kindness."
m. B: "he."
n. B C: "sin shall perish in darkness."

93 a. B: "it happened (that) Enoch began to recount
from the books." C: "Enoch gave me and seized me
[or "began"] to recount from the books."
b. According to Ethiopian commentators, Isaac.
c. B C: Enoch.
d. Or "sabbath."
e. Or "sabbath."
f. B C: "great evil (things)."
g. Or "sprout," "germinate."
h. C: "a law shall be made."
i. Or "sabbath."
j. Abraham, according to Ethiopian commentators.
k. Or "thereafter." Cf. EC, p. 195, n. 6, for
another interpretation.
l. This reading follows Ethiopian commentators
who consider Isaac as this other one.

m. B: "he shall come."
n. Or "sabbath."
o. Or "with an enclosure." Charles (*APOT*, vol. 2,
p. 263) thinks the enclosure to be Palestine; Ethiopian
commentators, "the fence of the Tabernacle." But
the key to the text may be m.Ab 1:1.
p. Or "sabbath."
q. So A. B and C read "at the completion of the
fifth sabbath, a house of glory."
r. Or "sabbath."
s. Or "the palace."
t. Or "sabbath."
u. Lit. "all its deeds."
v. 4QEn[g], following Milik (*The Books of Enoch*,
p. 266): "there shall be chosen the elect, for witness
to righteousness."
w. So B and C. A reads erroneously *'allā,* "but,"
instead of *'ella.*
x. Or "learning," "knowledge." 4QEn[g]: "wisdom and knowledge."
y. Or "fold," "acquisition," "possession." B
and C read "all his creation." 4QEn[g] omits "concerning all his flock."
z. Lit. "who is it, every son of man." B C:
"every son of the people."

One without being shaken? Who is there that is able to ponder his (deep) thoughts?
12 Who is there that can look directly at all the good[a2] deeds?[b2] •What kind of a person
is he that can (fully) understand the activities of heaven,[c2] so that he can see a soul,
or even perhaps a spirit—or, even if he ascended (into the heavens) and saw all (these
heavenly beings and) their wings[d2] and contemplated[e2] them; or, even if he can do
13 (what the heavenly beings) do?[f2]—and is able to live?[g2] •What kind of a person is
anyone that is able to understand the nature[h2] of the breadth and length of the earth?
14 To whom has the extent[i2] of all these[j2] been shown? •Is there perchance any human
being[k2] that is able to understand the length of heaven, the extent[l2] of its altitude,
upon what it is founded, the number of the stars, and (the place) where[m2] all the
luminaries rest?

Enoch's advice to his children and to the righteous

1 **94** "Now, my children,[a] I say to you: Love righteousness and walk therein! For the
ways of righteousness are worthy of being embraced; (but) the ways of wickedness
2 shall soon perish and diminish. •To (certain) known persons, the ways of injustice
and death shall be revealed as soon as they are born;[b] and they shall keep themselves
3 at a distance from (those ways) and would not follow them. •Now to you, those
righteous ones, I say: Do not walk in the evil way, or in the way of death! Do not
4 draw near to them lest you be destroyed! •But seek for yourselves and choose
righteousness and the elect life! Walk in the way of peace so that you shall have life
5 and be worthy! •Hold fast my words in the thoughts of your hearts; and let them not
be erased from your hearts! For I do know that sinners will counsel the people to
perform evil craft;[c] and every place will welcome it,[d] and every advice (of the sinners)[e]
may not diminish.

Woes unto the sinners

6 "Woe unto those who build oppression and injustice!
Who lay foundations for deceit.
They shall soon be demolished;
and they shall have no peace.
7 Woe unto those who build their houses with sin!
For they shall all be demolished from their foundations;
and they shall fall by the sword.
Those who amass[f] gold and silver;[g]
they shall quickly be destroyed.
8 Woe unto you, O rich people!
For you have put your trust in your wealth.
You shall ooze out[h] of your riches,
for you do not remember the Most High.
9 In the days of your affluence, you committed oppression,[i]
you have become ready for death, and for the day of darkness and the
day of great judgment.[j]

a2. Or "beautiful."
b2. B C: "at the heavenly deeds."
c2. C reads "What kind of a person is he that can
look directly into heaven and who is he that can
understand . . . ?"
d2. Or "wings," "borders," "corners," "limits," "extensions," "sides."
e2. Or "think," "contemplate."
f2. Lit. "do like them."
g2. B C: "is able to tell."
h2. Lit. "how."
i2. Or "size," "measure." 4QEn[g]: "shape."
j2. Lit. "all of them."
k2. Lit. "any man."
l2. Lit. "how."
m2. So B and C. A reads *ye'eti*, "she," "it,"
"this," instead of *'aytē.*

94 a. 4QEn[g]: "my sons."
b. B C: "from a generation."
c. Lit. "evil wisdom." The expression could also
be translated "evil magic," "evil deceit," "evil
cunning."
d. Lit. "receive her." B C: "no place will receive
her."
e. B C: "every trouble," "every temptation."
f. Lit. "acquire."
g. Or possibly "Those who build a fence of gold
and silver around it."
h. Lit. "come out," "exit."
i. B C: "you committed blasphemy and oppression."
j. B and C read "You have become ready for
slaughter [lit. "spilling blood"], for the day of
darkness and the day of great judgment."

10   Thus I speak and let you know:
        For he who has created you, he will also throw you down upon your
            own righteousness!ᵏ
        There shall be no mercy (for you).ˡ
11   And he, your Creator, shall rejoice at your destruction.
        (O God), your righteous ones shall be a reproachᵐ to the sinners and the
            wicked.

Enoch's sorrow and more woes unto the sinners

1 **95**   "Who would induceᵃ my eyes likeᵇ a cloud of waters;
        that I may weep over you,
        pouring my tears over you like a cloud of waters,
        so I would rest from the sorrow of my heart!
2   Who permits you to engage in evil fight?ᶜ
        Judgment will catch up with you, sinners.ᵈ
3   You righteous ones, fear not the sinners!
        For the Lord will again deliver them into your hands,
        so that you may carry out against them anythingᵉ that you desire.
4   Woe unto you who pronounce anathemasᶠ so that they may be neutralized!ᵍ
        (Salutary) remedyʰ is far from you, on account of your sins.ⁱ
5   Woe unto you who rewardʲ evil to your neighbors!
        For you shall be rewarded in accordance with your deeds.
6   Woe unto you, witnesses of falsehood!
        And unto those who prepare oppression!
        For you shall perish soon.
7   Woe unto you, sinners, for you persecute the righteous!
        For you shall be handed over and be persecuted through oppression.
        Its yokeᵏ shall be heavy upon you.

Hope for the righteous ones, more woes for the sinners

1 **96**   "Be hopeful, you righteous ones, for the sinners shall soon perish from
            before your presence.
        You shall be given authorityᵃ upon them, such (authority) as you may
            wish (to have).
2   In the day of the tribulation of the sinners,
        your children shall be raised high up and be made openly visibleᵇ like
            eagles,
        higherᶜ than the vultures will your dwelling place be,
        you shall ascend and enter the crevices of the earth and the clefts of the
            rock forever,
        like squirrels, before the face of the oppressors,
        the sirens shall be blown over you,
        wailing like the buzzing of wild bees.
3   But you, who have experienced pain, fear not,
        for there shall be a healing medicine for you,

k. B and C omit "upon your own righteousness."
See next n.
    l. B and C read "Upon your fall there shall be noˑ
mercy."
    m. B and C add "in those days."

95 a. Lit. "give."
    b. B C: "to be like."
    c. Or "evil hate." B C: "hate and evil."
    d. Text unclear.
    e. Lit. "all." B and C read "judgment."
    f. Lit. "anathematize anathemas."
    g. Lit. "unbound," "untied," "unfastened,"
"loosened." B and C read "so that they may not be

neutralized."
    h. Lit. "medicine," "cure," "drug that either
heals or hurts."
    i. At this point A adds "the matter [the word] is
where it has been left." This phrase is not found in
B, C, other MSS used by Charles, or those that I
have seen.
    j. Lit. "pay," "repay."
    k. Lit. "Her yoke."

96 a. Lit. "There shall be authority to you."
    b. B C: "be raised high up and rise."
    c. Lit. "exceeding."

a bright light shall enlighten you,
and a voice of rest you shall hear from heaven.

4   Woe unto you, you sinners!
For your money makes you appear like the righteous,
but your hearts do reprimand you like real sinners,
this very matter shall be a witness against you, as a record of your evil
    deeds.

5   Woe unto you who eat the best bread!d
And drink wine in large bowls,e
trampling upon the weak peoplef with your might.

6   Woe unto you who have water available to you all the time,g
for soon you shall be consumed and wither away,
for you have forsaken the fountain of life.

7   Woe unto you who carry out oppression, deceit, and blasphemy!
There shall be a record of evil against you.

8   Woe unto you, O powerful people!h
You who coercei the righteous with your power,
the dayj of your destruction is coming!
In those days, at the timek of your condemnation,
many and good days shall come for the righteous ones.

The sorrowful end of sinners, oppressors, and the rich; and more woes to them

1 **97**   "Be confident, you righteous ones!
For the sinners are due for a shame.
They shall perish on the day of (the judgment of) oppression.
Take for granteda this (indisputable) matter,

2   for the Most High shall record your destruction for you (O sinners),
and the angels of heaven shall rejoice over your destruction.

3   What do you intend to do, you sinners,
whitherb will you flee on that day of judgment,
when you hear the sound of the prayer of the righteous ones?

4   (In respect to your lot), you shall become like them,
(the ones) against whom you shall become witness(es),c
such is the fact:d You have become bedfellows with sinners.

5   In those days, the prayers of the righteous ones shall reach unto the Lord;
but for all of you, your days shall arrive.e

6   He shall read aloudf regarding every aspect of your mischief,
in the presence of the Great Holy One.
Then your faces shall be covered with shame,
and he will cast out every deed which is built upon oppression.g

7   Woe unto you, sinners, who are in the midst of the sea and on the dry
    land;
(you) whose records are (both) evil (and) against you.h

d. Lit. "the enriched [fattened] wheat."

e. I have followed in this case the emendation suggested by Charles. See EC, p. 201, n. 8. The text is corrupt and reads "the strength of the root of the fountain."

f. Lit. "the lowly ones."

g. Charles suggests emending the text: "who drink water from every fountain." See EC, p. 201, n. 10.

h. Or "powerful ones."

i. Or "force," "compel," "subject by force."

j. A reads "until the day." B and C read "for the day."

k. Lit. "on the day."

97 a. Lit. "Let this become a well-known fact for you."

b. So B and C. A reads ye'eti, "she," "she is," "it," "this," instead of 'aytē.

c. B: "(those) which becomes [sic] a witness against you." C: "(those) which becomes [sic] a witness against them."

d. Lit. "This is the matter."

e. Lit. "But for you, the days of all of you shall arrive." B C: "but for you, the days of your judgment shall arrive."

f. B C: "It shall be read aloud."

g. Cf. G. Nickelsburg, "Enoch 97–104: A Study of the Greek and Ethiopic Texts," Armenian and Biblical Studies, ed. M. E. Stone, supplementary vol. 1 to Sion (Jerusalem, 1976), p. 93.

h. Lit. "Whose records are evil—against you." Gp: "There is an evil record against you."

8   Woe unto you who gain silver and gold by unjust means;[i]
    you will then say, 'We have grown rich[j] and accumulated goods,
    we have acquired everything that we have desired.

9   So now let us do whatever we like;
    for we have gathered silver,
    we have filled our treasuries[k] (with money) like water.
    And many are the laborers[l] in our houses.'

10 Your lies flow like water.[m]
    For your wealth shall not endure
    but it shall take off from you quickly
    for you have acquired it all unjustly,
    and you shall be given over to a great curse.

Self-indulgence of the rich, origin of sins, more woes to sinners

1 **98** "Now I swear unto you, to the wise and to the foolish,[a]
    for you shall see many (things)[b] upon the earth.

2   For you men shall put on more jewelry[c] than[d] women, and more
    multicolored[e] ornaments than a virgin.
    In sovereignty, in grandeur, and in authority, (in) silver, in gold, in
    clothing, in honor, and in edibles—
    they shall be poured out like water.[f]

3   For this reason, they are devoid of knowledge and wisdom, so they shall
    perish thereby together with their goods[g] and together with all their
    glory and honor.
    Then in dishonor, in slaughter, and in great misery, their spirits[h] shall
    be cast away.[i]

4   I have sworn unto you, sinners: In the same manner that a mountain has
    never[j] turned into[k] a servant, nor shall a hill (ever) become a
    maidservant of a woman; likewise, neither has sin been exported[l]
    into the world. It is the people who have themselves invented it.
    And those who commit it shall come under a great curse.

5   Why[m] is a woman not given (a child)?
    On account of[n] the deeds of her own hands would she die without
    children.[o]

6   I swear to you, sinners, by the Holy Great One, that all your evil deeds
    are revealed[p] in the heavens.

7   "None of your (deeds of injustice are covered and hidden. •Think not in your
    spirit, nor say in your hearts)[q] that you neither know nor see[r] all our sins[s] being

i. Lit. "that which is not through justice [or
"right"],'' therefore, "unethically," "by violating
others' rights," "through wrongdoing."

j. B, C, and G[p]: " 'We have become rich with
riches.' ''

k. Lit. "storerooms."

l. G[p] reads "good things." Nickelsburg (*Armenian
and Biblical Studies*, p. 93) suggests correctly that
G[p] may be more accurate than the Eth. His suggestion
that the Eth. tradition is corrupted from *ḥerata* is not
convincing. The latter means "good persons," not
"good things."

m. G[p]: "You err."

98 a. G[p]: "not to the foolish."

b. G[p]: "many iniquities."

c. Or "ornaments," "adornments."

d. G[p]: "like."

e. G[p]: "fair color."

f. G[p] reads "They shall have silver and gold for
food, and in their houses they shall be poured out
like water."

g. G[p]: "you shall perish . . . with all your goods."

h. G[p]: "your spirits."

i. B and C add "into the furnace." G[p] is defective.

j. Lit. "not."

k. Lit. "become."

l. Lit. "sin has not been sent."

m. B and C read "Barrenness" instead of "Why."

n. B and C read "But on account of."

o. G[p] adds a whole verse before this one and reads
as follows: "Slavery was not given to a woman, but
because of the works of her hands; for it is not
ordained that a slave should become a slave. It was
not given from above, but it came about because of
oppression. Likewise neither was sin given from
above but from transgression. Likewise a woman was
not created barren, but because of her wrongdoing
she was punished with barrenness, childless shall she
die."

p. G[p]: "they will be revealed."

q. So B, C, and G[p]. The whole passage in
parentheses is missing from A, most probably due to
homoeoteleuton.

r. G[p] reads "that they do not know and do not
see."

s. B C: "every sin." G[p]: "your sins."

8 written down every day in the presence of the Most High. •From now on do know that all your injustices which you have committed unjustly are written down[t] every day until the day of your judgment.

9   "Woe unto you, fools, for you shall perish
through your folly!
You do not listen to[u] the wise, and you shall not receive good things.[v]

10   And now do know that you are ready for the day
of destruction.
Hope not that you shall live, you sinners,
you who[w] shall depart and die,
for you know for what (reason) you have been ready[x]
for the day of the great judgment,
for the day of anguish and great shame for your spirits.

11   Woe unto you obstinate of heart, who do evil and devour blood!
From where (will you find) good things that you may eat, drink, and be
satisfied?
Even from all the good things which the Lord, the Most High, stocked
in plenitude upon the whole earth?
No peace exists for you!

12   Woe unto you who love unrighteousness![y]
Why do you have hopes for good things for yourselves?
Do know that you shall be given over into the hands of the righteous
ones,
and they shall cut off your necks[z] and slay you, and they shall not have
compassion upon you.[a2]

13   Woe unto you who rejoice in the suffering of the righteous ones!
For no grave shall be dug[b2] for you.

14   Woe unto you who would set at nought the words of the righteous ones!
For you shall have no hope of life.[c2]

15   Woe unto you who write down false words and words of wickedness![d2]
For they write down their lies so that they (the people) may commit
wicked acts,[e2]
and they cause others to commit wicked acts.[f2]

16   They shall have no peace, but shall die quickly.[g2]

More woes unto the sinners

1 **99**   "Woe unto you who cause wickedness![a]
Who glorify and honor[b] false words,
you are lost, and you have no life[c] of good things;

2   woe unto you who alter the words of truth[d]
and pervert[e] the eternal law![f]
They reckon themselves not guilty[g] of sin,
they shall be trampled on upon the earth.

t. So B, C, and G^p. A reads "are arriving," "are coming."

u. So B and G^p. A: "You do not neglect." C: "You do neglect."

v. G^p adds "evils (in) you."

w. B and C read *alta*, "but," instead of *ella*.

x. B C: "For you know no ransom; for you are ready."

y. B C: "the deeds of unrighteousness [oppression]."

z. G^p omits "they shall cut off your necks."

a2. Nickelsburg's suggestion (*Armenian and Biblical Studies*, pp. 90–156) that *mehra* is a corruption for *mehka* is interesting and possible. But the distinctions in the present context are minimal.

b2. So B, C, and G^p. A reads "be revealed."

c2. G^p: "hope of salvation."

d2. G^p: "words of error."

e2. B C: "their lies so that they hear them and commit wicked acts." G^p: "they write down and they will lead many astray by their lies."

f2. Sentence omitted by G^p.

g2. G^p: "You yourselves err, and you shall have no joy; but you shall perish quickly."

99 a. G^p: "who cause errors."

b. C: "You glory and honor."

c. G^p: "salvation."

d. Or "uprightness."

e. Or "abolish," "delete," "do violence to."

f. G^p: "covenant."

g. So B, C, and G^p. A reads "They reckon themselves guilty."

3   "In those days, be ready, you righteous ones, to raise up your prayers as a memorial,
     and place them as a testimony before the angels; and they (the angels) shall bring the
4   sins of the sinners for a memorial before the Most High. •In those days, the nations
     shall be confounded, and the families of the nations shall rise in the day of the
5   destruction of the sinners.[h] •In those days, they (the women) shall become pregnant,[i]
     but they (the sinners) shall come out[j] and abort[k] their infants and cast them out from
     their midst; they shall (also) abandon[l] their (other) children,[m] casting their infants out
     while they are still suckling. They shall neither return to them (their babes) nor have
     compassion upon their beloved ones.
6   "Again I swear to you, you sinners, for sin has been prepared for the day of
7   unceasing blood. •(And those) who worship stones, and those who carve[n] images of
     gold and of silver and of wood and of clay,[o] and those who worship evil spirits[p] and
     demons, and all kinds of idols not according to knowledge,[q] they shall get no manner
8   of help in them.[r] • They shall become wicked[s] on account of the folly of their hearts;
     their eyes will be blindfolded on account of the fear of their hearts, the visions of
9   their dreams.[t] • They shall become wicked and fearful through them, for they wrought
10   all their deeds in falsehood and worshiped stone; so they shall perish instantly.[u] •In
     those days, blessed are they all who accept the words of wisdom and understand
     them, to follow[v] the path[w] of the Most High; they shall walk in the path of his
     righteousness and not become wicked with the wicked; and they shall be saved.

11   "Woe unto you who spread evil to your neighbors!
             For you shall be slain in Sheol.
12   Woe unto you who make sinful and deceitful measures!
             Who acquire worldly knowledge,[x]
             for you shall be consumed by it.[y]
13   Woe unto you who build your houses through the hard toil of others,[z]
             and your building materials are bricks and stones of sin,
             I tell you, you[a2] have no peace.[b2]
14   Woe unto you[c2] who reject the foundations[d2] and the eternal inheritance
                 of your (fore-) fathers!
             Who[e2] shall pursue after the wind—the idol;[f2]
             for there shall be no rest for you.[g2]
15   Woe unto you who engage in oppression and give aid to injustice!

h. G[p]: "of sin" or "of unrighteousness." B and
C have neither "of the sinners" nor "of sin."
   i. B: "those who become pregnant." C: "those
who become destitute."
   j. Nickelsburg (Armenian and Biblical Studies,
pp. 90–156) suggests yāwaṣe'u, in agreement with
the Gk. ekbalousin, "they shall cast out," instead
of yewaṣe'u.
   k. Nickelsburg (Armenian and Biblical Studies,
pp. 90–156) suggests "they shall sell," in agreement
with G. Zuntz, "Enoch on the Last Judgement,"
JTS 45 (1944) 66. Eth. masit means "to pluck out,"
"to tear out," "to remove violently," "to carry
off," and "to rob."
   l. B C: "they shall stumble," "they shall stam-
mer."
   m. G[p] has been restored to read "they that are
with child shall destroy their fruit." Nickelsburg
(Armenian and Biblical Studies, pp. 90–156) suggests
"they shall abort [yadaḥeṣu] their fruit."
   n. So B, C, and G[p]. A wrongly: "who cast out."
   o. G[p] adds: "and of stone." So does Tertullian
(De idolis 4).
   p. Lit. "evil souls."
   q. Or possibly "even if not according to knowledge." B reads "of statues."
   r. Cf. G[p] and Tertullian (De idolis 4). B and C

read "no help will be found [A wrongly: "every
help will be found"] in them."
   s. A wrongly: "They shall not become wicked."
   t. G[p] reads "and the visions of their dreams will
lead you astray."
   u. G[p] reads "You and the lying works that you
have made and fashioned of stone, you shall perish
together."
   v. Lit. "to do."
   w. G[p]: "the commandments."
   x. Lit. "Those who know [learn] upon the earth."
Text is not clear. B reads "Those who become bitter
upon the earth."
   y. G[p] omits vss. 11f.
   z. G[p]: "not (by) their own labor."
   a2. G[p]: "you foolish men."
   b2. Cf. Nickelsburg, Armenian and Biblical Studies, pp. 95f.
   c2. B C: "unto them."
   d2. So A and G[p]. B C: "the measures." Other
Eth. MSS: "princes."
   e2. Lit. "They."
   f2. Possibly this is a corruption for "the soul [or
"spirit"] of the idol [or "error"]." B and C read
"Their souls shall follow after idols." G[p] reads "A
spirit of error shall pursue you."
   g2. So A and G[p]. B C: "no rest for them."

Slaying your neighbors until the day of the great judgment,
because he shall debase your glory.

16 He will instill evil into your hearts.[h2]
He will arouse the anger of his spirit,[i2]
and destroy you all by the sword.
And all the holy and righteous ones shall remember your sins.

Final judgment of the sinners, the righteous, and the fallen angels. More woes.

1 **100** "In those days, the father will be beaten together with his sons, in one place;
and brothers shall fall together with their friends, in death, until a stream shall flow
2 with their blood. •For a man shall not be able to withhold his hands from his sons[a]
nor from (his) sons' sons[b] in order to kill them.[c] Nor is it possible for the sinner to
withhold his hands from his honored brother.[d] From dawn until the sun sets, they shall
3 slay each other.[e] •The horse shall walk through the blood of sinners up to his chest;
4 and the chariot shall sink down up to its top. •In those days, the angels shall descend
into the secret places. They shall gather together into one place all those who gave
aid to sin.[f] And the Most High will arise on that day of judgment in order to execute
5 a great judgment upon all the sinners.[g] •He will set a guard of holy angels over all
the righteous and holy ones, and they shall keep them[h] as the apple of the eye until
all evil and all sin[i] are brought to an end.[j] From that time on[k] the righteous ones shall
6 sleep a restful sleep,[l] and there shall be no one to make them afraid. •Then[m] the wise
people[n] shall see, and the sons of the earth shall give heed to all the words of this
book.[o] They shall know that their wealth shall not be able to save them at the place
where their sins shall collapse.

7 "Woe unto you, sinners, when you oppress[p]
the righteous ones, in the day of hard anguish,
and burn them[q] with fire!
You shall be recompensed according to your deeds.[r]

8 Woe unto you, you hard of heart,
who are watchful to devise evil![s]
Fear shall seize you,
and none shall come to your aid.[t]

9 Woe unto you, sinners, because of the words of your hands![u]
On account of the deeds of your wicked ones,[v]
in blazing flames worse than fire, it shall burn.[w]

10 "And now, do know that your deeds shall be investigated[x]—from the sun, from

---

h2. Sentence omitted by G[p].
i2. B: "the spirit of his anger." C: "his anger and his spirit." G[p]: "his anger."

100 a. G[p]: "his son."
b. G[p]: "his beloved."
c. Text: "to kill him." So G[p].
d. G[p]: "from a man of worth and his brother."
e. G[p]: "they shall be slain together."
f. So A, B, and G[p]. C reads "who brought down sin."
g. So A and B. C: "among the sinners." G[p]: "upon all."
h. G[p]: "they shall be kept."
i. G[p]: "tribulations and sin."
j. C: "he will bring to an end."
k. So G[p]. B C: 'emani, "and though [if]." A, 'emanu, is unclear, but could possibly be translated as "perhaps" or "whether." Nickelsburg may be right in suggesting that the Eth. original may have read 'emnēhu. Nickelsburg, *Armenian and Biblical Studies*, p. 98.
l. Or "a long sleep." Cf. G[p]: "a sweet sleep."

m. So G[p]. B reads "they." C reads "verily," "in certainty." Charles (*APOT*, vol. 2, p. 272) translates it "in security." A reads *'emanu*.
n. G[p]: "the wise among men."
o. G[p]: "these words of this letter."
p. Or "afflict," "make suffer."
q. G[p]: "guard them."
r. So B, C, and G[p]. A: "Their deeds shall be recompensed."
s. So B, C, and G[p]. A: "to eat evil."
t. G[p]: "none to take your part."
u. B and C read "Woe unto you, sinners, because of the words of your mouth and because of the deeds of your hands!" G[p] reads "Woe unto you, sinners, because of the works of your mouth! Woe unto you, all you sinners, because of the words of your mouth and of your hands."
v. Text unclear. B reads "which deeds you violated." C reads "which your wickedness wrought." G[p] reads "because you have gone astray from your holiness." Cf. Nickelsburg, *Armenian and Biblical Studies*, pp. 98f.
w. B: "you shall burn."
x. Or "examined," "inspected."

the moon, and from the stars—for heaven[y] by the angels, on account of your sins (which) were committed[z] upon the earth. The decree[a2] is with the righteous ones.
11 Every cloud, mist, dew, and rain shall witness against you;[b2] for they shall all be withheld from you, from descending for you; and they shall not give heed,[c2] because
12 of your sins. • So then offer gifts to the rain, that it be not hindered from descending for you; perhaps the dew may receive from you gold and silver in order to descend
13 for sure.[d2] • (In) descending,[e2] they shall fall upon you—the frost and the snow with their cold, and all the winds of the snow[f2] with their scourges—and in those days[g2] you cannot stand before them.

The fear of God that nature teaches

1 **101** "Examine the heaven, you sons of heaven,[a] and all the works of the Most High;
2 and be afraid to do evil in his presence. • If he closes the windows of heaven and hinders the rain and the dew from descending upon the earth because of you, what
3 will you do? • Or, if he sends his anger against you (and) your deeds,[b] is it not you who would entreat him?[c] Because[d] you utter bold[e] and hard (words)[f] against his
4 righteousness,[g] you shall have no peace. • Do you not see the sailors[h] of the ships, how their ships are tossed up and down by the billows[i] and are shaken by the winds, and
5 they become anxious? • On this account (it is evident that) they are seized by fear, for they will discharge all their valuable property[j]—the goods that are with them[k]—into the sea;[l] they think[m] in their hearts that the sea will swallow them up and they will
6 perish in it. • Is not the entire sea and all her waters and all her movements[n] the very work of the Most High? Has he not ordered[o] her courses of action and her waters—
7 (indeed) her totality—with sand? • At his rebuke they become frightened, and she dries up;[p] then her fish die[q] and all that is in her. But you, sinners, who are upon the earth,
8 fear him not! • Did he not make the heaven and the earth and all that is in them? Who gave the knowledge of wisdom[r] to all those who move upon the earth[s] and in
9 the sea? • Do not the sailors[t] of the ships fear the sea? Yet the sinners do not fear the Most High.[u]

Terror of the day of judgment: comfort to the suffering righteous ones

1 **102** "In those days,[a] when he hurls out against you[b] terror of fire,[c] where shall you flee, and where shall you find safety? When he flings his word[d] against you, will you
2 not faint[e] and fear?[f] • All the luminaries shall faint with great fear;[g] the whole earth[h]
3 shall faint[i] and tremble and panic.[j] • All the angels shall fulfill their orders.[k] The children of the earth will seek to hide themselves from the presence of the Great Glory,[l] trembling and confounded.[m] You, sinners, you are accursed forever; there is
4 no peace[n] for you! • But you, souls of the righteous, fear not; and be hopeful, you
5 souls that died in righteousness![o] • Be not sad because your souls have gone down into

y. B C: "in heaven."
z. B C: "which you committed."
a2. Or "judgment," "decision," "verdict."
b2. B and C read "He shall cause . . . to testify against you" instead of ". . . shall witness against you."
c2. C: "they shall give heed."
d2. Lit. "In order to descend descending." B and C read "In order to descend."
e2. B and C omit "(in) descending," and add "when."
f2. Lit. "the winds and the snow."
g2. G[p] omits "in those days."

101 a. B omits "you sons of heaven." G[p] reads "Consider then, you sons of men . . ."
b. B reads "and upon all your deeds." C reads "and because of your deeds."
c. G[p]: "will you not be entreating him?"
d. G[p]: "Why?"
e. Lit. "big," "great."

f. G[p] adds "with your mouth."
g. G[p]: "his greatness."
h. So G[p]. Eth. MSS: "kings." Halévy ("Recherches sur la langue de la rédaction primitive du livre d'Hénoch," *JA* 6.9[1867] 392) already suggested before the discovery of G[p] that the Eth. *nagast*, "kings," corresponds to the Heb. *malkēy*, which is corrupt for *malāḥēy*, "sailors."
i. Or "sea-waves," "tidal waves." A reads wrongly "by death." G[p] reads "billow and storm."
j. Lit. "good [beautiful, goodly] property."
k. G[p] reads "their goods and property."
l. Lit. "for all their valuable property . . . will come out into the sea." G[p]: "they will cast out into the sea . . ."
m. So G[p]. A, B, and C read "they do not think."
n. G[p] omits "her movements."
o. A is partially illegible. I have adjusted the three legible characters, *wa-rāḥa*, to read *wašerāḥa*. Eth. *šarḥo* means "to even," "to organize," "to arrange," "to set in order," "to adorn." The reading

Sheol in sorrow; or (because) your flesh[p] fared not well the[q] earthly existence[r] in accordance with your goodness;[s] indeed the time[t] you happened to be in existence was
6 (a time of) sinners,[u] a time of curse and a time of plague.[v] •When you die, the sinners will speak over you: 'As we die, so do the righteous die.[w] What then have they gained
7 by[x] their deeds? •Behold, like us they died in grief and in darkness,[y] and what have
8 they more than we? From now on we have become equal.[z] •What will they receive or what will they see forever? Behold they have surely died; and from now on they
9 shall never see light forever.'[a2] •Now I tell you, sinners, you have satiated yourselves with food and drink, robbing and sin, impoverishing people and gaining property,[b2]
10 and seeing good days.[c2] •Have you seen the righteous, how their end comes about,
11 for no injustice is found upon them until their death?[d2] •But they perished and became like those who were not, and descended into Sheol—and their spirits too[e2]—with anguish.[f2]

The two destinies of the righteous and the sinners: more woes unto the sinners

1 **103** "I now swear to you, righteous ones, by the glory of the Great One and by the
2 glory of his kingdom;[a] and I swear to you (even) by the Great One.[b] •For I know this[c] mystery; I have read the tablets of heaven and have seen the holy writings,[d] and I have
3 understood the writing in them; and they are inscribed[e] concerning you.[f] •For all good things, and joy and honor are prepared for and written down for the souls[g] of those who died in righteousness. Many and good things[h] shall be given to you—the offshoot
4 of your labors. Your lot exceeds even that of the living ones.[i] •The spirits of those

remains problematic. B has "All her course of action he sealed and bound." C has "He established all her course of action and bound . . ." G[p] has "He set their limits [so Bonner, *The Last Chapters of Enoch in Greek* (Studies and Documents 8; London, 1937) p. 57] and binds and sets it about . . ."

p. B C: "she becomes frightened and dries up." G[p]: "they become frightened and dry up . . ."

q. So A and G[p]. B C: "all her fish."

r. B C: "knowledge and wisdom." G[p]: "understanding."

s. G[p] omits "who move upon the earth."

t. Lit. "the kings." See n. h.

u. G[p] omits this sentence.

102 a. Omitted by G[p].

b. A wrongly reads "against them."

c. G[p]: "the surge of the fire of your burning."

d. Or "his voice."

e. G[p]: "be shaken."

f. G[p] adds "by the mighty sound."

g. This clause is omitted by G[p].

h. So B, C, and G[p]. A: "the earth and everything."

i. G[p]: "be shaken."

j. Lit. "be hasty," "be nervous," "be anxious." G[p]: "be confused."

k. So B and C. A: "their orders shall be fulfilled."

l. So B and C. A: "the Great One and glory."

m. G[p]: "the heaven and its lights shaken and trembling, all the sons of the earth."

n. G[p]: "no joy."

o. G[p]: "Be of good courage, souls of the just that are dead, the just and the pious."

p. Or "your body." G[p]: "the body of your flesh."

q. B, C, and G[p]: "your."

r. Lit. "in life" or "while alive."

s. G[p]: "your holiness."

t. Lit. "the day."

u. C has been adjusted to read "but wait for the

day of the judgment of sinners." G[p]: "the days that you lived were days of sinners."

v. G[p]: "days . . . of accursed men upon the earth."

w. G[p]: "the pious have died according to their fate."

x. So B, C, and G[p]. A: "and."

y. G[p]: "they have died like us. See now how they die in grief."

z. G[p]: "From now on let them rise and be saved."

a2. G[p] is abbreviated. It reads "and they shall forever see us eating and drinking." Cf. Bonner, *The Last Chapters of Enoch*, p. 61.

b2. Or "acquiring wealth."

c2. So B, C, and G[p]. A: "goods," "property," "wealth."

d2. G[p]: "Behold, now they who try to justify themselves, how great their downfall has been, because no righteousness was found in them until they died."

e2. B: "their souls descended." C: "their spirits descended."

f2. G[p]: "they were destroyed, and became as though they were not, and their souls went down in pain to . . ."

103 a. B: "I now swear . . . by this great glory and his honor and the honor of his kingdom." C: "I now swear . . . by the glory of the Great and Honored One (of) the mighty kingdom."

b. B C: "and I swear to you by his greatness."

c. So A, B, and G[p]. C omits "this."

d. B reads "the writing of the holy ones." C: "the holy writing." G[p]: "the writing of authority."

e. Lit. "engraved."

f. B reads "concerning them."

g. A: "for your souls."

h. B C: "many good things."

i. G[p] omits last two sentences.

who died in righteousness[j] shall live[k] and rejoice;[l] their spirits shall not perish,[m] nor their memorial from before the face of the Great One unto all the generations of the world. Therefore,[n] do not worry about their humiliation.

5 "Woe[o] unto you sinners who are dead![p] When you are dead in the wealth of your sins,[q] those who are like you[r] will say of you, 'Happy are you sinners![s] (The sinners)

6 have seen all their days.[t] •They have died now in prosperity and wealth.[u] They have not experienced struggle and battle in their lifetime.[v] They have died in glory, and

7 there was no judgment[w] in their lifetime.'[x] •You yourselves know that they will bring your souls[y] down to Sheol; and they shall experience evil and great tribulation—in

8 darkness, nets,[z] and burning flame. •Your souls shall enter[a2] into the great judgment; it shall be a great judgment in all the generations of the world. Woe unto you, for

9 there is no peace[b2] for you! •Now to the righteous and kind ones during their lifetime: Do not say, 'In the days of our[c2] toil,[d2] we have surely suffered hardships and have experienced every trouble.[e2] We have faced many evil things[f2] and have become consumed. We have died[g2] and become few, (characterized) by the littleness of our

10 spirit.[h2] •We have been destroyed;[i2] and we have found none whatsoever to help us with a word or otherwise.[j2] We have been tortured and destroyed,[k2] and could not even

11 hope to see life[l2] from one day to the other.[m2] •We hoped[n2] to be the head and have become the tail.[o2] We have moiled as we toiled,[p2] but had no authority over our own toil.[q2] We have become the victuals of the sinners and the oppressors;[r2] they[s2] have

12 made their yoke[t2] heavy upon us. •Those who hate us, while goading us and encompassing us,[u2] have become masters over us.[v2] We have bowed our necks to those[w2]

13 who hate us, but they had no pity on us.[x2] •We wanted to get away from them in order that we may escape and be at rest; but we found no place to which we might flee and

14 be safe from them.[y2] •Then, in our tribulation, we brought a charge against them before the authorities,[z2] and cried out against those who were devouring us,[a3] but they (the authorities) neither would pay attention to our cries nor wish to listen to our

15 voice. •But (on the contrary) they were assisting[b3] those who were robbing and devouring us, those who were causing us to diminish.[c3] They (the authorities) conceal

j. B C: "you who died in righteousness, your spirits." G^p: "their spirits."

k. G^p omits "shall live."

l. B and C read "shall rejoice and be glad."

m. B omits "shall not perish."

n. Or "So, now."

o. G^p omits "Woe."

p. B omits "who are dead."

q. G^p omits "in the wealth of your sins." B omits "wealth."

r. G^p omits "those who are like you."

s. B, C, and G^p: "Happy are the sinners!"

t. G^p: "all their days which they saw in their life."

u. G^p omits this sentence.

v. This sentence is omitted by G^p.

w. So C and G^p. A reads "there was judgment."

x. B omits this sentence.

y. So A and G^p. B and C read "their souls."

z. G^p: "in toils."

a2. A erroneously: "shall conquer."

b2. G^p: "joy."

c2. A: "their."

d2. G^p: "days of oppression."

e2. G^p omits "we have experienced every trouble."

f2. G^p omits "We have faced many evil things."

g2. So A. B, C, and G^p omit "We have died."

h2. Lit. "with our small [little] spirit." G^p omits "by the littleness of our spirit," and adds "we found none to take our part."

i2. G^p adds "we have been crushed."

j2. G^p omits this clause.

k2. Cf. Nickelsburg, *Armenian and Biblical Studies*, p. 102.

l2. G^p: "to know safety again."

m2. Lit. "from day to day."

n2. Or "expected."

o2. In A, the *na* in *zanab(a)*, "tail," has been dropped, and *zaba-*, the compound particle, has been joined to the immediately succeeding word, *ṣāmawena*, "we (have) toiled [labored]," to form *zabaṣāmawena.*

p2. Or "We have toiled as we worked [labored]."

q2. G^p: "we have not been the masters of our wages."

r2. G^p omits "the oppressors."

s2. G^p reads "the lawless ones."

t2. G^p: "the yoke."

u2. So A and G^p. B and C read "they that hate us and goad us."

v2. G^p reads "They who are our masters . . ."

w2. So B and C. A reads *wabo*, "there is [are]."

x2. G^p omits this sentence.

y2. G^p omits this clause.

z2. G^p omits this clause.

a3. G^p: "against those who insulted and outraged us."

b3. So B and C. A: *'ardā'ekewomu*, "you were assisting them," does not seem to make sense, though it agrees with reading of other early MSS.

c3. G^p reads "They did not take our part, finding no complaint against those who affront and devour us; but they harden against us those who slaughtered us and made us few."

their (the offenders') injustice and do not remove the yokes of those who devour us,[d3] scatter us, and murder us; they (the authorities) cover up our murder;[e3] and they (the authorities) do not remember (the fact) that they (the offenders) have lifted up their hands against us.'[f3]

1 **104** "I swear unto you that in heaven the angels will remember you for good[a] before
the glory of the Great One; and your names[b] shall be written before the glory of the
2 Great One.[c] •Be hopeful, because formerly you have pined away through evil and
toil. But now you shall shine[d] like the lights of heaven, and you shall be seen;[e] and
3 the windows of heaven shall be opened for you. Your cry shall be heard.[f] •Cry for
judgment, and it shall appear for you;[g] for all your tribulations shall be (demanded)
for investigation from the (responsible) authorities[h]—from everyone who assisted those
4 who plundered you.[i] •Be hopeful, and do not abandon your hope, because there shall
be a fire[j] for you; you are about to be making a great rejoicing like the angels of
5 heaven.[k] •You shall not have to hide on the day of the great judgment, and you shall
not be found as the sinners; but the eternal judgment shall be (far) away from you for
6 all the generations of the world.[l] •Now fear not, righteous ones, when you see the
sinners waxing strong and flourishing;[m] do not be partners with them, but keep far
away from those who lean onto their own injustice; [n] for you are to be partners with
7 the good-hearted people of heaven. •Now, you sinners, even if you say,[o] 'All our sins
shall not be investigated or written down,'[p] nevertheless, all your sins are being written
8 down every day. •So now I show unto you that light and darkness as well as day and
9 night witness[q] all your sins. •Do not become wicked in your hearts, or lie, or alter
the words of a just verdict,[r] or utter falsehood against the words of[s] the Great,[t] the
Holy One, or give praise to[u] your idols; for all your lies and all your wickedness are[v]
10 not for righteousness but for great sin.[w] •And now I know this mystery: For they (the
sinners) shall alter the just verdict[x] and many sinners will take it to heart;[y] they will
speak evil words and lie, and they will invent fictitious stories and write out my
11 Scriptures on the basis of their own words.[z] •And would that they had written down
all the words[a2] truthfully on the basis of their own speech,[b2] and neither alter nor take
12 away from my words, all of which I testify to them from the beginning! •Again know
another mystery!:[c2] that to the righteous and the wise[d2] shall be given the Scriptures

d3. So C. A reads "they do not remove their yokes; and they devour us." B reads "they do not remove their yokes but they devour us."

e3. "Our murder" is in the genitive objective case; in other words, the phrase should be read "the fact of our being murdered [slaughtered]."

f3. Gp: "concerning the sinners, they do not remember their sins."

104 a. Or the clause can be understood to mean "the angels will intercede for you in heaven."

b. So B and C. A reads "the names."

c. Gp omits this clause.

d. A wrongly reads *tefarehu*, "you (will) fear," instead of *tebarehu*.

e. C: "you shall shine and be seen."

f. So Gp. Eth. (as in A, B, and C) "And your cry" is incomplete.

g. Gp: "The judgment for which you cry shall also be made manifest against everything which helps against you for your oppression."

h. Lit. "your tribulations shall be investigated from the authorities."

i. Gp reads "from all who ate with those who affront and devour you."

j. B and C omit "fire"; v. 4 is altogether omitted in Gp.

k. So A and B. C: "for there shall be a great joy for you like the angels of heaven. What are you about to do?"

l. Gp: "(you sinners), shall be troubled; and there shall be eternal judgment upon you for all the generations of the world [ages]."

m. Or "prospering." Lit. "their way become befitting."

n. B, C, and Gp read "but keep far away from [Gp: "all"] their injustice."

o. Gp: "say not."

p. So B and C. A is not intelligible.

q. Lit. "see," "behold."

r. Or "the word of truth."

s. A omits "of."

t. Gp omits "Great."

u. A, B, and Gp. C reads "do not take account of."

v. Gp: "lead to."

w. A erroneously reads *hāṭe'an*, "sinners," instead of *haṭe'at*.

x. Or "the word of truth."

y. So A. B C: "Sinners will greatly [amply] alter and pervert the just verdict." Cf. also Nickelsburg, *Armenian and Biblical Studies*, p. 103. Gp: "sinners alter and write against . . . of truth and lead the many away."

z. So A. B C: "they will invent great inventions, and write books on the basis of their own words." Gp: "they lie and invent great falsehoods and write out the Scriptures in their names."

a2. So A and C. B Gp: "all my words."

b2. Gp: "in their names."

c2. So A. B C Gp: "I know another mystery."

d2. Gp adds "the holy."

13 of joy, for truth and great wisdom.[e2] •So to them shall be given the Scriptures;[f2] and they shall believe them and be glad in them; and all the righteous ones who learn from them the ways of truth shall rejoice.''[g2]

1 **105** In those days, he says, "The Lord will be patient and cause the children of the earth to hear. Reveal it to them with your wisdom,[a] for you are their guides; and (you 2 are) a reward[b] upon the whole earth. •Until[c] I and my son are united with them forever in the upright paths in their lifetime and there shall be peace unto you, rejoice, you children of truth.[d] Amen.''[e]

1 **106** And after some days my son, Methuselah, took a wife for his son Lamech,[a] and 2 she became pregnant by him[b] and bore him a son. •And his body was white as[c] snow and red as[d] a rose; the hair of his head[e] as white as wool[f] and his *demdema*[g] beautiful; and as for his eyes, when he opened them[h] the whole house glowed like the sun— 3 (rather) the whole house glowed even more exceedingly.[i] •And when[j] he arose from the hands of the midwife, he opened his mouth and spoke to the Lord with right- 4 eousness.[k] •And his father,[l] Lamech, was afraid of him and fled[m] and went to 5 Methuselah his father; • and he said to him, "I have begotten a strange son:[n] He is not like an (ordinary) human being, but he looks like the children of the angels of heaven to me;[o] his form is different, and he is not like us.[p] His eyes are like the rays of the 6 sun, and[q] his face glorious.[r] •It does not seem to me that he is of me,[s] but of angels;[t] and I fear[u] that a wondrous phenomenon[v] may take place upon the earth in his days.[w] 7 So I am beseeching you now, begging you in order that you may go to his (grand)father[x] Enoch, our father, and learn[y] from him the truth, for his dwelling place is among the 8 angels.''[z] •When Methuselah heard the words of his son,[a2] he came to us[b2] at the ends of the earth; for he had heard that I was there.[c2] He cried aloud, and I heard his voice and came to him;[d2] and I said to him, "Behold, my son, here I am, why[e2] have you 9 come here?''[f2] •Then he answered me and said, "On account of a great distress have 10 I come to you,[g2] on account of a grievous vision have I come near here.[h2] •Now, my

e2. So A. B C: ''for joy, truth, and great wisdom.'' G[p]: ''for the joy in the truth.''

f2. This clause is omitted by G[p].

g2. So A and G[p]. B C: ''shall be recompensed.''

105 a. So A? The text is partially illegible. B and C read ''The Lord says, they will cry out and testify in their wisdom to the children of the earth.''

b. Eth. *'esseyāt*, ''reward,'' ''wage.'' Possibly this may be a corruption of *'assat*, ''healing power,'' ''gift of healing,'' ''spiritual authority.''

c. So A. B C: ''For.''

d. Or ''uprightness.''

e. This ch. is missing from G[p]. Contrary to Charles's view, this short ch. seems to exist in the Aram. original. Cf. Milik, *The Books of Enoch*, p. 208.

106 a. G[p] reads ''I took a wife for my son, Methu-selah,'' and then adds ''and she bore him a son and called his name Lamech. Righteousness was brought low until that day. When he came of age, he took a wife for him.'' The Lat. fragment adds ''when he was three hundred fifty years old.''

b. G[p] omits ''she became pregnant by him.''

c. G[p]: ''whiter than.''

d. G[p]: ''redder than.''

e. G[p] omits ''of his head.''

f. G[p] adds ''and curly and glorious.''

g. This Eth. word has no equivalent in English. It refers to long and curly hair combed up straight, what one calls *gofārē* in several modern Ethiopian languages, or ''afro'' in colloquial English.

h. Lit. ''his eyes.''

i. G[p] omits this phrase.

j. G[p] omits ''when.''

k. So A. B and C read ''to the Lord of righteous-ness.'' G[p] reads ''he blessed the Lord.''

l. G[p] omits ''his father.''

m. Lat. omits ''and fled.''

n. G[p]: ''a strange child has been born to me.''

o. B, C, and G[p] omit ''to me.'' Lat. omits this clause.

p. Lat. omits this clause.

q. B and C omit ''and.''

r. Lat. omits this clause.

s. Lat. reads ''he is not born of me.''

t. G[p]: ''of an angel.''

u. A reads erroneously ''he did not fear.''

v. Lit. ''a wonder, miracle, wonderment.''

w. Lat. omits this clause.

x. B and C omit ''his (grand)father.''

y. Lit. ''hear.''

z. G[p] has a gap and misses this clause. Lat. reads ''he said to Methuselah: I am not able to know unless we go to our father Enoch.''

a2. Due to a gap, this clause is missing in G[p].

b2. B C G: ''to me.''

c2. G[p]: ''where he saw that I was then.''

d2. G[p]: ''He said to me, 'Father, give ear to my voice and come to me.' ''

e2. So G[p] and Lat. A B C: ''for.''

f2. So A. B C G[p] Lat.: ''why . . . come to me?''

g2. G[p] reads ''I have come here,'' and adds ''(my) father.''

h2. G[p] omits this clause. Lat. reads ''he said,'' omits vs. 9, and proceeds to vs. 10.

father, hear me:[i2] For unto my son Lamech a son[j2] has been born,[k2] one whose image and form are not like unto the characteristics of human beings; and his color is whiter than snow and redder than a rose,[l2] the hair of his head is whiter than white wool, and his eyes are like the rays of the sun; and (when) he opened his eyes the whole house

11 lighted up.[m2] •And (when) he rose up in the hands of the midwife, he opened his

12 mouth and blessed the Lord of heaven[n2] •Then his father, Lamech,[o2] became afraid[p2] and fled,[q2] and he did not believe that he (the child) was of him[r2] but of[s2] the image of the angels of heaven.[t2] And behold, I have come to you in order that you may make

13 me know the real truth.'' •Then I, Enoch,[u2] answered, saying to him, ''The Lord will surely make new things[v2] upon the earth; and I have already seen this matter in a vision and made it known to you. For in the generation[w2] of Jared, my father, they

14 transgressed the word of the Lord, (that is) the law of heaven.[x2] •And behold, they commit sin and transgress the commandment;[y2] they have united themselves with women and commit sin together with them; and they have married (wives) from among

15 them, and begotten children by them[z2] •There shall be a great destruction[a3] upon the

16 earth; and there shall be a deluge and a great destruction for one year. •And this son who has been born unto you shall be left upon the earth;[b3] and his three sons shall be

17 saved when they who are upon the earth are dead.[c3] •And upon the earth they shall give birth to giants,[d3] not of the spirit but of the flesh.[e3] There shall be a great plague

18 upon the earth, and the earth shall be washed clean[f3] from all the corruption.[g3] •Now, make known to your son[h3] Lamech that the son who has been born is indeed righteous;[i3] and call his name Noah, for he shall be the remnant for you; and he and his sons shall be saved from the corruption[j3] which shall come upon the earth on account of all the sin and oppression that existed, and it will be fulfilled upon the earth, in his days.[k3]

19 After that there shall occur still greater oppression than that which was fulfilled upon the earth the first time; for I do know the mysteries of the holy ones;[l3] for he, the Lord, has revealed (them) to me and made me know—and I have read (them) in the heavenly tablets.''

1 **107** Then I beheld the writing upon them that one generation shall be more wicked than the other,[a] until[b] a generation of righteous ones[c] shall arise, wickedness shall perish, sin shall disappear from upon the earth, and every good thing[d] shall come

---

i2. Gᵖ and Lat. omit this introductory clause.

j2. Gᵖ: ''a child.''

k2. Due to double haplography A reads *tawalda Lāmĕk waldya,* ''my son Lamech is born.''

l2. Lat. omits ''whose image . . . than a rose.''

m2. Gᵖ and Lat. omit the last clause.

n2. Gᵖ: ''the Lord of eternity.''

o2. Gᵖ: ''my son Lamech.''

p2. Lat. ''Lamech became afraid.'' The rest of vs. 12 is missing.

q2. B C and Gᵖ: ''he fled to me.''

r2. Gᵖ: ''that he is his son.''

s2. B C: ''from.''

t2. Gᵖ: ''but that (he is) from angels.''

u2. Gᵖ omits ''Enoch.''

v2. Lit. ''He will renew new things.'' Gᵖ: ''new order.''

w2. A erroneously: *waldu,* ''his son,'' instead of *teweledu.*

x2. Or ''the regulation or order [or ''rule,'' ''commandment,'' ''principle,'' ''custom''] of heaven''; so A. B and C read *'emal'elta samāy,* ''from the heights of heaven'' or ''from heaven above,'' instead of *'emser'āta samāy.* Gᵖ reads ''from the covenant of heaven.''

y2. Gᵖ: ''the custom.''

z2. See n. e3. Vss. 13f. missing in Lat.

a3. Gᵖ: ''wrath.''

b3. Gᵖ: ''this child that is born shall be left.''

c3. B and C add ''he and his children will be saved.'' Cf. 4QEnᶜ.

d3. Lit. ''those who are tall''; so A. B C: ''those who multiply.'' Gᵖ omits the phrase.

e3. In Gᵖ, this sentence is placed at the end of vs. 14. Charles in *APOT,* vol. 2, p. 279, decided to place it at the end of vs. 14. Milik also puts it at the end of vs. 14, in 4QEnᶜ.

f3. So 4QEnᶜ: ''be cleansed (from) great corruption.'' Gᵖ: ''he shall tame the earth.''

g3. So 4QEnᶜ. Gᵖ adds ''that is upon it.''

h3. Gᵖ omits ''your son.''

i3. Lit. ''he is righteous.'' B and C read ''the one who has been born is in truth his son.'' Gᵖ reads ''tell Lamech that he is his son in truth and holiness.''

j3. Or ''destruction.''

k3. Gᵖ reads ''whereupon you shall rest, and his sons, from the corruption of the earth and from all the sinners and from all the wickedness.'' Milik's reconstructing of this verse, according to 4QEnᶜ, as containing the triple explanation of Noah's names, is not convincing (see *The Books of Enoch,* p. cited).

l3. The preceding two clauses are missing in Gᵖ due to a gap.

107 a. Lit. ''generation.''

b. B: ''for,'' ''since,'' ''that.''

c. B C Gᵖ: ''righteousness.'' Cf. 4QEnᶜ.

d. Lit. ''good,'' ''beautiful,'' ''pleasant.''

2 upon her.[e] •"And now, my son, go[f] and make it known to your son Lamech that this
3 son[g] who has been born is his son in truth—and not in falsehood." •And when
Methuselah had heard the words of his father Enoch—for he revealed to him everything
in secret—he returned (home).[h] And he called the name of that son Noah, for he will
comfort the earth after all the destruction.[i]

1 **108** Another Book of Enoch—which he wrote for his son Methuselah and for those
2 who will come after him, observing the law in the last days. •You who have observed
(the law)[a] shall wait patiently in all the days[b] until (the time of) those who work evil
3 is completed,[c] and the power of the wicked ones is ended.•As for you, wait patiently
until sin passes away, for the names of (the sinners)[d] shall be blotted out from the
Book of Life[e] and the books of the Holy One;[f] their seeds shall be destroyed forever
and their spirits shall perish and die;[g] they shall cry and lament in a place that is an
invisible[h] wilderness and burn in the fire—for there exists[i] ground[j] there (as upon the
earth).
4 I also saw there something like an invisible cloud; (and) though I could see that it
was completely dark[k] yet I could not see[l] the flame of its fire because it was burning
brightly; and there were some things like bright mountains which formed a ring (around
5 it) and which were tossing it to and fro. •Then I asked one of the holy angels who
was with me, saying to him, "What is this bright thing? For it is not a heaven[m] but
merely the flame of a fire which is burning—and a voice of weeping, crying, and
6 lamenting as well as strong pain." •And he said unto me, "This place which you see,
into it shall be taken[n] the spirits of sinners, blasphemers, those who do evil, and those
who alter all the things which the Lord has done[o] through the mouth of the prophets,
7 all of which have to be fulfilled. •For some of (these things) were written and sealed
above in[p] heaven so that the angels may read[q] them (the things that are written) and
know that which is about to befall the sinners, the spirits of the ones who err,[r] as well
as those who defiled[s] their bodies, revenged themselves on[t] God,[u] and worked[v] together
8 with evil people. •Those who love God have loved neither gold nor silver, nor all the
good things which are in the world, but have given over their bodies to suffering—
9 who from the time of their very being have not longed after earthly food, and who[w]
regarded themselves[x] as a (mere) passing breath. And they have observed this matter,
the Lord having put them through much testing; then he received their pure spirits[y]
10 so that they should bless his name. •And I have recounted in the books all their
blessings. He has caused them to be recompensed,[z] for they were all[a2] found loving

e. Gp: "blessings shall come to them upon the earth."

f. Gp: "And now run, child."

g. Gp: "this child." 4QEnc: "this boy."

h. B: "he returned (home) having seen." C: "he returned (home) and revealed (them) to him." Gp omits this clause.

i. Gp: "And his name was called Noah, comforting the earth after the destruction."

108 a. Lit. "You who have worked [acted, done]." C: "You who have done the good."

b. So A. B and C read *la'ellu mawā'el*, "for those days," instead of *bakwellu mawā'el*.

c. B C: "until those who work evil are finished [consummated]."

d. Lit. "their names."

e. So C. A reads "from the book of." B omits the whole phrase.

f. B C: "of the holy ones."

g. So A. B C: "shall be killed."

h. Or "chaotic." Cf. Gen 1:2.

i. B C: "there is not."

j. Or "earth."

k. Lit. "I could see from its darkness." B and C are unintelligible: "for I could not see from its depth looking over."

l. B C: "I could see."

m. A could possibly be read *kamāya*, "like water."

n. B C: "shall be cast."

o. B C: "spoken."

p. So B and C. A omits "in."

q. So B and C. A reads "deposit," "preserve," "write down," or "put."

r. Or "the blunderers," "the falterers," "the lapsed," "the apostates." B and C and other MSS cited by Charles read *teḥutān*, "the humble ones," instead of *seḥutān*.

s. So A. B and C and other MSS cited by Charles, with the exception of his q, which is unintelligible, read *'aḥmamu*, "they made sick," "they afflicted," instead of *'aḥsamu*.

t. C: "by."

u. C reads "they were recompensed [revenged] by God."

v. B C: "diminished," "put to shame."

w. B C: "but."

x. So A and B. C: "their souls."

y. B C: "then their spirits were found pure."

z. B C: "he has recompensed them."

a2. B and C read *'ellu*, "they," "those," "those that," instead of *kwellu*.

God[b2] more than the fire of their eternal souls;[c2] and while they were being trodden upon by evil people, experiencing abuse and insult by them, they continued[d2] blessing
11 us.[e2] •So now I[f2] shall summon their spirits[g2] if they are born of light,[h2] and change those who are born in darkness—those whose bodies were not recompensed with
12 honor as they deserved for their faithfulness.[i2] •I shall bring them out into the bright light, those who have loved my holy name, and seat them each one by one upon the
13 throne of his honor;[j2] • and they shall be resplendent for ages[k2] that cannot be numbered;[l2] for the judgment of God is righteousness, because he will give faith[m2]—as well as the
14 paths of truth[n2]—to the faithful ones in the resting place.[o2] •Then they shall see[p2] those who were born in darkness being taken into darkness, while the righteous ones shall
15 be resplendent. •(The sinners) shall cry aloud, and they shall see the righteous ones[q2] being resplendent; they shall go to the place which was[r2] prescribed for them concerning[s2] the days and the seasons.'' Here ends the Revelation of the Secrets of Enoch.

b2. Lit. "heaven."

c2. B: "more than their eternal breath." C: "more than their breath in the world."

d2. Or "they remained," "they persisted." Lit. "they lived," "they settled down." B and C read *ḥasaru*, "they were shamed [slighted]," instead of *nabaru*.

e2. So A. B C: "me."

f2. It appears to me that the shift in personal pronouns may indicate some scribal effort at an interpretative commentary, or even an interpolation.

g2. B and C read "the spirits of the good [kind] ones."

h2. Lit. "if it is born of light"; A is difficult. It can possibly read "I shall call their spirits, if it is born of light," which agrees with some traditional Ethiopian commentaries, or "I shall call their spirits, mother of the one born of light . . ." B C: "from the generation of light."

i2. Or "faith."

j2. B: "in the throne of honor—his honor."

k2. Or "times," "seasons," "periods."

l2. Lit. "without number."

m2. Or "faithfulness."

n2. Or "uprightness."

o2. B C: "He will give faith to the faithful ones in the resting place of the paths of truth [or "uprightness"]."

p2. A erroneously adds "the righteous ones."

q2. B C: "the sinners."

r2. C: "were."

s2. B and C omit "concerning."

2 (Slavonic Apocalypse of) ENOCH

(Late First Century A.D.)

Appendix: 2 Enoch in *Merilo Pravednoe*

A NEW TRANSLATION AND INTRODUCTION*
BY F. I. ANDERSEN

This work is an amplification of Genesis 5:21–32; that is, it covers events from the life of Enoch to the onset of the Flood. The first and larger part, chapters 1–68, describes how Enoch was taken up to the Lord through the seven heavens and then returned to report to his family what he had learned. The second part, chapters 69–73, deals more briefly with the life of Enoch's successors, Methuselah and Nir, and ends with the story of the birth and ascension of Melchizedek, just prior to the Flood.

The book is basically a Midrash; but the sparse plot is almost lost in the large amount of apocalyptic material that it carries. The story of Enoch and his descendants provides the setting for a loosely assembled array of quite diverse ingredients, including cosmological speculations, ethical instruction, and prophecies of the future. Besides forecasting the Flood, these predictions extend to the fate of mankind, good and bad, after death. A basis for this eschatology was provided by the visits to Paradise and to the place of torment in the heavens. Angelology, astronomy, astrology, and calendrical systems all arise from the study of creation. The whole is suffused with teaching about God which is uncompromisingly monotheistic, notwithstanding the abundant mythology. The main doctrinal point, which is reiterated throughout, is that the Lord is the sole Creator. No other activity of God is celebrated, unless it is the last judgment. There is no interest in history. The author's posture is simple. His statements are unsupported by philosophical reasoning. Idolatry is denounced in conventional terms.

The ethical component is spread over the whole work, either as comments by the angels on why the occupants of heaven and hell are where they are, or as exhortations given by Enoch to his family. The cardinal virtues are care for the poor and needy, and sexual purity. Many other ideas, some quite strange, appear along the way; but the main concern is with the origin of things. While derived mainly from the biblical creation stories, the account of the cosmos has been elaborated in a quasi-scientific manner. The results are not altogether consistent; sometimes the picture is quite obscure. The most systematic description arises from the journey through the seven heavens. Then there is a distinct account of the origin of everything, presented as an extended story of the creation of the universe based on Genesis 1f., told by the Lord himself in the first person as autobiographical reminiscences. Some of this material is repeated when Enoch makes his report to his family on earth, in the form of lists, rather than narrative.[1]

---

* [The Introduction does not contain sections on "Relation to Canonical Books" or on "Relation to Apocryphal Books," because of the complex textural history of this document. J.H.C.]

[1] M. E. Stone, "Lists of Revealed Things in the Apocalyptic Literature," *Magnalia Dei: The Mighty Acts of God; Essays on the Bible and Archaeology in Memory of G. Ernest Wright*, eds. F. M. Cross, W. E. Lemke, and P. D. Miller, Jr. (Garden City, N.Y., 1976) pp. 414–52.

Texts

2 Enoch is known only from manuscripts in Old Slavonic.[2] Here is a list of known manuscripts, along with the symbols used to refer to them.

Manuscript	Our symbol	Sokolov	Bonwetsch	Vaillant	Charles
NLB 321	R	A(?)	S	R	
BAN 13.3.25	J	Я	J	J	
GIM Khlyudov	P	П	P	P	A
RM 3058	P^2			P^2	
BAN 45.13.4	A	Academy Chronograph (unpublished)			
GIM 3(18)	U	Ч	U	U	
TSS 793	Tr			Tr	
MS 387(3)	Syn			Syn	
GIM Barsov	B	Ь	B	B	
RM 578	Rum			Rum	
NLB 151/443	N	H	V^n	N	B
VL 125	V	B	V^v	V	
GIM Barsov²	B^2	$Ь^1$	B^1	B^2	
TSS 15	MPr		M	MPr	
TSS 253	TSS 253		(M)		
TSS 489	TSS 489		(M)		
TSS 682	TSS 682		(M)		
Gennadius	G		Genn.		
IHP 39	Chr			Chr	
RM 590	Chr^2		C	Chr^2	

The manuscripts differ widely in date and provenance. They are also quite diverse in scope and in individual readings. Not one of them is simply a text of 2 Enoch itself; in every case the Enoch material is either part of a larger·work or part of a collection of various pieces. Only a few of them have the text in any degree of completeness; most of them supply only brief extracts incorporated into different miscellanies, usually with drastic abbreviation or extensive reorganization. Four manuscripts (N, V, B², P) end with Enoch's second ascension. Five manuscripts (A, U, B, R, J) are more complete, since they go on to the subsequent events, including the legends of Methuselah and Melchizedek. J does not continue to the end, so that only A, U, B, R reach the rapture of Melchizedek and the Flood. The Melchizedek story is found also in Rum, which has extracted it from 2 Enoch, as the title shows. There is no evidence that the second part ever existed separately.[3]

Attempts have been made to classify the known manuscripts into textual families. Without critical editions of them all, this procedure is premature. A stemma of relationships is often very hard to work out in medieval manuscripts of this kind. To illustrate, M. I. Sokolov's impression that V is virtually identical with N, based on a cursory collation, has been repeated in much subsequent discussion; but it is false, and the several superior readings of V need to be included.[4] The fourteenth-century copy of *Merilo Pravednoe*, which is the oldest of all the manuscripts, is so far the only one that has been published in facsimile. But the extracts from 2 Enoch which have been incorporated into this ethical treatise have been

---

[2] The following abbreviations are used to refer to institutions holding MSS:

BAN Library of the Academy of Sciences of the U.S.S.R., Leningrad
GIM State Historical Museum, Moscow
IHP Institute of History and Philology, Nezhin
NLB National Library, Belgrade
RM Rumyantsev Museum
TSS Trinity-St. Sergius Monastery Library
[The last two collections are now in the Lenin Library, Moscow]
VL The Austrian National Library, Vienna

The editor and translator wish to express their gratitude to the Library of the Academy of Sciences in Leningrad for photographs of the unpublished MSS A and J; and to the Vienna Library for a photograph of the unpublished MS V.

[3] F. L. Horton (*The Melchizedek Tradition* [*SNTS* MS 30; Cambridge, 1976]) summarily dismisses 2En on the grounds that its Melchizedek materials are found in only one recension. This argument is not itself logical; but the facts are otherwise. The tradition is found in both recensions, in six MSS representing four text families.

[4] F. Repp, "Textkritische Untersuchungen zum Henoch-Apokryph des cod. slav. 125 der Österreichischen Nationalbibliothek," *Wiener slavistische Jahrbuch* 10 (1963) 58–68.

extensively rearranged, and this has to be balanced against its antiquity when its claims are measured (see following appendix).[5] Any attempt to write the textual history of 2 Enoch must wait until accurate copies of all manuscripts become available.

It is generally recognized that there is a longer and a shorter recension. This is a distinction in the character of the text, quite apart from the length of the extracts found in individual manuscripts. More precisely one can distinguish a very long recension (J, P, with P[2] as a brief extract of a text close to P), a long recension (R—physically longer even than J because it completes the Melchizedek section which J cuts short), a short recension (A, U, with Tr, Syn as extracts of the same kind of text), and a very short recension (B, N, V, B[2], with Rum as an extract in the same tradition). The other manuscripts, which are only extracts, belong to other text traditions.

Even manuscripts which are identified as being of the same kind are far from uniform among themselves. The closest pairs are P and P[2], A and U, V and N; but even these vary extensively in spelling. Quite apart from the mistakes made by scribes, or the liberties with which they expanded or condensed to suit their purposes, difficult readings due to other causes, including simple incomprehension of material from an alien culture, such as the calendar in 2 Enoch, have compounded the problems. It is likely that every manuscript has suffered from such influences to a greater or a less degree; not one can claim to be intrinsically superior to the others. Another result of this hazardous transmission is that while some sections have survived in many manuscripts, others are known from only a few copies. In the extreme case, a reading found only once might prove to be authentic, although such readings are often no more than a divergence in one manuscript. When it is so hard to tell whether a solitary reading is a sole survivor from the original or an interpolation, it is better to present all the evidence and suspend judgment. The common mistakes of counting witnesses as a measure of a reading's claim and dismissing a reading because of meager attestation are, accordingly, particularly detrimental in 2 Enoch research.

There are many indications that 2 Enoch is derived from sources foreign to Slavonic culture. Most, if not all, Slavonic literature of this kind was translated from Greek, and traces of such an origin may be discerned in 2 Enoch. But no Greek texts of 2 Enoch, or even parts of it, are known. This circumstance makes it all the more difficult to settle textual problems within the Slavonic manuscripts.

The extensive and substantial differences between manuscripts of the longer recension (R, J, P, P[2]—two or three families) and manuscripts of the shorter recension (the main ones are A, U, V, N, B[2], B—four or five families) constitute the major textual problem. The difference in length is due to two quite different features. There are blocks of text found only in the longer manuscripts; but even when the passages are parallel, the longer manuscripts tend to be more ample. At the same time there is so much verbal similarity when the passages correspond that a common source must be supposed; that is, we have recensions, not different versions. Furthermore, the very short manuscripts differ from the short ones in the same manner.

Quite contradictory explanations have been offered for these facts. Earlier investigators, notably Sokolov and R. H. Charles, accepted the longer texts as nearest to the original, and explained the shorter ones as the result of condensation.[6] N. Schmidt, A. Vaillant, and N. A. Meshchersky, in contrast, concluded that the longer texts were the result of expansion and heavy interpolation.[7] The extra material, therefore, tended to be discarded as probably inauthentic. These scholars, however, differ quite extensively in their arguments, and in their conclusions about the production of the book through its various stages. Reserve is called for. All of the material calls for reassessment. At the very least we should remain

[5] M. N. Tikhomirov, *Merilo pravednoe po rukopisi XIV veka* (Moscow, 1961).

[6] M. I. Sokolov, "Materialy i zamětki po starinnoĭ slavyanskoĭ literaturě," Vyp. 3, VII: *Slavyanskaya kniga Enokha: Tekst' s' latinskim' perevodom'. Chteniya v' obshchestve istorii i drevnosteĭ Rossiĭskikh* [*COIDR*] 4 (1899) 1–80. This is the text of R with variants from U and other MSS. Idem, "Slavyanskaya kniga Enokha pravednogo: Teksty, latinskiĭ perevod' i izsledovaniye," *COIDR* 4 (1910) [A] 111–82 (posthumous publication of the texts that Sokolov had collated); [B] 1–167 (his nn. on the texts). R. H. Charles, *The Book of the Secrets of Enoch* (Oxford, 1896).

[7] N. Schmidt, "The Two Recensions of Slavonic Enoch," *JAOS* 41 (1921) 307–12; A. Vaillant, *Le livre des secrets d'Hénoch: Texte slave et traduction française* (Paris, 1952); N. A. Meshchersky, "K istorii teksta slavyanskoĭ knigi Enokha (Sledy pamyatnikov Kumrana v vizantiĭskoĭ i staroslavyanskoĭ literaturě)," *Vizantiĭskiĭ vremennik* 24 (1964) 91–108; idem, "K voprosu ob istochnikakh slavyanskoĭ knigi Enokha," *Kratkiye soobshcheniya Instituta narodov Azii* 86 (Moscow, 1965) 72–78.

open to the possibility that some of the passages found only in manuscripts of the longer recension could preserve ancient traditions, some of which might well be original. Abbreviation as well as expansion has almost certainly taken place. In the present state of our knowledge, the genuineness of any disputed passage is difficult to judge.

The claims of the longer recension need special attention in the sections dealing with creation, chapters 24–33. These chapters contain many weird notions in the longer recension, some of which could be embellishments. But the shorter account is so incomplete and so disjointed that it seems more like the debris left after drastic revision than an original succinct account. Some, at least, of the creation passages found only in manuscripts of the longer recension are worthy of more serious attention than they have received.

Original language

Three possibilities have been defended by scholars. The work now exists only in Slavonic, and no certain trace of it has been found elsewhere. A. S. D. Maunder claimed that 2 Enoch was composed in Slavonic, and is a late medieval concoction.[8] But this is quite improbable. It is possible that some early Slav assembled these materials and translated them, but he is hardly likely to have composed them. And the extensive connection with 1 Enoch, however indirect, can hardly be denied. Most of the early religious literature in Slavonic was translated from Greek; 2 Enoch can hardly be an exception. Other cases are known of rare works surviving on the fringes of civilization, in languages such as Ethiopic and Armenian.

Greek is indicated as the language behind the Slavonic version, if not the language of the original composition, not only by the inherent historical possibilities of the case, but also by passages whose linguistic features preserve traces of Greek words and expressions. The best known of these are the anagram and the names of the planets in chapter 30. The anagram, which connects the name of Adam with the points of the compass, makes sense only in Greek. Yet such evidence is not entirely conclusive. First, this is an old tradition, and the Jews who mixed Greek science with their biblical studies took over this kind of terminology into Hebrew or Aramaic. Secondly, these key passages are missing from manuscripts of the shorter recension; so, if it could be shown that they are secondary interpolations, they do not prove that the original work as a whole was composed in Greek.

The text abounds in Semitisms; but several explanations of this are possible. It is theoretically possible that the book, or at least parts of it, came directly from Hebrew into Slavonic. This is what Meshchersky has argued for the shorter recension, which he takes to be the original work.[9] But it is more likely that the Semitisms are due to Hebrew (or Aramaic) sources behind the Greek version, or at least due to the cultivation of a biblical style in the Greek original. Now that it is known that parts of 1 Enoch existed in Aramaic in pre-Christian times,[10] it is more credible that 2 Enoch stands in another stream of Enoch traditions stemming from similar sources, and perhaps even of comparable antiquity. An original Semitic composition can still be suspected; but after two stages of translation through Greek to Slavonic, it is not now possible to tell how much written material in a Semitic language might lie behind those portions of the text which still have Semitisms, let alone to determine which Semitic language it might have been.

Date

Since no manuscripts older than the fourteenth century are known, any time before that is available as the date by which the book reached its present form. But evidence for the complete texts of the two main recensions is somewhat later than that, and the earliest evidence (that of *MPr*) different from both of them. This divergence is probably the result

---

[8] A. S. D. Maunder, "The Date and Place of Writing of the Slavonic Book of Enoch," *The Observatory* 41 (1918) 309–16.

[9] Sokolov, in his paper on the Phoenix, "Feniks' v' apokrifakh' ob' Enokhě i Varukhě," in *Novyĭ sbornik stateĭ po slavyanovedeniyu*, ed. V. I. Lamansky (St. Petersburg, 1905) pp. 395–405, pointed to pre-Christian writings in Heb. behind the Gk. text used by the Slav. translator. The suggestion that 2En (that is, the shorter recension, which he considers to be original) was actually translated directly from Heb. into Old Russian was first made, so far as I know, by N. A. Meshchersky in "Sledy pamyatnikov Kumrana v staroslavyanskoĭ i drevnerusskoĭ literaturě (K izucheniyu slavyanskikh versiĭ knigi Enokha)," *Trudy otdela drevnerusskoĭ literature [TODRL]* 19 (1963) 130–47; idem, "Problemy izucheniya slavyano-russkoĭ perevodnoĭ literatury XI–XV vv.," *TODRL* 20 (1964) 180–231; and in the papers cited in n. 7 above.

[10] J. T. Milik, *The Books of Enoch: Aramaic Fragments of Qumrân Cave 4* (Oxford, 1976).

of transmission in Slavonic, with extensive expansions and contractions (see nn. to the translation). The original translation could have been made in an early period of Slavic literacy, but even so the supposed Greek composition need not have been produced earlier than A.D. 1000. Of course the Greek author could have made use of ancient material, and almost certainly did. But the very freedom of the treatment makes it impossible to prove that any passage which resembles something in another work is a quotation, whether a quotation from 2 Enoch in some other work of known date (proving that 2En existed prior to the writing of the work which quotes it), or whether a quotation from some other work used by the author of 2 Enoch (proving that 2En must be later than the work which it quotes). And, quite apart from the elusive character of such evidence, even if it could be proved that 2 Enoch contains such a quotation, this might be no more than a late gloss, and not an integral part of the original work. Of this character are the references to the Julian calendar which are obvious glosses and settle nothing concerning the date of the main text. The suspected echoes of the New Testament seem to be of this kind, and betray more likely the hand of a Christian scribe than the mind of a Christian author. In view of this complicated situation, it is not surprising that dates ranging all the way from pre-Christian times to the late Middle Ages have been proposed for the production of 2 Enoch.

The rather improbable suggestion that 2 Enoch is no more than a medieval assemblage leaves uninvestigated the more important question of when and where these gathered materials were produced. Recognizing that the book is in all likelihood the result of a long and complex process of collecting and editing—a process which we cannot now reconstruct—the question of date becomes more complicated. The task is to date and locate the major stages (admittedly hypothetical) in the literary growth of the work. The questions of date and provenance thus go together.

Provenance

All attempts to locate the intellectual background of 2 Enoch have failed. There must be something very peculiar about a work when one scholar, Charles, concludes that it was written by a hellenized Jew in Alexandria in the first century B.C., while another, J. T. Milik, argues that it was written by a Christian monk in Byzantium in the ninth century A.D.

Affinities with the Qumran writings have been noticed; some of these can probably be explained by the use of 1 Enoch as the source of such features as the calendar. In spite of Milik's claims, and Vaillant's theory that 2 Enoch is a Christian revision of Jewish Enoch (1En), very little can be demonstrated by way of direct connection between the two works, and the divergences are numerous and substantial. In particular, 1 Enoch has an interest in history not present in 2 Enoch, while 2 Enoch has an interest in creation not present in 1 Enoch. Independent of this connection is the interest in Melchizedek, which was lively at Qumran.[11] If ancient, this part of 2 Enoch should be added to the Qumran Melchizedek traditions as background for the Christian treatment of this theme in Hebrews.[12]

The most remarkable token of continued puzzlement over this work is the failure of scholars to decide whether it came from Jewish or Christian circles. It hardly stands in the mainstream of either religion.

In spite of its evident biblical style, there is no point at which it can be shown to depend on the text of the New Testament, barring obvious Christian glosses, whose extraneous character is betrayed by their presence in only one manuscript or at most in manuscripts of one family. There is not a distinctively Christian idea in the book. Alleged use of it in the New Testament (evidence that it is a pre-Christian Jewish work) is in passing phrases of a very general kind; either 2 Enoch and the New Testament are drawing on a common background, or else a later author is vaguely influenced by such expressions.[13]

[11] In addition to Horton's monograph (cf. n. 3), see J. A. Fitzmyer, "Further Light on Melchizedek from Qumran Cave 11," *Essays on the Semitic Background of the New Testament* (London, 1971) pp. 245–67.

[12] For repeated arguments that the Melchizedek story in 2En is a pre-Christian Midrash see I. D. Amusin, "Uchitel' pravednosti kumranskoĭ obshchiny," *Yezhegodnik muzeya istorii religii i ateizma* 7 (1963) 253–77; idem, "Izbrannik boga v kumranskikh tekstakh," *Vestnik Drevneĭ Istorii* 1 (1966) 73–79; and esp. idem, "Novyĭ eskhatologicheskiĭ tekst iz Kumrana (11QMelchisedek)," *Vestnik Drevneĭ Istorii* 3 (1967) 45–62; idem, *Teksty Kumrana. Vypusk 1. Perevod s drevneyevreĭskogo i arameĭskogo, vvedeniye i kommentariĭ* (Pamyatniki pis'mennosti vostoka 33.1; Moscow, 1971).

[13] Apart from similarities to Jude and 2Pet, which are a distinct problem, 2En comes closer in language and ideas to Mt than to any other part of the NT; but it does not resemble Rev, as might have been expected. It is more likely that Mt and 2En have a similar milieu than that a later Christian author of 2En was influenced by only one book of the NT.

Vaillant's arguments that 2 Enoch is a Christian revision of 1 Enoch are unconvincing. Quite apart from the difference in scope, his main point is that 2 Enoch is not quite so hard on sinners! It could be argued, however, that the rabbis were more lenient than the apostles in this matter, and there is nothing in 2 Enoch as savage as Revelation. As already noted, the suspected quotations from the New Testament, adduced by Vaillant and others, do not amount to much; but more important is the total lack of a Christian Savior or scheme of salvation. On the contrary, Enoch occupies an exalted position as God's chosen and prime agent which is totally incompatible with Christian belief in Jesus as Messiah. Judaism and Christianity agree in highlighting God's justice in punishing the bad and rewarding the good; but a higher virtue is compassion expressed in mercy toward repentant sinners. According to the Christian Gospel, this mercy is mediated to mankind through the incarnate divine Redeemer, and secured by his atoning passion. In contrast, 2 Enoch is altogether severe. In spite of one extraordinary passage which says that Enoch takes away the sin of the world, there is another which denies any efficacy for mediatorial prayer, even Enoch's. A blessed afterlife is strictly a reward for right ethical behavior.

This does not mean that the work is Jewish; it lacks some of the most distinctive and definitive tenets of main-line Judaism. In fact, it knows nothing of developments between the Flood and the end of the world, so there is no place for Abraham, Moses, and the rest; there is no reference to the Torah. Instead, the writings attributed to Enoch are advanced as the essential guide to life and salvation; but the vital knowledge they convey does not go any further than belief in one God as the Creator, and the practice of a simple ethical code.

It would go a long way toward solving the mystery of 2 Enoch if we could discover a religious community that venerated it on its own terms. If the work is Jewish, it must have belonged to a fringe sect. If it was ever a sacred scripture of a real group, they could have been a community of God-fearers (the highest virtue in 2En 43:3), who were able to combine a strictly Jewish belief in one Creator-God (based on Gen, but combined with hellenistic metaphysics) and simple but strict ethical rules, with speculations about the cosmos, including a tincture of astrology. Add to this some typical sectarian concern about such things as tying the four legs of an animal when making a sacrifice, which is documented as a deviant practice on the margins of Judaism,[14] and a fanatical belief in the correctness of their own solar calendar (everything is regulated by astronomy, hence the week is not a unit in God's time and there is no interest in the sabbath).[15]

In some respects these features remind us of Philo's Therapeutae, whose simplicity Philo admired. But the Therapeutae, in contrast to the author of 2 Enoch, seem to have revered Moses.

If 2 Enoch does go back to the turn of the era, it is a source of the highest importance for the history of syncretism of selected parts of the Jewish faith with cosmological speculation. It has no intellectual strength, for there is no system, and the attempt to be philosophical is spoiled by unreflective folk notions. 2 Enoch could derive from any region in which Jewish, Greek, Egyptian, and other Near Eastern ideas mingled. Proto-gnostic speculations, such as the ordering of the ranks of heavenly beings, or the suggestion that Adam was originally a heavenly creature expelled from a heavenly Paradise after his fall, are hard to pin down. Egypt, or Syria-Palestine, or Asia Minor could have been the seedbed; but it is impossible to discern how early or how late such ideas were around. There are ingredients suspected of being Iranian in origin;[16] but in spite of claims sometimes made, the work is totally devoid of dualistic thinking, except for a passing belief that man is free to choose good or evil. There are, of course, fallen angels. As in 1 Enoch, they serve to explain Genesis 6:1–4; but there is nothing like the symmetry of the spirits of light and darkness as at Qumran.[17]

The Melchizedek legend constitutes a special problem. The fantastic details about this priest conflict both with Christian belief in Jesus as God's sole legitimate priest in heaven and with the Jewish idea that the descendants of Aaron (or Zadok) are God's sole legitimate

---

[14] S. Pines, *Types of Redemption*, pp. 72–87.

[15] A. Rubinstein, "Observations on the Slavonic Book of Enoch," *JJS* 15 (1962) 1–21.

[16] Cf. Pines, n. 14.

[17] J. H. Charlesworth, "A Critical Comparison of the Dualism in 1QS III, 13–IV, 26 and the 'Dualism' Contained in the Fourth Gospel," *NTS* 15 (1968–69) 389–418 (reprinted in *John and Qumran*, ed. J. H. Charlesworth [London, 1972] pp. 76–106).

priests on earth. The miraculous conception of Melchizedek without human father (not strictly virginal, and with no mention of a divine agent, such as the Holy Spirit) is a typical wonder story, made somewhat ridiculous to our taste by the circumstance of the spontaneous delivery of the infant from his mother's corpse. But it is certainly not an imitation of the account of Jesus' birth found in Matthew and Luke.[18] No Christian could have developed such a blasphemy (and we can imagine a scribe refusing to copy this part); and why should a Jew answer the Christians in this way when a more obvious and more scurrilous explanation of Mary's pregnancy was at hand? The Melchizedek materials from Qumran, regrettably fragmentary, do not line up with the Melchizedek story in 2 Enoch, except in the very general sense of being Midrashim. But this evidence at least shows that at the turn of the era Midrashic embellishments of terse biblical accounts could take on quite fantastic elements. The more sober treatment in Hebrews, while including features not derived from the Old Testament (but not demonstrably derived from any other known materials), could well be a fresh Christian attempt to say something on this current subject that would fit in with the Gospel.

If 2 Enoch does preserve ideas from an early setting in Palestine or nearby, its main importance would be its manner of interpreting the Torah. In particular, its various comments on the creation passages in Genesis could represent one of the earliest attempts to reconcile Scripture with science.

Historical importance

In every respect 2 Enoch remains an enigma. So long as the date and location remain unknown, no use can be made of it for historical purposes. The present writer is inclined to place the book—or at least its original nucleus—early rather than late; and in a Jewish rather than a Christian community. But by the very marginal if not deviant character of their beliefs, its users could have been gentile converts to moral monotheism based on belief in the antediluvian God of the Bible as Creator, but not as the God of Abraham or Moses.

Theological importance

Some passages sound as if there was a sect which accepted the Enoch writings as sacred scripture in the highest sense, but who they might have been we cannot now discern. The book is organized around the story of a journey and return, but it has no undergirding conceptual system. The monotheism is stark, but the God is altogether forbidding—not like the merciful father of all mankind that Jews and Christians believe in—and the attempts to describe him border on the ridiculous, although intended to be reverent and awesome. (The comparison with hot iron emitting sparks if we had only 22:1 could be judged an interpolation; for it occurs only in "longer" MSS. But it occurs again in 39:3, where it is found in *both* recensions.) Creation itself is explained by the extraordinary and quite unphilosophical notion that, when God alone existed, he was not at rest. A disproportionate amount of space is given to the duties of the innumerable angels in the various heavens, with the result that God himself is hardly involved in running the universe. In the longer recension the creation of man receives a lot of attention, and some analytical observations are made on his physiological and psychological constitution.

The ethics are general and humane. The traditional form of beatitude as the medium of moral exhortation is extensively used. Embedded in the conventional moralizing, alongside such quaint ideas as man's accountability for his treatment of animals, is an ethical idea as sublime as any found in Jewish or Christian teaching, an idea equal to the noblest doctrines of any ancient moralist. Man is the facsimile of God, God's visible face. Any disrespect for any human being is disrespect for God himself. This interpretation of the *imago dei* in ethical rather than metaphysical terms is quite enough to justify the inclusion of 2 Enoch within the Pseudepigrapha.

Translations

Sokolov attached a Latin translation to his 1899 edition of manuscript R. W. R. Morfill supplied the English translation from an eclectic text used in Charles's 1896 book. N. Forbes

---

[18] R. E. Brown, *The Birth of the Messiah* (Garden City, N.Y., 1977).

revised this for the *Apocrypha and Pseudepigrapha of the Old Testament,* separating the longer recension (Charles's A—from P) and the shorter (Charles's B—from N), and displaying them synoptically. Unfortunately the manuscripts used were the worst representatives of the two recensions.

G. N. Bonwetsch's German edition presented separate translations of the longer and shorter recensions based on all of Sokolov's published evidence.[19] He presented the Melchizedek legend separately. P. Riessler's edition contains another German version.[20] Vaillant's French edition, which highlights U, is the best working translation. He compiled ample textual and philological notes, but relegated to an *annexe* the material of the longer recension. Kahana made a Hebrew translation of R for his edition of the Pseudepigrapha.[21]

The reference system

There is no schema of chapters and verses common to the manuscripts, and no agreed convention among modern scholars. Sokolov introduced his own verse numbers, which have been followed by some. Charles's schema is different again. Vaillant's method of referring to a passage by the page and line number in his edition has little to commend it, since it depends on the accidents of typesetting.

The existing literature probably uses Charles's schema more than any other, so this has been retained here as much as possible. We have made the following minimal but necessary adjustments: (1) The chapter enumeration has been taken from the longer, rather than the shorter, recension, from which some whole chapters are missing and in which, at one point, the chapters come in a different sequence. (2) The chapter enumeration has been continued into the Melchizedek appendix, rather than numbering this as a distinct work. (3) Where Charles's verse numbers follow an abnormal verse sequence, we have changed the sequence to the text of A as a standard. (4) We have tried to mark the verse boundaries more precisely than Charles, and to make them the same for both recensions where they match. (5) We have supplied verse numbers for the long preface for convenience of reference.

The translation and its presentation

The translation tries to achieve three goals. It provides an idiomatic English translation of two prime manuscripts of 2 Enoch. It seeks to reproduce the peculiarities of the original sources as precisely as English will permit, even though the result might not be elegant. And it displays the two recensions side by side so that their similarities and differences may be viewed synoptically.

These aims sometimes conflict. The two manuscripts chosen are A (for the shorter recension) and J (for the longer). Since they are not always complete or superior, they need to be supplemented at some points by the readings in other manuscripts. When a portion of the text is lacking in A or J, it will be supplied from another source of the same recension. When another manuscript has an important variant to a reading present in A or J, this alternative will be supplied in a footnote. All such supplementary material will be clearly identified. The main text always corresponds to either A or J, even when their readings are inferior or erroneous or unintelligible. When necessary an ambiguous passage is clarified in a note. Space forbids the provision of a full textual apparatus, which would be very large because of the endless variations in spelling. Variant readings have been restricted to those in which a material difference is involved. We have resisted the temptation to make the English more readable by smoothing out textual difficulties.

A has been chosen to represent the shorter recension without prejudice as to its overall superiority. It was chosen for three reasons. First, because up to now it has never been published or used, and its very existence has escaped the attention of Western scholars; secondly, because the availability of photographs of A enables this lack to be remedied; thirdly, A is virtually identical with U, whose importance as an exemplar of the shorter recension is generally recognized. When another manuscript of the shorter recension has a

---

[19] G. N. Bonwetsch, *Die Bücher der Geheimnisse Henochs: Das sogenannte slavische Henochbuch* (TU 44; Leipzig, 1922).
[20] Riessler, pp. 452–73, 1297f.
[21] A. Kahana, *Ha-Sefarim ha-Ḥitṣonim le-Torah* (Jerusalem, 1936–37; reprinted 1978).

reading where A has nothing, this additional text is added to the translation of A, again without prejudice as to its claims to authenticity. Such passages could be either additions that have been made to A's kind of text, or original material that has been lost in A's line of transmission. Sometimes it will be obvious which of these explanations is more likely; but often it is not. It is wise at this time to leave such questions open.

Quite a few manuscripts which stem from the shorter tradition are only excerpts; but there are some which preserve a more ample text, although not as complete as that of A and U. There are two main kinds. To keep the picture simple, only two additional manuscripts, one of each kind, have been used to supply supplementary material in the translation itself. Such extras obtained from B are put in ⟨. . .⟩. Manuscript V is the best representative of the third kind of shorter manuscript; its special readings are shown in |. . .|. A further reason for using V is the fact that it has never been published; hitherto we have depended on its inferior congener N, the source of Charles's B. In short, the translation of the shorter recension presented here is the text of A supplemented by B and V.

A similar policy has been followed with the longer recension. J has been given pride of place for three reasons. First, because the full text has not been published before; secondly, because J is generally superior to P, its nearest congener, which has been prominent up to now as the source of Charles's A; thirdly, because J and P are further away from the shorter recension than R, the only other reasonably complete manuscript of the longer kind. We thus present the evidence of the most divergent texts. In addition, J goes on to the Melchizedek Midrash, which P lacks. Even so, it ends abruptly, and after 71:5 R is the only witness to the Melchizedek story in the longer tradition. Since P² is virtually identical with P its readings hardly matter. Hence it is possible to present all the textual evidence for the longer recension by supplying supplementary readings from R in ⟨. . .⟩ and supplementary readings from P in |. . .|. The most common occasions for the latter are the chapter titles, including often the enumeration "Word '1.' " These are peculiar to P and obviously secondary, even within the longer tradition. Sometimes they interrupt the text in a most unsuitable way; see, for instance, the transition between chapters 47 and 48, 53 and 54, 56 and 57, and the chapter heading between verses 1 and 2 of chapter 60.

Textual variants in the notes are alternatives, not supplements to what is in the main translations. Trivialities, such as the article, which does not exist in Slavonic, have not been included in this schema. {. . .} enclose a passage which is considered erroneous in the original manuscript, usually due to dittography.

The translation is as literal as English will tolerate. An attempt has been made to preserve distinctions in the vocabulary of the original by always rendering the same Slavonic word by the same English word. This information is often important for textual history. The name for the deity is mainly *gospodĭ*, which is always rendered "LORD." The occasional *vladykŭ* is "Lord," and *bogŭ* is "God." Since English has only one word for "Paradise," we have used it for *poroda* (a loan) and translated the native *rai* as "paradise." Without the aid of a concordance, we cannot guarantee complete success, since there are many pairs of synonyms of minor importance. The intensification of adjectives by means of the prefix *prĕ-*, which seems to be due to efflorescence in transmission of the text, is generally shown by means of "very" or, when it seems to be elative, "supremely." There was no convenient way to avoid thereby obscuring the use of the adverb *zĕlo*, "very."

Our presentation of numbers as either words or numerals reproduces the peculiarities of the manuscripts. We have even preserved some peculiarities of spelling, where they are of interest. Thus the various spellings of proper nouns, like Mathusalam and Edem, are exactly as found in the originals.

The synoptic display introduces numerous unsightly gaps into the printed text, especially in the shorter recension. We hope that the gain in facility for comparative study will outweigh the aesthetic loss.

In addition to the abbreviations listed at the beginning of this collection, noteworthy for this contribution are the following:

MSD   Sreznevskiĭ, I. I. *Materialy dlya slovarya drevnerusskogo yazyka.* 3 vols. St. Petersburg, 1893–1903.

OE   Vostokov, A. *Ostromirogo Evangelie 1056–57 goda.* St. Petersburg, 1843. [Repr.

O. Harrassowitz, vol. 1 of *Monumenta Linguae Slavicae Dialecti Veteris Fontes et Dissertationes*, eds. R. Aitzetmüller, J. Matl, L. Sadnik.]
SJS   Kurz, J., ed. *Slovník Jazyka Staroslověnského* (Lexicon Linguae Palaeo-Slovenicae). Prague, 1966– .
SRY   Barkhudarov, S. G., ed. *Slovar' russkogo yazyka XI–XVII vv.* Moscow, 1975– .
US   Kotkov, S. I., ed. *Uspenskiĭ Sbornik XII–XIII vv.* Moscow, 1971.

Translator's note

The purely provisional state of the present treatment of 2 Enoch must be underscored, at every level: text, translation, and notes. In spite of years of endeavor, including a visit to the U.S.S.R. in search of manuscripts, many needed materials are still not available. In particular, a thorough study of the *Disputatio* is essential, and it is an embarrassment that the present contribution must go forth before this task is accomplished.

The progress we have made would have been impossible without the continual encouragement of Professor James H. Charlesworth. Thanks to his tenacity, we were able to secure microfilms of the manuscripts A and J which are the basis of this edition. As editor, he and his staff have had an unusually difficult job in preparing these unfamiliar materials for the press. Although some will still maintain that 2 Enoch is a work of dubious authenticity (as a pseudepigraphon of the Old Testament, belonging with the other works in this volume, that is) and of doubtful value, all that has still to be debated thoroughly. Professor Charlesworth has insisted that a new attack on these problems requires a fresh presentation of the evidence. This translator wishes to acknowledge gratefully his share in the final production.

SELECT BIBLIOGRAPHY

Charlesworth, *PMR*, pp. 103–6.
Delling, *Bibliographie*, p. 160.
Denis, *Introduction*, pp. 28f.

Bonwetsch, G. N. *Die Bücher der Geheimnisse Henochs: Das sogenannte slavische Henochbuch.* TU 44; Leipzig, 1922.
Charles, R. H., and W. R. Morfill. *The Book of the Secrets of Enoch.* Oxford, 1896.
Meshchersky, N. A. "Concerning the History of the Text of the Slavonic Book of Enoch," *Vizantiĭskiĭ vremennik* 24 (1964) 91–108. (In Russian.)
———. "Concerning the Problem of the Sources of the Slavonic Book of Enoch," *Kratkiye Soobshcheniya Instituta narodov Azii* 86 (1965) 72–78. (In Russian.)
Pines, S. "Eschatology and the Concept of Time in the Slavonic Book of Enoch," *Types of Redemption*, eds. R. J. Z. Werblowsky and C. J. Bleeker. Supp. Numen 18; Leiden, 1970; pp. 72–87.
Vaillant, A. *Le livre des secrets d'Hénoch: Texte slave et traduction française.* Paris, 1952; repr. Paris, 1976. (Cf. my review in *RSR* 6 [1980] 74.)

2 (Slavonic Apocalypse of) ENOCH
[A] the shorter [J] the longer recension

2 ENOCH [J]

1a The story of Enoch:[a] how the LORD took him to heaven

|There was| a wise man and a great artisan whom the LORD took away.[d]   1
And he loved him so that he might see the highest realms;[f]   2
and of the most wise[g] and great and inconceivable and unchanging   3
kingdom[h] of God almighty, •and of the most marvelous and glorious and shining   4
and many-eyed[i] station of the LORD's servants, and of the LORD's immovable
throne,[j]

1a a. The titles in the MSS show a great variety.
U is the same as A; J P R have a preface of similar
form and scope, but with many differences. Rum
has essentially the same text as theirs through vs.
2 of the preface. P and P[2] begin: "The Book
(about) the secrets of Enoch, the son of Ared,"
after which P[2] adds "from The Pearl of Great
Price" and goes on immediately to the creation
story in ch. 28, whereas P continues "a man wise
and loved by God." In R the work is called "The
book of the holy secrets of Enoch, a man . . .,"
continuing in P. J's term "story" (*slovo*, lit.
"word") is the same as that used by P for the
individual chs. It can mean a literary work, or
simply "tale" as in *Slovo o polku Igoreve*, "The
Tale of Igor's Expedition."

Some titles do not have the word "secret." *MPr:*
"From the book of righteous Enoch"; B: "The
life of righteous Enoch, a man . . ." The latter—
bytija—is reminiscent of Gen. P's title is very long;
it designates Enoch as "a wise man and beloved
by God" followed by a detailed note about the
place and circumstances of making this copy. [The
notes to 2En are more extensive than our general
rule. This divergence is intentional because of the
importance of the recently discovered MSS, and
the refined methodology. J.H.C.]

b. The titles vary between "book" and "books."
Thus Tr: "which are called The Secret Books of
Enoch"; and V N: "And these are the books
(called) The Secrets of God, a revelation to Enoch";
B[2] is similar, but singular. This fluctuation could
reflect a tradition that there were several, or many
Enoch books and that this one is (1) a many-
volumed work; or (2) one of these books (*ot of* A
U is partitive); or (3) extracted from them. The last
is appropriate when we have a deliberate excerpt,
as in *MPr*. The other two meanings can be covered
by the fact that this is at once an account of the
origin of the many known books of Enoch and also
one of them, although not one of the set which
Enoch himself made in heaven.

Great importance is attached to the books that
Enoch wrote in heaven. God emphasizes their key
role for the last generation (chs. 33, 35, 36) and
Enoch repeats this several times in his final charge
(chs. 47, 48, 50, 53, 54). These could be the secret
books hidden away until the end-time (68:2). 2En
is then the book that tells the story of these books.
This awareness of a corpus of Enoch writings wider
than 2En itself, but dealing with subjects which
are listed in 2En, suggests that 2En was written
with immediate and detailed knowledge of such

books. It was an introduction to them. The repeated
emphasis on the importance of these books for the
spiritual well-being of the community of "the last
generation"—"the men of truth" (35:2), who will
study and obey these writings (36:1)—makes sense
only if such works were actually available in the
circles that produced 2En. The works which fit this
best are the books now collected under 1En; the
community that revered them must have been
something like the Qumran community. But the
community that generated them is not Qumran
itself, for the surviving fragments of Enoch books
in Aram. are older than the foundation at Qumran
and the outlook of 2En is quite different from that
at Qumran, except in the matter of the calendar.

c. A galaxy of epithets has gathered around
Enoch in the titles. Without tracing each one to its
MS, they include (1) wise man, (2) great scribe,
(3) great artificer, (4) righteous, (5) beloved by
God. The additional appellative in A U resembles
Gi blĝvi oče, which is conventional in titles to
extracts from the lives of saints in Christian miscellanies. A scribe evidently considered 2En to be
a similar hagiographical composition. He is, however, called *vladyko*, "master," rather than "father."
It is more likely that this refers to Enoch than to
God. A double name for the deity is rare in 2En;
then it is *gospodinŭ bogŭ*, "LORD God."

d. The MSS have so many different readings
that it is hard to decide which is best. The more
ample text of P is clear and logical, but Vaillant
(*Le livre des secrets d'Hénoch: Texte slave et
traduction française*, p. xvii), supposing it to result
from the corrections of a reviser, reconstructs the
textual history as follows:.

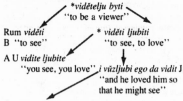

       *vidětelju byti
       "to be a viewer"

Rum *viděti*   * *viděti ljubiti*
B "to see"   "to see, to love"

A U *vidite ljubite*
"you see, you love" *i vŭzljubi ego da vidit* J
          "and he loved him so
          that he might see"

P *ego vozljuby, i prijati ego gdī da vidit*
"the Lord conceived love for him and received
him, that he should behold . . ." (*APOT*, vol. 2,
p. 431)

A difficulty in Vaillant's restoration is that it
supposes a different noun from the one at the end
of the paragraph. This could be overcome by

2 ENOCH [A]

1a From the secret book(s)[b] about the taking away of Enoch the just,[c]

1   a wise man,   a great scholar, whom the LORD took away.
2   to see,[e]   to love   the highest realm;
3 and of the most wise and great,   unchanging
4 and almighty sovereignty of God, •and of the very great
many-eyed
and immovable throne of the LORD, and of the brightly shining[k]

---

reading *viděcǐ* at both places; but the form in -*l* is essential for his theory that the verb "love" has arisen by misdivision.

There can be no doubt that the statement goes back ultimately to Gen 5:24: "Enoch walked with God. Then he vanished because God took him." This is altogether laconic. It could mean no more than an explanation of Enoch's premature death as an act of God. In Job 1:21 the same idiom means removal by death. In Gen 42:36 *'ēnennû,* "he is not," means "he is dead." In 2Kgs 2:3 the Lord "took" Elijah to heaven without dying, and it was easy to see this as supplying the missing details of Enoch's translation. This becomes explicit in Heb 11:5, and in 1Clem 9—he "was translated, and death was never known to happen to him." LXX is literal—*hoti metethēken auton ho theos.* Sir 44:16 and Heb 11:5 use the passive *metetethē,* a pious convention already evident in 1En 12:1 (*elēmphthē*). In this respect 2En is more primitive, or at least closer to the Heb. than these later accounts. In any case Charles's "received" is uncertain, if it is not his reception but his removal.

e. The words "to see . . ." and ". . . to be a witness" (vs. 6) constitute an inclusion around the long list of noun phrases which describe what Enoch saw. Strictly speaking the comprehensive term "the upper(-most) realm" is the object of "see" and all the rest is the object of "witness." Morfill's original division of the list was mistaken (*The Book of the Secrets of Enoch* [Oxford, 1896] p. 1). The list itself is carelessly compiled. It covers only a small part of the contents of the book, since it corresponds mainly to the seventh heaven.

f. Sokolov solved the textual problem discussed above by emending to *ljubitelja.* Enoch is to become a *lover* of the upper regions. This is altogether improbable. The phrase *vyšnjag(o) žitia* of A is plural in J P. Hence "the heavenly abodes" (Morfill, *Secrets of Enoch,* p. 1) or "uppermost dwellings" (Forbes, *APOT,* vol. 2, p. 431), *miškěnôt měrômîm* (Kahana, *Ha-Sefarim ha-Ḥitsonim le-Torah* [Jerusalem, 1936–37; reprinted 1978]). There is no need to compare this with Jn 14:2. The plural could have arisen from within the book itself, which does talk about eternal residences prepared for both good and bad. In ch. 61, however, three quite different words are used—*khranilišta,* "shelters," *khraminy,* "residences," *domy,* "houses." Here the singular is correct. Like *politeuma* (Phil 3:20) *žitie* can refer to manner of life, with an emphasis on order. This is its sense in 68:4—"this present life."

B has a gloss—*nižnjaja i vyšnjaja,* "lower and upper." 2En did not include a subterranean hell in its cosmos. In fact, one of the remarkable things about 2En is that its nearest equivalent to a traditional hell is a region in the north of the third heaven (ch. 10). But there are some passages which are under pressure to include the netherworld (18:7). The gloss in the preface of B is another result of the same tendency. It does not fit, because Enoch makes no visit to any lower region. But cf. 40:12.

g. Slav. *premoudryi* "wise" (A), is not a suitable attribute of "kingdom" (cěsarīstvo [A]) unless the latter means "reign" (*cěsarīstvije* [J]). It applies to God, where J uses *mudryi,* which suits Enoch (see n. c).

h. "Sovereignty" or "kingdom." *Cěsarstvo* can be abstract or concrete, like the Gk. *basileia,* which it habitually translates.

i. This epithet has a different referent in each list. The variation between the recensions in the use of the adjective "many-eyed" may reflect conflicting traditions about its appropriate use. The normal spelling is *mŭnogo-očityi.* P (*mnogoočitago*) is better than U (*mnogočitaᵍ*).

This, like other words in the preface, echoes Christian liturgical terms. In Ezek 4 the four creatures who are God's seat and vehicle are "full of eyes" (4:18). Their connection with the throne is clear from Rev 4:6, but 2En distinguishes the throne from the "station" of the Lord's servants, and J P ascribe "many-eyed" to the latter, A U to the former. Ezek 10:12 has a more extravagant description of creatures whose bodies are covered with eyes. The preface keeps the seraphim and cherubim distinct from these, and from each other. The latter are connected with singing, the former are probably intended by the fourth item, for they are either "bodiless" (J) or "fireborn" (A). In other texts they are associated as "many-eyed" and "six-winged," e.g. *mŭnogoočitii kherovimi i šestokrilataea serafima* (*SJS,* vol. 2, p. 241).

j. R at this point lacks five words and portions of two others. A space is left. One fragment supports J's *nepodvižimago* ("immovable") against P's *nepostižimago* ("incomprehensible"). Vaillant interprets it as "immobile," but Ezek 1 suggests the opposite. The idea is closer to Heb 12:28. Unlike AscenIs, which has a throne in each heaven, 2En knows only the throne of God in the seventh heaven.

k. A U do not use 2En's characteristic "glorious," found in J P R, but their *presvětla,* "very bright," is a synonym.

[J]

•and of the ranks and organization of the bodiless 5 armies, and of the indescribable composition of[m] the multitude[n] of elements, •and of the variegated appearance[o] and indescribable 6 singing of the army[p] of the cherubim,[q] and of the light without measure,[r] to be an eyewitness.[s]

1 |Concerning Enoch's dream|

At that time[a] he said, When 165 years were complete for me, I fathered my son 1 Methusala; and after that I lived 200 years.
I completed all the years of my life, 365 years. • In the first month,[c] on the 2 assigned day[d] of the first month, I was in my house alone.

---

l. Lit. "fireborn." Unless reflected in this word, the seraphim are not included in the list of the preface. They are present in 20:1, 21:1 in long MSS. Fire and light are fundamental elements in the physics of 2En. Fire enjoys varying prominence in the several creation sections of the book. Light is primary, fire derivative. Darkness comes first (ch. 24), then light (ch. 25). Water is made from light (ch. 27), rock is made from water (ch. 28), and fire comes from rock (ch. 29). The angels are created from this fire (29:3).

m. The term "ministration" (*APOT*, vol. 2, p. 431) derives from P's *služenia*. This is a mistake due to the frequency of *slouženije* elsewhere in 2En, where it refers to the liturgy rather than, say, the service of administrative duties. No other MS has it. All the rest read *složenīja*. It is true that the heavenly beings are called "elements" at various points, and the preface is mainly interested in angels, not physics; but these are not the primal matter—four "elements" or even one. They are multitudinous. Slav. *složenije* could be the indescribable "composition" of any one of these elements (in that case they would not be elementary); or else the innumerable formulae by which the elements combine to make the diverse materials of the universe.

Here, as elsewhere in 2En, it is hard to decide whether the texts have drifted from scientific terminology ("combination of elements") to something more mythological (the organization of the various ranks of beings), or the reverse.

n. Slav. *mŭnožīstvo* normally renders the Gk. *plēthos*. Does the longer reading of A U represent the biblicism "myriad myriad"? The word "element" (*stikhii* or *stoukhii*) could be the physical elements or "ranks" of angelic beings. We cannot tell how close this is to the *stoikheia* of the NT. In 2En 13:9 the *stoukhii* are angels of some kind.

o. The recensions differ at this point. R is defective. J P: *ob'javlenie*, "manifestations" (?).

p. Or "host," Heb. *ṣābā'* and *ṣēbā'ôt*. This terminology pervades 2En. The military character of the Lord's heavenly retinue goes back to the war theology of early Israel. 2En still knows of "armed" troops, but no combat is reported. Some angels serve as guards of prisoners, even as tor-

turers. Otherwise the parade order is that of a choir. Little can now be discerned of a chain of command, although there seems to be an echelon of officers. It is no longer possible to discern the human army upon which this celestial counterpart might have been modeled.

q. As in the West, the Heb. plural has been taken as the stem, and repluralized with Slav. suffixes.

r. The idea of boundless light occurs in *Pistis Sophia*.

s. The translation "eyewitness" attempts to distinguish the variant *samovidecĭ* from *vidēcĭ* or *viditelĭ*.

1 a. The reading from Jn 3 in *OE* begins with such a phrase, which is not in the Gk. But the position of the adjective there (*vŭ ono vrěmja*) is not as Hebraic as 2En 1:1. This abrupt beginning sounds like the continuation of some preceding narrative, and suggests that 2En is part of a larger work, a Midrash on Gen. But note that the second Lat. recension of the GBart begins in exactly the same way.

The ending of 2En is similarly abrupt since a continuation into the story of the Flood is called for. The story presupposes that the reader knows the background, but no explanation is given of Enoch's grief. The book does not even repeat the one thing that Gen says (twice!) about Enoch, namely, that he walked with God.

This unprepared onset makes it necessary to supply some kind of title. The one now present is clearly artificial, and its limited attestation and wide variation shows that it is an addition; but it cannot be a late addition, since it is found in MSS of both recensions which have already diverged substantially in details.

We can suppose, then, the extraction from a larger Midrash of the history from Enoch to the Flood, and its designation, rather inexactly, "the Book of Enoch" or the like. This is a misnomer, except for those MSS which end with the second ascension of Enoch. This has led to an altogether prejudiced assessment of the Melchizedek portion. While the Enoch story occurs without the Methuselah, Nir, Melchizedek continuation, the latter

[A]

5 station of the LORD's servants, •and of the ranks of the powerful, fireborn,[1] heavenly armies, the indescribable combination of a

6 great multitude of elements, •and of the variegated appearance and indescribable singing of the army of the cherubim, and of the light without measure, to be a witness.

1

1 And at that time Enoch said, When 365[b] years were complete for me,   Gen 5:21–23

2   •in the first month, on the assigned day of the first month, I was in my house alone,

never occurs except as part of the Book of Enoch. There is continuity; and the references back to Enoch in the Melchizedek section, as well as the similarity of style, suggest an original and integral work. Charles's omission of this Melchizedek material is thus unfortunate and mistaken.

b. Cf. Gen 5:23. A connection with the solar year has been suspected in this figure. But the solar year in 2En was originally 364 days.

c. V N read "second." Morgenstern (1924) has shown that at least three different calendars were used in ancient Israel. In the first (based on the solar year), the Canaanite names of the months were used. In the second system, the months were designated by number, the first corresponding to a New Year in the fall. The third system was the Babylonian lunar-solar calendar (still in use), and the Babylonian names were used. These appear also in 2En 73, complicated by the presence of Egyptian month names as well.

This feature of 2En is thus typically Jewish. But this does not mean that 2En is to be explained in terms of the Jewish liturgical year as we know it from biblical or rabbinic sources. In fact, its defiant use of a solar calendar points away from this. Its first month, which probably means the New Year month, could begin with the spring equinox. Since this calendar divides the year into four equal seasons, this would mean that Enoch finally went to heaven at the summer solstice, a suitable time for such an event. If Morgenstern is right in his argument that the latest priestly legislation embodied in biblical rules for observing both Passover and Sukkoth has swung into line with the Babylonian lunar calendar in which the first full moon after the autumn equinox takes place on the fifteenth day of the first month, with an intercalated month from time to time as needed, then 2En's calendar is different in many respects. 2En has only a trace of the Metonic cycle of nineteen years, found also in the Babylonian calendar, and accordingly passed on to Christians as well. But 16:8 is an evident gloss.

2En is heterodox in the matter of the calendar, but not unique. Quite apart from its possible dependence on 1En for such details, its agreement with Jub suggests similar antiquity. Yet in other

respects it diverges from Jub and Qumran. It has no interest in a seven-day week nor in the sabbath observance. The few references are glosses never integrated with prime texts. So we cannot tell whether 2En is a later reflex of this interest in a 364-day solar calendar, and that of a rather academic kind, found only among scribes; or whether it is archaic and conservative, and of vital importance to a community that tried to use such a calendar.

J. Morgenstern ("The Three Calendars of Ancient Israel," *HUCA* 1 [1924] 13–78, esp. p. 65) definitely thinks that the calendar of 1En and of Jub, in spite of the unworkable 364-day year, is related to the old Canaanite solar calendar. In fact, Jub 6:36–38 contains a polemic against the lunar calendar as an innovation. 2En does not contain such polemic, but its lunar calendar is geared to the solar year.

At least it can be said that the Enoch writings have a solar year with New Year at the vernal equinox, and this sets the date for Enoch's first translation.

d. The best MSS of both recensions agree that the day is *naročitiĭ*. R has a unique gloss which effects repetition of the whole expression—"in the first month, on the intended day of the first month, on the first day." It uses the numeral ã, but the adjective *prŭvyi* each time with "month." A U,
however, have *mc ã a*, with š ğ above the *a*, and this numeral could have produced R's numeral, since the sequence is the same. J has a reading much closer to A U, except that, like P and R, it reverses the noun-adjective sequence. This agreement of A U J then gives the best reading—"in the first month, on the designated day of the first month." In P this has been simplified to "on the 1st day of the first month," thus eliminating the obscure technical word. We cannot assume that it was a Jewish New Year's Day. Indeed, Jewish custom rules this out. According to Megillat Ta'anit (17b, 18a) 1–8 Nisan was a period in which it was forbidden to mourn or to use penitential self-mortification, and the first in particular, a new-moon day, could not be other than joyous. The scribal error "first" could only arise from ignorance of Jewish practice, unless 2En is heterodox.

[J]

And I lay on my bed, sleeping. •And, while I slept, a great distress entered my 3
heart, and I was weeping[e] with my eyes in a dream.[g] And I could not figure out
what this distress might be, |nor| what might be
happening to me. •Then two[h] huge[i] men[j] appeared to me, the like of which I had 4
never seen on earth.

Their faces were like the shining sun; 5
their eyes were[k] like burning lamps;
from their mouths fire[l] was coming forth;
their clothing was various singing;[m]
their wings[n] were more glistering than gold;[o]
their hands were whiter than snow.

And they stood at the head of my bed[p] and called me by my name.[q]
Then I awoke[r] from my sleep, and saw those men, standing in front of me, in 6
actuality.[s] •Then I bowed down[u] to them; and I was terrified; and the appearance 7
of my face was changed[v] because of fear. •Then those men said to me, "Be 8

e. There is a tradition that apocalyptists are upset
by evil in the world, or by inability to understand
the plan of God (Dan 7:15; Rev 5:4; 4Ezra 3). 1En
83:3 explains that Enoch was already distressed by
the evil brought upon the world by the fallen
Watchers. But a presupposition that this lies behind
Enoch's unexplained grief in 2En is not needed.
The motif could have been derived from a traditional
convention.

f. The sequence A U is inferior. V N read "I
was distressed, weeping with my eyes," a better
idiom.

g. R lacks nine words found in J P ("in a dream
[or sleep] and I could not understand what is
distress"), so that the remaining words ("This
which might be to me") are quite unintelligible. P
replaces *li* with *ili*. A U lack this statement entirely,
and, furthermore, have a much simpler picture:
Enoch is lamenting (no reason is given) and falls
asleep. Then the two men appear. J P, however,
and R in part, have a more complex development.
The weeping is part of the dream. If this is true,
then there is less need to look for some liturgical
setting for an act of penitence. After all, Enoch is
alone, in his house, on his bed.

But the recensions are different in this respect.
A gives the impression that first Enoch was weeping
alone in his house. No reason is given. Worn out
by grief, he lies down and falls asleep. He dreams
that he sees two men. In J the onset of distress
occurs after he falls asleep, again with no hint as
to its cause.

The place of this dream in the story is hard to
assess. The two "men" first appear in the dream,
then, when he wakes up, they are present in reality.
They could just as easily have come for him while
he was awake, so Enoch's dream contributes nothing to the plot.

h. Some MSS have the numeral. In what follows
the better MSS often use dual forms; but we have
refrained from translating this pedantically as "the
pair of men."

i. The appearance of figures of gigantic size is
a common motif in apocalypses of the early period.
Compare 4Ezra and the Gospel of Eve. In GPet
the two young men (!) who appeared at the tomb

of Jesus were tall ("their heads reached into
heaven") and the risen Lord was even taller (*ANT*,
p. 92). V agrees with J P R in reading *prěvelika
zělo*, "very big indeed," but A lacks the prefix.

j. Note the fluctuation between "man" and
"angel" in Zech 1. We are to suppose angels in
human form taken for the occasion. Their names
are given, rather casually, in 33:6. Even so, their
dimensions, and the following description, show
that this was not a disguise. In fact human form
need not be implied and "man" might mean,
simply, "person." The coming of angels in pairs
is an ancient tradition, going back to the two
"messengers" who conventionally accompany a
god on a journey in Canaanite mythology. Hence
the two "men" who accompany the Lord on his
visit to Abraham (Gen 18f.; cf. Gen 32:25). Compare the "two men" at the empty tomb (Lk 24:4).
Compare Acts 1:10 and 2Mac 3:26 ("There also
appeared to Heliodorus two young men of surpassing strength and glorious beauty, splendidly
dressed"). The "two young men" are angels. Cf.
2En 33:11.

k. A U lack the words supplied, which are found
not only in J P R, but also in other MSS of the
short recension (V N B B²). The loss is due to
homoeoteleuton of repeated *jako*. A U's reading
"his mouth" is clearly inferior; *ego* can be explained as a corruption of the dual (*j)eju* (which V
N R use correctly), which B and others have
replaced by plural *ikh*. J P have the dative. A U
have also moderated the concrete imagery by adding
"like" to fire, not found in B B².

l. The addition of *jako* to A U is inferior, since
other "short" MSS lack it.

m. The text at this point seems to be incorrigibly
corrupt. The MSS agree with surprising unanimity,
since the variants are mainly orthographical:

A	pěniju	razdaaniju
U	pěniju	razdajaniju
B	pěnija	razdnaja
B²	pěrĭe	različno
V	i penie	različno
N	pěnie	različ'no
R	pěnie	razděanie
J	pěnie	razdanie

[A]

3   4Ezra 3:1

weeping and grieving[f] with my eyes.
When I had lain down on my bed, I fell asleep.

4   •And two huge men appeared to me, the like of which I had   Dan 8:15
never seen on earth.

5

      Their faces 〈|were like the shining sun;   4Ezra 7:79;
      their eyes were|〉 like burning lamps;   Rev 1:16
      from his mouth (something) like fire was coming forth;   Dan 10:6;
      their clothing was various singing;   Rev 1:14; 19:12
      and their arms   Rev 9:17; 11:15
                 were like wings of gold—

at the head of my bed. And they called 〈me〉 by my name.

6,7   I got up from my sleep, and the men were standing with me in actuality. •Then   Dan 5:6,9,10;
I hurried[t] and stood up and bowed down to them;   Mt 14:27;
                                                   Acts 23:11
           and the appearance of my face was glittering because of fear.   2Kgs 1:15

P   i pĕniemŭ razdajanija
(P V have "and" between "clothing" and "singing").

Singing is a common theme in this book; at least it is a characteristic activity of the angels in the heavens. But it seems out of place at this point, where the whole interest is in the appearance of the men, and, specifically, their clothing. The matter is complicated by variation in the adjective that goes with "singing," although here the agreement of A and J is weighty.

n. At this point MSS of the shorter recension read like a garbled abbreviation; they have confused "the arms" and "the wings."

o. Compare the bird in the story of the ascension of Alexander, who forbids him to enter heaven.

p. This is the conventional stance of a dream visitor in relation to a sleeper. This is how the Lord stood "beside" Jacob in his dream at Bethel (Gen 28:12f.) as in NAB, not RSV, where the Lord is placed above the ladder. Compare 1Sam 3:10.

q. When the Lord appears in a vision he often addresses the person by name.

r. The MSS differ in the verb used to describe Enoch's arousal; and they do not divide into long and short. Both alternatives are found in MSS of both recensions, as V *vizbnouv* shows, while P has *vostakh*, closer to A U. Something similar happens with "my" in "my sleep"; V (short) agrees with R (long) in reading *svoego;* J P (long) agree with A U (short) in *moego*. A has the participle "having stood up."

s. The term "actuality" implies objectivity, not a dream. It means that what he saw on waking was exactly the same as what he had seen in his dream, as just described.

t. Slav. *az že uskorikh i vstakh*. The awkwardness of the construction, which seems to be a Hebraism (*w'mhr w'qm*), is shown by the chaos of MS readings. The normal idiom in Slav. is *uskoriti* plus the infinitive, which means "to speed up," not just "to act quickly." One variant (V N R) is *oujadri*, also followed by an infinitive. But R has dropped the second verb, and reads "I hastened to them," while J P have dropped the first verb. V

changed *vstakh* to the participle *vŭstavi*, which reverses the sequence of actions.

u. Unlike John's angelic guide, who rebuked him for such behavior (Rev 19:10), and the angel in AscenIs, Enoch's visitors accept the homage. Cf. Gen 18:2.

v. The MSS differ considerably in their description of Enoch's reaction to the appearance of the men, making it difficult to establish what the original author might have said. There is agreement that his basic response was one of fear, and longer MSS have the verb *oužasokhsja* as well as the noun *strakhŭ*. This is part of the conventional response to such an epiphany. The traditional accounts of such events have doubtless molded the account here. The following words of assurance are also part of the scenario. Such stories have probably contaminated the text in transmission.

The longer text of J is the most general: "and the appearance of my face was changed *ot strakha* (*apo phobou*)." There are variants corresponding to the words "appearance" and "changed."

The simple *vidĕnie* of J (*vĕdĕnie* of P) matches *pridĕnije* of A U. Vaillant (*Secrets*, p. 4, n. 16) incorrectly states that both these similar readings derive from R's original *zrĕnjem*, from which he goes on to restore the unattested original * *srĕniemĭ*, suggesting a cold, rather than a bloody, sweat. But "hoar-frost" is hardly acceptable; the emendation is too conjectural. Such a change could be due to the fact that "the appearance of my face" is redundant. Other MSS, notably B, read simply "my face." R's variant *zrĕnje* suggests that Enoch's vision was blurred; but this contradicts the statement that the men were plainly visible. More likely it means "my face changed at the vision," hence the instrumental; *zīrĕnije*, "sight," can be subjective or objective (*SJS*, vol. 1, p. 691). A's variant points in the same direction since *pridĕnije* (*SJS*, vol. 3, p. 261) has the connotation of "apparition" (*phantasma*); hence the instrumental case.

There are several variants of the verb. R could mean "I covered up my face from fear." Compare APOT, vol. 2, p. 431 (derived from N). B says "my face was covered with tears (*rydaniem*)," but B[2] has *rdeniemŭ*. The image is incongruous, since

[J]

brave, Enoch! In truth,[w] do not fear! The eternal God has sent us to you. And behold, you will ascend with us to heaven today.[x] •And tell your sons, ⟨|and all the members of your household,|⟩ everything that they must do in your house while they are without you on the earth. And let no one search for you until the LORD returns you to them." •And I hurried and[y] obeyed them; and I went out of my house and I shut the doors as I had been ordered. And I called my sons, Methusalam and Regim and Gaidad.[z] And I declared to them all the marvels that those men had told me.

2 |The instruction. How Enoch instructed his sons. "1."|[a]

"Listen, my children![c] I do not know where I am going, . nor what will confront me. •Now, my children, |I say to you|:

> Do not turn away from God.
> Walk before his face,
> and keep his commandments.[d]
> Do not abhor the prayers of your salvation,[e]
> so that the LORD will not curtail the work of your hands.
> And do not be ungenerous with the LORD's gifts, and the LORD will not be ungenerous with his donations and love-gifts in your storehouses.[f]
> And bless the LORD with the firstborn[g] of your herds and the firstborn of your children, and a blessing will be on you forever.
> And do not turn away from the LORD, and do not worship vain[h] gods, gods who did not create the heaven and the earth or any other created thing;[i] for they will perish, and so will those who worship them.

And may God make your hearts true in reverence for him.[j]
And now, my children, no one must search for me until the LORD returns me to you."

---

oblijati (*SJS*, vol. 2, p. 477) means to cover by pouring something over something. Thus the story of Boris and Gleb includes the words: *i vĭsĭ slĭzami oblijavŭ sja reče*, "and with all tears covering himself, he said:" (*US* 12b: 25–27). Compare *i vodoju oblijati lice jeja*, "and with water to cover her face" (*US* 138b:18–19). So we have the idiom "my face was bathed with sweat."

The reading of A U, *bleštac(a)*, suggests that his face was shining (or blanched?). The verb really means "to be radiant," and it is not part of the vocabulary usual for the terror response to an epiphany of this kind (*SRY*, vol. 1, p. 238). It would be more appropriate for the visitors. Thus the translation of Luke's version of the resurrection story in the Ostromir Gospel describes the two men in dazzling apparel (24:4), *vŭ rizakhŭ blištjaštakhŭ sja*. The women are terrified and fall to the ground. In view of the mobility of the vowels, and their frequent omission in spelling, we suggest either that A U means "and they were dazzling [white]" or that it should read * *bělěstasja* or the like, meaning "the appearance of my face turned white."

w. R agrees with J, "in truth." This additional phrase resembles a reading of Zech 8:13 found in Glagoliica Iosephi Vajs: *dr'zaite v istinu i krěpěte ruki vaše*. R has "LORD" instead of God, found in other MSS. B and V agree in the variant "youth" for "Enoch." Cf. ch. 10, n. j.

x. The word order corresponds to differences in MSS of the two recensions.

y. A Hebraism, both in the idiom (*mhr*) and in the semantics of "hear" = obey as Heb. *šm'*.

z. A has Methusalom and Regim as Enoch's sons. J adds Gaidad, who is *'îrād*, son of Enoch in the genealogy of Gen 4:18. In 2En 57:2 the sons of Enoch are:

A Mefusailom, Regim, Rim, Asukhan, Khermion

J Methosalam, Regim, Riman, Ukhan, Khermion, Gaidad

At each place the longer recension has added Gaidad from LXX.

2 a. The numerals in the ch. titles are reproduced here exactly as they are used in MS P. Sometimes the ch. is called *slovo*, "word."

b. The reading "I know" (A U) seems to be a

[A]

8 And the men said to me, "Be brave, Enoch!   Do not fear! The eternal
LORD has sent us to you. And behold, today you will ascend with us to heaven.
9 And you will tell your sons ⟨|and the members of your household|⟩ everything that   Gen 4:18;
they must do in your house   on the earth. And of your house let no one   2En 57:2
10 search for you until the LORD returns you to them." •And I   obeyed
them, and I went off.
      I called my sons, Methusalom and Rigim.
And I declared to them all   that the men had told me.

2

1 "And behold, I know^b ⟨my⟩ children, I do not know where I am going,   2En 7:5
2 nor what will confront me. •And now, my children: 1Sam 12:20

> Do not turn away from God,
> and walk before the face of the LORD,
> and keep his judgments.
> And do not diminish the sacrifice of your salvation,
> and the LORD will not diminish the work of your hands.
> Do not be ungenerous with the LORD's gifts; the LORD will not
> be ungenerous with his donations   in your storehouses.
> Bless the LORD with the firstborn of your herds and
> of your children, and you will be blessed by the LORD forever.
> Do not turn away from the LORD, nor worship unreal gods,
> who did not create either the heaven or the earth.

> ⟨They will perish.⟩   Jer 10:11

3 And may the LORD make your hearts true in reverence for him.
4 And now, my children, no one must search for me until the LORD returns me to
you."

---

simple error, since it is immediately contradicted.

  c. The readings in A and V are dual (compare
1:10) because two sons of Enoch are known in the
short recension. But the next occurrence is plural.
MSS of the longer recension have three sons in
1:10 and plural "children." Dual forms are also
used fairly consistently to refer to Enoch's two
angelic escorts. Of the seven injunctions, V has
only the first three and the last. It is remarkable,
but perhaps coincidental, that this omission corresponds roughly to the lacuna in P.

  d. Slav. *sudby*, "judgments," is the better reading, since R agrees with A U. P has a large lacuna
at this point; hence Charles's A text. J reads
zapovědi, "commandments." This is a significant
variant, for it draws attention to the difficulty felt
with the original *sudůby*. The latter is a palpable
Semitism, obviously *mišpāṭîm*, often used in the
OT to include ethical instructions or moral customs.
But for scribes who knew *sudůby* = Gk. *krimata*
the meaning of "verdicts, punishments" does not
suit; hence the change to the word that translates
entolai.

  e. Perhaps J R mean "make your prayers for

salvation odious (to God)." In any case the reading
is inferior. The original was intended for a community which practiced sacrifice.

  f. B adds "Bless the LORD!"

  g. R J repeat "firstborn." The identity of the
second item is not clear. Vaillant's "oxen" is the
result of emendation. The dominant *yunot* (R) or
yunošĭ (B) (agreement between long and short MSS
is important) is not intrinsically difficult (Ex 13:2;
22:29f.; 34:19f.). J reads *vnučjat*, "grandchil-
dren," which, however curious, at least confirms
that they are human. A U agree in *nuty*, "oxen";
but it is more likely that this easier reading is
secondary, since there are accompanying alterations.

  h. The translations "vain" (*pustošnyi*) and "unreal" (*suetnyi*) represent quite different, although
synonymous, words in the original.

  i. J agrees with R in the additional "nor any
other created thing," but P lacks it. V N B B² add
"they will perish," found also in long MSS, which
have further, "and those who worship them."

  j. P reads *vo stranakh svoikh*, "in your places."

[J]

3 |About the taking away of Enoch; how the angels took him on to the 1st heaven. "2."|[a]

And it came about,[c] when I had spoken to my sons, those men[d] called me. And 1 they took me up onto their wings, and carried me up to the first heaven,[e] and placed me on the clouds. •And, behold, they were moving. And there I perceived 2 the air higher up, and higher still I saw the ether. •And they placed me on the first 3 heaven. And they showed me a vast ocean, much bigger than the earthly ocean.[f]

4 |About the angels who govern the stars. "3."|

They led before my face the elders,[a] the rulers of the stellar orders. 1

And they showed me the 200 angels who govern the stars and the heavenly combinations. • 2

---

3 a. Only P has regular ch. headings. They are sporadic in other MSS. Their secondary character is shown by two features. They often use language identical with the text that follows, which brings about repetition; or they introduce new (later) terms not found in prime texts. MSS which have a title at this point vary between *vzjatie* (P) and *vŭskhoženie* (V). A U have *vŭskhyštenije* at the beginning. The translation "assumption" (*APOT*, vol. 2, p. 432) is scarcely warranted. *SJS* (vol. 1, p. 298) lists *vŭzjatie* as occurring only in Euchologium Sinaiticum. The corresponding verb *vŭzjati*, which is simply *lāqaḥ* or *lambanein*, is common in 2En and is generally used when the two men "take" Enoch from place to place. *Vŭskhož(d)enije* is *anabasis*, while *vŭskhyštenije* is "rapture."

b. With no other indication of a new ch., A has .ã. in the middle of the line. V completes the line with :•~ :•~ :•~ and then has a rubric—*vŭskhoženie enokhovo na .a.-e n̄bo*, which has a certain affinity with P's ch. heading.

c. The Hebraic character of the narrative composition is manifest in the abundant parataxis, and especially in the opening "and it was" (= *wayĕhî*). The unacceptable character of this idiom is shown by its alteration, either by dropping "and" (R P) or by changing *bystī* to *bykhŭ*, "I was" (A U). The latter is influenced by the autobiographical form, which is sustained in this ch. But P has changed "me" to "him" through the whole of vs. 1 (*APOT* A), against all other witnesses. It reverts to first person in vs. 2.

d. At this point A has *a n̄bo* in the margin, and a very large *I* to begin the next section. B has a similar ch. heading.

e. It should be noted that P is the only MS that calls the "men" "angels" at this point. All agree that they have wings. In the longer MSS the journey has two stages: First Enoch is placed on the clouds, then on the first heaven (same idiom). The clouds are a vantage point, not a vehicle. Although J supports R's "they were moving," P's "I looked" is superior. In describing the two stages the words "and they placed me on" occur twice. The intervening material is lacking in short MSS, an obvious instance of loss by homoeoteleuton, which is very

common in these MSS. But Vaillant considers extra material an inept addition by the reviser. But the text of P (*APOT*) is garbled; J and R agree that Enoch distinguished the air *vŭzdukh* from the *aierī*, borrowing this Gk. word to designate the ether. According to Eph 2:2 this is Satan's domain. Compare 2En 29:5. If the text of 2En came from a Gk. original, the correct sequence would be *aēr aithēr*. Having translated the first by *vozdukh*, the second would have been borrowed. Hence the ignorant use of the loan suggests composition in Slav. This distinction between atmosphere and stratosphere is already present in Homer. Made more systematic by later philosophers, ether becomes the fifth element. 2En is thus nearer to Homer than to Aristotle.

These layers are met in a six-tier scheme in a prayer in ActsJn (112).

f. This verse is 4:2 in A U. Several motifs of 2En 3 are found in TAb 7:19–8:3.

4 a. The *šestodnevtsa* (No. 238) of Prince P. P. Vyazemsky calls the ten archangels, whose names it gives, who are commanders of the ten orders of angelic powers, "the elders of the heavenly forces." 2En's elders are distinct from the two hundred angels who govern the stars. There seems to be a chain of command; so the elders could be senior angels, but in early Jewish and Christian literature the elders in heaven seem to be human. (A. Feuillet, "Les vingt-quatre vieillards de l'Apocalypse," *RB* 65 [1958] 5–32). 2En does not say how many elders there were. They are not the same as the "leaders" of 1En 82, for they are in charge of the seasons (four) and months (twelve), whereas the elders in 2En are "lords of the starry divisions." The location of angels on this first (the lowest) heaven is contrary to the usual astronomy which locates the (fixed) stars above the spheres of the seven planets. In 2En also (21:6—long MSS only) the stars and "the heavenly houses of the 12 zodiacs" are in the ninth heaven. This contradicts ch. 4, and also the account of creation in ch. 30, where the stars are placed in the lowest heaven, with the moon, or even below that in the air (30:4). The missing link between Rev and 2En could be

[A]

3 |The ascension of Enoch to the first heaven.|[b]

1 And it came about, when I had spoken to my sons, the men called me. And they Acts 1:9
took me up onto their wings, and carried me up to the first heaven.   And they
2 put me down there. •
3   Rev 4:6; 15:2;
                                                                               TLevi 2:7

4

1 They led before my face the elders, the rulers of the stellar orders. And they Rev. 4:4
showed me their movements[b] and their aberrations from year to year. And they
showed me in the light[c] the angels who govern the stars, the heavenly combinations.[d]
2 And they showed me there a vast ocean,[e] much bigger than the earthly ocean.
And the angels were flying with their wings.

---

supplied by the Beth Alpha mosaic. In its center circle the sun is surrounded by twenty-three stars and the crescent moon. Putting stars and the moon together corresponds to 2En 30:4. The number twenty-four corresponds to the number of elders in Rev.

It is important to emphasize that although ch. 30 is almost totally lacking from short MSS, they do have the stars in the first heaven in 4:1.

b. The correlative terms *šestvije* and *prekhoženije* occur again in 11:1 (with many variants in the latter term among the MSS). They invite a search for something precise by way of astronomical terminology. In describing the various cycles of nature, the verbs "go in" (*vŭkhod*) and "go out" (*izkhod*) are used, along with many variants, such as *vǐskhod-, proiskhod-, prikhod-, obkhod-*. At most points the MSS display great uncertainty as to which verb to use. Thus 5:2 describes the movements of clouds. According to J they go out and they go in; according to A they go in and they go out.

Two pictures are possible. Either the clouds go into the treasuries and then go out into the sky, or they come out into the sky and then return to the treasuries. The latter is probably intended, because the rising and setting of the sun and moon are described by the verbs *vkhoditi* ("he enters") and *iskhodit* ("he leaves"), although even this language is not used consistently. Thus in ch. 13 the rising of the sun for half the annual cycle is *iskhodit*, but *vkhodit* for the remainder (which Vaillant, *Secrets*, p. 12, wants to correct to *vŭskhoditŭ*). It could depend on the point of view of the observer. As we see it, the sun comes *into* the world in the morning and goes *out* at night. From the sun's point of view, he goes *out* into the world when he rises and goes back *in* at night.

Both *šīstvije* and *prěkhož[d]enije* can denote movement in general; but *obkhoženije* probably connotes "return." Note that in 13:4 *obūšīstvije* is the seasonal turning of the year.

So the terms might refer to the waxing and waning of the moon (although the month lengths do not fit that) or to the recession of the sun up to midwinter and his return up to midsummer, a

phenomenon described in 48:3.

We conclude that *šestvije* describes regular movement, such as the rising and setting of the sun; and *prekhoženije* describes a perturbation imposed on that, such as the annual movement of sunrise point across the horizon that lies behind ch. 13. The "aberrations" of the stars, referred to here, would then be another way of looking at *hai tropai hēliou*. Thus Cancer is in conjunction with the sun at the summer solstice; and so on.

The following phrase, "from year to year," can thus be taken literally. Vaillant's translation, *d'un temps à un autre* (*Secrets*, p. 7), recognizes a stage in the language when *godŭ* still meant simply "time" and not yet precisely "year." But the phrase used here seems to mean "annually" (*SJS*, vol. 1, p. 414). This fits in with the calendrical interests of 2En, which describes the movements of the sun and moon through the course of a year, but does not go into conjunctions and eclipses which vary from year to year.

We cannot be certain; because ch. 4 might be speaking only about the planets, not the fixed stars. But note 30:4.

c. Slav. *vu světě* (A), *vo světe* (U). This reading is demonstrably in error, since all long MSS (J P R) read *.č.*, the numeral 200, and so do V N. B B² have the word *dvěsti*. Vaillant plausibly supposes an intermediate * *.v. stě* (for *dŭvě sŭtě*, both duals), which some scribe has misread as an abbreviation of *vŭ světě*, "in the light." It is important to emphasize that the same error has given rise to the spurious "Lord of light" in 2En 18:3 (*APOT*, vol. 2, pp. 439f.); see the n. there.

d. "Combinations." P's reading. Slav. *služenija*, "services" (*APOT*, vol. 2, p. 432), must be discarded, although it is found in B also. All other MSS agree in *složenia*. See the same confusion in 1a:5. Vaillant's translation *combinaisons des cieux* may be questioned, especially since he annotates: *sans doute les constellations*. Except for a reference to the zodiac in 21:6 (probably spurious), 2En does not discuss the constellations, and here the "combinations" are probably the conjunctions of the planets.

e. In J P R this comes in 3:3.

[J]

And they fly with their wings, and do the rounds of all the planets.[f]

5 |About how the angels guard[a] the storehouses[b] of the snow. Word "4."|

And there I perceived the treasuries of the snow and the ice,[c]   1
and the angels who guard their terrible storehouses, •   2
and the treasury[d] of the clouds, from which they[e] come out and go in.

6 |About the dew and about olive oil and various flowers. Word "5."|

And they showed me the treasuries of the dew, like olive oil.   1
And the appearance of its image was like every kind of earthly flower, only more
numerous; and the angels who guard their treasuries, how they are shut and
opened.

7 |About how Enoch was taken to the 2nd heaven. Word "6."|[a]

And those men picked me up[b] and brought me up to the second heaven. And they   1
showed me, and I saw a darkness greater than earthly darkness. And there I
perceived prisoners[c] under guard,[d] hanging up,[e] waiting for[f] the measureless
judgment. •And those angels have the appearance of darkness itself, more than   2
earthly darkness. And unceasingly they made weeping, all the day long. And I

f. Vaillant's interpretation (*Secrets*, p. 9) of this obscure phrase, found only in the longer recension, is an improvement on the previous "and come around all those who sail" ("swimmers," *APOT*, vol. 2, p. 432).

It is true that *plavati* primarily describes swimming or marine navigation, but I have not found any other occurrences of the planets as "swimmers" in heaven. It seems unlikely that these angels have jurisdiction over travel on the great celestial ocean that has just been described. The immediate context, in longer MSS at least, is the government of stars. The idea that angels supervise the heavenly bodies in their movements is prominent in 2En. The verb *obŭkhoditi*, "go around, surround," fits the picture. We are to imagine that the *obŭkhodĭnikŭ* (= *periodeutēs*, an itinerant inspector) "does the rounds" of the "stars" making sure that they are functioning properly. Regularity is not automatic; there are no fixed laws of nature identical with the will of God or the truths of mathematics. But since the planets have been given their normal name "stars" in vs. 1, we cannot be sure that *plavajuštikhŭ* means "planets" precisely, but only those who might wander from the right path. Here we might have the idea that all is orderly in the upper *kosmos*, but in the lower *ouranos* things are sometimes irregular.

Note that all MSS have "they fly with their wings," but in the short tradition this reads like a fragment.

5 a. Slav. *dĭržati* normally means "keep" in the sense of "hold." But *MSD*, vol. 1, p. 775 lists *vladĕtĭ, pravitĭ* as meanings. Cf. *SJS*, vol. 1, p. 521.

b. The word "storehouses" used in the title (*khranilište*) is not the same as the word in the text

(*sŭkrovište*). Both come together in 5:1 in A U.

c. A has *khladnaa*, U essentially the same. But B has *golotnaja* and so do V N (which, however, have vs. 1 after vs. 2). Hence "cold" in *APOT*, vol. 2, p. 433. Originally * *kholdŭ*, the form in A is Slav. (Russ. *kholodnyĭ* [as in B²]), but it is not used for one of the elements in the lists in biblical texts. Since A has *golotnaja* at 40:10 in agreement with other MSS, its variant at 5:1 must be secondary. Slav. *golotnaja* corresponds to "frost." Cf. Ps 148:8.

d. A and U have an identical dittography at this point.

e. Presumably the subject is the snow and the frost, not the angels. On the verbs of motion, see n. b to ch. 4. Similar confusion occurs here. The variants represent two different ways of looking at the movement of the clouds. According to A, the elements first *go in* (*vkhodjat*) to the treasuries, and then go out (*iskhodjat*). But the relative adverb *otnjuduže* (or *otkuduže*—P's inferior reading) applies to "come out," but not to "go out." So the translation "into which they go" (*APOT*, vol. 2, p. 433) is incorrect. The awkwardness of A's idiom could account for the inversion of the verbs in R P. J has gone one step further, reading "go up and go in." Its first verb *vŭskodit* corresponds also to V N (all singular). Hence "goes up" (*APOT*, vol. 2, p. 433). The picture in R P is more like the way we view the rain cycle. The clouds first come out and then the water goes back in. In J the water goes up and goes back in. In V N, apparently, the clouds go up and come out. According to the Bible, the rain and snow come down from heaven and do not go back there (Isa 55:10). In the scheme of A U, the angels prepare the clouds and put them into the storehouse, ready to *go out* into the world.

[A]

5

1 And they showed me there the treasuries of the snow and the cold,   Job 38:22
2 terrible angels are guarding the treasuries. •And they   showed me there those guarding the treasuries; {and they showed me there the treasuries} of the clouds, from which they go in and come out.

6

1 And they showed me the treasuries of the dew, like olive oil. Angels were guarding their treasuries; and their appearance was like every earthly flower.

7 ⟨2 heaven.⟩

1 And those men   took me up to the second heaven. And they set me down   2Pet 2:4; Jude 6; on the second heaven. And they showed me   2En 18:4

2   prisoners under guard, in measureless judgment. •And there I saw the condemned angels,

7 a. A has *nbo* B [= 2] in the margin in large letters at this point.

b. Lit. "took me." Various verbs are used to describe the activities of the "men" in transporting Enoch from place to place. As many as three stages may be reported—(1) "picked me up"; (2) "carried me to"; (3) "put me down." As the story proceeds, there is a tendency to shorten the formula, generally by omitting the third item.

c. Slav. *užniky* (A, compare U) or *užiki* (B), that is *užinikŭ* = *desmios*; J P *veryžniki*, better *verižni* (R). The latter, attested in *SRY* (vol. 2, p. 89) but not in *SJS*, is probably East Slavic. Cf. *uzilišt*, *užilnicy užnici* at 10:3. The term points to angels (*desmophylaks*). It does not seem to be Christian vocabulary for damned spirits in the eschatological sense. But is it Jewish? In any case, the imagery is that of fetters, not "dungeons" (*APOT*, vol. 2, p. 433).

d. Slav. *bljudomy*, passive participle of *bljusti* (*SJS*, vol. 1, p. 117; *SRY*, vol. 1, p. 248; *MSD*, vol. 1, p. 121) = *phylattein, phylassein*. The passage resembles 2Pet 2:4 and Jude 6, but the correspondence of vocabulary is not complete enough to sustain a hypothesis of borrowing. Possible influence of Christian Scriptures on the transmission of 2En should be kept in mind as well. The longer and shorter MSS differ. The usual source of *tīma* (J) is *skotos* (*MSD* sub *tīma*). In J the adjective "great" modifies "judgment," not "day" as in Jude; "day" is lacking in 2En; but elsewhere "the day of the great judgment" is found. Both recensions have more in common with Jude than with 2Pet. To put it another way, they have nothing that is in 2Pet that is not in Jude, and the *siros* of 2Pet has no counterpart in the other texts. And there is nothing in the short MSS that is not also in long ones, except the different word for "prisoner," which does, however, bring in the idea of fetters

(cf. Jude). The evidence is not clear-cut enough to permit the explanation that the long recension is an expansion of the short one under the influence of Jude. For even the short recension already has affinities with Jude. In fact, the only point at which the long recension and Jude agree against short MSS is in the word "great," and even then the ideas are not quite the same, for Jude has "great day," 2En J "great judgment." Furthermore, and more seriously, "great" is found only in P— "measureless" is the better reading (all MSS); and 2En has the angels "weeping," J, in addition, "hanging" and "waiting."

e. Without any modification, we cannot be certain what *visjaša* means here. *Viséti* means either "to depend upon" or "to be suspended." (On the possible "wisdom" link between these two meanings, see W. F. Arndt and F. W. Gingrich, *A Greek English Lexicon of the New Testament* [Chicago, 1952] p. 451.) This verb is used of hanging (= crucifixion) in Lk 23:39; Acts 5:30; 10:39, and so describes suspension of an executed criminal (either in punishment or exposure), not of one awaiting sentence, as here. Has the idea come in from ApPet (7:22), which also has such things as "darkness" and the river of fire? At least the tradition is similar—but those are human sinners. Blasphemers are hung up by the tongue (*ek tēs glōssēs kremamenoi*), loose women by the hair, fornicators by the penis (surely!—not "thighs" as in HSW, vol. 2, p. 673—for this is a Hebraism from *raglayim*, "genitals").

f. This feature is curious because *žīdati* usually describes hopeful expectation with fervent longing; but "hope" would not fit. That such revaluation of *elpis* is distinctively Christian, see Zimmerli, *Man and His Hope*, and Bultmann on *elpis* in *TDNT*.

[J]

said to the men who were with me, "Why are these ones being tormented unceasingly?" •Those men answered me, "These are those who turned away[g] 3 from the LORD, who did not obey the LORD's commandments, but of their own will plotted together and turned away with their prince and with those who are under restraint[h] in the fifth heaven."[i] •And I felt very sorry for them; and those 4 angels bowed down to me and said to me, "Man of God,[j] pray for us to the LORD!"

And I answered them and said, "Who am I, a mortal man, that I should pray for 5 angels? Who knows where I am going[k] and what will confront me? Or who indeed will pray for me?"

8 |About the taking of Enoch to the 3rd heaven. Word "7."|[a]

And those men took me from there, and they brought me up to the third heaven, 1 and set me down |there|. Then I looked downward,[b] and I saw Paradise.[c] And that place is inconceivably pleasant.

And I saw the trees in full flower. And their fruits were ripe[e] and pleasant-smelling, with every food in yield and giving off profusely a pleasant fragrance. 2

And in the midst (of them was) the tree of life, at that place where the 3 LORD takes a rest when he goes[g] into paradise.[h] And that tree is indescribable for pleasantness and fine fragrance, and more beautiful than any (other)

created thing that exists. •And from every direction it has an appearance which is 4 gold-looking and crimson,[i] and with the form of fire. And it covers the whole of Paradise.[j] And it has something of every orchard tree and of every fruit. And its

---

g. The rebellion of Satanail and his followers is described in ch. 29 (long MSS only). These are "apostates," so literally *otŭstupiniku* (= *apostatēs*). The reading of A U, *zlostupnicy*, I have not found anywhere else. The intensified *prěstupiĭniku* is familiar, but the spelling points to the prefix *zŭlo-*, "evil," rather than *dzělo*, "very." The former follows the analogy of words intensified by *blago-*, "good." Hence "evil" is adjectival; the compound does not mean "those who turned aside to evil."

h. The nuance of *utvrŭždeni* is hard to establish ("confined," Morfill, *The Book of the Secrets of Enoch*, p. 6; "fastened," *APOT*, vol. 2, p. 433), for *utvĭržati* means "support," "strengthen."

i. This detail is lacking in short MSS, although the relevant information is present in them at ch. 18. In 2En 18:7 all traditions state that these fallen angels are "under the earth," a detail found also in 1En 10. (The second heaven in 2En is like the third heaven in ApPaul.) The scheme can be harmonized if the present location of fallen angels in the second heaven is temporary. After the judgment on "the Lord's great day" they will be consigned to a subterranean hell, anticipated in 2En 18:7. Cf. the conventional hell of 2En 40:13–42:2, occupied by damned humans.

In 2En there seem to be four grades of evil angels: (1) their prince, Satanail, apparently in the fifth heaven with (2) the Watchers, who consorted with women at Ermon; (3) the apostate angels of the second heaven; and (perhaps) (4) the ones condemned to be "under the earth." The NT also knows of hosts of wicked in heavenly places. Even Origen did not succeed in categorizing the various species of fallen angels. Two principles operate

oppositely. On the one hand, since the worst is the corruption of the best, the depth of all is proportional to original rank. Satan was one of the highest archangels; the Watchers, who commit the vile sins of Gen 6, become devils; the minor angels, who merely follow, become demons. But in 2En the heavens are in an ascending scale, and the wicked angels in the fifth heaven are worse than those in the second.

The characterization of the latter is vague. They evidently hope for salvation; they arouse Enoch's compassion. They request him to pray for them. This is not dismissed as impossible because their doom is inevitable. Rather he excuses himself with evasive replies: He is a man; he doesn't know where he is going; he doesn't have anyone to pray for him. Enoch's visit to the second heaven ends on this vague note.

j. J P have the variant *člče* for *mužu* of other MSS. V U say "to God," doubtless under the influence of the preceding title.

k. P agrees with A U etc., against the other short MSS, which have "and . . . or" rather than "or . . . or." P has *ili . . . albo*, the latter Old Ukrainian (*Slovnik staroukraïns' koï movi xiv-xv st.* (Kiev, 1977) vol. 1, p. 69).

8 a. A has G NBO, "3 Heaven" in large letters in the text; U in the margin.

b. This detail is only in J P. R agrees with short MSS. This literal translation suggests that he is still flying *sŭgljadavŭ krugŭmĭ = periblepsamenos*. In 2En 42 the paradise of Edem is located in the east as in the Bible, at least in the longer recension. In fact it is east of where the sun rises (42:4). It seems to be on the same level as the earth, since

[A]

weeping.   And I said to the men who were with me,
3 "Why are they tormented?" •The men answered me, "They are evil rebels
against the LORD, who did not listen to the voice of the LORD, but they consulted
their own will."
4   •And I felt   sorry for them.   The angels bowed down to me.   Deut 33:1
They said   , "Man of God, please pray for us to the LORD!"

5 And I answered them and said, "Who am I, a mortal man, that I should pray for
angels? And who knows where I am going or what will confront me? Or who
will pray for me?"

8

1 And the men took me from there. They brought me up to the   third heaven. 2Cor 12:2,4
And they placed me in the midst of   Paradise. And that place has an
appearance of pleasantness that has never been seen.[d]
2 Every tree was in full flower. Every fruit was ripe, every food was in yield Gen 2:9; Rev
profusely; every fragrance was pleasant. And the four rivers were flowing past Gen 2:9; 3:22;
with gentle movement, with every kind of garden producing every kind of good Prov 3:18;
3 food. •And the tree of life is in that place, under which the LORD takes a rest 15:4; 22:2,14;
when the LORD takes a walk[f] in Paradise. And that tree is indescribable for Rev 2:7; 4Ezra
pleasantness of fragrance.   ApMos 22:4

4

---

it is open as far as the third heaven (42:3).

The traditions about Paradise in 1En are similarly mixed. It has the "garden of life" (60:23; 61:12), "the garden where the elect and just live" (60:8), "the garden of justice" (77:3). It is across the ocean (77:3) "at the extremities of the earth" (106:7–8). This sounds like the place where Gilgamesh goes to consult Utnapishtim. This is where Enoch himself eventually goes (1En 60:8), and presumably the paradise to which Michael took Melkizedek in 2En 72:9. This is where Methuselah and Noah go to consult Enoch (1En 65:2).

Paradise is differently located in other parts of 1En. In chs. 37–71 he goes to the west (52:1), "to the extremity of the skies" (39:3). But in 70:1–4 he goes northwest. In the mythological journey of Enoch in 1En 17f., 23–25, Paradise is a marvelous garden to the northwest, near the divine mountain. It has the tree of life, and rivers come from it.

c. The Persian loan word has passed into many languages as a proper noun, Paradise. Originally Eden was the location of the garden, and Sumerian *Edin* means "steppe." Domestication into Heb. produced the etymology "pleasant." Hence *jannāt 'an-na'īm* or *jannāt 'adn* in the Koran, and the adjective *blag-* in 2En.

The designation of the heavenly paradise (*jannā 'āliyâ*) as "the garden of Eden" is a Jewish rather than a Christian tradition (Palache 1920). On the other hand, the transformation to *Edem* is LXX, while *Edom* is the Eth. term.

2En uses the term "garden" (= *gan*) only occasionally; but the connection is still there, especially in the emphasis on trees and fragrances.

d. A U read *nevidimo*. Other MSS (of several families) agree in *nesŭvĕdimo*. The reading of A U could be an error, influenced by the following *vidĕnija* (all MSS of the shorter recension), whereas

J etc. have *vidĕkhŭ*, "I saw." This emphasis on seeing throws doubt on A U's statement that Paradise has never been seen, unless it means that it was not like anything seen on the earth (3:3; 7:2). *SJS* gives a range of meanings for *nesŭvĕdomŭ*, including "indescribable."

e. P alone reads *zrĕkhŭ*, "I beheld," against *zrĕlŭ* (A and the rest), "ripe."

f. The tradition of Gen 3:8. But here it sounds like a continual practice, since this Paradise is part of the heavenly complex. Ezek 28:13 calls Eden "the garden of God," and Gen 13:10 knows about "Yahweh's garden," which is the ultimate in fertility and prosperity.

g. The reading *vŭskhoditī* of J P R V N contrasts with *vkhoditī* of B B² and is more difficult. U reads erroneously *khvoditī*. A reads *khoditŭ*, a secondary simplification (?). There is a similar difficulty in describing the movement of the clouds in 5:2. The idea of the LORD "ascending" into Paradise is incongruous with his usual location in the seventh heaven. *Vŭskhoditī* is the standard translation of *anabainein*; *voskhoždenije*, "the rising (of the sun)" is a characteristic derivative. The idea of return to origins or periodic return could be present.

h. The spelling "paradise" corresponds to *rai*, the native word.

i. The exact shade of *črŭvenno* is hard to establish. It could be dark red, crimson, or purple.

j. Slav. *ves porod* in which J P R agree. As Vaillant has pointed out (*Secrets*, pp. xvii and 88), this is a grammatical error. It should be *vsu poradu*, as if a scribe has replaced *rai* by *poroda* without adjusting the gender. The corresponding passage in the 1384 version of the *Disputatio* is *pokryvajetī vesī rai*. So there is no doubt that *porod* is secondary in 2En at this point.

[J]

root is in Paradise at the exit[k] that leads to the earth.

And paradise is in between the corruptible and the incorruptible.[l] And two streams 5
come forth, one a source of honey and milk, and a source which produces oil and
wine. And it is divided into 4 parts, and they go around with a quiet movement.
And they come out[m] into the paradise of Edem, between the corruptible and the 6
incorruptible. And from there they pass along and divide into 40 parts.[n] And it
proceeds in descent along the earth, and they have a revolution in their cycle, just
like the other atmospheric elements.

And there is no unfruitful tree there, and every tree is well fruited, and every 7
place is blessed.

And there are 300 angels, very bright, who look after Paradise; and with never- 8
ceasing voice and pleasant singing they worship the LORD every day and hour.
And I said, "How very pleasant is this place!" And those men said to me:

9 |The revelation to Enoch of the place of those who are righteous and kind.
Word "8."|[a]

"This place,[b] Enoch,[c] has been prepared[d] for the righteous, 1

> who suffer every kind of calamity[e] in their life
> and who afflict their souls,
> and who avert their eyes from injustice,
> and who carry out righteous judgment,
> and who give bread to the hungry,
> and who cover the naked with clothing,
> and who lift up the fallen,

k. It is hard to get the picture. Perhaps "extremity" is meant as in 1En 106:7f. Normally *iskhodŭ* (= *exodus*) means "going out" in the verbal rather than the substantive sense. I have not been able to find any equivalent of the phrase "the exodus of the earth." There is one clue, however. By a series of associations *iskhodŭ* can refer to the place where the sun rises (*môṣā'*). In Ps 75:7 (= 74.7), for instance, the MSS vary among *iskhodŭ vŭskodŭ vĭstaka* (= east). This agrees with 2En 42:4 (J).

These details are lacking in A etc., both in ch. 8 and in ch. 42. Either a scribe has added them to an original resembling A, not worrying about the inconsistency in the location; or else a scribe has removed them from a MS like J in order to alleviate the inconsistency. The position of the reference to the four rivers in 8:2 (A) seems awkward, since it interrupts the description of the fruitfulness of the trees. The description of Paradise in ch. 42 in A etc. seems rather vague contrasted with the details in the longer MSS. The notice about the olive tree (8:5, A etc.) seems unnecessary after the remark that the garden contains every kind of fruit tree. It seems to be debris from J's fuller account of the four rivers.

l. While this might suggest that Paradise is in a zone between heaven (incorruptible) and earth (corruptible), another explanation is possible. Ancient astronomy distinguished between *kosmos*, where order prevailed, and *ouranos*, where things were more irregular, or, at least, where change was possible. If, in the cosmology of 2En, heavens 1 and 2 are the region of change, and heavens 4–7 are changeless, Paradise, in the third heaven, is in between. But since there are fallen angels in both the second and the fifth heaven, and both good and bad human beings in the third heaven, this Paradise is not between two clearly defined levels of good and evil. The concept of "corruptible" does not seem to be moral.

The words *tĭlĕnije* and *netlĕnije* translate *to phtharton* and *aphtharsia* in 1Cor 15:53. The apostle switches from concrete to abstract, a fine but important point. The corruptible does not become incorruptible, it puts on incorruptibility.

m. P's reading *niskhodjatŭ*, "descend," is secondary and inferior. P has also lost by homoeoteleuton the words "and they divide themselves into 40 parts and proceed." In the next verse it has lost the words "and every tree is well fruited and every place" by the same process. It has also lost the adjective "atmospheric."

n. As a gloss, this seems to be unmotivated. Is it a reminiscence of the "Spring of 40," *Neba'el'Arba'in*, between Byblos and Baalbek, a notorious cult center in antiquity? The spring at Pella of the Decapolis is called *'Um 'Arba'in*, "mother of forty (outlets?)."

o. "God." A U. All other MSS have "LORD."

p. Plural; i.e. every day, but also for the whole of every day.

9 a. J agrees with P in having a new ch. begin at this unsuitable point. There is no break in A.

b. This ch. has notable affinities with Mt 25:31–46: (1) the designation "righteous"; (2) the idea of a "prepared" place; (3) the ethical measures; (4) the arrangement of the virtuous actions in pairs. There are also substantial differences, apart from

[A]

5 Gen 2:10–14

And another tree is near it, an olive, flowing with oil continually.

6

7 •And every tree is well fruited. Ezek 31:8
There is no tree there without fruit, and every place is blessed.
8 And the angels guarding Paradise are very splendid.
With never-ceasing voice and pleasant singing they worship God° throughout the
whole day.ᴾ And I said, "How very pleasant is this place!" The men answered
me:

9

1 "This place has been prepared, Enoch, for the righteous, Mt 25:34

who suffer every kind of tribulation in this life
and who afflict their souls,
and who avert their eyes from injustice, Isa 33:15; Ps 119:37
and who carry out righteous judgment,
to give bread to the hungry, Ezek 18:7; Isa 58:7; Mt 25:35, 37; 4 Ezra 2:20; Tob 4:16 Isa 1:17; Jer 22:3
and to cover the naked with clothing,
and to lift up the fallen,

the capital one that the Son of Man is the Judge: (1) the setting is quite different; (2) the good deeds in Mt are exclusively humanitarian, whereas 2En has religious duties and the endurance of persecution; (3) in fact there are only two in common—relieving hunger and nakedness. The community which used 2En 9 as its code was more self-consciously pious than the community of Mt 25. Its simple ethical monotheism would fit "God-fearers" anywhere; and it underscores 2En's constant theme—exclusive worship of the LORD as the only God.

c. The longer version is more orderly than the shorter; but most of the differences seem to be due to simplification of the original rhetoric or the addition of homiletical glosses. Thus the block of humane acts in the middle are stated with infinitives in A. These have been extended to the following injunctions in V, but in J all but the first have been normalized to relative clauses. This process is complete in P; but R retains the pattern of A U. The importance of this doubtless more authentic arrangement is that these four practices define what is meant by "righteous judgment." The absence of "and" in A U V N confirms this.

Other stylistic changes include:

1. Movement of "Enoch," since the vocative is delayed (V N agree with R J P in putting it earlier). In B it even occurs twice: *město ce, junoše, predivnymŭ i enokhu ugotovanno estĭ.* The variant "youth" occurs in B again in the matching statement in 10:4. Note also B's careless error in reading *pravednikomŭ* ("righteous") as *predivnymŭ* ("marvelous"); and the dative *enokhu* leads to an incongruous result: "This place has been prepared for

the righteous (and for) Enoch." But A U also have the apparent dative.

2. Rearranging clauses so that the verb comes first; thus R J P all have "before the face of the Lord" after "walk"; but P alone has moved "naked" to follow "clothe." Note that the construction "has been prepared," behind which a Gk. perfect participle probably lies, bothered the scribes.

Glosses include the addition of "every kind" to "calamity" (R J P), the addition of the words "and [not P, hence the translation (A) in *APOT*, vol. 2, p. 434] orphans" to "injured" (J R); the addition of "without a defect" to "walk" (R J P). V N have expanded "and naked cover with a garment" (in which A U agree with R J) to "and the naked dress and cover with a garment" (hence the translation [B] in *APOT*, vol. 2, p. 434). It can be seen from this that both MSS used in *APOT* represent extreme deviations from the main line. Minor variations include the change of "this life" (*žitii semŭ* [A]) to "their life" (*svoemĭ*—V as well as J R; the phrase is missing from P). Also V reads *životĕ.* A U lack the word "place" at the end, but since it is present in V N, this is a blemish in A U. P gives a unique theological twist to the second point by reading "from those who afflict" instead of "and who afflict" (compare *APOT*, vol. 2, p. 434). This moves away from the idea, in all other MSS, that self-inflicted sufferings are meritorious.

d. The same word is used for the place of torment (10:4) and also the place of judgment (49:2).

e. Slav. *napastĭ* = Gk. *epeireia,* "abuse."

[J]

and who help the injured and the orphans,
and who walk without a defect before the face of the LORD,
and who worship him only—

even for them this place has been prepared as an eternal inheritance."[f]

10 |Here they showed Enoch the frightful place and various tortures. Word "9."|

And those men carried me   1
to the northern[a] region; and they showed me there a very frightful place;
and all kinds of torture and torment are in that place, cruel darkness and lightless   2
gloom.[b] And there is no light there, and a black fire blazes[c] up perpetually,[d] with
a river of fire[e] that comes out over the whole place, fire here,[f] freezing ice[g] there,
and it dries up and it freezes;[h]
and very cruel places of detention and dark and merciless angels, carrying   3
instruments of atrocities[i] torturing without pity.
And I said, "Woe, woe! How very frightful this place is!" And those men said   4
to me, "This place, Enoch, has been prepared for those[k] who do not glorify God,
who practice on the earth the sin |which is against nature, which is child corruption
in the anus in the manner of Sodom|,[l] of witchcraft, enchantments,[m] divinations,
trafficking with demons, who boast about their evil deeds—|stealing, lying,
insulting, coveting, resentment, fornication, murder|[n]— •and who steal the souls   5
of men secretly, seizing the poor by the throat,
taking away their possessions,
enriching themselves from the possessions of others, defrauding them; who, when
they are able to provide sustenance, bring about the death of the hungry[p] by
starvation; and, when they are able to provide clothing, take away the last garment

f. Cf. Mt 25:34. 2En seems to be an independent
treatment of this theme which in the Gospel has
been radically Christianized. It is not likely that
2En 9 is a de-Christianized version of Mt 25. If
the author of 2En knew Mt 25, we would have
expected more specific resemblances.

10 a. The Essenes believed that Paradise was in
the north. The reading in J P R (*stranu = storonu*)
has the same ambivalence as Heb. *gĕbûl*, "boundary" or "region." In modern Russian this has
become differentiated into *strana*, "country," and
storona, "side," and hence "side" (*APOT*, vol.
2, p. 435). But earlier they were mere variants,
both covering all these meanings. Original *khōra*
(?).
   b. J P R agree against the other MSS in the
adjectives added to "darkness" and "gloom."
   c. Instead of "a black fire . . . with a river of
fire," in which both long and short MSS agree,
V N read "fire and flame and blackness."
   d. P's variant *prisno* is merely a synonym.
   e. The "river of fire" is first met in Dan 7:10.
The imagery of a volcano is present as "the lake
of fire" in Rev 19:20; 20:10, 14f.; 21:8. 1En 14:19
is still like Dan, while in 2En the fiery stream is
not yet the place and means of punishment as in
Rev. Compare SibOr 2.196–200; 252f.; 286; 3.84;
8.411; ApPet 8; ApPaul. Phillip prays before his
martyrdom to be delivered from "the waters of
fire" (*ANT*, p. 450), but this could come from
Rev.
   f. In 1En 14:3 the house of God is "hot as fire

and cold as ice." In 2En God is compared to
blazing fire. The idea that "the soul is a cold
element" is found in Aristotle (*De anima* 1.2.405b).
Origen (*On First Principles* 2.8.3), struggling to
establish the meaning of the word "soul" by
etymology, speculates that a fall from virtue is a
cooling of ardor for God, so cold is the natural
state of evil things. The Second Council of Constantinople condemned the opinion (attributed to
Origen) that demons have "cold and murky bodies"
as a result of sin.
   g. Other MSS do not confirm the "and" in P
which gave "frost and ice" in *APOT*, vol. 2,
p. 435.
   h. For P's nouns ("thirst and shivering" [*APOT*,
vol. 2, p. 435]), J and R agree in using verbs.
Because of its agreement with P, we have adopted
R's order rather than J's. The rhyme *zebet* (*zjabti*),
žežet (*žaždati*) explains the spelling, in which J and
R agree. This cold heat in one action parches and
chills.
   i. We prefer other short MSS, e.g. *i mučešte*
(V), to A U *imušte*, "having," which is clearly
an error.
   j. The remarkable reading *yunoše*, clearly legible
in A, supports the evidence of V, which has this
variant four times (not here), and of other MSS,
that there was a tradition in which Enoch was
addressed in this way. The similarity to the vocative
enoše might explain the variant as purely scribal
slip. But it is surprising that it is only in address,
never in description, that the term is used. The
variant *jenokhŭ* is rare. There is no phonetic reason

[A]

and   to help the injured,
      who walk   before the face of the LORD,
      and who worship him only—

Lk 1:6

for them this ⟨|place|⟩ has been prepared as an eternal inheritance.''

10

1 And the men carried me away from there, and they made me go up to the
northern heaven; and they showed me there a very frightful place;

2 every kind of torture and torment is in that place, and darkness and   gloom.
And there is no light there, but a black fire blazes up perpetually, and a river of
fire is coming out over the whole place,   with cold ice;

Dan 7:10; Rev 19:20; 20:10–15; 21:8

3   •and places of detention
and cruel angels and carriers of torture implements, tormenting without pity.

4 And I said,   "How very terrible this place is!" And the men answered me,
"This place, youth,[j] has been prepared for those who   practice godless
uncleanness on the earth,
      who perform witchcraft and |enchantments|,[m]
and who boast about their deeds.

Mt 25:41

Rom 1:32

5 They steal souls   secretly;
who untie the yoke[o] that has been secured;
who enrich themselves by fraud from the possessions of others,
and bring about the death of the hungry by starvation;
not being able to provide sustenance; and not being able

Rev 21:8

---

why the first vowel should change to *ju; *junokhŭ* is never found. But it cannot be a coincidence that this title is identical with that of Enoch (= Metatron) in 3En. [See the discussion on "Metatron" by P. Alexander in 3 Enoch. —J.H.C.]

k. The vices for which the wicked are in the place of torture are not simply the opposite of the virtues in ch. 9, nor corresponding sins of omission, except for starving the hungry, stripping the destitute naked, and idolatry. Even so the schemes are compatible, at least when the glosses are removed; but here the black arts are forbidden. The more specific Jewish duties—circumcision, sabbath-keeping, food taboos, sex taboos (as distinct from fornication and deviant practices)—are not listed. There is nothing here that any god-fearer, Jew or Christian, would not affirm.

l. The reference to sodomy is found only in P, which has similar additions in ch. 34. On *prokhodŭ* = *otverstie* ("aperture") see *MSD*, vol. 2, p. 1604. Slav. *zadneprokhodnoe otverstie* = "anus."

m. V N agree with J P R as reading *obajanije*, which means "magic" or more precisely "sorcery." The reading of A U (*obaženija*, "calumnies") is inferior.

n. The list of vices at the end of vs. 4 is found only in P.

o. The reference is quite obscure, and J P R do not have it. Elsewhere the yoke is a symbol of accepting God's authority. See the n. on 34:1. In a context which is talking about fraud, the sin could be tampering with the scales. See 44:5; *zugos* could be *měrilo*.

There could be a confusion in the verbs. Is it *rěšati* or *rěšiti*? The latter, indicated by *rěšeti* (V) (*MSD*, vol. 3, p. 227), means "unbind, untie." But *rěšatŭ* (A U) can refer to some of the worst sacrilege, such as taking away from the newly baptized the baptismal robe and washing that part of the body which had been anointed with the holy oil. The word is used like this in the Sermon on the Cross in the Dubensky Sbornik. It describes in terms of the utmost abhorrence something "unthinkably evil" that is done to the cross. If the "yoke" does not point to dishonesty in the use of scales, but rather to the violation of a sacred moral obligation, then we have no idea what it might be referring to.

p. There is a discrepancy between the two recensions, and considerable difference in word order. J P R say they are "able to supply sustenance"; but A U B read "not able" (twice in A U, once only in B). Here V and N agree with longer MSS, although V reads *nakrīmity* (a synonym of *nasytiti*, in which other MSS agree). P's solitary reading *gladnija* makes "the empty" the object of "satisfy," but *gladom*, "hunger," of J R, as well as the different word order of other MSS, shows that this is instrumental with "kill." Two distinct words are used here, each of which can render *limos—gladŭ* or *alŭčī* (f. *alŭča*). Either *alčuštija* or *gladnija* can mean "starvation." The coexistence of the synonyms in all MSS shows that such pairs do not necessarily contract dialects or traditions.

[J]

of the naked; •who do not acknowledge their Creator, but bow down to idols^q 6
which have no souls, which can neither see nor hear, vain gods; constructing
images, and bowing down to vile things made by hands—for all these this place
has been prepared as an eternal reward."^r

11 |Here they took Enoch to the 4th heaven, where the solar and lunar tracks
are. Word "10."|^a
And those men took me   and they carried^b me up to the fourth heaven. And 1
they showed me there all the movements and sequences,^c and all the rays of solar
and lunar light. •And I measured their movements and I compared their light. 2
And I saw that the sun has a light seven times greater than the moon. And I saw
his circle and his wheels^e on which he always goes,^f going past always like the
wind with quite marvelous speed. And his coming and his return give him no
rest,^g day and night.
And 4^h great stars, each star having 1000 stars under it, on the right-hand side of 3
the sun's chariot, and 4 on the left-hand side, each one having 1000 stars under
it, all together 8000, going with the sun perpetually.
And 150,000 |angels| accompany him in the daytime, and at night 1000. And 4
|100| angels go in front of the sun's chariot, six-winged, in flaming fire;

and the sun blazes up and sets the 100 angels on fire. 5

q. The word "idols" only in J. R P agree with other MSS in reading "gods." The gloss "which can neither see nor hear" only in J P. The epithet *istukanny* (*glyptoi*) only in P.

r. Slav. *dostoanie*. Contrast *naslěde*, "inheritance" (9:1). Both words are used in the Gospels to translate *klēronomia*.

11 a. At this point A has *D* (= 4) *NB̌O* (= heaven) in the margin in huge letters. In the text the MSS vary between the numeral (e.g. A) and the word (e.g. U).

b. The opening statement illustrates the kind of variation that takes place continually in these MSS. Most MSS have two verbs (in V they are *vŭzdvygnusta* and *vŭznesosta,* cf. N B etc.; in J *vuzjasta* and *vozvedošu,* cf. P R), but A U have only *vozdvigosta,* a simple case of loss by homoioarkton.

c. It is not clear what astronomical realities are meant by *prěkhoždenia,* "transitions." A U have probably simplified the text for this reason. By omitting "and" P arrives at "successive goings," but it reads *predkhodnaja.* Perhaps the original was a hendiadys.

d. The hesitation of scribes over the use of synonyms is illustrated at this point. Gk. is particularly rich in words for "light." Slav. has *luča* (best *aktis*) or *světŭ* (best *phōs,* opposite of "darkness"). But the latter also has the wider meaning of "world," "life," "age" (*'ólām, aiōn*). Here both are used in MSS of several families, but it is a question whether "rays of light" is glossed or whether "rays" (A U B) represents a simplification. In what follows *světŭ* is used by all. Another confusion arises in the word for "moon." Short MSS have nouns, "sun and moon"; long ones have switched to adjectives, "solar and lunar." The apparently original *měca* (*měsjacī*) developed into "month," while the synonym *luna* remains "moon." R still has *měsjačnago* but J P have *lunnago.* The secondary character of the readings with *lun-* is proved by the error in A U in vs. 2—"greater than the sun (!)"—it should be "moon"; and *měa,* as read by R and by all short MSS except

A U, explains the other readings. In J P it has been replaced by its synonym *luny;* while *slňca* (A U) is a misreading of the identical ending, a mistake not so easily made with *luny.* The idea seems to be an exegetical inference from Isa 30:26; see also 2En 66:7f.

e. The textual problems at this point may be illustrated by a few representative readings:

A	krǔ^g ea	i kolesnica
R	krugī eju	i kolesnicja eju
J P	krǔ^g emu	i kolěsi emu
V	i krǔ^g eju	kolesnyca

The picture seems to be that of a circuit (*krugŭ* = *kyklos*) around which the sun and the moon drive their chariots. That both heavenly bodies are in mind is shown by *kožđo eju,* "each of the two of them," which follows, and which the agreement of R V A proves to be superior. J P read "always." By the same token, R V, which read "their (dual) circle," are better than A U B² ("her") or J P B Chr ("his"). The grouping of both long and short MSS on both sides suggests that similar errors have developed independently. The feminine pronoun of A U is unaccountable, unless by simple error for the dual, since *sŭlnce* is neuter in Slav. But "moon" is feminine; see ch. 16. In any case the singular shows that J P are already talking only about the sun at this point. J's replacement of "chariot" by "wheels" (*kolo, koleso* also means "circle" and so is a near synonym of *krugŭ*) could be deliberate demythologization, since it occurs again in ch. 14; but most of the picture is still intact. In 11:2, 4, J P read *kolo* against *kolesnica* of other MSS, and this is probably intended as a synonym, since *kola* can also translate *hamaksa.* In 2En 16 *krugŭ* seems to mean "cycle" (of day and night), but there A U (not long MSS) retain the discussion of the moon's chariot. At 12:2 short MSS and R (but not J P) describe the angels "who pull the chariot of the sun," which is more concrete than J P. See the next n.

[A]

6 to supply clothing, take away the last garment of the naked; •who do not acknowledge their Creator, but bow down to vain gods, constructing images, and bowing down to something made by hand— And for all these this place has been prepared as an eternal reward."

11

1 And ⟨|the men|⟩ lifted me up from there ⟨|and they carried me up|⟩ to the 4th heaven. And they showed me there all the movements ⟨|and displacements|⟩, and 2 all the rays ⟨|of light|⟩ᵈ of the sun and the moon. • I measured their movements. I compared their light. And I saw that the sun has a light seven times greater than the sun(!). Their circle and their chariots on which each of them rides, passing like the wind. And there is no rest for them by day and by night, as they go off and come back.

3 And four great stars, holding onto the right-hand side of the sun's chariot, 4 on the left-hand side,

4 ⟨going⟩ with the sun perpetually, •

and angels

going in front of the sun's chariot,

5

f. By changing the original *ezditŭ*, "drives," to *šestvuetĭ*, "moves," J P have diminished the mythological content. At the end of vs. 2, J P have nouns where other MSS have verbs. A similar adjustment has been made in 12:2, where the verb *mučet* (*vehunt*)—original as R's agreement with short MSS shows—has become "accompany and run" in J P, which lack the reference to the chariot as well. This is the more remarkable, because otherwise long MSS have (retain?) mythological details lacking (censored?) in short MSS.

g. Once more the singular *emu*, "to him" (of J P), contrasts with the better dual (*ima*) of all other MSS. This seems to contradict the statement in 24:5 that "the sun has rest." It could mean no more than that he never stops moving; but in view of gnostic interest in "rest" something more significant could be involved. It suggests that "the Sun" is a self-conscious being.

It is difficult to establish from the descriptions of the sun, moon, and stars in these sections whether they are imagined to be living celestial beings or not. The vivid dramatic descriptions of their movements could be no more than personification for literary purposes. The strictly mechanical timetable does not suggest free rational beings (Origen equates freedom and rationality). The accompanying angels serve as the rational causes of the regular motions, the theological equivalents of "natural laws."

Origen, assuming that all creatures are capable of development, and therefore good and evil, does not exempt the heavenly bodies from this rule. Almost the whole of *On First Principles* 1.7 is devoted to the idea that the heavenly stars are souls in fiery bodies. He quotes Job 25:5 as a proof that stars can be tainted with sin (*On First Principles* 1.7.2).

Belief that the stars are living beings goes back to the old polytheism, and retains sophisticated expression by Plato, who called the stars "divine" (*Timaeus* 30b). Philo (*De mundi opif.*) taught that the stars, being heavenly beings, were incapable of defection. (See our discussion of "incorruptible" in the n. on 8:5 above.) Origen's other opinion (cf. Jude 13) arises from *a priori* notions, and an

irresistible desire to systematize. There is no doubt that he thought that the sun, moon, and stars were rational beings (compare *Contra Celsum* 5.11). His main argument is the mere fact of their movement as such. This is supported by Scriptures in which commands are addressed to stars as if to responsible beings. But he had it both ways: The very precision of their movements is seen as proof of the highest reason (*On First Principles* 1.7.3).

2En is on a much lower level of sophistication. It is content to describe the movement of sun and moon in terms of calendrical facts, with a little cosmology, or rather astronomy, about gates. The angels are the causes. The mechanism of locomotion, whether on wheels or in a chariot or on a circular orbit, is not clear. But in any case it is fairly crude in conceptuality.

Origen's views on this subject were attacked with vigor by Jerome and Justinian, and belief that the sun, moon, and stars were living beings became unorthodox. Since 2En decribes Sun and Moon at least in such a mythological way, its use in Christian circles could signify either (1) agreement with Origen against Jerome on this point; or (2) acceptance of 2En at a time after the controversy was forgotten; or (3) innocuous use of fairy-tale ways of talking about the sun and the moon.

h. The picture does not suit a quadriga, traditional for sun deities, for here there are four stars on each side of the chariot, making eight in all. All long MSS have the additional feature of one thousand angels for each of these eight.

In short MSS these verses have been drastically condensed by removing the extravagant figures, or else J P have been embellished. R is different again. It agrees at vs. 3 that each of the eight stars has one thousand stars under it. It continues: "And 15 myriad angels conduct him in the daytime, but at night a thousand angels, each angel with six wings, who go in front of the chariot, and one hundred angels give him fire." In J P the verbs seem to be singular, with the sun as subject. The sun enkindles and sets on fire (the words are synonyms) the one hundred angels. But in R the angels stoke up the sun.

[J]

12 |About the very wonderful solar elements. Word "11."|[a]

And |I looked and saw| flying spirits, the solar elements,[b] called phoenixes[c] and 1
khalkedras,[d] strange[e] and wonderful. For their form[f] was that of a lion, their tail
that of a . . . , and their head that of a crocodile. Their appearance was multicolored, like a rainbow. •Their size was 900[g] measures. Their wings were those 2
of angels, but they have 12 wings each. They accompany and run with the sun,
carrying heat and dew, ⟨and⟩ whatever is commanded |them| from God.
          Thus he goes through a cycle, and he goes down and he rises up 3
across the sky and beneath the earth[h] with the light of his rays. And he was there,
on the track,[i] unceasingly.

13 |The angels picked Enoch up and set him down in the East, at the solar
gates. Word "12."|[a]

And those men carried me away[b] to the east ⟨of that heaven⟩.   1
⟨|And they showed me|⟩ the solar gates[c] through which the sun comes out[d] according
to the appointment[e] of the seasons and according to the phases of the moon,[f] for
the entire year, and according to
the numbers on the horologe, day and night. •And I saw 6 open[g] gates, each gate 2
having 61 stadia and a quarter of a stadium. And I measured carefully and I

12 a. The divergences in the MS evidence for this
ch. cannot be described simply by reference to
long and short recensions; for there are substantial
differences within these two main kinds of text.
The short MSS are brief and scrappy to the point
of incoherence. They leave unclear such questions
concerning the celestial birds as:
   (1) Their relation to the "stars" that go with
the sun in ch. 11 (the continuity of short MSS at
this point suggests that they are the same, in fact
they are called "angels," and the talk to the contrary
in long MSS, which is all about phoenixes and the
khalkedras, is lacking).
   (2) Their number (the repetition of the numeral
in V N B² suggests that there are twelve of them,
while R |short| has the unique detail that there are
two).
   (3) Their anatomy (short MSS have only the
detail of twelve wings each |all agree in this|
whereas long MSS go into considerable detail; R
says merely that one was *like* a phoenix, the other
like a khalkedra, whereas J P identify them as these
creatures).
   (4) Their function (they "pull" the chariot; the
weakening of this to "accompany" in J P only is
clearly secondary).
   (5) Their task in conveying heat and dew to the
earth (obscure in all texts).
   (6) Their course (they descend to the earth in
short MSS, they go around under the earth in long
MSS, and this is probably the original picture).

   b. This terminology is a peculiarity of J P within
the long recension. See 1a, n. n.
   c. The plural (also in 19:6—both recensions) is
unexampled in all literature, and suggests ignorance
of the ancient and widespread traditions about this
bird which everywhere else is *sui generis*. Fur-

thermore, here the role of the phoenix(es) as the
bird of the sun is quite general. Charles (*APOT*,
vol. 2, p. 436) claimed that Lactantius' knowledge
of the phoenix is dependent on 2En. Van den Broek
(*The Myth of the Phoenix*, trans. I. Seeger [Leiden,
1972] p. 285, n. 1) denies this, with good reason.
Among many details, 2En evidently does not know
about the rejuvenating immersion of the phoenix
at sunrise. At the same time, van den Broek (*Myth*,
p. 260) agrees with Charles to the extent of
recognizing that 2En's ideas about the phoenix
must have originated at Alexandria.
   d. These are brass serpents; they are associated
with cherubim in 1En 20:7, compare 2En 19. In
the description which follows, phoenixes and khalkedras seem to be the same.
   e. P reads *čudni*, J *studnyi*, not "cold" (*stu-
denyi*), nor "shameful" (*studĭnyi*). The word in
P's preface, *prečudnykh*, is even more secondary.
   f. Knowledge of the anatomy of phoenix or
khalkedra gained from elsewhere cannot be used
safely here, for there is no indication that the author
of 2En knew any more than the names of these
creatures. Nor does Ezek 1:5–11 solve the problem.
R J P agree in the details, but each of the three
uses the conjunction "and" differently. P (*APOT*,
vol. 2, p. 436) suggests that feet and tails were
leonine; but R (Vaillant, *Secrets*, p. 91) suggests
that feet, tail, and head are crocodilian, so that the
body is that of a lion. This is not strictly the
meaning of *obrazŭ*, "shape."
   g. R uses the words "nine" and "hundred"; J
has the numeral 900; P has 900 and "hundred."
The value of the "measure," *měra*, is not defined.
In translation literature it is either *metron* or *batos*
("volume"); or *'ēpāh* or *bath* in OT texts (both
"volume"). The most obvious unit is the cubit,
the unit in the *Disputatio* (*hōs apo pēkhōn ennea*).

[A]

12

1 . . . flying spirits,

Ps 110:3

2
with 12 wings like those of angels, who pull the chariot of the sun, carrying the dew and the heat, when the LORD gives the command to descend to the earth,

3

with the sun's rays.

13

1 And the   men carried me away to the east of   heaven.
And they showed me the   gates through which the sun goes out according to the appointed   seasons and according to the cycle of the months, for the entire year, and according to
2 the shortening of the duration of the days ⟨|and of the nights|⟩. •6 gates, one (of which was) open, about thirty 1 stadia. Carefully I measured their size. And I

---

h. P and R have each leveled the prepositions; P reads *pod nbsi i pod zemlju*, "under the heaven and under the earth." R reads *po nbsi i po zemli*, "along the heaven and along the earth." J is best, with *po nbsi i pod zemleju*. The confusion could be due to a clash of models of the universe, either a series of horizontal levels or a set of spheres concentrically around the earth. Perhaps the two can be combined, with the seven "circles" in between an upper zone of light and a nether zone of darkness. In ch. 14 the sun travels from west to east under the earth in darkness every night.
     i. Cf. the heading of ch. 12 in P. In Akkadian westward movement is called *harrān šamši* (*ANET*, p. 89, n. 152).

13 a. This chapter is a highly condensed version of 1En 72.
     b. J P add the preposition *ot-*, "from," to the verb.
     c. The Slav. word *vrata* has no singular. In the oldest Mesopotamian traditions Šamaš comes out through a gate in the east. In Parmenides' poem *On Nature* the gates of the sun, which are described quite literally, are opened by Justice, holder of the keys of retribution.
     The adjective "solar" modifying "gates" is found only in J P. 3Bar has 365 gates in heaven by which the sun rises.
     d. The MSS use a variety of verbs to describe the sun's egress at its rising.
     e. MSS with the adjective are better. As a modifier of *vrěmja*, *ustavīnyi* has the idea of divine ordering. It translates *horismenos*, which in 1Clem 20:3 describes the appointed courses along which the heavenly bodies "roll."
     f. Since 2En is not specifically interested in the

phases of the moon as an astronomical phenomenon, what is meant here is probably the annual round of months (cf. ch. 16, n. e). The MSS agree in general, but fluctuate between singular (which suggests the moon [Vaillant, *Secrets*, p. 13]) or plural (which suggests the months). That an annual cycle is in mind is shown by the following remarks about the shortening of the days (short MSS), and by the phrase "the entire year." But the latter is not present in V, which reads *i po obikhoždeniemī š mca vcego*, "according to the round of every month." V is also superior to A in what follows— "and after shortening to (!) lengthening of days and nights." The correct *udliženiju* of V has become *prikhoždeniju*, which really means "arrival." It has been influenced by the preceding *obkhoždeniemi měsjaca*. B Chr read *uloženiju*, "diminution." Long MSS support "day and night." Before rejecting the reference to the sundial (all long MSS), note its occurrence in short MSS at 15:3.
     g. R says that the gates were "big," once more in significant agreement with V and N. All MSS agree in its occurrence in 14:1. It could mean "wide" or "tall." The same applies to the noun *velikota*, "bigness," which follows. At this point all MSS seem to be corrupt; at least it is not possible to work out what the dimensions of the gates were in the source documents. It is more probable that the measure is the width, not the distance away (Vaillant). We are to imagine six openings along the eastern horizon (perhaps an actual structure), which, when viewed from the proper point, make the place of sunrise move one stadium (or two) each day.
     The MSS disagree as to whether Enoch did or did not grasp the size of these gateways.

[J]

figured out their size to be so much—through which the sun comes out[h] and goes off to the west.

And it becomes even[i] and goes in through all the months.   3

⟨And the 1st gate he comes out for 42 days,[j]

the second	35 days,
the third	35 days,
the fourth	35 days,
the fifth	35 days,
the sixth	42 days.⟩

And then once more he does an about-turn and goes back the other way from the   4 sixth gate, according to the round of the seasons:

⟨And he goes in through the fifth gate 35 days,

the 4th	35 days,
the 3rd	35 days,
the second	35 days⟩.

And so ⟨the days of⟩ the whole year are completed, according to the cycle of the   5 four seasons.

14 |They carried Enoch to the west. Word "13."|

And then those men carried me away to the west of the heaven,[a] and they showed   1 me six[b] large open gates, corresponding to the circuit of the eastern gates, opposite them, where the sun sets according to the number of the days,[c] 365 and 1/4.[d]

Thus he goes back once again to the eastern gates, under the earth.[e] ⟨And when   2 he goes out from the western gates⟩, he takes off his light, the splendor which is his radiance, ⟨and four hundred angels take his

---

h. The MSS use different verbs to describe the sun's movements:

	comes out (vss. 3, 4)	goes off (vs. 3)	goes in (vss. 3, 5)
J P	iskhodit	idet	vŭskodit
R	iskhodit	idet	vŭkhodit
A U	vkhodit (3) iskhodit (4)	idet	vkhodit

S. Novaković ("Apokrif o Enohu," *Stárine XVI* [Zagrele (Agram)] pp. 65–81) reports *vískhoditi* as the first verb in the Belgrade MS; but V reads *víkhôdytí*. It is easy to see how *vŭskhodit*, "ascend," has crept in. The same split occurs in vs. 5 between R and J P. That is, A U are wrong in vs. 3; J P are wrong in vs. 3 (they are defective in vs. 5). The scribes were looking at sunrise from the human point of view; but the originals describe it from the sun's point of view. He "goes out" in the morning and "goes in" at night. In ch. 14 a different verb again, *zakhodit*, describes sunset.

i. Does this refer to the equinox? The reference to the four seasons (vs. 5) suggests that the year might begin on such a date, but the picture of the sun rising through successive gates and then work-

ing his way back through them suggests the movement of the point of sunrise across the horizon from solstice to solstice.

j. Most MSS are defective in the full details of the ten periods spent in the six gates each year. But the complete agreement of R (long) with A U (short), not only in the full list, but also in the number of days, proves their authenticity. Their correlation either with a working calendar or with astronomical facts is another matter. A scheme of this kind is not known elsewhere; but the system of gates is familiar from 1En, including the astronomical sections of the Aram. fragments from Qumran. The 364-day year is a certain link with these old treatises. 2En 13 is either another solar scheme that has survived, or else a garbled relic.

14 a. At 2En 10:1 all short MSS read "northern region" instead of "northern heaven." Here P alone has the variant "western regions" (but only "west" in its chapter title).

b. A U read *šestera*, and P has the numeral Ž = 6. But R reads *petora*, which J confirms with ě, apparently "5." The explanation is that the letter e is the numeral 6 in Glagolitic. It is notable

[A]

3 could not comprehend their size— •those by which the sun goes in and goes off
to the west.

The 1st gate he comes out for 42 days,
the second   35 days,
the third   35 days,
the fourth   35 days,
the fifth   35 days,
the sixth   42 days.

4 And again, turning around
at the sixth gate, according to the round of the seasons:

And he goes in through the fifth gate   35 days,
the fourth gate 35 days,
the third gate 35 days,
the second   35 days.

5 And the days of the   year are completed, according to the cycle of the
seasons.

14

1 And the   men   led   me away to the west of the heaven, and there
they showed me six large open gates, corresponding to the circuit of the eastern
heaven, opposite, by which the sun sets, corresponding to his rising by the eastern
2 gates and corresponding to the number of the day. •Thus he sets through the
western gates. And when he goes out from the western gates,
then four angels take away his crown,

that this primitive feature survives in two short
MSS. B has a similar reading at 16:8. At 70:1
similar confusion among numerals can be explained
in terms of Glagolitic originals.

c. The singular, "the day," in A U, which is
confirmed by B and V, is important evidence against
the reading of J P R, in which the length of the
year according to the Julian calendar is evidently
a gloss. The figure is purely theoretical. What is
being said is that the place where the sun sets in
the west matches the place where it rises in the
east, depending on the count of the day concerned.
V is different. Instead of "corresponding to the
circuit [*obkhodu*] of the eastern gates" in which
MSS of both recensions agree, it reads "corresponding to the eastern entrance" (*vīkhodu*—a word
which comes a little later in most MSS). And it
agrees with J R (against other MSS) in reading
"which it sets there," a palpable Hebraism (*tu* =
šām). Where others have "rising" (*vkhodu* =
entrance), it has "ascent" (*vīskhodu*). In vs. 3,
instead of "travels" (*ide*[*t*]), it has "goes out"
(*izydetī*).

d. The following information, found only in
MSS of the longer recension, is probably interpolated and cannot be used to date the main texts.

(1) The Julian year of 365¼ days (14:1; cf. 16:4
and 16:6).

(2) The calendrical cycle of twenty-eight years
(15:4) when all the days of the month fall again
on the same day of the week.

(3) The Metonic cycle of nineteen years during
which seven lunar months must be intercalated
(16:8).

(4) The lunar epacts (16:5) because twelve lunar
months fall short of one solar year by about twelve
days. The lunar epacts are first named in a Lat.
treatise on the computation of Easter, dated A.D.
243.

(5) The great cycle of 532 years (28 × 19) after
which all movable ecclesiastical festivals come on
the same day of the month and the same day of
the week (16:5).

e. J has developed a different picture, seeing
sunset (in the west, as described by all other MSS)
as a return to the eastern gates. This movement
"under the earth" has already been described in
12:3, although only J has got it correctly. P agrees
with J in using the preposition *ko*, but it has
"western gates."

[J]

crown[f] and carry it to the LORD⟩. •For, since his shining crown is with God,[g]   3
with 400 angels guarding it, the sun ⟨turns his chariot around⟩ and goes back
under the earth[h] on wheels, without the great light which is his great radiance and
ornament. |And he remains| for seven great hours in night. And the chariot spends
half its time under the earth. And when he comes to the eastern approaches, in
the 8th hour of the night, ⟨the angels, the 4 hundred angels, bring back the crown,
and crown him⟩. And his brightness and the shining of his crown are seen before[i]
sunrise. And the sun blazes out more than fire does.

15 |The solar elements, the phoenixes and the khalkedras, burst into song.|[a]

And then the solar elements, called phoenixes[b] and khalkedras, burst into song.   1
That is why every bird flaps its wings, rejoicing at the giver of light. And they
burst into song at the LORD's command:

> The light-giver is coming,   2
> to give radiance to the whole world;
> and the morning watch appears,
> which is the sun's rays.
> And the sun comes out over the face of the earth,
> and retrieves his radiance,
> to give light to all the face of the earth.

And they showed me this calculation[c] of the sun's movement, and the gates by   3
which he goes in and goes out; for these are the great gates which God created to
be an annual horologe.[d]
This is why the sun has the greater heat; and the cycle for him goes on for 28   4
years, and begins once more from the start.[e]

16 |They picked Enoch up and placed him once more in the east at the orbit of
the moon. Word "15."|

And another calculation[a] those men showed me, that of the moon, and all the   1
movements and phases;

f. Traditionally, representations of Helios show a crown or nimbus with seven rays. This is true also of figures associated with the sun, such as the phoenix. There is no indication that this use of 7 is any more than another occurrence of this sacred mystical or magical number. Nor is it invariant as a sun symbol, at least so far as coronal rays are concerned. Numbers 4, 5, 6, 9, and 12 are also found.

g. P reads "in heaven with the LORD." The brevity and obscurity of A U suggest that the text has been abbreviated by removing some of the more fantastic features. R differs considerably from J P in this ch.; but either or both might well preserve readings with a claim to authenticity. Since even A U describe the removal of the sun's crown at sunset, its replacement before sunrise is to be expected. We have presented all the evidence by conflating R's peculiar readings with the text of J. This does not mean that the textual problems are to be solved by such a maximizing procedure. In particular our interpretation of J's unique *provide* is dubious. See n. i.

h. The sun has daily turning points (*tropai*) if the movement is considered to be back and forth. There are also seasonal *tropai* corresponding to the solstices.

i. R says that "the 4 hundred angels bring (*prinoset*) the crown and crown him." P has the similar *privoditŭ*, suggesting that J (*provide*) is an error.

15 a. The expected ch. enumeration of P ("word '14' ") is missing. This shows that these headings were copied from another MS, and not made up just for P.

b. The superior reading of R avoids the plural.

c. The MSS vary extensively in the word used here and in 16:1, 8. Note the following:

	15:3	16:1	16:8
A	*raštenie*	*raštee* ñ	*raštinenie* ž
U		*raštinie* ñ	*raštinenie* ž
B	*razčinenie*	*razčinenie*	*razčinenie*
V	*razčinjenie*	*rasčynjenie*	*rasčinjenie*
Chr	*različenie*	*različenie*	*razlučenija*
J P R	*rasčitanie*	*rasčitenie*	*rasčetenie*

Vaillant (*Secrets*, p. 14) conjectures an original *raštitenie* at 15:3, but prefers R's *razčitenie* at 16:1. There are three or four terms, variously spelled. Longer MSS read *rasčitanie* throughout, except that P alone deviates to *rastečenie* in ch. 16—hence "course" (*APOT*, vol. 2, p. 438).

[A]

3 and carry it up to the LORD. •   Josh 10:12
        But the sun turns his chariot around
and travels   without   light;

and they place the crown on him there.

15

1

2

3 And they showed me this augmentation of the sun
and the gates by which he goes in and goes out; for these gates
        the LORD created to be an annual horologe.

4

16

1 But the moon has a different augmentation. They showed me all her movements
and all her phases. The men showed me the gates, and they showed me 12 gates

Rasčitanie ("calculation" [*APOT*, vol. 2, p. 438]), whether process or result, is not suitable, for the data in this ch. are not calculated. V similarly has only one word throughout, *razčinjenie,* and other MSS (N B) agree. This is the source of "disposition" in *APOT* (vol. 2, p. 438), but "order" or "routine" would be better, and suits. The fact that *diataksis* or *diatagē* could lie behind this word makes comparison with Acts 7:53 interesting. The variant *raštinenije* is attested, and all the words in A U could be the same. But *raštenie* (*auksēsis*), "increase," is also suitable in an astronomical treatise. Vaillant's emendation to "deduction" does not seem necessary. The variant of Chr—"difference," or "separation," assuming that *razlučenija* at 16:8 is not merely a scribal slip—has little claim to authenticity, but it does suggest that the text was not understood.

d. The annual movement of the sun serves as a kind of cosmic clock. From the time of Hesiod a farmer's almanac took its date from the annual movement of the sun through the ecliptic. This is due to the fact that the sidereal day is slightly shorter (by about four minutes) than the solar day. This means that the stars gradually overtake and surpass the sun. Roughly this permits the year to be divided into intervals, depending on what stars

the sun is near. The crudest system divides the zone into twelve zodiacs. The Egyptians recognized thirty-six constellations or decans of ten days each. By accurate observation of the risings (heliacal or acronycal) and settings (cosmical or heliacal) of individual stars, more exact indications are possible. In 2En all the recensions agree in the idea that the gates through which the sun rises and sets keep track of the days of the year in the same way as a sundial keeps track of the hours of the day. J, R, and P go on to affirm that this is why the sun is the greatest created thing. This statement is lacking in A U, except for the words *slnce skazaetī,* "the sun says," which are unintelligible. Yet something like them is found in other MSS. Even so, the divergence among the three MSS of the longer recension at this point leaves the whole matter obscure. J's "heat," *varī,* is clearly a corruption of *tvar,* "creature" (P). This strong statement about the sun is intended to reinforce the adherence of this group to the solar calendar.

e. A U share at this point the stray words *slnce skazaetī.* Other MSS have the same words in inverted order, as with *skazuetū solnce* (B). The corruption is irreparable.

16 a. See ch. 15, n. c.

[J]

⟨and⟩ 12 big gates, crowned[b] from the west to the east, through which the moon goes in and goes out, in accordance with the regular seasons.
She goes in by the first western gate, in the place of the sun—   2

> by the 1st[c] gate for 31[d] days exactly,[e]
> the 2nd   for 35 days exactly,
> the 3rd   for 30 days exactly,
> the 4th   for 30 days exactly,
> ⟨|the 5th   for 31 days|⟩ ⟨extraordinarily⟩ / |exactly|,
> ⟨|the 6th   for 31 days exactly,|⟩
> the 7th   for 30 days exactly,
> the 8th   for 31 days extraordinarily,
> the 9th   for 31 |35| days ⟨accurately⟩,
> the 10th   for 30 days exactly,
> the 11th   for 31 days exactly,
> the 12th   for 22 |28| days exactly.

Thus likewise by the western gates in accordance with the cycle, and in accordance   3
with the number of the eastern gates.

b. The picture is far from clear. There are twelve gates, each corresponding to one month of the solar year (but these months are not those of any known calendar). The disposition of the gates is not clear, whether "to the east" (A) or "from the west to the east" (J P). The movement of the moon is "going in and going out" through these gates. These gates are not the same as the gates of the sun—six in the east, six in the west—and the months connected with those gates are quite different in their division of the year. A further problem is the apparent description of these gates as a "crown." Parmenides conceived of the universe as a system of concentric rings of fire (cf. 2En 27:3), called *stefanai*. Is this word an intrusion of the word "crown" from the description of the sun? The word has a good claim to authenticity since A U read *věnca*. J P have the participle *věn'čan(n)a*, from which R's *věčnaa*, "eternal," is best explained as a corruption. Yet some short MSS also have this variant, e.g. V, identically *věčnaa*. Vaillant (*Secrets*, pp. 15f.) suspects that Ps 24 (Slav. 23):7, 9 with *vrata věč'naja* has contaminated the text. Vaillant emends the text extensively to arrive at twelve gates "crowned" in the east and twelve similar gates in the west. But the preposition *ko*, "to," which persists in all MSS, is awkward, except in J P—"from the west to the east."

If we are to imagine a complete circlet ("crown") of gates "from the west to the east," perhaps something like "the houses of the zodiacs" is in mind. But the language of vs. 3 suggests that there are two sets of gates, one set in the east, one set in the west, and that the moon behaves similarly in each set. This is the picture in 1En 72. J P clearly identify the first gate as "western," "in the place of the sun," the latter phrase being found in R as well. This is one of several details in which 1En can still be recognized behind 2En (e.g. 1En 73:4). But 1En (72:3) uses the same gates (six in the east, six in the west) to describe the movements of both sun and moon. 1En 75, however, describes a system of twelve gates in another connection,

and this could be the source of 2En's muddled account. The presence of fragments of ideas from 1En in longer MSS, and their absence from shorter MSS, disproves the theory that longer MSS have been interpolated. Many differences can only be explained if the shorter MSS have been abbreviated.

c. The designation of a month by a number rather than a name corresponds to Qumran practice. 1En and Jub similarly never use month names. Month names appear at 2En 48:2 and in chs. 68 and 73.

d. Another problem is the number of days to be assigned to each of the twelve months. R is the only MS with twelve numbers intact and they add up to 363. These agree fairly well with other MSS where they have the numbers, notably with A U. In fact, if we prefer A to R at the one point where they disagree (31 days for the third month), and supply A with R's figure for the twelfth month (22 days—a figure confirmed by J), the total is 364, which is probably original. But the lengths of the months do not line up with any known calendar.

The calendar in 16:2 according to the various MSS is as follows:

	P	J	R	A, U	B	1En Jub
1	(3)1	31	31	31	30	30
2	35	35	35	35	35	30
3	30	30	30	31	30	31
4	30	30	30	30	30	30
5	31	—	31	31	30	30
6	31	—	31	31	31	31
7	30	30	30	30	30	30
8	31	31	31	31	31	30
9	35	31	31	31	31	31
10	30	30	30	30	—	30
11	31	31	31	31	—	30
12	28	22	22	[22]	—	31
Total	373		363	[364]		364

The numerals in Vaillant (*Secrets*, pp. 15f.) correspond to U, except that month 12 is missing, and he has restored it (22 days) from R. *APOT* (vol. 2, p. 438), following Morfill (*Secrets of Enoch*, p. 18), "corrected" the

[A]

to the east, a crown, by which the moon goes in and goes out, in accordance with the regular seasons.

2

By the first gate to the east	31 days exactly,
and by the second	35 days exactly,
and by the third	31 days exceptionally,
and by the fourth	30 days exactly,
and by the fifth	31 days extraordinarily,
and by the sixth	31 days exactly,
by the 7th	30 days exactly,
by the eighth	31 days extraordinarily,
and by the 9th	31 days accurately,
and by the tenth	30 days exactly,
by the 11th	31 days exceptionally,
by the 12th gate she goes	22 days exactly.

3 Thus likewise by the western gates in accordance with the cycle, and in accordance with the number of the eastern gates.

---

figures in P. Besides the obvious correction of the first month from 1 to 31, they changed P's two 35-day months to 31 days each, thus securing a total of 365 days. But even so, the series *31 *31 30 30 31 31 30 31 *31 30 31 28 does not match the Julian calendar, and 2En does not use a 365-day year in any case. J agrees with R as far as it goes, and both preserve the vital information about the twelfth month. When this is supplied to A U the correct total is obtained. R is the only MS with figures for twelve months but its total is wrong. R agrees with U at every point except in the third month, where its value (30 days) explains why it is one day short. A U are accordingly the best witnesses. B has only nine months and only six of them agree with A U. But its agreement that the second month has 35 days is important evidence. In fact all MSS agree with this information.

e. The meaning of the adverbs used to characterize the behavior of the moon in each month is obscure. The discovery of the pattern is made harder by the wide disagreement among the MSS. Four different adverbs are used. Note the following translations: *invĕstno*, "exactly"; *ispytno*, "accurately" ("perfectly"?); *izjaštenŭ*, "exceptionally"; *izrjadenŭ*, "extraordinarily." The adverbs are altogether lacking in B. Only A U use all four. R has three; J P only two, with a marked trend to label most months "exactly." This accounts for the two months (3 and 11) for which R J P agree together against A U. Note the following:

Month	A U	R
1	exactly	exactly
2	exactly	exactly
3	exceptionally	exactly
4	exactly	exactly
5	extraordinarily	extraordinarily
6	exactly	exactly
7	exactly	exactly
8	extraordinarily	extraordinarily
9	accurately	accurately
10	exactly	exactly
11	exceptionally	exactly
12	exactly	exactly

Month	J	P
1	exactly	exactly
2	exactly	exactly
3	exactly	exactly
4	exactly	exactly
5	—	exactly
6	—	exactly
7	exactly	exactly
8	extraordinarily	extraordinarily
9	exactly	exactly
10	exactly	extraordinarily
11	exactly	exactly
12	exactly	exactly

Otherwise R agrees with A U (against J P) where this leveling has not occurred (5, 9). All agree in labeling the eighth month "extraordinarily." The textual evidence indicates that A U have the best readings. A clue is probably found in 16:6, which says that there are four "extraordinary" months each year. This has something to do with the waxing and waning of the moon in relation to the calendar months, although it is possible that the "diminution" and "augmentation" mentioned there refer to those periods of the year in which the days are getting shorter and longer. A U have lost some of the text at this point by homoioarkton, but restoration can be made from B. In J P R the scribes seem to have got the matter confused with the cycle of bisextile years.

The calendar of 1En begins the year at the spring equinox, when day and night are equal and the days are getting longer. This means that for roughly six months (10, 11, 12, 1, 2, 3) the days are lengthening, and this period includes the two "exceptional" months. In the other months the days are getting shorter, and this period includes the two "extraordinary" months. On a very short night it is possible that the moon will not be seen at all. On a very long night it can be seen, set, and rise again before the sun does.

[J]

And thus she goes,   and completes the solar year 365 and ½ of one day.[f]   4
But the lunar year has 354, making 12 months, ⟨calculated⟩ in accordance with   5
29 days. And it lacks 12 days of the solar cycle, which are the lunar epacts for
each year. Also the great cycle contains 532 years.
It passes by the quarters for three years, and the fourth completes it exactly. For   6
this reason they are taken away, outside heaven, for three years; and they are not
added to the number of the days, because these ones change the seasons of the
year—two new moons in augmentation,
two others in diminution.   •And when the western gates are completed, she   7
turns around and goes to the eastern ones with ⟨her⟩ light. Thus she goes, day and
night, in accordance with the heavenly cycles, lower than all the cycles, swifter
than the heavenly winds, and spirits and elements and flying angels, with 6
wings to each angel. •And the moon has a sevenfold intercalation, and a period of   8
revolution of 19 years. And she begins once again from the start.

17 |About the angelic songs which it is not possible to describe. Word "16."|

In the middle of the heaven I saw armed troops, worshiping the LORD with tympani   1
and pipes and unceasing voices, and pleasant |voices and pleasant and unceasing|
and various songs, which it is impossible to describe. And every mind would be
quite astonished, so marvelous and wonderful is the singing of these angels. And
I was delighted, listening to them.

18 |About the taking of Enoch to the fifth heaven. Word "17."|

And those men took me up on their wings and placed me on the fifth heaven.   1
And I saw there many innumerable armies called Grigori.[a] And their appearance
was like the appearance of a human being, and their size was larger than that of
large giants. •And their faces were dejected,[b] and the silence of their mouths was   2
perpetual. And there was no liturgy in the fifth heaven. ⟨|And I said to the men
who were with me, "What is the explanation that these ones are so very dejected,
and their faces miserable, and their mouths silent? And (why) is there no liturgy
in this heaven?"|⟩ •And those men answered me, "These are the Grigori, who turned   3
aside from the LORD,[c] 200 myriads,[d] together with their prince Satanail. And similar to
them are those who went down as prisoners in their train, who are in the second heaven,
imprisoned in great darkness.
And three of them descended to the earth from the LORD's Throne onto the place   4

---

f. A U read "365." The actual total of the
preceding numbers is 364, which is the correct
length of the Qumran-En-Jub solar calendar. But
other MSS read "364" (B V N B²).

18 a. The Gk. word for "Watchers" is not translated. There is a vast amount of lore concerning
these beings. According to Philo Byblos, Sanchuniathon described the creation of "some living
beings who had no perception, out of whom
intelligent living beings came into existence, and
they were called *Zophasemin* (= Heb. *ṣōpê-šā-
mayim,* that is, "Watchers of Heaven"). And they
were formed like the shape of an egg" (*PrEv*
1.10.1–2). 1En devotes a lot of attention to the fall

of the "Watchers." For parallels between 1En and
1QapGen, see E. L. Sukenik, *The Dead Sea Scrolls
of the Hebrew University* (ed. N. Avigad and Y.
Yadin; Jerusalem, 1955), pp. 16f. In 3En the *ʿîrîn*
and *qaddîšîn* are found in the Council of the
Almighty. These must be unfallen "Watchers."
They are law-enforcement officers who stand in
the presence of the Judge—*whn ʿyryn qdyšyn
ʿwmdyn lpnyv kšwṭryn lpny hšwpṭ* (3En 28:8). In
the Book of John the Evangelist, the angels seduced
by Satan are in the fifth heaven, a significant link
with 2En.

b. After the word *ounyla,* "dejected," A has a
line and a half which had to be crossed out before
continuing with the correct *lica ikh,* "their faces."

[A]

4 Thus she goes in also by the western gates. And she completes the year,
5 365 days. •

6 With four exceptional ones she goes in the year.
   That is why they are excepted, outside heaven and the year;
   and in the number of the days they are not counted, for they
   exceed the duration of a year—2 new moons in her augmentation,
7 |two other new moons in her diminution|.   •   When the western gates are
   completed, then she turns around and goes to the eastern ones with her light. Thus
   she goes, day and night, in   a cycle, her orbit similar to heaven, and
   the chariot on which she ascends is a wind, passing along, pulling her chariot,
8 with her flying spirits, six wings to each angel. •
   This is the account of the moon.

17

1 In the middle of the heaven I saw armed troops, worshiping God with tympani
   and pipes and unceasing voices,

                              ⟨And I was delighted, listening⟩.

18 5th heaven.

1 And the men picked me up from there and carried me away to the fifth heaven.
   And I saw there many   armies and Grigori. And |their| appearance was like
   the appearance of a human being, and their size was larger than that of large giants.
2 And their faces were dejected, and the silence of their mouths . . .
   And there was no liturgy ⟨taking place in the fifth heaven⟩. And I said to the men
   who were with me, "For what reason are they   so   dejected,
   and their faces miserable, and their mouths silent? And (why) is there no liturgy

3 in this heaven?" •And the men answered me, "These are the Grigori, 200 princes
   of whom turned aside,
   200
   walking in their train,
4 and they descended to the earth,   Gen 6:1–4

The break comes exactly at the end of fol. 628r. in U. This suggests that the copy was being made from U, but at this point the scribe lost his place. He does not seem to have resumed at the top of a later column.

c. Forbes's (*APOT*, vol. 2, pp. 439f.) "the Lord of light" is to be rejected. Such titles are not used. "Lord" is never modified in 2En. The reading derives solely from P, *gã sĩa*, misread as an abbreviation of *svĕta*. But all other MSS which preserve the passage (it is much abbreviated in V N) read simply the numeral .S̆. (= 200).

d. The MSS differ in their estimates of the scale of this rebellion. J P R name Satanail as the ringleader. (1En names Senayaza [6:3; 9:7] but also Azazel [9:6].) J P (but not R!) accuse only "three of them" of the ultimate sin. It is hard to know what to do with B's *dvĕ knjazja i dvĕsti khodivšikhŭ vo slĕdĭ ikhŭ*, "two princes and two hundred walking in their train." The last detail (two hundred) is known from 1En 6:6 along with several other substantial details of the episode. The whole story is merely another version of the legend, but hardly intelligible without a knowledge of the more ample variants. 2En 18:5 (lacking in the shorter MSS) is so close to 1En 9:9 that it may be taken as original, showing that the shorter recension has censored out such details, not that the longer recension has interpolated the text, in this place at least. A U, however, read .S̆. (200) twice.

[J]

Ermon.[e] And they broke the promise on the shoulder[f] of Mount Ermon. And they saw the daughters of men, how beautiful they were; and they took wives for themselves, and the earth was defiled by their deeds.

Who ⟨and the wives of men created great evil⟩ in the entire time of this age acted 5 lawlessly and practiced miscegenation and gave birth to giants and great monsters and great enmity.

And that is why God has judged them with a great judgment; and they mourn 6 their brothers, and they will be outraged on the great day of the LORD." •And I 7 said to the Grigori, "I have seen your brothers and their deeds and their torments ⟨and⟩ their great ⟨prayers⟩; and I have prayed for them. But the LORD has sentenced them under the earth[g] until heaven and earth are ended forever." •And I said, 8 "Why are you waiting for your brothers? And why don't you perform the liturgy before the face of the LORD? Start up your liturgy, and perform the liturgy before the face of the LORD,[h] so that you do not enrage your LORD ⟨God⟩ to the limit."

And they responded to   my recommendation, and they stood in four 9 regiments in this heaven. And behold, while I was standing with those men, 4 trumpets trumpeted in unison with a great sound, and the Grigori burst into singing in unison. And their voice rose in front of the face of the LORD, piteously and touchingly.

19 |About the taking of Enoch to the 6th heaven. Word "18."|

And those men took me from there, and they carried me up to the 6th heaven. 1 And I saw there 7 groups of angels, brilliant and very glorious. And their faces were more radiant than the radiance of the sun, and there was no difference between their faces or in their dimensions or in the style of their clothing.[a]

And these groups carry out and carefully study the movements of the stars, and 2 the revolution of the sun and the phases of the moon, and the well-being of the cosmos.

And when they see any evil activity,   they put the commandments 3 and instructions in order, and the sweet choral singing[c] and every kind of glorious praise. These are the archangels who are over the angels; and they harmonize all existence, heavenly and earthly;

and angels who are over seasons and years, and angels who are over rivers and 4 the ocean, and angels who are over the fruits of the earth and over every kind of grass, and who give every kind of food to every kind of living thing;

and angels who record all human souls, and all their deeds,[d] and their lives before 5 the face of the LORD.

---

e. Mount Hermon as the scene of this wickedness probably goes back to a polemic against the cult of *Ba'al-Harmon*. See my note in *BASOR* 198 (1970), 41. It probably has a reflex in the god *Hārām-bêt-'ēl* of Elephantine. Vincent (*La Religion des Judéo-araméens à Éléphantine* [Paris, 1937] pp. 593–621) draws attention to the motif of sexual relations between divine beings and women as a link between this cult and the use of the word "Hermon" in the Enoch corpus: "Il est vraisemblable que si l'auteur du livre d'Hénoch a placé cette scène du serment des anges sur le sommet de l'Hermon, c'est précisément parce qu'une pratique de serment rituel avait rendu celui-ci célèbre" (p. 602).

f. A: *na ramĕ*. 1En 6:6 says that the oath was sworn on the summit *eis tēn koryphēn* of Mount Hermon. B has the interesting reading *na arame*. There are many possible explanations of these

variants. A major shift from the source in 1En is the inversion of the oath; originally the fallen angels swore to sin. Here "they broke the promise."

g. Since A and U confirm the reading "under the earth" found only hitherto in longer MSS (it is not in V N, hence lacking in Charles's B text in *APOT*), its genuineness cannot be doubted, although it simply does not fit the cosmography of the rest of the book, and even contradicts this very ch., which locates the other fallen angels in the second heaven. According to Plato (*Phaedrus* 248e–249b, 257a, 615a, b) the location of souls between incarnations is *hypo gēs*.

h. The reading of A U, "in the name of fire," *vo imja ogne*, is a corruption of "in front of the Lord." MSS of the longer recension agree in *prĕd lice Gospodne*. Since *ğŋ* is a common abbreviation for "LORD," corruption to "fire" is readily explained. The preposition in this "biblical" phrase,

[A]

and they broke the promise on the
shoulder of Mount Hermon,

5 to defile themselves with human wives. •

6 And, when they had defiled themselves, the LORD condemned them. And these
ones mourn for their brothers and for the outrage
7 which has happened." •But I, I said to the Grigori, "I, I have seen your brothers
and I have understood their accomplishments and I knew their prayers; and I have
prayed for them. And now the LORD has sentenced them under the earth until
8 heaven and earth are ended. •But   why are you waiting for your brothers?
And why don't you perform the liturgy before the face of the LORD? Start up the
former liturgy. Perform the liturgy in the name of fire, lest you
annoy the LORD your God (so that) he throws you down from this place."
9 ⟨And they heeded the earnestness of   my recommendation,   and they
stood in four regiments in   heaven. And behold,⟩ while I was standing,
they sounded with 4 trumpets in unison,   and the Grigori began to perform
the liturgy as with one voice. And their voices rose up into the LORD's presence.

19 6th heaven.

1 And the men took me away from there, and they brought me up to the 6th heaven.
And I saw there 7 angels, grouped together, brilliant and very glorious. And their
radiance was like the radiance of the sun when it shines.   There was no
difference between their faces or in their dimensions or in the mode of their being.
2 These ones regulate, they study the peaceful order of the stars, the birth[b] of the
sun and the moon.

3 And they are the leaders of the angels and of celestial speech. And they make all
celestial life peaceful; and they preserve the commandments and instructions, and
sweet voices and singing, every kind of praise and glory.

4 And there are angels over seasons and years, and there are also angels over rivers   Rev 16:5
and oceans, angels over fruit
and grass, and of everything that breeds;
5 and angels of all people, and all their life they organize and write it down before
the face of the LORD.

---

lipnê Yhwh = enōpion tou Kyriou, varies in
translation. It can be prĕdŭ, na, or vo/vŭ/v and B
agrees in reading vo. But how "name" came from
"face" is hard to explain. Perhaps it is original,
and "in the name of the LORD" became "in the
name of fire" in A U and "in (front of) the face
of the LORD" in other MSS.

19 a. Where longer MSS have (so)pri/eloženia
odeždi, or the like, shorter MSS present a variety
of readings for the first word, some agreeing with
those in J P R, some more abstract. V N and other
shorter MSS agree that the second word is odežde,
but A U have the difficult ŏdrŭža, which could
mean something like "power" but is probably just
a mistake.

b. A U agree in roženie. B tĕčenie; others
khoždenie, "movement," which is perhaps correct.
Yet it is possible that we are here rather close to

an astrology, grounded in polytheism. The participle kipjaštim (19:4) suggests growth if not birth.
These angels, managers of seasonal fertility, are
not far removed from the old nature gods, but
acceptable to Jewish-Christian thought because they
are now heavenly creatures, subservient to the will
of the one true God.

c. This motif, which derives from Isa 6, is
common in the apocalypses. They differ widely in
the location and scope of this music. In AscenIs it
takes place in every heaven. According to Epistula
Apostolorum 13 the angels perform the liturgy daily
at "the altar of the Father" in the highest heaven.

d. The task of these recording angels is carried
out by Enoch himself, according to 2En 43; and
2En 65:4 suggests that God himself keeps a journal
of every person's activities from birth to death.
These records will be produced on judgment day
(52:15; cf. 40:13).

[J]

And in the midst of them are 7 phoenixes[e] and 7 cherubim and 7[f] six-winged 6
beings, having but one voice and singing in unison. And their song is not to be
reported;[g] and the LORD is[h] delighted by his footstool.

20 |From there they took Enoch into the 7th heaven. Word "19."|[a]

And those men lifted me up from there, and they carried me up to the 7th heaven. 1
And I saw there an exceptionally great light, and all the fiery armies of the great
archangels, and the incorporeal forces and the dominions and the origins and the
authorities, the cherubim and the seraphim and the many-eyed thrones; (and) 5
{9|P|, 10⟨R⟩} regiments and the shining *otanim* stations.[b] And I was terrified, and
I trembled with a great fear.

And those men picked me up and led me into their ⟨midst⟩.[c] And they said to me, 2
"Be brave, Enoch! Don't be frightened!"

And they showed (me) the LORD, from a distance, sitting on his exceedingly high 3
throne. For what |is on the 10th heaven, since the LORD is present there? And on
the 10th heaven| is God, and it is called in the Hebrew language Aravoth.[d] And
all the heavenly armies came and stood on the ten steps, corresponding to their
ranks, and they did obeisance to the LORD.

And then they   went to   their places in joy and merriment and in 4
immeasurable light, singing songs with soft and gentle voices, while presenting
the liturgy to him gloriously.

21 |About how here the angels left Enoch at the edge of the 7th heaven, and
departed from him invisibly. Word "20."|[a]

And they do not leave by night, nor depart by day, standing in front of the face 1
of the LORD, and carrying out his will—cherubim and seraphim standing all around
his throne,   six-winged and many-eyed;[b] |and| they cover his entire throne,
singing with gentle voice in front of the face of the LORD.

> Holy, Holy, Holy, LORD |Lord| Sabaoth,
> Heaven and earth are full of his glory.

And when I had seen all these things, those men said to me, "Enoch, up to this 2
point we have been commanded to travel with you."[c] And the men went away
from me, and from then on I did not see them anymore. But I, I remained alone
at the edge of the seventh heaven. And I became terrified; and I fell on my face,
and I said in myself, "Woe to me! What has happened to me?"[d]

---

e. This is the only place in all literature where
the phoenix is not *sui generis*. The spelling varies,
finikī (R), *finizi* (P), but *funikŭ* (A).

f. In A U the lack of the words "and 7" makes
"six-winged" an attribute of "cherubim." Other
MSS (long and short) make the six-winged a third
group. Since the "six-winged" are seraphim in Isa
6, these, although not named as such, are probably
intended here. I don't know why Charles says that
there were six of each of these (*APOT* [A] vol. 2,
p. 441).

g. By adding *mošti* (V) or *moštno* (P), "their
song is not possible to describe." Other texts
suggest that it is forbidden.

h. While singular and plural are not always
distinguished in the spelling, the MSS tend to agree
that "the LORD rejoices," and the reflexive pronoun shows that this is correct. P, however, adds
the preposition *po*, and both J and P have *emu*,
making the angels rejoice. Instead of *raduet*, V
has *velit*—"the LORD makes merry"!

20 a. The main differences between the two recensions in this ch. are undoubtedly the result of
a revision that incorporated into the antecedent of
longer MSS details about three more heavens which
are incompatible with the scheme of seven heavens.
Even so, the genuine Heb. words which occur in
these interpolations show that they are not medieval
Slav. notions. The full textual assessment is complicated by the differences between J, P, and R in
these details. In addition to 20:3, these farther
heavens are mentioned by longer MSS at 21:6–
22:1.

At the other extreme, shorter MSS seem incoherent, as if they have been mutilated. In particular,
the tradition of ten ranks of angels in the seventh
heaven with corresponding lists has a better claim
to be authentic than the scheme of ten heavens,
even though these details also are now found only
in longer MSS. And even then, there are discrep-
ancies. All longer MSS agree in vs. 3 that there
are ten "steps" (*stepeni*) (shorter MSS have no
numeral at this point), but in vs. 1 each MS has a

[A]

6. And in the midst of them are 7 phoenixes and 7 cherubim,   six-winged beings, having but one voice and singing in themselves.   Their song is not to be reported; the LORD is delighted by his footstool(s).

20

1 And the men lifted me up from there, and they carried me up to   the seventh heaven. And I saw   a   great light, and all the fiery armies of the incorporeal ones, archangels,
angels,
and
the shining *otanim* stations. And I was terrified, and I trembled.

2   •And the men picked me up with their . . .
And they said to me, "Be brave, Enoch! Don't be frightened!"

3 And they showed me from a distance   the LORD,   sitting on his throne.

                    And all the heavenly armies assembled, according to rank, advancing and doing obeisance to the LORD.

4 And then they withdrew and went to their places in joy and merriment,   in immeasurable light,
but gloriously serving him . . .

1Kgs 22:19; Isa
6; Ezek1; Rev 4;
Col 1:16

2En 1:8

Isa 6:1; Rev 4:2;
5:1; 19:4; 21:3

21

1 . . . by night, nor departing by day, standing in front of the face of the LORD,   carrying out his will—with all the army of cherubim around his throne, never departing, and the six-winged ones covering his throne, singing in front of the face of the LORD.

Isa 6:2,3

2 And when I had seen all these things,
                    the men went away from me, and from then on I did not see them anymore. They placed me   at the edge of   heaven, alone. And I became terrified;   I fell on my face.

different number of "regiments" (*polŭkovŭ*)—5 in J, 9 in P, 10 in R. Elsewhere the term "rank" (*činŭ*) or "order" is used. Ten is probably correct, not only because of the ten steps in vs. 3, but because there is a Jewish and Christian tradition that there are ten or nine ranks of beings in the highest heaven. For the former see Maimonides, *Mishneh Torah* (S. 1); for the latter see below. Both Jewish and Christian lists vary extensively in both the identity and the hierarchical sequence of these ten (or nine). We cannot assume that chance lists are meant to give relative ranking.

b. The difficulties experienced by Slav. scribes with these quite genuine Heb. words are shown in the MSS. The worst readings are those of V N (*ostanimskoe*) and P (*ioanitskoe*) and B (*serafimskoe*). U, whether by accident or knowledge, is closest to the Heb. (*'ôpānîm*) with *ofanimiskoe* (it has added the Slav. adjectival ending to the Heb. plural), while A has the variant *othanimskoe;* and J R are still close with *oanim'skoe*, whose writing accounts for P as an error requiring no comment.

c. The readings of A U, *vŭ stredu*, is unintelligible. Either * *sled-* (J P read *slĕdŭ*), "in their train," that is, Enoch followed the two "men," or *sred-* (R reads *srĕdju*), "in their midst," that is, Enoch was taken right in among the regiments listed in vs. 1.

d. Shorter MSS lack the reference to the Heb. *Aravot* (here J is better than P's *aravatŭ*) here and in 22:1. Since these passages are missing from R as well, they are clearly interpolations.

21 a. Shorter MSS have no indication of any ch. break at this point. Although J does not have a ch. heading (these are found only in P) it does have a break, in spite of the continuous syntax.

b. The attribute "many-eyed" is only in J P, and, like the following *trisagion*, is probably an intrusion from Christian liturgy.

c. It is hard to tell if the farewell speech of "the men" is an addition to longer MSS or an omission from shorter ones.

d. Only longer MSS have an expression of misery at this point. All have it in vs. 4.

[J]

And the LORD sent one of his glorious ones, the archangel Gabriel.ᵉ And he said 3
to me, "Be brave, Enoch!ᶠ Don't be frightened! Stand up, and come with me and
stand in front of the face of the LORD forever."

And I answered him and said, "Woe to me,ᵍ my LORD!ʰ My soul has departed 4
from me from fear and horror. And call ⟨to me⟩ the two men who brought me to
this place, because I have put my confidenceⁱ in them, and with them I will go
before the face of the LORD." •⟨|And Gabriel carried me up, like a leaf carried 5
up by the wind.| He moved me along⟩ and put me down in front of the face of
the LORD. •And I saw the eighth heaven, which is called in the Hebrew language 6
Muzaloth, the changer of the seasons, of dry and of wet, and the 12 zodiacs,
which are above the seventh heaven. And I saw the ninth heaven, which in the
Hebrew language is called Kukhavim, where the heavenly houses of the 12 zodiacs
are.ʲ

22 |In the 10th heaven the archangel Michael brought Enoch in front of the face
of the LORD. Word "21."|

And on the 10th heaven, Aravoth,ᵇ I saw the view of the face of the LORD, like 1
iron made burning hot in a fire |and| brought out, and it emits sparks and is
incandescent.ᶜ Thus even I saw the face of the LORD.ᵈ But the face of the LORD
is not to be talked about, it is so very marvelous and supremely awesome and
supremely frightening. • |And| who am I to give an account of the incomprehensibleᵉ 2
being of the LORD, and of his face, so extremely strange and indescribable? And
how many are his commands,ᶠ and his multiple voice, and the LORD's throne,
supremely great and not made by hands, and the choir stalls all around him, the
cherubim and the seraphim armies, and their never-silent singing.

Who can give an account of his beautiful appearance, never changing 3
and indescribable, and his great glory? •And I fell down flat and did 4
obeisance to the LORD.ᵍ •And the LORD, with his own mouth, said to me,ʰ "Be 5

---

e. Gabriel's role here resembles that of Michael
in 22:6. In the earliest Jewish and Christian Midrashim on biblical themes there is a decided preference for Michael as the Lord's chief executive
officer—*arkhistratig* in 2En. Almost any unnamed
angel in the Bible is likely to be identified with
him. According to 1QapGen (22:1, 2), the *pālīṭ* of
Gen 14:13 who brought the report to Abraham was
a shepherd whom Abraham had given to Lot. In
other Midrashim it is King Og. According to PRE
it was Michael. In ApAb it is Michael who conducts
the patriarch to the gate of heaven; cf. the role of
Michael in transporting Melkizedek in 2En 72
(longer MSS). In 3Bar Michael is the Mediator
(cf. 2En 33:10) who conveys the prayers of the
righteous to God and who takes back rewards to
the faithful. And so on. In 1En it is Michael who
does the honors, and even in 2En, Gabriel seems
to have a lesser role, and is called merely "one of
his glorious ones," but longer MSS add "archangel." In view of the popularity of the cult of
Michael in the Christian East, his prominence in
2En does not help to settle the religious setting of
this document. But "Gabriel" could come from a
Christian hand, at least when he ousts Michael, as
in A and U's variant readings in ch. 72. Gabriel
as the Christian favorite is already competing for
Michael's honors in Origen's claim that Gabriel
supervises wars (*On First Principles* 1.8.1).

f. In V Gabriel addresses Enoch as "youth!"

g. MSS of both long and short traditions present
the alternatives *ouvy mně*, "Woe to me!" (V N B²

J—*oukhī* of R is equivalent to *ouvy*) and *vo mně*,
"in me" (A U B P). The latter is meaningless, but
should not be rejected as a corruption (Vaillant,
Secrets, p. 22). It is undoubtedly authentic. Its
association with "my lord" points to the Hebrew
bî 'ǎdōnî (*'ǎdōnāy*). The exclamation *bî*, entreaty
rather than dismay, is used twelve times in OT,
always followed by "my lord" and nearly always
speech initial. In the LXX Pentateuch it is translated
deomai (plural Gen 43:20) but elsewhere by an
absurd misunderstanding of *bî, en emoi*. This
misunderstanding is found here in 2En. Either 2En
has repeated the mistake of LXX (Heb. original)
or it has reproduced a LXX text (Gk. original).
False correction of "in me" to "Woe to me"
followed inevitably within the Slav. transmission.

h. It is remarkable that Enoch addresses the
archangel as "my LORD," the title used exclusively
for God. A U lack "my."

i. Most MSS read *upoěavakh*, "I have hoped";
but A *povědakh*.

j. Vs. 6 is lacking in R, the other longer
recension. Its status as an interpolation is thus
different from material which R shares with J
and P.

22 a. A U have the same ch. heading twice.

b. Shorter MSS lack these secondary references
to the tenth heaven.

c. The state of the MSS betray the embarrassment of scribes over this attempt to describe the
appearance of the Lord. Two tendencies may be

[A]

3 And the LORD sent one of his glorious ones to me,   Gabril. And he said to me, "Be brave, Enoch! Don't be frightened! Stand up, and come with me and stand in front of the face of the LORD forever."
4 And I answered him and said, "⟨Woe⟩ to me,   LORD! My soul has departed from me from fear   . And call to me the two men who brought me to this place, because I have   spoken   to them, and with them I will go before
5 the face of the LORD." •And Gabril carried me up, like a leaf carried up by the
6 wind. He moved me along and put me down in front of the face of the LORD. •

22 About the appearance of the LORD.[a]

1 I saw the LORD.

His face was strong and very glorious
and terrible.
2   •Who (is) to give an account of the dimensions of the being of the face of the LORD, strong and very terrible? Or his many-eyed ones and
many-voiced ones, and the supremely great throne of the LORD, not
made by hands, or those who are in attendance all around him, the cherubim and
3 the seraphim armies,   or how unvarying and indescribable •and never-silent and glorious is his service.
4   •And I fell down flat and did
5 obeisance to the LORD. •And the LORD, with his own mouth, called to me, "Be

observed. One tries to expurgate the physical imagery, especially the comparison with scintillating iron. This has been heavily censored in short MSS, but V N have omitted vss. 1–3 altogether; hence their absence from the B text in *APOT*. V N also go on to say that Enoch fell on his face and did not even look at the Lord. The survival of the same details in both recensions at 39:3 shows that the comparison with hot iron is original; but here (22:1) it is lacking in all shorter MSS. This shows that sometimes J P might be the only MSS preserving authentic readings. In contrast shorter MSS have moved toward more abstract ideas (e.g. "the extent of the Lord's being"), yet even here the MSS falter. A, for instance, seems to read *iobijatŭ* with an illegible letter, like *fi*, above the omega. The spelling of U suggests that an infinitive was intended, with the result "who am I [or who is able] to describe the extent [*amplexus*] of the Lord's face as it is [*suštee*]." The latter is the participle (used as an adjective meaning "actual"), whereas all longer MSS have *suštestvo*, "being" in the abstract sense of "existence." Vaillant (*Secrets*, p. 26) restores *suštie (ousia, substantia)* as an intermediate reading.

But it is more likely that behind this language lies mystical speculation about the physical size of God (see ch. 39).

R is sufficiently distinct to be reproduced separately: "And I saw the LORD in the face. And his face is strong and very glorious [here R agrees with A U], marvelous and supremely frightening

[-*užas*-, where A U have *straš*-], terrible and horrifying [here R has *pritranno*, where J P have *prestrasno*]."

d. Cf. the face of fire seen by Jacob at the top of the ladder in LadJac. In the Book of John the Evangelist Satan's face becomes like heated iron.

e. Longer MSS incline to "the way of negation," using *neispovedimoe* (three times in J P but also in A U at the end of vs. 3). Yet the emphasis is not that God is unknowable, or even inconceivable, but rather indescribable, and then, not because it is impossible, but because it is forbidden. The Slav. connotations of *ispovedati* are with *eksomologein* but *neispovedimoe* is closer to *anekdiēgētos*. J R also have *neobětoe* ("not to be betrayed"?) and P reads *neizrečennoe (afatos, anekfrastos)*.

f. J P R agree in the reading *mnogo-učenii ego*, "his abundant knowledge" (*multum eruditum*), which is probably inferior to A U *mnogo-očnoe*. The former is not suitable, since the connections of *učenie* are with imparted teaching rather than inherent wisdom. Hence "instructions" (*APOT*, vol. 2, p. 443). But here the narrator has retreated, as biblical writers so often do, from describing God to depicting his splendid supernal setting (vs. 2).

g. In V N the sequence of events is different: Vss. 8–10 come before vs. 5, and vs. 11 follows vs. 7 (see *APOT* B).

h. The Lord's speech of welcome is identical in all MSS, except for the verb. A U have "called me"; J P R "said to me"; while V N read "called me and said."

[J]

brave, Enoch! Don't be frightened! Stand up, and stand in front of my face forever." • And Michael, the LORD's archistratig,[i] lifted me up and brought me in 6 front of the face of the LORD. And the LORD said to his servants,[j] sounding them out, "Let Enoch join in and stand in front of my face forever!"[k] • And the LORD's 7 glorious ones did obeisance and said, "Let Enoch yield[l] in accordance with your word, O LORD!"

And the LORD said to Michael, "Go, and extract[m] Enoch from |his| earthly 8 clothing. And anoint him with my delightful oil, and put him into the clothes of my glory."[n] • And so Michael did, just as the LORD had said to him. He anointed 9 me[o] and he clothed me. And the appearance of that oil is greater than the greatest light, and its ointment is like sweet dew, and its fragrance　　　myrrh;

and it is like the rays of the glittering sun. • And I looked at myself, and I had 10 become like one of his glorious ones,[p] and there was no observable difference.[q]

---

i. Slav. "archistratig." Michael's military functions are anciently attested. In IQM he is the one who overthrows the Kittim. In spite of the title used in 2En, there are no combat motifs in this book. A U have replaced the title with "great archangel." But *arkhistratigŭ* (J P R B V N B²) is certainly correct. A's variant comes from Dan 11:1 (*ho aggelos ho megas*), where the adjective is elative, making Michael at least an archangel, if not the senior one.

j. This act of the Lord in consulting the heavenly assembly is very significant. But it is difficult to know where to place it in the history of ideas. The ancient Mesopotamians believed it was impossible for a human to gain permanent admittance to the community of divine beings. Gilgamesh is asked,

Now who will call the gods for you to assembly,
that you may find the life you are seeking
(*Gilgamesh* 11:197f.).

The motif recurs in many stories of futile attempts of desperate or presumptuous mortals to scale the height of heaven, or of the achievement of a transient visit as the limit of possibility. The discussion in the divine assembly provides the starting point of many OT oracles, and prophets participate in some way, if only in a vision.

The scene in 2En 22 retains quite a lot of this mythology. There is no real debate. The Lord makes a proposal and the angels concur. The verb *iskusiti/iskusati*, found in both recensions, is strange, since it means "test" or "tempt." The question is whether a human as such should be admitted or whether Enoch should become an angel. The sequel shows that it is the latter. Note the backdrop of Gilgamesh:

When the gods created mankind
death for mankind they set aside
life in their own hands retaining
(10.3:3–5).

Ps 115:16 also affirms that

Heaven belongs to Yahweh
while he gave the earth to mankind.

The inevitability of death is one thing; possible admittance to heaven after death is another. In the case of Enoch the impression is given that entrance to heaven is possible only if death is circumvented. On the other hand, the events in ch. 22 might secure a release from the body essentially the same as death. In Egyptian Christian tradition, as found in the History of Joseph the Carpenter (ch. 31), in order to stress the universality of death, Jesus teaches that even Enoch and Elijah will have to

die in due course. Note the introductory comment to the extract from 2En in *MPr*, "he is still alive."

k. In a prayer to Boris and Gleb, the martyred princes, Yaroslav the Wise says, *Blagodatiju živa esta i gospodevi predŭstoita*, "By grace you (two) are alive, and stand in front of the Lord" (*Skazanie o Borise i Glebe*). Note the contrast of the native idiom here with the Semitism in 2En—*stoati prědŭ licě Gi*. The persistence of this simple but primitive and Hebraic anthropomorphism "in front of the face of God" is all the more striking since the movement to more abstract language is already in full swing in LXX. Thus Pss 17:15; 63:3 become in Gk. "to appear before God" (LXX 16:15; 62:3) instead of "to see the face of God."

l. The state of the MSS at vs. 7 shows that the scribes, if not the angels, were embarrassed by the proposal. In short MSS the response is simple, "Let him ascend," using the same word as the question. Longer MSS have become more ceremonial. But in J R the reply is *ustupit*. Since *MSD* (vol. 3, p. 1291) gives *otstupit'* as a meaning of *ustupiti*, P's reading (*otstupit*) could be no more than a gloss, although mistaken, since it seems to mean "retreat" or "depart," "withdraw," while *da ustupit*, "let him keep away," or any other of its several meanings, does not fit since "in accordance with your word" implies acquiescence.

m. The imagery of extracting a person from his garment is close to the terminology of Dan 7:15, "my spirit was upset inside its sheath." The same idea is found in 1QapGen 2:10, *wnšmty lgw ndnh'*, "and my breath within its sheath." Aram. *nĕdān* is a loan from Persian *nidāni*, "container."

In 2En there is no explicit talk about soul and body. But the identification (or at least a simile) is made in the 1076 *Sbornik* (p. 237, ll. 5–6): *tělo bo naše jestī aky riza*, "for our body is like a garment." Enoch is not simply liberated from his "clothing"; he has to be clothed upon (2Cor 5:3). In Rev the saints wear white robes (Rev 6:11; 7:9, 13, 14); these are not identified as a transformed body, but they are white by virtue of Christ's atonement, a need not recognized in 2En. In the Chaldean oracles the soul, as it travels through the planetary spheres, puts on successive garments corresponding to the qualities of the stars.

n. "The clothes of my glory" is a transparent Hebraism.

o. There is not enough detail about this chrism to betray the influence of baptismal practice. The symbolism is compatible with Christian ritual, but

[A]

brave, Enoch! Don't be frightened! Stand up, and stand in front of my face
6 forever." •And Michael, the LORD's greatest archangel, lifted me up and brought
me in front of the face of the LORD. And the LORD sounded out his servants. The
7 LORD said, "Let Enoch come up and stand in front of my face forever!" •And
the   glorious ones did obeisance and said, "Let   him   come up!"
8   •The LORD said to Michael, "Take Enoch, and extract (him) from   Zech 3:4,5;
the earthly clothing. And anoint him with the delightful oil, and put (him) into   2Ezra 2:39,45; 2Cor 5:3,4

9 the clothes of   glory." •And   Michael extracted me from my clothes. He   Rev 3:4,5,18;
anointed me with the delightful oil; and the appearance of that oil is greater than   4:4; 6:11; 7:9,13,14
the greatest light, its ointment is like sweet dew, and its fragrance like myrrh;
10 and its shining is like the sun. •And I gazed at all of myself, and I had become   Mt 13:43
like one of the glorious ones, and there was no observable difference. And the

there is no washing. It is the effulgent oil that gives Enoch the radiant countenance, dangerous to human beholders. This motif seems to have been influenced by the legend of Moses, whose shining face was a reflection of God's magnificent glory.

Philip, in his prayer before martyrdom, and evidently anticipating the heavenly condition (cf. Acts 6:15), says, "Clothe me in thy glorious robe and thy seal of light that ever shineth" (James, *ANT*, p. 450). Cf. Mt 13:43. Origen (*On First Principles* 2.3.7) speaks of the best and purest spirits, who must have some kind of body, being changed according to their degree of merit into an ethereal condition, and interprets "change" in 1Cor 15:52 as "shining with light."

p. At Qumran the souls of the righteous after death live with God "like angels" while the souls of the wicked go to join the spirits of Belial (1QS 4:6–8, 11–13; 1QM 12:1–7). This could indicate little more than their final location. The Christians resurrected are "like the angels in heaven" (Mt 22:30); but again this touches only the question of sexuality.

Epiphanius' account of Ebionite Christology casts Christ in a role not unlike that of Enoch in 2En, although the latter does not use adoptionist terminology.

Note the following: "They say that he was not begotten of God the Father, but created as one of the archangels . . . that he rules over the angels and all the creatures of the Almighty" (*AdvHaer* 30.16.4f.). It is not clear whether this act of "creation" explains the origination of Christ; but it does not say precisely that Christ was one of the originally created archangels, but made (to be) like one of them. Elsewhere in Ebionite teaching, according to the same Epiphanius, Jesus was constituted as Christ by the union of the Holy Spirit with the man. In any case the installation of Enoch does not seem to be contaminated at any point by Christian ascension doctrine. It is hard to tell how far 2En goes in the transmutation of a human to an angelic being. In the Christian synthesis with Gk. belief in the immortality of the soul as the main thing, the resurrection of the body dwindled in significance; at least the body was spiritualized so as to be hardly human any longer. This point could have been reached by Origen, although what he actually believed is hard to retrieve behind Rufinus' translation. To judge from the Gk. fragment preserved by Justinian (*Ep. ad Mennam*), Rufinus has accurately represented Origen's views

in *On First Principles* 1.6.2. A righteous soul may merit "the rank of angel." Jerome is, accordingly, probably perverse when he accuses Origen of "mixing everything up" (*Ep. ad Avitum* 3) by teaching "that one who is now a man may in another world become a demon," while a demon may become a man or an angel. He does not specifically accuse Origen of teaching that a man may become an angel, but complains about the idea of changing an archangel into a devil. Here Jerome goes too far, for Origen is on safe scriptural ground. He has avoided the trap in his statement that "the end is always like the beginning" (1.6.2) because he has recoiled from the logical inference that God originally made demons as such and that they "inherit this realm of darkness . . . from the necessity of their creation" (1.5.3). On the contrary, the differentiation in the hierarchy of moral beings is entirely due to the freedom of their rational natures. Origen falls back on the Bible when he expounds the fall of Lucifer (see also 1. Preface. 6). But he is in real difficulty by regarding all three species of rational creatures as having a common mode of being in moral freedom, especially since he regards this as constitutionally all-important. For, placing man in between angel and demon, he sees him capable of improvement or deterioration. Having admitted the fall of Satan, he finds it hard to teach the indefectibility of the loyal angels. Having admitted that man may be restored to his former state, it is hard for him to exclude demons from the same possibility. Hence his alleged heresy that Satan would be saved.

Enoch not only attains the rank (i.e. location and function) of an angel; he becomes like the members of the highest echelon in the seventh heaven. If Origen had known this tradition, it might have suited him to quote it. The problem seems to be behind the obscure language of 2En 31. It is not clear how much the events in 2En 18 imply the salvation of the angels in the fifth heaven. Those in the second heaven don't appear to have such a prospect; and all humans, blessed and cursed, are in between, in the third heaven.

q. The emphasis is physical. His face is incandescent (37:2); he has lost all desire for food (56:2), an effect ascribed directly to the oil of glory (but 42:5 speaks of feasting in eternal life); he does not seem to need sleep (23:3; cf. Rev 4:8); and there are statements elsewhere that suggest that he has become omniscient. In *Gilgamesh* (1.4.34, cf. 1. 29) and in the Bible (Gen 3:22) it is the acquisition

[J]

And the LORD summoned one of his archangels, Vrevoil[r] by name, who was swifter[s] in wisdom than the other archangels,

and who records all the LORD's deeds. •And the LORD said to Vrevoil, "Bring 11 out the books from my storehouses, and fetch a pen for speed-writing, and give it to Enoch and read him the books."[t] (And Vrevoil hurried and brought me the books,) a knife(?), and ink(?). And he gave me the pen for speed-writing from his hand.

23 |About Enoch's writing; how he wrote about his marvelous travels and what the heavens look like. And he himself wrote 360 and 6 books. Word "22."|[a]

And he was telling me all the things of heaven[b] and earth and sea and all the 1 elements and the movements and their courses, and the living thunder, the sun and the moon and the stars, their courses[c] and their changes, and seasons and years and days and hours, and

the coming of the clouds and the blowing of the winds, and the number of the angels and the songs of the armed troops;

and every kind of human thing, and every kind of language (and) singing, and 2 human life and rules and instructions and sweet-voiced singing, and everything that it is appropriate to learn.

And Vrevoil instructed me for 30 days and 30 nights, and his mouth never stopped 3 speaking. And, as for me, I did not rest,[d] writing

all the symbols and all the creatures.[e] •And when I had finished 30 days and 30 4 nights, Vrevoil said to me, "These things, whatever I have taught you, whatever you have learned, and whatever we have written down, you sit down |and| write— all the souls of men, whatever of them are not yet born, and their places, prepared for eternity.[f]

For all the souls are prepared for eternity, before the composition 5 of the earth." •And I sat down for a second period of 30 days and 30 nights, and 6 I wrote everything accurately. And I wrote[g] 366 books.[h]

24 |About the great secrets of God, which God revealed and related to Enoch; and he spoke with him face to face. Word "23."|

---

of wisdom or knowledge that makes a human "like God."

r. P's reading *Pravail* is deviant. The other numerous variations in spelling are not material. The name is otherwise unknown, and remains unexplained. As an archangel, he resembles Uriel, and the names are not unlike. As the scholar archangel, is Vrevoil modeled upon Thoth = Hermes = Mercury in the Egyptian-Phoenician tradition as reported by Sanchuniathon (Philo Byblos—Eusebius)? According to Diodorus, Thoth was scribe to Osiris, and tomb paintings often illustrate this. The tradition is that Sanchuniathon obtained his theology from the books of Thoth, just as Enoch got his from Vrevoil. Vrevoil's epithet here (swift in wisdom) agrees with Hermes' reputation for nimble wit. But the idea that a human learns the secrets of existence (or even acquires power) by gaining access to the heavenly tablets (of destiny) is an ancient one in Mesopotamia (the Adapa myth has much in common with the Enoch legends). And Eusebius connects Manetho's history with Thõ(y)th, who inscribed it first on some pillars in the land of Seriad, and after the cataclysm they were translated into Gk.

s. The epithet reminds us of *māhîr*, an epithet of the greatest scribes, beginning with Ezra.

t. The apocryphal documents contain numerous references to books in heaven; these ideas evolved out of the OT.

23 a. The commencement of a new ch. here in longer MSS is not suitable. Other MSS do not provide a break when Vrevoil is introduced at 22:10. But A begins a new section in the middle of 23:1.

b. The reading "LORD" (A U) is secondary, since other short MSS agree with long ones in the series "heaven and earth and sea."

c. The longer list of topics in J P R has high claim for authenticity. A U represent an intermediate stage of abbreviation between this and such MSS as V N (compare B in *APOT*, vol. 2, pp. 443f.). In contrast to the orderly list in J, the text of A U—"earthly commands and instructions and sweet-voiced singing"—seems garbled and, in fact, unintelligible compared with vs. 2 in J. Note that P has lost by simple scribal error the reference to clouds.

The reference to "the Hebrew language" is a

[A]

LORD summoned Vereveil, one of his archangels, who was wise,

11   who records all the LORD's deeds. •And the LORD said to Vereveil, "Bring out the books from the storehouses, and give a pen
               to Enoch and read him the books." And Vereveil hurried and brought me the books mottled with myrrh. And he gave me the pen   from his hand.

23

1 And he was telling me all the deeds of the LORD, the earth and the sea, and all the elements and the courses and the life,

and the changes of the years and the movements of the days, and the earthly commands and instructions, and the sweet-voiced singing and the coming of the clouds and the blowing of the winds,
2 and the Hebrew language, every kind of language of the new song of the armed troops,
and everything that it is appropriate to learn.
3 And Vereveil instructed me for 30 days and 30 nights, and his mouth never stopped speaking. And, as for me, I did not rest for 30 days and
4 30 nights, writing all the symbols. •And when I had finished, Vereveil said to me,

"You sit down; write everything that I have explained to you."

5   Mt 25:34
6   •And I sat down for a second period of 30 days and 30 nights, and I wrote accurately. And I expounded 300 and 60 books.

24

gloss peculiar to A and U. Vs. 2 refers to "all the languages."

d. The agreement of A U with J R (against P), and its fuller reading contrasted with the other short MSS, restores a better text. It makes it clearer that the work was done in two stages of thirty days each.

e. R and J agree in the addition "and all the creatures," implying the compiling of lists of created things. The term *znamenia* suggests that the copyist copied omen texts.

f. Short MSS lack the details about human souls and their destinies. The phrase "formation of the earth" (*zemlŭnago*) is reminiscent of Mt 24:34, and could be a Christian gloss. But the passage implies the pre-existence as well as the predestination of all souls. Even Adam existed before he was sent to the earth (ch. 32). A knowledgeable Christian scribe would recognize here the views of Origen on the subject condemned by the Second Council of Constantinople. That is, short MSS look more like orthodox censorship than long ones look like Christian interpolation.

g. A U: *ispovědakh*, "expounded"; other MSS

simply *izpisakh, napisakh,* or simply *pisakh,* "wrote (down)."

h. The recensions divide consistently over the number of books produced, whether 360 (short MSS) or 366 (long). When Popov published the 1679 Poltava copy (P) in 1880, he searched for evidence of the earlier circulation of this hitherto unknown work. He found a book called "Enoch" mentioned in a list of "disapproved" (i.e. non-canonical) books in a 14th-cent. MS; and a later list mentions: *Enokhŭ—o Enosě, čto bylŭ na pjatomŭ nevesi i ipisalŭ 300 knigŭ,* "Enoch—about Enoch, who was at the fifth [!] heaven and wrote 300 books." I have not been able to confirm this information.

There is a deviant Enoch tradition in the Book of St. John, allegedly Bogomil. In this work it is Satan who creates the world, and the angels who came to Enoch were his emissaries. They took him up into the firmament to behold his |Satan's| godhead. "And he commanded pen and ink to be given him, and he sat down and wrote 67 books" (James, *ANT,* p. 190).

[J]

And the Lord called me; and he said to me, "Enoch, sit to the left of me[a] with 1
Gabriel."   And I did obeisance to the LORD.
And the LORD spoke to me: "Enoch |Beloved|, whatever you see and whatever 2
things are standing still or moving about were brought to perfection by me. And
I myself will explain it to you.

Before anything existed at all, from the very beginning, whatever exists I created[c]
from the non-existent, and from the invisible the visible.
|Listen, Enoch, and pay attention to these words of mine!| For not even to my 3
angels[d] have I explained my secrets, nor related to them their origin, nor my
endlessness (and inconceivableness), as I devise the creatures,
as I am making them known to you today. •For, before any visible things had 4
come into existence,
     I, the ONE,[f] moved around in the invisible things, like the sun,
           from east to west and from west to east.
But the sun has rest in himself; yet I did not find rest,[h] because everything was 5
not yet created. And I thought up the idea[i] of establishing a foundation, to create
a visible creation.

25 |God explains to Enoch how the visible and the invisible come down from
the very lowest darkness. Word "24."|[a]

---

24 a. In 2En 24:1 Enoch sits at God's left hand,
next to Gabriel. No explanation is given of what
he is doing there, or why he is on the left. Nothing
is said about who is on the right-hand side. The
position assigned to Enoch elsewhere is different:
"standing in front of the face of the Lord."

b. This chapter heading, a rarity in A U, is in
the text of A, followed by a large letter. A Gk. *pi*
is in the margin of U.

c. The genre of recasting a biblical story into
autobiographical form is already present in the
reminiscences of Wisdom in Prov 8. But Wisdom
describes creation as carried out by God. God's
own account is given by the author of Job 38.

d. Cf. 40:3. In the NT the mystery that the
angels are curious about is the Gospel. Here it is
the story of creation. This is the only subject on
which the Lord himself discourses to Enoch. According to *Epistula apostolorum* (19) believers have
privileges denied to angels.

e. Vaillant's "birth" (*Secrets*, p. 29), which is
not a suitable word for the origin of angels in any
work remotely connected with the Bible, comes
from a purely conjectural emendation, *vŭstavlenija*,
behind which he sees *anastasis*.

f. The texts of the two recensions are not the
same at this vital point; but the picture is not
altogether clear in either of them. Both agree (vs.
5) that creation arose from a restlessness or lack
of equilibrium in God himself at the very first, in
contrast to the stability of the sun's movement.
J P R seem closer to the doctrine of creation *ex
nihilo* than the others, since they say more absolutely "I was (the only) One," whereas A U say
"like one (of them?)." V is quite clear in its
reading, "like one of the invisible things." Even
so, the impression remains that God was not the
only existent being or thing from the very first,
although each recension gives this impression in

its own way. Both agree that God made the existent
out of the non-existent, the visible out of the non-
visible. So the invisible things coexisted with God
before he began to make anything. (Contrast Christian belief that God made all things visible and
invisible.) Vs. 4 is quite explicit on this point:
Before any of the visible things had come into
existence, God was moving around among the
invisible things.

g. 2En's cosmology does not derive all existence
from one original substance, such as water (Thales)
or fire (Heraclitus), or a common indeterminate
substance (Anaximander) or mist (Anaximenes);
nor from four: fire, air, water, earth. Even so, an
attempt is made to account for these elements, and
the idea of mixture is present. But the biblical
process of differentiation and separation is still
recognized. Unlike the original, this version of Gen
1 gives prominence to fire, but it is quite derivative.

Some other unidentified mythology is given more
room than Gk. physics. Out of the original invisible
things, God calls two beings: Adoil, from whom
is born the great light, and Arukhas, from whom
comes the darkness. Water is made by thickening
a mixture of light and darkness. But light, if
anything, is the great elemental substance.

h. The primal restlessness of God contrasts with
the main trends of philosophy, especially those of
an absolute idealism, where by definition, God,
the perfect being, knows no change, and, of course,
has no needs. In gnostic thought, God is perfect
rest, and to this restless souls may themselves
attain.

That God himself is seeking repose comes out
already in Eccl. The restlessness of God is expressed
in the age-long quest of Wisdom or of the Holy
Spirit for a place of permanent rest. Eccl 24:7
represents Wisdom as seeking *anapausis* "from
generation to generation, passing into holy souls"

[A]

1 And the Lord called me; and he placed me   to the left of himself closer than Gabriel.   And I did obeisance to the LORD.

2 And the LORD spoke to me: "Whatever you see, Enoch,   things Heb 11:3
     standing still and moving about and which were brought to perfection by me,   I myself will explain it to you.

About the construction of creation.[b]

Before anything existed at all, from the very beginning, whatever is I created from non-being into being, and from the invisible things into the visible.

3   •And not even 1Pet 1:12;
                                                             Sir 42:17
to my angels have I explained my secrets, nor related to them their composition,[e] nor my endless   and inconceivable creation which I conceived,

4   as I am making them known to you today. •   Before any visible things had come into existence, and the light had not yet opened up,   I, in the midst of the light,[g] moved around in the invisible things, like one of them, as the sun moves around from east to west and from west to east.

5 But the sun has rest   ; yet I did not find rest, because everything was not yet created. And I thought up the idea of establishing a foundation, to create a visible creation.

25

(WisSol 7:27). Similarly, according to the Pseudo-Clement Homily III 20:2, the *Kerygmata Petrou* (a Jewish-Christian gnostic work) represents the pre-existent redeemer as spending the ages "changing his form at the same time as his name" until he becomes incarnate in Jesus, and so attains to eternal rest.

According to GHeb, a similar eschatological rest is attained by the Holy Spirit when the Son comes forth, and the Spirit "rests" upon him. The Spirit declares, "You are my rest."

The idea of rest is central in the Pseudo-Clementines, and their ultimate statement about God is "You are rest." Here then is a metaphysical counterpart (God is *anapausis*) to match the Christian "God is *agape* (love)."

2En sees the restlessness of God as the fact behind creation. It does not say how (or even whether) the creation satisfied God's need for rest. It seems to be building up for an interpretation of Gen 2:2f, which says that God rested on the seventh day.

The connection with creation is found also in the Apocryphon of John, where it is likened to the restlessness of Sophia at the beginning. This explains "moving over" in Gen 1:2. Wisdom was moving around at the first in the darkness of ignorance.

i. Philo's idea is that God "conceived beforehand the models of its parts, and that out of these he constituted and brought to completion a world discernable only by the mind (*Kosmos noētos*) and then, with that for a pattern, the world which our senses can perceive" (*On the Creation* 19). Cf. 24:2, which says that God made the visible out of the invisible.

25 a. If the sources behind this portion of 2En are ancient, it could represent one of the earliest

attempts to reconcile the Bible with science. It tries to integrate Gk. physics with Gen 1. Yet it does not have an avowed apologetic intention.

The cosmic-creative processes in 2En can be summarized as follows:

1. *Disintegration*, of light from Adoil (25:2), of darkness from Arukhas (26:2).

2. *Solidification* or thickening, the light solidifies into the upper foundation (25:4); the darkness solidifies into the lower foundation (26:3). In fact, this process of solidification (consolidation) seems to take place in two stages. To judge from 26:1 Arukhas is solidified from the original invisible things; but ch. 25 does not begin with a matching statement that Adoil (the light-bearer) was a consolidation of originally visible things, for original existence consisted of invisible things only. Water, in turn, results from the consolidation of a mixture of light and darkness (27:2); the heavenly circles (28:1) and earthly rocks (28:2) are solidified from water. Fire is one stage further in the solidification of rock (29:2).

3. *Mixing*, of light and darkness in order to produce water (27:2); the seven crystalline circles are a mixture of wet and dry; lightning is a mixture of water and fire (29:1). Finally the constitution of man involves more complex mixtures, which are discussed in several different ways.

At some points Gen is simply paraphrased with little embellishment, as on the rather uneventful fifth day (30:7), except that animals, as well as fish and birds, are made then, leaving man alone to be created on the sixth day. At other places there is not only embellishing but also drastic restructuring, as in the elaborate account of the creation of man (almost completely lacking in short MSS); or the bringing in of other biblical materials to enlarge the picture (the creation of angels and the fall of Satanail on the second day). Most of

[J]

"And I commanded the lowest things:[b] 'Let one of the invisible things descend 1
visibly!' And Adoil descended, extremely large. And I looked at him, and, behold,
in his belly he had a great light.[c] •And I said to him, 'Disintegrate yourself,[d] 2
Adoil, and let what is born from you become visible.' And he disintegrated
himself, and there came out a very
great light. •And I was in the midst of the |great| light. And light out of light is 3
carried thus. And the great age came out, and it revealed all the creation which I
had thought up to create. And I saw how good it was.
And I placed for myself a throne, and I sat down on it. And then to the light I 4
spoke: 'You go up higher ⟨than the throne⟩,[e] and be solidified |much higher than
the throne|, and become the foundation for the highest things.'
And there is nothing higher than the light, except nothing itself. And again I 5
bowed(?)[f] myself, and I looked upward from my throne.[g]

26 |God summons from the very lowest things a second time, so that Arkhas,
both heavy and red, should come out. Word "25."|

"And I called out a second time into the very lowest things, and I said, 'Let one 1
of the (in)visible[a] things come out visibly, solid.'
|And| Arkhas[b] came out, solid and heavy and very red.[c] •And I said, 'Open 2
yourself up, Arkhas, and let what is born from you become visible!' And he
disintegrated himself. There came out an age, dark, very large, carrying the
creation of all lower things. And I saw how good it was.
And I said to him, 'Come down low and become solid! And become the foundation 3
of the lowest things!' |And it came about.| And he came down and became solid.
And he became the foundation of the lowest things. And there is nothing lower
than the darkness, except nothing itself.[d]

27 |About how God founded the water, and surrounded it with light, and
established on it seven islands. Word "26."|[a]

the events of the first three days in Gen 1 take
place on the first day in 2En, leaving the second
day for making angels; the third day is devoted
entirely to the creation of Paradise. The two accounts are in phase at the fourth day.
   Even when biblical vocabulary is used it is
sometimes given a different "scientific" meaning.
On the third day, according to Gen 1, God separated
the sea from the land by "gathering" the water
together, so that the dry land "appeared." In 2En
(day one!) this "collection" is interpreted as the
solidification of water into rock.
   b. R reads "highest," which is more symmetrical.
   c. There are three readings: *věka velikago*, "great
age" (A U B Chr); *kamyka prěvelikaago*, "very
large stone" (V N B²); *světa* (J P R).
   d. Or "let (something) visible be loosed from
you." P lacks the repeated word, and J R *raždaemo*
seems to have used the root "to give birth." See
n. i to my translation of *MPr*.
   e. See Eccl 24:4f.
   f. The significance of this action remains obscure. It evidently puzzled the scribes, since the
MSS vary widely. First, the unsuitable chapter
division has isolated this statement, making it the
last action of the preceding episode rather than the
first action of the next one. Secondly, the sequence
of actions varies in the MSS. All culminate in the
second creative command (26:2) and the two preceding actions could be preparation for this. Prior

to the first command, God was moving around;
prior to the second he was seated on his throne.
Thirdly, the verb is usually associated with obeisance in worship, *vùskloniti* being the opposite of
nakloniti. Fourthly, on top of the mystery of the
Lord bending or straightening himself, the associated activity—before this in short MSS, after it in
long ones—is described by several different verbs:
vùzrěkhŭ, "gazed" (J P R); *zrěkhŭ*, "looked" (B
Chr); *rěkh*, "said" (A U); *viděkhŭ*, "saw" (V N).
   g. Much of the creation story now in long MSS
could be original, allowing also that short MSS
have sustained heavy losses and long ones probably
contain some interpolations.

   26 a. The connection between "visible" and "invisible" is not clear. The confusion in the MSS
reflects a tension between telling the stories of
Adoil and Arkhas along the same lines, as against
the idea that Arkhas produces darkness and so,
perhaps, is never visible. In this cosmogony, then,
both light and darkness come out of the original
"invisible," each becoming visible in its own way.
In Gen 1:3 God commands the light to shine into
pre-existent darkness; in 2Cor 4:6 the light shines
out of darkness.
   b. The name Arkhas invites identification with
Gk. *arkhē*, not unexpected in cosmology. *Arkhē* is
one of the most fundamental concepts of pre-
Socratic physics, and it remained in currency right
down through the Neoplatonists. The ending *-as*,

[A]

1 "And I commanded the lowest things: 'Let one of the invisible things come out visibly!' And Adail descended, extremely large. And I looked at him, and, behold, Heb 11:3; WisSol 11:17
2 in his belly he had a great age. •And I said to him, 'Disintegrate yourself, Adail, and let what is disintegrated from you become visible.' And he disintegrated himself,
3 Gen 1:12

and there came out from him the great age. And thus it carried all the creation which I had wished to create. And I saw how good it was.
4 And I placed for myself a throne, and I sat down on it. Prov 8:27(LXX)
To the light I spoke: 'You go up higher and be solidified and become the foundation for the highest things.'
5 And there is nothing higher than the light, except nothing itself. And I spoke, I straightened myself upward from my throne.

26

1 "And I called out a second time into the lowest things, and I said, 'Let one of the invisible things come out solid and visible.'
2 There came out Arukhas, solid and heavy and very black. •

And I saw how suitable he was.
3 And I said to him, 'Come down low and become solid! And become the foundation of the lowest things!' And he came down and became solid. And he became the foundation of the lowest things. And there is nothing lower than the darkness, except nothing itself.

27

however, which is not Slav., poses a doubt. The plural is met when two or more primal beings or substances are in mind; but the translator of 2En knew to render this literally as "beginnings." It is worth noting that Damascius, last of the pagan Neoplatonic philosophers, quotes from the Babylonian creation epic and identifies the two ultimate principles of Babylonian cosmology, the primal water elements, Apsu and Tiamat (abyss), as *arkhai*. But the Bible could have supplied the vocabulary of this section. Thus Prov 8:22–26 mentions *arkhē* (twice) as well as *tas abyssas*. On the other hand the spelling Arukhas suggests a Heb. word *'ārûk*, "extended"; but it is not a creation word.

c. Slav. *čermenŭ* ("red," long) or *črŭnŭ* ("black," short).

d. Together with 25:5 this makes a symmetrical picture of the cosmos.

Nothing

Adoil → the great light → Upper Foundation

Ar(u)khas → darkness → Lower Foundation

Nothing

The dualism of light and darkness arises from two primal beings, Adoil and Ar(u)khas. 2En does not say that God created them, but they are clearly under his control. This light and darkness are cosmophysical, not spiritual or ethical. They cannot be connected with the dualism of the Bogomils, which is quite outright—*dva načala* (= *arkhai*)

suti: edino ubo blago, drugoe zlo, "There are two *originals:* one good, the other evil" (cf. G. Wild, "Die bogumilische Häresie in einigen südslavischen Volksliedern," *Die Welt der Slaven* 9 [1964] 258–76).

27 a. From this point onward short MSS are fragmentary compared to the full and coherent account of creation that continues in long MSS. Except for trivial details, J, P, and R agree completely in the present chapter, whereas A, U, etc. have only a few words which scarcely make sense. At the very least we would expect the narrative to follow the thread provided by Gen 1; and this is present in vs. 4, even if the other material concerning the origin of water and the system of seven stellar circuits is extraneous. The former (vss. 1–3a) is quite in line with the fundamental cosmology of 2En. The latter (vs. 3b) does not fit the celestial structures described in chs. 3–21, but it does agree with 30:2a–3. At the present stage of research it is impossible to decide which, if either, of the two recensions is closer to the original. Even if vs. 3b in J, P, and R is an interpolation, vs. 4 must surely be original, and A, U, etc. lost this unobjectionable biblical material when the body of the chapter was excised. The mutilated state of the short MSS has produced further disorder. Comparison of A with V is enough to show that. Closer study indicates even more significantly that the key word *put*, "orbit" (for a planet), survives in V N as the

[J]

"And I gave the command: 'Let there be taken some of the light and   1
some of the darkness.' •And I said, 'Become thickened, and be wrapped around   2
with light!' And I spread it out, and it became water. And I
spread it out above the darkness, below the light.[b] •And thus I made the solid   3
waters, that is to say, the Bottomless. And I made a foundation of light around
the water. And I created seven great circles inside it, and I gave them an appearance
of crystal, wet and dry, that is to say glass and ice, and to be the circuit for water
and the other elements. And I pointed out to each one |of them| his route, to the
seven stars, each one of them in his own heaven, so that they might travel
accordingly.
And I saw how good it was. •And I made a division[c] between the light and   4
between the darkness,[d] that is to say, in the middle of the waters, this way and
that way. And I said to the light that it should be day, and to the darkness ⟨I
commanded⟩ that it should be night. And evening came, and ⟨again⟩ morning
came, ⟨that is⟩ the first day.[e]

28 |The week in which God showed Enoch all his wisdom and strength,
throughout all of the seven days; how he created all the forces of heaven and
earth, and every kind of thing that moves itself, even up to man.|[a]

"And thus I made solid the heavenly circles.[b] And ⟨I said⟩, 'Let the lower water,   1
which is below heaven, collect itself ⟨|into|⟩ one collection,[c] and let its waves
become dry.' And it happened like that.
And from the waves I created rocks, solid and big. And from the rocks I assembled[d]   2
the dry land; and I called the dry land Earth.[e]
And what was in the middle of the earth I called chasm, that is to   3
say, Bottomless.[f] •The sea I gathered into one place, and I bound it with a yoke.[g]   4
And I said to the sea: 'Behold, I give you an eternal boundary. And you will not
break through from your own waters.' And so I fixed the solid structure and
established[h] it above the waters.
This first-created day I named for myself. Then evening came and ⟨|again|⟩   5
morning, and it was the second day.

---

meaningless "road of water" lost completely from
A U.
    From another angle, the importance which Vail-
lant attaches to the use of the verb *grjasti* (*Secrets*,
p. xiv) as evidence of 10th-cent. translation into a
Western dialect can be noted. He cites only its
occurrence in 2:1, where only P (not even J R) has
the isogloss *idu*. The use of the same verb (*grjadut*)
in 27:3 to describe the movement of the planets is,
by the same token, in favor of the authenticity of
the passage.
    b. In 2En 27 there is a symmetrical universe in
layers rather than concentric spheres. Some light
and darkness, mingled in the intermediate zone,
are thickened and spread out to make water, "above
the darkness, below the light." This central zone—
"the bottomless" abyss—is encompassed with light;
and this part of the cosmos is more like the
Pythagorean system. Within this watery zone are
seven crystalline circles (compare the crystal sea
in Rev 4:6 and perhaps 1En 14:9–11, which also
mentions "the path of the stars," another point in
favor of the authenticity of 2En 27:3). This system
has nothing to do with the seven heavens in 2En
3–22, for those do not have a planet each, as in
Ptolemaic celestial mechanics, and they are tiers
not spheres. In ch. 27, however, each "star" has

its own *kruga*, "circle," or *puti*, "route."
    c. Only in the center zone do light and darkness
meet, making day and night. Here the account
picks up Gen 1.
    d. J P, but not R, preserve the Heb. repetition
of the preposition.
    e. The schedule of creation days, marked by the
refrain from Gen 1, is augmented here by supplying
the Slav. names for the days of the week in the
secondary ch. headings. Instead of marking the
close of daily work, it now marks the commencement of a new day. The formula "evening and
morning" certainly gives that impression; but the
original scheme is considerably changed as a result.
Note the following development of thought:

Preliminary acts—Conceptualization (ch. 24)
Adoil (ch. 25)   (light)
Ar(u)khas (ch. 26)   (darkness)
Water and the seven circles (ch. 27)
Day 1 Sea and land (ch. 28)
Day 2 Fire, angels, fall of Satan (ch. 29)
Day 3 Vegetation (ch. 30:1–2a)
Day 4 Heavenly bodies (ch. 30:2b–6)
Day 5 Fish, birds, reptiles, animals (ch. 30:7)
Day 6 Creation of Adam and Eve; their fall and
     expulsion (ch. 30:8–32:1)

[A]

1 "Then encompassing (myself?) with the light of the ether,　　　　　Gen 1:4
2 　　　　　　　　　　　•I thickened it.

3 I stretched it above the darkness. •

4

28

1 　　　　　　　　　　　　　　　　　　　　　　　　　Gen 1:90

2 "Then from the waters I hardened big stones, and the
clouds of the depths I commanded to dry themselves.
3 And I did not name what fell to the lowest places.　　　　　Gen 7:11; 8:2
4 　　　　　　　　•Gathering the ocean into one place, I bound it　Jer 5:22; Ps
with a yoke.　　　I gave to the sea　　　　　　　　　an eternal　24:2; 104:9;
Prov 8:29;
boundary, which will not be broken through by the waters.　　Job 26:10; 38:11
The solid structure I fixed and established it above the waters.
5

Day 7 Rest (ch. 32:2)
Day 8 Determination of the millennia (ch. 33)

28 a. MS P² begins at this point. It replicates P
through ch. 32 with minor textual deviations and
trivial orthographic variants.
　b. P P² read singular (cf. *APOT*, vol. 2, p. 446).
　c. "Collection" reflects LXX rather than MT;
but the Heb. "one place" is used in vs. 4.
　d. There is a variation between J (P P²) *sŭgru-
zikhĭ* (*contraxi*) and R *sŭgrězikh* (*commiscui*).
　e. The impression given by Gen 1 is that originally the land surface was covered by water, a
condition to which it reverted as a result of the
Deluge. On the third day the water was drained
away so that the dry land was exposed. 2En 28:2
has an opposite approach. Here land was made by
condensing and solidifying the primeval water. Is
this intended to explain the undulations on the
earth's surface? Philo's position (*On the Creation*
38) is between these two: originally "earth and
water being mingled together and kneaded, like a
mass of dough, into a single element, without shape
or distinction of its parts." The salt water was
taken out to one place, but sweet water remains in
the earth's pores to keep the soil fertile.
　f. Once more the shorter MSS are fragmentary,

inferior, and in considerable disagreement among
themselves. The negation in A U is an error,
reading *ne-* from *narekokh* of other MSS. The
terminology for the "bottomless" (*bezdnu/a*,
"abyss") varies: *upadok*, "fallen" (R—cf. *upad*
in A U, but V has *upadoki*), but *propastĭ*, "gulf"
(J P P²). On the etymology of *abyssos*, cf. Philo
(*On the Creation* 29), "for *to kenon* is a region of
immensity and vast depths."
　g. The yoke restraining the ocean could be a
fragment of mythology going back to the harness
(muzzle?) by which *yām* (Heb. "sea") was restrained in the Canaanite myth. In Job 38:10 the
ever-threatening ocean is kept back by a barricade.
But in 2En 28:4 the earth has become a solid shield
above the lower deeps to keep them from surging
up (e.g. Ps 24:2; Gen 7:11; 49:25).
　The MSS describe this threat differently. Where
J R have "from your own waters," P P² have
sostavŭ, "composition" ("component parts," cf.
APOT, vol. 2, p. 446). But all other MSS are
unanimous in having "water." A U, supported by
V N, read simply *ot vod(y)*, lit. "from water."
　h. "Established" has the same root as "foundation" (cf. 24:5). The imagery is problematical,
since we do not usually think of a firm upper
structure as a "foundation."

[J]

29 |Monday is the day. The fiery substance.|[a]

"And for all my own[b] heavens I shaped a shape from the fiery substance. My eye 1 looked at the solid[c] and very hard rock. And from the flash[d] of my eye I took the |marvelous| substance of lightning, both fire

in water and water in fire; •neither does this one extinguish that one, nor does 2 that one dry out this one. That is why lightning is sharper and brighter than the shining of the sun, and softer than water, more solid than the hardest rock.

And from the rock I cut off[e] a great fire,[f] and from the fire I created the ranks of 3 the bodiless armies—ten myriad angels—and their weapons are fiery and their clothes are burning flames. And I gave orders that each should stand in his own rank.

|Here Satanail[h] was hurled from the height, together with his angels.|[i]

But one from the order of the archangels deviated, together with the division that 4 was under his authority. He thought up the impossible idea, that he might place his throne higher than the clouds[j] which are above the earth, and that he might become equal to my power.

And I hurled him out from the height, together with his angels. And he was flying 5 around in the air, ceaselessly, above the Bottomless.

And thus I created the entire heavens. And the third day came. 6

30 |Tuesday.|

"And on the third day I commanded the earth to make trees grow, large and fruit- 1 bearing; and the mountains—all kinds of ⟨sweet grass and all kinds of⟩ sown seed. And I laid out paradise as a garden, and I enclosed it; and I placed armed guards,[a] angels aflame with fire. And thus I created the renewal of the earth.

And then evening came and morning came—the fourth day. 2

|Wednesday.|

And on the fourth day I commanded: 'Let there be great lamps on the heavenly circles.'

On the first, the highest circle, I placed the star Kronos;[b] 3

---

29 a. The two recensions are very different at this point, yet they agree in the central fact that fire was derived from rock and angels were made out of fire.

b. J agrees with R in this reading (not shown in Sokolov's Lat. translation); but A U agree with P P[2] in "armies." There is no preposition, so "fiery essence" could be the complement; i.e. he made them a fiery substance.

c. The same word, "solid," was used in 28:4 to denote the celestial firmament. Perhaps the same is meant here. But *o(t)*, "from," is often missing from words beginning with *o-* (haplography); this phenomenon occurs in the following words in the text, "(from) the flash," in P P[2], but not in J R. So it is "rock," not the firmament, that the great fire is cut from in vs. 2.

d. The translation follows P P[2]. Yet J R have a good claim of being the superior reading, since they agree against P (whereas P usually agrees with J against R). Yet their reading, "from the flash of my eye the lightning also received the watery (not

"marvelous" [P]) essense," is difficult; and P P[2] could be the result of reducing the difficulty. The theory is that lightning is a mixture of fire and water, but how the flash of God's eye supplies the aqueous component is not evident.

e. Perhaps "nipped," since the verb comes from brickmaking.

f. "Fire" is not an element in Gen 1; hence it is important to seek for the background of this thought in 2En (it is present in both recensions). The Chaldean oracles state that everything comes from fire: *eisin panta henos pyros ekgegaōta* (É. des Places, *Oracles Chaldaïques avec un choix de commentaires anciens* [Paris, 1971] p. 69). But Ezek 28:16 has a connection between stones and fire, and the myth behind this could have Canaanite connections, as well as supplying the form of the Lucifer myth found here in 2En. Even so, the derivation of fire from rock seems unparalleled; the reference to lightning suggests that the model is the striking of fire from flint. Cf. Akkadian (*abnu*) *išāti*, "fire (-stone)." Note that 2En's

[A]

29

1 "And for all the armies I fashioned the heavens,
the sun from the great light. And I placed it in the sky
so that it might shine onto the earth.

Ps 104:4; Heb 1:7

2

3   •From the rock I cut off a
great fire, and ⟨from⟩ the fire I created all the armies of the bodiless ones, and all
the armies of the stars and cherubim and seraphim and ophanim,ᵍ and all these
from the fire I cut out.

4   Isa 14:14

5   Eph 2:2

6

30

1 "And the earth I commanded to make all kinds of trees grow, and all kinds of
mountains, and all kinds of living grass, and all kinds of living seeds, producing
seeds; so that
before I created living souls, I prepared food for them.

Gen 1:11. Ps 147:8

2   Gen 1:14–19

3

---

derivation of fire does not accord with the Gk.
belief in fire as one of the four (or even the only)
primal element. In the Jewish tradition Gen 1
safeguarded the primacy of water. Even though
Gen 1 does not mention fire, the commentators
brought it in (cf. Rashi on Gen 1:8).

g. Short MSS have Heb. names for the angels.
A differs from U in reading *serathims* and *othanims*.

h. The name Satanail is present here only in P's
(secondary) ch. headings. But see 30:4.

i. Christian explanations of the origin of evil
linked Lk 10:18 with Isa 14 and Ezek 28, and
eventually Gen 3. So vs. 4 could be a Christian
interpolation. In the Byzantine tradition Satan's
revolt took place on the fourth day, not the second,
as here. Jewish theology concentrated on Gen 6,
and this is prominent in the Enoch cycle as in other
apocalypses.

j. The Book of John the Evangelist describes
Satan's presumption in similar language: "He set
his seat above the clouds of heaven" (James, *ANT*,
p. 188). GBart (4:24) explains that although Satan
was the first angel created, he refused to worship

Adam as the image of God. Later on it records his
revolt: "'I will set my throne over against his
throne" (4:55).

30 a. This conflation with Gen 3:25 flouts the
biblical chronology and obscures the significance
of this arrangement as a consequence of sin.

b. The scheme could be no better than a garbled
Almagest by some uninformed individual. Only a
few of the planets are on Ptolemy's levels. In 2En
the disposition of seven planets on seven heavenly
circles has nothing to do with the cosmology of
chs. 3–21. It is not even clear that the seven
crystalline circles of 2En 27:3 are the same as the
Pythagorean or Ptolemaic spheres. In any case the
seven heavens of the apocalypses represent layers;
2En 4:1 gives the impression that there are stars in
the first heaven (cf. 30:4); but chs. 11–17 place
sun and moon together in the fourth heaven. Note
also that these planetary orbits are counted from
the top down, whereas the heavens are numbered
from the bottom up.

[J]

on the 2nd,	⟨lower down,	I placed⟩	Afridit;
on the 3rd			Arris;
on the 4th			the sun;[c]
on the fifth			Zeous;
on the 6th			Ermis;
and on the 7th, the lowest,			the moon.

And with the lowest stars I beautified the air below.[d]   4
And I appointed the sun over the illumination of the day, but the   5
moon and stars over the illumination of the night. • And the sun goes in accordance   6
with each animal, and the twelve animals are the succession of the months. And
I assigned their names and the animals of their seasons,[e] and their connection with
the newborn, and their horoscopes,
and how they revolve. • Then evening came and morning came—the fifth day.   7

|Thursday.|

And on the 5th day I commanded the sea to engender fishes[f] and feathered birds
of many different kinds, and every kind of reptile that creeps on the earth and
that walks on the earth on four legs and that flies through the air—male sex and
female—and every kind of soul that breathes
the breath of all living things. • And evening came and morning came—the sixth   8
day.

|Friday.|

And on the sixth day I commanded my wisdom to create man out of the seven
components:

|1|[g]	his flesh from earth;
|second|	his blood from dew and from the sun;
|third|	his eyes from the bottomless sea;[h]
|fourth|	his bones from stone;
|fifth|	his reason from the mobility[i] of angels and from clouds;
|sixth|	his veins and hair from grass of the earth;
|seventh|	his spirit from my spirit and from wind.

And I gave him 7 properties:[j]   9

hearing	to the flesh;
sight	to the eyes;
smell	to the spirit;
touch	to the veins;
taste	to the blood;
to the bones—	endurance;
to the reason—	sweetness.

Behold, I have thought up an ingenious poem to recite: 10

c. P has lost the reference to the sun (cf. *APOT*, vol. 2, p. 448). It also lacks the word "air" in vs. 4, except for the letter *a*, which, interpreted as the conjunction, makes it appear that sun, moon, and stars are all together in the lowest heaven. But J confirms "air" in R, and "and" in R shows that

vs. 5 is a new section closer to Gen 1. But stars are not usually in the "air" zone in ancient cosmologies.
    d. On the stars as a beautiful adornment for the sky see Philo, *On the Creation* 17 (§53).
    e. The unique reading of P²; the others have

[A]

4

5

6

7   Gen 1:20–26

And the sea I commanded to engender its fish
                and every reptile that creeps on
the earth   and every bird that flies.

8   Prov 8:30;
                                                                     WisSol 9:4

When I had finished all this, I commanded my wisdom to create man.

9   Sir 17:5

10

''thundering.''   vol. 1, p. 392).
  f. A reads *raby*.   j. The noun used for the seven senses, *estestvŭ*,
  g. P uses numerals, P² words, to count the   means ''nature'' or ''substance'' in Russ. It was
components. J R do not have either.   used earlier for the fiery ''essence.'' In the next
  h. P P² derive man's eyes from the sun. vs. it is translated as ''substance,'' and in vs. 16
  i. Slav. *brŭzosti*, ''speed, impetuosity'' (*SRY*, as ''nature.''

[J]

From invisible and visible substances I created man.
From both his natures come both death and life.[k]
And (as my) image he knows the word like (no) other creature.
But even at his greatest he is small,
and again at his smallest he is great.

And on the earth I assigned him to be a second angel, honored and   11
great and glorious. •And I assigned him to be a king,[l] to reign |on| the earth, |and| 12
to have my wisdom. And there was nothing comparable to
him on the earth, even among my creatures that exist. •And I assigned to him a   13
name from the four components:[m]

from East — (A)	
from West — (D)	
from North — (A)	|South| — (M)
from South — (M)	|North| — (A).

And I assigned to him four special[n] stars, and called his name Adam.   14
And I gave him his free will; and I pointed out to him the two ways—[o] light and   15
darkness. And I said to him, 'This is good for you, but that is bad'; so that I
might come to know[p] whether he has love toward me or abhorrence, and so that
it might become plain who among his race loves me.
Whereas I have come to know his nature, he does not know his own nature. That   16
is why ignorance is more lamentable than the sin such as it is in him to sin. And
I said, 'After sin there is nothing for it but death.'
And I assigned a shade for him;[q] and I imposed sleep upon him, and he fell   17
asleep. And while he was sleeping, I took from him a rib. And I created for him
a wife, so that death[r] might come ⟨|to him|⟩ by his wife.
And I took his last word, and I called her name Mother, that is to say, Euva.[s]   18

31 |God hands over paradise to Adam, and gives him a command to look upon
the heavens, open, and that he might look upon the angels, singing the triumphal
song. Word "27."|[a]

"Adam—Mother; earthly and life. And I created a garden in Edem, in the east,   1
so that he might keep the agreement and preserve the commandment.
And I created for him an open heaven, so that he might look upon the angels,   2

---

k. Cf. Gregory's oration on his brother Caesarius
(PG, vol. 35, p. 785).

l. The MSS are all different in small details.
This verse could mean: "And I appointed him king
of the earth, to have a kingdom, by my wisdom."

m. The letters of the anagram are supplied as if
from Gk. P P[2] have South and North the wrong
way around. The same error occurs in SibOr 3:26.
Yet J R—a good combination—have it correctly.
If the reading of J R is original (which is likely,
since it is correct), the coincidence of the error of
P P[2] with SibOr is intriguing. If P P[2] is original
(an error innocently derived from SibOr) then J R
results from correction (in Slav.!) by someone who
knew the solution to the riddle in Gk.

n. The attribute of the day on which the story
began (1:2).

o. The two ways correspond to the ethical dualism of the NT, especially that of Jn. The exact
terminology is found in EpBar 17. In 2En "light"
and "darkness" have more ethical significance at

the end of the world (ch. 65) than at the beginning
(chs. 25f.). The hells in 2En are dark (7:1; 10:2),
but not the fifth heaven.

p. The translation "come to know" requires an
emendation, since all MSS read "I saw." P continues the verb consistently, "he does not *see* his
own nature; that is why non-*seeing* is . . ." But J
and R agree in reading "He does not *know* . . .
ignorance . . ." Hence it seems that the first verb
should also be "know." Confusion between *vid-*
and *věd-* occurs easily, and turns up in other
connections. One wonders if 40:1 was originally
"I have *seen* everything"; at least one cannot say
confidently that the book teaches that Enoch acquired omniscience. See the notes on 2En 36:3. In
40:3 the reading of A (*svědjatŭ;* cf. U) is confirmed
by J (*vědja\t*), R (*věℓdti*); but P has *vydjtŭ*, "see,"
the opposite error introduced here from other places
in which it is correct. The same problem occurs in
8:1, where some MSS (A U) read *nevidimo,*
"unseen," others (V N) *nesvědomo,* "unknown."

[A]

11
12   Gen 1:26,28

13

14
15   Gen 2:17; Deut
                                                13:3

16   Gen 2:17; Rom
                                                6:23

17   Sir 25:34; 1Tim
                                                2:14

18

31

1

2

The former could be the error, influenced by the following *vidĕnija*. But, on the other hand, the second Slav. recension of the *Disputatio* (A. Popov, *Istoriko-literaturnyĭ obzor drevne-russkikh polemičeskikh sočinenic protiv Latinjan (xi-xv v.)* [Moscow, 1875]) reads *es v rai sladostĭ toja že oko ne vidĕ i oukho ne slyša ni na Sr∧dce člku ne vzyde.* This favors the reading of A U at 8:1, even though 2En has not reproduced the quotation from 1Cor 2:9. In view of this, and remembering the identification of Enoch as an "eyewitness" in the Preface, 2En continues the tradition of 1En 41:1, "I *saw* all the secrets of the heavens . . ." This finely balanced textual question warrants thorough study, since the question of whether Enoch is a model "gnostic" has become an important one.

q. The reading "from him" is according to P P². J R read "for him," perhaps under the influence of the preceding text.

r. Charles (*APOT*, vol. 2, p. 450) connects this with Eccl 25:23 (i.e. 24). But the earliest extant

Slav. translation of this passage (*Izbornik* 1076g.181) reads (*o)tŭ ž⟨eny n⟩ ačjatŭkŭ grĕkhu: i toju vĭsi oumira⟨jem⟩ŭ.* There does not seem to be any verbal connection with 2En through either channel. 1Tim 2:14 is also not in this tradition, except as another speculation on Eve's role.

s. The play on words goes back to Heb., where the word "mother" (*'ēm*) is made out of the first and last letters of *'ādām*. So "his last word" means "the last letter (or syllable) of his name." The play has been developed in Slav., connecting *mati*, "mother," with *-am* of Adam or even with *-ma* (in P's anagram). This paronomasia has come a long way, since the firm link with "mother" is possibly only in Sumerian.

31 a. With the truncation of the story of the creation of man at 30:6, short MSS are void to 33:3. It must be admitted that much of what remains in (or was added to) long MSS is unintelligible, or at best weird.

[J]

singing the triumphal song.[b] And the light which is never darkened was perpetually in paradise.[c] •And the devil understood how I wished to create another world, so 3 that everything could be subjected to Adam on the earth, to rule and reign over it. •The devil is of the lowest places. And he will become a demon,[d] because he 4 fled from heaven; Sotona, because his name was Satanail. •In this way he became 5 different from the angels.[e] His nature did not change, ⟨but⟩ his thought did, since his consciousness of righteous and sinful things changed. •And he became aware 6 of his condemnation and of the sin which he sinned previously. And that is why he thought up the scheme against Adam. In such a form he entered paradise, and corrupted Eve. But Adam he did not contact.

But on account of ⟨her⟩ nescience I cursed them. But those whom I had blessed 7 previously, them I did not curse; ⟨and those whom I had not blessed previously, even them I did not curse⟩—neither mankind I cursed, nor the earth, nor any other creature, but only mankind's evil fruit-bearing.

This is why the fruit of doing good is sweat and exertion.   8

32 |After[a] Adam's transgression, God expels him into the earth from which he had been taken. But he does not wish to destroy him in the age to come. Word "28."|

"And I said |to him|, 'You are earth,[b] and into the earth once again you will go, 1 out of which I took you. And I will not destroy you, but I will send you away to what I took you from. Then I can take you once again at my second coming.'[c] And I blessed all my creatures, visible and invisible. And Adam was in paradise for 5 hours and a half.

And I blessed the 7th day |which is the sabbath| in which I rested from all my 2 doings.[d]

---

b. P² reads "the song for below the heaven" here and in vs. 2. But J R agree with P in reading "triumphal."

c. According to 2En 42:3 the earthly paradise was open to the third heaven, making connection with the heavenly paradise. It was an issue for debate among the Fathers whether Adam could *see* angels. Here Adam both sees and hears them. Philo taught that hearing is lower than seeing (*Cher* 8; *Sobr* 8). Origen was criticized for teaching that men could not see angels (Epiphanius, *Adv Haer* 64.4; Justinian, *Ep. ad Mennam*; Jerome, *Ep. ad Avitum* 2). Origen reasoned thus:

Angels are spirits which share with God the property of invisibility; that is, it is impossible for the human sense of sight to react with any body except one possessing color, shape, and size (*First Principles* 1.1.7).

Origen would have found 2En in error at this point, unless, of course, at this stage, Adam is still a celestial being. Hence this detail does not settle the unsolved question of Origen's acquaintance with a book of Enoch that deals with the subject of creation. The idea that Adam was demoted from a heavenly paradise to earth (2En 32:1) is found in Origen.

[For similar traditions re Adam, see especially the CavTr TAdam, and *Vita*. J.H.C.]

d. The MSS all disagree in small details, but even the omission of a conjunction can make a big difference to the connections of phrases and sentences. Vaillant's translation (*Secrets*, p. 103) is based on extensive emendation. In particular, his putting Satan in charge of the lower regions is highly conjectural. It is unknown how Charles (*APOT*, vol. 2, p. 450) obtained Satomail, for all MSS read Satanail in contrast to Sotona (J P; R— P² has Satana). The double use of *jako* suggests that two puns are involved.

First, "The devil" will become a *demon* (*bĕsĭ*) because he *fled* (*bĕže*). The parallelism of this wordplay to the following pun on "Satan" throws doubt on Vaillant's (*Secrets*, p. 103) emendation of *bĕsĭ* (attested by all four MSS, and quite a suitable word). Secondly, he will be Sotona because his name was Satanail. (The GBart, 4:24, records the change of name from Satanael to Satanao.) The difficulty lies with the intervening words, where each MS is different:

R	sŭtvorilĭ		sŭ	nbse
J	sŭtvori		sŭ	nbsĭ
P	sŭtvori sŭtvori		s	nbsŭ
P²	i	sotvori	sie	bĕsŭ

The word "create" is undeniable. One suspects a play on its first syllable (*sŭt-* or *sot-*) and the name Sotona. This paronomasia points to Slav. soil. The statement that Satan created "heaven" (or at least his own, the lowest, heaven) could have originated with the Bogomils. It is therefore a matter of considerable importance to recover the precise form

[A]

3   WisSol 2:24

4

5

6   Gen 3:6; 2Cor 11:3

7

8

32

1   WisSol 3:7

2

and possible origin of the Satan legend in 2En. P²
appears to have moved from this possibility by
changing "heaven" to "demon." But the creation
of a demon as such cannot be an act of God unless
this is P²'s way of saying that God punished Satan
by turning him into a demon. The theoretical
observations presented in the remainder of this ch.
only make the matter more obscure.

In general, 2En's strong overarching monotheism
keeps its dualistic tendencies within limit. The
Satan passages do not amount to a coherent or
systematic doctrine of evil. In particular, a wicked
ruler of the darkness of this world is never mentioned as enticing to sin in the ethical sections
(unless 34:2, 76:6, 25—the depravity before the
Flood); nor does he have a hand in the climactic
wickedness of the end time; nor is he the prince
of hell in the places of torment in 2En; nor is he
located in a domain of darkness, as opposed to
God's realm of light. 2En 29:4–5 describes the
revolt of an archangel (identified as Satan only in
P's secondary ch. heading), who is hurled from
heaven by God. In 18:3, on the contrary, the rebel
leader's descent to earth is willful and contrary to
God. 2En 31:4 is different again, casting Satan in
the role of rival to Adam as ruler of the earth. We
have, then, fragments of Satan stories loosely
mixed, with no evident concern to link them into
a consistent whole. This intellectual confusion
prevails generally in 2En.

e. The MSS are virtually identical, but the
meaning is quite obscure.

32 a. The use of *po*, "after," in the title could
be an error for *o*, "about." The noun is apparently
locative. The idiom settles nothing, since it translates no fewer than seven different Gk. prepositions.

b. This curious exegesis of Gen 3:19b seems to
be unique. It implies that Adam, made in a heavenly
Paradise from materials brought from the earth, is
now sent back to his native element to live there.
Were it not for P's ch. heading, no connection
with sin would be indicated. 2En 31:9 tends to
blunt the edge of the biblical curse; Adam is
blameless. Here Eve is not mentioned as banished
to Earth with Adam. Similarly Gen 3:22–24 mentions Adam only, not Eve. It cannot be proved that
this stage in man's destiny owes anything to the
theory of man's descent to bodily existence ascribed
to Origen. We have only to remember that in the
Koran (Sura 2:35–36), Adam and his wife begin
in a garden not of this world.

c. This familiar phrase need not be a Christian
touch. It is not found in the NT, although Justin
already uses it. It is scarcely conceivable that the
writer of 2En, with his stark monotheism, at this
point identifies the Lord as Jesus. On the contrary,
the idea is present in Jub 1:26, where *God* descends
at the end of the world, and lives with his purified
children for eternity.

d. P² ends here.

[J]

33 |God shows Enoch the epoch of this world, the existence of 7000 years, and the eighth thousand is the end, neither years nor months nor weeks nor days. Word "29."|

"On the 8th day I likewise appointed, so that the 8th day might be the 1st, the 1 first-created of my week,[a] and that it should revolve in the revolution of 7000; ⟨|so that the 8000|⟩ might be in the beginning of a time not reckoned and unending, 2 neither years, nor months, nor weeks, nor days, nor hours ⟨like the first day of the week, so also that the eighth day[b] of the week might return continually⟩.

And now, Enoch,[c] whatever I have told you, and whatever you have understood, 3 and whatever you have seen in the heavens, and whatever you have seen on the earth, and whatever I have written in the books—by my supreme wisdom all these things I planned to accomplish. And I created them from the highest foundation to the lowest, and to the end.

And there is no adviser[d] and no successor[e] to my creation. I am self-eternal and 4 not made by hands.[e] My thought is without change. My wisdom is my adviser and my deed is my word. And my eyes look at all things. ⟨If I look at all things⟩, then they stand still and shake with terror;[f] but, if I should turn my face away, then all things would perish.

Apply your mind, Enoch, and acknowledge the One who is speaking |to you|. 5 And you take the books which you yourself have written.

And I give you Samoila[g] and Raguila, who brought you up to me. And you go 6 down onto the earth and tell your sons all that I have told you and everything that you have seen, from the lowest heavens up to my throne.

|For| I created all the armies ⟨and⟩ all the forces. And there is no one who opposes 7 me or who is insubordinate to me; for all submit themselves to my sole rule and work my sole dominion.

And give them[h] the books in your handwriting, and they will read them and they 8 will acknowledge me as the Creator of everything. And they will understand that there is no other God except myself.

And let them distribute[i] the books in your handwriting,   9
children to children and family to family and kinsfolk to kinsfolk.

                                                            •And I will give you, 10
Enoch, my mediator, my archistratig, Michael, on account of your handwritings and the handwritings of your fathers—Adam and Sith[j] and Enos and Kainan and Maleleil and Ared your father. •And they will not be destroyed until the final 11

age.[k] So I have commanded my angels, Ariukh and Pariukh,[l] •whom I have 12 appointed on the earth as their guardians, and I have commanded the seasons, so that they might preserve them so that they might not perish in the future flood which I shall create in your generation.

---

33 a. For the correct *nedĕla* (J R) P has *na(d) dĕla*, "over (my) work." Vaillant (*Secrets*, pp. xx, 102) thinks that there is a pun on *ne-dĕlo*, "non-work."

b. The interest in the eighth day as "the Lord's day" could be Christian. 2En 28:5 has already indicated the naming of the first day for the Lord. Besides Rev 1:10, which is not conclusive, the idea turns up in quite early Christian writers.

c. Chr. reads "O man!" Slav. *enoš(e)* is the vocative form of Enoch; *'enōš* is a Semitic noun for "man."

d. On the solitary creator, compare Philo, *On the Creation* 23.

e. Vaillant (*Secrets*, p. 33) thinks that *nerukot-vorenŭ* means "not working with (my) hands," i.e. God creates by thought and speech. But see

the reference to God's hands in ch. 65. The point here is that God is self-existent, he is not dependent or a derived being. There could be an implied contrast with idols which are handmade. The punctuation of the MSS (which cannot be used with much confidence), and even more the gender of the adjective "without change," point to several possible meanings: (1) "I am eternal, not hand-made, unchanging; my thought is my counselor . . ."; (2) "I am eternal, not handmade; my thought is unchanging"; (3) ". . . my unchanging thought is my counselor."

f. Ps 104:29 says that when God *hides* his face, the creatures are troubled. 2En is closer to Hab 3:10 in the Gr. translation of the Barberini MSS: "When you looked, the mountains were agitated."

[A]

33

1

2

3 "And now, Enoch, whatever I have explained to you, and whatever you have seen in the heavens, and whatever you have seen on earth, and whatever I have written in the books—by my supreme wisdom   I have contrived it all—I created from the lowest foundation and up to the highest and out to their end.

4 There is no counselor and no successor, only myself, eternal, not made by hands. My unchanging thought is (my) counselor, and my word is (my) deed. And my eyes behold all things.
If I turn my face away, then all falls into destruction; but if I look at it, then all is stable.

5   •Apply your mind, Enoch, and acknowledge the One who is speaking to you. And you take the books which   I(!)   have written.

6 And I give you Semeila and Rasuila, who brought you up to me. And you go down onto the earth and tell your sons all that I have told you,   everything that   I(!)   have seen, from the lowest heavens up to my throne.

7 All the army I created.
There is no one who opposes me or who is insubordinate   ; and all submit themselves to my sole rule and work my sole dominion.

8 And deliver to them the books in your handwriting, and they will read them and know their Creator.   And they will understand this also how that there is no other Creator except myself.

9 And   distribute the books in your handwriting to your children and (your) children to (their) children; and the parents

10 will read (them) from generation to generation. •For I will give you an intercessor, Enoch, my archistratig, Michail, on account of your handwritings and the handwritings of your fathers—Adam and Seth.

11   •They will not be destroyed until the final age. For I have commanded my angels, Ariokh and

12 Mariokh, •whom I have appointed on the earth to guard them and to command the things of time to preserve the handwritings of your fathers so that they might not perish in the impending flood which I will create in your generation.

Margin references:
Isa 40:13; 46:10;
Sir 42:21; Rom
11:34;
Num 23:19;
1Sam 15:29;
Ezek 24:14; Jas
1:17;
Ps 33:9; Sir
42:15; Jn 1:1;
2Pet 3:5

Deut 32:39; Isa
44:6; 45:5,6;
46:9

1Chr 1:1

Gen 14:1,9; Dan
2:14

---

g. In some Jewish traditions Samoil is another name for Satan.

h. A does not agree with U, but the text is difficult to understand.

i. Cf. 2En 48:7 and 2En 54. The command to disseminate the revealed teaching contrasts with the typical gnostic injunctions to conceal the mysteries and impart them only to the worthy. 2En is similar to the Mesopotamian tradition. According to Berossus, Xisuthros (Sisithros = Ziusudra, the Babylonian Noah) was instructed to bury in Sippar all available writings, to preserve them during the Deluge. When it was over, Xisuthros tells the survivors "to rescue the writings from Sippar and disseminate them to mankind" (W. Lambert and A. Millard, *Atra-Hāsis* [Oxford, 1969] p. 136).

j. A *ositha;* U *osifa.*

k. On the preservation of these documents "until the final age" see 35:1.

l. P lacks vss. 11f., but J R have them, and are virtually identical. Both read "Ariukh" and "Pariukh." A U agree in *Ariōkh* and *Mariōkh* but V has *Ōriokh* and *Mariōkh.* It cannot be shown that this pair of angels are to be equaled with Hārūt and Mārūt of the Koran (Sura 2:96–104). Milik's arguments (*The Books of Enoch* [Oxford, 1976] p. 110), relying on alleged Slav. rendition of Gk. consonants, only go to show how very weak the links in this chain are. According to the Koran, the blasphemers were not Solomon, but the evil ones, teaching men magic and such things as came down at Babylon to the angels Hārūt and Mārūt. This is not altogether clear. It gives the impression that these two angels taught magic and in particular the use of love potions.

[J]

34 |God convicts the persons who are idol worshipers and sodomite fornicators, and for this reason he brings down the flood upon them. Word "30."|

"For I know the wickedness of mankind, how |they have rejected my commandments and| they will not carry the yoke[a] which I have placed on them.

But they will[b] cast off my yoke, and they will accept a different yoke. And they will sow worthless seed,[c] |not fearing God and not worshiping me, but they began to| worship vain gods, and they renounced my uniqueness.

And all the world will be reduced to confusion by iniquities and wickednesses 2 and |abominable| fornications |that is, friend with friend in the anus, and every other kind of wicked uncleanness which it is disgusting to report|, and the worship of (the) evil (one).

And that is why I shall bring down the flood onto the earth, |and I shall destroy 3 everything|, and the earth itself will collapse in great darkness.

35 |God leaves one righteous man of Enoch's tribe, together with all his house, who pleased God in accordance with his will. Word "31."|[a]

"And I will leave[b] a righteous man[c] from your tribe, together with all his house, 1 who will act in accordance with my will. And from his seed another generation will arise, the last of many,[d] but even out of those the majority will be very insatiable.

And I shall raise up[e] for that generation someone who will reveal to them the 2 books in your handwriting and those of your fathers. And he will have to point out to them the guard tower of the earth, truthful men, and those who carry out my will, who do not invoke my name invalidly.

And you[g] will tell that generation;[h] and they, when they have read (them), will 3 be more glorified in the end than in the beginning.

---

34 a. The imagery of the yoke is already developed in the OT, where obedience to God is wearing his yoke like a docile draft animal, and rebellion is the opposite. The Torah as yoke is a familiar idea in Judaism and Jesus defined discipleship as taking *his* yoke (Mt 11:29), which could be a Christian counterstatement. Similarly Clement spoke of "the yoke of his grace" (1Clem 16: end) as if in contrast to the yoke of law. 2En 48:8, in its turn, identifies the yoke with obedience to Enoch's writings. But here (ch. 34) the language is vague to the point of obscurity. It is of importance to discover whether this yoke joins two partners, and refers to marriage. The injunction about seed is then in strict poetic parallelism. The baffling passage in 2Cor 6:14–7:1 has affinities with Qumran as with 2En 34. In the OT idolatry and sexual immorality are hardly separable. In 2En 34 idolatry and miscegenation were the two main provocations of the Deluge. Sodomy (a gloss in P in vs. 2) is a later addition confusing the traditions from Gen 18f.

b. The inconsistency of the MSS (even within individual copies) in the use of verb tense forms shows up in the various translations. It remains uncertain whether the speech is prophetic prediction or describes what has already occurred. When are the events of 2En 18 to be dated in 2En's chronology? Since 2En 70:1 describes a golden age in the lifetime of Methuselah, that is, between Enoch and the Flood, 2En 34 corresponds to Gen 6:1–4, and is still future. But against this is the Paleja tradition that Enoch's righteousness was his refusal of the counsel of the giants, already abroad in his lifetime.

c. This transparent and age-old metaphor of sexual rectitude, present also in 42:11, is required by the context. It has not been recognized by modern scholars, and it eluded some scribe in the line of long MSS who omitted the clause. The poetic structure, preserved in A U etc., suggests that "yoke" and "seed" are metaphors of the same thing.

35 a. Very little is claimed for the translation of ch. 35 in either recension. The texts are parallel, but the numerous minor variations and uncertainty over the clause boundaries make all MSS rather unintelligible. In the present stage of research all individual readings should be kept in mind as options. Comparison with CD 1.11f. is especially inviting now that we know that Enoch books were in use at Qumran.

Kahana's translation is worth considering, even though it smooths over many difficulties:

"And there will stand up from his seed another generation, the very last, and from them many will be very lustful. And in that last generation I will show to them the books written by your hand and by the hands of your fathers. And the keepers of the earth will show them to faithful men, those who do my will [cf. Lk 2:14], who do not call upon my name in vain; and they will report to that generation, and they, after they call upon them will be more glorious in the end than at the beginning."

b. P has taken the opening words and placed them in its secondary ch. heading.

[A]

34

1 "I know the wickedness of mankind,
how they will not carry the yoke which I have placed on them.
Nor do they sow the seed which I have given them; but they have renounced my
yoke, and they will take on another yoke; and they will sow worthless seed,
and do obeisance to vain gods. And they will reject my sole rule.
And all the world will sin by injustices and crimes and
2 adulteries

and idolatries.

3 •Then I shall bring down the flood onto the earth,
and the earth itself will be overwhelmed by a great quantity of mud.

Mt 11:29; 2Cor 6:14

Eph 5:12

Gen 6:17

35

1 "And I will leave a righteous man (a member) of your tribe, together with all his
house, who will act in accordance with my will.
And from their seed will arise a generation, the last of many,
and very rapacious.
2 Then at the conclusion of that generation the books in your handwriting will be
revealed, and those of your fathers, by means of which the guardians[f] of the earth
will show themselves to the faithful men.

Gen 6:9

3 And they will be recounted to that generation, and they
will be glorified in the end more than at the first.

---

c. Lit. from Heb. *'iš ṣaddîq* (Gen 6:9).

d. If the phrase "last generation" can be recovered from the chaotic readings—the agreement of A U with J P in this detail (apart from punctuation) is impressive—then we have a very firm link with Qumran, where *dôr 'aḥărôn* is a specialized term for the end-time. With a few exceptions its biblical occurrences refer to "the next generation" or vaguely to the future. Eschatological connotation arises from symmetry with *dôr ri'šôn* (Job 8:8), "the olden days." Of further importance is the construction of "many" with the preceding adjective, not as in a new clause, as the usual translations have it. The postpositive conjunction leaves this in doubt. But if it is *rabbîm* with the meaning "all," then the whole phrase means "the last generation of all."

e. The opening words of vs. 2 are unintelligible, in spite of a fair measure of MS agreement. Vaillant (*Secrets*, p. 37) connects *izvode* with *eksagōgē* (*cours*). Other attempts—"the extinction of that family" (Charles, *The Book of the Secrets of Enoch*, 1896); "he who has brought up that race" (*APOT*, vol. 2, p. 453), etc.—are no more satisfying. R agrees with short MSS (*izvodē*) whereas J P have merged the preceding preposition *vo* to make *vozvodja*. The development could go in either direction. The context requires the introduction of an authoritative teacher along with the restitution of the books of Enoch, to provide for the needs of the faithful in the end-time. We suggest that this is an act of God. In this setting *izvodī(stvo)* =

ekbasis is not as suitable as *vozvodi*, which has the connotation of "raise up" (*SRY*, vol. 2, p. 273). Cf. *ēgeiren* (Lk 1:69), *wyqm* (CD 1.11). Cf. *otstavlju* (vs. 1).

f. The "guardians" are not identified. One suspects angels, since various duties have been assigned to them, notably the preservation of the books for use in the end-time. But the expression is obscure. The context does not clarify the relationship between the "righteous man" and the "truthful men." The key is the meaning of *strazie*, in which the MSS agree. Is it "guard tower" or "watchman"? Is it the teacher-interpreter, or are the writings themselves regarded as defense works against the evils of the last age? More problematical is the meaning of *zemstei*, for here the MSS are not agreed. Most MSS, in fact, have the more familiar adjective *zemnii*, *zemlēnii*, or the noun *zemli* (V N); the latter is the easiest reading, "of earth."

g. The ambiguity of *ty*, which translates either Gk. *sy* or *ekeinos*, is reflected in the verbs which go with it. J has *skaži*; P R *skažjut*. B lacks the pronoun. In the former case, it is Enoch himself (either *redivivus* [although the term is hardly suitable] or through his preserved and rediscovered writings) who will teach the last generation; in the second, "truthful men" (the same as the "guardians of the earth"?) who will do this. A U, reading a passive verb, imply that the books will be read to (or by) that generation.

h. P has "another generation."

[J]

36 |God commanded Enoch to live on the earth for 30 days, to impart knowledge to his sons and to his children's children. After 30 days he was taken up to heaven once more. Word "32."|[a]

"And now, Enoch, I am giving you a waiting period of 30 days to set your house 1 in order |and| to instruct your sons 〈|and all the members of your household|〉 about everything from me personally, so that they may obey what is said to them by you. And they will read and understand that there is no other God apart from myself, so that they may carry out all your instructions and study the books in your handwriting |accurately and attentively|.
And after 30 days[b] I shall send for you my angel, and he will take you up from 2 the earth and from your sons to me."

3

4

See 39:1.

37 |Here God summons an angel. Word "33."|[a]

And the LORD called one of the senior angels,[b] terrifying and frightful, and he 1 made him stand with me. And the appearance of that angel was as white as snow, and his hands like ice, having the appearance[c] of great frigidity. And he chilled my face, because I could not endure the terror of the LORD, just as it is not possible to endure the fire of a stove and the heat of the sun and the frost of death.[d]
And the LORD said to me, "Enoch, if your face had not been chilled here, no 2 human being would be able to look at your face."

38 |Mathusal, having hope, also waited for his father, Enoch, at his bed, day and night. Word "34."|[a]

And the LORD said to those men[b] who had brought me up at the first, "Let Enoch 1 descend onto the earth with you. And wait for him until the specified day." •And

---

36 a. The sequence of material in the next four chs. is hard to establish. There are major differences between the MSS. We have followed the sequence of the chs. as found in MSS of the longer recension (R J P). Other MSS which have the text at this point lack ch. 38 and have apparently reversed the sequence of chs. 37 and 39. The result in short MSS—36, 39, 37, 40—is not as suitable as the ordering in the longer recension. Furthermore, ch. 38 is surely authentic; at least it does not fit the common theory that such additional materials are interpolations put in by the so-called "reviser" who produced the longer recension. Its place in the narrative is vital, and the shorter MSS are crippled without it. The disarray of the text at this point is shown further by the peculiar material which A U have at the end of ch. 36 (see vss. 3f., lacking in J P R). Even Vaillant recognizes that this is a patch job which makes U inferior. But it

is not so certain that it is only an interpolation, as Vaillant (*Secrets*, p. 37) says concerning 36:3f., which he omits from his translation. At least vs. 3 has a claim to authenticity (see 67:2), even though vs. 4 is premature at this point. The placement of ch. 37 between chs. 39 and 40 in A can be understood. It explains how Enoch, who had, in fact, endured this ordeal, but who had himself become radiant as a result of his close exposure to the divine incandescence, was cooled down to protect ordinary mortals from the effects of his acquired effulgence.
Hence we follow the ch. sequence of J (which is the same as the sequence which Charles, in *APOT*, obtained from P), and rearrange the sequence of the text of A to fit it.

c. A had originally "thy," which has been corrected to "my."

d. Both A U read *vǐd*. Vaillant (*Secrets*, p. 37)

[A]

36

1 "And now, Enoch, I am giving you a respite period of 30 days to spend in your house and to speak to your sons about me, and to the members of your house and to all those who are guarding their hearts. Deut 32:39; Isa 44:6; 45:5; 46:9
And let them read and know that there is none
except myself.

2 And in 30 days I shall send the angels for you, and they will take you to me from the earth and from your sons and they will bring you to me.
3 Because a place has been prepared for you, and you will be in front of my face[c] from now and forever. And you will be seeing[d] my secrets, and you will be scribe for my servants, since you will be writing down everything that has happened on earth and that exists on earth and in the heavens, and you will be for me a witness of the judgment of the great age." All this the LORD said to me, as a man talks to his neighbor.
4 And now, my sons, listen to the voice of your father, and to all that I enjoin on you today, so that you might walk before the face of the LORD and so that whatever you do might be in accordance with the will of the LORD.

37

1 But the LORD called (one) of his senior angels, a terrifying one, and
he made him stand with me. And the appearance of that angel (was) snow,
and his hands ice,
And he refreshed my face, because I could not endure the terror of
the burning of the fire.

2 Ex 32:29
And it is thus that the LORD spoke to me all his words.

38

1

emends to *vĕd(y/ja)*, hence *connaissant*. This is not indicated. The balance favors "see." See the n. on 30:16.

37 a. The coherence and cogency of the long recension in contrast to the fragmentary character of even the best short MSS give them a better claim, since the rule *lectio difficilior potior* could only be applied mechanically if texts never suffered damage. The two explanations of the need of refrigeration by the ice angel are not contradictory. In the first place Enoch was in personal danger of being sizzled by the Lord's incandescence. But it seems very late in the story to solve this survival problem. In fact the transformation achieved in ch. 22 has already adapted him to this environment. What is needed now is to cool Enoch down so that he would not be fatally radiant when he returns to human company.

b. Lit. "elders." I have not been able to find any basis for Charles's "Tartarus" (*APOT*, vol. 2, p. 453).

c. Does *vidĕnije* in its first occurrence mean "face"?

d. P R read "air." J's reading *bezdušnago*, which is quite clear, could be a mistake.

38 a. There is no reason why this ch., which is quite lucid, and in the correct place, should not be accepted as authentic. Without such a ch., short MSS have no explanation of how Enoch returned to earth. In 36:3f. in A U, God is talking to Enoch one moment, and Enoch is talking to his children the next moment. In long MSS the transition is quite smooth.

b. In 1En 81:5, three angels lead Enoch back to earth.

[J]

they placed me at nighttime on my bed.^{c} •And Methusalam was anticipating my ₂
arrival, mounting strict guard at my bed.^{c} And he was terrified when he heard my ₃
arrival. And I said to him, "Let all the members of my household come down."
Then I said to them:

39 |The mournful^a admonition of Enoch to his sons; with weeping and great
sorrow he spoke to them. Word "35."|

"|O my children, my beloved ones!| Give heed, my children, |to the admonition ₅
of your father|, to whatever is in accordance with the will of the LORD. •I have
been sent today to you from the lips of the LORD, to speak to you whatever has
been and whatever is now and whatever will be until the day of judgment.^{b} •
Listen, my children, |for| it is not from my own lips that I am reporting to you
today, but from the lips of the LORD I have been sent to you. For you hear my
words, out of my lips, a human being^c created exactly equal to yourselves; but I
have heard from the fiery lips of the LORD. For the lips of the LORD are a furnace
of fire, and his angels are the flames^d which come out. But you, my children, see
my face, a human being created just like yourselves; but I am one who has seen
the face of the LORD, like iron^e made burning hot by a fire, and it is brought out
and it emits sparks and it is incandescent. •But you gaze into my eyes, a human
being equal in significance to yourselves; but I have gazed into the eyes of the
LORD, shining like the rays of the sun and terrifying the eyes of a human being.
But you, my children, see the right hand of one who helps you, a human being
created identical to yourselves;^{f} but I have seen the right hand of the LORD,
helping me and filling heaven.
But you see the scope of my activity,^{g} the same as your own; but I have seen the ₆
scope of the LORD, without limit and without analogy, and to which there is no
end.

c. In 1En, as Milik suggests (*The Books of
Enoch*, p. 14, n. 5), the angels bring Enoch back
and deposit him "on the earth in front of the door
of my house." This corresponds to the point of
departure in 2En 1:10, for he had risen from his
bed and gone outside and shut the door. The
circumstance that Methuselah is waiting at the
bedside suggests another version, in which the
patriarch is taken away in his sleep. Or even in
which the whole experience takes place in a prolonged dream. (See nn. on 2En 1:3.) His return to
his bed is then the fairy-tale equivalent of waking
from such a dream.

39 a. The sentimental title (cf. the title to ch. 55)

reflects a passing fashion in old Rusian literature.
b. The day of judgment as the end point of
history is a key idea in 2En. A number of different
terms are used, designating it as "the Lord's"
judgment or as "great."
c. Enoch's protestations that he is merely human
accord ill with the transformation described in ch.
22, in spite of the precautionary measures applied
in ch. 38. ·
d. Are these flames "words" (A etc.) or "angels" (J etc.)? The latter could be a mistake,
influenced by Ps 104:4 (= Heb 1:7). But the
"angels" written *a(g)ğly* could easily be misread
as "words," written *ğly*. The fire from which
angels are made in 2En 29 has a different origin.

[A]

2

3

39

1

See 36:4.

". . . so that whatever you do might be in accordance with the
2 will of the LORD. •For, as for me, I have been sent from the lips of the LORD to   Rev. 1:19
you, to speak to you whatever is now and whatever will be until the day of
3 judgment. •And now, my children,   it is not from my own lips that I am
reporting to you today, but from the lips of the LORD who has   sent me to
you. As for you, you hear my words, out of my lips, a human being created
equal to yourselves; but I, I have heard the words from the fiery lips of the LORD.
For the lips of the LORD are a furnace of fire, and his words are the fiery flames
which come out. You, my children, you see my face, a human being created just
like yourselves; I, I am one who has seen the face of the LORD, like iron made
burning hot by a fire, emitting sparks.
4   •For you gaze into (my) eyes, a human being created just like
yourselves; but I have gazed into the eyes of the LORD, like the rays of the shining
sun and terrifying the eyes of a human being.
5   •You, ⟨my⟩ children, you see my right hand beckoning you,
a human being created identical to ⟨y⟩ourselves;[f] but I, I have seen the right hand
of the LORD, beckoning me, who fills heaven.

6 You, you see the extent of my body,   the same as your own; but I, I have   48:5
seen the extent of the LORD, without measure and without analogy,   who
has no end.

---

e. On the simile, see the n. on 22:1.

f. A U share the curious error *nami* against *vami*
of all other MSS.

g. There should be no doubt that the reading in
A U—*tĕla*, "body"—found also in B, is correct.
It fits into the inventory of lips, face, eyes, right
hand, and body. The word *õbijatie* (A's consistent
spelling is better than that in the short MSS) is a
rare word, meaning "range" or "compass." When
the first-known long (P) and short (N) MSS (versions A and B in *APOT*) are placed side by side,
it is possible to suggest that the rather tedious
recitation in P represents a tasteless expansion of
the "reviser," and that the short is original. But
now A U **have a** virtually identical text to P,

including the ideas most offensive to theological
taste, esp. the remark about the size of the Lord's
body (cruder than the short version) and the puerile
simile in vs. 3 (which short MSS censored out in
22:1). One can see why Sokolov maintained that
U (to which we must now add A, not known to
Sokolov) represented an "intermediate" recension.
Furthermore, one can see the mind of scribes at
work on the changes. The ancestor of short MSS
defused the idea by changing one letter, *tĕla*
("body") to *dĕla* ("affairs, deeds"), making it
abstract. But the ancestor of V N etc. has simply
excised the whole passage. On the visibility of
God, cf. 48:5.

[J]

For you hear the sayings of my lips, but I have heard the LORD speaking like loud 7
thunder, when there is a continual disturbance in the clouds. •And now, my 8
children, listen to the discourses[h] of your earthly father. Frightening and dangerous
it is to stand before the face of an earthly king, terrifying and very dangerous it
is, because the will of the king is death and the will of the king is life. How much
more terrifying |and dangerous| it is to stand before the face of the King of earthly
kings and of the heavenly armies, |the regulator of the living and of the dead|.
Who can endure that endless misery?

40 |Enoch admonishes his children in all things truthfully from the lips of
the LORD, just as he saw them and heard them and wrote them down. Word
"36."|[a]

"And now therefore, my children, I know everything;[b] for either from the lips of 1
the LORD or else my eyes have seen from the beginning even to the end, and from
the end to the recommencement.
I know everything,[c] and everything I have written down in books, the heavens 2
and their boundaries and their contents. And all the armies and their movements
I have measured. And I have recorded the stars and the multitude of multitudes
innumerable. •What human being can see[d] their cycles and their phases? 3

For not even the angels know their number. But I have
written down all their names.[e] •The solar circle I have measured, and its rays[f] |I 4
have measured, the hours| I have counted; and its entrances in all the months, and

its departures, and all its movements—their names I have written down. •The 5
lunar circle I have measured, and its movements which are in accordance with
each day, and the diminution which it undergoes during each day and night in
accordance with all the hours.
I[g] appointed 4 seasons, and from the seasons I created 4 cycles, and in the cycles 6
I appointed the year, and I appointed months, and from the months I counted
days, and from the days I measured off the hours and I counted them and wrote
them down. •And everything that is nourished on the earth I have investigated 7
and written down, and every seed, sown and not sown, which grows from the
earth, and all the garden plants, and all the grasses, and all the flowers, and their
delightful fragrances and their names.

h. A U seem to be at fault here in using the
participle "discoursing." The switch to imperative
is certain: "Listen to the one who is giving you
advice about an earthly king!" Other short MSS
(V N B B²) read the noun "advice about an earthly
king"; or, perhaps, "the parable of the earthly
king," which makes a comparison *a fortiori* with
the heavenly king, a strategy familiar enough from
the Gospels. But the contrast is between instruction
from an earthly king, which is terrifying enough,
and teaching from the King of Kings. This only
works if the earthly king is Enoch himself, who
has been the other pole of the contrast all the way
through the chapter. R J P have eased this problem
by reading "earthly father." The contrasting title
of God has many forms in the MSS. A U read
simply "the king" and V N B² are similarly brief.
B has "King of Kings." J is more elaborate still.
The conjunctions in R point to "the King of Kings
and of both earthly and heavenly armies." P's
reference to "living and dead" could be a Christian
gloss, since a similar passage occurs in Gregory's
oration on his brother Caesarius, namely the in-

vocation *o zōēs kai thanatou Kyrie!* (PG, vol. 35,
p. 788).
i. The question at the end of this ch. in long
MSS is unanswered, rhetorical. In short MSS it
receives an apparent answer, because ch. 37 follows
at this point. The conjunction *no*, "but," marks
the link. Enoch was able to endure because an
angel of ice cooled him down when he was in the
presence of the Lord, and "that is how the Lord
spoke all his words to me" (37:2). Short MSS thus
have a flashback to an incident not reported in the
preceding narrative. The problem is not recognized
during the sixty days Enoch spent in the seventh
heaven, including a *tête-à-tête* seated next to the
Lord. As pointed out in the notes on chs. 37 and
38, the long recension is more logical, whether
original or not.

40 a. The two recensions are substantially the
same, except for a small lacuna at the end of vs.
3 in long MSS (a list of six nouns shortened to
two) and larger lacunae (or non-interpolations) at
vss. 6f. and 12 in short MSS (A U). Once more

[A]

7 As for you, you hear the words of my lips, but I, I have heard the words of the
8 LORD, like loud thunder, when there is a continual agitation in the clouds. •And now, my children, listen to the discourses of an earthly king(!). It is dangerous and perilous to stand before the face of an earthly king, terrifying ⟨and very perilous⟩ it is, because the will of the king is death and the will of the king is life.   To stand before the face of the King ⟨of   kings⟩,
who will be able to endure the infinite terror ⟨of that⟩, or of the great burnings?ⁱ

40

1   "Now therefore, my children, I know everything; some from the lips of the   WisSol 7:17–20
LORD, others my eyes have seen from the beginning even to the end, and from the end to the recommencement.
2 I, I know everything, and   I have written down in books the extremities of the heavens and their contents.   I, I have measured their movements and I know their armies.   I have fully counted the stars, a great multitude
3 innumerable. •What human being can conceive the circuits of their changes or their movements or their returns or their guides or the guided ones?
           The angels themselves do not know even their numbers. But I, I have
4 written down   their names. •And I, I have measured the solar circle, and its ⟨rays⟩   I have counted; and its entrances
           and its departures, and all its movements; ⟨and⟩ I have written down their names.
5 And I, I have measured the lunar circle and its daily movements, and the diminution of its light every day and hour. And I have written down its names.

6

7

these are intermediate between J P R and the much shorter V N. Vaillant's (*Secrets*, pp. 105f.) mechanical assignment of these long readings (he uses R) to an *annexe* as "additions of the reviser" is unwise, because of the textual phenomena of the ch. For these are obvious "losses" due to homoeoteleuton, a mistake which abounds in these MSS. At vss. 6f. it is due to the repetition of "names" at the end of vs. 5 and vs. 7, while half of vs. 12 has been lost by repetition of the word "earth." Exactly the same thing has happened in P, where vss. 4b–6 have fallen out between the repeated word "I counted." There is no reason why everything in the longest MSS, J and R, should not be accepted as authentic.

   b. The list includes many things noted in chs. 3–21, but there is no trace of the system of seven heavens, although the seventh heaven is mentioned in vs. 12. Apart from this and the concluding note on hell, all the phenomena are scientific and terrestrial. Compare the essay on the order of creation in 1Clem 20.

   c. Here there can be no doubt that Enoch asserts:

"I *know* everything," for he distinguishes what he has "seen" from what the Lord told him.

   d. The superior reading of A, *smyslitŭ*, "understand," has become, by error, *smotrit*, "look," in R J; and P has reverted to the common *vidĕ*, "see." More significant is A's commencement of *Prevratnyja* (the word in J P R is different, but both probably mean *paratropē* or "declination," although it is doubtful if an astronomical technicality of such precision is in mind) with a huge capital letter.

   e. The word "names" was written twice in A, but one was crossed out.

   f. A shares with U the erroneous reading *lica*, "face," for *luča*, "rays."

   g. Vs. 6 would be more appropriate in the mouth of the Creator. It gives the impression that the "seasons" and "cycles" are units larger than a year; and the number 4 could point to the bisextile year of the Julian calendar. Philo did not interpret the "appointed times" of Gen 1:14 liturgically (their original meaning), but as the four seasons in the year (*On the Creation* §59).

[J]

And the dwelling places of the clouds, their organization and their wings,[h] and 8 how they carry the rain and the raindrops—all this I investigated.

And I wrote down the rumble of the thunder and the lightning; and they showed 9 me the keys and their keepers, and the places where they go, where they go in and where they go out, by measure. They are raised by means of a chain, and they are lowered by means of a chain, so that he does not drop the clouds of anger with terrible injuries and violence, and destroy everything on the earth.

I wrote down the treasuries of the snow,   and the storehouses of the 10 cold, and the frosty winds. And I observed how, depending on the season, their custodians fill up the clouds with them, and their treasuries are not emptied.

I wrote down the sleeping chambers of the winds, and I observed and I saw how 11 their custodians carry scales and measures. And first they[i] place them in the scales, and secondly in the measure, and it is by measure that they release them skillfully into all the earth, lest the earth should be rocked by violent gusts.

I measured all the earth, and its mountains and hills and fields and woods and 12 stones and rivers, and everything that exists. I wrote down the height from the earth to the seventh heaven, and the depth to the lowermost hell,[j] and the place of condemnation,[k] and the supremely large hell, open and weeping.

And I saw[l] how the prisoners were in pain, looking forward to endless punishment; 13 and I recorded all those who have been condemned by the judge, and all their sentences and all their corresponding deeds.

41 |About how Enoch grieved over the sin of Adam.|[a]

"|And| I saw all those from the age of my ancestors, with Adam and Eve.[b] And 1 I sighed and burst into tears. |And I said| concerning their disreputable depravity, 'Oh how miserable for me is my incapacity |and that of|[c] my ancestors!'

And I thought in my heart and I said, 'How blessed is the person who has not 2 been born, or who, having been born, has not sinned before the face of the LORD, so that he will not come into this place nor carry the yoke of this place.'[d]

42 |About how Enoch saw the key-holders and the guards of the gates of hell standing.|[a]

"And I saw the key-holders and the guards of the gates of hell standing, as large 1 as serpents, with their faces like lamps that have been extinguished, and their eyes aflame, and their teeth naked down to their breasts.[b]

And I said to their faces, 'It would have been better if I had not seen you, nor 2

---

h. The reading of J R (*oustavy*) could be correct, yielding both *sostavi* (P) and *usta* (A), "mouths."

i. A U have the inferior reading "he" for "they."

j. The texts of long MSS remain open to the possibility that this "hell" is in one of the heavens. There is no earlier episode in which Enoch was "brought down" to a more conventional subterranean hell.

k. B reads, not *sudnoe* but *studenoe*, "icy"; cf. ch. 10. In any case, 2En does not know about hell as a place of fire and brimstone, but it does feature fire in heaven.

l. A begins with "and I saw" written twice, with the second one crossed out. The verse ends

with *ouvidĕkh*, "I observed," but other MSS read *ouvĕdakh*, "I knew"; this fluctuation occurs in other places (cf. ch. 8, n. d; ch. 30, n. p; ch. 40, n. c).

m. A U read *bole*. But *pole* (B etc.) is better. The error has gone further in J R: *bolit*.

41 a. To judge from Popov's 1880 edition of P, the enumeration of Words 37 and 38 was lost. It resumes correctly with "Word 39" (our ch. 43).

b. The mention of Adam and Eve could be a Christian touch. Early legends about the harrowing of hell usually note that Adam and Eve were waiting for the arrival of the Ransomer. See also 42:5. But if "the last one" is Christ, his identity is well concealed.

[A]

8 And the dwelling places of the clouds, and their mouths and their wings, and
their rains and their raindrops—I, I investigated them.

9 And I wrote down the rumble of the thunder and the marvel of the lightning; and
I have been shown their keepers, and the routes by which they go up
by measure. It is with a chain that they rise, and it
is with a chain that they fall, so that with harsh violence they do not pull the
clouds away and do not cause what is on the earth to perish.

10 I, I wrote down the repositories of the snows, and the storehouses of the ice, and Job 38:22
of every spirit of the cold. And I, I observed how, at certain seasons, their
custodians fill up the clouds with them, and the treasuries are not emptied.

11 I, I wrote down the   chambers of the winds, and I, I observed and I
saw how their custodians carry scales and measures.   ⟨First they place
them in the scales⟩, and secondly in the measure, and it is by measure that they
release them   into all the earth, so that by a severe blow ⟨they⟩ do not
12 shake the earth. •

From there I was brought down and I came to
the place of condemnation, and I saw   hell open,
13   and I saw there a certain ⟨plain⟩,ᵐ like a prison,   an unbounded Jude 13
judgment. And I descended and I wrote down all the judgments of the judged,
and I knew all their accusations.

41

1

"And I sighed and I wept over the perdition of the impious.

2   And I said in my heart,
'How blessed is   he   who has not been born, or who, having been born,
has not sinned before the face of the LORD, so that he will not come into this
place nor carry the yoke of this place.'

42

1 "And I saw the guardians of the keys of hell, standing by the very large doors, Rev 9:1; 20:1
their faces like those of very large snakes, their eyes like extinguished lamps, and
their teeth naked down to their breasts.

2 And I said to them to their faces, 'Would to heaven   that I had not seen

---

c. By introducing "and" twice, P makes Enoch
deplore both his own weakness and that of his
forebears. In J's better reading, confirmed by R,
he bewails the misery that has come to him because
of his ancestor's failure. Similar moral puzzlement
over the disparity between sin and its punishment
is expressed in 42:2b, a passage not well attested.

d. 2En does not admit the possibility of any
remedy for sin through repentance and reparation
from the human side, let alone compassion and
forgiveness from the divine side. It does not accept
the rich OT and rabbinic teaching that mercy is
God's essential attribute, more ultimate even than
justice. Its harsh legalism is equally untouched by
the Christian message that God in his love has

provided a Savior for all mankind.

42 a. The state of the MSS in this ch. gives
another good illustration of what happens to these
texts in transmission. This time it is P (a long MS)
that has lost a huge chunk (vss. 2b–13) at this
point. Fortunately, the complete text has been
preserved in J, confirmed by R word for word. A
U are almost as long. The lacunae in vss. 2b, 7b,
10b, which could be Christian glosses in J R, and
the longer one of vss. 4f., which are almost certainly
that (cf. 31:2, 41:1), correspond to other short MSS
as well, except that V N have suffered further
dislocation.

b. With these guardians compare the Scorpion
Men in Gilgamesh 9.2:1–9.

[J]

heard about your activities, nor that any member of my tribe had been brought to you. To what a small extent they have sinned in this life, but in the eternal life they will suffer forever.'

•And I ascended to the east, into the 3 paradise of Edem, where rest is prepared for the righteous. And it is open as far as the 3rd heaven; but it is closed off from this world.ᶜ

And the guards are appointed at the very large gates to the east of the sun, angels 4 of flame, singing victory songs, never silent, rejoicing at the arrival of the righteous.

When the last oneᵈ arrives, he will bring out Adam, together with the ancestors; 5 and he will bring them in there, so that they may be filled with joy; just as a person invites his best friends to have dinner with him and they arrive with joy, and they talk together in front of that man's palace, waiting with joyful anticipation to have dinner with delightful enjoyments and riches that cannot be measured, and joy

and happiness in eternal light and life; •and I say to you, my children:ᵉ Happy is 6 the person who reverences the name of the LORD, and who serves in front of his face always, and who organizes his gifts with fear, offerings of life,ᵍ and who in this life lives and dies correctly!

Happy is he who carries out righteous judgment, not for the sake of payment, but 7 for justice, not expecting anything whatever as a result; and the result will be that judgment without favoritism will follow for him.

Happy is he who clothes the naked with his garment, and to the 8 hungry gives his bread! •Happy is he who judges righteous judgment for orphan 9 and widow, and who helps anyone who has been treated unjustly!

Happy is he who turns aside from the secular path of this vain world, and walks 10 in the right paths, and who lives that life which is without end!

Happy is he who sows right seed,ʰ for he shall harvest sevenfold! 11

Happy is he in whom is the truth, so that he may speak the truth to his neighbor! 12

Happy is he who has compassion on his lips and gentleness in his heart! 13

Happy is he who understands all the works of the LORD, performedⁱ by the LORD,ʲ 14 and glorifies him! For the works of the LORD are right, but the works of mankind— some are good, but others are evil; and by their works those who speak lying blasphemies are recognized.

43 |Enoch shows his sons how he has sounded out and written down the decrees of God. Word "39."|ᵃ

"I, my children, every just deed and every just decree and every just decision I 1

---

c. The language suggests that this paradise is on the level of earth, even though Enoch "ascends" to it. Its location in the east, beyond where the sun rises, is more like the abode of the blessed in Mesopotamian tradition than anything said about Paradise in the rest of Enoch. It has connections with the paradise in the third heaven already described in chs. 8 and 9 (a harmonizing gloss?). Cf. 2En 31:2 and 2Cor 12:1–3. Cf. ch. 8, n. b.

d. Vaillant (*Secrets*, p. 107) thinks that "the last one" is a maladroit reference to Christ. Although this interpretation is possible, one would wish to ask why a Christian would be so coy. Vs. 4 gives the impression that it is the privilege of the last righteous person (the last Adam of 1Cor 15:45) who completes the tally of the elect, and so brings

the history of mankind to an end, to bring out the first man and the first sinner.

e. The form of moral instruction by beatitude, familiar from the NT, has a strong eschatological thrust. It represents a remarkable fusion of the wisdom and apocalyptic traditions. It relates the form of the eternal reward to a person's temporal behavior. The same pattern applies to punishment. The golden rule is turned around; what you did to others (good or bad) will be done to you.

f. A U, lacking "and," probably mean, more correctly, that serving in front of the Lord's face forever is the reward for fearing his name.

g. The obscure expression is rendered more problematical by the textual variants (note the following):

[A]

you, nor heard about your activities, nor that any member of my tribe had been
brought to you!'

Paradise

3 •And from there I went up into the Gen 2:8
paradise, even of the righteous, and there I saw a blessed place, and every creature Mt 25:34;
is blessed, |and| all live there in joy and in   2Cor 12:2

4   Gen 3:24

5   Lk 13:28–29;
                                                                                        14:16

gladness and in an immeasurable light and in eternal life.
6 Then I said, my children, |and now| I say it to you:
Happy is he   who reverences the name of the LORD, ⟨and⟩ who serves[f]
ceaselessly in front of his face, and who organizes the gifts, offerings of life, and
who will live his life and dies !
7 Happy is he who carries out righteous judgment!   Ezek 18:8;
                                                                                        Zech 7:9

8   (Happy is he who) clothes the naked with   a   garment, and to the
9 hungry gives his bread! •Happy is he who judges righteous judgment for orphan   Ps 10:18;
and widow, and who helps anyone who has been treated unjustly!   Isa 1:17;
                                                                                        Jer 22:3;
10 Happy is he who turns aside from the   path of   change,   Zech 7:10
and walks in the right paths!   Prov 4:11
11 Happy is he who sows right seed, for he shall harvest it sevenfold!   Job 4:8;
                                                                                        Prov 22:8;
                                                                                        Hos 10:13;
                                                                                        Gal 6:7
12 Happy is he in whom is the truth, so that he may speak the truth to his neighbor!   Lev 19:11;
                                                                                        Zech 8:16;
13 Happy is he who has compassion, truth, and gentleness in his lips!   Eph 4:25
14 Happy is he who understands all the works of the LORD,   Prov 31:26
                        ⟨and glorifies him⟩;
and, because of his works, knows the Creator!

43

1 "And behold, my children, having experienced[b] the things that have been ordered

A U *prinosy žizni*
J   *prn\so seja žizny*
R   *srn\so sie žizni*
A U *krai po zemli*
MPr *pravlemaja*
B²   *kormstvuemaja*
N V *korystvuemaa*
B   *skorstujaja*

(Vaillant's [*Secrets*, p. 45] ascription of *krŭmstvuema* to R is not confirmed by Sokolov's 1899
edition. Long MSS are all quite different.) Vaillant
(*Secrets*, p. 45) conjectures *krŭmstvuemaja*, although the verb *krŭmĭstvovati* is not attested. He
suggests a variant of *krŭmĭčĭstvovati* (*basanizō*);

but it is hardly suitable. A U suggest that Enoch
mapped the bounds of earth.
  h. Cf. Eccl 7:1–3.
  i. Lit. "created." Once again 2En's knowledge
of God is confined to creation; there is no interest
in history.
  j. V N read "Lord God" at the end of vs. 14b
and again in 43:1.

43 a. Here the recensions diverge. Short MSS are
more ample in vs. 1; long MSS are more ample in
vs. 2. (A seems to have a mutilated version of
this.) A U retain the reference to the balance in
vs. 1; long MSS have lost it, but they pick it up
again in 44:5.
  b. The MSS differ widely:

[J]

have checked out and written down,[c]

just as the LORD commanded me.
And in all these things I discovered differences. •For, just as one year is more 2
honorable than another year,
⟨|so one person is more honorable than another person|⟩—

some   because of much property;
some again because of wisdom of the heart;[g]
some again because of singular intelligence;
some again because of craftiness;
some again because of silence of the lips;
some again because of purity;
some again because of strength;
some again because of handsome appearance;
some again because of youth;
some again because of a penetrating mind;
some again because of bodily appearance;
some again because of abundant feelings.

Even though these sayings are heard on every side, nevertheless there is no one 3
better than he who fears God. He will be the most glorious in that age.[h]

44 |Enoch teaches his sons so that they might not insult the face of any person,
small or great. Word "40."|[a]

"The LORD with his own two hands created mankind; in a facsimile of his own 1
face,[b] both small and great,[c] the LORD created |them|.
And whoever insults a person's face, insults the face of a king, and treats the face 2
of the LORD with repugnance.
He who treats with contempt the face of any person treats the face of the LORD
with contempt.
He who expresses anger to any person without provocation will reap anger in the 3
great judgment. He who spits on any person's face, insultingly, will reap the same
at the LORD's great judgment.
Happy is the person who does not direct his heart[d] with malice toward any person, 4
but who helps |the offended and| the condemned, and lifts up those who have
been crushed, and shows compassion on the needy.
Because on the day of[e] the great judgment.   5

c. A's reading *ispisakhŭ* is confirmed by *MPr*
and R, against U's *ispytakh*. V N read *napisakh*.

d. V now confirms the already known variant
of N: *zymu i lěto*, "winter and summer," making
the latter more specific than its normal "year."

e. Enoch's organization of time makes him
sound like the Creator.

f. It is probable that the full list of twelve causes
of diversity among human beings is original. It is
not systematic; but A's version of the first five
seems but a fragment. U N are even more mutilated.

g. For "wisdom" (*mu(t)rosti*) of other MSS V
(N) reads *ml(s)ti*, "mercy."

h. The problem of diversity and inequality among
men received the attention of the rabbis: "Are not
all men created in the form of Adam, the first man?
And still the form of each man is different from
that of anybody else. Therefore can each and every
one say: It is for me that the world was created"
(Sanh 4:5; Yad Sanh 12:3).

44 a. This is the noblest ch. in the apocalypse.
Portions of it have been incorporated into *MPr*.
See the nn. there. Once more the text of A U,
which does not differ much from J P R (which are
virtually identical, although P has a few flaws), is

[A]

on the earth, I have written them down. I, I have arranged the whole year.[d] And from the year I have calculated the months, and from the months I have ticked off the days, and from the day I have ticked off the hours. I, I have measured and noted the hours.[e] And I have distinguished every seed on the earth, and every measure and every righteous scale. I, I have measured and recorded them, ⟨just as the LORD commanded me.

2 And in　　　the　　things I discovered differences⟩. •　　　　　　　One year is better than another year, and one day than another day, and one hour than another hour. Similarly one person is　　　　better　　　than another person—[f]

one	because of much property;	
another	because of wisdom of the heart;	
another	because of	intelligence;
(and)		craftiness;
and		silence of the lips;

3   Sir 10:22

(But there is) no one better than he who fears the LORD; for those who fear the LORD will be glorious forever.

44

1 "The LORD with his own two hands created mankind; and in a facsimile of his　Jas 3:9 own face.　　　　　Small and great the LORD created.

2 Whoever insults a person's face insults the face of the LORD; whoever treats a　Prov 14:31; Mt person's face with repugnance treats the face of the LORD with repugnance.　5:22 Whoever treats with contempt the face of any person treats the face of the LORD

3 with contempt. •　　　　(There is) anger
　　　　　　　　　　　　　　　　　and great judgment
(for) whoever spits on a person's face.

4　　　　　　　　　•Happy is he who directs ⟨|his heart|⟩ toward every person, such as bringing help to him who has been condemned, and by giving support to him who has been broken, and by giving to the needy.　Mt 7:2; Lk 6:38

5 Because on ⟨|the day of|⟩ the great judgment every deed of mankind will be

---

"intermediate" between those long MSS and the considerably abbreviated V N.

b. The idea is remarkable from any point of view. The universal kinship of the human race is both biological and theological. Whatever the diversity (ch. 43), every individual is "the face of the LORD." Here the *imago dei* is the basis for universalistic humane ethics. This is not the original meaning of *ṣelem*. Did it arise in Slav.? The text uses *podobii lica*, not *obrazŭ* or *videnije*, the usual terms for "image."

c. This imitates Gen 1:27, as the word order shows:

God created man in the image of himself,
　in the image of God he created him,
　male and female he created them.

The clause could be a quotation from WisSol 6:8, *hoti mikron kai megan autos epoiēsen*. In its original context this referred to difference in rank and responsibility. The thought thus resembles 2En 43:2, but not 2En 30:10.

d. A U lack "heart," which is present in all other MSS which have the passage.

e. The loss of "the day of" from A U is a simple scribal error.

[J]

every weight
and every measure and every set of scales will be just as they are in the market.
That is to say, each will be weighed in the balance, and each will stand in the
market, and each will find out his own measure and ⟨|in accordance with that
measurement|⟩ each shall receive his own reward.

45 |God points out that he does not want from people sacrifices and burnt
offerings, but hearts that are pure and crushed. Word "41."|

"If anyone is prompt in performing a good oblation in front of the face of the   1
LORD, then the LORD |also| will be prompt to accept it on his account, and he
will not perform righteous judgment for him.[a]
If anyone makes lamps numerous in front of the face of the LORD, then the LORD   2
will make his treasure stores numerous in the highest kingdom.
Does the LORD demand bread or lamps or sheep or oxen or any kind of sacrifices   3
at all? That is nothing, but he |God| demands pure hearts, and by means of all
those things he tests people's hearts.

46 |About how an earthly king does not accept gifts from people who are
disgusting or impure. So how much more is God disgusted with impure gifts;
but rather he rejects (the giver) with wrath, and he does not accept the gifts.
Word "42."|[a]

"|Listen, my people, and give heed to the utterance of my lips!| If to an earthly   1
king someone should bring some kinds of gifts, if he is thinking treachery in his
heart, and the king perceives it, will he not be angry with |him? And will he not
spurn| his gifts?
And will he not hand him over for judgment? •If any person seduces another   2
person into untruth by fair speech, but his heart is evil, will he not be conscious
|of the treachery| of his heart, and (will he not) judge himself in himself, whether
or not his judgment be true |how his untruthfulness is obvious to everyone|?[b]
And when the LORD sends out the great light,[c] in that (light)[d] there will be true   3
judgment, without favoritism, for true and untrue alike; and no one will be able
to hide himself then.

47 |Enoch instructs his sons from God's lips; and he hands over to them these
handwritten books. Word "43."|[a]

45 a. J has the fullest text, the basis of our
translation. P lacks "for him" and R lacks the
negative. The whole clause (vs. 1b) is missing
from A U.

46 a. V is identical with N (B in *APOT*) in having
a huge lacuna after the end of ch. 45. It resumes
at 49:2. A U, on the other hand, while much
shorter than J P R, have parallels in all chs. A U
lack 46:1f.; 47:2b; 48:1–4; 49:1. Once more Sokolov's term "intermediate" is appropriate. At
least it is no longer possible to regard 46:1–49:1
as a "long" interpolation. Just how much of the
material now found only in long MSS of chs. 46–
49 is original and how much was added by scribes

is still an open question.

b. Besides the main differences between P and
J R which we have supplied in the translation of
vs. 2, P has other differences from J R in vs. 3.
These can be seen in the A text of *APOT*. A U
also differ in many details.

c. If "the great light" is considered to be a
veiled Christian allusion to Christ as the last judge,
it is very indirect. And it should be emphasized
that it is present in MSS of both recensions side
by side with many differences.

d. Note the confusion between "light" and
"darkness." MSS such as J, which read *vŭ to\m*,
with wide support (including *MPr*) require a par-

[A]

restored by means of the written record. Happy is he whose measure will prove to be just and whose weight just and scales just! Because on the day of the great judgment every measure and every weight and every scale will be exposed as in the market;   and each one will recognize his measure, and, according to measure, each shall receive his reward.

45

1 "He who is prompt   with   his   oblations in front of the face of the LORD, the LORD will be prompt with his compensations.

2   •He who   makes lamps numerous in front of the face of the LORD, the LORD will make his treasure stores numerous.

3   •Does the LORD need bread or lamps or sheep or oxen? But with this the LORD tests the hearts of mankind.

Ps 40:6; 51:16; Isa 1:11; Mic 6:6–8; Sir 35:1–3
Ps 51:10; Mt 5:8 Deut 8:2; 2Chr 32:31; Ps 22:6; 139:23

46

1

2

3 For then the LORD will send out his great light, and in darkness the judgment will take place. And who, there, will be hidden?

Isa 9:2; Jn 1:8; 3:19–21; 5:35; 8:12

47

aphrase, either "in that (light)" or "at that (time)." But A reads *vŭ tmou*, which could mean "in darkness" (the *yer* is omitted also at 65:9 and 67:1). In *OE vŭ tĭmu = eis to skotos*, and its translation of Mt 25:46 *eis kolasin* reads *tĭmu* instead of *muku*.

47 a. This ch. illustrates the textual relationships between MSS of the various traditions. As noted above, it is quite lacking in V N. A U have essentially the same content as long J P R. The latter have a little more detail, and the differences can be explained by the usual mistakes of copyists. A typical case is the list in vs. 5, which is as follows:

the dust of the earth
the sand of the sea
the drops of the rain
the dew of the clouds
the blowing of the wind

R, J, and P have each lost a word or two here, but A U's loss has produced "the drops . . . of the clouds"! The loss of the passage about the books in vs. 2b (A U) is clearly due to homoeoteleuton, because "LORD" is repeated. There is no reason why this should not be accepted as authentic; Vaillant's (*Secrets,* p. 109) assignment of vs. 2b to the *annexe* is not warranted.

[J]

"And now, my children, place the thought on your hearts, and give heed to the 1
sayings of your father which I am making known to you from the lips of the
LORD. •And receive these books in your father's handwriting, and read them. |For 2
the books are many;| and in them you will learn all the deeds of the LORD. There
have been many books since the beginning of creation, and there will be until the
end of the age; but not one of them will make things as plain to you as ⟨the books
in⟩ my handwriting. If you hold on firmly to them, you will not sin against the
LORD.

For there is no other besides the LORD, neither in heaven, nor on the earth, nor 3
in the deepest places, nor in the one foundation.[b]
The LORD is the one who laid the foundations upon the unknown[c] things,[c] and he 4
is the one who spread out the heavens above the visible and the invisible things.
And the earth he solidified above the waters, and the waters he based upon the 5
unfixed things; and he (alone) created the uncountable creatures. |And| who is it
who has counted the dust of the earth or the sand of the sea or the drops of rain
or the dew ⟨of the clouds⟩[d] or the blowing of the wind?
Who is it who has plaited the land and the sea together with indissoluble bonds,[e] 6
and cut the stars out of fire, and decorated the sky and put in the midst of
them . . .

48 |About the solar movement along the seven circles. Word "44."|[a]

". . . the sun,[b] so that he might travel along the seven celestial[c] circles, which 1
are appointed with 182 thrones so that he might descend to the shortest day, and
once more 182 so that he might descend to the longest day.
He also has two great thrones[d] where he pauses when he turns around in this 2
direction and in the other direction, higher than the lunar thrones. From the month
Tsivan, from the 17th day, he descends until the month Theved; and from the
17th day of Theved he ascends.[e]
And in this way the sun moves along all the celestial circles. When he comes 3
close to the earth, then the earth is merry and makes its fruit grow. But when he
goes away, then the earth laments, and the trees and all fruits have no productivity.
All this is by measurement, and by the most precise measurement of the hours. 4
He fixed it by measure, by his own wisdom, ⟨that is everything⟩ visible and
invisible. •From the invisible things and the visible things he created all the visible 5
things; |and| he himself is invisible.
Thus I am making it known to you, my children; |and| you must hand over the 6
books to your children, and throughout all your generations, ⟨and to
(your) relatives⟩, •and |among| all nations who are discerning so that they may 7
fear God, and so that they may accept them. And they will be more enjoyable
than any delightful food on earth.
And they will read them and adhere to them. •But those who are undiscerning 8

---

b. The portions of this vs. found only in long
MSS correspond to the structure of the cosmos
described in chs. 24–33. The "foundation" is that
in 24:5, where A U also attest it!

c. The MSS agree in *na bezǐvěs[t]nykh*. We
would expect "invisible." Perhaps the confusion
between "know" and "see" has occurred here
also.

d. This is R's reading, confirmed to some extent
by A U. P has "morning"; J has "of the wind,"
a duplicate from the next phrase.

e. On the beautification of heaven see 30:4.

48 a. The ch. heading of P seems to interrupt the

list of created things, which in A U breaks off at
this point. Even J has a major stop at this point
with a large capital letter to mark a new ch.

b. Vs. 1 contains another version of the 364-
day year. This should be quite enough to vindicate
its authenticity.

c. Are the seven heavenly circles (see also vs.
3a) connected with the sun different from the ones
for the planets in 30:2? Do they mark the lines
between the six tracks across the sky from the six
eastern gates to the western gates?

d. If the two additional thrones are specific days
in addition to 364 in vs. 1, they are obviously the
solstices. The 364-day calendar could have been

[A]

1 ''And now, my children, place the thought on your hearts, and give heed to the
sayings of your father (and) all which I am making known to you from the lips
2 of the LORD. •And receive these books, the books in your father's handwriting,
and read them.

　　　　　　　　　　　And in them you will learn　　　　the deeds of the LORD,

3 that there is no one besides the LORD alone, •

Deut 32:39; Isa
44:6; 45:5; 46:9

4　　　　　　　　　　　　　　who laid the foundations upon the unknown things,
and　　　　　　　　who spread out the heavens above the　　　　invisible things.

Ps 104:2; Isa
40:22; 42:5;
44:24; 55:13;

5 And the earth he solidified above the waters,
　　　basing it　　　upon the unfixed things; and who alone
created the uncountable creatures.　　　Who is it who has counted
the dust of the earth or the sand of the sea or the drops　　　of the clouds?

Zech 12:1
2Pet 3:5

Job 36:27; Isa
40:12; Sir 1:2

6 Who has plaited the land and the sea together with indissoluble bonds. Who
caused the unknowable beauty ⟨of the stars⟩ to spring forth from the fire, and with
them has adorned the sky.ᵉ

48

1

2

3

4

5　　　　　''Who has made from the invisible things
all the visible things,　　　being himself invisible.

Heb 11:3

6　　　　　　　　　　　　　　And deliver
these books to your children, and the children to the children, and to
7 ⟨all⟩ your relatives, •and　　　　all your generations,

Rev 22:18,19

who have the wisdom and who will fear the LORD, and they will accept them.
And they will be more enjoyable to them than any delightful food.
8 And they will read them and adhere to them. •But the

---

reconciled with the solar year, or with the 365¼
days Julian calendar. The surplus days (the extra
thrones for the sun) could be regarded as non-days,
to be ignored in calendrical computations. This
problem was mentioned in 16:6; if these days were
''added to the number of the days'' they would
''change the seasons.'' If the 364-day calendar
were used for any length of time, it would quickly
produce chaos. Its excellent intention was to have
all festivals fall on the same day of the week each
year.

　e. Here the solar calendar is presented synoptically with the names of the Babylonian (lunar)
months. The third month is Babylonian *simanu*,

Heb. *sîwān*, Gk. *daisios* (R also knows the Egyptian
Pamovus[a]). Cf. *Siouan* in 1Bar 1:8. Note that
Semitic *samekh* would not have given Slav. *C*
through Gk. Here we are close to Heb. sources.
The month is roughly May or June, but being lunar
it moves in relation to the fixed annual solar points
of equinoxes and solstices. For 17 Tsivan to be
Midsummer Day, it would have to be well into
June, and it could not possibly happen annually.
In fact the summer solstice is normally in Tammuz.
The tenth month is *Ṭēbēt* (Audunaios), which is
close to J (*Theveda*) and R (*Thivitha*). P has *Thevana*
to rhyme with *Civana*, but in the immediate repetition of the word P has the more correct *Thevada*.

[J]

and who do not understand ⟨|the LORD|⟩[f] neither fear God nor accept them, but renounce them, and regard themselves as burdened by them—|a terrible judgment is awaiting them|. •Happy is |the person| who puts their yoke on and carries it 9 around; for he will plow[g] on the day of the great judgment.

49 |Enoch teaches his sons not to use an oath, neither by heaven nor by earth. And he points out the covenant of God, while they are even in their mother's womb. Word "45."|[a]

"For I am swearing to you, my children— But look! I am not swearing by any 1 oath at all, neither by heaven nor by earth nor by any other creature which the LORD created. For ⟨|the LORD|⟩ said, 'There is no oath in me, nor any unrighteousness, but only truth.' So, if there is no truth in human beings, then let them make an oath by means of the words 'Yes, Yes!' or, if it should be the other way around, 'No, No!'

And I make an oath to you—'Yes, Yes!'—that even before any person was in his 2 mother's womb, individually a place I prepared[b] for each soul, as well as a set of scales and a measurement of how long he intends him to live in this world, so

that each person may be investigated with it. •Yes, children, do not deceive 3 yourselves; |for| ahead of the time a place has been prepared there for each human soul.

50 |About how no one can hide himself who is born on the earth; nor can his achievement be kept secret. But he commands to be meek, to endure assaults and insults, and not to harm widows and orphans. Word "46."|

"I have set down the achievements of each person in the writings,[a] and no one 1 can ⟨|hide himself|⟩ who is born on the earth, nor |can| his achievement be kept secret. I see everything, as if in a mirror.

Now therefore, my children, in patience and meekness abide[b] for the number of 2 your days, so that you may inherit the final endless age[c] that is coming.

Every assault and every persecution and every evil   word |endure for the sake 3 of the LORD|. •If the injury and persecution happen to you on account of the LORD, 4 then endure them all for the sake of the LORD.[c] And if you are able to take vengeance with a hundredfold revenge, do not take vengeance, neither on one who is close to you nor on one who is distant from you. For the LORD is the one who takes vengeance, and he will be the avenger for you on the day of the great judgment, so that there may be no acts of retribution here from human beings, but only from the LORD.

f. J reads "God" twice. We have restored "the LORD" from P R.

g. Neither of the competing readings ("plow" or "find") seems to make sense.

49 a. The textual problems presented by the differences between the MSS are not easily solved. On the one side, the blunt declaration of an oath in short MSS seems pointless. Why should Enoch feel obliged to swear to this statement on predestination, a point already made in ch. 23? On the other hand, the longer version reads like a tortuous bit of casuistry, needed to account for the fact that a godly person like Enoch takes an oath, which is a forbidden thing. Dependence on Mt 5:34f. or Jas 5:12 appears obvious, but not certain. The statement

that God does not use oaths is not true, so far as the OT is concerned. In fact the teaching of Jesus seems to be that "Yes" or "No" should be enough. The repetition explained in 2En reflects the Jewish legal opinion that "Yes" or "No" became oaths when they were repeated (b.Sanh 36a).

b. The idea of a place "prepared" turns up several times in 2En. The statement of individual predestination seems to be particularly strong in long MSS. The balances mentioned in 49:2, however, seem to be different from those in 44:5. The former is closer to Dan 5:27; the latter close to Mt 7:2.

50 a. This casts Enoch in the role of a recording

[A]

undiscerning,   who do not understand the LORD,   will
not accept them, but will renounce them,   for their yoke will
9 weigh them down.   •Happy
is he who bears their yoke, ⟨and⟩ grasps it; for he will find it on the day of the
great judgment.

49

1 "For I, I am swearing to you, my children,

Sir 23:7–11; Mt
5:34,35; Jas
5:12

2   that before any
person existed, a place of judgment was prepared
for him, and the scale and the weight by means of which
a person
3 will be tested were prepared there
ahead of the time.

50

1 "And, as for me, I have put into writing the achievements of every person, ⟨and⟩
no one can escape.

2 Now therefore,   my children, live in patience and meekness for the number of   Lk 21:19
your days, so that you may inherit the   endless age that is coming.
3 ⟨And⟩ every assault and every wound and   burn[d]

Sir 2:4; 2Tim
4:5; Heb 10:32;
Jas 1:12; 1Pet
2:19

4 and every evil word, •if they
happen to you on account of the LORD, endure them;
and, being able to pay them back,

Deut 32:35;
Prov 20:22;
24:29; Sir 28:1;
Rom 12:19; Heb
10:30

do not repay them to ⟨your⟩ neighbor,
                 because it is the LORD who repays, and he will be
the avenger for you on the day of the great judgment.

---

angel, a task requiring virtual omniscience. All
long MSS read clearly *viždu,* "see" (not "know,"
which competes with this word in other places).
Even so, the extravagance of the claim could
account for excision from short MSS. But they did
not expurgate this idea everywhere.

  b. Slav. *prebudite* ("abide, live"), found in
both recensions, has the connotations of *meneite,*
as used, for instance, in Jn 15. P's *provoždaite* has
slipped into the common idiom "pass (the time)."

  c. The MSS differ in the number of attributes
of "age," *hā'ôlām habbā'* (?). P has one; A U V
N two; R J three. With the extra word of the last
pair, *poslědnici* (J), cf. "that generation" in 35:2.

  d. Vaillant (*Secrets,* p. 51) by inference from
Rev 7:16, restores the words "of the sun." There

is no textual support for this, even though V N
agree with A U in *znoi.* They confirm also the
absence of *vsjako,* "every," before this apparent
noun, a sign of common damage. This makes *jazva*
(V has *eza,* the spelling in the Hexaemeron of John
the Exarch) and *znoi* a pair. But the problem is
solved by the reading which J and R share against
the rest, even against P (*izgonit,* from which *znoi*
could be an error; yet J R are not satisfactory; for
izgoniti usually translates *ekballein*). This could be
why P has replaced it by *terpěte,* "endure," which
J and R (but not P) have in vs. 4, along with short
MSS. Note that similar equivocation exists in 51:3
over the same verb, *poterpite.*

  e. The additional material in long MSS could
be no more than homiletical embellishment.

[J]

Let each one of you put up with the loss of ⟨his⟩ gold and silver on account of a 5
brother, so that he may receive a full treasury in that age.

                                •Widows and orphans   and foreigners 6
|do not distress, so that God's anger does not come upon you;| . . .

51 |Enoch teaches his sons that they should not hide away treasure in the earth,
but he commands to give alms to the poor. Word "47."|ᵃ

". . . stretch out your hands |to the needy| in accordance with your   1

strength. •|Do not hide your silver in the earth.| Help a believer in affliction, and 2
then affliction will not find you, in your treasuries and in
the time of your work. •Every kind of afflictive and burdensome yoke, if it comes 3
upon you for the sake of the LORD, carry everything and putᵇ it off. And thus you
will find your reward on the day of judgment.
In the morning of the day and in the middle of the day and in the evening of the 4
day it is good to go to the LORD's templeᶜ |on account
of| ⟨|the glory of|⟩ |your| ⟨|creator|⟩. •For every kind of spirit glorifies him and 5
every kind of creature, visible and invisible, |praises (him)|.

52 |God teaches those who believe in him how they have to praise his name.
Word "48."|

"Happy is the person who opens his lipsᵃ for praise |of the God of   1
Sabaoth|,ᵇ and praises the LORD with his whole heart. •And cursed is |every 2
person| who opens his heart for insulting, and insults the poor and slanders his
neighbor, |because that person slanders God|.
Happy is he who opens his lips, both blessing and praising God.ᶜ   3
Cursed is |he who| opens his lips for cursing and blasphemy, before the face of 4
the LORD all his days.ᵈ
Happy—who blessesᵉ all the works of the LORD.   5
Cursed—who despises any of the LORD's creatures.   6
Happy—who looks carefullyᶠ to the raising up of the works of his own hand.ᵍ   7
Cursed—who looks |and is jealous| to destroy another.   8

f. The reading of A U, *sokrovište* (= *thēsauros*)
plotno (which corresponds to *sarks*), does not make
sense, and cannot be rescued by adding {not}
(Vaillant, *Secrets*, p. 51), for which there is no
textual support. The MSS are in chaos at this point.
See n. rr on *MPr*. A U are in error. V N *neoskudno*,
"inexhaustible" (cf. B *neoskudĕemo*), is probably
a secondary correction. J P R agree in something
like *plŭno*, "full" (J is slightly damaged at this
point), and this is surely correct. The general
principle is that future rewards as well as punishments will correspond to behavior in this life. A
U could then be trying to say that the future
treasures will match the present use of wealth
according to the flesh. The idea that he who gives
alms deposits treasure in heaven is an ethical
commonplace in Judaism and Christianity.

51 a. Detailed comparison of the MSS indicates

once more the intermediate character of A U, for
they share with long MSS the full text of vs. 3,
most of which is missing from V N (omitted
because the point has already been made in 50:4?).
Similarly vs. 2 could have been dropped from all
short MSS because the idea is present in 50:5.
Even so, vs. 2 could be a Christian homiletical
embellishment. Note, however, that the term "be-
liever" is *vĕrnyi* (*pistos*), not *vĕrujuštii* (*pisteuōn*).
Doubtless it means a coreligionist. The practice
enjoined in vs. 4 seems more Jewish than Christian;
but vs. 5 is probably a Christian gloss. "Don't
hide your silver in the ground" is a mere conceit
of some scribe behind P; yet, in spite of its solitary
attestation in the worst of all MSS, it could preserve
details derived originally from Eccl 29:10.
b. The variants cross recension lines; note the
following:

P   *terpĕte*   cf. 50:3f.

[A]

5
Lose   gold and silver for   your brother, so

Prov 19:17; Sir 29:10; Lk 6:38; 14:14

that you may receive a treasure (not) according to the flesh[f] on the day of judgment.

6 ⟨And⟩ stretch out your hands to the orphan and to the widows, and according to   Zech 7:10
(your) strength help the wretched, and they will be like a shelter at the time of
the test.

51

1

Prov 31:20; Sir 7:32; 14:13; 29:20

2

Sir 29:10

3   "Every kind of afflictive and burdensome yoke,   1Pet 2:19; 3:14
if it comes upon you for the sake of the LORD,   unfasten it.
And thus you will find your reward on the day of judgment.

4 In the morning   and at noon   and in the   Ps 55:17; Dan 6:10
evening of the day it is good to go to the LORD's temple

5 to glorify the Author of all things. •   Acts 2:15; 3:1; 10:9
Ps 150:6

52

1 "Happy is he who opens his heart for praise,

2   and praises the LORD.   •Cursed is
            he who opens his heart to insults,
and to slander against his neighbor.

3 Happy is he who opens his lips, both blessing and praising   the LORD.

4 Cursed is he who opens his lips for cursing and blasphemy,
before the face of the LORD .

5 Happy—is he who glorifies all the works of the LORD.   Sir 39:14

6 Cursed is he who insults the creatures of the LORD.

7 Happy is he who organizes the works of his hand, so as to raise them up.

8 Cursed—who looks   to obliterate the works of others.

J R   *ponesěte   i otrěžite*
B   *poterpite*   cf. P
A U   *otrešite*
MPr   *otrěšite*

See n. tt on *MPr otŭrězati = afairein or apokoptein;
otreši = athetein*, so either could be a variant of
the other. If J R represent conflation, they highlight
the contradiction that arises from 2En's ambiguous
use of the imagery of the yoke.

c. A U agree with J P R in reading *Khram*,
"temple." This must be original. V has *domĭ bžji*,
"house of God," and B has *cerkovĭ gospodnji*,
"the Lord's church," an obvious drift to Christian
terminology.

52 a. A U read "heart." For once B agrees against
them with J P R, which have "lips." V N B² have
"his heart and lips." In J P R the word "heart"
comes later on.

b. "God of Sabaoth" is a gloss of P. See 21:1.
So is its comment on vs. 2, in the spirit of ch. 44.
The use of "God" rather than "LORD" betrays
the Christian scribe.

c. At the end of vs. 3 J P R read *khvalja*,
"praising," whereas A U have *slavja*, "glorifying." See also vs. 5.

d. The wording "before [*prěd*] the face of the
LORD all his days" is common to all long MSS.

e. The reading of V, *slaven* (N also), is intermediate between A U *MPr slavja*, "glorifies," and
J P R *blagoslovjai*, "blesses."

f. The MSS differ widely in the verb used in
this benediction. A has *skladaja*; J has *sŭgljadajui*.
All agree that the corresponding verb in vs. 8 is
gljadaa (A), apart from the usual range of orthographic variants.

g. Instead of "the works of his own hand," P
(alone) has "the fallen."

[J]

Happy—who preserves the foundations of his most ancient fathers, |made firm 9
from the beginning|.

Cursed—he who breaks down the institutions of his ancestors and fathers. 10

Happy—who cultivates the love of peace. 11

Cursed—who disturbs those who are peaceful by means of love. 12

Happy ⟨is he who⟩ even though he does not speak peace with his tongue, 13
nevertheless in his heart there is peace toward all.

Cursed—who with his tongue speaks peace, but in his heart there is no peace |but 14
a sword|.[h]

|For| all these things (will be weighed) in the balances and exposed in the books 15
on the great[i] judgment day.[j]

53 |Let us not say, 'Our father is in front of God; he will appear {in front of
God} for us on the day of judgment.' For there a father cannot help a son, nor
yet a son a father. Word "49."|

                                                      1

"So now, my children, do not say, 'Our father is with God, and he will stand in
front of ⟨God⟩ for us, and he will pray for us
concerning our sins.' •|For| there is no helper there—not even for any one person 2
who has sinned.[b] See how I have written down all the deeds of every person
before the creation, and I am writing down what is done among all persons forever.

And no one can contradict my handwriting; because the LORD sees all the evil 3
thoughts of mankind, how vain they are, where they lie in the treasuries of the
heart.

So now, my children,[c] pay close attention to all your father's sayings, whatever 4
I say to you, so that you will not be sorry, saying, 'Our father{s} warned
us . . .'

54 |Enoch instructs his sons so that they may hand on the books to others also.
Word "50."|[a]

". . . at that time, about this ignorance of ours, so that they may be for your 1
inheritance of peace. The books which I have given to you,   do not hide
them. To all who wish, recite them, so that they may know[b] about the extremely
marvelous works of the LORD.

---

h. The gloss "but a sword" is unique to P.

i. A U characterize the judgment day as *gordago*, "majestic" or "terrible." All other MSS have *velikago*, "great," as commonly in this work.

j. The words which Charles took to be the conclusion of this exhortation (52:16 of text B in *APOT*) we regard as the beginning of a new section (53:1 in our A). The text of V is continuous at this point, but A marks the onset of a new section quite clearly. In any case the words are a formula for beginning discourse. The grammar points to *nyni de* rather than *wĕ'attāh* or *wk'(n)(t)* of Aram. epistolatory address. The vs. is entirely missing from long MSS, which begin a new ch. here. (P has its usual synopsis of the coming ch.) The words could have been lost by homoeoteleuton of "my children," at the beginning of vs. 1b.

53 a. See ch. 52, n. j. The MSS are divergent, and the original text hard to guess. Note the variants:

  V *da stavilo svĕta naslĕduete*
  B *da stavi svĕta naslĕduetŭ*
  A *na stavilo svĕta naslĕduite*

If some satisfactory explanation for "balance" could be found, V offers the best hope, since *da*, "so that," is better than *na*, "on." But the promise ("so that you may inherit the balance of light for eternity") is not clear. Hence A U have attached the word "balance" to "injustice." I doubt if *svĕtŭ* has acquired its secondary meaning of "world" in these texts, or, rather, it retains its exclusive connotation of *this* earthly world. The best interpretation is "light for eternity" (cf. 65:10). Ch.

[A]

9 Happy is he who preserves the foundations of the   fathers,
where they have been made sure.
10 Cursed is he who destroys the rules and restrictions of his fathers.   Mt 5:9
11 Happy is he who establishes peace.
12 Cursed is he who strikes down those who are in peace.   Sir 28:9.13
13 Happy is he who speaks peace,   Ps 120:7
and he possesses peace.
14 Cursed is he who speaks peace, but there is no peace in his heart.   Ps 28:3; 55:21; 62:4

15 All this will make itself known in the scales
in the book on the great judgment day.

53

1 "Now, therefore, my children, keep your hearts from every   2Mac 15:14
injustice in the balance; inherit the light for eternity.ᵃ
you will not say, my children, '⟨Our⟩ father is with the LORD,
and by his prayers
2 he will keep us free from sin.' •
You see that the works of every
person, I, even I, am writing them down.
3   •And no one will destroy my hand-   Ps 94:11; Sir 17:15.20; Heb 4:3
writing, because the LORD sees everything.

4 ⟨And⟩ now, therefore, my children, pay close attention to all your father's sayings,
whatever I say to you, . . .

54

1   •". . . so that they   Job 37:14.16; Ps 71:17; 139:14; Acts 2:11
may be peace for you in (your) inheritance. And the books which I have given to
you |from the LORD| do not mark them. For you will explain them to all who
wish it, so that you(!) will learn the works of the LORD.

49 has already made the point that in the last judgment all will be weighed up in their own balance. This will be known, because all their actions will be recorded in Enoch's handwriting.

b. It is hard to believe that a medieval Christian "reviser" making a copy of the ancestor of J P R from a *Vorlage* similar to A U V etc. would have interpolated the first sentence in vs. 2, so categorically inimical of the Christian doctrine of Christ's effectual mediation, unless he went too far in denying Enoch's intercessory power. It is easier to understand a scrupulous scribe, writing the ancestor of short MSS, eliminating such an objectionable doctrine—that there is not help of any kind for sinners.

c. Notwithstanding P's ch. division and heading,

J begins a major new section with this conventional opener. See ch. 52, n. j. (J is damaged at the bottom of the page, but the key readings are certain.)

54 a. In view of the insoluble problems in ch. 35, it is a pity that its companion (ch. 54) is in such an unreliable state. What are they to do with the books? Since J R have the same reading as V N, they are not to hide the books (*potaite*). P, omitting the negative, has the unique reading *podavaïte*, "give them away." B seems to say "drink them in" (*napite*) ("sing them"?), but the first syllable is a mistaken reading of negative *ne* of other MSS.

b. The reading of A U, *uvědaite*, "you will know," is inferior. All other MSS have *uvědajuti*, "so that they may know."

[J]

55 |Here Enoch shows his sons and with tears speaks to them: My children, the hour for me to go up to heaven has arrived. Behold, the angels are standing in front of me. Word "51."|

"For behold, my children, the prescribed[a] day has arrived, and the appointed time 1
confronts me. It urges me on to my departure |from you|; and the angels who
wish to go with me are standing on the earth, waiting for what they have been
told. •|For| tomorrow morning I shall go up to the highest heaven, |into the highest 2
Jerusalem|,[b]   into my eternal inheritance.
That is why I am commanding you, my children, so that you may do all that is 3
well-pleasing[c] before the face of the LORD."

56 |Methosalam asks from his father a blessing, so that he may prepare some
food for him to eat. Word "52."|[a]

Methusalam answered his father and said, "What is pleasing in your eyes, Enoch?[b] 1
Let us prepare food in front of your face, so that you may bless our houses and
your children ⟨and all your household⟩; and |your| people will be glorified by you.
And thus, after that, you will go away, as the LORD wills."
Enoch answered his son |Methasalam| and said, "Listen, child! Since the time 2
when the LORD[c] anointed me with the ointment of his glory, food[d] has not come
into me, and earthly pleasure my soul does not remember; nor do I desire anything
earthly.

57 |Enoch commands his son Methosalam to summon all his brothers. Word
"53."|[a]

"But |my child, Methasalam|, call |all| your brothers, and all the members of 1
your[b] households, and the elders of the people, so that I may speak to them and
depart, as it has been predetermined for me."
And Methusalam hurried and summoned his brothers,[c] Regim and Riman and 2
Ukhan and Khermion and Gaidad, and the elders of all the people. And he
summoned them before the face of his father Enoch, and they prostrated themselves
in front of his face, and Enoch looked upon them. And he blessed them; and he
spoke to them, saying:

58 |Enoch's instructions to his sons. Word "54."|[a]

"Listen, |to me| |my| children |today|! In the days of our father Adam, the LORD 1
came down onto the earth |on account of Adam|. And he inspected all his creatures
which he himself had created in the beginning of the thousand ages and when
after all those he had created Adam.

55 a. See ch. 1, n. d.
   b. The identification of the highest heaven as
Jerusalem is a peculiarity of P.
   c. We cannot agree with Vaillant (*Secrets*, p.
54) on setting aside the reading of U (*blagoslověnie*,
"blessing"), now confirmed by A, on the strength
of alleged agreement of B R in *blagovolěnie*, "good
will," across the recensions! But Sokolov (*COIDR*
[1910], p. 140) reports B as *blagoslověnie*. While
V's abbreviated reading is neutral, it seems to have
an *S*, justifying Novaković's normalization of N
(which we can no longer check) to *blagoslověnie*.
In other words, it is a clearly divided reading
between all long and all short MSS. Whether the

short reading is intrinsically inferior is another
matter.

56 a. The scene is reminiscent of Gen 27.
   b. It is startling to hear Methuselah address his
father by his given name (J R). P agrees with short
MSS in the conventional "father."
   c. The action here ascribed directly to the Lord
was performed on his behalf by Michael (ch. 22).
   d. There is confusion between *brašno*, "food,"
and *strašno* (A U), "unpleasant." It could be a
secondary pun within the Slav. tradition, since
other MSS read "food" solely. But all long MSS

[A]

55

1 "For   now, my children, the prescribed day approaches,
and the appointed time constrains (me).
             And the angels who   will   go with me are standing in
2 front of my face.   •And I, tomorrow
I shall go up to the highest heaven,
3   my eternal inheritance. •That is why I am commanding you, my children, to
do everything with a good will before the face of the LORD."

56

1 Mefusalom answered his father Enoch and said, "What is pleasing in your eyes,   Gen 27:4
Father, so that we may prepare food in front of your face, so that you may bless
our houses and your children and all the people of your house? And you will
glorify your people. And thus, after that, you will go away."
2 And Enoch answered his son   and said, "Listen, my child! Since the
time when the LORD anointed me with the ointment of my glory, it has been
horrible for me, and food is not agreeable to me, and I have no desire for earthly
food.

57

1 "But   call your brothers
and all the people of {my} house and the elders of the people,
so that I may speak to them and so that I may depart."
2 And Methusal   hurried and summoned his brothers, Regim and Ariim and
Akhazukhan and Kharimion   and the elders of all the people. And he
led them before the face of his father Enoch, and   they prostrated themselves
in front of him   , and Enoch welcomed   them. And he blessed them; and
he answered them, saying:

58

1 "Listen,   children   ! In the days of ⟨y⟩our father Adam, the
LORD came down onto the earth   and he   inspected all
his creatures which he himself had created.

---

read "anything earthly" instead of "earthly food."
The matter is complicated by inconsistent use of
the negative and variations in the idiomatic use of
the cases. Enoch's categorical disavowal seems to
imply that there is no eating in heaven, but there
are fruit trees in Paradise, and ch. 42:5 has the
traditional heavenly banquet of Jewish and Christian
eschatology.

57 a. Enoch's impending departure provides the
occasion for another round of teachings, this time
addressed to a wider circle.
   b. The MSS are divided between "our" and
"your" and A has "my," crossed out and followed

by "our," which is U's reading.
   c. Enoch's children are as follows:

1:10A	1:10J	57:2A	57:2J
Methusalom	Methusalam	Methusal	Methusalam
Regim	Regim	Regim	Regim
—		Ariim	Riman
—		Akhazukhan	Ukhan
—		Kharimion	Khermion
	Gaidad		Gaidad

58 a. Since this ch. has been incorporated into
MPr, albeit with considerable rearrangement, see
the nn. given there.

[J]

And the LORD summoned all the animals of the earth and all the reptiles of the   2
earth and all the birds that fly in the air, and he brought them all before the face
of our father Adam, so that he might pronounce names for all the quadrupeds;
and |Adam| named everything that lives on the earth.

And the LORD appointed him over everything ⟨|as king|⟩,[b] and he subjected   3
everything to him in subservience under his hand, both the dumb and the deaf, to
be commanded and for submission and for every servitude. So also to every
human being. The LORD created mankind to be the lord[d] of all his possessions.

And the LORD will not judge a single animal soul for the sake of man; but human   4
souls he will judge for the sake of the souls of their animals.[e] •In the great   5

age[f] there is a special place for human beings.   •And just as every   6
human soul is according to number, so also it is with animal souls. And not a
single soul which the LORD has created will perish until the great judgment.[g] And
every kind of animal soul will accuse the human beings who have fed them badly.

59 |Enoch teaches all his sons why they should not touch an ox, because of
the outflow. Word "55."|[a]

"He who acts lawlessly with the soul of an animal acts lawlessly   1
with his own soul. •For a person brings one of the clean animals to make a   2
sacrifice on account of sin, so that he may have healing for his soul. If he brings
it to the sacrifice from clean animals and birds ⟨and cereals⟩, then there is healing
for that person, and he will heal his soul.[b]

Everything that has been given to you for food, bind by four legs, so as to perform   3
the healing properly. And there is

healing and he will heal his soul. •|And| he who puts to death any kind of animal   4
without bonds,[c] ⟨|puts his own soul to death|⟩ and acts lawlessly with his own
flesh. •|And| he who does any kind of harm whatsoever to any kind of animal in   5
secret, it is an evil custom, and he acts lawlessly with his own soul.

---

b. The word "king" is found in both R and P, but at different points. See 30:12.

c. Slav. *povinovenie,* "obedience," of other MSS is preferable to *pominovanie* (A U).

d. The position of the word "lord" suggests that it is the subject of the verb, not the complement. It would be remarkable to give to man a title which, in this book, is used exclusively as the personal name of God. Nevertheless, the analogy of Ps 104:21 (LXX) makes it possible that J P R, which have *gospodina,* could be correct. In secular use the word is common enough as "master." But B agrees with A U in lacking it, while V N have *vlastela,* "overlord," perhaps to diminish the exalted title without adopting A U's drastic measures and excising it.

e. In 2En 58:4 the souls of animals will be preserved to testify against humans; but they are not themselves considered to be morally accountable. This contradicts Jewish, Muslim, and even medieval Christian belief. The responsibility of animals is established by the prescription of penalties for their crimes (Gen 9:5; Ex 21:28). From these texts considerable jurisprudence developed. The Mishnah begins with rules for the constitution of courts for the trial of accused animals (Sanh ch. 1).

f. R reads *vu věcě velicěm,* "in the great age"; cf. 25:1 (A!). P has *vǔ věcě cemǔ,* "in that age." J, by a simple error, reads *vǔ velicěm velicě.* Exactly the same thing happens in J at 61:2, but not at 65:8, where all MSS agree.

g. A U share a careless reading, the repetition of *do suda* (but A spells it differently—with *izica*— on the second occasion). Most MSS read *čelověka,* "man" (person), in one form or another; but B reads curiously *do sada,* "to the garden," instead of *do suda,* "until judgment."

59 a. Morfill (*Secrets of Enoch,* p. 75) inferred from the language of the ch. heading that its author believed that the crime being warned against was bestiality. Charles subsequently denied any such reference (*APOT,* vol. 2, p. 465). Each of the key words in the heading presents a distinct problem. Instead of the general term for "beast" (*skot*), used in the text, it has *govjado;* and for this noun SRY (vol. 4, p. 54) gives the meaning "ox," as distinct from sheep. But R. M. Tseïtlin (*Leksika staroslavyanskogo yazyka* [Moscow, 1977] pp. 21f.) does not consider it so specific. Its absence from G. P. Klepikova's discussion (*Slavyanskaya pastušes-*

[A]

2 ⟨And⟩ the LORD summoned all the animals of the earth and all the reptiles Gen 2:19
of the earth and all the winged birds, and he brought them before the face
of ⟨y⟩our father Adam, so that he might give names
to everything on the earth.

3 And the LORD left them with him, Gen 1:28; 2:19;
and he subjected everything beneath him, Sir 17:4
in the second place, having likewise made it deaf, for all submission[c] Ps 104:21
and for obedience to man. For the LORD made man (LXX)

4 the (lord) of all his possessions. •Over them there will be no judgment for every Gen 9:5
5 living soul, but for (that of) man alone. •For all the souls of the beasts there is
in the great

6 age a single place and a single paddock and a single pasture. •For
the souls of the animals
which the LORD has created will not be excluded until the judgment. And all those
souls will accuse ⟨man⟩ {until judgment}. He who grazes the souls ⟨of the
beasts⟩ badly commits iniquity against his own soul.

59

1
2 •"But he who brings a sacrifice of clean beasts,
it is healing, he heals
his soul. ⟨And he who brings a sacrifice of clean birds, it is healing, he heals his

3 soul. •And everything which you have for food, bind it by four legs;
there is

4 healing, he heals his soul.⟩ •He who puts to death any animal without binding it,

5 it is an evil custom; he acts lawlessly with his own soul. •Whoever does harm
to any animal in secret, it is an evil custom; he acts lawlessly with his own soul.

kaya terminologiya [Moscow, 1974]) confirms SRY. *Etimologičeskii slovar' slavyanskikh yazykov* (ed. O. N. Trubačev [Moscow, 1980] vol. 7, pp. 74ff.) points in the same direction. There is no warrant, accordingly, for Morfill's "Flesh of Cattle" (p. 75), let alone Charles's "beef" (*APOT*, vol. 2, p. 465). But why should the scribe have selected such a specific term unless he had in mind, not offenses against animals in general, but something done specifically to a "bull"? Even more problematical is the reason given for this injunction—"because of the outflow." *Isticanije* is a rare word. It is not listed in SJS. MSD (vol. 1, col. 1146) records two occurrences, unglossed. SRY supplies two meanings: (1) "outflow," especially of blood; (2) [*istecanie*] "going beyond bounds." If the former (a synonym of *istečenie*) is intended, then the nature of this outpouring is not clear. It requires reading between the lines to discover a reference to the "bull's" penis, which is not to be touched. The choice of this verb also has to be explained. Three aspects of the improper treatment of animals are dealt with: feeding badly (58:6), sacrificing wrongly (59:2–4), and whatever unlawful acts are referred to in 59:1 and 5. The emphasis on secrecy in the latter, and the severity of the penalty (loss of one's

own soul), show that something more wicked than neglect or even cruelty is involved. In biblical usage, both Heb. and Gk., "touch" can connote "injure," "taste" (food), or "sexual activity" (e.g. Prov 6:29; 1Cor 7:1). P's ch. heading resembles the latter in idiom, so bestiality is not excluded. This is the most likely evil to be done to an animal in secret (vs. 5). But the secret will come out at the last judgment, because the animal will lay charges. This suggests that *isticanije* should be connected with *istecŭ*, "plaintiff," and refers to the "accusation" made by the victim, as in 58:6.

b. Embarrassment over the topic, or simple incomprehension, could explain the differences among short MSS, for each family seems to have abbreviated it differently. V N have only vss. 1, 2a; B has only 2a, 2b, 3 (and then jumps to 60:4); A U have 2a, 4, 5. So among them, these three short families have preserved everything that is in long MSS.

c. It is not clear whether this slaughter is dietary, cultic, or magical. The rule for tying the beast, and the idea of "healing" (rather than say "forgiveness"—an idea not found in 2En) suggests magic.

[J]

60[a]

"He who does harm to a human soul creates harm for his own soul, and there is 1 for him no healing of his flesh, nor any forgiveness for eternity.

|How it is not proper to kill a human being, neither by weapon, nor by tongue. Word "56."|

He who carries out the murder of a human soul causes the death of his own soul, 2 and murders his own body; and there is no healing for him for eternity. •He who lies in wait for a person with any kind of trap, he himself will 3 be entangled in it; and there is no healing for him for eternity. •He who lies in 4 wait for a person in judgment, his retribution will not be slackened in the great judgment for eternity.

He who acts perversely, or says anything against any soul, righteousness will not 5 be created for him for eternity.

61 |Enoch admonishes his sons to keep themselves from unrighteousness and to extend their hands to the poor often, to give them some of their works. Word "57."|[a]

"So now, my children, keep your hearts from every 1 unrighteous deed which the LORD hates.[b]

And just as 2 a person makes request for his own soul from God,[d] in the same manner let him behave toward every living soul, because in the great age I will find out everything.[e] Many shelters have been prepared for people, good ones for the good, but bad ones for the bad, many, without number.

Happy is he who enters into the blessed houses;[f] for in the bad ones there is no 3 rest, nor returning.[g]

Listen, my children, old and young![h] A person, when he places a vow upon his 4 heart to bring gifts before the face of the LORD from his own works,[i] and his hands did not make that thing, then the LORD will turn away his face from the

works of his hands, ⟨|and|⟩ he will not find the works of his hands. •But even if 5 his hands did make it, but his heart is complaining, the illness of his heart will not cease; making complaint without ceasing, he shall not have even a single benefit.

---

60 a. Most of this ch. has been incorporated into *MPr*. See the nn. there.

61 a. In the synopsis supplied in P by way of ch. heading, the good deed enjoined in vs. 2 is identified as almsgiving. The following text is not so specific. In fact the "gift" discussed in vs. 3 sounds more like a votive offering. The weak exegesis in P's annotations throws doubt on our interpretation of the ch. 59 heading as well.

In this chapter A U are once more intermediate in scope between V N (vss. 1–3a) and J P R. In fact A U have a sentence (vs. 1b) lost from long MSS.

b. Some short MSS share with long ones the lack of the prefix *voz-* on this verb (A U V N).

c. All long MSS have lost the second half of vs. 1b by homoeoteleuton, due to repetition of "LORD," the last word in each clause.

d. All long MSS read "God" versus "LORD" in the rest.

e. Slav. (*cŭ-*)*věmi*, "find out, know." This claim to virtual omniscience could have been deliberately left out of short MSS.

f. Three different words are used for "dwelling" in this verse—*khranilišta*, "shelters"; *khraminy* (A U) or *khramy* (B V N B²), "temples"; *domy*, "houses." See n. e on the Preface. These residences are not located explicitly in either of the paradises mentioned elsewhere in 2En.

2En 61:2, by emphasizing how numerous they are, suggests that these are individual apartments for each departed soul, and the housing arrangements for good and bad are symmetrical.

Origen (*On First Principles* 2.11.6) describes the ascent of the soul through the various heavens. The journey has a superficial resemblance to En-

[A]

60

1 "Whoever does harm to a human soul creates harm for his own soul,   1Thes 4:6
and there is no healing for him for eternity.

2 ⟨Whoever carries out a murder   causes the death of his
own soul   ; and there is no healing for him for
3 eternity⟩. •Whoever pushes a person into a trap, he   Ps 7:16; 9:15;
4 catches himself in it; and there is no healing for him for eternity. •And whoever   35:8; 57:6; Prov
pushes   a person into judgment, his retribution will not fail for eternity.   26:27; 28:10; Sir
                                                                          27:29

5   Ps 101:5

61

1   "Now therefore, my children, keep your hearts from every unrighteous deed   Sir 15:11,13
which the LORD hates, and above all from every living soul, as many as the LORD
2 has created.ᶜ •That which   Jn 14:2; Sir
a person makes request from the LORD for his own soul, in the same manner let   39:25
him behave toward every living soul, because in the great age
                          many shelters have been prepared for people, very good houses
                                    ,   bad houses without number.
3 Happy is he who enters into the blessed dwellings; and indeed in the bad ones
there is no conversion.
4   A person, when he places a
vow upon his heart to bring a gift before the face of the LORD,
                                    and his hands did not   do it,   then
the LORD will turn away   the works of his hands, and he will not obtain
5 (anything).   •Even if his hands did do it, but his heart is complaining, and   2Cor 9:7
the illness of his heart does not cease,
the complaint is without benefit.

och's (cf. the AscenIs, 3Bar, and the TLevi); but
its meaning is altogether different, being purely
allegorical. Origen does not enumerate the heavens.
He does, however, call each heaven a sphere or
globe; but this shape does not derive from physical
astronomy; rather it is a purely rational deduction,
for the sphere is the most perfect shape. Origen
finds a biblical basis for all this by reasoning that
each successive heaven is one of the "resting
places" of Jn 14:2. The process is essentially
intellectual. The soul's ascent is a process of
education as it passes to higher and higher grades
of enlightenment. 2En bears no trace of such
synthesis with Gnosticism, unless it be in Enoch's
reiterated claim that he has acquired knowledge of
"everything." But there seem to be only two sets
of living quarters, the final homes of good and
bad.

g. All long MSS have "no rest" as well as
"nor returning." The fact that *pokaanije* (*metanoia*)
is not used points up once more the total absence
from 2En of the fundamental Jewish-Christian
belief in human repentance and divine forgiveness
as the prime factors in man's salvation. But see
62:3 and the n. there.
h. Lit. "big and little"; which is a pure Hebraism. P R reverse the sequence, and could be more
original.
i. R repeats the last clause; but not in identical
words, so it is not a case of simple dittography. It
has *ego* first time, *svoeju* the second, as in J P's
one statement. There could be a distinction between
"the works of *his* (the person's) hands" and "the
work of *his own* (God's) hands," just as there is
a comparison between the face of a person and the
face of God.

[J]

62 |About how it is appropriate to bring one's gift with faith. And that there is no repentance after death. Word "58."|[a]

"Happy is the person who, in his suffering, brings |his| gifts |with faith|[b] before 1 the face of the LORD, ⟨and⟩ sacrifices them and then receives remission of sins.[c] But if, before the time[d] comes, he should retract his vows, there is no repentance 2 for him.

If the ⟨|time|⟩ specified elapses, |and ⟨then⟩ he does it|,

he will not be accepted,[e] and there is no repentance after death.[f] •Because everything before the time and after the time 3 which a person does, both are a scandal before men and a sin before God.[g]

63 |About how not to despise the poor, but to share equally with them, so that you will not have a complaint before God. Word "59."|[a]

"A person, when he clothes the naked or gives his bread to the 1 hungry, then he will obtain a reward |from God|. •If his heart should murmur, it 2 is a twofold evil that he creates for himself. It is a loss that he creates in respect to that which he gives, and he will not have any obtaining of remuneration because of it.

And the poor man, when his heart is satisfied or his body is clothed,[b] and he 3 performs an act of contempt, then he will ruin all his endurance of poverty, and he will not obtain the reward for his good deeds. ·

For the LORD detests every kind of contemptuous person, and every person who 4 makes himself out to be great, and every untruthful word, stimulated by injustice;[c] and it[d] will be cut out with the blade of the sword of death, |and thrown into the fire.[e] And it will burn|; and this cutting out has no healing unto eternity."

---

62 a. While 2En teaches a noble humane ethic in general terms (ch. 44), its doctrine of judgment is rigorous legalism (ch. 61). This strictness continues in the short text of ch. 62. If the extant text is essentially original it deals precisely with the necessity for the punctual fulfillment of vows. If the longer text of vs. 3 in J P R is authentic, the point is that vows must be performed immediately (cf. Num 30:2). Even worse is the retraction of vows; the person is not allowed to change his mind. If this is what *pokajanije* means, then it holds to the literal meaning of *metanoia*, and does not imply contrition. The point is important, and it goes with the problem of the meaning of *otdanije* also used here. The problem is that this word translates both *antidosis* and *afesis*. The original meaning seems to be strictly one of repayment, whether reward or retribution, as in 63:1. At the end of vs. 1, where long MSS have glossed *otdaanie* with *grěkhom*, V N have *pokaanie adaniju*, "repentance for remission." Here "repentance" is an intrusion, betraying the same drift to Christian vocabulary, even in short MSS.

Except for vs. 3a, which has a good claim on being authentic, at least in its opening words, most of the additional material in the long MSS appear to be expansions by a Christian. This is certainly the case with the interpolations found only in P, notorious for such glosses.

In early Rus the conventional Christian teaching on penance took firm hold. The Testimony of Vladimir Monomakh (1115) emphasizes repentance, tears, and almsgiving (cf. 2En 63:1) (PVL Part 1:153–163; see *Adrianova-Perets* [1950]). The main movement of long MSS in this direction is achieved by adding the phrase "for sin" to *otdanie*, thus achieving the phrase used in the Gospels: "remission of sins." It should be noted however that V (and N) also read *adaanie grěkhovi*.

b. The phrase "with faith," in the ch. heading and in vs. 1, is a Christian gloss peculiar to P.

c. Since the nature of the "gifts" is not specified, it is not clear whether they are sacrifices or any kind of votive offering. Compare 59:2, 61:4. Unfortunately we cannot reconstruct the cultic practices of the community which used 2En as sacred scripture, whether in actuality or only in the author's imagination. Hence we do not know whether *ti sotvoriti* (here A U confirm the reading of J R, not in P), "he performs it," means "sacrifices" or simply "does."

d. The reading "before the time," preserved only by long MSS, completes the picture summed up in vs. 3. He cannot revise his vow before the deadline; nor can he count on an extension. Punctuality becomes the supreme virtue, in keeping with 2En's fascination with the exact measurement of time.

e. The difference between *blagoslovitcja* (A U) and *blagovolitcja* (J P R) occurs here just as in

[A]

62

1 "Happy is the person who, in his suffering, brings   a gift

2 before the face of the LORD, for he will find remuneration. •

                                                And a person

when with his mouth he appoints a time to bring a gift before
the face of the LORD, and he does it, then he will find
remuneration. But if the time specified elapses, and he
carries out his promise, his repentance will not be accepted,

3   •because every delay
                                 creates a scandal.

63

1 "⟨And⟩ a person, when he clothes the naked ⟨and⟩ gives his bread to the   Isa 58:7; Ezek
2 hungry,   will find remuneration.   •But if his heart   18:7
should murmur,
then he makes a loss,
and nothing will be obtained.

3 And when the poor man is satisfied,
and his heart is contemptuous, then he forfeits all his good work,
and he will not obtain (anything).

4 For the LORD detests every kind of contemptuous person."   Prov 6:16–17

55:3. See the n. there. V has a different reading
again: *vŭspiimeti* (cf. N). This contradicts the others
flatly. "He (presumably God) will accept the
(belated) change of mind."

f. The addition "after death" is common to all
long MSS; it is also in P's ch. heading. The point
(confirmed by vs. 3, even in long MSS) is that it
is too late to fulfill a vow after the specified time.

g. While the first part of vs. 3 in long MSS has
a claim to authenticity, the concluding phrase
"before men and a sin before God" is dubious.
The word "God" attracts suspicion.

63 a. This ch. shows more interest in spiritual
inwardness than any other part of 2En. It could,
however, be intended to counteract grumbling
against rules of sharing in a community.

b. It is hard to tell what has happened at the
beginning of vs. 3. There are two main traditions.
B has a drastically abbreviated text, consisting only
of vss. 1 and 2. It introduces the qualification by
ašte že, not *ašte li*, which is generally used in other
MSS. It is possible that the reading of A U
significantly agreeing with J P R (apart from minor
spelling variations), *iništi*, is a mistake for this.
If so, the ch. deals with only one matter—the
spiritual conditions for effective almsgiving. This
good deed can be ruined if the donor grudges the
gift, or despises the receiver. This is the presentation
of V N, which have *ašte li egda* at the beginning

of vs. 3. But if the evidence of A U J P R is
considered more original, then there are two sides
of almsgiving in view. The receiver, when his
misery is relieved, must not become haughty;
otherwise he forfeits his reward for his previous
endurance of poverty. The latter point is made only
in J P R, either a gloss there or a loss from the
other MSS.

c. The much longer text of J P R is probably
due to a scribe. Note the use of *muž*, not *čelověkŭ*,
for the second "man" (J R, not P); but A U V N
use *mužĭ* for "person" the first time, so the
abbreviation could be scribal.

d. Apparently the offending member, the tongue,
is cut out. Strictly speaking, *ostrota* is the point or
edge, and *ostrotoju* could be intended as an adjective, "sharp." But one suspects behind this a word
play, characteristic of the lurid punishments in early
Christian horror accounts of hell (see n. e on ch.
7). The tongue must be punished by the "tongue"
(the usual Heb. term) of the sword.

e. Since the reference to "fire" is a deviant
reading in P only, it does not indicate that 2En has
a conventional hell of torment in fire. See, however,
2En 10:2. The punishment of a vicious tongue with
fire could derive from Ps 120:3; but Dives' reference
to his tongue (Lk 16:24) could be germane, since
he was guilty of contempt for the poor, just like
the malefactor in 2En 63.

[J]

64 |About how the LORD calls Enoch up. And the people agreed together to go to kiss him at the place called Akhuzan. Word "60."|

⟨And⟩ when Enoch had spoken |these words| to his sons and to the princes of the 1 people, and all his people, near and far, having heard that the LORD was calling Enoch, they consulted one another, saying,

"Let us go, let us kiss Enoch." •And they came together, up to 2000ᵃ men, and 2 they arrived at the place

Akhuzanᵇ where Enoch was, and his sons. •And the elders of the people and all 3 the community came and prostrated themselves and kissed Enoch.

And they said to him, "O our father, Enoch! May you be blessed by the LORD, 4 the eternal king! And now, bless your ⟨|sons|⟩, and all the people, so that we may be glorified in front of your face today.

For you will be glorified in front of the face ⟨|of the LORD for eternity|⟩, because 5 you are the one whom the LORD chose in preference to all the people upon the earth;ᶜ and he appointed you to be the one who makes a written record of all his creation, visible and invisible, and the one who carried away the sin of mankindᵈ

and the helper of your own household." •|And Enoch answered his people, saying 6 to all of them|:

65 |About Enoch's instruction to his sons. Word "61."|ᵃ

"Listen, my children! Before ever anything existed, and before 1
ever any created thing was created, the LORD
            created the whole of his creation, visible and invisible.
And however much time there was went by. Understand how, on account of this, 2
he constituted man in his own form, in accordance with a similarity. And he gave
him

eyes	to see,
and ears	to hear,
and heart	to think,
and reason	to argue.ᵇ

And the LORD set everything forth for the sake of man, and he created the whole 3
of creation for his sake. And he divided it into times:

And from time	he established years;ᶜ
and from the years	he settled months;
and from the months	he settled days;
and from the days	he settled 7;
and in those	he settled the hours;
and the hours	he measured exactly,

so that a person might think about time, and so that he might count the years and
the months and the days and the hours and the perturbations and the beginnings
and the endings, and that he might keep countᵈ of his own life from the beginning

64 a. V and some other MSS read *četyrityčušti muži*, "four thousand men."

b. A actually reads Azukhan, but the other MSS are unanimous that it is Akhuzan.

c. This astounding encomium, for which the early extravagances of the book scarcely prepare the readers, could hardly please a Christian or a Jew. The turbulence of the MSS betrays the em-

barrassment of the scribes, and short MSS have obviously been pruned. Even so, the key term (*ōtetelja grěvī*, V's form) survives. The noun does not seem to be otherwise attested; neither the Prague Lexicon nor Sreznevskiĭ's dictionary list it. But the verb is common enough, rendering *eksairein*, *afairein*, etc. J P R use a different root, *otimiteli*; *otimati* also renders *afairein*. Here he carries off "the sins of mankind," so neither reproduces the

[A]

64

1 And it came about, when Enoch had spoken to his children and to the princes of
the people, that all his people and all his neighbors heard that the LORD was
calling Enoch. And they all consulted one another, saying,
2 "Let us go and   let us kiss Enoch." •And they gathered together, up to two
thousand men, and they arrived at the place
3 Azukhan where Enoch was, and his sons, •and the elders of the people.

And they kissed Enoch,

4 saying, "Blessed is the
LORD, the eternal king. Bless now your
people, and glorify ⟨us⟩ to the face of the LORD.

5   Jn 1:29

For the LORD has chosen you,
|to appoint you to be|
the one who reveals,
who carries away our sins."
6 |And| Enoch answered his people, saying:

65

1 "Listen, my children! Before   all   things existed, (and) before all creation
came about, the LORD established the age of creation, and after that he created
all his creation, visible and invisible.

2   Gen 1:27; Sir
                                                                     17:3–7
And after all that he created man according to his image,
and put in him

eyes	to see,
ears	to hear,
heart	to think,
and reason	to argue.

3 Then the LORD delivered the age for the sake of man,

and he divided it into times:

4   and into hours,   WisSol 7:18

so that a person might think about the |changes| of the periods and their ends, the
beginnings and the endings of the years and the months and the days and the
hours, and so that he might

---

wording of Jn 1:29, to which they are otherwise
startlingly close. While A has the verb (*ōtjati grěkh
našikhŭ*), it preserves the previous title *povedateli*,
"revealer," or at least *martyr* or *keryks*, whereas
J P R have the more innocuous *napistali*.
    d. The last statement seems to deny ch. 53.

65 a. Much of this ch. has been incorporated into

MPr. See the nn. there.
    b. Philo (*On the Creation* 62) recognizes the
traditional five senses: sight, hearing, taste, smell,
touch.
    c. Short MSS have a version of this information
in 43:1, a passage missing from long MSS.
    d. On vs. 4 see notes on *MPr*, which supplies
the superior reading "calculate."

[J]

unto death, and think of his sins, and so that he might write his own achievement, both evil and good.

For no achievement is hidden in front of the LORD, so that every person might 5 know his own achievement and so that he might not transgress any one of his commandments at all and so that he might hold onto what my hand has written in generation and generation.[e]

And when the whole of creation,[f] visible and invisible, which the LORD has 6 created, shall come to an end, then each person will go to

the LORD's great judgment. •|And| then |all| time will perish, and afterward there 7 will be neither years nor months nor days nor hours. They will be dissipated,[g] and after that they will not be reckoned.

But they will constitute a single age. And all the righteous, who escape from the 8 LORD's great judgment, will be collected together into the great age. And the great age will come about for the righteous, and it will be eternal.[h]

And after that there will be among them neither weariness ⟨|nor sickness|⟩ nor 9 affliction nor worry |nor| want nor debilitation nor night nor darkness.

But they will have a great light, a great indestructible light, and paradise, great 10 and incorruptible. For everything corruptible will pass away, and the incorruptible will come into being, and will be the shelter of the eternal residences.

11

66 |Enoch teaches his sons and all the elders of the people how they should walk with fear and trembling in front of the LORD, and worship him alone and not bow down to idols, but to the God who created heaven and earth and every kind of creature—and to his image. Word "62."|[a]

"Now therefore, my children, guard your souls from every kind of 1 injustice, such as the LORD hates.[b] •And walk in front of his face with fear |and 2 trembling|, and worship him alone. |To the true God bow down, not to idols which have no voice, but bow down to his statue|. And every kind of oblation present justly in front of the face of the LORD; but what is unjust the LORD detests.

For the LORD sees everything that a person thinks in his heart. Then reason advises 3 him. ⟨For⟩ every thought is presented before the LORD |who made the earth firm and settled all the creatures upon it|.

If you[c] look upon the sky, behold, the LORD is there; for the LORD created the 4 sky. If you look upon the earth, then the LORD is there; for the LORD founded the earth, and placed upon it all his creatures. If you meditate upon the depths of the ocean and on all that is beneath the earth, then the LORD is there. Because the LORD created all things.

Do not bow down to anything created by man, nor to anything created by God, 5 so committing apostasy against the LORD of all creation. For no kind of deed is hidden from the face of the LORD.

---

e. The obscure vs. 5 is missing from short MSS.

f. Here "creation" is time; its termination corresponds to the day of judgment.

g. The MSS vary: *rasipljatcja* (R); *rasypletcja* (J); *prilĕpitcja* (P = Gk. *synapagesthai*).

h. "Life" is a mere gloss in P.

i. Vs. 11, missing from short MSS, is attested by *MPr*. Vs. 11 is identical with 66:7 in J P R.

66 a. The preface of P includes a qualification, corresponding to a gloss found only in P in vs. 2. Two different words are used. The ch. heading is *vyobraženiju*; vs. 2 has *načertaniju*. These are rare,

affected, words, different from the simpler terms *obrazŭ* (= *skhēma, kharaktēr, morfē*, etc.) and *podobije* (= *homoiōma*). Both these words are used in Scripture to describe man as the image of God. By contrast *načertanije* refers more specifically to a work of art, i.e. a picture or statue. In P's curious gloss to 67:3, *načertanie* is an inscription on a *svitokŭ* (= *biblion*). I have not found a listing of *vyobraženije* in any lexicon or glossary. The comments are evidently due to a Christian (?) ikon-worshiper, and contradict one of 2En's fundamental tenets. Yet vs. 2 contrasts this lawful worship with idolatry (pagan).

[A]

|calculate| the death of his own life.

5

6   When the whole of creation,   which the LORD
has created, shall come to an end, and when each person will go to
7 the LORD's great judgment,   •then the time periods will perish, and
there will be neither years nor months nor days, and hours will no longer be
counted;
8 But they will constitute a single age. And all the righteous, who escape from the Mt 13:43
LORD's great judgment, will be collected together with the great age. And ⟨the
age⟩ at the same time   will unite with the righteous, and they will be eternal.
9 And   there will be among them neither weariness nor suffering nor affliction Rev 21:4
nor expectation of violence   nor the pain of the night nor darkness.
10 But they will have a great light for eternity, ⟨and⟩ an indestructible wall,   and
they will have a great paradise,
the shelter of an eternal residence.
11 How happy are the righteous who will escape the LORD's great judgment, for Mt 13:43
their faces will shine forth like the sun.[i]

66

1 "Now therefore, my children, guard your souls from every kind of   WisSol 14:9
2 injustice, from everything which the LORD hates. •   Walk in front of the face Phil 2:12; Eph
of the LORD,   and worship him alone.   6:5

                              And bring every oblation in
front of the face of the LORD.

3   1Chr 38:9; 2Chr
                                              6:30; Ps 94:11;
                                              Prov 15:11

4 For if ⟨you⟩ look ⟨upon the sky⟩, the LORD is there; for the LORD created the sky. Ps 139:8–12
If ⟨you⟩ look upon the earth

and upon the ocean, and if ⟨you⟩ meditate upon the things beneath the earth, the
LORD is there as well. For the LORD created all things.

5   Jer 16:17; Sir
                                              17:15

And no deeds are hidden from the face of the LORD.

b. V N have only vs. 1 (B in *APOT*). But A U have material which parallels most of the long text preserved by J P R. A considerable amount of these extras are doubtless due to later expansion, which has gone even further in P. Vss. 3 and 8 are probably commentary. Vs. 7 is identical with 65:11 in A. In vss. 4–6, A U present all the signs of being abbreviated from the more coherent, if somewhat verbose text in J P R. Thus the items in vs. 4 make a good set; and it is not likely that this was achieved merely by adding to the list in A U. It is worth emphasizing that, in contrast to J R, which agree throughout (J usually agrees with P

against R). P has a shorter version of vs. 4, but its abbreviation has taken place differently. The fragmentary condition of P could have been suspected even before J R supplied the correct text. While certainty is scarcely to be hoped for in such loose transmission, many of the long readings have a good claim to be authentic, especially when, as here, we can see the process of abbreviation at work in short MSS. In the case of the mere inventory in vs. 6 it is more difficult to decide whether A U are truncated or J P R have been expanded.

c. In A U the verbs are third person.

[J]

Walk, my children,   6

> in long-suffering,
> in meekness |honesty|,
> in affliction,
> in distress,
> in faithfulness,
> in truth,
> in hope,
> in weakness,
> in derision,
> in assaults,
> in temptation,
> in deprivation,
> in nakedness,

having love for one another, until you go out from this age of suffering, so that you may become inheritors of the never-ending age.

How happy are the righteous who shall escape the LORD's great judgment; for   7 they will be made to shine seven times brighter than the sun.

For in that age everything is estimated sevenfold[d]—light and darkness and food   8 and enjoyment and misery and paradise and tortures |fire, frost, et cetera|. All this I have put down in writing, so that you might read it and think about it."

67 |The LORD sent out darkness onto the earth, and it covered the people and Enoch. And he was taken up to the highest heaven. And it became light. Word "63."|

And when Enoch had spoken to his people,   1

⟨|the LORD|⟩ sent the gloom onto the earth, and it became dark[a] and covered the men who were standing |and talking| with Enoch. •And the angels hurried[b] and grasped Enoch and carried   2 him up to the highest heaven, where the LORD received him and made him stand in front of his face for eternity. Then the darkness departed from the earth, and it became light.

And the people looked, but they could not[c] figure out how Enoch had been taken   3 away. And they glorified God. |And they found a scroll on which was inscribed: THE INVISIBLE GOD.|[d] And then they |all| went to their homes.[e]

---

d. The factor of seven is commonly used in the biblical tradition. The present passage seems to be inspired by Isa 30:26, which predicts that the eschatological sun will be seven times brighter than the present one. In 65:11 (A) the righteous will shine ''like the sun.'' Several Christian apocalypses predict that at the parousia or in his present glory the face of Jesus is seven times brighter than the sun (*Epistula Apostolorum* 16; ApPet 7; ActsPhil § 20).

67 a. The veiling of the mysterious event in darkness resembles the evangelists' reports on the circumstances of Jesus' death. They do not have a correspondingly dramatic account of the return of the light. The GPet (6:22) does record the return of sunlight after the death of Jesus. The opposite is met in the Ebionite version of Jesus' baptism, according to Epiphanius (*AdvHaer* 30.13.7f., after the divine pronouncement of Ps 2:7 as in Lk 3:23) ''and immediately a great light shone round about the place.'' There is no preceding darkness, but

[A]

In long-suffering,
  in meekness,
and in the affliction
  of your distresses,

                          go out from this age of
suffering.''

7

8

67

1 While Enoch was talking to his people,

About the taking away of Enoch

                                 the LORD sent
darkness onto the earth, and it became dark and covered the men who were
2 standing   with Enoch. •And the angels hurried
and ⟨the angels⟩ grasped Enoch and carried him up to the highest heaven, and the
LORD received him and made him stand in front of his face for eternity. And the
darkness departed from the earth, and it became light.
3 And the people looked, and they understood   how Enoch had been taken
away. And they glorified God.
                           And they went away into their
homes.

the light is not simply an evidence of the closer
approach of the divine glory, for the descent of the
dove and the voice from heaven have already taken
place. On the light of Jesus' baptism, see W.
Bauer, *Das Leben Jesu* (Tübingen, 1909) pp. 134–
39.
  b. The words "and the angels hurried and grasped
Enoch" have been lost from P by homoeoteleuton.
  c. A U differ from all other MSS in omitting
"not," thus reversing the meaning. Luke (Acts
1:9) emphasizes that Jesus' ascension took place

in full view of the disciples.
  d. The significance of P's curious gloss about
the scroll is lost. In view of the many instances
in which the roots *vid* and *věd* are confused in
these texts, we might suspect *nevědimŭ bgŭ
(Acts 17:23). Was there a tradition that the Greeks
had profited by the missionary work hinted at in
chs. 35, 54 and 70:1?

  e. V N end at this point, with a suitable ascription: "To our God be glory forever. Amen."

[J]

68ª

Enoch was born on the 6th day of the month Tsivan,[b] and he lived for 365 years. 1
|And| he was taken up to heaven ⟨|in the month|⟩ Nitsan, on the 1st day. And he
remained in heaven for 60 days, •writing down all |those| notes about all the 2
creatures which the LORD had created. And he wrote 366 books and he handed
them over to his sons. And he remained on the earth for 30 days, talking with
them. •And then he was taken up to heaven again in the month of Tsivan |on the 3
6th day|,[c] on the very same 6th day on which he was even born, and at the very
same hour.
And just as every person has as his nature the darkness of this present life, so 4
also he has his conception and birth and departure from this life. In |the hour in|
which he was conceived, in that hour also he is born, |and| in that also he departs.

                And Methusalam and his brothers and all 5
the sons of Enoch hurried, and they constructed an altar at the place |called|
Akhuzan, |whence and| where Enoch had been taken up |to heaven|.
And they obtained sheep and oxen, and they summoned all the people, and they 6
sacrificed sacrifices in front of the face of the LORD.
And |all| the people |and the elders of the people and the whole assembly| came 7
to them to the festival, and brought offerings[d] for the sons of Enoch. And they
made a |great| festival, rejoicing and making merriment for three days, |praising
God who had given them such a sign through Enoch, his own favored servant,
even so that they might hand it on to their own sons, from generation to generation,
from age to age. AMEN|.[e]

69ª

And on the third day, in the time of the evening, the elders of the people spoke 1
to Methusalam, saying, "Stand in front of the face of the LORD and in front of
the face of all the people and in front of the face of the altar of the LORD, and
you will be glorified in your people."
And Methusalam answered his people:[c] "Wait, O men, until ⟨the LORD⟩, the God 2

68 a. The chronological information, much of
which is found elsewhere in the book, is lacking
in A U B. Was it dropped because of the tincture
of astrology in vss. 3 and 4?

b. Here, as in 48:2, the names rather than the
numbers, as in 1:2. As at 48:2, R has *Pamovousa*
(vss. 1 and 3) instead of *Civana*. P erroneously
says that Enoch was taken up on the first day of
Tsivan, but both J and R agree that it was Nisan
|(J has *Nicana*). According to this reckoning,
Enoch's first ascent was at the vernal equinox, or
near it (1:2).

c. The day of Enoch's second ascension was
the portentous date of the Festival of Firstfruits. J.
Morgenstern points out that "A far larger number
of events in the traditional early history of Israel
are linked to this day than to any other festival"
("The Calendar of the Book of Jubilees," *VT* 5
[1955] 56). How could a medieval Slav. scribe, or
even a Byzantine monk, have known such a fact,
and chosen such a date?

d. A U read "created," which could mean that
"the people who had come with them to the festival
also *made* (sacrifices)."

e. P ends here, with its own summary, shown in
|. . .|.

69 a. The Midrashim of Enoch's descendants,
mainly Methuselah and Melchizedek, occupy the
remaining five chs. This appeared first in English
as an appendix to the Morfill-Charles edition of
1896; but it was dropped from *APOT*. Bonwetsch
also presented it as a distinct work. Vaillant followed Sokolov in recognizing its integral place as
a continuation of 2En. It has no MS existence as
a distinct work. For this reason we have continued
the ch. enumeration. From ch. 69 five MSS (A U
B J R) supply the text. Rum begins at 70:13, but
J ends at 71:4. Charles did not identify the MS
source of his translation, but it is evidently R.
Vaillant's main text is U, with the variants of R in
his *annexe*. Since we present A and J in our two
versions, the complete information about these four
witnesses is now available.

In ch. 69 the textual differences between long
(J R) and short (A U) MSS are minor. Even so,
they are worthy of close attention. The Hebraic (or
at least pseudobiblical) character of the original is
abundantly manifest and the exotic character of the
Semitic idioms, due to literal translation, created
strains in Slav. syntax. Scribal alterations often
brought the language closer to the native style. One

[A]

68

1

2

3

4

⟨About the taking up of Enoch once more to heaven, where he had been.⟩

5   ⟨And⟩ Methusalem and his brothers,
the sons of Enoch, hurried, and they constructed an altar at the place
         Azukhan, whence   Enoch had been taken up.
6 And ⟨with them⟩ they obtained sheep and oxen,
and they sacrificed   in front of the face of the LORD.
7 And they ⟨summoned⟩ all the people
         to come with them to the festival; and the people brought offerings
for the sons of Enoch. And they made a   festival,
and made merriment for 3 days.

69

1 And on the 3rd day, |in| the time of the evening, the elders of the people spoke
to Mathusalem, saying, "Come and stand in front of the face of the LORD and |in
front| of the face of your people,[b] ⟨and in front of the altar of the LORD, and be
glorified in your people."
2 And Mefusalam answered the people:⟩

of the most obvious Semitisms is the repetition of a preposition in a series of coordinations, rather than using the preposition only once to govern a series of coordinated nouns. Thus vs. 1 was originally: "Stand in front of the face of the LORD and in front of the face of all the people and in front of the face of the altar of the LORD." This is literal translation of *lipnê*, repeated three times.

The noun "face" is redundant, since *lipnê* means "in front of." If *enōpion* were the original of this *prĕd* would have been enough. The long MSS (J R), which are identical word for word, preserve the Heb. idiom perfectly; but short A U have not only lost the third phrase at the beginning of a considerable lacuna, they have simplified the idiom. They dropped the preposition and kept the redundant noun: "Stand in front of the face of the Lord and the face of his people." B has naturalized the idiom differently, but the telltale noun "face" remains. "Come with us to (*na*) the face of the Lord and to (*na*) the face of your people and in (*vŭ*) the face of the altar of the Lord." In vs. 5 (cf. 17 and 70:14, 18) J R retain *prĕd*, but B A U

switch to *v:* "*in* front of them and *in* front of my altar." The fluctuation of *svoego/tvoego* is also revealing, since this option does not exist in Heb.

Other palpable Hebraisms are "the time of evening," "the elders of the people," and "the altar of the Lord." In fact one has only to glance at Kahana's translation to realize that literal back-translation into Heb. yields perfect classical narrative prose.

An important principle of text criticism follows from these observations, which could be multiplied indefinitely. The "correctness," i.e. originality of a reading, should not be tested by conformity to the norms of Slav. syntax. It is the opposite. The more Semitic idiom has the better claim, the more Slav. idiom is the result of domestication subsequent to translation.

b. The lacuna in A U at this point is made up by B.

c. B retains the Hebraic ethic dative, and *kŭ* with indirect object; J R have adjusted to the simple dative. In vs. 5 it is the other way: B J R keep *kŭ*, but A U have dropped it.

[J]

of my[d] father Enoch, shall himself raise up for himself
a priest[e] over his own people." •And the people waited until that night   3
in vain at the place Akhuzan.[f] •And Methusalam remained near the altar and   4
prayed to the LORD and said, "O LORD, the only One of the whole world,[g] who
has taken away my father Enoch, you raise up[h] a priest for ⟨your⟩ people, and
give their heart understanding to fear your glory and to perform everything in
accordance with your will."
Methusalam fell asleep,[j] and the LORD appeared to him in a night vision and said   5
to him,[k] "Listen, Methusalam! I am the LORD, the God of your father Enoch.
Give heed to the voice of these people and stand in front   of my altar,
and I shall glorify you in front of the face of all the people, and you will be
glorified
all the days of your life, and I shall bless you." •And Methusalam got up from   6
his sleep and blessed the LORD who had appeared to him.
And the elders of the people hurried[l] to Methusalam,[m]   7
and the LORD God directed Methusalam's heart to give heed to the voice of the
people. And he said to them, "The LORD God[n] is the one who has
given grace to these people in front of my eyes today." •And Sarkhasan[o] and   8
Kharmis and Zazas, the elders of the people, hurried and attired Methusalam in
the designated garments and placed a blazing crown on his head.
And the people hurried, and they brought sheep and oxen and some birds,[p] all of   9
them having passed inspection, for Methusalam to sacrifice in the name of the
LORD and in the name of the people.
And Methusalam came up to the LORD's altar, and his face was radiant, like the   10
sun at midday rising up, with all the
people in procession behind him.[q] •And Methusalam stood in front of the altar[r]   11
of the LORD, with all the people standing around the place of sacrifice.
And when the elders of the people had taken sheep and oxen, they tied their four   12
legs together,[s] and placed them at the head of the altar.[t]
And they said to Methusalam, "Pick up the knife! And slaughter   13
them in the required manner in the face of the LORD." •And Methusalam stretched   14
out his hands to heaven[u] and he called out to the LORD thus, saying, "Accept
⟨me⟩, O LORD! Who am I, to stand at the head of your
place of sacrifice and over the head of these people? •And now, O LORD, look   15
upon your servant[v] ⟨and⟩ upon all these people. Now all the inquiries, let them
come to pass! And give a blessing[w] to your servant in front of the face of all the
people, so that they may realize that you are the one who has appointed ⟨me⟩ to
be priest over your people."
And it happened, when Methusalam had prayed, that the altar was shaken, and   16
the knife rose up from the altar, and leaped into Methusalam's hand in front of
the face of all the people.[x] And the people trembled and glorified God.
And Methusalam was honored in front of the face of the LORD and in front of the   17
face of all the people from that day.

---

d. B agrees with J R that Methuselah is talking about "my" father; not addressed by the people—"your" father (A U).

e. Short MSS have *ereja*, long ones *žrŭca*. The same things occur in vs. 15.

f. The recensions divide consistently over *Azukhan/Akhuzan*.

g. Only B has a sound text: *Gospodi vsego věka, cyĭ edinŭ*. J is essentially the same, but R is defective. A U have only *vsego sña*. They have also misread *oca* J, "father," as *ŏt oca*.

h. With the idiom of "raise up" cf. 35:2. A U read *javi*, "reveal." It anticipates the verb in vs. 5.

i. The addition of the negative makes A U's reading inferior.

j. At the beginning of vs. 5, J alone has adjusted the Semitic syntax by putting the subject before the verb.

k. These details imitate the patriarchal narratives of Gen.

l. "Hurried" is a Hebraism, still present in A U, at vs. 8 (but B has *jadriša* there).

m. The use of *kŭ* (= *'el*) with a verb of motion is another Hebraism. This phenomenon abounds (with frequent adjustments to Slav. as textual variants). No more examples will be cited.

[A]

"Oh the LORD the God of your father Enoch, it is he himself who will raise up
3 a priest over his own people." •And the people waited all that night
4   at the place Azukhan. •And Mathusalom remained {the LORD} near the   1Sa 2:35
altar and prayed to the LORD and said,   "the whole
dream(?), who has selected {from} our father Enoch, you LORD, make known a
priest for your people, and   in a   heart that does not[i] understand   your
glory and to perform everything in accordance with your will."
5 And Mekhusalom fell asleep, and the LORD appeared to him in a night vision and   1Kgs 3:13
said to him, "Listen, Mefusalom! I am the LORD, the God of your father Enoch.
Give heed to the voice of your people and stand in front of them and in front of
my altar,   and I shall glorify you in front of the face of this people of
mine
6 all the days of your life."   •And Mefusalom got
up from his sleep and blessed   him   who had appeared to him.
7 And the elders of the people came up to Mefusalom in the morning, and the LORD
God directed Mefusalom's heart to give heed to the voice of the people. And he
said to them, "The LORD our God,   what is good
8 in his eyes, may he do it over this people of his." •And Sarsan and Kharmis and
Zazas, the elders of the people, hurried and attired Mefusalom in the choice
garment and placed a blazing crown on his head.
9 And the people hurried, and the people brought sheep and oxen and some birds,
all of them having passed inspection, for Mefusalim to sacrifice in front of the
face of the LORD and in front of the face of the people.
10 And Mefusalim came up to the LORD's altar, like the morning star when it   Sir 50:5-11
rises,   with all the
11 people in procession behind him. •And Methusalom stood in front of
the altar   with all the people   around the altar.
12   And   the elders of the people,   taking sheep and oxen,
           tied (their)   4   legs together, and placed (them) at the head of the
13 altar. •And the people said to Methusalim, "Pick up the knife! And slaughter
14 them in the required manner in the face of the LORD." •And Mefusalom stretching   1Kgs 8:22,54
out his hands to heaven,   called out to the LORD,   saying, "Alas for
me, O LORD! Who am I, to stand at the head of your
15 altar   (and) at the head of all your people? •And now, O LORD, LORD,
look favorably upon your servant and upon the head of all your people, and upon
all (their) tiny cares. And give grace to your servant in front of the face of this
people, so that they may realize that you are the one who has appointed   a
priest for your people."
16 And it happened that, while Methusalom was praying,   the altar was shaken,
and the knife rose up from the altar, and leaped into Methusalom's hands in front
of the face of all the people. And the people trembled and glorified the LORD.
17 And Methusalom was honored in front of the face of the LORD and in front of the
face of all the people from that day.

---

n. B has "your" where A U have "our." J R
lack the pronoun.

o. R agrees with other MSS that the name of
the first elder is Sarsan. B has only two: Sarsi and
Kharlis. Short MSS have "and," so the elders are
additional to the persons named.

p. The partitive use of *ot* (= *min*, "from"),
"some," is a Hebraism.

q. Several features of the following ceremonial
are reminiscent of the account in 1Kgs 8.

r. All MSS use *oltarja* the first time and most
again in vs. 12, but only A U the second. The
others have *zertvenniků*, i.e. B agrees with J R in
this variant. Cf. the corresponding pair of words

used for "priest."

s. The rule of 59:3. See 70:20.

t. "The head of the altar" is a literal Hebraism.

u. A similar gesture, described in the same
words, is performed by John at the raising of
Stacteus, an incident in the Acts of John (James,
ANT, p. 260).

v. B shares with J R the retention of the self-
designation "your slave," another Hebraism.

w. There is an interesting textual split here:
"Blessing" is read by J (long) and B (short);
"grace" is read by R (long) and A U (short).

x. The syntax of this verse is biblical Heb.

[J]

And Methusalam took the knife[y] and slaughtered all that had been brought by the 18
people. And ⟨the people⟩ rejoiced greatly, and they made merry in front of the
face of the LORD and in front of the face of Methusalam on that day. •And then 19
the people went off to their own shelters, each one of them.[z]

70

And Methusalam began to stand[a] at the altar in front of the face of the LORD, and 1
all the people, from that day for 10 years, hoping in an eternal inheritance, and
having thoroughly taught all the earth and all his own people.[c]

                                                And there was not found one single person
turning himself away in vanity from the LORD during all the days that
Methusalam lived. •And the LORD blessed Methusalam and was gratified by his 2
sacrifices and by his gifts and by every kind of service which he performed in
front of the face of the LORD. •And when the time of the departure days of 3
Methusalam arrived, the LORD appeared to him in a night vision and said to him,
"Listen, Methusalam! I am the LORD, the God of your father Enoch. I want you
to know[d] that the days of your life have come to an end, and the day of your rest
has come close.[e]
Call Nir, the second son of your son Lamekh, born after Noe, and invest him in 4
the garments of your consecration.[f] And make him stand at my altar. And tell
him everything that will happen in his days, for the time of the destruction of all
the earth, and of every human being and of everything that lives[g] on

the earth, is drawing near. •For in his days there will be a very great breakdown 5
on the earth, for each one has begun to envy his neighbor, and people against
people have destroyed boundaries, and the nation wages war. And all the earth is
filled with vileness
and blood and every kind of evil. •⟨And⟩ even more than that, they have abandoned 6
their LORD,[h] and they will do obeisance to unreal gods, and to the vault above
the sky, and to what moves above the earth, and to the waves of the sea. And
the adversary[i] will make himself great and will be delighted with his deeds, to
my great provocation.[j]
And all the earth will change its seasons ⟨and every tree and every fruit will 7
change their seeds⟩[k] anticipating the time of destruction. And all the races will
change on the earth by my conflagration.
Then I shall give the command. The Bottomless will be poured out over the earth,[l] 8

---

y. Short MSS faithfully reproduce the brachyl-
ogy of the anaphoric pronoun object which is
standard grammar of the Heb. verb *lāqaḥ*. J R have
been obliged to supply the object "knife."

z. The language of 1Kgs 8:66. The Heb. distributive construction is preserved, along with the
term "tent." This time it is A U that have adapted
to *domy*, "houses." B has removed the distributive
pronoun, but retains *krovy*, "shelters," showing
that this is original.

70 a. The verb form "began to stand" is a Hebraism lost from short MSS. On the other hand
short MSS have retained the Heb. idiom "head,"
which J R have either eliminated or changed to
"face."

b. Vaillant (*Secrets*, pp. xv, 68) has tried to
reconstruct the original numeral from *ŭpv* (B), a

Cyrillic numeral, since it uses *ižica*, or *ŭčv* (U),
ččv (A); assuming Glagolitic, 482, 492, 1092,
respectively, assuming A to be a careless writing
of *čuv*. A confirms Vaillant's suspicion that the
first numeral was 1000. He emended to **čupv* =
1482. This is close to the dating (*anno mundi*) of
Enoch in LXX figures. But the use of *ižica* forbids
the reading of *č* as Glagolitic.

c. B supports A U's variant "those who believe
in the Lord" (not in J R), and in addition repeats
"and there was not found a person deserting the
Lord" between this and the following remark about
converting apostates. The shorter texts can thus be
explained by the usual causes already mentioned.

d. We have followed B, *vĕdĕti ti velju*, because
it agrees in general with J R. The reading in which
A U agree—*vidite* ("see") *volju* ("will," a noun)—
seems to be a meaningless corruption of the other.

[A]

18 And Methusalom took the knife and slaughtered all that had been brought by the people. And the people rejoiced   and they made merry in front of the face
19 of the LORD and in front of the face of Methusalom on that day. •And then   1Kgs 8:66
they   went off to their houses.

70

1 And Mefusalom stood at the head of the altar and at the head of all the people
from that day onward.   In   492ᵇ
he explored the earth, and he sought out all those who had
believed in the LORD.   And those who had apostatized he corrected them and
converted them.   And there was not found one person
turning himself away   from the LORD during all the days that
2 Methusalom lived. •And the LORD blessed Methusalom ⟨and was gratified⟩ by his
sacrifices and by his gifts and by every kind of service which he performed in
3 front of the face of the LORD. •And after the ending of   the   days
of Methusalom,   the LORD appeared to him in a night vision and
said to him, "Listen, Methusalom! I am ⟨the LORD⟩, the God of your father
Enoch. ⟨I want you to know⟩ that the days of your life have come to an end, and
the day of your rest has come close.
4 Call Nir, the second son of your son Lamekh,
          and invest him in the garments of your consecration. And
make him stand at my altar. And you will tell him everything that will happen
⟨to him⟩ in his days, for the time is drawing near for the destruction of all the
earth, and of every human being and of everything that moves on
5 the earth.   ·   •For in his days there will be a
          great confusion on the earth, for each person has become envious
of his neighbor, and people will sin against people.
And nation will wage war against nation. And all the earth will be filled
6 with blood and with very   evil confusion. •Even more than that, they will
abandon their Creator, and they will do obeisance to that which is fixed in the
sky, and to what moves above the earth, and   the waves of the sea. And the
adversary will make himself great and will be delighted with their deeds, to my
provocation.
7 All the earth will change its order, and every fruit and every herb will change
their times, for they will anticipate the time of destruction. And all the nations
will change on the earth, and all my desire.
8 And then I, I shall   command the Bottomless. It will come out and rush out Gen 7:11

e. Note the poetic parallelism at the end of vs.
3.

f. "The garments of your consecration" is a
Hebraism.

g. J has lost a phrase by homoeoteleuton, due
to repetition of "earth." R agrees with A U B,
except that it reads "lives" instead of "moves."

h. "Creator" (*tvorca*) although not used elsewhere, is better than "LORD" (J), the usual term:
(1) because R has it; (2) because "LORD" is not
usually modified in any way, being used as a pure
proper noun.

i. Slav. *protivnik*, "adversary," or "opponent," is a rare title for the devil.

j. The variations in spelling of the related words
at the ends of vss. 6f. illustrate the point that slight
changes in spelling can cause substantial changes
in meaning; and sometimes a MS otherwise inferior

(here J) might have the best reading.

	vs. 6	vs. 7	
J	*raždeženia*	*žeženie*	vexation
R	*raždalenia*	*želanie*	
A	*raždelenie*	*želanie*	desire
U	*raždelenie*	*želanie*	
B	*raždenie*	*žalĕnie*	sorrow

k. R says that each fruit will change its "seed"
(*sĕmena*), not "time" (*vrĕmena*). J's loss of all
words between the two occurrences of the phrase
vrĕmena cvoja (homoeoteleuton once again) proves
that this is the correct reading. Furthermore, it is
this disruption of "time" that would impress hold-
ers of 2En's doctrine that the end was near. Was
this disruption of time due to the use of the
impossibly theoretical 364-day year calendar? But
see our qualifying notes on ch. 48.

l. The imagery of vs. 8 is drawn from Gen 7:11.

[J]

and the great storages of the waters of heaven will come down onto the earth ⟨in a great substance and in accordance with the first substance⟩.[m]

And the whole constitution of the earth will perish, and all the earth will quake, 9 and it will be deprived of its strength from that day. •Then I will preserve the son 10 of your son Lamekh, his first son, Noe. And from his seed I will raise up another world, and his seed will exist forever, until the second destruction when once again[n] mankind will have committed sin in front of my face.''

And Methusalam leaped up from his sleep, and his dream was very disturbing. 11 And he summoned all the elders of the people, and recounted to them all that the LORD had said to him and all the vision that had been revealed to him by the LORD. •And all the people were disturbed by his vision. And they answered him, 12 ''The LORD is lord, and he will act in accordance with his own will. And now, Methusalam, you do everything just as the LORD has told you.''[o]

And Methusalam summoned Nir, the son of Lamekh,[p] Noe's younger brother, 13 and he invested him with the vestments of priesthood in front of the face of all the people, and made him stand at the head of the altar of the LORD. And he taught him everything that he would have to do among the people.

⟨And Methusalam spoke to the people:⟩ ''Here is Nir. He will be in front of your 14 face from the present day as a prince and a leader.''

And the people said to Methusalam, ''Let it be so ⟨for us⟩ in accordance with 15 your word. And you be the voice of the LORD, just as he said to you.''

And when Methusalam had spoken to the people in front of the altar, his spirit 16 was convulsed, and, having knelt on his knees, he stretched out his hands to heaven, and prayed to the LORD. And, as he was praying to him, his spirit went

out in accordance with ⟨the will of⟩ the LORD. •And Nir and all the people hurried 17 and constructed a sepulcher[r] for Methusalam in the place Akhuzan, very thoughtfully adorned with all holy things, with lamps.

And Nir came with many praises, and the people lifted up Methusalam's body, 18 glorifying ⟨God⟩; they performed the service for him at the sepulcher which they had made for him and they covered him over.

And they said, ''⟨How⟩ blessed was Methusalam in front of the face of the LORD 19 and in front of the face of all the people!'' And when they wanted to go away to their own places, Nir said to the people, ''Hurry up today and bring sheep and bulls and turtledoves and pigeons, so that you may make a sacrifice in front of the face of the LORD today.

And then go away to your houses.'' •And the people gave heed to Nir the priest,[s] 20 and they hurried and they brought ⟨them⟩ and tied ⟨them⟩ up at the head of the altar. •And Nir took the knife of sacrifice, and slaughtered all that had been 21 brought to be sacrificed in front of the face of the LORD. •And all the people made merry in front of the face of the LORD, and on that day they glorified the 22 LORD, the God of heaven and earth, ⟨the God⟩ of Nir. And from that day there

---

m. J has lost twelve words from vss. 8b–9a by homoeoteleuton (''earth'' is repeated).

n. For comparison of the days of Noah with the end of the world see Mt 24:37; Lk 17:26.

o. Rum begins at this point, where the story of Melchizedek commences. Its title is: ''From the secret books of Enoch: the story about the priest Melchizedek, how he was born from the dead Sothonim.'' After a few words from the Preface,

it says: ''And when Enoch was on the earth, he fathered sons, Methusalam and Regim. And Methusalam became the priest on earth.'' Vs. 13 follows.

p. The spelling of Lamech at this point is enough to show that no safe inference can be made from such details about the original form of proper nouns, as Milik has done with Ariokh and Mariokh.

[A]

over the earth, and the   storages of the waters of heaven will rush ⟨from above⟩ onto the earth in a great substance in accordance with the first substance.
9 And the whole constitution of the earth will perish, and all the earth will quake,
10 and it will be deprived of its strength even from that day. •Then I, I will preserve Noe, the firstborn son of your son Lamekh. And I will make another world rise up from his seed, and his seed will exist throughout the ages.''
11   And Methusalom, getting up from his sleep, grieved greatly over the dream. And he summoned all the elders of the people, and recounted to them all that the LORD had said to him and   the vision that had been revealed to him by the LORD.
12 And   the people   grieved over   the vision. ⟨And⟩ ⟨the people⟩ answered him, ''The LORD   rules so as to act in accordance with his own will. And now,   do everything just as the LORD
13 has told you.'' •⟨And⟩ Methusalom summoned Nir, the second son of Lamekh,
                         and he invested him with the vestments of priesthood in front of the face of all the people, and made (him) stand at the head of the altar
          And he taught him everything that he would have to do among the people.

About the passing away of Methusal[q]

14 And Methusalom said to the people, ''Here is Nir. He will be in front of your face from the present day as the guide of the princes.''
15 And the people answered Methusalom, ''Let it be so for us,
          and let the word of the LORD be just as he said to you.''
16 And while Methusalom was speaking to the   1Kgs 8:22,54
people   his spirit was convulsed, and, kneeling on his knees, he stretched out his hands to heaven,
          praying to the LORD. And, as he was praying to him, his spirit
17 went out.   •And Nir and
all the people hurried and constructed a sepulcher for Methusalim and they placed for him incense and reeds and many holy things.
18 And Nir came with many praises, and the people lifted up Methusalam's body, glorifying ⟨God⟩; they performed the service for him at the sepulcher which they had made for him and they covered him over.
19 And the people said, ''How blessed is Methusalom in front of the face of the LORD and in front of the face of all the people!'' And from there they assembled,
                    and Nir said to the people, ''Hurry up today. Bring sheep and bulls and turtledoves and pigeons, so that we may make a sacrifice in front of the face of the LORD and rejoice today.
20 And then go away to your houses.'' •And the people gave heed to Nir the priest, ⟨and⟩ they hurried and they brought ⟨them⟩ and tied them up at the head of the
21 altar. •And Nir took the knife of sacrifice and slaughtered (them) in front of the face of the LORD.
22 And   the people hurried and did it and made merry in front of the face of the LORD all that day. They glorified the LORD God, the savior[t] of Nir. And in

B has *Lamekha*. Others have the Slav. adjective suffix *-ova*. J R *Lamekhova;* U *Lamefova;* A *Lamethova*. The point is that the fluidity of *kh, th, f* takes place within Slav. Methuselah shows similar fluctuations. We have carefully reproduced A's usage. U is more consistent, with Methusalom most of the time, but occasionally Methusalim, and once Methekhousalom. The same thing happens with Sofonim (U) in ch. 71—Sothonim (A). B has both.

J R agree in Sopanim.

q. A U provide a ch. heading before vs. 14.

r. B has *khramū*, ''temple'' (= shrine?), where the others have *grob*, ''grave.'' But at the end of vs. 18 B has ''grave.'' Cf. 71:22.

s. Here J R have not replaced *ierea* with *žrŭc*.

t. The word ''savior'' (A U) is secondary. B reads ''heaven'' as J R.

[J]

was peace and order over all the earth in the days of Nir—202 years.

And then the people turned away from the LORD, and they began to be envious 23
one against another, and people went to war against people, and race rose up
against race and struggled and insulted one another.

Even if the lips were the same, nevertheless the hearts chose different 24
things. •For the devil^u became ruler for the third time. The first was before 25
paradise; the second time was in paradise; the third time was after paradise, ⟨and⟩
continuing right up to the Flood.

And there arose disputation and great turbulence. And Nir the priest heard and 26
was greatly aggrieved. And he said in his heart, "In truth I have come to
understand how the time has arrived and the saying which the LORD said to
Methusalam, the father of my father Lamekh."^v

71

Behold, the wife of Nir, ⟨whose⟩ name was Sopanim, being sterile and never 1
having at any time given birth to a child^b by Nir—

And Sopanim was in the time of her old age, and in the day of her death. She 2
conceived in her womb, but Nir the priest had not slept with her,^c nor had he
touched her, from the day that the LORD had appointed him to conduct the liturgy
in front of the face of the people.^d

And when Sopanim saw her pregnancy, she was ashamed and embarrassed, and 3
she hid herself during all the days until she gave birth. And not

one of the people knew about it. •And when 282 days had been completed, and 4
the day of birth had begun to approach, and Nir remembered his wife, and he
called her to himself in his house,^e so that he might converse with her.^f

⟨And⟩ Sopanim came to Nir, her husband; and, behold, she was pregnant, and 5
the day appointed for giving birth was drawing near.

And Nir saw her, and he became very ashamed. And he said to her, "What is 6
this that you have done, O wife?^g And (why) have you disgraced me in front of
the face of these people? And now, depart from me, and go where you began the
disgrace of your womb, so that I might not defile my hand on account of you,
and sin in front of the face of the LORD."

And Sopanim spoke to Nir, her husband, saying, "O my lord!^h Behold, it is the 7
time of my old age, and the day of my death has arrived.

I do not understand how my

---

u. Vss. 24f., with the reference to the devil
(*Diavol*), not a character in 2En, are secondary.

v. B glosses "Methusalah"; J R "Lamekh."

71 a. A U have the same heading.

b. On childlessness, see our note on 2En 42:11.
Sopanim (J) was not a virgin.

c. This is a literal translation of the Slav. Scholars who have seen this story as an imitation of the
Gospel accounts of the virginal conception of Jesus
have been hasty and superficial. Every detail needs
careful assessment. Conventional stories of the
miraculous origin of a wonder-child generally have
such an element. There are always similarities in
obvious points which could hardly be absent.
Vaillant (*Secrets*, p. 75, n. 18) is inclined to see
in the language of this verse, *vo črevě imušti* =
en gastri ekhousa (Mt 1:18), a comparison between
Sopanim and the Blessed Virgin Mary. But the
phrase is a cliché for describing pregnancy.

There are many differences between 2En and
the NT; and the essentials of the NT account are
lacking. There is little resemblance between a young
betrothed virgin and an old sterile married woman.
While several barren wives in the OT eventually
give birth with divine aid, the natural role of the
husband is always recognized. The case of Sarah
is made extreme only by her old age. Philo, in
discussing Isaac's birth (in *Congr* 1–24 and *Somn*
2.10), contrasts Abraham's having a child by
Hagar, which he identifies with the propaedeutic
and profane sciences, with the acquisition of true
wisdom, which is implanted directly in the soul by
God. (The idea that virtue is a divine seed implanted
directly in the soul is found in the Clementine
Homily 3:27.) Hence God was the sole cause of
Isaac's conception. This, of course, is pure allegory.

Another story along the same lines is the birth
of Noah in 1En 106. The circumstances of Melchizedek's conception are closer to those of the

[A]

front of the face of the people, and from that day there was peace and order over all the earth in the days of Nir—202 years.

23 And after that the people changed, turned away from the LORD, and they began   Mt 24:7
to be envious one against another, and people went to war against people, and race rose up against race.

24

25   Gen 11:1

26 And there arose   great turbulence. And Nir the priest
heard and was greatly aggrieved. And he said in his heart,
"The time has arrived, please God, and the saying
which the LORD said to Methusalom, the father of my father."

71 About Nir's wife[a]

1 And behold, the wife of Nir,   Sothonim, being
sterile and never having   given birth to a child by Nir—
2 And Sothonim was in the time of   old age, and in the day
of   death. And she conceived in her womb, but Nir the priest had not slept
with her,   from the day that the LORD had appointed
him   in front of the face of the people.
3 ⟨And⟩ Sothonim   was ashamed,
and she hid herself during all the days.   And not
4 one of the people knew about it. •
And she was at the day of birth,   and Nir remembered his wife,
and he called her to himself in the temple, so that he might converse with her.
5 And Sothonim came to Nir, her husband; ⟨and⟩, behold, she was pregnant, and at the time for giving birth.
6 And Nir saw her, and he became very ashamed about her. And he said to her, "What is this that you have done, O wife? And why have you disgraced me in front of the face of all the people? And now, depart from me,   go where you conceived the disgrace of your womb, so that I might not defile my hand on account of you, and sin in front of the face of the LORD."
7 And Sothonim answered Nir, her husband, saying, "O my lord! Behold, it is the time of my old age, and there was not in me any (ardor of) youth   and I do not know how the indecency of my womb has been conceived."

conception of Mary herself in the Book of James (James, *ANT*, p. 20). Anna is an old but childless married woman. Her husband Joachim is a priest. They give themselves to spiritual exercises in isolation from each other. Joachim goes into the desert for forty days to fast and pray. While he is absent, Anna becomes pregnant. Her husband has it all explained to him by an angel, so there is no crisis (Book of James 4:2).

d. Sacral abstinence from sex while engaged with the holy mysteries is not a rule exclusive to Christian clergy of the Eastern churches. (1) The angels of heaven, in contrast to the Watchers, have never been defiled with women; hence sexual activity is banned in their presence (1En 15:3f.). (2) There was to be no sex for three days during assembly at Qumran (1QSa 1.26). (3) This is related to the warrior's sacral abstinence (1Sam 21:5). The Qumran community emphasized that there was to be no sex during war, "because the

holy angels accompany the armies" (1QM 7.3–7). (4) The Temple Scroll prohibited sex within the holy city Jerusalem (1QTem 45–47). (5) Moses refrained from sex after the Lord appeared to him (R. Bloch, "Quels aspects de la figure de Moïse dans la tradition rabbinique," *Moïse, homme de l'alliance* [Cahiers Sioniens] [Paris, 1955] pp. 93–167).

e. B Rum say he called her to the *khram* to himself. The word can mean "temple" or "house." By omitting the pronoun, A U incline to the former; by changing it to "his," J R incline to the latter.

f. J ends abruptly at the end of vs. 4. From here to the end we use R as the long MS.

g. Cf. Joseph's reproach of Mary in the Book of James (ch. 13).

h. She addresses her husband with the title used as the name of God elsewhere. [In *Vita* Eve repeatedly calls Adam "my Lord"; cf. *Vita* 1.2. J.H.C.]

[J]

menopause and the barrenness of my womb have been reversed.''

And Nir did not believe his wife, and for the second time he said to her, ''Depart 8
from me, or else I might assault you, and commit a sin in front of the face of the
LORD.''

And it came to pass, when Nir had spoken to his wife, Sopanim, that Sopanim 9
fell down at Nir's feet and died.[i]

Nir was extremely distressed; and he said in his heart, ''Could this have happened 10
because of my word, since by word and thought a person can sin in front of the
face of the LORD?

Now may God have mercy upon me! I know in truth in my heart that my hand 11
was not upon her. And so I say,[j] 'Glory to you, O LORD, because no one among
mankind knows about this deed which the LORD has done.' ''

And Nir hurried, and he shut the door of his house, and he went to Noe his 12
brother, and he reported to him everything that had happened in connection with
his wife. •And Noe hurried. He came with Nir his brother; he came into Nir's 13
house, because of the death of Sopanim, and they discussed between themselves
how her womb

was at the time of giving birth. •And Noe said to Nir, ''Don't let yourself be 14
sorrowful, Nir, my brother! For the LORD today has covered up our scandal, in
that nobody from the people knows this.

Now, let us go quickly and let us bury her secretly, and the LORD will 15
cover up the scandal of our shame.'' •And they placed Sopanim on the bed, and 16
they wrapped her around with black garments, and shut her in the

house, prepared for burial. They dug a grave in secret. • 17

And a child came out from the dead Sopanim.[k] And he sat on the bed at her side.
And Noe and Nir came in to bury Sopanim, and they saw the child

sitting beside the dead Sopanim, and wiping his clothing. •And Noe and Nir were 18
very terrified with a great fear, because the child was fully developed physically,
like a three-year-old. And he spoke with

his lips, and he blessed the LORD.[l] •And Noe and Nir looked at him, 19
and behold,

the badge of priesthood was on his chest, and it was glorious in appearance.

And Noe and Nir said, ''Behold, God is renewing the priesthood from blood 20
related to us, just as he pleases.'' •And Noe and Nir hurried, and they washed 21
the child, and they dressed him in the garments of priesthood, and they gave him
the holy bread and he ate it. And they called his name Melkisedek.

And Noe and Nir lifted up the body of Sopanim, and divested her of the black 22
garments, and they washed her, and they clothed her in exceptionally bright
garments, and they built a shrine for her.

Noe and Nir and Melkisedek came, and they buried her publicly. And Noe said 23
to his brother Nir, ''Look after this child in secret until the time, because people
will become treacherous in all the earth, and they will begin to turn away from
God, and having become totally ignorant, they will put him to death.''

And then Noe went away to his own place.

---

i. Cf. Acts 5:5, 10, according to which instantaneous death follows at a word of rebuke.

j. The ascription is peculiar to R. The passage about Gabriel is clearly secondary in A U; it is not in B Rum R.

k. I am not acquainted with any parallel to this extraordinary and sensational circumstance.

l. Similar prodigies are found in many legends. In the Acts of Peter (ch. 15) a seven-month-old child gives a remarkably mature lecture. In an infancy narrative the baby Jesus is able to cope with some dragons that threaten the family in a cave (James, *ANT*, p. 75). In the Apostolic History of Abdias (ch. 18) there is an incident in which a deacon in Babylon, Euphrosinus by name, was

[A]

8 ⟨And⟩ Nir did not believe her, and for the second time Nir said to her, "Depart from me, or else I might assault you, and commit a sin in front of the face of the

9 LORD." •And it came to pass, when Nir had spoken to his wife,
    that Sothonim fell down at Nir's feet and died.

10 Nir was extremely distressed; and he said in his heart, "Could this have happened because of my word?

11 And now, merciful is the eternal LORD,   because my hand was not upon her."

And the archangel Gabriel appeared to Nir, and said to him, "Do not think that your wife Sofonim has died because of (your) error; but this child which is to be born of her is a righteous fruit, and one whom I shall receive into paradise, so that you will not be the father of a gift of God."

12 And Nir hurried, and he shut the door of his house, and he went to Noe his brother, and he reported to him everything that had happened in connection with

13 his wife. •And Noe hurried to the room of his brother. And the appearance of his brother's wife was in death and her womb

14 was at the time of giving birth. •And Noe said to Nir, "Don't let yourself be sorrowful, Nir, my brother! For the LORD today has covered up our scandal, in that nobody from the people knows this.

15 And now, let us go quickly and let us bury her,   and the LORD will

16 cover up the scandal of our shame." •And they placed Sothonim on the bed, and they wrapped her around with black garments, and shut the door.

17 And they dug a grave in secret. •And when they had gone out
    toward the sepulcher, a child came out from the dead Sothonim. And he sat on the bed. And Noe and Nir came in to bury Sothonim, and they saw the child

18 sitting beside the corpse, and having his clothing on him. •And Noe and Nir were very terrified,   because the child was fully developed physically.   And he spoke with

19 his lips, and he blessed the LORD. •And Noe and Nir looked at him closely, saying, "This is from the LORD, my brother." And behold, the badge of priesthood was on his chest, and it was glorious in appearance.

20 And Noe said to Nir, "Behold, God is renewing the continuation of the blood

21 of the priesthood after us." •And Noe and Nir hurried, and they washed the child, and they dressed him in the garments of priesthood, and they gave him the holy bread and he ate it. And they called his name Melkisedek.

22 And Noe and Nir lifted up the body of Sothonim, and divested her of the black garments, and they washed her body, and they clothed her in   bright choice garments, and they built a grave for her.

23 And Noe and Nir and Melkisedek came,
    and they buried her publicly. And Noe said to his brother Nir, "Look after this child   until the time in secret, because people have become treacherous in all the earth, and in some way when they see him, they will put him to death."
    And   Noe went away to his own place.

---

falsely accused of fornication by a woman who was covering up for her real lover. When the child was born the apostles, on the day of its birth, questioned it, and the infant said that Euphrosinus was not its father.

The trivial legends about the infant Jesus showing off his erudition to schoolteachers, such as we have in the GThom. are merely projections back to early childhood of the tradition of Lk 2:41–52; but they have lost all restraint and dignity. The legend of Melchizedek goes to the extreme, for the newborn is mature physically as well as intellectually. [Cf. the Koran, Sura Mary, according to which Jesus, as a newborn infant from a virgin, delivers an oration. J.H.C.]

[J]

And great lawlessness began to become abundant over all the earth in the 24
days of Nir. •And Nir began to worry excessively, especially about the child, 25
saying,[m]

"How
miserable it is for me, eternal LORD, that in my days all lawlessness has begun
to become abundant over the earth. And I realize how much nearer our end is,
{and} over all the earth, on account of the lawlessness of the people.
And now, LORD, what is the vision about this child, and what is his destiny, and 26
what will I do for him? Is it possible that he too will be joined with us in the
destruction?" •And the LORD heeded Nir, and appeared to him in a night vision. 27
He said to him, "Nir,
the great lawlessness which has come about on the earth among the
multitude {which} I shall not tolerate.
And behold, I desire now to send out a great destruction onto the earth, and
everything that stands on the earth shall perish.
But, concerning the child, don't be anxious, Nir; because in a short while I shall 28
send my archistratig, Michael. And he will take the child, and put him in the
paradise of Edem, in the Paradise where Adam was formerly for 7 years, having
heaven open all the time up until when he sinned.[n]
And this child will not perish along with those who are perishing in this generation, 29
as I have revealed it, so that Melkisedek will be the priest to all holy priests, and
I will establish him so that
he will be the head of the priests of the future." •And Nir arose from his sleep 30
and blessed the LORD who had appeared to him, saying,

"Blessed be the LORD, the God of my fathers,

who has told me how he has made a great priest in my day,
in the womb of Sapanim, my wife.
Because I had no child in this tribe who might become the great 31
priest, but this is
my son and your servant, and you are the great God.

Therefore honor him together with your servants and great priests, with Sit, and 32
Enos, and Rusi, and Amilam, and Prasidam, and Maleleil, and Serokh, and
Arusan, and Aleem, and Enoch, and Methusalam, and me, your servant Nir.[o]
And behold, Melkisedek will be the head of the 13 priests 33
who existed before. •And afterward, in the last generation, there will be another 34
Melkisedek, the first of 12 priests. And the last will be the head of all, a great
archpriest, the Word and Power of God, who will perform
miracles, greater and more glorious than all the previous ones. •He, Melkisedek, 35
will be priest and king in the place Akhuzan, that is to say, in the center of the
earth, where Adam was created, and there will
be his final grave. •And in connection with that archpriest it is written how he 36
also will be buried there, where the center of the earth is, just as Adam also buried
his own son there—Abel, whom his brother Cain murdered; for he lay for 3 years
unburied, until he saw a bird called Jackdaw, how it buried its own young.[p]
I know that great confusion has come and in confusion this generation will come 37
to an end; and everyone will perish, except   that Noe, my brother, will be
preserved. And afterward there will be a planting from his tribe, and there will

m. The loss from R is homoeoteleuton between
the two occurrences of "saying."
n. Is this a gloss? It contradicts 32:1.
o. In the NT (Jude 14), Enoch is the seventh
from Adam. This is the case with Gen 5 (= 1Chr

1) and 2En 33:10. But this list has too many
names—to make Melchizedek the thirteenth? A
U's list varies in spelling, with two omissions, and
B is different again.
p. Vss. 34–37, only in R, are interpolated, and

[A]

24 And behold, all lawlessness   ⟨became abundant⟩ over all the earth in the
25 days of Nir. •And Nir began to worry excessively   about the
child, saying, "What will I do with him?" And stretching out his
hands toward heaven, Nir called out to the LORD, saying, "How
miserable it is for me, eternal LORD, that   all lawlessness has
begun to become abundant over the earth in my days! And I, I realize how much
nearer our end is.

26   And now, LORD, what is the vision about this child, and what
is his destiny, or what will I do for him, so   that he too will not be joined
27 with us in this destruction?" •And the LORD heeded Nir, (and) appeared to him
in a night vision. And he said to him, "Behold already, Nir, the great lawlessness
which has come about on the earth so that I will not suffer it anymore (and) I will
not tolerate it anymore. Behold, I plan now to send down a great destruction onto
the earth.

28 But, concerning the child, don't be anxious, Nir; because I, in a short while I
shall send my archangel Gabriel. And he will take the child, and put him in the
paradise of Edem.

29 And   he will not perish along with those who must
perish.   And as I have revealed it,   and Melkisedek
will be my priest to all   priests, and I will sanctify him and I
30 will change him into a great people who will sanctify me." •And Nir arose from
his sleep and blessed the LORD who had appeared to him, saying,

> "Blessed be the LORD, the God of my fathers,
> who has not condemned my priesthood and the priesthood of my fathers,
> because by his word he has created a great priest,
> in the womb of Safonim, my wife.
31 For I have no descendants.
> So let this child take the place of my descendants and become as my
> own son, and you will count him in the number of your servants,

32
with Sonfi, and Onokh, and Rusi, and Milam, and Serukh, and Arusan, and Nail,
and Enoch, and Methusail, and your servant Nir.
33 And   Melkisedek will be the head of the
34 priests in another generation.

35

36

37 For I know indeed that this race will end in confusion,
          and everyone will perish, except that Noe, my brother,
will be preserved in that generation for procreation.

---

include an incident (vs. 36) borrowed from the
cycle of Adam legends.

q. In a Christian legend, when Jesus goes to

school and confounds his teacher Levi with his
erudition, Levi exclaims, "I think he must have
been born before the Flood, before the Deluge."
(Cf. James, *ANT*, p. 77.)

[J]

be other people, and there will be another Melkisedek,q the head of priests reigning over the people, and performing the liturgy for the LORD.''

72

And when the child had been 40 days in Nir's tent, the LORD said to Michael,a 1 "Go down onto the earth to Nir the priest, and take my child Melkisedek, who is with him, and place him in the paradise of Edem for preservation. For the time is approaching, and I will pour out all the water onto the earth, and everything that is on the earth will perish."

2

Michael hurried, 3 and he came down when it was night, and Nir was sleeping on his bed. And Michael appeared to him, and said to him, "Thus says the LORD: 'Nir! Send the child to me whom I entrusted to you.'"c

And Nir did not realize who was speaking to him, and his heart was confused. 4 And he said, "When the people find out about the child, then they will seize him and kill him, because the heart of these people is deceitful in front of the face of the LORD." Nir said to the one who was speaking, "The child is not with me, and I don't know who you are."

And he who was speaking to me answered, "Don't be frightened, Nir! I am the 5 LORD's archistratig. The LORD has sent me, and behold, I shall take your child today. I will go with him and I will place him in the paradise of Edem, and there he will be forever.

And when the twelfth generation shall come into being, and there will be one 6 thousand and 70 years, and there will be born in that generation a righteous man. And the LORD will tell him that he should go out to that mountain where stands the ark of Noe, your brother. And he will find there another Melkisedek, who has been living there for 7 years, hiding himself from the people who sacrifice to idols, so that they might not kill him. He will bring him out, and he will be the first priest and king in the city Salim in the style of this Melkisedek, the originator of the priests. The years will be completed up to that time—3 thousand and 4 hundred and 32—

from the beginning and the creation of Adam. •And from that Melkisedek the 7 priests will be 12 in number until the great Igumen, that is to say, Leader, will bring out everything visible and invisible.''d

And Nir understood the first dream and believed it. And having answered Michael 8 he said, "Blessed be the LORD who has glorified you today for me! And now, bless your servant Nir! For we are coming close to departure from this world. And take the child, and do to him just as the LORD said

to you." •And Michael took the child on the same night on which he had come 9 down; and he took him on his wings,e and he placed him in the paradise

of Edom. •And Nir got up in the morning. He went into his tent and he did not 10 find the child. And there was instead of joy very

great grief, because he had no other son except this one.f •Thus Nir ended his 11 life. And after him there was no priest among the people. And from that time great confusion arose on the earth.

---

72 a. B is virtually identical with A U, except that the latter have systematically substituted Gabriel for Michael.

b. This verse, not in R, repeats 71:33.

c. Michael takes care of Melchizedek. In a similar fashion, Michael, "a mighty power in heaven," is charged by the good Father with the care of Christ, according to a Cop. translation of a discourse ascribed to Cyril of Jerusalem. Note also the presence of Michael in the vicinity of Rev 12:1–6, especially vs. 5. See E. A. W. Budge, *Miscellaneous Coptic Texts* (London, 1915) p. 637.

[A]

And from his tribe there will arise numerous people, and
Melkisedek will become the head of priests reigning over a
royal people who serve you, O LORD.''

72

1 And it happened, when the child had completed 40 days in Nir's tent, the LORD
said to the archangel Gabril, "Go down onto the earth to Nir the priest, and take
the child Melkisedek, who is with him, and place him in the paradise of Edem
for preservation. For the time is already approaching, and I, I will pour out all
the water onto the earth, and everything that is on the earth will perish.
2 And I will raise it up again in another generation, and Melkisedek
3 will be the head of the priests in that generation."[b] •And Gabriel hurried and he
came flying down when it was night, and Nir was sleeping on his bed that night.
And Gabriel appeared to him, (and) said to him, "Thus says the LORD: 'Nir!
Restore the child to me whom I entrusted to you.'''
4 And Nir did not realize who was speaking to him, and his heart was confused.
And he said, "When the people find out about the child, then they will seize him
and kill him, because the heart of these people is deceitful in front of the face of
the LORD." And he answered Gabriel and said, "The child is not with me, and
I don't know who is speaking to me."
5 And Gabriel answered him, "Don't be frightened, Nir! I am the archangel Gabriel.
The LORD sent me and behold, I shall take your child today. I will go with him
and I will place him in the paradise of Edem."

6

7

8 And Nir remembered the first dream and believed it. And he answered Gabriel,
"Blessed be the LORD who has sent you to me today!
And now, bless your servant Nir!
　　　　　　　　　　　　　　　And take the child, and do to him all that has been said
9 to you." •And Gabriel took the child Melkisedek on the same night
　　　　　　　　　　　　　　　　　　on his wings, and he placed him in the paradise
10 of Edem. •And Nir got up in the morning, and he went into his tent and he did
not find the child. And there was great joy and
11 grief for Nir because he had the child in the place of a son. •

(But this power is also equated with Mary.)
　d. In vss. 6f. a Christian scribe has brought in
various items of learning from the Gk. chronog-
raphers.

　e. In the GHeb, according to Origen (in *CommJn*
2.12; cf. HSW, vol. 1, p. 120), Jesus was carried

by the Holy Spirit up to Mount Tabor by one hair
of his head (documentation in HSW, vol. 1, p.
164).

　f. Rum ends with vs. 10 and has its own
conclusion. B ends here too. A U have a final
ascription which we have placed at the end of ch.
73.

[J]

73ᵃ

And the LORD called Noe onto the mount Ararat, between Assyria and Armenia, 1 in the land of Arabia, beside the ocean. And he said to him, "Make there an ark with 300 laketsᵇ in length and in width 50 lakets and in height 30. And two stories in the middle, and its doors of one laket.

And of their lakets 300, but of ours also 15 thousand; and so of theirs 50, but of 2 ours 2000 and 500, and so of theirs 30, but of ours 900, and of theirs one laket, but of ours 50."ᶜ •In agreement with this numeral the Jews keep their measurements 3 of Noe's ark, just as the LORD said to him, and they carry out all their measurements in the same way and all their regulations, even up to the present.

The LORD God opened the doors of heaven. Rain came onto the earth for 150 4 days, and all flesh died.ᵈ

And Noe was in the year 500. He fathered 3 sons: Sim, Kham, Afet. •After 100 5,6 years, after the birth of his three sons, he went into the ark in the month, according to the Hebrews, Iuars, according to the Egyptians, Famenoth, on the 18th day.ᵉ And the ark floated for 40 days. And in all they were in the ark for 120 days. 7 And he went into the ark, a son of 600 years, and in the six hundred first year of 8 his life he went out from the ark in the month Farmout according to the Egyptians, but according to the Hebrews Nisan, on the 28th day. •After the Flood he lived 9 350 years, and he died. He lived in all 950 years, according to the LORD our God.

> And to him be glory, from the beginning and now
> and until the end of the whole era.   AMEN +

---

73 a. Vaillant (*Secrets*, pp. xxif., 117f.) is on firm ground when he ascribes this concluding ch. to a Christian "reviser." The origin of this ch. is a question in its own right. It does not prove that other materials, found only in long MSS, all came from the same hand. The evidence of ch. 73 does create a presumption that similar additions were made elsewhere; but each case must be judged separately on its own merits.

b. *Lakūtī* is the Slav. term for "ell." It has nothing to do with the Heb. dry volume measure *leket*. The dimensions (in cubits) are the same in Gen 6:15.

c. Vaillant (*Secrets*, pp. xxif.) has demonstrated the derivation of some of these details from George Hamartolos.

d. Cf. Gen 7:11.

e. The integration of biblical data with material gleaned from other sources is made more difficult by problems within the Gen account itself. The name of the second month is correct. The reason for changing the biblical figures 17 and 27 to 18 and 28 is not explained. These details are not in the passages of George Hamartolos and the Kiev Chronicle, quoted by Vaillant (*Secrets*, pp. xxii–xxiv).

[A]

73

Gen 6:15

1

2

3

Gen 7:11

4

5

6

Gen 7:12,17
Gen 8:3
Gen 8:4

7

8

Gen 9:28

9

And to our God be glory always and now and always and in the ages of the ages.   AMEN.

	Gen	2En	Kiev Chron-icle	George Hamartolos
Went in	17/2	18 Iuars		
It rained	(40) (7:4, 12, 17)	150	40	40 days
The ark floated		40		
Earth covered	150 (7:24; 8:3)		120	120
In the ark		120 days	12 months 11 days	
Went out	27/2	28 Nisan		

Doubtless the entire period of the Flood was intended to be one solar year, which the Kiev Chronicle has computed from Gen 7:11 and 8:14. Vaillant gives the impression that 2En's erroneous figure of 120 days came from the Chronicle (*Secrets*, p. 119, n. 7). But neither of his identified sources make such a statement. It has been worked out that Gen contains two schedules for the Flood. According to P the waters prevail for 150 days. In J the period of 40 days is mentioned three times (7:4, 17; 8:6). Assuming that this is the same period each time, followed by three intervals of one week each, the total duration of the flood in J has been computed as 61 days. But the three 40's are probably the source of the figure 120 in all three Slav. texts. This is in flat contradiction to the biblical 150 (7:24; 8:3), which 2En reports as the period of rain.

APPENDIX: 2 ENOCH IN *MERILO PRAVEDNOE*

A NEW TRANSLATION AND INTRODUCTION
BY F. I. ANDERSEN

Merilo Pravednoe ("The Just Balance")[1] is the name of a celebrated collection of juridical and ethical writings of East Slavic provenance. A reference to Simeon, Bishop of Tver, who died A.D. 1288, as well as other evidence, shows that it was compiled in the thirteenth century. One of the sources was 2 Enoch. Material was excerpted from several different places in that work and rearranged to make a veritable *pasticcio*.[2]

The manuscripts of *Merilo Pravednoe* have been described by Lyubimovy[3] and Tikhomirov.[4] Vaillant, following Sokolov, lists four copies of *Merilo Pravednoe*: manuscripts numbered 15, 489, 682, 253 in the Trinity-St. Sergius Monastery,[5] now housed in the Lenin Library, Moscow. Tikhomirov stated that there were three copies of *Merilo Pravednoe*;[6] Meshchersky now reports five.[7]

In any case *Merilo Pravednoe* occupies a special place in 2 Enoch studies. It was in this miscellany that the existence of a Slavonic Book of Enoch was first made public.[8] It was also the first text of 2 Enoch ever printed; a transcription of TSS 15 appeared in Tikhonravov's *Pamyatniki*.[9] Collation with the photos shows a few errors in this first publication. This manuscript was also the first (and is still the only) witness to 2 Enoch to be published photographically in facsimile.[10] This copy was made in the middle of the fourteenth century, and so is the oldest known evidence for the text. The prestige deserved by this manuscript because of its antiquity is offset by the fact that the text has been rewritten with such extreme liberty. Yet even though the original narrative was separated and reassembled in a completely different pattern, there is no indication that any of the actual words were changed. In individual cases, then, its readings could have a superior claim to originality.

For these many reasons, a translation of TSS 15 is appended to the contribution on 2 Enoch.

---

[1] The title goes back to *zygos dikaios, mŏ'zĕnê-ṣedeq* (Job 31:6).

[2] The section from chs. 41 to 65 supplies the material, which has actually been sorted out. Statements on the same subject, scattered in 2En, are gathered into one place to make a collage which in some ways is more coherent than the original.

[3] V. P. Lyubimovy, *Pravda Russkaja*, vol. 1, ed. B. D. Grekov (Moscow-Leningrad, 1940) pp. 89–103.

[4] M. N. Tikhomirov, *Issledovaniye o «Russkoi pravda». Proiskhoždeniye tekstov* (Moscow-Leningrad, 1941) pp. 88–99; "Vossozdaniye russkoĭ pis' mennoĭ traditsii v perviye desyatiletiya tatarskogo iga," *Vestnik Istorii Mirovoĭ Kuľtury* 3 (1957) 3–13.

[5] The textual problems of the *MPr* tradition are discussed in detail by Sokolov in *COIDR* 4 (1910) 106–18.

[6] M. N. Tikhomirov, *Merilo pravednoe po rukopisi XIV veka* (Moscow, 1961) p. v.

[7] N. A. Meshchersky, "K istorii teksta slavyanskoĭ knigi Enokha," *Vizantiĭskiĭ Vremennik* 24 (1964) 24.

[8] A. V. Gorskiĭ and K. I. Nevostruyev, *Opisanie slavyanskikh rukopiseĭ Moskovskoĭ Sinodaľnoĭ Biblioteki* 2.2 (1859) 626–27. (Reference in Sokolov, *COIDR* 4 [1910] 89, n. 2; cf. Vaillant, *Secrets*, p. iii.) They listed TSS 253 and TSS 489.

Gorsky already observed the difference between this work and 1En; but Popov, in his 1880 edition of the Poltava MS, thought they were the same, and the matter completely escaped the attention of Western scholars for decades.

[9] N. S. Tikhonravov, *Pamyatniki otrečennoĭ russkoĭ literatury Tom* I (St. Petersburg, 1863) [= *Slavistic Printings and Reprintings*, ed. C. H. van Schooneveld, No. 184/1 (The Hague-Paris, 1970)] pp. 20–23. To be exact, a text published by A. N. Pypin in 1862 (documented by Sokolov in *COIDR* 4 [1910] 2, n. 2, but not confirmed by the present writer, and not entirely clear because of changes in the catalogue numbers), a page of a MS called No. 238 by Sokolov, was the very first.

[10] N. 6 above. The Enoch extracts occupy ff. 36–380b, six pages.

ENOCH TRADITIONS PRESERVED IN *MERILO PRAVEDNOE*

From the books of Enoch the righteous[a] before the Flood, and now he is (still) alive.

Listen, my children! Even before all things did not exist, the LORD[c] established [65:1][b] the age of creation. And after that he created the whole creation, visible and invisible;[d] and after all that he created man according to his own image, with his own two [65:2] hands,[e] small and great,[f,g] and he appointed for him eyes to see and ears to hear[h] and reason to argue.

Then the LORD released[i] the age for the sake of man; and he divided it into seasons [65:3] and years,[j] into months and days and hours; •so that a person might think about the [65:4] changes of the seasons, the beginnings and the endings,[k] so that he might estimate his own life and death.

a. This title is different from those of all other MSS.

b. The ch. and vs. references correspond to those of J used as a standard.

c. A U have the opposite sequence, verb = subject.

d. This stock phrase is probably used unreflectingly, and does not imply a sequence. In the Fathers, the invisible creation of spirit beings is completed first. Thus Basil, in his *Hexaemeron* (I § 5), argues that there was a whole invisible order, including angels, created before the visible order. Other schemes include the creation of angels on one of the six days. In 2En, since angels are created out of fire, they come rather late in the story.

e. The phrase "with his own two hands" is found in A U at 44:1.

f. The phrase "small and great" is found in A U at 44:1, but not contiguous with the preceding one. Furthermore, that text says "in the likeness of his face."

g. This phrase replaces the original "male and female."

h. *MPr* lacks the reference to the heart found in other MSS.

i. Slav. *razdrěši* in *MPr*. The scribes evidently had difficulty with this term, which is very important for understanding 2En's doctrine of creation. It occurs again in 25:2, which also has to do with the creation of "the great age" and where the MSS are similarly confused. There such a term comes three times. Adoil is commanded to *dissolve* himself so that the visible might be *dissolved* from him (or so that what was yielded by this action might become visible) and he *dissolved* himself, and "the great age," which had previously been in his belly, came out. This great age became the carrier of all the creation that the Lord wished to create.

Vaillant (*Secrets*, p. 31) equates the Slav. verb with *luesthai* but with the metaphorical sense of *accouchement*. This certainly finds support in the imagery of the great age in Adoil's belly and in the verb "came out." The latter, however, does not prove that Adoil gave birth to the great age. It seems rather from the language of 25:1 that there were stages, more physical in concept than successive emanations. First Adoil "came out [or "down"]" from the depths; then the great age "came out" from Adoil. Then (65:3) the great age was divided up into segments of time. Here we seem to have a more abstract Neoplatonic theory of the creation of particulars by dispersion, rather than a version of the egg theory of primeval creation. Nevertheless, the imagery of birth has been found in the language. V N read *raždaemoe* for *razrěšaemoe* in 25:2, and this reading, although poorly attested and best explained as secondary, is preferred by Vaillant because of his acceptance of the birth theory. The use of the dominant verb *razdrěšiti* in *MPr*'s text of 65:3 is therefore important. For there God is the subject of the verb, and it is hardly likely that any myth in the monotheistic tradition of 2En would teach that God gave birth to the world. Furthermore, as the text continues, it makes it clear that this act of God, performed on the age for the sake of man, consisted precisely of breaking it up into discrete portions. The verb *razděliti* is quite unambiguous in this respect.

The equation of *razdrěšiti* with *lusai* can be accepted, but not the inference that it means birth. The verb in A U, *razrěšiti*, also means *lusai* in the sense of "undo" (a shoelace), "release" (from sins, i.e. forgive). In fact *razdrěšiti* is simply a Russian variant, as shown, e.g. by systematic differences in the Ostromir Gospels (see the quotations from Mk 1:7 and Mt 18:18 in *MSD*, vol. 3, pp. 37, 52). But, so far as I can ascertain, it is never used to describe the release of a child in birth. A meaning somewhere between "relinquish" and "annihilate" is required. The control is supplied by the exposition which follows. Time is divided; and this is done for the sake of man. That is, time was differentiated, and made the medium of change so that man could be given his creaturely and fallen existence in such time, and so work his way to salvation as timeless existence, the climax of *MPr*, as its closing lines show.

j. The MSS differ extensively as to the units of time and their ordering: year, season, month, day, hour. The lack of interest in the "week" as a unit of time is conspicuous, but quite characteristic of 2En, which is a point against locating it in mainline Judaism. The term "seasons" is not cleanly used because it is evidently mixed up between *vremya* meaning "time" (in extension) or "season" (of the year), as well as all the range of ideas covered by *chronos* and *kairos*, both of which it translates. In addition to the possibilities of "(stretch of) time" and "(point in) time," 2En is interested in the beginning and ending of an epoch in time, especially the human life-span, with an astrological concern for the instant of birth and the instant of death.

k. A U are more ample at this point, with a reference to "years and months and days and hours," which *MPr* has in vs. 3, where A U lack the phrase. This could be a simple example of textual dislocation. But A U also read plurals. Vaillant (*Secrets*, p. 62) thinks that U is better. But the focus seems to be on death as the end of life and the sobering reflection on the inevitable termination of all time periods.

And behold, my children, I am the manager[l] of the arrangements on earth. I wrote [43:1] (them) down. And the whole year I combined,[m] and the hours of the day. And the hours I measured; and I wrote down every seed on earth.[n] And I compared every measure and the[o] just balance I measured. And I wrote[p] (them) down, just as the LORD commanded. •And in everything I discovered differences: (One) year is more [43:2] worthy[q] than (another) year, and day (than) day and hour (than) hour. Similarly also (one) person is more worthy than (another) person: one because of much property; another[r] because of superlative wisdom[s] of the heart; and another because of intelligence

l. The MSS are very divergent in their reading of this verb, upon which so much depends at this crucial point; for it defines Enoch's cosmic role. The variations probably betray theological embarrassment among the scribes. The unusual word order compounds the difficulty. The reading of the second verb in A is *pamĕtaa*, "remembering"; U reads *pometaya*, which could represent *riptein*. Enoch casts away the things of earth. But other MSS (B N) agree with *MPr*. V reads *promĕtaemaa* (= N); *MPr* has *promitaya*. Sreznevskiĭ (*MSD*, vol. 2, p. 1544) was unable to suggest a meaning for *promitati*. Vaillant (*Secrets*, p. 45) accepts *p(r)ometaya*, which he identifies as a rare verb corresponding to *basanizō*. The meaning is not quite suitable, and it does not correspond to Enoch's research earlier in the book. It casts Enoch in the role of investigator as well as recorder. The simplest solution is that Enoch observed the way things had been arranged on earth, and recorded his observations. But this is unobjectionable, and, if original, would hardly have upset the scribes. Other passages suggest that Enoch himself was in charge of these arrangements, which could have been objected to as an intrusion on divine prerogatives. It is also unclear whose deeds "on earth" he scrutinized, those of God, or those of men. If the former, then Enoch is the chronicler of creation as in ch. 40; Vaillant (*Secrets*, p. 45), citing WisSol 13:2, thinks it alludes to the way God has directed events on earth, in contrast to the theory that they are controlled by natural forces, wrongly considered divine. If the latter, Enoch is compiling the records to be used in the last assize, as in 50:1.

The evidence for the first verb is even more mixed. A and U read *i krai*, which makes no sense. Vaillant's notes imply the following schema:

krŭmičĭstvuemaya

krŭmstvuemaya ⟶ *krŭmstvuema* (R)
kormstvuemaya (B²)
korystvuemaya (V N)
skorstvuyaya (B)
pravlemaya (*MPr*)
i krai (A U)

N's reading yielded "the things that can be used on earth." The verb is not recognized by the Prague lexicon; the attestation given by Sreznevskiĭ suggests it is a Rusism. *MPr* seems to be an interpretation: the things that have been ordered on earth, i.e. by God. Vaillant (*Secrets*, p. 45) admits that the verb *krŭmĭstvovati* is otherwise unattested, but he interprets it as a "plausible" variant of *krŭmĭčĕstvovati*.

m. *MPr* has condensed the text at this point, omitting the breakdown of time into smaller units:

year, month, day, hour.

n. The MSS show considerable variation in the use and placement of the conjunction *i*, "and." This variation makes a big difference to clause boundaries, and connects verbs with different objects. The trouble seems to be caused by stress in the syntax, whether it is better to have the object before or after the verb. In the present instance the effect is to make "seed" the object either of the preceding verb ("I wrote down") or of the following verb ("compared").

In view of the exposition which follows, two ideas are being developed. There is the division of time into small units, and the differentiation of these units, so that no two days are the same. In a similar way the dispersal of seed produces individual human beings, all different. The thought begins with the act of the Creator, who made a variety of "seed on the earth," not the many species of animals and plants each created and reproducing "after its kind," according to Gen 1, but the variety of the common seed of mankind. We have already seen in *MPr* 36:8 (= 65:2) the alteration of Gen 1's "male and female" into "small and great," and this thought receives more attention here. There is tension in the MSS between describing such facts as something either God or Enoch arranged. Sometimes it comes out as the latter, as if he is some kind of manager of the cosmos. The reading of A U, *raznestvovakh*, probably means "dispersed," i.e. differentiated. The variant in *MPr*, *izrovno-vakhŭ*, is unique (it provides the only entry in *MSD*), and probably means "compared." Changes in the conjunctions make its object, not "every seed on earth," namely all mankind, but "every measure and the just balance."

o. Other MSS read "every" at this point.

p. *MPr* shares the reading *ispisakhŭ*, "wrote," with B, against *ispytak*, "probed," of other MSS.

q. It is hard to know what English equivalent to use for *čĭstĭnyi*. It is well illustrated by its use to translate *entimos* (Lk 7:2) or *entimoteros* (Lk 14:8). Even so, the moral connotation is not secured, whether this difference in "honor" is in the estimate of others, due to different grades of achievement, or due to differences in nature (whether by accident or divine decree). The following analysis does not settle the point since it is a mixture of these.

r. Whereas A U etc. list the series with
obŭ . . . ob že . . . ob že . . . i . . . i . . .
MPr has
ōbŭ . . . inŭ . . . a inŭ . . . i . . .
s. *prmdrti* = *prĕmudrosti*, while V N have *milosti*, "kindness." The common reading is simply *mudrosti*.

and, it could be, silence of the lips.[t] •But no one is better than the person who fears [43:3] the LORD. He who fears the LORD will be glorified forever. •Listen, children! In [58:1] the days of our father Adam, the LORD came down onto the earth, and he inspected[u] all[v] the creatures which he himself had created. •And the LORD[w] summoned all the [58:2] animals of the earth and the beasts[x] and all the flying birds.[y] And he brought them before the face of our father Adam, so that he might pronounce names[z] for all. And Adam named everything on earth.[a2] • And he subjected to him everything in inferiority.[b2] [58:3] And he made them deaf for all submission and obedience. •For every animal soul in [58:5] that age[c2] there is one place,[d2] one fold, and ⟨one⟩ paddock. •For the soul of an animal [58:6] which the LORD created will not be shut up until the judgment. • The LORD appointed[e2] [58:3b] mankind[f2] to all his own property.[g2] •Concerning this there will not be judgment for [58:4] every living soul,[h2] but for man alone. •And all the souls[i2] will accuse humans.[j2] •He [58:66][59:5] who does wickedness to an animal in secret, it is a lawless evil.[k2] He acts lawlessly against his own soul. •He who does wickedness to a human soul commits wickedness [60:1] against his own soul. •He who commits murder puts his own soul to death, and there [60:2] is no healing for him for eternity. •And he who lies in wait for a person with a net [60:3]

---

t. V reads *i khytrosti i mlīčania ezyka i ustnu*. A U have *khitrosti i molčaniya ustennago*. V thus agrees with A in adding "cunning" to "intelligence" (but A lacks the conjunction). But *MPr* agrees with A in having "silence of the lips," where V (N also) adds "tongue and" lips. *MPr*, however, has *prosto* instead of *khitrosti*. It is not obvious what nuance this introduces. At the end of the list, it could mean "perhaps," or "simply" (*haplōs*). Note, however, that *MPr* has *prěmudrosti* and the *prosto-* could be a similar prefix. Hence Sreznevsiī thinks it means "complete silence" (*MSD*, vol. 2, p. 1577).

u. At the very least *episkopein* lies behind this word. But behind it again is surely *lipqōd* (the variants point to an original supine). But the associations of either judgment or redemption are not present in the descent of the LORD.

v. Other MSS read *svoeya*, "his" creatures.

w. V reads "the LORD God" as in Gen.

x. It is hard to recover the original tradition behind this list of names. The difficulty with *MPr* is that both *skotŭ* and *zvěrĭ* mean "animal," with a distinction corresponding to Heb. *běhēmāh* (domestic) and *ḥayyāh* (wild). But the use of both to represent *thērion* is illustrated by a paraphrase of Gen 3:14: *proklata ty otŭ vŭsěkhŭ skotŭ i zvěrei zemŭskykŭ*. MSS like A which read *gad zemnyi*, "reptiles of the earth," are doubtless better. It is like the list in Acts 10:12; but this too has variants, such as *vī neuže běkhu vca četvrěnoga zemle i zvěri i gadi i ptice nebesneye* (*SJS*, vol. 1, p. 388).

y. This idiom does not seem to derive from the OT directly. Cf. *glagole ki vsimī pticamī pareštimī* (Rev 19:17). Note that R also has *parjaštei po vozdukh(u)*. Cf. J P. But A U have *pernatyya* ("feathered").

z. The Heb. idioms are more palpable here, but this could come through Gk. The text does not correspond to Gen 2:19 in these details, and LXX follows the Heb. literally. We have, then, an independent Midrash on Gen 2:19.

a2. *MPr* is closer to MSS of the longer recension than to those of the shorter recension at this point. This suggests that sometimes their longer readings might preserve something original that has been lost from the shorter recension.

b2. This is followed by the numeral *.v̄.ye* in

MPr. This is written fully in A and V (*vtoroe*), and the punctuation of both suggests that it goes with the preceding noun, not after a comma, as in Vaillant's edition. Still its significance is not clear. It could be a corruption of *pod rucě ego* (J), "under his hand."

c2. Slav. *vŭ věcě semī*. Other MSS have "the great age."

d2. The main variants are as follows:

> B *edino město estĭ i košarě edinago*
>   *i ograda edina i pastvina*
> A U *edino město estĭ*
>   *i ograda edina i pastvina edina*
> V *edino město ĕ̄ i košarī edinī*
> MPr *yedino město* *košara yedina*
>   *i pastvina*

B	place	pen	
		yard	pasture
A U	place	yard	pasture
V	place	pen	
MPr	place	pen	pasture

e2. A U read "created" and V has the same verb. V continues *vlastela vsemu stežaniyu* (see n. g2) *svoemu*. A U lack the first word "lord."

f2. Slav. *člvka*, not Adam.

g2. If Vaillant (*Secrets*, p. 57) is correct that this passage imitates Ps 105:21, then we must conclude that it comes directly from Heb., not Gk. The passage, however, is not very close to Ps 105:21 (104:21 in LXX): (1) It is not an individual (Adam) but mankind that is appointed to the Lord's property, so there is no analogy of king and vizier. (2) No title is used, as in 30:12; but V does use *vlastela*, which could reflect *'ādôn* rather than *kurios*, while J has *gna*, "lord." The agreement of a long and a short MSS in supplying a title must be offset by the fact that each has a different title. (3) A number of Heb. words lie behind *ktēsis*, and this fluctuates with *ktisis* in the Gk. MSS.

h2. A Hebraism, *nepeš ḥayyāh*, "animal." Gen 9 could be behind the interpretation attempted in 2En.

i2. That is, of animals.

j2. There is a considerable omission here.

k2. Slav. *zlobezakoniye*. But A U read *zlozakonie*, "evil-law," or, perhaps, "making the law evil," and B is similar. R has *zlo zakoni*.

will himself be entangled in it.[12] •He who seethes a person in a caldron, his judgment [60:4] will not come to an end for eternity.[m2] • He who insults and misprises the face of a [44:2] human person insults and misprises the face of the LORD. •Anger and great judgment [44:3] for whoever spits in a person's face[n2] •Happy is he who directs his heart to every kind [44:4] of person, and helps him who has been condemned, and gives support to him who has been broken;[o2] • for in the great judgment day every measure and weight in the [44:5] market will be exposed, and each one will recognize his own measure, and in it he will receive his reward. •And the LORD will send out his great light, and in it will [46:3] be the judgment, so that who, there, will hide?

Before mankind existed, a place of judgment, ahead of time, was prepared for them, [49:2] and scales[p2] and weights by means of which a person will be tested. •I the doings of [50:1] each person will put down, and no one will hide;[q2] •because the LORD is the one who [50:4] pays, and he will be the avenger on the great judgment day. •Gold and silver lose for [50:5] the sake of your brother, and you will receive a treasure without end[r2] on the day of judgment. •To orphan and widow stretch out your hands, and in accordance with your [50:6] strength help the wretched, and you will be a shelter in the time of testing.

Every yoke, afflictive[s2] and burdensome, which comes upon you, loose it[12] for the [51:3] LORD's sake, and you will receive a reward on the day of judgment. •Happy (is he [52:5]

---

12. Not all MSS preserve the parallel statements found in *MPr*. There seems to be a play on the sound of similar words, if not outright puns. If the latter could be proved, it would show that this passage at least was composed in Slav.

vrěya člěka v sětī samŭ oubyazayetī

vrěya člěka v sudŭ ne oskuděyetī sŭ yegō vŭ věki
(with superscript *d*)
The first word in both statements has more than one possible meaning.

1. First, we note the reading of P, *vlagayai*, the source of Charles's "put" (*APOT*, vol. 2, p. 465). Since this is not supported even by R and J, it may be set aside as a corruption. Note, however, *vlagati vŭ stydŭ* (*SRY*, vol. 2, p. 207).

2. The spelling in *MPr* (*vrěya*) (cf. A U) leaves undetermined the stem vowel. It could be the verb *vrěyati* (or *vrěvati*) (*SRY*, vol. 3, p. 111): "shove," "push" or "throw." It could be *vrěti*, one of whose meanings is "boil," "seethe." The significance of this possible meaning, at first sight improbable, is its correlation with (*so*)*sud* (*SRY*, vol. 3, p. 109). Its variant is *verěti* (*SRY*, vol. 2, p. 87).

3. On the other hand, J has the reading *varěyui*. *SRY* (vol. 2, p. 23) gives this meaning "lie in wait" (*podsteregat'*), but it also means "forestall," "anticipate."

4. The reading in V (*vīrai*) is closer to *MPr* than to J; but the similarity is insignificant, since the *yers* tend to be used indiscriminately. The unique text of P, which has a different verb in each statement (as if explicating the pun), also uses the unambiguous *sosud*, "vessel," which is neither a corruption nor an interpretation, but a resolution of the original homonym *sud* (this is both the ordinary word "judgment" and also the archaic equivalent of *sosud*). P thus resolves the ambiguity which is apparently present in *MPr*: "He who lies in wait for a person with a net . . ." "He who forestalls a person in judgment . . ." (or "He who boils a person in a caldron").

5. There is no question about the wordplay in the second statement (*so*)*sud* . . . *-skud-* . . . *sud*. *Sud* is a straight pun, reading *vrěya* for *vīrai* or *vereya* or *vareya*. There is secondary play on *seti* ("net")/*sud* ("vessel" or "judgment"), but this is lost when there is only one statement. Even so,

since the second statement in its more obvious meaning is a solution to the riddle in the first statement, it is less likely that it conceals another enigma in its own double meaning. Since MSS of 2En are the result of a fluid tradition, we cannot settle the "correct" reading of such sayings by reverting to the earliest text known to us. For all we know, *MPr* might already have leveled the verbs which are still distinct in P. The idea is commonplace (Ps 9:16; Eccl 27:26), but these biblical passages are not the immediate source of the wording in 2En. The Slav. verbs do not match the originals. Eccl 27:26 has *ho histōn pagida en autē halōsetai*. This is more succinct, more down to earth, less eschatological than 2En. By adding the word "person" 2En lowers the enigmatic content. And the impression remains that the word-play was concocted in Slav.

m2. Note that 44:1 has already been used in effect at 58:3b above. See nn. e and f. Vaillant (*Secrets*, p. vi) says that this section is "abridged" in *MPr*; but one wonders if A U already show signs of glossing.

n2. The more ample texts have four rude gestures, each separately stated. The last, spitting, is detached from the others. In this detail the text of *MPr* is similar to A U, except that the latter have plural ("they spit") against the preferable singular of all other MSS which have the passage. Yet, in spite of this agreement, the longer reading of 44:3 in R J P seems to be better.

o2. A third category is mentioned in A U.

p2. The word in the title of the miscellany.

q2. *MPr* has the same word here as in 46:3. There it is the same as A, but here A reads *niktože ne možeti ukrasti sye*, "no one will be able to sneak away."

r2. Here *MPr neoskudno* has the same root as the verb in 37ob:3 [60:4], and this gives it preference over other MS readings, particularly A (*plotno*), which seems to be a corruption of *nlŭno* (R). Furthermore, *MPr* is supported by B (*neoskuděemo*).

s2. A reads *vsyakogo skorbī*, "every kind of affliction," thus losing the allusion to the yoke. There is a marked difference between the outlook in this advice and that in Mt 11:28–30.

who) praises the works of the LORD •and preserves the foundations of the most [52:9]
ancient ancestors, •and who cultivates peace and who has peace.   [52:11]

Cursed (is he who) despises the creation of the LORD •and (who) looks to destroy [52:6][52:8]
the works of (his) neighbor •and (who) breaks down the rules and restrictions of his [52:10]
ancestors •and (who) speaks peace but there is not peace in his heart. •All this in the [52:14][52:15]
balance and in the books will be convicted on the day of the great^{v2} judgment. •Happy [42:9]
(is he) who judges righteous judgment for orphan and widow, and (who) helps
everyone who has been oppressed.

Happy (is he) in whom is truth, and who speaks truth to his neighbor,^{w2} and there [42:12]
is kindness in his lips and gentleness.

Happy (is he who) sows righteous seed, and he will reap sevenfold, •and (who) [42:11]
creates righteous judgment, •the naked he clothes with a garment, and to the hungry [42:7][42:8]
he gives bread.

Happy (is he who) understands the works of the LORD, and glorifies him and (who) [42:14]
because of his works, acknowledges (their) creator.

I arrived at the place of judgment, and I saw hell open. •And I saw there something [40:12][40:13]
more,^{x2} like a prison, judgment unmeasured. And I descended, and I wrote down all
the judgments of the judged, and all their accusations I knew.^{y2} •And I sighed and I [41:1]
wept over the perdition of the impious. •And I said in my heart, "Happy is he who [41:2]
has never been born, or (who), having been born, has not sinned against^{z2} the face
of the LORD, so that he did not come into this place,^{a3} nor endure the stench^{b3} of this
place." •And I saw the guardians of hell standing at the large gates, their faces like [42:1]
those of great serpents and their eyes like extinguished lamps, and their fangs exposed
down to their breasts. •And I said in their presence,^{c3} "It would have been better if [42:2]
I had not seen you, nor heard^{d3} of your activities, nor that any member of my race
had been brought to you."

t2. The MSS are quite confused over what to do with this yoke, whether to accept it or to get rid of it. In the latter case there is a suggestion that it is a work of charity to remove the heavy yoke from another. The different positions of the phrase "for the LORD's sake" also secure different nuances; either the yoke comes on to you on account of the LORD or otherwise repudiate it for the LORD's sake.

The main readings are: *MPr*, A *ōtrĕšite* (U has *otrĕšite*). *Otŭrĕšiti*, if genuine, reflects *luein*, but this does not seem to suit the spirit of the passage. The reading in B (*poterpite*) fits better, for it could mean "endure." P has *terpĕte*, but J has *vŭsĕ ponesete i otrĕžati e*, which is essentially the same as R. So there are four verbs:

otŭrĕšiti	(*MPr* A U)	renounce or loose
otrĕžiti	(J R)	cut off
(po)terpiti	(B P)	endure
ponesiti	(J R)	carry

Perhaps there are only two, those in J R being variants of the ones found only singly in other MSS. Even so, the two ideas seem to be opposed: ridding oneself of the yoke or bearing it patiently. The yoke is not the yoke of obedience to Torah nor the yoke of Christian discipleship, neither of which was considered a burden. It is persecution. There seems to be no logical way of combining the recommended responses, unless *otŭrĕžati* means "release" the yoke from someone else, or *otŭrĕšiti* means "forgive" your persecutors.

u2. *MPr* lacks two pairs of blessing and cursing found in longer MSS at this point.

v2. A U have the variant *gordago*, "terrible."

w2. Slav. *skreninōmu*, with initial *i* added in correction by another hand.

x2. The diverse readings at this point show that the scribes have lost control of the text. *MPr* (*yetero*

bole) should be retained for three text-critical reasons: because it is old, because it is difficult, because the others can be derived from it. *Yetero* corresponds to *tis* and becomes variously *nekoe, nekotorye* (A). The main alternative to *bole* is *pole* (B) and seems to mean "field" (*pedion, campus*). Vaillant (*Secrets*, p. 42) accepts this reading and meaning (*une certaine plaine*), but the language does not suit the imagery of a prison. MSS otherwise divergent agree in *bole*. The reading in A is very clear, since it writes the *b* in an unusual way. So it has a strong claim. But what does it mean? The stem *bol-* is found in words meaning either "sick" (hence R J P *kako bolit*) or "great," neither of which makes sense. If *pole* is preferred, but the meaning "field" causes difficulty, perhaps it derives from *polĕti* = *phlegein*. The language is remarkably like Codex Supraslensis 142:26, *šedŭ na mĕsto ideže bĕaše ogni raždŭženŭ. Vidĕvŭ plameni polyašti.* Cf. Dan 7:9, *prĕstolŭ ognenŭ-yemu kolesa yego ogni polya (pur phlegon).* Hell is a place of flaming fire.

y2. Slav. *ouvĕdakhŭ*. A U have *ouvidĕkh*, "I saw."

z2. *MPr* (also B) reads *na*, not the usual *pred*.

a3. This passage highlights the total lack of any scheme of salvation for sinners in 2En.

b3. *MPr*'s *smrada* is preferable, and is probably the source of *yarma* (A), "yoke," not *igo*, the usual term in 2En.

c3. Lit. "face."

d3. *MPr*: *vnyalŭ*. A reads *voni radi*, which seems to mean "on account of the stench," but is probably corrupt. From the similar reading of U Vaillant (*Secrets*, p. 44, n. 1) restores *vŭnradilŭ*, which is supported by *vnyadrilŭ* (B). See the details in *SJS*, vol. 1, pp. 305–6; *vŭnadriti ~ vŭnaraditi* means "behold." *MPr* is preferable; cf. n. y2 above.

Do not say, my children, "Our father is with God,[e3] and he will pray us out of [53:1]
sin." •You know,[f3] all the deeds of every person I continually record;[g3] •and no one [53:2]
can destroy[h3] what I have written, because the LORD sees everything, •so that you [55:3]
might do what is good[i3] in the face[j3] of the LORD, •most of all, to every living soul. [61:1b]
Just as one asks for his own soul from the LORD, so let him do to every living soul. [61:2]
Now preserve your heart[k3] from every unrighteous deed, so that you might inherit [61:1a]
the anchor of light[l3] forever. •And it will be yours in an inheritance of peace •when [54:1][65:6]
all creation shall come to an end, which the LORD created, each person will go to
the LORD's great judgment. •Then the seasons[m3] will perish and they will no longer [65:7]
constitute the year. Days and hours will not be reckoned. But it[n3] will be a single age.
And all the righteous will escape the great judgment. And they will gain the great [65:8]
age,[o3] and the age will gain[p3] the righteous, and they will be eternal. •And none of [65:9]
them will have weariness nor sickness nor affliction nor fear of violence nor exhaustion
nor night nor darkness; •but the great light (will be) in them,[q3] and the great age, an [65:10]
indestructible wall and a shelter, a great and eternal Paradise. • Happy are the righteous, [65:11]
who will escape the LORD's great judgment. And they will shine forth like even the
sun.

e3. Other MSS read "the LORD."

f3. *MPr* reads *V[D]ITE*, which could be either
vidite (A), "You see," or *vēdite*, "you know."
The latter is more suitable; but see n. y2, where
the opposite happens.

g3. Vaillant (*Secrets*, p. 54, n.5) does not note
the distinctive reading of *MPr napisyvayu*, which
emphasizes that this is Enoch's ongoing task. Note
the elaboration in the longer MSS.

h3. Vaillant's (*Secrets*, p. 55) interpretation of
raskaziti as *détruire* must be rejected. Strictly
speaking, it is *raskazati* (this is the reading in V)
that means *uničtožat'* (*MSD*, vol. 3, p. 72). Cf.
raskažati, "damage." Sreznevskiĭ gives *narušat/
narušit*, "violate," as possible meanings of both
raskažati (*MSD*, vol. 3, p. 71) and *raskaziti* (vol.
3, p. 72). But the latter is used, significantly with
"books" as object, meaning "profane," "repudiate." The point is not that Enoch's writings,
bequeathed to his descendants, cannot be destroyed
(although that idea is expressed elsewhere [ch. 35]);
his records of all the deeds of all mankind, which
are kept in heaven (for the day of judgment, see
52:15), cannot be gainsaid.

i3. *MPr* has the unique reading *dôbroye*.

j3. The usual Heb. idiom is "good in the eyes."

k3. Other MSS read "soul" but 53:1 has "heart"
and 53:1 and 61:1 seem to be conflated here.

13. The phrase is unintelligible. *Stavilo* also
means "measure," "weight." B reads *da stavi*,
but the exact agreement of V with *MPr* at this
point gives status to their reading. Sokolov's synoptic study (*COIDR* 4 [1910] p. 117) shows that
MPr has verbal affinities with 53:4 and 54:1 as
well as with both 53:1 and 61:1. But A, while
punctuated similarly, reads *na stavile svēta. Da* is
better than *na;* and the latter leads to the paraphrase
"injustice on the balance." But *nepravdy* is not
modified in 61:1; yet what does "the anchor of
light" mean? See 65:10 and 46:3.

m3. Slav. *vremena* as in 65:3 at the beginning
of *MPr*.

n3. That is, time.

o3. The absence of the reflexive pronoun in *MPr*
makes a big difference. In J (vol. 3, p. 279)
prikupiti[1] means "gain." It translates *kerdēsomen*
in Jas 4:13. But *prikupiti*[2] passive means "to be
united," as in A, which sustains the analogy of
fall (dispersion) versus salvation (reassembly) for
both time and for human souls. It is not easy to
tell whether this view of time is Neoplatonism or
Zoroastrianism.

p3. Again A has passive/reflexive.

q3. Slav. *vôinu*, "army" (?), or "in another"
(?).

3 (Hebrew Apocalypse of) Enoch

(FIFTH–SIXTH CENTURY A.D.)

A NEW TRANSLATION AND INTRODUCTION
BY P. ALEXANDER

3 Enoch purports to be an account by R. Ishmael of how he journeyed into heaven, saw God's throne and chariot, received revelations from the archangel Metatron, and viewed the wonders of the upper world. It falls into four main sections.

(1) Chapters 1–2, "The Ascension of Ishmael": Having passed through six heavenly palaces, one within the other, Ishmael is challenged by the guardian angels at the gate of the seventh, innermost palace. In response to his prayer for help God sends him the archangel Metatron, who ushers him into the seventh palace and presents him before God's throne. God graciously receives him and he joins the angels that attend the throne in reciting the Sanctus (the Qeduššah). (2) Chapters 3–16, "The Exaltation of Enoch": Metatron informs Ishmael that he is none other than Enoch the son of Jared (mentioned in Gen 5:18–24), whom God translated from earth to heaven and elevated over all the angels as his vice-regent. Metatron explains how and why he was taken up, and reveals in detail the steps by which he was transformed in mind and body from a human being into an angel; he describes his insignia and the heavenly functions he now performs. (3) Chapters 17–40, "The Heavenly Household": Metatron discourses to Ishmael on the organization and activities of the heavenly world. He gives an elaborate account of the angelic hierarchies, and describes a session of the heavenly assize and the performance of the climactic act of the angelic liturgy—the recitation of the celestial Sanctus. (4) Chapters 41–48, "The Sights of Heaven": Metatron takes Ishmael and shows him various heavenly marvels. These have to do with three main topics: (a) Cosmology: Ishmael sees the cosmic letters by which the world was created. He is also shown cosmic "opposites" (such as fire and water) held in balance by the power of divine names. (b) Eschatology: Ishmael sees the curtain (*pargôd*) that hangs before God's face, and represented on that curtain the whole course of human history from Adam until the coming of the Messiah. He also sees the right hand of God, behind his throne, waiting the appointed time of Israel's redemption. (c) Psychology: Ishmael is shown various souls; the souls of the righteous enjoying God's presence; the souls of the wicked and the intermediate in Sheol; the souls of the Patriarchs interceding for Israel; the souls of the stars; and the souls of the angels who have failed in the performance of the Sanctus, banished from God's presence and incarcerated behind fiery walls.

This summary of 3 Enoch is based on the contents of manuscripts A and B. The form of the work in these two manuscripts shows clear signs of editing; if we exclude the patently additional chapters 23–24 and 48BCD, then the overall structure of the work is reasonably coherent, and thematically related materials have been grouped together. It is evident, however, on closer investigation, that 3 Enoch has arisen through the combination of many separate traditions: it tends to break down into smaller "self-contained" units which probably existed prior to their incorporation into the present work. In the process of being brought together these pre-existing units of tradition were accommodated to each other only minimally, and so the work contains not a few cases of overlapping, inconsistency, and even contradiction. Manuscripts A and B give the longest recension of 3 Enoch. It is not clear whether the shorter recensions found in the other text-witnesses are abbreviations of this long recension, or whether, at least in some cases, they represent earlier stages in the growth of the work; the traditions may not all have been assembled at once, but could have come together in stages. There is some evidence to suggest that chapters 3–15 on the exaltation of Enoch are the oldest section of the work and formed the core around which the present A B text crystallized.[1]

Texts

The original title of 3 Enoch appears to have been Seper Hekalot (The Book of the Palaces), but it has also been known as The Chapters of Rabbi Ishmael, and The Book of Rabbi Ishmael the High Priest; one manuscript refers to chapters 3–15 as "The Elevation of Meṭaṭron." The name 3 Enoch was coined by H. Odeberg for his edition of 1928.

The text of 3 Enoch is in considerable confusion. Odeberg's attempted critical edition has many serious flaws. The translation offered in the present study draws on the following manuscripts and editions (a number of which were unknown to Odeberg):

Siglum	Location	Chapters
A	Vatican City: Biblioteca Apostolica Vaticana 228/4 (Assemanus).	1–48ABCD
B	Oxford: Bodleian Library 1656/2 (Neubauer).	1–48ABCD
C	Oxford: Bodleian Library 2257/4 (Neubauer).	3–16; 22–24; + 15B; 22BC
D	Oxford: Bodleian Library 1748/2 (Neubauer).	3–12; 15
E	Munich: Bayerische Staatsbibliothek 40/10 (Steinschneider).	1–15; 23–48AB
F	Rome: Biblioteca Casanatense 180/5 (Sacerdote).	1–15; 23–48AB
G	Vatican City: Biblioteca Apostolica Vaticana 228/3 (Assemanus). A manuscript of the Alphabet of Aqiba in the same hand as A.	48BCD
Crac	Alphabet of Aqiba, published in Cracow, 1579, as printed in BHM, vol. 2, pp. 114–17.	48BCD
Eleazar	London: The British Museum Library, MS Add. 27199 (Margoliouth 737). A manuscript of the writings of Eleazar of Worms. (See 15B, n. a; 22C, n. a.)	15B; 22C
Lemb	Seper Hekalot, published in Lemberg (Lvov), 1864. Cited only occasionally.	1:1–28:5; 48BC (beginning)
Mus	S. Musajoff, Merkabah Šelemah (Jerusalem, 1921) fols. 9a–14b.	1:9–20:2; 22:1, 11
Wert	Alphabet of Aqiba in Wertheimer, BM, vol. 2, pp. 350–55.	48BCD

The sigla used here are *not* the same as in Odeberg's edition. Other manuscripts of 3 Enoch not cited are: Florence, Biblioteca Medicea-Laurenziana, Plut. 44.13/18 (Biscionius), containing chapters 1:1–35:6, and 44:1–48A:9; and Jerusalem, The Jewish National and University Library 4/4 (Scholem) = MS 8° 381, which contains chapters 1:9–23:1. The Lemberg edition was reprinted at Warsaw in 1875, and the Warsaw edition at Piotrkow in 1883. The oldest printed text of 3 Enoch appears to be Deruš Pirqe Hekalot. It covers 3:1–12:5 and 15:1–2, and is dated by A. E. Cowley (*Catalogue of Hebrew Printed Books in the Bodleian Library* [Oxford, 1929] p. 241) to around 1650.

The translation of chapters 1–48A (except for 15B and 22BC) is based on B, despite the many errors of this manuscript, since the only critical edition of 3 Enoch available at present

---

[1] MS D and *Deruš Pirqe Hekalot* both contain effectively only the account of the exaltation of Enoch (see below on "Texts"). The earliest surely attested section of 3En is chs. 3–15; these chs. may have circulated once under the name of R. Aqiba, and it was for this reason that a summary of them was included in the Alphabet of Aqiba (see below on "Date"). On the literary structure of 3En see further ch. 1, n. a; 3, n. a; 16, n. a; 17, n. a; 41, n. a; 15B, n. a; 22B, n. a; 22C, n. a; 23, n. a; 48B, n. a. [Unless otherwise specified the OT quotations in Alexander's Introduction and notes are according to his own translations. This procedure was necessary because JB and other English versions often do not follow the Jewish tradition, and the significance of a quotation might have been lost. —J.H.C.]

is Odeberg's and that is the text which he prints. However, B has been freely emended from the readings of the other manuscripts and editions. Particular weight has been given to manuscript A, since it belongs to the same textual tradition as B but gives superior readings.

The base text for 15B and 22BC is manuscript C, as in Odeberg. For 15B the text-witnesses are C and Eleazar (see 15B, n. a); for 22B they are C, Ma'aśeh Merkabah, Hekalot Rabbati, and a Haggadic Fragment printed by Jellinek (see 22B, n. a); for 22C they are C, Eleazar, Ma'aśeh Merkabah, and the Haggadic Fragment (see 22C, n. a).

The translation of 48BCD is based on Wert since B, which Odeberg prints, is hopelessly corrupt. For 48BCD the text witnesses are: A, B, E (for 48B only), F (for 48B only), G, Crac, Wert.

A selection of variant readings is given in the notes. These readings are intended (1) to indicate the authority or authorities for departures from the base manuscripts, and (2) to record the more substantial variants.

For ease of reference the numbering of chapters and verses follows Odeberg. The chapter numbers derive ultimately from manuscript B.

A cautious attempt has been made to recover the original form of the A B recension of the text and so the obviously additional chapters 23–24 and 48BCD have been relegated to an appendix. The chapters numbered 15B and 22BC by Odeberg, which contain additional material not found in A or B, have also been put in this appendix.

Original language

3 Enoch is written in Hebrew. The exact character of its language has never been investigated, though Odeberg's "Index to the Hebrew Text" (*3 Enoch*, Pt. 4, pp. 3–18, esp. 14–18) provides a ready basis for analysis. There is no reason to suppose that the work has been translated into Hebrew from another language, such as Aramaic, in which some Merkabah traditions were written down. (Note, however, that the title "great and honored prince" in 18:5, 6 is in Aram.) There are loanwords from Latin (*familia*, 12:5) and Greek (e.g. *glōssokomon*, 27:2).

The style of 3 Enoch and of the related Merkabah literature is highly distinctive. It is marked by extreme redundancy: Note the piling up of synonyms in such a typical sentence as "He enlightened my eyes and my heart to utter psalm, praise, jubilation, thanksgiving, song, glory, majesty, laud, and strength" (1:12). It also indulges in the repeated use of such highly emotive words as "glory, majesty, power, greatness" (see e.g. 19:1), and it manifests a tendency to fall into rhythmic prose (see e.g. 22B:8). These characteristics of style find their ultimate expression in the Merkabah hymns. G. G. Scholem has aptly spoken of the "polylogy" of these compositions.[2] They lie at the very heart of Merkabah mysticism and were almost certainly a feature of the Merkabah movement from an early stage; they formed part of the technique by which the adepts made their ascent to the Merkabah, and the practical function of their repetitiveness was to induce ecstasy (see below). It is probable that the redundant style belonged originally to the Merkabah hymns but came in the end to pervade the whole of the Merkabah literature.[3]

Date

3 Enoch—like a number of other Merkabah texts—is attributed to Rabbi Ishmael, the famous Palestinian scholar who died shortly before the outbreak of the Bar Kokhba War in

---

[2] G. G. Scholem, *Major Trends in Jewish Mysticism*, p. 60. Merkabah hymns are not, in fact, found in 3En. See further, A. Altmann, "Hymns of Sanctification in Early Hekalot Literature," *Melilah* 2 (1946) 1–24 (in Heb.); Scholem, *Major Trends*, pp. 57–63; G. G. Scholem, *Jewish Gnosticism, Merkabah Mysticism and Talmudic Tradition*, pp. 20–30; J. Maier, "'Attāh hû' 'ādôn (Hekalot rabbati XXVI, 5)," *Judaica* 21 (1965) 123–33; J. Maier, "Hekalot rabbati XXVII 2–5," *Judaica* 22 (1966) 209–17; J. Maier, "Poetisch-liturgische Stücke aus dem 'Buch der Geheimnisse,'" *Judaica* 24 (1968) 172–81; J. Maier, "Serienbildung und 'Numinoser' Eindruckseffekt in den poetischen Stücken der Hekalot-Literatur," *Semitics* 3 (1973) 36–66.

[3] It should be noted, however, that redundancy is a feature of liturgical language in general: see e.g. the Qaddiš: "Blessed, praised and glorified, exalted, extolled and honoured, magnified and lauded be the name of the Holy One, blessed be he" (S. Singer, *The Authorised Daily Prayer Book* [London, 1962] p. 78). Also the benediction Yištabbaḥ: "Unto thee, O Lord our God, and God of our fathers, song and praise are becoming, hymn and psalm, strength and dominion, victory, greatness and might, renown and glory, holiness and sovereignty, blessings and thanksgivings from now even for ever" (Singer, *Authorised Prayer Book*, p. 37; cf. E. D. Goldschmidt, *The Passover Haggadah* [Jerusalem, 1960] p. 135; see also b.Pes 118).

A.D. 132 (see 1:1, n. b). Though some of the traditions of 3 Enoch can be traced back to Ishmael's time (and even earlier), there can be no question of accepting this attribution at its face value; the work is a pseudepigraphon and Ishmael is simply the master whose authority the author or redactor of 3 Enoch wished to claim. The question of the real date of 3 Enoch has elicited from scholars very different answers.

In the nineteenth and early twentieth centuries, though 3 Enoch itself was not well known, the tendency was to assign the type of literature to which it belongs to the gaonic era (7th–11th cent. A.D.). This view gained currency through the influence of L. Zunz's *Die gottesdienstlichen Vorträge der Juden* (Berlin, 1832; Frankfurt am Main, 1892²) pp. 165–79. It was H. Graetz, however, who first tried to establish this position by detailed argument (see "Die mystische Literatur in der gaonäischen Epoche," *MGWJ* 8 [1859] 67–78, 103–18, 140–53). Graetz reasoned that this Jewish mystical literature must be post-talmudic on the grounds that "the leading ideas contained therein were unknown in the talmudic age, and would have been abhorrent to talmudic authorities" (p. 104). In his view these Jewish mystical texts came into being in the ninth century under the influence of ideas current at that period in Islam. Thus he argued that the glorification of Enoch by the mystics (e.g. chs. 3–15), in contrast to his denigration in classic Midrashim (GenR 25:1; TargOnk to Gen 5:24⁴), reflects the favorable attitude to Enoch in Islamic tradition, which identifies him with righteous Idris of the Koran (Sura 19.57/56–58/57; 21.85f.; Masʿudi, *Murudj* 3, ed. Meynard-Courteille, vol. 1, p. 73). The nub of Graetz's case, however, was the contention that the crudely anthropomorphic doctrine of Šiʿur Qomah, found in the Jewish mystical literature (see below), is dependent on the teaching of Islamic *mushabbiha* sects, such as the Mughiriyya, followers of the heretic al-Mughira b. Saʿid al-ʿIdjli (Shahrastani, *Kitab al-Milal wal-Niḥal*, ed. Cureton, pt. 1 [1842] pp. 134f.; ed. Al-Wakil [Cairo, 1968] pp. 176–78; trans. Haar-brücker, vol. 1 [1851] pp. 203f.). Graetz's position is indefensible. There was no need to invoke Islam to explain the mystics' favorable views of Enoch; they were simply carrying on an indigenous Jewish tradition with its roots in Palestinian apocalyptic in the Maccabean period, if not earlier (see below). As for Šiʿur Qomah, Scholem and Lieberman have pointed to probable allusions to the doctrine already in the talmudic period (see below).

H. Odeberg (*3 Enoch*) took a very different line from that of Graetz. He maintained that the earliest stratum of material in 3 Enoch (9:2–13:2, which appears to describe Meṭaṭron as a primordial being) dates from a time not later than the first century A.D. (pt. 1, p. 188). The main body of the text, however, chs. 3–48A, was redacted in the latter half of the third century A.D. The rest of the material (chs. 1–2, 15B, 22BC, and 48BC) is all pre-Islamic (pt. 1, pp. 41f.).

Odeberg's main arguments are as follows: (1) A comparison of 3 Enoch with Ḥagigah 11b–16a suggests that 3 Enoch is not later than that text (pt. 1, p. 32). (2) The language of 3 Enoch is "most akin to that of the earlier haggadic dicta of the Babylonian Talmud, or, in general, that of the dicta attributed to the tannaitic teachers and earlier Amoras" (pt. 1, p., 37). (3) The reference to Sammaʾel, the Prince of Rome, and Dubbiʾel, the Prince of Persia (26:12), points to the origin of the work in pre-Islamic times, when Rome and Persia divided the world between themselves (pt. 1, p. 37). (4) The irenic attitude of 3 Enoch toward the nations suggests a period of good relations with the ruling power such as the Jewish colonies in Babylonia enjoyed under Sassanian Persia in the third and fourth centuries A.D. (pt. 1, pp. 37f.). (5) The form of the Qeduššah in 3 Enoch takes us back to a time when it had not yet received any of the amplifications attested in the Gemara of the Babylonian Talmud, or been associated with the ʿAmidah (pt. 1, p. 38). (6) The reference to the Messiah, the son of Joseph, in 45:5 dates the document after the time of Hadrian (pt. 1, p. 38). (7) Similarly the reference to the pre-existence of the soul (ch. 43) "may perhaps be taken as evidence for the origin of that section not much earlier than the beginning of the third century A.D.," if Billerbeck's opinion is correct that this idea first penetrated rabbinic Judaism then (pt. 1, pp. 38, 180). (8) The relationship which Odeberg perceived between 3 Enoch and the other Merkabah texts also played a part in his dating. He regarded 3 Enoch as one of the earliest of these texts, older, for example, than Hekalot Rabbati (pt. 2, pp. 54, 159),

---

⁴ However, the text of Onkelos at this point is not altogether certain; see I. Gruenwald, "Knowledge and Vision," *Israel Oriental Studies* 3 (1973) 66, n. 20; P. S. Alexander, "The Historical Setting of the Hebrew Book of Enoch," *JJS* 28 (1977) 176, n. 40.

and since he was still influenced by the nineteenth-century dating of this literature as post-talmudic, he tended to push 3 Enoch back into the talmudic period.

These arguments are not all of equal weight. The fourth is subjective and of little value. The third is weak, though not entirely lacking in force. The fifth is interesting: It is certainly noteworthy that the forms of the Qeduššah in 3 Enoch are simpler than those used in the synagogue liturgy; but it is very doubtful whether we can deduce from this that the sections of 3 Enoch which quote the heavenly Sanctus originated before the synagogue Qeduššot were composed. The second argument looks as if it might provide a strong case, but Odeberg offers no evidence beyond bald assertion, and, in fact, our knowledge of rabbinic Hebrew is hardly so exact as to allow us to draw such a precise conclusion. Arguments six and seven are possibly correct, and may indicate a date (or dates) after which 3 Enoch must have been finally redacted.[5] The crucial arguments are, however, the first and the eighth, and in both cases it seems that Odeberg made a fundamental misjudgment. As Scholem subsequently demonstrated, 3 Enoch is probably one of the later, not one of the earlier Merkabah texts. And while Odeberg was justified in maintaining that 3 Enoch contains traditions as old as, if not older than, talmudic Maʿaśeh Merkabah, he failed to see that occasionally it makes use of talmudic material, and so its final editing is presumably post-talmudic.[6]

Scholem dates 3 Enoch to the fifth or sixth century A.D., though he concedes that "much of the material is old and important" (*Gnosticism*, p. 17, n. 19). He does not systematically argue his case;[7] he surveys the Merkabah literature and offers a reconstruction of the development of Merkabah mysticism from the first to the tenth century A.D., and it is from this that his dating of 3 Enoch emerges. 3 Enoch is a highly complex and involved Merkabah text and so it should be assigned a place fairly late in the history of Merkabah mysticism (after Hekalot Zuṭarti and Hekalot Rabbati). Scholem maintains that "3 Enoch already reinterprets, and wrongly, some older Merkabah traditions that a third-century writer could not have misunderstood"[8] (*Gnosticism*, p. 7, n. 19). The following appear to be examples of what he means by reinterpretation. (1) One of Meṭaṭron's most distinctive titles is *Naʿar*. Originally this was used in the sense of "servant" and it referred to Meṭaṭron's role as the high priest of the heavenly sanctuary; its equivalent in one Aramaic text is *šammāšāʾ reḥîmāʾ* = "the beloved servant." (Cf. Meṭaṭron's common title *ʿebed* = "servant" [10:3].) In 3 Enoch 4, however, *Naʿar* is taken in the sense of "Youth" and linked with the notion that Meṭaṭron is translated Enoch: as the youngest of the angel-princes he is known among them as "Youth" (4:10) (*Gnosticism*, p. 66). (2) Another possible instance of reinterpretation is the name ʾAzbogah. In origin this was a secret name of God, possibly related to the gnostic concept of the Ogdoad, the eighth heavenly sphere. (ʾAzbogah is made up of three groups of consonants, each of which adds up by gematria to eight.) But in 3 Enoch 18:22 ʾAzbogah has become simply the name of one of the angels, and it is taken as a kind of abbreviation (notarikon) for *ʾozēr bigdê ḥayyîm* = "the one who girds (the righteous) with the garments of life" (*Gnosticism*, pp. 65f.).

A very late date for 3 Enoch has recently been advanced by J. T. Milik.[9] He holds that the work cannot have been composed earlier than the ninth or tenth century A.D., and that, in fact, the greater part of it was written between the twelfth and fifteenth centuries A.D. (pp. 126f.). His arguments run as follows: (1) 3 Enoch draws on 2 Enoch, which, in its Greek original, must be dated to the ninth or tenth century A.D. (2) On the incantation bowls

---

[5] J. Heinemann, "The Messiah of Ephraim and the Premature Exodus of the Tribe of Ephraim," *HTR* 68 (1975) 1–15, argues that the idea of the Messiah of Ephraim is pre-Hadrianic but that it underwent a transformation after the death of Bar Kokhba. On the pre-existence of the soul see E. E. Urbach, *The Sages: Their Concepts and Beliefs* (Jerusalem, 1975) vol. 1, p. 236: "Support for this concept is to be found only in dicta of the Palestinian Amoraim of the second half of the third century."

[6] See 4:6, n. l; 16:1–5, n. a; 31:2, n. e; 45:2, n. h. On the problem of the relationship of 3En to the Talmud see further below on "Historical importance."

[7] This is unfortunate. His arguments have to be culled from *Major Trends*, pp. 40–79, and from *Gnosticism*. It should be noted that *Gnosticism* gives earlier dates for the Hekalot texts than does *Major Trends* (see *Gnosticism*, p. 8). Thus in *Major Trends*, p. 45, Scholem appears to date 3En later than the 6th cent. A.D. The 5th/6th-cent. date assigned to it in *Gnosticism* presumably applies only to the bulk of the work (chs. 1–48A), and Scholem still stands by his view, put forward in *Major Trends*, p. 68, that the list of the seventy names of Meṭaṭron in 3En 48D is from the Gaonic era.

[8] I.e. if Odeberg's 3rd-cent. date for 3En were correct.

[9] J. T. Milik, "Enoch in Cabbalistic Literature," *The Books of Enoch: Aramaic Fragments of Qumran Cave 4* (Oxford, 1976) pp. 123–35.

which date from the seventh or eighth century, or even from the ninth century A.D., Meṭaṭron is not yet identified with Enoch (p. 128); Enoch is still a purely human figure and there is no hint of the central teaching of 3 Enoch that he was elevated to the rank of archangel (p. 133). (3) The name Meṭaṭron is to be derived from the Latin *metator*, via Greek *mētatōr*, *mitatōr* (p. 131). But this loanword could hardly have entered Hebrew and Judeo-Aramaic before the fifth or sixth century A.D., for it was then that Latin borrowings, especially of administrative and military terms, entered these languages *en bloc* (pp. 133f.). (4) 3 Enoch was influenced by the Arabic Hermetic tradition of the eighth to tenth centuries A.D. The Arabic Hermeticists identified Hermes with Enoch; the incantation bowls identify Hermes with Meṭaṭron. The author or redactor of 3 Enoch, receiving both these traditions, deduced that Enoch was the same as Meṭaṭron (p. 134). (5) "Cabbalistic theories, including the figure of Metatron-Enoch in his role as lieutenant of God, do not appear in Western Europe until the twelfth century (A.D.)" (p. 134).

Milik's arguments will not stand up to close scrutiny. The first of them depends on a dating for 2 Enoch which does not command much scholarly assent, and it requires us to posit a close and exclusive relationship between 2 Enoch and 3 Enoch such as does not, in fact, exist. In the second argument Milik's dating of the incantation bowls is open to question. Many of the bowls cannot be dated with certainty, but those from Nippur (among which are some of our most informative texts on Meṭaṭron) were found in stratified deposits and have been dated archaeologically to the seventh century A.D. *at the very latest*.[10] Moreover, the fact that Enoch is not identified with Meṭaṭron on the bowls proves little. It is unlikely that the circles from which 3 Enoch emanated were the same as those which produced the bowls. The failure of the magicians to equate Enoch and Meṭaṭron does not prove that the equation had not already been made by the Merkabah mystics either in Babylonia or in Palestine.

As for the third argument, Milik is rather overconfident about the derivation of the angelic name Meṭaṭron from the Latin *metator* (see below). His assertion that *metator* can hardly have entered Judeo-Aramaic or Hebrew before the fifth or sixth century A.D. does not accord with the evidence: it is found in what would appear to be much earlier Jewish material.[11] The appeal in Milik's fourth argument to Arabic Hermetic traditions to explain the equation between Meṭaṭron and Enoch is unnecessary. The identification can be explained as a natural development within the mystical tradition. It is very curious, if Milik is correct, that the impact of Arabic Hermeticism is not more evident in 3 Enoch or in the other Merkabah tracts. Out of the scores of names for Meṭaṭron found in the Merkabah traditions Hermes does not appear to be attested. Milik's final argument is simply mistaken. It assumes that 3 Enoch was written in western Europe. In fact it was almost certainly written in the East—either in Babylonia or in Palestine (see below on "Provenance"). It can be shown conclusively that the vast majority of the ideas contained in 3 Enoch, including the Enoch-Meṭaṭron doctrine, were known in both these centers long before the twelfth century A.D.

It is impossible to reach a very firm conclusion as to the date of 3 Enoch. The main problem is the literary character of the work: it is not the total product of a single author at a particular point in time, but the deposit of a "school tradition" which incorporates elements from widely different periods. Certain rough chronological limits can, however, be established. (1) 3 Enoch can hardly have been written later than the tenth century A.D., since it is clear from the writings of Sa'adya, Sherira and Hai, and the Karaites Jacob al-Qirqisani and Salmon b. Yeruḥim that the Merkabah literature was circulating widely among Rabbanites at that period and was regarded as being of considerable antiquity and authority.[12] Particularly interesting is the fact that Jacob al-Qirqisani knew the short account of the elevation of

---

[10] See J. A. Montgomery, *Aramaic Incantation Texts from Nippur* (Philadelphia, 1913) pp. 103f.; see further n. 18 below.

[11] The Latin *metator* is found in a dictum attributed to Eliezer b. Hyrcanus (late 1st/early 2nd cent. A.D.) in SifDeut 338 (ed. Finkelstein, p. 388), on which see n. 17 below. It occurs also in a dictum which, according to GenR 5:4, was cited by R. Levi (late 3rd cent. A.D.) in the name of Ben Azzai and Ben Zoma (1st half of the 2nd cent. A.D.). The angelic name Meṭaṭron occurs in a dictum which Rab Naḥman b. Isaac (died mid 4th cent. A.D.) attributed to Rab Idi (early 4th cent. A.D.) (b.Sanh 38b). Note also its occurrence in the 4th-cent. work Re'uyot Yeḥezqe'l, BM, vol. 2, p. 132 (ed. Gruenwald, p. 130).

[12] Sa'adya, see *'Oṣar hagge'onim*, ed. Lewin, *Berakot*, Responsa sec.; p. 17; Sherira and Hai, see *'Oṣar hagge'onim* (ed. Lewin, *Ḥagigah*, Responsa sec., pp. 10–12, 13–15); Jacob al-Qirqisani, see *Kitab al-Anwar* 1.3 and 4 (ed. Nemoy, vol. 1, pp. 14, 31); Salmon b. Yeruḥim, see *Seper Milḥamot 'Adonai* 15–17 (ed. Davidson, pp. 114–32).

Enoch found in certain recensions of the Alphabet of Aqiba and in 3 Enoch 48C (*Kitab al-Anwar* 1.4.2, ed. Nemoy, vol. 1, p. 31, 15). This short account appears to be a summary of a longer version of the elevation of Enoch closely akin to 3 Enoch 3–15. (2) If we are right in surmising that 3 Enoch has drawn some of its materials from the Babylonian Talmud,[13] then its final redaction can hardly be earlier than the fifth century A.D. (3) The magical bowls from Nippur show that many of 3 Enoch's ideas about Meṭaṭron and about the heavenly world were known in magical circles in the sixth and seventh centuries A.D. All things considered, then, though 3 Enoch contains some very old traditions and stands in direct line with developments which had already begun in the Maccabean era, a date for its final redaction in the fifth or the sixth century A.D. cannot be far from the truth.[14]

Provenance

In the period to which we have dated 3 Enoch there appear to have been two main centers of Merkabah mysticism—Palestine and Babylonia.[15] It is far from easy to determine in which of these two regions 3 Enoch was finally edited. The work draws extensively on Palestinian apocalyptic traditions about Enoch (see below), and some of its distinctive ideas can be paralleled in Palestinian sources; e.g. the identity of Enoch and Meṭaṭron is attested in one of the Palestinian Targumim (TarJon to Gen 5:24),[16] and "Miṭaṭron" occurs as a secret name of the prince of the third heaven in the fourth-century Palestinian work Re'uyot Yeḥezqe'l (BM, vol. 2, p. 132; ed. Gruenwald, p. 130).[17] On the other hand, there are also close parallels to 3 Enoch in texts of Babylonian provenance. Meṭaṭron is mentioned a number of times in the incantation bowls from Babylonia, and invoked as "the Great Prince," "the Great Prince of God's Throne," "the Great Prince of the Whole World"; one Mandaean bowl speaks of "Meṭaṭron . . . who serves before the curtain [*brgwd'*]."[18] There are three highly suggestive references to Meṭaṭron in the Babylonian Talmud (b.Sanh 38b; b.Ḥag 15a; b.AZ 3b). Particularly significant is the close relationship between the account of the humbling of Meṭaṭron in 3 Enoch 16 and that in Ḥagigah 15a. If, as seems to be the case, this story is of Babylonian origin, then it is reasonable to locate the final redaction of 3 Enoch in Babylonia.[19]

Historical importance

Classic rabbinic literature makes it clear that there was an esoteric doctrine in talmudic Judaism. It was concerned with two subjects—the Account of Creation (*Ma'aseh Bere'sit*)

---

[13] See n. 6 above.

[14] I. Gruenwald is of the opinion that 3En may be later than the 6th cent. A.D., though he agrees that it contains much older material, some of which may go back to the 2nd or 3rd cent. A.D., or even earlier; see "Jewish Sources for the Gnostic Texts from Nag Hammadi?" *Proceedings of the Sixth World Congress of Jewish Studies* (Jerusalem, 1977) vol. 3, p. 50.

[15] In the Middle Ages Merkabah texts were known in Europe and North Africa. Several Merkabah texts were discovered in the Cairo Genizah (Re'uyot Yeḥezqe'l, a Hekalot text, a fragment of Ši'ur Qomah, and the related magical tract Seper HaRazim). In the 10th cent. Ši'ur Qomah texts were known to the Jews of Fez in Morocco (Responsum of Sherira and Hai, '*Oṣar hagge'onim*, [ed. Lewin, *Ḥagigah*, Responsa sec., pp. 10–12]). Merkabah mysticism may have been known in southern Italy as early as the 9th cent. A.D.; by the 10th it was known in the Rhineland; and by the 13th in Spain. What we cannot be certain of is when the Merkabah teachings first began to spread from the East to the West, and how exactly they were transmitted.

[16] Cf. TarJon to Deut 34:6. These two references to Meṭaṭron probably belong to a late stratum of the Targum; the other two recensions of the Palestinian Targum make no reference to Meṭaṭron. It is well known that the final redaction of TarJon to the Pentateuch cannot have been earlier than the 7th cent. A.D., because of the allusion to a wife and daughter of Mohammed in Gen 21:21.

[17] SifDeut 338 (ed. Finkelstein, p. 388) does not allude to Meṭaṭron the archangel, contrary to what Odeberg, *3 Enoch*, pt. 1, pp. 91f., supposes: see Alexander, *JJS* 28 (1977) 163, n. 15.

[18] For the texts see Montgomery, *Aramaic Incantation Texts from Nippur*; C. D. Isbell, *Corpus of Aramaic Incantation Bowls*, SBL Dissertation Series 17 (Missoula, Mont., 1975); M. J. Geller, "Two Incantation Bowls Inscribed in Syriac and Aramaic," *BSOAS* 39 (1976) 422–27. It must be stressed that the decipherment of these texts is often acutely problematic; cf. with Montgomery's readings the readings proposed by J. N. Epstein, "Gloses babylo-araméens," *REJ* 73 (1921) 27–58; 74 (1922) 40–72. For discussion, see B. A. Levine, "The Language of the Magical Bowls," in J. Neusner, *A History of the Jews in Babylonia* (Leiden, 1970) vol. 5, pp. 343–75; L. H. Schiffman, "A Forty-two Letter Divine Name in the Aramaic Magic Bowls," *Bulletin of the Institute of Jewish Studies* 1 (1973) 97–102; Milik, *The Books of Enoch*, pp. 128–30; Alexander, *JJS* 28 (1977) 165–67.

[19] Odeberg reached the same conclusion, though for rather different reasons: see *3 Enoch*, pt. 1, pp. 37f.

and the Account of the Chariot (*Maʿaśeh Merkabah*). All study and discussion of these topics in public was banned.[20] The Mishnah rules that "the Account of Creation may not be expounded before two or more persons, nor the Chariot before even one, unless he is a scholar who understands of his own knowledge" (m.Ḥag 2:1). Those who ignored these injunctions did so at their peril. The story was told of a certain Galilean who announced that he would publicly lecture on the Merkabah, but who was stung by a wasp and died (b.Shab 80b). A young scholar who dabbled prematurely in chariot lore was said to have been smitten with leprosy (y.Ḥag 77a.46); another perceived the *ḥašmal* and was consumed by fire (b.Ḥag 13a).

Despite efforts to keep Merkabah teaching secret, we are not entirely in the dark as to its contents in the talmudic period; some elements of it are disclosed. The most extensive single text in classical rabbinic literature Ḥagigah 11b–16a. This gives an account of the seven heavens and their contents (strictly a motif of Maʿaśeh Bereʾšit), discusses the safeguards to be applied in studying and teaching Maʿaśeh Merkabah, and relates stories of the great masters and adepts.

The ideas which are explicitly put forward in Ḥagigah 11b–16a can hardly be the sum total of talmudic Merkabah mysticism; in view of the Mishnaic ruling it is reasonable to suppose that there were more esoteric doctrines which have not been made public. These deeper teachings are hinted at in a number of places. One of these is the story of the four who entered Pardes:

> Four entered Pardes, and these are they: Ben Azzai, Ben Zoma, ʾAḥer, and Rabbi Aqiba. Rabbi Aqiba said to them: When you reach the stones of pure marble do not say, "Water! Water!" for it is written, "He that speaks falsehood shall not be established before my eyes" (Ps 101:7). Ben Azzai looked and died: Scripture says of him, "Precious in the sight of the Lord is the death of his saints" (Ps 116:15). Ben Zoma looked and went mad: Scripture says of him, "Have you found honey? Eat so much as is sufficient for you lest you be sated with it and vomit it up" (Prov 25:16). ʾAḥer cut down the young plants. Rabbi Aqiba went out in peace.[21]

Pardes is a designation of the place to which the souls of the righteous go after death.[22] Here, however, the reference cannot be to the final departure of the souls of the four to that blissful abode; it must allude to a mystical entry into Pardes which took place while they were still alive; note how Aqiba not only enters but comes out again.[23] Pardes was sometimes located on earth, sometimes in heaven. Which of these traditions lies behind this passage cannot now be determined with certainty; however, a reference to a celestial Pardes is likely. The parallel in 2 Corinthians 12:1–7 points in this direction, and it is evident that—whatever its original meaning—the text was already being read in amoraic times in terms of a mystical ascent to heaven. Its setting in the Gemara should be noted; it occurs in a context dealing with the heavenly world, and in Ḥagigah 15a the enigmatic remark about ʾAḥer cutting down the young plants is apparently explained by a story about an encounter between ʾAḥer and the angel Meṭaṭron which is supposed to have taken place "on high," i.e. in heaven

---

[20] m.Ḥag 2:1 also forbids public discussion of the laws regarding incest: see P. S. Alexander, "The Rabbinic Lists of Forbidden Targumim," *JJS* 27 (1976) 185.

[21] b.Ḥag 14b. The parallels contain a number of variants: see t.Ḥag 2:3–4; y.Ḥag 77b.8–23; SongR 1:4.1. For discussion see A. Neher, "Le voyage mystique des quatre," *RHR* 140 (1951) 59–82; Scholem, *Major Trends*, pp. 52f.; Scholem, *Gnosticism*, pp. 14–19; I. Gruenwald, "Yannai and Hekhaloth Literature," *Tarbis* 36 (1966/67) 261–65; E. E. Urbach, "The Traditions About Merkabah Mysticism in the Tannaitic Period," *Festschrift Scholem* (1967) Heb. sec., pp. 12–16.

[22] Usually this place is referred to as Gan ʿEden in rabbinic literature; see 3En 5:5, n. f. Another suggestion is that Pardes is a cryptic designation for mystical or metaphysical speculation, this term having been chosen because it was in Paradise that the tree of knowledge was to be found (Gen 2:17) (Strack-Billerbeck, vol. 4, p. 1119; Scholem, *Major Trends*, p. 361, n. 45). "To enter Pardes," then, would mean to engage in a certain kind of esoteric study. In biblical and rabbinic Heb. *pardēs* means "a park," "a garden" (Neh 2:8; Eccl 2:5; Song 4:13; t.BMeṣ 1:10; b.Soṭ 10a). Like the Gk. *paradeisos* (the root of the English "paradise"), it is derived from the Persian *pairidaēza*, "an enclosure." See further I. de Vuippens, *Le paradis au troisième ciel* (Paris, 1925); Strack-Billerbeck, vol. 4, pp. 118–1165; H. Bietenhard, *Die himmlische Welt im Urchristentum und Spätjudentum* (Tübingen, 1951) pp. 161–85.

[23] The ending of the story in the Yerušalmi Talmud, the Tosepta (Erfurt MS), and SongR is clear on this point: "R. Aqiba entered in peace and went out in peace." The version in the Babylonian Talmud abbreviates. The Vienna MS of the Tosepta has an interesting variant: "R. Aqiba *ascended* in peace and *descended* in peace."

(cf. 3En 16).[24] If this interpretation of the story of the four who entered Pardes is correct, then it would seem that in talmudic times Ma'aśeh Merkabah contained a doctrine of mystical ascent to heaven.

Another element of the Merkabah tradition in the talmudic period may be disclosed by an early rabbinic gloss on 1 Samuel 6:12. Rabbinic exegetes derived the unusual verbal form *wayyiśśarnāh* in 1 Samuel 6:12 not from the root *yśr* in the sense of "go straight," but from *śyr*, "to sing." They took the text to mean that the cows sang a hymn as they pulled the cart bearing the Ark of the Covenant back along the road from Philistia to Israel. Various suggestions were made as to the song they sang; some identified it with the Song at the Sea (Ex 15), others with biblical Psalms (Pss 93, 98, 99), but the Palestinian haggadist R. Isaac Nappaḥa (mid 3rd cent. A.D.) stated that it was a non-biblical composition which ran as follows:

> Rejoice, rejoice, acacia shrine,
> Flaunt yourself in your abundant glory,
> Bound in embroideries of gold,
> Praised in the sanctum of the Temple,
> Resplendent in the finest of ornaments.[25]

As Scholem has pointed out, the whole force of this exegesis turns upon an allusion to the Merkabah hymns: Just as the ḥayyot (the holy creatures) bearing up the Merkabah sing hymns to the Merkabah, so the kine bearing up the Ark sang hymns to the Ark. The song of the kine has a number of affinities to some of the surviving Merkabah hymns (see Hekalot Rabbati 2:4, *BHM*, vol. 3, p. 84; Cairo Genizah Hekalot B/1, 33, ed. Gruenwald, p. 369). It would appear, then, that R. Isaac and his audience were acquainted with hymns of the Merkabah type and with their mystical setting.[26]

A patristic text appears to indicate that students of Ma'aśeh Merkabah were already speculating in the talmudic period on the mystical body of God. In the prologue of his commentary on the Song of Songs (cf. Jerome, *Commentary on Ezekiel*, 1 Praefatio, and Epistle 53, *ad Paulinum*), Origen informs us that in his day Jews did not study the beginning of Genesis, the beginning and end of Ezekiel, and the Song of Songs, until they had mastered the rest of Scripture and the oral law. Scholem has argued that the inclusion of the Song of Songs along with these other mystical texts shows that already in the early third century A.D. Ši'ur Qomah speculation had been attached to the description of the Beloved in the Song of Songs 5:10–16 (cf. Hekalot Rabbati 12, BM, vol. 1, p. 87: Merkabah Šelemah 38a). An analysis of certain tannaitic and amoraic statements about the Song of Songs undertaken by Lieberman tends to confirm Scholem's view.[27]

From this discussion it seems reasonable to conclude that, in addition to the explicit teachings given in Ḥagigah and in other classic rabbinic texts, Merkabah mysticism in the talmudic period contained the following three elements: (1) an idea of mystical ascent to heaven; (2) Merkabah hymns; and (3) speculation of the Ši'ur Qomah type. It is clear, then, that all the leading ideas in the Merkabah tracts such as Hekalot Rabbati and 3 Enoch were already present in Merkabah mysticism in the talmudic period. An important question now arises: What is the relationship between the talmudic Merkabah texts and the Merkabah tracts? Two views are possible. On the one hand we could argue that the mystical tracts are post-talmudic and have grown out of attempts to understand and to explain talmudic Ma'aśeh

---

[24] Later Jewish scholars certainly interpreted the story as referring to an ascent to heaven: see Hai, *'Oṣar hagge'onim*, ed. Lewin, *Ḥagigah*, Responsa sec., pp. 13–15, and esp. p. 14; Rabbenu Ḥanan'el to b.Ḥag 14b (cf. *'Aruk haśśalem* under *pardēs*); Rashi to b.Ḥag 14b; Tosapot to b.Ḥag 14b, *niknesu*.

[25] So b.AZ 24b; the parallels have a number of important variations: see GenR 54:4; Seder 'Eliyahu Rabbah 12 (11) (ed. Friedmann, p. 58); Midraš Semu'el 12:3 (ed. Buber, p. 40).

[26] Scholem, *Gnosticism*, pp. 20–30; I. Gruenwald, "A Technique of the *Midrash*: Linkage by Sound-Patterns," *Ha-Sifrut* 1 (1968/69) 726 (in Heb.). J. Goldin, *The Song at the Sea* (New Haven, 1971) pp. 80f., suggests that there are some ancient hymnic fragments embedded in Mekilta' deRabbi 'Išma'el, *Širah* 1 (ed. Horovitz-Rabin, p. 119). The hymns he reconstructs are in some respects similar to the Merkabah hymns.

[27] See Scholem, *Gnosticism*, pp. 38–40; Lieberman, app. D in Scholem's *Gnosticism*, esp. p. 123. For an application of Song 5:10–16 very explicitly to God see Mekilta' deRabbi 'Išma'el, *Širah* 3 (ed. Horovitz-Rabin, p. 127); Goldin, *The Song at the Sea*, pp. 115–20. Scholem's suggestion (*Gnosticism*, p. 40) that the reference to the "length of the nose being as the length of the little finger" in b.Bek 44a is a quotation from the Ši'ur Qomah (cf. Merkabah Šelemah 38a; Lieberman, *Shkiin* [Jerusalem, 1970²] p. 12) is unconvincing.

Merkabah materials. Or we could argue that the Merkabah tracts and the talmudic Merkabah texts belong to one unbroken mystical movement and that in some cases the traditions in the mystical tracts may go back to the talmudic period or may even be anterior to the talmudic Merkabah traditions.

Of these two views the second seems to fit the facts better. There are many elements in the Merkabah tracts (such as 3 Enoch's account of the elevation of Enoch)[28] which cannot easily be explained as Midrashim on talmudic Maʿaśeh Merkabah; clearly the writers of the tracts had access to Merkabah traditions other than those contained in classic rabbinic sources. Moreover, in certain cases the mystical tracts appear to contain in fuller form traditions alluded to only obscurely in the Talmud. For example, the statement attributed to R. Aqiba in the story of the four who entered Pardes, "When you reach the stones of pure marble do not say, 'Water! Water!' for it is written, 'He that speaks falsehood shall not be established before my eyes,' " has baffled exegetes both ancient and modern. Parallels to it, however, are found in the mystical tracts Hekalot Zuṭarti and Hekalot Rabbati, and there it is stated that Aqiba's remark refers to a stage in the ascent of the mystic to the Merkabah: When he reaches the sixth palace he sees a glittering pavement of pure marble flags, and it seems to him that they are waves of water threatening to swallow him up. He must be careful, however, not to cry out, "Water! Water!" for by uttering this falsehood he lays himself open to angelic attack. Though at certain points later elements may have crept into the tradition in Hekalot Zuṭarti and Hekalot Rabbati about the stones of pure marble, Scholem is surely right in seeing here the key to the enigmatic talmudic statement. If this is so, then it follows that in this case the mystical tracts contain Merkabah material as old as that in the Talmud.[29]

It would seem, then, that Merkabah mysticism was a movement which continued in unbroken existence from tannaitic to gaonic times. The movement originated in Palestine. This may be deduced from a number of facts. Merkabah doctrines are found in early Palestinian texts (e.g. t.Ḥag 2:1–6 and y.Ḥag 2, 77a). We should also note that the four who entered Pardes—Ben Zoma, Ben Azzai, Aqiba, and Elisha b. Abuya (ʾAḥer)—were all Palestinian scholars of the second century A.D. Merkabah literature itself claims Palestinian roots, for it cites as its authorities Tannaim belonging mainly to the circle of Yoḥanan b. Zakkai's disciples. Some of the surviving Merkabah texts contain what would appear to be identifiably Palestinian elements. Thus 3 Enoch's Meṭatron embodies Palestinian apocalyptic traditions about Enoch. In a vivid description of the guardian angels of the seventh palace Hekalot Rabbati refers to "the mangers of Caesarea" (presumably those attached to the hippodrome at Caesarea Maritima, Josephus, Ant 16.137), to the "gate of Caesarea," and to the "water-pipe in the Valley of Kidron" near Jerusalem (Hekalot Rabbati 16:1–2, BHM, vol. 3, pp. 94f.). The story about R. Ḥananyah b. Teradyon and Lupinus Caesar in Hekalot Rabbati 5–6 (BHM, vol. 3, pp. 87f., BM, vol. 1, pp. 80f.) is also, in all probability, of Palestinian origin. Merkabah mysticism spread from Palestine to the Jewish communities in Babylonia; cultural contacts between the two centers were close, so it is not difficult to see how the Merkabah ideas could have been carried to Babylonia.[30] We have already remarked on the presence of Merkabah materials in texts of Babylonian provenance such as the Babylonian Talmud and the incantation bowls. It is a fact that the Merkabah traditions in the Babylonian Talmud are richer and fuller than those in the classic Palestinian rabbinic texts (cf. y.Ḥag 2, 77a with b.Ḥag 11b–16a). There are two possible explanations of this fact: it is possible that the Babylonian mystics were less inhibited than their Palestinian counterparts about disclosing the contents of Maʿaśeh Merkabah; or else the Babylonian Talmud may contain further developments of the Merkabah tradition which originated among the Babylonian mystics.

---

[28] It is well known that classic rabbinic sources have very little to say about Enoch: he is not mentioned even once in the two Talmuds or the tannaitic Midrashim (see Ginzberg, Legends, vol. 5, p. 156, n. 58); the references to him in GenR are generally denigratory.

[29] See Major Trends, pp. 52f.; Gnosticism, pp. 14–16; see further Gruenwald, Tarbiṣ 36 (1966/67) 262–66; Urbach, Scholem Festschrift, pp. 15–17. Hai Gaon had already explained the talmudic text from Hekalot Zuṭarti in the 10th cent.: see ʾOṣar hagge'onim, ed. Lewin, Ḥagigah, Responsa sec., p. 14, and cf. Rabbenu Ḥanan'el to b.Ḥag 14b.

[30] E.g. the Babylonian scholar Rab (early 3rd cent. A.D.), who appears to have had an interest in esoteric lore, studied in Palestine, and the Palestinian Isaac Nappaḥa, who quoted the song of the kine (see n. 25 above), was in Babylonia for some time.

The Merkabah mystics came to be known as *Yôredê Merkābāh,* "those who descend to the Chariot,"[31] and in certain cases they appear to have been organized into regular conventicles. From a close reading of the Merkabah literature it is possible to sketch the profile of these conventicles. Particularly valuable is Hekalot Rabbati 13–18 (*BHM,* vol. 3, pp. 93–97), which appears to be a thinly disguised description of a Merkabah séance. Each group was gathered round a master who not only initiated his disciples into the mystical lore, but demonstrated the ascent to the Merkabah. The achieving of a "vision of the Merkabah" (*ṣepiyyat hammerkābāh*) (see 3En 1:1), either by the master himself or by another adept in the group, was probably the central act of a session of a conventicle.[32]

The technique of the ascent had two aspects. First, preparation: For some days prior to the ascent the adept made himself ready by fasting, eating special food, or bathing (Responsum of Hai Gaon, *'Oṣar hagge'onim,* ed. Lewin, *Ḥagigah,* Responsa sec., p. 14; Ma'aśeh Merkabah 19, ed. Scholem, p. 111; cf. Seper HaRazim 2:6–11, ed. Margalioth, p. 81). Secondly, there was the ascent itself. This was effected by the recitation of (1) Merkabah hymns or prayers (Ma'aśeh Merkabah 27, ed. Scholem, p. 113); (2) magic formulae; or (3) invocations of God or of the archangels by magical names (Hekalot Rabbati 14:4, *BHM,* vol. 3, p. 94).[33] These hymns, prayers, formulae, and invocations have one thing in common: they all involve the rhythmic repetition of certain words, or sounds, or ideas. Given the rigorous preparations for the ascent, the sense of anticipation and the aura of mystery and awe with which the act was surrounded, this repetition would have been potent enough to have sent the adepts into trance. Its efficacy would have been magnified if, as Hai Gaon asserts, the mystics recited the hymns with their heads between their knees, in the manner of Elijah on Mount Carmel (cf. 1Kgs 18:42), thus constricting their breathing.[34]

The Merkabah texts stress the dangers of the ascent: To reach the throne of God the mystic had to pass through seven gates guarded by awesome archangels. He must have the right "seals" to show them and he must know the names of the angels (Hekalot Rabbati 15 and 17, *BHM,* vol. 3, pp. 94f.; Ma'aśeh Merkabah 23, ed. Scholem, p. 112; cf. 3En 48D:5). The sixth gate was regarded as especially perilous (Hekalot Rabbati 17:6, *BHM,* vol. 3, p. 96). The adept had to be marked by certain qualities and he had to make the ascent in a condition of ritual and spiritual purity (Responsum of Hai Gaon, *Oṣar hagge'onim,* ed. Lewin, *Ḥagigah,* Responsa sec., p. 14; Hekalot Rabbati 13:2–3, *BHM,* vol. 3, p. 93; 20:1, *BHM,* vol. 3, p. 98; Cairo Genizah Hekalot A/2, 12–13, ed. Gruenwald, p. 362; Ma'aśeh Merkabah 1, ed. Scholem, p. 103). Hekalot Rabbati 18:2 (*BHM,* vol. 3, p. 96) describes an elaborate technique for terminating a trance which was probably used when things appeared to be going awry.[35]

---

[31] For the expression *Yôredê Merkābāh* see Hekalot Rabbati 9:2 (*BHM,* vol. 3, p. 90, l. 18); 10 (p. 91, l. 14); 16:3 (p. 95, l. 8); 17:6 (p. 96, l. 22); 18:4 (p. 97, l. 11); 26:1 (BM, vol. 1, p. 107, l. 11 = *BHM,* vol. 3, p. 102, l. 11); Cairo Genizah Hekalot A/2, ll. 3, 8 (ed. Gruenwald, p. 361); cf. Seder Rab Amram Gaon, ed. N. N. Coronel (Warsaw, 1865) pt. 1, p. 4a, with 9:2 above. (The passage is not in the edition of Hedegård. Note also p. 4b, which inserts Merkabah material.) Hekalot Rabbati uses the terms "fellowship" (*ḥabûrāh*) (see 18:1, *BHM,* vol. 3, p. 96, l. 28) and "members of the fellowship" (*ḥaberîm*) (see 18:4, *BHM,* vol. 3, p. 97, l. 17; 5:2, *BHM,* vol. 3, p. 87, l. 21) with regard to the mystical groups. From such expressions as *hayyôrēd lammerkābāh* (Hekalot Rabbati 20:1, *BHM,* vol. 3, p. 98, l. 14) and *lêrēd lammerkābāh* (*BHM,* vol. 3, p. 102, l. 9; BM, vol. 1, p. 107, l. 9, reads *lêrēd bammerkābāh*) it is clear that *Yôredê Merkābāh* means "those who descend to the chariot." The expression "*descend* to the Merkabah" is odd; the mystical tracts speak also of "ascending": see e.g. Hekalot Rabbati 16:3 (*BHM,* vol. 3, p. 95, l. 8): "All the masters of the Yôredê Merkābāh were *ascending* and were not being harmed, and they were seeing all this palace [i.e. the 7th palace], and were *descending* in peace." Scholem suggests that the liturgical phrase "go down before the Ark" (*yārad lipne hattēbāh*) may have influenced the terminology of "descending" to the Merkabah: see *Major Trends,* pp. 46f., and *Gnosticism,* p. 20, n. 1.

[32] See further Alexander, *JJS* 28 (1977) 169–73.

[33] See further Gruenwald, *Israel Oriental Studies* 3 (1973) 89f.

[34] "He [the mystic] sits fasting for a specified period of time and places his head between his knees and whispers earthwards many hymns and praises . . ." (*'Oṣar hagge'onim,* ed. Lewin, *Ḥagigah,* Responsa sec., p. 14). Cf. the posture of Ḥaninah b. Dosa in b.Ber 34b.

[35] Scholem, *Gnosticism,* pp. 10–12; L. H. Schiffman, "The Recall of Rabbi Neḥuniah b. Ha-Qanah from Ecstasy in the Hekalot Rabbati," *Association for Jewish Studies Review* 1 (1976) 268–82. Cf. J. Maier, "Das Gefährdungsmotiv bei der Himmelsreise in der jüdischen Apokalyptik und in der 'jüdischen Gnosis,'" *Kairos* 5 (1963) 18–40. The mystical ascent is compared to climbing a ladder in Hekalot Rabbati 13:2 (*BHM,* vol. 3, p. 93, l. 11) and 20:3 (p. 98, l. 31). According to Pereq mippirqe merkabah (*BHM,* vol. 3, p. 162, l. 12), the angels ascend a ladder to reach the throne of glory. There may be an allusion to Jacob's ladder (Gen 28:12); however, the ladder is a common mystical symbol: see A. Altmann, "The Ladder of Ascension," *Festschrift Scholem* (1967) pp. 1–32; E. R. Dodds, *Pagan and Christian in an Age of Anxiety* (Cambridge, 1965) pp. 50–53.

According to Hekalot Rabbati 18:4 (*BHM*, vol. 3, p. 97) the adept was expected to speak during the trance and scribes were placed to write down what he said, for his utterances were taken to be revelations of what was happening in the heavenly world. It is not clear whether any of these utterances have been incorporated directly into the Merkabah texts; it is possible that some of the angelic names and magical formulae are glossolalia.[36] Most of the material, however, probably arose from later reflection, by the adept himself, or by other members of his fellowship, on his trance experiences. These vivid experiences clearly cried out for some interpretation, and this was usually supplied by attempting to correlate them with Ezekiel's vision of the Merkabah.

Scholem and Gruenwald have published certain physiognomic texts which apparently emanated from the Merkabah circles. It would seem from these that, like the Pythagoreans (at least according to Iamblichus, *De vita Pythagorica* 17.71, 74) and possibly also the Qumran Essenes, the Merkabah mystics controlled entrance to their conventicles by using physiognomy.

A number of influential talmudic sages are known to have studied the Merkabah lore, so it would appear that the mystical movement was at home at the very heart of rabbinic Judaism. The Merkabah texts as they stand may be described broadly as "orthodox" in that they remain within the bounds of monotheism and pay due respect to Torah. However, there are clear signs that at least some rabbinic authorities were uneasy about Merkabah mysticism. It is possible that their concern was occasioned by a more extreme form of the teaching than we find in the extant texts. On the other hand it must be admitted that there is enough in the surviving literature to provoke misgivings.

In the first place, the practice of mystical ascent to God's throne is potentially dangerous to rabbinic Judaism. It is not at all clear why the adepts wanted to make the ascent to the Merkabah. In some cases the motive may have been purely religious: They wished to view the glory of God and to join in the heavenly Qeduššah (cf. 3En 1:11). Sometimes, however, they were convinced that the exercise would bring them very mundane benefits: They would discover what was about to happen in the world; they would see all that men do, even in their innermost chambers; they would gain the protection of the heavenly law court (Hekalot Rabbati 1:1–2:2, *BHM*, vol. 3, pp. 83f.). The adepts appear to have functioned on occasion like the pagan oracles and the pagan and Christian prophets of late antiquity. An interesting example of a typically oracular use of an adept is found in Hekalot Rabbati 5:5 (BM, vol. 1, p. 74).[37] There we are told that when Rome issued a decree to seize the leading Jewish scholars in Palestine, R. Nehunyah b. Ha-Qanah sent R. Ishmael down to the Merkabah to inquire of Suriʾel, Prince of the Divine Presence, why this had been allowed to happen.

So long as the adepts confined themselves to pronouncements on non-controversial matters there was little danger. If, however, they had begun to pronounce on ultimate issues, they could have come to be regarded as channels of revelation on a par with the written and the oral law. Pagan theurgists certainly exploited mediums as a way of discovering ultimate truths, and the Christian Montanists apparently collected the oracles of their prophets into a sort of Third Testament, equal in authority to the Old and New Testaments. Just as the Montanist principle of continuous revelation posed a serious threat to the Christian establishment, so too the Merkabah mystics, by resorting to ecstatic experience, *could have* threatened the stability of rabbinic Judaism with its commitment to the sufficiency of Torah.

It is not clear whether there was ever any attempt to impose an absolute ban on Merkabah mysticism in rabbinic circles, but strong efforts were certainly directed toward containing it: It was hedged about with safeguards and clamped firmly in a vise of orthodoxy. It was to be studied only by mature scholars (m.Hag 2:1; b.Hag 14a). According to Hekalot Rabbati 20:1 (*BHM*, vol. 3, p. 98) only those who have mastered Bible, Mishnah, Halakot, and Haggadot, and who observe all the laws revealed to Moses on Sinai, are allowed to descend to the Merkabah. This stress on the classical disciplines as a necessary propaedeutic was doubtless aimed at neutralizing the danger inherent in the mystics' practice of ascending to the throne of God; the mystics' minds would have been so imbued with an orthodox world view that they would have tended to assign orthodox values to their mystical experiences.

---

[36] A similar suggestion has been made about some of the formulae and unintelligible names in the magical papyri; see Dodds, *Pagan and Christian*, p. 55, n. 1.

[37] See BM, vol. 1, p. 74, n. 25; the text in *BHM*, vol. 3, p. 87, is rather different.

It was not only the mystics' methods but also some of their doctrines which caused concern. It is noteworthy that two out of the three references to Metatron in the Talmud are critical; some of the rabbis apparently thought that the position assigned to him, at least by some mystics, amounted to dualism (see b.Sanh 38b; b.Hag 15a; the neutral reference is b.AZ 3b). This is hardly surprising in view of the title "The lesser YHWH" which Metatron carries in the mystical literature (see 3En 12:5). Moreover, the extreme glorification of Enoch in certain mystical circles (cf. 3En 3–15) stands in pointed contrast to the striking silence about him in the two Talmuds and the hostile notices of him in classic Midrashim.[38]

It is possible to detect signs of uneasiness about the Merkabah traditions in our current texts of 3 Enoch. There appears to have been an orthodox tendency at work in the redaction of this tract. There are several attempts to diminish the powers of Metatron: 3 Enoch 16 contains a version of the humbling of Metatron (cf. b.Hag 15a), and there is an "orthodox" gloss aimed at demoting Metatron in 3 Enoch 10:3. It is possible that the marked absence of theurgy in 3 Enoch is to be explained in the same way. We are nowhere told in 3 Enoch how to make the ascent to the throne (the ascent itself is covered in one verse, 3En 1:1), and there is a striking lack of Merkabah hymns. It is even possible that a list of the seventy names of Metatron (which could have been used to invoke him) has been edited out of 3 Enoch 4:1 (see ch. 16, n. a).

A large number of elements in the Merkabah texts can be paralleled in apocalyptic literature, and yet, despite these shared traditions, the ethos of Merkabah mysticism is rather different from that of apocalyptic. The Merkabah texts concentrate overwhelmingly on the mysteries of heaven and on the description of God's throne: They show little interest in eschatological themes such as the last judgment, the resurrection of the dead, the messianic kingdom, and the world to come, all of which figure in classic apocalyptic. The differentiation is a matter of emphasis. The Merkabah texts do have some eschatology (see e.g. 3En 45:5), and apocalyptic literature does contain Maʿaśeh Merkabah (see e.g. 1En 14:8–25); but there is definitely much less eschatological interest in the Merkabah texts than in apocalyptic literature. So, too, we find cosmology treated in both kinds of text (see e.g. 1En 72–80 and 3En 18:4–7; 41–42); on the whole, however, cosmology bulks larger in apocalyptic than in Merkabah mysticism. In the talmudic period the tendency was to regard cosmology as belonging to a distinct though related esoteric tradition—to Maʿaśeh Bereʾšit rather than to Maʿaśeh Merkabah. Finally, we should note that although there is some evidence (particularly in later apocalyptic texts) that trances were experienced by the apocalyptists and that trance-inducing techniques were occasionally used by them, the theurgic element is much more explicit and overt in the Merkabah tradition: A number of the Merkabah treatises are taken up largely with the techniques for ascending to the throne of glory.[39]

Maʿaśeh Merkabah forms one of the strands of apocalyptic literature prior to A.D. 70; what is not clear, however, is whether at that period it was studied without reference to eschatology and had a literature and tradition of its own. It is tempting to argue that Merkabah mysticism did not have a separate existence outside of apocalyptic till after A.D. 70 and that it was the events of the years A.D. 70–135 in Palestine which brought about a reorientation of apocalyptic and gave rise to a more or less independent Merkabah movement. It is interesting to note that Hekalot Rabbati 13:1 (*BHM,* vol. 3, p. 93) appears to place the birth of the Merkabah movement just prior to the destruction of the Temple in A.D. 70. The destruction of the Temple removed a powerful, visible symbol of the divine presence and could have fostered the transcendent view of God that we find in the Merkabah texts. The war against Rome also dampened eschatological fervor: Messianic hopes were signally dashed and soberer spirits must surely have turned their backs on the apocalyptic fanaticism that had so aggravated the disasters of the Jewish people.[40] Apocalyptic hopes were shattered further sixty years later with the debacle of Bar Kokhba and the conversion of Jerusalem into

[38] GenR 25:1; TargOnk to Gen 5:24; see n. 4 above.

[39] For theurgy in apocalyptic see Gruenwald, *Israel Oriental Studies* 3 (1973) 89f.; and for an attempt to characterize Merkabah mysticism and apocalyptic see I. Gruenwald, "The Jewish Esoteric Literature in the Time of the Mishnah and the Talmud," *Immanuel* 4 (1974) 37–46.

[40] This new coolness toward eschatological hopes is perhaps classically illustrated by the dictum attributed to Yoḥanan b. Zakkai: "If you have a sapling in your hand, and it is said to you, 'Behold, there is the Messiah'—go on with your planting, and afterwards go out and receive him. And if the youths say to you, 'Let us go up and build the Temple,' do not listen to them . . .'" (ARN B 31, ed. Schechter, 34a).

a pagan city. As a result it is possible that in certain circles the eschatological element in apocalyptic was played down and a form of the tradition arose which was much less concerned with the future and more interested in the mysteries of the heavenly world. It can hardly be disputed that the destruction of the Temple in A.D. 70 created a profound crisis in apocalyptic, and it may have given an impetus to Merkabah mysticism, but we should note—in opposition to the view we have just put forward—that in the Angelic Liturgy from Qumran (4QŠirŠabb) we may have a pre-70 text devoted exclusively to classic Maʿaśeh Merkabah themes. If this is so—and we cannot be certain since the text is so fragmentary—then it would seem that already in the period before the destruction of the Temple, Maʿaśeh Merkabah had a literature of its own and was being treated as a subject in its own right.[41]

Our sketch of the development of Merkabah mysticism would be incomplete if we were to see it only in the light of Jewish religious history. To do so would be to lose sight of the important fact that it displays a number of affinities with certain non-Jewish religious world views of late antiquity. Undoubtedly the closest parallels are with Gnosticism. Indeed, Scholem has argued that Merkabah mysticism is to be regarded as "Jewish Gnosticism" (*Gnosticism*, pp. 2–3, 10). "Gnosticism" is notoriously difficult to define, for there are many variations in detail between the various gnostic systems, but a typical system would speak of God as a transcendent, supreme power; of a second power (sometimes called the demiurge) that created the world; of a series of spheres (or aeons) separating man from the supreme power, each under the control of a hostile spirit (or archon); of the divinity of the human soul and its ascent to the supreme power; and of the secret knowledge (*gnōsis*) by which this ascent is to be achieved.

In its broad outlines this structure invites comparison with the Merkabah texts. These speak of a transcendent God, and of God who reveals himself on the throne of glory; God as he reveals himself is sometimes referred to as *Yôṣēr Berēʾšît*, "the Creator" (cf. 3En 11:1). Separating God and man are a series of regions controlled by angels whose business it is to stop man from approaching God. The Merkabah texts also speak of the heavenly origin of the human soul (3En 43:3), and of an ascent to heaven, and they claim that they contain the secret of how this ascent can be made.

It has long been observed that there is a strong Jewish component in Gnosticism.[42] In some cases the Jewish elements in Gnosticism can be found also in the Merkabah texts. The correspondences between Merkabah mysticism and Gnosticism may be illustrated from two works. The first is *The Hypostasis of the Archons* (NHC 2/4).[43] The second section of this treatise follows a pattern found commonly in apocalyptic works (and also in 3En): that of a revelation of secrets by an angel. Eleleth, Sagacity, the Great Angel who stands in the presence of the Holy Spirit, comes down from heaven to instruct Norea about the origin of the archons. Chapter 94, 8–13 (Labib 142, 8–13) refers to a "veil" (*katapetasma*) that divides "the World Above and the realms that are below." Chapter 95, 19–22 (Labib 143, 19–22) makes it clear that this veil separates the seventh and eighth heavens. A parallel passage in the Untitled Work (NHC 2/5) refers to a "veil" (*parapetasma*) that separates man from the celestials (98, 22; Labib 146, 22). The Merkabah texts also mention heavenly veils: according to one tradition the first heaven, Wilon, is a veil, and we read of a curtain (*pargôd/pārôket*) that hangs before the throne of God (see 3En 17:3; 45:1). At 94, 25–26 (Labib 142, 25–26) we read that the first archon who came into existence was "Samael (which is, ʿgod of the blind')." Sammaʾel is the Prince of the Accusers in 3 Enoch 14:2 and 26:12. The Semitic etymology in the gnostic text is noteworthy: Samael is derived from the Hebrew/Aramaic root *smʾ*, "to be blind," and *ʾēl*, "God."[44]

---

[41] It appears that a number of glosses have been incorporated into the text of Ezek 1. These may be evidence of very early interest in Maʿaśeh Merkabah in its own right: see W. Zimmerli, *Ezechiel* (Biblischer Kommentar Altes Testament 13/1; 1969) esp. pp. 23–30.

[42] On the Jewish element in Gnosticism see G. W. MacRae, "The Jewish Background of the Gnostic Sophia Myth," *NovT* 12 (1970) 86–101; J. Quispel, *Gnostic Studies* (Istanbul, 1974) vol. 1, pp. 173–239; R. McL. Wilson, "Jewish Gnosis and Gnostic Origins: A Survey," *HUCA* 44 (1973) 89–118; B. A. Pearson, "Biblical Exegesis in Gnostic Literature," *Armenian and Biblical Studies*, ed. M. Stone, supp. vol. 1 to *Sion*, the Journal of the Armenian Patriarchate of Jerusalem (Jerusalem, 1976) 70–80.

[43] For editions see R. A. Bullard, *The Hypostasis of the Archons*, Patristische Texte und Studien 10 (Berlin, 1970); B. Layton, "The Hypostasis of the Archons," *HTR* 67 (1974) 351–426. Layton's translation has been quoted.

[44] Bullard offers the alternative translation " 'Samael,' that is, the blind god."

When Samael blasphemously proclaims to his seven offspring, "It is I who am the god of the Entirety," he is rebuked by Life (Zōē), the daughter of Faith-Wisdom (Pistis-Sophia). Then "she breathed into his face, and her breath became a fiery angel for her; and that angel bound Yaldabaoth (i.e. Samael) and cast him down into Tartaros below the Abyss" (95, 8–13; Labib 143, 8–13). It is perhaps not inappropriate to compare with this the Merkabah idea that the angels are created by the utterance (*dibbûr*) of God (see 3En 40:4; cf. 27:3). When Sabaoth, one of Yaldabaoth's offspring, sees the punishment meted out to his father, he repents, condemns his father and his mother, Matter, and praises Wisdom (Sophia) and Life (Zōē). Wisdom and Life thereupon take him up and give him charge over the seventh heaven. Sabaoth makes for himself "a great four-faced chariot [*harma*] of cherubim [*cheroubin*] and infinitely many angels to act as ministers, and also harps and lyres. And Wisdom took her daughter Life, and had her sit upon his right to teach him the things that exist in the Eighth (Heaven)" (95, 13–34; Labib 143, 13–34). This description of the elevation of Sabaoth is rather reminiscent of the account of the elevation of Enoch in 3 Enoch 4–15. Compare, for example, the instruction of Sabaoth with 3 Enoch 10:5, where we read that God committed the Prince of Wisdom and the Prince of Understanding to Enoch "to teach him the wisdom of those above and of those below, the wisdom of this world and of the world to come." Sabaoth's chariot naturally recalls Ezekiel's Merkabah: for the expression, "a chariot of cherubim," compare 3 Enoch 24:1 and 22:11. The allusion in the gnostic text to choirs of angels is also easily paralleled in the Merkabah texts; see 3 Enoch 35–40.[45]

The second text which we shall compare with Merkabah mysticism is Origen's summary of the teachings of the gnostic "sect of the Ophians" in the *Contra Celsum* 6:24–38.[46] Origen's account is garbled but a number of points are reasonably clear. An important part of the Ophian teaching was concerned with the ascent of the soul to heaven after death (6:27). To reach its goal in the realm of the Father and the Son the soul had to pass through a "Barrier of Evil," which is defined as "the gates of the archons which are shut for ever" (6:31). There are seven archons controlling the gates; in ascending order they are: Horaeus, Aiolaeus, Astaphaeus, (Adonaeus), Sabaoth, Iao, and Ialdabaoth.[47] To persuade the archons to let him pass, the soul must address them by name, recite the correct formula, and show to each of them a "symbol" (*symbolon*). These symbols are perhaps to be connected with the "seal" (*sphragis*) which, according to 6:27, was bestowed by the Father on the "Youth and Son." Seals are certainly mentioned in the context of passage through the aeons in the Naassene hymn quoted by Hippolytus, *Refutation of All Heresies* 5.10.2. Having passed through the realms of the seven archons the soul reaches the eighth sphere—the Ogdoad (6:31), which is ruled over by a nameless being hailed as "first power." The soul would appear to have effectively reached its goal since the Ogdoad seems to lie within the realm of the Father and the Son: "From here on," announces the ascending soul, "I am sent forth pure, being already part of the light of the Son and the Father" (6:31). The Ogdoad, or eighth heaven, is mentioned elsewhere in the gnostic texts; see, for example, *The Hypostasis of the Archons* 95, 34 (Labib 143, 34).

This whole passage should be compared with the ascent to the Merkabah described in Hekalot Rabbati 17:1–20:3 (*BHM*, vol. 3, pp. 95–98). According to this text the adept on his ascent to the Merkabah must pass through seven doors (the doors of the heavenly palaces), each of them controlled by powerful angels (cf. 3En 18:3). To pass through the doors the adept must know the names of the doorkeepers, and he must show them the appropriate seals (cf. 3En 48D:5). The concept of the eighth heaven can also be matched in the Merkabah texts. Ogdoad is sometimes found in the gnostic texts as a name of the supreme power; Scholem has argued that its analogue in the Merkabah texts may be the divine name ʾAzbogah, which is made up of three sets of consonants each of which adds up by gematria to eight

---

[45] The account of the elevation of Sabāoth in the Untitled Work (NHC 2/5) provides some further points of comparison with the Merkabah texts (see 103, 32–106, 18; Labib 151, 32–154, 18). See Gruenwald, *Proceedings of the Sixth World Congress of Jewish Studies*, vol. 3, pp. 45f.

[46] Edited by P. Koetschau in GCS; translated by H. Chadwick, *Origen: Contra Celsum* (Cambridge, 1953); also in W. Foerster, *Gnosis: A Selection of Gnostic Texts* (Oxford, 1972) vol. 1, pp. 94–99.

[47] Origen curiously lists them in descending order. "Adonaeus" has accidentally dropped out of the text; see 6:32. It is to be supplied between Astaphaeus and Sabaoth following the suggestion of Bouhéreau (see Koetschau's *apparatus criticus*); cf. Chadwick, *Origen: Contra Celsum*, p. 348, n. 1.

(*Gnosticism*, pp. 65–71; cf. 3En 18:22). The name of the archon of the fourth aeon in the gnostic text is noteworthy; as Origen recognized, Iao is probably derived from a form of the tetragram YHWH. In the gnostic works *Pistis Sophia* and the *Book of Jeu* we encounter the "Great Iao" and the "Little Iao" (*Pistis Sophia*, chs. 7 [twice], 86, 140; *Book of Jeu*, ch. 50). These may correspond to the titles "greater YHWH" and "lesser YHWH" found in the Merkabah texts (3En 48B:1[44]; 48D:1[90]) (cf. Odeberg, *3 Enoch*, pt. 1, app. 2, pp. 188–92).[48]

It is far from clear how we are to explain these parallels between Merkabah mysticism and Gnosticism. Has Merkabah mysticism in its early stages influenced Gnosticism? Or have both systems drawn on a common ancestral tradition, such as Palestinian apocalyptic? Or has some third party, such as syncretistic magic, mediated between them and transferred ideas from one tradition to the other? In the present state of our knowledge it is impossible to say. We must be careful not to read too much into these parallels. There are important theological differences between Merkabah mysticism and Gnosticism which should not be ignored. In Gnosticism there is normally a sharp conflict between the good supreme power and the evil demiurge; there is no such opposition between God in his transcendence and God as he reveals himself on the throne of glory in the Merkabah texts. We should also note that in Gnosticism the ascent to heaven is made after death whereas in Merkabah mysticism it is made during life and can be repeated many times over. It must also be recognized that parallels to Merkabah mysticism can be found not only in Gnosticism but also in the Hermetic writings, the Chaldean Oracles, the magical papyri (such as the so-called "Great Magical Papyrus of Paris"),[49] and more remotely in Roman Mithraism and Neoplatonism. Even the paganism of late antiquity was closer to Merkabah ideas than we might at first suppose, for, as E. R. Dodds points out, there were many pious pagans who, by the second century A.D., had come to regard the gods of classical Greek mythology as "no more than mediating daemons, satraps of an invisible, supramundane King."[50]

When we consider Merkabah mysticism in the light of these non-Jewish religious world views of late antiquity we can see how completely it fits into the religious climate of its time. It is not a purely Jewish religious phenomenon, but has been shaped by forces generally at work in the political and social history of late antiquity. Identifying those forces is an extremely delicate task. E. R. Dodds suggested that the disturbed social, political, and economic conditions in the period from Marcus Aurelius to Constantine had a profound effect on the development of several of the religious world views to which we may compare Merkabah mysticism. He quotes with approval a dictum of Festugière: "Misery and mysticism are related facts."[51] To some degree Dodds may be right. It is interesting to note that the Merkabah texts themselves make the point that Merkabah mysticism was a source of comfort and reassurance in times of crisis and stress (Hekalot Rabbati 4:4–5, *BHM*, vol. 3, pp. 86f.; cf. BM, vol. 1, pp. 74f.; and Hekalot Rabbati 13, *BHM*, vol. 3, p. 93). But a simple correlation of misery and mysticism cannot represent the whole story; we must also account for the fact that Merkabah mysticism continued to flourish and develop not only in Palestine but also in Babylonia right down to the eighth or ninth century A.D.

If we focus our attention on the phenomenon of trance, which appears to have played a significant role in Merkabah mysticism, we may perhaps gain a deeper understanding of the sociological function of Maʿaśeh Merkabah. It is true that there is a significantly high incidence of trance phenomena in very poor societies, but here we must note a crucial difference. When trance correlates with poverty as a catharsis, it is usually a public business: for it to be effective large numbers must go into trance or participate closely in the trances of those who do. The Merkabah mystics, on the other hand, were apparently few in number,

---

[48] Scholem (*Gnosticism*, pp. 37f.) has suggested that there are close parallels between the Merkabah doctrine of Šiʿur Qomah and the gnostic thinker Marcus' description of the "Body of Truth"; see Irenaeus, *Adversus Haereses* 1.14.3 = Epiphanius, *Panarion* 34.5 (Foerster, *Gnosis*, vol. 1, p. 205).

[49] See M. Smith, "Observations on Hekhalot Rabbati" in *Biblical and Other Studies*, ed. A. Altmann (Cambridge, Mass., 1963) pp. 142–60.

[50] Dodds, *Pagan and Christian*, p. 38; see also p. 57. Further, M. P. Nilsson, "The New Conception of the Universe in Late Greek Paganism," *Eranos* 44 (1946) 20–27; M. P. Nilsson, "Das Weltbild in der spätantiken Religion," *Geschichte der Griechischen Religion* (Munich, 1961²) vol. 2, pp. 702–11.

[51] A. J. Festugière, "Cadre de la mystique hellénistique," *Aux sources de la tradition chretiénne: Mélanges offerts à Maurice Goguel* (Neuchâtel/Paris, 1950), pp. 74–85; Dodds, *Pagan and Christian*, pp. 100f.

and their trances occurred in small, closely guarded conventicles. Trance outside this setting was presumably regarded as demon possession. The fact that the Merkabah trances were confined to a small elite within society suggests that their modern analogue would be shamanistic trance. In shamanistic societies trance is confined to a few and it serves two purposes: First, it marks off the trance-subjects as special and distinctive within the group; and, second, it is an integral part of the role which these people play toward society. Merkabah trances may have had a similar function within rabbinic society. They bolstered the authority of the adepts, who were rabbis, and they marked them off as holy men, like the holy men of the surrounding religions. Knowledge of the Merkabah mysteries had great prestige value: It is described as "a great matter," greater than a mastery of the intricacies of halakah (see b.Sukk 28a; Midraš Mišle 10, ed. Buber, 34a). But trance phenomena were also closely related to the rabbis' role in society. The rabbi was no mere academic: He was a holy man who through his knowledge and his power could protect society from demonic attack; he had a mediatorial role between God and man; he prayed for rain in times of drought, and, because of his holiness, had an especially close relationship to God. The ability to ascend to heaven and to reach God's throne would have been regarded as facilitating his work. It may, then, have been the continuing importance of the rabbi in the Jewish community that kept Merkabah mysticism alive for so long.[52]

Theological importance

COSMOLOGY

Though cosmology is strictly a motif of Ma'aśeh Bere'šit, a certain number of cosmological motifs are to be found in the Ma'aśeh Merkabah texts. One function of this cosmological element in Ma'aśeh Merkabah appears to be to provide a definite location in the universe for God's throne and to bring it into spatial relationship to man on earth.

According to 3 Enoch 17:1–3 and 18:1–2 there are seven heavens above the earth. This tradition of seven heavens is almost universal in classic rabbinic literature (e.g. b.Hag 12b; cf. PRE 19), in the Merkabah texts (e.g. Masseket Hekalot 4, *BHM*, vol. 2, p. 42; Re'uyot Yehezqe'l, BM, vol. 2, p. 130; ed. Gruenwald, p. 115), and in texts of the Ma'aśeh Bere'šit tradition (e.g. Midraš Konen, *BHM*, vol. 2, p. 53; cf. Seder Rabbah diBere'šit, BM, vol. 1, p. 29; Baraita' diMa'aśeh Bere'šit, ed. Séd, A 72–123, 296–369; B 60–112, 263–304). However, other views are occasionally found. Thus Hagigah 12b records an opinion that there are only two heavens, while Midraš Tehillim 114:2 (ed. Buber, 236a) states that some held that there are three. Within the Merkabah tradition itself speculation arose as to the possibility of heavens beyond the seventh. An eighth was postulated on the basis of the reference in Ezekiel 1:22 to a firmament *above* the heads of the creatures (b.Hag 13a).[53] Most extreme was the view that there are 955 heavens above the seventh (3En 48A:1; Masseket Hekalot 7, *BHM*, vol. 2, p. 45).

In 3 Enoch 18 the heavens are merely enumerated ("first heaven," "second heaven," etc.); in chapter 17, however, they each carry a special name ('Arabot, Ma'on, etc.) (cf. 3En 38:1). These names are found in other texts, though there is some difference of opinion as to which name goes with which heaven (see b.Hag 12b; LevR 29:11; ARN A 37, ed. Schechter 55b; Re'uyot Yehezqe'l, BM, vol. 2, pp. 131–33; ed. Gruenwald, pp. 121–37; Yannai, Qerobot leSeper Bere'šit 5/8, 112–14, ed. Zulay, p. 15). 3 Enoch 17 agrees precisely with the list in Hagigah 12b, which is attributed there to the third-century Palestinian authority Resh Laqish.[54] The first heaven is called Wilon, the "Veil." It separates the lower and the upper worlds, and its opening and shutting may have been regarded as causing the alternation of light and darkness.[55]

---

[52] On the role of the rabbi see J. Neusner, "The Phenomenon of the Rabbi in Late Antiquity," *Numen* 16 (1969) 1–20.

[53] For a possible connection between the 8th heaven in the Merkabah texts and the gnostic Ogdoad see above on "Historical importance."

[54] See Gruenwald, *Tarbiṣ* 36 (1966/67) 269f.

[55] See 3En 17:3, n. f.

Further cosmological material is to be found in 3 Enoch as follows: (1) 17:4–7, a short astronomical passage in which the heavenly bodies are described as inert masses moved through the heavens by angels; (2) 14:3–4, a list of angels who control the elemental forces of the world (fire, rain, thunder, etc.); (3) 41:1–3, speculation on the letters by which the world was created; (4) 42:1–7, speculation on the power of divine names to hold in balance opposed elemental forces such as cold and heat.

THE HEAVENLY WORLD

In the seventh heaven stands God's abode—a series of seven palaces (hêkālôt) arranged concentrically (3En 18:3; cf. 1:1–2; 7; 37:1; Hekalot Rabbati 15–16, BHM, vol. 3, p. 94; Masseket Hekalot 4, BHM, vol. 2, p. 42). The word for palace, hêkāl (pl. hêkālôt), denotes both "palace" and "temple" and so has overtones both of royalty and of holiness. The motif of the seven hêkālôt is peculiar to the Merkabah tradition, though it is not found in all the Merkabah texts; thus it is notably absent from the early work Re'uyot Yeḥezqe'l. It does not appear overtly in Ḥagigah 11b–16a, though, as we noted above, there may be an allusion to it in Aqiba's reference to "the stones of pure marble" (14a). Analogous ideas to the seven hêkālôt occur in a number of places: Seper HaRazim speaks of seven heavenly dwellings (meʿônôt) (Petiḥah 6, ed. Margalioth, p. 65; 7:19, 25, ed. Margalioth, p. 108; cf. 3En 17:3), and Ḥagigah 13a of God's "inner houses" and "outer houses"; the description of God's heavenly abode in 1En 14:10–17 (cf. 1En 71:5–9) as a house within a house is strongly reminiscent of the language used in Merkabah literature to describe the seven palaces. The seven palaces are essentially an idea of Maʿaśeh Merkabah, that of the seven heavens probably arose from cosmological speculation; 3En 18, which combines the two ideas by locating the seven palaces in the seventh heaven, probably marks the confluence of two originally independent streams of tradition.

The centerpiece of the heavenly world is the Merkabah, which stands in the innermost of the seven palaces and bears the throne of glory (kissēʾ hakkābôd). The physical aspects of the Merkabah are not clearly visualized (though see 3En 25:5 and cf. 22:12 and 48C:4). The topography of heaven is in general sketched very impressionistically (see 3En 37) and the aim appears to be simply to create an atmosphere of awesome majesty. The whole enormous structure of the Merkabah is defined in terms of angelic hierarchies. There is a tendency to spiritualize its physical elements: Thus the 'opannim, "wheels," and the ḥašmal (JB, "bronze") of Ezekiel 1 become orders of angels in 3 Enoch (see e.g. ch. 7).

A curtain (pargôd) hangs before God's throne separating his immediate presence from the rest of the heavenly world. This curtain shields the angels from the full glare of the divine glory. It also symbolizes the ultimate inscrutability of God and of the mysteries known only to him. In 3 Enoch 45 Meṭaṭron shows Ishmael the whole course of human history, from Adam to the messianic age, embroidered on the curtain.[56]

Following Daniel 7:10 the Merkabah texts speak of a River of Fire that flows out from beneath the throne of glory (3En 36:1). Occasionally more than one River of Fire is mentioned (3En 19:4; 33:4; 37:1). The River of Fire functions in a number of contexts: It is used in accounts of the divine judgment as a symbol of the wrath of God (18:19, 21; 33:4–5); it also forms part of the descriptions of the celestial Sanctus: The angels bathe in the River of Fire before they perform the Qeduššah (36:2).[57] A development of this motif is the speculation on the bridges that span the River of Fire (22B:1, with n. b; 22C:1).

In the celestial palaces are many treasuries and storehouses. Some of these contain natural phenomena such as snow (22B:3, 4) and lightning (37:2). In others are "spiritual gifts" such as wisdom, peace, and "the fear of heaven" (48D:2, varia lectio; cf. 1:11; 8:1). There are also the archives (27:1), where the records of the heavenly law court are kept, and in 43:3 there is a reference to a storehouse of beings.

---

[56] See 3En 45:1, n. a. Cf. the heavenly veils in the gnostic texts, on which see above on "Historical importance"; cf. also Wilon, the first heaven. See further O. Hofius, Der Vorhang vor dem Thron Gottes, Wissenschaftliche Untersuchungen zum Neuen Testament 14 (Tübingen, 1972); Gruenwald, Proceedings of the Sixth World Congress of Jewish Studies, vol. 3, pp. 49–51; Bietenhard, Die himmlische Welt in Urchristentum und Spätjudentum, pp. 73f.

[57] See 3En 18:19, n. aa.

GOD

The basic assertion about God in 3 Enoch and in the other Merkabah texts is that he is transcendent. The divine attributes most persistently stressed, God's holiness and his glory, are conceived of as attributes of transcendence, expressing his "otherness." God's transcendence is stated in three main ways.

First, God is said to be spatially remote from man. This idea is implicit in the cosmology: God dwells in the seventh palace in the seventh heaven. It is a standard theme of the Merkabah texts that the distances between the different heavens are almost inconceivably vast; see Ḥagigah 13a; Masseket Hekalot 4 (*BHM*, vol. 2, p. 43); Reʾuyot Yeḥezqeʾl (BM, vol. 2, p. 131; ed. Gruenwald, p. 121). There are elements of this motif of the dimensions of the heavens in 3 Enoch 22C.

Second, God is represented as being well-nigh inaccessible to man. His throne stands in the innermost of the seven concentric palaces and the way to it is barred by fierce guardian angels at the gate of each palace. Not only the gatekeepers but the angels in general are opposed to man (3En 1:6–7; 2:2; 5:10; 6:2; 15B:2). The hostile angels form a protective circle round God's throne; in a sense they are hypostatizations of his holiness.[58]

Third, God's transcendence is expressed through the story in 3 Enoch 5:10–14 of the withdrawal of his Šekinah from the earth. The Šekinah is the divine presence which takes up its abode in a place or with a person or group of people. Where God is experienced as present, there his Šekinah is said to dwell. 3 Enoch pictures the Šekinah in very concrete terms: It is a bright light, a luminous cloud, like the cloud that manifested God's presence in the Temple and the Tabernacle (1Kgs 8:10; Lev 16:2; cf. NumR 12:4; SongR 3:8). According to 3 Enoch 5:1–14, after Adam was expelled from Eden, the Šekinah remained on earth, but since the generation of Enosh (the third in line from Adam) it has been residing in the highest heaven.[59]

The Merkabah mystics were greatly exercised by the problem of who (or what) occupies the throne of glory, and how he (or it) should be represented. According to 3 Enoch it is the Šekinah that dwells on the throne (see e.g. 18:19, 24; 22:13, 16; 24:15; 28:2; 37:1; 39:1). However, we gather this fact only in passing, for 3 Enoch shrinks from dwelling on the appearance on the throne. This reticence contrasts sharply with the detailed descriptions which it offers of the higher orders of angels, and it rather sets 3 Enoch off from the Šiʿur Qomah strand of the mystical tradition. In Šiʿur Qomah a form is given to the divine glory: It is envisaged as a colossal human figure and the dimensions of its limbs are computed. Of this speculation there is hardly a trace in 3 Enoch.[60]

The Merkabah texts represent God and his angels under the image of an emperor and his court. God has his heavenly palace, his throne, and, in Meṭaṭron, his grand vizier; he has also his treasuries and storehouses. The image of God as the heavenly king is by no means an innovation of the Merkabah texts, but it is possible that the heavenly court of 3 Enoch reflects something of the earthly courts of its time. Noteworthy is the designation of the angelic hosts as "the heavenly household" (*pamalyaʾ šelemaʿalāh*: 3En 18:21; cf. 12:5; 16:1). This would appear to be an allusion to the *familia Caesaris*, the body of imperial slaves and

---

[58] On angelic opposition to man see A. Marmorstein, "Controversies Between the Angels and the Creator," *Melilah* 3–4 (1950) 93–102 (in Heb.); J. P. Schultz, "Angelic Opposition to the Ascension of Moses and the Revelation of the Law," *JQR* 61 (1970/71) 282–307; P. Schäfer, *Rivalität zwischen Engeln und Menschen: Untersuchungen zur rabbinischen Engelvorstellung* (Berlin, 1975); P. Schäfer, "The Rivalry Between Angels and Men in the *Prayer of Joseph* and Rabbinic Literature" (in Heb.), *Proceedings of the Sixth World Congress of Jewish Studies* (Jerusalem, 1973) vol. 3, pp. 511–15.

[59] The problem of divine immanence and transcendence in early Jewish religious thought is highly complex: for discussion see Urbach, *The Sages*, vol. 1, pp. 37–79; A. M. Goldberg, *Untersuchungen über die Vorstellung von der Schekinah in der frühen rabbinischen Literatur*, Studia Judaica 5 (Berlin, 1969).

[60] For Šiʿur Qomah texts see below on "Relation to Earlier Pseudepigrapha, Dead Sea Scrolls, and Merkabah Literature." Note also the very short passages in Hekalot Rabbati 12 (BM, vol. 1, p. 87) and Midraš Mišle 10 (ed. Buber, 34a). For studies see M. Gaster, "Das Schiur Komah," *Studies and Texts* (London, 1925–28) vol. 2, pp. 1330–53; A. Altmann, "Moses Narboni's 'Epistle on Shiʿur Qomah,'" *Jewish Mediaeval and Renaissance Studies*, ed. A. Altmann (Cambridge, Mass., 1967) pp. 225–88; R. Loewe, "The Divine Garment and Shiʿur Qomah," *HTR* 58 (1965) 153–60; Scholem, *Gnosticism*, pp. 36–42; Scholem, "Shiʿur Komah," *EncyJud* 14, cols. 1417–19; Scholem, *Von der mystischen Gestalt der Gottheit* (Zurich, 1962) pp. 7–47; Lieberman, *Shkiin*, pp. 11–14, 98f.

freedmen who formed the Roman civil service; the angels are God's imperial executive. The organization of the heavenly world in the Merkabah texts may reflect the image of an absolute monarchy with a complex bureaucracy; the emperor was only to be approached through intermediaries or with elaborate protocols. Perhaps this picture corresponds best to the image cast by the monarchy in the Byzantine era.[61]

THE HEAVENLY HOUSEHOLD

Although the angels play a central role in Merkabah mysticism, there is no uniform angelology in the Merkabah texts. Even within 3 Enoch itself we find three different angelologies incorporated more or less intact (ch. 17; ch. 18; chs. 19–22 and 25:1–28:6), and fragments of several other systems as well.

3 Enoch agrees with the standard rabbinic view that angels are of a fiery substance (chs. 7 and 15). The higher angels at least have human form: They are pictured as huge warriors armed with swords and bows; see 3 Enoch 22 and the vivid descriptions in Masseket Hekalot 4 (*BHM*, vol. 2, p. 42) and Hekalot Rabbati 15:8–16:2 (*BHM*, vol. 3, pp. 74f.) and 20:3 (p. 98); compare Seper HaRazim 2:14–16 (ed. Margalioth, p. 82) and 2:131–33 (ed. Margalioth, p. 88). In 3 Enoch 47:2f. the analogy with humankind is taken to the extent of seeing angels as composed both of "body" and "soul."

The countless myriads of angels are grouped into classes and the classes ordered into hierarchies. The angelology of 3 Enoch 19–22, 25:1–28:6 has the following grades (in ascending order of rank): common angels (*mešāretîm, maPākJm*, etc.), galgallim, creatures (*ḥayyot*), cherubim, ophanim, seraphim, Watchers and holy ones (*ʿirin* and *qaddišin*). Other angelic classes are mentioned elsewhere: ḥašmallim and šin'anim (ch. 7); 'elim, 'erʾellim, and ṭapsarim (14:1); and 'elohim (15B:1, n. c).[62]

Merkabah mysticism is greatly interested in the names of the angels. This interest was partly theurgical: To know the angels' names was to have the power to invoke them (see e.g. Hekalot Rabbati 14:4, *BHM*, vol. 3, p. 94). Merkabah texts are replete with angelic names. These are of various kinds: (1) Some, such as Michael and Gabriel, are biblical and traditional. Others are formed on the analogy of these and consist of a stem element and *ʾēl*, "God." In many cases the stem contains an allusion to the function of the angel who bears the name; Baraqi'el is the angel of lightning, *bārāq* (3En 14:4). In other cases, however, the stem does not appear to have any meaning. Some names are compounded with *yah*, "Lord," e.g. Suryah. (2) Another group comprises names constructed by using techniques of letter and number magic such as gematria, temurah, and notarikon. A case in point is 'Azbogah (3En 18:22). This name is made up of three pairs of consonants, each of which adds up by gematria to eight. (3) Some of the names may be corruptions of foreign words, particularly Greek. (4) Some may have originated as glossolalia.

There are a number of important angelic offices mentioned in the Merkabah texts. Different angels fill these offices in different traditions, but the offices themselves remain constant.

1. Prince of the Divine Presence (*Śar happānîm*): an angel who has the privilege of serving in God's immediate presence; see 3 Enoch 8:1; 48C:7; Hekalot Rabbati 11:1 (*BHM*, vol. 3, p. 91). It is possible that the idea of the Prince of the Divine Presence may be connected with that of the curtain: note Masseket Hekalot 7 (*BHM*, vol. 2, p. 46). 3 Enoch frequently calls Meṭaṭron Prince of the Divine Presence, but others, such as Suryah in Hekalot Rabbati 14:4 (*BHM*, vol. 3, p. 94), also bear the title. It is probable that the title is derived from Isaiah 63:9: "In all their affliction he was afflicted, and the angel of his presence [*maPak pānāyw*] saved them"; cf. Tobit 12:15; Jubilees 1:27; Hekalot Rabbati 3:3 (*BHM*, vol. 3, p. 85); Cairo Genizah Hekalot B/1, 36 (ed. Gruenwald, p. 369). Note also

---

[61] However, it should be borne in mind that it is very hard, first, to establish how the Byzantine ideology of kingship worked itself out in practice, and, second, to discover what image the monarchy would have cast in the minds of its subjects. As a Christian example of the correlation of the emperor and his court with God and his angels we may take the Byzantine mosaic from the Church of the Assumption, Nicâea, Turkey, which shows the archangels in the garb of court officials carrying military standards inscribed with the Sanctus; see further Louis Réau, *Iconographie de l'art chrétien*, vol. 2.1 (Paris, 1965) p. 35.

[62] Maimonides, *Yad. Yesode Torah* 2:7, lists ten orders of angels. In ascending order of rank they are: ḥayyot, ophanim, 'er'ellim, ḥašmallim, seraphim, mal'akim, 'elohim, bene 'elohim, cherubim, 'išim. The Zohar, Masseket 'Aṣilut, and Berit Menuḥah all have different systems, but the number ten remains constant. Christian writers, following Dionysius the Areopagite's Celestial Hierarchies, usually have nine orders; see Dante, *Paradiso*, Canto 28.

Esther 1:14, which refers to the seven princes (*śārîm*) of Persia and Media "who saw the king's face."

2. Prince of Torah (*Śar Tôrāh*): an angel who can help one to understand Torah (particularly its deeper, mystical aspects), and can prevent one from forgetting what one has learned (Hekalot Rabbati 30:2, *BHM*, vol. 3, p. 107; Ma'aśeh Merkabah 13, ed. Scholem, p. 109). In 3 Enoch 48D:4 the Prince of Torah is called Yepipyah. He is shown there in a typical role, assisting Moses to remember the Law he received on Sinai. Variations on the title Prince of Torah are "Prince of Learning" (*Śar Talmûd*) (Cairo Genizah Hekalot B/1, 20, ed. Gruenwald, p. 369) and "Prince of Wisdom" (*Śar ḥokmāh*) (3En 10:5; 48D:1[93]). Cairo Genizah Hekalot B/1, 37 (ed. Gruenwald, p. 369) speaks of "Princes of Torah" (*Śārê Tôrāh*).

3. Princes of kingdoms (*Śārê malkuyyôt*). Developing the thought of Daniel 10:20–21, 3 Enoch assigns to each nation on earth its angelic representative in heaven (cf. 1En 89:59), who speaks on its behalf in the heavenly law court (3En 30; cf. 17:8). The only princes of kingdoms to emerge in 3 Enoch as individuals are Samma'el, the Prince of Rome, Dubbi'el, the Prince of Persia (26:12), and Michael, the Prince of Israel (44:10).

4. Prince of the World (*Śar hā'ôlām*): an angel, distinct from the princes of kingdoms, who is in charge of the world as a whole. He is mentioned in rabbinic texts, but is a rather nebulous figure (b.Yeb 16b; b.Ḥull 60a; b.Sanh 94a; ExR 17:4). 3 Enoch 30:2 states that he has authority over the princes of kingdoms and he pleads for the world at the heavenly assize. In 3 Enoch 38:3 he appears to be the ruler of the heavenly bodies. He is not clearly identified in 3 Enoch. Metatron fulfills some of his functions (3:2; 10:3), and in later texts is equated with him explicitly (Tosapot to Yeb 16b and to Ḥull 60a). Some circles regarded Michael as the Prince of the World (PRE 27; cf. Yalquṭ Sim'oni Gen 132). The Prince of the World in the Merkabah texts is not an evil figure as in John 12:31 and 16:11.

5. The guardians of the doors (*Śômerê happetāḥîm*): angels who guard the gates of the seven palaces. Hekalot Rabbati 22:1 (*BHM*, vol. 3, p. 99) states that there are eight at each gate, and each group has its leader. In 3 Enoch 18:3, in contrast to Hekalot Rabbati, the gatekeepers are not given names; 3 Enoch 1:3, however, alludes to the chief of the gatekeepers of the seventh palace, Prince Qaspi'el. Cairo Genizah Hekalot A/1, 35 (ed. Gruenwald, p. 359) refers to "guardians of the palaces" (*Śômerê hêkālôt*), which is presumably a variant of "guardians of the doors."

By far the most significant angel in 3 Enoch is Metatron. Metatron's position in the heavenly world is briefly and accurately summed up in the title "The lesser YHWH" (3En 12:5; 48C:7; 48D:1[90]); he is the highest of the archangels and God's vice-regent (3En 10:3–6). Like the Holy One himself, he has a throne and presides over a celestial law court (3En 16:1).

There has been a great deal of speculation about the meaning of the name Metatron. The name actually occurs in two forms, Mṭṭrwn and Myṭṭrwn. Various etymologies for it have been suggested. The more plausible are as follows: (1) Latin *metator*: This word originally designated the officer who went ahead of the army to prepare its camp, but it was then used generally of anyone who prepares the way. In favor of this explanation is the fact that *metator* is clearly attested as a loanword in Hebrew and Jewish Aramaic.[63] (2) Greek *metaturannos* = "the one next to the ruler," i.e. next to God, or, assuming this is equivalent to *sunthronos*, "the one enthroned with (God)." (3) Greek (*ho*) *meta thronon* = "(the throne) next to the (divine) throne," "the second throne." None of the etymologies suggested is really satisfactory. It should be remembered that an angelic name such as Metatron does not necessarily have an etymology; it could be gibberish, like the magical names 'Adiriron and Dapdapiron.

Metatron in 3 Enoch is a complex figure with a long history behind him. It is possible to trace some of the stages of his development. Metatron is, in a number of respects, similar to the archangel Michael: Both angels were known as "the Great Prince"; both were said to serve in the heavenly sanctuary; both were guardian angels of Israel; what is said in one text about Michael is said in another about Metatron.[64] A possible explanation of these

---

[63] See n. 11 above. On the uses of *metator* in Lat. and Gk. see Milik, *The Books of Enoch*, pp. 131–33.
[64] See Ginzberg, *Legends*, vol. 5, p. 20, n. 91; p. 170, n. 10; p. 305, n. 248; vol. 6 (1928), p. 74, n. 381; Lieberman, *Shkiin*, pp. 11–15, 99f.; Alexander, *JJS* 28 (1977) 162f.

similarities would be that originally Meṭaṭron and Michael were one and the same angel: Michael was the angel's common name, Meṭaṭron one of his esoteric, magical names.[65] At some point, however, the connection between Meṭaṭron and Michael was obscured, and a new, independent archangel with many of Michael's powers came into being. The connection may not have been entirely lost, for we find that in some late texts the identity of the two angels is asserted: see e.g. Seper Zerubbabel, BM, vol. 2, p. 498 (the text in *BHM*, vol. 2, p. 55, is slightly different).

Meṭaṭron was merged with two other heavenly figures, (1) the archangel Yaho'el, and (2) translated Enoch. Meṭaṭron bears the name Yaho'el in 3 Enoch 48D:1(1). From other texts, however, we know of an angel Yaho'el quite independent of Meṭaṭron (Seper HaRazim 2:38, ed. Margalioth, p. 83; 2:140, ed. Margalioth, p. 89; Ma'aśeh Merkabah 20, ed. Scholem, p. 111, l. 29; Slavonic LAE 32:1f.; ApMos 43:4; and especially Slavonic ApAb 10). The archangel Yaho'el probably originated in speculation about the angel in whom God's name resides, according to Exodus 23:20f. (note in this connection ApAb 10). In 3 Enoch 12:5 and Sanhedrin 38b the angel of Exodus 23:20 is identified as Meṭaṭron. The title "lesser YHWH" (3En 12:5) may have belonged originally to Yaho'el; it certainly seems to be attested independently of Meṭaṭron in gnostic texts.

Meṭaṭron's absorption of translated Enoch could only have taken place in circles acquainted with the Palestinian apocalyptic Enoch traditions. The apocalyptic texts do not seem to go so far as to say that Enoch was transformed into an archangel when he was translated into heaven, but some of them speak of his exaltation in language which could be taken to imply this (see esp. 2En 22:8).

There were evidently mystics who laid great store by Meṭaṭron. It is not hard to see why he attracted them. He was a human being who had been elevated over all the angels, and was living proof that man could overcome angelic opposition and approach God. He was a powerful "friend at court." The transformation of Enoch in 3 Enoch 15 may reflect something of the experiences of the mystics themselves as they ascended to behold the Merkabah. Others, of more orthodox leanings, were not enamored of Meṭaṭron and considered that the powers ascribed to him bordered on dualism (b.Sanh 38b; b.Ḥag 15a). There are traces of criticism of the doctrine of Meṭaṭron in 3 Enoch 16 and 10:3.[66]

THE ACTIVITIES OF THE HEAVENLY WORLD

The heavenly law court
Building on such biblical texts as 1 Kings 22:19–22, Psalm 82; Job 1:6–12, and especially Daniel 7:9f., the rabbis taught that there is a heavenly law court (*bêt dîn šelema'alāh* or *pamalyā' šelema'alāh*, in its narrower sense) over which God presides (b.Sanh 38b; ExR 30:18; LevR 24:2). It was regarded as the heavenly counterpart of the earthly Sanhedrin (b.Sanh 99b; b.Ber 16b/17a), and there was earnest discussion as to the relative jurisdictions of the two courts (b.Makk 23b; Pesiqta' deRab Kahana 5:13, ed. Buber, 48a; cf. DeutR 5:5; GenR 26:6). The heavenly law court is one of the main themes of 3 Enoch, and its sessions are covered in detail. There are three main blocks of material: (1) 28:7–10; 30:1–33:2; (2) 26:12; and (3) 18:19–21. It is characteristic of 3 Enoch that the heavenly assize is not the eschatological last judgment, after the resurrection of the dead (cf. b.Sanh 91b; LevR 4:5), but a judgment that takes place daily (3En 28:7, 9; 26:12; cf. GenR 50:3). According to 3 Enoch 30:1f. the court is made up of seventy-two princes of kingdoms and the Prince of the

[65] Scholem, *Gnosticism*, p. 46, suggests that evidence of this is to be found in Re'uyot Yeḥezqe'l, BM, vol. 2, p. 132 (ed. Gruenwald, pp. 128f.): "The Prince dwells nowhere but in Zebul [the 3rd heaven] . . . And what is his name? . . . Miṭaṭron, like the name of the Power." He suggests the "Prince" here is Michael on the grounds that Michael is called "the great prince" in Dan 12:1; cf. b.Ḥag 12b; b.Men 110a; b.Zeb 62a. For strong arguments to the contrary see Gruenwald's note in *Temirin* 1 (1972) 128.

[66] On Meṭaṭron see Odeberg, *3 Enoch*, pt. 1, pp. 79–146; Scholem, *Gnosticism*, pp. 42–55; Scholem, "Metatron," *EncyJud* 11, cols. 1443–46; R. Margalioth, *Mal'ake 'Elyon* (Jerusalem, 1945) pp. 73–108; Bietenhard, *Die himmlische Welt im Urchristentum und Spätjudentum*, pp. 143–60; M. Black, "The Origin of the Name Metatron," *VT* 1 (1951) 217–19; A. Murtonen, "The Figure of Metatron," *VT* 3 (1953) 409–11; Urbach, *The Sages*, vol. 1, pp. 138f.; Alexander, *JSS* 28 (1977) 159–65. Lieberman, "Metatron, the Meaning of His Name and His Functions," in I. Gruenwald, *Apocalyptic and Merkavah Mysticism*, pp. 235–41.

World. Satan and his two representatives, Samma'el, the Prince of Rome, and Dubbi'el, the Prince of Persia, appear as the accusers in 26:12.

The heavenly academy

3 Enoch 18:15f. contains a passing reference to the rabbinic idea that Torah is studied in heaven in the heavenly academy (*yešîbāh šelemaʿalāh*), just as it is studied in the academies on earth (b.BM 86a; b.Giṭṭ 68a; b.Taʿan 21b; cf. b.Ber 64a).

The celestial Qeduššah

3 Enoch represents the celebration of God's holiness through the recitation of the Qeduššah (the Sanctus) as the central act of heavenly worship. 3 Enoch 35–40 is devoted entirely to this subject. The celestial Qeduššah takes a number of different forms in 3 Enoch: see (1) 22B:8; (2) 1:12; 20:2; (3) 39:1–2; 48B:2.

There is a marked absence in 3 Enoch of Merkabah hymns, which are such a striking feature of some Merkabah texts (e.g. Hekalot Rabbati and Maʿaśeh Merkabah). The only heavenly hymns in 3 Enoch are, like the Qeduššah, traditional and biblical. As we have already noted, the Merkabah hymns had a theurgical use and their total absence from 3 Enoch may point to an anti-theurgical tendency in the final redaction of this work.

MAN

3 Enoch is interested in the human soul, its origin, and its fate after death (see esp. 43:1–44:7). Men are divided into three classes—the righteous, the intermediate, and the wicked (cf. b.RH 16b/17a; b.Shab 152b; t.Sanh 13:3). The souls of the righteous ascend to the throne of glory after death and there enjoy God's presence: according to 3 Enoch 43:2 they fly above the throne; in Sanhedrin 152b they are stored in treasuries beneath the throne. The intermediate are purified in the purgatorial fires of Sheol and then, presumably, allowed to join the righteous above. The wicked are consigned to the flames of Gehinnom (3En 44:3). 3 Enoch is silent as to their ultimate fate, and the point was much disputed among the rabbis. Many regarded their punishment as of limited duration; after a brief period they would be annihilated (b.RH 17a; cf. m.ʿEduy 2:10; b.Shab 33b; LamR 1:40). Some taught, however, that certain types of sinners would be punished eternally (b.RH 17a).

3 Enoch is not explicit as to when the division into classes takes place. Two views are given in Rosh Hashanah 16b/17a: According to the one it takes place at a heavenly assize held on each New Year's Day (cf. m.RH 1:2; t.RH 2:11–13); according to the other it is done at the final day of judgment, when the dead are raised (b.RH 17a, with Tosapot *leyôm*). 3 Enoch has no interest in the last judgment, so it is probable that its view is that the division into classes takes place at the judgment which each man undergoes immediately after death. (For a fanciful description of this "judgment of the grave" see Masseket ḥibbuṭ haqqeber, *BHM*, vol. 1, pp. 151f.; cf. also *BHM*, vol. 5, pp. 49–51.) This is the judgment spoken of in 3 Enoch 31:2.

According to 3 Enoch the human soul not only survives the body, and, at least in the case of the righteous, goes up to the heavenly regions, but it pre-exists the body as well, and descends from the heavenly storehouse of souls to enter the body at birth (3En 43:3; cf. b.Yeb 62a and parallels: 63b, b.AZ 5a; b.Nidd 13b; GenR 24:4; LevR 15:1; further b.Ḥag 12b). Unborn souls have done no wrong and so may be classified loosely as "righteous" (3En 43:1). Some rabbis went so far as to hold that the soul was intrinsically pure (see b.Ber 10a; LevR 4:8; Tanḥuma', ed. Buber, vol. 3 [*Wayyiqra'*], 4a/b). The stress in 3 Enoch is on the idea of immortality; typically there is no reference to the eschatological notion of the resurrection of the dead.

Relation to the canonical books

OLD TESTAMENT

The mystics were steeped in the Bible and their picture of the heavenly world was formed by harmonizing the Old Testament references to (1) theophanies, (2) angels, and (3) ascensions to heaven.

1. *Theophanies:* The visions of the Merkabah in Ezekiel 1; 3:12–15, 22–24; 8:1–4; 10:1–22; and 43:1–7 were their basic texts. These provided them with such fundamental elements as the Merkabah (3En 1:1, 5–7); the wheels (ophanim; 3En 25); the four creatures (*ḥayyot*; 3En 20f.); the throne of glory (3En 1:10, 12); the *ḥašmal* (3En 36:2, 7); the cherubim (3En 22). Daniel 7:9–10 and Isaiah 6 were incorporated into Ezekiel's picture. Daniel 7 records a vision of God seated on a fiery throne which has wheels of flame. It furnishes the additional motifs of the heavenly law court (3En 28:7), the River of Fire (3En 18:19–21; 19:4; 33:4; 36:1–2; 37:1), and the hosts of attendant angels (cf. 3En 19:6). Isaiah 6 contains a vision of God seated on a high and exalted throne (cf. 3En 26:12). Isaiah 6 contributes to the total picture the seraphim (3En 26) and the Qeduššah (3En 1:12; 20:2). Note also the vision of heaven in 1 Kings 22:19–22, in which the Lord is seen seated on his throne with all the array of heaven standing before him. Ezekiel employs the language of the nature theophanies ("fire, lightning, storm") to express the appearance of God's glory. The Merkabah texts expand this imagery by drawing on other Old Testament accounts of nature theophanies, particularly God's appearance to Israel at Sinai (Ex 19:16–18; cf. 1Kgs 19:11–13; Pss 18:7–15 and 97:2–5). For combinations of these elements see 3 Enoch 34 and 37.

2. *Angels*: Such Old Testament phrases as "the host of heaven" (1Kgs 22:19) and "the host of the height" (Isa 24:31) suggest that the number of the angels is virtually infinite (cf. 3En 19:6). The Old Testament appplies various names to the angels: seraphim (Isa 6:2, 6); cherubim (Ezek 10); creatures (*ḥayyot*) (Ezek 1); Watchers and holy ones (*'irin* and *qaddišin*) (Dan 4:14). 3 Enoch takes these names as designations of different orders of angels (3En 19–22; 25–28:6). The angels are represented in Genesis 19:1f. and Daniel 8:15f. as having human form, and in Joshua 5:13; Numbers 22:23; and 1 Chronicles 21:16, 30 as being armed with weapons; cf. 3 Enoch 22:3–9. The powerful "angel of the Lord" in the Old Testament (who is sometimes hard to distinguish from God himself) may be the prototype of 3 Enoch's Meṭaṭron (cf. Ex 23:20–23 with Judg 2:1–5, and see 3En 12:5 and b.Sanh 38b).

3. *Ascensions to Heaven*: The most obvious case in the Bible of someone ascending to heaven is Elijah (2Kgs 2:11). Following a very old tradition 3 Enoch states that Enoch also was translated. Genesis 5:24 is ambiguous on this point, but the occurrence there and in 2 Kings 2:9 of the Hebrew verb *lāqaḥ* ("to take")[67] was used in rabbinic exegesis to show that Enoch departed in the same manner as Elijah. Note how 3 Enoch 6:1 describes Enoch's translation to heaven in the same terms as the Bible uses of Elijah's ascent.

THE NEW TESTAMENT

In view of the date of its final redaction there can be no possibility of 3 Enoch as a work having directly influenced the New Testament. However, it and the other Merkabah texts throw light on certain aspects of the New Testament.

1. *The Colossian "Heresy"*: The ideas of the Merkabah mystics provide some interesting parallels to the Colossian "heresy." The Colossian "heretics" stressed the role of angels as mediators between God and man (Col 2:8, 18; cf. Col 1:13–20 and 2:15) and visions played an important part in their religious life (Col 2:18). At the same time they appear to have had a legalistic strand to their teaching: They enjoined the observance of religious festivals, new moons and sabbaths, and the Jewish dietary laws (Col 2:16, 21); they may also have demanded circumcision from converts (cf. Col 2:11). New Testament scholars have described the Colossian "heresy" vaguely as "gnosticizing Judaism," or as "syncretistic Judaism," or have attempted to link it with Qumran and Essenes. They appear to be agreed that (despite its legalistic side) it cannot be linked with the Pharisaic movement. However, the Merkabah texts make it clear that these ideas can exist side by side with strict Torah-observant Judaism.

2. *Paul in Paradise*: According to 2 Corinthians 12:1–7 Paul himself experienced ascent to heaven. He describes it as being "caught up to the third heaven" and as being "caught up to paradise." The term "paradise" here recalls the expression "to enter Pardes," which was used early on in the Merkabah movement to designate the mystical ascent. Like the Merkabah mystics Paul is reluctant to speak of his experiences, though his reticence may

---

[67] On this verb see the references in n. 4.

be rather stronger than theirs; the words he heard in heaven were "so secret that human lips may not repeat them" (2Cor 12:4, NEB). Paul speaks of his ascension as "visions and revelations of the Lord" (2Cor 12:1). The genitive here may be objective: Just as the Merkabah mystics saw God enthroned at the climax of their ecstasy, so Paul may have seen Christ enthroned. However, certain differences between 2 Corinthians 12:1–7 and the Merkabah texts should be noted. Paul's cosmology may allow only for three heavens, as against seven in Merkabah mysticism, while his use of the verb "to be caught up" (*harpazesthai*) suggests involuntary rapture in contrast to the Merkabah mystics' use of trance-inducing techniques.

3. *The Book of Revelation*: The Book of Revelation is basically an apocalypse (a vision of the end-time) but it does contain material related to Ma'aśeh Merkabah. The description of God's throne in Revelation 4 harmonizes elements from Ezekiel 1, Daniel 7, and Isaiah 6, just as the Merkabah texts do. The heavenly hymns in Revelation form, perhaps, the most interesting link with the Merkabah texts. Their repetition of emotive words such as "praise," "honor," "glory," "might," "power," and "wealth" are rather reminiscent of some of the Merkabah hymns. See especially Revelation 4:11; 5:12, 13; 7:12; 15:3f.

4. *God's "House" and "Family"*: The reference in John 14:1 to God's "house" with its many "rooms" recalls the Merkabah traditions about God's heavenly "palaces" and "dwellings" with their many "chambers" (see 3En 1:1, n. d). Ephesians 3:14 appears to imply that there are "families" in heaven as well as on earth. This idea may be illuminated by the Merkabah designation of the angels as "the celestial family" (*pamalyā' šelema'alāh*), in contrast to God's "earthly family" (*pamalyā' šelemaṭṭāh*), Israel. The Merkabah texts also speak of "families" of angels (see 12:5, n. f).

Relation to earlier pseudepigrapha, Dead Sea Scrolls, and Merkabah literature

PSEUDEPIGRAPHA

The close links between the Merkabah literature and the Pseudepigrapha may be illustrated from five apocalyptic texts: 1 Enoch, 2 Enoch, Testament of Levi, Ascension of Isaiah 6–11, and Apocalypse of Abraham 15–29. The last two of these works (both dating probably from the second century A.D.) in certain respects form a bridge between apocalyptic and the Merkabah texts.

1 Enoch

1 Enoch has the same kind of complex angelology as we find in Merkabah mysticism; note, for example, the different orders of angels listed in 1 Enoch 61:10–12. 1 Enoch 20 mentions seven archangels: Uriel, Raphael, Raguel, Michael, Saraqael, Gabriel, and Remiel; cf. the angels of the seven heavens in 3 Enoch 17. There is a fair number of angelic names in 1 Enoch; besides the archangels just mentioned, note the list of fallen angels in 1 Enoch 6:7: Kokab'el (4QEnª 1 iii, 1. 7), Baraq'el (4QEnª 1 iii, 1. 8), Ziqi'el (4QEnᶜ 1 ii, 1. 26), etc. (cf. 1En 8:3; 69:2). Angelic names of precisely this type are well attested in the Merkabah texts: Ziqi'el occurs in 3 Enoch 14:4; compare further 1 Enoch's Kokab'el and Baraq'el with the slightly different forms in 3 Enoch—Kokabi'el (3En 14:4; 17:7) and Baraqi'el (3En 14:4). There are two Merkabah passages in 1 Enoch, viz. 14:8–25 and 71:5–11; the latter appears to be dependent on the former, which draws on Ezekiel 1 and 10, Isaiah 6, and Daniel 7:9f. Particularly interesting is the reference to the two heavenly houses, one apparently inside the other, with God's throne standing in the inner one. This is probably an anticipation of the idea of the seven concentric heavenly palaces which we find in the Merkabah texts (3En 1:1–2). 1 Enoch's treatment of the final translation of Enoch is also noteworthy (see chs. 70f): Enoch is exalted to the heaven of heavens and by some mysterious process ends up as the Son of Man (1En 71:14). This may perhaps be compared with the metamorphosis of Enoch into the archangel Meṭaṭron in 3 Enoch 3–15.

2 Enoch

2 Enoch is in some ways even closer to 3 Enoch than is 1 Enoch. Its basic scheme is as follows: Under the protection of two heavenly guides Enoch passes through the seven heavens and views the contents of each heaven. He comes to God's throne, is transformed (by being

stripped of his earthly garments and anointed with holy oil), and then is brought by the archangel Michael before God's face (2En 22). He is instructed by the archangels Vreveil and Gabriel about various subjects, particularly the workings of nature and the story of creation. The cosmology of the seven heavens found in 2 Enoch is fundamental to the Merkabah texts. The description of the contents of the seven heavens is also a standard Merkabah motif (cf. Re'uyot Yeḥezqe'l, BM, vol. 2, p. 131; ed. Gruenwald, p. 121; Seper HaRazim; b.Ḥag 12b). Enoch's ascent through the seven heavens to God's throne, where he receives instruction from the archangels in various mysteries, is parallel to Ishmael's journey in 3 Enoch. The transformation of Enoch in 2 Enoch 22 provides the closest approximation, outside Merkabah literature, to Enoch's transformation in 3 Enoch 3–15.

Testament of Levi

The Testament of Levi 2:6–5:3 tells of how Levi ascended through the heavens to the "throne of glory," where he received his priestly commissioning from God (5:1–2) and learned mysteries which he was to declare to men (2:10). Levi's heavenly journey was made under the protection of an angelic guide whom he questions about the wonders that he sees (2:8–9). Among the many motifs in this account which can be paralleled in the Merkabah texts, the following are particularly noteworthy:

The title of God, "The Great Glory" (3:4), is found in its Aramaic equivalent Ziwa' Rabba' as a title of Meṭaṭron in 3 Enoch 48D:1(88).

The designation of God's heavenly throne as the "throne of glory" (TLevi 5:1, following the text-witnesses beta, A[efg] and S in Charles's edition) is found very frequently in the Merkabah texts; see e.g. 3 Enoch 1:6.

The "Angels of the Presence of the Lord" in Testament of Levi 2:5–7 should be compared with the "Princes of the Divine Presence" in the Merkabah texts (e.g. 3En 8:1).

With the allusion to the heavenly choirs in Testament of Levi 3:8, cf. 3 Enoch 35f.

The "gates of heaven" in Testament of Levi 5:1 (4QTLevi arᵃ 2:18, tr'y šmy') recall the "gates" (petāḥîm / še'ārîm) of the heavenly palaces (hêkālôt) in the Merkabah texts (3En 1:2; Hekalot Rabbati 17:1, BHM, vol. 3, p. 95).

There is perhaps an allusion to the treasuries of fire, ice, and snow in Testament of Levi 3:2; cf. 3 Enoch 22B: 3, 4; 37:2.

The motif of the sea suspended in the first heaven, Testament of Levi 2:7, occurs again in Re'uyot Yeḥezqe'l (BM, vol. 2, p. 131; ed. Gruenwald, p. 123).

Ascension of Isaiah

The structure of Ascension of Isaiah 6–11 is very similar to that of 2 Enoch and Testament of Levi 2–5: Isaiah is conducted by a heavenly guide through the seven heavens to God's throne, where he receives the revelation of a mystery. Several details call for comment.

In each heaven, except the sixth, Isaiah sees a throne, with angels to its right and to its left, and "one sitting on the throne" (see e.g. AscenIs 7:18–20). These thrones may represent the angels in charge of the various heavens (cf. 3En 17), or they may be related to the idea that there is a Merkabah in each heaven (Re'uyot Yeḥezqe'l, BM, vol. 2, p. 131; ed. Gruenwald, p. 119).

In Ascension of Isaiah 7:18–23, 28–31 we find the motif of the dimensions of the heavens, which occurs also in the Merkabah tradition (Re'uyot Yeḥezqe'l, BM, vol. 2, p. 131; ed. Gruenwald, p. 121; b.Ḥag 13a).

Ascension of Isaiah 10:24–31 mentions angelic guardians of the gates of the various palaces, to whom passwords have to be given. This recalls the Merkabah notion of the gatekeepers of the seven heavenly palaces, to whom "seals" have to be shown by the mystic on his way up to heaven (Hekalot Rabbati 17:1–20:3, BHM, vol. 3, pp. 95–98).

With the angelic challenge to Isaiah as he ascends to heaven, "How far shall he ascend who dwells among aliens?" (AscenIs 9:1f.), cf. 3 Enoch 2:1f. and 6:2.

The theme of the angels praising God "with one voice," found in Ascension of Isaiah 7:15, 8:18, and 9:28, is paralleled in the Merkabah tradition (see Scholem, Gnosticism, pp. 29f.). With Isaiah's participation in the celestial hymns, cf. 3 Enoch 1:11.

Perhaps most significant of all is the setting which Ascension of Isaiah gives for Isaiah's vision (see 6:1–11). Isaiah makes his ascent in the presence of the king, his counselors, and forty prophets and sons of prophets; there is a clear description of him falling into a trance (6:10f.), and it is stressed (6:17) that he did not impart his heavenly vision to anyone but the inner circle of Hezekiah, Jasub, and the remaining prophets. This whole picture is strongly reminiscent of the description of the Merkabah conventicle in Hekalot Rabbati 13–20 (*BHM*, vol. 3, pp. 93–98).

Apocalypse of Abraham 15–29

In this work we find once again the pattern of an ascension through the seven heavens (ApAb 19) to God's throne, followed by a revelation of secrets. Abraham's heavenly guide is the archangel Jaoel, whose name (in the form Yaho'el) appears as one of the names of Metatron in 3 Enoch 48D:1. When God approaches Abraham in a frightening theophany, Abraham recites a hymn taught to him by Jaoel. Like the Merkabah hymns this is theurgical in character: It protects him from being consumed and it opens up the way to a vision of the Merkabah (ApAb 17–18). The Merkabah is described mainly in terms of Ezekiel 1 and Isaiah 6. The revelation that Abraham receives is a vision of the seven heavens, the earth, the garden of Eden, and the whole course of human history from Adam to the Messiah (ApAb 19–29; cf. this last element with 3En 45:3–5).

THE DEAD SEA SCROLLS

The Merkabah literature has links also with Qumran. Perhaps the closest parallels are in the following texts:

The angelic liturgy (4QŠirŠabb)

This poorly preserved text[68] appears to give an elaborate account of the liturgy used by the angels in the heavenly temple. The first of the published fragments alludes to various orders of angels and mentions in particular seven "sovereign princes" (*neśî'ê rôš*), i.e. archangels. The Qumran text uses the Hebrew term *neśî'îm* for the angels; the Merkabah texts normally call them *śārîm*; however, we find the expression *neśî'ê kābôd* ("glorious princes") in Seper HaRazim 5:4 (ed. Margalioth, p. 100). The second fragment contains a Merkabah piece, which is based on Ezekiel 1, but includes elements derived from Daniel 7 and 1 Kings 19. In line 1 it uses "the Glory" (*hakkābôd*) as a title of God (cf. above on TLevi 3:4) and it appears to refer to a heavenly tabernacle (*miškān*); this may be compared with the tabernacle of Metatron in 3 Enoch 15B:1. It brings in from 1 Kings 19:12 (RSV) the "still small voice"; this motif is prominent in the Merkabah texts (see 3En 22C:5, n. m). Line 2 appears to read, "there is a murmur of jubilation when they [i.e. the cherubim] raise their wings." The idea here may be similar to that in 3 Enoch 22:15: The cherubim raise their wings to praise God. Line 2 also refers to God's throne as the "throne [*kissē'*] of the Merkabah" and the "seat of his glory" (*mwšb kbwdw*); cf. the Merkabah designations "throne of glory" (*kissē' hakkābôd*) and "seat of his glory" (*mošab hadārô, mošab yeqārô*) (see 3En 1:6, n. j, and 22:12, n. t). Ezekiel 1:26 and 10:1 only refer to a "throne" (*kissē'*). Lines 4–5 seem to distinguish between the galgallim and the ophanim (cf. 3En 19 and 25). Line 5 possibly refers to "streams of fire";[69] cf. the "river(s) of fire" in the Merkabah texts (e.g. 3En 19:4). Finally, we should note in line 8 the reference to "the camps of the 'elohim" (*mhny 'lwhym*). Here 'elohim is probably not a designation of God but of the angels in general or of an angelic order (cf. 3En 15B:1, n. c); the idea is probably as in the Merkabah texts (3En 1:6, n. i) that the angelic choirs are organized into "camps."

The heavenly Melchizedek (11QMelch)

In this text[70] Melchizedek appears as being exalted over all the angels. It is stated that he will preside over a heavenly assize and exact punishment, with the help of the other angels,

---

[68] J. Strugnell, "The Angelic Liturgy at Qumran," *VT* Sup 7 (1959) 318–45. A fragment of the same work was unearthed at Masada (MasŠirŠabb): see Y. Yadin, "The Excavations at Masada," *IEJ* 15 (1965) 81f., 105–8. There are other, unpublished Merkabah fragments from cave 4 at Qumran.

[69] If this is, indeed, what is meant by *šybyly 'š* or *šbwly 'š*; Strugnell reports that later, in an unpublished fragment, there is a reference to *nhry 'wr*, "rivers of fire."

[70] A. S. van der Woude, "Melchisedek als himmlische Erlösergestalt," OTS 14 (1965) 354–73; J. T. Milik, "*Milkî-ṣedeq* et *Milkî-reša'* dans les anciens écrits juifs et chrétiens," *JJS* 23 (1972) 96–109; F. L. Horton, *The Melchizedek Tradition* (Cambridge, 1976) pp. 64–82.

from Belial and his minions. In view of the priestly functions of Melchizedek in the Bible (Gen 14:8; Ps 110:4), van der Woude has conjectured that at Qumran Melchizedek may have been regarded as the high priest of the heavenly Temple and identified with the archangel Michael, who fulfills the role of the heavenly high priest in rabbinic tradition (Ḥagigah 12b; cf. Midraš hanneʿelam, *Lek leka*, quoted in M. M. Kasher, *Torah Šelemah*, Genesis, vol. 3 [Jerusalem, 1931] p. 615, no. 111; Yalquṭ Ḥadaš, *Malʾakim* no. 19 [Warsaw, 1879] p.122).[71] However, all of this is very uncertain. A number of clear parallels between the heavenly Melchizedek of Qumran and the Meṭaṭron of 3 Enoch at once suggest themselves: both figures hold exalted, if not pre-eminent, positions among the angels; both are heavenly judges (for Meṭaṭron's court see 3En 16:1), and both, apparently, had earthly lives prior to their exalted, heavenly states.

Physiognomies (4QCryptic)

Like the Merkabah mystics the Qumran community was interested in physiognomy. 4QCryptic contains fragments of several texts which apparently attempted to establish that there is a significant relationship between a man's physical features, the astrological conditions prevalent at the time of his birth, and the number of parts his spirit possesses in the House of Light and in the Pit of Darkness.[72] Another text from Qumran cave 4 (4QMess ar) refers to the distinguishing physical marks of someone who is called "the elect of God"; the first editor of this fragment thought that the reference is to the Messiah.[73] Gruenwald has published some physiognomies which apparently emanated from Merkabah circles (see *Tarbiṣ* 40 [1971] 301–19). He has attempted to show that there are significant parallels between these Merkabah physiognomies and 4QCryptic (pp. 304f.). For example, his second fragment, 3/1 line 3 (p. 317), and 4QCryptic (1) 3:4 both seem to speak of "thick legs" (*šôqayim ʿābôt*) as an important distinguishing physical trait. He has further pointed out that the lentil-shaped marks (*tlwpḥyn*) on the body, mentioned in the Qumran messianic text (4QMess ar 1:2) are paralleled in a Merkabah physiognomy published by Scholem (*Seper Assap* [Jerusalem, 1953] p. 491, l. 1: "And the signs, some are like lentils [ʿadāšāh] and some are like the seeds of cucumbers"), though the precise word for lentil is different in each case.

MERKABAH LITERATURE

3 Enoch cannot be fully understood unless it is related to the corpus of Merkabah texts of which it forms a part. The parallels between 3 Enoch and the other Merkabah tracts will not be pursued here; they are amply covered elsewhere, in the introduction and in the notes to the translation. Some of the texts still remain in manuscript, or have been published only in part, or in very faulty editions. The more important printed editions are as follows:

1. Reʾuyot Yeḥezqeʾl ("The Visions of Ezekiel"): BM, vol. 2, pp. 127–34; I. Gruenwald, *Temirin. Texts and Studies in Kabbalah and Hasidism*, ed. I. Weinstock (Jerusalem, 1972) vol. 1, pp. 101–39. ET in L. Jacobs, *Jewish Mystical Testimonies* (New York, 1977) pp. 27–31.

2. Hekalot Zuṭarti ("The Lesser Hekalot"): fragment in S. Musajoff, *Merkabah Šelemah* (Jerusalem, 1921) fols. 6a–8b.

3. Hekalot Rabbati ("The Greater Hekalot"): *BHM*, vol. 3, pp. 83–108; BM, vol. 1, pp. 63–136; cf. M. Smith, "Observations on Hekalot Rabbati," in *Biblical and Other Studies*, ed. A. Altmann (Cambridge, Mass., 1963) pp. 142–60, which summarizes the text.

4. Masseket Hekalot: *BHM*, vol. 2, pp. 40–47; BM, vol. 1, pp. 55–62. German translation in A. Wünsche, *Aus Israels Lehrhallen*, vol. 3 (Leipzig, 1909) pp. 33–47.

5. Maʿaśeh Merkabah: Scholem, *Gnosticism*, pp. 101–17.

6. Šiʿur Qomah: fragments in *Seper Raziʾel* (Amsterdam, 1701) fols. 37a–38b; Musajoff, *Merkabah Šelemah*, fols. 32a–33b, 34a–43b.

---

[71] Meṭaṭron also fulfilled the role of the heavenly high priest; see 3En 15B:1.

[72] See J. M. Allegro and A. A. Anderson in DJD, vol. 5, pp. 88–91.

[73] J. Starcky, "Un texte messianique araméen de la grotte 4 de Qumrân," *École des langues orientales anciennes de l'Institut Catholique de Paris: Mémorial du cinquantenaire 1914–1964* (Paris, 1964) pp. 51–66.

7. Merkabah Rabbah: Musajoff, *Merkabah Šelemah*, fols. 1–6. See further, P. Schäfer, "Prolegomena zu einer kritischen Edition und Analyse der Merkavah Rabba," *Frankfurter Judäische Beiträge* 5 (1977) 65–99.

8. Cairo Genizah Hekalot: fragments published by I. Gruenwald, *Tarbiṣ* 38 (1969) 354–73; 39 (1970) 216f.

9. Tosepta Targumica to Ezekiel 1: BM, vol. 2, pp. 135–40.

10. Physiognomies: Scholem, in *Seper Assap* (Jerusalem, 1953) pp. 459–95; Scholem in *Liber Amicorum: Studies in Honour of C. J. Bleeker* (Leiden, 1969) pp. 175–93 (contains a German translation of one of the fragments published in *Seper Assap*); I. Gruenwald, *Tarbiṣ* 40 (1970–71) 301–19.

11. Seper HaRazim: M. Margalioth, *Sepher Ha-Razim* (Jerusalem, 1966). See further, J. Maier, " 'Das Buch der Geheimnisse.' Zu einer neu entdeckten Schrift aus talmudischer Zeit," *Judaica* 24 (1968) 98–111; J. Maier, "Poetisch-liturgische Stücke aus dem 'Buch der Geheimnisse,' " *Judaica* 24 (1968) 172–81; N. Séd, "Le Sefer Ha-Razim et la méthode de 'Combination des lettres,' " *REJ* 130 (1971) 295–300; J. H. Niggermeyer, *Beschwörungsformeln aus dem 'Buch der Geheimnisse'* (Hildesheim and New York, 1975).

12. Baraita' deMaʿaśeh Bereʾšit: this work contains Merkabah material; BM, vol. 1, pp. 19–48; cf. also pp. 365–69; N. Séd, *REJ* 123 (1964) 259–305; N. Séd, *REJ* 124 (1965) 22–123 (includes French translation).

13. *Śar happānîm*: P. Schäfer, "Die Beschwörung des *Sar ha-panim*: Kritisch Edition und Übersetzung," *Frankfurter Judäische Beiträge* 6 (1978) 107–45.

Cultural importance

WITHIN JUDAISM

Merkabah mysticism has made a contribution to Jewish life and thought in three main areas: (1) the liturgy of the synagogue; (2) the mystical theology of the Ḥaside ʾAškenaz; and (3) the Spanish Qabbalah.

The synagogue liturgy

The Merkabah mystics had some influence on the development of synagogue hymnology. Two synagogue hymns will serve to illustrate this point. The first is *ʾĒl ʾādôn ʿal kol hammaʿaśîm* ("God, the Lord over all works"), which is used in the morning service for sabbaths; it is found in all the prayer books, apart from Saʿadya's *Siddur*. This hymn praises God as the one who is "exalted above the holy creatures [*ḥayyot*] and is adorned in glory above the Merkabah"; it speaks of "purity and rectitude before his throne, loving-kindness and mercy before his glory," and it ends, "All the hosts on high render praise to him, the seraphim, the ophanim, the holy creatures ascribing glory and greatness." This is probably an example of a hymn composed by a poet who was acquainted with Merkabah ideas and used them to enrich his composition.

The second example seems to provide a clear case of a Merkabah hymn which was composed within the mystical circles, but later appropriated for public use. It is the *Haʾadderet wehāʾemûnāh leḥay ʿôlāmîm* ("Excellence and faithfulness are his who lives for ever"), which is found in the ʾAškenazi prayer books as the sixteenth section of the Qerobah *ʾEmeykā nāśāʾtî* for the morning service on Yom Kippur. The Qerobah is attributed to Meshullam b. Kalonymus (10th–11th cent. A.D.), but it seems that he did not compose this particular hymn; he simply lifted it bodily from the Merkabah traditions with which he was acquainted. It can be found in Hekalot Rabbati 26:7 (*BHM*, vol. 3, p. 103).[74] There is nothing obviously

---

[74] See I. Davidson, *Thesaurus of Mediaeval Hebrew Poetry* (New York, 1924) vol. 1, p. 139, n. 2976, and vol. 2 (1929) p. 116, n. 16.

mystical about this composition; however, it is a classic example of the "polylogy" of the Merkabah hymns, which was the basis of their theurgic power.[75]

The Ḥaside ʾAškenaz

Merkabah literature played a central role in shaping the theology of the medieval German-Jewish mystics known as the Ḥaside ʾAškenaz. For example, Eleazar b. Judah of Worms (c. A.D. 1165–c.1230) frequently quotes the Merkabah tracts in his voluminous writings (see esp. his *Sode Razayyaʾ*, pt. 2, *Sod hammerkabah*, published by Israel Kamelhar [Bilgoraj, 1936] under the title *Sode Razayyaʾ*). He gives many substantial and exact quotations from 3 Enoch. The interest of the Ḥaside ʾAškenaz in these mystical tracts is evidenced by the fact that the vast majority of our surviving Hekalot texts exist in late medieval copies that emanated from their circle. German Jewry may have been first introduced to the Merkabah literature by the Kalonymus family, which emigrated from southern Italy to the Rhineland in the ninth century, and which came to hold an eminent position among German Jews (Eleazar was a Kalonymide). It is possible that the Merkabah texts were first brought to southern Italy by Aaron of Baghdad, who arrived there in the ninth century. Tradition has it that Aaron was a great master of mystical lore (see Megillat ʾAḥimaʿaṣ, ed. A. Neubauer, *Mediaeval Jewish Chronicles*, vol. 2 [Oxford, 1895] p. 112; ed. B. Klar [Jerusalem, 1944] p. 13), and Eleazar bears witness that Aaron met Moses b. Kalonymus at Lucca and transmitted to him "all his secrets."[76]

The Spanish Qabbalah

The influence of the Merkabah traditions on the development of Jewish mysticism in medieval Spain may be illustrated from the Zohar, the most important text of the Spanish Qabbalah (composed probably by Moses de Leon in the late 13th cent. A.D.). There can be no doubt that the author of this work was acquainted with Merkabah traditions and that they helped to shape his thought. Thus in two passages he reworks, at considerable length, the Merkabah teachings about the seven heavenly palaces (Zohar *Berēʾšit* 1.38a–45a, and *Peqûdê* 2.244b–262b). Meṭaṭron is also frequently mentioned in the Zohar (e.g. Zohar *Wayeḥî* 1.223b: "From beneath her feet went forth a Youth [*Naʿar* = Meṭaṭron] who stretched from one end of the world to the other . . . and who is called 'Enoch, the son of Yared'"). But in many instances the concept of Meṭaṭron has been developed far beyond the comparatively simple ideas of the Merkabah mystics (see e.g. Zohar *Mišpāṭîm* 2.94a/b).[77] The author of the Zohar often refers to the "Book of Enoch" as one of his authorities; some of these references correspond reasonably well to 3 Enoch (see e.g. Zohar *Wayeḥî* 1.223b, and *Berēʾšit* 1.37b); however, the correspondences are never very exact, and there is much material attributed to this "Book of Enoch" which could never conceivably have formed part of 3 Enoch (see e.g. Zohar *Prologue* 1.13a, and *Mišpāṭîm* 2.100a).[78]

[75] On the influence of the Merkabah mystics on the synagogue liturgy see I. Elbogen, *Der jüdische Gottesdienst in seiner geschichtliche Entwicklung* (Frankfurt am Main, 1931) pp. 377–81; P. Bloch, "Die Yorede Merkābāh, die Mystiker der Gaonenzeit, und ihr Einfluss auf die Liturgie," *MGWJ* 37 (1893) 18–25, 69–74, 257–66, 305–11. Gruenwald and others have argued for the influence of Merkabah traditions on the early Palestinian liturgical poet Yannai; see Gruenwald, *Tarbiṣ* 36 (1966/67) 257–77; cf. Z. M. Rabbinowitz, "The Relationship of the Payyetan Yannai to Hekhalot and Merkabah Literature," *Tarbiṣ* 36 (1966/67) 402–5 (in Heb.). The influence is hard to deny; see e.g. Yannai's Qedušta' for Yom Kippur, which begins Missôd ḥakāmîm ûmillemed ḥabērîm (ed. Zulay, pp. 328–42, no. 132).

[76] See A. Neubauer, *REJ* 23 (1891) 230–37; see H. Gross, in *MGWJ* 49 (1905) 692–700. On the influence of Merkabah mysticism on medieval German Hasidism see Scholem, *Major Trends*, pp. 84–87; J. Dan, *The Mysticism of the Ḥaside ʾAskenaz* (Jerusalem, 1968) (in Heb.).

[77] On Meṭaṭron in the Zohar and in related mystical texts, see Odeberg, *3 Enoch*, pt. 1, pp. 111–25; Margalioth, *Malʾake ʿElyon*, pp. 73–108.

[78] For references to this "Book of Enoch" in the Zohar see Odeberg, *3 Enoch*, pt. 1, p. 22; Margalioth, *Malʾake ʿElyon*, pp. 80–3; *BHM*, vol. 3, pp. 195f. Moses de Leon in his *Miškan haʿedut* also has a long quotation from a "Book of Enoch": for the text see *BHM*, vol. 2, p. xxxi.

The influence of Merkabah mysticism outside the Jewish tradition is extremely hard to document. Its possible links with Gnosticism were explored above. The following are some notes on other areas which would be worth investigating.

Odeberg (*3 Enoch*, pt. 1, pp. 64–79) tried to establish that there are significant parallels between 3 Enoch and the literature of the Mandaean community of southern Iraq. J. Greenfield is skeptical about these parallels and asserts that they "are mostly verbal and are on the whole meaningless" (prolegomenon to KTAV reprint of Odeberg's *3 Enoch*, p. xxxix). Two things should, however, be borne in mind: first, Meṭaṭron and the curtain (*pargôd*) have turned up on a Mandaean incantation bowl; and, second, the Mandaeans were, for several centuries, in close historical contact with the rabbinic communities of Babylonia in which Merkabah mysticism flourished.

Following N. Séd's interesting study "Les hymns sur le paradis de Saint Ephrem et les traditions juives," *Le Muséon* 81 (1968) 455–501, it would seem to be worth investigating the possibility of Jewish Merkabah speculation having had some influence on Syriac Christian writers.

As we noted above, H. Graetz argued that the Merkabah doctrine of Šiʿur Qomah was influenced by anthropomorphic views of God held by certain Islamic thinkers. Though this is a mistaken notion, the parallels to which he pointed remain. It is possible that the influence worked in the other direction, and that the Islamic *mushabbiha* thinkers drew on Jewish Merkabah traditions.

SELECT BIBLIOGRAPHY

Charlesworth, *PMR*, pp. 106f.
Denis, *Introduction*, p. 28.

Alexander, P. S. "The Historical Setting of the Hebrew Book of Enoch," *JJS* 28 (1977) 156–80.
Blumenthal, D. R. *Understanding Jewish Mysticism: The Merkabah Tradition and the Zoharic Tradition*. New York, 1977.
Goldberg, A. "Der Vortrag des Maᶜasse Merkawa, Eine Vermutung zur frühen Merkawamystik," *Judaica* 29 (1973) 4–23.
――――. "Einige Bemerkungen zu den Quellen und redaktionellen Einheiten der Grossen Hekhalot," *Frankfurter Judaïstische Beiträge* 1 (1973) 1–49.
――――. "Der verkannte Gott: Prüfung und Scheitern der Adepten in der Merkawamystik," *ZRGG* 26 (1974) 17–29.
――――. "Rabban Yoḥanans Traum: Der Sinai in der frühen Merkawamystik," *Frankfurter Judaïstische Beiträge* 3 (1975) 1–27.
Gruenwald, I. "Yannai and Hekhaloth Literature," *Tarbiṣ* 36 (1966/67) 257–77. (In Hebrew.)
――――. "Knowledge and Vision: Towards the Clarification of Two 'Gnostic' Concepts in the Light of their Alleged Origins," *Israel Oriental Studies* 3 (1973) 63–107.
――――. "The Jewish Esoteric Literature in the Time of the Mishnah and the Talmud," *Immanuel* 4 (1974) 37–46.
――――. *Apocalyptic and Merkabah Mysticism*. AGAJU 14; Leiden, 1980.
Halperin, D. J. *The Merkabah in Rabbinic Literature*. American Oriental Series 62; New Haven, 1980.
Maier, J. *Vom Kultus zur Gnosis. Studien zur Vor- und Frühgeschichte der "jüdischen Gnosis"*. Kairos: Religionswissenschaftliche Studien 1; Salzburg, 1964.
Odeberg, H. *3 Enoch*. Cambridge, 1928. (This volume contains text, translation, commentary, and introduction; despite its weaknesses it remains valuable. It has been reprinted by KTAV [New York, 1973] with a useful prolegomenon by J. Greenfield.)
Schäfer, P. "Engel und Menschen in der Hekhalot-Literatur," *Kairos* 3–4 (1980) 201–25.
Scholem, G. G. *Major Trends in Jewish Mysticism*. New York, 1954³. .
――――. *Jewish Gnosticism, Merkabah Mysticism and Talmudic Tradition*. New York, 1965².
――――. *Kabbalah*. Library of Jewish Knowledge; Jerusalem, 1974. (This work collects together Scholem's numerous articles on mystical subjects in the *EncyJud*.)
Séd, N. "Les traditions secrètes et les disciples de Rabban Yoḥanan b. Zakkai," *RHR* 184 (1973) 49–66.
Urbach, E. E. "The Traditions About Merkabah Mysticism in the Tannaitic Period," *Studies in Mysticism and Religion Presented to G. G. Scholem*. Jerusalem, 1967. Hebrew section, pp. 1–28.
Wewers, G. A. *Geheimnis und Geheimhaltung im rabbinischen Judentum*. Religionsgeschichtliche Versuche und Vorarbeiten 35; Berlin, 1975.

THE BOOK OF ENOCH
BY RABBI ISHMAEL THE HIGH PRIEST

Ishmael enters the seventh palace[a]

"Enoch walked with God. Then he vanished because God took him."   Gen 5:24

1 **1** Rabbi Ishmael[b] said:
When I ascended to the height to behold the vision of the chariot,[c] I entered   Ezek 1
2 six palaces, one inside the other,[d] •and when I reached the door of the seventh   18:3
palace I paused in prayer before the Holy One, blessed be he; I looked up and
3 said: •"Lord of the Universe, grant, I beseech you, that the merit of Aaron,
son of Amram, lover of peace and pursuer of peace,[e] who received on Mount   Ex 24:9f.; 28:1
Sinai the crown of priesthood in the presence of your glory, may avail for me
now, so that Prince Qaspi'el,[f] and the angels with him, may not prevail over

1 a. Chs. 1f. provide a setting for the revelations that follow. It is not clear whether they were added to chs. 3–48A by the final redactor of 3En, or whether they had already been introduced at an earlier stage as a preface to a shorter form of the work (e.g. chs. 3–15/16). Chs. 1f. contain many parallels to the rest of the book. Two are particularly striking: (1) the way in which Ishmael, when he ascends to heaven, is challenged by the archangels and defended by God is similar to the challenge and defense of Enoch on his ascent (cf. 1:7f. and 2:1–3 with 4:7f. and 6:2f.); (2) the bestowal of spiritual gifts on Ishmael is exactly matched by the bestowal of spiritual gifts on Enoch (cf. 1:11f. with 8:1f.). It is possible that chs. 1f. have been pieced together from material lifted from the rest of the work. On the other hand, the parallelism could have deeper significance: It may be meant to suggest that the ascent of Ishmael (and so of every adept) is in certain respects analogous to the elevation of Enoch.

b. A famous Palestinian scholar who died before A.D. 132. There is a rabbinic tradition that he was of priestly descent (b.Ket 105b; b.Hull 49a; t.Hall 1:10), but he cannot have been high priest since he was only a child when the Temple was destroyed in A.D 70 (b.Gitt 58a). In view of the privileged relationship of the high priest to God, the mystics had a vested interest in claiming that their master held the supreme priestly office. Ishmael's name was early linked with mystical lore: b.Ber 7a claims that as high priest he had a vision in the Holy of Holies of " 'Aktari'el Yah, the Lord of Hosts, sitting on a high and lofty throne'' (cf. 3En 15B:4), and b.Ber 51a mentions three things which he is supposed to have learned from the Prince of the Divine Presence; note further the interpretation of 'Aza'zel (Lev 16:8) attributed to "the school of Ishmael" in b.Yoma 67b. R. Ishmael appears

as the narrator in a number of other Merkabah texts; see Hekalot Rabbati, Ma'aseh Merkabah (though in this work he is closely associated with R. Aqiba), and the Cairo Genizah Hekalot (note e.g. A/2, 34, ed. Gruenwald, p. 366, and B/1, 18, ed. Gruenwald, p. 368).

c. "To behold the vision of the chariot," F; "to behold in my vision the chariot," A. For the technical phrase, "the vision of the chariot" (sepiyyat hammerkābāh), see 16:2; Ma'aseh Merkabah 9 and 33 (ed. Scholem, pp. 107, 116); Hekalot Rabbati 1:1 (BHM, vol. 3, p. 83, l. 3); 2:3 (BHM, vol. 3, p. 84, l. 17).

d. Lit. "chamber within chamber" (heder betôk heder), i.e. concentrically; cf. Hekalot Rabbati 15:1 (BHM, vol. 3, p. 94): "Tôtôrsî'î YHWH, the God of Israel, dwells in seven palaces [hêkālôt], one within the other [heder betôk heder]." 3En combines here the tradition about the heavenly palaces (hêkālôt) (18:3; 37:1) with the tradition about the heavenly chambers (hadārîm) (18:18; 38:1; Hekalot Rabbati 3:1 [BHM, vol. 3, p. 85, l. 9]; 6:3 [BM, vol. 1, p. 76, l. 4 = BHM, vol. 5, p. 167, l. 20]; 7:2 [BHM, vol. 3, p. 89, l. 6]; 7:4 [BHM, vol. 3, p. 89, l. 13]; 7:5 [BHM, vol. 3, p. 89, l. 19]; Ma'aseh Merkabah 6 and 7 [ed. Scholem, pp. 106f.]; Tanhuma' ed. Buber, vol. 1, 71a). In 3En 7 the heavenly palaces are designated by the Lat. loanword palatium or praetorium (see ch. 7, n. d).

e. Cf. m.Ab 1:12: "Hillel said: Be of the disciples of Aaron, loving peace and pursuing peace."

f. "Qaspi'el," A E F, is correct as against B's "Qapsi'el," since the name is derived from the root qsp, "to be angry." Qesep is the name of an angel of destruction in TarJon to Num 17:11. In Hekalot Rabbati 15:7 (BHM, vol. 3, p. 94, l. 26) Qaspi'el is a gatekeeper of the sixth palace; in Seper HaRazim 4:2 (ed. Margalioth,

4 me and cast me from heaven." • At once the Holy One, blessed be he, summoned
to my aid his servant, the angel Meṭaṭron, Prince of the Divine Presence.[g] He
5 flew out to meet me with great alacrity, to save me from their power. • He
grasped me with his hand before their eyes and said to me, "Come in peace
into the presence of the high and exalted King[h] to behold the likeness of the
6 chariot." • Then I entered the seventh palace and he led me to the camp of the
Šekinah[i] and presented me before the throne of glory[j] so that I might behold
7 the chariot. • But as soon as the princes of the chariot[k] looked at me and the
fiery seraphim fixed their gaze on me, I shrank back trembling and fell down,[l]
stunned by the radiant appearance of their eyes and the bright vision of their
8 faces, until the Holy One, blessed be he, rebuked them and said, • "My servants,
my seraphim, my cherubim, and my ophanim, hide your eyes from Ishmael
my beloved son and honored friend, so that he does not shrink and tremble
9 so." • At once Meṭaṭron, Prince of the Divine Presence, came and revived me
10 and raised me to my feet, • but still I had not strength enough to sing a hymn[m]
before the glorious throne of the glorious King, the mightiest of kings, the most
11 splendid of potentates, until an hour had passed. • But after an hour the Holy
One, blessed be he, opened to me gates of Šekinah,[n] gates of peace, gates of
wisdom, gates of strength, gates of might, gates of speech, gates of song, gates
12 of sanctifying praise,[o] gates of chant. • He enlightened my eyes and my heart
to utter psalm, praise, jubilation, thanksgiving, song, glory, majesty, laud,[p]
and strength. And when I opened my mouth and sang praises before the throne

(margin references:) 18:4   22:10   Dan 8:17f.; 10:9,10,15   Rev 1:17   4:6; 6:2,3   8:1

---

p. 97) he is one of the angels who guide the sun during the night. For the motif of the angels attacking the adept as he ascends to the Merkabah, see b.Ḥag 15b: "And R. Aqiba too the ministering angels sought to thrust away; the Holy One, blessed be he, said to them: Let this elder be, for he is worthy to avail himself of my glory." See further 15B:2; Hekalot Rabbati 17:6 (*BHM*, vol. 3, p. 96); 24 (*BHM*, vol. 3, p. 102, ll. 11–19 = BM, vol. 1, pp. 107f.).

g. "Prince of the Divine Presence": the title of an angel who serves in God's immediate presence, within the curtain; see "Theological Importance."

h. "The high and exalted King" (*melek rām weniśśāʾ*), E F; A B have simply *rām weniśśāʾ*, "the high and exalted (One)." The expression *rām weniśśāʾ* is common in the Merkabah texts. It is sometimes used absolutely as a title of God (cf. Isa 57:15), and sometimes in the phrases "high and exalted King" and "high and exalted throne" (cf. Isa 6:1): see Masseket Hekalot 1 (*BHM*, vol. 2, p. 40); Hekalot Rabbati 7:2 (*BHM*, vol. 3, p. 89); Seper HaRazim 5:24 (ed. Margalioth, p. 102).

i. "Camp [*maḥanēh*] of the Šekinah," A and probably B; "sight [or "vision"] [*marēh*] of the Šekinah," E F. Normally we find "camps" in the plural; thus "four camps" in 18:4; 37:1; 40:3; Masseket Hekalot 6 (*BHM*, vol. 2, pp. 43f.); "seven camps" in Seper HaRazim 1:16 (ed. Margalioth, p. 67); "camps" in 22:2; 34:2; 36:1. But 35:5 also speaks of the "camp of the Šekinah"; the same expression is used as a designation of the inner court and the holy place in the Temple; see t.KelBQ 1:12; SifNum 1 (ed. Horovitz, p. 4, ll. 7–9); b.Zeb 116b; NumR 7:8. The camps are companies of angels, sometimes identified with the heavenly choirs; see further

18:4, n. h, and 35:1, n. c. The idea may be derived from Gen 32:1f.: "While Jacob was going on his way angels of God met him, and on seeing them he said, 'This is God's camp [*maḥanēh ʾelōhîm*],' and he named the place Maḥanayim [The Two Camps]." The Šekinah is the visible manifestation of God's presence; see "Theological Importance."

j. "The throne of glory" (*kissēʾ hakkābôd*), A E F; "the Holy One, blessed be he," B. God's celestial throne is most commonly called *kissēʾ hakkābôd* in the Merkabah texts, though various expressions with *môšāb* are also found; see 22:12, n. t.

k. The angels who minister to the chariot.

l. For the motif of fainting and being revived see the margin and 1En 71:11; ApAb 10.

m. At the climax of his ecstasy the mystic worships God in song; see Hekalot Rabbati 24:1 (*BHM*, vol 3, p. 100): "When he (the mystic) stands before the throne of glory, he begins to recite the hymn which the throne of glory sings each day"; cf. Maʿaśeh Merkabah 8 (ed. Scholem, p. 107, l. 15). The Merkabah hymns (see "Original Language") are examples of the hymns which the throne sings.

n. "Gates of Šekinah": the gates belong to the heavenly treasuries (see "Theological Importance"). "Šekinah" is the reading of A B E F Mus; Jellinek (*BHM*, vol. 5, p. 171) conjectures "understanding" (*bînāh*), presumably because Šekinah is not something that can be stored in treasuries. Note, however, 8:1, where A D E F Mus have "gates of Šekinah," and 5:4, where Šekinah is spoken of as if it were a beneficial substance.

o. "Sanctifying praise" = Qeduššah.

p. "Laud" (*hillûl*), A E F (cf. Mus); B repeats "psalm" (*tehillāh*).

of glory[q] the holy creatures below the throne of glory[r] and above the throne responded after me, saying,

Holy, holy, holy,   Isa 6:3

and,

Blessed be the glory of the Lord in his dwelling place.[s]   Ezek 3:12

Metatron vouches for Ishmael

1 **2** R. Ishmael said:
Then the eagles[a] of the chariot, the flaming ophanim[b] and the cherubim of   25:1
2 devouring fire, asked Metatron, •"Youth,[c] why have you allowed one born of   Ezek 1:16
woman to come in and behold the chariot? From what nation is he? From what   6:2; Job 15:14; 25:4
3 tribe? What is his character?" • Metatron replied, "He is of the nation of Israel,
whom the Holy One, blessed be he, chose from the seventy nations[d] to be his   3:2; 17:8; 30:2; Gen
people. He is of the tribe of Levi, which presents the offering[e] to his name. He 10
is of the family of Aaron, whom the Holy One, blessed be he, chose to minister
in his presence and on whose head he himself placed the priestly crown on
4 Sinai." • At once they began to say, "This one is certainly worthy to behold   4:9
the chariot, as it is written,[f]

Happy is the nation of whom this is true,   Ps 144:15
happy is the nation whose God is the Lord."

Ishmael questions Metatron[a]

1 **3** R. Ishmael said:
Then I questioned the angel Metatron, Prince of the Divine Presence. I said to
2 him, "What is your name?" • He answered, "I have seventy names, corresponding to the seventy nations of the world, and all of them are based on[b] the   48D:1; 2:3
name of the King of the kings of kings;[c] however, my King calls me 'Youth.'"[d]   48C:9; 29:1

---

q. "Before the throne of glory," A Mus; "before the Holy One, blessed be he," B; cf. n. j above.

r. "Below the throne of glory," B; "below the throne of the King of Glory," A E F. It is odd to have the creatures both above and below the throne. Mus is corrupt, but it suggests a reading, "[The holy creatures below the throne of the King of Glory/throne of glory], and the holy seraphim above the throne of glory." This may be the original text.

s. Like a synagogue precentor Ishmael leads the angels in the chanting of the Qeduššah; see "Theological Importance."

2 a. "Eagles" (nišrê), A B Mus; "attendants" (na'arê), E F. For eaglelike angels see 24:11; 26:3; 44:5, and for the expression "eagles of the Merkabah" see Alphabet of Aqiba (BHM, vol. 3, p. 26, l. 21); note also that one of the creatures is an eagle (Ezek 1:10; 10:14). Nevertheless the expression is strange; perhaps read "princes" (śārê) as in 1:7; 22:10.

b. "The flaming ophanim," A B E; F omits.

c. "Youth": see 4:10.

d. "From the seventy nations," A Mus; compare 17:8.

e. "Which presents the offering" (še-mērîm terûmāh), Odeberg's conjecture. For the idiom see Num 15:19; Ezek 45:1. A B have only terûmāh and E has only mērîm; Mus omits.

f. "As it is written," A E; "and they said," B.

3 a. Chs. 3–15, on the elevation of Enoch, may have formed the earliest edited section of 3En, and may have formed the core round which the rest of the work crystallized. They develop essentially as an answer to Ishmael's question why Metatron is called "Youth." Chs. 4–7 describe the ascent of Enoch to heaven; chs. 8–15, his transformation into an archangel. As elsewhere in 3En diverse earlier traditions have been utilized and adapted: see 4:1, n. a; 4:3, n. d; 4:6, n. l; 10:3, n. i; 14:4, n. d.

b. "And all of them are based on" (wekûllām 'al), A B E F; "and similar to" (ûke'ên), C D Mus; see the margin and cf. 10:3; 12:5; 30:1; further n. c below.

c. "The name of the King of the kings of kings," A E F; "the name of my King and my Creator," C; "the name of my King, the Holy One, blessed be he," D; "the name of my King," Mus; "the name of Metatron, the Angel of the Divine Presence," B. Three things are asserted in this verse: (1) Metatron has seventy names; for a list of them see 48D:1. (2) The number of the names corresponds to the number of the nations of the world. The idea probably is that Metatron is the Prince of the World, in charge of the seventy princes of kingdoms (see "Theological Importance"). (3) The names are "based on" the name of God. The natural interpretation of this would be that they are derived (by temurah, gematria, and other systems of letter and number magic) from the tetragram YHWH. However, according to 48C:9, 48D:5,

Metatron is Enoch

1 **4** R. Ishmael said:

I said to Metatron, "Why are you called by the name of your Creator[a] with 3:2
seventy names? You are greater than all the princes, more exalted than all the
angels, more beloved than all the ministers, more honored than all the hosts,
and elevated over all potentates in sovereignty, greatness, and glory; why, then,
2 do they call you 'Youth'[b] in the heavenly heights?" •He answered, "Because Gen 5:18–24
3 I am Enoch, the son of Jared.[c] •When the generation of the Flood sinned and Gen 6:1–7
turned to evil deeds, and said to God, 'Go away! We do not choose to learn
your ways,' the Holy One, blessed be he, took me[d] from their midst to be a Job 21:14
witness against them in the heavenly height to all who should come into the
4 world,[e] so that they should not say, 'The Merciful One is cruel![f] •Did *all* those
multitudes of people sin? And even if *they* sinned, what sin did their wives,
their sons, and their daughters commit? And what of their horses, their mules,
their beasts, their cattle, and all the birds of the world which the Holy One
destroyed with them in the waters of the Flood—what sin did *they* commit that
5 they should have perished as well?"[g] •Therefore the Holy One, blessed be he, 6:1,3; 7
brought me up in their lifetime, before their very eyes, to the heavenly height,
to be a witness against them to future generations.[h] And the Holy One, blessed
be he, appointed me[i] in the height as a prince and a ruler among the ministering
angels.

6 "Then three of the ministering angels, ʿUzzah, ʿAzzah, and ʿAzaʾel,[j] came 5:9
and laid charges against me in the heavenly height. They said before the Holy Job 1:6

the idea is that they were seventy of God's own
names which he bestowed on Metatron (thus
symbolizing the transfer to Metatron of some of
his power). This is probably the sense of the
reading "seventy names . . . similar to the name
of the King" (see n. b above). Cf. b.Sanh 38b,
"Metatron . . . whose name is similar to that of
his Master," and Re'uyot Yeḥezqe'l, BM, vol.
2, p. 132, l. 14 (ed. Gruenwald, p. 130), where
the name of the angel of the third heaven is said
to be "Miṭaṭron, like the name of the Almighty
[*haggebûrāh*]." The simplest explanation of
b.Sanh and Re'uyot Yeḥezqe'l is that "Metatron"
was not only the angel's name, but a secret name
of God as well.

     d. "Youth"; see 4:10.

4 a. "Why are you called by the name of your
Creator?" A Mus; "Why is your name like the
name of your Creator?" C. There is no answer
to this question; a passage containing a discussion
of the seventy names of Metatron has probably
been edited out. Its omission would be in keeping
with the anti-theurgical tendency of the final
redaction of 3En (see "Historical Importance").

     b. "Youth"; see 4:10.

     c. "Because I am Enoch, the son of Jared,"
A C D E Mus; cf. TarJon to Gen 5:24: "Enoch
was taken up and ascended to heaven and his
name was called Metatron, the great scribe."
The identification of Enoch and Metatron is
probably a late development (see "Theological
Importance").

     d. "Took me," A B; "took me up," C D
Mus; "rescued me," E F. There are three
different traditions concerning Enoch's elevation
in 3En: (1) ch. 4, Enoch is elevated to be "a

witness" (4:3, 5), but the manner of his ascent
is unspecified; (2) ch. 6, he is carried up in a
fiery chariot (6:1), to be God's "reward"[e] (6:3);
(3) ch. 7, he ascends on the wings of the Šekinah,
and is set to serve the throne of glory day by
day.

     e. "All who should come into the world" or
"all the inhabitants of the world": Heb. *bāʾê
hāʿôlām.*

     f. "So that . . . cruel," A.

     g. "Did *all* those multitudes . . . perished as
well?" reconstructed text. There are a great many
variations in the MSS and all forms of the text
are more or less corrupt. The charge is that God
destroyed the innocent with the guilty; cf. GenR
28:8; b.Sanh 108a (both references concerned
with the Flood). See further PRE 14: "If Adam
sinned, what sin did the earth commit that it
should be cursed?"; b.Yoma 22b, with regard
to God's command to wipe out the Amalekites:
"If the humans sinned, what sin did the cattle
commit? If the adults sinned, what sin did the
little ones commit?"

     h. Lit. "to the world to come" (*lāʿôlām
habbāʾ*), here the new world after the Flood, not
the messianic age.

     i. "Appointed me" (*netānanî*), Mus; A E F
have *ziwweganî* = (?) "took me into partner-
ship."

     j. "ʿUzzah, ʿAzzah, and ʿAzaʾel," A B;
"ʿIzzah, ʿUzzah, and ʿAzaʾel," E F; "ʿAzzah,
ʿAzziʾel, and ʿUzziʾel," Mus; "ʿAzzah, and
ʿAzaʾel," C D. These angels are probably evil
agencies, in view of the fact that they "laid
charges" (*hāyû maśṭînîm*) against Enoch; cf.
14:2, "Sammaʾel, Prince of the Accusers" (*śar
hammaśṭînîm*). They are certainly bad in 5:9.

One, blessed be he, 'Lord of the Universe,[k] did not the primeval ones[l] give you good advice when they said, Do not create man!' The Holy One, blessed be he, replied,[m] 'I have made and will sustain him; I will carry and deliver him.'[n] Isa 46:4

7 When they saw me they said before him, 'Lord of the Universe, what right 2:2; 6:2 has this one to ascend to the height of heights? Is he not descended from[o] those who perished in the waters[p] of the Flood? What right has he to be in heaven?'

8 Again the Holy One, blessed be he, replied,[q] and said to them, 'What right have you to interrupt me?[r] I have chosen this one in preference to all of you,

9 to be a prince and a ruler over you in the heavenly heights.' • At once they all arose and went to meet me and prostrated themselves before me, saying, 'Happy 2:4 are you, and happy your parents, because your Creator has favored you.'

10 Because I am young in their company[s] and a mere youth among them in days 2:2; 3:2; 4:1; and months and years—therefore they call me 'Youth.' "[t] 48D:1(89)

God removes the Šekinah

1 **5** R. Ishmael said: Meṭaṭron, Prince of the Divine Presence, said to me: From the day that the Holy One, blessed be he, banished the first man from Gen 3:23f. the garden of Eden, the Šekinah[a] resided on a cherub beneath the tree of life.

2 The ministering angels used to muster and come down from heaven in companies, and in bands and cohorts from heaven, to execute his will in all the

3 earth. • The first man and his generation dwelt at the gate of the garden of Eden so that they might gaze at the bright image of the Šekinah, or the brilliance of the Šekinah radiated from one end of the world to the other, 365,000[b] times 22:7,13; 28:2

4 more brightly than the sun; • anyone who gazed at[c] the brightness of the Šekinah 22B:7

k. "Lord of the Universe," C D E F Mus; A B omit.

l. "The primeval ones": The tradition behind this is found in b.Sanh 38b: When God wanted to create man, he first created a company of angels and asked their advice. They opposed the creation of man, so God destroyed them. The same fate befell a second company, but a third company allowed man to be created. However, when the generation of the Flood came, these angels said: "Lord of the Universe, did not the first company of angels speak aright?" God replied, "Even to old age I am the same, and even to grey hairs will I carry" (Isa 46:4). This tradition has been adapted here: (1) The third company of angels is identified with 'Uzzah, 'Azzah, and 'Aza'el; (2) the charge brought against mankind in general is incongruously applied specifically to Enoch; (3) the point of the expression "the first ones" (i.e. the first company of angels) has been obscured. The talmudic form of the tradition clearly has priority; what we have in 3En is a rather clumsy reworking of it. On the theme of angelic opposition to man, see 1:3, n. f, and 5:10, n. 1.

m. "Replied," C D Mus; "replied again" ('ôd mēšîb), A B E F; cf. n. q below.

n. The sense given to the biblical verse is either: "I will sustain man—you angels will not be troubled"; or: "I will be long-suffering with man."

o. "Descended from," lit. "one of the sons of the sons of"; so A B Mus and, substantially, C D. But the chronology is awry; according to Gen 5:21–24 and 7:11 Enoch was translated 669 years before the Flood.

p. "Waters," C D Mus; "days," A B E F.

q. "Again . . . replied" ('ôd mēšîb), A B E;

C D F Mus omit "Again"; cf. n. m above.

r. "To interrupt me," lit. "to enter into my words." For the idiom of m.Ab 5:7, "The wise man . . . does not break in upon the words of his fellow" (Danby, p. 456).

s. "Young in their company" (qāṭān betô-kām), A E; "young" (qāṭān), B.

t. "Youth" (Na'ar): a standard title of Meṭaṭron; see margin. Originally it meant "servant," and may have referred to Meṭaṭron's service in the heavenly sanctuary; for the use of na'ar for a temple servant see Ex 24:5; 1Sam 2:13. However, the name is reinterpreted here, in the context of the equation of Meṭaṭron with Enoch, to mean "youth" (see "Date"). Cf. b.Yeb 16b: "The following verse was uttered by the Prince of the World, 'I have been a youth (na'ar) and now I am old' " (Ps 37:25).

5 a. The visible manifestation of God's presence; see "Theological Importance." In the garden of Eden the Šekinah resided in a cherub; in heaven it resides on the throne of glory.

b. "365,000," C D; "65,000," A B E F Mus. For the number see 9:4.

c. "Gazed at," E F; "made use of," A B C Mus. The second reading is not out of the question, since Šekinah could be regarded as a luminous substance; see 1:11. For the Šekinah as a protection against demons see NumR 12:3, "Before the Tabernacle was erected demons vexed mankind, but from the moment the Tabernacle was erected, and the Šekinah took up its residence here below, the demons were exterminated from the world." According to b.Ber 17a, the righteous will feast on the brightness of the Šekinah in the world to come. Note also the tradition that the angels feed on the radiance of the Šekinah (see 22:7).

was not troubled by flies or gnats, by sickness or pain; malicious demons were
5 not able to harm him,[d] and even the angels[e] had no power over him. • When the
Holy One, blessed be he, went out and in from the garden to Eden, and from
Eden to the garden, from the garden to heaven, and from heaven to the garden   Gen 2:8,10
of Eden,[f] all gazed at the bright image of his Šekinah and were unharmed   Gen 4:26
6 —until the coming of the generation of Enosh,[g] who was the chief of all the
idolators in the world.
7   What did the men of Enosh's generation do? They roamed the world from
end to end, and each of them amassed silver, gold, precious stones, and pearls
in mountainous heaps and piles. In the four quarters of the world they fashioned
them into idols, and in each quarter they set up idols about 1,000 parasangs[h]
8 in height. • They brought down the sun, the moon, the stars and the constellations
and stationed them before the idols, to their right and to their left, to serve them
in the way they served the Holy One,[i] blessed be he, as it is written, "All the   1Kgs 22:19
9 array of heaven stood in his presence, to his right and to his left." • How was
it that they had the strength to bring them down? It was only because ʿUzzah,
ʿAzzah, and ʿAzaʾel[j] taught them sorceries that they brought them down and   4:6
employed them, for otherwise they would not have been able to bring them
down.
10   Thereupon the ministering angels conspired to bring a complaint[k] before the   4:6; Job 1:6
Holy One, blessed be he. They said in his presence, "Lord of the Universe,
what business have you with men, as it is written, 'What is man (ʾenoš) that   Ps 8:4
you should spare a thought for him?' It does not say here, 'What is Adam?'
11 but, 'What is Enosh?' because Enosh is the chief of the idolators.[l] • Why did you
leave the heaven of heavens above, the abode of your glory,[m] the high and
exalted throne which is in the height of ʿArabot,[n] and come and lodge[o] with
men who worship idols? Now you are on the earth, and the idols are on the   17:3
12 earth; • what is your business among the idolatrous inhabitants of the earth?"
Immediately the Holy One, blessed be he, took up his Šekinah from the earth,   6:1

---

d. "Malicious demons were not able to harm him," A and, substantially, C D Mus; "malicious demons had no power over him and were not able to harm him," B.

e. "Even the angels," A C Mus; B E F omit "even"; the reference is to good angels as opposed to demons.

f. "From heaven to the garden of Eden," A B; "from heaven to the upper garden," D. The D reading alludes to the tradition that there is both a terrestrial and a celestial garden of Eden; see Seder Gan ʿEden, *BHM*, vol. 3, pp. 137f. For the distinction in the text between "Eden" and "the garden" see b.Ber 34b: "Perhaps you will say, The garden and Eden are the same. Not so! For the text says, 'A river went out from Eden to water the garden [Gen 2:10]'; the garden is one thing and Eden is another." Cf. b.Sanh 99a; b.Taʿan 10a; GenR 15:2; note also Milton, *Paradise Lost*, bk. 12, ll. 624–29.

g. It is a standard theme of rabbinic Midrash that idolatry began in the time of Enosh; see e.g. b.Shab 118b; GenR 23:6f. This view is based on a forced interpretation of Gen 4:26, in which the unique form *hûhal* is linked with *hullîn* = "profane things" (see Rashi). 3En makes Enosh himself an idolator; most Midrashim speak only of his generation as idolators. According to Philo, *Abr* 7–14, Enosh was righteous.

h. "Parasang": a Persian measure of length (= 3.88 miles), used frequently in Hekalot texts.

i. "They served the Holy One," A F; "they served before the Holy One," E (cf. Mus); "they

serve before the Holy One," C D.

j. "ʿUzzah," B C; "ʿUzzaʾ," A. "ʿAzzah and ʿAzaʾel," A; "ʿAzzah and ʿAzziʾel," B C. In E the three names are: "ʿAzzaʾ, ʿUzzai, and ʿAzaʾel"; in F: "ʿAzzaʾ, ʿUzzai, and ʿAzziʾel"; and in Mus: "ʿAzzaʾ, ʿAzziʾel, and ʿUzziʾel." These angels are definitely evil agencies here; cf. 4:6. According to TarJon to Gen 6:4, ʿAzaʾel was one of the "Sons of God" who fell from heaven; cf. b.Yoma 67a; 1En 6–8.

k. "Conspired to bring a complaint": Heb. *qāšerû qaṭegor*; so A B C D Mus. For the same phrase see ARN A 2, ed. Schechter 5b: "The ministering angels conspired to bring a complaint against Moses." E F have here *qāreʾû qaṭegor* ≠ "recited a complaint." Note also Reʾuyot Yeḥezqeʾl, BM, vol. 2, p. 127, l. 9 (ed. Gruenwald, p. 105): "Ezekiel began to complain [*hithil qaṭegor*] before God."

l. Angelic opposition to man is an important theme of the Hekalot texts: see 1:3, 7; 2:1f.; 4:6f.; 6:2; 15B:2; Hekalot Rabbati 29:1 (*BHM*, vol. 3, p. 105); see "Theological Importance." Further, PRE 13. The hostility was shown supremely when the angels attempted to stop the Law being revealed to Moses: see 3En 15B:2, n. e; 48D:7.

m. "Your glory," E F Mus; "the glory of your name," A B.

n. "ʿArabot": the seventh heaven; see "Theological Importance."

o. "Come and lodge," A F.

14 from their midst.ᵖ •Then the ministering angels came, and the cohorts of the hosts, and the armies of ʿArabot, one thousand companies strong, and myriads of hosts. They took trumpets and seized horns and surrounded the Šekinah with psalms and songs, and it ascended to the heavenly heights, as it is written,   Ps 47:5

> God went up to the sound of horns,
> the Lord went up with a fanfare of trumpets.

The Angels object to Enoch's elevation

1 **6** R. Ishmael said: The angel Meṭaṭron, Prince of the Divine Presence, said to me:

When the Holy One, blessed be he, desired to bring me upᵃ to the height, he 16:5; 18:18
sent me Prince ʿAnapiʾel YHWHᵇ and he took me from their midst, before their
very eyes, and he conveyed me in great glory on a fiery chariot, with fiery 2Kgs 2:11
horses and glorious attendants,ᶜ and he brought me up with the Šekinah to the 4:3.5; 5:13
2 heavenly heights. •As soon as I reached the heavenly heights, the holy creatures,
the ophanim, the seraphim, the cherubim, the wheels of the chariot and the 21:1–4; 25:5–7;
ministers of consuming fire, smelled my odor 365,000 myriads of parasangs 26:9–12; 22:11–16; 19:2f.
offᵈ; they said, "What is this smell of one born of a woman? Why does a white Job 14:1; 15:14
3 dropᵉ ascend on high and serveᶠ among those who cleave the flames?"ᵍ •The 2:2; 4:7
Holy One, blessed be he, replied and said to them, "My ministers, my hosts, 1:8
my cherubim, my ophanim, and my seraphim, do not be displeased at this, for
all mankind has rejected me and my great kingdom and has gone off and
worshiped idols. So I have taken up my Šekinah from their midst and brought
it upʰ to the height. And this one whom I have removed from them is the
choicest of them allⁱ and worth them all in faith,ʲ righteousness, and fitting
conduct. This one whom I have taken is my sole reward from my whole world
under heaven."ᵏ

  4:3; 7

---

p. The removal of the Šekinah in 3En appears to be absolute and final; this would accord with the emphasis in Merkabah mysticism on the transcendence of God (see "Theological Importance"). In some rabbinic traditions it is taught that the Šekinah returned to earth from heaven at various points in history; see e.g. GenR 19:7; LamR proem 24; Pesiqta' deRab Kahana 1:1 (ed. Buber, 1b).

6 a. "To bring me up," A.
b. " 'Anapiʾel YHWH": an archangel. This same angel punishes Meṭaṭron in 16:5, and an etymology of his name is offered in 18:18. According to Hekalot Rabbati 23:1 (*BHM*, vol. 3, p. 100) he is one of the gatekeepers of the seventh palace. A variant form of the name— 'Anapʾel—is attested in Cairo Genizah Hekalot A/2, 45–49 (ed. Gruenwald, p. 367), but the parallel passage in Hekalot Zuṭarti (Bodleian MS 1531, fol. 45b) speaks of 'Anapiʾel, as in 3En. The highest archangels all carry the tetragram YHWH as part of their names; see 10:3; 12:5, n. e.
c. "He conveyed me . . . glorious attendants," A; "he conveyed me on a great cherub with fiery chariots and fiery horses and glorious attendants," Mus. Enoch's translation is described in terms borrowed from the account of Elijah's translation in 2Kgs 2:11f.: see "Relation to Canonical Books."

d. "365,000 myriads of parasangs off," A. For the number see 9:5, n. f.
e. "One born of woman . . . a white drop": the language is contemptuous. The expression "one born of woman" is derived from Job 14:1 and 15:14, where it has a denigratory connotation; the angels are often represented as using it in derogatory reference to mankind. The "white drop" recalls m.Ab 3:1, "Akabya b. Mehalalel said: Consider . . . from which you have come— from a putrid drop!" See further b.Shab 88b; PR 20:4 (ed. Friedmann, 96b, ll. 27f.); LevR 14:2; Peṭirat Mošeh, BM, vol. 1, p. 287, l. 5; AscenIs 9:1; 3En 48D:8.
f. "And serve," F; "and a gnat (come)," B.
g. "Those who cleave the flames": a name for the angels derived from Ps 29:7, "The voice of the Lord cleaves the flames of fire"; cf. Alphabet of Aqiba, *BHM*, vol. 3, p. 45, l. 10, where it is used of God's voice. The reading "those who cleave [ḥôṣebê] the flames" is supported by A B C E F; D Mus, however, have "those hewn out of [ḥaṣûbê] flames"; this form of the phrase is found in the early liturgical poets; see further 15:2 and 22B:6.
h. "My Šekinah . . . and brought it up," A.
i. "Choicest of them all," E Mus; "choicest in the world," A.
j. "Faith," A E F.
k. "From my whole world under heaven"; following the reading of Mus.

14

On the wings of the Šekinah

1 **7** R. Ishmael said: The angel Meṭaṭron, Prince of the Divine Presence, said to me:
When the Holy One, blessed be he, removed me from[a] the generation of the 4:3; 6:1
Flood, he bore me up[b] on the stormy wings of the Šekinah[c] to the highest heaven
and brought me into the great palaces[d] in the height of the heaven of ʿArabot, 17:3
where the glorious throne of the Šekinah[e] is found, and the chariot, the cohorts
of wrath, the hosts of fury, the fiery šin'anim,[f] the blazing cherubim, the 22:11–16; 25:5–7
smoldering ophanim, the ministers of flame, the lightning ḥašmallim and the 26:4
flashing seraphim.[g] He stationed me there to serve the throne of glory[h] day by 26:9–12
day.

The heavenly treasuries

1 **8** R. Ishmael said: Meṭaṭron, Prince of the Divine Presence, said to me:
Before the Holy One, blessed be he, set me to serve the throne of glory, he 48C:4
opened for me
　　300,000 gates[a] of understanding, 1:11
　　300,000 gates of prudence, 48D:2f.
　　300,000 gates of life,
　　300,000 gates of grace and favor,
　　300,000 gates of love,
　　300,000 gates of Torah,[b]
　　300,000 gates of humility,

7 a. "From" (*mibbên*), C D Mus; "from the
sons of" (*mibbenê*), A B E F.
　b. "When the Holy one, blessed be he, removed me . . . he bore me up," A C D F Mus.
　c. "Wings of the Šekinah": the proper context
for this expression is conversion to Judaism;
proselytes are said to be brought "under the
wings of the Šekinah"; see b.Shab 31a; b.Yeb
46b; RuthR 5:4. (In LevR 2:9 backsliding Israelites are also said to be brought back "under
the wings of the Šekinah.") The phrase is derived
from Ruth 2:12. Here it has been fancifully
adapted; cf. b.Soṭ 13b: "Moses was borne to
burial on the wings of the Šekinah." Note also
Hekalot Rabbati 2:4 (*BHM*, vol. 3, p. 84, l. 28),
"I came to take refuge under the shadow of your
wings," which echoes Pss 36:7 and 57:1.
　d. "Palaces," AE = *palṭorin*, from the Lat.
praetorium, "a palace, magnificent residence"
(in post-Augustan usage). C has *palṭin*, from the
Lat. *palatium*, "a palace." On the heavenly
palaces see 1:1, n. d, and "Theological Importance."
　e. "The glorious throne of the Šekinah," A
B; "the throne of glory and the Šekinah (are
found)," E F; "the glory of the Šekinah," C D
Mus.
　f. "Šin'anim," A B C E F Mus; "šeṭanim"
(= "Satans," "Accusers"), D.
　g. "The cohorts of wrath . . . seraphim":
orders of angels; see margin and "Theological
Importance." The šin'anim are derived from the
phrase *'alpê šin'ān* in Ps 68:18 (English text
68:17). This is commonly interpreted to mean
"thousands of repetition" i.e. thousands upon
thousands, but an early Jewish exegetical tradition takes *šin'ān* as a name for the angels; see
Midraš Tehillim, ed. Buber, 159b (to Ps 68:18);
Seper HaRazim 6:2 (ed. Margalioth, p. 104);

and the Targum for the verse; the KJV follows
this tradition: "thousands of angels." See also
24:6.
　h. "To serve the throne of glory": cf. 48C:4
and Hekalot Rabbati 11:1 (*BHM*, vol. 3, p. 91),
"The Angel of the Divine Presence enters to
adorn and arrange the throne of glory, and to
prepare a seat for the Mighty One of Jacob."

8 a. These are the gates into the heavenly treasuries; see "Theological Importance." The list
of treasuries varies greatly from MS to MS; B
has been followed. A D E F Mus all mention
"300,000 gates of Šekinah"; see 1:11. Cf.
48D:2f. and Alphabet of Aqiba, *BHM*, vol. 3,
p. 16: "5,000 gates of wisdom were opened to
Moses on Sinai, corresponding to the five books
of Torah; 8,000 gates of understanding, corresponding to the eight prophets; 11,000 gates of
knowledge, corresponding to the eleven Writings." The qualities stored in the treasuries
("understanding, prudence," etc.) correspond
roughly (1) to the qualities by which the world
was created (b.Ḥag 12a: "By ten things was the
world created, by wisdom, by understanding, by
knowledge, by strength, by rebuke, by might,
by righteousness, by judgment, by grace, and by
mercy"); and (2) to the qualities by which the
world is sustained (see 41:2; m.Ab 1:2; Alphabet
of Aqiba, *BHM*, vol. 3, p. 20). Note also the
"seven qualities that minister before the throne
of glory—wisdom, righteousness, justice, loving-kindness and compassion, truth and peace"
(ARN A 37, ed. Schechter 55b).
　b. "Torah": see 48D:2f.; Alphabet of Aqiba,
BHM, vol. 3, pp. 43f.; perhaps cf. Col 2:3;
contrast DeutR 8:6: no part of Torah was left in
heaven when it was revealed to Moses on Sinai.

300,000 gates of sustenance,
300,000 gates of mercy,
300,000 gates of reverence.

2 Then the Holy One, blessed be he, bestowed upon me wisdom[c] heaped upon 10:6; 41:3
wisdom, understanding upon understanding, prudence upon prudence, knowledge upon knowledge, mercy upon mercy, Torah upon Torah, love upon love,
grace upon grace, beauty upon beauty, humility upon humility, might upon
might, strength upon strength, power upon power, splendor upon splendor,
loveliness upon loveliness, comeliness upon comeliness; and I was honored
and adorned with all these excellent, praiseworthy qualities more than all the
denizens of the heights.

Enoch is enlarged

1 **9** R. Ishmael said: Meṭaṭron, Prince of the Divine Presence, said to me:
In addition to all these qualities,[a] the Holy One, blessed be he, laid his hand
2 on me and blessed me with 1,365,000[b] blessings. • I was enlarged[c] and increased 21:1; 22:3; 25:4; 26:4
3 in size till I matched the world in length and breadth. • He made to grow on
me 72 wings, 36 on one side and 36 on the other,[d] and each single wing covered
4 the entire world.[e] • He fixed in me 365,000[f] eyes and each eye was like the 21:1,2; 26:5
5 Great Light. • There was no sort of splendor, brilliance, brightness, or beauty Ezek 1:17; 22:8; 25:2
in the luminaries of the world[g] that he failed to fix in me.

Enoch's throne

1 **10** R. Ishmael said: Meṭaṭron, Prince of Divine Presence, said to me:
After all this, the Holy One, blessed be he, made for me[a] a throne like the 16:1
throne of glory,[b] and he spread over it[c] a coverlet[d] of splendor, brilliance,

---

c. "Wisdom": God bestows on Enoch the
contents of the treasuries. The MSS vary a little
in the list of qualities; B is followed.

9 a. "In addition to all these qualities," A C F
Mus.
b. "1,365,000," A E F; "1,305,000," B;
"500,360," C D; "5,360," Mus.
c. "I was enlarged," D Mus. The vast size
of the angels is a theme of 3En; see margin and
b.Ḥag 13a; Ma'yan Ḥokmah, *BHM*, vol. 1, p.
58, l. 10; Gedullat Mošeh 4 (BM, vol. 1, p.
278). According to 48C:5, Meṭaṭron's height, in
keeping with his supreme rank, is greater than
that of all the other angels. In the Hekalot texts
size conveys the idea of majesty and sublimity.
It is found not only in the motif of the measurements of the angels, but in Ši'ur Qomah, the
measurements of the body of God, and in the
motif of the dimensions of the heavens (see 22C:2
and "Theological Importance").
d. "On the one side . . . on the other," B C
E; "on the right side . . . on the left side," D.
The number 72 corresponds to the number of the
princes of kingdoms in 17:8; the idea may be
that, as Prince of the World, Meṭaṭron is in
charge of the princes of kingdoms; see 3:2.
e. "Covered the entire world," lit. "(was)
the fullness of the world"; so A E F. For the
expression see margin and Re'uyot Yeḥezqe'l,
BM, vol. 2, p. 132 (ed. Gruenwald, p. 128):
"The Prince . . . is the fullness of Zebul"; cf.
Isa 6:3, "his glory fills the whole earth."
f. "365,000," A B E F; "500,360," C Mus;
"5,360," D. The number 365 and multiples of
it are common in the mystical texts; see e.g. 5:3;

6:2; 17:7. The number 365 is most obviously
connected with the number of days in the solar
year.
g. "In the luminaries of the world": emending
to *še-bamme'ôrôt še-bā'ôlām*.

10 a. "After all this . . . made for me," D;
"All this the Holy One, blessed be he, made for
me: he made for me," E F; "All this the Holy
One, blessed be he, made for me," A B.
b. "A throne like the throne of glory": According to a dictum in b.Ḥag 15a no one is
allowed to sit in heaven except God; cf. 3En
18:24 and GenR 65:21; LevR 6:3; y.Ber 2c.23;
PR 22:6 (ed. Friedmann, 114a). Meṭaṭron, therefore, is highly privileged to have a throne. In
Masseket Hekalot 7 (*BHM*, vol. 2, p. 46) the
seven angels who were created first are said to
sit in front of the curtain; note also the angels
with thrones in Seper HaRazim 3:2–3 (ed. Margalioth, p. 92) and 5:4 (ed. Margalioth, p. 101).
c. "Over it," Mus; "over me," A B E F;
see n. d.
d. "A coverlet": this is the natural sense of
the word *perāś* (usually spelled *perās*), if we
follow Mus's reading "over it" (see n. c). For
this meaning of *perāś* see Masseket Ṣiṣit 2 (ed.
Higger, p. 50): "Evening garments and bed-
covers [*pirsê mittāh*] are exempt from fringes."
On the other hand, if we adopt A B E F's reading
"over me," the *perāś* would presumably be a
canopy; cf. NumR 10:4: "Pharaoh's daughter
spread a sort of canopy [*perās*] above him (i.e.
Solomon) and set therein all kinds of precious
stones and pearls which glittered like constellations."

brightness, beauty, loveliness, and grace, like the coverlet of the throne of glory, in which all the varied splendor of the luminaries that are in the world 9:5; 12:1
2 is set.ᵉ •He placed it at the door of the seventh palace and sat me down upon 16:1; 48C:8
3 it. •And the heraldᶠ went out into every heaven and announced concerning me: "I have appointed Meṭaṭron my servantᵍ as a prince and a ruler over all the 1:4; 44:9; 48C:1; 48D:1(12)
denizens of the heights, apart from the eight great, honored, and terrible princesʰ
4 who are called YHWH by the name of their King.ⁱ •Any angel and any prince 3:2; 12:5; 30:1
who has anything to say in my presence should go before him and speak to
5 him. •Whatever he says to you in my name you must observe and do, because Ex 23:20–22
I have committed to himʲ the Prince of Wisdom and the Prince of Understanding, 48D:1(93)
to teach him the wisdom of those above and of those below, the wisdom of this
6 world and of the world to come. •Moreover I have put him in charge of all the 1:1
stores of the palacesᵏ of ʿArabot, and all the treasuries that are in the heavenly 17:3; 8:1
heights.''

God reveals secrets to Enoch

1 **11** R. Ishmael said: The angel Meṭaṭron, Prince of the Divine Presence, said to me:
The Holy One, blessed be he, revealed to me from that time onwardᵃ all the mysteries of wisdom, all the depths of the perfect Torahᵇ and all the thoughts of men's hearts. All the mysteries of the world and all the orders of natureᶜ 13:1
2 stand revealed before me as they stand revealed before the Creator.ᵈ •From that timeᵉ onward I looked and beheld deep secrets and wonderful mysteries.ᶠ Before 45:3
3 a man thinks in secret, I see his thought; before he acts, I see his act.ᵍ •There 10:5; 48C:4,7
is nothing in heaven above or deep within the earth concealed from me.ʰ

---

e. ''All the varied splendor . . . is set,'' A E F Mus; ''all the kinds of luminaries that are in the world are set,'' B C.

f. For the herald see Hekalot Rabbati 6:4 (BHM, vol. 3, p. 88); Haggadat Šemaʿ Yiśraʾel, BHM, vol. 5, p. 165, l. 29; Cairo Genizah Hekalot A/2, 13 (ed. Gruenwald, p. 362); PR 33:10 (ed. Friedmann, 154b).

g. ''My servant'': for ''servant'' (ʿebed) as a title of Meṭaṭron see the margin. It is borne also by Surya', the Prince of the Divine Presence, in Hekalot Rabbati 13:1 (BHM, vol. 3, p. 93, l. 10), and by the angel 'Ozahyah in Cairo Genizah Hekalot A/2, 11 (ed. Gruenwald, p. 362). Its full form, ''servant of the Lord'' (ʿebed YHWH) occurs in Hekalot Rabbati 26:8 (BHM, vol. 3, p. 104, l. 17); cf. Isa 49:3. In one Merkabah text Meṭaṭron is referred to as the ''beloved servant'' (šammāšāʾ reḥîmāʾ); see ''Date.''

h. ''The eight great, honored, and terrible princes,'' A, and, substantially, D Mus.

i. ''YHWH by the name of their King,'' A; ''Yah, Yah, 'Ah, 'Ah by the name of their King,'' Mus; ''YHWH like the name of their King,'' D. ''Apart from . . . their King'' appears to be a gloss aimed at demoting Meṭaṭron; see ''Theological Importance.'' It is not stated who the eight princes are, but from 16:5 we may deduce that 'Anapi'el is one of them.

j. ''I have committed to him'' (mesartîm lô), A; but B D E F have mešāretîm lô = ''(the Prince of Wisdom and the Prince of Understanding) (are) his servants.''

k. ''Palaces,'' C Mus; ''palace,'' A D E F.

11 a. ''From that time onward'' (mēʾāz), A B E F; cf. n. e below; C D Mus have maʿyan = ''the wellspring (of all the secrets of Torah).''

b. ''Wisdom, all the depths of the perfect Torah,'' C Mus; ''perfect wisdom,'' B. Torah has both its outer and its inner meanings: cf. m.Ab 6:1, ''Whosoever engages in the study of Torah for its own sake merits many things . . . to him are revealed the secrets [rāzê] of Torah.'' The expression ''perfect Torah'' is derived from Ps 19:8 (English text 19:7); it occurs again in Alphabet of Aqiba, BHM, vol. 3, p. 14: ''But for the perfect Torah the whole world would not endure; but for the whole world the perfect Torah would not endure.''

c. ''The orders of nature'': Heb. sidrê berêʾšît; so A C D Mus. For the phrase see b.Shab 53b: ''Rab Judah observed: How difficult are man's wants that the orders of nature had to be changed for him''; further 3En 13:1; Alphabet of Aqiba, BHM, vol. 3, p. 13, l. 7; Hekalot Rabbati 9:5 (BHM, vol. 3, p. 91, l. 3). E has here ''all the secrets [sitrê] of nature''; B F have ''all the mysteries [rāzê] of nature.''

d. ''The Creator'' (yôṣēr berêʾšît), A B C E F; ''the Maker of all'' (yôṣēr hakkôl), Mus; ''the Maker of the work of creation'' (yôṣēr maʿaśêh berêʾšît), D.

e. ''From that time onward'' (mēʾāz), E F; cf. n. a above. A B have meʾôd; C D Mus omit.

f. ''Deep secrets and wonderful mysteries'': emending to berāzîm ʿamuqqîm ûbesôdôt muplāʾîm.

g. ''Before a man thinks . . . I see his act,'' A; ''before a man thinks, I know his thought; before a man thinks in secret, I see his thought; before he acts, I know his act,'' C Mus.

h. It is a fundamental idea of 3En that Meṭaṭron knows all mysteries; see margin. His relationship to Ishmael is that of revealer of secrets.

Enoch's robe, crown, and name

1 **12** R. Ishmael said: Meṭaṭron, Prince of the Divine Presence, said to me:
Out of the love which he had for me, more than for all the denizens of the
heights, the Holy One, blessed be he, fashioned for me a majestic robe,ᵃ in

2 which all kinds of luminaries were set,ᵇ and he clothed me in it. •He fashioned | 9:5; 10:1
for me a glorious cloak in which brightness, brilliance, splendor, and luster of

3 every kind were fixed, and he wrapped me in it.ᶜ •He fashioned for me a kingly | 16:1f.; 18:1

4 crownᵈ in which 49 refulgent stones were placed, each like the sun's orb, •and
its brilliance shone into the four quarters of the heaven of ʿArabot, into the
seven heavens, and into the four quarters of the world. He set it upon my head | 17:3

5 and he called me, "The lesser YHWH"ᵉ in the presence of his whole household | 48C:7; 48D:1(90)
in the height,ᶠ as it is written, "My name is in him." | Ex 23:21

The crown is inscribed

1 **13** R. Ishmael said: The angel Meṭaṭron, Prince of the Divine Presence, the
glory of highest heaven,ᵃ said to me:
Out of the abundant loveᵇ and great compassion wherewith the Holy One,
blessed be he, loved and cherished me more than all the denizens of the heights,
he wrote with his finger, as with a pen of flame, upon the crown which was | 18:25; 29:1; 39:1; 41:4
on my head,
the lettersᶜ by which heaven and earth were created; | 41:1
the letters by which seas and rivers were created;
the letters by which mountains and hills were created;
the letters by which stars and constellations, lightning

---

12 a. "A majestic robe," D and, substantially,
C; cf. 2En 22:8 (A and B); Alphabet of Meṭaṭron:
"Meṭaṭron is clad in eight garments made out of
the splendor of the Šekinah" (quoted from Odeberg). The eight garments here allude to the eight
garments of the high priest (m.Yoma 7:5); for
Meṭaṭron as the high priest of the heavenly
sanctuary see 15B:1. Meṭaṭron's robe may be
analogous to the robe (ḥālûq) of God; on this
see Hekalot Rabbati 3:4 (BHM, vol. 3, p. 86, l.
1); 24:3 (BHM, vol. 3, p. 101, l. 15—reading
ḥalûqô for hylwqw); Hekalot Zuṭarti (MS Bod.
1531, fol. 45a); see further 3En 16:1, n. a.
However, it is a common idea that the celestials
in general wear glorious garments; 1En 62:15;
Alphabet of Aqiba, BHM, vol. 3, pp. 33f.; see
further 18:22, n. i2.
b. "In which all kinds of luminaries were
set," A E F Mus and, substantially, D. C points
to the reading "in which all the varied brightness,
brilliance, and luster of the luminaries (was set)."
c. "And he wrapped me in it," A C D and,
substantially, E Mus.
d. "A kingly crown": this probably corresponds to God's "terrible crown" (29:1). For
crowned archangels see margin and Hekalot
Rabbati 11:1 (BHM, vol. 3, p. 91). The crowns
may be a sort of turban; see 16:2, n. f.
e. "The lesser YHWH": Meṭaṭron's most
revealing name, given to him as God's vice-
regent. 48B:1(44) has the corresponding divine
title, "The greater YHWH." From the quotation
of Ex 23:21 here and elsewhere, it is clear that
the concept of the "lesser YHWH" arose through
speculation about the angel of the Lord in whom
God's name resides; see "Theological Importance," and 30:1, n. d.
f. "Household [pamalyâ'] in the height":

Rabbinic texts refer to the angels in general, or
the heavenly law court in particular, as God's
"heavenly household" (pamalyâ' šelemaʿalâh),
in contrast to Israel or the sages—God's "earthly
household" (pamalyâ' šelemaṭṭâh). The use of
the Lat. loanword familia suggests that there is
an allusion to the familia Caesaris (see "Theological Importance"). Sometimes the Merkabah
texts speak of "families" of angels (see "Relation to the Canonical Books"). See 16:1; 18:21;
Cairo Genizah Hekalot A/1, 37 (ed. Gruenwald,
p. 359); Pereq mippirqe hekalot, BHM, vol. 3,
p. 161, ll. 7f.; Peṭirat Mošeh, BM, vol. 1, p.
287, l. 6; below 30:1, n. b.

13 a. "The glory of highest heaven": a title of
Meṭaṭron repeated in 15:1; 16:1; and 24:1. In
Hekalot Rabbati 6:3 (BM, vol. 1, p. 76, ll.
2–3) the archangel Segansag'el is addressed as
"the glory of the splendor of the height."
b. "Abundant love," A C E F.
c. The twenty-two letters of the Heb. alphabet;
cf. the "twenty-two seals" (B, "twenty-two
letters") in 48D:5. The classic statement of this
doctrine is in Seper Yeṣirah 2:2 (ed. Gruenwald,
Israel Oriental Studies 1 (1971) 148, no. 19):
"The twenty-two letters: God carved them and
shaped them, weighed them, changed them round
and combined them and created with them the
soul of all that has been created, and the soul of
all that will be created." See also b.Ber 55a:
"Rab Judah said in the name of Rab: Bezalel
[Ex 31:2] knew how to combine the letters by
which the heavens and the earth were created."
For creation of the world by the letter beth see
y.Ḥag 77c.41; GenR 1:10; for creation by the
letters of the divine name Yah see b.Men 29b;
Masseket Hekalot 7 (BHM, vol. 2, p. 46).

and wind, thunder and thunderclaps, snow and hail,
   hurricane and tempest were created;
the letters by which all the necessities of the world and
   all the orders of creation[d] were created.   11:1

2 Each letter flashed time after time like lightnings, time after time like torches,
time after time like flames, time after time like the rising of the sun, moon, and
stars.

Enoch receives homage

1 **14** R. Ishmael said: The angel Meṭaṭron, Prince of the Divine Presence, said
to me:
When the Holy One, blessed be he, placed this crown upon my head, all the   17:8; 18:2; 30:2
princes of kingdoms who are in the height of the heaven of ʿArabot and all the 17:3
legions of every heaven trembled at me. Even the princes of the ʾelim, the
princes of the ʾerʾellim and the princes of the ṭapsarim,[a] who are greater than 39:2
all the ministering angels that serve before the throne of glory, trembled and   26:12; Job 1:6; Zech
2 shrank from me when they saw me. • Even Sammaʾel, the Prince of the Accusers,[b]   3:1
who is greater than all the princes of kingdoms that are in the height, was afraid
3 and shuddered at me. • Even the angel of fire, the angel of hail, the angel of
wind, the angel of lightning, the angel of whirlwind,[c] the angel of thunder, the
angel of snow, the angel of rain, the angel of day, the angel of night, the angel
of the sun, the angel of the moon, the angel of the stars, the angel of the
constellations, who guide the world by their direction, trembled and shrank
back in alarm from me when they saw me.
4   These are the names of the princes[d] who guide the world:

---

d. "The letters by which heaven . . . all the
orders of creation," A Mus. A B Mus have
"orders [*sidrê*] of creation"; E F, "secrets [*sitrê*]
of creation"; see 11:1, n. c.

14 a. "ʾElim . . . ʾerʾellim . . . ṭapsarim": classes
of angels. The ʾelim are derived from passages
such as Ex 15:11: "Who among the ʾelim [JB,
"gods"] is your like, Lord." The Mekilta'
deRabbi 'Išmaʾel paraphrases this: "Who is your
like among those who serve before you in heaven"
(Bešallaḥ 8, ed. Horovitz-Rabin, p. 142, l. 14).
Cf. also the use of ʾelim in Ps 29:1; 89:7; Dan
11:36. The ʾerʾellim are derived from Isa 33:7:
"Look, the ʾerʾellim [JB fn., "their brave men"]
cry in the streets; the angels [JB, "ambassadors"]
of peace weep bitterly." *Tipsār*, plural *ṭapsārîm*,
occurs twice in the Bible as a designation of
rank: in Jer 51:27 JB translates it "officer," and
in Nah 3:17, "scribe." In neither passage does
there seem to be anything which could connect
the word with the heavenly world. However, in
the early synagogue poets (the *payṭanim*) and in
the Hekalot texts it was used of the angels, and
in 3En it denotes a distinct order of angels.
ʾErʾellim and ṭapsarim are mentioned together in
39:2; Masseket Hekalot 5 (*BHM*, vol. 2, p. 43,
l. 30) and 6 (*BHM*, vol. 2, p. 45, l. 11). For
ʾelim and ʾerʾellim see Seder Rabbah diBereʾšit,
BM, vol. 7, p. 45, l. 7. ʾErʾellim on their own
are found in b.Ket 104a; Midraš Konen, *BHM*,
vol. 2, p. 25, l. 20; Gedullat Mošeh 7 (BM, vol.
1, p. 179, l. 16).

b. "Sammaʾel, the Prince of the Accusers [*śar
hammaṣtînîm*]," A B; "Sammaʾel, the Prince of
all the Accusers," C Mus; "Wicked Sammaʾel,
the Prince of all the Accusers," F. Sammaʾel,

the leader of the wicked angels, is one of the
most important figures of talmudic and post-
talmudic angelology. DeutR 11:10 describes him
as "Head of the Accusers [*śeṭānîm*]"; cf. 3En
4:6, n. j. In 26:12 he appears as the Prince of
Rome, who, along with Dubbiʾel, the Prince of
Persia, acts as Satan's assistant in bringing accusations against Israel in the heavenly law court.
His identification with the Prince of Rome, the
great earthly adversary of Israel, is natural; cf.
Hekalot Rabbati 4:5 (*BHM*, vol. 3, p. 87, l. 2).
On Sammaʾel see also 3Bar 4:8; AscenIs 11:41;
b.Soṭ 10b; GenR 56:4; ExR 18:5; 21:7; PRE 13
and 46; Midraš "ʾElleh ʾezkerāh," *BHM*, vol.
3, p. 66, l. 1.

c. "Whirlwind" (*zaʿam*): the Heb. word usually means "wrath," "anger," but in this context
it must refer to a natural phenomenon; cf. the
double sense of the semantically related word
zaʿap, which can mean either (1) "anger,"
"rage," or (2) "storm," "hurricane." For this
latter sense of *zaʿap* see vs. 4: "Zaʿapiʾel, who
is in charge of hurricane [*zaʿap*]"; cf. Jonah 1:15
and m.Taʾan 3:8.

d. "The princes," A E F; "the angels," Mus.
The list of angels is a secondary gloss on vs. 3.
The angelic names here are composed of a stem
which indicates the phenomenon over which the
angel has control, plus the theophoric ending *ēl*;
e.g. Ruḥiʾel is *rûaḥ*, "wind," plus *ʾēl*, "God";
see "Theological Importance." The only exceptions to this pattern are the names Šimšiʾel and
Gabriel, in which the stem does not correspond
to the natural element which the angel rules; see
nn. e and g below. For a similar list of angelic
names see 1En 6:7; 8:3f.

Gabriel,[e] the angel of fire;   Dan 8:16
Baradi'el, the angel of hail;
Ruḥi'el, who is in charge of wind;
Baraqi'el, who is in charge of lightning;
Za'ami'el, who is charge of whirlwind;
Ziqi'el, who is in charge of comets;   42:7
Zi'i'el,[f] who is charge of tremors;
Za'api'el, who is in charge of hurricane;
Ra'ami'el, who is charge of thunder;
Ra'aši'el, who is in charge of earthquakes;
Šalgi'el, who is charge of snow;
Maṭari'el, who is in charge of rain;
Šimši'el,[g] who is in charge of day;
Laili'el, who is in charge of night;
Galgalli'el, who is in charge of the orb of the sun;   17:4
'Opanni'el,[h] who is in charge of the disk[i] of the moon;   17:5
Kokabi'el,[j] who is in charge of the stars;   17:7
Rahaṭi'el, who is in charge of the constellations.   17:6

5 They all fell prostrate when they saw me and could not look at me because of
the majesty, splendor, beauty, brightness, brilliance, and radiance of the glorious   12:3
crown which was on my head.

Enoch is transformed into fire

1 *15 R. Ishmael said: The angel Meṭaṭron, Prince of the Divine Presence, the
glory of highest heaven, said to me:
When the Holy One, blessed be he, took me to serve[a] the throne of glory, the   7
wheels of the chariot and all the needs of the Šekinah, at once my flesh turned   19:2
to flame, my sinews to blazing fire, my bones to juniper coals, my eyelashes[b]   22:4; 26:4
to lightning flashes, my eyeballs to fiery torches,[c] the hairs of my head to hot   9:2
flames, all my limbs to wings of burning fire,[d] and the substance of my body
2 to blazing fire. •On my right—those who cleave flames of fire—on my left—   6:2
burning brands[e]—round about me[f] swept wind, tempest, and storm; and the
roar of earthquake upon earthquake[g] was before and behind me.

---

e. "Gabriel," A B E F. For Gabriel as the
angel of fire see b.Pes 118a. Mus, however, has
"Nuri'el," which corresponds more closely to
the rest of the angelic names in the list; *nûrā'* is
the Aram. for "fire." See n. d above and n. g
below.
f. "Zi'i'el": so A B E F, but the form of the
name is probably corrupt. Perhaps read
"Zewa'i'el" to correspond more closely to
zewā'āh, "earthquake."
g. "Šimši'el," A B C E Mus; the name is
derived from *šemeš*, "the sun"; cf. Gen 1:16. F
has "Yomi'el" from *yôm*, "day."
h. " 'Opanni'el," A E F Mus.
i. "Disk," E F; cf. 17:5; but A B Mus have
"disks," presumably in reference to the phases
of the moon.
j. "Kokabi'el," A F Mus.

15 * For chapter 15B see the Appendix.
a. "To serve," C D Mus; "in service to
serve," A B E F.
b. "My eyelashes": Heb. *'ap'appay;* so C D

Mus. The Heb. word basically means "eyelids,"
but this hardly fits the context here. It can also
be used as a synonym for *'ênayim*, "eyes"; see
Jer 9:17. The reading of A B E F, *'ôr 'ap'appay*,
demands the translation "the light of my *eyes*."
c. "Fiery torches," D E F; A B have the
singular, "a fiery torch." Cf. the description of
the transformation of Enoch here with the transformation of Moses in Gedullat Mošeh 2 (BM,
vol. 1, p. 277).
d. "Burning fire," A C E F.
e. "Burning brands" (*bô'arîm lappîdim*), C
D. Note the attributive adjective is in an unusual
position before the noun. This is perhaps the best
of the variant readings, but it does not supply a
fully satisfactory complement to "those who
cleave flames of fire." Should we read *bôqe'ê
lappîdê 'êš* = "those who split firebrands [or
"tongues of flame"]"?
f. "Round about me," A Mus; "round about,"
B E F.
g. "Earthquake upon earthquake," A C E F
Mus; "thunder upon earthquake," B.

Metatron dethroned

1 **16** R. Ishmael said: The angel Metatron, Prince of the Divine Presence, the glory of highest heaven, said to me:[a]
At first I sat upon a great throne[b] at the door of the seventh palace, and I judged 10:1
all the denizens of the heights[c] on the authority of the Holy One, blessed be 17:3
he. I assigned greatness, royalty, rank, sovereignty, glory, praise, diadem, crown, and honor to all the princes of kingdoms, when I sat in the heavenly 10:3
court.[d] The princes of kingdoms stood beside me, to my right and to my left, 28:7-9
2 by authority of the Holy One, blessed be he. •But when 'Aher[e] came to behold 1:1
the vision of the chariot and set eyes upon me, he was afraid and trembled 1:7
before me. His soul was alarmed to the point of leaving him because of his fear, dread, and terror of me, when he saw me seated upon a throne like a king, with ministering angels standing beside me as servants and all the princes of
3 kingdoms crowned with crowns[f] surrounding me. •Then he opened his mouth 12:3; 18:1
4 and said, "There are indeed two powers in heaven!"[g] •Immediately a divine voice[h] came out from the presence of the Šekinah[i] and said, "Come back to
5 me, apostate sons—apart from 'Aher!" •Then 'Anapi'el[j] YHWH, the honored, Jer 3:22
glorified, beloved, wonderful, terrible, and dreadful Prince, came at the com- 6:1
mand of the Holy One, blessed be he, and struck me with sixty lashes of fire[k] and made me stand to my feet.

16 a. Ch. 16 is probably a secondary addition to chs. 3–15: It runs counter to the whole tenor of the foregoing description of the role of Metatron, and is probably aimed at minimizing his powers: cf. the gloss at 10:3, and see further "Historical Importance" for evidence of concern over the powers of Metatron. Such a story would hardly have originated in the mystical circles responsible for the traditions in chs. 3–15; it must have come from elsewhere. Its most obvious source is the account of the humbling of Metatron in b.Hag 15a. The talmudic version of the story probably has priority over the one quoted here. Allusions to the humbling of Metatron and to many other ideas in 3–16 are found in Cairo Genizah Hekalot A/2, 13–18 (ed. Gruenwald, pp. 362f.): "A youth [na'ar] comes out to meet you from behind the throne of glory. Do not bow down to him—for his crown is as the crown of his King, and the sandals on his feet are as the sandals of his King, and the robe [ḥālûq] upon him is as the robe [ḥālûq] of his King . . . his eyes blaze like torches, his eyeballs burn like lamps; his brilliance is as the brilliance of his King, his glory is as the glory of his Maker—Zehobadyah is his name."
b. "A great throne," A C Mus. (A, in fact, reads, "a great throne of glory," but cancels "of glory.")
c. "Denizens of the heights," C Mus; "denizens of the heights, the heavenly household," A B.
d. "The heavenly court [yešîbāh]": Metatron's court is analogous to God's heavenly law court (bêt dîn); cf. 28:7.
e. " 'Aher," A B; "Elisha b. Abuya," Mus; "Elisha b. Abuya, and he stood behind YHWH," C. Elisha b. Abuya was a Palestinian scholar of the late 1st and early 2nd cents. A.D. He was one of the four who entered Pardes (b.Hag 14b;

"Historical Importance"). He came to be regarded as the arch-heretic and was referred to contemptuously as 'Aher, "Another." (For another explanation of the name see b.Hag 15a.)
f. "Crowned with crowns," lit. "bound with crowns." The Merkabah texts normally speak of "binding" in connection with the heavenly crowns; see 12:4; 16:2; 17:8; 18:25; 21:4; Hekalot Rabbati 3:2 (BHM, vol. 3, p. 85, l. 15); 11:1 (BHM, vol. 3, p. 91). The idiom is found also in b.Hag 13b: "Sandalpon . . . stands behind the chariot and binds crowns on his Creator." The "crowns" may be diadems or turbans, or else "bind" has magical significance.

g. "Two powers in heaven": i.e. Elisha denied the unity of God. The precise nature of the dualism involved in asserting that there are two powers in heaven is not clear; for the expression, see b.Ber 33b; b.Meg 25a; SifDeut 329 (ed. Finkelstein, p. 379); Mekilta' deRabbi 'Išma'el, Šîrāh 4 (ed. Horovitz-Rabin, p. 130), Yitrô 5 (p. 220). m.Sanh 4:5 (cf. b.Sanh 38a) mentions heretics who speak of many powers in heaven.
h. "A divine voice": Heb. bat qôl, the voice that on special occasions mysteriously announces God's will (b.Yoma 9b; b.'Erub 13b; b.AZ 18a; b.Ber 61b).
i. "From the presence of the Šekinah," A C Mus; "from heaven, from the presence of the Šekinah," B.
j. " 'Anapi'el," A Mus; on this angel see above 6:1, n. b. B has here " 'Aniyyel"; cf. the angel 'Ani'el in Zohar Pequûdê 1.247b, and Seper Razi'el (Amsterdam, 1701) 5b, l. 12, and the angel 'An'el in Zohar Hadaš Yitrô 38b and Judah b. Barzillai's commentary on Seper Yeṣirah (ed. Halberstam [Berlin, 1885]) p. 247, l. 27.
k. In b.Yoma 77a Gabriel is punished with forty lashes of fire.

The princes of the seven heavens

1 **17** R. Ishmael said: The angel Meṭaṭron, Prince of the Divine Presence, the glory of highest heaven, said to me:[a]
There are seven great, beautiful, wonderful, and honored princes[b] who are in charge of the seven heavens. They are, Michael, Gabriel, Šatqiʾel, Šaḥaqiʾel,
2 Baradiʾel, Baraqiʾel, and Sidriʾel.[c] •Each of them is a prince over a heavenly host, and every one of them is attended by 496,000 myriads of ministering   35:1; 40:3
angels.
3 Michael, the Great Prince, is in charge of the seventh heaven, the highest,   33:5; 38:1
which is in ʿArabot.[d]
Gabriel, Prince of the Host, is in charge of the sixth heaven, which is in   14:4
Makon.
Šatqiʾel, Prince of the Host, is in charge of the fifth heaven, which is in
Maʿon.
Šaḥaqiʾel, Prince of the Host, is in charge of the fourth heaven, which is in
Zebul.
Baradiʾel, Prince of the Host, is in charge of the third heaven, which is in   14:4
Šeḥaqim.
Baraqiʾel, Prince of the Host, is in charge of the second heaven, which is   14:4
in Raqiaʿ.[e]
Sidriʾel, Prince of the Host, is in charge of the first heaven, which is in
Wilon.[f]
4 Under them is Galgalliʾel,[g] the Prince, who is in charge of the orb of the sun,   14:4
and with him are 96 angels, mighty and honored, who make the sun's orb run[h]   9:5
365,000 parasangs[i] through Raqiaʿ every day.

17 a. Chs. 17–40, which form the third major division of 3En, contain the discourses of Meṭaṭron on the heavenly world. The material falls into three rough sections: Chs. 17–28/29 deal with the angelic hierarchies; chs. 29/30–33 describe the sessions of the heavenly law court; chs. 34–40 are concerned with the recitation of the celestial Sanctus. Once again disparate traditions have been combined: There are three originally distinct angelologies (the first in ch. 17; the second in ch. 18; the third in 19–22; 25:1–28:6) and several different accounts of the heavenly assize, and of the performance of the celestial Qeduššah. See further 18:1, n. a; 18:24, n. p2; 19:1, n. a; 23:1, n. a; 28:7, n. g; 29:1, n. a; 30:1, n. a; 34:1, n. a; 35:1, n. a.

b. "Seven . . . princes": the idea that there are seven archangels is very old; see 1En 20 and 4QŠirŠabb. Cf. the "seven angels who were created first" in Masseket Hekalot 7 (BHM, vol. 2, p. 46, l. 30), and the seven Prōtoktistoi in Clement of Alexandria, Eclogae propheticae 57.1.

c. "Michael . . . Sidriʾel": the list of angels here and in vs. 3 follows A and, substantially, Mus. As usual, the vocalization of some names is uncertain.

d. On the seven heavens see "Theological Importance." It is clear from the parallel passage in b.Ḥag 12b that, apart from Wilon (on which see n. f below), the various names of the heavens are derived by exegesis from Scripture.

e. "Which is in Raqiaʿ," Lemb; "which is in the height of Raqiaʿ," A B; "which is in Šamayim," Mus.

f. "The first heaven, which is in Wilon," Mus; "the first heaven, which is in Wilon, which is in Šamayim," A. Wilon as a name for the

first heaven appears to have originated among Babylonian Jews, whereas Šamayim is the standard Palestinian term. Wilon, derived from the Lat. *velum*, "curtain," "veil," denotes an ordinary door curtain in rabbinic Heb. (m.Kel 20:6; m.Neg 11:11). It would seem, then, that the first heaven is regarded as a sort of veil or curtain which either conceals the heavenly world from human eyes, or which, by being opened and shut, is the cause of daylight and darkness. b.Ḥag 12b describes its function thus: "It does not serve for anything, but enters in the morning and leaves in the evening and renews every day the work of creation" (cf. Midraš Konen, BHM, vol. 2, pp. 36f.; Seder Rabbah diBereʾšit, BM, vol. 1, p. 39; Baraitaʾ di Maʿaseh Bereʾšit, ed. Séd, A 70–72; B 58f.). Note also Midraš 'aseret hadibberot (BHM, vol. 1, pp. 63f.): "The Holy One, blessed be he, created seven heavens. The lowest of them is called Wilon and it is like a curtain [wîlôn] drawn across the doorway of a house, so that those within can see those without, but those without cannot see those within." See further, b.Ber 58b; ARN A 37 (ed. Schechter, 55b); Midraš Tehillim 19:6 (ed. Buber, 83a–b), and 114:2 (ed. Buber, 236a). On the other heavenly curtain, the pargôd, see 3En 45:1, n. a.

g. "Under them is Galalliʾel": The angels who move the heavenly bodies (Galalliʾel, ʾOpanniʾel, Rahaṭiʾel, and Kokabiʾel) are subordinate to the angels of the seven heavens.

h. "Make . . . run," A Mus; "make descend," B. The expression is repeated in vss. 5 and 7.

i. "365,000 parasangs"; an obvious multiple of the number of days in the solar year. In the astronomical passage in vss. 4–7 the heavenly

5   Under them[j] is ʾOpanniʾel, the Prince, who is in charge of the globe of the moon, and with him are 88 angels[k] who make the moon's globe run 354,000[l] parasangs every night, whenever the moon stands in the east at its turning point. When does the moon stand[m] in the east at its turning point? Answer: On the 15th day of every month.[n]

6   Under them is Rahaṭiʾel, the Prince, who is in charge of the constellations, and with him are 72 angels, great and honored. Why is his name called Rahaṭiʾel?   14:4 Because he makes the constellations run 339,000 parasangs in their cycles and orbits[o] each night, from the east to the west and from the west to the east. For the Holy One, blessed be he, made for them all, for the sun, the moon, and the constellations, a tent to move in[p] by night from the west to the east.   Isa 40:22

7   Under them is Kokabiʾel, the Prince, who is in charge of all the stars, and with him are 365,000 myriads of ministering angels, great and honored, who   9:2 make the stars run from city to city and from state to state in the Raqiaʿ of the   Deut 4:19 heavens.

8   Above them[q] are 72 princes of kingdoms in the height, corresponding to the   30:2; 3:2; 48D:3 72 nations[r] in the world. All of them are crowned with kingly crowns, clothed   18:1 in regal dress, and decked with royal jewels.[s] All of them ride on royal horses   Zech 1:8 and grasp kingly scepters in their hands. Before each of them, when he travels through the Raqiaʿ, royal servants[t] run, with great honor and much pomp, just as kings travel on earth in chariots attended by horsemen and great armies, in glory, greatness, praise, acclamation, and splendor.

An angelic hierarchy

1   **18** R. Ishmael said: Meṭaṭron, Prince of the Divine Presence, the glory of highest heaven, said to me:
The angels of the first heaven, when they see their Prince, they dismount from   17:3 their horses[a] and fall prostrate.   Zech 1:8

---

bodies are classified into four groups: sun, moon, constellations, and stars (i.e. planets). They are assigned to the second heaven (Raqiaʿ), and their orbits (in diminishing length) are given. In 46:1–4 and probably also in 5:8, the heavenly bodies are animate beings; here they are inert masses which the angels trundle through the heavens. For this latter idea see 1En 80:1; 4Ezra 6:3; 3Bar 6:2. Astronomy forms an element in some apocalyptic texts; see e.g. 1En 72–82. It is, strictly speaking, a motif of Maʿaśeh Bereʾšit (see "Theological Importance").

   j. "Under them," A Mus.
   k. "88 angels," A B; "85 angels," Mus.
   l. "354,000": This figure is a multiple of the number of days in the lunar year (1 lunar month = 29½ days).
   m. "When does the moon stand," A Mus; "when does the moon sit," B.
   n. The words within parentheses are a gloss.
   o. "In their cycles and orbits," A.
   p. "To move in," A Mus.
   q. "Above them": either above the angels in charge of the heavenly bodies or above the angels in charge of the seven heavens. In favor of the former view is the fact that the princes of kingdoms, like the angels of the heavenly bodies, are here located in the second heaven. Note also 38:3, where the Prince of the World (who in 30:2 is said to be the leader of the princes of kingdoms) exercises authority over the heavenly bodies. In favor of the latter view is the fact that

in 18:2 the princes of kingdoms are placed on the hierarchical ladder above the seven princes of the seven heavens.
   r. "72 nations," B; "70 nations," A Mus. The division of mankind into seventy or seventy-two nations is based on a count of the names in the Table of the Nations in Gen 10. The normal rabbinic reckoning is seventy (b.Sukk 55b; NumR 14:12; Midraš Tehillim 68:6 [to Ps 68:12], ed. Buber, 159a; cf. m.Soṭ 7:5; b.Shab 88b), and this idea may be as old as 1En 89:59 (the "seventy shepherds"). However, there are variations: e.g. Midraš Haggadol to Gen 10:1 reckons sixty nations, but to Gen 10:32 speaks of seventy-two languages; normally the number of languages correlates with the number of nations in the world; see margin.
   s. "Decked with royal jewels," A and, substantially, Mus.
   t. "Royal servants," A Mus.

18 a. "Horses": emending to *sûsîm;* A B have the singular "horse" (*sûs*). For angelic horsemen see Hekalot Rabbati 15:8–16:2 (*BHM*, vol. 3, pp. 94f.); Masseket Hekalot 4 (*BHM*, vol. 2, p. 46); Seper HaRazim 2:132f. (ed. Margalioth, p. 88). The angelology of ch. 18 was originally independent of that in ch. 17. Two differences are noteworthy: (1) Ch. 17 goes in descending order, from the highest angels to the lowest, but ch. 18 in ascending order; (2) the heavenly palaces are mentioned in ch. 18, but not in ch. 17.

The Prince of the first heaven, when he sees[b] the Prince of the second heaven,   12:3; 16:2
he removes[c] the glorious crown[d] from his head and falls prostrate.
The Prince of the second heaven, when he sees the Prince of the third heaven,
he removes the glorious crown from his head and falls prostrate.
The Prince of the third heaven, when he sees the Prince of the fourth heaven,
he removes the glorious crown from his head and falls prostrate.
The Prince of the fourth heaven, when he sees the Prince of the fifth heaven,
he removes the glorious crown from his head and falls prostrate.
The Prince of the fifth heaven, when he sees the Prince of the sixth heaven,
he removes the glorious crown from his head and falls prostrate.
The Prince of the sixth heaven, when he sees the Prince of the seventh heaven,
he removes the glorious crown from his head and falls prostrate.

2 The Prince of the seventh heaven, when he sees the 72 princes of kingdoms,[e]   30:2
he removes the glorious crown from his head and falls prostrate.

3 The 72 princes of kingdoms, when they see the guardians of the door[f] of the   1:1
first palace which is in ʿArabot, the highest heaven, they remove the kingly
crowns[g] from their heads and fall prostrate.
The guardians of the door of the first palace, when they see the guardians of
the door of the second palace, they remove their glorious crowns from their
heads and fall prostrate.
The guardians of the door of the second palace, when they see the guardians
of the door of the third palace, they remove their glorious crowns and fall
prostrate.
The guardians of the door of the third palace, when they see the guardians of
the door of the fourth palace, they remove their glorious crowns and fall
prostrate.
The guardians of the door of the fourth palace, when they see the guardians
of the door of the fifth palace, they remove their glorious crowns and fall
prostrate.
The guardians of the door of the fifth palace, when they see the guardians of
the door of the sixth palace, they remove their glorious crowns and fall prostrate.
The guardians of the door of the sixth palace, when they see the guardians of   1:3
the door of the seventh palace, they remove their glorious crowns and fall
prostrate.

4 The guardians of the door of the seventh palace, when they see the four great
and honored princes who are in charge of the four camps of the Šekinah,[h] they   1:6; 37:1
remove their glorious crowns and fall prostrate.

---

b. "When he sees," A Mus.

c. "He removes," A Mus.

d. "The glorious crown": Contrast the "kingly crowns" assigned to the two highest princes (vs. 25), and to the princes of kingdoms (vs. 3). Note also the "crown of holiness" in 22:5. For doffing the crown as a mark of homage see Rev 4:4, 10 and Alphabet of Aqiba, *BHM*, vol. 3, p. 61, l. 32.

e. "The 72 princes of kingdoms": see 30:2, n. e, and "Theological Importance." Like the number of nations in the world (see 17:8, n. r), the princes of kingdoms are usually reckoned as seventy in number: so e.g. 1En 89:59 (the "seventy shepherds"), and PRE 24: "The Holy One, blessed be he, descended with the seventy angels that surround the Throne of Glory, and they confounded their [i.e. men's] speech into seventy nations and seventy languages."

f. "The guardians of the door": These angels are given names in Hekalot Rabbati 15:2–7; 25:1 (*BHM*, vol. 3, pp. 94, 99); see also Maʿaśeh Merkabah 23 (ed. Scholem, p. 112); Masseket Hekalot 4 (*BHM*, vol. 2, p. 42, l. 29). Qaspiʾel,

the leader of the guardians of the seventh palace, is mentioned by name in 3En 1:3. See further "Theological Importance."

g. "Kingly crowns," A B; "glorious crowns," Mus. A B Mus, in fact, have the singular "crown" (*keter*), but A Mus give the plural *kitrê* in vss. 4 and 5, and this should be read also in vs. 3.

h. "The four . . . princes . . . four camps of the Šekinah": Cf. 37:1, "four chariots . . . and . . . four camps of the Šekinah"; 35:3, angels grouped into four rows, with a mighty Prince at the head of each row; Masseket Hekalot 6 (*BHM*, vol. 2, p. 43f.), "Four companies of ministering angels utter praises before the Holy One, blessed be he. The first camp, on the right, is Michael's; the second camp, on the left, is Gabriel's; the third camp, in front of him, is ʾUriʾel's; and the fourth camp, behind him, is Raphael's; and the Šekinah of the Holy One is in the middle." Further, PRE 4; 1En 40:8–10, the Four Presences, Michael, Raphael, Gabriel, and Phanuel; 2En 18:9 (A), the four ranks in heaven. See 1:6 n. i and 35:1, n. c.

5 The four great princes, when they see Tagʿaṣ,[i] the Prince, great and honored in song and praise at the head of all the celestials, they remove the glorious crowns from their heads and fall prostrate.

6 Tagʿaṣ, the great and honored Prince,[j] when he sees Baratṭiʾel,[k] the great Prince, upon the tops of whose fingers ʿArabot is spread out,[l] he removes the glorious crown from his head and falls prostrate.   Dan 12:1 33:3

7 Baratṭiʾel, the great Prince, when he sees Hamon, the great, terrible, honored, beautiful, and dreaded Prince, who makes all the denizens of the heights quake when the time comes to recite the Qeduššah, as it is written, "At the voice of Hamon[m] the peoples flee, when you arise, the nations scatter", he removes the glorious crown from his head and falls prostrate.   19:6; 35:5; 38:1 Isa 33:3

8 Hamon, the great Prince, when he sees Ṭaṭrasiʾel[n] YHWH, the great Prince, he removes the glorious crown from his head and falls prostrate.

9 Ṭaṭrasiʾel YHWH, the great Prince, when he sees ʾAṭrugiʾel[o] YHWH, the great Prince, he removes the glorious crown from his head and falls prostrate.

10 ʾAṭrugiʾel YHWH, the great Prince, when he sees Naʿaririʾel[p] YHWH, the great Prince, he removes the glorious crown from his head and falls prostrate.

11 Naʿaririʾel YHWH, the great Prince, when he sees Sasnigiʾel[q] YHWH, the great Prince, he removes the glorious crown from his head and falls prostrate.

12 Sasnigiʾel YHWH, the Prince, when he sees Zazriʾel YHWH, the great Prince, he removes the glorious crown from his head and falls prostrate.

13 Zazriʾel YHWH, the Prince, when he sees Geburatiʾel YHWH, the Prince, he removes the glorious crown from his head and falls prostrate.

14 Geburatiʾel YHWH, the Prince, when he sees ʿArapiʾel[r] YHWH, the Prince, he removes the glorious crown from his head and falls prostrate.

15 ʿArapiʾel YHWH, the Prince, when he sees ʾAšroilu[s] YHWH, the Prince, he removes the glorious crown from his head and falls prostrate.

16 ʾAšroilu YHWH, the Prince, the head of every session of the heavenly academy,[t] when he sees Galliṣur YHWH, the Prince, who reveals all the secrets of Torah,[u] he removes the glorious crown from his head and falls prostrate.   48D:2-4

---

i. "Tagʿaṣ": Many of the angelic names in this chapter occur again in Hekalot Rabbati 15 (*BHM*, vol. 3, p. 94). The vocalization of most of them is uncertain, and there are numerous variants. The forms followed in the text are those of B. The meanings of many of the names are obscure and some of them are undoubtedly corrupt. On the formation of angelic names see "Theological Importance."

j. "The great and honored Prince": This phrase is in Aram. In Dan 12:1 Michael is called "the great prince" but the title is in Heb.

k. "Baratṭiʾel," B; "ʾAtatiʾel," A; "ʿAtapiʾel," Mus.

l. "Upon the tops of whose fingers ʿArabot is spread out," Mus; "of three fingers in the height of ʿArabot, the highest heaven," A B.

m. JB: "At the sound of your threat." RSV: "At the thunderous noise."

n. "Ṭaṭrasiʾel," A B; "Ṭuṭrasiʾel," Mus. Variant forms of the name appear as names of God in Hekalot Rabbati 11:2 (*BHM*, vol. 3, p. 91); 12:3f. (*BHM*, vol. 3, p. 92); 13:2 (*BHM*, vol. 3, p. 93). The *ṭaṭras* element may be the Gk. *tetras* (= the number four); the reference could then be to the tetragram YHWH.

o. "ʾAtrugiel," B; "ʾAṭarguniʾel," Mus; "ʾAṭruggiʾel," A.

p. "Naʿaririʾel," B; "Naʿaruriʾel," A. Cf. Meṭatron's title *Naʿar*, on which see 4:10.

q. "Sasnigiʾel": a variant of Meṭatron's name

Seganzagʾel in 48D:1(93).

r. "ʿArapiʾel," A B; "Nirpiʾel," Mus.

s. "ʾAšroilu," B; "ʾAšroili," A; "ʾAšroilai," Mus. Cf. the divine name 'Ašrawlun in Maʿaseh Merkabah 31 (ed. Scholem, p. 115, l. 18), and the divine name ʾAšroiliʾi in Hekalot Rabbati 12:4 (*BHM*, vol. 3, p. 92). In Hekalot Rabbati 30:3 (*BHM*, vol. 3, p. 10, l. 17) 'Ašroiliʾiʾel is the name of an angel.

t. "The head of every session of the heavenly academy," lit. "the head of every session [or "chapter"] of the denizens of the heights"; Heb. *rōʾš kol pereq benê mᵉrômîm*. The rabbinical Heb. *pereq* and the Jewish Aram. *pirqāʾ* can be used in the sense of a session of an academy; see b.Pes 100a: "I visited the session [*pirqāʾ*] of R. Phineas." *Rōʾš happereq* was a title of the heads of academies in the gaonic era. Lemb reads here "the head of the students of the heavenly academy" (*rōʾš ʿal benê pereq merômîm*); cf. b.Ket 62a. Mus omits the clause altogether. On the heavenly academy see "Theological Importance." It is possible, however, that the text means nothing more than "the most honored of the celestials"; cf. DeutR 4:8, "we too are aware of your good deeds, and we have made you head of the chapter [*rōʾš pereq*]" (cf. y.Hor 48a.39–55; LevR 5:4).

u. "Galliṣur YHWH . . . who reveals all the secrets of Torah"; cf. PR 20:4 (ed. Friedmann, 97b): "Galliṣur . . . reveals the reasons of God [*ṣûr*]."

17 Galliṣur YHWH, the Prince, when he sees Zakzaki'el YHWH, the Prince, who is appointed to record the merits of Israel[v] upon the throne of glory, he removes the glorious crown from his head and falls prostrate.

18 Zakzaki'el YHWH, the great Prince, when he sees 'Anapi'el[w] YHWH, the Prince, who keeps the keys of the palaces of the heaven of 'Arabot, he removes the glorious crown from his head and falls prostrate. Why is his name called 'Anapi'el? Because the bough of his majesty, glory, crown, brilliance, and splendor overshadows[x] all the chambers of 'Arabot,[y] the highest heaven, like the glory of the Creator of the World. As it is written of the Creator of the world, "His majesty veils the heavens, and the earth is filled with his glory," so does the majesty and glory of 'Anapi'el YHWH, the Prince, overshadow all the chambers of highest 'Arabot.

19 'Anapi'el YHWH, the Prince, when he sees Soteraši'el[z] YHWH, the great, terrible, and honored Prince, he removes the glorious crown from his head and falls prostrate. Why is his name called Soteraši'el? Because he is appointed to serve in the Divine Presence over the four heads of the River of Fire, opposite the throne of glory, and any prince who wishes to leave or to enter the presence of the Šekinah may do so only by his permission, because the seals of the four heads of the River of Fire[a2] are entrusted to his keeping. Further, he is called Soteraši'el because his height is 70,000 myriads of parasangs and he stirs up the fire of the River of Fire, and he leaves and enters the presence of the Šekinah to explain the records[b2] concerning the inhabitants of the earth, as it is written, "A court was held and the books were opened."

20 Soteraši'el YHWH, the Prince, when he sees Šoqedḥozi YHWH, the great, mighty, terrible, and honored Prince, he removes the glorious crown[c2] from his head and falls prostrate. Why is his name called Šoqedḥozi? Because he weighs men's merits in scales in the presence of the Holy One, blessed be he.

21 Šoqedḥozi YHWH, the Prince, when he sees[d2] Zehanpuryu[e2] YHWH, the Prince, great, mighty, honored, glorified, and dreaded in the whole heavenly household, he removes the glorious crown from his head and falls prostrate. Why is his name called Zehanpuryu? Because he is angry at the River of Fire and quenches it in its place.

Margin references: 6:1; 16:5 / 17:3 / Hab 3:3 / Gen 2:10; Dan 7:10 / Dan 7:10 / 31:1f.; 33:1f.

---

v. "The merits of Israel," Mus; "the merits of Israel, which they perform," A B.

w. " 'Anapi'el": The MSS vary between this form and " 'Anap'el." The name is here connected with the word 'ānāp, "a bough."

x. "Overshadows," A Mus.

y. "The chambers [ḥadrê] of 'Arabot," Mus. The concept of the heavenly "chambers" is similar to that of the heavenly "palaces"; see 1:1, n. d. The chambers may include the heavenly treasuries over which Meṭaṭron has charge; see 10:6. A B read "the glories [hadrê] of 'Arabot." "Glories" may refer to the angels; cf. Meṭaṭron's title "the glory [hadar] of highest heaven" (13:1).

z. "Soteraši'el": The name is pointed thus in A B. The remaining angels of this ch. belong to the heavenly law court. Soteraši'el is the accuser who stands for strict justice; he seeks to punish men by burning them in the River of Fire; Zehanpuryu is the defender who represents mercy; he quenches the River of Fire; Šoqedḥozi impartially weighs men's merits in the balance; 'Azbogah rewards those who have been adjudged righteous; Soperi'el YHWH and Šoperi'el YHWH are the two recording scribes of the court. Note that in the hierarchy mercy dominates over justice. On the heavenly law court see the margin and "Theological Importance."

a2. "The seals of the four heads of the River of Fire," A; "the seals of the four rivers of fire," B; "the seals of the River of Fire," Mus. The River of Fire is a standard motif in the descriptions of the Merkabah; it is derived from Dan 7:10. We find references to one River of Fire (A Mus and 36:1); four rivers of fire (B and 19:4; 37:1); and seven rivers of fire (33:4). The usual name for the River of Fire is Nehar diNûr, which is taken from Dan 7:10, but it is also called Rigyon. The meaning of the latter name is uncertain. The bridges which span the River of Fire were a subject of speculation; see 3En 22B:1; 22C:1. On the River of Fire see 1En 14:19; GenR 78:1; b.Ḥag 14a; Hekalot Rabbati 13:1 (BHM, vol. 3, p. 93, l. 7); Ma'yan Ḥokmah, BHM, vol. 1, pp. 59f.; Seder Rabbah diBere'šit 46 (BM, vol. 1, p. 45); Haggadat Šema' Yiśra'el, BHM, vol. 5, p. 165, l. 20; Masseket Hekalot 6 (BHM, vol. 2, pp. 44f.); Ma'aśeh Merkabah 3 (ed. Scholem, p. 103); Seper HaRazim 7:7 (ed. Margalioth, p. 107); PR 20:4 (ed. Friedmann, 97a, l. 25). See further n. u2 below; 33:3, n. e, and 33:4, n. h.

b2. "To explain the records," A Mus.

c2. "The glorious crown," A Mus.

d2. "Šoqedḥozi YHWH . . . when he sees," A and, substantially, Mus; "and when he sees," B. For Šoqedḥozi see Ma'aśeh Merkabah (ed. Scholem, p. 108, l. 21); Cairo Genizah Hekalot B/1, 37 (ed. Gruenwald, p. 369).

e2. "Zehanpuryu," B; "Zehapnurai," A;

22 Zehanpuryu YHWH, the Prince, when he sees[f2] ʾAzbogah[g2] YHWH, the Prince, great, mighty, terrible, honored, glorified, wonderful, beloved, and dreaded among the princes who know the secrets[h2] of the throne of glory, he removes the glorious crown from his head and falls prostrate. Why is his name called ʾAzbogah? Because he girds men with garments of life[i2] and in time to come he will wrap the righteous and pious of the world in robes of life, so that clad in them they may enjoy eternal life.

23 ʾAzbogah YHWH, the Prince, when he sees[j2] the two great, sovereign, and honored princes who stand above him, he removes the glorious crown from his head and falls prostrate. These are the names of the two princes:[k2] Soperiʾel YHWH, who puts to death, the great, honored, glorified, pure, ancient, and mighty Prince; and Śoperiʾel YHWH, who makes alive, the great, honored,

24 glorified, pure, ancient, and mighty Prince. •Why is the name of the one called Soperiʾel YHWH, who puts to death? Because he is in charge of the books of the dead, for he records in the books of the dead everyone whose day of death has come. Why is the name of the other called Śoperiʾel YWHW, who makes alive? Because he is in charge of the books of the living,[12] for he records in the books of the living everyone whom the Holy One, blessed be he, is pleased to bring into life,[m2] by authority of the Omnipresent One.[n2] So that you should not suppose that since the Holy One, blessed be he, sits on a throne, they too sit and write; Scripture states, "The whole host of heaven stood beside him." It does not say, "host of heaven" but "the *whole* host of heaven,"[o2] which teaches that even the great princes who are without peer in the heavenly height only attend to the needs of the Šekinah while standing.[p2]

25 But how can they write while standing?
The one stands upon wheels of storm; the other stands upon wheels of storm.[q2]
The one is clothed in a royal robe;[r2] the other is clothed in a royal robe.

Margin references: 27:2; 28:7; 30:2; 32:1; 44:9 — 45:1,6 — 1Kgs 22:19; 2Chr 18:18 — 12:1; 17:8

"Zehapṭai," Mus. A variant of this name appears as the name of the Prince of the Divine Presence in Hekalot Rabbati 17:5 (*BHM*, vol. 3, p. 96), and as the name of one of the gatekeepers of the seventh palace in Hekalot Rabbati 22:1 (*BHM*, vol. 3, p. 99).

f2. "Zehanpuryu YHWH . . . when he sees," A and, substantially, Mus; "and when he sees," B.

g2. " ʾAzbogah": Like several other angelic names in 3En, ʾAzbogah also occurs as a secret name of God; see e.g. Hekalot Rabbati 30:4 (*BHM*, vol. 3, p. 107, l. 23), where it is called a "great seal." It is explained in 3En as a kind of notarikon for "He who girds men with the garments of life" (*ʾôzēr bigdê ḥayyîm*); see n. i2 below. The original significance of the name, however, lay in the fact that it is made up of three groups of letters which each add up to eight; see "Date."

h2. "The secrets," A Mus; "the secret," B. The reference is probably to the seven angels who serve within the curtain and are party to the deepest secrets of God; see Masseket Hekalot 7 (*BHM*, vol. 2, p. 46).

i2. "He girds men with garments of life," A Mus; "he is girt with garments of life," B. The "garments of life" and the "robes of life" are the immortal bodies which the righteous receive in heaven; cf. 1En 62:15, 16; AscenIs 9:9; 2Cor 5:1–5; 2En 22:8 (A B).

j2. " ʾAzbogah YHWH . . . when he sees," A and, substantially, Mus; "and when he sees," B.

k2. "These are the names of the two princes," B.

A Mus. The various elements that make up the description of these two angels are almost all found elsewhere in 3En; see margin.

12. "Books of the dead" and "books of the living": In this context these books appear to record the moment when each man should be born, and the moment he should die. Usually, however, such books are supposed to contain the names of those destined for eternal perdition, and of those destined for immortality; see Dan 12:1f.; 1En 47:3; 108:3; Rev 3:5; 20:12.

m2. "Everyone whom the Holy One . . . is pleased to bring into life (*lehaḥayôtô*)," Lemb. It would be also possible to translate ". . . is pleased to raise from the dead"; see n. 12 above. A B have here: "everyone with whom the Holy One, blessed be he, is pleased in life."

n2. "The Omnipresent One," lit. "the Place" (*hammāqôm*). This is a common rabbinic name of God. It is explained in GenR 68:9: "He is the place of the world, but the world is not his place." See also m.Taʿan 3:8; t.Naz 4:7. In 3En it is characteristic of chs. 40–48; see 44:3; 45:1, 6; 47:1, 4; 48A:1, 4, 5; 48D:8.

o2. "It does not say, 'host of heaven' but 'the *whole* host of heaven,' " A Mus.

p2. ". . . while standing": It is a standard rabbinic idea that the angels do not, or cannot, sit; see 10:1. Vs. 25 is probably a secondary addition: the connection between it and vs. 24 is rather awkward.

q2. "Wheels of storm," Lemb; "wheels of tempest," A B Mus.

r2. "Royal robe," A Mus; "robe of angels," B.

The one is wrapped in a cloak of majesty; the other is wrapped in a cloak of majesty.

The one wears a kingly crown; the other wears a kingly crown.

The body of the one is full of eyes; the body of the other is full of eyes.   22:8; Ezek 1:18

The appearance of the one is like lightning; the appearance of the other is like lightning.

The eyes of the one are like the sun in its strength; the eyes of the other are like the sun in its strength.

The splendor of the one is as the splendor of the throne of glory; the splendor of the other is as the splendor of the throne of glory.ˢ²

The height¹² of the one is as the seven heavens; the height of the other is as   17:3
the seven heavens.

The wings of the one are as the days of the year; the wings of the other are as the days of the year.

The wings of the one are as the breadth of a heaven; the wings of the other   9:3
are as the breadth of a heaven.

The lips of the one are like the gates of the east; the lips of the other are like the gates of the east.

The tongue of the one is as high as the sea's waves; the tongue of the other is as high as the sea's waves.

From the mouth of the one flames issue; from the mouth of the other flames   22:4
issue.

From the mouth of the one lightnings shoot out; from the mouth of the other lightnings shoot out.

From the sweat of the one fire is kindled; from the sweat of the other fire   33:4
is kindled.ᵘ²

The tongue of the one is a blazing torch; the tongue of the other is a blazing torch.

On the head of the one is a sapphire stone; on the head of the other is a   26:5
sapphire stone.

On the shoulder of the one is the wheel of a swift cherub; on the shoulder   24:17
of the other is the wheel of a swift cherub.

In the hand of the one is a burning scroll; in the hand of the other is a burning scroll.

In the hand of the one is a pen of flame; in the hand of the other is a pen   13:1; 29:1; 39:1; 41:4
of flame.

The length of the scroll is 3,000 myriads of parasangs; the height of the pen is 3,000 parasangs;ᵛ² and the height of each single letter that they write is 365 parasangs.

Rikbi'el, prince of the wheels

1 **19** R. Ishmael said: The angel Meṭaṭron, Prince of the Divine Presence, said to me:
Above these two great princesᵃ is a prince, distinguished, honored, noble, glorified, adorned, dreaded, valiant, mighty, great, magnified, potent, crowned, wonderful, exalted, pure, beloved, sovereign, proud, elevated, ancient, and

---

s2. "The splendor of the one . . . throne of glory," A and, substantially, Mus; B omits.

t2. "The height," A.

u2. "From the sweat . . . fire is kindled": Cf. the idea that the River of Fire is formed from the sweat of the creatures as they strain to carry the throne; see 33:3f.

v2. "3,000 parasangs," Mus; "3,000 myriads of parasangs," A B.

19 a. "Above these two great princes," A Mus.

The connection with ch. 18 is awkward; note that B reads "Above these three angels." Chs. 19–22; 25:1–28:6 contain a new angelology which was originally independent of the angelologies in chs. 17 and 18; see 17:1, n. a. The three significant facts about this new angelology are: (1) It is concerned only with the Merkabah angels; (2) it lists those angels in ascending order of rank; (3) unlike the angelologies of chs. 17 and 18 it does not have a cosmological element.

strong, without a peer among all the princes. His name is Rikbi'el[b] YHWH, the great and terrible Prince. •Why is his name called Rikbi'el? Because he is

2 in charge of the wheels[c] of the chariot, and they are committed to his keeping.   Ezek 10:3; 6:2; 15:1; 41:2

3 How many wheels are there? Eight—two for each direction. Four winds enclose them in a circle, and these are their names: Storm, Tempest, Hurricane,

4 and Gale. •Four rivers of fire flow out from beneath them, one on each side.   18:19 Between them, forming a circle, four clouds stand, opposite their wheels.[d] These are their names: Clouds of Fire, Clouds of Firebrand, Clouds of Glowing

5 Coal, and Clouds of Brimstone. •The feet of the creatures rest on the wheels

6 and between one wheel and another earthquake roars and thunder rumbles. •   21:1–4 When the time comes to recite the song,[e] the multitude of the wheels trembles, the multitude of the clouds shudders, all the captains[f] tremble, all the horsemen   18:7; 35:5; 38:1 are agitated, all the valiant shiver,[g] all the hosts quake, all the legions are afraid,[h] all the overseers are terrified, all the princes and armies are alarmed,

7 all the ministers faint, all the angels and cohorts writhe in agony. •And one wheel utters a voice to another,[i] cherub to cherub, creature to creature, ophan to ophan, and seraph to seraph, saying, "Extol him who rides in the 'Arabot,[j]   Isa 6:3 whose name is the Lord, and exult before him."

                                      Ps 68:4

Hayli'el, prince of the holy creatures

1 **20** R. Ishmael said: The angel Metatron, Prince of the Divine Presence, said to me:
Above them[a] is a great and powerful prince, Hayli'el[b] YHWH is his name, a prince noble and terrible, a prince sovereign and mighty,[c] a prince great and dreaded, a prince from whom all the celestials shrink back, a prince who is able

---

b. "Rikbi'el," A Mus. The construction of the angelic names in chs. 19–22 and 25–28 (apart from Radweri'el in 27:1) is transparent: They are made up of an element corresponding to the function of the angel plus the theophoric ending 'el. Thus Rikbi'el is *rekeb*, "chariot" (a synonym of *merkābāh*), plus 'el, "God." On the formation of the angelic names see 14:4, n. d, and "Theological Importance." However, since Rikbi'el is in charge of the "wheels of the chariot" (*galgallê hammerkābāh*), the name Galgalli'el would have been more obvious; see 14:4; 17:4.

c. "The wheels" (*galgallîm*) are derived from Ezek 10:13, where it is implied that they are the same as the ophanim. In the present angelological system they are different from ophanim; see 25:5–7. In the Hekalot texts the word *galgal* has several senses: (1) It denotes the literal wheels of the chariot (see 15:1; 41:2; Masseket Hekalot 7, *BHM*, vol. 2, p. 45, l. 20; this is probably the meaning here); (2) it denotes a class of angels (see 6:2; Masseket Hekalot 5, *BHM*, vol. 2, p. 43, l. 17); (3) it denotes the "orb" (*galgal*) of the sun, in contrast to the "globe" (*'ôpān*) of the moon (see 17:4f.). In medieval Jewish texts the *galgallîm* are the heavenly spheres; see e.g. Ibn Gabirol, *Keter Malkut* 14, l. 131, and cf. b.BB 74a.

d. "Between them . . . their wheels": The exact sense is obscure; "forming a circle . . . stand" is *muqqāpîn we'ômedîm* in Heb., but the *muqqāpîn*, "forming a circle," is redundant. Cf. b.Yoma 25a: "The chamber of hewn stone was built like a large basilica. The count [*payis*] took place on the eastern side, with the elder sitting on the west and the priests standing around

[*muqqāpîn we'ômedîn*] in the form of a spiral"; cf. 33:3; 34:1; 37:2.

e. "The song": the heavenly Qeduššah; see "Theological Importance." For commotion at the recitation of the Qeduššah see margin and Ma'yan Hokmah, *BHM*, vol. 1, p. 59, ll. 15–22.

f. "Captains . . .": The various names for the angels in vs. 6 are mostly derived from Scripture; cf. Masseket Hekalot 5 (*BHM*, vol. 2, p. 43).

g. "All the valiant shiver," A.

h. "All the legions are afraid," Lemb.

i. "One wheel utters a voice to another": Cf. Masseket Hekalot 7 (*BHM*, vol. 2, p. 45, l. 23): "A heavenly voice [*bat qôl*] stands beside one wheel, and a heavenly voice stands beside another wheel."

j. "In the 'Arabot," A Mus. The JB translates *'arābôt* as "clouds": "Build a road for the Rider of the Clouds" (Ps 68:4). Rabbinic exegesis took it as a name for heaven, specifically the seventh heaven; see the Targum: "Praise him who sits on the throne of his glory in 'Arabot," and Midraš Tehillim 68:3 (to Ps 68:4) (ed. Buber, 158b). The KJV follows the rabbinic tradition: "Extol him that rideth upon the heavens."

20 a. "Above them"; i.e. above Rikbi'el and the galgallim of ch. 19.

b. "Hayli'el": This name is supposed to be derived from *hayyāh*, "a creature" (for the *hayyot*, "the creatures," see ch. 21), but, in fact, it is derived from *hayil*, "an army." The term "armies" (*hayālîm*) is sometimes applied to the angelic hosts; see 19:6.

c. "A prince sovereign and mighty," A Mus.

2 to swallow the whole world at one gulp. •Why is his name called Ḥayli'el?[d]   21:1-4
Because he is in charge of the creatures and he whips them with lashes of fire.[e]   16:5
He extols them when they utter praise and glory, and he makes them hasten   1:12; 35:1-36:2
to say,   Isa 6:3

and,   Holy,[f] holy, holy,
Blessed he the glory of the Lord in his dwelling place.   Ezek 3:12

The holy creatures

1 **21** R. Ishmael said: The angel Meṭaṭron, Prince of the Divine Presence, said
to me:
There are four creatures[a] facing the four winds. Each single creature would fill   Ezek 1:5
the whole world.[b] Each of them has four faces and every single face looks like   9:3
2 the sunrise. •Each creature has four wings and every single wing would cover
3 the world.[c] •Each one of them has faces within faces and wings within wings.[d]   Ezek 1:16
4 The size of a face is 248 faces, and the size of a wing is 365 wings. •Each   33:4
creature is crowned with 2,000 crowns and every crown is like the rainbow;   16:2
its brightness is as the brightness of the sun's orb[e] and the rays which shine   Gen 9:14; Ezek 1:28
from each separate crown are as the brightness of the morning star in the east.

Kerubi'el, prince of the cherubim

1 ***22** R. Ishmael said: The angel Meṭaṭron, Prince of the Divine Presence,
said to me:
Above them is a prince, noble,[a] wonderful, mighty, praised with all manner
of praise: Kerubi'el[b] YHWH is his name, a valiant prince, full of boundless
power; a majestic prince, with whom is majesty;[c] a righteous prince, with whom
is righteousness; a holy prince, with whom is holiness; a prince glorified by
2 thousands of hosts, a prince extolled by countless legions. •At his wrath[d] the
earth quakes; at his rage the camps tremble; the foundations shudder from fear   18:4
3 of him and ʿArabot quakes at his rebuke. •His body is full of burning coals;   17:3
it is as high as the seven heavens, as broad as the seven heavens, as wide as   9:2
4 the seven heavens. •The opening of his mouth blazes like a fiery torch,[e] and his   15:1
tongue is a consuming fire. His eyelashes are as the splendor of lightning, his   16:2; 18:1,3
5 eyes like brilliant sparks, and his face looks like a blazing fire. •A crown of •

---

d. "Ḥayli'el," Mus.

e. "Because he is in charge . . . lashes of
fire," A and, substantially, Mus.

f. "To say, 'Holy,' " B; "to say after him,
'Holy,' " Mus; i.e. Ḥayli'el acts as the heavenly
precentor (cf. 1:12); "to say after 'Holy' . . .
Blessed . . .," A. On the celestial Qeduššah see
margin and "Theological Importance."

21 a. "Creatures": Heb. ḥayyot, derived from
Ezek 1:5; cf. the description of the ḥayyot in
Masseket Hekalot 6 (*BHM*, vol. 2, p. 44).

b. "Would fill the whole world," lit. "is as
the fullness of the whole world"; for the expression see 9:3, n. e. On the vast dimensions of the
angels in general see 9:1, and of the creatures in
particular see b.Ḥag 13a.

c. "Would cover the world," lit. "is as the
covering of the world"; cf. n. b above.

d. "Faces within faces and wings within
wings": Cf. Ezek 1:16, "a wheel within a
wheel."

e. "The sun's orb," Lemb; "the orb," A B.

22 *For chapters 22B, 22C, 23, and 24 see the
Appendix.

a. "Noble," A C Mus.

b. "Kerubi'el": According to 1En 20:7 it is
Gabriel who is in charge of the cherubim.

c. "A majestic prince, with whom is majesty": emending to śar gē'eh weg'awāh 'immô;
the MSS are corrupt.

d. "At his wrath," A C.

e. "The opening . . . a fiery torch," A. It is
a common idea that the angels are formed out of
fiery matter; see e.g. 2En 29:3 (A B); PR 33:10
(ed. Friedmann, 154a/b); Seper HaRazim 6:3–8
(ed. Margalioth, p. 104). The idea is derived
from Ps 104:4. For other descriptions of the
angels see Hekalot Rabbati 15:8–16:2 (*BHM*,
vol. 3, pp. 94f.); Masseket Hekalot 4 (*BHM*,
vol. 2, p. 42); Messeket ḥibbuṭ haqqeber l (*BHM*,
vol. 1, p. 150); 2En 1:4f. (A B). See further
"Theological Importance."

holiness[f] is on his head, with the sacred name[g] engraved upon it, from which
6 lightning flickers. The bow of the Šekinah is across his shoulders; •his sword,
like a lightning flash,[h] is on his thigh; his arrows,[i] like lightning flashes, are in
his belt; a breastplate of consuming fire hangs round his neck, and coals of
7 juniper encompass him. •The splendor of the Šekinah is on his face;[j] horns of
8 majesty[k] are on his wheels, and a royal turban crowns his head. •His whole
9 body is full of eyes;[l] from head to toe he is covered with wings. •On his right
hand a flame blazes; on his left hand fire burns; coals blaze from his body and
firebrands shoot from him; lightnings flash from his face. He is always
accompanied by thunderclap upon thunderclap; earthquake upon earthquake
10 are ever with him, •and the two princes of the chariot[m] dwell with him.
11   Why is his name called Kerubi'el?[n] Because he is in charge of the chariots
of the cherubim[o] and the mighty cherubim are committed to his keeping. He
shines the crowns on their heads,[p] and furbishes the diadems on their foreheads;
12 he promotes the praise of their form,[q] and adorns[r] their majestic beauty; he
makes them, very lovely as they are, still lovelier, and increases their great
glory;[s] he sings the song of their praise, and recites the strength of their beauty;
he makes their glorious splendor gleam, and the glory of their comeliness and
grace he makes more fair; he decks their dazzling loveliness, and beautifies
their gracious beauty; he honors their majestic rectitude, and extols the order
of their praise—so as to prepare a throne[t] for him who sits upon the cherubim.
13   The cherubim stand beside the holy creatures and their wings are raised up
to the height of their heads. The Šekinah rests upon their backs, the splendor
of the glory is on their faces,[u] and song and praise are in their mouths. Their
hands are under their wings and their feet are covered by their wings, and horns
of glory are on their heads. The brilliance of the Šekinah is on their countenances,
and the Šekinah rests upon their backs. Sapphire stones surround them; pillars
14 of fire are on their four sides; pillars of flame flank them. •A sapphire stone

Right margin references:
13:1; 39:1
22C:4,6f.
Gen 3:24; Josh 5×13
5:4
22:13; 29:2
Isa 62:3
9:4; 18:25; 25:2,6; 26:6; Ezek 1:18
1:7; 2:1
24:1; Ps 18:10
1Sam 4:4; Ezek 10:1
22:7
Isa 6:2
22:7; 29:2
18:25; 25:6,7; 26:5

---

f. "Crown of holiness": Cf. "glorious crown" of 18:1, and the "kingly crowns" of 18:3. For angelic crowns see 16:2.

g. "The sacred name," i.e. God's name *par excellence*—YHWH.

h. "His sword, like a lightning flash," A C; "his sword," B.

i. "His arrows": emending to *ḥiṣṣāyw;* "his arrow," A; "arrows," C.

j. "The splendor of the Šekinah": The sense probably is that Kerubi'el stands in full view of the Šekinah and its light is reflected from his face; cf. vs. 13 below, and note Ex 34:29. According to PR 16:2 (ed. Friedmann, 80a); 48:3 (ed. Friedmann, 194a), the angels draw nourishment from the radiance of the Šekinah.

k. "Horns of majesty" or "rays of majesty": Heb. *qarnê hahôd;* see margin and Masseket Hekalot 5 (*BHM*, vol. 2, p. 43, l. 24); Seper HaRazim 2:178f. (ed. Margalioth, p. 90). For the use of *qeren* in the sense of a ray of light see Hab 3:4 and note the verb *qāran* in Ex 34:29, 30, 35. (JB translates it "was radiant" and "shone.")

l. "His whole body," A; "his body," B C. For the "eyes" see margin and Hekalot Rabbati 22:5 (*BHM*, vol. 3, p. 100); 23:1 (*BHM*, vol. 3, p. 100); Masseket Hekalot 5 (*BHM*, vol. 2, p. 43, l. 23). Hekalot Rabbati 3:4 (*BHM*, vol. 3, p. 86, l. 7) speaks of "eyes" in God's robe (*ḥālûq*).

m. "The two princes of the chariot," A C; cf. Hekalot Rabbati 30:4 (*BHM*, vol. 3, p. 107,

l. 20): "Sarbi'el, one of the princes of the chariot"; Alphabet of Aqiba, *BHM*, vol. 3, p. 36, l. 13.

n. "Kerubi'el," Lemb; "Kerubi'el YHWH, the Prince," A B C.

o. "Chariots of the cherubim," B; "chariots of the creatures," C. See 24:1, n. d.

p. With Kerubi'el's functions as described here cf. the angel who, according to Hekalot Zuṭarti (MS Bod. 1531, fol. 45a), "arranges the throne and clothes (the glory with) the garment, and adorns the *ḥašmal*, and opens the gates of salvation."

q. "The praise of their form," A.

r. "Adorns" (*mehaddēr*), Lemb.

s. "He makes them . . . great glory," Lemb; other texts are more or less corrupt.

t. "A throne": Heb. *môšāb.* For the use of this term for the throne of glory see 4QŠirŠabb, *môšab kebôdô*, "the seat of his glory"; Hekalot Rabbati 2:4, *môšāb 'elyôn*, "lofty seat"; so the text should read: *BHM*, vol. 3, p. 84, l. 25; BM, vol. 1, p. 70, l. 4; Masseket Hekalot 3 (*BHM*, vol. 2, p. 41, l. 20; BM, vol. 1, p. 56, l. 8) and Midraš 'Alpa' Betot, BM, vol. 2, p. 423, l. 15, *môšab yeqārô*, "the seat of his honor"; Seper HaRazim 7:32 (ed. Margalioth, p. 109), *môšab hadārô*, "the seat of his splendor"; cf. Hekalot Rabbati 10:1 (BM, vol. 1, p. 84, l. 1; *BHM*, vol. 3, p. 89, l. 28).

u. "The splendor of the glory is on their faces": See n. j above.

stands on one side and a sapphire stone on the other,ᵛ and beneath the sapphires,ʷ
15 coals of juniper.ˣ •A cherub stands on one side and a cherub on the other, and
the wings of the cherubim enfold each other in glory above their heads. They
spread themʸ to sing with them the song to him who dwells in clouds, and to
praise with them the glory of the King of kings.ᶻ

Ezek 10:5
Ps 97:2

16 Kerubi'el YHWH, the Prince, who is in charge of them, marshals them into
pleasing, fine, and beautiful array, and extols them with all kinds of praise,
glory, and honor. He makes them haste with glory and strength to do the will
of their Creator at every moment, for on top of their heads abides perpetually
the glory of the high and exalted King^a2 who dwells upon the cherubim.

1Sam 4:4; Ezek 10:1

'Opanni'el, prince of the ophanim

1 **25** R. Ishmael said: The angel Meṭaṭron, Prince of the Divine Presence, said
to me:
Above them is a prince, great, terrible, mighty, exalted, distinguished, dreaded,
2 ancient, and strong: 'Opanni'el YHWH is his name. •He has sixteen faces, four
on each side, and 100 wings on each side. He has 8,766 eyes, corresponding
3 to the number of hours in a year, 2,191 on each side.ᵃ •In each pair of eyes
in each of his faces lightnings flash; from every eye torches blaze, and no one
4 can lookᵇ on them, for anyone who looks at them is at once consumed. •The
height of his body is a journey of 2,500 years;ᶜ no eye can see it.ᵈ No mouth
can tell the mighty strength of his power,ᵉ save only the King of the kings of
kings, the Holy One, blessed be he.

14:4; 17:5
9:3

9:2

5 Why is his name called^f 'Opanni'el? Because he is appointed to tend the
ophanim,ᵍ and the ophanim are entrusted to his keeping.ʰ Every day he stands
over them and tends them and beautifies them: he praises and arranges their
running;ⁱ he polishes their platforms; he adorns their compartments; he makes
their turnings smooth, and cleans their seats. Early and late, day and night, he

Ezek 1:15; 10:12f.

---

v. "A sapphire stone . . . on the other," A
C.
w. "The sapphires," A.
x. "Coals of juniper," A C.
y. "Enfold each other in glory above their
heads. They spread them," C, substantially. The
idea is that the cherubim sing by moving their
wings; cf. Hekalot Rabbati 11:4 (*BHM*, vol. 3,
p. 92, l. 11); Pesiqta' deRab Kahana 9:3 (ed.
Mandelbaum, p. 151, l. 17); PRE 4 (end); 'Arugat
habbośem, ed. Urbach, vol. 1, p. 213. The idea
is based on Ezek 10:5. For the singing of the
cherubim see 2En 19:6 (A B).
z. "The King of kings," A.
a2. "The glory of the high and exalted King,"
C; "the great glory of the King," B; "the glory
of the great King" (?), A,

25 a. "He has 8,766 eyes . . . 2,191 on each
side": The MSS appear to be all more or less
corrupt. "8,766," A = 365¼ × 24; "8,769,"
E F; "8,466," B; "according to the number
of," A E F. "Hours in a year" (*śe'ôt yemôt
haśśānāh*) is a conjecture of Jellinek *BHM*, vol.5,
p.178), which can be easily derived from the
text of A E F (*śśt* to *ś'wt*); cf. Masseket Hekalot
2 (*BHM*, vol. 2, p. 42): "In every palace are
8,766 gates of lightnings corresponding to the
number of hours in the days of the year."
"2,191" is read by all the MSS (though all add
the unintelligible words "and sixteen" after it).
However, 8,766 divided by 4 is 2191½. The eyes

must cover the whole body (cf. 22:8 and vs. 6
below), since, according to vs. 3, there is only
one pair of eyes in each face.
b. "Can look," A E F; "can stand and look,"
B.
c. "A journey of 2,500 years": Measurements
in terms of a year's journey are a variation on
measurements by parasangs (5:7); see b.Ḥag 13a;
Re'uyot Yeḥezqe'l, BM, vol. 2, p. 131 (ed.
Gruenwald, p. 121).
d. "No eye can see it," A.
e. "Strength of his power," A E F.
f. "Why is his name called," A E F.

g. "The ophanim": derived from Ezek 1:15
and 10:12f. In Ezek 10:13 the ophanim and the
galgallim are identified, but they are usually
distinguished from the galgallim in the Merkabah
tracts, and taken as a distinct class of angels (see
19:2). The description of the ophanim in this
passage is inconsistent: Vs. 6 speaks of them as
living beings, but the language of vs. 5 ("their
running," "their platforms," etc.) seems more
in keeping with their original function as simply
wheels or a wheeled vehicle. In 4QŠirŠabb the
ophanim appear to be literal wheels, but they are
a class of angels in 1En 61:10; 71:7; 2En 29:3
(B); b.RH 24b; Midraš Konen, BHM, vol. 2, p.
25, l. 21.
h. A B add "and he is appointed to attend the
ophanim"; text follows E F.
i. "Their running," A E F.

tends them, so as to increase their beauty, to magnify their majesty, and to make them swift in the praise of their Creator.

6   All the ophanim are full of eyes and full of wings, eyes corresponding to 22:8 wings and wings corresponding to eyes. From them light shines, like the light Ezek 1:18 of the morning star.ʲ Seventy-two sapphire stones are set in their garments, on 9:3; 17:6,8; 18:2,3 the right side of each of them; seventy-two sapphire stones are set in their

7 garments, on the left side of each of them, •and four emeraldsᵏ are set in each 16:1 one's crown, the brightness of which shines into the four corners of ʿArabot, just as the brightness of the sun's orb shines into the four corners of the world.ˡ 17:3 Pavilions of brilliance, pavilions of splendor, pavilions of light, sapphire, and 29:2 emerald envelop them, so that no one should see the appearance of their eyes and of their faces.ᵐ

Serapiʾel, prince of the seraphim

1 **26** R. Ishmael said: The angel Meṭaṭron, Prince of the Divine Presence, said to me:
Above themᵃ is a prince, wonderful, noble, great, respected, mighty, lordly,
2 a captain and a leader,ᵇ glorified, honored, and beloved. • He is all full of brightness; all full of praise and radiance; all full of splendor; all full of light; all full of beauty; all full of loveliness; all full of greatness and magnificence.ᶜ
3 His face is like the face of angels, and his body is like the body of eagles.ᵈ
4 His brillianceᵉ is like lightning, his appearance is like firebrands, his beauty 44:5; 47:4 like lightning flashes, his majesty like fiery coals, his adornment like *ḥašmallim*,ᶠ his radiance like the light of the morning star, his image like the greater light, Gen 1:16
5 his height as the seven heavens, the light of his eyes like sevenfold light.ᵍ •The 9:2; 17:3; 15:1 sapphire stone on his head is the size of the whole world and like the brilliance Isa 30:26
6 of the heavens themselves in clarity. •His body is full of eyes like the stars of 22:8; Ezek 1:18 heaven, beyond reckoning, without number, and each eye is like the morning star. Some of them are like the lesser light, some like the greater light. From Gen 1:16 his ankles to his knees they resemble stars of lightning; from his knees to his thighs, the morning star; from his thighs to his waist, the light of the moon; from his waist to his neck, the light of the sun; and from his neck to his forehead, "unfading light." Zeph 3:5
7 The crown on his head is radiant like the throne of glory, and the height of the 16:2 crown is a journey of 502 years. There is no kind of radiance, no kind of 25:4 splendor, no kind of brilliance, no kind of light in the world which is not placed

---

j. "All the ophanim . . . the morning star," E F, substantially.

k. "Emeralds," A; "sapphires," B.

l. A F (and B E in corrupt form) add a gloss: "Why is its name called 'emerald' [*bāreqet*]? Because its splendor is like the appearance of lightning [*bārāq*]."

m. "Pavilions of brilliance . . . their faces," A; E F omit "and of their faces." The "pavilions" shield the other angels from the destructive glare of the ophanim; see 29:2. Cf. the function of the clouds in 34:2, and of the *pargôd* (see 45:1; 22B:6, n. g; "Theological Importance"). Note, too, how Galliṣur shields the other angels from the River of Fire (PRE 4), and from the fiery breath of the creatures (PR 20:4, ed. Friedmann, 97b).

26 a. "Above them," A E F.

b. "A leader," E F; "a leader and a ready scribe," A B.

c. "All full of loveliness . . . magnificence," A.

d. "His face . . . the body of eagles": "Face"

is *demût*, which denotes appearance or likeness in general. Here, however, it is contrasted with "body" (*gûp*), and so must have the restricted sense of the appearance of the face (*demût pānāyw*); cf. 35:2; 44:5; 47:4; and Ezek 1:10. For other descriptions of the appearance of angels see 22:4, n. e.

e. "His brilliance," A E F.

f. "*Ḥašmallim*": derived from the word *ḥašmal* in Ezek 1:27, where the JB translates it "bronze." In the Hekalot-Merkabah texts, however, *ḥašmal* denotes either (1) a heavenly substance of dazzling appearance (so here and in 36:2), or (2) an order of angels (so ch. 7; Midraš Konen, *BHM*, vol. 2, p. 25, l. 1; Haggadat Šemaʿ Yiśraʾel, *BHM*, vol. 5, p. 165, l. 17; Maʿyan Ḥokmah, *BHM*, vol. 1, p. 59, l. 25). In b.Ḥag 13b *ḥašmal* is taken as a kind of abbreviation (notarikon) for "the creatures speaking fire" (*ḥayyôt ʾēš memallelôt*).

g. "Sevenfold light": from Isa 30:26. Cf. Seder Rabbah diBereʾšit, BM, vol. 1, p. 47, l. 3; Seper HaRazim 7:1 (ed. Margalioth, p. 107).

8 in that crown. •Serapi'el is the name of that prince, and the name of the crown
on his head is "Prince of Peace." Why is his name called Serapi'el?[h] Because   Isa 9:5
he is in charge of the seraphim,[i] and the seraphim of flame are committed to   Isa 6:2
his care. He stands over them day and night and teaches them song, psalm,
eulogy, might, and majesty, so that they might glorify their king with all manner
of praise and sanctifying song.

9   How many[j] seraphim are there? Four, corresponding to the four winds of the
world. How many wings have each of them? Six, corresponding to the six days   Gen 1
of creation. How many faces have they? Sixteen, four facing in each direction.[k]

10 The measure of the seraphim and the height of each of them corresponds to the
seven heavens. The size of each wing is as the fullness of a heaven, and the   9:2; 17:3

11 size of each face is like the rising sun. •Every one of them radiates light like   21:1
the splendor of the throne of glory,[l] so that even the holy creatures, the majestic   21:1-4; 25:5-7;
ophanim, and the glorious cherubim cannot look on that light, for the eyes of   22:11-15
anyone who looks on it grow dim from its great brilliance.   25:7

12   Why is their name called seraphim? Because they burn the tablets of Satan.[m]   14:2; Job 1:6;
Every day Satan sits with Samma'el, Prince of Rome, and with Dubbi'el, Prince   Zech 3:1f.
of Persia, and they write[n] down the sins of Israel on tablets and give them to
the seraphim to bring them before the Holy One, blessed be he, so that he
should destroy Israel from the world. But the seraphim know the secrets of the
Holy One, blessed be he, that he does not desire[o] that this nation of Israel[p]
should fall. What, then, do the seraphim do? Every day they take the tablets
from Satan's hand and burn them in the blazing fire that stands opposite the
high and exalted throne,[q] so that they should not come into[r] the presence of the
Holy One, blessed be he, when he sits upon the throne of judgment and judges   31:1; 33:1
the whole world in truth.

Radweri'el, the heavenly archivist

1 **27** R. Ishmael said: The angel Metatron, Prince of the Divine Presence, said
to me:
Above the seraphim is a prince, more exalted than all princes, more wonderful

h. "And the name of the crown . . . Serapi'el," A B; E F omit. Cf. God's crown which
has the name *Keter Nora'* (29:1). "Prince-of-
Peace" is a title of the Messiah in Isa 9:5.

i. "In charge of the seraphim," A E F; "in
charge of the seraphim, and the holy seraphim,"
B. In Isa 6 it is the seraphim who sing the
Qeduššah, so it is natural that they should be
regarded as singing angels. On the seraphim see
1En 61:10; 71:7; 2En 19:6 (A B); 29:3 (B);
b.Ḥag 12b; RuthR 5:4; DeutR 11:10.

j. "How many," A E F.

k. "Four facing in each direction," E F.

l. "Every one of them . . . throne of glory,"
A E F.

m. "Why is their name . . . tablets of Satan,"
A B E; "Why is his name called Serapi'el?
Because he burns the tablets of Satan," F. Here
Satan is the Prince of the Accusers, and his
assistants are the princes of the two great political
enemies of the Jews—Rome and Persia. For
Samma'el see 14:2, n. b. Here he is an angel
distinct from Satan; in some texts Samma'el is
simply a name of Satan. For Dubbi'el see b.Yoma
77a. This name may be derived from the word
dôb, "a bear," the symbol of the Persians (Dan
7:5; b.Meg 11a; b.Kid 72a; b.AZ 2b). Instead
of "Dubbi'el" (which is read by A B), F has

"Dummi'el," for which angel see Hekalot Rabbati 18:6 (*BHM*, vol. 3, p. 97); Seper HaRazim
2:91 (ed. Margalioth, p. 86); see further 3En
22C:5, n. m. For Satan see 23:16; 1En 53:3;
54:6. Note also the use of the root *s/śṭn* in 4:6;
14:2. 3En appears to be the only Merkabah text
which mentions Satan by name. The context here
is the heavenly law court (see "Theological
Importance"). The accusers are excluded from
God's immediate presence (cf. 1En 40:7) and so
are not party to his innermost secrets. Their
accusations are burnt by the seraphim and never
reach God. This explanation of the name seraphim turns on the fact that the Hebrew root *śrp*
means "to burn."

n. "And they write," B F; "and he writes,"
A E.

o. "That he does not desire," A E F.

p. "This nation of Israel," A; "this Israelite
nation," B; "this nation of the Holy One, blessed
be he, Israel," E and, substantially, F.

q. "High and exalted throne," A E; "high
and exalted throne of glory," B F.

r. "So that they should not come into," E F;
"so that he [Satan?] should not bring them
into," A B.

than all ministers, Radweri'el[a] YHWH is his name, and he is in charge of the 18:24; 28:7; 30:2;
2 archives. •He takes out the scroll box[b] in which[c] the book of records[d] is kept, 32:1; Esth 6:1
and brings it into the presence of the Holy One, blessed be he. He breaks the
seals of the scroll box, opens it, takes out[e] the scrolls and puts them in the hand
of the Holy One, blessed be he.[f] The Holy One receives them from his hand 18:23–25; 33:2
and places them before the scribes,[g] so that they might read them out to the 18:19–25; 28:9;
Great Law Court which is in the height of the heaven of 'Arabot, in the presence 30–32
3 of the heavenly household.[h] •Why is his name called Radweri'el? Because from 17:3
every utterance that issues from his mouth an angel is formed,[i] and it joins in 40:4
the songs[j] of the ministering angels, and recites the song before the Holy One, 22B:8; 35–40
blessed be he, when the time comes[k] to say "Holy."[l]

The Watchers and the holy ones

1 **28** R. Ishmael said: The angel Metatron, Prince of the Divine Presence, said
to me:
Above all these are four great princes called Watchers and holy ones,[a] high, Dan 4:13,17
honored, terrible, beloved, wonderful, noble, and greater than all the celestials,
and among all the ministers there is none equal to them, for each of them singly
2 is a match for all the others together. •Their abode is opposite the throne of
glory, and their station is facing the Holy One, blessed be he, so that the
splendor of their abode resembles the splendor of the throne of glory, and the
3 brilliance of their image is as the brilliance of the Šekinah. •They receive glory
from the glory of the Almighty,[b] and are praised with the praise of the Šekinah. 22:7

---

27 a. "Radweri'el," B Lemb (Lemb gives the
pointing); "Dadweri'el," A; "Daryo'el," E;
"Daryoi'el," F. The etymology of the name is
completely obscure and the explanation of it in
vs. 3 does not fit its form. The angel Vreveil in
2En 22:11, 12 (A B) and 23:6 (A B) performs a
similar function to Radweri'el's.

b. "Scroll box": Heb. *delûsqûm šel ketābîm*,
lit. "box" or "chest of writings." The reference
is probably to a kind of bucket or box (known
as a *capsa* in Lat.) which was used in antiquity
for storing scrolls. *Delûsqûm* is the Gk. word
glôssokomon (see Jn 12:6; 13:29). It is found a
number of times in rabbinic texts (e.g. m.Gitt
3:3; b.Meg 26b); it sometimes means "sarcoph-
agus" (see b.MK 24b).

c. "In which," Lemb.

d. "The book of records": For the expression
see Esth 6:1. The book contains the record of all
men's deeds and forms the basis of God's judgment in the heavenly law court (see "Theological
Importance").

e. "Takes out," A E F.

f. "In the hand of the Holy One, blessed be
he," A E F; "(and places them) before the Holy
One, blessed be he," B.

g. "Before the scribes": emendation; "before
him, before the scribes," A B; "before him into
the hands of the Holy One," E F. In 18:23–25 and
33:2 (E F) two scribes are mentioned; in 33:2
(A B) and Hekalot Rabbati 5:1 (*BHM*, vol. 3,
p. 87, l. 9), only one. Masseket ḥibbut haqqeber,
BHM, vol. 1, p. 150, speaks of "A scribe and
one appointed with him." The majority ruling
in m.Sanh 4:3 states that there should be two
recording scribes in a court; R. Judah rules that
there should be three. According to MSS A B to
26:1 Šerapi'el is "a ready scribe"; Hekalot
Rabbati 20:2 (*BHM*, vol. 3, p. 98, l. 19) designates Gabriel "the scribe"; Metatron is the
heavenly scribe in b.Ḥag 15a and TarJon to Gen

5:24. With the scene as described here cf. the
account of Moses and Aaron's audience with
Pharaoh in Alphabet of Aqiba, *BHM*, vol. 3, p.
45, l. 24.

h. "Heavenly household": *pamalyā' šelema'alāh*—here used in the restricted sense of
the members of the heavenly law court; see
"Theological Importance."

i. "An angel is formed": This power is usually
attributed to God; see 40:4.

j. "Joins in the songs," lit. "stands in the
songs [*šîrôt*]"; cf. the language of 40:4, "Each
of them stands in song before his throne of
glory." It is tempting to emend to "stands in
the rows [*šûrôt*]," in the light of 35:3; 36:2; cf.
m.Pes 5:4, "The priests stood row upon row
[*šûrôt šûrôt*]."

k. "When the time comes," A E.

l. That is, to recite the celestial Qeduššah; see
"Theological Importance."

28 a. "Watchers and holy ones": derived from
Dan 4:10, 14. The Watchers and the holy ones
are a separate order of angels in the Merkabah
texts (see e.g. Gedullat Mošeh 8, BM, vol. 1,
p. 279), and in the early liturgical poets, the
paytanim (see Yannai's *piyyut*, *'Eḥād 'attāh ûmî
yešîbāk*, ed. Zulay, p. 242, no. 101, l. 85), but
apparently not in talmudic angelology (see the
texts in n. c below). They play a notable part in
1En: There they are taken either as fallen angels
(see 1En 1:5; 10:9, 15; 12:4; 13:10; etc.; 1QapGen
2:1, 16), or as angels close to God's throne (1En
12:2, 3; 20:1; 39:12, 13). In 3En they function
in the context of divine judgment.

b. "From the glory of the Almighty [*Gebûrāh*]," A B; "from the glory of the Šekinah,"
E F. *Gebûrāh*, "the power," is a frequent title
of God in the rabbinic texts; see b.Yeb 105b;
b.Shab 88b; and cf. Mt 26:64.

4 Moreover the Holy One, blessed be he, does nothing in his world without first 4:6
taking counsel with them; then he acts, as it is written, "Such is the sentence
proclaimed by the Watchers, the verdict announced by the holy ones."ᶜ   Dan 4:17
5 There are two Watchers and two holy ones.ᵈ How do they stand before the
Holy One, blessed be he? It is taught that a Watcher stands on one side and a
holy one on the other, and a Watcher stands on one side and a holy one on
6 the other.ᵉ •They abase the arrogant to the earth and exalt the lowly on high.ᶠ 48C:9
7 Every day when the Holy One, blessed be he, sits on the throne of judgment
and judges all the world,ᵍ with the books of the living and the books of the 18:24
dead open before him, all the celestials stand before him in fear, dread, terror,
and trembling. When the Holy One, blessed be he, sits in judgmentʰ on the
throne of judgment, his garment is white like snow, the hair of his head is as
pure wool, his whole robeⁱ shines like a dazzling light and he is covered all Dan 7:9;
8 over with righteousness as with a coat of mail. •The Watchers and the holy Rev 20:11
ones stand before him like court officers before the judge;ʲ they take up and Isa 59:17
debate every single matter and they close each case that comes for judgment
before the Holy One, blessed be he, as it is written, "Such is the sentence
9 proclaimed by the Watchers, the verdict announced by the holy ones." •Some
of them decide the cases; some of them issue the verdicts in the great court in Dan 4:17
ʿArabot; some of them raise the questions in the presence of the Almighty;ᵏ 17:3
some complete the cases before the One Above,ˡ and some carry out the
sentences on the earth beneath,ᵐ as it is written,

> Behold, a Watcher and a holy one came down from heaven.
> At the top of his voice he shouted,
> "Cut the tree down, lop off its branches,
> strip off its leaves, throw away its fruit;
> let the animals flee from its shelter
> and the birds from its branches."
> Dan 4:10f. (MT)

10   Why are their names called Watchers and holy ones? Because they sanctify 16:5; 20:2

c. Cf. b.Sanh 38b: "The Holy One, blessed
be he, does nothing without consulting his heavenly law court, for it is written, 'Such is the
sentence proclaimed by the Watchers . . .' "
Note, however, that in b.Sanh 38b the biblical
"Watchers and holy ones" are taken as the whole
heavenly law court, and not as a distinct class
of angels; see n. a above and further Midraš
Tehillim 119:35 (to Ps 119:89) (ed. Buber, 249a).
For God consulting his angels see 4:6, and further
GenR 8:4f.; LevR 29:1; Midraš Konen, BHM,
vol. 2, p. 26, l. 30.
d. "Two Watchers . . . two holy ones": These
numbers are hardly consistent with the functions
the angels perform according to vss. 8f. 1En
implies that the Watchers are numerous; cf. 1En
6:6; 10:9.
e. "It is taught . . . on the other," A; "It is
taught that a Watcher stands on one side and a
Watcher on the other, and a holy one stands on
one side and a holy one on the other," B; "A
Watcher stands on one side and a holy one on
the other," E F. The E F reading implies that
there is only one Watcher and only one holy
one.
f. "They abase . . . the lowly on high":
emended text. A B add before this: "They are
always exalting"; and E F add, "They are always
exalting the lowly." F subsequently omits "and
exalt the lowly on high," thus avoiding the
repetition. For the theme of humbling and raising

see 48C:9 and Hekalot Rabbati 1:2 (BHM, vol.
3, p. 83).
g. With vs. 7 begins a section on divine
judgment which (with the possible exception of
ch. 29) runs to 33:5. Judgment takes place daily
(cf. R. Yosi's view in t.RH 1:13), and is concerned with (1) adjusting affairs among the living
(so vss. 8f.), and (2) with passing judgment on
those who have just died (vs. 10). The concept
of a final, eschatological judgment (for which
see the fragment in BHM, vol. 6, pp. 152f.) is
absent from 3En; see "Historical Importance"
and "Theological Importance."
h. "Sits in judgment," A and, substantially,
B F; "sits as a judge," E. The description is
based on Dan 7:9; cf. 1En 47:3; 90:20; 4Ezra
7:33; Rev 20:11; LevR 29:3.

i. "His whole robe" (meʿîl), A E F. On God's
"robe" (hālûq) see 12:1, n. a.
j. "Like court officers before the judge": See
m.Kid 4:5 (with b.Kid 76b); t.Sanh 3:9; 8:2.
Masseket Hekalot 7 (BHM, vol. 2, p. 46, l. 31)
speaks of seven heavenly "court officers."
k. "The Almighty," A E F marg; see n. b
above.
l. "The One Above" (Maʿalāh): For this title
of God see b.Ber 19a; m.RH 3:8.
m. "Some carry out the sentences," F; "some
complete, descend, and carry out the sentences,"
A B.

the body and the soul with lashes of fire on the third day of judgment,[n] as it is written,[o] "After two days he will revive us, on the third day he will raise us and we shall live in his presence."

The names of the Watchers and the holy ones

1 **29** R. Ishmael said: The angel Metatron, Prince of the Divine Presence, said to me:

Each one of them[a] has seventy names corresponding to the seventy languages   3:2; 17:8; 48D that are in the world,[b] and all of them are based on the name of the Holy One,[c]   3:2; 48C:9 blessed be he. Every single name is written with a pen of flame[d] upon the   13:1; 39:1; 41:4

2 terrible crown[e] that is on the head of the high and exalted King. •From each   26:8 of them sparks and lightnings shoot forth; from each of them rays[f] of splendor stream out, and from each of them lights flash; pavilions and tents of brilliance[g]   25:7 surround them, for even the seraphim and the creatures, who are greater than all the celestials, cannot look on them.

The heavenly Law Court

1 **30** R. Ishmael said: The angel Metatron, Prince of the Divine Presence, said to me:[a]

Whenever the Great Law Court[b] sits in the height of the heaven of 'Arabot,[c] only the great princes who are called YHWH[d] by the name of the Holy One,   17:3; 10:3

---

n. The reference here is to the "judgment of the grave" (*dîn haqqeber*), which each man undergoes when he dies; see Masseket ḥibbuṭ haqqeber 2 (*BHM*, vol. 1, pp. 150f.): "The ministering angels [= 3En's Watchers and holy ones] come . . . and smite him [i.e. the dead man] a third time and exact from him judgment, and judge him in respect of every quality the first day, and the second day likewise they judge him; the third day they judge him with blows." Cf. further *BHM*, vol. 5, pp. 49–51. On the lashes of fire see margin and cf. the "chain half-fire, half-iron" with which the Angel of Death beats the dead man (*BHM*, vol. 1, p. 151, ll. 1f.); also Ma'aśeh deRabbi Yehośua' b. Levi, *BHM*, vol. 2, p. 50, l. 33. The punishment is purgatorial, aimed at fitting men for God's presence.

o. "As it is written," A E.

29 a. "Each one of them": i.e. of the Watchers and holy ones. It is probable, however, that originally this ch. was an independent fragment which described another class of angels.

b. "That are in the world," A B; E F omit.

c. "Based on the name of the Holy One": See 3:2, n. c.

d. "A pen of flame," A E F; "an iron pen of flame," B.

e. "The terrible crown": Heb. *keter nôrā'*, a technical name for God's crown. See Alphabet of Aqiba, *BHM*, vol. 3, p. 50, ll. 1–3: "R. Aqiba said, 'These are the 22 letters in which the whole Torah was given to the tribes of Israel, and they are written with a pen of flame upon the terrible and awful crown of the Holy One, blessed be he.' " Further, b.Ḥag 13b; PR 20:4 (ed. Friedmann, 97a); Ma'yan Ḥokmah, *BHM*, vol. 1, p. 59; Masseket Hekalot 1 (*BHM*, vol. 2, p. 46, l. 28). According to 26:8 Śerapi'el's crown is called "Prince of Peace."

f. "From each of them rays," A E F.

g. "Brilliance" (*nôgah*), A B; "wisdom" (*bînāh*), E; F omits.

30 a. Ch. 29 is intrusive (see 29:1, n. a), and so at an earlier stage in the evolution of 3En the account of the heavenly assize in chs. 30–33 probably followed directly on the account of the same subject in 28:7–10. The passage on the divine judgment in 28:7–10 forms the climax of the angelology of chs. 19–28. Different traditions have been combined in chs. 30–33: Contrast 31:1 with 33:1 (see 33:1, n. a); it seems very likely that each of the present chs. originally formed an independent unit of tradition.

b. "The Great Law Court" (*Bêt dîn haggā-dôl*): The heavenly law court is called either *Bêt dîn šelema'alāh* or *Pamalyā' šelema'alāh*. For the equivalence of these expressions (in certain contexts) cf. the form of R. Yoḥanan's dictum in y.Sanh 18a.59 with that in b.Sanh 38b; see further 12:5, n. f. The heavenly law court is mentioned frequently in rabbinic texts: See y.Ber 14c.16; b.RH 8b; b.Makk 13b, 14a; b.Shab 21a; b.Ter 3a/b; b.Sanh 99b; GenR 12:1; EcclR 2:12.1; LevR 29:4. In 3En 30 the heavenly law court is said to meet at a fixed time daily; cf. 28:7 and contrast b.RH 16a, which speaks of judgment being passed on New Year's Day. The court is made up of the seventy-two princes of kingdoms: Contrast the accounts of the workings of the heavenly law court in 18:20–24; 26:12; and 28:7–9. See further "Theological Importance."

c. "In the height of the heaven on 'Arabot," A E F.

d. "The great princes who are called YHWH": i.e. the high archangels who, like 'Anapi'el YHWH (6:1), bear the tetragram as part of their names; see the margin and Hekalot Rabbati 22:1, 3 (*BHM*, vol. 3, pp. 99f.). Cf. Pesiqta' deRab Kahana 12:22 (ed. Mandelbaum, p. 221): "Resh Laqish said: There is a tablet upon the heart of every angel and the name of the Holy One, blessed be he, is engraved on it, together with

2 blessed be he, are permitted to speak. •How many princes are there? There are 17:8; 18:2f.;
72 princes of kingdoms[c] in the world, not counting the Prince of the World,[f] 26:12
who speaks in favor of the world before the Holy One, blessed be he, every 38:3
day at the hour when the book is opened in which every deed in the world is 18:24
recorded, as it is written, "A court was held, and the books were opened." Dan 7:10

Justice, Mercy, Truth

1 **31** R. Ishmael said: The angel Meṭaṭron, Prince of the Divine Presence, said
to me:
When the Holy One, blessed be he, sits on the throne of judgment, Justice 33:1;
stands on his right hand, Mercy on his left,[a] and Truth stands[b] directly facing 18:19-21;
2 him. • When a man[c] enters his presence for judgment,[d] a staff, as it were,[e] Ps 89:14
extends toward him from the splendor of Mercy and takes up a position in front
of him. At once the man falls prostrate, and all the angels of destruction[f] fear 32:1; 33:1; 44:2
and shrink from him, as it is written, "His throne is established through Mercy
and he sits upon it in truth." Isa 16:5

---

that of the angel—Michael, Gabriel, Raphael'';
see also Midraš Tehillim 68:10 (to Ps 68:17,
"The Lord is in them") (ed. Buber, 160a). There
is presumably a difference between being "called
YHWH" and having a name "based on" the
name YHWH (see 29:1; 3:2).

e. "Princes of kingdoms": See margin and
"Theological Importance." For the idea that
each nation has its angelic representative see
Mekilta' deRabbi 'Išma'el, *Širah* 2 (ed. Horovitz-
Rabin, p. 124f.); ExR 21:5; LevR 29:2; DeutR
1:22; Song 8:14.1; PRE 24; TarJon to Gen 11:7–
18. The earthly Sanhedrin had only seventy or
seventy-one members according to m.Sanh 1:6,
but m.Zeb 1:3 and m.Yad 4:2 speak of "72
members of the college."

f. "The Prince of the World," A B E; "one
Prince," F. If we take this vs. in conjunction
with 10:3 it would appear that Meṭaṭron is the
Prince of the World; see "Theological Importance."

31 a. "Justice [*ṣedeq*] . . . Mercy [*ḥesed*]": Cf.
Ps 89:14: "Righteousness [*ṣedeq*] and Justice
support your throne, Love [*ḥesed*] and Faithfulness are your attendants." The relationship between the divine attributes of "justice" (*din*) and
"compassion (*raḥamim*)" is a common problem
of rabbinic texts; see b.Ber 7a; GenR 8:4; ARN
A 37 (ed. Schechter, 55b). The name YHWH is
linked with "mercy" and 'Elohim with "justice"; see SifDeut 26 (ed. Finkelstein, p.
41); GenR 33:3; but contrast Mekilta' deRabbi
'Išma'el, *Širah* 3 (ed. Horovitz-Rabin, p. 128, l.
6). For the conflict between Mercy and Justice
in the divine judgment see 3En 18:19–21 and
33:1. Note further the idea of God's two thrones—
one of Justice and one of Mercy (b.Ḥag 14a;
b.Sanh 38b; b.AZ 3b; LevR 39:3). Mercy usually
triumphs over Justice; Mekilta' deRabbi 'Išma'el,
Mišpaṭim 18 (ed. Horovitz-Rabin, p. 314); cf.
t.Soṭ 4:1 and contrast GenR 26:6 (end). The
procedures of the earthly Sanhedrin leaned to the
side of leniency; see m.Sanh 1:6; 5:5. For
hypostatization of the divine attribute of justice
see b.Shab 55a; Alphabet of Aqiba, *BHM*, vol.
3, p. 50, l. 19 (cf. b.Sanh 97b; 103a; b.Pes
119a).

b. "And Truth stands," A E F.

c. "A man," B; "a wicked man," A E F.

d. "For judgment": presumably just after
death; see 28:10.

e. "A staff, as it were": Heb. *kemaqqēl*. The
idea obviously is that Mercy extends to the man
its protection, but the language is awkward.
Perhaps read *zíw* for *mizzíw:* "The splendor of
Mercy extends towards him, like a staff, and
takes up position in front of him." There appears
to be an allusion here to a passage in b.Sanh
108a. b.Sanh 108a quotes Ezek 7:11: "Violence
is risen up into a rod of wickedness [*lemaṭṭēh
reša*']; none of them shall remain, nor of their
multitude, nor of their wealth: neither shall there
be wailing for them." Then it cites a comment
of R. Eleazar on this obscure verse: "This teaches
that violence erected itself like a staff [*kemaqqēl*],
stood before the Holy One, blessed be he, and
said before him: 'Lord of the Universe, none of
them shall remain, nor of their multitude, nor of
their wealth: neither shall there be wailing for
them!' " Violence personified is here seen as
accusing the generation of the Flood in the
heavenly law court; the staff is presumably a
symbol of chastisement. In 3En 31, however,
the idea has been transposed: The staff is now
wielded by Mercy in the heavenly court and has
become a symbol of protection. The connection
between "violence" and "staff" in b.Sanh 108a
must surely be original, since the connection was
derived from Ezek 7:11. 3En 31 presupposes R.
Eleazar's exegesis in b.Sanh 108a.

f. "Angels of destruction": mentioned frequently in rabbinic texts. They have two main
functions: (1) to exact punishment from the
wicked in this world; see 32:1; 33:1; b.Shab 55a,
88a; b.Pes 112b; Hekalot Rabbati 5:3 (*BHM*,
vol. 3, p. 87); Alphabet of Aqiba, *BHM*, vol. 3,
pp. 50f. and p. 62, l. 3; cf. 1En 53:3; 56:1; 63:1;
(2) to act as warders, torturers (and purifiers) of
the souls in hell; see 44:2; b.Ket 104a; b.Sanh
106b; Masseket Gehinnom 1 (*BHM*, vol. 1, p.
147, l. 19); Midraš Konen, *BHM*, vol. 2, p. 32;
cf. 2En 10:3 (Vaillant 5). Ma'yan Ḥokmah
(*BHM*, vol. 1, p. 58, l. 4) names Qemu'el as
"the angel appointed over the 12,000 angels of
destruction who stand at the gates of heaven."
See also 3En 1:3, n. f.

The sword of judgment

1 **32** R. Ishmael said: The angel Metatron, Prince of the Divine Presence, said to me:

When the Holy One, blessed be he, opens the book[a] half of which is fire and half flame, the angels of destruction[b] go out from his presence moment by moment to execute judgment against the wicked with the unsheathed sword of God,[c] the brilliance of which flashes like lightning and passes through the world from end to end, as it is written,

> For by fire will the Lord execute judgment,
> and by his sword, against all mankind.

18:24; 27:2; 28:7; 30:2; 44:9

Isa 66:16

2 All the inhabitants of the world are fearful before him when they see his sword sharpened and gleaming like lightning from one end of the world to the other,[d] and rays and sparks shooting from it as big as the stars of heaven, as it is written, "When I have sharpened the lightning of my sword."

Deut 32:41

The heavenly assize

1 **33** R. Ishmael said: The angel Metatron, Prince of the Divine Presence, said to me:

When the Holy One, blessed be he, sits on the throne of judgment, the angels of mercy stand on his right, the angels of peace stand on his left, and the angels
2 of destruction stand facing him.[a] •A scribe stands below him and a scribe stands
3 above him.[b] • Glorious seraphim surround the throne on its four sides with walls of lightning, and the ophanim surround them like torches, round the throne of glory,[c] and clouds of fire and clouds of flame are round about them,[d] to the right and to the left. Beneath them the holy creatures bear up the throne of glory,[e] each with three fingers,[f] and the height of each finger is 8,766 parasangs.[g]

31:1
31:2
18:23f.; 27:2
26:8–12
25:5–7
19:4; 34:1f.; 37:2
21:1–4

---

32 a. "When the Holy One, blessed be he, opens the book," A B; "When they open the book before the Holy One, blessed be he," E F. For fiery books see Seper HaRazim 7:7 (ed. Margalioth, p. 107).

b. "The angels of destruction": supplied; the texts simply say, "they (go out)"; see 31:2.

c. "With the sword of God," lit. "with his sword"; so B; but A E F have, "and his sword" (which makes the construction of the sentence awkward). In Alphabet of Aqiba, *BHM*, vol. 3, p. 62, l. 4, the angels of destruction are said to wield a sword. The sword (*ḥereb*) of God is a common end-time image in the OT; see Deut 32:41; Isa 27:1; 34:5; 66:16; Ezek 21:3. Cf. the "great sword" that was given to the sheep (Israel) to wreak God's judgment on their enemies in 1En 90:19, 34; 91:11; see also 1En 88:2 and Rev 19:15. For God's sword in rabbinic texts see SifDeut 40 (ed. Finkelstein, p. 84); DeutR 4:2 (both cases *sayip*); Maḥzor Vitry, ed. Hurwitz, p. 54, l. 13 (*ḥereb*). In GenR 21:9 the fiery sword of Gen 3:24 is personified as fiery angels.

d. The language is reminiscent of descriptions of the end-time (cf. Rev 6:15f.), but the judgment is represented as taking place "moment by moment" (vs. 1).

33 a. "Angels of mercy [*raḥamîm*] . . . angels of peace [*šālôm*] . . . angels of destruction [*ḥab-bālāh*]": corresponding respectively to Mercy, Truth, and Justice in 31:1f. Here the agencies of mercy are on the right and those of justice on the left; there the position is reversed. For the

conflict between Mercy and Justice see 31:1. For angels of mercy see Hilkot hakkisse' (BM, add. 27199, fol. 139a): "211 myriads of angels of mercy are standing beside the Throne and they plead in favour of Israel" (quoted from Odeberg). The angels of peace are derived from Isa 33:7; cf. b.Ḥag 5b; 1En 40:8. For the angels of destruction see 31:2.

b. "A scribe stands below him and a scribe stands above him," E and, substantially, F; "a scribe stands above him and a cherub stands above him," A B.

c. "Glorious seraphim . . . round the throne of glory," A and, substantially, E F.

d. "Clouds of fire . . . are round about them [*muqqāpîm*]": The idea of concentric circles round the throne is treated more elaborately in ch. 34. Once again the precise sense of *muqqāpîm* is obscure; see 19:4, n. d, and 34:1, n. b.

e. "The holy creatures bear up the throne of glory": See b.Ḥag 13b; GenR 78:1; LamR 3:23.8; and Ma'yan Ḥokmah, *BHM*, vol. 1, p. 60, ll. 1f., where it is stated that the River of Fire is formed from the perspiration of the creatures as they bear up the throne (see vs. 4 below and cf. 18:25).

f. "Each with three fingers," E margin; A B repeat "each with three fingers"; see 18:6, n. 1.

g. "8,766 parasangs": emendation. The MSS are confused: A has "8,766,000"; B, "800,766,000"; and E, "8,706,000"—all surely too large. The emendation is achieved by omitting the second *'alāpîm*.

4 From under the feet of the holy creatures seven rivers of fire[h] flow out: the 18:19
breadth of each river is 365,000 parasangs; its depth is 248,000 myriads[i] of 21:3
5 parasangs; its length cannot be reckoned or measured. •Each river flows round
in an arc[j] through the four quarters of the heaven of ʿArabot; then each one[k] 17:3; 38:1
falls into Maʿon; from Maʿon it descends to Zebul; from Zebul to Šeḥaqim;
from Šeḥaqim to Raqiaʿ; from Raqiaʿ to Šamayim;[l] from Šamayim it falls on
the heads of the wicked in Gehinnom, as it is written,

> Now a storm of the Lord breaks,
> a tempest whirls,
> it bursts over the head of the wicked. Jer 23:19

The circles round the creatures

1 **34** R. Ishmael said: The angel Meṭaṭron, Prince of the Divine Presence, said
to me:[a]
The hooves of the creatures[b] are encircled[c] by seven clouds of burning coal. 19:4; 33:3; 37:2
The clouds of burning coal are encircled by seven walls of flame.[d] The seven
walls of flame are encircled by seven walls of firebrands. The seven walls of
firebrands are encircled by seven walls of hailstones.[e] The seven walls of
hailstones are encircled by stones of hail. The stones of hail are encircled by
stones of hurricane blasts.[f] The stones of hurricane blasts are encircled by 37:2; 47:3
environs of flame. The environs of flame are encircled by the upper chambers
of storm wind. The upper chambers of storm wind are encircled by fire and 42:7

h. "Seven rivers of fire": See 18:19, n. a2. For the notion that the fiery rivers fall on the heads of the wicked in Gehinnom see b.Ḥag 13b; Masseket Gehinnom 4 (*BHM*, vol. 1, p. 149, l. 7) and cf. 2En 10:2 (A), where the idea may have been linked with the Greek idea of Pyriphlegethon, one of the rivers of the Underworld (Homer, *Odyssey* 10.513; Plato, *Phaedo* 114a).

i. "365,000 . . . 248,000": 365 is the number of the negative commandments, and 248 the number of the positive (see b.Makk 23b; and cf. 3En 21:3). Such dimensions for the river of judgment are appropriate.

j. "In an arc": Heb. *kemîn kippāh*, lit. "like a dome or a skullcap." The image is not clear. In GenR 4:5 and b.Meg 11a (end) *kippāh* denotes the vault of the heavens (cf. Midraš Konen, *BHM*, vol. 2, p. 33); in b.Yeb 80b it denotes the arc described in the air by spurting liquid. The closest parallel is Seder Rabbah diBereʾšit, BM, vol. 1, p. 27, l. 22: "Some say that the world is round and the sea goes round the world like a skullcap [*kemîn kippāh*]." There it means "in a circle." Note also b.Ḥag 14b: "The heavens became overcast and a kind of bow [*kemîn qešet*] appeared in the cloud."

k. "Each one": emendation, reading *kōl* '(*eḥad*) for B's unintelligible *wkl* ' and A E F's *wklh*.

l. " ʿArabot . . . Šamayim": The list of heavens agrees more or less with that in 17:3, but (1) Makon (the sixth heaven) has been accidentally omitted; (2) the first heaven here is Šamayim, but there it is Wilon (see, however, 17:3, n. f). See further "Theological Importance."

34 a. Ch. 34, which depicts the phenomena of heaven as arranged in concentric circles round the Merkabah (see n. c below), was linked to ch. 33 on the catchword principle: Cf. 34:1, "The hooves of the creatures," with 33:4, "the feet of the holy creatures." Ch. 34 ends with a

reference to the celestial Qeduššah. This leads naturally into a section (chs. 35–40) concerned with the same subject.

b. "The hooves of the creatures": Heb. *parsat raglê haḥayyôt;* so A E F. But the singular *parsat*, "hoof," is rather odd; contrast the plural in t.Mik 5:1, *parsôt raglê habbehēmāh*, "the hooves of the animal"; note also Masseket Hekalot 6 (*BHM*, vol. 2, p. 44, l. 29), where again the plural is found. However, we find the singular in the phrase *parsat haḥayyôt*, which occurs in Hekalot Zuṭarti (MS Bodleian 1531, fol. 41a), and in Reʾuyot Yeḥezqeʾl, ed. Gruenwald, p. 137 (BM, vol. 2, p. 133, l. 22, has a different text). The syntax of this chapter is confused in all the MSS. It is necessary to read throughout *lipnê . . . muqqāpîm*, lit. "in front of X, Y forms a circle" (cf. 19:4, n. d; 33:3, n. d; 37:2, n. b). For the idiom see Maimonides, *Yad. Hilkot Talmud Torah* 4:2: "The teacher sits at the head, and the pupils in front of him form a circle [*lepānāyw muqqāpîm*] like a crown." See also Masseket Hekalot 6 (*BHM*, vol. 2, pp. 44f.).

c. "Encircled": For the idea that heaven is arranged in concentric circles round the Merkabah see the margin and Masseket Hekalot 6 (*BHM*, vol. 2, pp. 44f.). In Midraš Konen (*BHM*, vol. 2, pp. 33f.) and Seder Rabbah diBereʾšit (BM, vol. 1, pp. 30f.) this principle is extended to the whole cosmos.

d. "Walls of flame": Cf. 1En 14:9–16; 71:5; Masseket Hekalot 4 (*BHM*, vol. 2, p. 42).

e. "Hailstones": *ʾabnê ʾelgābîš*—an expression taken from Ezek 13:11, 13; cf. b.Ber 54b; Seder Rabbah diBereʾšit, BM, vol. 1, p. 45, l. 7.

f. "Stones of hurricane blasts," lit. "stones of the wings of hurricane"—presumably another name for hailstones. For "wings of storm" see margin and Midraš Konen, *BHM*, vol. 2, p. 32 (bottom line).

2 water.ᵍ •Fire and water are encircled by those who say "Holy." Those who 1:12; 20:2; 35:4
say "Holy" are encircled by those who say "Blessed."ʰ Those who say
"Blessed" are encircled by bright clouds. The bright clouds are encircled by
coals of juniper. The coals of juniper are encircled by a thousand camps of fire 1:6; 18:4
and myriads of hosts of flame, and between each camp and each host a cloud 25:7
stands, so that they should not burn each other with fire.

The camps of the angels

1 **35** R. Ishmael said: The angel Meṭaṭron, Prince of the Divine Presence, said
to me:ᵃ
The Holy One, blessed be he, has 496,000ᵇ myriads of campsᶜ in the height 17:2; 40:3;
2 of the heaven of ʿArabot, and in each camp are 496,000 angels. •Every angel 1:6; 18:4
is as the Great Seaᵈ in height, and the appearance of their faces is like lightning; 17:3
their eyes are like torches of fire; their arms and feet look like burnished bronze, Dan 10:6
and the roar of their voices when they speak is as the sound of a multitude.
3 They all stand before the throne of glory in four rows and mighty princes stand 27:3; 36:2
4 at the head of each row.ᵉ •Some of them say "Holy" and some of them say 34:2
"Blessed";ᶠ some run on missions and some stand and serve, as it is written,

> A thousand thousand waited on him,
> ten thousand times ten thousand stood before him.
> A court was held
> and the books were opened.   Dan 7:10

5   When the time comes to say "Holy," a storm wind first goes out from the 18:7; 19:6; 38:1
presence of the Holy One, blessed be he, and falls on the campsᵍ of the Šekinah, 1:6; 18:4
and a great storm arises among them, as it is written,

> Now a storm of the Lord breaks,
> a tempest whirls.   Jer 30:23

6 Thereupon a thousand thousand of them become sparks, a thousand thousand 40:3; 47:1f.
firebrands, a thousand thousand glowing coals, a thousand thousand flames, a
thousand thousand males, a thousand thousand females, a thousand thousand
winds, a thousand thousand blazing fires, a thousand thousand flames, a thousand
thousand sparks, a thousand thousand ḥašmallim of light,ʰ until they accept the 7; 26:4; 36:2

---

g. "Fire and water," A B; "walls of fire and
water," E F.
   h. "Those who say 'Holy' . . . those who say
'Blessed' ": i.e. the angels who recite the heavenly Qeduššah in the form of versicle and response; see margin and "Theological Importance."

35 a. Chs. 35–40 contain an account of the
performance of the celestial Sanctus by the
angelic choirs. A number of internal contradictions suggests that diverse traditions have been
combined (cf. 35:1; 37:1; and 40:1; see 40:3, n.
h). It seems very probable that each of the present
chs. was originally an independent unit of tradition.
   b. "496,000," A E F; "506,000," B.
   c. "Camps": Cf. Alphabet of Aqiba, BHM,
vol. 3, p. 21, l. 21: "1,018 camps stand before
the Šekinah in the sanctuary which is in Šebaqim
[= the third heaven, as in 3En 17:3], and say
before him every day, 'Holy,' and in every camp
are (1008) (?1018) myriads of ministering angels." See further 1:6, n. i, and 18:4, n. h.

d. "The great sea": either the Mediterranean
(Num 34:6f.) or the primeval ocean (Midraš
Konen, BHM, vol. 2, p. 32, l. 14).
   e. "Four rows and mighty princes stand at
the head of each row": Cf. the four camps of
the Šekinah and their respective princes in 18:4.
   f. "Some of them say 'Holy' and some of
them say 'Blessed' ": i.e. they recite the celestial
Qeduššah; see the margin and "Theological
Importance."
   g. "Camps": emending to maḥanê; B has the
singular maḥanēh, for which see 1:6, n. i.
   h. "Thereupon a thousand thousand . . . ḥašmallim of light," A and, substantially, E F. Cf.
GenR 21:9: "The angels turn about: sometimes
they appear as men, sometimes as women, sometimes as spirits, sometimes as angels"; Midraš
Haggadol to Gen 3:24 (ed. Margulies, p. 111);
ExR 25:2; Yannai, Qerobot leSeper Bere'šit, ed.
Zulay, p. 16; no. 5/8; ll. 118–22. Maimonides,
Moreh Nebukim 1.49. In 40:3 and 47:1f. it states
that the angels are punished for not reciting the
Qeduššah properly, but here apparently they are
disciplined before they have even begun to recite.

yoke of the kingdom[i] of the High and Exalted One who created them all,[j] in   Isa 57:15
dread, in fear, in awe, with shuddering, quaking, anguish, terror, and trembling.
Then they return to their original state.[k] Thus the fear of their King is kept
before them every hour, so that they should set their hearts to recite the song
every hour, as it is written, "One called to another and said."   Isa 6:3

The angels bathe in the River of Fire

1 **36** R. Ishmael said: The angel Meṭaṭron, Prince of the Divine Presence, said
to me:
When the ministering angels desire to recite the song, the River of Fire rises,   18:19; 33:4
and its fires increase in strength a thousand thousand and myriads of myriads
of times,[a] and it flows out from beneath[b] the throne of glory between the
2 camps[c] of ministering angels and cohorts of ʿArabot. •All the ministering   1:6; 18:4; 35:1
angels first go down into the River of Fire and bathe themselves[d] in the fire of   17:3
the River of Fire,[e] and dip their tongues and their mouths seven times in the   2Kgs 5:10,14
River of Fire, and afterward they get out and don garments of ḥašmal,[f] and   26:4
they stand in four rows over against the throne of glory in every heaven.[g]   35:3
  37:1

The four chariots of the Šekinah

1 **37** R. Ishmael said: The angel Meṭaṭron, Prince of the Divine Presence, said
to me:

i. "The yoke of the kingdom": To accept
"the yoke of the kingdom of heaven" is to
acknowledge God's sovereignty. Cf. the Yoṣer
prayer: "Be Thou blessed, O our Rock . . .
Creator of ministering spirits, all of whom stand
in the heights of the universe, and proclaim with
awe and unison aloud the words of the living
God and everlasting King . . . And they all take
upon themselves the yoke of the kingdom of
heaven" (Singer, pp. 39f.). Jews accept the yoke
when they recite the Šemaʿ (m.Ber 2:2; SifNum
115, ed. Horovitz, p. 126). The Šemaʿ benediction, "Blessed be the name of his glorious
kingdom for ever and ever" (t.Taʿan 1:13; b.Pes
56a), is introduced into the celestial Qeduššah in
3En 39:2; cf. 48B:2.
j. "The kingdom of the High and Exalted One
who created them all": Heb. malkût rām weniśśāʾ
yôṣēr kullām; so A E F. B has malkût šāmayim
rām weniśśāʾ yôṣēr kullām. For rām weniśśāʾ as
a title of God see Isa 57:15 and Alphabet of
Aqiba, BHM, vol. 3, p. 37, l. 11.
k. "Their original state," A E F.

36 a. A paraphrase of rather obscure Heb.,
following the A E F text. The idea appears to be
that the River of Fire increases both in volume
and intensity to provide more effective cleansing
for the angels. Verbally the language recalls Dan
7:10.
b. "From beneath," A E F.
c. "The camps," A E F; "camp," B.
d. "Bathe themselves": a literal "baptism of
fire"; cf. Seder Rabbah diBereʾšit, BM, vol. 1,
p. 46; Maʿyan Ḥokmah, BHM, vol. 1, p. 59;
Hilkot Malʾakim, BM MS, Add. 27199, fol.
125a: "All the angels and all the camps bathe in
fiery rivers seven times and restore themselves
365 times" (quoted from Odeberg). See further
Seper HaRazim 7:16 (ed. Margalioth, p. 108);

ʿArugat habbośem, ed. Urbach, vol. 2, p. 184
(cf. Pereq mippirqe hekalot, BHM, vol. 3, p.
162). Contrast Reʾuyot Yeḥezqeʾl (BM, vol. 2,
p. 132; ed. Gruenwald, p. 126): "The angels
stretch out their hands and take some fire from
the River of Fire and cleanse their lips and their
tongues" (note the echo of Isa 6:6f.).
e. "In the fire of the River of Fire," A E F;
"in the fire," B.
f. "And don garments of ḥašmal": the text
contains several unintelligible words. A (which
is well supported by the other MSS) reads:
welôbešîn lebûš mḥmqy sml weʾôtepîn ṭply ḥašmal, "and don garments of . . . and wrap
themselves in . . . of ḥašmal." All that it seems
possible to say is that mḥmqy sml must conceal
the name of a substance parallel to ḥašmal and
ṭply a word corresponding to lebûš. Perhaps for
the latter read meʿîlê ("and wrap themselves in
cloaks of ḥašmal"); cf. 17:8; 18:25; Seder Rabbah diBereʾšit, BM, vol. 1, p. 46, l. 20; Seper
HaRazim 7:16f. (ed. Margalioth, p. 108); Reqanati's quotation from Seper Hekalot in BHM,
vol. 2, p. xvii.
g. "In every heaven": It is not clear whether
this goes with "stand" or with "throne of glory."
If it is construed with the former then the sense
would be that the angels in every heaven line up
facing the throne of glory in the seventh heaven.
If it is construed with the latter then the sense
would be that there is a throne of glory in each
of the seven heavens, and that the angels stand
facing the throne in their respective heavens. The
second interpretation is supported by the tradition
that there is a Merkabah in each heaven (see
37:1, n. a). According to AscenIs 7:13–9:2 there
is a throne in every heaven (except the sixth),
though it is not clear whether these thrones belong
to God, or to the angelic princes who rule over
the various heavens (cf. 3En 17).

Four chariots of the Šekinah stand in the seven palaces,[a] and before each of
them stand four camps of the Šekinah. Between one camp and another a River
2 of Fire flows along. •Between one river and another is a circle of bright clouds,[b]
and between each cloud[c] pillars of sulfur stand fixed; between one pillar and
another stands a circle of fiery wheels; between one wheel and another is a
circle of tongues of flame; between one tongue and another is a circle of
treasuries of lightning; behind the treasuries of lightning is a circle of hurricane
blasts; behind the hurricane blasts is a circle of storehouses of storm; behind
the storehouses of storm is a circle of winds, thunderclaps, thunders, and
sparks; behind the sparks is a circle of tremors.[d]

             1:1; 18:3
             1:6; 18:4; 35:1
             18:19; 33:4
             25:7; 34:2
             19:2f
             10:6; Jer 10:13
             34:1

Cosmic commotion at the singing of the Qeduššah

1 **38** R. Ishmael said: Meṭaṭron said to me:
When the ministering angels utter the "Holy," all the pillars of the heavens
and their bases shake, and the gates of the palaces of the heaven of ʿArabot
quiver; the foundations of the earth and of Šeḥaqim shudder; the chambers of
Maʿon[a] and the chambers of Makon[b] writhe, and all the orders of Raqiaʿ,[c] the
constellations and the stars, are alarmed; the orb of the sun and the orb of the
moon[d] hurry from their paths[e] in flight and, running backward[f] 12,000 parasangs,
2 seek to fling themselves from heaven, •because of the thunder of their voices,[g]
and the sparks and lightning flashes that shoot from their mouths,[h] as it is
written,

             18:7; 19:6;
             35:5f.; Isa 6:3f.
             17:3; 18:3; 33:5
             17:4–8
             22B:8

> Your thunder crashed as it rolled,
> your lightning lit up the world,
> the earth shuddered and quaked.

         Ps 77:18

3 But the Prince of the World calls to them and says, "Stay at rest in your places;
be not afraid because the ministering angels recite the song before the Holy
One, blessed be he," as it is written,

         30:2

> When all the stars of the morning were singing with joy,
> and the Sons of God in chorus were chanting praise.

         Job 38:7

Sacred names fly off from the throne of glory

1 **39** R. Ishmael said: The angel Meṭaṭron, Prince of the Divine Presence, said
to me:
When the ministering angels recite the "Holy," all the sacred names[a] engraved

         41:4; 48B:1;
         48D:5

---

37 a. "Four chariots . . . in the seven palaces":
Cf. Re'uyot Yeḥezqe'l, BM, vol. 2, p. 130 (ed.
Gruenwald, p. 119): "The Holy One, blessed be
he, created seven heavens and seven chariots in
them." For a list of the chariots of God see ch.
24.

b. "A circle of bright clouds": The description in this chapter is confused and the problem
is created once again by an obscure use of the
verb nqp (cf. 19:4, n. d; 33:3, n. d; 34:1, n. b).
Here two distinct formulae are employed: (1)
"Between one X and another X, Y forms a circle
[maqqîpîm/muqqāpîm]." (2) "Behind X, Y forms
a circle [maqqîpîm]." This second formula is
found in Midraš Konen, BHM, vol. 2, pp. 33f.;
Seder Rabbah diBere'šit, BM, vol. 1, pp. 30f.
As in ch. 34 the idea appears to be of phenomena
arranged concentrically around the Merkabah.

c. "Between each cloud" or "between each
river," lit. "between each one": so A E F.

d. "Behind the sparks is a circle of tremors,"
E F.

38 a. "The chambers of Maʿon," A E F; "the
orders of Maʿon," B. For the heavenly chambers
see 1:1, n. d.

b. "The chambers of Makon," A B; "the
palaces of Makon," E. Against E's reading is
the fact that the palaces are usually located in
'Arabot; see 18:3 and "Theological Importance."

c. "Orders [sidrê] of Raqiaʿ," A B; "secrets
[sitrê] of Raqia' "; cf. 13:1, n. d.

d. "The orb of the sun and the orb of the
moon," A E F.

e. "Their paths," A E F.

f. "Running backwards," A E F.

g. "Their voices," A E F; A B add (in
asyndeton) "their chanting"; text follows E F.

h. "From their mouths," A E F; "from their
faces," B.

39 a. "Sacred names": either (1) the name
YHWH inscribed many times over on the throne
(cf. 22:5); or (2) many different names, all
permutations of the name YHWH (cf. 48B:1).

with a pen of flame on the throne of glory fly off like eagles,[b] with sixteen
wings, and encompass and surround the Holy One, blessed be he, on the four
2 sides of the abode of his glorious Šekinah. •The angels of the host, the fiery 25:5-7
ministers, the ophanim of power,[c] the cherubim of the Šekinah, the holy 22:11-16;
creatures, the seraphim, the ʾerellim and ṭapsarim, the cohorts of flame and the 21:1-4; 26:8-12; 14:1
cohorts of devouring fire,[d] the ranks of firebrands, the hosts of flame, the holy 16:2
princes,[e] crowned with crowns, robed with royalty, covered with glory, girded
with beauty, girt with magnificence, girdled with majesty, fall prostrate three
times[f] and say, "Blessed be the name of his glorious kingdom for ever and 48B:2
ever."[g]

The proper order for the Qeduššah

1 **40** R. Ishmael said: Meṭaṭron said to me:
When the ministering angels say "Holy" according to its proper order before
the Holy One, blessed be he, the ministers of his throne and the servants of his
2 glory go out with great joy from under the throne of glory. •Each of them
has in his hands[a] a thousand thousand and myriads of myriads of starry crowns 16:2
like the brilliance of the morning star in appearance. They put them on the
heads of the ministering angels and the great princes. Those that say "Holy"
receive three crowns: one for saying "Holy,"[b] one for saying "Holy, Holy,"
and one for saying "Holy, Holy, Holy, YHWH of Hosts."[c] Isa 6:3
3 Whenever they do not recite the "Holy" according to its proper order,
devouring fire[d] goes out from the little finger of the Holy One,[e] blessed be he. 47:1
It falls[f] on their ranks, and splits[g] into 496,000 myriads of parts corresponding 17:2
to the four camps[h] of the ministering angels, and devours them at a stroke, as 1:6; 18:4; 35:1
it is written,

A fire precedes him as he goes,
devouring all enemies around him. Ps 97:3

4 Then the Holy One, blessed be he, opens his mouth, and, with one word,

---

See margin and Alphabet of Aqiba, *BHM*, vol.
3, p. 25: "The seals of the Holy One, blessed
be he, by which were sealed all the sacred names
which are on the throne of glory." See also the
quotation from the Alphabet of Aqiba quoted in
n. b below.

b. "Like eagles": Cf. Alphabet of Aqiba,
BHM, vol. 3, p. 26 (BM, vol. 2, p. 366): "But
God revealed to Moses all the names, whether
sacred names, or names engraved upon the kingly
crown on his head, or names engraved upon the
throne of glory, or names engraved upon the ring
on his hand, or names which stand like pillars
of fire around his chariots, or names which
surround the Šekinah like the eagles of the chariot
[cf. 3En 2:1], or names by which were sealed
heaven and earth [cf. 3En 48D:5] . . ." See also
b.AZ 18a (letters flying off from a burning Torah
scroll); b.Pes 87b (letters flying from the tables
of the Law). The angels are sometimes described
as being like eagles; see 2:1; 24:11; 26:3; 47:4.

e. "The ophanim of power": i.e. "the powerful ophanim" or "the ophanim of the Almighty
[*Gebûrāh*]"; see 28:3, n. b.

d. "Cohorts of devouring fire": emending to
gedûdê ʾēš ʾôkelāh.

e. "The holy princes": emending to *śārîm
qedôšîm*.

f. "Fall prostrate three times," A E F.

g. This is normally a response for the Šemaʿ,
not the Qeduššah; see "Theological Importance."

40 a. "In his hands," A E F. For crowned
angels chanting the Qeduššah see Seder Rabbah
diBereʾšit, BM, vol. 1, p. 46, l. 19. Cf. the
story of the crowning of Israel at Sinai in b.Shab
88a.

b. "One for saying 'Holy,' " E F.

c. For a similar division of the Qeduššah see
Seder Rabbah diBereʾšit, BM, vol. 1, p. 47, and
Seder Rab Amram Gaon, ed. Coronel 4b, pt. 1,
p. 18a.

d. "Devouring fire": Here the fire that punishes the angels proceeds directly from God; in
47:2 they are burned in the River of Fire. For
punishment of the angels for wrongly reciting
the Qeduššah see Hekalot Rabbati 30 (*BHM*, vol.
3, p. 108); Seder Rabbah diBereʾšit, BM, vol.
1, p. 47; Reqanati's quotation from Seper Hekalot
in *BHM*, vol. 2, p. xvii; Hilkot Malʾakim, BM,
MS Add. 27199, fol. 123a (the angels are lashed
by Ḥayliʾel with lashes of fire) (quoted from
Odeberg).

e. "The little finger of the Holy One, blessed
be he"; cf. margin and Midraš Konen, *BHM*,
vol. 2, p. 25, l. 12. The measurement of God's
little finger is an element of Šiʿur Qomah; see
"Historical Importance."

f. "It falls" (*wenôpelet*), A E F.

g. "And splits," A.

h. "Four camps": Two ideas have been combined here: (1) that there are four camps (see
18:4; 37:1), and (2) that there are 496,000
myriads of camps (see 35:1).

creates new ones like them to take their place.[i] Each of them stands in song before his throne of glory and recites "Holy," as it is written,

> Every morning they are renewed;
> great is his faithfulness.[j]

Lam 3:23

The cosmic letters

1 **41** R. Ishmael said: Meṭaṭron said to me:[a]
Come and I will show you[b]
    the letters[c] by which heaven and earth were created;   13:1; 48D:5
    the letters by which seas and rivers were created;
    the letters by which mountains and hills were created;
    the letters by which trees and grasses were created;
    the letters by which stars and constellations were created;
    the letters by which the orb of the moon and the disk of the sun, Orion and
       the Pleiades, and all the various luminaries of Raqia[c] were created;   17:3,4,7; 33:5; 38:1
2   the letters by which the ministering angels were created;   26:8–12
    the letters by which the seraphim and the creatures were created;[d]   21:1–4
    the letters by which the throne of glory and the wheels of the chariot were   19:2–4
      created;
    the letters by which the necessities of the world[e] were created;
    the letters by which wisdom and understanding, knowledge and intelligence,
      humility and rectitude were created, by which the whole world is   8:1
      sustained.[f]
3 I went with him and he took me by his hand, bore me up on his wings, and showed me those letters,[g] engraved with a pen of flame upon the throne of   13:1; 29:1; 39:1 glory, and sparks and lightnings[h] shoot from them and cover all the chambers[i]   17:3 of ʿArabot.

The cosmic power of divine names

1 **42** R. Ishmael said: Meṭaṭron said to me:
Come and I will show you
    where water is suspended in the height of Raqia[c];[a]   Gen 1:6f.

i. "New ones like them to take their place," E F; "others, new ones, like them to take their place," A B. Angels are created in two ways: (1) from the utterance (*dibbûr*) of God (see 27:3, n. i); (2) from the River of Fire. On the creation of the angels see b.Ḥag 14a; Re'uyot Yeḥezqe'l, BM, vol. 2, p. 132 (ed. Gruenwald, p. 126); ExR 15:6; GenR 78:1; LamR 3:23.8.

j. According to one view the angels endure only for a day and the creation of new ones each morning is a natural consequence of this fact, and not connected with the idea of them being punished for not reciting the Qeduššah properly; see the references in n. i above.

41 a. Chs. 41–48A are the final section of 3En. They contain a series of revelations by Meṭaṭron to Ishmael, in which Meṭaṭron fulfills his function of disclosing secrets (cf. 48D:2f.). The characteristic formula of the section is: "Come and I will show you . . . I went with him and he took me by his hand, bore me up on his wings, and showed me." Chs. 41f. are cosmological and belong to Ma'aśeh Bere'šit speculation. Chs. 43–44 and 46–47 are concerned with "souls." Ch. 45 interrupts this subject and may be a later intrusion. Chs. 45 and 48 have basically to do with the end-time. The book ends with a vision of the messianic age.
b. "I will show you," E F; "see," A B.

c. "The letters": the twenty-two letters of the Heb. alphabet; see 13:1, n. c; 48D:5.
d. "The letters by which the ministering angels . . . and the creatures were created, A E and, substantially, F; B omits.
e. "The world," A E F; "the worlds," B.
f. "Wisdom and understanding . . . by which the whole world is sustained": Cf. the heavenly treasuries in 8:1.
g. "Those letters," A and, substantially, E F.
h. "Sparks and lightnings," A E F; "sparks," B.
i. "All the chambers [*ḥadrê*]," F (cf. 1:1, n. d; 38:1); "all the glories [*ḥadrê*]," A (cf. 18:18, n. y); "all the inhabitants [*dārê*]," B.

42 a. "In the height of Raqia' " (*berûm rāqia'*): Odeberg's conjecture for the reading of A B (*brwm rmym*); cf. vs. 2: "I saw water suspended in the height of the heaven of ʿArabot [*berûm 'arābôt rāqia'*]"; and the Yoṣer prayer: "Creator of ministering spirits, all of whom stand in the height of the universe [*berûm 'ôlām*]" (Singer, p. 39). The reference is to the "upper waters," above the firmament (Gen 1:6f.); see Jub 2:4; TLevi 2:6, 7; GenR 2:4; 4:4, 5, 7; b.Pes 104a; b.Ḥag 15a; b.Ta'an 9b; Seder Rabbah diBere'šit, BM, vol. 1, p. 25. See also n. f below.

where fire burns in the midst of hail;[b]
where lightnings flash in the midst of mountains of snow;
where thunders rumble in the highest heights;
where flame blazes[c] in the midst of burning fire;
where voices can be heard[d] above thunder and earthquake.[e]

2 I went with him, and, taking me by his hand, he bore me up on his wings and showed me all these things. I saw water suspended in the height of the heaven 17:3 of 'Arabot, through the power of the name Yah, I am that I am, and its fruits Ex 15:2, 3:14 were descending from heaven[f] and watering the surface of the earth, as it is written,

From your palace you water the uplands,
the earth is full of the fruit of your works.   Ps 104:13

3 I saw fire, snow, and hailstones enclosed[g] one within the other, without one Ex 9:24 destroying the other, through the power of the the the name A Consuming Fire,
4 as it is written, "For YHWH your God is a consuming fire." •I saw lightnings Deut 4:24 flashing in the midst of mountains of snow, without being quenched, through the power of the name Yah, YHWH,[h] the Everlasting Rock, as it is written,
5 "Yah, YHWH is the everlasting Rock." •I saw thunders and voices roaring Isa 26:4 in the midst of flames of fire, without being overwhelmed, through the power
6 of the name Great God Almighty, as it is written, "I am God Almighty." •I Gen 17:1 saw flames of fire flaring and burning in the midst of blazing fire without being swallowed up, through the power of the name A Hand upon the Throne of
7 Yah, as it is written, "And he said: a hand upon the throne of Yah." •I saw rivers of fire in the midst of rivers of water, and rivers of water in the midst Ex 17:16 of rivers of fire,[i] through the power of the name He Keeps the Peace, as it is 18:19 written, "He keeps the peace in his heights";[j] He keeps peace between fire Job 25:2 and water, between hail and fire, between wind and cloud, between tremors and comets.[k]

The souls of the righteous

1 **43** R. Ishmael said: Metatron said to me:
Come and I will show you the souls[a] of the righteous who have already been created and have returned,[b] and the souls of the righteous who have not yet

---

b. "Hail" (*bārād*), A B; " *'abnê 'elgābiš*," E F: For the E F reading see 34:1, n. e.

c. "Blazes," A and, substantially, E F.

d. "Voices can be heard," A B F; "his voice can be heard," E. The E reading makes an appropriate reference to the "still, small voice" (1Kgs 19:12); see 4QŠirŠabb; Midraš Konen, *BHM*, vol. 2, p. 34, l. 14; Seder Rabbah di-Bere'šit, BM, vol. 1, p. 30, l. 9, and p. 47, l. 11.

e. "Thunder and earthquake," A E.

f. "And its fruits were descending from heaven," A B; "and from it rain was descending," E F. Cf. b.Ta'an 10a: "The upper waters are suspended by the word of God and their fruits are the rain waters." There may be an allusion to the idea that the upper waters are masculine and the lower waters feminine: See 1En 54:8; GenR 13:13; Seder Rabbah diBere'šit, BM, vol. 1, p. 25; Zohar 1 (*Bere'šit*) 29b (end).

g. "Enclosed," A E; cf. Ex 9:24, "The hail fell, and lightning flashing in the midst of it."

h. "Yah, YHWH," A E F.

i. "And rivers of water in the midst of rivers of fire," A E F. For the juxtaposition of fire and water see 34:1; 2En 29:1f. (A); y.RH 58a.37; b.Hag 12a; GenR 4:9; 10:3; SongR 3:11.1.

j. "His heights": so MT; the MSS read "the heights."

k. "Tremors and comets" (*ben zewā'îm* [= *zewā'ôt*] *lezîqîm*): The sense is not certain. The context demands two natural phenomena thought to be connected in some way. For comets as portending disasters see b.Ber 58b; Pliny, *Naturalis historia* 2.96f. Seneca, *Quaestiones naturales* 7. For *zîq* = "comet" see b.Ber 58b; *zîq* can also mean "a gust of wind": See b.Ber 60b, "a gust of wind [*zîqā'*] came and put out the lamp." For the juxtaposition of *zîqîm* and *zewā'ôt* see m.Ber 9:2 and b.Hull 86a.

43 a. "I will show you the souls," A E F: "Soul" here is *nešāmāh*; for the term see 47:1, n. a. On the ideas in chs. 43f. see, in general, "Theological Importance."

b. "Have returned": Cf. vss. 2f. For the abode of the righteous after death see b.Hag 12b, " 'Arabot, in which are . . . the souls of the righteous and the spirits and souls which are yet to be created [i.e. to be born]"; b.Shab 152b, "The souls of the righteous dead are hidden under the throne of glory"; EcclR 3:21.1, "The souls of the righteous ascend after death and are placed in the divine treasury"; SifDeut 344 (ed.

2 been created.ᶜ •He bore me up with him, and, taking me by his hand, he led meᵈ to the throne of gloryᵉ and showed me those souls which have already been created and have returned, flying above the throne of glory in the presence of 46:2
3 the Holy One, blessed be he.ᶠ •Then I went and expounded this verse, and found with regard to the text "The spirit shall clothe itself in my presence, and the souls which I have made," that "the spirit shall clothe itself in my presence"ᵍ Isa 57:16 refers to the souls of the righteousʰ which have already been created in the storehouse of beingsⁱ and have returned to the presence of God; and "the souls which I have made"ʲ refers to the souls of the righteousᵏ which have not yet been created in the storehouse.

The souls of the wicked and the intermediate

1 **44** R. Ishmael said: Meṭaṭron said to me:
Come and I will show you where the souls of the wicked stand, and where the souls of the intermediate stand; whither the souls of the intermediateᵃ descend, and whither the souls of the wicked descend.ᵇ
2 He said to me:
The souls of the wicked are brought down to Sheolᶜ by two angels of destruction, 31:2

Finkelstein, p. 401); ARN A 12 (ed. Schechter, 25b); Alphabet of Aqiba, *BHM*, vol. 3, p. 26, l. 25, "the treasuries of spirits and the treasuries of the souls of the living and of the dead"; Seper HaRazim 6:1f. (ed. Margalioth, p. 104); 7:2f. (p. 107). Contrast the "treasuries/chambers" in which the souls of the righteous are kept in Sheol till the resurrection according to 2Bar 21:23; 30:2; 4Ezra 4:35, 42; 7:32, 80, 95; cf. 1En 22:2f.

c. The pre-existence of the soul is implied throughout this chapter. There are three possible explanations why unborn souls may be called "righteous": (1) Souls may be created "righteous" and "unrighteous"; see WisSol 8:19f.; 4Mac 18:23; GenR 8:7; cf. b.BB 16a, "God creates both the righteous and the wicked." (2) Unborn souls may be designated as "righteous" by God in virtue of his foreknowledge of the righteous lives they live on earth; so GenR 8:7 (on another interpretation). (3) "Righteous" may be loosely used to express the idea that all souls before birth are pure; see b.Shab 152b; EcclR 12:7.1; and the benediction *'Elōhay nešāmāh*, recited on waking from sleep: "O my God, the soul which thou gavest me is pure" (Singer, p. 5; cf. b.Ber 60b).

d. "He led me," E F; "he bore me up," A B.

e. "To the throne of glory": A B add "to the abode of the Šekinah, and he revealed to the throne of glory." The text follows E F.

f. Ishmael is not shown the unborn souls as promised in vs. 1. There may be a lacuna in the text.

g. "That 'the spirit shall clothe itself in my presence,'" A F.

h. "The souls of the righteous": emendation (cf. vs. 1). The MSS misplace the expression after "of beings."

i. "The storehouse of beings": Heb. *gûp habberiyyôt*. This storehouse is mentioned in b.Yeb 62a; 63b; b.AZ 5a; b.Nidd 13b. Rashi explains the idea thus: "There is a treasure-house [*'ôṣār*] called *gûp*, and at the time of creation all souls destined to be born were formed and placed

there" (to b.AZ 5a). "*Gûp:* A chamber like a body [*gûp*]; the name for the special place for souls which are about to be born" (to b.Nidd 13b). "*Gûp:* A curtain [*pargôd*] which forms a partition between the Šekinah and the angels, and there are placed spirits and souls created since the six days of creation, which are to be put into bodies yet to be created" (to b.Yeb 63b). When this ch. of 3En speaks of "souls which have been created" and "souls which have not yet been created" it cannot mean creation in any absolute sense, but must refer to the entry of the soul into the body. Cf. b.Ḥag 12b, quoted in n. b above; see further Re'uyot Yeḥezqe'l, BM, vol. 2, p. 133, l. 18 (ed. Gruenwald, p. 136).

j. Isa 57:16 is used in connection with speculation on the soul in b.Yeb 62a; 63b; b.Nidd 5a; b.Ḥag 12b.

k. "Souls of the righteous," A B E; "souls", F. See vs. 1, n. c.

44 a. "The intermediate" (*bênôniyyîm*); see Maimonides, *Yad. Hilkot Tešubah* 3.1: "Every human being has both merits and iniquities. He whose merits are greater than his iniquities is righteous; he whose iniquities are greater than his merits is wicked; he in whom merits and iniquities are evenly balanced is intermediate." Cf. b.RH 16b; b.Ber 61b; b.Yoma 75a; ARN A 41 (ed. Schechter, 67a); t.Sanh 13:3.

b. "Where the souls of the wicked stand . . . the wicked descend," A and, substantially, B.

c. "Brought down to Sheol": Like descriptions of heaven, descriptions of hell and its torments form a distinct genre of Jewish Midrash; see Masseket ḥibbuṭ haqqeber, *BHM*, vol. 1, pp. 150–52; Masseket Gehinnom, *BHM*, vol. 1, pp. 147–49; Gan 'Eden weGehinnom, *BHM*, vol. 5, pp. 42–51; Ma'aśeh deRabbi Yehošua' b. Levi, *BHM*, vol. 2, pp. 50f.; Midraš Konen, *BHM*, vol. 2, pp. 30f., 35f. (cf. BM, vol. 1, pp. 33–38); Šib'ah hekalot haṭṭum'ah, BM, vol. 1, pp. 123–26; Gedullat Mošeh, BM, vol. 1, pp. 281–85.

3 Za'api'el and Samki'el.[d] •Samki'el is in charge of the souls of the intermediate, to support them and purify them from sin, through the abundant mercies of the Omnipresent One.[e] Za'api'el is appointed to bring down the souls of the wicked from the presence of the Holy One, blessed be he, from the judgment of the Šekinah,[f] to Sheol,[g] to punish them with fire in Gehinnom,[h] with rods of burning 2Kgs 23:10;
Mk 9:45; 28:10
4 coal. •I went with him, and, taking me by his hand, he bore me up and showed
5 them all to me with his fingers. •I saw that their faces looked like human faces, 47:4 but their bodies were like eagles.[i] Moreover, the faces of the intermediate were a greenish color,[j] on account of their deeds, for they are tainted until purified
6 of their iniquity by fire. •And the faces of the wicked souls were as black as the bottom of a pot,[k] because of the multitude of their wicked deeds.[l]

The souls of the patriarchs[m]

7 I saw the souls of the fathers of the world, Abraham, Isaac, and Jacob, and the rest of the righteous, who had been raised from their graves and had ascended into heaven. They were praying before the Holy One, blessed be he, and saying in prayer, "Lord of the Universe, how long will you sit upon your throne, as a mourner sits[n] in the days of his mourning, with your right hand 48A:1,2,4,5;
Ps 20:6 behind you,[o] and not redeem your sons and reveal your kingdom in the world? Do you not pity your sons who are enslaved among the nations of the world? Do you not pity your right hand behind you, by which you stretched out and Isa 42:5; 48:13;
Ezek 1:22;
Jer 10:12 spread[p] the heavens, the earth, and the heaven of heavens? Have you no pity?"
8 Then the Holy One, blessed be he, answered each and every one of them and said: "Since these wicked ones have sinned thus and thus,[q] and have transgressed thus and thus before me, how can I deliver my sons from among the nations of the world, reveal my kingdom in the world before the eyes of the gentiles and deliver[r] my great right hand, which has been brought low[s] by them."
9 Then Meṭaṭron, the servant of YHWH, called me and said to me:[t] "Take the 18:24

---

d. "Angels of destruction, Za'api'el and Samki'el": Za'api'el's name is derived from *za'ap*, "wrath," and Samki'el's from *semek*, "support." Note that Samki'el's function is to "support" the intermediate. On the angels of destruction see 31:2, n. f.

e. "Mercies of the Omnipresent One," A E F. For the divine title "Omnipresent One" see 18:24, n. n2. After purgation the intermediate are allowed to ascend to join the righteous; cf. b.RH 16b; ARN A 41 (ed. Schechter, 67a); cf. Se'udat Gan 'Eden, *BHM*, vol. 5, p. 46, l. 30; Pirqe Mašiaḥ, *BHM*, vol. 3, p. 75, l. 28. According to one view the wicked are ultimately annihilated; see b.Shab 33b; b.RH 16b/17a.

f. "From the judgment of the Šekinah," A E F; "from the splendor of the Šekinah," B. The judgment is the judgment that takes place after a man's death; see 28:10, n. n.

g. "To Sheol," A E.

h. "To punish them with fire in Gehinnom," E; "to punish them in the fire of Gehinnom," F.

i. "Their bodies were like eagles": The souls possess a sort of "spiritual" body distinct from the ordinary, physical bodies which they tenant during their earthly life. Cf. the idea of the "astral body" in spiritism, and the *ochēma*, "vehicle," of the soul in Neoplatonism (Proclus, *Institutio theologica* 205). Angels are represented as being like eagles; see 2:1; 24:11; 26:3.

j. "A greenish color" (*yarqût*), A E F.

k. "Black as the bottom of a pot": For the phrase see b.Meg 11a; b.Shab 30a; b.Sanh 107b.

For its use to describe the wicked in hell see b.RH 17a; Masseket Gehinnom 4 (*BHM*, vol. 7, p. 149, l. 4); Pirqe Mašiaḥ, *BHM*, vol. 3, p. 75, l. 29.

l. "Wicked deeds," E F and, substantially, A.

m. 44:7–10 is an apocalyptic fragment only loosely connected with the theme of the fate of souls. It is based on Ps 20:6 (MT 20:7); cf. Ex 15:6, 12.

n. "As a mourner sits," A E.

o. "Behind you," E: the place of forgetfulness and rejection; see 47:2f.; 48A:1.

p. "And spread," A E F.

q. The implication is that the sins of Israel delay the messianic redemption; see y.Ta'an 64a.29: "Rabbi Aḇa said in the name of R. Tanḥum b. Rabbi: If Israel would repent for only one day, immediately the Son of David would come." Cf. b.Sanh 98a; ExR 5:18; LamR proem 21.

r. "My sons . . . and deliver," E and, substantially, F; A B omit by homoeoteleuton.

s. "Which has been brought low": emending the A B text to *hammuppelet*; E has "fallen and brought low" (*nepîlāh umuppelet*).

t. "Then Meṭaṭron . . . and said to me": following the E text in the main, but emending *'abdî*, "my servant," to *'ebed Y*, "the servant of YHWH." For this title of Meṭaṭron see 10:3, n. g. Cf. Alphabet of Aqiba, *BHM*, vol. 3, p. 33, l. 27: "At once the Holy One, blessed be he, called to Meṭaṭron and said, My servant, go . . ." Odeberg (following the B text) trans-books and read their wicked deeds.'' At once I took the books and read their deeds, and it was recorded that each and every one of those wicked ones had incurred extirpation[u] thirty-six times over. Moreover, it was recorded that they had transgressed against all the letters of the Torah,[v] as it is written. "The whole of Israel has transgressed your Torah.'' It does not say here "against   Dan 9:11 your Torah,'' but simply "your Torah,'' because they transgressed it from ⁵Alep to Taw,[w] and incurred extirpation thirty-six[x] times over for each letter.

10 At once Abraham, Isaac, and Jacob began to weep. Then the Holy One, blessed be he, said to them: "Abraham, my friend, Isaac, my chosen one, Jacob, my firstborn,[y] how can I save them at this time from among the nations of the world?'' Thereupon Michael, the Prince of Israel,[z] cried out and lamented   Dan 12:1 in a loud voice, saying, "Lord, why do you stand aside?''   Ps 10:1

The heavenly curtain

1 **45** R. Ishmael said: Meṭaṭron said to me:
Come and I will show you the curtain[a] of the Omnipresent One, which is spread[b] before the Holy One, blessed be he, and on which are printed all the generations of the world and all their deeds, whether done or to be done, till the last
2 generation. •I went and he showed them to me[c] with his fingers,[d] like a father teaching his son the letters of the Torah; and I saw:[e]
each generation and its potentates;[f]

---

lates: "Meṭaṭron called and spake to me: 'My servant! Take the books . . .' '' But it is unlikely that Meṭaṭron would call Ishmael "My servant.'' The text may imply that Meṭaṭron is in charge of the heavenly records; b.Ḥag 15a states that Meṭaṭron is the heavenly scribe.

u. "Extirpation'': Heb. *kārēt*. This term refers, strictly speaking, to premature death inflicted by God for certain sins (b.MK 28a; y.Bikk 64c.37). Here, however, it is not used literally, but to indicate the enormity of Israel's transgressions. For "thirty-six'' see m.Ker 1:1: "For thirty-six transgressions is *kārēt* prescribed in the Law.''

v. "Moreover, it was recorded that they . . . all the letters of the Torah'': a paraphrase of obscure Heb. following the E text. The other MSS appear to be corrupt.

w. " ⁵*Alep to Taw*'': the first and last letters of the Heb. alphabet. Cf. LamR proem 24, where the twenty-two letters of the alphabet come to testify against Israel's transgressions of the Law.

x. "Thirty-six,'' A E F; "forty,'' B.

y. "Then the Holy One, blessed be he, said to them . . . Jacob, my firstborn,'' A E and, substantially, F.

z. "Michael, the Prince of Israel'': Dan 12:1; b.Yoma 77a. Cf. PR 44:10 (ed. Friedmann, 185a.27), where Michael pleads for Israel before God.

45 a. "The curtain [*pargôd*] of the Omnipresent One'': This curtain is the heavenly counterpart of the Veil which divided the Holy Place from the Holy of Holies in the earthly Tabernacle and Temple (Ex 26:31; 2Chr 3:14). The earthly veil is called the *pārôket;* the heavenly veil, though sometimes called a *pārôket,* is more commonly designated the *pargôd. Pargôd* is a loanword from Persian: Cf. the Pahlavi *pardag,* "curtain,'' "veil,'' and the cognate Hindustani *pardah,* from which the English "purdah'' is derived. The heavenly *pargôd* separates the immediate pres-

ence of God from the rest of heaven. It shields the angels from the destructive glare of the divine glory (Targum Job 26:9; cf. 3En 22B:6), and it conceals the ultimate mysteries of the deity; only the Prince of the Divine Presence is allowed to go within the curtain (cf. b.Yoma 77a). Sometimes secrets are announced by a heavenly voice "from behind the curtain'' (b.Ber 18b; b.Ḥag 15a; 16a; b.Sanh 89b; Ma'yan Ḥokmah, *BHM,* vol. 1, p. 60, l. 10; Ma'aśeh 'aśarah haruge malkut, *BHM,* vol. 6, p. 21, l. 32, and p. 31, l. 28; Midraš " 'Ēlleh 'ezkerāh,'' *BHM,* vol. 3, p. 65, l. 25; Midraš 'aśeret hadibberot, *BHM,* vol. 1, p. 81, ll. 3f.; Haggadat Šema' Yiśra'el, *BHM,* vol. 5, p. 165, ll. 29f.; Masseket ḥibbuṭ haqqeber 4; *BHM,* vol. 1, p. 152, l. 10). The idea in 3En 45 appears to be that the whole course of human history is already worked out "in blueprint'' in the heavenly realm, and has been totally foreordained by God. Cf. the heavenly tablets on which, according to Hekalot Rabbati 6:3 (BM, vol. 1, p. 76), all the trials foreordained for Israel are already recorded. On the *pargôd* see further b.Soṭ 49a; b.BM 59a; PRE 4; Masseket Hekalot 7 (*BHM,* vol. 2, p. 46, l. 30); Alphabet of Aqiba, *BHM,* vol. 3, p. 44, ll. 3, 9, and 16 (= BM, vol. 2, p. 388); Seder Gan 'Eden, *BHM,* vol. 3, p. 135, l. 25, and p. 138, l. 3; Rashi to b.Yeb 63b, catchword *gûp.* The first heaven, Wilon, is also regarded as a celestial veil; see 17:3, n. f.

b. "Which is spread,'' A E F.

c. "Showed them to me'': Cf. Alphabet of Aqiba, BM, vol. 2, p. 388, where R. Aqiba is shown by the angel Segansag'el the future sages of Israel in "the curtain of the Omnipresent One''; b.Sanh 38b: "The Holy One, blessed be he, showed to Adam every generation and its expositors, every generation and its sages.''

d. "With his fingers,'' A E F.

e. "Like a father . . . and I saw,'' A E F.

f. "Each generation and its potentates,'' A E F; B omits.

each generation and its heads;
each generation and its shepherds;
each generation and its keepers;
each generation and its oppressors;[g]
each generation and its tormentors;[h]
each generation and its officials;[i]
each generation and its judges;
each generation and its officers;
each generation and its teachers;
each generation and those who establish it;
each generation and the heads of them all;
each generation and the heads of its academies;[j]
each generation and its magistrates;
each generation and its princes;
each generation and its spokesmen;
each generation and its chiefs;
each generation and its nobles;
each generation and its elders;
each generation and its leaders.

3 And I saw:

Adam and his generation, their deeds and their thoughts;
Noah and the generation of the Flood, their deeds and their thoughts;[k] Gen 2:19
Nimrod and the generation of the division of tongues,[l] their deeds and their Gen 6:8
   thoughts; Gen 10:8; 11:9
Abraham and his generation, their deeds and their thoughts; Gen 17:5
Isaac and his generation, their deeds and their thoughts; Gen 17:19
Ishmael and his generation, their deeds and their thoughts; Gen 16:11
Jacob and his generation, their deeds and their thoughts; Gen 25:26
   the twelve tribes and their generations,[m] their deeds and their thoughts;
'Amram and his generation, their deeds and their thoughts; Num 26:59
Moses and his generation, their deeds and their thoughts;

4 Aaron and Miriam [and their generation],[n] their deeds and their acts;[o] Ex 15:20
the princes and the elders [and their generations],[p] their deeds and their acts;
Joshua and his generation, their deeds and their acts; Ex 17:9
the judges and their generations, their deeds and their acts;
Eli and his generation, their deeds and their acts; 1Sam 1:3
Phineas and his generation, their deeds and their acts;
Elkanah and his generation, their deeds and their acts; 1Sam 1:1
Samuel and his generation, their deeds and their acts; 1Sam 1:20
the kings of Judah and their generations, their deeds and their acts;
the kings of Israel and their generations, their deeds and their acts;

---

g. "Oppressors" (*nôgéśêhem*): See Ex 5:6; Isa 9:3; 60:17.

h. "Tormentors": emending to *sôreqêhem* (the E text is nearest to this). The verb *sāraq* means lit. "to comb"; however, in view of the parallelism with "oppressors," it must have a metaphorical sense here. It probably means "to torment," "to torture"; there may be allusion to the story of the martyrdom of Aqiba: "They brought out R. Aqiba to kill him, and they combed [*sôreqîn*] his flesh with combs of iron" (b.Ber 61b). The reference is to the Roman torture of hanging up a victim naked and scraping his body with "claws" (*ungulae*). Cf. b.Sanh 96b; b.Giṭṭ 57b.

i. "Officials" (*pequddôtêhem*): For this usage see 2Kgs 11:18; Ezek 44:11; Isa 60:17.

j. "Its teachers . . . the heads of its academies," B, but emending (with A) *rō'š* to *rā'šê*,

"heads (of them all)." A E F have a different text.

k. "Noah and the generations of the Flood, their deeds and their thoughts," A E F.

l. "Nimrod and the generation of the division of tongues," E. The "division of tongues" is associated in the Bible with the tower of Babel (Gen 11:1-9). Nimrod is usually linked in Jewish Midrash with the building of the tower of Babel (b.Hull 89a; b.AZ 53b).

m. "The twelve tribes and their generations," A E.

n. "[And their generation]" (*wedôrān*): has accidentally fallen out of the MSS.

o. "Their deeds and their acts": The formula changes here from "their deeds and their thoughts."

p. "[And their generations]" (*wedôrān*): has accidentally fallen out of the MSS.

the kings of the gentiles[q] and their generations, their deeds and their acts;
the rulers of Israel and their generations, their deeds and their acts;
the rulers of the gentiles and their generations, their deeds and their acts;
the heads of the academies of Israel and their generations, their deeds and
their acts;
the heads of the academies of the gentiles and their generations, their deeds
and their acts;
the princes of Israel and their generations, their deeds and their acts;
the princes of the gentiles and their generations, their deeds and their acts;
the chiefs of Israel and their generations, their deeds and their acts;
the chiefs of the gentiles and their generations, their deeds and their acts;
the men of renown of Israel and their generations, their deeds and their acts;
the men of renown of the gentiles and their generations, their deeds and their
acts;
the judges of Israel and their generations, their deeds and their acts;
the judges of the gentiles and their generations, their deeds and their acts;
the teachers of children in Israel and their generations, their deeds and their
acts;
the teachers of the children of the gentiles and their generations, their deeds
and their acts;
the spokesmen of Israel and their generations, their deeds and their acts;
the spokesmen of the gentiles and their generations, their deeds and their
acts;
all the prophets of Israel and their generations, their deeds and their acts;
all the prophets of the gentiles and their generations, their deeds and their
acts;
5 and every battle in the wars[r] which the gentiles fight with Israel[s] in the days
of their dominion.
And I saw:
the Messiah the son of Joseph[t] and his generation, and all that they will do
to the gentiles.
And I saw:
the Messiah the son of David and his generation, and all the battles and
wars, and all that they will do to Israel whether for good or bad.
And I saw:
all the battles and wars which Gog and Magog[u] will fight with Israel in the   Ezek 38:2; 39:6
days of the Messiah, and all that the Holy One, blessed be he, will do to
them in the time to come.
6 All the rest of the leaders of every generation and every deed of every generation
both of Israel and of the gentiles, whether done or to be done in the time to

---

q. "The kings of the gentiles": From here to
the end of the vs. the MSS have many variants
and inconsistencies. B is followed, but its inconsistencies are eliminated.

r. "Every battle in the wars," A.

s. "Which the gentiles fight with Israel," E
F and, substantially, A.

t. "Messiah the son of Joseph": a forerunner
of the Messiah the son of David who will fight
against Israel's enemies at the end-time and fall
in battle. In earlier texts he is a rather nebulous
figure, but he is treated fully in the late apocalypses: See b.Sukk 52a/b; TarJon to Ex 40:11
("Messiah son of Ephraim . . . at whose hand
Israel will triumph over Gog and his allies at the
end of days"); GenR 75:6; 95 (= MS Vatican
Ebr. 30 fols. 175b/176a); 99:2; NumR 14:1;
SongR 2:13.4; PR 36:1f. (ed. Friedmann, 161b.8;
162a.7); Pesiqta' deRab Kahana 5:9 (ed. Buber,

51a.16); Midraš Tehillim 87:6 (to Ps 87:5) (ed.
Buber, 189b); Midraš Tanḥuma', ed. Buber, vol.
1, 103a; Targumic Tosepta' to Zech 12:10 (Sper-
ber, vol. 3, p. 495); Targum Song 4:5 (cf. 7:4);
Seper Zerubbabel, BHM, vol. 2, p. 55; Ništarot
R. Šim'on b. Yoḥai, BHM, vol. 3, p. 80; 'Otot
hammašiaḥ, BHM, vol. 2, p. 60; Tepillat R.
Šim'on b. Yoḥai, BHM, vol. 4, p. 124; Midraš
Wayyoša', BHM, vol. 1, pp. 55f.; 'Aggadat
Mašiaḥ, BHM, vol. 3, p. 141; Pirqe mašiaḥ,
BHM, vol.3, pp. 71–73; Pereq R. Yo'šiyyahu,
BHM, vol. 6, p. 115; Sa'adya, 'Emunot weDe'ot
8.5f.

u. "Gog and Magog": Ezek 38:2; 39:6. The
leaders of the gentile nations in their final,
concerted attack on Israel in the end-time. Their
defeat marks the establishment of the messianic
kingdom: Rev 20:8; SifDeut 343 (ed. Finkelstein,
p. 398); m.'Eduy 2:10; b.AZ 3b; b.Ber 7b.

come, to all generations, till the end of time, were all printed on the curtain[v] of the Omnipresent One. I saw them all with my own eyes, and when I had seen[w] them I opened my mouth and said in praise of the Omnipresent One, "For the word of the king is paramount, and who dare say to him, 'Why do that?' He who obeys the command will come to no harm."[x] And I said, "Lord, Eccl 8:4f. what variety you have created," and, "Great are your achievements, Lord."[y] Ps 104:24

The spirits of the stars

1 **46** R. Ishmael said: Metatron said to me:
[Come and I will show you][a] the spirits[b] of the stars, which stand in the Raqia[c] every night in fear[c] of the Omnipresent One—where they go and where they 17:3,7
2 stand. •I went with him, and, taking me by his hand, he showed me them all with his fingers. They were standing like fiery sparks around the chariots of the Omnipresent One.[d] What did Metatron do? At once he clapped his hands and 24:1; 37:1 chased[e] them all from their places. Immediately they flew up[f] on wings of flame and fled to the four sides of the throne of the chariot, and he told me the name of each of them,[g] as it is written,

> He counts the number of the stars
> and gives each of them a name. Ps 147:4

This teaches us that the Holy One, blessed be he, has given to every single star
13 a name.[h] •They are all counted in to the Raqia[c] of the heavens by Rahati'el, 14:4; 17:6 to serve the world;[i] and they are counted out,[j] to go and glorify the Holy One, 6:8 blessed be he, with songs and praises, as it is written,

> The heavens declare the glory of God,
> and the vault of heaven proclaims his handiwork. Ps 19:1

14 In time to come the Holy One, blessed be he, will create them anew, as it is 40:4; Lam 3:23 written, "Every morning they are renewed." They open their mouths and recite a song. What is the song they recite? "I look up at your heavens, made by your fingers." Ps 8:3

The spirits of the punished angels

1 **47** R. Ishmael said: Metatron said to me:
Come and I will show you the souls of the angels and the spirits of the ministers[a]

v. "Printed on the curtain," A E F.
w. "And when I had seen," A E F.
x. "For the word of the king . . . come to no harm": giving the quotation indicated by A.
y. "And, 'Great are your achievements, Lord,' " A E F.

46 a. "[Come and I will show you]": (bō' we'ar'kā); these words have accidentally fallen out of the MSS.
b. "The spirits (rûḥān) of the stars," A E F; "the plain" or "space" (riwḥān) "of the stars," B. The A E F reading is supported by the fact that (1) this section of 3En (chs. 43f., 46f.) is largely concerned with "spirits/souls"; and (2) the stars are clearly regarded as animate beings, like angels, and so can be said to possess "spirits." Like angels they have fiery bodies (vs. 2: "They were standing like fiery sparks"); they have wings (vs. 2); they perform songs before God (vs. 4); and Lam 3:23 is applied to them (vs. 4; cf. 40:4). For stars with animate form see also 1En 88:1; 90:21. Here the stars are sentient beings (cf. 5:8; b.AZ 42b; 43a; 43b; Maimonides, *Moreh Nebukim* 2.5); but in 14:4 and 17:6 they

appear to be regarded as inert masses of matter that are moved by the angels.
c. "In fear," lit. "in wrath" (za'am).
d. "The chariots of the Omnipresent One," A E; "the chariot of the Omnipresent One," F.
e. "And chased," A E F.
f. "Immediately they flew up": A E add "from their places"; text follows B.
g. "And he told me the name of each one of them," B (but adding "(to) me" with A E F); "and each of them told me its name and its surname [kinnúy]," A E F. Cf. 1En 43:1; 69:21.
h. "To every single star a name," A E F.
i. "To serve the world": Cf. 4Ezra 6:46.
j. "Counted in . . . counted out": I.e. in the evening they enter the sky to give light to the world; in the morning they depart and ascend to the throne to praise God. Cf. Midraš Tehillim 19:7 (to Ps 19:3) (ed. Buber, 83b) for the stars worshiping God during the day.

47 a. "The souls of the angels and the spirits of the ministers," A; "the souls and spirits of the ministers," E F. The constitution of the angels in this ch. is exactly parallel to that of men in chs. 43f.; they possess both "body"

whose bodies have been burned in the fire of the Omnipresent One, which goes
out from his little finger. They are turned to fiery coals in the middle of the 40:3
2 River of Fire,[b] but their spirits and souls stand behind the Šekinah. •Whenever 18:19,21; 44:7;
the ministering angels do not recite the song at the right time or in a proper and 48A:1
35:6; 40:3f.
fitting manner,[c] they are burned[d] and consumed by the fire of their Maker and
by the flames of their Creator in their places,[e] and a storm wind blows on them 35:5
and casts[f] them into the River of Fire, and they are reduced there to mountains
of burning coal. But their spirits and souls return to their Creator and all of
them stand behind their Maker.
3   I went with him,[g] and, taking me by his hand, he showed me all the souls
of the angels and the spirits of the ministers, which stand behind the Šekinah
4 upon storm blasts,[h] surrounded by walls of fire. •Then Meṭaṭron opened for me
the gates in the walls of fire, within which they were standing, behind the
Šekinah. At once I looked up and saw that their faces were like angels' faces,
and their wings like birds' wings, made of flame and wrought in burning fire.[i] 44:5
Then I opened my mouth in praise of the Omnipresent One, and I said, "Great
are your achievements, Lord."   Ps 92:5

The right hand of God

                                                    Ex 15:6;
1 ***48A** R. Ishmael said: Meṭaṭron said to me: Ps 78:54
44:7; 47:1
Come and I will show you the right hand of the Omnipresent One,[a] which has
been banished behind him[b] because of the destruction of the Temple.[c] From it
all kinds of brilliant lights shine, and by it the 955 heavens[d] were created. Even 26:8–12; 25:5–7
the seraphim and the ophanim are not allowed to look[e] on it, till the day of
salvation comes.
2   I went with him, and, taking me by his hand, he bore me up on his wings
and showed it[f] to me, with all kinds of praise, jubilation, and psalm: No mouth
can tell its praise,[g] no eye behold it, because of the magnitude of its greatness,
3 its praise, its glory, its honor, and its beauty. •Moreover, all the souls of the
righteous who are worthy to see the joy of Jerusalem[h] stand beside it, praising Neh 12:43
and entreating it, saying three times every day,

(*gûp*) and "spirit/soul" (*rûaḥ/nesāmāh*). The
former is consumed in the River of Fire; the
latter "returns to God" (cf. 43:1–3). The spirit/
soul has its own peculiar bodily shape: It has a
human face and a birdlike body (cf. 44:5, n. i).
    b. "They are turned . . . River of Fire":
According to one view all the angels return to
the River of Fire (from which they emerged)
after reciting the Qeduššah; see 40:4, n. i.
    c. "Or in a proper and fitting manner," A E.
    d. "They are burned," A E F.
    e. "In their places," A E F.
    f. "And casts," A E F.
    g. "With him," A E F.
    h. "Upon storm blasts," lit. "upon wings of
storm" (*kanpê se'ārāh*): Odeberg's conjecture;
cf. 34:1, n. f. The angels are often associated
with phenomena of storm and fire; see 18:25;
22:13; 33:3.
    i. "Burning fire," A E F.

48A * For chapters 48BCD see the Appendix.
    a. "The right hand of the Omnipresent One":
With the material about the end-time in this ch.
cf. 44:7–10. The end-time plays only a small
part in Merkabah texts; see "Theological Importance." The hypostatized right hand of God
in this ch. should be compared with the representations of God's hand in Jewish synagogue
art in late antiquity (e.g. in the synagogues of
Beth 'Alpha and Dura-Europos).

b. "Behind him": the place of forgetfulness
or rejection.
    c. "The Temple," A E F. The idea seems to
be that God's right hand cannot operate till the
Temple is restored.
    d. "The 955 heavens": Contrast the seven
heavens of 17:3 and 18:1f. Cf. Masseket Hekalot
7 (*BHM*, vol. 2, p. 45): "The Holy One, blessed
be he, descends from the upper heaven of heavens, from 955 heavens, and sits in 'Arabot on
the throne of his glory." The number 955 is
derived by gematria from the word "heavens"
(*šāmayim*, final *mēm* = 600). See "Theological
Importance."
    e. "Are not allowed to look," A E F.
    f. "Showed it," A E F.
    g. "Its praise," A F.
    h. "The joy of Jerusalem": Either (1) they
are granted a vision of the future glory of the
terrestrial Jerusalem (cf. Pesiqta' deRab Kahana
20:7, ed. Buber, 143a; PR 41:1–5, ed. Friedmann, 172b); or (2) they see the heavenly Jerusalem *Yerûšalayim šelema'alāh*—the celestial
counterpart of the earthly city which, according
to one view, would descend to earth at the end
of time: See 1En 90:28f.; 2Bar 4:2–7; 4Ezra
7:26; Gal 4:26; Rev 21:2; b.Ta'an 5a; b.Ḥag
12b; Alphabet of Aqiba, *BHM*, vol. 3, p. 67, l.
30; Ništarot R. Šim'on b. Yoḥai, *BHM*, vol. 3,
p. 80, l. 26; Re'uyot Yeḥezqe'l, BM, vol. 2, p.
133 (ed. Gruenwald, p. 132).

"Awake, awake! Clothe yourself in strength,
arm of the Lord, Isa 51:9

as it is written, 'He made his glorious arm go at the right hand of Moses.' " Isa 63:12
4 Then the right hand of the Omnipresent One wept, and five rivers of tears flowed[i] from its five fingers, and, falling into the Great Sea, made the whole world quake,[j] as it is written,

The earth will split into fragments,
the earth will be riven and rent.
The earth will shiver and shake,
the earth will stagger like a drunkard,
sway like a shanty Isa 24:19f.

—five times, corresponding to the five fingers of his great right hand.
5   But when the Holy One, blessed be he, shall see that there is none righteous in that generation,[k] none pious on the earth, no righteousness in men's hands, no one like Moses, no intercessor like Samuel, who could entreat[l] the Omnipresent One for salvation, for redemption, for his kingdom to be manifested in the whole world, for his great right hand to be set before him once again,
6 so that he might effect with it a great deliverance for Israel; • then the Holy One, blessed be he, will at once remember his own righteousness, merit, mercy, and grace, and, for his own sake, will deliver his great arm, and his own righteousness will support him, as it is written, "He saw that there was no Isa 59:16 one"—like Moses, who sought mercy many times for Israel in the wilderness and annulled the decree[m] against them—"and he was astonished that there was no intercessor"—like Samuel, who interceded with the Holy One, blessed be he, and cried to him; and the Holy One answered him,[n] and did what he wanted, even what was not foreordained,[o] as it is written, "It is now wheat harvest, is
7 it not? I will call on the Lord and he shall send thunder and rain." •Moreover, 1Sam 12:17 Samuel is linked with Moses,[p] as it is written, "Moses and Aaron among his priests, and Samuel among those who invoke his name"; moreover, Scripture Ps 99:6
8 says, "Even if Moses and Samuel were standing in my presence." • "My own Jer 15:1 arm brought me salvation": the Holy One, blessed be he, will say then, "How Isa 63:5 long shall I expect the children of men to work salvation for my arm[q] by their righteousness?[r] For my own sake, for the sake of my own merit and righteousness, I shall deliver my arm, and by it save my sons[s] from among the gentiles," as it is written, "For my own sake and my sake alone[t] shall I act—
9 is my name to be profaned?" •Then the Holy One, blessed be he, will reveal Isa 48:11 his great arm in the world,[u] and show it to the gentiles: it shall be as long as the world and as broad as the world,[v] and the glory of its splendor shall be like 32:1
10 the brilliant light of the noonday sun at the summer solstice.[w] • At once Israel

i. "Flowed," A E F.
j. "And, falling into the great sea . . . quake," A E and, substantially, F.
k. The idea is that the final redemption will begin in an age of great iniquity; m.Soṭ 9:15; SongR 2:13.4; b.Sanh 97a; 2Thes 2:7–12; Lk 21:28; cf. 44.8, n. q.
l. "Who could entreat," A B; "who entreated," E F. Samuel is frequently compared to Moses in the haggadah, and is sometimes even regarded as his superior; see ExR 16:4; PR 43:7 (ed. Friedmann, 182a); Midraš Tehillim 1:3 (to Ps 1:3) (ed. Buber, 2b); Pesiqta' deRab Kahana 4:5 (ed. Buber, 38a).
m. "And annulled the decree," A and, substantially, B; "and annulled the decrees," E and, substantially, F.
n. "Answered him," A E F.
o. "Foreordained" or "fitting": Heb. rā'ûy. In 1Sam 12:17 Samuel commands an event out

of the natural order of things, such as rain at harvest time.
p. "Linked with Moses": A B add, "in every place"; text follows E F. See n. 1 above.
q. "For my arm," A E F.
r. "By their righteousness," A.
s. "And by it save my sons," A.
t. "For my own sake and my sake alone," A E F = MT.
u. "In the world," A E F; B omits.
v. "It shall be as long . . . as broad as the world," F. Cf. 32:1f., where the splendor of God's sword pervades the world from end to end.

w. "The brilliant light of the noonday sun at the summer solstice," lit. "the light of the sun in its strength (Judg 5:31) at its turning point in Tammuz (June–July)." "Turning point" (tequpat) is the reading of A E F. See PRE 6.

shall be saved from among the gentiles and the Messiah shall appear to them
and bring them up to Jerusalem with great joy. Moreover, the kingdom of   Isa 66:20
Israel, gathered from the four quarters of the world, shall eat with the Messiah,[x]
and the gentiles shall eat[y] with them, as it is written,

> The Lord bares his holy arm
> in the sight of all the nations,
> and all the ends of the earth shall see
> the salvation of our God;   Isa 52:10

and it also says,

> The Lord alone is his guide,
> with him is no alien god;   Deut 32:12

and it says,[z]

> The Lord will be King of the whole world.   Zech 14:9

---

x. "Moreover, the kingdom of Israel . . . with the Messiah," E; "moreover, their kingdom shall extend to the end of the world," F. A B appear to be corrupt. The reference is to the Messianic banquet: See 1En 62:14; 2Bar 29:3f.; Mt 8:11; Lk 22:30; Rev 19:9; Pesiqta' deRab Kahana 29 (= Additional Pisqa' for Sukkot) (ed. Buber, 188b); Ništarot R. Šim'on b. Yoḥai, *BHM*, vol. 3, p. 80; Pirqe Mašiaḥ, *BHM*, vol. 3, p. 76, l. 32; Se'udat Liwyatan, *BHM*, vol. 6, pp. 150f.

y. "Eat," A E F.

z. "And it says," E.

APPENDIX TO 3 ENOCH

CHAPTERS 15B, 22B, 22C, 23, 24, 48B, 48C, 48D, WITH NOTES

The ascension of Moses[a]

1 **15B** Meṭaṭron is Prince over all princes,[b] and stands before him who is exalted above all gods.[c] He goes beneath the throne of glory, where he has a great heavenly tabernacle of light,[d] and brings out the deafening fire, and puts it in the ears of the holy creatures, so that they should not hear the sound of the utterance that issues from the mouth of the Almighty. Ps 82:1 · 21:1–4

2 When Moses ascended to the height,[e] he fasted 121 fasts,[f] until the dwellings of the *ḥašmal*[g] were opened to him, and lo, his heart was as the heart of a lion;[h] he saw countless legions of the hosts surrounding him,[i] and they desired to consume him, but Moses besought mercy,[j] first for Israel and then for himself, and he who sits on the chariot opened the windows[k] which are above the heads of the cherubim and 1,800,000 advocates for Israel[l] came out to meet Moses, Ex 19:3 · 7; 26:4; 36:2 · 2Sam 17:10 · 1:7; 48D:7 · Gen 7:11; 22:11–16

15B a. A difficult and fragmentary chapter; it is found only in C and in Eleazar, fol. 116ab. Vs. 1 is concerned with the heavenly tabernacle of Meṭaṭron; vss. 2, 4, and 5, with the ascension of Moses to heaven to receive the Law; vs. 3 is a mystical fragment about the Šemaʿ.

b. "Meṭaṭron is Prince over all princes," Eleazar; C has "R. Ishmael said to me, Meṭaṭron, Prince of the Divine Presence and Prince over all princes, said to me"; but C has an awkward sentence structure, which appears to provide no object-clause for the verb "said."

c. "Gods": Heb. *'elohim:* a class of angels; see 4QŠirŠabb; Maimonides, *Yad. Yesode hattorah* 2.7; "Theological Importance."

d. "A great heavenly tabernacle of light": For Meṭaṭron as the high priest of the heavenly tabernacle see NumR 12:12: "When the Holy One, blessed be he, told Israel to set up the tabernacle, he intimated to the ministering angels that they also should make a tabernacle, and when the one was erected below, the other was erected on high. The latter was the tabernacle of the youth (*naʿar*), whose name is Meṭaṭron, and there he offers up the souls of the righteous to atone for Israel in the days of their exile."

e. The connection between vss. 1 and 2 probably is the idea that when Moses ascended to heaven to receive the Law, it was Meṭaṭron whom he met; see 48D:7; b.Sanh 38b. For other accounts of the ascension of Moses and the opposition of the angels to it, see b.Shab 88b–89a; Midraš Tanḥumaʾ, ed. Buber, vol. 3, 56b; Gedullat Mošeh, BM, vol. 1, pp. 281–85; Haggadat Šemaʿ Yiśraʾel, *BHM*, vol. 5, pp. 165f.; Maʿyan Ḥokmah, *BHM*, vol. 1, pp. 58–61; PR 20:4 (ed. Friedmann, 96b); 25:3 (ed. Friedmann, 128a); Midraš Tehillim 8:2 (ed. Buber, 37a–38a); PRE

46; SongR 8:11.2.

f. "121 fasts": i.e. he fasted for 121 days.

g. "Dwellings of the *ḥašmal*": i.e. the innermost of the celestial palaces. On *ḥašmal* see 26:4, n. f.

h. "And lo [*ûre'ēh*], his heart was as the heart of a lion," C. Cf. 2Sam 17:10, where David is said to have had a heart like the heart of a lion. Here the expression refers to Moses' steadfastness when confronted by the threatening hosts of heaven. The text, however, is rather difficult. Odeberg translates: "and he saw the heart within the heart of the Lion." He identifies the lion with one of the four creatures (Ezek 1:10). Eleazar reads: "and he saw [*werā'āh*] that it was white [*lābān;* or, repointing *libbān,* "(that) their heart (was)"] like the heart of the lion." The lion has magical significance; see Seper HaRazim 1:133–35 (ed. Margalioth, p. 74): "And put the heart of the lion over your heart." Note also the description of the angels in Seper HaRazim 2:105 (ed. Margalioth, p. 87): "Their strength is like that of a lion."

i. "Surrounding it," i.e. the *ḥašmal*.

j. "Mercy," Eleazar.

k. "The windows" (*ḥallônôt*): Cf. the "windows" (*'arubbôt*) of heaven in Gen 7:11. See 1En 72:3, 7; 75:5, 7; 101:2; Gedullat Mošeh, BM, vol. 1, p. 278, l. 2; Midraš 'aśeret hadibberot, *BHM*, vol. 1, p. 64, ll. 3f.

l. "For Israel," Eleazar; C omits. The context here is the heavenly assize; cf. 28:7–33:2 and "Theological Importance." For Meṭaṭron as a heavenly advocate see Yalquṭ Re'ubeni 1.62b; as Israel's advocate, see in particular Šemot šel Meṭaṭron, Bodleian MS 1748, fols. 33b and 40b. Michael is usually Israel's heavenly representative; see 44:10, n. z.

and with them was Meṭaṭron, Prince of the Divine Presence. They received the prayers of Israel and placed them as a crown[m] on the head of the Holy One, 3 blessed be he. •And he (Meṭaṭron) said,[n] "Hear, Israel, the Lord our God, the Deut 6:4 Lord is one!," and the face of the Šekinah[o] rejoiced and was glad. They (the hosts) said to Meṭaṭron, "Who are these (the advocates), and to whom do they give all this honor and glory?" They received answer,[p] "To the Majestic One of the House of Israel." They (the hosts) said, "Hear, Israel, the Lord our God, the Lord is one! To whom ought glory and greatness to be given more than to you, Lord of greatness and of power, God and King, living and eternal?" 4 Then ʾAktariʾel Yah YHWD of hosts[q] answered and said to Meṭaṭron, Prince of the Divine Presence, "Fulfill every request he makes of me. Hear his prayer 5 and do what he wants, whether great or small."[r] •At once Meṭaṭron, Prince of the Divine Presence, said to Moses, "Son of Amram, fear not! for already God favors you. Ask what you will[s] with confidence and boldness, for light shines from the skin of your face from one end of the world to the other." But Moses Ex 34:29f. said to him, "Not so! lest I incur guilt." Meṭaṭron said to him, "Receive the letters[t] of an oath which cannot be broken!"

Heavenly numbers[a]

1 **22B** R. Ishmael said: Meṭaṭron, Prince of the Divine Presence, said to me: How do the angels stand on high?
He said to me:
Just as a bridge is laid across a river and everyone crosses over it, so a bridge 2 is laid from the beginning of the entrance[b] to its end, •and the ministering angels[c] go over it and recite the song before YHWH, the God of Israel. In his 35:1-40:4 presence[d] fearsome warriors and dread captains stand. A thousand thousand and myriads of myriads chant praise and laud before YHWH, the God of Israel. 3 How many bridges are there? How many rivers of fire? How many rivers of 18:19; Dan 7:10 4 hail? How many treasuries of snow? How many wheels of fire? •How many Job 38:22

---

m. "They received the prayers of Israel and placed them as a crown," C; "they received his (Moses') prayer and placed it as a crown," Eleazar. According to one tradition it is the angel Sandalpon who places the prayers of Israel as a crown on God's head; see b.Ḥag 13b; PR 20:4 (ed. Friedmann, 97a); Midraš Tehillim 19:7 (to Ps 19:3) (ed. Buber, 84a); Maʿyan Ḥokmah, BHM, vol. 1, p. 59; Midraš Konen, BHM, vol. 2, p. 26, l. 24; Yalquṭ Ḥadaš, Malʾakim no. 9 (Warsaw, 1879) p. 122.

n. "And he (Meṭaṭron) said . . ."; vs. 3 is a highly confused fragment; it is impossible to say for certain who are the subjects of the verbs. The question "Who are these?" is not answered. Something may be missing.

o. "The face of the Šekinah," Eleazar.

p. "They received answer" or "they answered." But if the latter translation is adopted, who is the subject?

q. " ʾAktariʾel Yah, YHWD of hosts": YHWD is a pious substitute for YHWH. ʾAktariʾel is here a name for God as he manifests himself on the throne; so b.Ber 7a. It is found also as the name of an angel; cf. Zohar Terumah, 2.146b; Yalquṭ Ḥadaš, Malʾakim no. 25 (Warsaw, 1879) p. 122. In origin it was probably the name of a crown (keter) of God; see 29:1, n. e.

r. "Small," Eleazar. On Meṭaṭron as God's executor see 10:3.

s. "What you will," C; "what you need," Eleazar.

t. "The letters": Probably the letters of the divine name; see 13:1.

22B a. 22B is a fragment found as a whole only in C. Vss. 1–5 occur again in Maʿaseh Merkabah 3 (ed. Scholem, p. 103) and in the Haggadic Fragment in BHM, vol. 6, pp. 153f. Vs. 8 occurs again in Hekalot Rabbati 8:4 (BHM, vol. 3, p. 90; BM, vol. 1, p. 85). The fragment originally took the form of a question from R. Ishmael ("How do the angels stand on high?"), followed by the answer of his heavenly mentor ("He said to me . . ."). "Meṭaṭron, Prince of the Divine Presence" was later inserted to bring the opening of the passage into conformity with the openings of chs. 5–22.

b. "The entrance" (mābôy): This leads into God's immediate presence. According to vs. 4 there are several entrances. The gates of the palaces are called petāḥîm (Hekalot Rabbati 15:2, BHM, vol. 3, p. 94, l. 15) or šeʿārîm (Masseket Hekalot 4, BHM, vol. 2, p. 42, l. 17). Cf. the ladder by which the angels ascend into God's presence in Pereq mippirqe hekalot, BHM, vol. 3, p. 162, l. 12 (cf. Gen 28:12). The bridge spans the river(s) of fire; cf. 22C:1; Hekalot Rabbati 13:1 (BHM, vol. 3, p. 93); Midraš Mišle 10 (ed. Buber, 34a).

c. "And the ministering angels," Maʿaseh Merkabah and the Haggadic Fragment.

d. "In his presence," C; "upon it" (i.e. upon the bridge), Maʿaseh Merkabah.

ministering angels? There are 12,000 myriads of bridges, six above and six 19:2–7
below; 12,000 myriads of rivers of fire, six above and six below; 12,000
treasuries of snow, six above and six below; 24,000 myriads of wheels of fire,
twelve above and twelve below, surrounding the bridges, the rivers of fire, the
rivers of hail, the treasuries of snow, and the ministering angels.ᵉ How many
ministering angels are at each entrance? Six for every single human being, and
they stand in the midst of the entrances, facing the paths of heaven.ᶠ

5   What does YHWH, the God of Israel, the glorious King, do? The great God,
6 mighty in power, covers his face. • In ʿArabot there are 660 thousands of myriads 17:3
of glorious angels, hewn out of flaming fire, standing opposite the throne of 6:2; 15:2
glory. The glorious King covers his face,ᵍ otherwise the heaven of ʿArabot
would burst open in the middle, because of the glorious brilliance, beautiful 17:3
brightness, lovely splendor, and radiant praises of the appearance of the Holy
One,ʰ blessed be he.

7   How many ministers do his will? How many angels?ⁱ How many princes in
the ʿArabot of his delight, feared among the potentates of the Most High,
favored and glorified in song and beloved, fleeing from the splendor of the
Šekinah, with eyes grown dim from the light of the radiant beauty of their
King, with faces black and strength grown feeble?

The Heavenly Qeduššah

Rivers of joy, rivers of rejoicing, rivers of gladness, rivers of exultation, rivers 35:1–40:4
of love, rivers of friendship pour outʲ from the throne of glory, and, gathering
strength, flow through the gates of the paths of the heavenᵏ of ʿArabot, at the 17:3
melodious sound of his creatures' harps, at the exultant sound of the drums of 21:1–4
his wheels, at the sound of the cymbal music of his cherubim. The soundˡ swells 19:2–7
and bursts out in a mighty rush— 22:11–16

> Holy, holy, holy, Lord of hosts,
> the whole earth is full of his glory.ᵐ   Isa 6:3

Heavenly measurementsᵃ

1 **22C** R. Ishmael said: Meṭaṭron, Prince of the Divine Presence, said to me:ᵇ
What is the distance between one bridge and another?ᶜ 12 myriads of parasangs:ᵈ

---

e. "How many bridges . . . ministering angels," Maʿaśeh Merkabah.

f. "Six for every single human being . . . the
paths of heaven": emending to *w' lekôl biryāh
biryāh weʿômedîn beṭôkām; w' lekôl* is from C's
wlkwl; weʿômedîn is read by Maʿaśeh Merkabah,
and *beṭôkām* by the Haggadic Fragment. However, the text is very uncertain.

g. "Covers his face": a reference to the
heavenly curtain (see 45:1), or to the thick
darkness with which God surrounds himself
(b.Ḥag 12b end, quoting Ps 18:2; Masseket
Hekalot 3, *BHM*, vol. 2, p. 41). See further
45:1, n. a, and 25:7, n. m.

h. "The Holy One": inserting *haqqādôš*.

i. "Angels": emending to *malʾākim.*

j. "Pour out," Hekalot Rabbati (*BHM* and
BM).

k. "Paths of heaven": See 4QŠirŠabb (*šbyly
'š* or *šbwly 'š*); Yannai, Qedušta' for Yom Kippur
(ed. Zulay, p. 333, l. 97), "Environs of fire . . .
paths of water"; Cairo Genizah Hekalot A/2, 3
(ed. Gruenwald, p. 361).

l. "The sound," Hekalot Rabbati (*BHM* and
BM).

m. "Holy . . . his glory," C; "with Qeduššah, when Israel recites before him, Holy, holy,
holy," Hekalot Rabbati (*BHM;* BM omits "with
Qeduššah").

22C a. A fragment found in C. Vss. 1–3 occur
also in Maʿaśeh Merkabah 10 (ed. Scholem, p.
108); in the Haggadic Fragment in *BHM,* vol.
6, p. 154, and in a quotation by Eleazar (fol.
126a). Vss. 4–7 are also quoted by Eleazar (fol.
78a). Vss. 1–3 deal with the subject of the
dimensions of the heavens; vss. 4–7 form a
distinct unit of material concerned with the
heavenly rainbow.

b. "R. Ishmael said: Meṭaṭron . . . said to
me," C; "R. Ishmael said: I said to Aqiba,"
Haggadic Fragment.

c. For the motif of the dimensions of the
heavens see b.Ḥag 13a; Reʾuyot Yeḥezqeʾl, BM,
vol. 2, p. 131, ed. Gruenwald, p. 121; Masseket
Hekalot 2 (*BHM*, vol. 2, p. 41).

d. "12 myriads of parasangs," C, Maʿaśeh
Merkabah; the Haggadic Fragment omits.

in their ascent 12 myriads of parasangs, and in their descent[e] 12 myriads of
2 parasangs. •Between the rivers of fear and the rivers of dread, 22 myriads of
parasangs; between the rivers of hail and the rivers of darkness[f], 36 myriads
of parasangs; between the chambers of hail[g] and the clouds of mercy, 42 ⟨34:1; 37:2⟩
myriads of parasangs; between the clouds of mercy and the chariot, 84 myriads ⟨19:4; 33:3⟩
of parasangs; between the chariot and the cherubim, 148 myriads of parasangs; ⟨22:11–16⟩
between the cherubim and the ophanim, 24 myriads of parasangs; between the ⟨25:5–7⟩
ophanim and the chambers of chambers, 24 myriads of parasangs;[h] between
the chambers of chambers and the holy creatures, 40,000[i] parasangs; between ⟨21:1–4⟩
one wing and another, 12 myriads of parasangs, and their breadth is the same;
3 between the holy creatures and the throne of glory, 30,000[j] parasangs; •from
the foot of the throne of glory to the place where he sits, 40,000 parasangs,[k]
and his name is sanctified there.

The celestial rainbow

4 The arches of the bow rest upon 'Arabot, 1,000 thousand and a myriad of ⟨17:3⟩
myriads of measures high, by the measure of the Watchers and the holy ones, ⟨28:1–10⟩
as it is written, "I have set my bow in the clouds." Now, "I will set in the ⟨Gen 9:13⟩
clouds" is not written here, but "I have set"—already, in the clouds that
encircle the throne of glory, when his clouds pass by the angels of hail and the
coals of fire.[l]
5 The fire of the voice descends to[m] the holy creatures, and because of the ⟨Ezek 1:25⟩
breath of that voice they "run" to another place, fearing lest it should bid them ⟨21:1–4⟩
go; and they "return," lest it should harm them on the other side; therefore
"they run and return." ⟨Ezek 1:14⟩
6 Those arches of the bow are fairer and brighter than the whiteness of the ⟨17:5; 48A:9⟩
sun at the summer solstice;[n] they are whiter than blazing fire, and they are
7 great and fair. •Above them[o] the wheels of the ophanim rest upon the arches
of the bow, 1,000 thousand and one myriad of myriads high, according to the ⟨25:5–7⟩
measure of the seraphim and the legions. ⟨26:8–12⟩

e. "Ascent . . . descent": The distinction
between "ascent" and "descent" here recalls
the distinction between the angelic gatekeepers
on the ascent to the Merkabah and the descent
in Hekalot Rabbati 22:3 (*BHM*, vol. 3, p. 99).
    f. "Darkness," Eleazar (1), Ma'aseh Mer-
kabah, Haggadic Fragment.
    g. "Chambers of hail," C, Ma'aseh Merkabah
(the reference is to the heavenly storehouses; see
10:6 and "Theological Importance"); "orders of
hail," Eleazar (1), Haggadic Fragment.
    h. "Parasangs," Eleazar (1), Ma'aseh Mer-
kabah.
    i. "40,000," Eleazar (1), Ma'aseh Merkabah,
Haggadic Fragment.
    j. "30,000," Ma'aseh Merkabah.
    k. Cf. Hekalot Rabbati 10 (*BHM*, vol. 3, p.
91): "From the throne of his glory and upwards
is a distance of 180,000 myriads of parasangs."
    l. "When his clouds . . . coals of fire": The
text is very obscure. Odeberg translates: "As his
clouds pass by, the angels of hail (turn into)
burning coal."
    m. "To" ('*ēṣel*), Eleazar (2); "from" (*mē'ēṣel*),
C. Cf. Ezek 1:15: "There was a wheel on the
ground beside the creatures ('*ēṣel haḥayyôt*)."
The voice, which presumably belongs to God,

is derived from Ezek 1:25: "And there was a
voice from above the firmament over their [i.e.
the creatures'] heads." In Hekalot Rabbati 4:1
(*BHM*, vol. 3, p. 86) this idea has been elaborated
into six heavenly voices which no one can endure
to hear. Cf. also the "still small voice" (*qôl
demāmāh daqqāh*) (1Kgs 19:12) which denotes
in the Merkabah texts sometimes a divine voice,
and sometimes the singing of the heavenly choirs;
see 4QŠirŠabb (see "Relation to Earlier Pseudepigrapha"); Midraš Konen, *BHM*, vol. 2, p.
34, 1. 24; Hekalot Rabbati 26:8 (*BHM*, vol. 3,
p. 104, l. 6). Note also the "palace of silence"
(*hêkal demāmāh*) (Hekalot Rabbati 3:1, *BHM*,
vol. 3, p. 85, l. 10); "the angels of silence"
(*mal'akê demāmāh*) (Seper HaRazim 2:21, ed.
Margalioth, p. 82); and the angel "Dummi'el,"
"silence of God" (3En 26:12, n. m). The reading
"from the creatures" in C may have been
influenced by the etymology of *ḥayyôt* in b.Ḥag
13b as "the creatures speaking fire"; this would
suggest that the fire issues *from* the creatures.

n. "The sun at the summer solstice," lit. "the
sun at the turning point in Tammuz." See the
margin.

o. "Above them," Eleazar (2).

The winds of god[a]

1 **23** R. Ishmael said: The angel Meṭaṭron, Prince of the Divine Presence, said
to me:
How many[b] winds blow from under the wings of the cherubim? From there the   22:11–16
hovering wind blows,[c] as it is written, "God's wind hovered over the water." Gen 1:2

2 From there the strong wind[d] blows, as it is written, "The Lord drove back the
sea with a strong easterly wind all night."   Ex 14:21

3 From there the east wind[e] blows,[f] as it is written, "The east wind brought the Ex 10:13
locusts."

4 From there the wind of quails blows, as it is written, "A wind came from the Num 11:31
Lord and it drove quails in."

5 From there the wind of jealousy blows, as it is written, "If a wind of jealousy Num 5:14
comes upon him."

6 From there the wind of earthquake blows, as it is written, "Afterwards the
wind of earthquake, but the Lord was not in the earthquake."   1Kgs 19:11

7 From there the wind of YHWH blows, as it is written, "He carried me away Ezek 37:1
by the wind of the Lord and set me down."

8 From there the evil wind blows, as it is written, "And the evil wind left him." 1Sam 16:23

9 From there the wind of wisdom and insight, the wind of counsel and power,[g]
and the wind of knowledge and the fear of YHWH blow, as it is written,

> On him the wind of the Lord rests,
> a wind of wisdom and insight,
> a wind of counsel and power,
> a wind of knowledge and of the fear of the Lord.   Isa 11:2

10 From there the wind of rain blows, as it is written, "The rain is born of the Prov 25:23
north wind."

11 From there the wind of lightning blows, as it is written,

> He makes the lightning flash for the downpour
> and brings the wind out of his storehouses.   Jer 10:13

12 From there the wind that shatters the rocks blows, as it is written, "Then the
Lord himself went by. There came a mighty wind, so strong it tore the
mountains and shattered the rocks before the Lord."   1Kgs 19:11

13 From there the wind of the abatement of the waters[h] blows, as it is written,
"God sent a wind across the earth and the waters abated."   Gen 8:1

14 From there the wind of wrath and sorrow[i] blows, as it is written, "Suddenly
from the wilderness a gale sprang up, and it battered all four corners of the
house, which fell in on the young people."   Job 1:19

15 From there the storm wind blows, as it is written, "Storm wind that obeys his Ps 148:8
decree."

16 Satan stands among these winds, for there is no storm wind that is not sent by
Satan.[j] All these winds blow only from beneath the wings of the cherubim, as
it is written, "He mounted a cherub and flew, and soared on the wings of the   Ps 18:10;
wind."   2Sam 22:11

---

23 a. Chs. 23–24 are secondary since they interrupt the angelological system of 19–22, 25–
28. Ch. 22 is on the cherubim and ch. 23 got
attached to it because of the reference to the
cherubim in 23:1. In the biblical quotations in
ch. 23 the key word is *rûaḥ*. This means both
"wind" and "spirit." In several of the texts it
must have the latter sense (see e.g. vs. 5), but
it has been taken fancifully to mean "wind"
throughout. For similar enumerations see Masseket Hekalot 1 (*BHM*, vol. 2, p. 40); Alphabet
of Aqiba, *BHM*, vol. 1, p. 27.

b. "How many," A B E F; "I will tell you
how many," C.

c. "Blows," A E F.
d. "Strong wind," A C E F.
e. "East wind," A C E F.
f. "Blows," A E F.
g. "The wind of counsel and power," C.
h. "Waters," A E F; "sea," B.
i. "Wrath and sorrow," A E F.

j. "There is no storm wind that is not sent by
Satan," lit. "there is no storm wind but the
storm wind of Satan"; so A. FLemb have: "there
is no storm wind but Satan" (?). Perhaps the
background to this statement is Job 1 (see esp.
vss. 12 and 19).

17   Whither do all these winds go? It is taught that they go out from under the
wings of the cherubim and fall on the orb of the sun, as it is written, "Southward
goes the wind, then turns to the north; it turns and turns again; back then to
its circling goes the wind.''ᵏ From the orb of the sun they go round and fall   Eccl 1:6
upon the mountains and the hills, as it is written, "For he it is who formed the
18 mountains, created the wind." •From the mountains and hills they go round   Amos 4:13
and fall upon seas and rivers; from the seas and rivers they go round and fall
upon towns and cities; from towns and cities they go round and fall upon the
garden, and from the garden they go round and fall upon Eden, as it is written,
"He walked in the garden at the time of the daily wind." In the midst of the   Gen 3:8
garden they mingle and blow from one side to the other. They become fragrant
from the perfumes of the garden and from the spices of Eden,ˡ until scattering,
saturated with the scent of pure perfume,ᵐ they bring the scent of the spices of
the gardenⁿ and the perfumes of Eden before the righteous and the godly who
shall inherit the garden of Eden and the tree of life in time to come, as it is
written,   Gen 3:22

> Awake, north wind,
> come, wind from the south!
> Breathe over my garden,
> to spread its sweet smell around.
> Let my beloved come into his garden,
> let him taste its rarest fruit.   Song 4:16

The chariots of Godᵃ

1 **24** R. Ishmael said: The angel Meṭaṭron, Prince of the Divine Presence, the
glory of highest heaven,ᵇ said to me: 13:1
How manyᶜ chariots has the Holy One, blessed be he?
He has the chariots of the cherubim,ᵈ as it is written, "He mounted a cherub   Ps. 18:10;
and flew."   2Sam 22:11
2 He has the chariots of wind, as it is written, "He soared on the wings of the
wind."   Ps 18:10
3 He has the chariots of swift cloud, as it is written, "See! the Lord comes,
riding a swift cloud."   Isa 19:1
4 He has the chariots of clouds, as it is written, "I am coming to you in a dense
cloud."   Ex 19:9
5 He has the chariots of the altar, as it is written, "I saw the Lord standing upon
the altar."   Amos 9:1
6 He has the chariots of twice ten thousand, as it is written, "The chariots of God
are twice ten thousand, thousands of angels."ᵉ   Ps 68:17
7 He has the chariots of the tent, as it is written, "The Lord showed himself in
the tent, in a pillar of cloud."   Deut 31:15

k. "Southward . . . goes the wind": The
quotation is given after A E.
l. "Spices of Eden," A E and, substantially,
F. For the distinction between Eden and the
garden see 5:5. The fragrance of the garden of
Eden is mentioned in b.BB 75a; NumR 13:2;
Midraš Konen, *BHM*, vol. 2, p. 28.
    m. "Scent of pure perfume," E F.
    n. "Spices of the garden," A E F.

24 a. See ch. 23 n. a. Ch. 24 was introduced
after 23 because (1) it contains a list similar to
the one in ch. 23, and because (2) 24:1 mentions
the cherubim; cf. 23:1 and 22:16.
    b. "The glory of highest heaven": Heb. *hadar
merôm kōl;* so A E. For this title of Meṭaṭron

see 13:1, n. a.
    c. "How many," A B E F; "I will tell you
how many," C.
    d. "Chariots of the cherubim," A B C; "char-
iots of the cherub," E F; cf. 22:11. According
to 37:1 God has four chariots; according to
Re'uyot Yeḥezqe'l, BM, vol. 2, p. 130 (ed.
Gruenwald, p. 119), he has seven, one of which
is the "chariot of the cherub." See further 37:1,
n. a.

    e. The JB translates Ps 68:17, "With thou-
sands of divine chariots the Lord has left Sinai
for his sanctuary." For the translation given in
the text see Midraš Tehillim 68:10 (to Ps 68:17)
(ed. Buber, 159b) and 3En 7, n. g.

8 He has the chariots of the tent of meeting, as it is written, "The Lord addressed
Moses from the tent of meeting."   Lev 1:1

9 He has the chariots of the mercy seat, as it is written, "He heard a voice that
spoke to him from above the throne of mercy."   Num 7:89

10 He has the chariots of sapphire stone, as it is written, "Beneath his feet there
was, it seemed, a sapphire pavement."   Ex 24:10

11 He has the chariots of eagles, as it is written, "I carried you on eagles' wings."
They are not eagles but fly like eagles.[f]   Ex 19:4

12 He has the chariots of acclamation, as it is written, "God has gone up in
acclamation."   Ps 47:5

13 He has the chariots of ʿArabot, as it is written, "Extol him who rides in the   17:3; 19:7
ʿArabot."   Ps 68:4

14 He has the chariots of clouds, as it is written, "He makes the clouds his
chariots."   Ps 104:3

15 He has the chariots of the creatures,[g] as it is written, "The creatures ran and
returned"—they run by permission and return by permission, for the Šekinah   Ezek 1:14
is above their heads.   22:13

16 He has the chariots of the wheels, as it is written, "Go in between the wheels."   Ezek 10:2

17 He has the chariots of the swift cherub, as it is written, "Riding upon a swift   Ps 18:10; Isa 19:1
cherub."[h] When he rides upon the swift cherub, between placing one foot on
its back and placing the other foot on it, he perceives 18,000 worlds[i] at a glance;
he discerns and sees into all of them, and knows all that is in them, as it is
written, "Eighteen thousand round about."[j]   Ezek 48:35
How do we know that he views every one of them each day? Because it is
written,

> The Lord is looking down from heaven
>   at the sons of men,
> to see if a single one is wise,
>   if a single one is seeking God.   Ps 14:2

18 He has the chariots of the ophanim, as it is written, "The ophanim were covered
all over in eyes."   Ezek 10:12

19 He has the chariots of the holy throne, as it is written, "God sits on his holy
throne."   Ps 47:8

20 He has the chariots of the throne of Yah, as it is written, "A hand upon the
throne of Yah."   Ex 17:16

21 He has the chariots of the throne of judgment, as it is written, "The Lord of
hosts shall be exalted in judgment."   Isa 5:16

22 He has the chariots of the throne of glory, as it is written, "A throne of glory,
set high from the beginning."   Jer 17:12

23 He has the chariots of the high and exalted throne, as it is written, "I saw the
Lord sitting on a high and exalted throne."[k]   Isa 6:1

---

f. "They are not eagles but fly like eagles,"
A B (the subject is "the chariots"); C E F omit.
The words are an obvious gloss.

g. "The creatures," C E F; "life," A B.

h. "Swift cherub" (kerûb qal): a fusion of
the "cherub" (kerûb) of Ps 18:11 (ET, 18:10)
and the "swift cloud" (ʿāb qal) of Isa 19:1. The
"swift cherub" is mentioned also in b.AZ 3b;
cf. PRE 4 (ed. Friedlander, p. 25, n. 3).

i. "18,000 worlds": perhaps to be identified
with the worlds which God created and rejected
prior to the creation of the present world; see
GenR 3:7: "The Holy One, blessed be he, went
on creating worlds and destroying them until he
created this one and declared, 'This one pleases

me; those did not please me.' " In other texts,
however, the 18,000 worlds clearly coexist with
the present world, but they constitute a region
of ultimate mystery into which God alone can
penetrate; see b.AZ 3b; Midraš Konen, BHM,
vol. 2, p. 34, l. 16; Baraita' diMaʿaśeh Bereʾšit,
ed. Séd, p. 72; Seder Gan ʿEden, BHM, vol. 3,
p. 139.

j. "When he rides . . . round about," A.

k. Vss. 15–23 contain a short angelological
system which runs (in ascending rank): creatures
— wheels — cherubim — ophanim — thrones.
With the list of thrones in vss. 19–23 cf. Masseket
Hekalot 1 (BHM, vol. 2, p. 40).

The names of God[a]

1 **48**B The Holy One, blessed be he, has seventy names[b] which may be ex-   3:2; 29:1; 48C:9
pressed, and the rest, which may not be expressed, are unsearchable and without
number. These are the names which may be expressed:[c]

(1) Hadiriron[d] YHWH of Hosts, Holy, Holy, Holy; (2) Meromiron;
(3) Beroradin; (4) Nec̆uriron; (5) Gebiriron; (6) Kebiriron; (7) Dorriron;
(8) Sebiroron; (9) Zehiroron; (10) Hadidron; (11) Webidriron;
(12) Wediriron; (13) Peruriron; (14) Hisiridon; (15) Ledoriron;
(16) Ṭatbiron; (17) Ṣaṭriron; (18) ʿAdiriron; (19) Dekiriron; (20) Lediriron;
(21) Šeririron; (22) Tebiriron; (23) Taptapiron; (24) ʾApʾapiron;
(25) Šapšapiron; (26) Ṣapṣapiron; (27) Gapgapiron; (28) Raprapiron;
(29) Dapdapiron; (30) Qapqapuron; (31) Haphapiron; (32) Wapwapiron;
(33) Pappapiron; (34) Zapzapiron; (35) Ṭaptapiron; (36) ʿApʿapiron;
(37) Mapmapiron; (38) Sapsapiron; (39) Napnapiron; (40) Laplapiron;
(41) Wapwapiron; (42) Kapkapiron; (43) Ḥaphapiron;[e] (44) Tabtabib, that
is Yah, the greater YHWH;[f] (45) ʾAbʾabib; (46) Qabqabib; (47) Šabšabib;   12:5; 48D:1(90)
(48) Babbabib; (49) Ṣabṣabib; (50) Gabgabib; (51) Rabrabib;
(52) Ḥarabrabib; (53) Pabpabib; (54) Habhabib; (55) ʿAbʿabib;
(56) Zabzabib; (57) Sabsabib; (58) Ḥashasib; (59) Ṭabṭabib; (60) Wesisib;
(61) Pabpabib; (62) Basbasib; (63) Papnabib; (64) Lablabib;
(65) Mabmabib; (66) Nupkabib; (67) Mammambib; (68) Nupnubib;
(69) Paspabib; (70) Ṣaṣṣib.[g]

These are the names of the Holy One, blessed be he, which go forth adorned
with many crowns[h] of fire, with many crowns of flame, with many crowns of   16:2
lightning, with many crowns of *ḥašmal,* with many crowns of lightning flash,   7; 26:4; 36:2
from before the throne of glory, and with them go a thousand camps of Šekinah,   1:6; 18:4; 37:1
and myriads of myriads of the hosts of the Almighty, conducting them like a
king, with trembling, terror, fear, and quaking, with praise, glory, and dread,
with trepidation, greatness, honor, and dignity, with strength and with great
jubilation and singing, with pillars of fire and pillars of flame, with bright
2 lightning flashes and with the appearance of *ḥašmal.* •They give to them glory
and strength, and cry before them, "Holy, holy, holy," as it is written, "And   Isa 6:3
one cried to another and said, Holy, holy, holy." They roll them through every
heaven in the height, like the sons of kings,[i] noble and revered, and when they

48B a. The translation of chs. 48BCD is based
on Wert; see "Texts." These chs. did not belong
originally to 3En; they were taken from the
Alphabet of Aqiba and attached to 3En in the A
B recension of the text. See further 48C, n. a.

b. "Seventy names": See margin and cf. the
Targum to Song 2:17, and the *piyyuṭ* for *musap*
on the second day of Šabuʿot: "God is called by
seventy names and his people he chose from
seventy nations." Midraš Haggadol to Gen 46:8
gives a list of seventy non-mystical names of
God. NumR 14:5 refers to a seventy-letter or
seventy-syllable divine name ("*Seventy shekels* . . . alludes to the fact that Gabriel came and
added to Joseph's name one letter from the name
of the Holy One . . . and taught him seventy
languages"). However, a seventy-two-letter
magical name of God is more common; see PR
15:17 (ed. Friedmann, 76b); Pesiqta' deRab
Kahana 5:11 (ed. Buber, 52b); Rashi to b.Sukk
45a; Seper Razi'el 24b.

c. The list which follows is found only in
Wert. Crac omits it, but has the editorial note
"Here are written 22 names according to the
alphabet *'albam;* 22 according to the alphabet
'atbaš; and 22 according to *tašraq.*" This infor-

mation does not appear to be correct; the names
are not based on *temurot.*

d. "Hadiriron . . .": The vocalization of many
of the names on this list is uncertain.

e. Names 2–43 are all followed by "YHWH
of Hosts, Holy, Holy, Holy" in the MS, but for
the sake of brevity this formula is omitted.

f. "The greater YHWH," or "great YHWH":
The name corresponds to Meṭatron's title "the
lesser YHWH"; see 12:5; 48D:1(90).

g. Names 45–70 are all followed by "that is
Yah, the greater YHWH," in the MSS, but for
the sake of brevity this formula is omitted.

h. "Adorned with many crowns": Cf. Alphabet of Aqiba, BHM, vol. 3, p. 24: "the letters
of the divine name are adorned with crowns of
lightning"; Alphabet of Aqiba, BHM, vol. 3, p.
36: "The letters on the chariot go out to meet
the Holy One with songs . . . and the Holy One
crowns each one with two crowns"; Alphabet of
Aqiba, BHM, vol. 3, p. 25: "The Holy One,
blessed be he, sits on a fiery throne and round
about him stand sacred names like pillars of
fire."

i. "Like the sons of kings," A G Crac; "like
the sons of angels," B E F.

bring them back to the place of the throne of glory, all the creatures of the　21:1–4
chariot open their mouths in praise of the glorious name of the Holy One,
blessed be he, and say, "Blessed be the glory of the Lord in his dwelling
place."ʲ　　　　　　　　　　　　　　　　　　　　　　　　　　　　Ezek 3:12

Short account of the elevation of Enochᵃ

1 **48C** *'Alep:* The Holy One, blessed be he, said: I made him strong, I took　10:3
him, I appointed him, namely Meṭaṭron my servant, who is unique among all
the denizens of the heights.

　　'Ālep: "I made him strong"ᵇ in the generation of the first man. When I saw　5:1; Gen 1:27
that the men of the generation of the Flood were behaving corruptly, I cameᶜ　4:3
and removed my Šekinah from their midst, and I brought itᵈ up with the sound　5:14
of the horn and with shouting to the height above, as it is written,

　　　　God went up to the sound of horns,
　　　　the Lord went up with a fanfare of trumpets.　　　　　　Ps 47:5

2　*Lamed:* "I took him"—Enoch the son of Jared, from their midst, and brought　4:3
him up with the sound of the trumpet and with shouting to the height, to be　4:5
my witness, together with the four creatures of the chariot, to the world to　21:1–4
come.

3　*Peh:* "I appointed him"—over all the storehouses and treasuries which I　10:6
have in every heaven, and I entrusted to him the keys of each of them. I set　4:5
4　him as a prince over all the princes,ᵉ •and made him a minister of the throne　7
of glory. [I set him over]ᶠ the palaces of 'Arabot, to open for me their doors;　17:3
over the throne of glory, to deck and arrange it; over the holy creatures,ᵍ to　22:11f.
adorn their heads with crowns; over the glorious ophanim, to crown them with　25:5–7
strength and honor, over the majestic cherubim, to clothe them with glory;　22:11–16
over the bright sparks,ʰ to make them shineⁱ with brilliant radiance; over the　26:8–12
flaming seraphim, to wrap them in majesty; over the *ḥašmallim* of light, to　7; 26:4; 36:2
gird them with radiance every morning, so as to prepare for me a seat, when
I sit upon my throne in honor and dignity, to increase my honor and my
strength in the height. I committed to him wisdom and understanding, so that　10:5; 11:1f.
he should beholdʲ the secrets of heaven above and earth beneath.

---

j. "Blessed be the glory . . . dwelling place,"
Wert; "Blessed be the name of his glorious
kingdom for ever and ever," A B E F G Crac.
For the responsa of the Qeduššah see "Theological Importance."

48C a. The material taken over from the Alphabet of Aqiba and attached to the end of the
A B recension of 3En (see 48B, n. a) consists
of two main components. First, 48C:1–9: These
verses are structured in the form of an acrostic
on the first letter of the Heb. alphabet ('Ālep)
and evidently constitute the core of the Alphabet
of Aqiba traditions. Second, 48B, 48C:10–12,
and 48D: This material contains secondary expansions of the acrostic section.

　b. "I made him strong" or "I made him pre-
eminent": Heb. *'ibbartîw*, from *'abbîr* = (1)
"strong"; (2) "eminent." Since Enoch's elevation is not treated till later, *'ibbartîw* must refer
to something that took place during his lifetime.
The verb *'ibbēr* is used of hardening one's heart
in b.Sanh 109b; perhaps it refers here to Enoch's
determination to be righteous in a sinful generation. The verb also occurs in Midraš 'Alpa'

Betot 2 end (BM, vol. 2, p. 427, l. 27); the use
there is very similar to that here, but the sense
is equally uncertain. Here the "generation of the
first man" is regarded as extending down to the
time of the Flood; cf. the tradition that Adam
lived till the time of Enoch and was buried by
him (Seder 'Olam 1, ed. Neubauer, p. 26). For
the expression "the first man" ('ādām hāri'šôn)
see b.BB 75a.

　c. "I came": emending to *bā'tî*.

　d. "I brought it up," B; "I brought him up,"
A G; "I went up," Wert Crac.

　e. "Princes," A B G Crac; "heavens," Wert.

　f. "[I set him over]"; (*weśamtîw 'al*), or a
similar phrase, has accidentally fallen out of the
MSS.

　g. "Over the holy creatures": Cf. Hekalot
Rabbati 11:1 (*BHM*, vol. 3, p. 91): "When the
Angel of the Presence enters to exalt and arrange
the throne of God's glory and to prepare a seat
for the Mighty One of Jacob, he adorns the
ophanim of glory with a thousand thousand
crowns . . ."

　h. "The bright sparks," Crac.

　i. "To make them shine," A B.

　j. "I committed . . . should behold," Crac.

5 I increased his stature by seventy thousand parasangs,[k] above every height, 9:1
among those who are tall of stature. I magnified his throne from the majesty 10:1; 16:1
6 of my throne. I increased his honor from the glory of my honor. •I turned his
flesh to fiery torches and all the bones of his body to coals of light. I made the 15:1f.
appearance of his eyes[l] like the appearance of lightning, and the light of his
eyes like "light unfailing."[m] I caused his face to shine like the brilliant light 26:6
of the sun, the brightness of his eyes like the brilliance of the throne of glory.
7 I made honor, majesty, and glory his garment; beauty, pride, and strength, 12:1-4
his outer robe, and a kingly crown, 500 times 500 parasangs, his diadem. I
bestowed on him some of my majesty, some of my magnificence, some of the
splendor of my glory, which is on the throne of glory, and I called him by my
name,[n] "The lesser YHWH, Prince of the Divine Presence, knower of secrets."[o] 12:5; 48D:1(90)
Every secret I have revealed to him in love, every mystery I have made known
to him in uprightness.
8 I have fixed his throne at the door of my palace, on the outside,[p] so that he 16:1
might sit and execute judgment over all my household in the height. I made
every prince stand before him to receive authority from him and to do his will.[q] 12:3-5
9 I took seventy of my names and called him by them, so as to increase his 3:2; 48D:1
honor. I gave seventy princes into his hand, to issue to them my commandments 17:8; 48D:3
in every language; to abase the arrogant to the earth at his word; to elevate the 28:6
humble to the height at the utterance of his lips;[r] to smite kings at his command;
to subdue rulers and presumptuous men at his bidding; to remove kings from
their kingdoms, and to exalt rulers over their dominions, as it is written,

> He controls the procession of times and seasons;
> he makes and unmakes kings; Dan 2:21

to give wisdom to all the wise of the world, and understanding and knowledge
to those who understand, as it is written,

> He confers wisdom on the wise,
> and knowledge on those with wit to discern; Dan 2:21

to reveal to them the secrets of my word, and to instruct them in the decree of
10 my judgment, •as it is written, "So the word that goes from my mouth does
not return to me empty: he carries out my will." It does not say here, "I carry Isa 55:11
out," but, "he carries out,"[s] which teaches us that Metatron stands[t] and carries
out every word and every utterance that issues from the mouth of the Holy
One, blessed be he, and executes the decree of the Holy One.
11 It is written,[u] "He shall prosper to whom I send it"; "I shall prosper"[v] is Isa 55:11
not written here, but "he shall prosper": This teaches that every decree that
goes out from[w] the Holy One, blessed be he, against a man, when he repents,
it is not executed against him, but against another, wicked man,[x] as it is written,

---

k. "Seventy thousand parasangs": Cf. 9:2, though the measurement is not given there. The relative stature of the angels is an indication of their rank; see PR 20:4 (ed. Friedmann, p. 97a): "The angel Hadarni'el, who is sixty myriads of parasangs taller than his fellows."

l. "The appearance of his eyes": emending to *mar'ēh 'ênāyw;* otherwise read *mar'ēhû,* "his appearance," with G.

m. "Light unfailing," A B G Crac; Wert omits.

n. "By my name," A Crac Wert; B omits.

o. "Knower of secrets": Cf. Hekalot Rabbati 26:8 (*BHM,* vol. 3, p. 104, l. 17): "Metatron . . . wise in secrets."

p. "On the outside," A G Crac Wert; B omits.

q. "To do his will," B G Crac; "to do my will," A Wert.

r. "At his word . . . at the utterance of his lips": emended text; Wert has, "at my word . . . at the utterance of my lips."

s. "He carries out": The English versions (e.g. RSV, JB) construe "(unless) it [i.e. God's word] carries out."

t. "Metatron stands": There is perhaps a stress on Metatron's standing posture; cf. 10:1, n. b, and 16:5.

u. A gloss catching up the exposition of Isa 55:11 in the previous verse.

v. "I shall prosper," A B G.

w. "From," lit. "from before"; so A B Wert; "from the mouth of," G Crac.

The virtuous man escapes misfortune,
the wicked man incurs it instead.

Prov 11:8

12   Moreover, Meṭaṭron sits for three hours every day in the heavens above, and assembles all the souls of the dead that have died in their mothers' wombs, and of the babes that have died at their mothers' breasts, and of the schoolchildren that have died while studying the five books of the Torah. He brings them beneath the throne of glory,ʸ and sits them down around him in classes, in 15B:1 companies, and in groups, and teaches them Torah, and wisdom, and haggadah, and tradition, and he completes for them their study of the scroll of the Law, as it is written,

To whom shall one teach knowledge,
whom shall one instruct in the tradition?
Them that are weaned from the milk,
them that are taken from the breasts.ᶻ

Isa 28:9

The seventy names of Meṭaṭron

1 **48**D Meṭaṭron has seventy names,ᵃ and these are they: 3:2; 4:1; 48C:9
(1) Yaho'elᵇ Yah; (2) Yoppi'el; (3) 'Apap'el; (4) Margay'el; (5) Geyor'el;
(6) Ṭandu'el; (7) Ṭaṭnadi'el; (8) Ṭaṭri'el; (9) Ṭabṭabi'el; (10) 'Ozahyah;
(11) Zahzahyah; (12) ʿEbed;ᶜ (13) Zebuli'el; (14) Ṣapṣapi'el; (15) Sopri'el;
(16) Paṣpaṣi'el; (17) Senigron; (18) Sarpupirin; (20) Miṭaṭron;ᵈ
(20) Sigron; (21) 'Adrigon; (22) 'Asṭas; (23) Saqpas; (24) Saqpas;
(25) Mikon; (26) Miṭon; (27) Ruaḥ Pisqonit;ᵉ (28) 'Aṭaṭyah;ᶠ
(29) 'Asasyah; (30) Zagzagyah; (31) Paṣpaṣyah; (32) Meṣamyah;
(33) Maṣmaṣyah; (34) 'Abṣannis; (35) Mebargaš; (36) Bardaš;
(37) Mekarkar; (38) Maṣpad; (39) Tašgaš; (40) Tašbaš; (41) Meṭarpiṭaš;
(42) Paspiṣahu; (43) Beṣihi; (44) 'Iṭmon; (45) Pisqon; (46) Ṣapṣapyah;
(47) Zeraḥ Zeraḥyah; (48) 'Ab'abyah; (49) Habhabyah; (50) Pepaṭpalyah;
(51) Rakrakyah; (52) Ḥashasyah; (53) Ṭapṭapyah; (54) Tamtamyah;
(55) Ṣahṣahyah; (56) ʿArʿaryah; (57) ʿAlʿalyah; (58) Zazruyah;
(59) ʿAramyah; (60) Sebar Suhasyah; (61) Razrazyah; (62) Taḥsanyah;
(63) Sasrasyah; (64) Ṣabṣebibyah; (65) Qeliqalyah; (66) Hahhahyah;
(67) Warwahyah; (68) Zakzakyah; (69) Ṭiṭrisyah; (70) Sewiryah;
(71) Zehapnuryah; (72) Zaʿzaʿyah; (73) Galrazyah; (74) Melakmelapyah;
(75) ʿAṭṭaryah; (76) Perišyah; (77) ʿAmqaqyah; (78) Ṣalṣalyah;

x. "Another, wicked man," A B; "another man," Crac Wert and, substantially, G.

y. "Beneath the throne of glory": Meṭaṭron's tabernacle is located beneath the throne; see 15B:1.

z. Cf. the tradition in b. AZ 23b that God also instructs the prematurely dead.

48D a. "Seventy names," A B G Wert; "seventy-two names," Crac. B adds: "which the Holy One, blessed be he, took from his own name and bestowed on him." The list of names is based on Wert. The other MSS have many variants and Crac gives only the last name. On the forms of the names see "Theological Importance." Though the text records that there are seventy names, the actual list has more than seventy. There are two possible explanations of this fact: The original list of seventy has been expanded at various stages in the course of its transmission. Or, the list given here is not original but was added to the text at a late date, after the original list had dropped out. See n. n below. Lists of the names of Meṭaṭron, some of them

with elaborate commentaries, are a distinct genre of mystical literature (see e.g. Seper Haḥešeq, BM MS Add. 27120, and Šemot šel Meṭaṭron, Bodleian MS 1748). In Hekalot Rabbati 26:8 (*BHM*, vol. 3, p. 104, l. 13) we find an early list of eight names of Meṭaṭron.

b. "Yaho'el": See "Theological Importance."

c. "ʿEbed": short for "ʿEbed YHWH," "the Servant of the Lord"; see 10:3, n. g.

d. "Miṭaṭron": a common variant form of Meṭaṭron; see e.g. Re'uyot Yeḥezqe'l, BM, vol. 2, p. 132, l. 14 (ed. Gruenwald, p. 130).

e. "Ruaḥ Pisqonit": i.e. "the interceding [or "arguing"] spirit." The expression occurs again in b.Sanh 44b: "the interceding spirit said before the Holy One, blessed be he . . . ." The Tosapot identify this spirit as Gabriel. b.Sanh 44b also quotes the view of R. Ḥanina that the interceding spirit has three names: "*Pisqon*, because he argues [*pôsēq debārîm*] against the Most High; *'Iṭmon*, because he hides ['ōṭēm] the sins of Israel; and *Sigron*, because when he closes [*sôgēr*] a matter none can reopen it."

(79) Ṣabṣabyah; (80) Geʿiṭ Zeʿiṭyah; (81) Geʿiṭyah; (82) Perišperišyah; (83) Šepaṭ Šepaṭyah; (84) Ḥasamyah; (85) Śar Śaryah; (86) Gebir Geburyah; (87) Gurṭaryah; (88) Ziwaʾ Rabbaʾ;ᵍ (89) Naʿar Neʾeman;ʰ   12:5
(90) lesser YHWH, after the name of his Master, as it is written, "My name is in him"; (91) Rabrakiʾel; (92) Neʿamiʾel; (93) Seganzagʾel, Prince of Wisdom.ⁱ

2   Why is his name called Seganzagʾel? Because all the storehouses of wisdom
3 were committed into his hand. •All of them were opened for Moses on Sinai,   8:1f.;10:6
until he had learned, in the forty days that he stood on the mount,   Ex 34:28
Torah in the seventy aspects of the seventy languages;   29:1
the Prophets in the seventy aspects of the seventy languages;
the Writings in the seventy aspects of the seventy languages;
halakot in the seventy aspects of the seventy languages;
haggadot in the seventy aspects of the seventy languages;
traditions in the seventy aspects of the seventy languages;
toseptas in the seventy aspects of the seventy languages.

4 As soon as they were completed, at the end of forty days, he forgot them all in a moment—until the Holy One, blessed be he, summoned Yepipyah, the Prince of Torah,ʲ and he gave them as a giftᵏ to Moses, as it is written, "The Lord gave them to me." After that he remembered the Torah.ˡ How do we   Deut 10:4
know he remembered it? Because it is written, "Remember the Torah of my servant Moses, to whom at Horeb I prescribed laws and customs for the whole of Israel": "the Torah of Moses" refers to the Torah, the Prophets, and the   Mal 4:4
Writings; "laws" refers to halakot and traditions; "customs" refers to haggadot and toseptas; all these were given to Moses on Sinai.ᵐ

5   These are the seventyⁿ names—each of them like the sacred name on the chariot, engravedᵒ on the throne of glory—which the Holy One, blessed be   39:1
he, took from his sacred name and bestowed on Meṭaṭron—seventy names by which the ministering angels address the King of the kings of kings in heaven above. He bestowed on him the twenty-two sealsᵖ which were struck outᑫ by   13:1
his finger, by which all the orders of the heaven of ʿArabot were sealed; by

f. " 'Aṭaṭyah": found as a name of the angel of the third heaven (= ? Michael) in Re'uyot Yeḥezqe'el, BM, vol. 2, p. 132, l. 14 (ed. Gruenwald, p. 130).

g. "Ziwa' Rabba' ": i.e. "the Great Glory." This was originally a title of God; see TLevi 3:4; 1En 14:20, 102:3. The expression occurs also in Mandaean texts, e.g. Right Ginza 76:1, *aiar ziua rba*, "the Great Radiant Ether."

h. "Na'ar Ne'eman": i.e. "the faithful servant"; see 4:10, n. t for Meṭaṭron's title *Na'ar;* note further the "faithful servant" (*'ebed ne'emān*) in Hekalot Rabbati 3:1 (*BHM*, vol. 3, p. 85).

i. "Seganzag'el," Wert; "Segansag'el," B. This angelic name (with many variations) is found frequently in the Merkabah texts and sometimes designates an angel distinct from Meṭaṭron: See Cairo Genizah Hekalot B/1, 17 and 40 (ed. Gruenwald, pp. 368 and 370); Hekalot Rabbati 6:3 (BM, vol. 1, p. 75). The title "Prince of Wisdom" appears to be equivalent to "Prince of Torah": See n. j below.

j. "The Prince of Torah": Wert adds "As it is written, 'Of all men you are the most handsome [*yopyāpitā*, with a play on *Yepipyah*], your lips are moist with grace, for God has blessed you for ever' " (Ps 45:2). The text follows A B G Crac. TarJon to Deut 34:6 names Meṭaṭron, Yopi'el, 'Uri'el, and Yepipyah as "Princes of Wisdom," i.e. Princes of Torah; see "Theological Importance." According to the parallel passage in Ma'yan Ḥokmah, *BHM*, vol. 1, p. 61, it was the fear of the angels that caused Moses

to forget the Law. On the theme of angelic opposition to the revelation of the Law to Moses see 3En 15B:2, n. e.

k. "As a gift": See b.Ned 38a: "At first Moses used to study the Torah and forget it, until it was given him as a gift."

l. "Remembered the Torah": Wert adds "and did not forget it again." Text follows A B G Crac.

m. "On Sinai," Wert; B has "In the height [*mārôm*], on Sinai." Both the oral and the written Torah were given to Moses on Sinai; see ExR 47:1; b.Ber 5a.

n. "Seventy," B; "ninety-two," A G Crac Wert. See n. a above.

o. "Engraved": Wert Crac (which are followed in the text) have a singular participle which must agree with "the sacred name." B has a plural participle which goes with "the seventy names."

p. "Twenty-two seals," A G Crac Wert; "twenty-two letters," B. The seals are magical divine names; see Alphabet of Aqiba, *BHM*, vol. 3, p. 25 (cited in 39:1, n. a); Hekalot Rabbati 17:1–5 (*BHM*, vol. 3, pp. 95f.); Masseket Hekalot 4 (*BHM*, vol. 2, p. 43, l. 4); cf. 7 (*BHM*, vol. 2, p. 47); Ma'aśeh Merkabah 11 (ed. Scholem, p. 108, l. 17); 15 (p. 109, l. 28). In incantation texts these seals are used to bind the powers of angels or demons.

q. "Struck out": The Heb. verb *ṭb'* is used of minting coins.

which the destinies[r] of the princes of kingdoms in the height, with regard to **17:3**
sovereignty, dominion, greatness,[s] and majesty, were sealed; by which the
destinies of the Angel of Death and the destinies of every nation and kingdom
were sealed.

6　The angel Meṭaṭron, Prince of the Divine Presence, Prince of Torah; the
angel, Prince of Wisdom; the angel, Prince of Understanding; the angel, Prince
of Glory; the angel, Prince of the Palace; the angel, Prince of Kings; the angel,
Prince of Rulers; the angel, Prince of the exalted, lofty, great and honored
7　Princes, who are in heaven and earth, said, • "YHWH the God of Israel is my
witness that when I revealed this secret to Moses, all the armies of the height,
8　in every heaven, were angry with me. They said to me, • "Why are you revealing
this secret to mankind, born of woman, blemished, unclean, defiled by blood **2:2; 6:2**
and impure flux, men who excrete putrid drops—that secret[t] by which heaven **13:1**
and earth were created, the sea and the dry land, mountains and hills, rivers
and springs, Gehinnom, fire and hail, the garden of Eden and the tree of life? **Gen 2:8**
By it Adam was formed, the cattle and the beasts of the field, the birds of **Gen 3:22; 1:26**
heaven and the fish of the sea, Behemoth and Leviathan, the unclean creatures **Job 40:15; 41:4**
and reptiles, the creeping things of the sea and the reptiles of the deserts, Torah,
wisdom, knowledge, thought, the understanding of things above, and the fear
of heaven. Why are you revealing it to flesh and blood?' "
I said to them, "Because the Omnipresent One has given me authority from
the high and exalted throne, from which all the sacred names proceed with **39:1; 48B:1**
9　fiery lightnings, with brilliant sparks[u] and flaming ḥašmallim." •But their minds **7; 26:4; 36:2**
were not set at ease until the Holy One, blessed be he, rebuked them and drove **4:8; 6:3**
them out of his presence with a rebuke, saying to them, "I wished, I desired,
I ordered it, and entrusted it to Meṭaṭron my servant alone, because he is unique
10　among all the denizens of the heights. • Meṭaṭron brought it out from my **8:1; 10:6**
storehouses and committed it to Moses,[v] and Moses to Joshua, Joshua to the
Elders, the Elders to the Prophets, the Prophets to the Men of the Great
Synagogue, the Men of the Great Synagogue to Ezra the Scribe, Ezra the Scribe
to Hillel the Elder, Hillel the Elder to R. Abbahu, R. Abbahu to R. Zira, R.
Zira to the Men of Faith, and the Men of Faith to the Faithful—so that they
should use it to admonish men and to heal the diseases that befall the world,
as it is written, 'Then he said, If you listen carefully to the voice of the Lord
your God and do what is right in his eyes, if you pay attention to his
commandments, and keep his statutes, I shall inflict on you none of the diseases
that I inflicted on the Egyptians, for it is I, the Lord, who gives you healing.' "[w] **Ex 15:26**

---

r. "Destinies," lit. "lots" (*peṭāqîm*). Cf.
Alphabet of Aqiba, *BHM*, vol. 3, p. 63, l. 18:
The destinies of every nation, save Israel, are in
the keeping of Negarsan'el, the angel of Gehinnom.

s. "Greatness," A B Crac.

t. "That secret": The secret could be either
(1) the Torah, or (2) the secret names of God.
For the cosmic power of the Torah see GenR
1:1, and for angelic opposition to the revelation
of Torah see 5:10, n. l. The identification of the
secret with the Torah appears to be excluded by
the fact that Torah is one of the things created
by the secret. On the theme of the cosmic power
of divine names see 42:1–7; Alphabet of Aqiba,
BHM, vol. 3, p. 26: "Names by which heaven
and earth were sealed, sea and dry land . . ."

u. "With brilliant sparks": emending to *ûbe-
zîqê*.

v. Vs. 10 gives a chain of mystical tradition
similar to the chains of tradents of the oral law:
Cf. m.Ab 1:1. The chain, however, has many
missing links since Ezra lived in the mid-5th
cent. B.C., Hillel in the late 1st cent. B.C., and
Abbahu in the late 3rd cent. A.D.! Hillel was a

prominent Palestinian Pharisaic teacher; Abbahu
was head of the rabbinic academy at Caesarea
Maritima; Zira (= Ze'ira) was a Babylonian who
associated with Abbahu. The expressions "men
of faith" (*'anšê 'emûnāh*) and "faithful" (*ba'alê
'emûnāh*) appear to be quasi-technical terms for
the mystics: See Hekalot Rabbati 26:3 (*BHM*,
vol. 3, p. 103, l. 10); cf. "Men of Knowledge"
(*'anšê maddā'*) in Seper HaRazim 1:199f. (ed.
Margalioth, p. 72). According to the Alphabet
of Aqiba, *BHM*, vol. 3, p. 29, l. 11, "the men
of faith" constitute a distinct category of the
righteous in the world to come.

w. The use of Ex 15:26 as an incantation is
condemned in m.Sanh 10:1: "R. Aqiba says,
'He that utters a charm over a wound and says,
"I will inflict on you none of the diseases . . .
[Ex 15:26]," . . . has no part in the world to
come.' " According to Ma'yan Ḥokmah, *BHM*,
vol. 1, p. 61, l. 18, "a word of healing" was
one of the secrets committed to Moses when he
ascended to heaven to receive the Torah. In an
Aram. incantation text Meṭaṭron is called "The
Great Healer" (*'syh rb'*).

SIBYLLINE ORACLES

(Second Century B.C.–Seventh Century A.D.)

A NEW TRANSLATION AND INTRODUCTION
BY J. J. COLLINS

Sibylline oracles are a widely attested phenomenon in the ancient world. They are found invariably in epic Greek hexameters (perhaps under the influence of the Delphic oracle) but the phenomenon was not peculiar to Greece. Many of the alleged Sibyls were Asiatic and their type of prophecy is widely assumed to have come to Greece from the East, although there is no clear evidence to support (or refute) this view.[1] No satisfactory etymology of the word "Sibyl" has been proposed,[2] so no light is thrown on the phenomenon from this source. In the earliest attestations, from the fifth and fourth centuries B.C., the word "Sibyl" refers to a single individual.[3] It is quite possible that the word was originally the proper name of a prophetess.

The Sibyl is always depicted as an aged woman uttering ecstatic prophecies. Ovid tells us that she was granted by Apollo that she might live as many years as there were grains of sand on the seashore. However, she did not ask for youth, so she remained for thousands of years a shriveled, shrunken old woman.[4] According to Heracleides Ponticus (c. 360–25 B.C.) the Sibyl was older than Orpheus.[5] If any historical prophetess ever underlay the figure of the Sibyl, she was already lost in the mists of legend by the fifth century. According to Heraclitus she "reaches through thousands of years" with her voice.[6] Her prophecy was even said to continue after her death, while her soul revolved in the face of the moon.[7] She was sometimes thought to be intermediate between the divine and human state, and a coin from Erythrea refers to her as *Thea Sibylla*, "the Goddess Sibyl."[8] In Jewish tradition she was said to be a daughter (or daughter-in-law) of Noah.[9]

As from the fourth century B.C. we read of a number of Sibyls.[10] The most famous Sibyls were those of Erythrea and Marpessus in Asia Minor and of Cumae in Italy.[11] Various attempts were made in late antiquity to reduce the chaotic plurality to order by making lists. The most influential list was that of Varro, who enumerated ten, Persian, Libyan, Delphic, Cimmerian, Erythrean, Samian, Cumean, Hellespontian, Phrygian, and Tiburtine.[12] Notably the Hebrew, Chaldean, and Egyptian Sibyls are omitted from this list. The Suda and the anonymous Prologue to the present collection of Sibylline Oracles repeat this list but identify the Persian Sibyl with the Hebrew. In the Middle Ages the number was increased to twelve,

---

[1] See A. Rzach, "Sibyllen," Pauly-Wissowa 2A (1923), cols. 2073f.

[2] See the discussion of the various proposed etymologies by V. Nikiprowetzky, *La Troisième Sibylle*, p. 2.

[3] So Heraclitus, in Plutarch, *De Pythiae oraculis* 6 (397a); Aristophanes, *Peace* 1095–117; Plato, *Phaedrus* 244b.

[4] Ovid, *Metamorphoses* 14.132.

[5] Clement, *Strom* 1.108.1. Cf. ShepHerm Vis 1.2.2 where an aged woman appears who at first is thought to be the Sibyl, but then is identified as the Church (Vis 2.4.1).

[6] Plutarch, *De Pythiae oraculis* 6 (397a).

[7] See further Rzach, Pauly-Wissowa 2A, col. 2079.

[8] Ibid., col. 2078.

[9] Cf. SibOr, Prologue 33, 1.289, 3.827.

[10] Cf. Aristotle, *Problemata* 954a, and Heracleides Ponticus in Clement, *Strom* 1.108.1.

[11] On the individual Sibyls see especially the discussion by Rzach, Pauly-Wissowa 2A, cols. 2081–103. Also A.-M. Kurfess, *Sibyllinische Weissagungen*, pp. 9–16.

[12] Lactantius, *DivInst* 1.6.

to correspond to the twelve apostles.[13] We find a shorter list in Pausanias 10.12.1–9 where only four are mentioned: the Libyan Sibyl, Herophile of Marpessus (whom he identifies with the Delphic Erythrean and Samian Sibyls), Demo of Cumae, and Sabbe of the Hebrews (whom some call Babylonian, some Egyptian). The name of the Hebrew Sibyl, Sabbe or Sambethe (so the Suda and the anonymous Prologue to the Sibylline Oracles), is as enigmatic as the term "Sibyl." Derivations range from Sibtu, Queen of Mari and the Queen of Sheba, to the Jewish sabbath or the divine epithet Sabaoth.[14] There is no conclusive evidence to tie the name to any one etymology.

Also obscure is the relation between the Hebrew Sibyl and the Babylonian (or Chaldean). Pausanias reports that some people identified Sabbe as a Babylonian Sibyl and said that she was daughter of Berossus. Berossus was a Chaldean priest who lived in the first quarter of the third century B.C. He was said to be an astrologer, and he wrote a history of Babylonia which began with the myths of the creation of the world and ended with a prediction of cosmic destruction.[15] Such a well-known historical figure could not possibly be the father of the legendary Sabbe.

In Sibylline Oracles 3.809f. the Sibyl says that she has come from Babylon. The same book, Sibylline Oracles 3.97–161, contains a description of the fall of the tower of Babel and a euhemeristic account of Greek mythology. Since the work of Bousset and Geffcken this passage has been widely accepted as a fragment of the Babylonian Sibyl.[16] The relation of that Sibyl to Berossus is then explained by postulating that Berossus derived material from the Sibyl or vice versa. However, close examination of the passage in Sibylline Oracles 3 reveals no evidence of Babylonian origin.[17] The story of the fall of the tower is a natural expansion of the biblical narrative. The euhemeristic account of Greek mythology may well be a borrowing from another source but there is no reason to suspect that the source was Babylonian. In fact there is no extant oracle or fragment that can be attributed to a Babylonian Sibyl.[18] Such a Sibyl may possibly have existed but any alleged relationship to the Jewish Sibyl or to Berossus must be purely hypothetical. The outline of Berossus' history, which has a cosmic sweep from creation to final destruction, bears obvious analogy to many of the Sibylline books. This analogy may be due to a historical influence which cannot now be traced, but the analogy itself may have been enough to give rise to the supposed relationship between the Sibyl and Berossus.

The nature of Sibylline oracles

The most characteristic feature of Sibylline oracles is the prediction of woes and disasters to come upon mankind. In the words of the Erythrean Sibyl, the Sibyl was "foreseeing on behalf of men hardships difficult to bear." In this they show some similarity to the Old Testament prophets, since "from remote times the prophets . . . prophesied war, famine and plague for many countries and for great kingdoms" (Jer 28:8). Further, like the prophets, their words of doom are often directed against specific peoples and cities, and occasionally, at least, a ray of hope does penetrate their message, indicating restoration after the destruction. The disasters are due to the wrath of the gods, which can be incurred by ritual offenses, but also, especially in the Jewish and Christian oracles, by ethical violations. The fragments of the pagan Sibyls which have survived are relatively brief and describe either the Sibyl herself and her relationship with the gods—especially Apollo—or woes to come upon specific

[13] So the *Chronicum paschale*, ed. L. Dindorfius (Bonn, 1832), 1.201f.

[14] See the discussion of Nikiprowetzky, *La Troisième Sibylle*, pp. 12–16, and most recently J. M. Rosenstiehl and J. G. Heintz, "De Sibtu, la reine de Mari, à Sambethe," *RHPR* 52 (1972) 13–15.

[15] See P. Schnabel, *Berossos und die babylonisch-hellenistische Literatur* (Leipzig, 1923). The authenticity of the passage that refers to cosmic destruction (Seneca, *Naturales quaestiones* 3.29.1) has been questioned by Jacoby (*FGH*, vol. 3C, pp. 395–97) and others because it is the first such reference in Babylonian literature. However, this is not an adequate reason to reject the attribution. Berossus may well have derived the idea from a non-Babylonian source.

[16] W. Bousset, "Die Beziehungen der ältesten jüdischen Sibylle zur Chaldäischen," *ZNW* 3 (1902) 23–50; J. Geffcken, "Die Babylonische Sibylle," *Nachrichten der königlichen Gesellschaft der Wissenschaften zu Göttingen*, Phil.-Hist. Kl. (1900) 88–102.

[17] See the detailed discussion of Nikiprowetzky, *La Troisième Sibylle*, pp. 15–36.

[18] SibOr 3.381–87 is ascribed to a Babylonian Sibyl by S. K. Eddy, *The King Is Dead*, p. 127. The same passage is attributed to a Persian Sibyl by J. Geffcken, *Komposition und Entstehungszeit*. Neither attribution has any basis other than the reference to the destruction of Babylon.

places.[19] None of them is extensive enough to show the pretended outline of the entire course of world history which we find in some of the Jewish and Christian books.

For this reason some scholars tend to distinguish sharply between the early Sibylline oracles and the longer continuous oracles found in our collection, and see the prototype of the later Sibylline oracles in the long poem attributed to Lycophron, the *Alexandra*.[20] Lycophron lived in the first half of the third century B.C., but since vss. 1446–50 of the poem seem to refer to the battle of Cynoscephalae in 197 B.C., many scholars think the attribution is false. The *Alexandra* consists of an allegorical *ex eventu* prophecy, put in the mouth of Alexandra or Cassandra, daughter of Priam, which dwells at length on the fate of the heroes after the Trojan War, but also (in vss. 1412–50) deals with Greek and Roman history in the hellenistic age. The poem is notoriously difficult, partly because of the allegorical language, which can be highly confusing—Agamemnon is referred to as Zeus and vice versa. The poem has a clear political tendenz. It glorifies the Trojans and prophesies the exaltation of their descendants, the Romans. Yet the prophetic form of the poem is a clear literary fiction—no one ever suggested that it was a real prophecy of Cassandra.

The *Alexandra* shows a number of features characteristic of the later Sibylline oracles which are not found in the extant pagan fragments, most notably extended *ex eventu* prophecy, which might be taken as an attempt to cover the whole course of world history, from the earliest known events to the present time. It also emphasizes the theme of the conflict between East and West, a favorite subject of the Sibylline oracles.[21] Yet it is by no means clear that this poem was the prototype of the Sibylline oracles. *Ex eventu* prophecy was a common device in Greek drama—Cassandra herself figured in the *Oresteia* of Aeschylus. Also the Erythrean (or Marpessan) Sibyl was said to have prophesied about Helen, the war between Asia and Europe, and the fall of Troy;[22] therefore, most probably, an *ex eventu* prophecy of some length was ascribed to her. It is more likely that Lycophron, or Pseudo-Lycophron, modeled his poem on the Sibylline form than vice versa.

Neither the *Alexandra* nor the Erythrean Sibyl divide world history into a set number of periods, in the manner typical of the later Sibylline oracles. However, such periodization of history was certainly a feature of the pagan Sibyls as can be seen by Virgil's reference to the *ultima aetas*, "final age," of the Cumean Sibyl in the Fourth Eclogue. The periodization of history was probably a relatively late development in the Sibylline tradition (i.e. after 400 B.C.) under Persian influence.[23]

The Roman Sibylline oracles

The most famous collection of Sibylline oracles in antiquity was the official one at Rome. Legend places the origin of these oracles in the time of Tarquinius Priscus.[24] This probably indicates that the Romans had acquired a collection of oracles in Greek hexameters before the fall of the monarchy.[25] These oracles were entrusted to special keepers, first two men, then ten, finally fifteen.[26] They were consulted only in time of crisis for the state, and the consultation had to be authorized by a decree of the senate. No other body of literature was accorded such official authority in the Greco-Roman world.

[19] The fragments of the pagan Sibyls can be found in C. Alexandre, *Oracula Sibyllina*, vol. 2, pp. 118–47. To these should be added the Oslo fragment published by G. Crönert, "Oraculorum Sibyllinorum fragmentum Osloense," *Symbolae Osloenses* 6 (1928) 57–59.

[20] So especially M. J. Wolff, "Sibyllen und Sibyllinen," *Archiv fur Kulturgeschichte* 24 (1934) 312–25. Cf. also Kurfess, *Sibyllinische Weissagungen*, pp. 19f. On the *Alexandra* see J. J. Collins, *The Sibylline Oracles of Egyptian Judaism*, pp. 8, 128 n. 67.

[21] *Alexandra* 1283–450. See E. Kocsis, "Ost-West Gegensatz in den jüdischen Sibyllinen," *NovT* 5 (1962) 105–10.

[22] Pausanias 10.12.1–9.

[23] See K. Kerenyi, "Das Persische Millennium im Mahabharta, bei der Sibylle und Vergil," *Klio* 29 (1936) 1–35; D. Flusser, "The Four Empires in the Fourth Sibyl and in the Book of Daniel," *Israel Oriental Studies* 2 (1972) 148–75.

[24] The legend is recounted in the anonymous Prologue to the Sibylline Oracles. See also Dionysius of Halicarnassus, *Roman Antiquities* 4.62.

[25] On the Roman Sibylline oracles see Hermann Diels, *Sibyllinische Blätter* (Berlin, 1890); A. Rzach, Pauly-Wissowa 2A, cols. 2103–16; W. Hoffmann, *Wandel und Herkunft der Sibyllinische Bücher in Rom* (diss., Leipzig, 1933); and most recently R. Bloch, "L'Origine des Livres Sibyllins à Rome: Méthode de recherche et critique du récit des annalistes anciens," *Neue Beiträge zur Geschichte der Alten Welt* (Berlin, 1965) Bd. 2, pp. 281–92.

[26] See Rzach, Pauly-Wissowa 2A, col. 2106.

When the temple of Jupiter was burned down in 83 B.C. the Sibylline books were destroyed. When the temple was rebuilt in 76 B.C. oracles were collected from various Sibylline centers, especially Erythrea.[27] In view of the diverse origins of these oracles it is probable that the collection was made up of short oracles rather than long continuous ones. The content of these oracles may have varied. Tibullus, 2.5.66–78, suggests that they were preoccupied with prodigies and portents. One of the main extant examples of Roman Sibyllines deals with the birth of an androgyne, who will have "all the male characteristics and those which young girls show forth," and the other prescribes rituals for the occasion of the founding of the *Ludi Saeculares,* "Secular Games."[28] The use to which these oracles were put could vary too. In the early fifth century the Sibylline oracles were used as the authority for founding temples to Greek gods.[29] In 173 B.C. they were consulted when the Romans were alarmed by prodigies during a war with Macedonia.[30] In general they were consulted in serious crises of any kind.

The function of Sibylline oracles

Besides the superstitious fascination with prodigies to which they attest, Sibylline oracles (like other oracles and prophecies) seem to have functioned widely as political propaganda.[31] Callisthenes wrote that both Apollo of Didyma and the Erythrean Sibyl prophesied Alexander's coming kingship.[32] Nicanor, who like Callisthenes accompanied Alexander on his campaigns, is cited by Varro for the statement that the Persian Sibyl was oldest of all.[33] Nicanor's interest in the Sibyl strongly suggests that there were Sibylline oracles that had a bearing on Alexander's campaign. Plutarch associates Sibylline oracles primarily with political upheavals.[34] In A.D. 12 the Emperor Augustus destroyed more than two thousand prophetic verses, including some Sibylline verses, because he found them politically subversive.[35] The fact that some Sibylline books were spared by exception shows that their prestige in Rome was exceptional, but does not mean that they were devoid of political significance. It should also be remembered that the idea of a golden age, which Virgil apparently derived from the Cumean Sibyl, was closely bound to the expectation of an ideal monarch. Accordingly, it lent itself readily to political propaganda, whether or not the relevant Sibylline sources had such a purpose.

All the Sibylline oracles were, of course, essentially religious. Prodigies, portents, and political crises were all related to the will of the gods and often related to matters of right worship (so, for example, the extant Roman Sibylline oracles). The pagan Sibyl spoke for Apollo, as surely as her Jewish counterpart spoke for Yahweh.

The Sibylline oracles, like all oracles in antiquity, were subject to interpolation, falsification, and manipulation.[36] This fact was well known in the ancient world. The Sibyls were mercilessly parodied by Aristophanes and Lucian,[37] while Cicero and even Plutarch show themselves aware of the deceptions of oracle-mongers.[38] Nevertheless, the prestige of these oracles was enormous. It was doubtless because of the high esteem in which these prophecies were held that Jewish and Christian writers used the form so extensively to present their own messages.

Text

The present collection of Sibylline oracles is composed of two distinct collections in

[27] Dionysius of Halicarnassus 4.62.5f.

[28] For the text of these oracles see Jacoby, *FGH,* vol. 2B, pp. 1179–91, also Alexandre, *Oracula Sibyllina,* vol. 2, pp. 242–52. For bibliography see Collins, *The Sibylline Oracles,* p. 124, nn. 33f.

[29] See H. W. Parke, *Greek Oracles* (London, 1967), p. 52.

[30] Livy 42.2.6.

[31] See Collins, *The Sibylline Oracles,* ch. 1.

[32] Strabo 17.1.43 (814).

[33] Lactantius, *DivInst* 1.6. See Eddy, *The King Is Dead,* p. 11.

[34] Plutarch, *De Pythiae oraculis* 398.

[35] Suetonius, *Augustus* 31.1.

[36] See especially A. D. Nock, "Oracles théologiques," *Revue des études anciennes* 30 (1928) 280–90, and "Religious Attitudes of the Ancient Greeks," *Proceedings of the American Philosophical Society* 85 (1942) 472–82.

[37] See the texts in Alexandre, *Oracula Sibyllina,* vol. 2, pp. 140–47.

[38] Cicero, *De divinatione* 2.54.110f.; Plutarch, *De Pythiis oraculis* 25.

manuscript.[39] The first consists of the two manuscript groups usually referred to as φ and ψ and contains books 1–8. In group φ only, these are preceded by the anonymous Prologue. The collection in φ begins with the present book 1, which gives an account of creation, while ψ begins with book 8, which has a strong interest in Christology. φ lacks 8.487–500.

The second collection consists of the group of manuscripts known as Ω. This begins with a ninth book, made up of material already found in the first collection: book 6, then a single verse, which has been placed at the beginning of book 7 since the edition of Alexandre, then 8.218–428. Then follows book 10, which is identical with book 4 of the first collection, and then books 11–14. The first two books of the second collection should be numbered 9 and 10, in sequence after the first collection. Since these books merely reduplicate material found in books 1–8 they are omitted in the editions, but the numbering of books 11–14 is retained. Hence the anomaly whereby there are no books 9 and 10 in the present collection.

The chief manuscripts in each group are:

Ω:

M: Codex Ambrosianus E64 sup.	(15th cent.)	
Q: Codex Vaticanus 1120	(14th cent.)	
V: Codex Vaticanus 743	(14th cent.)	
H: Codex Monacensis gr. 312	(1541)	
Z: Codex Hierosolymitanus Sabaiticus 419	(end of 14th cent.)	

φ:

A: Codex Vindobonensis hist gr. XCVI 6	(15th cent.)
P: Codex Monacensis 351	(15th cent.)
B: Codex Bodleianus Baroccianus 109	(end of 15th cent.)
S: Codex Scorialensis II Σ 7	(end of 15th cent.)
D: Codex Vallicellianus gr. 46	(16th cent.)

ψ:

F: Codex Laurentianus plut. XI 17	(15th cent.)
R: Codex Parisinus 2851	(end of 15th cent.)
L: Codex Parisinus 2850	(1475)
T: Codex Toletanus Cat 99.44	(c. 1500)

The abundant quotations in the Church Fathers also provide important evidence to the text.

The first edition was published in Basel in 1545 by Xystus Betuleius (Sixtus Birken). It was based on manuscript P and contained only the first eight books. Only in the nineteenth century were books 11–14 first published, when Angelo Mai discovered manuscripts M, Q, and V (1817–28). The first complete edition was that of C. Alexandre, who published the Prologue and books 1–8 and the fragments in 1841, and books 11–14 in 1853. The two major editions are those of A. Rzach, *Oracula Sibyllina* (1891) and J. Geffcken (who incorporated suggestions of K. Buresch, L. Mendelssohn, and U. Wilamowitz-Möllendorf), *Die Oracula Sibyllina* (1902). Opinions are divided as to which is the better edition. In general, Rzach prints emendations more readily, which gives a smoother text, but one which on occasion improves the manuscripts unduly. Geffcken is more cautious. His work is also more extensively informed by other oracular literature. The present translation is based on Geffcken's text. Occasions where other readings are followed (those of Rzach, those suggested in Geffcken's apparatus or others) are listed in the notes.

Mention should be made of the contributions of A.-M. Kurfess in *Sibyllinische Weissagungen* (1951), which gives a text and German translation of books 1–11, and in several articles.[40] For book 3 see V. Nikiprowetzky, *La Troisième Sibylle* (1970).

---

[39] For full discussion of the text of the Sibylline Oracles see J. Geffcken, *Die Oracula Sibyllina*, pp. XXI–LIII. Also Rzach, Pauly-Wissowa 2A, cols. 2119–22.

[40] See especially Kurfess, "Ad Oracula Sibyllina ed. Geffcken (1902)," *Symbolae Osloenses* 28 (1950) 95–104; 29 (1952) 54–77; "Zu den Oracula Sibyllina," *Colligere Fragmenta* (A. Dold Festschrift; Beuron, 1952) pp. 75–83.

Date

The dates of the various Sibylline books range from the mid-second century B.C. to the seventh century A.D. The dates of the individual books will be discussed in the separate introductions that follow. Books 3, 4, and 5 and the fragments were known to Clement of Alexandria at the end of the second century. These, and books 6, 7, and 8 were known to Lactantius about A.D. 300. The Prologue must be dated about A.D. 500, since it depends on the Theosophy, which contains at the end a chronicle from Adam to Caesar Zenon (474–91) and therefore was written after or during the latter's reign. The Prologue was probably composed for the first collection of Sibylline oracles as found in φ.[41]

Provenance

The provenance of the individual books will also be discussed in the separate introductions that follow. Approximately half the collection can be ascribed to Egypt—books 3, 5, 11–14. Other books can be traced (with varying degrees of probability) to Syria (4, 6, 7), to Asia Minor (1/2), or only to an undetermined region of the Near East (most of SibOr 8).

Historical importance

Despite their wealth of historical allusions, the Sibylline oracles cannot be expected to provide reliable chronological or factual data. Some books, especially the later ones, show only the vaguest knowledge of the events they describe. The stylized presentation of the oracles is in any case not intended for factual reporting. The main historical value of the books lies in their representation of popular attitudes in the realm of politics, the legend-laden view of kings and empires, and the hopes and fears of Eastern peoples under first Greek and then, for most of the books, Roman rule. In particular they are a major source for the ideology of resistance to Rome throughout the Near East.[42] Historical interest is notably lesser in the oracles that are clearly Christian (6, 7, and parts of 1, 2, and 8).

Theological importance

The theological importance of the Sibylline oracles lies perhaps less in their actual content than in the phenomenon which they represent—the attribution of inspired Jewish and Christian oracles to the pagan Sibyl. It is true, of course, that the Sibyl was identified as the daughter (or daughter-in-law) of Noah. However, Christian apologists explicitly emphasized that she was pagan, hoping thereby to establish her as an independent witness to the truth of the Christian faith. The logic of this position is clearly stated by Lactantius, _Epitome Institutionum_ 68 (73):

> Therefore since all these things are true and certain, foretold by the harmonious prediction of all the prophets, since Trismegistus, Hystaspes and the Sibyl all uttered the same things, it is impossible to doubt that hope of all life and salvation resides in the one religion of god . . .

Even before Christian writers adapted the Sibyls for their apologetic purposes, the oracles represented a remarkable attempt to find a mode of expression common to Jews (or Christians) and gentiles. As such the Jewish Sibylline oracles originated in the apologetic literature of hellenistic Judaism. The willingness to incorporate material from pagan oracles shows a significant readiness to build on the common human basis of Jews and gentiles. At least the earliest oracles in Sibylline Oracles 3 express a very positive attitude to their gentile neighbors. Later, after the destruction of the Temple, the Jewish oracles, e.g. Sibylline Oracles 5, adopt a more negative attitude but persist in using the international Sibylline form.

---

[41] See Rzach, Pauly-Wissowa 2A, cols. 2119f.

[42] See especially H. Fuchs, _Der geistige Widerstand gegen Rom in der antiken Welt_; Eddy, _The King Is Dead_; and R. MacMullen, _Enemies of the Roman Order_ (Cambridge, 1966) pp. 128–62.

[43] See F. Christ, _Die Römische Weltherrschaft in der antiken Dichtung_ (Stuttgart, 1938).

ESCHATOLOGY

In content, the Sibylline oracles are dominated by eschatology. The only books that do not contain significant eschatological passages are Sibylline Oracles 11–13, and even there eschatological passages may well have been lost or displaced. The eschatology of the Jewish oracles is political in nature: It is concerned with the advent of a glorious kingdom and the transformation of the earth. As such it was a suitable medium of propaganda for the hellenistic world. A similar interest in the transformation of the earth under an ideal ruler is also found throughout the hellenistic world. The most famous example is Virgil's Fourth Eclogue, and, in general, such an earthly eschatology was well harnessed in the service of Roman propaganda.[43] However, political eschatology also functioned widely in the ideology of resistance to Rome (and earlier to Greece) in the Near East. The best-known examples are the Egyptian Demotic Chronicle and Potter's Oracle, and the Persian Oracle of Hystaspes and Bahman Yasht, and of course the Jewish apocalyptic literature.[44]

The negative side of this eschatology is the threat of the destruction of the world, usually by fire. Here again plentiful parallels can be found in the pagan world, especially in Persian eschatology and in the Stoic concept of the *ekpurōsis*, "conflagration."[45] The idea of the conflagration is often associated with the Flood, as the two great destructions which punctuate the history of the world. (So especially SibOr 1/2 and 4.) The idea of a twofold destruction of the world is related to that of the Great Year, which is attested in some Greek writings.[46]

Periodization is ubiquitous in the Sibylline Oracles. Usually history is divided into ten generations, but the pattern of four kingdoms also occurs, at least in Sibylline Oracles 4. The division of history into ten periods ultimately derives from Persian religion,[47] but it is also found widely in Jewish apocalyptic.[48]

The affinities of the Sibylline Oracles with pagan eschatology are further augmented by the incorporation of popular motifs and legends. The most famous example is the legend that Nero would return as an eschatological adversary at the head of a Parthian host, which is especially prominent in Sibylline Oracles 4, 5, and 8.[49] Another example is provided by the schema of four kingdoms in Sibylline Oracles 4.[50]

Only in the Christian books do we find extensive interest in the fate of the individual after death. Belief in a resurrection is attested in the Jewish Sibylline Oracles 4 but only very tersely. There is some doubt as to how much of the judgment scene in Sibylline Oracles 2 is Jewish or Christian. However, the developed interest in the sufferings of the condemned is most prominently displayed in Sibylline Oracles 2, which is largely Christian, the Christian Sibylline Oracles 7, and the Christian parts of Sibylline Oracles 8. Sibylline Oracles 2 is especially characterized by its detailed interest in the fiery sufferings of the damned. Even in the Christian books, however, the paradise of the resurrected saints is an earthly one, depicted in terms of a transformation of the earth.

MORAL EXHORTATION

The eschatology of the Sibylline Oracles usually provides a framework for exhortation. Destruction is a punishment for sins and can be avoided by certain righteous actions. The sins in which the Sibyl expresses most interest are idolatry and sexual offenses, while most of the standard ethical prohibitions of injustice, violence, etc., are also present. The polemic against idolatry is found throughout and is related to the Sibyl's repeated insistence on monotheism. All forms of sexual offenses are condemned, but special reproach is poured on homosexuality. It should be noted that the sexual polemics usually are not inspired by asceticism but rather by a concern for natural law. Only in Sibylline Oracles 2.51, in a Christian passage, is virginity commended as a virtue. While both polemic against idolatry and against homosexuality are typical features of Jewish apologetic, both can also be paralleled amply in the preachings of gentile moralists.

---

[44] See Collins, *The Sibylline Oracles,* ch. 1.
[45] Ibid., ch. 6.
[46] Ibid., pp. 101f.
[47] Cf. n. 23 above.
[48] Especially the Apocalypse of Weeks in 1En 93; 91:12–17; and 11QMelch. See n. b on SibOr 2.15.
[49] Collins, *The Sibylline Oracles,* pp. 80–87.
[50] See especially Flusser, *Israel Oriental Studies* 2 (1972) 148–75.

One further vice that is frequently condemned, especially in Sibylline Oracles 8, is greed. At this point the religious polemic of the oracles is more directly related to the political polemic that often surrounds it.

Cultural significance

The impact of the Sibylline oracles on the culture of the West lies mainly in their impact on the theological tradition. The oracles are quoted hundreds of times in the Church Fathers.[51] They were important enough to find a place in the Emperor Constantine's "Speech to the Saints."[52] More significant, however, was the fact that production of Sibylline oracles continued down through the Middle Ages, and had an important influence on millenarian thinking, notably on Joachim of Fiore.[53] The Tiburtine Sibyl was especially popular in the Middle Ages.[54] In liturgical circles the fame of the Sibyl was perpetuated by her mention in the *Dies irae* of Tomas a Celano. About 1600, Orlando di Lasso composed a polyphonic arrangement of Sibylline prophecies.[55]

The impact of the oracles on secular culture was not great and was probably most significant in the Latin poets. In addition to Virgil's use of the Cumean Sibyl, echoes of the oracles have been found in Horace and Juvenal, although it is not certain that there was literary dependence.[56] The depictions of the tortures of the damned in Sibylline Oracles 2 are echoed in a long tradition of Western writing, most notably in Dante's *Inferno*. However, this tradition is not specifically indebted to the Sibyl, but to the broader phenomenon of apocalyptic literature.

One final area in which the influence of the Sibylline oracles should be noted is that of art. Michelangelo juxtaposed five Sibyls (Persian, Erythrean, Delphic, Cumean, and Libyan) with the Old Testament prophets in the Sistine Chapel. Raphael used four Sibyls (Cumean, Persian, Phrygian, and Tiburtine) to adorn Santa Maria della Pace in Rome. Various other painters depicted individual Sibyls.[57] Eschatological motifs of the Sibylline tradition such as the Antichrist figure also appear in medieval art, but specific influence of the Sibyl is more difficult to establish in these cases.

---

[51] See B. Thompson, "Patristic Use of the Sibylline Oracles," *The Review of Religion* 6 (1952) 115–36.

[52] Kurfess, *Sibyllinische Weissagungen,* pp. 208–22.

[53] B. McGinn, "Joachim and the Sibyl," *Citeaux* 24 (1973) 97–138; Kurfess, *Sibyllinische Weissagungen,* pp. 344–48: Rzach, Pauly-Wissowa 2A, cols. 2169–83.

[54] For the text of the Tiburtine Sibyl see E. Sackur, *Sibyllinische Texte und Forschungen* (Halle, 1898) pp. 177–87; Kurfess, *Sibyllinische Weissagungen,* pp. 262–78. See also P. J. Alexander, *The Oracle of Baalbek: The Tiburtine Sibyl in Greek Dress* (Dumbarton Oaks Studies 10; Washington, 1967).

[55] On the influence of the oracles on the Western Church see further E. S. Demougeot, "Jérôme, les oracles sibyllins et Stilicon," *Revue des études anciennes* 54 (1952) 83–92; K. Prummn, "Der Prophetenamt der Sibyllen in kirchlichen Literatur," *Scholastik* 2 (1929) 54–77, 221–46, 498–533.

[56] See especially a series of articles by A.-M. Kurfess: "Horaz und die Sibyllinen," *ZRGG* 8 (1956) 253–56; "Juvenal und die Sibylle," *Judaica* 10 (1954) 60–63 (also *Historisches Jahrbuch* 76 [1957] 79–83); "Virgil's vierte Ekloge und die Oracula Sibyllina," *Historisches Jahrbuch* 73 (1954) 120–27; and "Virgil's 4 Ekloge und die christlichen Sibyllinen," *Gymnasium* 62 (1955) 110–12. See also F. Dornseiff, "Die sibyllinischen Orakel in der augusteischen Dichtung," *Römische Dichtung der augusteischen Zeit* (Berlin, 1960) pp. 43–51. For traces of the Sibyl in medieval English literature see W. L. Kinter, *Prophetess and Fay. A Study of the Ancient and Mediaeval Tradition of the Sibyl* (Ph.D. diss.; Columbia, New York, 1958). Rzach, Pauly-Wissowa 2A, cols. 2180f., cites a few instances of Sibylline influence on German literature.

[57] Rzach, Pauly-Wissowa 2A, cols. 2181f.

SELECT BIBLIOGRAPHY

Charlesworth, *PMR*, pp. 184–88.
Delling, *Bibliographie*, pp. 155f.
Denis, *Introduction*, pp. 111–22.

TEXTS

Alexandre, C. *Oracula Sibyllina I*. Paris, 1841 (Part 1), 1853 (Part 2). (Text, Lat. translation and nn. to the entire twelve books and fragments.)

Geffcken. J. *Die Oracula Sibyllina*. GCS 8; Leipzig, 1902. (Gk. text and apparatus. It also contains a valuable apparatus of religio-historical parallels.)

Rzach, A. *Oracula Sibyllina*. Leipzig, 1891. (Gk. text and apparatus, with a list of parallels to Homer and Hesiod.)

TRANSLATIONS

Bate, H. N. *The Sibylline Oracles, Books III–V*. London, 1918. (Introduction, translation, and nn. to SibOr 3–5.)

Kurfess, A.-M., and McL. Wilson, R. "Christian Sibyllines," HSW, vol. 2, pp. 703–45. (Translation of SibOr 1.323–400; 2.34–55, 149–347; books 6–8; and the Latin *Prophetia sibillae magnae* from the 4th or 5th cent. A.D. with biblical cross-references.)

Lanchester, H. C. O. "The Sibylline Oracles," *APOT*, vol. 2, pp. 368–406. (Introduction, translation, and nn. to SibOr 3–5.)

Terry, M. S. *The Sibylline Oracles*. New York, 1890. (Translation of the twelve books into English blank verse.)

THE MOST IMPORTANT OTHER TRANSLATIONS ARE

Blass, F. "Die Sibyllinischen Orakel," *APAT*, vol. 2, pp. 177–217. (Introduction, translation, and nn. to books 3–5.)

Kurfess, A.-M. *Sibyllinische Weissagungen*. Berlin, 1951. (Gk. text [without apparatus], German translation, and nn. to SibOr 1–11. Also contains other relevant texts—Virgil's Fourth Eclogue, Constantine's Speech, extracts from Lactantius and the Theosophy, and the Tiburtine Sibyl.)

A new German translation of "Sibyllinen," by Dr. Merkel for *JSHRZ*, was announced but not yet available when this manuscript was sent to press.

STUDIES

Alexandre, C. *Oracula Sibyllina II*. Paris, 1856. (A collection of excursus on particular topics with a useful collection of the pagan Sibylline fragments.)

Bousset, W. "Sibyllen und Sibyllinische Bücher," *Real-Encyclopedie der protestantische Theologie und Kirche* 18 (1906) 265–80. (A review of the phenomenon of Sibylline prophecy and of the individual books.)

———. *The Antichrist Legend*. London, 1896. (An important collection of eschatological passages from Christian writers which frequently parallel the Sibylline Oracles.)

Collins, J. J. *The Sibylline Oracles of Egyptian Judaism*. SBLDS 13; Missoula, 1974. (Date, provenance, context, and motifs of SibOr 3–5.)

Eddy, S. K. *The King Is Dead*. Lincoln, Nebraska, 1961. (Important though erratic study of the resistance literature of the hellenistic Near East.)

Fuchs, H. *Der geistige Widerstand gegen Rom in der antiken Welt*. Berlin, 1938. (Brief but richly documented study of Near Eastern resistance literature in the Roman period.)

Geffcken, J. *Komposition und Entstehungszeit der Oracula Sibyllina*. TU N.F. 8.1; Leipzig, 1902. (Date and provenance of each of the twelve books.)

Nikiprowetzky, V. *La Troisième Sibylle*. Etudes Juives 9; Paris, 1970. (Extensive introduction, Gk. text, French translation, and nn. to SibOr 3.)

Peretti, A. *La Sibilla Babilonese nella propaganda ellenistica*. Firenze, 1943. (A study of SibOr 3 against the background of Near Eastern propaganda such as Berossus.)

Pincherle, A. *Gli Oracoli Sibillini Giudaici*. Rome, 1922. (Merits mention as one of the few book-length studies, but contributes little to the discussion.)

Rzach, A. "Sibyllinische Orakel," "Sibyllen," Pauly-Wissowa 2A (1923), cols. 2073–183. (Extensive review of the phenomenon of Sibylline prophecy and of the individual Sibylline books.)

Further bibliography on particular books and topics will be found in the notes to the introductions of the individual books. The older literature on the oracles is listed by Lanchester, *APOT*, vol. 2, p. 376. At the time this manuscript was sent to press studies by V. Nikiprowetzky, "La Sibylle Juive depuis Ch. Alexandre," for *ANRW*, and by J. J. Collins, "The Development of the Sibylline Tradition," for the same volume, were announced but not yet available.

An extensive bibliography can be found in Collins, *The Sibylline Oracles*.

Introduction

The Prologue is found only in manuscript group φ. It is anonymous and its exact provenance is unknown. It can be dated no earlier than the sixth century A.D. since it depends on the Theosophy, which in turn refers to Caesar Zenon (474–91) and can be no earlier than the end of the fifth century.[1]

The Prologue explains briefly why its author decided to collect the Sibylline Oracles. It then gives a list of ten Sibyls and recounts the legendary origin of the Sibylline books at Rome. It appeals to Lactantius for a defense of the value of the oracles. Finally it concludes by citing a few parallels in Sibylline Oracles 3.1–45, in the Sibylline fragments, and in the Pseudo-Orphic fragments.

SIBYLLINE ORACLES

Prologue

If the hard labor involved in reading Greek literature produces great benefit for those who accomplish it, inasmuch as it is able to make those who toil at these things very learned, it befits the wise much more to busy themselves with the sacred writings—inasmuch as they
5 treat of God and the things which provide spiritual benefit— •and gain from that source a double profit throughout being able to benefit both themselves and those who meet them. For these reasons, therefore, I decided to set forth the oracles called Sibylline, which are
10 found scattered and confusedly read and recognized, •in one continuous and connected book, so that they might be easily reviewed by the readers and award their benefit to them, by expounding a not inconsiderable number of necessary and useful things, and making the
15 study at once more valuable and more diversified. •For they expound very clearly about Father, Son, and Holy Spirit, the divine Trinity, source of life;[a] about the incarnate career of our Lord and God and Savior Jesus Christ; the birth, I mean, from an unchanging virgin,[b]
20 and the healings performed by him; •similarly his life-giving passion and resurrection from the dead on the third day and the judgment which will take place, and the retribution for what we all have done in this life. In addition to these things they clearly recount the things which are expounded in the Mosaic writings and the books of the prophets, about the creation
25 of the world, •the fashioning of man and the expulsion from the garden and again the new formation. In manifold ways they tell of certain past history, and equally, foretell future events, and, to speak simply, they can profit those who read them in no small way.

The name "Sibyl"

30 "Sibyl" is a Latin word, interpreted as "prophetess," that is to say "seer." •Therefore the female seers were called by one name. Now Sibyls, as many have written, have lived in various times and places, and are ten in number.[c] First, then, the Chaldean, that is to say the Persian, who is called by the proper name Sambethe,[d] who is of the family of the most
35 blessed Noah. She is said to have prophesied the career of Alexander the Macedonian.[e] • SibOr 1.289; 3.827

---

[1] Rzach, Pauly-Wissowa 2A, col. 2120.
a. Or "which rules over life."
b. Lit. "without flux." The expression is used with reference to the son in trinitarian discussions, so the flux in question can scarcely be physical.
c. So also Varro in Lactantius, *DivInst* 1.6; Tübingen Theosophy, 75.
d. So the Suda (C. Alexandre, *Oracula Sibyllina II*, Excursus 1, 84).
e. Callisthenes, in Strabo 17.1.43 (814).

Nicanor, who wrote the life of Alexander, mentions her.[f] Second, the Libyan, of whom Euripides made mention in the prologue of the *Lamia*. Third, the Delphian, who was born in Delphi, of whom Chrysippus spoke in the treatise on divinity. Fourth, the Italian, at

40 Cimmeria in Italy, whose son was Evander •who founded the shrine of Pan at Rome which is called Lupercum.[g] Fifth, the Erythrean, who also prophesied about the Trojan war.[h] Apollodorus the Erythrean confirms her. Sixth, the Samian, who is called by the proper name Phyto, about whom Eratosthenes wrote. Seventh, the Cumean, who is called Amaltheia

45 who is also Erophile, but with some, Taraxandra. Virgil calls the Cumean Deiphobe, daughter of Glaucus.[i] Eighth, the Hellespontian, born in the village Marmessus, around the small town Gergition. She was once within the boundaries of Troy in the times of Solon and Cyrus, as Heracleides Ponticus wrote.[j] Ninth, the Phrygian. Tenth, the Tiburtian, Abounaea by name.

The Cumean Sibyl

50   They say that the Cumean brought nine books of her own prophecies to Tarquinius Priscus, who then ruled the Roman state, and asked three hundred didrachms for them.[k] She was

55 slighted, and was not asked what was contained in them •so she consigned three of them to the fire. Again, in another approach to the king, she brought forward the six books and asked the same sum. She was considered of no account, so she again burned three more. Then, a third time, she approached, bringing the three that were left, and asked the same

60 price, saying that if he did not accept she would burn them also. •Then, they say, the king read them and was amazed. He gave a hundred didrachms for them and took them, and he entreated her about the others. When she answered that she did not have the equivalent of what had been burned, and could not know anything of the sort without inspiration, but that sometimes certain people had selected from various cities and regions what they considered

65 necessary and beneficial •and that a collection must be made from them, they did this also with all speed. For that which was given by God did not escape notice, though it truly lay hidden in a nook. The books of all the Sibyls were deposited in the Capitol of ancient Rome.

70 Those of the Cumean were concealed and not released to many •since they expressed what would happen in Italy very precisely and clearly, but those of the others were known to all. Those of the Erythrean have as superscription this name by which she is called, derived from the region. But the others are not inscribed as to what belongs to whom, but are not

75 distinguished. •Now Firmianus,[l] a not inconsiderable philosopher, and priest of the afore-mentioned Capitol, looking toward Christ, our eternal light, set forth in his own works what had been said by the Sibyls about the ineffable glory, and capably refuted the absurdity of

80 Greek error. His powerful commentary •was in Latin, but the Sibylline verses were set forth in Greek. That this may not appear incredible, I will provide a testimony of the aforementioned man as follows:[m] When the Sibylline verses found with us can easily be despised by those who are knowledgeable in Greek culture, not only because they are easily available (for

85 things which are rare are thought valuable) •but also because not all the verses preserve metrical accuracy, he has a rather clear argument. This is the fault of the secretaries, who did not keep pace with the flow of speech or even were ignorant, not of the prophetess. For the memory of what had been said ceased with the inspiration. With regard to this even Plato

90 said •that they describe many great things accurately while knowing nothing of what they say.[n]

   For my part, therefore, I will set forth as much as possible of what has been handed on in Rome by the elders.

   Now she expounded about the God who had no beginning, as follows:

f. Varro, in Lactantius, *DivInst* 1.6.
g. Ovid, *Fasti* 2.279f.
h. Lactantius, *DivInst* 1.6; Pausanias 10.2.2.
i. Virgil, *Aeneid* 6.36.
j. Clement, *Strom* 1.108.1–3.
k. Dionysius of Halicarnassus, *Roman Antiquities* 4.62.
l. Better known as Lactantius. He is not otherwise known to have been a priest of the Capitol.
m. Kurfess, following Erbse, conjectures that some Lat. words are missing here.
   n. *Meno* 99d. Vss. 86–91 appear to be derived, not from Lactantius, but from Justin, *Cohortatio ad Graecos* 37.15 (Geffcken). For vss. 91–100, however, see Lactantius, *DivInst* 1.6.

One God, the creator

One God, who alone rules, exceedingly great unbegotten

but God alone, one highest of all, who made•
heaven and sun and stars and moon
and fruitful earth and waves of water of sea
who alone is God, abiding as indomitable creator.
He himself established the shape of the form of mortals.
He himself mixed the nature of all, begetter of life.

Which she said, meaning either that they join° by coming together into one flesh or that he made both the world under heaven and man from the four elements which are opposed to each other.

---

o. Reading *prosginontai* (Alexandre). Geffcken retains the MSS reading *patros* (*prs*). The sense is clear enough. Two explanations are offered for the phrase "He mixed the nature of all"—the coupling involved in the act of procreation or the blending of the four elements.

THE SIBYLLINE ORACLES, BOOKS 1 AND 2

Introduction

The first two books of the Sibylline Oracles are not separated in the manuscripts and, in fact, constitute a unit.[1] The work consists of an original Jewish oracle and an extensive Christian redaction. The Jewish oracle was structured on the familiar Sibylline division of world history into ten generations. The first seven generations are preserved without interpolation in Sibylline Oracles 1.1–323.[2] Then follows a Christian passage on the incarnation and career of Christ in 1.324–400. After a transitional passage in 2.1–5 the original sequence is resumed in 2.6–33. However, a considerable portion of the Jewish oracle has been lost, as there is no reference to the eighth or ninth generations, but we are thrust immediately into the climactic events of the tenth (2.15).

The remainder of Sibylline Oracles 2 (vss. 34–347) is an account of eschatological crises and the last judgment. It shows clear signs of Christian redaction but is probably not an original Christian composition. Rather the Christian Sibyllist modified the eschatological conclusion of the Jewish work by interpolations. The extent of the redactor's work is difficult to determine exactly. One passage, 2.154–76, is surely Jewish, as it culminates in the universal rule of the Hebrews (175). A number of passages are certainly Christian:

> 2.45–55 refers to Christ and allots a special place to virgins and martyrs.[3]
> 2.177–83 is based on the parable of the watchful servant (Mt 24:46–51; Lk 12:36–40).
> 2.190–92 (cf. Mark 13:17): It is possible that both Mark and Sibylline Oracles 2 could have derived this motif independently from Jewish tradition.
> 2.238–51: For the coming of Christ in glory with his angels cf. Matthew 25:31. The condemnation of the Hebrews in verse 250 is obviously Christian.
> 2.311f.: These verses refer to the intercession of the virgin.
> 2.264: This verse refers to presbyters and deacons. It is part of a catalog of sins condemned at the judgment (255–83). The rest of the passage is not necessarily Christian.[4]

The remainder of Sibylline Oracles 2 could have been written by either a Jew or a Christian. Most scholars incline to the opinion that such passages were taken over as part of the Jewish original.

In the ψ group of manuscripts, Sibylline Oracles 2 contains a lengthy insert from the sayings of Pseudo-Phocylides[5] (vss. 56–148). These verses contain a number of clear indications of Jewish authorship or redaction. We find references to the Old Testament in verse 82—"God wants not sacrifice but mercy instead of sacrifice" (cf. Hos 6:6)—and in 100f., which warns against transgressing boundaries (cf. Ex 22:5; Deut 19:14). The polemic against homosexuality (vs. 73), while less conclusive, is also typically Jewish. Nothing in these verses is necessarily Christian. However, they form part of the longer passage on the contest for entry into heaven, of which at least verses 45–55 are Christian. While Jewish in authorship, the verses may have been first inserted into the Sibylline Oracles by a Christian.

---

[1] The main discussions of these books are those of Geffcken, *Komposition und Entstehungszeit*, pp. 47–53; Rzach, Pauly-Wissowa 2A, cols. 2146–52; A. Kurfess, "Oracula Sibyllina I/II," *ZNW* 40 (1941) 151–65.

[2] Geffcken, *Komposition und Entstehungszeit*, p. 48, argued that SibOr 1 175–79 and 193–96 were Christian interpolations based on SibOr 8.184–87 and 7.7, 9–12 respectively, but he has been convincingly refuted by Kurfess, *ZNW* 40 (1941) 151–60.

[3] For the association of martyrdom and virginity in the early Church see H. von Campenhausen, *Die Idee des Martyriums in der alten Kirche* (Göttingen, 1964) pp. 139f. They are already the two chief distinguishing marks of the elect in Rev.

[4] Geffcken inclined to Christian authorship because of the parallels with such Christian writings as ApPaul (*Komposition und Entstehungszeit*, p. 52).

[5] See especially A. Kurfess, "Das Mahngedicht des sogenannten Phokylides im zweiten Buch der Oracula Sibyllina," *ZNW* 38 (1939) 171–81. For a more complete study of Ps-Phoc see the work of P. van der Horst in this volume, and in *The Sentences of Pseudo-Phocylides with Introduction and Commentary* (SVTP 4; Leiden, 1978).

Date

Such evidence as we have for the date of Sibylline Oracles 1 and 2 is scanty and less than conclusive. There are two major opinions:

1. Geffcken dated both Jewish and Christian stages in the third century A.D.[6] For the Jewish stage he advanced three arguments:

a. The Sibyl and Noah are depicted on coins from Apamea-Kibotos in the third century. However, this proves only that the association of the Sibyl and Noah was known in Asia Minor in the third century. It does not prove that it was not known earlier. The Sibyl and Noah were associated already in Sibylline Oracles 3.827, in the second century B.C. This criterion must be considered inconclusive.

b. Certain metrical peculiarities in the book find their closest analogies in book 12, which dates from the third century. However, given the metrical irregularity of the entire Sibylline corpus,[7] no firm conclusion can be based on this.

c. Geffcken's third argument is the author's poor style. This again cannot be said to point to any particular date.

For the Christian redaction Geffcken posits dependence on Sibylline Oracles 8, which was written in the late second century. This dependence, as we shall see, is open to question.

2. The second major position on the date of this book is that of Kurfess.[8] Kurfess dates the Jewish stage about the turn of the era and the Christian stage before A.D. 150.

For the Jewish stage the latest possible date is supplied by the comparison with Sibylline Oracles 7, which is usually dated in the mid-second century A.D. Now Sibylline Oracles 7.7, 9–12 correspond exactly to Sibylline Oracles 1.183, 193–96. Since these verses are well integrated in their context in book 1 and are part of a fragmentary isolated oracle in book 7 we must assume the priority of Sibylline Oracles 1.[9] The date of Sibylline Oracles 7, however, is by no means certain, but since it is quoted by Lactantius we can at least take the mid-third century A.D. as the latest possible date for Sibylline Oracles 1.

The earliest possible date for the Jewish stage is supplied by the fact that Rome is the only power singled out for destruction in the tenth generation (SibOr 2.18). Rome was prominent in Asia Minor from the beginning of the second century B.C., but the fact that it is the only power mentioned suggests that the oracle was written at a time when Roman power in the Near East was consolidated, therefore no earlier than 30 B.C. This gives a period from 30 B.C. to A.D. 250 within which the oracle could have been written.

This period can probably be limited further. The Jewish stage contains no reference to the destruction of Jerusalem, and there is no reference in book 2 to the favorite Sibylline theme of Nero's return. There is a reference to the fall of Jerusalem in 1.393–96. However, it is passed over briefly without any recrimination against Rome, and there is no reference to it in the context of the tenth generation. In fact, the only offense mentioned in connection with the destruction of Rome is idolatry (2.17). It is unlikely that a Jew writing after A.D. 70, who is at all concerned with historical events, would pass over the destruction of the Temple so lightly. Therefore the consensus of scholars that 1.387–400 is part of the Christian redaction is probably right. These verses are the only part of the Christian addition to book 1 that do not deal with the career of Christ. Presumably they were added to bring the oracle up to date. If this is so, the original Jewish oracle probably carried its review of history no later than the time of Augustus, and so the dating suggested by Kurfess, about the turn of the era, is most likely correct.

The earliest possible date for the Christian redaction is the fall of Jerusalem. The latest possible date is more difficult to find. Kurfess argues that the book must be earlier than Sibylline Oracles 7 and 8.[10] There is in fact no reason to posit literary dependence between

---

[6] Geffcken, *Komposition und Entstehungszeit*, p. 49.

[7] See A. Rzach, *Metrische Studien zu den Sibyllinischen Orakel* (Wien, 1892); Bousset, "Sibyllen und Sibyllinische Bücher," p. 274.

[8] Kurfess, *ZNW* 40 (1941) 151–65. A similar position was maintained by H. Dechent, *Über das 1, 2 und 11 Buch der Sibyllinische Weissagungen* (Frankfurt am Main: diss., Jena, 1873).

[9] Contra Geffcken, *Komposition und Entstehungszeit*, p. 48.

[10] Kurfess, *ZNW* 40 (1941) 165.

the Christian redaction of books 1 and 2 and book 7, but the parallels between books 2 and 8 are too numerous for mere coincidence:

2.305–12	cf. 8.350–58
2.318–21	cf. 8.208–12
2.322–24	cf. 8.110f., 121
2.325–27, 329	cf. 8.424–27

The direction of the influence is disputed. Geffcken presumes the priority of book 8, Kurfess of book 2. There is no clear conclusive evidence either way. The contention of Kurfess that the verses are more likely to be original in the sustained eschatological treatise of book 2 seems to carry the greater probability. In any case, the highly developed eschatology of the book is presumably later than the Revelation of John. Since no other historical event is mentioned after the destruction of Jerusalem, the Christian redaction should probably be dated no later than A.D. 150.[11]

Provenance

At least the Jewish substratum of Sibylline Oracles 1 and 2 comes from Phrygia.[12] This is indicated by 1.196–98, where Phrygia is said to be the first land to emerge after the Flood, and to become the nurse of restored humanity in the sixth generation. Also, in 1.261f., Ararat is located in Phrygia. The prominence thus given to Phrygia is the only indication of local provenance. There is nothing to indicate the provenance of the Christian redaction. The speech of Noah in 1.150–98 underlines the hortatory function of the book, but there is nothing to indicate its actual setting in life.

Historical importance

If the early dating proposed for both Jewish and Christian stages of Sibylline Oracles 1 and 2 is correct, then these books acquire considerable historical importance. The Jewish substratum is the only extensive document we have from the Judaism of Asia Minor in this period. The historical importance of the Jewish stage is somewhat diminished by the doubt as to whether much of book 2 is Jewish or Christian, but it remains a substantial source for an area of Judaism of which little is known. The book is remarkable among the Sibylline Oracles for its lack of reference to particular cities and events (though such references may have been part of the lost account of the eighth and ninth generations). Accordingly it is more difficult to relate to a specific historical situation than the other Sibylline books.

Theological importance

The main theological interest of Sibylline Oracles 1 lies in its use of the schematization of history into ten generations. Such a schematization is presupposed in several Sibylline Oracles, including those of the Cumean Sibyl of Virgil's Fourth Eclogue,[13] but it is most elaborately developed here and in Sibylline Oracles 4.[14] In Sibylline Oracles 1 it is combined with the idea of the Great Year. The first five generations end with a destruction by flood; the second five with a destruction by fire.[15]

ETHICS

The schematization of history is used by the Sibyllist as a framework for exhortation. The

[11] Ibid., p. 165.

[12] Geffcken, *Komposition und Entstehungszeit*, p. 50.

[13] See especially the commentary of Servius, who identified the "last age" of Virgil's Sibyl as the tenth, *Servii Grammatici qui feruntur in Vergilia Bucolica et Georgica commentarii* (ed. G. Thilo; Leipzig, 1887) pp. 44f.; D. Flusser, "The Four Empires in the Fourth Sibyl and in the Book of Daniel," *Israel Oriental Studies* 2 (1972) 163.

[14] On the schematization of world history in SibOr 1 see A. Rzach, "Sibyllinische Weltalter," *Wiener Studien* 34 (1912) 114f. Cf. also the Apocalypse of Weeks (1En 93; 91:12–17) and 11QMelch.

[15] See Collins, *The Sibylline Oracles*, pp. 101f. Such a doctrine of two world cycles seems to be implicit in Hesiod, and is explicit in Heraclitus and Plato (see esp. *Politicus* 273 b–c). For such a belief in Judaism see especially *Vita* 49; Josephus, *Ant* 1.2.3 (70f.). See further I. Chaine, "Cosmogonie aquatique et conflagration finale d'après la secunda Petri," *RB* 46 (1937) 207–16. Cf. also the late Apocalypse of Asclepius, from Egypt.

impending destruction of the world provides an occasion for presenting the crucial ethical values on which the judgment is based. So in Sibylline Oracles 1.150–70 and again in 174–98 Noah preaches to his contemporaries about the sins which lead to destruction and the ways to avoid it. The sins mentioned are obvious ones—violence (155–57, 176), deceit (177), adultery and slander (178), and lack of reverence for God (179). The remedy is simple—repentance and supplication (167–69). Because of the Christian redaction it is not clear whether humanity is given a similar warning before the final destruction by fire.

ESCHATOLOGY

It is also uncertain how far the eschatological rewards and punishments of Sibylline Oracles 2 can be ascribed to the Jewish oracle. At least 2.154–76 appears to be Jewish. This passage describes the eschatological dominion of the Hebrews "as of old," therefore presumably an earthly kingdom of the historical order.

The description of the resurrection in 2.214–37 is quite possibly Jewish. The four archangels, Michael, Gabriel, Raphael, and Uriel, are familiar from Jewish sources.[16] The reference to the Giants (2.231f.) is an explicit point of contact with book 1. The actual description of resurrection, with its very physical conjunction of bones and flesh, recalls Ezekiel 37. The natural sequel to such a resurrection is not a heavenly state but rather a transformation of the earth, which we find in 2.317–29. The punishment of the wicked by fire (2.285–310) is of course attested as early as Isaiah 66:24 and was common in intertestamental Judaism,[17] so it too could have formed part of the Jewish work.

THE CHRISTIAN REDACTION

The Christian redactor was interested primarily in the eschatology of the book. His impatience with the earlier history is shown by his omission of the eighth and ninth generations.

The redactor also makes use of the end-time for a hortatory purpose. The ethical instruction is presented in two passages:

1. The contest for entry into heaven (2.39–153) provides a framework for exhortation. Much of this is taken up (at least in the ψ MSS) by the sayings of Pseudo-Phocylides, which consist of the rather banal commonalities of Greek and Near Eastern folk wisdom with a few distinctly Jewish verses.[18] Of course the inclusion of this material is significant as an indication of the Sibyl's willingness to find common ground for gentile, Jew, and Christian. The most significant indication of the values of the Christian redactor, however, is found in 2.46–48, where two classes are singled out for special honor—martyrs and virgins. This combination is quite typical of early Christianity.[19] Other virtues specifically mentioned are justice, monotheistic worship, and marital fidelity (2.49–52).

2. The second passage important for the ethics of the redactor is found in 2.255–83.[20] This is a catalog of sins for which people are condemned. In addition to the usual condemnation of idolatry, violence, injustice, etc., special emphasis is laid on the treatment of widows and orphans (2.270–73) and of parents (273–76) and on sexual offenses and abortion (279–82).

Much more emphasis is laid on the punishment of the bad than on the reward of the good. The plight of the damned in the fiery underworld is described in lurid detail in 2.285–310. The detailed interest in punishment after death and the use of the wisdom teachings of Pseudo-Phocylides reflect an interest in the judgment of the individual rather than a political notion of the end-time focused on the overthrow of Rome. Yet the Christian redaction retains much of the Jewish oracle, and salvation is ultimately presented as a transformation of the earth rather than as a heavenly state. Neither the Jewish nor the Christian stage attaches any significance to a distinction between soul and body.

One final feature of the eschatology is worthy of note. According to 2.330–38 the blessed

---

[16] E.g. 1En 9:1; ApMos 40:1. See Y. Yadin, *The Scroll of the War of the Sons of Light Against the Sons of Darkness* (Oxford,1962) p. 238.

[17] E.g. 1QS 2:8; 1En 21. See Collins, *The Sibylline Oracles*, p. 109.

[18] [See the different evaluation of Ps-Phoc by P. van der Horst found herein. —J.H.C.]

[19] Cf. n. 3 above.

[20] This passage could conceivably be Jewish. Cf. n. 4 above.

can obtain the release of some condemned souls by intercession. In a gloss in the ψ manuscripts this doctrine is condemned and attributed to Origen.

Relation to other literature

The most conspicuous parallels in these books to a biblical text are found in the account of the Flood, which draws heavily on the Septuagint.[21] However, even here the Sibyllist is not solely dependent on biblical tradition, since some details of the story correspond, not with Genesis, but with Babylonian myth.[22] Rzach suggests that the Sibyl may have been influenced by Berossus, who shows a similar sweep of cosmic history from creation to the end.

Various parallels are found in the Jewish stratum of the work to the intertestamental writings of Judaism. The most significant perhaps are the parallels to the Watchers in 1 Enoch.[23] Sibylline Oracles 1 and 2 is more obviously related to the rest of the Sibylline literature, especially book 4, in its organization of history into periods, and to book 8 in the eschatology of the Christian redaction.

A conspicuous feature of Sibylline Oracles 1 and 2 is the extent of the influence of Hesiod, especially the *Works and Days*.[24] In book 1 each half of world history is divided into four declining ages, followed by a fifth in which the world is actually destroyed. The sixth generation, the first after the Flood, is said to be golden (1.284). The schema, and several verbal parallels, reflects direct use of Hesiod by the Sibyl.

Finally the eschatology of Sibylline Oracles 2, with its heavy concentration on the punishments of hell, is paralleled in late Jewish and early Christian apocalypses—especially the apocalypses of Zephaniah, Peter, and Paul.[25] The idea of punishment in Orphism (e.g. Plato, *Republic* 10.614–21, *Gorgias* 523) and some Greek influence is probable in book 2. However, the most prominent feature of the Sibylline writing is the fiery character of the netherworld. The destruction of the world by fire, and the attendant destruction of sinners, was very prominent in the Persian notion of the end and throughout the Sibylline tradition. Kurfess has emphasised the parallels between Sibylline Oracles 2 and the Oracle of Hystaspes.[26] However, the distinctive character of the eschatology of Sibylline Oracles 2 is a fiery hell as an eternal place of punishment. This concept appears to be a Jewish development. The Watchers in 1 Enoch are consigned to a fiery abyss, and the sinners in the judgment share a like fate (e.g. 1En 90:23f.). Eternal fiery punishment of the wicked is a standard feature of the concept of the end-time of intertestamental Judaism. Descriptions of the tortures of the damned receive great attention in Christian literature down through the Middle Ages. The climactic product of the genre is of course Dante's *Inferno*.

---

[21] See Rzach, Pauly-Wissowa 2A, cols. 2146f.

[22] Rzach, Pauly-Wissowa 2A, col. 2148. In both the SibOr and the Babylonian myth the raven is sent out third, and the dove rests on the ground before returning with the olive twig.

[23] E.g. the Watchers in 1En 1–16; SibOr 1.87–103.

[24] For the detailed parallels see A. Kurfess, "Homer und Hesiod im 1 Buch der Oracula Sibyllina," *Philologus* 100 (1956) 147–53.

[25] See A. Kurfess, "Dies irae," *Historisches Jahrbuch* 77 (1958) 328–38.

[26] Kurfess, ibid., p. 328; also Kurfess, *Sibyllinische Weissagungen*, pp. 282–86. On the Oracle of Hystaspes see H. Windisch, *Die Orakel des Hystaspes* (Amsterdam, 1929), and J. R. Hinnells, "The Zoroastrian Doctrine of Salvation in the Roman World," *Man and His Salvation: Studies in Memory of S. G. F. Brandon* (Manchester, 1973) pp. 125–48.

THE SIBYLLINE ORACLES
Book 1

FROM THE FIRST BOOK

The Sibyl's introduction

Beginning from the first generation of articulate men
down to the last, I will prophesy all in turn,
such things as were before, as are, and as will come upon
the world through the impiety of men.

The creation

5 First God bids me tell truly how the world
came to be. But you, devious mortal, so that you may never neglect my
    commands,
attentively make known the most high king. It was he who created
the whole world, saying, "let it come to be" and it came to be.   Gen 1
For he established the earth, draping it around with   Ps 93:1; cf.
10 Tartarus,[a] and he himself gave sweet light.   Ps 97:2
He elevated heaven, and stretched out the gleaming sea,
and he crowned the vault of heaven amply with bright-shining stars
and decorated the earth with plants. He mixed the sea
with rivers, pouring them in, and with the air he mingled fragrances,
15 and dewy clouds. He placed another species,
fish, in the seas, and gave birds to the winds;
to the woods, also, shaggy wild beasts, and creeping
serpents to the earth; and all things which now are seen.
He himself made these things with a word, and all came to be,   WisSol 9:1;
20 swiftly and truly. For he is self-begotten   Ps 33:6
    Frag 3
looking down from heaven. Under him the world has been brought to
    completion.
And then later he again fashioned an animate object,
making a copy from his own image, youthful man,   Gen 1:26; WisSol 2:23
beautiful, wonderful.[b] He bade him live in an   Sir 17:3
    CavTr (ed. Budge), p. 52
25 ambrosial garden, so that he might be concerned with beautiful works.
But he being alone in the luxuriant plantation of the garden
desired conversation, and prayed to behold another form
like his own. God himself indeed took a bone from his   Gen 2:21f.
flank and made Eve, a wonderful maidenly
30 spouse, whom he gave to this man to live with him in the garden.
And he, when he saw her, was suddenly greatly   Philo, *Op* 152 (53)
amazed in spirit, rejoicing, such a corresponding
copy did he see. They conversed with wise words
which flowed spontaneously, for God had taken care of everything.
35 For they neither covered their minds with licentiousness
nor felt shame, but were far removed from evil heart;
and they walked like wild beasts with uncovered limbs.

The Fall

To these did God then address commands

a. The nether world.   *ends of the Jews* (Philadelphia, 1909–25) vol. 1, pp.
b. On the beauty of Adam see L. Ginzberg, *Leg-*   59–62; vol. 6, pp. 78–80.

and instruct them not to touch the tree. But a very horrible
40 snake craftily deceived them to go to the fate   Gen 3:1–6
of death and receive knowledge of good and evil.
But the woman first became a betrayer to him.   Sir 25:24;
She gave, and persuaded him to sin in his ignorance.   1Tim 2:14;
     Philo, *Op*
He was persuaded by the woman's words, forgot   151 (53)
45 about his immortal creator, and neglected clear commands.
Therefore, instead of good they received evil, as they had done.
And then they sewed the leaves of the sweet fig tree
and made clothes and put them on each other.
They concealed their plans, because shame had come upon them.
50 The Immortal became angry with them and expelled them
from the place of immortals. For it had been decreed
that they remain in a mortal place, since they had not kept
the command of the great immortal God, and attended to it.
But they, immediately, going out on the fruitful earth
55 wept with tears and groans. Then
the immortal God himself spoke to them for the better:
"Increase, multiply,ᶜ and work on earth   Gen 1:28
with skill, so that by sweat you may have your fill of food."   Gen 3:19
Thus he spoke, but he made the serpent, cause of the deceit,
60 press the earth with belly and flank,   Gen 3:14
having bitterly driven him out. He aroused a dire enmity
between them. The one guards his head
to save it, the other his heel, for death is at hand
in the proximity of men and malignant poisonous snakes.

The first generation

65 And then the race multiplied as the universal ruler
himself commanded, and innumerable peoples grew
one after another. They constructed all sorts
of houses and also made cities and walls,
well and with understanding. To these he granted
70 a lengthy day for a very lovely life. For they did not
die worn out with troubles, but as if overcome by sleep.ᵈ   1.301
Blessed were the great-hearted mortals, whom the
immortal savior king, God, loved. But they also
sinned, smitten with folly. For they shamelessly
75 ridiculed their fathers and dishonored their mothers.
Plotters against their brothers, they did not know their familiar friends.
They were polluted, sated with the blood of people,
and they made wars. Upon them came a final
ruin, cast from heaven, which removed them,
80 terrible ones, from life. But Hades received them.
They called it Hades, since Adam first went (there)
having tasted death, and earth covered him.
Therefore all men who are born on earth
are said to go to the House of Hades.ᵉ
85 But all these, even when they went to Hades,
had honor, since they were the first race.

---

c. The command to multiply is given here *after* the Fall.

d. Vss. 65–124 show close contacts with Hesiod, *Works and Days* 109–74, both in ideas and in terminology. The division of this segment of history into five generations is, of course, inspired by Hesiod.

e. The attempt to associate Hades with Adam is apparently original to the Sibyl. Needless to say it is without foundation.

The second generation

But when it had received these, he fashioned again
another very diverse second race from the most righteous men who were
    left.
These were concerned with
90 fair deeds, noble pursuits, proud honor,
and shrewd wisdom. They practiced skills
of all kinds, discovering inventions by their needs.   1En 6–16; 69:4–15
One discovered how to till the earth with plows,
another, carpentry, another was concerned with sailing,
95 another, astronomy and divination by birds,
another, medicine, again another, magic.
Different ones devised that with which they were each concerned,
enterprising Watchers,ᶠ who received this appellation
because they had a sleepless mind in their hearts
100 and an insatiable personality. They were mighty, of great form,
but nevertheless they went under the dread house of Tartarus
guarded by unbreakable bonds, to make retribution,
to Gehenna of terrible, raging, undying fire.   2.292

The third generation

After these again a third race, mighty in spirit,
105 of overbearing terrible men appeared,
who performed many evils among themselves.
Wars, slaughters, and battles destroyed theseᵍ
continually, men of proud heart.

The fourth generation

After these things, in succession came another race of men,
110 late of fulfilment, the youngest, bloodthirsty, indiscriminate,
in the fourth generation.ʰ They shed much blood,
neither fearing God nor respecting men.
For a raging wrath and grievous impiety
was indeed inflicted on them.
115 Wars and slaughters and battles
cast some to the netherworld, though they were miserable
impious men. Others the heavenly God himself
later removed from his world in wrath,
draping them around with great Tartarus, under the base of the earth.

The fifth generation

120 Again he made afterward another far inferior race of men,
for whom thereafter immortal God fashioned no good,
since they suffered many evils.
For they were insolent, much more than those Giants,ⁱ
crooked ones, abominably pouring forth slander.

---

f. In 1En 6–16 the "Watchers" are identified with
the fallen "sons of God" of Gen 6. Fragments of
the myth are also found in 1En 69, 86–88; Jub 5;
2En 18:7 (rec. A); TReu 5:6f.; TNaph 3:5; CD 2:18;
1QapGen 2:1; 2Pet 2:4; Jude 6, etc. In SibOr 1 the
"Watchers" are a generation of humans, but their
mastery of diverse skills is paralleled in 1En 7f., 69,
and their punishment in a "Gehenna of fire" in 1En
10:7, 13. On Gehenna see SibOr 2.293. The term
ʿîr, "Watcher," is found in Dan 4:10, 14, 20.
    g. Cf. Hesiod, *Theogony* 228.
    h. In Hesiod, *Works and Days* 156–60, the fourth

generation is "nobler and more righteous."
    i. In Hesiod, *Theogony* 185, the Giants spring from
the Earth when it is impregnated by the blood of
Heaven, who had been castrated by Cronos. They are
also mentioned in Homer, *Odyssey* 7.59; 10.120. In
Gen 6:4 (LXX) the Giants are begotten by the fallen
"sons of God." Here in SibOr 1 the Giants are simply
identified with the Watchers. See also Philo's allegorical treatment of the Giants in *De gigantibus*. The
analogy between Gen 6 and the Giants of Greek
mythology is noted by Josephus, *Ant* 1.3.1 (73).

Noah bidden prepare for the Flood

125 Noah alone among all was most upright and true,
a most trustworthy man, concerned for noble deeds.[j]
To him God himself spoke as follows from heaven:
"Noah, embolden yourself, and proclaim repentance
to all the peoples, so that all may be saved.
130 But if they do not heed, since they have a shameless spirit,
I will destroy the entire race with great floods of waters.
But I bid you to construct quickly an imperishable
wooden house, flourishing with unthirsting roots.
I will place a mind in your breast, and crafty
135 skill, and (will put) measures in your lap; I will take care of everything
so that you and as many as live with you will be saved.

Gen 6:9;
WisSol 10:4f.
Sir 44:17

3.403; 1.185; 5.185

A riddle on the name of God

I am the one who is, but you consider in your heart:[k]
I am robed with heaven, draped around with sea,
the earth is the support of my feet, around my body is poured
140 the air, the entire chorus of stars revolves around me.
I have nine letters, I am of four syllables. Consider me.[l]
The first three have two letters each.
The last has the rest, and five are consonants.
The entire number is: twice eight
145 plus three hundred, three tens and seven. If you know who I am
you will not be uninitiated in my wisdom.

Frag. 1.7; 8.429–36; 3.20
Ex 3:14

Isa 66:1

1.326–30; 5.1–51; 8.148;
11–14 (passim);
Rev 13:18; EBar 9:8

Noah preaches repentance

Thus he spoke, but an immeasurable fear seized the man, such a thing
     did he hear.
And then, having craftily devised all in turn,
he entreated the peoples and began to speak in words like these:[m]
150 "Men sated with faithlessness, smitten with a great madness,
what you did will not escape the notice of God, for he knows all things,
the immortal savior, who oversees everything, who commanded me
to announce to you, so that you may not be destroyed by your hearts.
Be sober, cut off evils, and stop fighting violently
155 with each other, having a bloodthirsty heart,
drenching much earth with human blood.
Mortals, stand in awe of the exceedingly great, fearless
heavenly creator, imperishable God, who inhabits the vault of heaven,
and entreat him, all of you—for he is good—
160 for life, cities, and the whole world,
four-footed animals and birds, so that he will be gracious to all.
For the time will come when the whole immense world of men
perishing by waters will wail with a dread refrain.
Suddenly you will find the air in confusion
165 and the wrath of the great God will come upon you from heaven.
It will truly come to pass that the immortal savior

2Pet 2:5

---

j. Philo, *Congr* 90, says that Noah was the first
righteous man.
     k. Vss. 137–46 are found in the Tübingen The-
osophy 81. Cf. also the Ps-Orph fragments preserved
by Aristobulus in Eusebius, *PrEv* 13.12.5. Similar
formulations are also found in the magical papyri.
     l. The riddle remains problematic. Kurfess plau-

sibly identifies the letters as *monogenēs*, but the numerical values do not produce the required total.
Other unsuccessful proposals noted by Geffcken are
theos sōtēr and *zōēs buthos*. For a parody of gematria
see Lucian, *Alexander*, 11.
     m. For Noah as a preacher see Josephus, *Ant* 1.3.1
(74); 2Pet 2:5; ApPaul 50.

will cast forth upon men[n] . . . unless you propitiate God
and repent as from now, and no longer anyone
do anything ill-tempered or evil, lawlessly against one another
170 but be guarded in holy life.''
When they heard him they sneered at him, each one,   ApPaul 50
calling him demented, a man gone mad.
Then again Noah cried out a refrain:
"O very wretched, evil-hearted fickle men,[o]   8.184–87;
175 abandoning modesty, desiring shamelessness,   cf. 2.254–83; 3.36–45;
Rom 1:29–31; 13:13;
tyrants in fickleness and violent sinners,   1Cor 5:10f.; 6:9f.
liars, sated with faithlessness, evildoers, truthful in nothing,
adulterers, ingenious at pouring out slander,
not fearing the anger of the most high God,
180 you who were preserved till the fifth generation to make retribution.
You do not bewail each other, cruel ones, but laugh.
You will laugh with a bitter smile when this comes to pass,
I say, the terrible and strange water of God.   7.7
Whenever the abominable race of Rheia,[p] a perennial shoot   3.402–9
185 on the earth, flourishing with unthirsting roots,   1.133, etc.
disappears root and all in a single night,
and the earth-shaking land-quaker will scatter cities
complete with their inhabitants, and the hiding places of the earth and
    will undo walls,
then also the entire world of innumerable men
190 will die. But as for me, how much will I lament, how much will I weep
in my wooden house, how many tears will I mingle with the waves?
For if this water commanded by God comes on,
earth will swim, mountains will swim, even the sky will swim.   7.9–12
All will be water and all things will perish in water.
195 Winds will stop, and there will be a second age.
O Phrygia, you will emerge first from the surface of the water.
You, first, will nourish another generation of men
as it begins again. You will be nurse for all.''

Noah enters the Ark

But when he had spoken these things in vain to a lawless generation
200 the Most High appeared. He again cried out and spoke.
"Now the time is at hand, Noah, (to say all in turn),
to do to the immense world everything
which on that day I promised and indicated to you,
as much as the myriad evils generations did previously, on account of
    a faithless people.
205 But quickly go on board with your sons and wife   Gen 7:7;
and daughters-in-law. Call as many as I bid you to address,   1Pet 3:20
species of four-footed animals, and serpents and birds.
I will subsequently put in the breasts
of as many as I apportion life to go willingly.''
210 Thus he spoke. But the man went, cried out loudly and spoke
and then his spouse and sons and daughters-in-law
entered the wooden house. But then
the other creatures went in turn, as many as God wished to save.[q]

n. Geffcken assumes a lacuna here: "It will truly come to pass that He will cast forth upon . . . the immortal savior . . .''

o. Lists of vices recur frequently in the Sibylline corpus, NT, Philo, and other hellenistic and Jewish writings. See H. Conzelmann, *I Corinthians* (Philadelphia, 1975) p. 100.

p. Rheia, or Rhea, was daughter of Ouranos and Gaia, wife of Cronos, mother of Zeus and the gods. Here the "race of Rheia" should probably be understood as those who worship the pagan gods.

q. Reading *rhusai* for *rhexai* (Hase, listed by Geffcken).

But when the joining bolt was about the shutter,
215 fitted to a side in the polished wall,
    then indeed the plan of the heavenly God was accomplished.

The Flood

He threw clouds together and hid the brightly gleaming disk.
Having covered the moon, together with the stars, and the crown of
      heaven
all around, he thundered loudly, a terror to mortals,
220 sending out hurricanes. All the storm winds were gathered together
    and all the springs of waters were released
    as the great cataracts were opened from heaven,
    and from the recesses of the earth and the endless abyss
    measureless waters appeared and the entire immense earth was covered.
225 The wondrous house itself swam on the flood.
    Battered by many raging waves and swimming   CavTr (ed. Budge), p. 114
    under the impact of the winds, it surged terribly.
    The keel cut immense foam
    as the rushing waters were moved.
230 But when God had deluged the entire world with rains   Gen 8:6
    then Noah considered that he might look on
    the counsel of the immortal, and see the Hades of Nereus.[r]
    He quickly opened the shutter from the polished wall,
    fixed as it was skillfully with fastenings opposite each other.
235 Beholding the great mass of limitless waters,
    Noah was struck with terror to see with his eyes
    only death on all sides,[s] and he quivered greatly at heart.
    And then the air drew back a little, since it had labored many days
    drenching the whole world, and showed then the great vault
240 of heaven at evening, as it were bloodied, greenish-yellow,
    and the brightly gleaming disk hard pressed. Noah barely maintained
      his courage.
    And then taking one dove aside,[t]
    he cast it out, so that he might know in his heart
    whether firm land had yet appeared. But she, laboring with her wings,
245 having flown all over, returned again; for the water
    was not receding, but rather it had filled everything.
    But he waited again some days and sent a dove once more,
    so that he might know if the great waters had ceased.
    But she, flying, winged her way and went on the land.
250 Having rested herself a little on the damp land,
    she returned to Noah again, bringing an olive twig,
    a great sign of her message. Courage
    and great joy seized them all because they were hoping to see land.
    And then afterward he sent out quickly another black-winged
255 bird. But this one, trusting in his wings,
    flew prudently, and when he came to the land he stayed there.
    And Noah knew that land was near, closer by.

r. Nereus was an old sea-god.

s. The text is corrupt. I read *moron monon ophthalmoisin* with Alexandre.

t. Vss. 233–57 diverge from the biblical narrative and are more closely related to Babylonian traditions. (Izdubar Epic Tablet XI; A. Jeremias in W. Roscher, *Ausführliches Lexikon der griechischen und römischen Mythologie* [Leipzig, 1909] vol. 2, p. 798.) In Gen Noah sends first a raven, then a dove, three times. Here he sends two doves and then a "black-winged bird," or raven. The latter is the sequence in the Babylonian account. In both Babylonian and Sibylline accounts the second bird touches the ground. This detail is also found in Josephus, *Ant* 1.3.5 (92) and in Berossus F 4:15 (Jacoby, *FGH*, vol. 3C, p. 380). In the Gilgamesh epic (*ANET*, p. 95) the second bird finds no resting place. In Gen 8:11 the second bird brings back an olive twig. This detail is also picked up in SibOr 1.251.

But when the heavenly craft had swum to and fro
on the dashing waves, by the billows of the sea,
260 it was fastened on a small beach and made fast.

The Ark lands in Phrygia

There is a certain tall lofty mountain on the dark
mainland of Phrygia.ᵘ It is called Ararat.
When all were about to be saved on it,
thereupon there was a great heartfelt longing.
265 There the springs of the great river Marsyos had sprung up.
In this place the Ark remained on lofty summits
when the waters had subsided. Then again from heaven
the wondrous voice of the great God cried out
as follows: "Noah, trustworthy righteous man who has been preserved,   7.8
270 go forth boldly with your sons and wife
and three daughters-in-law and fill the whole earth
increasing and multiplying, dealing justly   1.57; Gen 9:1
with each other, to generations of generations, until
the whole race of men comes to trial, when there will be judgment for
    all.''
275 Thus the heavenly voice spoke. But Noah took courage
and jumped to the land from the Ark, and his sons with him
and his wife, and daughters-in-law and serpents and birds,
the species of four-footed animals and all the other creatures together
went out of the wooden house into one place.
280 And then Noah, most righteous of men,
came out eighth, having fulfilled forty-one dawns   Gen 7:17
on the waters, through the counsels of the great God.

The sixth generation

Then again a new generation of life dawned,
the first golden,ᵛ excellent one, which is the sixth
285 since the time of the first formed man. Its name is
"heavenly," for God will take care of everything.
O the first race of the sixth generation! O great joy!
in which I later shared,ʷ when I escaped dire destruction,
having been much buffeted by waves, suffering terrible things with my   3.823–27; Prologue 33
    husband and brothers-in-law,
290 and father-in-law and mother-in-law, and fellow brides.
I will tell exactly. There will be a multicolored flower
on the fig tree. Time will be at its midpoint. There will be
a royal scepter-bearing rule. For three great-spirited kings,ˣ   3.110–15
most righteous men, will destroy the fates
295 and will rule for a period of many years, administering justice
to men. They will be concerned with labor, and fair deeds.
The earth will rejoice, sprouting with many
spontaneous fruits, overladen with offspring.
Those who give nourishment will be ageless, always.

---

u. The usual location of Ararat in Armenia is given
by Josephus, *Ant* 1.3.5 (90). Africanus, reported by
Syncellus, located it in Parthia, but recorded that
some thought it was in Phrygia (Geffcken). Berossus
F 4:16 locates the landing place of the ark in Armenia.

v. On vss. 283–314 cf. Hesiod, *Works and Days*
108–39.

w. In Constantine's "Speech to the Saints," 18
(Kurfess, *Sibyllinische Weissagungen*, p. 208) the

Erythrean Sibyl is said to have lived in the sixth
generation after the Flood and to have been a priestess
of Apollo. The relationship to Noah is also noted in
the scholion to the *Phaedrus* 244b.

x. The three sons of Noah: Shem, Ham, and Japheth (Gen 6:9). In SibOr 3.110–15 the three are
identified as Cronos, Titan, and Iapetus. Presumably
the similarity of the names Japheth and Iapetus fa-
cilitated the equation.

300 Free from hard raging diseases
　　they will die, smitten by sleep, and will go away   1.71
　　to Acheron in the halls of Hades, and there
　　they will have honor, since they were a race of blessed ones,
　　happy men, to whom Sabaoth gave a noble mind.
305 To these also he always confided his counsels.
　　But they will be blessed, even entering Hades.

The seventh generation: the Titans

　　Then thereafter another grievous, mighty second
　　race of earthborn men (will arise),
　　the Titans.[y] Each individual will have a similar form,   3.147–58
310 appearance, and size; there will be one nature and one language,
　　as God previously put in their breasts, from the first generation.
　　But they also will have a proud heart
　　and finally rushing toward destruction will plot
　　to fight in opposition against the starry heaven.[z]   Dan 8:10f.;
315 And then the rushing of the mighty ocean of raging waters[a2]   Isa 14:13;
　　will be among them. But the great Sabaoth in anger   Rev 12:4
　　　　　　　　　　　　　　　　　　　　　　　　　　　　　　　Isa 17:12;
　　will shut them out, preventing them, because he promised   Ps 65:7
　　not to make a flood again against evil-spirited men.
　　But when he will make the immense billow of many waters   Gen 9:11;
　　　　　　　　　　　　　　　　　　　　　　　　　　　　　　　Isa 54:9f.
320 of a wave surging this way and that,   Sir 44:19
　　to cease from anger, the great loud thundering God will reduce   Job 38:
　　the depths of the sea to other measures, having defined it   8–11; Prov
　　　　　　　　　　　　　　　　　　　　　　　　　　　　　　　8:29; Pss
　　around the land with harbors and rough shores.   65:7; 104:9;
　　　　　　　　　　　　　　　　　　　　　　　　　　　　　　　PrMan 3

Christian passage on the incarnation and life of Christ

　　Then indeed the son of the great God will come,[b2]
325 incarnate, likened to mortal men on earth,
　　bearing four vowels, and the consonants in him are two.   1.141–45,
　　I will state explicitly the entire number for you.   etc.
　　For eight units, and equal number of tens in addition to these,
　　and eight hundreds will reveal the name[c2]
330 to men who are sated with faithlessness. But you, consider in your heart
　　Christ, the son of the most high, immortal God.
　　He will fulfill the law of God—he will not destroy it—   Mt 5:17
　　bearing a likeness which corresponds to types,[d2] and he will teach
　　　　everything.
　　Priests will bring gifts to him, bringing forward gold,   Mt 2:11
335 myrrh, and incense. For he will also do all these things.
　　But when a certain voice will come through the desert land   Mt 3:1–6;
　　bringing tidings to mortals, and will cry out to all   Mk 1:1–6;
　　　　　　　　　　　　　　　　　　　　　　　　　　　　　　　Lk 3:1–6;
　　to make the paths straight and cast away   Jn 1:23

---

y. The Titans in Greek mythology were children of Heaven and Earth. Cronos was the youngest of the Titans and their leader. The revolt of the Titans against Zeus is recounted in Hesiod, *Theogony* 618–885, Apollodorus, *Library* 1.2.1; 6.3.

z. In Hesiod, *Theogony* 687–735, the Titans were defeated by the thunderbolt of Zeus and imprisoned at the ends of the earth. In the more elaborate account of the revolt against Zeus by Nonnos of Panopolis in Egypt (5th cent. A.D.) the revolt includes an attack by Typhon on the stars (*Dionysiaca* 2.361f.). The revolt against the stars in the biblical tradition may

be related to the fragmentary Ugaritic myth of Athtar's attempt to occupy the throne of Baal (*ANET*, p. 140).

a2. The rushing of the ocean must be seen against a long background of the metaphorical use of the sea as a symbol of chaos in the OT, which derives ultimately from the role of Yamm in the Ugaritic myths. Cf. Hab 3:15; Isa 7:12–14.

b2. Vss. 324–400 are Christian. Cf. Tübingen *Theosophy*, 83.

c2. *Iēsous* has a numerical equivalence of 888.

d2. I.e. which fulfills the implicit prophecies of the OT. On vss. 332–82, cf. SibOr 8.269–320.

evils from the heart, and that every human person

340 be illumined by waters, so that, being born from above   Jn 3:3

they may no longer in any respect at all transgress justice

—but a man with barbarous mind, enslaved to dances   Mk 6:17–29;

will cut out this voice and give it as a reward—   Mt 14:3–12

then there will suddenly be a sign to mortals when a beautiful

345 stone which has been preserved will come from the land of Egypt.   1Pet 2:4; Mt 2:20

Against this the people of the Hebrews will stumble. But the gentiles   1Pet 2:4 (Isa 8:14f.)

will be gathered under his leadership.

For they will also recognize God who rules on high

on account of this man's path in common light.

For he will show eternal life to chosen men

350 but will bring the fire upon the lawless for (all) ages.   Mt 11:2–6;

Then indeed he will cure the sick and all who are   Lk 7:18–23

blemished, as many as put faith in him.

The blind will see, and the lame will walk.   8.205–7

The deaf will hear; those who cannot speak will speak.

355 He will drive out demons, there will be a resurrection of the dead;

he will walk the waves, and in a desert place   6.13; Mk 6:45–51; Mt 14:22–33

he will satisfy five thousand from five loaves   8.275–78; Mt 14:13–21;

and a fish of the sea, and the leftovers of these   Mk 6:30–44; 8:1–10;

will fill twelve baskets for the hope of the peoples.[e2]   Lk 9:10–17; Jn 6:1–13

360 And then Israel, intoxicated, will not perceive[f2]   Isa 6:9f.; Mt 13:13–15;

nor yet will she hear, afflicted with weak ears.   Mk 4:12; Lk 8:10;

But when the raging wrath of the Most High comes upon the Hebrews   Jn 12:40; Acts 28:26

it will also take faith away from them,

because they did harm to the son of the heavenly God.

365 Then indeed Israel, with abominable lips

and poisonous spittings, will give this man blows.

For food they will give him gall and for drink

unmixed vinegar, impiously, smitten in breast   Mt 27:34

and heart with an evil craze, not seeing with their eyes

370 more blind than blind rats, more terrible than poisonous

creeping beasts, shackled with heavy sleep.[g2]

But when he will stretch out his hands and measure all,

and bear the crown of thorns—and they will stab

his side with reeds—on account of this, for three hours   Mt 27:27–31; Mk 15:16–20;

375 there will be monstrous dark night in midday.   Jn 19:1–3 Mt 27:45;

And then indeed the temple of Solomon will effect[h2]   Mk 15:33; Lk 23:44

a great sign for men, when he goes to the house of Adonis[i2]   8.305f.; Mt 27:51;

announcing the resurrection to the dead.   Mk 15:38; Lk 23:45

But when he comes to light again in three days   1Pet 3:19 (Eph 4:9?)

380 and shows a model to men and teaches all things,

he will mount on clouds and journey to the house of heaven   Acts 1:9

leaving to the world the account of the gospel.

Named after him, a new shoot will sprout

from the nations, of those who follow the law of the Great One.

385 But also after these things there will be wise leaders,

and then there will be thereafter a cessation of prophets.

---

e2. Geffcken assumes a lacuna here. One MS, ψ, inserts: "Then, in addition to what has been said, the Erythrean adduces the account of the mad and unforgivable outrage of the killers of the Lord and of the movement of all this which took place on this account and the resurrection of the dead as follows:"

f2. On vss. 360–80, cf. SibOr 8.287–320.

g2. Cf. the widespread metaphor of sleep and waking in gnostic literature—e.g. Berlin Codex 58:16–59:1, but also Eph 5:14.

h2. Reading *ektelesē* (ψ, Alexandre, Rzach) for *ekelesei*.

i2. I.e. Hades. For the myth of Adonis see Ovid, *Metamorphoses* 10.298–559, 708–39.

Prophecy of dispersion of the Jews

Then when the Hebrews reap the bad harvest,
a Roman king will ravage much gold and silver.[j2]
Thereafter there will be other kingdoms
390 continuously, as kingdoms perish,
and they will afflict mortals. But there will be
a great fall for those men when they launch on unjust haughtiness.
But when the temple of Solomon falls in the illustrious land
cast down by men of barbarian speech
395 with bronze breastplates, the Hebrews will be driven from their land;
wandering, being slaughtered, they will mix much darnel in their wheat.
There will be evil strife for all men;
and the cities, violated in turn,
will weep for each other on receiving the wrath of the great
400 God in their bosom, since they committed an evil deed.

2.164;
14.356; Mt
13:36–43;
Rev 14:15

Mt 24:7;
Mk 13:8;
Lk 21:10

---

j2. An obvious reference to the defeat of the Jews in A.D. 70. Vs. 393 refers to the same event. The "other kingdoms" of vs. 389 are probably an oracular cliché. In any case, they do not precede the fall of the Temple.

THE SIBYLLINE ORACLES
Book 2

The inspiration of the Sibyl

When indeed God stopped my most perfectly wise song
as I prayed many things, he also again placed in my breast
a delightful utterance of wondrous words.
I will speak the following with my whole person in ecstasy
5 For I do not know what I say,[a] but God bids me utter each thing.

2.346f;
3.1–7,
295–300,
489–91;
11.322–24;
12.293–95;
13.172f.

Prophecy of disasters in the tenth generation

Mt. 24:7;
Mk 13:8;
Lk 21:10;
4Ezra
5:1–7, etc.

But when on earth there are raging earthquakes
and thunderbolts, thunders, and lightnings . . . and mildew of the land
and frenzy of jackals and wolves, and slaughters
and destructions of men and bellowing oxen,
10 four-footed cattle and laboring mules
and goats and sheep, then much farmland
will be left barren through neglect,
and fruits will fail. Selling of free men into slavery
will be practiced among very many people, and robbing of temples.
15 Then indeed the tenth generation of men[b] will also appear

3.156–61; 4.20.47,86; 7.97;
8.199; 1En 91:15; 11QMelch 7

after these things, when the earth-shaking lightning-giver[c]
will break the glory of idols and shake the people of

8.37–49

seven-hilled Rome.[d] Great wealth will perish,
burned in a great fire by the flame of Hephaestus.[e]

3.350–62; 5.159,177f.,
367,434–46; 8.37–49;
Rev 17f.

20 Then there will be bloody precipitation from heaven . . .
but the entire world of innumerable men

4.134; 12.56f.; 14.89

will kill each other in madness. In the tumult
God will impose famines and pestilence[f] and thunderbolts
on men who adjudicate without justice.

Mt 24:7; Mk 13:8; Lk 21:10;
Lactantius, *DivInst* 7.15.10
3.332; 8.175;
11.46, 240; 12.114

25 There will be a scarcity of men throughout the whole world
so that if one were to see a man's footprint on the ground, one would
    wonder.

4Ezra 16:27

Then further, the great God who lives in the sky
will be a savior of pious men in all respects.
Then also there will be deep peace and understanding,

3.619–23; 744–56;
2Bar 29:5–8; 1En 10:18–20;
SibOr 8.209–12

30 and the fruitful earth will again bear more numerous fruits,
being neither divided nor in servitude any longer.
Every harbor, every port will be free for men
as it was before, and shamelessness will perish.
And then again God will perform a great sign,

5.155

---

a. Cf. Plato, *Meno* 99d; Prologue to SibOr, 90.

b. At this point the original numerical sequence of the Jewish oracle is resumed. In the commentary on Virgil's Eclogue 4:4, Servius (c. A.D. 400) states that the Cumean Sibyl divided history into ten generations. In addition to the Jewish and Christian passages listed in the margin, the idea is also found in the Persian *Zand-I Vohūman Yasn* (Bahman Yasht) 1:11; 3:29; 4:1, etc., and the rabbinic *PRE 11*, Targum to Esther (beginning) and second Targum to Esther (beginning). See further in the general introduction to SibOr 2.

Note also that the Flood took place in the tenth

generation from Adam (cf. Gen 5). For Philo's reflections on the number 10 see *Congr* 90–121; *Dec* 20–31.

c. "Earth-shaker" was a traditional epithet of Poseidon, "lightning-giver" of Zeus.

d. So also the Oracle of Hystaspes in Lactantius, *DivInst* 7.15.19. For references in later Christian literature to the destruction of Rome see Bousset, *The Antichrist Legend*, pp. 121–32.

e. The Greek god of fire.

f. A proverbial cliché since Hesiod, *Works and Days* 243. Cf. Herodotus 7.171; Thucydides 2.54, etc. It is especially common in oracular literature.

35 for a star will shine like a resplendent crown,[g]
resplendent, gleaming from the radiant heaven
for no small number of days. For then he will show
from heaven a crown to men who strive in contest.

The heavenly contest

1Cor 9:24; Heb 12:1; 2Tim 4:7;
Gal 5:7; Phil 2:16;
4Mac 17:11–14; 6:10; TJob 27

Then again[h] there will be a great contest for entry
40 to the heavenly city.[i] It will be universal for all
men, holding the glory of immortality.
Then every people will strive for the immortal prizes
of most noble victory. For no one there can shamelessly
buy a crown for silver.
45 For holy Christ will make just awards to these
and crown the worthy. But to martyrs he will give
an immortal treasure, to those who pursue the contest even to death.
He will give an imperishable prize from the treasure
to virgins who run well and to all men
50 who perform justice and to diverse nations
who live piously and acknowledge one God,
who love marriage and refrain from adultery.
He will give rich gifts and eternal hope to these also.
For every soul of mortals is a gracious gift of God
55 and it is not lawful for men to defile it with any grievous things.

[Extract from Pseudo-Phocylides:[j]]

On justice

Do not gain wealth unjustly, but live from legitimate things.
Be satisfied with what is available, and refrain from what belongs to
    others.
Do not tell lies, but preserve[k] all truths.
(Do not revere idols, to no good purpose, but always the imperishable
    one.)
60 First, honor God, then your parents.
Dispense all things justly, and do not come to an unjust judgment.[l]
Do not unjustly cast down poverty. Do not be partial in judgment.
If you judge badly, God will judge you later.
Avoid false witness. Adjudicate justly.
65 Guard that which is deposited with you. Preserve love[m] in all things.
Give just measures, but an overmeasure to all[n] is good.
Do not cheat in measuring, but weigh evenly.
Do not commit perjury either in ignorance or willingly.
God detests a perjurer, whatever one swears.[o]

---

g. Such astral phenomena are frequently under-stood as signs of great changes and upheavals in the hellenistic age. The astrological writings of Nechepso and Petosiris from Egypt in the 2nd cent. B.C. consist of the interpretation of such signs. Cf. the star and comet which appear before the fall of Jerusalem in Josephus, *War* 6.5.3 (289).

h. Reading *kai tote men megas autis agōn* (Rzach) for *kai tothmai megas gar agōn*.

i. The *agōn*, or "contest," motif is derived from Stoicism (V. C. Pfitzner, *Paul and the Agon-Motif* [Leiden, 1967] pp. 23–37). It is also used extensively by Philo, *Agr* 113, 119; *Praem* 52; *Mut* 106; *Abr* 48. Also in later Christian literature: Clement of Alexandria, *Quis dives salvetur* 3; Tertullian, *Ad martyras* 3, etc.

j. See P. van der Horst, "Pseudo-Phocylides," in this vol., and *The Sentences of Pseudo-Phocylides with Introduction and Commentary* (SVTP 4; Leiden, 1978) for a more complete treatment. The translation offered here is an independent rendering of Geffcken's text. Nn. are added only where the sentences diverge from the edition of Young (D. Young, *Theognis, Ps.-Pythagoras, Ps.-Phocylides* [Leipzig, 1961, 1971]), which is used by van der Horst. Verses not in Young's edition are put in parentheses here. The first four verses of Young are omitted in SibOr 2.

k. Young: "Speak."

l. Young: "judgment for favor."

m. Young: "faith."

n. Young: "of all."

o. Young: "the immortal God . . . whoever swears."

70 (Never accept in your hand a gift which derives from unjust deeds.)
Do not steal seeds. Whoever takes for himself is accursed
(to generations of generations, to the scattering of life.
Do not practice homosexuality, do not betray information, do not
    murder.)
Give one who has labored his wage. Do not oppress a poor man.
75 Take heed of your speech. Keep a secret matter in your heart.
(Make provision for ophans and widows and those in need.)
Do not be willing to act unjustly, and therefore do not give leave to one
    who is acting unjustly.

On mercy

Give to the poor[p] at once and do not tell them to come tomorrow.
(With perspiring hand give a portion of corn to one who is in need.[q]   Did 1:6
80 Whoever gives alms knows that he is lending to God.
Mercy saves from death when judgment comes.
God wants not sacrifice but mercy instead of sacrifice.   8.390; Hos 6:6;
Therefore clothe the naked. Give the hungry a share of your bread.)   Mt 9:13; 12:7
Receive the homeless into your house and lead the blind.   8.404; Isa 58:7
85 Pity the shipwrecked, for the voyage is uncertain.
Give a hand to one who has fallen. Save a solitary man.
All have a common lot, the wheel of life,[r] unstable prosperity.
If you have wealth, stretch out your hand to the poor.
The things which God gave you, give of them to one in need.[s]
90 Every life of men is common, but falls out unequally.[t]
(When you see a poor man, never mock him with words
and do not verbally abuse a person who is at fault.
Life is assessed in death. Whether one acted
lawlessly or righteously will be distinguished when one comes to judg-
    ment.

On moderation

95 Do not damage your mind with wine or drink to excess.)   Tob 4:16
Do not eat blood. Abstain from what is sacrificed to idols.   Acts 15:20,
Gird on the sword, not for killing but for defense.   29; 21:25;
May you not use[u] it either lawlessly or righteously.   1Cor 8:10
For even if you kill an enemy, you defile your own hand.
100 Keep off a neighboring field. Do not trespass.   Ex 22:5;
(Every boundary is just; but trespass is grievous.)[v]   Deut 19:14
The acquisition of legitimate things is profitable, but that of unjust things
    is bad.
Do not damage any fruit of the soil when it is growing.
Let strangers have equal honor among citizens,
105 for all will experience exile of many hardships[w]
(as guests of each other. But no one will be a stranger among you
since you are all mortals of one blood),[x]   3.247
and a country has no secure place for men.[y]

---

p. Young has the singular "poor man" here.
q. Young (vs. 23): "It will fill your hand, give alms to the needy."
r. Young: "life is a wheel."
s. Young has the plural "needy."
t. Young (vs. 30): "Let all of life be in common and all things be in agreement."

u. Young: "need."
v. Young: "Measure is best of all, excesses are grievous."
w. Young (vs. 40): "we all experience poverty that makes one wander."
x. This is a common Stoic sentiment.
y. Slightly different wording in Young.

On money

(Neither wish to be wealthy nor pray for it. But pray for this:
110 to live on a little, having nothing unjust.)
The love of money is mother *of all evil.*
(Have no desire for gold or silver. Also in these
there will be double-edged iron which destroys the spirit.)
Gold and silver are always a deception for men.
115 Life-destroying gold, originator of evils, crushing all things,
would that you were not a desired affliction for men,
for because of you are battles, plunderings, murders,
children hostile to their parents and brothers to their kindred.

7.89;
Theognis
1155
3.325, 641;
8.17; 1Tim
6:10

On honesty and moderation

(Do not weave plots, and do not arm your heart against a friend.)
120 Do not hide one thought in your heart while you say another.
Do not change in your place like a many-footed creature which clings
    to rock.
Be straightforward with all. Speak what comes from your soul.
Whoever deliberately does injustice is an evil man. As for one who acts
    under compulsion,
I will not pronounce his end. But let the counsel of each man be straight.
125 Do not boast of wisdom or strength or wealth.
There is One, God, at once wise, powerful, and rich.
Do not wear out your heart[z] with passing evils
for that which has happened can no longer be undone.
Be not precipitous to the hand. Bridle wild anger,
130 for often one who struck a blow unintentionally committed murder.
Let your passions be normal, neither great nor excessive.
Abundant profit is not a good thing for mortals.
Much luxury draws toward inordinate desires.
Great wealth is proud, and it fosters arrogance.
135 Ire, when it takes the initiative,[a2] fashions a destructive frenzy.
Anger is a propensity, but wrath goes to excess.
The zeal of the good is noble, but that of the bad is bad.[b2]
The daring of the wicked is destructive, but that of the good brings
    glory.[c2]
Love of virtue is revered, but that of Aphrodite augments disgrace.
140 A man who is too simple is called a fool among the citizens.[d2]
Eat, drink, and discourse in moderation.
Of all things, moderation is best, but excess is grievous.[e2]
(Be not envious or faithless or a slanderer
or of evil mind, or an inordinate deceiver.)
145 Practice temperance. Refrain from base deeds.[f2]
Do not imitate evil but leave vengeance to justice,
for persuasion is a profit, but strife engenders strife in turn.
Do not trust quickly, before you see the end with certainty.
          [End of passage from Ps-Phoc]

Conclusion of the contest

This is the contest, these are the prizes, these the awards.

---

z. Young: "liver."
a2. Young: "steals over one."
b2. Young: "monstrous."
c2. Young: "greatly helps a man who labors at
noble deeds."

d2. Following Young's reading *hēdus agan
aphrōn* for *hēdus aganophrōn* (ψ).
e2. Young has the plural: "excesses."
f2. Young's vss. 70–75 are missing here. SibOr
2.145–48 corresponds to Young's 76–79.

150 This is the gate of life and entry to immortality
   which the heavenly God appointed as reward of victory
   for most righteous men. But they, when they receive
   the crown, will pass through this in glory.

Mt 21:13;
TAb 10
(rec. A), 9
(rec. B)

Signs of the end

But whenever this sign appears throughout the world,
155 children born with gray temples from birth,[g2]
   afflictions of men, famines, pestilence, and wars,
   change of times, lamentations, many tears;
   alas, how many people's children in the countries will feed
   on their parents, with piteous lamentations. They will place
160 their flesh in cloaks and bury them in the ground, mother of peoples,
   defiled with blood and dust. O very wretched
   dread evildoers of the last generation,
   infantile, who do not understand that when the species of females
   does not give birth,[h2] the harvest of articulate men has come.
165 The gathering together is near when some deceivers,
   in place of prophets, approach, speaking on earth.
   Beliar also will come[i2] and will do many signs
   for men.[j2] Then indeed there will be confusion of holy
   chosen and faithful men, and there will be a plundering
170 of these and of the Hebrews. A terrible wrath will come upon them
   when a people of ten tribes will come from the east
   to seek the people, which the shoot of Assyria destroyed,
   of their fellow Hebrews. Nations will perish after these things.

4Ezra 6:21
2.23, etc.
8.214;
14.298a

1.387, etc.
14.365

Mk 13:22; Mt 24:11,24;
Did 16; ApEl 1:12
3.63; 73; 2Cor 6:15;
AscenIs 2:4; 4:2; 1QM 13:10f.
3.66; ApEl 3; Did 16
3.69

4Ezra 13:40; AsMos 4:9;
Ant 11.5.2 (133)

Eschatological rule of the Hebrews

Later the faithful chosen Hebrews will rule over
175 exceedingly mighty men, having subjected them
   as of old, since power will never fail.
   The Most High, who oversees all, living in the sky,
   will spread sleep over men, having closed their eyes.
   O blessed servants, as many as the master, when he comes,
180 finds awake; for they have all stayed awake
   all the time looking expectantly with sleepless eyes.
   For he will come, at dawn, or evening, or midday.
   He will certainly come, and it will be as I say.
   It will come to pass for future generations, when from the starry heaven
185 all the stars appear in midday to all,
   with the two luminaries, as time presses on.

ApEl 3:45f.

Mt
24:45–51;
25:1–13; Lk
12:42–46
Did 16

3.804;
8.204; War
6.5.3 (288);
4Ezra 5:4

Coming of Elijah and other signs

Then the Thesbite,[k2] driving a heavenly chariot at full stretch from
heaven, will come on earth and then display three signs[l2]
to the whole world, as life perishes.

Mal 3:23;
ApEl 3:25;
Mt 11:14;
16:14;
17:10

---

g2. The oldest attestation of this sign is in Hesiod, *Works and Days* 181. It is also found in Stoic writings and in the Christian *Testamentum domini* 7.

h2. Cf. GEgyp; Clement of Alexandria, *Strom* 3.6.45; Tiburtine Sibyl (ed. Sackur), p. 181.

i2. Beliar (Belial) occurs more than thirty times as the demonic adversary in the Qumran scrolls.

j2. See further Bousset, *The Antichrist Legend,*

pp. 175–81.

k2. Elijah. Cf. Commodian, *Carmen apologeticum* 833; Lactantius, *DivInst* 7.17.1; Bousset, *The Antichrist Legend*, pp. 203–8.

l2. Did 16:6: "And then shall appear the signs of the truth. First the sign spread out in heaven, then the sign of the sound of the trumpet, and thirdly the resurrection of the dead."

190 Alas, for as many as are found bearing in the womb
on that day, for as many as suckle
infant children, for as many as dwell upon the wave;
alas, for as many as will see that day.
For a dark mist will cover the boundless world
195 east and west and south and north.

Mt 24:19;
Mk 13:17;
Lk 21:23;
ApEl 2:30

Destruction by fire

And then a great river of blazing fire
will flow from heaven,[m2] and will consume every place,
land and great ocean and gleaming sea,
lakes and rivers, springs and implacable Hades
200 and the heavenly vault. But the heavenly luminaries
will crash together, also into an utterly desolate form.[n2]
For all the stars will fall together from heaven on the sea.
All the souls of men will gnash their teeth,
burning in a river, and brimstone and a rush of fire
205 in a fiery plain, and ashes will cover all.[o2]
And then all the elements of the world will be bereft—
air, land, sea, light, vault of heaven, days, nights.
No longer will innumerable birds fly in the air.
Swimming creatures will no longer swim the sea at all.
210 No laden ship will voyage on the waves.
No guiding oxen will plow the soil.
No sound of trees under the winds. But at once all
will melt into one and separate into clear air.

2.286;
3.54, 72,
83; 7.121;
8.243, 338;
1En 52:6;
1QH
3:29–33

5.512–31;
8.340; 2Pet
3:12

8.190, 341; Mt 24:29;
Mk 13:25
2.305; 8.105, 231, 350;
Mt 14:12

4.179; ApEl 3:83
3.80f.; 8.337; Rev 6:12

ApEl
3:62f.

3.87; 8.412

The judgment

Then the imperishable angels of immortal God,
215 Michael, Gabriel, Raphael, and Uriel,[p2]
who know what evils anyone did previously,
lead all the souls of men from the murky dark
to judgment, to the tribunal of the great
immortal God.[q2] For one alone is imperishable,
220 the universal ruler, himself, who will be judge of mortals.

ApMos 40:3; 1En 9:1

1En 109:7; AscenIs 7:27

TAb 10–11 (rec. A)
9–10 (rec. B)

Resurrection of the dead

Then the heavenly one will give souls and breath and
voice to the dead and bones fastened
with all kinds of joinings . . . flesh and sinews
and veins and skin about the flesh, and the former hairs.
225 Bodies of humans, made solid in heavenly manner,
breathing and set in motion, will be raised on a single day.

4.181; Ezek
37:1–10;
ApPet 4

m2. The river of fire is a standard element in Persian eschatology, e.g. Bundahishn 30:19; Cf. also ApPet 5–6.

n2. This conception is found in Stoicism (e.g. Seneca, *Consolatio ad Marciam* 26:6) and in Berossus (Seneca, *Naturales quaestiones* 3.29.1).

o2. This passage refers to the sufferings involved in the destruction of the world by fire, not yet the eternal punishment of the damned. On vss. 200–13, cf. SibOr 8.337–50.

p2. So ψ, Kurfess. Geffcken, following φ with emendations, reads "Barakiel, Ramiel, Uriel, Samiel, Azael." Michael, Gabriel, Uriel, and Raphael,

in varying sequence, are the most usual archangels: 1En 9:1; ApMos 40:3; NumR 2:10; PR 46; PRE 4. Uriel is replaced by Phanuel in 1En 40:9; 54:6; 71:8, and by Sariel in 1QM 9:14–16. Barakiel, Ramiel, and Azael are fallen angels in Gen 6–13. Sammael is an evil angel in AscenIs.

q2. For the tribunal of God, cf. Dan 7, where the Ancient of Days presides. In TAb, Abel has the role of judge. In the Similitudes of 1En the "Son of Man" is judge. In Mt 19:28 the apostles will sit as judges. In 1Cor 2:6 all the faithful will judge. Most often, as here, God himself is judge.

Then Uriel, the great angel, will break the gigantic bolts,
of unyielding and unbreakable steel, of the gates
of Hades, not forged of metal; he will throw them wide open[r2]
230 and will lead all the mournful forms to judgment,
especially those of ancient phantoms, Titans
and the Giants and such as the Flood destroyed.
Also those whom the wave of the sea destroyed in the oceans,
and as many as wild beasts and serpents and birds
235 devoured; all these he will call to the tribunal.
Again, those whom the flesh-devouring fire destroyed by flame,
these also he will gather and set at the tribunal of God.
When Sabaoth Adonai, who thunders on high, dissolves fate
and raises the dead, and takes his seat
240 on a heavenly throne, and establishes a great pillar,[s2]
Christ, imperishable himself, will come in glory on a cloud
toward the imperishable one with the blameless angels.
He will sit on the right of the Great One, judging at the tribunal
the life of pious men and the way of impious men.
245 Moses, the great friend of the Most High, also will come,
having put on flesh. Great Abraham himself will come,
Isaac and Jacob, Joshua, Daniel and Elijah,
Habbakuk and Jonah, and those whom the Hebrews killed.
He will destroy all the Hebrews after Jeremiah,
250 judged on the tribunal, so that they may receive and make
appropriate retribution for as much as anyone did in mortal life.

Distinction of righteous and wicked

And then all will pass through the blazing river
and the unquenchable flame.[t2] All the righteous
will be saved, but the impious will then be destroyed
255 for all ages, as many as formerly did evil[u2]
or committed murders, and as many as are accomplices,
liars, and crafty thieves, and dread destroyers of houses,
parasites, and adulterers, who pour out slander,
terrible violent men, and lawless ones, and idol worshipers;
260 as many as abandoned the great immortal God
and became blasphemers and ravagers of the pious,
breakers of faith and murderers of the righteous men,
and as many elders and reverend deacons
as, by crafty and shameless duplicity regard[v2] . . .
265 judge with respect, dealing unjustly with others,
trusting in deceitful statements . . .
More destructive than leopards and wolves, and most wicked;
or as many as are very arrogant or are usurers,

Side references:

ApZeph
6–7; ApPet
4; cf.
Hesiod,
Theogony
732–33

1.91, 103;
2En 18

1En 61:5

7.27
Mt 25:31;
24:30;
16:27; Mk
8:38; 13:26;
ApPet 1;
ApEl 3:97;
Lk 9:26

Acts 7:56;
ApPet 6

4Ezra 1:39;
Mt 23:34,
37; Lk
11:49–51;
ApIoan (ed.
Tischendorf) p. 22

8.411;
ApPaul 31,
34, 39;
ApPet 6, 12

ApPet
8–12;
ApPaul
31–43;
GkApEzra
4:1–24
1.175, etc.
Rev 21:8

ApPaul
35–36

---

r2. Lit. "straight." Uriel plays a similar role in
the judgment in ApPet 4.
s2. In Plato, *Republic* 10.616b (myth of Er), the
place of judgment is marked by a "straight light like
a pillar, most nearly resembling a rainbow." Its
fastenings held together the entire vault of heaven,
and from the extremities was stretched the spindle of
necessity. The concept is most probably Orphic. In
ApPet 9 a pillar of fire is an instrument of torture.
t2. The idea of a river ordeal is ancient in the
Near East and underlies many passages in the Psalms
(Ps 69:2f.; Ps 18:5; Jonah 2:4, 6). However, the river
of fire derives from Persian belief about the end-time
where it serves to distinguish the good from the bad.

Cf. Bundahishn 30:19f. (tr. West, *Sacred Books of
the East*, vol. 5, p. 125f.): "Afterwards the fire and
halo melt the Shatvairo in the hills and mountains,
and it remains on this earth like a river. Then all men
will pass into that melted metal and become pure;
when one is righteous, then it seems to him just as
though he walks continually in warm milk; but when
wicked, then it seems to him in such as manner as
though, in the world, he walks continually in melted
metal." Cf. Lactantius, *DivInst* 7.21.6, who may be
dependent on the Persian Oracle of Hystaspes.
u2. On lists of vices cf. n. on SibOr 1.174.
v2. Lacuna: presumably "regard persons."

who gather interest upon interest in their homes
270 and harm in each case orphans and widows,
or as many as give to widows and orphans
what derives from unjust deeds, and as many as make reproach
when they give from the fruit of their own labors; as many as
abandoned their parents in old age, not making return at all, not providing
275 nourishment to their parents in turn.[w2] Also as many as disobeyed
or answered back an unruly word to their parents,
or as many as denied pledges they had taken, and
such servants as turned against their masters.
Again, those who defiled the flesh by licentiousness,
280 or as many as undid the girdle of virginity
by secret intercourse, as many as aborted
what they carried in the womb, as many as cast forth their offspring
unlawfully.

Margin notes:
EpBar 19:11; ShepHerm Sim 9.24.2

3.765; ApPet 8; EpBar 19:5; Did 2; ApPaul 40

Punishment of the wicked

These and the sorcerers and sorceresses in addition to them
will the anger of the heavenly imperishable God
285 also bring near to the pillar, around which an undying
fiery river flows in a circle. All these at once
the angels of the immortal, everlasting God will
punish terribly from above with whips of flame,
having bound them around with fiery chains
290 and unbreakable bonds. Then, in the dead of night,
they will be thrown under many terrible infernal beasts
in Gehenna,[x2] where there is immeasurable darkness.
But when they have inflicted many punishments
on all whose heart was evil, then later
295 a fiery wheel from the great river will press them hard
all around, because they were concerned with wicked deeds.
Then they will wail here and there at a distance
in most piteous fate, fathers and infant children,
mothers and weeping children at the breast.
300 They will not have their fill of tears, nor will their voice
be heard as they lament piteously here and there,
but in distress they will shout at length
below dark, dank Tartarus. In places unholy
they will repay threefold what evil deed they committed,
305 burning in much fire. They will all gnash their teeth,[y2]
wasting away with thirst and raging violence.
They will call death fair, and it will evade them.
No longer will death or night give these rest.
Often they will request God, who rules on high in vain,

Margin notes:
2.240, 252

ApZeph 5; GkApEzra 4:1–24

1.103; 4.43 Mt 5:22; AsMos 10:10

ApPet 12

Hesiod, Theogony 736–39 8.350–58

Rev 9:6; ApEl 2:24

---

w2. This is one of the outrages of the fifth generation in Hesiod, *Works and Days* 186f.

x2. In the OT, Gehenna refers to a valley outside Jerusalem where, on occasion, incense was burned and children were sacrificed to "Molech" (2Kgs 23:10; Jer 7:31; 32:35). It refers to a place of punishment for the dead in AsMos 10:10 and Mt 5:22. Cf. also 1En 27:2f.; 54:1–2, where the "valley" is not named.

The idea of a place of punishment in the netherworld was prominent in Orphism (e.g. Plato, *Republic* 10.614–21; *Gorgias* 523). The destruction of the wicked by fire is prominent in Persian belief about the end, but it is not an eternal punishment in the

netherworld. The idea of a fiery hell seems to be a Jewish development. It is suggested by Isa 66:24, but that passage does not imply that the wicked will be alive to feel the flames. The fallen "Watchers" are consigned to a fiery abyss consistently in 1En 10:13; 18:11, etc., and this punishment was extended to sinful humans (90:23f.; cf. 54:1f.). A place of fiery eternal punishment is presupposed in the Qumran scrolls (e.g. 1QS 2) and is ubiquitous in later apocalypses (e.g. Rev 19:20; 20:14f.). Darkness and gloom are characteristic of Tartarus in Hesiod, *Theogony* 736–39.

y2. Vss. 305–12 correspond to SibOr 8.350–58.

310 and then he will manifestly turn away his face from them.
    For he gave seven days of ages to erring men   4Ezra 7:101
    for repentance through the intercession[z2] of the holy virgin.[a3]

Rewards of the righteous

But as for the others, as many as were concerned with justice and noble
    deeds,
and piety and most righteous thoughts,
315 angels will lift them through the blazing river   ApPet 13
    and bring them to light and to life without care,
    in which is the immortal path of the great God
    and three springs of wine, honey, and milk.[b3]   8.208–12;
    The earth will belong equally to all, undivided by walls   3.622f.;
                                                                      5.282f.
320 or fences. It will then bear more abundant fruits
    spontaneously. Lives will be in common and wealth will have no   Virgil,
        division.   Eclogue
                                                                      4.18–22
    For there will be no poor man there, no rich, and no tyrant,   8.110f., 121
    no slave. Further, no one will be either great or small anymore.
    No kings, no leaders. All will be on a par together.
325 No longer will anyone say at all "night has come" or "tomorrow"   8.424–27
    or "it happened yesterday," or worry about many days.
    No spring, no summer, no winter, no autumn,
    no marriage, no death, no sales, no purchases,
    no sunset, no sunrise. For he will make a long day.
330 To these pious ones imperishable God, the universal ruler, will also
        give
    another thing.[c3] Whenever they ask the imperishable God
    to save men from the raging fire and deathless gnashing
    he will grant it, and he will do this.
    For he will pick them out again from the undying fire
335 and set them elsewhere and send them on account of his own people
    ᵗto another eternal life with the immortals
    in the Elysian plain where he has the long waves   ApPet 14;
    of the deep perennial Acherusian lake.[d3]   ApPaul 22

Confession of the Sibyl

Alas for me, wretched one. What will become of me on that day
340 in return for what I sinned, ill-minded one,   7.151–55
    busying myself about everything but caring neither for marriage nor for
        reasons?
    But also in my dwelling, which was that of a very wealthy man,
    I shut out those in need; and formerly I committed lawless deeds
    knowingly. But you, savior, rescue me, a brazen one,
345 from my scourges, though I have done shameless deeds.
    I beseech you to give me a little rest from the refrain,
    holy giver of manna, king of a great kingdom.

z2. Lit. "through the hand of."

a3. In 4Ezra 7:101 the souls of the dead have seven days of freedom after they separate from their bodies to see the eschatological secrets. Then they shall go to their destined abodes. 4Ezra goes on to say that there will be no intercession at the judgment. SibOr 2 apparently knew this tradition and so assigned the seven days to the intercession of the Virgin.

b3. Vss. 318–21—cf. SibOr 8.208–12. On the general concept of the transformation of the earth, cf. Isa 11 and Virgil's Fourth Eclogue.

c3. In ψ a refutation is inserted here: "Plainly false. For the fire which tortures the condemned will never cease. Even I would pray that this be so, though I am marked with very great scars of faults, which have need of very great mercy. But let babbling Origen be ashamed of saying that there is a limit to punishment." Cf. Origen, Princ 2.10.5, 6; Contra 5.15.

d3. The Elysian fields or Isles of the Blest appear in Homer, Odyssey 4.561–69 and Hesiod, Works and Days 167–73. They figured prominently in Orphic eschatology.

THE SIBYLLINE ORACLES, BOOK 3

Introduction

The third Sibyl is the only book of the collection that has received extensive scholarly attention.[1] The composite nature of the book has been recognized by virtually all scholars,[2] but the fragmentation of the book proposed by Geffcken[3] is certainly excessive. In fact we may distinguish three stages in the book:[4]
1. The main corpus: verses 97–349 and 489–829.
2. Oracles against various nations: 350–488.
3. Verses 1–96, which probably constitute the conclusion of a different book.
One verse (776) must be regarded as a Christian interpolation.[5]

1. The main corpus

In the main corpus of the book five oracles may be distinguished: (1) 97–161; (2) 162–95; (3) 196–294; (4) 545–656; (5) 657–808. The first of these, 97–161, stands apart from the rest of the book. It contains: (a) the fall of the tower of Babylon (97–104); (b) a euhemeristic account of the war of the Titans against Cronos and his sons (105–55); (c) a list of world empires (156–61).

The description of the fall of the tower has been widely thought to be a fragment from a collection of oracles of a Babylonian sibyl, perhaps influenced by Berossus, but this theory has been soundly refuted by Nikiprowetzky.[6] There is nothing in the Sibylline account that could not be developed from Genesis.

The euhemeristic account of Greek mythology is exceptional in Sibylline Oracles 3, and may possibly be borrowed from a non-Jewish source but, on the other hand, is not incompatible with anything else in the book.

The list of world empires is, of course, a typical Sibylline feature. Sibylline Oracles 3.156–61 lists eight kingdoms, but we should assume that the kingdom of Cronos is presupposed as a first kingdom and that a tenth, final kingdom is expected. The passage therefore conforms to the typical Sibylline division of history into ten periods.[7]

The entire section 3.97–161 serves as an introduction to the remaining portions of the book. It introduces the theme of world kingship and shows that it was a cause of strife from the beginning. It therefore provides a context for the oracles about the end-time that are in the rest of the book.

The other four sections present a recurring pattern: (a) sin, usually idolatry, which leads to (b) disaster and tribulation, which is terminated by (c) the advent of a king or kingdom. The third section of the book (196–294) differs from the others insofar as it is not about the end-time but describes the Babylonian exile and restoration. In the second section (162–95) the king who terminates the period of disasters is identified as the seventh king of Egypt from the Greek dynasty and in the fourth section (545–656) as a king "from the sun," which should be taken as a reference to an Egyptian king.[8] In the final section the reference is to a kingdom raised up by God (767).

DATE

The date of the main corpus is fixed by three references to the seventh king of Egypt in

---

[1] See especially the studies of A. Peretti, *La Sibilla Babilonese nella propaganda ellenistica*; V. Nikiprowetzky, *La Troisième Sibylle*; J. J. Collins, *The Sibylline Oracles of Egyptian Judaism*, pp. 21–71.

[2] See Collins, *The Sibylline Oracles*, p. 21. The only significant exception is Nikiprowetzky.

[3] Geffcken, *Komposition und Entstehungszeit*, pp. 1–17.

[4] Collins, *The Sibylline Oracles*, p. 28.

[5] Geffcken, *Komposition und Entstehungszeit*, p. 14. Nikiprowetzky, *La Troisième Sibylle*, p. 329, apparently takes the verse as Jewish and understands "son of God" as a reference to the Temple.

[6] Nikiprowetzky, *La Troisième Sibylle*, pp. 17–36.

[7] See H. Jeanmaire, *La Sibylle et le retour de l'âge d'or* (Paris, 1939) p. 103.

[8] Collins, *The Sibylline Oracles*, pp. 40f.

verses 193, 318, and 608. While seven was a sacred number, thus perhaps describing the seventh king as the ideal king, the number could not have been introduced, with any credibility, later than the reign of the seventh Ptolemy.[9] The identification of the seventh Ptolemy is not, however, unambiguous. There are three possible identifications:

> Ptolemy 6, Philometor, who reigned from 180–64, 163–45;
> Ptolemy 7, Neos Philopator, 145–44;
> Ptolemy 8, Physcon (also called Euergetes II), 170–64, 164–63, and 144–17.

Philometor and Physcon were co-regents from 170–64 and Physcon replaced Philometor for a time in 164–63. The enumeration of the kings is further confused by the possibility that Alexander was counted as the first king. Finally, the Sibylline oracle may have been written either during the reign of the seventh king or during that of the sixth, when the seventh was proximately expected. Accordingly, the reference to the seventh king could conceivably point to a date at any time in the second century B.C. down to the death of Physcon in 117 B.C.

However, this period can be further defined. The prominence of the Romans in verses 175–90 requires a date after the battle of Magnesia in 190 B.C. and probably after Rome's intervention in the affairs of Egypt in the time of Antiochus Epiphanes. This already brings us down to the time of Philometor, and so the oracles were most probably written at some time during the reigns of Philometor and Physcon. In view of the remarkable confidence which the Sibyl places in the Ptolemaic kings and of the celebrated relations of Philometor with the Jews,[10] it is most probable that the Sibyl wrote in the period 163–45 B.C.[11]

PROVENANCE

There is no doubt that Sibylline Oracles 3 was written in Egypt. This is clear from the double reference to Egypt in 155–61, in which the kingdom of Macedonia is followed by a kingdom of Egypt, and from the repeated references to the seventh king of Egypt.

Within Egypt the work has been usually located in Alexandrian Judaism. However, there is reason to believe that it was written in the circles associated with the priest Onias, founder of the temple at Leontopolis.

The strongest clue to the provenance of Sibylline Oracles 3 is the enthusiastic endorsement of a Ptolemaic king as a savior figure who will put an end to war and usher in a reign of peace. The emphasis on warfare and politics throughout the book contrasts sharply with the spiritualizing tendencies usually associated with Alexandrian Judaism. However, it seems entirely appropriate for a follower of Onias, who was a prominent general in the army of Philometor.[12] The hailing of a Ptolemaic king (either Philometor or his expected heir) as a virtual messiah points also to the circles of Onias, who benefited most obviously from the

---

[9] The only dissenter from this view is Nikiprowetzky (*La Troisième Sibylle*, p. 215). He identifies the seventh king as Queen Cleopatra VII (!). It is very doubtful whether the numeral 7 was associated with Cleopatra in antiquity. In any case, whatever the queen's manly qualities, history leaves little possibility that she could have been mistaken for a king.

[10] Josephus, *Apion* 2:49, claims that Philometor entrusted his whole realm to the Jews. While this is certainly an exaggeration there must have been some basis for the statement. The Jewish temple at Leontopolis was built under Philometor (*War* 1.1.1 and 7.10.2 [432]; *Ant* 12.9.7 [382f.] and 13.3.1 [62f.]). Also, the Jewish philosopher Aristobulus was said to have been teacher of Philometor or at least to have dedicated a book to him (2Mac 1:10). See J. J. Collins, "The Provenance of the Third Sibylline Oracle," *Bulletin of the Institute of Jewish Studies* 2 (1974) 8f.

[11] Nikiprowetzky, *La Troisième Sibylle*, pp. 209–12, argues for a 1st-cent. date mainly on the basis of the prominence of Rome in vss. 175–90. However, that oracle makes special note of Roman outrages in Macedonia (190). This reference points not to a 1st-cent. date but rather to the Macedonian wars in the 2nd cent. B.C. Peretti, *La Sibilla Babilonese*, p. 190, regarded the references to the Romans as a late insertion. J. Nolland, "Sib Or III. 265–94, An Early Maccabean Messianic Oracle," *JTS* 30 (1979) 158–67, argues that vss. 282–94, which ostensibly refer to the restoration under Cyrus, refer typologically to the author's own day, which he identifies as the time when the Temple was profaned by Antiochus Epiphanes. Since he takes the oracle to refer to a Davidic messiah, and since it does not refer to the Maccabees, he dates it "prior to significant Maccabean success." However, even if we accept the typological interpretation of the passage, which is not certain, the only individual king mentioned in the passage is Cyrus. Typologically, the passage suggests that a gentile king will fill the messianic role. Silence on the Maccabees may be due to a lack of sympathy with them, and the Maccabean restoration of the Temple may not have been recognized.

[12] Josephus, *Apion* 2.149.

patronage of Philometor, rather than to any academic circles in Alexandria. Further, the third Sibyl displays an interest in the Temple which is unparalleled in any document from Egyptian Judaism[13]—see verses 286–94, 564–67, 657–59, 715–18. This interest in the Temple does not require priestly origins but is obviously highly compatible with the attitudes of a follower of Onias.

The Temple to which Sibylline Oracles 3 refers is certainly the Jerusalem Temple. This fact, and the lack of any explicit reference to Leontopolis, might be thought to constitute an objection to provenance in the circles of Onias. The objection, however, is not a serious one, and rather provides a closer indication of the date of the work. The temple of Leontopolis was not built until several years after Onias arrived in Egypt.[14] The land for the temple was probably given in recognition of services over a number of years.[15] Sibylline Oracles 3 was probably written in this period before the new temple was built—therefore approximately 160–50 B.C. We should note moreover that there is no reason why the community of Leontopolis should not have continued to look on Jerusalem as the ideal temple even after the new shrine was built, just as the Qumran community continued to look to the Jerusalem Temple after they had severed connections with it.[16]

HISTORICAL IMPORTANCE

The main historical interest of Sibylline Oracles 3 lies in its attestation of a Jewish community that could hail a Ptolemaic king as a savior figure or Messiah. The transformation at the end-time is dated to the reign of the seventh king of Egypt in verses 193, 318, and 608, but the most striking instance is found in verses 652–56. There we read that a "king from the sun" will bring peace to the earth by the counsels of God. The phrase "a king from the sun" is also found in the closely contemporary Egyptian Potter's Oracle,[17] where it clearly refers to an Egyptian king. In Egyptian mythology the king was thought to be an incarnation of the sun-god.[18] There is nothing to indicate that Sibylline Oracles 3 endorsed the Egyptian mythology, but in view of the frequency with which the Egyptian kings (including the Ptolemies) were associated with the sun,[19] verse 652 must be taken as a reference to an Egyptian king. This Egyptian "king from the sun" cannot be held distinct from the "seventh king" of the Greeks in whose reign war will cease. In short, Sibylline Oracles 3 looked upon the seventh Ptolemaic king, whether present or still future, as a messiah sent by God. Such veneration of a gentile king was not without precedent in Jewish tradition but strikingly recalls how Deutero-Isaiah hailed Cyrus as messiah (Isa 45:1).

A work that hails a Ptolemaic king as a savior figure must be presumed to have at least in part a propagandistic purpose. The work might at least hope to ingratiate the royal house and show that Jews and gentiles could share a common hope.

[13] Collins, The Sibylline Oracles, pp. 48f.; Bulletin of the Institute of Jewish Studies, pp. 11f. A. Momigliano, "La portata storica dei vaticini sul settimo re nel terzo libro degli Oracoli Sibillini," in Forma futuri: Studi in onore del Cardinale Michele Pellegrino (Turin, 1975) pp. 1077–84, argues that SibOr 3 was writen to assert the unity of Egyptian and Palestinian Judaism after the Maccabean revolt. He sees a reference to the revolt in vss. 194f.: "And then the people of the great God will again be strong." This allusion, however, is far too vague and should be understood as future hope, not accomplished fact. There is nothing in SibOr 3 that indicates sympathy with the Maccabees. The emphasis placed on a king of Egypt is quite alien to the nationalism of the Maccabees, but is strikingly compatible with the politics of the Oniads both before and after the revolt.

[14] See M. Delcor, "Le Temple d'Onias en Egypte," RB 125 (1968) 196.

[15] V. Tcherikover, Corpus papyrorum Judaicorum (Cambridge, 1957) vol. 1, p. 45.

[16] Collins, Bulletin of the Institute of Jewish Studies, pp. 15f.; The Sibylline Oracles, p. 51.

[17] See L. Koenen, "Die Prophezeiungen des 'Töpfers,' " Zeitschrift fur Papyrologie und Epigraphik 2 (1968) 178–209; idem, "The Prophecies of a Potter: A Prophecy of World Renewal Becomes an Apocalypse," Proceedings of the Twelfth International Congress of Papyrology, ed. D. H. Samuels (Proceedings of the 12th International Congress of Papyrology, 1970) pp. 249–54; F. Dunand, "L'Oracle du Potier et la formation de l'apocalyptique en Egypte," L'Apocalyptique (Études d'Histoire des Religions 3; Paris, 1977) pp. 39–67.

[18] See J. Bergman, Ich bin Isis (Uppsala, Sweden, 1969) p. 67.

[19] In a hieroglyphic stele dated to 311 B.C., Alexander IV is described as "chosen of the sun, son of the sun." On the Rosetta Stone, Ptolemy V Euergetes is described as the son of the sun "to whom the sun has given victory." See E. R. Bevan, A History of Egypt under the Ptolemaic Dynasty (London, 1927) pp. 28, 30, 263; W. Dittenberger, Orientis Graeci inscriptiones selectae (Hildesheim, Germany, 1960) vol. 1, p. 143; A. Momigliano, Forma futuri: Studi in onore del Cardinale Michele Pellegrino, pp. 1077–84, suggests that in SibOr 3, as in the Potter's Oracle, the king from the sun is anti-Ptolemaic. This view ignores the association of sun mythology with the Ptolemies and makes a strained distinction between the seventh king and the king from the sun. Momigliano's thesis that the oracle was written in support of the Maccabean revolt suffers from the lack of any clear reference to the Maccabees.

THEOLOGICAL IMPORTANCE

As usual in the Sibylline Oracles the concept of the end-time provides a framework for exhortation. Certain types of action lead to destruction, certain others to deliverance. In section 2 (vss. 162–95) the main cause of destruction is the misconduct of the Romans, especially homosexuality (185–86) and covetousness (189). In section 3 (196–294) the Babylonian exile is a direct punishment for idolatry (275–85). In the fourth section (545–656) the Greeks are endangered because of idolatry (545–55) but can avoid disaster by sending sacrifices to the Temple (565). They are contrasted with the Jews, who honor the Temple with sacrifices and avoid idolatry (575–90), adultery and homosexuality (595–600). Again in verses 601–7 the gentiles are said to be in danger because of homosexuality and idolatry. Finally in the last section (657–808) the Sibyl again appeals to the Greeks to refrain from idolatry, adultery, and homosexuality (762–66) and prophesies that people from all countries will send gifts to the Temple (715–19, 772f.). The main message of Sibylline Oracles 3 then would seem to lie in the denunciation of idolatry and sexual abuses and in the advocacy of the Temple. This message is explicitly directed to the gentiles but no doubt was intended for Jewish readers as well.

One brief passage (vss. 591–95) gives us a glimpse of some of the more specific practices of this branch of Judaism. They raise their arms in prayer to God at dawn and take ritual baths (or wash their hands ritually).[20] Despite occasional attempts to relate these practices to the Essenes or Pythagoreans, the evidence is not specific enough to warrant the identification of a sect.[21]

The eschatology of Sibylline Oracles 3 centers on the expectation of an ideal king or kingdom. The enemies of that king will be killed or subdued by oaths (654). The state of salvation is envisaged in political earthly terms, as a transformation of the earth and exaltation of the Temple (701–61, 767–95).

Before this ideal king comes there will be a period of chaotic tribulation. In verses 611–15 this is brought about in part by a king from Asia, the traditional threat to Egypt.[22] In verses 660–701 a final period of confusion is caused by the attack of the gentiles on Jerusalem. They are destroyed directly by God by various means, including brimstone from heaven.

RELATION TO OTHER BOOKS

The ethics of Sibylline Oracles 3 are commonplace in the Judaism of the hellenistic age. Similar polemics against sexual aberrations are found, for example, in Epistle of Aristeas 152, Philo, *Abr* 135; *SpecLeg* 2.50, 3.37; and Romans 1:26. Polemic against idolatry is ubiquitous in Jewish writing after Deutero-Isaiah. The polemic against astrology and Chaldean divination in verses 220–28 is paralleled in Jubilees 12:16–18 and 1 Enoch 80:7.

The eschatology of Sibylline Oracles 3 finds its closest parallels in pre-exilic Jewish literature such as Isaiah and the Psalms. The assault of the gentiles on Jerusalem is especially reminiscent of Psalms 2 and 48, while the transformation of the earth in verses 785–95 is obviously dependent on Isaiah 11. The idea of the pilgrimage of the gentiles at the end-time to Jerusalem is found in Isaiah 2:1–4, Micah 4:1–4, and Zechariah 14:16–21.

The expectation of an ideal king, followed by a transformation of the earth, is also paralleled in a number of contemporary gentile writings, most notably the Potter's Oracle and (somewhat later) Virgil's Fourth Eclogue. Sibylline Oracles 3 shows no sign of a belief in resurrection or afterlife typical of the apocalyptic writings of the period.

2. Sibylline Oracles 3.350–488. Oracles Against Various Nations

Verses 350–480 consist of four diverse oracles that lack any ethical exhortation and are included because of the general Sibylline interest in political oracles. The four oracles are vss. 350–80, 381–87, 388–400, 401–88.

---

[20] According to a quotation in Clement (*Protrepticus* 6:70) they purify their *flesh* by washing. According to the MSS they wash their hands.

[21] See the discussion by Nikiprowetzky, *La Troisième Sibylle*, pp. 238–59. Nikiprowetzky errs in trying to eliminate the differences between SibOr 3 and SibOr 4.

[22] See Collins, *The Sibylline Oracles*, pp. 39f. Peretti, *La Sibilla Babilonese*, mistakenly takes the king from Asia as a messianic figure.

This oracle is distinguished from the rest of the book by the fact that the antithetical powers are Rome and Asia, whereas the rest of the book deals with internal Egyptian matters and presents a contrast between Rome and Egypt or Asia and Egypt. The theme of the oracle is the vengeance of Asia on Rome, which will be exacted by a lady, a *despoina*. The lady in question should be identified as Cleopatra, representing also Egypt, of which she was queen, and the goddess Isis, whom she claimed to incarnate.[23] The only serious alternative to this interpretation, which has been put forward,[24] is that the oracle was part of the propaganda of Mithridates (in which case the *despoina* must be identified as Asia). However, one detail of the oracle renders this interpretation highly unlikely. Not only is the destruction of Rome envisaged but also its restoration (361) and an ultimate state of harmony (375). Such an idea of reconciliation had no place in Mithridates' war to the death against Rome.[25] Cleopatra's ambition, however, was to rule over the Roman Empire, not to destroy it. She stood in the tradition of Alexander—her son by Antony was called Alexander Helios—and therefore in a tradition which envisaged the unity of East and West.[26]

Date and provenance

This oracle must have been written shortly before the battle of Actium (31 B.C.) and, presumably, in Egypt. There is nothing specifically Jewish in these verses but, whether they were composed by a Jew or only taken over, we must note that they are quite in harmony with the enthusiasm for the Ptolemaic house noted in the main corpus of Sibylline Oracles 3. It is true that relations between Cleopatra and the Jews were not always cordial. The queen wanted to restore Egyptian rule in Palestine, a desire naturally resented by Herod.[27] There is also a report, of less than complete reliability, that she withheld corn from the Jews in time of famine.[28] However, there is no reason to suppose that Cleopatra was at odds with all Jews or that some of them could not have espoused her cause, especially those who had a tradition of loyalty to the Ptolemaic house.

Significance and relation to other literature

The importance of this oracle lies in its attestation of Near Eastern anti-Roman propaganda. The fact that at least one strand of Egyptian Judaism could espouse such an oracle is also of interest.

Two traditions are important for understanding this oracle. The first is an old tradition, common to the entire eastern Mediterranean, which saw world history as an ongoing conflict between East and West, Asia and Europe. This theme is found in Herodotus 1.4 and is used in the Alexandra of Lycophron, in oracles preserved by Phlegon which are said to have been uttered at the time of the battle of Magnesia,[29] and above all in the Oracle of Hystaspes.[30] It also finds mention in Tacitus' account of the Jewish war.[31] Significantly, Cleopatra's campaign against Rome was presented as a world conflict between East and West not only by the Roman poets Virgil (Aeneid 8.685f.) and Florus (2.21) but most explicitly by the Egyptian Jew Philo (*Legatio ad Gaium* 144).[32]

The second tradition is native to Egypt. According to Egyptian tradition every queen was an incarnation of Isis. This claim was made explicitly by Cleopatra.[33] Many aspects of the

---

[23] Collins, *The Sibylline Oracles*, pp. 57–71.

[24] So Geffcken, *Komposition und Entstehungszeit*, p. 8; Lanchester, "The Sibylline Oracles," p. 372; Peretti, *La Sibilla Babilonese*, p. 340.

[25] See H. Jeanmaire, *La Sibylle et la retour de l'Âge d'or*, p. 58. On the Mithridatic wars see E. Will, *Histoire politique du monde hellenistique, 323–30 av. J.C.* (Nancy, France, 1967) vol. 2, pp. 387–422.

[26] See especially W. W. Tarn, "Alexander Helios and the Golden Age," *Journal of Roman Studies* 22 (1932) 135–59.

[27] Josephus, *Ant* 15.4.2 (96ff.).

[28] This report is attributed by Josephus to Apion, who used it in anti-Jewish polemic. *Apion* 2.56–61.

[29] F. Jacoby, *FGH*, vol. 2B, pp. 1174–77; Collins, *The Sibylline Oracles*, p. 7.

[30] Especially Lactantius, *DivInst* 7.15.11.

[31] Tacitus, *Histories* 5.13.

[32] See E. M. Smallwood, *Legatio ad Gaium* (Leiden, 1970) p. 228.

[33] Collins, *The Sibylline Oracles*, pp. 170f.

final state envisaged in this Sibylline oracle are paralleled in the Isis aretalogies—the title *despoina*, abolition of war and slaughter, introduction of harmony and justice.[34] The Jewish Sibyllist need not have endorsed the worship of Isis, but the endorsement of the queen reflects the same cordial attitude to the Egyptian royal house that was attested in the oracles from the time of Philometor.

VERSES 381–87

These verses are ascribed to a Persian Sibyl by Geffcken because they predict the fall of the Macedonian kingdom after the conquest of Babylon.[35] They are ascribed to a Babylonian Sibyl by S. K. Eddy for exactly the same reason.[36] At least the existence of a Persian Sibyl is attested.[37] (The existence of the Babylonian Sibyl is more dubious.) However, the evidence for attributing this oracle to a specific situation is simply inadequate. It could have been written by anyone hostile to the Macedonians at any time after the fall of Babylon to Alexander.

VERSES 388–400

This oracle is again directed against the Macedonians. The man, clad in purple, who will come to Asia is certainly Alexander.[38] This oracle was updated by a Jewish Sibyllist who added references to the root with ten horns and the horn growing on the side, clearly alluding to Daniel 7. Since all the oracles in verses 350–488 were apparently late additions to Sibylline Oracles 3, the reference to Daniel is of no help in dating the book. The oracle stands as an isolated piece of anti-hellenistic propaganda.

VERSES 401–88

These verses have been plausibly attributed by Geffcken to the Erythrean Sibyl.[39] Varro tells us that the Sibyl of Erythrea prophesied that Troy would fall and that Homer would write falsehoods,[40] and Pausanias (10.2.2) says that she sang of Helen and the Trojan War. These are precisely the themes we find in Sibylline Oracles 3.401–32. Further, this is the only section of Sibylline Oracles 3 where there are regular references to places in Asia Minor.

The only indications of date are in verses 464–69, where there is clear reference to a Roman civil war, and in 470, which speaks of a man from Italy who goes to Asia. The man from Italy has been identified by Lanchester as Sulla.[41] This oracle might well be associated with the Mithridatic wars.

The oracles in verses 350–480 show no ethical interest. They were presumably inserted to bring Sibylline Oracles 3 up to date and to add to its Sibylline flavor by increasing the prophecies of destruction against particular cities.

3. The oracles in Sibylline Oracles 3.1–96

The first ninety-six verses of Sibylline Oracles 3 are dissociated from the rest of the book by all scholars except Nikiprowetzky.[42] Even the manuscripts contain indications that these verses are part of a separate work. In most manuscripts the present Sibylline Oracles 3 is introduced as an extract from the "second book, about God." Before verse 93 three manuscripts in the class ψ insert the note "seek here the remnants of the second book and the beginning of the third."[43] Sibylline Oracles 3.1–45 are quite different from anything else

---

[34] Tarn, "Alexander Helios," pp. 139–48; Collins, *The Sibylline Oracles*, p. 62.

[35] Geffcken, *Komposition und Entstehungszeit*, p. 13.

[36] Eddy, *The King Is Dead*, p. 127.

[37] Varro, cited by Lactantius, *DivInst* 1.6.

[38] So Eddy, *The King Is Dead*, p. 12, following Bousset, "Die Beziehungen der ältesten jüdischen Sibylle zur Chaldäischen," *ZNW* 3 (1902) 23–50. H. H. Rowley, "The Interpretation and Date of the Sibylline Oracles, III, 388–400," *ZAW* 44 (1926) 324–27, suggests Antiochus Epiphanes. Eddy considers this oracle Persian in origin, but his opinion rests on no firm basis.

[39] Geffcken, *Komposition und Entstehungszeit*, p. 13.

[40] Lactantius, *DivInst* 1.6.

[41] Lanchester, "The Sibylline Oracles," p. 387.

[42] See his discussion, *La Troisième Sibylle*, pp. 60–66, 217–25.

[43] Vss. 93–96 form a distinct oracle which may or may not have been associated with the preceding section.

in Sibylline Oracles 3 and find their closest analogues in the fragments found in Theophilus and in the verses cited in the Prologue. Kurfess has suggested that the first three fragments with verses 1–92 make up the original second book of the collection.[44] This suggestion is attractive insofar as verses 46–92 would then form the conclusion of a book, whereas they now stand rather incongruously at the beginning of a book.[45] There must, however, be some doubt as to whether verses 46–96 really belong with verses 1–45 at all. Also verses 63–74 must be considered later than the rest of the material.

DATE

Verses 1–45 and the fragments in Theophilus are direct hortatory material that are concerned chiefly with monotheism and polemic against idolatry. This material finds its closest parallels in the Jewish Orphic fragments, which probably date to the second century B.C.,[46] and also in Philo. In themselves, they could have been composed at any time in the late hellenistic or early Roman periods. If we may assume that they originally formed a unit with any part of verses 46–92 we can fix their date more precisely.

Verses 46–92 consist of three oracles: 46–62, 63–74, 75–92. Verses 46–62 must be dated shortly after the battle of Actium. Verse 52 refers to the second triumvirate.[47] Verses 46f. presuppose that Rome has already gained control over Egypt.

Verses 75–92 were also written shortly after the battle of Actium. This oracle is dominated by the figure of Cleopatra, the "widow" of verse 77.[48] Here she is no longer the glorious queen of Sibylline Oracles 3.350–80 but the widow who has brought disaster upon the world. The oracle reflects the disillusionment of the Egyptian Jews after the defeat of Cleopatra.

Verses 63–74 relate the coming of Beliar, the signs he will perform, and his eventual destruction. He is said to come "*ek Sebastēnōn*." Two main interpretations of this phrase have been proposed:

a. It means: from the people of Sebaste, the name given to Samaria by Herod in 25 B.C. in honor of Augustus. Beliar is then identified with Simon Magus or simply said to be associated with Samaria as an anti-Messiah.[49] In fact, however, there is no parallel for an anti-Messiah from Samaria in Jewish writings.

b. The phrase "*ek Sebastēnōn*" means "from the line of the Augusti."[50] In this case Beliar can be most plausibly identified with Nero. This interpretation is supported by two parallels. First there is the prominence of Nero as an eschatological adversary throughout the Sibylline corpus.[51] Second, in the Ascension of Isaiah 4:1, Beliar is clearly said to come in the likeness of Nero ("a lawless king, the slayer of his mother").

Most probably, then, Sibylline Oracles 3.63–74 should be taken as a reference to Nero. It was added sometime after A.D. 70 to bring this collection up to date with current eschatological expectations. Even if we were to understand verse 63 as a reference to Sebaste we would have to assume that it was a late insertion in its present context.

PROVENANCE

The interest in Cleopatra points to an Egyptian setting for verses 75–92, and this is confirmed by the reference to Egypt in verse 46. Nothing in the other passages is incompatible with Egyptian provenance.

HISTORICAL AND THEOLOGICAL IMPORTANCE

The opening forty-five verses of Sibylline Oracles 3 and the fragments are important as

---

[44] A. Kurfess, "Christian Sibyllines" in HSW, vol. 2, p. 707. On the other fragments see A. Kurfess, "Wie sind die Fragmente der Oracula Sibyllina Einzuordnen?" *Aevum* 26 (1952) 228–35.

[45] Nikiprowetzky attempts to include in SibOr 3 not only the present vss. 1–96 but also the fragments found in Theophilus and the fragment of Ps-Phoc from SibOr 2 (*La Troisième Sibylle*, p. 65). See the critique by Collins, *The Sibylline Oracles*, p. 25.

[46] See N. Walter, *Der Thoraausleger Aristobulus* (Berlin, 1964).

[47] So Friedlieb, Geffcken, Jeanmaire, Kurfess; Collins, *The Sibylline Oracles*, p. 65.

[48] So Friedlieb, Jeanmaire, Bousset, Tarn. For full discussion see Collins, *The Sibylline Oracles*, pp. 66–70.

[49] Nikiprowetzky, *La Troisième Sibylle*, pp. 140–43.

[50] So Bousset, Lanchester, Charles. See Collins, *The Sibylline Oracles*, p. 86.

[51] See Collins, *The Sibylline Oracles*, pp. 80–87.

an attestation of a highly spiritual idea of God, similar to that found in the Orphic fragments and Philo. God is eternal (3.15), self-begotten, and invisible (3.11). Great emphasis is laid on the contrast between perishable and imperishable (frags. 1–3) and on the unity and uniqueness of God. Idolatry is the supreme sin because it is not in accordance with truth. This highly spiritual religion is not, however, adverse to sacrificial cult but insists only that it be offered to the true God (frag. 1:20–22).

The passages 46–62 and 75–92, referring to the end-time, are important indicators of the reaction of some Egyptian Jews to the defeat of Cleopatra. The tone in each oracle is one of bitter disillusionment. The main emphasis falls on a day of destruction—with brimstone from heaven in 3.60f. and the collapse of the heavens, accompanied by a stream of fire from heaven in verses 80–85. It is noteworthy that here, after the battle of Actium, the horizons of the Sibyl are no longer confined to Egypt but extend to the whole world. The "holy prince" of 3.49 will gain sway over the whole earth. This conception of the savior figure may well be influenced by Roman propaganda, which emphasized the universality and eternity of the empire.[52]

Again in verses 75–92 the Sibyl is concerned with the whole universe, but this time there is no mention of a savior figure. Drawing on the language of Isaiah 34:4, the Sibyl envisages the collapse of the heavens and a final conflagration. The widow Cleopatra brings widowhood and desolation on the universe. Like Babylon in Isaiah 47:8f., her claim to universal rule is made void by her widowhood.

The destruction of the heavens is an important recurring theme in the Sibylline Oracles. The most striking elaboration is found in Sibylline Oracles 5.512–31. It also occurs in apocalyptic writings such as Revelation 6:13–14.

---

[52] Ibid., pp. 65f.

THE SIBYLLINE ORACLES
Book 3

FROM THE SECOND BOOK CONCERNING GOD

The inspiration of the Sibyl

Blessed, heavenly one, who thunders on high, who have the cherubim
as your throne,[a] I entreat you to give a little rest
to me who have prophesied unfailing truth, for my heart is tired within.
But why does my heart shake again? and why is my spirit
5 lashed by a whip, compelled from within to proclaim
an oracle to all? But I will utter everything again,
as much as God bids me say to men.

Ps 80:1;
99:1, etc.

3.295–300;
489–91;
698–701;
818; 2.1–5,
etc.

Praise of God and denunciation of idolatry

Men, who have the form which God molded in his image,[b]
why do you wander in vain, and not walk the straight path
10 ever mindful of the immortal creator?
There is one God, sole ruler, ineffable, who lives in the sky,
self-begotten, invisible, who himself sees all things.
No sculptor's hand made him, nor does a cast
of gold or ivory reveal him, by the crafts of man,
15 but he himself, eternal, revealed himself
as existing now, and formerly and again in the future.
For who, being mortal, is able to see God with eyes?
or who will be able even to hear only
the name of the great heavenly God who rules the world?
20 who created everything by a word, heaven and sea,
untiring sun, full moon,
shining stars, strong mother Tethys,[c]
springs and rivers, imperishable fire, days, nights.
Indeed it is God himself who fashioned Adam, of four letters,
25 the first-formed man, fulfilling by his name
east and west and south and north.
He himself fixed the shape of the form of men
and made wild beasts and serpents and birds.
You neither revere nor fear God, but wander to no purpose,
30 worshiping snakes and sacrificing to cats,[d]
speechless idols, and stone statues of people;
and sitting in front of the doors at godless temples[e]
you do not fear[f] the existing God who guards all things.
You rejoice in the evil of stones, forgetting the judgment
35 of the immortal savior who created heaven and earth.
Alas for a race which rejoices in blood, a crafty and evil race

2.126; 3.629,760; 8.377

4.12

Isa 40:18–26
WisSol 13:10–19
LetAris 135–38; 2En 33
(A&B);
Ps-Heraclitus Letter 4
Philo, Dec 76–80

Ex 33:20; Judg 13:22; 1Jn 4:12

1.19; WisSol 9:1
Ps 33:6

2En 30:13

WisSol
15:18
Ezek 9:17

a. Lit. "who have the cherubim, enthroned" (following Geffcken).

b. On vss. 8–45 cf. SibOr frags. 1 and 3 and the Ps-Orph fragments in Eusebius, *PrEv* 13.12.5.

c. Tethys was a sea-goddess and therefore personified the sea.

d. The polemic is specifically directed against the Egyptians. Cf. LetAris 138; Philo, *Dec* 76; WisSol 15:18.

e. Nikiprowetzky, *La Troisième Sibylle*, p. 229, convincingly explains this verse with reference to the cult of Isis. Cf. Ovid, *Tristes* 296f.: *Isidis aede sedens vir ante fores*, "A man sitting in front of the doors in the shrine of Isis."

f. Reading *ou tremete* (Geffcken) for *tēreite*.

of impious and false double-tongued men and immoral
adulterous idol worshipers who plot deceit.
There is wickedness in their breasts, a frenzy raging within.
40 They ravage booty for themselves and have a shameless spirit.
For no one who is rich and has possessions will give a share to another
but there will be terrible wickedness among all mortals.
They will have no fidelity at all. Many widowed women   1Tim 5:13
will love other men secretly for gain;
45 and those who have^g husbands will not keep hold of the rope of life.

Universal rule of Rome, followed by eschatological destruction

But when Rome will also rule over Egypt
guiding it toward a single goal,^h then indeed the most great kingdom   AsMos
of the immortal king will become manifest over men.   10;1; PssSol 17:4
For a holy prince will come to gain sway over the scepters of the earth   PssSol
50 forever, as time presses on.   17:32–34; 8.169
Then also implacable wrath will fall upon Latin men.
Three will destroy Rome with piteous fate.ⁱ
All men will perish in their own dwellings
when the fiery cataract flows from heaven.   2.196, etc.
55 Alas, wretched one, when will that day come,
and the judgment of the great king immortal God?
Yet, just for the present, be founded, cities, and all   8.123; 13.64
be embellished with temples and stadia, markets and golden
silver and stone statues so that you may come to the bitter day.
60 For it will come, when the smell of brimstone spreads   3.462; 7.142
among all men. But I will tell all in turn,
in how many cities mortals will endure evil.

The advent of Beliar

Then Beliar will come from the *Sebastēnoi*^j   2.167, etc. AscenIs 2:4; 4:2
and he will raise up the height of mountains, he will raise up the sea,   AscenIs 4:5; ApEl 3:7
65 the great fiery sun and shining moon,   Ephrem Syrus 9; Ps-Methodius 93B; ApPet 2
and he will raise up the dead,^k and perform many signs   Ps-Hippolytus 23.106.
for men. But they will not be effective in him.   14,24
But he will, indeed, also lead men astray, and he will lead astray
many faithful, chosen Hebrews, and also other lawless men
70 who have not yet listened to the word of God.
But whenever the threats of the great God draws nigh
and a burning power comes through the sea to land   3.54,84, etc.
it will also burn Beliar and all overbearing men,
as many as put faith in him.

Cosmic destruction in the reign of Cleopatra

75 Then indeed the world will be governed under the hands of a woman,^l
and be obedient in everything.
Then when a widow reigns over the whole world,   11.279,
and throws gold and silver into the wondrous brine   290; Isa 47:8f.; Rev 18:7–8

g. Reading *hai lachousai* (φ, ψ, Nikiprowetzky)
for *lelachousa*.

h. Reading *eis hen ithunousa* (ψ, Nikiprowetzky).
The reference is to Rome's conquest of Egypt after
the battle of Actium in 31 B.C.

i. This should be read as a reference to the second
triumvirate (Antony, Lepidus, and Octavian).

j. I.e. Nero will come from the line of Augustus.
See the Introduction to SibOr 3.

k. Contrast ApEl 3:10f., where the Antichrist is
distinguished from the Messiah precisely by his inability to raise the dead.

l. The woman here and widow in vs. 76 should
be identified as Cleopatra.

and casts the bronze and iron of ephemeral men
80 into the sea, then all the elements of the universe   2.206;
will be bereft, when God who dwells in the sky   8.337
rolls up the heaven as a scroll is rolled,   8.413
and the whole variegated vault of heaven falls   Isa 34:4;
on the wondrous earth and ocean. An undying cataract   Rev 6:14
85 of raging fire will flow, and burn earth, burn sea,   3.54;
and melt the heavenly vault and days and creation itself   2.196, etc.
into one and separate them into clear air.   2.213
There will no longer be twinkling spheres of luminaries,
no night, no dawn, no numerous days of care,
90 no spring, no summer, no winter, no autumn.   2.326;
And then indeed the judgment of the great God   8.425f.
will come into the midst of the great world, when all these things 2En 65 (B)
    happen.

Fragmentary oracle

O, O for the floating waters and all dry land,
and the rising sun which will never set again.   Mal 4:2
95 All will obey him as he enters the world again
because it was the first to recognize his power also.[m]

The tower of Babel

But when the threats of the great God are fulfilled
with which he once threatened men when they built the tower   Gen 11:1-9; Jub 10:19-26
in the land of Assyria[n] . . . They were all of one language   Ant 1.4.3 (118); Ps-Eup F1,
100 and they wanted to go up to starry heaven.   F2 (PrEv 9:17,18)
But immediately the immortal one imposed a great compulsion[o]
on the winds. Then the winds cast down the great tower   Jub 10:26; Ant 1.4.3 (118)
from on high, and stirred up strife for mortals among themselves.
Therefore humans gave the city the name Babylon.   Gen 11:9
105 But when the tower fell, and the tongues of men
were diversified by various sounds, the whole
earth of humans was filled with fragmenting kingdoms.
Then was the tenth generation of articulate men,   2.15, etc.
from the time when the Flood came upon the men of old.

The Titans

110 Cronos and Titan and Iapetus reigned,[p]   1.293
the best children of Gaia and Ouranos, whom men called
earth and heaven, giving them a name
because they were the first of articulate men.
The portions of the earth were threefold, according to the lot of each
115 and each one reigned, having his share, and they did not fight
for there were oaths imposed by their father, and the divisions were
    just.
When the full time, the old age of the father, came,
he also died, and the sons made a dire

---

m. This fragment is enigmatic. It is sometimes regarded as Christian.

n. Anakoluothon.

o. The parallel passage in Josephus, *Ant* 1.4.3 (118), uses the plural "gods." This has often been taken to reflect a pagan source, probably Berossus. Josephus explicitly claims to be citing the Sibyl at this point. Even if Josephus had access to a Babylonian source it does not follow that the Sibyl also drew on that source.

p. The account of the Titans is paralleled in Hesiod, *Theogony* 421ff., but differs in details and is interpreted euhemeristically to refer to human beings.

transgression of oaths and stirred up strife against each other
120 as to who should have royal honor and reign over all men.

Hesiod,
Theogony
629f.

Cronos and Titan fought against each other
but Rhea, Gaia, Aphrodite who loves crowns,
Demeter, Hestia, and fair-tressed Dione
brought them to friendship, having assembled
125 all the kings, kindred and brothers, and other men
who were of the same blood and parents.
And they chose Cronos king to rule over all
because he was eldest and best in appearance.
But Titan, for his part, imposed great oaths on Cronos
130 that he should not rear a family of male children, so that
he himself might reign when old age and fate came upon Cronos.
Whenever Rhea gave birth, the Titans sat by her,
and they tore apart all male children,
but they allowed the females to live and be reared with their mother.
135 But when Lady Rhea gave birth in the third[q] child-bearing
she brought forth Hera first. When they saw
with their eyes the female species, the Titans, savage men,
went home. Then Rhea bore a male child,
whom she quickly sent away to be reared secretly and in private,
140 to Phrygia, having taken three Cretan men under oath.
Therefore they named him Zeus, because he was sent away.[r]
Similarly she sent away Poseidon secretly.
Further, the third time, Rhea, marvel of women, bore Pluto
as she went past Dodona, whence the watery paths
145 of the river Europus flowed and the water ran to the sea
mingled with the Peneius, and they call it Stygian.[s]
When the Titans heard that children existed

1.310–17

in secret, whom Cronos had begotten with Rhea, his consort,
Titan assembled sixty sons
150 and held Cronos and Rhea, his consort, in fetters.[t]
He hid them in the earth and guarded them in bonds.
Then indeed the sons of mighty Cronos heard it
and they stirred up great war and din of battle against him.
This is the beginning of war for all mortals
155 for this is the first beginning of war for mortals.

A list of kingdoms

Then God inflicted evil upon the Titans

3.199–201

and all the descendants of Titans and of Cronos
died. But then as time pursued its cyclic course
the kingdom of Egypt arose, then that of the Persians,

4.49–104;
8:6–9

160 Medes, and Ethiopians, and Assyrian Babylon,
then that of the Macedonians, of Egypt again, then of Rome.[u]

A further prophecy of world kingdoms

Then the utterance of the great God rose in my breast

3.297–99;
490f.; 698f.

q. Gk. *tē tritatē geneē* (φ, ψ, Nikiprowetzky) for
tēn tritatēn geneēn.

r. A pun on the Gk. word *dia,* accusative of Zeus,
but also a preposition. Cf. Cornutus 2: *hoti di' auton
ginetai kai sōzetai panta,* "because on account of
him all things come into being and are saved." So
also LetAris 16. This etymology is Stoic in origin.
The usual story of the birth of Zeus says that he was
sent to Crete.

s. The Styx was one of the rivers of the underworld.

t. For the revolt of the Titans against Zeus see
Hesiod, *Theogony* 618–885; Apollodorus, *Library*
1.2.1; 6.3.

u. If we include the kingdom of Cronos and an
anticipated kingdom of the end-time, this list gives
the usual number 10.

and bade me prophesy concerning every land
and remind kings of the things that are to be.
165 And God first put this in my mind:
How many kingdoms of men will be raised up?
The house of Solomon will rule first of all,
and the Phoenicians, who disembark on Asia and other
islands, and the race of Pamphylians, and Persians and Phrygians,
170 Carians and Mysians, and the race of the Lydians, rich in gold.
Then the overbearing and impious Greeks:
Another, great diverse race, of Macedonia, will rule,
who will come as a terrible cloud of war on mortals.
But heavenly God will destroy them from the depth.
175 But then will be the beginning[v] of another kingdom,
white and many-headed from the western sea.[w]
It will rule over much land, and will shake many,
and will thereafter cause fear to all kings.
It will destroy much gold and silver
180 from many cities. But there will again be gold
on the wondrous earth, and then silver also and ornament.
They will also oppress mortals. But those men
will have a great fall when they launch on a course of unjust haughtiness.
Immediately compulsion to impiety will come upon these men.
185 Male will have intercourse with male and they will set up boys
in houses of ill-fame and in those days
there will be a great affliction among men and it will throw everything
　　　into confusion.
It will cut up everything and fill everything with evils
with disgraceful love of gain, ill-gotten wealth,
190 in many places, but especially in Macedonia.[x]
It will stir up hatred. Every kind of deceit will be found among them
until the seventh reign, when
a king of Egypt, who will be of the Greeks by race, will rule.[y]
And then the people of the great God will again be strong
195 who will be guides in life for all mortals.

Reference column:
2.73; 3.596,764; 4.34; 5.166, 387,430; LetAris 152
Philo, *Abr* 135
SpecLeg 2.50; 3.37
Rom 1:26; 1Cor 6:9f.

3.613

3.318; 608

1.385

A prophecy of various woes

But why did God also prompt me to say this:
What first, what next, what will be the final evil
on all men, what will be the beginning of these things?
First God will inflict evil upon the Titans
200 for they will make retribution to the sons of mighty Cronos,
because they bound Cronos and the noble mother.
Second, the Greeks will have tyrannies and proud
kings overbearing and impious,
adulterous[z] and wicked in all respects. There will no longer
205 be respite from war for mortals. All the terrible Phrygians
will perish, and evil will come upon Troy on that day.
Immediately evil will also come upon the Persians and Assyrians,
all Egypt, Libya, and the Ethiopians,

3.156

11.53–55

v. Or: "dominion."
w. Rome. The reference is to the Senate. As Lanchester notes, Rome still appears here as a remote and unfamiliar power. The passage fits the impression of Rome in the East after the battle of Magnesia (190 B.C.).
x. Macedonia was divided after the battle of Pydna in 168 B.C. and was made a Roman province in 147 B.C.
y. Most probably either Ptolemy VI Philometor (if Alexander is counted as the first king) or his anticipated successor. See the Introduction to SibOr 3.
z. A possible reference to Helen of Troy.

so that great evil will be shared[a2] among the Carians and Pamphylians
210 and all men. But why should I narrate them individually?
But when the first things reach an end, immediately
the second things will come upon men. I will proclaim to you first of
    all:
Evil will come upon the pious men who live around
the great Temple of Solomon, and who are the offspring
215 of righteous men. Nevertheless I will also proclaim the race
of these; and the genealogy of their fathers, and the people of them all,
all very thoughtfully, O devious, crafty mortal.

Praise of the Jews

There is a city . . . in the land of Ur of the Chaldeans,   Gen 11:1–9; Jub 12; *LAB* 6:18;
whence comes a race of most righteous men.   Ps-Eup F1 (*PrEv* 9:17); Deut
18:10; Lev 19:31; 20:6,27
220 They are always concerned with good counsel and noble works
for they do not worry about the cyclic course of the sun
or the moon or monstrous things under the earth
nor the depth of the grim sea, Oceanus,
nor portents of sneezes, nor birds of augurers,   Isa 47:12;
Did 3:4
225 nor seers, nor sorcerers, nor soothsayers,
nor the deceits of foolish words of ventriloquists.
Neither do they practice the astrological predictions of the Chaldeans[b2]   Deut 4:19;
nor astronomy. For all these things are erroneous,   Jer 8:2;
2Kgs 23:
such as foolish men inquire into day by day,   24f.
Isa 8:19f.;
230 exercising themselves at a profitless task.   44:25
And indeed they have taught errors to shameful men   1.95; 1En 8
from which many evils come upon mortals on earth
so that they are misled as to good ways and righteous deeds.
But they care for righteousness and virtue[c2]
235 and not love of money, which begets innumerable evils   2.111f.,
114f.;
for mortal men, war, and limitless famine.   3.641; 8.17
They have just measurements in fields and cities   2.66
and they do not carry out robberies at night against each other
nor drive off herds of oxen, sheep, or goats,
240 nor does neighbor move the boundaries of neighbor,   2.100; Ex
22:5; Deut
nor does a very rich man grieve a lesser man   19:14
nor oppress widows in any respect, but rather helps them,   2.76
always going to their aid with corn, wine and oil.   Hos 2:8
Always a prosperous man among the people gives a share
245 of the harvest to those who have nothing, but are poor,   2.79
fulfilling the word of the great God, the hymn of the law,
for the Heavenly One gave the earth in common to all.[d2]   2.319
But when the people of twelve tribes leaves Egypt
and travels the path with leaders sent by God
250 traveling along at night with a pillar of fire   Ex 13:21;
WisSol
and travels by day, every dawn, with a pillar of cloud,   18:3
he will appoint a great man, as leader for this people,
Moses, whom the queen found by the marsh, took home,   Ex 2:5–10
reared, and called her son. But when he came
255 leading this people, which God led from Egypt

a2. Gk. *kakon mega koinōthēnai* (Geffcken) for *metakinēthēnai*.

b2. Ps-Eup claimed that Abraham not only practiced "Chaldean science" but discovered it, and so the present passage has often been understood as a polemic against that view. Abraham also rejects the observation of the stars in Jub 12:17. Cf. Philo, *Abr* 84; *Migr* 187f.

c2. On vss. 234–47 cf. the extract from Ps-Phoc in SibOr 2.

d2. A common Stoic idea.

to the mountain, Sinai, God also gave forth   Ex 19
the Law from heaven, having written all just ordinances on two tablets
and enjoined them to perform it. And if anyone should disobey
he would pay the penalty by law, whether at human hands
260 or escaping men; he would be utterly destroyed in all justice.
[For the Heavenly One gave the earth in common to all   3.247
and fidelity, and excellent reason in their breasts.]
For these alone the fertile soil yields fruit
from one- to a hundredfold, and the measures of God are produced.

Exile and restoration

265 But on these also evil will come, and they will not escape
pestilence. And you will surely flee, leaving the very beautiful
temple, since it is your fate to leave the holy plain.
You will be led to the Assyrians[e2] and you will see
innocent children and wives in slavery   Deut
270 to hostile men. All means of livelihood and wealth will perish.   28:30–33
The whole earth will be filled with you and every sea.
Everyone will be offended at your customs.   Deut 28:37
Your whole land will be desolate; your fortified altar   Deut
and temple of the great God and long walls   29:21–23
275 will all fall to the ground, because you did not obey in your heart Deut
the holy law of the immortal God, but in error   29:25–28;
you worshiped unseemly idols and you did not fear   Jer 5:19;
the immortal Begetter of gods and of all men   16:11
but were not willing to honor him. But you honored the idols of mortals.
280 Therefore for seven decades of times all your fruitful earth   Jer 25:11
and the wonders of the Temple will be desolate.
But a good end and very great glory await you
as immortal God decreed for you. But, you, remain,
trusting in the holy laws of the great God,
285 whenever he may lift your wearied knee upright to the light.   5.108; Isa 44:27–45:1
And then the heavenly God will send a king[f2]   Potter's Oracle, col. 3
and will judge each man in blood and the gleam of fire.   Oracle of Hystaspes, DivInst
There is a certain royal tribe whose race will never stumble.   7.17.15
This too, as time pursues its cyclic course,   Ezek 38:22; Isa 66:16
290 will reign, and it will begin to raise up a new temple of God.   Ezra 5–6; Hag 1–2
All the kings of the Persians will bring to their aid   Ezra 1:7–11; 7:14–23
gold and bronze and much-wrought iron.
For God himself will give a holy dream by night   Joel 3:1
and then indeed the temple will again be as it was before.

Woes against various nations

295 When indeed my spirit ceased the inspired hymn,   3.1–5, etc.
and I entreated the great Begetter that I might have respite from com-
        pulsion,
the word of the great God rose again in my breast
and bade me prophesy concerning every land   3.162–64,
and remind kings of the things that are to be.   etc.
300 God prompted me to say this first,
how many grievous woes the Immortal devised
for Babylon, because it destroyed his great Temple.   5.434;
Woe to you, Babylon, and race of Assyrian men.   11.204; Isa
                                                                      13:47; Jer
                                                                      50f.; cf.
                                                                      Rev 18

e2. The Assyrians and Babylonians are regarded   f2. Most probably Cyrus is meant. The royal tribe
as equivalent: Cf. SibOr 3.160.   in 288 is the people of the Jews.

At some time a rushing destruction will come upon the whole land of
    sinners
305 and a tumult will destroy the entire land of mortals
and an affliction of the great God, leader of hymns.
For a heavenly eternal destruction will come upon you, Babylon,
one day, from above, and on the children of wrath,
(but it will come down upon you from heaven from the holy ones).
310 Then you will be as you were before, as if you had not been.   2Bar 31:5
Then you will be filled with blood, as you yourself formerly
poured out the blood of good men and righteous men,
whose blood even now cries out to high heaven.   Gen 4:10; 2Mac 8:3
A great affliction will come upon you, Egypt, against your homes,   Rev 6:10; Deut 32:43
    Isa 19
315 a terrible one which you never expected to come upon you,
for a sword will pass through your midst[g2]   7.18
and scattering and death and famine will lay hold of you
in the seventh generation of kings, and then you will rest.   3.192f.,608
Woe to you, land of Gog and Magog, situated in the midst   3.512; Rev 20:7–10; Ezek 38:1
320 of Ethiopian rivers.[h2] How great an effusion of blood you will receive
and you will be called a habitation of judgment among men
and your dewy earth will drink black blood.
Woe to you, Libya,[i2] woe to sea and land,
daughters of the west, how you have come to a bitter day.
325 You will also come pursued by a hard struggle,
terrible and hard. There will again be a terrible judgment,
and you will all of necessity go to destruction
because you have utterly destroyed the great house of the Immortal
and have chewed it terribly with iron teeth.   Dan 7:7
330 Therefore you will see your land full of corpses,
some (slain) by war and every assault of the demon
of famine and pestilence, others by barbarous-spirited enemies.   2.23, etc.
All your land will be desolate and your cities desolate ruins.
But in the west a star will shine which they call "Comētēs,"[j2]   8.191;
    Nechepso-
335 a sign to mortals of sword, famine, and death,   Petosiris
destruction of leaders and of great illustrious men.   (ed. Riess)
There will again be very great signs among men.   p. 345
The deep-flowing Tanais will leave Lake Maeotis[k2]
and there will be the track of a fertile furrow down
340 the deep stream, while the immense current occupies a narrow channel.
There will be chasms and yawning pits. Many cities[l2]
will fall with their inhabitants: in Asia: Iassus,
Cebren, Pandonia, Colophon, Ephesus, Nicaea,
Antioch, Tanagra, Sinope, Smyrna, Maros,
345 prosperous Gaza, Hierapolis, Astypalaea;
of Europe: famous Cyagra, royal Meropeia,
Antigone, Magnesia, divine Mycenae.
Know then that the destructive race of Egypt is near destruction
and then for the Alexandrians the year which has passed will be the
    better one.

g2. Probably a reference to the civil war between Ptolemy VI Philometor and Ptolemy VIII Euergetes II.

h2. The association of Gog and Magog with Ethiopia is probably due to the mention of Cush in Ezek 38:5.

i2. The Lybians are listed in Ezek 38:5 among those who follow Gog.

j2. Lanchester relates this comet to that mentioned in Seneca, Naturales quaestiones 7:15, as occurring at the death of Demetrius, king of Syria, but astral phenomena are a favorite topic of such oracles. See especially Nechepso-Petosiris.

k2. Tanais is the river Don, Lake Maeotis the sea of Azov.

l2. A few of these places, Maros, Cyagra, and Meropea, are unknown. The others are located in Asia Minor and Greece.

An oracle against Rome

350 However much wealth Rome received from tribute-bearing Asia,
Asia will receive three times that much again
from Rome and will repay her deadly arrogance to her.
Whatever number from Asia served the house of Italians,
twenty times that number of Italians will be serfs
355 in Asia, in poverty, and they will be liable to pay ten-thousandfold.
O luxurious golden offspring of Latium, Rome,
virgin, often drunken with your weddings with many suitors,[m2]
as a slave will you be wed, without decorum.
Often the mistress[n2] will cut your delicate hair
360 and, dispensing justice, will cast you from heaven to earth,
but from earth will again raise you up to heaven,
because mortals are involved in a wretched and unjust life.
Samos will be sand, and Delos will become inconspicuous,
Rome will be a street. All the oracles will be fulfilled.
365 Smyrna will perish and there will be no mention of it. There will be an
　　avenger,
but for the bad counsels and the wickedness of its leaders . . .
Serene peace will return to the Asian land,
and Europe will then be blessed. The air will be good for pasture
for many years, bracing, free from storms and hail,
370 producing everything—including birds and creeping beasts of the earth.
O most blessed, whatever man or woman will live to what time!
There will be report of the blessed ones, as among countryfolk.[o2]
For all good order and righteous dealing will come
upon men from starry heaven and with it
375 temperate concord, best of all things for men
and love, faithfulness and friendship even from strangers.
Bad government, blame, envy, anger, folly,
poverty will flee from men, and constraint will flee,[p2]
and murder, accursed strife, and grievous quarrels,
380 night robberies, and every evil in those days.

An oracle on Alexander the Great

But Macedonia will bring forth a great affliction for Asia
and a very great grief for Europe will spring up
from the race of Cronos, the progeny of bastards and slaves.[q2]
She will conquer[r2] even the fortified city of Babylon.
385 Having been called mistress of every land which the sun beholds,
　she will perish by evil fate,
leaving a name among her much-wandering posterity.

An oracle on Alexander and his descendants

Also at a certain time there will come to the prosperous land of Asia
a faithless man[s2] clad with a purple cloak on his shoulders,

Margin references:
4.145;
8.72;
Oracle of Hystaspes,
DivInst
7.15.11

5.162–78

Isa 47:1;
Jer 25:27;
48:26

Isa
14:13–16

4.91;
8.165f.; 7.4

3.619–23; 751–59; 11.79,237;
12.87,172; Philo, Praem
90–92; Horace, Epode 16.53ff.

4.192; Virgil, Eclogue 4.53

5.6f.;
11.195–203

11.215–18

---

m2. Possibly a response to Roman taunts at the multiple weddings of Cleopatra.

n2. The mistress should be identified as Cleopatra (who also identified with Isis).

o2. Gk. *makarōn ken eē phatis hōs en agraulois* (Geffcken). Geffcken regards this as a Christian interpolation, referring to the shepherds of Luke 2. It may however simply refer to rustic credulity on matters of supernatural apparitions.

p2. In the Isis aretalogies Isis was said to hold sway over fate. The utopian picture of peace and justice presented here is also paralleled in the Isis aretalogies.

q2. Alexander claimed to be a son of Zeus Ammon after his visit to the shrine of the God in Egypt in 332 B.C.

r2. Gk. *dedamēseî* (Badt) for *dedomēseî*.

s2. This reference is widely disputed but should be taken to refer to Alexander.

390 savage, stranger to justice, fiery. For a thunderbolt beforehand
   raised him[t2] up, a man. But all Asia
   will bear an evil yoke, and the earth, deluged, will imbibe much gore.
   But even so Hades will attend him in everything though he knows it
      not.
   Those whose race he wished to destroy,
395 by them will his own race be destroyed.
   Yet leaving one root, which the destroyer will also cut off
   from ten horns, he will sprout another shoot on the side.[u2]   Dan 7:7
   He will smite a warrior and begetter of a royal race   11.250–53
   and he himself will perish at the hands of his descendants in a conspiracy
      of war,[v2]
400 and then the horn growing on the side will reign.   Dan 7:8

Prophecies of various catastrophes (from the Erythrean Sibyl)

   There will also be immediately a sign for fertile Phrygia,
   when the abominable race of Rhea,[w2] a perennial shoot   1.184
   in the earth, flourishing with unthirsting roots,   1.133, etc.
   will disappear stump and all in a single night[x2]
405 in the city of the earthquaking land-shaker, complete with its inhabit-
      ants,[y2]
   which they will at one time call by the name Dorylaeon[z2]
   of ancient, much-lamented dark Phrygia.
   That time is by name "earth-shaker."
   It will scatter the hiding places of the earth and undo walls.
410 The signs will be a beginning, not of good, but of evil.
   It will have princes who are knowledgeable in the war of all tribes,
   producing native[a3] descendants of Aeneas, kindred blood.
   But thereafter you will be a prey to men who are lovers.[b3]
   Ilium, I pity you. For a fury will sprout in Sparta,[c3]   11.125–40
415 a very beautiful, famous, most excellent shoot,
   leaving the widespread wave of Asia and Europe.
   It will bring lamentations and labors and groans
   and inflict them especially on you, but your fame will be ageless for
      future generations.
   There will also be again a certain false writer, an old man,[d3]   11.163–71
420 of falsified fatherland. The light will go out in his eyes.
   He will have much intelligence and will have speech well proportioned
      to his thoughts,
   blended under two names. He will call himself a Chian
   and write the story of Ilium, not truthfully
   but cleverly. For he will master my words and meters.

---

t2. Gk. *auton* (φ, ψ, Kurfess, Nikiprowetzky); Geffcken suggests *autou*, "raised up a man before him."

u2. The reference to the ten horns and the eleventh that sprouts on the side is a Jewish addition to this oracle, based, of course, on Dan 7. The identity of the final "shoot" is open to a wide variety of interpretations; Alexander Balas is perhaps the most probable one.

v2. Gk. *huph huiōnōn en homophrosunēsin Areōs* (Geffcken) for *huph huiōn hōn es homophrona aision arrēs*. The reference is to the fratricidal struggles for the Syrian throne in the decades following Antiochus Epiphanes. It is not possible to authenticate the reference with regard to any individual king. Alexander Balas was assassinated, though not literally by his descendants.

w2. Cf. SibOr 3.140. When Rhea gave birth to Zeus she sent him to Phrygia.

x2. The fall of Troy.

y2. The walls of Troy were built by Poseidon.

z2. Dorylaeon is in Phrygia, on the Thymbris.

a3. Gk. *autochthonas* (Lanchester) for *autochthonos*.

b3. Menelaus and the Greeks, motivated by the love of Helen.

c3. Helen. Pausanias 10.12.2 says the Erythrean Sibyl sang of Helen.

d3. Homer. Lactantius, *DivInst* 1.6.9, mentions that the Erythrean Sibyl prophesied that Homer would write falsehoods. Cf. also Diodorus Siculus 4.66.

425 He will be the first to unfold my books with his hands,
but he will especially embellish the helmeted men of war,
Hector, son of Priam, and Achilles, son of Peleus,
and the others, as many as cared for warlike deeds.
He will also make gods to stand by these
430 writing falsely, in every way, about empty-headed men.
It will also be great glory for these to die at Ilium,
but he himself will also receive appropriate recompense.
For Lycia also the race of Locrus will engender many evils.
Chalcedon, to whose lot has fallen the way of the sea strait,
435 you also will an Aetolian youth at some time come and destroy.
Cyzicus, the sea will also break off your great wealth.
You, Byzantium, will love war in Asia
and receive groans and blood beyond reckoning.
Cragos, also, lofty mountain of Lycia, water will rush
440 from your peaks when the rock has been opened in a chasm,
until it stops even the prophetic signs of Patara.[e3]
Cyzicus, inhabitant of wine-selling Propontis,
the crested wave of Rhyndacus will crash around you.
You also, Rhodes, will indeed be free from slavery for a long time,   7.1
445 daughter of a day, and you will have great wealth thereafter,
and you will have power at sea surpassing others.
But afterward you will be a prey to lovers
in beauty and wealth. You will place a terrible yoke on your neck.[f3]
A Lydian earthquake will destroy the affairs of Persia,
450 causing most dire disasters for Europe and Asia.
The destructive king of the Sidonians and the battle cry of others
will bring deadly destruction by sea on the Samians.
The plain will sweep to the sea with the blood of
perishing men. Wives with splendidly robed maidens
455 will cry aloud their private unseemly outrage,
some for the dead, some for sons who are perishing.
A sign for Cyprus; an earthquake will destroy the ravines
and Hades will receive many souls at once.
Trallis, the neighbor of Ephesus, will undo by an earthquake   5.289
460 her well-made walls, and a people of grave-minded men.
The earth will flood with boiling water, then the earth,
weighed down, will drink of it. There will be a smell of brimstone.   3.60; 7.142
Samos also will build royal palaces in due time.[g3]
Italy, no foreign war will come to you
465 but native blood, much bemoaned, inexhaustible,[h3]
notorious, will ravage you, shameless one;
and you yourself, stretched out by the warm ashes,
will kill yourself with no foresight in your breast.
You will not be mother of good people, but nurse of wild beasts.
470 But when a destructive man comes from Italy[i3]   4.107;
then, Laodicea, dashed down headlong   5.290;
by the wonderful water of Lycus, beautiful town of the Carians,   7.22;
you will bemoan your famous parent[j3] and be silent.   12.280;
The Thracian Crobyzi will rise up throughout Haemus.   14.85
475 Chattering of teeth comes upon the Campanians
because of the famine which destroys cities.[k3]

e3. Patara had a famous oracle of Apollo.
f3. Rhodes was subdued by Rome in 167 B.C.
g3. Samos was conquered by the Ptolemies in the
early 3rd cent. B.C.
h3. This might refer to the Slave Wars, Social
War, or the civil war of Marius and Sulla, from the
late 2nd cent./early 1st cent. B.C.
i3. Sulla, who sailed for Greece in 87 B.C. to fight
Mithridates.
j3. Zeus, who often appears on coins of Laodicea.
k3. Gk. *ptoliporthon* (Castalio) for *polukarpon*.

Cyrnus, bemoaning its aged parent,[13] and Sardinia, will sink in the wave 7.96
with sea-children, amid great storms of winter
and afflictions of the holy God throughout the depths of the sea.
480 Alas for all the virgins whom Hades will wed
and unburied youths whom the deep will attend.
Alas for infant children floating in the sea, and great wealth.
The blessed land of Mysians will suddenly produce a royal race.
Truly Carthage will not survive long.[m3]
485 There will be lamentation with many groans among the Galatians.   4.106
A final but greatest disaster will come upon Tenedus.
Brazen Sicyon, and you,[n3] Corinth, will boast   4.105; 7.60
over all, with howls, and the flute will sound equally.

A further prophecy of various disasters

When indeed my spirit stopped its inspired hymn   3.1–7, etc.
490 the utterance of the great God again rose in my breast
and bade me prophesy concerning the earth.
Woe to the race of Phoenician men and women   5.456; 7.64; 12.105, 153;
and all the maritime cities, none of you   14.80
will come to the sunlight in common light.
495 No longer will there be a number and tribe alive
because of the unjust tongue and lawless, unholy life
which all have carried out, opening an unholy mouth;
and they composed terrible words, false and unjust,
and stood before God the great king,
500 and they opened their loathsome mouth falsely. Therefore God
will terribly subdue them with afflictions beyond all
the earth, and send a bitter fate upon them,
burning their cities from the ground, and many foundations.
Woe to you, Crete, of many sorrows. To you will come
505 affliction and fearful, eternal destruction.[o3]
The whole earth will again see you smoking
and fire will not leave you forever, but you will burn.
Woe to you, Thrace, how you will come to a yoke of slavery!
when Galatians mingled with Dardanidae
510 ravage[p3] Greece with a swoop, then will evil come upon you.
You will give to another land and will receive nothing.
Woe to you, Gog and Magog, and to all in turn   3.319, etc.
of the Marsians and Angians. How many evils fate brings upon you!
Many too upon the sons of Lycians and Mysians and Phrygians.
515 Many peoples of Pamphylians and Lydians will fall,
Maurians and Ethiopians and strange-speaking peoples,
Cappadocians and Arabs. Why indeed should I proclaim each one
according to its fate? for on all peoples, as many as inhabit the earth
will the Most High send a terrible affliction.
520 But when a vast barbarian people comes against the Greeks[q3]
it will destroy many heads of chosen men.
They will ravage many fat flocks, which belong to mortal men,
and herds of horses and mules, and loud-bellowing oxen.
They will burn well-constructed houses lawlessly with fire

---

13. Gk. *poluetē* (ψ, Nikiprowetzky) for *poluue-*
teis.
m3. Fall of Carthage in 146 B.C.
n3. Gk. *su* for *se* (Kurfess).
o3. Gk. *exalapaxis* (Wilamowitz) for *exalapaxei*.
p3. Gk. *persousi* (Rzach) for *portheontes*. The

reference is to the invasion by the Gauls in 280 B.C.
q3. Probably the Roman invasion that led to the
capture of Corinth in 146 B.C. It is possible that the
reference is to the invasion of the Gauls.

525 and will take many slaves to another land by compulsion,
　　children and broad-girdled women,
　　delicate ones from the chambers, falling forward on tender feet.　　Deut 28:56
　　They will see themselves suffering every terrible outrage
　　in fetters at the hand of strange-speaking enemies,
530 and they will have no one to ward off a war a little or be a helper in
　　　　life.
　　They will see the enemy enjoying their private possessions
　　and all their wealth. They will tremble beneath the knees.
　　A hundred will flee, but one will destroy them all.　　Isa 30:17;
　　Five will stir up grievous wrath but shamefully　　Deut 32:30
535 coming to grips with each other in terrible war and din of battle
　　they will cause joy to their enemies, but grief to the Greeks.
　　A yoke of slavery will come upon all Greece.
　　At once war and pestilence will come upon all.　　3.603; Frag. 3.20
　　God will make a great bronze heaven on high　　Deut 28:23;
540 and cause drought over the whole earth, and make the earth iron.　　1En 80:2
　　But then all mortals will weep terribly
　　for the lack of sowing and plowing, and the one who created heaven　5.276
　　　　and earth
　　will set down much lamented[r3] fire on the earth.　　5.274,377
　　One third of all mankind will survive.　　5.103; Zech 13:8
　　　　　　　　　　　　　　　　　　　　　　　　　　　　　　Rev 9:15, 18; Cf. Ezek 5:12

Exhortation to the Greeks

545 Greece, why do you rely on mortal leaders　　Lactantius,
　　who are not able to flee the end of death?　　Divlnst
　　To what purpose do you give vain gifts to the dead　　1.15.15
　　and sacrifice to idols? Who put error in your heart　　Lactantius,
　　that you should abandon the face of the great God and do these things?　Divlnst
　　　　　　　　　　　　　　　　　　　　　　　　　　　　　　1.15.15;
550 Revere the name of the one who has begotten all, and do not forget it.　WisSol
　　It is a thousand years and five hundred more　　14:12–20
　　since the overbearing kings of the Greeks
　　reigned, who began the first evils for mortals,
　　setting up[s3] many idols of dead gods.　　WisSol 13:10; 14:12
555 On account of them you have been taught vain thinking.
　　But when the wrath of the great God comes upon you,
　　then indeed you will recognize the face of the great God.
　　All the souls of men will groan mightily and
　　stretch out their hands straight to broad heaven　　Oracle of
560 and begin to call on the great king as protector　　Hystaspes,
　　and seek who will be a deliverer from great wrath.　　Divlnst
　　But come and learn this and place it in your heart,　　7.17.18
　　how many woes there will be as the years circle on.
　　Greece, also, by offering the holocausts of oxen
565 and loud-bellowing bulls, which she has sacrificed, at the Temple of the
　　　　great God,
　　will escape the din of war and panic and pestilence
　　and will again escape the yoke of slavery.
　　But the race of impious men will survive up to this point:
　　whenever this fated day comes to pass.
570 You will certainly not sacrifice to God until everything happens.　　4Ezra
　　What God alone has planned will not go unfulfilled.　　5:45–49;
　　A strong necessity will insist that everything be fulfilled.　　2Thes 2:3;
　　　　　　　　　　　　　　　　　　　　　　　　　　　　　　1QpHab 6,
　　　　　　　　　　　　　　　　　　　　　　　　　　　　　　etc.

r3. Gk. *polyn oikton* (Alexandre) for *polun histon.*
s3. Gk. *anathentes* (Alexandre) for *thaneontōn.*

Eulogy of the Jews

3.218–20

There will again be a sacred race of pious men
who attend to the counsels and intention of the Most High,
575　who fully honor the temple of the great God
with drink offering and burnt offering and sacred hecatombs,
sacrifices of well-fed bulls, unblemished rams,
and firstborn sheep, offering as holocausts fat flocks of lambs
on a great altar, in holy manner.
580　Sharing in the righteousness of the law of the Most High,
they will inhabit cities and rich fields in prosperity,
themselves exalted as prophets by the Immortal
and bringing great joy to all mortals.
For to them alone did the great God give wise counsel
585　and faith and excellent understanding in their breasts.
They do not honor with empty deceits works of men,
either gold or bronze, or silver or ivory,
or wooden, stone, or clay idols of dead gods,
red-painted likenesses of beasts,
590　such as mortals honor with empty-minded counsel.
For on the contrary, at dawn they lift up holy arms
toward heaven, from their beds, always sanctifying their flesh[13]
with water, and they honor only the Immortal who always rules,
and then their parents. Greatly, surpassing all men,
595　they are mindful of holy wedlock,
and they do not engage in impious intercourse with male children,
as do Phoenicians, Egyptians, and Romans,
spacious Greece and many nations of others,
Persians and Galatians and all Asia, transgressing
600　the holy law of immortal God, which they transgressed.

Side notes:
4.45,136; 5.281

WisSol
13–15; Isa
44:8–20,
etc.

Ezek 8:10

4.165f.;
PssSol 6:6;
War 2.8.5
(128)

2.60

3.185, etc.

Prophecy of judgment

Therefore the Immortal will inflict on all mortals
disaster and famine and woes and groans
and war and pestilence and lamentable ills,
because they were not willing to piously honor the immortal begetter
605　of all men, but honored idols
made by hand, revering them, which mortals themselves will cast away,
hiding them in clefts of rocks, through shame,
whenever the young[u3] seventh king of Egypt rules
his own land, numbered from the dynasty of the Greeks,
610　which the Macedonians, wonderful men, will found.
A great king will come from Asia,[v3] a blazing eagle,
who will cover the whole land with infantry and cavalry.
He will cut up everything and fill everything with evils.
He will overthrow the kingdom of Egypt. He will take out
615　all its possessions and ride on the broad back of the sea.
Then they will bend a white knee on the fertile ground
to God the great immortal king
but all handmade works will fall in a flame of fire.

Side notes:
Frag. 3.20

8.224; 11.88; Isa 31:7
1En 91.9

Isa 2:18–20

3.318,193

Potter's Oracle, col. 1
Nechepso-Petosiris
(ed. Riess), p. 339
AsMos 3:1
3.188; 5.365

Lactantius,
DivInst
7.19.9

---

t3. So Clement, *Protrepticus* 6.70; MSS read "hands."

u3. The youth of Philometor at the time when Antiochus Epiphanes invaded Egypt is emphasized in the classical accounts of the incident: e.g. Livy 42.29.5–7. "Young" (*neos*) was also an epithet of Horus.

v3. A "king from Asia" was a traditional enemy of Egypt; e.g. the Hyksos, who were still remembered in hellenistic times (Josephus, *Apion* 1.74–92). The tradition was reinforced by the careers of Cambyses and Artaxerxes III and again by Antiochus Epiphanes. The present passage may be influenced by the relatively recent memory of Antiochus, but should be taken as a more general reference.

Transformation of the earth

And then God will give great joy to men,
620 for earth and trees and countless flocks of sheep

2.29–32,
etc.

will give to men the true fruit
of wine, sweet honey and white milk
and corn, which is best of all for mortals.

2.318;
8.211;
5.282

Philo,
SpecLeg
2.181

Appeal for conversion

But you, devious mortal, do not tarry in hesitation
625 but turn back, converted, and propitiate God.

Clement,
Protrepticus
7.74

Sacrifice to God hundreds of bulls and firstborn lambs
and goats at the recurring times.
But propitiate him, the immortal God, so that he may have pity

Deut 4:35
Isa 43:11; 45:5.14, etc.

for he alone is God and there is no other.
630 Honor righteousness and oppress no one,

2.56f.

for so the Immortal bids wretched mortals.
But you, guard against the wrath of the great God,
whenever the culmination of pestilence comes upon all mortals
and they are subdued and meet with terrible justice.

Eschatological woes

1En 99:4;
2Bar 70:3;
4Ezra 6:24;
9:3;

635 King will lay hold of king and take away territory.
Peoples will ravage peoples, and potentates, tribes.

13:30f.; Mt
24:6f.; Mk
13:8; Lk
21:10

All leaders will flee to another land.
The land will have a change of men and foreign rule
will ravage all Greece and drain off
640 the rich land of its wealth, and men will come
face to face in strife among themselves because of gold and silver.
Love of gain will be shepherd of evils for cities.

2.111;
3.235; 8.17

All will be unburied in a foreign country.
Vultures and wild beasts of the earth
645 will ravage the flesh of some. Indeed when this is completed
the huge earth will consume the remains of the dead.
It itself will be completely unsown and unplowed,

3.542;
5.276

wretched, proclaiming the curse of innumerable men,
(for many lengths of yearly recurring times—

Ezek 39:9

650 light shields, long shields, javelins and diverse weapons
and not even wood will be cut from a thicket for the flame of the fire.[w3])

The savior king

3.286; 5.109; 13.151, 164
Potter's Oracle, col. 2
ApEl 2:39

And then God will send a King from the sun[x3]
who will stop the entire earth from evil war,
killing some, imposing oaths of loyalty on others;
655 and he will not do all these things by his private plans

Jn 6:38; Mt 26:39, etc.

but in obedience to the noble teachings of the great God.

The final assault on the Temple

The Temple[y3] of the great God (will be) laden with very beautiful wealth,

---

w3. Vss. 649–51 are probably intrusive. Cf. vss. 728, 729, 731.

x3. I.e. an Egyptian king. Cf. Potter's Oracle, col. 2, Rosetta Stone, etc., and the Introduction to SibOr 3.

the aretalogies (Andros, 158). In the Potter's Oracle the king from the sun is sent by Isis.

y3. Following Geffcken and Rzach, and the context. Nikiprowetzky has *laos* "people" (φ).

gold, silver, and purple ornament,
and earth (will be) productive and sea full
660 of good things. And kings will begin
to be angry with each other, requiting evils with spirit. 1En 56:7
Envy is not good for wretched mortals.
But again the kings of the peoples will launch an attack Ps 2; 4Ezra
together against this land, bringing doom upon themselves, 13:33
    Ezek 38–39
665 for they will want to destroy the Temple of the great God
and most excellent men when they enter the land.
The abominable kings, each one with his throne Jer 1:15
and faithless people, will set them up around the city. Oracle of Hystaspes, *DivInst*
    7:17

Cosmic judgment

And God will speak, with a great voice,
670 to the entire ignorant empty-minded people, and
judgment will come upon them from the great God, and all will perish
at the hand of the Immortal. Fiery swords will fall Oracle of Hystaspes, *DivInst*
from heaven on the earth. Torches, great gleams, 7:19; SibOr 3.798
    War 6.5.3 (288)
will come shining into the midst of men.
675 The all-bearing earth will be shaken in those days Ps 18:7; Judg 5:4f.; Hab 3:6
by the hand of the Immortal, and the fish in the sea AsMos 10:4
and all the wild beasts of the earth and innumerable tribes of birds, Ezek 38:20
all the souls of men and all the sea
will shudder before the face of the Immortal and there will be a terror.
680 He will break the lofty summits of the mountains and the mounds of 1En 1:6;
    giants Micah 1:4;
    Isa 40:4
and the dark abyss will appear to all. 3.409
High ravines in lofty mountains Isa 30:25
will be full of corpses. Rocks will flow 3.804
with blood and every torrent will fill the plain.
685 All well-constructed walls of hostile men
will fall to the ground, because they knew neither the law
nor the judgment of the great God, but with mindless spirit
you all launched an attack and raised spears against the sanctuary.
God will judge all men by war and sword
690 and fire and torrential rain. There will also 5.377; Ezek 38:22
be brimstone from heaven and stone and much Isa 30:30; 29:6
    Ps 11:6
grievous hail. Death will come upon four-footed creatures.
Then they will recognize the immortal God who judges these things. Ezek 38:23
Wailing and tumult will spread throughout the boundless earth
695 at the death of men. All the impious will bathe in blood.
The earth itself will also drink
of the blood of the dying; wild beasts will be sated with flesh.
God himself, the great eternal one, told me 3.1–7, etc.
to prophesy all these things. These things will not go unfilfilled.
700 Nor is anything left unaccomplished that he so much as puts in mind
for the spirit of God which knows no falsehood is throughout the world. WisSol 1:7

The salvation of the elect

But the sons of the great God will all live Hos 11:1; WisSol 2:13,16
peacefully around the Temple, rejoicing in these things
which the Creator, just judge and sole ruler, will give.
705 For he alone will shield them, standing by them magnificently
as if he had a wall of blazing fire round about. Zech 2:5
They will be free from war in towns and country.
No hand of evil war, but rather the Immortal himself

and the hand of the Holy One will be fighting for them.   Ex 14:25; Isa 41:10
                                                                  2Mac 8:24
710 And then all islands and cities will say,   Isa 49:1; 51:5
    "How much the Immortal loves those men!
    for everything fights on their side and helps them,   WisSol 16:24; 5:17–23
    heaven, divinely driven sun and moon"
    (but the all-bearing earth will be shaken in those days).   3.675
715 They will bring forth from their mouths a delightful utterance in hymns,
    "Come, let us all fall on the ground and entreat   Ps 95:6
    the immortal king, the great eternal God.
    Let us send to the Temple, since he alone is sovereign   5.493–500; Ps 122:1
    and let us all ponder the Law of the Most High God,   Isa 2:3; Micah 4:2
720 who is most righteous of all throughout the earth.
    But we had wandered from the path of the Immortal.   3.9; Isa 53:6
    With mindless spirit we revered things made by hand,   WisSol 5:6
    idols and statues of dead men."   3.554; WisSol 13:10; 14:12
    The souls of faithful men will cry out as follows:
725 "Come, let us fall on our faces throughout the people of God,
    and let us delight with hymns God the begetter, throughout our homes,
    gathering the weapons of enemies throughout all the land   Ezek 39:9f.
    for seven lengths of annually recurring times,   3.649
    light shields and long shields, helmets, many diverse arms, 3.650
730 a large number of bows also, and an abundance of unjust weapons.
    For not even wood will be cut from a thicket for the flame of the fire." 3.651

Exhortation to the Greeks

    But wretched Greece, desist from proud thoughts.
    Entreat the great-hearted Immortal and take precautions.
    Do not send against this city your thoughtless people
735 which is not from the holy land of the Great One.
    Do not disturb Camarina, for it is better undisturbed.[z3]
    (Do not disturb) a leopard from its lair lest evil befall you,
    but keep away from it. Do not have a proud overbearing
    spirit in your breast, making ready for a hard contest.
740 Serve the great God so that you may have a share in these things.

The day of judgment

    When indeed this fated day also reaches its consummation   Lactantius, *DivInst* 7.20.1
    and the judgment of immortal God comes upon mortals,   Amos 5:18; Isa 2:12, etc.
    a great judgment and dominion will come upon men.
    For the all-bearing earth will give the most excellent unlimited fruit 3.620–23; 2.29–32, etc.
745 to mortals, of grain, wine, and oil   3.243; Hos 2:8
    and a delightful drink of sweet honey from heaven,
    trees, fruit of the top branches, and rich flocks
    and herds and lambs of sheep and kids of goats.
    And it will break forth sweet fountains of white milk.
750 The cities will be full of good things and the fields will
    be rich. There will be no sword on earth or din of battle,   3.367–80
    and the earth will no longer be shaken, groaning deeply.
    There will no longer be war or drought on earth,
    no famine or hail, damaging to fruits,
755 but there will be great peace throughout the whole earth.
    King will be friend to king to the end of the age.
    The Immortal in the starry heaven will put in effect

---

z3. This vs. is an old proverb. Quoted by Servius
in his commentary on Virgil's *Aeneid* 3.701.

a common law[a4] for men throughout the whole earth
for all that is done among wretched mortals.

760 For he himself alone is God and there is no other,
and he himself will burn with fire a race of grievous men.

3.629, etc.

2.196; Ps
97:3; Isa
66:16

Moral exhortation

But urge on your minds in your breasts
and shun unlawful worship. Worship the Living One.
Avoid adultery and indiscriminate intercourse with males.

765 Rear your own offspring and do not kill it,
for the Immortal is angry at whoever commits these sins.

3.184–86,
etc.
2.280f.

The eschatological kingdom

And then, indeed, he will raise up a kingdom for all
ages among men, he who once gave the holy Law
to the pious, to all of whom he promised to open the earth

770 and the world and the gates of the blessed and all joys
and immortal intellect and eternal cheer.
From every land they will bring incense and gifts
to the house of the great God. There will be no other
house among men, even for future generations to know,

775 except the one which God gave to faithful men to honor
(for mortals will invoke the son of the great God).[b4]
All the paths of the plain and rugged cliffs,
lofty mountains, and wild waves of the sea
will be easy to climb or sail in those days,

780 for all peace will come upon the land of the good.
Prophets of the great God will take away the sword
for they themselves are judges of men and righteous kings.[c4]
There will also be just wealth among men
for this is the judgment and dominion of the great God.

785 Rejoice, maiden, and be glad, for to you the one
who created heaven and earth has given the joy of the age.
He will dwell in you. You will have immortal light.
Wolves and lambs will eat grass together in the mountains.
Leopards will feed together with kids.

790 Roving bears will spend the night with calves.
The flesh-eating lion will eat husks at the manger
like an ox, and mere infant children will lead them
with ropes. For he will make the beasts on earth harmless.
Serpents and asps will sleep with babies

795 and will not harm them, for the hand of God will be upon them.

Dan 2:44;
7:27

Isa 2:3;
Micah 4:2;
Zech 14:16

Lactantius,
DivInst
4.6.5

2.29–32,
etc.

Zech 2:10;
Isa 12:6
8.324, etc.
Isa 60:1

Isa 11:6–8;
65:25; 2Bar
73:6; Philo,
Praem
85–90;
Virgil,
Eclogue
4:18–25

Lactantius,
DivInst
7:24

The signs of the end

I will tell you a very clear sign, so that you may know
when the end of all things comes to pass on earth:
when swords are seen at night in starry heaven
toward evening and toward dawn,

800 and again dust is brought forth from heaven
upon the earth and all[d4] the light of the sun

2.185; 3.672; Oracle of
Hystaspes, *DivInst* 7:19
War 6.5.3 (288)

2.185, etc.;
Joel 2:10

---

a4. A common Stoic notion—cf. the last vs. of
Cleanthes' "Hymn to Zeus."

b4. This vs. must be regarded as a Christian
interpolation.

c4. The idea that prophets will rule in a kingdom
at the end-time is unusual, but cf. the role assigned

to prophets in 1Mac 14:41. In *Vita Mos* 2:1 Philo
says that Moses is both prophet and king. The Hasmonean king John Hyrcanus was also said to have
the gift of prophecy (Josephus, *Ant* 13.10.7 [299]).

d4. Gk. *kai hapan* (Wilamowitz) for *hapan kai
hoi*.

is eclipsed in the middle from heaven, and the rays
of the moon appear and return to the earth.
There will be a sign from the rocks, with blood and drops of gore.   3.683
805 You will see a battle of infantry and cavalry in the clouds,   2Mac 5:2; War 6.5.3 (288)
like a hunt of wild beasts, like a mist.   Tacitus, History 5.13
This is the end of war which God, who inhabits heaven, is accomplishing.
But all must sacrifice to the great king.

The Sibyl's conclusion

(I say) these things to you, having left   Lactantius,
810 the long Babylonian walls of Assyria, frenzied, a fire sent to Greece, DivInst
prophesying the disclosures[e4] of God to all mortals,   1.6.13
so that I prophesy divine riddles to men.
Throughout Greece mortals will say that I am of another country,
a shameless one, born of Erythrae.[f4] Some will say that
815 I am Sibylla born of Circe[g4] as mother and Gnostos as father,
a crazy liar. But when everything comes to pass,   11.317; Lactantius,
then you will remember me and no longer will anyone   DivInst 4.15.29
say that I am crazy, I who am a prophetess of the great God.   3.1–7, etc.
For he did not reveal to me what he had revealed before to my parents
820 but what happened first, these things my father[h4] told me,
and God put all of the future in my mind
so that I prophesy both future and former things
and tell them to mortals. For when the world was deluged
with waters, and a certain single approved man was left   1.287;
825 floating on the waters in a house of hewn wood   Prologue 33
with beasts, and birds, so that the world might be filled again,
I was his daughter-in-law and I was of his blood.
The first things happened to him and all the latter things have been
        revealed,
so let all these things from my mouth be accounted true.

e4. Gk. *mēnumata* (ψ) for *mēnimata*. On the
supposed Babylonian origin of the Sibyl cf. Pausanias
10.12.9 and Justin, *Cohortatio ad Graecos* 37, who
also say that she was daughter of Berossus. See the
general introduction.

f4. Lactantius also identifies the Sibyl of SibOr 3
with the Erythrean Sibyl.

g4. Circe was the magic-working goddess who
changed Odysseus' men into swine (*Odyssey* 10.210;
Aeneid 7.19–20). According to Virgil, *Aeneid* 6.36,

Deiphobe, the Cumean Sibyl, was daughter of Glaucus. Gnostos is enigmatic. Kurfess emends to
agnōstoio, "of an unknown father." Nikiprowetzky
gives the name as *Gnostēs*, which might mean
"diviner" or "one who knows." Epiphanius, *AdvHaer*
26.1, says the gnostics attributed certain books to
Noriah, the wife of Noah. In SibOr 3.827 the Sibyl
is daughter-in-law of Noah.

h4. Gk. *genetēs*, "father" (Wilamowitz).

THE SIBYLLINE ORACLES, BOOK 4

Introduction

Sibylline Oracles 4 is a composite oracle which consists of a political oracle from the hellenistic age updated by a Jew in the late first century A.D., and adapted for specifically religious purposes.[1] The older hellenistic oracle is structured by a twofold division of history into ten generations and four kingdoms. This is found in Sibylline Oracles 4.49–101. There we read that the Assyrians will rule for six generations, the Medes for two, and the Persians for one. Then the tenth generation and fourth kingdom coincide in the Macedonian Empire. We should expect that this climactic generation would be followed by a definitive kingdom or judgment, but instead we find history prolonged to refer to Rome and its eventual downfall (145–48). Since Rome is not integrated into the numerical schematization of history we must assume that verses 102–51 are a later addition, and that the original oracle referred to no historical empire after Macedonia. We should expect, however, that the original oracle built up to some conclusion, which is not now contained in verses 49–101. It is quite possible that the conclusion now found in verses 173–92, which tells about the end-time, also formed the conclusion of the original oracle, but this, of course, cannot be conclusively demonstrated.[2]

The second stage of the oracle is found in verses 1–48 and 102–72 (and possibly 173–92). Verses 102–51 are a collection of oracles relating to particular events and legends that bring the older oracle up to date. Verses 1–48 and 152–72 give the moral and religious teachings of the redactor. There is no trace of Christian redaction in Sibylline Oracles 4.

Date and provenance

The original oracle was probably written not long after the time of Alexander.[3] The Macedonian Empire is thought to have lasted only one generation, and there is no clear reference to any events between the death of Alexander and the rise of Rome.

In schematizations of history of this sort the last enumerated kingdom/generation is either a glorious one (e.g. the seventh king in SibOr 3) or is especially marked out for destruction (as in Dan 2 and 7). Since the Macedonians do not in any sense usher in a glorious age in Sibylline Oracles 4 we must assume that the oracle was anti-Macedonian in tendency. If the present conclusion was part of the original oracle, then Macedonia would have been the immediate victim of the judgment of God. Such an oracle could have been written in any place that was subject to Macedonia. Although the schematization of history may reflect Persian influence,[4] the oracle is not likely to be Persian, since the Persians are allotted only one generation of world empire, and the author shows no special sympathy for them. Nothing in the oracle necessarily requires Jewish authorship. Even the passage about the end-time, 173–92, while it probably contains at least Jewish redactional elements, could have been largely composed by a gentile, as both the destruction of the world by fire and the resurrection of the dead could be derived from Persian doctrines.[5] Also the reference to the Flood in verses 51–53 could be derived from Babylonian or even Greek tradition. The particular

---

[1] The most important discussions of SibOr 4 are those of Geffcken, *Komposition und Entstehungszeit*, pp. 18–21; J. Thomas, *Le Mouvement baptiste en Palestine et Syrie* (Gembloux, Belgium, 1938) pp. 46–60; V. Nikiprowetzky, "Réflexions sur quelques problèmes du quatrième et du cinquième livre des Oracles Sibyllins," *HUCA* 43 (1972) 29–76; A. Peretti, "Echi di dottrine esseniche negli Oracoli Sibillini Giudaici," *La parola del passato* 17 (1962) 247–95; D. Flusser, *Israel Oriental Studies* 2 (1972) 148–75; and J. J. Collins, "The Place of the Fourth Sibyl in the Development of the Jewish Sibyllina," *JJS* 25 (1974) 365–80.

[2] Collins, *JJS* 25 (1974) 373–75.

[3] Geffcken, *Komposition und Entstehungszeit*, p. 20, suggests a date after A.D. 60 on the basis of the reference to an earthquake in vs. 107. However, that vs. is probably part of the later redaction and, in any case, the identification of the earthquake in question is doubtful. Cf. Lanchester, *APOT*, vol. 2, p. 395.

[4] See Flusser, *Israel Oriental Studies* 2 (1972) 162–74.

[5] See Collins, *JJS* 25 (1974) 374. On the role of the conflagration in Zoroastrianism see R. Mayer, *Die biblische Vorstellung vom Weltbrand* (Bonn, 1956) pp. 1–79. The belief in resurrection is attributed to the Persians by Diogenes Laertius (*Proem* 9), who derives his statement from Theopompus (3rd cent. B.C.).

enumeration of world kingdoms, Assyria, Media, Persia, Macedonia, cannot be derived from the Book of Daniel, where the first empire is Babylon; it is paralleled in Tobit 14 and in Roman sources[6] and so was widely known in the eastern Mediterranean. While Jewish authorship remains as plausible as any other, there is nothing distinctively Jewish about the original oracle.

The redaction of Sibylline Oracles 4 can be located with more precision. It refers to the destruction of the Jerusalem Temple (116), the legend of Nero's flight to the Parthians and future return (119–24, 138–39),[7] and the eruption of Vesuvius in A.D. 79 (130–35). All scholars agree that it was written shortly after the last datable event mentioned—therefore about A.D. 80. Its Jewish character is revealed by its doctrines and most specifically by the fact that it understands the eruption of Vesuvius as a punishment for the destruction of Jerusalem (136).

The geographical provenance of the first-century redaction is more controversial. Most scholars locate it in Syria or the Jordan Valley because of the importance attached to baptism,[8] and, while the evidence is less than conclusive, this position carries the balance of probability. Recently Nikiprowetzky has attempted to associate it with Sibylline Oracles 3 and 5, and therefore to assign it to Egypt.[9] However, Sibylline Oracles 4 shows an attitude to the Temple diametrically opposed to what we find in Sibylline Oracles 3 and 5. In the latter two books the Temple plays a central role. In Sibylline Oracles 4.5–12 and 27–30 there is a complete rejection of temple worship.[10] Since Sibylline Oracles 5 must be dated later than Sibylline Oracles 4, the difference in attitude to temple worship cannot be explained by the fact that the Jewish Temple was no longer in existence when book 4 was written. Sibylline Oracles 4 also attaches far greater importance to baptism than either books 3 or 5. Since the only reference to Egypt in book 4 (vs. 72) is part of the hellenistic oracle,[11] there is no basis whatever for Egyptian provenance.

Historical and theological importance

The hellenistic oracle is important as a specimen of anti-Macedonian political prophecy. Our appreciation of the hellenistic oracle is, however, hindered by doubt as to how it originally concluded.

The periodization of the hellenistic oracle has multiple parallels in Jewish apocalyptic. The ten generations appear in the Apocalypse of Weeks in 1 Enoch, the Melchizedek text from Qumran Cave 11, Sibylline Oracles 1 and 2, but also in the Cumean Sibyl, as reported by Servius in his commentary on the Fourth Eclogue.[12] The four kingdoms are best known from Daniel 2 and 7, but are also found in Aemilius Sura and the Persian Zand-ī Vohūman Yasn.[13] It should be noted that Sibylline Oracles 4 is concerned with world history only since the Flood (vss. 51–53). Therefore, its four kingdoms, followed presumably by a destruction of fire, are analogous to the four generations that come between the Flood and the destruction by fire in Sibylline Oracles 1 and 2. The view of the end-time of Sibylline Oracles 4, with its emphasis on bodily resurrection, finds its closest parallel in Sibylline Oracles 2. In both Sibylline books the good are restored to life on earth while the wicked are condemned to the underworld. The description in Sibylline Oracles 2 is, however, much more elaborate and probably represents a later stage of this tradition about the end-time. The Jewish first-century redaction used the schematization of history as a framework for exhortation. In verses 161–77 we get a concise summary of what is necessary to avert disaster—to refrain from violence, "wash your whole bodies in perennial rivers" and supplicate God. The rejection of violence is, of course, commonplace, although we should note that deeds of violence are

[6] See Flusser, *Israel Oriental Studies* 2 (1972) 153–62; J. W. Swain, "The Theory of Four Monarchies, Opposition History Under the Roman Empire," *Classical Philology* 25 (1940) 1–21.
[7] On the Nero legend in the Sibylline Oracles see Collins, *The Sibylline Oracles*, pp. 80–87.
[8] See Thomas, *Le Mouvement baptiste*, pp. 48f.; Collins, *JJS* 25 (1974) 379. Asia Minor has also been suggested.
[9] Nikiprowetzky, *La Troisième Sibylle*, pp. 232f.; idem, *HUCA* 43 (1972) 59. Also B. Noack, "Are the Essenes Referred to in the Sibylline Oracles?" *Studia Theologica* 17 (1963) 92–102.
[10] See further Collins, *JJS* 25 (1974) 366–69.
[11] Contra Noack, *Studia Theologica* 17 (1963) 97.
[12] See further Flusser, *Israel Oriental Studies* 2 (1972) 162–74.
[13] Ibid., pp. 153–62.

blamed for the fall of Jerusalem (118), so the book may reflect a quietist attitude. However, the distinctive requirement, if disaster is to be averted, is baptism. The role of baptism here and its relation to the judgment is strikingly reminiscent of John the Baptist and quite different from the ritual washings of Sibylline Oracles 3.592f., which are not presented in an eschatological context. This baptism is also quite different from the ritual washings of the Essenes despite the efforts of scholars to identify them.[14]

Our knowledge of the doctrines of the Jewish first-century redactor is supplemented by verses 1–48. There we find polemic against idolatry (6f.), sexual offenses (33f.), injustice, and violence. Monotheism and God's power as creator are emphasized. The distinctive doctrine of these verses, however, is the rejection of temple worship. According to verses 8–11, God does not have a temple of stone, but one which is not made by hands. According to verses 27–30, the pious reject all temples and sacrificial cults. While these passages are not specifically an attack on the Jewish Temple (which no longer existed), they undermine the very idea of temple worship and make no allowance for the possibility of an acceptable temple. This rejection of temple worship has its parallels in the Bible, most proximately in the speech of Stephen in Acts 7.

The distinctive doctrines of Sibylline Oracles 4 then are baptism, as a prerequisite for salvation, and the rejection of temple cults. To these must be added a lively expectation of the end. This complex of doctrines finds its closest parallels in the beliefs of the Christian Ebionites and Elcasaites.[15] There is nothing in Sibylline Oracles 4 to suggest Christian authorship, but the book was presumably written in Jewish baptist circles, of a kind similar to those Christian sectarian movements and perhaps historically related to them.

---

[14] Most recently Peretti, *La parola del passato* 17 (1962) 247–95, and Noack, *Studia Theologica* 17 (1963) 92–102. See the thorough critique of this position by Nikiprowetzky, *HUCA* 43 (1972) 29–57.

[15] Collins, *JJS* 25 (1974) 379.

THE SYBILLINE ORACLES
Book 4

Proclamation of the Sibyl

People of boastful Asia and Europe, give ear
to the unfailing truths that I am about to prophesy   2.1–5, etc.
through my honey-voiced mouth from our shrine.
I am not an oracle-monger of false Phoebus, whom vain   Clement,
5 men called a god, and falsely described as a seer,[a]   Protr 4.50

Polemic against idolatry and temples

but of the great God, whom no hands of men fashioned   3.12ff., etc.
in the likeness of speechless idols of polished stone.
For he does not have a house, a stone set up as a temple,[b]   Acts 7:48f.
dumb and toothless, a bane which brings many woes to men,   (cf. Isa 66:1–2)
10 but one which it is not possible to see from earth nor to measure   Heb 8:1–5; 9:11f.; Ex 25:40
with mortal eyes, since it was not fashioned by mortal hand.   Acts 7:44
He sees all at once but is seen by no one himself.   3.12
Dark night is his, and day, sun and   3.20–23
stars, moon and fish-filled sea,
15 and land and rivers and source of perennial springs,
things created for life, also showers which engender   WisSol 1:14
the fruit of the soil, and trees, both vine and olive.
He it is who drove a whip through my heart within,
to narrate accurately to men what now is,   3.162–64,
20 and what will yet be, from the first generation   etc.
until the tenth comes. For he himself will prove everything   2.15, etc. 3.700
by accomplishing it. But you, people, listen to the Sibyl in all things
as she pours forth true speech from her holy mouth.

Praise of the righteous

Happy will be those of mankind on earth   Justin,
25 who will love the great God, blessing him   Cohort ad Graec 16;
before drinking and eating, putting their trust in piety.   3.573–96
They will reject all temples when they see them;[c]   Clement,
altars too, useless foundations of dumb stones   Protr 4:62
28a (and stone statues and handmade images)[d]
defiled with blood of animate creatures, and sacrifices   7.78
30 of four-footed animals. They will look to the great glory of the one God
and commit no wicked murder, nor deal in
dishonest gain, which are most horrible things.
Neither have they disgraceful desire for another's spouse   3.764
     3.184–86, etc.

a. Pausanias 10.12.6 says that the Sibyl is a prophetess of Phoebus (Apollo).

b. Gk. *naon lithon hidruthenta* (ψ) for *naō lithon helkusthenta*.

c. This rejection of temple worship and animal sacrifice is characteristic of the Ebionites. See the PseudClemRec 1.54–65. The rejection of bloody sacrifices is also characteristic of the Elcasaites (Epiphanius, *Panarion Haeresium* 19.3). The attitudes of the Essenes to temple worship are more complex. Philo (*Quod Omn* 75) says they expressed their devotion "not by sacrificing animals but by determining to render their own minds holy." Josephus (*Ant* 18.1.5 [19]) says that they sent gifts to the temple but offered sacrifices by themselves. While the question as to whether sacrifices were offered at Qumran is disputed, temple worship is never rejected in principle in the scrolls. The custom of saying grace before meals is attested for both the Essenes (*War* 2.8.5 [131]) and the Pharisees (m.Ber 3).

d. This vs. is found only in Clement and is rejected by Geffcken.

or for hateful and repulsive abuse of a male.
35 Other men will never imitate their way
or piety or customs, because they desire shamelessness.
On the contrary, they deride them with mockery and laughter.   1.171
Infantile in their foolishness, they will falsely attribute to those
what wicked and evil deeds they themselves commit.

The coming judgment

40 For the entire race of men is slow of faith. But when   Lactantius,
the judgment of the world and of mortals has already come,   *DivInst*
7.23.4
which God himself will perform, judging impious and pious at once,
then he will also send the impious down into the gloom in fire,[e]   2.292
and then they will realize what impiety they committed.
45 But the pious will remain on the fertile soil,   2.313–38; 3.573
and God will give them spirit and life and favor at once.   4.189
All these things will be accomplished in the tenth generation,   2.15, etc.
but now, the things which will happen from the first generation,
these will I say.

The first kingdom

First, the Assyrians will rule over all mortals,[f]
50 holding the world in their dominion for six generations
from the time when the heavenly God was in wrath   Lactantius,
De ira Dei
with the cities themselves and all men,   23.4
and the sea covered the earth when the Flood burst forth.

The second kingdom

These will the Medes destroy,[g] and boast on their thrones.
55 They will have only two generations. In their time the following things
will take place:
There will be dark night in the mid-hour of day;[h]   1.375, etc.
the stars and the circles of the moon will disappear from heaven;   5.347;
8.204
the earth, shaken by the turmoil of a great earthquake,   8.433;
will cast down headlong many cities and works of men.   3.675,714,
752
60 Then islands will emerge from the depth of the sea.
But when the great Euphrates is flooded with blood,
then indeed a terrible din of battle will arise for the Medes
and Persians in war. The Medes will fall under the spears
of the Persians and flee over the great water of the Tigris.[i]

The third kingdom

65 The power of the Persians will be the greatest of the whole world.
They are destined to have one generation of very prosperous rule.
All evils which men pray to be spared will come to pass:
battles and murders, dissensions and exiles,   12.113;
13.9,107; 14.122
headlong crashes of towers and overthrow of cities,

e. On the idea of a fiery hell see n. x2 to SibOr 2.292.
f. For discussion and bibliography on the four kingdoms see the Introduction to SibOr 4. The succession of Assyrian, Median, and Persian empires is found in Herodotus 1.95, 130, in Ctesias, Diodorus Siculus 2.1–34. It is also implied in Tob 14.
g. Nineveh fell to an alliance of Medes and Babylonians in 612 B.C.
h. Lanchester sees here a reference to a phenomenon said to have occurred during a battle between Medes and Lydians in 585 B.C. (Herodotus 1.71). Such portents are common in oracular literature, e.g. Nechepso-Petosiris.
i. Cyrus the Persian had conquered Media by 550 B.C.

70 when boastful Greece sails to the wide Hellespont
bringing grievous doom to the Phrygians and Asia.ʲ
Further, famine and failure of crops will visit
much-furrowed wheat-bearing Egypt, for a twenty-year cycle,
when the Nile, which nourishes corn, hides
75 its dark water somewhere else under the earth.
A king will come from Asia, brandishing a great spear,   3.611
with countless ships.ᵏ He will walk the watery paths
of the deep, and will cut through a lofty mountain as he sails.
Him will wretched Asia receive as a fugitive from war.
80 When the flame of Aetna belches forth a stream of great fire   7.6
it will burn all miserable Sicily,
and the great city Croton will fall into the deep stream.
There will be strife in Greece.ˡ Raging against each other,
they will cast many cities down headlong and will destroy many men
85 by fighting. But the strife will have equal effect on all parties.
But when the race of men comes to the tenth generation   2.15
then there will also be yokes of slavery and terror for the Persians.

The fourth kingdom

But when the Macedonians boast of scepters,
thereafter there will also be dire capture for Thebes.ᵐ   8.161
90 The Carians will inhabit Tyre, and the Tyrians will perish.ⁿ
Sand will cover all Samos under beaches.   3.363;
Delos will no longer be visible, and all the affairs of Delos will be   8.166
     inconspicuous.
Babylon, great in appearance but insignificant in battle,ᵒ
will stand, built on useless hopes.
95 Macedonians will colonize Bactria, but the people ofᵖ Bactria
and Susa will all flee to the land of Greece.
It will come to pass in future generations that Pyramus of the silver
     current,�q
pouring forward its shoreline, will reach the sacred island,
and you, Baris, will fall, and Cyzicus, when cities slide   3.442
100 as the earth is shaken by earthquakes.   4.58, etc.
Upon the Rhodians, too, a final, but greatest, disaster will come.   8.160

The rise of Rome

Nor will the power of Macedonia survive, but from the west
a great Italian war will bloomʳ under which the world
will serve, bearing the yoke of slavery for the Italians.
105 You also, miserable Corinth, will one day behold your capture.
Carthage, your tower will also bend the knee to the ground.ˢ
Wretched Laodicea, at some time an earthquake will throw you headlongᵗ   3.471
and spread you flat, but you will be founded again as a city, and stand.
Beautiful Myra of Lycia, the shuddering earth will no longer
110 support you, but falling down headlong on the earth,

---

j. A reference to the Greek assistance to the Ionian revolt against Persia in 499 B.C.

k. The invasions of Greece by Xerxes in 480 B.C. Xerxes made a bridge of boats across the Hellespont and cut a canal through the Athos Peninsula.

l. A reference to the continual wars among the Greeks, but especially the Peloponnesian War of 431–404 B.C.

m. Thebes was captured by Alexander in 335 B.C.

n. Tyre was captured in 332 B.C.

o. Babylon was captured without resistance in 331 B.C.

p. Reading apo (Rzach) for hupo.

q. The Pyramus is a Cilician river. This oracle is also found in Strabo 1.3.7 and 12.2.4.

r. The Macedonian wars, beginning in 214 B.C. and culminating in the battle of Pydna in 168 B.C.

s. Carthage and Corinth fell in 146 B.C.

t. Tacitus, Annals 14.27, reports an earthquake at Laodicea in A.D. 60.

you will pray to flee to another land as an exile
when the Lord[u] spreads out the dark water of the sea
with thunderings and earthquakes because of the impieties of Patara.
Armenia, the compulsion of slavery awaits you also.[v]

The destruction of Jerusalem

115 An evil storm of war will also come upon Jerusalem   5.154,
    from Italy, and it will sack the great Temple of God,   398–409
    whenever they put their trust in folly and cast off piety
    and commit repulsive murders in front of the Temple.[w]
    Then a great king will flee from Italy like a runaway slave[x]   5.143,216;
120 unseen and unheard over the channel of the Euphrates,   12.81–94
    when he dares to incur a maternal curse for repulsive murder[y]   5.30,145,
    and many other things, confidently, with wicked hand.   363; 8.71;
    When he runs away, beyond the Parthian land,   AscenIs 4:2
    many will bloody the ground for the throne of Rome.[z]
125 A leader of Rome will come to Syria[a2] who will burn
    the Temple of Jerusalem with fire, at the same time slaughter   4.116, etc.
    many men and destroy the great land of the Jews with its broad roads.
    Then indeed an earthquake will destroy at once Salamis and Paphos
    when the dark water overwhelms Cyprus, which is washed by many   4.143;
        waves.   5.450–51;
                                                         7.5

Various disturbances

130 But when a firebrand, turned away from a cleft in the earth
    in the land of Italy, reaches to broad heaven,[b2]
    it will burn many cities and destroy men.
    Much smoking ashes will fill the great sky,
    and showers will fall from heaven like red earth.
135 Know then the wrath of the heavenly God,
    because they will destroy the blameless tribe of the pious.
    Then the strife of war being aroused will come to the west,
    and the fugitive from Rome will also come, brandishing a great spear,[c2] 5.28–34,138–53,215–24,
    having crossed the Euphrates with many myriads.   363–70; 3.63–74; 8.70–72,
                                                        140–47; Rev 17:11
140 Wretched Antioch, they will no longer call you a city   AscenIs 4:1–2
    when you fall under spears by your own folly;   13.125
    and then pestilence and terrible din of battle will destroy Cyprus.   13.126
    Woe to miserable Cyprus, a broad wave of the sea   4.129
    will cover you when you have been tossed up by wintry blasts.
145 Great wealth will come to Asia, which Rome itself   3.350–55; 8.72; Oracle of
    once plundered and deposited in her house of many possessions.   Hystaspes, *DivInst* 17.15.11
    She will then pay back twice as much and more

---

u. Gk. *ho medōn* (Lanchester) for *homadon*. The
Lord in question could be Poseidon.
    v. The Armenian wars of A.D. 43–66.
    w. The reference is most probably to the Romans,
but possibly to the Zealots.
    x. Nero. The emperor committed suicide in A.D.
68, but there was a widespread belief that he had fled
to the Parthians and would return. See further vs.
138.
    y. Nero had his mother put to death (Suetonius,
Nero 34; cf. 39).
    z. A reference to the rapid succession of emperors,
Galba, Otho, Vitellius, and Vespasian, and the accompanying strife.

a2. Titus.
    b2. The eruption of Vesuvius which destroyed
Pompeii in A.D. 79.
    c2. The legend of Nero's return arose from the
belief that he had fled to the Parthians and was boosted
by a series of impostors who claimed to be the returned
emperor. At least two such impostors are known, one
in A.D. 69 (Tacitus, *Historiae* 2.8, 9; Dio Cassius
64.9) and the other about twenty years later (Suetonius, *Nero* 57). At first Nero was believed to be still
alive and operating on a human level. In the Jewish
tradition, however, he is mythicized and even identified with Belial in SibOr 3.63–74 and AscenIs 4:1–2.

to Asia, and then there will be a surfeit of war.[d2]
A bitter famine will destroy the cities of the Carians,
150 which are very beautifully turreted, by the waters of the Maeander,
whenever the Maeander hides its dark water.

Impiety of the last times

But when faith in piety perishes from among men,
and justice is hidden in the world,
untrustworthy men, living for unholy deeds,   Clement,
155 will commit outrage, wicked and evil deeds.   *Paid* 3.3.15
No one will take account of the pious, but they will even   Lactantius,
destroy them all, by foolishness, very infantile people,   *Divlnst*
rejoicing in outrages and applying their hands to blood.   7.17.8
Even then know that God is no longer benign   Lactantius,
160 but gnashing his teeth in wrath and destroying the entire   *De ira Dei*
race of men at once by a great conflagration.   23.5
                                                                4.176

Exhortation to conversion and baptism

Ah, wretched mortals, change these things, and do not   Lactantius,
lead the great God to all sorts of anger, but abandon   *De ira Dei*
daggers and groanings, murders and outrages,   23.7
165 and wash your whole bodies in perennial rivers.[e2]   Isa 1:16; Mt 3:1–6; Mk 1:4f.
Stretch out your hands to heaven and ask forgiveness   Lk 3:3f.
for your previous deeds and make propitiation   3.591, etc.
for bitter impiety with words of praise; God will grant repentance
and will not destroy. He will stop his wrath again if you all
170 practice honorable piety in your hearts.

The conflagration

But if you do not obey me, evil-minded ones, but love
impiety, and receive all these things with evil ears,
there will be fire throughout the whole world,[f2] and a very great sign   2.186, etc.
with sword and trumpet at the rising of the sun.   4.161
175 The whole world will hear a bellowing noise and mighty sound.
He will burn the whole earth, and will destroy the whole race of men
and all cities and rivers at once, and the sea.
He will destroy everything by fire, and it will be smoking dust.

d2. This should not be interpreted with Lanchester as a reference to a specific event. As in the parallel Sibylline passages, it attests the common Asiatic hope for vengeance on Rome. See the Introduction to SibOr 3 on vss. 350–80.

e2. The most obvious parallel to the baptism of SibOr 4 is provided by John the Baptist, who also preached a baptism of repentance in the face of imminent eschatological destruction. Baptism and eschatology are also linked in the Ebionite and Elcasaite sects (PseudClemRec 1.54–65; Hippolytus, *Ref* 9; Epiphanius, *AdvHaer* 19, 30). The baptism of SibOr 4 shows little resemblance to the ritual washings of the Essenes. All that we know of the baths of the Essenes from Josephus or from the Qumran scrolls points to daily purifications, not to a baptism of repentance. The ritual washings in SibOr 3.591–93 also refer to daily purifications.

f2. The destruction of the world by fire was part of several traditions in the hellenistic age. In Stoicism, the *ekpurosis*, "conflagration," would reduce every-thing to its primal substance. The doctrine of the Great Year, found already in Heraclitus and Plato, envisaged two great cycles, one ending in a flood, the other in a conflagration (e.g. Plato, *Timaeus*, 22b). This idea is found in Berossus (Seneca, *Naturales quaestiones* 3.29.1) and may have influenced SibOr 1 and 2 and even SibOr 4, which deals only with the period after the Flood. It is also found in *Vita* 49, Josephus, *Ant* 1.2.3 (70f.), and 2Pet 3:6f. Fire as a stream of molten metal is a standard feature of Persian eschatology. In the Bundahishn this stream of fire melts mountains and makes the earth level. The Oracle of Hystaspes also predicted the destruction of the world by fire (Justin, *Apologies* 1.20). In the biblical tradition fire is an instrument of Yahweh's judgment (Amos 7:4; Isa 66:16, etc.). The belief in a final conflagration is attributed to both the Essenes and the Pharisees by Hippolytus (*Ref* 9). It is attested in 1QH 3.29–33; 1En 52:6; and Ps-Sophocles (Ps-Justin *De Monarchia* 3; Clement, *Strom* 5.121.4–122.1).

Resurrection and judgment

But when everything is already dusty ashes,
180 and God puts to sleep the unspeakable fire, even as he kindled it,
God himself will again fashion the bones and ashes of men   2.221; Ezek 37:1–10
and he will raise up mortals again[g2] as they were before.   ApPet 4
4Ezra 7:32; 2Bar 50:2
And then there will be a judgment over which God himself will preside,   2.218f., etc.
judging the world again. As many as sinned by impiety,
185 these will a mound of earth cover,
and broad Tartarus and the repulsive recesses of Gehenna.
But as many as are pious, they will live on earth again   Lactantius, *DivInst* 7.23.4
when God gives spirit and life and favor   4.46
190 to these pious ones.[h2] Then they will all see themselves
beholding the delightful and pleasant light of the sun.
Oh most blessed, whatever man will live to that time.   3.371; 8.164
Virgil, Eclogue 4:53

g2. Belief in resurrection is attributed to Persian religion by Theopompus (Diogenes Laertius, *Proem* 9) but is, of course, also widely attested in Jewish texts.

h2. Vs. 188 "and the imperishable wealth of the great God" is rejected by Geffcken and Rzach.

THE SIBYLLINE ORACLES, BOOK 5

Introduction

Sibylline Oracle 5 is made up of six oracles (or in some cases collections) which may or may not have been composed to form a unified whole, but in any case are held together by certain recurring themes.[1] They are: (1) Verses 1–51: an introduction to the book, which reviews history from Alexander to Hadrian (or, if vs. 51 be original, Marcus Aurelius).[2] The emperors are not referred to explicitly but by gematria (the numbers represented by their initials).

The next four oracles are (2) 52–110; (3) 111–78; (4) 179–285; (5) 286–434. These show a common pattern:

  a. Oracles against various nations. In (2) and (4) the oracles are mainly against Egypt, in (3) and (5) against Asiatic countries.

  b. The return of Nero as an eschatological adversary.

  c. The advent of a savior figure.

  d. A destruction, usually by fire. (The manner of destruction is not specified in [2].)

Finally, there is a concluding oracle (6), verses 435–530. This oracle is largely concerned with Egypt. Verses 493–504 describe the building of a temple to the one true God in the land of Egypt and its subsequent destruction by the Ethiopians. The oracle concludes with an elaborate battle of the stars (512–53).

The only passage in Sibylline Oracles 5 that reflects Christian redaction is verses 256–59. Even here it is probable that a reference to a Jewish savior figure in the original Jewish oracle has been modified only by an allusion to the crucifixion.[3]

Date

The prominence of the Nero legend in (2), (3), (4), and (5) requires a date no earlier than A.D. 70 but more probably later than 80. The latest possible date for the collection is supplied by the favorable reference to Hadrian in verses 46–50, which must have been written before the Jewish revolt of A.D. 132. Not all sections of the book were necessarily written at the same time. The bitterness of complaint about the destruction of the Temple (cf. esp. vss. 398–413) suggests that at least the central oracles—(2), (3), (4), and (5)—were not far removed in time from that event. By analogy with 4 Ezra and 2 Baruch we might suggest a date in the last years of the first century A.D. Expectation of Nero's return is also likely to have flourished at that time. One detail may give a closer indication of date. In a number of places the Sibyl speaks of the destruction or dereliction of pagan temples (52–59, 484–91). The destruction of pagan temples was a notable feature of the Jewish revolt in the Diaspora of A.D. 115.[4] We may see in these Sibylline oracles an indication of the atmosphere which fostered that revolt in the early years of the second century. The opening oracle, (1), which refers to Hadrian, must be dated after the revolt. The concluding oracle, (6), which has no reference to a saving figure and is considerably more pessimistic in tone than the other oracles, may also be thought to reflect the failure of the revolt.[5]

Provenance

The Egyptian origin of Sibylline Oracles 5 is not disputed. Sections (2) and (4) deal

[1] See especially Collins, *The Sibylline Oracles*, pp. 73–95. SibOr 5 is discussed by Geffcken, *Komposition und Entstehungszeit*, pp. 22–30; Rzach, Pauly-Wissowa 2A, cols. 2134–40; Nikiprowetzky, *HUCA* 43 (1972) 30–33.

[2] See Lanchester, *APOT*, vol. 2, p. 373. The objection to vs. 51 is that a Jew who wrote of Hadrian in favorable terms must have written before the Jewish revolt of A.D. 132.

[3] Collins, *The Sibylline Oracles*, p. 88, following Lanchester, *APOT*, vol. 2, p. 402; B. Noack, "Der hervorragende Mann und der Beste der Hebraer (SibOr 5.256–59)," *Annual of the Swedish Theological Institute* 3 (1964) 122–46; Kurfess, *Sibyllinische Weissagungen*, p. 310, takes the passage as Jewish, consisting of a hybrid reference to Moses and Joshua.

[4] See A. Fuks, "Aspects of the Jewish Revolt in A.D. 115–117," *Journal of Roman Studies* 51 (1961) 98–104.

[5] See Collins, *The Sibylline Oracles*, pp. 94f. There is little substantial disagreement on the date of SibOr 5. All scholars date it between A.D. 80 and 130.

primarily with Egypt. In verse 53 (2) the Sibyl claims to be the familiar friend of Isis. The opening section, (1), begins with a reference to Egypt and includes a reference (vss. 17–18) to Cleopatra. The final section of the book, (6), includes a direct address to Isis (484) and Sarapis (487) and looks forward to the erection of a temple to the true God in the land of Egypt. Egyptian references are lacking in sections (3) and (4), but there is nothing in these sections incompatible with Egyptian authorship. The manner in which Sibylline Oracles 5 alternates its emphasis on Egypt and Asia suggests deliberate arrangement.

Sibylline Oracles 5 continues the major themes of Sibylline Oracles 3—interest in the Temple, expectation of a savior figure, the eschatological adversary (cf. SibOr 3.611; 75–92). Like Sibylline Oracles 3, it has little of the formal periodization characteristic of books 1 and 2 and 4. Sibylline Oracles 3 and 5 can be seen as the two extremities of one tradition in Egyptian Judaism. In Sibylline Oracles 5.501–3 we read that there will be a temple to the true God in the land of Egypt,[6] which will be destroyed by an Ethiopian invasion. It is not clear, however, whether the Sibyl actually envisages an invasion from Ethiopia. The Ethiopians are said to leave the Triballi, who were properly a tribe in Thrace, and this makes little geographical sense. In Sibylline Oracles 3.319f. the Ethiopians are identified with Gog and Magog and so may be understood as a general name for eschatological adversaries. It is possible then that the destruction of the temple in Egypt, which precipitates the battle of the stars, is actually the destruction of Leontopolis by the Romans. However, even if we should understand both the temple and its destruction as eschatological, the idea would be more intelligible if the Sibyllist stood in a tradition once related to Leontopolis.

Historical and theological significance

Sibylline Oracles 5 is an important witness to at least one strand of Egyptian Judaism in the period between the Jewish revolts. By contrast with Sibylline Oracles 3, book 5 shows advanced alienation from all its gentile neighbors. In the period between the two books relations between Jews and gentiles in Egypt had deteriorated considerably.[7] Whereas Sibylline Oracles 3 could look to the Ptolemaic house with enthusiasm, Sibylline Oracles 5 shows clear antipathy to the Egyptians (e.g. vss. 82–85 and 484–96) and their persecution of the Jews (vss. 68f.). Consequently two sections, (2) and (4), are dominated by oracles of doom for Egypt.

Much more powerful, however, is the Sibyl's animosity toward Rome. The outburst against Rome in verses 162–78 is unparalleled in bitterness anywhere in the Sibylline Oracles. Rome is denounced because of immorality, adultery, and homosexuality (166), but more significantly because of the destruction of Jerusalem (160–61). Ultimately Rome had laid claim to divine honors—"you said, 'I alone am, and no one will ravage me.' " (vs. 173) For this reason she must be cast down.[8]

The great adversary of the end-time in Sibylline Oracles 5 is the Roman emperor Nero. Utilizing the popular legend that Nero had fled to Parthia and would one day return, the Sibyl presents him both as king of Rome (vs. 139) and as leading an attack on Rome in the eschatological time (vs. 367). It should be noted that Nero was expected to return from the Parthians, not (at least explicitly) from the dead.[9] In verse 147 he is said to go to the Persians. In verse 93 he is referred to as a Persian. In verse 363 he is said to come from the ends of the earth. He is not yet identified with Belial as he is in Sibylline Oracles 3.63–74 and in Ascension of Isaiah 4:1, but his wickedness consists, in large part, of his claim to be God (vss. 34, 139f.). In fact the evil of Nero has the same three dimensions as the evil of Rome: he is morally evil,[10] he was responsible for the destruction of Jerusalem (vs. 150), since the Jewish war began in his reign, and he claimed to be God.

The four central oracles, (2), (3), (4), (5), contain references to a savior figure—in verses 108f., 155–61, 256–59, and 414–25. The striking feature of this figure is that he is depicted

---

[6] The idea had a biblical basis in Isa 19:19 but is nevertheless highly unorthodox.

[7] See Collins, *The Sibylline Oracles*, pp. 76f.

[8] Ibid., p. 79.

[9] See A. Yarbro Collins, *The Combat Myth in the Book of Revelation* (Harvard Dissertation Series; Missoula, Mont., 1976) p. 177.

[10] His major crime was matricide (vss. 30, 142, and 363) but he is also accused of violence and of "sinning against spouses" (146).

as coming from heaven. This is most explicit in 414, where he is said to come "from the expanses of heaven." In verse 256 the savior figure is said to come "from the sky," but since verse 257 is clearly Christian, 256 may also be redactional. In verse 108 the savior figure is a king "from God" who is sent against Nero. This figure is not necessarily heavenly (cf. SibOr 3.286) but obviously could be. In section (3) the function of the savior is exercised by "a great star" that comes from heaven and burns the sea and Babylon (158f.). Stars were frequently associated with savior figures in the hellenistic world.[11] Messianic figures in Judaism could be designated as stars by application of the Oracle of Balaam.[12] The leader of the Jewish revolt in A.D. 132 was given the name Bar Kokhba, son of the star. Stars were frequently identified with angels in Jewish tradition.[13] The star that destroys the sea and Babylon (here a metaphor for Rome) in Sibylline Oracles 5.158f. must be seen in the Jewish tradition of angelic or heavenly savior figures represented by Michael in the Book of Daniel, in the War Scroll from Qumran Cave 1, and Melchizedek in the text from Qumran Cave 11.[14]

The heavenly character of the savior figure in Sibylline Oracles 5 reflects the alienation of the Jewish community from its environment. In Sibylline Oracles 3 the Sibyllist could hope for a savior figure from the Ptolemaic house. In Sibylline Oracles 5 he must look outside the earthly realm for a heavenly figure.

Two passages in Sibylline Oracles 5 envisage a restored and glorious Jerusalem (vss. 249–55 and 420–27). In each case the restoration is upon the earth. According to verse 251 the wall of Jerusalem will extend as far as Joppa. Both passages emphasize that Jerusalem will be admired by other nations. There is no question here of resurrection of the dead.

The emphasis in Sibylline Oracles 5, however, falls not on restoration but on destruction. This is most strikingly evident in the final section of the book. Even the temple of the true God in Egypt will be destroyed by the Ethiopians (vs. 507). The books ends with a conflagration of the earth and desolation of the heavens, without any sign of further hope.

ETHICS

The ethics of Sibylline Oracles 5 are reflected chiefly in the vices for which the nations are condemned. As elsewhere in the Sibylline Oracles we find polemic against idolatry (vss. 75–85, 278–80, 353–56, 403–5, 495f.) and sexual offenses, especially homosexuality (vss. 386–93, 430). The most striking feature of the piety of Sibylline Oracles 5, however, is its emphasis on the Temple and cultic piety. Verses 406f. recall the sacrifices offered to God in the Temple and, in the final section, a temple in Egypt is envisaged where sacrifices will be offered. This interest in sacrifices is remarkable in view of the fact that the Temple had been destroyed for several years. It shows the gulf that separates the tradition in which Sibylline Oracles 5 stands from that of Sibylline Oracles 4.

Relation to other literature

Apart from its relation to Sibylline Oracles 3, book 5 has its most significant contacts with the Revelation of John. While the total eschatological conceptions of the two books are quite different, they share a number of important motifs.[15] Chief of these are the use of the Nero legend (Rev 13:3, 18; 17:11), the designation "Babylon" applied to Rome (SibOr 5.159; Rev 18), the contrast of the two cities, Rome and Jerusalem (cf. SibOr 5.418–25; in Rev contrast ch. 18 with ch. 21), and certain astral imagery (SibOr 5.155–59; Rev 8:10; 9:1).

The final conflagration and battle of the stars finds it closest parallel in Seneca, *Consolatio ad Marciam* 26.6, which is influenced by Stoic doctrines but can also be understood against the biblical background of such passages as Isaiah 34:4.

The opening oracle in Sibylline Oracles 5.1–11 is a summary of Sibylline Oracles 11 but the two books share little beyond this. See the introduction to Sibylline Oracles 11.

[11] See Collins, *The Sibylline Oracles*, pp. 90–92.

[12] Num 24:17; cf. TJud 24:1. At Qumran the Oracle of Balaam is used in both CD and 4QTest.

[13] E.g. Judg 5:20; Job 38:7; 1En 80:6; 2Bar 51:10; Dan 8:10. See W. Foerster, "Astēr," *TDNT*, vol. 1, pp. 503–5.

[14] See J. J. Collins, "The Son of Man and the Saints of the Most High in the Book of Daniel," *JBL* 93 (1974) 64–66.

[15] See C. Holzinger, *Erklärungen zu einigen der umstrittensten Stellen der Offenbarung Johannis und der Sibyllinische Orakel* (Sitzungsbericht der Akad. der Wiss, Ph.-Hist. Kl. 216, 3; Wien, 1936); Yarbro Collins, *Combat Myth*, ch. 4.

THE SIBYLLINE ORACLES
Book 5

A review of history

But come, hear my woeful history of the Latin race.	12.1–11
First of all, indeed, after the death of the kings	
of Egypt, all of whom the evenhanded earth took under,	
and after the citizen of Pella, to whom	
5 all the East and prosperous West were subjected,	
whom Babylon tested and held out as a corpse to Philip,	
alleged, not truly to be descended from Zeus or Ammon,[a]	3.383; 11.197
and after the one of the race and blood of Assaracus,	11.144
who came from Troy, who split the onslaught of fire,[b]	
10 and after many princes, after warlike people,	
and after infants, children of the flock-devouring beast,[c]	11.110–17
there will be the first prince who will sum up twice ten[d]	1.141, etc.
with his initial letter. He will conquer long in wars.	
He will have his first letter of ten,[e] so that after him	
15 will reign whoever obtained as initial the first of the alphabet.[f]	
Thrace will crouch before him and Sicily, then Memphis.	12.20–23
Memphis, cast down headlong through the wickedness of its leaders	8.162
and of an indomitable woman who fell upon the wave.[g]	
He will give laws to the peoples and subordinate all things.	
20 After a long time he will hand over sovereignty to another,	
who will present a first letter of three hundred,	12.39
and the beloved name of a river.[h] He will rule over Persians	
and Babylon. He will indeed then conquer the Medes with the spear.	
Then whoever obtained an initial of three will rule.[i]	
25 Next, a prince who will have twice ten on his first letter.[j]	
But he will reach the farthest water of Oceanus	12.88f.
cleaving[k] the tide under the Ausonians.	
One who has fifty as an initial[l] will be commander,	12.78–86
a terrible snake, breathing out grievous war, who one day	
30 will lay hands on his own family and slay them, and throw everything	4.121, etc.
into confusion,	
athlete, charioteer, murderer, one who dares ten thousand things.	Juvenal 8.224
He will also cut the mountain between two seas and defile it with gore.	
But even when he disappears he will be destructive. Then he will return	
declaring himself equal to God. But he will prove that he is not.	4.138, etc.
35 Three princes after him will perish at each others' hands.[m]	12.95–101

a. Alexander the Great. He died of fever in Babylon in 323 B.C. Clement, *Protrepticus* 10.96, quotes part of vs. 6. After his visit to the shrine of Zeus Ammon in 332 B.C., Alexander claimed to be son of that god.

b. Aeneas, who escaped from burning Troy. Assaracus, king of Phrygia, was his great-grandfather.

c. Romulus and Remus.

d. *K*aisar (Caesar); K is 20.

e. *I*ulius.

f. Augustus.

g. A reference to the defeat of Cleopatra at Actium.

h. Tiberius.

i. Gaios (Caligula).

j. Klaudios (Claudius).

k. Gk. *daixas* (Rzach) for *aixas*. The reference is to Claudius' expedition against Britain. Ausonia is strictly southern Italy, but is used poetically for the whole country.

l. Nero. Vs. 31 refers to his competing as a charioteer in the Olympian games; vs. 32 to his attempt to cut through the Isthmus of Corinth in A.D. 66–67. The fact that he is called a snake may be influenced by the story that a serpent was found around his neck when he was an infant (Tacitus, *Annals* 11:11), but it may be a more general derogatory term. On the legend of Nero's return see SibOr 4.138, etc., and SibOr 4, n. c2.

m. Galba, Otho, and Vitellius.

Then will come a certain great destroyer of pious men,
who show a clear initial of seven times ten.[n]
His son, with a first initial of three hundred, will get the better of him[o]
and take away his power. After him will be a commander,
40 with an initial of four, a cursed man,[p] but then　　　　　　　12.125
a revered man, of the number fifty.[q] After him　　　　　　　12.143
one who obtained a marked initial of three hundred,[r]　　　　12.147-64
a Celtic mountaineer, hastening to an Eastern war.
He will not avoid an unseemly fate, but will die.
45 Foreign dust will cover him, a corpse, but dust which
has the name of the Nemean flower. After him another will reign,
a silver-headed man. He will have the name of a sea.[s]　　　8.52; 12.164
He will also be a most excellent man and he will consider everything.
And in your time, most excellent, outstanding, dark-haired one,
50 and in the days of your descendants, all these days will come to pass.　8.136
After him three will rule, but the third will come to power late in life.[t]　12.176
　　　　　　　　　　　　　　　　　　　　　　　　　　　　　　　　8.65

Prophecies of destruction against Egypt

Thrice-wretched one, I am weary of putting an utterance of disaster in　3.1-7, etc.
　　my heart
and the inspired chant of oracles, I who am the familiar friend of Isis.　5.484
First, indeed, around the steps of your much-lamented temple
55 maenads will dart, and you will be in bad hands
on that day, when the Nile traverses　　　　　　　　　　　　14.119f.
the whole land of Egypt up to sixteen cubits,　　　　　　　　Artapanus
　　　　　　　　　　　　　　　　　　　　　　　　　　　　　　(*PrEv* 9.27)
so as to flood the whole land and drench it with streams.
The beauty of the land and glory of its appearance will disappear.
60 Memphis, you indeed will weep most of all over Egypt,　　　5.180
for formerly you were the one who mightily ruled the land,
wretched one, so that even he who rejoices in thunder will cry out
from heaven with a great voice, "Mighty Memphis,
who formerly boasted most to wretched mortals,
65 you will weep in dire straits and disastrous fate,
so that the eternal immortal God will notice you in the clouds.
Where is your sturdy spirit among men?
Because you raged against my children who were anointed by God[u]
and incited evil against good men,
70 you in return have such a nurse[v] for recompense.
You will no longer have any right openly among the blessed.
You have fallen from the stars, you will not go up to heaven."　　Isa 14:12
These things God bade me declare to Egypt
in the final time when men will be utterly evil.
75 But the wicked endure evil, awaiting
the anger of the immortal deep-sounding heavenly one.　　　　3.30-35, etc.;
They worship stones and brute beasts instead of God,　　　　WisSol 13-15

---

n. *Ouespasianos* (Vespasian), who conducted the war against the Jews.

o. Titus. Suetonius, *Titus* 5, reports an ungrounded suspicion that Titus plotted to overthrow his father.

p. Reading *ephtharmenos* (Lanchester) for *ephthos moros*. The reference is to Domitian. For a sharply different assessment of Domitian see SibOr 12.124-42.

q. Nerva.

r. Trajan, who was born in Spain. He died at Selinus in Cilicia. The word *selinon* means "parsley," which was used in the victory wreath at the Nemean games.

s. Hadrian (Adriatic Sea).

t. Marcus Aurelius. The other two are Antoninus Pius and Lucius Verus. Hadrian had no children, but he adopted Antoninus. Antoninus in turn adopted Marcus Aurelius and Lucius Verus.

u. The reference is a general one to the traditional enmity of Israel and Egypt from the time of the Exodus, and more proximately the feuds in the 1st cent. A.D.

v. Presumably Rome.

revering very many things, one here another there, which have no
    reason,
or mind or hearing, and things which it is not even lawful for me to   Frag. 3.31
    mention,
80 the particular types of idols, brought into being by the hands of mortals.   Isa 44:9–20;
From their own labors and wicked notions,   40:19f.
men have accepted gods of wood and stone.
They have made them of bronze and gold and silver, vain,
lifeless, dumb, and smelted in fire,   5.356; 8.47
85 vainly putting their trust in such as these.
Thmouis and Xouis are oppressed,ʷ the counsel of Heracles,
Zeus, and Hermes is cut off,
and you, Alexandria, famous nurse of cities,   11.234
war will not leave you . . .
90 You will make retribution for pride, the things you formerly did.
You will be silent for a long age, and the day of return . . .
and the luxurious drink will no longer flow for youˣ . . .

The return of Nero

For the Persian will come onto your soilʸ like hail,   4.138, etc.
and he will destroy your land and evil-devising men   1En 56:5f.
                                           Rev 9:13–18
95 with blood and corpses, by terrible altars,
a savage-minded mighty man, much-bloodied, raving nonsense,
with a full host numerous as sand, bringing destruction on you.ᶻ
And then, most prosperous of cities,ᵃ² you will be in great distress.   5.88
All Asia, falling to the ground, will lament for the gifts she enjoyed
    from you
100 when she wore a crown on her head.
But the one who obtained the land of the Persians will fight,
and killing every man he will destroy all life
so that a one-third portion will remain for wretched mortals.   3.544; Zech 13:8; Rev 9:15,18
He himself will rush in with a light bound from the West,ᵇ²   5.371
105 besieging the entire land, laying it all waste.
But when he attains a formidable height and unseemly daring,
he will also come, wishing to destroy the city of the blessed ones,
and then a certain king sent from God against him   3.286; 3.652; 5.414; Oracle of
will destroy all the great kings and noble men.   Hystaspes, *DivInst* 7.17;
                                       Lactantius, *DivInst* 7.18.5
110 Thus there will be judgment on men by the imperishable one.

Prophecies of destruction against various Eastern places

Alas for you, wretched heart, why do you provoke me   5.286
to show these things to Egypt, a grievous multiplicity of sovereignty?
Go to the East, to the mindless tribes of the Persians,
and show them what now is and what will be.
115 The current of the river Euphrates will bring on a flood
and will destroy Persians, Iberians, and Babylonians
and Massagetae, who love war and trust in bows.
All Asia will blaze, burned with fire as far as the islands.

---

w. Towns in lower Egypt.
   x. I.e. the Nile will dry up. Contrast SibOr 5.56,
but cf. Isa 19:5–8.
   y. Gk. *pedon* for *dapos* (Geffcken). The Persian
is Nero, returning from the Parthians. See SibOr 4,
n. c2. 1En 56:5f. also refers to a Parthian invasion
but is probably influenced by the historical invasion
of Palestine by the Parthians in 40 B.C.

z. Gk. *epaxōn* (Geffcken) for *apaixōn*.
   a2. The reference is apparently to Alexandria—cf.
vs. 88.
   b2. Presumably he will have conquered the West
first. Nero acts as king of Rome (SibOr 5.139) but
is also attacking Rome (SibOr 5.367). When he
comes from the West he must be understood to have
come from Rome.

Pergamos, which was formerly revered, will perish like a bunch of
    grapes,
120 and Pitane will appear totally desolate among men.
All Lesbos will sink in the deep abyss, so as to perish.   5.316
Smyrna will one day weep, rolled down the cliffs.
She who was once revered and famous will perish.
Bithynians will bewail their land, reduced to ashes,
125 and great Syria, and Phoenicia of many tribes.
Woe to you, Lycia, how many evils the sea
devises against you, spontaneously encroaching on the grievous land,
so that it will flood with a bad earthquake and bitter streams
the watery[c2] shore of Lycia which once breathed perfume.
130 A terrible wrath will also come upon Phrygia because of the pain
for which Rhea, mother of Zeus, came and remained there.[d2]
The sea will destroy the race and savage people of the Tauri,
and will destroy the plain of the Lapiths and break it off down from the
    earth.[e2]
A deep-eddying river, deep-flowing Peneius, will destroy the land of 7.56
    Thessaly,
135 chasing men[f2] from the land,
(Eridanus,[g2] which claims to have once begotten forms of wild beasts).

The career of Nero and his flight to the East

The poets will bewail thrice-wretched Greece
when a great king of great Rome, a godlike man   4.119
from Italy, will cut the ridge of the isthmus.   5.32,218; 8.155; 12.84
140 Him, they say, Zeus himself begot and lady Hera.[h2]   8.153
Playing at theatricals with honey-sweet songs rendered   12.92 Suetonius; Nero 20
with melodious voice, he will destroy many men, and his wretched
    mother.
He will flee from Babylon,[i2] a terrible and shameless prince
whom all mortals and noble men despise.
145 For he destroyed many men and laid hands on the womb.   4.121, etc.
He sinned against spouses, and was sprung from abominable people.   Suetonius, Nero 34,39
He will come to the Medes and to the kings of the Persians,
those whom he first desired and to whom he gave glory,[j2]
lurking with these evil ones against a true people.
150 He seized the divinely built Temple and burned the citizens[k2]
and peoples who went into it, men whom I rightly praised.
For on his appearance the whole creation was shaken
and kings perished,[l2] and those in whom sovereignty remained
destroyed a great city and righteous people.

c2. Or: unperfumed. The pun is presumably intentional and is also playing on the name of Myra,
the chief city of Lycia.

d2. In SibOr 3.140 Rhea sent the infant Zeus to
Phrygia. In the usual form of the myth she sent him
to Crete.

e2. Reading: exolesas Lapithōn dapedon kata gēs
aporēxei (Rzach). The Lapiths were a wild tribe living
in Thessaly in heroic times.

f2. Gk. meropas for morphas (Lanchester).

g2. Geffcken reads Epidanus for the MS Eridanus.
The reference is enigmatic and probably corrupt.
Eridanus was the name of a mythical river, later
identified with the Po.

h2. Blatantly sarcastic. For the mysterious occurrences at Nero's birth see Suetonius, Nero 6.

i2. For Babylon as a symbolic name for Rome see

especially Rev 14:8; 16:19; 18:2, 21, 22. The analogy
between Babylon and Rome, both of which destroyed
Jerusalem and the Temple, underlies the fictional
setting of 4Ezra and 2Bar.

j2. See SibOr 4, n. c2. In A.D. 63 Nero crowned
Tiridates of Parthia as king of Armenia, thereby ceding to him, in effect, the province of Armenia. Tiridates hailed Nero as imperator and made obeisance
to him as an emanation of Mithras. Nero's popularity
with the Parthians endured after his death.

k2. Nero did not, of course, capture Jerusalem,
but the war began in his reign.

l2. Possibly a reference to Galba, Otho, and
Vitellius, but it may be more general. Lanchester
emends to read "when he died," thaneontos for
prophanentos, but the passage does not suppose that
Nero had in fact died.

Cosmic destruction

155 But when after the fourth year a great star shines[m2]   Rev 8:10; 9:1
    which alone will destroy the whole earth, because of
    the honor which they first gave to Poseidon of the sea,[n2]
    a great star will come from heaven to the wondrous sea
    and will burn the deep sea and Babylon[o2] itself   5.143
160 and the land of Italy, because of which many
    holy faithful Hebrews and a true people perished.

Oracle against Rome

    You will be among evil mortals, suffering evils,   3.356–62; Rev 18
    but you will remain utterly desolate for all ages yet,   5.342
    (it will exist, but it will remain utterly desolate forever),
165 despising your soil, because you desired sorcery.
    With you are found adulteries and illicit intercourse with boys.   3.764,185; Clement, *Paid* 2.10.99
    Effeminate and unjust, evil city, ill-fated above all.
    Alas, city of the Latin land, unclean in all things,
    maenad, rejoicing in vipers,[p2] as a widow you will sit   Rev 18:7; Isa 47:9
170 by the banks, and the river Tiber will weep for you, its consort.
    You have a murderous heart and impious spirit.
    Did you not know what God can do, what he devises?
    But you said, "I alone am,"[q2] and no one will ravage me."   Rev 18:7; Isa 47:8; Isa 14:3
    But now God, who is forever, will destroy you and all your people, Ezek 28:2
175 and there will no longer be any sign of you in that land,
    as there was formerly, when the great God found your honors.
    Remain alone, lawless one. Mingled with burning fire,   8.101; Isa 14:15
    inhabit the lawless nether region of Hades.

Oracles of destruction against Egypt

    Now again, Egypt, I will bewail your fate.
180 Memphis, you will be leader of labors, smitten on the ankles.   5.60
    In you the pyramids will utter a shameless sound.
    Python, rightly called "double-city" of old,   Ex 1:11
    be silent forever, so that you may desist from wickedness.   (Pithom)
    Arrogance, treasury of evil labors, maenad of many laments,   5.231
185 dire sufferer, tearful one, you will remain a widow forever.
    For many years you alone were ruler of the world.
    But when Barca[r2] puts on a white skirt
    over a dirty one, may I neither be nor come into being.
    O Thebes, where is your great strength? A savage man
190 will destroy your people. But you will take gray garments
    and lament, wretched one, alone, and will make retribution for everything
    which you did before, having a shameless spirit.
    They will see lamentation because of lawless deeds.
    A great man of the Ethiopians will destroy Syene.[s2]

---

m2. The "fourth year" is an equivalent of the "three and a half times" of Dan 7:25; 12:7, at the end of which comes deliverance from persecution. The star here performs the role of destroying angel in accordance with the widespread identification of stars and angels in the OT and intertestamental writings. See the Introduction to SibOr 5.

n2. Poseidon was god of the sea. In the OT the sea is frequently a symbol of chaos and hostility to God: Hab 3:15; Isa 7:12–14, etc. On the destruction of the sea here cf. Rev 21:1.

o2. I.e. Rome. Above, n. i2.

p2. This remark is clearly pejorative but its precise relevance is enigmatic. Lanchester suggests the analogy of the death of Cleopatra, which might also be suggested by the term "widow." (Cf. SibOr 3.77.)

q2. Cf. the divine claim, Ex 3:14; Isa 43:11; 44:6; 45:7.

r2. A city captured by the Persians in the time of Darius. The kilt was a Persian garment, so this may be an old oracle.

s2. There was an Ethiopian invasion of Egypt in 24 B.C., but the Ethiopians had always been a threat to the southern part of the country.

195 Dark-skinned Indians will occupy Teuchira[t2] by force.
Pentapolis, you will weep, but a very mighty man will destroy you.
Much lamented Libya, who will narrate your doom?
Cyrene, who of men will weep piteously for you?
You will not desist from hideous lamentation until the time of destruction.

An oracle against the Gauls

200 Among the Britains[u2] and wealthy Gauls
the ocean will be resounding, filled with much blood,
for they also did evil to the children of God
when the purple king led a great Gallic host
from Syria against the Sidonians.[v2] He will also kill you,
205 Ravenna, and lead you to slaughter.

Destruction for the Ethiopians

Indians, have no courage, and great-spirited Ethiopians;[w2]
for when the wheel of arched[x2] Axis, Capricorn　　　　　5.512–31, etc.
and Taurus amid Gemini, revolves in mid-heaven,
Virgo, coming forth, and the sun, fixing a belt
210 all about its brow, shall lead.
There will be a greatly heavenly conflagration on earth
and from the battling stars[y2] a new nature will emerge,
so that the whole land of the Ethiopians will perish in fire and groanings.

The return of Nero

You, too, Corinth, bewail the mournful destruction within you.　　　7.60
215 For when the three sister Fates, spinning with twisted threads,
lead the one who is (now) fleeing deceitfully[z2]　　　　　4.119f.; 5.143
beyond the bank of the isthmus on high so that all may see him,
who formerly cut out the rock with ductile bronze,　　　　　5.139, etc.
he will destroy and ravage your land also, as is decreed.
220 For to him God gave strength to perform　　　　　3.66; ApEl 3:6–10
things like no previous one of all the kings.
For, first of all, cutting off[a3] the roots from three heads　　　　　Dan 7:8
mightily with a blow, he will give them to others to eat,
so that they will eat the flesh of the parents of the impious king.[b3]
225 For murder and terrors are in store for all men
because of the great city and righteous people which is　　　　　5.154
preserved throughout everything, which Providence held in special place.

Denunciation of arrogance

Arrogance, unstable one of evil counsels, surrounded by evil fates,

---

t2. Also known as Arsinoe.

u2. Gk. *Brutessi* for *Brugessi* (φ, ψ).

v2. Most probably a reference to Vespasian, who had Gauls in his army.

w2. Ancient geographers were confused on the relation of India and Ethiopia and sometimes claimed that there were two Ethiopias, one in Africa, one in India. Cf. Strabo 1.2. The same confusion is found in SibOr 11.61–79.

x2. Gk. *kurton* for *toutous* (Lanchester).

y2. Gk. *astrōn d'ek machimōn* for *en machimois* (Geffcken). The tradition of an astral battle is reflected in diverse sources, such as Judg 5:20; Isa 14:12; Dan 8:10; Seneca, *Consolatio ad Marciam* 26.6; *Hercules*

furens 944–52; Nonnus, *Dionysiaca* 38.347–409.

z2. Nero, see SibOr 4, n. c2.

a3. Gk. *schissamenos* for *stēsamenos* (Rzach). This detail recurs in several forms of the Antichrist legend—e.g. Commodian, *Carmen apologeticum* 911; Hippolytus, *De Christo et Antichristo* 52. (See Bousset, *The Antichrist Legend*, p. 159.) The origin of the tradition lies apparently in the conflation of the three uprooted horns of Dan 7:8 and the three defeated powers, Egyptians, Libyans, and Cushites, in Dan 11:43.

b3. Possibly a reference to Nero's murder of his mother.

beginning and great end of toil for men   5.244
230 when creation is damaged and saved again by the Fates.   5.245
      Leader of evils and great affliction to men,   5.184
      which of mortals desired you, who did not resent you within.
      By you a certain king, cast down, destroyed his revered life.[c3]
      You arranged all things badly and brought on a full flood of evil,
235 and through you the beautiful folds of the world were changed.
      Put forward these causes for our strife, perhaps they are the last.
      How and what do you say? I will persuade you and even if I blame you
            somewhat I will speak.

Praise and exaltation of the Jews

There was once among men a shining light of the sun   3.218–60,
      when the harmonious ray of the prophets was being spread abroad,   573–600
240 a tongue dripping a beautiful drink for all mortals with honeyed sweet-
            ness;
      it made manifest, offered and effected gentle things for all.
      Therefore, narrow-minded leader of greatest evils,
      the reaping hook and grief will come in that day.   1.387, etc.
      Beginning and great end of toil for men,   5.229
245 when creation is damaged and saved again by the Fates.   5.230
      Give ear to the bitter harsh-sounding speech, you affliction to men.
      But whenever the Persian land desists from war,
      pestilence, and groaning, then on that day it will come to pass that   Lactantius,
      the divine and heavenly race of the blessed Jews,   DivInst 4.20.11
250 who live around the city of God in the middle of the earth,   LetAris 83f.
      are raised up even to the dark clouds,   5.424f.
      having built a great wall round about, as far as Joppa.
      No longer will trumpet whistle the sound of war,   8.117
      and no longer will they perish at raging hostile hands,
255 but they will set up[d3] trophies won from the wicked, forever.
      There will again be one exceptional man from the sky   5.414,108, etc.; Oracle of
      (who stretched out his hands on the fruitful wood),[e3]   Hystaspes, DivInst 7.17
      the best of the Hebrews, who will one day cause the sun to stand,   Dan 7:13; 4Ezra 13:3
      speaking with fair speech and holy lips.   Josh 10:12
260 Blessed one, no longer weary your spirit in your breast,
      divinely born, wealthy, sole-desired flower,
      good light, holy shoot, beloved plant,[f3]   CD 1:3;
      delightful Judea, fair city, inspired with hymns.   1Cor 3:6
      No longer will the unclean foot of Greeks
265 revel around your land but they will have a mind in their breasts that
            conforms to your laws.
      But glorious children will honor you exceedingly,
      and they will attend table with devout music,
      all sorts of sacrifices and with prayers honoring God.   5.407
      Such righteous men as endured toils will receive
270 greater, pleasant things in exchange[g3] for a little distress.
      But the wicked, who dispatched lawless utterance against heaven,
      will desist from speaking against each other
      but will hide themselves until the world is changed.
      There will be a shower of blazing fire from the clouds,   3.543; 5.377
275 and mortals will no longer enjoy bright corn from the earth.
      All will remain unsown and unplowed until mortal men   3.542

---

c3. Presumably Nero.   telos poepthēmenon hagnos.
d3. Gk. anastēsousi for stēsamenos (Rzach).   g3. Gk. enallaxousi for kalon arxousi (Mendels-
e3. At least this verse is Christian.   sohn).
f3. Gk. semnon te thalos, pephilēmenon ernos for

pay attention to the immortal eternal God, ruler of all,
and no longer honor mortal things,
neither dogs nor vultures, which Egypt taught
280 men to revere with vain mouths and foolish lips.
But the holy land of the pious alone will bear all these things:
a honey-sweet stream from rock and spring,
and heavenly milk will flow for all the righteous.
For with great piety and faith they put their hope
285 in the one begetter, God, who alone is eminent.

Woes for Asia

But why does my clever mind suggest these things to me?
Now, wretched Asia, I bewail you piteously
and the race of Ionians, Carians, and Lydians rich in gold.
Woe to you, Sardis,[h3] woe lovely Trallis,
290 woe Laodicea, beautiful city, how you will perish
destroyed by earthquakes and changed to dust.
To dark Asia . . .
The well-built shrine of Artemis of Ephesus
with cleavings and earthquakes will fall to the wondrous sea,
295 headlong, as storm winds overwhelm ships.
Ephesus, supine, will wail, weeping on the shores,
seeking the temple which is no longer there.
And then the imperishable God who dwells in the sky in anger
will cast a lightning bolt from heaven against the power of the impious.
300 Instead of winter there will be summer on that day
and then indeed there will be great affliction[i3] for mortal men
for the One who thunders on high will destroy all shameless men
with thunders and lightnings and blazing thunderbolts
on hostile men, and he will destroy the impious in such a manner
305 that corpses will remain on earth more numerous than sand.
Smyrna also will come, bewailing its musician,[j3]
to the gates of Ephesus, and she herself will truly perish.
Foolish Cyme, with her divinely inspired streams,[k3]
cast down at the hands of godless, unjust and lawless men,
310 will no longer take her chariot forward to such a height
but will remain, a corpse, in swelling[l3] streams.
And then they will cry out at once, awaiting evil.
The difficult people and shameless tribe of the Cumaeans
will have a sign and know because of what it labored.
315 Then when they bewail a wicked land reduced to ashes,
Lesbos will be destroyed forever by Eridanus.
Woe to you, Cibyra,[m3] fair city, desist from revelry.
Hierapolis also, the only land which has mingled with Pluton,[n3]
you will have what you have desired to have, a land of many tears,
320 piling a mound on the earth by the streams of Thermodon.
Rock-clinging Tripolis by the waters of the Maeander,
apportioned to nightly waves on the shore,
the providence of God will one day destroy you utterly.
May I never willingly take the land which is neighbor to Phoebus.[o3]

Marginal references:
3.30, etc.; WisSol 15:18
Lactantius, DivInst 7.24.14
3.622
8.211
5.111
3.459
3.471
Acts 19:28
Clement, Protr 4.50
2.157; 8.215; 14.299
5.122
5.121,136
12.280
4.4

---

h3. Sardis was destroyed by an earthquake in A.D. 17.

i3. Gk. *mega pēm'* for *metepeit'* (Rzach).

j3. Gk. *lurourgon* for *lukourgon* (Geffcken). The reference is to Homer.

k3. The inspired streams suggest the Sibylline shrine at Cumae in Italy, but the context favors the Cumae in Asia.

l3. Gk. *kumainousi* for *kumēoisi* (Lanchester).

m3. Gk. *kibura* for *kerkura* (Mendelssohn).

n3. Pluton was god of the underworld; Plutus was god of wealth. Presumably the pun is intended.

o3. Pausanias 10.12.5 says the Sibyl Herophile went to Claros, the famous oracular shrine of Phoebus Apollo.

325 A lightning bolt from above will one day destroy luxurious Miletus
     because it chose the deceitful strain of Phoebus
     and the clever practice of men and prudent counsel.

Prayer for Judea

Be gracious, begetter of all, to the fertile, luxurious,
great land of Judea, so that we may behold your plans.
330 For you knew this one first, God, with favors,
     so that she seemed to be your special gift to all men
     and to attend as God enjoined.

Woes for Europe

Thrice wretched one, I desire to see the affairs of the Thracians
and the wall between two seas swept down in the dust
335 by Ares (sweeping) like a river on a fishing diver.[p3]
     Wretched Hellespont, one day the offspring of the Assyrians will put
         a yoke on you.[q3]
     The battle of the Thracians against you will utterly destroy your mighty
         strength.
     An Egyptian king seizes Macedonia,
     and a foreign region will cast down the strength of leaders.[r3]
340 Lydians and Galatians, Pamphylians and Pisidians
     en masse will conquer, armed in evil strife.
     Thrice-wretched Italy, all desolate, unwept, you will await
     a destructive beast in a blooming land, to be destroyed.
     It will be possible to hear a heavenly crash of thunder, the voice of God
345 throughout broad heaven above.[s3]

     The imperishable flames of the sun itself will no longer be,   5.477
     nor will the shining light of the moon be anymore   5.480
     in the last time, when God assumes command.
     Everything will be blackened, there will be darkness throughout the
         earth,
350 and blind men, evil wild beasts, and woe.
     That day will last a long time, so that men
     will take note of God himself, the prince who oversees all from heaven.
     Then he will not pity hostile men
     who sacrifice herds of lambs and sheep, and loud-bellowing bulls,
355 and great golden-horned calves
     to lifeless Hermes and gods of stone.   3.31; Ezek 9:17
     But let law, wisdom, and glory rule over the righteous,
     lest one day the imperishable God in anger destroy   Lactantius, *De ira Dei* 23.8
     the livelihood of men with every race[t3] and a shameless tribe.
360 It is necessary to love God, the wise eternal begetter.

The return of Nero

There will come to pass in the last time about the waning of the moon
a war which will throw the world into confusion and be deceptive in
     guile.

---

p3. The wall in question spanned the isthmus on which Byzantium stood. Ares was the god of war.

q3. Xerxes' bridge across the Hellespont in 481 B.C.

r3. Seleucus I defeated Lysimachus of Thrace at the battle of Corupedion in 281 B.C. but was himself murdered by Ptolemy Keraunos. The latter, in turn, was defeated and killed by the Gauls in 280 B.C.

s3. Reading: *estai d'aitherion ana ouranon eurun huperthen* (Geffcken).

t3. Gk. *paggenei* for *pan genos* (Wilamowitz).

A man who is a matricide will come from the ends of the earth   4.138, etc.; 4.121, etc.
in flight and devising penetrating schemes in his mind.   AscenIs 4:2
365 He will destroy every land and conquer all
and consider all things more wisely than all men.
He will immediately seize the one because of whom he himself perished.   8.142
He will destroy many men and great rulers,
and he will set fire to all men as no one else ever did.
370 Through zeal he will raise up those who were crouched in fear.
There will come upon men a great war from the West.   5.104
Blood will flow up to the bank of deep-eddying rivers.   Lactantius, *DivInst* 7.19.5
Wrath will drip in the plains of Macedonia,   1En 100:3
an alliance to the people[u3] from the West, but destruction for the king.
375 Then a wintry blast will blow throughout the land,
and the plain will be filled again with evil war.
For fire will rain on men from the floors of heaven,   3.543; 5.274
fire and blood, water, lightning bolt, darkness, heavenly night,
and destruction in war, and a mist over the slain
380 will destroy at once all kings and noble men.
Then the piteous destruction of war will cease thus   3.653,727–30; Isa 2:4
and no longer will anyone fight with swords or iron   Ps 46:9; Ezek 39:9
or with weapons at all, which will no longer be lawful.
A wise people which is left will have peace,
385 having experienced evil so that it might later rejoice.

Admonition to the Romans

Matricides, desist from boldness and evil daring,   5.363
you who formerly impiously catered for pederasty   3.185, etc.
and set up in houses prostitutes who were pure before,
with insults and punishment and toilsome disgrace.
390 For in you mother had intercourse with child unlawfully,   7.43–45
and daughter was joined with her begetter as bride.
In you also kings defiled their ill-fated mouths.
In you also evil men practiced bestiality.
Be silent, most lamentable evil city, which indulges in revelry.
395 For no longer in you will virgin maidens
tend the divine fire of sacred nourishing wood.[v3]

Destruction of the Temple

The desired Temple has long ago been extinguished by you,
When I saw the second Temple cast headlong,
soaked in fire by an impious hand,
400 the ever-flourishing, watchful Temple of God
made by holy people and hoped
by their[w3] soul and body to be always imperishable.
For among them no one carelessly praises a god   3.13, etc.
of insignificant clay, nor did a clever sculptor make one from rock,
405 nor worship ornament of gold, a deception of souls.
But they honored the great God, begetter of all
who have God-given breath, with holy sacrifices and hecatombs.   5.268
But now a certain insignificant and impious king
has gone up, cast it down, and left it in ruins
410 with a great horde and illustrious men.

---

u3. Gk. *leō(i)* for *dō d̄* (Geffcken).   of Vesta in A.D. 64.
v3. Gk. *para soi g'hierēs* for *para soio tēn tēs*   w3. Gk. *autōn* for *autou* (Rzach). The reference
(Rzach). The reference is to the burning of the temple   is, of course, to Herod's Temple.

He himself perished at immortal hands when he left the land,[x3]
and no such sign has yet been performed among men
that others should think to sack a great city.

The advent of a savior figure

For a blessed man came from the expanses of heaven[y3]   5.256, etc.
415 with a scepter in his hands which God gave him,
and he gained sway over all things well, and gave back the wealth
to all the good, which previous men had taken.
He destroyed every city from its foundations with much fire
and burned nations of mortals who were formerly evildoers.
420 And the city which God desired, this he made   5.261; Lactantius, *DivInst* 7.24.6
more brilliant than stars and sun and moon,
and he provided ornament and made a holy temple,[z3]
exceedingly beautiful in its fair shrine,[a4] and he fashioned
a great and immense tower over many stadia
425 touching even the clouds and visible to all,   5.251f.
so that all faithful and all righteous people could see
the glory of eternal God, a form desired.
East and West sang out the glory of God.   Ps 19:1
For terrible things no longer happen to wretched mortals,
430 no adulteries or illicit love of boys,   3.764
no murder, or din of battle, but competition is fair among all.
It is the last time of holy people when God, who thunders on high,
founder of the greatest temple, accomplishes these things.

An oracle against Babylon

Woe to you, Babylon, of golden throne and golden sandal.   3.303, etc. Isa 13; Jer 51
435 For many years you were the sole kingdom ruling over the world.
You who were formerly great and universal, you will no longer lie   Isa 47:5
on golden mountains and streams of the Euphrates.
You will be spread out flat by the turmoil of an earthquake. Terrible
    Parthians
made you shake[b4] all over. Restrain your mouth with a bridle,
440 impious race of Babylonians. Neither ask nor take thought
how you will rule over the Persians or how you will hold sway over the
    Medes.
Because of your dominion which you had, you will send to Rome
hostages, even those who were in bondage to Asia.[c4]
So also, though thinking as a queen, you will come
445 under the judgment of your adversaries on whose account you sent
    ransom.
You will pay a bitter reckoning to your enemies in return for your
    crooked words.

Eschatological upheavals

In the last time, one day the sea will be dry,   Rev 21:1
and ships will then no longer sail to Italy.   8.237,348

---

x3. Reading *chersin hup' athanatois apobas gēs* (Geffcken). The king is Titus, but his death was not in any way miraculous.

y3. The past tense is used by anticipation. The heavenly origin of the savior figure accords with the consistent expectation of SibOr 5.

z3. Gk. *hagion t'oikon*; (Rzach: *oikon* ["house" or "temple"] is added).

a4. Gk. *en sēkō kalō* for *ensarkon kalon* (Lanchester). Contrast the new Jerusalem in Rev 21:22 in which there is no temple.

b4. Gk. *krotein* for *kratein* (Lanchester).

c4. A possible reference to Roman prisoners captured at Carrhae and recovered by Augustus.

Great Asia then will be water, bearing all cargo,
450 and Crete a plain. Cyprus will have a great affliction,   4.128f.
and Paphus will bewail a terrible fate so that even
the great city of Salamis, suffering a great affliction, will notice it.
Now there will again be barren dry land on the shore.
A not inconsiderable swarm of locusts will destroy the land of Cyprus.
455 Ill-fated men, you will weep when you look toward Tyre.   7.62; 14.87
Phoenicia, terrible wrath awaits you, until you fall   3.492
a bad fall so that the Sirens may truly weep.   2Bar 10:8
It will come to pass in the fifth generation when the destruction of Egypt
ceases, when the shameless kings intermingle.
460 The clans of the Pamphylians will settle in Egypt
and in Macedonia, and in Asia, and among the Lycians
there will be a bloody war throwing the world into confusion in dust,
which a king of Rome and the potentates of the West will stop.[d4]
Whenever a wintry blast drips as snow,
465 when a great river and the biggest lakes are frozen over,
immediately a barbarian throng will march to the land of Asia[e4]
and will destroy the race of terrible Thracians as if it were weak.
Then desperate men weakened by famine
will devour their parents and gulp them down as food.
470 Wild beasts will devour the table[f4] from all dwellings.
Even birds will devour all mortals.
The bloody ocean will be filled with flesh
and blood of the senseless, from evil war.
There will be such weakness on earth   2.25
475 that it will be possible to know the number of men and count of women.
A wretched generation will groan ten thousandfold at the end
when the sun is setting so that it never rise again,   5.346; 3.94
remaining to be plunged in the waters of the ocean,
for it saw the impious wickedness of many men.
480 There will be moonless night round the great heaven itself.   5.347
No small mist will cover the folds of the world about,
a second time. But then the light of God will lead   WisSol 18:1
the good men, as many as sang out the praise of God.

The conversion of Egypt

Isis, thrice-wretched goddess, you will remain by the streams of the   5.53; Clement,
      Nile   *Protr* 4.50
485 alone, a speechless maenad on the sands of the Acheron.[g4]
No longer will memory of you remain throughout the whole earth.
And you, Sarapis, reposing on many unwrought stones,
will lie, a very great casualty in thrice-wretched Egypt.
But as many as brought the desire of Egypt to you will all
490 bewail you bitterly, turning their attention to the imperishable God.
Those who sang out your praises as a god will know that you are nothing.
Then a man clad in linen, one of the priests, will say,
"Come, let us erect a sanctuary of the true God.   3.716-31
Come, let us change the terrible custom we have received from our
      ancestors

---

d4. This rather confused passage seems to refer to the defeat of Antony and Cleopatra. The "fifth generation" may be analogous to the tenth generation of SibOr 2.15, etc.—i.e. the fifth generation after the Flood.

e4. Geffcken compares an oracle in Pausanias 10.15.3 on the invasion of the Gauls. This may be an old oracle from the time of the Gaulish invasions in the early third century B.C.

f4. (The Gk. noun reflects metonymy; "food" would be preferable, but it has already been used in the preceding sentence. —J.H.C.)

g4. I.e. in Hades.

495 on account of which they performed processions and rites   3.30,14, etc.
    to gods of stone and earthenware, and were devoid of sense.
    Let us turn our souls, singing out the praises of the imperishable God
    himself, the begetter who is eternal,
    the ruler of all, the true one, the king,
500 the begetter who nourishes souls, the great eternal God.''
    Then there will be a great holy temple in Egypt,[h4]   Isa 19:19
    and a people fashioned by God will bring sacrifices to it.
    To them the imperishable God will grant to reside there.
    But when the Ethiopians leave the shameless tribes of the Triballi
505 and are about to till the land[i4] of Egypt,
    they will launch on a course of wickedness, so that all the later things
          may come to pass,
    for they will destroy the great temple of the land of Egypt.   War 7.10.2
    God will rain on them a terrible wrath, down on earth,   (420–36)
                                                                      5.373
    so as to destroy all the wicked and all the lawless.
510 There will no longer be any sparing in that land,
    because they did not guard what God entrusted to them.

The battle of the stars

    I saw the threat of the burning sun among the stars   3.207–13;
    and the terrible wrath of the moon among the lightning flashes.   2.200–1, etc.
    The stars travailed in battle;[j4] God bade them fight.
515 For over against the sun long flames were in strife,
    and the two-horned rush of the moon was changed.
    Lucifer fought, mounted on the back of Leo.
    Capricorn smote the ankle of the young Taurus,
    and Taurus deprived Capricorn of his day of return.
520 Orion removed Libra so that it remained no more.
    Virgo changed the destiny of Gemini in Aries.
    The Pleiad no longer appeared and Draco rejected its belt.
    Pisces submerged themselves in the girdle of Leo.
    Cancer did not stand its ground, for it feared Orion.
525 Scorpio got under the tail[k4] because of terrible Leo,
    and the dog star perished by the flame of the sun.
    The strength of the mighty day star burned up Aquarius.
    Heaven itself was roused until it shook the fighters.
    In anger it cast them headlong to earth.
530 Accordingly, stricken into the baths of ocean,   2.202, etc.
    they quickly kindled the whole earth. But the sky remained starless.   7.125

h4. This idea may have been influenced by the historical temple at Leontopolis. It is even possible that the passage refers to that temple directly.

i4. Gk. *Aiguptou gaian* for *Aiguptou heēn* (Alexandre). The Triballi were properly a tribe in Thrace. The Ethiopians were traditional enemies of Egypt. Their eschatological role is suggested in SibOr 3.319f. where they are identified with Gog and Magog. It is not clear then whether the Ethiopians are literally Ethiopians or just a name for the eschatological adversary. If the latter is the case, then it is possible that the destruction in question is the destruction of the Leontopolis temple by the Romans.

Otherwise, both the temple and the invasion must be taken as eschatological.

j4. Cf. n. y2 above. Cf. especially the conflagration in Seneca, *Consolatio ad Marciam* 26.6; *Thyestes*, 844–74; *Naturales quaestiones* 3.29.1 (which he attributes to Berossus); Nonnus, *Dionysiaca* 38.347–409. The collision of the stars here may be understood as a parallel to the apocalyptic battle in heaven (Rev 12:7) expressed in more cosmological terms. Here, however, *all* the stars are cast down.

k4. Gk. *oura(i) hupēlthe* (Geffcken) for *ouran epēlthe*.

THE SIBYLLINE ORACLES, BOOK 6

Introduction

The twenty-eight verses which make up Sibylline Oracles 6 are not even presented as a Sibylline oracle but are quite simply a hymn to Christ. There is nothing to indicate a Jewish or pagan substratum in this book. It consists of a brief account of the career of Christ, beginning with his baptism and concluding with an apostrophe to the cross.

The hymn has been designated heretical by Geffcken[1] because of the association of fire with the baptism of Christ in verse 6, which is paralleled in Sibylline Oracles 7.84. Geffcken sees a parallel here to the Gospel of the Ebionites, but there the reference is to a light which shone around Christ rather than to fire.[2] The Gospel of the Ebionites also begins with the baptism of Christ, but the evidence is not sufficient to support a literary relationship between the two works. Kurfess has rightly protested that the association of fire with the baptism of Christ is not necessarily sectarian in any case.[3]

The latest possible date for this hymn is fixed by the fact that Lactantius (c. A.D. 300) cites it. Geffcken very tentatively proposes a second-century date, because the meter is better than is usual in third-century works.[4] This criterion must be considered dubious. Kurfess posits that Sibylline Oracles 7 depends on Sibylline Oracles 6 for the association of fire with the baptism of Christ, but in fact there is nothing to suggest literary dependence between the two books.[5] At most the parallel would suggest that the books come from similar milieus.

The interest in baptism in the Jordan might suggest that Sibylline Oracles 6 originated near the Jordan Valley, but this again is by no means necessary. Ultimately all we can say with confidence about the provenance of Sibylline Oracles 6 is that it was written by a Christian before the time of Lactantius.

The idea expressed in verse 37, that the cross would be taken up to heaven, was popular in later Christian writings.[6]

---

[1] Geffcken, *Komposition und Entstehungszeit*, p. 31, following Alexandre and Mendelssohn.

[2] Epiphanius, *AdvHaer* 30.13.

[3] Kurfess, *Sibyllinische Weissagungen*, p. 313.

[4] Geffcken, *Komposition und Entstehungszeit*, p. 32.

[5] Kurfess, HSW, vol. 2, p. 708. Geffcken, *Komposition und Entstehungszeit*, p. 32, already argued against literary dependence here.

[6] See Rzach, Pauly-Wissowa 2A, col. 2141.

THE SIBYLLINE ORACLES
Book 6

A hymn to Christ

I speak from my heart of the great famous son of the Immortal,
to whom the Most High, his begetter, gave a throne to possess
before he was born, since he was raised up the second time   8.264
according to the flesh, when he had washed in the streams of the river   7.66–67; Mt 3:16–17
5 Jordan, which moves with gleaming foot, sweeping the waves.   Mk 1:9–11; Lk 3:21–22
Jn 1:31–32
He will escape the fire and be the first to see delightful God   7.84; Epiphanius, AdvHaer
coming in the spirit on the white wings of a dove.   30.13.7 (GEbion)
Lactantius, DivInst 4.15.3
A pure flower will bloom, fountains will burst forth.   Isa 11:1; Lactantius,
He will show ways to men; he will show heavenly paths.   DivInst 4.13.21
10 He will teach all with wise words.
He will come to judgment and persuade a disobedient people,   1.204
boasting praiseworthy descent from the Heavenly Father.   1.356, etc.; 1.351; Lactantius,
He will walk the waves; he will undo the sickness of men;   DivInst 4.15.25; Mt 14:26
Mk 6:48; Jn 6:19
he will raise the dead. He will repel many woes.   1.355; 8.205; Mt 11:5; Lk 7:22
15 From one wallet men will have surfeit of bread   1.357, etc.
when the house of David brings forth a shoot. In his hand   7.31; Isa 11:1
are the whole world and earth and heaven and sea.
He will flash like lightning on the earth   Mt 24:27; Lk 17:24
as the two begotten from each other's sides once saw him when he first
shone forth.[a]
20 It will come to pass when earth rejoices in the hope of a child.   ProtJames 18
For you alone, land of Sodom, evil afflictions are in store.   Rev 11:8
For with your hostile mind you did not perceive your God   Lactantius, DivInst 4.18.20
when he came before mortal eyes. But you crowned him
with a crown from the thornbush, and you mixed terrible gall   8.303; 1.367; Mt 27:29,34
25 for insult and drink.[b] That will cause great afflictions for you.   Mk 15:18,23; Lk 23:36
Ps 69:21
O wood, o most blessed, on which God was stretched out;   5.257
earth will not contain you, but you will see heaven as home   GPet 39–42
when your fiery eye, o God, flashes like lightning.   Rev 1:14; 19:12

---

a. The Sibyl asserts that Adam and Eve saw Christ.
Cf. John 8:56: "Your father Abraham rejoiced to
think that he would see my Day; he saw it and was

glad."
b. Gk. *pōma* for *pneuma* (Alexandre).

THE SIBYLLINE ORACLES, BOOK 7

Introduction

Sibylline Oracles 7 is poorly preserved and at best seems to be a loosely structured collection of oracles.[1] The collection is framed by passages that deal with the Flood (7–15)[2] and by an extended eschatological tableau that predicts a conflagration, eternal punishment of sinners by fire, and the restoration of the earth (118–51). Much of the intervening section is taken up with oracles against various nations and places: verses 1–6, 16–23, 40–63, 96–117. These could very well have been derived from pagan oracles. The sequence of references is chaotic. So verses 40–50 refer to a war of Rome with the Parthians, which ended in the rout of the Romans, possibly at Carrhae. This is followed by an oracle on Troy (51–54). Later the Sibyl returns to Rome (vss. 108–11), but the reference is to the rise of Rome after the fall of Macedonia.

These oracles of destruction are interrupted by an eschatological passage in 24–39, which includes a conflagration (24–28) and a messianic prophecy (29–39), and by a passage on the baptism of Christ, followed by certain ritual prescriptions in 64–95. The latter passage contains the most distinctive doctrines of Sibylline Oracles 7. The book concludes with a confession of the Sibyl.[3]

Since the book is framed by passages on the Flood and conflagration it corresponds approximately to the second half of Sibylline Oracles 1 and 2 and, less directly, Sibylline Oracles 4. However, one important feature is missing. The periodization, which was the main structuring element in the earlier oracles, is completely lacking. The eschatology of in Sibylline Oracles 7 has close affinities with both Sibylline Oracles 4 and Sibylline Oracles 2.

There is nothing to suggest a Jewish substratum in the book. The hope in the house of David (29–39) does not envisage an earthly kingdom but the enthronement of Christ above the angels.

Date

Most scholars have dated Sibylline Oracles 7 to the second century,[4] but there is no clear evidence. The latest possible date is provided by Lactantius.[5] The vague and disordered historical prophecies provide no clear allusion later than the time of Christ. The second-century date has been proposed mainly on the basis of the alleged Jewish-Christian and gnostic character of the book. In fact, there is nothing in the book to enable us to fix its date with any precision within the second and third centuries.

Provenance

The provenance of the book is equally elusive. The interest in the baptism of Christ and the fact that Christ is introduced in an oracle against Coele-Syria and Phoenicia might suggest that Sibylline Oracles 7 was composed somewhere in Syria, but this is very far from conclusive.

Theological and historical importance

The book has been designated "gnostic" and "Jewish-Christian" by Geffcken and

---

[1] The main discussions of SibOr 7 are: Geffcken, *Komposition und Entstehungszeit*, pp. 33–37; Rzach, Pauly-Wissowa 2A, cols. 2141f.; Kurfess, *Sibyllinische Weissagungen*, pp. 313–16; and J. G. Gager, "Some Attempts to Label the Oracula Sibyllina, Book 7," *HTR* 65 (1972) 91–97.

[2] This section is heavily dependent on SibOr 1. See Kurfess, "Oracula Sibyllina, I/II," *ZNW* 40 (1941) 151–65.

[3] Kurfess, "Die Sibylle über sich selbst," *Mnemosyne* (1941) pp. 195–98.

[4] Geffcken, *Komposition und Entstehungszeit*, p. 36; Kurfess, *Sibyllinische Weissagungen*, pp. 313f.; Rzach, Pauly-Wissowa 2A, col. 2142, prefers the third century.

[5] Cf. Lactantius, *DivInst* 7.16.13; SibOr 7.123.

Kurfess, but both designations have been challenged by Gager.[6] The evidence for "Jewish-Christianity" consists of the reference to the Davidic house in verses 29–39 and the condemnation in verses 134–35 of those who claim to be Hebrews when that is not their race. Neither of these references in a Christian context in the second or third century need necessarily imply affinity with Judaism. The house of David is summed up in an individual figure, presumably Christ, who is enthroned above the angels (32–35). The term "Hebrews" may well be used in a spiritual sense or merely be an allusion to Revelation 2:9; 3:9.[7] Of course, the possibility that Sibylline Oracles 7 was produced by people who were Jews by race cannot be ruled out, but the evidence is inconclusive.

A number of unusual references in the book have gnostic parallels:[8]

1. On the towers in verse 71, compare Acts of Thomas 17–23, where Thomas builds a spiritual palace (cf. ShepHerm Vis 3.3.3, 4.1).

2. On Uranus as a mythological person (vs. 71) compare Epiphanius, *AdvHaer* 31.3.

3. On God's noble "mothers" (Hope, Piety, and Holiness, vss. 72–73) compare Irenaeus 1.5.2f., Epiphanius, *AdvHaer* 31.5 (also ShepHerm Vis 3:8).

4. On the "third lot" (vs. 139) compare Pistis Sophia (244–45).

5. On the "Ogdoad" (vs. 140) compare Epiphanius, *AdvHaer* 31.6.

These allusions are isolated in Sibylline Oracles 7 and, at least in the case of the Ogdoad, quite out of context. Gager is surely right in insisting that they do not make the book gnostic in any clearly defined sense. They show that this Sibyl, who drew freely on gentile oracles, was familiar with some gnostic terminology and could draw on it too. Ultimately we cannot identify Sibylline Oracles 7 with any known sect.

Yet the interest of the book is considerable if only as a specimen of the diversity within second- or third-century Christianity. The author is clearly Christian, however unusual his Christianity, and is also monotheistic, as his polemic against idolatry shows (vss. 14, 21, 129–31).[9] Sacrifice is replaced by a strange rite commemorating the baptism of Christ (76–84). Water is sprinkled on fire and a dove released to heaven, which is said to symbolize the begetting of the Logos by the Father. Here, as in Sibylline Oracles 6, the begetting of Christ is closely associated, if not identified, with his baptism and also with a theophany by fire.

The ritualism of verses 76–84 is continued in verses 85–91, where a rite is prescribed for accepting supplicants. Strikingly, the Sibyl does not enjoin that anything be given to the beggars but only that a prayer be recited over them. Geffcken rightly draws attention to the implications of magic here,[10] but they are not sufficient to associate the Sibyl with any particular sect.

The eschatology of Sibylline Oracles 7 is closely modeled on Sibylline Oracles 2[11] and Sibylline Oracles 4. The world will be destroyed by a conflagration, and the wicked will not simply perish but will be tortured by fire forever. The infernal punishment is somewhat more elaborate here than in Sibylline Oracles 4 but does not approach the vividness and detail of Sibylline Oracles 2. As in Sibylline Oracles 4 and Sibylline Oracles 2 the just are rewarded, not by a heavenly life, but by the resurrection and transformation of the earth. Sibylline Oracles 7 does not make an explicit connection between its ritual prescriptions and its eschatology. We should note that sacrifices are also rejected in Sibylline Oracles 4, and the importance attached to the baptism of Christ in book 7 also recalls the importance of baptism in book 4.

The final confession of the Sibyl (150–62) is obviously related to the concluding verses of Sibylline Oracles 2.

[6] Gager, *HTR* 65 (1972) 91–97.

[7] In Rev 2:9 the reference is probably to people who were Jews by race but whom the author did not consider heirs to the promises of Judaism.

[8] See especially Kurfess, HSW, vol. 2, p. 707.

[9] Gager's emphasis on the syncretism of the Sibyl must be qualified by this fact.

[10] Geffcken, *Komposition und Entstehungszeit*, p. 34.

[11] On the priority of SibOr 2 to SibOr 7 see the introduction to books 1 and 2 and Kurfess, *ZNW* 40 (1941) 151–65.

THE SIBYLLINE ORACLES
Book 7

Destruction of various places

O Rhodes, you wretched one, for you first will I weep.   3.444
You are first of cities, but you will perish first,
widowed of men, completely failing to gain a livelihood.[a]   3.363; 4.92; 8.165
Delos, you will swim and be unstable on the water.   Herodotus 6.98
5 Cyprus, one day the wave of the gleaming sea will destroy you.   4.129,143: 5.450–51
Sicily, the fire that flares beneath you will burn you up.   4.81
       *   *   *

The Flood

This I say, the terrible and strange water of God.   1.183
       *   *   *

A certain Noah came, a solitary fugitive from all men.   1.125, etc.
       *   *   *

Earth will swim, mountains will swim, even the sky will swim.   1.193–96
10 All will be water and all things will perish in waters.
Winds will stop, and there will be a second age.
O Phrygia, you will shine forth first from the surface of the water,
but you, the same, first to impiety, will reject God;
pleasing to speechless idols, which will destroy you,   3.30,14, etc.
15 wretched one, as many years pursue their cyclic course.

Further oracles of destruction

The unfortunate Ethiopians, also suffering piteous woes,[b]   5.206
will be smitten with swords under the skin as they crouch in fear.
Civil strife among themselves will destroy sleek Egypt,   3.316
always concerned with corn blades, which the Nile
20 saturates with seven swimming streams. Thence, unexpectedly,
men will drive out Apis, who is not a god to men.[c]
Alas, Laodicea, daring one, you will speak falsehood,   3.471, etc.
you who have never seen God. The wave of Lycus will dash over you.
The great God himself, the begetter,[d] will make many stars
25 and will hang an axis through the middle of the sky
and set up a great terror for men to behold on high,
an immense[e] pillar, with great fire, from which   2.240; Plato,
drops will destroy the evil races of men who have done harm.   *Republic* 10.616b

A messianic oracle

For one day that time will come to pass when once for all men
30 will beseech God, but will not stop fruitless
troubles. But all will be fulfilled through the house of David.   6.16
For God entrusted and gave a throne to him.[f]   2Sam 7:16; Pss 132:11; 89:36
The angels will sleep under his feet—   Heb 1:4–14
those who cause fires to gleam and those who pour forth[g] rivers,   ShepHerm Vis 3.4.1

---

a. Gk. *ateuktos* for *adeukēs* (Geffcken).
b. Gk. *id' algea* for *hyp' algea* (Geffcken).
c. Apis was the sacred bull worshiped at Memphis.
d. Gk. *ho gennetēs* for *gennētheis* (Buresch).
e. Gk. *kion' ametrēton* for *kiona metrēsas* (cf. Kurfess, HSW, vol. 2, p. 721).

f. In view of the following vs., the reference is most probably to Christ rather than to David.
g. Gk. *procheousi* for *phainousi* (Kurfess). On the angels of the elements see further Strack-Billerbeck 3:818.

35 those who protect cities and those who send out storm winds.   Rev 16:5; 1En 60:12–22;
   A difficult life will come upon many men,   82:10–14; Jub 2:2
   entering souls and changing hearts of men.   2En 4–6; 19:4; 40:9
   But when a young shoot puts forth eyes from the root,   6.16; Isa 11:1
   which once distributed abundant nurture to all branches . . .[h]
        *   *   *

Oracles against various nations

40 These things will further be in time. But when others
   rule over the tribe of warlike Persians[i] then there will be
   terrible weddings of brides because of lawless tribes.
   For mother will have her own son also as husband. Son   5.390–91
   will have intercourse with mother.[j] Daughter, reclining on father,
45 will sleep according to this savage custom. Later
   a Roman Ares will shine out on them from many a lance.   12.71,278;
   They will mix much earth with human blood.   13.35
   A prince of Italy will then flee from the might of the spear.[k]   1.156
   They will leave on the ground a flower engraved with gold,
50 which always bears an unholy sign when it goes forth.[l]
   It will come to pass when Ilias, all evil and ill-fated,
   piteously drinks deep not marriage but the tomb, then brides
   will weep deeply, because they did not take thought of God
   but always made noise with cymbals and rattling sounds.
55 Prophesy, Colophon, a great terrible fire hangs over you.
   Ill-wedded Thessaly, the earth will no longer see you,   5.134
   even as ashes, but you will sail alone, a fugitive from the mainland.
   Thus,[m] O wretched one, you will be the mournful refuse of war,
   O one who falls to dogs and rivers and swords.
60 O wretched Corinth, you will receive grievous war about yourself,   5.214
   miserable one, and you will perish at each other's hands.
   Tyre, you alone will receive so great a fate, for you will excel   5.455; 14.87
   in small-mindedness, bereft of pious men.

Baptism of Christ

   Ah, Coele-Syria, last possession of the Phoenician men   3.492
65 on whom the brine of Beirut lies belched up,
   wretched one, you did not recognize your God, whom once Jordan   6.4–5, etc.
      washed
   in its streams,[n] and the spirit flew like a dove.   6.7
   He, before either earth or starry heaven,
   was sovereign Word, with the Father and Holy Spirit.   Jn 1:1
70 He put on flesh but quickly flew to his Father's home.
   Great heaven established three towers for him[o]   Acts of Thomas 17–23
   in which the noble mothers of God now live: ShepHerm Vis 3.3.3;
                      3.4.1, etc.

---

h. Gk. *klēmasin* for *tēn ktisin* (Geffcken).

i. Gk. *Persōn machimōn phul'* (Rzach) for *Persai machimōn phulon*.

j. Gk. *homilēsei* for *dēlēsei* (Kurfess).

k. The most famous defeat of Romans by Parthians was at Carrhae in 53 B.C. The Roman leader on that occasion, Crassus, was killed after he had surrendered, but that detail may have been overlooked by the Sibyl. Alexandre, Excursus V, 385, sees here a reference to the campaign of Alexander Severus to recover Mesopotamia from the Parthians in A.D. 231. The success of that campaign is disputed but Meso-

potamia was recovered. A reference to Carrhae seems more likely here.

l. Gk. *ekpromolon to pheron g'aiei sēmeion anagnon* for *ekpromolonta pheron g'aei sēmeion anagkēs* (Geffcken). Cf. the Jewish reaction to Roman standards in *War* 2.9.2 (169–71); *Ant* 18.3.1 (55–59).

m. Gk. *houtōs* for *autois* (Alexandre).

n. Gk. *prochoēsi* for *tritatoisi* (Fabricius).

o. For Uranos as a mythological person cf. Epiphanius, *AdvHaer* 31.3. See the Introduction to SibOr 7.

hope and piety and desirable holiness.
They do not rejoice in gold or silver but in reverential acts
75 of men, sacrifices, and most righteous thoughts.

Irenaeus 1.5.2; ShepHerm Vis
3.8; Epiphanius, *AdvHaer* 31.5

Ritual prescriptions

You shall sacrifice to the immortal great noble God,
not by melting a lump of incense in fire or striking
a shaggy ram with a sacrificial knife, but with all
who bear your blood, by taking a wild dove,[p]
80 praying, and sending it off, while gazing to heaven.
You shall pour a libation of water on pure fire, crying out as follows:
"As the father begot you, the Word, so[q] I have dispatched a bird,
a word which is swift reporter of words, sprinkling
with holy waters your baptism, through which you were revealed out
of fire.
85 You shall not shut the door when some other stranger
comes, begging you to ward off poverty and hunger.
But take the head of this man, sprinkle it with water,
and pray three times. Cry out to your God as follows:
'I do not desire wealth. I am poor and I have received a poor man.'
90 You, father, provider, deign to listen to both."
He will give to you when you pray.

4.29–30

6.6

Ps-Phoc 22f.
Did 1:5; 4:5

2.56,109

Mt 7:7

Fragmentary verses

91a Thereafter a man led away . . .
      *   *   *

Do not afflict me, sacred and righteous holiness of God
(holy, indomitable, proved concerning the offspring . . .)[r]
Father, check my wretched heart. I have looked to you,
95 to you, the undefiled, whom no hands made.
      *   *   *

3.1–5, etc.

3.14, etc.

Oracles against various nations

Sardinia, you who are powerful now, will be changed to ashes.
You will no longer be an island, when the tenth time comes.
Sailing on the waters they will seek you, who no longer exist.
Kingfishers will wail a piteous lament over you.
100 Rugged Mygdonia, beacon of the sea, difficult of exit,
you will boast for an age; you will perish through ages,
entirely, with a hot wind. You will rage with many ills.
Celtic land, upon your mountain beyond the Alps, which are difficult
    to cross,
deep sand will make a mound over you entirely. You will no longer
    give tribute,
105 corn, or fodder. You will be desolate without people,
forever frozen with icy crystals.
You will make amends for the outrage, impious one, which you had not
    noticed.
Sturdy-spirited Rome, after the Macedonian spear
you will flash like lightning to Olympus. But God will make you
110 utterly unknown when you will seem in appearances

3.447

2.15, etc.

3.161,175

3.350, etc;
Oracle of
Hystaspes,
DivInst 7.15.11

---

p. Gk. *agriēn su peleian* for *agriēna peteina*
(Geffcken). The origins and extent of this ritual
remain enigmatic.

q. Gk. *hōs* for *pater* (Geffcken).

r. This vs. is defective in the MSS.

to remain much better established. Then I will cry out to you as follows:
"You who once gleamed[s] brightly will lift your voice as you perish."
Further, Rome, I will again utter further things to you.
Now you, wretched Syria, will I bewail piteously.   13.119
115 Thebes of ill counsel, an evil sound will come upon you,
with the voice of flutes. A trumpet will sound a bad sound
for you. You will see the whole land perishing.

Cosmic destruction

Woe to you, wretched one, woe, evil-spirited sea.
You will all be devoured by fire, and you will destroy people with brine.   5.159
120 For there will be as much fire raging on the earth   2.196, etc.
as water, and it will flow and destroy the whole earth.
It will burn up mountains, burn rivers and empty springs.   4.176;
The world will be chaos when men perish.   1En 52:6;
    1QH 3:29–33
Then wretched men, burning badly, will look   Lactantius,
    DivInst 7.16.3
125 on heaven, void of stars but overcome by fire.   5.531
They will not be destroyed quickly but, being burned in spirit
by their perishing flesh for the years of ages
forever, they will know, by dire tortures, that it is not possible
to deceive the law of God. The earth, under constraint,
130 has perceived that whichever of the gods she dared to accept
in falsehood on her altars was smoke, misty[t] through the sky.

False prophets

But they will endure extreme toil who, for gain,
will prophesy base things, augmenting an evil time;
who putting on the shaggy hides of sheep   Mt 7:15
135 will falsely claim to be Hebrews, which is not their race.   Rev 2:9; 3:9
But speaking with words, making profit by woes,
they will not change their life and will not persuade the righteous
and those who propitiate God through the heart, most faithfully.

Restoration of the world

In the third lot of circling years,   Pistis Sophia
    244f.
140 of the first ogdoad, another world is seen again.   Epiphanius,
    AdvHaer 31.4
All will be night, long and unyielding,
and then a terrible smell of brimstone will extend   3.60,462
announcing murders, when those men perish
by night and famine. Then he will beget a pure mind
145 of men and will set up your race as it was before for you.   4.182
No longer will anyone cut a deep furrow with a crooked plow;   Virgil, Eclogue
    4.40–45
no oxen will plunge down the guiding iron.
There will be no vine branches or ear of corn, but all, at once,   1En 10:18–19; 2Bar 29:5–8
will eat the dewy manna with white teeth.   Ex 16

Confession of the Sibyl

150 God will then be with them, who will teach you,
even as me, the sorrowful one. For what evils   2.339–47
I formerly did, knowingly! and I performed many other things badly
    through neglect.

---

s. Gk. *marmairousa* for *kai marmaran se*   t. Gk. *achlunthenta* for *algēthenta* (Wilamowitz).
(Geffcken).

I have known innumerable beds, but no marriage concerned me.
Utterly faithless, I imposed a savage oath on all.

155 I shut out those in need, and going among those who go forth
to a shady^u glen, I did not observe the oracle of God.
Therefore fire has eaten and will devour me. For I myself will not
live, but an evil time will destroy me, when men who pass by
will fashion a tomb for me by the sea;

160 and they will destroy me with stones, for when I was speaking to the
Father
he communicated to me the dear son.^v May you stone me! Stone me all
of you!
For thus will I live and fix my eyes on heaven.

Ovid, *Metamorphoses* 14.142

---

u. Gk. *euskion* for *ikelon* (Geffcken).
v. Gk. *epi moi gar patri lalousē(i) huia philon*
metedōke; so φ, except that it reads *lalousa* not *lalousē(i)*.

THE SIBYLLINE ORACLES, BOOK 8

Introduction

The eighth book is clearly composite and falls obviously into two quite different sections.[1] Verses 1–216 are mainly concerned with political prophecies, especially directed against Rome. Verses 217–500, by contrast, are largely taken up with Christology, the incarnation, and the praises of God. The political concerns that dominated the first half of the book are completely lacking in the second.

Within each half of the book there are a number of loosely structured oracles. In verses 1–216 we find:

> 1–16 refer to the fall of the tower of Babylon and repeat substantially the list of kingdoms found in Sibylline Oracles 3.159–61.
> There follows (17–36) an admonition against greed. Next we find a series of oracles against Rome:
> 37–49 attack Rome for idolatry.
> 50–72 present an attack on Hadrian and expect the return of Nero.
> 73–130 describe the woes to come upon Rome and the equality of all in the eschatological time.
> 131–38 predict power and stability for the fifteenth king of Egypt in the sixth generation of Latin kings—i.e. Hadrian.[2]
> 139–50 again pick up the Nero legend.
> 151–59 present yet another prophecy of the return of Nero.
> 160–68 consist of oracles against various gentile nations.
> 169–93 describe eschatological upheavals, which, in part at least (vs. 171), have special relevance for Rome.
> 194–216 relate the eschatological reign of a woman in the tenth generation.

Geffcken ascribes three passages to a pagan Sibyl. He rightly notes that verses 131–38, which are favorable to Hadrian, are incompatible with verses 50–72 and are the work of an Egyptian Sibyllist (Hadrian is called the fifteenth king of Egypt). This Sibyllist may have been either a pagan or a Christian, but certainly not a Jew. The oracle was inserted here to counteract or correct the attack on Hadrian in the earlier passage. Geffcken also ascribes verses 160–68 to a pagan Sibyl. These are typical Sibylline verses, the clichés of the genre. They could indeed be taken over from a pagan Sibyl but could just as easily have been composed by a Jew or Christian. In fact, several of the verses seem to be taken from, or modeled on, earlier Jewish Sibyls—160 from Sibylline Oracles 4.101; 162 from 5.17; 164, cf. 3.371; 165f. from 3.363f. A third passage that Geffcken ascribes to a pagan Sibyl is the Nero oracle in verses 151–59. Geffcken rightly notes that Nero is here presented in historical terms with little mythological elaboration.[3] However, this is equally true of the other Nero passages in Sibylline Oracles 8 and does not necessarily require gentile authorship.

In the rest of the first half of the book Geffcken distinguishes the work of two Christian authors, one in verses 1–49 and 73–130, the other in 50–72, 139–50, 169–216, 337–58. This enables him to unite the two Nero passages (50–72 and 139–50), but the differences which he alleges between the two sets of oracles are exceedingly vague. The persistent interest in Rome rather suggests that the entire first half of the book, except for verses 131–38, is a unified work.

Geffcken assumes that all this material is Christian.[4] The only evidence to support this view consists of a few random parallels with Christian apologists. Rzach prefers to see the work as Jewish, while admitting that the eschatological reign of the woman (vss. 194–216)

---

[1] The most important discussions are those of Geffcken, *Komposition und Entstehungszeit*, pp. 38–46 and Rzach, Pauly-Wissowa 2A, cols. 2142–46. Also Kurfess, *Sibyllinische Weissagungen*, pp. 316–33.

[2] See Geffcken, *Komposition und Entstehungszeit*, p. 39.

[3] Ibid., p. 39. See also his "Studien zur älteren Nerossage," *Nachrichten der Göttingen Gesellschaft der Wissenschaften* (1899) 433.

[4] Geffcken, *Komposition und Entstehungszeit*, p. 44. So also Bousset, *Real-Encyclopedie*, p. 277.

could be Christian, under the influence of Revelation 17–18 and 21.[5] The eschatological woman in Sibylline Oracles 8 could equally well be modeled on the oracle about Cleopatra in Sibylline Oracles 3.75–92, which was written by a Jew, but verses 196f., which refer to "the sacred child" who "destroys the malignant abyss," seem clearly to presuppose the New Testament apocalypse. The eschatological passage in verses 205–8 also probably depends on Matthew 11:5 or alternatively on a Christian passage in Sibylline Oracles 1.353–55. However, the indications of Christian origin are confined to the eschatological passage in 194–216.

Jewish authorship of the remainder of the first section of Sibylline Oracles 8 is supported by the animosity toward Hadrian in verses 50–59, although no explicit reference is made to the Jewish revolt. More significant is the fact that Nero in verse 141 is said to attack specifically "the nation of the Hebrews." This reference excludes gentile authorship, though not necessarily Christian. Since Sibylline Oracles 8.1–193 contains nothing that is specifically either Jewish or Christian, the question of authorship cannot be decisively settled.[6] However, in view of the prominence of Christology in the rest of the book and in the Christian Sibylline Oracles in general, the lack of Christian elements may be a significant indication of non-Christian authorship.

We may conclude then that a slight balance of probability favors the Jewish authorship of Sibylline Oracles 8:1–216, with the exception of the gentile oracle in verses 131–38 and the Christian eschatological section in 194–216.

Verses 217–500

The second half of the book consists again of a collection of oracles, although separate authorship is not necessarily implied. We find:

217–50: an acrostic poem that spells out with the initials of each line the words *Iēsous Christos Theou Huios Sōtēr Stauros*, "Jesus Christ, Son of God, Savior, Cross."[7]
251–336: a long poem on Christ, including a sketch of his earthly career.
337–58: a description of eschatological disturbances.
359–428: a speech of God that concentrates on denunciation of idolatry.
429–55: a hymn in praise of God.
456–79: the incarnation.
480–500 conclude the book with ethical and ritual exhortation.

Geffcken wished to ascribe the eschatological section in verses 337–58 to the author of the first half of the book.[8] However, there is no positive reason for this attribution. Since a number of verses in this passage recall the Christian Sibylline Oracles 2, especially in the punishment of the damned (vss. 350–58),[9] it should be thought to belong with the clearly Christian second half of the book.

Date

The date of verses 1–216 can be fixed with some precision. Verses 65–74 envisage the return of Nero during the reign of Marcus Aurelius. Therefore this oracle must have been written before the death of that emperor in A.D. 180. Verses 148f. say that Rome will have completed 948 years before it is destroyed. Strictly speaking, that should point to a date of A.D. 195. However, given that this destruction of Rome is still in the future, and that Sibylline chronology is never exact,[10] this statement is quite compatible with a date about A.D. 175.

The latest possible date for the second half of the book is provided by Lactantius, who quotes extensively from the entire book. There is no closer indication of date. Geffcken

---

[5] Rzach, Pauly-Wissowa 2A, col. 2144.

[6] SibOr 8.205–7 might seem to depend on SibOr 1.353–55 or Mt 11:5 and therefore be Christian, but this has been disputed by Kurfess, *ZNW* 40 (1941) 159. None of the alleged cases of dependence on the NT cited by H. Fuchs, *Geistige Widerstand*, p. 79, are necessarily so.

[7] The first five initials, of course, spell the famous Christian cryptogram *Ichthus*, "fish."

[8] Geffcken, *Komposition und Entstehungszeit*, p. 41.

[9] See Geffcken, *Die Oracula Sibyllina*, pp. 164f.

[10] See Geffcken, *Komposition und Entstehungszeit*, p. 40.

notes similarity of style thoughout the book and suggests that there was no great lapse of time between the various parts.[11]

Provenance

There is nothing to indicate the place of origin of Sibylline Oracles 8. Verses 131–38 were obviously written in Egypt (vs. 138), but the rest of the work could have been written in any part of the Near East that was subject to Rome.

Historical and theological importance

Sibylline Oracles 8.1–216 is a striking example of anti-Roman prophecy, which surpasses even Sibylline Oracles 5 in vehemence. The explicit basis for this polemic is not, as we might expect, Rome's violation of the sovereignty of any particular people (even the Jews) but rather her greed and social injustice (vss. 18–36). In this respect, and also in the opposition of Rome and Asia (e.g. vs. 72), Sibylline Oracles 8 continues the tradition of Sibylline Oracles 3.350–80. Rome is also attacked for idolatry (vss. 43–49), but the sexual polemic of the earlier Sibylline Oracles is missing. The fate of Rome is that she will be cast down to the underworld, where she will be punished in fire and brimstone (102). This punishment is evidently modeled on the individual tortures described, for example, in Sibylline Oracles 2.305. It is followed by a description of Hades, as the place where all are equal, recalling the description of Sheol in Job 3:17–19. There are references to the resurrection of the dead in verses 83 and 170, but this section of Sibylline Oracles 8 shows little interest in the afterlife. The main theme is the coming destruction of Rome and the removal of its wickedness.

The acrostic poem in verses 217–50 is the only example of this phenomenon in the Sibylline Oracles, although acrostics were considered criteria for the authenticity of pagan Sibylline Oracles.[12] The use of acrostics here reflects the desire of the Christian author to present his work as a gentile oracle. Chritian forgeries and interpolations of this sort aroused bitter disputes in apologetic debates.[13]

The remainder of the Christian oracles contain no striking doctrinal peculiarities. There is a polemic against idolatry in verses 377–98. Verses 404–8 recommend almsgiving and charity as a substitute for sacrifice. In verses 480–500 the commandments to love God and neighbor are repeated, and sacrifices are replaced by hymns and pure minds.

Sibylline Oracles 8 makes extensive use of the first five Sibylline books. The oracles against Rome are especially close to the tradition of Sibylline Oracles 3.350–80 and Sibylline Oracles 5. They also find close parallels in the *Carmen apologeticum* of Commodian, a Christian apologist of the fifth century A.D.[14]

---

[11] Ibid., p. 44.

[12] Cicero, *De divinatione* 2.54, 111, 112. SibOr 11 claims to give an acrostic but does not.

[13] See especially Origen, *Contra Celsum* 7.53.

[14] Geffcken, *Komposition und Entstehungszeit*, p. 40; Bousset, *Antichrist Legend*, pp. 79–81; Fuchs, *Geistige Widerstand*, p. 79.

THE SIBYLLINE ORACLES
Book 8

Prophecy of world kingdoms and destruction

As the great wrath comes upon the disobedient world
I show forth the wrath of God to the last age,
prophesying to all men, city by city.
From the time when the tower fell and the tongues of men
5 were divided into many dialects of mortals,
first the Egyptian kingdom, then that of the Persians,
Medes, Ethiopians, and Assyrian Babylon,
then that of Macedonia, which boasted in great arrogance,
then, fifth, the famous lawless kingdom of the Italians[a]
10 last of all, will show many evils to all men
and will expend the toils of the men of all the earth.
It will lead untiring kings of nations to the west
and will legislate for peoples and subdue all things.
The mills of God grind fine flour, though late.[b]
15 Then fire will destroy everything and reduce to fine dust
the heads of lofty mountains and of all flesh.

Lactantius, *De ira Dei* 23.3
1Thes 1:10; Mt 3:7; Lk 3:7
3.811

3.105; Gen 11:1–9

3.159–61; 4.49–104

2.196; 4.173;
7.120, etc.
7.122, etc.

Admonition against greed

The beginning of evils for all will be love of gain and folly
for there will be a desire for deceitful gold and silver.
For there is nothing that mortals preferred to these,
20 not the light of the sun, not heaven nor sea
nor the broad earth whence everything grows
nor God who gives everything, begetter of all.
Nor did they prefer faith and piety to these.
It is the source of impiety and forerunner of disorder,
25 deviser of wars, hostile troubler of peace
which alienates parents from their children and children from their
    parents.
Even marriage will never be wholly honored apart from gold.
Earth will have boundaries and all the sea guards,
craftily divided among those who have gold.
30 As if wishing to have the much-nurturing earth forever
they will ravage the poor, so that they themselves may acquire
additional land and subject them by imposture.
If the huge earth did not have its throne
far from starry heaven, men would not have equal light
35 but it would be marketed for gold and would belong to the rich,
and God would have prepared another world for beggars.

2.111, etc.;
1Tim 6:10

Oracle against Rome

One day, proud Rome, there will come upon you from above
an equal heavenly affliction, and you will first bend the neck
and be razed to the ground, and fire will consume you, altogether

3.350, etc.

---

a. Babylon is presumably distinguished from the Persian Empire but placed after it in chronological sequence. The Roman Empire is also fifth in SibOr 4, but there the number is not attached to it and the reference belongs to the second, redactional, stage of the oracle.

b. An old proverb, found in a number of Gk. sources.

40 laid low on your floors, and wealth will perish
and wolves and foxes will dwell in your foundations. Isa 34:11–15
Then you will be utterly desolate, as if you had never been. 3.310;
Where then will be the Palladium?^c What sort of God will save you? 2Bar 31:5
One of gold, or stone or bronze? Or where then will be your
45 senatorial decrees? Where the race of Rhea or Cronos
or Zeus and of all those whom you revered? 3.122, 547–48,
Lifeless demons, likenesses of dead corpses, 554; 8:393;
whose tombs ill-fated Crete will have as boast,^d Lactantius,
worshiping senseless corpses with ritual enthronements. *DivInst* 1.11.47

Hadrian

50 But when, luxurious one, you have had fifteen kings 8.138
who enslaved the world from east to west,
there will be a gray-haired prince with the name of a nearby sea,^e 5.47; 12.164
inspecting the world with polluted foot,^f giving gifts.
Having abundant gold, he will also gather more
55 silver from his enemies and strip and undo them.
He will participate in all the mysteries of magic shrines.^g 12.169
He will display a child as god,^h and undo all objects of reverence.
From the beginning he will open up the mysteries of error to all.
Then will be a woeful time, because "the woeful" himself will perish.
60 One day the people will say, "Your great power, o city, will fall,"
knowing that the fated evil day is immediately at hand.
Then fathers and infant children will mourn together,
regarding your most piteous fate.
Mournful, they will raise dirges by the banks of Tiber.
65 After him, three will ruleⁱ who have the last day of all, 5.51; 12.176
fulfilling the name of the heavenly God,
whose power is both now and for all ages.

The return of Nero in the time of Marcus Aurelius

One, an old man,^j will control dominions far and wide,
a most piteous king, who will shut up and guard all the wealth
70 of the world in his home, so that when the blazing
matricidal exile returns from the ends of the earth 4.119–24;
he will give these things to all and award great wealth to Asia.^k 138–39, etc.
3.350, etc.

Woes to come upon Rome

Then you will mourn, doffing the garment^l of leaders,
with its broad purple border, and wearing a garment of mourning.
75 O proud queen, offspring of Latin Rome. 3.356, etc.
No longer will you have the fame of your pride

c. The Palladium was a sacred image of Pallas Athene, said to have been brought from Troy and kept in the temple of Vesta. It was believed to protect the city and was credited with saving Rome from the Gauls in 390 B.C.

d. Crete laid claim not only to the cave where Zeus was hidden as a child but also to his grave.

e. Contrast the negative presentation of Hadrian here with the positive attitude of SibOr 5.47f. and SibOr 8.131–38. SibOr 12.164–75 is also basically positive.

f. Hadrian toured the provinces of the empire in the years A.D. 120–31.

g. Hadrian was one of several emperors initiated at Eleusis, and oriental religions flourished in his reign.

h. Antinous, the favorite of Hadrian, was deified upon his death, by drowning, in Egypt in A.D. 130.

i. See SibOr 5, n. t. The three are Lucius Verus, Antoninus Pius, and Marcus Aurelius.

j. Marcus Aurelius.

k. On the contrast between East and West, Asia and Europe, see the Introduction to SibOr 3 on vss. 350–55.

l. Gk. *zōsma* for *phōs* (Geffcken).

nor will you ever be lifted up, ill-fated one, but you will be laid low.
For the glory of the eagle-bearing legions will also fall.
Where then is your strength? What sort of land will be an ally
80 which has been lawlessly enslaved by your vain thoughts?
For then there will be confusion of all the land of mortals,
when the universal ruler himself comes and judges on the tribunal   Lanctantius, *DivInst* 7.24.1; 2.218,239–43, etc.; Dan 7:9–10
the souls of the living and dead, and the whole world.
Neither will parents be friendly to children nor children to parents   1En 56:7; 99:5; 100:2 Micah 7:6; Mt 10:35–36
85 because of impiety and affliction beyond hope.   Lk 12:53
Then you will have gnashing of teeth and scattering and capture   8.105,125; Mt 8:12; Lk 13:28
when the fall of cities comes and yawning gaps in the earth.
When the purple dragon comes on the waves,[m]   Rev 12:3; 13:1
pregnant with a host, and will nurture your children
90 when famine and civil war are at hand;
then the end of the world and the last day is near,
and the judgment of the immortal God for the approved elect.
First there will be implacable wrath of Romans.
A bloodthirsty time, and wretched life will come.
95 Woe to you, Italian land, great savage nation.
You did not perceive whence you came, naked and unworthy   8.108; Job 1:21; Eccl 5:14; Rev 17:16
to the light of the sun, so that you might go again naked
to the same place and later come to judgment
because you judge unjustly . . .
100 By gigantic hands, alone in the whole world,   5.178; Isa 14:15
you will come from a height and dwell under the earth
in naphtha and asphalt and brimstone and much fire,   Rev 19:20; 20:10; 21:8
and you will disappear and will be blazing dust
forever. Everyone who looks will hear a mournful
105 great bellowing from Hades and gnashing of teeth   8.86; 2.203, etc. 2.302
as you strike your godless breast with your hands.
Night is equal to all at once, to those who have wealth
and to beggars. Coming naked from the earth, going naked again   8.97, etc.
to the earth, they cease from life, having completed their time.

The equality of all in the eschatological time

110 No one is slave there, no lord, no tyrant,[n]   2.322–24; 2En 65:8–9
no kings, no leaders who are very arrogant,
no forensic rhetoricians, no ruler judging for money.   2.62
They do not pour blood on altars in libations of sacrifices.   4.29–30; 7.78
No drum sounds, no cymbal,
115 no flute of many holes, which has a sound that damages the heart,   Rev 18:22
no pipe, which bears an imitation of the crooked serpent,
no savage-sounding trumpet, herald of wars,   5.253
none who are drunk in lawless revels or dances,
no sound of the lyre, no evil-working device,
120 no strife, no anger, in its diverse kinds; nor will there be a knife
beside the dead, but the age will be common to all.
        *   *   *
Key-bearer of the great enclosure on the tribunal of God . . .   2.227
        *   *   *

---

m. The dragon and the sea are symbols of chaos in Near Eastern religion, deriving from Yamm in Ugaritic myth, Tiamat in Babylonian myth, etc. The dragon in Rev 12 and beast from the sea in Rev 13 provide the most obvious parallels for the eschatological use of this symbolism (but cf. Isa 27:1; Dan 7f.). It is not clear whether any more specific reference is intended here. It is possible that the returning Nero is here identified with the dragon, as he is identified with the beast in Rev 13.

n. Originally a Stoic notion—e.g. Seneca, *Consolatio ad Marciam* 26.4.

Destruction of Rome

and with statues of gold and silver and stone,°	3.58
be beautiful, so that you may come to a bitter day,	3.59
125 to see your punishment first, Rome, and the gnashing of teeth.	8.86, etc.

No longer will Syrian, Greek, or foreigner, or any other nation,
place their neck under your yoke of slavery.
You will be utterly ravaged and destroyed for what you did.

| Groaning in panic, you will give until you have repaid all, | 3.350–55, etc.; |
| 130 and you will be a triumph-spectacle to the world and a reproach of all. | 12.227 |

An encomium on Hadrian

| Then the sixth generation of Latin kings | 1.284 |

will complete its last life and abandon the scepters.
Another king of the same race will reign[p]
who will rule the whole earth and gain sway over dominions.
135 He will rule by the counsels of the great God without contamination,
his children and the race of his unshaken children.
For thus it is prophesied, in the cyclic course of time,

| whenever there will have been fifteen kings of Egypt.[q] | 8.50 |

The return of Nero

Then when comes the time of the Phoenix, of the fifth period[r] . . .

*   *   *

140 he will come to ravage the race of peoples, undistinguished tribes,	4.119, etc.; 138,
the nation of the Hebrews. Then Ares[s] will take Ares captive.	etc.
He himself will destroy the overbearing threat of the Romans.[t]	5.361

For the empire of Rome, which then flourished, has perished,
the ancient queen over the surrounding cities.
145 No longer will the plain of luxuriant Rome be victorious
when he comes from Asia, conquering with Ares.
Having done all these things, he will come to the trampled town.
You will fulfill thrice three hundred and forty-eight
years[u] when an evil violent fate

| 150 will come upon you fulfilling your name. | 13.46–47; |
| | 1.141, etc. |

Another oracle on the return of Nero

Alas for me, thrice-wretched one, when will I see that day,	3.55
destructive indeed to you,[v] Rome, and especially to all Latins?	
Celebrate, if you wish, the man of secret birth,	5.140

riding a Trojan chariot from the land of Asia

| 155 with the spirit of fire. But when he cuts through the isthmus | 5.139, etc. |

glancing about, going against everyone, having crossed the sea,
then dark blood will pursue the great beast.

---

o. Alexandre would fill the lacuna between 123 and 124 by inserting SibOr 3.57: "Yet just for the present, be founded, cities, all be embellished."

p. The reference is to Hadrian. Contrast SibOr 8.50–72 and see the Introduction to SibOr 8.

q. I.e. Roman kings, beginning with Julius Caesar and counting Galba, Otho, and Vitellius.

r. The reference to the fifth period must be seen in the context of the division of history into ten periods, divided by the Flood in the fifth, which underlies SibOr 1 and 2 and SibOr 4. The reference here is to the fifth period *after* the Flood, when the conflagration will take place, and mankind will rise again from the ashes—cf. SibOr 4.179–82.

s. The god of war.

t. Cf. Rev 17:16 where the beast and its horns reject the prostitute and devour her. On the complex relations between the returned Nero and Rome see further Bousset, *The Antichrist Legend*, pp. 81f.

u. Strictly speaking this should give the date A.D. 195, but the Sibyl's chronology is less than reliable. See the Introduction to SibOr 8.

v. Gk. *soi g'oloon* for *seio pote* (Rzach).

The hound pursued the lion that was destroying the herdsmen.   14.17
They will take away dominion, and he will pass over to Hades.

Oracles against various nations

160 A final but greatest evil will come upon the Rhodians,   4.101
and for the Thebans evil captivity awaits thereafter.   4.89
Egypt will be destroyed by the wickedness of its rulers.   5.17
(Also, like the men who afterward fled dire destruction,
thrice happy was the man, and four times blessed.)[w]   3.371
165 Rome will be a street and Delos inconspicuous   3.363–64
and Samos sand . . .
Then later, also, evil will come upon the Persians.
In return for overbearing pride, all arrogance will be destroyed.

Eschatological upheavals

Then a holy prince[x] will gain control of the scepters of the whole world   3.49
170 for all ages, he who raised the dead.
The Most High will lead three, then, in piteous fate at Rome,[y]   3.52
and all men will perish in their own dwellings.
But they will not be persuaded, which would be much better.
But whenever there rises upon all the evil day
175 of famine and pestilence, hard to bear, and tumult,   2.23, etc.
and then again the former wretched lord[z]
will assemble the council and deliberate how he will destroy[a2] . . .

                    *   *   *

The withered will bloom, appearing together with leaves.   Lactantius,
The floor of heaven will rain[b2] on the hard rock   DivInst 7.16.6
180 shower and flame and many breezes on the earth
and an abundance of poisonous seeds throughout the whole earth.
But they will act again with shameless spirit,
not fearing the wrath of God or of men,   1.175–79
abandoning modesty, desiring shamelessness,
185 tyrants in fickleness and violent sinners,
liars, lovers of faithlessness, evildoers, truthful in nothing,   3.36–40
breakers of faith, ingenious at pouring out slander.
They will not have surfeit of wealth, but shamelessly
they will collect more. Under the sway of tyrants they will perish.
190 All the stars will fall directly into the sea,   2.202, etc.; 5.530; 8.341
all in turn,[c2] and men will call a shining comet   Commodian, Carmen
                                                                               apologeticum 1011
"the star," a sign of much impending toil,   3.334; Nechepso-Petosiris
war, and slaughter.   (ed. Riess), p. 345
May I not be alive when the abominable woman[d2] reigns,   3.75; Rev 17; 8.200

w. Geffcken puts these vss. in parentheses because
of their incoherence.

x. Geffcken and Kurfess identify this figure as
Elijah and cite Commodian, Carmen apologeticum
839, 850, as a parallel. However, in the context here
the more natural interpretation is to identify him as
God himself.

y. The precise reference of the "three" is not
possible to determine. The verse is clearly modeled
on SibOr 3.52, where the reference was to the second
triumvirate. We may also compare the three heads
of the eagle in 4Ezra 11–12. Commodian, Carmen
apologeticum 871, says that the returned Nero adopts
two Caesars, and in 911 the Antichrist slays three
kings. We may conclude that three Romans figure
widely in apocalyptic traditions, but their role and

precise reference may vary.
z. Nero redivivus. Cf. Commodian, Carmen apologeticum 910.
a2. Geffcken supposes that the passage which has
been lost here narrated Elijah's murder by Nero (cf.
Commodian, 858). There is, however, no clear
reference to Elijah here. Nero's victims may have
been diverse.
b2. Gk. brexei for deixei (Geffcken).
c2. Gk. panta mala hexeiēs atar for polla men
hexēs astra (Rzach).
d2. This is not a reference to a historical figure
but to an eschatological one modeled on the whore
of Babylon of Rev 17 or the widow of SibOr 3.75.
For the contrast between this woman and "heavenly
grace" cf. the contrasts between Babylon in Rev 18

195 but rather then, when heavenly grace comes to rule,
and whenever the sacred child, the destroyer[e2] of all, Rev 12:5
destroys the malignant abyss with bonds, opening it up. Rev 20:2–3
Suddenly a wooden house will cover men round about. 11.135;
But when the tenth generation is within the house of Hades, 1.132–33
 2.15, etc.
200 thereafter the power of the female will be great. God himself 8.194, etc.
will increase many evils for her when she is crowned and
receives royal honor. The entire year will be an age turned upside
  down.[f2]
The sun, seeing dimly,[g2] shines at night. 3.801, etc. 4Ezra 5:4
Stars will leave the vault of heaven. A raging storm with many a
  hurricane 8.190, etc.
205 will lay the earth desolate. There will be a resurrection of the dead 1.353–55; Mt
and most swift racing of the lame, and the deaf will hear 11:5; Lactantius,
 DivInst 4.15.15
and blind will see, those who cannot speak will speak,
and life and wealth will be common to all. 2.318–21
The earth will equally belong to all, not divided
210 by walls or fences, and will then bear more abundant fruits.
It will give fountains of sweet wine and white milk
and honey . . . 5.282f.;
 3.620–23;
 *   *   * Virgil, Eclogue
 4.18–22; ApPaul
and judgment of the immortal God . . . 25f.
but when God changes the times . . . 2.157; 14.298a,
 299; Lactantius,
215 making winter summer, then all the oracles are fulfilled. DivInst 7.16.9
But when the world perished . . .

Acrostic poem on the judgment

Jesus Christ, son of God, savior, cross.[h2]
The earth will sweat when there will be a sign of judgment.
A king will come from heaven who is to judge 5.108, etc.
all flesh and the whole world forever when he comes.
220 Both faithful and faithless men will see God
the Most High with the holy ones at the end of time.
He will judge the souls of flesh-bearing men on the tribunal 8.82; 2.218,
when the whole world becomes barren land and thorns. 239–43, etc.
Men will throw away idols and all wealth. 3.606; Isa 2:18; Lactantius,
 DivInst 7.19.9
225 Fire will burn up land, heaven, and sea, 2.196, etc.; 4.176
pursuing the hunt, and will break the gates of the confines of Hades. 2.227
Then all the flesh of the dead, of the holy ones, will come
to the free light. The fire will torture the lawless forever. 2.291f.
Whatever one did secretly, he will then say everything,
230 for God will open dark breasts with lights.
A lament will rise from all and gnashing of teeth. 2.305; 8.350; Mt 8:12; 13:42
The light of the sun will be eclipsed and the troupes of stars. Lk 13:28
 4.57, etc.
He will roll up heaven. The light of the moon will perish. 3.82; Isa 34:4; Rev 6:12–14
He will elevate ravines, and destroy the heights of hills. Isa 40:4; AsMos 10:4; 1En 1:6
235 No longer will mournful height appear among men.
Mountains will be equal to plains, and all the sea

---

and the New Jerusalem in Rev 21, and between
Rome and the *despoina* in SibOr 3.356–62.

e2. Gk. *delēmon'* for *dolophōn.* The reference is
to the "iron scepter" of Rev 12:5 and the subsequent
destructive role of the Messiah in Rev 19–21. Contrast
the peaceful rule of the child in Virgil, Eclogue
4.11–17.

f2. Gk. *huptios* for *hēpios* (Geffcken).

g2. Gk. *amaura blepōn* for *auchmēra trechōn*
(Rzach).

h2. This line is not a vs., but is the title for the
following vss. (218–50), which form an acrostic in
Gk. The first letters of the lines spell out *Iēsous
Chreistos (H)uios Sōtēr Stauros.* It is not possible to
reproduce the acrostic in English. A Lat. rendering
is found in Augustine's *De civitate Dei* 18.23. See
also Constantine's "Speech to the Saints," 18–19.

will no longer bear voyage. For earth will then be parched
with its springs. Bubbling rivers will fail.
A trumpet from heaven will issue a most mournful sound,
240 wailing for the defilement of limbs and the woes of the world.
The gaping earth will then show the abyss of the nether world.
All will come to the tribunal of God the king.
A river of fire and brimstone will flow from heaven.
There will then be a sign for all men, a most clear seal:[i2]
245 the wood among the faithful, the desired horn,
the life of pious men, but the scandal of the world,
illuminating the elect with waters in twelve streams.[j2]
An iron shepherd's rod will prevail.
This is our God, now proclaimed in acrostics,
250 the king, the immortal savior, who suffered for us.

Margin references:
8.348; 5.447f.
1Thes 4:16; Mt 24:31; 1Cor 15:52
Lactantius, *DivInst* 7.20.3 2.218,243; 8.82, etc.
2.196, etc.
Lk 1:68
1Cor 1:17–25; Rom 9:33 1Pet 2:6–8
Ps 2:9; Rev 2:27; 12:5; 19:15

A poem on Christ

Moses prefigured him, stretching out his holy arms,
conquering Amalek by faith so that the people might know
that he is elect and precious with God his father,
the staff of David and the stone he promised.
255 The one who has believed in him will have eternal life.
For he will come to creation not in glory, but as a man,
pitiable, without honor or form, so that he might give hope to the
        pitiable.
He will give form to perishable flesh and heavenly faith to the
        faithless,
and he will fashion the original man,
260 formed by the holy hands of God,
whom the snake craftily caused to err, to go to the fate
of death and receive knowledge of good and evil,
so as to abandon God and serve mortal customs.
For the universal ruler took him into his counsel
265 first of all from the beginning and said, "Let us both, child,
make mortal tribes, copying our likeness.
Now I with my hands, then you with a word, will tend
our form so that we may produce a common construct."
Mindful therefore of this resolution, he will come to creation
270 bearing a corresponding copy to the holy virgin,
illuminating by water, at the same time through the hands of elders,
doing all with a word, healing every disease.
He will stop the winds with a word. He will calm
the raging sea by walking on it with feet of peace and with faith.
275 From five loaves and a fish of the sea
he will satisfy five thousand men in the desert,
and taking all the leftover fragments,
he will fill twelve baskets for the hope of the peoples.
He will call on the souls of the blessed; he will love the wretched,
280 who will do good in return for evil when they are mocked,
beaten, and whipped, desiring poverty.
Perceiving everything and seeing everything and listening to everything,
he will observe the heart and lay it bare for trial.
He himself is the hearing and mind and sight and reason

Margin references:
Ex 17:11; EpBar 12:2
Isa 11:1; 1Pet 2:6; Jn 3:36
Isa 53:2–3; Lactantius, *DivInst* 4.16.17
Rom 5:15; 1Cor 15:45; Justin, *Cohortatio ad Graecos* 38:1
Gen 3:1–13; 1.40
8.439f.; ShepHerm Sim 9.12.2
8.442; Gen 1:26
8.247; Jn 4:1f.
Lactantius, *DivInst* 4.15.9 Mt 15:30f.; 1.356, etc.
Mk 4:35–41; 6:48–52; Jn 6:18–21 Lactantius, *DivInst* 4.15.24 1.357–59, etc.

---

i2. Cf. the seven seals in Rev 6.
j2. The language of illumination is commonly
used for baptism from the second half of the 2nd
cent. A.D., e.g. Justin, *Apologies* 1.61.14.

285 of all, who creates forms, to whom everything is subject,
 who saves the dead and cures every disease.
 Later he will come into the hands of lawless and faithless men,[k2]   1.366
 and they will give blows to God with unholy hands
 and poisonous spittings with polluted mouths.
290 Then he will stretch out his back and give it to the whips   Isa 50:6
 (for he will hand over to the world the holy virgin).[12]   Jn 19:26f.
 Beaten, he will be silent, lest anyone recognize   Lactantius,
 who he is, whose son, and whence he came, so that he may speak to   *DivInst* 4.18.17
       the dead;
 and he will wear the crown of thorns. For, made of thorns,   1.373
295 the crown of chosen men is an eternal delight.
 They will stab his sides with a reed on account of their law.
 For by winds shaken by another wind   Mt 11:7
 the inclinations[m2] of the soul are turned from wrath and change.
 But when all these things of which I have spoken are fulfilled,   Lactantius,
300 then for him every law will be dissolved which from the beginning *DivInst* 4.17.4
 was given in teachings to men, on account of a disobedient people.   Rom 7:1–6
 He will stretch out his hands and measure the entire world.   1.372
 They gave him gall for food and vinegar to drink.   1.367; Ps 69:21
 They will show forth this table of inhospitality.
305 The veil of the Temple will be rent, and in midday   1.375f., etc.
 there will be dark monstrous night for three hours.
 For no longer with secret law and temple must one serve
 the phantoms of the world. That which had been hidden was again
       made manifest
 when the eternal sovereign came down to earth.
310 He will come to Hades announcing hope for all   1.378; 1Pet 3:19; 4:6
 the holy ones, the end of ages and last day,
 and he will complete the fate of death when he has slept the third day.
 And then, returning from the dead, he will come to light,
 first of the resurrection, showing a beginning to the elect,   1Cor 15:20
315 having washed off their former vices with the waters
 of an immortal spring, so that, born from above,   Jn 3:3,7
 they may no longer serve the lawless customs of the world.
 First, then, the Lord was seen clearly by his own,
 incarnate as he was before, and he will show in hands and feet
320 four marks fixed in his own limbs,   Jn 20:27
 east and west and south and north.   3.26
 For so many kingdoms of the world will accomplish
 the unlawful blameworthy action as our archetype.
 Rejoice, holy daughter Sion, who have suffered much.   3.785
325 Your king himself comes in, mounted on a foal,   Jn 12:15; Mt 21:5; Zech 9:9
 appearing gentle to all so that he may lift our yoke   Mt 11:29
 of slavery, hard to bear, which lies on our neck
 and undo the godless ordinances and constraining bonds.
 Know that he is your God, as he is son of God.
330 Honor him and keep him in your heart
 and love him from your soul and bear his name.
 Set aside the former (customs) and wash from his blood,
 for he is not propitiated by your laments or prayers.
 Since he is imperishable he pays no attention to perishable sacrifices,   4.29f.; 7.78; 8.390; Hos 6:6
335 except when intelligent mouths bring forth a hymn.[n2]   Mt 9:13
 Know who he is, and then you will see the begetter.   8.498

---

k2. On the account of the passion (287–320) see
SibOr 1.360–80 and the parallels there listed. SibOr
8.287–90 are quoted by Lactantius, *DivInst* 4.18.15.

12. Kurfess omits this verse as doubtful.
m2. Gk. *prosklimata* for *pros krimata* (Rzach).
n2. Gk. *ekpropherontōn* for *ekpropherontes*.

Eschatological disturbances

Then in time all the elements of the world will be bereft,   3.80; 2.206, etc.
air, land, sea, light of blazing fire,
and heavenly dome and night and all days
340 will rush together into one, into an utterly desolate form.   2.201
For all the stars of luminaries will fall from heaven   8.190, etc.
and no longer will well-winged birds fly on the air   4Ezra 5:6;
nor will there be walking on earth, for all wild beasts will perish.   Lactantius, DivInst 7.16.8
There will be no voices of men, or beasts, or birds.
345 The world, in disorder, will hear no useful sound.
The deep sea will resound with a great sound of threat.
All the swimming creatures of the sea will die, trembling.
No longer will a ship bearing cargo sail on the waves.   8.237, etc.
The earth, being bloodied by wars, will bellow.
350 All the souls of men will gnash their teeth   8.231, etc.
with the wailings and panic of the lawless souls,
dissolving with thirst and famine and pestilence and murders,
and they will call death fair and it will evade them.   2.305f.; 13.118; ApEl 2:24
For no longer will death give rest to those, or night.   Rev 9:6
355 Often will they make request of God who rules on high, in vain,   2.309-12
and then he will manifestly turn away his face from them.
For he gave seven days of ages for repentance
to erring men, through the intercession of the holy virgin.[o2]

A speech of God against idolatry

God himself showed me all these things in my mind,   3.1-7, etc.
360 and he will fulfill all the things which are spoken through my mouth:
"I know the number of sand and the measures of sea.   Job 38-41
I know the recesses of earth and murky Tartarus.   4Ezra 4
I know the numbers of stars and trees and how many tribes
of four-footed animals, swimming creatures, and birds that fly,
365 and men that are, and that will be, and the dead.
For I myself fashioned the forms and minds of men,   3.27
and I gave right reason, and I taught understanding,
I who formed eyes and ears, seeing and hearing
and knowing every thought, and sharing the knowledge of all.   Ps 94:9
370 Being within, I am silent, and later I myself will test
and bring about . . . whatever any one of mortals did in secret   WisSol 1:11
coming also to the tribunal of God and telling to mortals . . .
I understand the dumb, and I hear one who does not speak
and how much is the total height from earth to heaven.
375 Beginning and end I know; I who created heaven and earth
for all things are from him, he knows what is from the beginning to the
    end.
For I alone am God, and there is no other God.   3.11, etc.; Isa 44:6; 45:5
They decree an image, fashioned of wood, to be mine,   Lactantius, DivInst 1.6.16
and shaping it with their hands, a speechless idol;   Isa 44:9-20; WisSol 13:11
380 they honor it with prayers and unholy worship.
Abandoning the Creator, they worshiped licentiousness.
All have gifts from me but give them to useless things,   Hos 2:8 (10)
and they think all these things useful, like my honors,
making burnt offerings at meals, as to their own dead.   WisSol 14:15, 20
385 For they burn flesh and, sacrificing bones full of marrow
on altars, they pour blood to demons
and light lamps for me, the giver of light.

o2. See SibOr 2.312, n. z2.

Mortals pour libations of wine as if to a thristy god,
getting drunk to no purpose, for useless idols.

390 I have no need of your sacrifice or libation   8.333f., etc. Isa 1:11
or polluted burnt offerings or most hated blood.
For they will do these things to the memory of kings and tyrants,   WisSol 14:15–21
for dead demons, as if they were heavenly beings,   8.47, etc. Frag. 1.22
performing a godless and destructive worship.

395 Godless ones also call their images gods,
abandoning the Creator, thinking to have
all hope and life from them. Trusting
in dumb and speechless things with evil result, they are ignorant of good
    end.
I myself proposed two ways, of life and death,[p2]   Did 1–6; EpBar 18–21
400 and proposed to the judgment to choose good life.   Deut 30:15; TAsh 1:3–8
But they turned eagerly to death and eternal fire.
Man is my image, having right reason.[q2]   1.23, etc. Gen 1:26
Set for him, you, a pure and unbloodied table,   2.96, etc. Lev 17:10
having filled it with good things, and give the bread to the hungry   2.83f., etc.
405 and drink to the thirsty and clothes to the naked body,
supplying them from your own labors with holy hands.
Accept the afflicted and stand by the suffering
and provide for me, the living one, a living sacrifice.   Rom 12:1
Sowing now on water,[r2] so that I also may one day give you
410 immortal fruits, and you will have eternal light
and unfading life, when I test all by fire.   2.252, etc.
For I will melt all things and separate them into clear air.   2.213; 3.87
I will roll up heaven, open the recesses of the earth,   3.82; Isa 34:4; Rev 6:14
and then I will raise the dead, having undone fate   Lactantius, DivInst 7.20.4
                                                               4.182, etc.
415 and the sting of death, and later I will come to judgment, 1Cor 15:55
judging the life of pious and impious men.   2.244
I will set ram by ram and shepherd by shepherd   Mt 25:32f.
and calf by calf, near each other for trial.
Whoever are convicted in the trial because they were exalted   2.255, etc.
420 and stopped the mouth of all so that they in envy
could equally subject those who act in holy manner,
ordering them to be silent, pressing on for gain,
will all depart then, as not[s2] approved by me.
No longer will you say in sorrow "it will be tomorrow,"   2.325–27,29; 3.89
425 or "it happened yesterday," nor worry about many days,
nor spring, nor winter, nor summer, nor autumn,
nor sunset, nor sunrise. For I will make a long day
forever; light will be desired.

                        *   *   *

Hymn to God

Self-begotten, undefiled, everlasting, eternal,[t2]   Frag. 1.17; 3.12; Ps-Orph, vs.
430 master of heaven in might, measuring the fiery breath.   10 (ed. Denis), 3.20–23
He holds the scepter of thunder with a rough firebrand,   Pss 93; 97; 148
and he soothes the peals of deep-sounding thunderbolts,

---

p2. The doctrine of the two ways has its roots in
the ethics of the OT, especially in the Wisdom
tradition—Prov 4:10–14; Ps 1:6—but also in the
Deuteronomic covenant (Deut 30:15). A similar contrast is found in Hesiod, Works and Days 287–92.
The two ways recur in T12P and in early Christian
instructions, but cf. also the contrast of the "ways"
of the Two Spirits in 1QS 4.

q2. Cf. Philo, Op 69: "It is in respect of the
Mind, the sovereign element of the soul, that the
word 'image' is used."
r2. A Gk. proverb. See Geffcken's apparatus.
s2. Gk. ou for kai (Rzach).
t2. This conception of deity is also found in pagan
writings. See the Tübingen Theosophy, 18–21.

storming the earth, he restrains the rushing noises, Micah 1:3–4;
and he dulls the fiery whips of lightnings; Hab 3:6;
1En 1:3–6;
435 he contains the unspeakable pourings of showers and storms of icy AsMos 10:1–4
hail, missiles of clouds and attacks of winter.

*　　*　　*

For they bear witness to each thing
that you yourself decide to do and approve in your mind.
With your son, before all creation, you shared deliberations 8.264f.
440 with equal breasts, fashioner of men and creator of life.
Him you addressed with the first sweet voice from your mouth:
"Look, let us make a man like in all respects to our 8.265, etc.
form, and let us give him the life-supporting breath to have.
Though he is mortal all the things of the world will serve him;
445 when he is fashioned of clay we will subject all things to him." 1Cor 15:47
These things you said to the Word, and all was done in your heart.
All the elements together obeyed your command, WisSol 19:18
and eternal creation was arranged for a mortal creature:
heaven, air, fire, earth, land and sea current,
450 sun, moon, chorus of stars, mountains, 3.20–23
night, day, sleep, waking, spirit and motion,
soul and intellect, skill and voice and strength
and wild tribes of living creatures, those of swimming creatures and
　　birds,
walking creatures and amphibians and serpents and things of double
　　nature;
455 for all things were arranged spontaneously[u2] under your leadership.

The incarnation

In the last times he changed the earth and, coming late[v2]
as a new light, he rose from the womb of the Virgin Mary.
Coming from heaven, he put on a mortal form.
First, then Gabriel was revealed in his strong and holy person. Lk 1:26
460 Second, the archangel also addressed the maiden in speech:
"Receive God, Virgin, in your immaculate bosom."
Thus speaking, he breathed in the grace of God,[w2] even to one who was Lk 1:31–36
　　always a maiden.
Fear and, at the same time, wonder seized her as she listened.
She stood trembling. Her mind fluttered
465 while her heart was shaken by the unfamiliar things she heard.
But again she rejoiced, and her heart was healed by the voice.
The maiden laughed and reddened her cheek, ProtJames 17
rejoicing with joy and enchanted in heart with awe.
Courage also came over her. A word flew to her womb.
470 In time it was made flesh and came to life in the womb, Jn 1:14
and was fashioned in mortal form and became a boy
by virgin birth. For this is a great wonder to men,
but nothing is a great wonder for God the Father and God the Son.
The joyful earth fluttered to the child at its birth.
475 The heavenly throne laughed and the world rejoiced.
A wondrous, new-shining star was venerated by Magi. Mt 2:2
The newborn child was revealed in a manger to those who obey God: Lk 2:7f.
cowherds and goatherds and shepherds of sheep.
And Bethlehem was said to be the divinely named homeland of the Micah 5:1f.
　　Word.

u2. Gk. *automatōs* for *autos soi* (Rzach).
v2. Gk. *bradus* for *brachus* (Rzach).
w2. Gk. *theou* for *theos* (Rzach).

Ethical and ritual exhortation

480 Be humble in heart, hate bitter power,
and, above all, love your neighbor as yourself,
and love God from the soul and serve him.
Therefore we are also of the holy heavenly race
of Christ, and are called brethren.
485 Having a remembrance of joy in worship,
we walk the paths of piety and truth.
We are never allowed to approach the sanctuaries of temples
nor to pour libations to statues nor to honor them with prayers,
nor with delightful scents of flowers nor with gleams
490 of lamps, nor even to embellish them with offerings,
nor with breaths of incense sending up a flame on altars[x2]
nor with libations from the sacrifice of bulls, rejoicing in gore,[y2]
to send blood from the slaughter of sheep as propitiatory offerings for
     earthly penalty;
nor to defile the light of the sky with smoke from burnt offerings
495 and polluted breezes from a fire that burns flesh.
But rejoicing with holy minds and glad spirit,
abundant love and hands that bring good gifts
with gracious psalms and songs appropriate to God,
we are bidden to sing your praises as imperishable and pure from all
     deceit,
500 God, wise begetter of all.

Mt 22:37–39;
Mk 12:29–31;
Lk 10:27

4.8, etc.

8.335;
Eph 5:19;
Col 3:16

21

x2. Gk. *bōmois* for *bōmon* (Geffcken).
y2. Gk. *luthrochareis* for *lutrochareis*.

THE SIBYLLINE ORACLES, BOOK 11

Introduction

The last four books of the Sibylline collection (11–14) provide a more or less continuous outline of history from the Flood down to the Arab conquest, with a very brief eschatological conclusion in Sibylline Oracles 14.351–61. The end of each book is marked by a prayer of the Sibyl (SibOr 11.315–24, 12.293–99, 13.172f.), and there are similar introductory verses at the beginning of each book. However, the contents of the oracles in each book pick up where the preceding one left off. No one would suggest that all this material was composed by the same author at one time. Rather we have an ongoing tradition that was repeatedly updated. Since every stage presumably had an eschatological conclusion, it is probable that the present ending of Sibylline Oracles 14 was composed early and repeatedly moved back.[1]

Sibylline Oracles 11 reviews history from the Flood to the death of Cleopatra.[2] References to historical figures are not direct but veiled thinly by gematria—i.e. the numbers represented by the letters of a name or only by the initial. Kurfess has suggested that the sequence of kingdoms is modeled on Sibylline Oracles 3.159–61,[3] and this seems essentially correct. The first kingdom is the Egyptian (vss. 19–32). Then we find the unhistorical sequence of Persia (47–50), Media (51–60), Ethiopia (61–79),[4] Assyria (80–105), Macedonia (186–223), Egypt (232–60), and Rome (261–314). Within this framework Sibylline Oracles 11 has made some modifications. Between the first rule of Egypt and that of Persia there is inserted a Hebrew kingdom (33–41) ruled by Moses. Next, the kingdom of the Assyrians contains no reference to Babylon (unlike SibOr 3.160) and is described in remarkably favorable terms. The Assyrian king is a champion of the law of God (vss. 81–82) and will build the temple of God (vs. 87)! In fact we must understand Assyrians here as a name for the Jews and the king as Solomon.[5]

Verses 109–71 are a digression on Romulus and Remus (vss. 109–71), the Trojan War (122–43), Aeneas (144–62), and Virgil (163–71).[6] A confused passage that includes a reference to the Persian invasion of Greece (179–82) intervenes before the rise of the Macedonians.

The account of the Ptolemaic Empire dwells at length on the time of Cleopatra (vss. 243–60), and the book culminates in an oracle on the conquest of Egypt by the Romans.

Date

There is no agreement as to the date of Sibylline Oracles 11. J. Strugnell contends that the present book is not an independent piece but is continued directly in Sibylline Oracles 12.[7] Even those who accept the book as an independent unit disagree on its date. Geffcken dates it after A.D. 226 because verse 161 presupposes the fall of the Parthians.[8] However, the tense of the verb in question is disputed. Geffcken reads *mēkuneto*, "tarried," but Kurfess emends to *mēkuneth*, which he interprets as a present tense, *mēkunetai*, following Bousset. Even if we retain *mēkuneto*, the use of tenses in the Sibylline Oracles does not permit a firm conclusion that the event in question was already past. Rzach accepts the present tense, "where the Parthian tarries," but still argues for a later date.[9] He assumes

---

[1] See esp. W. Scott, "The Last Sibylline Oracle of Alexandria," *The Classical Quarterly* 9 (1915) 144–47.

[2] The main discussions are those of H. Dechent, *Über das erste, zweite und elfte Buch*, pp. 49–88; Geffcken, *Komposition und Entstehungszeit*, pp. 64–66; Rzach, Pauly-Wissowa 2A, cols. 2152–55; Bousset, *Real-Encyclopedie*, p. 278; Kurfess, *Sibyllinische Weissagungen*, pp. 333–41; "Oracula Sibyllina XI (IX)–XIV (XII), Nicht Christlich sondern Jüdisch," *ZRGG* 7 (1955) 270–72.

[3] Kurfess, *Sibyllinische Weissagungen*, p. 333.

[4] Ethiopia and India are often confused in the SibOr. Cf. SibOr 5.206. See Kurfess, *Sibyllinische Weissagungen*, p. 334.

[5] Geffcken, *Komposition und Entstehungszeit*, p. 66.

[6] This passage is modeled on the figure of Homer in SibOr 3.419–25.

[7] Private communication. See Collins, *The Sibylline Oracles*, p. 181.

[8] Geffcken, *Komposition und Entstehungszeit*, p. 66.

[9] Pauly-Wissowa 2A, col. 2154.

that the prophecy of the Roman conquest of Mesopotamia (vss. 159–60) is a *vaticinium ex eventu*, " 'prophecy' after the actual event." Mesopotamia was first conquered under Trajan but was lost again in the time of Hadrian and not reconquered until the reign of Septimius Severus. Accordingly, Rzach accepts Geffcken's dating of the book to the third century. Both scholars support this date with references to stylistic considerations and to the similarity of Sibylline Oracles 11 to books 12–14.

Over against this position, Dechent, Bousset, and Kurfess have argued for a date in the first century A.D. Dechent's position rests on the extremely dubious argument that the word *geneē*, "race," in verse 159 refers to the Julio-Claudian house, and that the oracle must therefore have been written before the death of Nero.[10] It is more natural, however, to understand the *geneē* in verse 159 with reference to Aeneas and the Roman race. Bousset's argument is simply that the oracle would not have stopped with Cleopatra if it were written much later.[11] Kurfess supports this argument with further considerations. There is no reference in the book to peoples with whom Rome came into conflict in the second century. There is no reference to the fall of the Temple, and there is little real hostility to Rome. The main object of the Sibyl's wrath is Egypt (298–314). Kurfess infers that the book was written under Augustus or Tiberius, before relations between Jews and Romans in Egypt began to deteriorate in the time of Caligula.[12]

The argument of Bousset, that an oracle which ends with Cleopatra must be presumed to be written soon after her death, would be conclusive if it were certain that Sibylline Oracles 11 was composed as an independent unit. However, Strugnell's suggestion that Sibylline Oracles 11 and 12 were composed as a unit deserves careful consideration. The date proposed for Sibylline Oracles 11 by Geffcken and Rzach, sometime in the third century, not long after the conquest of Mesopotamia by Septimius Severus, is also a plausible date for Sibylline Oracles 12, which concludes with the death of Alexander Severus. Further, Sibylline Oracles 12.1–11 may be considered a summary of Sibylline Oracles 11, since it singles out the "citizen of Pella" (cf. SibOr 11.219: "Pellaean Ares"), who falsely claimed descent from Zeus Ammon (11.197), Aeneas, the descendant of Assaracus (11.144), and the "children of the flock-devouring beast," Romulus and Remus (SibOr 11.110–17). Further, Sibylline Oracles 12 picks up where Sibylline Oracles 11 leaves off, has a similarly positive attitude to the Romans, and shows equally little interest in moral and religious questions.

However, the question is complicated by the fact that Sibylline Oracles 12.1–11, which provide the summary of Sibylline Oracles 11, are taken directly from Sibylline Oracles 5. Two possibilities therefore emerge:

1. Sibylline Oracles 11 may have drawn on Sibylline Oracles 5. We have seen that much of Sibylline Oracles 11 is built on the list of kingdoms in Sibylline Oracles 3.159–61. Further, the passage on Virgil in verses 163–71 is based on Sibylline Oracles 3.419–25 and even the passages on Cleopatra in 250–53 and the conquest of Egypt in 285–90 are modeled on Sibylline Oracles 3.397–400 and 350–60 respectively. On this hypothesis Sibylline Oracles 11 would be virtually completely composed by borrowings and expansions of earlier Sibyls.

2. Alernatively, Sibylline Oracles 5.1–11 may already have been a summary of Sibylline Oracles 11. Both Sibylline Oracles 5 and 12 are interested primarily in the period after the battle of Actium. Verses 1–11 (common to both books) are distinctly a summary. However, some of the details in that summary, the references to the "son of Assaracus" and the "children of the beast," do not occur in any Sibyl earlier than Sibylline Oracles 5, unless we assume an earlier date for Sibylline Oracles 11. The references to the Roman origins could be supplied in Sibylline Oracles 11 from popular lore (or in some part from Virgil) and would have been sought out to complement the Sibylline history of the East.

Neither of these hypotheses can be established with certainty, but the second seems the more probable. The choice of details in Sibylline Oracles 5.1–11 is more easily understandable if that passage is summarizing an earlier Sibyl. Further support for an earlier dating can be found in Sibylline Oracles 11.171, which says that Virgil will conceal the Sibyl's writings until after his death. This reference makes most sense if the book was written shortly after Virgil's death in 19 B.C. The anti-Egyptian attitude of Sibylline Oracles 11 fits well with the

---

[10] Dechent, *Uber das erste, zweite und elfte Buch*, pp. 49–88.

[11] Bousset, *Real-Encyclopedie*, p. 278.

[12] Kurfess, *Sibyllinische Weissagungen*, p. 339.

picture of Alexandrian Judaism found in such works as 3 Maccabees and the Wisdom of Solomon. Finally, the book is intelligible in itself as an oracle which culminates in the conquest of Egypt and has been recognized by the tradition as an independent book. The fact that Sibylline Oracles 12 picks up where Sibylline Oracles 11 leaves off may be somewhat coincidental, since that is the beginning of the Roman Empire, the subject matter of Sibylline Oracles 12. Otherwise Sibylline Oracles 12 is not conspicuously dependent on book 11 and draws much more directly on Sibylline Oracles 5.

The reference to the Parthians in verse 161 should then be understood as a real prophecy. The Parthians were already prominent as a threat to Rome in the East in the first century B.C. An oracle that proclaimed the universal rule of Rome might very naturally prophesy the conquest of the Parthians to complete the ideal extent of Roman dominion.

The stylistic arguments for a later date were adequately refuted by Bousset. Sibyllists at all times and places were capable of poor style and faulty meter.[13]

Sibylline Oracles 11 then should be dated tentatively about the turn of the era.

Provenance

There is no doubt that this book was written in Egypt. Its review of history begins with Egypt and ends there, and the culmination of the book is an oracle on the destruction of Egypt.

The reference to the foundation of Alexandria in verses 219f. and the eulogy in verses 232–35 suggest that the Sibyllist wrote in that city. Despite the parallels in Sibylline Oracles 3 and Sibylline Oracles 5.1–11 noted above, Sibylline Oracles 11 lacks most of the concerns of books 3 and 5—interest in the Temple, expectation of a savior figure and eschatological judgment, polemic against idolatry and sexual abuses. The motif of widowhood with references to Cleopatra recalls Sibylline Oracles 3.75–92, but this does not require literary dependence as the motif would arise naturally in the context of Cleopatra's defeat. The use of gematria is paralleled in Sibylline Oracles 5.1–51, but this, of course, is not peculiar to the Sibylline Oracles.[14]

The book is Jewish, as is shown by the references to Joseph (29f.), Moses (38–40), Solomon (80–103) and by the fact that Egypt is said to be finally destroyed because it oppressed God's chosen people (307). There is nothing to indicate a Christian origin or redaction. The oracle may well have been written before the origin of Christianity.

The book does not seem to belong to the same tradition as Sibylline Oracles 3 or 5. Yet it can be located in the development of Egyptian Judaism by reference to these other Sibyls. It stands closest to Sibylline Oracles 3.75–92 by its antipathy to Cleopatra, while it lacks the vehemence of that passage. It shows no sign of the resentment against Rome that burns in Sibylline Oracles 5. In fact, the book lacks any criticism of Rome, even such as we find in the earliest stage of Sibylline Oracles 3 (vss. 175–91).

Historical and theological importance

The only theological interpretation offered in Sibylline Oracles 11 is in verses 307–10, which say that Egypt will be subjected because of its treatment of the Jews. The obvious reference here is to the sojourn in Egypt before the Exodus, but it probably also suggests strained relations between the Egyptians and the community that the Sibyl represents. Otherwise, Sibylline Oracles 11, like books 12–14, is remarkably void of theology. There is no eschatological conclusion. There may have been one, and it is possible that Sibylline Oracles 14.351–61 originally stood at the end of Sibylline Oracles 11 and was moved back gradually as additions were made. Even that passage, however, contains nothing more specific than the hope that the Jewish people would rule the whole earth. There is no description of a judgment, and the review of history is not used to frame ethical and ritual exhortations as is often the case in books 1–5.

The historical value of the book is extremely scant. The author's ignorance of history is

[13] Bousett, *Real-Encyclopedie*, p. 278.
[14] See F. Dornseiff, *Das Alphabet in Mystik und Magie* (Leipzig, 1922).

amazing. Not only does he list Persian, Median, and Ethiopian kingdoms before the time of Solomon, but he can blandly identify Jews and Assyrians and completely ignore the Babylonian kingdom. Nearer his own time he describes the rulers of Rome as Caesars even before Julius and Augustus (vs. 265), and he gives the number of kings of Egypt before Cleopatra as eight (243). The only period on which he seems reasonably well informed is that of Cleopatra, and even there he gives few specific data.

The only literary contact of note is with Sibylline Oracles 3, which it echoes in many places, most notably in the list of kingdoms and in the account of Virgil in verses 163–69, which is modeled on Homer in the earlier Sibyl.

Unlike most of the other Sibylline Oracles, Book 11 is not a vehicle for religious exhortation. The most obvious function of the book lies in its anti-Egyptian propaganda. Verses 277–97 can be read as a direct rejoinder to the pro-Cleopatran ideology in Sibylline Oracles 3.350–61. In view of its attention to Aeneas and his progeny, the book might be said to be pro-Roman, but it shows no explicit enthusiasm for Rome and is much more interested in the discomfiture of Egypt.

THE SIBYLLINE ORACLES
Book 11

Introduction of the Sibyl

World of widespread men, long walls,
great cities, and innumerable nations
of east, west, south, and north,   2.195
divided in many diverse languages and kingdoms,
5 to you[a] I am about to speak the most disastrous tidings.

The tower of Babylon

For from the time when the Flood came upon the men of old   3.109
and destroyed that[b] generation with many waters,
the universal ruler himself furnished another race
of restless men, who in opposition to heaven
10 built a tower to an awful height. The tongues   3.99, etc.
of all[c] were loosed, but on them came the wrath   Gen 11:1-9
of the Most High God, hurled down, and the wondrous tower
fell. For they roused evil strife against each other.
Then also was the tenth generation of articulate men.   3.108; 2.15, etc.
15 From the time when these things happened, the entire earth was divided
between diverse men and all sorts of dialects
of which I will tell the numbers and name them in acrostics,[d]
according to the first initial, and I will reveal the name.

The rule of Egypt

First Egypt will receive royal dominion
20 outstanding and just. Then many counseling
men will govern in her. But then
a terrible man will rule, a very mighty skirmisher.
His name will have the letter of the acrostic.
Swords[e] will he extend against pious men.
25 While he wields power this[f] great sign will be
in the land of Egypt. In great glory she
will then feed with corn people who are perishing by famine.
The same man, prisoner and judge, will nurture the East   Gen 39-41
and the race of Assyrian men. Know his name
30 . . . of the measure of the tenth number.[g]
But when the affliction of ten plagues comes upon Egypt   Ex 7:14-12:34
from shining heaven, then I will again proclaim these things to you.
Woe to you, Memphis, woe, great kingdom.
The Red Sea will destroy a great multitude of you.   Ex 14-15
35 Then when the people of twelve tribes, bidden by the Immortal,
leave the fruitful plain of destruction[h]

---

a. Gk. *alla per eis hymas* for *alP haper humōn* (Rzach).

b. Gk. *keinēn* for *peniēn* (Rzach).

c. Gk. *hapantōn* for *ap'allōn* (Rzach).

d. The list of kingdoms is apparently based on SibOr 3.159-61. There is no real acrostic in SibOr 11, although rulers are indicated by their initial letters.

e. The Gk. word for swords here is *phasgana*, which has the same initial as Pharoah.

f. Gk. *d'eseitai ekeino* for *d'estai ekeinō* (Alexandre).

g. I is 10. The name is *losēph*, Joseph. SibOr 11.80 also uses the name "Assyrians" for the Israelites.

h. Gk. *olethrou* for *olethron* (Rzach). The plain in question is, of course, Egypt.

and God himself, the prince, gives a law to men,   Ex 19-20
then a great, great-spirited king will rule the Hebrews,
one who has a name from sandy Egypt,[i]
40 a man falsely thought to have Thebes as his homeland.
But a terrible snake will love Memphis, and will devour[j] many things
    in wars.

The rule of Persia

In the twelfth decade of revolving kingship
in the seventeenth century of years, when five more
are left,[k] then will be the empire of Persia.
45 Then there will be darkness upon the Jews, and they will not escape   Amos 5:18
famine and pestilence, which is hard to bear, on that day.[l]   2.23, etc.
But when a Persian rules and leaves the scepters
to the sons of his grandson[m] as the years pursue their cyclic course,
for only five times four and a hundred in addition to these,[n]
50 you will complete[o] a hundred enneads and make amends for all.

The rule of Media

Then, Persia, you will be given as a servant to the Medes,
perishing with afflictions through mighty war.
Immediately disaster will come upon Persians and Assyrians,   3.207-9
all Egypt, Libyans and Ethiopians.
55 Carians and Pamphylians, and all other mortals.
Then he will give the royal empire to descendants
who again will lay waste races for many spoils,
ravaging the entire earth without sympathy.
Mournful, the Persians will wail dirges by the Tigris.   8.64
60 Egypt will moisten much earth with tears.
Then a very rich Indian will cause many evils   5.206
for you, Median land, until you make amends for all
which you had formerly done with shameless spirit.
Woe to you, Median nation, thereafter you will serve
65 Ethiopian men[p] beyond the land of Merois.
You will complete a hundred years from the beginning, wretched one,
adding seven to these, and you will place your neck under the yoke.

The rule of India/Ethiopia

Then thereafter there will arise a dark-skinned, gray-haired,

---

i. Kurfess sees here a pun on "sandy" (*psa-mathōdeos*) and a reference to Psammetichus, mistaken here for a Hebrew. However, the reference is surely to Moses, whose name was Egyptian and who had been treated like a son by Pharaoh's daughter (Ex 2:10).

j. Gk. *laphuxetai* for *phulaxetai* (Buresch). Geffcken sees here a further reference to Moses, who is depicted by Artapanus (a Jewish-Egyptian historian of the 2nd cent. B.C.) as an Egyptian general and also as the founder of the animal cults. Alexandre takes the snake in this passage to represent "wisdom" and so to be applicable to Moses. The phrase "terrible snake" is, however, most naturally understood in a pejorative sense. It refers to Nero in SibOr 5.29 and 12.81 and to Severus in 12.264. The phrase may refer to some unspecified Pharaoh or rather be a general derogatory reference to the Egyptian monarchy.

k. In view of the chaotic sequence of kingdoms

no real chronological value can be attached to these numbers.

l. Dechent saw here a reference to the destructions of Samaria and Jerusalem, but the verse is not specific.

m. Gk. *huiōnoio huiois* for *huios huiōnoio* (Geffcken). The Persian may be Cyrus or Cambyses, the conqueror of Egypt.

n. Gk. *hekaton d'epi tautais* for *dekateusei de tautas* (Rzach). Here again the numbers have no historical value. The Persians, in fact, overthrew the Medes, not vice versa.

o. Gk. *teleseis* for *teletheis* (Rzach).

p. On the confusion of India and Ethiopia see SibOr 5.206, n. w2. The confusion in Jewish sources may have been increased by the fact that India and Ethiopia are mentioned together in Esth 8:9 as the limits of the Persian Empire. The geographical indication "beyond . . . Merois" (65) shows that the author had the African country in mind.

great-spirited Indian prince^q who will cause many evils
70 to the East through mighty war,
and he will damage you, or rather destroy you beyond all.
But when he reigns twenty years and ten
plus seven and ten, then every nation
of the royal empire will rage and display freedom,^r
75 abandoning slave blood for three single years.
But he will come again and every nation of men
will place its neck under the yoke for the mighty one again   3.448
as it was formerly subject to the king, and it will willingly be subordinate.
There will be great peace throughout the whole world.   3.755; 11.237

The rule of the "Assyrians"

80 Then a great man will be king over the Assyrians.^s
He will rule and persuade everyone to speak according to his mind
what God disposed in laws. Then all the kings
will fear this man. They who plume themselves with spears,
fearful and speechless, exceedingly mighty and lovely to behold,
85 will serve this man, through the plans of the great God.
For he will persuade everything by speech and subdue everything,
and he will mightily build the temple of the great God   1Kgs 5-8
and the lovely altar, and he will cast down idols.   3.606, etc.
He will gather tribes and the generation of fathers
90 and infant children into one place as settlers and build a wall around   1Kgs 9:15
    them.
He will have a name of the number two hundred,   12.258
and will show the signs of an initial of eighteen.
But whenever he prevails, as decades pursue their cyclic course,
for two plus five, coming to the end of (his) time,
95 there will be as many kings as tribes of men,
as clans, as cities, and as islands,
lands of the blessed and fields of shining fruit,
but there will be one great king over them, a leader of men.
Many great-spirited kings will yield to him.
100 They will give to him and his sons and prosperous grandsons
portions of the kingdom for empire
until eight decades of decades and six single years^t
in addition to these. He will rule even those who are his opponents to
    the end.

The advent of Macedonia

But when a strong wild beast comes with mighty Ares,^u

q. Kurfess take the Indians of SibOr 11 as the Persians and the prince as Ahasuerus (Artaxerxes) of the Book of Esther. While it is true that the author may have been influenced by Esth 8:9, the passage is too confused to permit identifications.

r. Kurfess sees a reference to revolts under Xerxes, but there are no historical data that correspond to the statements here.

s. Solomon, who built the Temple (vs. 87) and the wall of Jerusalem (vs. 90, cf. 1Kgs 9:15), and whose initial (S) has a numerical value of 200 (vs. 91) and is the eighteenth letter of the alphabet (vs. 92). Kurfess, following Dechent, takes the Assyrians as Persians and the king as the Artaxerxes of Ezra 7:11 who "did much" for the Temple and in whose reign Ezra and Nehemiah reorganized Jerusalem. Kurfess is obliged to regard vss. 91f. as an insert modeled on

SibOr 12.258. However, the parallel in SibOr 12 is only partial. Even with the emendation Kurfess is still obliged to say that Artaxerxes built the Temple, which is simply untenable. The history of SibOr 11 is muddled on any interpretation. If we accept the present text we must take this passage as a reference to Solomon. The term "Assyrians" is also used for the Israelites in SibOr 11.29.

t. As usual in SibOr 11 the numbers make no historical sense.

u. Ares was god of war. Alexandre and Kurfess plausibly see here a reference to Alexander, who overthrew the Persians. It does not, however, follow that the previous vss. also referred to the Persians. The sequence of kingdoms is not chronological but is determined by SibOr 3.159–61.

105 then for you also, royal land, will wrath spring up.
Woe to you, Persian land, how many effusions you will receive
of human blood when that man of mighty spirit
comes to you. Then again I will proclaim these things to you.ᵛ

Romulus and Remus

But when Italy produces a great marvel for men,
110 a murmuring of infants by an unpolluted spring,   5.11
in a shady cave, children of a flock-devouring beast,
who, when they have become men, will cast down headlong
many who have shameless spirit on seven strong hills.   Rev 17:9
Both number a hundred.ʷ Their name will show them
115 a great sign of things to come.ˣ They will build strong walls
on seven hills and will set up grievous war
about them. Then there will be an insurrection of men
springing up about you, great land of beautiful corn,
great-spirited Egypt.ʸ But I will again proclaim these things,
120 and in additionᶻ you will receive a great affliction in your homes,   3.314
and again you will have an insurrection of your own men.

The Trojan War

Now you, wretched Phrygia, do I bewail piteously,
for on you will come captivity from Greece, which subdues horses,
and terrible war, through mighty battles.
125 Ilium, I pity you, for a fury from Spartaᵃ²   3.414-18
will come to your dwelling, mingled with a destructive star.
It will especially cause you toils, labors, groanings, and wailings
when skilled men begin battle,
the heroes of the Greeks, by far the best of those who love war.
130 One of these, a mighty warrior, will be king.ᵇ²
For the sake of his brother he will perform most evil deeds.
They will destroy the famous walls of Troy of the Phrygians,
when the son of Cronosᶜ² for twice five revolving years
fulfills the murderous deeds of war.
135 Suddenly a wooden deceitᵈ² will cover men around,   8.198
and the one of deep grief will receive it, on her knees,
not perceiving that it is an ambush pregnant with Greeks.
Alas, how many Hades will receive in one night!
How much spoils will it carry off from the old man of many tears!ᵉ²
140 but there will be ageless glory in future generations.
A great man from Zeus,ᶠ² a king, will have the name
of the first letter. He, when he has returned home,
will then fall at the hand of a deceitful woman.

---

v. The digressions on Romulus and Remus, the Trojan War, Aeneas, and Virgil are explained by Kurfess as a résumé of Western history to prepare the reader for the final conflict of East and West. It is probably true that the Sibyl digresses at this point to fill in some of the more significant historical traditions for which the list of kingdoms makes no provision. It is typical of the historical confusion of the book that two conflicting accounts of the foundation of Rome are juxtaposed (115, 155).

w. *R*, the initial of both Romulus and Remus, has a numerical value of 100.

x. I.e. by suggesting the name Rome.

y. This reference is quite enigmatic and indicative of the confusion of the book.

z. Gk. *proseti* for *pros epi* (Rzach).

a2. Helen.

b2. Agamemnon, and his brother Menelaus.

c2. Zeus.

d2. Gk. *dolos* for *domos* (Ω, Rzach). The reference is to the Trojan horse. The phrase echoes SibOr 8.198, where the word *domos* refers to a means of salvation, modeled on the Ark in SibOr 1.133.

e2. Priam, king of Troy.

f2. Agamemnon, murdered by his wife, Clytemnestra.

A famous child of heroes from the race and blood
145 of Assaracus will rule,[g2] a mighty and brave man.　　　　　5.8; Virgil,
He will come from Troy when it has been destroyed by a great fire,　　*Aeneid* 6.778
fleeing from his fatherland on account of the turmoil of Ares.
Carrying on his shoulders his elderly father,　　　　　　　Virgil, *Aeneid* 6.110
holding his only son by the hand, he will perform　　　　　Virgil, *Aeneid* 2.723
150 a pious deed, glancing around, he who split the onslaught
of the fire of blazing Troy, and pressing on through the throng.　　5.9
In fear he will cross the land and frightful sea.
He will have a name of three syllables; for the first letter
is not insignificant but reveals the supreme man.[h2]
155 Then he will set up the mighty city of the Latins.[i2]
In the fifteenth year on the depths of brine
perishing on the waters he will meet the end of death.[j2]
But even when he dies the nations of men will not forget him.
For the race of this man will later rule over all
160 as far as the rivers Euphrates and Tigris, in the midst
of the land of the Assyrians, where the Parthian tarried.[k2]
It will come to pass in future generations when all these things happen.

Virgil

There will be again a certain elderly wise man, a bard,　　　　3.419-25
whom all call the wisest among men,
165 by whose noble mind the whole world will be educated.
For he will write the chief points with power and intelligence[l2]
and at various times he will write clearly, very wondrous things,
having mastered my words and meters and phrases.
For he will be the very first to unfold my books.
170 Afterward he will also conceal them and will no longer show them to
men[m2]
until the goal of wretched death, the end of life.

Prophecies of confusion and tumult

But whenever these things are accomplished of which I spoke,
the Greeks will again fight against each other.
Assyrians and Arabs, and further, quiver-bearing Medes,
175 Persians and Sicilians and Lydians will rise up,
Thracians and Bithynians and those who inhabit the land
of beautiful corn by the streams of the Nile. Imperishable
God will cause tumult among them all at once. But an Assyrian man,
a bastard Ethiopian, will very terribly come, suddenly,
180 with the spirit of a wild beast, and he will cut through the entire isthmus[n2]　8.155f.

g2. Aeneas. Assaracus, his great-grandfather, was
king of Phrygia.

h2. A pun on the coincidence of the initials of
Aeneas and Adam.

i2. Aeneas was usually considered founder not of
Rome itself but of Lavinium, head of the Latin league.
Romulus and Remus are usually said to come after
Aeneas. SibOr 11 presents, in effect, a double found-
ing of Rome.

j2. This tradition is found in Dionysius of Halicarnassus, *Roman Antiquities* 1.64.4; *Origo gentis
Romanae* 14.3; *Scholion Veronense ad Vergili Aeneid*
1.259.

k2. The tense of this verb is disputed. Kurfess
reads *mēkuneth*, "tarries." In any case, since the
whole passage is prophetic, no firm conclusions as
to the date of the book can be based on the use of the

past tense.

l2. Supply *kata* before *dunamin* (Alexandre). The
passage is modeled on SibOr 3.419-25, where the
reference is to Homer. Kurfess notes that the distinctive references to Homer's blindness and place of
origin are omitted and that the content of his songs
concerns Aeneas more immediately than the fall of
Troy. Accordingly, the passage should be taken as
a reference to Virgil. From this it follows that the
Sibyl wrote later than Virgil's death in 19 B.C.

m2. The fiction that the pseudepigraphical writings
were hidden in antiquity is common in Jewish apocalyptic—cf. Dan 12:4, 9; 4Ezra 14:46.

n2. The reference is most probably to Xerxes'
invasion of Greece in 480 and to his canal through
the Athos Peninsula, but cf. the description of Nero's
return in SibOr 8.155f.

glancing about, going against everyone, and will sail across the sea.
Then very many things will happen to you, faithless Greece.
Woe to you, wretched Greece, how many lamentations you must make!
For seven and eighty revolving years
185 you will be the mournful refuse of frightful war of all the tribes.

The rise of Macedonia

Then again the affliction of the Macedonians will come upon Greece,   3.381; 4.88
and it will destroy all Thrace and the turmoil of Ares,
in islands and mainlands and among the Triballi,o2 who love war.
            *   *   *
He will be among the foremost fighters, and will have this name,
190 an initial which shows the number fifty ten times.p2
He will have swift fate in empire, but he will leave behind
a very great kingdom throughout the boundless earth.
He himself will fall at the hand of a bad counselor, a spear-bearer,
having lived as a leader with fair windq2 as no one else.

Alexander

195 Thereafter the great-spirited son of this man will rule,
of the first letter.r2 There will be a detailed account of his race.
Although this man was not born of Zeus or Ammon, all   5.7; 3.383
will nevertheless declare him to be, and will depict him as a bastard of
    the son of Cronos.
He will lay waste the cities of many articulate men,
200 but the greatest wound will spring up for Europe.   3.382
This man will also afflict the city of Babylon with pestilence,   3.384
and every land on which the sun looks,
in the East. He alone will sail the world.
Woe to you, Babylon, you will be in servitude at triumphal processions, 3.303, etc.
205 you who were called mistress. Ares will come to Asia.
He will truly come and will kill many of your children.
Then you will send out your royal man
whose name is of the number four,s2 fighter with the spear,
and terrible arrow-shooter, with mighty warriors.
210 Then indeed famine and war will seize the midst of
Cilicians and Assyrians. But great-spirited kings
will drape themselves in terrible conflict of spirit-destroying strife.
But you, flee the former king12 and abandon him.
Do not wish to remain and do not be ashamed to be cowardly,   Herodotus 1.55
215 for a terrible lion will come upon you, a carnivorous beast,
wild, stranger to justice wearing a cloak about his shoulders.   3.389-92
Flee the man who is like a thunderbolt. An evil yoke will come to Asia,
and the whole earth will drink inundating murder.
But whenever Pellaean Ares will establish
220 the great city of Egypt, giver of wealth, and name it for himself,u2
betrayed deceitfully by his companions, (he will undergo) fate and
    death . . .

---

o2. Gk. *Triballois* for *toratrois* (Rzach).

p2. Philip of Macedon. He did not extend his empire beyond Greece but laid the foundations for Alexander's conquests. He was assassinated in 336 B.C. at the age of forty-six.

q2. Gk. *ouria* for *suria* (Geffcken).

r2. Alexander. He claimed to be son of Zeus Ammon after he visited the shrine of that god in Egypt in 332 B.C.

s2. Darius III, the Persian king defeated by Alexander.

t2. Gk. *pheugōn proteron basilēa* for *phuge peron ton basilēa* (Rzach).

u2. I.e. when Alexander founds Alexandria. Alexander was not, however, assassinated, but died of fever in Babylon in 323 B.C.

For when he leaves the Indians and goes to Babylon,
foreign murder will destroy him about the tables.

The Diadochi

Thereafter others will rule each individual tribe,
225 kings who are devourers of the people and ovebearing and faithless
for a few years; then a great-spirited leader
who will glean all[v2] Europe bare
from the time when the whole earth drinks the blood of all the tribes,
but he will leave life, having undone it by his own fate.[w2]
230 There will be other kings, twice four men
from his race, all of whom have the same name.

The second rule of Egypt

Then Egypt will be a ruling bride
and the great city of the Macedonian prince,
revered Alexandria, famous nurse of cities,   5.88; 11.302
235 glittering with beauty, will alone be metropolis.
Then let Memphis blame its rulers.[x2]   5.17; 8.162
There will be deep peace throughout the whole world,   3.755; 11.79
and the earth of dark soil will then give more abundant fruits.
And then evil will come upon the Jews, and they will not escape
240 famine and pestilence on that day which is hard to bear,[y2]   2.23, etc.
but the ambrosial earth, dark-soiled with its beautiful corn,
newly adorned, will receive many dying men.

Cleopatra

But eight kings of marshy Egypt
will complete numbers of years three and thirty
245 plus two hundred.[z2] But their race will be destroyed,   3.395f.
not of them all, but a root will grow out,
a female, destructive of mortals, betrayer of her own kingdom.
But thereafter they will perform evil deeds
among themselves in wickedness, and one will destroy another.
250 A royal son will cut down a warrior father,   3.397-400
and he himself will fail at the hands of his son, but before that
he will sprout another plant. A root will shoot up thereafter
spontaneously. From it there will be a race that grows on the side.[a3]
For there will be a queen of the land by the streams of the Nile,
255 which advances to the sea with sevenfold mouths;
she will have a much-loved name of the number twenty.[b3]

---

v2. Gk. *hos hapasan* for *hos pasin* (Geffcken).
Antiochus the Great invaded Europe in 196 B.C., but
his campaign ended in failure. There were eight Seleucid kings named Antiochus counting from Antiochus I (vs. 230). Alexandre suggested that the reference is to Antigonus, but there never were eight
kings by that name (in the same dynasty).

w2. Gk. *leipsei atar bioton moirē(i) idiē(i) ana-
lusas* (Geffcken) for *biotou morphēn idian*.

x2. The reference is to the decline of the traditional
centers of Egyptian power in favor of Alexandria. Cf.
the Potter's Oracle, col. 1, which prophesies that the
Agathos Daimōn, "Good Spirit," will leave Alexandria and return to Memphis.

y2. The reference is obscure but Josephus (*Apion*

2.56–61) claimed that in time of famine Cleopatra
withheld corn from the Jews.

z2. Here again the numbers are inaccurate. There
were more than eight Ptolemies before Cleopatra.
However, the time from the death of Ptolemy I to the
rise of Cleopatra was approximately 231 years.

a3. These vss. are modeled on SibOr 3.397–400,
prompted by the association of the "root growing on
the side." They do not, however, fit the historical
situation which led up to the reign of Cleopatra.

b3. *Kleopatra.* Her popularity in Egypt is widely
attested. For Cleopatra in the earlier Sibylline tradition
see SibOr 3.350–61 (which shows enthusiasm for
her) and 75–92 (which is very negative).

She will make innumerable requests and collect all wealth   3.78f.
of gold and silver. There will indeed be treachery against her
from her own men.[c3] Then again, blessed land, you will have
260 wars and battles and slaughters of men.   4.68, etc.

Julius Caesar

But when many rule luxuriant Rome,
in no respect chosen from the blessed but tyrants,
leaders of thousands and myriads,
supervisors of lawful assemblies and most great
265 Caesars will rule in succession all the days.
Last of these, of the number ten,
Caesar will rule last, who[d3] will be struck in dread war
by hostile men, and stretch out his limbs on the ground.
The children of Rome will carry him in their own hands
270 and bury him piously and pour a mound on him
sharing favor to his memory, because of his friendship.
But when the end of the time of the age is at hand
fulfilling twice three hundred[e3] and twice ten   12.12
from the time when your founder, the son of the beast, was leader,[f3]   11.109-21
275 no longer will a dictator be a limited ruler
but a prince will be king, a godlike man.   3.49

The conquest of Egypt

Know then, Egypt, that a king is coming against you.
He will truly come, a terrible Ares with gleaming helmet.
Then for you, widow,[g3] there will thereafter be captivity.   3.77
280 For there will be wars which cause evils, terrible and raging
in force around the walls of the land. In wars
you yourself, suffering mournfully, will flee, wretched one,
over the newly slain. Later you will come to bed
with the terrible one himself. The conclusion is the joining marriage.[h3]
285 Woe to you, ill-wed maiden, you will give
the royal rule to a Roman king and will make amends   12.18
for all you formerly did in wars of men.[i3]
You will give your whole land as a dowry to a powerful man
as far as inner Libya and dark-skinned men.
290 You will no longer be a widow,[j3] but you will live with a lion,
a man-eating, terrible warrior of the war cry.
And then, wretched one (you will be) inconspicuous to all among men
for you will depart with shameless spirit.
A tomb like a circular mound well-wrought,

---

c3. We know of no conspiracy against Cleopatra, but some of Antony's followers defected after Actium.

d3. Gk. *Kaisar hos* for *Kaisaros* (Alexandre). Apparently the Sibyl thought all Roman consuls were called Caesar, so Julius (*Iulus*) is said to be *last*. Caesar was not, of course, killed in battle but was assassinated.

e3. Gk. *Triēkosious* for *diēkosiōn* (Alexandre). Here and in SibOr 12.12 the age of Rome at the time of Caesar's death is given as 620 years. The usual date for the founding of Rome was 753 B.C., which would give the age of Rome as 709 at the time of Caesar's death.

f3. Romulus.

g3. The widow is at once bereaved Egypt and Cleopatra.

h3. The king is evidently Octavian, the prince of vs. 276, not Antony (as claimed by Kurfess). Since Cleopatra did not marry Octavian, we must conclude either that the Sibyllist is giving a figurative account of the conquest of Egypt or, as in so many other passages in this book, is referring to Cleopatra but embellishing fact with legend. The symbolic reference to Egypt remains, of course, in any case.

i3. This passage seems to be a direct inversion of SibOr 3.350-61.

j3. Widowhood is usually conceived as an ultimate disaster (Isa 47:8f.; Rev 18:7f.), but here the "union" with victorious Rome is, ironically, a worse fate.

295 fitted with pinnacles, will receive you alive within it, in a snare[k3]
cleverly made . . . A great people will mourn you,
and a king will raise a terrible piteous lament for you.

Punishment for Egypt

Then also Egypt of many labors will be a servant,
which for many years brought spoils from the Indians.
300 She will disgracefully be enslaved and will mingle tears in the river,
the fruit-bearing Nile, because when she has acquired wealth
and abundance of all goods, nurse of cities,   11.234
she will nourish the race of the devourer of flocks, of terrible men.   13.43-49
Alas, to how many wild beasts will you be servant and booty,
305 prosperous Egypt, lawgiver to peoples.
You who formerly also rejoiced in great kings
will be slave to peoples, wretched one, on account of that people
which formerly, when it was living piously, you brought to great   Ex 1:8-22
    affliction[13]
of labors and lamentations, and you placed on its neck
310 the yoke of a plow and you moistened the fields with tears of mortals.
Therefore God himself, the imperishable prince who lives in the sky,   5.298
will utterly destroy you and impel you to lamentation,
and you will make amends for what you formerly did lawlessly.
At last you will realize that the anger of God has come upon you.

Conclusion of the Sibyl

315 But I will go to Pytho[m3] and well-built Panopeia.
There all will pronounce me a true
seer, chanter of oracles,[n3] though someone will call me[o3]   3.816
a messenger with frenzied spirit. But when he approaches the books
let him not shrink from them. He will know both all that is to be and 3.820-22
    that was before
320 from our words. Then no longer will anyone call
the divinely possessed seer an oracle-monger of necessity.
But, prince, now stop my very lovely speech,
thrust away the frenzy and the true inspired voice   3.1-7, etc.
and the terrible madness, but grant a pleasant refrain.   13.173; 12.297

---

k3. These two lines are hopelessly corrupt. I follow
Kurfess:

*kai labetai se mnēma, peridromos hoia te tumbos
zōsan esō, husplegxin epharmostos koruphaisin.*

The reference is to the death of Cleopatra.

l3. The reference is to the oppression of the Hebrews before the Exodus.

m3. Pausanias 10.12.6 says that the Sibyl is a
prophetess of Apollo, but this is expressly denied in
SibOr 4.4f.

n3. Gk. *chrēsmōdon* for *chrēsmō* (Friedlieb).

o3. Supply *est' ereōn tis,* "someone will call,"
in vs. 318 after *aggelon* (Kurfess).

THE SIBYLLINE ORACLES, BOOK 12

Introduction

Sibylline Oracles 12 continues the political review of book 11, in the same style.[1] The first eleven verses are borrowed directly from Sibylline Oracles 5, and the influence of Sibylline Oracles 5.1–51 is evident down to verse 176. After the introductory verses 1–11 the review of history proper begins with Augustus (i.e. where SibOr 11 left off) and outlines the history of the emperors to the death of Alexander Severus.

There are Christian insertions in verses 30–34 and 232, but the book as a whole is Jewish not Christian. It is unthinkable that a Christian would have written of Domitian in such glowing terms as we find in Sibylline Oracles 12.124–38.[2] The references to the Jews in verses 99–104 and 152 and the name Sabaoth for God in verse 132 reflect Jewish rather than pagan authorship. The book concludes with the Sibyl's account of her own inspiration (vss. 293–99).

Date and provenance

The book is dated by its latest reference, the death of Alexander Severus in A.D. 235 (vs. 288). Like books 11 and 13–14, with which it forms a tradition, it was most probably written in Alexandria—compare the reference to "the city of Egypt," in verse 42, and to Egypt as the "land of splendid fruit" (vs. 17).

Theological and historical importance

Like the other late Sibylline Oracles, the book contains little material of theological interest. It does, however, echo the traditional Sibylline polemic against idolatry (vss. 111f. and 292).

The historical interest of the book is considerable as it provides a rare witness to the popular perception of Roman emperors in the eastern provinces. Fact is mixed with legend and error throughout. Tiberius is erroneously said to have been murdered (vs. 47). Titus is said to have been murdered by his soldiers (122f.). The Sibyl reports bloody drops from heaven in the time of Caligula (vss. 56f.), rain of stone in the reign of Claudius (vs. 75), and miraculous rain in the time of Marcus Aurelius (vs. 200). The latter emperor is said to have been granted whatever he asked by God. The Sibyl gives negative accounts of emperors who were widely unpopular—Caligula (vss. 50–67), Nero (vss. 78–94), Nerva (vss. 142–46), Commodus (vss. 206–28), Septimius Severus (vss. 256–68). However, the general attitude to the emperors is favorable. Praise is lavished on Augustus (vss. 12–35), Domitian (vss. 124–38), Hadrian (vss. 163–75), and Marcus Aurelius (vss. 187–205). Most significant is the treatment of the emperors who suppressed Jewish revolts. Vespasian is admittedly a destroyer of pious men (vs. 99), but greatest attention is paid to his destruction of Phoenicia and Syria (vss. 105–12), and these countries are said to be punished for idolatry. Vespasian himself is described at the end as "noble" and "excellent" (vss. 115f.). Trajan's suppression of the Jewish revolt of A.D. 115–17 is passed over as briefly as possible (vs. 152), and again the emphasis falls on the destruction of Phoenicia and Syria (vss. 153–55). The account of Hadrian makes no reference whatever to a Jewish revolt and contrasts sharply with the hostile account in Sibylline Oracles 8.52–59 on which it is partly based. It should also be noted that the description of Nero, while based on Sibylline Oracles 5.28–34, contains no reference to

---

[1] The only extensive discussion of SibOr 12 is that of Geffcken, "Römische Kaiser im Volksmunde der Provinz," *Nachrichten von der königlichen Gesellschaft der Wissenschaften zu Göttingen*, Phil-Hist. Kl. (Göttingen, 1901) pp. 183–95. See also *Komposition und Entstehungszeit*, pp. 56–58; Rzach, Pauly-Wissowa 2A, cols. 2155–58; Kurfess, *ZRGG* 7 (1955) 271.

[2] Cf. Bousset, *Real-Encyclopedie*, p. 278.

the legend of Nero's return which played so prominent a part in the earlier books. In all, Geffcken's opinion is well-founded that this Sibyllist placed loyalty to Rome above his Judaism.[3]

The book must be classified as political propaganda, although its immediate objective is not clear. It does little more than record popular recollections of the emperors in a traditional form.

The main literary parallels are in the earlier Sibylline Oracles, especially books 3, 5, and 8.

---

[3] Geffcken, *Nachrichten*, pp. 183f.

THE SIBYLLINE ORACLES
Book 12

A review of history

But come, hear my woeful history of the Latin race.[a]   5.1-11
First of all, indeed, after the death of the kings
of Egypt, all of whom the evenhanded earth took under,
and after the citizen of Pella, to whom
5 all the East and prosperous West were subjected,
whom Babylon tested and held out as a corpse to Philip,
alleged, not truly to be descended from Zeus or Ammon,[b]   3.383; 11.197
and after the one of the race and blood of Assaracus,   11.144
who came from Troy, who split the onslaught of fire,[c]
10 and after many princes, after warlike people,
and after infants, children of the flock-devouring beast,[d]   11.110-17
and after the passage of six hundred years   11.273
and two decades of the dictatorship of Rome,

Augustus

will be the very first man from the western sea,   5.12; 3.176
15 great lord of Rome and a brave warrior
who obtained the first of the letters.[e] When he has shackled you,
land of splendid fruit, he will be sated with man-slaying war.[f]
You will make amends for the outrage which you have willingly   11.286f.
   unleashed.
For he, the great-spirited one, will be best in wars.
20 Thrace will crouch in fear before him and Sicily and Memphis;   5.16-19
Memphis, cast down headlong on account of the wickedness of its   8.162; 13.53
   leaders
and of an indomitable woman[g] who fell beneath the spear.
He will give laws to the peoples and subordinate all things.
With mighty glory he will control dominions far and wide.
25 For no other scepter-bearing king of the Romans
will ever exceed this man, even for a little time,
not for one hour, because God approved all for this man;
and indeed he manifested wonderful great times
on the wondrous earth, and in them he showed signs.

Christian insertion

30 But whenever a bright star most like the sun   8.476; Mt 2:2
shines forth from heaven in midday,
then indeed the secret word of the Most High will come   Jn 1:14
wearing flesh like mortals. But with him
the power of Rome will increase, and of the famous Latins,

---

a. Vss. 1–11 are taken directly from 5.1–11.

b. Alexander, who claimed to be son of Zeus Ammon after he visited the shrine of that god in Egypt in 332 B.C.

c. Aeneas. Assaracus, king of Phrygia, was his great-grandfather.

d. Romulus and Remus.

e. Augustus.

f. Gk. *plēsthēsetai* for *pagēsetai* (Rzach). The reference is to the conquest of Egypt.

g. Cleopatra.

Death of Augustus

35 but the great king himself will die by his own fate,
having handed on the royal dominion to another.

Tiberius

After this man there will be a certain mighty warrior.　　　12.124
He will rule, wearing a purple cloak on his shoulders,　　　3.389
and he will be of the number three hundred on his first initial.　5.21f.

　　　　　*　　　*　　　*

40 He will destroy Medes and also arrow-shooting Parthians.
In his might he will destroy a city of high gates,
and evil will come upon the city of Egypt and the Assyrians,
Colchians, Heniochians, and the Germans who live by the streams
of the Rhine beyond the sandy banks.
45 He will also sack thereafter the city with high gates
near the Eridanus,[h] which was devising evils,　　　5.136
and then he will fall, smitten with glittering iron.[i]

Gaius (Caligula)

Thereafter another man, with deceitful locks, will rule,
who has obtained the number three. The initial will show　　5.24
50 his name. He will collect much gold.
There will be no surfeit from much gold but shamelessly
he will ravage more and deposit it throughout all the earth.
There will be peace, and Ares will rest from wars.
He will reveal many things, having the greatest faith　　　Suetonius,
55 in prophecies for the sake of livelihood and life. But on him　*Caligula* 51
there will come a most great sign. Bloody drops　　　　2.20, etc.;
will flow from heaven on[j] the dying king.　　　　　　Suetonius,
He will do many lawless things. Trusting in prophecies,　　*Caligula* 57
he will place woes about the neck for the Romans.
60 He will kill the heads of the senate. Famine will seize　　Suetonius,
Campanians and Thracians, Macedonians, Italians.　　　*Caligula* 26
Egypt alone will nourish numerous tribes.
The prince himself will deceitfully bring to ruin a virgin maiden,
having used the mystery in utter deception.[k] But citizens
65 will mourn and bury her. All will be in wrath
against the prince and will deceitfully maltreat him.
A mighty man, he will perish at the hands of mighty men in flourishing
　　Rome.[l]

Claudius

Another lord will rule again of the number twice ten.　　　5.25
Then wars and mournful cares will come upon
70 the Sauromatae and Thracians and the javelin-throwing Triballi.
The Roman Ares will destroy all.
There will be a terrible sign when this man rules　　　　11.25
over the land of the Italians and Pannonians. Around them

---

h. The reference is not clear. Geffcken suggests Augustodunum near the Rhone. The Eridanus was a mythical river. Cf. SibOr 5.136.

i. This assertion is erroneous.

j. Gk. *kat'* for *kai* (Rzach).

k. This reference is obscure, but presumably refers to the seduction of a vestal virgin. The Sibyllist possibly confused Caligula with Nero, who is known to have raped a vestal virgin (Suetonius, *Nero* 28).

l. Caligula was assassinated in A.D. 41.

there will be dark night in the mid-hour of day[m]   4.56, etc.
75 and rain of stone from heaven. But then   14.235
a mighty lord and judge of the Italians
will go to the halls of Hades by his own fate.[n]

Nero

Another man of the number fifty will come again,   5.28
terrible and frightful. He will destroy many
80 who are outstanding in wealth from all the cities,
a terrible snake, breathing grievous war,[o] who one day   5.29
will lay hands on his own family[p] and kill them and perform many things
as athlete, charioteer, murderer, one who dares ten thousand things.   5.31
He will also cut the mountain between two seas and will defile it with   5.32
    gore.
85 But he will be destructive to the Italians, even when he has disappeared.   5.33
Making himself equal to God, he will convince a willing people.   5.34
There will be deep peace when this man rules   3.755; 12.172
and quaking of men. Cleaving the tide[q] under the Ausonians,   5.26f.
he will reach[r] the strange water from the streams of Oceanus.
90 Glancing about him, he will set up many contests for peoples,
and he himself will compete as a contestant   Suetonius, *Nero*
with voice and lyre, singing a song accompanied by strings.   22-25
Later he will flee, abandoning the royal dominion.
Perishing wretchedly, he will make amends for what he did.   4.119, etc.

Galba, Otho, and Vitellius

95 After him three will rule, two lords who have obtained   5.35
in their names the number seventy, and in addition to these one
of the third letter.[s] They will perish, one here, another there,
in mighty war, at the hands of an army.

Vespasian

Then will come a certain lord, a great destroyer   5.36
100 of pious men,[t] a man of mighty spirit, an Ares who wields the spear,
who will clearly show an initial seven times ten.   5.37
He will destroy Phoenicia and bring Syria to destruction.
A sword will also come upon the land of Solyma
as far as the last turning of the sea of Tiberias.
105 Alas, Phoenicia, how much you will endure, one of great sorrows.   12.153
You will be bound with cords[u] and every nation will trample you.
Alas, you will come to the Assyrians and will see   3.268, etc.
infant children in slavery among hostile men,
and wives also and your whole livelihood. Wealth will perish.
110 For the anger of God will come upon you, one of great sorrows,

---

m. There were, in fact, four solar eclipses in the reign of Claudius, but none of them was noted in Italy.

n. According to Suetonius, *Claudius* 44: "Most people think Claudius was poisoned."

o. Gk. *phusōn polemon barun* for *phuseōs ho brachus logos* (Rzach). Cf. SibOr 5.29.

p. Gk. *hēs geneēs* for *hēgemonas* (Rzach). Cf. SibOr 5.30.

q. Gk. *daixas* for *d'aixas* (Rzach).

r. Gk. *hixeth'* for *eixen* (Rzach). Vss. 88f. seem

to be misplaced here. They refer to Claudius' expedition against Britain in SibOr 5. Ausonians is a poetic name for Italians.

s. I.e. Galba. Otho and Vitellius (*Ouietellios*) have the same initial in Gk.

t. While SibOr 12 recognizes that Vespasian suppressed the Jewish revolt, he stresses rather the destruction of Phoenicia and Syria.

u. Gk. *sphigchtēsē stropheiois* for *sphiktē(i)si tropaiēsi* (Geffcken).

because they did not keep his law but served   3.275-77
all idols with disgraceful devices.
There will be many wars, battles and slaughters,   4.68, etc.
famines and pestilence, and upheavals of cities.   2.23, etc.
115 At the end of life a noble great-spirited king,
excellent himself, will fall by compulsion of the army.ᵛ

Titus

Thereafter two other princesʷ will rule,
loving the memory of their father the great king,
winning much glory among spear-wielding warriors.
120 One man of these will be a noble lord.
He will have the name of three hundred, but he   5.38
will fall by deceit, stretched out, even among the ranks
smitten on the soil of Rome with double-edged bronze.ˣ

Domitian

Also after him a certain man, a mighty warrior,   12.37
125 with an initial four will rule a great kingdom,   5.40
whom all mortals will love throughout the boundless earth.ʸ
Then there will be respite from war throughout the whole world.
From West to East all will serve this man
willingly, not by compulsion,
130 and cities will spontaneously be subject or subordinate.
For heavenly Sabaoth, the imperishable God who dwells in the sky,
will especially confer glory on him.
Then famine will diminish Pannonia and all
the Celtic land, and will destroy them on top of each other.
135 The Assyrians, whom the Orontes floods,
will have buildings and embellishment and anything that may seem
        greater.ᶻ
These the great king will love, and he will cherish them
beyond the other citizens. But he himself
will receive a great wound in the middle of his breast
140 at the end of life, taken deceitfully by a companion.
Within the wondrous, great palace of the kingdom
he will fall, slain.ᵃ² After him will be a lord,

Nerva

a majestic man, of the number fifty who will destroy   5.41
many townsmen and citizens of Rome, for every reason.
145 But he will have short rule,ᵇ² for on account of the former king
he will go, slain, thereafter,ᶜ² to the halls of Hades.

---

v. Vespasian was not, in fact, assassinated.

w. Titus and Domitian.

x. This is incorrect. Titus died of fever.

y. Contrast the terse comment in SibOr 5.40: "a cursed man."

z. Domitian was famous as a benefactor of the provinces.

a2. Domitian was assassinated in A.D. 96. His wife, Domitia, was one of the conspirators.

b2. This translation of *oligarchēsei*, "he will have a short rule," seems to be demanded by the context. The word normally means "he will form/participate in an oligarchy."

c2. Nerva ruled for only sixteen months but he was not assassinated. He lacked support in the army, and rapidly lost prestige, but he was morally blameless. Geffcken suspects that the charges leveled against him here are tendentious. Nerva had his greatest problems with those who resented the murder of Domitian.

Trajan

Then immediately there will be another king and mighty warrior
who has obtained the marked initial of three hundred.   5.42
He will rule and ravage the diverse land
150 of the Thracians and the Germans who inhabit
the savage extremities of the Rhine, and the arrow-shooting Iberians.
Immediately another very great evil will come upon the Jews,[d2]
and Phoenicia, after these things, will drink torrential slaughter.   12.105
The walls of the Assyrians will fall with many warriors.
155 Again a spirit-destroying man will destroy these.
Thereafter will be the threats of the powerful God,   3.71
earthquakes and great famines throughout the whole earth,
and snowstorms out of season and fierce thunderbolts.
Then also a king, the great Celtic mountaineer,   5.43
160 rushing through the tumult of war to the strife of battle,
will not escape an unseemly fate but will die.
Foreign dust, which has the name of a Nemeian flower,[e2]   5.45f.
will cover him, a corpse. After him another will be prince,

Hadrian

a silver-headed man. He will have the name of a sea,   5.47; 8.52
165 presenting the beginning of the alphabet, an Ares of four syllables.
He will also dedicate temples in all cities,
inspecting the world on his own foot, bringing gifts.   8.53-56
Gold and much alloy he will give to many.
He will also master all the mysteries of
170 the magic shrines. Indeed the thunderbolt
will give a much better ruler to men.[f2]
There will be long peace when this prince   3.755; 12.87
will be. He will also be a singer of splendid voice,   Spartian,
sharer in lawful things, and just legislator.   Hadrian 14;
                                                          16; 26
175 He will fall, undone by his own fate.

The Antonines

After him three will rule, but the third will come to power late in life,[g2]   5.51; 8.65
containing three decades. But another prince will rule
again, of the first unit.[h2] After him another lord,
of seven decades.[i2] They will have noble names.
180 They will destroy much-spotted men,
Britons and Moors, great Dacians and Arabs.

---

d2. The Jewish revolt in the Diaspora in A.D. 115.
Again the Sibyllist touches lightly on the unpleasant
chapters in Jewish-Roman relations and stresses the
destruction in Phoenicia and Syria.

e2. Gk. *alla Nemeiēs* for *ounoma d'eiē* (Rzach).
The wreath at the Nemean games was parsley,
"*selinon*." Trajan died at Selinus in Cilicia. He is
called Celtic because he was born in Spain.

f2. Some words are missing in this vs. The passage
is a deliberate inversion of the attack on Hadrian in
SibOr 8.50–59. In SibOr 8 Hadrian travels with *polluted* foot, here on his own foot. In SibOr 8 he will
collect money, here he will bestow it. Even the mysteries in SibOr 12 are no longer "mysteries of error"
(SibOr 8.58). The deification of Antinous is omitted.
See further the warm praise of Hadrian in SibOr

8.131–38. The thunderbolt is associated with Zeus
and is here a sign of divine approval. Spartian, *Hadrian* 14.3, claims that a thunderbolt once burned the
victim when Hadrian was sacrificing.

g2. In SibOr 5 the third is Marcus Aurelius. The
other two are Antoninus Pius and Lucius Verus.
Hadrian had no children, but he adopted Antoninus.
Antoninus in turn adopted Marcus Aurelius and Lucius Verus. However, in SibOr 11 the third is apparently Lucius (L = 30), although the reference is
not appropriate, since he was ten years younger than
Marcus Aurelius.

h2. Antoninus Pius.

i2. V = 70. The reference is to M. Annius Verus,
or, as he was subsequently and more usually called,
Marcus Aurelius.

But whenever the youngest of these[j2] perishes,
then indeed terrible Ares will come upon Parthia[k2]
again, who formerly wounded it and will finally utterly destroy it.
Then also the prince himself will be felled by a deceitful beast
while exercising his hands.[l2] This is the alleged cause of death.

Marcus Aurelius

After him another man will rule, who knows many wise things,
with the name of the first powerful king,
of the first unit.[m2] He will be good and great.
190 A mighty man, he will accomplish many things for the great Latins,
for the sake of his father's memory. He will immediately decorate
the walls of Rome with gold and silver and ivory,
going in the marketplaces and temples with strong light.[n2]
One day also a most terrible wound will spring up
195 for the Romans in wars. He will utterly destroy[o2]
the entire land of the Germans whenever the great sign of God
appears from heaven, and saves bronze-helmeted men
who are being worn out on account of the piety of the king.
For the heavenly God will indeed hearken to him in everything.
200 At his prayer he will shower rainwater out of season.[p2]
But when those things of which I spoke are completed
then also the famous kingdom of the great pious prince
will fail with the revolving years.
At the end of his life, having displayed his son
205 rising to kingship, he will die by his own fate,

13.66;
14.131,211

Commodus

leaving the royal dominion to a fair-haired lord,
who will have the name of two decades.[q2] A king from birth,
he will receive dominion from his father.
This man will contain all things with extraordinary calculation.
210 He will emulate the very great-spirited mighty Heracles,[r2]
and he will excel with mighty weapons, having
the greatest glory in hunts with dogs and horse riding.
He will live dangerously, quite alone.
There will be a terrible sign when this man rules.
215 On the soil of Rome there will be cloud and mist
so that no one of mortals can see another who is near him.[s2]
Then indeed there will be simultaneously wars and mournful cares,
whenever the prince himself, the madman crazed with love,[t2]
will come shaming his race, base, on ill-advised
220 couches in unholy wedlock.
Then indeed a great destructive man, concealed in bereavement,
incurring wrath, will suffer evil[u2] in the bath,
a murderous man, shackled by deceptive fate.

Ex 10:21-23

j2. Lucius Verus.

k2. Avidius Cassius, who conquered Mesopotamia in A.D. 165–66. L. Verus died in 169.

l2. Avidius proclaimed himself emperor in A.D. 175, but was assassinated three months later. The reference to the beast is, of course, legendary.

m2. The famous philosopher king succeeded as Emperor in 161 as M. Aurelius Antoninus. The reference here is to the name Antoninus.

n2. M. Aurelius was not noted for building in Rome, but he did build roads in the provinces.

o2. Gk. *men* for *min* (Alexandre).

p2. The Sibyl follows pagan tradition here—cf. *Vita Marci* 24.

q2. *Kommodos*. He had been gradually promoted and became joint ruler in 177 at the age of sixteen.

r2. Commodus claimed to be Heracles incarnate as Hercules Romanus.

s2. This legend is recorded in Lampridius, *Commodus* 16.2.

t2. Commodus is said to have lived incestuously with his sisters (Lampridius, *Commodus* 5.8).

u2. Gk. *kaka peisetai* for *kaka chōsetai* (Rzach).

Confusion after the death of Commodus

Know then that the destructive time of Rome is near
225 because of the passion of the ruler. Many will perish
in the halls of the Palladium[v2] at the hands of Ares.
Then Rome will be bereft and make amends for all
that it alone did formerly in many wars.
My heart weeps, it weeps within me.
230 For from the time when the first king,[w2] proud Rome,
a single man, gave a noble law to earthly men
and the word of the great immortal God came to earth[x2]
until the end of the nineteenth kingdom,[y2]
the time of years has been fulfilled: twice a hundred,
235 twice twenty and twice two, plus six months.[z2] Then

8.43

8.129;
3.350–55, etc.
5.169f., etc.

12.32; Jn 1:14

Pertinax

the twentieth king will bereave the race, because in his dwelling
he will shed his blood, smitten with a sharp bronze sword,
having an initial of the number eighty,[a3] which shows his name[b3]
and grievous old age. But he will make a widow
240 in a short time when there will be many warriors,
many destructions, and murders and slaughters,
destructive strife and woes for the sake of conquest
of the lordship, and many horses and men in confusion
will fall on the ground, rent asunder by wars.

Didius Iulianus

245 Then another man will come, having the sign of his name
of the number ten,[c3] and he will inflict many
griefs and groanings and he will destroy many.
He himself will again have swift fate and he will fall
in mighty war, smitten with glittering iron.

Pescennius Niger

250 Another warrior of the number fifty will come,[d3]
roused from the East for the sake of the lordship.
A warlike Ares, he will come as far as Thrace,
but will flee thereafter and come to the plain of Bithynians
and the soil of Cilicians. Brazen, spirit-destroying Ares
255 will quickly destroy him on the Assyrian plains.

Septimius Severus

Then a resourceful man who craftily knows what is expedient
will come to power,[e3] roused from the West.

v2. The Palladium was a sacred image of Pallas
Athene, said to have been brought from Troy and
kept in the temple of Vesta. It was believed to protect
the city and was credited with saving Rome from the
Gauls in 390 B.C.

w2. Augustus.

x2. A Christian insertion.

y2. As the emperors have been enumerated (including Avidius Cassius) Commodus is the nineteenth.

z2. This calculation is not quite correct. The death
of Commodus took place in A.D. 193.

a3. Reading vs. 238 with Rzach: *thēsei ogdoēkont'
arithmōn* for *ogdoēkont' arithmon eteos*.

b3. Pertinax ruled for only three months. He was
assassinated. Vss. 237–44 refer to the tumult of the
times, not to any deeds of Pertinax.

c3. *Iulianos*. He was also assassinated after three
months. The statement that he "will destroy many"
is without basis.

d3. Pescennius *Niger*. He was proclaimed emperor
by his legions in Syria when Pertinax was murdered.
He was defeated by Septimius Severus.

e3. Gk. *kratēsei* for *kratēsai*.

His name will have the sign of the number two hundred.[f3]   11.91
Much more will he contrive war for the sake
260 of royal dominion, having gathered his whole army
against the men of Assyria,[g3] and he will subordinate everything.
The great power will rule for the Romans. In his heart
will be many a scheme, the wrath of destructive Ares.
A terrible snake, grievous in war, who will destroy all   5.29; 12.81;
265 earthly men who have become exalted.   11.41
Having killed noble men for the sake of wealth, like a star,   5.155, etc.
and having ravaged the whole earth of perishing men,
he. will go[h3] to the East, and every deceit will be his.[i3]

Alexander Severus

Then when an infant Caesar reigns with him,
270 having the name of the mighty Macedonian prince
of the first letter, there will be tumult around him.[j3]
He will escape the dread deceit of the advancing king
in the bosom of the army.[k3] But the temple-warden[l3]
ruler, of savage customs, will suddenly
275 perish in mighty war, overcome by glittering iron.
Even when he is dead the people will rend him in pieces.   14.169
Then indeed the kings of the Persians will rise up[m3]   13.13,110
. . . a Roman Ares . . . a Roman prince.
Phrygia of many flocks will also groan with earthquakes.
280 Alas, Laodiceia, alas, wretched Hierapolis,   3.471;
for you first did the yawning earth receive . . .[n3]   5.290,318
         *   *   *

. . . will wail as men perish
285 in the hands of Ares. But an evil fate of men
will come upon you. But then, as he hastens
through the eastern route to see Italy, he will fall,
by glittering iron, stripped, having aroused hatred because of his
     mother.[o3]

Conclusion

For there are all sorts of seasons and each contains something different[p3]   Eccl 2:1–8
290 . . . but not all know it at once.
For not all things belong to all. Only those
who honor God and forget idols will have joy.   3.14,30, etc.
But now, prince of the world, king of every kingdom,   3.1–7, etc.
immortal one without falsehood—for you placed an ambrosial voice
295 in my heart—stop my speech. For I do not know   Prologue 90
what I say. For it is you who utter everything in me.
Let me rest a little and grant a pleasant refrain   11.324
of my heart. For my heart within is wearied
of oracular words, proclaiming royal dominions.

f3. Septimius, a native of Africa, was governor of Upper Pannonia and saluted as emperor at Carnuntum after the death of Pertinax.

g3. I.e. against the army of Pescennius in the East.

h3. Gk. *bēset'* for *thēsei* (Rzach).

i3. Gk. *autō(i)* for *autois* (Rzach). There is evidently a lacuna here. The accounts of Caracalla and Elagabalus are lost.

j3. Gk. *huparxei* for *apaxas* (Geffcken). The reference is to Alexander Severus (Alexianus), adopted by Elagabalus and entrusted with the secular administration in A.D. 221.

k3. Alexander's mother bribed the Pretorians to murder Elagabalus in A.D. 222.

l3. Elagabalus was priest of the sun-god, also named Elagabalus, in his native Emesa in Syria.

m3. In 231 the Persian king, Artaxerxes, invaded Mesopotamia.

n3. The next two lines are hopelessly fragmentary.

o3. Alexander and his mother were murdered in A.D. 235.

p3. Gk. *pantoiai hekastē* for *panta . . . tartē* (Alexandre).

THE SIBYLLINE ORACLES, BOOK 13

Introduction

Sibylline Oracles 13 continues the historical sequence of Sibylline Oracles 12.[1] Some verses are lost at the beginning, before verse 7, but the first clear reference is to Gordianus III (A.D. 240–44) in verses 13–20. The review of history is very brief and extends only to the time of Odenath of Palmyra, in the reign of Gallienus (A.D. 260–68) in verses 150–73.

The reference to the persecution of Decius in verses 87f. is assumed by all commentators to have been written by a Christian. Geffcken assumed that the entire work is Christian. Against this, Rzach, followed by Kurfess, has pointed out that there is no reference to the persecution under Valerian or to his capture by the Persians, which a Christian might have seen as a punishment of God.[2] Verses 87f. could easily have been inserted later. There is nothing else in the book to suggest Christian authorship. If, then, the book was not written by a Christian, it is probably Jewish, not pagan. This is indicated by the references to divine providence in verse 112, the wrath of the great God (vs. 54) or of the Most High (vs. 109) and the polemic against astrology in verses 69–73 (cf. SibOr 3.227f.).[3]

Date and provenance

Since Sibylline Oracles 13 does not refer to the deaths of either Gallienus or Odenath, it can be dated with some confidence about A.D. 265. The place of origin is less certain. The enthusiasm shown for Odenath of Palmyra might suggest an origin somewhere in Syria, but there is also a eulogy of Egypt and Alexandria in verses 43–49. Since the other Sibylline books with which Sibylline Oracles 13 is in continuity come from Alexandria, this book was probably written there too.

Historical and theological importance

Apart from the few indications of Jewish authorship listed above, Sibylline Oracles 13 is quite without theological interest. Its historical interest is, however, considerable. Most important are the references to Mareades (also called Kyriades), a Roman traitor who twice tried to lead Parthian forces against Rome and of whom little is known.[4] As presented in Sibylline Oracles 13.89–100 and 119–30, this figure is modeled on the Nero legend.[5] For the Sibyllist the legend of Nero's return, which was no longer alive in its original form, was actualized in Mareades.

The hero of the book is ultimately Odenath of Palmyra, who fought for the Romans against the Parthians. He is twice described as *heliopemptos*, "sent from the sun" (vss. 151, 164), and while the title derives from the association of the sun with Palmyra, the phrase also recalls the savior king of Sibylline Oracles 3.652 and suggests that Odenath too was a savior figure.[6] At the end the Sibyl prophesies that Odenath will be "intact, unblemished, and great," and will rule over the Romans (vss. 170f.). The oracle then can be understood as political propaganda in praise of Odenath.

The most significant literary contacts are with the earlier Sibyls; but there are also a number of parallels to the Apocalypse of Elijah.[7]

---

[1] SibOr 13 is discussed by Geffcken, *Komposition und Entstehungszeit*, pp. 59–63; Rzach, Pauly-Wissowa 2A, cols. 2158–62; Kurfess, *ZRGG* 7 (1955) 271f.; Bousset, *Real-Encyclopedie*, p. 278.

[2] Rzach, Pauly-Wissowa 2A, col. 2161.

[3] Ibid., cols. 2160f.; Kurfess, *ZRGG* 7 (1955) 272.

[4] The only other source is Trebellius Pollio. See Geffcken, *Komposition und Entstehungszeit*, p. 60.

[5] See Rzach, Pauly-Wissowa 2A, col. 2159. SibOr 12.122f. are taken from SibOr 4.138f.

[6] Compare also ApEl 2:39, which refers to a king from "the city of the sun," (Palmyra or, possibly, Heliopolis). See J. M. Rosenstiehl, *L'Apocalypse d'Elie* (Paris, 1972) pp. 63f.

[7] See Rosenstiehl, *L'Apocalypse d'Elie*, p. 65:

ApEl 2:28; cf. SibOr 13.62
ApEl 2:24; cf. SibOr 13.118
ApEl 2:39; cf. SibOr 13.151, 164.

THE SIBYLLINE ORACLES
Book 13

The Sibyl's introduction

The holy immortal imperishable God bids me again   2.1-5, etc.
sing a great wondrous word.[a] He who gave power
to kings, and took it away again, and delimited for them   Lk 1:52
a time of both things, of life and of wretched death.
5 The heavenly God also presses me hard, though I am reluctant,
to proclaim these things to kings about royal dominion.

         *   *   *

A period of strife

Ares, furious with the spear.[b] At his hand all will perish—
the infant child and the elder who legislates[c] for assemblies.
For there will be many wars and battles and slaughters,   4.68, etc.
10 famines and pestilence, earthquakes and fierce thunderbolts,   2.6f., etc.
and many volleys of lightnings[d] throughout the whole world,
and plundering and despoiling of temples.

Gordianus III

Then indeed there will be an insurrection of enterprising Persians,   12.277; 13.110
Indians, Armenians, and Arabs, simultaneously, and round about these
15 a Roman king will approach, insatiable for war,
a young Ares,[e] leading on warriors even against Assyrians.
The warlike Ares will stretch out his spear, sending
as far as the deep-flowing, silver-eddying Euphrates
for the sake of retribution.[f] For, betrayed by a companion,[g]
20 he will fall in the rank, smitten with glittering iron.

Philippus

Immediately a warrior who loves the purple will rule,
appearing from Syria,[h] a terror of war, and with Caesar,
the son, he will also ravage the whole earth. Both
will have the one name, five hundred added
25 to the first letter and the twentieth.[i] But when these
lead in wars and become adjudicators,
there will be rest from war for a little while, not for long.
But when the wolf pledges oaths to the flock   14.348;
against the white-fanged dogs, then it will do mischief,   Isa 11:6
30 hurting the wool-fleeced sheep, and will cast off the oaths.[j]

---

a. Gk. *thespesion* for *theon*, and add *autis* (Rzach).

b. Presumably a reference to the civil strife in the year A.D. 238 when the emperors Gordianus I and II, Bulbinus, and Pupienus Maximus all met their deaths.

c. Gk. *geraos te themisteuôn* for *gegaôs te themisteuei* (Alexandre).

d. Gk. *asteropôn te phorai pollai* for *assuriôn te poroi polloi* (Geffcken).

e. Gordianus III (A.D. 238–44) became emperor at thirteen. In his time Goths and Persians were defeated by Rome.

f. Gk. *nemeseôs* for *ideteôs* (Wilamowitz).

g. Gordianus III was assassinated in A.D. 244.

h. Julius Verus Philippus conspired to have Gordianus III assassinated and replaced him as emperor. In 247 he elevated his son to the rank of Augustus. Both were killed in a battle at Verona in A.D. 249.

i. *A* for Augustus (1), *K* for Kaisar (20), and *Ph* for Philippus (500).

j. The reference is to a treaty with the Parthians which was not fully observed.

Then also there will be lawless strife of overbearing kings
in wars. Syrians will perish terribly.
Indians, Armenians, Arabs, Persians, and Babylonians
will destroy each other through mighty war.
35 But when the Roman Ares destroys the German,[k]
having conquered the spirit-destroying Ares of the ocean,
then also the Persians, overbearing men,
will have war for many years, but they will not have victory.
For as a fish does not swim on the summit of a lofty rock
40 with many ridges, windy and high,
nor does a tortoise fly, nor an eagle swim in water,
so also the Persians are far from victory[l]
on that day, insofar as the dear nurturer of Italians,
which lies in the plain of the Nile by the wondrous water,
45 dispatches a seasonal tribute to seven-hilled Rome.   2.18; Rev 17:9
These things are fated. For as much, Rome, as your name   8.150
contains in numbers of counted time,
for that many years the marvelous great city
of the Macedonian prince will willingly supply you with corn.[m]   11.303

Prophecies of woe against various peoples

50 But I will sing another toilsome distress for the Alexandrians,
who will perish through strife of shameful men:
males, cowardly and without courage,
who will love peace by preference, on account of the wickedness of   3.366; 5.17;
their leaders.   8.162; 12.21
The wrath of the great God will also come upon the Assyrians,
55 and a winter flood of a river will destroy them, (a river) which will
come
to the cities of Caesar and harm the Canaanites.[n]
The Pyramus will water the city of Mopsos,[o] where the Aegeans
will fall on account of the strife of exceedingly mighty men.
Wretched Antioch, grievous Ares will not leave you,   4.140; 13.125
60 when Assyrian war presses around you.
For in your halls a leader of men[p] will dwell
who will fight all the arrow-shooting Persians,   ApEl 2:28
himself sprung from the royal dominion of the Romans.
Now cities of Arabs, be embellished with temples and stadia   3.57; 8.123f.
65 and broad marketplaces and resplendent wealth,
and statues of gold and silver and ivory,
but above all Bostra and Philippopolis, though given to learning,[q]
that you may come to great grief.
For neither the joyful spheres of the circular zodiac,   3.221-30
70 Aries, Taurus, and Gemini,
nor those stars, regulating time, which appear
with these in heaven, in which you, wretched one, have trusted much,
will profit you when that day which is yours approaches hereafter.
Now I will sing most terrible wars for the Alexandrians,
75 who love war. A great people will perish

k. The Goths. They were not, however, defeated
by Philippus.

l. The Sibyl is not referring to a historical defeat
of the Parthians but is affirming a belief that Rome
will eventually overcome them.

m. Alexandria. Egypt was historically a major
source of corn.

n. The reference is enigmatic. Presumably the Palestinian Caesareas, not the Cappadocian or Maure-
tanian, are intended.

o. Mopsuestia in Cilicia.

p. Alexandre suggests Philippus, who was a native
of Arabia, but this is by no means certain.

q. These cities were not especially known for astrological or astronomical learning, but there is nothing implausible in the assertion.

when townsmen are destroyed by opposing citizens,
who fight for the sake of hateful strife.
Darting around these, Ares, terrible in appearance, will stir up (the strife)
  of war.
Then also the great-spirited one will fall, with his mighty son,
80 by deceit on account of an older king.[r]

Decius

After him another great-spirited prince, skilled in the art
of warfare, will rule mighty, flourishing Rome.
Emerging from the Dacians, he will be of the number
three hundred, with an initial of four.[s] He will destroy many.
85 And then the king will indeed slay all his kinsmen and
friends, and as kings perish
there will be immediately plunderings and murders of faithful men,[t]
suddenly, because of the former king.

Mareades/Kyriades

Then when a deceitful man comes, a foreign ally,[u]   13.119-30
90 appearing as a bandit from Syria, an inconspicuous Roman,
he will also deceitfully approach the race of Cappadocians
and will besiege them and press them hard,[v] insatiable for war.
Then you, Tyana and Mazaka, will experience captivity.
You will be in servitude, and will place your neck under the yoke for
  this man.
95 Syria also will weep when men perish,
nor will Selenaea then save its sacred town.
But when a wanton man flees[w] from Syria in anticipation before
the Romans, fleeing through the streams of the Euphrates,   4.119f., etc.
no longer like the Romans but like the proud arrow-shooting

Death of Decius

100 Persians, then a lord of Italians,[x]
will fall in the rank, smitten by glittering iron,
letting go his decorum. His sons will perish in addition to him.

Trebonianus Gallus

But when another king rules Rome
then also nations in agitation will come against the Romans;
105 a destructive Ares, with a bastard child, against the walls of Rome.[y]   13.142
Then indeed there will be famines, pestilence, and fierce thunderbolts,

---

r. Philippus and his son were killed in battle (above, n. h). Decius had already been acclaimed emperor by his troops. He had pledged loyalty to Philippus, but his sincerity was doubted.

s. *Decius* (4) took the name *Trajan* (300) when he became emperor.

t. Decius persecuted Christianity because he wished to revive the state religion. Vss. 87–88 are usually assumed to be written by a Christian.

u. Gk. *epiklētos* for *epi klinēs* (Rzach). The reference is to Mareades/Kyriades, a traitor who twice tried to lead Parthian forces against Rome. See the Introduction to SibOr 13.

v. Gk. *piesei* for *pesetai* (Rzach).

w. Gk. *prophugēsin aselgēs* for *periphuxana-selgēn* (Rzach). Mareades takes on some characteristics of the Nero legend of SibOr 4 and 5.

x. Decius and his son were killed fighting against the Goths.

y. Trebonianus Gallus was a lieutenant who betrayed Decius but succeeded him as emperor in A.D. 251. His reign was a disaster. The Parthians overran Mesopotamia, the Goths again invaded, and plague was rampant. Gallus' son Volusianus was raised to the rank "Augustus," but he is not known to be illegitimate. Geffcken refers to an illegitimate son, Hostilianus.

and terrible wars and upheavals of cities,   4.68, etc.
suddenly. Syrians will perish frightfully.
For great wrath from the Most High will come upon them.
110 Immediately there will be an insurrection of enterprising Persians.   12.277; 13.13
Syrians, mingled with Persians, will slay Romans,
but nevertheless they will not conquer by the divinely decreed plan.
Alas, for as many as sprung from the East will flee,   3.392
with their possessions, to strange-tongued men.
115 Alas, of how many men will the earth drink dark blood.
For this will be the time when the living one day
will pronounce a blessing on the dead with their mouths
and will say that death is fair, and it will evade them.   2.307, etc.;
                                                                              8.353
                                                                              ApEl 2:24

The return of Mareades/Kyriades

Now, wretched Syria, I bewail you piteously.
120 On you too will come an affliction from arrow-shooting men,
a terrible one, which you never expected to come upon you.   3.315
For the fugitive of Rome will come, brandishing a spear,[z]   4.138f.
having crossed the Euphrates with many myriads,
who will burn you down and dispose everything badly.
125 Wretched Antioch, they will no longer call you a city   4.140f.; 13.59
when you fall under spears by your own folly.
When he has completely plundered and stripped you he will abandon
    you,
exposed and uninhabited. Suddenly whoever sees you will weep.
And you, Hierapolis, will be a triumph-spectacle, and you, Beroea,
130 you will weep with Chalcis for her newly slain children.

Further woes in the reign of Gallus

Alas, for as many as dwell on towering Mount Casius
and as many as are in Amanus and those whom Lycus deluges,
and Marsyas and silver-eddying Pyramus.
For they will dedicate spoils as far as the ends of Asia,
135 having stripped cities, and they will take away the images of all
and cast down temples on the fertile earth.
Then there will be great affliction for Gallia and Pannonia,
Mysians and Bithynians, when the warrior comes.
O Lycians, Lycians, a wolf is coming to lick blood
140 when the Sanni come with Ares, sacker of cities,
and the Carpians approach to fight against the Ausonians.
And then a bastard son, by his shameless daring,   13.105
will destroy a king but will immediately perish himself,
because of impiety.[a2] Afterward again another will rule,
145 bearing dominion in his names. He will fall quickly,[b2]
smitten in mighty war with glittering iron.

Odenath

Again the world will be in chaos as men perish
by pestilence and war. Persians will again set out
to the tumult of Ares, raging against the Ausonians.

---

z. Vss. 122f. are borrowed from SibOr 4.138–39,
where they are used of the return of Nero.
    a2. The Sibyl mistakenly asserts that Gallus was
murdered by his son. Both Gallus and Volusianus
were murdered by their troops in A.D. 253.

b2. Aemilianus was acclaimed emperor by his
troops in Moesia in A.D. 252 and was accepted in
Italy after the death of Gallus. However, he was
murdered by his troops after only three months, when
Valerian was proclaimed emperor.

150 Then there will be a flight of Romans,[c2] but afterward   3.652, etc.
the last priest of all will come, sent from the sun,[d2]   13.164
appearing from Syria, and he will accomplish everything with deceit.   ApEl 2:39
Then there will be a city of the sun.[e2] Around it
Persians will endure terrible threats of Phoenicians.[f2]

155 When two men, lords swift in war, rule over
the exceedingly mighty Romans, the one will present
the number seventy, the other will be of the number three,[g2]
then also a stately bull[h2] digging the earth
with its hoofs and raising dust with its two horns

160 will do many evils to the dark-skinned serpent[i2]
which drags its coils on its scales. But he himself will perish with it.
After him another, a well-horned stag,[j2] will come again,
hungering in the mountains, desiring in its belly to eat
venomous beasts. Then will come, sent from the sun,   13.151; 3.652

165 a lion, terrible and frightful, breathing a great flame.[k2]   ApEl 2:39
Then indeed he will destroy with much shameless daring
the stag, well-horned and swift, and the greatest beast,
the frightful venemous one which issues many hissing noises,
and the goat which goes sideways.[l2] Him will glory attend.

170 He himself intact, unblemished and great,
will rule over the Romans, and the Persians will be powerless.[m2]

Conclusion

But God, prince, king of the world, stop the refrain   11.323f.;
of our words, but grant a pleasant refrain.   3.1-7, etc.

c2. Valerian was captured by the Parthians and died in captivity (A.D. 260).

d2. Odenath of Palmyra, who assumed the title of king when Valerian was captured. He inflicted several defeats on the Persians and was given the title "Imperator" by Gallienus with authority over the entire Near East. He is not known to have been a priest. Perhaps the Sibyl assumes the coincidence of priesthood and kingship in an oriental ruler.

e2. Palmyra.

f2. The Palmyreans are called Phoenicians here, probably because they were great traders, possibly because of a legend that they were descended from Solomon.

g2. *Valerian* (70) and his son *Gallienus* (3). Gallienus was co-regent with his father from A.D. 253 and subsequently succeeded him.

h2. Valerian. Cf. the animal imagery in Dan 7–8; 1En 83–90; 4Ezra 11–12, etc.

i2. The Parthians, in general, or their king, Shapur.

j2. Either Macrianus, sent to the East by Valerian, or his son Quietus. Quietus was killed by Odenath.

k2. Odenath, who not only defeated the Parthians but also disposed of his Roman rivals.

l2. Some rival of Odenath, possibly Balista.

m2. Odenath was murdered in A.D. 267 (possibly by his wife, Zenobia). SibOr 13 was apparently written before that date.

THE SIBYLLINE ORACLES, BOOK 14

Introduction

For anyone who has labored through the first eleven books of the Sibylline Oracles, the twelfth (bk. 14) must seem the ultimate *reductio ad absurdum* of a genre never noted for its rationality.[1] Alexandre's despairing conclusion was that the book was composed "either in insane zeal for prophecy or . . . in hope of profit."[2] Geffcken's indignant outburst was worthy of a Sibyl: The Sibyllist was a "Phantast . . . an ignoramus who knew nothing except the names of peoples, countries and cities, and arbitrarily mixes these, now with one, now with another traditional motif, playing mindlessly," and his prophecy was "general raving."[3] Even W. Scott, who was heavily committed to finding authentic historical references in the book, can do no better than suggest "that each of the several paragraphs was originally composed as an account of some known ruler, but that they were not originally connected together in one series, and that their present arrangement is merely accidental."[4] Precedent can be found for such random collections of oracles (e.g. SibOr 3.381–489), but in Sibylline Oracles 14 it comprises very nearly the entire book, at least verses 1–283. Since the text is also hopelessly corrupt, the book has little meaning, let alone importance.

It is possible to discern that verses 1–283 are, like the preceding books, concerned with Roman emperors, but scarcely any can be identified with any certainty.[5] The later part of the book (vss. 284 to the end) is concerned with Egypt rather than Rome. Scott has advanced an elaborate interpretation of these verses with reference to the Arab conquest of Egypt in the seventh century. He relies heavily on emendations, and while no one can doubt that the text he emends is corrupt, that which he produces has only a dubious relation to the tradition and can scarcely serve as the basis for historical inferences.

The most interesting part of the book is in verses 340–49, which refer to a battle involving Jews, Arabs, and "Fair heads" (Europeans of some sort). Scott sees here the conquest of Alexandria by the Arabs and assumes Jewish collaboration with the conquerers.[6] No more plausible identification has been advanced.

Date and provenance

If Scott's interpretation is correct, the book took its final form no earlier than the seventh century. In any case it seems to be the latest of the Sibylline collection and certainly cannot be earlier than the third century. The poor state of the text and uncertainty of the references prevent any definite conclusion.

There is consensus that the book was written by an Alexandrian Jew. The Alexandrian setting is obvious in verses 284–349. The Judaism of the author is reflected chiefly in the eschatological conclusion (vss. 350–61). There is nothing to suggest Christian authorship.[7]

Historical and theological importance

If Scott's interpretation is accepted, Sibylline Oracles 14 acquires some significance with reference to the Arab conquest of Egypt, but the uncertainties are too great for the oracle to have any real importance. The eschatological conclusion portrays a rather communistic

---

[1] The main discussions of SibOr 14 are those of Geffcken, *Komposition und Entstehungszeit*, pp. 66–68; Rzach, Pauly-Wissowa 2A, cols. 2162–65; and W. Scott, "The Last Sibylline Oracle of Alexandria," *Classical Quarterly* 9 (1915) 144–66, 207–28; and 10 (1916) 7–16.

[2] Quoted by Rzach, Pauly-Wissowa 2A, cols. 2162f.

[3] Geffcken, *Komposition und Entstehungszeit*, p. 66.

[4] Scott, *Classical Quarterly* 9 (1915) 146f. For an earlier attempt to find historical references in the book see A. Wirth, "Das vierzehnte Buch der Sibyllinen," *Wiener Studien* 14 (1892) 35–50.

[5] See the summary by Rzach, Pauly-Wissowa 2A, cols. 2163f.

[6] Scott, *Classical Quarterly* 9 (1915) 223f.

[7] Bousset, *Real-Encyclopedie*, p. 279, strangely assumes, without argument, that the book is Christian.

golden age when there will be no more wealth or poverty, a theme reminiscent of some earlier Sibylline passages: for example, Sibylline Oracles 2.319f.; 8.17–36, 110. The ultimate ideal, tersely expressed in verse 360, is the universal dominion of the Jews. The main theological point of the book is expressed in the opening verses: God brings to naught the pride of kings.

The main literary parallels of the book are with the earlier Sibylline Oracles.[8]

---

[8] See Rzach, Pauly-Wissowa 2A, col. 2165.

THE SIBYLLINE ORACLES
Book 14

Against the pride of kings

Men, why do you vainly think excessively proud thoughts
as if you were immortals, though your lordship is short,
and all wish to reign over mortals,
not perceiving that God himself hates
5 the love of lordship, and especially insatiable kings,
terrible and impious. He stirs up darkness against these,
because instead of good deeds and righteous thoughts
they all prefer purple mantles and cloaks,
desiring the wars, woes, and murders.
10 Imperishable God, who dwells in the sky, will utterly destroy these men
and make them short-lived, and will slay one here, another there.

3.8-11;
Frag. 1.1-11

Philo, *Somn* 2.7
(53)

Prophecies of various rulers

But whenever the destroyer of bulls,[a] trusting in his strength,
comes, with beautiful shaggy hair, and destroys all
and crushes the shepherds, they will have no strength
15 unless the young dogs, with fleetness of feet, come to the strife
through the glens, eager to pursue.
The hound pursued the lion which was destroying the herdsmen.
Then there will also be a prince of four syllables,[b] trusting in his strength,
manifest from a unit. Brazen Ares will quickly destroy him
20 on account of the strife of insatiable men.
Thereafter two other men, princes, will rule,
both of the number forty.[c] In their time there will be
great peace of the world and on all the people,
and law and justice. But men with gleaming helmets,
25 in need of gold and silver, because of this
will kill them impiously, taking them in their hands.
Then again a terrible young warrior will rule,
a lord of the number seventy, a fiery destroyer of spirits,
who will impiously hand over to an army the people of Rome,
30 which is being slain in wickedness on account of the wrath of kings,
when he has cast down the entire famous city of the Latins.
It is no longer possible to see Rome, nor is it possible to hear,
in such form as another[d] bypasser saw her a short time before.
For all this will lie in ashes, and there will be no
35 sparing of works. For the destructive[e] one himself will come
from heaven. Immortal God will send lightning bolts and thunderbolts
from the sky against men. Some he will destroy
with blazing lightnings, others with fierce[f] thunderbolts.
Then the infants of mighty Rome and the famous[g] Latins
40 will kill the dread shameless lord.

13.158-69

8.158

12.117

4.179

5.302f.

---

a. The animal imagery of this passage (12–17) recalls Dan 7–8 and the Animal Apocalypse of 1En, but especially SibOr 13.158–69. Accordingly, Alexandre sees here a reference to Odenath.

b. Perhaps Aureolus, proclaimed emperor in A.D. 268 and assassinated in the same year.

c. I.e. with the initial *M*. No identification is pos-

sible here or in the majority of the references in this book.

d. Gk. *allos* for *toian* (Rzach).

e. Gk. *oloos* for *holos* (Alexandre).

f. Gk. *maleroisi* for *krueroisi* (Rzach).

g. Gk. *kleinoi* for *Rhōmēs* (Geffcken).

Nor will light dust lie around him when he is dead,
but he will be a plaything for dogs and birds and wolves,
because he despoiled a warlike people.
After him another famous man of the number forty will rule,[h]
45 a destroyer of Parthians and Germans, who unleashed
terrible manslaying beasts which harass constantly
on the streams of the ocean and Euphrates.
And then Rome will be again as it was before.
But when a great wolf comes on his soil,
50 a prince risen from the West will thereafter die,
cloven by sharp bronze in mighty war.
Then another Ares of mighty spirit will rule
the exceedingly mighty Romans, manifested from Assyria.
He will be of the first letter and will subordinate everything in wars.
55 He and his armies simultaneously will display dominion
and establish laws. Brazen Ares will quickly destroy him
when he falls in the deceitful ranks.
After him three who have a proud heart will rule,[i]　　　5.51; 8.65;
one with the number of a unit, one of three decades,　　　12.176
60 the other, a prince, will share in three hundred.
Wretched ones, who will melt gold and silver
in a great fire, the statues of temples made by hands,　　　3.606,618
and they will give them to the armies, furnishing them
with money for the sake of victory, dividing great and noble treasures.
65 Desiring base things, they will equally ravage
the arrow-shooting Parthians of the deep-flowing Euphrates
and hostile Medes and Massagetae, warriors with delicate hair,
and Persians, men who carry quivers.
But whenever the king comes to an end by his own fate,
70 leaving his royal scepter to his younger sons　　　3.115-21
and imposing law, they will immediately forget
the injunctions of the father, arm their hands for war,
and set out for strife for royal dominion.[j]
The another single prince of the number three will rule
75 again, and he will quickly see fate, smitten with a spear.
After him, then, many will perish on top of each other,
mighty men, for royal dominion.
One great-spirited man will rule over the exceedingly mighty Romans,
an elderly man of the number four, and he will arrange all things well.
80 Then war and strife will come upon Phoenicia
when the nations of the arrow-shooting Persians come near.
Alas, how much will fall at the hands of savage-speaking men:
Sidon and Tripoli and proud Beirut
will see each other amid corpses and blood.
85 Wretched Laodicea, you will raise up about yourself　　　3.471, etc.
a great unsuccessful war through the impiety of men.
Alas, wretched Tyrians, you will reap the bad harvest　　　1.387, etc.
whenever the sun which gives light to men fails in the day,

h. Rzach sees here a reference to Marcus Aurelius, who at various times was known as Parthicus Maximus and as Germanicus. Such a reference is quite out of context here.

i. This passage (58–64) recalls the treatment of the Antonines in SibOr 8 and 12. the letters *A* and *L* might refer to Antoninus Pius and Lucius Verus. The third initial, *T*, makes no sense, but the distribution of gold and silver recalls the prophecy in SibOr

8.68–72 that Marcus Aurelius would surrender the wealth of the world to the returned Nero. It is impossible to attach any meaning to the passage in its present context.

j. Rzach sees here a reference to the brothers Caracalla and Geta (the prince of the number 3 in vs. 74). Caracalla assassinated Geta and became sole emperor in defiance of their father's wishes.

and the disk does not shine. Bloody drops will come on the earth   2.20, etc.
90 thick and frequent from heaven.
Then a king will die, betrayed by his companions.
After him many shameless leaders
will kill each other, carrying on wicked strife.
Then there will be a majestic prince of many counsels,
95 with a name of the number five, relying on great armies,
whom men will love for the sake of royal dominion.
Having a noble name, he will associate it with noble deeds.
There will be a terrible sign. When he holds sway   14.179
between Taurus and snowy Amanus,
100 one certain city will perish from the land of the Cilicians,
a beautiful and strong city of a mighty river.
There will be many earthquakes in Propontis and Phrygia.
A famous king will lose his life
in a consumptive disease of death, by his own fate.
105 After this man, two princely kings will rule,
the one presenting a number of three hundred, the other of three.
Therefore he will also destroy many, for the city
of seven-hilled Rome, on account of the mighty kingdom.   2.18, etc.
Then evil will come upon the senate, and it will not escape
110 when the angry king is in wrath against it.
There will be a sign among all earthly men.
There will be numerous showers of snow. Hail
will destroy the fruits of cattle on the boundless earth.
They themselves will fall overcome in wars
115 by mighty Ares because of the war of Italians.
Then another resourceful king will rule,
having gathered the entire army and divided money
between those with bronze breastplates for the sake of war. But then
the Nile beyond fruitful Libya of the mainland   5.56
120 will water for two years the black plain of Egypt
and arable land. But famine will prevail over everything;
and war and bandits, murders and slaughters.   4.68, etc.
Many cities will be destroyed by warrior men
with demolitions at the hands of an army.
125 He himself will fall by glittering iron, betrayed.
After him one who obtained an initial of the number three hundred
will rule the Romans and exceedingly powerful men.
He will stretch out a spirit-destroying spear against the Armenians,
Parthians, Assyrians, and Persians, steadfast in battle,
130 and then will the foundation of splendidly built Rome be
raised up with gold and alloy and silver   14.211; 12.192
and ivory ornament. A great people of all the East
and prosperous West will live in her.
A king will impose other laws on her.
135 Afterward wretched death and powerful fate
will receive him again on a huge island.
Another man will rule of ten times three, like to a beast
with beautiful shaggy hair. He will be from the Greeks by race.
Then the town of Phthia of the Molossians, which nurtures much,
140 and Larissa will be laid low[k] on the banks of the Peneius.
Then there will be an insurrection of horse-grazing Scythia
and a terrible war by the waters of Lake Maiotis,
on the streams by the furthest source of the spring
of Phasis, with moist foliage in the flowery meadow.

k. Gk. *klithēset'* for *klutē kai* (Rzach).

145 Many will fall at the hands of mighty warriors.
Alas, wretched ones, as many as Ares takes with bronze.
Then the king, having utterly destroyed the Scythian race,
will die by his own fate, having undone his life.
Another terrible man will rule thereafter, revealed
150 by the number four, whom all the Armenians,
who drink the thick ice of the very swift-flowing Araxis,
and the great-spirited Persians will fear in wars.
In the midst of the Colchians and mighty Pelasgians
there will be terrible wars and slaughters.
155 Also the Phrygian land and the towns of the land of Propontis,
baring double-edged swords from their scabbards,
will strike each other on account of grievous impieties.
Then God will show a great sign to mortal men   2.34; 14.220
from heaven, with the revolving years,
160 a bat, a portent of impending evil war.
Then indeed the king will not escape the hands of the army   14.168
but will die, overcome by the hand with glittering iron.
After him another will reign again, of the number fifty,
manifested from Asia, a terrible cause of panic, a warrior,
165 and he will wage war even against the splendid walls of Rome,
on Colchians, Heniochians, and milk-drinking Agathyrsians,
the Euxenian Sea, and the sandy Gulf of Thrace.
Then indeed the king will not escape the hands of the army.   14.161
Even when he is dead, a corpse, they will rend him asunder.   12.276
170 Then indeed when the king has perished, Rome, famed for men,
will be desolate, and a great people will perish.
Then a terrible and frightful man from most great Egypt
will rule and will destroy the great-spirited Parthians,
Medians, Germans, Bosporidans and Agathyrsians,
175 Britons, Iernaeans[l] and quiver-bearing Iberians,
crooked Massagetae, and overbearing Persians.
Then a splendid man will look upon all Greece
at enmity with[m] Scythia and the windy Caucusus.
There will be a mighty sign. When he holds sway   14.98
180 crowns will rise from heaven in south and north   2.34f.
very like shining stars.
Then he will leave the royal dominion to his son,
who is of the first letter, when by his own fate
the manly king goes in the halls of Hades.   12.77
185 But when this man's son rules in the land of Rome,
manifested by a unit, there will be great, very lovely
peace throughout the whole earth. The Latins will   3.755; 11.79,
love this king because of the honor of his father.   etc.
When he is hastening to go to East and West
190 the Romans will restrain him, even when he is not willing,
as lord of Rome, because all had a friendly spirit
for the king, the very illustrious prince.
But after a short time wretched death
will snatch him away from life, betrayed in his own fate.
195 Thereafter again other mighty warriors
will smite each other, carrying on evil strife,
having, not a princely kingdom, but one of tyrants.
They will indeed perform many evil things in the whole world,

l. Gk. *Iernaious* for *Permanious* (Rzach).
m. Gk. *echthrainōn* for *echthairōn* (Geffcken).

especially to the Romans, until the third Dionysus,[n]
200 until an armed Ares comes from Egypt
    whom they call by name Prince Dionysus.
    But when a murderous lion and murderous lioness
    rend the illustrious purple royal garment,
    the winds will snatch up the kingdom as it falls in ruins.[o]
205 Then a holy prince, who obtained the first of the alphabet,   5.15
    pressing hard[p] on hostile rulers for victory,
    will abandon them to dogs and birds to eat.
    Woe to you, city burned with fire, mighty Rome!   3.356-62;
    How many things you must suffer when all these things come to pass.   5.162-78;
                                                      Rev 18, etc.
210 But a great king, who is very famous for
    gold and alloy and silver and ivory,   14.131
    will rouse you up completely, and you will be first in the world
    with possessions and temples, marketplaces, riches, and stadia.   13.64f.; 3.58, etc.
    Then again you will be a light to all, as you were before.   Isa 49:6; 60:1
215 Alas, wretched Cecropians, Cadmeans, and Laconians,
    who are around Peneius and Molossos, deep grown with rushes,
    Trike, Dodona, and high-built Ithone,
    the Pierican mountain pass around the greak peak of Olympus,
    Ossa, Larissa, and Calydon of high gates.
220 But when God performs a great sign for men,   14.158
    a dark night over the world in daytime,
    then, king, an end will come upon you and you will not escape
    the swift bow of your brother shot at you.
    Then a man will rule, spirit-destroying, unspeakable, fiery,
225 of royal birth, who will have his race from Egypt.
    Younger, but much better than his brother,
    he has obtained the marked initial of the number eighty.
    Then the entire world will receive the grievous wrath
    of the immortal God in its bosom, because of honor.
230 For there will come upon articulate, ephemeral man   4.68, etc.;
    famines and pestilence, wars and slaughters   2.23, etc.
    and inexhaustible darkness on the earth, mother of peoples,
    and disturbance of times and implacable anger
    from heaven, and earthquakes and burning thunderbolts   2.6
235 and showers of stones and squalid drops.   12.75
    The lofty hilltops of the Phrygian land shook.
    The feet of the Scythian mountains were shaken, towns trembled,
    the entire ground of the land of Greece shook with them,
    and many cities will fall with headlong crashes
240 under the blazing thunderbolts, and with lamentations
    when God is greatly in wrath.[q] It is not possible to flee the wrath or to
        escape it.
    Then a king will fall, smitten by the hand of the army,
    by his own men, like no one else.
    After him many men of the Latins will again
245 rise up draped with a purple cloak on their shoulders,   3.389; 12.38
    who will love to obtain the royal dominion as their lot.
    Then there will be three kings on the splendid walls of Rome.
    Two will have the first number,

---

n. Even this reference is uncertain, despite the use
of the personal name. An Egyptian ruler is evidently
intended. Geffcken suggests Mark Antony, who
claimed to be Dionysus, and was the third ruler to
take the name in the Ptolemaic period.

    o. Gk. *pneumata summarpsousin ereipomenēn*

basileian for *pneumoni summarpsousin epeigomenēs
basileiēs* (Geffcken).

    p. Gk. *epeigomenos* for *ameipsamenos* (Rzach).

    q. The change in tense is in the Gk., and is typical
of the inconsistency, even incoherence, of book 14.

but one will bear the name "strife"[r] like no one else.
250 They will love Rome and the whole world,
   caring for men. But they will accomplish nothing.
   For God was not propitious to the world, nor will he be
   gentle to men, because they performed many evil things.
   Therefore he will bring a disgraceful spirit upon kings
255 much worse than leopards and wolves. For men with bronze breastplates,   2.267
   taking them unsparingly in their own hands,
   will destroy princes, complete with their scepters,
   who are impotently subdued and stengthless like women.
   Alas, wretched men, the cream of famous Rome,
260 relying on false oaths, you will be destroyed.
   Then many men who are lords of the spear
   will launch an attack which is not proper and
   will take away the offspring of the firstborn men with blood.
   Then the Most High will bring upon them a fate twice as terrible[s]   14.304
265 and he will destroy all men by their own deeds.
   But again God will lead those who have a shameless heart
   to come to judgment, as many as have designed evils.   2.217
   They are shut up, shooting at each other,
   heading even to the judgment[t] of evil.
269a All stars will fall directly into the sea,   8.190-93
270 many stars in turn, and men will call
270a a shining comet "the star," a sign of
   much impending toil, war, and slaughter.
                    *   *   *
   When he gathers many oracles from[u] islands
   which declare[v] to strangers battle and grievous
   strife and destruction of temples,[w] he will tell them to gather
275 with all speed wheat and barley in the houses of Rome,
   as he eagerly seeks abundance for twelve months.
   The city will be wretched in those days.
   But immediately it will again be prosperous in no small way.
   There will be calm, whenever the dominating force is destroyed.
280 Then the race of the Latins will be reigning last,
   and no[x] other kingdom will sprout after it.
   Children and the race of children will be unshaken.   8.136
   For it will be well known,[y] since God himself will govern.

Conquest of Egypt by the Persians

   There is a certain dear land, a nurturer for men,
285 lying in the plain. The Nile sets limits all about it,
   flowing by Libya and Ethiopia.
   Short-lived Syrians will ravage hither and thither
   all the spoil from this land. It will have a great
   noble, princely king, eager to send evils upon thieves.[z]

r. Rzach sees here a reference to the two Augusti, Pupienus and Balbinus (A.D. 238), and Gordianus III, who shared authority with them. However, he reads "twenty" (K for Kaisar) instead of "strife" to permit the identification of Gordianus.

s. Gk. dis toinun hupsistos agoi moirēn tote deinēn for toiēn d'ou prōton agein oiktrēn tote daimōn (Geffcken).

t. Gk. autēn este krisin for eisoikrisin (Geffcken).

u. Gk. para for peri (Geffcken). Sibylline oracles

were collected after the official oracles at Rome had been destroyed when the temple of Jupiter was destroyed in 83 B.C. (Dionysius of Halicarnassus 4.62.6).

v. Gk. phrazontas for phrazomenoi (Rzach).

w. Gk. hierōn for hieron (Alexandre).

x. Gk. k'ou for kai (Geffcken).

y. Omit hoi.

z. Gk. speudōn kaka phōresi pempein for paidōn kai phōtesi pempōn (Gutschmidt).

290 With terrible thought he will bring[a2] mighty help
  to all of the land of proud Italy
  in the most terrible situations. When he comes on the wine-dark sea
  from Assyria and destroys the Phoenicians in their homes
  to fetter evil war and dread battle din,
295 there will be one lord of the land of two lordships.[b2]
  Now I will sing the laborious end of the Alexandrians.
  The barbarians will inhabit sacred Egypt,
  the carefree unshaken one, when envy comes from somewhere.
298a But when God changes times . . .
  He makes winter summer; then all the oracles will be fulfilled.   8.215
300 But when three children win Olympian victories,
  even if he tells those who ponder[c2] to purify[d2]
  first the famous oracles with the blood of a suckling animal,[e2]
  the Most High, who[f2] stretches out a long spear of mourning against all,
  will bring a fate three times more terrible.   14.264
305 Much barbarian blood will then flow in the dust
  when the city is sacked by unsociable guests.[g2]
  Blessed whoever died, and blessed whoever is childless.   13.116f.;
  For then[h2] he who formerly ruled over free people, of which he was   2.190
    namesake,[i2]
  will place his neck under the yoke of slavery.   3.350-61
310 The prince, who was formerly very famous, will no longer[j2]
  evolve plans but will incur such mournful[k2] slavery.

The recapture of Egypt by the Romans

Then indeed an ill-fated army of Sicilians[l2] will come immediately,
  bringing terror, when a great barbarian nation advances.
  If they grow fruit, they will ravage the fields.
315 To these God, who thunders on high, will give evil instead of good.
  Stranger will always plunder the hateful gold of stranger.

The Arab invasion

But when all see the blood of the flesh-eating lion
  and the murderous lioness comes upon the body,
  she will tear away the scepter from him, even from his head.[m2]
320 All the peoples in Egypt will taste as at a friendly feast
  and will accomplish mighty deeds.
  One wards off another, but there will be a great cry of battle among
    them.

a2. Gk. *oisei* for *hoisin* in vs. 291 (Alexandre).

b2. Scott suggests that the king in question is Chosroes II of Persia, who conquered Syria and Phoenicia and occupied Egypt and boasted that the Roman Empire was his (A.D. 616–18).

c2. Gk. *phrazomenoisi* for *dē phrazōsi* (Rzach). Scott reads "Persians" for "children" and applies vs. 300 to the conquest of Caesarea, Jerusalem, and Alexandria. The following vss. are hopelessly corrupt.

d2. Gk. *kathērai* for *kathērē* (Rzach).

e2. Scott sees here a symbolic reference to "some shedding of Jewish blood." He takes the animal as a lamb, symbolic of Jews as in 1En 90, and notes the parallel with Rev 7:14 for "to wash in the blood of the Lamb."

f2. Gk. *hos* for *ou* (Rzach).

g2. Alexandria was captured by force three times in the 7th cent., by the Persians in A.D. 617, by the Romans in 645, and by the Arabs in 646. The latter two are described in vss. 312–47. This passage refers to the first conquest. The "barbarian blood" is Roman.

h2. Gk. *dē tote gar* for *ton gar dē* (Geffcken).

i2. Gk. *epōnumos* for *epōnumon* (Rzach). The reference is to some Roman ruler.

j2. Gk. *meg' aoidimos ouk eth'* for *men aoidimon houtos* (Rzach).

k2. Gk. *poludakron* for *poluedron* (Rzach).

l2. Scott sees here a reference to the recapture of Egypt, about A.D. 627, but emends *Sikelōn* to *ek Kilikōn*, "out of Cilicia," the conjectural base from which the army set out. The emendation is very dubious, but the Sibyl is quite capable of referring to a Roman army as Sicilian.

m2. Scott suggests that the lion is Rome and the lioness the invading Arabs (A.D. 639). This is plausible, though conjectural.

Similarly fear of raging strife will come
upon men and many others will perish,
325 slaying each other by mighty battle.
Then one will come with thick dark scales.[n2]   13.160f.
Two others will come in agreement with each other
and third to them a great ram from Cyrene,
whom I previously mentioned as having fled from battle by the banks
     of the Nile.[o2]
330 But not all will complete even an ineffectual journey.
Then with the great revolving years
there will be a great length of very peaceful time. But then
a second war will come upon[p2] them in Egypt again.
It will be a naval war, and they will not be victorious.
335 O wretched ones, there will be a conquest of an illustrious city
and it will be spoiled in wars, but not for long.
Then neighboring men, wretched ones, will flee
from a great land, and will lead their gray-haired parents.
Again they will fall on a land,[q2] greatly victorious.
340 The Jews[r2] will destroy men steadfast in battle,
ravaging in wars as far as the gray sea,
taking vengeance for[s2] fatherland and parents.
He will set a race of spoil-bearing men[t2] among the dead.
Alas, how many men will swim around the waves,
345 for many will fall on the sandy shores.
Fair heads will fall to Egyptian birds.[u2]
Then the blood of mortals will be among the Arabs.[v2]
But whenever wolves pledge oaths to dogs   13.28
on the sea-girt island, then there will be a raising of towers.
350 Men will inhabit the city which suffered much.[w2]

Eschatological prophecy

No longer will there be deceitful gold or silver   8.17-36,110-21; 2.319-24, etc.
or acquisition of land, or laborious slavery,
but one friendship and one manner for a merry people.
All will be in common, and one equal light of life.
355 On earth evil will sink into the wondrous sea.
Then the harvest of articulate men is near.   2.164, etc.
A strong necessity insists that these things be accomplished.   3.572
Then no other chance wayfarer will say
that the race of articulate men will cease to be, though they perish.
360 Then the holy nation will hold sway over the whole earth   2.174-76;
for all ages, with their mighty children.[x2]   3:49; 8:169;
                                                                       Dan 2:44; 7:27

n2. Presumably 'Amr, the Arab leader.
o2. There is no (clear) previous reference. The
three are on the Roman side in the conflict. Scott
interprets the ram as the Patriarch Cyrus and takes
Cyrene as "Cyrus-land." Cyrus was a bishop in
Colchis before he was appointed Patriarch and Governor of Egypt in A.D. 631. Vs. 330 refers to the
failure of Cyrus to expel the invaders.
p2. Gk. *esset'* for *thēset'* (Wilamowitz). After an
armistice in A.D. 641 there was peace for four years.
In A.D. 645 the Romans broke the truce by a surprise
attack on Alexandria.
q2. Gk. *gaia(i)* for *paida* (Buresch). The reference
is to the return of the Arabs.
r2. Gk. *Ioudaioi* for *Ioudaious* (Scott). Since the
Sibyl is clearly favorable to the Arabs, she would not
refer to any Jews who may have been killed by the

invaders.
s2. Gk. *poinēn arnumenoi* for *poimene ampho-
teroi* (Scott). Scott suggests that the Jews were fighting to avenge Jerusalem.
t2. The Romans. "He" is presumably 'Amr.
u2. "Fair heads" refers to Germanic people in the
Roman army. "Egyptian birds" is a pun, since *aig-
uptios* also means vulture.
v2. Gk. *tous Arabas* for *tōn Arabōn* (Geffcken).
w2. The reference is clearly to Alexandria, although Scott entertains the possibility that it refers
to Jerusalem.
x2. Gk. *tekessi* for *tokeusin* (Rzach). The reference, of course, is to the eschatological kingdom of
the Jews. The concluding eschatological oracle may
be older than the remainder of SibOr 14.

THE SIBYLLINE ORACLES, FRAGMENTS

Introduction

As noted in the introduction to Sibylline Oracles 3, fragments 1–3 are probably part of the lost book 2 and belong with Sibylline Oracles 3.1–45. The major dissenter from this view is Geffcken, who regards them as Christian forgeries by Theophilus, but there is nothing in the fragments that requires Christian authorship.[1] Kurfess has attempted to locate the other fragments within the Sibylline corpus, but they are too brief to admit of confident identification.[2]

The theological significance of the fragments lies in their insistence on monotheism and denunciation of idolatry, a common theme in the Sibylline Oracles. They show no trace of the political concerns that dominate the other Jewish books and emphasize the spirituality and eternity of God in a manner reminiscent of Pseudo-Orpheus and Philo. The eschatology of the fragments is presented most fully in fragment 3 and has a strong otherworldly character. The wicked will be burned with torches for all eternity while the righteous will enjoy life in paradise. This emphasis on individual afterlife is quite atypical of the Jewish Sibylline Oracles and is most closely paralleled in the Christian redaction of Sibylline Oracles 2.

The fragments are found in Theophilus, *Ad Autolycum* 2.36 (frags. 1 and 3) and 2.3 (frag. 2) with some parallels in Clement and Lactantius. Fragments 4–7 are from Lactantius and fragment 8 is from Constantine's "Speech to the Saints."

---

[1] Geffcken, *Komposition und Entstehungszeit*, pp. 69–75. See the criticisms of Rzach, Pauly-Wissowa 2A, cols. 2129f.

[2] Kurfess, "Wie sind die Fragmenta der Oracula Sibyllina einzuordnen?" *Aevum* 26 (1952) 228–35.

THE SIBYLLINE ORACLES
Fragment One

Affirmation of monotheism

Mortal and fleshly men, who are nothing,   Frag. 3.21;

how do you so quickly exalt yourselves, while disregarding the end of   3.8-11, etc.; Clement, *Strom*

life?   3.3.14

You do not fear or revere God, who oversees you,   3.29

the Most High, the knowing, all-seeing, witness of everything,   2.177

5 the Creator who nourishes all, who put a sweet spirit   Lactantius, *DivInst* 4.6.5

in all and made it a guide for all mortals?   WisSol 1:7; 12:1

There is one God, who rules alone, exceedingly great, unbegotten,   3.11, etc; Prologue 95

universal ruler, invisible, who himself sees all things.   Lactantius, *DivInst* 1.6.15 3.12; Ps-Orph vs. 12

He is not seen by any mortal flesh.   (ed. Denis)

10 For what flesh can see with eyes the true and heavenly   3.17; 4.10-11; Frag. 3.15

immortal God, who inhabits the vault of heaven?   1Jn 4:12; Ps-Orph vs. 13 (ed. Denis), etc.

But men, who are mortal, are not even able   EpBar 5:10

to stand against the rays of the sun,[a]

men who are veins and flesh on bones.

15 Revere him who alone is ruler of the world.   Lactantius,

He is alone, from age to age,   *DivInst* 1.6.16

self-generated, unbegotten, ruling everything throughout.   3.12; 8.429, etc.

Administering judgment to all mortals in common light.   Ps-Orph vs. 10

You will have the appropriate reward of wickedness

20 because you abandoned the true and eternal God

and (ceased) to honor him and sacrifice sacred hecatombs

but made the sacrifices to the demons in Hades.   3.547; 8.393,47

You walk in affectation and madness, and, having abandoned   3.9f.,721; Clement, *Protr* 2:27

the straight, right path, you went away and wandered

25 through thorns and stakes. Vain mortals,

stop roaming in darkness and black night without light

and leave the darkness of night and take hold of light.   Jn 1:4-9; 8:12; 1Jn 1:6-7

Behold, he is clear and unwavering for all.   1QS 3

Come, do not always follow darkness and gloom.   Clement, *Strom* 5.14.116

30 Behold, the sweet light of the sun shines outstandingly.

Put wisdom in your breasts and have knowledge.

There is one God who sends showers, winds, and earthquakes,   Frag. 1.7, etc.

lightnings, famines, pestilence, and mournful woes,   2.23, etc.

snowstorms, and ice. Why do I name them individually?

35 He rules heaven; holds sway over earth, he himself exists.

Fragment Two

If gods beget and yet remain immortal   Constantine's

there would have been more gods born than men,   "Speech to the Saints," 4

and mortals would never even have a place to stand.

Fragment Three

Against idolatry

But if that which comes into being also absolutely perishes,   Lactantius, *DivInst* 1.8.3

---

a. Geffcken lists several Gk. parallels to this idea, notably Clement, *Protrepticus* 6.71, where such an idea is ascribed to Socrates.

a god cannot be formed from the thighs of man and a womb.
But God (is) alone, unique, supreme over all. He has made
heaven and sun and stars and moon,

5 fruitful earth and waves of water of the sea,
lofty mountains, perennial streams of springs.
Again, he begets an innumerable multitude of water creatures.
He sustains serpents which move on the earth
and diverse kinds of birds, shrill, lisping,

10 trilling, chirping, disturbing the air with their wings.
He placed a wild brood of beasts in the valleys of mountains
and made all cattle subject to us mortals.
He established a divinely fashioned ruler of all
and subordinated to man things diverse and incomprehensible.

15 For what flesh of mortals is able to know all these things?
But he alone knows, who made these things from the beginning,
the eternal incorruptible Creator who lives in the sky,
who provides for the good a much greater good as reward,
but stirs up wrath and anger against the wicked and unjust

20 and war and pestilence and tearful woes.
Men, why do you vainly exalt yourselves so that you will be rooted
    out?
Be ashamed of deifying polecats and brute beasts.[b]
Does not madness and frenzy take away the sense of the mind
if gods steal dishes and plunder pots?

25 And instead of living in the golden boundless vault of heaven
they appear moth-eaten and are woven with thick cobwebs.
Mindless ones, adoring snakes, dogs, and cats,
you revere birds and wild serpents of the earth
and stone statues and handmade images

30 and heaps of stones by the roads. These things you revere
and many other vain things which it is disgraceful even to mention.
There are gods which by deceit are leaders of mindless men,
from whose mouths pour deadly poison.
But he is life and imperishable eternal light,

35 and he pours out a delight sweeter than honey for men[c] . . .
Bend the neck to him alone
and you will incline your path among the pious ages.
Leaving all these things, you all with foolishness
and frenzied spirit quaffed a goblet full of judgment,

40 very pure, strong, well fortified, quite unmixed.
You are not willing to become sober and come to a prudent mind
and know God the king who oversees all.
Therefore the gleam of blazing fire comes upon you.
You will be burned with torches all day, thoughout eternity,

45 shamed by lies on account of useless idols.
But those who honor the true eternal God
inherit life, dwelling in the luxuriant garden
of Paradise for the time of eternity,
feasting on sweet bread from starry heaven.

Frag. 1.7, etc. Prologue 93-97
3.20-23

Gen 1:20-21

Gen 1:22

Gen 1:26;
Philo, *Op* 28
(84-86);
Ps 8:5-8

Job 38-42

Lactantius,
De ira Dei 22:7
Sir 39:25

3.603;
Ps-Orph vs. 16
(ed. Denis)
Frag. 1.2, etc.

3.30;
WisSol 15:18;
12:24

Frag. 3.22, etc.

3.31, etc.

5.77-79

1Jn 1:5;
Dan 2:22

Isa 51:17; Ps 60:3; Jer 25:15
Rev 14:8

Frag. 1.4,15,17,35

2.196, etc.

2.292, etc.

Lactantius, *DivInst* 2.12.19
Mt 19:29; Mk 10:17; Lk 18:18

2.316-38

2Bar 29:8; Ex 16:4; Jn 6:31-33

Fragment Four

Listen to me, articulate men, the eternal king reigns.

---

b. The worship of cats was a specifically Egyptian   c. Some words are missing in vss. 35f.
form of idolatry.

Fragment Five

Who alone is God, the invincible Creator.
He himself established the form of the shape of mortals.
He mingled the nature of all, begetter of life.

Prologue 98-100

Fragment Six

. . . whenever it comes
there will be fire in the dark middle of black night.

2.196, etc.

Fragment Seven

Uncreated God.

Fragment Eight

The Erythrean, then, to God: "Why, she says, O master,
do you inflict the compulsion of prophecy on me and
not rather guard me, lifted high above the earth,
until the day of your most blessed coming?"

3.1-5, etc.
3.296, etc.

Mal 3:2

TREATISE OF SHEM

(First Century B.C.)

A NEW TRANSLATION AND INTRODUCTION

BY J. H. CHARLESWORTH

This pseudepigraphon, attributed to Shem, the son of Noah, describes the characteristics of the year according to the house of the zodiac in which it begins. Documents like this one, which are technically called calendologia, are also attributed to other biblical personalities; one of these is called the *Revelatio Esdrae de qualitatibus anni*.[1] The Treatise of Shem contains twelve chapters, following the twelve signs of the zodiac running counterclockwise from Aries to Capricorn, but reversing the order of the last two so that Pisces precedes Aquarius. This inverted order was caused by a scribe who omitted a chapter in his haste to finish, but eventually added the missing chapter at the end. The scribe who copied the only extant manuscript, or an earlier scribe, warns the reader that a copyist's mistake places Aquarius after Pisces. Originally the twelve chapters were in an ascending order of desirable features, beginning with Aries, in which apparently the worst year begins, and culminating with Pisces, in which clearly the best year originates: "there will be peace and prosperity among men, and love and harmony among all the kings who are on the entire earth" (TrShem 11:18).

Text

The Treatise of Shem is preserved in a fifteenth-century Syriac manuscript, unbound, in the John Rylands University Library of Manchester (Syr. MS 44, fols. 81b–83b). The base for the present translation[2] is a critical edition I am preparing for the SBL Texts and Translations, Pseudepigrapha Series.

Original language

The four Greek loan words found in the Syriac text are not indicative that the original language is Greek. Each of them (see nn. a to ch. 3, c to ch. 5, d and k to ch. 7, d and g to ch. 11), with the possible exception of *harmonia*, "well-ordered" (see n. d to ch. 7), early passed into and became customary in Syriac. The original language seems to be Semitic

---

[1] See the contribution by D. A. Fiensy and the Introduction ("Theological importance") to the GkApEzra by M. E. Stone herein. Also see James, *LAOT*, pp. 80f., and Charlesworth, *PMR*, pp. 182–84. Reliable books are F. Cumont's *Astrology and Religion Among the Greeks and Romans*, trans. J. B. Baker (New York, 1912; repr. 1960); O. Neugebauer's *The Exact Sciences in Antiquity* (New York, 1957[2]); F. Cumont's *L'Égypte des astrologues* (Brussels, 1937); F. Boll's *Sternglaube und Sterndeutung: Die Geschichte und das Wesen der Astrologie*, ed. W. Gundel (Leipzig, Berlin, 1931[4]; repr. 1966 with additions by H. G. Gundel). I am grateful to Professors R. E. Brown and J. F. Oates for significant advice on improving the Introduction.

[2] The translation attempts to expose the meaning behind the cryptic language without becoming a subjective paraphrase. It is generally an idiomatic rendering; when necessary the literal meaning is supplied in the notes. Parentheses denote words necessary in idiomatic English; brackets circumscribe the boundaries of a textual restoration. I have attempted to be consistent: 'nš', "people," is distinguished from bnynš', "men"; agricultural terms are translated by the same word, tmrʾ, "date," ʿbwrʾ, "produce," prdtʾ, "rye," ʿlltʾ, "harvest," zrʿ, "grain," ḥṭʾ, "wheat," dqʾ, "dried peas," sʿrʾ, "barley," dwzʾ, "rice." Chs. and vss. are provided herein for the first time.

since there are abundant Semitisms that appear to be original and personal names are defined according to the Semitic alphabet (chs. 2, 6, 7, 8, 9, 10, 11, 12). Because of the lacunae and the corrupt nature of the Syriac text[3] it is impossible to discern whether the original language is Hebrew or Aramaic (Syr.). If the provenance is Alexandrian, then Aramaic would be a little more probable.

Date

It is impossible to date this document precisely and certainly; but it is logically justifiable to assume that the notations are not fictitious but historically based. If this assumption is correct, then the references to the Romans (1:5; 3:6f.; 11:12) would indicate that the document was composed in the Roman period. A. Mingana speculated that this treatise was composed after the ravaging of Palestine by Vespasian or Hadrian.[4] His suggestion is unlikely; by that time (c. A.D. 69–138) peace had been established in the Roman Empire, and the singular most notable feature regarding a date of composition is the pervasive references to wars, usually against the Romans (3:6f.; 1:9; 2:2; 3:3; 7:8, 18; 10:10f.; cf. 5:7; 6:13; 12:8). This concern coincides with the terror of war that characterized the eastern portion of the Empire during the first two thirds of the first century B.C., and until Octavian defeated Antony in 31 B.C. at Actium.[5] Octavian's own inscriptions and Virgil's writings demonstrate that Octavian was popularly conceived as the one who put an end to war.[6] The fear of war between Rome and Egypt—"And the king of the Romans will not remain in one place . . . a great war and misery (will occur) on all the earth, and especially in the land of Egypt" (1:5–9)—adequately describes the period when Antony was associated with Alexandria and "married according to Egyptian law" to Cleopatra (37–30 B.C.). This passage may also refer obliquely to the suicides of Antony and Cleopatra, and the merciless acts by Octavian in Alexandria in 30 B.C. The claim that the Romans will defeat the Parthians (3:6f.), if our restoration of the text is accurate, indicates a date shortly after Antony's victory over the Armenians, Medes, and Parthians, and the celebration of this triumph in Alexandria (not in Rome as tradition demanded) in the fall of 34 B.C. Likewise the reference in 12:4—"And Egypt (will rule) over Palestine"—also fits nicely into 34 B.C., because in that year Antony, out of his exigencies, especially his need for Cleopatra's money, granted her the rule over Palestine. Then she along with her son Caesarion began a joint reign over it.[7]

The second most notable feature regarding the date of composition is the reference to and fear of "robbers," "thieves," or "marauders" (cf. 7:20; 10:7; 11:11; 12:1; cf. 6:1; 10:1; 11:1). This concern recalls the period before Octavian strengthened the Empire, built impressive and extensive highways, and established a military police, which secured relatively speedy and safe travel within the Empire. These observations cumulatively suggest that the Treatise of Shem was composed in the last third of the first century B.C., probably sometime after the events in the thirties but when the memories of the preceding era were still fresh.

It is possible to speculate further regarding the date of composition. Antony or Cleopatra may be the subject of 2:3: "And a wind will go out from Egypt and will fill the entire earth."[8] A reference to the battle at Actium between Antony and Octavian may be couched

---

[3] See nn. f to ch. 2, e, g, and i to ch. 5, e to ch. 6, e, j, and o to ch. 7, d and g to ch. 8.

[4] *Some Early Judaeo-Christian Documents in the John Rylands University Library: Syriac Texts* (Manchester, 1917; pp. 20–29, 52–59; repr. from *BJRL* 4 [1917] 59–118).

[5] Conspicuously absent are references to the internal struggles within the Roman Empire during the 1st cent. A.D., Claudius' charge to the Alexandrians to be "tolerant and friendly to the Jews" (London Papyrus, 1912), the *Nero redivivus* myth, the two great Jewish wars (A.D. 66–70, 132–35), both of which exacted great costs in Alexandria—50,000 Jewish lives were lost there in the first war and the synagogue was burned in the second. No significant historical event after 30 B.C. seems to be portrayed in the TrShem.

[6] An inscription at Priene, which is just south of Ephesus in Asia Minor, dated 9 B.C., refers to Octavian as the "savior, who . . . put an end to war and . . . set everything in order." In his *Res gestae divi Augusti,* Octavian himself spoke of Actium as "the crowning victory," and pointed with justifiable pride at the peace he had established in the Empire: "I restored peace to all the provinces of Gaul and Spain and to Germany, to all . . ." With phrases reminiscent of the dream of a blessed future described in Isa 11, Virgil in his Fourth Eclogue (19–22) spoke of the age Octavian had inaugurated: "He shall receive the life of gods, and see/Heroes with gods commingling, and himself/Be seen of them, and with his father's worth/Reign o'er a world at peace." A reliable edition of the last two texts is contained in C. K. Barrett's *The New Testament Background: Selected Documents* (London, 1956; New York, 1961).

[7] See A. E. Samuel, *Ptolemaic Chronology* (MBPAR 43; Munich, 1962) p. 159.

[8] For a reliable discussion of Antony and Cleopatra, who are often presented romantically, see R. Syme, *The Roman*

in 2:10: "two kings will oppose one another." Antony's defeat by Octavian in the sea battle at Actium, and his subsequent suicide in Alexandria, may be mentioned in 6:13–17: "And the king [the Roman Emperor Octavian] will strive with a king [Antony] and will slay him. And Alexandria will be lost . . . And many ships will be wrecked." Another reference to the results of this battle may be found in the next chapter, 7:16f.: "And the king [Octavian] will stay in one place [Octavian ends the intermittent wars and resides in Rome]. And power will leave the land [Egypt will become the personal possession of Octavian, the first Roman king of Egypt].⁹ And the nobles will flee to the sea, and there will be between (them) [in the sea] a severe war." If these conjectures are sound, then our author was thinking about the vicissitudes of life evoked by the defeat of the seemingly invincible Antony and Cleopatra. Although they commanded nearly twice as many men and ships as Octavian, they both deserted Actium before the battle was decided; ironically this is one of the greatest non-battles of history.¹⁰ Hence, it appears that a Jew composed this astrological document after 31 B.C.,¹¹ probably by the late twenties, when the victory at Actium had become a major part of Roman propaganda.¹²

Provenance

The two most likely places in which this text was composed are Egypt (mentioned in chs. 1, 2, 7, 8, 9, 12) and Palestine (specified in chs. 4, 6, 11). The latter is improbable since there is a reference to robbers who come *from* Palestine ("And robbers will come from Palestine" [11:11]). The numerous references to the Nile (chs. 1, 2, 3, 4, 5, 6 [restored], 7, 8, 12) demonstrate that the provenance is probably Egyptian; and the products, wheat, barley, peas, are certainly Egyptian crops. The references to irrigation (1:4; 10:18) and illnesses caused by winds bearing desert sands (4:7) increase this probability. References to the city Alexandria (4:3 and 6:14) imply that the provenance may be Alexandrian. The description of the beneficial effects of the north wind (3:1; 5:1; 8:1), the harmful characteristics of the east wind (7:3; 10:2), and the continuous references to the sea (1:10; 2:12 [twice]; 3:7; 4:5; 7:18 [twice, once restored]; 11:5; cf. 10:5), the [se]acoast (10:15), fishing (11:5), and ships (1:10; 2:12; 3:7; 4:5; 6:16; 11:6) denote that the Treatise of Shem was composed probably in Alexandria.¹³

Revolution (Oxford, 1939) and H. H. Scullard, *From the Gracchi to Nero* (London, 1970). An attractive account of Alexandria is presented in E. M. Forster's *Alexandria: A History and a Guide* (Garden City, N.Y., 1961). Scholarly discussions of Jewish life in Alexandria can be found in V. Tcherikover's *Hellenistic Civilization and the Jews*, trans. S. Applebaum (New York, 1959; repr. 1970); in M. Stern's "The Jewish Diaspora," *The Jewish People in the First Century*, ed. S. Safrai and M. Stern (Assen, 1974) vol. 1, pp. 117–83; see also pp. 184–215; and in P. M. Fraser's *Ptolemaic Alexandria*, 3 vols. (Oxford, 1972).

⁹ According to Samuel, the Ptolemaic kingdom ended on August 3, 30 B.C.; the following year Octavian began to reign (*Ptolemaic Chronology*, p. 160).

¹⁰ "The battle of Actium was decided before it was fought" (Syme, *The Roman Revolution*, p. 296).

¹¹ Some critics will claim the obvious has not been stated emphatically, affirming the date suggested by pointing to the voluminous astrological treatises pseudonymously attributed to King Nechepso and his priest, Petosiris, that were composed in Alexandria sometime in the 2nd cent. B.C. (Boll, *Sternglaube*, p. 24; Fraser, *Ptolemaic Alexandria*, vol. 1, pp. 436f., vol. 2, pp. 632f.; M. Nilsson, *Geschichte der Griechischen Religion* [Handbuch der Altertums-wissenschaft 5.2.; Munich, 1955–61²] vol. 2, p. 269; earlier scholars dated these texts to the second third of the 1st cent. B.C., e.g. W. Kroll, "Nechepso," Pauly-Wissowa 16.2, cols. 2160–67; and E. Riess, "Astrologie," Pauly-Wissowa 2.2, cols. 1802–28, especially cols. 1816f.). Dating the TrShem in the last third of the 1st cent. B.C. fits nicely with the observation that astrology began to be popular about the time of Jesus' birth (Nilsson, *Geschichte*, vol. 2, p. 276).

¹² For the myth of Actium see Syme, *The Roman Revolution*, pp. 297, 440f. Professor J. F. Oates, who read this contribution, opinioned in a letter of February 22, 1978: "I was convinced that this is the area in which we must date it. It must come after 63 B.C., Pompeii's settlement of the East, and before A.D. 69, the Jewish revolt. Within that time period the whole set of references to particular Roman activity, as well as the movement of the vernal equinox from the House of Aires to Pisces at exactly this time, convinces me that we are talking about a period in the late 20's B.C." The severe earthquake in Palestine, which occurred during the battle at Actium, may also have been in the author's mind when he composed 7:19 (see n. k to ch. 7).

¹³ Alexandria during the hellenistic period was characterized by its astrological ideas (cf. especially Cumont, *L'Egypte des astrologues*; Nilsson, *Geschichte der Griechischen Religion*, vol. 2, pp. 268–81; Fraser, *Ptolemaic Alexandria*, vol. 1, pp. 434f.). For examples of zodiacal papyri in late Ptolemaic and early Roman Egypt see O. Neugebauer and R. A. Parker, *Egyptian Astronomical Texts*, 4 vols. (London, 1960–69; especially see vol. 3, pp. 203–12 and vol. 4, plates 46, 47, and 48). As usual, there are problems that preclude certainty regarding a provenance. Rain is mentioned throughout the treatise, and it almost never rains in Egypt. Perhaps such comments are a convention of this type of writing, or an aspect of the author's dream for a better day (in Jub 12:16–18 Abraham is portrayed as looking to the signs of the stars to see what the year would bring in terms of rain).

Historical importance

A few decades ago historians had no clear evidence that Jews composed astrological tracts at the time of Jesus; many good scholars thought this interest surfaced only late in medieval Jewish mysticism. Even quite recently the erudite and informed editors of the *Encyclopedia Judaica* reported that the zodiac is "first mentioned in the *Sefer Yeẓirah*," a document dated somewhere between the third and sixth centuries (*EncyJud*, vol. 16, col. 1191).

Jewish interest in astrology and the zodiac is at least so early as Jesus of Nazareth.[14] This new insight is demonstrated by the early date of the Jewish Sibylline Oracles, especially 5.512–31,[15] and the discovery among the Dead Sea Scrolls of two Jewish astrological documents, one called 4QCryptic (formerly 4Q186)[16] and the other still unnamed and unpublished.[17]

The clearest and fullest evidence for an early Jewish interest in astrology had been unknown to scholars, although it has been shelved for most of this century in the famous John Rylands University Library of Manchester, England. The document is of course the Treatise of Shem, and like 4QCryptic the concern is not with daily manipulations of nature and man by the stars but with the determination of the year or of people (cf. TrShem 8:12) according to the zodiacal house in which they originate or are born.

If the historical reconstruction attempted above is accurate, we have a significant and unparalleled Jewish response to one of the most significant and epoch-making sea battles in the history of our culture. Jewish soldiers from King Herod of Judea along with troops from throughout the Eastern Empire united under Antony. Octavian won the battle, nevertheless, and his success at Actium enabled him to unite the "civilized" world and to lay the foundations for the greatness of the Roman Empire. He received the title that had been reserved for the gods, and even today he is known as Augustus ("the exalted one"). Significant for an understanding of many passages in the Treatise of Shem is the recognition that Augustus Caesar took Egypt as his own personal possession and began to export Egyptian grain to Rome.

Theological importance

The contention that if the year begins in Virgo then a Jew whose name contains a *y*, *s*, *b*, and *n* will be robbed and forced to flee his home contradicts the ancient tradition that the Jewish home is protected by God (e.g. cf. Ex 12:13, 22) and each member in it is protected by the solidarity of the family (cf. Lev 25:25; 47–49; Gen 4:23f.). The pervasive idea that fortune, the rise of the Nile, the movement of the stars and the moon, health, and a good harvest depend upon the power of the zodiac flagrantly compromises the ancient tradition that God is lord of the universe (cf. Pss 24, 29) and actively involved in the processes of history (e.g. cf. the cultic confession of faith in Deut 26:5–9; cf. Ps 8). The claim that ample rain depends upon the house of the zodiac in which the year begins compromises the belief that God controls the rain (e.g. cf. Amos 4:7; Zech 10:1), a central Jewish belief popularized by the colorful account of Elijah's successful prayer for rain on Mount Carmel (1Kgs 18:1, 41–46),[18] and contradicts the idea that people can effect the amount of rain by petition(s), prayers, and other actions (TrShem 10:17).

In the Pseudepigrapha this biblical perspective is reaffirmed in an antiastrological context. The author of Jubilees, who venerated Shem (cf. Jub 7:10–18; 8:18; 10:13f.; 19:24f.),

---

[14] See my "Jewish Astrology in the Talmud, Pseudepigrapha, the Dead Sea Scrolls and Early Palestinian Synagogues," *HTR* 70 (1977) 183–200.

[15] See the discussion and translation of the SibOr herein by J. J. Collins. Book 5 was composed early in the 2nd cent. A.D. The TrShem is at least a century older, according to our dating.

[16] Published by J. M. Allegro in "An Astrological Cryptic Document from Qumran," *JSS* 9 (1964) 291–94; repr. DJD 5, 88–91, plate XXXI. See J. Carmignac, "Les Horoscopes de Qumran," *RQ* 5 (1965) 199–217.

[17] See J. T. Milik, *Ten Years of Discovery in the Wilderness of Judaea*, trans. J. Strugnell (SBT 26; London, 1959) p. 42.

[18] The only scholar who has read and commented on the TrShem besides Mingana, E. R. Goodenough, claims correctly that the thin veneer of Judaism in the TrShem discloses that the author did not relate his astrological beliefs to his Jewish faith; he writes, "a Jew would seem to have believed in both Judaism and astrology but to have been content to join the two together thus loosely rather than try really to fuse them." See his *Jewish Symbols in the Greco-Roman Period* (New York, 1958) vol. 8, p. 199.

explicitly rejected[19] ideas characteristic of the Treatise of Shem.

> And in the sixth week, in its fifth year, Abram sat up during
> the night on the first of the seventh month,[20] so that he might observe the
> stars from evening until daybreak so that he might see what
> the nature of the year would be with respect to rain.
> And he was sitting alone and making observations;
> And a word came into his heart, saying:
> "All of the signs of the stars and the signs of the sun and the
> moon are in the hand of the LORD. Why am I seeking?
> > If he desires, he will make rain morning and evening,
> > And if he desires he will not send (it) down;
> > And everything is in his hand." (Jub 12:16–18)

While Jubilees 12, of course, was not written against the Treatise of Shem, it was directed against the astrological claims that the zodiac determined yearly rainfall, an idea expressed, for example, in the Treatise at 5:1: "*And if the year begins in Leo*: there will be spring rains, then the soil will be deprived of the north winds."

The author clearly contradicts his astrological ideas when he affirms the older tradition that God is efficacious; he hears petitions and prayers for rain (8:3; 10:17; cf. 12:9). It is significant that the author refers to God only three times (8:3; 11:17; 12:9) and that twice he uses the phrase "the living God."

The author of the Treatise of Shem was apparently a Jew. Some hellenistic Jews considerably compromised ancient traditions as they became accommodated to foreign lands and customs. Diasporic Judaism, and even Palestinian Judaism, was not guided by an established orthodoxy. The Treatise of Shem significantly improves our perception of the variegated nature of intertestamental Judaism; mere possession of it should invalidate the recent claim that astrology in Judaism was never more than a Qumranite or sectarian aberration.[21]

Noticeably absent in this document are references to angels, a belief in immortality or a resurrection from the dead, and the various levels of heaven. No Jewish festivals are noted except Passover (1:8; 6:12) and the references to it may simply be another indication of the Egyptian provenance.

The author (or a later copyist) may have attributed this document to Shem because he was the oldest son of Noah (Gen 10:21; cf. Jub 4:33), was greatly blessed and loved by his father

---

[19] Other significant arguments against astrology are as follows: According to the author of the early chapters of 1En, astrology is an evil and demoniac idea since it was taught to men by one of the fallen angels, Baraqiyal (1En 8:3). The third book of the SibOr (c. 2nd cent. B.C.) in ll. 220–36 praises righteous men who neither search the mystical meaning of the movements of the heavenly bodies nor are deceived by the predictions of Chaldean astrology. Philo of Alexandria (c. 25 B.C.–A.D. 45) attempted to refute the ideas of the astrologers and argued that Moses, although he apparently had a concept of the universe similar to that of the astrologers, taught that God alone is in control of creation, but he never suggested that the "stars or their motions" affected the fate of men (*Migr* 32). Josephus mentions that the veil of the Temple, which was composed of Babylonian tapestry, "typified the universe" and possessed "mystic meaning," but although it "portrayed a panorama of the heavens, the signs of the zodiac" were not represented (*War* 5.212–14; cf. *War* 6.228–92). Later R. Johanan argued against Jewish interest in astrology by teaching that Israel is immune from planetary influence (b.Shab. 156a). The entire fourth book of Hippolytus' *Ref* is directed against astrology and speculations regarding the influence of the zodiac; his attention is directed against the belief that one's fate is determined by the house of the zodiac that is rising over the horizon at the moment of birth, an idea different from the thoughts in the TrShem but similar to those in 4QCryptic. For an informative account of the attempts by Octavian and others to control the volatile speculations of the astrologers, see R. MacMullen, "Astrologers, Diviners, and Prophets," *Enemies of the Roman Order* (Cambridge, Mass., 1966) pp. 128–62. For further discussion see *HTR* 70 (1977) 183–200.

[20] I.e. Tishri, the beginning of the Jewish year. "There are four 'New Year' days: on the 1st of Nisan . . . on the 1st of Elul . . . on the 1st of Tishri is the New Year for [the reckoning of] the years [of foreign kings], of the Years of Release and Jubilee years, for the planting [of trees] and for vegetables; and the 1st of Shebat . . ." (RH 1.1). H. Danby, *The Mishnah* (Oxford, 1933) p. 188. Danby notes that Tishri "is alone spoken of throughout the rest of the tractate as 'the New Year.' "

[21] M. R. Lehman, using the outmoded paradigm of "normative Judaism," claims solely on the basis of 4QCryptic and an enigmatic passage in the Talmud that "astrology never got a permanent foothold in Judaism, since it was, from the beginning, fraught with sectarian overtones." See his "New Light on Astrology in Qumran and the Talmud," *RQ* 32 (1975) 599–602. It should be added that astrology did make a "foothold in Judaism" as demonstrated by R. P. Hanina b. Hama: "The stars make one wise, the stars make one rich, and there are stars for Israel" (b.Shab. 156a). For an excellent survey of astrology in Judaism see A. Altman, "Astrology," *EncyJud* 3, cols. 788–95. Also see my article on the subject in *HTR* 70 (1977) 183–200.

(Gen 9:26; Jub 7:11f.; 8:18; 10:14; cf. TSim 6:5), was considered "highly honored" (Sir 49:16), and was a major figure in the sacred line that runs from Adam to Abraham (Gen 11:10–33; Jub 19:24–31). He receives as an inheritance "the middle of the earth" (Jub 8:12–30), which included the Promised Land and the three dwellings of God, the garden of Eden, Mount Sinai, and Mount Zion (Jub 8:18f.). Moreover, according to some ancient traditions, the angels taught Noah every kind of medicine and the cure for diseases; he in turn wrote all these things in a book and gave it to Shem (Jub 10:10–14). These traditions could easily have caused a Jew to attribute the ideas contained in the present document to Shem.[22]

Relation to canonical books

Intermittently throughout the preceding discussion the Treatise of Shem has been compared with the Old Testament. The few parallels emphasize a difference in perspective. For example, the Old Testament prophets prophesy about what is soon to happen because of God's involvement in history; the author of the Treatise of Shem predicts events potentially far distant in the future because of the effect of the zodiac upon earthly cycles. The Old Testament writers saw the stars as obeying God's commands and displaying his glory;[23] the author of the Treatise of Shem claimed the heavenly bodies caused events to happen on the earth.

One passage in the New Testament[24] receives new illumination because of the discovery of Jewish interest in astrology prior to Jesus and his followers. Matthew 2:2 mentions that the wise men (*magoi*) came to Judea to see a newly born King of the Jews because "we have seen his star in the East . . ." (RSV). An alternative and better translation is "we saw his star as it rose . . ." (JB) or "we saw his star when it came up in the east . . ." (GNMM).[25] With either translation, and especially with the latter, it is conceivable that the author of this tradition—either Matthew himself or more probably[26] another Jewish Christian before him—was influenced by astrological predictions. So strong were the astrological overtones in this verse (and Mt 2:9) that some early Christians claimed it proved "that astrology may be depended on."[27] Eventually St. John Chrysostom in the fourth and St. Augustine in the fifth century were forced to direct one or more sermons against an astrological interpretation of Matthew 2:1–12. St. Augustine became embroiled in a heated controversy and the influence of his opponents can be surmised by the words he used: "This star confounded the meaningless reckonings and prognostications of the astrologers when it showed these worshippers of stars

---

[22] Shem was also accorded a significant place in holy history in later Jewish writings; cf. N. Pavoncello, "La scuola di Shem e di Ever nella tradizione rabbinica," *RevistB* 27 (1979) 325–29. The TrShem is significantly different from other documents attributed to Shem. Most notable among these are the gnostic Paraphrase of Shem (Nag Hammadi Codex VII, 1) and the medieval *Kitāb al-Ikhtilājāt* (T-S A45.21), or the "Book of Twitches" composed by Shem (ed. by S. Hopkins, *A Miscellany of Literary Pieces from the Cambridge Genizah Collections* [Cambridge University Library Genizah Series 3; Cambridge, 1978] pp. 69–71).

[23] Cf. especially Isa 40:26; 45:12; Pss 19:1, 5f.; 148:3. The concept reappears in the Pseudepigrapha: 2Bar 3:34f.; 1En 18:13–16; 21:1–6; 41:5; 86:1–6; 4Ezra 6:3. I am indebted here to W. Foerster, "*astēr, astron*," *TDNT* 1 (1964) 503–5. King Josiah deposed the priests "who offered sacrifice to Baal, to the sun, the moon, the constellations and the whole array of heaven" (2Kgs 23:5, JB).

[24] Rev 4:6–8, which describes the four living creatures that surround the heavenly throne, and Rev 12:1, which describes a woman crowned with "twelve stars," are usually interpreted in terms of the zodiac. The first passage represents the four main zodiacal constellations (Taurus, Leo, Scorpio, Aquarius), the second portrays the twelve signs of the zodiac. See R. H. Charles, *The Revelation of St. John*, 2 vols. (ICC; Edinburgh, 1920, repr. 1963 and 1966) vol. 1, pp. 122f., 315f.

[25] The GNMM is the translation behind E. Schweizer's *The Good News According to Matthew*, trans. D. E. Green (Atlanta, 1975).

[26] Schweizer correctly sees two traditions behind Mt 2:1–12, one that emphasized the struggle between Herod and the newborn king and another that had as its motif "the homage offered by the astrologers." These traditions were of different origin, and "Matthew was probably the first to link the two traditions." *Good News According to Matthew*, pp. 36f. Another careful argument for the independent prior character of the tradition about the wise men has been published recently by F. Zinniker, *Probleme der sogenannten Kindheitsgeschichte bei Mattäus* (Freiburg, 1972) cf. especially p. 167.

[27] The quotation from these Christians is preserved by St. John Chrysostom; *Homilies on the Gospel of Saint Matthew*, trans. G. Prevost, rev. M. B. Riddle (Nicene and Post-Nicene Fathers 10; New York, 1894) Homily 6, p. 36. Gk.: *hoper esti sēmeion tou tēn astrologian einai bebaian.*

that the Creator of heaven and earth was worthier of adoration.''[28] In an earlier sermon St. Augustine claimed that ''the star did not determine the marvels of Christ's birth, but Christ determined the appearance of the star among His other miracles.''[29]

The new evidence for astrology among the Jews and the early astrological interpretation of Matthew 2:1–12 should demonstrate that merely discussing the obviously striking parallels between these verses and the tradition about Balaam as recorded in Numbers 22:1–24:25, which have been demonstrated by A. Paul and R. E. Brown,[30] does not totally exhaust the rich complexities in Matthew. It is no longer justifiable to approach Matthew 2 with the assumption that all Jews believed the stars intervened in man's destiny *only* in line with God's will; and it is unwise to presuppose that Matthew's wise men *must* be pagans because of their astrological beliefs.[31] Astrological speculation could well have been linked with Jesus' birth by Jewish Christians before Matthew wrote.[32] At his birth (or close to it)[33] Jupiter and Saturn over a period of *eight months* were in conjunction three times in Pisces, the Hebrew zodiacal sign and the sign of the last days.[34] Later Jewish and Jewish-Christian astrologers could well have noted the significance: Jupiter, the ''star''[35] that denoted kingship, was linked with Saturn, the ''star'' that represented Israel (or Palestine). A derived meaning

---

[28] St. Augustine, *Sermons on the Liturgical Seasons,* trans. M. S. Muldowney (The Fathers of the Church 38; New York, 1959) Sermon for the Epiphany, Sermon 201, p. 67.

[29] Ibid., Sermon 199, p. 62.

[30] A. Paul correctly argues that this ''coincidence is certainly not fortuitous.'' See his list of six parallels between Mt and Num; *L'Évangile de l'enfance selon saint Matthieu* (Lire la Bible 17; Paris, 1968) pp. 100–4. See R. E. Brown, ''The Balaam Narrative,'' *The Birth of the Messiah* (Garden City, N.Y., 1977) pp. 190–96.

[31] These assumptions are expressed either explicitly or implicitly by A. Paul, who eventually reaffirms the ancient tradition that the wise men were disciples of Zarathustra (*L'Évangile de l'enfance,* pp. 104–12, 116–25). R. A. Oriti incorrectly states, ''Since the Jews were not believers in astrology, they would attribute no special significance to the chance grouping of planets.'' ''The Star of Bethlehem,'' *Griffith Observer* 39 (1975) 9–14. The wise men are called Zoroastrians in Leeds Arabic MS No. 184 (c. 18th cent.), which is a four..h version (Arabic four) of the oriental form of the Tiburtine Sibyl: ''The Zoroastrians shall come from the east, bearing gifts for him'' (p. 293). While there is no literary dependence between this text and the TrShem, there are some interesting similarities. Note, for example, vs. 9: ''The ninth sun is the ninth age, in which the Lion Cub shall come out of the west, and rebuild the earth's ruins, and the world shall be prosperous and the fruit of the earth shall multiply . . .'' (pp. 302f.). See E. Y. Ebied and M. J. L. Young, ''An Unrecorded Arabic Version of a Sibylline Prophecy,'' *Orientalia Christiana Periodica* 43 (1977) 279–307.

[32] A cuneiform tablet, the Celestial Almanac of Sippar, predicted the triple conjunction of Saturn, Jupiter, and Mars in 7 B.C. Hence, astrologers and astronomers eagerly anticipated the celestial wonder. See the discussion and bibliographical notes in E. Stauffer, *Jesus and His Story,* trans. R. and C. Winston (New York, 1960); especially see pp. 32–34, 217.

[33] Jesus' birth, according to critical research, is placed between 8 and 6 B.C.; in 7 B.C. there was a conjunction of Jupiter and Saturn three times (thanks to the optical illusion of retrograde motion) in Pisces: in late May and early June, throughout October, and in early December. See the astronomical tables published by W. D. Stahlman and O. Gingerich, *Solar and Planetary Longitudes for Years −2500 to +2000 by 10-Day Intervals* (Madison, Wisc., 1963) p. 306. Shortly after this threefold conjunction, on February 19, 6 B.C., Mars was in conjunction with Saturn, ''but the Magi, though they were expecting it, probably were prevented from observing it because the sun had by now moved into the area and all three planets were almost certainly lost in the glare of sunset.'' R. S. Knapp, *A Star of Wonder* (Chapel Hill, N.C., 1967) p. 15. For assistance in this research I am grateful to R. S. Knapp and J. P. Charlesworth, both of the Morehead Planetarium.

[34] W. Sinnott claims that Matthew's star was probably the conjunction of Venus with Jupiter on June 17, 2 B.C., which occurred in Leo (a lion according to early Semitic records, and Judah is called a ''lion's whelp'' in Gen 49:9f.) with the planets equidistant from the star Regulus (prince), which always remains between Leo's feet (cf. Gen 49:9f.). See his ''Thoughts on the Star of Bethlehem,'' *Sky and Telescope* (December 1968) 384–86. Also see the response to Sinnott by the editor in chief, C. A. Federer, who offers the opinion ''that Ensign Sinnott's results make the Star of Bethlehem more plausible astronomically than it has seemed heretofore.'' ''Rambling Through December Skies,'' *Sky and Telescope* (December 1968) 390, 396.

[35] Mt uses the noun *astēr,* ''star,'' not *astron,* ''star, constellation.'' Ignatius (Eph 19.2) also uses the noun *astēr.* R. Rodman argues that *astēr* should not be taken to denote a conjunction of planets because *astron* would more appropriately represent ''conjunction'' and *planēs* ''planet.'' (''A Linguistic Note on the Christmas Star,'' *Griffith Observer* 40 [1976] 8f.) *Astron,* however, does not mean ''conjunction,'' and *astēr* does mean ''planet'' only when combined with *planēs,* as Rodman reports: *planēs astēr* means ''wandering star.'' But Mt, who was a Semite not a Greek, did not originate the account (see n. 21), rather he adapted the earlier tradition in line with his pervasive emphasis upon the fulfillment of messianic prophecies. One should remember that *astēr* is generic and might even represent a ''comet,'' since Origen, who obviously wrote in Gk., claimed that the star was ''a new star'' (*astera en tē anatolē kainon*) like a comet or meteor. He claims that Chaeremon the Stoic's *Treatise on Comets* shows that comets occasionally did portend *good* things (*Contra Celsum,* bk. 1, 58f.). It seems unlikely, however, that *astēr* denoted the conjunction of two planets; it is more likely that the author of the tradition, if he used *astēr,* was focusing upon the unique behavior of Saturn, the star of Israel.

seems clear: In the last days a great king shall be born in Israel.[36] Proof of astrological speculations among the Jews prior to the birth of Christianity, as now demonstrated by the recovery of the Treatise of Shem, coupled with the indisputable fact of a "most unusual celestial display"[37] near the time of Jesus' birth by no means prove that Matthew 2 preserves reliable historical information; but it is now more difficult to claim that Matthew's star was created purely out of a myth.

Cultural importance

It is significant that the Treatise of Shem was composed about the time that the vernal equinox (the traditional beginning of the year, the start of spring) moved from Aries to Pisces, where it has been ever since, although it is about to move into Aquarius. This change, G. de Santillana has argued, would have evoked strong "astrological emotion" since one age was succeeding another.[38] It is certainly not clear, however, that this phenomenon was perceived or comprehended in antiquity. If it was, then the Treatise of Shem would be an unparalleled record of this monumental shift, the Precession of the Equinoxes.

The cultural importance of this document is even greater if, indeed, it reflects the unexpected demise of Antony and Cleopatra at Actium and their subsequent suicides in Alexandria. It becomes the first link in that literary chain of classics that features and exposes the paradigm of Antony and Cleopatra's paradoxical lives and love. It would be difficult to overestimate the influence upon our culture of such masterpieces as Plutarch's *Life of Marcus Antonius*, Shakespeare's *The Tragedy of Antony and Cleopatra*, Dryden's *All for Love*, and Shaw's *Caesar and Cleopatra*.

SELECT BIBLIOGRAPHY

Charlesworth, *PMR*, pp. 182–84.

Charlesworth, J. H. "Rylands Syriac MS 44 and a New Addition to the Pseudepigrapha: The Treatise of Shem," *BJRULM* 60 (1978) 376–403.
————. "Jewish Astrology in the Talmud, Pseudepigrapha, Dead Sea Scrolls, and Early Palestinian Synagogues," *HTR* 70 (1977) 183–200.
Mingana, A. "The Book of Shem Son of Noah," *Some Early Judaeo-Christian Documents in the John Rylands Library: Syriac Texts.* Manchester, 1917; pp. 20–29 (intro. and ET), 52–59 (text); reprint from *BJRL* 4 (1917) 59–118.

---

[36] This interpretation has been defended repeatedly and has been reasserted recently by E. Nellessen (*Das Kind und seine Mutter: Struktur und Verkündigung des 2. Kapitels im Matthäusevangelium* [Stuttgarter Bibelstudien 39; Stuttgart, 1969] pp. 117–19, and Zinniker [*Probleme*] pp. 111–15).

[37] For Matthew's wise men this phenomenon would have been "a powerful and awesome omen, (in fact this kind of planet arrangement takes place only every eight centuries)." Knapp, *A Star of Wonder*, p. 15.

[38] G. de Santillana, *Hamlet's Mill: An Essay on Myth and the Frame of Time* (Boston, Mass., 1969) p. 145.

THE TREATISE COMPOSED BY SHEM, THE SON OF NOAH, CONCERNING THE BEGINNING OF THE YEAR AND WHATEVER[a] OCCURS IN IT[b]

1,2 **1** *If the year begins in Aries*[c]: The year will be lean. •Even[d] its four-footed (animals) will
3 die; and many clouds will neither be visible nor appear.[e] •And grain will not reach (the
4 necessary) height,[f] but its[g] rye will (reach good height) and will ripen. •And the river Nile
5 will overflow[h] (at) a good rate. •And the king of the Romans will not remain in one place.
6 And the stars of heaven will be dispersed as sparks of fire;[i] and the moon will be eclipsed.[j]
7,8 And the first grain will die, but the last grain will be harvested. •And from Passover [until
9 the New Year][k] produce will have a blight.[l] •And the year will be bad, for a great war and
10 misery (will occur) on all the earth, and especially in the land of Egypt. •And many ships
11 will be wrecked when the sea billows. •And oil will be valued in Africa; but wheat will be
12 reduced in value in Damascus and Hauran; but in Palestine it[m] will be valued. •And (in that
13 region there will be) various diseases, and sicknesses, even fighting[n] will occur in it.[o] •But
it will be allowed to escape from it[p] and be delivered.

1 **2** *And if the year begins in Taurus*: Everyone whose name contains a Bēth, or Yūdh, or
2 Kāph will become ill, or be wounded by an iron (weapon). •And there will be fighting.[a]
3,4 And a wind will go out from Egypt and will fill the entire earth. •And in that (year)[b] there
will be wheat and abundant rains, but the nobles[c] of the land and of the surrounding region
5 will destroy (the crops).[d] •And [the rain][e] of (this) year will be withheld for three months,
6 and afterward produce will be exceedingly expensive for thirty-six days. •And many people
7 will die from diseases of the throat, then leanness will cease.[f] •And the first grain will perish

---

1 a. MS: *w'lm'*, "world, age"; ed. corr.: *wklm'*, "whatever." According to the author of Jub, Shem inherited Palestine when the earth was distributed among the sons of Noah. The land given to Ham is hot, that to Japheth is cold, but that to Shem is neither hot nor cold (see Jub 8:12–30, esp. vs. 18). According to the Book of the Bee (ch. 21), Noah commands Shem "to see the sources of the rivers and the seas and the structure of the earth." ET: E. A. W. Budge, *The Book of the Bee* (Anecdota Oxoniensia, Semitic Semes 1.2; Oxford, 1886) p. 35.

b. Nothing—not even a dot or space—distinguishes the title from the body of the text; both are on the same line and in red ink.

c. Italics denote red lettering in the MS. The author obviously is thinking about the houses (geoarc) of the zodiac, which change approximately every two hours as the earth daily rotates on its axis. He is not referring to the signs (heliarc) of the zodiac, which divide the year into twelve parts as the earth revolves around the sun. Each year begins in a different house, but years begin in the same sign for intervals of approximately two thousand years. Since the beginning of recorded history years have begun in only three signs: Taurus, Aries, and Pisces.

d. *Waw* copula is translated in numerous ways: "then," "and," "although," "but," "even," "for." In a more idiomatic translation the superfluous *Waw* would be omitted.

e. Lit. "come to pass."

f. Lit. "And grain, height will not be to it."

g. The pronoun refers back to Aries.

h. Fol. 81b ends. Lit. "will overflow a good overflow."

i. Perhaps this sentence means that there will be meteor showers.

j. In this text *nez'ar*, "it will become feeble," means "it will be eclipsed." See 4:4. In Syr. "the waning moon" is *sahrâ khadh ḥassîr*.

k. A lacuna of 50 mm., room for approximately fourteen letters. Ed. proposes: [*'dmt lwt ryš š]ñt'*, "until the New Year."

l. Or, "mildew."

m. Lit. "they will be valued"; but "wheat" is lit. "grains of wheat."

n. Syr. *wzyn'* means "and weapons" but in some phrases denotes "war." However, our author in 1:9 uses *qrb'* to denote war. Mingana suggested emending the text to *zw'*, "earthquake."

o. I.e. Palestine.

p. The MS incorrectly has a dot over the *H*.

2 a. See n. n, ch. 1. Mingana emended the text to *zw'*, "earthquake."

b. Lit. "it."

c. "Abundant" and "nobles" are both from *rawr'bhâ*.

d. Lit. "them."

e. A lacuna of 10 mm., which is approximately the size of *mṭr'* in the preceding line. Parts of the *m* and *'a* are barely visible. *wmṭr'*, "and rain," moreover, is written in the margin.

f. This phrase is unattractive and unsophisticated in Syr. *qṭynwt'*, "leanness," is usually a word with good connotations: "fineness." *'bd*, "cease," lit. means "perish" (see the next verb in the text).

8 in like manner, but the last grain will be harvested.ᵍ •And barleyʰ and dried peasⁱ will (also)
9,10 be harvested. •And devils will attack men but will not harm them in any way. •And two
11,12 kings will oppose one another. •And the large river Nile will rise above its banks.ʲ •Those
who are on a ship in the midst of the sea or people who are on the sea will be in severe
13 misery. •But at the close of the year there will be great blessing.

1 **3** *And if the year begins in Gemini*: The moon will be beautiful and a north wind will blow
2 and rain will come from it. •And everyone whose name has a Taw, or Ḥēth, or Mīm will
3 have on his faceᵃ leprosyᵇ or a mark. •And in the beginning of the year there will be a harsh
4 war.ᶜ •And there will be spring rains and grain [will be good]ᵈ and beautiful, and especially
5,6 the grain that has been irrigated. •And miceᵉ will multiplyᶠ on the earth. •And the Romans
7 [and the Parthian]sᵍ will make severe wars with each other. •And the Romans will proceed
8 by ships on the sea, then they will cause a war and destroy the (Parthians).ʰ •And evil people
will proceed in this world and they will do evil;ⁱ then there will be anxiety and harsh misery.
9 But at the end of the year there will be prosperity; even the river Nile will overflow
exceedingly.

1 **4** *And if the year begins in Cancer*: In the beginning of the year there will be a sufficiency
2 of produce and people will be healthy.ᵃ •And the Nile will overflow half its (usual) rate.ᵇ
3,4 And Alexandria will be afflicted, and misery from the plague will be in it. •And the stars
5 will shine magnificently for the moon will be eclipsed.ᶜ •And many ships will be wrecked
6,7 in the sea.ᵈ •And in the beginning of the ye[ar wheat and barley will be expensive.]ᵉ •And
winds will increase, then many people will be ill from sties (of the eyes) and from coughing
8 and vomiting.ᶠ •And wine will be abundant, but bulls, and sheep, and small cattle will perish,
9,10 even dried peas will perish. •But oil will compensate (for) them.ᵍ •Then at the end of the
11 year the harvest will be wearisomeʰ for nine days, but afterward there will be rain. •And
great blessing will be in (this year).ⁱ

---

g. Cf. 1:7 in which the verb *ʿt* is an imperfect; here
it is an active participle with passive meaning.
h. A plural noun in Syr.
i. *Legumen aridum*, cf. R. Payne Smith's *Thesaurus Syriacus*, vol. 1, cols. 297f. Also see R. Köbert's
Vocabularium Syriacum, p. 45. Mingana, incorrectly:
"the watered cereals."
j. Lit. "its measure."

3 a. Gk. *prosōpon*.
b. There may be a play on words between *garbᵉyâ*,
"north," and *garbâ*, "leprosy."
c. The scribe errs and writes twice "a harsh war."
d. A lacuna of approximately 12 mm., just enough
room for *ntʾb*, "will be good." The scribe extends
the *T* far above the other consonants and here it is
visible above the lacuna.
e. Syr. *wᶜqwbrʾ* is an error for *wᶜwqbrʾ*. In Syr.
MSS the consonants *q* and *w* are easily confused; in
MS 44 they are distinguishable.
f. Mingana was surprised by this verb form; it is
an Aphel active participle masculine plural: *masgîn*.
g. A lacuna of approximately 13 mm., or enough
room for five or six consonants plus the final *ʾA*,
which is barely visible. Mingana restored *wprsyʾ*,
"and the Persians." This restoration is philologically
possible, but the Romans fought the Egyptians and
Parthians. "Egyptians" is unlikely as a restoration
because the bottom of the *ṣ* in *mṣryʾ* would have been
visible since the lacuna does not extend far enough
below the line to absorb the long infralinear tail (see
mṣryn in l. 9 of the same folio). Restore: [*wprtwy*]ʾ,
"[and the Parthian]s."
h. Lit. "them."

i. The verbs and their forms in this sentence are
identical with the first two verbs in the preceding
sentence.

4 a. Fol. 82a ends.
b. Lit. "And the Nile will ascend half its ascent."
c. See n. j, ch. 1.
d. Mingana forgot to translate this sentence.
e. A lacuna of approximately 50 mm. A hand
different from the original scribe's has added these
words in the right margin of fol. 82b. This hand
appears to have written *nʾqdn*, "will be burned,"
instead of *nʾqrn*, "will be expensive." See 2:5,
"produce will be exceedingly expensive."
f. The word in the MS, *wrsᶜʾ*, is not found in the
Syr. lexicons by R. Payne Smith and R. Köbert (but
cf. C. Brockelmann, p. 737). Emend the *r* to a *d* by
simply moving a dot, *wdsᶜʾ*; and compare the Ar.
dasᶜatun, "vomiting" (E. W. Lane, bk. 1, pt. 3, p.
879). Mingana (without explanation): "back aches."
g. Lit. "will make them equal"; taking *nšwʾ* as
an Aphel imperfect. Mingana: "will make up for
them."
h. Mingana reported incorrectly that the MS has
tʾbd; it has *tʾqd*, which should be emended to *tʾqr*,
"wearisome" (cf. 2:5). Strictly speaking this restoration is not an emendation since a consonant is not
altered; only one diacritical dot is moved.
i. Lit. "it."

1 **5** *And if the year begins in Leo*: There will be spring rains, then the soil will be deprived
2 of[a] the north winds. •And grain will be enjoyed[b], for[c] indeed the food of men will be good.
3,4 And wheat and rice and dried peas will be expensive, and wheat must be irrigated. •And
5,6 oil and dates will be expensive. • And there will be disease among men. • And pregnant
7,8 (females)[d] and small cattle will die. •And the king[e] will strive with a king. •And the large
locust(s)[f] will come and will not subside; but somewhat [gradually][g] they will swirl in circles[h]
9,10 and shrink (back) together.[i] •And the river Nile will overflow its highest rate.[j] •And people
11 will have headache(s). •Then at the end of the year there will be much rain.

1 **6** *And if the year begins in Virgo*: Everyone whose name contain Yūdhs or Semkath, and
2 Bēth, and Nūn will be diseased and robbed, and will flee from his home. • And (this
3 misfortune) will occur in the beginning of the year.[a] •And shortage of water will be in every
4,5 circle.[b] • And the first grain will not prosper. • And people will suffer (many) miseries[c] in
6,7 winter and summer. •But the last grain will be harvested and it will be good. •And produce
will be expensive in Hauran and Bithynia,[d] but at the end of the year it[e] will be inexpensive.[f]
8,9,10 Even wine will be less (expensive) and pleasant. •And dates will be abundant. •But oil
11 will be expensive. •And wheat and barley will be valued, but dried pea(s) will be reduced
12 in value. •And rain will be late and will not fall upon the earth until[g] thirty days before the
13,14 Passover [feast].[h] •And the king[i] will strive with a king and will slay him. •And Alexandria

---

5 a. Mingana: "will be scorched by." Although *mn*
often denotes the agent of an action, *mn* with *'bd*
means "to be deprived of." If this document was
written in Alexandria, then the loss of the north wind
would also mean the loss of rain. Clouds heavy with
water would form over the Mediterranean to the north
of this city and not over the desert in the south. It is
noteworthy that 3:1 refers to rain coming from the
north wind.

b. Lit. "be beloved." Mingana: "corn will not be
injured."

c. Gk. *de*.

d. Apparently, because of the context, only animals are meant. No distinction is drawn between
men and women; the Syr. noun *bnynš'*, translated
"men" in 5:2, 5:5, and elsewhere, is generic.

e. Cf. 6:13 and 12:8. The MS has the plural
"kings" but the verb is clearly singular. If the dots
for the plural are not ignored—as they should be since
they appeared relatively late in Syr. MSS—and if the
verb is emended to the plural—by merely affixing
wn—then the sentence would mean "And kings will
strive with the king (the Roman Emperor)."

f. Here and in 7:7 "locust" is singular. Collective
nouns representing animals in Syr. can take singular
or plural verbs (cf. T. Nöldeke's *Compendious Syriac
Grammar*, pp. 251f.), but is is odd to have in one
sentence both singular ("it will come and it will not
subside") and plural verbs ("they will swirl . . . they
will shrink [back]").

g. The lacuna measures 11 mm. or enough space
for four or five consonants. The final *'ā* is visible and
is attached to a preceding consonant. The top of an
l may be discerned. Restore probably [*qlyl*]' (*qallîlâ*),
which with the previous *qallil* means "little by little"
or "gradually."

h. Mingana misread the MS, which has *dwr' ldwr'*
not *dwk' ldwk'*.

i. Lit. "And the large locust will come (3 masc.
sing.), and it (*sic*) will not decrease, but somewhat
little [by little] they will turn back from circle to circle
and they will shrink one with another." Mingana:
"A considerable number of locusts will make their
appearance and their number will decrease but slightly
. . . (Mingana's desire not to emend) they will turn

from one place to another and they will be gathered
together." The Syr. is difficult to translate because
of the conflicting verbs, idioms, cryptic style, and
lacuna.

j. Lit. "its highest overflow."

6 a. Mingana claimed that there "are evidently some
words missing here," and left the sentence open:
"And there will be at the beginning of the year
[. . .]" The line in the MS ends with "in the beginning of the year" and the author refers frequently to
the "beginning," "middle," and "end" of the year;
it is possible that a line or more has been omitted
inadvertently due to the repetition of identical words.
In fact, three lines below this one the last word is
"year." Another line could have ended in "year"
and the copyist could have inadvertently omitted it
as his eye returned to "the year" which ended it,
thinking it was the one he had just copied. This error
is one of the most frequently committed by Syriac
scribes. Nevertheless, there is no evidence in the MS
that some words have been omitted. Scribes corrected
this MS (cf. n. e, ch. 4, and d, ch. 8), and the phrase
can be translated sensibly to refer to what precedes.
There is, therefore, no need to suppose that some
words are missing.

b. Mingana misread the MS: "in some places."
See n. h, ch. 5.

c. Lit. "will have miseries." Mingana: "will be
in distress and sickness."

d. Linking a plain in Transjordan with a region in
northwest Asia Minor seems odd. Note that in 1:11
Hauran is joined in thought with Damascus. Perhaps
"Bithynia" was originally "Batanaea," which is just
north of Hauran.

e. Following the correction of "they" to "it."

f. Lit. "be valued little."

g. Lit. "the thirty days to Passover." Mingana:
"during thirty days down to the time of Passover."

h. At this point the MS has a lacuna of 13 mm.,
which is space for five or six consonants. Restore
['*adh* '*idhâ*]:[feast]. Cf. Jn 2:23.

i. The MS has a plural noun; ignore the dots for
the plural because the following singular pronoun
demands a singular antecedent. Cf. 5:7 and 12:8.

15,16 will be lost.^j •And [the Nil]e^k will not overflow well. •And many ships will be wrecked.
17 But at the end of the year there will be a sufficiency about everything.^l

1,2 **7** *And if the year begins in Libra*: There will be spring rains. • And the year will be
3,4 transformed. •And people will be spared^a from the east wind. •And fig trees will not produce
5,6,7 fruit.^b •But dates and oil will be plentiful. •But wine will be expensive. •And wheat will be
8,9 valued greatly. And the locust^c will appear. •And a severe war will occur in Africa. •And
10 men will have severe diseases. •And in the middle of the year rain will be held back (for)
11,12,13 twenty days. •And cultivated^d wheat will not ripen^e well. •And all lands will be good. •And
everyone whose name has a Yūdh or Bēth will be sick, and he will have anxiety, and will
14,15 go into exile^f from his land. •And wine will be damaged. •And adultery will increase, and
16,17 (licentious) desire^g will increase. • And the king^h will stay in one place. •And power will
18 leave the land.^i •And the nobles will flee to the sea, and there will be between (them) [in]
19,20 the [sea]^j a severe war. •And there will be in Galilee a severe earthquake.^k •And robbers^l
21 will gather^m in Hauran and in Damascus.^n •And the river Nile will overflow (at) its highest
22 rate.^o •And a severe plague will occur in Egypt, and it will be in [Gali]lee^p as in Beth Bardune
23 (the Place of Mules?).^q •People will be troubled because of (the lack of) rain.

1 **8** *And if the year begins in Scorpio*: The north wind will blow in the beginning of the year,
2 and there will be many spring rains. •And at the end of the year everything will be expensive.
3 And rain will diminish^a until people recite^b petition(s) and prayer(s), and beseech with alms
4,5 the living God.^c •And there will be disease among women who are pregnant. •And many
6 men on account of affliction [will migrate]^d from their countries. •And wheat and barley will
7 be harvested very little, but dried peas will be harvested. •And there will be (sufficient) wine
8,9 and oil. •And ulcers will develop within the bodies of men but will not injure^e them. •And
10 the Nile will overflow half of its (usual) rate.^f •And (there will be) whispers (of hope) for

j. Mingana: "Living in Alexandria will be dear."
k. The lacuna measures 12 mm. and a final Semkath is partly visible. There is room for an *l. nylws*, "Nile," occupies the required amount of space in l. 12 of this fol. If further confirmation for the restoration is needed, *slq*, "to overflow," is used above to describe the rise of the Nile in 1:4; 2:11; 3:9; 4:2; and 5:9. Restore *w[nylw]s*, "and [the Nil]e."
l. Another possible translation: "worth for everything." Mingana: "moderation in everything."

7 a. Lit. "will spare from the east wind." Perhaps the verb form should be changed to the Ethpa'al, "They will make supplication to the east wind."
b. Lit. "they will not have in them fruits."
c. Fol. 82b ends.
d. The Syr. noun seems to be a Gk. loan word, *harmonia*, which can mean "well-ordered." Since the Gk. word also denotes "means of joining" the expression may denote a hybrid wheat. The Gk. noun, however, is not reported to have been used in an agricultural sense. Mingana merely transliterated the word.
e. Emend the text as Mingana suggested. Although the '*ē* is clear in this particular word it is easily confused with the *n*.
f. Another possible translation: "into captivity." A more expert Syriac translator (or author) perhaps might have used simply one word and not four, since *qallî*, the Pas'el of *g^elâ*, means "go into exile (or captivity)." Mingana: "and will emigrate from his country."
g. Syr. *yû'ābhâ*, "earnest desire," usually has a good connotation.
h. The Roman Emperor is probably meant; cf. 1:5.
i. The same word as in 7:13. Possibly "earth" is meant (so Mingana).
j. Restore [*bym*]', "[in] the [sea]." The last consonant looks like an *'ā*. The lacuna is 10 mm., the precise size of the preceding *bym'*. As seen repeatedly

(cf. 7:15), the author tends to repeat the same word. Mingana does not attempt a restoration and gives no indication in the translation that there is a lacuna. Although the space is ideal for *bynt[hwn]*, "between [them]," *the final 'ā* resists this restoration.
k. In the spring of 31 B.C., when the battle at Actium was in full force (*akmazontos de tou peri Aktion polemou*. Josephus, *War* 1. 370), there was a severe earthquake in Palestine (cf. Josephus, *War* ll. 369–72; *Ant.* 15.121–26).
l. Gk. *lēstēs*.
m. Mingana emended the text to *npqwn*, "will appear."
n. Cf. 1:11 and 10:15, in which the scribe spells Hauran correctly and Damascus without the *w* after *m*.
o. Lit. "all of it its overflow." Cf. 1:4.
p. Restore probably *b[ǧly]b*, in [Gali]lee;" the first and last two consonants and the bottom of the *g* are visible.
q. This sentence is problematical. Contrast Mingana: "In Egypt there will be a cruel pest, which will be in . . . that is to say mules." Further research on this document should clear up some textual problems.

8 a. This verb was used in 1:6 and 4:4 to describe the eclipse of the moon.
b. "People" is a true plural and should take a plural verb. See Nöldeke's *Compendious Syriac Grammar*, p. 251.
c. Mingana's translation is an expanded paraphrase: "and rain will be so scarce that people will address prayers and supplications to the living God, for the sake of food."
d. This lacuna of 13 mm. can be restored easily because a later hand has written the missing words in the left margin. Restore *n[šnwn mn]*, "th[ey will migrate]."
e. The verb is singular; it should be plural.
f. Lit. "overflow half of its overflow." Cf. 4:2.

11 small cattle.ᵍ •And everyone whose name has a Taw or Yūdh will become sick, but will
12 recover health. •And everyone born in Scorpio (will) survive (his birth),ʰ but at the end of
the year he will be killed.

1 **9** *And if the year begins in Sagittarius*: Everyone whose name contains a Bēth or Pē will
have misery and a severe disease, and in the beginning of the year it will increase in severity.
2,3 And men in many places will be troubled. •And in the land of Egypt there will be sown
4,5 only a (very) little.ᵃ •And in the middle of the year there will be much rain. •But men will
6 gather produce into granaries because of the (following) drought.ᵇ •And grain will not be
7,8 pleasing. •Even at the end of the year it will not be good.ᶜ •But wine and oil will be
9 considered good. •And adultery will increase and small cattle will die.

1 **10** *And if the year begins in Capricorn*: Everyone whose name contains a Qōph will become
2 sick and be plundered and wounded with a sword. •And the eastᵃ wind (will) ruleᵇ the year.
3,4 And everyone (should) sow (early); the last (to sow) will be unsuccessful. •And in the
5 beginning of the yearᶜ [everything]ᵈ will be expensive. •Waves and storms will increase,
6 (so that) they (who are on the sea)ᵉ will die. •And in the middle of the year produce will
7,8,9 be expensive. •And thieves will increase. •And governmental officials will be cruel. •Even
10 wasps and (small)ᶠ reptiles of the earth will increase, and they will harm many people. •And
11 many people (will move)ᵍ from one place to another because of the existing war. •And wars
12,13 will increase on the earth. •Then at the end of the year rain will diminish. •And in (some)
14 places grain will be harvested, but in (other) places grain will perish. •And there will be a
15 disease in Damascus and in Hauran. •And there [will be]ʰ a famine along the [se]acoast.
16,17 And adultery will increase. •And people will reciteⁱ petition(s) and prayers and (observe) a
18 fast and (give) alm(s) (in hope for) rain. •And irrigated grain will be good.

1 **11** *And if the year begins in Pisces*: Everyone whose name contains a Kāph or Mīm (will)
2,3 become sick and (eventually) slain.ᵃ •The year will be good. •And the grain (will be) good
4,5 and healthy. •And there will be spring rains. •And fishing in the sea will be [prosper]ous.ᵇ
6,7,8 And when (the sea) billows ships will be wrecked. •And (people)ᶜ will become sick. •And

g. Mingana stated concerning 8:10, which he omitted from his translation, "There is here a Syr. sentence for which I cannot find any satisfactory meaning." Cf. 5:6 and 9:9. R. Payne Smith (col. 672) lists under *gawgâ* the following: *"locutio secreta, . . .* prayers, recommendations." We have reserved "prayer" to represent *ṣlwt'*.

h. Lit. "he is alive." According to 8:12 the author believes that the zodiac determines not only the characteristics of each year but also the fate of people according to the time of their birth, an idea featured in 4QCryptic (see the Introduction).

9 a. Lit. "And the land of Egypt they will not sow in it anything except a little of something."

b. Lit. "failure of rain."

c. Usually the author reserves something good for the end of the year.

10 a. The original scribe observed that he had omitted the *n* in this word and restored it above the line.

b. This verb and the next one are participles.

c. Fol. 83a ends.

d. When the scribe turned the fol. over and began to copy the text on the back he apparently omitted the noun. Following 8:2 restore [*klmdm*], "[everything]."

e. Cf. 2:12 and 1:10. Mingana thought the subject again had been omitted. Perhaps it has, but the text is cryptic and is comprehensible as extant.

f. Syr. *šerṣâ* denotes vermin, and small creeping things like snakes and mice; large reptiles are represented by *raḥshâ*.

g. Mingana claimed that a verb has been omitted. But a verb is not demanded; the cryptic style and the prepositional phrase "from place to place" can justify a non-verbal sentence.

h. Mingana restored this lacuna with *bspr[ym']*, which is impossible. A *y* clearly and *m* partly are visible. A lacuna of 10 mm. remains after which there is a *w* and *'ā*; restore *bspr ym[' nh]w'*, "there [will be] along the [se]acoast."

i. Mingana attempted to emend the text to *nsqwn*, "they will offer," and placed this verb in the text itself. The text should not be altered; cf. 8:3, in which *npq* also means "to recite."

11 a. Mingana thought the text contained *wmtdbyz*, relegated this reading to the nn. with *"sic!,"* and placed *wmtbzz* in his text. The text is not written neatly but seems to contain *wmtdbḥ*, "and (will) be slain."

b. A lacuna of 5 mm.; restore, with Mingana: *n[s]g̊wn*. The top of the *g* is visible. Lit. "And sea fishing will [inc]rease."

c. Mingana claimed that the "subject has been omitted by the copyist." But "people" may be presupposed because of the numerous preceding phrases; cf. e.g. 10:10, 17; 9:2, 5; 8:3. Note especially 7:9, "And people will have severe diseases." Nonspecialists in Syr. should be informed that Syr. verbs contain subjects, although they are indefinite pronouns. The present verb means "they will become sick."

9,10   wine and oil and wheat, each of them, shall be pleasing. •Then[d] grain will be good.[e] •There
will be wars and much desolation in cities; and villages will be transferred and displaced
11   from one place to another.[f] •And robbers[g] will come from Palestine and [many will wa]ge[h]
12   a great war against three cities. • And the Romans (sometimes will be) victorious and
13,14   (sometimes) easily overcome. •And there will be a great disease among men. •And there
15   will come forth a black man who seeks the kingdom. •And the house of the kingdom will
16   perish. •And the king will seek to understand what men are saying, and (will) lay waste
17   many cities. •And no one will be able to stop him; and the fear of God and his mercies (will)
18   be absent from him. •Then at the end of the year there will be peace and prosperity among
men, and love and harmony among all the kings who are on the entire earth.[i]

1   **12** [The section on][a] Aquarius, which (of course) is before Pisces, nevertheless because of
a mistake, was copied in the (following) manner:[b] When[c] the year begins in Aquarius,
everyone whose name contains a Lāmadh or Pē (will) become sick or utterly ruined by
2,3   marauders.[d] •And in the beginning of the year rain will increase. •And the Nile will overflow
4,5,6   its full rate.[e] • And Egypt (will rule)[f] over Palestine. • [Barley][g] will be harvested. • And
7,8   lamb(s) and sheep will prosper. •And the west wind (will) govern the year. •And the king
9   will fight with a king.[h] • And the first grain will prosper; but dried pea(s) will not sprout
(very) much although they[i] (will) be harvested. And merchants (will) seek help[j] from the
living God.[k]

d. Gk. de.

e. Mingana misread the text; ignore his "(sic)."

f. Lit. "from place to place."

g. Gk. lēstēs.

h. Mingana failed to note in his text that there is
here a lacuna of 12 mm. Clearly visible is the following: w[   ]ṁḥwn. Mingana placed in his text
wrmḥwn. A nun, which takes up only 2mm., will not
fill the lacuna, which needs from four to six letters.
dyn, "then," plus n is attractive in terms of space,
but dyn does not begin a sentence. In 3:6 and 3:7
"will make" wars is nʿbdwn, but this is impossible
here because of the extant m and ḥ. A key is supplied
by the remnant of a Sᵉyāmē, and g or l above the
space; restore w[šg̱yʾn]ṁḥwn, "and [many will
wa]ge." sgyʾ fits neatly; see the third line on this
fol.

i. The document originally ended on this very
positive note. The ending of the twelve years according to the zodiac is influenced, perhaps, by the
emphasis of the author's contemporaries: The fast-

approaching future age would be one of peace and
prosperity upon the entire earth.

12 a. Syr. [nwgrʾd], "the section on," appears to
be hidden behind penciled marks.

b. This opening was added by a copyist.

c. The usual introductory formula is broken, probably by the copyist who added the preface.

d. Lit. "from plundering."

e. Lit. "overflow its full overflow."

f. The preposition "over" indicates the meaning
suggested above. Mingana claimed a verb had been
omitted.

g. Restore [sʿrʾ], "[barley]." The noun must be
feminine because the verb is feminine. Cf. 2:8.

h. Cf. 5:7 and 6:13.

i. Lit. "it (will) be harvested."

j. Change mʿdrnʾ, "helpers," to mʿdrnwtʾ,
"helps."

k. See n. i, ch. 11.

APOCRYPHON OF EZEKIEL

(First Century B.C.–First Century A.D.)

A NEW TRANSLATION AND INTRODUCTION

BY J. R. MUELLER and S. E. ROBINSON

The Apocryphon of Ezekiel has not survived intact; four fragments preserved in secondary sources and one small fragment of the apocryphon itself, which is also quoted by Clement of Alexandria, are all that remain. Of these five fragments, the only one long enough to require summarization here is the story of the lame man and the blind man found in rabbinic literature and in the writings of Epiphanius.

In this story a certain king invites everyone in his kingdom except two cripples, the lame man and the blind man, to attend a great feast. Understandably offended, the two cripples devise a plan to get even. The lame man braids a rope and, throwing it to the blind man, leads the latter to himself. He then climbs onto the shoulders of the blind man. Thus equipped with the eyes of the lame man and the legs of the blind, the two men enter the garden of the king and, presumably, tear down the fruit trees or, as in the Hebrew version, eat the choice fruit. When the deed is discovered, the lame man and the blind man are brought before the king. Each appeals to his particular infirmity as proof that he could not be the guilty party. Then the wise king has the lame man placed on the shoulders of the blind, and having thus demonstrated how the deed was performed, orders them to be flogged together before him. As they are flogged, each accuses the other of being primarily responsible for the crime. The moral which is drawn from the story is that body and soul, like the lame man and the blind man, cooperate in all the deeds performed in mortality; hence, at the judgment of God, body and soul must be reunited in a resurrection so that both may receive their just deserts.

Texts

The texts for fragment 1, the story of the lame man and the blind, are found in Epiphanius' *Against Heresies* 64.70, 5–17 (ed. Holl), and in rabbinic literature at Sanhedrin 91a, b (attributed to R. Judah ha-Nasi, c. A.D. 200), Leviticus Rabbah 4:5 (attributed to R. Ishmael, c. A.D. 130), and in the Mekhilta on Exodus 15:1 (also attributed to R. Ishmael). The translations below are taken from K. Holl's edition of Epiphanius[1] and from the Soncino Hebrew-English edition of the Babylonian Talmud.[2]

Fragment 2 is found in several places, the earliest of which is the text of 1 Clement 8:2f. The translation of fragment 2 below is taken from K. Lake's edition of 1 Clement.[3] Other versions of this fragment are found in Clement of Alexandria (*Paid* 1.10),[4] and in the Coptic Exegesis on the Soul from Nag Hammadi.[5] There is also an allusion to this passage in *Quis dives salvetur* 39.2 by Clement of Alexandria.[6]

---

[1] *Epiphanius: Ancoratus und Panarion,* ed. K. Holl (GCS 31; Leipzig, 1915) vol. 2, pp. 515–17.

[2] *Sanhedrin,* ed. I. Epstein (London, 1969) vol. 9, § 91a, b.

[3] K. Lake, *The Apostolic Fathers* (LCL; London, 1912) p. 20.

[4] GCS 12, p. 143, l. 20.

[5] CG II, 6; see *The Nag Hammadi Library,* ed. J. M. Robinson (San Francisco, 1977) p. 186. For the view that ApocEzek did not exist as an entity prior to the time of Epiphanius, cf. B. Dehandschutter, "L'Apocryphe d'Ézéchiel: Source de l'Exégèse sur l'âme, p. 135, 31–136, 4?" *Orientalia Lovaniensia Periodica* 10 (1979) 227–35.

[6] GCS 17, p. 185. A.-M. Denis (*Introduction,* p. 189) attributes this citation to ApocEzek, but it is an allusion

Fragment 3 is also found in Clement of Alexandria (*Strom* 7.16),[7] and in Tertullian (*De carni Christi* 23),[8] the Acts of Peter 24,[9] Epiphanius (*AdvHaer* 30.30),[10] and Gregory of Nyssa (*Against the Jews* 3).[11] Because this fragment takes on various forms in citation, obscuring the original form, all citations are translated below.

The fourth surviving fragment of the Apocryphon of Ezekiel is cited in no fewer than thirty-two secondary sources, which date from the second century A.D. well into the Middle Ages. The earliest and most important of these citations is found in Justin Martyr's *Dialogue with Trypho* 47.5, from which the translation below is taken.[12]

Slightly varying versions of fragment 5 are found in Clement of Alexandria (*Strom* 1.9),[13] in Origen (*Homilies on Jeremiah* 18.9),[14] and in the Manichaean Psalmbook (Psalm 239:5f.).[15] The sole surviving fragment of a manuscript of the Apocryphon of Ezekiel itself, as opposed to a citation of the apocryphon found in secondary sources, contains this fifth fragment. This manuscript fragment was identified and edited by C. Bonner from among the Chester Beatty Papyri.[16] This fragment confirms that the citation of Clement is from the apocryphon; the translation is based on the fragmentary text of the papyrus and the complete text of Clement.

Original language

It is extremely hazardous to speculate on the original language of compositions that are no longer extant or that are known by only a few fragments. Bearing this in mind, one may, however, hypothesize that Greek and Hebrew are the most likely candidates for the original language of the apocryphon. On the one hand, Greek might be suggested by the fact that it was so widely spoken in the intertestamental period and by the fact that the only surviving manuscript fragment of the apocryphon is written in Greek. On the other hand, Hebrew might be suggested by the appearance of a Hebrew version of fragment 1 in the rabbinic literature and by the statement of Josephus that there were in his day two books of Ezekiel, the natural inference being that he considered these companion pieces, and hence written in the same language, i.e. Hebrew. However, both of these possibilities are threads too slender to bear much weight, and in the absence of more manuscript evidence, the question of the original language of the Apocryphon of Ezekiel should be left open.

Date

The Apocryphon of Ezekiel cannot be dated later than the end of the first century A.D. 1 Clement (c. A.D. 95) uses the Apocryphon as one of its sources, and the Jewish historian Flavius Josephus noted (*Ant* 10.5.1) that Ezekiel had left behind two books, of which we may assume one to have been the apocryphon. The earliest possible date cannot be determined as precisely, although the conjecture of K. Holl[17] and J.-B. Frey,[18] placing the composition of the document between 50 B.C. and A.D. 50, has been generally accepted.

---

rather than a citation. Influence from ApocEzek can be seen throughout this chapter: (1) the presence of the term "blacker" in what appears to be a quotation from Isa 1:18, which destroys the synonymous parallelism; (2) the emphasis upon repentance "with the whole heart"; and (3) the use of the appellation "Father" (infrequently used in the treatise except on the lips of Jesus) in close conjunction with the theme of repentance.

[7] GCS 17, p. 66, l. 25.

[8] PL 2, col. 836.

[9] See M. R. James, *ANT*, p. 325.

[10] GCS 25, p. 371, l. 16.

[11] PG 46, col. 208.

[12] Corpus Apologetarum 2, p. 160. For a full listing of citations, cf. A. Resch, *Agrapha* (TU 30.3–4, pp. 102, 322–24). A corrective to Resch has been proposed by A. Baker, "Justin's Agraphon in the Dialogue with Trypho," *JBL* 87 (1968) 277–87.

[13] GCS 12, p. 139, ll. 16–27.

[14] GCS 6, p. 163.

[15] Cf. C. R. C. Allberry, *A Manichaean Psalm-Book* (Stuttgart, 1938) vol. 2, p. 39; and W. D. Stroker, "The Source of an Agraphon in the Manichaean Psalm-Book," *JTS* 28 (1977) 114–18.

[16] C. Bonner, *The Homily on the Passion by Melito, Bishop of Sardis, and Some Fragments of the Apocryphal Ezekiel*, p. 186.

[17] "Das Apokryphon Ezechiel," *Aus Schrift und Geschichte*, pp. 85–98; cf. especially p. 92.

Provenance

The fragmentary nature of the extant apocryphon makes a determination of its provenance very hazardous. Although some of the fragments may indicate a Christian redaction of the apocryphon, there is little doubt that the original was Jewish in character.[19]

Historical importance

Historically, the Apocryphon of Ezekiel is another example of an intertestamental text that, though Jewish in origin, has been preserved, albeit fragmentarily, only in Christian sources. This common phenomenon serves to remind the reader that intertestamental Judaism was not nearly as monolithic in its theology nor as homogenous in its literary tradition as the rabbinic Judaism of a slightly later time. Moreover, the wide popularity of the Apocryphon of Ezekiel in early Christian sources witnesses a certain latitude in the concept of canon that became less common as the Church became less and less diversified in later centuries. The transmission history of fragment 4 illustrates how an apt saying, even from an apocryphal source, could find its way into general usage and become a Christian maxim long after its origins had been forgotten.[20]

Theological importance

The first and longest fragment is an eloquent statement of the doctrine of the resurrection and of the judgment of God in the end-time. In both the Hebrew and Greek versions the message is clear: God will reunite body and spirit in a future judgment in order to dispense justly either reward or punishment. The resurrection envisioned is a literal reunion of the departed spirit with its former body. Man is neither a spirit in a body, nor a body with a spirit, but both a body and a spirit. Without both, the identity of the individual is incomplete and he cannot be judged. Also, the individual is clearly judged as an individual and not as a member of a people or of a community. In both the Hebrew and Greek versions the criterion for judgment is the deeds performed in mortality. However, the Greek version may reflect the belief that those who were in the service of the king in the parable (Christians?) are exempt from the judgment, or that only those who are not enlisted in the king's service would perform deeds worthy of condemnation, for the Greek version has no judgment of those invited to the banquet.

Relation to canonical books

It has been suggested by some scholars that the Apocryphon of Ezekiel never existed as a separate document, but only as an expanded version of, or Midrash on, canonical Ezekiel.[21] If we were dealing only with fragments 2, 4, and 5, this suggestion would be very attractive, for these fragments do bear some similarity to passages from the canonical Ezekiel. However, it is very difficult to understand where fragments 1 and 3 would fit in such an expanded or paraphrased text, for they are totally unlike anything in the canonical Ezekiel. Also, Epiphanius explicitly identifies fragment 1 as coming from "Ezekiel's own apocryphon."[22] Moreover, any theory that the Apocryphon of Ezekiel is merely an expanded or paraphrased Christian version of canonical Ezekiel must ignore the notice in Josephus (*Ant* 10.5.1) that

[18] *DBSup*, vol. 1, cols. 458–60.

[19] Denis, *Introduction*, p. 190; K.-G. Eckart, "Das Apokryphon Ezechiel," *JSHRZ* 5.1 (1974) 47, 49; Holl, *Aus Schrift und Geschichte*, pp. 93f.; T. Zahn, *Forschungen zur Geschichte des neutestamentlichen Kanons und der altkirchlichen Literatur* 6 (1900) 311; J.-B. Frey, *DBSup*, vol. 1, col. 460. For the opposite opinion, cf. M. R. James, "The Apocryphal Ezekiel," *JTS* 15 (1914) 243, and A. Resch, *Agrapha*, pp. 381–84.

[20] A. Baker, *JBL* 87 (1968) 285. J. Jeremias disputes the claim that Justin has improperly attributed this saying to Jesus (*Unknown Sayings of Jesus*, pp. 86f.; the second English edition cited in Bibliography was translated from the substantially revised third German edition of 1963). He proposed that the *Liber graduum* preserved the most original form of the saying and attributed it clearly to Jesus, just as Justin did. The attribution to Ezekiel appears later only as a result of a change in the form of the citation that brings it into close alignment with Ezek 33:12–20.

[21] See J. Danielou, *The Theology of Jewish Christianity* (London, 1964) pp. 105–7, and more recently, Baker, *JBL* 87 (1968) 285f. Resch (*Agrapha*, pp. 381–84) suggests that the fragments are actually from a Christian reworking of the canonical Ezekiel.

[22] Epiphanius, *AdvHaer* 64.70.

the Jewish historian knew of two books attributed to that prophet. The five fragments presently extant and the testimony of Jewish and Christian writers in antiquity weigh heavily in favor of the separate existence of the Apocryphon of Ezekiel. A more detailed statement of its relationship to canonical literature must unfortunately await the discovery of a more complete text of the apocryphon.

Relation to apocryphal books

The Apocryphon of Ezekiel seems to have enjoyed a certain amount of popularity in the first centuries of the present era. Besides the numerous quotations from the apocryphon in the patristic literature, fragment 2 is quoted in the Exegesis on the Soul from the gnostic library at Nag Hammadi;[23] fragment 3 is found in the Acts of Peter;[24] and fragment 5 is found in the Manichaean Psalmbook.[25]

The Ascension of Isaiah may also have known the apocryphon, for in chapter 11, as the rumor of Mary's maternity is spread throughout Bethlehem, some affirm and some deny the report. This is quite reminiscent of fragment 3, especially as preserved by Epiphanius.[26] The characterization of the Messiah's mother as a heifer probably finds its precedent in Jewish literature at 1 Enoch 90:37. Here Enoch symbolically represents the coming of a Messiah by the birth of a white bull. Our apocryphon has taken over this motif and has logically assumed that Enoch's white bull would have been born from a heifer. This motif of the heifer who bears the Messiah is taken up by the Church Fathers in later controversies over the virginity of Mary.[27]

SELECT BIBLIOGRAPHY

Charlesworth, *PMR*, pp. 109f.
Delling, *Bibliographie*, p. 165.
Denis, *Introduction*, pp. 187–91.

Baker, A. "Justin's Agraphon in the Dialogue with Trypho," *JBL* 87 (1968) 277–87.
Bellinzoni, A. J. *The Sayings of Jesus in the Writings of Justin Martyr. NovT*Sup 17; Leiden, 1967; ch. 5, pp. 131–34.
Bonner, C. *The Homily on the Passion by Melito, Bishop of Sardis, and Some Fragments of the Apocryphal Ezekiel.* Studies and Documents 12; London, 1940; pp. 183–202.
Eckart, K.-G. "Das Apokryphon Ezechiel," *JSHRZ* 5.1 (1974) 45–54.
Holl, K. "Das Apokryphon Ezechiel," *Aus Schrift und Geschichte. Theologische Abhandlungen, Adolf Schlatter zum seinem 70. Geburtstage.* Stuttgart, 1922; pp. 85–98. (Reprinted in *Gesammelte Aufsätze zur Kirchengeschichte.* Tübingen, 1928; vol. 2, pp. 33–43.)
James, M. R. "The Apocryphal Ezekiel," *JTS* 15 (1914) 236–43.
———. "Ezekiel," *LAOT.* New York, 1920; pp. 64–70.
Jeremias, J. *Unknown Sayings of Jesus.* London, 1964; pp. 83–88.
Stroker, W. D. "The Source of an Agraphon in the Manichaean Psalm-Book," *JTS* 28 (1977) 114–18.

---

[23] Robinson, *The Nag Hammadi Library*, p. 186.
[24] See James, *ANT*, p. 325.
[25] See Allberry, *A Manichaean Psalm-Book*, vol. 2, p. 39.
[26] *AdvHaer* 30:30.
[27] All citations of fragment 3 are examples of this use of ApocEzek.

THE APOCRYHON OF EZEKIEL
FRAGMENTS

THE APOCRYPHON OF EZEKIEL

Fragment 1

Epiphanius, *Against Heresies* 64.70, 5–17[a]

Introduction

"*For the dead will be raised and those in the tombs will be lifted up,*" speaks   Isa 26:19 (LXX)
the prophet. And also, so that I might not pass over in silence the things mentioned
about the resurrection by Ezekiel the prophet in his own apocryphon,[b] I will present
them here also. For speaking enigmatically, he refers to the righteous judgment,
in which soul and body share:[c]

The lame and blind men in the garden

1 **1** A certain king had everyone in his kingdom drafted,[d] and had no civilians[e]
except two only: one lame man and one blind man, and each one sat by himself
2 and lived by himself. •And when the king was preparing a wedding feast for his   Mt 22:2
own son, he invited all those in his kingdom, but he snubbed the two civilians,   Lk 14:16
3 the lame man and the blind man. •And they were indignant within themselves and
resolved to carry out a plot against the king.
4   Now the king had a garden[f] and the blind man called out from a distance to the
lame man, saying, "How much would our crumb of bread have been among the
crowds who were invited to the party? So come on, just as he did to us, let us
5,6 retaliate (against) him." •But the other asked, "In what way?" •And he said, "Let
7 us go into his garden and there destroy the things of the garden." •But he said,
8 "But how can I, being lame and unable to crawl?" •And the blind one spoke,
"What am I able to do myself, unable to see where I am going? But let us use
subterfuge."
9   Plucking the grass near him and braiding a rope, he threw (it) to the blind man
10 and said, "Take hold and come along the rope to me." •And he did as he (the
lame man) had urged (and) when he approached, he said, "Come to me, be (my)
feet and carry me, and I will be your eyes, guiding you from above to the right
11,12 and left." •And doing this they went down into the garden. •Furthermore, whether
they damaged or did not damage (anything), nevertheless the footprints were visible
in the garden.
13   Now when the partygoers dispersed from the wedding feast, going down into
14 the garden they were amazed to find the footprints in the garden. •And they reported
these things to the king, saying, "Everyone in your kingdom is a soldier and no
one is a civilian. So how then are there footprints of civilians in the garden?"
15 And he was astounded.

Parenthetic remark by Epiphanius

So says the parable of the apocryphon, making it clear that it refers to a man,
for God is ignorant of nothing. For the story says:

The judgment of the intruders

1 **2** He summoned the lame man and the blind man, and he asked the blind man,
2 "Did you not come down into the garden?" •And he replied, "Who, me, lord?
3 You see our inability, you know that I cannot see where I walk." •Then approaching

Babylonian Talmud, Sanhedrin 91a, b[g]

Introduction

Antoninus said to Rabbi,[h] "The body and the spirit are both able to escape from judgment. How? The body says, 'The spirit sinned, for from the day it separated ApMos 37-39 from me, behold, I have been lying like a silent stone in the grave.' Also the spirit can say, 'The body sinned, for from the day I separated from it, behold, I have QuesEzra 6(B) been flying in the air like a bird.' " And he (Rabbi) said to him, "I will give you an illustration:

The lame and blind men in the garden

"To what may this be compared? To a king of flesh and blood who possessed a beautiful garden[i] which had beautiful early figs. And he set in it two guards, one lame and one blind.[j] The lame man said to the blind man, 'I see beautiful early figs in the garden. Come and carry me on your back, and we will gather (them) to eat them.' The lame man rode upon the blind man and they gathered them and ate them.

"After a few days the owner of the garden came. He said to them, 'Where are those beautiful early figs?' Then the lame man said to him, 'Do I have feet to walk with?' Then the blind man said to him, 'Do I have eyes to see with?'

"What did he (the king) do? He made the lame man ride upon the blind and he judged them as one. So the Holy One, blessed be he, brings the spirit and Ps 50:4 placing it in the body, he also judges them as one. For it is said, '*He will call* 4Ezra 7:28-44 *to the heavens from above and to the earth, so he might judge his people.*' '*He* TAb 20 *will call to the heavens from above*'—this to the spirit. '*And the earth so he* ApMos 41:1-3 *might judge his people*'—this to the body."[k] ApPaul 14
QuesEzra 12-14(B)

---

1 a. GCS 31, pp. 515–17. See also the possible allusion to the story by Epiphanius (64.17), by George Cedrenus (PG 121, cols. 225f.), by George Hamartolos (PG 110, cols. 268f.), and in the History of Peter (cf. E. A. Budge, *Contendings of the Apostles* 2:8–18) and the Palatine Anthology 9:11–13.

b. Gk. *en tō idiō apokruphō*; it is from this phrase that the title "Apocryphon of Ezekiel" has been derived. Epiphanius' statement substantiates the witness of Josephus (*Ant* 10.6) to a second book of Ezekiel. Such a book is also listed among the OT Apocrypha in the stichometry of Nicephorus.

c. Epiphanius' introduction surely indicates that in the ApocEzek the story and the interpretation are inextricably bound, just as they are in the rabbinic parallel (see below).

d. I.e. into the army.

e. Gk. *paganoi*; this term is significant for the dating of the ApocEzek: Its presence, if original, confirms an earliest possible date for ApocEzek of 63 B.C., the date of the Roman occupation of Palestine. For a full discussion of the term, cf. T. Zahn, "Paganus," *Neue kirchlichen Zeitschrift* 10 (1899)

18–43; and B. Altaner, "Paganus," *ZKG* 58 (1939) 130–41.

f. Gk. *paradeisos*. The Heb. form of this word is found in the rabbinic parallel (see below n. i).

g. Cf. the parallels in Mekhilta Shirata 2 and LevR 4:5.

h. This story is part of a fictitious dialogue between Marcus Aurelius and Judah the Prince. Cf. L. Wallach, "The Parable of the Blind and the Lame," *JBL* 62 (1943) 333–39.

i. Heb. *prds*.

j. In the form of the story preserved in the Tanḥuma (Wayyikra 12) the problems associated with the choosing of a blind man and a lame man to guard the king's garden are alleviated; the king reasons that a healthy man would see the beautiful fruits and eat them for himself. Thus to save the fruits he decides to appoint the lame man and the blind man as guardians.

k. In Sifra on Deut 32:2 the appendix to the story in which Ps 50:4 is cited is attributed to Simai, a disciple of Judah. Cf. Wallach, *JBL* 62 (1943) 337.

4 the lame man, he asked him also, "Did you come down into my garden?" •And
answering, he said, "O lord, do you wish to embitter my soul in the matter of my
5 inability?" •And finally the judgment was delayed.

6   What then does the just judge do? Realizing in what manner both had been   Lk 20:15
joined, he places the lame man on the blind man and examines both under the   2Tim 4:8
7,8 lash. • And they are unable to deny; they each convict the other. • The lame man
on the one hand saying to the blind man, "Did you not carry me and lead me
9 away?" •And the blind man to the lame, "Did you yourself not become my eyes?"
10 In the same way the body is connected to the soul and the soul to the body, to   4Ezra 7:28-44
11 convict (them) of (their) common deeds. • And the judgment becomes final for   TAb 20
both body and soul, for the works they have done whether good or evil.   TJob 4:9
                                                                                ApMos 41:1-3
                                                                                ApPaul 14
                                                                                QuesEzra 12-
                                                                                14(B)

Fragment 2

1 Clement 8:3[a]

Repent, house of Israel, from your lawlessness. I say to the children of my people,   Ezek 39:22
"If your sins reach from the earth to heaven, and if they are redder than scarlet   Isa 1:18
or blacker than sackcloth, and you turn back to me with a whole heart and say,   Rev 6:12
'Father,' I will heed you as a holy people."   Jer 3:19
                                                                                Ezek 3:16-21;
                                                                                18:31
                                                                                Rom 8:15
                                                                                Gal 4:6
                                                                                Mk 14:36
                                                                                Jub 1:24

Fragment 3

Tertullian, *De carne Christi* 23

We read also in the writings of Ezekiel[a] concerning that cow which has given   1En 90:37
birth and has not given birth.

Epiphanius, *Panarion Haeresies* 30.30, 3

And again in another place he says, "And the heifer[b] gave birth and they said,
'She has not given birth.' "

Gregory of Nyssa, *Against the Jews* 3

Behold, the heifer has given birth, and has not given birth.

Clement of Alexandria, *Stromata* 7:16

She has given birth and she has not given birth, say the Scriptures.   AscenIs 11:14
                                                                                Isa 7:14

Acts of Peter 24

And again he (the prophet) said, "She has given birth and has not given birth."   AscenIs 11
                                                                                Isa 7:14

---

2 a. The last portion of this citation can also be found
in Clement, *Paid* 1.10, and is cited in full in the Nag
Hammadi *Exegesis on the Soul*. For a discussion of
the latter, cf. A. Guillaumont, "Une Citation de
l'apocryphe d'Ézéchiel dans l'exégèse au sujet de
l'âme," in *Essays on the Nag Hammadi Texts*, ed.
M. Krause (NHS 6; Leiden, 1975) pp. 35–39; M.
Scopello, "Les Citations d'Homère dans le traité de
l'exégèse de l'âme," in *Gnosis and Gnosticism: Papers Read at the Seventh International Conference
on Patristic Studies*, ed. M. Krause (NHS 8; Leiden,
1978) pp. 3–12; and M. Scopello, "Les 'Testimonia'
dans le traité de 'L'exégèse de l'âme' (Nag Hammadi,
II, 6)," *RHR* 191 (1977) 159–71; and B. Dehandschutter, *Orientalia Lovaniensia Periodica* 10 (1979)
227–35.

3 a. Tertullian is the only ancient author who ascribes this saying to Ezekiel.
   b. K.-G. Eckart has argued that the form of the
saying as found in Epiphanius is original based upon
Epiphanius' familiarity with ApocEzek (see fragment
1) and his faithful quotation of the story of the lame
man and the blind man ("Die Kuh des apokryphen
Ezechiel," *Antwort aus der Geschichte*, ed. W. Sommer and H. Ruppel [Berlin, 1969] pp. 44–48). This
conclusion is unconvincing because of the uncertainty
surrounding the transmission history of fragment 1
(compare the two versions above); Epiphanius may
have embellished the simple story with references to
such NT passages as the parable of the great feast
(Mt 22:2; Lk 14:16).

Fragment 4

Justin Martyr, *Dialogue with Trypho* 47[a]

Wherefore also our Lord Jesus Christ[b] said, "In the things which I find[c] you, in these also I will judge (you)."

Ezek 18:30;
33:12-20
4Ezra 7:102-15
1En 50:4
2Bar 85:12
QuesEzra 5(B)

Fragment 5

Clement of Alexandria, *Paedagogus* 1:9[a]

Therefore he says by Ezekiel . . ., "And the lame I will bind up, and that which is troubled I will heal, and that which is led astray I will return, and I will feed them on my holy mountain . . . and I will be," he says, "their shepherd and I will be near to them as the garment to their skin."

Ezek 34:14-16

Jer 13:11; 23:23

---

4 a. Cf. n. 12 to the Introduction.

b. Justin is the only ancient author to attribute this saying to Jesus. K. Holl proposed that this ascription is false; he postulated that the saying was originally attributed to "the prophets" (cf. the citations by Elias of Crete and in Pseudo-Athanasius) and that Justin mistakenly read the *kurios*, "Lord," of the original as Jesus Christ instead of God (*Aus Schrift und Geschichte*, p. 95).

The only authors to attribute the agraphon to Ezekiel are Evagrius of Antioch in his Lat. translation of the Life of Antony 16 (c. 375 A.D.; cf. PL 26, col.

869) and John Climacus (c. 649 A.D.). J. Jeremias claims that the ascription to Ezekiel is secondary and is based upon the similarity of the agraphon to Ezek 33:12–20 (cf. above, "Texts").

c. Gk. *katalabō*, "overtake, find upon arrival."

5 a. Cf. also the fragmentary text preserved in the Chester Beatty Papyri (cf. n. 16 to the Introduction). Misspellings abound in the papyrus fragment; they have not been noted here because they do not represent significant departures from the text found in Clement.

APOCALYPSE OF ZEPHANIAH

(First Century B.C.–First Century A.D.)

A NEW TRANSLATION AND INTRODUCTION
BY O. S. WINTERMUTE

If the calculations of Carl Schmidt are correct, only about one fourth of the text of the Apocalypse of Zephaniah has been preserved, with a lacuna of over one half of the text at the beginning.[1] Even the text that survived is not continuous. There is preserved: (1) a short Greek quotation cited by Clement of Alexandria,[2] (2) two pages of a Sahidic manuscript, and (3) eighteen pages of Akhmimic text, broken by a lacuna after page 12.

Despite the fragmentary nature of the text, the genre and structure are quite obvious: It is an apocalypse; more specifically it shares the greatest number of literary features with other apocalyptic writings such as 1 Enoch, 2 Enoch, 3 Baruch, and The Apocalypse of Paul (cf. Nag Hammadi CG V, 2.).[3] Each of these works contains the first-person account of a seer who is led through heavenly spheres by an angelic guide or guides and bears witness to the splendor of various heavenly glories (cf. TLevi and AscenIs) as well as terrifying scenes of sinners as they suffer the torment of their just punishment. Such writings normally have an episodic structure consisting of a series of short vignettes and dialogue strung together or set side by side with other independent literary units inside the loose framework of a "cosmic journey." The isolated episodes or scenes that make up such a work are frequently complete and self-consistent. Consequently they are readily subject to modification. They may be expanded upon, abbreviated, omitted, or supplemented by the addition of new episodes. Thus various episodes or scenes within 1 Enoch have been assigned correctly to different authors from different periods of time. In 3 Baruch, which is a fairly straightforward trip through five heavens, the seer can pause along the way to include one digression on the tree (actually a grape vine) of Paradise and another on the Phoenix, as well as lesser concerns. In the case of 2 Enoch, a simple comparison of the translations of the two main Slavonic manuscripts illustrates how easily the separate scenes may be modified, abbreviated, expanded upon, or omitted without doing serious violence to the overall structure of the work. The Apocalypse of Paul, moreover, contains doublets that are found in the seer's journeys to the promised land and his subsequent visit to Paradise, suggesting that the writer drew into his account episodes from separate, overlapping sources.

The Apocalypse of Zephaniah undoubtedly had a similar structure. Within the surviving fragments there are indications of repetition and overlapping. The sea of fire first appears in 6:1, but it is taken up again in 10:3, where the author describes the torment of the souls who sink in the sea. The punishment of sinners that is discussed in 10:4–9 is also the concern of the first eight lines of the Sahidic fragment.

This type of literature is composed of self-contained scenes and episodes that are loosely

---

[1] C. Schmidt, "Der Kolophon des Ms. Orient. 7594 des Britischen Museums; eine Untersuchung zur Elias-Apokalypse," *Sitzungsberichte der Preussischen Akademie der Wissenschaften*, pp. 312–21. Schmidt said that he was assisted in reconstructing the MS by Ibscher.

[2] *Strom* 5.11.77.

[3] This newly discovered text from Nag Hammadi CG V, 2 is also titled "The Apocalypse of Paul," but it is a gnostic text which should not be confused with the previously cited apocalypse which has the same name. See n. 12 below.

joined rather than tightly woven into a developing plot or interconnected sequence of events; hence, it is virtually impossible to guess what the initial forty-six pages[4] of missing text contained. Most likely they recorded a general description of Zephaniah's cosmic travels, in which he saw both heavenly glories and the torments of hell. This rather safe conjecture is supported by the contrasting content of Clement's quotation about the fifth heaven and the Sahidic fragment's description of a tortured soul in Hades; both of these may have been located somewhere in the first half of the text. There is a positive aspect to the self-contained nature of the episodes: We can understand the surviving fragments of the Akhmimic text quite well, despite having only the most general understanding of what preceded it.

The surviving text begins with a brief glimpse of angelic glory in the fifth heaven. After a lacuna of unknown length, the seer describes a vision of the scourging of a soul in Hades and his own terrified response. This is followed by an angelic exhortation to prevail over the accuser so that the seer might come up from Hades. Subsequently, the seer journeys with the angel of the Lord to a great broad place in which further visions begin.

The Akhmimic manuscript contains the largest portion of surviving text. It may be divided into two major sections: (1) scenes from the travelogue, and (2) trumpet scenes.

The travelogue describes the seer's movements, which introduce a new setting for the visions and dialogue that follow. The first travel notice is found at 2:1: "Now I went with the angel of the Lord and he took me up (over) all my city." The scenes and dialogue from on high continue until 3:1, where the second travel notice begins with the sentence: "The angel of the Lord said to me, 'Come, let me show you the place of righteousness.' And he took me up upon Mount Seir . . ." Other travel notices appear in 4:1, 5:1, 6:1, and 8:1, where the seer is transported by boat to the site of the trumpet scenes. Both the quotation cited by Clement and the Sahidic text (B8) contain similar travel notes. The author of the text used the travel notices to break up his travelogue into a number of episodes. If we count the brief introductory fragment dealing with burial, there are seven such episodes:

1. A brief fragment dealing with burial (ch. 1).

2. Scenes from some heavenly location above Jerusalem (ch. 2). Here the seer witnesses scenes of city life, discusses the nature of the continous light that shines with the righteous, and sees men in torment.

3. Scenes from Mount Seir (ch. 3). A vision of three men led by two angels provides the starting point for a dialogue in which the angel who accompanies the seer describes the manner in which angels record the good and evil deeds of men on a manuscript for the time of judgment.

4. Scenes outside the heavenly city (ch. 4). Here Zephaniah sees the terrifying angels who bring the souls of evil men to their eternal punishment. He prays for deliverance, and his petition is heard.

5. Scenes within the city (ch. 5). Here the seer's attention is centered on the gates and the city square. He also witnesses the transformation of his angelic guide.

6. Scenes from Hades (chs. 6f.). After turning back, Zephaniah observes a sea of fire. Subsequently he is confronted by the accuser, who has his manuscript of sins and short-comings, and Eremiel, who has a record of his good deeds.

7. Scene in a boat (ch. 8). At this point the seer puts on an angelic garment and joins the angelic host.

The text ends with four trumpet scenes in which the episodes are introduced by a great angel who blows on a golden trumpet. The scenes appear in the following order:

1. The trumpet that heralds the seer's triumph over the accuser (ch. 9). This episode describes the seer's wish to embrace the angel, and the angel's conversation with Old Testament saints (Abraham, Isaac, etc.).

2. The trumpet that heralds the opening of heaven (ch. 10). In this episode the seer once again sees the fiery sea and the sinners who are tormented in it. He also sees bodies with hair and learns that the Lord provides body and hair.

3. The trumpet that calls the saints to intercessory prayer (ch. 11). In this scene, the seer sees a pious multitude interceding for those in torment; he is told that the pious assemble for prayer daily when the trumpet sounds.

---

[4] The pagination which is noted here is based on Schmidt's analysis of the text. See n. 1 above for bibliography.

4. The trumpet that introduces a discussion of the end (ch. 12). The seer is told about a trumpet that will be blown in the future and hears about God's coming wrath.

Title

The title, the Apocalypse of Zephaniah, is not preserved in either of the surviving Coptic manuscripts, but the Sahidic manuscript contains the following statement: "Truly, I, Zephaniah, saw these things in my vision." That statement together with the general content of the text is sufficient to classify the work as an Apocalypse of Zephaniah.

It is not entirely clear from the content of the surviving portions of text why the author selected Zephaniah as the name of the seer. There are some parallels with the biblical Book of Zephaniah (cf. the nn. to the translation), but there are stronger parallels to Zechariah. The strongest parallels to Zephaniah in the surviving text are the concern for apostate priests in 3:2–6 (cf. Zeph 1:4) and the mention of God's coming wrath in 12:5–8 (cf. Zeph 1:14–18). Since a considerable amount of text is missing, it is quite probable that some lost episode near the beginning of the text provided a literary tie to the biblical prophet Zephaniah.

Texts

The text of the Apocalypse of Zephaniah has been partially preserved in two separate manuscripts that come from the White Monastery of Shenuda near Sohag. The earlier manuscript, which Steindorff dated at the end of the fourth century, is written in Akhmimic; the second manuscript, which Steindorff dated at the beginning of the fifth century, is written in Sahidic.[5] Both manuscripts contain the text of the Apocalypse of Elijah as well as the Apocalypse of Zephaniah.

Since the surviving text was purchased for European libraries leaf by leaf in two separate lots, there was originally a considerable amount of confusion about the identity and the content of these texts. The first group of papyri, which was purchased by Maspero between 1881 and 1884, contained not only two pages of the text of the Apocalypse of Zephaniah and twelve pages of the text of the Apocalypse of Elijah from the Sahidic manuscript but also fourteen pages of the Apocalypse of Elijah from the Akhmimic manuscript. That group of papyri is now in the Bibliothèque Nationale, inventory number *Copte* 135.

A second lot of papyri from the same Akhmimic manuscript was uncovered in 1888 by K. Reinhardt. That collection consisted of sixteen pages of text: four from the Apocalypse of Zephaniah and twelve from the Apocalypse of Elijah. The papyri are now located in the Egyptological section of the State Museum of Berlin (German Democratic Republic), inventory number P 1862.

The Greek text of Clement's citation has been published in Stählin's edition of the *Stromata*, book 5.11.77.[6] In addition to that quotation, there are three ancient witnesses who mention an Apocalypse of Zephaniah. Since they simply list the title without quoting from the document, there is some uncertainty about the relationship between the Coptic apocalypse and the work cited in those three lists.

The first of these is the stichometry that was appended to the chronography of Nicephorus, Patriarch of Constantinople (806–15). That list, which may be several centuries older than the work of Nicephorus, includes a text entitled "(The Book of the) Prophet Zephaniah," which contained 600 stichoi. The listing of the Zephaniah title immediately follows a work entitled "(The Book of the) Prophet Elijah." The proximity of the works attributed to Zephaniah and Elijah in the stichometry and the fact that the works appear together in two separate Coptic manuscripts lend some support to the assumption that the Coptic works are to be identified with the ancient works mentioned in the stichometry. Nevertheless, it would appear that we do not have texts in the recension used for counting stichoi, since the calculations of Schmidt reveal that the text of Elijah is a bit short for the suggested 316 stichoi and the space needed for the text of Zephaniah is a bit more than the suggested 600 stichoi.

The second ancient witness is the *Synopsis scripturae sacrae* of Pseudo-Athanasius, an

---

[5] G. Steindorff, *Die Apokalypse des Elias, eine unbekannte Apokalypse und Bruchstücke der Sophonias-Apokalypse.*
[6] *Clemens Alexandrinus,* ed. O. Stählin (GCS 15).

early list (perhaps 6th cent.) which Zahn treated as an independent tradition.[7] The list of books in general is similar to that found in the stichometry of Nicephorus, but there is no stichometry provided. The works assigned to Elijah and Zephaniah appear in precisely the same order and with the same title that was given to them in the stichometry of Nicephorus.

The third writing is the anonymous *Catalogue of the Sixty Canonical Books*. It lists the Apocalypse of Elijah, the Vision of Isaiah, and the Apocalypse of Zephaniah in that order. Here the works attributed to Elijah and Zephaniah are both designated as apocalypses, and the Vision of Isaiah is placed between them. Nevertheless, there is nothing in this listing of the two works that prevents their being identified with the parallel works mentioned in the previous lists. In fact, the probability lies with their being the same.

It has generally been assumed that the ancient lists refer to the same work cited by Clement. Be that as it may, a more important question to consider is the relationship between Clement's citation and the Coptic texts. There are details in the quotation that both parallel and contradict data in the Coptic fragments. The most striking parallel is that both quotations deal with angels and describe them as singing hymns before God (as in the AscenIs). Contradictory features are most noticeable in the description of the deity; he is called "the ineffable most high God" in the Clement citation, but the "Lord Almighty" in the Coptic text. The "Holy Spirit" is mentioned in Clement's quotation, but not in the Coptic fragments. The quotation also assigns the spirit a role in transporting the seer; the Coptic fragments portray the seer traveling with the angel of the Lord. None of these contradictory features excludes the possibility that the quotation was taken from the same text as the Coptic fragments. Variation between Clement and the Coptic text may occur because Clement had a Christian recension of the text. Variation may also exist because the author of the apocalypse was following a different source in writing about the fifth heaven. Nevertheless, the majority of scholars appear to have followed the lead of E. Schürer and assumed that this quotation was taken from the same Apocalypse of Zephaniah as that preserved in the surviving Coptic fragments.[8] Thus the simplest hypothesis is to assume that there was a single ancient text entitled "The Apocalypse of Zephaniah," which was attested by the four ancient witnesses listed above, and the Coptic fragments represent two different versions of that text.

Original language

It is generally assumed that the Coptic texts of the Apocalypse of Zephaniah are translations of a Greek original. There is no reason to suspect a pre-Greek stage of writing behind any of the surviving fragments. On the contrary, there is reason to believe that the writer did not fully understand Hebrew (compare the note regarding "Eloe, Lord, Adonai, Sabaoth" at 6:7).

Date

If the quotation by Clement of Alexandria is part of the apocalypse, then there are distinct limits for the time within which the text is to be dated. The earliest date for the Apocalypse of Zephaniah is sometime after the story of Susanna was circulated in Greek as part of the Book of Daniel. In 6:10 the author of the apocalypse appeals to the accounts of Susanna, Shadrach, Meshach, and Abednego as examples of God's power to deliver. Unfortunately, the date and even the original language of composition of the tale of Susanna are still matters of debate, but one could assume with some certainty that the text would be well known in Alexandria as part of the Book of Daniel during the first century B.C. The latest date is, of course, the time of Clement of Alexandria's *Stromata*. If we are correct in assuming that Clement accepted the work as that of the biblical prophet Zephaniah, it must have circulated long enough to have acquired that prestige. That would set the latest date sometime before the last quarter of the second century of the Christian era.

As a result of the preceding arguments we can fix the date of this writing somewhere between 100 B.C. and A.D. 175. In commenting on the author's use of Mount Seir in 3:2 we have speculated about the historical period in which such a setting would be most apt to

---

[7] T. Zahn, *Geschichte des Neutestamentlichen Kanons* (Erlangen, 1889) vol. 2, pp. 302–18.

[8] E. Schürer, Review of *Die Apokalypse des Elias* by Steindorff in *TLZ* 24 (1899) cols. 4–8.

occur, concluding that motives for a pro-Edomite tradition may have persisted until the fall of Jerusalem in A.D. 70. If the author of this text is responsible for the tradition that places the seer's vision on Mount Seir, then he probably wrote before A.D. 70.

Provenance

We have no knowledge of the author apart from what we can deduce from his work. Although the claim is made that these are the visions of Zephaniah, reported in the first person, the well-known literary conventions of apocalyptic writing have led scholars to disregard that claim. Zephaniah is generally considered to be a pseudonym used by an anonymous writer who either believed that he was writing in the spirit of the biblical prophet Zephaniah or simply wished to enhance the prestige of his own ideas by invoking the name of an illustrious man of God.

Whatever his name, it is fairly clear that the writer was a Jew. In the surviving portions of the text that deal with doctrines as basic as judgment for sin, intercessory prayer, and life after death, there is nothing distinctively Christian. The lack of Christian elements is even somewhat surprising when we remember that the manuscripts came from the library of a Christian monastery. They were preserved by monks, and in all probability copied by monks from earlier manuscripts that had been translated from Greek to Coptic within a Christian community. Over a period of one or two centuries of transmission by Christian scribes there are a number of ways that Christian concerns might have entered the document short of a conscious redaction of the text: (1) a Christian translator might have assumed that certain Greek terms in the document he was translating had a "Christian" meaning; (2) a Christian copyist might unconsciously have expanded a phrase or reformulated a sentence to agree with a familiar liturgical statement drawn from a Christian context; or (3) a monk might even have been tempted to add the name of Jesus or Paul to the list of righteous saints in Paradise. As a matter of fact, however, there is no clear example of any such modification of the text. The closest point of contact with Christian writings is found in the Akhmimic text. At 2:1–4 there is a close parallel to Matthew 24:40f. and Luke 17:34–36. At 6:11–15 there is a description of the angel Eremiel that has several features in common with descriptions of angels in Revelation. At 10:9 there is a quotation containing the word *katēchoumenos,* which is used in a sense frequent in patristic texts. Nevertheless, each of these parallels may be rather easily explained as due to a common Jewish-Christian heritage. The most important point to observe is that in the surviving fragments there is no evidence of any Christian modification of any of the major theological concerns expressed in the work.

Further study of the document by other scholars who are more knowledgeable about the sectarian divisions of ancient Judaism will be required before it is possible finally to set this apocalypse in its proper sociological context, but the following preliminary statements may be set forth. The author, who was concerned about the question of life after death, was not a Sadducee. His dualism is not compatible with that of Qumran. There is no zealot theology in evidence. He comes across as a gentle man, concerned for intercession on behalf of those in torment. He has concern for proper fulfillment of priestly ordinances (3:3f.) and times of daily prayer (11:5f.), but there is no reason to believe that the author himself was a priest. As a writer of apocalyptic, he shares features with a wide range of similar writings, a number of which are indicated in the accompanying notes, but his writing is also illuminated by referring to the Old Testament and to books within the Apocrypha such as Tobit, the Wisdom of Solomon, and the additions to Daniel.

Since the author wrote in Greek, he may well have resided in a Jewish community outside of Palestine, somewhere in the hellenistic world. Evidence favoring Egypt is strongest. Two separate manuscripts have survived in Egypt. The Coptic (Budge) Apocalypse of Paul probably contains a quotation from a third Egyptian manuscript (see fragment B, n. c), attesting to the popularity of the text in Egypt. The only remaining Greek fragment of the work is the quotation by Clement of Alexandria. Consequently, it is reasonable to assume that the work was produced in that city. The comment regarding the weighing of good and evil (see ch. 8, n. b) also reminds one of an Egyptian motif, but such a comment could scarcely be decisive.

Theological importance

A basic theme present in all of the Coptic fragments is that of a divine judgment which faces all men. The Sahidic fragment, for example, contains a description of the scourging of a soul that was found in lawlessness. The same theme provides a connecting link joining the separate episodes in the travelogue. In 3:1 the angel of the Lord says, "Come, let me show you the place of righteousness." If the translation "place of righteousness" is correct, it probably refers to the heavenly realm beyond the river of Hades, in which dwell the righteous men of old: Abraham, Isaac, Jacob, Enoch, Elijah, and David. In order to reach that place it is necessary for the seer to travel the route of a departed soul, which involves a harrowing confrontation with the accuser in Hades. The journey is carried out in stages. At the first stage, on Mount Seir, the seer learns how the evidence for and against a man is collected by angels who sit upon the gate. At the second stage, which is outside the heavenly city, he sees the terrifying angels who bring up the souls of ungodly men to their justly deserved eternal punishment. They cannot touch Zephaniah, however, because he is pure. The third stopping point is within the city before the gates, where fire is being cast forth. After withdrawing from there, the seer finds himself in Hades, where he encounters both Eremiel and the accuser. Eremiel is clearly a beneficent angel who cares for the souls imprisoned there, but the accuser, true to his title, seeks to condemn men before the Lord. Thus he functions as a prosecutor in the final judgment of men. It is also in Hades that the seer recognizes his own manuscripts, which contain testimony for and against him. When he finally prevails over the accuser and is judged victorious, he joins the ranks of angelic beings and summarizes his experience by saying, "Now, moreover, my sons, this is the trial because it is necessary that the good and the evil be weighed in a balance" (8:5).

In the trumpet scenes there are further descriptions of punishment for sinful souls and mention of a final day "when the Lord will judge," but the theme of intercessory prayer by the righteous becomes equally prominent. The concern of the righteous for those in torment appears in several passages. In 2:8f. Zephaniah sees the souls of men in torment and he offers a strong intercessory appeal which prompts the angel of the Lord to show him the place of righteousness. Along the way he observes two angels weeping over the three sons of Joatham because they have no righteous deeds to record. Nevertheless, this theme reaches its climax in the third trumpet scene, where we read of "multitudes" (including Abraham, Isaac, and Jacob) and "all the righteous" who intercede daily for those in torment.

The intercessory prayers are addressed to a God who is capable of mercy (11:2), who remains with his saints, and has compassion on behalf of the world (2:9). A similar conception of God lies behind Zepaniah's prayer for his own deliverance. In 6:10 he appeals to the God whose faithfulness to his saints is illustrated by his salvation of Israel, Susanna, Shadrach, Meshach, and Abednego. In 7:8 he appeals to God's mercy, which is "in every place and has filled every space."

A corollary of God's mercy and patience is his willingness to permit repentance, which could spare man the punishment he justly deserves. In the second trumpet scene the seer is shown the torment of sinful souls. When he has seen them, he asks, "do they not have repentance here?" The answer is "yes," and the opportunity continues right up until "the day when the Lord will judge." This text is written with a strong appeal for repentance. The two most extended and specific descriptions of the torment of sinners are found in the second trumpet scene and in the Sahidic fragment. Each time the description is closed with a comment about repentance. The comment from the second trumpet scene was discussed above and encourages repentance by emphasizing God's patience. The comment at the end of the torments described in the Sahidic fragment encourages repentance by warning that the soul is being tormented because it was "found in its lawlessness" and taken from its body before "it attained to repenting."

Despite the emphasis on God's mercy and his willingness to accept repentance, the author never forgets that God is the final judge, and that those found wanting will be subject to his wrath. The Akhmimic fragment is broken off after page 18, just as the author begins his final description of God's wrath. It is reasonable to assume that the four missing pages of the Akhmimic manuscript described the eschatological woes that are to be expected at the end of the age.

God's glory is presented indirectly in the Coptic texts. His transcendence is preserved throughout, but the splendor of his angel, Eremiel, is so great that the seer assumes that he is God and falls down to worship him. He is soon corrected by the angel, but one implication of the encounter is that if one could see him, God would be even more glorious than his great angel. In the quotation preserved by Clement, the angelic thrones in the fifth heaven are described as being "sevenfold more (brilliant) than the light of the rising sun." By implication, the glory of God, who is far above the fifth heaven, is beyond description, a view explicit in the name for God: "the ineffable most high God" (fragment A).

In contrast to Clement's quotation, the Akhmimic text refers to God as "Lord Almighty" (*pjaeis pantokrator* = Gk. *kurios pantokratōr*). This Greek phrase is consistently used in the Septuagint to render the Hebrew *Yahweh Ṣᵉbaʾôt*, the "Lord of Hosts." In the pre-exilic period this expression identified Yahweh as the God of the Armies (Hosts) of Israel, but by the time of the Exile "the Hosts" were identified with heavenly beings (cf. Isa 13:4f.). Thus it is natural in a text that places so much emphasis on the angelic hosts to confront the phrase "Lord of Hosts."

The angelology was very important for the author's understanding of the divine world. God is everywhere assumed to be an absolutely sovereign monotheistic deity; yet the author's angelology allows him to deal with data that is moderately dualistic. There are basically two types of angels: (1) beautiful angels, who praise God and assist righteous men, and (2) ugly angels, who are sent to terrify evil men, transport their souls to eternal punishment, and torment them. The ugly angels are not described as demons or evil angels but as "servants of all creation" (4:6), and hence servants of the God of all creation, the *pantokratōr*. The ugliest angel is "the accuser," but there is nothing to suggest that he is either a fallen angel or a lord of demons. His task remains much the same as that of Satan in the Book of Zechariah, a document that extensively influenced the author of this apocalypse.

One of the important tasks of the angels in the Akhmimic text is to watch men and record every deed, both good and bad. Ultimately the writer is dealing with the omniscience of God, the righteous judge, who knows our every deed, but he deals with it in a very homely figure. Ugly angels write down all the evil deeds of men and take them to the accuser, who records them in order to accuse men before God. The beautiful angels write down all the good deeds of the righteous and give them to the great angel—Zephaniah's guide—and he takes them to God, who enrolls them in the Book of the Living. In this mode of operation we can see two groups of angels serving in different camps. One group works for the great angel and the other works for the accuser. The great angel and the accuser appear to be on a level of parity before the Lord Almighty. A similar picture may be drawn from the scene in Hades, where Eremiel, the guardian of souls, appears vis-à-vis the accuser of souls. There are striking parallels between the structure presented here and similar views that appear in the Qumran Manual of Discipline (1QS 3.13–4.26), where God created two spirits to govern the affairs of men: a spirit of truth and a spirit of falsehood. The significant difference, however, is that the ugly angels in the Apocalypse of Zephaniah are not commissioned to deceive men or to contribute to their downfall; they merely report it.

The anthropology of the text has already been touched upon in dealing with theology and angelology. Here we may summarize. There are two ways open to men. One leads to enrollment in the Book of the Living (9:2), investiture in angelic garments (8:3), participation in angelic liturgy, and communion with the righteous, including the patriarchs, Enoch, Elijah, and David. The other way leads to eternal punishment (4:6f.). Every man is judged on the basis of his earthly deeds, and the righteous are delivered from Hades. Repentance is capable of changing the ultimate destiny of man. In all of this, man is represented as being free to make moral choices. He is not deceived or misled by evil spirits. On the contrary, there is evidence that the angels and the righteous continually seek to intercede with prayers and weeping on behalf of the fallen.

Relation to canonical books

Inasmuch as the Apocalypse of Zephaniah was written within a Jewish community, the author was familiar with the Old Testament and also expected his readers to be. It seems likely that he was familiar with the Pentateuch, prophets, and a number of the writings. The edition of Daniel that he used contained the story of Susanna. At 2:5 the description of a drop suspended from a bucket is probably dependent on Isaiah 40:15.

Elsewhere, the author's use of the Old Testament is less specifically related to a particular text. He knows a number of epithets for God (6:7), the names of patriarchs (11:4; 9:4), heroes (6:10; 9:4), and the prophet Zephaniah (fragment B, 7). He also mentions Psalms (1:2) and the Book of the Living (3:7; 9:2; cf. Ps 69:28). The manner in which the dialogue between the prophet and his angelic interpreter is described follows the model found in Zechariah 1–6. The use of such data does not suggest that thè author was a particularly careful student of the Scriptures who would rank with Paul, Philo, or the author of Jubilees. His knowledge is the casual sort available to a layman in the Jewish community. He is not interested in either studying the Scriptures directly or using them to support his theological position. The Old Testament simply provides him with a literary model for a portion of the angelic discourse, a number of well-known characters, a few ethical concerns, and incidental descriptive details.

The author's limited use of the Old Testament is determined by his concern for postmortem judgment of souls, a concern virtually unmentioned in the Old Testament. Conversely, many significant concerns of the Old Testament are barely noted by the author. From the Pentateuch he is familiar with the phrase "commandments and ordinances" (3:4), but the phrase is split up so that the "commandment" is that of a priest Joatham, and the ordinances are from the Lord. The writer mentions the sons of Israel (7:7), but there is no mention of covenant, election, or land. He lists the patriarchs (9:4), but treats them merely as examples of pious men who were saved. He mentions God's mighty act of saving Israel from Pharaoh (6:10), but reveals no theological feeling for sacred history.

The historical texts of the Old Testament have little interest for our author. He mentions David and Elijah simply as examples of holy men. He is somewhat more interested in the prophets, but both Zephaniah, who appears as the central figure in the apocalypse, and Zechariah, whose angelic dialogue serves as a model, are portrayed here, not as messengers of God's judgment or blessing, but as apocalyptic seers to their own age.

The author's interest in angels, thrones, and apocalyptic judgment represents a more direct influence from the later Old Testament collection of writings, particularly Daniel and Psalms. The sins of omission that are listed on the seer's manuscript (7:3–8) are expressed in a form (i.e. "If I did not . . .") reminiscent of Job 31:16, 20. Both Job and the present text ultimately reflect the "Negative Confessions," which are found in the Egyptian Book of the Dead, confessions to be made in the underworld at the judgment of the soul. The ethical concern for the widow and orphan (7:4f.) is found throughout the Old Testament (Deut 24:17; Isa 1:17; Job 31:16f.), and so is the mention of prayer and fasting (Judg 20:26; 1Kgs 21:9; Ezra 8:21), but the concern for turning to the sons of Israel reflects a post-exilic setting when life within a non-Jewish environment has singled out the children of Israel as a distinctive group among the nations for whom the pious express continual concern. Although the author of the present apocalypse has no interest in Nehemiah's political hopes for his people, he accepts the model of piety expressed in Nehemiah 1:4–6. In that passage Nehemiah is described as engaging in daily fasting and intercessory prayer for the children of Israel.

Since there is little reason to believe that the present text was influenced by the New Testament, any parallels that occur are due to borrowing from a common milieu or a New Testament dependence on the present work. One of the most striking parallels is the seer's vision of two women grinding at a mill (2:3; cf. Mt 24:41). In that case, we are probably dealing with a well-known proverbial expression that was used by both the author of the present apocalypse and the evangelist.

At 6:14f. there is a significant parallel to Revelation 19:10 (cf. 22:8f.). In both cases the seer falls down to worship an angel, and in both cases he is told not to worship the angel because he is not God. The context in which the adoration occurs in the present text is clear and logical. The seer was so awed by the splendor of the angel Eremiel that he mistook him for God. The author may have wished to indicate the surpassing majesty of God by suggesting that what might appear to men to attain the level of divine glory does not rise above the level of angelic splendor. The motif is repeated twice in Revelation (19:10; 22:8f.) in a context that is less clear. The angel who appears there describes himself as merely a fellow servant of the seer. The New Testament author may be dependent on a tradition that wishes to combat the worship of angels.

In the Apocalypse of Zephaniah the angel who is worshiped is both identified and described

(6:11–15) in a passage that is strikingly similar to Revelation 1:13–18. The passage is obviously based on the description of a figure appearing in Daniel 10:5–14. The fact that the figure in Daniel is not identified undoubtedly generated a considerable amount of speculation. His legs are burnished bronze like those of the divine figure described in Ezekiel 1:27. He also claims to have been aided by Michael in resisting the Persians. It would appear from the description that Daniel saw either God or one of his highest angels. Whoever seeks to solve the problem of Daniel's vision must decide that issue, and if he decides that it is an angel he is then obliged to try to identify him. In the present text the issue is resolved when Zephaniah encounters the same figure that Daniel saw and identifies him as Eremiel, denying that he is the Lord Almighty.

The author, or the source on which he relies, has both edited and expanded Daniel's vision at points. He eliminates Daniel's reference to the figure as a man and also the notice of his linen garment because he is not interested in his human features. He adds a notice that his face was shining like the sun and reports that he is responsible for those imprisoned in the abyss and Hades. What is surprising is to find the two added details in Revelation 1:11–18.

There are, of course, differences in the vision that is preserved in Revelation. The human features of Daniel's figure have been retained because the Christian tradition has identified the man in Daniel 10:5 with the Son of Man in Daniel 7. The Christian tradition is probably also responsible for providing the figure in Revelation 1:11–18 with white hair, a portrayal taken from the description of the Ancient of Days in Daniel 7.

Despite the differences, however, the descriptions of Eremiel and the figure of the Son of Man in Revelation are strikingly similar. The figures also share a benevolent concern for the souls in Hades. On the basis of the parallels, it is reasonable to assume that the Apocalypse of Zephaniah bears witness to a Jewish tradition that portrays Eremiel, the good angel of Sheol, in imagery based on Daniel 10:5–12, which was subsequently expanded. When the Christians began to identify the figure in Daniel 10:5–7 with the Son of Man, they used that expanded description of Eremiel to portray the risen Christ in his role as one who has power over death and Sheol.

Relation to apocryphal books

The Apocalypse of Zephaniah is dependent upon a tradition of apocalyptic writing that is concerned with demonstrating God's justice and mercy by permitting a seer to witness scenes of postmortem judgment and places of blessing prepared for the righteous. One of the earliest of these writings is found in 1 Enoch 21–25, a portion of "The Book of Watchers," which Milik dates "towards the middle of the third century B.C."[9] Subsequent treatments of the same theme in Jewish and Christian circles involved the seer's ascent through three, four, seven, eight, or ten heavens to the throne of God. As Bousset has shown in his study of *Die Himmelsreise der Seele*, later elaborations of the form involved many additional details, such as the removal of earthly garments and investiture with heavenly ones, sacramental anointing, and magical defense against demons who threaten the seer's ascent to the highest heaven.[10] There also appears to be a clear shift of emphasis from a simple display of God's justice toward a direct focus on the experiences of the seer as a prototype of the postmortem trials of a pious soul as it advances toward the throne of the Almighty.

The surviving portions of the Apocalypse of Zephaniah reflect a relatively early stage in the evolution of the type of apocalypse outlined above. Its closest parallels in both form and content are to be found in the apocalyptic portions of 1 Enoch, 2 Enoch, 3 Baruch, the Apocalypse of Paul, and the Nag Hammadi text CG V, 2,[11] which also bears the title "The Apocalypse of Paul." To a lesser extent there is also a formal parallel to be seen with the Testament of Levi and the Ascension of Isaiah. Specific parallels in content between the Apocalypse of Zephaniah and the apocalyptic writings listed above will be found in the notes that accompany the text.

---

[9] J. T. Milik, *The Books of Enoch* (Oxford, 1976) p. 28.

[10] W. Bousset, *Die Himmelsreise der Seele* (Darmstadt, 1960; a reprint of essays first published in 1901).

[11] An ET by G. MacRae and W. Murdock is now available in NHL, pp. 239–41.

The Coptic (Budge) Apocalypse of Paul[12] contains a number of unique readings or expansions. In two passages there are expressions that contain literal parallels to the Apocalypse of Zephaniah. Since the expansions in the manuscript that Budge published are undoubtedly later than the Apocalypse of Zephaniah, there is good reason to suspect some sort of dependence. Both parallels are discussed in the notes that accompany the present text (see fragment B, n. c and ch. 3, n. a).

BIBLIOGRAPHY

Charlesworth, *PMR*, pp. 220–23.
Denis, *Introduction*, pp. 192f.

Bouriant, U. "Les papyrus d'Akhmim," *Mémoires publiées par les membres de la mission archéologique française au Caire,* 1.2 (1885) 260–79. (This was the first publication of the Papyri purchased by Maspero and subsequently preserved in the Bibliothèque Nationale.)

Houghton, H. P. "The Coptic Apocalypse," *Aegyptus* 39 (1959) 43–67, 177–210. (Houghton's work consists of a transliteration of Steindorff's text with a literal translation.)

James, M. R. *The Lost Apocrypha of the Old Testament.* London, 1920; pp. 72–74. (James provides a brief appraisal of the text similar to the work of Schürer and Lods.)

Lacau, P. "Remarques sur le manuscrit akhmimique des apocalypses de Sophonie et d'Élie," *JA* 254 (1966) 169–95. (Lacau's work is the most extensive and most recent linguistic study of the ApZeph. It represents a significant advance in the study of the text.)

Lods, A. *Histoire de la littérature hébraïque et juive.* Paris, 1950; pp. 943f. (A brief survey of the text of ApZeph.)

Riessler, P. *Altjüdisches Schrifttum ausserhalb der Bibel.* Augsburg, 1928 (repr. 1966); pp. 114–25. (This German translation is good, but is scarcely an advance on the pioneering work of Steindorff.)

Schmidt, C. "Der Kolophon des Ms. Orient. 7594 des Britischen Museums; eine Untersuchung zur Elias-Apokalypse," *Sitzungsberichte der Preussischen Akademie der Wissenschaften.* Philosophisch-Historische Klasse, Berlin, 1925; pp. 312–21. (In this study, Schmidt sought to reconstruct the original order and length of the Akhmimic MS.)

Schürer, E. Review of *Die Apokalypse des Elias* by Steindorff in *TLZ* 24 (1899) cols. 4–8. (Schürer's review of Steindorff's work provided an important response and correction; he insisted that Steindorff's "anonymous Apocalypse" was part of ApZeph.)

Steindorff, G. *Die Apokalypse des Elias, eine unbekannte Apokalypse und Bruchstücke der Sophonias-Apokalypse.* TU 17.3a; Leipzig, 1899. (Steindorff was the first to sort out the confusing textual problems of ApZeph and ApEl; he was able to publish all of the pp. of both documents in their proper order. All subsequent studies are indebted to him.)

Stern, L. "Die koptische Apokalypse des Sophonias, mit einem Anhang über den untersahidischen Dialect," *Zeitschrift für ägyptische Sprache und Altertumskunde* 24 (1886) 115–29. (Stern produced a helpful grammatical study and translation of the texts published by Bouriant.)

---

[12] E. A. W. Budge, *Miscellaneous Coptic Texts in the Dialect of Upper Egypt* (London, 1915) pp. 534–74. The Nag Hammadi ApPaul must be carefully distinguished from the previously known ApPaul. The Nag Hammadi text might be designated "II Apocalypse of Paul" or "The Gnostic Apocalypse of Paul." Although it survives in Cop., it should not be referred to as "The Coptic Apocalypse of Paul" because there is also a Cop. version of the previously known ApPaul which was published by Budge in *Miscellaneous Coptic Texts in the Dialect of Upper Egypt.*

Till, W. "Bemerkungen und Erganzungen zu den achmimischen Textausgaben," *Zeitschrift für ägyptische Sprache und Altertumskunde* 63 (1928) 90f. (Till's brief comments deal primarily with minor grammatical points.)

Von Lemm, O. "Kleine koptische Studien, X, 1–3," *Bulletin de l'académie impériale des sciences de Saint-Pétersbourg* 13 (1900) 1–11. (In this study, Von Lemm identified several obscure words and made a significant start toward the restoration of lacunae at the beginning of the text.)

————. "Kleine koptische Studien, XXVI, 7–12," *Bulletin de l'académie impériale des sciences de Saint-Pétersbourg* 21 (1904) 41–45. (Another brief linguistic study of ApZeph.)

THE APOCALYPSE OF ZEPHANIAH

Clement, *Stromata* 5.11.77

The scene in the fifth heaven

A And a spirit took me and brought me up into the fifth heaven. And I saw angels who are called "lords,"[a] and the diadem was set upon them in the Holy Spirit,[b] and the throne of each of them was sevenfold more (brilliant) than the light of the rising sun.[c] (And they were) dwelling in the temples of salvation and singing hymns to the ineffable[d] most high God.[e]

Ezek 11:1
2En 18
3Bar 11
AscenIs 7:32-37
TLevi 3
Rev 19:12
1Kgs 22:19
Isa 6:1-8
Ezra 1:26-28

Sahidic fragment

The seer's vision of a soul in torment

1 **B** [I s]aw a s[ou]l which five thousand angels punished [?][a] [an]d gua[rded].
2 They took [it] to the East and they brought it to the West. They beat its . . . they
3 gave it a hundred . . . lashes for each one[b] daily. •I was afraid and I cast myself
4 up[o]n my face so that my joints dissolved. •The angel helped me. He said to me,
"Be strong, O one who will triumph,[c] and prevail so that you will triumph[d] over
5 the accuser and you will come up from Hades." •And after I arose I said, "Who
6 is this whom they are punishing?" •He said to me, "This is [a] soul which was
found in its lawlessness." And before it attained to repenting it was [vi]sited, and
7 taken out of its body. •Truly, I, Zephaniah, saw these things in my vision.

Rev 22:8

A a. In 2En 18 the seer also finds a host in the fifth heaven. In that text they are called "Egoroi" ("Gregori" in text A). Charles identifies them with the Aram. *'irim* who appear in Dan. That word is translated into Gk. as *egrēgoroi*, "watchers" (Aquila, Symmachus). When Enoch first saw them, they were lamenting for their fallen brethren, but he persuaded them to praise God with their singing, as the "lords" are doing in the present passage. The background for designating an angelic host as "lords" may be sought in the LXX version of Deut 10:14–17 where the God of the heavens is described as "God of gods and Lord of lords." The mention of "many gods and many lords" in 1Cor 8:5 may also be related to Deut 10:17, but it is basically pejorative in its thrust and consequently belongs to a different tradition than the present work.

b. We have capitalized the Holy Spirit because the spirit is undoubtedly that of God. Nevertheless, there is no need to understand this in a trinitarian or Christian sense as Clement may have done. There is sufficient attestation of the use in Jewish sources: Cf. WisSol 9:17; MartIs 5:14; 4Ezra 14:22; PssSol 17:42; CD 2.10.

c. In Dan 7:9 there is mention of "thrones" being set up for a scene of judgment. The use of the plural suggests that members of the heavenly host are also to be enthroned beside the Ancient of Days. The same passage provides an OT background for the brilliant, luminous quality of the thrones portrayed in the present text. Cf. Col 1:16; Rev 4:4; AscenIs 7:13.

d. The Gk. *arrētos*, "ineffable," may be used of

God in two senses: (1) one who is indescribable because he is beyond comprehension, and (2) one whose name ought not to be spoken because it is prohibited outside of a limited cultic setting. It is difficult to know which sense is intended here because of the lack of context. Both uses were current in Jewish sources.

e. The Gk. *hupsistos*, "most high," was used in the LXX to render the Heb. *'elyon*. It was subsequently rather widely used in the apocrypha and pseudepigrapha as a divine name. Cf. Tob 1:4, 13; Jdt 13:13; 2Mac 3:31; 3Mac 6:2. See also *TWOT*, vol. 8, p. 618.

B a. The meaning of the Cop. word used here and in vs. 5 is uncertain.

b. "Each one" must refer to the angels.

c. There is a similar phrase on fol. 35b of the Cop. version of the ApPaul edited by Budge. It reads, "Be strong, O one who will triumph and you will triumph over the accuser, who will come up from Hades." The text of ApPaul must represent either a quotation from the present text or a borrowing from a common stock of liturgical expressions. The version in ApPaul has been corrupted so that it appears that the accuser is the one who will come up from Hades, but when it is corrected to agree with the wording of the present apocalypse the sense of ApPaul is improved.

The reading "O one who will triumph" in the present text requires reading the Cop. *peknajro* as *petnajro*.

d. Reading *jeknajro* for *petnajro*.

The scene in a broad place

8   And the angel of the Lord[e] went with me. I saw a great broad place, thousands of thousands surrounded [it] on its left side and myriads of myriads on its right
9   [side]. The form[f] of [each] one was different. • Their hair was loose[g] like that belonging to women. [Their] teeth were like the teeth of . . .[h]

The Akhmimic Text

Fragment dealing with burial

1,2 **1** . . . dead. We will bury him like any man.[a] • Whenever he dies, we will carry him out playing the cithara before [him] and chanting psalms and odes[b] over his body.

Scenes from above the seer's city

1   **2** Now I went with the angel of the Lord, and he took me up (over) all my city.[a]
2   There was nothing[b] before my eyes. • Then I saw two men walking togeth[er] on   Mt 24:40f.
3   one road.[c] I watched [them] as they ta[lk]ed. • And, moreover, I also saw two   Lk 17:34f.

e. The angel of the Lord appears in the OT as a figure closely identified with Yahweh. In the earlier portions of the OT he is sent to deliver a message from God or to assist Israel in time of distress. With the prophet Zechariah, however, the angel of the Lord becomes a guide and interlocutor who explained the visions that the prophet saw. It is in that role that the angel of the Lord appears in the present text.

f. The Cop. word can also represent the Gk. words *genos*, "genus," or *phusis*, "nature."

g. The same phrase is found at vs. 4:4.

h. The remainder of the text is broken off. The reverse side of the papyrus is illegible, except for isolated words.

1 a. The author may be explaining what the burial practice in a typical situation is. That would contrast with the seer's own transformation. It is also possible that the seer is here quoting someone else who is describing the seer's own body, which appeared to be dead. In *PJ* there is an account of what happened when Jeremiah was undergoing a visionary experience. Those who were left on the earth thought that he was dead and considered preparing his body for burial. The Cop. word that is used in the present passage means either "to bury" or "to prepare the corpse for burial." In the Nag Hammadi ApPaul (CG V, 19, 27–29), Paul is apparently told to look back and see his own "[likeness]" upon the earth. Unfortunately the text must be restored at that critical point.

b. This description of the funeral rite is so brief that it is not possible to tell whether it is Christian or Jewish. The pattern clearly conforms to very early Christian practice, but that does not exclude the possibility of it being Jewish. In 2Sam 3:31–4, King David provides a prototype for Jewish funeral processions together with the accompanying lamentation. Josephus (*Apion* 2.27) describes the appropriate response of pious Jews of his time to a passing funeral procession. The recitation of Ps 91 during the procession is apparently very ancient.

2 a. Jerusalem would be the most likely city to appear in an apocalypse of Zephaniah. Note God's word in Zeph 1:10–13. It is also of interest to note Zech-

ariah's considerable interest in Jerusalem since our author is greatly indebted to that prophet.

b. Possibly "no one."

c. The present passage is obviously related to the words of Jesus reported in Mt 24:40f. and Lk 17:34f. (cf. GThom 91, 23). Unfortunately, the nature of the relationship is not easy to determine. If we agree with P. Lacau, "remarques sur le manuscrit akhmimique des apocalypses de Sophonie et d'Élie," *JA* 254 (1966) 176, that the quotation "two men . . . on one road" is simply a variant of the "two men . . . in the field," which appears at Mt 24:40, then we may compare the three versions in the following manner: (1) two men on one road (= field)—two women grinding at the mill—two in one bed (ApZeph), (2) two men in the field—two women grinding at the mill (Mt), (3) two in one bed—two women grinding—[two men in the field] (Lk). The ApZeph contains the fullest account. It mentions the "mill" of Mt and the "bed" of Lk.

A simple solution might be to assume that the version of ApZeph is a conflation of the Gospel passages, but there are a number of reasons for rejecting that position. Lacau has already noted that this would then be the only passage in the apocalypse that could be specifically identified as Christian.

The structure of the saying suggests a carefully worked proverbial phrase, similar to the proverb about the drop on the bucket that follows. In the present saying, the action moves from two men on the road to two women who are presumably straining together in a common effort to turn the upper millstone, and then, finally, to a couple in bed. The scene becomes progressively more intimate as the saying continues. It begins with two men, turns to two women, and concludes with a couple (presumably a man and a woman). The fact that the proverb is so well constructed and complete in its present form means that it is not a simple conflation. One is not obliged to accept the opinion that it is derived from the Gospel accounts. In fact, one could argue that Mt and Lk provide abbreviated variants of a longer parable. It is our opinion that this was a familiar parable that was used in the present work and alluded to by Mt, Lk, and the author of GThom.

The proverbial nature of the saying is also apparent

4 women grinding together at a mill. And I watched them[d] as they talked. •And I
  [also] saw two upon a bed, [each] one of them acting for their (mutual) . . .[e] upon
5 a bed. •And [I saw] the whole inhabited world ha[nging] like a drop of wa[ter],   Isa 40:15
6 which is suspended[f] from a buc[ket] when it comes up from[g] a well. •I said to the   WisSol 11:22
7 angel of the Lord, "Then does darkness or night not exist in this place?"[h] •He said   Ps 139:12
  to me, "No, because darkness does not exist in that place where the righteous and
  the saints are, but rather they always exist in the light."

8,9   And I saw all the souls of men as they existed in punishment. •And I cried out   Isa 57:15
  to the Lord Almighty,[i] ["O Go]d, if[j] you remain with the [sa]ints, you (certainly)   1Clem 59:3
  have compassion[k] on behalf of the world [and] the souls which are in [this]
  punishment."

Vision of recording angels from Mount Seir

1 **3** The angel of the Lord said to me, "Come, let me show you the [place (?)] of   Eccl 3:16
2 righteousness."[a] •And he took me [up] upon Mount Seir[b] and he [showed me]   Deut 33:2
3 three men, as two angels walked with them rejoicing and exulting over them. •I   Isa 21:11
                                                                                     Judg 5:4

from the manner in which it is used by the author.
Although there is a slight lacuna at the end of the
statement, it is hardly large enough to permit the
author to explain his saying; he reasonably expected
his readers to understand the saying as a familiar
proverb dealing with the frailty of life and its inevitable end. It is a vision that follows his discussion of
a typical funeral procession; the reader was expected
to supply a traditional understanding of the visitation
of the Angel of Death, who would remove one of the
partners in each of these vignettes (cf. GThom 91,
24). In order for the writer to assume that sort of
reading, the proverb must have circulated in a form
that made it readily applicable to the *typical* human
experience. The Gospel quotations will not meet that
requirement because they are set in the context of the
sudden appearance of an eschatological age.

The motif of a seer ascending and looking back to
see events on earth is also found in ApPaul 13. The
seer in that text watches men at the point of death as
the soul leaves the body. Compare Nag Hammadi CG
V, 19, 29–32.

d. The pronoun must be restored in the text.

e. The translation of "[each] one of them acting
for their (mutual) . . . upon a bed," is uncertain. If
we were certain of the reading "on a bed," or if we
were able to restore the word that fits in the lacuna,
we could then be more confident about reading the
rest of the phrase. The word in the lacuna is a Gk.
word ending in *ia*. We also know that it was feminine
singular. Lacau suggested *adikia, anomia,* or some
word suggesting repose. The list of words could be
extended to include words meaning "harmony,"
"pleasure," or "accord." The parallel from the
GThom describes the two as "resting" or "being at
repose" upon a bed.

f. There are two scribal errors in this sentence. In
the phrase "which is suspended," the scribe wrote
a *chai* instead of an *e*.

g. In the phrase "up from," he wrote an *e* instead
of a *chai*. The translation of 2:3–5 depends upon
reconstructions of the text suggested by Lacau in *JA*
254 (1966) 169–95.

h. The question appears to be a non sequitur in
the present context, where it follows proverbial observations on the tenuous nature of human existence.
It is possible that there was a lacuna in the MS from
which the present text was copied, or perhaps the
abrupt change is simply a witness to a rather crude
conflation of sources.

In its present setting, the question concerning the
absence of darkness is introduced by the comment
that "There was nothing before my eyes," and examples of the seer's unusual vision as he observes
people engaged in various activities from his location
high above the city.

i. The term *pantokratōr* was well established in
Jewish writings on the basis of its use for translating
ṣᵉbaʾôt and *šaddai* in the LXX. Although the term
gains currency among the patristic writers, its use in
the NT is strictly limited. Apart from an OT quotation
in 2Cor 6:18, it is found only in Rev. For its use
within the OT see "Theological Importance."

j. There is a scribal error at this point. He wrote
o instead of *e* at the beginning of the word for "if."

k. A slight emendation is required to permit the
reading "you (certainly) have compassion."

3 a. A feminine noun that describes a location is
needed at this point. There is a similar phrase in the
Cop. (Budge) ApPaul, a work that appears to depend
on the present text in several places. The Cop. text
published by Budge (*Miscellaneous Coptic Texts in
the Dialect of Upper Egypt,* p. 568) records the
following command by Paul's guiding angel: "Rise
up now and follow me and let me show you your
place." The angel then leads Paul into Paradise.

b. Probably Edomite Seir, which is closely associated with Mount Sinai in the theophanies that appear
in the Song of Deborah (Judg 5:4f. and Deut 33:2).
Throughout the OT, Edom is treated as a model of
villainy, but after the conquest of Edom by John
Hyrcanus, the Idumeans begin to be fully involved
in the affairs of Judah. During the period of Antipater
and the Herodians, pro-Edomite sentiment undoubtedly flourished. Despite the fact that hatred for those
Idumean monarchs only intensified the traditional
mistrust of Edom among certain Jewish parties, there
were others who sought their favor. For example,
Josephus reports in his *War* (4.4) that the Idumeans
came to Jerusalem to assist the Zealots shortly before
that city fell to the Romans. The most likely period
for this pro-Edomite portion of the narrative that
locates the prophet's vision on Mount Seir is between
128 B.C. and A.D. 70, when there was a reasonable
motive for recalling positive references to Mount Seir
in the OT or for making it the locus of a new vision.

In the Nag Hammadi ApPaul, the ascent of the
apostle takes place from the mountain of Jericho. CG
V, 19, 12.

4 said to the angel, "Of what sort are these?" •He said to me, "These are the three
sons of Joatham,[c] the priest, who neither kept the commandment of their father   Deut 6:1
nor observed the ordinances of the Lord."   Lk 1:6
                                                                                    Ps 119:4
5 Then I saw two other angels weeping[d] over the three sons of Joatham, the priest.
6 I said, "O angel, who are these?" He said, "These are the angels of the Lord
Almighty. They write down all the good deeds[e] of the righteous upon their
7 manuscript[f] as they watch at the gate of heaven. •And I take them from their hands
and bring them up before the Lord Almighty; he writes their name in the Book of
8 the Living.[g] •Also the angels of the accuser who is upon the earth,[h] they also write
9 down all of the sins of men upon their manuscript. • They also sit at the gate of
heaven. They tell the accuser and he writes them upon his manuscript so that he
might accuse them when they come out of the world (and) down there."[i]

Vision of ugly angels who carry off the souls of ungodly men

1 **4** Then I walked with the angel of the Lord. I looked before me and I saw a place   Dan 7:10
2 there. • [Thousands] of thousands and myriads of myriads of an[gels] entered   Rev 5:11
                                                                                        1En 40:1
3 through [it]. • Their faces were like a leopar[d], their tusks being outside their   60:1
4 mouth [like] the wild boars. • Their eyes were mixed with blood. Their hair was
5 loose like the hair of women, and fiery scourges were in their hands. •When I saw
them, I was afraid. I said to that angel who walked with me, "Of what sort are
6 these?" •He said to me, "These are the servants of all creation who come to the
7 souls of ungodly men and bring them and leave them in this place. • They spend
three days going around with them in the air before they bring them and cast them
into their eternal punishment."
8 I said, "I beseech you, O Lord, don't give them authority to come to me."
9 The angel said, "Don't fea[r]. I will not permit them to come to [you] because
you are pure[a] before the Lord. I will not permit them to come to you because the
10 Lord Almighty sent me to you because ⟨you⟩ are pure before him." • Then he
beckoned to them, and they withdrew themselves and they ran from me.

---

c. This passage might possibly be decisive for dating the apocalypse if we could identify Joatham and his sons. Unfortunately, that is not a simple matter. The name Joatham appears in Josephus as a spelling for Jotham (cf. spelling of Jotham in Mt 1:9). Josephus identifies two high priests by that name. In a list that parallels 1Chr 6:4–8, 50–53, and Ezra 7:2–5, Josephus (*Ant* 8.12) has inserted Joatham at the point where the biblical writers list Uzzi and Zerahiah as ancestors of Solomon's priest, Zadok.

A second Jotham, son of Juelus, is mentioned in a list of high priests who held office between the time of Solomon and the Babylonian captivity. Jotham is the tenth priest in line. Using an average of twenty years for the length of a high priest's tenure, Jotham, son of Juelus, would have served sometime during the period of Ahaz or Hezekiah. It is conceivable that his sons might have disgraced themselves during the reign of Manasseh and Amon. The biblical Zephaniah, who provided the pseudonym for the present work, and who began his labors shortly after the reign of Amon, delivered an important oracle (Zeph 1:1–6) against the priests in Jerusalem, who are charged with swearing by both Yahweh and Milcom (vss. 4f.). In the Heb. text, the errant priests are called *kemarîm*, a term not used for legitimate priests of Yahweh, the Heb. text also adds the phrase "with the priests." Zephaniah threatened to remove the names of those priests.

At best any argument for identifying the Jotham of this text with either of the priests mentioned by

Josephus remains a fragile hypothesis. It is equally possible that the author has in mind some lesser priest whose family affairs were notorious among the contemporaries of the author of ApZeph.

d. There may be a temporal sequence here, with two angels rejoicing before the three sons sin (3:2–4) and two others weeping afterward. It is also possible that the text simply describes two different angelic responses. Two bad angels rejoice in wickedness and two good angels weep.

e. Compare ApPaul, chs. 7, 9, and 10. In that text angels bring forth deeds of men, whether good or evil, at sunset. One angel goes forth rejoicing and another goes out with a sad face.

f. "Their manuscript" is corrected from scribal "his manuscript." The plural pronoun refers to the angels. The plural is correctly used in 3:8, and the singular is correctly used in 3:9, where the pronoun refers to the accuser.

g. Compare Ps 69:28, where the Book of the Living is parallel to those "enrolled among the righteous." Compare also Ex 32:32f.; Ps 40:7; Isa 34:16; Dan 7:10; 12:1; Mal 3:16; Phil 4:3; Rev 3:5; 13:8.

h. It may also be read "who is over the earth," in the sense of authority, or it could refer to the angels who are upon or over the earth.

i. The Cop. construction is adverbial, describing the direction of the verb of motion. Perhaps the region of the accuser is "down there."

4 a. The word for "pure" also means "saint."

Vision of the heavenly city

1 **5** But I went with the angel of the Lord, and I looked in front of me and I saw
2 gates. •Then when I approached them I discovered that they were bronze gates.
3 The angel touched them and they opened before him. I entered with him and
4 found its whole square like a beautiful city, and I walked in its midst. •Then the
angel of the Lord transformed himself[a] beside me in that place.
5   Now I looked at them, and I discovered that they were bronze gates and bronze   Isa 45:2
6 bolts and iron bars. •Now my mouth was shut[b] therein. I beheld the bronze gates   Ps 107:16
in front of me[c] as fire was being cast forth for about fifty stadia.

Vision of the accuser and the angel Eremiel in Hades

1,2 **6** Again I turned back and walked, and I saw a great sea. •But I thought that it   1En 67:13
was a sea of water. I discovered that it was entirely a sea of flame like a slime   ApPet 23
3 which casts forth much flame and whose waves burn sulfur and bitumen. •They   Rev 19:20
began to approach me.
4,5   Then I thought that the Lord Almighty had come to visit me. •Then when I saw,
6 I fell upon my face before him in order that I might worship him. •I was very   Dan 10:10; 8:17
7 much afraid, and I entreated him that he might save me from this distress. •I cried
out, saying, "Eloe, Lord, Adonai, Sabaoth,[a] I beseech you to save me from this
distress because it has befallen me."
8   That same instant I stood up, and I saw a great angel before me. His hair was
spread out like the lionesses'.[b] His teeth were outside his mouth like a bear. His
hair was spread out like women's. His body was like the serpent's when he wished
9 to swallow me. •And when I saw him, I was afraid of him so that all of my parts   1En 21:9

---

5 a. In AscenIs there are a number of transformations. At 9:30 Isaiah is apparently transformed to appear like an angel. In 10:18–27 Isaiah witnesses the various transformations of the Lord as he descends from heaven to heaven. The reader is reminded of the transfiguration scenes in Mk 9:2f.; Mt 17:2; Lk 9:28f.; or the theological commentary of 2Cor 3:18. The ancestor of the transfiguration motif in Judaism may ultimately be the translation of Elijah in 2Kgs 2:11 or the account of Moses' shining face in Ex 34:29. The expectation that all who are righteous will be transfigured is based on Dan 12. The theme is enthusiastically expanded in apocalyptic literature. Compare 4Ezra 7:97, 125; 2Bar 51:3, 10; 1En 39:7; 104:2. The writers also conceived of a continuum between the angels and men who would become like the angels. Cf. 1En 104:6 and 2Bar 51:10. Consequently, angels might also be subject to transformations. Angelic messengers faced the same problem that confronted Moses when he was forced to veil and unveil his face as he moved between God and men in Ex 34:33–35. Apparently the angels dealt with the problem through a series of transformations.

b. This translation assumes that the sights within the city were not meant to be revealed. Compare ApPaul 21, where Paul is prohibited from revealing what he has seen in the third heaven. ApPaul is obviously dependent on Paul's note in 2Cor 12:1–4. Nevertheless, the idea of secret lore, sealed books, hidden knowledge is the stock-in-trade of Jewish apocrypha (= hidden matters) generally. Compare 4Ezra 14:4–6, 44–46; Dan 12:4.

If the seer's mouth was closed with respect to mysteries seen within the city, that would explain why very little is described beyond the gates and the overall beauty of the square. The reader has been led to expect a report of the seer's vision and an angelic explanation of each scene, but that is missing from the episode within the city.

c. In most of the apocalyptic writings gates are described as part of the heavenly city, but in TAb 11 (rec. A), there are two gates within the first gate of heaven. One leads on a narrow way for the blessed and one leads to a wide path for those who are evil. An earlier ancestor of that scene is to be found in the Myth of Er in Plato's *Republic* 614–21. Plato does not describe the entrances to heaven and Hades as gates, but TAb provides evidence that such a feature was known in apocalyptic writings. The gates which our seer beheld with fire being cast forth could possibly be the gates opening up from Hades.

6 a. Steindorff suggests that this represents a Heb. phrase, *ᵓlōhay, ᵓᵃdōnay, ᵓᵃdōnay ṣᵉbaᵓôt*, which would be translated "My God, my Lord, Lord of Hosts." That looks like a curious expression indeed. It is hard to imagine that it would be constructed in a Heb.-speaking community. It is also strange that anyone would translate the first *ᵓᵃdōnay* and transcribe the second. It would appear that the author of this text was not well acquainted with Heb. He apparently knew two Heb. Epithets: "Eloe" and "Adonai Sabaoth." He used the two of them together with his own Gk. term *kurios* to address God by means of three of his titles: "Eloe, Kurios, Adonai Sabaoth." The Cop. translator translated the Gk. and left the Heb. transcriptions in place.

b. This vs. also contains the phrase "his hair was spread out like women's." One of these descriptions appears to be redundant. Steindorff suggested that there might have been a description of his face which was like "the lionesses'." At this point he compared a text from Cod. Bruc. 227, l. 6, in which the description of the face of the figure precedes the description of its teeth. Cf. also 4:3f., above, and Rev 9:8.

10 of my body were loosened and I fell upon my face. •I was unable to stand, and
I prayed before the Lord Almighty, "You will save me from this distress. You
are the one who saved Israel from the hand of Pharaoh, the king of Egypt. You
saved Susanna from the hand of the elders of injustice. You saved the three holy
men, Shadrach, Meshach, Abednego, from the furnace of burning fire. I beg you
to save me from this distress."

11 Then I arose and stood, and I saw a great angel standing before me with his face
shining like the rays of the sun in its glory since his face is like that which is
12 perfected in its glory. •And he was girded as if a golden girdle were upon his   Rev 1:13-15
13 breast. His feet were like bronze which is melted in a fire. •And when I saw him,   Dan 10:5f.
14 I rejoiced, for I thought that the Lord Almighty had come to visit me. •I fell upon   Rev 2:18
15 my face, and I worshiped him. •He said to me, "Take heed. Don't worship me.   Rev 19:10;
I am not the Lord Almighty, but I am the great angel, Eremiel,[c] who is over the   22:8f.
Ascenls 7:21
abyss and Hades, the one in which all of the souls are imprisoned from the end
of the Flood, which came upon the earth, until this day."

16 Then I inquired of the angel, "What is the place to which I have come?"[d] He
17 said to me, "It is Hades." •Then I asked him, "Who is the great angel who stands
thus, whom I saw?" He said, "This is the one who accuses men in the presence
of the Lord."

Vision of the two manuscripts

1 **7** Then I looked, and I saw him with a manuscript in his hand. He began to unroll   ApPaul 17
2 it. •Now after he spread it out, I read it in my (own) language. I found that all my
sins which I had done were written in it, those which I had done from my youth
3 until this day. •They were all written upon that manuscript of mine without there
4 being a false word in them. •If I did not go to visit a sick man or a widow, I found   Job 31
5 it written down as a shortcoming upon my manuscript. •If I did not visit an orphan,
6 it was found written down as a shortcoming on my manuscript. •A day on which
I did not fast (or) pray in the time of prayer I found written down as a failing   Dan 6:10
7 upon my manuscript. •And a day when I did not turn to the sons of Israel—since
8 it is a shortcoming—I found written down upon my manuscript[a] •so that I threw
myself upon my face and prayed before the Lord Almighty, "May your mercy
reach me and may you wipe out my manuscript because your mercy has [co]me
to be in every place and has filled every [p]lace."

9 Then I arose and stood, and I saw a great angel before me saying to me,
"Triumph, prevail because you have prevailed and have triumphed[b] over the
accuser, and you have come up from Hades and the abyss. You will now cross
over the crossing place."

10,11 Again he brought another manuscript which was written by hand. •He began
to unroll it, and I read it, and found it written in my (own) language . . .

    TWO PAGES MISSING

    (In the missing pages the author probably discussed the content of the
    second manuscript, which should have recorded the good deeds of the seer.
    If the missing material is parallel to the preceding section, the reading of

---

c. This is the angel whose duty it is to watch over
the souls in Hades. The same figure appears in 4Ezra
4:36 as Jeremiel. In that text Ezra asks how long he
must wait until the new age, and he is informed that
the righteous are in the underworld and in the chambers of the souls, which are like a womb that will
bear when its time is filled. In 2Bar 55:3 and 63:6
the name is spelled Ramiel. He is described in that
text as "the angel . . . who presides over true visions"
(55:3). In 1En 20, the spelling is Remiel. He is listed
as one of the seven archangels; he is set over "those
who rise."
d. The Cop. phrase is ambiguous. It could mean

"which I have come up to" (so Steindorff) or "which
I have come down to." The seer is in Hades, but the
location is not clear.

7 a. The grammar of this last notice of sin differs
from the others. Perhaps it is done for climactic effect.
b. A slight emendation would make this passage
conform more closely to the parallel texts by reading
"triumph, prevail so that you will prevail and
triumph." Such an emendation does little to improve
the sense, however, and there is reason to believe that
this statement was meant to express the vindication
of the seer, who has already triumphed.

the manuscript would be followed by a prayer—possibly a prayer of thanksgiving—and a pronouncement of triumph by a great angel. That would be followed by preparations for crossing over the river in a journey out of Hades. The section that follows begins after the arrival of a boat.)

1,2 **8** . . . They helped me and set me on that boat. • Thousands of thousands and
3 myriads of myriads of angels gave praise before me. •I, myself, put on an angelic
4 garment. I saw all of those angels praying. •I, myself, prayed together with them,
5 I knew their language, which they spoke with me. •Now, moreover, my sons,[a] this is the trial because it is necessary that the good and the evil be weighed in a balance.[b]

The first trumpet, a proclamation of triumph and visitation of the righteous

1 **9** Then a great angel came forth having a golden trumpet in his hand, and he blew it three times over my head, saying, "Be courageous! O one who has triumphed. Prevail! O one who has prevailed. For you have triumphed over the accuser, and
2 you have escaped from the abyss and Hades. •You will now cross over the crossing
3 place. For your name is written in the Book of the Living." •I wanted to embrace him, (but) I was unable to embrace the great angel because his glory is great.
4   Then he ran to all the righteous ones, namely, Abraham and Isaac and Jacob
5 and Enoch and Elijah and David.[a] •He spoke with them as friend to friend speaking with one another.

Gen 18
Jas 2:23

A second trumpet, the openimg of heaven, a vision of souls in torment

1 **10** Then the great angel came to me with the golden trumpet in his hand, and he
2 blew it up to heaven. •Heaven opened from the place where the sun rises to where
3 it sets, from the north to the south. •I saw the sea which I had seen at the bottom

---

8 a. This sentence is an attempt to sum up the preceding episode. It is addressed to the hearers, who are identified as "my sons." The homiletical aside suggests that this portion of the text was prepared for use within an organized religious community that assembled to hear lectures or sermons. It is not possible to determine whether the text was originally written for that purpose or simply used in that manner by later generations.

b. The mention of weighing good and evil in a balance reminds one of the Egyptian prototype for judgment in the underworld.

9 a. "Abraham, Isaac, Jacob, Enoch, Elijah, and David." These six righteous ones have a special status for the writer of ApZeph. After leaving Hades, where Eremiel watches over the souls entrusted to him, the seer enters the realm of the righteous and meets those who did not sojourn in Hades. In this group, Enoch serves as the prototype for others. The statement that "Enoch walked with God. Then he vanished because God took him" (Gen 5:24) gave rise to early speculation about where he was taken. Jub 4:23 reports that he was conducted to the garden of Eden, where he writes down all the wickedness of the children of men. In 1En 70 we are told that his name was raised aloft and he saw angels measuring the place for the elect and righteous. He also saw the first fathers and the righteous who dwelt there. Unfortunately, that ch. in 1En cannot be dated. According to J. T. Milik, *The Books of Enoch*, p. 4, it is from a portion of 1En which was not attested at Qumran.

The removal of the patriarchs and David to Paradise presented a more severe problem because their death and burial was an accepted fact, and their tombs were available as shrines. TAb, TIsaac, and TJac, which are relatively late documents, preserve an account of how it was done. The body of each patriarch was buried, but his soul was removed to be with God (cf. ApMos for the removal of Adam's soul). An earlier witness to that tradition may possibly be seen in Jesus' argument preserved in Mt 22:29–33. The climax of the argument is found in vs. 32, "I am the God of Abraham, the God of Isaac and the God of Jacob? God is God, not of the dead, but of the living."

Apparently a similar removal was accorded King David, whose eternal presence was required as a musician who leads the praise of God with his harp and song (cf. ApPaul 29). See also the Cop. (Budge) ApPaul, fol. 36a. The motivation for David's transfer to a heavenly scene is probably to be located in a text such as the LXX version of Ps 16(LXX 15):10, in which it is stated that God would not leave his (i.e. David's) soul in Hades. It is also quite possible that the author of Acts 2:25–36 was arguing against a popular Jewish opinion that the soul of David was in Paradise while his uncorruptible body remained in the tomb. The author of Acts would be opposed to the theology of the present text because he explicitly states that "David did not ascend into the heavens." It is interesting to note that the Christian addition to 4Ezra, commonly referred to as 5Ezra, contains a list of Jewish heroes that begins with Abraham, Isaac, Jacob, Elijah, and Enoch. It then adds the names of the prophets, but it does not mention David.

The number of righteous persons in the heavenly Paradise described in our text is not obvious. Ch. 11:1 mentions "multitudes," but it is not clear that they are presently in Paradise.

4 of Hades. Its waves came up to the clouds. •I saw all the souls sinking in it. I saw
some whose hands were bound to their neck, with their hands and feet being
5 fettered. •I said, "Who are these?" He said to me, "These are the ones who were
bribed[a] and they were given gold and silver until the souls of men were led astray."
6,7 And I saw others covered with mats of fire. •I said, "Who are these?" He said
to me, "These are the ones who give money at interest, and they receive interest
8 for interest." •And I also saw some blind ones crying out. And I was amazed　Zeph 1:17
9 when I saw all these works of God. •I said, "Who are these?" He said to me,　Jas 1:22
"These are catechumens who heard the word of God, but they were not perfected
10 in the work which they heard."[b] •And I said to him, "Then do they not have
11 repentance here?" He said, "Yes." •I said, "How long?" He said to me, "Until
12 the day when the Lord will judge." •And I saw others with their hair on them.
13,14 I said, "Then there is hair and body in this place?" •He said, "Yes, the Lord
gives body and hair to them as he desires."　　　　　　　　　　　　　　　1Cor 15:38

The intercession of the saints for those in torment

1,2 **11** And I also saw multitudes. He brought them forth. •As they looked at all of
the torments they called out, praying before the Lord Almighty, saying, "We pray
to you on account of those who are in all these torments so that you might have
3 mercy on all of them." •And when I saw them, I said to the angel who spoke with
4 me, "⟨Who are these?⟩" •He said, "These who beseech the Lord are Abraham
5 and Isaac and Jacob. •Then at a certain hour daily they come forth with the great
6 angel. He sounds a trumpet up to heaven and another sound upon the earth. •All
the righteous hear the sound. They come running, praying to the Lord Almighty
daily on behalf of these who are in all these torments."

Another trumpet blast heralding the coming wrath of God

1 **12** And again the great angel comes forth with the golden trumpet in his hand
2 blowing over the earth. •They hear (it) from the place of the sunrise to the place
3 of the sunset and from the southern regions to the northern region. •And again he
4 blows up to heaven and his sound is heard. •I said, "O Lord, why did you not
5 leave me until I saw all of them?" •He said to me, "I do not have authority to
show them to you until the Lord Almighty rises up in his wrath to destroy the　Zeph 1:15
6 earth and the heavens. •They will see and be disturbed, and they will all cry out,
saying, 'All flesh which is ascribed to you we will give to you on the day of the　Rev 6:17
7 Lord.' •Who will stand in his presence when he rises in his wrath ⟨to destroy⟩ the　Mal 3:2
8 earth ⟨and the heaven?⟩ •Every tree which grows upon the earth will be plucked
up with their roots and fall down. And every high tower and the birds which fly[a]
will fall . . ."

FOUR PAGES MISSING

10 a. The Gk. word for "bribed" had to be restored
because the scribe confused it with a Gk. word meaning "to wear."

b. The quotation could certainly pass as a Christian
statement with its use of the word *katechoumenos* in
close proximity to *metanoia* in vs. 10 and joined to
a discussion of ones who were not "perfected,"
which probably reflects a *Vorlage* containing *teleioi*.
But one is not compelled to read it that way. The
word *metanoia* received from the intertestamental
Jewish writings many of the nuances that it has in the
NT (cf. WisSol 12:10, 19; PrMan 8).

The idea of the perfection of just men has a wider
history. It has philosophical antecedents as well as
currency to describe initiates in mystery religions.
Furthermore, the use of *telios* in the LXX to translate
tamin and *shalem* gave it wide currency in Jewish
writings. Thus Noah is designated "perfect" in the
LXX of Gen 6:9 in the sense of wholeness, so too
Enoch was described as perfected in WisSol 4:13,
16.

Consequently the only word that is not fully current
in Jewish writings is *katechoumenos*, but that does
not exclude its possible use by a Jewish author. There
was a considerable degree of continuity between Jewish and Christian methods of instruction. The verb
katecheō was used by both Philo and Josephus in the
sense of giving information. It would therefore not
be too surprising to discover a Jewish writer who
used the passive participle to describe those who were
taught. Finally, there is one element in Christian
usage which is not clearly present in this text. In
Christian usage, the term often refers to instruction
of proselytes, but there is no reason to assume that
those who were instructed in this text were any other
than members of the community who had been fully
informed of the significance of their own tradition.

12 a. After "fly" the scribe has created a dittography
by repeating the phrase "upon the earth and every
high tower."

TABLE OF TITLES GIVEN TO BOOKS ASSOCIATED WITH
EZRA (AND NEHEMIAH) IN SELECTED VERSIONS

Document Version	Old Testament Book of Ezra	Old Testament Book of Nehemiah	Paraphrase of 2 Chronicles chs. 35-36; the whole Book of Ezra; Nehemiah 7:38-8:12; plus a tale about Darius's bodyguards	A Latin Apocalypse
Septuagint	II Esdras		I Esdras	
Latin Vulgate	I Esdras	II Esdras	III Esdras	IV Esdras
Many later Latin Manuscripts	I Esdras		III Esdras	II Esdras =chs. 1-2 IV Esdras = chs. 3-14 V Esdras = chs. 15-16
Great Bible (1539) Douay Bible (1609-1610)	I Esdras	II Esdras	III Esdras	IV Esdras
Russian Bible, Moscow Patriarchate (1956)	I Esdras	Nehemiah	II Esdras	III Esdras
Geneva Bible (1560) Bishops' Bible (1568) King James Version (1611) Revised Standard Version (1957)	The Book of Ezra	The Book of Nehemiah	I Esdras	II Esdras

THE FOURTH BOOK OF EZRA

(Late First Century A.D.)

With the Four Additional Chapters

A NEW TRANSLATION AND INTRODUCTION

BY B. M. METZGER

The treatise identified in Latin manuscripts as 4 Ezra (*Esdrae liber IV*) comprises chapters 3–14 of an expanded form of the book traditionally included among the Apocrypha of English Bibles under the title 2 Esdras. This expanded form includes a Christian framework, comprising chapters 1f. and 15f., commonly called 2 and 5 Esdras in the later Latin manuscripts.[1] For the convenience of the reader, the following pages provide a translation of the entire sixteen chapters. The accompanying chart shows the confused and confusing nomenclature of the diverse titles applied to the work.

The opening two chapters set forth a divine call to Ezra, a man of priestly descent (1:1–3), to reprove the Jewish people for their waywardness despite God's repeated mercies (1:4–2:32). Rejected by Israel, Ezra turns to the gentiles (2:33–41) and is granted a vision of a great multitude that stands on Mount Zion, each receiving a crown from "the Son of God, whom they confessed in the world" (2:42–48). Following this Christian introduction, the main body of the book (chs. 3–14), written by a Jewish author and preserved in several Oriental versions (see "Texts"), sets forth seven visions granted to Salathiel, also called Ezra, in Babylon. In the first vision (3:1–5:19), presented in dialogue form, Ezra bewails the fate of his people and raises perplexing questions concerning the origins of the world's sin and suffering. He is assured that the end of the age is near.

In the second vision (5:21–6:34), after reiterating his complaint that God has abandoned his own chosen people to the gentiles, Ezra raises a new problem concerning the lot of those who die before the present age has passed away (5:41) and is assured that their lot will be similar to that of those living at the inauguration of the new age (5:42–6:10). There follows a list of the signs of the end of the age (6:11–28).

The lengthy third vision (6:35–9:25) describes the final judgment and the future state of the righteous and the wicked (7:26–[131]). Expressing great compassion for the lost, Ezra struggles with the problem of reconciling God's mercy with the destruction of the wicked (7:[132–40]) and once again makes intercession to God on their behalf (8:4–36). This is followed by an admonition that Ezra, who is destined for eternal bliss, would do better to think about his own future than to brood over the lot of sinners, which they deserve (8:37–62). The vision concludes with a recapitulation of the signs that will precede the end (8:63–9:25).

The fourth vision (9:26–10:59) depicts a woman in deep mourning for her only son and describes her suffering (9:38–10:4). She is suddenly transformed into a glorious city, identified as heavenly Zion in the day of salvation (10:25–59).

The fifth vision (11:1–12:39) is an elaborate allegory illustrating the course of future history by means of an eagle rising from the sea (11:1–35). The eagle, Ezra is told, represents the Roman Empire, which will be punished by God's Messiah for persecuting his elect (12:10–34).

In the sixth vision (13:1–58) Ezra sees one like a man rising from the sea, who, with the

---

[1] Modern scholars sometimes designate chs. 1–2 as 5 Ezra and chs. 15–16 as 6 Ezra.

clouds of heaven at the head of a great army, annihilates his enemies with a stream of fire issuing from his mouth.

The seventh and final vision (14:1–48) is an account of how an angel commissions Ezra to dictate for forty days to five men, who produce in this manner ninety-four books, namely twenty-four canonical books and seventy esoteric books that will remain hidden.

At this point the Oriental versions of the book come to an end (see "Texts"). The Christian form of the book, preserved in Latin manuscripts, continues with a kind of appendix comprising chapters 15 and 16. These contain denunciations against the enemies of God's people and exhortations for the chosen people to put their trust in God.

Texts

The following translation is made from the Latin text edited by R. L. Bensly, *The Fourth Book of Ezra*. In general the translation follows the rendering of the Revised Standard Version of the book (the initial draft of which was prepared by the present writer), but is modified by minor alterations and corrections.

The Latin manuscripts cited by Bensly are the following:

1. Codex Sangermanensis, A.D. 822, formerly in the Library of the Benedictine Abbey of S. Germain des Prés at Paris, now in the Bibliothèque Nationale, number 11505 Fonds Latin. This, the oldest known copy of 4 Ezra, lacks 7:[36]–[105] and is the parent of the vast majority of extant manuscripts.[2] The missing section had at one time been contained on a leaf that had been cut out in early times. Since the passage contains an emphatic denial of the value of prayers for the dead (7:[105]), it is probable that the excision was made deliberately for dogmatic reasons.

2. Codex Ambianensis, a Carolingian minuscule of the ninth century is number 10 in the Bibliothèque Communale of Amiens. This manuscript contains the "missing" section (7:[36]–[105]).[3]

3. Codex Complutensis, written in a Visigothic hand and dating from the ninth to tenth centuries, formerly of Complutum (Alcalá de Heñares), is now MS 31 in the Library of the Central University at Madrid.

4. Codex Mazarinaeus is in two volumes, dating from the eleventh century, numbered 3 and 4 (formerly 6, 7) in the Bibliothèque Mazarine at Paris. The text of 4 Ezra is given in the sequence of chapters 3–16, 1 and 2.

The types of text of 4 Ezra in these and other Latin manuscripts fall into two main families: the French group (represented by MSS S and A) and the Spanish group (represented by MSS C and M). In general the French family presents a superior text.

Other versions of 4 Ezra (chs. 3–14) are the Syriac, Ethiopic, Armenian, and two independent Arabic versions; the last three are rather free renderings, of little value in reconstructing the original text. In addition, fragments of a Coptic and of a Georgian version are extant. The following are the chief editions of these seven Oriental versions.[4]

Syriac: *The Old Testament in Syriac According to the Peshiṭta Version,* edited on behalf of the International Organization for the Study of the Old Testament by the Peshiṭta Institute of the University of Leiden (eds. P. A. H. de Boer and W. Baars) part IV, fascicle 3, *Apocalypse of Baruch. 4 Esdras,* ed. R. J. Bidawid (Leiden, 1973).

Ethiopic: *Veteris Testamenti Aethiopici,* ed. A. Dillmann, tomus V, *Libri apocryphi* (Berlin, 1894) pp. 152–93, based on ten manuscripts.

Armenian: J. Zohrab's text of 4 Ezra, included in his edition of the Armenian Bible

---

[2] So M. R. James in R. L. Bensly, *The Fourth Book of Ezra,* p. xiii. For a convenient list of eleven Lat. MSS containing 4Ezra see L. Gry, *Les Dires prophétiques d'Esdras (IV. Esdras),* vol. 1, pp. xi–xiii. For information concerning other Lat. MSS containing excerpts and paraphrases of 4Ezra, see M. McNamara, *The Apocrypha in the Irish Church* (Dublin, 1975) p. 27.

[3] See R. L. Bensly, *The Missing Fragment of the Fourth Book of Ezra* (Cambridge, 1875). Actually, the text of the so-called missing section had been published in Ar. and in German in preceding centuries; see B. M. Metzger, "The 'Lost' Section of II Esdras (=IV Ezra)," *JBL* 76 (1957) 153–57; reprinted in B. M. Metzger, *Historical and Literary Studies, Pagan, Jewish, and Christian* (Leiden, 1963) pp. 48–51.

[4] A convenient edition, printed in parallel columns, is B. Violet's *Die Ezra-Apokalypse (IV. Ezra)* I. Teil: *Die Überlieferung.* This provides a critical Lat. text with German translations of the Syr., Eth., and two Ar. versions, and a Lat. translation of the Arm. version.

(Venice, 1805) and translated into English by J. Issaverdens, *Uncanonical Writings of the Old Testament* (Venice, 1901) pp. 481–691, is superseded now by M. E. Stone's edition (based on twenty-two MSS) and English translation, *The Armenian Version of IV Ezra* (University of Pennsylvania Armenian Texts and Studies, 1; Missoula, Mt., 1979).[5]

Arabic: The version known as Arab 1 is preserved in two manuscripts, the original and a copy of it. The original is Bodleian MS Or 251 (cat. Nicoll, p. 13, no. VI) of A.D. 1354,[6] and the copy is in the Vatican (Arab. 3). The Arabic text was published by E. G. A. Ewalt in "Das vierte Ezrabuch nach seinem Zeitalter, seinen arabischen Ubersetzungen und einer neuen Wiederherstellung," in *Abhandlungen der Königlichen Gesellschaft der Wissenschaften zu Göttingen*, vol. XI (1863). A second Arabic version, known as Arab 2, exists in a complete form in a Vatican manuscript (Arab. 462) of the fourteenth century and in partial form in two other manuscripts. The Vatican manuscript was edited with a Latin translation by J. Gildemeister, *Esdrae liber quartus arabice e codice Vaticano* (Bonn, 1877). Two further fragments of an Arabic version independent of Arab 1 and Arab 2 are also known.[7]

Coptic (Sahidic): A fragmentary parchment leaf, dating from the sixth to the eighth centuries, was edited by J. Leipoldt and B. Violet, "Ein saidisches Bruchstück des vierten Esrabuches," *Zeitschrift für ägyptische Sprache und Altertumskunde* 41 (1904) 138–40. The leaf contains 4 Ezra 3:29–46.

Georgian: Portions of 4 Ezra are contained in two manuscripts: one preserved in the Library of the Greek Patriarchate at Jerusalem (MS 7 + 11 written A.D. 1050), and the other—containing excerpts comprising about two thirds of the book—in the lavra of Iveron on Mount Athos (written A.D. 978). The two manuscripts, according to Blake, "go back to the same archetype, and that by no means a remote one" (*HTR* 19 [1926] 303). See R. P. Blake, "The Georgian Version of Fourth Esdras from the Jerusalem Manuscript," *HTR* 19 (1926) 299–375, and "The Georgian Text of Fourth Esdras from the Athos MS," *HTR* 22 (1929) 57–105. Blake is of the opinion that the Georgian and the Ethiopic versions go back to a single Greek archetype (*HTR* 19 [1926] 309). In a more recent study Kourtsikidzé finds that the Georgian texts edited by Blake are represented also by a fragment of the Paris Lectionary (ed. M. Tarchnichvili).[8]

Greek: A tiny scrap of papyrus found at Oxyrhynchus, dating from about the fourth century (POxy 1010), preserves the text of 15:57–59.

There is also a condensation in Greek of chapters 11 and 12 contained in a manuscript dated A.D. 1656, which is in the Library of the Greek Orthodox Patriarchate at Jerusalem (no. 160). When the text is compared with that of the several versions of 4 Ezra, it appears that the condensation was made from the current Latin form of the book.[9]

Original language

The relation of the extant versions of the Ezra Apocalypse (chs. 3–14) to each other and to a lost original has received prolonged and repeated study. Not a few instances have been collected in which differences between the several versions (with the possible exception of

[5] Textural problems in the Arm. version of 4Ezra are dealt with by Stone in *Muséon* 79 (1966) 387–400; *HTR* 60 (1967) 107–15; and *Textus* 6 (1968) 48–61; see also Stone's *Concordance and Texts of the Armenian Version of IV Ezra* (Oriental Notes and Studies 11; Jerusalem, 1971).

[6] In 1646, John Gregory of Christ Church, Oxford, called attention to this MS as preserving "the most authenticke remaine" of 4Ezra. At the beginning of the 18th cent., at the request of William Whiston, Simon Ockley, the noted Arabist at Oxford, prepared an ET of this version for inclusion in the former's curious work entitled *Primitive Christianity Reviv'd* (London, 1711) vol. 4. On the continent J. A. Fabricius made a Lat. translation of Ockley's rendering for his *Codicis pseudepigraphi Veteris Testamenti* (Hamburg, 1723) vol. 2, pp. 173–307, and J. H. Haug made a German translation (probably from Fabricius) of the "missing" section of ch. 7 for the Berleburg Bibel (1742) vol. 8, pp. 105f.

[7] For details, see Violet, *Die Ezra-Apokalypse*, p. xxxix, and G. Graf, *Geschichte der christlichen arabischen Literatur* (Vatican City, 1944) vol. 1, pp. 219–21. For details of a newly identified witness, see M. E. Stone, "A New Manuscript of the Syrio-Arabic Version of the Fourth Book of Ezra," *JSJ* 8 (1977) 183f.

[8] Ts. Kourtsikidzé, *Versions géorgiennes des livres apocryphes de l'Ancien Testament* (Académie des sciences de Géorgie, Institut des manuscrits, Metsniereba; Tiflis, 1973) vol. 2, pp. 270–308 [in Georgian, with Russ. résumé, pp. 309–43]. According to B. Outtier (*Bedi Kartlisa* 33 [1975] 382), this study represents, with some changes and corrections, Kourtsikidzé's work that appeared in *Mravaltavi* 1 (1971) 93–109.

[9] So R. Rubinkiewicz, "Un Fragment grec du IVᵉ Livre d'Esdras (chapitres XI et XII), *Muséon* 89 (1976) 75–87.

the Armenian) can be explained by presupposing corruptions in or misunderstanding of a Greek text underlying them. For example, in 8:6 the Latin *locum* obviously arose from misreading Greek *typon* as *topon*, and in 9:19 the Latin and Oriental versions took *nomos* (accented on the first syllable) as "law," which does not fit the context, instead of *nomos* (accented on the last syllable) as "pasture." Likewise the internal evidence of versions often suggests dependence upon an underlying Greek text. For example, the Latin sometimes reproduces Greek constructions (e.g. the genitive absolute) or Greek genders that are unknown to Latin grammar. Furthermore, quotations of 4 Ezra included in Greek patristic and apocryphal documents presuppose knowledge of a Greek version of the book.[10] In modern times Hilgenfeld, with the assistance of Lagarde and H. Rönsch, reconstructed the lost Greek text from the Latin version.[11]

There remain, however, many other phenomena that suggest a Semitic original lying behind the lost Greek text. Several scholars have argued that this was Aramaic.[12] On the other hand, the presence of instances of notable Hebraisms (such as the infinitive absolute construction) has led most modern scholars to postulate a Hebrew original underlying the Greek.[13]

Date

According to most scholars,[14] the original Jewish document known today as 4 Ezra was composed about A.D. 100. This opinion rests upon a more or less plausible interpretation of the opening sentence, which states that "in the thirtieth year after the destruction of our city" Salathiel, who is also called Ezra, was in Babylon and underwent the experiences recounted in the visions that follow (3:1). Although this purports to be in the thirtieth year after the destruction of Jerusalem by Nebuchadnezzar in 586 B.C., it becomes obvious when one begins to study the book that this statement is intended to refer cryptically to the fall of Jerusalem in A.D. 70 (3:2; 6:19; 10:48; and elsewhere).

Since it is difficult to believe that a Jewish book of this kind could have found its way into Christian circles after the Bar-Kokhba revolt, when Church and Synogogue had become hopelessly alienated, the date of the completion of the Hebrew original cannot be placed much after A.D. 120. This would allow time for the Greek version to have been made and taken up in Christian circles.

Near the middle or in the second half of the third century four chapters were added, two at the beginning and two at the end, by one or more unknown Christian writers.

Provenance

Although several scholars have thought that the core of 4 Ezra was composed in Rome among the Jewish Diaspora (the reference to Babylon [3:1] being understood as a cryptic reference to Rome), the obviously Semitic coloration of the work rather suggests Palestine as the place of writing and publication of the Hebrew original. There is no trace of any influence from Egyptian Judaism or from the Qumran community.

Theological importance

Among the more prominent theological ideas presented in 4 Ezra is the author's belief in God as the one and only Creator (3:4; 6:38–55; 6:1–6). The term by which he usually refers

---

[10] For the quotations, see e.g. Denis, *Introduction*, pp. 194f.

[11] A. Hilgenfeld, *Messias Judaeorum* (Leipzig, 1869) pp. 36–113.

[12] E.g. Gry, *Les Dires prophétiques d'Esdras*, pp. xxiii–lxxvi; C. C. Torrey, *Apoc. Lit.*, p. 122; J. Bloch, "The Ezra Apocalypse: Was It Written in Hebrew, Greek, or Aramaic?" *JQR* 48 (1957–58) 279–94.

[13] See especially G. H. Box, *The Ezra-Apocalypse*, pp. xiii–xix; A. Kaminka, "Beiträge zur Erklärung der Esra-Apokalypse und zur Rekonstruktion ihres hebräischen Urtextes," *MGWJ* 76 (1932) 121–38, 206–12, 494–511, 604–7; 77 (1933) 339–55; and F. Zimmerman, "Underlying Documents of IV Ezra," *JQR* 51 (1960–61) 107–34. Editions of the reconstructed Heb. text of 4Ezra have been published by A. Kaminka, *Sefer Ḥazonot Assir Shealtiel* (Tel Aviv, 1936) and by J. Licht, *Sefer Ḥazon ʿEzra* (Jerusalem, 1968).

[14] See, *inter alia*, J. M. Myers, *I and II Esdras*, pp. 129–31; and J. A. T. Robinson, *Redating the New Testament* (Philadelphia, 1976) pp. 247, 315.

to God is the Most High (*altissimus*); it occurs sixty-eight times in the apocalypse proper, but not once in the Christian additions. Besides being Judge at the final judgment (6:1–6), God is merciful and compassionate (7:[132–38]). The Law is a divine gift to Israel (3:19f.; 9:31f.). It had indeed been offered to the other nations of the world but was deliberately rejected by them (7:23f., [72]); Israel, on the other hand, had accepted it. It was for this reason, the writer holds, that Israel was elected by God to be his special possession and chosen people.

It is here that the particular pathos of the book emerges as the author wrestles with the question: Why has God delivered his people into the hands of their enemies? What puzzles the author is that God should permit Israel's oppressors to be in prosperity, while his own people, who are at least no worse than these, he leaves to perish (3:30, 32). It is with this question bearing on divine justice that the seer agonizes, seeking "to justify the ways of God to man." In the end, however, the author concludes that God's ways are inscrutable.

The teaching of 4 Ezra on the subject of mankind and human free will is basically pessimistic. Sin is conceived as consisting essentially in unfaithfulness to the Law (9:36), resulting in alienation and estrangement from God (7:[48]). Although free will is definitely asserted in a few passages (e.g. 3:8; 8:56–58), the seer believed that inevitably all have turned away from God. This defection is due, in some way, to the sin of Adam (7:[118]), who possessed an evil heart (*cor malignum*, 3:20) in which a grain of evil seed (*granum seminis mali*) had been sown (4:30). Since all of Adam's descendants have followed his example in clothing themselves with an evil heart (3:26), each is morally responsible.[15] It will be seen that this view corresponds to the rabbinic doctrine of the evil inclination or impulse (*yeṣer ha-raʿ*).

The eschatological speculations of the book are extensive and somewhat involved. The author's consideration of the traditional belief in a messianic kingdom set up on earth, a kingdom which in his view will endure for four hundred years (7:28f.), is overshadowed by concern to penetrate the mystery of the world to come and the conditions of the afterlife. The dawn of the end of the age will be heralded by wonderful and terrible signs—physical, moral, and political (4:52–5:13a; 6:11–29; 7:26–[44]; 8:63–9:12). After the resurrection (5:45; 7:32, [37]) and the judgment (7:33–35; 7:[105, 115]) the wicked will go to the furnace of Hell and the righteous to the Paradise of delight (7:36, [78–101]).

In addition to these otherworldly speculations, 4 Ezra also contains, in other sections of the book, quite different eschatological teachings. In the Eagle Vision (ch. 12) a purely political eschatology is concerned with release from the tyranny of Rome, secured by the Messiah, who will then set up the Kingdom of God upon earth (12:32–34; cf. 11:44–46). Different again is the eschatology of the Vision of the Man rising from the Sea (ch. 13); in this vision the pre-existent Messiah, after annihilating all his enemies, gathers a peaceful multitude (the ten "lost" tribes of Israel) to himself.

In this connection a comment may be added as to the role of the Messiah in the total eschatological thought of 4 Ezra. This role, as Stone points out,[16] is difficult to assess. Besides taking up the whole attention of chapter 13 and playing a significant role in chapters 11–12, the Messiah is mentioned elsewhere in the book only at 7:28f. Stone conjectures that the reason for the relative paucity of references to the Messiah may be that he was not the answer to the questions that Ezra was asking. At the same time, though the Messiah is not the exclusive center of the seer's aspirations, he plays a significant role in the author's eschatological scheme.

One other feature of the seer's theological outlook deserves comment. This is his universalism, shown in his world-embracing solicitude not only for his own nation, but for all people whose wickedness will bring them to a tragic fate in the next life. His pathetic lament concerns humanity as a whole, regardless of racial origins (7:[62–69]). In fact, the compassion of Ezra for the lost seems at times to exceed that attributed by the author to God himself (cf. 8:37–62), for when he makes intercession at length in behalf of the mass of mankind who, as sinners, will be doomed, his prayer is in vain. He is told bluntly, "Many have been created, but few will be saved" (8:3).

---

[15] For the most recent discussion of this doctrine see A. L. Thompson, *Responsibility for Evil in the Theodicy of IV Ezra*.

[16] M. E. Stone, "The Concept of the Messiah in IV Ezra," Goodenough Festschrift, pp. 295–312.

Unity of the book

From what has been said in the preceding section concerning the eschatological features of 4 Ezra 3–14, it can be seen that quite disparate elements are represented. There has been, therefore, not a little debate as to whether the book is the product of a redactor who combined the diverse productions of several authors,[17] or whether, despite more or less minor inconsistencies arising from the utilization of varying traditions, the artistry of the book suggests the hand of a single author who managed to fit heterogeneous details into a more or less coherent scheme.[18] Although such a question cannot, perhaps, be regarded as permanently settled, many scholars today tend to regard chapters 3–14 as representing the author's own conception and handiwork.

Relation to canonical books

A number of resemblances in thought and diction with the New Testament occur in the Ezra Apocalypse (chs. 3–14), but none of them suggests direct dependence. In 7:7 the writer speaks of the narrow entrance that leads to the abode of the righteous, a concept that occurs also in Matthew 7:13f. With the statement "Many have been created, but few will be saved" (8:3) compare Matthew 22:14 and Luke 13:23f. In 4:33 the seer asks, in reference to the time when the new age will come, "How long and when will these things be?"—with which may be compared the words of the disciples to Jesus in Luke 21:7.

Parallels with Pauline theology occur in the seer's treatment of the evil *yeṣer* (see "Theological importance") as compared with Romans 5:12–22, and the personification of Zion as "the mother of us all" (10:7) as compared with Galatians 4:26, "the Jerusalem that is above . . . is our mother."

The transiency of human life as described in 7:[61], "the multitude . . . are now like a mist, and are similar to a flame and smoke," may be compared with James 4:14: "What is your life? For you are a mist that appears for a little time and then vanishes."

In 4 Ezra 12:42 the comparison of Ezra as being "like a lamp in a dark place" reminds one of the exhortation to pay attention to the prophetic word "as to a lamp shining in a dark place" (2Pet 2:19). The Messiah's destruction of a hostile multitude by the breath of his mouth (13:10f.) finds a parallel in 2 Thessalonians 2:8.

The reader will find a considerable number of parallels between 4 Ezra and the Book of Revelation.[19] Among these are the noteworthy similarities between the account in 13:32–39 and the context of Revelation 7:9 and 14:1. The former refers to the messianic woes followed by the coming of the Son of Man, who will stand on Mount Zion and gather to himself "a multitude that was peaceable."

Relation to apocryphal books

Many scholars have pointed to a very considerable number of parallel passages between 4 Ezra and 2 Baruch, which is also sometimes called the (Syriac) Apocalypse of Baruch.[20] The latter work, which on the whole represents a point of view and a theological outlook somewhat more in accordance with later rabbinical Judaism than 4 Ezra, appears to have been written as an answer to the perplexities mentioned by the seer.

Several striking parallels can be found between 4 Ezra and 1 Enoch, particularly the latest section of 1 Enoch (i.e. chs. 37–71, the Similitudes of Enoch). These include 4 Ezra 6:49–52 and 1 Enoch 60:7–9; 4 Ezra 7:32f. and 1 Enoch 51:1, 3; 4 Ezra 7:[37] and 1 Enoch 62:1.

[17] See e.g. R. Kabisch, *Das vierte Buch Esra* (Göttingen, 1889), who identified two basic documents and three minor ones that were combined by a redactor; Box, *The Ezra-Apocalypse*, pp. xxii–xxxiii; W. O. E. Osterley, *II Esdras*, pp. xif.; and Torrey, *Apoc. Lit.*, pp. 116–23; and "A Twice-Buried Apocalypse," *Munera Studiosa*, eds. M. H. Shepherd, Jr., and S. E. Johnson (Cambridge, Mass., 1946) pp. 23–39.

[18] See e.g. H. Gunkel in Kautzsch's *APAT*; W. Sanday in Box, *The Ezra-Apocalypse*, pp. 5*–8*; M. R. James, "Salathiel qui est Esdras," *JTS* 19 (1918) 347–49; Gry, *Les Dires prophétiques d'Esdras*, pp. cxiii–cxxiv; Pfeiffer, *History*, pp. 81–86; and Myers, *I and II Esdras*, pp. 119–21.

[19] For two dozen parallels see the index to passages in Box, *The Ezra-Apocalypse*, p. 377.

[20] See e.g. P. Bogaert, *Apocalypse de Baruch. Introduction, traduction du syriaque et commentaire* (SC 144; Paris, 1969) vol. 1, pp. 58–67; cf. also Thompson, *Responsibility for Evil*, pp. 121–27.

The author of 4 Ezra seems to have been acquainted also with the Psalms of Solomon, though the similarity of the phraseology of the parallel passages is hardly close enough to justify the view that the seer borrowed from the earlier work.[21]

Cultural importance

Among ancient Jewish apocalyptic works, the cultural importance of 4 Ezra over the centuries is noteworthy. A few extracts from it are still used in the Christian liturgy; e.g. the Introit of the Mass for the Dead in the Roman Missal (*Requiem aeternam . . .*) is based on 2:34f. The dying words of Bishop Latimer spoken to his brother martyr when, in 1555, both were about to be burned at the stake in front of Balliol College, Oxford ("Be of good comfort, Master Ridley. Play the man. We shall this day light such a candle, by God's grace, in England, as I trust shall never be put out.") echo the traditional rendering of 14:25.

Of greater significance is the remarkable influence of 4 Ezra on Christopher Columbus, William Whiston, and John Ruskin.[22] A passage from "the prophet Ezra" encouraged Columbus to venture to set sail. In 6:42 a comment is made about God's work of creation: "On the third day you commanded the waters to be gathered together in the seventh part of the earth; six parts you dried up and kept so that some of them might be planted and cultivated and be of service before you." Although, of course, the proportion of water to dry land is nearly the reverse of Ezra's figures, Columbus was heartened by Ezra's erroneous comment on Genesis. In fact, it was partly by quoting this verse to the hesitant sovereigns of Spain that Columbus finally obtained financial support for his several voyages.

In the first half of the eighteenth century the learned and eccentric William Whiston, Sir Isaac Newton's successor as Lucasian Professor of Mathematics in Cambridge University, drew up a list of ninety-nine "proofs" that the end of the age was at hand. One third of these signs come from 4 Ezra (5:1–13; 6:20–24; 9:1–8) and are quite general, resembling similar predictions in the canonical Scriptures. For example, the forty-sixth and the sixty-fifth "Signals" in his total list are that "Wickedness should be vastly encreas'd beyond Measure of former Ages" and that "Incontinency, Vileness, and Wickedness, shall be increased upon the Earth." Much more specific was Whiston's interpretation of the significance of the rumor, circulating in 1726, that an illiterate farm woman of Surrey, named Mary Toft, had given birth to a litter of rabbits. To the torrent of pamphlets and editorials written for and against the truth of the story, Whiston added his impassioned defense—for he was convinced that here was a signal fulfillment of Ezra's prophecy that at the end of the age "women shall bring forth monsters" (5:8).

Among the books of the Apocrypha to which Milton gave repeated attention was 4 Ezra, which he referred to as 2 Esdras. On the occasion of writing the introduction to his *Deucalion*, he says:

> It chanced, this morning, as I sat down to finish my preface that I had, for my introductory reading, the fifth chapter of the second book of Esdras; in which, though often read carefully before, I had never enough noticed the curious verse, "Blood shall drop out of wood, and the stone shall give his voice, and the people shall be troubled" [5:5]. Of which verse, so far as I can gather the meaning from the context, and from the rest of the chapter, the intent is, that in the time spoken of by the prophet, which, if not our own, is one exactly corresponding to it, the deadness of men to all noble things shall be so great, that the sap of trees shall be more truly blood, in God's sight, than their hearts' blood; and the silence of men, in praise of all noble things, so great, that the stones shall cry out, in God's hearing, instead of their tongues . . .

---

[21] For a list of nearer and more remote parallels, see H. E. Ryle and M. R. James, *Psalms of the Pharisees, commonly called the Psalms of Solomon* (Cambridge, 1891) pp. lxvi–lxix.

[22] For more detailed information about the influence of 4Ezra on each of these three, see Metzger, *Intr. to the Apoc.*, pp. 232–38.

BIBLIOGRAPHY

Charlesworth, *PMR*, pp. 111–16.
Delling, *Bibliographie*, pp. 160–62.
Denis, *Introduction*, pp. 194–200.

Bensly, R. L., ed. *The Fourth Book of Ezra, the Latin Version Edited from the MSS.* T&S
    3.2; Cambridge, 1895. (The edition of the Lat. version from which the present translation
    was made.)
Box, G. H. *The Ezra-Apocalypse, being chapters 3–14 of the Book commonly known as 4
    Ezra (or II Esdras).* London, 1912. (A thorough investigation, with commentary.)
———. "4 Ezra," *The Apocrypha and Pseudepigrapha of the Old Testament,* ed. R. H.
    Charles, Oxford, 1913; vol. 2, pp. 542–624. (A condensation of the preceding work.)
Gray, M. L. *Towards the Reconstruction of 4 Esdras and the Establishment of Its Contem-
    porary Context.* Unpublished B. Litt. thesis, Oxford, 1976. (The people in Israel for
    whom the author wrote did not survive; we do not know who he was or to which group
    he belonged.)
Gry, L. *Les Dires prophétiques d'Esdras (IV. Esdras).* Paris, 1938. 2 vols. (A comprehensive
    study of the Lat. text.)
Myers, J. M. *I and II Esdras: Introduction, Translation and Commentary.* Anchor Bible 42;
    Garden City, N.Y., 1974. (A fresh translation, with full textural nn. and commentary.)
Oesterley, W. O. E. *II Esdras (the Ezra Apocalypse), with Introduction and Notes.* London,
    1933. (A brief commentary based on the Revised Version [1896] of II Esdras.)
Thompson, A. L. *Responsibility for Evil in the Theodicy of IV Ezra.* SBLDS 29; Missoula,
    Mont., 1977. (An informative study of the theology of 4Ezra.)
Violet, B. *Die Ezra-Apokalypse (IV. Ezra)* I. Teil: *Die Überlieferung.* GCS 18; Leipzig,
    1910. (Convenient edition of the Lat. text with translations of the several Eastern
    versions in parallel columns, with textural nn.)

THE FOURTH BOOK OF EZRA

The genealogy of Ezra

1 1 The second[a] book of the prophet Ezra the son of Seraiah, son of Azariah, son
2 of Hilkiah, son of Shallum, son of Zadok, son of Ahitub, •son of Ahijah, son of
Phinehas, son of Eli, son of Amariah, son of Azariah, son of Meraioth, son of
Arna, son of Uzzi, son of Borith, son of Abishua, son of Phinehas, son of Eleazar,
3 son of Aaron, of the tribe of Levi, who was a captive in the country of the Medes
in the reign of Artaxerxes, king of the Persians.

Ezra's prophetic call

4,5 The word of the Lord came to me, saying, •"Go and declare to my people their
evil deeds, and to their children the iniquities which they have committed against Isa 58:1
6 me, so that they may tell their children's children •that the sins of their parents
have increased in them, for they have forgotten me and have offered sacrifices to
7 strange gods. •Was it not I who brought them out of the land of Egypt, out of the
8 house of bondage? But they have angered me and despised my counsels. •Pull out
the hair of your head and hurl all evils upon them, for they have not obeyed my
9 law; they are a rebellious people. •How long shall I endure them, on whom I have
10 bestowed such great benefits? •For their sake I have overthrown many kings; I Ex 14:2
11 struck down Pharaoh with his servants, and all his army. •I have destroyed all
nations before them, and scattered in the east the people of two provinces, Tyre
and Sidon;[b] I have slain all their enemies.

Summary of God's mercies to Israel

12,13 "But speak to them and say, Thus says the Lord: •Surely it was I who brought
you through the sea, and made safe highways for you where there was no road; Ex 14:29
14 I gave you Moses as leader and Aaron as priest; •I provided light for you from a Ex 13:21
pillar of fire, and did great wonders among you. Yet you have forgotten me, says
the Lord.
15 "Thus says the Lord Almighty: The quails were a sign to you; I gave you camps Ex 16:13
16 for your protection, and in them you complained. •You have not exulted in my
17 name at the destruction of your enemies, but to this day you still complain. •Where
are the benefits which I bestowed on you? When you were hungry and thirsty in
18 the wilderness, did you not cry out to me, •saying, 'Why hast thou led us into this Neh 14:3
wilderness to kill us? It would have been better for us to serve the Egyptians than
19 to die in this wilderness.' •I pitied your groanings and gave you manna for food; Ps 78:25
20 you ate the bread of angels. •When you were thirsty, did I not cleave the rock so WisSol 16:20
that waters flowed in abundance? Because of the heat I covered you with the leaves WisSol 11:4
21 of trees. •I divided fertile lands among you; I drove out the Canaanites, the
Perizzites, and the Philistines before you. What more can I do for you? says the
22 Lord. •Thus says the Lord Almighty: When you were in the wilderness, at the
23 bitter stream, thirsty and blaspheming my name, •I did not send fire upon you for Ex 15:22-25
your blasphemies, but threw a tree into the water and made the stream sweet.

---

1 a. Codex Ambianensis omits "second" here and
reads "third" in the title of the book.

  b. The author is confused; Tyre and Sidon were

cities (not provinces) lying west (not east) of the
country of the Medes (vs. 3).

God's appeal to Israel

24 "What shall I do to you, O Jacob? You would not obey me, O Judah. I will
turn to other nations and will give them my name, that they may keep my statutes.
25 Because you have forsaken me, I also will forsake you. When you beg mercy of
26 me, I will show you no mercy. •When you call upon me, I will not listen to you; Isa 1:15; 5
for you have defiled you hands with blood, and your feet are swift to commit
27 murder. •It is not as though you had forsaken me; you have forsaken yourselves,
says the Lord.
28 "Thus says the Lord Almighty: Have I not entreated you as a father entreats his
29 sons or a mother her daughters or a nurse her children, •that you should be my Jer 24:7
people and I should be your God, and that you should be my sons and I should Heb 8:10
30 be your father? •I gathered you as a hen gathers her brood under her wings. But Mt 23:37
31 now, what shall I do to you? I will cast you out from my presence. •When you Lk 13:34
offer oblations to me, I will turn my face from you; for I have rejected your feast
32 days, and new moons, and circumcisions of the flesh. •I sent to you my servants
the prophets, but you have taken and slain them and torn their bodies in pieces;
their blood I will require of you, says the Lord.

A new people

33 "Thus says the Lord Almighty: Your house is desolate; I will drive you out as
34 the wind drives straw; •and your sons will have no children, because with you they
35 have neglected my commandment and have done what is evil in my sight. •I will
give your houses to a people that will come, who without having heard me will
believe. Those to whom I have shown no signs will do what I have commanded.
36,37 They have seen no prophets, yet will recall their former state.[c] •I call to witness
the gratitude of the people that is to come, whose children rejoice with gladness;
though they do not see me with bodily eyes, yet with the spirit they will believe Jn 20:29
the things I have said.
38 "And now, father,[d] look with pride and see the people coming from the east;
39 to them I will give as leaders Abraham, Isaac, and Jacob and Hosea and Amos
40 and Micah and Joel and Obadiah and Jonah •and Nahum and Habakkuk, Zephaniah,
Haggai, Zechariah, and Malachi,[e] who is also called the messenger of the Lord.

Divine judgment upon Israel

1 **2** "Thus says the Lord: I brought this people out of bondage, and I gave them
commandments through my servants the prophets; but they would not listen to
2 them, and made my counsels void. •The mother[a] who bore them says to them, Isa 54:1
3 'Go, my children, because I am a widow and forsaken. •I brought you up with 1Bar 4:19
gladness; but with mourning and sorrow I have lost you, because you have sinned
4 before the Lord God and have done what is evil in my sight. •But now what can 1Bar 4:11
I do for you? For I am a widow and forsaken. Go, my children, and ask for mercy
5 from the Lord.' •I call upon you, father,[b] as a witness in addition to the mother
6 of the children, because they would not keep my covenant, •that you may bring
confusion upon them and bring their mother to ruin, so that they may have no
7 offspring. •Let them be scattered among the nations, let their names be blotted out
from the earth, because they have despised my covenant.
8 "Woe to you, Assyria, who conceal the unrighteous in your midst! O wicked Gen 19:24
9 nation, remember what I did to Sodom and Gomorrah, •whose land lies in lumps
of pitch and heaps of ashes. So I will do to those who have not listened to me,
says the Lord Almighty."

c. Other authorities read "their iniquities."
d. God is represented as addressing Ezra as 　　2 a. I.e. Jerusalem.
"father" of the nation (cf. 2:5).　　　　　　　　　b. The author addresses Ezra as "father" (cf.
e. The minor prophets are arranged in the order　1:38).
of the LXX.

10   Thus says the Lord to Ezra: "Tell my people that I will give them the kingdom
11 of Jerusalem, which I was going to give to Israel. •Moreover, I will take back to
   myself their glory, and will give to these others the everlasting habitations, which Lk 16:9
12 I had prepared for Israel.ᶜ •The tree of life shall give them fragrant perfume, and Rev 2:7; 22:2,14
13 they shall neither toil nor become weary. •Ask and you will receive; pray that your Mt 25:34
   days may be few, that they may be shortened. The kingdom is already prepared
14 for you; watch! •Call, O call heaven and earth to witness, for I left out evil and
   created good, because I live, says the Lord.

Exhortation to good works

15   "Mother,ᵈ embrace your sons; bring them up with gladness, as does the dove;
16 establish their feet, because I have chosen you, says the Lord. •And I will raise
   up the dead from their places, and will bring them out from their tombs, because
17 I recognize my name in them. •Do not fear, mother of the sons, for I have chosen
18 you, says the Lord. •I will send you help, my servants Isaiah and Jeremiah.
   According to their counsel I have consecrated and prepared for you twelve trees
19 loaded with various fruits, •and the same number of springs flowing with milk and Rev 22:2
   honey, and seven mighty mountains on which roses and lilies grow; by these I will Deut 31:20
20 fill your children with joy. •Guard the rights of the widow, secure justice for the
21 fatherless, give to the needy, defend the orphan, clothe the naked, •care for the
   injured and the weak, do not ridicule a lame man, protect the maimed, and let the
22 blind man have a vision of my glory. •Protect the old and the young within your
23 walls; •when you find any who are dead, commit them to the grave and mark it,ᵉ
24 and I will give you the first place in my resurrection. •Pause and be quiet, my
25 people, because your rest will come. •Good nurse, nourish your sons, and strengthen
26 their feet. •Not one of the servants whom I have given you will perish, for I will
27 require them from among your number. •Do not be anxious, for when the day of
   tribulation and anguish comes, others shall weep and be sorrowful, but you shall
28 rejoice and have abundance. •The nations shall envy you but they shall not be able
29 to do anything against you, says the Lord. •My hands will cover you, that your
30 sons may not see Gehenna. •Rejoice, O mother, with your sons, because I will
31 deliver you, says the Lord. •Remember your sons that sleep, because I will bring
   them out of the hiding places of the earth, and will show mercy to them; for I am
32 merciful, says the Lord Almighty. •Embrace your children until I come, and
   proclaim mercy to them; because my springs run over, and my grace will not fail."

Rejected by Israel, Ezra turns to the gentiles

33   I, Ezra, received a command from the Lord on Mount Horeb to go to Israel.
   When I came to them they rejected me and refused the Lord's commandment.
34 Therefore I say to you, O nations that hear and understand, "Await your shepherd;
   he will give you everlasting rest, because he who will come at the end of the age
35 is close at hand. •Be ready for the rewards of the kingdom, because the eternal Isa 60:20
36 light will shine upon you forevermore. •Flee from the shadow of this age, receive Rev 21:23; 22:5
37 the joy of your glory; I publicly call on my Savior to witness.ᶠ •Receive what the
   Lord has entrusted to you and be joyful, giving thanks to him who has called you
38 to heavenly kingdoms. •Rise and stand, and see at the feast of the Lord the number
39 of those who have been sealed. •Those who have departed from the shadow of this
40 age have received glorious garments from the Lord. •Take again your full number,
   O Zion, and conclude the list of your people who are clothed in white, who have Rev 3:4; 6:11;
41 fulfilled the law of the Lord. •The number of your children whom you desired is 7:1

---

c. Lat. "those."
   d. "Mother," probably a reference to the
Church.
   e. Or "seal it"; or "mark them and commit

them to the grave."
   f. Other authorities read "I testify that my Savior
has been commissioned by the Lord."

full; beseech the Lord's power that your people, who have been called from the
beginning, may be made holy.'' 4:36f.
Rev 6:11

Ezra's vision of a great multitude

42　I, Ezra, saw on Mount Zion a great multitude, which I could not number, and Rev 7:9
43　they all were praising the Lord with songs. • In their midst was a young man of
great stature, taller than any of the others, and on the head of each of them he 1En 46:1
placed a crown, but he was more exalted than they. And I was held spellbound.
44,45　Then I asked an angel, ''Who are these, my lord?'' •He answered and said to me,
''These are they who have put off mortal clothing and put on the immortal, and
they have confessed the name of God; now they are being crowned, and receive
46　palms.'' •Then I said to the angel, ''Who is that young man who places crowns
47　on them and puts palms in their hands?'' •He answered and said to me, ''He is
the Son of God, whom they confessed in the world.'' So I began to praise those
48　who had stood valiantly for the name of the Lord. •Then the angel said to me,
''Go, tell my people how great and many are the wonders of the Lord God which
you have seen.''

THE EZRA APOCALYPSE

The first vision

1　**3** In the thirtieth year after the destruction of our city, I, Salathiel,[a] who am also 2Kgs 25:1f.
called Ezra, was in Babylon. I was troubled as I lay on my bed, and my thoughts
2　welled up in my heart, •because I saw the desolation of Zion and the wealth of
3　those who lived in Babylon. •My spirit was greatly agitated, and I began to speak
4　anxious words to the Most High, and said, •''O sovereign Lord, did you not speak
at the beginning when you formed the earth—and that without help—and com-
5　manded the dust[b] • and it gave[c] you Adam, a lifeless body? Yet he was the
workmanship of your hands, and you breathed into him the breath of life, and he
6　was made alive in your presence. •And you led him into the garden which your
7　right hand had planted before the earth appeared. •And you laid upon him one
commandment of yours; but he transgressed it, and immediately you appointed WisSol 1:13f.;
2:23f.
death for him and for his descendants. From him there sprang nations and tribes,
8　peoples and clans, without number. •And every nation walked after its own will Gen 6:12
and did ungodly things before you and scorned you, and you did not hinder them.
9　But again, in its time you brought the flood upon the inhabitants of the world and Gen 6:1f.
10　destroyed them. •And the same fate befell them: As death came upon Adam, so
11　the flood upon them. •But you left one of them, Noah with his household, and all
the righteous who have descended from him.

The patriarchs

12　''When those who dwelt on earth began to multiply, they produced children and
peoples and many nations, and again they began to be more ungodly than were
13　their ancestors. •And when they were committing iniquity before you, you chose
14　for yourself one of them, whose name was Abraham; •and you loved him and to Gen 12:1
15　him only you revealed the end of the times, secretly by night. • You made with Gen 15:5,12,17
him an everlasting covenant, and promised him that you would never forsake his
descendants; and you gave to him Isaac, and to Isaac you gave Jacob and Esau.
16　And you set apart Jacob for yourself, but Esau you rejected; and Jacob became
17　a great multitude. •And when you led his descendants out of Egypt, you brought
18　them to Mount Sinai. •You bent down the heavens and shook[d] the earth, and moved Ex 19:16-18
Ps 68:7f.

---

3 a. ''Salathiel'' is the Gk. form of Shealtiel (the
father of Zerubbabel, Ezra 3:2; 5:2; Neh 12:1).
b. Syr., Eth.

c. Syr.
d. Syr. Eth., Arab 1, Georgian; Lat. ''set fast.''

19 the world, and made the depths to tremble, and trouble the times. •And your glory passed through the four gates of fire and earthquake and wind and ice, to give the Law to the descendants of Jacob, and your commandment to the posterity of Israel.

The evil heart

20 "Yet you did not take away from them their evil heart, so that your Law might
21 bring forth fruit in them. •For the first Adam, burdened with an evil heart, transgressed and was overcome, as were also all who were descended from him.
22 Thus the disease became permanent; the law was in the people's heart along with
23 the evil root, but what was good departed, and the evil remained. •So the times passed and the years were completed, and you raised up for yourself a servant,
24 named David. •And you commanded him to build a city for your name, and in
25 it to offer you oblations from what is yours. •This was done for many years; but
26 the inhabitants of the city transgressed, •in everything doing as Adam and all his
27 descendants had done, for they also had the evil heart. •So you delivered the city into the hands of your enemies.

Babylon compared with Zion

28 "Then I said in my heart, Are the deeds of those who inhabit Babylon any
29 better? Is that why she has gained dominion over Zion? •For when I came here I saw ungodly deeds without number, and my soul has seen many sinners during
30 these thirty years.[e] And my heart failed me, •for I have seen how you endure those who sin, and have spared those who act wickedly, and have destroyed your people,
31 and have preserved your enemies, •and have not shown to anyone how your way
32 may be comprehended.[f] Are the deeds of Babylon better than those of Zion? •Or has another nation known you besides Israel? Or what tribes have so believed your
33 covenants as these tribes of Jacob? •Yet their reward has not appeared and their labor has borne no fruit. For I have traveled widely among the nations and have seen that they abound in wealth, though they are unmindful of your commandments.
34 Now therefore weigh in a balance our iniquities and those of the inhabitants of the   Job 31:6
world; and so it will be found which way the turn of the scale will incline.   Ps 62:9
Prov 16:2
35 When have the inhabitants of the earth not sinned in your sight? Or what nation   1En 41:1; 61:8
36 has kept your commandments so well? •You may indeed find individual men who have kept your commandments, but nations you will not find."

Uriel's reply: God's ways are inscrutable

1,2 **4** Then the angel that had been sent to me, whose name was Uriel, answered •and
said to me, "Your understanding has utterly failed regarding this world, and do   1En 20:2
3 you think you can comprehend the way of the Most High?" •Then I said, "Yes, my lord." And he replied to me, "I have been sent to show you three problems.
4 If you can solve one of them for me, I also will show you the way you desire to see, and will teach you why the heart is evil."
5 I said, "Speak on, my lord."
And he said to me, "Go, weigh for me the weight of fire, or measure for me a measure[a] of wind, or call back for me the day that is past."
6 I answered and said, "Who of those that have been born can do this, that you ask me concerning these things?"
7 And he said to me, "If I had asked you, 'How many dwellings are in the heart of the sea, or how many streams are at the source of the deep, or how many streams are above the firmament, or which are the exits of hell, or which are the
8 entrances[b] of Paradise?' •perhaps you would have said to me, 'I never went down

---

e. Eth., Arab 1, Arm.; Lat., Syr. "in this thirtieth year."
f. Syr.; Lat. "how this way should be forsaken."

4 a. Syr., Eth., Ar., Georgian; Lat. "a blast."
b. Syr.; cf. Eth., Arab 2, Arm.; Lat. omits "of
hell, or which are the entrances."

9　into the deep, nor as yet into hell, neither did I ever ascend into heaven.' •But now
I have asked you only about fire and wind and the day, things through which you
have passed and without which you cannot exist,[c] and you have given me no
10　answer about them!" •And he said to me, "You cannot understand the things with
11　which you have grown up; •how then can your mind comprehend the way of the
Most High? And how can one who is already worn out[d] by the corrupt world
12　understand incorruption?"[e] When I heard this, I fell on my face[f] •and said to him,
"It would be better for us not to be here than to come here and live in ungodliness,
and to suffer and not understand why."

Parable of conflict between forest and sea

13　He answered me and said, "I went into a forest of trees of the plain, and they　Isa 55:8f.
14　made a plan •and said, 'Come, let us go and make war against the sea, that it may
15　recede before us, and that we may make for ourselves more forests.' •And in like
manner the waves of the sea also made a plan and said, 'Come, let us go up and
subdue the forest of the plain so that there also we may gain more territory for
16　ourselves. •But the plan of the forest was in vain, for the fire came and consumed
17　it; •likewise also the plan of the waves of the sea, for the sand stood firm and
18　stopped them. •If now you were a judge between them, which would you undertake
to justify, and which to condemn?"
19　I answered and said, "Each has made a foolish plan, for the land is assigned
to the forest, and to the sea is assigned a place to carry its waves."
20　He answered me and said, "You have judged rightly, but why have you not
21　judged so in your own case? •For as the land is assigned to the forest and the sea
to its waves, so also those who dwell upon earth can understand only what is on
earth, and he who is above the heavens can understand what is above the height
of the heavens."

Why Israel has become a reproach

22　Then I answered and said, "I beseech you, my lord, why[g] have I been endowed
23　with the power of understanding? •For I did not wish to inquire about the ways
above, but about those things which we daily experience: why Israel has been
given over to the gentiles as a reproach; why the people whom you loved has been
given to godless tribes, and the Law of our fathers has been made of no effect and
24　the written covenants no longer exist; •and why we pass from the world like
25　locusts, and our life is like a mist,[h] and we are not worthy to obtain mercy. •But
what will he do for his name, by which we are called? It is about these things that
I have asked."

The near approach of the end of the age

26　He answered me and said, "If you are alive, you will see, and if you live long,[i]
27　you will often marvel, because the age is hastening swiftly to its end. •For it will
not be able to bring the things that have been promised to the righteous in their
28　appointed times, because this age is full of sadness and infirmities. •For the evil
about which[j] you ask me has been sown, but the harvest of it has not yet come.
29　If therefore that which has been sown is not reaped, and if the place where the
evil has been sown does not pass away, the field where the good has been sown
30　will not come. •For a grain of evil seed[k] was sown in Adam's heart from the

c. Other Lat. MSS read "from which you cannot
be separated."
　d. The text here is uncertain.
　e. Syr., Eth. "the way of the incorruptible?"
　f. Syr., Eth., Arab 1; Lat. is corrupt.
　g. Syr., Eth., Arm.; Lat. is corrupt.

h. Syr., Eth., Ar., Georgian; Lat. "a trembling."
　i. Syr.; Lat. "live."
　j. Syr., Eth.; Lat. is uncertain.
　k. I.e. evil *yeṣer*.

beginning, and how much ungodliness it has produced until now, and will produce
31 until the time of threshing comes! •Consider now for yourself how much fruit of
32 ungodliness a grain of evil seed has produced. • When heads of grain without
number are sown, how great a threshing floor they will fill!''

When will the new age come?

33 Then I answered and said, ''How long[l] and when will these things be? Why are
34 our years few and evil?'' •He answered me and said, ''You do not hasten faster
than the Most High, for your haste is for yourself,[m] but the Highest hastens on
35 behalf of many. •Did not the souls of the righteous in their chambers ask about
these matters, saying, 'How long are we to remain here?[n] And when will come
36 the harvest of our reward?' •And Jeremiel[o] the archangel answered them and said,
'When the number of those like yourselves is completed;[p] for he has weighed the
37 age in the balance, •and measured the times by measure, and numbered the times
by number; and he will not move or arouse them until that measure is fulfilled.' ''
38 Then I answered and said, ''O sovereign Lord, but all of us also are full of
39 ungodliness. • And it is perhaps on account of us that the time of threshing is
delayed for the righteous—on account of the sins of those who dwell on earth.''
40 He answered me and said, ''Go and ask a woman who is with child if, when
her nine months have been completed, her womb can keep the child within her
any longer.''
41 ''No, my lord,'' I said, ''it cannot.''
42 He said to me, ''In Hades the chambers of the souls are like the womb. •For
just as a woman who is in travail makes haste to escape the pangs of birth, so also
do these places hasten to give back those things that were committed to them from
43 the beginning. •Then the things that you desire to see will be disclosed to you.''

How much time remains?

44 I answered and said, ''If I have found favor in your sight, and if it is possible,
45 and if I am worthy, •show me this also: whether more time is to come than has
46 passed, or whether for us the greater part has gone by. •For I know what has gone
by, but I do not know what is to come.''
47 He said to me, ''Stand at my right side, and I will show you the interpretation
of a parable.''
48 So I stood and looked, and behold a flaming furnace passed by before me, and
49 when the flame had gone by I looked, and behold, the smoke remained. •And after
this a cloud full of water passed before me and poured down a heavy and violent
rain, and when the rainstorm had passed, drops remained in the cloud.
50 And he said to me, ''Consider it for yourself; for as the rain is more than the
drops, and the fire is greater than the smoke, so the quantity that passed was far
greater; but drops and smoke remained.''
51 Then I prayed and said, ''Do you think that I shall live until those days? Or who
will be alive in those days?''
52 He answered me and said, ''Concerning the signs about which you ask me, I
can tell you in part; but I was not sent to tell you concerning your life, for I do
not know.

Signs of the approaching end of the age

1 **5** ''Now concerning the signs: Behold, the days are coming when those who dwell

---

l. Syr., Eth.; Lat. is uncertain.
m. Syr., Eth., Ar., Arm.; Lat. is corrupt.
n. Syr., Eth., Arab 2, Georgian; Lat. ''How
long do I hope thus?''

o. Syr. *Remiel*; cf. the seventh of the seven
archangels listed in 1En 20:1–8.
p. Syr., Eth., Arab 2; Lat. ''number of seeds
is completed for you.''

on earth shall be seized with great terror,[a] and the way of truth shall be hidden,
2 and the land shall be barren of faith. • And unrighteousness shall be increased   Mt 24:1
3 beyond what you yourself see, and beyond what you heard of formerly. • And the
land[b] which you now see ruling shall be waste and untrodden,[c] and men shall see
4 it desolate. • But if the Most High grants that you live, you shall see it thrown into
confusion after the third period;[d]

> and the sun shall suddenly shine forth at night,
>> and the moon during the day.
5 Blood shall drip from wood,   Hab 2:11
>> and the stone shall utter its voice;   Lk 19:40
> the peoples shall be troubled,
>> and the stars shall fall.[e]

6 And one shall reign whom those who dwell on earth do not expect, and the birds
7 shall fly away together; • and the sea of Sodom[f] shall cast up fish; and one whom
the many do not know shall make his voice heard by night, and all shall hear his
8 voice.[g] • There shall be chaos also in many places,[h] and fire shall often break out,
and the wild beasts shall roam beyond their haunts, and menstruous women shall
9 bring forth monsters. • And salt waters shall be found in the sweet, and all friends
shall conquer one another; then shall reason hide itself, and wisdom shall withdraw
10 into its chamber, • and it shall be sought by many but shall not be found, and
11 unrighteousness and unrestraint shall increase on earth. • And one country shall ask   Isa 59:14f.
its neighbor, 'Has righteousness, or anyone who does right, passed through you?'
12 And it will answer, 'No.' • And at that time men shall hope but not obtain; they
13 shall labor but their ways shall not prosper. • These are the signs which I am
permitted to tell you, and if you pray again, and weep as you do now, and fast   5:20; 6:35;
for seven days, you shall hear yet greater things than these."   12:51

Conclusion of the vision

14 Then I awoke, and my body shuddered violently, and my soul was so troubled
15 that it fainted. • But the angel who had come and talked with me held me and
strengthened me and set me on my feet.
16 Now on the second night Phaltiel, a chief of the people, came to me and said,
17 "Where have you been? And why is your face sad? • Or do you not know that
18 Israel has been entrusted to you in the land of their exile? • Rise therefore and eat
some bread, so that you may not forsake us, like a shepherd who leaves his flock
in the power of savage wolves."
19 Then I said to him, "Depart from me and do not come near me for seven days,
and then you may come to me."
20 He heard what I said and left me. • So I fasted seven days, mourning and
weeping, as Uriel the angel had commanded me.

THE SECOND VISION

Ezra reiterates his complaints of divine inequity

21 And after seven days the thoughts of my heart were very grievous to me again.
22 Then my soul recovered the spirit of understanding, and I began once more to

---

5 a. Syr.; Eth. "confusion"; Lat. is uncertain.
  b. I.e. the Roman Empire.
  c. Syr.; Lat. is corrupt.
  d. Lit. "after the third"; Eth. "after three months"; Arm. "after the third vision"; Georgian "after the third day."
  e. Eth.; cf. Syr. and Ar.; Lat. is uncertain.

f. I.e. the Dead Sea.
  g. Bensly's correction; Lat. "fish; and it shall make its voice heard by night, which the many have not known, but all shall hear its voice."
  h. Syr. "a fissure shall arise over wide regions" (cf. Zech 14:4).

23 speak words in the presence of the Most High. •And I said, "O sovereign Lord, from every forest of the earth and from all its trees you have chosen one vine, Ps 80:8
24 and from all the lands of the world you have chosen for yourself one region,[i] and
25 from all the flowers of the world you have chosen for yourself one lily, •and from Song 2:2 all the depths of the sea you have filled for yourself one river, and from all the Hos 14:5
26 cities that have been built you have consecrated Zion for yourself, •and from all Ps 132:13 the birds that have been created you have named for yourself one dove, and from Ps 74:19 all the flocks that have been fashioned you have provided for yourself one sheep, Ps 79:13
27 and from all the multitude of people you have gotten for yourself one people; and to this people, whom you have loved, you have given the Law which is approved
28 by all. •And now, O Lord, why have you given over the one to the many, and dishonored[j] the one root beyond the others, and scattered your only one among the 1En 93:8
29 many? •And those who opposed your promises have trodden down on those who
30 believed your covenants. •If you really hate your people, they should be punished at your own hands."

Response to Ezra's complaints

31   When I had spoken these words, the angel who had come to me on a previous
32 night was sent to me, •and he said to me, "Listen to me, and I will instruct you; pay attention to me, and I will tell you more."
33   "Speak on, my lord," I said. And he said to me, "Are you greatly disturbed in mind over Israel?[k] Or do you love him more than his Maker does?"   8:47
34   "No, my lord," I said, "but because of my grief I have spoken; for every hour I suffer agonies of heart, while I strive to understand the way of the Most High and to search out part of his judgment."
35   He said to me, "You cannot." And I said, "Why not, my lord? Why then was Job 3:11; I born? Or why did not my mother's womb become my grave, that I might not 10:18-19 see the travail of Jacob and the exhaustion of the people of Israel?"
36   He said to me, "Count up for me those who have not yet come, and gather for me the scattered raindrops, and make the withered flowers bloom again for me;
37 open for me the closed chambers, and bring forth for me the winds shut up in them, or show me the picture of a voice; and then I will explain to you the travail that you ask to understand."[l]
38   "O sovereign Lord," I said, "who is able to know these things except he whose
39 dwelling is not with men? •As for me, I am without wisdom, and how can I speak concerning the things which you have asked me?"
40   He said to me, "Just as you cannot do one of the things that were mentioned, so you cannot discover my judgment, or the goal of the love that I have promised my people."

Why successive generations have been created

41   I said, "Yet behold, O Lord, you have charge of those who are alive at the end, but what will those do who were before us, or we, or those who come after us?"
42   He said to me, "I shall liken my judgment to a circle;[m] just as for those who are last there is now slowness, so for those who are first there is no haste."
43   Then I answered and said, "Could you not have created at one time those who have been and those who are and those who will be, that you might show your judgment the sooner?"
44   He replied to me and said, "The creation cannot make more haste than the Creator, neither can the world hold at one time those who have been created in it."
45   And I said, "How have you said to your servant that you[n] will certainly give

---

i. Eth.; Lat. "pit."
j. Syr., Eth., Ar.; Lat. "prepared."
k. Or "You are greatly distracted in mind over Israel."

l. Lat. "see."
m. Or "crown."
n. Syr., Eth., Arab 1; Lat. is uncertain.

life at one time to your creation? If therefore all creatures will live at one time[o] and the creation will sustain them, it might even now be able to support all of them present at one time."

46   He said to me, "Ask a woman's womb, and say to it, 'If you bear ten[p] children, why one after another?' Request it therefore to produce ten at one time."

47   I said, "Of course it cannot, but only each in its own time."

48   He said to me, "Even so have I given the womb of the earth to those who from 49 time to time are sown in it. •For as an infant does not bring forth, and a woman who has become old does not bring forth any longer, so have I organized the world which I created."

50   Then I inquired and said, "Since you have now given me the opportunity, let me speak before you. Is our mother, of whom you have told me, still young? Or is she now approaching old age?"

51   He replied to me, "Ask a woman who bears children, and she will tell you. 52 Say to her, 'Why are those whom you have borne recently not like those whom you 53 bore before, but smaller in stature?' •And she herself will answer you, 'Those born in the strength of youth are different from those born during the time of old 54 age, when the womb is failing.' •Therefore you also should consider that you and 55 your contemporaries are smaller in stature than those who were before you. •And those who come after you will be smaller than you, as born of a creation which already is aging and passing the strength of youth."

The end of the age

56   I said, "O Lord, I beseech you, if I have found favor in your sight, show your servant through whom you are going to visit your creation."

1 **6** He said to me, "At the beginning of the circle of the earth,[a] before the portals 2 of the world were in place, and before the assembled winds blew, •and before the rumblings of thunder sounded, and before the flashes of lightning shone, and before 3 the foundations of Paradise were laid, •and before the beautiful flowers were seen, and before the powers of movement[b] were established, and before the innumerable 4 hosts of angels were gathered together, •and before the heights of the air were lifted up, and before the measures of the firmaments were named, and before the 5 footstool of Zion was established, •and before the present years were reckoned, and before the imaginations of those who now sin were estranged, and before those 6 who stored up treasures of faith were sealed—•then I planned these things, and they were made through me and not through another, just as the end shall come through me and not through another."

The division of the times

7   I answered and said, "What will be the dividing of the times? Or when will be the end of the first age and the beginning of the age that follows?"

8   He said to me, "From Abraham to Isaac,[c] because from him were born Jacob 9 and Esau, for Jacob's hand held Esau's heel from the beginning. •For Esau is the 10 end of this age, and Jacob is the beginning of the age that follows. •For the beginning of a man is his hand, and the end of a man is his heel,[d] between the heel and the hand seek for nothing else, Ezra!"

---

o. Lat. omits "If . . . one time."

p. Syr., Eth., Arab 2, Arm.; Lat. is corrupt.

6 a. The text is uncertain; cf. Syr.: "The beginning by the hand of man, but the end by my own hands. For as before the land of the world existed there, and before"; Eth.: "At first by the Son of Man, and afterwards I myself. For before the earth and the lands were created, and before."

b. Or "earthquake."

c. Other authorities read "Abraham."

d. Syr.; Lat. is defective here.

Signs of the end of the age

11 I answered and said, "O sovereign Lord, if I have found favor in your sight,
12 show your servant the end of your signs which you showed me in part on a previous 4:51-5:13
night."

13 He answered and said to me, "Rise to your feet and you will hear a full,
14 resounding voice. •And if the place where you are standing is greatly shaken
15 while the voice is speaking, do not be terrified; because the word concerns the end,
16 and the foundations of the earth will understand •that the speech concerns them.
They will tremble and be shaken, for they know that their end must be changed."

17 When I heard this, I rose to my feet and listened, and behold, a voice was
18 speaking, and its sound was like the sound of many waters. •And it said, "Behold,
the days are coming, and it shall be that when I draw near to visit the inhabitants
19 of the earth, •and when I require from the doers of iniquity the penalty of their
20 iniquity, and when the humiliation of Zion is complete, • and when the seal is
placed upon the age which is about to pass away, then I will show these signs: The
21 books shall be opened before the firmament, and all shall see it together. •Infants Dan 7:10; 12:1
a year old shall speak with their voices, and women with child shall give birth to Mal 3:16
22 premature children at three or four months, and these shall live and dance. •Sown Rev 20:12
places shall suddenly appear unsown, and full storehouses shall suddenly be found
23 to be empty; •and the trumpet shall sound aloud, and when all hear it, they shall 1Cor 15:52
24 suddenly be terrified. •At that time friends shall make war on friends like enemies, 1Thes 4:16
and the earth and those who inhabit it shall be terrified, and the springs of the
fountains shall stand still, so that for three hours they shall not flow.
25 "It shall be that whoever remains after all that I have foretold to you shall be
26 saved and shall see my salvation and the end of my world. • And they shall see Gen 5:24
the men who were taken up, who from their birth have not tasted death; and the 2Kgs 2:11f.
heart of the earth's[e] inhabitants shall be changed and converted to a different spirit.
27,28 For evil shall be blotted out, and deceit shall be quenched; • faithfulness shall
flourish, and corruption shall be overcome, and the truth, which has been so long
without fruit, shall be revealed.

Conclusion of the vision

29 While he spoke to me, behold, little by little the place where I was standing
30 began to rock to and fro.[f] •And he said to me, "I have come to show you these
31 things this night.[g] •If therefore you will pray again and fast again for seven days,
32 I will again declare to you greater things than these,[h] •because your voice has
surely been heard before the Most High; for the Mighty One has seen your
uprightness and has also observed the purity which you have maintained from your
33 youth. •Therefore he has sent me to show you all these things, and to say to you:
34 'Believe and do not be afraid! •Do not be quick to think vain thoughts concerning
the former things, lest you be hasty concerning the last times.' "

THE THIRD VISION

35 Now after this I wept again and fasted seven days as before, in order to complete
36 the three weeks as I had been told. •And on the eighth night my heart was troubled
37 within me again, and I began to speak in the presence of the Most High. •For my
spirit was greatly aroused, and my soul was in distress.

---

e. Syr.; cf. Eth., Arab 1, Arm.; Lat. omits
"earth's."

f. Syr., Eth.; cf. Ar., Arm.; Lat. is corrupt.

g. Syr.; cf. Eth.; Lat. is corrupt.

h. Syr., Eth., Arab 1, Arm.; Lat. adds "by
day."

God's work in creation

38 I said, "O Lord, you spoke at the beginning of creation, and said on the first Gen 1:1-4
39 day, 'Let heaven and earth be made,' and your word accomplished the work. •And
then the Spirit was hovering, and darkness and silence embraced everything; the
40 sound of man's voice was not yet there.[i] •Then you commanded that a ray of light
be brought forth from your treasuries, so that your works might then appear.
41 "Again, on the second day, you created the spirit of the firmament, and
commanded him to divide and separate the waters, that one part might move
upward and the other part remain beneath.
42 "On the third day you commanded the waters to be gathered together in the
seventh part of the earth; six parts you dried up and kept so that some of them
43 might be planted and cultivated and be of service before you. •For your word went
44 forth, and at once the work was done. •For immediately fruit came forth in endless
abundance and of varied appeal to the taste; and flowers of inimitable color; and
odors of inexpressible fragrance. These were made on the third day.
45 "On the fourth day you commanded the brightness of the sun, the light of the
46 moon, and the arrangement of the stars to come into being; •and you commanded
them to serve man, who was about to be formed. Ps 8:6-8
47 "On the fifth day you commanded the seventh part, where the water had been
gathered together, to bring forth living creatures, birds, and fishes; and so it was
48 done. • The dumb and lifeless water produced living creatures, as it was commanded,[j] that thereafter the nations might declare thy wondrous works.
49 "Then you kept in existence two living creatures;[k] the name of one you called
50 Behemoth and the name of the other Leviathan. •And you separated one from the Job 7:12;
other, for the seventh part where the water had been gathered together could not 26:12f.
Ps 74:12-15
51 hold them both. •And you gave Behemoth one of the parts which had been dried Isa 30:7;
52 up on the third day, to live in it, where there are a thousand mountains; •but to 51:9f.
Leviathan you have the seventh part, the watery part; and you have kept them to
be eaten by whom you wish, and when you wish.
53 "On the sixth day you commanded the earth to bring forth before you cattle,
54 beasts, and creeping things; •and over these you placed Adam as ruler over all the
works which you had made; and from him we have all come, the people from
whom you have chosen.

Why does Israel not possess her inheritance?

55 "All this I have spoken before you, O Lord, because you have said that it was
56 for us that you created this world.[l] •As for the other nations which have descended
from Adam, you have said that they are nothing, and that they are like spittle, and
57 you have compared their abundance to a drop from a bucket. •And now, O Lord, Isa 40:15
behold, these nations, which are reputed as nothing, domineer over us and devour
58 us. •But we your people, whom you have called your first-born, only begotten,
59 zealous for you,[m] and most dear, have been given into their hands. •If the world
has indeed been created for us, why do we not possess our world as an inheritance?
How long will this be so?"

Response to Ezra's questions

1 **7** When I had finished speaking these words, the angel who had been sent to me
2 on the former nights was sent to me again, •and he said to me, "Rise, Ezra, and
listen to the words that I have come to speak to you."
3 I said, "Speak, my lord." And he said to me, "There is a sea set in a wide

---

i. Syr., Eth.; Lat. "was not yet from you."
j. The text of this verse is uncertain.
k. Syr., Eth.; Lat. "two souls."

l. Syr., Eth., Arab 2; Lat. "the first-born
world." Compare Arab 1 "first world."
m. The meaning of the Lat. text is obscure.

4 expanse so that it is broad[a] and vast, •but it has an entrance set in a narrow place,
5 so that it is like a river. •If anyone, then, wishes to reach the sea, to look at it or
   to navigate it, how can he come to the broad part unless he passes through the
6 narrow part? •Another example: There is a city built and set on a plain, and it is
7 full of all good things; •but the entrance to it is narrow and set in a precipitous
8 place, so that there is fire on the right hand and deep water on the left; •and there
   is only one path lying between them, that is, between the fire and the water, so
9 that only one man can walk upon that path. •If now that city is given to a man for
   an inheritance, how will the heir receive his inheritance unless he passes through
   the danger set before him?''

10,11 I said, "He cannot, lord." And he said to me, "So also is Israel's portion. •For
   I made the world for their sake, and when Adam transgressed my statutes, what
12 had been made was judged. •And so the entrances[b] of this world were made narrow
   and sorrowful and toilsome; they are few and evil, full of dangers and involved
13 in great hardships. •But the entrances of the greater[c] world are broad and safe, and
14 really yield the fruit of immortality. •Therefore unless the living pass through the
   difficult and vain experiences, they can never receive those things that have been
15 reserved for them. •But now why are you disturbed, seeing that you are to perish? 1Cor 2:9
16 And why are you moved, seeing that you are mortal? • And why have you not
   considered in your mind what is to come, rather than what is now present?''
17 Then I answered and said, "O sovereign Lord, behold, you have ordained in
   your Law that the righteous shall inherit these things, but that the ungodly shall
18 perish. •The righteous therefore can endure difficult circumstances while hoping
   for easier ones; but those who have done wickedly have suffered the difficult
   circumstances and will not see the easier ones."
19 He said to me, "You are not a better judge than God, or wiser than the Most
20 High! •Let many perish who are now living, rather than that the law of God which
21 is set before them be disregarded! •For God strictly commanded those who came
   into the world, when they came, what they should do to live, and what they should
22 observe to avoid punishment. •Nevertheless they were not obedient, and spoke
   against him;

      they devised for themselves vain thoughts,
23   and proposed to themselves wicked frauds;
      they even declared that the Most High does not exist,
      and they ignored his ways!
24   They scorned his Law, and denied his covenants;
      they have been unfaithful to his statutes
      and have not performed his works.

25 "Therefore, Ezra, empty things are for the empty, and full things for the full.

The temporary messianic kingdom and the end of the world

26 "For behold, the time will come, when the signs which I have foretold to you 6:20-24
   will come to pass; the city which now is not seen shall appear,[d] and the land which
27 now is hidden shall be disclosed. •And everyone who has been delivered from the
28 evils that I have foretold shall see my wonders. •For my son the Messiah[e] shall
   be revealed with those who are with him, and those who remain shall rejoice four
29 hundred years.[f] •And after these years my son the Messiah shall die, and all who
30 draw human breath. •And the world shall be turned back to primeval silence for
31 seven days, as it was at the first beginnings; so that no one shall be left. •And after
   seven days the world, which is not yet awake, shall be roused, and that which is

---

7 a. Syr.; cf. Eth., Arab 1; Lat. "deep."
   b. Eth. "the ways."
   c. Syr. "future."
   d. Arm.; Lat., Syr. "that the bride shall appear,
   even the city appearing."

   e. Syr., Arab 1; Eth. "my Messiah"; Arab 2
   "the Messiah"; Arm. "the Messiah of God"; Georgian "the elect my Messiah"; Lat. "my son Jesus."
   f. Lat., Arab 1; Syr. "thirty years"; Arab 2
   "one thousand years"; Eth., Arm. omit.

32 corruptible shall perish. • And the earth shall give up those who are asleep in it;   Dan 12:2
and the chambers shall give up the souls which have been committed to them.
33 And the Most High shall be revealed upon the seat of judgment,^{g} and compassion
34 shall pass away,^{h} and patience shall be withdrawn;^{i} • but judgment alone shall
35 remain, truth shall stand, and faithfulness shall grow strong. • And recompense
shall follow, and the reward shall be manifested; righteous deeds shall awake, and
[36] unrighteous deeds shall not sleep.^{j} • Then the pit^k of torment shall appear, and   Rev 9:2
opposite it shall be the place of rest; and the furnace of Hell^l shall be disclosed,   Lk 16:23f.
[37] and opposite it the Paradise of delight. • Then the Most High will say to the nations
that have been raised from the dead, 'Look now, and understand whom you have
denied, whom you have not served, whose commandments you have despised!
[38] Look on this side and on that; here are delight and rest, and there are fire and
[39] torments!' Thus he will^m speak to them on the day of judgment——• a day that has
[40] no sun or moon or stars, • or cloud or thunder or lightning or wind or water or air,
[41] or darkness or evening or morning, • or summer or spring or heat or winter^n or frost
[42] or cold or hail or rain or dew, • or noon or night, or dawn or shining or brightness
or light, but only the splendor of the glory of the Most High, by which all shall
[43] see what has been determined for them. • For it will last for about a week of years.
[44] This is my judgment and its prescribed order; and to you alone have I shown these
things.''

The small number of the saved

[45]   I answered and said, "O sovereign Lord, I said then and I say now:^{o} Blessed
[46] are those who are alive and keep your commandments! • But what of those for
whom I prayed? For who among the living is there that has not sinned, or who
[47] among men that has not transgressed your covenant? • And now I see that the world
[48] to come will bring delight to few, but torments to many. • For an evil heart has
grown up in us, which has alienated us from God,^{p} and has brought us into
corruption and the ways of death, and has shown us the paths of perdition and
removed us far from life——and that not just a few of us but almost all who have
been created!''
[49]   He answered me and said, "Listen to me, Ezra,^{q} and I will instruct you, and
[50] will admonish you yet again. • For this reason the Most High has made not one   5:32
[51] world but two. • For whereas you have said that the righteous are not many but
few, while the ungodly abound, hear the explanation for this.
[52]   "If you have just a few precious stones, will you add to them lead and clay?"^{r}
[53]   I said, "Lord, how could that be?"
[54]   And he said to me, "Not only that, but ask the earth and she will tell you; defer
[55] to her, and she will declare it to you. • Say to her, 'You produce gold and silver
[56] and brass, and also iron and lead and clay; • but silver is more abundant than gold,
and brass than silver, and iron than brass, and lead than iron, and clay than lead.'
[57] Judge therefore which things are precious and desirable, those that are abundant
or those that are rare?"
[58]   I said, "O sovereign Lord, what is plentiful is of less worth, for what is more
rare is more precious."
[59]   He answered me and said, "Weigh within yourself^s what you have thought, for
he who has what is hard to get rejoices more than he who has what is plentiful.
[60] So also will be the judgment^t which I have promised; for I will rejoice over the

g. Syr. adds "and then comes the end."
h. Syr. adds "and pity shall be far off."
i. Lat. "gather together."
j. The passage from vs. [36] to vs. [105], formerly missing in the Lat. MSS used for editions of the Vulgate, has been restored (see "Texts").
k. Syr., Eth.; Lat. "place."
l. Lat. "gehenna."
m. Syr., Eth., Arab 1; Lat. "you shall."
n. Or "storm."

o. Syr.; Lat. "And I answered, 'I said then, O Lord, and I say now: . . . .' "
p. Bensly's correction; Lat., Syr., Eth. "from these."
q. Syr., Arab 1, Georgian; Lat., Eth. omit "Ezra."
r. Arab 1; Lat., Syr., Eth. are corrupt.
s. Syr., Eth., Arab 1; Lat. is corrupt here.
t. Syr., Arab 1; Lat. "creation."

few who shall be saved, because it is they who have made my glory to prevail
[61] now, and through them my name has now been honored. •And I will not grieve
over the multitude of those who perish; for it is they who are now like a mist, and
are similar to a flame and smoke—they are set on fire and burn hotly, and are
extinguished.''

Lamentation of Ezra, with response

[62]   I replied and said, ''O earth, what have you brought forth, if the mind is made
[63] out of the dust like the other created things! •For it would have been better if the   4:12
dust itself had not been born, so that the mind might not have been made from it.
[64] But now the mind grows with us, and therefore we are tormented, because we
[65] perish and know it. •Let the human race lament, but let the beasts of the field be
glad; let all who have been born lament, but let the four-footed beasts and the
[66] flocks rejoice! •For it is much better with them than with us; for they do not look
for a judgment, nor do they know of any torment or salvation promised to them
[67] after death. •For what does it profit us that we shall be preserved alive but cruelly
[68] tormented? •For all who have been born are involved in iniquities, and are full of
[69] sins and burdened with transgressions. •And if we were not to come into judgment
after death, perhaps it would have been better for us.''
[70]   He answered me and said, ''When the Most High made the world and Adam
and all who have come from him, he first prepared the judgment and the things
[71] that pertain to the judgment. •And now understand from your own words, for you
[72] have said that the mind grows with us. • For this reason, therefore, those who
dwell on earth shall be tormented, because though they had understanding they
committed iniquity, and though they received the commandments they did not keep
them, and though they obtained the Law they dealt unfaithfully with what they
[73] received. •What, then, will they have to say in the judgment, or how will they
[74] answer in the last times? •For how long the time is that the Most High has been
patient with those who inhabit the world, and not for their sake, but because of
the times which he has foreordained!''

The state of the departed before the judgment

[75]   I answered and said, ''If I have found favor in your sight, my lord, show this
also to your servant: whether after death, as soon as every one of us yields up his
soul, we shall be kept in rest until those times come when you will renew the
creation, or whether we shall be tormented at once?''
[76]   He answered me and said, ''I will show you that also, but do not be associated
with those who have shown scorn, nor number yourself among those who are
[77] tormented. •For you have a treasure of works laid up with the Most High; but it   8:33,36
[78] will not be shown to you until the last times. •Now, concerning death, the teaching
is: When the decisive decree has gone forth from the Most High that a man shall
die, as the spirit leaves the body to return again to him who gave it, first of all
[79] it adores the glory of the Most High. •And if it is one of those who have shown
scorn and have not kept the way of the Most High, and who have despised his
[80] Law, and who have hated those who fear God—•such spirits shall not enter into
habitations, but shall immediately wander about in torments, ever grieving and
[81] sad, in seven ways. •The first way, because they have scorned the Law of the
[82] Most High. •The second way, because they cannot now make a good repentance
[83] that they may live. •The third way, they shall see the reward laid up for those
[84] who have trusted the covenants of the Most High. •The fourth way, they shall
[85] consider the torment laid up for themselves in the last days. •The fifth way, they
shall see how the habitations of the others are guarded by angels in profound
[86] quiet. •The sixth way, they shall see how some of them will pass over[u] into

u. Bensly's correction; the text of this vs. is
corrupt.

[87] torments. •The seventh way, which is worse[v] than all the ways that have been mentioned, because they shall utterly waste away in confusion and be consumed with shame,[w] and shall wither with fear at seeing the glory of the Most High before whom they sinned while they were alive, and before whom they are to be judged in the last times.

[88] "Now this is the order of those who have kept the ways of the Most High,
[89] when they shall be separated from their mortal body.[x] •During the time that they lived in it,[y] they laboriously served the Most High, and withstood danger every
[90] hour, that they might keep the Law of the Lawgiver perfectly. •Therefore this is
[91] the teaching concerning them: •First of all, they shall see with great joy the glory
[92] of him who receives them, for they shall have rest in seven orders. •The first order, because they have striven with great effort to overcome the evil thought[z] which was formed with them, that it might not lead them astray from life into
[93] death. •The second order, because they see the perplexity in which the souls of
[94] the ungodly wander, and the punishment that waits them. •The third order, they see the witness which he who formed them bears concerning them, that while
[95] they were alive they kept the Law which was given them in trust. •The fourth order, they understand the rest which they now enjoy, being gathered into their chambers and guarded by angels in profound quiet, and the glory which awaits
[96] them in the last days. •The fifth order, they rejoice that they have now escaped what is mortal, and shall inherit what is to come; and besides they see the straits and toil[a2] from which they have been delivered, and the spacious liberty which
[97] they are to receive and enjoy in immortality. •The sixth order, when it is shown to them how their face is to shine like the sun, and how they are to be made like Dan 12:3
[98] the light of the stars, being incorruptible from then on. •The seventh order, which Mt 13:43 is greater than all that have been mentioned, because they shall rejoice with boldness, and shall be confident without confusion, and shall be glad without fear, for they hasten to behold the face of him whom they served in life and from Mt 5:8
[99] whom they are to receive their reward when glorified. •This is the order of the Rev 22:4 souls of the righteous, as henceforth is announced,[b2] and the aforesaid are the 1Cor 3:14 ways of torment which those who would not give heed shall suffer hereafter." Rev 22:12
[100] I answered and said, "Will time therefore be given to the souls after they have been separated from the bodies, to see what you have described to me?"
[101] He said to me, "They shall have freedom for seven days, so that during these seven days they may see the things of which you have been told, and afterward they shall be gathered in their habitations."

May the righteous intercede for the ungodly?

[102] I answered and said, "If I have found favor in your sight, show further to me, your servant, whether on the day of judgment the righteous will be able to intercede
[103] for the ungodly or to entreat the Most High for them, •fathers for sons or sons for parents, brothers for brothers, relatives for their kinsmen, or friends[c2] for those who are most dear."
[104] He answered me and said, "Since you have found favor in my sight, I will show you this also. The day of judgment is decisive[d2] and displays to all the seal of truth. Just as now a father does not send his son, or a son his father, or a master his servant, or a friend his dearest friend, to be ill[e2] or sleep or eat or be healed
[105] in his stead, •so no one shall ever pray for another on that day, neither shall anyone lay a burden on another;[f2] for then everyone shall bear his own righteousness or unrighteousness."

v. Lat. "greater."
w. Syr., Eth.; Lat. is corrupt.
x. Lit. "the corruptible vessel."
y. Syr., Eth.; Lat. is corrupt.
z. I.e. evil *yeṣer*.
a2. Syr., Eth.; Lat. "fulness."
b2. Syr.; Lat. is corrupt here.

c2. Syr., Eth., Arab 1; Lat. "kinsmen for their nearest, friends [lit. 'the confident'] for their dearest."
d2. Lat. "bold."
e2. Syr., Eth., Arm.; Lat. "understand."
f2. Syr.; Lat. omits "on that . . . another."

36[106] I answered and said, "How then do we find that first Abraham prayed for the   Gen 18:23
37[107] people of Sodom, and Moses for our fathers who sinned in the desert, •and Joshua   Ex 32:11
Josh 7:6f.
38[108] after him for Israel in the days of Achan, •and Samuel in the days of Saul,g2 and   1Sam 7:9; 12:23
39[109] David for the plague, and Solomon for those in the sanctuary, •and Elijah for those   2Sam 24:17
1Kgs 8:22f.,30
40[110] who received the rain, and for the one who was dead, that he might live, •and   1Kgs 18:42; 45
Hezekiah for the people in the days of Sennacherib, and many others prayed for   17:20f.
2Kgs 19:15-19
41[111] many? •If therefore the righteous have prayed for the ungodly now, when corruption
has increased and unrighteousness has multiplied, why will it not be so then as
well?"

42[112] He answered me and said, "This present world is not the end; the full glory
43[113] does noth2 abide in it;i2 therefore those who were strong prayed for the weak. •But
the day of judgment will be the end of this age and the beginningj2 of the immortal
44[114] age to come, in which corruption has passed away, •sinful indulgence has come
to an end, unbelief has been cut off, and righteousness has increased and truth has
45[115] appeared. •Therefore no one will then be able to have mercy on him who has been
condemned in the judgment, or to harmk2 him who is victorious."

Lamentation over the fate of the mass of humanity

46[116] I answered and said, "This is my first and last word: It would have been better
if the earth had not produced Adam, or else, when it had produced him, had
47[117] restrained him from sinning. •For what good is it to all that they live in sorrow
48[118] now and expect punishment after death? • O Adam, what have you done? For
though it was you who sinned, the fall was not yours alone, but ours also who are
49[119] your descendants. •For what good is it to us, if an eternal age has been promised
50[120] to us, but we have done deeds that bring death? • And what good is it that an
51[121] everlasting hope has been promised us, but we have miserably failed? •Or that safe
and healthful habitations have been reserved for us, but we have lived wickedly?
52[122] Or that the glory of the Most High will defend those who have led a pure life,
53[123] but we have walked in the most wicked ways? •Or that a paradise shall be revealed,
whose fruit remains unspoiled and in which are abundance and healing, but we
54[124]
55[125] shall not enter it, •because we have lived in unseemly places? •Or that the faces
of those who practiced self-control shall shine more than the stars but our faces   Dan 12:3
56[126] shall be blacker than darkness? •For while we lived and committed iniquity we did
not consider what we should suffer after death."

57[127] He answered and said, "This is the meaning of the contest which every man
58[128] who is born on earth shall wage, •that if he is defeated he shall suffer what you
59[129] have said, but if he is victorious he shall receive what I have said.l2 •For this is
the way of which Moses, while he was alive, spoke to the people, saying, 'Choose
60[130] for yourself life, that you may live!' •But they did not believe him, or the prophets
61[131] after him, or even myself who have spoken to them. • Therefore there shall not
bem2 grief at their damnation, so much as joy over those to whom salvation is
assured."

Enumeration of seven divine attributes: an implicit appeal to God's mercy

62[132] I answered and said, "I know, my lord, that the Most High is now called
merciful, because he has mercy on those who have not yet come into the world;
63[133] and gracious, because he is gracious to those who turn in repentance to his law;
64[134] and patient, because he shows patience toward those who have sinned, since they
65[135] are his own works; •and bountiful, because he would rather give than take away;n2

g2. Syr., Eth., Arab 1; Lat. omits "in the days   j2. Lat. omits "the beginning."
of Saul."   k2. Syr., Eth.; Lat. "overwhelm."
  h2. Lat. omits "not."   l2. Syr., Eth., Arab 1; Lat. "I say."
  i2. Or "the glory does not continuously abide   m2. Syr.; Lat. "was not."
in it."   n2. Or "is ready to give according to requests."

66[136] and abundant in compassion, because he makes his compassions abound more and more to those now living and to those who are gone and to those yet to come,
67[137] for if he did not make them abound, the world with those who inhabit it would
68[138] not have life; •and he is called giver, because if he did not give out of his goodness so that those who have committed iniquities might be relieved of them, not one
69[139] ten-thousandth of mankind could have life; •and judge, because if he did not pardon those who were created by his word and blot out the multitude of their sins,[o2]
70[140] there would probably be left only very few of the innumerable multitude.''

1 **8** He answered me and said, ''The Most High made this world for the sake of
2 many, but the world to come for the sake of few. •But I will tell you a parable, Ezra. Just as, when you ask the earth, it will tell you that it provides very much clay from which earthenware is made, but only a little dust from which gold comes;
3 so is the course of the present world. •Many have been created, but few will be saved.''

Ezra implores God to show mercy to his creation

4 I answered and said, ''Then drink your fill of understanding, O my soul, and
5 drink wisdom, O my heart![a] •For not of your own will did you come into the world,[b] and against your will you depart, for you have been given only a short
6 time to live. •O Lord who art over us, grant to your servant that we may pray before you, and give us seed for our heart and cultivation of our understanding so that fruit may be produced, by which every mortal who bears the likeness[c] of a
7 human being may be able to live. •For you alone exist, and we are of your hands,　Isa 44:6; 45:11;
8 as you have declared. • And because you give life to the body which is now　60:21
fashioned in the womb, and furnish it with members, what you have created is preserved in fire and water, and for nine months the womb that you have fashioned[d]
9 bears your creation which has been created in it. •But that which keeps and that which is kept shall both be kept by your keeping.[e] And when the womb gives up
10 again what has been created in it, •you have commanded that from the members themselves (that is, from the breasts) milk should be supplied, which is the fruit
11 of the breasts, •so that what has been fashioned may be nourished for a time; and
12 afterward you will guide him in your mercy. •You have brought him up in your righteousness, and instructed him in your law, and reproved him in your wisdom.
13 You will take away his life, for he is your creation; and you will make him live,
14 for he is your work. •If then you suddenly and quickly[f] destroy him who with so
15 great labor was fashioned by your command, to what purpose was he made? •And　Ps 139:14f.
now I will speak out: About mankind you know best; but I will speak about your
16 people, for whom I am grieved, •and about your inheritance, for whom I lament,　Ps 28:9
and about Israel, for whom I am sad, and about the seed of Jacob, for whom I am
17 troubled. •Therefore I will pray before you for myself and for them, for I see the
18 failings of us who dwell in the land, •and[g] I have heard of the swiftness of the
19 judgment that is to come. •Therefore hear my voice, and understand my words, and I will speak before you.''
The beginning of the work of Ezra's prayer, before he was taken up. He said,
20 ''O Lord who inhabits eternity,[h] whose eyes are exalted[i] and whose upper chambers
21 are in the air, •whose throne is beyond measure and whose glory is beyond
22 comprehension, before whom the hosts of angels stand trembling •and at whose command they are changed to wind and fire,[j] whose word is sure and whose　Ps 104:4
　　　　　　　　　　　　　　　　　　　　　　　　　　　　　　　　　　　　　　Heb 1:7

o2. Lat. ''contempts.''

8 a. Syr.; Lat. ''let it feed on what it understands.''
　b. Syr.; Lat. is corrupt here.
　c. Syr.; Lat. ''place'' (see Introduction, ''Original language'').
　d. Lit. ''for nine months your fashioning.''
　e. Syr.; Lat. is corrupt here.

f. Syr.; Lat. ''will with a light command.''
g. Lit. ''but.''
h. Or ''abide forever.''
i. Another Lat. text reads ''whose are the highest heavens.''
j. Syr.; Lat. ''they whose service takes the form of wind and fire.''

utterances are certain, whose ordinance is strong and whose command is terrible,
23 whose look dries up the depths and whose indignation makes the mountains melt Isa 50:2; 51:10
24 away, and whose truth is established forever[k]—·hear, O Lord, the prayer of your Micah 1:4
Sir 16:18f.
25 servant, and give ear to the petition of your creature; attend to my words. ·For as
26 long as I live I will speak, and as long as I have understanding I will answer. ·O
   look not upon the sins of your people, but at those who have served you in truth.
27 Regard not the endeavors of those who act wickedly, but the endeavors of those
28 who have kept your covenants amid afflictions. · Think not on those who have
   lived wickedly, in your sight; but remember those who have willingly acknowledged
29 that you are to be feared. ·Let it not be your will to destroy those who have had
30 the ways of cattle; but regard those who have gloriously taught your Law.[l] ·Be not
   angry with those who are deemed worse than beasts; but love those who have
31 always put their trust in your glory. ·For we and our fathers have passed our lives
   in ways that bring death,[m] but you, because of us sinners, are called merciful.
32 For if you have desired to have pity on us, who have no works of righteousness,
33 then you will be called merciful. · For the righteous, who have many works laid
34 up with you, shall receive their reward in consequence of their own deeds. ·But
   what is man, that you are angry with him; or what is a mortal race, that you are
35 so bitter against it? ·For in truth there is no one among those who have been born
   who has not acted wickedly, and among those who have existed[n] there is no one
36 who has not transgressed. ·For in this, O Lord, your righteousness and goodness
   will be declared, when you are merciful to those who have no store of good
   works.''

Response to Ezra's prayer

37   He answered me and said, ''Some things you have spoken rightly, and it will
38 come to pass according to your words. ·For indeed I will not concern myself about
   the fashioning of those who have sinned, or about their death, their judgment, or
39 their damnation; · but I will rejoice over the creation of the righteous, over their
40 pilgrimage also, and their salvation, and their receiving their reward. · As you[o]
   have spoken, therefore, so it shall be.

Humankind is compared with seeds and plants

41   ''For just as the farmer sows many seeds upon the ground and plants a multitude
   of seedlings, and yet not all that have been sown will come up[p] in due season, and
   not all that were planted will take root; so all those who have been sown in the
   world will not be saved.''
42,43   I answered and said, ''If I have found favor before you, let me speak.[q] ·For if
   the farmer's seed does not come up, because it has not received your rain in due
44 season, or if it has been ruined by too much rain, it perishes.[r] ·But man, who has
   been formed by your hands and is called your own image because he is made like
   you, and for whose sake you have formed all things—have you also made him like
45 the farmer's seed? ·No, O Lord[s] who are over us! But spare your people and mercy Joel 2:17
   on your inheritance, for you have mercy on your own creation.''

The final divine answer

46   He answered me and said, ''Things that are present are for those who live now,
47 and things that are future are for those who will live hereafter. ·For you come far

---

k. Arab 2; other authorities read ''bears witness.''
l. Syr. ''have received the brightness of your
law.''
m. Syr., Eth.; the Lat. is uncertain.
n. Syr.; the Lat. is uncertain.
o. Eth. ''you''; Lat. ''I.''

p. Syr., Eth. ''will live''; Lat. ''will be saved.''
q. Or ''If I have found favor, let me speak before
you.''
r. Bensly's correction; cf. Syr., Arab 1, Arm.;
the Lat. is corrupt.
s. Eth., Ar.; cf. Syr.; Lat. omits ''O Lord.''

short of being able to love my creation more than I love it. But you have often
48 compared yourself[t] to the unrighteous. Never do so! •But even in this respect you
49 will be praiseworthy before the Most High, •because you humble yourself, as is
becoming for you, and have not deemed yourself to be among the righteous in
50 order to receive[u] the greatest glory. • For many miseries will affect those who
51 inhabit the world in the last times, because they have walked in great pride. •But
think of your own case, and inquire concerning the glory of those who are like
52 yourself, •because it is for you that Paradise is opened, the tree of life is planted,　Rev 2:7; 22:2
the age to come is prepared, plenty is provided, a city is built, rest is appointed,[v]
53 goodness is established and wisdom perfected beforehand. • The root of evil is
sealed up from you, illness is banished from you, and death[w] is hidden; hell has
54 fled and corruption has been forgotten;[x] •sorrows have passed away, and in the end
55 the treasure of immortality is made manifest. • Therefore do not ask any more
56 questions about the multitude of those who perish. •For they also received freedom,
but they despised the Most High, and were contemptuous of his Law, and forsook
57,58 his ways. •Moreover they have even trampled upon his righteous ones, •and said
in their hearts that there is no God—though knowing full well that they must die.　Pss 14:1; 53:1
59 For just as the things which I have predicted await[y] you, so the thirst and torment
which are prepared await them. For the Most High did not intend that men should
60 be destroyed; •but they themselves who were created have defiled the name of him
who made them, and have been ungrateful to him who prepared life for them.
61,62 Therefore my judgment is now drawing near; •I have not shown this to all men,
but only to you and a few like you.''

The end, and the signs preceding it

63　　Then I answered and said, • ''Behold, O Lord, you have now shown me a
multitude of the signs which you will do in the last times, but you have not shown
me when you will do them.''

1　**9** He answered me and said, ''Measure carefully in your mind, and when you see
2 that a certain part of the predicted signs are past, •then you will know that it is
the very time when the Most High is about to visit the world which he has made.
3 So when there shall appear in the world earthquakes, tumult of peoples, intrigues
4 of nations, wavering of leaders, confusion of princes, •then you will know that
it was of these that the Most High spoke from the days that were of old, from the
5 beginning. •For just as with everything that has occurred in the world, the beginning
6 is evident,[a] and the end is manifest; •so also are the times of the Most High: The
beginnings are manifest in wonders and mighty works, and the end in requital[b] and
7 signs. •And it shall be that everyone who will be saved and will be able to escape
8 on account of his works, or on account of the faith by which he has believed, •will
survive the dangers that have been predicted, and will see my salvation in my land
and within my borders, which I have sanctified for myself from the beginning.
9 Then those who have now abused my ways shall be amazed, and those who have
10 rejected them with contempt shall dwell in torments. • For as many as did not
11 acknowledge me in their lifetime, although they received my benefits, • and as
many as scorned my Law while they still had freedom, and did not understand but
12 despised it[c] while an opportunity of repentance was still open to them, •these must
13 in torment acknowledge it[d] after death. •Therefore, do not continue to be curious

t. Syr., Eth.; Lat. ''brought yourself near.''
u. Or ''righteous; so that you will receive.''
v. Syr.; Lat. ''allowed.''
w. Syr., Eth., Arm.; Lat. omits ''death.''
x. Syr.; Lat. ''Hades and corruption have fled
into oblivion'' or ''corruption has fled into Hades
to be forgotten.''

y. Syr.; Lat. ''will receive.''

9 a. Syr.; Eth. ''in the world''; Lat. is corrupt.
b. Syr.; Lat., Eth. ''in effects.''
c. Or ''me.''
d. Or ''me.''

as to how the ungodly will be punished; but inquire how the righteous will be saved, those to whom the age belongs and for whose sake the age was made."[e]

The fate of the wicked

14,15 I answered and said, •"I said before, and I say now, and will say it again: There
16 are more who perish than those who will be saved, •as a wave is greater than a drop of water."
17 He answered me and said, "As is the field, so is the seed; and as are the flowers, so are the colors; and as is the work, so is the product; and as is the farmer, so
18 is the threshing floor. •For there was a time in this age when I was preparing for those who now exist, before the world was made for them to dwell in, and no one
19 opposed me then, for no one existed. •But now those who have been created in this world, which is supplied both with an unfailing table and an inexhaustible
20 pasture,[f] have become corrupt in their ways. • So I considered my world, and behold, it was lost, and my earth, and behold, it was in peril because of the devices
21 of those who[g] had come into it. •And I saw and spared some[h] with great difficulty, and saved for myself one grape out of a cluster, and one plant out of a great forest.[i]
22 So let the multitude perish which has been born in vain, but let my grape and my
23 plant be saved, because with much labor I have perfected them. •But if you will
24 let seven days more pass—do not fast during them, however; •but go into a field of flowers where no house has been built, and eat only of the flowers of the field,
25 and taste no meat and drink no wine, but eat only flowers, •and pray to the Most High continually—then I will come and talk with you."

THE FOURTH VISION

The abiding glory of the Mosaic Law

26 So I went, as he directed me, into the field which is called Ardat;[j] and there I sat among the flowers and ate of the plants of the field, and the nourishment they
27 afforded satisfied me. •And after seven days, as I lay on the grass, my heart was
28 troubled again as it was before. •And my mouth was opened, and I began to speak
29 before the Most High, and said, •"O Lord, you showed yourself among us, to our fathers in the wilderness when they came out from Egypt and when they came into   Ex 19:9; 24:10
30 the untrodden and unfruitful wilderness; •and you said, 'Hear me, O Israel, and   Deut 4:12
31 give heed to my words, O descendants of Jacob. •For behold, I sow my Law in
32 you, and you shall be glorified through it forever.' •But though our fathers received the Law, they did not keep it, and did not observe the statutes; yet the fruit of the
33 Law did not perish—for it could not, because it was yours. •Yet those who received
34 it perished, because they did not keep what had been sown in them. •And behold, it is the rule that, when the ground has received seed, or the sea a ship, or any dish food or drink, and when it happens that what was sown or what was launched or
35 what was put in is destroyed, •they are destroyed, but the things that held them
36 remain; yet with us it has not been so. •For we who have received the Law and
37 sinned will perish, as well as our heart which received it; •the Law, however, does not perish but remains in its glory."

The vision of a dependent woman

38 When I said these things in my heart, I lifted up my eyes[k] and saw a woman

---

e. Syr.; Lat. "saved, and whose is the age and for whose sake the age was made."
   f. Bensly's correction. Lat. "law" (see Introduction, "Original language").
   g. Bensly's correction. Lat. "devices which."

h. Lat. "them."
i. Syr., Eth., Arab 1; Lat. "tribe."
j. Syr., Eth., "Arpad"; Arm. "Ardab."
k. Syr., Ar., Arm.; Lat. "I looked about me with my eyes."

on my right, and behold, she was mourning and weeping with a loud voice, and was deeply grieved at heart, and her clothes were rent, and there were ashes on
39 her head. • Then I dismissed the thoughts with which I had been engaged, and
40 turned to her • and said to her, "Why are you weeping, and why are you grieved at heart?"
41 "Let me alone, my lord," she said, "that I may weep for myself and continue to mourn, for I am greatly embittered in spirit and deeply afflicted."
42 And I said to her, "What has happened to you? Tell me."
43 She said to me, "Your servant was barren and had no child, though I lived with
44 my husband thirty years. • And every hour and every day during those thirty years
45 I besought the Most High, night and day. • And after thirty years God heard your handmaid, and looked upon my low estate, and considered my distress, and gave me a son. And I rejoiced greatly over him, I and my husband and all my neighbors,[1]
46 and we gave great glory to the Mighty One. • And I brought him up with much
47 care. • So when he grew up and I came to take a wife for him, I set a day for the marriage feast.

1 **10** "But it happened that when my son entered his wedding chamber, he fell
2 down and died. • Then we all put out the lamps, and all my neighbors[a] attempted
3 to console me; and I remained quiet until evening of the second day. • But when they all had stopped consoling me, that I might be quiet, I got up in the night and
4 fled, and came to this field, as you see. • And now I intend not to return to the city, but to stay here, and I will neither eat nor drink, but without ceasing mourn and fast until I die."
5 Then I broke off the reflections with which I was still engaged, and answered
6 her in anger and said, • "You most foolish of women, do you not see our mourning,
7 and what has happened to us? • For Zion, the mother of us all, is in deep grief and Gal 4:26
8 great humiliation. • It is most appropriate to mourn now, because we are all mourning, and to be sorrowful, because we are all sorrowing; you are sorrowing
9 for one son, but we, the whole world, for our mother.[b] • Now ask the earth, and she will tell you that it is she who ought to mourn over so many who have come
10 into being upon her. • And from the beginning all have been born of her, and others will come; and behold, almost all go to perdition, and a multitude of them are
11 destined for destruction. • Who then ought to mourn the more, she[c] who lost so
12 great a multitude, or you who are grieving for one? • But if you say to me, 'My lamentation is not like the earth's, for I have lost the fruit of my womb, which I
13 brought forth in pain and bore in sorrow; • but it is with the earth according to the
14 way of the earth—the multitude that is now in it goes as it came'; • then I say to you, 'As you brought forth in sorrow, so the earth also has from the beginning
15 given her fruit, that is, man, to him who made her.' • Now, therefore, keep your
16 sorrow to yourself, and bear bravely the troubles that have come upon you. • For if you acknowledge the decree of God to be just, you will receive your son back
17 in due time. • Therefore go into the city to your husband."
18 She said to me, "I will not do so; I will not go into the city, but I will die here."

Further remonstrance of Ezra

19,20 So I spoke again to her, and said, • "Do not say that, but let yourself be persuaded because of the troubles of Zion, and be consoled because of the sorrow of Jerusalem.
21 For you see that our sanctuary has been laid waste, our altar thrown down, our
22 temple destroyed; • our harp has been laid low, our song has been silenced, and our rejoicing has been ended; the light of our lampstand has been put out, the ark of our covenant has been plundered, our holy things have been polluted, and the name by which we are called has been profaned; our free men[d] have suffered abuse,

---

1. Lit. "all my fellow citizens."

10 a. Lit. "all my fellow citizens."

b. Cf. Syr.; Lat. is corrupt.
c. Syr.
d. Or "children."

our priests have been burned to death, our Levites have gone into captivity, our virgins have been defiled, and our wives have been ravished; our righteous men have been carried off, our little ones have been cast out, our young men have been
23 enslaved and our strong men made powerless. •And, what is more than all, the seal of Zion—for she has now lost the seal of her glory, and has been given over
24 into the hands of those that hate us. •Therefore shake off your great sadness and lay aside your many sorrows, so that the Mighty One may be merciful to you again, and the Most High may give you rest, a relief from your troubles.''

A vision of the heavenly Jerusalem

25   While I was talking to her, behold, her face suddenly shone exceedingly, and her countenance flashed like lightning, so that I was too frightened to approach
26 her, and my heart was terrified. While[e] I was wondering what this meant, •behold, she suddenly uttered a loud and fearful cry, so that the earth shook at the sound.
27 And I looked, and behold, the woman was no longer visible to me, but there was an established city,[f] and a place of huge foundations showed itself. Then I was   Heb 11:10
28 afraid, and cried with a loud voice and said, • ''Where is the angel Uriel, who   Rev 21:9-21 came to me at first? For it was he who brought me into this overpowering 4:1 bewilderment; my end has become corruption, and my prayer a reproach.''

Interpretation of the vision

29   As I was speaking these words, behold, the angel who had come to me at first
30 came to me, and he looked upon me; •and behold, I lay there like a corpse and   Rev 1:17 I was deprived of my understanding. Then he grasped my right hand and strength-
31 ened me and set me on my feet, and said to me, • ''What is the matter with you? And why are you troubled? And why are your understanding and the thoughts of your mind troubled?''
32   I said, ''Because you have forsaken me! I did as you directed, and went out into the field, and behold, I saw, and still see, what I am unable to explain.''
33   He said to me, ''Stand up like a man, and I will instruct you.''   5:15; 6:13,17
34   I said, ''Speak, my lord; only do not forsake me, lest I die before my time.[g]
35 For I have seen what I did not know, and I have heard what I do not understand.
36,37 Or is my mind deceived, and my soul dreaming? •Now therefore I entreat you to give your servant an explanation of this bewildering vision.''
38   He answered me and said, ''Listen to me and I will inform you, and tell you about the things which you fear, for the Most High has revealed many secrets to
39 you. •For he has seen your righteous conduct, that you have sorrowed continually
40 for your people, and mourned greatly over Zion. •This therefore is the meaning
41 of the vision. •The woman who appeared to you a little while ago, whom you saw
42 mourning and began to console—•but you do not now see the form of a woman,
43 but an established city[h] has appeared to you—•and as for her telling you about the
44 misfortune of her son, this is the interpretation: •This woman whom you saw,
45 whom you now behold as an established city, is Zion.[i] •And as for her telling you that she was barren for thirty years, it is because there were three thousand[i] years
46 in the world before any offering was offered in it.[j] •And after three thousand[i] years Solomon built the city, and offered offerings; then it was that the barren woman
47 bore a son. •And as for her telling you that she brought him up with much care,
48 that was the period of residence in Jerusalem. •And as for her saying to you, 'When my son entered his wedding chamber he died,' and that misfortune had overtaken
49 her,[k] that was the destruction which befell Jerusalem. •And behold, you saw her likeness, how she mourned for her son, and you began to console her for what had

---

e. Syr., Eth., Arab 1; Lat. omits ''I was too . . . terrified. While.''
f. Syr., Eth., Ar.; Lat. ''a city was being built.''
g. Syr., Eth., Ar.; Lat. ''die to no purpose.''
h. Syr., Eth., Ar.; Lat. ''a city to be built.''

i. Syr., Eth., Ar., Arm.; Lat. is corrupt.
j. Bensly's correction. Lat., Syr., Ar., Arm. ''her.''
k. Or ''him.''

50 happened.[1] • For now the Most High, seeing that you are sincerely grieved and
profoundly distressed for her, has shown you the brightness of her glory, and the
51 loveliness of her beauty. • Therefore I told you to remain in the field where no
52 house had been built, • for I knew that the Most High would reveal these things
53 to you. • Therefore I told you to go into the field where there was no foundation
54 of any building, • for no work of man's building could endure in a place where the
city of the Most High was to be revealed.

55   "Therefore do not be afraid, and do not let your heart be terrified; but go in and
see the splendor and vastness of the building, as far as it is possible for your eyes
56,57 to see it, • and afterward you will hear as much as your ears can hear. • For you
are more blessed than many, and you have been called[m] before the Most High, as
58,59 but few have been. • But tomorrow night you shall remain here, • and the Most
High will show you in those dream visions what the Most High will do to those
who dwell on earth in the last days."
     So I slept that night and the following one, as he had commanded me.

THE FIFTH VISION

(The Eagle Vision)

1 **11** On the second night I had a dream, and behold, there came up from the sea
2 an eagle that had twelve feathered wings and three heads. • And I looked, and
behold, he spread his wings over[a] all the earth, and all the winds of heaven blew
3 upon him, and the clouds were gathered about him.[b] • And I looked, and out of
4 his wings there grew opposing wings; but they became little, puny wings. • But
his heads were at rest; the middle head was larger than the other heads, but it also
5 was at rest with them. • And I looked, and behold, the eagle flew with his wings,
6 to reign over the earth and over those who dwell in it. • And I saw how all things
under heaven were subjected to him, and no one spoke against him, not even one
7 creature that was on the earth. • And I looked, and behold, the eagle rose upon his
8 talons, and uttered a cry to his wings, saying, • "Do not all watch at the same time;
9 let each sleep in his own place, and watch in his turn; • but let the heads be reserved
for the last."
10   And I looked, and behold, the voice did not come from his heads, but from the
11 midst of his body. • And I counted his opposing wings, and behold, there were
12 eight of them. • And I looked, and behold, on the right side one wing arose, and
13 it reigned over all the earth. • And while it was reigning it came to its end and
disappeared, so that its place was not seen. Then the next wing arose and reigned,
14 and it continued to reign a long time. • And while it was reigning its end came also,
15 so that it disappeared like the first. • And behold, a voice sounded, saying to it,
16 "Hear me, you who have ruled the earth all this time; I announce this to you
17 before you disappear. • After you no one shall rule as long as you, or even half
as long."
18   Then the third wing raised itself up, and held the rule like the former ones, and
19 it also disappeared. • And so it went with all the wings; they wielded power one
20 after another and then were never seen again. • And I looked, and behold, in due
course the wings that followed[c] also rose up on the right[d] side in order to rule.
21 There were some of them that ruled, yet disappeared suddenly; • and others of
them rose up, but did not hold the rule.
22   After this I looked and behold, the twelve wings and the two little wings
23 disappeared; • and nothing remained on the eagle's body except the three heads that

Dan 7:3
Rev 13:1

---

l. Most Lat. MSS and Arab 1 add "these were
the things to be opened to you."
m. Arab 1 "your name is known."

11 a. Arab 2, Arm.; Lat., Syr. "in."

b. Syr.; cf. Eth., Ar.; Lat. omits "the clouds"
and "about him."
c. Syr., Arab 2 "the little wings."
d. Some Eth. MSS read "left."

24 were at rest and six little wings. •And I looked, and behold, two little wings separated from the six and remained under the head that was on the right side; but
25 four remained in their place. •And I looked, and behold, these little wings[e] planned
26 to set themselves up and hold the rule. •And I looked, and behold, one was set
27 up, but suddenly disappeared; •a second also, and this disappeared more quickly
28 than the first. •And I looked, and behold, the two that remained were planning
29 between themselves to reign together; •and while they were planning, behold, one of the heads that were at rest (the one which was in the middle) awoke; for it was
30 greater than the other two heads. •And I saw how it allied the two heads with
31 itself, •and behold, the head turned with those that were with it, and it devoured
32 the two little wings[f] which were planning to reign. •Moreover this head gained control of the whole earth, and with much oppression dominated its inhabitants; and it had greater power over the world than all the wings that had gone before.

33 After this I looked, and behold, the middle head also suddenly disappeared, just
34 as the wings had done. •But the two heads remained, which also ruled over the
35 earth and its inhabitants. •And I looked, and behold, the head on the right side devoured the one on the left.

36 Then I heard a voice saying to me, "Look before you and consider what you
37 see." •And I looked, and behold, a creature like a lion was aroused out of the forest, roaring; and I heard how he uttered a man's voice to the eagle, and spoke,
38,39 saying, •"Listen and I will speak to you. The Most High says to you, •'Are you not the one that remains of the four beasts which I had made to reign in my world,
40 so that the end of my times might come through them? •You, the fourth that has come, have conquered all the beasts that have gone before; and you have held sway over the world with much terror, and over all the earth with grievous
41 oppression; and for so long you have dwelt on the earth with deceit.[g] •And you
42 have judged the earth, but not with truth; •for you have afflicted the meek and injured the peaceable; you have hated those who tell the truth, and have loved liars; you have destroyed the dwellings of those who brought forth fruit, and have
43 laid low the walls of those who did you no harm. •And so your insolence has come
44 up before the Most High, and your pride to the Mighty One. •And the Most High has looked upon his times, and behold, they are ended, and his ages are completed!
45 Therefore you will surely disappear, you eagle, and your terrifying wings, and your most evil little wings, and your malicious heads, and your most evil talons,
46 and your whole worthless body, •so that the whole earth, freed from your violence, may be refreshed and relieved, and may hope for the judgment and mercy of him who made it.' "

1,2 **12** While the lion was saying these words to the eagle, I looked, •and behold, the remaining head disappeared. And the two wings that had gone over to it arose[a]
3 and set themselves up to reign, and their reign was brief and full of tumult. •And I looked, and behold, they also disappeared, and the whole body of the eagle was burned, and the earth was exceedingly terrified.

Ezra asks for an interpretation of the vision

Then I awoke in great perplexity of mind and great fear, and I said to my spirit,
4 "Behold, you have brought this upon me, because you search out the ways of
5 the Most High. •Behold, I am still weary in mind and very weak in my spirit, and not even a little strength is left in me, because of the great fear with which I have
6 been terrified this night. •Therefore I will now beseech the Most High that he may strengthen me to the end."
7 So I said, "O sovereign Lord, if I have found favor in your sight, and if I have

---

e. Syr.; Lat. "underwings."
f. Syr.; Lat. "underwings."
g. Syr., Ar., Arm.; Lat., Eth. "The fourth came, however, and conquered . . . and held sway . . .

and for so long dwelt."

12 a. Eth.; Lat. omits "arose."

been accounted righteous before you beyond many others, and if my prayer has
8 indeed come up before your face, •strengthen me and show me, your servant, the
interpretation and meaning of this terrifying vision, that you may fully comfort my
9 soul. •For you have judged me worthy to be shown the end of the times and the
last events of the time.''

The interpretation of the vision

10 He said to me, ''This is the interpretation of this vision which you have seen:
11 The eagle which you saw coming up from the sea is the fourth kingdom[b] which
12 appeared in a vision to your brother Daniel. •But it was not explained to him as
13 I now explain or have explained it to you. •Behold, the days are coming when a
kingdom shall arise on earth, and it shall be more terrifying than all the kingdoms
14 that have been before it. •And twelve kings shall reign in it, one after another.
15 But the second that is to reign shall hold sway for a longer time than any other
16,17 of the twelve. •This is the interpretation of the twelve wings which you saw. •As
for your hearing a voice that spoke, coming not from the eagle's[c] heads but from   11:10
18 the midst of his body, this is the interpretation: •In the midst of[d] the time of that
kingdom great struggles shall arise, and it shall be in danger of falling; nevertheless
19 it shall not fall then, but shall regain its former power.[e] •As for your seeing eight
20 little wings[f] clinging to his wings, this is the interpretation: •Eight kings shall arise   11:3,11
21 in it, whose times shall be short and their years swift; •and two of them shall
perish when the middle of its time draws near; and four shall be kept for the time
22 when its end approaches; but two shall be kept until the end. •As for your seeing
23 three heads at rest, this is the interpretation: •In its last days the Most High will   11:30-52
raise up three kings,[g] and they[h] shall renew many things in it, and shall rule the
24 earth •and its inhabitants more oppressively than all who were before them; therefore
25 they are called the heads of the eagle. • For it is they who shall sum up his
26 wickedness and perform his last actions. •As for your seeing that the large head
27 disappeared, one of the kings[i] shall die in his bed, but in agonies. •But as for the
28 two who remained, the sword shall devour them. • For the sword of one shall
devour him who was with him; but he also shall fall by the sword in the last days.
29 As for your seeing two little wings[j] passing over to[k] the head which was on the
30 right side, •this is the interpretation: It is these whom the Most High has kept for
the eagle's[l] end; this was the reign which was brief and full of tumult, as you have
seen.
31 ''And as for the lion that you saw rousing up out of the forest and roaring and   11:37f.
speaking to the eagle and reproving him for his unrighteousness, and as for all his
32 words that you have heard, •this is the Messiah[m] whom the Most High has kept   Dan 7:13-14
until the end of days, who will arise from the posterity of David, and will come   1En 48:6; 62:7
and speak to them;[n] he will denounce them for their ungodliness and for their
33 wickedness, and will cast up before them their contemptuous dealings. •For first
he will set them living before his judgment seat, and when he has reproved them,
34 then he will destroy them. •But he will deliver in mercy the remnant of my people,
those who have been saved throughout my borders, and he will make them joyful   7:2
until the end comes, the day of judgment, of which I spoke to you at the beginning.
35,36 This is the dream that you saw, and this is its interpretation. •And you alone were   11:1
37 worthy to learn this secret of the Most High. •Therefore write all these things that
38 you have seen in a book, and put it in a hidden place; •and you shall teach them
to the wise among your people, whose hearts you know are able to comprehend

b. In Daniel's vision (Dan 7:7) the fourth kingdom symbolized the Greek or Macedonian Empire;
here it is reinterpreted (vs. 12) as the Roman Empire.
  c. Lat. ''his.''
  d. Syr., Arm.; Lat. ''After.''
  e. Eth., Arab 1, Arm.; Lat., Syr. ''beginning.''
  f. Syr.; Lat. ''underwings.''

g. Syr., Eth., Ar., Arm.; Lat. ''kingdoms.''
h. Syr., Eth., Arm.; Lat. ''he.''
i. Lat. ''them.''
j. Arab 1; Lat. ''underwings.''
k. Syr., Eth.; Lat. omits ''to.''
l. Lat. ''his.''
m. Lit. ''anointed one.''
n. Syr.; Lat. omits ''of days . . . and speak.''

39 and keep these secrets. •But wait here seven days more, so that you may be shown whatever it pleases the Most High to show you.'' Then he left me.

Grief over Ezra's absence

40   When all the people heard that the seven days were past and I had not returned to the city, they all gathered together, from the least to the greatest, and came to 41 me and spoke to me, saying, •''How have we offended you, and what harm have 42 we done you, that you have forsaken us and sit in this place? • For of all the prophets you alone are left to us, like a cluster of grapes from the vintage, and like 43 a lamp in a dark place, and like a haven for a ship saved from a storm. •Are not 2Pet 1:19 44 the evils which have befallen us sufficient? •Therefore if you forsake us, how much better it would have been for us if we also had been consumed in the burning of 45 Zion! •For we are no better than those who died there.'' And they wept with a loud voice.

Ezra comforts his people

46   Then I answered them and said, • ''Take courage, O Israel; and do not be 8 47 sorrowful, O house of Jacob; •for the Most High has you in remembrance, and 48 the Mighty One has not forgotten you in your struggle. •As for me, I have neither forsaken you nor withdrawn from you; but I have come to this place to pray on account of the desolation of Zion and to seek mercy on account of the humiliation 49 of our° sanctuary. •Now go, every one of you to his house, and after these days 50,51 I will come to you.'' •So the people went into the city, as I told them to do. •But I sat in the field seven days, as the angel^p had commanded me; and I ate only of the flowers of the field, and my food was of plants during those days.

THE SIXTH VISION

(The Man from the Sea)

1,2 **13** After seven days I dreamed a dream in the night; •and behold, a wind arose 3 from the sea and stirred up all its waves. • And I looked, and behold, this wind made something like the figure of a man come up out of the heart of the sea. And I looked, and behold,^a that man flew^b with the clouds of heaven; and wherever he 4 turned his face to look, everything under his gaze trembled, • and whenever his voice issued from his mouth, all who heard his voice melted as wax melts^c when Micah 1:4 it feels the fire.   Jdt 16:15 5   After this I looked, and behold, an innumerable multitude of men were gathered together from the four winds of heaven to make war against the man who came 6 up out of the sea. • And I looked, and behold, he carved out for himself a great Dan 2:4 7 mountain, and flew up upon it. •And I tried to see the region or place from which the mountain was carved, but I could not. 8   After this I looked, and behold, all who had gathered together against him, to 9 wage war with him, were much afraid, yet dared to fight. •And behold, when he saw the onrush of the approaching multitude, he neither lifted his hand nor held 10 a spear or any weapon of war; •but I saw only how he sent forth from his mouth as it were a stream of fire, and from his lips a flaming breath, and from his tongue Isa 11:4 11 he shot forth a storm of sparks.^d •All these were mingled together, the stream of fire and the flaming breath and the great storm, and fell on the onrushing multitude which was prepared to fight, and burned them all up, so that suddenly nothing was

o. Syr., Eth.; Lat. ''your.''
p. Lit. ''he.''

13 a. Syr.; Lat. omits ''this wind . . . and be-

hold.''
b. Syr., Eth., Ar., Arm.; Lat. ''grew strong.''
c. Syr.; Lat. ''burned as the earth rests.''
d. The text is uncertain.

seen of the innumerable multitude but only the dust of ashes and the smell of smoke. When I saw it, I was amazed.

12 After this I saw the same man come down from the mountain and call to him
13 another multitude which was peaceable. •Then many people[e] came to him, some of whom were joyful and some sorrowful; some of them were bound, and some were bringing others as offerings.

Request for interpretation of the vision

14 Then in great fear I awoke; and I besought the Most High, and said, •"From the beginning you have shown your servant these wonders, and have deemed me
15 worthy to have my prayer heard by you; •now show me also the interpretation of
16 this dream. •For as I consider it in my mind, woe to those who will survive in
17 those days! And still more, woe to those who do not survive! •For those who do
18 not survive will be sorrowful, •because they understand what is in store for the
19 last days, but not attaining it. •But woe also to those who do survive, for this reason—they shall see great dangers and much distress, as these dreams show.
20 Yet it is better[f] to come into these things,[g] though incurring peril, than to pass from the world like a cloud, and not to see what shall happen in the last days."

The interpretation of the vision

21 He answered me and said, •"I will tell you the interpretation of the vision, and
22 I will also explain to you the things which you have mentioned. •As for what you
23 said about those who are left,[h] this is the interpretation: •He who brings the peril at that time will himself protect those who fall into peril, who have works and
24 have faith in the Almighty. •Understand therefore that those who are left are more
25 blessed than those who have died. •This is the interpretation of the vision: As for
26 your seeing a man come up from the heart of the sea, •this is he whom the Most High has been keeping for many ages, who will himself deliver his creation; and
27 he will direct those who are left. •And as for your seeing wind and fire and a storm
28 coming out of his mouth, •and as for his not holding spear or weapon of war, yet destroying the onrushing multitude which came to conquer him, this is the inter-
29 pretation: •Behold, the days are coming when the Most High will deliver those
30 who are on the earth. •And bewilderment of mind shall come over those who
31 dwell on the earth. •And they shall plan to make war against one another, city against city, place against place, people against people, and kingdom against   Isa 19:2
32 kingdom. •And when these things come to pass and the signs occur which I showed   Mt 24:7 you before, then my son will be revealed, whom you saw as a man coming up
33 from the sea.[i] •And when all the nations hear his voice, every man shall leave his
34 own land and the warfare that they have against one another; •and an innumerable   Rev 16:16; multitude shall be gathered together, as you saw, desiring to come and conquer   19:19
35,36 him. •But he will stand on the top of Mount Zion. •And Zion will come and be made manifest to all people, prepared and built, as you saw the mountain carved
37 out without hands. •And he, my Son, will reprove the assembled nations for their   Dan 2:34,45
38 ungodliness (this was symbolized by the storm), •and will reproach them to their face with their evil thoughts and with the torments with which they are to be tortured (which were symbolized by the flames); and he will destroy them without
39 effort by the law[j] (which was symbolized by the fire). •And as for your seeing him
40 gather to himself another multitude that was peaceable, •these are the ten tribes   2Kgs 17:1-6 which were led away from their own land into captivity in the days of King Hoshea, whom Shalmaneser the king of the Assyrians led captive; he took them across the
41 river, and they were taken into another land. •But they formed this plan for

e. Lat., Syr., Arab 2 lit. "the faces of many people."

f. Eth.; cf. Arab 2; Lat. "easier."

g. Syr.; Lat. "this."

h. Syr., Arab 1 add "and of those that do not survive."

i. Syr. and most Lat. MSS omit "from the sea."

j. Syr.; Lat. "and the law."

themselves, that they would leave the multitude of the nations and go to a more
42 distant region, where mankind had never lived, •that there at least they might keep
43 their statutes which they had not kept in their own land. •And they went in by the
44 narrow passages of the Euphrates River. •For at that time the Most High performed   Josh 3:14-16
signs for them, and stopped the channels of the river until they had passed over.
45 Through that region there was a long way to go, a journey of a year and a half;
and that country is called Arzareth.[k]

46 "Then they dwelt there until the last times; and now, when they are about to
47 come again, •the Most High will stop[l] the channels of the river again, so that they   Isa 11:15f.
may be able to pass over. Therefore you saw the multitude gathered together in
48 peace. • But those who are left of your people, who are found within my holy
49 borders, shall be saved.[m] •Therefore when he destroys the multitude of the nations
50 that are gathered together, he will defend the people who remain. •And then he
will show them very many wonders."

51 I said, "O sovereign Lord, explain this to me: Why did I see the man coming
up from the heart of the sea?"
52 He said to me, "Just as no one can explore or know what is in the depths of
the sea, so no one on earth can see my Son or those who are with him, except in
53 the time of his day.[n] •This is the interpretation of the dream which you saw. And
54 you alone have been enlightened about this, •because you have forsaken your own
55 ways and have applied yourself to mine, and have searched out my law; •for you
56 have devoted your life to wisdom, and called understanding your mother. •Therefore
I have shown you this, for there is a reward laid up with the Most High. And after
three more days I will tell you other things, and explain weighty and wondrous
matters to you."

57 Then I arose and walked in the field, giving great glory and praise to the Most
58 High because of his wonders, which he did from time to time, •and because he
governs the times and whatever things come to pass in their seasons. And I stayed
there three days.

THE SEVENTH VISION

The Lord commissions Ezra

1 **14** On the third day, while I was sitting under an oak, behold, a voice came out
2 of a bush opposite me and said, "Ezra, Ezra." •And I said, "Here I am, Lord,"   Ex 3:4
3 and I rose to my feet. •Then he said to me, "I revealed myself in a bush and spoke
4 to Moses when my people were in bondage in Egypt; •and I sent him and led[a] my
people out of Egypt; and I led him up on Mount Sinai, where I kept him with me
5 many days; •and I told him many wondrous things, and showed him the secrets
of the times and declared to him[b] the end of the times. Then I commanded him,
6 saying, •'These words you shall publish openly, and these you shall keep secret.'
7,8 And now I say to you: •Lay up in your heart the signs that I have shown you,
9 the dreams that you have seen, and the interpretations that you have heard; •for
you shall be taken up from among men, and henceforth you shall live with my Son
10 and with those who are like you, until the times are ended. •For the age has lost   5:50-55
11 its youth, and the times begin to grow old. • For the age is divided into twelve
12 parts, and nine[c] of its parts have already passed, •as well as half of the tenth part;
13 so two of its parts remain, besides half of the tenth part.[d] •Now therefore, set your

---

k. Heb. for "another land."
l. Syr.; Lat. "stops."
m. Syr.; Lat. omits "shall be saved."
n. Syr.; Eth. "except when his time and his day
have come"; Lat. omits "his."

14 a. Other authorities read "he led."

b. Syr., Eth., Ar., Arm.; Lat. omits "declared
to him."
c. Bensly's correction. Lat., Eth. "ten."
d. Syr. omits vss. 11, 12; Eth. "For the world
is divided into ten parts, and has come to the tenth,
and half of the tenth remains. Now . . ."

house in order, and reprove your people; comfort the lowly among them, and
14 instruct those that are wise.[e] And now renounce the life that is corruptible • and
put away from you mortal thoughts; cast away from you the burdens of man, and
15 divest yourself now of your weak nature, • and lay to one side the thoughts that   2Cor 5:4
16 are most grievous to you, and hasten to escape from these times. • For evils worse
17 than those which you have now seen happen shall be done hereafter. • For the
weaker the world becomes through old age, the more shall evils be multipled
18 among[f] its inhabitants. • For truth shall go farther away, and falsehood shall come
near. For the eagle[g] which you saw in the vision is already hastening to come."   11:1f.

Ezra's prayer for inspiration to restore the Scriptures

19,20   Then I answered and said, "Let me speak in your presence, Lord.[h] • For behold,
I will go, as you have commanded me, and I will reprove the people who are now
living; but who will warn those who will be born hereafter? For the world lies in
21 darkness, and its inhabitants are without light. • For your Law has been burned,
and so no one knows the things which have been done or will be done by you.
22 If then I have found favor before you, send the Holy Spirit to me, and I will write
everything that has happened in the world from the beginning, the things which
were written in your Law, that men may be able to find the path, and that those
who wish to live in the last days may live."
23   He answered me and said, "Go and gather the people, and tell them not to seek
24 you for forty days. • But prepare for yourself many writing tablets, and take with   Ex 24:18; 34:28
you Sarea, Dabria, Selemia, Ethanus, and Asiel—these five, because they are
25 trained to write rapidly; • and you shall come here, and I will light in your heart
the lamp of understanding, which shall not be put out until what you are about to
26 write is finished. • And when you have finished, some things you shall make public,
and some you shall deliver in secret to the wise; tomorrow at this hour you shall
begin to write."

Ezra's address to the people

27   Then I went as he commanded me, and I gathered all the people together, and
28,29 said, • "Hear these words, O Israel. • At first our fathers dwelt as aliens in Egypt,
30 and they were delivered from there, • and received the Law of life, which they did
31 not keep, which you also have transgressed after them. • Then land was given to
you for a possession in the land of Zion; but you and your fathers committed
32 iniquity and did not keep the ways which the Most High commanded you. • And
because he is a righteous judge, in due time he took from you what he had given.
33,34 And now you are here, and your brethren are farther in the interior.[i] • If you, then,   13:45
will rule over your minds and discipline your hearts, you shall be kept alive, and
35 after death you shall obtain mercy. • For after death the judgment will come, when
we shall live again; and then the names of the righteous will become manifest, and
36 the deeds of the ungodly will be disclosed. • But let no one seek me for forty
days."

Ezra's experience in the field

37   So I took the five men, as he commanded me, and we proceeded to the field,
38 and remained there. • And on the next day, behold, a voice called me, saying,
39 "Ezra, open your mouth and drink what I give you to drink." • Then I opened my
mouth, and behold, a full cup was offered to me; it was full of something like
40 water, but its color was like fire. • And I took it and drank; and when I had drunk
it, my heart poured forth understanding, and wisdom increased in my breast, for

e. Lat. omits "and . . . wise."
f. Lit. "upon."
g. Syr., Eth., Ar., Arm.; Lat. is corrupt.

h. Most Lat. MSS omit "Let me speak."
i. Syr., Eth., Arm.; Lat. "are among you."

41 my spirit retained its memory; •and my mouth was opened, and was no longer
42 closed. •And the Most High gave understanding to the five men, and by turns they
wrote what was dictated, in characters[j] which they did not know.[k] They sat forty
43 days, and wrote during the daytime, and ate their bread at night. •As for me, I
44 spoke in the daytime and was not silent at night. •So during the forty days ninety-
45 four[l] books were written. •And when the forty days were ended, the Most High
spoke to me, saying, "Make public the twenty-four[m] books[n] that you wrote first
46 and let the worthy and the unworthy read them; •but keep the seventy[o] that were
47 written last, in order to give them to the wise among your people. •For in them
is the spring of understanding, the fountain of wisdom, and the river of knowledge."
48 And I did so.[p]

AN APPENDIX

1 **15**[a] The Lord says, "Behold, speak in the ears of my people the words of the
2 prophecy which I will put in your mouth, •and cause them to be written on paper;   Isa 51:16
3 for they are trustworthy and true. •Do not fear the plots against you, and do not   Jer 1:9
4 be troubled by the unbelief of those who oppose you. •For every unbeliever shall
die in his unbelief."

God's vengeance upon the wicked

5   "Behold," says the Lord, "I bring evils upon the world, the sword and famine
6 and death and destruction. •For iniquity has spread throughout every land, and
7,8 their harmful deeds have reached their limit. •Therefore," says the Lord, •"'I will
be silent no longer concerning their ungodly deeds which they impiously commit,
neither will I tolerate their wicked practices. Behold, innocent and righteous blood
9 cries out to me, and the souls of the righteous cry out continually. •I will surely
avenge them," says the Lord, "and will receive to myself all the innocent blood
10 from among them. •Behold, my people is led like a flock to the slaughter; I will   Ps 44:22
11 not allow them to live any longer in the land of Egypt, •but I will bring them out   Isa 53:7
with a mighty hand and with an uplifted arm, and will smite Egypt[b] with plagues,
as before, and will destroy all its land."

Denunciation against oppression of Israel

12   Let Egypt mourn, and its foundations, for the plague of chastisement and
13 punishment that the Lord will bring upon it. •Let the farmers that till the ground
mourn, because their seed shall fail and their trees shall be ruined by blight and
14 hail and by a terrible tempest. •Alas for the world and for those who live in it!
15 For the sword and misery draw near them, and nation shall rise up to fight against   Mt 24:7
16 nation, with swords in their hands. •For there shall be unrest among men; growing   Mk 13:8
                                                                                        Lk 21:10

---

j. I.e. in a new script, the Aram. (square) characters.

k. Syr.; cf. Eth., Arab 2, Arm.; Lat. is corrupt.

l. Syr., Eth., Arab 1, Arm.; Lat. is corrupt.

m. Syr., Arab 1; Lat. omits "twenty-four."

n. I.e. the books of the Hebrew canon, comprising the five books of the Law (Gen, Ex, Lev,
Num, Deut), eight books of the Prophets (the
former prophets, Josh, Judg, 1 and 2Sam [as one
book], 1 and 2Kgs [as one book]; the latter prophets,
Isa, Jer, Ezek, and the Twelve [counted as one
book]), and eleven books of the Writings (Pss,
Prov, Job, Song, Ruth, Lam, Eccl, Esth, Dan,
Ezra-Neh [as one book], 1 and 2Chr [as one book]).

o. I.e. esoteric, apocalyptic books.

p. Syr. adds "in the seventh year of the sixth

week, five thousand years and three months and
twelve days after creation.

"At that time Ezra was caught up, and taken to
the place of those who are like him, after he had
written all these things. And he was called the
Scribe of the knowledge of the Most High for ever
and ever." Eth., Arab 1, Arm. have a similar
ending.

15 a. Chs. 15 and 16 (except 15:57–59, which has
been found in Gk.) are extant only in Lat.

b. Perhaps an allusion to the occurrence during
the reign of Galienus (A.D. 260–68) of a terrible
famine, followed by a plague, which killed two
thirds of the population of Alexandria.

strong against one another, they shall in their might have no respect for their king
17 or the chief of their leaders. •For a man will desire to go into a city, and shall not
18 be able. •For because of their pride the cities shall be in confusion, the houses Lk 21:26
19 shall be destroyed, and people shall be afraid. •A man shall have no pity upon his
neighbors, but shall make an assault upon their houses with the sword, and plunder
their goods, because of hunger for bread and because of great tribulation.

Denunciation against sinners

20   "Behold," says God, "I call together all the kings of the earth to fear me, from
the rising sun and from the south, from the east and from Lebanon; to turn and
21 repay what they have given them. •Just as they have done to my chosen people
until this day, so I will do, and will repay into their bosom." Thus says the Lord
22 God: •"My right hand will not spare the sinners, and my sword will not cease
23 from those who shed innocent blood on the earth." •And a fire will go forth from
his wrath, and will consume the foundations of the earth, and the sinners, like
24 straw that is kindled. •"Woe to those who sin and do not observe my command-
25 ments," says the Lord; •"I will not spare them. Depart, you faithless children!
26 Do not pollute my sanctuary." •For the Lord knows all who transgress against
27 him; therefore he will hand them over to death and slaughter. •For now calamities
have come upon the whole earth, and you shall remain in them; for God will not
deliver you, because you have sinned against him.

A vision of terrifying warfare

28,29   Behold, a terrifying sight, appearing from the east! •The nations of the dragons
of Arabia shall come out with many chariots, and from the day that they set out,
their hissing shall spread over the earth, so that all who hear them fear and tremble.
30 Also the Carmonians,[c] raging in wrath, shall go forth like wild boars of the forest, Ps 80:13
and with great power they shall come, and engage them in battle, and shall devastate
31 a portion of the land of the Assyrians with their teeth. •And then the dragons,
remembering their origin, shall become still stronger; and if they combine in great
32 power and turn to pursue them, •then these shall be disorganized and silenced by
33 their power, and shall turn and flee. •And from the land of the Assyrians an enemy
in ambush shall beset them and destroy one of them, and fear and trembling shall
come upon their army, and indecision upon their kings.

Ominous storm clouds

34   Behold, clouds from the east, and from the north to the south; and their appearance
35 is very threatening, full of wrath and storm. •They shall dash against one another
and shall pour out a heavy tempest upon the earth, and their own tempest; and
36 there shall be blood from the sword as high as a horse's belly •and a man's thigh Rev 14:20
37 and a camel's hock. •And there shall be fear and great trembling upon the earth;
and those who see that wrath shall be horror-stricken, and they shall be seized with
38 trembling. •And, after that, heavy storm clouds shall be stirred up from the south,
39 and from the north, and another part from the west. •And the winds from the east
shall prevail over the cloud that was[d] raised in wrath, and shall dispel it; and the
tempest that was to cause destruction by the east wind shall be driven violently
40 toward the south and west. •And great and mighty clouds, full of wrath and
tempest, shall rise, to destroy all the earth and its inhabitants, and shall pour out
41 upon every high and lofty place[e] a terrible tempest, •fire and hail and flying swords
and floods of water, that all the fields and all the streams may be filled with the
42 abundance of those waters. •And they shall destroy cities and walls, mountains

---

c. Carmania (Kirman) was the northern province
of the Parthian Empire.

d. Lit. "that he."

e. Or "eminent person."

43 and hills, trees of the forests, and grass of the meadows, and their grain. •And
44 they shall go on steadily to Babylon,[f] and shall destroy her. •They shall come to
her and surround her; they shall pour out the tempest and all its wrath upon her;
then the dust and smoke shall go up to heaven, and all who are about her shall wail
45 over her. •And those who survive shall serve those who have destroyed her.

Asia has become like Babylon

46 And you, O Asia, who share in the glamour of Babylon and the glory of her
47 person—•woe to you, miserable wretch! For you have made yourself like her; you　Rev 14:8; 17:4f.
have decked out your daughters in harlotry to please and glory in your lovers, who
48 have always lusted after you. • You have imitated that hateful harlot in all her
49 deeds and devices; therefore God says, •''I will send evils upon you, widowhood,
poverty, famine, sword, and pestilence, to lay waste your houses and bring you　Rev 18:7f.
50 to destruction and death. •And the glory of your power shall wither like a flower,
51 when the heat rises that is sent upon you. •You shall be weakened like a wretched
woman who is beaten and wounded, so that you cannot receive your mighty lovers.
52,53 Would I have dealt with you so violently,'' says the Lord, •''if you had not always
killed my chosen people, exulting and clapping your hands and talking about their
54,55 death when you were drunk? •Trick out the beauty of your face! •The reward of
56 a harlot is in your bosom, therefore you shall receive your recompense. •As you
will do to my chosen people,'' says the Lord, ''so God will do to you, and will
57 hand you over to adversities. •Your children shall die of hunger, and you shall fall
by the sword, and your cities shall be wiped out, and all your people who are in
58 the open country shall fall by the sword. •And those who are in the mountains and
highlands[g] shall perish of hunger, and they shall eat their own flesh in hunger for
59 bread and drink their own blood in thirst for water. •Unhappy above all others,
60 you shall come and suffer fresh afflictions. •And as they pass they shall wreck the
hateful[h] city, and shall destroy a part of your land and abolish a portion of your
61 glory, as they return from devastated Babylon. •And you shall be broken down
62 by them like stubble, and they shall be like fire to you. •And they shall devour
you and your cities, your land and your mountains; they shall burn with fire all
63 your forests and your fruitful trees. •They shall carry your children away captive,
and shall plunder your wealth, and abolish the glory of your countenance.''

Denunciation of Babylon, Asia, Egypt, and Syria

1,2 **16** Woe to you, Babylon[a] and Asia! Woe to you, Egypt and Syria! •Gird yourselves
with sackcloth and haircloth, and wail for your children, and lament for them; for
3 your destruction is at hand. •The sword has been sent upon you, and who is there
4 to turn it back? •A fire has been sent upon you, and who is there to quench it?
5,6 Calamities have been sent upon you, and who is there to drive them away? •Can
one drive off a hungry lion in the forest, or quench a fire in the stubble, when once
7,8 it has begun to burn? •Can one turn back an arrow shot by a strong archer? •The
9 Lord God sends calamities, and who will drive them away? • Fire will go forth
10 from his wrath, and who is there to quench it? •He will flash lightning, and who
11 will not be afraid? He will thunder, and who will not be terrified? •The Lord will
12 threaten, and who will not be utterly shattered at his presence? •The earth and its　Ps 18:15
foundations quake, the sea is churned up from the depths, and its waves and the
fish also shall be troubled at the presence of the Lord and before the glory of his
13 power. •For his right hand that bends the bow is strong, and his arrows that he
shoots are sharp and will not miss when they begin to be shot to the ends of the
14 world. •Behold, calamities are sent forth and shall not return until they come over

---

h. Another reading is ''idle'' or ''unprofitable.''

f. I.e. Rome.
g. Gk.; Lat. omits ''and highlands.''

16 a. I.e. Rome.

15 the earth. • The fire is kindled, and shall not be put out until it consumes the
16 foundations of the earth. • Just as an arrow shot by a mighty archer does not return,
17 so the calamities that are sent upon the earth shall not return. • Alas for me! Who
will deliver me in those days?

The beginning of calamities

18   The beginning of sorrows, when there shall be much lamentation; the beginning
of famine, when many shall perish; the beginning of wars, when the powers shall
be terrified; the beginning of calamities, when all shall tremble. What shall they
19 do in these circumstances, when the calamities come? • Behold, famine and plague,
20 tribulation and anguish are sent as scourges for the correction of men. • Yet for all
this they will not turn from their iniquities, nor be always mindful of the scourges.
21 Behold, provisions will be so cheap upon earth that men will imagine that peace
is assured for them, and then the calamities shall spring up on the earth—the sword,
22 famine, and great confusion. • For many of those who live on the earth shall perish
23 by famine; and those who survive the famine shall die by the sword. • And the
dead shall be cast out like dung, and there shall be no one to console them; for
24 the earth shall be left desolate, and its cities shall be demolished. • No one shall
25 be left to cultivate the earth or to sow it. • The trees shall bear fruit, and who will
26 gather it? • The grapes shall ripen, and who will tread them? For in all places there
27 shall be great solitude; • one man will long to see another, or even to hear his
28 voice. • For out of a city, ten shall be left; and out of the field, two who have
29 hidden themselves in thick groves and clefts in the rocks. • As in an olive orchard   Isa 17:6
30 three or four olives may be left on every tree, • or as when a vineyard is gathered
some clusters may be left by those who search carefully through the vineyard,
31 so in those days three or four shall be left by those who search their houses with
32 the sword. • And the earth shall be left desolate, and its fields shall be for briers,
and its roads and all its paths shall bring forth thorns, because no sheep will go
33 along them. • Virgins shall mourn because they have no bridegrooms; women shall
mourn because they have no husbands; their daughters shall mourn because they
34 have no helpers. • Their bridegrooms shall be killed in war, and their husbands
shall perish of famine.

Warnings of impending disasters

35   Listen now to these things, and understand them, O servants of the Lord.
36 Behold the word of the Lord, receive it; do not disbelieve what the Lord says.[b]
37,38 Behold, the calamities draw near, and are not delayed. • Just as a woman with
child, in the ninth month, when the time of her delivery draws near, has great pains   4:40
about her womb for two or three hours beforehand, and when the child comes
39 forth from the womb, there will not be a moment's delay, • so the calamities will
not delay in coming forth upon the earth, and the world will groan, and pains will
seize it on every side.
40   "Hear my words, O my people; prepare for battle, and in the midst of the
41 calamities be like strangers on the earth. • Let him that sells be like one who will   1Cor 7:29-31
42 flee; let him that buys be like one who will lose; • let him that does business be
like one who will not make a profit; and let him that builds a house be like one
43 who will not live in it; • let him that sows be like one who will not reap; so also
44 him that prunes the vines, like one who will not gather the grapes; • them that
marry, like those who will have no children; and them that do not marry, like
45,46 those that are widowed. • Because those who labor, labor in vain; • for strangers
shall gather their fruits, and plunder their goods, and overthrow their houses, and
take their children captive; for in captivity and famine they will beget their children.

b. Bensly's correction. Lat. "do not believe the   d. Lit. "consent to them shall be for these in."
gods of whom the Lord speaks."   e. The Lat. is uncertain.
     c. Lit. "he."   f. Another reading is "seed."

47 Those who conduct business do it only to be plundered; the more they adorn their
48 cities, their houses and possessions, and their persons, •the more angry I will be
49 with them for their sins," says the Lord. •Just as a respectable and virtuous woman
50 abhors a harlot, •so righteousness shall abhor iniquity, when she decks herself out,
and shall accuse her to her face, when he comes who will defend him who searches
out every sin on earth.

The power and wisdom of God

51,52 Therefore do not be like her or her works. •For behold, just a little while, and
53 iniquity will be removed from the earth, and righteousness will reign over us. •Let
no sinner say that he has not sinned; for God[c] will burn coals of fire on the head
54 of him who says, "I have not sinned before God and his glory." •Behold, the
Lord knows all the works of men, their imaginations and their thoughts and their
55 hearts. •He said, "Let the earth be made," and it was made; "Let the heaven be
56 made," and it was made. •At his word the stars were fixed, and he knows the
57 number of the stars. •It is he who searches the deep and its treasures, who has
58 measured the sea and its contents; •who has enclosed the sea in the midst of the
59 waters, and by his word has suspended the earth over the water; •who has spread
60 out the heaven like an arch, and founded it upon the waters; •who has put springs
of water in the desert, and pools on the tops of the mountains, to send rivers from
61 the heights to water the earth; •who formed man, and put a heart in the midst of
62 his body, and gave him breath and life and understanding •and the spirit of Almighty
63 God; who made all things and searches out hidden things in hidden places. •Surely
he knows your imaginations and what you think in your hearts! Woe to those who
64 sin and want to hide their sins! •Because the Lord will strictly examine all their
65 works, and will make a public spectacle of all of you. •And when your sins come
out before men, you shall be put to shame; and your own iniquities shall stand as
66 your accusers in that day. •What will you do? Or how will you hide your sins
67 before God and his angels? •Behold, God is the judge, fear him! Cease from your
sins, and forget your iniquities, never to commit them again; so God will lead
you forth and deliver you from all tribulation.

Impending persecution of the chosen people

68 For behold, the burning wrath of a great multitude is kindled over you, and they
69 shall carry off some of you and shall feed you what was sacrificed to idols. •And
those who consent to eat shall be held in[d] derision and contempt, and be trodden
70 under foot. •For in many places[e] and in neighboring cities there shall be a great
71 insurrection against those who fear the Lord. •They shall be like madmen, sparing
72 no one, but plundering and destroying those who continue to fear the Lord. •For
they shall destroy and plunder their goods, and drive them out of their houses.
73 Then the tested quality of my chosen people shall be manifest, as gold that is   Zech 13:9
tested by fire.   1Pet 1:7

Promise of divine deliverance

74 "Hear, my chosen people," says the Lord. "Behold, the days of tribulation are
75 at hand, and I will deliver you from them. •Do not fear or doubt, for God is your
76 guide. • You who keep my commandments and precepts," says the Lord God,
77 "do not let your sins pull you down, or your iniquities prevail over you." •Woe
to those who are choked by their sins and overwhelmed by their iniquities, as a
field is choked with underbrush and its path[f] overwhelmed with thorns, so that no
78 one can pass through! •It is shut off and given up to be consumed by fire.

GREEK APOCALYPSE OF EZRA

(Second to Ninth Century A.D.)

A NEW TRANSLATION AND INTRODUCTION
BY M. E. STONE

The Greek Apocalypse of Ezra contains the visions received by Ezra, who had fasted and prayed to have the mysteries of God revealed to him. His prayer is answered; and he is taken up into heaven, where he intercedes for the sinners whom he sees being punished. God replies that he rewards the righteous for their righteousness (1). Ezra once again prays, expressing deep questions about the righteousness of the world and the punishment of sinners. Angels appear to him and he again prays for the sinners. Adam's sin, he is told, was due to Satan, but Ezra observes that "If you had not given him Eve, the serpent would never have deceived her" (2:16). Ezra again remonstrates with God, requesting mercy for mankind (2:18–25). He asks for a vision of the day of judgment; it is granted (2:26–3:7). The signs of the approaching end, particularly internecine strife, are set before him.

In chapter 4, Ezra is led down into Tartarus. He sees Herod being punished; then he descends to the bottom of hell. There he sees various sorts of sinners being punished as befits their crimes. Next, he sees the Antichrist; his appearance and his signs are described. Subsequently, he sees further cases of punishments and is taken to heaven (5:1–7). The wonders of the development of the fetus are set forth before him, emphasizing Ezra's doubts about the creation of man (5:12–14). He then sees the saints in heaven, certain cosmological secrets, and some details of the judgment. The final part of the writing contains an account of Ezra's struggle with the angel for his own soul, a description of God's comfort to him as death approaches, his concluding prayer, and the narrative of his death and burial. The whole concludes with a doxology (chs. 6 and 7).

Text

The writing was first published in 1866 by C. Tischendorf from a fifteenth-century Greek manuscript preserved in Paris (Cod. Par. Graec. 929), although scholars earlier had noted its existence.[1] It has been translated into English and German.[2] There doubtless exist a number of other manuscripts, and at least one further has already been noted.[3] The text of the manuscript upon which Tischendorf based his edition also serves as the base of the present translation. The manuscript, unfortunately, is both faulty and corrupt at a number of points. Tischendorf suggested numerous emendations, most of which have been accepted herein. In a number of cases additional emendations have been suggested. Sometimes his suggestions have been rejected, changed, or modified (the more significant of these are placed in the notes to the translation).[4] The Greek language of the writing is late in character. It is notable for a number of anomalous forms and usages: among them, *kolasasthai*, "condemn," in 1:11; *anapausōmai*, "I shall give rest," and *kathestēka*, "I am," in 1:12;

---

[1] C. von Tischendorf, *Apocalypses Apocryphae*, pp. 24–33. On earlier scholars, see his Introduction, pp. xii–xiv.

[2] A. Walker, "The Revelation of Esdras," *ANF*, vol. 8, pp. 571–74. P. Riessler, pp. 126–37 and brief nn. on p. 1273.

[3] Cod. Par. Graec. 390, 16th cent., noted by A.-M. Denis, *Introduction*, p. 92. Denis's chapter on this work is the only attempt at a study of the apocalypse and contains much valuable information; see his *Introduction*, pp. 91–96.

[4] These will be published by M. E. Stone in "The Metamorphosis of Ezra: Jewish Apocalypse and Mediaeval Vision," *JTS* N.S. 33 (1982) 17f.

dikazesthai en, "presses suit against," in 2:6; *pisteuei,* "let him believe," in 4:11; and *apheis,* "you permit," in 4:34. The Greek style is inelegant and the single published manuscript often unclear or clumsy. The English translation, in such cases, is inevitably somewhat rough; efforts have been made to make it as clear as possible within the limits of faithfulness to the text. Such cases are particularly prominent in 2:16 and 3:11.

Composition

The Greek Apocalypse of Ezra as extant is a Christian composition in which a series of sources, Jewish and Christian, have been utilized.[5] The whole has been put together in a somewhat crude fashion and the writing is characterized by literary unevenness and inconsistency, repetitions, and a measure of incoherence. Many of these features are discussed in the following paragraphs, others are pointed out in the notes. The corrupt state of the Paris manuscript makes it possible that amelioration of the text by recourse to a broader range of witnesses might obviate some clumsy passages. Yet their abundance makes it unlikely that they are all the result of textual corruption. Furthermore, the careless nature of the final editor has on occasion resulted in a strange or fanciful utilization of a source which has led to an absurdity or at least a measure of the bizarre. For example, in 1:5, Ezra is said to fast for 120 weeks, a somewhat excessive period based on the seven one-week fasts in 4 Ezra. Other examples are found in the commentary.

A study of the apocalypse enables the attentive reader to recover certain stages of the editor's work. It is best to start from the descriptions of heaven and Tartarus in chapters 4–5. In 4:5, very abruptly, Ezra asks to be shown "the lower parts of Tartarus." He descends, with angels, and sees Herod (9–12), a fiery place of punishment (13–14), the disobedient (16–18), the unsleeping worm and consuming fire (20). By now he has reached the foundation of hell and is led to the south. He sees first "hanging" punishment there (22–24) and is then led to the north, where he sees the Antichrist, who is described in detail (25–33). In this connection a prophecy about the end-time is pronounced and its explanation given (35–43). Then, bracketed by two prayers for pity (5:1, 6), follows one more "hanging" punishment and a description of the terrors of hell (5: 2–4). The seer is then returned to heaven (5:7), where he sees many punishments and gives vent to his feeling of the futility of the birth of man (8–11). The wonders of conception and birth and their purpose are described (12–14).

So far, at least on the face of it, the narrative is moderately coherent; 5:1–6, however, is a section that does not fit in its present position but would better follow 4:22–24. In 5:20–28 confusion reigns. In 5:20, Ezra asks to see punishments and Paradise. He is taken to the east (21) and sees Paradise and the righteous, some meteorological phenomena, and "eternal punishments." Then, in 5:27, he is apparently back in Tartarus for he sees a "hanging" punishment and is led "further down into Tartarus," where he sees the sinners mourning (5:24–28).

This confusion is the result of the combination of diverse sources. The first source describes a descent into Tartarus (4:5–21); the seer descends to the lowest level of Tartarus, called *apōleia,* "destruction." This section is straightforward and self-contained. The remaining types of material occurring here are also found combined in other apocalypses.[6] These are (1) the descriptions of the "hanging" punishments; (2) the physiognomy of the Antichrist;[7] and (3) the description of Paradise. These may have originally been represented by the following fragments: (1) "hanging" punishments: 4:22–25; 5:2–4 (5–7?), 8–11, 24–25 (26?); (2) Antichrist and prophecy about the end-time: 4:25–43; and (3) Paradise: 5:20–23. Fragment 1 in particular was broken up and combined by redactional links with the first source but, like fragments 2 and 3, it is of an indubitably ancient character. It is this redactional work that has caused the various inconsistencies in the text. This analysis finds considerable support from an examination of the Vision of Ezra, which contains another form of the "hanging" punishments, Tartarus, and Paradise material found in the Greek Apocalypse of Ezra. A

---

[5] The problem of definition of Jewish and Christian materials in such works as this is referred to by R. A. Kraft, "The Multiform Jewish Heritage of Early Christianity," *Christianity, Judaism and Other Graeco-Roman Cults,* ed. J. Neusner (Leiden, 1975) pp. 174–99, particularly pp. 184–87.

[6] The best examples are to be found in the fragmentary Elijah apocryphon; see M. E. Stone and J. Strugnell, *The Books of Elijah: Parts 1–2* (T&T 18, Pseudepigrapha No. 8; Missoula, Mont., 1979).

[7] See further discussion, "Theological importance."

comparison of the two writings clearly indicates that they shared common sources but each used them differently.

It may be observed further that 5:7–11 fits very well with 1:7f. A difficulty of the latter passage is that it refers to the "first heaven," where no more follow, while its references to "judgments" and to the voices of the wicked imploring Ezra's intercession are nicely complemented by 5:9–11 in which the sinners tell Ezra that "since you came here . . . we have obtained a slight respite." Both passages are typified by the seer's exclamation "It were better that man was not born . . ." (1:6; 5:8). Observe also that 1:9, Ezra's prayer on behalf of the sinners, is still in the first person with which the book opens. Ezra's speech is introduced in 1:10 and follows immediately upon his prayer in 1:9; but it is in the third person: "And Ezra said." Again a clear sign of the literary "seam" can be discerned.[8]

A final observation in this connection is that 3:11–15 may be an originally independent piece of text as is indicated by the two second plural verbs found only there in the book.[9]

Original language

It follows from the above that the writing was composed in Greek. Riessler suggested that the supposed Jewish source was written in Hebrew. His chief examples adduced to support this view are as follows: 1:20 contains a corruption of a hypothetical *mdr* to *gdr;* in 2:12 a supposed *barah*, "to eat" was confused with *bara*, "to do"; in 4:21, *apōleia*, supposedly from Hebrew *sht*, was misinterpreted in context; it should mean "grave"; in 5:23, *kolasis* is a mistranslation of *pqwdh*. All these examples are unlikely, unnecessary, or unconvincing. Most scholars correctly contend that the writing as extant is Christian and was originally written in Greek.[10]

Date and provenance

The dependence of the writing on (presumably the Greek version of) 4 Ezra and its Christian character indicate a date sometime in the first millennium. If James is correct and this is the writing referred to in the Canon of Nicephorus (c. A.D. 850), then a date sometime between A.D. 150 and 850 is probable. Its provenance cannot be discerned.[11]

Historical importance and literary implications

This writing clearly conveys no historical information in the ordinary sense of the word. In the broader context of Byzantine apocalyptic writing, it is an important witness of the way in which older Jewish apocalyptic traditions were taken over and reused by the Church. It may be appropriate in this context to observe that there are a number of other Christian compositions connected with this writing. One is the Armenian Questions of Ezra and another is most probably the Apocalypse of Sedrach (see the contribution herein). Other Ezra writings exist in Syriac, Ethiopic, Latin, and Greek.

1. Syriac Apocalypse of Ezra. It includes a vision of Four Empires, an account of the Antichrist, and other material.[12]

2. Ethiopic Apocalypse of Ezra. This Falasha work preserves details of judgment, historical prediction, and related legends. It is clearly dependent upon 4 Ezra and Jubilees. If the latter part is original, it was composed in Ethiopic. It does not belong to the cycle of Ezra books

---

[8] It should be observed that the vacillation between first- and third-person narrative occurs frequently in the book. It indicates its composite and poorly authored character but cannot serve on its own as a criterion for literary analysis.

[9] See nn. to 3:11–15. Riessler suggested that GkApEzra is a composite work containing an older Jewish source that has been Christianized. In his view, the Jewish sections are 1:1–3:10; 3:16–4:8; 4:16–21; 5:6–6:2 and the Christian passages are 3:11–15; 4:9–15; 4:22–5:5; 6:6–7:16. This analysis is incompatible with the analysis suggested above. See the next section.

[10] Denis, *Introduction,* pp. 91f., presents a summary of views.

[11] M. R. James, "Introduction," *The Fourth Book of Ezra,* p. lxxxvii. Certain general observations are made by H. Weinel, "Die spätere christliche Apokalyptik," Gunkel Festschrift, pp. 157–60, but he offers no firm conclusions or even hypotheses.

[12] A. Baethgen, "Beschreibung der Syrischen HS 'Sachau 131,' " *ZAW* 6 (1886) 199–211; more fully in J.-B. Chabot, "L'Apocalypse d'Esdras," *RevSem* 2 (1894) 242–50, 333–46. Further on this work see Denis, *Introduction,* p. 94.

to which the Greek Apocalypse of Ezra appertains and does not contain dialogues between the seer and God.[13]

3. *Visio Beati Esdrae,* "The Vision of the Blessed Ezra." The Vision of Ezra belongs to the same body of literature as our Apocalypse of Ezra. It contains a fuller form of the descent into Tartarus and the "hanging" punishments, without the material on the Antichrist. Several features indicate it to have been translated from Greek; Mercati claims that there are almost no New Testament references in it.[14] For the sake of clarity it should be noted that there are some references to the New Testament, particularly in the description of Herod's slaying of the infants. Thus no particular presumption of antiquity vis-à-vis the Greek Apocalypse of Ezra and the Apocalypse of Sedrach seems to follow. Many features of the apocalypse are lacking.

4. *Revelatio Esdrae de qualitatibus anni,* "The Revelation to Ezra Concerning the Characteristics of the Year." This is an astrological treatise, presumably belonging to the same category of astrological-divinatory literature associated with Ezra of which Tischendorf gave some Greek excerpts and of which James noted some texts in Old English. To the Latin texts, Mercati added some fragments in Italian, while Nau discussed some futher Greek versions.[15] Charlesworth has recently drawn our attention to an astrological document in Syriac attributed to Shem which is similar to this document (see the contribution herein).

5. A Greek calendar of events of patriarchal history, combined with astrological portents and auguries arranged by days of the lunar month, is also attributed to Ezra.[16]

6. Finally, mention should be made of chapters 1–2 and 15–16 of 4 Ezra, which occur only in the Latin Vulgate. These chapters, fragments of which have been discovered in Greek, are sometimes called 3 and 5 Ezra respectively (see Metzger's contribution herein).[17]

Theological importance

GOD

God is mentioned in the work chiefly in dialogue with the seer. Ezra remonstrates with him, invoking his mercy (1:20, 12; etc.), and God responds, admitting his merciful character but insisting that he must punish the wicked for their sins. This idea returns throughout the first part of the work, and is perhaps most clearly expressed by the exclamation "Your sins exceed my kindness" (2:21). One of the sins against God is the crucifixion: "they gave me vinegar and gall to drink" (2:25; 7:1). This statement, of course, implies, as does 6:16 (cf. 6:17), a Christological view, but the book refrains from any reference to salvation through Christ. Other noteworthy Christian features are the mention of Paul and John (1:20) and of "the Christian people" (1:6; 2:7; 5:1; etc.), and the idea that Antichrist turned the stones into bread and water into wine (4:27).

God is entitled usually "Lord" (*passim*), but he is also called "Most High" (1:2), merciful, greatly pitying one (1:10), and Father (2:22). He is associated with the cherubim (2:26) and is the one who drives the cherubim (7:6). He is opposed by Satan. The most striking feature of the concept of God is that he can be argued with. The seer can reproach him, remonstrate with him, and beseech him on behalf of mankind. This feature is inherited from 4 Ezra.

---

[13] James, *Fourth Ezra,* p. lxxxvii, refers to its occurrence in BM Eth. No. 27.7, fol., 67a–71b, and BM Eth. No. 61.1, fols. 1–7r. It was published with a French translation by J. Halévy, *Tĕʾĕzâza Sanbat* (Bibl. Ec. Hautes Études 137; Paris, 1902).

[14] G. Mercati, *Note di letteratura biblica e cristiana,* pp. 70–73. Translation is found in Riessler, pp. 350–54. Denis concludes from the claimed absence of NT references that it is older than GkApEzra, ApSedr, and certain other works (*Introduction,* p. 93). In this he follows the view of Mercati, p. 66. P. Dinzelbacher, "Die Vision Alberichs und die Esdras-Apokryphe," *Studien und Mitteilungen zur Geschichte der Benediktiner-Ordens* (Othobeuen, 1976) pp. 435–42, points to the older printing of an inferior longer rec. of the Visio B. Esdrae and some of its relationships in medieval apocalyptic literature.

[15] G. Mercati, *Note di letteratura biblica e cristiana,* pp. 74–79; Tischendorf, *Apocalypses Apocryphae,* pp. xiii–xiv; James, *Fourth Ezra,* pp. lxxxvii–lxxxix; F. Nau, "Analyse de deux opuscules astrologiques attribués au Prophète Esdras . . .," *ROC* 12 (1907) 14–16. The Eth. text published by S. Grébaut, *ROC* 18 (1913) 97f., seems not to be closely related to the above.

[16] Nau, *ROC* 12 (1907) 16–21.

[17] For more extensive bibliography on Ezra literature, see Denis, *Introduction,* pp. 91–96. For older works see E. Schurer, *Geschichte des jüdischen Volkes* (Leipiz, 1898³) vol. 3, p. 330.

MANKIND AND CREATION

Mankind, the book stresses, is a special creation by God. In 1:10; 2:10–11, 23, as also in 4 Ezra and the Apocalypse of Sedrach, God's direct responsibility for the creation of mankind is stressed (see 1:10 margin). The same idea also occurs elsewhere.[18] This emphasis makes even more acute the seer's reproach of God for the perilous state of things. In 5:19 this concept is developed further: The world was created for the sake of mankind (see also 4Ezra 6:55; 7:11; 8:44; and 2Bar 14:19).[19]

Great emphasis is placed in the book on mankind's sinfulness and the rigor of their punishment. This stress is, of course, inherent to the seer's argument with God and is a sustained theme of the writing. Not only are the punishments of the sinners repeatedly stressed (1:7–11, 18; 4:9–20; 5:1–6), but the very point of the creation or birth of sinful mankind is repeatedly questioned. The expression of this theme derives from 4 Ezra (see 1:6 margin) and it recurs in various forms in many sources: for example, 2 Baruch 3:1, 4 Ezra 7:69, Babylonian Talmud 'Erubin 13b. Adam, who was created by God, sinned as a result of Satan's activity, although the name of Satan does not occur (2:12–14). The prophet's observation that without the creation of Eve by God, the serpent would not have deceived her, and that God creates and destroys whom he wishes (2:16f.), receives no response. The emphasis on Eve may be a reminiscence of the minimization of Adam's responsibility for the Fall to be found in the Adam books (contrast especially 4 Ezra 3:20f.).

Mankind is weak and limited; their knowledge is such that they cannot answer divine challenges. This is expressed by a "riddle" question posed in 2:32: "count the stars and the sand of the sea," to which Ezra responds that he, being merely human, finds this beyond his ability (3:2). A similar question occurs in 4:2 and the seer's response is likewise similar (cf. 4:4). These questions are clearly inspired by similar questions preserved in 4 Ezra (4:3–9 and 5:36–38). In the Bible the idea that the stars cannot be counted is commonplace, yet the number of stars was revealed to an apocalyptic seer in 1 Enoch 43:1–4 and in 2 Enoch 40:2–3. The use of such questions is extensive and goes back to biblical roots in Job and elsewhere. While using expressions designed to deny the possibility of men achieving secret knowledge, the Apocalypse of Ezra is in fact full of revelations of such mysteries, including natural phenomena (5:23).[20] This situation naturally indicates a tension between the theme of mankind's limited nature (derived from 4 Ezra) and the disclosure of secrets to them (not from 4 Ezra). Yet the basic and pervasive concept is mankind's limitations.

Humans are composed of soul and body; on death the soul leaves the body and departs for heaven, while the body returns to the earth (7:3). It would seem to follow, perhaps only by implication, that all those whom Ezra sees being punished are in fact the souls of the sinners. The contrast of the soul and body comes out most explicitly in the passage in 6:5–15 in which Ezra argues with the angel about giving up his soul. This theme—the unwillingness of the righteous man to yield up his soul—is widespread. The most extensive example preserved and one which resembles the Greek Apocalypse of Ezra in many ways is the Testament of Abraham, the whole of which is formed around this theme. In that work the angel fails to bring forth Abraham's soul, hence Death is sent. Different from the Greek Apocalypse of Ezra and the Testament of Abraham is Origen's description of the struggle between the good and evil angels over Abraham's soul (HLk 35). In the two former works the righteous man himself is the protagonist. Most recently J. T. Milik related the source referred to by Origen with the Visions of Amram from Qumran Cave 4. Be this as it may, the common theme of the Greek Apocalypse of Ezra and the Testament of Abraham also recurs in the Apocalypse of Sedrach 9, there sharing a source with the Apocalypse of Ezra.

---

[18] 2En 44:1; Alpha Beta de R. Akiba (A. Jellinek, *Bet ha-Midrasch* [repr. Jerusalem, 1938] vol. 3, p. 59): "for the whole world was created by the speech of the Holy One, Blessed be He, and man by his hand"; and ApMos 37:2; Philo, *De somniis* 210.

[19] For similar rabbinic views see E. E. Urbach, *The Sages, Their Concepts and Beliefs*, trans. I. Abrahams (Jerusalem, 1975) vol. 1, pp. 214f. It is also clearly brought out in the ApSedr 3; cf. here 5:19.

[20] The development of the "riddle" questions is traced in detail in M. E. Stone, "Lists of Revealed Things in Apocalyptic Literature," *Magnalia Dei*, eds. F. M. Cross, W. E. Lemke, P. D. Miller (New York, 1976) pp. 414–52. The development of the language of denial of possible secret knowledge is discussed in M. E. Stone, "Paradise in IV Ezra iv:8 and vii:3b, viii:52," *JJS* 17 (1966) 85–88.

A similar situation relating to Moses is contained in the Armenian Life of Moses; and a situation like Origen's quotation and 4Q Visions of Amram is referred to in Jude 9.[21]

The protagonist is Ezra, who is the figure known from the biblical Book of Ezra. Here he is called "the prophet" and not "the scribe"; this shift occurs either because of the later Christian tendency to make every biblical author into a prophet or because of his role as a recipient of visions. The selection of Ezra as the seer is due to 4 Ezra, the book which has inspired the present writing. In 6:5ff. Ezra is assimilated to Moses. This identification is found in other sources, of which some chief ones are: (1) the interpretation of 4 Ezra 14 as a second Sinai event; (2) rabbinic dicta such as that of R. Jose: "Ezra was worthy that the Torah be given by him had not Moses preceded him" (Tosefta Sanhedrin 4:7 and par.); (3) Armenian traditions developing this view.[22] Many of the verses in which Ezra appears referred originally to Moses. The intercessory function which Ezra fulfills throughout the book bears a similarity to that of Enoch in 1 Enoch 12 (see Isaac's contribution herein).

Angels play a large role in the book. The cherubim associated with God were mentioned above. In addition to the tasks already mentioned, the cherubim guard the tree of life (2:14). A chief function of the angels in this apocalypse, however, is the common one of guide and interpreter for the seer. There is considerable variation in the names and titles of these guides: 1:3 Michael the archangel; 1:4 the archistrategos Raphael; 2:1 Michael and Gabriel and all the apostles; 4:7 Michael and Gabriel and thirty-four other angels; 4:24 Michael the archistrategos; in 6:2 Michael, Gabriel, Raphael, Uriel, and five other angels with strange (some Greek-sounding) names are mentioned. In 4 Ezra it is Uriel who reveals the secrets; in the Vision of Ezra, Ezra is led to Tartarus by seven angels of Tartarus (l. 2) and to heaven by Michael and Gabriel (l. 79).

The title "archistrategos" (1:4 and commentary) most frequently refers to Michael, as it does in older sources: Testament of Abraham; Joseph and Asenath 14; Daniel 8:11; 2 Enoch 22:6f.; 33:10f.; 3 Baruch 11:1f.[23] In *Sefer Zerubbabel* (Even-Shmuel, *Midreshe-Ge'ula*, p. 73) variant readings are "Michael" and "chief of the army of the Lord." The five strange names in 6:2 are not readily paralleled. Aker might be compared with *'kyr* in *Sefer Harazim* (ed. Margalioth, Index, s.v.) and an angel Zebuleon might be related to Hebrew *zebul*.

In 1:7 reference is made to a "great command of angels" who come and lead the seer to the judgments. In 2:13 Adam is said to have been guarded by an angel, and the tree of life by a cherub. In 3:8 the angels are said to be destined to glorify God, and in 4:22 angels beat a wicked man. The nine angels in 6:2 are "over the consummation." These tasks, like that of an angelic guide, are in no way extraordinary in a writing as late as the Apocalypse of Ezra.

The book clearly foresees a final judgment, whose character is set forth in some detail (2:26). On that day there will be no rain upon the earth (2:29) but only merciful judgment (2:30). There is a strict judgment (see 1:16; 5:17; cf. also 2:30); God eventually will assemble wicked men in the valley of Jehosaphat and annihilate them and the world (3:5f.). Moreover, the book refers to the signs and portents that will precede that day, namely the breakdown

---

[21] An extensive discussion of TAb and related issues is in M. R. James, *Testament of Abraham* (T&S 2.2; Cambridge, 1892) pp. 14–29. 4QʿAmram was published by J. T. Milik, "4Q Visions de ʿAmram et une citation d'Origène," *RB* 79 (1972) 77–97. The Arm. Life of Moses was published by M. E. Stone, "Three Armenian Accounts of the Death of Moses," *Studies on the Testament of Moses*, ed. G. W. E. Nickelsburg (SCS 4; Missoula, Mont., 1973) pp. 118–21. The same theme occurs in the Heb. *Peṭirath Mose* ("Death of Moses") in Jellinek, *BHM*, vol. 1, pp. 115–29, and in some rabbinic sources.

[22] See M. E. Stone, "The Apocryphal Literature in the Armenian Tradition," *Proceedings Israel Academy* 4 (1971) 67.

[23] Compare also J. Z. Smith, "The Prayer of Joseph," *Religions in Antiquity*, ed. J. Neusner (Leiden, 1968) p. 269 and nn. there. Also see Smith's contribution herein.

of society and human relationships, and the appearance of the Antichrist. This is most clearly expressed in 3:12, where well-known language and literary forms are involved. The same occur, with some changes, in Armenian 4 Ezra 5:9; 6:4; and elsewhere (see Mt 10:21; 1En 100:1; Melito, *Paschal Homily* 51; Hesiod, *Works and Days,* 183–90; Ovid, *Metamorphoses* 1.144–46; m.Soṭah 9:16; Tiburtine Sibyl 36f.).[24]

Next the Antichrist will appear. He is first mentioned in the book in 3:15, where it says that he will come up from Tartarus and show many things to men. In connection with the extensive Antichrist passage in chapter 4, reference is also made to the final judgment (4:36–43). This event is described in the following way: the Antichrist will come and perform signs by which he will lead astray the race of men (4:32–34). Then a trumpet will sound, the graves will be opened, and the dead will rise (4:36). The Antichrist will hide in the outer darkness and then heaven and earth and sea will perish—heaven will be burned for eighty cubits and earth for eight hundred cubits; this melting of the earth and men results because of the hiding of the Antichrist (4:37–39, 43).

The idea of the burning of the heavens and the earth in a conflagration at the end of days is ancient and widespread; see, for example: Josephus, *Antiquities* 1.70; Philo, *Vita Mosis* 2, 263; Life of Adam and Eve 49f.; 2 Peter 3:10; and Agadat Bereshit (Jellinek, *Bet ha-Midrasch,* vol. 4, p. 1).[25] No exact parallel is known to the measurements given for the conflagration. The manuscript is sadly corrupt at the point where the sin of the heavens should be mentioned, but the sin of the earth is the hiding of the Antichrist.

All of 4:25–43 is an extensive description of the Antichrist and his activities; Ezra has reached the lowest level of Tartarus. He sees a "hanging" punishment. Then he proceeds to the north, where he sees the imprisoned Antichrist. The chief themes expressed in this section are:

1. the imitation of Christ (4:27)
2. the danger of men being led astray (4:28)
3. the details of the physiognomy of the Antichrist (4:29–31)
4. the "Lucifer" theme (4:32)
5. the Antichrist becomes a child and an old man (4:33)
6. divine warning and the signs of the end (4:34–43):
   a. the trumpet (4:36)
   b. graves open and the dead rise (4:36)
   c. Antichrist hides (4:37)
   d. heaven, earth, and sea perish (4:38)
   e. heaven burns for eighty cubits and earth for eight-hundred and the reasons for this (4:39–43)

A body of themes are gathered here that have old, widespread roots. The idea of the wicked king of the last generation may already be found in Ezekiel 28:2; Daniel 7:24f.; and that of the leader of the forces of evil in the last battle in 1QM 18:1; 1QS 4:18f.; Testament of Levi 3:3; Testament of Dan 5:6, 10f.; and Assumption of Moses 8. In the New Testament the term "Antichrist" is first encountered (1Jn 2:18, 22; 4:3; 2Jn 7). This figure is also probably the "son of perdition" and the "man of lawlessness" in 2 Thessalonians 2:2–4.

A particularly Christian development is that the Antichrist will take on features in imitation of those of Christ in order to deceive men. This idea is clear in the Apocalypse of Ezra 4:27 and the warning against it comes out once again in 4:35. Another particularly clear example is in the Seventh Vision of Daniel, where the Antichrist is described as "a wonder-worker having near him the souls of the lost, drawing bread out of stones," and giving sight to the blind. All this is said to be in resemblance (that is, of Christ). The passage concludes with a lament for those who believe in him. Earlier in the same section he is said to be born of an unholy virgin and to turn many away from the worship of God. The same theme may also be observed in the Coptic Apocalypse of Elijah 3:1–11 and other sources.[26]

---

[24] P. J. Alexander, *The Oracle of Baalbek* (Washington, 1967) p. 10.

[25] There are numerous texts giving lists of cosmic signs which will precede the end-time. Many such have been assembled in M. E. Stone, *Signs of the Judgement, Onomastica Sacra and the Generations from Adam* (University of Pa. Arm. Texts and Studies 3; Chico, Cal., 1981), pp. 2–57. Compare also the ApThom. For one text with widespread ramifications see W. W. Heist, *The Fifteen Signs Before Doomsday* (East Lansing, 1954).

[26] E.g. the Seventh Vision of Daniel (see J. Issaverdens, *The Uncanonical Writings of the Old Testament* [Venice, 1934] p. 263). See ApEl in J.-M. Rosenstiehl, *L'Apocalypse d'Élie* (Textes et Études 1; Paris, 1972) pp. 95–98.

The description of the physiognomy of the Antichrist is to be found in a series of different sources. Most similar to the Apocalypse of Ezra (4:29–32) is the description in the Greek Apocalypse of Ioannis (according to Tischendorf, *Apocalypses Apocryphae*, pp. 74f.):

> The appearance of his face is gloomy; the hairs of his hand are sharp as missiles, his eyebrows like those of a wild man, his right eye like the star which rises at dawn and the other like that of a lion; his mouth (is as wide) as one cubit, his teeth a span long, his fingers like scythes; the soles of his feet (are) two span; and on his forehead (is) an inscription: "Antichrist." He will be exalted up to heaven, he will descend as far as Hades, performing false apparitions.

This description draws upon the same source as the Apocalypse of Ezra, and apparently not on the Apocalypse of Ezra itself.[27] Another description is that occurring in a Greek fragment attributed to an Elijah apocalypse which has numerous parallel forms.[28] Likewise, such descriptions are to be found in the Coptic Apocalypse of Elijah, which goes back to a Greek original, 3:12f.,[29] in *Sefer Eliyahu* (ed. M. Buttenwieser, p. 16), in *Sefer Zerubbabel* (ed. Even-Shmuel, *Midreshe-Ge'ula*, p. 79), and in a series of other sources. This type of description of the features of the face and body, in combination with astrological indications of the character is to be found in 4Q186 (DJD, vol. 5, pp. 88–91). This is presumably to be related to Jewish physiognomic literature of a somewhat later date, Hebrew texts of which have been preserved.[30] It should also be set in the broader context of the physiognomic literature in Greek, which is sadly fragmentarily preserved.

The "Lucifer" features are the presumption of the Antichrist to set himself above God. The old mythical fragment in Isaiah 14:12–15 has had a decisive influence on later developments of this theme. It is clearly found in the description of the "little horn" in Daniel 7:8, 20, 25, an important early "Antichrist" text. The theme of the primordial pride that led to the fall of Satan is clear in the *Vita Adae et Evae* and in certain later forms of this story.[31] These features are appropriately assigned herein to the Antichrist.

The relationship between these events and the punishments that Ezra sees in the course of his descent to Tartarus is not clear. The "hanging" punishments, typical of this section, are widespread, the two oldest texts dealing with them being the Apocalypse of Peter (22–24) and the Elijah apocryphon.[32] They are also to be found in the Apocalypse of Paul 39f. and the Apocalypse of the Virgin 9f. Both these writings also contain material on the Antichrist, that in the Elijah apocryphon being a physiognomic description. These punishments might be seen, then, as forming an intermediate state between death and final judgment. This possibility is not stated, however, and their occurrence in the Apocalypse of Ezra may be due either to the combination of diverse sources or to the combination of just such material in 4 Ezra. The same factors have doubtless led to the confusion about the place of punishment, which is sometimes located in the heavenly spheres and sometimes in the abyss (see n. to 1:7).

Relationship to canonical and apocryphal books

While the Apocalypse of Ezra uses the biblical writings of both the Old and New Testaments, it is difficult to signal any particular biblical books with which it shows special

---

[27] On further possible relationships of this description see W. Bousset, *The Antichrist Legend*, trans. A. K. Keane (London, 1896) p. 42. This work contains an invaluable study of the legend of the Antichrist and a wealth of sources are cited.

[28] See Stone and Strugnell, *The Books of Elijah*, and the Gk. fragment published by F. Nau in *JA* 11 (1917) 454. The parallel texts are all adduced in the former work. See also J.-M. Rosenstiehl, "Le Portrait de l'Antichrist," *Pseudépigraphes de l'Ancien Testament et manuscrits de la Mer Morte*, ed. M. Philonenko (Paris, 1967) pp. 45–60.

[29] See most recently J.-M. Rosenstiehl, *L'Apocalypse d'Élie*.

[30] G. Scholem, "Physiognomy and Chiromancy," *Sefer Asaf* (Jerusalem, 1953) pp. 459–95 [in Heb.]; idem, "Ein Fragment zur Physiognomik und Chiromantik aus der Tradition der spätantiken jüdishen Esoterik," *Liber amicorum C. J. Bleeker* (Leiden, 1969) p. 181; I. Gruenwald, "Further Jewish Physiognomic and Chiromantic Fragments," *Tarbiz* 40 (1971) 301–19 [in Heb.].

[31] Particularly the unpublished Gk. Discourse Concerning the Four Archangels contained in a number of MSS presently under study. This document contains details of the ancient attempt by Samael (or Satan) to seat himself as God and of his defeat.

[32] See Stone and Strugnell, *The Books of Elijah*; cf. also ActsThom 56.

connections.[33] A number of cases appear to point to a dependence on the Septuagint.

The relationship of the work with 4 Ezra is intimate. First, the very form of the writing, a dialogue between the prophet Ezra and an angel (or God) in which the seer taxes his interlocutor with telling questions, doubtlessly derives from that writing.[34] Second, a number of the topics raised are clearly taken from 4 Ezra, even though the Apocalypse of Ezra treats or expresses them differently.[35] Such are not merely the questions about the purpose and nature of creation or the repeated calls for God's mercy, appealing to his own self-predication, but the "riddle" questions (2:32–3:2; 4:2–4; cf. 4Ezra 4:3–9; 5:36–38), the description of the development of the fetus (5:12f.; cf. 4Ezra 8:6–13) and of the messianic woes (3:11–14; cf. 4Ezra 5:1–13; 6:21–24; 9:3). In a number of cases there is more or less a literal use of the text of 4 Ezra (see margins),[36] and many words and expressions strongly resemble 4 Ezra. Moreover, the literary framework is perfunctory, a fact which emphasizes the dependence of the Apocalypse of Ezra upon 4 Ezra.

The Apocalypse of Sedrach and the Vision of Ezra are both closely related to the Apocalypse of Ezra and 4 Ezra.[37] The Apocalypse of Sedrach has expressions in common with the Apocalypse of Ezra that do not occur in 4 Ezra, while nearly all its allusions to 4 Ezra also occur in the Apocalypse. It is, therefore, tempting to think of the Apocalypse of Sedrach as based on another form of the materials in the Apocalypse of Ezra, perhaps with some "access to 4 Ezra."[38] A similar situation was observed above to obtain as to the relationship between the Apocalypse of Ezra and the Vision of Ezra. The chief parallels between the Apocalypse of Ezra and the Apocalypse of Sedrach are noted in the margins (the references are according to James's paragraph division). The most striking parallel between the Apocalypse of Sedrach and 4 Ezra not found in the Apocalypse of Ezra is the passage about the choice representative of each kind (ApSedr 8; 4Ezra 5:23–27). There are also some parallels with the Armenian Questions of Ezra (see the contribution herein), but it seems unwise to state that the Armenian is "a version of the apocryphon."[39] The independent relations between the Questions of Ezra and the Apocalypse of Sedrach do indicate, however, that the Questions of Ezra belongs to the same literary tradition.

SELECT BIBLIOGRAPHY

Charlesworth, *PMR*, pp. 116f.
Denis, *Introduction*, pp. 91–96.

TEXT

Tischendorf, C. von. *Apocalypses Apocryphae.* Leipzig, 1866; pp. xii–xiv, 24–33.

TRANSLATIONS

Riessler, P. *Altjüdisches Schrifttum ausserhalb der Bibel.* Augsburg, 1928; pp. 127–37, 1237.
Walker, A. "The Revelation of Esdras," *ANF*, vol. 8, pp. 571–74.

---

[33] This observation, naturally, refers to special literary relationships. The origins of the figure Ezra in the canonical Ezra have been discussed above ("Theological importance").

[34] Tischendorf, *Apocalypses Apocryphae*, p. xii.

[35] See also note on 7:5ff.

[36] Parallels are conveniently set forth by B. Violet, *Die Ezra-Apokalypse*, pp. l–lix. Many of his "parallels" are in fact collections of associated terminology in similar contexts. Particularly striking, however, is the parallel between the ApEzra 1:10–18 and 4Ezra 7:133–38, both writings utilizing language drawn from Ex 34:6–7. Note the use of *eusplagchnos*, "compassionate," in ApEzra 1:10 and see the observations by M. E. Stone, "Apocryphal Notes and Readings," *Israel Oriental Studies* 1 (1971) 127–29.

[37] On the Vision of Ezra see "Historical importance and literary implications."

[38] M. R. James, *Apocrypha Anecdota* (T&S 2.3; Cambridge, 1893) p. 129.

[39] Denis, *Introduction*, p. 93.

STUDIES

James, M. R. Introduction, *The Fourth Book of Ezra*, ed. R. L. Bensly. T&S 3.3; Cambridge, 1895; pp. lxxxvi–lxxxix.
Mercati, G. *Note di letteratura biblica e cristiana antica.* Studi e Testi 5; Rome, 1901; pp. 61–69.
Violet, B. *Die Ezra-Apokalypse.* GCS 18; Leipzig, 1910; pp. l–lx.

[After the preparation of this contribution, the following appeared:
Müller, U. *Die griechische Ezra-Apokalypse. JSHRZ* 5; Gütersloh, 1976. (German translation)
Wahl, O. *Apocalypsis Esdrae, Apocalypsis Sedrach, Visio Beati Esdrae.* PVTG 4; Leiden, 1977. (text)]

CRITICAL SIGNS

(10△348)	word/s added
[#973UL]	lacuna in manuscript or text, or incomprehensible letters; words within brackets are restorations
⟨10△348⟩	emendations
⌈#973UR⌉	uncorrected corruption of the text

THE GREEK APOCALYPSE OF EZRA[a]

Introduction and prayer

1,2 **1** It came to pass in the thirtieth year on the twenty-second of the month,[b] •I was in my house and I cried out, saying to the Most High, "Lord, grant (me) glory so 3 that I may see your mysteries." •When night fell the angel Michael, the archangel, came and said to me, "Prophet Ezra,[c] lay aside bread for seventy weeks."[d] And 4 I fasted just as he told me. • And the architstrategos[e] Raphael came and gave me 5 a storax staff,[f] •and I fasted twice sixty weeks, and I saw the mysteries of God 6 and his angels. •And I said to them, "I wish to plead[g] with God concerning the Christian people. It were better that man were not born than that he entered the world."[h]

(margin: 4Ezra 3:1)
(margin: Gen 30:37(LXX))
(margin: 2:7,31; 4:1,4; 6:20; 5:1; 1:21; 5:9,14 / 4Ezra 4:12; 7:62-68,116 / 2Bar 10:6 / ApSedr 4)

Ezra taken up to heaven: his prayer for mercy

7 Therefore, I was taken up into heaven and I saw in the first heaven[i] a great 8 command of angels and they led me to the judgments. •And I heard a voice saying 9 to me, "Have pity upon us, Ezra elect of God."[j] •Then I began to say, "Woe to the sinners when they see the righteous man (elevated) above angels, and they are 10 for fiery Gehenna."[k] •And Ezra said, "Have pity upon the works of your hands,[l] 11 merciful and greatly pitying one.[m] • Condemn me rather than the souls of the sinners, for it is better to punish[n] one soul and not to bring the whole world to 12 destruction." •And God said, "I shall give rest to the righteous in Paradise and 13 I am merciful." •And Ezra said, "Lord, why do you show favor to the righteous? 14 For as a hired man completes his time of service and goes away, and again a slave serves his masters in order to receive his wage,[o] thus the righteous man receives 15 his reward in the heavens.[p] •But, have mercy upon the sinners for we know that

(margin: 5:7)
(margin: 4Ezra 7:85f.)
(margin: 2:11,23 / 4Ezra 3:5; 7:132-39 / ApSedr 3)
(margin: 5:6; 2:24 / ApVirg 26)

---

1 a. The title in the MS is "Treatise and Revelation of Esdras [Ezra] the Holy Prophet and Beloved of God." This title is frequently numbered as vs. 1.

b. The date in years, but not that in days, derives from 4Ezra 3:1; this dependency explains why the phrase "the thirtieth year" appears without proper clarification.

c. For the emendation behind this translation see Stone, "Metamorphosis of Ezra."

d. The seventy weeks are perhaps inspired by the prophet's seven weeks' fasting in 4Ezra and 2Bar, in both of which a week's fast intervenes between each vision.

e. Architstrategos—lit. "commander-in-chief of an army"—is an angelic title most frequently used of the angel Michael; cf. Introduction.

f. The significance of this gift to the seer is unclear. M. Himmelfarb has drawn my attention to the storax rod of the pearl merchant in the *Acts of Peter and the Twelve Apostles* (CG VI,1) 2:25.

g. The legal character of Ezra's disputation with God here and below (see margin) may derive from expressions such as those in 4Ezra 7:19. See also ApSedr 3.

h. This expression, drawn from 4Ezra, recurs a number of times in GkApEzra. See margin.

i. This reference to a first heaven probably reflects a source which contained a vision of a number of heavenly spheres. Here in GkApEzra the sinners are said to be punished in the heavens (cf. 5:7–11, 24–26; 2En 7:10). This is confused with another view placing the place of punishment in Tartarus

or the abyss. See in detail Introduction.

j. This title has become commonplace in late pseudepigrapha.

k. The word "elevated" is supplied only for the sake of translation. B. Violet's suggestion that *phroureisthai*, "guarded," should be supplied on the basis of 4Ezra 7:85f. seems gratuitous. The idea that the vision of the punishment of the sinners is part of the reward of the righteous, and the reverse, is found in 4Ezra 7:83–86, 93f.; 2Bar 51:5. Cf. 4Ezra 7:38.

l. Here, in 2:10f., 23 and in various places in 4Ezra and ApSedr (see margin), it is stressed that God himself is directly reponsible for the creation of man not with his word, but with his very hand. See also the note to 5:19.

m. The Gk. word for "merciful" is uncommon, but occurs in certain sources in connection with *polyeleas*, "greatly pitying," as a rendering of the divine attributes listed in Ex 34:6f.; Jonah 4:2; Joel 2:13; Ps 86:16. See Introduction and n. 34.

n. "To punish"—lit. "to be punished."

o. The sense of the Gk. verb (*epituchein*) is difficult here. The translation follows a suggestion of T. Korteweg; for the sense see 6:22. Korteweg would read *artou* for *autou* preceding, but for the absolute use, see Jas 4:2.

p. For the image of the wage, a common one also in the NT, see 4Ezra 8:33. Cf. particularly Mt 20:1–15 and see M. Smith, *Tannaitic Parallels to the Gospels* (SBLMS 6; Philadelphia, 1968²) pp. 49–70 and nn.

16,17 you are merciful." •And God said, "I have no way to be merciful to them." •And
18 Ezra said, "(Be merciful) because they cannot sustain your anger."q •And God   4Ezra 8:34
said, "(I am wrathful) because such (are the deserts) of such (men) as these."
19,20 And God said, "I wish to keep you as both Paul and John. •You have given me
uncorrupted the inviolate treasury, the treasure of virginity, the wall of men."r

Ezra's second prayer

21   And Ezra said, "It were better if man were not born; it were well if he were
22 not alive. •The dumb beasts are a better thing than man, for they do not have
23,24 punishment. •[You to]oks us and delivered us to judgment. •Woe to the sinners
in the world to come, for their condemnation is endless and the flame unquenched."

v. 21
1:6; 5:9,14
4Ezra 4:12;
7:62–68,116
2Bar 10:6
ApSedr 4
v. 22
4Ezra 7:65-67
QuesEzra A5
v. 24
Isa 66:24

Ezra remonstrates with God: the sin of Adam

1 **2** As I said this to him, Michael and Gabriel and all the apostles came and said,
2,3,4 "Greetings!" •[And Ezra said, "Faithful man of God!] •Arise and come hither (vs. 3) 2:18,26
with me, O Lord, to judgment."a And God said, "Behold I am giving you my
5 covenant, both mine and yours, so that you will accept it." •And Ezra said, "We
6 shall plead our case in your ear(s)." •And God said, "Ask Abraham your father ApSedr 2
what kind of son presses suit against his fatherb and come and plead the case with
7 us." •And Ezra said, "As the Lord lives, I shall never cease pleading the case 1:6; 2:13; 4:1,4;
8 with you on account of the Christian people. •Where are your former mercies, O 6:20
9 Lord? Where your long-suffering?" •And God said, "As I made night and day I ApSedr 4
made the righteous and the sinner and it were fitting to conduct yourself like the
10 righteous man." •And the prophet said, "Who made Adam, the protoplast, the WisSol 7:1; 10:1
11 first one?" •And God said, "My immaculate hands,c and I placed him in Paradise 1:10; 2:23
12 to guard the region of the tree of life."d •[. . .] "Since he who established ApSedr 4
13 disobedience made this (man) sin."e •And the prophet said, "Was he not guarded Gen 2:9,15-19
14 by an angel?f •And was life not preserved (by) the cherubim for the endless age? 4Ezra 3:5
15 And how was he deceived who was guarded by angels (whom) you commanded v. 12
16 to be present whatever happened?g Attend also to that which I say! •If you had ApSedr 4
17 not given him Eve, the serpent would never have deceived her.h •If you save v. 13
whom you wish you will also destroy whom you wish."

v. 13
LAE 33:1f.
ApMos 7:2
ApSedr 8
v. 14
Gen 3; 24
v. 15
ApSedr 4

q. The idea that mankind cannot sustain God's wrath is analogous to 4Ezra 8:34, where it says that man, being corruptible, is not a fitting object of divine anger.

r. Riessler suggests that these vss. are an interpolation. They do seem to interrupt the course of the dialogue and, more notably, are divine speech following directly upon divine speech.

s. In Gk. only the beginning of this word is preserved by the MS and the restoration is uncertain.

2 a. Clearly this vs. is not a response to vs. 2 nor a continuation of it. It appears that the speaker must be Ezra, and that more than the introductory formula, which has been restored here, was actually lost.

b. The sense is obscure here. ApSedr 3 has "the son has a lawsuit with [?] the father" (cf. Plato, *Euthyphro* 4e). Apparently Abraham is invoked to testify about some specific past case of a son pressing suit against his father, but it remains uncertain to which event reference is made. Abraham's dialogue with God about Sodom and Gomorrah (Gen 18) does not seem to fit here.

c. The expression "immaculate hands" is common to GkApEzra and ApSedr in connection with the creation of man but does not occur in 4Ezra.

d. Or "the food of the tree of life"; cf. Walker, *ANF* 8, p. 571. 4Ezra does not mention any task assigned to Adam in the garden of Eden. The Bible (Gen 2:15) says "to till it and keep it." In Gk-ApEzra 5:21 the tree of life is in the East, i.e. in Eden (Gen 2:8). Cf. 1En 24:3f.

e. He who established disobedience is Satan. The vs. is not a response to the question in vs. 10. T. Korteweg suggests the loss of something like "And the prophet said, 'Why are we now separated from the tree of life?' And God said . . ." This may have been due to scribal error. The text lying behind the translation is discussed in detail in Stone, "Metamorphosis of Ezra."

f. *Vita* 33:1f. reports that Adam and Eve had guardian angels and the Fall took place at the hour when these angels had ascended to heaven to pray. This is related of Eve alone in ApMos 7:2. ApSedr 8 relates that angels guarded Adam continually.

g. Tischendorf has numerous emendations for vss. 14f.; nearly all are accepted. See in detail Stone, "Metamorphosis of Ezra."

h. This vs. seems tautological but it may in fact preserve a reminiscence of the minimizing of Adam's responsibility for the Fall, stressed in LAE and *Vita*.

Ezra remonstrates with God: the sins of men

18 　And the prophet said, "O my Lord, let us continue to a second judgment."

19,20 And God said, "I cast fire upon Sodom and Gomorrah." •And the prophet said,

21 　"Lord, you bring upon us what we deserve." •And God said, "Your sins exceed

22 　my kindness." • And the prophet said, "Remember Scripture, my father, who

23 　measured out Jerusalem and rebuilt her.[i] •Pity, Lord, the sinners, pity your own

24 　molding,[j] have mercy upon your works." •Then God remembered his works and

25 　said to the prophet, "How can I have mercy upon them? •They gave me vinegar

and gall to drink and [. . .][k] they repented."

The day of judgment

26 　And the prophet said, "Reveal your cherubim[l] and let us go together to judgment,

27,28 and show me what is the character of the day of judgment." •And God said, "You

29 　have digressed, Ezra, •for such is the day of judgment upon which there is no rain

30,31 on the earth, •for there is a merciful judgment during that day."[m] •And the prophet

said, "I shall never cease to argue the case with you until I see the day of

32 　consummation." •(And God said,) "Count the stars and the sand of the sea and

if you will be able to count this, you will also be able to argue the case with me.'"[n]

1,2 **3** And the prophet said, "Lord, you know that I bear human flesh. •And how can

3 　I count the stars of heaven and the sand of the sea?" •And God said, "O my elect

prophet, no man will know that great day and the manifestation which prevails to

4 　judge the world. •For your sake, O my prophet, I told you the day, but the hour

5,6 　I told you not."[a] •And the prophet said, "Lord, tell me also the years." •And God

said, "If I see that the justice of the world has become abundant, I will be long-

suffering toward them.[b] If not, I will stretch out my hand and I will grasp the

Margin references:
2:3,26
Gen 19:24
v. **23**
1:10; 2:11
4Ezra 8:24;
7:134
ApSedr 3
v. **24**
1:16
ApVirg 27
v.**25**
7:1
Ps 69:21
Mt 27:34
Mk 15:36
Lk 23:36
ApVirg 29

7:6; 2:3,18
4Ezra 7:39,41
1:6; 2:7; 4:1,4;
6:20

Jer 33:22
Sir 1:2
Gen 15:5; 32:13
Heb 11:12

4:4
4Ezra 4:6

Joel 4:2,12
1En 53:1
MidPs 8:10

---

i. The vs. is difficult. The Gk. actually reads "memorial of writings." The text reflected by the translation is as emended by Tischendorf but he has not avoided all difficulties, notably the nominative case of "father." The vs. might be emended to "through the recollection of Scripture, O my Father, you measured out Jerusalem and rebuilt her." This would be better Gk. and does not require very extensive tampering with the transmitted text. Yet it does involve accepting four distinct changes in it and, at the present stage of textual knowledge (see n. g above), perhaps Tischendorf's more conservative suggestion is to be preferred. The actual statement is somewhat odd, if the reference is to be the pseudepigraphic background of Ezra, for he was one of those responsible for the rebuilding of Jerusalem. Perhaps our author was thinking of the angelic guide in Ezek 40–48 and the angel in Zech 2:5–9. The underlying idea may be that God, who, in accordance with the scriptural promises of restoration, rebuilt Jerusalem in his mercy, will also have mercy upon the sinners.

j. The Gk. *plasis* is used in EpBar 6:9 much as it is here, apparently meaning "creation."

k. The Gk. has four corrupt words here that cannot be read. Tischendorf emends, dubiously, to "and not then." This is certainly a Christian reference. The apparent denial of divine mercy, justified by citing the crucifixion as evidence for the wickedness of mankind, seems strange. In ApPaul 44 a similar reproach precedes Christ's statement that he will grant some respite to the suffering sinners.

l. God's cherub throne; cf. e.g. Ezek 1.

m. Certainly a corrupted text based upon 4Ezra 7:39–42, where the phenomena of nature are said to be removed on the day of judgment. ApIoan

(Tischendorf, *Apocalypses Apocryphae*, p. 75) speaks of the removal of dew, clouds, and winds. It is unclear why GkApEzra should have singled out the rain alone from this list. Compare, however, the Daniel Apocalypse according to A. Vassiliev, *Anecdota Graeco-Byzantina Pars Prior* (Moscow, 1893) p. 47. The statement in vs. 30 is strange. In 4Ezra great emphasis is laid upon the view that, although divine compassion and human prayer can bring forgiveness and mercy in this age (most strikingly in 7:106–12), the day of judgment will be characterized by the strictest divine justice. This is particularly clear in 4Ezra 7:33, the latter part of which might have been misunderstood by GkApEzra. In fact, in 1:16 and 5:17 GkApEzra refers to strict judgment. The same view as in 4Ezra is also found in 2Bar 85:12. Compare also TAbr, rec. A, 13. See also the note to 5:10. Walker's translation (*ANF* 8, p. 572) is "for such is the day of judgment as that in which there is no rain upon the earth; for it is a merciful tribunal as compared with that day." This is barely possible on the basis of the Gk.

n. The similarity between these questions and those in 4:2–4, the answers to which are beyond human knowledge, and those in 4Ezra 4:3–9 and 5:36–38 is noted in the Introduction. They come to show the limitations of man, yet of course GkApEzra is actually full of special revelations, including meteorological ones in 5:23.

3 a. This vs. stands in evident contradiction with vs. 3. Compare Mk 13:32: "But of that day and hour no one knows."

b. The import of these vss. is unclear. If even the days and hours have been revealed (vs. 5), then

inhabited world from its four corners and I will gather them all together to the valley of Jehosaphat and I will wipe out the human race and the world will be no
7 more.'' •And the prophet said, ''And how will your right hand be glorified?''
8 And God said, ''I will be glorified by my angels.''

Why was man created?

9   And the prophet said, ''Lord, if this was your calculation, why did you form   4Ezra 8:7,44
10 man? •You said to Abraham our father, *'I will surely multiply your seed as the*   ApSedr 4
   stars of the heaven and as the sand along the shore of the sea.'[c] And where is your   Gen 22:17(LXX)
   promise?''

Signs of the end

11   And God said, ''First I shall cause by shaking[d] the fall of four-footed beasts and
12 men. •And when you see that brother delivers brother over to death and children   4Ezra 6:24
13 will rise up against parents and a wife abandons her own husband, •and when   4Ezra 9:3;
   nation will rise up against nation in war, then you shall know that the end is near.[e]   13:31f.
14 And then brother will not have mercy upon brother, nor man upon his wife, nor   4Ezra 7:102f.
15 children upon parents, nor friends upon friends, nor slave upon master.[f] •For the
   opponent of men[g] himself will come up from Tartarus and will show many things
16 to men. •What shall I do to you, Ezra, and will you argue the case with me?''

Ezra descends to Tartarus

1 **4** And the prophet said, ''Lord, I shall never cease arguing the case with you.''   1:6; 2:7,31; 6:20
2,3 And God said, ''Count the flowers of the earth. •If you can count them you also   4Ezra 5:36
   will be able to argue the case with me.''[a]   3:1
4   And the prophet said, ''Lord, I cannot count them—I bear human flesh—but
5 neither will I stop arguing the case with you. •I wish, Lord, to see the lower parts
6,7 of Tartarus.'' •And God said, ''Go down and see!'' •And he gave me Michael
8 and Gabriel and thirty-four other angels,[b] •and I descended eighty-five steps and
   they led me down five hundred steps.

The punishment of Herod

9   And I saw a fiery throne and an old man seated on it, and his punishment was   VisEzra 50-55
10,11 merciless. •And I said to the angels, ''Who is this and what is his sin?'' •And they   Mt 2:16
   said to me, ''This is Herod, who was king for a time, and he commanded to kill
12 the infants two years old or under.'' •And I said, ''Woe upon his soul!''

The disobedient and the abyss

13   And again they led me down thirty steps. And I saw boiling fires there, and a   VisEzra 16,30-35

why should the prophet wish to know the years? The response, in vs. 6, is that the length of the years is determined by human conduct.

c. The quotation is the LXX of Gen 22:17. The point made resembles 4Ezra 3:4–16.

d. Tischendorf's emendation of this phrase *siesmou ptosin*, ''the falling . . . through shaking,'' to *seismon eis ptosin*, ''shaking for falling,'' is rejected. The phrase is difficult to translate.

e. The picture of internecine strife given in vs. 12 is a commonplace; see Introduction. On the verbs in vss. 12f., see Introduction.

f. Although this list is related to that in vs. 12, it stems apparently from a different source as is indicated particularly by the phrase ''nor slave upon master.'' This phrase occurs in 4Ezra 7:102–4 and

not in the other passages that probably stand behind vs. 12. 4Ezra 7:102–4 proclaim that on the day of judgment no man, however intimately related, will be able to pray for his fellow. In GkApEzra, intercessory prayer has become ''to have mercy upon.'' The original intent of the verses is preserved in the Ethiopic Ezra Apocalypse (cf. Halévy, *Tĕᵓĕzāza Sanbat*, p. 182).

g. The opponent of men is the Antichrist; see 4:37. The reproach of God implied here resembles 4Ezra 3:4–7.

4 a. See n. on 2:32.

b. In VisEzra there are seven angels of Tartarus. In 6:2, Michael and Gabriel appear together with seven other angels; see also ApVirg 4.

14 multitude of sinners in them. •And I heard their voices, but I did not perceive their VisEzra 29
15 forms.[c] •And they led me down deeper many steps which I was unable to count.
16,17 And I saw old men there, and fiery axles were revolving upon their ears.[d] •And
18 I said, "Who are these and what is their sin?" •And they said to me, "These are Isa 66:24
19,20 the eavesdroppers."[e] •And again they led me down five hundred other steps. •And Mk 9:48
21 there I saw the unsleeping worm and fire consuming the sinners. •And they led ApPaul 12 VisEzra 44
me down to the foundation of Apoleia (Destruction)[f] and there I saw the twelvefold
22 blow of the abyss.[g] •And they led me away to the south and there I saw a man VisEzra 24-28
23 hanging from his eyelids and the angels were beating him. •And I asked, "Who
24 is this and what is his sin?" •And Michael the archistrategos said to me, "This
man is incestuous; having carried out a small lust, this man was commanded to
be hanged."

The Antichrist

25 And they led me away to the north and I saw a man there restrained[h] with iron
26,27 bars. •And I asked, "Who is this?" And he said to me, •"This is the one who
says, 'I am the son of God and he who made stones bread and water wine.' "[i]
28 And the prophet said, "Make known to me what sort of appearance he has and
29 I will inform the race of men lest they believe in him."[j] •And he said to me, "The Isa 14:12(LXX)
appearance of his face is as of a wild man. His right eye is like a star rising at
30 dawn and the other is unmoving. •His mouth is one cubit, his teeth are a span
31 long, •his fingers like scythes, the soles of his feet two span, and on his forehead
32 an inscription 'Antichrist.'[k] •He was exalted up to heaven, he will descend as far Isa 14:13-15
33,34 as Hades.[l] •One time he will be a child, another an old man."[m] •And the prophet
35 said, "Lord, how do you permit the race of men to stray?" •And God said, "Hear,
my prophet! He becomes a child and an old man and let no one believe that
36 he is my beloved son. •And after these things a trumpet, and the graves will be 1Cor 15:52
37 opened and the dead will rise up uncorrupted.[n] •Then the opponent, having heard

c. See 5:10, n.

d. The text is emended at this point; see Stone, "Metamorphosis of Ezra."

e. The eavesdroppers are a class of sinners well known in visions of punishments like this; cf. ApVirg 10. Other sources are collected by S. Lieberman, "On Sins and Their Punishment," *L. Ginzberg Jubilee Volume* (New York, 1945) vol. 2, p. 258 (in Heb.). The particular punishment in GkApEzra here is paralleled in certain of the medieval Heb. sources he cites.

f. Is the description of the Antichrist introduced following this section because of his title "Son of Perdition" (*apoleias*) derived from 2Thes 2:3? This title is not found in GkApEzra, but see the Daniel Apocalypse, published by Vassiliev, *Anecdota Graeco-Byzantina*, p. 43. See in general Bousset-Keane, *Antichrist*.

g. The Gk. word is rare. Lampe (*Patristic Greek Lexicon*) offers "the twelve last plagues of hell" with no further support (cf. also ApIoan in Tischendorf, *Apocalypses Apocryphae*, p. 94).

h. The Gk. word here, *katecho*, is that generally used for the imprisonment or restraint of the Antichrist; see 2Thes 2:6, 7 and the remarks of Vielhauer according to HSW, vol. 2, pp. 614f.

i. The Antichrist claims to be Christ and performs his miracles; see Seventh Vision of Daniel (Introduction), Cop. ApEl 3:1, 8–10. There is denied him only the resurrection of the dead. Cf. also the Daniel Apocalypse published by Vassiliev, *Anecdota Graeco-Byzantina*, p. 43.

j. The idea that the purpose of the revelation of the signs of the Antichrist is that the seer might

warn men against him is also to be found; e.g. Cop. ApEl 3:2ff.

k. The chief physiognomic descriptions are noted in the Introduction. They do not bear particular resemblance in detail to what we find here except for ApIoan. The same style and the same literary type are, however, clearly observable. Note the "high" soles of his feet in *Sefer Eliyahu*, p. 16.

l. See the discussion of this theme in the Introduction. It is also prominent in the Vision of Enoch the Just (ed. Issaverdens, *Uncanonical Writings*, pp. 245f.).

m. This detail also recurs in the Cop. ApEl, 3:14. Its source and significance are not clear. See also Tiburtine Sibyl 190–92 (Alexander, *Oracle of Baalbek*, p. 113, n. 54). The matter is discussed with suggestions as to its origins in Bousset-Keane, *Antichrist*, pp. 150–53.

n. The trumpet announces the redemption; see Isa 27:13; Zech 9:14; Mt 24:31; 1Thes 4:16f.; Did 16:6. The closest parallel is, however, 1Cor 15:52, upon which GkApEzra depends entirely.

The graves are opened and the dead arise uncorrupted. This is the general resurrection of the dead and not the grisly portent which is the falling of the dead bodies from their graves. This latter is to be found in Signs of the Judgement XI (Stone, *Signs of the Judgement*, pp. 26f.) and probably also in Mt 27:51. The sources for the resurrection are manifold, but here, again, GkApEzra seems directly dependent on 1Cor 15:52. Parallels to these two events in later literature are abundant and are not cited.

38 the terrible threat, will hide himself in the outer darkness.° •Then the heaven and
39 the earth and the sea will perish.ᴾ •Then I shall burn the heaven for eighty cubits
40 and the earth for eight hundred cubits.'' •And the prophet said, ''And (in) what
41,42 did the heaven sin?'' •And God said, ''Since [. . .] is the evil.''�q •And the prophet
43 said, ''Lord, (in) what did the earth sin?'' •And God said, ''Since the opponent
having heard my terrible threat will hide (in it), and because of that I shall melt
the earth and with it the rebel of the race of men.''ʳ

Further punishments

1,2 **5** And the prophet said, ''Pity, O Lord, the race of Christians.'' •And I saw a   1:6
3 woman suspended and four wild beasts were sucking upon her breasts.ᵃ •And the
angels said to me, ''She begrudged giving her milk but also cast infants into the
4,5 rivers.'' •And I saw terrible darkness and night without stars or moon. •There is
there neither young nor old, neither brother with brother nor mother with child nor
6 wife with husband. •And I wept and said, ''O Lord, Lord, have mercy upon the   1:15
sinners.''

Ezra taken to heaven

7   And as I said these things a cloudᵇ came and seized me and took me up again   1:7f.
8,9 to the heavens. •And I saw many judgments and I wept bitterly and I said, •''It   1:6,21; 5:14
10 were better if man did not come forth from his mother's belly.'' •Those who were   ApSedr 4
4Ezra 4:12;
in punishment called out, saying, ''Since you came here, holy one of God, we   7:62-68,116
2Bar 10:6
11 have obtained a slight respite.''ᶜ •And the prophet said, ''Blessed are they who
bewail their own sins.''

Birth and its purpose

12   And God said, ''Hear Ezra, beloved one! Just as a farmer casts down the seed
13 of corn into the earth, so a man casts down his seed into a woman's place.ᵈ •In

o. The opponent hides himself in outer darkness.
If vs. 43 is correctly understood, the ''outer darkness'' must be somewhere on earth since the earth
is burned in order to melt the hidden Antichrist.
The term occurs in contexts not particularly significant for the present text in the NT (Mt 8:12;
22:13; 25:30). In a context not unlike the present
it occurs in QuesEzra, rec. A, 3; cf. also ApPaul
16.

p. There is some contradiction here between the
perishing of heaven, earth, and sea (vs. 38) and the
burning of heaven and earth to various measures
(of breadth? of depth?) in vss. 39–43. A similar
contradiction is to be observed in the Arm. version
of Signs of the Judgement between the signs cited
below:
   1. Heaven, earth, and sea perish; cf. Arm. Signs
of the Judgement VII.
   2. Heaven is burned for 80 cubits and earth for
800; cf. Signs of the Judgement XIV.
Earth is burned for 30 (variant 33) cubits: ApDaniel
published by Tischendorf, *Apocalypses Apocry-*
phae, p. xxxii, and Vassiliev, *Anecdota Graeco-*
Byzantina, p. 47; Eth. Ezra Apocalypse according
to Halévy, *Tĕ'ĕzāza Sanbat*, p. 178; and 8,500
(variants: 500, 1,800, 660, 30) cubits in ApIoan
14 (Tischendorf, *Apocalypses Apocryphae*, p. 81);
72 cubits Cop. ApEl 3:83.
   The idea of a general conflagration at the end of
days is found in quite early sources; see Josephus,
Ant 1.70; Philo, *Vita Mos* 2:263; *Vita* 49f.; cf. 2Bar
70:8; 2Pet 3:10. The idea has been attributed to

Stoic origins.
   q. The sin of heaven is unclear due to textual
corruption.
   r. The sin of the earth is that in it is hidden the
rebel (for the title compare Vision of Enoch the Just
[ed. Issaverdens, *Uncanonical Writings*, pp.
246f.]).

5 a. Cf. ApVirg 20, where this punishment is recorded for a different sin, one of ecclesiastical
character. The first sin here appears to be complemented by the punishment, although a second sin
has been added. The ecclesiastical character of the
sins in ApVirg indicates that work to be later in
character than GkApEzra. See also 4:13f. (margin)
for a similar case.
   b. The idea of a cloud taking the seer up to
heaven occurs elsewhere, e.g. 1En 14:8; ApIoan
(Tischendorf, *Apocalypses Apocryphae*, pp. 71,
93); TAb, rec. A, 9, 15; rec. B, 8, 10, etc.; cf. Isa
19:1 (of God).
   c. The view that the prayer of the righteous can
be instrumental in gaining some respite for the
suffering sinner is, of course, clear in TAb and
ApPaul 44. It also bears on the concluding section
of QuesEzra. The term for respite is not that of
ApPaul, regarding which see Lieberman, *Ginzberg*
Volume, vol. 2, p. 252; see 2:30 n.
   d. The image of mankind as the husbandman's
seed is to be found in 4Ezra 8:41–44; cf. the parable
of the sower, Mt 13:1–9 and parallels. Note the
literalistic treatment of the image in GkApEzra.

the first (month) it is a whole, in the second it is swollen, in the third it grows hair, in the fourth it grows nails, in the fifth it becomes milky, in the sixth it is ready and quickened, in the seventh it is prepared, [in the eighth . . .], in the ninth the bars of the gateways of the woman are opened and it is born healthy on the earth.''

4,15 And the prophet said, "It were better for man not to have been born. • Alas, O
16 human race, at that time when you come to judgment!'' • And I said to the Lord,
17 "Lord, why did you create man and give him over to judgment?'' • And God said in his exalted pronouncement, "I will not pardon those who transgress my cov-
8,19 enant.'' • And the prophet said, "Lord, where is your goodness?'' • And God said, "I prepared everything because of man and man does not keep my commandments."[e]

1:6,21; 5:9
ApSedr 4
ApSedr 6

4Ezra 4:12
7:62-68,116
2Bar 10:6

4Ezra 6:55;
7:11; 8:44
ApSedr 3

Punishments and rewards

20   And the prophet said, "Lord, reveal to me the punishments and Paradise.''
21,22 And the angels led me away to the east[f] and I saw the tree of life. • And I saw there
Enoch and Elijah and Moses and Peter and Paul and Luke and Matthew and all
23 the righteous and the patriarchs.[g] • And I saw there the [punishment] of the air and the blowing of the winds and the storehouses of the ice and the eternal
24,25 punishments. • And I saw there a man hanging by his skull. • And they said to me,
26 "This one transferred boundaries.'' • And there I saw great judgments and said to
27 the Lord, "O Lord, Lord, which of men, having been born, did not sin?'' • And they led me farther down in Tartarus and I saw all the sinners lamenting and
28 weeping and evil mourning. • And I too wept, seeing the race of men punished thus.

2:11

QuesEzra A4

4Ezra 7:68
8:35; cf.
4Ezra 3:35f.

1 **6** Then God said to me, "Ezra, do you know the names of the angels who are
2 over the consummation: • Michael, Gabriel, Uriel, Raphael, Gabuthelon, Aker, Arphugitonos, Beburos, Zebuleon?''[a]

Ezra struggles for his soul

3   Then a voice came to me, "Come here, die, Ezra, my beloved! Give back that
4 which has been entrusted (to you).''[b] • And the prophet said, "And whence can
5 you bring forth my soul?''[c] • And the angels said, "We can cast it forth through
6 your mouth.'' • And the prophet said, "I spoke mouth to mouth with God and it
7 will not go forth from there.'' • And the angels said, "We will bring it forth through
8 your nostrils.'' • And the prophet said, "My nostrils smelled the glory of God.''[d]
9,10 And the angels said, "We can bring it forth through your eyes.'' • And the prophet
11 said, "My eyes have seen the back of God.'' • And the angels said, "We can bring
12 it forth through your head.'' • [. . . And the angels said, "We can bring it forth through your feet.''] And the prophet said, "I walked with Moses on the mountain,
13 and it will not come forth from there.''[e] • And the angels said, "We can cast it

Num 12:8(LXX)
ApSedr 2

OdesSol 11:15
Ex 33:23

e. Here the view is not only that man is the special creation of God (see 1:10, commentary) but that creation was for the sake of man. See "Theological Importance.''

f. Paradise is in the East; cf. Gen 2:8.

g. Paul meets the patriarchs in Paradise, ApPaul 47.

6 a. On the angelic name, see "Theological Importance.''

b. The term "that which is entrusted'' refers to the soul; see also vss. 17, 21. It occurs also in 1Tim 6:20; 2Tim 1:12, 14; cf. ShepHerm, Mand. 3:2.

c. On this theme, the struggle for the soul of the righteous, see "Theological Importance.''

d. The idea of smelling the glory of God is to be found elsewhere. Note in particular OdesSol 11:15: "And my breath was refreshed/By the fragrance of the Lord'' (trans. Charlesworth). Another

parallel is the Arm. Life of Moses, where Moses says, "My mouth spoke with God and my eyes saw the light of the Godhead and my nostrils smelt the fragrance of sweetness . . .'' (Stone in SCS 4, pp. 118f.). 1En 24f. has the idea of the fragrance of the tree of life, which stands near the divine throne. Cf. also P. A. H. de Boer, "An Aspect of Sacrifice, II: God's Fragrance,'' *Studies in the Religion of Ancient Israel* (VTSup 23; Leiden, 1972) pp. 37–47. To this passage in which each member of the body is tested as to the departure of the soul, cf. ApSedr 10.

e. If this is a response to vs. 11, it is incoherent. Presumably something has been lost between vss. 12 and 13, perhaps the response to vs. 11 and the question that provoked vs. 12. The reconstruction here claims only to convey the apparent sense of that lost sentence.

14 forth through the tips of your (toe)nails." •And the prophet said, "My feet walked
15 in the sanctuary." • And the angels departed unsuccessful, saying, "Lord, we
16 cannot receive his soul." •Then he said to his only begotten son, "Go down, my   ApSedr 9
beloved son, with a numerous host of angels, taking the soul of my beloved Ezra."
17 For the Lord, having taken a numerous army of many angels, said to the prophet,   6:21
"Give me that deposit which I entrusted to you. The crown is readied for you."ᶠ   OdesSol 1:1-5;
18 And the prophet said, "Lord, if you take my soul from me, who will you have   9:8f.,11; 17:1;
                                                                                      20:7f.
19 left to plead on behalf of the race of men?" •And God said, "You who are mortal   4Ezra 4:11
20 and earthly, do not plead the case with me." •And the prophet said, "I shall never 1:6; 2:7,31;
21 cease pleading." •And God said, "Give, in the meanwhile, that which is entrusted   4:1,4; 6:17
                                                                                      QuesEzra A6
22 (to you). The crown is readied for you. •Come here, die, so that you may attain   OdesSol 1:1-5;
23 it." •Then the prophet began to speak with tears, "O Lord, what profits it that I 9:8f.,11; 17:1;
                                                                                      20:7f.
24 plead the case with you, and I am going to fall to the earth? •Woe, woe! for I will
25 be consumed by worms. •Bewail me, all holy and pious ones, I plead greatly and
26 am delivered over to death! •Bewail me, all holy and just ones, because I have
entered the bowl of Hades."ᵍ

Soul and body

1 **7** And God said to him, "Hear, Ezra, my beloved one. I, being immortal, received 2:25
2 a cross, I tasted vinegar and gall, I was set down in a grave. •And I raised up my   Ps 69:21
                                                                                        Mt 27:34
elect ones and I summoned up Adam from Hades so that the race of men   Mk 15:36
3 [. . .].ᵃ Therefore, fear not death. • For that which is from me, that is the soul,   Lk 23:36
                                                                                        4Ezra 7:32
departs for heaven. That which is from the earth, that is the body, departs for the
4 earth from which it was taken." •And the prophet said, "Woe, woe! What shall
I do? How shall I act? I know not."

Concluding prayerᵇ

5 And then the blessed Ezra began to say, "O eternal God, Creator of the whole   Isa 40:12(LXX)
creation, who measured out the heaven with a span and contained the earth in his   2:26
                                                                                     2Sam 22:11
6 hand,ᶜ •who drives the cherubim, who took the prophet Elijah to the heavens in   Ps 18:11
                                                                                   v. 6
7 a fiery chariot, •who gives nurture to all flesh, whom all things fear and tremble 2Kgs 2:11f.
8,9 from the face of your power, •hear me who pleads greatly •and give to all who   Sir 48:9
                                                                                     v. 7
copy this book and preserve it and recall my name and preserve my memory fully,   Ps 136(135):25
10 give them blessing from heaven. •And bless all of his things, just as the ends of 4Ezra 8:21-23
11,12 Joseph.ᵈ •And remember not his previous sins on the day of his judgment. •Those
13 who do ñot believe this book will be burned like Sodom and Gomorrah." •And

f. The crown or garland of the righteous at the
end of days. The origins of the idea are found in
Isa 28:5; 62:3; Ezek 28:12 (LXX); 1Cor 9:25; 2Tim
4:8; Jas 1:12; 1Pet 5:4; Rev 2:10; 3:11. This is
doubtless the "crown of glory" of the righteous in
1QS 4.7, 1QH 9.25, and "crown with great glory"
in 2Bar 15:8. Cf. also Sir 45:12; TBenj 4:1; WisSol
5:16; AscenIs 7:22; 9:24. Cf. also the Sabbath
morning Amidah, which states of Moses "you
placed a crown of glory on his head" (*The Authorised Daily Prayer Book*, with commentary by
J. H. Hertz [London, 1947] p. 456). The concept
of the crown is prevalent in the OdesSol; note the
parallels cited in the margin to the translation and
especially OdesSol 9:8-11 (see the translation by
Charlesworth herein).

g. The expression "bowl of Hades" is unusual
and not of biblical origin. Can it be compared with
the "hollow places" in which the souls reside
according to 1En 22? The Gk. words differ in the
two sources.

7 a. A reference to the descent into hell, the oldest
extended narrative of which is in the GNic 5(21):1ff.
This idea is also perhaps referred to by Eph 4:8f.
and in OdesSol 42:11f.

b. Violet, *Ezra-Apokalypse*, p. li, suggests a
number of phrases in this section to be similar to
4Ezra 8:20-36. These are not particularly striking
but the overall resemblance of the two passages in
tone and function is noteworthy.

c. Gk. *draken*. This form is untranslatable; perhaps read *drakin*, "hand"; cf. Isa 40:11 (LXX).

d. The import of the vs. as it stands is unclear.
The reference might be to Joseph's flourishing in
Egypt or to the story of the bearing off of his
remains by the departing Israelites (Ex 13:19).
R. A. Kraft suggests that "Joseph" is the result
of a scribe's misreading of "Job" as an abbreviation
for Joseph. This is confirmed by Paris MS 390,
which reads *ta eschata tou Iob*, "the ends of Job."
If this is so, the vs. refers to the restoration of
Job's prosperity after his sufferings.

a voice came to him saying, "Ezra, my beloved, I shall grant to each one the things which you asked."

Death and burial of Ezra

14 And at once he gave over his precious soul with much honor on the eighteenth
15 of the month of October. • And they buried him with incense and psalms. His precious and holy body provides unceasingly strengthening of souls and bodies for those who approach him willingly.

Doxology

16 Glory, might, honor, and worship to him for whom it is fitting, for the Father and the Son and the Holy Spirit, now and always and for ever and ever. Amen.

VISION OF EZRA

(Fourth to Seventh Century A.D.)

A NEW TRANSLATION AND INTRODUCTION
BY J. R. MUELLER and G. A. ROBBINS

Although this pseudepigraphon is thoroughly Christian[1] and has as its closest parallels certain New Testament apocrypha,[2] its place within the Old Testament Pseudepigrapha is assured for two reasons: (1) its attribution to the figure of Ezra; and (2) its affinities with the other Ezra-related pseudepigrapha, most notably 4 Ezra, the Greek Apocalypse of Ezra, and the Apocalypse of Sedrach.[3]

The Vision opens abruptly. Unlike the Greek Apocalypse of Ezra, there is no preparation for the petition that Ezra makes in the first verse: "Grant me, O Lord, courage that I might not fear when I see the judgments of the sinners." That Ezra will receive a vision of the damnation of the wicked is presupposed. His entreaty is scarcely uttered before he is transported by seven angels of hell to the infernal regions.

The series of visions commences with Ezra's arrival at the fiery gates of hell (vss. 3–11). Here Ezra sees the just passing untouched through the flaming portals. When the damned attempt to do likewise, they are ripped apart by the dogs (or in some MSS, lions) that lie in front of the gates and are consumed by the fire. It is a recurrent feature of the vision that the just pass through the infernal regions unscathed, whereas the damned are unable to escape.

After passing through the gates, Ezra begins his descent into Tartarus. The account of this descent is fuller (vss. 12–55) than that of the Greek Apocalypse of Ezra. He sees the torments of adulterers, both men and women (vss. 12–18); of incestuous mothers and sons (vss. 19–22); of those who failed to make confession, who were niggardly in almsgiving, who were inhospitable to the sojourner (vss. 23–26); of Herod, on account of his slaughter of the holy innocents (vss. 37–39); of false teachers (vss. 40–42, 45–47); of unchaste virgins (vss. 43f.); of unjust rulers (vss. 48f.); of disrespectful children (vs. 50); of unfair masters (vs. 50); and of women who murdered the children they conceived in adultery (vss. 51–55).

Having witnessed all the "judgments of sins," Ezra enters into Paradise. Escorted no longer by the angels of hell, but rather by Michael and Gabriel (vs. 56), he catches a glimpse of the heavenly habitations and their splendor. Before placing him in the presence of God, the angels of heaven beg Ezra to plead the case of the sinners whose punishments he has recently witnessed. Ezra does intercede on their behalf, but is assured by God that they are receiving "according to their works" (vs. 61), just as the elect, who made good confession, who were penitent, who gave alms freely (vss. 26, 64), receive theirs, i.e. "eternal rest" in the kingdom of heaven (vss. 64, 66).

Texts

The Vision of Ezra is preserved in seven Latin manuscripts, which date from the eleventh

---

[1] Cf. vss. 10 (the Lord's day); 37–39 (Herod and the slaughter of the infants in Bethlehem); and the numerous allusions to the NT noted in the margins (see also "Relation to canonical books").

[2] E.g. ApPet, ApVirg, ApJohn, ApPaul (VisPaul). Cf. "Relation to apocryphal books."

[3] Cf. "Relation to apocryphal books."

to the thirteenth centuries. While at least three of these may be considered major witnesses, the present translation is based upon a manuscript preserved in the Vatican Library, Vat. lat. 3838, fols. 59ᵃ–61ᵃ (12th cent.; referred to below as V).[4] This text is to be preferred because its language is closer to the earlier, classical Latin than any of the other manuscripts, which suffer from numerous vulgarities of language, syntax, and spelling common to the medieval period. They also are interpolated at five points in the narrative. At least one of these interpolations could not have been possible before the late sixth century, which rules out any claim that the manuscripts in which it appears represent the original form of the document.[5]

The second and third major witnesses both represent this longer, interpolated tradition. Their alternate readings and additions are included in the notes to the translation. The first of these witnesses is a twelfth-century manuscript from Heiligenkreuz, Austria, Codex 11, fols. 272ᵇ–73ᵃ (referred to below as H).[6] The second witness to the longer traditions is MS AI/6 (Hs 1) from the Bibliothek des Priesterseminars in Linz, Austria (11th cent.; referred to as L below).[7] Manuscript L is distinct from the remainder of the manuscripts in that Ezra speaks in the first person.[8]

In addition to the above, O. Wahl has recently discovered in Austria four new manuscripts that contain the Vision of Ezra: (1) Klosterneuburg, Stiftsbibliothek, Codex 714, fols. 139ᵇᵃ–41ᵇᵃ (12th cent.; referred to below as K); (2) Lilienfeld, Stiftsbibliothek, Codex 145, fols. 70ᵃᵃ–70ᵇᵇ (13th cent.; referred to below as Lf); (3) Melk, Stiftsbibliothek, Codex 310.F.8, fols. 208ᵇ–9ᵇ (13th cent.; referred to below as M); and (4) Lilienfeld, Stiftsbibliothek, Codex 134 Klein-Maria-Zell, fols. 109ᵃᵇ–10ᵃᵃ (13th cent.; referred to below as Z).[9]

These manuscripts contain innumerable textual variants, few of which significantly alter the sense of the three major witnesses. The variants are primarily spelling differences, word omissions and transpositions, and minor additions.[10]

Original language

There is almost unanimous agreement that the extant Latin of the Vision of Ezra is a translation from an earlier Greek tradition.[11] Two points favor this conclusion: (1) the tangible literary kinship with the Greek Apocalypse of Ezra (see the contribution by M. E. Stone herein) and the Apocalypse of Sedrach (see the contribution by S. Agourides herein), both extant in Greek;[12] and (2) variations within the witnesses to the Vision itself, which are most easily explained as variant translations of a Greek original. The following may be adduced as examples: (1) verse 2, V: *portaverunt*, "they carried"; L: *levaverunt*, "they lifted"; (2) verse 4, L, V: *tangebat*, "it touched"; Lf: *nocuit*, "it injured"; (3) verse 10, V: *peccaverunt*, "they sinned"; L: *manserunt*, "they remained"; (4) verse 13, V: *flagellis*, "with scourges"; L: *vectibus*, "with bars"; (5) verse 14, V: *nolite parcere*, "refuse to have mercy"; L: *non parcite*, "do not have mercy"; (6) verse 23, V: *fluctuabat*, "it was roiling"; L: *inundabat*, "it was overflowing"; (7) verse 26, V: *faciebant*, "were making"; L: *proficiebant*, "were offering"; (8) verse 28, V: *miserere*, "have pity"; L: *parce*, "have mercy"; (9) verse 31, V: *elemosinam non fecerunt*, "they did not give alms"; L: *elemosinas nullas fecerunt*, "they gave no alms"; (10) verse 34, V: *immortalem*, "immortal"; L: *inexstinguibilem*, "inextinguishable"; (11) verse 35, V: *quasi*, "like"; L: *sicut*, "as"; (12) verse 37, V: *hominem*, "person"; L: *virum*, "man"; (13) verse 38, V: *per multa temporum*, "for a long time"; L: *multum tempus annorum*, "for many years"; (14) verse 44, V: *violaverunt*, "they violated"; L: *disruperunt*, "they disrupted"; (15) verse 49, V: *laedebant*, "they wounded";

---

[4] G. Mercati, *Note di letteratura biblica e cristiana antica*, pp. 70–73.

[5] Cf. the arguments of P. Dinzelbacher, "Die Vision Alberichs und die Esdras-Apokryphe," *Studien und Mitteilungen zur Geschichte des Benediktiner-Ordens* 87 (1976) 435–42 and n. 2. For the view that the longer text is the more original, cf. O. Wahl, "Vier neue Textzeugen der Visio Beati Esdrae," *Salesianum* 40 (1978) 583–89.

[6] A. Mussafia, "Sulla visione di Tundalo," *Sitzungsberichte d. phil.-hist. Klasse d. Kaiserl. Akademie d. Wissenschaften* 67 (1871) 157–206.

[7] O. Wahl, *Apocalypsis Esdrae—Apocalypsis Sedrach—Visio beati Esdrae*, pp. 49–61.

[8] But cf. vss. 1, 11, 15, 30, 36, 38, 39, 65, where the third person form *is* found; this inconsistency points to the secondary nature of this MS.

[9] Wahl, *Salesianum* 40 (1978) 584.

[10] Ibid., 587–89.

[11] Cf. Mercati, *Note*, p. 67; and Wahl, *Salesianum* 40 (1978) 586f.

[12] Cf. "Relation to apocryphal books."

L: *laeserunt,* "they injured"; (16) verse 53, V: *accusabant,* "they accused"; L: *interpellant,* "they accosted"; (17) verse 58, V: *duxerunt,* "they led"; L: *deposuerunt,* "they brought"; (18) verse 65, V: *intrent in,* "they enter in"; L: *acceperunt,* "they receive"; (19) verse 66, V: *fecerit,* "he performed"; L: *servierit,* "he served." While none of these examples could carry the weight of the hypothesis of a Greek original on its own, collectively they are capable of bearing such weight.

O. Wahl has also noted a few verses that he claims represent Semitisms, most notably verse 7 (cf. also vss. 17, 21): *bonum desiderium desideraverunt,* "they desired a good desire."[13] Wahl makes no explicit claims that these few examples represent evidence for a Semitic original, yet his mention of them implies that the possibility might be entertained. Such a possibility is doubtful for two reasons: (1) the previously mentioned literary relationships to works known only in Greek, and (2) the likelihood that phrases like *desiderium desideraverunt* may be biblicisms or "Vulgatisms" (cf. Ps 115:14) rather than Semitisms.

Date and provenance

There are no historical allusions in the Vision of Ezra that would yield an approximate date for the work. Given the numerous allusions to the New Testament, especially the Herod episode (vss. 37–39), the earliest possible date would be the late first century A.D. That a medieval work, the Vision of Alberich, is literarily dependent both on the shorter (MS V) and the longer versions of the Vision (MSS H and L), which would mean that they had to be available prior to A.D. 1111, the latest possible date would be the early twelfth century (even earlier if the eleventh-century date of MS L is accurate).[14] The upper limit may be reduced slightly to allow time for the original to circulate in translation before being interpolated. This seems especially applicable here, as the Latin translations witness to both a longer and a shorter tradition. The lower limit may be raised for two reasons: (1) the Vision lacks many features of classical intertestamental apocalyptic works such as 4 Ezra and 2 Baruch; its features are derivative, not originative; (2) the Vision shares features, such as the "hanging" punishments and the journey through the underworld, with many New Testament apocrypha. While no literary dependence need be postulated, the Vision certainly shares the *Zeitgeist,* "ethos," of their era, the third and fourth centuries A.D. For these reasons, the Greek original of the Vision of Ezra, whose Latin translations assured it an important role in later medieval literature, should probably be dated from A.D. 350–600.

Apocalyptic works, especially those that do not recount history and do not have other historical allusions, are nearly impossible to locate geographically and culturally. All that may be said in the case of the Vision of Ezra is that it is a Christian document of unknown origin circulated in medieval times in the West.[15]

Historical and theological importance

It is a commonly held notion that, by the beginning of the second century A.D., apocalypticism had died out in Christianity. As the early Church attempted to come to grips with the continued delay of the Parousia (the second coming of Christ), with waning hopes for an imminent end of history, and with the implications this realization had for a longer-than-anticipated institutional life, the apocalyptic tradition, it is argued, a tradition inherited from Judaism and incorporated into the very fabric of the Church's daily existence, its worship and its authoritative writings, was largely abandoned.[16]

As recent studies have shown,[17] such an opinion cannot be maintained. While apocalyptic expectations underwent numerous transformations, both in content and in the manner in

---

[13] Wahl, *Salesianum* 40 (1978) 586.

[14] Dinzelbacher, *Studien* 87 (1976) 440.

[15] Ibid., 435–42.

[16] B. McGinn, in *Visions of the End: Apocalyptic Traditions in the Middle Ages* (New York, 1979) p. 16, quotes M. Werner as the foremost proponent of this view: "The delay of the Parousia of Jesus, which after his Death became increasingly obvious, must, in view of the non-fulfillment of the eschatological expectation, have grown into a problem which was conducive to the transformation of the original eschatological doctrine." See Werner, *The Formation of Christian Dogma* (New York, 1957) p. 22.

[17] E.g. J. Pelikan, *The Emergence of the Catholic Tradition, 100–600* (Chicago, 1971) pp. 123–32; N. Cohn, *The Pursuit of the Millennium,* rev. ed. (New York, 1970); and McGinn, *Visions.*

which those expectations were given expression, apocalypticism remained a vital component of the Catholic faith not only in the patristic period but throughout the Middle Ages as well. In the second through the fourth centuries A.D., those hopes were preserved and fostered by such writers as Irenaeus, Commodian, and Lactantius. Even those early Church Fathers who were opposed to overt apocalypticism—Eusebius, Jerome, Augustine, and Tyconius—witnessed to its resiliency, and often served as sources of information for later medieval views with which they would have found little sympathy.

B. McGinn[18] has noted that classical apocalypticism had twin offspring. On the one hand, a visionary literature was produced which increasingly centered on the fate of the individual soul, on the personal afterlife, with a detailed account of the pains of hell and the joys of heaven. Although such visions could exhibit the common eschatological pattern of crisis, judgment and salvation, and include speculation about the career of the Antichrist, interest in history as a unitary structure was not strong. On the other hand, there also existed a variety of texts more closely linked to apocalyptic proper which evinced explicit historical concerns, especially a view of the present as a moment of supreme crisis, and a fervent hope of an imminent judgment that would vindicate the just. Texts of the latter sort frequently, though not invariably, incorporated concern with the structure of history, usually in terms of a theory of world ages.

The Vision of Ezra can best be understood as belonging to the first of McGinn's categories, to that visionary literature which laid stress on the personal afterlife. Unlike the Greek Apocalypse of Ezra, to which it is clearly related, the Vision of Ezra makes no mention of the Antichrist. Christ himself is referred to only obliquely (vss. 38, 46). There is no concern for the number and duration of the ages of the world or with Christ's thousand-year reign (Rev 20:4–6). Nor does the document address itself to an impending eschatological crisis. Rather, the primary concern of the Vision of Ezra is the punishment of sinners, the contrast between their torments and the beatitude of the just. The punishments and rewards in the afterlife correspond directly to the sin(s) or good deed(s) wrought on this side of the grave. Moreover, God's judgment of the sinners is unimpeachable. When Ezra bewails humanity's fate before God, God thunders back with the central theme of the Vision: "In my image I have formed man and I have commanded that they not sin, and they sinned. Therefore they are in torments" (vs. 63; cf. GkApEzra 5:12–19; ApSedr 4).

How does such a vision function in the life of a community? Sociologists are inclined to view millenarian movements as agents of social change, as prepolitical phenomena, at times as protorevolutionary ones. The literature they produce functions, then, as a critique of social, political, and economic institutions. But if the Vision of Ezra is not a millenarian text, as we have argued above, then the sociological stereotypes used to characterize such literature probably will not apply. McGinn has correctly observed that apocalypticism is broader than either millenarianism or messianism, and its literature can have more than one function.[19] Though he does not discuss this document, the Vision of Ezra aptly illustrates McGinn's point. By correlating as it does the punishments and rewards in the afterlife with actions committed in the earthly sphere, the Vision confronts us with an apocalyptic tradition intended to support and recommend the existing values and mores espoused by the institutional Church. The Church of the seer, opposing reprobates within and without, will not compromise its long-held demands of almsgiving, fidelity in marriage, confession, hospitality, chastity, right teaching, the just use of power, and respect of parents. Rather, by means of the Vision, those values receive divine imprimatur, eternal validation. The elect who "go into eternal rest" do so on account of "confession, penitence, and largesse in almsgiving" (vs. 64), by maintaining the Church's ethical norms. To do otherwise is to "sin" (vs. 63) and "enter into judgment" (vs. 65).

Relation to canonical books

Beyond the name, Ezra, the Vision displays no contact with the canonical books of the Old Testament. Mercati also claimed that there were practically no New Testament references

---

[18] McGinn, *Visions*, pp. 14f.
[19] Ibid., pp. 28–36. McGinn's critique and corrective of Cohn's analysis of medieval millenarian movements and those of other anthropologists who study millenarianism in primitive societies are trenchant. We are indebted to him for the remarks that follow.

or allusions in the Vision.[20] M. E. Stone (see contribution herein) has rightly noted that there are indeed some references to the New Testament discernible in the text. He cites the description of Herod's slaughter of the infants (vs. 38 = Mt 2:16–18) as a clear example. It may be that, in this instance, the Vision is relying more on the Greek Apocalypse of Ezra (4:9–12), which also mentions Herod in this context, than on the New Testament directly. The emphasis placed on largesse in almsgiving (vss. 7, 26, 31, 64) probably derives from injunctions in Matthew 6:2–4, but especially in Acts 9:36, 10:2, and 24:17. The doctors of the Law in verse 46, "who were teaching with words, but they did not spur on to work," bear resemblance to the scribes and Pharisees in Matthew 23:1–7, "who sit on Moses' seat," who "preach but do not practice." In verse 57b of manuscript H, "those who altered the last things and spoke false testimony" suffer the sort of fate Revelation 22:19 promises for the "one who takes away from the words of the book of this prophecy." Other allusions are noted in the margins and in the notes to the text.

Relation to apocryphal books

The strongest and most consistent links with any other apocryphal works occur between the Vision and the other literature of the Ezra cycle: 4 Ezra, the Greek Apocalypse of Ezra, the Questions of Ezra, and the Apocalypse of Sedrach.[21] But even these links, with one notable exception, are not close enough to postulate any theory of literary dependence one way or the other. They all share in the *Zeitgeist* of the collapse of classical apocalyptic during the fall of the Roman Empire. All share, to varying degrees, the pessimism of their progenitor, 4 Ezra, and are built around the figure of Ezra and his complaints against God. These complaints are somewhat muted in the Vision of Ezra. There is really only one complaint in the Vision of Ezra (paralleled in the Greek Apocalypse of Ezra): that the animals are better off than humans because they are not required to praise God yet do no sin (vs. 62).

The one episode in the Vision of Ezra that is closely paralleled in the Greek Apocalypse of Ezra is the scene in which Herod is seated upon a throne and being tortured (VisEzra 37–39; GkApEzra 4:9–12). In this one instance literary dependence could be posited, but the brevity and singleness of this example, coupled with the elusiveness of establishing dates for the two documents, leave the question open as to which document served as the source for the other.[22]

Numerous other parallels exist between the Vision and the Greek Apocalypse of Ezra (especially 4:5–5:6), but, again, these are general in nature and preclude any attempt to establish priority. The situation in this regard is further complicated by the parallels all the Ezra literature displays with the New Testament apocryphal works (ApPet, ApPaul, ApVirg, VisPaul). The common features include the journey through hell and heaven and the "hanging" punishments of the sinners in hell (cf. the marginal references). It is unlikely that any theory of literary dependence would account for the similarities; often individual sins and their punishments occur in different combinations in all the documents.

Cultural importance

It has been noted repeatedly that Dante Alighieri's *Divine Comedy*, the supreme literary creation of the Middle Ages, bears striking resemblance to the apocalyptic literature of its own and earlier centuries. What were the sources for Dante's compelling vision of *inferno, purgatorio,* and *paradiso*? Surprisingly, the Vision of Ezra may be put forward. P. Dinzelbacher has recently demonstrated that the medieval Vision of Alberich, a treatise recognized by Dante scholars since its publication in the early nineteenth century as a sure source and inspiration for Dante, had itself relied on both shorter and longer recensions of the Vision of Ezra.[23]

---

[20] Mercati, *Note*, p. 66.

[21] Cf. Müller, "Die Griechische Esra-Apokalypse," *JSHRZ* 5.2 (1976) 88; Wahl, *Apocalypsis Esdrae*, pp. 2–7. For a general survey of extant Ezra literature, cf. R. A. Kraft, " 'Ezra' Materials in Judaism and Christianity," *ANRW* II.19.1 (1979) 119–36.

[22] Mercati, *Note*, pp. 65–68, has suggested that VisEzra may be older than the GkApEzra and ApSedr. This opinion has been generally disregarded by most modern scholars. Cf. Wahl, *Apocalypsis Esdrae*, p. 8.

[23] Dinzelbacher, *Studien* 87 (1976) 435–42. For a discussion of vision literature in the medieval period, see Dinzelbacher, *Vision und Visionliteratur im Mittelalter* (Monographien zur Geschichte des Mittelalters 23, Stuttgart, 1981).

SELECT BIBLIOGRAPHY

Charlesworth, *PMR*, p. 119.
Denis, *Introduction*, p. 93.

Dinzelbacher, P. "Die Vision Alberichs und die Esdras-Apokryphe," *Studien und Mitteilungen zur Geschichte des Benediktiner-Ordens* 87 (1976) 435–42.
Mercati, G. *Note di letteratura biblica e cristiana antica.* Studi e Testi 5; Rome, 1901; pp. 61–73.
Mussafia, A. "Sulla visione di Tundalo," *Sitzungsberichte d. phil.-hist. Klasse d. Kaiserl. Akademie d. Wissenschaften* 67 (1871) 157–206.
Wahl, O., ed. *Apocalypsis Esdrae—Apocalypsis Sedrach—Visio beati Esdrae.* PVTG 4; Leiden, 1977.
———. "Vier neue Textzeugen der Visio Beati Esdrae," *Salesianum* 40 (1978) 583–89.

VISION OF THE BLESSED EZRA

1 Ezra[a] prayed to the Lord, saying, "Grant me courage, O Lord, that I might not
2 fear when I see the judgments[b] of the sinners." • And there were granted to him[c]
 seven angels of hell[d] who carried[e] him beyond the seventieth grade in the infernal
3 regions. • And he saw[f] fiery gates,[g] and at these gates he saw two lions lying there
 from whose mouth and nostrils[h] and eyes proceeded the most powerful flames.
4 The most powerful[i] men were entering[j] and passing through the fire, and it did
5,6 not touch[k] them. • And Ezra[l] said, "Who are they, who advance so safely?"[m] • The
 angels said to him,[n] "They are the just[o] whose repute has ascended to heaven,
7 who gave alms generously, clothed[p] the naked, and desired a good desire."
8 And others[q] were entering[r] that they might pass through the gates, and dogs[s]
9 were ripping them apart[t] and fire was consuming them.[u] • And Ezra[v] said,[w] "Who
10 are they?"[x] The angels said,[y] • "They denied the Lord[z] and sinned[a2] with women
11 on the Lord's Day."[b2] • And Ezra[c2] said, "Lord, have mercy on the sinners!"
12 And they led him lower beyond the fiftieth[d2] grade, and he saw in that place
13 men standing in torments.[e2] • Some[f2] were throwing fire in their faces;[g2] others,
14 however, were whipping them with fiery scourges.[h2] • And the earth cried aloud,[i2]
 saying, "Whip them and refuse to have mercy[j2] on them, because they worked
15 impiety upon me." • And Ezra said,[k2] "Who are they, who are in such torments
16,17 daily?" • The angels said,[l2] 'They dwelled with married women; • the married
 women are those who adorned themselves not for their husbands, but that they
18 might please others, desiring an evil desire.'"[m2] • Ezra said,[n2] "Lord, have mercy
 on the sinners!"

27,40
TAb 13.11
ApPaul 16

v. 5,6
Acts 9:36; 10:2;
24:17
Mt 6:2f.
2En 42:8

Mt 25:36
Jas 2:15f.
Ps 105:14

Rev 14:4
18,20,22,33,42,
47,55,61
GkApEzra 1:15,
5:6
v. 12
GkApEzra 4:18

ApPet 32
VisPaul (Syr.) 6

v. 16,17
GkApEzra 4:24
VisPaul 38f.
ApPet 23
TAb B 12:2
11,20,22,33,42,
47,55,61
GkApEzra 1:15;
5:6

a. L: "When the blessed Ezra."

b. L: "all the judgments."

c. H K M Lf V; omitted in Z L.

d. Cf. ApPaul 16, 18: angelo tartarucho, qui prepositus est penis, "the angel Tartaruchus that is set over the torments." This similarity probably does not represent anything more than a shared Zeitgeist; the parallels here are general in nature and do not give reason to suspect literary dependence. In fact, both works may have no relation to one another; the phrase may be derived from earlier works such as TAb.

e. V H K M Z Lf: portaverunt; L: levaverunt, "lift, elevate, support." This variation suggests a Gk. Vorlage pherō, "to bear, lift, carry."

f. L: vidi, "I saw." The major difference between L and the rest of the MSS is the first-person presentation; but even L is inconsistent in its usage (cf. vss. 1, 8a, 11, 15, 30, 36, 38, 39, 65).

g. L adds ingrediebatur per flammam eius, et LXX duos pedes foras portam, "He was entering through this flame, and 72 foot-soldiers outside the gate."

h. L: auribus, "ears."

i. L: magni, "great."

j. L adds per se, "by themselves."

k. L V: tangebat (H K M Z: tetigit); Lf: nocuit, "to hurt, injure, harm."

l. L: "And I asked the angels who were leading me."

m. L: cum tanto gaudio, "with such great joy."

n. L: mihi, 'to me.' Cf. n. f.

o. H omits iusti, "the just."

p. L K M add et calciaverunt, "and shod."

q. L: "other men."

r. L adds per se, "by themselves."

s. V obscure: eanes; read with H K M Z L: canes. Mercati (p. 70), unaware of the existence

of other MSS of VisEzra, proposed leones (cf. vs. 3).

t. H K M Z V Lf: a canibus laniabantur, "and they were being mangled by dogs."

u. H K M Z V Lf: ab igne comburebantur, "they were being consumed by the fire"; L omits the clause. H L add, following vs. 8, "And Ezra said [L: "And the blessed Ezra was saying to the Lord"], 'Lord, have mercy on the sinners!' And he did not have pity on them." Cf. 2Pet 2:4.

v. H omits "Ezra."

w. L: "And I asked the angels who were leading me." Cf. n. 1.

x. H L K M Z add "who are in such pain and such torment"; Lf: "who are in such torments."

y. L adds mihi, "to me." Cf. n. n.

z. So V; H: deum, "God."

a2. V H L^corr: peccaverunt; L: manserunt, "remained."

b2. L H add ante missam, "before the Mass." L also adds "and for that reason they are in such torment."

c2. L: "Blessed Ezra."

d2. H K M Z V Lf: "forty."

e2. L: "And they bore me downward toward a grade in the infernal regions, and I saw (people) being thrown downward."

f2. L H add angeli, "of the angels."

g2. L: "Some of the angels were ministering."

h2. V: flagellis; L: vectibus, "with bars."

i2. L: "And the earth interrupted."

j2. V: nolite parcere; L H: non parcite, "do not have mercy."

k2. L: "And the blessed Ezra asked the angels."

l2. L: "And they said to me."

m2. Lat.: malum desiderium desiderantes. Cf. Ps 105:14 in the Vulgate and vs. 7.

n2. L: "And I said."

19 And again they brought him to the south,[o2] and he saw a fire, and poor ones and
20 also women hanging,[p2] and angels[q2] were whipping them with fiery clubs.[r2] •And
21 Ezra said, "Lord, have mercy on the sinners![s2] Who are they?" •And the angels
22 said, "They dwelled with their mothers, desiring an evil desire." •And Ezra
said,[t2] "Lord, have mercy on the sinners!"

23 And they led (him)[u2] downward in the infernal regions,[v2] and he saw a caldron[w2]
in which were[x2] sulfur and bitumen, and it was roiling[y2] just like the waves of the
24 sea. •And the just were entering,[z2] and in the midst of it they were walking over
the fiery waves, praising greatly the name of the Lord, just like those who walk
25 over dew or cold water.[a3] •And Ezra said,[b3] "Who are they?"[c3] The angels said,[d3]
26 "They are the ones who daily were making[e3] better confession before God and
27 the holy priests, freely bringing alms[f3] (and) resisting sins."[g3] •And the sinners
came, wishing to pass over, and the angels of hell came and submerged them in
28 the fiery stream.[h3] •And from the fire they cried out, saying, "Lord, have pity[i3]
29 on us!" But he did not have pity.[j3] •A voice was heard, but a body was not seen
30,31 because of the fire and the anguish. •And Ezra said,[k3] "Who are they?" •The
angels said,[l3] "They were brought down by lust all their days;[m3] they did not
32 receive strangers;[n3] they did not give alms;[o3] •they took unjustly the things of
others for themselves;[p3] they had an evil desire; therefore, they are in anguish."[q3]
33 And Ezra said,[r3] "Lord, have mercy on the sinners!"

34 And he walked as before and he saw[s3] in an obscure place an immortal[t3] worm,
35 its magnitude he was not able to reckon.[u3] •And in front of its mouth stood many[v3]
sinners, and when it drew in a breath, like[w3] flies they entered into its mouth; then,
36 when it exhaled, they all exited a different color. •And Ezra said,[x3] "Who are
they?" And they said,[y3] "They were full of every bad thing and they went about
without confession or penitence."[z3]

GkApEzra 4:22-24

11,18,22,33,42, 47,55,61
GkApEzra 1:15; 5:6
11,18,20,33,42, 47,55,61
GkApErza 1:15; 5:6

GkApEzra 4:13-18 1,40
GkApEzra 1:8
VisPaul 32

VisPaul 40

11,18,20,22,42, 47,55,61
GkApEzra 1:15; 5:6

GkApEzra 4:21
ApJohn
Mk 9:48
Isa 66:24
ApPaul 12
ApPet 24,26
VisPaul 42

o2. "And they bore me downward and brought me to the south."

p2. L: "And I saw poor people hanging over the fire, (both) women and men"; H K M Z: "And he saw men and women hanging in a fire."

q2. H: *quattuor*, "four"; L: *quaterni*, "four at a time."

r2. V: *fustibus;* H: *vectibus*, "with clubs"; L omits last prepositional phrase.

s2. H L omit.

t2. L: "And I said."

u2. V omits; H supplies.

v2. V: *Et assumpserunt me deorsum II quingentos gradus*, "And they took me downward II five-hundredth grades."

w2. L adds "and large, the height of it was 200 cubits."

x2. L H add *ardebat*, "were burning."

y2. V: *fluctuabat*, L: *inundabat*, "overflowing."

z2. V: *veniebant;* L H: *venerunt*, "entered."

a3. L omits "or cold water."

b3. H omits "Ezra"; L: "And I asked the angels."

c3. L adds "who proceed in such joy?"

d3. L adds *mihi*, "to me."

e3. V: *faciebant;* H: *proficiebant*, "were offering."

f3. H adds "freely."

g3. Vs. 26 in L reads "Those are the ones who gave alms generously and clothed the naked" (cf. vs. 7).

h3. Vs. 27 in L reads "And the sinners came; and they made them heavy, so that they who did not wish to sink might sink. They were pressing them down with fiery yokes on their necks."

i3. V H: *miserere;* L: *parce*, "have mercy." Cf. the refrain of Ezra which L connects with the sinners' plea in this vs.

j3. H K M Lf add *eis*, "on them."

k3. L: "And the blessed Ezra said to the angels." Cf. n. f.

l3. L: "And they said to me."

m3. L: "Those were in lust and ravishing all the days of their lives."

n3. H L add *et hospites*, "and sojourners."

o3. V H: *elemosinam non fecerunt;* L: *elemosinas nullas fecerunt*, "they gave no alms."

p3. L reverses the order of the clauses in this vs.; the transposition does not significantly alter the sense.

q3. L adds *dimersi*, "plunged."

r3. L omits the beginning of this vs.

s3. L: "And I walked and I saw."

t3. V: *immortalem;* L H: *inexstinguibilem*, "inextinguishable."

u3. L: "Its length and height I was not able to reckon, at least seventy cubits."

v3. L adds *milia*, "thousands."

w3. V: *quasi;* L: *sicut*, "as, just like."

x3. L: "And the blessed Ezra said to the angels"; H: "And Ezra said to the angels."

y3. L adds *mihi*, "to me."

z3. L omits the last clause. H K M Z Lf and L then add: "And I walked as before and I saw a fiery stream, (and) a great bridge was over it, its width able to accommodate equally seventy oxen. When the just were coming, they went across with joy and exultation. And truly, when the sinners were coming, the bridge shook itself into fragility like a string of thread. (And) they were falling into that river acknowledging their own sins, saying, 'Because we did every evil thing, for that reason we were delivered into this torment.' And they requested pity and not one of them received (it)." For a detailed discussion of this theme in medieval literature, cf. P. Dinzelbacher, *Studien und Mitteilungen* 87 (1976) 435–42; and idem, *Die Jenseitsbrücke im Mittelalter* (Ph.D. dissertation; Wien, 1973).

37   And[a4] he saw[b4] a person[c4] sitting on a fiery throne, and his counselors stood   GkApEzra 4:9-
around him in the fire, and they served him from the fire and out of every[d4] side.   12

38   And Ezra said,[e4] "Who is that?"[f4] And the angels said,[g4] "That man, whose name
is Herod, was king for a long time,[h4] who, in Bethlehem of Judea, slew[i4] the infant   Mt 2:16

39   males on account of the Lord."[j4] •And Ezra[k4] said, "Lord, judge a right   VisPaul 18
judgment!"[l4]   Jn 7:24

40   And he walked and saw[m4] men who were bound and the angels of hell were
41 pricking their eyes with thorns. •And Ezra said,[n4] "Who are they?" The angels
42 said,[o4] "They showed strange paths to those wandering." •Ezra said,[p4] "Lord, have   ApPet 33
43 mercy on the sinners!" •And he saw virgins with five-hundred-pound neck irons[q4]   v. 42
on, as if near death, coming[r4] to the west. And Ezra said, "Who are they?"   11,18,20,22,33,
   47,55,61
44,45 And the angels said,[s4] "They violated[t4] their virginity before marriage." •And   GkApEzra 1:15;
there was[u4] a multitude of old men, lying prostrate, and over them molten iron   5:6
   VisPaul 39
46 and lead were being poured.[v4] And he said, "Who are they?" •And the angels
said,[w4] "They are the doctors of the Law[x4] who confused baptism and the law of   Mt 23:1-3
the Lord, because they were teaching with words, but they did not spur on to
47 work;[y4] and in this they are judged."[z4] •And Ezra said,[a5] "Lord, have mercy on   11,18,20,22,33,
the sinners!"   42,55,61
   GkApEzra 1:15;
48   And he saw visions of a furnace, against the setting sun, burning with great   5:6
49 fire, into which were sent many kings and princes of this world;[b5] •and many
thousands of poor people were accusing[c5] them and saying, "They, through their
50 power, wounded[d5] us and dragged free men into servitude." •And he saw[e5] another   Rom 1:30
furnace, burning with pitch and sulfur,[f5] into which sons were cast who acted
wretchedly at the hands of their parents[g5] and caused injury by means of their   ApPet 23,25
51 mouth.[h5] •And he saw[i5] in a most obscure place another furnace burning, into   VisPaul 40
52 which many women[j5] were cast. And he said,[k5] "Who are they?"[l5] •And the
53 angels[m5] said, "They[n5] had sons in adultery and killed them." •And those little
ones themselves accused[o5] them, saying, "Lord, the souls which you gave to us

---

a4. L adds an introductory clause (cf. previous note): "And I walked as before." H also adds "And he walked farther." These introductory clauses form an inclusion with the beginning of the long addition cited in the previous note; this sort of literary device is commonly found at points where the text has been interpolated.

b4. L: "I saw."

c4. V: *hominem;* L H: *virum* (L: *bonum*), "man" (H), "good man" (L).

d4. V: *omni;* L H: *utraque,* "both sides."

e4. L: "And the blessed Ezra asked."

f4. "Who are they?" (cf. vss. 5, 9, 15, 20, 30, 36, 43, 45, 51, 54). The question is not exceptional inasmuch as it is regularly repeated throughout the VisEzra. It is not appropriate here, however, as the answer demonstrates. The singular of V is to be preferred.

g4. L adds *mihi,* "to me."

h4. V: *per multa temporum;* L: *multum tempus annorum,* "for many years."

i4. Read with L H: *interfecit;* V omits the verb.

j4. L reads instead "on account of the name of the Lord."

k4. L: "blessed Ezra."

l4. All MSS: *rectum iudicium iudicasti;* possibly a Semitism, but more likely a biblicism.

m4. L: "And I walked and I saw."

n4. L: "And I asked the angels."

o4. L: "And they said to me."

p4. L: "And I said."

q4. V H: *bogiis;* L: *pogines,* "neck irons." The text of this vs. is quite corrupt.

r4. L H add *clamando,* "crying out."

s4. L adds *mihi,* "to me."

t4. V: *violaverunt* (H: *violabant*); L: *disruperunt,* "disrupted."

u4. H: *vidit,* "he saw"; L: *vidi,* "I saw." V omits the verb.

v4. L reads "I went out as before and I saw a baptismal pool and the pushing of multitudes before that baptismal pool and many thousands were pouring molten iron and lead over them."

w4. L adds *mihi,* "to me."

x4. L adds "and the corrupters of God."

y4. L reads simply "who corrupted baptism."

z4. V: *et in hoc iudicantur;* L: *et ideo iudicantur,* "and for that reason they are judged."

a5. L: "And I said."

b5. L: "And I walked as before toward the setting sun, (and) I saw men descending into a burning furnace of fire where kings and princes were being sent."

c5. L reads "were standing and accosting."

d5. V: *laedebant;* L: *laeserunt,* "injured."

e5. L: "I saw there."

f5. L adds "and bitumen."

g5. V: *qui in parentes manus miserunt;* L: *qui in parentes manserunt,* "who dwelled with (their) parents."

h5. L H add "Also there were sent there those who denied God, and who did not give servants justice [H: "just recompense"]."

i5. L: "And I saw."

j5. V: *multae mulieres;* L: *multi,* "many (men)."

k5. L: "The blessed Ezra asked the angels."

l5. V: *istae;* L: *isti,* "they" (masculine).

m5. L: *dixerunt,* "they said."

n5. All MSS use the feminine *istae;* the feminine is consistently used in V.

o5. V: *accusabant;* L: *interpellant,* "accosted" (cf. n. c5).

54 these (women) took away.''[p5] •And he said,[q5] "Who are they?" And the angels
55 said,[r5] "They killed their sons."[s5] •And Ezra said,[t5] "Lord, have mercy on the
   sinners!''[u5]
56   Then Michael and Gabriel came and said to him,[v5] "Come into heaven!''[w5]
57 And Ezra said,[x5] "As my Lord lives, I may not come until I see[y5] every judgment
58 of sinners.''[z5] •And they led[a6] him downward into the infernal regions beyond the
   fourteenth level. And he saw[b6] lions and little dogs[c6] lying around fiery flames.
59 And the just came through them and they crossed over into Paradise. •And he saw
   many thousands of the just and their habitations were the most splendid of any
   time.[d6]
60   And after he saw this, he was lifted up into heaven, and he came to a multitude
   of angels, and they said to him, "Pray to the Lord for the sinners." And they put
61 him down within the sight of the Lord.[e6] •And he said,[f6] "Lord, have mercy on
   the sinners!" And the Lord said,[g6] "Ezra, let them receive according to their
62 works." •And Ezra said,[h6] "Lord, you have shown more clemency to the animals,[i6]
   which eat the grass and have not returned you praise, than to us; they die and have
63 no sin; however, you torture us, living and dead." •And the Lord said,[j6] "In my
   image I have formed man and I have commanded that they not sin and they sinned;
64 therefore they are in torments. •And the elect are those who go into eternal[k6] rest
65 on account of confession,[l6] penitence, and largesse in almsgiving." •And Ezra
   said,[m6] "Lord, what do the just do in order that they may not enter into[n6] judgment?"
66 And the Lord said to him, "(Just as) the servant who performed[o6] well for his
   master will receive liberty, so too (will) the just in the kingdom of heaven." Amen.

11,18,20,22,
33,42,47,61
GkApEzra 1:15;
5:6

GkApEzra 1:12

11,18,20,22,
33,42,47,55
GkApEzra 1:15;
5:6
GkApEzra 1:18
ApSedr 4
4Ezra 4:12;
7:62-68,116
GkApEzra
1:6,21f.; 5:9,14
2Bar 10:6
v. 62
VisPaul 15,42
QuesEzra 6(A),
3(B)
v. 63
GkApEzra 5:19
4Ezra 6:55;
7:11; 8:44
ApSedr 3

GkApEzra 1:14

p5. L H add "And I saw [H: "he saw"] other
women hanging in the fire and serpents were sucking
their breasts" (cf. GkApEzra 5:2).

q5. L: "And I said to the angels."

r5. L: "And they said to me."

s5. L H add "And they did not give suck to other
orphans."

t5. L: "And I said"; H: "and the blessed Ezra
said."

u5. L adds "And he did not have pity upon them"
(cf. vs. 28).

v5. L: "Then the angels, Michael and Gabriel,
came and said to me."

w5. L adds "so that we might make the Paschal
feast."

x5. L: "And I said."

y5. V: videam; L: videro, "I will see."

z5. L adds "And I walked as before and I saw the
beasts ripping them apart. And I said, 'Who are they?'
And the angels said to me, 'These are the ones who
altered the last things [Rev 22:18] and spoke false
testimony.'" H also adds this section, but follows
the third-person format of MS V over against the first
person of MS L.

a6. V: duxerunt; L: deposuerunt, "brought
down."

b6. L: "I saw."

c6. V: caniculos; L H: camelos, "camels."

d6. L adds "Here is light and joy and rejoicing
and salvation (Mt 13:42); (and those) who did good
things upon the earth; and there was no sorrow for
them; and heavenly manna nourished them because
they gave alms generously. Many are (here) who did
not give because they did not have any (thing) from
which to give (for) they have suffered on account of

poverty. The needy, because they did not have any
(alms) from which to give, said a good word; they
were more firm in piety than others who did many
good things. They praised the Lord who loved justice,
for the great alm which will be around him is acceptable." H adds similarly "Here is light, joy, and
health. And daily they have manna from heaven
because they gave alms generously on earth. And
many are here who did not give because they did not
have any (thing) from which to give. Nevertheless,
they also have a similar rest on account of the good
will which they had. And therefore they praise the
Lord, our God, who loved justice."

e6. Vs. 60 in MS L reads "And I saw all the
judgments of sinners; and Michael, Gabriel, (and)
Uriel came and pushed me into a flaming cloud and
lifted me above one heaven and they lifted me above
seven, and many thousands of angels came because
I saw God's judgment of sinners, asking, 'Beseech
the Lord on behalf of the sinners.' And they lifted
me into the seventieth heaven to the entrance of the
Lord, my God, (but) I have not merited to see another
heaven" (cf. GkApEzra 5:7-11).

f6. L: "And I said."

g6. L: ad me, "to me." Cf. the usual mihi, nn.
n, y, 12, d3, 13, y3, g4, o4, s4, w4, r5.

h6. L omits "And Ezra said."

i6. L: "You made it better for the animals than
for people."

j6. L omits "And the Lord said."

k6. L omits "eternal."

l6. L adds orationem, "prayer."

m6. L: "And the blessed Ezra asked."

n6. V: intrent; L: acceperunt, "receive."

o6. V: fecerit; L: servierit, "serves."

QUESTIONS OF EZRA

(Date Unknown)

A NEW TRANSLATION AND INTRODUCTION
BY M. E. STONE

The Questions of Ezra is a work that purports to relate a dialogue between the prophet Ezar and the angel of the Lord. The subject of the dialogue, which survived in two recensions, is the fate of the souls of men after death. The prophet asks about the fate of the righteous and sinners—the righteous are destined, he is told, for "great joy and eternal light" and the sinners for "the outer darkness and the eternal fire" (vs. 3). Next follows Ezra's question about the fate of the sinners and the fact that nearly all men are sinners. What will be the fate of the souls, he asks, immediately after death (vs. 10)? A page is missing from the manuscript of one recension at this point, but from the second it can be surmised that there followed a discussion of the purpose of creation and the temporary places of the sinners (they are imprisoned by demons in the lower atmosphere) and the righteous (they rise to the Divinity in the upper atmosphere). There follows a characterization of the seven steps up to the Divinity and of the guardians of the divine throne (vss. 19–30) abounding in vivid and bizarre descriptions. The freeing of the souls from the hands of Satan through expiatory prayers is then discussed and, in recension B, the document concludes with a prediction of the resurrection and final judgment.

Texts

The Questions of Ezra is extant in two textual forms. The first is that published by Yovsēpʻiancʻ in his edition of the Armenian apocrypha[1] and first translated into English by J. Issaverdens.[2] Yovsēpʻiancʻ based his edition on a single manuscript, a Maštocʻ (Ritual), manuscript number 570 of the Library of the Mechitarist Fathers in Venice.[3] The manuscript was written in A.D. 1208, and the Questions of Ezra occurs on folios 203r–206v.

In the present translation a second form of the Questions of Ezra is added to the published information. This is found in the Menologium (Lives of Saints) of the Armenian Church, in the fourth recension thereof, that was printed in Constantinople in 1730 (pp. 424–25).[4] This printed text was compared with that of a seventeenth-century manuscript in the Bodleian Library, Oxford (MS Marsh 438, vol. 3, fol. 402). No major differences were to be observed between these two witnesses.[5]

The Venice text is here given first as recension A and the Menologium text as recension B. B differs from A in several respects:

1. It is much shorter but, even where the texts are parallel, it contains a number of details not in the longer A text.

---

[1] S. Yovsēpʻiancʻ, *Uncanonical Books of the Old Testament*, pp. 300–3 [in Arm.].

[2] J. Issaverdens, *The Uncanonical Writings of the Old Testament*, pp. 505–9.

[3] B. Sargissian and S. Sargsian, *Grand Catalogue of the Armenian Manuscripts of the Mechitarist Library in Venice*, vol. 2 (Venice, 1966) pp. 55–66 (in Arm.).

[4] On the Armenian *Menologium*, see J. Mércérian, "Introduction à l'étude des synaxaires arméniens," *Bulletin arménologique* (Mélanges de l'Université de S. Joseph 40; Beirut, 1953).

[5] Clearly a broad collation of MSS might produce some significant variants. See Stone, *Sion* 52 (1978) 54–60, where the text is published.

2. It seems to preserve text in two places where there is a physical lacuna in A: following verse 10 of A and following verse 40 of A.

3. It lacks verses 11–30 of A.

Original language and date

There is insufficient evidence to determine whether the writing was originally composed in Armenian or whether it was translated into Armenian from another language. Possible arguments based on literary considerations will be adduced in the next section. There seems no clear basis for establishing the date except to say that the writing is a Christian composition clearly based on Jewish models. There is no indication of provenance.

Composition and literary affinities

The Questions of Ezra should be viewed in the context of the apocryphal Ezra literature. Its general inspiration derives clearly from 4 Ezra, which may also have provided certain patterns of the questions posed. (See the marginal notes to the translation.) The amount of verbal parallelism is very limited, however, and decisive evidence whether dependence is on the extant Armenian version or on the lost Greek version of 4 Ezra is unclear. The contacts between the two writings are shared general ideas and not direct parallels. Special note should be taken of the seven steps or ways of ascent of the souls in the Questions of Ezra A 19–21, and the similar material in 4 Ezra 7:81–98. Beyond this, however, the very dialogue style and the subject matter indicate the dependence on 4 Ezra.

The general resemblance to the Greek Apocalypse of Ezra is also quite striking; both writings center on questions about the fate of the souls and share the dialogue form. The Latin Vision of Ezra is another form of this writing. The third body of apocryphal Ezra material with which the Questions of Ezra should be related is the extensive expansionary passages found in the Armenian version of 4 Ezra. These passages are dialogues on various theological issues inserted into the dialogue of 4 Ezra.[6] Taken together, these writings constitute a fairly extensive body of literature, inspired by 4 Ezra and preserved in the Armenian tradition. (The apocryphal Ezra writings in various languages are discussed in the Introduction to GkApEzra.)

In a study of the Questions of Ezra published in Armenian in 1898, B. Sargissian pointed out certain parallels between it and two other Armenian texts, the Inquiries of St. Gregory the Illuminator and the Martyrdom of St. Kalistratos.[7] He published the chief parallels with these writings in his work. Both contain dialogues concerning the fate of the souls of men. Sargissian is of the opinion that the Inquiries of Gregory is later than the Questions of Ezra of which he knew only recension A, but that the Martyrdom of Kalistratos is an Armenian translation of an older Greek source that may also have served the Questions of Ezra.[8] Although the Martyrdom of Kalistratos contains closer verbal parallels to the Questions of Ezra than does the Inquiries of St. Gregory, it also has close parallels with this latter work. It is by no means certain, however, that this implies that it served as a source for the Questions of Ezra.[9] This is particularly so in view of the affinities of the latter with the Ezra literature noted above, as well as with the text of recension B.

Concerning the composition of the writing, Sargissian suggests that the section A 31–40 is a later addition to an older description of the heavens. Moreover, he considers this older description to have some features in common with Zoroastrianism. This theory requires reevaluation in view of the new information to be gained from recension B. On the basis

---

[6] See the publication of one such dialogue: M. E. Stone, "Some Features of the Armenian Version of IV Ezra," *Le Muséon* 79 (1966) 395–400. A translation based on an inadequate text may be found in Issaverdens, *Uncanonical Writings*, pp. 361–501. See now M. E. Stone, *The Armenian Version of IV Ezra* (Univ. of Pennsylvania Armenian Texts and Studies 1; Missoula, Mont., 1979).

[7] B. Sargissian, *Studies on the Uncanonical Writings of the Old Testament*, pp. 452–82 (in Arm.). The text of parts of the Inquiries of St. Gregory is on pp. 465–69; that of extracts from the Martyrdom of St. Kalistratos is on pp. 475–78. The latter may also be found in P. Awgerian, *Complete Lives and Martyrdoms of the Saints* (Venice, 1810–14) vol. 6, pp. 489–94 (in Arm.).

[8] Sargissian, *Studies*, pp. 469–77.

[9] The final resolution of these issues must await the full publication of the Arm. texts involved.

of a comparison of the two recensions it may be suggested that the cosmological description from verses 16 to 30 is derived from a separate source, although the supposed Zoroastrian features are not as striking as Sargissian thought. This section is not represented in B.

The comparison of A and B thus seems to imply that two source documents are involved. The first contained the dialogue between the prophet and the angel concerning the fate of the souls. It comprised six parts: (1) A 1–10; (2) the section upon which B 4 is based, which fell in the lacuna after verse A 10; (3) A 11–15; (4) the section upon which B 6 is based; (5) A 31–40; and (6) a section corresponding to B 10–14. The second document comprised the dialogue about the ascent of the soul corresponding to A 16–30. This section is distinctive in its views and contains a pastiche of ideas drawn from older sources.

This analysis would contradict the view of Sargissian referred to above, for it is clear that the discussion of the fate of the souls belonged in the same document as the indubitably Christian section dealing with the freeing of the souls from Satan. This means that the writing as extant is Christian; but it probably draws upon older sources. The point in its development at which the description of the ascent of the souls was combined with the dialogue about the fate of the righteous and the wicked is unclear. If recension B was based on a form of the text in which this section did not occur, then we must say that it was incorporated subsequently into the original composition. If, on the other hand, the epitomist of B simply left it out, as he did other isolated verses of A, then this material may go back to an older source utilized by the person who put the Questions of Ezra together in its present shape in recension A.

The forty-day period of repentance (A 32) appears in a somewhat different form in another of the documents associated with the pseudepigraphical Ezra literature, the Apocalypse of Sedrach 13–14. In that writing there is emphasis on prayer and service of God that in general resembles that in the Questions of Ezra. This may, however, reflect merely a common concern and a similar response of monastic piety to similar issues (see vss. 31ff., n. q). In the Introduction to the Greek Apocalypse of Ezra the relationship between the Ezra apocrypha is discussed.

Theological importance

The central issue of this document is the fate of the souls of men after death and at the end of time. This issue devolves naturally from certain assumptions about the nature of God as revealed in his dealings with men. On the first hand God requites the righteous and wicked after death for their actions. Emphasis is laid on the fact that this requital is just and fitting "and those things in which God finds man, by those is he judged" (B 4). Yet God's mercy is displayed; by means of prayer, repentance, and due memorial service, it is possible to gain release of the souls of men from the power of Satan who punishes them (A 31–36; B 9f.).

According to A 16–30, God is seated in the highest heaven, surrounded by angelic hosts, and his glory is such that sinful man in his weakness can only approach the throne of God; even the angels cannot see his face (A 24–26). The throne of God is situated opposite the garden (the heavenly paradise), and there is sublime light (A 21). He is surrounded by seraphim who sing the Trisagion to him perpetually (A 24), a picture derived ultimately, of course, from Isaiah, chapter 6.

Man is sinful and only the martyrs who died in tortures for the sake of God are seen to be righteous (A 7).

The details of the cosmological view of the document, based as it is on common hellenistic assumptions, have been set forth in the notes to A 16–20. There are seven heavenly spheres, the lower ones characterized by evil, negative traits, the upper ones by fiery, positive ones. Hell is in the third sphere. The soul of the righteous is led by an angel through these spheres until it reaches the presence of the Divinity. Apparently, in A 16, various fearsome and dangerous areas are described through which the soul passes with its angelic guide until it

---

[10] The idea that the souls of the wicked find no rest until judgment, but wander about, is found in 4Ezra 7:80. This may have provided an impetus in the tradition for the introduction of these concepts, but the views are by no means identical.

commences the ascent through the heavenly spheres. There is no suggestion of the inhabitants of the heavenly spheres beyond the list of the guardians around the divine throne (A 27–30).

On the other hand there are two quite distinctive angelological views that should be mentioned. The first is the idea of the good and evil angels who will come after death to take the souls of the righteous and the wicked, respectively. This idea bears a certain resemblance to Zoroastrianism, as pointed out in the note to A 15; however, clear parallels in older Jewish sources and some later Christian ones are also shown to exist, but the view, as it occurs here, is not to be found exactly in any other source. The other view touches on demonology. In the description of the intermediate state of the souls in B 6, it says that the souls of the righteous rise to the upper atmosphere, while those of the wicked are imprisoned in the lower atmosphere, held by demons. This idea is not found in the ancient Jewish sources and it seems to represent an adaptation of concepts of hellenistic religion in which the atmosphere is thought to be full of semidivine beings both good and bad, and according to which the soul of the righteous rises to the supralunar spheres. These ideas have been taken over and adapted to a description of the intermediate state of the souls, between death and resurrection. The punishment of the souls of the wicked in this intermediate state is then thought to be in the hands of demons or of Satan (A 31–33; B 12).[10]

This indicates that the dualistic views in which there is a contrast between angels and demons, corresponding to the contrast between the righteous and the sinners, are well established in this writing. What is not clear is the extent of cosmic dualism. At one level, there is a clear contrast of the earthly sphere and the heavenly spheres above it. At another, there is the expectation of an end-time, which suggests an opposition between this world and that to come, But neither of these views is developed as a dominant one in the document.

It is clear, from recension B in particular, that an end-time is expected, and that it is thought of in conventional terms. Gabriel will sound the trumpet, the souls will be reunited with the bodies, and the resurrected will pass in judgment before Christ at the time of his return (B 11–14). What is more distinctive is the view of the intermediate state, which includes the punishment of the souls of the wicked by demons in the atmosphere and the ascent of the souls of the righteous who will see the throne of God. The view of an intermediate state is derived, in general, from 4 Ezra, but here has received a special development.

Cultural importance

The Questions of Ezra is an interesting example of the development and Christianization of themes deriving from the great Jewish apocalypses of the period of the second Temple. The questions with which it deals, the fate of the souls of men and reward and punishment, are among those that have always aroused men to thought and speculation. This work is one of those developments that show the way in which various Christian churches developed and amplified themes of special interest to them.

BIBLIOGRAPHY

Charlesworth, *PMR*, pp. 117f.

TEXTS

Recension A

Yovsēpʿiancʿ, S. *Uncanonical Books of the Old Testament.* Venice, 1896; pp. 300–3. (In Arm.)

Recension B

Stone, M. E. "Two New Discoveries Concerning the Uncanonical Ezra Books," *Sion* 52 (1978) 54–60. (In Arm.)

TRANSLATION

Issaverdens, J. *The Uncanonical Writings of the Old Testament*. Venice, 1934^2; pp. 505–9.

STUDIES

Sargissian, B. *Studies on the Uncanonical Writings of the Old Testament*. Venice, 1898; pp. 452–84. (In Arm.)
Stone, M. E. "The Apocryphal Literature in the Armenian Tradition," *Proceedings of the Israel Academy of Sciences and Humanities* 4 (1971) 59–77, 371–72.

THE QUESTIONS OF THE PROPHET EZRA OF THE ANGEL OF THE LORD CONCERNING THE SOULS OF MEN

Recension A

What is the fate of the righteous and the sinners?

1 Ezra the prophet saw the angel of God and asked him one question after another.[a] B 1
2 And the angel approached him and said what will be at the consummation. •The 10, 4Ezra 7:75
prophet asked the angel and said, "What has God prepared for the righteous and
the sinners? And at the time at which the day of the end arrives, what will become
3 of them? Where do they go, to honor or to tortures?"[b] •The angel replied and said B 2; 4Ezra 7:38
to the prophet, "Great joy and eternal light have been prepared for the righteous GkApEzra 1:24
and for the sinners there have been prepared the outer darkness[c] and the eternal
4 fire." •The prophet said to the angel, "Lord, who of the living has not sinned 4Ezra 3:35
5 against God? •And if that is so, then blessed are the beasts and the birds who do GkApEzra 5:26
B 3; 4Ezra
6 not await resurrection and have not expected the end.[d] •If you will crown the 7:65ff.
righteous, who have endured all tortures, and the prophets and the martyrs when GkApEzra 1:21-
23
they were taking stones and with a hammer were pounding their faces until their GkApEzra 6:21
7 innards were seen, •they were tortured for your sake. Have mercy upon us sinners 31
who have been occupied and have been seized by Satan."[e]

The prophet rebuked

8 The angel replied and said, "If there is someone above you, do not talk with
9 him anymore, otherwise great evil will befall you." •The prophet said to the angel,
10 "Lord, I would speak a little more with you, reply to me! •When the day of the 2; 4Ezra 7:75
end arrives and he takes the soul, will he assign it to the place of punishment or
to the place of honor until the Parousia? [. . .]ᶠ"

The day of the endᵍ

11 The angel replied and said, "Do not wait until the day of the end, but like a
12 flying eagle hasten to do good deeds and mercy. •For that day is fearsome, urgent,
13 and exacting. It does not permit care of children or of possessions. •It comes and
arrives suddenly like someone merciless and impartial, it takes a captive unexpectedly, surely. Whether he weeps or mourns, it will have no mercy.

The good and evil angels

14 "But when the day of the end arrives, a good angel comes to the good soul and B 6
an evil one to the evil. Just as someone sent by the kings to doers of evil deeds

---

a. Lit. "matter by matter."

b. Here and in vs. 3 the reference appears to be
to final rewards and punishments. Yet vss. 14–17
perhaps refer to an intermediate state; see particularly B 6–8, 11–14. This seems to be further evident
from vs. 10.

c. See GkApEzra 4:38, n.

d. The form of this common expression here is
closer to 4Ezra 7:65ff. than the similar sentiment
as formulated in GkApEzra 1:21–23.

e. Compare the idea, expressed here in Christian
terms, with 4Ezra 8:26–28.

f. Following this vs., according to Sargissian in
Studies, p. 453, a page of MS has been lost. The
text contained by B 8 probably derives from the
missing section (see Introduction). The Parousia is
the second coming of Christ, expected to occur at
the end of days.

g. The idea of the impartiality of the day of
judgment expressed in vss. 11–13 is prominent in
4Ezra, but it is formulated there in different terms:
See 4Ezra 5:42; 7:33–35, 66, 102–15. There, moreover, intercessory prayer is denied as a possibility;
here vss. 31–40 are a paean of praise to it.

15 and good deeds recompenses good to the good and evil to the evil, •even in the   B 6
   same way a good angel comes to the good soul and an evil one to the evil.[h] Not
16 that the angel is evil, but each (man's) deeds (are evil).[i] •He takes the soul, brings
   it to the east; they pass through frost, through snow, through darkness, through
   hail, through ice, through storm, through hosts of Satan, through streams, through
   the winds of terrible rains, through terrible and astounding paths, through narrow
17 defiles, and through high mountains.[j] •O wondrous way, for one foot is behind the   4Ezra 7:7-8
18 other and before it are fiery rivers!'' •The prophet was amazed and said, "O, that
   wondrous and terrible way!''

The seven steps to the Divinity[k]

19   The angel said, "To that way there are seven camps and seven steps to the   4Ezra 7:81-99
20 Divinity, if I can make (someone) pass along it. •Because the first lodgings are   22,28
   bad and wondrous; the second fearsome and indescribable; the third hell and icy
   cold; the fourth quarrels and wars;[l] in the fifth, then, investigation—if he is just,
   he shines, and if he is a sinner, he is darkened; in the sixth, then, the soul of the
21 righteous man sparkles like the sun; •in the seventh, then, having brought (him)
   I make him approach the great throne of the Divinity, opposite the garden, facing
   the glory of God[m] where the sublime light is.''

h. ApPaul 11–16 describes groups of good and evil angels who receive the souls of the righteous and wicked men: Cf. 2Bar 51:1–6; TAb A 17, B 13. The idea of personification of a man's deeds in the form of two women occurs commonly in Zoroastrianism; see J. Duchesne-Guillemin, *La Religion de l'Iran ancien* (Paris, 1962) pp. 332f. This is not necessarily the direct source of the passage here. Other features of Iranian eschatology, notably the *Činvat* bridge of testing, are noticeably absent. Cf. the rather different story in Xenophon (*Memorabilia* 2.1.20ff.).

i. This observation may be compared with Armenian 4Ezra 8:62L, there emphasizing the essential goodness of creation: "That which was created for good, he did not use well and he (man) sinned. Not that I created anything evil, but everything which I created was very good; each thing which existed, existed for its own purpose, just as iron existed not that it might kill, but that it might work the ground and be of use to all."

j. This description apparently refers either to the first part of the ascent through the heavenly spheres (see vss. 20–21) or, more likely, to some preliminary stage. The east as the direction in which the soul is led should be contrasted with GkApEzra 5:21 (see also n.). There east is the direction of Paradise. In 1En 22:1 Sheol is in the west (cf. also 23:1), while the gardens of spices are in the east (chs. 28–32) and Paradise in the north (ch. 32). In 2En, hell is on the northern side. The presence of the meteorological phenomena in the lower heavens is commonplace, e.g. 2En 5; TLevi 3:2. With the list of phenomena in 2En 40:1–11, cf. 1En 34; 41:3f.

k. ApPaul 14, 16 relates how the angels lead the souls to the presence of God. The idea of seven steps of ascent to the Divinity (which correspond to seven heavens) is widely known. On the seven heavens, see H. Bietenhard, *Die himmlische Welt im Urchristentum und Spätjudentum* (WUNT 2; Tübingen, 1951) pp. 3–8, for the chief sources. The idea of the seven spheres that bear the planets and that form stages for the ascent of the soul is common in hellenistic thought, and these are sometimes described as the steps of a ladder; see the sources assembled by H. Lewy, *The Chaldean*

Oracles and Theurgy (Cairo, 1956) p. 413. The term "lodging" is not a common expression in this context but may perhaps be compared with "habitations" (used differently) in 4Ezra 7:80. The seven lodgings here are comparable with the seven "ways" or "orders" of the ascent of the soul after death in 4Ezra 7:80–98. Are the "lodgings" the same as the *mansiones* or "way stations" of Roman travel and route descriptions, such as the Peutinger Table?

l. In this description, the lower stages, apparently lower heavens, have a negative character. Such may also be observed in the description of the heavens, e.g. in 2En and 3Bar. Hell, in the sources that bear this character, is often in the third heaven, so 3Bar 4:1–6; 2En 10; TIsaac (*apud* G. H. Box, *Testament of Abraham* [London, 1927] pp. 67–70). The idea of hell's being associated with icy cold may be compared with TLevi 3:2; ApPaul 42. The description in this vs. is paralleled by that in vs. 22, which refers to terrors, quarrels and wars, burning heat. A similar series of terms also occurs in vs. 28—"quarrels, wars, burning heat''—but there it is preceded by "thunders, earthquakes." The "burning heat" of vss. 22 and 28 is not referred to in vs. 20, and the term may refer to the fiery environs of the Godhead; cf. Dan 7:9–10; 1En 14:19; 71:5–6; etc. Alternatively it might refer to hell, but then it would be in the wrong position in the series. The "thunder" and "earthquakes" of vs. 28 are not echoes of anything in either vs. 20 or vs. 22. The heavenly repositories of meteorological phenomena are widely known. Elements of this description may be drawn from 4Ezra 3:19, in which vs. God's descent on Sinai is described: "And your glory passed through the four gates of fire and earthquake and wind and ice." In the present text only "wind" is missing. Cf. also the order of elements in the list of revealed things in 2Bar 59:11—innumerable angels, flaming hosts, splendor of the lightnings, voice of thunders, chiefs of the angels, treasuries of light, etc.

m. The glory of God is also the climax of the ascent of the souls through the seven "ways" or "orders" according to 4Ezra 7:87, 98, and elsewhere.

God cannot be seen

22 The prophet said to the angel, "My lord, when you cause him to pass through 20,28
such terrors, through quarrels, through wars, through burning heat, why do you
not cause him to meet the Divinity, rather than causing him to approach only the
23 throne?" •The angel said to the prophet, "You are one of the foolish men and you 4Ezra 4:10-11
24 think according to human nature. •I am an angel and I perpetually serve God, and
I have not seen the face of God. How do you say that sinful man should be caused
25 to meet the Divinity? •For the Divinity is fearful and wondrous and who dares to
26 look toward the uncreated Divinity? •If a man should look he will melt like wax 30; 4Ezra 13:4
before the face of God: for the Divinity is fiery and wondrous. For such guardians ApSedr 2
stand around the throne of the Divinity.

Those around the divine throne

27 "There are stations, . . .,[n] hollows, fiery ones, girdle wearers, (and) lanterns.
28 At that place there are thunders, earthquakes, quarrels, wars, burning heat,[o] fire 20,22
29 wearers, flame-swarming ones, (and) fiery hosts. • Around him are incorporeal Isa 6:1-3
seraphim, six-winged cherubim: With two wings they cover their face, and with
two wings their feet, and flying with two, they cry, 'Holy, Holy, (Holy) Lord of
30 Hosts, the heaven and earth are full of your glory.'[p] •Such guardians stand around 26
the throne of the Divinity."

Freeing of the soul from Satan

31 The prophet asked the angel and said, "Lord, what will become of us, for we 7; B 7
are all sinners and seized in the hands of Satan? Now, by what means are we
32 delivered or who will bring us forth from his hands?" •The angel answered and B 8-9
said, "If someone remains after death, father or mother or brother or sister or son 4Ezra 7:102-5
1Cor 15:29
or daughter or any other Christian, and he offers prayers,[q] with fasts, for forty
33 days, there will be great rest and mercy through the sacrifice of Christ. •For Christ B 9
was sacrificed for our sake upon the cross and for six ages he delivered (our) soul LAE 44
34 from the hands of Satan. •How the soul is delivered through that offered reverently
35 by a priest, if he fulfills the forty days in such a way as is pleasing to God![r] For
forty days he will remain in the church not going in the public places, but from
36 time to time will recite the Psalms of David together with prayers. •It is this which
brings us forth from the hands of Satan. If not, give to the poor.

The nature of prayer

37 "For your prayers are thus: just as a farmer goes forth, comes to sow, and the Mt 13:22
shoot comes forth joyous and graceful and desires to produce numerous fruit, and ApSedr 13-14
thorn and weeds also come forth and choke (it) and do not let numerous fruit be

---

n. The Arm. word occurring at this point is
unknown and does not have a clear etymology.
Sargissian (*Studies*, pp. 470f.) suggests that the
word *manasruank'* derives from Avestan *manah*
+ *sravha*, apparently supposed to mean "beautiful
spirits." A forced Arm. etymology might be derived from the stem *man-*, "spin," and the word
sur, "sword," i.e. "those of spinning swords."
The rest of the strange terms in this vs. and in the
latter part of vs. 28 seem to refer to classes of
angels, but they are unparalleled in the descriptions
of the guardians of the divine throne. Sargissian
reports that the Inquiries of St. Gregory substitutes
the symbols of the Four Evangelists for the difficult
angelic names. Throughout vs. 27, the Armenian
reads lit. "these are hollow, these are fiery ones,"
etc. In vs. 28 it reads "these are earthquakes" and

similarly up to "burning heat." From "burning
heat" until the end of the vs. it reads "there are
fire wearers," etc. Note also that the word "heat"
is lit. plural in vs. 22 and vs. 28.
o. The words from "thunders" to "burning
heat" appear to be out of place. The list of beings
surrounding the throne of God is distorted by these
features that apparently appertain to the lower heavens; see vs. 20, n.
p. This vs. is almost a quotation of Isa 6:2–3,
adapted so as to fit the literary context.
q. On the prayer of the righteous man as efficacious in bringing repentance, see GkApEzra 5:10
commentary and ApPaul 44.
r. The original is highly confusing; thus, the
non-verbal sentence.

38 assembled.ˢ •Similarly, also you, when you go inside the church and desire to
   offer prayers before the Divinity, the cares of this world and the deceit of greatness
39 (wealth) come forth and choke you and do not let numerous fruit be sown. •For
   if your prayer were such as Moses wept for forty days and spoke with God mouth
40 to mouth, •likewise also Elijah was taken up to heaven in a fiery chariot, likewise
   Daniel also pray[ed] in the li[ons'] den [. . ."]

Ex 24:18
Num 12:8
Ex 33:11
v. 40
2Kgs 2:11f.
Dan 6

(See Recension B, 10–14.)

Recension B

1   He saw the angel of God and asked concerning the righteous and sinners when
2 they go forth from this world. •The angel said, "For the righteous there is light
3 and rest, eternal life, but for the sinners, unending tortures." •Ezra said, "If that
   is so, then blessed are the animals and the beasts of the field and the creeping
4 things and the birds of heaven who do not await resurrection and judgment." •The
   angel said, "You sin in saying this, for God has made everything for the sake of
   man and man for the sake of God. And those things in which God finds man, by
5 those is he judged." •Ezra said, "When you take the souls of men, where will
6 you bring them?" •The angel said, "I bring the souls of the righteous to worship
   God and establish them in the upper atmosphere, and the souls of the sinners are
7 seized by the demons who are imprisoned in the atmosphere." •And Ezra said,
8 "And when will the soul which is seized by Satan be delivered?" •The angel said,
   "When' the soul has someone as a good memorial in this world, (this) one releases
9 it from Satan through prayer and (acts of) mercy." •Ezra said, "By what means?"
   The angel said, "By prayer, by (acts of) mercy, and by sacrifices." (Ezra said)
10 "If the sinner's soul has no good memorial, which helps him, what will happen
11 to him?" •The angel said to him, "Such a one is in the hand of Satan until the
12 coming of Christ, when the trumpet of Gabriel sounds. •Then the souls are freed
13 from the hands of Satan and soar down from the atmosphere. •And they come and
   are united each with its body which had been returned to dust and which the sound
14 of the trumpet had built and aroused and renewed. •And it raises (it) up before
   Christ our God who comes to judge (those on) the earth, that is the righteous and
   the wicked, and requites each for his deeds."

A 1-2
A 3
A 5

A 14-15

A 31
A 32

A 32-33

13

11; Mt 24:31
1Cor 15:51f.
1Thes 4:16

   Through the petition of your divinely narrated prophets, have pity upon the
readers of this writing.

---

s. A similar problem as previous footnote: It is
impossible to clarify it with original text.
   t. Lit. "if the soul . . . who releases it . . ."

REVELATION OF EZRA

(prior to Ninth Century A.D.)

A NEW TRANSLATION AND INTRODUCTION
BY D. A. FIENSY

The Revelation of Ezra is a *kálandologion*,[1] or almanac describing the nature of the year depending on the day of the week on which the year begins. Natural conditions such as rainfall and drought, the severity of winter, and the abundance of crops can be predicted; while the fate of national rulers can also be foreseen.

Text

G. Mercati[2] edited three Latin manuscripts in 1901 that purported to be revelations of Ezra. His oldest manuscript (MS A),[3] which is translated here, was produced in the ninth century.[4]

Original language

There is no reason to conclude that this text is a translation. Grammatical and syntactical evidence is lacking for a Greek or Semitic original.[5] The original language, then, is probably Latin.

Date

The latest possible date for this text is the ninth century, since the earliest extant manuscript comes from that period. However, *kalandologia* were obviously composed prior to the ninth century and had become very popular by that time. Nicephorus (c. 806–15) condemned the use of certain "profane" books, among them *brontologia*,[6] *selēnodromia*,[7] and *kalandologia*.[8] Thus the composition of this text may have been well before the ninth century.

---

[1] See A. A. Sophocles, *Greek Lexicon of the Roman and Byzantine Periods* (Cambridge, 1914) p. 621; F. Boll and C. Bezold, *Sternglaube und Sterndeutung* (Leipzig, 1931) pp. 159, 186.

[2] *Note di letteratura biblica e cristiana antica*, pp. 74–79.

[3] Palat. Lat. 1449, fol. 119ᵛ–120.

[4] Mercati's MSS B and C (which are actually later recs.) date from the 12th and 15th cent. respectively. For Gk. MSS see F. Boll, F. Cumont, G. Kroll, and A. Olivieri, eds., *Catalogus codicum astrologicorum Graecorum* (Brussels, 1898–1932). The *kalandologia* listed in it attributed to Ezra range from the 12th to the 16th cent., three hundred or more years after Mercati's MS A. Although these texts are similar in form to the Lat., they are altogether different compositions.

[5] It must be asked whether the document is a translation due to the many astrological texts extant in Gk. (see Boll et al., *Catalogus*) and to the numerous Heb. and Ar. astrological texts that were translated into Lat. See K. Kohler, "Astrology," *JE*, vol. 2, pp. 241–45, and the bibliography given there, especially M. Steinschneider, *Die Hebraischen Übersetzungen des Mittelalters und die Juden als Dolmetscher* (Graz, 1956) pp. 186, 501–649, 666.

[6] Predictions based on thunder. See Sophocles, *Lexicon*. An example is found in Boll et al., *Catalogus*, vol. 10, pp. 58f.

[7] Predictions based on the course of the moon. See Sophocles, *Lexicon*. An example is found in Boll et al., *Catalogus*, vol. 10, pp. 243–47.

[8] I translate literally the text found in PG 100, p. 852, Canon 3: "The Apocalypse of Paul and those (books) called brontologies, selenodromies, and calendologies must not be received, for they are profane." See the comments of J. A. Fabricius, *Codex apocryphus Novi Testamenti* (Hamburg, 1703) vol. 2, pp. 952f., on this passage.

Provenance

If the work was composed in Latin it originated from Western Europe or North Africa. The work is evidently the product of a Christian, since the author uses the expression "the Lord's Day."

Historical importance

The Revelation of Ezra demonstrates the importance of Ezra as an astrological figure. It was probably due to the popularity of 4 Ezra[9] that "Ezra" became the most common pseudonym for prognosticators in the Middle Ages.[10] In addition to the Latin manuscripts edited by Mercati there are numerous Greek texts[11] as well as English and Old French prognostications that claim Ezra as their author.[12]

Relation to non-canonical literature[13]

The Revelation of Ezra is strikingly similar to the Treatise of Shem. Both documents attest to the same belief: The beginning of the year determines the nature of the year. The difference between the two is that in Shem it is the zodiacal sign that determines the year, while in Ezra it is the day of the week. If Shem was composed in the first century B.C. (see the contribution in this volume), it may be the prototype of the genre to which the Revelation of Ezra belongs.

The Revelation of Ezra also bears a resemblance to the Testament of Solomon. As Solomon became for Jews the magician par excellence, so at a later period Ezra's name was associated with astrology and he became for Christians (and perhaps for Jews) the prognosticator par excellence.

The best parallels to the Revelation of Ezra are other medieval *kalandologia*. A Latin text attributed to Bede[14] and several anonymous Greek *kalandologia*[15] are extant in addition to those attributed to Ezra cited above. Although they differ in details, they are identical in structure.[16] They begin with something like: If the first of January is on Sunday, such and such will occur during the year. The formula is then repeated for each day of the week. The authors share the same interests: the success of the harvest, the weather, wars, plagues, and the fate of national rulers.

---

[9] According to M. R. James, *The Fourth Book of Ezra* (T&S 3.2; Cambridge, 1895) p. lxxxix.

[10] See Boll and Bezold, *Sternglaube*, p. 175, who say that although the names Aristotle, Melampus, Adam, David, and Solomon were used, Ezra's name was most popular.

[11] Gk. astrological texts similar to our Revelation of Ezra (and attributed to Ezra) are cited and extracted by: C. Tischendorf, *Apocalypses Apocryphae* (Hildesheim, 1866, 1966) pp. xiif. This same MS is described by F. Nau, "Opuscules astrologiques d'Esdras," *Revue de l'Orient chrétien* 2, second series (1907) 15f.; J. A. Fabricius, *Codex pseudepigraphus Veteris Testamenti* (Hamburg, 1722) p. 1162; C. Tischendorf, "Versuch einer vollständigen Einleitung in die Offenbarung des Johannes und die apokalyptische Literatur überhaupt," *Theologische Studien und Kritiken* 24 (1851) 430f.; and numerous places in Boll et al., *Catalogus*, for example, vol. 4, pp. 44, 77; vol. 5, part 4, pp. 23, 69, 106, 156; vol. 8, part 3, pp. 17, 26, 75, 88; vol. 12, pp. 23, 46 etc. (see the index to each vol.).

[12] See R. L. Bensley, *The Missing Fragment* (Cambridge, 1875) pp. 80f., who gives bibliography for the English and French texts and argues that the "Erra Pater" of the English books is a corruption of "Ezra Pater." E. F. Bosanquet, *English Printed Almanacks and Prognostications* (London, 1917) p. 163, extracts a text of Erra Pater: "Pronostycacion For euer of Erra Pater: A Iewe borne in Iewery."

[13] See J. H. Charlesworth, "Jewish Astrology in the Talmud, Pseudepigrapha, the Dead Sea Scrolls, and Early Palestinian Synagogues" *HTR* 70 (1977) 183–200, for the influence of astrology on the pseudepigrapha as well as on ancient Jewish literature in general.

[14] PL 90, p. 951. Bede lived in the 8th cent.

[15] See the text edited by R. Wünsch, "Zu Lydus de Ostentis," *Byzantinische Zeitschrift* 5 (1896) 419f. (Codex Vaticanus gr. 1823, fol. 103ᵛ); Boll et al., *Catalogus*, vol. 7, p. 126; vol. 10, pp. 151f., 153f. C. D. F. Du Cange, "*Kalandologion*" *glossarium ad scriptores mediae et infimae graecitatis* (Lugduni, 1688) vol. 1, p. 548, also prints on anonymous *kalandologion*.

[16] But I have only had access to the following texts: the text attributed to Bede, Du Cange's text, the texts printed in the appendices of *Catalogus*, vol. 7, p. 126 (Codex Monacensis 7, fol. 132ᵛ), and vol. 10, pp. 151f. (Codex Atheniensis 11, fol. 24), that printed by Wünsch, *Byzantinische Zeitschrift* 5 (1896) 419f., and extracts in Tischendorf, *Apocalypses*, pp. xiiif. and *Theologische Studien und Kritiken* 24 (1851) 430f. The other *kalandologia* to which I refer are listed and described in various publications already cited.

Theological emphasis

The author believed that the nature of the year was predetermined by the day of the week on which it began. Though the author may have been at least nominally Christian, he made no attempt to reconcile such fatalism with Christian belief.[17]

SELECT BIBLIOGRAPHY

Charlesworth, *PMR*, pp. 118f.
Denis, *Introduction*, pp. 94f.

Mercati, G. *Note di letteratura biblica e cristiana antica*. Studi e Testi 5; Rome, 1901.

---

[17] As we find in Clementine Recognitions 10.12 (*ANF* 3) and Firmicius Maternus, *Mathesis*, where the stars can only influence one's behavior but the final choice is one's own. See C. McIntosh, *The Astrologers and their Creed: an Historical Outline* (New York, 1969) pp. 59–62.

THE REVELATION OF EZRA

The revelation which was made to Ezra and the children of Israel concerning the nature of the year through[a] the beginning of January.

1 If the first day of January comes on the Lord's Day,[b] it makes a warm winter, a wet spring, a windy autumn, good crops, abundance of cattle, sufficient honey, good vintages, plenty of beans, successful gardens. (But) young men will die, there will be battles and great robberies, (and) something new will be heard about kings and rulers.

2 The Day of the Moon (Monday) makes both winter (and) summer moderate.[c] There will be great floods and sickness, infantry warfare,[d] changes of rulers, many wives will sit in lamentation, there will be much ice,[e] kings will die, (there will be) a good vintage, bees will die.

3 The Day of Mars (Tuesday) makes a severe and gloomy winter, spring snow, rainy summer, (and) a dry autumn. Grain will be high-priced. (There will be) a destruction of pigs, (and) a sudden plague among cattle. Sailing (will be) dangerous, (and) honey sufficient; flax (will be) high-priced, fires (will be) numerous, beans, garden vegetables, (and) oil will be abundant. Women will die and kings (also will die). The vintage (will be) troubled.

4 The Day of Mercury (Wednesday): productiveness of crops, a good vintage, lack of fruits, success in business, a destruction of men, a warm winter. Autumn will be moderate. (There will be) dangers from the sword, plenty of oil, looseness of the bowels and entrails. Women will die, there will be famine in diverse places (and) a good summer. Something new will be heard (and) there will be no honey.

5 The Day of Jupiter (Thursday): (There will be) worthlessness of grain; meat (will be) high-priced (and there will be an) abundance of fruits. There will be less honey; winter (will be) moderate, spring windy, autumn good, summer good. (There will be) a destruction of pigs (and) much rain; rivers will flood.[f] There will be sufficient oil, the crop will spoil, beans will be mixed,[g] and (there will be) peace.

6 The Day of Venus (Friday) makes a moderate winter, a bad summer, dry autumn, worthless grain, a good vintage, inflammation of the eyes. Infants will die, there will be an earthquake, (there will be) peril for kings; oil (will be) abundant, sheep and bees will perish.

7 The Day of Saturn (Saturday) makes a windy winter, a bad spring, a summer (which) changes as it is harassed by storms, a dry autumn, scarcity of grain (and) high-priced flax. Fevers will spread,[h] people will be harassed by various ailments, old men will die.[i]

---

a. Lat. *per*, "through" or "by means of." The meaning is that the nature of the year is determined on the first day or beginning of January.

b. The days of the week are named after the seven planets except for the first day where *dies dominicus* replaced *solis dies*. Thus the *dies Lunae* is Monday, etc. See the contributions on "Week" in *The Oxford Dictionary of the Christian Church* (ed. F. L. Cross and E. A. Livingstone, London, 1974) p. 1464, and in *Harper's Dictionary of Classical Literature and Antiquities* (ed. H. T. Peck, New York, 1897) p. 1669. Also see R. L. Poole, *Medieval Reckonings of Time* (London, 1935) pp. 17f.

c. Lat. *facit hiemem aestatem communem temperatam*. Mercati's later recs. have produced two different readings: MS B, *erit hyens communis, vernus et estas temperati*, "Winter will be ordinary, spring and summer moderate." MS C, *hyems erit aspera,* *ver communis et estas ventosa*, "Winter will be harsh, spring ordinary, and summer windy."

d. Lat. *bella militum*, "wars of foot soldiers."

e. This seems to conflict with the moderate winter mentioned just above.

f. Lat. *exeo*, "to spread abroad," usually of a report. See A. Souter, *A Glossary of Later Latin* (Oxford, 1949) p. 136.

g. Lat. *promiscua*. Perhaps it means that several varieties of beans will grow together.

h. Lat. *dominentur*, "will have dominion."

i. The outlook for a year beginning on Saturday is wholly gloomy, while the other days bring mixed expectations. Perhaps this is due to the ancients' belief that the planet Saturn's influence was only baneful. See Firmicius Maternus, *Mathesis* 3.2, Marcus Manilius, *Astronomicon* 2.

APOCALYPSE OF SEDRACH

(Second to Fifth Century A.D.)

A NEW TRANSLATION AND INTRODUCTION

BY S. AGOURIDES

The Apocalypse of Sedrach begins with a sermon by Sedrach on the necessity of unfeigned love and on its paradigmatic expression in the sacrifice of the Son of God. At the conclusion of the sermon, Sedrach hears the voice of an angel and is taken up into the presence of the Lord. Sedrach asks the Lord why the world was created, and when the Lord replies that it was created for man, Sedrach reproaches him for the condition of man in the world. Sedrach's objections are centered on the problem of evil in the world, while the answers offered by the Lord in reply to Sedrach's charges are centered on man's own responsibility for evil. In the end, Sedrach pleads that the Lord will be merciful to men.

At this point, the Lord directs his only begotten Son to take the soul of Sedrach and place it in Paradise. Sedrach resists the attempt with a series of questions and lamentations. Christ reminds Sedrach that he has been promised Paradise, but still Sedrach resists, for he is concerned with the fate of sinners. The Lord promises Sedrach that if a man lives a hundred years of sin and then repents for only three years, he will be saved. Then Sedrach, with the help of the archangel Michael, gradually persuades the Lord to reduce the required period of repentance to twenty days. Having been thus satisfied, Sedrach allows his soul to be taken to Paradise.

Although the word "apocalypse" is not found in either the title or the body of the text, the ascent of the seer into heaven to speak with God face to face certainly justifies the classification of this work as an apocalypse. The seer is identified only as Sedrach; but, since the only Sedrach known to Byzantine writers was the character from Daniel 3:12, it is probable that he is intended as the author.

Text

The Apocalypse of Sedrach is preserved in only one fifteenth-century Greek manuscript, which is located in the Bodleian Library: Cod. Misc. Gr. 56, fols. 92–100. The text was published in part by M. R. James.[1] James omitted as irrelevant to the main theme of the work the largest part of the sermon on love with which the manuscript begins. The text published by James was translated into English by A. Rutherford.[2] The text published here issues from an independent reading of the Greek and differs with that of James in several respects, the principal difference being that the text of the sermon is here included in its entirety.

Original language

There is no reason to doubt that Greek was the original language of the Apocalypse of

---

[1] I am grateful to the editor and his staff for polishing this introduction. M. R. James, *Apocrypha anecdota*, pp. 130–37.
[2] A. Rutherford, "The Apocalypse of Sedrach," *ANF*, vol. 10, pp. 175–80.

Sedrach. The extant Greek text is replete with patristic and Byzantine vocabulary and syntax, although elements of modern Greek also appear.

Date

Although there is general agreement that the Apocalypse of Sedrach dates, in its final redacted form, to the Byzantine period, the probability that the apocalypse is shaped out of much earlier material is accepted by most scholars. It is the opinion of M. R. James and A.-M. Denis that the Apocalypse of Sedrach received its final form around the tenth or eleventh century A.D., but that the author drew upon materials which extended back to an earlier age.[3] M. E. Stone and J. H. Charlesworth have argued that the materials so used must have dated from the early centuries of the present era.[4]

Much of the doctrinal content of Sedrach is atypical of medieval Christianity and many other elements of the Apocalypse are more Jewish than Christian (see below, "Provenance"). Where "Christ" is briefly mentioned, the term seems to be a substitute for the name of the Jewish archangel Michael. While no precise dates can be given, it appears that the Apocalypse was originally composed between A.D. 150 and 500, and that it was joined together with the sermon on love and received its final form shortly after A.D. 1000.

Provenance

The Apocalypse of Sedrach appears to be from a Jewish original for the following reasons: First, the role of Sedrach as explorer of the divine will and mediator for divine compassion does not fit the Christian tradition of either the earlier or later period. In popular Christian tradition this role is attributed to Mary, the mother of God. For example, in the Apocalypse of Mary, she travels through hell, sees the torments of the sinners, and tearfully pleads with her son for them. As a result he grants them a respite of fifty days in Paradise between Easter and Pentecost.

Second, the final period of twenty days' repentance agreed to by the Lord at Sedrach's pleading seems to be in conflict with much of later Church discipline. Most of the serious sins in the later Church require several years of repentance.[5]

Third, Christian elements such as the incarnation or the cross are conspicuously absent. Christ plays practically no role at all. He is sent for Sedrach's soul; but this motif probably originates with the role of Michael,[6] who appears elsewhere in the text. The Christian redactor here has substituted the figure of Christ for the figure of Michael.

Fourth, one can detect a change not only in content but in style, when moving from the first section to the last. The difference between the bombastic rhetoric of the sermon on love and the more subtle tones of the apocalypse itself is readily apparent. The contrast is accentuated by a sudden transition from the sermon to the ascent of Sedrach. All of these indicate that the author of the second section is not the author of the Christian homily.

Fifth, the theme of man's debate with God is typically Jewish and the reluctant reduction of the period of penitence at the badgering of the favored seer qualifies as the leit-motif of the Apocalypse of Sedrach. Other Jewish features of the Apocalypse are the *bat qol* received by the seer, and the belief that the soul filled the entire body.[7] The tradition about the creation of Adam and Eve, and their comparison to the sun and the moon, is typically Jewish as is also the angelology of this document. Finally, those things represented as most beloved by God are: "among the rivers, (the) Jordan; among the cities, Jerusalem."[8]

It appears that the original Sedrach apocalypse was at some time put together with one or more Christian sermons on love, repentance, orthodoxy, and the second coming of Christ. In the course of time all but the sermon on love and the apocalypse itself dropped out, with the remainder of the collection still bearing the more inclusive title, but now being attributed to the main character, Sedrach.

[3] James, *Apocrypha anecdota*, p. 128f.; and A.-M. Denis, *Introduction*, p. 98.
[4] M. E. Stone, "Prophets, Lives of the," *EncyJud*, vol. 13, cols. 1149f.; and J. H. Charlesworth, *PMR*, p. 178.
[5] See J. Nicolaides, ed., *The Rudder*, trans. D. Cummings (Chicago, 1957) pp. 931–52.
[6] As it is, for example, in TAb.
[7] As R. Meier relates in GenR 14:9.
[8] ApSedr 8:2.

It may be fairly stated that the sermon on love is a product of Byzantine Christianity and that the apocalypse itself originated in Jewish circles, but nothing further can be said about the place of composition.

Theological importance

The main theme of the Apocalypse of Sedrach is the love of God and his compassion for the sinner and full understanding of man's weakness. This theme ties together both the sermon and apocalypse portions of the text and gives them a thematic unity which M. R. James did not recognize. Particular emphasis is placed on the mercy of God, who reduces the period of repentance required of even the most inveterate sinner, and who, in a unique passage (14:5), grants salvation even to the unbaptized. The mercy of God, for the author of Sedrach, overcomes all confessional barriers if only man will repent. Even man's capacity to sin, the gift of free will, is granted to man as a result of God's unbounded love. Thus God's love and mercy are emphasized in three ways: first, in his granting to humans their freedom of choice; second, in his accepting of long-delayed repentance; and third, in his granting salvation to the unbaptized. The universalism evident in the unrestricted application of God's mercy to all is contradictory to most contemporaneous Christian views on the subject, and only serves to emphasize how thin the Christian veneer on this document is.

The analogy of a prodigal son found in the apocalypse has a most un-Christian twist to it: The father does not forgive, but takes back the inheritance from the prodigal and casts him out. It is uncertain whether this analogy is related to the famous parable of Jesus, but if it is, it may represent a Jewish form of the parable that was later adapted by Jesus to make a different point.

Finally, the description of the beauty of the human body (". . . your hair is known from Theman, your eyes from Bosra . . .")[9] and the lamentation over the prospect of separation from it would surely have brought a blush to the cheek of many Christian ascetics. Sedrach laments over the human body that decays in the grave as one laments over the body of his sweetheart. This glorification of the body seems anomalous with the ascetic ideal of later Christianity.

Relation to canonical and non-canonical books

Scholars recognize the indebtedness of the Apocalypse of Sedrach to the canonical book of Job, the Apocalypse of Baruch, and the Testament of Abraham. The most striking parallels, however, are to the book of 4 Ezra. James cites many resemblances in language and subject matter, and there is no question that the author of the Apocalypse of Sedrach has borrowed from 4 Ezra.[10] There are major differences between Ezra and Sedrach. The latter is not set against a background of biblical events, not even those relating to the person of Sedrach. There is no eschatological interest about the end-time, and the national problems of the Jews are not mentioned. However, the main theme of the Apocalypse of Sedrach, namely, the compassion of God for the lost sinner, is also one of the main themes of 4 Ezra.

The idea that man was created superior to the angels, who were invited to worship him, and that Satan's refusal to prostrate himself led to his exile from heaven, is found in the Life of Adam and Eve.[11]

The statement of J. H. Charlesworth that "very little critical work has been published on this pseudepigraphon" is woefully correct.[12] A more complete introduction and a commentary to the text of Sedrach are needed. It is hoped that the present translation will stimulate further research on this rich but neglected document.

---

[9] ApSedr 11:1.

[10] James, *Apocrypha anecdota*, pp. 128f.

[11] *Vita* (ApMos) 16.

[12] Charlesworth, *PMR*, p. 178.

SELECT BIBLIOGRAPHY

Charlesworth, J. H., *PMR*, pp. 178–82.
Delling, *Bibliographie*, p. 165.
Denis, *Introduction*, pp. 97–99.

James, M. R. *Apocrypha anecdota*, T&S 2.3; Cambridge, 1893; repr. 1963; pp. 130–37.
Knippenberg, R. "Sedrachapokalypse," *BHH*, vol. 3, col. 1754.
Meier, R. "Sedrach-Apokalypse," *RGG*³, vol. 5, col. 1631.
Rutherford, A. "The Apocalypse of Sedrach," *ANF*, vol. 10, pp. 175–80.
Stone, M. E. "Prophets, Lives of the," *EncyJud*, vol. 13, cols. 1149f.

THE APOCALYPSE OF SEDRACH

A sermon by the holy and blessed Sedrach on love, and repentance, and Orthodox Christians, and on the second coming of our Lord Jesus Christ. Master, grant (thy) blessing.

1,2 **1** Beloved, we must prefer nothing more than unfeigned love. •We commit many faults every hour, day and night, and for this reason let us acquire love, because
3 it *covers a multitude of sins.* • What do we gain, my children, if we possess   1Pet 4:8
4 everything yet do not have saving love? •How does one benefit, my children, if   1Cor 13:1-3
one gives a great banquet and invites king and nobleman and prepares every sort of expensive fare in order that nothing should be missing; nevertheless, if there is no salt, that banquet cannot be eaten; and one not only bears the expense but
5 one also wastes (his) efforts and is disgraced by the guests. •It is the same in our situation, my brethren; what will we profit, for what grace do we possess without
6 love? •Our every deed is false, even if one has virginity and fasts and keeps vigil
7 and prays and gives a banquet for the poor. •And if one brings gifts to God, or offers the first fruits of all his goods, or builds churches or does anything else without love, it shall be counted by God as nothing, for (these things) are not
8 acceptable. •Thus the prophet says: "*The sacrifice of the impious is an abomination*   Prov 15:8
9,10 *to the Lord.*" •Do not be advised to do anything without love. •If you say, "*I hate my brother but I love* Christ," you are a *liar,* and John the Theologian rebukes   1Jn 4:20
you, for how can one who *does not love his brother whom he has seen, love God*   1Jn 4:20
11 *whom he has not seen?* •It is clear that anyone who hates his brother but thinks
12 that he loves Christ is a liar and is deluding himself. •For John the Theologian says that we have this commandment from God, that *he who loves God should also love*   1Jn 4:21
13 *his brother.* •And again the Lord himself says, "*Upon these two (commandments)*
14 *depend all the law and the prophets.*" •Oh, how extraordinary and paradoxical   Mt 22:40
is the miracle that he who has love fulfills all the law; *love is the fulfilment of the*   Rom 13:10
15 *law.* •Oh, power of love beyond imagination; oh, power of love beyond measure!
16 There is nothing more honorable than love, nor is there anything greater either
17 in heaven or on the earth. •This divine love is the capital (virtue); among all the
18 virtues love is the highest perfection in the world.[a] •It dwelt in the heart of Abel; it worked together with the Patriarchs; it guarded Moses; it made David the dwelling
19 place of the Holy Spirit; it strengthened Joseph. •But why do I say these things?   TJos 17:1f.
20 The most important is that this love brought the Son of God down from heaven.
21 Through love all good things were revealed; death was trampled down, Hades was made captive, Adam was recalled (from death), and through love one flock
22 was made thereafter of angels and men. •Through love Paradise has been opened; the kingdom of heaven is promised; the waste places it made[b] (into) cities, and filled[b] the mountains and the caves with song; it taught men and women who were
23 treading the narrow and sorrowful path. • But how long shall we prolong this sermon on the achievements of love which even the angels cannot accomplish?
,25 Oh, blessed love which bestows all good things! •Blessed is the man who possesses true faith and unfeigned love; for, as the Master said, nothing is greater than love *for which a man lays down (his) life for his friends.*   Jn 15:13

1 **2** And he heard a hidden[a] voice in his ears: "Here, Sedrach, you who wish and   Rev 1:12
desire to talk with God and to ask him to reveal to you the things that you wish

---

1 a. Gk. *to telos tou kosmou,* "the ideal (or goal) of the world."

b. The translations "made" and "filled" are from the same Gk. word *anadeiknumi,* lit. "ex-

hibit." See Lampe.

2 a. Lit. "he received a voice invisibly (*aoratōs*)."

2,3 to ask." •And Sedrach said, "What (is it), my Lord?" •And the voice said to him,
4 "I was sent to you that I may carry you up into heaven." •And he said, "I want
to speak to God face to face,[b] but I am not able, Lord, to ascend into the heavens."
5 But the angel, having stretched out his wings, took him and went up into the
heavens, and took him up as far as the third heaven, and the flame of the divinity
stood there.

1,2 **3** And the Lord said to him, "Welcome, my dear Sedrach. •What kind of complaint
do you have against the God who created you, for you have said, 'I want to speak
3 with God face to face'?" • Sedrach said to him, "Indeed, the son does have a
4 complaint against the Father: My Lord, what did you create the earth for?" •The
5 Lord said to him, "For man." •Sedrach said, "What did you create the sea for
6 and why did you spread every good thing upon the earth?" •The Lord said, "For
7 man." •Sedrach said to him, "If you have done these things, why did you destroy
8 man?" •And the Lord said, "Man is my work and the creature of my hands, and
I discipline[a] him as I find it right."

1 **4** Sedrach said to him, "Your discipline[a] is punishment[b] and fire; and they are
2,3 very bitter, my Lord. •It would be better for man if he were not born. •Indeed,   4Ezra 4:12;
what have you done, my Lord; for what reason did you labor with your spotless   7:[64]; 7:46
4 hands and create man, since you did not desire to have mercy upon him?" •God
said to him, "I created the first man, Adam, and placed him in Paradise in the
midst of (which is) the tree of life, and I said to him, 'Eat of all the fruit, only
5 beware of the tree of life, for if you eat from it you will surely die.' •However,
he disobeyed my commandment and having been deceived by the devil he ate
from the tree."

1 **5** Sedrach said to him, "It was by your will that Adam was deceived, my Master.
2 You commanded your angels to worship Adam, but he who was first among the   *Vita* 13:1-14:3
angels disobeyed your order and did not worship him; and so you banished him,
because he transgressed your commandment and did not come forth (to worship)
3 the creation of your hands. •If you loved man, why did you not kill the devil, the
4,5 artificer of all iniquity? •Who can fight against an invisible spirit? •He enters the
6 hearts of men like a smoke and teaches them all kinds of sin. •He even fights
7 against you, the immortal God, and so what can pitiful man do against him? •Yet
have mercy, Master, and destroy punishment; otherwise receive me also with the
sinners, for if you will not be merciful with the sinners, where are your mercies
and where is your compassion, O Lord?"

1 **6** And God said to him, "Be it known to you, that everything which I commanded
2 man to do was within his reach. •I made him wise and the heir of heaven and
earth, and I subordinated everything under him and every living thing flees from
3 him and from his face. •Having received my gifts, however, he became an alien,
4 an adulterer and sinner. •Tell me, what sort of a father would give an inheritance   Lk 15:11-24
to his son, and having received the money (the son) goes away leaving his father,
5 and becomes an alien and in the service of aliens. •The father then, seeing that
the son has forsaken him (and gone away), darkens his heart and going away, he
retrieves his wealth and banishes his son from his glory because he forsook his
6 father. •How is it that I, the wondrous and jealous God, have given everything to
him, but he, having received them, became an adulterer and sinner?"

1 **7** Sedrach said to him, "You, Master, created man; you know the low state of

---

b. Or "mouth to mouth."   4 a. Or "education," *paideusis*.
                                             b. *Kolasis* should not be translated as "hell,"
3 a. Or "educate," *paideuein*.   but as "punishment."

his will and his knowledge[a] and you send man into punishment on a false pretext;
2,3 so remove him. •Am I alone supposed to fill the celestial realms? •If that is not
4 so, Lord, save man also. •Pitiful man has transgressed by your will,[b] O Lord.''
5,6 ''Why do you throw words around me as if they were a net, Sedrach? •I created
Adam and his wife and the sun and I said, 'Look at each other (to see) who is
7 illuminated.' •And the sun and Adam were of one character, but the wife of Adam
8 was brighter than the moon in beauty, and she gave life to her.'' •Sedrach said,
9 ''What is the use of beautiful things if they wither away to dust? •How is it that
10 you said, Lord, 'Do not repay *evil for evil*'? •How is it, Master, for the word of   Rom 12:17
11 your divinity never lies? •And why did you thus repay man, if you do not wish   1Thes 5:15
1Pet 3:9
12 (to return) evil for evil? •I know that among the four-footed beasts the mule is a
crafty animal,[c] it is none other; yet, with the bridle we turn it where we wish.
13 You have angels; send them to watch (over man) and when he makes a move
toward sin hold onto his foot, and he will not go where he wants.''   4Ezra 7:46

1 **8** God said to him, ''If I hold his foot, he says, 'You have given me no grace in
the world,' and so I left him to his own desires because I loved him and thus I sent
2 my righteous angels to watch him night and day.'' •Sedrach said, ''I know that
among your own creatures, Master, you loved man first; among the four-footed   4Ezra 5:23-27
creatures, the sheep; among trees, the olive; among plants which bear fruit, the
vine; among things that fly, the bee; among the rivers, (the) Jordan; among the
3,4 cities, Jerusalem. •But man also loves all these, Master.'' •God said to Sedrach,
''I will ask you one thing, Sedrach; if you can answer me, then you have rightly
5 challenged me, although you have tempted your creator.'' •Sedrach said, ''Speak.''
6 The Lord God said, ''Since I created everything, how many people have been   4Ezra 4:7; 5:36f.
born, and how many have died and how many shall die and how many hairs do
7 they have? •Tell me, Sedrach, since the heaven and the earth have been created,
how many trees have been made in the world, and how many shall fall and how
8 many shall be made, and how many leaves do they have? •Tell me, Sedrach, since
I made the sea how many waves have billowed, and how many have rolled slightly,
and how many will arise, and how many winds blow near the shore of the sea?
9 Tell me, Sedrach, since the creation of the world of the ages when the air is full
of rain, how many drops have fallen upon the world and how many shall fall?''
10 And Sedrach said, ''You alone know all these things, Lord; you alone are
acquainted with all of these; I only beg you to make man free from punishment,
for otherwise I myself am going to punishment and am not separated from our
race.''

1 **9** And God said to his only begotten Son, ''Go, take the soul of my beloved
2 Sedrach, and put it in Paradise.'' •The only begotten Son said to Sedrach, ''Give
me that which our Father deposited in the womb of your mother in your holy
3 dwelling place since you were born.'' •Sedrach said, ''I will not give you my   TAb 16-20
4 soul.'' •God said to him, ''And why was I sent, and why did I come here, and
5 you make a pretense[a] to me? •I was commanded by my father not to hesitate in
taking your soul; hence, give me your most desired soul.''

1 **10** And Sedrach said to God, ''From where will you take my soul, from which

---

7 a. Lit. ''of what kind of will and what kind of knowledge we are.''

b. [Or ''Pitiful man has transgressed your will, O Lord.'' Within the present context alone, *sou thelematos hemarten* would be translated normally with *sou thelematos* (your will) as the object of the transitive verb *hemarten* (to sin). However, this phrase should be viewed in conjunction with a similar occurrence in 5:1, in which *sou thelematos* appears with a passive verb and is rendered ''by your will.'' The double occurrence of this phrase

suggests that *sou thelematos* is an idiomatic expression used by the author to indicate means or agent. The verb *hemarten* in 7:4 should probably be understood as intransitive. This rendering of 7:4 suits the overall spirit of the present document and provides a better climax for the argument that Sedrach is developing in 7:1-4. —J.H.C.]

c. The Gk. is *alogon*. See Lampe.

9 a. Or ''an excuse,'' *prophasizein*.

2 member?'' •And God said to him, "Do you not know that it is placed in the middle
3 of your lungs and your heart and that it is spread out to all the members? •It is
removed through the pharynx and larynx and the mouth; and whenever it is due
to go out (from the body) it is drawn with difficulty at the beginning and as it
comes together from the fingernails and from all the members there is, of necessity,
a great strain[a] in being separated from the body and detached from the heart.''
4 When he had heard all these things, and recalled the memory of death, Sedrach
was very troubled and he said to God, "Lord, give me a little while that I may
cry, for I have heard that tears accomplish much and can become a sufficient cure
for the humble body of your creatures.''

1 **11** And crying and lamenting he started saying, "O wondrous head, ornamented
like heaven; O sunlight upon heaven and earth; your hair is known from Theman,
your eyes from Bosra, your ears from thunder, your tongue from bugle, and your
brain is a small creation; the head, the movement of the whole body, is trustworthy
and very beautiful, beloved of all but as soon as it falls in the earth it is unrecognized.
2 O hands which hold so well, which are easily taught and hard-working, through
3 which the body is fed. • O hands so adept, gathering materials, together you
4 ornamented houses. •O fingers, beautified and adorned with gold and silver; even
great structures are made by the fingers; the three joints stretch the palms and they
gather good things together; but now you have become strangers to this world.
5 O feet, which walk so well, moving by themselves so very quickly and untiring.
6 O knees, thus joined, without you the body does not move; the feet run together
with the sun and the moon, night and day, gathering all things together, food and
7 drink which nourish the body. •O feet, so swift and well moving, stirring up the
8 face of the earth and ornamenting houses with every good thing. •O feet, which
bear the whole body, which walk straightway to the temples,[a] making repentance
9 and supplicating the saints, and now suddenly you are to remain unmoved. •O
10 head, hands, and feet, till now I have held you fast. •O soul, what placed you in
11 the humble and wretched body? •Yet now, separated from it, you ascend where
12 the Lord calls you and the wretched body goes away for judgment. •O beautiful
13 body, hair shed by the stars, head like heaven adorned. •O face sweet-smelling,[b]
eyes like windows, a voice like a bugle's sound, a tongue which talks so easily,
a beard well trimmed, hair like the stars, head high as heaven, a body adorned,
the illuminator[c] elegant and renowned, yet now after falling within the earth, your
beauty beneath the earth is unseen.''

1 **12** Christ said to him, "Stop, Sedrach, how long will you shed tears and groan?
2,3 Paradise has been opened to you, and after dying you will live.'' •Sedrach said   4Ezra 8:52
to him, "Once more will I speak to you, Lord, while I live, before I die; and do
4,5 not ignore my supplication.'' •The Lord said to him, "Speak, Sedrach.'' •(And
Sedrach said,) "If man lives eighty or ninety or a hundred years, and lives them   Gen 18:22-33
in sin but in the end is converted and the man lives in repentance, for how many
6 days of repentance do you forgive (him) his sins?'' •God said to him, "If he returns
after living one hundred or eighty years and repents for three years and bears the
fruit of righteousness and death should reach him, then shall I not remember all
his sins.''

1,2 **13** Sedrach said to him, "Three years are too many, my Lord. • His death
3 perchance will arrive and he will not fulfill his repentance. •Have mercy, Lord,
4 upon your image and be compassionate, because three years are too many.'' •God
said to him, "If, after a hundred years, a man lives and remembers his death and
confesses before men, and I find him, after one year[a] I will forgive all his sins.''

---

10 a. Lit. "there is great force in being separated . . .''

11 a. The Gk. is *naoi*, "temples''; cf. 14:10.
  b. Lit. "well anointed with sweet oil.''

c. The Gk. is *to phōtagōgon*. This is also translated in the same verse as "window.''

13 a. *Chronos*, "a time.''

5 Again Sedrach said, "Lord, I beg for your mercy again upon your creature; one year is much, and his death will perchance arrive and suddenly snatch him away."
6 The Savior said to him, "Sedrach, my beloved, one question will I ask you, then you can resume your inquiries; if the sinner repents for forty days, shall I not indeed remember all the sins he has done?"

1 **14** And Sedrach said to the archangel Michael, "Hear me, strong protector; help
2 me and intercede that God may be merciful to the world." •And falling upon their faces, they besought God and said, "Lord, teach us in what way and through what
3 repentance man may be saved, or by what labor." •God said, "By repentances,
4 supplications, and liturgies, through draining tears and fervent groanings. •Do you not know that my prophet David (was saved) because of tears, and that the rest
5 were saved in one moment? • You know, Sedrach, that there are nations which have no law, yet fulfill the law; they are not baptized, but my divine spirit enters them and they are converted to my baptism, and I receive them with my righteous
6 ones in the bosom of Abraham. •And there are some baptized with my baptism   Lk 16:22 and anointed with my divine myrrh, but they have become full of despair and they
7 will not change their mind. •Yet I await them with much pity and much rich mercy,
8 that they may repent. •But they do that which my divinity hates, and they did not
9 hear the wise man who asked and said, 'We in no way justify the sinner.' • Are you not at all aware that it is written, 'And those who have repented will not see
10 punishment'?[a] •And they heard neither the apostles nor my word in the Gospels and they cause sorrow to my angels, and of a certainty in my meetings and in my liturgies they do not heed my angel and they do not stand in my holy churches;[b] they stand and do not prostrate (themselves) in fear and trembling but they pronounce long words[c] which neither I nor my angels accept."

1 **15** Sedrach said to God, "Lord, you alone are without sin and very merciful, showing pity and grace to sinners, but your divinity said, *'I did not come to call*
2 *the righteous but sinners* to repentance.' " •And the Lord said to Sedrach, "Do   Mt 9:13 you not know, Sedrach, that after changing his mind the robber was saved in one   Lk 23:43
3 instant? •Do you not know that even my apostle and evangelist was saved in an instant? [. . . but sinners are not saved][a] because their hearts are like decayed stone; they are those who walk along impious paths and who perish with the Antichrist."
4 Sedrach said, "My Lord, you also said, 'My divine spirit entered the nations   Rom 2:14
5 which though having no law yet do the things of the law.' •However, as the robber and the apostle and evangelist and the rest who have stumbled (are) in your kingdom, my Lord, in the same manner forgive those who in recent days[b] have sinned against you, Lord, because life is full of toil and (is) obdurate."

1 **16** The Lord said to Sedrach, "I made man in three stages; when he is young, I overlook his mistakes because of his youth; again, when he is a man I watch over his mind; again, when he grows old I preserve him so that he may repent."
2 Sedrach said, "Lord, you know and are acquainted with all this; yet have compassion
3 with sinners." •The Lord said to him, "My beloved Sedrach, I promise to have compassion even less than forty days, as far as twenty, and whoever remembers your name will not see the place of punishment but he will be with the just ones in a place of refreshment and rest, and the sin of him who copies this admirable
4 sermon will not be reckoned for ever and ever." •And Sedrach said, "Lord, also whoever preforms a liturgy in honor of your servant, rescue him, Lord, from all
5 evil." •And the servant of God, Sedrach, said, "Now, Master, take my soul."
6,7 And God took him and put him in Paradise with all the saints. •To him be glory and power for ever and ever, amen.

---

14 a. The source for the two quotations is unknown.
   b. The Gk. here is *ekklēsiai.* Cf. n. 11.a.

c. Or "boast of things," *megalorēmonein.*
15 a. The clause in brackets is in Lat.
   b. *ep' eschatōn,* lit. "in the last (days)."

2 (Syriac Apocalypse of) BARUCH

(early Second Century A.D.)

A NEW TRANSLATION AND INTRODUCTION

BY A. F. J. KLIJN

Although the destruction of Jerusalem in 587 B.C. is given by the apocalyptist as the occasion for writing this work, it was in fact written after the fall of Jerusalem in A.D. 70. 2 Baruch is a work with varied contents consisting of lamentations, prayers, questions with answers, apocalypses with explanations, addresses to the people, and a letter to Jews in the Dispersion. The contents can be summarized as follows:

1:1–8:5. Jerusalem is destroyed by the Babylonians after the angels remove the holy vessels from the Temple.

9:1–12:4. After fasting for seven days, Baruch sends up a lamentation to God.

12:5–20:4. Baruch fasts for seven days. Questions follow concerning the usefulness of being righteous and living a long life with the answer that man must not direct himself to corruption.

20:5–30:5. Baruch fasts for seven days, and after praying, declares that God will finish that which he began. Twelve disasters are announced, followed by the coming of the Anointed One, the resurrection of the dead, and the final judgment.

31:1–34:1. Baruch warns the people that disasters will come before the end of time.

35:1–43:3. In the Holy of Holies Baruch receives a vision of a forest and a plain surrounded by mountains. The forest changes into a cedar; then he sees a vine and a spring. The vision is explained and those who will live to see its consummation are named.

44:1–46:7. Baruch speaks to the people about God's judgment.

47:1–48:50. Baruch fasts for seven days. In a prayer he expresses his conviction that everything is determined by God.

49:1–52:7. Baruch asks about the outward appearance of the righteous ones after the resurrection.

53:1–74:4. Baruch sees a vision of a cloud from which bright and dark waters alternately pour. The vision is explained.

75:1–77:26. Baruch thanks God, then speaks to the people a third time about the righteous ones who will be saved.

78:1–87:1. The work concludes with a letter to the nine and a half tribes in which the Jews of the Dispersion are exhorted to obey God's commandments and to trust in God.

Text

The textual tradition regarding chapters 1–77, the apocalypse proper, must be dealt with separately from that of chapters 78–87, the attached letter.

The text of the apocalypse is known from one Syriac manuscript: *Bibliotheca Ambrosiana* B. 21 Inf. in Milan, fols. 257a–265b, dated from the sixth or seventh century. Three small excerpts are known from Jacobite lectionaries: BM Add. 14.686, dated 1255, fol. 77a, c. 1, l. 14–77b, c. 2, l. 9, contains 44:9–15; BM Add. 14.687, dated 1256, fol. 157b, c. 1, l. 6–158a, c. 2, l. 3, contains 72:1–73:2, and fol. 175a, c. 2, l. 12–176a, c. 1, l. 1, also contains 72:1–73:2. A fourth portion is mentioned for the first time in D. Dedering's edition:

"Pampakuda [in Kerala, India]. A. Konath Libr., MS 77. The MS is dated A.D. 1423: 44:9–15; 72:1–73:2."[1]

Recently an Arabic version of the apocalypse has been discovered (Sinai No. 589), but the text has not yet been published. Preliminary observations show that this manuscript is a translation of a Syriac document, but probably not the same text as present in *Bibliotheca Ambrosiana* B. 21 Inf. The translation is rather free and thoroughly adapted to Muslim ideas. The recently discovered manuscript does not significantly improve our understanding of the Syriac text, but it is sometimes useful in evaluating conjectured improvements to the Syriac proposed by former editors of this pseudepigraphon.

One fragment, verso and recto, is known in Greek among the *Oxyrhynchus Papyri*: 12:1–13:2 (verso) and 13:11–14:3 (recto) from the fourth or fifth century.[2]

There are thirty-six different texts of the letter in Syriac. The translation below follows the text of *Bibliotheca Ambrosiana*, fols. 265b–267a, which is the letter as it is attached to the apocalypse. In the following translation, this text is indicated by the *siglum* c while the other manuscripts are cited according to the *sigla* presented in the *List of Old Testament Pershiṭta Manuscripts*.[3] Only in a few cases are readings of other manuscripts preferred over c.

Original language

The heading of the Syriac text states that the document has been translated from Greek; the report is certainly true. The existence of a Greek version is proved by the fragment of this work discovered among the *Oxyrhynchus Papyri* (see also 3:6). The extant Greek is different from the Syriac and seems to be a free rendering.

The Greek version, most of which is lost, appears to have been translated from Hebrew. An original Hebrew version should be accepted because of the many parallels between 2 Baruch and other Jewish writings composed in Hebrew or Aramaic. In some cases the Syriac text is intelligible only after translating it into Hebrew. Finally, a translation of the Syriac text into Hebrew restores a play on words apparently contained in the original.[4]

Date

Several passages help determine the probable date of the Apocalypse of Baruch.

32:2–4 states that "after a short time the building of Zion will be shaken in order that it will be rebuilt. But that building will not remain because it will again be uprooted"; finally a new Temple will appear that will last forever. In this passage two destructions are presupposed, indicating that the author lived after the destruction of the second Temple in A.D. 70.

In 67:1, the author speaks about the disaster that befalls "Zion now." In 68:5, he writes about the restoration of the Temple. If he assumes the view of Baruch, the author speaks about the destruction of the Temple in 587 B.C. and the building of the second Temple without mentioning its destruction. In that case the author used a source that has to be dated before A.D. 70. If, however, he is referring to the restoration of the Temple which probably took place in A.D. 130 during the time of Hadrian, then the "last black waters," mentioned in chapters 69 and 70, might refer to the time of Bar Kokhba.[5]

In 28:2, it is said: "For the measure and the calculation of that time will be two parts:

[1] S. Dedering, *Apocalypse of Baruch*, p. iii. The present translation is based on Dedering's edition. The existence of an Ar. version of this work was announced by P. S. van Koningsveld, "An Arabic Manuscript of the Apocalypse of Baruch," *JSS* 6 (1975) 205–7. The Ar. MS is being studied for publication by G. J. H. van Gelder, A. F. J. Klijn, and F. Leemhuis.

[2] *The Oxyrhynchus Papyri*, part III, ed. B. P. Grenfell and A. S. Hunt (London, 1903) pp. 4–7 (12:1–13:2 on 4–5; 13:11–14:3 on 5).

[3] *List of Old Testament Peshiṭta Manuscripts (Preliminary Issue)*. (Peshiṭta Institute, Leiden, 1961) p. 99.

[4] See F. Zimmermann, "Textual Observations on the Apocalypse of Baruch," *JTS* 40 (1939) 151–56; and F. Zimmermann, "Translation and Mistranslation in the Apocalypse of Baruch," *Studies and Essays in Honour of Abraham A. Neuman*, ed. by M. Ben-Horin, *et al.* (Leiden, 1962) pp. 580–87.

[5] See H. Bientenhard, "Die Freiheitskriege der Juden unter den Kaisern Trajan und Hadrian und der messianische Tempelbau," *Judaica* 4 (1948) 164–66.

weeks of seven weeks.'' This passage is thoroughly unclear and cannot be used to arrive at a date of origin.[6]

The passage 61:7 is quoted in Barnabas 11:9, an indication that the author of Barnabas knew this work. It is, however, not quite clear when Barnabas was written. Two proposed dates are A.D. 117 and 132.[7]

These passages point to a date after A.D. 70, although the author probably made use of earlier sources.

In this connection the relation with 4 Ezra is significant. If this work is dependent on 4 Ezra, a date around A.D. 100 is probable. A dependence, however, of both writings on a common source seems the most acceptable hypothesis. 2 Baruch is probably later than 4 Ezra, since it appears to show an advanced stage of theological development.

Therefore, the Apocalypse of Baruch seems to come from the first or second decade of the second century.

Provenance

There are three reasons why this work was probably written in Palestine. The original language, Hebrew, indicates this region. Also, the work shows a close acquaintance with Jewish rabbinical literature. Finally, the author takes his stand with the inhabitants of Palestine, who, especially in the final letter, try to exhort and encourage the Jews in the Dispersion.

Historical importance

The work shows a composite character. The first part is characterized by certain, sometimes conflicting, traditions about the Temple. In chapter 4 the author used a tradition in which a new, already existing Temple from heaven will appear on earth. This differs from the tradition used in chapter 6 in which angels are sent from heaven to take away the vessels from the Temple in order to preserve them in the earth "until the last times, so that you may restore them when you are ordered" (6:8).[8] Here a restoration of the second Temple is supposed. Both traditions about the Temple have parallels in Jewish literature before A.D. 70.[9] They show that in the Jewish world many ideas existed with regard to the future of the Temple.

But the author of this work was not himself interested in the Temple. The destruction was for him a suitable starting point from which to raise a general lamentation about Israel's fate after the disaster in 70. Subsequent to a narrative section the author starts, in chapter 10, a long passage in which Baruch speaks about Israel's sorrows but ironically does not mention the Temple. It is striking that in the final letter, the author speaks about the destruction and writes that the angels came from heaven to remove the vessels "lest they be polluted" (80:2), which only means that he does not expect a restoration of the Temple.

An important part of the apocalypse is devoted to the three visions (27:1–30:5; 36:1–40:4; and 53:1–76:5). These visions contain the announcement of the appearance of the Anointed One, after whose appearance there will be a time of abundance. While the importance of the land of Israel is emphasized, nothing is said about the Temple. Here we are dealing with traditions which apparently predate A.D. 70. At the same time, we should note that the author inserts these visions into his work explaining them in his own way. In addresses to the people after the visions, he does not mention their contents. After the first vision (31:1–32:6), Baruch emphasizes that disasters will come at the end of time (31:5); in the address after the second vision (44:1–46:7), he tells the people that everyone will be judged according to

---

[6] L. Gry, "La Date de la fin des temps, selon les révélations ou les calcula du Pseudo-Philo et de Baruch (Apocalypse syriaque)," *RB* 48 (1939) 337–56.

[7] This depends on Barnabas 16:4, from which no certain conclusions can be drawn because its text is corrupt.

[8] In PR 26:6 we read that an angel breached the walls of Jerusalem so that the enemies cannot boast that they have vanquished the city, but nothing is said about the holy vessels. See W. G. Braude *Pesikta rabbati* (Yale Judaica Series 18; New Haven, London, 1968) pp. 524, 534f. In 2Bar two traditions are brought together.

[9] For the concept of a temple in heaven see 1En 90:28f.; 1Q32; 2Q24; 5Q15; 4QFlor; Tob 14:5; SibOr 5.402, 414–44; Jub 1:27–29. For the concept of vessels hidden in the earth, see 2Mac 2:4f.

his work (46:6); and after the third vision (77:1–26), he says that the righteous ones will be saved (77:26). In the final letter nothing is said about an Anointed One. Here the author speaks about the corruptibility of the world, the final judgment, and the necessity of living according to the Law.

From this we may gather that the importance of this work lies in the manner in which the author deals with traditional material. He knows of traditions concerning the Temple and the Messiah, but was not himself influenced by these ideas. He was impressed by the holiness of God and his inscrutable ways. He was convinced that God's judgment has confronted Israel and will come over the whole world; the only way to survive is to live according to God's commandments. Without losing his belief in a coming judgment, he has separated himself from all speculations about the way this judgment will arrive.

Theological importance

A description of the theological importance includes the traditions about the Temple; the apocalyptic parts of the writing; passages in which the author speaks by means of addresses, prayers, answers and questions; and the final letter. With regard to the visions, the following particulars are of importance:

The Anointed One will be revealed after the tribulation, which will afflict the earth (29:3). In two of the visions the Anointed One shows a warlike character. He will execute the last ruler over the earth (39:7–40:2), allowing some nations to survive but destroying others (70:9 and 72:2).

The first and the third visions present the idea of a great abundance on the earth after the appearance of the Anointed One (29:4–7 and 73:2–74:4).

All the visions express the idea that the land of Israel will be protected during the culmination of the tribulations (29:2; 40:2; and 71:1).

In the second and third visions it is revealed that the Anointed One will either judge or destroy the nations (39:7–8; 40:1; and 72:2).

The rest of the work contains the following concepts:

God is the creator (14:17; 21:4–5; 54:13; 78:3; 82:2) who rules his creation (21:5; 54:2–4) and will judge it in the future (5:2–3; 48:27, 39; 83:7; 85:9). God's government is not always evident because he is inscrutable (14:8; 21:9–10; 44:6; 75:2–5). However, he knows the times and periods and has appointed a day on which to judge the earth (21:8; 48:2; 54:1). He also knows the number of men on the earth (21:10; 23:4; 48:6, 46). He will fulfill everything he promised in the past (44:13; 83:5; 84:6), and he will avenge himself on the enemies of Israel (82:2, 4–9). He is merciful to those who show themselves to be righteous (24:2; 75:1; 78:13; 85:8).

Israel is loved by God (5:1; 21:21; 78:3) but cannot be compared with the other nations since she was elected by God (48:20; 77:5). For that reason she is separated from the other nations (42:5). Israel has Abraham as her father (78:4) and is not mixed with the other nations (48:23). She has acquired for herself some privileges and received others: She possesses righteous men (14:7), the righteousness of the fathers (84:10), God's promises (78:7), knowledge (14:5), and the Law (48:24; 77:3). This has created more responsibility for Israel (15:6; 19:3). However, she did not sin in the same way as the other nations (14:5), although she trespassed certain of the commandments (1:2; 77:8–10). For this reason she will be punished for some time (4:1; 6:9; 13:9; 78:3; 79:2). Israel deserved this suffering (78:5; 79:2). Her punishment will be the destruction of the Temple and the Dispersion among the nations (1:4). However, all of this shows that God did not reject his people, and the disasters reconcile her sins (13:9–10). Therefore, Israel should rejoice in her sufferings (52:6). After the destruction of the city, Israel has nothing left other than God and his Law (85:3), which will last for ever and ever (77:5). Some Jews separated themselves from Israel (41:3) and mixed themselves with other nations (42:4); they will be rejected. Those who live according to the Law will be gathered together (78:7), will take part in the resurrection of the dead, and will enjoy life on a new earth (30:1–2).

The *Law* is a lamp given by Moses (17:4) on the occasion of the establishment of the covenant (19:1). The Law illuminates (38:1–2; 54:5) and divides between life and death (46:3). Darkness is the result of Adam's sin (18:2). Everyone is free to choose between light and darkness (54:15, 19; 85:7). He who chooses to live according to the Law will receive eternal life (32:1; 38:1; 48:22; 51:3, 4–7; 54:15), the good things (44:7), and grace and truth (44:14). The Law should be explained and expounded (3:6; 46:3) and will last for ever and ever (46:4; 77:16). Wisdom and intelligence are given in order to scrutinize God's Law (44:14; 46:5; 48:24; 51:3), and to understand God's actions, especially those at the end of time (54:5). But many wise men will be silent at that time (70:5; cf. 48:36). The Law has to be learned (32:1; 84:1–9) so that Israel will live according to God's will in the future (44:3; 46:5; 82:6).

The *nations* have rejected God's goodness (13:12). Although they know that they act unrighteously, still they resist God (82:9). They have become "their own Adam" (54:15, 19). They may live happily (12:3–4; 82:3–9) and boast before their own gods (5:1; 7:2; 67:2; 80:3), but, in fact, they served the God of Israel when they destroyed Jerusalem (5:3; 7:2–3). They acted out of their hatred for Israel (3:5); therefore, they await unknowingly their just punishment (5:1; 12:4; 13:5–7; 48:32). They dispersed Israel, but this will benefit both of them (1:4; 41:4). Only a few individuals have joined Israel (41:4f.; 42:5), but eventually all nations will be subjected to Israel (72:5).

The *world* was created by God because of man (14:18), the righteous ones (15:7), or the Patriarchs (21:24). Death rules over all men because of Adam's sin (17:3; 19:8; 23:4; 48:42–43). Therefore, life is a struggle (15:8; 16:1) and full of pain (48:50). Nothing is more bitter than the world (21:13). Creation will be destroyed (21:4, 83), being subject to corruption (21:9; 28:5; 40:3; 42:2; 44:9; 74:2; 83:9–11; 85:5). The world is only temporary (85:10), but will be renewed (32:6; 44:12; 57:2).

At the time of the *judgment* God will vindicate himself (5:2; 48:27; 85:9). Before that time (83:2–7), however, the number to be borne must be completed (23:4f.), because everything has its own time (22:1–8). The destruction of Jerusalem is only one of the things that will happen at the end (20:2); horror will cover the whole earth (25:3; 32:1; 48:30f.). Then one will know that the end is near (23:7; 82:2; 83:1). God will not tarry (20:15; 54:1; 83:1). On the day of judgment the books will be opened (24:1). Until that day the righteous will sleep in the earth, the realm of death and the treasure of souls (11:4; 21:23–24; 31:1–2). These righteous possess a treasure of good works (14:12; 24:1). They will rise from the dust (21:23; 31:1–2), no longer corruptible (40:3; 85:5). Their outward appearance will be changed (50–51), and they will receive the world that was promised to them (14:13; 44:13; 84:6). They will be like angels (51:10), but even more excellent than the angels (51:12). Sinners will waste away in the fire (30:4–5; 44:15; 51:6; 54:14, 21–22).

The author's clear theological concepts were shaped by reinterpreting traditions passed down to him. He rejected the idea of a messianic kingdom on earth. He awaits God's judgment; only the Law, which is known to Israel alone, is efficacious. The author tried to show the individual Jews living all over the world that at present nothing is left apart from God and his Law (80:3).

Relation to canonical books

The number of quotations from the Old Testament is small. In 4:2 Isaiah 49:16 is quoted according to the text of the Peshiṭta. There might also be quotations in 5:1 (Josh 7:9), 13:2 (Ezek 2:1), and 64:3 (2Chr 33:7), but it is not certain that the author really quoted since he is deeply steeped in the usage of the Old Testament and its contents. He continually uses Old Testament expressions and easily shifts from alluding to them to quoting them. It is, therefore, to be expected that the author often refers to the books of Kings and Chronicles and alludes to the prophet Jeremiah in the final letter to Baruch.

It is striking that there are many parallels to the New Testament. It is, of course, impossible to prove dependency on the part of the author. He most likely shared with the New Testament authors a dependency on apocalyptic imagery. The parallels are especially striking with the Pauline Epistles, in particular Romans and 1 and 2 Corinthians.

Relation to apocryphal books

The work shows a great number of parallels with 4 Ezra and Pseudo-Philo. The parallels with Pseudo-Philo are too incidental to suppose dependency, and are explicable from a common knowledge of haggadic material. The parallels with 4 Ezra are attributed by many scholars to a dependence by 2 Baruch on 4 Ezra; but since the theological ideas of the two writings differ widely, a common source is also more likely here. This source might be written, but it is also possible that we are dealing with common knowledge and teaching popular in the synagogues.

Some parallels with 4 Baruch apparently are due to dependence by the author of 4 Baruch on 2 Baruch.

There are, in addition, a number of parallels with 1 and 2 Enoch, but only in isolated passages.

Cultural importance

2 Baruch is extremely important for an understanding of early Judaism since it copes with the catastrophe of A.D. 70. After the destruction of the Temple, a new period arrived that was characterized by the influence of the rabbis. The author opened a way for studying the Law after a period of apocalyptic expectations. He was an expert on both apocalyptic imagery and rabbinic teaching, and, as such, was one of the Jews who managed to bring Judaism into a new era.

SELECT BIBLIOGRAPHY

Charlesworth, *PMR*, pp. 83–86.
Delling, *Bibliographie*, pp. 162f.
Denis, *Introduction*, pp. 182–86.

Bogaert, P. *Apocalypse de Baruch, introduction, traduction du Syriaque et commentaire.* SC 144 and 145; Paris, 1969.
Charles, R. H. *The Apocalypse of Baruch Translated from the Syriac.* London, 1896. (An old but still useful work.)
Dedering, S. *Apocalypse of Baruch.* Peshiṭta Institute, part IV, fasc. 3; Leiden, 1973. (The Syr. text of the apocalypse proper.)
Ginzberg, L. "Apocalypse of Baruch (Syriac)," *Jewish Encyclopedia*, ed. I. Singer. New York, 1902; cols. 551–56. (Important for the relationship of 2Bar to rabbinic literature.)
Harnisch, W. *Verhängnis und Verheissung der Geschichte. Untersuchungen zum Zeit- und Geschichtsverständnis im 4. Buch Esra und in der syr. Baruchapokalypse.* FRLANT 97; Göttingen, 1969. (Useful for understanding the theological background of 2Bar.)
Klijn, A. F. J. "The Sources and the Redaction of the Syriac Apocalypse of Baruch," *JSS* 1 (1970) 65–76.
Kmosko, M. *Epistola Baruch filli Neriae.* Patrologia Syriaca, Pars Prima, Tomus secundus, accurante R. Graffin; Paris, 1907; cols. 1215–36. (The Syr. text of the letter.)

THE BOOK OF THE APOCALYPSE OF BARUCH
THE SON OF NERIAH

translated from the Greek into Syriac

Jerusalem will be destroyed*

1 **1** And it happened in the twenty-fifth year of Jeconiah[a], the king of Judah, that
2 the word of the Lord came to Baruch, the son of Neriah, •and said to him:

Have you seen all that this people are doing to me, the evil things which the
two tribes which remained have done—more than the ten tribes[b] which were carried
3 away into captivity? •For the former tribes were forced by their kings to sin, but
4 these two have themselves forced and compelled their kings to sin.[c] • Behold,
therefore, I shall bring evil upon this city and its inhabitants. And it will be taken
away from before my presence for a time. And I shall scatter this people among
5 the nations that they may do good to the nations.[d] • And my people will be
chastened, and the time will come that they will look for that which can make their
times prosperous.[e]

1 **2** This, then, I have said to you that you may say to Jeremiah[a] and all those who
are like you that you may retire from this city.[b] For your works are for this city
like a firm pillar and your prayers like a strong wall.

1 **3** And I said:

O Lord, my Lord,[a] have I therefore come into the world to see the evil things
2 of my mother? •No, my Lord. If I have found grace in your eyes, take away my
spirit first that I may go to my fathers and I may not see the destruction of my
3 mother. •For from two sides I am hard pressed: I cannot resist you, but my soul
4 also cannot behold the evil of my mother. • But one thing I shall say in your
5 presence, O Lord: Now, what will happen after these things? •For if you destroy
your city and deliver up your country to those who hate us, how will the name of
6 Israel be remembered again? •Or how shall we speak again about your glorious
7 deeds? Or to whom again will that which is in your Law be explained? •Or will
the universe[b] return to its nature and the world go back to its original silence?
8 And will the multitude of the souls be taken away and will not the nature of man
9 be mentioned again? •And where is all that which you said to Moses about us?

Marginal references:
10:1
Jer 1:1-3
Ezek 1:1-3
Hos 1:1
Jer 32:12-16;
36:4,8,14,32;
43:3-6; 45:1;
51:59
2Kgs 17:21-23
2Kgs 22:16
2Chr 34:28
Jer 6:19; 19:3
Dan 11:29,35
2Kgs 23:27;
24:3
Jer 32:31

21:24; 57:1;
59:1; 66:7
4Ezra 4:36; 8:51
14:7
Jer 1:18; 15:20

14:8,16; 16:1;
23:1; 38:1;
48:45
4Ezra 3:4; 5:23
Isa 50:1
Jer 50:12
Hos 4:5
4Ezra 10:6-7
28:6
Gen 6:8
4Ezra 5:56;
7:102; 8:42;
12:7
1Kgs 19:4
44:2
Gen 15:15
Phil 1:23
Rom 9:19
46:3-4
83:13,14,16,21
4Ezra 7:30

1 * [A. F. J. Klijn has aimed at an idiomatic translation. Some vss. in the Syr. are, as R. H. Charles
stated, clearly "unintelligible." No attempt has
been made to rewrite or improve the document.
The reader needs to be informed that Klijn's translation "the Anointed One" could also have been
rendered "the Messiah"; cf. e.g. 30:1; 39:7; 40:1;
70:9; and 72:2. —J.H.C.]

a. This is King Jehoiachin, Jechonias in 2Chr
36:9 (LXX) and Josephus, *Ant* 6.103, who became
king in his eighteenth year, i.e. 597 B.C., according
to 2Kgs 24:8. In the eighth year of his reign King
Nebuchadnezzar came to Jerusalem and carried
away Jehoiachin to Babylon (2Kgs 24:12). This is
in agreement with "the twenty-fifth year of Jeconiah" in 1:1 (cf. 6:1), but not with 8:5, where the
imprisonment of Zedekiah is mentioned. This can
refer only to the devastation of Jerusalem ca. 587
B.C. This discrepancy is not due to different sources
used by the author but to inaccuracy on his part.

b. In 62:5; 77:19; 78:1 the nine and a half tribes
are mentioned. The same is found in 4Ezra 13:40
in the Syr., Eth., and Ar. translations. This can be

explained if one accepts that west of the river Jordan
nine and a half tribes were living, i.e. the twelve
apart from those of Reuben, Gad, and the half of
Manasseh.

c. Contrary to 2Kgs 24:9 Jehoiachin was "kind
and just" according to Josephus, *Ant* 10.100, and
"a noble example" according to his *War* 6.106.
See also b.Arak 17a.

d. The verb *ntʿb* is used. The Jews in the Dispersion make known the God of Israel to the nations,
cf. 41:4 and 42:5.

e. Lit. ". . . will look for their prosperity of
their time."

2 a. According to Jer 37:11–16 and 38:23 Jeremiah
was taken captive after the capture of the city.

b. Also in 4Bar 1:1 and PR 26:6.

3 a. Probably from the Gk. *despota kyrie* as in
Gen 15:1 and 8.

b. In the Syr. text we find the word *tzbytʾ*,
"ornament." This is obviously a mistranslation
from the Gk. word *kosmos*.

The New Jerusalem

1 **4** And the Lord said to me:

> This city will be delivered up for a time,   1:4
> And the people will be chastened for a time,   3:5-7
> And the world will not be forgotten.

2 Or do you think that this is the city of which I said: *On the palms of my hands*   Isa 49:16
3 *I have carved you*[a]? • It is not this building that is in your midst now; it is that   6:9; 32:4
Ex 25:9,40
which will be revealed, with me, that was already prepared from the moment that   Mk 14:58
I decided to create Paradise.[b] And I showed it to Adam before he sinned.[c] But
when he transgressed the commandment, it was taken away from him—as also
4 Paradise. • After these things I showed it to my servant Abraham in the night   54:4
5 between the portions of the victims.[d] • And again I showed it also to Moses on   4Ezra 3:13-14
Mount Sinai[e] when I showed him the likeness of the tabernacle and all its vessels.   Ex 25:9,40
6,7 Behold, now it is preserved with me—as also Paradise.[f] • Now go away and do   51:11; 59:8
4Ezra 7:123;
as I command you.   8:52
2Cor 12:4
Rev 2:7

Preparation made by the angels before the enemies arrive

1 **5** And I answered and said:

> So then I shall be guilty[a] in Zion,
> that your haters will come to this place and pollute your sanctuary,
> and carry off your heritage into captivity,   Deut 9:26,29
> and rule over them whom you love.
> And then they will go away again to the land of their idols,
> and boast before them.[b]   7:1; 67:2; 80:3
> And what have you done to your great name?

2 And the Lord said to me: Josh 7:9
4Ezra 4:25;
10:22
> My name and my glory shall last unto eternity.   Pss 135:13;
> My judgment, however, shall assert its rights in its own time.   48:27; 85:9;
3 And you shall see with your eyes that the   6:4ff.
enemy shall not destroy Zion and burn Jerusalem,
but that they shall serve the Judge for a time.
4 You, however, go away and do all which I have
said to you.

5 And I went away and took with me Jeremiah and Adu and Seraiah and Jabish[c] and   2:1
Gedaliah and all the nobles of the people. And I brought them to the valley of   4Ezra 8:17
Neh 12:4
6 Kidron and told them all which had been said to me. • And they raised their voices   Jer 51:59,61
7 and they all lamented. • And we sat there and fasted until the evening.   44:1
Jer 38:1; 40:14
22:1; 31:2

1 **6** Now it happened on the following day that, behold, an army of the Chaldeans   10:1; 31:3; 32:7;
44-46; 77:1-17
surrounded the city.[a] And in the evening I, Baruch, left the people, went outside,   9:2; 12:5; 20:5;
2 and set myself by an oak. • And I was grieving over Zion and sighed because of   21:1; 43:3; 47:2
4Ezra 5:20;
3 the captivity which had come upon the people. • And behold, suddenly a strong   6:35; 9:26-27;
4 spirit[b] lifted me and carried me above the wall of Jerusalem. • And I saw, and   12:51
1:1
behold, there were standing four angels at the four corners of the city, each of   55:1; 77:18
4Ezra 14:1

Ez 3:12,14
Acts 8:38

---

4 a. The quotation is according to the Peshiṭṭa   e. See Ps-Philo 11:15.
version of the Old Testament.   f. See Ps-Philo 19:10.
  b. According to b.Pes 54a the Temple is one of
the seven things created before the creation of the   5 a. Is it because his prayer was not heard (cf. ch.
world. See for a temple in heaven TLevi 5 and Wis   3), or because he leaves the city (cf. 2:1)?
9:8, cf. Heb 8:2.   b. Cf. 4Bar 1:5 and 4:7.
  c. About revelations given to Adam see 2En   c. This name is unknown.
31:2; Ps-Philo 13:8–9; 26:6; LAE 25:1–28:4.
  d. See Ps-Philo 23:6 and GenR 44:12.   6 a. Cf. 4Bar 4:1.
                                                          b. Or "wind."

5 them with a burning torch in his hands.[c] •And another angel came down from
6 heaven and said to them, "Hold your torches and do not light them before I say
7 it to you.[d] •Because I was sent first to speak a word to the earth and then to deposit
in it what the Lord, the Most High, has commanded me." •And I saw that he
descended in the Holy of Holies and that he took from there the veil, the holy
ephod, the mercy seat, the two tables, the holy raiment of the priests, the altar of
incense,[e] the forty-eight precious stones[f] with which the priests were clothed, and
8 all the holy vessels of the tabernacle. •And he said to the earth with a loud voice:

> Earth, earth, earth, hear the word of the mighty God,
> and receive the things which I commit to you,
> and guard them until the last times,
> so that you may restore them when you are ordered,
> so that strangers may not get possession of them.
> 9 For the time has arrived when Jerusalem will also be
> delivered up for a time,
> until the moment that it will be said that it will be restored forever.

> And the earth opened its mouth and swallowed them up.

(margin references: Exod 26:31; 29:5; 25:17; Deut 10:5; Ex 29:5; Jer 22:29; 80:2; 2Mac 2:5; 10:19; 4:2; 32:4)

1 **7** And after these things I heard this angel saying to the angels who held the
torches:
Now destroy the walls and overthrow them to their foundations so that the
enemies do not boast and say, "We have overthrown the wall of Zion and we
have burnt down the place of the mighty God." And they restored me to the place
where I once stood.

(margin reference: 5:1)

The enemies enter the city

1 **8** Now the angels did as he had commanded them; and when they had broken up
the corners of the wall, a voice was heard from the midst of the temple after the
wall had fallen, saying:
2 Enter, enemies, and come, adversaries, because he who guarded the house has
left it.[a]
3,4 And I, Baruch, went away. •And it happened after these things that the army
5 of the Chaldeans entered and seized the house and all that is around it. •And they
carried away the people into captivity and killed some of them. And they put King
Zedekiah in irons and sent him to the king of Babylon.

(margin references: 2Kgs 25:3-4; Jer 34:2; 2Kgs 25:7,11; Jer 39:5,9)

1 **9** And I, Baruch, came with Jeremiah, whose heart was found to be pure from
2 sins, and who was not captured during the seizure of the city; •and we rent our
garments, and wept and mourned, and fasted for seven days.

(margin references: Jer 39:14; 40:6; 5:6)

Baruch's lamentation

1 **10** And it happened after seven days that the word of God came to me and said
to me:
2,3 Tell Jeremiah to go away in order to support the captives unto Babylon.[a] •You,
however, stay here in the desolation of Zion and I shall show you after these days
what will happen at the end of days.

(margin references: 1:1; Rev 1:1; 4:1)

---

c. Cf. 4Bar 3:2–4 and PR 26:6.
d. Cf. 4Bar 3:4.
e. Syr. *pyrm³*, lit. "censer," Gk. *thymiatērion*.
In Philo, *Heres* 226; *Vita Mos* 2.94; Josephus, *Ant*
3.147 and 198; and *War* 5.218, the Gk. word means
"altar of incense."
f. Nothing is known about this number of precious stones; cf. Ex 28:21 speaking about twelve
precious stones.

8 a. Cf. 4Bar 4:1. The same tradition in Josephus,
War 6.300 and Tacitus, *Histories* 5.13.

10 a. The word *ngym* can be translated as "support" only. Jer 43:6–7 reports that Jeremiah went
to Egypt. Bar 1:1 states that he is in Babylon.
According to 4Bar 4:5, he also went to Babylon.
PR 26:6 states that he was sent to Babylon, but that
he returned to Jerusalem; cf. 33:1–2.

4,5   And I spoke to Jeremiah as the Lord commanded me. •He, then, went away
       with the people, but I, Baruch, came back and sat in front of the doors of the 35:1,4
       Temple, and I raised the following lamentation over Zion and said:

6   Blessed is he who was not born,   Jer 20:14
           or he who was born and died.[b]   4Ezra 4:12
                                                                                        Mt 26:24
7   But we, the living, woe to us,
           because we have seen those afflictions of Zion,
           and that which has befallen Jerusalem.

8   I shall call the Sirens[c] from the sea,   Isa 13:21; 34:13;
           and you, Lilin,[d] come from the desert,   43:20
                                                                                        Mic 1:8 (LXX)
           and you, demons[e] and dragons[f] from the woods.   Isa 34:14
           Awake and gird up your loins to mourn,
           and raise lamentations with me,
           and mourn with me.

9   You, farmers, sow not again.
           And you, O earth, why do you give the fruit of your harvest?[g]
           Keep within you the sweetness of your sustenance.

10   And you, vine, why do you still give your wine?
           For an offering will not be given again from you in Zion,
           and the first fruits will not again be offered.

11   And you, heaven, keep your dew within you,
           and do not open the treasuries of rain.

12   And you, sun, keep the light of your rays within you.
           And you, moon, extinguish the multitude of your light.
           For why should the light rise again,
           where the light of Zion is darkened?

13   And you, bridegrooms, do not enter,
           and do not let the brides adorn themselves.
           And you, wives, do not pray to bear children,

14   for the barren will rejoice more.   Mt 24:19
           And those who have no children will be glad,   Isa 54:1
           and those who have children will be sad.   Lk 23:29

15   For why do they bear in pains only to bury in grief?

16   Or why should men have children again?
           Or why should the generation of their kind be named again,
           where this mother is lonely,
           and her children have been carried away in captivity?

17   Henceforth, do not speak anymore of beauty,
           and do not talk about gracefulness.

18   You, priests, take the keys of the sanctuary,
           and cast them to the highest heaven,
           and give them to the Lord and say,
           "Guard your house yourself,
           because, behold, we have been found to be false stewards."[h]

19   And you, virgins who spin fine linen,
           and silk with gold of Ophir,
           make haste and take all things,
           and cast them into the fire,
           so that it may carry them to him who made them.

b. Cf. 2En 41:2; 1En 38:2; and b.ʿErub 13b.   f. Syr. *yrwrʾ*. The word is used in the Peshitta
c. Syr. *syrynws* as in 1En 19:2 (Gk. version). version of the Old Testament in Isa 13:22 and
Mic 1:8 (LXX) mentions *seirenēs*.   43:20.
d. Syr. *llyʾ* are mentioned in Isa 34:14 (Heb.);   g. See for the following b.Soṭ 9:12 and b.BB
see also b.Shab 151b.   60b.
e. Syr. *šʾdʾ*. In Deut 32:17 and Ps 106:37, they   h. Cf. 4Bar 4:3–4; b.Taʿan 29a; LevR 19:6; and
are identified with idols.   PR 131b.

And the flame sends them to him who created them,
so that the enemies do not take possession of them.[i]

1 **11** Now this I, Baruch, say to you, O Babylon:
If you had lived in happiness and Zion in its glory, it would have been a great
2 sorrow to us that you had been equal to Zion. •But now, behold, the grief is infinite
and the lamentation is unmeasurable, because, behold, you are happy and Zion
3 has been destroyed. • Who will judge over these things? Or to whom shall we
complain about that which has befallen us?
4 O Lord, how have you borne it? Our fathers went to rest without grief and, 4Ezra 3:30
5 behold, the righteous sleep at rest in the earth. •For they did not know this anguish 21:24; 30:1-2
6 nor did they hear that which has befallen us.[a] •Would that you had ears, O earth, 4Ezra 7:32
and would that you had a heart, O dust, so that you might go and announce in Eccl 9:5
7 the realm of death and say to the dead, •"You are more happy than we who
live."

1 **12** But[a] I shall say as I think and I shall speak to you, O land, that which is
happy.
2 The afternoon will not always burn nor will the rays of the sun always give
3 light. •Do not think and do not expect that you will always have happiness and
4 joy, and do not raise yourself too much and do not oppress.[b] •For surely wrath will
arise against you in its own time, because long-suffering is now held back, as it
were, by reins.
5 And having said these things, I fasted for seven days. 5:6

The nations will be judged

1 **13** And after these things, it happened that I, Baruch, was standing on Mount 21:2; 47:2;
Zion and, behold, a voice came from the high heavens, saying to me: 48-72
2,3 Stand upon your feet, Baruch, and hear the word of the mighty God. •Because Ezek 2:1
you have been astonished at that which has befallen Zion, you will surely be
4 preserved until the end of times[a] to be for a testimony. •This means that if these 25:1
happy cities will ever say, "Why has the mighty God brought upon us this Mk 6:11; 13:9
5 retribution?", •you and those who are like you, those who have seen this evil and and par.
retribution coming over you and your nation in their own time, may say to them
6,7 that the nations will be thoroughly punished." •And this they may expect. •And
when they say in that time, "When?", you will say to them:

8 You who have drunk the clarified wine,
you now drink its dregs,
for the judgment of the Most High is impartial. Ps 75:9
9 Therefore, he did not spare his own sons first, 44:4
but he afflicted them as his enemies because they sinned. Deut 10:17
10 Therefore, they were once punished, Prov 3:11-12
that they might be forgiven.[b] Rom 11:21
Heb 12:4-11
11 But[c] now, you nations and tribes, you are guilty, 78:3
because you have trodden the earth all this time, Wis 12:2
and because you have used creation unrighteously. 2Mac 6:13-15;
7:16-17, 33
Jdt 8:22
82:3
2Mac 6:14

---

i. Cf. b.Ket 106a; PR 26:6; ProtJames 10.

11 a. Cf. 4Bar 4:9.

12 a. 12:1–13:2 is available in Gk.
b. 12:3 reads in Gk. as follows: "And do not
expect to have joy and do not excessively oppress."

13 a. The same in 25:1, but in 43:2; 44:2; 46:7;

78:5; and 84:1 Baruch is said to die before long;
cf. 4Ezra 14:9, where the death of Ezra is announced.
b. Especially in PssSol this idea is met; cf. 3:3–4;
7:8; ch. 10; and 13:8.
c. 13:11–14:3 is available in Gk.: "You have
trodden the earth and misused the created things in
it. For you were always ungrateful."

12   For I have always benefited you,
    and you have always denied the beneficence.

What is the profit of being righteous?

1 **14** And I answered and said:
    Behold, you have shown me the course of times,[a] and that which will happen   20:6; 48:2; 56:2
2 after these things. •And you have told me that the retribution of that which has
been spoken by you will come upon the nations. And now, I know there are many
who have sinned and who have lived in happiness and who have left the world,
but there will be few nations left in those times to which those words can be spoken
3 which you said. •For what is the advantage (of this), or what evil worse than that
4 which we have seen befall us can we expect to see? •But I will continue to speak   Rom 3:1
5 before you. •What have they profited who have knowledge before you, and who
did not walk in vanity like the rest of the nations, and who did not say to the dead: Jer 2:5
6 "Give life to us," but always feared you and did not leave your ways? •And,   Isa 8:19
behold, they have been diligent and, nevertheless, you had no mercy on Zion on
7 their account. •And if there are others who did evil, Zion should have been forgiven   2:2; 84:10
on account of the works of those who did good works and should not have been   Gen 18:22-25
8 overwhelmed because of the works of those who acted unrighteously. •O Lord,
my Lord, who can understand your judgment? Or who can explore the depth of
9 your way? •Or who can discern the majesty of your path? Or who can discern
your incomprehensible counsel? Or who of those who are born has ever discovered
10 the beginning and the end of your wisdom? •For we all have been made like   Ps 146:4
11 breath. •For as breath ascends without human control and vanishes, so it is with   Job 7:7 / Jas 4:14
the nature of men, who do not go away according to their own will, and who do   48:15
12 not know what will happen to them in the end. •For the righteous justly have   4Ezra 8:5
good hope for the end and go away from this habitation without fear because they   24:1
possess with you a store of good works which is preserved in treasuries.   4Ezra 7:77 / 8:33
13 Therefore, they leave this world without fear and are confident of the world which   Tob 4:9 / Mt 6:19-20
14 you have promised to them with an expectation full of joy. •But woe to those of   15:7; 44:15; 51:3
us who have also now been treated shamefully and who await evils at that time.
15 But you know exactly what you have made of your servants, for we are not able
16 to understand that which is good like you, our Creator. •I shall continue to speak   Gen 1:6-7
17 before your presence, O Lord, my Lord. •When in the beginning the world did   Pss 33:6 / 4Ezra 6:38
not exist with its inhabitants, you devised and spoke by means of your word and   Heb 11:3
18 at the same time the works of your creation stood before you. •And you said that   15:7
you would make a man for this world as a guardian over your works that it should
19 be known that he was not created for the world, but the world for him. •And
now, I see that the world which was made for us, behold, it remains; but we, for
whom it was made, depart.

1 **15** And the Lord answered and said to me:
    You are rightly astonished about man's departure, but your judgment about the
2 evils which befell those who sin is incorrect. •And with regard to what you say
about the righteous who are taken away and the wicked ones who are happy,   Rom 4:15
3,4 and with regard to what you say that man does not know your judgment, •for this
reason, now, listen and I shall speak to you; pay attention and I shall let my   19:3; 48:40; 55:2 / 4Ezra 7:72
5 words be heard. •It is true that man would not have understood my judgment if   EBar 5:4
he had not received the Law and if he were not instructed with understanding.   14:18; 21:24
6 But now, because he trespassed, having understanding, he will be punished   4Ezra 6:55-59;
7 because he has understanding. •And with regard to the righteous ones, those   8:1,44; 9:13
whom you said the world has come on their account, yes, also that which is   48:50; 51:14 / 4Ezra 7:3-14,
8 coming is on their account. •For this world is to them a struggle and an effort   127-128
with much trouble. And that accordingly which will come, a crown with great   Rom 8:18 / 2Cor 4:17
glory.   4Mac 17:15 / 1Cor 9:25

---

14 a. Syr. *dwbrhwn dzbn'*, in Gk. *kairon taxeis*.
In 59:4 we have to render the first word by "ways"
(of the Law) and in 93:3 and 4 by "kinds." Cf.

1QpHab 7:13: *kwl qysy 'l ybw'w ltkwnm*, "all times
of God come according to their order"; see also
1Cor 15:23.

2Tim 4:8 / Jas 1:12 / 1Pet 5:4 / Rev 2:10

1 **16** And I answered and said:

O Lord, my Lord, behold, the present years are few and evil, and who can inherit that which is unmeasurable in this short time?

Gen 47:9
Pss 90:9-10

Gen 5:5

1 **17** And the Lord answered and said to me:

2 With the Most High no account is taken of much time and of few years. •For what did it profit Adam that he lived nine hundred and thirty years and transgressed 3 that which he was commanded? •Therefore, the multitude of time that he lived did not profit him, but it brought death and cut off the years of those who were born 4 from him. •Or what did it harm Moses that he lived only one hundred and twenty years and, because he subjected himself to him who created him, he brought the Law to the descendants of Jacob and he lighted a lamp to the generation of Israel?[a]

19:8; 23:4;
48:42-43; 54:15-
19; 56:5-6
4Ezra 3:7, 21-
22; 4:30; 7:118-
121
Rom 5:12
1Cor 15:21
Deut 34:7
31:3; 46:4
4Ezra 3:19; 9:30
59:2
Ps 119:105

1 **18** And I answered and said:

2 He who lighted took from the light, and there are few who imitated him. •But many whom he illuminated took from the darkness of Adam and did not rejoice in the light of the lamp.

Jn 1:9
Jn 3:19; 5:35

1 **19** And he answered and said to me:

Therefore he appointed a covenant for them at that time and said, "Behold, I appoint for you life and death," and he called heaven and earth as a witness against 2 them. •For he knew that his time was short, but that heaven and earth will stay 3 forever. •They, however, sinned and trespassed after his death, although they knew that they had the Law to reprove them and that light in which nothing could err, apart from the spheres, which witnessed, and me. And I judge everything 4 that exists. •You, however, should not think about this in your heart and you 5 should not be afflicted because of the things which have been. •For now the end of times is at stake whether it be property, happiness, or shame; and not its 6 beginning. •For when a man is happy in his youth and is treated badly in his old 7 age, he forgets all happiness he possessed. •And further, when a man is badly treated in his youth but will be happy in the end, he does not remember his 8 disgrace anymore.[a] •And further, listen: Even if everyone had been happy continually since the day death was decreed against those who trespassed, but was destroyed in the end, everything would have been in vain.

84:2
Deut 30:19;
31:28
AsMos 3:12

17:3

1 **20** Therefore, behold, the days will come and the times will hasten, more than the former, and the periods will hasten more than those which are gone, and the 2 years will pass more quickly than the present ones.[a] •Therefore, I now took away 3 Zion to visit the world in its own time more speedily. •Now, however, remember 4 everything which I commanded you and seal it in the interior of your mind. •And 5 then I shall show you my strong judgment and my unexplorable ways. •Therefore, go away and sanctify yourself for seven days and do not eat bread and do not 6 drink water and do not speak to anybody. •And after this time come to this place, and I shall reveal myself to you, and I shall speak to you true things, and I shall command you with regard to the course of times, for they will come and will not tarry.

54:1; 83:1
4Ezra 4:26

4Ezra 5:56;
6:18; 9:2

5:5

14:1

Prayer of Baruch, the Son of Neriah

1 **21** I went from there and sat in the valley of Kidron in a cave of the earth and sanctified myself there and ate no bread, but I was not hungry; I drank no water, but I was not thirsty. And I stayed there until the seventh day as he had commanded 2,3 me. •And after this I came to the place where he had spoken with me. •And it

5:5

5:6

13:1; 20:5

---

17 a. Cf. Ps-Philo 9:8; 15:6; and 19:4.   1–3; and Euripides, *Andromache* 100–3.

19 a. The same idea is found in classical Gk.   **20** a. Cf. Ps-Philo 19:13.
writers; cf. Herodotus 1.32; Sophocles, *Trachiniae*

happened at sunset that my soul received many thoughts, and I began to speak in
the presence of the Mighty One, and said:

4 O hear me, you who created the earth, the one who fixed the firmament by the
word[a] and fastened the height of heaven by the spirit, the one who in the beginning
5 of the world called that which did not yet exist and they obeyed you. •You who
gave commandments to the air with your sign and have seen the things which are
6 to come as well as those which have passed.[b] •You who reign with great thoughts
over the powers which stand before you, and who rules with indignation[c] the
countless holy beings, who are flame and fire,[d] whom you created from the
7 beginning, those who stand around your throne. •For you alone (all) this exists
8 so that you may create at once all that you want. •You are the one who causes the
rain to fall on earth with a specific number of raindrops. You alone know the end
9 of times before it has arrived. Hear my prayer. •For only you can sustain those
who exist, those who have gone and those who will come, those who sin and those
who have proved themselves to be righteous,[e] since you are the Living One, the
10 Inscrutable One. •For you are the only Living One, the Immortal One and the
11 Inscrutable One, and you know the number of men. •And while many have sinned
once, many others have proved themselves to be righteous.

12 You know where you have preserved the end of those who have sinned or the
13 fulfillment of those who have proved themselves to be righteous. •For if only this
life exists which everyone possesses here, nothing could be more bitter than this.
14 For of what help is strength which changes into weakness, or food in abundance
15 which changes into famine, or beauty which changes into ugliness? •For the nature
16 of men is always changeable. •For as we were once, we are no longer, and as we
17 are now, we shall not remain in the future. •For if an end of all things had not been
18 prepared, their beginning would have been senseless. • But let me know all that
which comes from you, and regarding that which I ask you, enlighten me.

19 How long will corruption remain, and until when will the time of mortals be
happy, and until when will those who pass away be polluted by the great wickedness
20 in this world?[f] •Therefore, command mercifully and confirm all that you have said
that you would do so that your power will be recognized by those who believe that
21 your long-suffering means weakness. • And now show it to them, those who do
not know, but who have seen that which has befallen us and our city, up to now,
that it is in agreement with the long-suffering of your power, because you called
22 us a beloved people on account of your name. •From now, therefore, everything
23 is in a state of dying. •Therefore, reprove the angel of death,[g] and let your glory
appear, and let the greatness of your beauty be known, and let the realm of death
be sealed[h] so that it may not receive the dead from this time, and let the treasuries
24 of the souls[i] restore those who are enclosed in them. • For as many years have
passed as those which passed since the days of Abraham, Isaac, and Jacob and all
those who were like them, who sleep in the earth—those on whose account you
25 have said you have created the world. • And now, show your glory soon and do
not postpone that which was promised by you.

26 And it happened that when I had ended the words of this prayer, I became very
weak.

Marginal references:
Ps 33:6
Jer 10:12; 51:15
48:8
2Mac 7:28
Rom 4:17
48:8,10; 54:2
48:10
4Ezra 8:21
Dan 7:9f.
Ps 104:4
Isa 6:1-2
48:8
4Ezra 8:23
59:5
48:2; 54:1
Rev 1:8
21:11,12;
24:1,2; 51:1,3; 62:7
14:9
23:4; 48:6,46
1Cor 15:19
48:35; 88:11-21
28:5
4Ezra 6:7
2Pet 3:9
Jer 14:9; 15:16
30:2
4Ezra 4:35-41;
7:32,95
11:4
14:18; 15:7
44:13; 51:3;
83:4,5

---

21 a. The MS reads *bmlᵉh,* "in his fullness,"
which is corrected into *bmlth.*

b. The MS reads *dᶜbd,* "that which you are
doing"; corrected by Kmosko and Dedering.

c. Syr. *bzᶜypwtᵃ.* The same word is found in
4Ezra 8:23: "whose indignation melts the mountains." This sentence was quoted in *AposCons* 8:7:
kai hē apeilē tēkei horē. The Gk. *apeilē* is used as
a translation of the Heb. *gᶜrᵃ* in the LXX; cf. Isa
50:2, which is also rendered by *epitimēsis,* an important word in the NT, cf. Mt 8:26; Lk 4:39;
9:42. The eschatological overtone is also seen in
AsMos 10:3: "And he will go forth from his holy

habitation with indignation and wrath on account
of his sons."

d. Cf. 2En 29:3.

e. In Syr. the *Ethpael* of the verb *zdq* is used.
This is usually translated "to act righteously," but
the above translation seems to be better; cf. also
11, 12; 24:1 and 2; 51:1 and 3; and 62:7.

f. Answers are given in 23:7–24:1.

g. See for the angel of death Strack-Billerbeck,
vol. 1, pp. 144–49.

h. Cf. Ps-Philo 3:10.

i. Cf. Ps-Philo 32:13.

1 **22** And afterward it happened that, behold, the heaven was opened, and I saw, _{48:25}
and strength was given to me, and a voice was heard from on high which said to
me:

2,3   Baruch, Baruch, why are you disturbed? •Who starts on a journey and does not
complete it? Or who will be comforted making a sea voyage unless he can reach
4 a harbor? •Or he who promises to give a present to somebody—is it not a theft,
5 unless it is fulfilled? •Or he who sows the earth—does he not lose everything unless
6 he reaps its harvest in its own time? •Or he who plants a vineyard—does the planter
7 expect to receive fruit from it, unless it grows until its appointed time? • Or a
woman who has conceived—does she not surely kill the child when she bears
8 untimely? •Or he who builds a house, can it be called a house, unless it is provided
with a roof and is finished? Tell this to me first.

Margin references for ch. 22: 4Ezra 5:14; 12:5 / Dan 10:17 / Ezek 1:1 / Acts 7:57 / Mt 3:16; 17:5 and par.; pass. / Rev 4:1

1 **23** And I answered and said:
    No, Lord, my Lord.
2   And he answered and said to me:
    Why, then, are you disturbed about that which you do not know, and why are
3 you restless about that of which you do not possess any knowledge? •For as you
have not forgotten men who exist and who have passed away, I remember those
4 who will come. •For when Adam sinned and death was decreed against those who _{17:3}
were to be born, the multitude of those who would be born was numbered. And _{21:10}
for that number a place was prepared where the living ones might live and where
5 the dead might be preserved.[a] •No creature will live again unless the number that _{4Ezra 4:33-36}
has been appointed is completed. For my spirit creates the living, and the realm _{Rom 11:25 / Rev 6:11}
6 of death receives the dead. •And further, it is given to you to hear that which will
7 come after these times. •For truly, my salvation which comes has drawn near[b] _{Rev 4:1}
and is not as far away as before. _{82:2 / Lk 21:28 / 1Pet 4:7 / Jas 5:3}

1 **24** For behold, the days are coming, and the books will be opened in which are
written the sins of all those who have sinned,[a] and moreover, also the treasuries _{4Ezra 6:20 / 1Dan 7:10}
in which are brought together the righteousness of all those who have proven _{1En 90:20}
2 themselves to be righteous. •And it will happen at that time that you shall see, and _{Rev 20:12 / 14:12}
many with you, the long-suffering of the Most High, which lasts from generation _{21:9}
to generation, who has been long-suffering toward all who are born, both those _{21:20 / Rom 9:22}
who sinned and those who proved themselves to be righteous.
3   And I answered and said:
    But, behold, O Lord, a man does not know the number of things which pass _{21:9}
4 away nor those which come. •For behold, I also know what has befallen me; but
that which will happen with our enemies, I do not know, or when you will command
your works.

1 **25** And he answered and said to me:
    You also will be preserved until that time, namely until that sign which the Most _{13:3}
2 High will bring about before the inhabitants of the earth at the end of days. •This
3 then will be the sign:[a] •When horror seizes the inhabitants of earth, and they fall _{Mt 24:30}
4 into many tribulations and further, they fall into great torments. •And it will happen _{Mk 13:4 / Lk 21:7; 11:25}
that they will say in their thoughts because of their great tribulations, "The Mighty _{Rev 12:1-3}
One does not anymore remember the earth"; It will happen when they lose hope, _{70:2 / 4Ezra 13:30}
that the time will awake. _{Lk 21:25-26}

---

23 a. Cf. 2En 49:2 and b.Hag 15a.
    b. Cf. 1En 51:2.
24 a. 1En 90:20.

25 a. About signs announcing the coming judgment, cf. 4Ezra 4:51–5:13; 8:63–9:6; 1En 99:4–7;
Jub 23:22–31; SibOr 3.796–808.

The apocalypse of the twelve calamities and the coming of the Messiah

1 **26** And I answered and said:
That tribulation which will be will it last a long time; and that distress,[a] will it embrace many years?

1 **27** And he answered and said to me:
That time will be divided into twelve parts, and each part has been preserved
2 for that for which it was appointed. •In the first part: the beginning of commotions.[a] 53:6
3,4 In the second part: the slaughtering of the great. • In the third part: the fall of 4Ezra 14:11-12 Mt 24:8
5,6 many into death. •In the fourth part: the drawing of the sword. •In the fifth part: Rev 15:1
7 famine and the withholding of rain. • In the sixth part: earthquakes and terrors. 70:8
9,10 In the eighth part:[b] a multitude of ghosts[c] and the appearances of demons. •In the Mt 24:7 Mk 13:8
11,12 ninth part: the fall of fire. •In the tenth part: rape and much violence. •In the Lk 21:11
13 eleventh part: injustice and unchastity. •In the twelfth part: disorder and a mixture 10:8
14 of all that has been before. •These parts of that time will be preserved and will 70:8
15 be mixed, one with another, and they will minister to each other. •For some of 4Ezra 5:18
these parts will withhold a part of themselves and take from others and will accomplish that which belongs to them and to others; hence, those who live on earth in those days will not understand that it is the end of times. 48:32

1,2 **28** But everyone who will understand will be wise at that time. •For the measure Dan 12:10
and the calculation of that time will be two parts: weeks of seven weeks.[a] Mt 24:15
3 And I answered and said:
It is good that man should come so far and see, but it is better that he should 4Ezra 13:16-20
4,5 not come so far lest he fall. •But I shall also say this: •Will he who is incorruptible
despise those who are corruptible, and will he despise what happens with those 40:3; 43:2; 44:9; 74:2; 85:5
who are corruptible so that he might only look to those who are not corruptible? 4Ezra 4:11; 7:31,114
6 But when, O Lord, these things will surely come of which you spoke to me before,
7 let me also know this, if I have found grace in your eyes: •Is it in one place or Gen 6:8; 19:19
in one part of the earth that these things will come or will they be noticed by the 4Ezra 4:56
whole earth?

1 **29** And he answered and said to me:
That which will happen at that time bears upon the whole earth. Therefore, all
2 who live will notice it. •For at that time I shall only protect those found in this 69:1
3 land at that time.[a] •And it will happen that when all that which should come to 40:2; 71:1
pass in these parts has been accomplished, the Anointed One will begin to be 4Ezra 9:8; 12:48-49
4 revealed.[b] •And Behemoth will reveal itself from its place, and Leviathan will 39:7; 72:2
come from the sea, the two great monsters which I created on the fifth day of 4Ezra 7:27-28; 12:32; 13:32
creation and which I shall have kept until that time. And they will be nourishment[c] Isa 27:1
5 for all who are left.[d] •The earth will also yield fruits ten thousandfold.[e] And on 4Ezra 6:49-52
one vine will be a thousand branches, and one branch will produce a thousand 4Ezra 6:25; 7:28; 9:8; 12:34; 13:24,26
clusters, and one cluster will produce a thousand grapes, and one grape will
6 produce a cor of wine.[f] •And those who are hungry will enjoy themselves and they
7 will, moreover, see marvels every day. •For winds will go out in front of me 4Ezra 7:28; 12:34; 13:50
every morning to bring the fragrance of aromatic fruits and clouds at the end of

---

26 a. Syr. 'nnq' from the Gk. anagkē; cf. Lk 21:23.

27 a. Syr. zw°, which in the Syr. translations of the NT is used to render the Gk. seismos, "earthquake"; cf. Lk 21:11; Mt 24:71; and Mk 13:5.
  b. The seventh part is absent.
  c. Syr. pntsy'; cf. Gk. phantasia, also in 48:34.

28 a. This indication is not clear.

29 a. Cf. Ps-Philo 7:4 and b.Pes 113a.
  b. In PssSol the Anointed One is mentioned in 18:6; cf. 17:23ff. about the Son of David and the Servant. See also 1En 48:10 and 52:4. About the "appearance" of the Anointed One, see Jn 1:31 and 2Thes 1:7.
  c. See Strack-Billerbeck, vol. 4, pp. 1156f.
  d. Cf. 1En 90:30; SibOr 5: 384; and PssSol 18:7.
  e. We find a close parallel in Irenaeus, Adv Haer 5.33.3–4, see also 1En 10:19.
  f. See for this measure Josephus, Ant 15.14.

8 the day to distill the dew of health.^g •And it will happen at that time that the
treasury of manna will come down again from on high, and they will eat of it in
those years^h because these are they who will have arrived at the consummation
of time.ⁱ

73:2
Isa 26:19
4Ezra 7:12;
8:52ff.
Ps 78:25
Rev 2:17

1 **30** And it will happen after these things when the time of the appearance^a of the
Anointed One has been fulfilled and he returns with glory,^b that then all who
2 sleep in hope of him will rise. •And it will happen at that time that those treasuries
will be opened in which the number of the souls of the righteous were kept,^c and
they will go out and the multitudes of the souls will appear together, in one
assemblage, of one mind. And the first ones will enjoy themselves and the last
3 ones will not be sad. •For they know that the time has come of which it is said
4 that it is the end of times. •But the souls of the wicked will the more waste away^d
5 when they shall see all these things. •For they know that their torment has come
and that their perditions have arrived.

48:22

21:23; 50:2

1Cor 15:52

51:5

Baruch speaks to the people

1 **31** And it happened after these things, that I went to the people and said to them:
Assemble to me all our elders and I shall speak words to you.
2,3   And they all assembled in the valley of the Kidron. •And I began to speak and
said to them:
Hear, O Israel, and I shall speak to you, and you, O seed of Jacob, pay attention,
4 and I shall teach you. •Do not forget Zion but remember the distress of Jerusalem.
5 For, behold, the days are coming, that all that has been will be taken away to be
destroyed, and it will become as though it had not been.

5:5; 44:1

5:5

17:4

1 **32** You, however, if you prepare your minds to sow into them the fruits of the
law,^a he shall protect you in the time in which the Mighty One shall shake the
2 entire creation. •For after a short time, the building of Zion will be shaken in order
3 that it will be rebuilt. •That building will not remain; but it will again be uprooted
4 after some time and will remain desolate for a time. •And after that it is necessary
5 that it will be renewed in glory and that it will be perfected into eternity.^b •We
should not, therefore, be so sad regarding the evil which has come now, but much
6 more (distressed) regarding that which is in the future. •For greater than the two
7 evils will be the trial when the Mighty One will renew his creation.^c •And now,
do not draw near to me for some days and do not call upon me until I shall come
to you.
8   And it happened after having said all these words to them that I, Baruch, went
my way. And when the people saw that I went away, they raised their voices and
lamented and said:
9   Where are you going from us, Baruch, and do you leave us as a father who
leaves his children as orphans and goes away from them?

46:5
Job 11:13
4Ezra 9:31

4:2

ch. 27
44:12; 57:2
Isa 65:17
4Ezra 7:75

4Ezra 5:1

4Ezra 5:18

1 **33** These are the commands which your friend Jeremiah, the prophet, gave to
2 you. And he said to you, •"Look to this people during the time I am absent, while
I help the rest of our brothers in Babylon, against whom has been declared the
3 sentence that they should be carried away into captivity." •And now, if you

10:2

4Ezra 17:40

---

g. About dew as an eschatological gift see 1En
60:20; cf. 34:1–2; 36:1; and 75:5; and cf. b.Ḥag
12b.
  h. SibOr 3.746; Ps-Philo 19:10; and b.Ḥag 12b.
  i. Syr. *šwlmh dzbnʾ;* see Gal 4:4.

30 a. Syr. *mʾtyṭ*, Gk. *parousia;* see Mt 24:37.
  b. The Anointed One is pre-existent; cf. 1En
46:1–2; 48:3; 62:7; 4Ezra 12:32 and 13:26.
  c. Cf. Ps-Philo 3:10; 11:6; 19:2; and 51:5.

d. Cf. Ps-Philo 16:3.

32 a. Lit. "to sow in them." The Law as source
of life, cf. 38:2 and 48:24; cf. also Sir 17:11; 32:24;
45:5; 1Bar 4:1; WisSol 6:18; 7:14; PssSol 14:2; and
4Ezra 7:45.
  b. See Introduction.
  c. Transformation of the creation is in 1En
45:4–5, and about a new heaven and earth see 1En
72:1 and 91:15–16.

abandon us too, it would have been better for all of us that we shall die first, and
that then you should abandon us.

1 **34** And I answered and said to the people:
Heaven forbid that I should abandon you or that I should go away from you.
But I shall go to the Holy of Holies to ask from the Mighty One on behalf of you 10:5
and Zion so that I may receive in some ways more light, and after that I shall
return to you.

The apocalypse of the forest, the vine, the fountain, and the cedar

1 **35** And I, Baruch, went to the holy place and sat on the ruins and wept and said:

2   O that my eyes were springs,   Jer 9:1
    and my eyelids, that they were a fountain of tears.
3   For how shall I be sad over Zion,
4   and lament over Jerusalem?
    For at the place where now I am prostrate,
    the high priests used to offer holy sacrifices,
    and placed thereon incense of fragrant spices.
    Now, however, that of which we are proud has become dust,
    and that which our soul desired is ashes.

1 **36** And when I had said this, I fell asleep at that place and saw a vision in the Zech 1:8
2 night. •And behold there was a forest with trees that was planted on the plain and
surrounded by high mountains and rugged rocks. And the forest occupied much Ezek 17:3-9
3 space. •And behold, over against it a vine arose, and from under it a fountain (ran)
4 peacefully. •And that fountain came to the forest and changed into great waves,
and those waves submerged the forest and suddenly uprooted the entire forest and
5 overthrew all the mountains which surrounded it. • And the height of the forest
became low, and that top of the mountains became low. And that fountain became
6 so strong that it left nothing of the great forest except one cedar. •When it had also
cast that one down, it destroyed the entire forest and uprooted it so that nothing Ps 29:5
was left of it, and its place was not even known anymore. Then that vine arrived
with the fountain in peace and in great tranquillity and arrived at a place which
was not far away from the cedar, and they brought to him that cedar which had
7 been cast down. •And I saw, and behold, that vine opened its mouth and spoke
and said to the cedar, "Are you not that cedar which remained of the forest of
wickedness? Because of you, wickedness remained and has been done during all
8 these years, but never goodness. •And you possessed power over that which did
not belong to you; you did not even show compassion to that which did belong
to you. And you extended your power over those who were living far from you,
and you keep those who are close to you in the nets of your wickedness, and you
9 uplift your soul always like one who could not be uprooted. •But now your time
10 has hastened and your hour has come. •Therefore O cedar, follow the forest which
has departed before you and become ashes with it, and let your earth be mixed
11 together. •And now, sleep in distress and rest in pain until your last time comes
in which you will return to be tormented even more."

1 **37** And after these things I saw that the cedar was burning and the vine growing,
while it and all around it became a valley full of unfading flowers. And I awoke
and arose.

Interpretation of the apocalypse

1 **38** And I prayed and said: 44:14; 46:5;
    O Lord, my Lord, you are the one who has always enlightened those who   48:24,36; 51:3;
54:5; 59:7
Prov 16:22

2 conduct themselves with understanding. •Your Law is life, and your wisdom is 32:1
3,4 the right way. •Now, show me the explanation of this vision. •For you know that Prov 4:11
my soul has always been associated with your Law, and that I did not depart from Mk 10:20
your wisdom from my earliest days. Lk 18:21

1 **39** And he answered and said to me:
2 Baruch, this is the explanation of the vision which you have seen. •As you have
seen the great forest surrounded by high and rocky mountains, this is the word:
3 Behold, the days will come when this kingdom that destroyed Zion once will be
4 destroyed and that it will be subjected to that which will come after it. •This again
will also be destroyed after some time. And another, a third, will rise and also that
5 will possess power in its own time and will be destroyed. • After that a fourth
kingdom[a] arises whose power is harsher and more evil than those which were
before it, and it will reign a multitude of times like the trees on the plain, and it
6 will rule[b] the times and exalt itself more than the cedars of Lebanon. • And the 4Ezra 5:1
truth will hide itself in this and all who are polluted with unrighteousness will flee to it
7 like the evil beasts flee and creep into the forest. • And it will happen when the
time of its fulfillment is approaching in which it will fall, that at that time the
dominion of my Anointed One which is like the fountain and the vine, will be 29:3
Jn 15:1
revealed. And when it has revealed itself, it will uproot the multitude of its host. 40:2
8 And that which you have seen, namely the tall cedar, which remained of that
forest, and with regard to the words which the vine said to it which you heard,
this is the meaning.

1 **40** The last ruler who is left alive at that time will be bound, whereas the entire
host will be destroyed. And they will carry him on Mount Zion, and my Anointed
One will convict him of all his wicked deeds and will assemble and set before him 4Ezra 12:32;
2 all the works of his hosts. •And after these things he will kill him[a] and protect the 13:37
3 rest of my people who will be found in the place that I have chosen. •And his 29:2
Dan 7:27
dominion will last forever until the world of corruption has ended[b] and until the 28:4; 30:1
4 times which have been mentioned before have been fulfilled. •This is your vision, Gal 4:4
and this is its explanation. Tob 14:5
4Ezra 11:44

About the apostates and the believers

1 **41** And I answered and said:
For whom and for how many will these things be? Or who will be worthy to
2 live in that time? •I shall now say before you everything that I think, and I shall
3 ask you about the things of which I meditate. • For behold, I see many of your
people who separated themselves from your statutes and who have cast away from
4 them the yoke of your Law.[a] •Further, I have seen others who left behind their
5 vanity[b] and who have fled under your wings.[c] •What will, therefore, happen with 1:4
6 those? Or how will that last time receive them? • Their time will surely not be Ps 36:8; 57:2
Ruth 2:12
weighed exactly, and they will certainly not be judged as the scale indicates?

1 **42** And he answered and said to me:
2 Also these things I shall show you. As for what you said: ''To whom and to
how many will these things be?'' The good that was mentioned before will be to
those who have believed,[a] and the opposite of these things will be to those who

39 a. Apparently Babylon, Persia, Greece, and
Rome are meant; cf. Dan 7.
b. The verb *'ḥd* is used; cf. 48:8, ''to take'' or
''to seize.''

40 a. The Messiah as warrior, cf. 72:2; Isa 11:4;
1En 46:3–6; 62:2. See also the Targum of Ps.
Jonathan on Genesis 49:11.
b. The rule of the Anointed One seems to be of
a limited time.

41 a. This applies to Christians from the Jews; see
for the expression ''yoke of the Law'' Ab 3:5 and
b.Sanh 94b.
b. The heathen idols are meant; cf. Deut 32:2.
c. The author refers to proselytes; see for the
expression ''to flee under your wings'' Pss 36:8;
57:2; and Ruth 2:12.

42 a. To believe in God is to live according to the
Law. Cf. 54:5 and 21; 59:2; 4Ezra 6:27, 28; 9:7–8;
and 1En 47:8.

3 have despised.[b] • And as for that which you said with regard to those who have
4 drawn near[c] and to those who have withdrawn, this is the explanation. • As for
those who have first subjected themselves and have withdrawn later and who
mingled themselves with the seed of the mingled nations,[d] their first time will be
5 considered as mountains. • And those who first did not know life and who later
knew it exactly and who mingled with the seed of the people who have separated
6 themselves, their first time will be considered as mountains.[e] • And times will
inherit times, and periods periods, and they will receive from one another. And
then, with a view to the end, all will be compared according to the length of times
7 and the hours of periods.[f] • For corruption will take away those who belong to it,
8 and life those who belong to it. • And dust will be called, and told, "Give back
that which does not belong to you and raise up all that you have kept until its own   30:1-2
time."

1 **43** You, however, Baruch, strengthen your heart with a view to that which has
been said to you, and understand that which has been revealed to you because you
2 have many consolations which will last forever. • For you will go away from this
place and leave the regions which are now before your eyes. And you shall forget   13:3
that which is corruptible and not again remember that which is among the mortal   21:19; 28:5
3 ones. • Go away, therefore, and command your people and come to this place and
afterward fast seven days. And then I shall come to you and speak with you.   5:6

Baruch speaks to the people

1 **44** And I, Baruch, went from there and came to my people and called my first-   46:1
born son and the Gedaliahs, my friends, and seven of the elders of the people and   5:1; 5:6; 46:1
said to them:
2,3   Behold, I go to my fathers in accordance with the way of the whole earth. • You,   3:2; 13:3
however, do not withdraw from the way of the Law, but guard and admonish the   Gen 15:15
people who are left lest they withdraw from the commandments of the Mighty   Josh 23:14
4 One. • For you see that he whom we serve is righteous and that our Creator is   1Kgs 2:2
5,6 impartial. • And see what has befallen Zion and what happened to Jerusalem, • that   13:8
the judgment of the Mighty One will be made known, as well as his ways which
7 are inscrutable and right. • For when you endure and persevere in his fear and do   14:9
not forget his Law, the time again will take a turn for the better for you.[a] And they
8 will participate in the consolation of Zion. • For that which is now is nothing. But   Lk 2:25
9 that which is in the future will be very great. • For[b] everything will pass away   28:4
which is corruptible, and everything that dies will go away, and all present time
will be forgotten, and there will be no remembrance of the present time which is
10 polluted by evils. • For he who runs now runs in vain and he who is happy will
11 fall quickly and be humiliated. • For that which will be in the future, that is what
one will look for, and that which comes later, that is what we shall hope for. For
12 there is a time that does not pass away. • And that period is coming which will
remain forever; and there is the new world which does not carry back to corruption   32:6
those who enter into its beginning, and which has no mercy on those who come
13 into torment or those who are living in it, and it does not carry to perdition. • For
those are the ones who will inherit this time of which it is spoken, and to these
14 is the heritage of the promised time. • These are they who prepared for themselves   21:25

---

b. Cf. for the destruction of sinners 4Ezra 7:93;
9:9–12; 1En 53:2; 56:1–4; 60:6; 69:27; 90:3–10;
and 102:1–3.
    c. See for the expression "to draw near" Eph
2:13 and 17; cf. Strack-Billerbeck, vol. 3, pp. 585f.
    d. See for the expression Ex 30:5 and Jer 25:20;
cf. Jub 30:7; TLevi 9:10; Philo, *Spec Leg* 3.29,
about the prohibition of mixed marriages.
    e. As in v. 4, we find the expression *wrmt*ʾ
mthsb, which is unknown and cannot be satisfac-

torily emended. The author wants to say that the
periods before the conversion no longer have significance.
    f. It seems that the length of time during which
one has been disobedient is taken into consideration.

44 a. The same promise in 46:5–6; 84:2; 85:4; Jub
1:22–23; 5:17; 23:26; and TJud 26:1.
    b. 9–15 also in BM Add. 14.686 and A. Konath
Library MS 77; see Introduction.

treasures of wisdom. And stores of insight are found with them. And they have　28:1-2
15 not withdrawn from mercy and they have preserved the truth of the Law. •For
the coming world will be given to these, but the habitation of the many[c] others
will be in the fire.[d]

1 **45** You, therefore, admonish the people as much as you can. For this is our work.
2 For, when you instruct them, you will make them alive.

1 **46** And my son and the elders of the people said to me:　　　　44:1
Did the Mighty One humiliate us to such an extent that he will take you away
2 from us quickly? •And shall we truly be in darkness, and will there be no light
3 anymore for that people who are left? •For where shall we again investigate the　3:6
Law, or who will distinguish between death and life for us?　　　Ps 119:92-93
　　　　　　　　　　　　　　　　　　　　　　　　　　　　Prov 13:14
4 And I said to them:　　　　　　　　　　　　　　　　　　　　4Ezra 14:20-21
I cannot resist the throne of the Mighty One. But Israel will not be in want of　Jer 14:21; 17:12
5 a wise man, nor the tribe of Jacob, a son of the Law.[a] •But only prepare your heart　17:4; 77:16
so that you obey the Law, and be subject to those who are wise and understanding
6 with fear. And prepare your soul that you shall not depart from them. •If you do　32:1
this, those good tidings will come to you of which I spoke to you earlier, and you　38:1-2
7 will not fall into the torment of which I spoke to you earlier. •But with regard to　44:7
the word that I shall be taken up, I did not let it be known to them at that time,　13:3; 48:13
not even to my son.　　　　　　　　　　　　　　　　　　　　4Ezra 14:50

1 **47** And after I had left, having dismissed them, I returned from there and said
to them:
Behold, I go to Hebron, for to there the Mighty One has sent me.
2 And I arrived at that place where the word was spoken to me, and I sat there
and fasted seven days.　　　　　　　　　　　　　　　　　　5:6

Prayer of Baruch

1 **48** And it happened after seven days that I prayed before the Mighty One and
said:

2 O Lord, you summon the coming of the times,
and they stand before you.
You cause the display of power of the worlds to pass away
and they do not resist you.
You arrange the course of the periods,　　　　　　　　　14:1
and they obey you.
3 Only you know the length of the generations,
and you do not reveal your secrets to many.
4 You make known the multitude of the fire,
and you weigh the lightness of the wind.
5 You investigate the end of the heights,
and you scrutinize the depths of darkness.
6 You command the number which will pass away, and which will be　21:10
preserved.
And you prepare a house for those who will be.　　　　　Jn 14:2
　　　　　　　　　　　　　　　　　　　　　　　　　　　2Cor 5:1-2
7 You remember the beginning which you created,
and you do not forget that destruction which will come.
8 With signs of fear and threat you command the flames,　　　21:5-6
and they change into winds.
And with the word you bring to life that which does not exist,

---

c. The word "many" is absent in the two MSS　　46 a. In b.Shab 139b we meet "the disciples of
mentioned under n. b.　　　　　　　　　　　the wise men," but it is not certain that they are
　d. Cf. 4Ezra 7:36; 1En 90:26f.; 100:9; TZeb　identical with the unknown "son of the Law."
10:3; and 4Mac 12:12.

and with great power you hold[a] that which has not yet come.

9   You instruct the creation with your understanding,   21:6,4
and you give wisdom to the spheres so that they minister according to their
positions.[b]   51:11

10   Innumerable hosts[c] stand before you,
and serve peacefully your sign according to their positions.   48:8

11   Hear your servant,
and regard my appeal.

12   For we are born in a short time,
and in a short time we return.

13   With you, however, the hours are like times,
and the days like generations.

14   Be, therefore, not angry at man because he is nothing;
and do not take count of our works;
for what are we?

15   For behold, by your gift we come into the world,
and we do go not of our own will.   14:11

16   For we did not say to our parents: "Beget us,"
nor have we sent to the realm of death saying: "Receive us."

17   What therefore is our strength that we can bear your wrath,
or what are we that we can endure your judgment?

18   Protect us in your grace,
and in your mercy help us.

19   Look at the small ones who submit to you,   Mt 10:42;
and save all those who come to you.   18:6,10
And do not take away the hope of our people,
and do not make short the times of our help.

20   For these are the people whom you have elected,
and this is the nation of which you found no equal.

21   But I shall speak to you now,
and I shall say as my heart thinks.

22   In you we have put our trust, because, behold, your Law is with us,
and we know that we do not fall as long as we keep your statutes.   44:7; 77:3

23   We shall always be blessed; at least, we did not mingle with the nations.
For we are all a people of the Name;   42:4

24   we, who received one Law from the One.
And that Law that is among us will help us,   78:4; 85:4
and that excellent wisdom which is in us will support us.   Eph 4:4-6
     38:1-2

25 And when I had prayed these things I became very weak.   21:26
26 And he answered and said to me:

You have prayed honestly, Baruch,
and all your words have been heard.

27   But my judgment asks for its own,
and my Law demands its right.

28   For from your words I shall answer you,
and from your prayer I shall speak with you.

29   Because it is as follows: There is nothing that will be destroyed unless it acted
wickedly, if it had been able to do something without remembering my goodness
and accepting my long-suffering.

30,31   For this reason surely you will be taken up, as I said to you before. •And the 46:7
time will come of which I spoke to you and that time is appearing which brings
affliction. For it will come and pass away with enormous vehemence; and arriving

---

48 a. See 29:5.

b. Cf. 1En 2:1 and 1Clem 20; see also Jude 6.

c. 2En 20:1–3.

32 in the heat of indignation, it will be turbulent. •And it will be in those days that
all inhabitants of the earth will live with each other in peace, because they do not [27:15]
33 know that my judgment has come near.[d] •For in that time there will not be found [Jer 6:14; 8:11] [Ezek 13:10]
many wise men and there will also be not many intelligent ones, but, in addition,
34 they who know will be silent more and more.[e] •And there will be many tidings [ch. 28; 70; 5]
and not a few rumors, and the works of the phantoms will be visible, and not a [Mt 24:6,11,24]
35 few promises will be told, some idle and others affirmed.[f] •And honor will change [27:9]
itself into shame, and strength will be humiliated to contempt, and the strong one
36 will be broken down, and beauty will become contemptible. •And many will say
to many in that time, "Where did the multitude of intelligence hide itself and [38:1-2; 70:5]
37 where did the multitude of wisdom depart?"[g] •And when one thinks about these [4Ezra 5:9-11]
things, jealousy will arise in those who did not think much of themselves; and
passion will take hold of those who were peaceful; and many will be agitated by [70:6]
wrath to injure many; and they will raise armies to shed blood; and they will [Mt 24:6]
38 perish with those at the end. •And it will happen in that time that a change of [44:7]
times will reveal itself openly for the eyes of everyone because they polluted
themselves in all those times and caused oppression, and each one walked in his [4Ezra 3:8]
39 own works and did not remember the Law of the Mighty One. •Therefore, a fire
will consume their thoughts, and with a flame the meditations of their kidneys[h] [Ps 7:10]
40 will be examined. For the Judge will come and will not hesitate. •For each of the [Jer 11:20; 17:10; 20:12]
inhabitants of the earth knew when he acted unrighteously, and they did not know [Sir 35:18] [2Pet 3:9]
41 my Law because of their pride. •But many will surely weep at that time—more, [Rom 2:14-15]
however, because of the living ones than of the dead.

42 And I answered and said:
O Adam, what did you do to all who were born after you? And what will be [17:3]
43 said of the first Eve who obeyed the serpent, •so that this whole multitude is going
to corruption? And countless are those whom the fire devours.
44 But again I shall speak before you.
45,46 You, O Lord, my Lord, you know that which is in your creation, •for you
commanded the dust one day to produce Adam; and you knew the number of those
who are born from him and how they sinned before you, those who existed and
47 who did not recognize you as their Creator. •And concerning all of those, their
end will put them to shame, and your Law which they transgressed will repay
them on your day.
48 But now, let us cease talking about the wicked and inquire about the righteous.
49 And I will tell about their blessedness and I shall not be silent about their glory
50 which is kept for them. •For surely, as you endured much labor in the short time
in which you live in this passing world, so you will receive great light in that [2Cor 4:17]
world which has no end.

1 **49** But further, I ask you, O Mighty One; and I shall ask grace from him who
2 created all things. •In which shape will the living live in your day? Or how will
3 remain their splendor which will be after that? •Will they, perhaps, take again this
present form, and will they put on the chained[a] members which are in evil and by
which evils are accomplished? Or will you perhaps change these things which have
been in the world, as also the world itself? [1Cor 15:51]

1 **50** And he answered and said to me:
Listen, Baruch, to this word and write down in the memory of your heart all

---

d. [Klijn has accurately represented the Syr.
Charles saw a problem with this verse and emended
the Syr. so as to obtain "shall be moved one against
the other, because they know not that my judgement
has drawn nigh." *APOT*, vol. 2, p. 506. —J.H.C.]
e. 33 is quoted in Cyprian, *Testimoniorum libri
III ad Quirinium* 3.29.
f. 34 is quoted in Cyprian, *Testimoniorum libri
III ad Quirinium* 3.29.

g. 36 is quoted in Cyprian, *Testimoniorum libri
III ad Quirinium* 3.29.
h. This Syr. idiom means "the meditations of
their innermost self."

49 a. Cf. OdesSol 17:4: "My chains were cut off
by his hands" and 21:2: "Because he cast off my
bonds for me." [The Syr. text here is difficult to
understand. —J.H.C.]

2 that you shall learn. •For the earth will surely give back the dead at that time; it 30:2
receives them now in order to keep them, not changing anything in their form. But
as it has received them so it will give them back. And as I have delivered them
3 to it so it will raise them. •For then it will be necessary to show those who live
that the dead are living again, and that those who went away have come back.
4 And it will be that when they have recognized each other,[a] those who know each
other at this moment, then my judgment will be strong, and those things which
have been spoken of before will come.

1 **51** And it will happen after this day which he appointed is over that both the
shape of those who are found to be guilty as also the glory of those who have 1Cor 15:51
1Cor 15:41
2 proved to be righteous will be changed. •For the shape of those who now act 21:9
wickedly will be made more evil than it is (now) so that they shall suffer torment.
3 Also, as for the glory of those who proved to be righteous on account of my law, 21:9
those who possessed intelligence in their life, and those who planted the root of
wisdom in their heart—their splendor will then be glorified by transformations, 33:1-2
and the shape of their face will be changed into the light of their beauty so that Sir 1:6,20
Wis 3:15
they may acquire and receive the undying world which is promised to them. 4Ezra 7:97
4 Therefore, especially they who will then come will be sad, because they despised Mt 17:2
Phil 3:21
my Law[a] and stopped their ears lest they hear wisdom and receive intelligence. 74:2
5 When they, therefore, will see that those over whom they are exalted now will 21:25
then be more exalted and glorified than they, then both these and those will be Zech 7:11
changed, these into the splendor of angels and those into startling visions and
6 horrible shapes; and they will waste away even more. •For they will first see and 30:4
then they will go away to be tormented.
7 Miracles, however, will appear at their own time to those who are saved because
of their works and for whom the Law is now a hope, and intelligence, expectation, 51:3
8 and wisdom a trust. •For they shall see that world which is now invisible to them,
9 and they will see a time which is now hidden to them. •And time will no longer Lk 20:36
10 make them older. •For they will live in the heights of that world and they will be
like the angels[b] and be equal to the stars.[c] And they will be changed into any shape
which they wished, from beauty to loveliness, and from light to the splendor of
11 glory. •For the extents of Paradise will be spread out for them, and to them will 4:7
be shown the beauty of the majesty of the living beings under the throne,[d] as well 48:10
as all the hosts of the angels, those who are held by my word now lest they show 48:10
themselves, and those who are withheld by my command so that they may stand
12 at their places until their coming has arrived. •And the excellence of the righteous
13 will then be greater than that of the angels. •For the first will receive the last, those
whom they expected; and the last, those of whom they had heard that they had
14 gone away. •For they have been saved from this world of affliction and have put
15 down the burden of anguishes. •Because of which men lost their life and for what 15:8
16 have those who were on the earth exchanged their soul? •For once they chose for Mt 16:26
themselves that time which cannot pass away without afflictions. And they chose
for themselves that time of which the end is full of lamentations and evils. And
they have denied the world that does not make those who come to it older. And
they have rejected the time which causes glory so that they are not coming to the
glory of which I spoke to you before.

---

50 a. Cf. Ps-Philo 62:9.

51 a. This can be compared with 1QpHab 1:11
and 5:11–12.

 b. According to 1En 62:13–16 "the righteous
and elect" will be clothed with "garments of
glory," and according to 104:4 their joy will be
as that of the angels of heaven; see also Strack-

Billerbeck, vol. 1, p. 891.
 c. Cf. Dan 12:3 and 1En 104:2; see also 2En
66:7.
 d. b.Shab 152b speaks about the souls under the
throne. If we have to accept that "the living beings"
are standing lower than the throne, we can refer to
Rev 6:4 or 7:11.

1 **52** And I answered and said:

2 How shall we forget[a] those for whom at that time woe is preserved? •And why are we again sad for those who die? Or why do we weep for those who go into 3 the realm of death? •The lamentations should be kept for the beginning of that coming torment; let the tears be laid down for the coming of that destruction which 4,5 will then come. •But with a view of these things, I shall also speak. •And concerning 6 the righteous ones, what will they do now? •Enjoy yourselves in the suffering which you suffer now.[b] For why do you look for the decline of your enemies? 7 Prepare your souls for that which is kept for you, and make ready your souls for the reward which is preserved for you.

And when I had said this I fell asleep there.

The apocalypse of the clouds

1 **53** And I saw a vision. And behold, a cloud was coming up from the great sea. And I was looking at it, and behold, it was entirely filled with black water and there were many colors in that water. And something like great lightning appeared 2 at its top. •And I saw that the cloud was rapidly passing in a quick run and covering 3 the whole earth. •And it happened after this that the cloud began to pour the water 4 that it contained upon the earth. •And I saw that the water which descended from 5 it was not of the same likeness. •For at first, it was very black until a certain time. And then, I saw that the water became bright, but there was not much of it. And after this, I saw black water again, and after this bright again, and black again and 6 bright again. •This, now, happened twelve times, but the black were always more 27:1 7 than the bright. •And it happened at the end of the cloud that, behold, it poured black water and it was much darker than all the water that had been before. And fire was mingled with it. And where that water descended, it brought about 8 devastation and destruction. •And after this I saw how the lightning which I had 9 seen at the top of the cloud seized it and pressed it down to the earth. •That lightning shone much more, so that it lighted the whole earth and healed the regions Mt 24:17 where the last waters had descended and where it had brought about destruction. 10,11 And it occupied the whole earth and took command of it. •And after this I saw, behold, twelve rivers[a] came from the sea and surrounded the lightning and became 12 subject to it. •And because of my fear I awoke.

Prayer of Baruch

1 **54** And I asked the Mighty One and said:

You alone, O Lord, knew the heights of the world beforehand and that which will happen in the times which you bring about by your word. And against the 20:1 works of the inhabitants of the earth you hasten the beginnings of the times. And 21:8 2 the ends of the periods you alone know. •You are the one for whom nothing is Jer 32:17,27 3 hard; but you are, however, the one who easily accomplishes all by a sign. •You Lk 1:37 are the one to whom both the depths and the heights come together, and whose 21:5 4 word the beginnings of the periods serve. •You are the one who reveals to those 5 who fear that which is prepared for them so that you may comfort them. •You show your mighty works to those who do not know. You pull down the enclosure Eph 2:14 for those who have no experience and enlighten the darknesses, and reveal the secrets to those who are spotless, to those who subjected themselves to you and 38:1-2 your Law in faith. Sir 42:19

6,7 You showed this vision to your servant; open to me its exposition also. •For 42:2

---

52 a. MS *ṭ'yn*, "how will they forget," but with the editions of Charles, Ryssel, and Kmosko *ṭ'ynn* must be read.

b. About the joy to suffer see 4Mac 15:24; 16:17ff.; 17:2; 9f.; b.Sanh 101a; GenR 33:1; Mt

5:10; Acts 5:41; Jas 1:2.

53 a. The rivers can refer either to Israel or the nations.

I know that I have recieved the answer regarding the subjects about which I asked you, and that you gave me a revelation about that which I asked, and that you have let me know with what voice I should honor you or from which members I should
8 cause glory and praise to go up to you. •For if my members should be mouths and the hairs of my head voices, even so I should not be able to honor you properly; and I should not be able to utter your glory or to express the excellence of your
9 beauty.[a] •For who am I among men or what is my significance among those who are more excellent than I that I have heard all these marvelous things from the
10 Most High and innumerable promises from him who created me? •Blessed is my mother among those who bear, and praised among women is she who bore me.
11 For I shall not be silent in honoring the Mighty One but with the voice of glory
12 I shall narrate his marvelous works. •For who is able to imitate[b] your miracles, O God, or who understands your deep thoughts of life?
13 For with your counsel, you reign over all creation which your right hand has created, and you have established the whole fountain of light with yourself, and
14 you have prepared under your throne the treasures of wisdom. •And those who do not love your Law are justly perishing. And the torment of judgment will fall upon
15 those who have not subjected themselves to your power. •For, although Adam sinned first and has brought death upon all who were not in his own time, yet each of them who has been born from him has prepared for himself the coming torment.
16 And further, each of them has chosen for himself the coming glory. •For truly, the one who believes will receive reward.
17 But now, turn yourselves to destruction, you unrighteous ones who are living now, for you will be visited suddenly, since you have once rejected the under-
18 standing of the Most High. •For his works have not taught you, nor has the artful
19 work of his creation which has existed always persuaded you.[c] •Adam is, therefore, not the cause, except only for himself, but each of us has become our own Adam.
20 You, however, O Lord, explain to me what you have revealed to me. And
21 inform me about that which I asked you. •For at the end of the world, a retribution will be demanded with regard to those who have done wickedly in accordance with their wickedness, and you will glorify the faithful ones in accordance with
22 their faith. •For those who are among your own, you rule; and those who sin, you blot out among your own.

Judg 5:24
Lk 1:42; 11:27
Ps 107:22

75:1
Ps 40:6
Sir 18:4-5; 42:17
4Ezra 3:5

17:3
Rom 5:12

Hab 2:4
Rom 1:17
Heb 10:38

Wis 13:1-9
Rom 1:20-21
54:15

42:2

Interpretation of the apocalypse

1 **55** And it happened that when I had finished the words of this prayer, I sat down
2 there under a tree to rest in the shadow of its branches. •And I was surprised and astonished, and I pondered in my thoughts about the multitude of the goodness which the sinners who are on earth have rejected from them, and about the great punishment which they have despised, when they knew that they should be punished
3 because of the sins they have committed. •And while I was pondering these and similar things, behold, Ramael,[a] the angel who is set over true visions, was sent to me and said to me:
4 Why does your heart trouble you, Baruch, and why are you disturbed by your
5 thought? •For if you are already disturbed, only hearing about the judgment, what
6 about when you see it with your eyes openly? •And if you are already so disturbed by the expectation with which you expect the day of the Mighty One, what about
7 when you arrive at its coming? •And if you are so fully terrified by the words of the announcement of the punishment of those who have transgressed, how much
8 more when this event itself will reveal marvelous things? •And if you have heard the names of the good and evil things which will come at that time, and if you are

6:1

15:6

63:6
4Ezra 4:36

---

54 a. PssSol 15:3 and OdesSol 26:4.

b. Syr. *mtdm*, also in 75:1, can be translated as "to imagine" and "to imitate." Both translations are possible here.

c. Cf. 1En 36:4.

55 a. In 4Ezra 4:36 he is called Jeremiel, but in the Syr. translation he is also named Ramael; cf. SibOr 2.215–17 and 1En 20:8, where he is one of the archangels.

grieved, what about when you will see what the Majesty will reveal, who will convince some and cause others to rejoice?

1 **56** But now, since you have asked the Most High to reveal to you the explanation
2 of the vision which you have seen, I have been sent to say to you •that the Mighty
One has let you know the course of times, namely those which have passed and 14:1
those which in his world will come to pass, from the beginning of his creation
3 until the end, (the times) which are known by deceit and by truth. •For as you saw
a great cloud which came up from the sea and went and covered the earth; this is
the length of the world which the Mighty One has created when he took counsel
4 in order to create the world.[a] •And it happened when the word had gone out from
him, that the length of the world was standing as something small, and it was
established[b] in accordance with the abundance of the intelligence of him who let
5 it go forth. •And as you first saw the black waters on the top of the cloud which
first came down upon the earth; this is the transgression which Adam, the first
6 man, committed. •For when he transgressed, untimely death came into being, 17:3
mourning was mentioned, affliction was prepared, illness was created, labor
accomplished, pride began to come into existence, the realm of death began to ask Prov 27:20
to be renewed with blood, the conception of children came about, the passion of Isa 5:14
the parents was produced, the loftiness of men was humiliated, and goodness Gen 3:16
7 vanished. •What could, therefore, have been blacker and darker than these things?
8,9 This is the beginning of the black waters which you have seen. •And from these
10 black waters again black were born, and very dark darkness originated. •For he
11 who was a danger to himself was also a danger to the angels. •For they possessed
12 freedom in that time in which they were created. •And some of them came down
13 and mingled themselves with women. •At that time they who acted like this were Gen 6:1-4
14 tormented in chains.[c] •But the rest of the multitude of angels, who have no number,
15 restrained themselves. •And those living on earth perished together through the
16 waters of the flood. •Those are the first black waters.

1 **57** And after these you saw the bright waters; that is the fountain of Abraham and
his generation, and the coming of his son, and the son of his son, and of those
2 who are like them. •For at that time the unwritten law was in force[a] among them,
and the works of the commandments were accomplished at that time, and the belief 32:6
in the coming judgment was brought about, and the hope of the world which will
be renewed was built at that time, and the promise of the life that will come later
3 was planted. •Those are the bright waters which you have seen.

1 **58** And the third black waters you have seen; that is the mingling of all sins
which the nations committed afterward, after the death of those righteous men,
and the wickedness of the land of Egypt, in which they acted wickedly in the
2 oppression with which they oppressed their sons. •But also these perished at the Ex 1:14
end.

1 **59** And the fourth bright waters which you have seen; that is the coming of Ex 2:10
Moses, and of Aaron, and of Miriam, and of Joshua, the son of Nun, and of Ex 4:14; 15:20
Ex 17:9
2 Caleb, and all those who are like these. •For at that time the lamp of the eternal Num 13:6
law which exists forever and ever illuminated all those who sat in darkness. This 17:4
(lamp) will announce to those who believe the promise of their reward and to those
3 who deny the punishment of the fire which is kept for them. •But also the heaven 42:2
will be shaken from its place at that time; that is, the heavens which are under the
throne of the Mighty One were severely shaken when he took Moses with him.[a] Ex 24:12-18

---

56 a. The cloud exists of thirteen parts: twelve parts alternately black and bright and finally one very black part.

b. [Klijn here follows Charles, who accepted Ceriani's emendation of the Syr., and rendered this verb as "was established." —J.H.C.]

c. Cf. 1En 10:4; see also 2En 18:4–6 and Sir 44:20.

57 a. See Jub 23:10 and b.Yoma 28b.

59 a. Cf. Ps-Philo 19:16.

4 For he showed him many warnings together with the ways of the Law and the
   end of time, as also to you; and then further, also the likeness of Zion with its 4:5
   measurements which was to be made after the likeness of the present sanctuary. Ex 25:40; 26:30
5 But he also showed him, at that time, the measures of fire, the depths of the abyss,[b] Heb 8:5
6 the weight of the winds,[c] the number of the raindrops,[d] •the suppression of wrath,
7 the abundance of long-suffering, the truth of judgment, •the root of wisdom, the 51:3
8 richness of understanding, the fountain of knowledge, •the height of the air,[e] the 27:1-2
                                                                                          Bar 3:12
   greatness of Paradise, the end of the periods, the beginning of the day of judg- 4Ezra 14:47
                                                                                          Sir 1:3
9,10 ment,[f] •the number of offerings,[g] the worlds which have not yet come, •the 4:7
   mouth of hell,[h] the standing place of vengeance, the place of faith, the region of
11 hope, •the picture of the coming punishment, the multitude of the angels which
   cannot be counted, the powers of the flame, the splendor of lightnings,[i] the voice
   of the thunders, the orders of the archangels,[j] the treasuries of the light, the changes
12 of the times,[k] and the inquiries into the Law. •These are the fourth bright waters
   you have seen.

1 **60** And the fifth black waters which you have seen poured down; those are the
   works which the Amorites have done, and the invocations of their incantations
   which they wrought, and the wickedness of their mysteries, and the mingling of Josh 24:18
2 their pollutions.[a] • But even Israel was polluted with sins in these days of the Judg 3:5
   judges, although they saw many signs which were from him who created them.

1 **61** And the sixth bright waters which you have seen; this is the time in which
2 David and Solomon were born. •And at that time the building of Zion took place, 1Kgs 8:1ff
   and the dedication of the sanctuary, and the shedding of much blood of the nations
   which sinned at that time, and the many offerings which were offered at that time
3 at the inauguration of the sanctuary. • And rest and peace reigned at that time. 1Kgs 8:62-63
4 And wisdom was heard in the assembly, and the richness of understanding was
5 magnified in the congregations. •And the holy festivals were fulfilled in happiness 1Kgs 3:12
6 and much joy. •And the judgment of the rulers was seen at that time without deceit,
   and the righteousness of the commandments of the Mighty One was accomplished 21:9
7 in truth. • And the land which then received mercy, since its inhabitants did not
   sin, was praised above all countries, and the city of Zion ruled over all countries EBar 11:9
8 and regions at that time. •These are those bright waters you have seen.

1 **62** And the seventh black waters you have seen; that is the perversion of the ideas
2 of Jeroboam who planned to make two golden calves, • and all the iniquities 1Kgs 12:32
3 accomplished by the kings who succeeded him, •and the curse of Jezebel, and the 1Kgs 18:4
4 idolatry which Israel practiced at that time, •and the withholding of rain, and the
5 famines of such a kind that the women ate the fruits of their womb, •and the time 2Kgs 6:28-29
   of their exile which befell the nine and a half tribes because they lived in many 1:2
6 sins. •And Salmanassar, the king of the Assyrians, came and carried them away 1:2
7 into captivity. •And concerning the nations much could be said: how they acted 2Kgs 17:3-6
                                                                                          4Ezra 13:40
   unrighteously and wickedly, and how they never proved themselves to be righteous. 21:9
8 These are those seventh black waters you have seen.

1 **63** And the eighth bright waters you have seen; that is the righteousness and the
2 integrity of Hezekiah, King of Judah, and the grace which came upon him. •For 2Kgs 16:20
   at that time Sennacherib was moved to destroy, and his wrath roused him, and also 2Kgs 18:13-37
3 the multitude of the nations which were with him in order to destroy; • when
   Hezekiah the king heard that which the Assyrian king devised, namely, to come

b. Cf. 1En 18:11 and 21:7–10.
c. Cf. 1En 41:4 and 2En 40:11.
d. Cf. Sir 1:2; 2En 47:5; and Ps-Philo 19:10.
e. Cf. 1En 40:12.
f. Cf. 2En 65:7–10.
g. Cf. Ps-Philo 19:10.

h. Cf. 1En 27:2f.; 54:1–6; and 90:26f.
i. Cf. 1En 41:3; 43:1f.; 60:13–15; and 2En 40:9.
j. Cf. 1En 61:10; 71:7–9; and 2En 30:1 and 3.
k. Cf. 1En 82:11–20; 2En 13:5; and 40:6.

60 a. Cf. Jub 29:11 and Ps-Philo 25:10–13.

and seize him and destroy his people—the two and a half tribes which were left—
and that he also wanted to destroy Zion, then Hezekiah trusted upon his works,
and hoped upon his righteousnesses, and spoke with the Mighty One and said: 21:9
4 "Pay attention, behold, Sennacherib is ready to destroy us, and he will boast and
5 be uplifted when he has destroyed Zion." • And the Mighty One heard him for 2Kgs 19:14-19
6 Hezekiah was wise, and he paid attention to his prayers for he was righteous. • And
7 the Mighty One then commanded Ramael, his angel who speaks with you. • And 55:3
I went away and destroyed their multitude, of which the number of the chiefs
alone was one hundred and eighty-five thousand, and each of them had an equal
8 number.ᵃ • And at that time I burned their bodies within, but I preserved their
clothes and their arms on the outside so that still more of the marvelous works of
the Mighty One might be seen, and so that his name might be mentioned throughout
9 the entire earth.ᵇ • Thus Zion was saved, and Jerusalem was delivered from its
10 tribulations. • And all those who were in the holy land rejoiced, and the name of
11 the Mighty One was praised so that it was spoken of. • These are those bright
waters which you have seen.

1 **64** And the ninth black waters you have seen; that is, the wickedness that existed
2 in the days of Manasseh, the son of Hezekiah. • For he acted very wickedly, and 2Kgs 21:2
killed the righteous, and perverted judgment, and shed innocent blood, and violently
polluted married women, and overturned altars, and abolished their offerings, and
3 drove away the priests lest they minister in the sanctuary. • And he made a statue
with five faces: Four of them looked into the direction of the four winds, and the
fifth was on the top of the statue so as to challenge the zeal of the Mighty One.ᵃ
4 And then the wrath of the Mighty One went out so that Zion should be uprooted
5 as has also happened in your days. • But also the judgment went out against the
two and a half tribes so that they also should be carried away into captivity as
6 you have now seen. • And the impiety of Manasseh increased to such a degree
7 that the glory of the Most High removed itself from the sanctuary.ᵇ • Therefore,
Manasseh was called the impious one in that time, and finally his habitation was
8 in the fire. • For although the Most High had heard his prayer, in the end when he
fell into the brazen horse and the brazen horse was melted, it became to him as
9 a sign regarding the hour (which was to come).ᶜ • For he had not lived perfectly
since he was not worthy, but (the sign was given to him) that he might know
10 henceforth by whom he should be punished at the end. • For he who is able to
benefit is also able to punish.

1 **65** This Manasseh sinned and he thought in his time that the Mighty One would
2 not call account for these things.ᵃ • These are those ninth black waters you have
seen.

1 **66** And the tenth bright waters you have seen; that is the purity of the generation 2Kgs 22:1
of Josiah, the king of Judah, who was the only one in his time who subjected
2 himself to the Mighty One with his whole heart and his whole soul. • He purified 2Kgs 23:4-30
the country from the idols, sanctified all the vessels which were polluted, restored
the offerings to the altar, raised the horn of the holy, exalted the righteous, and
honored all those who were wise with understanding. He brought the priests back
to their ministry, and destroyed and removed the magicians, enchanters, and

---

63 a. 2Kgs 19:35–36; 2Mac 8:19 and 15:22 mention a number of one hundred and eighty-five thousand killed. 2Chr 32:21 does not speak about a particular number, but b.Sanh 95b writes about a baraitha giving the number as two thousand and six hundred million "less one."
  b. Cf. b.Sanh 94a.

64 a. The same or a similar tradition is available in the Peshiṭta version of 2Chr 33:7 and also in the Commentary on the Diatessaron by Ephraem Syrus; see L. Leloir (ed.), *Commentaire de L'Évangile Concordant ou Diatessaron* (SC 121; Paris, 1966) p. 200. See also b.Sanh 103b.
  b. Cf. b.Sanh 103b.
  c. Cf. 2Chr 33:10–13 and Targum 2Chr 33:11.

65 a. Cf. b.Sanh 90a.

3 diviners from the land. •And he not only killed the impious who were living, but
4 also the bones were taken from the graves of the dead and burned with fire. •And
   he established the festivals and the sabbaths with their holy practices, and he
   burned the polluted with fire, and as for the lying prophets who deceived the
   people, also these he burned with fire. He cast the people who obeyed them, as
5 long as they lived, into the Kidron valley, and heaped stones upon them. •And
   he was zealous with the zeal of the Mighty One with his whole soul, and he alone
   was strong in the Law at that time so that he left no one un-circumcised or anyone
6 who acted wickedly in the whole country all the days of his life. •He, then, is
   one who shall receive reward forever and ever and be honored with the Mighty
7 One more than many in the last time. •For on his account and on account of those
   who are like him, the precious glories have been created and prepared which were
8 spoken to you earlier. •These are those bright waters which you have seen.

1 **67** And the eleventh black waters you have seen; that is the disaster which has
2 befallen Zion now. •Do you think that there is no mourning among the angels
   before the Mighty One, that Zion is delivered up in this way? Behold, the nations   5:1
   rejoice in their hearts, and the multitudes are before their idols and say, "She who
   has trodden others down for such a long time has been trodden down; and she who
3 has subjugated has been subjugated." •Do you think that the Most High rejoices
4 in these things or that his name has been glorified? •But how will it be with his
5 righteous judgment? •But after these things those scattered among the nations will
6 be taken hold of by tribulations and live in shame in every place. •For so far as
   Zion has been delivered up and Jerusalem laid waste, the idols in the cities of the
   nations are happy and the flavor of the smoke of the incense of the righteousness
   of the Law has been extinguished everywhere in the region of Zion; behold, the   21:9
7 smoke of the impiety is there. •But the king of Babylon will arise, the one who   Rom 10:5
   now has destroyed Zion, and he will boast over the people and speak haughtily   Phil 3:6
8,9 in his heart before the Most High. •And he too will fall finally. •These are those
   black waters.

1,2 **68** And the twelfth bright waters which you have seen; this is the word. •For
   there will come a time after these things, and your people will fall into such a
3 distress so that they are all together in danger of perishing. •They, however, will
4 be saved, and their enemies will fall before them.[a] •And to them will fall much
5 joy one day. •And at that time, after a short time, Zion will be rebuilt again, and
   the offerings will be restored, and the priests will again return to their ministry.[b]
6,7 And the nations will again come to honor it.[c] •But not as fully as before. •But it   Ezra 3:12
8 will happen after these things that there will be a fall of many nations. •These are
   the bright waters you have seen.

1 **69** With regard to the last waters you have seen which are blacker than all those
   preceding which came after the twelfth, those which were brought together; they
2 apply to the whole world. •For the Most High made a division at the beginning   29:1
3 for only he knows what will happen in the future. •For with regard to the evils of
4 the coming impieties which occurred before him, he saw six kinds. •And of the
   good works of the righteous which would be accomplished before him, he foresaw
   six kinds, with the exclusion of that which he should accomplish himself at the
5 end of the world. •These are, therefore, not black waters with black, nor bright
   with bright. For that is the end.

1 **70** Therefore, hear the exposition of the last black waters which will come after
2 the black waters. This is the word. •Behold, the days are coming and it will happen
   when the time of the world has ripened and the harvest of the seed of the evil ones

---

68 a. This might refer to Esther.
b. This refers to the restoration of the Temple

after the exile in Babylon.
c. Cf. Tob 14:5–6.

and the good ones has come that the Mighty One will cause to come over the earth and its inhabitants and its rulers confusion of the spirit and amazement of the heart.
3 And they will hate one another and provoke one another to fight. And the despised ^{25:3} ^{4Ezra 6:24} will rule over the honorable, and the unworthy will raise themselves over the
4 illustrious. •And many will be delivered to the few, those who were nothing will rule over the strong, the poor will be greater in number than the rich, and the
5 impious will exalt themselves over the brave. •The wise will be silent, and the foolish will speak. And the thought of men will not be realized then, nor the 48:33,36
6 counsel of the strong, and the hope of those who hope will not be realized. •Then 4Ezra 5:12 it will happen when those things occur which have been said before will come to pass, that confusion will fall upon all men. And some of them will fall in war, and others will perish in tribulations, and again others of them will be troubled by their 48:37
7 own. •The Most High will then give a sign to those nations which he has prepared before, and they will come and wage war with the rulers who will then remain.
8 And it will happen that everyone who saves himself from the war will die in an 27:7,10,6 earthquake, and he who saves himself from the earthquake will be burned by fire, 4Ezra 9:3; 13:29-32
9 and he who saves himself from the fire will perish by famine. •And it will happen that everyone who will save himself and escape from all things which have been said before—both those who have won and those who have been overcome—that
10 all will be delivered into the hands of my Servant, the Anointed One. •For the Isa 21:9; 42:1; 42:9; 43:10; whole earth will devour its inhabitants. 44:21; 49:3 Acts 3:13,26; 4:27,

1 **71** And the holy land will have mercy on its own and will protect its inhabitants 29:2
2 at that time. •This is the vision which you have seen, and this is its explanation. For I have come to tell you these things since your prayer has been heard by the Most High.

1 **72** Now,[a] hear also about the bright waters which come at the end after these
2 black ones. This is the word. •After the signs have come of which I have spoken to you before, when the nations are moved and the time of my Anointed One comes, he will call all nations, and some of them he will spare, and others he will
3,4 kill.[b] •These things will befall the nations which will be spared by him. •Every nation which has not known Israel and which has not trodden down the seed of
5 Jacob will live. •And this is because some from all the nations have been subjected
6 to your people. •All those,[c] now, who have ruled over you or have known you, will be delivered up to the sword.

1 **73** And it will happen that after he has brought down everything which is in the 1Cor 15:24-25 world, and has sat down in eternal peace on the throne of the kingdom,[a] then joy Heb 4:3
2 will be revealed and rest will appear.[b] •And then health will descend in dew, and 29:7 illness will vanish, and fear and tribulation and lamentation will pass away from Rev 21:4
3 among men, and joy will encompass the earth. • And nobody will again die 54:15 Rev 21:4
4 untimely, nor will any adversity take place suddenly. •Judgment, condemnations, contentions, revenges, blood, passions, zeal, hate, and all such things will go into
5 condemnation since they will be uprooted.[c] •For these are the things that have filled this earth with evils, and because of them life of men came in yet greater
6 confusion. •And the wild beasts will come from the wood and serve men, and the asps and dragons will come out of their holes to subject themselves to a child.[d]

---

72 a. 72:1–73:2 also in BM Add. 14.687 twice and A. Konath Library MS 77; see Introduction.

b. The Messiah as warrior, see 39:7–40:2. Concerning his dominion over the nations, see Ps 72:11 and 17; Isa 14:2; 66:12; 19–21; 4Ezra 13:37–38 and 49; AsMos 10; TJud 24:6; 1En 90:30; and PssSol 17:32.

c. The second text of BM Add. 14.687 omits the words "who ruled . . . [73:1] brought down everything."

73 a. Cf. Rev 21:5; 1En 69:27 and 29; 61:8.

b. Cf. Jub 23:29; 1En 5:7–9; 25:6; 51:6; TLevi 18:4; and TJud 24:1.

c. Cf. 4Ezra 6:26–28; SibOr 3.376–80 and 751–55.

d. See also the quotation from Papias in Irenaeus, *Adv Haer* 5.33.3–4.

7 And women will no longer have pain when they bear, nor will they be tormented Isa 11:6-9
when they yield the fruits of their womb.ᵉ

1 **74** And it will happen in those days that the reapers will not become tired, and
the farmers will not wear themselves out, because the products of themselves will
shoot out speedily, during the time that they work on them in full tranquillity.
2 For that time is the end of that which is corruptible and the beginning of that which
3 is incorruptible. •Therefore, the things which were said before will happen in it. 28:4
Therefore, it is far away from the evil things and near to those which do not die.
4 Those are the last bright waters which have come after the last dark waters.

1 **75** And I answered and said:

Who can equal your goodness, O Lord?
for it is incomprehensible.
2 Or who can fathom your grace 54:12
which is without end? 14:8f.
Isa 40:13f.
3 Or who can understand your intelligence?
4 Or who can narrate the thoughts of your spirit?
5 Or who of those born can hope to arrive at these things,
apart from those to whom you are merciful and gracious?
6 For if you were not merciful to men, 4Ezra 7:132-34;
those who are under your right hand, 8:31f.,36,45;
12:48
they were not able to come to them,
apart from those who are named among the famous number.ᵃ
7 But we who exist, when we know why we have come,
and then subject ourselves to him who brought us out of Egypt,
we shall come againᵇ and remember those things which have passed away,
and rejoice with regard to the things which have been.
8 But if we do not know now why we have come,
and do not recognize the sovereignty of him who brought us up from Egypt,
we will come again and ask for that which has now occurred,
and shall be severely grieved because of that which has happened.

1 **76** And he answered and said to me:
Since the revelation of this vision has been explained to you as you prayed for,
hear the word of the Most High that you know that which will happen to you after
2 these things. •For you will surely depart from this world, nevertheless not to death
3 but to be kept unto (the end) of times. •Therefore, go up to the top of this mountain, 13:3
and all countries of this earth will pass before you, as well as the likeness of the
inhabited world, and the top of the mountains, and the depths of the valleys, and Deut 34:1-3
Mt 4:8
the depths of the seas, and the number of rivers, so that you may see that which 3:3
4,5 you leave and whither you go. •This will happen after forty days. •Go, therefore, Ex 24:18; 34:28
Deut 9:9,18
now during these days and instruct the people as much as you can so that they may 4Ezra 14:23,
learn lest they die in the last times, but may learn so that they live in the last times. 43,45

Baruch speaks to the people

1 **77** And I, Baruch, went away from there and came to the people, and assembled
them from the greatest to the smallest and said to them:
2 Hear, O children of Israel, behold how many are left from the twelve tribes of Jer 6:13; 8:10;
3,4 Israel. •To you and to your fathers the Lord gave the Law above all nations. •And 31:34
because your brothers have transgressed the commandments of the Most High, he 48:22
brought vengeance upon you and upon them and did not spare the ancestors, but 1Bar 3:37; 4:4
4Ezra 5:27

e. Cf. LevR 14:9.

75 a. The elect ones, cf. 1Clem 2:4.
b. At the resurrection of the dead.

he also gave the descendants into captivity and did not leave a remnant of them.
5,6 And, behold, you are here, with me. •If, therefore, you will make straight your
ways, you will not go away as your brothers went away, but they will come to 78:7
7 you. •For he is merciful whom you honor, and gracious in whom you hope, and
8 true so that he will do good to you and not evil. •Have you not seen what has
9 befallen Zion? •Or do you think that the place has sinned and that it has been
destroyed for this reason, or that the country has done some crime and that it is
10 delivered up for that reason? •And do you not know that because of you who
sinned the one who did not sin was destroyed, and that because of those who acted
unrighteously, the one who has not gone astray has been delivered up to the
enemies?   Bar 2:26

The people invite Baruch to write a letter

11   And the whole people answered and they said to me:
      Everything which we can remember of the good things which the Mighty One
      has done to us we shall remember, and that which we do not remember he knows
12 in his grace. •But do this for us, your people: Write also to our brothers in Babylon
      a letter of doctrine and a roll of hope so that you might strengthen them also before
13 you go away from us.ᵃ •For the shepherds of Israel have perished, and the lamps
      which gave light are extinguished, and the fountains from which we used to drink
14 have withheld their streams. •Now we have been left in the darkness and in the
      thick forest and in the aridness of the desert.
15   And I answered and said to them:
      Shepherds and lamps and fountains came from the Law and when we go away,
16 the Law will abide. •If you, therefore, look upon the Law and are intent upon   46:4
      wisdom, then the lamp will not be wanting and the shepherd will not give way and   4Ezra 9:37
17 the fountain will not dry up. •Nevertheless, I shall also write to your brothers in   46:4
      Babylon, as you have said to me, and I shall send it by means of men. Also I shall
      write to the nine and a half tribes, and send it by means of a bird.
18   And it happened on the twenty-first day of the ninth month that I, Baruch, came
      and sat down under the oak in the shadow of the branches, and nobody was with   6:1
19 me; I was alone. •And I wrote two letters. One I sent by means of an eagleᵇ to
      the nine and a half tribes, and the other I sent by means of three men to those who   1:2
20 were in Babylon. •And I called an eagle and said to him these words:
21   You have been created by the Most High that you should be higher than any
22 other bird. •But now go and do not stay in any place, do not go into a nest, do
      not sit on any tree until you have flown over the breadth of the many waters of
      the river Euphrates and have come to the people that live there and cast down to
23 them this letter. •Remember that Noah at the time of the flood received the fruit
24 of the olive tree from a dove when he sent it away from the ark. •And also the   Gen 8:11
      ravens served Elijah when they brought food to him as they were commanded.
25 Also Solomon, in the time of his kingship, commanded a bird whither he wanted   1Kgs 17:6
      to send a letter and in whatever he was in need of and it obeyed him as he
26 commanded it.ᶜ •And do not be reluctant and do not deviate to the right nor to the
      left, but fly and go straight awayᵈ that you may preserve the command of the
      Mighty One as I said to you.

The letter to the nine and a half tribes

1 **78** The letter of Baruch, the son of Neriah which he wrote to the nine and a half
      tribes.ᵃ

---

77 a. This letter is unknown.
   b. Cf. 4Bar 7:3.
   c. Cf. EcclR 2.25.
   d. Cf. 4Bar 7:12.

78 a. This is the heading of the text as it is found
attached to the apocalypse. This text is generally
followed in the translation; see Introduction. In
other texts of this letter different headings are available.

These are[b] the words of the letter[c] which Baruch, the son of Neriah, sent to the [1:2] nine and a half tribes which were across the river[d] in which were written the following things:

2 Thus speaks Baruch, the son of Neriah, to the brothers who were carried away 3 in captivity: •Grace and peace be with you.[e] I remember, my brothers, the love [Rom 1:7] of him who created me,[f] who loved us from the beginning and who never hated [1Cor 1:3] [2Cor 1:2] 4 us but, on the contrary,[g] chastised us. •And truly I know: Are we not all,[h] the [1:5; 4:1; 13:10] twelve tribes, bound by one captivity as we also descend from one father? [48:24] 5 Therefore, I have been the more diligent to leave you the words of this letter before I die so that you may be comforted regarding the evils[i] which have befallen you, [13:3] and you may also be grieved with regard to the evils which have befallen your brothers, and then further, so that you may consider the judgment of him who decreed it against you to be righteous,[j] namely, that you should be carried away into captivity, for what you have suffered is smaller than what you have done, in 6 order that you may be found worthy of your fathers in the last times. •Therefore, if you think about the things you have suffered now for your good so that you may not be condemned at the end and be tormented, you shall receive hope which lasts [83:8] forever and ever, particularly if you remove from your hearts the idle error for 7 which you went away from here. •For if you do these things in this way, he shall [77:6] continually remember you. He is the one who always promised on our behalf to [Deut 30:3] [Jer 23:3] those who are more excellent than we[k] that he will not forever forget or forsake[l] [Bar 4:36-37; 5,6] our offspring, but with much mercy assemble all those[m] again who were dispersed.[n] [2Mac 2:18] [Tob 13:13] [4Ezra 13:12f.]

1 **79** Therefore, my brothers, learn first what befell Zion, namely, that Nebucad- 2 nezzar, the king of Babylon, came up against us. •For we had sinned against him [1:3] who created us, and had not observed the commandments[a] which he ordered us. [Bar 1:15-23] 3,4 And yet he has not chastised us as we deserved. •For what befell you, we suffered even more,[b] for it befell us also.

1 **80** And now, my brothers,[a] when the enemies had surrounded the city, angels were sent from the Most High. And they demolished the fortification[b] of the strong wall, and he destroyed[c] their solid iron corners which could not be loosened. [7:1-2] 2 Nevertheless, they hid the holy vessels[d] lest they be polluted[e] by the enemies. [6:7-8] 3 And when they had done these things,[f] they left the demolished wall, the looted house, the burned temple, and the people who were overcome to the enemies, for [7:1] they were delivered up lest the enemies should boast and say, "We have overcome[g] 4 to such an extent that we have even destroyed the house of the Most High." •They have also bound your brothers and carried them away to Babylon and have caused [8:5] 5,6 them to live there. •And we have been left here with very few. •That is the 7 affliction about which I write to you. •For truly I know that the inhabitants[h] of

---

b. "These are," l; "and these are," c *solus*.

c. "Of the letter," l; om., c *solus*.

d. "The river," l; "the river Euphrates," c *solus*.

e. "Be with you," l; om., c *solus*.

f. "Me," l; "us," c *solus*.

g. MSS 17a1/2/3/4 p w 16g6 12a1 17/15a1 omit "on the contrary."

h. "Are we not all," l; "that, behold . . .," c *solus*.

i. "The evils," l; "the evil," c *solus*.

j. Cf. 4Ezra 10:16 and PssSol 3:3; 4:9; 8:7.

k. The Patriarchs.

l. "That he will . . . forsake," l; "that he will never forget or forsake us," c *solus*.

m. "All those," l; "those," c *solus*.

n. Cf. 1En 90:33 and PssSol 17:50.

79 a. "The commandments," l; "the command-

ment," c *solus*.

b. "For what . . . us also": The various readings in the MSS are all corrupt, but the meaning of the text is clear.

80 a. "I make known to you that" *post* "brothers," c *solus* omits.

b. "Fortification," l; "fortifications," c *solus*.

c. "He destroyed," l; "they destroyed," c *solus*.

d. "The holy vessels," l; "the vessels of the holy vessels," c *solus*.

e. "Destroyed," l; "polluted," 17a2; "taken," l; "polluted," 17a3 p w 16g6 17/15a1.

f. "And when these things had gone by," l; "And when they had done these things," c *solus* (wrong reading).

g. "Overcome," l; "overcome with power," c *solus*.

h. "Inhabitants," l; "habitation," 7a1 and c.

Zion were a comfort to you. As long[i] as you knew that they were happy, this was more important than the affliction you endured being separated from them.

1,2 **81** But also hear the word of consolation. •For I mourned with regard to Zion `Heb 13:22`
3 and asked grace from the Most High and said, •"Will these things exist for us
4 until the end?[a] •And will these evils befall us always?" And the Mighty One did according to the multitude of his grace,[b] and the Most High according to the magnitude of his mercy, and he revealed to me a word that I might be comforted, and showed me visions that I might not be again sorrowful, and made known to me the mysteries[c] of the times, and showed me the coming of the periods.

1 **82** My brothers, therefore I have written to you that you may find consolation
2 with regard to the multitude of tribulations.[a] •But you ought to know that our Creator will surely[b] avenge us on all our brothers according to everything which `13:10-12` they have done against us and among us; in particular that the end which the Most `Bar 4:30-35` High prepared is near, and that his grace is coming,[c] and that the fulfillment of
3 his judgment is not far. •For now we see[d] the multitude of the happiness of the
4 nations although they have acted wickedly; but they are like a vapor.[e] •And we behold the multitude of their power while they act impiously; but they will be `4Ezra 7:61`
5 made like a drop.[f] •And we see the strength of their power[g] while they resist the `Isa 40:15`
6 Mighty One every hour;[h] but they will be reckoned like spittle.[i] •And we will `4Ezra 6:56` ponder about the glory of their majesty while they do not keep the statutes[j] of the
7 Most High; but as smoke they will pass away. •And we think about the beauty of their gracefulness[k] while they go down in impurities;[l] but like grass which is `Isa 40:6-7`
8 withering, they will fade away. •And we ponder about the strength of their cruelty while they themselves do not think about the end; but they will be broken like a
9 passing wave. •And we notice the pride[m] of their power while they deny the goodness of God[n] by whom it was given to them; but as a passing cloud[o] they will vanish.

1 **83** For the Most High will surely hasten his times, and he will certainly cause `20:1`
2 his periods to arrive. •And he will surely judge[a] those who are in his world, and `20:2` will truly inquire into everything with regard to all their works which were sins.[b]
3 He will certainly investigate the secret thoughts and everything which is lying in the inner chambers of all their members[c] which are in sin.[d] And he will make them `Jer 17:9`
4 manifest in the presence of everyone with blame. •Therefore,[e] nothing of the `1Cor 4:5; 14:25` present things should come into your heart, but they should, on the contrary, be `Heb 4:12` `21:25`
5 expected, since that which was promised[f] will come. •And we should[g] not look

---

i. "So far," l; "As long," f w p.

81 a. "Will these . . . the end," l; "How long will these things exist for us," c *solus*.
b. "His grace," l; "grace," 7a1 c 6h14 10g1 12d2 17/15a1.
c. "Mysteries," l; "mystery," c 12d2 17/15a1.

82 a. "Tribulations," l; "your tribulations" (or: "your tribulation," 17a1/2/3/4 16g6 12a1 17/15a1 w p), c *solus*.
b. "Surely," l; "surely . . . us," c *solus*.
c. Cf. Did 10:6.
d. "For now we see," l; "For, see, we see," c *solus*.
e. "Like impure," l; "like a vapor," c *solus* (wrong reading).
f. "Impurity," l; "drop," c *solus* (wrong reading).
g. "Truth," l; "power," c *solus* (wrong reading).
h. "Every year," l; "every hour," c *solus*

(wrong reading).
i. Cf. Isa 40:15 (LXX); 4Ezra 6:56; and Ps-Philo 7:3.
j. "Statutes," l; "commandments," c *solus*.
k. "Their gracefulness," l; "their life," c *solus*.
l. "Impurities," l; "impurity," c *solus*.
m. "Pride," l; "beauty," c *solus*.
n. "Of God," l; om., c *solus*.
o. Cf. Ps-Philo 19:13.

83 a. "And our God will judge," l; "And he . . . judge," 6h14 10g1.
b. "Which were sins," l; "which were hidden," c *solus*.
c. "In the inner chambers of all their members," l; "which is in the inner chamber ["chambers," 17a2/3/4 16g6 w p] which is in all their members," c *solus*.
d. "Which are in sin," l; "of man," c *solus*.
e. "Therefore," l; "For therefore," 7a1 c.
f. "Promised," l; "promised us," c *solus*.
g. "We should," l; "we should now," c *solus*.

upon the delights of the present[h] nations, but let us think about that which has been
6 promised to us regarding the end. •For the ends of the times and the periods will
7 surely pass away and all which is in them together. •The end[i] of the world will
then show the great power of our Ruler since everything will come to judgment.
8 You should, therefore, prepare your hearts for that which you have believed
before, lest you should be excluded from both worlds, namely, that you were
9 carried away into captivity here and tormented there.[j] •For that which exists now
or that which has passed away or that which will come, in all of that, neither the
10 evil in it is fully evil, nor the good is even fully good. •For all sorts of health
11 which exist now changes into illnesses.[k] •And every might which exists now
changes into weakness, and every power that exists now changes into miseries,[l]
12 and every youthful energy changes into old age and consummation. And every
beauty of gracefulness which exists now changes into withering and ugliness.
13 And every infantile pride[m] which exists now changes into lowliness and shame.
And every glory of haughtiness which exists now changes into the shame of
14 silence. •And every delight and all splendor which exists now changes into ruin
15 of silence. •And every joy and every delight[n] which exist now change into rejection
16,17 and ruin.[o] •And every clamor of pride[p] changes into silent dust.[q] •And every
possession of richness[r] which exists now changes into the realm of death alone.
18 And every seizing[s] desire which exists now changes into involuntary death, and
19 every desire of lust[t] changes into the judgment of punishment. •And every
20 capability of deceit[u] which exists now changes into refutation by truth. •And every
sweetness of ointments which exists now changes into judgment and condemnation.
21,22 And every friendship[v] changes into silent[w] defamations.[x] •Since all these things
23 happened now, do you think[y] that they will not be avenged? •But the end of
everything will come to light.[z]

1 **84** Now, I gave you knowledge,[a] while I still live. For I have said that you should
particularly learn my mighty commandments[b] which he has instructed you. And
I shall set before you some of the commandments of his judgment before I die. 13:3
2 Remember that once Moses called heaven and earth to witness against you and 19:1-3
said, "If you trespass the law, you shall be dispersed. And if you shall keep it, ·Deut 33:19-20
3 you shall be planted."[c] •And also[d] other things he said to you when you were in Isa 60:21
4 the desert as twelve tribes together. •And after his death you cast it away from
5 you and, therefore,[e] that which has been said before has come upon you.[f] •And Bar 2:14-20
now, Moses spoke to you before it befell you and, behold, it has befallen you for
6 you have forsaken the Law. •Also I, behold, I say to you after you suffered that
if you obey the things which I have said to you, you shall receive from the Mighty
7 One everything which has been prepared and has been preserved for you. •Therefore,

h. "The present," l; "the," c *solus*.

i. "The end," l; "And the end" (17a3), or:
"In the end," c *solus*.

j. "That you were . . . tormented there," l;
"that will be carried away in captivity now and be
tormented thereupon," c *solus*.

k. "Illness," l; "illnesses," 17a1/2/4 15/17a1
w p.

l. "Miseries," l; "misery," c *solus*.

m. "Infantile pride," l; "dominion and vanity,"
c *solus*.

n. "Every joy and every delight," l; singular,
c *solus*.

o. "Ruin," l; "worms," c *solus*.

p. "Pride," l; "pride which is now," c *solus*.

q. "Silent dust," l; "dust and silence," c *solus*.

r. "Of richness," l; "and richness," c 7a1/2/3/
4 16g6 w p.

s. "Seizing," l; plural, 17a1/3 6h14 w p.

t. Lit., "lusts," l; singular, c 17a1/3 6h14 10g1

12d2; "which now (are)" *post* "lusts," c *solus*
omits.

u. "Deceit," l; plural, c *solus*.

v. "Of treachery" *post* "friendship," c *solus*
omits (wrong reading).

w. "Silent," l; "true," c *solus*.

x. "Defamations," l; singular, c *solus*.

y. "Do you think," l; "does anyone think," c
solus.

z. Lit. "truth."

84 a. "I gave you," l; "behold, I gave you," c
solus.

b. "My mighty commandments," l; "the commandments of the Mighty One," c *solus*.

c. "Be planted," l; "be preserved," c *solus*.

d. "And also," l; "But also," c *solus*.

e. "And therefore," l; "therefore," c 12d2.

f. See for 2–4: 19:1–3; Deut 30:19–20; Isa 60:21;
1QS 8.5 and 11.8; Jub 7:34; 1En 84:6; and PssSol
14:3.

let this letter be a witness between me and you that you may remember the commandments of the Mighty One, and that it also may serve as my defense in
8 the presence of him who has sent me. •And remember Zion and the Law[g] and the holy land and your brothers and the covenant and your fathers,[h] and do not forget
9 the festivals and the sabbaths. •And give this letter and the traditions[i] of the Law
10 to your children after you as also your fathers handed down to you. •And ask always[j] and pray seriously with your whole soul that the Mighty One may accept you in mercy and that he may not reckon the multitude of your sinners,[k] but   4Ezra 10:24
11 remember the integrity of your fathers. •For if he judges us not according to the   14:7 multitude of his grace, woe to all us who are born.[l]   75:6

1 **85** Further, know that our fathers in former times and former generations had
2 helpers, righteous prophets and holy men.[a] •But we were also in our country, and   Mt 13:17 they helped us when we sinned, and they intervened for us with him who has created us since they trusted in their works. And the Mighty One heard them[b] and
3 purged us from our sins. •But now, the righteous have been assembled, and the prophets are sleeping.[c] Also we[d] have left our land, and Zion has been taken away   1Mac 9:27 from us, and we have nothing now apart from the Mighty One and his Law.[e]
4 Therefore, if we direct and dispose our hearts, we shall receive everything which
5 we lost again by many times.[f] •For that which we lost was subjected to corruption,   44:7
6 and that which we receive will not be corruptible. •We also have written to our   28:4
7 brothers in Babylon so that I may[g] attest to them these things also. •And these things which I have said earlier should be before your eyes always, since we are
8 still in the spirit of the power[h] of our liberty. •And further, the Most High is also[i]   4Ezra 8:56; 9:11 long-suffering to us here and has shown to us that which comes and has not
9 concealed from us what will happen at the end. •Therefore, before his judgment[j] exacts his own and truth of that[k] which is its due, let us prepare ourselves that we   5:2 may possess and not be possessed, and that we may hope and not be put to shame, and that we may rest with our fathers and not be punished with those who hate us.
10 For the youth of this world has passed away, and the power of creation is   4Ezra 5:50-56; already exhausted, and the coming of the times is very near and has passed by.   14:10-16 And the pitcher is near the well, and the ship to the harbor, and the journey to the
11 city, and life to its end. •Further, prepare yourselves so that, when you sail and ascend from the ship, you may have rest and not be condemned when you have
12 gone away. •For behold, the Most High will cause all these things to come. There will[l] not be an opportunity to repent[m] anymore, nor a limit to the times, nor a duration of the periods, nor a change to rest,[n] nor an opportunity to prayer, nor sending up petition, nor giving knowledge,[o] nor giving love, nor opportunity of repentence, nor supplicating[p] for offenses, nor prayers[q] of the fathers, nor in-

---

g. "Zion and the Law," l; "the Law and Zion," c *solus*.

h. "And your fathers," l; "of your fathers," c *solus*.

i. "Traditions," l; "tradition," c *solus*.

j. "Always," l; "always continuously," c *solus*.

k. "Sinners," l; "sins," c *solus*.

l. Cf. Ps-Philo 19:9 and 28:5.

85 a. "Prophets and holy men," l; "holy prophets," c *solus*.

b. "Them," l; "their prayer," c *solus*.

c. Cf. b.Sanh 11a.

d. "Also we," l; "And also we," c *solus*.

e. Cf. b.Sot 49ab.

f. "We shall receive . . . by many times," l; "shall we receive again everything which we lost, and much more than we lost, by many times," c

solus.

g. "That I may . . .," l; "And I may," c *solus*.

h. "Of the power," l; "and in the power," c *solus*.

i. "Also," l; om., c *solus*.

j. "His judgment," l; "the judgment," 7a1, or "the Judge," c *solus*.

k. "Of that," l; "that," 7a1 c.

l. ". . . the Most High . . . There will . . .," l; "when the Most High . . ., there will . . .," c *solus*.

m. 4Ezra 7:82 and 9:12 and 2En 62:2.

n. "To rest," l; "for the ways," 6h14 10g1 w p; "for the way," 17a2/3/4 15/17a1 16g6; "for the souls," 12d2, 7a1 c 17a1 10ml.

o. "Nor giving of knowledge," l; "nor a giver," 17a2 c.

p. "Supplicating," l; "supplication," c *solus*.

q. "Prayers," l; "prayer," c *solus*.

13 tercessions of the prophets, nor help of the righteous.[r] •There is the proclamation
   of judgment to corruption,[s] regarding the way[t] to the fire and the path that leads   Mt 7:13
14 to the glowing coals.[u] •Therefore, there is one Law by One, one world and an end   48:24
15 for all those who exist. •Then[v] he will make alive those whom he has found, and[w]
   he will purge them from sins, and at the same time he will destroy those who are
   polluted with sins.

1 **86** When you, therefore, receive the letter,[a] read it carefully in your assemblies.
   And think about it, in particular, however,[b] on the days of your fasts. And   Bar 1:14
   remember me by means of this letter in the same way as I remember you by means   Col 4:16
   of this, and always.[c]   1Mac 12:11
   Rom 1:9

1 **87** And[a] it happened when I had finished all the words of this letter and had
   written it carefully until the end, I folded it, sealed it cautiously, and bound it to
   the neck of the eagle. And I let it go and sent it away.
   The end of the letter of Baruch, the son of Neriah.

---

r. Cf. Ps-Philo 33:5.
s. "To corruption," l; "of corruption," c *solus*.
t. "Regarding the way," l; "and the way," c
solus.
u. "To the glowing coals," l; "to the realm of
death," c *solus*.
v. "Then," l; "And then," 6h14 10g1 12d2 c.
w. "Has found and . . .," l; "has found

that . . .," c *solus*.

86 a. "The letter," l; "this my letter," c *solus*.
b. "However," l; om., c *solus*.
c. "And always," l; "and it may fare you well
always," c *solus*.

87 a. This ch. is available in c only.

3 (Greek Apocalypse of) BARUCH

(First to Third Century A.D.)

A NEW TRANSLATION AND INTRODUCTION
BY H. E. GAYLORD, JR.

In this pseudepigraphon, Baruch, the scribe of Jeremiah, weeps over the destruction of Jerusalem and its Temple and the mockery of its heathen destroyers. The Lord sends an angel to comfort him and to guide him through the heavens and show him their mysteries. This angel then leads Baruch through five heavens:

1. The first contains a plain where those being punished for waging war against God are found (ch. 2).

2. The second contains a plain where those who forced others to build a tower to heaven in order to discover its contents are found (ch. 3).

3. The third contains a plain in which are a snake, a sea, and primal rivers, as well as the garden of Eden (perhaps Hades), the sun with the Phoenix, and the moon (chs. 4–9).

4. The fourth contains a plain on which are a pool and exotic birds, and the gathering place of the souls of the righteous (ch. 10).

5. The fifth is where the angels responsible for men on earth bring the gifts of men to Michael, who presents them to God. Baruch does not pass inside the gates of this heaven; they remain closed. In these chapters, three classes of mankind are mentioned: the righteous, the insufficiently righteous, and the sinners. In the Slavonic version, Baruch is granted permission to intercede for the suffering sinners (chs. 11–16).

After his heavenly journey, Baruch is returned to earth to relate what he has seen to his fellow men (ch. 17).

Texts

3 Baruch is found in both Greek and Slavonic. The Slavonic is a translation from a lost Greek original.

GREEK MANUSCRIPTS

1. BM MS Add. 10073. This manuscript is dated from the late fifteenth to the early sixteenth century. It is described by M. R. James.[1]

2. Andros, Monastery of the Hagia, MS 46; dated by J.-C. Picard to the beginning of the fifteenth century.

On the relation between these manuscripts, Picard concludes that they "were both copied from the same manuscript, today lost." [2]

---

[1] *Apocrypha Anecdota II.*

[2] J.-C. Picard, *Apocalypsis Baruchi Graeci*, p. 69. MS 46 is described in P. Lambros, "Katalogus ton en te kata ten Andron mone tes Hagias Kodikon," *Epeteris tou Parnassou 2* (1898) pp. 180–83, and A. Ehrhard, *Überlieferung und Bestand der hagiographischen und homiletischen Literatur der Griechischen Kirche* (Leipzig, 1939–1952), 1.3, pp. 587, 839. The first sixty-two fols. contain homilies, but it should be noted that all subsequent items of this MS are also contained in BM MS Add. 10073.

SLAVONIC MANUSCRIPTS

Family stemma: A   B¹   B²

The Slavonic manuscript tradition is preserved in at least twelve manuscripts; these can be divided into two major families, one of which is composed of two subfamilies. In most respects the more original readings have been preserved in family A. Clear revisions can be found in family B as a whole, and further redaction has led to its subfamilies. Until now, subfamily B¹ has been used for comparison with the Greek manuscript tradition, with the exception of a comment by W. Lüdtke.[3] The translation below is based on family A wherever possible. Unfortunately, its best representatives, manuscripts L and T, both lack the sections 1:2–2:2 and 16:8–17:1, and these have been supplied by family B.

Family A:

L. Leningrad Greek 70 fols. 105–111v and St. Catherine's Monastery Slavonic 34 fols. 27–29v. One large manuscript, formerly in St. Catherine's Monastery, Sinai, has been split into four parts. One part (Slavonic 34) remains there, and the other three were removed to Russia and are now in the Salykov-Ščedrin State Library of Leningrad. The folios containing 3 Baruch were misbound into two of the parts of this manuscript. B. M. Zagrebin has recently discovered the relationship of these parts and described the contents of the original manuscript.[4] The manuscript was written by several scribes; the portion containing 3 Baruch dates from the thirteenth century. This scribe copied a number of apocrypha. A tentative list includes the Abgar Legend, 3 Baruch, and 4 Baruch. The proper sequence of folios in 3 Baruch as now recovered is Greek 70 fols. 105–108; Slavonic 34 fols. 27–29; Greek 70 fols. 109–111v. Three gaps still damage the text of this manuscript. 1:2–2:2a is missing (fols. 105v and 106r [first half] are blank). The order of 2:7–4:5a and 4:5b–5:2a is reversed because of a confusion in an antecedent manuscript, and this is probably what caused the loss of text at 5:2b–12a. The third missing portion is from 16:8 to the end. Both L and T contain an addition before 5:1, and end with an expanded version of the prayer of Baruch in chapter 16. The ending (16:8 to the end) is contained only in the manuscripts of family B. For further details on this manuscript and a diplomatic edition of it, see my forthcoming edition.

T. Theological Academy of Moscow No. 363/679, reportedly now in the Historical Museum of Moscow. This manuscript from the fifteenth century was published by N. Tichonravov (see bibliography). In addition to the faults it has in common with L, this manuscript shares with manuscript B the loss of 1:1–3:1, and an addition at the end of 5:3. (This seems to be a fragment from *Vita* 13–17, otherwise unknown in Slavonic.) Both T and B omit 3:8b. T omits 6:6–10:5.

B. Originally in the Barsov collection, this manuscript has passed into the Theological Academy of Kiev. It was written in A.D. 1701 and was published by M. Sokolov (see bibliography). Its language is very late, and it summarizes and rephrases passages freely. Manuscript B ends with a summary conclusion after chapter 9.

Family B:

The effects of the redaction behind this group can be clearly seen at a number of points:
1. 2:6 is omitted.
2. An interpolation occurs at 3:5.

---

[3] W. Lüdtke, "Beiträge zu slavischen Apokryphen: 2 Apokalypse des Baruch," *ZAW* (1911) 220: "Stimmt T [in family A] mehr fach genauer mit G [Gk.] überein als S [in family B¹]." MS N, a very inferior MS of family B¹, is the basis for the earlier translations of Bonwetsch ("Das slavisch erhaltene Baruchbuch," *Nachrichten von der Königlichen Gesellschaft der Wissenschaften zu Göttingen: philologische-historische Klasse* [1896] 91–101) and W. R. Morfill (in *Apocrypha Anecdota II*, pp. 95–102), and MS S, the best representative of family B¹, was used by W. Hage for his more recent translation in *JSHRZ* 5.1. For a fuller description of the MSS, see E. Turdeanu ("L'Apocalypse de Baruch en slave," *Revue des études slaves* 48 [1969] 23–48) and H. E. Gaylord (*The Slavonic Version of 3 Baruch* [forthcoming]).

[4] This important discovery was announced in B. M. Zagrebin, "O proischoždenii i sud'be nekotorych slavjanskich palimpsestov Sinaja," in *Iz istorii rukopisnych i staropečatnych sobranij Otdela rukopisej i redkich knig GPB* (Issledovanija, obzory, publikacii; Sbornik naučnych trudov; Leningrad, 1979) pp. 61–80.

3. 3:8 is revised and has an interpolation.

4. 4:1–2a is omitted.

5. 4:5b is revised in two respects.

This is not an exhaustive list; there are also a large number of small variants that support this grouping. The arrangement of subfamilies B^1 and B^2 is largely based on small variants. A full description of the manuscripts in family B can be found in Gaylord (see n. 3).

THE TEXTUAL BASIS FOR THE TRANSLATIONS

The translation below of the Greek is based on the texts of M. R. James and J.-C. Picard. The translation of the Slavonic is based on my forthcoming edition. In that edition manuscript L has been used as the base text, emended when necessary on the basis of a thorough comparison of all the known manuscripts, as described above. When manuscripts L and T are absent (1:2–2:2 and 16:8 to the end), an eclectic text has been made. T and family B are used for 5:2b–12a.

News of the discovery of the Sinai manuscript portion of L reached me only after this work was completed. I have had time only to make a preliminary examination of it and a provisional translation. My definitive analysis and translation, especially of 6:6–11:3, will be found in my critical edition.

Parallel translations of the Greek and Slavonic texts are presented rather than an eclectic one for several reasons. Firstly, the divergences between the two textual traditions are so many and so great that the apparatus would rapidly be filled with variants alone. Secondly, the systematic variations and tendencies of each tradition should be examined not only on individual readings, but as a whole. Furthermore, the divergence of the textual tradition of present Greek manuscripts and the Greek basis of the present Slavonic tradition occurred not later than the tenth century, approximately five hundred years before the earliest extant Greek manuscript. In several important differences, a strong argument for the priority of the Slavonic exists:

1. The possible dependencies of the Greek on 4 Baruch in the introduction and chapter 1 are omitted in the Slavonic.

2. Explicit New Testament citations in the Greek (4:15; 5:3(?); 15:4; 16:2), and the phrase "through Jesus Christ Emmanuel" at 4:15 are all lacking in the Slavonic.

3. The story of the planting of the garden by angels in the Slavonic, lacking in the Greek, is worthy of consideration as original.

4. The structure and content of chapter 4.

These matters are discussed below.

Original language

The Slavonic version is a translation from Greek. A few linguistic features of the Greek could be explained by supposing a Semitic base text but are not unknown in later Koine Greek usage. There is no convincing argument that the Greek is a translation from another language.

Date and provenance

The dating and assignment of a historical context for 3 Baruch have been the subject of considerable discussion. M. R. James[5] was the first to suggest a reference to this work in Origen, *De principiis* 2.3.6: "Finally they appeal to the book of the prophet Baruch to bear witness to this assertion, because in it there are very clear indications of the seven worlds or heavens."[6] If this identification is correct then the latest possible date for the writing of 3 Baruch would be A.D. 231. The suggestion that the earliest possible date may be set by 4 Baruch because of allusions to it in 3 Baruch (introduction and chapter 1) has been cautioned against by James himself.[7] James concluded that 3 Baruch is "a Christian Apocalypse of

---

[5] James, *Apocrypha Anecdota II*, p. li.

[6] Translation by G. W. Butterworth, *Origen on First Principles* (London, 1936; repr. New York, 1966) p. 91.

[7] James, *Apocrypha Anecdota II*, p. lv.

the second century."[8] L. Ginsberg argued that it is a Jewish-gnostic work from the beginning of the second century.[9] H. M. Hughes maintained that the original version is a second-century Jewish work that has been modified by Christian redactors.[10] J.-C. Picard claimed that it is a product of Jewish mysticism in the Diaspora from the first or second century with very minor Christian interpolations.[11] The most recent statement concerning the provenance is that it is a product of Syrian Jewry.[12]

Origen's statement does not help us to determine the latest possible date for our present work. Either he knew a version other than the present one (i.e. one with seven heavens), or he is speaking about another work altogether that has not survived. The only clear references to 3 Baruch are of a much later date, namely the use of 3 Baruch, chapter 2, in the History of the Rechabites[13] and in later Slavonic literature.[14] Nor is the suggested earliest possible date reliable since the possible references to 4 Baruch (absent in the Slavonic version) are probably secondary.[15]

Another argument for the earliest possible date is the dependency of 3 Baruch on 2 Baruch 76:3, in which Baruch is promised a vision.[16] However, the interests of the author of 3 Baruch suggest that he belongs to a group completely other than that of the author of 2 Baruch. There is no apocalyptic notion of an end-time in 3 Baruch, nor would that interest him. Furthermore, his interest would seem to be focused on heavenly realities and not on those on earth. A timeless heavenly service in which the good deeds or prayers of men are offered by Michael on the altar is his chief answer to the crisis caused by the destruction of the earthly temple, and not a patient waiting for the new temple (whether in heaven or in Jerusalem) at the end of days.

Chapters 11–16 have often been singled out as having Christian characteristics, and even as being a secondary Christian conclusion replacing the earlier Jewish one. Yet many of these Christian elements are lacking in the Slavonic version, e.g. the citation of Matthew 25:23 in 15:4, Romans 10:19 or Deuteronomy 32:21 in 16:2, the monastic expression *pneumatikous pateras* in 13:4 (although it does contain references to the Church here and in chs. 15 and 16). The Slavonic also lacks the reference to Christian priests, Greek version 16:4. The Greek version would also appear to show a Christianizing tendency at the end of 5:3 (cf. Slavonic 5:3; the phrase as in the Slavonic also appears in 1:6 and 2:6), cf. also 4:15 in the Greek. One definitely sees Christian editing in chapters 11–16 in the Slavonic and even more in the Greek. Christian revision of the Greek manuscript tradition may also be seen in 4:3–6 and 4:15.

One cannot be certain about a time and place of composition for 3 Baruch. The alternatives are that it is a Christian composition that has made use of Jewish traditions, which may or may not have been later reworked, or that it is a basically Jewish composition that has undergone Christian reworking. The most likely dating of the initial composition in the latter case would be during the first two centuries after Christ; in the former, the dating would be very difficult. However, the scholarly dichotomy of Jewish and Christian writings in the first two centuries, like the earlier one between Diaspora and Palestinian Jewry, may be a misleading attempt to distinguish what is closely interrelated.

Historical importance

The greatest problem in establishing a historical context for this work is the evaluation

---

[8] Ibid., p. lxxi.

[9] L. Ginsberg, "Greek Apocalypse of Baruch," *JE*, vol. 2, p. 551.

[10] H. M. Hughes, "The Greek Apocalypse of Baruch," *APOT*, vol. 2, pp. 529f.; accepted by W. Hage, *Die griechische Baruch-Apokalypse, JSHRZ* 5.1, pp. 19f.

[11] Picard, *Apocalypsis Baruchi*, pp. 75–78; and "Observations sur l'Apocalypse grecque de Baruch," *Sem* 20 (1970) 100–3.

[12] L. Rost, *Einleitung in die alttestamentlichen Apokryphen und Pseudepigraphen einschliesslich der grossen Qumran-Handschriften* (Heidelberg, 1971) p. 88.

[13] Formerly called the Apocalypse of Zosimus. Cf. especially chs. 2f.; see James, *Apocrypha Anecdota II*, pp. lvif. [Also see HistRech discussed and translated in the present collection. —J.H.C.]

[14] See Turdeanu, *Revue des études slaves* 48 (1969) 36–38, 44–48.

[15] The points in common with the 4th cent. ApPaul chs. 7–11 do not necessarily reflect a literary relationship, but see Introduction, "Historical importance."

[16] James, *Apocrypha Anecdota II*, p. liv.; P. Bogaert, *Apocalypse de Baruch* (SC; Paris, 1969) vol. 1, p. 455.

of the two versions. Previously it has been argued that the Slavonic is a rewritten version of the Greek. With the new manuscript evidence it can be seen that the Slavonic represents in the main the same text as the Greek. At some points it is shorter and at others it is longer.

Three sections (chs. 4f., 10, and 11–16) are most important in judging the two versions. The Slavonic places the resting place of the righteous and hell apparently elsewhere than in the first four heavens. The Greek version places hell in the third heaven (cf. chs. 4f.), and the resting place of the righteous in the fourth (ch. 10). In chapters 4 and 5 the Slavonic concentrates upon the incidents associated with the Fall: the garden of Eden and the serpent being punished for his role in the Fall. Further, in chapter 10 the inhabitants of the fourth heaven are not the righteous but probably angels singing the praises of God. Yet in both places it can be argued that those passages occurring only in the Greek are a reworking of the original construction, which is better represented by the Slavonic version.

In his introduction to the Greek text, M. R. James raised the issue of the relation between 3 Baruch and the fourth-century Apocalypse of Paul and suggested the possibility that the Apocalypse of Paul in chapters 9–18 was dependent on a version of 3 Baruch, chapters 11–16, closer to the original than the present Greek version.[17] The Slavonic version of these chapters would reflect such a text, which includes the same sequence at that point as the Apocalypse of Paul. Another possibility would be the dependence of both 3 Baruch and the Apocalypse of Paul on a common original.

If the contents of the concluding chapters of the Slavonic version are more original than the Greek, then the earlier chapters 4 and 5 and chapter 10 also must be considered more original. Furthermore it is precisely in chapters 4f. and 11–16 that the Greek has suffered the most at the hands of Christian scribes. Wine is identified as the "blood of God" (4:15); "spiritual fathers" (mentioned in 13:4) is a Christian term especially used for monastics and bishops, and the function of the priests in 16:4 would also suggest a Christian context. Moreover, the New Testament is explicitly cited in the Greek at 15:4 and perhaps at 16:2. Yet the Slavonic itself is not free from Christian elements (cf. 13:4 and 16:2).

While there is evidence of Christian reworking of this apocalypse, there is also strong evidence of its original writing being Jewish or early Christian. The many parallels with Jewish traditions are not likely to have been known after the clear separation between Jewish and Christian communities. Therefore the original work should probably be dated in the first two centuries A.D.

Theological importance

The visions found in 3 Baruch share elements with many Jewish and Graeco-Roman traditions, yet differ from their parallels at crucial points.

The supreme episode in most heavenly visits in the apocryphal and mystical (Merkabah) literature is the appearance before the throne of God. Although the throne is mentioned twice in 3 Baruch (6:8[S]; 9:4[S]), this element is missing in the journey. The gates of the fifth heaven remain closed to Baruch, and he does not see the throne. It is possible, however, that the original text contained descriptions of further heavens, but the original form cannot be reconstructed from the extant versions.

There seem to be two differing views concerning God in this work. He acts directly against the two sets of tower builders (2:7; 3:6, 8), but in the later chapters he intervenes only through intermediaries, meting out rewards and punishments (chs. 11–16). Angels implement the will of God in the creation of the garden of Eden and in the daily care of the sun and moon. Moreover, another group of angels render daily (?) account of the activities of men to their commander-in-chief Michael. He receives from them the good works of men, which he as high priest then takes to the temple in an upper heaven to offer upon the altar. The same angels then give rewards and punishments to the men in their charge.

This work has a wealth of angels. Two angelic messengers are mentioned: Phanael is described as an archangel (10:1[G]), an angel of hosts (2:6[G]; 10:1[S]), and an interpreter of revelations (11:7[G]). An otherwise unknown angel, Sarasael, delivers a revelation to Noah (4:15). The central angelic figure in 3 Baruch is Michael, who is addressed as the

---

[17] A close relation between ApPaul and 3Bar was first suggested by N. Bonwetsch, *Nachrichten*, pp. 92f. Cf. also James, *Apocrypha Anecdota II*, pp. 70f.; Turdeanu, *Revue des études slaves* 48 (1969) 42. 3Bar has many other parallels with ApPaul. An edition of the Slavonic version of ApPaul would aid in sorting out this problem.

commander-in-chief of all the angels (see n. to 11:4). Yet his activities are even broader: He holds the keys to the gates of the upper heavens, the kingdom of God or heaven (11:2), and functions as priest in the heavenly temple. In chapters 11–16 he is also the single intermediary between God and the angels overseeing men.

Five angels are mentioned by name in the Slavonic version of 3 Baruch: Michael, Gabriel, Uriel, Raphael, and Satanael (the MSS of family A), and Michael, Gabriel, Raphael, Phanuel, and Satanael (the MSS of family B). The name Satanael, modeled upon the -EL element in other angels' names, is changed to Satan when he loses his favored status. Satanael is mentioned in several other works as well. The earliest is 2 Enoch 18, 31, where he is the chief of the fallen Watchers. Moreover, he is probably identified with the figure in Isaiah 14:13f. who falls from heaven. A parallel account is also found in the Gospel of Bartholomew 3:25–29 and in the Book of the Cave of Treasures.[18] Yet the name Satanael in the Slavonic is probably secondary to the name Samael in the Greek version. Samael became a centralizing figure in the later rabbinic literature, incorporating the functions of several angels. Yet Diabolos, or Satan, functioned in the same manner among Christians, and we find little record of Samael in Christian literature. The first four archangels in the two lists are each paralleled in early Jewish and Christian sources (see n. to 4:7[S]). The name Samael is very common as the chief of evil angels in rabbinic literature and some apocryphal works. Possible etymologies are the poison of God (cf. the poison administered by the Angel of Death, b.AZ 20b), or the blind one.

Both versions of 3 Baruch are confused in their treatment of Samael and the vine. In the Greek they are both cursed before the fall of Adam and Eve, but the vine is to be transformed for the good (4:15). In the Slavonic version the vine is first identified with "sinful desire which Satanael spread over Eve and Adam," and then Noah is told to "alter its name and change it for the better." Implied in both versions is disobedience among the angels before that of Adam and Eve. At least three different backgrounds are possible for the account of Samael here, and it is impossible to make a definitive judgment. Though the vine was planted by Samael and cursed by God, in the new creation after the Flood the vine and its fruit remain useful, within reason.

By his disobedience Adam lost "the glory of God" (4:16[G]), which may have been comparable to that of angels (cf. 13:4[S]). The reward of the righteous is oil, possibly the sign of the glory of God, which the angel-guide promises to show Baruch several times in this text (6:12; 7:2; 11:2; 16:3[S]). It is hardly accidental that there are traditions that Adam sought to receive the "oil of mercy" at the point of death, and that Enoch was transformed by the "oil of his glory" (see n. to 15:1). The angel describes the resting place of the righteous as one of glory (16:4[S]), but Baruch does not visit it.

The story about the phoenix bird, known in classical, Jewish, and Christian antiquity, also appears here.[19] Many of the details correspond to the classical tradition. Early Christianity used this story as a symbolic representation of the resurrection of Jesus: the new phoenix rising out of the ashes of its predecessor. Yet here, without parallel, the phoenix is the protector of the world, shielding its inhabitants from the fierce pure rays of the sun, which would destroy them and their impure deeds were it not for this mediator.

Two central themes run through the entirety of 3 Baruch. At the opening, Baruch is crying over the destruction of Jerusalem and the Temple. The angel tells him not to be concerned for the salvation of Jerusalem (1:3), and he promises to show Baruch the mysteries of God. These mysteries concern obedience and disobedience to God's commands and their results. Another aspect of the mysteries that Baruch encounters at many points is the wonders of the natural, albeit heavenly world. He observes the workings of the sun and moon and, most clearly in the Slavonic, observes other wonders too: the snake that keeps the great sea in balance and the origin of fruitful rains. Baruch sees the punishment of those who waged war with God (ch. 2), of those who forced others to build a tower to the heavens (ch. 3), of the serpent who participated in the temptation of Adam and Eve (ch. 4), of the moon that helped Samael in the temptation (ch. 9), and the punishment of men who disobey God's commands

---

[18] See E. A. W. Budge, *The Book of the Cave of the Treasures* (London, 1927) pp. 56f.

[19] [See the recent and very important work on the phoenix—and the discussion of the phoenix in 3Bar (especially pp. 261–304)—by R. van den Broek, *The Myth of the Phoenix* (Leiden, 1972); also cf. nn. d, e, h, j, and k to ch. 6 below. —J.H.C.]

(ch. 16). Moreover, Adam himself lost the "glory of God" because of his disobedience (4:13, 16). In chapters 11–16 the focus is shifted to those presently living. No final Day of Judgment is even hinted at (except in Baruch's remark in 1:7). It appears that angels take a daily account of the lives of men and receive new instructions concerning them. Those who have lived virtuously receive their reward, and those who have clearly been disobedient are punished for committing the sins listed at several points in the text (chs. 4, 8, 13). The two versions give differing accounts of those who have insufficient accomplishments.

Baruch's initial concern would seem to be about the proper functioning of the Temple in Jerusalem. How can the proper relation between God and men be maintained without the sacrifices of the Temple? The answer becomes clear: There is a heavenly temple in which the prayers, virtues, and good deeds are offered by Michael. The rewards, the oil (of mercy) and the glory of God, will not be withheld because of the absence of the Temple in Jerusalem. This answer is quite different from others given in this period. Here there is no mention of a messiah, no division between Israel and the other nations (except possibly in Baruch's opening lament), and no notion of two ages.

Relation to canonical books

The opening chapters of 3 Baruch are most closely bound to stories from the Book of Genesis, but these are expanded and reworked in a manner common to much of the literature of second Temple Judaism.

A good example of this is the treatment of the tower of Babel (Gen 11:1–9). Two different groups of men seem to be distinguished here.[20] The first group attempted to reach heaven in order to wage war with God and are punished in the first heaven. The second group, imprisoned in the second heaven, forced others to build a tower so as to discover the composition of heaven. Here several elements of the Egyptian enslavement of Israel are incorporated into the story. The store cities (fortified cities in LXX) of Exodus 1:11 may here have been interpreted as a tower. The story of the woman forced to work while giving birth is elsewhere told of the Egyptian period (see n. to 3:5). Bricks are also a strong element of the account in Exodus 1. The punishment with blindness is mentioned in Genesis 19:11 in relation to the citizens of Sodom and Gomorrah, but it is suggested already in the Wisdom of Solomon 19:17 that the plague of darkness (Ex 10:21–23) was also blindness.

Again, the story of the garden of Eden is expanded here. The planting of the garden was not done directly by God but by his angels, and the angel who caused Adam and Eve to sin was one of these angels. The punishment of the snake (Gen 3:14f.) takes place in the third heaven, where, according to the Slavonic version, he "eats earth like grass" (4:3). The giants who, we are told, were drowned in the Flood may be the children of the unions described in Genesis 6:1–4 (cf. e.g. 1En 6–16). A strong typological relation is set up between Adam and Noah, who discovers a piece of the vine through which Adam and Eve sinned washed out of the garden by the receding floodwaters. Afraid to provoke God's wrath, Noah hesitates to plant the vine, but the angel Sarasael is sent to instruct him to do so.[21]

Relation to apocryphal books

Baruch, a minor figure in the Book of Jeremiah, became an important pseudonym in the second Temple period of Jewish history. In the second century B.C., 1 Baruch 1:1–3:8 was written. After A.D. 70 the works 2 and 4 Baruch were written. These books attributed to Baruch are not the work of a single school, but this name brought associations of the fall of Jerusalem and the destruction of the Temple in 587 B.C. and the crisis that resulted. Furthermore, there is a Christian Apocalypse of Baruch in Ethiopic which was adapted by

---

[20] A threefold division of tower builders is mentioned in rabbinic sources: "Rabbi Jeremiah ben Eleazar said, 'They (the builders) were split into three groups.' One said, 'Let us go up and dwell there,' and one said, 'Let us go up and practise idolatry,' and one said, 'Let us go up and make war.' " The first group is dispersed, the second is stopped when God confuses their tongues, and the third group is changed into apes, evil spirits, and demons (b.Sanh 109a).

[21] The two versions diverge greatly here (5:15). The Gk. "and its fruit . . ." is a Christian addition, but its opening and closing phrases may be original.

the Falashas.[22] Justin the Gnostic in the second century also had a book of Baruch.[23] James thinks that still another book of Baruch was known to Cyprian.[24] One can see by the last three books the degree to which Baruch's name was used for very different purposes: He is even identified as an angel by Justin the Gnostic.

3 Baruch is one of a number of books concerning the visions of a man conducted through the various heavens. Similar visions are recorded in the Testament of Abraham, the Apocalypse of Abraham, 1 Enoch, 2 Enoch, the Testament of Levi, the Vision of Isaiah, and the Merkabah literature. Lists of seven heavens and their contents are also given in rabbinic sources. These lists are far from uniform, and different items occur in the various works.

On many specific points common traditions are shared between 3 Baruch and other apocryphal literature, and these are mentioned in the notes below. Among these is the tradition about Adam's pre-Fall glory, which he lost (4:16[G]). This important tradition is closely related to the books concerning Adam and Eve. The secondary references to Satanael in the Slavonic version have probably been influenced by Christian traditions; this may also be true of the mention of Satanael in 2 Enoch. Still, it is possible that this myth, based on Isaiah 14:12–14, and found in the Latin *Vita Adae et Evae* as well as in one late rabbinic source, is much older than is sometimes thought.

In what A. Vaillant considers the oldest version of 2 Enoch[25] seven phoenixes are located in the sixth heaven (2En 19:6). However, in the long text, phoenixes and chalkydii accompany the sun in the fourth heaven (2En 12:1–3). Moreover, they announce to the earthly birds the entrance of the sun at dawn (2En 15:1). Yet the main function of the phoenix in 3 Baruch, guardian of the world, has no parallel.

Cultural importance

This work has not made a great impact in later history. It is possible that it has influenced certain parts of the Apocalypse of Paul and the History of the Rechabites. Origen may cite it at one point.

Yet in Slavic literature it has had some importance, as witnessed by the fact that twelve known manuscripts exist today. The Slavonic version was reedited before the fourteenth century (MSS of family B). Moreover, it gave rise to a Bulgarian folktale known from the eighteenth century.[26] There are also Russian manuscripts (15th–17th cent.) of a moral discourse against the abuse of wine, which uses chapters 4 and 5 of 3 Baruch to confirm its point.[27]

Thus while in Western Europe and Greece 3 Baruch has lain in libraries unread until the late nineteenth century, it has been in popular and religious use among Slavic peoples.

---

[22] Cf. W. Leslau, *Falasha Anthology* (New Haven, 1951) pp. 57–76.

[23] Cf. Hippolytus, *Ref* 5.24.

[24] Cyprian *Testimonia* 3.29. See M. R. James, LAOT, pp. 77f. [Also see S. E. Robinson's discussion of Baruch in 4Bar in the present collection. —J.H.C.]

[25] See A. Vaillant, *Le Livre des Secrets d'Hénoch* (Paris, 1952). [But regarding Vaillant's methods and conclusions see the contribution herein on 2En by F. Andersen. —J.H.C.]

[26] Published by P. Lavrov, in *Sbornik otd. russk. jaz. i slov.* 67 (1899) 149–51.

[27] See Turdeanu, *Revue des études slaves* 48 (1969) 36–38, 44–48.

ANNOTATED BIBLIOGRAPHY

Charlesworth, *PMR*, pp. 86f.
Delling, *Bibliographie*, p. 163.
Denis, *Introduction*, pp. 79–84.

GREEK TEXT

James, M. R. *Apocrypha Anecdota II*, ed. J. A. Robinson. T&S 5; Cambridge, 1899.
(Introduction, pp. li–lxxi; Gk. text, pp. 83–94. This is the first edition of the Gk. text
based on BM MS Add. 10073, and the Introduction is still an important study of 3Bar
and its themes. Repr. Kraus, 1967. For a translation of Slavonic MS N see W. R.
Morfill's work in the same vol., pp. 95–102.)
Picard, J.-C. *Apocalypsis Baruchi Graece*, ed. A.-M. Denis and M. de Jonge. PVTG 2;
Leiden, 1967. (Picard's text is based upon the two extant MSS.)

SLAVONIC TEXT

Hercigonia, E. " 'Videnje Varuhovo' u Petrisovu Zborniku iz 1468 Godine," in *Zbornik
za filologiju i lingvistiku* N.S. 7 (1964) 63–93. (Transcription of MS Z, textual com-
mentary including comparisons with MSS S and N, and linguistic discussion of MS Z.)
Novaković, S. "Otkrivene Varuhovo," in *Starine* 18 (1886) 203–9. (Transcription of
MS N.)
Sokolov, M. I. "Apokrifičeskoe otkrovenie Varuka," *Drevnosti, Trudi slavjanskoj kommissi
imp. Moskovskago archeologičeskago obščestva* 4 (1907) 201–58. (Transcriptions of
MSS S, P, and B are included in this study, the only extensive comparison of Gk. and
Slavonic traditions.)
Tichonravov, N. "Otkrovenie Varuka," in *Sbornik otd. russk. jas. i slov.* 58 (1894) 48–54.
(Transcription of MS T.)
Turdeanu, E. "L'Apocalypse de Baruch en slave," *Revue des études slaves* 48 (1969)
23–48.

STUDIES

Bonwetsch, N. "Das slavisch erhaltene Baruchbuch," *Nachrichten von der Königlichen
Gesellschaft der Wissenschaften zu Göttingen: philologische-historische Klasse* (1896)
91–101. (Translation and discussion of Slavonic MS N.)
Ginsberg, L. "Greek Apocalypse of Baruch," *JE*, vol. 2, pp. 549–51. (Argues for a Jewish
origin. This article is still quite valuable.)
Hage, W. *Die griechische Baruch-Apokalypse*. JSHRZ 5.1; Gütersloh, 1974; pp. 15–44.
(Translation of Slavonic MS S.)
Hughes, H. M. "The Greek Apocalypse of Baruch," *APOT*, vol. 2, pp. 527–41.
Picard, J.-C. "Observations sur l'Apocalypse grecque de Baruch," *Sem* 20 (1970) 77–103.
Riessler, P. *Altjüdisches Schrifttum ausserhalb der Bibel*. Heidelberg, 1928; repr. Heidelberg,
1966; pp. 40–54, 1269f.
Turdeanu, E. "Apocryphes bogomiles et apocryphes pseudo-bogomiles," *Revue de l'histoire
des religions* 69 (1950) 22–52, 176–218. (For 3Bar, see especially pp. 177–81.)
———. "Les apocryphes slaves et roumains: Leur apport à la connaissance des apocryphes
grecs," *Studi bizantini e neoellenici* 8 (1953) 47–52. (For 3Bar, see especially 50–52.)

APOCALYPSE OF BARUCH

Slavonic

when the angel Phanuel[c] was sent to him on the holy mountain Zion[d] beside the river, as he cried over the captivity of Jerusalem. Lord, give thy blessing.[e]

1 **1** When King Nebuchadnezzar captured Jerusalem and enriched Babylon,[a] then I Baruch cried loudly and said,

2 "Lord, in what way was King Nebuchadnezzar righteous?[d] Why did you not spare your city Jerusalem which is your vineyard of glory?[c] Why have you acted so, Lord?"

3 And behold, as I was crying to myself, an angel of the Lord appeared and said to me, "Be silent, O man of his pleasure![e] Jerusalem had to suffer this. But thus speaks the Lord Almighty to you,

4 and he sent me before your face so that I could show you all the mysteries of God.[g]

5 For both your tears and your voice entered the ears of the Almighty God.

6 Only tell me that you will neither add nor omit (anything), and I will show you mysteries which no man has ever seen."

7 And I Baruch said to the angel, "As the Lord God lives, if you will show me, I will listen; I will not subtract nor will I add one word.[h] If I do omit (anything), then Deut 4:2 may the Lord pass judgment upon me on the Day of Judgment."

a. The Gk. contains two introductions. The first has signs of being a medieval creation. On "narration" cf. e.g. ApMos, introduction; TAb (both versions), introduction.

b. This term differs from that in the body of this work, mystery, cf. 1:4(S); 1:6; 1:8(G); 2:6; 5:3(S).

c. The name of Baruch's angelic guide is mentioned also at 2:5. This is one of the four archangels in the Parables of Enoch. See Introduction, "Theological Importance."

d. This is also the place of revelation to Baruch in 2Bar 13:1f.

e. The invocation in an introduction is a common patristic device, e.g. ActsThom, introduction; ActsJn, introduction; ApZos(=HistRech), introduction; ApSed, introduction. Cf. Lampe, *eulogeō ad loc.*

f. M. R. James emends the Gk. *gel* to read *Kedrōn*, lacking in the Slavonic. The geographical reference would be to the eastern side of the Temple mount, facing the Kidron brook. Cf. 2Bar 5:5; 21:1; 31:1.

g. The second introduction of the Gk. seems influenced by 4Bar 3:14. The background of these stories of Abimelek is in Jer 38:7–13 and 39:15–18.

h. Possibly the gates of Nicanor, cf. Josephus, *War* 5.201–6; m.Middot 1:4; t.Yoma 2:4; and A. Schalit, *König Herodes* (Berlin, 1969) p. 389, n. 834. These gates may be referred to in Acts 3:10. Baruch also laments before the Temple gates in 2Bar 10:5.

i. This is the place of revelations in 2Bar 34:1;

APOCALYPSE OF BARUCH

Greek

1. Narration[a] and Apocalypse of Baruch concerning the secret things[b] he saw by the command of God. Lord, give thy blessing.[e]

2. Apocalypse of Baruch who is by the Kidron River[f] weeping over the captivity of Jerusalem while Abimelek was safeguarded in the estate of Agrippa by the hand of God,[g] and who was seated by the beautiful gates[h] where the Holy of Holies[i] stood.

1 Woe, now I Baruch (was) weeping in my mind[b] and considering the people and how King Nebuchadnezzar was permitted by God to plunder his city, saying,

2 "Lord, why have you set fire to your vineyard and laid it waste?[c] Why have you done this? And why, Lord, did you not requite us with another punishment, but rather handed us over to such heathen so that they reproach us saying, 'Where is their God?' "

3 And behold, while I was weeping and saying such things, I saw an angel of the Lord coming and saying to me, "Know, O man, greatly beloved man,[e] and do not concern yourself so much over the salvation of Jerusalem.[f] For thus says the Lord God Almighty,

4 and he sent me before you in order that I should proclaim and disclose to you all things of God.[g]

5 For your prayer has been heard before him and has entered the ears of the Lord God."

6 And when he told me these things, I became calm, and the angel said to me, "Cease irritating God, and I will disclose to you other mysteries greater than these."[i]

7 And I Baruch said, "As the Lord lives, if you disclose a word to me and I hear it from you, I shall speak no further. May God add to me punishment on the Day of Judgment if I speak in the future."

8 [j]And the angel of hosts[k] said to me, "Come and I shall disclose to you the mysteries of God."

Marginal references:
Isa 5;
Ezek 15;
Ps 80:8–16
Pss 42:3,10;
79:10; 115:2;
Joel 2:17;
Micah 7:10

35:1. The Gk. contains three conflicting geographical references. The Holy of Holies was set apart by a curtain, not gates. Between it and the end of the Temple mount stood the gates of Nicanor. The Slavonic has a plausible geographic reference.

1 a. The opening of 4Ezra 3:2 voices the same contrast. Cf. also 2Bar 11:1f.

b. Cf. also 2Bar 6:2; 10:5; 35:1.

c. This theme is also prominent in 2Bar 3:5; 5:1; 4Ezra 3:27–36; 5:28–30.

d. Cf. 4Ezra 3:28.

e. Dan 10:11 Θ. There also an angel is sent to announce God's hearing of a prayer.

f. In the Slavonic this seems to be misplaced

from here to 2:3.

g. The Slavonic may conflate Gk. vss. 4 and 8b here. The mysteries are mentioned at 1:4(S), 6, 8(G); 2:6; 5:3(S); 17:1(S).

h. The requirement of precise transmission of revelations is also mentioned in Deut 4:2; 13:1 and Rev 22:18.

i. None has been mentioned except perhaps the salvation of Jerusalem. Cf. also 4Ezra 5:13 and ApPaul (Lat.) 40 [end].

j. Lacking in S. Cf. vs. 4.

k. Cf. 2:1(S). This class of the angelic guide is also mentioned in 2:6(G); 10:1(S); elsewhere cf. 1En 20:1(G⁸); 61:10; TAb (A) 9, 14; 2Thes 1:7; Josh 5:14 LXX.

1 **2** And the angel of hosts took me and carried me where the firmament of heaven[a] is.

2 And it was the first heaven,[d] and in that heaven he showed me very large doors.[e] And the angel said to me, "Let us pass through these doors." And we passed through like the passing of 30 days. He showed me salvation.[g]

3 And I saw a plain;[h] there were men[i] living there whose faces were those of cattle, with the horns of deer, the feet of goats, and the loins of rams.

4 And I Baruch asked the angel, "Tell me what is the thickness of the heaven which we have crossed, and what is the plain, so that I can tell the sons of men."

5 Phanael[k] said to me, "The gates which you saw are as large as (the distance) from east to west; the thickness of heaven is equal to the distance from earth to heaven, the plain where we are standing is equal to its width (i.e. heaven's)."

6 He said to me, "Go and I will show you the mysteries."

7 I said to the angel, "Lord, who are these strangely shaped creatures?" And the angel said to me, "These are those who built the tower of the war against God.[l] The Lord threw them out."

1 **3** And the angel took me and led me to the second heaven and showed me large open[a] doors, and the angel said to me, "Let us pass through them."

2 And we passed through, flying like the passing of 7 days.[b]

3 And he showed me a great prison,[c] and there were strangely shaped creatures living in it, with the faces of dogs, the horns of deer, and the feet of goats.[d]

4 And I asked the angel of the Lord, "Who are these?"

5 And he said to me, "These are the ones who had planned[e] to build the tower, for at that time they forced men and a multitude of women to make bricks.[f] Among them was one woman who was near to giving birth, and they did not release her, but, working, she gave birth, and took her cloak and wrapped the infant, and left her infant, and made bricks again.

6 And the Lord God appeared to them and confused their languages.[g] And they built their tower 80 thousand cubits in height, and in width 5 hundred and twenty.

7 They took an auger so that they could proceed to bore heaven so that they could see whether heaven is (made) of stone or of glass or of copper.

8 And God saw them and did not heed them, but he chastened them invisibly."[i]

---

2 a. The heavens rest upon the firmament, cf. 1En 18:5; 33:2. This is the *Rāqiaʿ* in the creation story, Gen 1:6–8, which separates the upper and lower waters.

b. Identified as the ocean in ApPaul 21 and TAb (B) 8, or possibly the Upper Waters (Gen 1:6–8), which are discussed in GenR 4:3 and b.Ḥag 15a and elsewhere. In the ApZos 2 the Eumeles River is mentioned at this juncture. This work is very similar to 3Bar here and possibly dependent on it. In the heavenly journey of TLevi 2:7 a "hanging sea" is mentioned under the first heaven. Further a river of fire and the ocean appear also in 1En 17:5.

c. Gk. *pnoē* can also mean "living creature" as in 8:7 and e.g. LXX Ps 40:6; 24:12. Cf. ApZos 2, where the cloud over the waters says, "Through

me passes no bird, nor breath of wind . . ." [See the contribution herein on ApZos = HistRech. —J.H.C.]

d. See Introduction on the arrangement of the heavens. This formulation is repeated in 3:1f.; 4:2. The entrances to other heavens are at 10:1(G) and 11:1f.

e. Cf. Ps 78:23 and also below 3:1; 11:1.

f. Lacking in the Slavonic. "Flying" is mentioned at 3:2. The winds carry Enoch to heaven in 1En 14:8. Cf. also ApZos 2.

g. Probably a misplaced fragment in Slavonic from 1:3.

h. Plains are mentioned in chs. 2, 3 (second heaven), 4 (third heaven), and 10 (fourth heaven).

i. Cf. 3:3. Cf. the rabbinic division into three groups, mentioned in the Introduction.

1 **2** And taking me, he led me to where the heaven was set fast[a] and where there was a river[b] which no one is able to cross, not even one of the foreign winds[c] which God created.

2 And taking me, he led me up to the first heaven[d] and showed me a very large door.[e] And he said to me, "Let us enter through it." And we entered as on wings[f] about the distance of 30 days' journey.

3 And he showed me a plain[h] within the heaven. And there were men[i] dwelling on it with faces of cattle and horns of deer and feet of goats and loins of sheep.

4 And I Baruch asked the angel, "Tell me, I pray you,[j] what is the thickness of this heaven in which we have journeyed, and what is its width, and what is this plain, that I may report these to the sons of men."

5 And the angel, whose name was Phamael,[k] said to me, "This door which you see is (the door) of heaven, and (its thickness) is as great as the distance from earth to heaven, and the width of the plain which you saw is the same (distance) again."

6 And again the angel of hosts said to me, "Come and I will show you greater mysteries."

7 And I said, "I pray you, show me what those men are." And he said to me, "These are the ones who built the tower of the war against God,[l] and the Lord removed them."

1 **3** And taking me, the angel of the Lord led me to a second heaven. And he showed me there a door similar to the first. And he said, "Let us enter through it."

2 And we entered, flying about the distance of 60 days' journey.

3 And he showed me there also a plain, and it was full of men, and their appearance was like (that) of dogs, and their feet (like those) of deer.

4 And I asked the angel, "I pray you, lord, tell me who these are."

5 And he said, "These are the ones who plotted[e] to build the tower. These whom you see forced many men and women to make bricks.[f] Among them one woman was making bricks in the time of her delivery; they did not permit her to be released, but while making bricks she gave birth. And she carried her child in her cloak and continued making bricks.

6 And appearing to them, the Lord changed their languages;[g] by that time they had built the tower 463 cubits (high).

7 And taking an auger, they attempted to pierce the heaven, saying, 'Let us see whether the heaven is (made) of clay or copper or iron.'

8 Seeing these things, God did not permit them (to continue), but struck them with blindness[h] and with confusion of tongues, and he made them be as you see."

---

j. Oft-used phrase in Gk., lacking in Slavonic. Cf. also 2:7; 3:4; 4:8; 4:14.

k. Mentioned in the Introduction (S). Phamael is probably a corruption, the Slavonic MSS vary between Phanael and Phanuel.

l. Gen 11:1–9. Cf. Introduction.

3 a. Perhaps an addition under the influence of 11:1.

b. Probably confusion of letters that were used as numbers.

c. The Slavonic reading here is based upon a Gk. uncial error, *PEDION/KELLION*. This would indicate that the Gk. *Vorlage* of the Slavonic and the present Gk. MS family diverged during the period when uncials were still being written.

d. Contamination from 2:3.

e. This second group planned the tower and forced others to build it. This also is an expansion of Gen 11. Cf. also b.Sanh 109a and parallels and Introduction above.

f. A similar story about the Egyptian enslavement is told in PRE 48 and TarJon to Ex 24:10.

g. Cf. Gen 11:7f.

h. This seems to be the ninth plague against the Egyptians (Ex 10:21–23), which is reinterpreted as blindness. The men of Sodom received this punishment (Gen 19:11), and WisSol 19:17 makes this interpretation explicit.

i. Slavonic has misunderstood the point here. The confusion of tongues is mentioned twice in the Gk. (vss. 6, 8), but only once in Slavonic.

1 **4** And I Baruch said, "The Lord has shown me great (things)."

2 And the angel said, "Come and let us pass through these doors; you will see the glory of God."[b] And I passed through with the angel like the passing of 187 days.

3 And he showed me a plain, and there was a serpent on a stone mountain.[d] And it drinks one cubit of water from the sea every day, and it eats earth like grass.[e]

4 And I Baruch said to the angel, "Lord, does he drink one cubit from the sea?"

5 The angel said to me, "Listen, Baruch, the Lord God made 353 rivers,[i] and the first river is the Alpheia, the second Aboura, the third Agirenik, the fourth Dounab, the fifth Ephrat, the sixth Zephon, the seventh Matepus, the eighth Arenous, the ninth Pelkuri. And there are 354 others flowing into the sea, and thus it is washed,[j] and it does not diminish[k] because his heart is enflamed."

6 And I Baruch said to the angel, "Show me the tree[l] which deceived Adam."[m]

7 And the angel said to me, "When God made the garden and commanded Michael to gather two hundred thousand and three angels so that they could plant the garden, Michael[n] planted the olive and Gabriel, the apple; Uriel, the nut; Raphael, the melon; and Satanael,[o] the vine. For at first his name in former times was Satanael, and similarly all the angels planted the various trees."

8 And again I Baruch said to the angel, "Lord, show me the tree through which the serpent[p] deceived Eve and Adam." And the angel said to me, "Listen, Baruch. In the first place, the tree was the vine,[q] but secondly, the tree (is) sinful desire which Satanael spread over Eve and Adam, and because of this God has cursed the vine because Satanael had planted it, and by that he deceived the protoplast Adam and Eve."

9 And I Baruch said to the angel, "Lord, if God has cursed the vine and its seed, then how can it be of use now?"

10 And the angel said to me, "Rightly you ask me. When God made the Flood upon the earth, he drowned every firstling, and he destroyed 104 thousand giants,[u] and the water rose above the highest mountains 20 cubits above the mountains, and the water entered into the garden, bringing out one shoot from the vine as God withdrew the waters.[v]

11 And there was dry land, and Noah went out from the ark

12 and found the vine lying on the ground, and did not recognize it having only heard about it and its form.

13 He thought to himself, saying, 'This is truly the vine which Satanael planted in the middle of the garden, by which he deceived Eve and Adam; because of this God cursed it and its seed. So if I plant it, then will God not be angry with me?'

---

4 a. Cf. Slavonic. The Gk. may be a Christian addition reflecting Rev 15:1, 3. Cf. n. on 5:3.

b. Omission due to homoeoteleuton; text preserved in the Slavonic.

c. James has suggested that this figure as presented in the Gk. version is related to the huge dragon that is the outer darkness of Pistis Sophia ch. 126. The Slavonic presents the serpent of Gen 3 being punished for its part in the fall of Adam.

d. Text corrupt. James et al. emend the text to read "two hundred plethra in length."

e. One of the punishments of the serpent in Gen 3:14; cf. also Isa 65:25. James suggests the background of LXX Ex 15:7.

f. Vss. 3–6 in the Gk. are perhaps later additions concerning Hades and punishments, absent from the Slavonic. Here the serpent is distinct from

Hades, but in 5:3(G) Hades is identified as the belly of the serpent.

g. Or "in which also." This may be the rough seam of an interpolation. Cf. Slavonic "like a stone mountain and it drinks . . .''

h. In time or importance.

i. An acrostic may lie behind the list of rivers, cf. H. Jacobson, "A Note on the Greek Apocalypse of Baruch," *JSJ* 7 (1976) 201–3.

j. Cleansed?

k. The sense requires "does not increase."

l. Here the tree deceives Adam, but in vs. 8 it is the serpent and Satanael (or Samael) who deceive.

m. The following section in Slavonic may have fallen out of the Gk. by homoeoteleuton, or may be an addition. The story is not preserved elsewhere

1 **4** And I Baruch said, "Behold, lord, you have shown me great and wondrous[a] things. Now show me all, for the Lord's sake."

2 And the angel said to me, "Come, let us go through"[b] . . . with the angel from that place, a journey of about 185 days.

3 And he showed me a plain and a serpent[c] who appeared to be stone.[d] And he showed me Hades,[f] and its appearance was gloomy and unclean.

4 And I said, "What is this dragon and this monster around it?"

5 And the angel said, "This dragon is the one which eats the bodies of those who pass through their lives badly, and he is nourished by them.

6 And this is Hades which is like him, in that[g] also he drinks about one cubit from the sea, and nothing is diminished from it (i.e. the sea)."

7 Baruch said, "And how is that?" And the angel said, "Listen, the Lord God made 360 rivers, the primary[h] ones of them being the Alphias, the Aburos, and the Gerikos, and because of these the sea is not diminished."

8 And I said, "I pray you, show me which is the tree[i] which caused Adam to stray." And the angel said, "It is the vine[q] which the angel Samael[r] planted by which the Lord God became angered, and he cursed him and his plantling. For this reason he did not permit Adam to touch it.[s] And because of this the devil became envious,[t] and tricked him by means of his vine."

9 And I Baruch said, "And since the vine became the cause of such evil and was cursed by God and (was) the destruction of the first formed, how is it now of such great use?"

10 And the angel said, "Rightly you ask; when God caused the Flood over the earth and destroyed all flesh and 409,000 giants,[u] and the water rose over the heights 15 cubits, the water entered Paradise and killed every flower, but it removed the sprig of the vine completely and brought it outside.[v]

11 And when the earth appeared from the water and Noah left the ark, he started to plant (some) of the discovered plants.

12 He also found the sprig, and taking it, he considered in his mind what it was. And I came and told him about it.

13 And he said, 'Should I plant it, or what (should I do with it)? Since Adam was destroyed by means of it,[w] will I also encounter the anger of God through this?' And while saying these things, he prayed for God to reveal to him what he should do with this.

---

except in a Slavonic fable based on this story (see Introduction).

n. The order of the angels here follows MS family A. The list in family B is: Michael, Gabriel, Raphael, and Phanuel (corrupt in all MSS). The first four angels of A correspond with the list in ApMos 40:1 and in 1En 9:1(Gk.), as well as rabbinic lists. The list in family B is paralleled by the Parables of Enoch: 1En 40:9; 54:6; 71:8, 9, 13.

o. He lost his title, -EL, when he was exiled. Cf. Isa 14:12.

p. Is this the same serpent as in ch. 4?

q. This tree is identified as the vine by 2nd-cent. sages as well: R. Meir (b.Sanh 70a) and R. Judah b.Ilai (GenR 15:7). It is also mentioned in ApAb 23:5 and the *Palea Historica* (ed. Vassiliev, p. 190).

r. The Gk. MSS read Samuel, as in the *Palea Historica* (ed. Vassiliev, p. 258), but this is most probably a mistake for Samael, cf. 9:7. Samael is probably the original name. He is the chief of the evil angels in rabbinic literature, and appears in AscenIs 7:9; 11:41(Eth.); and TarJon on Gen 3:6. In the Acts of Andrew and Matthew 24 both names are attested in MSS.

s. Omitted in Slavonic. In the biblical account God commands Adam not to eat from it (Gen 2:17), but Eve tells the serpent that they may not even touch it (Gen 3:3).

t. WisSol 2:24; *Vita* 12:1.

u. The offspring in Gen 6:1–4.

v. TarJon on Gen 9:20.

w. Connection established between Adam and Noah.

14 And he knelt down on (his) knees and fasted 40 days. Praying and crying, he said, 'Lord, if I plant this, what will happen?'

15 And the Lord sent the angel Sarasael; he declared to him, 'Rise, Noah, and plant the vine, and alter its name, and change it for the better.'

16 "But beware, Baruch: The tree still possesses its evil.

17 Those who drink wine in excess do all evil: Brother does not show mercy to brother, nor father to son, nor son to father. And from the evil of wine comes forth murder and adultery, fornication and cursing, as much evil as exists, because of wine."

Micah 7:6
Mk 13:12
Mt 10:21

1 **5** I Baruch said to the angel, "Let me ask you, lord, about one thing still which you said to me:

2 that the serpent drinks one cubit of water from the sea a day: How great then is its stomach that it drinks so much?"

3 And the angel said to me, "As great as is its stomach, so great is Hades."[b] And he said to me, "If you wish, come and I will show you mysteries greater than these."

1 **6** And the angel took me where the sun goes forth.[a]

2 And he showed me a chariot-of-four, and the horses were flaming, for the horses were winged angels. And upon this chariot sat a man wearing a fiery crown.[b] And the chariot was drawn by forty angels,[c] and (there was) also a bird[d] flying, large as a mountain.

3 I said to the angel, "Lord, what is this bird?" And he said to me, "This is the guardian of the world."[f]

4 And I said, "For what purpose is it the guardian of the world? Show me!"

5 And the angel said to me, "This bird which goes before the sun stretches out its wings and hides the burning rays of the sun.

6 For if he did not hide the rays of the sun, the human race and every creature on earth would not survive because of the flames of the sun. Thus God has commanded this bird to serve the world.

7 But look on the right wing, at what is written." And he commanded the bird to spread his wings, and I saw letters, greater than a threshing floor on earth of 4000. Those letters were pure gold.

8 And he said to me, "Read them aloud!" And they said thus: "The earth has not borne me, nor has the heaven, but wings of fire bear me. And the birds wait for me."

x. Such pairs occur also in Isa 5:20. Cf. also 4Bar 9:18.

y. The Gk. version is the result of considerable reworking.

z. This emendation by James is quite probable. However, the vs. conflicts with vs. 9. Several scholars have viewed this vs. as a Christian interpolation.

5 a. Cf. ApPaul 32.

b. The Slavonic compares the serpent's stomach with Hades, rather than identifying them. Cf. 4:3(G) which seems to conflict with this vs.

c. Mysteries have been consistently promised. The Gk. may be a Christian revision; cf. Jn 5:20.

6 a. The sun and moon appear to be in the third heaven, cf. 7:2; 10:1.

b. This hellenistic conception of a crowned sun, riding in a chariot, was incorporated into Jewish art as well. Such a representation is found in the 4th-cent.-A.D. mosaic on a synagogue floor at Hammat Tiberias. The 6th-cent.-A.D. synagogue floor at Beth Alpha contains a depiction of Helios in a

14 And in 40 days he completed his prayer and entreating much and crying, he said, 'Lord, I implore you to reveal to me what I should do with this plant.'

15 And God sent the angel Sarasael, and he said to him, 'Rise, Noah, plant the sprig, for the Lord says this: "Its bitterness will be changed into sweetness, and its curse will become a blessing,ˣ and its fruit will become the blood of God, and just as the race of men have been condemned through it, so through Jesus Christ Emmanuel in it (they) will receive a calling and entrance into Paradise." 'ʸ

16 Then know, Baruch, that just as Adam through this tree was condemned and was stripped of the glory of God, thus men now who insatiably drink the wine deriving from it transgress worse than Adam, and become distant from the glory of God, and will secure for themselves eternal fire.

17 For (no)ᶻ good derives from it. For those who drink excessively do these things: Brother does not have mercy on brother, nor father on son, nor children on parents, but by means of the Fall through wine come forth all (these): murder, adultery, fornication, perjury, theft, and similar things. And nothing good is accomplished through it."

Micah 7:6
Mk 13:12
Mt 10:21

₁ **5** And I Baruch said to the angel, "May I ask you one question, lord?

₂ Since you told me that the serpent drinks one cubit from the sea, tell me how large its belly is."

₃ And the angel said, "Its belly is Hades. As far as 300 men can throw a weight,ᵃ so great is his belly.ᵇ Come now and I will show you worksᶜ greater than these."

₁ **6** And taking me, he led me where the sun goes forth.ᵃ

₂ And he showed me a chariot drawn by four horses and fire underneath it. And upon the chariot sat a man wearing a fiery crown.ᵇ The chariot was drawn by forty angels.ᶜ And behold, a birdᵈ runs along before the sun, as large as nine mountains.ᵉ

₃ And I said to the angel, "What is this bird?" And he said to me, "This is the guardian of the world."ᶠ

₄ And I said, "Lord, how is it the guardian of the world? Teach me."

₅ And the angel said to me, "This bird accompanies the sun and spreading its wings absorbs its fire-shaped rays.

₆ For if it did not absorb them, none of the race of men would survive, nor anything else that lives, so God appointed this bird."

₇ And he unfolded his wings, and I saw on his right wing very large letters like the place of a threshing floor, having the space of 4000 modia,ᵍ and the letters were gold.

₈ And the angel said to me, "Read them." And I read, and they said thus: "Neither earth nor heaven bear me, but the wings of fire bear me."

---

chariot, pulled by four horses.

c. In 1En 72:4f. this chariot is driven by the winds, but in 2En 11 it seems to be drawn by angels. Cf. also PRE 6.

d. Phoenixes and chalkydii accompany the sun in 2En 12 (A) and seven more phoenixes are in the sixth heaven. On the phoenix in antiquity, see R. Van den Broek, *The Myth of the Phoenix* (Leiden, 1972).

e. This is James's conjecture on the corrupt text, partially confirmed by the Slavonic. Another sug-

gestion is to emend in the light of 2En 12 (A): "about nine hundred measures" or with Discourse of the Paniogate, "about nine cubits" (Hughes, *APOT*, vol. 2, p. 536). The most interesting suggestion is by Moulton in Hughes to read *hōs oreuōn*, "as a guardian," cf. vs. 3. Cf. also V. d. Broek, *The Myth of the Phoenix*, p. 252.

f. This title and function of the phoenix is not attested elsewhere.

g. About 24,000 feet.

9 I Baruch said, "Lord, what is the name of this bird?"

10 And he said to me, "Phoenix."

11 I Baruch said, "What does he eat?" And the angel said, "Heavenly manna."[h]

12 And I said, "Does he produce excrement?" He said to me, "He produces it."[i] And again he said to me, "You will observe the glory of God[m]; see what this bird is going to become." He went past in front of the sun.

13 And while we were singing, there was a noise, great as 30 cows, and the place where we stood shook. And I Baruch said, "What is this noise, my lord?" And he said to me, "The angels are opening the 65 gates of heaven, and light is being separated from darkness."[p]

14 And the sun entered (the chariot)[q] and a voice came, "O Sun, giver of light, give splendor to the world."[r] The bird spread his wings and covered the rays of the sun and it flapped its wings and there was a noise like thunder and the bird cried out, saying, "O giver of light, give splendor to the world."

15 As I heard the voice of the bird, I said, "What is that sound?"

16 And he said, "This is the cocks on earth beginning to waken in the world. At the first call they call out, knowing that the sun is rising. And the cocks cry out."[t]

1 **7** I Baruch said, "Does the sun rest much?" And the angel said to me, "From when the cocks crow until the light comes."

2 And the angel said to me, "Listen, Baruch, what I have shown you is in the first and second heavens, but this place in heaven (is where) the sun goes and it is where he gives light to the world." And he said to me, "Be patient and you will see the glory of God."[a]

1 **8** And the sun came with the crown and 36 angels and also the bird, exhausted.

3 And I said, "Lord, where are they carrying the crown of the sun, and why is the bird exhausted?"

4 And the angel said to me, "The crown of the sun which he wears during the day, 4 angels take and carry to heaven. They cleanse the rays of the sun from the earth."

---

h. On the food of the phoenix, cf. V. d. Broek, *The Myth of the Phoenix*, pp. 335–56. The dew of heaven is mentioned in 10:9.

i. Family B² of the Slavonic contains the following here: "Its excrement becomes black cumin, and with this kings are anointed, and without cumin he is not king, not having (it) in a vessel when the king is enthroned." For fuller details, see H. E. Gaylord, *The Slavonic Version of 3 Baruch* (forthcoming).

j. See V. d. Broek, *The Myth of the Phoenix*, pp. 187, 214–16.

k. This is an element of the phoenix's nest in the classical tradition. Cf. V. d. Broek, *The Myth of the Phoenix*, pp. 164–70.

l. Is this for coronation or embalming?

m. Cf. 7:2; 11:2; 16:4(S).

n. Lit. "thunder like the sound of thunder."

o. This must relate to the solar calendar. The solar year contains 364 days according to 1En 72:32. However, in 1En 72–82 and 2En 13f. there are only six gates in the east and six in the west. The 300 has dropped out of S.

9 And I said, "Lord, what is this bird, and what is its name?"

10 And the angel told me, "His name is Phoenix."

11 "And what does he eat?" And he told me, "The manna of heaven and the dew of earth.[h]

12 And I said, "Does the bird excrete?" And he said to me, "He excretes a worm, and from the excretion, this worm,[j] cinnamon[k] comes into existence, which kings and princes use.[l] But wait and you will see the glory of God."[m]

13 And while he was speaking, there was a thunderclap[n] and the place where we stood was shaken. And I asked the angel, "My lord, what is this sound?" And the angel said to me, "The angels are opening the 365 gates[o] of heaven now, and light is separating itself from darkness."[p]

14 And a voice came saying, "Light giver, give splendor to the world!"[r]

15 And hearing the sound of the bird, I said, "Lord, what is this sound?"

16 And he said, "This is what wakens the cocks on earth, for just as articulate beings do,[s] thus also the cock informs those on the earth according to its own tongue. For the sun is being prepared by the angels and the cock is crowing."[t]

1 **7** And I said, "And where does the sun begin to work after the cock crows?"

2 And the angel said to me, "Listen, Baruch, everything I have shown you is in the first and second heaven; and in the third heaven the sun passes through and gives splendor to the world. But wait and you will see the glory of God."

3 And while I was speaking to him, I saw the bird, and he appeared ahead and grew little by little, and became full sized.

4 And after him (I saw) the sun gleaming and with him angels carrying (him) and a crown on his head; we were not able to look directly into this sight and see.

5 And at the same time as the sun shone out, the phoenix spread out its wings. Seeing such glory, I became overcome with a great fear and fled and hid in the wings of the angel.

6 And the angel said to me, "Do not fear, Baruch, but wait and you will see them setting."[b]

1 **8** And taking me, he led me to the west. And when the time of the setting (of the sun) came, I saw again the bird coming in front and the sun coming with the angels. When he came, I saw the angels, and they removed the crown from his head.

2 And the bird was overcome and let his wings droop.

3 And when I saw these things, I said, "Why do they remove the crown from his head and why is the bird so overcome?"

4 And the angel said to me, "When the day is completed, 4 angels take the crown of the sun and carry it to heaven and renew it because it and its rays are defiled upon earth. And every day it is renewed."[a]

---

p. According to the Syr. TAdam (ed. Kmosko, *Pat. Syriaca*, I.2, p. 1337) in the eleventh hour of the night. [See the contribution herein on TAdam. —J.H.C.]

q. The translation "entered (the chariot)" is a rare meaning for this word. It often means "set, go down"; but this meaning does not fit here.

r. 2En 15:2(A).

s. This is the conjectural translation of James; Ryssel, *APAT*, proposes "just as men do through the mouth."

t. Family B of the Slavonic for vss. 15f. read "And I said to the angel, 'What is this bird singing?' The angel said to me, 'He excites your cocks on earth, and the cocks sing when the sun rises.' "

7 a. S refers to the setting of the sun here and probably should be placed with 8:1f.(G).

b. See parallel in S 8:5.

8 a. 2En 14:2.

b. In S family B preserves vs. 6 as follows: "It

5 And the angel said to me, "The sun sees all the lawlessness in the world; he does not countenance lewdness, adultery, jealousy, rivalry, theft, murder, all of which are not acceptable to God. And also the bird is exhausted, just as one of the earthly birds; it takes up the fiery rays of the sun and is exhausted by them."

And then the angels brought the crown of the sun. And I saw such glory, I was frightened, I fled into the wings of the angel. And the angel said, "Do not fear, Baruch, the Lord is with you, but be comforted."

2 **9** And I said to the angel of the Lord, "Teach me what the moon is."

3 And he said to me, "It is like a woman, sitting on a chariot, and twenty angels are leading the chariot by means of oxen, and the oxen are angels. The form of the moon is like a woman."[b]

5 And I Baruch said, "Lord, why does it sometimes wax and sometimes wane?"

6 And he said to me, "Listen, Baruch, it was beautiful.

7 But when the first-created Adam sinned, having listened to Satanael, when he covered himself with the serpent, it (i.e. the moon) did not hide but shone forth, and God was angered by it. He lay bare its days to affliction."

1,2 **10** And the angel of power took me to a very wide mountain, and in the middle of the mountain was a large lake of water.[b]

3 And there were birds from all heaven. But the very large ones were not like these (ones), they were similar to a crane. And there were other birds larger than those.
4 And I asked the angel, "Lord, what is this lake in the midst of the mountain and what are these birds?"
5 And he said to me, "The birds are ready day and night, praising God ceaselessly.[c]

6 And the clouds take the water from here and rain upon the earth, and plants sprout."

is overcome because of the burning heat and warmth of the sun."
   c. Cf. 6:6; TLevi 3:1; ApPaul 4.

9 a. Ryssel, *APAT*, emends to read "the chariot of the moon."
   b. This representation of the moon is hellenistic and has no parallel in Jewish literature of the period. In the Book of the Luminaries, 1En 72–82, the sun rides in a chariot and by implication so does the moon. 2En 16:7 explicitly states that the moon rides in a chariot pulled by angels.
   c. The term "the first Adam" is very common in rabbinic literature and need not imply the Pauline second Adam.

5 And I Baruch said, "Lord, by what are its rays defiled upon earth?" And the angel said to me, "By the sight of the lawlessness and unrighteousness of men committing fornication, adultery, theft, robbery, idol-worship, drunkenness, murder, discord, jealousy, slander, murmuring, gossip, divination, and other things which are unacceptable to God. By means of these it is defiled, and because of this it is renewed.

6 And now, concerning how the bird becomes overcome: It is overcome because it checks the rays of the sun and the fire and burning the whole day.[b]

7 For if its wings did not draw around the rays of the sun as earlier said, no living being would survive."[c]

1 **9** And when they had withdrawn, night arrived, and with it the moon[a] and the stars.

2 And I Baruch said, "Lord, explain this also to me, please. How does it depart and where is it going, and in what pattern does it travel?"

3 And the angel said, "Wait and you will see this shortly." And on the morrow I saw this also in the form of a woman, seated in a wheeled chariot. And in front of it were oxen and lambs near the chariot, and also many angels.[b]

4 And I said, "Lord, what are the oxen and lambs?" And he said to me, "These are angels also."

5 And again I asked, "Why does it sometimes grow larger and sometimes grow smaller?"

6 "Listen, O Baruch: This which you see was designed by God to be beautiful without peer.

7 And during the transgression of the first Adam,[c] she gave light to Samael when he took the serpent as a garment, and did not hide, but on the contrary, waxed. And God was angered with her, and diminished her and shortened her days."

8 And I said, "And why does she not shine all the time, but only at night?" And the angel said, "Listen: Just as servants are unable to speak freely before kings, so also before the sun, the moon and stars are unable to shine. For the stars are permanently suspended, but they are dispersed by the sun; and the moon, while being safe, is exhausted by the heat of the sun."

1 **10** And when I had been taught all these things by the archangel, he took me to a third[a] heaven.

2 And I saw an unbroken plain and in the middle of it was a lake of water.[b]

3 And in it were many birds of every species but unlike those here. But I saw a crane, like large oxen. And all were great, excelling those on earth.

4 And I asked the angel, "What is the plain and what is the lake and what are the multitude of birds around it?"

5 And the angel said, "Listen, Baruch: This plain which surrounds the lake, and in which are other mysteries, is the place where the souls of the righteous[d] come when they assemble, living together choir by choir.

6 And the water is that which the clouds receive to send as rain upon the earth, and (then) fruit grows."

---

10 a. Lit. "third," but this must be the entrance to the fourth heaven. They entered the third in ch. 4, cf. also 7:2.

  b. James and others identify this as the Acher-usian lake; cf. ApMos 37:3; SibOr 2:334–38; ApPet 14; ApPaul 22.

  c. Cf. TLevi 3:8; 2En 17:1; ApZeph (in *Strom* 5.11.77) for angelic choirs in the heavens.

  d. It is not clear from the text if these are the birds. Various Jewish and Christian traditions portray the righteous souls as birds. On the Jewish traditions concerning the soul represented as a bird, cf. V. Aptowitzer, "Die Seele als Vogel," *MGWJ* 69 (1925) 150–69.

8 And I said, "How is it that men say that clouds come to the sea and take water and rain?"

9 And the angel said to me, "The race of men is ignorant, for all the water of the sea is salty so that if it rained because of the sea, no plant would sprout on earth. But know that they come from that lake and the clouds rain."

1 **11** And the angel of power took me and led me to the fifth heaven.

2 And he showed me large gates, and names of men were written (on them),[a] and they were closed. And I said, "Lord, will these gates open so that we can enter through them?" And the angel said to me, "It is not possible to enter through them until Michael, the holder of the keys of the kingdom,[b] comes." And the angel said to me, "Wait and you will see the glory of God."

3 And while we were waiting, there was a noise from the highest heaven like triple thunder. And I Baruch said, "Lord, what is this noise?"

4 And he said to me, "Michael is descending to accept the prayers of men."[d]

5 And then a voice came, saying that the gates should open, and they opened. And there was a great noise, greater than the first.

6 And Michael came, and the angel who was with me met him and bowed to him.

7 And I saw him holding a very large receptacle, and its depth was that from heaven to earth, and its width that from east to west.

8 And I said, "Lord, what is Michael holding?"

9 And he said to me, "This is where the prayers of men go."[h]

1 **12** And while he was speaking to me, angels came, carrying gifts full of flowers.[a]

2 And I said, "Lord, who are these?"

3 And he said to me, "These are the angels who are in the service of men."[b]

4 And Michael took the gifts from them and put them in the receptacle.

5 And I saw other angels carrying gifts, and they were dejected and did not dare to draw near because they did not have (sufficient) measure.

6 And Michael called, saying, "Come also, you angels, bring what you have brought."

7 And Michael cried greatly over the [un]filled receptacle.[e]

---

11 a. Cf. ApPaul 19.

b. Cf. 4Bar 9:5. Peter as the heavenly major-domo, cf. Mt 16:19.

c. This is the rank of Michael in several works, cf. e.g. Dan 10:13, 21; 2En 22:6; 33:10(A); TAb(A) *passim*, (B) 14. Cf. Josh 5:14 LXX.

d. These he apparently offers on the altar of the heavenly temple, which is mentioned in TLevi 5:1 and elsewhere. See also b.Ḥag 12b: "In it (the fourth heaven) is Jerusalem and the temple and an altar constructed and Michael, the great commander, stands and offers sacrifices on it." On the rabbinic sources for this idea, see V. Aptowitzer,

"The Heavenly Temple in the Agada," *Tarbiz* 2 (1931) 137–53, 257–77. TLevi 3:6 mentions "a reasonable and bloodless offering." On prayer and good deeds as the proper sacrifice at Qumran, cf. CD 11:20f., 1QS 9.4f. Cf. also the words of R. Johanan ben Zakkai in ARN A ch. 4.

e. This function is also ascribed to other angels, e.g. Ramiel in 2Bar 55:3 and Gabriel in Dan 9:23.

f. Contrasted with those portrayed in 4:5(G).

g. Probably the bowl for offerings at the heavenly altar. The LXX uses this term for sprinkling pans used in the Temple worship. The prayers of the saints are offered in such golden bowls in Rev

7 And again I said to the angel of the Lord, "What are the birds?" And he said to me, "These are the ones who continuously praise the Lord."c

8 And I Baruch said, "Lord, why do men say that the water which rains is from the sea?"

9 And the angel said, "There is rain from the sea and from water on earth; but that which produces the fruits is from here. Know from now on that what is called the dew of heaven comes from here."

1 **11** And taking me from this, the angel led me to the fifth heaven.

2 And the gate was closed. And I said, "Lord, will the gate be opened so that we can enter?" And the angel said to me, "We are not able to enter until Michael the holder of the keys of the kingdom of heavenb comes. But wait and you will see the glory of God."

3 And there was a great noise like thunder, and I said, "Lord, what is this noise?"

4 And he said to me, "The commander-in-chiefc Michael is descending to receive the prayers of men."d

5 And behold a voice came: "Let the gate be opened!" And they opened, and there was a shriek as from thunder.

6 And Michael came, and the angel with me went to meet him and made obeisance to him and said, "Hail, commander-in-chief of all our regiment."

7 And the commander-in-chief Michael said, "Hail thou also, our brother, interpreter of revelationse to those who pass through life rightly."f

8 And after they greeted each other, they stood still. And I saw the commander-in-chief Michael take hold of a very large bowl,g its depth being so great as from heaven to earth, and its width so great as from north to south. And I said, "Lord, what is it that Michael the archangel is holding?"

9 And he said to me, "This is where the virtues of the righteous and the good works which they do are carried,h which are brought by him before the heavenly God."

1 **12** And while I was speaking with them, behold angels came carrying baskets filled with flowers,a and they gave them to Michael.

2 And I asked the angel, "Lord, who are these and what is it that they are carrying?"

3 And he said to me, "These are the angels over the principalities."b

4 And taking the baskets, the archangel emptied them into his bowl.

5 And the angel said to me, "These above-mentioned flowers are the virtues of the righteous."

6 And I saw other angels carrying baskets which were less than full.c And they came distressed, and did not dare to approach, for they did not achieve the full prizes.d

7 And Michael cried out, saying, "Come also, you angels, bring what you have brought."

8 And Michael was greatly distressed and so was the angel with me, because they had not filled the bowl.

5:8, cf. also Rev 8:3.
  h. Slavonic seems influenced by vs. 4.

12 a. James (in his introduction to R. L. Bensley, *The Fourth Book of Ezra* [Cambridge, 1895] pp. lii–liii) noticed that twelve angels with flowers are mentioned in the Spanish MSS of 4Ezra 1:40, a Christian work.
  b. Angels of power and angels of principalities, cf. 1En 61:10. The powers and principalities in lists of heavenly forces are mentioned several times in

the NT and in other sources, e.g. TLevi 3:8. Angels of hosts are mentioned in 1:8(G) and 10:1(S). The relation between these different heavenly forces is unclear.
  c. Hughes, *APOT*, emended this to read "neither empty nor full." The text is uncertain but the meaning clear.
  d. Ryssel, *APAT*, first suggested that the Gk. is here dependent on Phil 3:14; 1Cor 9:24.
  e. The negative has dropped out of S.

1 **13** And I saw others coming and crying, and they were trembling with fear, saying, "Woe to us, darkened ones, that we have been handed over to places of demons and of men. And we want to depart from them, if possible."
2 And Michael said, "You are not able to depart from them, but tell me what you want."
3 And they said to him, "We entreat you, Michael our chief, transfer us from them, for we do not want to remain with the disobedient, unreasonable men.

4 Their wives flee to the church, and from thence they bring them out to jealousy and to fornication and envy, and they sin in many other ways, which you, O Glorious One,[b] know."

5 And Michael answered and said, "Be patient until I ask God what he commands concerning you."

1 **14** Michael ascended and the gates closed; there was thunder as if there (were) 40 oxen.[a]
2 And I said to the angel, "What is the noise?" And he said to me, "Now Michael is bringing the prayers[b] of men."

1 **15** And at that time Michael descended and brought the first angels full mercy.[a]

2 And he said, "Come, angels, and receive mercies; just as you brought prayers to God, so receive. In the measure that men requested, thus give to them."

3 And Michael called out again, "Come, you angels who brought lesser gifts. Just as you brought, thus receive, in the measure that men offered prayers. Announce it to them and be not negligent. But (they should) prostrate themselves in prayer in the holy church."[d]

1 **16** Michael again called the other angels who were crying, "Come also, you angels, and take (back) the petitions (and) what the Lord has prophesied about those men. There is no command for you to depart from them.
2 But bring them painful diseases and horrors and caterpillars and locusts and storms, thunder and hail and devastation to their cities, and demons to strangle their children, because they do not fear God and they do not come to church and to the place of prayers. Bring them curses, and no success in good, and murder."
3 The angels took their commands from Michael; trembling and crying they went.

---

13 a. This expression is used to refer to monastics and Christian leaders, especially bishops, cf. Lampe, p. 1105b. Note that both versions are Christian.

b. It would appear that Michael is referred to as "Glorious One."

14 a. See 10:3(G).

b. The Slavonic calls the offerings "prayers" consistently, but the Gk. version refers to them as "prayers" and "virtues" and "good works," cf. 11:4, 9; 12:5; 15:2f.

15 a. The Slavonic version may have misread

1 **13** And then similarly came other angels crying and lamenting and saying with fear, "See how we are, blackened, Lord, for we are handed over to evil men, and we want to be withdrawn from them."

2 And Michael said, "So that the enemy will not dominate at the end, you must not withdraw from them. But tell me what you desire."

3 And they said, "We beg you, Michael our commander-in-chief, transfer us from them, for we are unable to remain with evil and foolish men. For there is no goodness in them, but only every unrighteousness and greediness.

4 Indeed we have seen them enter into no church, nor (go) to the spiritual fathers,[a] nor to anything good. But wherever there is murder, they are in the midst of it, and wherever there is fornication, adultery, theft, slander, perjury, envy, drunkenness, strife, jealousy, grumbling, gossip, idol worship, divination, and things similar to these. There are (with these men) works of such nature and worse; therefore we ask to be released from them."

5 And Michael said to the angels, "Wait until I learn from the Lord what is to happen."

1 **14** And at that time Michael departed and the doors closed. And a noise like thunder came.

2 And I asked the angel, "What is the noise?" And he said to me, "Now Michael is bringing the virtues[b] of men to God."

1 **15** And at that time Michael came down, and the gate opened, and he brought oil.[a]

2 And for the angels who had brought the full baskets, he filled (the baskets) with oil, saying, "Take, give a hundredfold reward[b] to our friends, and to those who have laboriously done good works.[c] For those who have sown well, harvest well."

3 And he said to those who had brought half-full baskets, "Come you also, receive the reward according to what you brought, and give it to the sons of men."

4 Then he said to those who brought the full (baskets) and those (who brought) the half-full (baskets), "Go, bless our friends and tell them that thus says the Lord: You have been faithful over a little, he will set you over much; enter into the delight of our Lord."[d]   Mt 25:23

1 **16** And turning, he said to those who had brought nothing, "Be not sad, and cry not, but do not let the sons of men alone.

2 But since they have provoked me to anger by their deeds, go and provoke them to jealousy, and provoke them to anger, and embitter them against those who are no nation, against a people without understanding.

3 Moreover, send forth caterpillars and locusts, rust and grasshoppers, hail with lightning and fury. Punish them with the sword and death, and their children with demons.   Deut 32:21 (LXX) Rom 10:19

---

elaion as eleos. Seth seeks the "oil of mercy" from the garden of Eden in ApMos 9:3; 13:1; cf. also 2En 8:1. Enoch is anointed before God with a "good oil" (2En 22:8), or the "oil of God's glory" (2En 56:2). Cf. E. Quinn, *The Quest of Seth for the Oil of Life* (Chicago, 1962) for other traditions concerning this oil.

b. Cf. Mt 19:29 and Mk 10:30.
c. Cf. nn. to 11:9 and 14:2.
d. The Gk. paraphrases the NT verse. The Slavonic parallel seems to be addressed to only those who brought an insufficient measure, but also appears to be Christian.

4 And the angel said to me, "By the command of the Ruler I say to you, Baruch, stand on the right side and you will see the glory of God.ᵃ And you will see the resting place of the righteous, glory and joy and rejoicing and celebration.ᵇ And you will see the torture of the impious, wailing and groans and lamentations and the eternal worm. Their voice goes up to heaven and implores, 'Have mercy on us, God.' "

5 And I Baruch said to the angel, "Lord, who are these?*"

6 And he said to me, "These are the sinners, having despised the command of God."

7 And I said to the angel, "Permit me, Lord, to cry on their behalf."

8 And the angel said to me, "You also may cry for them; perhaps the Lord God will hear your voice and have mercy on them."

1 **17** And a voice from heaven came, saying, "Bring Baruch down to the face of all the earth so that he will tell the sons of men that which he has seen and heard, and all the mysteries you have shown him. And glory be to our God forever." AMEN.

---

16 a. There appear to be three glories of God referred to in this work: that of the sun (6:12; 7:2; 7:5), that of Michael (11:2; 13:4[S]), and that of the righteous in their resting place (16:4). Note that Adam lost the glory of God in the Fall (4:16[G]).

b. This promise is not fulfilled.

4 For they did not listen to my voice, nor observe my commands, nor carry them out, but they despised my commands and my churches, and insulted the priests proclaiming my words to them.''

5

6

7

8

1 **17** And while he was speaking, the door closed and we withdrew.

2 And taking me, the angel returned me to where I was at the beginning.

3 And when I came to myself, I praised God, who had deemed me worthy of such honors.

4 And you, brethren, who happen upon these revelations, glorify God also so that he will glorify us now and forever to all eternity! AMEN.

APOCALYPSE OF ABRAHAM

(First to Second Century A.D.)

A NEW TRANSLATION AND INTRODUCTION
BY R. RUBINKIEWICZ

The theme of the Apocalypse of Abraham seems to be Israel's election and its covenant with God. The document can be divided into two parts, chapters 1–8 and chapters 9–32. Chapters 1–8 constitute a story of Abraham's youth and his perception of idolatry. Abraham concludes that his father's idols are not gods, because some stone idols are crushed and a wooden idol is accidentally consumed by fire. Abraham consequently beseeches God to reveal himself, whereupon he hears God's voice, which instructs Abraham to leave his father's house.

Abraham is commanded to offer a sacrifice so that God will reveal "great things which you have not seen . . ." (9:6). God sends his angel Iaoel to lead Abraham up to heaven (15:4), where he sees seven visions: the light and fiery angels (15:5–7), the fire (17:1–3), the throne (18:1–14), the firmaments (19:4–9), the world (21:2–7), the seven sins of the world (24:3–25:2), and the destruction of the Temple (27:1–3). Finally God announces the punishment of the gentiles through ten plagues (chs. 29f.) and the victory of the just (chs. 31f.).

Texts

The Apocalypse of Abraham is known only in an Old Slavonic translation, which has come down to us in several Russian redactions. The combined witness of six manuscripts that contain essentially the full text allows us to discern fairly clearly the original form of the Slavonic text, although many details remain obscure. Four manuscripts provide confirmatory evidence only for the first eight chapters. Other fragments, summaries, and reworkings are obviously derived from the older long form; they will not concern us here.

The apocalypse appears as a completely independent unit only in one manuscript, but basically the same text is found in a second manuscript with a slightly different beginning and a radically truncated ending. A slightly different redaction is reflected in the text that has been incorporated into the Explanatory Palaia (*Tolkovaja Paleja*), a broad account of Old Testament history interspersed with exegesis, much of it anti-Jewish polemic. These are the manuscripts:

S– Sil'vestrovskij sbornik, Moscow, Central'nyj Gosudarstvennyj Arkhiv Drevnikh Aktov, Sin. Tip. 53, fols. 164–83. 14th cent. Facsimile published as vol. 99, *Obščestvo ljubitelej drevnej pis'mennosti*, St. Petersburg, 1891. Published by N. S. Tikhonravov in *Pamjatniki otrečennoj russkoj literatury* (St. Petersburg, 1863) vol. 1, pp. 32–53.

D– A miscellany, Lenin Library, Moscow, Tikhonravov 704, fols. 70–79. 16th cent. Unpublished.

A– The Volokalamsk Paleja Tolkovaja, Moscow, Lenin Library, Mosk. Dukh. Akad. 172/549, fols. 85–101. 15th cent. Printed in N. S. Tikhonravov, *Pamjatniki*, vol. 1, pp. 54–77.

B– The Synodal Paleja Tolkovaja, Moscow, Gosudarstvennyj Istoričeskij Muzej, 869 (Sin. 211) fols. 76–90. 16th cent. Unpublished.

C– A Palaia, Lenin Library, Moscow, fond 173.III, No. 136, fols. 18–43. 16th cent.
Unpublished.

K– Solovec Palaia, Leningrad, Public Library, Kaz. Dukh. Akad. 431, fols. 79–95.
16th–17th cent. Published by I. J. Porfir'ev, in "Apokrifičeskie skazanija o vetkho-
zavetnykh licakh i sobytijakh po rukopisjam Soloveckoj biblioteki," *Sbornik Otd. russ.
jaz. i slov. Imp. Akad. Nauk* 17 (1877) 111–30.

We were able to consult the unpublished texts D, B, and C in microfilms, which were
made available through the cooperation of the libraries and museums of the U.S.S.R.[1]
The Palaia manuscripts, which contain the longer form of the Ladder of Jacob, have the
first eight chapters of the Apocalypse of Abraham; this is the later Palaia redaction. The
earlier redaction, represented by the Kolomna manuscript of A.D. 1406, has only a few
fragments of the Apocalypse of Abraham. An abbreviated text, summarizing chapters 1–12,
15, 17, 20, and 30, is found in two manuscripts, while a derived legend is found in seven.
They are not helpful in establishing the early Slavonic text.

Most critics have distinguished two parts to the Apocalypse of Abraham: chapters 1–8 and
chapters 9–32; they claim that the former did not belong to the original apocalyptic work
but was added later by an editor.[2] If our interpretation of the apocalypse 1–6 is correct, these
chapters form an integral part of the work and were written by the same author who composed
the rest of the apocalypse. It is generally accepted that the present text of the apocalypse has
many insertions which are due to Slavonic editors. All of chapter 7 seems to be redactional.[3]

Original language

A thorough investigation of the original language of the Apocalypse of Abraham has never
been undertaken. A. Rubinstein studied only ten passages from the apocalypse and concluded
that the document probably was written in Hebrew.[4] The Slavonic text of the Apocalypse
of Abraham contains several Hebrew names, words, and phrases. The most impressive
examples are the following: Ioavan is a Slavonic deformation of the Hebrew *ywn* (Greece);
Souzouch is probably a transcription of the name *kwrwŝ* (Cyrus); and Maroumat is an
abbreviation of the Hebrew *Martā Rômā*. The use of parts of the body instead of a simple
pronoun is frequent: "My heart was perplexed" (1:4), "Why now have you afflicted my
heart?" (27:6).[5] The parallelism of the verses reflects Semitic thought.[6]

The positive instead of a comparative betrays a Semitic original. "It was heavy of a big
stone" (1:5) renders the Semitic *kbd mn* (cf. also 6:9), which has to be translated: "heavier
than a big stone." Moreover, the prepositions are sometimes utilized according to Hebrew
rather than Slavonic syntax (for example: 8:4, "for the sins," lit. "in the sins"; 12:10, "you
will see all," lit. "you will see in all" [= Heb. *r'h bᵉ*][7]; 27:11, "to rule from them in
them," lit. "to rule in them" [= Heb. *hmŝylty bhm*]).

The syntax of the temporal phrases reflects the Hebrew original of our apocalypse.
Frequently a phrase is introduced by the verb *hyh*: "And it came to pass, that when I saw
it, my heart was perplexed . . ." (1:4; cf. e.g. 1:7; 2:5; 5:4; 5:10, 11; 8:5). Numerous other
examples could be cited. The foregoing suggests that the Apocalypse of Abraham was written
in a Semitic language, probably in Hebrew.

The Slavonic version of the Apocalypse of Abraham was made in the eleventh or twelfth

---

[1] A seventh text (Uvarov 85, fols. 297–313, Historical Museum, Moscow) turned out to be a copy of S and therefore
of no interest. E. Turdeanu, in his preliminary study of the MSS on the basis of published materials ("L'Apocalypse
d'Abraham en slave," *JSJ* 3 [1972] 156–64), did not know of MSS C and D, which we found during our work toward
a critical edition of the ApAb. He believed that MS Sin. 548 (Historical Museum, Moscow) contained ApAb; N. B.
Tikhomirov of the Lenin Library has kindly informed us that this is an error. I am grateful to the editor for polishing
the introduction and to H. G. Lunt for improving the English translation.

[2] Cf. N. Bonwetsch, *Die Apokalypse Abrahams: Das Testament der vierzig Märtyrer*, p. 41.

[3] Ch. 7 seems to be derived from *Palaea Tolkovaja* (Moscow, 1892) pp. 123–45.

[4] Cf. A. Rubinstein, "Hebraisms in the Slavonic 'Apocalypse of Abraham,' " *JJS* 4 (1953) 108–15; idem, "Hebraisms
in the 'Apocalypse of Abraham,' " *JJS* 5 (1954) 132–35. He analyzed ten examples: ApAb 8:4; 12:3, 10; 14:4, 6,
13; 29:8, 20; 31:1, 2.

[5] Cf. also 17:23; 22:2.

[6] Cf. especially 1:4; 3:1; 6:1, 11; 12:20; 21:3.

[7] Cf. also 31:4.

century A.D. in the south of the Slavic world, probably in Bulgaria. It may be that this pseudepigraphon was translated directly from Hebrew into Slavonic. Between 1108/9 and 1120 the archbishop of Ochride (Macedonia) was Leon Mung, a Jew converted to Christianity.[8] His teacher was Tobias b. Eleazar (11th cent.), the author of the Midrash Lekaḥ Tov. Bulgaria at that time had educated men who could make the translation from Hebrew into Slavonic. Further study needs to be made regarding this issue.

Date

It is commonly held that our pseudepigraphon was composed at the end of the first century A.D. No decisive argument, however, has been given in support of this date. In the following paragraphs the issue will be discussed first in terms of the external and then in terms of the internal data.

The testimonies of Nicephorus,[9] patriarch of Constantinople (806–15), of Pseudo-Athanasius (6th cent.),[10] and of the Apostolic Constitutions (4/5th cent.)[11] are very vague and nothing can be deduced from them in regard to our apocalypse. Epiphanius (4th cent.) speaks about some ''Apocalypse of Abraham'' used by the Sethians.[12] The same apocalypse was utilized by the Audiens and we know its content, thanks to Theodore bar Konai (8th cent.)[13] and Origen.[14] There can be no doubt, however, that the writing used by the Sethians and our pseudepigraphon are two different works.

The text of Recognitiones (2nd cent.) gives us at least two traditions. The first one presents Abraham as an astrologer (Rec. 32:3f.), the second one (33:1f.) may be an allusion to the Apocalypse of Abraham. These witnesses permit us to suggest that the Apocalypse of Abraham was possibly known by the second century.

Our pseudepigraphon was written after A.D. 70, because the author describes the destruction of Jerusalem (cf. ch. 27). Hence, the apocalypse—that is the early Jewish stratum—was composed sometime after A.D. 70 and before the middle of the second century.[15] It is unwise to speculate further regarding the date of the apocalypse in the present collection of documents.[16]

Provenance[17]

If the original language of the Apocalypse of Abraham is Hebrew, then it was most likely composed in Palestine. It is necessary to be conservative regarding the probable provenance of the apocalypse for two main reasons: First, it is preserved in Slavonic manuscripts that are far removed from the conjectured time and place of the original composition. Second, as stated herein by H. G. Lunt and F. I. Andersen respectively in the presentations of the Ladder of Jacob and 2 Enoch, pseudepigrapha preserved only in Slavonic may have been considerably altered by the Bogomils (a medieval dualist sect), who were influenced by passages in the pseudepigrapha and composed new ones.

---

[8] Cf. "Notitia Archiepiscopi Iannis Comneni," ed. in: *Fontes Historiae Bulgaricae* (Sofia, 1968) vol. 7, p. 110; see also: N. Snegarov, *Istirija na Ochridskata archiepiskopija* (Sofia, 1924) vol. 1, pp. 204f.; I. S. Emmanuel, *Histoire des Israélites de Salonique* (Paris, 1935) p. 34.

[9] PG, vol. 100, col. 1059.

[10] PG, vol. 28, col. 432.

[11] PG, vol. 1, col. 1100.

[12] PG, vol. 41, col. 669.

[13] Cf. H. Pognon, *Inscriptions mandaïtes des coupes de Khouabir* (Paris, 1892) p. 195; H. C. Puech, "Fragments retrouvés de l'Apocalypse d'Allogène," in *Mélanges Franz Cumont* (Brussels, 1936) pp. 937f.

[14] PG, vol. 13, col. 1889.

[15] L. Ginzberg ("Apocalypse of Abraham," *JE*, vol. 1, p. 92) placed the ApAb in "the last decades of the first century." G. H. Box and J. I. Landsman argued that the ApAb was composed between A.D. 70 and the first decades of the 2nd cent. See their discussion in *The Apocalypse of Abraham*, pp. xvf. This n. 15 and the sentence to which it is attached in the text have been added by J.H.C.

[16] [R. Rubinkiewicz speculates on the date for the composition of ApAb in *L'Apocalypse d'Abraham en slave. Édition critique du texte, introduction, traduction et commentaire*. He argues that plagues 1, 3, 5, 7, and 9 describe the events of the years A.D. 69 and 70, especially the war between the Jews and the Romans; and that plagues 2, 4, 6, 8, and 10 reflect the eruption of Vesuvius in A.D. 79. On the basis of these observations he suggests that the ApAb was written shortly after A.D. 79, perhaps between 79 and 81. —J.H.C.]

[17] The section of the introduction regarding provenance was written by J.H.C.

The Christian interpolations and gnostic glosses

Chapter 7 appears to be inserted from the legend of Abraham found in the Palaia. The interpolator of 29:3–13 was probably a Christian editor who had nothing to do with gnostic circles. However, the gloss in 22:5, the censure in 20:5, and the gloss in 20:7 reveal that their author wanted to indicate that the God of Abraham is a god of evil. This point of view is usually associated with the gnostics. The gloss in 22:5 and the censured text of 20:5, however, show that they could be made only in the Slavic world. The only Slavs who claimed that the God of the Old Testament was the god of evil were the Bogomils. Their founder was Pope Bogomil (10th cent. A.D.). According to the Bogomils, God had two sons: Satanael and Jesus. Satanael rebelled against God and created the visible world; everything described in the book of Genesis is the work of the devil. If then this world is created by Satanael (= god of the OT), one has to abstain from every contact with the material world. The Bogomils, therefore, condemned marriage, abstained from meat and wine, and did not believe in the resurrection of the body.[18]

The glosses in 20:5, 7 and 22:5 perfectly suit their doctrine. We can say the same about the interpolator of 29:3–13; he shows that Jesus came forth from the heathens and not from the Jews (= the people with Azazel!). Perhaps also inserted by a Bogomil were 9:7, an injunction against meat and wine, and 23:4–10, which claims that the sin of Adam and Eve consisted in the conjugal relation. Maybe the same Bogomil editor interpolated 10:6–12 and 17:8b–19. The general content of the account of the sin of Adam and Eve reveals that it comes from Jewish sources. It fit the Bogomil doctrine, however, and therefore was inserted into our apocalypse.

Theological importance

God. The God of eternity (9:3) is the God who protects Abraham and his descendants (9:4). He created the world (9:4), chose Israel, called this nation "my people" (22:5; 31:1), and will give it victory over its enemies (31:1f.).

Angelology. Angelology plays a large role in our apocalypse. The most important figure is the Angel of God, Iaoel. His fundamental role is to protect and strengthen Abraham (10:3).

Demonology. The chief of the fallen angels is Azazel (13:6). His power is over the earth, because he has chosen it for his dwelling place (13:7f.; 14:6). However, his power is limited (13:10) since God does not permit him to tempt all the righteous (13:11). For example, he cannot seduce Abraham (13:14), and he has no power over the body of the righteous (13:10).

Cosmology. God shows Abraham the firmaments in order that he may know that "on no single expanse is there any other but the one whom" Abraham has searched for or who has loved him (19:3). God says to Abraham: "Look now beneath your feet at the firmament and understand the creation that was depicted of old on this expanse" (21:1). Abraham sees then the earth with the wicked men, and the garden of Eden with the just, he sees the sea with Leviathan, and the waters over the firmaments; at last, he watches the men on the right and on the left side of the "picture of creation" (chs. 21f.). Abraham is told that as the world is divided into two parts: earth and Eden, the waters of the sea and the waters over the firmaments, so mankind is divided into the people of God and the heathens (21:3–7).

The numeration of the firmaments is due to editorial expansions, probably by a Slavic editor. The descriptions of the three heavens is similar to that in the Testament of Levi 3:1–4.

Dualism. In the Apocalypse of Abraham there is no ontological dualism. The created world is good before the eyes of God (22:2). There is no other God in the universe than "the one whom" Abraham has "searched for" and "who has loved" him (19:3).

There is evil in the world, but it is not inevitable. God has full control over the world and he does not permit the body of the just to remain in the hand of Azazel (13:10). Azazel is wrong if he thinks he can scorn justice and disperse the secret of heaven (14:4). He will be banished in the desert forever (14:5).

Eschatology. The age of ungodliness endures "twelve periods" (29:2). After the last

---

[18] Cf. D. Obolenski, *The Bogomils* (Cambridge, 1948); S. Runciman, *The Medieval Manichees* (Cambridge, 1947); D. Angelov, *Bogomilstvo vû Bûlgarija* (Sofia, 1961).

period comes the final judgment, which precedes the redemption of the just. God announces ten plagues (29:15; 30:2–8); when they pass, he will send his "chosen one" (31:1) who will gather the dispersed people. Together with him God will punish the heathens (31:2). The apostates will be burned through the fire of Azazel (31:6); the Temple and the sacrifices will be restored (29:17f.).

The doctrine of resurrection is noticeably absent, although it may be reflected in the symbol of the dew (19:4). The Apocalypse of Abraham, however, passed through the hands of the Bogomils, who did not believe in the resurrection of the body. It is possible that phrases mentioning the resurrection were omitted. It is clear, regardless of that possibility, that our author believed in life after death (cf. 21:6).

Relation to the canonical books[19]

The books of Genesis and Ezekiel play a fundamental role in the Apocalypse of Abraham. The author begins with the text of Genesis 20:13 (ApAb 1:1), which is quoted according to the exegesis of the Targums; he ends his work with the citation of Genesis 15:13–16 (= ApAb 32:1–3), but he changes the biblical "fourth generation" into "seventh," i.e. a perfect one.

The apocalypse at 8:4 and 9:1–4 reflects respectively Genesis 12:1 and 15:1 seen in the light of Psalm 20:2f. or Deuteronomy 33:29. The author quotes Genesis 15:9f. (ApAb 9:5), and Genesis 15:17a (ApAb 15:1). Apocalypse of Abraham 20:4 calls to mind Genesis 18:27; 20:6 is based on Genesis 18:30.

Chapters 1 and 10 of Ezekiel are behind chapters 18f. Abraham sees four living creatures (ApAb 18:5–11; Ezek 1:10; 10:14), the wheels full of eyes (ApAb 18:3, 12), the throne (ApAb 18:3; Ezek 1:23), and the divine chariot (ApAb 18:12; Ezek 10:6).

There is no direct relationship between the Apocalypse of Abraham and the New Testament. There are some parallel expressions, however, which may indicate that both drew from a shared tradition.

Relation to the apocryphal books

The author of the Apocalypse of Abraham follows the tradition of 1 Enoch 1–36. The chief of the fallen angels is Azazel, who rules the stars and most men. It is not difficult to find here the traditions of Genesis 6:1–4 developed according to the tradition of 1 Enoch. Azazel is the head of the angels who plotted against the Lord and who impregnated the daughters of men.[20] These angels are compared to the stars.[21] Azazel revealed the secrets of heaven and is banished to the desert.[22] Abraham, as Enoch, receives the power to drive away Satan.[23] All these connections show that the author of the Apocalypse of Abraham drew upon the tradition of 1 Enoch.

Cultural importance

The Apocalypse of Abraham is one of the most important works written after the destruction of the nation in A.D. 70. The importance of the apocalypse may be compared to that of 2 Baruch or 4 Ezra, but our author analyzes the causes of the destruction of Jerusalem from a different perspective: The defeat was caused by the infidelity of Israel toward the covenant with God and the opportunistic politics of some leaders.

The pseudepigraphon is written with great talent and with a good understanding of biblical exegesis. The symbolical language is clear, logical, and easy to understand. The Apocalypse of Abraham provides us with an insight into the literary "workshop" of the Palestinian

[19] For a full discussion see Rubinkiewicz, *L'Apocalypse d'Abraham.*
[20] ApAb 14:4; 1En 6:4 and ApAb 14:6; 1En 6:1f.; 10:4.
[21] ApAb 14:6; 1En 86:1.
[22] ApAb 14:4; 1En 8:1 and ApAb 14:5; 1En 10:4.
[23] ApAb 14:3; 1En 14:3.

writers of the first century A.D.; in consequence we may understand better the literary genres of that period.

The Apocalypse of Abraham was practically unknown for ten centuries. Neither the Semitic original nor the supposed Greek version has been found. Perhaps the latter never existed. Translated into Slavonic, our document circulated first in Bulgaria and afterward in Russia. Known only in the Orient, it had no influence on occidental literature.

The transmission of the Apocalypse of Abraham[24]

The Slavonic Apocalypse of Abraham is to be ascribed to the extraordinarily productive burst of cultural activity during the reign of Simeon of Bulgaria (893–927), when a prodigious amount of material was translated from Greek into Old Church Slavonic as part of the effort of the Bulgarian emperor to bring his realm to the level of Byzantium itself.[25] The translation contains Greek words well known from Old Church Slavonic (*adŭ*: "*haidēs*, Hades"; *aerŭ*: "*aēr*, air"; *stuxija*: "*stoicheion*, element"), along with the conventional bizarre rendering of Gehenna as "fiery race" (by a confusion of *géenna* with *geneá* or some other derivative of the Gk. root *gen*-) and numerous literalistic phrases that make better sense in Greek than in Slavonic. There can be no question that this text, like the whole Slavonic culture of Bulgaria of the time, was translated from Greek.[26] It is, then, fully realistic to assume that a Greek text of the Apocalypse of Abraham still existed in the Balkans as late as the ninth century, although no trace has yet been found in surviving Greek manuscripts.

The style is strongly Semitic but generally within the bounds of the biblical Greek that was presumably used by some hellenistic Jews for original works, e.g. Revelation. It is reasonable to hypothesize that the text was composed in Hebrew or Aramaic and rendered very literally into Greek. While no decisive arguments for a Semitic original have yet been advanced, the sheer number of Semitisms is best explained by this hypothesis. The quotation of the Divine Name *El, El, El, El* (retained only in copy S) and *Eli* (glossed "that is, my God"; replaced, except in copy S, by the spelling *Ili*, in line with the accepted form in Mt 27:46) is suggestive but inconclusive. Final *-il* for Hebrew *'ēl* in the names Azazel, Iaoel, and Michael indicates Greek mediation. Perhaps the strange wording of 9:4 reflects the Hebrew of Genesis 15:1 (see n. b to ch. 9). It is not impossible that *putĭ zemĭnŭ* (10:4) reflects *drk 'rṣ* in the sense of "manners, morality," but it may be an inept way of expressing "the road to the (promised) land." This meager evidence may suggest a Hebrew original.

The Slavonic text has come down to us in relatively full form in six manuscripts, the oldest from the early fourteenth century, the second from the fifteenth, and the others from the sixteenth century. The chief distinction among the copies is that four contain the apocalypse more or less integrated into the Explanatory Palaia, while two present the text as an independent (copy S) or nearly independent unit (copy D). The Palaia variants contain long interpolations of anti-Jewish polemical passages, but otherwise the text is so close to S D that only in chapter 7 is a new redaction indicated. The oldest copy, S, is unfortunately extremely faulty, with numerous omissions of syllables, sentences, and even paragraphs; with frequent distortions even of obvious words; and with unsuccessful efforts to update the archaic language, the forms and vocabulary of which were often not understood by the

---

[24] [Due to the complicated history of transmission of ApAb, the following remarks by H. G. Lunt are intended to supplement the work of R. Rubinkiewicz. —J.H.C.]

[25] The translation of ApAb could be slightly earlier, from the last years of the initial period of Slavonic culture, viz., the Moravian mission of Cyril and Methodius (863–84), and its Bulgarian offshoot after 864; for it appears that the translation was made into an occidental version of OCS and then, like most texts that have come down to us through East Slavic mediation, adapted to the more eastern norm that was elaborated under Simeon. It is impossible, however, to exclude a dating up to about 1050, the end of the OCS period. In any case, the archaic language of ApAb makes Turdeanu's ascription of the translation to the 13th cent. unacceptable (cf. E. Turdeanu, *JSJ* 3 [1972] 156–64). The combined evidence of such works as 1En, the Palaia, and the VisIs requires us to posit Slavonic versions of many apocryphal and pseudepigraphic works—along with a remarkable store of more orthodox texts—before the final Byzantine military triumph of 1018 and the rapid withering of Slavonic cultural activity in the Balkans. See H. G. Lunt, "On the Language of the Slavonic Apocalypse of Abraham," *Festschrift for Moshé Altbauer* (Slavica Hierosolymitana; in press).

[26] A few translations from Lat., made in Moravia (or Pannonia or perhaps Dalmatia), may have been in use in Macedonia and Bulgaria, e.g. the GNic. The products of western Slavonic culture are somewhat better represented in Russia, where they were introduced between about 988 and 1100.

scribe.[27] Copy D stems ultimately from the same *Vorlage* as copy S, but unfortunately the scribe, clearly not at home in the style and special sphere of apocalyptic tradition and allusions, gave up well before the end and simply omitted most of the apocalyptic vision (from 26:5 on), reducing all of it to a few phrases. On the other hand, the Palaia texts A B C K continue beyond the end of S (in 31:3).[28] Tikhonravov[29] apparently chose to exclude a paragraph (ch. 32) that Porfir'ev,[30] probably rightly, assigns to this text rather than to the subsequent episode in the Palaia account of Abraham's life.

It is reasonable to assume that all six copies stem originally from a single old manuscript (very likely with some faults) representing the archaic language in South Slavic orthography. All copies reflect Novgorod phonetics at some state in their history; this shows up in 6:7 (*učinen*: "appointed, installed") of A B C K instead of S D's correct *učenen*: "valued." B is, overall, the most reliable text, occasionally agreeing with S D against A C K (e.g. in retaining in 17:2 *pokljače*, "knelt," a word not known in Russian, against the replacement *ponik*, "having bowed his head," of A C K). A and C often go together,[31] but they have independent omissions and distortions. K, the youngest copy, shows many clarifying paraphrases or lexical substitutions that are illuminating even when they only show precisely in what way the scribe understood the old text. B has as marginal notes materials K incorporates into the text. The picure is approximately as follows:

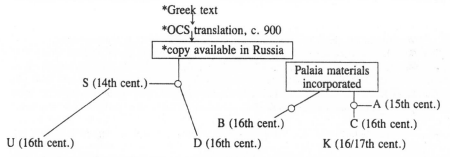

Agreement of S D B provides the most reliable readings. On the whole, variations are minor and a plausible text can be established, but there are important passages where the textual corruptive cannot be repaired.

The German translation by Bonwetsch[32] and the English one by Box, assisted by Landsman,[33] were based on rather indiscriminate selections of variants from the published texts of S A K. Neither translator was fully acquainted with the medieval language, and both made a number of conjectures and emendations based on modern Russian rather than Old Slavonic. Since these translations have been the basis of much of the work on the apocalypse, we have felt it necessary to point out some of their mistakes in our notes.

The aim of the present translation is to give readers the clearest possible picture of the complicated Slavonic text we believe to have been available in Russia in the thirteenth or fourteenth century. The history of that text back to about A.D. 900 and of its Greek model or models of earlier date remains a matter for speculation. It is quite possible that individual component parts have very diverse origins.

The translation follows the chapter divisions established by Bonwetsch and, with a few exceptions, the verses used by Rubinkiewicz in his Rome dissertation. The song in chapter 17 is treated as verse, but 21:3–7, which might be viewed as poetry, is set as prose.

---

[27] The scribe mistreats in the same way the other texts in the codex; however, some of these are far less exotic in theme and archaic in language. Thus no editorial purpose is to be discerned for the odd omissions and distortions in S, although of course they must be noted in cases where we must depend on the witness of other MSS.

[28] The scribe of S ends another text in mid-sentence.

[29] N. S. Tikhonravov, *Pamjatniki otrečennoj russkoj literatury*, vol. 1, p. 77.

[30] I. J. Porfir'ev, *Sbornik Otd. r. jaz. i slov.* 17 (1877) 130.

[31] E.g. the angel's headdress in 11:3 is *sudarí*, "handkerchief, sudarium," in A C, but *kidarí*, "kidaris," in S D B K. See also the variants discussed in n. c to ch. 8.

[32] N. Bonwetsch, *Die Apokalypse Abrahams.*

[33] In G. H. Box and J. I. Landsman, *The Apocalypse of Abraham* (London, 1918).

In view of the difficulty and obscurity of much of the text, the translation has adhered as closely as possible to the original, and the notes supply even more literal renderings when necessary. The notes also point out the most important cases where the translation is based on emendations of S, where various manuscripts have omissions, where significant variants occur, or where the text must be deemed corrupt. Words added in the text to obtain idiomatic English have been enclosed in parentheses.

SELECT BIBLIOGRAPHY

Charlesworth, *PMR,* pp. 68f.
Delling, *Bibliographie,* pp. 163f.
Denis, *Introduction,* pp. 37f.

Bonwetsch, G. N. *Die Apokalypse Abrahams. Das Testament der vierzig Märtyrer.* Studien zur Geschichte der Theologie und der Kirche, Bd. 1, Heft 1; Leipzig, 1897.
Box, G. H., and Landsman, J. I. *The Apocalypse of Abraham.* London, 1918.
Frey, J. B. "Abraham (Apocalypse d')," *DBSup,* vol. 1, cols. 28–38.
Ginzberg, L. "Abraham, Apocalypse of," *JE,* vol. 1, pp. 91f.
Rubinkiewicz, R. "Apokalipsa Abraham," *Ruch Biblijny i Liturgiczny* 27 (1974) 230–37.
———. *L'Apocalypse d'Abraham en slave. Édition critique du texte, introduction, traduction et commentaire.* Ph.D. diss.; Rome, 1977.
———. "Les Sémitismes dans l'Apocalypse d'Abraham," *Folia Orientalia* 21 (1980) 141–48.
———. "La Vision de l'histoire dans l'Apocalypse d'Abraham," *ANRW* II.19.1. Pp. 137–51.
Rubinstein, A. "Hebraisms in the Slavonic 'Apocalypse of Abraham,' " *JJS* 4 (1953) 108–15.
———. "Hebraisms in the 'Apocalypse of Abraham,' " *JJS* 5 (1954) 132–35.
———. "A Problematic Passage in the Apocalypse of Abraham," *JJS* 8 (1957) 45–50.
Turdeanu, E. "L'Apocalypse d'Abraham en slave," *JSJ* 3 (1972) 153–80.

THE APOCALYPSE OF ABRAHAM

TRANSLATED BY R. RUBINKIEWICZ
REVISED AND NOTES ADDED BY H. G. LUNT

The Book of the Apocalypse of Abraham, son of Terah, son of Nahor, son of Serug, son of Arphaxad, son of Shem, son of Noah, son of Lamech, son of Methuselah, son of Enoch, son of Jared.[a]

Abraham's rejection of idolatry

1 1 On the day I was guarding[b] the gods of my father Terah and the gods of my 2 brother Nahor, while I was testing (to find out) which god is in truth the strongest, I (then) Abraham, at the time when my lot came, when I was completing the 3 services of my father Terah's sacrifice to his gods of wood, of stone, of gold, of silver, of copper, and of iron, •having entered their temple for the service, I found a god named Marumath, carved from stone, fallen at the feet of the iron god 4 Nakhin.[c] •And it came to pass, that when I saw it my heart was perplexed and I thought in my mind that I, Abraham, could not put it back in its place alone, 5 because it was heavy, (being made) of a big stone. •But I went and told my father, 6 and he came in with me. •And when[d] we both lifted it to put it in its place, its head 7 fell off, even while I was holding it by its head. •And it came to pass, when my father saw that the head of his god Marumath had fallen, he said to me, "Abraham!" 8 And I said, "Here I am!" •And he said to me, "Bring me the axes and chisels[e] 9 from the house." And I brought them to him from the house.[f] •And he cut another Marumath from another stone, without a head, and he smashed the head that had fallen off Marumath and the rest of Marumath.

1 2 He made five other gods and he gave them to me and ordered me to sell them 2 outside on the town road. •I saddled my father's ass and loaded them on it and 3 went out on the highway to sell them. •And behold, merchants from Phandana[a] of Syria were coming with camels, on their way to Egypt to buy *kokonil*[b] from 4 the Nile. •I asked them a question and they answered me. And walking along I conversed with them. One of their camels screamed. The ass took fright and ran

Jub 12:12-14

---

1 a. The heading is only in S; the badly garbled names are normalized here. D contains instead a few introductory lines (following a completely different text, from the Chronicle of John Malalas), which may be rendered as follows: "Moses put together the following, which he wrote in the Book of the Small Genesis (= Jubilees), how Abraham came to know God. For previously he obeyed the gods of his father Terah the astrologist. And (while I was) guarding his gods and the gods of my brother Nahor, my father complained about me. And it came to pass on one of the days . . .''

In the Palaia MSS, A B C K, the preceding text briefly mentions Serug's idol-making and the beginning of idol worship by his son Nahor, continued (to the joy of the Devil) by Nahor's son Terah, father of Abraham. But Abraham perceives that the idols are of unfeeling wood and recalls Ps 115:5–7. Then ApAb begins.

In view of the abrupt opening in all three variants, it is possible that the original beginning of the story has been lost.

b. The verb is found in no other text. G. N. Bonwetsch (*Die Apokalypse Abrahams*) and G. H. Box and J. I. Landsman (*The Apocalypse of Abraham*) translated "planed," supposing the root *strug*, "scrape." Variant readings indicate rather *nastïrzajušču* here, with the root *sterg*, "guard."

c. S by error *naricena*, "named"; A *Nakhon*.

d. S *jegda*, "when"; D K *jedva* = A B C *odva*, "scarcely."

e. Exact sense uncertain, but etymologically *izïmalo* is "tool for taking (something) out."

f. A B C K omit.

2 a. Probably Paddan-aram, cf. Gen 25:20 and LadJac 4, n. b.

b. Unknown word, perhaps reflecting Gk. *kokkina*, "scarlet clothing," or *koukkinos*, "doum palm; fiber of palm." Bonwetsch's "papyrus" is a groundless conjecture.

away and threw off the gods. Three of them were crushed and two remained
5 (intact). •And it came to pass that when the Syrians saw that I had gods, they said
to me, "Why did you not tell us that you had gods? We would have bought them
6 before the ass heard the camel's voice and you would have had no loss. •Give us
7 at least the gods that remain and we will give you a suitable price." •I considered
it in my heart. And they paid both for the smashed gods and the gods which
8 remained. •For I had been grieving in my heart how I would bring payment to my
9 father. •I threw the three broken (gods) into the water of the river Gur, which was
in this place. And they sank into the depths of the river Gur and were no more.

1 **3** As I was still walking on the road, my heart was disturbed and my mind
2 distracted. •I said in my heart, "ᵃWhat is this inequalityᵇ of activity which my
3 father is doing? •Is it not he rather who is god for his gods, because they come
4 into being from his sculpting, his planing, and his skill? •They ought to honor my
father because they are his work. What is this foodᶜ of my father in his works?
5 Behold, Marumath fell and could not stand up in his sanctuary, nor could I myself
6 lift him until my father came and we raised him up. •And even so we were not
able (to do it) and his head fell off of him. And he put it on another stone of
7 another god, which he had made without a head. •And . . .ᵈ the other five gods
which got smashed (in falling) from the ass, who could not save themselves and   WisSol 13:10-16
injure the ass because it smashed them, nor did their shards come up out of the
8 river." •And I said to my heart,ᵉ "If it is so, how then can my father's god
Marumath, which has the head of another stone and which is made from another
stone, save a man, or hear a man's prayer, or give him any gift?"

1 **4** And thinking thus, I came to my father's house. And I watered the ass and gave
him hay. And I took out the silver and placed it in the hand of my father Terah.
2 And when he saw it, he was glad, and he said, "You are blessed, Abraham, by
the god of my gods, since you have brought me the price for the gods, so that my
3 labor was not (in) vain." •And answering I said to him, "Listen, father Terah!
The gods are blessed in you, because you are a god for them, because you made
4 them, for their blessing is their perdition and their power is vain. •They did not
5 help themselves; how then can they help you or bless me? •I was good for you
in this transaction,ᵃ for through my good sense I brought you the silver for the
6 smashed (gods)." •And when he heard my speech he became furiously angry with
me, because I had spoken harsh words against his gods.

1 **5** But having pondered my father's anger, I went out. And afterward when I had
2,3 gone out, he called me, saying, "Abraham!" •And I said, "Here I am!" •And
he said, "Up, gather wood chips, for I was making gods from fir before you came,
4 and prepare with them food for my midday meal." •And it came to pass, when
I was choosing the wooden chips, I found among them a small god which would
5,6 fitᵃ . . .ᵇ in my left hand.ᶜ •And on its forehead was written: god Barisat. •And
it came to pass when I put the chips on the fire in order to prepare the food for
my father, and going out to inquire about the food, I put Barisat near the enkindling

---

3 a. S omits through vs. 4.

b. Slav. *likhotĭ*, usually "excessiveness, super-
fluity," but it also represents Gk. "*anōmalia*,"
"unevenness."

c. Though grammatical, (*si*) *izĕdĭ*, "(this)
food," is probably corrupt; *izĕdĭ* usually renders
the Gk. *katabrōma*, i.e. "food for beasts." K
makes things worse by changing it to *estĭ zlo
prelĭsti*, "is the evil of deceit," but the pronoun
si does not fit.

d. Corrupt; perhaps "he made" is omitted.

e. Sic. Perhaps a Hebraism, meaning simply
"to myself."

4 a. Slav. *obrjašča*, probably for Gk. *heurēma*,
"what is found unexpectedly, piece of good luck;
sum realized by a sale."

5 a. S D; A B C K "(was)."

b. Slav. *vŭ oslony*, meaning unknown. Bonwetsch's (*Die Apokalypse Abrahams*) "in die
Streu" and Box and Landsman's (*The Apocalypse
of Abraham*) "among the brush-wood" are both
thoroughly implausible.

c. Slav. *vŭ šuici mi* cannot mean "on my left,"
as Bonwetsch and Box and Landsman render it.

7 fire,[d] saying to him threateningly,[e] • "Barisat, watch that the fire does not go out
8 before I come back! If the fire goes out, blow on it so it flares up." • I went out
9 and I made my counsel.[f] • When I returned, I found Barisat fallen on his back, his
10 feet enveloped by fire and burning fiercely. • And it came to pass when I saw it,
I laughed (and) said to myself, "Barisat, truly you know how to light a fire and
11 cook food!" • And it came to pass while saying this in my laughter,[g] I saw (that)
12 he burned up slowly from the fire and became ashes. • I carried the food to my
13 father to eat.[h] • I gave him wine and milk, and he drank and he enjoyed himself
14 and he blessed Marumath his god. • And I said to him, "Father Terah, do not bless
Marumath your god, do not praise him! Praise rather Barisat, your god, because,
as though loving you, he threw himself into the fire in order to cook your food."
16 And he said to me, "Then where is he now?" • And I said, "He has burned in
17 the fierceness of the fire and become dust." • And he said, "Great is the power
of Barisat! I will make another today, and tomorrow he will prepare my food."

1 **6** When I, Abraham, heard words like this from my father, I laughed in my mind,
2 and I groaned in the bitterness and anger of my soul. • I said, "How then is a
3 figment of a body made by him (Terah) an aid for my father? • Or can he have
subordinated (his) body to his soul, his soul to a spirit, and the spirit to stupidity
4 and ignorance?" • And I said, "It is only proper to endure evil that I may throw
5 my mind to purity and I will expose my thoughts clearly to him." • I answered and
said, "Father Terah, whichever of these gods you extol, you err in your thought.
6 Behold, the gods of my brother Nahor standing in the holy sanctuary are more
7 venerable than yours. • For behold, Zouchaios,[a] my brother Nahor's god is more
venerable than your god Marumath because he is made of gold, valued[b] by man.
8 And if he grows old with time, he will be remodeled, whereas Marumath, if he
9 is changed or broken, will not be renewed, because he is stone. • What about[c]
Ioav, the god on the other god,[c] who stands with Zouchaios?[d] For he is also more
venerable than the god Barisat; [e]he is carved from wood and forged from silver.[e]
Because he too is a term of comparison,[f] being valued by man according to external
11 experience. • But Barisat, your god, when he was still not carved,[g] • rooted[h] in the
12 earth, being great and wondrous, with branches[i] and flowers; and praise[j] . . . • But
13 you made him with an axe, and by your skill he was made a god. • And behold
14 he has already dried up and his fatness has perished. • He fell from the height to
15 the earth, he came from greatness to smallness, • and the appearance of his face
17 wasted away.[k] • And he himself was burned up by the fire • and he became ashes
18 and is no more. • And you say, Let me make another and tomorrow he will make
19 my food for me. • But in perishing [l]he left himself no strength[l] for his (own)
destruction."

---

d. Lit. "the enkindling (or catching) of the fire."

e. S *prěščeniemĭ*, "with a threat"; A B C K *prisěščeniemŭ* (D *prě-*), "with a visitation."

f. Old *sŭvětŭ*, "counsel, council, advice," is hopelessly confused orthographically with *světŭ*, "light," in all medieval Slav. MSS. We may posit here Gk. *epoiēsa boulēn* (or *phōs*). Box and Landsman suggest this phrase reflects Heb. *'sh 'sh* in the sense of "execute a plan."

g. S D; A B C K "in my mind and laughing."

h. S D; A B C K "and he ate it."

6 a. Here *zukhe*, below in vs. 9 *zukhej* or *zukhij* (or possibly *uzukhej*); a Gk. form *Zouchaios* is thus probable.

b. S D *ucěnen-*, "valued"; A B C K, by phonetic substitutions common in Novgorod texts, *učinen-*, "ordered, ordained."

c. S D corrupt; A B C K may reflect text altered

by scribal conjecture. Original possibly "Iao, the other god."

d. S omits from here through vs. 15.

e. D omits.

f. A B C *sŭprimirenie*, K *sŭprimĕrenie*; Gk. *symmetria, symmetrēsis*; D omits prefix, producing *primirenie,* "reconciliation."

g. D A C K lit. "before being worked"; B "before the division" or "separation."

h. Lit. "uprooted," surely from an early scribal error.

i. C *sŭ věiem*, B D *sŭ věem*; A K by error *sŭ věnem*, "with a bride-price" or "dowry."

j. S omits. The whole sentence is obscure, possibly corrupt.

k. Either *vŭ istjaknovenie* D or *vŭ istjasknovenii* B (others distorted), lit. "became in wasting-away."

l. S omits. The sentence is probably corrupt.

(S C)	(A B C K)
1 **7**[a] This I say:	Abraham, having thought this, came to his father and said, "Father Terah,
2 "Fire is more venerable in formation, for even the unsubdued (things) are subdued in it, and it	fire is more venerable than your gods, the gold and silver ones, and the stone and wooden ones, because the fire burns your gods. And your gods being burned obey the fire, and the fire
mocks that which perishes[b] easily by means of its	mocks them while it is consuming your gods.
3 burning.[c] •[d]But neither is it venerable, for it is subject[e] to the waters.[d]	But neither will I call it (fire) god, because it is subjugated to the waters.[f]
4 But rather the waters	The waters

4 are more venerable than it (fire), because they overcome fire and sweeten the earth
5 with fruits. •But I will not call them god either, for the waters subside under the
6 earth [g]and are subject to it.[g] •But I will not call it a goddess either, for it is dried
by the sun (and) subordinated to man for his work.

7 More venerable among the gods, I say, is the sun, for with its rays it illuminates the whole universe and the various airs.[h]	The sun I call more venerable than the earth, for with its rays it illuminates the whole universe.
8 Nor will I place among the gods the one who obscures his course by means of the moon and the clouds.[i]	But I will not call it a god because when night comes it becomes murky with darkness.

9 Nor again shall I call the moon or the stars gods, because they too at times during
the night dim their light.

10 Listen, Terah my father, I shall seek before you the God who created all the gods supposed by us (to exist).[j]	But hear this, Terah my father, let me proclaim to you the God who created all things.
11 For who is it, or which one is it who made the heavens crimson	But this is the true God who has made the heavens crimson

and the sun golden, who has given light to the moon and the stars with it, who
has dried the earth in the midst of the many waters, who set you yourself among
the things[k] and who has sought

me out in the perplexity of my thoughts?	me out now in the perplexity of my thoughts.

12 If [only]^l God will reveal himself by himself to us!"

---

7 a. Ch. 7 (plus 8:1) is the only part of ApAb that occurs in the early redaction of the Explanatory Palaia (represented by the 1406 Kolomna MS and its family), where it follows immediately after Abraham's paraphrase of Ps 115:5–7 that in the later type of Palaia (like A B C K) precedes the beginning of ApAb. The ch. was supplied with somewhat clearer opening lines than the obscure text witnessed by S D, and subsequent minor modifications clearly change the emphasis and, as far as can be judged from the faulty work of the scribes of S and D, simply remove difficult phrases. Later, when the first six chs. were inserted into the Palaia type that underlies A B C K, the modified text of ch. 7 was unchanged, even though in B C the third-person reference to Abraham at the beginning violates the first-person narration that precedes and follows.
b. Lit. plural "the things which perish."

c. Plural *palenii*, "burnings" (D by error *padenii*, "fallings").
d. S omits.
e. D by error *pokrovenŭ*, "covered," for *pokorenŭ*, "subjugated, subject."
f. The plural "waters" is probably a Hebraism.
g. A B C K omit.
h. Cf. *aer* in the sense of "atmosphere" or "firmament" in 15:5 below. D has an ungrammatical phrase which adds a form (instrumental plural?) of the word "man, human."
i. Both S and D are slightly corrupt here, but together they yield a plausible sentence.
j. Lit. "the, supposed by us, gods."
k. Slav. *vŭ g[lago]lĕxŭ*, "in the words," reflecting Gk. *rēmata* (or *logoi*) for Heb. *dbrym*.
l. Lit. merely "if," which would imply omission of a clause; the Palaia exegesis obviously considers this a complete sentence. Possibly Gk. *eiper* or *eithe* translated as simple *ei*.

1 **8** And it came to pass as I was thinking things like these with regard to my father
Terah in the court of my house,[a] the voice of the Mighty One came down[b] from
2 the heavens in a stream of fire, saying and calling, "Abraham, Abraham!" •And
3 I said, "Here I am." •And he said, "You are searching for the God of gods, the
4 Creator, in the understanding of your heart.[c] I am he. •Go out from Terah, your   Gen 12:1
father, and go out of the house, that you too may not be slain in the sins of your
5 father's house." •And I went out. And it came to pass as I went out—I was not
6 yet outside the entrance of the court— •that the sound of a great thunder came and
burned him and his house and everything in his house, down to the ground, forty
cubits.[d]

The Apocalypse

1,2 **9** Then a voice came speaking to me twice: "Abraham, Abraham!" •And I said,   Gen 15:1
3 "Here I am." •And he said, "Behold, it is I. Fear not, for I am Before-the-World
4 and Mighty, the God who created previously, before the light of the age.[a] •I am
5 the protector for you[b] and I am your helper. •Go, get me a three-year-old heifer,   Gen 15:9f.
a three-year-old she-goat, a three-year-old ram, a turtledove, and a pigeon, and
6 make me a pure sacrifice. And in this sacrifice I will place the ages.[c] •I will
announce to you guarded things[d] and you will see great things which you have not
7 seen, because you desired to search for me, and I called you my beloved. •But   Isa 41:8
for forty days abstain from every kind of food cooked by fire,[e] and from drinking   Jas 2:23
8 of wine and from anointing (yourself) with oil. •And then you shall set out for me   TAb 2
the sacrifice which I have commanded you, in the place which I will show you
9 on a high mountain. •And there I will show you the things which were made by
10 the ages and by my word, and affirmed, created, and renewed. •And I will announce
to you in them what will come upon those who have done evil and just things in
the race of man."

1 **10** And it came to pass when I heard the voice pronouncing such words to me
2 that I looked this way and that. •And behold there was no breath of man. And my
spirit was amazed, and my soul fled from me. And I became like a stone, and fell
face down upon the earth, for there was no longer strength in me to stand up on
3 the earth. •And while I was still face down on the ground, I heard the voice[a]
speaking, "Go, [b]Iaoel of the same name,[b] through the mediation of my ineffable
4 name, consecrate this man for me and strengthen him against his trembling." •The
angel he sent to me in the likeness of a man came, and he took me by my right

---

8 a. At this point, the text of A B C K is interrupted
by a long passage (identical to that in the older
redaction, cf. MS of 1406) with heterogeneous
material. There is some exegesis, then the story of
how Abraham burned Terah's sanctuary and his
brother Haran perished trying to save the gods
(derived from the Chronicle of George the Monk),
then more exegesis concerning the lineage from
Abraham to the Virgin Mary. Then the first part
of 8:1 is repeated and ApAb continues.
  b. Lit. "fell."
  c. Slav. *vŭ umě srdca svojego*, probably Gk. *"en
dianoia kardias sou*," "in the thought of your
heart." Since *umŭ* often means "mind," B K expanded to "in your mind and the thoughts of your
heart," while A C simplified to "in your mind."
  d. The syntax of the last two words is obscure.

9 a. D *iže preže pervěje stvorixŭ světa věka*; S
omits *preže*; A B C *preže s. pervěje sv. v.* (K
expands to "first created heaven and earth and then
the first light of the light and world"). Not fully
clear, for both *preže* and *pervěje* may mean "first

of all" and "previously." Further, *světŭ* may
represent older *sŭvětŭ*, "counsel, council." *Věkŭ*
reflects Gk. *aiōn*, "age, eternity," Heb. *'wlm*; both
can also mean "world."
  b. Probably Gen 15:1, *'nky mgn lk*, read as
mêgên 'alêka and translated absolutely literally.
  c. A B C K add "for you." *Věky*, "ages,"
perhaps replaces archaic *větŭ*, "word, pact, agreement, permission"; a similar conjecture was made
by the scribe of C, who substitutes *zavět*, "covenant," producing the plausible "I will set down a
covenant."
  d. Slav. *sŭbljudenaja*, possibly Gk. *(syn)tēr-
ēmena*.
  e. Lit. "which issues from fire."

10 a. A B C K add "of the Holy One."
  b. Slav. *ioailŭ tīze* can be restored from the
variants here, and at vss. 10:8, 13:1, and 17:7.
The element *-il-* in the angels' names shows Gk.
mediation, with *-ēl* for Heb. *'l*. Here *yhwh'l* is
indicated.

5 hand and stood me on my feet. •And he said to me, "Stand up, Abraham, friend
6 of God who has loved you, let human trembling not enfold you! •For lo! I am sent
to you to strengthen you and to bless you in the name of God, creator of heavenly
7,8 and earthly things, who has loved you. •Be bold and hasten to him. •I am Iaoel
and I was called so by him who causes those with me on the seventh expanse, on
the firmament,[c] to shake, a power through the medium of his ineffable[d] name in
9 me. •I am the one who has been charged according to his commandment, to restrain
the threats of the living creatures[e] of the cherubim[f] against one another, and I teach
those who carry the song[g] through the medium of man's night of the seventh hour.[h]
10 I am appointed to hold the Leviathans, because through me is subjugated the
11 attack and menace of every reptile. •I am ordered[i] to loosen Hades and to destroy
12 those who wondered[j] at the dead. •I am the one who ordered your father's house
13 to be burned with him, for he honored the dead. •I am sent to you now to bless
you and the land which he whom you have called the Eternal One has prepared
14,15 for you. •For your sake I have indicated the way of the land.[l] •Stand up, Abraham,
go boldly, be very joyful and rejoice. And I (also rejoice) with you, for a venerable[m]
16 honor has been prepared for you by the Eternal One. •Go, complete the sacrifice
of the command.[n] Behold, I am assigned (to be) with you and with the generation
17 which is predestined (to be born) from you.[o] •And with me Michael blesses you
forever. Be bold, go!"

1 **11** And I stood up and saw him who had taken my right hand and set me on my
2 feet. •The appearance of his body[a] was like sapphire, and the aspect of his face
3 was like chrysolite, and the hair of his head like snow. •And a kidaris[b] (was) on   Dan 7:9
his head, its look that of a rainbow, and the clothing of his garments (was) purple;   Rev 1:14
4 and a golden staff[c] (was) in his right hand. •And he said to me, "Abraham." And
I said, "Here is your servant!" And he said, "Let my appearance not frighten
5 you, nor my speech trouble your soul. Come with me! •And I will go with you
6 visible until the sacrifice, but after the sacrifice[d] invisible forever. •Be bold and
go!"

1,2 **12** And we went, the two of us alone together, forty days and nights. •And I ate
no bread and drank no water, because (my) food was to see the angel who was
3 with me, and his discourse with me was my drink. •We came to God's mountain,
4 glorious Horeb. •And I said to the angel, "Singer of the Eternal One, behold I have
no sacrifice with me, nor do I know a place for an altar on the mountain, so how
5,6 shall I make the sacrifice?" •And he said, "Look behind you." •And I looked

---

c. Slav. *na tverdi* is possibly a gloss explaining
"on the seventh expanse."

d. Only S has the negation; the others thus read
"speakable name."

e. I.e. Heb. *ḥywt*.

f. Or simply "the cherubim," an apposition
explaining "living creatures."

g. A B C K "his song."

h. Slav. *posrědĭstvomĭ člověčĭskyja nošči sed-
mago časa* is unclear, but Box and Landsman's
(*The Apocalypse of Abraham*) omission of "medium" and the inversion to produce "the song of
the seventh hour of the night of man" requires
justification. Perhaps "at the seventh hour" might
be possible. Cf. TAdam.

i. S D *povelěnŭ*, passive "having been commanded"; A B C K *povelěvyi*, active "who gave
the command."

j. The sentence is clear, but offers no clue as to
why these people merit destruction. The verb *diviti
sja* unambiguously means "wonder, be astonished
at" and often renders Gk. *thaumazein*. Perhaps the
Gk. version of ApAb had a related verb or phrase

denoting some wonder-working that involved
corpses, a practice abominated by pious Jews.

k. S omits from i to k through homoeoteleuton.

l. Conjecturing that *putĭ zemenŭ*, "the way of
the land," reflects Heb. *drk 'rṣ*, we may translate
"I have established manners (or morals) for you."

m. A B D K; S "eternal."

n. Probably means "the sacrifice which was
commanded," cf. 9:8.

o. Slav. *prougotovlenym is tebe*, lit. "pre-
prepared out of you."

11 a. S B *těla ego*; D A C K *těla nogu ego*,
perhaps "of his body (and) legs," or perhaps
sapphire refers only to the legs or feet and a separate
description of the body has been lost.

b. Kidaris in LXX is "headdress" (e.g. Ex
39:28), "turban" (e.g. Zech 3:5), and "cap" (e.g.
Ezek 45:18). A D by error *sudarĭ*, "handkerchief"
(Gk. *sudarion*), a word known to Slavs from Jn
20:7, but probably unclear in meaning.

c. Or "scepter."

d. B adds in margin "I will be for you."

behind me. And behold all the prescribed sacrifices were following us: the calf, Gen 15:9f.
7 the she-goat, the ram, the turtledove, and the pigeon. •And the angel said to me,
8 "Abraham." And I said, "Here I am." •And he said to me, "Slaughter all these
9 and divide the animals exactly into halves. But do not cut the birds apart. •And
give them to the men whom I will show you standing beside you, for they are the
10 altar on the mountain, to offer sacrifice to the Eternal One.[a] •The turtledove and
the pigeon you will give to me, for I will ascend on the wings of the birds to show
you (what)[b] is in the heavens, on the earth and in the sea, in the abyss, and in the
lower depths, in the garden of Eden and in its rivers, in the fullness of the universe.
And you will see its circles in all."[c]

1 **13** And I did everything according to the angel's command. And I gave the angels
who had come to us the divided parts of the animals. And the angel Iaoel[a] took
2,3 the two birds. •And I waited for the evening gift.[b] •And an unclean bird flew down Gen 15:11
4 on the carcasses, and I drove it away. •And the unclean bird spoke to me and said,
"What are you doing,[c] Abraham, on the holy heights, where no one eats or drinks,
nor is there upon them food for men. [d]But these all will be consumed by fire and
5 they will[d] burn you up. •[e]Leave the man who is with you and flee! For if you
6 ascend to the height, they will destroy you."[e] •And it came to pass when I saw
the bird speaking I said this to the angel: "What is this, my lord?" And he said,
7 "This is disgrace,[f] this is Azazel!" •[g]And he said to him, "Shame[h] on you,
8 Azazel![g] For Abraham's portion[i] is in heaven, and yours is on earth, •for you have
selected here, (and) become enamored of the dwelling place of your blemish.[j]
Therefore the Eternal Ruler, the Mighty One, has given you a dwelling[k] on earth.
9 Through you the all-evil spirit (is) a liar, and through you (are) wrath and trials
10 on the generations of men who live impiously. •For the Eternal, Mighty One did
not allow the bodies of the righteous to be in your hand, so through them the
11 righteous life is affirmed and the destruction of ungodliness. •Hear, counselor, be
12 shamed by me! You have no permission to tempt all the righteous.[l] •Depart from
13 this man! •You cannot deceive him, because he is the enemy of you and of those
14 who follow you and who love what you wish.[m] •For behold, the garment which
in heaven was formerly yours has been set aside for him, and the corruption which
was on him has gone over to you."

1 **14** And the angel said to me,[a] "Abraham!" And I said, "Here I am, your
2 servant." •And he said, "Know from this that the Eternal One whom you have
3 loved has chosen you. •Be bold and do through your authority whatever I order
4 you against him who reviles[b] justice. •Will I not be able to revile[b] him who has 1En 9:6
scattered about the earth the secrets of heaven[c] and who has taken counsel against
5 the Mighty One? •Say to him, 'May you be the firebrand[d] of the furnace of the

12 a. The men are the altar. The infinitival phrase
prinositi žertvu specifies no subject and its connection with the men remains unclear. Perhaps it
should be taken literally, "to carry the sacrifice to
the Eternal One."
  b. The sentence is incomplete.
  c. Obscure, perhaps corrupt. Possibly "in the
fullness of the universe and its circles, and you will
see . . . in all." Seems to look forward to ch. 21.

13 a. S D A C omit, B in margin.
  b. Or "reward"; Gk. *dōron, dōrea.*
  c. Or "what business do you have"; Gk. *ti soi.*
  d. S (D unclear); A B C K, with unspecified
subject, "they all will consume (you) with fire
and."
  e. Only in S.
  f. Gk. *atimia,* "dishonor," or *asebeia,* "im-

piety."
  g. S omits.
  h. Gk. *oneidos,* "reproach."
  i. Texts all have spellings reflecting *čisti,*
"honor," but surely *časti,* "part, portion," was
original.
  j. Or "filth."
  k. Texts faulty; emend acc. *tja* to dat. *ti* and
read *žitéli,* "dwelling-place" rather than ungrammatical *žiteli,* "dweller."
  l. Text odd, more literally "to be a tempter as
far as all just men are concerned."
  m. Or "want."

14 a. S omits from here through vs. 4.
  b. Or "mocks," "mock."
  c. Cf. 1En 9:6.
  d. Or "torch" or "burning coal"; Gk. *dolos* or
anthrax.

6 earth! Go, Azazel, into the untrodden parts of the earth.[e] •For your heritage is over
those who are with you, with the stars and with the men born by the clouds,[f]
7 whose portion you are, indeed they exist through your being.[g] •Enmity[h] is for you
8 a pious act.[i] Therefore through your own destruction be gone[j] from me!' " •And
9 I said the words as the angel had taught me. •And he said, "Abraham." And I
10 said, "Here I am, your servant!" •And the angel said to me, "Answer him not!"
11,12 [k]And he spoke to me a second time. •And the angel said, "Now, whatever he
13 says to you, answer him not,[k] lest his will run up to you.[l] •For the Eternal, Mighty
14 One gave him the gravity[m] and the will. Answer him not." •And I did what the
angel had commanded me. And whatever he said to me about the descent,[n] I
answered him not.[o]

1 **15** And it came to pass when the sun was setting, and behold a smoke like that Gen 15:17
of a furnace, and the angels who had the divided portions of the sacrifice ascended
2 from the top of the furnace of smoke. •And the angel took me with his right hand
and set me on the right wing of the pigeon and he himself sat on the left wing of
3 the turtledove, (both of) which were as if[a] neither slaughtered nor divided. •And
4 he carried me up to the edge of the fiery flames. •And we ascended[b] as if (carried)
5 by many winds to the heaven that is fixed on the expanses.[c] •And I saw on the air[d]
6 to whose height we had ascended a strong light which can[e] not be described. •And
behold, in this light a fiery Gehenna was enkindled,[f] and a great crowd in the
7 likeness of men.[g] •They all were changing in aspect and shape, running and
changing form and prostrating themselves and crying aloud words I did not know.

1 **16** And I said to the angel, "Why is it you now brought me here? For[a] now I can
2 no longer see, because I am weakened and my spirit is departing from me." •And
3 he said to me, "Remain with me, do not fear. •He whom you will see coming
directly toward us in a great sound[b] of sanctification[c] is the Eternal One who has
4 loved you. You will not look at him himself. •But let your spirit not weaken,[d] for
I am with you, strengthening you."

1 **17** And while he was still speaking, behold the fire coming toward us round
about, and a voice was in the fire like a voice of many waters, like a voice of the
2,3 sea in its uproar. •And the angel knelt down[a] with me and worshiped. •And I
wanted to fall face down on the earth. And the place of highness on which we

---

e. Vss. 6–14 are omitted by S, which has only
"And the angel said to me, 'Answer him not, for
God has given him freedom [lit. "will"] over those
who answer him.' "

f. I.e. men to whom the clouds gave birth.

g. Or "generation"; Gk. *to einai* or *genēsis*.
The whole sentence is obscure.

h. Possibly Gk. *echthra*, "hatred."

i. Probably Gk. *dikaiōma*, "just action," or
eusebeia, "piety." The sentence is unclear.

j. Lit. "may you have disappeared."

k. D omits.

l. Textual *pritečetĭ*, "runs up to," surely represents archaic *pritŭčetĭ*, "touch, come in contact
with": "lest his will affect you."

m. Probably Gk. *baros* for Heb. *kbd*, "honor,
glory."

n. Slav. *o sŭnitii* is clear (Landsman to the
contrary). The word usually reflects Gk. *katabasis*,
referring to Christ's descent into Hades, but it may
also be *synkatabasis* or *symbasis* in any meaning
possible.

o. S D negative; A C *věščax*, "I said, told," B
K *otvěščax*, "I answered."

15 a. S D omit "as if."

b. S omits from here to "ascended" in vs. 5.

c. Or "firmaments," see note to 19:3, below.

d. Slav. *na aere* presents the air as a surface.

e. S; others "could."

f. Text somewhat corrupt. Archaic gen. *ognĭna
rodu*, "of fiery Gehenna," misread as nom. *ognĭ
narodu*, "fire for the crowd (or nation)," and the
grammar was adjusted, possibly with the loss of a
word or two.

g. Lit. "of male shape, of male form."

16 a. S D *jako*; A B C K *zane jako*, "for it is as
though."

b. Lit. "in many voice," perhaps rendering Gk.
en polyphōnia.

c. Variants of S D A C establish *svjatĭby*, "of
sanctification." Gk. *hagiasmos*. B K understood
this old word in its narrower meaning "threefold
Sanctus" and modified the text to clarify it: "saying, 'holy, holy, holy' " (K adds "[is] the Lord").

d. A B C K add "because of the shouting."

17 a. S D B K; A C replace an unfamiliar verb
with "bent his head."

4 were standing now stopped on high, now rolled down low.[b] •And he said, "Only
5 worship, Abraham, and recite the song which I taught you." •Since there was no
ground to which I could fall prostrate, I only bowed down, and I recited the song
6,7 which he had taught me. •And he said, "Recite without ceasing." •And I recited,
and he himself recited the song:[c]

8 Eternal One, Mighty One, Holy El,[d] God autocrat
9 self-originate, incorruptible, immaculate,
unbegotten, spotless, immortal,
10 self-perfected,[e] self-devised,[f]
without mother, without father, ungenerated,[g]
11 exalted, fiery,
12 just, lover of men, benevolent, compassionate, bountiful,
jealous over me, patient one, most merciful.
13 Eli,[h] eternal, mighty one, holy, Sabaoth,
most glorious [i]El, El, El, El,[i] Iaoel,
14 you are he my soul has loved, my protector.
15 Eternal, fiery, shining,[j]
light-giving, thunder-voiced, lightning-visioned, many-eyed,
16 receiving the petitions of those who honor you[k]
and turning away from the petitions of those who restrain you
by the restraint[l] of their provocations,
17 redeemer of those who dwell in the midst of the wicked ones,
of those who are dispersed among the just of the world,
in the corruptible age.[m]
18 Showing forth[n] the age of the just,
you make the light shine[o]
before the morning[p] light upon your creation
[q]from your face[r]
to spend the day[s] on the earth,[q]
19 and in your heavenly dwelling place
(there is) an inexhaustible light of an invincible[t] dawning
from the light[u] of your face.
20 Accept my prayer [v]and delight in it,[v]
and (accept) also the sacrifice which you yourself made
to yourself through me as I searched for you.
21 Receive me favorably,
teach me, show me, and make known to your servant
what you have promised me.

b. That is, the surface is undulating up and down.
c. A B C K add "with me." B has a marginal note, incorporated into the text of K: "The first song of Abraham which the holy angel Iaoel taught him when he was traveling with him about the air, crying out like this:"
d. Only S retains "El."
e. Gk. *autoteleios* or *autotelēs*.
f. Assuming original *samosŭvětīne*, Gk. *autoboulētos*, rather than the derivationally implausible *samosvětīne*. An inept calque of the Gk. *autophōs* or *autophōtos*, "absolute light," is not impossible, however.
g. Slav. *bezrodīne* is probably Gk. *agennētos* or *agenealógētos* (cf. Heb 7:3), but it could also mean "without kin."
h. A B C K all distort this form and add a gloss: "that is, my God."
i. S only.
j. Possibly a compound, "shining with fire," Gk. *pyrophengēs, pyrophlogos*.

k. S omits from here to end of first clause in vs. 22.
l. Or "hold you by the compassing."
m. The translation of vss. 21f. can only be approximate, for the grammatical relations are ambiguous.
n. D *projavljaja*; A B C K *ponovljaja*, an innovated form for expected old *ponavljaja*, "renewing, restoring."
o. Or "you, the light, shine."
p. S *utrīnimŭ*; A B C D K *vnutrīnimŭ*, "inner."
q. S omits.
r. Or possibly "by your face, through the agency of your countenance."
s. Or "continue through the day."
t. D *nepobědima* (S *nepovědimo*, surely with *v* for *b*, and with incorrect ending); A B C K *neispovědima*, a late form (for *neispovědoma*), "indescribable, unexpressible."
u. A C; S D B K plural "lights."
v. S omits.

1 **18** And as I was still reciting the song, the mouth[a] of the fire which was on the
2 firmament[b] was rising up on high. •And I heard a voice like the roaring of the sea,
3 and it did not cease from the plenitude of the fire. •And as the fire rose up, soaring
to the highest point, I saw under the fire a throne of fire [c]and the many-eyed ones
round about, reciting the song, under the throne four fiery living creatures, singing. Ezek 1:6-12,23
4,5 And the appearance of each of them was the same, each having four faces. •And
this (was) the aspect of their faces: of a lion, of a man,[d] of an ox,[e] and of an eagle.
Each one had four heads [f]on its body so that the four living creatures had sixteen
6 faces. •And each one had[f] six wings: two on the shoulders, two halfway down, and
7 two at the loins. •With the wings which were on their shoulders they covered their
faces, with the wings at their loins they clothed their feet, and they would stretch
8 the two middle wings out and fly, erect.[g] •And when they finished singing, they
9 would look at one another and threaten one another. •And it came to pass when
the angel who was with me saw that they were threatening each other, he left me
10 and went running to them. •And he turned the face of each living creature from
the face which was opposite it so that they could not see each other's faces
11 threatening each other. •And he taught them the song of peace which the Eternal
12 One has in himself.[h] •And while I was still standing and watching, I saw behind[i]
the living creatures a chariot with fiery wheels. Each wheel was full of eyes round Ezek 1:15-25;
13 about. •And above the wheels was the throne which I had seen. And it was covered 10:6-12
with fire and the fire encircled it round about, and an indescribable light[j] surrounded
14 the fiery crowd.[k] •And I heard the voice of their sanctification[l] like the voice of Ezek 1:26-28
a single man.

1 **19** And a voice came to me out of the midst of the fire, saying, "Abraham,
2,3 Abraham!" •And I said, "Here I am!" •And he said, "Look at the expanses[a]
which are under the firmament to which you have now been directed and see that
on no single expanse is there any other but the one whom you have searched for
4 or who has loved you." •And while he was still speaking, behold, the expanses
under me, the heavens, opened and I saw on the seventh firmament upon which
I stood a fire spread out[b] and a light[c] and dew[d] and a multitude of angels and a host
of the invisible glory, [e]and up above[e] the living creatures I had seen; I saw no one
5 else there. •And I looked from on high, where I was standing, downward to the
6 sixth firmament. •And I saw there a multitude of spiritual angels, incorporeal,
carrying out the orders of the fiery angels who were on the eighth[f] firmament, as

---

18 a. Perhaps for Gk. *cheilos* in the sense of
"edge, brink," i.e. the fire is envisioned as a
brimming lake or river.

b. Or "expanse," see n. to 19:3, below.

c. Ambiguous as to whether *ot ognja*, "from
fire," describes the throne or the "many-eyed
ones" (Gk. *polyommatoi*), or both; or perhaps the
creatures were standing at a distance, "away from
the fire."

d. S *člvci* for *človĕčĭ*, "of a human being"; D
A B C K *mužesk*, "of a male," placed after "of
an ox," perhaps under the influence of Rev 4:7.

e. As in Heb. Ezek 1:10; LXX has "calf," as
does Rev 4:7.

f. S omits because of homoeoteleuton.

g. The last clause is faulty and obscure. The
final word is *prosti*, "simple," but may mean
"upright."

h. Obscure; unclear whether "self" refers to the
Eternal One or the angel, and whether "which"
refers to "song" or "peace."

i. Or "following after."

j. If *svĕtŭ*; possibly, however, *sŭvĕtŭ*, "council."

k. Or "nation." Also possible: "an indescribable light (or council) of the fiery crowd (or nation)

surrounded (it)." The text is probably corrupt.

l. Or "acclamation," Gk. *hagiasmos*, cf. 16:3
above.

19 a. Three Slav. roots underlie synonyms for
"heaven" that probably stand for three Gk. words.
Tvĭrdĭ (19:6, well-known elsewhere) and *tvĭrdĭstvo*
(19:4) with a variant *tvĭrdĭstvie* (19:8), both known
only from ApAb, surely translate *stereōma*, "firmament." *Protjaženie*, "a pulling out tightly,"
and *prostĭrtie*, "a spreading out broadly," doubtless
reflect forms based on Gk. *ten*. Here *prostĭrtie* is
rendered "firmament" (18:1; 19:3, 6; 21:1, 2) and
protjaženie "expanse" (19:3, 4; 21:1); but the
plural, *prostĭrtija*, at 15:4 is rendered "expanses."

b. Or "a widespread fire."

c. B adds "great" in the margin; K places it in
the text. Cf. n. c to 17:7.

d. Slav. *rosu*; D *ručku*, "vessel, container."

e. S A C K *ot svyše*, D *i tŭ svyše*, B *i svyše*;
perhaps something has been omitted.

f. Surely for "sixth"; the Glagolitic letter-sym-
bol for *8* corresponds to the Cyrillic letter whose
numerical value is *6*. S has other indications of a
fore-text written in Glagolitic.

7 I was standing on its elevation (?)[g]. •And lo, neither on this firmament was there
8 in any shape any other host, but only the spiritual angels. •And the host I saw on
9 the seventh firmament commanded the sixth firmament and it removed itself.[h] •I
saw there, on the fifth (firmament), hosts[i] of stars, and the orders they were
commanded to carry out, and the elements[j] of earth obeying them.

1,2 **20** And the Eternal, Mighty One said to me, "Abraham, Abraham!" •And I said,
3 "Here I am!" •And he said, "Look from on high[a] at the stars which are beneath   Gen 15:5
4 you and count them for me and tell me their number!" •And I said, "When can
5 I? For I am a man."[b] •And he said to me, "As the number of the stars and their   Gen 18:27
power[c] so shall I place for[d] your seed the nations and men, set apart for me in my
6 lot with Azazel."[e] •And I said, "Eternal and Mighty One. Let your servant speak   Gen 18:30
7 before you and let your fury not rage against your chosen one. •Behold, before
you led me up, Azazel[f] insulted me. How then, since he is now not before you,
did you establish[g] yourself with them?"[h]

1 **21** And he said to me, "Look now beneath your feet at the firmament and
understand the creation that was depicted of old[a] on this expanse, (and) the creatures
2 which are in it[b] and the age[c] prepared after it."[d] •And I looked beneath the
firmament at my feet and I saw the likeness of heaven[e] and the things that were
therein.
3 And (I saw) there the earth and its fruit, and its moving things and its things
that had souls, and its host[f] of men and the impiety of their souls and their
justification, [g]and their pursuit[h] of their works[g] [i]and the abyss and its torments,[i]
4 and its lower depths and (the) perdition in it. •And I saw there the sea and its
islands, and its cattle and its fish, and Leviathan and his realm and his bed and
his lairs, and the world[j] which lay upon him, and his motions and the destruction
5 he caused the world.[k] •I saw there the rivers and their upper (reaches) and their
circles.
6 And I saw there the garden[l] of Eden and its fruits, and the source and the river
flowing from it, and its trees and their flowering, making fruits, and I saw men
doing justice[m] in it, their food and their rest.
7 And I saw there a great crowd of men and women and children, half of them

---

g. Unclear; the word appears to mean lit. "suspensions."

h. Or "to remove itself."

i. "Hosts" here and "host" in vss. 4, 7, 8 above could be translated "powers" or "power."

j. Gk. *stoicheia*.

20 a. Explicitly contrasts with the "look up" of Gen 15:5.

b. B K add "earth and ashes" from LXX Gen 18:27. A C harmonize further by omitting "man."

c. Or "host."

d. Or "to," or perhaps "under."

e. Possibly "the lot [Gk. *klēros*] belonging to me and Azazel." S is slightly corrupt, and the others may represent some sort of modification of the original text.

f. Possibly "before Azazel led me up, he."

g. "support" or "secure."

h. S D *sŭ nimi*; (A?) B C K *sŭ nimŭ* "with him." The whole sentence is obscure.

21 a. Lit. "formerly shadowed," with a unique verb (D *stěnovanuju*, S corrupt, A B C K *stěnevanuju*, cf. *stěnĭ*, "shadow") which may be a clumsy calque of Gk. *skiagraphein*, "sketch, outline, depict; prefigure, foreshadow."

b. Viz. "creation."

c. S (D "unto the age, forever"); A B C K "ages."

d. Or "according to it (creation)." The sentence is obscure, not least because *tvari* is used apparently both for "creation" and "creature."

e. D A B C K *podobie nebesa*; S corrupt, *podŭ 6 nbsě*, roughly "under 6th heaven" (less likely "under 6 heavens"), but ungrammatical. The original text was surely acc. *podŭnebesie*, Gk. *tēn hyp' ouranon*, i.e. "I saw (the terrestrial world) beneath the sky."

f. Or "power."

g. S omits because of homoeoteleuton.

h. Gk. *epitēdeumata*.

i. Perhaps a gloss; in S it stands after "lower depths and perdition."

j. Or "inhabited world," *oikoumenē*.

k. Lit. "destructions to the world because of him."

l. Slav. *sadŭ*, usually "plant," Gk. *phyton*; "tree," Gk. *dendron*; here probably "newly planted area." At 12:10 Eden is *vertepŭ*, *kēpos*, at 23:4 *ovoščĭnikŭ*, "orchard."

m. Slav. *pravdu dějuščixŭ* is not found elsewhere. *Pravĭda* is "righteousness, justice, rule, truth"; *dikaiosynē, dikaion, dikaiōma, alētheia*.

on the right side of the portrayal, and half of them on the left side of the portrayal.[n]

1,2 **22** And I said, "Eternal, Mighty One! What is this picture of creation?" •And he said to me, "This is my will with regard to what is[a] in the light[b] and it was[c] good before my face. And then, afterward, I gave them[d] a command by my word and Ps 33:9 they came into existence. Whatever I had decreed was to exist had already been outlined[e] in this[f] and all the previously created (things) you have seen stood[g] before 3 me." •And I said, "O sovereign, mighty and eternal! Why are the people in this 4 picture on this side and on that?" •And he said to me, "These who are on the left side are a multitude of tribes who existed previously . . . and after you[h] some (who have been) prepared for judgment and order,[i] others for revenge and perdition 5 at the end of the age. •Those on the right side of the picture are the people set apart for me of the people with Azazel; these are the ones I have prepared to be born of you and to be called my people.

1 **23** "Look[a] again at the picture: Who is the one who seduced Eve, and what is Gen 3 2 the fruit of the tree?[b] •And you will know what will be [c]and how much will be for 3 your seed[c] in the last days. •And what you cannot understand,[d] I will make known to you because you have been pleasing before my face and I will tell you what[e] 4 I have kept in my heart." •And I looked at the picture, and my eyes ran to the 5 side of the garden of Eden. •And I saw there a man very great in height and terrible in breadth, incomparable in aspect, entwined with a woman who was also equal 6 to the man in aspect and size. •And they were standing under a tree[f] of Eden, and 7 the fruit of the tree was like the appearance of a bunch of grapes of the vine.[g] •And behind the tree was standing (something) like a dragon in form, but having hands 8 and feet like a man's, on his back six wings on the right and six on the left. •And he was holding the grapes of the tree[f] and feeding[h] them to the two I saw entwined 9 with each other. •And I said, "Who are these two entwined with each other, or who is this between them, and what is the fruit which they are eating, Mighty 10 One, Eternal?" •And he said, "This is the world[i] of men,[j] this is Adam and this 11 is their thought[k] on earth, this is Eve. •And he who is between them is the impiety 12 of their behavior[l] [m]unto[n] perdition, Azazel himself."[m] • And I said, "Eternal,

---

n. Slav. *obrazĭstvo*, attested only here, must be more than *obrazŭ*, "image," Gk. *eikōn, typos*, implying a suffixed Gk. form like *eikonisma* or *eikonismos*.

22 a. Slav. *kŭ suščemu*, lit. "toward that which is (or exists)," possible Gk. *pros* (or *eis, epi) to onta*.
b. If *světŭ*; possibly *sŭvětŭ*, "council, counsel."
c. Lit. "became, came to be."
d. The text of the previous sentence is probably corrupt; in any case it provides no clear referent for this plural pronoun.
e. S *načerta sja*; others inappropriately *načertaša*, "they outlined."
f. S B K imply original *vŭ semĭ*, although the reference is not clear; distorted in D A C to *vsěmŭ*, "to all."
g. Or "came to stand, took position."
h. Or "because of, through you." The following phrases are in the acc., so loss of a preceding verb must be assumed.
i. Slav. *ustrojenie*, "ordering, being put in order; restoration."

23 a. D A B C K *posmotri*; S *po smotrenii*, "after a look."
b. Slav. *dreva*; A C *črěva*, "of the womb."
c. S differs: "for your name among people."

d. S "days of the age, or how one cannot understand."
e. Or "the things that."
f. Slav. *sadŭ*, not specifically a tree, cf. n. 1 to ch. 21.
g. Slav. *viničina*, probably "of a wild vine"; A K *finična*, "of the palm [Gk. *phoinix*]," is surely secondary within Slav.
h. B C *zalagaše*, a verb with the specialized sense "put morsels of food into the mouth of someone" (a meaning preserved in Serbo-Croatian), other MSS distorted because this meaning was unknown. Bonwetsch (*Die Apokalypse Abrahams*) and Box and Landsman (*The Apocalypse of Abraham*) ignored the grammar and completely mistranslated the sentence. Here the serpent explicitly is feeding the fruit both to Adam and to Eve.
i. Slav. *světŭ* only rarely means "world," Gk. *kosmos*, ordinarily rendering "light," *phōs, phengos, photismos*. Or this may be *sŭvětŭ*, "council, counsel."
j. Or "of man, human."
k. Slav. *pomyšlenie* is "thought" in any possible sense, including "intention, plan" or negative "plot, evil design," and "desire."
l. Slav. *načinanija*, lit. "deed, act, doing."
m. D omits.
n. S A K *vŭ*; B C omit, making "perdition" an apposition with "impiety" and "Azazel."

Mighty One, why then did you adjudge him such dominion that through his works
13 he could ruin humankind on earth?'' •And he said to me, ''Hear, Abraham! Those
who desire evil, and °all whom I have hated as they commit° them^p—over them
14 did I give him dominion, and he was to be beloved of them.'' •And I answered
and said, ''Eternal, Mighty One! Why did it please you to bring it about that evil
should be desired in the heart of man, because you are angered^q at what was chosen
by you^r . . . him who does useless things^s in your light (?).''^t

1 **24** And he said to me thus, ''Close^a to the nations . . . for your sake and for the
sake of those set apart after you, the people of your tribe, as you will see in the
2 picture, what is burdened on^b them. •And I will explain to you what will be, and
3 everything that will be in the last days. •Look now at everything in the picture.''
4 And I looked and saw there ^cthe creatures that had come into being^c before me.
5 And I saw, as it were,^d Adam, and Eve who was with him, and with them the
crafty adversary and Cain, who had been led by the adversary to break the law,
and (I saw) the murdered Abel (and) the perdition brought on him and given
6 through the lawless one.^e •And I saw there fornication^f and those who desired it,
and its defilement and their zeal; and the fire of their corruption in the lower depths
7 of the earth. •And I saw there theft and those who hasten after it, and the system
8 of their ^gretribution, the judgment of the great court.^g •I saw there naked men,
forehead to forehead, and their shame and the harm (they wrought) against their
9 friends and their retribution. •And I saw there desire,^h and in her hand (was) the
head of every kind of lawlessness; ^iand her torment^j and her dispersal^k destined^l
to destruction.

1 **25**. I saw there the likeness of the idol of jealousy, like a carpenter's figure such
as my father used to make, and its body was of glittering copper,^a and before it
2 a man, and he was worshiping it. •And (there was) an altar opposite it and boys
3 being slaughtered on it in the face of the idol. •And I said to him, ''What is this
idol, or what is the altar, or who are those being sacrificed, or who is the sacrificer,
or what is the handsome temple which I see, the art and beauty^b of your glory that
4 lies beneath your throne?'' •And he said, ''Hear, Abraham! This temple which

---

o. Reading *vŭtvorjaščixŭ* as acc. plural, whereby the sense of the prefix is unclear. Or perhaps ''everything I hated in those who commit,'' reading *vŭ tvorjaščixŭ* as a prepositional phrase.

p. The plural pronoun has no obvious referent; it might be an error and somehow refer to ''evil,'' or there may be an omission here.

q. The rest of the sentence is obscure, probably corrupt.

r. S D *na izvolenoe tebě*; A B C K *na izvolenie tebě* is meaningless.

s. Slav. *dělajuščemu nepoleznoje* is clear, but the only possible dat. that could agree is *tebě*, which would mean ''by you who are doing useless things.'' Could Abraham be upbraiding God? If not, there must be a lacuna here.

t. S has *nŭ světĭstvojemĭ*, which could be emended to a plausible *světĭstvijemĭ* and mean ''but through your radiance''; this phrase precedes *dělajuščemu*. The D A B C K *vŭ světě tvojemĭ*, ''in your light [or world; or counsel, council],'' could well be secondary, an attempt to repair an incomprehensible passage.

24 a. The text is corrupt and at some point there must be omissions. Perhaps ''thus'' goes with ''close.'' The notion of anger introduced by Bonwetsch and copied by Box and Landsman is totally absent from the passage.

b. Slav. *utjažĭčenaja*, possibly ''things which have been made grievous against''; grammatical connection with the preceding text is not clear.

c. Or ''what had come into being in creation.''

d. Slav. *jako*, ''as,'' Gk. *hōs*.

e. Slav. *bezakonĭnikomĭ*, presumably an echo of the description of Cain just before, *vragomĭ bezakonĭnovavŭšago Kaina*.

f. I.e. Gk. *porneia*.

g. S omits.

h. Slav. *želanie*, a neuter, but the following possessives are feminine, surely reflecting mechanical translation of pronouns referring to Gk. *epithymia*.

i. S omits to end of the sentence.

j. D *mučenie*, Gk. *martyrion, basanos, timōria*; A B C K *molčanie*, ''silence,'' Gk. *hēsychia*, is surely secondary, a scribal slip in the fore-text common to the Palaia MSS.

k. Slav. *rastočenie*, usually renders the Gk. *diaskorpismos*, but also possibly ''alienation,'' *ekpoiēsis*, or ''abortion.''

l. Slav. *predajemo*, lit. ''being given over.''

25 a. Or ''bronze,'' Gk. *chalkos*.

b. None of the MSS is quite grammatical. Perhaps emend to *dobrolěpĭnu xytrostĭju i krasotoju*, ''handsome [Gk. *euprepēs*] with the art and beauty.''

you have seen, the altar and the works of art, this is my idea of the priesthood of the name of my glory, where every petition of man[c] will enter and dwell; the ascent of kings[d] and prophets and whatever sacrifice I decree to be made for me 5 among my coming people, even of your tribe. • And the body[e] you saw is my anger, because the people who will come to me out of you will make me angry. 6 And the man you saw slaughtering is he who angers me, and the sacrifice is a killing of those who are for me a testimony of the judgment of the completion at the beginning of creation."

1 **26** And I said, "Eternal, Mighty One! Why did you establish it to be so and to 2 call on the testimonies of this one?" • And he said to me, "Hear, Abraham, and 3 understand what I will explain to you, and answer whatever I ask you. • Why did your father Terah not obey your voice and abandon the demonic worship of idols 4 until he perished, and all his house with him?" • And I said, "Eternal, Mighty One, surely because it did not please him to obey me, nor did I follow his works." 5 And he said to me, "Hear, Abraham. As the counsel[a] of your father is in him, as 6 your counsel is in you, so also the counsel of my will is ready.[b] • In days[c] to come you will not know them in advance, nor the future (men) you will see with your 7 own eyes that[d] they are of your seed. • Look at the picture!"

1 **27** And I looked and I saw, and behold the picture swayed. And from its left side a crowd of heathens[a] ran out and they captured the men, women, and children who 2 were on its right side. • [b]And some they slaughtered[b] and others they kept with 3 them. • Behold, I saw (them) running to them[c] by way of four ascents[d] and they burned the Temple with fire, and they plundered the holy things that were in it. 4 And I said, "Eternal One, the people you received from me are being robbed by 5 the hordes of the heathen. • They are killing some and holding others as aliens, and they burned the Temple with fire and they are stealing [e]and destroying[e] the beautiful 6 things which are in it. • Eternal, Mighty One! If this is so, why now[f] have you 7 afflicted my heart and why will it be so?" • And he said to me, "Listen, Abraham, all that you have seen will happen on account of your seed who will (continually) provoke me because of the body[g] which you saw and the murder in what was 8 depicted in the Temple of jealousy, and everything you saw [h]will be so."[h] • And I said, "Eternal, Mighty One! Let the evil works (done) in iniquity now pass by; 9 but make commandments in them[i] more than his[j] just works. • For you can do 10 this." • And he said to me, "Again the time of justice will come upon them, at 11 first through the holiness[k] of kings. • And I will judge with justice[l] those whom I 12 created earlier,[m] to rule from them in them. • And from these same ones will come men who will have regard for[n] them, as[o] I announced to you and you saw."

c. Specifically "male."

d. S D; A B K "kingdoms"; C by error "temple."

e. Or "statue."

26 a. S D A C have *světŭ*, "light," but B specifies *sŭvĕt* and K the newer spelling *sŭvĕtŭ*, "counsel, council." B K thus believed that "light" was inappropriate here.

b. Or "prepared."

c. From this point D departs radically from other MSS, reducing the rest of the work to a dozen lines made up of recognizable phrases from later chs., but utterly incoherent and therefore useless for our purposes.

d. Or "for, since." The sentence is not clear.

27 a. Or "a heathen people."

b. S omits because of homoeoteleuton.

c. Slav. *pritekšaja*, "(them) running," probably is the heathen, while "to them" denotes the victims; but the passage is not clear.

d. S *sŭxody*, "descents, goings down"; A B C

K *vŭxody*, "entrances, goings in"; philologically also *vŭsxody*, "ascents, goings up," or *isxody*, "exits, goings out," are justifiable, cf. also 28:4, 5 below and LadJac 5, n. d. The acc. numeral *četyri* here makes no sense ("four descents running"); instrumental *četyrĭmi* is to be posited.

e. S omits.

f. A B C K "from now."

g. Or "statue."

h. A B C K omit.

i. S *zapovĕdi stvori vŭ nixŭ*, probably corrupt. Others are not much better, *zapovĕdi stvorivŭšixŭ*, "those who have made commandments"; but neither acc. nor gen. fits the context.

j. Reference unclear. This whole sentence is garbled and probably has lost words or phrases.

k. Archaic *prĕpodobie*, Gk. *hosiotĕs*, simplified in A B C K to *podobie*, "semblance."

l. Slav. *vŭ pravdĕ*, lit. "in justice."

m. Or "at first."

n. Slav. *potŭščati*, probably Gk. *spoudazein*.

o. Or "inasmuch as."

28 And I answered and said, "Mighty, Eternal One, you who are sanctified by
your power, be merciful in my petition, since for this you informed me [a]and
showed me. •Since you have brought me up on to your height, therefore inform
me,[a] your beloved, about whatever I ask: Will what I saw be their lot[b] for long?"
And he showed me a multitude of his people. •And he said to me, "For this
reason (it is) through the four ascents[c] you saw[d] (that) my anger will be because
of them,[e] and in them will be retribution[f] for their works. •And in the fourth ascent[g]
is one hundred years. And one hour of the age will also be one hundred years[h] in
evil among the heathen[i] and an hour in their mercy, even with reproaches as among
the heathen."[j]

29 And I said, "Eternal, Mighty[a] One! How long a time is an hour of the age?"
And he said, "I decreed to keep twelve periods of the impious age among the
heathens and [b]among your seed, and what you have seen will be[b] until the end of
time. •Count (it) up, and you will understand. •Look down at the picture." [c]And
I looked[c] and saw a man going out from the left, the heathen side. From the side
of the heathen went out men and women and children, a great crowd, and they
worshiped him. •And while I was still looking, those on the right side came out,
and some insulted this man, and some struck him and others worshiped him. •And
I saw that as they worshiped him Azazel ran and worshiped and, kissing his face,
he turned and stood behind him. •And I said, "Eternal, Mighty One! Who is this
man insulted and beaten by the heathen, with Azazel worshiped?"[d] •And he
answered and said, "Hear, Abraham, the man whom you saw insulted and beaten
and again worshiped is the liberation[e] from the heathen for the people who will
be (born) from you. •In the last days, in this twelfth hour of impiety, in the twelfth
period of the age of my fulfillment,[f] I will set up this man from your tribe, the one
whom you have seen from my people. •All will imitate him, . . . (you) consider[g]
him as one called by me . . . (they) are changed[h] in their counsels.[i] •And those
you saw coming out from the left side of the picture and worshiping him, this
(means that) many of the heathen will trust in him. •And those of your seed you
saw on the right side, some insulting him, some beating him, and others worshiping
him, many of them shall be offended[j] because of him. •It is he who will test those
of your seed who have worshiped him in the fulfillment of the twelfth hour, in the

---

28 a. S omits because of homoeoteleuton.

b. Lit. "will what I saw be to them."

c. S B C K *sxody*, "descents"; A *isxody*,
"exists"; cf. n. d to ch. 27.

d. S A C K "which you saw"; B "as you saw."

e. Obscure. Lit. "will be to me from them anger
(or angering)."

f. S B C K *vŭzdanie*; A *vzderžanie*, "restraint."

g. S *sxodŭ*, "descent"; A B C K *vxod*, "entrance"; cf. n. c.

h. C omits to end of vs.; but a mark in the MS
leads one to expect a marginal note that is not
visible in the microfilm.

i. S omits rest of sentence because of homoeoteleuton.

j. Sense of last clause is obscure.

29 a. S omits.

b. Ambiguous, could be "what you have seen
will be among your seed even."

c. S omits.

d. This sentence is obscure and may well be
corrupt; the translation is strictly literal and retains
the original word order. Two opposite interpretations are possible. In one, the phrase "with Azazel"
is construed with "by the heathen" to mean that
the heathen are being aided by Azazel in insulting,

beating, and, presumably, also worshiping the man.
In the other, "with Azazel" is construed with the
following participle to mean that both Azazel and
the man are being worshiped.

e. Slav. *oslaba*, "liberation, security, relaxa-
tion," Gk. *adeia, anesis*.

f. Slav. *sŭkončanie*, "ending, completion, consummation," Gk. *symplērōsis, plērōsis, synteleia*.

g. Slav. *pritŭči*, apparently imperative of
pritŭknuti, "push, touch, prove," which furnishes
the stem for the noun *pritŭča*, "comparison, proverb," and related words. The connection of this
clause with the context is obscure.

h. This clause is corrupt, and omissions must
be assumed. The nom. plural present participle
preminujušče sja has no subject; and it requires
emendation. Assuming the Novgorod substitution
of *i* for *ě* (well attested in all MSS elsewhere),
prěměnujušče sja means "being exchanged for,
turning into." Alternatively, the reflexive particle
sja may be suppressed, yielding the sense "passing
by, going past."

i. The reflexive possessive may refer to the lost
subject of the participle, or to some other possessor
not preserved in the context. Instead of "counsels,"
the meaning may be "lights" or possibly "worlds."

j. Or "led into error," Gk. *skandalizontai*.

14 curtailing of the age of impiety. •Before the age of justice starts to grow,[k] my
judgment will come upon the heathen who have acted wickedly through the people
15 of your seed[l] who have been set apart for me. •In those days I will bring upon all
earthly creation ten plagues through evil and disease and the groaning of the
16 bitterness of their souls. •Such will I bring upon the generations of those who are
on it,[m] out of anger and corruption of their creation[n] with which they provoke me.
17 And then from your seed will be left the righteous men in their number, protected
by me, who strive[o] in[p] the glory of my name toward the place prepared beforehand
18 for them, which you saw deserted in the picture. •And they will live, being affirmed
19 by the sacrifices and the gifts of justice and truth in the age of justice. •And they
will rejoice forever in me, and they will destroy those who have destroyed them,
they will rebuke those who have rebuked them through their mockery, and they
20 will spit in their faces. •Those rebuked[q] by me when they are to see me rejoicing[r]
21 with my people for those who rejoice and receive and truly return[s] to me. •See,
Abraham, what you have seen, hear[t] what you have heard, know what you have
known.[u] Go to your inheritance! And behold I am with you forever."[v]

1 **30** And while he was still speaking, I found myself on the earth, and I said,
"Eternal, Mighty One, I am no longer in the glory in which I was above, and all
2 that my soul desired to understand in my heart I do not understand." •And he said
to me, "I will explain to you the things you desired in your heart, for you have
sought[a] to know the ten[b] plagues[c] which I prepared against the heathen, and I
3 prepared them beforehand in[d] the passing of the twelve hours on earth. •Hear what
4 I tell you, it will be thus. •The first: sorrow from much need. The second: fiery
5 conflagrations for the cities. •The third: destruction by pestilence[e] among the cattle.
6 The fourth: famine of the world, of their generation.[f] •The fifth: among the rulers,
destruction by earthquake and the sword. The sixth: increase of hail and snow.
7 The seventh: wild beasts will be their grave. The eighth: pestilence and hunger
8 will change their destruction.[g] •The ninth: execution by the sword and flight in
distress. The tenth: thunder, voices, and destroying earthquakes.

1 **31** "And then I will sound the trumpet out of the air, and I will send my chosen
one, having in him one measure of all my power, and he will summon my people,

---

k. This clause may belong to the preceding
sentence.
l. It is possible to read "of your seed" as
describing the heathen.
m. Presumably on earth.
n. Slav. *tvari*, "creation, creature, creatures";
but also Gk. *epitēdeuma*, perhaps then ultimately
here (as in Ezek 20:39) Heb. *glwlym*, "idols." Yet
the whole vs. is obscure, and may well be corrupt.
o. Or "hastening," Gk. *spoudazontes*.
p. S *vŭ*, "in"; A B C K *kŭ*, "toward." Either
could be secondary.
q. Passage unclear; it is possible that the ones
who "will be spitting in their faces" are identical
with those "being rebuked."
r. Grammatical agreement fails here and the
connections of this and the following participles
cannot be established with certainty; the whole
verse is corrupt.
s. S *obrazujuščix sja*, "forming themselves,
being formed (shaped, depicted)"; B K
obraščajuščix sja (acc. or gen.), A C *-im sja* (dat.),
"returning, turning back, converting."
t. S omits.
u. S omits.
v. At this point A B C K insert a long passage
beginning "And the Lord said to him from the
clouds: 'Abraham, I am the Lord himself, maker

of heaven and earth.' " In the earlier Palaia which
does not contain ApAb this passage is an independent unit, which is introduced by the sentence:
"This is written out of the Book of the Sons of
Jacob [*is knigŭ iže sutĭ Ijakoviči*]." The passage
has some echoes from earlier parts of ApAb, then
specific reference to 29:11f., 14, 15, 19, 20, but
simplified. (Porfir'ev prints this much in his edition
of K, p. 129.) These quotations, or rather paraphrases, are then explicated in the anti-Jewish
Christian polemic manner usual in the Palaia commentaries.

30 a. A B C K *iskalŭ*; S by error *skazalŭ*, "explained."
b. All *desjatyja*, acc. plural "tenth," surely by
error for *desjatĭ*, "ten," but perhaps this is a sign
of a more serious corruption.
c. S *vredy* (from *vrědŭ*), "wound, ulcer, illness;
hurt, harm," Gk. *blabē*; A B C K *věry*, "faiths."
The word translated "plague" in 29:15 is *jazva*,
"wound," Gk. *plēgē*.
d. A B C K *v*; S *po*, "after."
e. S gen. *mora*; A B C K nom. *morŭ*, making
it appositive to "destruction."
f. Obscure.
g. Obscure; possibly means "take turns in causing destruction," but this cannot be certain.

2 humiliated by the heathen. •And I will burn with fire[a] those who mocked them and
ruled over them in this age[b] and I will deliver those who have covered me with
3 mockery over to the scorn[c] of the coming[d] age. •Because I have prepared them[e]
(to be) food for the fire of Hades, and (to be) ceaseless soaring in the air of the
underworld (regions)[f] of the uttermost depths,[g] (to be) the contents[h] of a wormy
4 belly. •For the makers[i] will see in them[j] justice, (the makers) who have chosen my
desire and manifestly kept my commandments, and they will rejoice with mer-
rymaking over the downfall of the men who remain and who followed[k] after the
5 idols and after their murders. •For they shall putrefy in the belly of the crafty
6 worm Azazel, and be burned by the fire of Azazel's tongue. •For I waited so they
7 might come to me, and they did not deign to. •And they glorified an alien (god).
8 And they joined one to whom they had not been allotted, and they abandoned the
Lord who gave them strength.[l]

1 **32**."Therefore, hear, Abraham, and see, behold your seventh generation shall
2,3 go with you. •And they will go out into an alien land. •And they will enslave[a]   Gen 15:13
4 them and oppress them as for one hour of the impious age. •But of the nation
5 whom they shall serve[b] I am the judge."[c] •And the Lord said this too,[d] "Have you
heard, Abraham, what I told you, what your tribe will encounter in the last days?"
6 Abraham, having heard, accepted the words of God in his heart.

31 a. S *ognīmī*; A B C K *s nimī*, "with him."

b. Slav. *vŭ věkŭ*, "in an age, for an age" (or
"the age!"), but usually "forever," Gk. *eis aiōnion*.

c. Slav. *ukoriznīstvo*, unique to this passage; not
clearly different from usual *ukorŭ* or *ukorizna*,
"shame, mockery, derision, reproach."

d. S *nastajuščago*, a rare word; A B C K substitute the ordinary *nastojaščego*, "present" (which
is used for Gk. *epiousios* in the Lord's Prayer).

e. S *ty*; A B C K *to* "this."

f. S *podzemnymŭ*, dat. plural adjective, "underworld, subterrestrial"; A B C K *pod zemnymi*,
"under the earthly," with an instrumental plural
noun to be supplied.

g. S ends here; the rest of ApAb is transmitted
only in the Palaia texts.

h. C *napolnenie*, "filling"; B adds *ploda*,
"fruit," which might mean "fullness of/with fruit"
but the syntax is odd; A has past passive participle
napolneny (acc.), "filled"; K has nom. *napolneni*,
plus *ploda*, "filled with (the) fruit." Translation
assumes *plod* is a gloss to explain *napolnenie*.

i. Slav. *tvorīci*, "doers," Gk. *poiētoi*.

j. Reference unclear.

k. The participle *šedŭše* lacks agreement, but
this is a common fault of Slavonic MSS. It is
probably to be taken as gen. referring to the same
people as the previous clause. If it is nom. and
belongs with the next clause, then the conjunction
bo, "for," is inappropriate.

l. Accepting either A *vozmogšago ja*, "having

strengthened them," or C *vozmoguščago ja*,
"strengthening them"; B *vŭzmužĭšago sja*, "who
became a man [adult], gained courage," does not
fit; and K *vozmožaščago* is meaningless.

32 a. The text gives no clue that the subject of
this sentence is different from that of the preceding
and following sentences, but perhaps this represents
secondary harmonization with LXX Gen 15:13.

b. Lit. "to whom they will be slaves," not
exactly either LXX or Heb. Gen 15:14.

c. Lit. "I am the one who judges," reflecting
Heb. *dn* translated as (*ho*) *krinōn*.

d. The exact end of ApAb is not certain. Porfir'ev printed vss. 5, 6 in his edition of K (p. 130).
Tikhonravov, however, excluded them from his
edition of A, surely because he considered them
additions made by the editors of the Palaia. To be
sure, these two sentences do occur in the older
Palaia, following the text referred to above in n. v
to ch. 29, but in the absence of detailed studies of
the Abraham material in different redactions of the
Palaia, it is premature to make a final judgment.
After the two sentences, the older Palaia says:
"After this, it is said, Abraham rose up (to go) to
Egypt because of the famine," and continues with
a paraphrase of Gen 12:14–20 about Sarah and
Pharaoh. B C (and presumably A K, which are not
available), on the other hand, quote Gen 12:1–3
and paraphrase in some detail the following account.

APOCALYPSE OF ADAM

(First to Fourth Century A.D.)

A NEW TRANSLATION AND INTRODUCTION
BY G. MACRAE

The Apocalypse of Adam is a gnostic secret revelation or "apocalypse" communicated by Adam to his son Seth and destined to be preserved for Seth's posterity, the race of the gnostics. Because it is narrated by Adam immediately before his death, it also bears some of the literary characteristics of the genre testament. Adam first narrates the story of the Fall in a peculiarly gnostic version without much direct dependence on the Genesis garden story. In his fallen state of subservience to the creator God, without knowledge of the God of truth above, he receives a revelation of the future from three mysterious strangers, and it is this revelation that forms the substance of the remaining narrative. Adam then foretells the story of the Flood, of the resettlement of the world, and of a cosmic conflagration that is perhaps based on the destruction of Sodom and Gomorrah. These catastrophic events are interpreted as efforts on the part of the creator God to destroy the race of Seth, of which he is envious, but heavenly beings save them in each case. In a third episode a saving figure, called the "Illuminator of knowledge," comes and is persecuted by the powers of the world, who in their wrath are perplexed about his origin and their own ignorance. There follows a long poetic passage in which erroneous myths about his origin on the part of thirteen "kingdoms" are narrated in very stylized form. In contrast with these, the "kingless race" (i.e. the Sethian gnostics) know his true origin from above and are enlightened by him. The peoples of the earth then acknowledge their error and the supremacy of the gnostics, and a voice confirms both. In the formal conclusion of the work baptism is equated with gnosis, or knowledge.

Text

The Apocalypse of Adam is preserved in a unique manuscript in the collection of Coptic codices discovered near Nag Hammadi, Egypt, in 1946. It is the fifth and last treatise in Codex V (64,1–85,32), which also contains three Christian gnostic apocalypses and a speculative non-Christian gnostic tractate.[1] The codex may be dated to the second half of the fourth century A.D.; Codex VII of the same collection has been dated after A.D. 348 on the basis of documentary papyri embedded in its cover.[2] The codex is now preserved in the Coptic Museum at Old Cairo (inventory number 10548). Almost all of the pages of the Apocalypse of Adam have suffered damage at the bottom and sometimes at the top so that several lines of text are often missing.

Original language

The extant version of the Apocalypse of Adam is in the Sahidic dialect of Coptic with

---

[1] See the table of contents of the library in A. Böhlig and F. Wisse, *Nag Hammadi Codices III, 2 and IV, 2: The Gospel of the Egyptians* (NHS 4; Leiden, 1975) pp. xi–xii.
[2] J. W. B. Barns, "Greek and Coptic Papyri from the Covers of the Nag Hammadi Codices," in M. Krause, ed., *Essays on the Nag Hammadi Texts* (NHS 6; Leiden, 1975) pp. 9–18; see especially p. 12.

some other dialectal traits characteristic of the dominant language of the Nag Hammadi library. Like most Coptic literature of the early period, it is undoubtedly a translation from Greek, and there are no linguistic features in the work that would point to any other language underlying the Greek. In the rare cases where the apocalypse seems close to the biblical text, it is clearly the Septuagint version that it depends on.

Date

The only certain conclusion that may be drawn about the date of composition of the work is that it is older than the extant Coptic version. Because the form of the gnostic myth contained in it shows apparently primitive features, and because the work seems to be independent of Christian influence, some interpreters assign it a conjectural date in the first or early second century A.D.[3] One author detects in its description of the destruction by fire an allusion to the Vesuvius eruption in A.D. 79 and would date the work no earlier than the first decade of the second century.[4] The allusion is a doubtful one, however. The limits for dating are approximately the first to the fourth centuries A.D., and the document probably belongs earlier rather than later in this period. In addition, it may contain traditional elements that are much earlier.

Provenance

Some of the Nag Hammadi codices bear indications that they were copied in the vicinity of, and perhaps in close relation to, the monastic communities of Upper Egypt, especially Chenoboskion.[5] The site of the find confirms this location. If the Apocalypse of Adam is a late document, it might have originated in Egypt. But there is no positive reason to associate the Greek original with Egypt, and it might have been composed anywhere in the Mediterranean world. Epiphanius, writing his descriptive catalog of heresies around A.D. 375, describes a sect called the Archontics, whose teachings resemble the Apocalypse of Adam in several ways.[6] He locates this sect in his own time in the province of Palestine and in Armenia. The connection with the Archontics is not a strong one, but an earlier Palestinian origin for the apocalypse is not inherently improbable.

Historical importance

The Apocalypse of Adam, like the majority of gnostic documents that have come down to us, especially the many retellings and embellishments of the Genesis story, provides few if any clues to its milieu or function. It is generally assumed that such gnostic works were written for the edification of gnostic individuals or communities. It has been suggested that this one served as an elementary introduction to Gnosticism for initiates,[7] but it does not bear the marks of clearly propagandistic works such as the Letter of Ptolemy to Flora.[8] Its real importance lies in the absence of any unmistakably Christian influences in its depiction of the Illuminator of knowledge, opening up the possibility that the work reflects a transition from some form of apocalyptic Judaism to Gnosticism. Much greater specificity would be merely conjecture at the present stage of investigation into the problem of the origins of Gnosticism. Some scholars regard the work as a product of late Gnosticism, but such a view does not exclude the possibility that elements in it may be very much older.[9]

If the final pages of the document are an indication, it seems to reflect a polemical context

---

[3] E.g. M. Krause in W. Foerster, ed., *Gnosis: A Selection of Gnostic Texts*, vol. 2, p. 15.

[4] H. Goedicke, "An Unexpected Allusion to the Vesuvius Eruption in 79 A.D.," *American Journal of Philology* 90 (1969) 340–41.

[5] T. Säve-Söderbergh, "Holy Scriptures or Apologetic Documentations? The 'Sitz im Leben' of the Nag Hammadi Library," in J.-E. Ménard, ed., *Les Textes de Nag Hammadi* (NHS 7; Leiden, 1975) pp. 3–14.

[6] *Panarion* 40; Foerster, *Gnosis*, vol. 1, pp. 295–98.

[7] W. Beltz, *Die Adam-Apokalypse aus Codex V von Nag Hammadi: Jüdische Bausteine in gnostischen Systemen* (diss. Berlin, 1970).

[8] Epiphanius, *Panarion* 33.3–7; Foerster, *Gnosis*, vol. 1, pp. 155–61.

[9] See H.-M. Schenke, *OLZ* 61 (1966) col. 32; R. Haardt, *WZKM* 61 (1967) 153–59; R. McL. Wilson, *Gnosis and the New Testament* (Oxford, 1968) pp. 135–39.

in which the interpretation, if not perhaps even the practice, of baptism is a point of serious disagreement. Since nothing in the text clearly suggests Christian baptism, it is possible that the document reflects an encounter between Jewish practitioners of baptism and sectarian gnostics who diverge from them on this issue in particular.

The presence of repetitious and occasionally awkward transitions in the narrative suggests that the Apocalypse of Adam in its present form is the result of a process of growth in which several elements were combined or in which the narrative was expanded in successive stages. Such stages may reflect a progressively explicit gnosticizing of Jewish apocalyptic themes.

Theological importance

One of the most characteristic features of the Apocalypse of Adam, as of many other gnostic writings that retell the creation story, is the sharp distinction drawn between the creator God and the remote supreme God. The former is at times called "the ruler of the aeons and the powers," at times "God the Almighty," even "Sakla," a derisive name. The creator God, the God of Genesis, becomes a hostile power whose mission is to thwart the attempts of humanity to preserve a knowledge of the supreme God, the "God of truth" or "the eternal God." This radical dualism of the deity is a gnostic commonplace; it is uncommon, however, for a gnostic work to use the name "God" for both the Demiurge and the supreme Father.

Humanity in this conception is the creature of the Demiurge and normally lives in servitude to him and in ignorance of the eternal God, destined for death. But the Apocalypse of Adam also distinguishes two categories of people, the followers of the Demiurge and the descendants of Seth, the gnostics, in whom knowledge of the higher God is preserved and who are destined for imperishability:

> For the whole creation that came from the dead earth will be subject to the power of death. But those who reflect on the knowledge of the eternal God in their hearts will not perish.

The apocalypse does not speculate on the eternal or divine element in this type of man, as many gnostic works do, but it clearly seems to presuppose a qualitative difference. The encounter between the types of humanity that is resolved in the final pages of the work does not appear to hold out hope for the ultimate salvation of the non-gnostics. But beyond the promise of imperishability, the precise nature of salvation is not spelled out.

As in most gnostic systems, and indeed in many forms of ancient Judaism and Christianity, the cosmos of the Apocalypse of Adam is subject to the influence of a host of spiritual beings, both gracious and malevolent, variously called aeons, angels, and powers. The terms are not used consistently, but the powers are in general the minions of the creator God who oppress humanity and attempt to persecute the gnostics, while "the great eternal angels" or "the holy angels" are representatives of the eternal God who share the knowledge of the gnostic race and intervene in the world to save them from harm.

Relation to canonical books

Many gnostic cosmogonic treatises are closely dependent on the text of Genesis, which they paraphrase or comment on consciously and sometimes with careful attention to the original text.[10] The Apocalypse of Adam is unusual in that it is clearly dependent on the Genesis story but never quotes it exactly except for an occasional word or phrase. It has the character of a gnostic Midrash on the text, but a text already mediated by a Jewish exegetical tradition. There are no other exact allusions to Old Testament texts in the document, but there is evidence of an acquaintance with the Old Testament, especially with the figure of the Isaian servant of Yahweh in the depiction of the Illuminator of knowledge. Several New Testament passages may be cited as parallels to statements in the Apocalypse of Adam, but there is no reason to postulate dependence on the New Testament text.

---

[10] E.g. The Nature of the Archons, The Apocryphon of John, etc. See O. Wintermute, "A Study of Gnostic Exegesis of the Old Testament," in *The Use of the Old Testament in the New and Other Essays*, ed. J. M. Efird (Durham, N.C., 1972) pp. 241–70.

Relation to apocryphal books

Because the Apocalypse of Adam contains gnostic theology, it stands apart from most of the pseudepigrapha. Nevertheless, it is closely related to the extensive Adam literature and has many parallels to the Life of Adam and Eve in particular.[11] An exact identification of the work with any previously known document is not possible, however. Epiphanius mentions "apocalypses of Adam" as well as "books in the name of Seth" in use among the sectarians whom he calls the "gnostics,"[12] but nothing more specific is known of them. The Cologne Mani Codex quotes passages from an "Apocalypse of Adam,"[13] the first of a series of apocalypses in the names of Genesis figures, but the quotations have nothing in common with the Nag Hammadi work. Within gnostic literature itself the work shares many features with the Nag Hammadi Gospel of the Egyptians, an explicitly Christian gnostic treatise in the name of Seth. In addition, the Apocalypse of Adam shares its concern about the meaning of baptism and its various names of angels with gnostic writings, especially the Nag Hammadi tractates Zostrianos and Triple Protennoia, and an untitled work from the Bruce Codex.[14]

SELECT BIBLIOGRAPHY

Charlesworth, *PMR*, pp. 72–74.
Denis, *Introduction*, pp. 11–14.

Böhlig, A. "Jüdisches und iranisches in der Adamapokalypse des Codex V von Nag Hammadi," *Mysterion und Wahrheit: Gesammelte Beiträge zur spätantiken Religionsgeschichte.* AGAJU 6; Leiden, 1968; pp. 149–61.

Böhlig, A., and P. Labib. *Koptisch-gnostische Apokalypsen aus Codex V von Nag Hammadi im Koptischen Museum zu Alt-Kairo.* Halle-Wittenberg, 1963; pp. 86–117.

Foerster, W. (ed.). *Gnosis: A Selection of Gnostic Texts.* Oxford, 1972–74; vol. 2, pp. 13–20. (Brief introduction by M. Krause, and ET by R. McL. Wilson.)

Hedrick, C. W. *The Apocalypse of Adam. A Literary and Source Analysis.* SBLDS 46; Chico, Calif., 1980. (This book appeared after the present work was completed.)

Kasser, R. "Bibliothèque gnostique V: Apocalypse d'Adam," *RTP* 17 (1967) 316–33. (Introduction and French translation.)

MacRae, G. W. "The Apocalypse of Adam," in D. M. Parrott (ed.), *Nag Hammadi Codices V, 2–5 and VI with Papyrus Berolinensis 8502, 1 and 4.* NHS 11; Leiden, 1979; pp. 151–95. (Annotated text and translation.)

MacRae, G. W. "The Coptic Gnostic Apocalypse of Adam," *HeyJ* 6 (1965) 27–35.

MacRae, G. W., and D. M. Parrott. "The Apocalypse of Adam (V, 5)," in J. M. Robinson (ed.), *The Nag Hammadi Library in English.* San Francisco, 1977; pp. 256–64.

Robinson, J. M. (ed.). *The Facsimile Edition of the Nag Hammadi Codices: Codex V.* Leiden, 1975; pp. 66–85. (This edition contains photographs of the Cop. MS.)

Rudolph, K. "Gnosis und Gnostizismus, ein Forschungsbericht," *ThRu* 34 (1969) 160–69. (A detailed survey of the discussion about ApAdam in scholarship.)

Schottroff, L. "Animae naturaliter salvandae: Zum Problem der himmlischen Herkunft des Gnostikers," in W. Eltester (ed.), *Christentum und Gnosis.* BZNW 37; Berlin, 1969; pp. 65–97.

---

[11] See the contribution herein on LAE and ApMos.

[12] *Panarion* 26.8.1; Foerster, *Gnosis*, vol. 1, p. 320.

[13] 48, 16–50, 7; A. Henrichs and L. Koenen, "Der Kölner Mani-Codex (P. Colon. inv. nr. 4780)," *Zeitschrift für Papyrologie und Epigraphik* 19 (1975) 48–51.

[14] For the Bruce Codex tractate see C. A. Baynes, *A Coptic Gnostic Treatise Contained in the Codex Brucianus* (Cambridge, 1933). The Nag Hammadi tractates mentioned are published in translation in J. M. Robinson, ed., *The Nag Hammadi Library in English* (San Francisco, 1977).

Note on the translation

In the translation that follows, the division into paragraphs and the section titles have been introduced by the translator. Most of the explanations of the Illuminator's origin, however, are set off by paragraph signs in the margin of the manuscript. To facilitate references to the text, the page numbers of the original manuscript have been included in parentheses. Square brackets are used to indicate lacunae and to enclose words reconstructed by the translator. Occasional explanatory or interpretative phrases are included in parentheses.

(64) THE APOCALYPSE OF ADAM

1 **1** The revelation (apocalypse) which Adam taught his son Seth in the seven ^{Gen 5:4(LXX)}
2 hundredth year,[a] saying, "Listen to my words, my son Seth. •When God created ^{LAE 25:1}
me out of earth along with Eve your mother, I used to go about with her in a glory[b] ^{Gen 2:7}
3 which she had seen in the aeon[c] from which we had come. •She taught me a word
of knowledge of the eternal God. And we were like the great eternal angels, for
we were loftier than the God who created us and the powers that were with him,
whom we did not know.

The Fall

4 "Then God, the ruler of the aeons[c] and the powers, separated us[d] wrathfully.
5 Then we became two aeons, and the glory in our hearts deserted us, me and your ^{ApMos 20:1-2;}
6 mother Eve, along with the first knowledge that used to breathe within us. •And ^{21:6}
the glory fled from us, entering into other great [aeons] and another great [race],[e]
one that did not [come (65) from] the aeon that [we] came from, I and Eve your
7,8 mother. •But the knowledge entered into the seed of great aeons.[f] •That is why
I myself have called you by the name of that man who is the seed of the great race ^{Gen 5:3}
or from whom (it comes).[g]
9 "After those days the eternal knowledge of the God of truth withdrew from me
10 and your mother Eve. •Since that time we have learned about dead things, like
11 men. •Then we recognized the God who created us, for we were not strangers to
12 his powers, and we served him in fear and subjection. •And afterward our hearts ^{Deut 6:13;}
were darkened. ^{Ps 2:11}

Adam's vision

1 **2** "Now I was sleeping in the thought of my heart, and I saw before me three ^{Gen 18:2;}
men[a] whose appearance I could not recognize because they were not from the ^{TAb 6}
powers of the God who created me. They surpassed [those powers in their] glory.
2 The men [spoke], (66) saying to me, 'Rise up, Adam, from the sleep of death,[b]
and hear about the aeon and the seed of that man to whom life has come, the one
who came forth from you and from Eve your wife.'

---

1 a. The seven hundredth year, according to the LXX of Gen 5:4 (MT = 800), is the length of Adam's life after the birth of Seth; cf. Josephus, *Ant* 1.2.3. Thus the apocalypse is a deathbed "testament" of Adam.

b. Throughout, the word "glory" is a literal translation of the Cop. for Gk. *doxa*. It may sometimes refer to honor or dignity, sometimes to external splendor, as often in the LXX.

c. The word "aeon" in Gk., a loanword in Cop., is sometimes a temporal, sometimes a spatial concept. In addition, in gnostic literature it is also used for personal beings, whether spiritual or material. All these meanings occur in ApAdam, but the word is translated "aeon" throughout.

d. The primordial state of Adam and Eve, as often in gnostic literature, is seen as that of a single androgynous being. Here the androgyne myth is used to interpret Gen 2:21–23.

e. The Gk. word *genea*, a loanword in Cop., is variously translated here as "race," "nation," or "generation," according to the context.

f. The point may be to assert that the external splendor of Adam and Eve reverted to heavenly beings, but their knowledge (*gnōsis*) passed into the posterity of Seth. The words "glory" and "knowledge" are not in the text at this point but are inferred from the grammatical gender of the verbs. The "seed" is the posterity or offspring of Seth; two Gk. words, possibly reflecting different sources, and a Cop. word are all rendered "seed" throughout the translation.

g. The final phrase is obscure and may be an editorial gloss. Seth, perhaps a heavenly prototype of Seth, is the "man" referred to.

2 a. The appearance of three "men" is common in the Abraham legends and is frequent in gnostic literature, where it is sometimes interpreted in a trinitarian sense. In TAb 6 (rec. A) the strange appearance of the "men" is also emphasized.

b. The sleep of Adam and his awakening to a revelation of knowledge, which may be rooted in Gen 2:21, is a widespread gnostic motif.

3　　"When I heard these words from those great men who stood before me, we
4　sighed in our hearts, I and Eve. •And the Lord, the God who created us, stood　Gen 3:8
5　in our presence and said to us, 'Adam, why were you sighing in your hearts? •Do
　　you not know that I am God who created you, and that I breathed into you a spirit[c]　Isa 45:5ff.
　　of life for a living soul?'　　　　　　　　　　　　　　　　　　　　　　　Gen 2:7
6,7　　"Then darkness fell over our eyes. •Then the God who created us created a son
　　from himself [and Eve your mother] [. . . 3 lines missing].
8　　(67) "[Then I was defiled] in the thought of my heart. I recognized a sweet
9　desire for your mother. •Then the vigor of our eternal knowledge perished in us,
10　and feebleness pursued us. •For this reason the days of our life became few, for　Gen 6:3
　　I knew that I had become subject to the power of death.　　　　　　　　　Gen 3:19

The Flood

1　**3** "Now then, my son Seth, I will reveal to you what was revealed to me by those
2　men whom I once saw before me. • After I have completed the times of this
　　generation and the years of [the generation] have been fulfilled, then [. . . 3 lines
3　missing]. (69)[a] •Rain showers of God the Almighty will be poured forth so that　Gen 6:17
　　he may destroy all flesh from the earth because of the things it seeks after,[b]
　　including [those who] come from the seed of the men to whom the life of knowledge,
　　which went out from me and Eve your mother, was passed on. For they were
　　strangers to him.
4　　"Afterward great angels will come on high clouds to bring those men to the
　　place where the spirit of life dwells [. . . 7 lines missing] (70) from heaven to　Gen 6:17
5　earth. •[But] the whole [multitude] of flesh will be left behind in the [waters].
6,7　Then God will rest from his wrath. •He will cast his power upon the waters, and
　　he will give power to (Noah and his wife and)[c] his sons and their wives by means　Gen 6:18
　　of the ark, together with their animals, whichever he pleased, and the birds of　Gen 7:2-3
　　heaven, which he called[d] and placed upon the earth.
8　　"And God will say to Noah—whom the nations will call Deucalion[e]—'Behold,
　　I have guarded you in the ark, together with your wife and your sons and their
　　wives and their animals and the birds of heaven, which you called [and placed
9　upon the earth . . . 4 lines missing]. (71) •For this reason I shall give the [earth]　Gen 9:1-3
　　to you and your sons. In sovereignty you shall rule over it, you and your sons.
10　And from you no seed will come forth of the men who will not stand in my
　　presence in another glory.'[f]
11,12　　"Then they will be like the cloud of great light. •Those men will come, the ones
13　who were sent forth from the knowledge of the great aeons and the angels. •They
14　will stand in the presence of Noah and the aeons. • And God will say to Noah,
15　'Why have you departed from what I told you? • You have created another race
　　in order that you might scorn my power.'
16　　"Then Noah will reply, 'I shall bear witness before your might that it is not
　　from me that the race of these men has come, nor from [my sons . . . 5 lines
　　missing] (72) knowledge.'
17　　"And [he][g] will release those men and bring them into their proper land and

---

c. Or "breath," as in Gen 2:7.

3 a. P. 68 was left entirely blank by the copyist.
　b. The Flood is prompted by the desires and
pursuits of humanity.
　c. The words "Noah and his wife and" are not
in the text but are required if the creator God is the
subject of the verb "will give power."
　d. The verb for "called" (i.e. summoned) might
be rendered "named," in which case the allusion
would be to the naming of the animals, which in
Gen 2:19-20 is the task of Adam, not Noah.
　e. Deucalion, son of Prometheus, is the mythical

hero of the Greek flood story; see Apollodorus,
Bibliotheca, 1.7.2; Pseudo-Lucian, *De dea Syria*
12-13.
　f. Alternate rendering: "the men who will not
also stand in honor before me" (Krause-Wilson).
The awkward double negative may be an error on
the part of the Cop. translator.
　g. The antecedent of the pronoun is unclear
because of the preceding lacuna; it would make
most sense if it were Seth or some other heavenly
figure. For the 600-year sojourn in tranquillity,
see Josephus, *Ant* 1.3.9.

18 build them a holy dwelling place. •And they will be called by that name and will Jas 2:7
19 dwell there six hundred years in a knowledge of imperishability. •And angels of
20 the great light will dwell with them. •Nothing abominable will be in their hearts,
but only the knowledge of God.

The division of the earth

1 **4** "Then Noah will divide all the earth among his sons, Ham and Japheth and Gen 9:18-19
2 Shem. •He will say to them, 'My sons, hear my words. Behold, I have divided
3 the earth among you. •But serve him in fear and subjection all the days of your
4 life. •Do not let your seed depart from the face of God the Almighty[a] [. . . 5 lines
missing}.'
5 (73) "[Then Shem[b] the] son of Noah [will say, 'My] seed will be pleasing before
6 you and before your power. •Put a seal on it with your strong hand in fear and
commandment, so that all the seed that has come forth from me will not be inclined
away from you and God the Almighty, but they will serve in humility and fear of
their knowledge.'
7 "Then from the seed of Ham and Japheth others will go, four hundred thousand[c]
men, and will enter into another land and sojourn with those men who came forth
8 from the great eternal knowledge. •For the shadow of their power will guard those
who have sojourned among them from every evil deed and every foul desire.
9 Then the seed of Ham and Japheth will make twelve kingdoms,[d] and [their other] Gen 10:1ff
seed will enter the kingdom of another people [. . . 3 lines missing] (74) great (LXX); 49:28;
aeons of imperishability.   1Chr 1:1-16

The fire

1,2 **5** "And they will approach Sakla[a] their God. •They will go in to the powers,
3 making accusations against the great men who dwell in their glory. •They will say
to Sakla, 'What is the power of these men who have stood in your presence, the
ones who were taken from the seed of Ham and Japheth to become four hundred
4 (thousand)[b] men? •They have been received into another aeon, the one from which
they came forth, and they have overturned all the glory of your power and the
5 dominion of your hand. •For the seed of Noah from his son has done all your will
together with all the powers in the aeons over which your might rules, while both
those men and the ones who are sojourners in their glory have not done what you
6 wish. •Instead, they have turned aside your entire multitude.'
7 "Then the God of the aeons will give them some of those who serve him
8 [. . . 1 line missing]. •They will come to that land (75) where dwell the great men
9 who have not been defiled nor will be defiled by any desire. •For it is not from
a defiled hand that their soul has come, but it came from a great commandment

---

4 a. The title "God the Almighty" (Gk. *panto-*
kratōr), like "God who created us," clearly designates the inferior creator, or Demiurge. It is a
frequent epithet of God in the LXX.

b. The separate mention of Ham and Japheth a
few lines below makes the reconstruction of the
name of Shem very likely here. The story in Gen
9:20–27 singles out Ham negatively over against
Shem and Japheth; Canaan, Ham's son, is to be a
slave to Shem and Japheth and Japheth is to dwell
in the tents of Shem. By identifying Shem, ancestor
of the Israelites, so closely with Noah and God the
Almighty, ApAdam seems to show an anti-Jewish
bias that is not uncommon in gnostic sources.

c. The number 400,000 may be simply a large
round number. The Manichean *Homilies* 68.18 refers to "400,000 righteous," and Josephus (*Ant*
7.13.1) uses the same number of the tribe of Judah.

Here it apparently refers to non-Jewish converts to
the race of Sethian gnostics.

d. The twelve kingdoms may be modeled on the
twelve tribes of Israel. In the LXX of Gen 10:2
and 10:6 there are twelve sons of Japheth and Ham.
For the twelve plus one, cf. the thirteen kingdoms
mentioned below, which have parallels in the Nag
Hammadi documents such as the Gospel of the
Egyptians (Codex III, 63, 18: thirteen aeons) and
Marsanes (Codex X, 2, 14–4, 23: thirteen "seals").

5 a. Sakla or Saklas, probably from an Aram.
word for "fool," is a common derisive name for
the lower God in gnostic sources (e.g. Gospel of
the Egyptians, 58, 24).

b. The omission of "thousand" in the MS is
undoubtedly a scribal error.

10 of an eternal angel. •Then they will cast fire and sulfur and asphalt[c] upon those
men; and fire and mist will come over those aeons, and the eyes of the powers of
the luminaries[d] will be darkened so that the aeons may not see by them in those
days.

11 "And great clouds of light[e] will come down and other clouds of light will
12 descend on them from the great aeons. •Abrasax and Sablo and Gamaliel[f] will
come down to take those men out of the fire and the wrath and bring them above
13 the aeons and the rulers of the powers and take them away •[. . . 3 lines missing]
(76) dwelling place of the great ones [. . .] there with the holy angels and the
14 aeons. •The men will resemble those angels, for they are not strangers to them,
but they are at work in the imperishable seed.

Gen 19:24;
Ps 11:6

Gen 1:16;
Isa 13:10;
Mk 13:24 par.

TAb 9

The coming of the Illuminator

1 **6** "Again for the third time[a] the Illuminator[b] of knowledge will pass by in great
glory in order to leave a remnant of the seed of Noah and the sons of Ham and
2 Japheth so that he might leave behind for himself fruit-bearing trees.[c] •And he will
redeem their souls from the day of death, for the whole creation that came from
3 the dead earth will be subject to the power of death. •But those who reflect upon
4 the knowledge of the eternal God in their hearts will not perish. •For they have
not received spirit from this kingdom alone, but from an eternal angel they have
5 received (it) [. . . 4 lines missing] (77) of Seth. •And he will do signs and wonders
in order to scorn the powers and their ruler.

6 "Then the God of the powers will be disturbed, saying, 'What is the power of
7 the man who is loftier than we?' •Then he will stir up a great wrath against that
man, and the glory will withdraw and dwell in holy houses which it has chosen
8 for itself. • The powers will not see it with their eyes, nor will they see the
9 Illuminator either.[d] •Then they will punish the flesh[e] of the man upon whom the
holy spirit has come.[f]

10 "Then the angels and all the races of the powers will use the name in error,
asking, 'Where has it (the error) come from?' or 'Where have the words of
deception, which all the powers have failed to discover, come from?'

Ps 1:3;
Jer 17:8;
Mt 3:10 par.;
7:16-20 par.

Ex 7:3;
Mk 13:22;
Jn 4:48

1QpHab 9,2

c. The biblical model for the apocalyptic destruction by fire is the story of Sodom and Gomorrah in Gen 19:24–28. The scheme of destruction first by flood, then by fire, is well known in Jewish and Christian apocalyptic sources; cf. e.g. LAE 49:3–50:2. In *Ant* 1.2.3 Josephus portrays Adam as having predicted these events to Seth.

d. The "luminaries" or "lights" are the sun and the moon. The darkening of them is a common apocalyptic theme in biblical contexts.

e. Clouds of light or bright clouds are a common means of ascent to the heavens in the pseudepigrapha as well as in gnostic literature; cf. e.g. TAb 9 (rec. A).

f. In various combinations these three names occur frequently in the gnostic literature from Nag Hammadi and elsewhere, usually designating angelic beings in a gracious or protective role, e.g. Gospel of the Egyptians 52, 19–53, 9.

6 a. Though the coming of the Illuminator has not been mentioned previously, this is the "third time" in relation to the rescue of the race of Seth in the Flood and the fire. In an important parallel passage in the Gospel of the Egyptians (63, 4–8) the great Seth passes through "three Parousias": "the Flood, and the conflagration, and the judgment of the rulers and the powers and the authorities." In that work, Seth in his third Parousia is identified with

Jesus; here such an identification is not explicit if indeed it is intended at all.

b. The Gk. word, *phōstēr*, is used elsewhere in ApAdam to refer to the sun and the moon. As a title it is widely used in Christian, gnostic, and Manichean sources to refer to the savior figure, e.g. Hippolytus, *Refutation* 5.8.40; Letter of Peter to Philip (Codex VIII, 139, 15). Compare the phrases "the light of knowledge" in TLevi 4:3, the "light of the nations" in Isa 42:6, and "the light of the world" in Jn 8:12; 9:5.

c. The metaphor of fruit-bearing trees for people is found in the NT but is already traditional. See also PssSol 14:2[5] and OdesSol 11:16a–21.

d. The theme of the ignorance or blindness of the Demiurge and the powers in the presence of the heavenly redeemer is a favorite gnostic motif; see e.g. Paraphrase of Shem (Codex VII, 36, 2–24), where it appears without reference to Jesus. Cf. also 1Cor 2:6–8.

e. The scene of the punishment of the Illuminator presupposes the kind of Docetism familiar in gnostic accounts of the passion of Jesus. The expression "punish the flesh" does not necessarily imply this, however; at Qumran the wicked priest is said to suffer "vengeance in the body of his flesh."

f. Reference to the holy spirit recalls Isa 42:1, and there are other traces of servant imagery in the portrayal of the Illuminator.

The origin of the Illuminator

1   **7** "Now the first kingdom says of him,
'He came [. . . 3 lines missing] (78) a spirit [. . .] to heaven.

2   He was nourished in the heavens.

3   He received the glory of that one[a] and the power. He came to the bosom of his mother.

4   And thus he came to the water.'[b]

5   "And the second kingdom says about him,
'He came from a great prophet. And a bird came, took the child who was born, and carried him to a high mountain.

6   And he was nourished by the bird of heaven. An angel came forth there and said to him, "Rise up! God has given you glory."

7   He received glory and strength.

8   And thus he came to the water.'

9   "The third kingdom says of him,
'He came from a virgin womb. He was cast out of his city, he and his mother; he was taken to a desert place.   Rev 12:1-6

10   He was nourished there.[c]

11   He came and received glory and power.

12   And thus he came to the water.'

13   "The fourth kingdom says [of him]:
'He came [from a virgin . . . Solomon] (79) sought her, he and Phersalo and Sauel[d] and his armies which had been sent out. Solomon also sent his army of demons[e] to seek the virgin. And they did not find the one they   TSol *passim* sought, but the virgin who was given to them was the one they fetched.[f] Solomon took her. The virgin conceived and gave birth to the child there.

14   She nourished him on a border[g] of the desert. When he had been nourished,

15   He received glory and power from the seed from which he had been begotten.

16   And thus he came to the water.'

17   "And the fifth kingdom says of him,
'He came from a drop from heaven. He was cast into the sea. The abyss received him, brought him forth, and took him to heaven.[h]

18   He received glory and power.

19   And thus he came to [the water].'

20   "And the sixth kingdom says,
'[. . . 2 lines missing] (80) which is below, in order to [gather] flowers.

---

7 a. "Of that one" or possibly "of that place." For a parallel to this passage and several of the others, see the traditions of the Archontics about the birth and youth of Seth in Epiphanius, *Panarion* 40.7.1–3.

b. This puzzling refrain could be understood as a reference to baptism (cf. the baptism of Jesus in the Gospels). In other gnostic sources, however, "the descent to (or upon) the water" refers to coming into the world; cf. e.g. the Second Logos of the Great Seth (Codex VII, 50, 16–18).

c. The text reads: "he nourished him(self)"; it has been emended to conform to other instances in the list.

d. These two names are not attested elsewhere in gnostic or pseudepigraphical literature.

e. Solomon's army of demons is mentioned in magical and other gnostic sources; see TSol *passim*. Josephus (*Ant* 8.2.5) mentions Solomon's peculiar power over demons.

f. The substitution of the virgin recalls the gnostic myth of the substitution of the earthly or shadow Eve when the powers sought to defile the spiritual Eve: cf. e.g. Nature of the Archons (Codex II, 89, 18–31).

g. The exact meaning of the Cop. word translated "border" is uncertain.

h. The line about nourishing is omitted, possibly by accident.

She conceived from the desire of the flowers and gave birth to him in that place.

21   The angels of the flower garden[i] nourished him.
22   He received glory there and power.
23   And thus he came to the water.'

24   "And the seventh kingdom says of him,
'He is a drop. It came from heaven to earth. Dragons brought him down to caves.[j] He became a child. A spirit came upon him and took him on high to the place where the drop had come from.[k]
25   He received glory and power there.
26   And thus he came to the water.'

27   "And the eighth kingdom says of him,
'A cloud came upon the earth and enveloped a rock. He came from it.
28   The angels who were above the cloud nourished him.
29   He received glory and power there.
30   And [thus he] came [to the water].'

31   (81) "And the ninth kingdom says of him,
'Of the nine Muses one separated away.[l] She went to a high mountain and spent some time dwelling there so as to desire herself alone, that she might become androgynous. She fulfilled her desire and conceived from her desire. He was brought forth.
32   The angels who were over the desire nourished him.
33   And he received glory there and power.
34   And thus he came to the water.'

35   "The tenth kingdom says of him,
'His god loved a cloud of desire. He begot him in his hand and cast some of the drop upon the cloud near him.[m] And he was brought forth.[n]
36   He received glory and power there.
37   And thus he came to the water.'

38   "And the eleventh kingdom says,
'The father desired his own daughter. She also conceived from her father. She put [the child] in a tomb (82) out in the desert.
39   The angel nourished him there.[o]
40   And thus he came to the water.'

41   "The twelfth kingdom says of him,
'He came from two luminaries.[p]
42   He was nourished there.
43   He received glory and power.
44   And thus he came to the water.'

Gen 1:16

---

i. Translation uncertain; the Gk. word appears to be in the genitive case, *antheōnos*, which is very unusual in Cop.

j. In Gk. mythology the infant Zeus is said to have been hidden and nourished in a cave; cf. Apollodorus, *Bibliotheca* 1.1.6–7.

k. See n. h above.

l. This particular story is not told of the Muses in Gk. sources, but the motif of conception without intercourse is a common one, e.g. in the gnostic Sophia myth and in Gk. mythology; cf. Apollodorus, *Bibliotheca* 1.3.5 (Hera giving birth to He-phaestus).

m. The Cop. expression rendered "near him" is uncertain. The underlying myth is a common description of the creation of other beings by the Egyptian god Atum; cf. S. G. F. Brandon, *Creation Legends of the Ancient Near East* (London, 1963) pp. 21–23.

n. A line of the common refrain is missing and perhaps should be supplied.

o. See previous n.

p. The luminaries or lights are again the sun and the moon.

45　　　"And the thirteenth kingdom says of him,
　　　　　'Every birth of their ruler is a word.�q
46　　　And this word received a mandateʳ there.ˢ
47　　　He received glory and power.
48　　　And thus he came to the water—so that the desire of those powers might
　　　　be fulfilled."ᵗ

49　"But the race without a king over itᵘ says, 'God chose him from all the aeons.ᵛ
50,51 He made a knowledge of the undefiled one of truth exist in him. •He said, "[From]
52　an alien air [out of a] great aeon the [great] Illuminator has come forth. •And he
　　had made (83) the race of those men whom he chose for himself shine, so that they
　　should shine upon the whole aeon." 'ʷ

Dan 12:3;
Mt 13:43;
Phil 2:15;
LAE 29:9

The victory

1 **8** "Then the seed will fight against the power, those who will receive his name
2 upon the water, and of them all.ᵃ •And a cloud of darkness will come upon them.
3 Then the peoples will cry out with a loud voice, saying, 'Blessed is the soul of
4 those men because they have known God with a knowledge of the truth. •They
　will live for aeons of aeonsᵇ because they have not been corrupted in their desire
　with the angels, nor have they accomplished the works of the powers, but they
　have stood before him in a knowledge of God like light that has come out of fire
5,6 and blood. •But we have done every deed of the powers senselessly. •We have
7 gloried in the transgression of all our works. •We have cried out against [God
8 . . . 2 lines missing] (84) is eternal. [. . .] our spirits. •For now we know that our
　souls will surely die.'

The voice

9　"Then a voice came to them, saying—Micheu and Michar and Mnesinous,ᶜ
　who are over the holy baptism and the living water—'Why were you crying out
　against the living God with impious voices and tongues without law over them and
10 souls full of blood and abominable deeds? •You are full of works that are not of
11 the truth, but your ways are full of gladness and joy. •Having defiled the water
　of life, you have drawn it within the will of the powers to whom you have been
12 given to serve them. •And your thought does not resemble that of those men whom
　you persecute, [for] they have not [obeyed your] desires and (85) their fruit does
13 not wither. •But they will be known to the great aeons because the words they
　have kept, of the God of the aeons, were not set down in the book nor were they
14 written. •But angelic beings will bring them, words which all the generations of

---

q. Or logos; compare Jn 1:1–14 and the logos speculations of the hellenistic world.

r. The Cop. word rendered "mandate" has multiple meanings; one might possibly translate "received form there" or "was provided for there."

s. See n. n above.

t. This remark is apparently an editorial insertion referring to the context in which the passage was introduced.

u. "The kingless race (or generation)" is a frequent self-designation of the gnostics in the Nag Hammadi writings. It may be related to the biblical tradition reflected in 1Sam 8. This race's explanation contrasts with the others in form and content. It is the "true," gnostic explanation over against the speculations of the powers.

v. Ambiguous; perhaps "from eternity."

w. It is uncertain where to terminate the quotation.

8 a. The sentence is completely ambiguous and perhaps textually corrupt. The phrase "those who will receive" may refer either to the seed (the race of Seth) or the power (their opponents). Despite the antibaptism sentiments of the following passage, the former seems preferable. The final phrase may refer to the name (of Seth and) of all Sethians.

b. "Aeons of aeons" here clearly has the sense of "forever and ever."

c. In gnostic literature these names are regularly associated with baptism or water; cf. e.g. Gospel of the Egyptians 64, 14–20. Their syntactical function here is unclear, however. The voice may be addressing them directly or making a statement about them ("Micheu . . . are over the holy baptism"); or the mention of them may be an editorial remark or gloss identifying the voice.

men will not know, for they will be on a high mountain, upon a rock of truth.[d]
15 For this reason they will be called "the words of imperishability [and] truth,"
of those who know the eternal God in wisdom of knowledge and teaching of eternal
angels, for he knows all things.' "[e]

Conclusion

16   These are the revelations which Adam made known to Seth his son, and his son
17 taught his seed about them. • This is the secret knowledge of Adam which he
imparted to Seth, which is the holy baptism[f] of those who know the eternal
knowledge through the ones born of the word and the imperishable illuminators,
those who came from the holy seed: Jesseus, Mazareus, Jessedekeus, [the living
water].[g]

---

d. There is a tradition connected with Adam and
Seth concerning revelations written on stone and
brick to survive the Flood and the conflagration;
cf. Josephus, *Ant* 1.2.3; LAE 50:1–2. The Gospel
of the Egyptians (68, 1–13) is described as a book
written by Seth and placed on a hidden mountain.

e. The revelation spoken by Adam ends logically
here. Where to end the words of "the voice" is
uncertain.

f. The identification of knowledge with, or the
substitution of it for, baptism is known in gnostic
sources; cf. e.g. Epiphanius, *Panarion* 40.2.6; Paraphrase of Shem 30–31.

g. The phrase "the living water" is reconstructed from a parallel passage, involving the same
names, in Gospel of the Egyptians 66, 10–11. The
role of these figures in the present context, however,
is unclear.

APOCALYPSE OF ELIJAH

(First to Fourth Century A.D.)

A NEW TRANSLATION AND INTRODUCTION
BY O. S. WINTERMUTE

The Apocalypse of Elijah is a composite work that contains the following: an opening homiletical section that discusses prayer and fasting (ch. 1); a phophetic description of events that precede the advent of the Antichrist (ch. 2); a description of the Antichrist (ch. 3); an account of three martyrdoms (ch. 4); and oracles depicting events that are to occur "on that day" (ch. 5).

The title of the present work is given at the end of the Akhmimic text as *tiapoklupsis ēheleias*: "The Apocalypse of Elijah." That title might lead one to expect the work to contain an account of secret lore revealed by an angelic messenger to Elijah, but it does not. The work begins in the form of a prophecy spoken by a figure who is identified simply as "son of man," a title that was used of Ezekiel (Ezek 2:1) in the Old Testament. Within the text, Elijah is mentioned twice, both times in the third person and in association with Enoch. The fact that Elijah is mentioned in the text might explain why his name was joined to the title, but it will be argued below that the portions of text that refer to Elijah and Enoch are Christian interpolations added to an earlier Jewish work. If that is true, the title of the original Jewish work remains unknown.

The designation "apocalypse" is also a somewhat inadequate description of the basic document. An apocalypse, i.e. "revelation," usually contains the account of a secret revelation conveyed to a seer by an angelic messenger who directs that the revelation be written down for the benefit of those who will remain faithful in the last days. The present document does not have such a framework. The writer presents his opening statements as "the word of the Lord," which comes to him in a normal prophetic form (cf. Ezek 6:1; 12:1; 13:1). Although the point of view changes in the document, there is no evidence to suggest that the writer begins to assume the role of an apocalyptic seer.

The fact that the document is not written in apocalyptic form leads one to ask why it is called an apocalypse. The answer is to be sought in an examination of the type of material contained in the document. Much of the portrayal of the final days of the present age is typical of the apocalypses. In fact, there is reason to believe that the description of the martyrdom of Enoch and Elijah (in ch. 4) is strongly influenced by the account of two martyrs in Revelation 11:4–12. In other words, the present text, which is not written in the form of an apocalypse, contains passages that may rightly be described as apocalyptic inasmuch as they are similar to descriptions found in works constructed in the form of an apocalypse. Not only the Christian editor who inserted the Enoch-Elijah martydom but also other early readers would have been aware of its dependence on Revelation. Consequently, the final Christian edition of this text, which described the martyrdom of Elijah in an "apocalyptic" manner, came to be designated "The Apocalypse of Elijah."

A closer analysis of the structure of this work reveals its composite nature more clearly:

Chapter 1

The first chapter contains a prophetic homily encouraging fasting and prayer. This is possibly an early Jewish work that has been supplemented by a Christian editor. The original Jewish homily would have had the following structure:

1. Introduction: a description of the call of a prophet who is identified as a "son of man" (1:1).
2. Exhortation: "remember" what is prepared for the sealed and for the sinners (1:8–12).
3. Exhortation: "hear" about deceivers who will appear in the last days and oppose the fast (1:13f.).
4. Exhortation: "remember" the benefits of a pure fast, which was created by God (1:15–22).
5. Closing comment: the value of single-mindedness, and a simile comparing the farmer's tool and the soldier's breastplate to single-mindedness (1:23–27).

The Christian editor who added 1:3–7 was aware of the homiletical structure of the work and so he added his comments in a similar form. After the prophet's call, he also added a quotation from 1 John 2:15 (at 1:2), which contains an imperative that aptly suits the homiletical style.

Neither of these added comments have anything to do with fasting and prayer, which constituted the main concern of the earlier Jewish composition. They are, however, thematically related to the larger text, which deals with the judgment of the Antichrist and the salvation of the saints. That would indicate that the Christian editor had much of the present text before him when he began his editing.

It is obvious that additional verses in chapter 1, particularly 1:8–12, might be regarded as the work of a secondary Christian editor. In fact, there is nothing in any part of chapter 1 that could not be regarded as the work of a Christian writer. Nevertheless, it is clear that the verses that are most intrusive and irrelevant to the basic theme of prayer and fasting are verses 1:2–7 (possibly 8–12), which contain explicit quotations and themes drawn from the New Testament.

Chapter 2

The second chapter is the most difficult portion of the text to analyze. That is due in part to the fact that the recently published Chester Beatty Papyrus has added some fifteen verses (2:15b–30b) to the chapter, increasing its length by more than one fourth and drastically changing the presumed scenario. The scholarly community has not yet had an opportunity to examine the text and make its contribution to a study of the many tantalizing questions that it raises.

The difficulties involved in an attempt to understand this chapter are aggravated by the problem of identifying the genre involved. The chapter attempts to provide a description of events preceding the advent of the Antichrist. At first impression it appears to fit somewhere in the continuum of Jewish and Christian apocalyptic prophecies, which extend from Daniel to 6 Ezra. It seems to share with them a method of surveying history in the form of future predictions that make use of such coded expressions as "a king who rises in the north" (2:3, cf. Dan 11:6) or "in the west" (2:6, cf. Dan 8:5) or the three "kings of Persia" who will struggle with four "kings of Assyria" for three years (2:42). Since the code is unclear, both the interpretation and the dating of this chapter remain uncertain.

Chapter 2, together with chapter 5, also shares another literary feature with the type of apocalyptic prophecy found in Daniel. That is the tendency to repeat certain characteristic motifs and even to restate the same sequence of events in several different forms. Thus chapters 2, 7, 8, and 11 of Daniel abound in descriptions of beasts, kingdoms, and horns. They speak of powers arising with "four winds of heaven" (Dan 7:2; 8:8) and a kingdom that will never be destroyed (Dan 2:44; 7:14). The same chapters of Daniel provide four different descriptions of the sequence of Median-Persian, Greek, and Seleucid kingdoms which precede the final age.

In a similar manner chapter 2 of the Apocalypse of Elijah repeats the notice that "your children will be seized" (2:4, 30), the land or cities of Egypt "will groan" (2:4, 31), many will "desire death, but death will flee" (2:5, 32) from them, and good rulers will "take vengeance" (2:8, 48) on the land of Egypt. Chapter 2 also appears to give two different accounts of events preceding the advent of the son of lawlessness. The chapter begins with a description of the desperate plight of those who live in Egypt. The women who bear children are tormented and lament their giving birth. At that point Persian kings intervene and remove the Jews from Egypt to Jerusalem, and we are informed that "the son of perdition will soon come." The following oracle begins "In those days the lawless (one) will appear in the holy places," but at that point the text breaks off and the writer returns to discuss the Persian rise to power in much greater detail. This time the author describes how a native king from Heliopolis assisted the Persians in their conquest of Memphis. Finally, at the end of the chapter the king from Heliopolis is fully established in power and his reign is characterized by a short-lived era of peace, which immediately precedes the coming of the son of lawlessness.

The most difficult problem to be resolved in the study of the Apocalypse of Elijah is the historical significance of the various kings mentioned in the text. There are at least three possibilities:

1. All of the kings are drawn from a literary tradition, and the author himself believes or speculates that at some future date the first of these kings will appear.

2. Some of the kings had already appeared, but the author casts his work in the style of a seer who desires to warn his contemporaries of the imminent end of the age by joining their own history to that of the final age and casting it all in the form of a future prophecy.

3. The author has made use of a prior literary tradition or even a complete apocalypse from an earlier time, which he brought up to date by modifying details of the predicted future to conform more accurately to the actual course of history as he knew it.

Chapter 2 may be outlined in the following manner:

1. An introductory subtitle (2:1).
2. A description of historical events that will precede the advent of the Antichrist (2:2–28).
3. A lament for Egypt "in those days" (2:29–38).
4. A homiletical aside and announcement of the appearance of the lawless one (2:39f.).
5. A further description of historical events "in those days," which will precede the advent of the Antichrist (2:41–53).

The introductory subtitle in 2:1 introduces the remainder of the tractate, which begins with the discussion of an Assyrian king (2:3) and ends with a destruction of heaven and earth and the creation of new ones (5:23, 30, 38). If the subtitle has been correctly identified, its presence would suggest that the present work was created when an editor or writer joined the opening homily on fasting and prayer to an independent document that is described by this subtitle.

The first description of coming events, which begins at 2:2 and ends at 2:28, contains a series of references to kings who cannot be identified at this time. It clearly begins with an Assyrian king who is wicked. He is replaced by a pious king from the west. The new Chester Beatty Papyrus introduces an evil, demon-faced son (vs. 19), who seems to be responsible for the evil events described in verses 24–27.

The lament for Egypt begins in verse 2:29. It is characterized by a loose literary description of times of affliction, and (with the exception of a mention of three Persian kings in vs. 39) lacks specific allusion to political events. The lament is also characterized by the recurring phrase "in those days," which continues to the end of the chapter. This lament for Egypt begins immediately after the writer informs us that "the priests of the land will tear their clothes." The author may have intended the lament to represent the response of those priests. At the point where the lament ends, there is a homiletical aside addressed to the same priests of the land.

Verse 2:41 begins with the phrase "in those days," which generally introduces a larger paragraph. In this case, however, it simply contains an announcement that the lawless one will appear. One might expect the author to begin his treatment of that important figure at this point, but he immediately drops the subject and turns once again to events preceding the appearance of the son of lawlessness, whose more complete introduction is delayed until chapter 3.

Chapter 2 ends with the discussion of a war between Persians and Assyrians. In the midst of their struggle for Egypt, a native ruler appears at Heliopolis, sides with the Persians, and comes to power in Memphis as a righteous king. This portion of text is heavily influenced by a literary tradition that appears in the *Oracle of the Potter*,[1] an Egyptian text from the

---

[1] See C. C. McCown, "Egyptian Apocalyptic Literature," *HTR* 18 (1925) 397–400; L. Koenen, "Die Prophezeiungen des Töpfers," *Zeitschrift für Papyrologie und Epigraphie* 2 (1968) 178–209.

end of the third century B.C., surviving in three fragmentary Greek versions dated between the first and third centuries A.D. That text presents itself as an oracle given by a potter to King Amenophis concerning things that shall come to pass in Egypt. It was produced by native Egyptians who resented Greek domination of their land from Alexandria, which is referred to as "the city by the sea" that will be reduced to a place where fishermen dry their nets. Both the cities of Heliopolis, where the potter is buried in honor, and Memphis, where native rule should flourish, are mentioned favorably. The heart of the prophecy, however, is the prediction that a native king who will rule bountifully will appear from the sun and be established by Isis so that those who survive will call upon the dead to arise and share the good things with them. The literary tradition regarding that native king obviously plays a part in the righteous king from the "city of the sun" (2:46) who comes to power in Memphis and introduces "abundant well being" (2:52) so that the living will say to the dead, "Rise up and be with us in this rest" (2:53). It can be concluded, therefore, that in addition to apocalyptic motifs inherited from Jewish and Christian literature, the author has drawn on motifs attested in Egyptian apocalyptic writing.

Chapter 3
This chapter contains a discussion of the following matters:
1. The advent of the son of lawlessness (1:1).
2. The signs of the advent of the true Christ (1:2–4).
3. The works of the Antichrist (1:5–13).
4. The physical signs of the Antichrist (1:14–18).

The main concern of this section is the figure of the son of lawlessness, who falsely claims to be the Christ. His works are reported and his physical signs given. The description of the advent of the true Christ (1:2–4) is obviously a digression inserted by a Christian editor of this work. The descriptions of the physical signs of the Antichrist, however, are well known from such late Hebrew texts as the Apocalypse of Zerubbabel, the Prayer of Simon ben Yochai, the Signs of the Messiah, and Midrash Wayissou, which were published by A. Jellinek in his *Bet ha-Midrash*.[2] Although there are also parallel descriptions in later Christian texts, it is difficult to believe that Jewish writers would borrow their basic description of the physical appearance of the man of lawlessness from Christians. Therefore, it may be assumed that the parallel portions of our present text originated in Jewish circles. Of course, in its present form the entire section was reworked by a Christian editor who inserted the description of the true Christ and modified the description of the works of the Antichrist to agree with a Christian typology.

From chapter 3 we learn little about the speaker or his audience, which is addressed in a homiletical style (cf. e.g. 3:1, 13f., 18). There is also little evidence for dating this section; all that can be said is that the description of the true Christ is post-Christian, and that it is later than the Jewish document to which it was joined.

Chapter 4
This chapter may be outlined in the following manner:
1. The martyrdom of Tabitha (4:1–6).
2. The martyrdom of Elijah and Enoch (4:7–19).
3. The persecution of the righteous (4:20–29).
4. The martyrdom of the sixty righteous men (4:30–33).

One of the noticeable literary features of this section is the manner in which the martyrdoms parallel one another. The following chart displays the most obvious parallels:

TABITHA	ELIJAH-ENOCH	SIXTY MARTYRS
will hear that the shameless one has revealed himself in the holy place	will hear that the shameless one has revealed himself in the holy place	will hear
she will put on her garment		they will gird on the breastplate

[2] A. Jellinek, *Bet ha-Midrash* (Jerusalem, 1938) vol. 2, pp. 54–57 (Apocalypse of Zerubbabel); vol. 4, pp. 117–26 (Simon ben Yochai); vol. 2, pp. 58–63 (The Signs of the Messiah); vol. 3, pp. 1–5 (Midrash Wayissou).

she will pursue him up to Judea scolding him up to Jerusalem	they will come down and fight with him	they will run to Jerusalem and fight with the shameless one
Tabitha delivers a speech scolding the shameless one	Elijah and Enoch deliver a speech scolding the shameless one	the sixty deliver a speech scolding the shameless one
then the shameless one will be angry	the shameless one will hear and he will be angry	he will hear and he will be angry
description of martyrdom resurrection of Tabitha	description of martyrdom resurrection of Elijah and Enoch	description of martyrdom
a second scolding speech	a second scolding speech two additional episodes which include an ascension	

The Elijah-Enoch martyrdom, written in Christian circles, is strongly influenced by the martyrdom of the two witnesses in Revelation 11:1–12. Most interpreters of Revelation identify the two witnesses described there as Elijah and Moses, but from the time of Hippolytus onward a number of Church Fathers reinterpreted the passage in Revelation to apply to Enoch and Elijah, the two men who had never died. Since Elijah was taken to heaven in a fiery chariot (2Kgs 2:11), it was generally assumed that he never died. The case for Moses, although less clear, was made in certain Jewish circles because the burial place of Moses was never found (Deut 34:5f.). The case for Enoch was stronger than the one for Moses, and probably much older since it is clearly set forth in 1 Enoch. Consequently, it was possible for Christian exegetes to replace Moses with Enoch, particularly if they had misgivings about Moses' reputed longevity.[3]

The Martyrdom of Tabitha was also composed by a Christian author. The name, which means "gazelle," is that of a woman from Joppa, who was also known as Dorcas. In Acts 9:36–41 a story is told of the manner in which Peter raised her from the dead. Lacking any report of her subsequent death, it must have been assumed that she was still alive and would survive in order to serve as a witness in the last days. Her speeches are quite similar to those of Enoch and Elijah, and like them she is resurrected to deliver a concluding rebuke to the shameless one.

When we turn to the story of the sixty martyrs, the account is much simpler. It has nothing that marks it as distinctively Christian. There is no resurrection. There is nothing to suggest that the sixty men previously shared the "deathless" nature of the first three martyrs. When they speak of the powers of the shameless one, they liken them to the powers "which the prophets have done," a phrase that contrasts with a Christian version in 3:12, "He will do the works which the Christ did." The context in which the third martyrdom is set is smoother than that of the earlier martyrdoms. Tabitha heard about the appearance of the shameless one and accused him of being "hostile to all the saints," but the persecution of the saints had not yet been described. In the case of the sixty, however, they girded on their armor and fought with the shameless one in response to the persecution of the saints after it is fully described. The present location of this martyrdom is anticlimactic. The first two martyrdoms are far more spectacular. Tabitha was resurrected to scold a second time. Enoch and Elijah are resurrected, scold and fight again, and apparently ascend in full view of all the people of the world. It is difficult to see why anyone would want to add a relatively simple martyrdom tale concerning sixty pious men immediately after such a spectacular account. It is more reasonable to assume that the spectacular accounts were inserted into an original martyr tale written on a more modest scale.

In view of the preceding arguments, the present section may be understood to have

---

[3] For a brief discussion on the manner in which Enoch came to be more highly regarded in Christian circles than in early rabbinic circles cf. G. H. Box, *APOT*, vol. 1, p. 482; J. T. Milik, *The Books of Enoch: Aramaic Fragments of Qumran Cave 4* (Oxford, 1976) p. 7. Cf. also R. Bauckham, "The Martyrdom of Enoch and Elijah: Jewish or Christian?" *JBL* 95 (1976) 447–58.

originally contained a Jewish account of the persecution of the saints followed by the martyrdom of the sixty. A later Christian editor inserted the first two martyrdoms. There are also some features in the account of the persecution of the saints, such as the dominical words of the Christ in 4:27, that suggest that the Christian editor expanded the original persecution scene.

As with chapter 3 we learn little about the speaker, although he could be a prophet. This chapter lacks the type of direct address that was found in the previous chapter. It is written in a narrative style and was possibly intended for general circulation within the Jewish and Christian communities. The section does not contain any specific historical allusions that might be of significance for dating either its Christian or Jewish strata.

Chapter 5
The oracles in the final chapter describe the following events:
1. Many who witness the persecution of the righteous flee from the Antichrist and denounce him (5:1).
2. The Christ sends angels to save those who are sealed. Gabriel and Uriel lead them to paradise (5:2–6).
3. Cosmic signs occur and sinners rebuke the Antichrist because he misled them so that they are destined to suffer famine and thirst (5:7–14).
4. The Antichrist laments his end, pursues the saints, and fights against the angels (5:15–21).
5. There is a description of a cosmic fire (5:22f.).
6. The byways speak describing the coming judgment (5:24–29).
7. After a description of the Lord's judgment, Elijah and Enoch return to kill the son of lawlessness (5:30–32).
8. There is a description of the death of the Antichrist (5:33–35).
9. The chapter concludes with a description of the beginning of the millennium (5:36–39).

The series of oracles found in this section is somewhat difficult to analyze. There are no specific historical references. The material is drawn from traditional apocalyptic lore common to both Judaism and early Christianity. On the basis of what we have concluded about the admixture of Jewish and Christian materials in the previous sections, we are inclined to confront the present section with the *a priori* assumption that it contains an early Jewish stratum that has been supplemented by a Christian editor. Unfortunately, the process of disentangling the Jewish and Christian strata will require a considerable amount of further research. At this point in our research we can only point to isolated examples that support our *a priori* assumption.

One example of the mixing of Jewish and Christian strata may be seen at 5:2–6, where there appear to be two slightly different versions of the salvation of the saints. The second version may well be the earlier one. It describes the return of the saints to Eden in terms of the Exodus motif. "Gabriel and Uriel will become a pillar of light leading them into the holy land." The version that now stands first is somewhat more elaborate and betrays a Christian inclination. The Christ will send sixty-four thousand angels to save "those upon whose forehead the name of Christ is written." That statement should be contrasted with the statement in 1:9, where it is "the Lord" who is quoted as saying that "I will write my name upon their forehead." The reference in 5:11 to "the Christ who created us" also helps to identify this portion of the text as the work of a Christian writer.

A second example of the mixing of strata may be seen in the doublet concerning the burning of the earth. The earlier version occurs at 5:22f., where "the Lord" commands the fire that prevails over the earth in a manner reminiscent of the Flood story. The Christian version is found at 5:36f., where "the Christ" comes forth with his saints and it is reported that "He will burn the earth."

There is no clear identification of either the speaker or the audience in this chapter, but presumably it is intended to be taken as the word of a prophet addressed to the larger community of Christians and Jews. The chapter opens with people fleeing from the Antichrist, who persecuted sixty righteous men in Jerusalem; but the scene is enlarged in this section when the writers begin to describe the final events on a cosmic scale.

Text

Until recently, the two most important manuscripts of the Apocalypse of Elijah were those edited by G. Steindorff.[4] The earliest manuscript, which Steindorff dated in the fourth century, was written in Akhmimic, and the second manuscript, which he dated at the beginning of the fifth century, was written in Sahidic. In addition to the Apocalypse of Elijah, both manuscripts contained the text of the Apocalypse of Zephaniah. The history of both of these manuscripts was discussed in the introduction to the Apocalypse of Zephaniah, to which the reader is referred.

In addition to the two manuscripts published by Steindorff, fragments of two additional manuscripts have long been available. One was written in Sahidic and the other in Greek. The Sahidic fragment, which contains only the opening section of the text, was written at the end of a manuscript now preserved in the British Museum as *Orient.* 7594; it was published by E. A. W. Budge in 1912.[5] The manuscript contained the books of Deuteronomy, Jonah, and Acts. The Sahidic fragment itself was added in a later hand and has been dated in the first half of the fourth century.[6]

The Greek fragment contains only a few words that parallel the Akhmimic text at 5:30–32. Nevertheless, it is an important witness to support the assumption that there was a Greek text underlying the present Coptic texts. It also bears witness to the close relationship between the Greek text and the Akhmimic translation. The fragment, which was first published by E. Pistelli,[7] was also dated in the fourth century.

Of the manuscripts available at the time when the present translation was begun, the Akhmimic manuscript was the most complete. Consequently, the Akhmimic text was chosen as the basis for the translation presented here. After that translation was completed, a new papyrus manuscript (4th–5th cent.) from the Chester Beatty Library and Gallery of Oriental Art (inventory no. 1493) was edited by A. Pietersma, S. T. Comstock, and H. Attridge.[8] During the final stages of preparing the present work for publication, the editors of the Chester Beatty Papyrus very generously permitted me to make use of a prepublication version of their text so that it was possible to take advantage of many of its readings to supplement and improve the present translation. The Chester Beatty Papyrus is the most complete manuscript now available. It is written in Sahidic and covers ten folios, which contain the text of the Apocalypse of Elijah from verse 1:1 to 5:15a.

Inasmuch as the Akhmimic text contains three lacunae, it had to be supplemented by following the Sahidic text. The only manuscript evidence available for the Sahidic text at the time the translation was begun was the manuscript published by Steindorff,[9] and that was used to fill in two lacunae. It was not possible to fill in the third lacuna until a copy of the Chester Beatty Papyrus was made available, because it is the only manuscript that contains that portion of the text. As a result of the procedure that had to be followed, the basic text used for the present translation is the Akhmimic version, but it was supplemented by readings taken from Sahidic manuscripts in the following manner:

Chapter 1:1–2:15b	follows the Akhmimic text.
Chapter 2:15b–2:30a	follows the Chester Beatty Papyrus.
Chapter 2:30b–4:2	follows the Akhmimic text.
Chapter 4:3–4:15a	follows the Sahidic manuscript edited by Steindorff.
Chapter 4:15b–5:13a	follows the Akhmimic text.
Chapter 5:13b–5:23a	follows the Sahidic manuscript edited by Steindorff.
Chapter 5:23b–5:39	follows the Akhmimic text.

---

[4] *Die Apokalypse des Elias, eine unbekannte Apokalypse und Bruchstücke der Sophonias-Apokalypse.*
[5] *Coptic Biblical Texts in the Dialect of Upper Egypt,* pp. lv–lvii, 270f.
[6] See the review of Budge's work by W. E. Crum in *ZDMG* 66 (1912) 782.
[7] *Papiri greci e latini,* vol. 1, p. 16, no. 7.
[8] *The Apocalypse of Elijah: Based on Pap. Chester Beatty 1493.*
[9] *Die Apokalypse des Elias.*

Ancient witnesses

Both Steindorff[10] and J.-M. Rosenstiehl[11] have provided surveys of ancient witnesses to apocryphal works that have been attributed to Elijah. There are three types of witnesses: early lists of canonical and noncanonical works, citations in early Christian writings, and a complete Hebrew text also known as the Apocalypse of Elijah.

The most important lists are: the Stichometry of Nicephorus, the closely related Synopsis of Sacred Scripture of Pseudo-Athanasius, the Catalogue of the Sixty Canonical Books, and a list of ancient works preserved in the Apostolic Constitutions. Most lists do not provide much information about the text beyond the canonical status and the title, which may appear in a slightly different form from list to list. The Stichometry of Nicephorus, however, reports that the length of the work was 316 *stichoi* (lines). On the basis of that bit of information, Steindorff[12] noted that the work was approximately the same length as Paul's Epistle to the Galatians. He then compared the length of a Coptic (Bohairic) text of Galatians with the length of the Coptic (Akhmimic) text of the Apocalypse of Elijah and discovered that the Apocalypse of Elijah was about 7 percent shorter than Galatians. Nevertheless, Bohairic may be written a bit more pleonastically than Akhmimic, and the parallel is probably close enough to represent a recension of the Apocalypse of Elijah cited in the Stichometry of Nicephorus. An argument of that type merely establishes the *possibility* that the present text is the one mentioned by Nicephorus. The possibility is strengthened by two facts: First, it is significant that we have five surviving manuscripts of the present work. That would indicate that it was rather widely used, an important criterion for a work to be included in the ancient lists. Secondly, it should be noted that the present text circulated in two separate manuscripts with the Apocalypse of Zephaniah. In the lists of Nicephorus and Pseudo-Athanasius, the two works are listed side by side. In the Catalogue of the Sixty Canonical Books the order of books is: the Apocalypse of Elijah, the Vision of Isaiah, and the Apocalypse of Zephaniah.

At the present stage of research, we can only speak of the possibility that the ancient lists referred to the present Apocalypse of Elijah because citations in early Christian writings clearly bear witness to other works attributed to Elijah. In his *Commentary on Matthew* (27:9) Origen traced Paul's quotation in I Corinthians 2:9 to the Apocalypse of Elijah (*in Secretis Eliae*). Jerome (Epistle 101 to Pammachius and *Commentary on Isaiah*, vol. 17) did not deny that the quotation was to be found in the Apocalypse of Elijah, but he denies that Paul was dependent on an apocryphal work. The relevant point, however, is that the ancients were familiar with an Apocalypse of Elijah that spoke of things "which the eye has not seen nor the ear heard." No such phrase is to be found in our apocalypse.

Three ancient witnesses attribute citations to Elijah without specifically identifying the work that contained them as the Apocalypse of Elijah. The first of these is Epiphanius (*AdvHaer* 42), who claimed that the quotation in Ephesians 5:14 was circulated "in Elijah" (*empheretai para tōi Ēliai*). That quotation is not found in the Coptic Apocalypse of Elijah. The second witness is the writer of the Pseudo-Titus Epistle.[13] He attributed a description of souls tormented in Gehenna to "the prophet Elijah." No such description is found in the Coptic Apocalypse of Elijah. The third witness is a Greek fragment published by F. Nau,[14] which contains a description of the Antichrist quite similar to the description that appears in the Testament of the Lord; but the Greek description is introduced by the statement that "Elijah the prophet spoke concerning the Antichrist." In that case, the fragment parallels an episode in the Coptic Apocalypse of Elijah that contains a description of the Antichrist, but the details of the two descriptions are quite different.

The only other complete Apocalypse of Elijah to survive is a Hebrew text published by A. Jellinek.[15] The Hebrew text is significantly different from the Coptic work. It more nearly approximates the form of an apocalypse. The text begins with a detail from 1 Kings 19:5,

---

[10] Ibid., pp. 20–22.
[11] *L'Apocalypse d'Élie*, pp. 13–15.
[12] *Die Apokalypse des Elias*, p. 14.
[13] See HSW, vol. 2, p. 158.
[14] F. Nau, "Methodius-Clement-Andronicus," *Journal Asiatic* 9 (1917) 454.
[15] *Bet ha-Midrash*, vol. 3, pp. 65–68.

where we are told that Elijah "lay down and slept under a broom tree; and behold an angel touched him." The writer of the apocalypse then informs us that Michael, the Great Prince, revealed to Elijah on Mount Carmel a vision concerning the end. The vision begins with a brief spiritual tour of various heavenly regions, in which he sees a burning fire, stars in combat, and souls being judged according to their deeds. Then he is told that a false ruler (i.e. the Antichrist), who is known by many different names, will appear. A description of the "signs" of that ruler is given. This one section has close parallels with the Coptic Apocalypse of Elijah. Thereafter the Hebrew apocalypse describes the various kings who will appear at the end of the age, the advent of the Messiah, and various other eschatological events. Although both the Hebrew Apocalypse of Elijah and the Coptic Apocalypse of Elijah deal to some extent with similar matters, the only point of close verbal agreement is in the description of the signs of the Antichrist.

When Jellinek first published the text of the Hebrew Apocalypse of Elijah, he traced its composition to Persia in the Gaonic period,[16] but there is reason to believe that the writer made use of much earlier traditions. That possibility was rather clearly established with regard to the signs of the Antichrist by W. Bousset[17] and more recently by J.-M. Rosenstiehl.[18] One suspects that there are other antique traditions contained in the Hebrew Apocalypse of Elijah. Steindorff was probably correct in suggesting that it is possible that "both writings have been partially created out of the same Hebrew source."[19]

Original language

Portions of the text of the Apocalypse of Elijah have survived in both the Sahidic and Akhmimic dialects of Coptic as well as in Greek. It is generally assumed that the Apocalypse was translated from Greek, and there is no reason to deny that assumption, especially in light of the existence of a fragment of Greek text that has survived.

When Steindorff published his edition of *Die Apokalypse des Elias*, he offered convincing evidence that the Sahidic version was translated from Akhmimic.[20] The evidence was primarily in the form of unusual Akhmimic features that appeared in the Sahidic text which he edited. It seemed reasonable to assume that a translator of the Sahidic text found some puzzling constructions in the text from which he worked. Being unable to translate them or careless about translating every expression, he allowed them to enter the Sahidic text. In strong contrast to the Sahidic manuscript edited by Steindorff, the newly discovered Chester Beatty Papyrus provides a different sort of evidence. It contains essentially the same Sahidic text as that found in Steindorff's edition, but without the unusual Akhmimic features. It is also more extensive. On the basis of a limited study of the evidence provided by the new Chester Beatty Papyrus, it seems reasonable to conclude that the Akhmimic and Sahidic texts represent independent translations from the Greek. The problem deserves further study. The strange Akhmimic features in Steindorff's Sahidic manuscript remain puzzling. Perhaps they are due to a scribe whose native dialect was Akhmimic, thereby making him more familiar with the Akhmimic version.

Date

Since there are Coptic manuscripts of the present text dated to the early fourth century at the latest, the original Greek text can scarcely be later than the end of the third century. On the other hand, the text in its present form is obviously post-Christian. At verses 4:13f. there seems to be dependence on Revelation 11:8f. At verse 1:2 there is apparently a quotation from 1 John 2:15, a writing that shares with the Apocalypse of Elijah a concern for the last days and the coming of the Antichrist (1Jn 2:18). The dating of these documents from the Johannine circle remains a problem for New Testament scholars. Nevertheless, an extremely

---

[16] Ibid., p. xviii.

[17] *The Antichrist Legend*, trans. A. H. Keane (London, 1896) pp. 108f., 156.

[18] "Le Portrait de l'antichrist," *Pseudépigraphes de l'Ancien Testament et manuscrits de la mer mort*, vol. 1, pp. 45–63.

[19] *Die Apokalypse des Elias*, p. 22.

[20] Ibid., pp. 16–18, 23–31.

conservative guess at the date when both 1 John and Revelation might be available for use together by a Christian writer in Egypt would scarcely fall before the middle of the second century. Consequently, it is possible to set a reasonable date somewhere between A.D. 150 and 275 for the final composition of the present work. Such scholars as E. Schürer,[21] W. Bousset,[22] and J.-M. Rosenstiehl[23] have concluded that the work must be dated after the middle of the third century, and it is probable that the document was composed closer to 275 than to 150. Nevertheless, most of the evidence used for dating the text will need to be revised in terms of the additional information provided by the new Chester Beatty Papyrus. Although the new portion of text is not large, it radically changes our understanding of chapter 2, the primary chapter consulted by previous scholars in an attempt to discover historical allusions of value for dating. Until scholars have time to appraise carefully the new material, the date of the final composition should be left open.

Most scholars who have studied the Apocalypse of Elijah have concluded that it is a composite work containing both Jewish and Christian materials. The task of sorting out the various passages to be assigned to each group is still being pursued. Once that has reached a state of general consensus, it will be possible to examine the Jewish data separately and propose a date for its composition. That task should be carried out with a close examination of related Jewish works such as the Hebrew Apocalypse of Elijah,[24] in order to determine more precisely the nature of a possible common ancestor. Until that is done, any statement about a date for the earlier Jewish material in this tractate remains too conjectural. Nevertheless, the Jewish stratum seems to predate the destruction of the Jewish quarter in Alexandria in A.D. 117.

Provenance

The events described in chapters 3 and 4 are eschatological events that will take place in Jerusalem. They are part of the eschatological lore that anticipates the appearance of the Messiah in that city. Chapter 3, however, describes events that will occur in Egypt before the time of the Antichrist. It is that interest in Egypt which betrays the provenance of the writers of this work. The Jewish community in Alexandria may have been the home of the writer of the Jewish portions of the work. Chapter 2:15 apparently mentions the removal of "the wise men" to that city. It is quite possible that the Christian reworking of the document also took place in that city. One of the sources of the present work is the *Oracle of the Potter*,[25] which expresses a very hostile attitude toward "the city by the sea." In the present text, the hostility is removed, and the wise men are taken there in much the same way as Jews are returned to Jerusalem in 2:39.

Theological concerns

The theology of the present document is not the product of a single writer or community. It is only natural that a work that contains both Jewish and Christian strata would express different theological concerns in different parts of the document. Therefore, it is obvious that a simple survey of the various statements concerning God, angels, and men would scarcely do justice to the complexity of this important text. It is also obvious that no final statement can be made about the theological concerns of the several parts of the document until research on the present text reaches a point where there is general agreement on the respective Jewish and Christian components. Therefore, the following survey must be limited to an attempt to review the theological content of the text on the basis of our present understanding.

A discussion of the theology of the various chapters of this document must distinguish between the earlier Jewish stratum and the later Christian additions. From a literary point of view, it is probable that the Jewish document itself was composed of several different

---

[21] *Geschichte des jüdischen Volkes im Zeitalter Jesu Christi* (Leipzig, 1898–1901) vol. 3, p. 368.
[22] *Die Religion des Judentums in späthellenistischen Zeitalter* (Tübingen, 1926) p. 46.
[23] *L'Apocalypse d'Élie*, p. 75.
[24] Jellinek, *Bet ha-Midrash*, vol. 3, pp. 65–68.
[25] See n. 1.

sources. It is quite likely that chapter 1, which deals with prayer and fasting, was once an independent document. However, there are only very slight differences between the basic theological framework of the Jewish portion of chapter 1 and the theology expressed elsewhere in the Jewish stratum. Consequently, it is possible to describe the Jewish theology contained within this document as a unity.

The view of God expressed in the Jewish document is that he is the enthroned Creator of the heavens who has prepared a place for the righteous. One slight discrepancy between chapter 1 and the rest of the document is that in chapter 1 the place prepared with thrones and crowns is within a heavenly city. Elsewhere the place of the righteous is expressed in terms of Exodus typology as a "place of rest" or "the holy land," which is likened to the garden of Eden, where the tree of life is found.

The God who appears in the Jewish document may also be described as a Lord of history who raises up kingdoms and brings them down as he hastens this age to its end. The righteous kings are opposed to idols, confess that the name of God "is one," and care for his house. God demands that his Law be obeyed, and prepares his wrath for sinners who disobey. Under his command are angels—including Gabriel and Uriel—who lead the righteous to their place of reward. There are also thrones of death who bar the way for the unrighteous, and there are demons who probably served to punish sinners.

Within the world there is a dualism of good and evil. The righteous obey the Law and are part of the Covenant. The sinners disobey and are cut off from the Covenant so that they are under God's wrath. The kingdoms of the earth are also good or evil as each one follows in its turn. As history moves toward its culmination, two human leaders will appear. The one expected to lead the righteous is a prophet like Moses, who will perform signs and wonders. The text does not describe this messianic figure directly. Knowledge of the Messiah must be extrapolated from the figure of the lawless one, who is a false Messiah. The false Messiah, who rules as an earthly monarch, will also do the signs and wonders that the prophets did, but the righteous will be able to recognize him by the signs on his head. Although the forces of evil come to dominate at the end of the age under the rule of the lawless one who will torture and slay the righteous, this world is not regarded as totally evil. So long as the righteous remain in it, the sun will rise and the earth will bear fruit. It is only when the righteous are removed that natural calamities will abound and the sun will fail to rise.

In its discussion of the final destiny of the righteous, the Jewish document contains an apparent discrepancy between chapter 1 and later sections of the text. In chapter 1, the righteous who die are led to a heavenly city by the angels. Elsewhere we are told that those who flee the lawless one will "lie down as one who sleeps." Their spirit and soul returns to the Lord, but their body is turned into stone until the day of the great judgment when they will be resurrected and find a place of rest. Presumably the place of rest is the holy land, to which the righteous are led by Uriel and Gabriel. Although there is a conflict between this view and the one expressed in chapter 1, the Jewish writer who joined the two together apparently saw none. He could easily have interpreted the journey to the heavenly city as the route the soul followed after death to await the day of judgment and resurrection.

The destiny of the unrighteous is the opposite of that of the righteous. In chapter 1 they are prevented from reaching the heavenly city by the thrones of death. Elsewhere the wrath of God is brought upon them in the form of a final judgment by fire. They do not share in the rest. There is no way of knowing whether or not the writer expected the unrighteous to be resurrected for their final judgment. There is no specific mention of it.

It is important to note the recurrence of the Exodus motif in the latter part of the document. It seems reasonable to assume that the writer's thinking about the Messiah and false Messiah was stimulated by Deuteronomy 18:18, 20. In verse 18 God promises to send a prophet like Moses, but in verse 20 he speaks of the false prophet who "presumes to say in my name a thing I have not commanded him to say." The problem of discerning between the true and the false eschatological prophets was of crucial importance to the writer of this text.

The Christian theology expressed in this text is strikingly different. This is true despite the fact that the Christian editor must have accepted in a general way the Jewish theology contained in the document he emended. In the Christian text, the merciful God of glory is virtually identified with the Christ, the Son of God. Both God and Christ are hailed as

Creator, and it is God who "changed himself (to be) like a man when he was about to come to us so that he might save us."

The dualism within the Christian additions is not between good and evil men, but it is between God and Satan. The son of lawlessness, the Antichrist, is identified with Satan in the same way that the Christ is identified with God. Within the world, the Christ is God incarnate and the Antichrist is Satan incarnate. Therefore the struggles are no longer those of human adversaries, but a cosmic struggle between God and Satan in an effort to remove man from captivity of this age and bring him to the kingdom of the Christ. The Christ is consistently portrayed as a triumphant divine figure, walking upon the clouds, shining like the sun, commanding sixty-four thousand angels. The Antichrist is painted in similar colors. He acts against heaven and is hostile to the thrones. He has fallen from heaven. He can do all of the works the Christ did except for giving life.

In contrast to the Jewish theology, which saw the struggle between good and evil largely in terms of human adversaries who were righteous or sinful men, the Christian theology views man as virtually a helpless pawn in the larger cosmic struggle. The world is conceived of as totally evil. Men are captives. All that they can do is to refuse to love the world and *endure* in the face of martyrdom. Since this world is so dominated by evil, the chief concern of men is to escape. That is possible for the pious who have turned from the world to "live in the Lord." The Antichrist has power to torture them and even kill them, but he has no power over their spirit or soul.

The final destiny of the pious is to live in the kingdom of Christ in a new heaven and a new earth, which will replace this evil one. The fate of the Antichrist is to be destroyed in the judgment by Elijah and Enoch, but his death is no more final for him than it was for the pious. After death he is to be cast to the bottom of the abyss together with all who believe in him.

Relation to canonical books

In its present form the Apocalypse of Elijah reflects a familiarity with the major collections of books within both the Old and New Testaments. The Old Testament works most frequently alluded to are the books within the Pentateuch and Prophets. The Apocalypse of Elijah begins in the style of a prophetic writing. In the Akhmimic text the prophet is called "son of man" (1:1) in imitation of the prophet Ezekiel. At 5:5 there is an obvious use of the Exodus motif. From the collection of later writings, an allusion to Ecclesiastes 12:7 may appear at 4:25. The figure of the lawless one who will appear in the holy places is ultimately derived from the book of Daniel.

Turning to the New Testament, the gospel tradition is most clearly reflected in the list of works the Antichrist will do in imitation of the true Christ (3:9f.). The influence of the Pauline corpus may be noted at many points, but it is most clearly illustrated at 2:41 and 3:1, which make use of the description of the advent of the man of lawlessness in 2 Thessalonians. Literature from the Johannine circle is used at 1:2, which contains a quotation from 1 John 2:15, and at 4:13–14, which is dependent on Revelation 11:8f. In light of the breadth of literary allusions that appear in this text, it is quite probable that the writer knew most if not all of the books of the Old and New Testaments. We cannot, of course, draw any final conclusion about the extent of his canon on the basis of that observation.

Relation to apocryphal books

In the notes that follow, attention is called to parallels that may be found in the Wisdom of Solomon and Sirach. Nevertheless, the parallels are not of such a nature as to suggest that the author of the Apocalypse of Elijah relied on those works. There are no *a priori* reasons why he might not have known that group of works traditionally referred to as the Old Testament Apocrypha, but neither is there clear evidence that he did. A similar observation may be made with regard to the larger group of anonymous Jewish writings composed between 200 B.C. and A.D. 200. The author discusses Enoch, but there is no obvious dependence on the books of Enoch. He shares apocalyptic motifs with the Sibylline Oracles and the Psalms of Solomon, but the very nature of apocalyptic speculation makes the source of such material difficult to determine.

Introduction to the translation

The translation is based on the Akhmimic text of the Apocalypse of Elijah where that is extant. When it is lacking, it is necessary to follow one or another of the Sahidic manuscripts. Chapters 4:3–4:15a and 5:13b–5:23b follow the Sahidic manuscript edited by Steindorff in *Die Apokalypse des Elias*. Chapter 2:15b–2:30a follows the Chester Beatty Papyrus edited by A. Pietersma, S. T. Comstock, and H. W. Attridge.[26]

In the notes that follow, reference is made to the Akhmimic text, the Sahidic text, and the several Sahidic manuscripts. Since there is only one Akhmimic manuscript, the designation "Akhmimic text" clearly refers to that unique manuscript. The term "Sahidic text" is used in an unqualified manner only when all of the Sahidic manuscripts available for that portion of the text agree. Otherwise the separate Sahidic manuscripts are named.

BIBLIOGRAPHY

Charlesworth, *PMR*, pp. 95–98.
Denis, *Introduction*, pp. 163–69.

Bouriant, U. "Les Papyrus d'Akhmim," *Memoires publiés pas les membres de la mission archéologique française au Caire*. Paris, 1885; vol. 1, pp. 260–79. (A partial publication of the text based on leaves of the MSS available to Bouriant in 1885.)

Bousset, W. *Der Antichrist in der Überlieferung des Judenthums, des Neuen Testaments und der Alten Kirche*. Göttingen, 1895; ET 1896. (This work provides an excellent background study for chs. 3–5.)

———. "Beitrage zur Geschichte der Eschatologie," *Zeitschrift für Kirchengeschichte* 20 (1900) 103–12. (Published the year after Steindorff's text appeared, this article provides a first attempt to interpret the text. He suggested that the text had a Jewish background, attempted to identify the historical allusions in ch. 3, and called attention to a number of parallel texts.)

Budge, E. A. W. *Coptic Biblical Texts in the Dialect of Upper Egypt*. London, 1912; pp. lv–lvii and 270–71. (This is the first publication of the Sahidic text of Or. 7594 from the BM. At the end of the MS a later scribe has added the opening portion of the Sahidic text.)

Lacau, P. "Remarques sur le manuscrit akhmimique des Apocalypses de Sophonie et d'Élie," *Journal asiatique* 254 (1966) 169–95. (This work contains a large number of helpful grammatical nn. on the text.)

McNeil, B. "Coptic Evidence of Jewish Messianic Beliefs (Apocalypse of Elijah 2:5–6)," *Revista degli Studi Orientali* 51 (1977) 39–45. (This article traces the literary background of the figure of a king who walks on water and roars like a lion. He believes that the figure provides "evidence about Jewish messianic beliefs in the first century A.D.")

Pietersma, A., Comstock, S. T., and Attridge, H. W. *The Apocalypse of Elijah: Based on Pap. Chester Beatty 2018*. T&T p. 19, Pseudepigrapha Series 9; Chico, Calif., 1981 (p.) (This important publication makes available the Chester Beatty Papyrus for the first time. The authors have indicated variant readings from all other MSS in the footnotes. Future studies of the Apocalypse of Elijah should begin with this edition of the text.)

Pistelli, E. *Papiri greci e latini*. Florence, 1912; vol. 2, p. 16, no. 7.

Rosenstiehl, J.-M. *L'Apocalypse d'Élie*. Paris, 1972. (This is the most significant recent study of ApEl. It contains an important introduction to the work, a translation, and extensive nn.)

---

[26] *The Apocalypse of Elijah.*

————. "Le Portrait de l'antichrist," *Pseudépigraphes de l'Ancien Testament et manuscrits de la mer mort*, ed. M. Philonenko. Paris, 1967; vol. 1, pp. 45–63.

Schmidt, C. "Der Kolophon des Ms. Orient. 7594 des Britischen Museums: Eine Untersuchung zur Elias-Apokalypse," *Sitzungsberichte der Preussischen Akademie der Wissenschaften, philosophisch-historische Klass.* Berlin, 1925; pp. 312–21. (In this article, Schmidt makes sense of the Colophon published by Budge in his *Coptic Biblical Texts in the Dialect of Upper Egypt.*)

Steindorff, G. *Die Apokalypse des Elias, eine unbekannte Apokalypse und Bruchstücke der Sophonias-Apokalypse.* TU 17; Leipzig, 1899. (This masterful work made the full text available in an essentially correct order for the first time. It is the starting point for all subsequent studies of the text.)

Till, W. "Bemerkungen und Ergänzungen zu den achmîmischen Textausgaben," *Zeitschrift für ägyptische Sprache und Altertumskunde* 63 (1928) 90f. (This work contains some helpful grammatical nn. on the text.)

Von Lemm, O. "Kleine koptische Studien, XXVI, 13–18," *Bulletin de l'académie impériale des sciences de Saint-Pétersbourg*, 5ᵉ série, 21 (1904) 045–050.

THE APOCALYPSE OF ELIJAH

The call of the prophet

1 **1** The word of the Lord came to me,[a] saying,[b] "Son of man, say to this people, `ApPaul 3`
'Why do you add sin to[c] your sins and anger[d] the Lord God who created you?' "[e] `Ezek 33:1f, 6:1, 12:1, 13:1, 14:2`
2 Don't love the world or the things which are in the world,[f] for the boasting[g] of `Isa 30:1` `Sir 3:27`
the world and its destruction belong to the devil. `PssSol 3:6,10` `1Jn 2:15`

Deliverance from captivity is through the Incarnate Son

3 Remember[h] that the Lord of glory,[i] who created everything,[j] had mercy upon
4 you so that he might save us[k] from the captivity of this age.[l] •For many times the `1En 22:14, 25:3`

1 a. For the opening phrase compare Ezek 33:1–2; 6:1; 12:1; 13:1; 14:2. G. Steindorff in *Die Apokalypse des Elias*, p. 67, called attention to a very close parallel in the ApPaul, which reads: "The word of the Lord came to me, saying, 'Say to this people, "How long will you sin and add to the sin and anger the God who created you?" ' " (ApPaul 3).

The last part of this quotation is parallel to the LXX version of Isa 30:1, which reads, "to add sins to sins."

The opening portion of this text has been preserved in the Sahidic text written at the end of BM MS 7594. The best edition of that Sahidic text was provided by C. Schmidt in "Der Kolophon des Ms. Orient. 7594 des Britischen Museums: Eine Untersuchung zur Elias-Apokalypse," *Sitzungsberichte der Preussischen Akademie der Wissenschaften, Philosophisch-Historische Klasse*, pp. 312–21. The Sahidic text differs from the Akhmimic slightly and is somewhat closer to the ApPaul. It reads "The word of the Lord came to me, saying to me, 'Say to this people, "Why do you sin and add (reading ⟨n⟩tetnoueh, with Schmidt) sin to your sin and anger (reading ⟨n⟩tetntičont, with Schmidt) the Lord God who created you?" ' " In agreement with the ApPaul the text of BM MS 7594 does not include the phrase "son of man," but it does include the phrase "why do you sin?" A similar Sahidic text is provided by the new Chester Beatty Papyrus.

In writing the phrase "to me," the scribe corrected an original *a* to *r* in writing *šarai*. The siglum { } indicates words (or letters) in the Cop. text that are otiose and, therefore, not translated. The siglum [| |] indicates a letter eliminated by the Cop. scribe in antiquity. The siglum ⟨ ⟩ indicates a passage omitted by the scribe.

b. The text of BM MS 7594 adds "to me" at this point.

c. Reading *aj* {*et*} *n*.

d. The word for anger in the Akhmimic text is *tinouks*. BM MS 7594 and the Chester Beatty Papyrus read *tičõnt*.

e. The Akhmimic text reads *etahtene-tẽne*. BM MS 7594 is to be read *pentaftamie-tẽutn* (the scribe wrote *pentauftamie-tẽutn*) in agreement with the Chester Beatty Papyrus.

f. A quotation from 1Jn 2:15. Cf. 1En 108:8; Jas 1:27; 4:4.

g. An important motif in several gnostic texts from Nag Hammadi is the "boasting" of the chief ruler of this world. Cf. CG II 103, 9; 107, 30; 112,

28; 86, 30; 94, 21. The biblical background for the boasting of a demonic power may be traced to Dan 11:36–39; 2Thes 2:3–4. Cf. AscenIs 4:2. J.-M. Rosenstiehl in *L'Apocalypse d'Élie*, p. 79, called attention to a large number of parallel passages in the Pseudepigrapha as well as in other Jewish and Christian writings that share this writer's negative view of the present world and its domination by Satan.

h. The style of this first section is homiletical. It was written to be preached. The literary units in this section begin with exhortations to "remember" or "hear." These exhortations recall the rhetorical style of Deut. Cf. Deut 9:1; 6:4; 7:18; 8:2, 18; 20:3. Rosenstiehl, *L'Apocalypse d'Élie*, p. 29, has called attention to the similarity between 1:3 and 1:5. He thought that both sections were Christian interpolations, with intervening text from an earlier Jewish work. It is our opinion that the entire paragraph was introduced by the Christian editor.

i. The Akhmimic text reads "the Lord of glory." BM MS 7594 and the Chester Beatty Papyrus read only "the Lord." The expression "Lord of glory" is a frequent epithet in 1En. Cf. 1En 22:14; 25:3; 27:3, 5; 36:4; 40:3; 63:2; 75:3; 83:8. If Milik's reconstruction of the Qumran fragments of 1En 22:14 is correct, the original Ar. phrase read *mr' rbwt'*. See his work *The Books of Enoch: Aramaic Fragments* (Oxford, 1976) p. 218.

j. Reading *etahtano nho⟨b⟩ nim*. BM MS 7594 and the Chester Beatty Papyrus read *pentaftamie nka nim*. Rosenstiehl, *L'Apocalypse d'Élie*, p. 80, has called attention to the juxtaposition of the double motif of Creator who also delivers from captivity. He notes the parallels in Isa 44:24f.; 40:21–26; 41:17–20.

k. In the phrase "had mercy upon *you* so that he might save *us*," Rosenstiehl, *L'Apocalypse d'Élie*, p. 80, assumed that the shift of pronoun was due to a confusion between the Greek words *humin* and *hēmin*. It is also possible that a person writing in a homiletical style might have intended the shift. Compare the well-known pronominal change in the famous "credo" of Deut 26:5–10.

l. The idea of souls in captivity in this world was a widespread feature of gnostic theology. CG II 114, 20 contains a simple, basic statement of this doctrine. It reads "And these are the ones who are taken captive by the First Father according to lot. And thus they were shut up in the prisons of the moulded bodies until the consummation of the eon." Cf. Eph 4:8.

devil desired not to let the sun rise[m] above the earth and not to let the earth yield fruit,[n] since he desires to consume men like a fire[o] which rages in stubble,[p] and 5 he desires to swallow[q] them like water.[r] •Therefore, on account of this,[s] the God of glory[t] had mercy upon us, and he sent his son to the world[u] so that he might 6 save us from the captivity.[v] •He did not inform an angel or an archangel or any principality[w] when he was about to come to us,[x] but he changed himself to be like a man[y] when he was about to come to us so that he might[z] save us [from flesh].[a2] 7 Therefore become sons to him since he is a father to you.

Eph 4:8
Mal 4:1
Joel 2:5
Acts 7:2
Jn 3:17, 10:36
Phil 2:6-8

What is prepared for both the sealed and the sinners

8 Remember that he has prepared thrones and crowns[b2] for you in heaven, saying, "Everyone who will obey[c2] me will receive thrones and crowns among those who 9 are mine."[d2] •The Lord said, "I will write my name[e2] upon their forehead and I

Col 1:16; Jas 1:12
Rev 20:4
Rev 3:12, 7:3, 14:1, 7:16

---

m. Rosenstiehl, *L'Apocalypse d'Élie*, p. 80, calls attention to 5:18, where the writer claims that it is because of the saints that the sun shines above the earth. He also calls attention to a number of texts dealing with the deceits and plots of the devil.

The present text contains a number of features that suggest an Egyptian origin. At this point, one is reminded of the Apophis myth. Apophis was a serpent of the Underworld who continually sought to hinder the sun god on his daily journey. For the Christian editor of this text, the devil, who is incarnate as the Antichrist, may be conceived of as a serpent. Cf. 5:33, where the Antichrist is said to "perish like a serpent which has no breath in it."

n. Written *ati[|a|]karpos*. In 5:18 the fertility of the land is also attributed to the presence of the saints.

o. BM MS 7594 and the Chester Beatty Papyrus read "the fire."

p. Reading *etpēt ḫn ouróoui*, lit. "which runs within straw." The reading is supported by BM MS 7594 and the Chester Beatty Papyrus, which read *efpēt ḫn ourooue*, but the Akhmimic MS reads *efpēt ḫn ouḫray*," lit. "who runs with a shout" or "roar." Cf. 1Pet 5:8. Rosenstiehl, *L'Apocalypse d'Élie*, p. 115, has cited the following parallels for the figure of fire-destroying stubble: Ex 15:7; Isa 5:24; Nah 1:10; Mal 3:19; Joel 2:5; WisSol 3:7; 1En 48:9; 6Ezra 15:23; 1QM 11.10.

q. The Cop. word for "swallow" is *ōmk*. It was translated "consume" in the preceding line.

r. One tradition that developed in the OT was the view that the world, which had once been destroyed by a flood, was threatened with a future destruction by fire. Cf. Zeph 1:2-3, which recalls the flood imagery of Gen 7:4, 23, and Zeph 1:18. The fire imagery is a figure rooted in the practice of *ḥerem*, which involved burning all the booty after a holy war. When the wicked are finally destroyed in a cosmic holy war, all things will be consumed by fire. Cf. Joel 2:30; 2Pet 3:10. In the present text, however, it is the devil who is held responsible for the desire to consume men like fire and like water. Rosenstiehl, *L'Apocalypse d'Élie*, p. 80, sees the devil as the executive of God's wrath against Sodom (fire) and against the sinners of Noah's time (water). He also notes the imagery in Ex 15:4-7; Rev 12:15; and Hos 5:10, which is quoted in CD 19.15.

s. BM MS 7594 and the Chester Beatty Papyrus read "and on account of this." They lack "There-fore."

t. At 1:3 the Akhmimic text reads "Lord of glory," which is familiar from 1En. The expression "God of glory" is familiar from Acts 7:2 and Ps 29(LXX 28):3. The passage in Pss is based on a Heb. *'l hkbwd*. Contrast the phrase *mr' rbwt'*, which Milik, *Books of Enoch*, identified as the Ar. antecedent for "Lord of glory" in Enoch. See n. i above.

u. Reading *aftnnau* instead of the scribe's *aftnnaf*. The Chester Beatty Papyrus reads *afnatnnoou*, "He will send." Passages such as Jn 3:17 and 10:36 immediately come to mind. Rosenstiehl, *L'Apocalypse d'Élie*, pp. 49, 80, compares theology of Isa 63:8–9 (LXX) and cites a long list of Jewish texts that treat "Son of God" as a messianic title.

v. The scribe wrote *aijmalōsia* for *aichmalōsia* here and elsewhere.

w. The phrase "or any principality" is lacking in BM MS 7594 and the Chester Beatty Papyrus.

x. Steindorff, *Die Apokalypse des Elias*, p. 68, called attention to the parallel in *Ep. ad Diognetum* 7:2. Could this passage reflect a tradition contrary to the Lucan birth narratives?

y. Cf. Phil 2:6–8. Rosenstiehl, *L'Apocalypse d'Élie*, p. 81, called attention to several Christian interpolations in the T12P: TAsh 7:3; TSim 6:5, 7; TBenj 10:7.

z. BM MS 7594 breaks off at this point, except for a few fragments. It is lacking for about fourteen lines and resumes at vs. 1:13 of the Akhmimic text.

a2. There is a lacuna in the Akhmimic text. The Chester Beatty Papyrus has preserved the writing *[s]qrx*, which would neatly fill the Akhmimic lacuna when joined with the preposition *hn*.

b2. Cf. Rev 2:10; 20:4. Rosenstiehl, *L'Apocalypse d'Élie*, p. 81, has already called attention to WisSol 5:16; 1En 108:12; 4Ezra 2:46; AscenIs 9:25; and 1QS 4.7.

c2. The scribe began to write *eta*, but corrected the *a* to *n* and continued to write *etnacōtme nsōi*. The Chester Beatty Papyrus reads "everyone who will obey *his Voice*."

d2. "Those who are mine" are probably the righteous, but they might include angels.

e2. Cf. Rev 3:12; 7:3; 14:1; 20:4. Rosenstiehl, *L'Apocalypse d'Élie*, p. 49, calls attention to Ex 13:9; Deut 6:8. On p. 82 he cites passages that describe men, both good and evil, who were marked by God.

10 will seal their right hand, and they will not hunger or thirst.[f2] •Neither will the son   2Thes 2:3
of lawlessness[g2] prevail over them, nor will the thrones hinder them,[h2] but they
11 will walk with the angels[i2] up to my city.[j2]" •Now, as for the sinners, they will be   ApPaul 13:1, 14
shamed[k2] and they will not pass[l2] by the thrones, but the thrones of death[m2] will
12 seize them and rule over them because the angels will not agree with them. •They   ApPaul 15-16
have alienated themselves from his dwellings.

The deceivers who oppose the fast

13   Hear, O wise men of the land,[n2] concerning the deceivers[o2] who will multiply   2Tim 4:1-5
in the last times so that they will set down for themselves doctrines which do not
belong to God, setting aside the Law of God, those who have made their belly   Phil 3:19
their God,[p2] saying, "The fast[q2] does not exist, nor did God create it," making   3Mac 7:11
themselves strangers to the covenant of God[r2] and robbing[s2] themselves of the   Jer 22:9
14 glorious promises.[t2] •Now these are not ever correctly established[u2] in the firm   Eph 2:12
                                                                                        Jas 1:12, 2:5

f2. Cf. Isa 49:10; Rev 7:16.

g2. The "son of lawlessness" is the most fre-quent title used in this text to designate the An-tichrist. Cf. 3:1, 5, 13, 18; 4:2, 15, 20, 28, 31; 5:6, 10, 32. The Cop. reflects a Gk. *huios anomias*. That Gk. term is found in Ps 89:22 (LXX 88:22) in a context that speaks of David and his messianic heirs, assuring him that the son of lawlessness will not harm him again. The Heb. text reads *bn ʿwlh*, "son of wickedness," i.e. "a wicked person." "The man of lawlessness" in 2Thes 2:3 is obviously a similar figure.

h2. These thrones are members of the angelic host. Cf. Col 1:16. In vs. 1:11 they are characterized as "thrones of death," i.e. "angels of death," who seize sinners.

i2. Angels accompany the souls of the righteous as they leave the world. Cf. ApPaul 13, 14. In TAb the angel of death comes to Abraham disguised in beauty. In TIsaac and TJac, angels are sent for the souls of the Patriarchs. In the ApMos Gabriel re-moves the soul of Adam.

j2. "My city" is the heavenly Jerusalem. Cf. 4Ezra 8:52; 10:27; 2En 55:2; Heb 11:16; Phil 3:20.

k2. The Chester Beatty Papyrus lacks "they will be shamed."

l2. Reading *sena⟨ou⟩ōtbe*.

m2. Reading *nthronos mpmou*. The scribe wrote *ngmau*. These are the angels of death that confront the wicked. Cf. ApPaul 15f. for an example of the plight of a wicked soul after death.

n2. This phrase provides another example of the author's homiletical style. Rosenstiehl, *L'Apocalypse d'Élie*, p. 83, has called attention to "the wise" in Dan 11:33, 35; 12:3. He also noted the use of the term *mśkyl* in a technical sense at Qumran. At 2:15 below "the wise men" are taken to the metropolis by the sea.

o2. BM MS 7594 reads "these deceivers." Ro-senstiehl, *L'Apocalypse d'Élie*, p. 83, cites TJud 19:4 and other texts where Satan is described as "Prince of error." Cf. AsMos 7; Mt 24:11. 1Tim 4:1-5 provides an interesting counterpoint vis-à-vis the present text. Timothy describes those who en-join abstinence from foods as "giving heed to . . . doctrines of demons." In the present text, the author is attacking those who make their belly their God and fail to abstain.

p2. Reading ⟨e⟩*taueire ntouḥei nnounoute neu*. The scribe wrote *ntoune* instead of *nnoute*. BM MS 7594 and the Chester Beatty Papyrus read *ete peu-*

noute pe hētou, "whose belly is their God." Cf. Phil 3:19; 3Mac 7:11.

q2. Rosenstiehl, *L'Apocalypse d'Élie*, p. 83, has noted that this discussion of fasting may be ex-plained in a Jewish context. The most important single cultic fast in the OT is related to the Day of Atonement; compare Lev 16:29–31; 23:27–32; Num 29:7. The expression for fasting in those passages is "to afflict oneself." In *SpecLeg* 2.195, Philo says that a purpose of the fast that occurs on the Day of Atonement is to control the tongue, the belly, and the organs below the belly, a view of fasting similar to that of the present text.

There are a number of passages that deal with the fasting of individuals as a work of piety. Cf. Ezra 10:6; Neh 1:4; Dan 9:3; Jdt 8:5–6; TReu 1:10; TSim 3:4. The practice was enthusiastically sup-ported by the Pharisees and other Jewish sects (Lk 18:12; Mt 6:16–18), including the followers of John the Baptist (Mk 2:18–20). The fact that Jesus' earliest disciples were accused of not fasting sug-gests that during the life of Jesus the freedom to fast or not to fast was still a debatable issue.

r2. Reading *eueipe mmau ⟨n⟩śmmo atdiathēkē m⟨pnoute⟩* in agreement with BM MS 7594 and the Chester Beatty Papyrus. For references to alienation from the Covenant see Eph 2:12; 4:18; 1Clem 1:1; Deut 29:25; Jer 22:9; and frequently in the docu-ments from Qumran; cf. Rosenstiehl, *L'Apocalypse d'Élie*, p. 84. Both the sect of Qumran and the early Christians used "covenant" as a technical term to describe their community. Cf. Jer 31:31; Jub 23:16–21.

s2. The Akhmimic text uses the Gk. term *apos-terei*. BM MS 7594 and the Chester Beatty Papyrus have translated it as *fōče*.

t2. The Akhmimic text uses *špōp* for "prom-ises." BM MS 7594 and the Chester Beatty Papyrus have *erēt*. These promises probably refer to the "crowns" and "thrones" mentioned in line 1:8. Cf. PssSol 12:8; Jas 1:12; 2:5. The NT frequently links the promises to the covenants with Abraham, Moses, and David, which were realized in the coming of the Messiah. Cf. Heb 11:13, 39–40, or 2Pet 1:2–4, where the ethical implications are spelled out. The present text does not contain any suggestion that these promises are to be realized in a messianic figure.

u2. Reading *nei de sesmant en nouaeiš*. Stein-dorff, *Die Apokalypse des Elias*, p. 72, had mis-

faith.[v2] Therefore, don't let those people lead you astray.[w2]

Mt 24:4
Mk 13:5

The benefits of the fast

15　Remember that from the time when he created[x2] the heavens, the Lord created
the fast[y2] for a benefit to men on account of the passions and desires[z2] which fight
16　against you so that the evil[a3] will not inflame[b3] you. •"But it is a pure fast[c3] which

Jas 4:1

17　I[d3] have created," said the Lord. •The one who fasts continually[e3] will not sin

1Pet 2:11

18　although jealousy and strife are within him. •Let the pure one fast, but whenever
19　the one who fasts is not pure he has angered the Lord and also the angels. • And

Zeph 2:3,
1:15,18
Ezek 7:19
Rom 2:5

he has grieved his soul, gathering up wrath for himself for the day of wrath.

20　　　[f3]But a pure fast[g3] is what I[h3] created,
　　　　with a pure heart and pure hands.[i3]

Pss 24:4

21　　　It[j3] releases sin.[k3]

PssSol 3:8

　　　　It heals diseases.
　　　　It casts out demons.[l3]

22　　　It is effective up to the throne of God for an ointment[m3]
　　　　and for a release from sin by means of a pure prayer.

---

divided the reading as *semante nnoaeiš*, giving a positive rather than a negative reading, but the use of *an* in BM MS 7594 and the Chester Beatty Papyrus confirms the reading with *en*. The text of BM MS 7594 also requires some reconstruction. It should read *nai ete n⟨se⟩semont an ⟨n⟩ouoeiš nim*, "these who are not correctly established at all times." This reconstruction is supported by the Chester Beatty Papyrus.

v2. Reading *hn⟨t⟩pistis etajraeit*. BM MS 7594 reads *hn tpisti[s]*. It was also necessary to restore the article in the Akhmimic text because the relative clause requires a definite antecedent. The scribe originally wrote *hm pistis etachraeit*. The Chester Beatty Papyrus reads *hn tpistis ettajrēu*.

w2. Reading *nei etmmo* for "those people" with Schmidt, "Der Kolophon," p. 315. Steindorff, *Die Apokalypse des Elias*, p. 72, had read *netmmo*. BM MS 7594 reads [n]*ai etmmau*. A similar warning is found in Mt 24:4 and Mk 13:5.

x2. Reading ⟨j⟩*ntaftano*. BM MS 7594 reads *intaftamie*. The Chester Beatty Papyrus reads *jin taftamie*.

y2. Reading *rpmeeue ⟨je⟩ apjaeis cōnt n⟨t⟩nēstia*. Restored on the basis of the parallel with 1. 1:3, 8, BM MS 7594 and the Chester Beatty Papyrus.

z2. After the word "desires" the text of BM MS 7594 has a lacuna which is larger than the parallel Akhmimic text can supply. The Chester Beatty Papyrus contains the phrase "which change," i.e. "changing" or "fickle desires." For the sense of the passage cf. Jas 4:1; 1Pet 2:11; Tit 2:12. Rosenstiehl, *L'Apocalypse d'Élie*, p. 84, calls attention to Josephus, *War* 2.8.2, which speaks of the value the Essenes placed on resisting passions. Cf. TJos 4:8; 10:1f. The struggle against passions was a hellenistic commonplace. Cf. Plato, *Phaedo* 83b; Philo, *LegAll* 2.106; *SpecLeg* 2.195.

a3. Reading *ppo⟨nē⟩ros*. The reading has been confirmed by the Chester Beatty Papyrus. BM MS 7594 preserved . . .]*ēros* at this point. From here on the BM text breaks off, except for a few isolated letters. Schmidt, "Der Kolophon," p. 315, suggests that approximately thirteen lines were lost.

b3. The Cop. word *šobh* (Akhmimic *šōbh*) may be used to render the Gk. word *ekkaiō* in the figurative sense in which it appears in Rom 1:27. It could also reflect the Gk. word *phlegō*. The Chester

Beatty Papyrus reads "so that the evil [or evil one] will not deceive you."

c3. Instead of "a pure fast" one could read "clean" or "holy fast." In vs. 1:20, where the word is found again, the same adjective is used of "hands" and "heart." Joel 1:14; 2:15 speak of *sanctifying* a fast. Rosenstiehl, *L'Apocalypse d'Élie*, p. 84, has noted that the discussion of fasting in this text parallels Isa 58:1–11. In both cases a true fast involves avoiding sin, but the present emphasis on "purity" or "sanctity" of the fast is lacking in Isa.

d3. The Chester Beatty Papyrus reads "which he has created." The use of the first-person pronoun seems to require that the quotation precede the phrase "said the Lord." In reading the Sahidic text, it is possible to assume that the phrase "The Lord said" begins a new sentence, and that the phrase that follows is to be treated as a quotation.

e3. In the Chester Beatty Papyrus the expression "continually" follows and clearly modifies the verb "sin." In the Akhmimic text, the word order makes the reference of "continually" somewhat ambiguous. It could be rendered "The one who fasts will *never* sin," in agreement with the Chester Beatty Papyrus.

f3. The passage that follows is probably not poetry in the strict sense, but the saying is expressed in obvious parallel construction.

g3. Read ⟨ou⟩*nēstia*. Cf. 1:16. The reading is supported by the Chester Beatty Papyrus.

h3. The Chester Beatty Papyrus reads "what the Lord created."

i3. Reading *hnouhēt ⟨ef⟩ouaabe mn henčij⟨eu⟩-ouaabe* for grammatical reasons. The reading is supported by the Chester Beatty Papyrus. The sense recalls Ps 24:4.

j3. The Chester Beatty Papyrus reads "For the pure fast releases sin."

k3. A well-known purpose of fasting on the Day of Atonement is the release of sin. Cf. PssSol 3:8.

l3. Although the phrase "and fasting" is generally considered to be an addition to Jesus' discussion of casting out demons at Mk 9:29, it reflects an ancient view of the importance of fasting for an exorcist.

m3. The Chester Beatty Papyrus adds "for a fragrance."

The need for single-mindedness

23   Who[n3] among you, if he is honored in his craft, will go forth to the field[o3] without a tool in his hand? Or who will go forth to the battle to fight[p3] without a
24 breastplate on? •If he is found, will he not be killed because he despised[q3] the
25 service[r3] of the king? •Likewise no one is able to enter the holy place if he is
26 double-minded. • The one who is double-minded[s3] in his prayer[t3] is darkness to
27 himself.[u3] And even the angels do not trust him. •Therefore be[v3] single-minded in the Lord at all times so that you might know every moment.[w3]

Subtitle for the remaining portion of the text

1 **2** Furthermore,[a] concerning the kings of Assyria and the dissolution of the heaven and the earth[b] and the things beneath the earth:[c]

The Assyrian king of injustice

2   "Now therefore ⟨those who are mine⟩[d] will not be overcome" says the Lord,   Mk 13:7
3 "nor will they fear in the battle."[e] •When[f] they see [a king][g] who rises in the   Deut 1:29f, 7:18 north, [who will be called][h] "the king of [Assyria" and][h] "the king of injustice,"[i]   Dan 11:40

n3. Rosenstiehl, *L'Apocalypse d'Elie*, p. 86, viewed the extended figure of speech that begins here as an addition. He thought it had the nature of a *logion*, which remains unidentified. The peasant and the mercenary suggested to him an origin in the Ptolemaic period, but soldiers and farmers are standard figures in any age.

o3. Reading *atkai⟨e⟩ efjieau* with W. Till, "Bemerkungen und Ergänzungen zu den achmîmischen Textausgaben," *Zeitschrift für ägyptische Sprache und Altertumskunde* 63 (1928) 90. We have altered the word order for clearer sense in English.

p3. The words "to fight" are lacking in the Chester Beatty Papyrus.

q3. The parallel Sahidic text published by Steindorff, *Die Apokalypse des Elias*, pp. 114–45, begins at this point. This phrase is preceded by the words *mmof mmau*, "him there." This could be part of a slight variation of the Akhmimic sentence "Will he not be killed?"

r3. Steindorff, *Die Apokalypse des Elias*, p. 74, restored *ōph[ik]ion*. In Sahidic l. S3, 2, the form is *ophikion*. Steindorff correctly identified the word as the Gk. *ophphikion*, which represents Lat. *officium*. Rosenstiehl, *L'Apocalypse d'Élie*, suggested that the use of a Lat. official term indicated a date after Diocletian in the 3rd cent. A.D., but that is not necessarily true. There is no reason why such a common Lat. term could not have entered Egypt much earlier.

s3. Rosenstiehl, *L'Apocalypse d'Élie*, p. 86, has tracked down a long list of parallels for this passage, including 1QH 4.14; TAsh 3:1–4:1; Jas 4:8; and a very close parallel in the thirteenth canon published by A. Harnack in *Die Lehre der zwölf Apostel* (TU 2; Leipzig, 1886) p. 231.

t3. Reading ⟨ḫn⟩ *tfproseuchē* in agreement with the Sahidic text published by Steindorff, *Die Apokalypse des Elias*. The Chester Beatty Papyrus reads *hm teuproseuchē*.

u3. Reading *eie nkeke araf*. W. E. Crum, *A Coptic Dictionary* (Oxford, 1962) p. 101, lists several idioms involving darkness of the heart, i.e. mind. A similar use is probably intended here. To

make the mind dark suggests creating a shady, furtive mentality within a man so that the angels will not trust him.

v3. The Chester Beatty Papyrus reads "If you become single-minded always in the Lord *be wise in the time*." The phrase in italics is lacking in Akhmimic. The Sahidic text published by Steindorff, *Die Apokalypse des Elias*, reads *erri *ake hn pehroei*. **ake* should undoubtedly be read *sabe*, and *hroei* is quite possibly a corruption of the Akhmimic plural for the word *hoou*, "day." There are a number of Akhmimic forms in that Sahidic text.

w3. Translating *nhate nim*. The Sahidic text reads *hob nim*, "everything." It is possible that the Akhmimic text is corrupt. The point of single-mindedness is to keep the mind from clouding up in a darkening manner so that one will be able to perceive everything or perceive at every moment.

2 a. The Sahidic text omits "Furthermore." The abrupt transition clearly marks the introduction of a new source.

b. For the dissolution of the heaven and the earth cf. vss. 1:4; 4:28; 5:37.

c. The phrase "and the things beneath the earth" is omitted in the Sahidic text.

d. Restoring ⟨nete noui ne⟩ to agree with the Sahidic text. The phrase "Now therefore" is lacking in Sahidic. Rosenstiehl, *L'Apocalypse d'Élie*, p. 87, assumed that the Akhmimic "Now therefore" was a corruption of the phrase "those who are mine," which is found in Sahidic.

e. The Sahidic text reads "in a battle." Cf. Mk 13:7 and the synoptic parallels. The command not to fear is a traditional OT phrase derived from the institution of holy war. Cf. Deut 1:29f.; 7:18; 20:1.

f. The Sahidic text reads "and when."

g. Restored on the basis of the Sahidic text.

h. Restored on the basis of the Sahidic text.

i. King of injustice is a title of Beliar in AscenIs 4:2.

j. Restored on the basis of the Sahidic text.

4 [he will increase][j] his battles and his disturbances[k] against Egypt. •The land will
5 groan together[l] because[m] your children will be seized. •Many will desire death in Rev 9:6
those days, but death will flee from them.[n]

The western king of peace

6 And[o] a king who will be called "the king of peace" will rise up in the west.[p]
7,8 He will run upon the sea like a roaring lion.[q] •He will kill the king of injustice, 1Pet 5:8
and he will take vengeance on Egypt with battles[r] and much[s] bloodshed.
9 It[t] will come to pass in those days[u] that he will[v] command a p[eace][v] and a
10 [vain][v] gift in Egypt. •[He will give][v] peace to these who are holy, [saying],[w]
11 "The name of [God][x] is one."[y] •[He will][x] give honors to the s[aints[z] and] an Zech 14:9
12 exalting[a2] to the places of the saints.[b2] •He will give vain gifts to the house of God. Deut 6:4
13 He will wander around in the cities of Egypt with guile, without their knowing.
14 He will take count of the holy places. He will weigh the idols of the heathen. He
15 will take count of their wealth. He will establish priests for them. •He will command Dan 11:33
that the wise men and the great ones of the people be seized, and they will be
brought to the metropolis which is by the sea,[c2] saying,[d2] "There is but one

k. The Chester Beatty Papyrus reads "the disturbances."

l. Here "land" is used to represent the people who live in Egypt. The writer begins the sentence with this figure, treats the people in the third person, and then shifts to the second person to address them directly when he writes "your children will be seized." This is part of the homiletical style of the writer of this section. The hearers or readers are assumed to be the citizens of Egypt.

m. The word "because" is omitted in the Sahidic text.

n. The phrase "but death will flee from them" is lacking in the Sahidic text. Cf. vs. 2:32 below, which is a precise parallel of Rev 9:6.

o. For the word "and" the Sahidic text reads "then."

p. Rosenstiehl, *L'Apocalypse d'Élie*, p. 88, has called attention to the messianic attributes of the king of the west. He is king of peace (Isa 9:6), walks on water (?) (Mt 14:25), like a lion (Gen 49:9; 4Ezra 11:37; 12:31f.). He also noted the striking parallel with the description given in the Tiburtine Sibyl.

q. The same figure is used of the devil in 1Pet 5:8. Hippolytus, in his work *On the Antichrist*, ch. 6, speaks of both the Christ and the Antichrist as lions.

r. The Sahidic text has a singular form: "a battle," or "a war."

s. The word "much" is lacking in the Sahidic text published by Steindorff, *Die Apokalypse des Elias*.

t. The Sahidic text published by Steindorf, *Die Apokalypse des Elias*, begins the sentence with "And."

u. Reading ⟨*ḫ*⟩*nnhooue etmmo*. This is a standard phrase. Cf. vss. 2:31, 33, 35.

v. Restorations based on readings in the Sahidic text. The Akhmimic text reads "he commanded," a past tense.

w. Restored on the basis of sense. The Sahidic text reads "He will begin to say." There does not appear to be enough room in the Akhmimic text to permit restoration of all of that.

x. Restored on the basis of the Sahidic text published by Steindorff, *Die Apokalypse des Elias*.

y. Cf. Zech 14:9 and Deut 6:4. According to the *History of the Patriarchs, Patralogia Orientalis*, vol. 1, p. 142, Mark's first convert in Alexandria was a cobbler whom the evangelist heard shouting *heis ho theos*, "God is one." It is reported that Mark was surprised that the cobbler knew God's name. The story illustrates the fact that this formula had wide currency within both the Jewish and Christian communities and elsewhere in the hellenistic world. In his volume entitled *heis theos* (Göttingen, 1926), E. Peterson traced the use of this formula in both Christian and non-Christian circles. In Christian circles outside Egypt there was a strong tendency to expand the acclamation to include either the name of Christ or both the name of Christ and the name of the Holy Spirit.

z. The Sahidic text reads "He will give glory to the priests of God." Rosenstiehl, *L'Apocalypse d'Élie*, p. 89, was persuaded that the reading of the Akhmimic text was incorrect at this point. The Sahidic reading, "priests of God" instead of "saints," may be influenced by the use of these texts in monastic circles. The Akhmimic text used the expression "priests of the land" in vs. 2:40 to identify the audience addressed by the writer. The priests appear again at 4:21 together with the saints. The word that is translated "saints" is literally "the ones who are pure" or "holy." It is the word that one would use to designate either the "*ḥasîdîm*" of the OT or the "saints" of the NT.

a2. Rosenstiehl, *L'Apocalypse d'Élie*, p. 89, reads "restoration." The Cop. word is *jise*, which means "a lifting up," generally in the sense of "praise."

b2. The Sahidic text has "the holy places."

c2. This metropolis is generally considered to be Alexandria. Cf. The Oracle of the Potter.

d2. Both the Akhmimic and Sahidic texts published by Steindorff, *Die Apokalypse des Elias*, break off at this point. The Akhmimic text preserves only two letters, i.e. *ou*, from the quotation that follows. There is a single sheet (two pages) of papyrus missing from the Akhmimic text at this point. The lacuna in Steindorff's Sahidic text is larger and resumes its parallel at vs. 3:7 of the Akhmimic text.

16 language." •But when you hear, "Peace and joy exist," I will . . .[e2]

The evil son on the right

17,18 Now I will tell you his signs so that you might know him. •For he has two sons:
19 one on his right and one on his left. •The one on his right will receive a demonic
20 face, (and) he will fight against the name of God. •Now four kings will descend
21 from that king. •In his thirtieth year he will come up to Memphis, (and) he will
22 build a temple in Memphis. •On that day his own son will rise up against him and
23 kill him. •The whole land will be disturbed.
24 On that day he will issue an order over the whole land so that the priests of the
land and all of the saints will be seized, saying, "You will repay doubly every
25 gift and all of the good things which my father gave to you." •He will shut up
26 the holy places. He will take their houses. He will take their sons prisoner. •He
will order and sacrifices and abominations and bitter evils will be done in the
27,28 land. •He will appear before the sun and the moon. •On that day the priests of
the land will tear their clothes.

A lament for Egypt in those days

29,30 Woe to you, O rulers of Egypt, in those days because your day has passed. •The
violence (being done to) the poor will turn against you, and your children will be
31 seized as plunder. •In those days the cities of Egypt will groan for the voice of
the one who sells and the one who buys will not be heard. The markets of the   Rev 18:11
32 cities of Egypt[f2] will become dusty. •Those who are in Egypt will weep together.
They will desire death, (but) death will flee and leave them.[g2]   Rev 9:6
33 In those days,[h2] they will run up to the rocks and leap off, saying, "Fall upon   Hos 10:8
34 us." And still they will not die.[i2] • A double affliction will multiply upon[j2] the Lk 23:30
whole land.   Rev 6:16
35 In those days[k2] the king will command, and all the nursing women will be seized
and brought to him bound. They will suckle serpents. And their blood will be
36 drawn[l2] from their breasts, and it will be applied as poison to the arrows.[m2] •On
account of the distress of the cities,[n2] he will command again, and all the young
lads from twelve years and under will be seized and presented in order to teach
them to shoot[o2] arrows.

e2. The translation of the Chester Beatty Papyrus inserted at this point is based on the text provided by A. Pietersma, S. T. Comstock, and H. W. Attridge. They were kind enough to allow me to use the text that will appear under their names in the *Texts and Translations: Pseudepigrapha Series*, published by the Society of Biblical Literature.

f2. The Chester Beatty Papyrus has a different reading. There is a preposition "in" before "the markets" so that the complete phrase "in the markets of the cities of Egypt" is joined to the preceding sentence. A new sentence is then created by providing a new pronoun so that the following sentence reads "They will become dusty."

g2. Restoring ⟨te⟩pmou pōt fkaoue. Restoring the conjunctive helps the sense of the passage and provides a precise parallel for the Cop. version of Rev 9:6. The Chester Beatty Papyrus reads awō ntemou pōt nsabol mmoou, "and death will flee from them."

h2. The Chester Beatty Papyrus lacks the phrase "In those days."

i2. The Chester Beatty Papyrus adds "but death flees from them."

j2. The Chester Beatty Papyrus reads "round about the whole land."

k2. The Chester Beatty Papyrus adds "in that time."

l2. The Akhmimic text has the verb sōk abal, "draw forth." The Chester Beatty Papyrus has sōōng ebol, "suck out."

m2. O. Von Lemm, "Kleine koptische Studien, X, 4–6," *Bulletin de l'académie impériale des sciences de Saint-Pétersbourg*, 5ᵉ série, 13 (1900) X, 4, clearly identified the Cop. word klo as the word for "poison." In an extended discussion he concluded that it was a vegetable poison. The word that follows is sate, which could be the word for "arrow," "dart," or less likely an irregular Akhmimic spelling of the Sahidic sate, "fire," "fiery." Assuming that it means "arrow," the Sahidic form should be sote, but the Chester Beatty Papyrus has soto, a form more difficult to interpret.

n2. The Chester Beatty Papyrus reads "wars" instead of "cities."

o2. Reading at⟨s⟩ebau atik sate. The restoration is supported by the Chester Beatty Papyrus, which reads nsetsaboou enej.

37   [p2]The midwife who is upon the earth will grieve.[q2]

The woman who has given birth[r2] will lift her eyes to heaven,

saying, "Why did I sit upon the birthstool,[s2]

to bring forth a son to the earth?"

38   The barren woman and the virgin will rejoice,[t2]   Lk 23:29

saying, "It is our time to rejoice,   Isa 54:1

because we have no child upon the earth,   WisSol 3:13

but our children are in heaven."[u2]

The return of the Jews to Jerusalem

39   In those days, three kings will arise among the Persians, and they will take captive the Jews who are in Egypt. They will bring them to Jerusalem,[v2] and they will inhabit it and dwell there.[v2]

Homiletical aside

40   Then when you hear that there is security[w2] in Jerusalem, tear your garments,   1Thes 5:2f
O priests of the land,[x2] because the son of perdition[y2] will soon come.[z2]   Jn 17:12
                                                       2Thes 2:3

Truncated oracle mentioning the lawless one

41   [a3]In those days, the lawless one[b3] will appear in the holy places—   2Thes 2:8

Persian-Assyrian wars

42   In ⟨those⟩ days[c3] the kings of the Persians will hasten and they will stand to fight

---

p2. The passage that follows has a number of poetic characteristics. In addition to parallelism, there is a continual play on the contrast between "earth" and "heaven." The two words are set in antithetical parallelism in ll. 1 and 2, where "The midwife . . . upon the earth" is set in parallel with the mother who "will lift her eyes to heaven." There is a similar antithetical parallelism involving the same two words in the last two lines. By using the same type of parallelism in the opening and closing lines the writer has devised an enclosure that marks off the limits of the poem. The poem may be divided into two stanzas. The first four lines describe the lament of fertile women and the last four lines describe the rejoicing of childless women. The first stanza ends with the word "earth," and the second stanza ends with "heaven."

q2. The Chester Beatty Papyrus adds "then. And."

r2. Reading *tetasmise*. The scribe wrote *tatasmise*.

s2. Lit. "the brick." Cf. Ex 1:16, where the Heb. word *'bnym*, "stones," is used. They are translated "birthstools." The Egyptian hieroglyphic determinative for the word *msi*, "to give birth," clearly portrays a woman giving birth in the squatting position that was normal when she was seated on a birthstool.

t2. Lacau, "Remarques," 190, would restore *as⟨n⟩areśe*. For the sense of the passage cf. Isa 54:1; WisSol 3:13; 2Bar 10:14–15; Lk 23:29.

u2. The Akhmimic text writes "heaven" in the plural. The Chester Beatty Papyrus uses the singular.

v2. The Chester Beatty Papyrus reads "and they will populate it for them again."

w2. Rosenstiehl, *L'Apocalypse d'Elie*, p. 92, who followed an earlier reading of *pōrj*, "division," wished to relate this passage to "the house of division," which is apparently his translation of *byt plg* in CD 20, 22 and 4QpNah 4.1. The Chester Beatty Papyrus reads "when you hear that there is security and safety in Jerusalem." The word I have translated as "safety" is *asphaleia*, and its presence in the expanded reading of the Chester Beatty Papyrus together with a preceding definite article indicates that the preceding noun should be read as *ōrj*, "security," plus the definite article. The words *ōrj* and *asphaleia* are virtually identical in meaning.

x2. This is a homiletical aside to the reader or hearers of this text, who are called "priests of the land." This passage may simply reflect the use of the text in monastic circles.

y2. Reading ⟨p⟩*śēre mpteko*. Cf. Jn 17:12; 2Thes 2:3.

z2. Lit. the text reads "he will not delay before he comes."

a3. The Chester Beatty Papyrus begins this sentence with the word "Immediately."

b3. Cf. 2Thes 2:8. Perhaps this figure is to be identified with "the son of lawlessness" at 3:1, 5. In Semitic parlance "son of" can simply mean "one of" a particular class. "The son of lawlessness" could be rendered "the lawless one." The Cop. construction describing the appearance of the "lawless one" here is similar to that used in 3:5 to describe the appearance of the "son of lawlessness."

c3. Reading *hnnhooue⟨etmmo⟩* to make this phrase conform to the reading elsewhere in the text. Cf. 2:35, 39, 42. The Chester Beatty Papyrus also reads "In those days."

43 (?)[d3] with the kings of Assyria. Four kings will fight with three. •They will spend three years in that place until they carry off the wealth of the temple which is in that place.[e3]

44 In those days,[f3] blood will flow from Kos[g3] to Memphis. The river of Egypt will become blood, and they will not be able to drink from it for three days.

Gen 15:18
Ex 7:19f

45 Woe to Egypt and those who are in it.[h3]

46 In those days, a king will arise in the city which is called "the city of the sun,"[i3] and[j3] the whole land will be disturbed. ⟨He will⟩[k3] flee to Memphis ⟨with the Persians⟩.[l3]

The Persian triumph

47 In the sixth year, the Persian kings will plot an ambush in Memphis. They will 48 kill the Assyrian king. •The Persians will take vengeance on the land,[m3] and they[n3] will command to kill all the heathen and the lawless ones. They will command to 49 build the temples of the saints.[n3] •They will give double gifts to the house of God. 50 They[o3] will say, "The name of God is one." • The whole land will hail[p3] the Persians.

The reign of the righteous king from the city of the sun

51 Even the remnant, who did not die under the afflictions, will say, "The Lord has

---

d3. Reading ⟨se⟩ahe aretou with the word amiḥe implied. The scribe wrote aḥrēarit. Von Lemm, *Bulletin de l'académie impériale des sciences de Saint-Pétersbourg*, 5ᵉ série, 21 (1904) XXVI, 14, provided a number of examples of armies "standing to fight." He interpreted the idiomatic use of ōhe erat to mean "to stand over against hostilely." Lemm's emendation was fully justified on the basis of the Akhmimic text alone, but there is now evidence from the Chester Beatty Papyrus that makes Lemm's reading and that provided in the present translation questionable. Unfortunately the Chester Beatty reading contains a lacuna, but the remaining text reads [. .]r[. . . .] hrit, which does not agree with what Lemm proposed.

Lemm saw this section, with its battle between Persia and Assyria, as a recollection of Cyrus and Nebuchadnezzar. The mention of taking treasure from the temple in 2:43 recalled for him the activity of Nebuchadnezzar in Jer 52:19. The subsequent triumph over Assyrians in Memphis in 2:47 he attributed to the Persian kings who overthrew the Babylonians.

e3. The Chester Beatty Papyrus reads "carry off the wealth from that place."

f3. The phrase "In those days" is lacking from the Chester Beatty Papyrus.

g3. Steindorff, *Die Apokalypse des Elias*, pp. 84f., has identified this with the Arabic city of Qûṣ, the ancient Apollinopolis Parva. It is located a few kilometers south of Coptos on the eastern bank of the Nile.

h3. The Chester Beatty Papyrus reads "in Egypt."

i3. Most likely Heliopolis, biblical On. Cf. the LXX text of Gen 41:45; 46:20. The Cop. biblical texts translate the LXX form as tpolis mprē.

j3. Instead of "and" the Chester Beatty Papyrus reads "in those days."

k3. Reading ⟨fna⟩pōt with the Chester Beatty Papyrus.

l3. The Akhmimic text does not contain the phrase "with the Persians," but that is the sense of the passage. A native Egyptian king will arise in Heliopolis. By associating himself with the Persian kings and assisting them in the plot against Memphis, he will share in their triumph over the Assyrians and come to reign as the "righteous king." The sequence of events is made clear by the new Sahidic text provided by the Chester Beatty Papyrus. I would translate the relevant passages in the following manner: "In the sixth year of the kings, he will flee to Memphis *with* the Persians. *He* will plot an ambush in Memphis. *He* will kill the Assyrian kings. The Persians will take vengeance on the land."

By inserting a preposition and changing the personal pronoun to third masculine singular at two points, the Sahidic text provides a slightly different reading, which clarifies the role of the king from Heliopolis. The Akhmimic text may be interpreted in a similar way, but prior to the publication of the Chester Beatty Papyrus its meaning was not obvious.

m3. See n. l3 for the Sahidic translation up to this point.

n3. The Sahidic text continues to describe the close cooperation between the Persians and the king from Heliopolis. I would translate it as follows: "*He* will command and *they* will kill all the heathen and the lawless ones. *He* will command and *they* will plunder the temples of the heathen and *they* will exterminate the priests. *He* will command and *they* will build the temples of the saints." It should be noted that the Sahidic text is a bit longer than the Akhmimic text at this point.

o3. The Chester Beatty Papyrus reads "he."

p3. The Cop. word ouōšt can mean "worship." It was a normal practice to extend divine honors to the rulers of Egypt, whether natives or conquerors. For example, the Persian kings, Cambyses and Darius, and the Macedonian king, Alexander the Great, were all accorded divine honors.

52 sent us a righteous king so that the land will not become a desert." •He will Jer 50:12f
command that no royal matter be presented[q3] for three years and six months.[r3] The Dan 7:25
53 land will be full of good in an abundant well-being. •Those who are alive will go
to those who are dead, saying, "Rise up and be[s3] with us in this rest."[t3]

The advent of the son of lawlessness

1 **3** In the fourth year of that king,[a] the son of lawlessness[b] will appear, saying, Mt 24:5
"I am the Christ,"[c] although he is not. Don't believe him![d]

Digression concerning the advent of the true Christ

2   When the Christ comes, he will come in the manner of a covey of doves[e] with Mt 3:16
the crown[f] of doves surrounding him. He will walk upon the heaven's vaults with
3 the sign of the cross[g] leading him. •The whole world will behold him like the sun Isa 60:1-3
4 which shines from the eastern horizon to the western. •This is how he[h] will come, 2Thes 1:7
with all his angels surrounding him.[i]   Mt 24:27
                                                                       Lk 17:24

---

q3. This passage presents the translator with a crux. The Akhmimic text reads lit. "He will command not to give any royal thing (or person)." It has traditionally been emended to read "He will command not to give anything to the king," but the emendation is not supported by the new Chester Beatty Papyrus, which reads "He will command so that nothing royal will be given." One might speculate that the passage involves the suspension of certain royal taxes or royal honors.

r3. Josephus, *Ant* 12.3.3, reports on a three-year remission of taxes for Judah which was ordered by Antiochus the Great. Earlier in *Ant* 11.8.5 Josephus reported that Alexander the Great agreed to remit taxes during the sabbatical year.

s3. The Chester Beatty Papyrus reads "remain."

t3. Cf. Ps 95:11; Heb 3:11, 18; 4:1–11. The psalmist equates "the rest" with the attainment of the land of promise. Subsequently writers easily identified the rest with the realization of eschatological promises in other forms. At this point in the text, the present writer uses a figure close to that found in Ps 95:11, although he has reinterpreted the good land of rest to apply to Egypt. Cf. the following NHL text *On the Origin of the World*, II, 122:34, "These great signs appeared only in Egypt, signifying that it is like the Paradise of God." At 4:27 below, the author sets the place of rest in an eschatological context. Surprisingly, it is not part of the kingdom of the Messiah, but it is a lesser place. A writer who was in any way dependent on Heb. would probably not have made that sort of adjustment. It is our opinion that this discussion of "rest" goes back to the early Jewish stratum within the text. Cf. WisSol 4:7; TLevi 18:9; TDan 5:12.

3 a. The scribe left a space before the phrase "in the fourth year of that king." Steindorff, *Die Apokalypse des Elias*, p. 86, suggested that it might be the result of the scribe's attempt to indicate a new section. The Chester Beatty Papyrus has preserved a longer reading at the beginning, which I would restore as *hrai nteh[ē nt] mahfto nromp[e,* "In the beginning of the fourth year." Rosenstiehl, *L'Apocalypse d'Élie*, p. 95, has a long footnote attempting to pin down the significance of "the fourth year." He calls attention to the three and

one half years in Dan 7:25; Lk 4:25; Jas 5:17; Rev 11:3; 12:14; 13:5. But all of those refer to times of suffering for the saints in contrast to the three and one half years of bounty in our text. He then calls attention to the period of forty years in the Tiburtine Sibyl, but he comes to no firm conclusion.

b. "The son of lawlessness" is lacking from the Chester Beatty Papyrus.

c. The Cop. probably translates an *ego eimi* statement. Cf. Mt 24:5 and the synoptic parallels. This boast of the Messiah is also present in Heb. versions of the Antichrist legend. Cf. Jellinek, *Bet ha-Midrash*, vol. 2, p. 56 ('*ny hw' mśyḥ*) and vol. 4, p. 124 ('*ny mśyḥkm*).

d. Reading *pisteue ⟨a⟩raf*.

e. Cf. Mt 3:16 and the gospel parallels. Cf. also Mt 10:16 and 12:39 since the name Jonah means "dove." The translation "covey of doves" is supported by the Chester Beatty Papyrus, which I would restore to read *nnoumeh[ou]al ngrompe*. The word *mehoual* is listed by Crum, *Coptic Dictionary*, p. 208a, as meaning "nest, dovecot," but just as the word *ohe* means both "sheepfold" and "flock" the word for "nest" or "dovecot" may be extended to mean "covey" or "flock." The Akhmimic word that is translated "covey" is *samnt*. Crum, *Coptic Dictionary*, p. 339b, listed its meaning as "collecting place." It is also used of small bodies of water. I would suggest a semantic evaluation similar to that which occurred in the *mah*, "nest, brood." In Middle Egyptian the hieroglyphic determinative for *mḥ* is the picture of three ducklings in a pool. The duck pond is conceived of as a "brooding place." That expression may then be used for other "brooding places" and applied to other species of birds.

f. The Chester Beatty Papyrus reads "his crown."

g. Mt 24:30 speaks of the "sign of the son of man" appearing before him. W. Bousset in *The Antichrist Legend*, trans. A. H. Keane (London, 1896) pp. 232–36, traced the various apocalyptic descriptions of the sign of the son of man, particularly the sign of the cross.

h. The Chester Beatty Papyrus reads "the Christ."

i. Cf. 2Thes 1:7; Mk 8:38; Mt 16:27.

Works of the Antichrist

5 But the son of lawlessness[j] will begin to stand again in the holy places.[k]

6 [l]He will say to the sun,[m] "Fall," and it will fall.   Mt 24:29
He will say, "Shine," and it will do it.
He will say, "Darken," and it will do it.

7 He will say to the moon, "Become bloody," and it will do it.[n]   Joel 2:31

8 He will go forth with them from the sky.[o]   Rev 6:12
He will walk upon the sea and the rivers as upon dry land.[p]   Mk 6:48

9 He will cause the lame to walk.[q]   Mt 11:5
He will cause the deaf to hear.
He will cause the dumb to speak.
He will cause the blind to see.

10 The lepers he will cleanse.
The ill he will heal.
The demons he will cast out.[r]

,12 He will multiply his signs and his wonders in the presence of everyone. •He will
13 do the works which the Christ did,[s] except for raising the dead alone.[t] •In this
you will know that he is the son of lawlessness, because he is unable to give life.

Signs of the Antichrist

,15 For behold[u] I will tell you his signs[v] so that you might know him. •He is a

---

j. Cf. 2Thes 2:4. The figure can be traced to Dan 9:27; 11:31; 12:11. Cf. 1Mac 1:54; Mt 24:15; Mk 13:14. [Cf. also especially TAdam 3:1. — J.H.C.]

k. Reading ḥnmma ⟨e⟩touaabe. The Chester Beatty Papyrus reads "in the holy place."

l. The passage that follows is probably not poetry in the strict sense, but we have printed it in this form to call attention to the considerable amount of parallelism.

m. The Antichrist was generally expected to produce signs. Cf. 2Thes 2:9; Rev 13:13. Bousset discussed "the wonders of the Antichrist" at length in *The Antichrist Legend*, pp. 175–81.

n. This sentence is lacking in the Chester Beatty Papyrus. The two preceding sentences lack the phrase "he will say." The order is also reversed. The text reads: "darken, and it will; shine, and it will."

o. The Sahidic text published by Steindorff, *Die Apokalypse des Elias*, resumes its parallel at this point. That text has a difficult reading, which translates as follows: "saying, 'walk upon the dry land,' and you will walk upon the sea and the rivers as upon the dry land." The Chester Beatty Papyrus reads "and he will say 'walk upon the sea and the rivers as upon the dry land.' "

p. Reading šouŏou at Steindorff's suggestion in *Die Apokalypse des Elias*, p. 88. The scribe wrote šoušou.

q. The following list of miracles parallels Mt 11:5. Cf. TAdam 3:1.

r. When the author grants the Antichrist power to cast out demons, one is reminded of Jesus' statement concerning a house divided against itself, Mt 12:24–27.

s. The Sahidic text edited by Steindorff, *Die Apokalypse des Elias*, reads "which the Christ is going to do." The Chester Beatty Papyrus reads *chrēstos* in place of *Christos*. Cf. Jn 2:11; 2:23; 3:2. In 4:31 below the writer speaks of the Antichrist as doing "every power which the prophets did."

t. In the apocalyptic texts mustered by Bousset in *The Antichrist Legend*, pp. 176–81, there is a disagreement over the ability of the Antichrist to raise the dead. Some texts include that among his abilities as a sign of his power, but others explicitly deny it.

u. The Sahidic text edited by Steindorff, *Die Apokalypse des Elias*, lacks the word "for."

v. See Bousset, *The Antichrist Legend*, p. 156, for examples of "The Antichrist in the Character of a Monster." Bousset calls attention to the "original Jewish character" of our apocalypse at this point. Rosenstiehl has collected all of the relevant descriptions together in "Le Portrait de l'antichrist," which appears in *Pseudépigraphes de l'ancien testament et manuscrits de la mer mort* (Paris, 1967) vol. 1, pp. 45–63.

. . . of a skinny-legged young lad,[w] having a tuft of gray hair[x] at the front of his bald[y] head. His eyebrows[z] will reach to his ears. There is a leprous bare spot on
16 the front of his hands. •He will transform himself in the presence of those who
17 see him.[a2] He will become a young child. He will become old.[b2] •He will transform himself in every sign.[c2] But the signs of his head will not be able to change.[d2]
18 Therein you will know that he is the son of lawlessness.

The martyrdom of Tabitha

1 **4** The virgin, whose name is Tabitha,[a] will hear that the shameless one has revealed himself[b] in the holy places.[c] And she will put on her garment of fine
2 linen. •And she will pursue him up to Judea,[d] scolding him up to Jerusalem,[e]

w. The translation of this section is difficult and uncertain. The texts read as follows: Akhmimic, *oupelēč noušēm pe nḫr-šire nšam-ouerēte*; Sahidic (text published by Steindorff, *Die Apokalypse des Elias*), *oupelēk noukouei pe nsa-lašeie nšamaretf*; the Chester Beatty Papyrus, *oupelēč nou[koui pe nsalašeie] nšamaratf*.

The first word in the Akhmimic text, *pelēč* (=*pelēk*), is unknown, but it is probably a noun. Rosenstiehl, *L'Apocalypse d'Élie*, p. 98, transcribed the word as Peleg and treated it as a title for Hyrcanus II which was concealed in the Qumran references to *plg*. That thesis is a bit too speculative for us to follow. Although it must be admitted that if he was correct in interpreting the word "division" in 2:40 as a translation of the Heb. *plg* his argument would be strengthened, it is clever to say the least. Both references to the appearance of the Antichrist (2:40 and the present passage) contain a reference to Peleg according to his view.

The second word in the description of the Antichrist is a familiar word meaning "small, young." The Akhmimic *šēm* and the Sahidic *kouei* are synonyms. They normally precede the noun that they modify. Cf. W. Till's *Koptische Grammatik* (Leipzig, 1961²) p. 69.

The last word in the Akhmimic phrase given above is *šam-ouerēte*. The Sahidic *šamaretf šamaratf* is apparently a synonym. The words are written without an article and should normally be translated as an attribute of the preceding noun. The word *šamouerēte* is a compound expression composed of the word *šma*, "thin, light, subtle," and *ouerēte*, "foot, leg." Fortunately, we have a close Heb. parallel for this Cop. phrase. In the HebApEl (in *Bet ha-Midrash*, vol. 3, p. 65) we read that *šwqyw dqym*, "his legs are thin." The word *dq*, "thin, light, subtle," is the precise equivalent of the Cop. *šma*.

The noun which is modified by both "thin-legged" and "young" is not the same in Akhmimic and in Sahidic. In Akhmimic the word is *ḫr-šire*, "little servant, lad." When it is modified by the two attributives the phrase reads "a skinny-legged young lad." Rosenstiehl's translation (in *L'Apocalypse d'Élie*) of the complete phrase as "a little Peleg, young, with slender legs," assumes a less orthodox syntax on the part of the writer.

The noun in Sahidic is *sa-lašeie*. I know of no reason to ignore Crum's interpretation of this word as "tall," perhaps more lit. "grotesquely tall man." Compare the Ar. gloss indicating a "monstrous form" (Crum, *Coptic Dictionary*, pp. 333a and 148a). Thus the Sahidic text reads "a skinny-legged young grotesquely tall man." A mention of great height (sometimes ten or twelve cubits) is a

frequent characteristic of descriptions of the Antichrist. Cf. Rosenstiehl, *Pseudépigraphes*, p. 54.

x. The mark of Cain (?), Gen 4:15. The Antichrist cannot change this sign. See 3:17 below.

y. The Akhmimic word is *šatmehēl*, and the Sahidic word is *čaloubih*. Both forms of the word were discussed by Von Lemm, *Bulletin de l'académie impériale*.

z. The Chester Beatty Papyrus has *bouhe*, which Crum (*Coptic Dictionary*, p. 48a) lists as meaning "eyelid." W. Westendorff, *Koptisches Handwörterbuch* (Heidelberg, 1977) pp. 30, 496, has added the meaning "*Wimper*." It seems clear from its use in the present context that the meaning "eyebrow" should also be added.

a2. The Sahidic text reads "He will change himself in your presence."

b2. The Sahidic text published by Steindorff (*Die Apokalypse des Elias*) reads "Sometimes he will become old, but other times [reading *hinkesop* for *hinkeop*] he will become young again." The Chester Beatty Papyrus reads "Sometimes he will become old but sometimes he will become young again." An interesting theophany of Christ as a child and as an old man is found at the beginning of the Apocryphon of John from Nag Hammadi.

c2. The Sahidic text published by Steindorff (*Die Apokalypse des Elias*) reads "in his signs."

d2. The Sahidic text reads "he will not be able to change." Although they may be translated in the same way, the Sahidic text published by Steindorff and the Chester Beatty Papyrus use different forms to express the future tense. The former uses a negative first future and the latter uses a negative third future.

4 a. This is apparently the woman from Joppa, who was also known as Dorcas (Acts 9:36). Peter raised her from the dead. That would suggest that this martyr tale, which is closely parallel to those that follow, was the work of a Christian editor of a later time who may have sought to preserve an etiological detail about the healing blood of Tabitha by writing her story into a martyr tale that paralleled those that follow.

b. The Sahidic text published by Steindorff (*Die Apokalypse des Elias*) reads "The one who is shamed appeared."

c. The Sahidic text published by Steindorff (*Die Apokalypse des Elias*) reads "in the holy place."

d. Lit. "run after him up to Judea." The Sahidic text reads "and she will run up to Judea."

e. The Sahidic text published by Steindorff (*Die Apokalypse des Elias*) reads "and she will scold him. He (is) up to Jerusalem." The introduction of the pronoun "he" is an error.

saying,[f] "O shameless one, O son of lawlessness,[g] O you who have been hostile
to all the saints."[h]

3   Then the shameless one will be angry at the virgin. He will pursue her up to
4 the regions of the sunset.[i] He will suck her blood in the evening. •And he will
5 cast her upon the temple, and she will become a healing[j] for the people. •She
will rise up at dawn. And she will live and scold him, saying, "O shameless one,
you have no power against my soul or my body, because I live in the Lord
6 always.[k] •And also my blood which you have cast[l] upon the temple has become
a healing for the people."

The martyrdom of Elijah and Enoch

7   Then when Elijah and Enoch[m] hear that the shameless one has revealed himself
in the holy place,[n] they will come down and fight with him, saying,

8   [o]Are you indeed not ashamed?[p]
        When you attach yourself to the saints,[q]
        because you are always estranged.
9   You have been hostile to those who belong to heaven.
        You have acted against those belonging to[r] the earth.
10   You have been hostile to the thrones.[s]   2En 20:1
        You have acted against the angels.[t]   Rev 4:4
        You are always a stranger.   Col 1:16
11   You have fallen from heaven like the morning stars.[u]   Job 38:7

---

f. Reading (esjou mmas) je. The Sahidic text published by Steindorff (*Die Apokalypse des Elias*) has *esjō mmos je*. The Chester Beatty Papyrus reads *esjō m[mos] naf je*.

g. This phrase is the same one that is used by Enoch and Elijah in 4:15.

h. The Antichrist's hostility to all the saints, which Tabitha condemns here, is described in some detail in 4:20–29 below.

The Akhmimic text breaks off at this point. There is a single sheet (two pages) of Akhmimic text missing, but the Sahidic text continues uninterrupted and preserves a complete text until the Akhmimic text is resumed.

i. Rosenstiehl, *L'Apocalypse d'Élie*, p. 100, notes that Tabitha came from Joppa, in the extreme west with respect to Jerusalem.

j. The Cop. word *oujai* can also be translated "a salvation."

k. A similar statement is made by Elijah and Enoch in 4:15 below.

l. The reading at the beginning of this sentence is provided by the Chester Beatty Papyrus. The Sahidic text published by Steindorff (*Die Apokalypse des Elias*) reads simply "Even my blood you have cast."

m. The expectation that Elijah would return before the coming of the Messiah is based on Mal 4:5. The assumption that Enoch would return before the day of judgment is based on 1En 90:31, a part of the Book of Dreams. Bousset, *The Antichrist Legend*, pp. 203–8, assembled a large number of Christian texts dealing with the return of Elijah and Enoch. Although one assumes that the two witnesses in Rev 11 were probably intended by the author to represent Moses and Elijah, the Christian exegetes began to interpret them as Elijah and Enoch at a very early date, i.e. from the time of Irenaeus and Hippolytus (cf. Bousset, *The Antichrist Legend*, p. 27).

n. The Chester Beatty Papyrus reads "holy places."

o. The passage that follows has several poetic features in addition to the obvious parallelism in ll. 4f., 6f., 9f. The last three lines are parallel to the first three lines, providing an enclosure. In l. 2 there is a contrast between the Antichrist's attempt to *attach* himself to the saints and his standing *firmly against* God in l. 11. Within the poem the writer identifies the one who would attach himself to the saints as a devil. The poem has a symmetrical structure when the lines are grouped together in a sequence of three lines (1–3), two lines (4f.), three lines (6–8), two lines (9f.), three lines (11–13). When it is read this way the first group of three lines ends with the phrase "you are always estranged." The second group of three lines ends with the phrase "you are always a stranger," and the last group ends with "you are a devil."

p. Not necessarily a question. It could be read "you are indeed not ashamed."

q. Reading *enetouaab* for *nenetouaab*. Cf. the Sahidic text edited by Steindorff (*Die Apokalypse des Elias*) 7.22. This line is lacking from the Chester Beatty Papyrus.

r. The Chester Beatty Papyrus reads "those who are upon the earth."

s. In the third ch. of the TLevi, the author describes various ranks of angels, including a group described as "thrones." Cf. 2En 20:1; Col 1:16; Rev 4:4. At 1:10f. the "thrones" were conceived of as being potentially hostile to men. Here they are apparently good angels who deserve the respect of the shameless one.

t. The Chester Beatty Papyrus has a slightly different reading for the last two lines, i.e. "you have been hostile to the angels and the thrones."

u. Cf. Job 38:7; Isa 14:12. An elaboration of the fallen star motif is found in 1En 86:1; 88:1–3; 90:24; Jude 13.

You were changed, and your tribe[v] became dark for you.　　　Isa 14:12
12　But you are not ashamed,
　　when you stand firmly against God.
　　You are a devil.

13　The shameless one will hear and he will be angry, and he will fight with them in the market place of the great city.[w] And he will spend seven days fighting with　Rev 11:8
14　them.[x] •And they will spend three and one half days in the market place dead,[y] while all the people see them.

15　But on the fourth day they will rise up and they will scold him saying, "O shameless one,[z] O son of lawlessness.[a2] Are you indeed not ashamed of yourself since you are leading astray the people of God for whom you did not suffer?[b2] Do you not know that we live in the Lord?"

16　As the words were spoken, they prevailed over him, saying,[c2] "Furthermore, we will lay down the flesh for the spirit,[d2] and we will kill you since you are unable to speak on that day because we are always strong in the Lord.[e2] But you are always hostile to God."[f2]

17,18　The shameless one will hear, and he will be angry and fight with them. •And
19　the whole city will surround them. •On that day they will shout up to heaven as they shine[g2] while all the people and all the world see them.[h2]　　　Dan 12:3

The persecution of the saints

20　The son of lawlessness will not prevail over them. He will be angry[i2] at the
21　land, and he will seek to sin against the people.[j2] •He will pursue all of the saints.
22　They and the priests of the land will be brought back bound. •He will kill them and destroy them . . .[k2] them. And their eyes will be removed[l2] with iron spikes.
23　He will remove their skin from their heads.[m2] He will remove their nails one by one.[n2] He will command that vinegar and lime be put in their nose.

24　Now those who are unable to bear up under the tortures of that king will take

---

v. The reading "your tribe" is found in the Chester Beatty Papyrus. The Sahidic text published by Steindorff (Die Apokalypse des Elias) reads simply "tribe." The noun in both cases is the Gk. word phylē. The meaning of the sentence is not obvious.

w. The great city is undoubtedly Jerusalem, but Rosenstiehl, L'Apocalypse d'Élie, p. 43, notes that the epithet is frequently a pejorative expression based upon Jonah's use of the term for Nineveh. Although the term is used of Jerusalem in SibOr 5:154, 226, 413 and Jer 22:8, it is more frequently applied to the metropolis of a detested enemy. The use of the expression in Rev is a case in point. The author of that work always uses the term to refer to Rome, except in Rev 11:8 where it is used to describe the city in which the Lord was crucified. There are numerous parallels between the present passage and Rev 11:7–11 which presume a dependence on either the present text of Rev or one of its sources.

x. The Chester Beatty Papyrus adds "and he will kill them."

y. Reading eumoo(u)t in agreement with the Chester Beatty Papyrus.

z. Restoring [o pat]šipe in the Akhmimic text on the basis of the Sahidic. The Akhmimic text resumes at this point.

a2. The phrase "O son of lawlessness" is lacking in the Sahidic text.

b2. This need not be a question.

c2. This is a straightforward attempt to translate a passage which Steindorff, Die Apokalypse des

Elias, p. 93, and others have found incomprehensible. The Sahidic text reads "we live in the Lord in order to scold you always. When you say 'I have prevailed over these,' we will lay down the flesh of the body." Admittedly, the Sahidic text is a bit smoother.

d2. The Sahidic text reads "the flesh of the body." Cf. 5:32 below, where a doublet preserves a fuller form in which Elijah and Enoch put off the flesh of the world and receive spiritual flesh.

e2. The Sahidic text reads "We always live in the Lord." For the Akhmimic expression cf. Eph 6:10.

f2. The Sahidic text reads "because you are always hostile."

g2. Cf. Dan 12:12; Rev 11:12; Mt 13:43.

h2. The Sahidic text published by Steindorff (Die Apokalypse des Elias) reads "the whole world will see them." The Chester Beatty Papyrus reads "while the whole world sees them." Both lack reference to "all the people."

i2. Reading fnabō(l)k. The Sahidic parallel reads fnačōnt, "he will be angry."

j2. The next three sentences are lacking from the Sahidic text.

k2. This line is no longer legible in the Akhmimic text.

l2. The Sahidic text reads "He will command and their eyes be burned with an iron borer."

m2. This sentence is lacking from the Chester Beatty Papyrus.

n2. The Sahidic text published by Steindorff (Die Apokalypse des Elias) reads "separately."

gold and flee over the fords to the desert places.[o2] They will lie down as one[p2] who
25,26 sleeps. •The Lord will receive their spirits and their souls[q2] to himself. •Their flesh   Eccl 12:7
will petrify.[r2] No wild animals will eat them until the last day of the great
27 judgment.[s2] •And[t2] they will rise up and find a place of rest.[u2] But they will not
be in the kingdom of the Christ as those who have endured[v2] because the Lord
28 said,[w2] "I will grant[x2] to them that they sit on my right hand."[y2] •They will receive   Mk 12:36
favor over others,[z2] and they will triumph[a3] over the son of lawlessness. And they
29 will witness the dissolution of heaven and earth. •They will receive the thrones
of glory and the crowns.[b3]

The martyrdom of the sixty righteous

30,31   Sixty[c3] righteous ones[d3] who are prepared for this hour[e3] will hear.[f3] •And they   Isa 59:17
will gird on the breastplate of God,[g3] and they will run to Jerusalem and fight with   1Thes 5:8
the shameless one,[h3] saying, "All powers[i3] which the prophets have done from the
beginning[j3] you have done. But you were unable[k3] to raise the dead because you
have no power to give life.[l3] Therein we have known that you are the son of
32 lawlessness." •He will hear,[m3] and he will be angry and command to kindle
33 altars.[n3] •And the righteous ones will be bound. They will be lifted up and burned.

o2. The Sahidic text reads "flee upon the rivers saying 'ferry us across to the desert.' " Bousset, *The Antichrist Legend*, pp. 211–14, has collected a number of Christian texts dealing with the flight of the faithful. Mt 24:16–20; Lk 17:31–33; and Mk 13:14–19 preserve a picture of the flight of the faithful.

p2. The Chester Beatty Papyrus appears to have repeated the phrase "as one" twice.

q2. The Sahidic text published by Steindorff (*Die Apokalypse des Elias*) reads "the spirit and the soul." Cf. Eccl 12:7.

r2. Lit. "become rock." The Sahidic text published by Steindorff (*Die Apokalypse des Elias*) reads "taste like hams." The confusion arose in Gk. when someone wrote *perna*, "ham," for *petra*, "rock." Subsequently, the Cop. *šōpe*, "become," was changed to *tōpe*, "taste," and the preposition "like" was added. The Chester Beatty Papyrus has the word for "ham" following a lacuna.

s2. Reading *ša{ph}p̣ae nhooue*, "until the last day." The Sahidic text published by Steindorff (*Die Apokalypse des Elias*) reads "until the day of the great [reading *nt{č}nog*] judgment." For the day of judgment see 5:25 below.

t2. Reading *aou*. The scribe wrote *asu*. The Sahidic text lacks a word for "and."

u2. The Sahidic text published by Steindorff (*Die Apokalypse des Elias*) reads "receive a rest." The Chester Beatty Papyrus reads "receive a place of [rest]."

v2. The Sahidic text published by Steindorff (*Die Apokalypse des Elias*) reads "but they are able to come to a rest. Be with the Christ as those who have endured." The text is apparently confused. Steindorff, p. 128, suggested restoring the text to agree with the Akhmimic reading.

w2. The Chester Beatty Papyrus has a different reading at this point. It apparently reads "(as for) those who have endured, [the Lord said]."

x2. The Sahidic text published by Steindorff (*Die Apokalypse des Elias*) has *tasse*, "command, order, arrange." The Chester Beatty Papyrus unfortunately has a lacuna at this point.

y2. Reading *hiounem mmaei* with the Sahidic (*mmoei*). The scribe wrote *hiounem mmau*, "on their right." Cf. Mk 12:36 and the synoptic parallels.

z2. The phrase could be translated "favor for [i.e. on behalf of] others." The phrase is lacking in Sahidic.

a3. Reading *sena{č}čro*.

b3. Cf. 1:8 above and the footnotes at that point.

c3. Written *ḥnt-jouōt*, lit. "three twentys."

d3. The Chester Beatty Papyrus adds "in those days."

e3. Reading *atiou{ou}nou*. The Sahidic text published by Steindorff (*Die Apokalypse des Elias*) has *nnteuneuneu*, which is probably a corruption of *nteunou*. The Chester Beatty Papyrus has *eteun{ou}*.

f3. The Sahidic text published by Steindorff (*Die Apokalypse des Elias*) reads "will be chosen on that day." The Akhmimic text reads *sōtme*, "hear," but Steindorff, p. 96, and others had been convinced that it should be changed to *sōtp*, "choose," to agree with the Sahidic text. Each of the preceding martyr tales began with the martyr "hearing" that the shameless one revealed himself. Cf. 4:1 and 4:7. The parallelism among the three stories supports the reading "hear" at this point. The Chester Beatty Papyrus now supports the Akhmimic reading.

g3. Cf. Isa 59:17; WisSol 5:18; Eph 6:14; 1Thes 5:8.

h3. The Sahidic text published by Steindorff (*Die Apokalypse des Elias*) reads "Fight with them and the shameless one."

i3. Reading *čam* for the scribal *čim*. The parallel in the Sahidic text is *čom*.

j3. The phrase "from the beginning" is lacking in the Sahidic text.

k3. The Chester Beatty Papyrus apparently adds [*na*]*me*, "truly."

l3. The phrase "to give life" is lacking in Sahidic.

m3. The Sahidic text reads "the shameless one will hear," but the text published by Steindorff (*Die Apokalypse des Elias*) requires a slight emendation, i.e. *p{a}atšipe*.

n3. The phrase "to kindle altars" is lacking in the Sahidic text at this point; it reads "and they will place them on the altars." Rosenstiehl, *L'Apocalypse d'Élie*, p. 107, calls attention to a number of later Christian texts that describe the sacrifice of Elijah and Enoch on the altar of Zion.

Men flee from the Antichrist

1 **5** And on that day the heart[a] of many will harden[b] and they will flee from him,[c]
saying, "This is not the Christ. The Christ does not kill[d] the righteous. He does
not pursue men[e] so that he might seek them, but he persuades them[f] with signs and Deut 26:8, 29:2
wonders."[g]

The removal of the righteous

2 On that day[h] the Christ will pity those who are his own. And he will send from Isa 6:2
3 heaven[i] his sixty-four thousand angels, each of whom has six wings.[j] •The sound[k] Rev 4:8
4 will move heaven and earth when they give praise and glorify. •Now those upon
whose forehead the name of Christ is written and upon whose hand[l] is the seal,
both the small and the great,[m] will be taken up upon their wings and lifted up
before his wrath.
5 Then Gabriel and Uriel will become a pillar of light leading them into the holy Ex 13:21f
6 land.[n] •It will be granted to them to eat[o] from the tree of life. They will wear white Isa 49:10
garments[p] . . . [q]and angels will watch over them.[r] They will not thirst,[s] nor will Rev 7:16
the son of lawlessness be able to prevail over them.

Natural disasters which follow the removal of the righteous

7 And on that day the earth[t] will be disturbed, and the sun will darken, and peace
8,9 will be removed from the earth.[u] •The birds will fall on the earth, dead. •The earth
10 will be dry.[v] The waters of the sea will dry up. •The sinners will groan[w] upon the

---

5 a. The Sahidic text published by Steindorff (*Die
Apokalypse des Elias*) contains an example of dittography at this point. The text is written *hnpehoou
etmmau phēt {etmmau phēt.}*

b. Taking *arau* as an ethical dat. Cf. Von Lemm,
Bulletin de l'académie impériale. The Sahidic text
reads "many will turn aside."

c. The Sahidic text reads "they will remove
themselves from him," but the Sahidic text published by Steindorff (*Die Apokalypse des Elias*)
requires an emendation, i.e. read *sesahōou* for
seshōou.

d. Reading *ḥōtbe*. The scribe wrote *ḥōtḥe*.

e. The Sahidic text reads "true men."

f. The Sahidic text published by Steindorff (*Die
Apokalypse des Elias*) has a somewhat smoother
reading, "But does he not seek even more to persuade them?" The Chester Beatty Papyrus reads
"will he not seek to persuade them."

g. Cf. Deut 26:8; 29:2; and frequently throughout the OT. Cf. also WisSol 10:16; Jn 4:48; Acts
2:19, 22, 43; 4:30.

h. Reading in agreement with the Sahidic text.
The Akhmimic text has "In those days."

i. Reading *abal⟨ḥ⟩ntpe* in agreement with the
Sahidic text.

j. The scribe wrote *ntbh* and corrected it to *nth*.
For the sense of the passage cf. Isa 6:2; Rev 4:8;
2En 16:7; 19:6; 21:1; ApMos 37:3.

k. The phrase "the sound" could be rendered
"the voice." The Sahidic text reads "their sound."

l. The Sahidic text reads "right hand." For the
sealing of the righteous cf. Rev 3:12; 7:3; and vs.
1:9 above.

m. The Sahidic text reads "from their least to
their greatest." Cf. Rev 11:18; Jer 31:34; Ps 115:13.

n. The Sahidic text reads "and they will lead
them until they bring them into the holy place."

o. Reading *at⟨ou⟩ouōm*. For texts dealing with
eating from the tree of life cf. TLevi 18:11; 1En

25:5.

p. Reading *ser ph⟨orei⟩nhbsou [nouobḥ . . .]*.
The restoration is based on the Sahidic but the
lacuna in the Akhmimic text may be large enough
to accommodate an additional word. For white
garments cf. Rev 7:13 and perhaps Zech 3:4–5.

q. The last five lines on this page have been
successfully restored by C. Schmidt, *Sitzungsberichte*, p. 321. He was able to reconstruct the text
after discovering that the fragment of the text which
Steindorff, *Die Apokalypse des Elias*, p. 108, had
published at the end of his Akhmimic text actually
belonged at the bottom of p. 39, with its reverse
side fitting into p. 40, 12–16. Our readings in both
these sections are based on Schmidt's reconstruction
rather than Steindorff's text.

r. Reading *[se]rais arau če na[ggelos]*. The
scribe wrote *se* instead of *če*.

s. The Sahidic text reads "They will not hunger
or thirst." Cf. Isa 49:10; Rev 7:16.

t. The Chester Beatty Papyrus apparently reads
"the [who]le earth."

u. The Sahidic text continues "and the heaven. The trees
will be plucked up and they will fall. The wild
beasts and the cattle will die in a disturbance." In
the Sahidic text published by Steindorff, however,
the scribe wrote by mistake the words "the spirit"
instead of "the heaven."

v. Bousset, *The Antichrist Legend*, pp. 195–99,
has collected a large number of texts that describe
the final drought and famine. This sentence is lacking from the Chester Beatty Papyrus.

w. The Nag Hammadi tractate "On the Origin
of the World" II, 125, 34, provides the following
parallel: "Then the rulers will lament, crying out
on account of their death. The angels will mourn
for their men, and the demons will weep for their
times, and their men will mourn and cry out on
account of their death."

earth saying, "What have you done to us, O son of lawlessness, saying I am the
11 Christ,[x] when you are the devil?[y] •You are unable to save yourself[z] so that you
might save us. You produced signs[a2] in our presence until you alienated us from
12 the Christ who created us.[b2] Woe to us because we listened to you.[c2] •Lo now we
will die[d2] in a famine.[e2] Where indeed is now the trace of a righteous one[f2] and
we will worship him,[g2] or where indeed is the one who will teach us and we will
13 appeal to him. •Now indeed we will be wrathfully destroyed[h2] because we
14 disobeyed God. •We went to the deep places of the sea, and we did not find
water. We dug in the rivers and papyrus reeds,[i2] and we did not find water."

The lament of the Antichrist and the pursuit of the righteous

Then on that day, the shameless[j2] one will weep,[k2] saying, "Woe to me because
15 my time has passed by for me[l2] while I was saying that my time would not pass
16 by for me. •My years became months and my days have passed away[m2] as dust
17 passes away.[n2] Now therefore I will perish together with you. •Now therefore run
18 forth to the desert. Seize the robbers and kill them. •Bring up the saints.[o2] For
because of them, the earth yields fruit.[p2] For because of them the sun shines upon
19 the earth. For because of them the dew will come upon the earth." •The sinners
will weep saying, "You made us hostile to God. If you are able,[q2] rise up and
pursue them."
20   Then he will take his fiery wings[r2] and fly out after the saints. He will fight with
21 them again. •The angels will hear and come down. They will fight with him a
battle of many swords.[s2]

---

x. Cf. vs. 3:1.

y. The Sahidic text reads "you are the son of lawlessness." Lacau, *Journal asiatique* 254 (1966) 191, reconstructed the phrase "saying I am the Christ when you are the devil." He reads *ekjou mmas(je)anok pe pchs entak(pe)pdiabolos.* The Sahidic text published by Steindorff (*Die Apokalypse des Elias*) contains both *je* and the restored *pe.*

z. Rosenstiehl, *L'Apocalypse d'Élie*, p. 110, recognized this as a traditional reproach. Cf. Jer 2:28; Isa 46:2; Lk 23:37; Mk 15:31; Mt 27:42.

a2. The Sahidic reads "vain signs."

b2. The Chester Beatty Papyrus reads "who created every one."

c2. Reading [an]*cōtme nsōk.* The scribe wrote *nsoub* for the second word.

d2. Here again we begin the use of Schmidt's text, *Sitzungsberichte*, p. 321.

e2. Lacau, *Journal asiatique* 254 (1966) 191, restored *ḫnnouhebou[oune]* in place of Schmidt's *hebou[oun].* The Sahidic text adds "and an affliction." See Bousset, *The Antichrist Legend*, pp. 195–99, for examples of drought and famine.

f2. Rosenstiehl, *L'Apocalypse d'Élie*, p. 111, sees this as an intercessory appeal for a just man. He compares Gen 18:23–33 and 4Bar 1:1–3, which suggests that a city cannot fall if there are enough just men in it. He assembled a large number of citations.

g2. The Chester Beatty Papyrus reads "and we will worship you."

h2. The Akhmimic text breaks off at this point, but the Sahidic text published by Steindorff (*Die Apokalypse des Elias*) continues uninterrupted. That is the text being followed in this edition. The Akhmimic text lacks a single sheet (two pp.). The

Akhmimic text resumes at 5:25.

i2. This is certainly a figure of severe drought. When water is not available anywhere else, it is normally possible to find it beneath a riverbed. The reading "and papyrus reeds" is an attempt to make sense of *mmn nase mmahe.* Steindorff's emendation, in *Die Apokalypse des Elias*, to read *mmntase mmahe*, "sixteen cubits," seems unlikely in view of the spelling [m]*n nase* [*mmah*]*e* in the Chester Beatty Papyrus. I have taken *ase* to be a hitherto unattested form of the New Egyptian '*isy*, "reeds." The word *mahe* is well known in Cop. as "flax," a plant that requires abundant water. In Middle Egyptian the word for "flax" is *mḥy* and the word for "papyrus plant" is *mḥyt.* Either "papyrus" or "flax" would fit the present context.

j2. Reading *pat(ŝî)pe.*

k2. The reading is taken from the Chester Beatty Papyrus, where it is followed by a lacuna of nearly a full line. The Sahidic text published by Steindorff (*Die Apokalypse des Elias*) reads "the shameless one wept," without any lacuna.

l2. The Chester Beatty Papyrus ends at this point.

m2. Reading *anahooue ouōtb* for *anahooueetb.* For shortening of days see Bousset, *The Antichrist Legend*, pp. 218f.

n2. Reading *eŝauouōtb* for the scribe's *eŝŝafouōtb.*

o2. Reading {*a*}*netouaab anisou ah*{*h*}*rai.*

p2. The scribe accidentally repeated himself in writing this *ere pkah*{*ere pkah*} *tikarpos.*

q2. Reading *e*[*ŝōpe*] *ouncom* {*com*}.

r2. Reading *nef*{*n*}*tnh nkōht.*

s2. Bousset, *The Antichrist Legend*, p. 223, gathered texts describing the battles between the angels and the demons.

The cosmic fire

22   It will come to pass on that day that the Lord will hear and command the heaven
23 and the earth with great wrath. And they will send forth fire.[t2] •And the fire will
prevail over the earth seventy-two cubits. It will consume the sinners and the devils
24 like stubble. •A true judgment will occur.[u2]

Word of the coming judgment

25   On that day, the mountains and the earth will utter speech.[v2] The byways[w2] will
speak with one another, saying, "Have you heard today the voice of a man who
26 walks who has not come to the judgment of the Son of God."[x2] •The sins of each
one will stand against him[y2] in the place where they were committed, whether those
27 of the day or of the night.[z2] •Those who belong to the righteous[a3] and . . .
will see the sinners and those who persecuted them and those who handed them
over to death in their torments.

28,29   Then the sinners [in torment[b3]] will see the place of the righteous. •And thus
grace will occur. In those days, that which the righteous will ask for many times
will be given to them.

The judgment and the execution of the Antichrist

30   On that day, the Lord will judge the heaven and the earth.
          [c3]He will judge those who transgressed in heaven,
          and those who did so on earth.
31   He will judge the shepherds of the people.[d3]
          He will ask about the flock of sheep,
          and they will be given to him,
          without any deadly guile[e3] existing in them.

32   After these things, Elijah and Enoch will come down.[f3] They will lay down the
flesh of the world,[g3] and they will receive their spiritual flesh.[h3] They will pursue[i3]
the son of lawlessness and kill him since he is not able to speak.[j3]
33   On that day, he will dissolve in their presence like ice which was dissolved by
34 a fire. He will perish like a serpent[k3] which has no breath in it. •They will say to

---

t2. Bousset, *The Antichrist Legend*, pp. 237–44, has assembled a large number of texts dealing with the final conflagration.

u2. The Akhmimic text resumes at this point. It reads "[stubb]le with true judgment." Cf. Rev 16:7; 19:2; Rom 2:5; Jn 5:30; Ps 119:75.

v2. This recalls a detail of the ancient prophetic *rîv* motif, i.e. the courtroom trial. The heavens and the earth (Isa 1:2), the mountains and the foundations of the earth (Micah 6:2), who were original witnesses to the covenant, were called again to witness the lawsuit for breach of contract. It is only fitting that they should be present in the final judgment scene. Cf. 4Ezra 5:11.

w2. Till, *Zeitschrift für ägyptische Sprache und Altertumskunde* 63 (1928) 91, correctly identified this word as *ḥōou*, the plural of *ḥo*, "way, path." The Sahidic text edited by Steindorff (*Die Apokalypse des Elias*) lacks this word. The Sahidic text ends at this point with the reading "on [that] day."

x2. Rosenstiehl, *L'Apocalypse d'Élie*, p. 113, has provided a very long list of citations that describe the Messiah as Son of God or portray him as presiding over the judgment. Cf. for example 1En 105:2; 4QFlor 1, 11–13; 4Ezra 12:31–33; Jn 5:22, 27.

y2. Cf. WisSol 4:20. A picturesque version of this motif is found in ApPaul 16. Cf. ApPet 6.

z2. Cf. 1En 104:7f.

a3. Reading *na⟨n⟩dikaios*. The motif of sinners and righteous observing each other is widespread. Cf. 1En 108:14f.; 62:11f.; Jub 23:30; Lk 16:23–26.

b3. Reading *ḫ[nk]o[las]is*. We would prefer *ḫ[ntk]o[las]is* or *ḫ[nn]o[ukolas]is*, but there is apparently not enough room.

c3. This passage is characterized by a pronounced parallel structure. It may have been poetic.

d3. There is a fragment of Gk. text, published by E. Pistelli, *Papiri greci e latini*, p. 16, which contains a portion of this phrase, e.g. *poimenos tou* [*laou*]. The judgment of the shepherds is a dominant motif in Ezek 34 and 1En 90:1–26.

e3. The Gk. text contains the words *aneu dolu*, "without guile."

f3. The Gk. text reads *hote ēleias kai en[och]*.

g3. The Gk. text preserved *tou kosm [ou]*, "of the world."

h3. Cf. Paul's "spiritual body" in 1Cor 15:44.

i3. The Gk. fragment has only *kata[diōkousin]*. It ends at this point.

j3. Cf. Mk 1:34.

k3. Cf. TAsh 7:3. Satan was traditionally identified with the serpent that tempted Eve. Cf. ApMos 15–17.

him, "Your time has passed by[13] for you. Now therefore you and those who believe
35 you will perish." •They will be cast into the bottom of the abyss[m3] and it will be
closed[n3] for them.

The millennial age

36   On that day, the Christ, the king, and all his saints will come forth from heaven.[o3]
37,38 He will burn the earth. He will spend a thousand years[p3] upon it. •Because the
sinners prevailed over it, he will create a new heaven and a new earth.[q3] No deadly   Rev 21:1
39 devil[r3] will exist in them. •He will rule with his saints, ascending and descending,[s3]
while they are always with the angels and they are with the Christ for a thousand   Rev 20:4
years.

---

13. Reading ⟨ou⟩ine as suggested by Steindorff,
Die Apokalypse des Elias, p. 190.

m3. Cf. Rev 20:3.

n3. Reading *cehōjp mmas*. The scribe wrote
hōjč.

o3. Reading *nnēu abal⟨ḫ⟩ntpe*. Cf. Lacau, *Journal asiatique* 234 (1966) 192. Cf. 4Ezra 7:28; 1Thes
4:16; Mt 24:30.

p3. Cf. Rev 20:6. It is fitting that events "on
that day" should continue for a thousand years
since one day in the sight of the Lord is equal to
a thousand years. Cf. Ps 90:4; 2Pet 3:8; Jub 4:30.
By uniting Ps 90:4 with Gen 2:2, it was possible
to construct a view of the world which continues
for six thousand years before reaching the Sabbath,
i.e. "the rest" of one thousand years. Cf. 2En
32:1–33:2 and Irenaeus *AdvHaer* 5.28.3.

q3. Cf. Rev 21:1; 2Pet 3:10–13; Isa 65:17;
66:22; 1En 91:16; Jub 1:29.

r3. Reading *diabolos* [m] *ṃou* (?) If there were
space, the reading *diabolos* [mp] *ṃou*, "devil of
death," might make better sense. It would then be
a pejorative designation for the "angel of death."
Actually, Rosenstiehl's reading in *L'Apocalypse
d'Élie*, p. 116, makes good sense, "neither devil
[nor] death," but that would require reconstructing
a compound subject between the negative *mn* and
the verb *ḥoop*, a syntactic construction that is quite
unusual. Normally when a compound subject is
desired, one subject is set before the verb and the
second is joined after it. The reconstruction of
diabolos with an adjective is not entirely satisfactory, but it is more idiomatic than the attempt to
reconstruct a compound subject at this point.

For the elimination of death cf. Rev 21:4; Isa
25:8; 4Ezra 8:53; Rev 20:14.

s3. Reading [f]*nneu eḫrai*. Cf. Gen 28:12; Jn
1:51.

APOCALYPSE OF DANIEL

(Ninth Century A.D.)

A NEW TRANSLATION AND INTRODUCTION

BY G. T. ZERVOS

In its present form the Apocalypse of Daniel[1] is a comparatively late Byzantine apocalypse in which earlier traditions concerning the coming of the Antichrist and the end of the world are adapted to the particular historical situation of eighth-century Byzantium. Accordingly, the text may be divided into two major heterogeneous sections, the first of which (chs. 1–7) is based upon the historical events of the Byzantino-Arab wars of the eighth century and their aftermath leading up to the coronation of Charlemagne in Rome in A.D. 800, all of which the author relates in a cryptic manner and projects into the future as prophecies. The narrative leaves the historical sphere and enters the realm of apocalyptic with the beginning of the second major section (chs. 8–14) in which the author draws upon earlier traditions and sources and presents his own version of the end of the world as a direct continuation of the series of historical events described in chapters 1–7. The events of the last years of the world, which in this section also are recounted in the future tense as prophecies, are dominated by the figure of the Antichrist. Described in some detail are the origin and personal characteristics of the Antichrist as well as his rise to power as king and messiah of the Jewish nation, which has been previously restored in Judea. His brief reign—characterized by the deterioration of nature, the persecution of Christians, an unsuccessful attempt at a miracle, and confrontations first with a dragon and then with three holy men—is brought to an abrupt end by the coming of the day of judgment and the appearance of Christ.

Texts

The text of the Apocalypse of Daniel is preserved complete in each of two manuscripts and partially—and in a much freer rendering—in a third. The complete texts are found in a fifteenth- or sixteenth-century manuscript (MS M) in the School of Medicine at Montpellier, France (Nr. 405, fols. 105r–15), and in a fifteenth-century manuscript (MS B) in the Bodleian Library at Oxford (Codex Canonicianus Nr. 19, fols. 145–52). The partial text (MS V) is in the Bibliotheca Marciana in Venice (Marc. Grec. VII 22, fols. 14–16).[2] The present translation is derived from photographs of manuscript B. This manuscript was published by V. Istrin in *Otkrovenie Mefodie Patarskago i Apokrificheskie Vidienie Daniila* (Moscow, 1897) pp. 145–50; but a reexamination of the photographs revealed numerous errors in Istrin's edition, which reappeared recently in K. Berger's *Die griechische Daniel-Diegese*.[3]

Manuscript B is an extremely corrupt text with misspelled words in almost every line. The

---

[1] This particular apocalypse should not be confused with numerous other medieval works associated with the names of Daniel and Methodius. These are catalogued briefly by A.-M. Denis in "Les Apocalypses de Daniel," *Introduction*, pp. 309–14.

[2] MSS M and B were studied by photographs, V by reference to K. Berger, *Die griechische Daniel-Diegese*, pp. 8–11. I would like to express my appreciation to the Bodleian Library at Oxford and the School of Medicine at Montpellier for excellent photographs of these MSS, and to the International Center for the Study of Christian Origins at Duke University for access to them.

[3] Berger, *Daniel-Diegese*, pp. 12–23.

majority of these misspellings are obviously due to the confusion of the scribe over various groups of Greek letters and diphthongs that during the course of the development of the language have come to be pronounced identically.[4] Most of these misspellings or itacisms were corrected by Istrin and will receive no comment in the critical notes of the present translation. Other misspellings, omissions of words and phrases, and mistaken transcriptions by Istrin will be noted.

Original language

There is no apparent reason why the original language of the Apocalypse of Daniel should be considered to be other than Greek. This assertion is supported by the use of the Greek Septuagint text for Old Testament quotations (4:14; 5:12; 11:11; 14:12) and for Semitic proper names (Hagar in 1:2f.; Ishmael in 1:4), as well as for the reference to the "flinty rock" in 13:8 (cf. Deut 8:15).

The case for Semitic sources for parts of the apocalyptic section (chs. 8–14) would have to be built on such slight evidence as the occurrence of the odd Semitic place-name Gouzēth[5] (9:7), which may be contrasted with the easily identifiable Greek place-names in chapter 1, and the Semitism "sons of men" (14:5). This phrase, although unique in this document, could still be explained as the influence of the Septuagint or possibly even of the New Testament.

Of interest also within this context is the confusion of the manuscripts over the three letters on the forehead of the Antichrist (9:25). While manuscripts M and V have readings that are easily understandable in Greek, manuscript B has the letters *A K T*; the scribe is obviously hard-pressed to explain their significance.[6] This could suggest that this manuscript has preserved the original letters from an earlier source. It is not inconceivable that this source was written in a different, possibly Semitic, language, thus explaining an almost ridiculous attempt to elucidate the meaning in Greek of three letters transliterated from such a language as Aramaic or Syriac.[7] However, for lack of more conclusive evidence, the most that can be said is only that these three examples—Gouzēth in 9:7, "sons of men" in 14:5, and the three letters on the forehead of the Antichrist in manuscript B (9:25)—could conceivably be faint traces of an earlier, possibly Semitic, source or sources that underlie the whole or parts of the apocalyptic section of the Apocalypse of Daniel.

Date

The date of the present form of our apocalypse can be determined with some precision by identifying the last historical event to which it makes reference. This appears to be the transfer of the kingdom from Constantinople to Rome (7:14), which may with reasonable certainty be interpreted as an allusion to the coronation of Charlemagne as emperor in Rome on Christmas Day, A.D. 800. This interpretation is supported by the description of the last Byzantine ruler before this event took place as a woman (6:10f.), who corresponds to the historical figure of the Empress Irene, sole ruler of Byzantium from 797 to 802. It may therefore be concluded that the Apocalypse of Daniel was in all probability written between the early months of 801, allowing time for the news of Charlemagne's coronation to reach Byzantium, and the end of Irene's reign on October 31, 802.[8]

The determination of the date of any possible earlier traditions and sources of the apocalyptic section would be extremely difficult and would have to depend on the identification of passages of the present apocalypse with those found in known earlier works. As will be seen below, the Apocalypse of Daniel, and especially its apocalyptic section, contains elements parallel to such early documents as the Sibylline Oracles (books 3–5, 2nd cent. B.C. to 2nd cent. A.D.), 2 Baruch, 4 Ezra, and the Revelation of John (all late 1st cent. A.D.).

---

[4] These itacisms indicate that the scribe who copied MS B did so while hearing the original text being read orally.
[5] See n. 12.
[6] See ch. 9, n. d2.
[7] Aram. *'khth* is mentioned as a root associated with the meaning "venomous" or "vindictive" in M. Jastrow's *A Dictionary of the Targumim, the Talmud Babli and Yerushalmi, and the Midrashic Literature* (New York, 1903) vol. 1, p. 66. In Syriac *'chth* is a noun form meaning "wrath" or "lasting anger." Both of these Semitic words could apply as characteristics of the Antichrist.
[8] Cf. Berger, *Daniel-Diegese*, pp. 36f.

Furthermore, our apocalypse describes the conception of the Antichrist by a virgin who touches the head of a small fish into which the Antichrist has previously entered (ch. 9). This account resembles a cryptic Christian inscription of the late second century on the tomb of Aberkios of Hierapolis,[9] which depicts Christ as a fish that has been caught by a pure virgin. This parallel, in addition to those with the early pseudepigraphical works mentioned above, *could* indicate that the author of the Apocalypse of Daniel was familiar with early traditions and incorporated some of them into his own work. It may be concluded, therefore, that the original date of certain elements of this apocalypse could be centuries earlier than that of the document as a whole and that some of them could fit into the apocalyptic environment that produced such works as the Sibylline Oracles, 2 Baruch, 4 Ezra, and the Revelation of John.

Provenance

Berger's suggestion of a provenance in the Greek islands rather than in Byzantium itself, because of what he describes as the considerable role which the former play in the manuscripts of the apocalypse,[10] does not seem to be well founded. The word *nēsos* (island) occurs only twice each in manuscripts M (2:15; 5:9) and V (vss. 34, 36)[11] and three times in manuscript B (5:9; 11:8 twice). Such a paucity of references to the term "island" within the document could hardly warrant the conclusion of a provenance in the Greek islands. Even these few instances could perhaps be explained more satisfactorily as an example of the dependence of the Apocalypse of Daniel on the imagery of the Revelation of John (see "Relation to Canonical Books"), in which islands are mentioned three times (Rev 1:9; 6:14; 16:20). Rather, the overwhelming concern of the apocalypse for the city of Constantinople, at least throughout the historical section, suggests that the "mother of cities" (7:11), Constantinople itself, is the place of origin.

The change in the overall character of the Apocalypse of Daniel in proceeding from the historical to the apocalyptic section is also apparent in the corresponding geographical shift from Greek Byzantium to Hebrew Judea. This probably reflects the distinctive provenance of the supposed earlier sources of the apocalyptic section, but to determine this provenance with any degree of certainty would be most difficult. Aside from the references to Judea (8:1) and Jerusalem (8:5; 9:14), the only other geographical clue is the place-name Gouzēth (9:7), which Berger explains as the transcription of Kush, the Semitic name for Ethiopia. He concludes, however, that it is more satisfactorily identified as Egypt by a literary parallel occurring in another Christian apocalyptic work.[12] At any rate, on the basis of such meager information the most that can be said is that the provenance of the hypothetical sources of the apocalyptic section is perhaps in a Semitic rather than a Greek environment; Palestine and possibly Egypt are suggested by references in the text.

Historical importance

In its present form, the Apocalypse of Daniel has significance mainly within the context of late eighth-century Byzantine history. The author describes three Byzantine rulers, the first very favorably and the last two in a derogatory manner. The first emperor, as described in chapters 3–5, has characteristics of both Leo III (717–41) and his son Constantine V (741–75); but he is probably to be identified with the latter.[13] Both Leo III and Constantine

---

[9] Ibid., pp. 104–6.

[10] Ibid., p. 9.

[11] Ibid., p. 25.

[12] Ibid., p. 106. The place-name Gouzē is identified explicitly as the "land of the Egyptians" in the *Logos tou Kyriou hēmōn Iēsou Christou peri tēs antilogias tou diabolou*, which was published by A. Vassiliev in his *Anecdota Graeco-Byzantina*, Pars Prior (Moscow, 1893) p. 8. It is perhaps worthy of note that Jastrow identifies *Goza* as "a river or channel in Babylon" (*Dictionary*, vol. 1, p. 220).

[13] Concerning the complicated matter of the divergence of the MSS as to the succession of Byzantine emperors presented in ApDan, see Berger, *Daniel-Diegese*, pp. 32–39. It seems that the number of years of rule (thirty-four for Constantine V against thirty-six in 5:13 of ApDan), the mention of the two small boys in 3:15; 4:1, 4; 5:2, 18 (see ch. 3, n. r), and the letter "K" denoting the name of the emperor in 3:12 (see ch. 3, n. m) would strongly suggest that Constantine V is indeed the savior-king of ApDan, or at least of the version contained in MS B. This is verified by the descriptions of the two rulers who succeed him in ch. 6, who in fact correspond to the two historical successors of Constantine V—Leo IV and Irene.

V are notorious in Byzantine history, the former as the initiator and the latter as the most zealous proponent of the iconoclastic movement, which literally shook Byzantium to its very foundations for over a century until it was finally defeated in A.D. 842. On the contrary, the last two rulers, who are described so unfavorably in chapter 6, correspond to Leo IV (775–80) and Irene (797–802 as sole ruler), both of whom in varying degrees opposed the iconoclasts. Irene, in fact, convened the Seventh Ecumenical Synod which met at Nicea in 787 and officially reinstated the veneration of icons and condemned iconoclasm as heresy, acts for which she was later canonized by the Orthodox Church.

The extreme favoritism of the author of the Apocalypse of Daniel toward Constantine V and his obvious dislike of Leo IV and Irene perhaps betray his own iconoclastic tendencies. These, however, he never states in this work, possibly out of fear, since he probably wrote during Irene's reign after the decision of the Seventh Ecumenical Synod. Thus, a supporter of iconoclasm, writing at a time when his party was apparently defeated by what must have seemed to him as a heretic empress, could have viewed this development in connection with the rise of a new political power under Charlemagne as the beginning of a series of events that were expected to take place at the end of the world.[14] Accordingly, the author drew upon earlier traditions and sources dealing with the last days and composed his own version of what was supposed to follow in the near future. If this hypothesis is correct, it would explain the sudden leap in the story line of the Apocalypse of Daniel from the Byzantine political scene in 801 to the apocalyptic narrative concerning the Antichrist and the last days of the world.

Theological importance

Since the Apocalypse of Daniel is historically and politically oriented, there is relatively little theological material contained in it. God appears mainly when he intervenes in the political or military history of nations, as for example in chapter 3, in which he determines the outcome of the Byzantino-Arab wars (cf. 6:9 and 7:11); but he is also responsible for the abundance of the fruits of the earth in peacetime (5:16). Man also is shown chiefly in political and military situations; but in the sphere of religion he is divided into two camps according to faith: the Roman Christians and the misbelievers (especially the Arabs and Jews). World history is presented as proceeding toward a final "judgment and recompense" (14:14), but exactly what is to follow is not specified beyond a single statement concerning the flowering of Christ as "Lord and king of glory" (14:16). There is only one mention of an angel in 3:7, but this verse could be dependent on the imagery contained in chapter 16 of the Revelation of John (see "Relation to Canonical Books"). As far as can be ascertained from the description of the sinful rulers in chapter 6 and from the account of liturgical degeneration in chapter 2:5–8, the ethics of the apocalypse seem to be along the traditional lines that would be expected in a medieval Christian work.

The most important single theological aspect of the Apocalypse of Daniel—and which significantly seems to belong to the earlier underlying sources—is a relatively complex dualism centering on the figure of the Antichrist,[15] who is the leader of the final assault by the forces of evil against the Christians. Jews (ch. 11), demons (ch. 12), and even nature itself (chs. 11:5–11; 12:9–13) take part in this great persecution, while the whole affair is summarily described as "the deception of the devil" (14:15). Given in chapter 9 are important details about the origin of the Antichrist as well as a bizarre description of his person. The "theology" of the Antichrist as presented in this apocalypse is completed by the addition, in the last two chapters, of the accounts of his unsuccessful attempt at a miracle and his confrontation with three holy men leading up to his final downfall, which coincides with the coming of the day of judgment and the appearance of Christ.

---

[14] For a discussion of the belief that the fall of the Roman Empire, which to our author was the Byzantine Empire, would immediately precede the end of the world, see W. Bousset's *The Antichrist Legend*, pp. 123–32.

[15] Concerning the Antichrist tradition see Bousset, *Legend*, and more recently H. D. Rauh's *Das Bild des Antichrist im Mittelalter: von Tyconius zum deutschen Symbolismus* (Beiträge zur Geschichte der Philosophie und Theologie des Mittelalters N.F. 9; Münster, 1979); see especially pp. 145–52.

Relation to canonical books

Except for such scattered references to biblical books in 1:1 (Mk 13:7, 8, and parallels), 4:14 (Deut 32:30), 5:12 (Isa 2:4), 9:9f. (2Thes 2:3), 11:11 (Prov 11:32), 14:9 (Heb 11:38), and 14:12 (Ps 51:19), the Apocalypse of Daniel seems to be primarily dependent on the imagery and language of the Revelation of John. In fact, the overall framework of this apocalypse is reminiscent of the sixth and seventh bowls of God's wrath described in Revelation 16:12–21 and of the fall of the great harlot Babylon portrayed in chapters 17 and 18. In Revelation 16:12 we find the idea that the Euphrates River will dry up so that the way of the kings of the East may be prepared. Similarly, in the Apocalypse of Daniel 1:2 a bush that restrains the three sons of Hagar also dries up, and according to 1:3 these three figures enter Babylonia, the area around the Euphrates River. In Revelation 16:13–16 three unclean spirits go forth to gather the nations of the world to the great final battle of Armageddon. This brings to mind the three armies led by the three sons of Hagar against Byzantium, where they engage in a great war with the savior-king and his two small boys (chs. 1–4). A significant parallel may be seen at the climax of the attack by the respective forces of evil in each of the narratives in question. In both cases very similar statements occur concerning sounds and voices from heaven and a great earthquake, which seem to signal the turning point in the battle (Rev 16:17f.; ApDan 3:7). Finally, the description of the great harlot Babylon in Revelation (chs. 16–18) is obviously the prototype of the references to Babylon in our apocalypse (7:2, 5, 11). This is verified by similarities even in details such as the seven hills of the city Babylon (Rev 17:9; ApDan 7:2, 5) and the woes pronounced upon this city (Rev 18:10, 16, 19; ApDan 7:2, 5, 11).

Aside from the possibility that the historical structure of the Apocalypse of Daniel is dependent on the succession of events described in chapters 16–18 of the Revelation of John, there also seems to have been a certain amount of borrowing of specific images. For example, Revelation 14:20 presents the image of blood as deep as the bridles of horses, and the Apocalypse of Daniel 4:8 portrays horses as being submerged and drowning in blood. According to Revelation 9:6 men will seek death and desire to die, and according to our apocalypse 12:4f. people will be calling on death and will be blessing those who have already died. The drying up of all greenery, trees, and flowers and the description of the earth as being like copper according to the Apocalypse of Daniel 12:9–11 could be a reflection of the burning of one third of the trees and green grass on the earth that is depicted in Revelation 8:7. Finally, a striking parallel image in the two documents is the description in Revelation 6:15f. of the kings of the earth and magnates, among others, hiding themselves in the caves and the rocks of the mountains and calling on the mountains and rocks to fall on them. This seems to be reproduced in the Apocalypse of Daniel at 2:15, where it is written that rulers and magnates will "flee to the glens of the mountains" and in 12:6 (MS M only), where it is said that people will entreat and beg the mountains to cover them.

Finally, there are a number of parallel phrases and terms in the two works that would support a dependence of the Apocalypse of Daniel on the Book of Revelation. The most outstanding of these are the phrases "sand of the sea" used to describe the multitudes of the enemy in our apocalypse at 12:1 (cf. Rev 20:8), and "foundation of the world" found in our apocalypse at 4:6; 5:16; and 10:1 (cf. Rev 13:8). The terms "mountains" and "islands" are used together twice in Revelation (6:14; 16:20), while appearing also together in the present apocalypse at 5:9 and separately at 1:9; 2:15, 17; 11:8; and 14:9. Also of interest are the similes of the mourners of fallen Babylon as sailors in Revelation 18:17–19 and as merchants in 18:3, 11, and 15. Sailors will lament over fallen Babylon according to the Apocalypse of Daniel 7:13, merchants will do likewise according to 7:14 (MS M only). Each of these parallel terms and phrases would seem insignificant alone. However, when viewed together and in connection with the previously discussed similarities of historical structure and imagery, they strongly indicate a dependence of the Apocalypse of Daniel on the Revelation of John.

Relation to apocryphal books

The Apocalypse of Daniel is only one of a considerable number of similar apocalypses that are strangely reminiscent of the early Jewish pseudepigraphical works.[16] That the Apocalypse of Daniel either influenced or was influenced by one or more of these contemporary documents cannot be doubted, as this is evidenced by several examples of direct dependence.[17] It is beyond the scope of this introduction, however, to examine this matter in more detail. The most that will be done will be to point out some of the most significant parallels between this apocalypse and some early pseudepigrapha.

The reference to the king of the Romans by the initial letter of his name (ApDan 3:12) could stem from Sibylline Oracles 5.1–51, in which most of the Roman emperors from Julius Caesar to Marcus Aurelius are identified by the numerical value of the first Greek letter of their names. It is perhaps significant that among the names of these emperors, Caesar and Claudius begin in Greek with the letter K, which has the numerical value twenty, as is the case with the Roman king mentioned in the Apocalypse of Daniel 3:12. It should be noted that this apocalypse follows the motif of the Sibylline Oracles as opposed to that used in the Revelation of John 13:18, in which the figure represented by the second beast is identified by the number 666, the sum of the numerical values of all the letters of his name. In view of the probable dependence of this apocalypse on Revelation, as discussed in the preceding section, the method for denoting emperors could indicate that this particular element is borrowed from another source, possibly the Sibylline Oracles.

Another concept of the Sibylline Oracles worthy of note in relation to the Apocalypse of Daniel is that found in Book 3.75–77, in which a woman is described as the last ruler before the end of the world. This idea accords with 6:10f. of our apocalypse, which also presents a woman as the last ruler of the "Seven-hilled" city in an eschatological context (cf. Rev 17). The similarity between the two texts is strengthened by the appearance in both of a malevolent figure who will deceive people, especially the Jews. In Sibylline Oracles 3.63–69 the deceiver is Beliar, or Satan, and in our apocalypse the later chapters are concerned with the Antichrist, who will deceive the Jews into worshiping him as the Messiah.

A final motif of the Sibylline Oracles present also in the Apocalypse of Daniel is that expressed in 3:10 and concerns the savior-king of the Romans, "who people say is dead and useful for nothing, who people think died many years before." This is apparently a reference to the early *Nero redivivus* legend, which found its way repeatedly into the Sibylline Oracles (e.g. 4.119, 138f.; 5.33f., 101–7, 137–54) and is implied in Revelation 13:3. The essential difference between the use of this motif in the Sibylline Oracles and Revelation on the one hand and in the Apocalypse of Daniel on the other is that in the former two works it refers to the monstrous figure of Nero as an enemy of the people of God, and in the present apocalypse it is applied to the savior-king sent by God.

Chapter 10 of the Apocalypse of Daniel contains an interesting description of the fruitfulness of the earth just prior to the rise to power of the Antichrist. The phraseology in 10:3f. includes vine branches, grape clusters, and individual grapes; this cluster of images is strongly reminiscent of what R. H. Charles referred to as a "fragment of an old Apocalypse"[18] recorded in 1 Enoch 10:19, 2 Baruch 29:5, and later by Papias through a quotation preserved in Irenaeus, *Contra haereses* 5.33.3. Exactly which of these documents was the source of the parallel passage in our apocalypse cannot be determined with certainty. However, the occurrence of such a passage serves to demonstrate that the author of the Apocalypse of Daniel did at least take into consideration much earlier sources and in this particular case interpolated, although not without modification, early apocalyptic material into his own work.

Another possible case of the insertion of foreign material into the Apocalypse of Daniel may perhaps be seen in chapter 13, which concerns an unsuccessful attempt by the Antichrist to turn a stone into bread in the presence of his Jewish worshipers. There appear to be elements from another tradition interwoven into the fabric of this chapter. This is indicated

---

[16] See n. 1. Berger gives an extensive list of 188 apocryphal works, both early and medieval, in pp. xi–xxiii of *Daniel-Diegese*.

[17] Aside from the aforementioned parallel in the document published by Vassiliev, *Anecdota Graeco-Byzantina*, p. 8, there are also strong literary affinities between ApDan and the so-called "Apocalypse of John" published by C. Tischendorf in his *Apocalypses Apocryphae Mosis, Esdrae, Pauli, Iohannis, item Mariae Dormitio* (Leipzig, 1866) pp. 73–76. Berger (*Daniel-Diegese*) deals extensively with the matter of parallels between ApDan and other—especially medieval—apocryphal works in his commentary on the text of the Apocalypse of Daniel.

[18] *APOT*, vol. 2, p. 497.

by the use of two different Greek words—*lithos* (stone) in verses 1 and 2, and *petra* (rock) in verses 8 and 10—to describe the stone. Furthermore, the verses in which the term *petra* is located (vss. 8–13) stand apart from the rest of chapter 13 and from the apocalypse as a whole in two significant ways. First, these verses are written as a block in the present tense as opposed to the rest of the document, which, except for a very few scattered instances, is in the future tense.[19] Secondly, verses 8–13 relate a series of events that are theologically incompatible with the Book of Revelation, which has been shown to be a major source of the imagery in our apocalypse.

Verses 8–13 describe the Antichrist commanding a "flinty rock" to become bread in order to impress the Jews. Instead, the rock becomes a dragon and reviles him as iniquitous and unjust, thus shaming him before the Jews. This picture of a dragon as an enemy of the Antichrist is contrary to the portrayal of the dragon (Satan) in Revelation 13:2, 4, 11; and 16:13 as an ally of the two bestial Antichrist figures described in Revelation 13. The linguistic evidence of the two different Greek words for the stone used in the two sections of chapter 13, the grammatical peculiarity of the second section being in the present tense, and the theological incompatibility of this section with the main source of the imagery of the apocalypse as a whole, the Book of Revelation, would indicate that verses 8–13 of chapter 13 of the Apocalypse of Daniel are based on material originating from another source. The closest parallel to the imagery presented in these verses may be found in 4 Ezra 5:5, in which a stone is also said to "utter its voice" within an eschatological context closely resembling the woeful times preceding the end of the world as presented in the last chapters of the Apocalypse of Daniel.[20]

Finally, and of particular interest in connection with the relation of the Apocalypse of Daniel to other apocryphal works, is the suggestion made by W. Bousset[21] concerning the existence of a now lost apocalypse dealing with the Antichrist, which was entitled, according to Bousset, the Apocalypse of Daniel. Even more interesting is the possibility raised by Bousset[22] that this lost apocalypse was used as a source by the third-century Christian Father Hippolytus, thus bringing the date of this hypothetical document to a period approaching that of the early pseudepigrapha. An investigation of the possibility of the existence of such a document and its relation to the other medieval apocalypses would perhaps clear up many of the questions concerning the sources of the apocalyptic material preserved in the Apocalypse of Daniel.

Cultural importance

The present Apocalypse of Daniel was until very recently accessible only through the manuscripts themselves or through Istrin's rare edition of 1897, and then only to those with a knowledge of Greek. Berger's publication in 1976 made it available in German, while the present translation is the first appearance of this document in English. Under such circumstances the Apocalypse of Daniel can hardly be said to have exercised any significant influence on our culture. However, certain concepts embodied in this and similar Byzantine works, although originally intended for one specific period of history, have lived on through the popular beliefs and aspirations of those nations that have inherited the Byzantine spiritual tradition.

As the centuries passed, the Turks replaced the Arabs as the "sons of Hagar" and the "Ishmaelites" and became the relentless enemies of the Orthodox nations of the Balkans and eastern Europe. The Ottoman Empire eventually enveloped all these peoples, except the Russians, and took the "Seven-hilled" city of Constantinople in 1453. The subsequent decline of the Turkish Empire was paralleled by the emergence of Russia as a world power and later by the establishment of such independent and restive Balkan states as Greece, Bulgaria, Serbia, and Romania. Thus was created a political situation reminiscent of eighth-century Byzantium, with free Orthodox nations again in conflict with the "sons of Hagar."

A new significance was acquired by the old Byzantine apocalypses that told of a Roman

---

[19] See ch. 13, n. j.
[20] Cf. 4Bar 9:30.
[21] Bousset, *Legend*, pp. 68–72, 160.
[22] Ibid., pp. 82f.

king named Constantine who would defeat the Ishmaelites and drive them away from the "Seven-hilled" city. This concept was especially tantalizing to the Russians, who considered themselves to be the inheritors of the Roman sovereignty after the fall of the Byzantine Empire. The Russian rulers were called czars after the Caesars and Moscow was the Third Rome—after classical Rome and the New Rome, which was the official title of Constantinople. The centuries-long struggle of Russia to gain strategic access to the Mediterranean Sea also took on the nature of a holy war to liberate the old Byzantine imperial city of Constantinople, which happened to sit astride the Bosporus, the natural gateway from the Black Sea to the Mediterranean.

Catherine the Great went so far as to christen her second grandson Constantine in 1779 as part of a plan to drive the Turks out of the Balkans and Asia Minor and to reestablish the Byzantine Empire with her grandson as its ruler in Constantinople. The Romanov dynasty also pursued an aggressive foreign policy against the Turks throughout the nineteenth century. This culminated in World War I with the secret treaty of the Allies awarding Constantinople to Russia after victory. The Russian Revolution of 1917 intervened, however, and Russia withdrew from the war, thus losing by a matter of months the prize it had sought through centuries of wars and struggles. At any rate, this interest of the Russians in medieval apocalyptic traditions explains the appearance in the late nineteenth century of collections of Byzantine apocalypses in Russian editions, such as that of Istrin and the *Anecdota Graeco-Byzantina* of A. Vassiliev, which appeared in Moscow in 1893.

The influence of medieval apocalyptic traditions may also be seen in the case of modern Greece. The Greeks were the first of the Balkan peoples to achieve their independence from the Ottoman Empire in 1830 and have added traditional Greek territories to their state roughly every generation since that time at the expense of the ever-dwindling Turkish Empire. The old prophecies concerning a king named Constantine who would drive the Turks from Constantinople seemed to be coming true in the early 1920s when indeed King Constantine XII (twelfth in line from Constantine the Great) ruled Greece at a time when a Greek army of occupation had landed in Asia Minor and was moving eastward. Although the expedition failed and the Greeks were driven out of Asia Minor, there can be little doubt that the ancient popular traditions had played a not inconsiderable role in the formulation of the Greek war plans. Even today the belief is widespread among the Greek people, as the only remaining free Orthodox nation, that someday a Constantine will accomplish the reconquest of the "Queen of cities," which has until now eluded their grasp. The examples of Russia and Greece serve to demonstrate how Byzantine apocalyptic traditions, if not such works themselves as the Apocalypse of Daniel, have significantly influenced major historical events throughout the centuries and continue to have the potential to do so.

BIBLIOGRAPHY

Charlesworth, *PMR*, pp. 180–82.

Berger, K. *Die griechische Daniel-Diegese*. SPB 27; Leiden, 1976. (This is by far the most helpful work on the Apocalypse of Daniel with critical text, German translation, and exhaustive notes pointing out and analyzing parallels with numerous other apocryphal works.)

Bousset, W. *The Antichrist Legend*, trans. by A. H. Keane. London, 1896. (The usefulness of this book lies mainly in its discussion of the various elements of the Antichrist theme, which is so central to our apocalypse, as they developed from the earliest times through the medieval period.)

Istrin, V. *Otkrovenie Mefodie Patarskago i Apokrificheskie Vidienie Daniila*. Moscow, 1897. (This book is valuable for the text of MS B which it contains, although it must be used with caution because of Istrin's often heavy-handed corrections of the very corrupt MS.)

THE APOCALYPSE OF DANIEL[a]

)[b] (1)[b] 1 **1** According to the God-spoken word[c] which says: "*When you heard of wars and* Mk 13:7f.
rumors of wars,[e] nation will fight against nation, and kingdom against kingdom,
2 *earthquakes*, plagues and deviations[f] of stars."[g] •Then the bush which restrains
3 the sons of Hagar[h] will dry up. •And three sons of Hagar will go forth into great
Babylonia,[i] (whose) name(s) are) Ouachēs,[j] and another[k] Axiaphar, and the third
(2) 4 Morphosar. •And Ishmael will come down[l] the region of the land of swift passage.
5,6 And he will establish his camp in Chalcedon across from Byzantium. • And the
other one[m] will come to Antioch, Cilicia, and Iberian Anatolia, the Thrakysan
7 country and Smyrna[n] and as far as the Seven-hilled (city).[o] • And[p] he will spill
8 Roman[q] blood.[r] • And another[s] will come to the region of Persia and (to) the Galilean
9 country, the Armenian border, and the city of Trebizond. • And he will come to
10 the region of the land of the Meropes. •And he will massacre male children from Mt 2:16
11 two and three years old and younger.[t] • And he will consume them by the sword.
12 And the third one[u] will come down the regions of the north[v] and Mesiaspolis[w] and
Synopolis, and Zalichos, the regions of Chrysiapetra, and the well-lit valley and
Bithynia, and of Daphnousia, Chrysioupolis, and Damoulion and as far as the
Seven-hilled (city).[x]

(3) 1 **2** And therefore all these (will) slaughter an infinite multitude of Romans from
2 two and three years old[a] and younger.[b] • And they will gather together toward the

---

1 a. The title of MS B is: "The Discourse of Our
Holy Father Bishop Methodius Concerning the Last
Days and Concerning the Antichrist"; of MS M:
"Narrative Concerning the Days of the Antichrist,
How He Will Come to Be, and Concerning the End
of Time"; and of MS V: "The First Vision of
Daniel. The Vision and Apocalypse of Daniel the
Prophet." Only the more significant variations
among the MSS will be pointed out in the critical
notes. Translations from M that will appear in the
textual notes are often based upon corrupt passages.

b. In the margin the Roman numerals in parentheses denote the divisions of the text in V. Istrin's
edition, *Otkrovenie Mefodie Patarskago i Apokrificheskie Vidienie Daniila*; the regular numerals in
parentheses are K. Berger's chapter divisions in
Daniel-Diegese.

c. Lit. "voice."

d. Read *akousēte* for *akousate* in B.

e. Read *polemōn* for *polemon* in B. Istrin has
polemou.

f. Read *paratropai* with M for *epitropai* in B.

g. The first part of this quotation is an exact
rendering from Mk 13:7f., while the latter part
seems to reflect the concern with heavenly signs in
the parallel passage in Lk 21:10f.

h. Hagar was the maidservant of Sarah who gave
birth to Ishmael by Abraham (Gen 16). Hence, the
Byzantines commonly referred to the Arabs and
later to the Turks, whom they thought to be the
descendants of Hagar and Ishmael, as Agarenes and
Ishmaelites.

i. M: "And the nations and the three sons of
Hagar will go forth from great Babylonia," but it
may also be translated: "And the nations of great
Babylonia and the three sons of Hagar will go
forth."

j. As supported by the reading of this name as
Oualleis in M, this is probably a reference to the

Arab Caliph Walid I who ruled early in the 8th
cent. See Berger, *Daniel-Diegese*, pp. 47–49, for
a discussion of the identities of the three sons of
Hagar mentioned by name in this verse.

k. Istrin corrects the corrupt reading *ho hete* in
B to *ho heteros* (lit. "the other").

l. Istrin corrects the corrupt reading *kato meros*
in B to *katelthē to meros*. This is supported by M.

m. The three individuals vaguely referred to in
B as "the other one," "another," and "the third
one" are more clearly identified in M as the afore-
mentioned three sons of Hagar.

n. Read *Smyrnēn* for *Smirnin* in B. Istrin has
Smirnēn.

o. The "Seven-hilled" city which will be mentioned many times in this document is Constantinople (Byzantium), the capital of the Byzantine
Empire, which, like Rome, was built upon seven
hills.

p. B has *kai* twice.

q. The Byzantines considered themselves to be
the successors of the Roman Empire and therefore
as a rule referred to themselves as Romans.

r. Read *haima* for *haiman* in B.

s. Lit. "the other one." Istrin omits the article
ho in B. See n. m.

t. Lit. "from above."

u. See n. m.

v. Read the noun *borra* with M for the adjective
boreiou in B.

w. This is probably, with M, the city Amasia.

x. The geographical places mentioned in this
chapter correspond in general to those involved in
the Arab invasions of Asia Minor in the early 8th
cent.

2 a. The *tryetous* in Istrin's text is his correction
of an obscure reading in B.

b. Lit. "from above."

3,4 sea. •And in their ships[c] (will be) a myriad myriads. •And there will be other
5 infinite and innumerable multitudes. •And in that place many will deny our Lord
6 Jesus Christ and the holy gifts and will follow the apostates.[d] •And every sacrifice
7,8 will cease from the churches. •And the liturgy of God will be mocked.[e] •And the
9 priests will be as laymen.[f] •And Ishmael will cry out with a great voice, boasting[g]
10 and saying, •"Where is the God of the Romans? There is no one helping them,
(4) 11 for we have defeated them completely." •For truly[h] the three sons of Hagar will
12 roar[i] against the Romans. •And they will cross over against the Seven-hilled (city)
13,14 toward Byzantium. •And conferring, they will say (among) themselves, •"Come
and let us make a bridge in the sea[j] with boats and transport[k] horses for ourselves
15 to Byzantium, the Seven-hilled (city)." • But the rulers of the Romans and the   Rev 6:15
16 magnates of the Seven-hilled (city) will flee to the glens of the mountains.[l] •And
17 there will be fear and affliction. •And there will be much necessity of the moun-
18 tains.[m] •And the people of the Seven-hilled (city) will be afflicted by the sword.
19,20 Woe, woe then. •How will the orthodox faith of the Christians and the invincible
power of the honorable and life-giving cross be overcome?[n]

(5) 1,2 **3** But hear, brethren, that because of their iniquity God forbears. •And the first
3 will set up his couch across from Byzantium. •And he will strike and they will be
4,5 stricken. •And then the rulers of the Romans blaspheme, saying, •"Woe, woe,
6 neither in[a] heaven do we have a king[b] nor on the earth." •And with this word[c] the
Lord will incline his mercy toward the Romans and toward their revenge and will
7 repay[d] justice to his enemies. •And there will be a great sound from heaven and   Rev 16:17f.
8 a fearful earthquake and a voice from the angel from heaven. •And the Lord will
incline his head and will set his fury[e] against the sons of Hagar and upon the feet[f]
9 of Ishmael. •And the Lord will lift up the cowardice of the Romans and put[g] (it)
into the hearts of Ishmael, and the courage of the Ishmaelites into the hearts of the
10 Romans. •And the Lord will raise up a king of the Romans, who people say is
11 dead and useful for nothing, who people think[h] died many years before.[i] •The
12 Lord is reserving this man in the outer country[j] of Persia.[k] •This (is) his name: that   SibOr 5.1-51
13 which (begins with)[l] the letter K[m] of the alphabet. •And this man is coming to the
14,15 Seven-hilled city toward the evening.[n] •And he will prepare for his enemies. •And
on Saturday[o] morning, as the sun rises, he will engage in a great war with the

---

c. Istrin corrects *auklais* in B to *nauklais*.

d. Istrin corrects *hypostatais* in B to *apostatais*.

e. The obscure reading *hypomōxei* in B could possibly be a corrupt form of the verbal root *mōkaō* with the preposition *hypo*. Berger corrects this word as *hypochōrei* ("to recede").

f. Vss. 5–8 do not appear in M.

g. Read *egkauchōmenos* for *enkauchomenos* in B.

h. Istrin corrects *allēthōs* in B to *alēthōs*.

i. Read *bryxousin* for *bryzousin* in B. M supports this with *brixousin*.

j. Istrin corrects *thallassē* in B to *thalassē*.

k. Lit. "cross over" with causative meaning.

l. M: "will take refuge in the islands of the sea."

m. M: "of the Romans."

n. Istrin's text omits the preposition *kata* from before the verb *kyrieuthēsetai* in B. Vss. 19f. do not appear in M.

3 a. Istrin's text omits the article *tō* in B.

b. Read *basilea* for *basilean* in B.

c. Lit. "voice." In place of the present text up to this point in ch. 3, M has: "However, beloved ones, hear of the most compassionate philanthropy

of the all-merciful God. For as the son of Hagar and of godless Ishmael is roaring like wild lions against the Romans . . ."

d. Read *antapodōsei* for *anttapodosei* in B.

e. Istrin's text omits the phrase *kai thysei ton thymon autou* in B. Read *thēsei* for *thysei*.

f. M: "implacable race."

g. Read *balei* for *ballei* in B.

h. Read *nomizousin* ("to think") with M for *onomazousin* ("to name") in B.

i. This verse brings to mind the *Nero redivivus* legend. See "Relation to apocryphal books."

j. Istrin's text has the mistaken reading *ex eōchōran* for *eis exochōran* in B.

k. M: "in the inner country of the Persian and Syrian nations."

l. Lit. "that which (is) in the letter."

m. The letter "K" is the reading of M and probably refers to Constantine V. B has *Ē*, which, if referring to the Emperor Heraclius, could be the original reading from a more primitive tradition. See W. Bousset, *The Antichrist Legend*, p. 78.

n. M mentions that this man's entrance will occur on a Friday (*Paraskeuē*), which is an obvious play on the verb *paraskeuazō* ("to prepare") in the next verse.

o. Istrin corrects *Sabatō* in B to *Sabbatō*.

16 nation[p] and the sons of Hagar, both he and[q] the two small boys.[r] •And the rulers
17 of the Romans will gather together in Byzantium. •Then even the priests of the
Romans and the bishops and abbots who are found will bear weapons of war.

1 **4** And when he has gathered those together with (the) two small boys, that king
2 also will join[a] in a mighty war with the nation of the sons of Hagar.[b] •And he will
3 massacre them like the grass of a reed being burned by fire. •And from their blood
4 a three-year-old[c] bull will drown.[d] •And the king alone will pursue a thousand and
5 the two small boys myriads. •And Ishmael and the sons of Hagar will be butchered[e]
(6) 6 to the end. •And there will be war and great bloodshed such as has not been since
7 the foundation of the world. •The blood will be mixed[f] in the sea one and a half
8 miles.[g] •And in the streets of the Seven-hilled (city) horses will be submerged,[h] Rev 14:20
9 drowning in the blood. •And from that nation and from Ishmael there will remain[i]
10 only three tents of men. •And (the) sons of Ishmael will serve the Romans to the
end and will serve the chief donkey drivers[j] of the Seven-hilled (city for) thirty
11 years. •And the nature of Ishmael in the sword and in captivity is more bitter and
12 more grievous[k] beyond that of the Romans.[l] •And the Roman race will desire to
13 see[m] a trace of Ishmael and will not find (it). •And then the prophetic word will
14 be fulfilled (that says): •"*How will one pursue a thousand and two remove myriads* Deut 32:30LXX
unless[n] *the Lord God rejected them and the Lord gave them over?*"[o]

1 **5** And the king of the Romans will subdue every enemy and adversary under his
2 feet. •And the scepter of that king will be long-lived, likewise[a] (that) of the two
3,4 small boys. •And his fame will go forth from the east and the west. •And there
5 will be one empire.[b] •And no one will resist him because this man has come from
6,7 God and[c] he will cause all[d] war to cease. •And there will be great peace. •And
8 every city and fortresses will be built. •And there will be many altars acceptable
9 to God[e] in all the civilized world. •And all the islands[f] and the mountains will be
10 inhabited.[g] •And the bread and the wine and the olive oil and the gold and the
11 silver will increase[h] in all[i] the earth. •And that king will cause all hostility to cease Isa 2:4
12,13 upon the earth. •And they will make their weapons into scythes. •And his reign
14 will be (for) thirty-six years.[j] •And the rulers of the Romans will desire[k] to join

p. M: "Ishmael."
q. Istrin's text has this *kai* in parentheses unnecessarily, since it does occur in B.
r. Constantine V in fact did have two sons, besides Leo IV, by another wife.

4 a. Istrin corrects *synkrotēsei* in B to *sygkrotēsei*.
b. The phrase "of the sons of Hagar" is supplied from M.
c. Istrin corrects *tryotēs* in B to *trietēs*.
d. Read *pnigēsetai* for *pnigysētai* in B. Istrin has *pnigizetai*.
e. Read *sygkopēsetai* for *sygkopisētai* in B. Istrin has *synkopēsetai*.
f. Gk. *rasthēsetai* in B could conceivably be a corrupt form of the verb *rainō* ("to sprinkle"), but more probably the words *kai rasthēsetai* taken together are a mistaken writing of *kerasthēsetai* ("to mix"). This is supported by the reading *sygkerasthēsetai* of M.
g. Lit. "twelve stades" of about one-eighth mile each.
h. Istrin's reading of *kaphēsontai* for *baphēsontai* could be a mistake, since *b* and *k* are often written alike in B.
i. Read *mēnē* for *mynē* in B. Istrin has *menei*.
j. Gk. *archionēlatais* ("chief donkey drivers") has been suggested by Berger for the obscure reading *archoliōtais* in B.
k. Read *pikrotera kai odynērotera* for *pykrotera kai odynōtera* in B. Istrin has mistakenly written

pokrotera.
l. Vss. 10f. do not appear in M.
m. Read *idein* with M for *ē d' an* in B. V also supports M.
n. The reading *eimē* (unless) of M is more in accord with the text of this LXX quotation (Deut 32:30) than is the *oimoi* ("alas") of B.
o. Read *paredōken* with M for *eparedōken* in B.

5 a. Read *estai makroēmereuon homoiōs* for *estin makro hemerebontei ho misos* in B. Istrin has mistakenly written *makron*.
b. In place of this vs., M has: "And he will thrust his broadsword in the east and his bow into the sides of the north and the bear."
c. Read with M *apo tou theou houtōs* (correctly *houtos*) for *apo thē holos* in B. Istrin's text omits the phrase *apo thē holos elēlythen*.
d. Read *panta* for *pasa* in B.
e. The phrase "acceptable to God" does not appear in M.
f. Istrin corrects *nisai* in B to *nēsoi*.
g. For this vs. M reads: "The islands also will be inhabited."
h. Read *plēthynthēsetai* with M for the corrupt *planthēsetai* in B.
i. Read *pasē* for *mpasē* in B.
j. This vs. does not appear in M.
k. Read *epithymēsousin* for *epithymōsousin* in B.

15 in war but will not find (it).[l] •And all the perimeter(s) of the earth[m] will fear them.
16 And that king will glorify God because in his reign God gave to him the good
17 things of the earth which he did not give since the foundation of the world. •And
18 the king will fall asleep[n] in peace. •And his two small boys will be taken up[o] in
peace[p] after thirty-three years.[q]

(II) (7) 1,2   **6** And after him there will arise from the north[a] another king.[b] •And working
3 great impurities[c] and many injustices, he will also work great iniquities. •And he
4 will couple[d] mother and son and brother and sister. •And[e] he will bring the monks
out of the holy monasteries and will join the monasteries together[f] and will cause
5,6 the nuns[g] to lie with his nation. •And he will work great transgressions. •Woe,
7,8 woe then (to) the Christian race. •Woe to those who are pregnant.[h] •And the praises
9 of God also will cease. •And the Lord God will call fire from heaven and will
(8) 10 consume them.[i] •And after him a foul and alien woman[j] will reign in the Seven-   SibOr 3.75-77
11 hilled (city). •And she will settle on the southern side of the Seven-hilled (city).[k]

(9) 1,2   **7** And therefore woe (to) the Christian race. • And woe to you, Seven-hilled   Rev 18:10,16,19
3 Babylon, because the Byzantium of God will flee from you. •And your holiness
4,5 and your temples will flee from you. •And your glory will fall. •And woe to you,   Rev 17:9, 18
6 Seven-hilled Babylon, the new Byzantium. •And woe to you, the Christian race.
7 Again (there will be) an inroad of nations, again fear (among) the Romans, again
8 slaughters and disturbances (for) the Roman nation.[a] •Churches will be destroyed.
9,10 The faith[b] has been dissolved. • Women conceive[c] the babies of misbelievers.[d]
11 And therefore woe to you, wretched[e] Babylon, the mother of cities,[f] because God
12,13 will incline his wrath which emits fire. •And your[g] high walls will fall. •And there   Rev 18:17-19
will remain in you only one[h] pillar of Constantine the Great, so that they who sail

---

l. At this point M inserts: "And that king will be called by the name of a wild beast." This could be a reference to Leo III (717–41), father of Constantine V.

m. Lit. "all the circle of the earth."

n. Istrin mistakenly reads *synkoitēthēsetai* for *synkymēthisetai* in B (correct to *synkoimēthēsetai*).

o. Read *aparthōsin* for the obscure *apar*(?)*thōsin* in B.

p. M: "And he and his two small boys will fall asleep . . ." Istrin's text omits the whole phrase *kai ta dio autou myraki apar*(?)*thōsin en eirēnē* in B (correct to *kai ta dyo autou meirakia aparthōsin en eirēnē*).

q. The thirty-three years given in this vs. for the reign of the king conflict with the thirty-six given in vs. 13. This conflict does not exist in M, which omits vs. 13. Constantine V in fact ruled for thirty-four years (741–75).

6 a. Istrin corrects *bora* in B to *borra*.

b. This king from the north corresponds to Leo IV, who was known as the "Khazar" because he was the son of Constantine V and a princess of Khazaria, a kingdom to the north of Byzantium. He ruled from 775 to 780.

c. Istrin corrects *akartasias* in B to *akarthasias*.

d. Read *syzeuxei* for *synzeuxei* in B.

e. Istrin mistakenly reads *kai* for *ek* in B.

f. Istrin's text omits the phrase *kai synzeuxei ta monastēria* in B.

g. Read *monastrias* for *monēstērias* in B.

h. In place of vss. 4–7, M has: "And the iniquity of transgression will be accomplished and of licentiousness and of incest as the people will behave licentiously by his decrees."

i. M: "he (the king) will be shaken by heavenly fire."

j. This woman corresponds to the Empress Irene who ruled with her son Constantine VI from 780 to 797 then as sole ruler from 797 to 802.

k. Instead of vss. 10f., M has: "And after him a tall alien man will arise from the sides of the south. And he will reign in the Seven-hilled (city)." This reading upsets the chronology that has been established for B and raises the possibility of a different date, if not for the apocalypse as a whole, at least for the version of the text represented by M.

7 a. Istrin's text omits the phrase *to genos tōn Rōmaiōn* in B.

b. Istrin corrects *ai poistois* in B to *hē pistis*.

ç. Read *sylambanousin* for *synlambanousin* in B.

d. In place of vss. 1–10, M has: "And therefore woe to you, Seven-hilled Babylon, because your wealth and your glory will be proclaimed. For, boasting, you said, 'I am clothed in gold and in hyacinth and pearl and in scarlet raiment and in purple and in silver and amber and my hand is not [In place of the obscure phrase *ouk estin hē emi cheira*, V has: "there is nothing inferior in me"], because kings will reign in me and potentates will come in and go out and great rulers will reside in me.'" Cf. Rev 18:7, 16.

e. Read *talaipōre* for *talaipore* in B.

f. Istrin corrects *pollaiōn* in B to *poleōn*.

g. Istrin mistakenly writes a second *ta* for *sou* in B.

h. Istrin omits the *heis* in B.

14 the sea[i] may lament there. •And furthermore the kingdom will be taken up[j] from him[k] and will be given to Rome.[l]

1,2 **8** And another great scepter will arise from Judea. • And[a] his name (is) Dan.[b]
3 And then the Jews, the implacable Hebrew race, who are dispersed into cities and
4 countries, will be gathered together. •And they will be gathered together there.[c]
5,6 And they will come into Jerusalem toward their king.[d] •And they will afflict the
7 Christian race in all[e] the earth. •Woe, woe,[f] good people.[g]

)1 **9** With him[a] reigning, the Antichrist will go forth from the lower regions[b] and the
2,3 chasms of Hades. •And he will come into a small garidion[c] fish. •And he is coming
4,5 in the broad sea. •And he will be caught[d] by twelve fishermen. •And the fishermen
6 will become maddened[e] toward each other. •One will prevail over them, whose
7 name (is) Judas. •And he takes that fish for his inheritance and comes into a place Mt 26:14f.
8 named Gouzēth and there sells[f] the fish for[g] thirty silver pieces. •And a virgin girl
9 will buy the fish. •Her name (is) Injustice because the son of injustice will be born[h] 2Thes 2:3
,11 from her. •And her surname[i] will be Perdition. •For by touching[j] the[k] head of the
12 fish she will become pregnant[l] and will conceive the Antichrist himself. •And he
13 will be born from her (after) three months. •And he will suckle (from) her (for)
,15 four[m] months. •He comes into Jerusalem[n] and becomes a false teacher.[o] •And he AscenIs 4
16 will appear quiet and gentle[p] and guileless.[q] •The height of his stature (will be)
,18 fifteen feet.[r] •And the hairs of his head[s] (will reach) as far as his feet. •And he
,20 (will be) large and three-crested.[t] •And the track[u] of his feet (will be) large.[v] •His
eyes (will be) like the star which rises[w] in the morning, and his right (eye will be)
,22 like a lion's.[x] •His lower teeth[y] (will be) iron and his lower jaw diamond.[z] •And

---

i. Istrin corrects *thalasan* in B to *thalassan*.

j. Istrin mistakenly writes *aparthēsetai* for *eparthēsetai* in B.

k. M: "from you," and furthermore inserts at this point: "Your merchants will flee from you and will be lost. And every city and country will lament over you, the mother of cities. For at that time the kingdom will be lifted up from Byzantium . . ."

l. This is probably a reference to the coronation of Charlemagne as emperor in Rome on Christmas Day, 800.

8 a. Istrin omits this *kai* in B.

b. M adds at this point: "And he will reign in Jerusalem." Based upon the OT passages in Gen 49:17, Deut 33:22, and Jer 8, a tradition arose very early that associated the Antichrist with the tribe of Dan. Irenaeus attributes to this concept the omission in Rev 7:5–8 of the tribe of Dan from the list of the tribes of the sons of Israel who are sealed as servants of God (*Contra haereses* 5.30.2). For an earlier form of the tradition, see TDan 5:4–13.

c. M transposes to this point from the preceding vs. the phrase: "from every city and country."

d. Istrin corrects *basilean* in B to *basilea*.

e. Istrin corrects *mpasē* in B to *pasē*.

f. Istrin's text omits the second "woe" in B.

g. In place of this vs., M has: "And they will oppress the Romans unto death."

9 a. M specifies Dan.

b. Read *katachthoniōn* for *kakochthoniōn* in B. M supports this with *katachthonion*.

c. Istrin writes *garidion* for *gabridion* in B. The original spelling was probably *gauridion* and was doubtless the name of a particular type of fish.

d. Read *halieuthēsetai* for *hallieuthēsetai* in B.

e. Read *ekmaneis* for *egymaneis* in B. Istrin has

egmaneis.

f. Read *pōlei* for *pōllei* in B.

g. Istrin's text omits the preposition *eis* in B.

h. Read *gennēthēnai* for *genēthēnai* in B.

i. Read *epōnymon* for *epōnymian* in B.

j. Istrin mistakenly writes *hepsomenē* ("to cook") for *hapsamenoi* in B (correct to *hapsamenē*, "to touch").

k. Istrin's text omits the article *tēs* in B.

l. Read *eggyos* for *eggonos* ("grandson") in B. M and V support this reading.

m. M: "five months."

n. Read *Hierosolyma* for *Hierosolyman* in B.

o. Istrin corrects *parodaskalos* in B to *paradaskalos*. M: "teacher of children."

p. "Gentle" seems to be the general import of the obscure readings *praophylēs* (B) and *praophaleis* (M). Berger corrects this to *prosphilēs* ("beloved").

q. M further describes the Antichrist as "downcast" and "prosecuting transgressions."

r. Lit. "ten cubits" of about eighteen inches each.

s. "Head" is the reading of M. B repeats the *hēlikia* ("stature") of the preceding vs., probably by a scribal error.

t. B has the difficult reading *trikoryphos*, which may best be translated as "three-crested." M: "topped with hair." V supports B.

u. Istrin's text mistakenly has *ichnys* for *ichnos* in B.

v. M: "three cubits" (four and a half feet).

w. Istrin corrects *anatelōn* in B to *anatellōn*.

x. Istrin's text omits *kai ho dexios autou hōs leōntos* in B.

y. M and V: "the upper part of his teeth."

z. M has the correct neuter singular ending of the adjective "diamond"; B has the plural.

23 his right arm (will be) iron and his left copper. •And his right hand (will be) four
24 and a half feet (long).ᵃ² •(He will be) long-faced, long-nosed,ᵇ² and disorderly.ᶜ²
25,26 And he also has upon his forehead three letters: *A, K, T*.ᵈ² •And the *A* signifies:
"I deny," the *K*: "And I completely reject," the *T*: "The befouled dragon."ᵉ²
27 And the Antichrist will be teaching and being taught.ᶠ²

1 **10** At that time there will be an abundance of grain and wine and olive oil such
2 as has not been since the foundation of the world.ᵃ •And in those times theᵇ ear   2Bar 29:5
3 will pour out a half measure of grain.ᶜ •And the vine branchᵈ will put out a hundred
4 grape clusters. •And the grape cluster will bear ten thousandᵉ (grapes) and will pour
5,6 out a hundred measures.ᶠ •And the seed of the olive tree will be complete.ᵍ •And
7 there will be muchʰ fruitfulness of all kinds. •And the land will be fruitful and will
produce her fruits a hundredfold.ⁱ

(12) 1 **11** And the Jewish nation and the Jerusalemitesᵃ will take counselᵇ saying,
2,3 "Come, let us make this admirable man king."ᶜ •And they makeᵈ him king and
4,5 crown him (after) three days. •And he will reign (for) three years. •And in his first
6 yearᵉ all the grass upon the earth will fail. •And in the whole world there will not
7 be found a half measureᶠ of grain or a half jar of wine nor other fruit.ᵍ •Then there
8 will be a mightly plague. •And those on the mainland will flee to the islands and
9 those on the islands to the mainland. •And for a time a mannerʰ of disease will
be upon the whole earth and a great plague which has never occurred until that
10,11 era.ⁱ •And the people will be deadened. •If ʲ *the just man is barely saved, how will*   Prov 11:31LXX
the sinner appear?

---

a2. M: "His left hand (will be) three cubits
(long) and his right hand four cubits."

b2. Read *makrorinos* with M for the obscure
makroradēs in B.

c2. Istrin writes *eudiathetos* ("well-disposed")
for *adoiathetos* (correct to *adiathetos*, "disorderly") in B.

d2. M: "*A T Ch*, that is, Antichrist"; V: "Denying, *Ch X St*." The verb *arnoumai* ("to deny")
occurs in connection with the three letters on the
forehead of the Antichrist because the numerical
equivalents of the Gk. letters that make up this verb
spelled as *arnoume* add up to 666, the number of
the Antichrist figure in Rev 13:18. The numerical
values of the Gk. letters *Ch, X*, and *St* also add up
to 666. The letters *A K T*, however, which are
preserved in B, obviously puzzled even the scribe
of this MS. The *A* is explained adequately as representing *arnoumai*, but the *K* and *T* are presented
as signifying the conjunction *kai* ("and") and the
article *ton* ("the"), which introduce the phrases:
"And I completely reject" and "The befouled
dragon." This ludicrous explanation by the scribe
of B indicates that he is dealing with a set of letters
foreign to him—possibly from another source—for
which he concocts an obviously forced interpretation. For the possibility that these letters were originally from a Semitic source, see the Introduction,
n. 7.

e2. This vs. does not appear in M.

f2. In place of this vs., M has: "And when the
scepter of Dan has come to an end, the Antichrist
will be teaching and being taught, trying and being
tried." Cf. OdesSol 38:9f.

10 a. M inserts at this point: "For they who cultivated the good things of the world will be (for)
three years."

b. Istrin's text omits the article *tou* in B, which
has no grammatical place in the sentence.

c. Read *choinikon sitou* for *phoinikos* in B. This
is supported by M. A *choinix* was a dry measure
of about a quart.

d. My conjectured meaning: The reading *agkōn*
("angle" or "bend") suggested by M is preferable
to the *askos* ("wine skin") of B, although the
meaning is still obscure.

e. Lit. "will become a bearer of ten thousand."
Read *genēsetai* for *gennēsetai* in B and *myriagōgos*
for *myriorygos* in B.

f. M: "two measures of wine" (*oinon metra
dyo*).

g. M adds at this point: "the whole of it not
containing (extraneous) matter."

h. Istrin corrects *polē* in B to *pollē*.

i. At this point M adds: "And there will be much
elation, such as has not been from the foundation
of the world until those times should come."

11 a. Istrin corrects *hoi erosolymitai* in B to *hoi
Hierosolymitai*.

b. Read *symboulion* with M for *symboulon* in
B.

c. Read *basilea* for *basilean* in B.

d. Istrin corrects *poioun* in B to *poiousin*.

e. M: "first year of his reign."

f. Read *hēmichoinikon*, as suggested by the readings of M and V. B: "a half tablet" (*hēmison
pinakion*), which Istrin corrects to *hēmisyn pinakion*.

g. M: "And other fruit will not be found."

h. The phrase *kata spithamēn kai opēan* is extremely obscure.

i. In place of vss. 7–9, M has: "And there will
be upon the face of the earth a great famine, such
as has not been since the foundation of the world
until that time. For the earth will be worn out by
the plague."

j. Istrin's text omits *oi*, which should be read *ei*
("if").

1 **12** And then the unclean spirits and the demons will go forth like the sand[a] of
2 the sea, those in the abyss[b] and those in the crags and ravines.[c] •And they will
adhere to the Antichrist and they also will be[d] tempting the Christians[e] and killing[f]
3,4 the babies of the women. •And they themselves will suckle from them. •And then   Rev 9:6
the people will be calling upon death and digging up the tombs and saying,
5 "Blessed and thrice blessed are you who have already died,[g] because you did not
6 reach these days."[h] •And[i] they who go down to the sea also (will be) saying,
7 "May the fury of your waves swallow us also, O holy sea."[j] •And then all flesh
8 of the Romans will lament. •And while there will be temporary[k] joy[l] and exultation
of the Jews, (there will be) affliction and oppression of the Romans[m] from every
,10 necessity of the evil demons. •And the earth will become like copper. •And all
11 greenery will dry up. •And every tree and every flower upon the earth will fail.
,13 And the lakes and the rivers and the wells will dry up. •And the moisture[n] of the
waters will completely dry up.[o]

1,2 **13** And then the Antichrist will lift up a stone in his hands and say, •"Believe
3 in me and I will make these stones (into) bread." •And then (the)[a] Jews will
4 worship (him), who are saying, •"You are Christ for whom we pray and on
5 account of you the Christian race has grieved[b] us greatly."[c] •And then the Antichrist
6,7 will boast, saying to the Jews, •"Do not be grieved thus. •A little (while and) the
8 Christian race will see and will realize[d] who I am."[e] •And the Antichrist lifts up
9 (his) voice toward the[f] flinty rock,[g] saying,[h] •"Become bread before the Jews."   4Ezra 5:5
,11 And disobeying[i] him, the rock becomes a dragon. •And the dragon says to the
12 Antichrist, •"O you who are full of every iniquity and injustice, why do you do   4Bar 9:30
13 things which you are not able?" •And the dragon shames[j] him before[k] the Jews.

4) 1 **14** And then three men will go forth and will condemn[a] him (as) a liar and a
2 deceiver. •And these three men, two from heaven and one from the earth,[b] also

---

12 a. Istrin corrects *amos* in B to *ammos*.

b. Istrin corrects *abēsō* in B to *abyssō*.

c. In place of "ravines," M has: "in the lower regions, in the caves, in the lakes, in the springs, in the pools, and in the air."

d. Istrin's text omits *pros ton antuchruston* (correct to *antichriston*) *kai esontai* in B.

e. M: "people."

f. Read *anairountes* for *anairountai* in B. This is supported by M.

g. Istrin's text mistakenly has *protereutēsantes* for *proteleutēsantes* in B.

h. At this point M inserts: "final, grievous, and wholly evil (days), entreating and begging the mountains and saying, 'Cover us, O mountains.' "

i. Istrin's text omits *men* in B.

j. At this point M inserts: "And woe to those who suckle and are pregnant in those most evil days" (Mt 24:19; Mk 13:17; Lk 21:23).

k. Read *proskairos* for *proikeroi* in B. Istrin's text has *proskarē*.

l. Istrin's text mistakenly has *kara* for *chara* in B.

m. M: "Christians."

n. Read *ikmades* for *ekmades* in B. The plural is translated here as singular.

o. At this point M inserts: "And the faces of the people will be deadened by the coming plague."

13 a. Istrin corrects *oioudeoi* in B to *hoi Ioudaioi*.

b. Read *elypēsen* for *ellypēsen* in B.

c. At this point M inserts: "And the Jews will be in great joy then, speaking with the Antichrist."

d. The text of B is extremely corrupt at this point.

e. At this point M inserts: "The day will try you and I will tempt you."

f. Read *tēn* for *ton* in B.

g. Gk. *akrotomos petra* is the same phrase used in the LXX to describe the rock out of which Moses brought forth water miraculously in the wilderness (Deut 8:15).

h. Read *legōn* with M for *legontes* in B, which Istrin writes *legonta*. At this point M inserts: "I made heaven and earth. I say to you, the flinty rock . . ."

i. Istrin's text mistakenly has *parakalousa* for *parakousasa* in B.

j. Istrin has the verb *kataischynō* in the future tense with the accent on the last syllable. Since the spelling of this verb is exactly the same in the present tense, except for the accent being on the next to the last syllable, it is possible to translate it here in the present. MSS B and M support this interpretation; in B the ending of this verb is in an abbreviated form showing no accent, and in M it is clearly written in the present tense. Thus, this vs. is in harmony with the preceding five vss., which seem to constitute a distinct unit (see "Relation to apocryphal books").

k. Istrin corrects *enōpoi* in B to *enōpion*.

14 a. Istrin corrects *exelexousin* ("to choose") in B to *exelegxousin* ("to condemn").

b. The two men from heaven who will confront the Antichrist were already identified from early patristic times as Enoch and Elijah, the two biblical figures who did not suffer death but were taken up to heaven still living (Irenaeus, *Contra haereses*

3 walk before the Antichrist and say,[c] • "Woe to you, O worker of injustice and
4 inheritor[d] of eternal fire." • And they will walk in all the earth, crying out[e] and
5 saying to the afflicted Christians, • "Hear,[f] O sons of men, and do not worship AscenIs 4
him, because he is not the Christ nor[g] a God-fearing man, but he is the Antichrist."
6,7 And many Christians will run to the feet of the saints and say,[h] • "What shall we
8,9 do, O saints? • Where shall we Christians hide?" • And many of the Christians will Heb 11:38
hide in mountains and caves and in the holes of the earth (and) will be saved, so
10 that the treacherous Samuel[i] might not seize them. • And when the Antichrist finds
11 these three men[j] he will kill them by the sword. • Then that spoken by the prophet
12,13 David will be fulfilled: • *Then they will offer up bulls upon your altar.*"[k] • And Ps 51:19
(50:21LXX)
with the Antichrist reigning and with the demons persecuting, the Jews contriving
14 vanities[l] against the Christians, the great day of the Lord draws near. • And there
15,16 will be[m] judgment and recompense. • And the deception of the devil will fall. • And Jn 8:12
the light of the world, Christ our Lord[n] and king of glory, will flower, to whom
is due all glory and honor and dominion forever.[o] Amen.

5.5.1; cf. Gen 5:24; 2Kgs 2:11; Mal 4:5; Rev
11:3–13; 4Ezra 6:26). The third man from the earth,
John the Evangelist, was added in later times. For
a discussion of the three witnesses see Bousset's
The Antichrist Legend, pp. 203–11.
  c. Lit. "and saying."
  d. Read *klēronome* for *klērōnome* in B.
  e. Istrin's text mistakenly has *kraxontes* for *kra-
zontes* in B.
  f. Read *akousate* for *akousēte* in B. Istrin has
akousete.
  g. Lit. "but not."
  h. Lit. "and saying."

  i. M: "*Samaēl.*"
  j. M inserts at this point: "in the midst of the
altar . . ."
  k. This quote is from the LXX text of Ps 50:21.
  l. Read *kena meletountōn* for *kai namele touton*
in B.
  m. Read *genēsetai* for *gennēsetai* in B.
  n. M: "Christ our God."
  o. Lit. "unto the ages." M inserts a typical
liturgical formula: "Together with the Father and
the Son and the Holy Spirit, now and always and
unto the ages of ages."

TESTAMENTS

*OFTEN WITH APOCALYPTIC
SECTIONS*

INTRODUCTION

BY J. H. CHARLESWORTH

The traditions in the Old Testament provided the framework and most of the presuppositions for the following testaments. These documents represent a type of writing that was presaged in the Old Testament (cf. Gen 49), but which did not reach maturity until the time of the second Temple. Just as the Old Testament contains for Jews and Christians a record of God's covenant, testament, and will (nouns represented by one word in Gk., *diathēkē*), so the following compositions reputedly preserve the solemn last words and wills of model figures. No binding genre was employed by the authors of the testaments, but one can discern among them a loose format: The ideal figure faces death and causes his relatives and intimate friends to circle around his bed. He occasionally informs them of his fatal flaw and exhorts them to avoid certain temptations; he typically instructs them regarding the way of righteousness and utters blessings and curses. Often he illustrates his words—as the apocalyptic seer in the apocalypses—with descriptions of the future as it has been revealed to him in a dream or vision. The latter feature is common to apocalyptic literature and plays a significant role in some of the testaments, especially the Testaments of the Twelve Patriarchs, the Testament of Abraham, and the Testament of Moses. The unique features and peculiarities of some of these documents and the significant differences among them should not be overshadowed by their sharing of the title "testament." Some scholars, for example, have argued that the Testament of Abraham is not a testament because it lacks one of the form's reputed features: Abraham is not portrayed as preparing and giving a testament.

It is clear that the testaments do not represent a well-defined genre; moreover, the testamentary framework often includes, for example, apocalyptic, ethical, and Midrashic types of literature. Some works included under "Expansions of the 'Old Testament' and Other Legends" have even been called testaments; for example, Jubilees has been denominated "The Testament of Moses."

Also to be consulted when reading the testaments are the following: the Testament of Hezekiah (in the Martyrdom and Ascension of Isaiah), the Testament of Zosimus (an earlier name for the History of the Rechabites), and the Testament of Orpheus (cf. Orphica in the Supplement).

CONTENTS

TESTAMENTS OF THE TWELVE PATRIARCHS

(Second Century B.C.)

*

A NEW TRANSLATION AND INTRODUCTION

BY H. C. KEE

The Testaments of the Twelve Patriarchs purport to be the final utterances of the twelve sons of Jacob, on the model of Jacob's last words in Genesis 49. Just prior to his death, each of the sons is depicted as gathering around him his offspring, reflecting on aspects of his life, confessing his misdeeds, exhorting his family to avoid his sins and exemplify virtue, concluding with predictions about the future of Israel and giving instructions concerning his burial. In the process, each patriarch calls for special honor to be given to Levi and Judah, progenitors, respectively, of the priestly and kingly lines of the nation. The account in each case ends with a report of the burial of the patriarch. Most of the Testaments include a section in which the destiny of the nation is described according to a pattern of the nation's sin, its exile as divine judgment, and its restoration in glory in the eschatological future.[1]

Texts

GREEK
1. Vatican Library, Cod. Graec. 731, thirteenth century, complete (= *c*).
2. St. Catherine's Monastery, Mount Sinai, MS 547, seventeenth century, ends at the Testament of Joseph 15:7 (= *h*).
3. Bodleian Library, MS Baroccio 133, Oxford, fourteenth century, numerous omissions (= *a*).
4. Monastery of Koutloumousiou, Cod. 39, Mount Athos, tenth century (= *e*), includes extensive additions following the Testament of Levi 2:3; 18:2; the Testament of Asher 7:2. The second of these corresponds to the version of the Testament of Levi that exists in Aramaic fragments (see below).
5. University Library, Cambridge, MS Ff. 1.24, tenth century (= *b*).

In his edition of the Greek text of the Testaments, R. H. Charles assumed the existence of two ancient recensions of the work, one of which he designated α and the other β. He believed he could trace these two different textual traditions back to two recensions of what he thought to be the original Hebrew of the Testaments. For the most part the differences between the Greek textual traditions were accounted for by Charles as having arisen by chance, based in many cases on corruption in the process of translation. According to Charles, both α and β texts contain Christian interpolations, with a greater number in the

[1] My studies in T12P were initiated by my esteemed teachers at Yale, Millar Burrows and Clarence Tucker Craig. More recently I have benefited by way of stimulus, challenge, and criticism from the members of the Pseudepigrapha Seminars of the Society of Biblical Literature and the Studiorum Novi Testamenti Societas, especially M. de Jonge and J. H. Charlesworth. John Priest, of Florida State University, read a draft of this material and offered most helpful comments and criticism; Dr. Ellen Young likewise provided perceptive editorial assistance. To all of them I hereby express gratitude, in recognition that I bear responsibility for the results.

latter text tradition. Charles based his critical text primarily on the α text, but acknowledged that sometimes one tradition preserves the true text, and at times the other, so that the translator is obliged to move back and forth between α and β. M. de Jonge, on the other hand, based his critical text on the β tradition. H. J. de Jonge, in M. de Jonge, *Studies on the Testaments of the Twelve Patriarchs*, rejects the α/β classification of manuscripts and concludes that only manuscripts *b* and *k* (only contains excerpts) have preserved the oldest stage of the Greek archetype.

ARMENIAN

Nearly all of the twelve manuscripts of the Testaments in Armenian known to R. H. Charles were from western Europe (chiefly in the library of the Mechitarist Fathers in Venice); of these, nine were used by Charles in preparing his critical edition of the text. C. Burchard now lists forty-five manuscripts of the Testaments in Armenian, some of which are now in the Armenian Patriarchate in Jerusalem and which have been published in part by M. Stone in his critical study of the Testament of Levi. Until new evidence from previously unpublished manuscripts shows otherwise, however, the Armenian manuscripts are still to be classified as Aᵃ and Aᵝ, of which Aᵃ is an abbreviated text that includes readings of a secondary nature, although on the whole it stands closer to the α text of the Greek tradition. In addition, it represents several superior readings. The Armenian manuscripts remain translations from the Greek, however, and give no evidence of dependence on Semitic originals.

SLAVONIC

The Slavonic manuscripts are few and late, consisting mostly of material excerpted from Greek sources in which Old Testament narratives are retold in expanded form.

HEBREW

Late Hebrew fragments of a Testament of Judah and a complete Testament of Naphtali have long been known, but the Late Hebrew style in which they are written and their divergence in both structure and basic substance from the Greek Testaments exclude them from consideration as being merely late copies of an original Hebrew document that might underlie our Greek Testaments. They present only occasional and fragmentary verbal parallels with the Greek Testaments. An unpublished genealogy of Bilhah from Qumran Cave 4 seems to have an affinity with the Testament of Naphtali 1:6–12, but determination of the relationship must await publication of the text.

ARAMAIC

The fragments of an Aramaic Testament of Levi, discovered in the Cairo Genizah (a synagogue storeroom) and first published in 1910, have since been supplemented by a somewhat fuller Greek version of this same work found at the Monastery of Koutloumousiou on Mount Athos, and more recently by numerous fragments discovered at Qumran. The latter include possible parallels—their fragmentary nature precludes certainty—to the Testament of Levi 21 and to a Prayer of Levi which is not found in our Greek Testament of Levi but which does appear in the Athos version after Testament of Levi 2:3. All these fragments evidence kinship with the Testaments and at some points with the Jubilees, but the divergences in wording are so great as to exclude the possibility of a direct literary dependence of our Greek Testaments on this Aramaic material.

The textual basis for this translation is the critical edition of R. H. Charles, although some readings have been adopted from the β text published by M. de Jonge, usually in the interests of literary coherence or clarity of meaning. In addition, the edition of S. Agourides has been consulted. Where the weight of evidence between the two main text traditions seems to be balanced, or where one offers an interesting variant to the content of the other, both have been printed in parallel columns.

Original language

The discovery of fragments of testaments in Aramaic that are in some way akin to the Testaments of the Twelve Patriarchs has led some scholars to conclude that the Greek form of this work is dependent on a hypothetical Aramaic or Hebrew document that included testaments of all twelve of the patriarchs. The direct links between the Greek version and the Aramaic works are so few, however, and the absence from the Semitic fragments of some of the fundamental concepts of the Testaments presented here is so complete as to rule out an Aramaic original for our Testaments.

Charles sought to make a case for Hebrew as the original language of the Testaments on the grounds that (1) Hebrew idiom underlies the Greek text and (2) that awkward turns of speech, puzzling etymologies for personal and place-names, and seemingly unintelligible passages can best be accounted for by reconstructing a Hebrew original. But the Semitic idiom can just as well be explained as deriving from the language and style of the Septuagint in use among Greek-speaking Jews.

The evidence adduced for mistranslations from a Semitic original is purely hypothetical and is more than offset by the clear indication that our document is dependent on the Septuagint as Testament of Joseph 20:3 (*hippodromos*) shows, and by the occurrence of puns on Greek words (e.g. TLevi 6:1). The pervasive use of technical terms of hellenistic piety for which there are no exact counterparts in Hebrew or Aramaic, in addition to the influence of hellenistic romances on the style and scope of the narrative portions of the Testaments, points rather to the conclusion that they were originally written in Greek. There were possibly some additions to the text made by Greek-speaking Jews in the period around the turn of the eras; for example, Testament of Reuben 6:7 and Testament of Levi 18:9 may have been expanded by later Jewish (non-Essene) editors.

A large number of passages in the Testaments are messianic, but ten or more of them also sound specifically Christian. Examples of this are Testament of Levi 4:1; 14:2, which speak of laying hands (violently) on the "Son" or "the Savior of the world." In Testament of Asher 7:3, God is said to come eating and drinking, as a man. Testament of Benjamin 9:3 depicts the Lord entering "the first temple," after which he is "raised up on wood." Charles designated these passages as Christian interpolations into a basically Jewish document. M. de Jonge, on the other hand, asserted that the whole of the Testaments is Christian: building on Jewish traditions—the testaments of Levi and Naphtali, as well as other testaments which have survived in fragmentary form or in later copies—a Christian author produced the present complete set of twelve testaments around A.D. 200. His theory, however, seems both unwarranted and unnecessary.

The existence of the Aramaic fragments of a Testament of Levi and of the fragmentary Hebrew Testament of Naphtali at Qumran, together with the much later Hebrew testaments of Judah and Naphtali, shows that in the testamentary literature linked with the sons of Jacob and produced in the period of the second Temple we are dealing with a broad and free tradition. The genre "testament" is itself loosely defined, and its exemplars are transmitted in versions which vary in language and content. As a result of this generic and conceptual fluidity, it is not surprising that there are only very occasional points of verbal contact between the Greek Testaments and the Hebrew and Aramaic testaments. Literary dependence cannot be inferred, much less demonstrated. Rather, we must reckon with an author who, in writing the Testaments, is drawing on a free tradition and creating from it his own distinctive literary product. The peculiarities of the document can be accounted for fully if we assume that it was written originally in Greek, with Hebrew and Aramaic testaments serving loosely as models and perhaps to a very limited extent as sources for details. The Christian interpolations, which number not more than twelve, and which occur in the latter part of those testaments that contain them, are conceptually peripheral to the main thrust of the document and are literarily incongruous, so that they may be readily differentiated from the original Greek text.

Date

Apart from the Christian interpolations, which seem to have a special affinity with Johannine thought and probably date from the early second century A.D., the basic writing gives no evidence of having been composed by anyone other than a hellenized Jew. Its use of the Septuagint suggests that it was written after 250 B.C., which is the approximate year that the Septuagint translation was completed. Syria is the last world power to be mentioned in the sketch of successive world empires, and the lack of any unambiguous reference to the Maccabees might suggest a date before that nationalist revolt *circa* early second century B.C. If, however, the combination of prophetic, priestly, and kingly roles in Testament of Levi 18:2 is taken as a reference to John Hyrcanus (so R. H. Charles), then the Testaments may well have been written during his reign (137–107 B.C.). Others have inferred from some evidences of kinship between the Testaments and the Dead Sea writings that the former is Essene in origin (so M. Philonenko and A. Dupont-Sommer). Certainly the view in the Testaments of a dual messiahship, with an anointed king from Judah and an anointed priest from Levi, parallels the (not always consistent) messianic outlook at Qumran. And since the Qumran community seems to have flourished in the period beginning about 150 B.C., this link could also be taken as evidence pointing to the Maccabean period as the date of origin of the Testaments.

Provenance

Proponents of the Aramaic origin of the writing look to Palestine as its place of writing, although the marked differences between it and the Dead Sea Scrolls on the essence of obedience to the law rule out Qumran. Champions of a Christian origin for the Testaments have a wide range of options for provenance. The internal evidence, however, could be read as pointing to Egypt, because of the special interest in Joseph (which seems to have flourished among Egyptian Jews) and possibly because of the loose links between the Christian interpolations and Johannine thought, which is at times assigned to Alexandrine Christianity. More likely, however, is a Syrian provenance: It is Syria rather than the Ptolemies of Egypt that appears as the current world power in this writing; the knowledge of Palestinian place-names but the lack of accuracy as to their location may point to a neighboring land such as Syria, while almost certainly ruling out Palestine proper.

Historical importance

When the ten or twelve Christian interpolations are set aside, the basic document of the Testaments bears witness to the diversity of outlook that developed within Judaism in the period prior to the Maccabean Revolt and flourished throughout the Maccabean period. Secondarily, the Greek text as it has been preserved demonstrates the various ways in which the perspectives represented by this writing were appropriated by Jews and Christians in subsequent centuries. The oldest discernible stage of this writing represents (1) a synthesis of devotion to the Law of Moses and dyarchic messianism (king and priest); incorporated with that synthesis is (2) a piety employing the religious and ethical language and concepts of Hellenism. By the time the testaments were taken over by Christians, they included not only universal precepts of hellenistic ethics but apocalyptic expectations, ascetic exhortations, entertaining embellishments of the biographical sections of the book of Genesis, and a primitive kind of somatic psychology as well. The document demonstrates, therefore, the openness of one of several segments of Judaism during the period of the second Temple to non-Jewish cultural insights and influences, as well as to the inadequacy of the neat division of Jews into the "three philosophies" that historians have inherited from Josephus in his *Antiquities* (13.171–73).

Theological importance

God. Although God is represented as merciful and gracious (TIss 6:4; TJos 2:1; TJud 23:5), his qualities as emphasized in this document are his holiness (TLevi 3:4) and his wrath (TLevi 6:11). He effects judgments in the world (TLevi 4:1; 18:1f.; TJud 22:1; 23:3) and does so with such vengeance that the patriarchs intercede in behalf of others (TReu 1:7; 4:4; 6:6). In the end-time, he will dwell in the midst of Israel (TLevi 5:2; TJud 22:2; TZeb 9:8; TNaph 8:3).

Man is portrayed as possessing seven (or eight) spirits (i.e. the senses; TReu 2:2–9); these "are commingled" with seven other "spirits of error" (TReu 3:3–6). His organs function to influence his behavior by means of a kind of somatic psychology (TSim 2:4; TZeb 2:4;

TGad 5:11; TJos 15:3). Sleep leads him into fantasy and error, as well as to visions of death (TReu 3:1, 7). In contrast to women, men are basically pure in mind (TReu 6:2; see below under Ethics).

Cosmology. The universe is ceiled by three heavens, in ascending order: of water, of light, and of God's dwelling place (TLevi 2:7–10). It is essential to preserve natural order (TNaph 3:2–5), since natural law is identical with the Law of God (TNaph 3:4). The present age will end in the consummation of God's purpose (TReu 6:8).

Angels. The angels who instruct the righteous (TReu 5:3; TIss 2:1; TJud 15:5) are present in the first heaven, where they also serve as instruments of punishment on the wicked (TLevi 3:2–3). In the second heaven are the spirits of Beliar, and in the third are the archangels of the Lord's presence, who offer to him a bloodless oblation. The angel of peace enables Israel to withstand her enemies (TDan 6:5). In addition to interceding in behalf of Israel (TLevi 5:6), the angels offer special guidance to Levi and Judah (TLevi 5:4).

Dualism. Two kinds of spirits are abroad in the world: the spirits of truth and the spirits of error (TJud 20:1f.). This has been so since the beginning of time when the Watchers brought a curse on the earth by defying the natural order (TNaph 3:5). The fundamental split now manifests itself in the choice between Two Ways, one guided by the angels of the Lord and the other by the angels of Beliar (TAsh). It is Beliar who instigates human acts of sin (TDan 1:7; 3:6, where he is called Satan; 5:6; TBenj 6:1; 7:1f.), especially by taking advantage of human sexual urges (TReu 4:11; 6:3; 7:2). He will carry many off into apostasy in the last days (TIss 6:1), but will be defeated by God's agents of salvation (TDan 6:3; TJos 20:2).

Eschatological Agents and Events. Levi and Judah are central figures in the eschatology of the Testaments (TReu 6:8, 11; TSim 7:1; TIss 5:7–8; TJos 19:11; TNaph 5:1–5; 6:7; 8:2) with Judah as king (TJud 1:6; 24:1–6) but with Levi as his superior (TJos 19:4). As God's anointed priest, Levi will be the agent of redemption (TLevi 18:1–11) and will overcome Beliar (TLevi 18:12). After the temple has been destroyed in judgment (TLevi 10:3; 15:1; 16:4–5), it will be rebuilt in the end (TBenj 9:2). In some passages there appears (in addition to Levi and Judah) a unique prophet in the eschatological temple (TBenj 9:2), while in other texts there is a single agent "from Levi and Judah" who accomplishes redemption (TDan 5:10; TGad 8:1; TBenj 4:2). Finally, God himself will be revealed to all the nations (TLevi 4:4), among whom Israel will stand as a light (TLevi 14:34; TSim 7:2; TJud 22:3; 25:5; TBenj 9:5).

Ethics. Although there is throughout the Testaments a stress on obedience to the Law, the ethical appeal rarely refers to specific legal statutes of the Torah. Rather, universal virtues are presented in a manner strongly reminiscent of Stoicism: integrity (TSim 4:5; TLevi 13:1; TIss 3:2; 4:8; 5:1; 7:8; TJud 23:5), piety (TReu 6:4; TIss 7:5; TLevi 16:2), uprightness (TIss 13:1; 4:6, TGad 7:7; TSim 5:2), honesty (TDan 1:3), generosity (TIss 3:8; 4:2; 7:3), compassion (TIss 7:5; TJud 18:3; TZeb 2:4; 5:1–3; 7:1–4; 8:6), hard work (TIss 5:3–5), and self-control (TJos 4:1–2; 6:7; 9:2–3; 10:2–3). Conversely, the grossest sin is sexual promiscuity (TReu 1:6; 1:9; 3:10–4:2; 4:7–8; 5:3–4; 6:1; TLevi 9:9; 14:6; 17:11; TSim 5:3; TIss 4:4; 7:2; TJud 11:1–5; 12:1–9; 13:5–8; 17:1–3; 18:2–6), a failing that Beliar exploits (TReu 4:10). But sexual misdeeds are not linked to specific commandments; rather, they are handled by injuctions to temperance or asceticism, for which there is no basis in the Torah. Sin is instigated not only by Beliar directly (TReu 4:8, 10), but also by the power of anger (TDan 2:1–5:2), of envy (TDan 1:4; TGad 7:1–7; TSim 4:5, 7, 9; 6:2), and of greed (TJud 17:1; 19:103). Women are inherently evil (TReu 5:1) and entice men (TReu 5:1–7; TJud 10:3–5; 15:5f.) as well as the Watchers (TReu 5:6) to commit sin. The sabbath law does not figure in the Testaments and circumcision is mentioned only in connection with the enforced circumcising and subsequent slaughter of the Shechemites by Jacob's sons. The issue there is not circumcision, however, but cruelty to fellow human beings. The food laws are mentioned only as a metaphor of moral purity (TAsh 2:9; 4:5).

The resources for right living are God's spirit (TSim 4:4), one's conscience (TReu 4:3; TJos 20:2), God's fidelity (TJos 9:2), and the inherent power of good to overcome evil (TBenj 5). One of the highest virtues is brotherly love (TSim 4:7; TIss 5:2; TDan 5:4), which is instilled in the reader by both the negative example of the consequences of hatred of one's brother (TGad 3:1–5:11; TSim 2:6–7) and by the exemplary model of Joseph (TSim 4:5f.; TJos 17:2–8).

The Law is treated in the Testaments as a virtual synonym for wisdom (TLevi 13:1–9), as it is at times in rabbinical tradition. Unlike its function among the rabbis, however, in the Testaments, law (= wisdom) is universal in its application (TLevi 14:4) and is equated with natural law (TNaph 3). Accordingly, homosexuality and idolatry are condemned, not because they are specifically prohibited in the Torah, but because they are not compatible with the law of nature (TNaph 3:3–4). The linking of wisdom with natural law, including the movement of the heavenly bodies, goes beyond even the viewpoint expressed in Wisdom of Solomon 7. The understanding of law in the Testaments, with its movement away from legal requirements toward general moral ideals or to conscience, contrasts with that of the nascent Pharisaic movement of the period, the leaders of which were primarily concerned with the relevance of legal precepts to their daily lives, and with that of the Essenes, whose stringent interpretation of the Torah led them to withdraw from their Jewish co-religionists and from all outside contacts in order for them to maintain their Torah-demanded purity. The appeal to a universal law of nature in the Testaments is incompatible with the concept of the Torah as a protective wall of covenantal identity that characterized most of Jewish piety in the period of the second Temple and subsequently.

Afterlife. In much of the writing there is no clear evidence of a hope of an afterlife (TIss 4:3); in some passages, however, the resurrection of the faithful is affirmed (TJud 25:1–4; TZeb 10:2).

Relation to canonical books

The blending of ethical exhortations and eschatological expectations recalls the teaching of Jesus in the gospel tradition in a general way, but the one obvious common element is the uniting of love for God with love for one's neighbor. "Neighbor," however, seems to be understood in the Testaments as a fellow Israelite. The dyarchic (Levi and Judah) or triadic (Levi, Judah, the Prophet) messianic hopes of this writing are not present in the New Testament, although the messianic roles of prophet, priest, and king are assigned to Jesus in the various New Testament books (prophet in Lk 13:33; Jn 6:14; priest and king in Heb 7; king in Mt 2:2; Lk 19:38; Jn 1:49; Rev 19:16). The description of the high priest's investiture (TLevi 8:1–10) recalls the Christian's armor in Ephesians 6:13. It is only in the Christian interpolations that there are direct links—especially with Johannine thought and language—but these are, of course, secondary in nature and not part of the original document. The document offers rather different solutions for the same problems—messianic hope, eschatology, obedience to the Law—dealt with in the New Testament.

Relation to apocryphal books

This pseudepigraphon is the most extensively preserved representative of that part of the testamentary literature of the period of the second Temple that builds on Genesis 49 and the last words of Moses in order to serve as a vehicle for ethical and eschatological teaching. Closest to our work in specific content and literary method is Jubilees, although several fragments from the Dead Sea Scrolls show real kinship with the Testaments in detail (1QapGen, 4QPBless, 11QMelch, 4QPrNab ar, 4QFlor). Still closer in form, though manifesting only occasional fragmentary verbal links, are the testamentary fragments (4QTLevi ar[a]; a fragment of TNaph in Heb.). Behind both the Qumran material and the Testaments stands an oral tradition expressed in testamentary form, but the verbal and conceptual differences are so great as to rule out literary dependence of our Greek documents on these Semitic texts.

Cultural importance

In antiquity the most significant impact of the Testaments was on the Christians, who took them up and adapted them to their own purposes. The most striking modern example of romantic expansion of the patriarchal narratives is Thomas Mann's massive Joseph cycle, where Joseph appears as something of a prig, just as he does to modern eyes in the Testaments.

BIBLIOGRAPHY

Charlesworth, *PMR*, pp. 211–20.
Delling, *Bibliographie*, pp. 167–71.
Denis, *Introduction*, pp. 49–59.

Agourides, S. *Diathēkai tōn XII Patriarchōn*. Athens, 1973. (Brief critical introduction and text, based on the work of Charles and de Jonge, but incorporating readings from two MSS of T12P from the Great Laura at Athos.)

Becker, J. *Untersuchungen zur Entstehungsgeschichte der Testamente der Zwölf Patriarchen*. Leiden, 1970. (Perspicacious analysis of the document, including careful comparison with other testamentary literature, especially from Qumran. Concludes our document was written in Gk., and is not of Qumranian origin.)

Burchard, C., Jervell, J. and J. Thomas, *Studien zu den Testamenten der Zwölf Patriarchen*. Berlin, 1969.

Charles, R. H. *The Greek Versions of the Testaments of the Twelve Patriarchs*. Oxford, 1908; Hildesheim, 1960. (First and still the most valuable critical text, based primarily on the α MSS tradition.)

———. *The Testaments of the Twelve Patriarchs, Translated . . . with Notes*. London, 1908. (Unsurpassed nn., references to relevant biblical and apocryphal material.)

———. *Apocrypha and Pseudepigrapha of the Old Testament*. 2 vols. Oxford, 1913 (repr. 1963). (Summary of discussions found in his commentary, with translation of Gk., as well as of Heb. and Aram. fragments.)

de Jonge, M. (ed.). *Studies on the Testaments of the Twelve Patriarchs*. Leiden, 1975. (Technical studies primarily concerned with classification of the MS tradition and the relationship of the Gk. to the Arm. MSS.)

———. *Testamenta XII Patriarchum* (Pseudepigrapha Veteris Testamenti Graece 1). Leiden, 1964; a second edition of this *editio minima* appeared in 1970. (Gk. text and apparatus, assuming that the β MSS tradition is closer to the original.)

———. *The Testaments of the Twelve Patriarchs: A Study of Their Text, Composition, and Origin*. Leiden, 1953. (An earnest, learned, but unconvincing attempt to show the Christian origin of T12P.)

———. *The Testaments of the Twelve Patriarchs: A Critical Edition of the Greek Text*, with H. W. Hollander, H. J. de Jonge, and Th. Korteweg. (Pseudepigrapha Veteris Testamenti Graece 1.2). Leiden, 1978. (This *editio maior* appeared after Kee had completed his work on the T12P for the *OTP*. —J.H.C.)

Dupont-Sommer, A. *The Essene Writings from Qumran*, trans. G. Vermes. New York, 1962 (repr. Gloucester, Mass.: Peter Smith, 1973). (In ch. 9 Dupont-Sommer asserts that T12P originated at Qumran, though he offers no detailed analysis to support his theory.)

Kee, H. C. "The Ethical Dimensions of the Testaments of the XII as a Clue to Provenance," *NTS* 24 (1978) 259–70.

Philonenko, M. *Les Interpolations chrétiennes des Testaments des Douze Patriarches et les manuscrits de Qumran*. (Cahiers de la RHPR 35) Paris, 1960. (Reduces Christian interpolations to a minimum; sees basic kinship with Qumran documents.)

Stone, M. E. *The Testament of Levi: A First Study of the Armenian Manuscripts of the Testaments of the XII Patriarchs in the Convent of St. James, Jerusalem, with Text, Critical Apparatus, Notes and Translation*. Jerusalem: St. James, 1969.

TESTAMENTS OF THE TWELVE PATRIARCHS, THE SONS OF JACOB THE PATRIARCH

Testament of Reuben, the firstborn son of Jacob and Leah

1 ¹ A copy of the testament of Reuben: the things which he commanded to his sons ² before he died in the one hundred twenty-fifth year of his life.[a] •Two years after the death of Joseph, his brother Reuben became sick and there gathered to watch ³ over him[b] his sons and his sons' sons. •And he said to them, "My children, behold ⁴ I am dying, and I am going the way of my fathers." •When he saw Judah and Gad and Asher his brothers there he said to them, "Raise me up so that I can tell my brothers and my children the things that I have hidden in my heart, for behold I ⁵ am departing from you now." •And when he was raised up he kissed them and said to them, "Listen, my brothers and my sons; give heed to the things which ⁶ I, Reuben, your father, command you. •See here, I call the God of heaven to bear witness to you this day,[c] so that you will not behave yourselves in the ignorant ways of youth and sexual promiscuity in which I indulged myself and defiled the ⁷ marriage bed of my father, Jacob. •But I tell you he struck me with a severe wound in my loins for seven months, and if my father, Jacob, had not prayed to the Lord ⁸ in my behalf, the Lord would have destroyed me. •For I was thirty years old when I committed this evil deed in the sight of the Lord, and for seven months I was ⁹ an invalid on the brink of death. •And after this, with determination of soul, for ¹⁰ seven years I •repented before the Lord: I did not drink wine or liquor; meat did not enter my mouth, and I did not eat any pleasurable food. Rather, I was mourning over my sin, since it was so great. Never had anything like it been done in Israel.

2 ¹ "And now give heed to me, my children, concerning the things which I saw ² during my time of penitence, concerning the seven spirits of deceit.[a] •For seven spirits are established against mankind, and they are the sources of the deeds of youth. •And seven other spirits are given to man at creation so that by them •every ³,⁴ human deed (is done). First is the spirit of life, with which man is created as a composite being. The second is the spirit of seeing, with which comes desire. ⁵ The third is the spirit of hearing, with which comes instruction. The fourth is the ⁶ spirit of smell, with which is given taste for drawing air and breath. •The fifth is ⁷ the spirit of speech, with which comes knowledge. •The sixth is the spirit of taste for consuming food and drink; by it comes strength, because in food is the substance ⁸ of strength. •The seventh is the spirit of procreation and intercourse, with which ⁹ come sins through fondness for pleasure. For this reason, it was the last in the creation and the first in youth, because it is filled with ignorance; it leads the young person like a blind man into a ditch and like an animal over a cliff.

1 a. The simple fact that Reuben died is asserted in Jub 46:4, but no date for his demise is indicated.

b. The pattern for instructions and exhortations to one's posterity, together with predictions concerning the future, was set by the tradition attributed to Jacob (Gen 49).

c. Although the Law is the declared norm for ethical behavior in T12P, the details of moral obligation and the overall framework in which obedience to the Law is enjoined are shaped by Stoic virtues and by Stoic anthropological conceptions, and also by the dualistic notions of Jewish apocalypticism. Cf. TLevi 13:1–9; TIss 5:1, n.

2 a. The spirits of deceit seem to be human qualities, or at least each exploits some basic human quality (2:4–8). As such they are akin to the Stoic notion of spirits. Elsewhere in T12P, however, the evil spirits are personified, given specific names, and identified as the spirits of Beliar (alternate spelling, Belial; see n. on TReu 4:7), as in TIss 7:7, or as agents of Beliar, as in TAsh 6:4. Satan figures relatively infrequently in T12P (TDan 3:6; 5:6; 6:1; TGad 4:7; TAsh 6:4, in α text), whereas Beliar appears more than thirty times (depending on which textual tradition is used as the basis for the count). The devil (diabolos) is somewhat more common than Satan in T12P.

1 **3** "In addition to all is an eighth spirit: sleep, with which is created the ecstasy
2 of nature and the image of death. •With these are commingled the spirits of error.[a]
3,4 First, the spirit of promiscuity resides in the nature and the senses. • A second
spirit of insatiability, in the stomach; a third spirit of strife, in the liver and the
gall; a fourth spirit of flattery and trickery, in order that through excessive effort
5 one might appear to be at the height of his powers; •a fifth spirit of arrogance, that
one might be boastful and haughty; a sixth spirit of lying, which through destruc-
tiveness and rivalry, handles[b] his affairs smoothly and secretively even with his
6 relatives and his household. • A seventh spirit of injustice, with which are thefts
and crooked dealings, in order that one might gain his heart's desire. For injustice
7 works together with the other spirits through acceptance of bribes. •With all these
8 the spirit of sleep forms an alliance, which results in error and fantasy. •And thus
every young man is destroyed, darkening his mind from the truth, neither gaining
9 understanding in the Law of God nor heeding the advice of his fathers—•just this
was my plight in my youth. And now, my children, love truth and she will preserve
you. Give heed to the words of Reuben, your father.

10 "Do not devote your attention to a woman's looks,
nor live with a woman who is already married,
nor become involved in affairs with women.

11 "For if I had not seen Bilhah bathing in a sheltered place, I would not have fallen   Gen 35:22
12 into this great lawless act.[c] •For so absorbed were my senses by her naked femininity
13 that I was not able to sleep until I had performed this revolting act. •While our
father, Jacob, had gone off to visit his father, Isaac, and we were at Gader near
Ephratha in Bethlehem, Bilhah became drunk and was sound asleep, naked in her
14 bedchamber. •So when I came in and saw her nakedness, I performed the impious
deed without her being aware of it. Leaving her sleeping soundly, I went out.
15 And immediately a messenger from God revealed it to my father. He came and
made lamentation over me, and never again touched her.

1 **4** "Do not devote your attention to the beauty of women, my children, nor occupy
your minds with their activities. But live in integrity of heart[a] in the fear of the
Lord, and weary yourself in good deeds, in learning, and in tending your flocks,
until the Lord gives you the mate whom he wills, so that you do not suffer, as I
2 did. •For until my father's death I never had the courage to look him in the face
3 or speak to any of my brothers because of my disgraceful act. •Even until now my
4 conscience[b] harasses me because of my impious act. •And yet my father consoled
me greatly and prayed to the Lord in my behalf so that the Lord's anger would
pass me by—which is just how the Lord treated me. From that time until now I
5 have kept a careful watch and have not sinned. •So then, my children, observe all
6 the things that I command you •and do not sin, for the sin of promiscuity is the
pitfall of life, separating man from God and leading on toward idolatry, because
it is the deceiver of the mind and the perceptions, and leads youths down to hell
7 before their time. •For promiscuity has destroyed many. Whether a man is old,
well born, rich, or poor, he brings on himself disgrace among mankind and provides
8 Beliar[c] with an opportunity to cause him to stumble. •You heard how Joseph

---

3 a. Although in T12P there is no direct statement
of the inherent evil of the human body, the "spirits
of error" exploit human frailties for evil ends.
 b. Or "speaks."
 c. Another version is offered in Jub 33:1–9.

4 a. The highest virtue in TReu is integrity. But
cf. also TIss 4:1–5:1; TSim 4:5. Similarly in hellenistic Judaism (WisSol 1:1) and the later Pauline
tradition (Col 2:22; Eph 6:5).
 b. This is a Gk. (Stoic) conception, according
to which moral consciousness induces guilt; else-

where it is regarded as a force that aids in ethical
decisions and thus positively fosters moral rectitude. Cf. TJud 20:2 (reading with the α text).
 c. Beliar is prince of the demonic powers. He
appears in other writings of the period (MartIs 1:8;
2:4; 3:11) and is identical with Belial (CD 4.13;
Jub 1:20). In 2Cor 6:15 he is called Beliar. He is
to be overcome in the last days by God's anointed
agents (TLevi 18:12; TDan 5:10–11) and is to be
cast into the fire (TJud 25:3). In the present age the
righteous may be delivered from his power (TReu
4:11).

9 protected himself from a woman and purified his mind from all •promiscuity: He found favor before God and men. For the Egyptian woman did many things to him, summoned magicians, and brought potions for him, but his soul's deliberation 10 rejected evil desire. •For this reason the God of our fathers rescued him from every 11 visible or hidden death. •For if promiscuity does not triumph over your reason, then neither can Beliar conquer you.[d]

1 **5** "For women are evil, my children, and by reason of their lacking authority or power over man, they scheme treacherously how they might entice him to them- 2 selves by means of their looks. • And whomever they cannot enchant by their 3 appearance they conquer by a stratagem. •Indeed, the angel of the Lord told me and instructed me that women are more easily overcome by the spirit of promiscuity than are men. They contrive in their hearts against men, then by decking themselves out they lead men's minds astray, by a look they implant their poison, and finally 4 in the act itself they take them captive. •For a woman is not able to coerce a man 5 overtly, but by a harlot's manner she accomplishes her villainy. •Accordingly, my children, flee from sexual promiscuity, and order your wives and your daughters not to adorn their heads and their appearances so as to deceive men's sound minds. For every woman who schemes in these ways is destined for eternal punishment. 6 For it was thus that they charmed the Watchers, who were before the Flood.[a] As they continued looking at the women, they were filled with desire for them and   Gen 6:1-4 perpetrated the act in their minds. Then they were transformed into human males, and while the women were cohabiting with their husbands they appeared to them. Since the women's minds were filled with lust for these apparitions, they gave birth to giants. For the Watchers were disclosed to them as being as high as the heavens.

1 **6** "So guard yourself against sexual promiscuity, and if you want to remain pure 2 in your mind, protect your senses from women. •And tell them not to consort with 3 men, so that they too might be •pure in their minds. For even recurrent chance meetings—although the impious act itself is not committed—are for these women an incurable disease, but for us they are the plague of Beliar and an eternal disgrace. 4 Because in sexual promiscuity there is a place for neither understanding nor piety,[a] 5 and every passion dwells in its desire. •For this reason, I say to you, you will vie 6 with the sons of Levi and will seek •to be exalted above them, but you will not be able: For God will perform vengeance in their behalf, and you will die an evil 7 death, •since God gave Levi the authority, and to Judah with him, [as well as to 8 me and to Dan and to Joseph],[b] to be rulers. •It is for this reason that I command you to give heed to Levi,[c] because he will know the law of God and will give   Deut 33:8-10

d. Moral forces operate at two levels: the human and the demonic. If the human will is strong, Beliar is unable to gain control; if the will is weak, Beliar dominates.

5 a. In the story recounted in Gen 6:1–4, according to which sexual union between human females and heavenly male creatures violates the divine order, there is no clear assignment of blame. In Jub 4:15, where the narrative is elaborated, the heavenly Watchers come to offer moral instructions to the earthlings. But here blame is placed on the women, who are the villainesses, since they lure the Watch- ers into the illicit sexual relations, with dire con- sequences for the whole of the human race, as exemplified in their monstrous progeny. The Watchers appear in other texts of the period as well. Cf. CD 2.18; TNaph 3:5; Jub 4:22; 7:21; 8:3; 10:5; and often in the Enochic literature.

6 a. The blending of cultural backgrounds is evi-

dent here, in that *eusebeia*, which is a commonplace hellenistic ethical term for piety, is here used ap- parently as a translation of *hesed*, from which the Hasidim took their name.

b. Possibly a later Jewish interpolation, since Dan and Joseph did not have messianic significance in Hasidic or Essene circles, nor in early Christi- anity.

c. Levi has a multiple role here as both inter- preter of the Law and as officiator at the priestly sacrifices, just as in the Dead Sea Scrolls the func- tions of priest and teacher-prophet are at times linked closely. In CD 7.15–20, however, the in- terpreter of the Law is identified as the star of Num 24:17, while in the Psalms of Joshua the role of star and that of Levi are set side by side. The term for consummation of the ages is a technical one in apocalyptic literature (cf. TLevi 10:2). In TZeb 9:5 (*b d g* texts) the event is called simply "in the last days." Cf. Dan 9:27; 12:4, 13 (LXX); Mt 13:39, 40; Heb 9:26. Similar phrases in 1En 10:13; 16:1.

instructions concerning justice and concerning sacrifice for Israel until the con-
9   summation of times; he is the anointed priest of whom the Lord spoke. •I call to
witness the God of heaven that you do the truth, each to his neighbor, and that
10 you show love,[d] each to his brother. •Draw near to Levi in humility of your hearts
11 in order that you may receive blessing from his mouth. •For he will bless Israel
and Judah, since it is through him that the Lord has chosen to reign[e] in the presence
12 of all the people. •Prostrate yourselves before his posterity, because (his offspring)   TSim 5:5
will die in your behalf in wars visible and invisible. And he shall be among you
an eternal king.''

1,2 **7** And Reuben died, having spoken these commandments to his sons. •And they
placed him in a coffin until they carried him up from Egypt and buried him in
Hebron, in the cave where his father was.

Testament of Simeon, the second son of Jacob and Leah

1   **1** A copy of the words of Simeon, which he spoke to his sons before he died in
2   the hundred and twentieth year of his life, at the time when his brother •Joseph
died. While Simeon was sick his sons came to see him, and becoming stronger,
he sat up, kissed them, and said,

1   **2**   "Listen, my children, to Simeon, your father, and I shall tell you the
things which I have in my heart.
2   I was born of Jacob, a second son for my father; and Leah, my mother,
called me Simeon because the Lord had heard her prayer.   Gen 29:33
3   And I became extraordinarily strong; I did not hold back from any exploit,
nor did I fear anything.
4   My heart was firm,
my courage was high, and my feelings were dispassionate.

5,6 "For by the Most High, manly courage is given to men in soul and body. •In
the time of my youth I was jealous of Joseph, because my father loved him more
7   than all the rest of us. •I determined inwardly to destroy him, because the Prince
of Error[a] blinded my mind so that I did not consider him as a brother nor did I
8   spare Jacob, my father. •But his God and the God of our fathers sent his messenger
9   and delivered him from my hands. •For when I went to Shechem to procure an
unguent for the flocks, and Reuben went to Dothan where our supplies and stores   Gen 37:25-28
10 were, my brother Judah sold him to the Ishmaelites. •When Reuben heard this he
11 was sorrowful, for he wanted to restore him to his father. •But when I heard it,
I was furious with Judah because he had let him go away alive. For five months
12 I was angry with him. •The Lord bound my hands and feet, however, and thus
prevented my hands from performing their deeds, because for seven days my right
13 hand became partly withered. •I knew, children, that this had happened to me
because of Joseph, so I repented and wept. Then I prayed to the Lord God that

---

d. The appeal for brotherly love here contrasts
with that found in other testaments, where the injunction to love one's brother is accompanied by
the negative example according to which Joseph is
hated by his brothers. The opposite view of the
relationship among the twelve brothers is given as
well in Jub 46:1, where it is declared that
"They were of one accord . . . brother loved
brother . . .''
   e. Possibly "and Judah" is a Jewish interpolation, since the following pronouns are singular.

Apparently Levi is here seen as fulfilling the kingly
role, just as the eternal priest ''after the order of
Melchizedek'' does in Ps 110. Melchizedek, the
prototype of the priest-king, appears in canonical
texts only in a fragmentary passage in Gen
14:18–20, though he is also mentioned in numerous
apocryphal writings.

2 a. The Prince of Error (other MSS add "and the
spirit of jealousy") is here personified, unlike the
seven spirits of TReu 2:1–3:6.

my hand might be restored and that I might refrain from every defilement and grudge and from all folly, for I knew that I had contemplated an evil deed in the sight of the Lord and of Jacob, my father, on account of Joseph, my brother, because of my envying him.

1 **3** "And now, my children, pay heed to me. Beware of the spirit of deceit and
2 envy. •For envy dominates the whole of man's mind and does not permit him to
3 eat or drink or to do anything good. •Rather it keeps prodding him to destroy the one whom he envies. Whenever the one who is envied flourishes, the envious one
4 languishes. •Out of the fear of the Lord I chastened my soul by fasting for two years. And I came to know that liberation from envy occurs through fear of the
5 Lord. •If anyone flees to the Lord for refuge, the evil spirit will quickly depart
6 from him, and his mind will be eased. •From then on he has compassion on the one whom he envied and has sympathetic feelings with those who love him; thus his envy ceases.

1 **4** "Now my father was inquiring about me because he saw that I was sullen.
2 And I said to him, I am inwardly in pain, for I was more sorrowful than all of them
3 because it was I who was responsible for what had been done to Joseph. •And when we went down into Egypt and he placed me in fetters as a spy, I knew that
4 I was suffering justly, and I did not lament. •But Joseph was a good man, one who had within him the spirit of God, and being full of compassion and mercy he did   Gen 41:38
5 not bear ill will toward me, but loved me as well as my brothers. •Guard yourselves therefore, my children, from all jealousy and envy. Live in the integrity of your   TReu 4:1 heart, so that God might give you grace and glory and blessing upon your heads,
6 just as you have observed in Joseph. •In all his days he did not reproach us for this deed, but he loved us as his own life; he extolled us more than he did his own
7 sons, and he showered us with wealth, flocks, and produce. •And you, my children,   Gen 47:11 each of you love his brothers with a good heart, and the spirit of envy will depart
8 from you. •For that attitude makes the soul savage and corrupts the body; it foments wrath and conflict in the reason, excites to the shedding of blood, drives the mind
9 to distraction, arouses tumult in the soul and trembling in the body. •Even in sleep some passion for evil fills his fantasy and consumes him; by evil spirits it stirs up his soul and fills his body with terror. In distress it rouses his mind from sleep, and like an evil, penetrating spirit, so it manifests itself to human beings.

1 **5** "Because nothing evil resided in Joseph, he was attractive in appearance and   Gen 39:66
2 handsome to behold, for the face evidences any troubling of the spirit. •And now my children,[a]

> "Make your hearts virtuous in the Lord's sight,
> make your paths straight before men,
> and you shall continually find grace with the Lord and with men.
3 > Guard yourselves from sexual promiscuity because fornication is the mother of all wicked deeds;
> it separates from God and leads men to Beliar.

4 "For I have seen in a copy of the book of Enoch[b] that your sons will be ruined by
5 promiscuity, and they shall injure with a sword the sons of Levi. •But they shall   TLevi 6:12 not be able to withstand Levi, because he shall wage the Lord's war and will
6 triumph over all your battalions.[c] •These forces distributed among Levi and Judah

---

5 a. The piety here enjoined is closely akin to that of the wisdom literature (Ps 5:8; Prov 8:35): In Prov 6:23–35 and 7:1–17 there are solemn warnings about sexual indulgence with harlots.

b. Not in extant Enoch literature, although there is a similar outlook in 2En 34:2, where Enoch is told why God sent the Flood. Curiously, references to Enoch in T12P are frequently to otherwise unknown material.

c. Levi as warrior-leader may be a reference to the Maccabees or to the eschatological battle of the kind depicted in 1QM.

will be few in number, and from you there will be no one for leadership, just as
our father predicted in his blessings.[d]   Gen 49:7

1 **6** "See, I have told you everything, so that I might be exonerated with regard to
your sin.

2   "If you divest yourselves of envy and every hardness of heart,
      my bones will flourish as a rose[a] in Israel
      and my flesh as a lily in Jacob.
      My odor shall be like the odor of Lebanon.
      Holy ones shall be multiplied from me forever and ever,
      and their branches shall extend to a great distance.
3   Then the seed of Canaan will be destroyed,
      and there will be no posterity of Amalek.
      All the Cappadocians[b] shall be destroyed
      and all the Hittites shall be wholly obliterated.
4   The land of Ham shall be wanting,
      and all that people shall perish.
      Then the whole earth shall be at rest from trouble,
      and everything under heaven shall be free from war.

5 "Then Shem shall be glorified; because God the Lord, the Great One in Israel, will   Jub 7:12
6 be manifest upon the earth [as a man].[c] By himself will he save Adam. •Then all
the spirits of error shall be given over to being trampled underfoot. And men will
7 have mastery over the evil spirits. •Then I shall arise in gladness[d] and I shall bless
the Most High for his marvels, [because God has taken a body, eats with human
beings, and saves human beings[e]].

1 **7** "And now, my children, be obedient to Levi and to Judah. Do not exalt
yourselves above these two tribes, [because from them will arise the Savior come
2 from God]. •For the Lord will raise up from Levi someone as high priest and from
Judah someone as king[a] [God and man]. He will save all the gentiles and the tribe
3 of Israel. •For this reason I command these things to you and you command them
to your children, so that they may observe them in their successive generations."

1 **8** And when Simeon had finished his instructions to his sons, he fell asleep with
2 his fathers at the age of one hundred and twenty years. •They placed him in a
wooden coffin in order to carry his bones up to Hebron; they took them up in
3 secret during a war with Egypt. •The bones of Joseph the Egyptians kept in the
tombs of the kings, since their wizards told them that at the departure of Joseph's

---

d. Apart from an oblique reference in TLevi 6:6,
the factor of a curse on Levi is wholly suppressed
in T12P.

6 a. Imagery like this is found in both the prophetic
and wisdom traditions: Cf. Isa 35:1; Song 2:1;
especially Hos 14:5–7, where the fragrance of
Lebanon is specifically mentioned.
   b. The Cappadocians are mentioned also in
1QapGen 21:23, where this designation replaces
Ellasar (= Larsa) in the biblical text as Gen 14:9.
The names of the enemies as here given, therefore,
include both the traditional foes mentioned in the
biblical accounts (Ham, the Amalekites) as well as
those contemporary with the writer of the T12P.
   c. The MSS differ here in detail; some link the
glorification with Seth rather than Shem; some omit
the reference to God as "the Great One in Israel."
But all agree that God will be manifest "as a man."

Apparently, this is the first of the Christian interpolations. The theological viewpoint of these insertions stresses the humanity of the "body" that
"God has taken"—a view that was later denounced
by orthodox Christians as Patripassianism, since it
affirmed the suffering of the Father. The second
part of this interpolation (TSim 6:7b), in addition
to employing characteristically Christian language,
interrupts the flow of thought in the passage as a
whole.
   d. Possibly an affirmation of a doctrine of the
resurrection of the righteous at the end of the age.
Dan 12:2, on the other hand, teaches the resurrection of both the just and the unjust.
   e. See n. c above.

7 a. The kingly rule is here assigned to Judah, as
is traditional, but in contrast to TReu 6:12, where
Levi rules.

bones there would be darkness and gloom in the whole land and a great plague[a] Ex 10:21-23
on the Egyptians, so that even with a lamp no one could recognize his brother.

1,2 **9** And the sons of Simeon uttered lamentations for their father. •And they were
in Egypt until the day of their departure by the hand of Moses.

Testament of Levi, the third son of Jacob and Leah

1 **1** A copy of the words of Levi: the things that he decreed to his sons concerning
all they were to do, and the things that would happen to them until the day of
2 judgment.[a] •He was in good health when he summoned them to him, but it had
been revealed to him that he was about to die. When they all were gathered together
he said to them:

1,2 **2** "I, Levi, was born in Haran and came with my father to Shechem. •I was a
youth, about twenty years old. It was then that, together with Simeon, I performed
3 vengeance against Hamor because of our sister, Dinah.[a] •As I was tending the Gen 34:1-31
flocks in Abel-Maoul[b] a spirit of understanding from the Lord came upon me, and
I observed all human beings making their way in life deceitfully. Sin was erecting
4 walls and injustice was ensconced in towers. •I kept grieving over the race of the
5 sons of men, and I prayed to the Lord that I might be delivered. •Then sleep fell Gen 28:12
6 upon me, and I beheld a high mountain, and I was on it.[c] •And behold, the heavens Jub 32:1
7 were opened, and an angel of the Lord spoke to me: 'Levi, Levi, enter!' •And I
8 entered the first heaven,[d] and saw there much water suspended. •And again I saw
a second heaven much brighter and more lustrous, for there was a measureless
9 height in it. •And I said to the angel, 'Why are these things thus?' And the angel
said to me, 'Do not be amazed concerning this, for you shall see another heaven
10 more lustrous and beyond compare. •And when you have mounted there, you shall
stand near the Lord.[e] You shall be his priest and you shall tell forth his mysteries
11 to men. You shall announce the one who is about to redeem Israel. •Through you TSim 6:5
and Judah the Lord will be seen by men, [by himself saving every race of
12 humankind]. •Your life shall be from the Lord's provision; he shall be to you as
field and vineyard and produce, as silver and gold.

1 **3** " 'Listen, therefore, concerning the heavens which have been shown to you.

---

8 a. Perhaps the "great plague" is the death of the
firstborn (Ex 11:1-11), although the passage shifts
to the plague of darkness.

1 a. The real writer of TLevi obviously thinks that
he is standing near the day of judgment; hence his
eagerness to convey his warnings and promises.

2 a. The story of the vengeance against Hamor
and the men of Shechem (depicted as an individual)
for having defiled Dinah is told in Gen 34. Here
Levi is credited with having taken the initiative in
slaughtering the male inhabitants.

b. Abel-Maoul is apparently a variant spelling
for Abel-Meholah (Judg 7:22). In the biblical tradition, the gift of understanding, which was granted
to Solomon as king and archetypal wise man (1Kgs
3:12) and to Daniel as seer (Dan 1:17), is linked
with the spirit of the Lord and promised as a divine

gift to the shoot from the royal Davidic line in Isa
11:1-3.

c. The sleep, the vision, the mountain, the ascent
to the heavens and on to the throne of God are
standard elements in Merkabah (throne) mysticism.
Based on the visions of the divine dwelling place
in Isa 6 and Ezek 1 (cf. 1En 14 and 3En) as well
as on the mountaintop visions granted to Moses and
Elijah, this movement began to flourish in Judaism
during the hellenistic period and influenced both
apocalyptic and Jewish mystical tradition.

d. The vision originally included three heavens,
although in some forms of the text (α) 3:1-8 has
been modified and expanded in order to depict seven
heavens. Cf. 2Cor 12:2, where Paul ascends in a
vision to the "third heaven."

e. Similarly, when Daniel is taken up to the
divine throne (Dan 7:9-14), he is given a vision of
the end-time and of the eschatological conflict that
will precede the consummation.

2 The lowest is dark[a] for this reason: It sees all the injustices of humankind •and contains fire, snow, and ice, ready for the day determined by God's righteous judgment. In it are all the spirits[b] of those dispatched to achieve the punishment 3 of mankind. •In the second are the armies arrayed for the day of judgment to work vengeance on the spirits of error and of Beliar. Above them are the Holy Ones. 4 In the uppermost heaven of all dwells the Great Glory[c] in the Holy of Holies 5 superior to all holiness. •There with him are the archangels, who serve and offer propitiatory sacrifices to the Lord in behalf of all the sins of ignorance of the 6 righteous ones.[d] •They present to the Lord a pleasing odor, a rational and bloodless 7 oblation. •In the heaven below them are the messengers who carry the responses 8 to the angels of the Lord's presence. •There with him are thrones and authorities; 9 there praises to God are offered eternally. •So when the Lord looks upon us we all tremble. Even the heavens and earth and the abysses tremble[e] before the presence 10 of his majesty. •But the sons of men, being insensitive to these matters, keep sinning and provoking the anger of the Most High.

2Bar 53:5; 58:1
Rom 12:1
Col 1:16
Rev 4:1-11
Eph 6:12
Isa 6:4; 24:18-23
Hag 2:6-7,21-22

1 **4** " 'Know, then, that the Lord will effect judgment on the sons of men.

" 'For even when stones are split,
when the sun is extinguished,
the waters are dried up,
fire is cowed down,
all creation is distraught,
invisible spirits are vanishing,
and hell is snatching spoils by sufferance of the Most High,
men—unbelieving still—will persist in their wrongdoing.
Therefore they shall be condemned with punishment.

2 " 'The Most High has given heed to your prayer that you be delivered from wrongdoing, that you should become a son[a] to him, as minister and priest in his 3 presence. •The light of knowledge you shall kindle in Jacob, and you shall be as 4 the sun for all the posterity of Israel. •Blessing shall be given to you and to all your posterity until through his son's compassion the Lord shall visit all the nations forever, [although your sons will lay hands on him in order to impale him].[b] 5 Therefore counsel and understanding have been given to you so that you might 6 give understanding to your sons concerning this. •Because those who bless him shall be blessed, and those who curse him shall be destroyed.'

Isa 60:1-3
Dan 12:3
Mt 13:43
Jub 31:17;
Gen 12:3

1 **5** "At this moment the angel opened for me the gates of heaven and I saw the 2 Holy Most High sitting on the throne.[a] •And he said to me, 'Levi, to you I have given the blessing of the priesthood until I shall come and dwell in the midst of

Gen 28:17;
Isa 6:1-5;
Rev 21:5-22:5
TSim 6:5
TLevi 4:4
Hos 11:9

---

3 a. Following the so-called α text, which contains fewer evidences of expansion of the (original) account of the three heavens. The pervasion of the lower heaven by darkness is a common feature in apocalyptic literature; see 2Bar 53:5; 58:1; 60:1; cf. also 2Pet 2:4; Jude 13. The wintry elements held in reserve for the day of judgment appear also in 2En 5:1; 1En 60:17–18; cf. Jub 37:1–10.

b. Instruments of God's judgment; cf. Sir 39:28–31. The Holy Ones in 3:3 are angels.

c. Great Glory is a favorite name of God in Merkabah circles; cf. 1En 14:19; 102:3; similar titles in 1En 25:3, 7; 47:3 (from Isa 6).

d. The liturgy performed in the heavenly archetypal sanctuary corresponds to the offerings in the earthly temple, which is a copy of the heavenly temple (Ex 25:9, 40; 26:30; 27:8).

e. Isa 13:9–13, where the shaking occurs on the day of the Lord (= day of judgment); also in the

Isaiah apocalypse (Isa 24:17–20). In Hag 2:6f. God shakes loose from the nations their treasures.

4 a. "Son" is here a designation for the anointed priest, in parallel to the king who is God's son (Ps 2:7; cf. Ps 110, though there "son" is not referred to).

b. One of the clearest instances of a Christian interpolation: "impale" (= crucify). Probably "his son" is a Christian addition as well.

5 a. The climax of the vision comes when Levi sees God on his throne. In addition to texts cited in ch. 3, n. d, cf. Ps 24:7–10, where Yahweh enters the sanctuary.

b. The notion of God as visibly reigning on earth lent itself readily to Christian interpretation in relation to Christ, and to interpolations which make the links with the incarnation explicit, as in 4:4.

3 Israel.'[b] •Then the angel led me back to the earth, and gave me a shield and a
sword, and said to me, 'Perform vengeance on Shechem for the sake of Dinah,
4 your sister, and I shall be with you, for the Lord sent me.' •At that time I put an
5 end to the sons of Hamor, as is written in the tablets of the fathers.[c] •And I said
to him, 'I beg you, Lord, teach me your name, so that I may call on you in the
6 day of tribulation.' •And he said, 'I am the angel who makes intercession[d] for the
7 nation Israel, that they might not be beaten.' •And after this I awoke[e] and blessed
the Most High.

1 **6** "And as I was going to my father, I found a brass shield. Thus the name of
2 the mountain is Aspis, which is near Gebal to the right of Abima.[a] •And I guarded
3 these words in my heart. •Then I advised my father and Reuben that they tell the
sons of Hamor that they should not be circumcised,[b] because I was filled with zeal
4 on account of the abominable thing they had done to my sister. •And I destroyed
5 Shechem first, and Simeon destroyed Hamor. •Then my brothers came and destroyed   Gen 34:25-31
6 that city by the sword. •When my father heard of this he was angry and sorrowful,   Jub 30:1-26
because they had received circumcision and died,[c] and so he passed us by in his
7 blessings. •Thus we sinned in doing this contrary to his opinion, and he became
8 sick that very day. •But I saw that God's sentence was 'Guilty,' because they had
wanted to do the same thing to Sarah and Rebecca that they did to Dinah, our
9 sister. But the Lord prevented them. •They persecuted Abraham when he was a
nomad, and they harassed his flocks when they were pregnant, and they grossly
10 mistreated Eblaen,[d] who had been born in this house. •This is how they treated
11 the nomadic people, seizing their wives and murdering them. •But the wrath of   1Thes 2:16
God ultimately came upon them.

1 **7** "And I said to my father, Jacob, 'Through you the Lord will bring the Canaanites
2 to nothing and will give their land to you and your descendants after you. •For   Sir 50:25f.
from this day forward, Shechem shall be called "City of the Senseless,"[a] because
3 as one might scoff at a fool, so we scoffed at them, •because by defiling my sister   Deut 22:21
4 they committed folly in Israel,' •and we left there and came to Bethel.

1 **8** "There I again saw the vision as formerly,[a] after we had been there seventy

c. The tablets are thought of as the record of
divine historical decrees, which are fixed and im-
mutable, just as were the laws written by the hand
of God (Ex 24:12; 32:15f.; Deut 9:9, 11, 15).
d. The intercessory angel served a necessary
function at a time when stress on the notion of
God's transcendence distanced him from mankind,
as in this document. Michael fulfills this mediatorial
role in Dan 10:13, 21; 12:1 (cf. 1En 20:5). An
unnamed "one" intercedes in 1En 89:76 and in
90:14. The angel of peace aids the faithful in TDan
6:5; TAsh 6:4; TBenj 6:1; and in 1En 52:5; 53:4.
In 1En 40:8 the roles of Michael and that of the
angel of peace are linked. Cf. also Rev 12:7; TMos
10:1f.
e. The vision is ended, but the message is to be
guarded until the time appropriate for its disclosure
(6:2), with which is to be compared Dan 4:25
(LXX).

6 a. The common Gk. word *aspis* is unknown as
a place name, a phenomenon which suggests that
the text as we have it, including the names of the
locales, originated in a Gk.-speaking setting.
Abima, though not distinctively Gk, is also otherwise unknown. The wide range of textual variants
(*Abila, Amēba, Abēma, Abina*) and conjectural
readings (*Abilēnē*) show that the difficulty is an
ancient one.

b. In this passage—though not in Gen 34—
Levi's opposition to circumcising the Shechemites
was based on his determination to kill them in
revenge, but he wanted to do so without resort to
a subterfuge and without involving them, however
superficially, in the sacred rites of the covenant
people.
c. Circumcision is not mentioned in the accounts
of this incident in Jub 30 or Josephus, *Ant* 1.21,
apparently on the ground that it was wrong to kill
circumcised persons. In the Gen 49 account of
Jacob's deathbed pronouncements, Simeon and
Levi are cursed; in Deut 33, Moses' farewell blessings omit Simeon but promise Levi the roles of
priest and instructor in the Law of God (Deut
33:8–11).
d. Eblaen is otherwise unknown. The textual
tradition offers a wide range of variants.

7 a. Sir 50:25–26 declares that the "foolish people" of Shechem are a non-nation; cf. CD
13.23–14.2.

8 a. Jacob's vision (Gen 28:10–17; 35:9; Jub
27:19–27) is replaced—or supplemented—in TLevi
by Levi's vision. Jub 3:3–9, however, depicts
Levi as fulfilling the role of priest for his father and
the clan at Bethel.

2 days. •And I saw seven men[b] in white clothing, who were saying to me, 'Arise,
put on the vestments of the priesthood, the crown of righteousness, the oracle of   Ex 28:3-43;
understanding, the robe of truth, the breastplate of faith, the miter for the head,   Eph 6:13
3 and the apron for prophetic power.' •Each carried one of these and put them on
4 me and said, 'From now on be a priest, you and all your posterity.' •The first
5 anointed me with holy oil and gave me a staff.[c] •The second washed me with pure
water, fed me by hand with bread and holy wine, and put on me a holy and glorious
6,7 vestment. •The third put on me something made of linen, like an ephod. •The fourth
8 placed . . . around me a girdle which was like purple. •The fifth gave me a branch
9,10 of rich olive wood. •The sixth placed a wreath on my head. •The seventh placed
the priestly diadem on me and filled my hands with incense, in order that I might
11 serve as priest for the Lord God.[d] •And they said to me, 'Levi, your posterity shall
be divided into three offices as a sign of the glory of the Lord who is coming.
12,13 The first lot shall be great; no other shall be greater than it. •The second shall be
14 in the priestly role. •But the third shall be granted a new name, because from Judah
a king will arise and shall found a new priesthood in accord with the gentile model
15 and for all nations. •His presence is beloved, as a prophet of the Most High,[e] a
16 descendant of Abraham, our father. •To you and your posterity will be everything
desired in Israel, and you shall eat everything attractive to behold, and your
17 posterity will share among themselves the Lord's table. •From among them will
be priests, judges, and scribes, and by their word the sanctuary will be controlled.'
18,19 When I awoke, I understood that this was like the first dream. •And I hid this in
my heart as well, and I did not report it to any human being on the earth.

1 **9** "And after two days Judah and I went with our father, Jacob, to Isaac, our
2 grandfather. •And my father's father blessed me[a] in accord with the vision that I
3 had seen. And he did not want to go with us to Bethel. •When we came to Bethel   Gen 28:10-22
my father, Jacob, saw a vision[b] concerning me that I should be in the priesthood.
4,5 He arose early and paid tithes for all to the Lord, through me. •And thus we came
6 to Hebron to settle there. •And Isaac kept calling me continually to bring to my
7 remembrance the Law of the Lord,[c] just as the angel had shown me. •And he
taught me the law of the priesthood: sacrifices, holocausts, voluntary offerings of
8 the first produce, offerings for safe return. •Day by day he was informing me,
9 occupying himself with me. And he said to me, •'Be on guard against the spirit
of promiscuity, for it is constantly active and through your descendants it is about

b. Jub 32:3 represents Jacob as clothing Levi in
the priestly garments. The investiture here described
is performed by seven men (angels?) who are God's
agents, as are the six who execute judgment in Ezek
9:2. The scene is offered in a more elaborate form
in 4QŠirŠabb 39. Similar references to the seven
angels are found in 1En 20; 81:5; 87:2; 90:21; 3En
17–18. The basic biblical description of the priestly
garb is given in Ex 28:3–43; Sir 45:8–12 portrays
Aaron in a brief sketch. The virtues linked with the
various garments are reminiscent of Eph 6:13–17,
where the armor of God is described along similar
lines.
   c. The anointing, as in Ex 28:41–43; 29:1–8; Ps
133:2. The process of robing the high priest on the
Day of Atonement is described in Lev 16:1–34.
Bread and wine are Melchizedek's offering in Gen
14:18; cf. Ps 110:4. 1QapGen 22:14 retells the story
of Melchizedek's bringing food and drink to Abram,
but with no elaboration of the concise Genesis
account.
   d. The climax of the investiture of Levi as priest
is the giving of the priestly diadem, but that is
followed by an enigmatic reference to a threefold
office (8:11). The first office is "greater" than the
others; the second is the priesthood; the third is the

kingship, although it is granted to Judah rather than
to Levi (8:14) and is immediately defined as a "new
priesthood." That new role, which is said to follow
the model of the gentiles, may allude to the Maccabean priest-kings, with their increasingly secular
discharge of the dual role.
   e. Having blended priestly and kingly roles, the
office is associated with that of prophet, and then
with those of judge and scribe. Clearly the present
form of the text is confused, or at least has undergone substantial modification from the typical dyarchic pattern of Levi as priest and Judah as king.
But cf. Jub 31:14f.

9 a. The story parallels that of Isaac's blessing
Jacob and Esau (Gen 27) and is given in a more
elaborate form in Jub 31:8–23, where Levi is
blessed (as priest) by Isaac's right hand and Judah
by his left hand (as king).
   b. In Jub 32:1, it is Levi rather than Jacob who
has the dream vision at Bethel (Gen 28). The paying
of tithes recalls Abraham's payment to Melchizedek
in Gen 14:20.
   c. Isaac's instructions to Levi are a briefer version of those given by Abraham to Isaac in Jub
21:1–25.

10 to defile the sanctuary. • Therefore take for yourself a wife while you are still
young, a wife who is free of blame or profanation, who is not from the race of
11 alien nations. • Before you enter the sanctuary, bathe; while you are sacrificing,
12 wash; and again when the sacrifice is concluded, wash. • Present to the Lord the   Jub 21:12
13 twelve trees[d] that have leaves, as Abraham taught me. • And from every clean
14 living animal and bird, bring a sacrifice to the Lord • And of all your first produce
and wine bring the very first as a sacrifice to the Lord God. And salt with salt   Mk 9:49
every sacrificial offering.'

1 **10** "And now, my children, observe the things which I commanded you, since
2 what I heard from my ancestors I have told to you. • See, I am free of responsibility
for your impiety or for any transgression which you may commit until the consummation of the ages,[a] [against Christ, the Savior of the world] in leading Israel
3 astray and in fomenting in it great evils against the Lord. • And you shall act
lawlessly in Israel, with the result that Jerusalem cannot bear the presence of your
wickedness, but the curtain of the Temple will be torn,[b] so that it will no longer
4 conceal your shameful behavior. • You shall be scattered as captives among the
5 nations,[c] where you will be a disgrace and a curse. • For the house which the Lord
shall choose shall be called Jerusalem, as the book of Enoch the Righteous
maintains.[d]

1,2 **11** "I was twenty-eight when I took a wife; her name was Melcha. • She conceived
and gave birth to a son, and I gave him the name Gersom, because we were
3 sojourners in the land. • And I saw that, as concerns him, he would not be in the
4 first rank. • And Kohath was born in the thirty-fifth year of my life, before sunrise.
5 And in a vision I saw him standing in the heights, in the midst of the congregation.
6 This is why I called him Kohath, that is the Ruler of Majesty and Reconciliation.
7 And she bore me a third son, Merari, in the fortieth year of my life, and since
his mother bore him with great pain, I called him Merari; that is bitterness.
8 Jochebed was born in Egypt in the sixty-fourth year of my life, for by that time
I had a great reputation in the midst of my brothers.

1,2 **12** "And Gersom took a wife who bore him Lomni and Semei. • The sons of   Ex 6:16-25
3 Kohath were Abraham, Issachar, Hebron, and Ozeel. • And the sons of Merari
4 were Mooli and Moses. • And in my ninety-fourth year Abraham took Jochebed,   Ex 6:20
my daughter, as his wife, because he and my daughter had been born on the same
5 day. • I was eight years old when I entered the land of Canaan, and eighteen years   Jub 30:17-23
old when I killed Shechem. At nineteen years I served as a priest; at twenty-eight
years I took a wife; and at fourty-eight I entered Egypt. See, my children, you are
a third generation. During my one hundred eighteenth year Joseph died.

1 **13**   "And now, my children, I command you:[a]
Fear the Lord your God with your whole heart,
and walk according to his Law in integrity.
2   Teach your children letters also,
so that they might have understanding throughout all their lives

---

d. The twelve trees are named in Jub 21:12; cf.
the trees in the desert according to Ezek 47:12 and
the eschatological tree with the twelve kinds of fruit
in Rev 22:2.

10 a. The consummation is expected soon. Cf.
TLevi 5:2, "Until I (= God) shall come." The
bracketed words are a Christian interpolation, but
much of this ch. appears to have been modified by
a Christian hand.
b. The figure of speech here describing the temple veil as covering Israel's shame is awkward and

may have been altered by a Christian editor from
an original reference to "garment." That would be
consonant with the picture of God's judgment in
Hos 2:9–10, which may provide the background
for the imagery of this passage in TLevi.
c. The eschatological scattering of Israel, as announced in Zech 7:14; Ezek 12:15; Jer 9:16.
d. No known parallel in Enochic literature.

13 a. A poem in praise of devotion to the Law.
Compatible with Ps 1 and Sir 39, but the passage
seems intrusive here.

as they ceaselessly read the Law of God.

3 For everyone who knows the Law of God shall be honored
wherever he goes, he shall not be a stranger.

4 He shall acquire many more friends than his parents,
and many men will want to serve him and to hear the Law from his mouth.

5 Therefore, my sons, do righteousness on earth   Mt 6:20f.
in order that you might find it in heaven.

6 Sow good things in your souls   Prov 22:8
and you will find them in your lives.   Gal 6:7f.
If you sow evil,
you will reap every trouble and tribulation.

7 Acquire wisdom in fear of the Lord
because if a captivity occurs,
if cities and territories are laid waste,
if silver and gold and every possession are lost,
nothing can take away the wisdom of the wise man
except the blindness of impiety and the obtuseness of sin.

8 For if anyone preserves himself from these evil deeds,
his wisdom shall be glorious, even among his opponents;
it will be found to be a homeland in a foreign territory,
and a friend in the midst of his enemies.

9 Whoever teaches good things and practices them
shall be enthroned with kings,
as was Joseph my brother.

1 **14** "And now, my children,[a] I know from the writings of Enoch that in the end-
time you will act impiously against the Lord, setting your hands to every evil deed;
because of you, your brothers will be humiliated and among all the nations you
2 shall become the occasion for scorn. •For your father, Israel, is pure with respect
to all the impieties of the chief priests, [who laid their hands on the Savior of the
3 world,] •as heaven is pure above the earth; and you should be the lights of Israel[b]
4 as the sun and the moon. For what will all the nations do if you become darkened
with impiety? You will bring down a curse on our nation, because you want to
destroy the light of the Law which was granted to you for the enlightenment of
every man, teaching commandments which are opposed to God's just ordinances.
5 You plunder the Lord's offerings; from his share you steal choice parts, con-
6 temptuously eating them with whores. • You teach the Lord's commands out of   Micah 3:11
greed for gain; married women you profane; you have intercourse with whores and
adulteresses. You take gentile women for your wives and your sexual relations
7 will become like Sodom and Gomorrah. •You will be inflated with pride over your
priesthood, exalting yourselves not merely by human standards but contrary to the
8 commands of God. •With contempt and laughter you will deride the sacred things.

1 **15** "Therefore the sanctuary which the Lord chose shall become desolate through
2 your uncleanness, and you will be captives in all the nations.[a] •And you shall be
to them a revolting thing, and you shall receive scorn and eternal humiliation
3 through the just judgment of God. •All who hate you will rejoice at your destruction.
4 And unless you had received mercy through Abraham, Isaac, and Jacob, our
fathers, not a single one of your descendants would be left on the earth.

---

14 a. Here the priesthood is portrayed as corrupt,
self-serving, and sensual. Perhaps this reflects disillusionment with the increasingly secularized later
Maccabean priests, as suggested in the n. for
8:10–14 above. The passage may be later than the
rest of TLevi.

b. The α text adds "for all the nations"; the
same meaning is implied in the other MS readings.
Israel does not discharge her role as a light to the

nations (Isa 49:6).

15 a. 15:1–2; 16:1; 17:1. Both the predictions of
the pollution of the Temple and the announcement
of the divinely ordained chronology of seventy
cycles of seven years leading up to the appearance
of the eschatological priest show kinship with Dan
9:1–27. Apparently Dan 9 and TLevi are dependent
on a common apocalyptic tradition.

1 **16** "Now I have come to know that for seventy weeks you shall wander astray
2 and profane the priesthood and defile the sacrificial altars. •You shall set aside the
Law and nullify the words of the prophets by your wicked perversity. You persecute CD 1.15
just men: and you hate the pious; the word of the faithful you regard with revulsion.
3 A man who by the power of the Most High renews the Law you name 'Deceiver,' Mk 11:18; 14:1
and finally you shall plot to kill him,[a] not discerning his eminence; by your Mt 27:24f.
4 wickedness you take innocent blood on your heads. •I tell you, on account of him
5 your holy places shall be razed to the ground. • You shall have no place that is
clean, but you will be as a curse and a dispersion among the nations until he will
again have regard for you, and will take you back in compassion.

1 **17** "Because you have heard about the seventy weeks, listen also concerning the
2 priesthood. •In each jubilee there shall be a priesthood:[a] In the first jubilee the first
person to be anointed to the priesthood will be great, and he shall speak to God
as father; and his priesthood shall be fully satisfactory to the Lord, and in the days
3 of his joy, he shall rise up for the salvation of the world. •In the second jubilee the
Anointed One shall be conceived in sorrow of the beloved one, and his priesthood
4 shall be prized and shall be glorified by all. •The third priest shall be overtaken
5 by grief, and •the fourth priesthood shall be with sufferings, because injustice shall
be imposed upon him in a high degree, and all Israel shall hate each one his
6,7 neighbor. •The fifth shall be overcome by darkness; •likewise the sixth and the
8 seventh. •In the seventh there shall be pollution such as I am unable to declare in
the presence of human beings, because only the ones who do these things understand
9 such matters. •Therefore they shall be in captivity and will be preyed upon; both
10 their land and their possessions shall be stolen. •And in the fifth week they shall
return to the land of their desolation, and shall restore anew the house of the Lord.
11 In the seventh week there will come priests: idolators, adulterers, money lovers,
arrogant, lawless, voluptuaries, pederasts, those who practice bestiality.

1 **18**   "When vengeance will have come upon them from the Lord, the priesthood
          will lapse.
2   And then the Lord will raise up a new priest[a]
          to whom all the words of the Lord will be revealed.
          He shall effect the judgment of truth over the earth for many days.
3   And his star[b] shall rise in heaven like a king;
          kindling the light of knowledge as day is illumined by the sun.
          And he shall be extolled by the whole inhabited world.
4   This one will shine forth like the sun in the earth;
          he shall take away all darkness from under heaven,
          and there shall be peace in all the earth.
5 | The heavens shall greatly rejoice in his days   Isa 44:23
   | and the earth shall be glad;
   \   the clouds will be filled with joy
    \   and the knowledge of the Lord will be poured out on the earth like the Isa 11:9
              water of the seas.
          And the angels of glory of the Lord's presence will be made glad by him. 1En 51:4

---

16 a. As in TLevi 10, ch. 16 gives evidence, not
of interpolation, but of reworking by a Christian
editor in light of the gospel tradition about the
complicity of Jewish priests in the death of Jesus.

17 a. The progressive debasement of the priesthood is depicted as occurring in seven stages.

18 a. The glorious epoch of the eschatological
priest. Cf. Ps 110; his priesthood endures forever.
Much of what is predicted concerning him appears
in the prophetic tradition in relation to the king.

Some scholars see here allusions to one or another
of the Maccabean priest-kings.

b. The image of the star builds on Num 24:17;
the motif also appears in CD 7.18, where there is
a differentiation between the Star, who is the interpreter of the Law, and the Scepter, who is the
Messiah of Israel and a kingly figure (CD 7.19–20).
In 1QPs J 9–13 the Star is an eschatological figure—
presumably the king—and is distinguished from
Levi (1QPs J 14–18). The Num 24 passage is also
referred to in 1QM 9.6; 4QPBless 5.27. Cf. TJud
24:1.

6   The heavens will be opened,
and from the temple of glory sanctification will come upon him,
with a fatherly voice, as from Abraham to Isaac.

7   And the glory of the Most High shall burst forth upon him.
And the spirit of understanding and sanctification   Isa 11:2
shall rest upon him [in the water].[c]

8   For he shall give the majesty of the Lord to those who are his sons in truth
forever.
And there shall be no successor for him from generation to generation
forever.

9   And in his priesthood the nations shall be multiplied in knowledge on the
earth,
and they shall be illumined by the grace of the Lord,
but Israel shall be diminished by her ignorance
and darkened by her grief.
In his priesthood sin shall cease
and lawless men shall rest from their evil deeds,
and righteous men shall find rest in him.

10   And he shall open the gates of paradise;[d]
he shall remove the sword that has threatened since Adam,

11   and he will grant to the saints to eat of the tree of life.   Gen 2:9
The spirit of holiness shall be upon them.   Rev 22:2,4,19

12   And Beliar shall be bound[e] by him.
And he shall grant to his children the authority to trample on wicked spirits.

13   And the Lord will rejoice in his children;
he will be well pleased by his beloved ones forever.

14   Then Abraham, Isaac, and Jacob will rejoice,[f]
and I shall be glad, and all the saints shall be clothed in righteousness.

1 **19** "And now, my children, you have heard everything. Choose for yourselves
2 light or darkness, the Law of the Lord or the works of Beliar." •And his sons   Deut 30:15-20
3 replied, "Before the Lord we will live according to his Law." •And their father
said to them, "The Lord is my witness and his angels are witnesses, and you are
4 witnesses, and I am witness concerning the word from your mouth." •And his
sons said, "(We are) witnesses." Then Levi finished giving instructions to his
sons. He stretched out his feet on his bed and was gathered to his fathers, having
5 lived a hundred and thirty-seven years. •And they put him in a coffin and later
buried him in Hebron with Abraham, Isaac, and Jacob.

Judah, the fourth son of Jacob and Leah

1 **1** A copy of the words of Judah which he spoke to his sons before he died. When
2 they gathered together and came to him, he said to them, •"Listen, my children,
3 to Judah, your father. I was the fourth son born to my father, Jacob, and Leah,   Gen 29:35
4 my mother, named me Judah, saying, 'I give thanks to the Lord, because he has
5 given me a fourth son.' •In my youth I was keen; I obeyed my father •in accord
6 with his every word, and I honored my mother and her sister. •And it happened

c. "[In the water]" is apparently an interpolation
based on Jesus' having received the spirit at baptism
(Mk 1:9–11), which also linked with a heavenly
voice.

d. The primordial paradise is restored, its entrance guarded by a sword (Gen 3:24).

e. The binding of Beliar, as in Isa 24:22–23,

where the wicked angels are rendered powerless;
cf. Mk 3:27; Lk 11:14–22. The motif of trampling
on the evil spirits appears also in Lk 10:19; cf.
TSim 6:6; TZeb 9:8.

f. Cf. Jn 8:56; Mt 8:11, where the patriarchs
share in the eschatological blessings.

that as I matured, my father declared to me, 'You shall be king,[a] achieving success Gen 49:8-10
in every way.'

1 **2** "And the Lord bestowed on me grace in all my undertakings, in the field and
2 at home. •I know that I raced a deer, caught it, prepared it as food for my father,[a]
3 and he ate it. •By chasing it, I captured a gazelle, and everything that was in the
4 fields I overtook. •I killed a lion and removed a kid from its mouth. Seizing a bear
5 by the paw, I dropped it over a cliff and it was crushed. •I raced a wild boar and
6 as I ran, overtook it and dismembered it. •In Hebron a leopard leapt on a dog and
7 seized it; I snatched it by the tail and broke it in two on a rock. •I found a wild
ox grazing in the country; grasping it by the horns and brandishing it in a circle
until it was blind, I hurled it down and destroyed it.

1 **3** "When two armor-clad kings of the Canaanites came with a large force to seize
our flocks, I ran out alone[a] against one of the kings, struck him on his leg armor,
2 knocked him down, and killed him, •as I did the other, the king of Tappual, while
3 he was astride his horse, with the result that all his people were scattered. •Achor,
the king, a giant of a man, was shooting arrows before and behind while on a
horse; I lifted a stone of sixty pounds weight, hurled it at his horse, and killed it.
4 After I had fought with Achor for two hours, I killed him, cut his shield in two,
5 and hacked off his feet.[b] •While I was removing his breastplate, eight of his
6 companions started to attack me. •Wrapping my clothing in my hand, I slung
7 stones at them, killing four of them, and the rest fled. •My father, Jacob, killed 1Sam 17:4
Belisath, king of all kings, a giant of a man in strength, twelve cubits tall. 2Sam 21:19-22
8,9 Trembling seized them and they stopped attacking us, •so that my father had no
10 anxiety about battles so long as I was with my brothers. •For he saw in a vision
concerning me that a powerful angel accompanied me everywhere so that no one
might touch me.

1 **4** "After that, an attack against us occurred in the south that was greater than the
one at Shechem. After my brothers and I joined forces, we pursued a thousand
2 men and killed two hundred of them, and destroyed four kings. •I went up on the
wall and killed their king. Thus we liberated Hebron and took all the captives.

1 **5** "Next day we went off to Areton, a city secure and strong which threatened
2 us with death. •Gad and I went up from east of the city, while Reuben and Levi
3 came from the west. •Those who were on the wall, supposing that we were the sole
4 attackers, were drawn out against us. •And so, secretly, by means of pegs, my
brothers climbed up the wall on the other sides and invaded the city without their
5 knowing it.[a] •And we captured it with the edge of the sword; those on the walls
fled into a tower, which we set afire, and thereby took all of them and all their
6 possessions. •As we were leaving, the men of Tappual killed them and burned
their city, plundering everything that was in it.[b]

1 **6** "When I was in the waters of Chozeba, the men of Jabel launched an attack
2 against us. •And having joined battle with them, we put them to flight, slew their
3 allies from Siloam, and we left them with no means to attack us. •Again, on the
fifth day, the people of Macher attacked. Marshaling our forces, we triumphed

1 a. It is Judah's obedience that leads to his being
rewarded by his designation as king rather than an
arbitrary divine choice, as might be inferred from
Gen 49:8–10. Cf. TJud 17:5f.

2 a. This exploit sounds like an echo of Jacob's
undertaking in providing savory food for the aged
Isaac (Gen 27).

3 a. These stories of military strategy and triumph

over the Canaanites are similar to those told about
Jacob's battles with the Amorites in Jub 34:1–9,
as well as to David's exploits in 1Sam 17:1–54.
All this material is an expansion based on a brief
hint concerning Jacob's encounters with the Amorites in Gen 48:22.
  b. Missing in α text. Reading from β.

5 a. Reading from β.
  b. Reading from β.

over them in a mighty onslaught, and killed them even before they could withdraw
4 into their stronghold. •When we approached their city, the women rolled stones
from the crest of the hill on which the city was built. But Simeon and I, entering
the city secretly from behind, seized its heights and completely destroyed it as
well.

1 **7** "On the next day we were told that the king of the city of Gaash was coming
2 against us with a large force. •So Dan and I, pretending to be Amorites, entered
3 their city as allies. •In the depth of night our brothers came and we opened the
gates for them. All their possessions and all their loot we destroyed; their three
4,5 walls we razed. •We drew near to Thamna, where all their equipment was. •Then
since I was being insulted by them, I became angry and launched an attack against
6 them up to the heights, while they were slinging stones and shooting arrows. •Had
it not been that Dan, my brother, fought along with me, they would have killed
7 me. •We went out against them with wrath and they all fled. Proceeding by another
8 route, they petitioned my father, and he made peace with them; •we did them no
harm, but we kept them subject to tribute and returned to them the spoils taken
9,10 from them. •I built Thamna and my father built Rabael.[a] •I was twenty when this
11 battle occurred. •And the Canaanites were fearful of me and my brothers.

1,2 **8** "I had many cattle; I had Hiram the Adullamite as chief herdsman.[a] •When I Gen 38:1-5
approached him, I saw Barsaba, the king of Adullam. He conversed with us and
held a drinking party for us. When I urged him, he gave me his daughter, named
3 Saba, as a wife. •She bore me Er, Onan, and Shelom. The Lord took away two
of them, but Shelom lived.

1 **9** "For eighteen years my father was at peace with his brother Esau[a] and his sons
2 with us, after we had come out of Mesopotamia from Laban. •When the eighteen
years were completed, Esau, my father's brother, came up against us with a force
3 powerful and strong. •Jacob struck Esau with an arrow, and in death he was carried
4 up to Mount Seir. •We pursued Esau's sons, who had possession of a fortified city
5 which we were unable to enter. Encamping around it, we besieged it. •When they
had not opened to us after twenty days, I set up a ladder and, holding a shield in
6 position over my head, climbed up in spite of being hit by stones. •I killed four
7 of their powerful men while Reuben and Gad killed six others. •Then they asked
us for peace terms, and following consultation with our father we took them as
8 subjects under tribute. •They regularly gave us 200 cors of wheat and 500 baths
of oil and 500 measures of wine, until the famine, when we went down into
Egypt.

1 **10** "After this my son Er brought from Mesopotamia Tamar,[a] daughter of Aram,
2 as a wife for himself. •Er was wicked,[b] and a difficulty arose concerning Tamar, Gen 38:6-11

---

7 a. Reading from β.

8 a. The writer here introduces the background of
the narrative of Jacob and Tamar with its sensuality
and scheming (Gen 38:1–30); the story is developed
further in TJud 10–12.

9 a. The conflict between Jacob (and sons) and
Esau (and sons) is also reported, with minor variations, in Jub 38:1–24. Both accounts expand on
the biblical evidence for conflict between the sons
of Isaac (Gen 27) and on the personal and place-
names in the genealogy of Esau in Gen 36.

10 a. There are in TJud 10–13 three motifs in the
portrayal of the evils resulting from sexual irre-
sponsibility or promiscuity: (1) the scheming

mother theme in 10–12; (2) the seductive widow
in 12; (3) the plotting father-in-law, who not only
decks out his daughter for enticement purposes but
also offers wealth as an added inducement for taking
her (13). The confusion of names in the textual
tradition is only incidental; central is the delineation
of these modes of seduction.
   b. Here is specified why Er's wickedness led to
his death: Contrary to the divine priorities (as our
author discerns them), exogamy is a graver moral
issue for him and his mother than is his failure to
beget posterity (cf. 10:6). Also Er's death without
offspring and Onan's failure to fulfill his obligation
to his dead brother are blamed on the scheming,
xenophobic mother. It was because of her that he
and Onan failed to have intercourse with their wives
and thus were victims of divine judgment.

because she was not of the land of Canaan. An angel of the Lord took him away
3 on the third night. • He had not had intercourse with her, in keeping with his
mother's treacherous scheme, because he did not want to have children by her.
4 In the days designated for the bridal chamber, I assigned Onan to fulfill the marital
role with her, but in his wickedness he did not have intercourse with her even
5 though he was with her for a year. • When I threatened him, he lay with her, but
let his semen spill out on the ground, as his mother ordered him. He also died
6 through his wickedness. • I wanted to give Shelom to her also, but his mother
would not allow it. She did this evil thing because Tamar was not the daughter
of Canaan as she was.

1 **11** "And I knew that the race of the Canaanites was evil, but youthful impulses
2 blinded my reason, • and when I saw her, I was led astray by the strong drink and
3 had intercourse with her. • While I was absent, she went off and brought from
4 Canaan a wife for Shelom. • When I realized what she had done, I pronounced a
5 curse on her in the anguish of my soul, • and she died in her wickedness, together
with her children.

1 **12** "After this, while Tamar was a widow she heard two years later that I was   Gen 38:12-26
2 going up to shear sheep. • Decking herself in bridal array she sat at the entrance
of the inn in the city of Enan, for there was a law among the Amorites that a   Jub 41:8-23
3 woman who was widowed should sit in public like a whore. • Since I was drunk
with wine, I did not recognize her and her beauty enticed me because of her manner
4 of tricking herself out. • I bent down and said to her, 'I shall go in to you.' And
she said, 'What will you give me?' And I gave her my staff, my ring, my royal
5 crown as a pledge. So I had intercourse with her and she conceived. • Not
understanding what I had done, it was my wish to kill her. But she sent me secretly
6 the pledges and utterly humiliated me. • I summoned her and heard the words
spoken in a mystery, when I was drunk and sleeping with her. So I could not kill
7 her, because it was from the Lord. • I kept saying, 'What if she did it deceitfully,
8 having received the pledge from some other woman?' • But I did not go near her
again[a] until the end of my life because I had done this thing which was revolting
9 in all Israel. • Those who were in the city were saying that there had been no whore
at the gate, because she had come quickly from another district and sat at the gate.
10,11 So I supposed no one knew that I had gone in to her. • Afterward I went to Egypt
12 to Joseph on account of the famine. • I was forty-six years old and I spent seventy
years in Egypt.

1 **13** "And now, my children,[a] I command you give heed to Judah, your father, and
keep my words so as to perform all the Lord's just decrees and to obey the command
2 of God. • Do not pursue evil impelled by your lusts, by the arrogance of your
heart, and do not boast the exploits and strength of your youth because this too
3 is evil in the Lord's sight. • Since I had boasted that during a war not even a
beautifully formed woman's face would entice me, and I had scolded Reuben my
brother concerning Bilhah, my father's wife, the spirit of envy and promiscuity
plotted against me until I lay with Anan,[b] the Canaanite woman, and with Tamar,
4 who was pledged in marriage to my son. • For I said to my father-in-law, 'I will
confer with my father and then I will take your daughter.' But since he was
unwilling to delay, he showed me a measureless mass of gold which was in his
5 daughter's name. • He decked her in gold and pearls, and made her pour out wine
6 for us in a feast. • The wine perverted my eyesight; pleasure darkened my heart.

---

12 a. Although Tamar is said to have conceived
(12:4), there is no indication here of offspring,
much less of the names of children, as in Gen
38:27-30.

13. a. From 13:1–16:5 there is further expansion
of Gen 38, interspersed with hortatory features:

warning against youthful sensual urges, against
drunkenness, sexual promiscuity, and the power of
women over men.

     b. Anan, otherwise unknown (α text). β text has
Bathshua variously spelled. Tha name Anan is probably invented but Bathshua derives from Gen 38:12.

7 I longed for her and lay with her; thus I transgressed the Lord's command and
8 that of my father when I took her as my wife. •And the Lord repaid me according
to the rashness of my soul, because I had no delight in her children.

1 **14** "And now, my children, I tell you, Do not be drunk with wine, because wine
perverts the mind from the truth, arouses the impulses of desire, and leads the eyes Eph 5:18
2 into the path of error. •For the spirit of promiscuity has wine as its servant for the
3 indulgence of the mind: •If any one of you drinks wine to the point of drunkenness,
your mind is confused by sordid thoughts, and your body is kindled by pleasure
4 to commit adultery. Thus he commits sin and is unashamed. •Such is the drunkard,
5 my children; he who is drunken has respect for no one. •See, even I was deceived
so that I was not ashamed before the throng in the city, because before the eyes
of all I turned aside to Tamar and committed a great sin, and disclosed to my sons
6 my acts of uncleanness. • When I had drunk wine I flouted shamelessly God's
7 command and took the Canaanite woman. • He who drinks wine needs much
perception, my children, and this is the perception the wine drinker requires: So
8 long as he is decent, he may drink. •But if he exceeds the limit, the spirit of error
invades his mind and makes the drunkard become foul-mouthed and lawless; yet
rather than be ashamed, he boasts in his dishonorable action and considers it to
be fine.

1 **15** "The promiscuous man is unaware when he has been harmed and shameless
2 when he has been disgraced. •For even someone who is a king, if he is promiscuous,
is divested of his kingship, since he has been enslaved by sexual impulses, just
3 as I experienced. •For I gave my staff (that is, the stability of my tribe), my girdle
4 (that is, my power), and my crown (that is, the glory of my kingdom). •Since I
repented of these acts, I consumed neither wine nor meat until my old age, and
5 I saw no merriment at all. •And the angel of the Lord showed me that women have
6 the mastery over both king and poor man: •From the king they will take away his
glory; from the virile man, his power; and from the poor man, even the slight
support that he has in his poverty.

1 **16** "Take care to be temperate with wine, my children; for there are in it four
2 evil spirits: desire, heated passion, debauchery, and sordid greed. • If you drink
wine in merriment, showing due respect for the fear of God, you shall live. But
if you drink without restraint and the fear of God departs, the result is drunkenness
3 and shamelessness sneaks in. •But if you wish to live prudently, abstain completely
from drinking in order that you might not sin by uttering lewd words, by fighting,
by slander, by transgressing God's commands, then you shall not die before your
4 allotted time. •The mysteries of God and men wine discloses, just as I disclosed
to the Canaanite woman the commandments of God and the mysteries of Jacob,
my father, which God had told me not to reveal.[a]

1 **17** "And now, my children, I command you not to love money or to gaze on the
beauty of women.[a] Because it was on account of money and attractive appearance
2 that I was led astray to Bathshua the Canaanite. •And I know that on account of
3 these two things my tribe is doomed to wickedness. •For even the wise men from
among my sons will be changed for the worse, and the kingdom of Judah they
shall cause to be diminished, though the Lord gave it to me because of my obedience
4 to my father. • For at no time did I bring grief to Jacob, my father, because

16 a. The climax of Judah's confession is that
while drunk and indulging in sex with a Canaanite
(β text) he disclosed to a non-Israelite certain divine
commandments and mysteries. This detail points
toward the T12Ps having been written by a mystical
or esoteric sect.

17 a. The solemnity of the warning about sexual
promiscuity is intensified by the writer's showing
that even kings can fall victim to feminine wiles
and disgrace the kingdom.

5 everything he said, I did.[b] • And Abraham, my father's father, blessed me as
6 destined to be the king in Israel; and Jacob blessed me similarly. • And so I know
that through me the kingdom will be established.

1 **18** "For in the books of Enoch the Righteous I have read the evil things you will
2 do in the last days. • Guard yourselves therefore, my children, against sexual
3 promiscuity and love of money; • listen to Judah, your father, for these things
distance you from the Law of God, blind the direction of the soul, and teach
4 arrogance. They do not permit a man to show mercy to his neighbor. • They deprive
his soul of all goodness, and oppress him with hardships and grief, they take away
5 sleep from him and utterly waste his flesh. • They impede the sacrifices to God,
he does not remember the blessings of God, he does not obey the prophet when
6 he speaks, and he is offended by a pious word. • For two passions contrary to
God's commands enslave him, so that he is unable to obey God: They blind his
soul, and he goes about in the day as though it were night.

1 **19** "My children, love of money leads to idolatry, because once they are led   Eph 5:5
astray by money, they designate as gods those who are not gods. It makes anyone   Col 3:5
2 who has it go out of his mind. • On account of money I utterly lost my children,
and had it not been for the penitence of my flesh, the humility of my soul, and
3 the prayers of my father, Jacob, I would have met death childless. • But the God
of my fathers, who is compassionate and merciful, pardoned me because I acted
4 in ignorance. • The prince of error blinded me, and I was ignorant—as a human
being, as flesh, in my corrupt sins—until I learned of my own weakness after
supposing myself to be invincible.

1 **20** "So understand, my children, that two spirits await an opportunity with
2 humanity: the spirit of truth and the spirit of error. • In between is the conscience   TAsh 1:3-9;
  1QS 3:13-4:26
3 of the mind which inclines as it will.[a] • The things of truth and the things of error
4 are written in the affections of man, each one of whom the Lord knows. • There
is no moment in which man's works can be concealed, because they are written
5 on the heart in the Lord's sight. • And the spirit of truth testifies to all things and   Jn 16:7-13
brings all accusations. He who has sinned is consumed in his heart and cannot
raise his head to face the judge.

1 **21** "And now, children, love Levi so that you may endure. Do not be arrogant
2 toward him or you will be wholly destroyed. • To me God has given the kingship
and to him, the priesthood; and he has subjected the kingship to the priesthood.
3,4 To me he gave earthly matters and to Levi, heavenly matters. • As heaven is
superior to the earth, so is God's priesthood superior to the kingdom on earth,
unless through sin it falls away from the Lord and is dominated by the earthly
5 kingdom. • For the Lord chose him over you to draw near to him, to eat at his table
6 to present as offerings the costly things of the sons of Israel. • You shall be to them
like the sea; as in it the just and the unjust are tempest-tossed, some are taken
captive, some become rich, so shall it be in every race of mankind: Some shall
be exposed to danger, some taken captive, some shall grow rich by looting:

7   "Those who rule shall be like sea monsters,
       swallowing up human beings like fish.

---

b. Contrast 17:4 and 6. See n. for TJud 1:6. The
reasons for Judah's receiving the kingship and both
the extent and the durability of his kingdom are
inconsistently portrayed in TJud. This is perhaps
another indication that the document in its present
form has undergone modification by Jews with
views that differed from those of the original author.

20 a. Reading with β text.

23 a. Among the predictions of judgment upon
Israel in the last days is the destruction of the
Temple, which may be an authentic prediction on
the analogy of Dan 9, or it may be an interpolation
based on the Roman assault on city and Temple in
A.D. 66–70.

   b. Reading with β text.

Free sons and daughters they shall enslave;
houses, fields, flocks, goods they shall seize.

8   With the flesh of many persons they shall wickedly
gorge crows and cranes.
They shall make progress in evil; they shall
be exalted in avarice.

9   Like a whirlwind shall be the false prophets:
They shall harass the righteous.

1 **22** "The Lord will instigate among them factions set against each other and
2 conflicts will persist in Israel. •My rule shall be terminated by men of alien race,
until the salvation of Israel comes, until the coming of the God of righteousness,
3 so that Jacob may enjoy tranquility and peace, as well as all the nations. •He shall Gen 49:10;
preserve the power of my kingdom forever. With an oath the Lord swore to me Ps 89:1-4,34-37
that the rule would not cease for my posterity.

1 **23** "My grief is great, my children, on account of the licentiousness and witchcraft
and idolatry that you practice contrary to the kingship, following ventriloquists,
2 omen dispensers, and demons of deceit. • You shall make your daughters into
musicians and common women, and you will become involved in revolting gentile
3 affairs. •In response to this the Lord will bring you famine and plague, death and
the sword, punishment by a siege, scattering by enemies like dogs, the scorn of
friends, destruction and putrefaction of your eyes, slaughter of infants, the plunder
of your sustenance, the rape of your possessions, consumption of God's sanctuary
4 by fire,[a] a desolate land, and yourselves enslaved by the gentiles. •And they shall
5 castrate some of you as eunuchs for their wives, •until you return[b] to the Lord in
integrity of heart, penitent and living according to all the Lord's commands. Then
the Lord will be concerned for you in mercy and will free you from captivity under
your enemies.

1 **24** "And after this there shall arise for you a Star from Jacob[a] in peace: And a
man shall arise from my posterity like the Sun of righteousness, walking with the
2 sons of men in gentleness and righteousness, and in him will be found no sin. •And
the heavens will be opened upon him to pour out the spirit[b] as a blessing of the Joel 2:28-29
3 Holy Father. •And he will pour the spirit of grace on you. And you shall be sons Ps 45:1f.
4 in truth, and you will walk in his first and final decrees. •This is the Shoot of God[c]
5 Most High; this is the fountain for the life of all humanity. •Then he will illumine
6 the scepter of my kingdom, •and from your root will arise the Shoot, and through
it will arise the rod of righteousness for the nations, to judge and to save all that
call on the Lord.

25 "And after this Abraham, Isaac, and Jacob will be resurrected to life and I
1 and my brothers will be chiefs (wielding) our scepter in Israel: Levi, the first; I,
2 second; Joseph, third; Benjamin, fourth; Simeon, fifth; •Issachar, sixth; and all the
rest in their order. And the Lord blessed Levi; the Angel of the Presence blessed
me; the powers of glory blessed Simeon; the heaven blessed Reuben; the earth
blessed Issachar; the sea blessed Zebulon; the mountains blessed Joseph; the Tent
blessed Benjamin; the lights blessed Dan; luxury blessed Naphtali; the sun blessed
Gad; the olive tree blessed Asher.

---

24 a. A mosaic of eschatological expectations based on Num 24:17 (vs. 1a); Mal 4:2 (vs. 1b); Ps 45:4 in LXX (vs. 1c); Isa 53:9 (vs. 1d). Cf. CD 7.11–20, especially 19–20. For the Star, see TLevi 18:3, n.

  b. The outpouring of the spirit is linked with the advent of the ideal king (Isa 11:2), to the coming of the messenger bringing good news to the oppressed (Isa 61:11), and to the eschatological effusion of all humanity (Joel 3:1 in Heb.). The first

ordinances or decrees are mentioned in 1QS 9.10 and CD 20.31.

  c. The Shoot (= Branch) is the eschatological king: Isa 11:1; Jer 23:5; 33:15; Zech 3:8; 6:12; CD 1.7.

25 a. The adoption of one language restores the unity of mankind shattered since the divine judgment at the Tower of Babel confused the language of man (Gen 11:1–9). Cf. Jub 3:28.

3　　　"And you shall be one people of the Lord, with one language.[a] 　*Jn 17:22*
　　　There shall no more be Beliar's spirit of error, because he will be thrown *Eph 4:4* *Rev 20:2,14*
　　　into eternal fire.

4　　　And those who died in sorrow shall be raised in joy;
　　　and those who died in poverty for the Lord's sake shall be made rich;
　　　those who died on account of the Lord shall be wakened to life. 　*Dan 12:2;*
5　　　And the deer of Jacob shall run with gladness; 　*Rev 12:11;* *Rev 20:4*
　　　the eagles of Jacob shall fly with joy;
　　　the impious shall mourn and sinners shall weep, 　*Isa 40:28-31*
　　　but all peoples shall glorify the Lord forever.

1　**26** "Observe the whole Law of the Lord, therefore, my children, because it is
2　hope for all who pursue his way." •And he said to them, "At one hundred nineteen
3　years of age, I am dying before your eyes this day. •Do not bury me in expensive
　　clothing or disembowel me for embalming because that is what is done for royal
4　rulers. But take me up to Hebron with you." •When he had said this, Judah fell
　　asleep and his sons did everything as he had instructed them, and they buried him
　　in Hebron with his fathers.

Testament of Issachar, the fifth son of Jacob and Leah

1　**1** A copy of the words of Issachar. He called his sons to him and said, "Listen,
　　children, to Issachar, your father; give ear to the words of one who is beloved of
2　the Lord. •I was the fifth son to be born to Jacob as a payment for mandrakes,[a]
3　for when Reuben, my brother, brought in mandrakes from the field, Rachel met *Gen 30:1-24*
4　him on the way and took them. •Reuben wept, and at the sound of his voice his
5　mother, Leah, came out. •These were fragrant fruit produced in the land of Horan
6　in the high country below a waterfall. •Rachel said, 'I will not give you these
7　because they shall be mine in place of children.'[b] •There were two of the fruits.
　　Leah said, 'Is it not enough that you took the husband of my virginity? Must you
8　take these as well?' •And Rachel said, 'In exchange for your son's mandrakes let
9　Jacob be yours tonight.' •Leah replied to her, 'Do not boast, and do not hold too
　　high opinion of yourself, for Jacob is mine and I am the wife of his youth.'
10　Rachel said, 'What do you mean? I was prepared for marriage to him first and for
11　my sake he served our father fourteen years. •What can I do with you? Treachery
　　and human trickery are increasing, and treachery is spreading over the earth. If
12　that were not so, you would not see Jacob's face. •You are not his wife, but by
13　craftiness you were taken to him in my place. •My father deceived me and replaced
　　me that night, not allowing Jacob to see me. Because if I had been there this would
14　not have happened.' •Then Rachel said, 'In exchange for the mandrakes I will hire
　　out a woman to Jacob for one night.' And Jacob had intercourse with Leah; she
15　conceived and bore me. •And on account of the "hire," I was called Issachar.

1　**2** "Then an angel of the Lord appeared to Jacob and said, 'Rachel shall bear two
　　children, because she despised intercourse with her husband, choosing rather
2　continence.' •If Leah, my mother, had not given up the two fruits in exchange for
　　sexual intercourse, she would have borne eight sons. But accordingly, she bore
　　six and Rachel bore two, because through the use of mandrakes[a] the Lord had
3　regard for her. •For he perceived that she wanted to lie with Jacob for the sake

---

1 a. An herb with a large forked root, considered
to be a love philter and an aid to pregnancy.
　b. Or "they shall be mine as a means of getting
children."

2 a. TIss adds the curious explanation that God
listened to Rachel "because of the mandrakes" (cf.
Gen 30:22), as though the potency of the roots
invoked or encouraged divine intervention.

4 of children and not merely for sexual gratification. •In addition, she gave up Jacob
on the following day so that she might obtain the other mandrake. Thus it was
5 through the mandrakes that the Lord listened to Rachel. •Even though she longed
for them passionately, she did not eat them, but presented them in the house of
the Lord, offering them up to the priest of the Most High who was there at that
time.

1 **3** "Accordingly, when I grew up, my children, I lived my life in rectitude of
heart; I became a farmer for the benefit of my father and my brothers,[a] and I   Gen 49:15
2 brought the produce from the fields at their appropriate times. • And my father
3 blessed me, since he saw that I was living in integrity.[b] •I was no meddler in my
4 dealings, nor was I evil or slanderous to my neighbor. •I spoke against no one,
5 nor did I disparage the life of any human; •I lived my life with singleness of vision.
Accordingly, when I was thirty-five I took myself a wife because hard work
consumed my energy, and pleasure with a woman never came to my mind; rather
6 sleep overtook me because of my labor. •And my father was continually rejoicing
in my integrity. Whatever it was that I labored over at every harvest and whenever
there was a firstborn, I first made an offering to the Lord through the priest, then
7 for my father, and then for myself. •And the Lord doubled the good things in my
8 hands. Jacob knew that God collaborated with my integrity. •In the integrity of
my heart, I supplied everything from the good things of the earth to all the poor
and the oppressed.

1 **4**   "Now, listen to me, children, and live in integrity of heart,
          for in it I have observed everything that is well-pleasing to the Lord.
2   The genuine man does not desire gold,
           he does not defraud his neighbor,
           he does not long for fancy foods,
           nor does he want fine clothes.
3   He does not make plans to live a long life,
           but awaits only the will of God.
4   And the spirits of error have no power over him,
           since he does not include feminine beauty in the scope of his vision,
           lest by allowing distraction he might corrupt his mind.
5   Envy will not penetrate his thinking;
           no malice dissipates his soul;
           no avarice intrudes upon his integrity.
6   For he lives by the integrity of his soul,
           and perceives all things by the rectitude of his heart,
           making no place for an outlook made evil by this world's error,   Mt 6:22
           in order that he might envision no turning aside from any of the Lord's
              commands.

1 **5**   "Keep the Law of God, my children;
          achieve integrity; live without malice,
          not tinkering with God's commands or your neighbor's affairs.[a]
2   Love the Lord and your neighbor;   Lk 10:27
           be compassionate toward poverty and sickness.
3   Bend your back in farming,

---

3 a. An interpretation of Jacob's prediction in Gen
49:15 that places Issachar in a more favorable light
than what seems to be mindless submission to slavery and drudgery. LXX and the Targums similarly
modify Gen 49:15.

  b. Cf. n. to TReu 4:1. Integrity is the central
element in the portrait of Issachar (3:1–6) as well
as in the moral injunctions that follow in 4:1–6:1.

5 a. Although observance of the Law is affirmed
and obedience to certain provisions of it are enjoined, the basic ethical outlook here is that of
hellenistic morality, especially of the Stoic type,
with its stress on self-discipline and personal integrity. Similarly in 7:1–6, where there is added to
integrity, piety (*eusebeia*); cf. TReu 6:4; TJud 18:5.

perform the tasks of the soil in every kind of agriculture,   Gen 49:15
offering gifts gratefully to the Lord.

4 "Thus the Lord will bless you with the first fruits, as he has blessed all the saints
5 from Abel until the present. •For to you is given no other portion than the fertility   Gen 4:2-5
6 of the earth, from which comes produce through toil.[b] •Our father, Jacob, blessed
7 me by the blessing of the earth and of the first fruits. •And Levi and Judah were
glorified by the Lord among the sons of Jacob.[c] The Lord made choice among
8 them: To one he gave the priesthood and to the other, the kingship. •Subject
yourselves to them, and live in integrity as did your father, because to Gad[d] has
been assigned the rout of the attackers who are coming against Israel.

1 **6** "Understand, my children, that in the last times your sons will abandon sincerity
and align themselves with insatiable desire. Forsaking guilelessness, they will ally
themselves with villainy. Abandoning the commands of the Lord, they ally them-
2 selves with Beliar. •Giving up agriculture, they pursue their own evil schemes;[a]
3 they will be scattered among the nations and enslaved by their enemies. •Tell these
things to your children, therefore, so that even though they might sin, they may
4 speedily return to the Lord, •because he is merciful: He will set them free and
take them back to their land.

1 **7** "I am a hundred and twenty-two years old, and I am not aware of having   Jub 21:22
committed a sin unto death.   Jub 33:18
    1Jn 5:16f.

2   "I have not had intercourse with any woman other than my wife,
    nor was I promiscuous by lustful look.
3   I did not drink wine to the point of losing self-control.
    I was not passionately eager for any desirable possession of my neighbor.
4   There was no deceit in my heart;
    no lie passed through my lips.
5   I joined in lamentation with every oppressed human being,
    and shared my bread with the poor.
    I did not eat alone; I did not transgress boundaries;
6   I acted in piety and truth all my days.
    The Lord I loved with all my strength;
    likewise, I loved every human being as I love my children.[a]
7   You do these as well, my children,
    and every spirit of Beliar will flee from you,
    and no act of human evil will have power over you.
    Every wild creature you shall subdue,
    so long as you have the God of heaven with you,
    and walk with all mankind in sincerity of heart."

8 And he instructed them that they should take him up to Hebron and bury him there
9 in the cave with his fathers. •And he stretched his legs and died at a good old
age—the fifth son, with all his members sound and still strong; he slept the eternal
sleep.

---

b. A more positive view of human toil than that
of Gen 3:17, where the ground is cursed.

    c. The honor here demanded for Levi and Judah
is typical of the whole of the T12P.

    d. Mention of Gad seems intrusive and unsuit-
able here.

6 a. Implicit here is the ideal of agrarian life as
especially conducive to morality.

7 a. Universal love and brotherhood are here commanded rather than merely neighborly obligation
to one's fellow covenant member.

Zebulon, the sixth son of Jacob and Leah

1 **1** A copy of the testament of Zebulon, which he decreed for his sons in the one
hundred fourteenth year of his life, thirty-two years after the death of Joseph.
2 And he said to them, "Listen to me, sons of Zebulon; heed the words of your
3 father. •I am Zebulon, a good gift to my parents, for when I was born my father   Gen 30:20
prospered exceedingly, in flocks and herds, when he got his share of them by
4 means of the spotted rods.[a] •I am not aware, my children, that I have sinned in
5 all my days, except in my mind. •Nor do I recall having committed a transgression,
except what I did to Joseph in ignorance, because in a compact with my brothers
I kept from telling my father what had been done, although I wept much in secret.
6 I was afraid of my brothers because they had all agreed that, if any one disclosed
7 the secret, he should be killed by a sword. •Even when they wanted to kill him,
I exhorted them with tears not to commit this lawless act.[b]

1 **2** "Simeon and Gad came upon Joseph to kill him. Falling on his face, Joseph
2 began to say to them, •'Have mercy on me, my brothers; pity the deep feelings
of Jacob, our father. Do not put your hands on me to pour out innocent blood,
3 because I have not sinned against you. •If I have sinned, discipline me as one
trains a child, but do not lay your hand on me for the sake of our father, Jacob.'
4 As he was saying these words, I was moved to pity and began to weep; my
courage grew weak and all the substance of my inner being became faint within
5 my soul. •Joseph wept, and I with him; my heart pounded, the joints of my body   Jer 4:19
6 shook and I could not stand. •And when he saw me crying with him, while the
7 others were coming to kill him, he rushed behind me beseeching them. •Reuben   Gen 37:21f.
stood up and said, 'My brothers, let us not kill him, but let us throw him into one
of those dry cisterns which our fathers dug and in which there is to be found no
8 water.' •Accordingly, the Lord prohibited any water from rising up in them so that
Joseph's preservation might be accomplished.
9   And the Lord did this until the time when they sold him to the Ishmaelites.

1,2 **3** "I had no share in the price received for Joseph, my children. •But Simeon,   TarJon on Gen
Gad, and our other brothers accepted the money, bought shoes for themselves,   37:28
3 their wives, and their children. •'We will not use the money for eating, which is   Gen 37:20
the price of our brother's blood, but we will trample it underfoot in response to
his having said he would rule over us. Let us see what comes of his dreams.'
4 Accordingly, it is written in the book of the Law of Moses that anyone who is   Deut 25:5-10
unwilling to raise up posterity for his brother, his shoe should be removed and one
5 should spit in his face.[a] •Joseph's brothers did not want their brother to live, and
6 the Lord removed Joseph's shoe from them. •For when they arrived in Egypt their
shoes were removed by Joseph's servants before the gate, and thus they did
7 obeisance to Joseph in the manner of the Pharaoh. •Not only did they do obeisance,
but they were spit upon, prostrating themselves forthwith before him. And thus
8 they were humiliated before the Egyptians. •After that the Egyptians heard all the
wicked things that we had done to Joseph.

1,2 **4** "After they had thrown him into the pit,[a] they sat down and began to eat; •as
for me, I tasted nothing for two days and two nights, being moved with compassion

---

1 a. An allusion to the imitative magic by which
Jacob sought to guarantee the breeding of mottled
cattle in his deal with Laban (Gen 30:25–31:16).
Nothing in the Gen account links the narrative with
Zebulon, however.

b. The Gen 37 report of the sale of Joseph as
a slave gives no hint of a special role for Zebulon,

as does TZeb 2:1–4:13, or for Dan (as in 4:7–9).
TZeb exonerates Judah, however (cf. Gen 37:26f.).

3 a. A variant practice is attested in Ruth 4:7–8.

4 a. Reading with the β text to vs. 6.

for Joseph. And Judah joined me in abstaining from food; he stayed near the cistern, because he was afraid that Simeon and Gad might go out and kill Joseph.
3 When they observed that I was not eating, they assigned me to guard him until
4 he might be sold. •He remained in the cistern three days and three nights, so that
5 when he was sold he was starving. •When Reuben heard that Joseph had been sold while he was away, he tore his clothing in mourning, saying, 'How can I look my
6 father in the face?' •He took money and ran after the merchants, but found no one, since they had left the highway and had traveled by a shortcut through the region
7 of the Troglodytes.[b] •And Reuben ate no food that day. Then Dan came to him
8 and said, •'Do not weep; do not mourn, for I have found what we should say to
9 our father, Jacob. •Let us kill a goat's kid and dip Joseph's coat in its blood. Then
10 we shall say, "Do you recognize whether this is your son's garment?" ' •(For they had taken off from Joseph his father's coat when they were about to sell him
11 and put on him an old garment of a slave.) •Simeon had the garment and was unwilling to give it to him, preferring to cut it up with his sword, since he was
12 burning with anger that he had not killed him. •But we all rose in opposition to him and said, 'If you don't give it up we shall say you alone did this evil deed
13 in Israel.' •So he gave it up and they did as Dan had stated.

Jonah 1:17LXX
Mt 12:40
Gen 37:22,29

Gen 37:32

1 **5** "Now, my children, I tell you to keep the Lord's commands; show mercy to your neighbor, have compassion on all, not only human beings but to dumb
2 animals. •For these reasons the Lord blessed me, and when all my brothers were ill, I alone passed without sickness, for the Lord knows the purpose of each man.
3 Have mercy in your inner being, my children, because whatever anyone does to
4 his neighbor, the Lord will do to him. •For the sons of my brothers were sickly and died on account of Joseph, because they did not act in mercy out of their inner
5 compassion. •But you, my sons, were preserved free from illness, as you know. When I was in Canaan catching fish by the sea[a] for our father, Jacob, many were drowned in the sea, but I survived unharmed.

Gen 49:13

1 **6** "I was the first to make a boat to sail on the sea, because the Lord gave me
2 understanding and wisdom concerning it. •I positioned a rudder behind it, put up
3 a sail on a straight piece of wood in the middle. •In it I sailed along the shores,
4 catching fish for my father's household until we went to Egypt. •Being compas-
5 sionate, I gave some of my catch to every stranger. •If anyone were a traveler, or sick, or aged, I cooked the fish, prepared it well, and offered to each person
6 according to his need, being either convivial or consoling. •Therefore the Lord made my catch to be an abundance of fish; for whoever shares with his neighbor
7 receives multifold from the Lord. •I fished for five years, sharing with every person
8 whom I saw, and sufficing for my father's household. •Summers, I fished; winters, I tended the flock of my brothers.

1 **7** "Now I will tell you what I did. I saw a man suffering from nakedness in the wintertime and I had compassion on him: I stole a garment secretly from my own
2 household and gave it to the man in difficulty. •You, therefore, my children, on the basis of God's caring for you, without discrimination be compassionate and
3 merciful to all. Provide for every person with a kind heart. •If at any time you do not have anything to give to the one who is in need, be compassionate and merciful
4 in your inner self. •For when my hand could not find the means for contributing

---

b. Mention of "Troglodytes" (= cave dwellers), which is the meaning for Suki-im conjectured by the translators of 2Chr 12:3 (LXX). Since another Gk. version (Lucian) merely transliterates the name of this otherwise unknown people, we must assume that the word did not automatically mean cave dwellers and that T12P is using LXX, not the Heb. text.

5 a. Building on the words of Jacob about Zebulon's dwelling by the sea (Gen 49:13), the text here depicts him as an expert fisherman and a pioneer builder of seagoing boats.

to a needy person, I walked with him for seven stades,[a] weeping; my inner being was in torment with sympathy for him.

1 **8** "You also, my children, have compassion toward every person with mercy, in
2 order that the Lord may be compassionate and merciful to you. • In the last days God will send his compassion on the earth, and whenever he finds compassionate
3 mercy, in that person he will dwell. • To the extent that a man has compassion on   Mt 7:2
4 his neighbor, to that extent the Lord has mercy on him. • For when we went down   Gen 43:30; 45:1-
into Egypt, Joseph did not hold a grudge against us. When he saw me, he was   15
5 moved with compassion. • Whomever you see, do not harbor resentment, my children; love one another, and do not calculate the wrong done by each to his
6 brothers. • This shatters unity, and scatters all kinship, and stirs up the soul. He who recalls evil receives neither compassion nor mercy.

1 **9** "Pay heed to the streams: When they flow in the same channel[a] they carry
2 along stones, wood, and sand, • but if they are divided into many channels, the
3 earth swallows them and they become unproductive. • And you shall be thus if you
4 are divided. • Do not be divided into two heads, because everything the Lord has made has a single head. He provides two shoulders, two hands, two feet, but all
5 members obey one head. • In the writing of the fathers I came to know that in the last days you shall defect from the Lord, and you shall be divided in Israel, and you shall follow after two kings; you shall commit every abomination and worship
6 every idol. • Your enemies will take you captive and you shall reside among the
7 gentiles with all sorts of sickness and tribulation and oppression of soul. • And thereafter[b] you will remember the Lord and repent, and he will turn you around because he is merciful and compassionate; he does not bring a charge at wickedness against the sons of men, since they are flesh and the spirits of deceit lead them
8 astray in all their actions. • And thereafter the Lord himself will arise upon you,   Mal 4:2
the light of righteousness with healing and compassion in his wings. He will liberate every captive of the sons of men from Beliar, and every spirit of error will be trampled down. He will turn all nations to being zealous for him. And you shall see [God in a human form], he whom the Lord will choose: Jerusalem is his name.
9 You will provoke him to wrath by the wickedness of your works, and you will be rejected until the time of the end.

1 **10** "And now, my children, do not grieve because I am dying, nor be depressed
2 because I am leaving you. • I shall rise again[a] in your midst as a leader among your sons, and I shall be glad in the midst of my tribe—as many as keep the Law of
3 the Lord and the commandments of Zebulon, their father. • But the Lord shall bring   Ps 11:5f.
4 down fire on the impious[b] and will destroy them to all generations. • I am now   CD 2.5;
5 hurrying to my rest, like my fathers. • But you fear the Lord your God with all your   1En 90:24;
6 strength all the days of your life." • When he had said this, he fell into a beautiful   100:9; 108:3
sleep, and his sons placed him in a coffin. Later they carried him up to Hebron and buried him with his fathers.

---

7 a. Use of a Gk. unit of measure (= about 600 feet or less than one fifth of a kilometer) is a further indication of a provenance in a Gk.-speaking area for T12P.

9 a. Metaphors and prophecies in praise of unity, a corollary of personal integrity and a guarantee of corporate strength.

b. Reading with β; with *b d g* in vs. 8.

10 a. An apparent reference to the resurrection of the just; cf. TJud 25:1. Zebulon's own moral instructions are added to the general appeal to obey the law.

b. Cf. Ps 11:5f., as in the judgment that fell in patriarchal times in Gen 19:24.

The Testament of Dan, the seventh son of Jacob and Bilhah

1 A copy of the words of Dan, which he spoke to his sons at the last of his days, in the one hundred twenty-fifth year of his life. •Assembling his clan, he said, "Sons of Dan, hear my words; give heed to what is uttered by the mouth of your father. •I have made proof in my heart and in my life that truth with honest dealings is good and well-pleasing to God, while falsehood and anger are evil because they instruct mankind thoroughly in every evil.[a] •My children, I confess to you today that in my heart I rejoiced over the death of Joseph, a man who was true and good. I was glad about the sale of Joseph, because Father loved him more than the rest of us. •For the spirit of jealousy and pretentiousness kept saying to me, 'You too are his son.' •And one of the spirits of Beliar was at work within me, saying, `CD 12.2` 'Take this sword, and with it kill Joseph; once he is dead, your father will love you.' •This is the spirit of anger that persuaded me that as a leopard sucks the blood of a kid, so I should suck the blood of Joseph. •But the God of Jacob, our father, did not allow him to fall into my hands so that I might find him alone, nor did he permit me to accomplish this lawless act, lest two tribes be lost from Israel.

2 "And now, my children, I am dying, and I say to you in truth that if you do not guard yourselves against the spirit of falsehood and anger, and love truth and forbearance, you will perish. •There is blindness in anger, my children, and there is no angry person who can perceive the face of truth. •For even if one is his father or mother, he treats them as enemies; if it is a brother, he does not recognize him; if it is a prophet of the Lord, he misunderstands; if it is a just man, he is unaware of him; if a friend, he ignores him. •For the spirit of anger ensnares him in the `CD 4.15` nets of deceit, blinds his eyes literally, darkens his understanding by means of a lie, and provides him with its own peculiar perspective. •By what means does it ensnare the vision? By hatred in the heart, it gives him a peculiar disposition to envy his brother.

3 "Anger is evil, my children, for it becomes the motivating force of the soul itself.[a] •That force has strange effects on the body of the angry man; it dominates his soul, and provides the body with a peculiar power so that it can accomplish every lawless act. •When the soul acts, it justifies whatever is done since it lacks discernment. •So then whoever is angry, if he is a powerful person, has triple strength by reason of his anger: First through the power and support of his subordinates; second through his wealth, by which he can win by persuasive acts and triumph in injustice; third, he has the natural force of his own body, and through it he accomplishes evil. •But if the angry one is a weak person, his strength is twice that of nature, for anger always supports such persons in their transgression. This spirit always moves with falsehood at the right hand of Satan, in order that such deeds may be done through savagery and deception.

4 "Understand, then, the power of anger, that it is senseless. •First, it arouses by spoken word; then by actions it gives strength to the one who is aroused, by sharp losses it perturbs his mind, and thus arouses his soul with great anger. When anyone speaks against you, do not be moved to anger; and if anyone praises you as being kind, do not be elated, nor be carried away, neither by pleasure nor by shame. •First it is pleasant to hear and thus it sharpens the mind to be sensitive to some provocation; and then when anyone is aroused by anger, it makes him

---

1 a. Honesty and freedom from anger are the virtues upheld and exemplified in TDan, as the ensuing confession shows (1:4–6).

3 a. A mingling of moral injunctions and a kind of primitive psychology.

5 suppose his self-esteem is justified. • If you suffer a loss, if you undergo the destruction of anything, do not become alarmed, my children, because this spirit makes one desire what is transitory in order that he might be made angry over
6 what he is missing. •If you lose something, by your own action or otherwise, do
7 not be sorrowful, for grief arouses anger as well as deceit. •Anger and falsehood together are a double-edged evil, and work together to perturb the reason. And when the soul is continually perturbed, the Lord withdraws from it and Beliar rules it.

1 **5**   "Observe the Lord's commandments, then, my children,
      and keep his Law.[a]   TZeb 8:2
      Avoid wrath,
      and hate lying,
      in order that the Lord may dwell among you,
      and Beliar may flee from you.
2   Each of you speak truth clearly to his neighbor,   Zech 8:16f.
      and do not fall into pleasure and troublemaking,   1Thes 5:23
      but be at peace, holding to the God of peace.   Rom 15:33
      Thus no conflict will overwhelm you.   Heb 13:20f.
3   Throughout all your life love the Lord,
      and one another with a true heart.
4   For I know that in the last days you will defect from the Lord,   TIss 6:1
      you will be offended at Levi,   TZeb 9:5
      and revolt against Judah;   2Tim 3:1-5
      but you will not prevail over them.   2Pet 3:3
      An angel of the Lord guides them both,
      because by them Israel shall stand.

5 "To the extent that you abandon the Lord, you will live by every evil deed, committing the revolting acts of the gentiles, chasing after wives of lawless men,
6 and you are motivated to all wickedness by the spirits of deceit among you. •For I read in the Book of Enoch the Righteous that your prince[b] is Satan and that all the spirits of sexual promiscuity and of arrogance devote attention to the sons of Levi in the attempt to observe them closely and cause them to commit sin before the Lord.

7   "My sons will draw close to Levi,
      will participate with them[c] in all manner of sins;
      and with the sons of Judah they will share in greed,
      like lions snatching what belongs to others.
8   Accordingly you will be led off with them into captivity;
      there you will receive all the plagues of Egypt,
      and all the evils of the gentiles.
9   Therefore when you turn back to the Lord, you will receive mercy,
      and he will lead you into his holy place, proclaiming peace to you.
10   And there shall arise for you from the tribe of Judah and (the tribe of) Levi
        the Lord's salvation.[d]
      He will make war against Beliar;
      he will grant the vengeance of victory as our goal.
11   And he shall take from Beliar the captives, the souls of the saints;
      and he shall turn the hearts of the disobedient ones to the Lord,

---

5 a. The standard appeal to obey the Law. Cf. TDan 6:10.

b. No known Enochic text supports this, although Jewish and patristic speculation linked Dan and the Antichrist, possibly on the basis of the idolatry attributed to Dan in Judg 18:11–31 and the prophecies of judgment linked to Dan in Jer 8:16–17.

c. Curiously, Levi and Judah set the pattern for these evil acts of Dan. Perhaps 5:7 is a Jewish interpolation, since it contrasts sharply with 5:4 and 5:10.

d. The salvific tasks of Levi and Judah are not specified, but are loosely grouped as "the Lord's salvation." God is the agent in all that follows.

and grant eternal peace to those who call upon him.

12   And the saints shall refresh themselves in Eden;
the righteous shall rejoice in the New Jerusalem,
which shall be eternally for the glorification of God.

13   And Jerusalem shall no longer undergo desolation,
nor shall Israel be led into captivity,
because the Lord will be in her midst [living among human beings].[e]
The Holy One of Israel will rule over them in humility and poverty,
and he who trusts in him shall reign in truth in the heavens.

1 **6** "And now fear the Lord, my children, be on guard against Satan and his spirits.
2 Draw near to God and to the angel who intercedes for you,[a] because he is the
mediator between God and men for the peace of Israel. He shall stand in opposition
3 to the kingdom of the enemy. •Therefore the enemy is eager to trip up all who call
4 on the Lord, •because he knows that on the day in which Israel trusts, the enemy's
5 kingdom will be brought to an end. •This angel of peace will strengthen Israel so
6 that it will not succumb to an evil destiny. •But in Israel's period of lawlessness
it will be the Lord who will not depart from her and therefore she will seek to do
7 his will, for none of the angels is like him. •His name shall be everywhere
8 throughout Israel; [and the Savior will be known among the nations].[b] •Keep
yourselves from every evil work, my children, and cast aside anger and every lie;
9 love truth and patience. •What you have heard from your father pass on to your   Zech 9:9
children, so that the father of nations may accept you. For he is true and patient,
10 lowly and humble, exemplifying by his actions the Law of God. •Forsake all
11 unrighteousness and cling to the righteousness of the Law of God. •And bury me
near my fathers.''

1,2 **7** When he had said this, he kissed them and slept an eternal sleep. •And his sons
buried him and later they carried his bones to be near Abraham, Isaac, and Jacob.
3 Dan prophesied to them, however, that they would go astray from God's law,
that they would be estranged from their inheritance, from the race of Israel, and
from their patrimony; and that is what occurred.

The Testament of Naphtali, the eighth son of Jacob and Bilhah

1 **1** A copy of the testament of Naphtali, which he decreed at the time of his death
2 in the one hundred thirty-second year of his life. •When his sons were gathered
together in the seventh month, on the fourth day of the month, and he was in good
3 health, he gave a feast and drinking party. •After he awoke early the next morning,
4 he told them, "I am dying," but they did not believe him. •And while he was
blessing the Lord he confirmed that after the previous day's feast he would die.

---

e. Probably the detail of God's living among
mankind is a Christian interpolation.

6 a. The intercessory angel; see TLevi 5:5–6 and
the n. there. Cf. 1En 40:6; also Tit 2:5; Heb 9:15;

12:22–24.
    b. Possibly a Christian interpolation, although
the statement stands in poetic parallel to vs. 7a and
its universalism can be documented elsewhere in
T12P.

5 Then he began to say to his sons, "Listen, my children, sons of Naphtali, hear
6 your father's words. •I was born from Bilhah; Rachel acted by trickery, giving Gen 30:8
Bilhah to Jacob in place of herself, and she bore me on the knees of Rachel, for
7 which reason she called me Naphtali. •Rachel loved me because I was born in her
lap; while I was tender in appearance[a] she would kiss me and say, 'May I see a
8 brother of yours, like you, from my own womb!' •Thus Joseph was like me in
9 every way, in keeping with Rachel's prayer. •But my mother was Bilhah,[b] daughter
of Rotheos, Deborah's brother, nurse of Rebecca; she was born the very day on
10 which Rachel was born. •Rotheos was of Abraham's tribe, a Chaldean, one who
11 honored God, free and well-born, •but he was taken captive and bought by Laban,
who gave him Aina, his servant girl, as a wife. She bore a daughter and called
her Zelpha[c] from the name of the village in which he had been taken captive.
12 After that she bore Bilhah, saying, 'My daughter is ever eager for new things: No
sooner had she been born than she hurried to start sucking.'

1 **2** "Since I was light on my feet like a deer, my father, Jacob, appointed me for Gen 49:21
2 all missions and messages, and as a deer he blessed me. • For just as a potter
knows the pot, how much it holds, and brings clay for it accordingly, so also the
Lord forms the body in correspondence to the spirit,[a] and instills the spirit cor-
3 responding to the power of the body. • And from one to the other there is no
discrepancy, not so much as a third of a hair, for all the creation of the Most High
4 was according to height, measure, and standard. •And just as the potter knows the WisSol 11:20
use of each vessel and to what it is suited, so also the Lord knows the body to what
5 extent it will persist in goodness, and when it will be dominated by evil. •For there Gen 1:26f.
is no form or conception which the Lord does not know since he created every WisSol 2:23
6 human being according to his own image. •As a person's strength, so also is his 1Cor 11:7
work; as is his mind, so also is his skill. As is his plan, so also is his achievement;
as is his heart, so also is his speech; as is his eye, so also is his sleep; as is his soul,
so also is his thought, whether on the Law of the Lord or on the law of Beliar.
7 As there is a distinction between light and darkness, between seeing and hearing,
thus there is a distinction between man and man and between woman and woman.
8 One cannot say they are one in appearance or in rank, •for God made all things
good in their order: the five senses in the head; to the head he attached the neck,
in addition to the hair for the enhancement of appearance; then the heart for
prudence; the belly for excretion from the stomach; the windpipe for health; the
liver for anger; the gallbladder for bitterness; the spleen for laughter; the kidneys
for craftiness; the loins for power; the lungs for the chest; the hips for strength and
9 so on. •Thus my children you exist in accord with order for a good purpose in fear
of God; do nothing in a disorderly manner, arrogantly, or at an inappropriate time.
10 If you tell the eye to hear, it cannot; so you are unable to perform the works of
light while you are in darkness.

---

1 a. Following the text of β; other MSS are best
translated by simply "young."

b. It is important for the writer to prove that
Bilhah is a relative of the Abraham-Isaac-Jacob
clan in order that her son, Naphtali, may have a
proper place in that tribe's destiny. Here her ancestry is traced back to the time of Abraham, when
he was among the Chaldeans (Gen 11:27–28).

c. In Jub 28:9 Bilhah's sister's name is Zilpah;
she was given by Laban as a maidservant to Rachel.
In Gen 30:9–13 Zilpah is Leah's maid and the
mother of Asher and Gad, while Bilhah is Rachel's

maid and the mother of Dan and Naphtali, as here
(1:9).

2 a. More of the psychophysiology of T12P. All
that happens is in keeping with the divine plan,
which is especially suited by God for each individual. Phrases from 2:8 match a fragmentary Heb.
TNaph found in 12th–13th-cent. MSS. The possible
relationships of the Qumran TNaph fragment can
be determined only when the text is published.
Judging by the published TLevi text from Qumran,
we might expect only occasional overlapping.

1 **3** "Do not strive to corrupt your actions through avarice or to beguile your souls by empty phrases, because those who are silent in purity of heart will be able to 2 hold fast God's will and to shunt aside the will of Beliar. •Sun, moon, and stars do not alter their order; thus you should not alter the Law of God by the disorder 3 of your actions. •The gentiles, because they wandered astray and forsook the Lord, have changed the order, and have devoted themselves to stones and sticks, patterning 4 themselves after wandering spirits. •But you, my children, shall not be like that: In the firmament, in the earth, and in the sea, in all the products of his workmanship discern the Lord who made all things, so that you do not become like Sodom, 5 which departed from the order of nature. •Likewise the Watchers departed from nature's order; the Lord pronounced a curse on them at the Flood. On their account he ordered that the earth be without dweller or produce.

Deut 4:28
WisSol 14:21
Jude 22,23

Gen 19:1
Gen 6:1
TReu 5:6
Jude 7

1 **4** "I say these things, my children, because I have read in the writing of holy Enoch that you also will stray from the Lord, living in accord with every wickedness 2 of the gentiles and committing every lawlessness of Sodom. •The Lord will impose captivity upon you; you shall serve your enemies there and you will be engulfed 3 in hardship and difficulty until the Lord will wear you all out. •And after you have been decimated and reduced in number, you will return and acknowledge the Lord 4 your God. •And it shall happen that when they come into the land of their fathers, 5 they will again neglect the Lord and act impiously, •and the Lord will disperse them over the face of the whole earth until the mercy of the Lord comes, a man who effects righteousness,[a] and he will work mercy on all who are far and near.

1,2 **5** "In the fortieth year of my life, I saw on the Mount of Olives east of •Jerusalem[a] that the sun and the moon stood still. And behold, Isaac, my father's father, was saying to us, 'Run forth, seize them, each according to his capacity; to the one 3 who grasps them will the sun and the moon belong.' •All of them ran, but Levi seized the sun and Judah,[b] outstripping the others, grasped the moon. Thus they 4 were exalted above others. •When Levi became like the sun, a certain young man 5 gave him twelve date palms. •And Judah became luminous like the moon, and twelve rays were under his feet. Then running toward the others, Levi and Judah 6 seized them. •And behold, there was a bull on the earth[c] with two great horns and an eagle's wings on his back. They tried to lay hold of him, but were unable. 7 But Joseph overtook them and seized him and went up with him into the heights. 8 And I looked, since I was there, and behold a sacred writing appeared to us, which said, 'Assyrians, Medes, Persians, Elamites, Gelachians, Chaldeans, Syrians shall obtain a share in the twelve staffs of Israel through captivity.'

Zech 14:4-7
Gen 37:9
Rev 12:1

Ezek 1:10
Rev 4:7
Dan 8:5-8

---

4 a. There is here no identification by tribe or specific role of God's human agent to restore the disobedient nation.

5 a. The location of the vision on the Mount of Olives is in keeping with the late prophetic tradition which expects God's eschatological activity there both in judgment (Ezek 11:23, when the nimbus of glory abandons the Temple, departing from the mountain on the east) and in revelation (Ezek 43:2, when the glory returns). The final defeat of God's enemies is foreseen as occurring on this mountain as well (Zech 14, especially vss. 3–4). In the gospel tradition, the judgment of Israel is pronounced from a vantage point on the Mount of Olives (Mk 13:3f. and parallels). The place from which the New Jerusalem is seen in Rev 21:10 is called simply "a great, high mountain."

b. The ascendancy of Levi and Judah is here

depicted in imagery that recalls Ezek 11 and 43, with their descriptions of the departure and return of the divine glory (see n. 5a above) and the details of Joseph's dream (Gen 37:9–11). Here, however, it is not Joseph but Levi and Judah who receive the highest places.

c. The animal vision recalls the succession of earthly empires in Dan 10–11, where the series culminates in the kingdom of Greece (= Alexander), which then bifurcates into the kingdom of the south (= the Ptolemies in Egypt) and the kingdom of the north (= Seleucids in Syria). Here, however, Syria is the last nation to be named, which implies that it is the world power with which the writer and his contemporaries are confronted. The Chaldeans (= Babylonians?) are mentioned in what appears to be completely out of sequence, but they may simply be here because they are part of the tradition, as in Dan, where they figure as the

1 **6** "And again after seven months[a] I saw our father, Jacob, standing by the sea
2 at Jamnia and we, his sons, were with him. •And behold a ship came sailing past
3 full of dried fish, without sailor or pilot. •Inscribed on it was 'The Ship of Jacob.'
4 So our father said to us, 'Get into our boat.' •As we boarded it, a violent tempest
arose, a great windstorm, and our father, who had been holding us on course, was
5 snatched away from us. •After being tossed by the storm, the boat was filled with
6 water and carried along on the waves until it broke apart. •Joseph escaped in a
light boat while we were scattered about on ten planks; Levi and Judah were on
7,8 the same one. •Thus we were all dispersed, even to the outer limits. •Levi, putting
9 on sack cloth, prayed to the Lord in behalf of all of us. •When the storm ceased,
10 the ship reached the land, as though at peace. •Then Jacob, our father, approached,
and we all rejoiced with one accord.

1 **7** "These two dreams I recounted to my father, and he replied, 'These things
must be fulfilled at their appropriate time, once Israel has endured many things.'
2 Then my father said, 'I believe that Joseph is alive, for I continually see that the
3 Lord includes him in the number with you.' •And he kept saying tearfully, 'You
live, Joseph, my son, and I do not see you, nor do you behold Jacob who begot
4 you.' •He made me shed tears by these words of his. I was burning inwardly with
compassion to tell him that Joseph had been sold, but I was afraid of my brothers.

1 **8** "Behold, my children, I have shown you the last times, all things that will
happen in Israel.

2   "Command your children that they be in unity with Levi and Judah,[a]
          for through Judah will salvation arise for Israel,
          and in him will Jacob be blessed.
3   Through his kingly power God will appear [dwelling among men on the
               earth],
          to save the race of Israel,
          and to assemble the righteous from among the nations.
4   If you achieve the good, my children,
          men and angels will bless you;
          and God will be glorified through you among the gentiles.
          The devil will flee from you;
          wild animals will be afraid of you,
          and the angels will stand by you.[b]
5   Just as anyone who rears a child well is held in good esteem,
          so also there will be a virtuous recollection on the part of God for your
               good work.

---

national designation of the oppressors and the title
for the court wise men (Dan 2:2; 3:8; 4:7; 5:7; 11).
The bull is linked with Joseph in Deut 33:13–17.
The eagle's wings recall Ezek 17:3, while the eagle
image itself appears in Ezek 1:10 and is then taken
up in Rev 4:7 and 12:14. Here Joseph seeks to
control both bull and eagle. If these animals are to
be interpreted as representing earthly powers, then
possibly the bull is Alexander, the horns are the
Seleucids and the Ptolemies; the eagle is the Romans, a rising power in the west during the 2nd
and 1st cent. B.C. The Heb. TNaph (2–3) has a
more elaborate version of this vision.

6 a. As in the β text, perhaps seven months corresponds to Daniel's seventy *haptads*, or "weeks"

of years (Dan 9:24). The α text reads "seven days."
While maintaining the hegemony of Levi and Judah,
TNaph makes a special place for Joseph, who in
turn enjoys special favor with Jacob and with God.

8 a. More credit is given to Judah than to Levi
here as God's eschatological agent. The ambiguity
as to whether Levi or Judah has primacy is evident
in the Dead Sea texts as well as here. The interpolated phrase underscores the fact that God appears
among men "in human form," and hence that his
appearance benefits all humanity.
     b. The link between the devil and the wild an-
imals recalls the account of Jesus' temptation in the
synoptic gospel tradition (Mk 1:13).

6   The one who does not do the good,
men and angels will curse,
and God will be dishonored among the gentiles because of him;
the devil will inhabit him as his own instrument.
Every wild animal will dominate him,
and the Lord will hate him.

7   The commandments of the Lord are double,
and they are to be fulfilled with regularity.

8   There is a time for having intercourse with one's wife,   Eccl 3:5
and a time to abstain for the purpose of prayer.

9 "And there are the two commandments:[c] Unless they are performed in proper
sequence they leave one open to the greatest sin. It is the same with the other
10 commandments. •So be wise in the Lord and discerning, knowing the order of his
commandments, what is ordained for every act, so that the Lord will love you."

1 **9** He gave them many similar instructions, urging them to transfer his bones to
2 Hebron and bury him with his fathers. •He ate and drank in soulful glee, covered
his face, and died. And his sons acted in accord with the things commanded by
the father, Naphtali.

The Testament of Gad, the ninth son of Jacob and Zilpah

1 **1** A copy of the testament of Gad, concerning what he said to his sons in the one
2 hundred twenty-seventh year of his life, saying, •"I was Jacob's ninth son; among
3 the shepherds I was brave. •I guarded the flock at night, and when the lion came,   TJud 2:2
the wolf, the leopard, the bear or any other wild animal attacked the flock, I
pursued it, seized it by the foot with my hand, crushed and blinded it, and hurled
4 it a distance of twelve hundred feet. •Now Joseph[a] was tending the flocks with me
for about thirty days, and since he was delicate, he became faint from the heat,
5 and went back to Hebron to his father. •He made Joseph lie down close to him
6 because he loved him. •And Joseph said to his father, the sons of Zilpah and Bilhah   Gen 37:2
are killing the best animals and eating them against the advice of Judah and Reuben.
7 He saw that I had set free a lamb from the mouth of a bear, which I then killed,
but that I had killed the lamb when I was saddened to see that it was too weak to
8 live; and we had eaten it. •This he told our father. On this matter I bore a grudge
9 against Joseph until the day he was sold into Egypt; •the spirit of hatred was in
me, and I wanted to see or hear nothing of Joseph. He reproved us to our faces
because we had eaten the newborn of the flocks without Judah. And whatever
Joseph told our father, he believed him.

1 **2** "I now confess my sin, children, that frequently I wanted to kill him; to the
depth of my soul I hated him and any inner feeling of mercy toward him was
2 completely absent. •Because of his dreams my hatred toward him increased and
I wanted to gobble him up from among the living as an ox gobbles up grass from

---

c. No indication is given as to which are the
"two" commandments, and thus what the correct
sequence of obeying them is. One might infer from
8:1–8 that they are (1) loving God and (2) loving
neighbor. This sequence would then mean to give
obligation to God priority over responsibility to

fellow humans.

1 a. Unsympathetic expansion of the Joseph story
from Gen 37; here Joseph is portrayed as a tattler
and as one who misrepresents his brothers' actions
to his father.

3 the ground. •For this reason Judah and I[a] sold him to the Ishmaelites for thirty
pieces of gold; we hid ten pieces and showed only the twenty to our brothers.
4,5 Thus it was through greed that our plot to kill him was carried out. •But the God
of my fathers rescued him from my hands so that I might not perform a lawless
deed in Israel.

1 **3** "And now children, listen to the words of truth: to perform justice and every
law[a] of the Most High; not to be led astray by the spirit of hatred because it is evil
2 beyond all human deeds. •Whatever anyone does, he who hates is revolted; if he
3 fears the Lord and hopes for good things, the hater has no love for him. •The hater
disparages truth, envies the successful person, relishes slander, loves arrogance,
because hatred blinds his soul. It was in this way that I regarded Joseph.

1 **4** "Beware, my children, of those who hate, because it leads to lawlessness against
2 the Lord himself. •Hatred does not want to hear repeated his commands concerning
3 love of neighbor, and thus it sins against God. •For if a brother makes a false step,
immediately it wants to spread the tale to everyone, and is eager to have him
4 condemned for it, punished, and executed. •If the hater is a slave, he conspires
against his master, and whenever difficulty arises it plots how he might be killed.
5 Hatred collaborates with envy, when it sees or hears about the prosperity of those
6 who do well; it is perpetually peevish. •Just as love wants to bring the dead back
to life and to recall those under sentence of death, so hate wants to kill the living
and does not wish to preserve alive those who have committed the slightest sin.
7 For among all men the spirit of hatred works by Satan through human frailty for
the death of mankind; but the spirit of love works by the Law of God through
forbearance for the salvation of mankind.

1 **5** "Hatred is evil, since it continually consorts with lying, speaking against the
truth; it makes small things big, turns light into darkness, says that the sweet is
bitter, teaches slander, conflict, violence, and all manner of greed; it fills the heart
2 with diabolical venom. •I tell you this, my children, from experience, so that you
3 might escape hatred and cling to love of the Lord. •Righteousness expels hatred;
humility kills envy. For the person who is just and humble is ashamed to commit
an injustice, not because someone else will pass judgment on him but out of his
4 own heart, because the Lord considers his inner deliberations. •He will not denounce
5 a fellow man, since fear of the Most High ovecomes hatred. •Being concerned not
to arouse the Lord's anger, he is completely unwilling to wrong anyone, even in
6 his thoughts. •I understood this at the last, after I had repented concerning Joseph,
7 for according to God's truth, repentance destroys disobedience, puts darkness to
flight, illumines the vision, furnishes knowledge for the soul, and guides the
8 deliberative powers to salvation. •What it has not learned from human agency, it
9 understands through repentance. •For God brought on me a disease of the liver,[a]
and if it had not been for the prayers of Jacob, my father, he would shortly have
10 summoned from me my spirit. •For by whatever human capacity anyone trans-
11 gresses, by that he is also chastised. •Since my anger was merciless in opposition
to Joseph, through this anger of mine I suffered mercilessly, and was brought under
judgment for eleven months, as long as I had had it in for Joseph, until he was
sold.

---

2 a. Gad joins with Judah in the plan to sell Joseph
into slavery; cf. Gen 37:26. From 3a–5 we follow
the β text. The α text omits "for thirty . . .
brothers," which may be an indication of a Christian interpolation, based on Mt 26:15 and 27:3 (cf.
Zech 11:12), although it is possibly a direct allusion
to Ex 21:32, where this amount is the price of a
slave.

3 a. Although introduced by an appeal to obey the
Law, the main thrust of this hortatory section from
3:1–7:6 is the general ethical appeal for avoidance
of hatred, of which the manifestation of love and
forgiveness are the positive counterparts.

5 a. The liver was regarded as the seat of anger
and strong emotions.

1 **6** "Now, my children, each of you love his brother. Drive hatred out of your
2 hearts. Love one another in deed and word and inward thoughts. •For when I stood
before my father I would speak peaceably about Joseph, but when I went out, the
3 spirit of hatred darkened my mind and aroused my soul to kill him. •Love one
another from the heart, therefore, and if anyone sins against you, speak to him in
peace. Expel the venom of hatred, and do not harbor deceit in your heart. If anyone
4 confesses and repents, forgive him. •If anyone denies his guilt, do not be contentious
5 with him, otherwise he may start cursing, and you would be sinning doubly. •In
a dispute do not let an outsider hear your secrets, since out of hatred for you he
may become your enemy, and commit a great sin against you. He may talk to you
frequently but treacherously, or be much concerned with you, but for an evil end,
6 having absorbed from you the venom. •Even if he denies it and acts disgracefully
out of a sense of guilt, be quiet and do not become upset. For he who denies will
repent, and avoid offending you again; indeed he will honor you, will respect you
7 and be at peace. •But even if he is devoid of shame and persists in his wickedness,   Deut 32:35
forgive him from the heart and leave vengeance to God.   Rom 12:19

1 **7** "If anyone prospers more than you, do not be aggrieved, but pray for him that
2 he may prosper completely, for this is what is precisely to your advantage. •And
if he becomes even more exalted, do not be envious, but remember that all humanity
dies. Offer praise to the Lord who provides good and beneficial things for all
3 mankind. •Search out the Lord's judgments, and thus you shall gain an inheritance
4 and your mind will be at rest. •Even if someone becomes rich by evil schemes,
as did Esau, your father's brother, do not be jealous; wait for the Lord to set the
5 limits. •For if he takes away the things obtained by evil means, those who repent
6 receive forgiveness, and the impenitent one receives eternal punishment. •The man
who is poor but free from envy, who is grateful to the Lord for everything, is
richer than all, because he does not love the foolish things that are a temptation
7 common to mankind. •Drive hatred away from your souls, and love one another
in uprightness of heart.

1 **8** "Tell these things to your children as well, so that they will honor Judah and
2 Levi, because from them the Lord will raise up a Savior for Israel.[a] •I know that
at the end your children will depart from them and will live in all manner of
3 wickedness and evildoing and corruption in the sight of the Lord." •Then after
he had been silent for a brief time he said again to them, "My children, obey your
4 father. Bury me near my fathers." •He drew up his feet and fell asleep in peace.
And after five years they took him up and buried him in Hebron with his fathers.

The Testament of Asher, the tenth son of Jacob and Zilpah

1 **1** A copy of the testament of Asher, the things he spoke to his sons in the one
2 hundred twenty-fifth year of his life. •While he was still healthy he said to them,
"Listen, children of Asher, to your father, and I will show you everything that
3 is right in the sight of God. •God has granted two ways[a] to the sons of men, two

---

8 a. The special roles for Levi and Judah are a
feature shared by T12P and the Dead Sea documents, where a kingly and priestly Messiah are
awaited; cf. 1QS[a] 2.11–21; CD 11.23; 14.19; 19.10;
20.1. It is also implied in Zech 4:14.

1 a. In 1:3–5:4 is set forth an elaborate version of

the Doctrine of the Two Ways, an ethical tradition
which is anticipated in the choices set before Israel
by Moses (Deut 30:15) and by Joshua (Josh 24:15).
It is stated explicitly in Jer 21:8–14, and further
developed in Sir 15:11–17 and in 2En 30:15. In
earliest Christian writings it is echoed in Mt
7:13–14, elaborated in EpBar 17 and Did 1; in post-

4 mind-sets, two lines of action, two models, and two goals. •Accordingly, everything
5 is in pairs, the one over against the other. • The two ways are good and evil;
concerning them are two dispositions within our breasts that choose between them.
6 If the soul wants to follow the good way, all of its deeds are done in righteousness
7 and every sin is immediately repented. •Contemplating just deeds and rejecting
8 wickedness, the soul overcomes evil and uproots sin. •But if the mind is disposed
toward evil, all of its deeds are wicked; driving out the good, it accepts the evil
9 and is overmastered by Beliar, who, •even when good is undertaken, presses the
struggle so as to make the aim of his action into evil, since the devil's storehouse
is filled with the venom of the evil spirit.

1 **2** "The soul, they say, may in words express good for the sake of evil, but the
2 outcome of the action leads to evil. •There is a man who has no mercy on the one
who serves him in performing an evil deed; there are two aspects of this, but the
3 whole is wicked. •And there is a man who loves the one who does the evil, as he
is himself involved in evil, so that he would choose to die in evil for the evildoer's
4 sake. There are also two aspects of this, but the whole situation is evil. •Although
indeed love is there, yet in wickedness is evil concealed; in name it is as though
5 it were good, but the outcome of the act is to bring evil. •Someone steals, deals
unjustly, robs, cheats, but yet has pity on the poor. This also has two aspects, but
6 is evil as a whole. •He who cheats his neighbor provokes God's wrath; he who
serves falsely before the Most High, and yet has mercy on the poor, disregards
the Lord who uttered the Law's commands; he provokes him, and yet he alleviates
7 the plight of the poor day laborer. •He defiles the soul and takes pride in his own
body; he kills many, yet has pity on a few. This also has two aspects, but is evil
8 as a whole. •Someone else commits adultery and is sexually promiscuous, yet is
abstemious in his eating. While fasting, he is committing evil deeds. Through the
power of his wealth he ravages many, and yet in spite of his excessive evil, he
9 performs the commandments. •This also has two aspects, but is evil as a whole.
Such persons are hares, because although they are halfway clean, in truth they are Lev 11:6
10 unclean, •for this is what God has said on the tables of the commandments. Deut 14:7

1 **3** "But you, my children, do not be two-faced like them, one good and the other
evil; rather, cling only to goodness, because in it the Lord God is at rest, and men
2 aspire to it. •Flee from the evil tendency, destroying the devil by your good works.
For those who are two-faced are not of God, but they are enslaved to their evil
desires, so that they might be pleasing to Beliar and to persons like themselves.

1 **4** "For persons who are good, who are single-minded—even though they are
2 considered by the two-faced to be sinners—are righteous before God. •For many
who destroy the wicked perform two works—good and evil—but it is good as a
3 whole, because evil is uprooted and destroyed. •One person hates the man who,
though merciful, is also unjust, or who is an adulterer, even though he fasts, and
thus is two-faced. But his work is good as a whole, because he imitates the Lord,
4 not accepting the seeming good as though it were the truly good. •Another person
does not want to see any pleasant days among the convivial, lest they disgrace the
body and pollute the soul. This also has two aspects, but is good on the whole.
5 For such persons are like gazelles and stags: In appearance they seem wild and
unclean, but as a whole they are clean. They live by zeal for the Lord, abstaining
from what God hates and has forbidden through his commandments, staving off
evil by the good.

apostolic literature it is a popular motif: AposCon
7.1; Clementine Homilies 5.7; Clement of Alexandria, *Strom* 5.5. Notable here is the effort to set
authentic works of mercy over against merely external manifestations of piety.

₁ **5** "Children, you see how in everything there are two factors, one against the
other, one concealed by the other: In possessions is greed, in merriment is
₂ drunkenness, in laughter is lamentation, in marriage is dissoluteness. •Death is
successor to life, dishonor to glory, night to day, darkness to light, but all these
things lead ultimately to day: righteous actions to life, unjust actions to death,
₃ since eternal life wards off death. •One cannot say truth is a lie, nor a righteous
act is unjust, because all truth[a] is subject ultimately to the light, just as all things
₄ are subject ultimately to God. •I have demonstrated all these things in my life, and
have not strayed from the Lord's truth. I have searched out the commandments
of the Most High and lived them according to all my strength.

₁ **6** "You also, my children, give attention to the Lord's command, pursuing the
₂ truth with singleness of mind. •The two-faced are doubly punished because they
both practice evil and approve of others who practice it; they imitate the spirits of
₃ error and join in the struggle against mankind. •You therefore, my children, keep
the Law of the Lord; do not pay attention to evil as to good, but have regard for
what is really good and keep it thoroughly in all the Lord's commandments, taking
₄ it as your way of life and finding rest in it. •For the ultimate end of human beings
displays their righteousness, since they are made known to the angels of the Lord
₅ and of Beliar. •For when the evil soul departs, it is harassed by the evil spirit
which it served through its desires and evil works. But if anyone is peaceful with
joy he comes to know the angel of peace and enters eternal life.

₁ **7** "Do not become like Sodom, which did not recognize the Lord's angels and   Gen 19:1
₂ perished forever. •For I know that you will sin and be delivered into the hands of
your enemies; your land shall be made desolate and your sanctuary wholly polluted.
₃ You will be scattered to the four corners of the earth; in the dispersion you shall
be regarded as worthless, like useless water, until such time as the Most High
visits the earth. [He shall come as a man eating and drinking with human beings,][a]
crushing the dragon's head in the water. He will save Israel and all the nations,
₄ [God speaking like a man]. •Tell these things, my children, to your children, so
₅ that they will not disobey him. •For I know that you will be thoroughly disobedient,
that you will be thoroughly irreligious,[b] heeding not God's Law but human
₆ commandments, being corrupted by evil. •For this reason, you will be scattered
like Dan and Gad, my brothers, you shall not know your own lands, tribe, or
₇ language. •But he will gather you in faith through his compassion and on account
of Abraham, Isaac, and Jacob."

₁ **8** After he had said these things he gave instructions, saying, "Bury me in
₂ Hebron." And he died, having fallen into a beautiful sleep. •And his sons did as
he commanded them: They took him up to Hebron and buried him with his fathers.

5 a. The ground of this ethical appeal is an ultimate
quasi-philosophical judgment concerning abstract
realities such as truth and integrity rather than a
moral evaluation based simply on individual acts
performed in conformity to the commandments of
Jewish law; cf. 6:3–7:7.

7 a. Probably these references to the humanity of

the God who comes to save are Christian interpolations. The crushing of the dragon's head recalls
the water imagery of primordial chaos and the
serpent (Gen 1:7–9; 7:11; Ps 74:12–17; 148:7; Isa
27:1), which resurfaces in Rev 12:1–17; 20:2.

b. Typical of T12P is the stylized reference to
the Law mingled with the conventions of hellenistic
ethics (e.g. *asebountes*).

The Testament of Joseph, the eleventh son of Jacob and Rachel

1 **1** A copy of the testament of Joseph.[a] When he was about to die, he called his sons and his brothers and said to them:

2 "My brothers and my children.
Listen to Joseph, the one beloved of Israel.
Give ear to the words of my mouth.

3 In my life I have seen envy and death.
But I have not gone astray: I continued in the truth of the Lord.

4 These, my brothers, hated me but the Lord loved me.
They wanted to kill me, but the God of my fathers preserved me.
Into a cistern they lowered me; the Most High raised me up.

5 They sold me into slavery; the Lord of all set me free.   Mt 25:31-46
I was taken into captivity; the strength of his hand came to my aid.
I was overtaken by hunger; the Lord himself fed me generously.

6 I was alone, and God came to help me.
I was in weakness, and the Lord showed his concern for me.
I was in prison, and the Savior acted graciously in my behalf.
I was in bonds, and he loosed me;

7 falsely accused, and he testified in my behalf.
Assaulted by bitter words of the Egyptians, and he rescued me.
A slave, and he exalted me.

1,2 **2** "And this chief officer of Pharaoh entrusted to me his household. •I struggled with a shameless woman who kept prodding me to transgress with her, but the

3 God of my father rescued me from the burning flame. •I was jailed, I was whipped,   TJos 6:6
I was sneered at, but the Lord granted me mercy in the sight of the prison-keeper.

4 "For the Lord does not abandon those who fear him,
neither in darkness, or chains, or tribulation or direst need.

5 For God does not disappoint as does man,   Num 23:19
nor is he timorous like a son of man   Isa 40:28-31
nor like an earthborn is he weak or frightened away.

6 In all these matters he takes his stand,
and in various ways he offers assistance,
even though for a brief time he may stand aside in order to test the
disposition of the soul.

7 In ten testings[a] he showed that I was approved,   Jub 19:8
and in all of them I persevered,   Gen 22:1
because perseverance is a powerful medicine   Ab 5:3
and endurance provides many good things.

1 **3** "How often the Egyptian woman threatened me with death! How often, after turning me over to the tormentors she would call me back and threaten me! But

2 since I was unwilling to have intercourse with her, she kept saying to me, •'You will be master over me and all my household if you will only give yourself over

1 a. Consisting largely of an expansion on the narratives of Gen 37:39–45, TJos is probably composite in the form in which it appears in the present text. This is indicated, for example, by awkward syntactical shifts in the narration (from first to third person) in 14:3, 6; 16:3. After 10:4, the theme of chastity seems to be eclipsed by concern for manifestation of brotherliness, especially by safeguarding the reputation of one's brothers, but the anti-

sexual motif keeps appearing and no clear break is evident. At 19:3–7 the Arm. MSS offer a more complete version of the apocalyptic predictions, probably in the more original form. The other MS evidence diverges at that point, however, and there occurs one of the clearest instances of Christian interpolation.

2 a. Num 14:22 mentions Israel's ten testings of God.

3 to me; then you will be our ruler.' •But I recalled my father's words, went weeping
4 into my quarters, and prayed to the Lord. •For those seven years I fasted, and yet
seemed to the Egyptians like someone who was living luxuriously, for those who   Dan 1:8-16
5 fast for the sake of God receive graciousness of countenance. •If my master was
absent, I drank no wine; for three-day periods I would take no food but give it to
6 the poor and the ill. •I would awaken early and pray to the Lord, weeping over
the Egyptian woman of Memphis because she annoyed me exceedingly and
7 relentlessly. • In the night she would come in to me, pretending a mere visit.
8 Because she had no male child, she pretended to consider me as a son. •For a time
she would embrace me as a son, but then I realized later that she was trying to lure
9 me into a sexual relationship. •When I became aware of this I lamented to the
point of death. After she had gone out, I came to myself and mourned in her behalf
10 for many days, because I had recognized her deceit and her deviousness. •I spoke
to her the words of the Most High, hoping he might divert her from evil desire.

1 **4** "How often, then, did she flatter me with words as a holy man, deceitfully
praising my self-control through her words in the presence of her husband, but
2 when we were alone she sought to seduce me. •Publicly she honored me for my
self-control, while privately she said to me, 'Have no fear of my husband, for he
is convinced of your chastity so that even if someone were to tell him about you,
3 he would not believe it.' •During all these affairs I stretched out on the ground
4 praying God to rescue me from her treachery. •When she achieved nothing by
means of it, she began to approach me for instruction, so that she might learn the
5 Word of God. •And she kept saying to me, 'If you want me to abandon the idols,
have intercourse with me, and I shall persuade my husband to put away the idols,
6 and we shall live in the presence of your Lord.' •But I kept telling her that the
Lord did not want worshipers who come by means of uncleanness, nor would he
be pleased with adulterers, but with those who were pure in heart and undefiled
7,8 in speech. •She was consumed with jealousy, wanting to fulfill her desire. •But
I devoted myself the more to fasting and prayer that the Lord might rescue me
from her.

1 **5** "Again on another occasion she said to me, 'If you do not want to commit
2 adultery, I shall kill my husband by a drug and take you as my husband.' •When
I heard this, I tore my clothing and said to her, 'Woman, show reverence to God;
do not commit this wicked deed, lest you be utterly destroyed. For you should
3 know that I shall make it known to all that this is your scheme.' •Filled with fear,
4 she ordered me not to disclose her plan. •Then she withdrew, but kept trying to
entice me with gifts and every manner of pleasurable things.

1,2 **6** "Later she sent me food mixed with enchantments. •When the eunuch who was
carrying it arrived, I looked up and saw a frightening man who offered me a sword
3 along with a bowl. So I perceived it was a trick to lead me astray.[a] •When he
departed, I wept; I tasted neither one item nor the other of the food he brought.
4 A day later she came to me and said, when she recognized the food, 'Why didn't
5 you eat the food?' • And I said to her, 'Because you filled it with a deadly
enchantment. How can you say, "I do not go near the idols, but only to the Lord."
6 Now then understand that the God of my father revealed to me through an angel[b]
your wickedness, but I have kept it for this reason: to shame you if somehow by
7 seeing it you might repent. •In order for you to learn that the evil of the irreligious
will not triumph over those who exercise self-control in their worship of God, I
will take this and eat it in your presence.' When I had said that, I prayed aloud,

---

6 a. God's miraculous preservation of his servant
from the harmful effects of drugs or poison is a
recurrent theme in the biblical tradition, as in
Elisha's deliverance in 2Kgs 4:38–41 or in Paul's
immunity to the viper in Acts 28:1–6. Cf. the

additional ending to Mark (Mk 16:18).
  b. Abraham's "angel" in Gen 16:7 and
22:15–18 is a circumlocution for Yahweh himself,
but here the angel is a messenger or intermediary,
as in TLevi.

8 'May the God of my fathers and the angel of Abraham be with me.' •And I ate. When she saw this, she fell upon her face at my feet weeping. I raised her up and warned her, and she agreed with me that she should no longer commit this impiety.

1 **7** "But her heart was still inclined to evil and she turned over in her mind how she might entrap me. Shortly she was groaning and depressed, even though she 2 was not sick. •When her husband saw her, he said to her, 'Why are you so downcast?' She responded to him, 'I am suffering from a pain in my heart, and 3 groans of my spirit have taken hold of me.' •He tried to cure her with words. Then she seized the occasion and came running in to me, while her husband was still outside, and said to me, 'I shall hang myself, or hurl myself over the precipice 4 if you do not have intercourse with me.' •Since I perceived that the spirit of Beliar 5 was troubling her, I prayed to the Lord, but I said to her, •'Why, wretched female, are you troubled and disturbed, blinded by sin? Remember that if you kill yourself, Astetha, your husband's concubine, who is filled with envy of you, will beat your 6 children; thus you will destroy your memory from the earth.' •And she said, 'See, then, you do love me. That is enough. Only keep contending for my life and that 7 of my children, and I shall cling to my expectation of gaining my desire.' •She did not understand that I spoke in this way for the Lord's sake and not for hers. 8 For if anyone is subjected to the passion of desire and is enslaved by it, as she was, even when he hears something good bearing on that passion he receives it as aiding his wicked desire.

1 **8** "I tell you, my children, it was about the sixth hour when she left me. Bending my knees before the Lord, I prayed a whole day and a whole night. Toward dawn 2 I arose, crying and begging deliverance from her. •Finally, she grasped my clothing, Gen 39:12-20 3 determined to force me into having intercourse with her. •When I saw, therefore, that in her madness she had seized my garment, I shook loose and left it and fled 4 naked. •She held on to it, and brought false accusation against me. Her husband came and threw me in prison in his own house; then the next day he whipped me 5 and sent me to the Pharaoh's prison. •When I was in fetters, the Egyptian woman was overtaken with grief. She came and heard the report how I gave thanks to the Lord and sang praise in the house of darkness,[a] and how I rejoiced with cheerful voice, glorifying my God, because through her trumped-up charge I was set free from this Egyptian woman.

1 **9** "Many times she sent messages to me saying, 'Acquiesce in fulfilling my desire, 2 and I will release you from the fetters and liberate you from the darkness.' •Not even in my mind did I yield to her, for God loves more the one who is faithful in self-control in a dark cistern than the one who in royal chambers feasts on 3 delicacies with excess. •If a man strives for self-control and at the same time desires glory—and the Most High knows that it is appropriate for him—he brings 4 it about for him, even as he did for me. •How often, as though she were ill, she came down at odd hours and listened to my voice as I prayed! When I was aware 5 of her groanings, I fell silent. •For when I had been with her in her house, she would bare her arms and thighs so that I might lie with her. For she was wholly beautiful and splendidly decked out to entice me, but the Lord protected me from her manipulations.

1 **10** "So you see, my children, how great are the things that patience and prayer 2 with fasting accomplish. •You also, if you pursue self-control and purity with patience and prayer with fasting in humility of heart, the Lord will dwell among 3 you, because he loves self-control. •And where the Most High dwells, even if envy befall someone, or slavery or false accusation, the Lord who dwells with him

---

8 a. The praise of God sounding forth from prison appears in the story of Daniel in the lion's den (Dan 6) as well as in Acts 16:25–34.

on account of his self-control not only will rescue him from these evils, but will
4 exalt him and glorify him as he did for me. •For these problems beset all mankind
5 either in deed or word or thought. •For my brothers know how much my father
loved me, yet I was not puffed up in my thoughts. Even while I was a child I had
6 the fear of God in my heart, for I understood that all things pass away. •I did not
arouse myself with evil design, but honored my brothers, and out of regard for
them even when they sold me I was silent rather than tell the Ishmaelites that I
was the son of Jacob, a great and righteous man.

1 **11** "You, therefore, my children, in every act keep the fear of God before your
eyes and honor your brothers. For everyone who does the Law of the Lord will
2 be loved by him. •As I was going with the Ishmaelites, they kept asking me, 'Are
you a slave?' And I replied, 'I am a slave out of a household,' so as not to disgrace
3 my brothers. •The greatest of them said to me, 'You are not a slave; even your
4 appearance discloses that.' But I told them that I was a slave. •As we were reaching
Egypt they began to squabble over me as to which of them would put up the money
5 and take me. •Accordingly it seemed good to all of them that I should be left in
Egypt with a trader handling their trading post until they returned bringing their
6 merchandise. •The Lord granted me favor in the eyes of the trader and he entrusted
7 me with his household. •And God blessed him by my hand, and he prospered in
gold and silver and in business. And I was with him three months.

1 **12** "At that time the Memphian woman, Pentephris' wife, came down in a
palanquin with great splendor, because she had heard about me from one of her
2 eunuchs. •She said to her husband that through[a] a certain young Hebrew the trader
had become rich; they say that he surely stole him out of the land of Canaan.
3 Now, then, work justice concerning him; take the young man to your household,
and the God of the Hebrews will bless you, because grace from heaven is with
him.

1 **13** "Pentephris believed her words, ordered the trader to come, and said to him,
'What is this I hear about you, that you steal persons from the land of Canaan and
2 sell them as slaves?' •The trader fell at his feet and besought him saying, 'I pray
3 you, my lord, I do not know what you are saying.' •Pentephris said to him, 'Where
is this Hebrew from, then?' And he said, 'The Ishmaelites left him with me until
4 they return.' •But he did not believe the trader and ordered that he be stripped and
5 beaten. •But since he persisted in his statements, Pentephris said, 'Bring in the
young man.' When I entered I prostrated myself before Pentephris, for he was
6 third in rank among Pharaoh's officers. •And taking me aside from the trader he
7 said to me, 'Are you a slave or a freeman?' •I said to him, 'A slave.' He said,
8 'Of whom?' I replied, 'Of the Ishmaelites.' •He said, 'How did you become a
9 slave?' And I said, 'They bought me out of the land of Canaan.' •But he said to
me, 'You are really lying.' And immediately he ordered that I also be stripped and
whipped.

1 **14** "The Memphian woman was watching through the doors as they beat me, for
her residence was nearby. So she sent a message to him. 'Your sentence is unjust,
because you have punished as a wrongdoer someone who, though a freeman, was
2 stolen.' •But since I did not change my statement while they were beating me, he
ordered me to be imprisoned 'until,' he said, 'the masters of the servant boy
3 arrive.' •But the woman said to her husband, 'Why do you detain in bonds this
4 young man who, though a captive, is well-born? •Rather he should be set free and
attended to by servants.' She wanted to see me by reason of her sinful passion,

---

12 a. Lit. "by the hand(s) of."

17 a. The ground of harmony among brothers is
the concealment of the failures of others. God hon-

ors good intentions. The ethical outlook resembles
that enjoined in the Dead Sea community, according
to 1QS 10.17f.

5 but I was ignorant of all these things. •He said to her, 'It is not proper for Egyptians to take away what belongs to others before the evidence has been presented.' He said this concerning the trader, but the young man he kept incarcerated.

15 "Twenty-four days later the Ishmaelites came; they had heard that Jacob, my
2 father, was mourning greatly over me, and they came and told me. •'Why did you tell us that you were a slave? Look, we now know that you are the son of a great man in the land of Canaan, and that your father is mourning for you in sackcloth
3 and ashes.' •When I heard this my inner being was dissolved and my heart melted, and I wanted to weep very much, but I restrained myself so as not to bring disgrace
4 on my brothers. So I said to them, 'I know nothing; I am a slave.' •Then they conferred about selling me so that I might not be discovered in bondage to them,
5 for they feared my father, that he might come and avenge himself powerfully against them. They had heard that he was a great person in the sight of God and
6 men. •Then the trader said to them, 'Release me from Pentephris' judgment.' So they came and requested of me, 'Say that you were purchased by us with money, and then he will release us from responsibility.'

16 "The Memphian woman said to her husband, 'Buy the young man, for I hear
2 it said that they are selling him.' •Immediately she sent a eunuch to the Ishmaelites,
3 requesting them to sell me. •But the eunuch was not willing to buy me and came away after testing them out. He told his mistress that they were asking a great deal
4 of money for the boy. •She sent the eunuch back again and told him, 'Even if they are asking two minas; offer it. Do not be sparing of the gold; just buy the boy and
5 bring him to me.' •The eunuch went and gave them eighty pieces of gold and took me away, but he told the Egyptian woman he had paid a hundred. Although I knew the facts, I kept quiet in order not to bring the eunuch under disgrace.

17 "So you see, my children, how many things I endured in order not to bring
2 my brothers into disgrace.ª •You, therefore, love one another and in patient
3 endurance conceal one another's shortcomings. •God is delighted by harmony among brothers and by the intention of a kind heart that takes pleasure in goodness.
4 When my brothers came to Egypt they learned that I had returned their money   Gen 42:25-35
5 to them, that I did not scorn them, and that I sought to console them. •After the   Gen 50:19-21
death of Jacob, my father, I loved them beyond measure, and everything he had
6 wanted for them I did abundantly in their behalf. •I did not permit them to be troubled by the slightest matter, and everything I had under my control I gave to
7 them. •Their sons were mine, and mine were as their servants; their life was as my life, and every pain of theirs was my pain; every ailment of theirs was my
8 sickness; their wish was my wish. •I did not exalt myself above them arrogantly   Lk 22:27
because of my worldly position of glory, but I was among them as one of the least.

18 "If you live in accord with the Lord's commands, God will exalt you with
2 good things forever.ª •And if anyone wishes to do you harm, you should pray for him, along with doing good, and you will be rescued by the Lord from every evil.
3 Indeed you can see that on account of my humilityᵇ and patient endurance I took to myself a wife, the daughter of the priest of Heliopolis; a hundred talents of gold were given to me along with her, and my Lord caused them to be my servants.
4 And he also gave me mature beauty, more than those of mature beauty in Israel; he preserved me until old age with strength and beauty. In every way I was like Jacob.

---

18 a. Here ethical motivation is chiefly instru-
mentalist: Obedience to the Law guarantees that
God will exalt the obedient one.
   b. The reader is not impressed in this portrait

with Joseph's humility in spite of his claim to
possess it. His self-praise for possessing "mature
beauty" (18:4) does not sound strikingly humble.

1,2 **19** "Listen, my children, concerning the dream that I saw. •Twelve stags were grazing at a certain place; nine were scattered over the whole earth, and likewise also the three.[a]

A

3

4

5

6

7

bAnd as I looked, the three stags became three lambs; they cried out to the Lord, and the Lord led them into a fertile, well-watered place. He led them out of darkness into light. • And there they cried out to the Lord until the nine stags were gathered to him, and they all became like twelve sheep. After a short time they multiplied and became many herds. •Later as I was looking, twelve bulls were nursing from one cow, who furnished a sea of milk. • The twelve herds and the innumerable herds drank from it. And the horns of the fourth bull ascended to heaven and became as a rampart for the herds. And from between the two horns there sprouted forth yet another horn. •And I saw a heifer which surrounded them twelve times and which became to perfection an aide to the bulls.

8 And I saw that a virgin was born from Judah, wearing a linen stole; and from her was born a spotless lamb. At his left there was something like a lion, and all the wild animals rushed against him, but the lamb conquered them, and destroyed them, trampling them underfoot.

cAnd I saw in the midst of the horns a certain virgin wearing a multicolored stole; from her came forth a lamb. Rushing from the left were all sorts of wild animals and reptiles, and the lamb conquered them.

9 And the angels and mankind and all the earth rejoiced over him.

Because of him the bull rejoiced and the cow and the stags were also glad with them.

10 These things will take place in the last days.

These things must take place in their appropriate time.

11 You, therefore, my children, keep the Lord's commandments; honor Levi and Judah, because from their seed will arise the Lamb of God who will take away the sin of the world, and will save all the nations, as well as Israel.

And you, my children, honor Levi and Judah, because from them shall arise the salvation of Israel.

---

19 a. The division of the twelve tribes into nine and three, rather than the normal biblical ten and two (1Kgs 12:21), is paralleled in 1En 89:72 and 1QM 1:2, where the sons of Levi, Judah, and Benjamin receive special mention.

b. 19:3–7 is preserved only in Arm.; the Arm. version of 19:8–12 differs significantly from the Gk. as well. Since an important segment is available only in the Arm. version, this passage is textually problematic. 19:8–12 is preserved in different textual forms, and evidence of Christian interpolation seems clear. Everything is compatible with the

dyarchic eschatological expectations of the T12P until vs. 11b is reached; then follows characteristically Christian terminology.

c. The right-hand column continues the Arm. text; the left column is based on c, β. This ch. contains some of the most extended apocalyptic material in all the T12P. The animals may represent nations, but more likely they are individual rulers or leaders, as in the case with the "horns" of Dan 7:8. Possibly Maccabean rulers are intended, but sectarian leaders and their opponents could as well be depicted in this cryptic fashion.

12 For his kingdom is an everlasting kingdom which will not pass away. But my
kingdom will come to an end among
you, like a guard[d] in an orchard who
disappears at the end of the summer.

For my kingdom shall have an end
among you, like an orchard guard who
disappears after the summer.

1 **20** "For I know that after my death the Egyptians will oppress you, but God will
work vengeance on your behalf, and will lead you into the promises made to your
2 fathers. •You shall carry my bones along with you, for when you are taking my   Gen 50:25
bones up there, the Lord will be with you in the light, while Beliar will be with   Ex 13:19
3 the Egyptians in the dark. • Take Asenath, your mother, and bury her by the
hippodrome, near Rachel, your grandmother."[a]
4 And when he had said this he stretched out his feet and fell into a beautiful
5,6 sleep. •And all Israel and all Egypt mourned with great lamentation. •And at the
departure of the sons of Israel from Egypt, they took along Joseph's bones and
buried him in Hebron with his fathers. The years of his life were one hundred
ten.

The Testament of Benjamin, the twelfth son of Jacob and Rachel

1 **1** A copy of the words of Benjamin which he testified to his sons, having lived
2 one hundred twenty-five years. •He kissed them and said, "Just as Isaac was born
3 to Abraham in his old age, so I was born to Jacob. •Since Rachel, my mother, died   Gen 35:16-20
as she was bearing me, I had no milk from her, but was nursed instead by Bilhah,
4 her maid servant. •For after Rachel bore Joseph she was sterile for twelve years;
5 she prayed to the Lord, with fasting, •and conceived and gave birth to me. My
father loved Rachel exceedingly, and prayed that he might see two sons born from
6 her. •For this reason I was called Benjamin, that is 'son of days.'[a]

1 **2** "When I came to Joseph in Egypt and my brother recognized me, he said,
2 'What did they say to my father when they sold me?' •And I replied to him, 'They   Gen 37:31
spattered your shirt with blood and sent it to him and said, "Do you know if this   TZeb 4:9-11
3 shirt belongs to your son?" ' •And (Joseph) said to me, 'Yes, brother. When they
stripped off my shirt and gave me to the Ishmaelites, they gave me a loincloth,
4 beat me, and told me to run. •One of them who had whipped me was met by a
5 lion and it ate him. •So his partners were terrified and kept me under a looser rein.'

1 **3** "Now, my children, love the Lord God of heaven and earth; keep his com-
2 mandments; pattern your life after the good and pious man Joseph. • Let your
thoughts incline to the good, as you know to be so with me, because he who has
3 the right set of mind sees everything rightly. •Fear the Lord and love your neighbor.
Even if the spirits of Beliar seek to derange you with all sorts of wicked oppression,
they will not dominate you, any more than they dominated Joseph, my brother.
4 How many men wanted to destroy him, and God looked out for him! For the
person who fears God and loves his neighbor cannot be plagued by the spirit of
5 Beliar[a] since he is sheltered by the fear of God. •Neither man's schemes not those

d. The guard in the orchard recalls Isa 1:8; 5:2;
Mk 12:1, where a tower or booth serves to guard
the Lord's vineyard or grove. Apparently what is
contrasted here is the temporary nature of Joseph's
rule and the eternal duration of God's kingdom in
the end-time.

20 a. According to Gen 48:7, Rachel was buried

on the way to Ephrath, which in LXX = Hippodromos. The mention of the hippodrome here points
to a culturally hellenistic provenance for T12P.
1 a. This is one of a series of etymologies connected with Benjamin's name: "Son of days' =
"son of old age"(?); see Gen 44:20, "son of old
age"; Gen 35:18, "son of sorrow," "son of [my]
right hand."

of animals can prevail over him, for he is aided in living by this: by the love which
6 he has toward his neighbor. •Joseph also urged our father to pray for his brothers,
that the Lord would not hold them accountable for their sin which they so wickedly
7 committed against him. • And Jacob cried out, 'O noble child, you have crushed
the inner feelings of Jacob, your father.' He embraced him and kept kissing him
for two hours, saying,[b]

8 'Through you will be fulfilled the
heavenly prophecy concerning the Lamb
of God, the Savior of the world, because
the unspotted one will be betrayed by
lawless men, and the sinless one will
die for impious men by the blood of the
covenant for the salvation of the gentiles
and of Israel and the destruction of
Beliar and his servants.'

'In you will be fulfilled the heavenly
prophecy which says that the spotless
one will be defiled by lawless men and
the sinless one will die for the sake of
impious men.'

1 **4** "See then, my children, what is the goal of the good man. Be imitators of him
in his goodness because of his compassion, in order that you may wear crowns
2 of glory.[a] •For a good man does not have a blind eye, but he is merciful to all,
3 even though they may be sinners. •And even if persons plot against him for evil
ends, by doing good this man conquers evil, being watched over by God. He loves
4 those who wrong him as he loves his own life. • If anyone glorifies himself, he
holds no envy. If anyone becomes rich, he is not jealous. If anyone is brave, he
praises him. He loves the moderate person; he shows mercy to the impoverished;
5 to the ill he shows compassion; he fears God. •He loves the person who has the
gift of a good spirit as he loves his own life.

1 **5** "If your mind is set toward good,[a] even evil men will be at peace with you;
the dissolute will respect you and will turn back to the good. The greedy will not
only abstain from their passion but will give to the oppressed the things which they
2 covetously hold. •If you continue to do good, even the unclean spirits will flee
3 from you and wild animals will fear you. •For where someone has within himself
respect for good works and has light in the understanding, darkness will slink away
4 from that person. •For if anyone wantonly attacks a pious man, he repents, since
the pious man shows mercy to the one who abused him, and maintains silence.
And if anyone betrays a righteous man, the righteous man prays. Even though for
a brief time he may be humbled, later he will appear far more illustrious, as
happened with Joseph, my brother.

1 **6** "The deliberations of the good man are not in the control of the deceitful spirit, TLevi 5:6
2 Beliar, for the angel of peace guides his life.[a] •For he does not look with passionate TDan 6:5
longing at corruptible things, nor does he accumulate wealth out of love for TAsh 6:6
3 pleasure. •He does not find delight in pleasure, nor does he grieve his neighbor,
nor does he stuff himself with delicacies, nor is he led astray by visual excitement:
4 The Lord is his lot. •The good set of mind does not receive glory or dishonor from
men, nor does it know deceit, or lying, or conflict, or abuse. For the Lord dwells

---

3 a. On Beliar, see TReu 2:1, n.

b. On the left, c. β text; on the right, the Arm.
The major text traditions include a Christian interpolation at this point; one group of MSS refers
explicitly to "Lamb of God" (Jn 1:29). For the
destruction of Beliar in the end-time, see Lk 10:18;
Rev 12:9; 20:2.

4 a. Crowns of glory are a familiar image in Christian usage: 1Pet 5:4; 1Cor 9:25; 2Tim 4:8; Jas 1:12;
Rev 2:10.

5 a. Here, in contrast to other sections of T12P
where sin is defeated only by divine judgment or
by expulsion of Beliar, there is a wholly optimistic
view that good deeds will overcome the evil inclination of others.

6 a. Extols the hellenistic virtue of integrity, although it incorporates a dualistic view of mankind;
the unwary are subject to the control of Beliar.

in him, illumines his life, and he rejoices in everything at every appropriate time.
5 The good set of mind does not talk from both sides of its mouth: praises and curses, abuse and honor, calm and strife, hypocrisy and truth, poverty and wealth,
6 but it has one disposition, uncontaminated and pure, toward all men. •There is no duplicity in its perception or its hearing. Whatever it does, or speaks, or perceives,
7 it knows that the Lord is watching over its life, •for he cleanses his mind in order that he will not be suspected of wrongdoing either by men or by God. The works of Beliar are twofold, and have in them no integrity.

1 **7** "So I tell you, my children, flee from the evil of Beliar, because he offers a
2 sword to those who obey him. •And the sword is the mother of the seven evils:[a] it receives them through Beliar: The first is moral corruption, the second is destruction, the third is oppression, the fourth is captivity, the fifth is want, the
3 sixth is turmoil, the seventh is desolation. •It is for this reason that Cain was handed Gen 4:15 over by God for seven punishments, for in every hundredth year the Lord brought
4 upon him one plague. •When he was two hundred years old suffering began and in his nine hundredth year he was deprived of life. For he was condemned on account of Abel his brother as a result of all his evil deeds, but Lamech was Gen 4:24
5 condemned by seventy times seven.[b] •Until eternity those who are like Cain in their moral corruption and hatred of brother shall be punished with a similar judgment.

1,2 **8** "But you, my children, run from evil, corruption, and hatred of brothers; •cling to goodness and love. For the person with a mind that is pure with love does not
3 look on a woman for the purpose of having sexual relations. •He has no pollution in his heart, because upon him is resting the spirit of God. For just as the sun is unpolluted, though it touches dung and slime, but dries up both and drives off the bad odor, so also the pure mind, though involved with the corruptions of earth, edifies instead and is not itself corrupted.

1 **9** "From the words of Enoch the Righteous[a] I tell you that you will be sexually promiscuous like the promiscuity of the Sodomites and will perish, with few exceptions. You shall resume your actions with loose women, and the kingdom
2 of the Lord will not be among you, for he will take it away forthwith. •But in your Hag 2:9 allotted place will be the temple of God, and the latter temple will exceed the former in glory. The twelve tribes shall be gathered there and all the nations, until such time as the Most High shall send forth his salvation through the ministration
3 of the unique prophet.[b] •[He shall enter the first temple, and there the Lord will TLevi 10:3 be abused and will be raised up on wood. And the temple curtain shall be torn, and the spirit of God will move on to all the nations as a fire is poured out. And he shall ascend from Hades and shall pass on from earth to heaven. I understand how humble he will be on the earth, and how splendid in heaven.][c]

1 **10** "When Joseph was in Egypt I earnestly desired to see his appearance and the form of his face, and through my father Jacob's prayers I saw him, while I was awake during the day, just as he was, his whole appearance."

---

7 a. TBenj has its own version of the seven deadly sins, according to which stress falls on sexual indulgence.

b. Lamech's seventy times seven condemnation (Gen 4:24) contrasts precisely with Mt 18:22, where forgiveness is to be extended by an identical formula.

9 a. Not found in extant Enochic material.

b. The expectation of the eschatological prophet builds on Deut 18:15 and figures importantly at Qumran: 1QS 9.10–11; 1QSᵃ 2.11–12. Possibly the star, mentioned in CD 7.15–20 (which is based on Num 24:17) is the One Who Teaches Rightly (1QS

1.11), forerunner of the unique prophet of the endtime. The prophet is directly mentioned in PssJosh 5–8 (= 4QTestim) in a passage which leads into a declaration about the star. The text from Num 24 is quoted in Stephen's sermon (Acts 7:37), where it is taken to refer to Jesus as the eschatological prophet.

c. Perhaps the most explicit of all the Christian interpolations. The tearing of the Temple veil is mentioned in TLevi 10:3 and may be a "prediction" after the event of Jerusalem's fall in A.D. 70, or it could be an authentic predictive note that was exploited by Christians and expanded into the present extended interpolation.

2   After he had spoken these things to them he said, "You know then, my children,
3 that I am dying. Do the truth, each of you to his neighbor; •keep the Law of the
4 Lord and his commandments, •for I leave you these things instead of an inheritance.
Give them, then, to your children for an eternal possession; this is what Abraham,
5 Isaac, and Jacob did. •They gave us all these things as an inheritance, saying,
'Keep God's commandments until the Lord reveals his salvation to all the nations.'   TJud 25:4
6 And then you will see Enoch and Seth and Abraham and Isaac and Jacob being
7 raised up at the right hand in great joy.[a] •Then shall we also be raised, each of   Mt 19:28-30
us over our tribe, and we shall prostrate ourselves before the heavenly king.   Dan 12:2
8 Then all shall be changed, some destined for glory, others for dishonor, for the   1Cor 15:51
9 Lord first judges Israel for the wrong she has committed •and then he shall do the
10 same for all the nations. •Then he shall judge Israel by the chosen gentiles as he
tested Esau by the Midianites who loved their brothers. You, therefore, my
11 children, may your lot come to be with those who fear the Lord. •Therefore, my   Jer 31:31
children, if you live in holiness, in accord with the Lord's commands, you shall   Rom 11:26
again dwell with me in hope; all Israel will be gathered to the Lord.

1 **11** "And I shall no longer be called a rapacious wolf on account of your rapine,   Gen 49:27
2 but 'the Lord's worker' providing food for those who do good works. •And in later   Deut 33:12
   Isa 42:1
times there shall rise up the beloved of the Lord, from the lineage of Judah and
Levi, one who does his good pleasure by his mouth, enlightening all the nations
with new knowledge. The light of knowledge will mount up in Israel for her
salvation, seizing them like a wolf coming upon them, and gathering the gentiles.
3 Until the consummation of the ages he shall be in the congregations of the gentiles
4 and among the rulers, like a musical air in the mouths of all. •He shall be written
of in sacred books, both his work and his word. And he shall be God's Chosen
5 One forever. •He shall range widely among them, like my father, Jacob, saying,
'He shall fill up what was lacking of your tribe.' "

1 **12** "And when he had finished his statements he said, "I command you, my
children, carry my bones up out of Egypt; bury me in Hebron near my fathers."
2 Benjamin died last of all in his one hundred twenty-fifth year at a ripe old age,
3 and they placed him in a coffin. •And in the ninety-first year after the departure
of the sons of Israel for Egypt, they and their brothers took up the bones of their
fathers secretly, because of the war with Canaan, and buried them in Hebron by
4 the feet of their fathers. •Then they returned from the land of Canaan and resided
in Egypt until the day of the departure from Egypt.

---

10 a. A doctrine of the resurrection as in TJud
25:4; but here, as in Dan 12:2, there is the expectation that both the just and the unjust will be raised
in the last day. As the final doctrinal statement, the
passage serves as a fitting conclusion to the T12P,
with only the stylized account of Benjamin's death
as the actual end of the book.

TESTAMENT OF JOB

(First Century B.C.–First Century A.D.)

A NEW TRANSLATION AND INTRODUCTION
BY R. P. SPITTLER

The Testament of Job resembles the form and purpose of the better-known Testaments of the Twelve Patriarchs. It is slightly shorter than Paul's Letter to the Romans, and commends the virtue of endurance (or patience: *hypomonē*) based on the biblical character, Job. It is not equal to the literary and philosophic grandeur of the canonical book of Job but is prosaic and at times humorous.

A Prologue (ch. 1) gives the title and setting. An Epilogue (chs. 51–53) describes Job's death, soul ascent, and burial. The main body of the Testament (chs. 2–50) falls into four literary divisions: Job relates in turn to a revealing angel (chs. 2–5), to Satan (chs. 6–27), to the three kings (chs. 28–45), and to his three daughters (chs. 46–50). The bulk of the testament (1:4–45:4), embracing the first three of the four sections, is Job's first-person account of the cause and consequences of his sickness.

At the end of his life, the patriarch (identified as Jobab, a descendant of Esau, before God named him Job) gathers his children for last words of counsel and for distribution of his estate (ch. 1). Job's perplexity over the idolatry he sees (chs. 2f.) occasions the appearance of an angel, who promises catastrophe yet renown (ch. 4) should Job persist in his resolve to destroy the idol's shrine. He does (ch. 5).

Satan's consequent attack on Job (chs. 6–27) begins subtly with his disguise as a beggar (chs. 6–8) seeking to take advantage of Job's generosity and piety, which Job recounts at length (chs. 9–15). But the former charities are displaced by tragic losses (chs. 16–26) in property, family, and health. Nevertheless, Job endures nobly and when Satan finally confronts him directly, it is to surrender before the athlete of endurance (ch. 27).

The three kings appear, astonished at the extent of Job's calamities (chs. 28–30): Eliphas laments Job's losses (chs. 31–34). Baldad tests his sanity (35:1–38:5). Sophar offers their royal physicians (38:6–8). As a final blow, Job's grieving wife, Sitis, dies and is buried (chs. 39f.). Finally, Elihu speaks (ch. 41). The kings are forgiven by Job's intercession (ch. 42), while Elihu is cursed (ch. 43). Job recovers (ch. 44), gives final counsels, and divides the inheritance among his seven sons (ch. 45).

When the three daughters inquire about their share of the inheritance, Job calls for the triple-stranded phylactery by which he was cured when at God's direction he girded himself (ch. 46). As one of the magical cords is given to each of the daughters in turn, they lose interest in earthly concerns and begin to speak ecstatically in the language of angels (chs. 47–50), yielding hymns said to have been preserved by Nereus, Job's brother (ch. 51) and blessing God in their distinctive dialects as the soul of Job is carried off in a heavenly chariot (ch. 52). Finally (ch. 53), Job's body is buried with a proper lament.

Text

The Testament of Job survives in four Greek manuscripts, in an Old Church Slavonic version, and in an incomplete Coptic version. No Semitic witnesses to the text exist. Modern translations have appeared in French,[1] Serbo-Croatian (in part),[2] English,[3] German,[4] and modern Hebrew.[5]

P–   Paris, Bibliothèque Nationale, fonds grec 2658, complete; dated in the eleventh century. It was edited by M. R. James[6] and S. Brock.[7] As a whole, P is the best manuscript, although traces of Christian intrusions appear (Brock). A second manuscript in the same library, fonds grec 938, is a sixteenth-century copy of P.

S–   Messina, Sicily, San Salvatore 29, complete; dated A.D. 1307/1308. It was edited by A. Mancini[8] and (with V) by R. Kraft.[9] S apparently represents (with V?) a separate textual tradition from P.

V–   Rome, Vatican, Greek 1238, complete; a palimpsest manuscript dated A.D. 1195, with earlier writing in the same century. This manuscript restyles textual difficulties into smooth paraphrases, shows some evidence of Christian terminology, harmonizes chronological references, and frequently abbreviates. V is accessible now in the edition of Brock; it is the first manuscript published in modern times.[10]

Slav–   An Old Church Slavonic version was published by G. Polívka[11] based on a manuscript known once to have been owned by P. J. Šafarik (1795–1861) and apparently located in Prague. Two other manuscripts also were consulted by Polívka: Belgrade National Library, no. 149 (incomplete), and the Moscow Rumjancov Museum, no. 1472.

Coptic–   Papyrus Cologne 3221, incomplete and unevenly preserved. It is now being edited by M. Weber of the Institute for Antiquity at the University of Cologne. Preliminary details[12] show the Coptic text (Sahidic dialect, with Bohairic influence) differs from the Greek. This oldest (A.D. 5th cent.) of witnesses to the text of the Testament of Job will aid the production of a critical text.

Original language

Earlier modern scholars (Kohler, James, Riessler) held the work to have been written originally in Hebrew, even though no manuscript evidence of a Semitic origin exists. Strongest considerations supporting the possibility of a Hebrew original arise from hymnic portions of the text, where such phrases as "while crowns lead the way with praises" (43:14) may reflect Hebraisms.

An Aramaic origin was argued by C. C. Torrey,[13] on alleged linguistic grounds. But his arguments have convinced few modern scholars.[14]

Greek is most likely the language in which the Testament of Job was originally composed. No Semitic versions or manuscripts are known. Moreover, the close, though complicated, linguistic relation of the Testament to the Septuagint Book of Job provides the strongest argument in favor of original composition in Greek.

---

[1] J. Migne, *Dictionnaire des apocryphes* (Troisième et dernière encyclopédie théologique, t. 24; Paris, 1858) vol. 2, cols. 401–20; M. Philonenko, "Le Testament de Job, Introduction, traduction et notes," *Sem* 18 (1968) 1–75.

[2] S. Novaković, "Apocrifna priča o Jovu," *Starine* 10 (1878) 157–70. This work translates into Serbo-Croatian about half of TJob from Migne's earlier French translation, making up what was lacking in the one Old Church Slavonic MS known to the author.

[3] K. Kohler, "The Testament of Job," in G. Kohut, ed., *Semitic Studies in Memory of Rev. Dr. Alexander Kohut*, pp. 264–338; R. Spittler, *The Testament of Job: Introduction, Translation, and Notes*, Harvard University Ph.D. (1971) pp. 75–130; R. Kraft et al., eds., *The Testament of Job According to the SV Text*.

[4] P. Riessler, *Altjüdisches Schrifttum ausserhalb der Bibel übersetzt und erklärt* (Augsburg, 1928) pp. 1104–34, 1333f.; B. Schaller, "Das Testament Hiobs," in W. Kümmel et al., eds., *JSHRZ* (Gütersloh, 1979) vol. 3, pt. 3, pp. 325–74. [We are grateful to Schaller for sending us page proofs —J.H.C.]

[5] A. Kahana, *ha-Sefarim ha-Hitsonim* (Tel Aviv, 1936/37[1], 1956[2]) vol. 1, pp. 515–38; A. Hartom, *ha-Sefarim ha-Hitsonim* (Tel Aviv, 1965) vol. 6, pp. 1–42.

[6] M. R. James, *Apocrypha Anecdota, 2nd Series*, pp. lxxii–cii, 104–37.

[7] S. Brock, *Testamentum Iobi*.

[8] A. Mancini, "Per la critica del 'Testamentum Job,'" *Rendiconti della Reale Accademia dei Lincei, Classe di Scienzi Morali, Storiche e Filologiche*, Serie Quinta 20 (1911) 479–502.

[9] Kraft et al., *Testament of Job*.

[10] A. Mai, *Scriptorum veterum nova collectio e Vaticanis codicibus*, vol. 7, cols. 180–91.

[11] G. Polívka, "Apokrifna priča o Jovu," *Starine* 24 (1891) 135–55.

[12] Found in M. Philonenko, *Sem* 18 (1968) 9, 61–63.

[13] C. C. Torrey, *The Apocryphal Literature* (New Haven, 1945) p. 143.

[14] Earlier, an Aram. origin was affirmed by R. Pfeiffer, *History of New Testament Times* (New York, 1941) p. 70.

Relation to the Septuagint

The Septuagint Book of Job is 20 percent shorter than the underlying Masoretic text; nevertheless, the Greek at points considerably expands the Hebrew version. Especially is this true of the speech of Job's wife: Two sentences appear in the Hebrew text ("Do you hold fast your integrity? Curse God and die." Job 2:9). These become a plaintive paragraph in the Septuagint, while the Testament of Job (24f.) gives Job's wife a name (Sitis) and embellishes her speech even more.

Similarly, the Septuagint differs from the Masoretic text at the end of the Book of Job: The Greek version closes with a paragraph about Job's homeland and his ancestors (Job 42:17b–e LXX). This longer Septuagint ending shows correspondences with the Testament of Job. It also embodies marked parallels to an Aristeas fragment preserved by Alexander Polyhistor (in Eusebius, *PrEv* 9.25.1–4).

The Testament of Job draws mainly from the narrative framework of the Septuagint Book of Job, which appears at Job 1–2; 42:7–17. But in addition, Job 29–31 (LXX) furnished Testament of Job 9–16 with numerous concepts and phrases by which to amplify Job's wealth, piety, and generosity. At times, merely a phrase of the Septuagint language is worked into the Testament (seven thousand sheep: Job 1:3 LXX; TJob 9:3). In a few instances, more complete Septuagint quotations appear.

Reliance of the testament on the Septuagint is clear also from the testament's agreement with Septuagint passages where there is no Hebrew equivalent (e.g. TJob 13:5). As yet unresolved is the complicated problem of the textual relations between the several Greek manuscripts of the Testament of Job and the textual growth of the Septuagint Book of Job.

The testament genre

The mere phrase "My son(s)," found already in short units of wisdom literature (e.g. Prov 5:1, 7), implies the essence of the testament (*diathēkē*): A wise aged (and usually dying) father imparts final words of ethical counsel to his attentive offspring. In the major biblical instance—the blessing of Jacob on his twelve sons (Gen 47:29–50:14)—specific elements characteristic of the later Jewish testaments already appear: (1) An ill father (48:1), (2) near death (47:29), (3) and on his bed (47:31), (4) calls his sons (49:1), (5) disposes of his goods (48:22), and (6) issues a forecast of events to come (49:1, *et passim*). The father (7) dies (49:33) and (8) a lamentation ensues (50:2–14). Each of these features appears in the Testament of Job.

J. Munck[15] found a sufficient grouping of these features in late Jewish (e.g. Tob 14:3–11; 1En 91:1–19) as well as New Testament (Acts 20:17–38; 1Tim 4:1–16) literature to identify the "farewell address" as a widely used literary technique in which features of the testament genre show up in literature not in the testament form.

The notion of the term "testament" in the sense of a legal will, not to mention the derived notion of a spiritual legacy, was only possible as a hellenistic development. For the Hebrew language apparently has no specific word for "testament," even though inheritance laws flourished in Israel. The Hebrew term *bryt* refers to a covenant or a contract, not a will.

The first century B.C. and the first century A.D. were eminently the centuries of the testament. Some products of the genre of that era were absorbed into other works: The Testament of Moses, composed in the first century A.D., was absorbed into the Assumption of Moses. The Testament of Hezekiah, a Christian product, must have originated late in the first century A.D.; but since the second to fourth centuries A.D., it has been part of the Ascension of Isaiah (3:13b–4:18). In its Greek form, the Testament of Adam probably goes back to the environs of the first century A.D.

The Testament of Abraham is another first-century A.D. product. The fourth-century Christian document *Constitutiones apostolorum* (6.16.3) in its list of apocryphal works cites the "apocryphal books . . . of the three patriarchs," which presumably refers to the testaments of Abraham, Isaac, and Jacob, who are elsewhere widely remembered together.

In the Testament of Orpheus appears a Jewish-hellenistic text that called on the pagan mystagogue as a witness to monotheism.

---

[15] "Discours d'adieu dans le Nouveau Testament et dans la littérature biblique," in O. Cullmann and P. Menoud, eds., *Aux sources de la tradition chrétienne* (M. Goguel Festschrift) (Neuchatel/Paris, 1950) pp. 155–70.

Subsequent Christian testaments display tendencies: The third-century Testament of Solomon was a guide to magical exorcistic rites. The *Testamentum Domini* (extant only in Syr.) reflects ecclesiastical interests of the fourth and fifth centuries.

The strong ethical note of the earlier Jewish testaments endured throughout the Middle Ages, when Jewish scholars wrote (*non*pseudepigraphic) moral wills for their children. The earliest of these was the *Orhot Hayyim* ("Ways of Life"), written by Eliezer Ben Isaac Gershom around A.D. 1050. In his study *Jewish Magic and Superstition*, J. Trachtenberg[16] made use of very late representatives of this genre, including the Testament of Judah the Pius and the Testament of Shabbetae Horowitz, dated in the sixteenth century A.D.

Development also characterized the testament genre; it obtained the sense of a will, which legally specified the testator's wishes regarding the disposition of his estate following death. *Testamentum Platonis* (in Diogenes Laertius 3.41–43) provides a first-century B.C. example. The same classical author preserves (among others) the will of Theophrastus (Diogenes Laertius 5.51–57). Wealthy persons could designate the establishment of memorial cults or institutions, resulting in such epigraphic remains as the *Testamentum Galli*, the *Testamentum Epicuri*, and the *Testamentum Epictetae*. Showing the possibilities of evolving literary elaboration of this form, the Testament of Diogenes (c. A.D. 200) is a summary of the philosopher's parting words inscribed on a wall for travelers to see. Similarly, the third- or fourth-century A.D. *Testamentum Porcelli* was said by Jerome to amuse schoolboys, since it was a "satiric parody" of a will contrived by a pig named Grunnius Corocotta prior to his slaughter.

But it is above all the Testaments of the Twelve Patriarchs with which the Testament of Job most readily aligns. As do these, the Testament of Job (1) opens with a deathbed scene; (2) celebrates a virtue; (3) offers moral exhortations; and (4) closes with the death, burial, and lamentation scene.

But the Testament of Job embodies distinctive modifications of the testament genre. It treats but one biblical character, who was not from the Torah but from the wisdom literature. Of the features identified as characteristic of the testament genre, the Testament of Job may, in comparison with the Testaments of the Twelve Patriarchs, be said to be more haggadic, considerably less hortatory, and almost entirely devoid of any apocalyptic element.

It is fair to say that the biblical details have undergone considerably more haggadic embellishment in the Testament of Job than in the Testaments of the Twelve Patriarchs, which nowhere equal the hagiographic fantasy apparent in the extensive magnification of Job's generosity (TJob 9–15).

Exhortation in the Testament of Job is almost limited to 45:1–3, which may have been an original end to an earlier form of the testament. The "two-ways"—the way of righteousness and the way of evil—motif does not appear. Overall, the Testament of Job is a far more artistic tale—a "novelized" testament, one might say—than the Testaments of the Twelve Patriarchs.

Traditional apocalyptic features in the Testament of Job show through only slightly, such as in the description of the splendorous sashes Job bequeathed his daughters (TJob 46:7f.) or the appearance of the angel (TJob 3–5). There is no assumption to heaven (nor even seven or three heavens), no tour of celestial scenes with an angelic interpreter (the angel is not heard of again), and no foreboding promises of cosmic doom. There is, in the Testament of Job, no messianism (as in TLevi 18), no "Belial" nor any named angels, no sense of eschatological imminence, no concern for the end of the age, and no discontent with the present world. To the contrary, the praise of Job's philanthropy amounts to praise of social institutions. The Testament of Job does not indulge in portentous grotesque symbolism or in apocalyptic zoology.

Although it has been drawn up by one disinterested in the testament form, the Testament of Job more nearly retains testamentary elements than does, for example, the Testament of Abraham, the Testament of Isaac, or the Testament of Jacob. It clearly aligns more with the Testaments of the Twelve Patriarchs than with the legal or literary pagan "testaments" or the medieval Hebraic varieties.

---

[16] Cleveland/New York, 1961.

Provenance, purpose, and date

The Testament of Job was almost certainly written in Greek, probably during the first century B.C. or A.D., and possibly among the Egyptian Jewish sect called the Therapeutae, described extensively by Philo in his tract *Vita contemplativa*.

Although Christian editing is possible, the work is essentially Jewish in character. It draws heavily from the Septuagint Book of Job, to which text the Testament of Job also may have contributed. Characteristic features of the text include Job's affirmation of the "upper world" (*hypercosmios*), concerns for proper burial, and attention to women. Some aspects of the Testament of Job resemble those found in the sectarian Qumran texts, but more singular interests appear in its use of magic and "merkabah mysticism" (Jewish mystical speculation focusing on God's chariot, *mrkbh*).

The earliest modern opinion on the Testament of Job was that of Cardinal Mai,[17] who concluded that the work was produced by a Christian. James,[18] although suggesting that it may have had a Semitic origin, claimed that in its present form the work stems from a second-century A.D. Christian, born a Jew, who put the Hebrew original into Greek and added his own material (TJob 46–53 and the poetic pieces at TJob 25, 32, 33, 43).

A decade after James, F. Spitta[19] published an extensive study on the Testament of Job. He concluded that the testament is a piece of pre-Christian folk piety not attributable to the Essenes. He also argued that the tradition about Job lay behind the New Testament portrayal of Jesus as sufferer.

Similarly, D. Rahnenführer[20] views the Testament of Job as a pre-Christian, non-Essene text the purpose of which was to serve propagandistic missionary interests of hellenistic Judaism.

M. Delcor[21] suggests that the invasion of Palestine by the Persian general Pacorus in 40 B.C. may lie behind the reference to Satan's disguise as the "king of the Persians" (TJob 17:2). But J. Collins[22] tempers this proposal, noting that Persian kings were traditional enemies of Egyptian royalty. As the testament suggests a time of persecution, when the "patience" (or "endurance") it commends would be specially relevant, Collins proposes a first-century A.D. date as more likely. But the state of the evidence hardly permits any more precise dating than the first century B.C. or A.D.

About the same time as James, near the end of the last century, K. Kohler[23] described the Testament of Job as an Essene Midrash on the biblical Book of Job, possibly traceable to the Therapeutae.

More recently, M. Philonenko[24] re-evaluated Kohler's thesis in view of the Qumran finds. He concluded that the Egyptian Therapeutae are to be distinguished from the Qumran Essenes and that the former is a more likely source for the Testament of Job than the latter. While the Essenes were misogynists, the Therapeutae allowed women a significant role. Prayer toward the east (TJob 40:3) also characterizes the Therapeutae (*Vita cont* 89). Most importantly, Philo recounts (80) how spontaneous hymnic compositions sprang from sacred meetings of the Therapeutae, in which both men and women were present.

Several internal features of the testament appear to confirm an Egyptian origin. Job is called "the king of all Egypt" (TJob 28:7). The reference to Job's "fifty bakeries" (TJob 10:7) finds no Septuagint source, as do many of the quantities mentioned in the Testament. The Therapeutae held the number fifty in special reverence, perhaps as a reference to the Feast of Pentecost. Gem collecting, attributed to Job (TJob 28:4f.; 32:5; cf. Job 31:24 LXX), was an Egyptian royal pastime according to Theophrastus (*De lapidibus* 24.55).

A few considerations warrant hesitancy in accepting an Egyptian provenance among the

---

[17] Mai, *Scriptorum veterum nova collectio*, vol. 7, col. 191.

[18] *Apocrypha Anecdota*, pp. xciii–xciv.

[19] "Das Testament Hiobs und das Neue Testament," *Zur Geschichte und Literatur des Urchristentoms*, vol. 3, pt. 2, p. 165.

[20] "Das Testament des Hiob und das Neue Testament," *ZNW* 62 (1971) 88–93.

[21] "Le Testament de Job, la prière de Nabonide et les traditions targoumiques," in S. Wagner, ed., *Bibel und Qumran*, p. 72.

[22] "Structure and Meaning in the Testament of Job," in G. MacRae, ed., *Society of Biblical Literature: 1974 Seminar Papers*, vol. 1, p. 50.

[23] *Semitic Studies*, p. 273.

[24] *Sem* 18 (1968) 21–24.

Therapeutae. Philo made a special point (70–72) about the absence of slaves in the community of the Therapeutae; yet they are assumed in the Testament of Job, and are both male (13:4) and female (14:4). Philo does not mention any glossolalic hymn singing, as does the Testament of Job (48:3; 50:1). Nor does he include laments among the forms or purposes of the hymns of the Therapeutae. Even so, an origin of the Testament among the Egyptian Therapeutae seems very possible.

But has there been any Christian editing? Job's first-person address ends at chapter 45. Testament of Job 46–53 supplements 1–45 in reporting Job's recovery. Apocalyptic language more conspicuously appears in chapters 46–53, which contain no extended poetic piece to match those found in chapters 1–45. In the single reference to the devil found in 46–53, he is called "the enemy" (TJob 47:10), while the terms "Satan," the "devil," and the "evil one" appear in 1–45.

Spittler[25] suggested that the Testament may have been reworked in the second century by Montanists. Eusebius (HE 5.17.1–4) preserves the argument of an unnamed anti-Montanist who demanded to know where in the range of biblical history any precedent appeared for ecstatic prophecy. The descriptions of Job's daughters speaking in ecstasy (TJob 48–50) may have been a Montanist move to supply such a precedent. Furthermore, the document— or at least the tradition it preserves, that of Job's return of the escaping worm to his body (TJob 20:8f.)—is reflected in one of Tertullian's books (De anima 14.2–7) written just before his Montanist period.

The following reconstruction of the origin and development of the Testament of Job mingles probabilities with possibilities. The result is a scenario for the emergence of the Testament of Job that must be seen as conjectural; how in fact the Testament arose cannot be described with faultless historical accuracy.

Somewhere in the second half of the first century B.C., a member of the Therapeutae near Alexandria produced a "testament" in praise of patience, which is surely a "contemplative" virtue. Although he (or someone before him) may have used a Semitic original, his own work bore unmistakable evidences of a lover of the Septuagint. Having himself spontaneously composed hymns at the Therapeutae vigils, and with his poetic skills now refined by writing, he—or she—produced at least three (TJob 25, 32, 43; 33?) poetic pieces in the work. As the document left the Therapeutic community and found its way to the Phrygian regions, it was in Greek and consisted of the Testament of Job 1–45, a true "testament" of a tested servant (therapōn) of God.

The work was artful enough—at least so far as the speech of Job's wife (TJob 24) is concerned—to have been interlaced with the developing text of the Septuagint. If the Testament was influential enough to have affected the Septuagint text, or been affected by it, it may be no surprise to find it in Phrygian regions two centuries later.

When the new prophecy erupted, there was no contest over canon, scripture, or doctrine. When, however, the original Montanist trio passed and the foretold end had not yet come, the movement organized and prophetic ecstasy spread. Prophetic virgins constituted themselves into an institution. At one point—before A.D. 195—an anti-Montanist writer demanded of the Montanists where in scripture prophecy in ecstasy might be claimed. In an era of canonical flexibility, a Montanist apologist, probably of Jewish background, made use of a "testament" known to him and in which he found ideas compatible with his own species of Judaistic practice. By creating Testament of Job 46–53, possibly inserting chapter 33, and certain other restyling, the apologist for the new prophecy produced a text wherein the daughters of Job were charismatically, or magically, lifted into prophetic ecstasy, enabling them to speak in the language of angels.

The work remained in Montanist hands as a propaganda text, perhaps particularly useful for Jews. Tertullian, at any rate, came by the text even before he became a Montanist. He used this Jewish testament in praise of patience in producing his own work De patientia. The work may even have played some part in his attraction to the Montanist movement.

By the sixth century, the work appeared on a list of proscribed apocrypha, the Gelasian Decree. But even before then it had been translated into Coptic, showing its continued popularity in Egypt. By the tenth century, it had been translated into Slavonic. In spite of four late medieval Greek manuscripts, the work remained virtually unknown in the West till modern times.

[25] Spittler, Testament of Job, pp. 58–69.

Theological importance

As a whole, the theological outlook of the Testament of Job aligns with hellenistic Judaism. The living (37:2) and just (43:13) God is the one who created heaven, earth, the sea, and mankind (2:4). God is called the "Master of virtues" (*despotēs tōn aretōn* 50:2) as well as the "Demiurge" (39:12), but without subsequent gnostic notions attached to that term. The title "Father" (33:3, 9; 40:3; 47:11; cf. 50:3; 52:6; see n. i to 52) need not be viewed as a Christian intrusion (see n. g to 33). In the Testament, it is Job's zeal against an idol's shrine (2–5) that is made the occasion of the calamities that befall him. God is the receiver of praise (14:3) and present in praise (51:1). He is Job's source of healing, the creator of physicians (38:8), to the end that even at death Job felt no pain (52:1f.).

Human nature in the Testament of Job is subject to the deception of the devil (3:3), exemplified in the various disguises assumed by Satan in his opposition to Job (see n. c to 6). Job's wife, his servants, and he himself are the objects of Satan's attacks. Indeed, a highly developed doctrine of Satan marks the Testament. He is variously identified as Satan (6:4), the devil (3:3), the evil one (7:1 V), the enemy (47:10). He is not human (23:2; cf. 42:2) nor of flesh, as Job (27:2), but is a spirit (27:2) who was responsible for the nefarious inspiration of Elihu (41:5f.; cf. 17:1f.). As in the canonical account, Satan derives his limited authority from God (8:1–3; cf. Job 1:12; 2:6).

The notion of angels in the testament corresponds to Jewish and Christian thought. An interpreting angel, also called a "light" (4:1; cf. 3:1), figures in Testament of Job 2–5 in a manner characteristic of Jewish and Christian apocalyptic. Job's daughters speak in ecstasy the language of the angels (48:3), the archons (49:2), and the cherubim (50:2). Unidentified heavenly creatures (angels?), functioning as the psychopomps of Greek mythology, carry off Job's soul at his death (52:6–10; cf. 47:11).

Distinctive emphasis is given in the testament to a cosmological dualism that inculcates a certain otherworldliness. This motif most clearly appears in Job's psalm of affirmation, in which he boldly asserts, "My throne is in the upper world" (33:3). By contrast, this world and its kingdoms pass away (33:4, 8), a claim that infuriates the friendly kings who came to help (34:4). But the cosmic superiority of the upper world—which nowhere is elaborately described in the Testament of Job—also emerges in the effects of the charismatic sashes once they are donned by Job's daughters. Their hearts were changed, they no longer cared for earthly things, they used the tongues of angels (48–50). Even so, the testament celebrates Job's exemplary care for the poor (9–13), which is an earthbound enterprise to which he returns following his recovery (44:2–5).

Several eschatological ideas exist side by side in the testament. Among the rewards promised Job by the angel is participation in the resurrection (4:9; cf. n. c to 4). Job's children, who died when their house collapsed (39:8), however, need no burial; they were taken directly to heaven by their creator (39:8–40:3). Yet the testament ends with a description of Job's soul being carried off in a chariot (52:10); his body is buried a few days later (53:5–7).

In fact, burial concerns are a distinct interest of the testament, reflecting its Jewish origin. Not only did Job's wife, Sitis, plead for the burial of her children (39:1–10), her own burial is told in detail: the procession, the place, the lament used, even animals mourning her death (40:6–14). Similarly, Job's burial is described (53:5–7). The poetic compositions at Testament of Job 25 and 32 stem from the lament form, the life setting of which was the funeral.

A high interest in women marks the testament. This first appears in the names given to both Job's present wife (Dinah) and his earlier spouse (Sitis). Sitis, unnamed at Job 2:9f. in the canonical account, becomes a leading figure in the testament, which extensively elaborates her speech (TJob 24:1–25:10) compared to the Septuagint adjustment of the Masoretic text (TJob 24:1–25:10; Job 2:9a–d LXX). More than this, in Testament of Job 21–26 Sitis becomes something of a figure of pity, driven to enslavement and finally forced to sell her hair ignominiously to Satan. Even so, the Sitis cycle functions to accentuate Job's troubles. In the Testament of Job 39–40, she reappears on behalf of her deceased—but as yet unburied—children, three of whom were women.

No less than six words are used in the Testament of Job for female slave.[26] Widows, too,

---

[26] *Pais* (7:3); *doulē* (7:7); *therapainē* (14:4); *paidiskē* (21:2); *doulis* (21:3); *latris* (24:2); all are used with the feminine article.

make their appearance: Job is their champion. (His funeral dirge has the line "Gone is the clothing of widows!" 53:3.) And by his musical skills Job could quell their murmuring (14:1–5). At Testament of Job 13:4–6 (quoting Job 31:31 LXX) complaints against Job are attributed specifically to his male servants, apparently exonerating the female servants mentioned at Job 31:31 (LXX).

Aside from the wives, the widows, and the slaves, there are the daughters of Job already named in the canon and said to have had such beauty that "Throughout the land there were no women as beautiful as the daughters of Job" (Job 42:15). The fact that "their father gave them inheritance rights like their brothers" triggered a distinct section of the testament (46–50), where the earlier interest in patience has been displaced by a concern for ecstatic and perhaps magical participation in the upper world through glossolalia.

Finally, the motif of endurance, or patience (*hypomonē*), receives high praise in the testament. The degree to which this theme is worked into the testament is clear evidence of its kinship with the testament genre. Job is the hero of patience; he is born to it (1:5). If he is patient—the angel promises (4:6)—he will gain fame and be restored. On the dung heap, he invites his wife Sitis to endure with him (26:5). Underwriting the charitable exploits of others whose mismanagement led to bankruptcy, Job acceded to their pleas for patience (11:10). He would undergo whatever Satan could bring; that adversary finally learned Job could not be enticed away from patience to contempt (20:1). Job was like the underdog wrestler who nevertheless won the match "because he showed endurance and did not grow weary" (27:4). It was their prior knowledge of Job and his former happy estate—and not their patience—that led to the speechlessness of the king-friends upon their discovery of Job (28:5). Sitis bitterly condemns Job's dung heap motto: "Only a little longer!" (24:1). No more fitting summary of the hortatory intent of the testament could be quoted than 27:7: "Now then, my children, you also must be patient in everything that happens to you. For patience is better than anything."[27]

Cultural importance

Rejected by the rabbis and the Church, the Testament of Job not surprisingly has been virtually unnoticed till modern times and has had little detectable effect on the development of Western culture. Nothing in Archibald MacLeish's play *J.B.*, for example, suggests any roots traceable to the testament.

Early Church Fathers developed parallels between Job and Jesus as sufferers, a theme at times expressed in early medieval Christian art. Tertullian may have used the testament in some form of its literary history (see n. f to 20). According to Kohler[28] the Islamic tradition preserves features of the saga of Job distinctive to the testament. A few plays and works on the biblical book of Job from the sixteenth to the eighteenth century were cited over a century ago in a short preface to the first French translation of the testament.[29] Whether or not any of these reflects aspects of the story of Job distinctive to the testament remains to be investigated (as do possible relations between the text traditions of the testament and the Vulgate).

The chief contribution of the Testament of Job lies in its witness to the sectarian diversity of hellenistic Judaism. Much of its vocabulary and concepts it shares with the New Testament, as well as with other contemporary literature in the testament genre. Here in a single document, however, typical hellenistic Jewish monotheistic propaganda and moral exhortation mix with a primitive form of Merkabah mysticism, with the sharply dualistic outlook at Qumran (especially TJob 43), with the beginnings of Jewish magic (46:3–47:6), and with a Montanist-like interest in angelic glossolalia. The testament is in fact a valuable monument to the rich variety of hellenistic Jewish piety.

---

[27] Some of the T12P, rather than commending virtues, condemn vices, as TSim (envy), TJud (love of money, fornication). TJob incidentally depreciates arrogance (*alazoneia*, 15:8), exultation (*gauriama*, 33:6), boasting (*kaukēma*, 33:8), scorn (*kataphrōnēsis*, 15:6), contempt (*oligoria*, 20:1), pride (*hyperēphania*, 15:8); all are inconsistent with enduring patience.

[28] *Semitic Studies*, pp. 292–95.

[29] J. Migne, *Dictionnaire des apocryphes*, vol. 2, col. 402.

About the translation

The text employed is eclectic and has been critically reviewed, but it largely follows Brock and therefore reflects P. While a generally conservative stance has been taken toward the text, a conjectured reading of "Eliphas" for "Elihu" has been adopted at Testament of Job 31:1, 5; 32:1; 33:1. This choice is not supported in the extant Greek witnesses, but it draws partial support from the Coptic version as well as from the order of appearance of Job's friends in the Septuagint (see n. a to 31).

Versification follows that of Brock. Marginal references focus on parallels internal to the testament itself, although frequent reference is provided to likely Septuagint sources for the language of the Testament. All marginal references to Job are to the Septuagint version. A number standing by itself refers to the verse of that number in the same chapter. Where chapter and verse are given with no preceding book cited, the reference is to the Testament of Job itself.[30]

BIBLIOGRAPHY

Charlesworth, *PMR*, pp. 134–36.
Delling, *Bibliographie*, p. 167.
Denis, *Introduction*, pp. 100–4.

Brock, S. *Testamentum Iobi*. J. C. Picard, *Apocalypsis Baruchi graece*. PVTG 2; Leiden, 1967. (Re-edits MS P, noting all significant variations in S and V and selected variants in Slavonic. Useful introduction covering the characteristics and interrelations of the text witnesses.)

Collins, J. J. "Structure and Meaning in the Testament of Job," in G. MacRae, ed., *Society of Biblical Literature: 1974 Seminar Papers*. Cambridge, Mass., 1974; vol. 1, pp. 35–52. (Views TJob as a coherent 1st-cent. A.D. product of Egyptian Judaism. Valuable suggestions regarding opposition between Job and others [notably Satan, his friends, and his wife] as a possible clue to the underlying structural unity of the work.)

Delcor, M. "Le Testament de Job, la prière de Nabonide et les traditions targoumiques," in S. Wagner, ed., *Bibel und Qumran. Beiträge zur Erforschung der Beziehungen zwischen Bibel- und Qumranwissenschaft. Hans Bardtke zum 22.9.1966*. Berlin, 1968; pp. 57–74. (Concludes that the Gk. interpolation at Job 2:9 derives from TJob and that TJob 17:1 alludes to the invasion of Palestine by Pacorus in 40 B.C., after which TJob was composed.)

Jacobs, I. "Literary Motifs in the Testament of Job," *JJS* 21 (1970) 1–10. (Sees TJob as an early sample of Jewish martyr literature, distinctively featuring a convert who suffers for his faith.)

James, M. R. *Apocrypha Anecdota, 2nd Series*. T&S, 5.1, Cambridge, England, 1897; pp. lxxii–cii, 104–37. (Standard text, with ch. divisions, used until Brock. Helpful introductory material; biblical parallels cited.)

---

[30] Aiming for readability without violating the sense of the underlying text, the translation does not hesitate to omit Gk. particles and conjunctions (where these would not affect the sense), to exchange a singular for a plural (where more natural in English), to reorder sentence components (always, however, with the resulting ET vs. corresponding to the Gk. vs. of the same number). The terms "endurance" and "patience" are used interchangeably to translate the Testament's celebrated virtue, *hypomonē*.

The translation has had a circuitous history. At first part of my Harvard doctoral dissertation, it was placed at the disposal of R. Kraft to be revised as he and his staff were directed by their work in producing a preliminary text of the SV strand of the TJob text tradition. In the process, H. Attridge provided many helpful suggestions regarding both text and translation. Since I have had the benefit of their work, along with that of J. Timbie, I am expressly grateful not only for the distinct textual advances they have made but also for their concurrence in letting the translation once again be reworked for publication here. I have profited much from a critical reading of the work in the present form by B. Schaller of Göttingen. Inadequacies that remain are my own, of course.

Kee, H. C. "Satan, Magic, and Salvation in the Testament of Job," in G. MacRae, ed., *Society of Biblical Literature: 1974 Seminar Papers*. Cambridge, Mass., 1974; vol. 1, pp. 53–76. (TJob is a 1st-cent. A.D. text, originally Gk., most closely aligned with magical and mystical features of early merkabah mysticism. Its eschatology is a temporal process—modeled by Job's endurance—and hence not gnostic.)

Kohler, K. "The Testament of Job: An Essene Midrash on the Book of Job Reedited and Translated with Introductory and Exegetical Notes," in G. Kohut, ed., *Semitic Studies in Memory of Rev. Dr. Alexander Kohut*. Berlin, 1897; pp. 264–338. (Uses Mai's Gk. text [=V]. Kohler's ch. and vs. divisions differ from those of James. Introduction focuses on Semitic, especially rabbinic and Muslim, folklore about Job. Sees TJob as originating from Therapeutae "in the outskirts of Palestine in the land of Hauran, where the Nabatheans [*sic*] lived, and the Essene brotherhoods spread it all over the Arabian lands," p. 295.)

Kraft, R. A. (ed.), with H. Attridge, R. Spittler, J. Timbie. *The Testament of Job According to the SV Text*. T&T 5; Pseudepigrapha series 4: Missoula, Mont., 1974. (Valuable nn. on the textual history of the TJob and an extensive bibliography.)

Mai, A. *Scriptorum veterum nova collectio e Vaticanis codicibus*. Rome, 1833. (10 vols.; TJob = vol. 7, cols. 180–91; *editio princeps*, using the V text.)

Mancini, A. "Per la critica del 'Testamentum Job,' " *Rendiconti della Reale Accademia dei Lincei, Classe di Scienze Morali, Storiche e Filologiche*. Serie Quinta 20 (1911) 479–502. (Collation of S with P [James] and V [Mai], with some philological and text-critical observations.)

Philonenko, M. "Le Testament de Job, Introduction, traduction et notes," *Sem* 18 (1968) 1–75. (French translation with brief nn. and introduction. Original language of TJob not determined—at least parts come from Heb., e.g. ch. 43. An authentically Jewish writing of Egyptian Therapeutic origin, from 1st cent. A.D. [pre 70]. Also announces existence of the Cop. version. See also "Le Testament de Job et les Thérapeutes" *Sem* 8 [1958] 41–53, which supports Kohler's thesis of a Therapeutic origin by appealing to Qumran parallels.)

Polívka, G. "Apokrifna priča o Jovu," *Starine: Jugoslavenska Akademija Znaosti i Umjetnosti* ("Antiquities: for the Yugoslav Academy of Sciences and Humanities," Zagreb) 24 (1891) 135–55. (Edition of the three Slav. MSS.)

Rahnenführer, D. "Das Testament des Hiob und das Neue Testament," *ZNW* 62 (1971) 68–93. (Summarizes his 1967 doctoral dissertation at Halle-Wittenberg. Pre-Christian, originally Gk., example of hellenistic Jewish missionary literature. Useful data on the vocabulary of TJob and its affinities with the NT.)

Schaller, B. "Das Testament Hiobs," in W. Kümmel *et al.*, eds., *JSHRZ* (1979) 303–74 (seen in page proofs). (Highly useful introduction, translation with nn. TJob was composed in Gk. as a product of hellenistic Judaism; but it is not specifically attributable to the Therapeutae. Dated probably early to middle 2nd cent.)

Spitta, F. "Das Testament Hiobs und das Neue Testament," *Zur Geschichte und Literatur des Urchristentums*, vol. 3, pt. 2. Göttingen, 1907; pp. 139–206. (TJob is a pre-Christian, but not Essene, product of Jewish popular piety and furnished NT writers with a model for Jesus as sufferer. Includes some nn. provided by James correcting Mai's text of V.)

TESTAMENT OF JOB[a]

Prologue (1)

Title

1 **1** The book of the words of Job, the one called Jobab.[b]   Gen 36:33f.

Setting[c]

2   Now on the day when, having fallen ill,[d] he began to settle his affairs, he called
3 *his seven sons and his three daughters*,[e] •whose names[f] are Tersi, Choros, Hyon,   Job 1:2
4 Nike, Phoros, Phiphe, Phrouon, *Hemera*,[g] *Kasia, and Amaltheia's Horn*.[h] •And   Job 42:14
when he had called his children he said,[i] Gather round, my children. Gather round
me so that I may show you the things which the Lord did with me and all the
things which have happened[j] to me.
5   I am your father Job, fully engaged in endurance.[k] But you are a chosen and   Jas 5:11
6 honored race from the seed of Jacob,[l] the father of your mother. •For I am *from*   Job 42:17c
the sons of Esau, the brother of Jacob, of whom is your mother Dinah,[m] from

---

1 a. So P (*diathēkē*). "Testament (*diataxis*) of
Job," S; "Testament (*diathēkē*) of the Blameless,
Sorely Tried, and Blessed Job, His Life and a Copy
of His Testament," V; "Life and Conduct of the
Holy and Righteous Job," Slav.

b. Reference is made probably to the Jobab of
Gen 36:33f., who is described as the second king
of Edom. This suggests a setting in the patriarchal
era, confirmed by Job's genealogy "from the sons
of Esau" (TJob 1:6). Similarly, Job 42:17c LXX
describes Job as a descendant of Abraham and
speaks (in reverse order from TJob) of "Jobab, the
one called Job" (42:17d).

c. Following the testament form, 1:2–7 pictures
Job at the end of his life (248 years old, according
to 53:8 S V Slav), his children gathered around
him, about to urge endurance (*hypomonē*) by a
recital of his own famed perseverance.

d. But, according to 52:1, he fell ill without pain
or suffering, due to the miraculous effects of the
splendorous girdle (46:7f.) by which he had recovered from his earlier stroke (47:4–8). Among
the T12P, TReu (1:2) and TSim (1:2) likewise
describe their subjects as ill as part of the deathbed
scene, while TLevi (1:2), TNaph (1:2), and TAsh
(1:2) each expressly state the patriarch is in good
health even though—in conjunction with the testament form—about to die.

e. The second set of ten children: The first ten
(also seven sons and three daughters according to
Job 1:2, but not specifically so stated in TJob) were
all lost in Job's tragedy (TJob 1:6; 18:1; cf. Job
1:18f.). The total and the male-female ratio thus
agree with Job 42:13. On seven sons, cf. Ruth 4:15;
1Sam 2:51; Tob 14:3A. Job's 7,000 sheep and
3,000 camels (Job 1:3; cf. TJob 9:2–4) appear in
the same ratio.

f. V Slav omit all names. S omits the first five.
The seven sons, listed first, play no further role in
TJob (cf. 46:1f.), while the daughters figure prom-
inently in 46–53.

g. The last three names correspond to those given

Job's daughters at Job 42:14 LXX (cf. MT). The
sons are not named in canonical Job.

h. "Amaltheia's Horn" is the legendary horn
of plenty (*cornucopia*) ascribed in Gk. mythology
to the broken horn of the she-goat who nursed Zeus.
Gk. myth likewise knows of Nereus, the name of
Job's brother (see n. b to 51).

i. Job's own words begin here, and the first
person is used throughout TJob 1:4b–45:4. The
quotation marks appropriate here, and after TJob
45:4, are omitted to ease reading; inclusion also
would require initial quotation marks at every intervening paragraph and the introduction of need-
lessly complicating quotations within quotations.

j. Cf. 1:7. Contrast the similar but future phrase
characteristic of apocalypses (e.g. Rev 1:1; 22:6;
Dan 2:28, 45; 1En 1:2). Testaments tend to look
back, apocalypses ahead.

k. Or patience (*hypomonē*), the virtue celebrated
by TJob and that for which Job is remembered at
the only place where he is mentioned in the NT,
Jas 5:11: "You have heard of the patience of
Job . . ."

l. Job is distinguished by patient endurance, his
children by noble ancestry.

m. In canonical Job the first wife is unnamed
and the second unmentioned. In TJob the wife of
Job's trials is named Sitis (n. b to 25), while the
mother of the ten children just named and before
whom Job declares this "testament" is Dinah, the
daughter of Jacob and Leah (Gen 20:31; 46:15).
That makes Job an in-law to the twelve patriarchs
and thereby further legitimates a testament from
one outside the circle of patriarchal worthies, Abraham, Isaac, Jacob, and the twelve sons of Jacob.
Dinah as Job's wife is known elsewhere in the
Jewish tradition: Ps-Philo 8:7f.; Targum on Job 2:9;
jBB 15b; GenR 57:4; cf. 73:9 and 80:4. While no
more is heard of Dinah in TJob, Sitis plays a major
role (21–26, 39f.) and is the subject of an
extensive lament (25), which is one of several
carefully wrought poetic pieces in TJob.

whom I begot you. (My former wife died with the other ten children in a bitter death.)

7   So hear me, children, and I will show you the things which have befallen me. 4

I. Job and the Revealing Angel (2–5)[a]

Job's perplexity over idolatry

1,2 **2** Now I used to be Jobab before the Lord named me Job. •When I was called
3   Jobab, I lived quite near a venerated idol's temple.[b] •As I constantly saw whole-   3:6; 4:1,4; 5:2;
    burnt offerings being offered up there, I began reasoning within myself saying,   17:4
4   "Is this really the God who made heaven and earth, the sea too,[c] and our very
    selves? How shall I know?"

1   **3** One night as I was in bed a loud voice came to me in a very bright light saying,   4:1; 5:2; 18:5,8
2   "Jobab, Jobab!" •And I said, "Yes? Here I am." And he said, "Arise, and I will
3   show you who this is whom you wish to know. •This one whose whole-burnt
    offerings they bring and whose drink offerings they pour is not God. Rather, his
    is the power of the devil,[a] by whom human nature[b] is deceived."
4,5   When I heard these things, I fell on my bed worshiping and saying, •"My Lord,
6   who came for the salvation of my soul, •I beg you—if this is indeed the place of   47:11; 52:5,6,10
    Satan[c] by whom men are deceived—grant me authority to go and purge his place
7   so that I may put an end to the drink offerings being poured for him. Who is there
    to forbid me, since I rule this region?"[d]   28:7; 29:3

The angel's disclosure of impending calamities

1   **4** The light[a] answered me and said, "You shall be able to purge this place. But   3:1
    I am going to show you all the things which the Lord charged me to tell you."

2 a. TJob here (2–5) blends apocalyptic features into the testament form. A revealing angel responds in a night vision to Job's concern over a nearby idol's shrine. His destruction of it, authorized by the angel, becomes the cause of Satan's attack on Job. The nighttime sleep interrupted by a voice and a light, the perplexity motif, worship of the revealing angel, the call by name, all these are typical features of apocalypses roughly contemporary with TJob; e.g. 2En 1:2–9A; 4Ezra 3:1–4; 4:1f.; 3Bar 1:2–8; Rev 1:9–19. Such features are not common in the T12P, but cf. TLevi 2:4–6.

b. Elsewhere the pagan temples are called "the place of Satan" (3:6; 4:4), "the temple of the idol" (5:2), "the temple of the great god . . . the place of drink offerings . . . the house of god" (17:4). Opposition to idolatry in TJob 2–5 resembles the similar iconoclasm of Abraham (Jub 12:12).

c. Quite nearly a creedal formula at Ps 145 (146):6; Acts 4:24; 14:15; Rev 10:6; 14:7, probably arising from Ex 20:11; Neh 9:6 (2Ezra 19:6 LXX). Except for Rev 14:7 (which has "and every water-spring"), these all add "and all that is in them" (or similarly), for which TJob alone reads, "and our very selves." In all cases the order heaven, earth, and sea is retained. Cf. Jub 2:2 (where the addition is "all the spirits" [angels], which are then extensively enumerated); PrMan 2f.; Jdt 13:18.

3 a. Elsewhere "the devil" is called "Satan" (3:6), "the enemy" (47:10; cf. 7:11, Slav addition

to 53:8), and in V only "the evil one" (7:1; 20:2) and "wretched one" (27:1). Belial (or Beliar) does not appear. Satan as enemy: TDan 6:3f.; Mt 13:39; Lk 10:18f.

b. The phrase "human nature" occurs in the NT only at Jas 3:7, where various bestial natures are said to have been tamed by it. TJob elsewhere shows sensitivity to the distinction between human and beastly (39:10) or Satanic (7:5; 42:2) natures. Such deception by Satan later in TJob overtakes Job's doormaid (7:6), his wife (23:11), and threatens even Job himself (26:6).

c. The "place of Satan" is not as strongly polemic as the NT expression "synagogue of Satan" (Rev 2:9; 3:9) and "the place where Satan is enthroned" (Rev 2:13).

d. Where LXX had already called Job's friends "kings" (Job 2:11), TJob makes Job a king too, most strongly at 28:7, "Jobab, the king of all Egypt." The friends speak of him as their "fellow king" (29:3), and his throne—mentioned at 20:4— becomes the taunting refrain in the lament of Eliphas (32:2–12): "Where then is the splendor of your throne?" Perhaps the canonical Job 19:9 (cf. 31:36)—speaking already in the MT of Job's crown—implies he was there too considered a ruler (cf. 29:25, "like a king amid his armies . . ."").

4 a. I.e. the angel who appeared in "a very bright light" (3:1).

2 And I said, "Whatever he has charged me, his servant, I will hear and do."

3,4 Again he said, "Thus says the Lord: •If you attempt to purge the place of Satan, 2:2 he will rise up against you with wrath for battle. But he will be unable to bring 18:5; 27:1

5 death upon you. He will bring on you many plagues, •he will take away for himself 37:3f.

6 your goods, he will carry off your children. •But if you are patient, I will make your name renowned in all generations of the earth till the consummation of the 53:8

7 age.[b] •And I will return you again to your goods. It will be repaid to you doubly, 44:5

8 so you may know that the Lord is impartial—rendering good things to each one 43:13

9,10 who obeys. •*And you shall be raised up in the resurrection.*[c] •For you will be like Job 42:17a

11 a sparring athlete,[d] both enduring pains and winning the crown. •Then will you 27:3-5 know that the Lord is just, true, and strong, giving strength to his elect ones."

Job's destruction of the idol's shrine

1 **5** And I, my little children, replied to him, "Till death I will endure: I will not 1:4

2 step back at all." •After I had been sealed by the angel when he left me, my little 3:1 1:4 children, then—having arisen the next night—I took fifty youths with me, struck

3 off for the temple of the idol, and leveled it to the ground. •And so I withdrew 2:2 into my house, having ordered the doors to be secured.[a]

II. Job and Satan (6–27)[a]

A. SATAN'S ATTACK AND JOB'S TRAGEDY (6–8)[b]

Satan disguised as a beggar

1,2 **6** Listen, little children, and marvel. •For as soon as I entered into my house and

3 secured my doors, I charged my doormen thus, •"If anyone should seek me today, give no report; but say, 'He has no time, for he is inside concerned with an urgent matter.' "

4 So while I was inside Satan knocked at the door, having disguised himself as 17:2; 20:5; 23:1

---

b. Not in LXX, the expression "consummation of the age" occurs in the T12P and at Mt 13:39; Heb 9:26.

c. Both syntactically and doctrinally, this verse could qualify as a Christian interpolation: even more V's additional phrase "to eternal life." But LXX Job already taught a future resurrection, even apart from the interesting statement in the appendix (42:17a) "And it is written that he will rise again with those whom the Lord will raise up" (". . . whom the Lord raised up" reads V distinctively at TJob 53:8). Resurrection in 4:9 as well as in 53:8V (and Job 42:17a LXX) seems limited to the righteous, as in 2Mac 7:14. This contrasts with, e.g., TBenj 10:8, where "All shall arise—some to glory, and others to dishonor."

d. This phrase artfully anticipates 27:3–5, where similar athletic imagery marks the end of the episode of Satan and Job.

5 a. According to 6:2 and 9:7f., the doors ordinarily stood open for the benefit of the poor seeking food. The author has the habit of introducing a major section with a brief advance summary: 5:3 brings on 6–8, while 8:3 announces 9–26. Cf. 46:11 for 48–50.

6 a. Chiastic structure marks this section: 6–8 describe Satan's attack issuing in Job's tragedy, while the closing ch. (27) reverses the matter with Job conquering Satan. Where at 6:1–6 Job secludes himself from Satan, by 27:1f. it is Satan who is hiding from Job. The remaining chs. (9–26) appear to be modeled after the temporal contrast characteristic of certain mocking laments: 9–15 tells what Job *once was* (wealthy, philanthropic, hospitable, musically skilled, pious). Then 16–26 details what he *later became* (deprived of wealth, family, health).

b. Having just razed the idol's temple (5:2), Job conceals himself in his house shutting doors (5:3; 6:2f.) that usually stand open (9:7f.). Coming in disguise as a begger—many such beggers came to Job's house to share in his care for the poor (9:8)—Satan first asked an interview (6:5f.), then a loaf of bread (7:2). Denied both, with Job's assertion of his "estrangement" from him (7:4, 10), Satan negotiates authority over Job with God (8:1f.) and discomfits him (8:3). Throughout 6–8, Job is thoroughly insulated from Satan. Job is occupied within his house, all communication with Satan is relayed by the doormaid, who at first was unaware of Satan's true identity.

5 a beggar.[c] • And he said to the doormaid, "Tell Job I wish to meet with him."
6 When the doormaid came and told me these things, she heard me say to report that
I had no time just now.

1 **7** When he heard that, Satan departed and put a yoke[a] on his shoulders. And
2 when he arrived, he spoke to the doormaid saying, •"Say to Job, 'Give me a loaf
3 of bread from your hands, so I may eat.' " •So I gave a burnt loaf of bread to the
4 girl to give to him and said to him, •"Expect to eat my loaves no longer, for you
are estranged from me."
5   Then the doormaid, ashamed to give him the burnt and ashen loaf of bread
6 (for she did not know he was Satan), took the good loaf of her own and gave it   23:2; 27:2; 42:2
7 to him. •And when he received it and knew what had occurred he said to the girl,
"Off with you, evil servant. Bring the loaf of bread given you to be given to me."
8 The girl wept with deep grief, saying, "Truly, you well say I am an evil servant.
9 For if I were not, I would have done just as it was assigned to me by my master."   20:9
And when she returned, she brought him the burnt loaf of bread, saying to him,
10 "Thus says my lord, 'You shall no longer eat from my loaves at all, for I have
11 been estranged from you. • Yet I have given you this loaf of bread in order that
I may not be accused of providing nothing to a begging enemy.' "[b]   47:10; cf.
12   When he heard these things, Satan sent the girl back to me saying, "As this loaf   Prov 25:21
of bread is wholly burnt, so shall I do to your body also. For within the hour, I
13 will depart and devastate you." •And I replied to him, "Do what you will. For
if you intend to bring anything on me, I am prepared to undergo whatever you
inflict."

Satan implores the Lord for power over Job

1,2 **8** After he withdrew from me, when he had gone out under the firmament, •he
3 implored the Lord that he might receive authority over my goods. •And then, when   41:3
he had received the authority,[a] he came and took away all my wealth.   16:2,4

B. JOB'S GENEROSITY AND PIETY (9–15)[a]

His philanthropy

1 **9** So listen, for I will show you all the things which have befallen me, my losses.   1:4
2,3 For I used to have 130,000 *sheep*;[b] •of them I designated *7,000* to be sheared for   Job 1:3; 16:3; 32:2
the clothing of orphans and widows, the poor, and the helpless. And I had a pack

---

c. Satan in disguise appears elsewhere in TJob:
17:2 (as "king of the Persians"); 23:1 (as "bread
seller"). At 20:5 Satan also appeared as a "great
whirlwind." The motif serves a literary, rather
than a dogmatic, purpose: In each case what Satan
becomes suits the requirements of the narrative
context. Here, Satan appears as a beggar precisely
because it is beggars who gained ready entrance to
Job's house (9:8–10:4). TReu 5:6 refers to the
fallen angels who were disguised as men. Paul's
awareness that Satan disguises himself as an "angel
of light" leads him to view his opponents as fake
apostles (2Cor 11:13–15). Satan's impersonations
may have been among the designs of Satan known
to Paul (2Cor 2:11).

7 a. The meaning is unclear, since the word (*as-
salion*) is not found elsewhere in the Gk. of any
period. Since it goes on the shoulders, it must be
something worn or borne. Possibilities: garment,
shawl, wallet, basket, wineskin, water bag, shield.

That upon his return with the item Satan asks for
bread may suggest it was suited to carrying the
bread. Even that might be a garment with roomy
folds.
  b. The phrase possibly reflects Prov 25:21a,
"If your enemy is hungry, give him something to
eat; if thirsty, something to drink" (behind Rom
12:20).

8 a. Job likewise had to obtain authority to raze
the idol's shrine (3:6; 4:1).

9 a. Typical Midrashic embellishment characterizes this section magnifying the pious generosities
of Job. Job 29 and 31, both LXX (less so Job 30
LXX), clearly inform the author here, supplying
numerous details and actual language and illumin-
ing several textual problems in TJob 9–15.
  b. Cf. 10:5. Job 1:3 lists 7,000 sheep, 3,000
camels, 500 yoke of oxen, 500 she-asses, all
doubled following his recovery (42:10, 12). TJob,

of 80 *dogs* guarding *my flocks*.[c] I also had 200 other dogs guarding the house. Job 30:1

4 And I used to have 9,000 *camels*; from them I chose *3,000* to work in every city. Job 1:3; 16:3; 32:2

5 After I loaded them with good things, I sent them away into the cities and villages, charging them to go and distribute to the helpless, to the destitute, and to all the

6 widows. •And I used to have 140,000 *grazing she-asses*. From these I marked off Job 1:3 *500* and gave a standing order for their offspring to be sold and given to the poor and needy.

7 From all regions people began coming to me for a meeting. *The four doors*[d] of Job 31:32

8 my house *stood open*. •And I gave a standing order to my house servants that these doors should stand open, having this in view: Possibly, some would come asking alms and, because they might see me sitting at the door, would turn back ashamed, getting nothing. Instead, whenever they would see me sitting at one door, they could leave through another and take as much as they needed.

His hospitality

1 **10** And I established in my house thirty[a] tables spread at all hours, for strangers 25:5; 32:7

2,3 only. •I also used to maintain twelve[b] other tables set for the widows. •When any 13:4; 14:2 stranger approached to ask alms, he was required to be fed at my table before he

4 would receive his need. •Neither did I allow anyone *to go out of my door with an* 11:12; 12:4 *empty pocket*.[c]   Job 31:34

5 I used to have 3,500 *yoke of oxen*. And I chose from them *500 yoke* and Job 1:3; 16:3; 32:3 designated them for plowing, which they could do in any field of those who would

6,7 use them. •And I marked off their produce for the poor, for their table. •I also used to have fifty bakeries[d] from which I arranged for the ministry of the table for the poor.

His underwritten charities[a]

1 **11** There were also certain strangers[b] who saw my eagerness, and they too desired

2 to assist in this service. •And there were still others, at the time without resources and unable to invest a thing, who came and entreated me, saying, "We beg you,

3 may we also engage in this service. We own nothing, however. •Show mercy on 9:4 us and lend us money so we may leave for distant cities on business and be able

4 to do the poor a service. •And afterward we shall repay you what is yours."

5 When I heard these things, I would rejoice that they would take anything at all

in true Midrashic style, vastly expands the totals owned by Job, but the net of those specifically designated for the poor agrees exactly with the canonical totals. The figures in P S V all agree in the three places where they are given in TJob (9:2–6/10:5; 16:3; 32:2f.), except for V's two enlargements at 16:3 ("the multitude" for "the seven thousand") and 32:3 (3,000 for 1,000). The details about the dogs is parenthetical; none of them is said to be marked off for the poor, they do not appear in the lists at 16:3 or 32:2f.

c. Retain here the reading of S V ("guarding my flocks . . . guarding the house."). P has likely dropped out the line by a characteristic error in copying, the close proximity of the two occurrences of "guarding" in vs. 3. On the dogs, cf. Tob 5:16, 11:4 and see the surprising number of references in L. Ginzberg, *Legends of the Jews* (Philadelphia, 1967) vol. 7, pp. 115f.

d. A reason for this many doors is offered in the talmudic text, ARN 7:1, "And why did Job make four doors to his house? So that the poor should not have the trouble of going round the entire house. He who came from the north entered straight ahead, and he who came from the south entered

straight ahead, and so on all sides. For this reason Job made four doors to his house." Job 31:17, 20—which inform TJob 9–10—are also quoted at ARN 7:1.

10 a. This figure is doubled to sixty at 32:7, except for Slav, which reads fifty. Slav also attributes fifty such tables to Sitis (25:5), where P S V read seven. The wife of Job thus shared in his continuous hospitality.

b. So 13:4; 14:2; 15:1. Probably from such LXX sources as Job 22:9; 29:13b; 31:16b. Cf. NT care (1Tim 5:9–16) and feeding (Acts 6:1) of widows.

c. An LXX connection emerges in the similarity of this sentence to Job 31:34 LXX, which differs considerably from the MT.

d. As with the dogs of 9:3, these are added to the canonically listed property of Job.

11 a. Although parts of Job 29–31 appear in this section (e.g. 11:11f./Job 31:35f.), the Midrashic connection of TJob 11f. with Job 29–31 is not as evident as that of the other chs. in TJob 9–15.

b. The "strangers" are presumably among those whom he fed (10:1).

6 from me for the care of the poor. •And receiving their note eagerly, I would give
7 them as much as they wished, •taking no security from them except a written note.
8 So they would go out at my expense.
9,10   Sometimes they would succeed in business and give to the poor. •But at other
times, they would be robbed. And they would come and entreat me saying, "We
beg you, be patient with us. Let us find how we might be able to repay you."
11 Without delay, I would bring before them the note and *read it* granting cancellation   Job 31:36f.
as the crowning feature[c] and saying, "Since I trusted you for the benefit of the
12 poor, *I will take nothing back from you.*" •Nor would I take anything from my   10:4 12:4
debtor.[d]

1 **12** On occasion a man cheerful at heart[a] would come to me saying, "I am not
wealthy enough to help the destitute. Yet I wish to serve the poor today at your
2 table." •When it was agreed, he would serve and eat. At evening, as he was about
to leave for home, he would be compelled to take wages from me as I would say,
3 "I know you are a workingman counting on and *looking for your wages.* You   Job 7:2
4 must accept." •Nor did I allow the wage earner's pay to remain at home with me   10:4 11:12;
in my house.[b]   Lev 19:13

His fabulous wealth in cattle: the buttered mountains[a]

1 **13** Those who milked the cows grew weary, since *milk flowed in the mountains.*   Job 29:6
2 *Butter*[b] *spread over my roads,* and from its abundance my herds bedded down
3 in the rocks and mountains because of the births. •So *the mountains* were washed
4 over *with milk* and became as congealed butter. •And my servants,[c] who prepared
5 the meals for the widows and the poor, grew tired and •would curse me in contempt,   10:2
6 saying, "*Who will give us some of his meat cuts to be satisfied?*" •Nevertheless,   Job 31:31
I was quite kind.

His musical prowess

1,2 **14** And I used to have six psalms[a] and a ten-stringed *lyre.* •I would rouse myself   52:3
daily after the feeding of the widows, *take the lyre,* and play for them. And they   10:2 Job 21:12
3 would chant hymns. •And with *the psaltery* I would remind them of God so that   Job 21:12
4 they might glorify the Lord. •If my maidservants ever began murmuring, *I would*
5 *take up the psaltery* and strum as payment in return.[b] •And thus I would make
them stop murmuring in contempt.

---

c. "Granting . . . feature" tentatively translates
the unclear adaptation of Job 31:36 LXX. V characteristically smooths the text: ". . . And tearing
it up, I would free them of the debt," omitting the
vexing LXX word "crown" (*stephanos*) retained
in P S.

d. The phrase again draws on the same LXX
source, which radically differs from the MT at this
point (Job 31:37).

12 a. The words are reminiscent of Paul's "cheerful giver" (*hilaron . . . dotēn,* 2Cor 9:7), using
the language of Prov 22:8 LXX, which is a line
absent from the Heb. text.

b. Basic law at Lev 19:13. (Cf. Deut 24:135;
Tob 4:14; BMes 9:11f.; Mal 3:5; Jas 5:4.) Job 7:2
may be in view: ". . . the workman with no
thought but his wages" (cf. Job 31:39 LXX).

13 a. To portray Job's fabulous wealth in cattle,
the author utilizes the LXX version of Job 29:6
(cf. TJob 13:2f.) and 31:31 (cf. 13:5f.) drawn

from Job's final speech in the dialogue (Job
20:1–31:40)—itself a wishful longing for prior days
of affluence and status corresponding in mood to
the plaintive tone of TJob 9–15.

b. Bountiful milk led to lavish supplies of butter,
which is invariably linked with milk (Gen 18:8;
Judg 5:25) or honey (2Sam 17:29; Isa 7:15) or both
(Deut 32:13f.; Job 17:20) as a token of affluence.

c. While Job 31:31 LXX reports Job never
provoked his *female* servants to this complaint,
TJob makes it the content of the *male* servants'
exasperated curse. In the MT, males likewise are
in view.

14 a. Perhaps a repertoire specifically used to quell
murmuring among the widows, vs. 5. A Dead Sea
Scroll text (11QPs[a] 27:2–11) speaks of four psalms
of David "for making music over the stricken"
(trans. of J. A. Sanders, *The Dead Sea Psalms
Scroll* [Ithaca, 1967] p.137).

b. Lit. "the wages of repayment."

His familial piety[a]

1,2 **15** After the ministry of the service, my children daily[b] took their supper. •They 1:4
3 went in to *their older brother* to dine with him, •*taking along with them their three* Job 1:18; 1:4
4 *sisters also.* The urgent matters were left with the maidservants, •since my sons
also sat at table with the male slaves who served.[c]

I therefore early would offer up sacrifices on their behalf according to their Job 1:5
5 *number,* 300 doves, 50 goat's kids, and 12 sheep. •I issued a standing order for
all that remained after the rites to be furnished to the poor.[d] And I would say to 1Bar 6:27
them, "Take these things remaining after the rites, so that you may pray on behalf 4
6 of my children. •Possibly, my sons may have sinned before the Lord through
7 boasting by saying with disdain, •'We are sons of this rich man, and these goods
8 are ours. •Why then do we also serve?' " For pride[e] is an abomination before
9 God. •And again, I offered up a select calf on the altar of God, lest my sons may
have thought evil things in their heart toward God.

C. JOB'S LOSSES (16–26)[a]

1. His cattle

1 **16** As I was doing these things[b] during the seven years[c] after the angel had made
2 the disclosure to me, •then Satan—when he had received the authority—came 8:3
3 down unmercifully •and torched 7,000[d] sheep (which had been designated for the 9:3
clothing of the widows), the 3,000 camels, and the 500 she-asses, and the 500 9:4; 9:6; 10:1

15 a. Dependence on Job 1:1–4 LXX is evident in 15:1–9: LXX adds the calf to MT, and to the calf TJob adds the list of sacrificial animals (15:4; cf. Job 42:8). Thus in TJob even the domestic piety of Job—resulting in a recurring supply of fresh meat—contributes to his care for the poor.

b. TJob follows Job 1:4 LXX in making definitely daily banquets out of the probably annual celebrations mentioned in MT.

c. By slight emendation of the text (so Kraft), this sentence could read "and the sisters were attended by the maidservants, as my sons also were waited on by the male slaves who served them."

d. Contrasting with the stinginess of the Babylonian priests, LetJer 6:27, "Whatever is sacrificed to them [the idols], the priests re-sell and pocket the profit; while their wives salt down part of it, but give nothing to the poor or to the helpless."

e. While patience is the major virtue extolled in TJob, the leading vices it combats are pride (*hyperēphania,* 15:8), contempt (*oligōria,* 20:1), and arrogance (*alazoneia,* 21:3).

16 a. This reaction narrates the sequence of Job's losses: in turn, his cattle (16), his children (17–19), his health (20), finally his wife (21–26). The order follows that of the canonical story (Job 1:14–19). Literary exaggeration is used, but with restraint.

b. Doing what? Presumably Job is made to refer to the charitable practices just rehearsed in 9–15.

c. Chronological details appear elsewhere in the TJob at 21:1; 26:1; 27:6; 28:1, 8; 41:2; 52:1; 53:7; 53:8 S V Slav. Cf. Job 42:16, where MT agrees with LXX (V and S) against LXX (A) and TJob 53:8 S V Slav. According to P, Job spent at least forty-eight years on the dung heap outside the city (21:1). After eleven years (22:1) his bread ration

was reduced, producing a famine crisis that would have lasted six years since it was in the seventeenth year (26:1) that Sitis invited Job to blaspheme God and die (26:1). Again according to P, the visiting kings came in the twentieth year (28:1, 8), reviewed Job's situation for twenty-seven days (41:2; On this figure P S V agree), after which Job recovered (42:1; 44:1; 47:5–7; but how long is unspecified). P lacks the longer ending of 53:8 found in S, V, or Slav so that this witness is not bound by any length of years for Job's total life span. As for S, it is only by the addition of this longer ending—which resembles Job 42:16—that S varies from P in its chronology. With V the matter is quite otherwise: By omission (28:1 V; cf. 27:6 V) and alteration (16:1 V, 22:1 V) a believable seven-year period of testing is ascribed to Job (21:1 V) and uniformly maintained. For V, the spreading of incense took—not three days (as 31:4 P S)—but three hours (31:4 V). V's artistry emerges again in its own version of the longer ending: Only V calculates how long Job lived *before* his plague (85 years, apparently derived by halving the 170 years that, according to the major LXX MSS, Job lived after his recovery). That V's total for the years Job lived is not the expected sum of 255 but 248 finds V haplessly recording the traditional figure for the length of Job's life. This feature alone should preclude a wrongheaded expectation of chronological perfection in an apocryphon where the interest lies quite beyond mathematical accuracy. In summary, P's scheme is not really self-contradictory, although it is rather artless and certainly less believable than V's consistent seven-year scheme. S simply accords with P, except for its longer ending.

d. On this and the other figures in 16:3, see n. b to 9.

4 yoke of oxen. • All these he destroyed by himself, according to the authority he 8:3
had received against me.

5,6 The rest of my herds were confiscated by my fellow countrymen, who • had
been well treated by me, but who now rose up against me and took away the

7 remainder of my animals. • They reported to me the destruction of my goods, but
I glorified God and did not blaspheme.

cf. Job 1:22;
2:10

2. His children

1 **17** Then the devil, when he had come to know my heart, laid a plot against me. 20:1
2 Disguising himself as the king of the Persians,[a] he stood in my city gathering 6:4
3 together all the rogues in it. • And with a boast he spoke to them saying, "This 2Mac 1:20,33
man Jobab is the one who destroyed all the good things of the earth and left
nothing—the one who distributed to the beggars, to the blind, and to the lame—

4 yet the one who destroyed the temple of the great god and leveled the place of 2:2
drink offerings. Therefore, I also shall repay him according to what he did against
the house of god. Come along then and gather spoils for yourselves of all his 2:2
animals and whatever he has left on the earth."

5 They answered him and said, "He has *seven sons and three daughters*. Possibly 1:2
they might flee to other lands and plead against us as though we were tyrants and Job 1:2
in the end rise against us and kill us."

6 So he said to them, "Have no fear at all. Most of his possessions I have already
destroyed by fire. The others I confiscated. And as for his children, I shall slay
them."

1 **18** When he said these things to them, he departed and smashed *the house down* Job 1:19
2 *upon my children* and killed them.[a] • My fellow countrymen, when they saw that
what was said truly happened, pursued and attacked me and began to snatch up

3 everything in my house. • My eyes witnessed cheap and worthless men at my tables
and couches.[b]

4 I was unable to utter a thing; for I was exhausted—as a woman numbed in her

5 pelvic region by the magnitude of birth pangs[c]—• remembering most of all the
battle foretold by the Lord through his angel and the songs of victory which had 4:4 3:1
been told to me.

6 [d]And I became as one wishing to enter a certain city to discover its wealth and

17 a. This is the second disguise of Satan—here
the "devil" (see n. c to 6). Appropriately, only
another king could rally opposition to Job "the
king of all Egypt" (28:7; see n. d to 3). And what
better "king" (conveniently here left nameless,
however) than "the king of the Persians," who in
the person of Cyrus (Ezra 1:2–7)—to name but
one—had previously shown kindness to the Jews?
Disguised thus as a royal benefactor, Satan could
appeal to Job's countrymen the more convincingly.
Choice of the phrase may reflect the author's
conviction that Job lived in the Persian era. See
the Introduction above for a possible clue to date
of composition furnished by this reference to the
king of the Persians.

18 a. Again (as 17:6) Satan is blamed for the
tragedy attributed in Job 1:18f. to a great wind.

b. S here has an unusual longer reading: "My
eyes saw those who make lamps at my tables and
couches: Cheap and worthless men they were."

c. The same simile at 1Thes 5:3 stresses sud-
denness, rather than exhaustion as here.

d. The point of this striking parable of the beleaguered mariner (18:6–8) lies in Job's expressed
willingness to see his vast wealth plundered (18:2),
buoyed as he is by the hope of eventual improved

survival as the angel promised (4:6–11). It is tempting to wonder if the author of TJob may have
intended a connection with the promise of 4:9,
"You shall be raised up in the resurrection," in a
mood similar to Heb 11:8–16 (cf. 12:21f.). Although the notion of a heavenly citizenship—with
earthbound living thought of as a sojourn—emerges
strongly in Christian circles (Phil 3:20; Eph 2:19;
Rev 21:2; later Augustine, *De civitate dei*), Philo
speaks similarly (*Agr* 65). In yet another Alexandrian piece (4Mac 7:1–3), marine imagery very
similar to TJob 18:6–8 occurs. It may be merely
coincidental that the same three figures used in TJob
18:4–8 (parturient woman, valued city, beleaguered
ship) likewise describe personal distress in one of
the Qumran hymns: "And they made my soul like
a ship on the depths of the sea, and like a fortified
city before them that besiege it. And I was confined
like the woman about to bring forth at the time of
her first child-bearing" (1QH 3.6f.). The otherworldliness motif implied in the parable—relinquish any worldly goods necessary to reach the
destined port—also characterizes Job's psalm of
affirmation (33:2–4) and the "changed hearts" of
his daughters when they were in ecstasy (48:2; 49:1;
50:2).

7 gain a portion of its splendor, •and as one embarked with cargo in a seagoing ship. 4Mac 7:1-3
Seeing at mid-ocean the third wave[e] and the opposition of the wind, he threw the
cargo into the sea, saying, "I am willing to lose everything in order to enter this
8 city so that I might gain both the ship and things better than the payload." •Thus,
I also considered my goods as nothing compared to the city about which the angel 3:1
spoke to me.

1 **19** When the final messenger[a] came and showed me the loss of my children, I
2 was deeply disturbed. •And I tore my garments,[b] saying to the one who brought
3 the report, "How were you spared?" •And then when I understood what had
4 happened I cried aloud, saying, •*"The Lord gave, the Lord took away. As it seemed* Job 1:21b
good to the Lord, so it has happened. Blessed be the name of the Lord!"

3. His health

1 **20** So when all my goods were gone, Satan concluded that he was unable to 17:1
2 provoke me to contempt.[a] •When he left he asked my body from the Lord so he
3 might inflict the plague on me. •Then the Lord gave me over into his hands to be
used as he wished with respect to the body; but he did not give him authority over
my soul.
4   Then he came to me while I was sitting on my throne mourning the loss of my
5 children. •And he became like a great whirlwind and overturned my throne. For 6:4
6 three hours[b] I was beneath my throne[c] unable to escape. •And he struck me with
a severe plague *from head to toe.*[d]   Job 2:7f.
7,8   In great trouble and distress *I left the city,*[e] *and I sat on a dung heap* •*worm-* Job 7:5
ridden[f] *in body.* Discharges from my body wet *the ground* with moisture. Many
9 *worms were in my body,* •and if a worm ever sprang off, I would take it up and

e. Popularly (as sometimes the ninth, or tenth) held to be the most devastating one, as Plato, *Republic* 472a = 5:17.

19 a. The only messenger mentioned in TJob, while LXX describes four such envoys of disaster (1:14, 16, 17, 18).
b. As a sign of grief: See n. d to 28. The scene parallels Job 1:18–21 LXX, but there shaving of the head is included.

20 a. See n. e to 15.
b. Similar three-hour periods at 30:2; 31:4 V; cf. three days at 23:7; 24:9; 31:4 P S and three years at 27:6 P S.
c. P, followed by Slav, has Satan on the throne; V puts Job on the ground; S is followed in this translation as giving the necessary sense.
d. Lit. "From feet to head" P; "from pate to the toenails of my feet" S V Slav. Note reversal of order.
e. TJob follows LXX (Job 2:8) in locating Job outside the city; no such statement is made in the MT. The crucifixion of Jesus, in line with common practice, was effected outside the city (Jn 19:20). Cf. Heb 13:9–14.
f. Cf. 24:3. This detail of Job's illness seems to be worked into the narrative of TJob (perhaps from there to the LXX interpolation at Job 2:9) from the more poetic plaint of Job at Job 7:5. Worms, which were said to accompany certain cases of illness (Herodotus 4.205; 2Mac 9:9; Josephus, *Ant* 17.169 = 16.6.5; Acts 12:23; Eusebius, *HE* 2.10.1; Lu-

cian, *Alexander* 59), became a Jewish, then Christian, eschatological forecast for the ungodly (Isa 66:24; Jdt 16:17; Eccl 7:17; Mk 9:48). It is boils that afflict Job according to the LXX (*helkos*, Job 2:7) and the MT (*š⁺ḥîn*). But TJob speaks of Job as worm-ridden (*skōlēkobrōton to sōma*). A similar feature appears in *Visio Pauli* 49 (M. R. James, ed., *Apocrypha Anecdota* [T&S 2.3; Cambridge, 1893] p. xx). A similar reference appears in ARN, where the relevant passage may be translated, "And worms would crawl down him and worms would make holes, holes in his flesh, until one of the worms made a strife with its fellow. What did Job do? He took up one and laid it down upon its hole. And the other he laid down on its hole." (S. Schechter, ed., *Aboth de Rabbi Nathan* [New York, 1945] p. 164, ll. 26–28.) Even more significant, however, is the similar tradition in Tertullian, *De patientia* 14.2–7 (J. Borleffs, ed., pp. 42f.). In this work—written before he became a Montanist—Tertullian clearly reflects TJob 20:8f. in a vivid, if vulgar, passage: "How God laughed! How what was already lacerated was the more mangled when, with laughter, he would call the little beasts breaking forth back into the pits and pastures of his furrowed flesh!" (*De patientia*, 14.5). So much resembles the passage in ARN just listed; but *De patientia* shows other parallels to features of the Job story *not* found in LXX (*De patientia* 14.2/TJob 1:5; *De patientia* 14.4/TJob 24:4; 25:10c). It appears warranted to conclude Tertullian utilized a Jewish testament praising patience as a source for his own treatment of the same theme.

return it to its original place, saying, "Stay in the same place where you were put
until you are directed otherwise by your commander."[g]   7:9

4. His wife[a]

Sitis enslaved

1 **21** I spent forty-eight[b] years *on the dung heap outside the city* under the plague   Job 2:8
2 so that I saw •with my own eyes, my children,[c] my first[d] wife carrying water into
the house of a certain nobleman as a maidservant so she might get bread[e] and bring
3 it to me. •I was stunned. And I said, "The gall[f] of these city fathers! How can they
4 treat my wife like a female slave?" •After this I regained my senses.[g]   35:4-6

1 **22** After eleven years they kept even bread itself from me, barely allowing her   21:1
2 to have her own food. •And as she did get it, she would divide it between herself
and me, saying with pain, "Woe is me! Soon he will not even get enough bread!"[a]

Sitis sells her hair to Satan

3   She would not hesitate to go out into the market to beg bread from the bread   cf. 24:7-10
sellers so she might bring it to me so I could eat.

1,2 **23** When Satan knew this, he disguised himself[a] as a bread seller.[b] •It happened   6:4
by chance that my wife went to him and begged bread, thinking he was a man.[c]   7:6
3,4 And Satan said to her, "Pay the price and take what you like." •But she answered   24:8
him and said, "Where would I get money? Are you unaware of the evils that have
5 befallen us? •If you have any pity on me, show mercy; but if not, you shall see!"
6   And he answered her, saying, "Unless you deserved the evils, you would not
7 have received them in return.[d] •Now then if you have no money at hand, offer me

---

g. The worm's forced compliance with its ordained role shows a touch of humor on the part of
the author, who elsewhere associates animals and
humans by having the cattle mourn over the death
of Sitis (20:11; cf. Mk 1:13b). Acquiescence in
one's fate has links with a well-known Stoic principle, "Fate (*heimarmenē*) is said to be the cause
of all that is, the rational principle by which the
world is managed (Diogenes Laertius 7.149). The
incident of the replaced worms functions as but one
more way to extol the virtue of patience. Curiously,
while the "commander" is in the author's mind
assuredly God (cf. 26:4; Job 2:10), it is nevertheless
Satan to whom Job's plague was just attributed
(20:6; cf. n. a to 18).

21 a. According to the storytelling artistry of the
author, Job loses his first wife, Sitis, in three stages.
She is first driven to impoverished slavery in order
to support Job (21:1–22:2). When her owners re-
strict her food supply, she sells her hair to Satan
(22:3–23:11). Finally, in a passage closely resembling the LXX addition to Job 2:9, she makes a
prolonged and embittered speech inviting Job to
curse God and die (24; 25:9f.). Her speech is interrupted by a poetic lament for Sitis (25:1–8) and
followed by Job's "patient" response (26). The
account of Sitis is resumed and completed in 39f.
    b. So P S, but seven years in V Slav. See n. c
to 16.

c. Such direct address is characteristic of the
testament form. V reads "my *beloved* children."
    d. S V Slav read "my humiliated wife."
    e. Frequently mentioned in TJob, including Sa-
tan's disguise as a bread seller (22:3–23:2). The
LXX Job makes no mention of bread in connection
with Job's diet.
    f. Lit. "pretentious boastfulness." See n. e to
15.
    g. Lit. "I regained my patient capacity to rea-
son"; this is another reference to the patience motif.
At 35:4–6 Baldad undertakes an assessment of Job's
mental balance.

22 a. Unlike the speech of Sitis (24f.), these words
have no counterpart in the text of the LXX.

23 a. This is the third (or fourth? See n. c to 6)
disguise of Satan, who first (6:4) became a beggar,
a role now assumed by Job's wife. As in the first
disguise, Satan appears to a woman in Job's circle
(6:4, to his female servant; 23:2, to his wife). In
none of the disguised appearances (6:4; 17:2; 23:2)
does Satan encounter Job directly, which leads to
Job's challenge for confrontation at 27:1.
    b. P has simply "merchant."
    c. Cf. 7:6; 27:2; 42:2. NT also knows of the
confusion of angels with men: Acts 12:15; Heb
13:2; Rev 19:9f.
    d. Similar ideas abound in the biblical Job (e.g.
4:7f.; 11:6c; cf. Jn 9:2).

the hair of your head[e] and take three loaves of bread. Perhaps you will be able to
8 live for three more days." •Then she said to herself, "What good is the hair of
9 my head compared to my hungry husband?" •And so, showing disdain for her
hair, she said to him, "Go ahead, take it."

10   Then he took scissors, sheared off the hair of her head, and gave her three
11 loaves, while all were looking on. •When she got the loaves, she came and brought
them to me. Satan followed her along the road, walking stealthily, and leading her   25:10; 27:1;
heart astray.   48:2; 49:1; 50:2

The speech of Sitis: begun

1 **24** At once *my wife* drew near. Crying out with tears[a] *she said* to me, "Job, Job![b]   Job 2:8b-9d
How long will you sit *on the dung heap outside the city* thinking, *'Only a little*   20:7
2 *longer!' and awaiting the hope of your salvation?* •*As for me, I am a vagabond*
and a maidservant going round from place to place. Your memorial has been wiped   39:8; 40:4;
away *from the earth—my sons and the daughters of my womb for whom I toiled*   43:5,17
3 *with hardships in vain.*[c] •*And here you sit* in worm-infested[d] *rottenness, passing*   20:8
4 *the night in the open air.* •And I for my part am a wretch immersed in labor by
day and in pain by night, just so I might provide a loaf of bread and bring it to
5 you. •Any more I barely receive my own food, and I divide that between you and
6 me—•wondering in my heart that it is not bad enough for you to be ill, but neither
do you get your fill of bread.
7,8   [e]"So I ventured unashamedly to go into the market, •[f]even if I was pierced in   cf. 22:3-23:11
my heart to do so. And the bread seller said, 'Give money, and you shall receive.'
9 But I also showed him our straits and then heard from him, 'If you have no money,
woman, pay with the hair of your head and take three loaves. Perhaps you will
10 live for three more days.' •Being remiss, I said to him, 'Go ahead, cut my hair.'
So he arose and cut my hair disgracefully in the market, while the crowd stood
by and marveled."

e. No mention was made at TJob 19:2 of Job's
own head-shaving, listed among the grief reactions
at Job 1:20. Shaving of the head in TJob is not a
sign of grief but of disgrace (23:10; 24:10), as it
is also at 1Cor 11:6: "In fact, a woman who will
not wear a veil ought to have her hair cut off. If a
woman is ashamed to have her hair cut off or
shaved, she ought to wear a veil." The disgrace
might arise from cropped hair as (1) a mode of
humiliating punishment (Aristophanes, *Thesmo-
phoreazusae* 838: for rearing a cowardly son; or,
Tacitus, *Germania* 19: for adultery) or (2) the
practice of female homosexuals (Lucian, *Dialogi
meretricii* 290 = 5.3).

24 a. A sample of the high interest of TJob in
lamentation.
   b. The double vocative is repeated near the end
of Sitis' speech (25:9) but appears in neither the
LXX nor the MT.
   c. The very close agreement between TJob
24:1-3 and the longer LXX form of Job 2:9 (cf.
Job 2:8b-9e LXX) does not clearly settle the uncertain textual relation between the two.
   d. See n. f to 20.
   e. This paragraph repeats information in
23:2-10.
   f. TJob 24:8 is textually unclear. V smooths the
text, "And the bread seller said to me . . ."
Translation is conjectural.

A lament for Sitis[a]

1 **25** Who is not amazed that this is Sitis,[b] the wife of Job?   40:13

2   Who used to have fourteen draperies sheltering her chamber and a door
within doors, so that one was considered quite worthy merely to gain
admission to her presence:

3   Now she exchanges[c] her hair for loaves!

4   Whose camels, loaded with good things, used to go off into the regions of 9:4
the poor:
     Now she gives her hair in return for loaves!

5   Look at her who used to keep seven tables reserved at her house, at which 10:1
the poor and alien used too eat:
     Now she sells outright her hair for loaves!

6   See one who used to have a foot basin of gold and silver, and now she goes
along by foot:
     Even her hair she gives in exchange for loaves!

7   Observe, this is she who used to have clothing woven from linen with gold: 39:1,4
     But now she bears rags and gives her hair in exchange for loaves!

8   See her who used to own couches of gold and silver: 32:4
     But now she sells her hair for loaves!

The speech of Sitis: concluded

9   "Job, Job! Although many things have been said in general, I speak to you in
10 brief: •In the weakness of my heart, my bones are crushed.[d] Rise, take the loaves, 23:11
be satisfied. And then *speak some word against the Lord and die*.[e] Then I too shall Job 2:9e
be freed from weariness that issues from the pain of your body."

---

25 a. Possibly an interpolation, inserted at a logical point, just following the report of the reaction
of the crowd to the cutting of her hair (24:10).
Omission of the lament for Sitis (25:1–8) leaves
undisturbed the continuity of the narrative. Inclusion of poetic pieces appropriate to narrative context
but abruptly inserted without introduction is paralleled at 1Mac 1:24–28; 3:3–9, 45; 14:4–15; and
Lk 1:14–17, 32f. This lament for Sitis contrasts
her former wealth and charity with her present state
in a way very similar to the description of Job's
pious generosity (TJob 9–15), followed by the
recital of his losses (TJob 16–26), and corresponding exactly in form to the lament for Job (TJob
32:2–12). As Job commissioned charitable missions
to the poor (9:4f.) and set up free food centers in
his own home (10:1–4), Sitis did likewise (25:4f.).
While Job's wealth is described in terms of cattle
(9:1–6; 10:5; 13:1–3), bakeries (10:7), and jewels
(28:5f.), more feminine objects figure in the wealth
of Sitis: draperies (25:2), a gold and silver foot
basin (25:6), expensive clothing and furniture
(25:7f.). Such connections between the descriptions
of Sitis and Job argue against viewing 25:1–8 as
an interpolation, a point strengthened by the fact
that the similar lament for Job (32:2–12) is carefully
worked into the prose context (see especially 31:5–
32:1; 33:1). The abcb'db"e . . . pattern, which also
characterizes the lament for Job, appears elsewhere
in Jewish poetry: most clearly, Ps 136. While the
repetition of a line is found in the pure lament form
(e.g. 2Sam 1:19, 25, 27; cf. 1Mac 9:21), the
taunting quality of the refrain in the lament for
Sitis (25:3–8) more closely parallels the prophetic
mocking songs sampled in Rev 18, with its thrice-

repeated (18:10, 16–17a, 19) refrain of doom for
Babylon. The form of the lament for Sitis thus
represents none of the earlier, purer forms of funeral
dirges. In fact, the lament is occasioned not by
death but by disgrace (as that for Job was occasioned
by privation). Since laments were recorded and
passed on traditionally (TJob 40:14; 2Sam 1:18;
Jer 9:19 [20]; 2Chr 35:35), the appearance of the
lament for Sitis at this point in the TJob is not
surprising. TJob's own term is a "royal lament"
(*basilikos thrēnos*, 31:7), in which the refrain served
for antiphonal response (31:8; 33:1; 43:3). The
sharp temporal contrast between what one was and
what one has become (in a *tragic* direction) is used
at Ezek 27:32–36. What amounts to an inverse
lament—contrasting a former disparaged with a
present blessed state—appears in Christian literature (1Cor 6:9–11; Tit 3:3–7).

b. Variously spelled in P S V and everywhere
omitted by Slav. Apparently derived from Ausitis,
the LXX translation (Job 1:1; 42:17b, e LXX [A])
for Job's home city, called Uz (*ʿûṣ*) in the MT.
LXX, but not MT, links Elihu with the same region
(Job 32:2 LXX).

c. Reflecting TJob's characteristic interest in lexical variety, a different word for "exchange" is
used in the six references (25:3, 4, 5, 6, 8); vs. 7
uses the same term as vs. 6. V assures variety by
omitting the refrain ("Even . . . loaves") from vs.
6.

d. Or read, with S V, ". . . in brief: The
weakness of my heart crushed my bones."

e. "Speak . . . and die," Job 2:9e LXX (A).
The wording is a Heb. euphemism, actually inviting
Job to curse God.

Job's response

1 **26** So I answered her, "Look, I have lived seventeen[a] years in these plagues
2 submitting to the worms in my body, •and my soul has never been depressed by 20:8
my pains so much as by your statement, '*Speak some word against the Lord and* Job 2:9e
3 *die.*' •I do indeed suffer these things, and you suffer them too: the loss both of 25:10
our children and our goods.[b] Do you suggest that we should *say something against*
4 *the Lord*, and thus be alienated from the truly great wealth?[c] •Why have you not 33:2-9
remembered those many good things we used to have? *If we have received good* Job 2:10
5 *things from the hand of the Lord, should we not in turn* endure *evil things?* •Rather
let us be patient till the Lord, in pity, shows us mercy.
6 "Do you not see the devil standing behind you[d] and unsettling your reasoning
so that he might deceive me too? For he seeks to make an exhibit of you *as one* Job 2:10
of the senseless women who misguide their husbands' sincerity."[e]

D. JOB'S TRIUMPH AND SATAN'S DEFEAT (27)

1 **27** Again turning to Satan, who was behind my wife, I said, "Come up front! 23:11
Stop hiding yourself![a] Does a lion show his strength in a cage? Does a fledgling
take flight when it is in a basket?[b] Come out and fight!" 4:4
2 Then he came out from behind my wife. And as he stood, he wept, saying,
"Look, Job, I am weary and I withdraw from you, even though you are flesh and
3 I a spirit. You suffer a plague, but I am in deep distress. •I[c] became like one 7:6
athlete wrestling another, and one pinned the other. The upper one silenced the 4:10
4 lower one, by filling his mouth with sand[d] •and bruising his limbs. But because
he showed endurance and did not grow weary, at the end the upper one cried out
5 in defeat. •So you also, Job, were the one below and in a plague, but you conquered
my wrestling tactics which I brought on you."
6,7 Then Satan, ashamed, left me for three years. •Now then, my children, you also 27:7
must be patient in everything that happens to you. For patience is better than
anything.[e]

---

26 a. V Slav have "seven years." On chronology,
see n. c to 16.
b. The text is corrupt at this point, the translation
tentative.
c. Doubtless to be identified with Job's eternal
and supercosmic splendor and majesty celebrated
in Job's psalm of affirmation at 33:2–9.
d. The phrase with a similar ring at Mk 8:33
(cf. Mt 4:10; 16:23; Lk 4:8) wishes the devil out
of sight. Here, inspiration for the speech of Sitis
is attributed to Satan (going beyond LXX), who by
his location behind Sitis continues to be hidden
from Job. See n. a to 23.
e. Developed from a line in Job 2:10 LXX, the
same source as that used for the quotation at TJob
26:4.

27 a. Only here does Job meet Satan directly.

Hitherto, Satan appeared, largely in disguise, to
members of Job's circle: Now he is climactically
challenged by Job (cf. n. a to 23).
b. Neither the caged lion (as Ezek 19:9 LXX)
nor the boxed fledgling (cf. Eccl 11:30) can show
its full capabilities; likewise Satan cannot perform
his best in hiding.
c. Following S V: P has "You became . . ."
d. The wrestling was often done in sand pits
(e.g. Lucian, *Anacharsis* 2).
e. This paragraph concludes the first major section of the TJob, in which Job successfully withstood the indirect attacks of Satan, finally chal-
lenging him directly and conquering (27:5) the one
whom the angel promised would wage war against
Job (4:3). The concluding aphorism in praise of
patience is typical of the testament genre.

III. Job and the Three Kings (28–45)[a]

A. JOB RECOGNIZED AND THE KINGS ASTONISHED (28–30)

1,2 **28** After I had spent twenty years under the plague, •the kings[b] also *heard about* 21:1
what happened to me. They arose and came to me, each from his own country,[c] Job 2:11-13
3 so that they might encourage me by *a visit.* • But as they approached from a
distance, *they did not recognize me. And they cried out and wept, tearing their*
4 *garments and throwing dust.*[d] •*They sat beside me for seven days and nights. And* 29:4; 30:4; 31:1
5 *not one of them spoke to me.*[e] • It was not due to their patience[f] that they were 35:4
silent, but because they knew me before these evils when I lived in lavish wealth.
. For when I used to bring out for them *the precious stones,*[g] they would marvel, Job 31:24
clapping their hands, and say, "If the goods of our three kingdoms were gathered 32:5
into one at the same place, they would be no equal to the glorious stones of your
6 kingdom." •For *I was more noble*[h] *than those from the east.*
7 But when they came to Ausitis asking in the city, "Where is Jobab, the king Job 1:3
44:1 3:7
8 of all Egypt?"[i] they said to them about me, •"He sits on a dung heap outside the 20:7
9 city. For twenty years he has not returned to the city." •Then they asked about 21:1
my goods and the things which had befallen me were shown to them.

1 **29** When they heard that, they left the city together with the citizens. And my 20:7
2 fellow citizens showed me to them, •but they remonstrated, saying I was not Jobab.
3 Since they were still quite in doubt, *Eliphas—the king of the Temanites*[a]—turned Job 2:11
31:5; 32:12;

28 a. This second major section of the TJob retains the order of the canonical Job in bringing on the three friends only after the incident with Job's wife. The "friends" of MT (Job 2:11) in LXX already became kings (see n. d to 3), a shift shared by TJob. A bit of suspense characterizes this as the preceding and following sections: Only after a series of disguises does Satan meet Job head on (27:1f.); only after seven days of silence (28:4), extensive fumigation (31:2–4), and interrogation (31:1; 38:6) are the fellow kings convinced that the tragic figure before them is indeed Job in his right mind; only after donning the charismatic sashes do the daughters—and they alone—get to witness Job's ascent to heaven (47:11; 52:9). The sequence of the appearance of the kings follows that of the discourses in the biblical Job: Eliphas, Baldad, Sophar, Elihu.

b. See nn. d to 3 and a to 28.

c. See n. a to 29.

d. A customary symbol of grief, here done by the three friends, later by Job himself (29:4). The language in both places parallels Job 2:13 LXX, where, however, LXX omitted "toward heaven" of MT (cf. Acts 22:23). The custom of throwing the earth "toward heaven" or on one's head (TJob 29:4; cf. 2Mac 10:25; Jdt 9:1; Rev 18:19) may have originated with the conveyance in baskets carried on the head of earth used by grieving relatives to bury a deceased member of the family.

e. V adds here the names of the four kings, which contrasts with its omission of the names of the ten children at 1:3f., but agrees in both instances with LXX.

f. Job's patience is contrasted with the absence of that virtue in his friends.

g. Such as characterized Job's throne (32:5); cf. the disclaimer that he put his trust in them (Job 31:24 LXX). Josephus (*War* 2.8.136 = 7.137)

reports that the Essenes cherished among their esoteric interests "the works of the ancients" wherein "they study the healing of diseases, the roots offering protection, and the properties of stones." BB 16b preserves a tradition that "Abraham had a precious stone hung about his neck which brought immediate healing to any sick person who looked on it." But it is not such medicinal values of stones but their proof of wealth which is in view here. Collections of gems (*daktuliothēkē*) existed after Alexander, and the elder Pliny (*Historia naturalis* 37.5.11) names the first Roman gem collector (Scaurus). Is Job here portrayed as such a gem collector? Theophrastus (*De lapidibus* 24.55) refers, with some hesitation, to unspecified records that mention unusually large gems sent to Egyptian kings as gifts from Babylonian kings (24) and that describe royal Egyptian synthetic gem manufacture (55). If gemology was a feature of hellenistic Egyptian royalty, the argument for an Alexandrian provenance for TJob may thereby be strengthened.

h. "You are more noble" S V.

i. This phase may suggest an Egyptian origin for TJob. V's longer reading adds to Job's Egyptian kingdom "all this territory," suggesting V may have known that Ausitis was not to be located in Egypt. The reference to Egypt might also have arisen from the frequent appearance of the word in the T12P, probably well known to the author of TJob.

29 a. Only for Eliphas is the homeland of any of the kings identified in TJob. The ethnic references for the other kings given at Job 2:11 LXX may have been omitted in TJob because Teman was much better known than the other sites (Ezek 25:13; Amos 1:12) and was renowned for its wisdom (Jer 49:7; Obad 8, 9; 1Bar 3:22f.).

4 to me and said, "Are you Jobab, our fellow king?" • And I wept, shaking my 36:1; 3:7
head[b] and throwing dust on it. And I said to them, "I am indeed."[c] 28:3 31:6; 36:1

1 **30** When they saw me shaking my head, they dropped to the ground in a faint.
2 And their troops were disturbed at seeing their three kings collapsed on the ground 31:8; 34:5
3 as if dead, for three hours. • Then they arose and began saying to one another, 42:3
4 "We do not believe that this is he!" • Then they sat for seven days reviewing my 28:4
5 affairs, recalling my herds and goods and saying, • "Have we not known about the
many good things sent out by him into the cities and the surrounding villages[a] to 9:4
be distributed to the poor, besides those established at his house? How then has
he now fallen into such a deathly state?"

B. ELIPHAS: LAMENTS JOB'S LOSSES (31–34)

Eliphas confirms Job's identity

1 **31** And after seven days of such considerations, Eliphas[a] spoke up and said to 28:4
his fellow kings, "Let us approach him and question him carefully to see if it is 35:6
really he himself or not."
2 But since they were about a half stadion[b] distant from me because of the
stench[c] of my body, they arose and approached me with perfumes in their hands, 32:8; 34:4
3 while their soldiers accompanied them scattering incense[d] around me so they would 39:8
4 be able to approach me. • And they spent three days[e] furnishing the incense.
5 And when they had come near me, Eliphas spoke up and said to me,

> "Are you Jobab, our fellow king?[f] 29:3
> Are you the one who once had vast splendor?
> Are you the one who was like the sun by day in all the land?
> Are you the one who was like the moon and the stars that shine at midnight?"
6 And I said to him, "I am indeed." 29:4

A lament of Eliphas for Job

7 And so, after he had wept with a loud wailing, he called out a royal lament 40:14
8 while both the other kings and their troops sang in response.[g] 30:2 33:1; 43:3; 44:1

b. In both LXX (Job 16:14; Lam 2:15) and NT (Mt 27:39) references to shaking the head refer to scornful derision mounted by others; Job here in pained grief heaps scorn on himself.

c. Same language (*egō eimi*) as used of Jesus in the Gospels.

30 a. P reads "villages and the surrounding cities." The translation follows S V.

31 a. Confusion exists in the textual witnesses between the names of Elihu and Eliphas. P S V here all read Elious. At 29:3 Eliphas appears as the first of the royal interviewers, corresponding with the biblical order. Eliphas should dominate through TJob 34, after which Baldad appears. Indeed Eliphas is named at 34:2, 5 by P S V. Yet the same witnesses all read Elious at 31:1, 5; 32:1 (also 33:1 P S). Possibly, Elious (Elihu probably is intended) is a sort of pseudo-Satan figure standing behind and inspiring Eliphas (cf. 41:5; 42:2) so that either may be said to be the originator of the insulting words. This translation adopts the conjecture of Riessler (p. 1334) reading Eliphas for

Elihu at 31:1, 5; 32:1; 33:1, thereby unifying 29–34 as an Eliphas section. Eliphas at 31:1, at least, appears in the recently discovered 5th cent. A.D. Cop. translation of the TJob, Papyrus Colon 3221.

b. About 304 feet.

c. 2Mac 9:9–12 says the terminal illness of Antiochus IV was accompanied by worms and by an odor so revulsive to his troops that he could not be carried.

d. But without magical connotations of fumigation such as appear with the apotropaic effects of a smoke contrived from the heart and liver of a fish; cf. Tob 6:8.

e. V has "three hours."

f. The questions anticipate the poetic lament in ch. 32.

g. Antiphonal singing also at TJob 43:3; 44:1, but the references are absent in V at 31:8; 44:1. The refrains of the hymns at TJob 25, 32; 33, 43:4, 17 suit remarkably Philo's remark that the Therapeutae use traditional as well as newly composed hymns, at times joining in on "the last lines or the refrains" (*Vita cont* 80).

1 **32** Hear then the lament[a] of Eliphas as he celebrates for all[b] the wealth of Job:[c]

2　　"Are you the one who appointed 7,000 sheep for the clothing of the poor?[d] 9:3
　　Where then is the splendor of your throne?
　　Are you the one who appointed 3,000 camels for the transport of goods to 9:4
　　the needy?
　　Where then is the splendor of your throne?

3　　Are you the one who appointed the thousand[e] cattle for the needy to use 10:5
　　when plowing?
　　Where then is the splendor of your throne?

4　　Are you the one who had golden couches[f] but now sits on a dung heap? 25:8
　　Now where is the splendor of your throne?

5　　Are you the one who had a throne of precious stones, but now sits in 28:5
　　ashes?[g]
　　Now where is the splendor of your throne?

6　　[h]Who opposed you when you were in the midst of your children? For you cf. Job 29:5
　　were blooming as a sprout[i] of a fragrant fruit tree!
　　Now where is the splendor of your throne?

7　　Are you the one who established the sixty[k] tables set for the poor? 　　10:1
　　Now where is the splendor of your throne?

8　　Are you the one who had the censers of the fragrant assembly,[l] now you 52:4
　　live amid a foul stench? 　　　　　　　　　　　　　　　　　　　31:2

9　　Are you the one who had golden lamps on silver stands, but now you await
　　the light of the moon?
　　Where then is the splendor of your throne?

10　　Are you the one who had the ointment of frankincense,[m] but now you are
　　in straits?
　　Where then is the splendor of your throne?

11　　*Are you the one who jeered at the unjust* and the sinners, but now *you* too Job 5:22
　　have become a joke?[n] 　　　　　　　　　　　　　　　　　　Job 12:4
　　Now where is the splendor of your throne?

---

32 a. Possibly a development of a line at Job 29:20 LXX, "My splendor was newly upon me."

b. "For the children" in P, a change calling only for an additional iota (*paisin* for *pasin*).

c. S here adds "Where then is the splendor of his throne?" Use of the third person pronoun, in contrast to the second person refrain throughout the lament itself, may suggest S used the phrase as a title for the lament.

d. The question that introduces the refrain may be translated, with equal grammatical warrant, as an assertion tinged with sarcasm: "You are the one who appointed 7,000 sheep for the clothing of the poor: Where then is the splendor of your throne?" and similarly throughout 32:2–12.

e. Equivalent to the "500 yoke" mentioned at 10:5; 16:4; Job 1:3.

f. Sitis also was said to have had couches of gold and silver; cf. 25:8. Cf. Job's golden lamps on silver stands (32:9) and Sitis' clothing of gold-woven linen (25:7).

g. S. P reads "sits on the road."

h. This verse closely parallels in thought, if not in language, Job 29:5 LXX (lines reversed), a favorite source for the author: "When I was very fruitful and my children surrounded me . . ."

i. The Qumran hymns speak often (1QH 6:15; 7:19; 8:6, 8, 10) of the "sprout" (*nēṣer*), but apparently as a self-designation for their own community drawn from Isa 11:1; 60:21. Some of these passages have been taken to refer to the

Teacher of Righteousness and thus to a revered individual, as here (TJob 32:6) to Job.

j. S omits vs. 6. The obvious difference in style suggests these lines may have been added later.

k. But thirty according to 10:1—with twelve more for widows (10:2)—while Sitis is credited with seven (25:5). Slav evens the count, reading "fifty" for both Job (32:7) and Sitis (25:5).

l. The text is uncertain. References to Job's use of censers, lamps (32:9), and frankincense (32:10) appear to ascribe to him prerogatives held only by priests (cf. 2Chr 26:16–21). Use here of "assembly" (*ekklēsia*) may derive from Job 30:28 ("I stand up in the assembly" RSV), where Job contrasts his present cry for help with his former honored status in the city gate (Job 29:7–25, especially 29:7). It is difficult to say whether the assembly in view is cultic, juridical (as would suit Job 29:7–25), or even military (as TJob 31:2–4).

m. The parallelism here, which continues that in the two preceding verses, shows that the frankincense (*libanos*) is here a token of costliness, as it was in the two NT occurrences (Mt 2:11; Rev 18:13). See G. Van Beek, "Frankincense and Myrrh," *BA* 23 (1960) 70–95.

n. The word joke (*chleuē*) appears nowhere in LXX, but possibly stems from Job 12:4 LXX, "For a just and blameless man has become the object of mockery (*chleuasma*)." The idea, however, appears in the favored LXX source at Job 30:9; 31:30; cf. 30:1; 17:6.

12   Are you Job, the one who had vast splendor?   29:3
            Now where is the splendor of your throne?"°

Job's psalm of affirmation[a]

1 **33** After Eliphas[b] finished wailing while his fellow kings responded to him all   31:8
2 in a great commotion, •when the uproar died down, I said[c] to them, "Quiet! Now
   I will show you my throne with the splendor of its majesty, which is among the   43:6
   holy ones.[d]   43:10

3   [e]"My throne is in the upper world,[f] and its splendor and majesty come
           from the right hand of the Father.[g]
4   •The whole world shall pass away[h]   33:4
           and its splendor shall fade. And those who heed it shall share in its
           overthrow.
5   But my throne is in the holy land,[i] and its splendor is in the world of the   7
           changeless one.[j]   36:5

---

o. This vs. is found only in P, which—though
it uses "Job" here—employs the name Jobab at
31:5 (and Job again at 33:2). At 25:1, the very
similar taunting lament uses the name of Job's
wife; cf. "Elihu" at 43:5, 17. Thus of the four
poetic pieces in TJob, three are directed against
named individuals.

33 a. Directly responding to the reproachful refrain in Eliphas' mocking lament, Job asserts in
this psalm of affirmation (TJob 33:3–9) his alle-
giance to the supramundane (*hyperkosmios*, 33:3),
heavenly realm where—contrary to transient earthly
reigns (33:8)—he has an eternal kingdom (33:9).
In form, the seven-part poem alternates between
four assertions of the supercosmic permanence of
his "throne" (33:3, 5, 7, 9) and three evenly
interspersed derogations of mundane transience
(33:4, 6, 8). Each of the positive statements contains
some variation of "my throne," which is reminiscent of the refrain characteristic of the two earlier
poems (TJob 25, 32). The ascription of a heavenly
throne to a revered figure is a frequent hagiographic
technique in the literature of the period (Mt 19:28b
= Lk 22:30, and cf. Mt 20:21; Rev 4:4; 11:16;
20:4; neo-Heb. examples in H. Odeberg, *3 Enoch
or the Hebrew Book of Enoch* [Cambridge, 1928,
repr. 1973] p. 27, note to 3En 10:1, where Enoch
has just such a throne set for him as he is proclaimed
Metatron). But the rabbis felt anyone seated in
heaven gives affront to the Holy One (Hag 15a).
Job's claim to have a throne at the Father's right
is thus a daring one.
   b. Only V so reads. P has Elihu and S, Elious.
See n. a to 31.
   c. Dropping the first person, P reads "Job said."
   d. A striking resemblance to the Qumran concept
of the fellowship of the just with the angels (e.g.
1QH 3.21–23; 4.24f.; 11.10–12; 1QS 11.709; 1QSa
2.8f.) elsewhere in TJob expressed in his daughters'
charismatic access to the language of the angels
(48:3; 49:2; 50:2). Among the harsh (excommunicative?) judgments invoked on Elihu was the loss
of such fellowship: "And the holy ones abandoned
him" (43:10). Exactly as the Qumran members
were themselves called "men of holiness" (1QS
8.17, 23; 9.8; cf. 8.20), so may "the holy ones"
now rejoice at the discomfiture of Elihu (43:15; cf.
43:14). The whole of the hymn against Elihu (TJob
43:4–17), in fact, is replete with Qumran affinities.
   e. This vs. follows 33:4 in V.

f. Neither LXX nor MT uses this term (*hyperkosmios*), which first appears in 5th cent. Christian
(Cyril of Alexandria) or pagan (Iamblichus) mystical authors.
   g. Only P reads "Father" here. S has "God"
and V reads "Savior." S V speak of "the Father
in the heavens." S V Slav add the line "My throne
is eternal." Surprisingly, the phrase "from the
Father's right hand" is not readily paralleled in the
biblical tradition (MT, LXX, NT) though the
tendency apparent at Acts 2:33 and Eph 1:17, 20
emerges clearly in later Christian examples, including exactly this phrase in a variant reading for
Mk 16:19 (quoting Ps 109 [110]:1). The wide NT
use of Ps 109 (110):1 regularly appears with
"Lord" (as LXX), "God," or a circumlocution
such as "power" (Mt 26:64; but note conflation at
Lk 22:69: "at the right hand of the Power of God")
or "majesty" (Heb 1:3; 8:1). "Father" is used of
God nationally already at such places as Isa 63:16;
64:8; Mal 1:6; 2:10, and of God as the Father of
individuals at least since Eccl 23:4 (cf. 23:1):
"Lord Father and God of my life . . ."
   h. Both NT parallels (1Cor 7:31; 1Jn 2:17) use
the present tense. Cf. Did 10:6: "Let grace come
and this world pass on."
   i. "The holy land" as early as Zech 2:16; WisSol
12:3; 2Mac 1:8 refers to the promised land. But it
is apparently not until Origen (*Contra Celsum* 7:29)
that the term is used metaphorically of heaven,
though the meaning might be anticipated in such
places as Mt 5:5: "The gentle . . . shall have the
earth for their heritage." One motif in intertestamental literature is the special privilege that attaches
to those who live in Palestine (Joel 2:32; 4Ezra
13:48f.; 2Bar 29:3; 40:2). Charles, in a note to 2Bar
29:2 (*Apocalypse of Baruch* [London, 1896] pp.
51f.), summarizes rabbinic notions that (1) of them
who will inherit the coming world, one is he who
lives in Israel (Pes 113a); (2) leaving Israel forfeits
the accumulated merit of the fathers (BB 91a); (3)
he who dies in the Holy Land will rise first in the
resurrection (Jalkut Shimeoni; Bereshit 130); and
(4) the righteous dead, if they are to participate in
the resurrection, would have to roll through underground passageways to Palestine (Ket 111a).
   j. S V have "the unchangeable world." Parallelism with "Father" in 33:3, 9 suggests "the
changeless one" here is a title for God, but there
seems no firm reason to associate the title with a
similar expression for an eon ("endless and un-

6   •*Rivers will dry up*,   Job 14:11
     and the arrogance of their waves goes down into the depths of the abyss.
7   But the rivers of my land, where my throne is, do not dry up nor will they   5
     disappear, but they will exist forever.[k]
8   •These kings will pass away, and rulers come and go; but their splendor   34:4
     and boast shall be as in a mirror.[l]
9   But my kingdom is forever and ever, and its splendor and majesty are in
     the chariots of the Father."[m]   52:6,8,10

Eliphas' rejoinder

1,2 **34** As I was saying these things to them so they would be quiet, •Eliphas[a] became
     enraged and said to the other friends, "What good has it done that we have come
3   here with our armies to comfort him? •Look, now he accuses us! Let us then go   5
4   back to our own countries. •Here he sits in the misery of worms and foul odors;   28:2 20:8 31:2
     and yet he is piqued at us. 'Kingdoms pass away and so do their sovereigns.[b] But   33:8f.
5   as for my kingdom,' he says, 'it shall last forever.' " •So Eliphas, arising with
     great consternation, turned away from them in deep sadness and said, "I am
     leaving: We came to cheer him, and yet he demeans us in the presence of our   2
     troops."   30:2

C. BALDAD TESTS JOB'S SANITY (35:1–38:5)

1   **35** Then Baldad seized him[a] and said, "One should not speak that way to a man
2   who not only is in mourning but also is beset by many plagues. •Take note:
     Although we are quite healthy, we were not strong enough to approach him because   31:2-4
3   of the foul stench, except by the use of much perfume. •You there, Eliphas, do
4   you forget how you were when you fell ill[b] for two days? •Now then, let us be
     patient in order that we may discover his true condition. Perhaps he is emotionally   39:13; cf. Job
                                                                                           36:28b
     disturbed.[c] Perhaps he recalls his former prosperity and has become mentally   41:4
5   deranged. •For who would not be driven senseless and imbalanced when he is   21:4
6   sick? •But allow me to approach him, and I will determine his condition."   31:1

---

changing power") in Simonian Gnosticism (Hippolytus, *Ref* 6.17.7; cf. 6.12.4; 6.14.6).

k. The term "forever" (*eis to diēnekes*)—found in Heb 7:3; 10:1, 12, 14—is not elsewhere used in NT or LXX, but the 2nd-cent. A.D. historian Appian uses it to say Julius Caesar was made dictator "forever" (*Bella civilia* 1.4).

l. I.e. transient. The same feature (*not* opacity) characterizes the mirrors of 1Cor 13:12 and Jas 1:23.

m. This remarkable phrase, "the chariots of the Father," is attested in P S V, while "Father" is used elsewhere of God only by P (33:3; 40:2; 47:11 [possibly of God here also]; 52:12). The textual validity of "Father" at 33:3 draws some strength from its appearance here; for the result then has the term "Father" artfully arranged in the first and last units of the poem, in each of which Job says his splendor and majesty are associated with the "Father." The passage is commonly connected with the so-called Merkabah mysticism (mystical speculation about the "chariots" [*mrkbwt*] of God thriving on the fringe of hellenistic Judaism through and beyond NT times). Such speculations appear in a minor sectarian document from Qumran. Called the "Angelic Liturgy" (4QŠirŠabb 37–40), these fragmentary texts suggest an order of worship merging angelic cultic actions with the liturgy of the Qumran covenanters. But in contrast with these Qumran fragments, TJob has no sevenfold heaven nor is it even concerned with ecstatic descriptions of the throne or chariot as 4QŠirŠabb 40. In fact, TJob 33:9 asserts yet again the supramundane permanence of Job's own throne—not God's—by locating it with "the chariots of the Father." Perhaps an Alexandrianized early Merkabah tradition lies behind this unusual phrase.

34 a. Here, as not since 29:3, triply attested in P S V. See n. a to 31.

b. P has "administrations."

35 a. Seized Eliphas, that is, who according to 34:5 was about to leave. S V Slav add "by the hand."

b. There is no canonical reference to the illness of Eliphas, which may have been occasioned by the stench of Job's sickness.

c. The Gk. of chs. 35–38 shows a rich vocabulary for mental (in)stability which taxes the translator's ingenuity. The section may have been informed by Job 36:28b LXX: "In all these things your understanding was not deranged nor was your mind disturbed in your body."

1 **36** Then Baldad, when he had arisen, approached me and said, "Are you Job?" 29:3
And I said to him, "Yes." 29:4

2 And he said, "Is your heart untroubled?"

3 And I said to him, "My heart is not fixed on earthly concerns, since the earth 48:2; 49:1; 50:2
and those who dwell in it are unstable. But my heart is fixed on heavenly concerns, 47:3
for there is no upset in heaven."[a]

4 And Baldad replied and said, "We know the earth is unstable, since of course 33:4
it changes from time to time. Sometimes it steers an even course and is at peace;

5 there are also times of war. • But as for heaven, we hear that it stays calm. But 33:5

6 if you are truly sound of mind, I will ask you about something.[b] • And if you
answer me sensibly regarding the first query, I will ask you about a second matter.
And if you answer me calmly, it will be clear that you are not emotionally
disturbed."

1 **37** So he said, "In whom do you hope?"[a]

2 And I said, "In the God who lives."

3 And again he said to me, "Who destroyed[b] your goods or inflicted you with
these plagues?"

4 And I said, "God." 4:3-5

5 And again he replied and said, "Do you hope upon God? Then how do you
reckon him to be unfair[c] by inflicting you with all these plagues or destroying your

6 goods? • If he were to give and then take away, it would actually be better for him
not to have given anything. At no time does a king dishonor his own soldier who
bears arms well for him. Or who will ever understand the deep things[d] of the Lord

7 and his wisdom? Who dares to ascribe to the Lord an injustice? • Answer me this,
Job.

8 "And again I say to you, if you are sound of mind and have your wits about
you, tell me why we see the sun on the one hand rising in the east and setting in
the west, and again when we get up early we find it rising again in the east? Explain
these things to me if you are the servant of God."[e]

1 **38** And to all this I said, "I do have my wits about me, and my mind is sound.
Why then should I not speak out the magnificent things of the Lord?[a] Or should

---

36 a. The gist of Job's response—his alliance with
the stable "heavenly concerns"—accords with the
central theme of his psalm of affirmation (TJob 33).
There it was his throne, here it is his mind (kardia/
pseuchē). There it was the supramundane (hyperkosmios), here it is the "heavenlies" (epourania).
With this relate the glossolalic participation of Job's
daughters in the same upper world (TJob 48:3; 49:2;
50:2). The whole motif, furthermore, may be compared to the postresurrectional understanding of
Christian existence implied in Col 3:1f.: "Since you
have been brought back to true life with Christ, you
must look for the things that are in heaven, where
Christ is, sitting at God's right hand. Let your
thoughts be on heavenly things, not on the things
that are on the earth."

b. Putting riddles follows a typical wisdom motif
(cf. H. Torczyner, "The Riddle in the Bible,"
HUCA 1 [1924] 125–49). Job has his own riddle
to ask, 38:3f.

37 a. The question—now sincere, not rhetorical—
may arise from Job 17:15 LXX: "Where then is
my hope?" The longer recension of Tob—reflected
in the Vulgate as well as in the Heb. and Aram.
fragments of Tob from Qumran—says Tobit's
misfortune happened "so that the example of his
patience might be given to posterity, just as was
also that of saintly Job" (Tob 2:12 Vulgate; cf.

Jas 5:11: "You have heard of the patience of Job").
The same passage (not paralleled in the shorter Gk.
recension) also shows very high similarities with
certain elements in the TJob: "For just as the kings
would mock blessed Job, so also those who were
subject to him and his kin would laugh at his way
of life, saying, 'Where is your hope? To what end
did you give alms and perform burial rites?' "
(Tob 2:15f. Vulgate).

b. God here, but Satan at 4:3–5.

c. The text is corrupt. P reads "How then can
he be unfair by inflicting . . .?" Kraft conjectures,
"How then does he act unjustly when he judges,
inflicting . . .?"

d. This phrase is closer to NT expressions (1Cor
2:10) than to anything in LXX (but cf. Dan 2:22
LXX, "the deep and dark things").

e. In LXX (e.g. 1:8; 2:3), Job is frequently
called the "servant" (ho therapōn) of God. S V
Slav omit the "if" clause.

38 a. The phrase "the magnificent things (ta me-
galeia) of the Lord" has been suggested as the
title of a collection of angelic hymns. If so, Job
appears here (38:1f.) to say that recital of angelic
hymns, while entirely open to him in full possession
of his mental powers, is inappropriate as a demonstration of sanity. Rather, he will show mental
acuity in a way that will not offend the Lord, by

2 my mouth utterly blunder regarding the Master?[b] Never! •Who are we to be busying
ourselves with heavenly matters, seeing that we are fleshly, having *our lot in dust*   5 Job 30:19
and ashes?[c]

3   "Now then, so you may know that my heart is sound, here is my question for
you: Food enters the mouth, then water is drunk through the same mouth and sent
into the same throat. But whenever the two reach the latrine,[d] they are separated
from each other. Who divides them?"

4   And Baldad said, "I do not know."

5   Again I replied and said to him, "If you do not understand the functions[e] of the
body, how can you understand heavenly matters?"   2

D. SOPHAR: OFFERS THE ROYAL PHYSICIANS (38:6–8)

6   Then Sophar replied and said, "We are not inquiring after things beyond us,[f]
but we have sought to know if you are of sound mind. And now we truly know
7 that your intelligence has been unaffected. •What then do you wish us to do for   cf. Job 36:28b
you? Look, since we are traveling[g] we have brought along with us the physicians
of our three kingdoms. Do you wish to be treated by them? Perhaps you will find
relief."

8   But I answered and said, "My healing[h] and my treatment are from the Lord,   47:6
who also created the physicians."   Sir 38:1

E. SITIS: LAMENTS HER CHILDREN, DIES, AND IS BURIED (39–40)[a]

1 **39** While I was saying these things to them, my wife Sitis arrived in tattered   25:7
2 garments, • fleeing from the servitude of the official she served, since he had
3 forbidden her to leave lest the fellow kings see her and seize her. •When she came,
4 she threw herself at their feet and said weeping, •"Do you remember me, Eliphas—
you and your two friends—what sort of person I used to be among you and how
5 I used to dress? •But now look at my debut and my attire!"[b]   25:7

asking a counterriddle—which baffles Baldad
(38:3f.). "The great things" refers, in LXX, to
the mighty deeds of God, chiefly those displayed
at the Exodus (Deut 11:2; Ps 105 [106]:21). They
were to be recited widely (Ps 70 [71]:19; Eccl
36:7). So the "mighty deeds" became a praiseful
recital of the acts of God. Luke uses the same
phrase to describe the content of glossolalia heard
on the Day of Pentecost (Acts 2:11; cf. 10:46,
"Since they could hear them speaking strange
languages and proclaiming the greatness [*megalu-
noutōn*] of God"). As the companion of Paul, who
himself knew of tongues of angels (1Cor 13:1),
Luke, with Paul, may have been aware of some
tradition linking the glossolalic praise of God with
angelic hymnody. While there is not sufficient
evidence to say either Luke or Paul knew of the
TJob, the concern of all three with prophetic
experience at once ecstatic and angelic brings them
closer together on this point than any other contemporary texts.

b. "Master" (*despotēs*) appears only here in the
TJob. Cf. Job 5:8 LXX: "Lord and Master of all."

c. This view of the "nothingness" of mankind,
which permits neither ability nor right to meddle
in heavenly matters, is frequently expressed; it
constitutes the thrust of the God speeches in Job
38:1–41:25 (cf. especially Job's response at 42:3b,
"I have been holding forth on matters I cannot

understand, on marvels beyond me and my knowledge"). See further the conversations concluded
by 4Ezra 4:10f., 21 and Jn 3:12. TJob sees no
conflict between this anthropological abnegation—
reflected here in Job's own words—and Job's earlier
claim that he sides with the "heavenlies" (36:3).

d. Neither P, S, nor V adopts a euphemism for
"latrine" as Codex Bezae does for Mk 7:19 (= Mt
15:17, only here in NT) by reading ("sewer,
drain," *ochetos*).

e. "Foresight" in S.

f. Sophar's denial that he and his friends were
exploring inscrutables shows that the gist of Job's
remarks (38:1–5) was a caution against such speculation.

g. The text is uncertain.

h. In the ongoing narrative, Job's healing is not
detailed, though it must have occurred during the
appearance of God to Job "through a hurricane
and clouds" (42:1). Later (47:4–9), the effects of
the healing and the role of Job's charismatic
phylactery are recalled.

39 a. TJob 39f. resume and complete the Sitis
episode earlier treated at 21–26. On the name, see
n. b to 25.

b. TJob 39:4f. summarize the lament for Sitis
(25:1–8). Even the characteristic contrast ("But
now . . .") of the refrain is preserved.

6   Then, when they had made a great lamentation[c] and were doubly exhausted, 53:2
7   they fell silent • so that Eliphas seized his purple robe,[d] tore it off, and threw it
     about my wife.
8   But she began to beg them, saying, "I plead with you, order your soldiers to 31:3
     dig through the ruins of the house that fell on my children so that at least their 18:1
9   bones might be preserved as a memorial • since we cannot because of the expense. 24:2
10   Let us see them, even if it is only their bones. • Have I the womb of cattle or of
     a wild animal that my ten children have died and I have not arranged the burial 40:13
     of a single one of them?''
11   And they left to dig, but I forbade it, saying, "Do not trouble yourselves in
12   vain. • For you will not find my children, since they were taken up into heaven[e]
     by the Creator their King.''[f]
13   Then again they answered me and said, "Who then will not say you are demented 35:4
     and mad when you say,[g] 'My children have been taken up into heaven!' Tell us
     the truth now!''

1 **40**   And I replied to them and said, "Lift me up so I can stand erect." And they
2   lifted me up, supporting my arms on each side. • And then when I had stood up,
3   I sang praises to the Father.[a] • And after the prayer I said to them, "Look up with 50:3; 52:12

---

c. Jewish funereal interests apparent here are
illustrated at Tob 1:17–19 and Eccl 38:16–23.
Here, as also TJob 19:2; 20:4; 53:1–4, it is a
question of sincere and traditional laments (even
if, fantastically, the animals share in the lamentation, 40:10!), and not the mocking laments of TJob
25:1–8 and 32:1–12. See also n. d to 28.

d. This sign of royalty was placed even about
idols (LetJer 6:11, 71; cf. Jn 19:2, 5).

e. Body *and* soul, apparently, since (1) the
search for bones would be fruitless (39:11) and (2)
it is the *children*, not their souls, or spirits, merely,
that have been taken to heaven (39:12f.; 40:3). Yet
this seems to contradict the account of Job's demise,
where although his *soul* was borne off in a chariot
to the east (42:10), his *body* was at once prepared
(53:11) and buried after three days "in a beautiful
sleep" (53:7). At the outset of the story, the angel
had promised Job would be raised up in the
resurrection (4:9; see n. c to 4), an echo (or source?)
of Job 42:17a LXX. Though nothing direct is said
of the future of the wicked in the TJob, the hymn
against Elihu (TJob 43) speaks more of banishment,
of separation from the "holy ones," than it does
of extinction or of consignment to any special
abode of the wicked dead, either with or without
a resurrection. (See 43:5, 6, 10.) Except for the
assumption of the children, the view of life after
death expressed in these passages in TJob is not
unlike that of Jub 23:28–31; 1En 91:10; 92:3;
103:3f.; TAb B 7, in which the bones and the
bodies rest in the earth but the spirits rise in
conscious joy. If the ascent to heaven of the children
(leaving no bones behind!) seems inconsistent with
the other references, it is only because TJob reflects
a stage in the development of Jewish eschatology
where considerable diversity appeared. Compared
to Qumran thought, TJob openly asserts (as 4:9)
the resurrection of the righteous, where Qumran
(e.g. 1QH 3.19) tacitly assumes it, or, by virtue

of intense eschatological immediacy, obviates it.
TJob never reaches (at best, 43) the execratory
vocabulary of damnation for the wicked characteristic of the Qumran texts (e.g. 1QS 4.11–14).
Finally, Qumran knows nothing comparable to the
bodily assumption into heaven, following death,
of Job's deceased children. While ancient worthies
such as Elijah (without death, 2Kgs 2:9 LXX),
Abraham (TAb B 7), Paul (before death, 2Cor
12:2, 4) were said to have been "taken up"
(*analambanein/analēmpsis;* for 2Cor, *harpazein*),
the ascension of Jesus (Acts 1:11) should not be
overlooked in this case. With Jesus, there was no
discussion about body and/or soul, whereas Paul
twice (2Cor 12:2f.) wondered if he were "in the
body" during the ascent. The model of Jesus—
ascension after death, consequent to resurrection—
may betray a Christian hand somewhere in the
editorial history of TJob.

f. TJob employs some unusual divine titles: "the
great God" (17:4); "Master" (*despotēs*) (38:1);
"the Master of virtues" (50:2); "the Creator"
(*dēmiourgos*) and "King" here at 39:12. "Creator"
(*dēmiourgos*) is used in NT only at Heb 11:10.
None of the later gnostic contempt for the term
"creator" appears here.

g. V reads for the quotation, "for when we were
about to recover the bones of your children, you
forbad us, saying, 'They have been gathered up
and are kept by their Creator.' ''

40 a. So P; "I sang praises first to the Lord and
to God" S; " . . . to God first" V. Kraft conjectures
"I first gave thanks to the Lord." On "Father" in
TJob, see n. g to 33. Cf. singing praises to the
Father with a similar line in the speculative hellenistic theosophic tract *Poimandres* 1.26, which says
of the climax of the ascended soul upon its arrival
at the eighth sphere, "And it sings (*hymnei*) to the
Father with those who are there."

your eyes to the east[b] and see[c] my children crowned[d] with the splendor of the 52:10 43:14
heavenly one.''[e]

4 And when she saw that, Sitis my wife fell to the ground worshiping and said, 21:2
"Now I know that I have a memorial with the Lord. So I shall arise[f] and return 24:2
to the city and nap awhile and then refresh myself before the duties of my
5 servitude." •And when she left for the city she went to the cow shed of her oxen,
6 which had been confiscated by the rulers whom she served. •And she lay down
near a certain manger and died in good spirits.[g]   1:6

7,8 When her domineering ruler sought her but could not find her, •he went when
9 it was evening into the folds of the herds and found her sprawled out dead. •And
all who saw[h] cried out in an uproar of lament over her, and the sound reached
10 through the whole city. •When they rushed in to discover what had happened,
11 they found her dead and the living animals standing about weeping[i] over her.[j]

12 And so bearing her in procession, they attended to her burial, locating her near 52:12
13 the house that had collapsed on her children. •And the poor of the city made a 18:1 53:1,5f.
great lamentation, saying,[k] "Look! This is Sitis, the woman of pride and splendor! 25:1
She was not even considered worthy of a decent burial!''   39:10

14 So then you will find in "The Miscellanies"[l] the lament made for her.   41:6; 48:3; 49:3;
                                                                                     50:3; 51:4

F. JOB'S RECOVERY AND VINDICATION (41–45)

Elihu's insult

1 **41** Eliphas and the rest sat beside me after these things arguing and talking big
2 against me.[a] •After twenty-seven days, they were about to arise and go to their
3 own countries, •when they were implored by Elihu, saying, "*Stay here till* I clarify Job 36:2
this issue for him. You held on quite some time while Job boasted himself to be
4 a just man. •But I will not hold on. From the start I too made lamentation for him, 32:1
remembering his former prosperity.[b] And here now he speaks out in boastful 35:4

b. Same direction toward which Job is carried
off at death (52:10). At least at Lk 1:78, the "east"
(*anatolē*) had messianic connotations. Literal aid
from the east—fellow Jews in Babylon—was recalled in 1Bar 4:36; 5:5. Josephus (*War* 2.128 =
2.8.5) mentions the prayers of the Essenes directed
toward the sun; and according to Athanasius,
Quaestiones ad Antiochum 37 (PG 28.620A), the
Jews prayed toward the east. Christian practices in
patristic times included baptizing toward the east
and orienting churches in that direction. Contrast
the north-south orientation of most graves at Qumran.

c. S V Slav have "when they looked, they saw."

d. The anticipated future of the sons of truth,
according to 1QS 4.7, includes "the glorious
crown" (*kelîl kābôd*).

e. V has "the heavenly king."

f. This expression is not strong enough to suggest
that Sitis shares Job's hope of resurrection (TJob
4:9).

g. S V have ". . . died disheartened."

h. Probably the city folk, but possibly the mourning animals of vs. 11.

i. Sympathetic participation of animals is an
occasional feature of certain popular sectarian literature: the cooperative worm (20:9); Ignatius (Rom
4:2) seeks the aid of beasts in becoming the "pure
bread of Christ"; cf. Mk 1:13, Jesus with the wild
beasts; and 2En 58:6, where beasts are said to
survive to accuse their abusers. (See an extensive
n. to 2En 58:6 regarding Jewish and Greek notions
of the rationality of animals in Charles, *APOT*,
vol. 2, p. 464.

j. Vss. 9–11 show considerable disarray in the
text witness. S has twice written the words "and
the living animals . . . over her." V places vs. 9
after vs. 11.

k. The minuscule lament shows the same con-
trastive form as the longer laments of TJob 25, 32
(see n. a to 25).

l. Lit. "things omitted." Used in LXX as Gk.
title for the two books commonly called 1 and 2
Chr. So called, because the books of "Chronicles"
were to supply additional events omitted from 1
and 2 Kgs. TJob shows high interest in fabulous
"books." Besides these unidentified "Miscellanies," also mentioned are "The Miscellanies of
Eliphas" (41:6), the "Hymns of Kasia" (49:3),
and the "Prayers of Amaltheia's Horn" (50:3).
Parallels at 49:3 and 50:3 suggest "The Spirit" as
a title at 48:4. "The Great Things" (51:3; cf. 38:1;
51:4) could be yet another such title (see n. a to
38). The principle is anticipated by numerous
"lost" books mentioned in the canonical literature
(Num 21:14; Josh 10:13 MT; 2Sam 1:18; 1Kgs
11:41; 14:19, 29; 15:7; 1Chr 29:29; 2Chr 9:29;
12:15; 20:34; 26:22; 33:18f.; 35:25. Cf. 1Mac
16:24).

41 a. V has a lengthy restyling of vss. 1–3,
showing dramatic literary improvement: ". . . against
me, saying for 27 days that I had suffered this
justly due to many sins and that there was no hope
left for me. But I vigorously remonstrated. Filled
with anger, they arose to leave in a rage. Then
Elihu implored them . . ."

b. P adds here "And suddenly he has undertaken
to exalt himself."

5 grandeur, saying he has his throne in heaven. •Listen to me now, and I will tell   33:2-9
you about his imaginary estate.'' Then Elihu, inspired by Satan,[c] spoke out against
6 me insulting words, •which are written down in ''The Miscellanies of Eliphas.''[d]   40:14

The kings forgiven through Job's intercession

1 **42** *After* Elihu *ended* his arrogant speech, *the Lord*—having appeared plainly *to*   Job 38:1
2 *me through a hurricane and clouds*[a]—*spoke* • and censured Elihu,[b] showing me
3 that the one who spoke in him was not a human but a beast.[c] •And when the Lord   7:6
spoke to me through the cloud, the four kings also heard[d] the voice of him who   30:2   52:9
spoke.
4,5 [e]*After the Lord* finished *speaking to me, he said to Eliphas,* • ''You there,   Job 42:7-10
Eliphas—*you and your two friends*—why *did you sin? You have not spoken truly*
6 regarding *my servant Job.* •Arise and have him offer up sacrifices on your behalf
so your sin might be taken away. *Except for him, I would have destroyed you.''*
7,8 So they brought me the things for sacrifice. •And I took them and made an offering
on their behalf, and *the Lord* received it favorably and *forgave their sin.*   43:4

A hymn against Elihu

1 **43** Then when Eliphas, Baldad, and Sophar knew that the Lord had showed them
2 favor regarding their sin—but had not considered Elihu worthy—•Eliphas replied[a]
3 and spoke up with a hymn[b] •while the other friends and their troops sang to him
4 in response near the altar. •Eliphas[c] spoke in this manner:[d]   31:8

---

c. In the canonical Job, Elihu makes a very graphic and explicit claim to inspiration: ''For I am filled with words, choked by the rush of them within me. I have a feeling in my heart like new wine seeking a vent, and bursting a brand-new wineskin. Nothing will bring relief but speech, I will open my mouth and give my answer'' (Job 32:18–20; cf. 32:8, ''But now I know that it is a breath in man, the inspiration of Shaddai, that gives discernment''). While the biblical book attributes the inspiration to God (Job 32:8), TJob ascribes it to Satan (41:5; cf. 42:2).

d. See n. 1 to 40. The words of Elihu are preserved in the records of Eliphas perhaps because Elihu is the subject of execration (TJob 43) and any invitation to consult his own records would be inappropriate.

42 a. A less restrained apocryphon may well have easily or fabulously amplified this event mentioned at Job 38:1.

b. Beyond his speech, nothing is heard of Elihu in the canonical book.

c. Cf. 23:2; 27:2, all of which attest a developed yet restrained view of Satan not unlike that of NT (e.g. Eph 2:2).

d. V omits the whole verse. S reads ''. . . the cloud, they heard.''

e. TJob 42:4–8 slightly compresses Job 42:7–9 LXX, with the following differences: (1) LXX (42:7) says the kings did not speak the truth as Job did—TJob (42:5) says they did not speak truly *regarding* (*kata*) Job; (2) LXX (42:8) speaks of seven bullocks and seven rams, TJob (42:6) merely of ''sacrifices''; (3) the names of the kings (42:9) in LXX are omitted in TJob (42:9; but cf. 28:4 V, where V has the names); (4) unusually, TJob in one or two cases does not follow the Alexandrian text of LXX.

43 a. P reads ''Eliphas received a spirit . . .'' (or ''the Spirit''?) P here omits ''holy'' before ''spirit,'' but includes it at 51:2. The activity of the spirit here is associated with speaking (or singing) the hymn (cf. 1Cor 14:15; Eph 5:18f.), but not with the inspiration of composing the hymn. Describing the hymn composition of the Therapeutae, Philo mentions no ''spirit'' (*Vita cont* 29.80). On the other hand, the Holy Spirit (according to 51:2 P; S has ''holy angel,'' V omits) is present in Nereus' recording of the hymns (51:2 P). ''Spirit'' as inspiring agent is clear in such Jewish literature as 1En 91:1; MartIs 1:7; 5:14; TAb A 4; and 4Ezra 14:22. But in none of these examples is it a matter of hymn composition. But cf. Job's query of Baldad, found at Job 26:4 LXX: ''Whose breath is it that has come forth from you?''

b. See n. g to 31. Philo (*Vita cont* 80) identifies among the hymns of the Therapeutae those that were sung at the altar, as here and at 44:1, where in view is the altar where the sacrifices had just been offered by Job for his fellow kings (42:6–43:3).

c. Eliphas, as the leading one of the visiting kings, gives the hymn. He also is the only one identified as to homeland (29:3); was first to speak upon the kings' discovery of Job (29:3); and was first to be addressed by Sitis (39:4).

d. This hymn (43:4–17) is an imprecatory execration text given, according to TJob, at the altar when it became clear Elihu did not share in the forgiveness just mediated through Job's sacrificial offices (42:5–43:3). Something like a refrain appears as the opening and closing lines (43:4, 17); it is not impossible the refrain originally appeared in alternation with the remaining verses so as to approximate the form of the laments in TJob 25, 32 (see n. g to 25). Some parallels with other material in TJob appear: e.g. cf. 43:10 with 33:2

"Our sins were stripped off, and our lawlessness buried.   17; 42:8

5   Elihu, Elihu—the only evil one[c]—will have no memorial[f] among the   24:2
living.

His quenched lamp lost its luster,   Job 18:5

6   and the splendor of his lantern *will flee* from him into condemnation.
For this one is the one of darkness and not of light.
And the doorkeepers of darkness shall inherit his splendor and majesty.[g]   33:2

7   His kingdom is gone, his throne[h] is rotted.   33:3,5,7,9
And the honor of his tent[i] lies in Hades.   11

8   He loved the beauty of the *snake* and the scales of the *dragon*.   Job 20:16
Its venom and poison shall be his food.   12

9   He did not take to himself the Lord, nor did he fear him.
But even his honored ones[j] he provoked to anger.

10   The Lord has forgotten him, and the holy ones abandoned him.[k]   33:2

11   But wrath and anger shall be his tent.[l]   7
He has no hope in his heart, nor peace in his body.

12   He had the poison of *asps*[m] in his tongue.   Job 20:14

13   Righteous is the Lord, true are his judgments.
With him there is no favoritism. *He will judge us all together.*   Job 9:32

14   Behold the Lord has come! Behold his holy ones are prepared,   10
while crowns[n] lead the way with praises.   40:3

(for use of Job 18 LXX, see n. g to 43). Yet much of the language of the psalm is distinctive and its affinities with Qumran hymnody have been noted by Philonenko ("Le Testament de Job," *Sem* 18 [1968] 52f.). Even though it belongs to a considerably later period (5th to 6th cent. A.D.), a striking parallel is afforded by the Cop. gnostic apocryphon entitled Book of the Resurrection of Jesus Christ by Bartholomew the Apostle (ResBart). This text contains an execration against Judas Iscariot said to have been pronounced by Jesus in "Amente," an Egyptian mythological term for hell, where Jesus went following death and prior to resurrection and where he found Judas Iscariot. Both the Elihu hymn and the Judas invective (1) are poetic in form, (2) appear in the third person, (3) amount to an excommunicative curse, and (4) are uttered against a named individual. Striking conceptual similarities appear in the following paired excerpts (utilizing the present translation of TJob and, for ResBart, that of E. Budge, *Coptic Apocrypha* [London, 1913] p. 185; Cop. text, pp. 7–9 with plates VII–IX; excerpts from TJob are in textual sequence, those from ResBart are not):

TJob 43:5	Elihu . . . will have no memorial among the living
ResBart	Judas' inheritance has been taken away from among the living
TJob 43:5	his quenched lamp lost its luster
ResBart	the light departed and left him, and darkness came upon him
TJob 43:7	His kingdom is gone, his throne is rotted, and the honor of his tent lies in Hades
ResBart	his crown has been snatched away . . . the worm has inherited his substance . . . his house hath been left a desert
TJob 43:8	He loved the beauty of the snake and the scales of the dragon. Its venom and poison shall be his food.
ResBart	His mouth was filled with thirty snakes so that they might devour him

The Elihu hymn shows more literary finesse; it begins and ends with a similar couplet, for example. But both hymns must arise from the same literary stock, the roots of which reach through Job 18 LXX as far back as the "mocking dirges" in Isa 14 and Ezek 28.

e. Close the the Christian title for Satan, "the Evil One," which occurs at TJob 7:1 V; 20:2 V; cf. Mt 13:19 and 6:13.

f. The frequency of the expression "no memorial" in TJob (24:2; 39:8; 40:4; 43:5, 17) was anticipated by its occurrence at Job 18:17 LXX (cf. Job 2:9 with TJob 24:2 and see n. c to 24). With whom the "memorial" occurs varies: the earth (24:2; Job 2:9b), the living (43:5, 17), the Lord (40:4), or no such reference (39:8).

g. The themes and the language of 43:5f. appear in the LXX poem of Job: the vanished memorial (Job 18:17); the quenched lamp (Job 18:5f.; 21:17; 29:3); light/darkness motifs (Job 12:25; 17:12; 18:6, 18; 23:11; 26:10). Baldad's derisive description of the ungodly (Job 18:2–21 LXX), in particular, seems to inform TJob 43:5f.

h. The ill end of Elihu's "splendor and majesty" (vs. 6) and of his "throne" (vs. 7) contrast with the heavenly, supramundane character of Job's kingdom and throne (33:2, 3, 5, 9).

i. S V have "stateliness."

j. A title for angels, cf. 43:10, 14f.; 33:2.

k. The second member of a parallelism, first part of which is 43:9. Banishment, or excommunication, seems to be implied.

l. S V have "for emptiness."

m. S V Slav have "an asp."

n. Possibly angels.

15	Let the holy ones rejoice, let them leap for joy in their hearts,°	10
16	for they have received the splendor they awaited.	
17	Gone is our sin, cleansed is our lawlessness.	4; 42:8
	And the evil one Elihu has no memorial among the living."ᵖ	24:2

Job's restoration

1 **44** After Eliphas ended the hymn, while all were singing in response to him and 31:8
encircling the altar, we aroseᵃ and entered the cityᵇ where we now make our home. 28:7
2 And we held great festivities in the delight of the Lord. Once again I sought to 9:1-15:9; 45:2
do good works for the poor.
3 　And *all* my friends and *those who had known me* as a benefactor came to me. Job 42:10f.
4 ᶜAnd they queried me, saying, "What do you ask of us now?" And remembering
the poor again to do them good, I asked them, saying, "Let *each one* give me *a*
5 *lamb* for the clothing of the poor who are naked." • So then *every single one*
brought a *lamb and a gold coin.*ᵈ *And the Lord blessed* all the goods I owned,ᵉ
and *he doubled my estate.* 　　　　　　　　　　　　　　　　　　　　　　　4:7

Job's final counsels and the division of the inheritanceᵃ

1 **45** And now, my children, behold I am dying. Above all, do not forget the Lord. 1:4
2,3 Do good to the poor. Do not overlook the helpless. • Do not take to yourselves
4 wives from strangers.ᵇ • Look, my children, I am dividing among you everything 1:4 46:4
that is mine, so each one may have unrestricted control over his own share.ᶜ

---

o. Vs. 15 appears to describe, in poetic form, the more prosaic conclusion of 43:17, which virtually repeats 43:5. S V Slav read "Let their hearts leap for joy."

p. Eliphas, Baldad, and Sophar are thus forgiven and they may, with the "holy men," rejoice (43:15). But Elihu now stands under divine judgment, excluded from the group; he is not again heard of in TJob.

44 a. One expects at this point, or earlier, some description of Job's healing. But none is given, although 47:2–9 recounts how his recovery was effected through a triple-stranded band, or sash, Midrashically derived from a literal interpretation of the biblical injunction, "Gird your loins like a man" (Job 38:3; 40:7 RSV). The band is then split into three parts and given to the daughters as their inheritance.

b. Reference is made either probably to the unnamed city of the region of Ausitis (TJob 28:7 and Job 1:1; 42:17b, e A) or possibly to the city the angel mentioned (TJob 18:8).

c. TJob 44:3–5 restyles Job 42:10–12 so as to reflect Job's charitable deeds detailed earlier at TJob 9–15.

d. Lit. a "tetradrachma of gold." V makes it an alloy: ". . . of gold and silver." Cf. Job 42:11

LXX B, "a tetradrachma of uncoined gold."

e. V completes the verse with a characteristic and lengthy reading: "and within a few days I abounded in goods and cattle and the remaining things which I had lost. And I gained others in double quantity. And I took a wife, your mother, and I fathered the ten of you in lieu of my ten children who had died."

45 a. This paragraph is typical of the close of the usual "testament": the death scene, exhortations to the children, summary injunctions. But the death itself is not described (till 52:1–53:8), and there is no concern to take the bones back to Hebron (found in all T12P).

b. The essentially Jewish ban against foreign marriage has been widely recognized. From biblical roots (Gen 24:3, 37; 27:46–28:1; Num 36:8; Ezra 10:10; cf. Gen 26:34f.), it has spread to such texts as JosAsen 8:5; Tob 1:9; 3:15; 4:12f.; 6:10–12 (preeminently); Jub 20:4; 22:20; 25:1–10; 30:7–17; TLevi 9:10; Ps-Philo 9:15; 18:13; 43:5; AddEsth 4:17w, x.

c. This final sentence serves as a transition to the following (fourth and final) major section of TJob, 46–53. Here end Job's testamentary words to his children begun in the first person at 1:4b (see n. i to 1).

IV. Job and His Three Daughters (46–50)[a]

The daughters' inheritance: their father's phylactery

1 **46** And they brought forth the estate for distribution among the seven males[b] only.
2 For he did not present any of the goods to the females. They were grieved and said to their father, "Our father, sir, are we not also your children? Why then did you not give us some of your goods?"
3 But Job said to the females, "Do not be troubled, my daughters: I have not
4 forgotten you. •I have already designated for you *an inheritance* better than that of *your seven brothers.*"[c]   45:4; 47:1   Job 42:15
5 Then when he had called his daughter who was named Hemera he said to her, "Take the signet ring, go to the vault, and bring the three golden boxes, so that
6 I may give you your inheritance." •So she left and brought them back.
7 And he opened them and brought out three multicolored cords[d] whose appearance
8 was such that no man could describe, •since they were not from earth but from
9 heaven,[e] shimmering with fiery sparks like the rays of the sun.[f] •And he gave each one a cord, saying, "Place these about your breast, so it may go well with you all the days of your life."

1 **47** Then the other daughter, named Kasia,[a] said to him, "Father, is this the inheritance which you said was better than that of our brothers? Who has any use   46:4
for these unusual[b] cords?[c] We cannot gain a living from them, can we?"
2 And their father said to them, "Not only shall you gain a living from these,
3,4 but these cords will lead you into the better world, to live in the heavens.[d] •[e]Are   36:3
you then ignorant, my children, of the value of these strings? The Lord considered

---

46 a. Merely named (1:3 P) prior to this point in TJob, the three daughters dominate the final main section. Chs. 1–45 have been related in the first person; with 46:1, however, there is a sudden shift to third-person discourse, which is sustained through 50:3; thereafter the first person returns, but it is Job's brother Nereus who speaks throughout (51–53). Although such a shift may suggest compositional evolution, similar shifts of person occur in texts where unity is not in question, such as 2Ezra 6:28; Tob 3:7; and 1QapGen 21.23–30. While TJob 1–45 serves to commend the virtues of patience and philanthropy in a manner reminiscent of the T12P, TJob 46–53 seems rather to legitimate charismatic communion with the angels in a mode approaching Merkabah mysticism.

b. A similar interest in males occurs at 15:4. It may be possible to detect here rudimentary proto-gnostic interests, such as the process of "becoming male" as an expression for saving enlightenment.

c. The whole of TJob may be considered as a Midrashic development from Job 42:15b: "And their father gave them inheritance rights like their brothers." The daughters each receive as their portion one cord of the tri-stranded belt, or girdle, by which Job was miraculously cured (47:5). No particular theological use is made here of "inheritance."

d. S has "the multicolored objects." V has "three cordlike aprons." The meaning is unclear. Elsewhere it is called a cord (*spartē*, 48:1), cincture (*perizōsis*, 52:1), phylactery (47:11), while more likely words for "girdle" (*zōnē, kestos*) are not used. These terms suggest a sash, or cord, derived from the tri-stranded therapeutic girdle that God provided Job (47:5) when the challenge was given,

"Gird up your loins . . ." (Job 38:3; 40:7; cf. 42:4 RSV). By this object, Job was cured (47:4–8). Now each of the three daughters is given as her inheritance one of the three cordlike strands, which she is to don as a sash. These "cords" are possibly a magical device for fending off evil; see n. i to 47:11.

e. In accord with the earth/heaven bifurcation of TJob 33:2–9; 36:3.

f. 3En 29:2 describes a class of angels thus: "And from each of them sparks and lightnings shoot forth; from each of them rays of splendor stream out, and from each of them lights flash; pavilions and tents of brilliance surround them, for even the seraphim and the creatures who are greater than all the celestials cannot look on them."

47 a. Kasia and Hemera (46:5) have a part in the conversation with their father. But Amaltheia's Horn is not introduced till 50:1.

b. Or, "useless."

c. S Slav put the question: "What then is so unusual about these cords?"

d. As Job affirmed in his psalm (33:2–9) and asserted during his interrogation (36:3), the daughters too will now be enabled to share in the heavenly world, specifically by ecstatic utilization of the language of heavenly beings (48:3; 49:2; 50:2).

e. The account of Job's miraculous cure (vss. 4–9) occurs neither in the canonical book nor after TJob 42:3 or 43:17, where it might logically appear. From God's challenge to Job to arise and gird himself for divine interrogation (Job 38:3; 40:7; cf. 42:4), TJob in Midrashic style fashions the very "girdle" that now becomes the inheritance for the daughters.

me worthy of these in the day in which he wished to show me mercy and to rid
my body of the plagues and the worms.   20:8

5   "Calling me, he furnished me with these three cords and said, '*Arise, gird your*   Job 38:3; 40:2
loins like a man. I shall question you, and you answer me.'

6   "So I took them and put them on. And immediately from that time the worms   20:8
7 disappeared from my body and the plagues, too. •And then my body got strength   38:8
8 through the Lord as if I actually had not suffered a thing.[f] •I also forgot the pains   52:1
9 in my heart. •And the Lord spoke to me in power,[g] showing me things present and
things to come.

10   "Now then, my children, since you have these objects you will not have to face   1:4
11 the enemy at all,[h] but neither will you have worries of him in your mind, •since   7:11
it is a protective amulet[i] of the Father.[j] Rise then, gird yourselves with them before
I die in order that you may be able to see those who are coming for my soul, in   52:2
order that you may marvel over the creatures[k] of God."

The charismatic sashes[a]

1 **48** Thus, when the one called Hemera[b] arose, she wrapped around her own string[c]
2 just as her father said. •And she took on another heart—[d]no longer minded toward   23:11

---

f. See n. d to 1.

g. Probably this refers to the event described in
TJob 42:1–3 and Job 38:1 LXX. The scene is taken
as the origin of an apocalyptic vision disclosing
"things present and impending," a typical apocalyptic agenda (cf. Rev 1:1; see n. j to 1). Such
apocalyptic visions—more precisely the claims
based on them made by his opponents—led Paul
to his statement in Rom 8:38: "no angel, no prince,
nothing that exists, nothing still to come." Yet he
allowed even at Corinth a "revelation" (*apokalyp-
sis*) among the components of an ordered Christian
service (1Cor 14:26).

h. Cf. 7:11 and n. a to 3.

i. Lit. "phylactery" (*phylaktērion*). In view of
its therapeutic and evil-averting effects, this phylactery appears to stem from the sphere of magic.
No hint is given that this phylactery corresponds
to the usual arm and head cases for miniature
Scripture portions, examples of which (with slight
differences) have been found at Qumran. In common with the traditional Jewish phylacteries, those
of Job's daughters were to be tied on, or at least
donned (47:11; 48:1; 49:1; 50:1; 52:1). But it is
striking that they wore them at all, since talmudic
tradition exempted from the use of phylacteries
slaves, mourners, and females (Kid 34a; MK 15a;
Tefillin 3). Yet neither is it a pure magical amulet
(a written prescription for magically fending off
evil). It is thus a case of restrained Jewish magic,
resulting in a wearable "charm" Midrashic in origin
and capable of effects including those (1) therapeutic (47:5–7; 52:1); (2) economic (47:2); (3) evil-
averting (47:10); (4) glossolalic (48:3; 49:2; 50:2);
and (5) apocalyptic-visionary (47:2, 9, 11; 52:9).

j. Job, or God? The text is ambiguous. S V Slav

read "the Lord," understanding the term as a
divine title, as they also did at 40:2, where according
to P, Job "sang praises to the Father." "Father"
is a frequent title for Job in the immediate context:
47:1, 2; 48:1 (cf. 52:9, 12). The "father" here
seems to be Job, whose own phylactery he is about
to grant his daughters as their inheritance.

k. V has "wonders."

48 a. The accounts of the daughters putting on
their sashes (48–50) show several common elements: (1) the name of the daughter; (2) donning
the sash; (3) having the "heart changed"; (4) no
longer concerned with worldly things; (5) glossolalia in the language of specified heavenly beings;
(6) a brief characterization of the contents of glossolalia; and (7) reported preservation of the speeches
in mythical books (but see n. h to 48).

b. Lit. "Day." See nn. f, g, and h to 1.

c. S has "wrapped it around herself."

d. V heightens by adding "and at once she was
outside her own flesh," which parallels Paul's
ecstatic ascent; he twice wondered whether the
ascent was "in the body" or "outside the body"
(2Cor 12:2f.). The changed "heart" (cf. 49:1;
50:2) refers not to conversion but appears rather to
describe the onset of the ecstatic state, "the descent
to the Merkabah." When Saul was "also among
the prophets," it is said that "God gave him
another heart." Note the similarity to the language
of Montanus preserved in the 4th-cent. heresiologist
Epiphanius: "Behold! Humankind is like a harp,
and I strum as a plectrum; humans sleep, I am
awake. Behold! The Lord is the one who excites
the hearts of humans, the one who gives them a
heart" (*AdvHaer* 48.4.1).

3 earthly thingsᵉ—•but she spoke ecstatically in the angelic dialect,ᶠ sending up a
hymn to God in accord with the hymnic style of the angels. And as she spoke
ecstatically, she allowed "The Spirit"ᵍ to be inscribed on her garment.ʰ   40:14

1 **49** Then Kasia bound hers on and had her heart changed so that she no longer 23:11
2 regarded worldly things. •And her mouth took on the dialect of the archons and
3 she praised God for the creation of the heights. •So, if anyone wishes to know
"The Creation of the Heavens,"ᵃ he will be able to find it in "The Hymns of 40:14
Kasia."ᵇ

1 **50** Then the other one also, named Amaltheia's Horn, bound on her cord. And
2 her mouth spoke ecstatically in the dialect of those on high, •since her heart also 23:11
was changed, keeping aloof from worldly things. For she spoke in the dialect of
3 the cherubim, glorifying the Master of virtuesᵃ by exhibiting their splendor. •And
finally whoever wishes to grasp a traceᵇ of "The Paternal Splendor" will find it 40:3
written down in "The Prayers of Amaltheia's Horn."ᶜ   40:14

e. Cf. 49:1 and 50:2, but also 2En 56:2 A: "And Enoch answered his son and said, 'Listen, my child! Since the time when the LORD anointed me with the ointment of my glory, it has been horrible for me, and food is not agreeable to me, and I have no desire for earthly food.' " 2Clem 5:6 urges Christians "to regard worldly things (ta kosmika) as not their own." But 2Clem deals with "this world and the coming one" (2Clem 6:3), which is an eschatological dualism not central to the TJob. With this avoidance of "worldly things" can be related Job's own deprecation of "earthly things" (TJob 36:3; see n. a to 36) and especially his psalm of affirmation (TJob 33), where the heavenly throne is described as Job's present possession, an ontological rather than eschatological dualism. The ontology resembles Heb, especially 9:1 and 8:5: While eschatological events are not absent (Heb 9:28; TJob 4:9; 47:9) they play no major role. To the contrary, the enduring reality of the upper world is already realized (Heb 12:22–24, in community; TJob 48–50, by ecstatic access). Overall, TJob shows an eschatology closer to Heb. than to Qumran (or, for that matter, to the Montanists with their hope for the descending New Jerusalem; Epiphanius, AdvHaer 49.1.2f.).

f. Similarly, "the dialect of the archons" (49:2), "the dialect of those on high" (50:1), "the dialect of the cherubim (50:2), "the distinctive dialect" (52:7). The source of Paul's "tongues . . . of angels" (1Cor 13:1)? Paul, however, does not use "dialect" (dialektos), which in NT is Luke's word alone. In the account of the Pentecostal glossolalia, Luke uses the word expressly for humans (of varied nationality) and not for angels; contrast his use of "magnify" (megalunein; see n. a to 38). In ApAb 17, an angel teaches Abraham a heavenly song, recital of which leads him to a vision of the Merkabah. The singing of hymns by females ("virgins") in the language of the cherubim—as well as the notion of the "Chariot of the Father"—is known also to Resurrection of Bartholomew (ed. Budge, Coptic Apocrypha, pp. 11f., 189).

g. See n. a to 43. "Spirit" here could be the subject: "As she spoke ecstatically, the Spirit let it be inscribed on her garment." In view of parallel titles of poems at 49:3 and 50:3, Kraft—followed here—takes "The Spirit" as also a title of a poem or hymn. V omits the entire sentence.

h. For "on her garment (en stolē)," M. J. Schwartz (in Philonenko, Sem 18 [1968] 56) in-

geniously conjectures "in her epistle" (en epi stolē). The proposal has in its favor the provision of a book corresponding to the "Hymns of Kasia" (49:3) and the "Prayers of Amaltheia's Horn" (50:3). But the conjecture may be unnecessary. Philo (Vita cont 29) speaks of hymnic composition by the Therapeutae using the same term (charattō). The existence of mystically engraved gems pertaining to 3rd-cent. Gnosticism is well known (cf. C. Bonner, Studies in Magical Amulets [Ann Arbor, 1950] pp. 1–21). So are the "garments of glory" prepared for such persons as Isaiah (AscenIs 9:2–11); Metatron (3En 12:1); and Enoch (2En 22:8). Most interesting is the line in Hekhalot Rabbati 24, where God is described as "glorified with embroideries of songs" (hmhwdr brkmy syr; cf. G. Scholem, Jewish Gnosticism [New York, 1965²] p. 26; cf. p. 128 and n. to p. 26). Scholem (p. 24) also calls attention to AZ 24b, where animals addressing the ark sing a hymn containing the line describing the throne as "girdled in golden embroidery." Finally, Hekhalot Rabbati 3.4 says of God's garment, "And it is every part engraved from within and from without JHWH JHWH." These and other comparatively inaccessible texts grouped by Scholem disclose a motif of the "garment of God," sometimes said to be inscribed. While these sources are late (3rd. cent. A.D.), it may be possible to see in Hemera's inscribed skirt a development of early Merkabah traditions already present in 4QŠirŠabb 37–40.

49 a. Probably this is another title of a poem. Possibly "the creation of the heavens" was one of the various subjects of mystical inquiry featured in Merkabah mysticism.

b. Cf. Ps 71 (72):20, "the hymns of David, son of Jesse."

50 a. See n. f to 39.

b. The meaning is unclear. S omits the title in quotes. P obscurely adds "of Hemera." "Trace" (lit. "footprint") might mean (so Kraft) "poetic rhythm."

c. "Amaltheia's Horn," latinized then anglicized to "Cornucopia," is widely used as a book title, ancient and modern. But the 2nd-cent. A.D. grammarian Aulus Gellius expressly rejected this title for his own miscellany called Attic Nights (praefatio 6).

Epilogue (51–53)

Nereus' literary activity

1,2 **51** After the three had stopped singing hymns,[a] •while the Lord was present as
was I, Nereus,[b] the brother of Job, and while the holy angel[c] also was present, 53:1
3 I sat near Job on the couch. And I heard the magnificent things,[d] while each one
4 made explanation to[e] the other. •And I wrote out[f] a complete book of most of the 40:14
contents of hymns that issued from the three daughters of my brother, so that these
things would be preserved. For these are the magnificent things of God.

Job's death, soul ascent, and burial

1 **52** After three days, as Job fell ill[a] on his bed (without suffering or pain, however, 47:7
since suffering could no longer touch him on account of the omen of the sash he
2,3 wore), •after those three days he saw those who had come for his soul.[b] •And rising 5,6,8; 47:11
4 immediately he took a lyre[c] and gave it to his daughter Hemera. •To Kasia he gave 14:1f.
5 a censer,[d] and to Amaltheia's Horn he gave a kettle drum, • so that they might 32:8
6 bless those who had come for his soul. •And when they took them, they saw the 2
7 gleaming chariots[e] which had come for his soul.[f] •And they[g] blessed and glorified 33:9　2
God[h] each one in her own distinctive dialect.

8 　After these things the one who sat in the great chariot got off and greeted Job 33:9
9 as the three daughters and their father[i] himself looked on, though certain others

---

51 a. Here and at 51:4, as well as 52:12 (cf. 18:2:
songs of victory taught by the angel), the products
of the daughters' glossalalic speeches are described
as hymns, although they are called "prayers" at
50:3. What singing angels sound like, which presumably those using their language would resemble,
can be gauged from 2En 17:1 J: "In the middle of
the heaven, I saw armed troops, worshiping the
LORD with tympani and pipes, and unceasing
voices, and pleasant [voices and pleasant and
unceasing] and various songs which it is impossible
to describe. And every mind would be quite astonished, so marvelous and wonderful is the singing
of these angels. And I was delighted listening to
them."
　b. The shift back to first person (as TJob 1:4–
45:4)—but now to Nereus—affects at least 51:1–
4 and 53:1–4. See nn. i to l and a to 46. The
name "Nereus" is a Gk. mythological deity.
Nereus, sometimes said to be the oldest of the
gods, was an apt choice for the name of an oracular
recorder, since this god himself was said to have
had the gift of prophecy (Horace, *Carmina* 1.15).
Like Job, the god Nereus had daughters, the fifty
(number varies) Nereids, whose names were recorded. Like Satan, Nereus could transform himself
into many shapes (fire, water, etc., Apollodorus
2.5.11). Paul knew a Christian of this name at
Rome (Rom 16:15). Nereus is called Nahor (Naōr)
at TJob 1:6 S V Slav, where he is made a brother
to Esau by S and a brother to Job by V.
　c. Perhaps the same angel as the one who met
Job earlier, TJob 5:2 (cf. 18:5). P speaks here of
"the Holy Spirit," while V omits the whole phrase.
　d. See n. a to 38. V adds so as to read "the
magnificent things of the three daughters of my
brother."
　e. The translation is uncertain; possibly, "made
signs to each other," or "noted things down for
each other" (so Kraft).
　f. 2En knows of books written by angels (22:11)

and—at the angel's dictation—by Enoch (23:6; cf.
Rev 2:1 and Rom 16:22). 4Ezra 14:42, on the
other hand, has five men writing in unfamiliar
letters what Ezra himself uttered under inspiration.
In TJob, however, it is Nereus himself who takes
the literary initiative, even though both the Lord
and the "holy angel" (or, "Holy Spirit"?) were
present.

52 a. See n. d to 1.
　b. Regularly called angels by V (52:5, 6, 8;
47:11).
　c. According to 14:1f., Job had a ten-stringed
lyre with which he entertained the widows after
dinner.
　d. A censer as Job had in earlier days of glory
(32:8).
　e. The ascent of Job's soul is not unlike that
said of Enoch, where, however, there is no death
involved and no soul/body separation: 3En 6:1,
"When the Holy One, blessed be he, desired to
lift me up on high, he first sent 'Anaphiel H [H =
tetragrammaton], the Prince, and he took me from
their midst in their sight and carried me in great
glory upon a fiery chariot with fiery horses, servants
of glory. And he lifted me up to the high heavens
together with the Shekinah" (trans. H. Odeberg,
3 Enoch [Cambridge, 1928] p. 19). Biblical accounts of the ascensions of Enoch (Gen 5:24) and
Elijah (2Kgs 2:11) no doubt inform such descriptions. Similar also is Abraham's death, ascent, and
burial as told in TAb 20A.
　f. S omits "they saw the gleaming chariots
which had come for his soul."
　g. S has Job himself blessing God "in the
distinctive dialect," cf. TJob 40:2: "I [Job] sang
praises to the Father."
　h. Only S reads "God."
　i. Or, Father? Presumably Job, but see 52:12
and n. j to 47.

10 did not see.[j] •And taking the soul he flew up, embracing it, and mounted the chariot   42:3   33:9
11 and set off for the east.[k] •But his body, prepared for burial, was borne to the tomb   40:3   40:12
12 as his three daughters went ahead girded about and singing hymns to God.[l]   40:2

1 **53** And I Nereus, his brother, with the seven[a] male children accompanied by the   51:1   1:2
2 poor and the orphans[b] and all the helpless, we were weeping •and saying: 40:13

"[c]Woe to us today! A double woe!   39:6
Gone today is the strength *of the helpless!*   Job 29:15f.
3   Gone is the light *of the blind!*
Gone is *the father* of the orphans!
Gone is the host of strangers![d]
Gone is the clothing of widows!
4   Who then will not weep over the man of God?"

5   And as soon as they brought the body to the tomb, all the widows and orphans
6,7 circled about •forbidding it to be brought into the tomb. •But after three days they
8 laid him in the tomb in a beautiful sleep, •since he received a name renowned[e] in   4:6
all generations forever. AMEN.[f]

j. It was a property of the charismatic sash (47:11) that gave the daughters access to the vision. Restriction of the vision of the assumption also appears in an earlier, Gk. form of the AsMos (in Clement of Alexandria, *Strom* 6.15), where only Joshua and Caleb witness the sight. In the finally edited form, Moses' assumption is not mentioned and he dies in the presence of all the people, AsMos 1:15. Cf. 2Kgs 2:10–12; 6:17.

k. Where his former ten children already were. See n. b to 40.

l. S V Slav have "to God." P reads "hymns of the(ir) father."

53 a. S Slav omit.

b. The poor also made lamentation for Sitis (40:13). The mourners included those aided by Job's philanthropy (TJob 9–15; e.g. 9:3).

c. Cf. the lament for Sitis at 40:13f. The language of Job 29:15 LXX informs this lament: "I was the eye of the blind, the feet of the lame. I was a father to the weak. I tracked out a cause not my own." The lament contains numerous echoes of the earlier celebration of Job's philanthropy (TJob 9–15).

d. The texts read variously, including or combining such ll. as "Gone is the way of the heart," "Gone is the shelter/clothing of the naked," "Gone

is the protector of widows."

e. The angel's promise is fulfilled.

f. In place of the "Amen" with which P ends, S V provide longer endings close in content to Job 42:16 LXX. Noteworthy is the contrast between the *future* tense of Job 42:17a LXX ("And it is written that he will again rise with those whom the Lord raises up") and the *past* tense of TJob 53:8 V ("And it is written that he was raised up with those whom the Lord raised up"). Slav has a distinctive ending: "And Job lived after his plague and his sufferings 170 years. And the whole span of his life was 248 years. And he saw his sons and grandsons and great-grandsons, to the third generation. Do not believe his enemies forever, for just as honey makes wine bitter, so is his deceitfulness. And if he humbles himself before you and bows, make firm your heart and beware of him and guide him over yourself. Do not place him higher than yourself, lest he seek out your seat. And when you announce your thoughts to him with your own lips, your enemy will call you blessed, but in his heart he thinks of throwing you into a ditch. Your enemy sheds tears before you, but in his heart he thinks of drinking your blood. Glory be to our God forever. Amen." (Translation kindly supplied by J. Kolsti.)

TESTAMENTS OF THE THREE
PATRIARCHS

INTRODUCTION

BY E. P. SANDERS

The works that now bear the titles "The Testament of Abraham," "The Testament of Isaac," and "The Testament of Jacob" apparently spring from an apocryphal book, written in Greek during the first century by a Jewish author in Egypt, which dealt with the death of Abraham, his tour of the inhabited world, and his view of the judgment. It is no longer possible to ascertain the history of the story in Jewish usage, but it would appear that the story about Abraham developed into two distinct recensions before it was appropriated by Christians. The Testament of Isaac and the Testament of Jacob are derivative from the Testament of Abraham, perhaps being written to round out the stories of the deaths of the three patriarchs, and they were apparently written in that order: The Testament of Isaac refers to Michael's being sent to Abraham (2:1), as well as to the story of Abraham's death (8:1), while the Testament of Jacob refers to the commemoration of the deaths of both the other two patriarchs (1:2; 8:1). In addition, as the marginal references will make clear, the Testament of Jacob echoes many of the themes of the Testament of Isaac. As they now stand, the latter two testaments contain more Christian elements than the Testament of Abraham in either recension; but it cannot be said with certainty whether they were originally composed by Jews or Christians.

It is certain, however, that eventually all three were Christianized and became the exclusive property of the Church. They were for some centuries immensely popular in Christianity, as may be seen both from their wide distribution and from the influence of the Testament of Abraham on later Christian writing and art.

Because of the derivative and often repetitive character of the Testament of Isaac and the Testament of Jacob, principal interest attaches to the Testament of Abraham, which will receive a fuller introduction and notes than do the other two testaments.

TESTAMENT OF ABRAHAM

(First to Second Century A.D.)

A NEW TRANSLATION AND INTRODUCTION

BY E. P. SANDERS

The events preceding the death of the patriarch Abraham form the setting for the testament that bears his name. When it is time for Abraham to die, God sends the archangel Michael to inform him to prepare for death and to make a will. It is hoped that Abraham will voluntarily surrender his soul to Michael. Abraham, however, is recalcitrant and refuses to go, requesting first to be shown all the inhabited world. After consulting with God, Michael conducts Abraham on such a tour. Abraham, seeing people engaged in various sins, calls down death upon them, but God tells Michael to stop the tour; for he, unlike Abraham, is compassionate and postpones the death of sinners so that they may repent. Abraham is then conducted to the place of judgment to witness the fate of souls after they depart from their bodies, so that he may repent of his severity. He learns that souls are tried in three ways: by fire, by record, and by balance; and he learns that there are three judgments: by Abel, by the twelve tribes of Israel, and, finally, by God. Abraham intercedes on behalf of a soul that is judged to be neither wicked nor righteous and, repenting for his former harshness, he then pleads on behalf of those whom he had caused to die. God saves the former and restores the latter. Abraham is taken back home, but he still declines to surrender his soul. God finally sends Death, who shows Abraham his ferocity and who at last takes his soul by a deception. The soul of Abraham is conducted to heaven by angels.

Texts

The Testament of Abraham exists in two basic forms, a longer form, attested by several Greek manuscripts and supported on the whole by a Rumanian version (TAb A), and a shorter form, attested by several Greek manuscripts and supported on the whole by the Slavonic version, a Rumanian version, and by the Coptic, Arabic, and Ethiopic versions (TAb B).[1] The best witnesses for each of the two forms are the Greek manuscripts, although the versions are useful in shedding light on various points.[2] There are several minor and two major differences between the two Greek recensions, but it is likely that they have a common ancestor.

The only published critical text of the two recensions of the Testament of Abraham is that of M. R. James,[3] and the present translation is based on his text, taking into account some of the major variants. In his recent thesis, F. Schmidt has argued strongly that, for the shorter recension, manuscript E, which was not known to James, provides the best Greek text. The notes to B give special attention to the readings of E, a typed copy of which was kindly provided by Schmidt.

---

[1] The most complete discussion of the texts and versions is that by F. Schmidt, *Le Testament d'Abraham: Introduction, édition de la recension courte, traduction et notes*, vol. 1, pp. 1–20. See also A.-M. Denis, *Introduction*, pp. 32–34; M. Delcor, *Le Testament d'Abraham*, pp. 5–24. Delcor misstates the relationship of the northern versions, Slavonic and Rumanian, to the Gk. recs. on p. 23, although he describes it accurately on p. 16.

[2] Schmidt (*Le Testament d'Abraham*) has shown that one of the Slavonic versions is an important supporter of what may be the best MS of TAb B, Gk. MS E.

[3] M. R. James, *The Testament of Abraham*.

James based his text primarily on the following manuscripts:
A (the long recension)
MS A: Paris, Bibl. Nat. Fonds Grec 770, fols. 225^v–241^r, dated A.D. 1315.
MS B: Jerusalem, Saint Sepulcri 66, dated in the fifteenth century.
B (the short recension)
MS A: Paris, Bibl. Nat. Fonds Grec 1613, fols. 87^v–96^v, dated in the fifteenth century.
Now to be especially noted is MS E: Milan, Abrosienne Grec 405, fols. 164^r–171^r, dated in the eleventh or twelfth century.

Scholarly opinion is divided on the relative antiquity of the two forms of the Testament of Abraham.[4] With regard to the story, the Testament of Abraham B differs from the Testament of Abraham A in two major ways: First, in B Abraham's view of the judgment is before his tour of the world, not after; second, in B the judgment scene itself is much less fully described. Instead of the elaboration of A (three means of judgment; three judgments), there is only the story of the condemnation of a woman who was a heinous sinner. The style and vocabulary of B are simpler and less verbose than that of A. There are also fewer late words and fewer places where Christian influence is probable.[5]

The first editor of the Greek recensions, M. R. James, was of the opinion that A best represents the contents and order of the original composition, while B sometimes preserves earlier wording.[6] In spite of the difficulties inherent in any complicated solution, this still seems to be the soundest conclusion. But even though it is best to conclude that the contents and order of the original are better preserved in A, James's other point must also be emphasized: B lacks most of the late words of A in its present form, some of which are not evidenced before the fifth century A.D., and B lacks most of A's evidence of Christian influence.[7] The story itself is not substantially Christianized; the Messiah, or the Son of Man, or Christ, for example, does not appear in the judgment scene. The present form of A, however, does show some instances of Christian editing, such as a few verbal dependencies on the New Testament, and these are almost entirely absent from B. (See "Relation to canonical books.")

Although there are numerous differences among the various Greek manuscripts that support each recension, the difference between the two recensions is even more strongly marked, and it is necessary to postulate a separate *Vorlage* for each of them. These two *Vorlage* themselves probably have a common ancestor, but neither appears to be directly dependent on the other. The existence of an ultimate common ancestor is indicated not only by the general similarity of the story line but also by the high degree of verbatim agreement between the two recensions in some chapters and occasional striking verbatim agreements even in the sections where the order of events differs.[8] On the other hand, the existence of two separate intermediate ancestors is indicated by the consistency in style, syntax, and vocabulary within each recension.[9]

It appears that there was originally a book about Abraham that contained approximately the *contents* of the Greek Testament of Abraham A in the order given there. It was rewritten in at least two principal recensions, each one of which was translated into different languages and copied in Greek without close concern for exactitude. The later copyists were presumably Christians, with the result that some Christian phraseology crept into A and a Christian doxology was added to both recensions (so all MSS except E of rec. B). Different manuscripts and versions were Christianized to different degrees, but no thoroughly systematic Chris-

---

[4] It is debatable whether or not TAb A and TAb B are directly or indirectly related and even whether there is an original behind either or both of them. See R. A. Kraft, SCS 6, pp. 121–37. The present proposal is for an indirect and complicated relationship between the two recs. and for a common ancestor at some remove from the extant witnesses.

[5] The most thorough examination of the vocabulary of TAb and of parallels with the NT is that of N. Turner, *The Testament of Abraham: A Study of the Original Language, Place of Origin, Authorship, and Relevance*. See esp. pp. 242–48 on date of vocabulary, and pp. 14–48 on Christian influence.

[6] James, *Testament*, p. 49; so also G. H. Box, *The Testament of Abraham*, p. xiii; Delcor, *Le Testament d'Abraham*, p. 33; G. W. E. Nickelsburg, SCS 6, p. 92. Nickelsburg convincingly argues the case in favor of the priority of the story as it appears in A. See also n. b to B10 below.

[7] These points have been emphasized in the theses of Turner and Schmidt; cf. Nickelsburg, SCS 6, p. 92.

[8] The amount and the significance of verbatim agreement between the two recs. have been underestimated. See e.g. Kraft, SCS 6, pp. 123, 126 (citing Turner).

[9] A few of the details that support these two generalizations will be given in the nn. to the translations.

tianizing of the document was carried out, since it is still easily recoverable as a Jewish document. The precise *wording* of the original cannot be ascertained, although frequently it may be better represented by B.[10]

Original language

Among early scholars, L. Ginzberg and K. Kohler favored a Hebrew original of the Testament of Abraham, while G. H. Box maintained that the work was originally Palestinian and may have had a Semitic original, even though the present Greek does not read like a translation. N. Turner agreed with Box's view with regard to recension A, but argued that B was a translation from Hebrew, written not in Palestine but in Egypt. Schmidt has accepted the hypothesis of a Hebrew original for B.[11] Of the scholars mentioned, only Turner systematically and in detail tried to establish a Hebrew original for one of the recensions.[12] It is noteworthy that he first modified his position to the view that a Hebrew original is only slightly more likely than the alternative (that B was written in "Jewish Greek");[13] and he has now kindly indicated to the present writer that he "cannot believe either recension to be a translation."[14]

M. Delcor is the principal exponent of the view that the original was written in Greek.[15] He cites the closeness of much of the language to the later, or Alexandrian, books of the Septuagint and regards the Semitisms as being "Septuagintalisms." Delcor, however, based his study primarily on A. Turner had already noted that A shows knowledge of the Septuagint of Genesis, although he considered that B does not; and also that A, but not B, has "a strong linguistic similarity with 2, 3, 4 Maccabees."[16] Thus there is no dispute about the language of A: It is not based directly on a Hebrew original and it does reflect Alexandrian Greek. There is still, however, the question of B: Is the language, besides being simpler, also indicative of a Hebrew original?

The only weakness in Turner's original analysis points the way to the solution of the problem. He meticulously dated the Greek of both recensions (See "Date"), but not the Hebrew of his retroversion.[17] B can, for the most part, be smoothly translated into Hebrew, but it is the classical Hebrew of the early narrative sections of the Bible that emerges, not any form of late Hebrew as known from the late canonical books, the Dead Sea Scrolls, and rabbinic literature.

Thus what we have in B, and occasionally also in A, is an imitation of the classical biblical prose style, which the author doubtless thought was appropriate to his theme. The question of whether this sort of Jewish Greek existed as a spoken language among Jews of

---

[10] Although A contains more late words than B, and clearer evidence of Christian influence, it also has more terminological affinity with other Jewish literature of Egyptian provenance, as the nn. to the translation will show. The language of A cannot always be considered later than that of B, and room for conjecture as to the original wording will remain. The verbatim agreements between the two recs. should afford the best evidence for the original vocabulary and style.

[11] Schmidt, *Le Testament d'Abraham*, vol. 1, p. 120.

[12] No one has proposed an Aram. original, and Turner's study shows that the Semitisms are Hebraisms rather than Aramaisms. See his *The Testament of Abraham*, p. 57.

[13] Turner, "The 'Testament of Abraham': Problems in Biblical Greek," *NTS* 1 (1954/55) 222f.

[14] Letter of November 24, 1976. The reason for the change in Turner's view since he wrote his thesis in 1951 is that, in his comprehensive studies of the syntax and grammar of biblical Gk. (see n. 18 below), he repeatedly found the same Semitizing style that marks the Testament of Abraham, especially rec. B. In a further note to the present writer, dated November 10, 1977, he wrote in part, "I now think that books written freely in 'biblical Greek' were relatively representative phenomena among Jews and Christians who had tasted the influence of the synagogue and knew the Greek versions of the Bible very well . . . Like Professor Sanders I would think that both recensions were more likely to have been composed in this dialect of Greek than to have been literally rendered from a *Vorlage*; that the Semitic idioms had already infused the dialect known to the author, who was not consciously translating nor even thinking in one language and writing in another."

[15] Delcor, *Le Testament d'Abraham*, p. 34: written in Gk. in Alexandria. Cf. E. Janssen, "Testament Abrahams" (*JSHRZ* 3 [1975]) 193–256; see pp. 198–200: written in Gk. in Palestine.

[16] Turner, *NTS* 1 (1954/55) 221, summarizes the detailed demonstration in his thesis. In favor of the use of LXX in B, however, see the agreements noted in B2, nn. b, c; B5, n. a.

[17] A similar problem exists in the study by R. A. Martin, "Syntax Criticism of the Testament of Abraham," *SCS* 6, pp. 95–120. Many of the control texts used for establishing the characteristics of translation Gk. are the LXX translations of *classical* Heb.

the period is a large topic that cannot be broached here,[18] but the occurrence of the imitation· or partial imitation, of the classical biblical style in literary works composed in Greek ca· be well documented,[19] and this seems to be the best solution to the problem of the style o· B. It would be possible to imitate the classical style in Hebrew, but there are no clea· instances of such an imitation, even when biblical themes are being dealt with in lat· apocalypses.

It was earlier noted that there is extensive verbatim agreement between the two recensions· which in general seem to have had separate histories of transmission, and this fact argue· strongly in favor of Greek as the language of the original composition.[20] When we add t· this evidence the observation that the habit of composing in Semitizing Greek was widespread· the best conclusion is seen to be that both recensions had Greek originals.

Date

Estimates of the date of the Testament of Abraham have ranged very widely and for goo· reason. There are no references to historical events, the doctrines of the book are not databl· to any narrow historical period, and even the language of the work does not present a sur· criterion, since, on the one hand, it is doubtful that we have the original language; and, o· the other, B is written in a style partly imitative of classical biblical prose. James, wh· regarded the work as Christian, thought that it must have been later than the Apocalypse o· Peter[21] and earlier than Origen: "That it was written in the second century, that it embodie· legends earlier than that century, and that it received its present form perhaps in the nint· or tenth century, seems . . . a sufficiently probable estimate."[22] Turner's original estimat· of the date of the book was much earlier. He regarded it as having been written in Egyp· before the Septuagint was translated or in wide use, and when at least some Jews still spok· Hebrew. He dated the Greek translation represented by B to c. 200–165 B.C. and tha· represented by A to a period not much later, though perhaps as late as the second centur· A.D., with some late additions.[23] Schmidt, who regards the work as Palestinian, compose· in Hebrew in either Essene or related circles, dates the original to the first half of the firs· century A.D.[24] He argues that, since the Testament of Abraham is concerned with onl· individual eschatology, it must come after 4 Ezra, where both individual and collective o· national eschatology are matters of concern. Apart from the fact that it is impossible t· suppose that there was a steady progression from national eschatology to a mixture of nationa· and individual eschatology to purely individual eschatology,[25] the argument that the Testamen· of Abraham comes after 4 Ezra is itself in conflict with the pre-50 date, since 4 Ezra mus· be dated after the destruction of the Temple in A.D. 70.

On the assumption that the original work was written in Greek and comes from Egyp· (See "Provenance"), it is possible to make a reasonable conjecture of the date on the basi· of general considerations. It is doubtful if Egyptian, especially Alexandrian, Judaism wa· sufficiently intact after A.D. 117 to allow the production of such literature,[26] especially · work like the Testament of Abraham, which does not distinguish Jew from gentile in th· judgment. On the other hand, it is unlikely that the work is very early. It combines genre· and motifs that must have been known to the author from other literature: some aspects o·

---

[18] Most recently, see N. Turner, *A Grammar of New Testament Greek IV: Style* (Edinburgh, 1976) p. 7, and furthe· references there.

[19] For examples from Lk, ProtJames, Acts of Pilate, see E. P. Sanders, *The Tendencies of the Synoptic Traditio·* (Cambridge, 1969) pp. 200–02, 226, 228.

[20] Turner's original view, *The Testament of Abraham*, pp. 242–48, that A and B are independent translations, doe· not account for the verbatim agreement between them. Considering the gross differences between A and B, the degre· of verbatim agreement is remarkable and points toward a Gk. original.

[21] James's hypothesis about ApPet as a source for many traditions in TAb and elsewhere (*Testament*, p. 23) wa· not borne out when fragments of the lost work were subsequently found.

[22] James, *Testament*, p. 29.

[23] Turner, *The Testament of Abraham*, pp. 242, 248.

[24] Schmidt, *Le Testament d'Abraham*, p. 120.

[25] Note, for example, the late (3rd cent. or later) story of R. Joshua b. Levi (*BHM*, vol. 2, pp. 48–51) and th· still later apocalypse of Elia (*BHM*, vol. 2, pp. 65–68), where the expectation of Israel's victory over the gentiles i· the messianic time appears.

[26] For the date, see V. Tcherikover, *Hellenistic Civilization and the Jews* (Philadelphia, 1959) p. 356 and n. 65· where further references are given.

the testament genre, the "ascension" or heavenly tour genre, and the motif of resistance to death apparently borrowed from the Moses traditions. (See below.) Further, there is a concern, assuming that A preserves the original contents, to bring into one picture the different images of the judgment: fire, balance, and written records. It seems best to assume a date for the original of c. A.D. 100, plus or minus twenty-five years. The work was rewritten by more than one hand, and A in particular shows the traces of late redactional activity. The redactional activity that imparted to A, and to a lesser extent to B, late words and traces of New Testament passages, however, must be distinguished from the rewriting that produced the ancestors of the two recensions. If the late redactional activity had extended to rewriting, it would doubtless also have resulted in a pronounced Christianizing of the text, especially the judgment scene.[27] Despite being repeatedly copied by Christian scribes, the Testament of Abraham in both recensions remains unmistakably Jewish.

Provenance

If the Testament of Abraham is regarded as having been originally written in Greek, the most likely place of origin is Egypt.[28] The evidence for this may be summarized as follows: The vocabulary, especially of A, shows strong similarity to that of the late books of the Septuagint and to other Jewish books written in Greek in Egypt (e.g. 3Mac); the motif of the weighing of souls is most closely paralleled in late Egyptian depictions; the three levels of judgment may reflect the three levels of government in Egypt. These arguments are decisive only for recension A. Since it appears that the story as it is found in A, especially the account of the judgment scene, more accurately reflects the ultimate common ancestor (see above, n. 6, and references there), it is best to postulate Egyptian provenance for the original story. Recension B is as lacking in definite signs of its place of origin as it is in definite indications of its date. It would be reasonable to assume that the story was redacted where it first circulated, in Egypt, but there is nothing that would decisively rule out other Jewish centers in the Mediterranean basin.

In the discussion of provenance it is instructive to consider the connections between the Testament of Abraham and other Jewish literature. The closest parallels, both in terms of some of the major motifs and in terms of details, are to be found in the Testament of Job, 3 Baruch, 2 Enoch, and the Apocalypse of Moses. Some scholars have argued that each of these works originates from Egypt. The Egyptian origin of most of them (TJob is the exception) is now questioned.[29] If such works as 3 Baruch and the Apocalypse of Moses do not come from Egypt, their close resemblance to some aspects of the Testament of Abraham would seem to indicate the degree to which themes, motifs, and ideas "floated" around the Mediterranean world. In any case, as will be shown in more detail in the notes to the translation, there are more parallels between the Testament of Abraham and the works just named than between it and any other grouping of more or less contemporary literature.[30]

There have been repeated attempts to find a connection between the Testament of Abraham and one of the Jewish parties named by Josephus, particularly the Essenes. Ginzberg hesitated

---

[27] Thus even if the judgment scene in A is not original, it is still Jewish and comes from A.D. 100.

[28] Turner, even when arguing for a Heb. original, proposed Egypt as the country of origin, while Schmidt, who favors a Palestinian provenance for the original, considers A to be the result of an Egyptian redaction. See Turner, *The Testament of Abraham*, pp. 177–85; Schmidt, *Le Testament d'Abraham*, pp. 119–21. Janssen (*JSHRZ* 3, pp. 198f.) proposed Gk. composition and a Palestinian origin, but the latter rests on very weak grounds, e.g. that the interest in Mamre shows "palestinian coloring" (p. 199). The phrase "oak of Mamre" is derived from the LXX; see A1 n. a. For arguments in favor of Egyptian origin, see also Delcor, *Le Testament d'Abraham*, pp. 28–32, 59–62, 67f.

[29] In favor of the Egyptian origin of ApMos, see A.-M. Denis, *Introduction*, p. 6; on 2En (the long rec.), see J. H. Charlesworth, *PMR*, p. 104; on 3Bar, see J. C. Picard, *PVTG* 2, pp. 77f.; on TJob, see M. Philonenko, "Le Testament de Job," *Sem* 18 (1968) 24. For the latest views see the introductions to each work in the present edition.

[30] There are numerous parallels with regard to details in rabbinic and other Heb. and Aram. literature, but many of them are in late material; and, when the vast size of this material is considered, the proportion of parallels is seen to be relatively small. Kohler ("The Pre-Talmudic Haggada II: The Apocalypse of Abraham and its Kindred," *JQR* 7 [1895]) exaggerated the degree to which motifs of TAb are paralleled in rabbinic literature. Thus, for example, the passages referred to on p. 593 as showing that "the Midrash . . . preserved the memory of Abraham's ride above the vault of heaven" (GenR 48, 82) are not really to the point. Further, in considering the relation of TAb to rabbinic sources, the different and even contradictory motifs in the latter should be noted: E.g. Abraham was the first to dispose of his property in his lifetime (TanBub Noah 20, vol. 1, p. 47), a motif that is directly opposite one of the themes of TAb.

on whether to attribute the Testament of Abraham to the Pharisees or Essenes, while Kohler definitely attributed it to the Essenes. Recently Schmidt has called it "a writing springing from a popular Essenism,"[31] while Delcor also sees a link with Essenism, and concludes that the Testament of Abraham may come from the Therapeutae.[32] Kohler's evidence could now be dismissed were it not for the fact that recent scholars cite him as having shown that both the Testament of Abraham and the Testament of Job have Essene traits and continue to consider his outmoded list of Essene characteristics as accurate. Kohler's view of Essenism was eccentric in his own time[33] and now should be considered completely discredited; his finding of Essene "traits" (hospitality, cosmopolitanism, an emphasis on angels and the like) in the Testament of Abraham should no longer be cited as evidence for an Essene origin of the work.

Kohler mentioned that the eschatology of the Testament of Abraham was Essene without specifying why he came to this conclusion.[34] Recently Schmidt has argued that it is Essene because of the clear distinction between body and soul, a distinction Josephus attributes to the Essenes.[35] The evening prayers (B4:5),[36] the mention of a divine chariot, the elaborate angelology, and the mention of the "River Ocean" (B8:3)[37] have also been cited as showing some connection with Essenism. None of these points is convincing. Josephus also attributes belief in the immortality of the soul to the Pharisees, adding that they believed in the transmigration of souls (*War* 2.163). Josephus' comments demonstrate two points: First, supposing that his description is accurate, belief in the immortality of the soul was not peculiarly Essene; and, second, his attribution of a doctrine of transmigration to the Pharisees should make one cautious about relying very strictly on his descriptions. Morning and evening prayers are common in Judaism, and one learns more about merkabah ("chariot") speculation from rabbinic literature than from the Dead Sea Scrolls. A developed angelology is common in Judaism, and the angels of the Testament of Abraham have no particularly Essene traits.[38] Finally, in the Testament of Abraham, at least in B, Abraham lives in a city (B3:2), which would seem to rule out a connection with Philo's Therapeutae, who were strictly non-urban dwellers.[39]

The most important observation is that the Testament of Abraham, far from presenting the particular doctrines of some Jewish sect, represents a kind of lowest-common-denominator Judaism. In some ways its most characteristic feature is its characterlessness; it lacks peculiar traits.

Historical importance

The Testament of Abraham, along with 2 Enoch and 3 Baruch, bears witness to the existence of a universalistic and generalized Judaism, in which "good works" consisted of such obvious virtues as charity and hospitality, coupled with avoidance of obvious moral sins—murder, adultery, and robbery—and according to which all people, whether Jew or gentile, are judged according to how well they observe these ethical requirements. The Torah

---

[31] Schmidt, *Le Testament d'Abraham*, vol. 1, p. 120.

[32] Delcor, *Le Testament d'Abraham*, pp. 69–72.

[33] Kohler, for example, equated the *hasidim* ("pious") of rabbinic literature with the Essenes and thus greatly extended the range of "Essene traits." See Kohler, *JQR* 7 (1895); countered by A. Büchler, *Types of Jewish-Palestinian Piety from 70 B.C.E. to 70 C.E.: The Ancient Pious Men* (London, 1922). Kohler further thought that "Essenism" was represented by such leading rabbis of the post-Essene period as R. Eliezer the Great and R. Ishmael (*JQR* 7 [1895]), and he attributed to the Essenes the trait of universalism, just the opposite of the sectarianism that we now know was the characteristic of the sect. Kohler is still cited, however, as having shown the Essene traits of TAb and TJob by such modern scholars as Delcor, Schmidt, and Philonenko.

[34] Kohler, *JQR* 7 (1895).

[35] Schmidt, *Le Testament d'Abraham*, vol. 1, pp. 54f., referring to *War* 2.7. 154–58 and other passages such as 4Ezra 7:78. He must also then consider 4Ezra as related to Essenism (p. 55a).

[36] Schmidt, *Le Testament d'Abraham*, pp. 82f.

[37] Delcor, *Le Testament d'Abraham*, pp. 70f. Josephus, when describing the Essenes (*War* 2.155), writes, "Sharing the belief of the sons of Greece, they maintain that for virtuous souls there is reserved an abode beyond the ocean" (trans. H. Thackeray, LCL). Josephus clearly has in mind the Gk. "Isles of the Blessed," and it is precarious to see here vocabulary used by Essenes themselves. Delcor also refers to 3Bar 2:1: "A river which no one can cross," which shows how widely spread the supposed Essene influence must be on his hypothesis.

[38] On angelology, see recently A. Kolenkow, SCS 6, pp. 153–62.

[39] See Philo, *Vita cont* 18–20.

and the covenant of Israel seem to play no role. The Testament of Abraham is one of the few witnesses, and thus a very important one, to the existence in Egypt of a form of Judaism that stressed neither the philosophical interpretation of Judaism, as did Philo, nor the need to retain strictly the commandments that set Jews apart from gentiles, as did the author of Joseph and Asenath. Judaism is depicted here as a religion of commonplace moral values, which nevertheless insists both on the strictness of God's judgment and on his mercy and compassion.

Theological importance

The most striking feature of the Testament of Abraham is the one that has just been noted: the lowest-common-denominator universalism of its soteriology. This feature was especially noted by Kohler, who spoke of the work's "cosmopolitan humanity."[40] Other commentators have noted the universalism of the work but have not seen it as a particularly striking feature.[41] The principal component parts of the lowest-common-denominator universalistic soteriology are these: First, there is no distinction between Jew and gentile. The only reference to Israel is the one in A13:6, which mentions the judgment by the twelve tribes; this implies a special role for Israel, but Israel's importance is not developed and does not inform the rest of the book. Abraham looks down on the sins of "the inhabited world," (A10:1; cf. B12:12, "all the creation"); it is the souls of all mankind which will be judged, the descendants of Adam, not of Abraham or Jacob (A11:9; B8:12f.). The vast majority of Jewish documents provide a special place for Israel in the divine economy, either restricting salvation to Israel,[42] providing for the future restoration of the twelve tribes,[43] or allowing that some righteous gentiles will be saved along with faithful Israelites;[44] but in any case making a clear distinction.[45] The works that most closely parallel the universalism of the Testament of Abraham are 2 Enoch and 3 Baruch.[46] Second, the sins mentioned in the Testament of Abraham are heinous by anyone's definition; and no specifically Jewish transgressions, such as hiding circumcision, transgressing the Sabbath or the dietary laws, and the like, are mentioned—not even idolatry, which is condemned in 2 Enoch 10:6 and 3 Baruch 13:4. Third, everyone is judged by the same standard, whether the majority of his deeds be good or evil, and even Abraham's intercessory prayer is not specified as being for his descendants.[47] One hears nothing about the merits of the patriarchs aiding their descendants, God's forgiving observant Jews on the Day of Atonement, or anything of the sort. Fourth, the only means of atonement mentioned are repentance and premature death. Repentance plays a principal part in any Jewish work dealing with sin and atonement, and there are good rabbinic parallels for the idea that death, especially premature death, atones. Those whom God punishes by death will not be further punished.[48] But again this is not applied in the Testament of Abraham to those in the covenant, who need only to repent or be sufficiently punished in order to retain their share of the covenant promises; the atoning efficacy of repentance and premature death applies equally to all. This universalism stands in sharp contrast to the strong emphasis on converting to Judaism in the Egyptian work

---

[40] Kohler, *JQR* 7 (1895).

[41] Cf. Turner, *The Testament of Abraham*, pp. 149f. Turner saw the universalism as supporting an early date, since he thought that it soon disappeared from Judaism.

[42] E.g. AsMos 10:7f.; R. Eliezer in tSanh 13:2; JosAsen 8:5; 9:2; 15:3, 7f.; perhaps Philo: See Sanders, "The Covenant as a Soteriological Category and the Nature of Salvation in Palestinian and Hellenistic Judaism," *Jews, Greeks and Christians*, R. Hamerton-Kelly and R. Scroggs, eds. (Leiden, 1976) pp. 26–38.

[43] E.g. AsMos 4:6f.; Philo, *Praem* 162–72; 4Ezra 13:39f.

[44] E.g. R. Joshua in tSanh 13:2; ApAb 22; perhaps 1En 108:11 (note "those who were born in darkness").

[45] Note, for example, the prohibition of intermarriage: TJob 45:3; JosAsen 7:6; earlier, Jub 30:7.

[46] In 3Bar there is no clear distinction between Jews and gentiles. The lists of vices, for example, are quite general, although idolatry is mentioned (13:4). In 2En, note such phrases as "all the souls of mankind, however many are born" (23:4; cf. 43:1); race of Adam (30:15); *no one* shall escape notice in the day of judgment (46:3); *whoever* accepts and obeys (48:6–9). There are, however, some motifs that are more distinctly Jewish: sacrifices atone (59:2; but cf. 45:1–3); "upper Jerusalem" as a name for heaven (55:2). One can find a few other sentences in Jewish materials that put "all the children of the world" or "all nations" on equal terms at the end. See 1En 10:21; 91:14 (J. T. Milik, ed., *The Books of Enoch* [Oxford, 1976] p. 267).

[47] Contrast the prayer of Moses in AsMos 11:17; 12:6.

[48] E.g. Mek Bahodesh 7 (Lauterbach, vol. 2, pp. 249–51) and parallels; mYoma 8.8; SifNum 4 (Horovitz, 7). See E. P. Sanders, *Paul and Palestinian Judaism* (London, Philadelphia, 1977) pp. 159, 172–74.

Joseph and Asenath, or the emphasis on loyalty to the dietary laws in 4 Maccabees (see 1:33; 13:2), or Philo's insistence on the importance of being in the commonwealth of Israel,[49] or the repetition in the Testament of Job and even 2 Enoch of the significance of the Temple sacrifices.[50] Further, since Abraham is the subject, it is remarkable that nothing is said about proselytism, since Abraham was known as the first proselyte.[51]

Numerous other theological characteristics should be noted. The emphasis on judgment on the basis of deeds (A12f.; B9f.) is standard, both in Jewish and Christian literature,[52] although the literal depiction of it in the Testament of Abraham is unique. The efficacy of repentance and God's merciful inclination to delay the death of sinners until they repent are noteworthy, and the delay of death to allow for repentance is perhaps a unique motif.[53] God is the final judge, although recension A differs from most Jewish and Christian literature in interposing two prior levels of judgment. God can be directly prayed to and is directly concerned with men's conduct, although he uses angels as intermediaries. Michael, as often elsewhere, is the chief intermediary. Two angels not mentioned elsewhere are named: Dokiel, who weighs, and Puriel, who tests by fire. The idea that the soul separates from the body at the time of death, and that it is the soul that goes either to salvation or punishment, is relatively widespread. Recension A does not, as do some documents, explicitly provide for the future resurrection of the body and the reunion of body and soul, although B7:16, where the resurrection is mentioned, does imply such a reunion (see A20 n. h).

Since it appears likely that one of the main purposes of the original author was to describe the judgment scene (see "Genre and relation to other Jewish and Christian literature"), and thus to indicate on what basis all individuals would gain either life or punishment, this theme deserves further comment. As has been noted, the soteriology of A is simple: If sins not repented of or punished by premature death prior to the judgment outweigh or outnumber righteous deeds, the soul is sentenced to punishment. If righteous deeds predominate, the soul goes to life. If they are equally balanced, the implication of A14:6 seems to be that the balance can be tilted in favor of life by intercessory prayer. God is merciful and desires that sinners repent, but if they deserve punishment, he is righteous and will punish. All this is straightforward, and most of these themes are common in Jewish materials. The author's particular contribution is in having everyone, Jew or gentile, judged on the same basis and in describing the judgment concretely. The author brought together in graphic form three traditional images of judgment, although they are not actually harmonized or assigned separate roles in the testing of deeds. The operative means of testing appears to be the enumeration of deeds written in a book.

Further, the author harmonized three levels of judgment: the judgment of individual souls immediately after death, the traditional nationalistic theme of the judgment of gentiles by Israel (or of the wicked by the righteous), and the final apocalyptic judgment by God.

In both these cases—the presentation of three modes of judgment and the presentation of three levels of judgment—the author is reconciling separate traditional motifs, but the harmony is only pictorial and is not based on a systematic explanation of how the harmonization works.

---

[49] *Virt* 219 (on proselytes who join the [Jewish] commonwealth, which is "full of true life and vitality"). Cf. the importance of being initiated into the mysteries of Moses, *Virt* 178.

[50] TJob 15:9; 42:6–8; cf. 2En 59:2; 62:1.

[51] Delcor, *Le Testament d'Abraham*, p. 36, thinks that the reference to Abraham's hospitality implies his activity in proselytism, citing a rabbinic Midrash to that effect. Cf. Schmidt (*Le Testament d'Abraham*, vol. 1, p. 120). What is striking about TAb is that *proselytism is not mentioned at all;* nor is there need to refer to it, since all the race of Adam is judged by the same standard.

[52] E.g. Rom 2:13; 2Cor 5:10; Mt 25:31–46. For the theme of weighing deeds in Paul and Palestinian Jewish literature, and an argument to the effect that "weighing" does not, as it does in TAb, constitute soteriology in other literature, see Sanders, *Paul and Palestinian Judaism*, pp. 128–47, 515–88, 543.

[53] See A10:14 and n.

[54] The full evidence was set out by Turner; see n. 5 above. When one takes into account the probable date of composition, the late redactional activity, and the full evidence of the dependence of TAb on the NT in at least three places, it becomes impossible to accept the view of C. W. Fishburne, "ICor. iii 10–15 and the Testament of Abraham," *NTS* 17 (1970) 109–15, that Paul used TAb A13:13. Fishburne did not have access to Turner's study, nor did he note the numerous late elements in TAb A.

Relation to canonical books

Almost nothing of the Old Testament appears in the Testament of Abraham except the obvious references to Abraham in Genesis (see A1:5; 3:6; 4:11; 6:4; 8:5–7; see also 13:8; 11:12; B2:8–10; 6:10–13; see also 5:1). Recension A, as we now have it, has been influenced by the wording of the New Testament in at least three places (see A11:2, 10f.; 13:13 and nn.).[54] Recension B may also have been influenced by the wording of Matthew 7:13,[55] although the image of two gates probably does not depend on Matthew.

Genre and relation to other Jewish and Christian literature

The Testament of Abraham is not properly a testament.[56] Michael, at God's behest, instructs Abraham to make testamentary disposition of his goods, but no testament is made and there are no last words of advice to his son, although Isaac figures in the story. Nor is there any direct paraenesis, although the value of doing good works and avoiding evil is made prominent. The tour of earth and the view of the judgment are related to numerous other views of heaven, hell, the afterlife, and the like, which are usually called "apocalypses" or "ascensions." The third principal part of the work concerns Abraham's reluctance to die and a description of how his soul is taken. There are parallels to this motif, especially in stories about Moses.

The purpose of the book appears to be this: The author was concerned to present the judgment scene, in order to stress the value of good works, the efficacy of repentance, and God's justice and mercy, and in order to reconcile and depict the various images of judgment—by fire, balance, and deeds written in books. He chose as his medium a narrative that plays on the testamentary motif in order to provide an introduction: Michael goes to Abraham to advise him that it is time to draw up a will in view of his impending death. The author employs the theme of resisting death, borrowed from Moses traditions, as the *occasion* of Abraham's being given a tour of earth and subsequently a view of the judgment. Thus the judgment scene is central, and the other two principal motifs are employed to introduce it and provide a setting for it.

The only real connection with the testamentary literature is the emphasis on one virtue. Just as Job exemplifies endurance and charity, Abraham exemplifies hospitality.

The reluctance of the seer to die, as well as the connection of this motif with a vision, probably comes from Moses traditions. The exegetical base for the connection between resistance to death and revelations about the world to come seems to be Deuteronomy 34:1–4, which the earliest Midrashim interpret thus: God shows Moses "all the land" in compensation for not letting him enter, *after Moses had protested the restriction.* The rabbis understand the vision of the land to include its historical future: Moses saw the Temple and "the whole land" from the time of creation until the resurrection of the dead; while "the city of palm trees" (Deut 34:3) is understood to mean that Moses saw Paradise and the righteous leisurely strolling in it.[57] The Mekilta also mentions in this connection that God showed Abraham the land and some of its future history.[58] In later Midrashim, Moses is depicted as having been given a tour of heaven and hell, conducted by angels.[59] It may be that the motif of Michael's coming for Abraham's soul is also dependent on Moses traditions, and it is likely that a now lost "Assumption of Moses" told of Michael's being sent to bury Moses, Satan's opposition, and Michael's victory.[60] There is a twofold scene of Moses' disposition: His soul is taken to heaven and his body buried.[61] Moses' protest of death and his being given a view of the other world have a better exegetical grounding and are more widespread than the story about Abraham, and it is likely that Moses traditions influenced the Testament of Abraham.

---

[55] See B8 n. e.

[56] See recently Nickelsburg, SCS 6, pp. 85–88; A. Kolenkow, SCS 6, pp. 139–52.

[57] SifDeut 357 (to 34:1f.).

[58] Mek Amalek 2 (Lauterbach, vol. 2, pp. 151–54).

[59] See GedMos; "The Revelation of Moses," by M. Gaster, repr. in *Studies and Texts* (Jerusalem, 1971; ET first published 1893) pp. 125–41.

[60] See S. E. Loewenstamm, "The Death of Moses," SCS 6 (1976) p. 208: ". . . in all the midrashim that recognize the participation of the angels in the burial of Moses, Michael, the guardian angel of Israel, occupies the leading role."

[61] Clement, *Strom* 6.5. It is not unlikely that these Moses traditions also influenced the stories about Adam and Eve in ApMos.

There are, however, other stories about Abraham's being conducted on a heavenly tour or being shown a vision of the afterlife. In connection with the promise to Sarah (not, it is to be noted, in connection with Abraham's death), Pseudo-Philo wrote that God showed Abraham a vision of the place of fire for punishing the wicked and the torches for enlightening the righteous.[62] On the occasion of the sacrifice mentioned in Genesis 15:17 (again, not his death), the Apocalypse of Abraham 15–29 describes a heavenly tour in which Abraham sees the seven heavens and some historical events. There is a similar story in Targum Neophiti at the same point.[63] There are numerous other stories of ascensions and heavenly tours, but it still appears most likely that the author, in connecting a *protest against death* with a *heavenly tour*, was principally indebted to the Moses traditions.[64]

The heavenly tour of the Testament of Abraham must be distinguished from other "ascensions" and "apocalypses." It is not a tour of the different layers of heaven (usually seven), nor is it a tour of the place of repose of the righteous and the punishment of the wicked. It is a view primarily of the place of judgment to which souls go for sentencing. Thus the work lacks the paraenetic purpose of other "tour" works, which describe the awful torment of the damned and the bliss of the righteous.

The testament of Abraham is also related to works that give an account of the departure of the soul and the burial of the body, such as the Apocalypse of Moses, the Testament of Job, and the lost Assumption of Moses. Other comparisons and contrasts are cited in the notes.

Some of the themes—that angels do not eat, the heavenly tour, the departure of the soul and its ascent—are so widespread that direct influence is impossible to determine. The Testament of Abraham, however, does seem to have been used by the author of the Christian Apocalypse of Paul. Note, for example, God's repeated statement in chapters 4, 5, and 6 that his "patience bears with them until they are converted and repent" (cf. TAb A10:14; B12:13). It also appears to have been used by the author of the Christian Apocalypse of Sedrach. Other parallels are cited in the notes.

---

[62] Ps-Philo, *LAB* 23:6.

[63] See Delcor, *Le Testament d'Abraham*, p. 39. Delcor (p. 41) regards this as the point of departure for the story in TAb.

[64] In this as in many other matters it is difficult to decide whether one tradition influenced another or whether similar stories arose spontaneously. The date of the final redaction of the materials is not always decisive. In the present case, the final redaction of the materials in which the Moses stories appear is probably later than the date of the original composition of TAb. The arguments in favor in TAb's dependence on Moses traditions are as follows: The other Abraham traditions about a vision or heavenly tour do not connect it with a protest against death, while this is the standard connection in the Moses traditions; the connection of protest with tour or vision arises naturally from the biblical story of Moses' protest in Deut 34; although the earliest sources for the Moses tradition (SifDeut and Clement of Alexandria) are to be dated at the end of the 2nd cent., it is noteworthy that essentially the same tradition appears in both Palestine and Egypt; finally, Clement was drawing on an early (but now lost) work, while the exegesis of Deut 34:1 in SifDeut almost certainly antedates the final redaction of SifDeut.

BIBLIOGRAPHY

Charlesworth, *PMR*, pp. 70–72.
Delling, *Bibliographie*, pp. 166f.
Denis, *Introduction*, pp. 31–39.

EDITIONS: THE GREEK TEXT

James, M. R. *The Testament of Abraham: The Greek text now first edited with an introduction and notes.* T&S 2.2; Cambridge, 1892. (The edition contains W. E. Barnes's appendix, which gives in ET extracts from all three testaments in the Ar. version.)
Schmidt, F. *Le Testament d'Abraham: Introduction, édition de la recension courte, traduction et notes.* (Unpublished doctoral dissertation, University of Strasbourg, 1971, 2 vols.)
Stone, M. E., trans. *The Testament of Abraham: The Greek recensions.* T&T 2; Pseudepigrapha Series 2; Missoula, Mont., 1972. (A reprint of James's text with ET on facing pp.)

EDITIONS: ANNOTATED TRANSLATIONS

Box, G. H. *The Testament of Abraham.* TED; London, 1927.
Craigie, W. A. "The Testament of Abraham . . .," *ANF*, vol. 10, pp. 183–201. (The introduction and nn. are quite brief, but the two recs. are conveniently printed in parallel cols.)
Delcor, M. *Le Testament d'Abraham: Introduction, traduction du texte grec et commentaire de la recension grecque longe, suivie de la traduction des Testaments d'Abraham, d'Isaac et de Jacob d'après les versions orientales.* SVTP 2; Leiden, 1973. (This is the most nearly complete edition. Information on the most important editions and translations of the non-Gk. versions is given on pp. 15–22.)
Janssen, E. "Testament Abrahams," *JSHRZ* 3 (1975) 193–256.

GENERAL

Nickelsburg, G. W. E., Jr., ed. *Studies on the Testament of Abraham,* rev. ed. SCS 6; Missoula, Mont., 1976.
Turner, N. *The Testament of Abraham: A Study of the Original Language, Place of Origin, Authorship, and Relevance.* (Unpublished doctoral dissertation, London, 1953.)
————. "The 'Testament of Abraham': Problems in Biblical Greek," *NTS* 1 (1954/55) 219–23.

TESTAMENT OF ABRAHAM

Recension A

1 **1** Abraham lived the measure of his life, 995 years. All the years of his life he
lived in quietness, gentleness, and righteousness, and the righteous man was very
2 hospitable: •For he pitched his tent at the crossroads of the oak of Mamre[a] and bSot 10a
welcomed everyone—rich and poor, kings and rulers, the crippled and the helpless,
friends and strangers, neighbors and passersby—(all) on equal terms did the pious,
3 entirely holy, righteous, and hospitable Abraham welcome. •But even to him came
the common and inexorable bitter cup of death and the unforeseen end of life.
4 Therefore the Master God called his archangel Michael[b] and said to him, "Commander-in-chief[c] Michael, go down to Abraham and tell him about his death, so
5 that he may arrange for the disposition[d] of his possessions. •For I have blessed him
as the stars of heaven and as the sand by the seashore, and he lives in abundance,
(having) a large livelihood and many possessions, and he is very rich.[e] But above
all others he is righteous in all goodness, (having been) hospitable[f] and loving until
6 the end of his life. •But you, archangel Michael, go to Abraham, my beloved
7 friend,[g] announce his death to him, and give him this assurance, •'At this time you
are about to leave this vain world and depart from the body, and you will come
to your own Master[h] among the good.' "

1 **2** So the Commander-in-chief left the presence of God and went down to Abraham
at the oak of Mamre, and he found the righteous Abraham in the nearby field,
sitting beside yokes of plow oxen with the sons of Masek[a] and other servants,
2 twelve in number. And behold the Commander-in-chief came toward him. •When
Abraham saw the Commander-in-chief Michael coming from afar, in the manner
of a handsome soldier, then Abraham arose and met him, just as was his custom
3 to greet and welcome all strangers.[b] •And the Commander-in-chief saluted him
and said, "Hail, honored father, righteous soul elect of God, true friend of the
4 heavenly One." •And Abraham said to the Commander-in-chief, "Hail, honored
soldier, bright as the sun and most handsome, more than all the sons of men. Well
5 met! •Therefore I ask your presence whence has come your youthfulness of age.[c]
Teach me, your suppliant, whence and from what army and from what road your
6 beauty has come here." •The Commander-in-chief said, "Righteous Abraham, I
come from the great city. I have been sent from the great king to provide for the

---

1 a. In both recs., "oak" is always singular and
"Mamre" is treated as an adjective, as in LXX
Gen 18:1, both points in contrast to the Heb.

b. Michael as head of the angels and God's
principal messenger to men: ApMos 3:2; 13:2; 22:1;
Rev 12:7; perhaps AsMos 10:2; cf. Dan 12:1, especially Theodotion.

c. Gk. *archistratēgos;* a common title in A but
not B: See B14, n. b. The title is apparently Egyptian
Jewish: See also 3Bar 11:6; 13:3; 2En 22:6; 33:10
(both in MS A); JosAsen 14:7; GkApEzra 1:4; 4:24.
It appears to originate in the title LXX gives to the
sword-bearing man who is captain of the Lord's
army in Josh 5:13–15.

d. "Arrange for the disposition" is *diataxetai,*
the verb consistently used in A. See also 4:11; 8:11;
15:1. The verb does not appear in B: Note *dioikēsē*
(1:3) and *diatithēmi* (7:17).

e. Gen 22:17 is taken to refer to Abraham's
wealth rather than his descendants; so also 4:11.

The quotation is in precise agreement with LXX.

f. Gk. *philoxenos.* On *philoxenia* as the principal virtue, cf. ApPaul 27.

g. Isa 41:8LXX, "whom I loved"; Heb., "my
friend"; cf. also 2 Chron 20:7. On Abraham as the
friend *(philos)* of God: Jas 2:23; ApAb 9, 10; Philo,
Sobr 56 (adding "my friend" to Gen 18:17).

h. Gk. *despotēs* as a title for God: Gen
15:2, 8 LXX; and frequently in LXX.

2 a. Masek as proper name: Gen 15:2 LXX; contrast the Heb.

b. Cf. Heb 13:2: "And remember always to
welcome strangers, for by doing this, some people
have entertained angels without knowing it"; see
Gen 18:1f.; Tob 5:5–12:22; Homer, *Odyssey*
17.485f.; Ovid, *Metamorphoses* 8.626f.

c. Apparently, "you"; cf. "your presence,"
"your beauty."

7 succession of[d] a true friend of his, for the king summons him." •And Abraham said, "Come, my lord, go with me as far as my field." And the Commander-in-
8 chief said, "I am coming." •And so they went and sat in the plowed field beside
9 the company. •Abraham said to his servants, the sons of Masek, "Go to the herd of horses and get two gentle and tame horses, well broken, so that I and this
10 stranger may ride." •And the Commander-in-chief said, "No, my lord Abraham, do not let them bring horses, for I abstain from ever sitting on a four-footed animal.
11 For is not my king rich with great possessions, having authority over both men and every kind of beast?[e] But I abstain from ever sitting upon a four-footed animal.
12 Let us go then, righteous soul, walking in high spirits until (we reach) your house." And Abraham said, "Amen; let it be so."

,2 **3** As they were leaving the field in the direction of his house, •beside the road
3 there stood a cypress tree. •And by the command of God the tree cried out in a human voice and said, "Holy, holy, holy is the Lord God who is summoning him
4 to those who love him."[a] •Abraham hid the mystery, thinking that the Commander-
5 in-chief had not heard the voice of the tree. •Then they came near the house and sat in the courtyard. And when Isaac saw the face of the angel he said to Sarah his mother, "My lady mother, behold: The man who is sitting with my father
6 Abraham is no son of the race which dwells upon the earth." •And Isaac ran and did obeisance[b] to him and fell at the feet of the incorporeal one. And the incorporeal one blessed him and said, "The Lord God will bestow upon you his promise which   Gen 12:1-7; he gave to your father Abraham and to his seed, and he will also bestow upon   22:17
7 you the precious prayer[c] of your father and your mother." •Then Abraham said to Isaac his son, "Isaac, my child, draw water from the well and bring it to me in the vessel so that we may wash this stranger's feet; for he is tired, having come
8 to us from a long journey." •And so Isaac ran to the well and drew water into
9 the vessel and brought it to them. •Then Abraham went forward and washed the feet of the Commander-in-chief Michael. Abraham's heart was moved and he
10 wept over the stranger. •When Isaac saw his father crying, he also cried. When
11 the Commander-in-chief saw them crying, he too wept with them; •and the Commander-in-chief's tears fell to the vessel, into the water of the basin,[d] and
12 they became precious stones. •Abraham saw the wonder and was astonished, and he picked up the stones secretly and hid the mystery, keeping it in his heart alone.

1 **4** Then Abraham said to Isaac his son, "My beloved son, go into the guest room[a] and beautify it. Spread out for us there two couches, one for me and one for this
2 man who is staying as our guest today. • Prepare for us there a dining couch and a lampstand and a table with an abundance of everything good. Beautify the chamber, my child, and spread linens and purple cloth and silk[b] underfoot. Burn every valuable and prized incense, and bring fragrant plants from the garden to
3 fill our house. •Light seven lamps filled with oil so that we may make merry,

---

d. "Provide for the succession of": *diadochēn . . . komizomenos;* so also Schmidt. Box, Craigie, and Stone: "To take the place of"; Delcor: "Porteur d'une invitation." Delcor's translation gives a satisfactory translation of the participle, but neither translation makes good sense of *diadochēn.* The meaning apparently is that Michael's assignment is to encourage Abraham to make testamentary dispositions; see 1:4; 4:11; 8:11; 15:1.

e. In 2:10f. the words for "animal" and "beast" are *zōon* and *ktēnos* respectively. The same two words appear in B2:5, 12, in a different context and where there is little verbatim agreement.

3 a. The meaning is not completely clear, but it is probably "is summoning Abraham to be with those who love God." So Box.

b. Gk. *proskuneō*, which can vary in significance from "worship," "prostrate oneself before," and the like, to "salute." It is understood here in the stronger sense. Cf. Gen 18:2, where Abraham prostrates himself before the angels.

c. Gk. *euchē*, "prayer or vow," but usually "vow" in LXX. Gen mentions no relevant *euchē*, but cf. Jub 22:6–9, where Abraham prays for his descendants.

d. Gk. *niptēr*, for which LSJM cites only Jn 13:5.

4 a. Gk. *to tameian tou triklinou*, lit. "chamber with three couches." *Triklinos* is subsequently used for individual rooms and is translated "room."

b. Gk. *byssos*: LSJM: "flax," the linen made from it; Indian cotton; silk.

because this man who is staying as our guest today is more honorable than kings
4 and rulers; for even his appearance surpasses all the sons of men." •Isaac prepared
everything well. And Abraham, taking along the archangel Michael, went up to
the guest chamber, and they both sat on the couches, and he placed between them
5 a table with an abundance of everything good. •Then the Commander-in-chief rose
up and went outside, as if he needed to urinate; and he ascended into heaven in
6 the twinkling of an eye and stood before God and said to him: •"Master, Lord,[c] let
your might know that I cannot announce the mention of death to that righteous
man, because I have not seen upon earth a man like him—merciful, hospitable,
righteous, truthful, God-fearing, refraining from every evil deed. And so now
7 know, Lord, that I cannot announce the mention of death." •Then the Lord said,
"Michael, Commander-in-chief, go down to my friend Abraham, and whatever
he should say to you, this do;[d] and whatever he should eat you also eat with him.
8 And I shall send my holy spirit upon his son Isaac, •and I shall thrust the mention
of his death into Isaac's heart, so that he will see his father's death in a dream.
Then Isaac will relate the vision, you will interpret it, and he himself will come
9 to know his end." •And the Commander-in-chief said, "Lord, all the heavenly
spirits are incorporeal, and they neither eat nor drink.[e] Now he has set before me
a table with an abundance of all the good things which are earthly and perishable.
And now, Lord, what shall I do? How shall I escape his notice while I am sitting
10 at one table with him?" •The Lord said, "Go down to him, and do not be concerned
about this. For when you are seated with him I shall send upon you an all-devouring
spirit, and, from your hands and through your mouth, it will consume everything
11 which is on the table. Make merry with him in everything. •Only interpret well
the things of the vision, so that Abraham will come to know the sickle of death
and the unforeseen end of life, and so that he might make arrangements for the
disposition of all his belongings; for I have blessed him more than *the sand of the
sea* and *as the stars of heaven.*"[f]

1 **5** Then the Commander-in-chief went down to the house of Abraham and sat with
2 him at table, while Isaac served them. •When the supper was finished, Abraham
prayed, according to his custom, and the archangel prayed with him. Then they
3 rested, each on his couch. •Isaac said to his father, "Father, I too should like to
rest with you in this room, so that I too might hear your conversation. For I love
4 to hear the distinction of speech of this man who has every virtue." •But Abraham
said, "No, my son, but go to your own room and rest on your couch, so that we
5 should not become burdensome to this man." •Then Isaac received the blessing
from them and blessed them, and he went to his own room and rested on his
6 couch. •Then God thrust the mention of death into Isaac's heart as in a dream.
7 And around the third hour of the night Isaac woke up and rose from his couch and
8 went running up to the room where his father was asleep with the archangel. •Then
when Isaac reached the door he cried out saying, "Father Abraham, get up and
open (the door) immediately for me, so that I can come in and hang on your neck
9 and kiss you before they take you from me." •Then Abraham arose and opened
10 (the door) for him. Isaac entered, hung upon his neck, and began to cry in a loud
voice. •Then Abraham's heart was moved, and he too cried with him in a loud
11 voice. When the Commander-in-chief saw them crying he too cried. •Then Sarah,
who was in her tent, heard their crying and came running to them. She found them
12 embracing and crying. •And Sarah said with tears, "My lord Abraham, what are
13 you crying about? Tell me, my lord. •Did this brother who is staying as our guest

---

c. Gk. *despota kyrie*: Gen 15:2, 8 LXX; and
elsewhere.

d. Cf. Ma'aseh d'R. Joshua b. Levi, *BHM*, vol.
2, p. 48, top.

e. Angels neither eat nor drink: DeutR 11:4; cf.
bYoma 4b, top; 75b (where the question is debated).
The angels who visited Abraham only pretended

to eat: GenR 48:14; TarJon Gen 18:8 (Cf. TargOnk
18:8); cf. Tob 12:19. Angels' food is distinct from
animals': *Vita* 4:2; WisSol 16:20 (=manna);
JosAsen 16:8 (= the honey that gives immortality).

f. "More than": also 8:5. Cf. "as": Gen 22:17
LXX; 1:5 above.

today bring you news about your nephew Lot, that he has died? Is it for this that
14 your mourn thus?'' •Then the Commander-in-chief answered and said to her, ''No,
sister Sarah, it is not as you say. Rather, your son Isaac, it appears, had a dream
and came to us crying, and when we saw him our hearts were likewise moved,
and we cried.''

1 **6** When Sarah heard the Commander-in-chief's distinction of speech, she im-
2 mediately realized that the speaker was an angel of the Lord. •Then Sarah beckoned
Abraham to come to the door (and step) outside, and she said to him, ''My lord
3 Abraham, do you know who this man is?'' • Abraham said, ''I do not know.''
4 Sarah said, ''You must know, my lord, the three heavenly men who stayed as
guests[a] in our tent beside the oak of Mamre when you slaughtered the unblemished　Gen 18:1-8
5 calf and set a table for them. •After the meat had been eaten, the calf got up again
and exultantly suckled its mother. Do you not know, my lord Abraham, that they
gave us Isaac, the very fruit of my womb, as was promised to us? For this man
6 is one of those three holy men.'' •Then Abraham said, ''O Sarah, you have spoken
truly. Glory and blessing from (our) God and Father! For I too, late this evening,
when I was washing his feet in the vessel (which has) the wash basin,[b] said in my
heart, 'These feet are (those of one) of the three men that I washed previously.'
7 And later when his tears fell into the basin they became precious stones.'' And
(Abraham) took them out of his bosom and gave them to Sarah and said, ''If you
8 do not believe me, look at them.'' •Sarah took them and knelt down[c] and embraced
(him) and said, ''Glory be to God who shows us wonders. And now know, my
lord Abraham, that a revelation of something is among us, whether it be evil or
good.''

1 **7** Then Abraham left Sarah and entered the room and said to Isaac, ''Come, my
beloved son, tell me the truth. What were the things that you saw and what
2 happened to you that you came running to us thus?'' •Isaac answered and began
to say, ''My lord, I saw, this night, the sun and the moon above my head, and
3 its (i.e. the sun's) rays were encircling and shedding light on me. • And while I
was thus watching and exulting at these things, I saw heaven opened, and I saw
a light-bearing man coming down out of heaven, flashing (beams of light) more
4 than seven suns. •And that sunlike[a] man came up and took the sun from my head,
and he went up into the heavens, whence also he had come. And I was deeply
5 grieved that he had taken the sun from me, •and after a little while, as I was still
grieving and anguishing, I saw that man for a second time coming down out of
6 heaven. And he took from me also the moon from my head. •And I cried greatly
and I besought that light-bearing man and I said, 'No, my lord, do not take my
glory from me. Have mercy on me and heed me. And if you do take the sun from
7 me, at least leave the moon with me.' •But he said, 'Let them be taken up to the
king above, because he wants them there.' And he took them from me, but he left
the rays with me.''
8 　　The Commander-in-chief said, ''Hear, righteous Abraham: The sun which your
child saw is you, his father. And the moon similarly is his mother Sarah. And the
light-bearing man who came down from heaven, this is the one sent from God,
9 who is about to take your righteous soul from you. •And now know, most honored
Abraham, that at this time you are about to leave the earthly life and journey to
10 God.'' •And Abraham said to the Commander-in-chief, ''O most surprising wonder
11 of wonders! And is it you, then, who are about to take my soul from me?'' •The
Commander-in-chief said to him, ''I am Michael, the Commander-in-chief who

---

6 a. The verb is *epizenizomai,* which appears here
and in B6:10, but apparently nowhere else. See
Delcor, *Le Testament d'Abraham,* p. 112, n. 1.
　b. ''Basin'' is here apparently an adjectival
genitive, ''the wash-basin-vessel.'' The only other

construction (''the vessel of the basin'') would
make the vessel (*lekanē*) a part of the basin (*niptēr*),
contrary to the obvious sense of 3:11 above.
　c. Gk. *proskuneō.* See ch. 3, n. b.
7 a. Lit. ''sun-shaped.''

stands before God, and I was sent to you that I might announce to you the mention
12 of death. And then I shall return to him just as we were commanded." • And
Abraham said, "Now I do know that you are an angel of the Lord, and you were
sent to take my soul. Nevertheless, I will not by any means follow you, but you
do whatever he commands."

1 **8** When the Commander-in-chief heard this statement, he immediately became
invisible. And he went up into heaven and stood before God and told (him)
2 everything which he saw at Abraham's house. • And the Commander-in-chief also
said this to the master, "Your friend Abraham also said this, 'I will not by any
3 means follow you, but you do whatever he commands.' • Almighty Master, what
4 do your glory and (your) immortal kingship command now?" • God said to the
Commander-in-chief Michael, "Go to my friend Abraham one more time and say
5 this to him: • 'Thus says the Lord your God, who led you into the promised land,   Ex 6:8
6 who blessed you more than *the sand of the sea* and *the stars of heaven*, • who   Heb 11:9
Gen 22:17
opened the womb of the barren Sarah and graciously granted to you Isaac, the fruit   Gen 18:11-14
7 of the womb in old age. • Truly[a] I say to you that *blessing I will bless you and*
multiplying I will multiply your seed,[b] and I will give to you whatever you ask
8 of me; for I am the Lord your God and besides me there is no other.[c] • Tell me why
you are resisting me and why there is grief in you? And why have you resisted
9 my archangel Michael? • Do you not know that all those who (spring) from Adam
and Eve die? And not one of the prophets escaped death, and not one of those who
reign has been immortal. Not one of the forefathers has escaped the mystery of
death. All have died, all have departed into Hades, all have been gathered by the
10 sickle of Death.[d] • But to you I did not send Death. I did not allow a fatal disease
to befall you. I did not permit the sickle of Death to come upon you. I did not
allow the nets of Hades to entwine you. I did not ever want any evil to come upon
11 you. • But for (your) good comfort I sent my Commander-in-chief Michael to you,
in order that you might come to know of your departure from the world and that
you might make arrangements for the disposition of your house and everything
that belongs to you, and so that you might bless Isaac your beloved son. And now
12 know that I have done these things not wanting to grieve you. • And so why did
you say to my Commander-in-chief, "I will not by any means follow you"? Why
did you say these things? Do you not know that if I give permission to Death, and
he should come to you, then I should see whether you would come or not come?' "[e]

1 **9** The Commander-in-chief received the exhortations of the Lord and went down
to Abraham. When the righteous man saw him he fell upon his face on the ground
2 as one dead, • and the Commander-in-chief told him everything which he had heard
from the Most High. Then the pious and righteous Abraham stood up and with
many tears he fell at the feet of the incorporeal one and besought (him), saying,
3 "I beg you, Commander-in-chief of the powers above, since you have thought
it altogether worthy yourself to come to me, a sinner and your completely worthless
servant,[a] I beseech you now too, Commander-in-chief, to serve me (by delivering)
4 a communication yet once more to the Most High, and say to him; • 'Thus says
Abraham your slave: "Lord, Lord, in every deed and word which I have asked
5 of you you have heeded me, and you have fulfilled my every wish. • And now,

---

8 a. *Amēn.*

b. Gen 22:17, retaining verbatim the Hebraism
from LXX. The Heb. idiom means "I will surely
bless . . ."

c. Gk. *plēn emou ouk estin allos.* Cf. Ex 20:3
and Deut 5:7, *theoi heteroi plēn emou;* Deut 4:35,
39, *ouk estin eti [allos] plēn autou;* 2En 36:1.

d. Cf. the argument with Moses, PetMos, *BHM,*
vol. 1, p. 116 bottom.

e. Cf. PetMos, *BHM,* vol. 1, pp. 127f.; DeutR
11:10: God first commands his chief angels to take

Moses' soul, but they decline because they are not
great enough. Then Sammael, the angel of death,
goes but is unsuccessful. Finally God himself takes
Moses' soul.

9 a. It is common in Jewish sources for those who
are considered "righteous" to consider themselves
unworthy in prayer or in comparison with God. See
E. P. Sanders, *Paul and Palestinian Judaism,* pp.
224–28, 266f., 291f., 375, 395, 421f.

Lord, I do not resist your might, for I too know that I am not immortal, but rather mortal. Although, therefore, at your command everything yields and shudders and
6 trembles before your power, and I too fear, yet I ask one request of you. • And now, Master Lord, heed my plea: While I am yet in this body I wish to see all the inhabited world and all the created things which you established, master, through one word;[b] and when I have seen these things, then, if I depart from life, I shall
7 have no sorrow.' ' '' •The Commander-in-chief then went again and stood before God and told him everything, saying, "Thus says your friend Abraham, 'I wish
8 to behold all the inhabited world in my life, before I die.' '' •When the Most High heard these things, he again commanded the Commander-in-chief Michael and said to him, "Take a cloud of light, and the angels who have authority over the chariots, and go down and take the righteous Abraham on a chariot of cherubim and lift him up into the air of heaven so that he may see all the inhabited world."

1 **10** And the archangel Michael went down and took Abraham on a chariot of cherubim and lifted him up into the air of heaven and led him onto the cloud, as well as sixty angels. And on the carriage[a] Abraham soared over the entire inhabited
2 world. •And Abraham beheld the world as it was that day: Some were plowing, others leading wagons; in one place they were pasturing (flocks), elsewhere abiding (with their flocks) in the fields,[b] while dancing and sporting and playing the zither; in another place they were wrestling[c] and pleading at law; elsewhere they were
3 weeping, then also bearing the dead to the tomb. •And he also saw newlyweds being escorted in procession.[d] In a word, he saw everything which was happening
4 in the world, both good and evil. •Then continuing on, Abraham saw men bearing swords, who held in their hands sharpened swords, and Abraham asked the
5 Commander-in-chief, "Who are these?" • And the Commander-in-chief said, "These are robbers, who want to commit murder and rob and burn and destroy."
6 Abraham said, "Lord, Lord, heed my voice and command that wild beasts come
7 out of the thicket and devour them." •And as he was speaking wild beasts came
8 out of the thicket and devoured them. •And he saw in another place a man with
9 a woman, engaging in sexual immorality with each other, •and he said, "Lord, Lord, command that the earth open and swallow them up." And immediately the
10 earth split in two and swallowed them up. • And he saw in another place men
11 breaking into[e] a house and carrying off the possessions of others, •and he said, "Lord, Lord, command that fire come down from heaven and consume them."
12 And as he was speaking fire came down from heaven and consumed them. •And immediately a voice came down from heaven to the Commander-in-chief, speaking thus, "O Michael, Commander-in-chief, command the chariot to stop and turn
13 Abraham away, lest he should see the entire inhabited world. •For if he were to see all those who pass their lives in sin, he would destroy everything that exists.
14 For behold, Abraham has not sinned[f] and he has no mercy on sinners. •But I made   Ezek 53:11
the world, and I do not want to destroy any one of them; but I delay[g] the death   4Ezra 8:60

---

b. Cf. 1Clem 27:4, "By the word of his majesty he established all things"; Poimandres 31, "By a word you established all things"; similarly WisSol 9:1; SibOr 3:20; Jub 12:4; and elsewhere, apparently depending on Ps 33:6. Contrast Ab 5:1, "with ten words."

10 a. The "carriage" or "vehicle" is now apparently the cloud.
b. "Abiding in the fields," *agraulountas*. The word means "live out of doors," and LSJM gives only Lk 2:8 as applying it to shepherds. Thus the usage may here depend on Lk. Most translators add "by night" or "overnight."
c. For the evidence that Jews in the Diaspora watched and perhaps participated in sports and theater, see Philo, *Ebr* 177 (theater) and passages cited

by H. A. Wolfson, *Philo*, vol. 1, pp. 80f. (although Wolfson denies their significance).
d. Gk. *opsikeuō*, "escort in procession," a late word, cited by Lampe and Sophocles, but not LSJM. Cf. also below, 20:12, where the angels escort the soul of Abraham.
e. Lit. "digging" or "tunneling"; the word appears in Mt 6:19f.; 24:43.
f. Cf. Abraham's self-description in 9:3, "a sinner."
g. "Delay . . . until," *anamenō . . . heōs*. The usual translation of *anamenō* is "await," but LSJM gives "delay" as a possibility, and this yields better sense here. So also Box. Note that B has "my heart is moved (with compassion) . . . *so that* they may convert." The Slavonic has "for they may turn from their sins and save themselves" and the Ro-

15 of the sinner until he should convert and live. •Now conduct Abraham to the first gate of heaven, so that there he may see the judgments and the recompenses[h] and repent over[i] the souls of the sinners which he destroyed."

1 **11** Michael turned the chariot and brought Abraham toward the east, to the first Gen 2:8(LXX)
2 gate of heaven. •And Abraham saw two ways.[a] The first way was *strait* and *narrow* 1En 32:2
3 and the other *broad* and *spacious*.[b] •[And he saw there two gates. One gate was broad],[c] corresponding to the broad way, and one gate was strait, corresponding
4 to the strait way. •And outside the two gates of that place, they[d] saw a man seated on a golden throne. And the appearance of that man was terrifying, like the
5 Master's. •And they saw many souls being driven by angels and being led through the broad gate, and they saw a few other souls and they were being brought by
6 angels through the narrow gate. •And when the wondrous one who was seated on the throne of gold saw few entering through the strait gate, but many entering through the broad gate, immediately that wondrous man tore the hair of his head and the beard of his cheeks, and he threw himself on the ground from his throne
7 crying and wailing. •And when he saw many souls entering through the strait gate, then he arose from the earth and sat on his throne, very cheerfully rejoicing and
8 exulting. •Then Abraham asked the Commander-in-chief, "My lord Commander-in-chief, who is this most wondrous man, who is adorned in such glory, and
9 sometimes he crys and wails while other times he rejoices and exults?" •The incorporeal one said, "This is the first-formed[e] Adam who is in such glory, and
10 he looks at the world, since everyone has come from him. •And when he sees many souls *entering through* the strait gate, then he arises and sits on his throne rejoicing and exulting cheerfully, because this strait gate is (the gate) of the righteous, *which leads to life*, and those who enter through it come into Paradise. And on account of this the first-formed Adam rejoices, since he sees the souls
11 being saved. •And when he sees *many* souls *entering through* the broad gate, then he pulls the hair of his head and casts himself on the ground crying and wailing bitterly; for the broad gate is (the gate) of the sinners, *which leads to destruction and to eternal punishment*.[f] And on account of this the first-formed Adam falls from his throne, crying and wailing over the destruction of the sinners; for many
12 are the ones who are destroyed, while few are the ones who are saved. •For among seven thousand there is scarcely to be found one saved soul, righteous and undefiled."[g]

manian "I do not desire the death of the wicked, but that he should repent and live." Cf. ApPaul 4, 5, 6 ("bear with them . . . so that"). The idea that God postpones the punishment of sins in order to allow time for repentance is relatively widespread: Rom 2:4; 3:25; WisSol 11:23; 12:10; Philo, *LegAll* III.106; cf. the rabbinic view that God postpones the deserved punishment of the world for the sake of the patriarchs (Sifra Behuqqotai pereq 8:7; to Lev 26:42). Actually delaying death is a striking development of this theme.

h. Gk. *antapodosis* may have either a negative or a positive meaning.

i. Or, "change his mind about."

11 a. Two ways: see e.g. SifDeut 53 (Finkelstein, pp. 120f.); bBer 28b; Did 1:1; J. P. Audet, *La Didachè: Instructions des apôtres* (Paris, 1958): See Audet's index under "*Duae viae*."

b. The commentators correctly note that the theme of two ways is a common feature of Jewish literature. The verbatim agreement between this passage and Mt 7:13f., however, is marked: the combination of "gate" and "way," the use of precisely the same four adjectives (*stenē, tethlimmenē, plateia,* and *eurochōros*), and the phrases that appear later in this chapter, "which leads to

life" and "which leads to destruction." The compact and balanced form of Mt could hardly have been derived from TAb; and in view of other evidence of verbatim agreement between TAb A and the NT, the dependence of the former on the latter here seems indispensable. See "Relation to Canonical Books."

c. Following James's reconstruction.

d. Or "I." Either the person or the number of the verb changes here: from *eiden* to *idon*.

e. Gk. *ho prōtoplastos;* in LXX at WisSol 7:1; 10:1. LSJM cites in addition only Philo, *Fragmenta* 61 H (= *QE* 2.46); but so also the introduction to ApMos (referring to both Adam and Eve). Cf. also Philo, *Op* 27: *En archē* (Gen 1:1) means *prōtos;* the verb *plassein* appears in Gen 2:7 LXX. *Prōtos* and *plassein* are also connected in SibOr 3:25: *ton prōton plasthenta.*

f. Apparently conflating Mt 7:13 ("that leads to perdition") and Mt 25:46 ("eternal punishment").

g. For the "many" and "few" theme, cf. Mt 22:14; 4Ezra 8:3 (so Box, Delcor). The Romanian here is more severe: one saved in 7,000 years. Cf. the sevenfold of Gk. rec. B, where the Falasha has thirteen times. Cf. the "well nigh all that have been created" of 4Ezra 7:48 and 7:68: "all the earth-born are defiled with iniquities . . ."

12 While he was yet saying these things to me,[a] behold (there were) two angels, with fiery aspect and merciless intention and relentless look, and they drove myriads [1En 56:1] 2 of souls, mercilessly beating them with fiery lashes. •And the angel seized one 3 soul. And they drove all the souls into the broad gate toward destruction. •Then 4 we too followed the angels and we came inside that broad gate. •And between the two gates there stood a terrifying throne with the appearance of terrifying crystal, 5 flashing like fire. •And upon it sat a wondrous man, bright as the sun, like unto 6,7 a son of God. •Before him stood a table like crystal, all of gold and byssus.[b] •On the table lay a book whose thickness was six cubits, while its breadth was ten 8 cubits. •On its right and on its left stood two angels holding papyrus and ink and 9 pen. •In front of the table sat a light-bearing angel, holding a balance in his hand. 10 [On] (his) left there sat a fiery angel, altogether merciless and relentless, holding a trumpet in his hand, which contained within it an all-consuming fire (for) testing 11 the sinners.[c] •And the wondrous man who sat on the throne was the one who 12 judged and sentenced the souls. •The two angels on the right and on the left recorded. The one on the right recorded righteous deeds, while the one on the left 13 (recorded) sins.[d] •And the one who was in front of the table, who was holding the 14 balance, weighed[e] the souls.[f] •And the fiery angel, who held the fire, tested the 15 souls.[g] •And Abraham asked the Commander-in-chief Michael, "What are these things which we see?" And the Commander-in-chief said, "These things which 16 you see, pious Abraham, are judgment and recompense." •And behold, the angel 17 who held the soul in his hand brought it before the judge. •And the judge told one of the angels who served him, "Open for me this book and find for me the sins 18 of this soul." •And when he opened the book he found its sins and righteous deeds to be equally balanced,[h] and he neither turned it over to the torturers nor (placed it among) those who were being saved, but he set it in the middle.[i]

13 And Abraham said, "My lord Commander-in-chief, who is this all-wondrous judge? And who are the angels who are recording? And who is the sunlike angel 2 who holds the balance? And who is the fiery angel who holds the fire?" •The Commander-in-chief said, "Do you see, all-pious Abraham, the frightful man who

---

12 a. Here the change to the first person is clear.

b. See ch. 4 n. b.

c. MSS CDE read "sins," perhaps influenced by 13:13 below, which in turn seems to have been influenced by 1Cor 3:13–15. According to the Rumanian, the fiery angel holds not a trumpet with fire, but a page on which are written temptations and sins. Rec. B and the other versions do not have the passage.

d. Judgment by deeds written in a book or books: 1En 81:1f.; SifDeut 307; Ab 2:1; bNed 22a, top; RH 16b, 32b; 2En 52:15; and elsewhere. Contrast the books of the living or the book of life: Dan 12:1; Jub 30:20–22; 1En 47:3; 108:3; and elsewhere.

e. Gk. *zugiazō*, a verb unattested in LSJM and in Sophocles. Lampe cites only its two appearances in TAbA 12, 13. The "weighing" scene appears to have led the author to use neologisms. Cf. the n. on *zugias* below.

f. The *imagery* of weighing deeds, as distinct from this graphic description of weighing *souls*, is very widespread. In Jewish literature, see e.g. 1En 41:1; 4Ezra 3:34 (of nations); 2En 52:15 (combining balance and books). See further Pearson, SCS 6, pp. 244, 249–53. On the theme in rabbinic material, see Sanders, *Paul and Palestinian Judaism*, pp. 128–47. For evidence that emphasis on the strict weighing of deeds is closer to Iranian than rabbinic thought, see D. Winston, "The Iranian Component in the Bible, Apocrypha, and Qumran," *History*

of Religions 5 (1966) 195, n. 33. The depiction of weighing souls, however, is generally considered Egyptian; see Delcor ad loc.; Schmidt, *Le Testament d'Abraham*, vol. 1, pp. 72–76 (Egyptian, somewhat altered); Turner, *The Testament of Abraham*, pp. 177–85.

g. Fire as a means of testing, as distinct from being the means of punishing sinners, is not so common a judgment theme as weighing and recording. It is, however, indicated in such passages as Ps 66:10–12 (65:10–12 LXX): "You tested us, God, you refined us like silver . . . but now the ordeal by fire and water is over." Here "test" is *dokimazō*, the word used in TAb. So also Zech 13:9; Jer 6:29; WisSol 3:6. For refining by fire, see Mal 3:2. The image of testing (*dokimazō*) by fire is picked up by Paul (1Cor 3:13–15) and in 1Pet 1:7 (cf. also 1Pet 4:12, "for a test," *peirasmos*). For refining by fire, see Rev 3:18. The theme as such is readily explicable in TAb as an independent use of the motif of testing by fire, although the precise wording in 13:13 below seems to have been influenced by 1Cor.

h. Gk. *zugias . . . ex isou:* The adjective *zugios*, "balanced" or "balancing," is not found in this meaning in LSJM or Sophocles, and Lampe gives only this reference. "Balanced" is required by the context, but MSS A and B correct the neologism. Cf. n. e above. Here there is a striking agreement with B9:8: *isozugousas*, "evenly balanced."

i. "In the middle": Cf. tSanh 13:1.

is seated on the throne? This is the son of Adam, the first-formed, who is called
3 Abel, whom Cain the wicked killed. •And he sits here to judge the entire creation, Gen 4:8
examining both righteous and sinners. For God said, 'I do not judge you, but
4 every man is judged by man.' •On account of this he gave him judgment, to judge
the world until his great and glorious Parousia.[a] And then, righteous Abraham,
there will be perfect judgment and recompense, eternal and unalterable, which no
5 one can question. •For every person has sprung from the first-formed, and on
6 account of this they are first judged here by his son.[b] •And at the second Parousia
they will be judged by the twelve tribes of Israel,[c] both every breath and every
7 creature. •And, thirdly, they shall be judged by the Master God of all; and then
thereafter the fulfillment of that judgment will be near, and fearful will be the
8 sentence and there is none who can release. •And thus the judgment and recompense
of the world is made through three tribunals. And therefore a matter is not ultimately
established by one or two witnesses, but *every matter shall be established by three
witnesses.*[d]
9   "The two angels, the one on the right and the one on the left, these are those
who record sins and righteous deeds. The one on the right records righteous deeds,
10 while the one on the left (records) sins. •And the sunlike angel, who holds the
balance in his hand, this is the archangel Dokiel,[e] the righteous balance-bearer,
and he weighs the righteous deeds and the sins[f] with the righteousness of God.[g]
11 And the fiery and merciless angel, who holds the fire in his hand, this is the
archangel Purouel, who has authority over fire,[h] and he tests the work of men
12 through fire. •And if the fire burns up the work of anyone, immediately the angel
of judgment takes him and carries him away to the place of sinners, a most bitter
13 place of punishment. •But *if the fire tests the work of anyone*[i] and does not touch
it, this person is justified and the angel of righteousness takes him and carries him
14 up to be saved in the lot of the righteous. •And thus, most righteous Abraham,
all things in all people are tested by fire and balance."

1 **14** Abraham said to the Commander-in-chief, "My lord Commander-in-chief,
2 how was the soul which the angel held in his hand adjudged to the middle?" •The
Commander-in-chief said, "Hear, righteous Abraham: Since the judge found its
sins and its righteous deeds to be equal, then he handed it over neither to judgment
3 nor to be saved, until the judge of all should come." • Abraham said [to] the
Commander-in-chief, "And what is still lacking to that soul in order (for it) to be
4 saved?" •And the Commander-in-chief said, "If it could acquire one righteous deed

---

13 a. The final judgment will be held by God
when he comes; thus the traditional view of the
judgment is combined with judgment of individuals
immediately after death. On God's coming, see
2En 32:1 (where it implies the resurrection). The
final judgment is not connected with the word
parousia in LXX, although it is linked with God's
coming; e.g. Mal 3:2, *eisodos. Parousia* (usually
of Christ) is frequently linked with judgment in the
NT: e.g. 1Thes 4:15; 1Jn 2:28; for *parousia* used
of God, see Jas 5:7; 2Pet 3:12. The term was
probably more common in Jewish literature than
can now be directly demonstrated.
  b. For the assignment of individual souls to
torment or bliss immediately after death, without
waiting for the resurrection, see ApAb 21.
  c. This brings in and modifies another traditional
motif: the judgment of *gentiles* by Israel (or of the
wicked by the righteous, in which case the righteous
could be understood as Israel): Dan 7:22 LXX: "He
gave the judgment to the saints of the Most High,"
i.e. to Israel; Jub 32:19: "They (Israel) shall judge
all the nations . . ."; WisSol 3:8: "They (the
righteous) shall judge (the) Gentiles" (*ethnē*); 1QpHab
5.4: "God will give the judgment of the Gentiles

(*goyim*) into the hands of his elect"; cf. 1QS 5.6f.;
1QH 4.26; 1QM 6.6; 11.13f.; ApAb 22:29. The
theme is applied to the disciples in Mt 19:28, which
helps attest to its existence as a Jewish theme of
judgment. The present passage in TAb is the only
reference to Israel in the work.
  d. Deut 19:15 LXX. "By the mouth of two
witnesses, and by the mouth of three witnesses,
shall every matter be established."
  e. The name is elsewhere unattested, or virtually
so. See Delcor, ad loc. Box (ad loc.) proposed a
Heb. original, *dôqî'ēl*, which would refer to exactitude (in weighing). Schmidt (*Le Testament
d'Abraham*, vol. 1, p. 75) proposed that the original
was *Ṣedeqiel*, "justice of God."
  f. Note that instead of souls (12:13), deeds are
to be weighed. See ch. 12 n. f above.
  g. Gk. *en dikaiosunē theou:* i.e. with perfect
equity. Thus Delcor: "suivant la justice de Dieu."
But Stone takes *en* to mean "by means of."
  h. Fire in Gk. is *pur*. This is apparently a gre-
cized form of *Uriel*. Cf. 1En 20:2.
  i. The italicized words are found in a different
sequence in 1Cor 3:13f.

5 more than (its) sins, it would enter in to be saved."[a] • Abraham said to the
Commander-in-chief, "Come, Commander-in-chief Michael, let us offer a prayer
on behalf of this soul and see if God will heed us."[b] And the Commander-in-chief
6 said, "Amen, let it be so." • And they offered supplication and prayer on behalf
of the soul, and God heeded them, and when they arose from prayer they did not
7 see the soul standing there. • And Abraham said to the angel, "Where is the soul
8 which you were holding in the middle?" • And the angel said, "It was saved
through your righteous prayer, and behold a light-bearing angel took it and carried
9 it up to Paradise." • Abraham said, "I glorify the name of the Most High God and
10 his boundless mercy." • Abraham said to the Commander-in-chief, "I beg you,
archangel, heed my plea; and let us beseech the Lord yet (again) and let us prostrate
11 ourselves for his compassion • and beg his mercy on behalf of the souls of the
sinners whom I previously, being evil-minded, cursed and destroyed, whom the
earth swallowed up and whom the wild beasts rent asunder and whom the fire
12 consumed because of my words. • Now I have come to know that I sinned before
the Lord our God. Come, Michael, Commander-in-chief of the powers above,
come, let us beseech God with tears that he may foreigive me (my) sinful act and
13 grant them to me." • And the Commander-in-chief heeded him and they offered
supplication before God. When they had besought him for a long time, a voice
14 came out of heaven, saying, • "Abraham, Abraham,[c] I have heeded your voice
and your supplication and I forgive you (your) sin; and those whom you think
that I destroyed, I have called back, and I have led them into life by my great
15 goodness. • For I did punish them in judgment for a time. But those whom I destroy
while they are living on the earth, I do not requite in death."[d]

1 **15** The voice of the Lord said also (to) the Commander-in-chief, "Michael,
Michael, my servant, return Abraham to his house, because behold his end is near
and the measure of his life is completed, so that he may make arrangements for 1:1;
2 the disposition of everything. And then take him and conduct him up to me." • The ApMos 13:6
Commander-in-chief turned the chariot and the cloud around and conducted Abra-
3,4 ham to his house. • And he went to his room and sat on his couch. • And Sarah his
wife came and embraced the feet of the incorporeal one and made supplication,
saying, "I thank you, my lord, for bringing my lord Abraham. For behold, we
5 thought that (he) had been taken away from us." • Isaac his son also came and
embraced his neck. Similarly all his male and female servants also surrounded
6 Abraham in a circle and embraced him, glorifying God. • The incorporeal one
said to him, "Hear, righteous Abraham: Behold your wife Sarah, behold also your
beloved son Isaac, behold also all your male and female servants around you.
7 Make arrangements for the disposition of everything which you have, because the
day has drawn near on which you are to depart from the body and once again go
8 to the Lord." • Abraham said, "Did the Lord say so, or are you saying these things
9 on your own?"[a] • The Commander-in-chief said, "Hear, righteous Abraham: The
10 Master commanded and I tell (it) to you." • Abraham said, "I will by no means

14 a. One rabbinic tradition was that God himself
would remove an iniquity in the case of one whose
deeds were balanced. See yKid 1.10 (61d); bRH
17a. And note the similar view in the Cop. Enoch
apocryphon: B. Pearson, SCS 6, pp. 244, 275.

b. Note Abraham's intercession on behalf of
Sodom, Gen 18:22–33. On intercessory prayer as
such, see AsMos 11:17; 12:6 (Moses on behalf of
Israel); Ps-Philo, *LAB* 33:5 (effective only before
death); 2En 53:1 (efficacy denied); 4Ezra 7:102–15
(intercession at the time of judgment denied). This
may be the earliest instance in Jewish sources in
which intercessory prayer is considered effective
after the death of the person on whose behalf it is
offered. From later sources, see e.g. EcclR 4:1.
See further E. E. Urbach, *The Sages* (Jerusalem,

1975) pp. 508–10 and notes. On intercession generally, see R. le Déaut, "Aspects de l'intercession
dans le Judaïsme ancien," *JSJ* 1 (1970) 35–57.

c. Note the repetition, "Abraham, Abraham"
in Gen 22:11.

d. Cf. the well-known rabbinic view that those
who are punished with suffering or premature death
in this world are considered to have been sufficiently
punished and to have atoned for their sins, so that
they are not punished in the world to come: See
Sanders, *Paul and Palestinian Judaism*, pp.
168–74.

15 a. Cf. PetMos, *BHM* vol. 1, p. 127, bottom:
Moses asks Sammael: "Who sent you . . ."

11 follow you." •When the Commander-in-chief heard this statement, he immediately
left Abraham's presence and went up into the heavens and stood before the Most
12 High God and said, •"Lord Almighty, behold I have heeded your friend Abraham
with regard to everything that he mentioned to you and I have fulfilled his request:
I showed him your power and the entire earth under heaven as well as the sea; I
showed him judgment and recompense by means of a cloud and chariots. And
13 again he has said, 'I will not follow you.' " •And the Most High said to the angel,
14 "Does my friend Abraham say still again, 'I will not follow you'?" •The archangel
said, "Lord Almighty, thus he speaks, and I refrain from touching him because
from the beginning he has been your friend and he did everything which is pleasing
15 before you. • And there is no man like unto him on earth, not even Job, the
wondrous man.[b] And for this reason I refrain from touching him. Command, then,
immortal king, what is to be done."

1 **16** Then the Most High said, "Call Death here to me, who is called the (one of)
2 abominable countenance and merciless look."[a] •And the incorporeal Michael went
and said to Death, "Come! The Master of creation, the immortal king, calls you."
3 When Death heard, he shuddered and trembled, overcome by great cowardice;
and he came with great fear and stood before the unseen Father, shuddering,
4 moaning and trembling, awaiting the Master's command. •Then the unseen God
said to Death, "Come, bitter and fierce name of the world, hide your ferocity,
cover your decay, and cast off from yourself your bitterness, and put on your
5 youthful beauty and all your glory, •and go down to my friend Abraham and take
him and conduct him to me. But I also tell you now that you may not terrify him;
but rather you are to take him with soft speech, because he is my true friend."
6 When Death heard these things he left the presence of the Most High and donned
a most radiant robe and made his appearance sunlike and became more comely and
beautiful than the sons of men, assuming the form of an archangel, his cheeks
flashing with fire; and he went away to Abraham.
7 Now the righteous Abraham (had) come out of his room and (was) seated under
the trees of Mamre, holding his chin in his hand and waiting for the arrival of the
8 archangel Michael. •And behold a sweet odor[b] came to him and a radiance of light.[c]
And Abraham turned around and saw Death coming toward him in great glory and
youthful beauty. And Abraham arose and went to meet him, thinking that he was
9 the Commander-in-chief of God. •And when Death saw him he knelt[d] before him
and said, "Greetings,[e] honored Abraham, righteous soul, true friend of the Most
10 High God, and companion of the holy angels." •Abraham said to Death, "Greetings, you who are sunlike in appearance and form, most glorious assistant, bearer
of light, marvelous man. Whence comes your glory to us, and who are you and
11 whence have you come?" •Then Death said, "Most righteous Abraham, behold,
12 I tell you the truth. I am the bitter cup of death."[f] •Abraham said to him, "No,
rather you are the comeliness of the world, you are the glory and beauty of angels
and of men, you are the best formed of all forms. And you say, 'I am the bitter
cup of death,' and do you not rather say, 'I am the best formed of everything
13 good'?" •Death said, "I am telling you the truth. What God has named me, that
14,15 I tell you." •Abraham said, "Why have you come here?" •Death said, "I have
16 come for[g] your holy soul." •Then Abraham said, "I understand what you are

b. Note that TJob comes from approximately
the same time and place as TAb. On rabbinic views
about the relationship between Job and Abraham,
see A. Büchler, *Studies in Sin and Atonement in
the Rabbinic Literature of the First Century* (London, 1929; repr. 1967) pp. 130–50.

16 a. Cf. ch. 8 n. e above.
b. Gk. *osmē euōdias*, as in Gen 8:21.
c. Gk. *phōtos apaugasma;* cf. WisSol 7:26,
apaugasma . . . phōtos aidou.

d. Gk. *proskuneō;* see ch. 3 n. b above.
e. For *chairois* instead of *chaire* to mean "greetings," "hail," cf. 3Bar 11:6f.
f. The phrase "bitter cup of death" is often
taken to reflect one of the names of the angel of
death, Sammael, "the poison of God." So Box,
ad loc.; Delcor, ad loc. For Sammael, see DeutR
11:10 (Heb.); 3Bar 4:8; 9:7 (Gk.). In PetMos
(above, ch. 8 n. e), he is called simply *Sam.*
g. Or, "on account of"; so also 18:4 below.

saying, but I will by no means follow you." And Death became silent and did not answer him a word.

1 **17** Abraham arose and went into his house, and Death followed him there. Abraham went up into his room, and Death also went up with him. Abraham 2 reclined on his couch, and Death came and sat by his feet. •Then Abraham said, 3 "Leave, leave me, because I want to rest on my couch." •Death said, "I shall 4 not depart until I take your spirit[a] from you." •Abraham said to him, "By the immortal God I say to you that you must tell me the truth! Are you Death?" 5,6 Death said to him, "I am Death. I am the one who ravages the world." •Abraham said, "I beg you, since you are Death, tell me, do you also come to all thus, in 7 pleasing shape and glory and such youthful beauty?" •And Death said, "No, my lord Abraham; for your righteous deeds and the boundless sea of your hospitality and the greatness of your love for God have become a crown upon my head. In youthful beauty and very quietly and with soft speech I come to the righteous, 8 but to the sinners I come in much decay and ferocity and the greatest bitterness 9 and with a fierce and merciless look." •Abraham said, "I beg you, heed me and 10 show me your ferocity and all your decay and bitterness." •And Death said, "You could by no means bear to behold my ferocity, most righteous Abraham." 11 Abraham said, "Yes, I shall be able to behold all your ferocity, on account of the name of the living God, because the power of my heavenly God is with me." 12 Then Death put off all the bloom of youth and beauty and all the glory and the 13 sunlike form which he had worn, •and he put on (his) robe of tyranny, and he made his appearance gloomy and more ferocious than any kind of wild beast and more 14 unclean than any uncleanness. • And he showed Abraham seven fiery heads of dragons and fourteen faces: (one of) most brightly burning fire and great ferocity, and a dark face, and a most gloomy viper's face, and a face of a most horrible precipice, and a fiercer face than an asp's, and a face of a frightening lion, and 15 a face of a horned serpent[b] and of a cobra.[c] •And he showed him also the face of a fiery broad sword and a sword-bearing face[d] and a face of lightning flashing 16 frighteningly and a noise of frightening thunder.[d] •And he showed him also another face, of a fierce, storm-tossed sea and a fierce, turbulent river and a frightening 17 three-headed dragon and a mixed cup of poisons; •and, in a word, he showed him great ferocity and unbearable bitterness and every fatal disease as of the odor of 18 death. • And from the great bitterness and ferocity, male and female servants, 19 numbering about seven thousand, died. •And the righteous Abraham entered the depression of death,[e] so that his spirit failed.

1 **18** And when the all-holy Abraham saw these things, he said to Death, "I beg you, all-destroying Death, hide your ferocity and put on the youthful beauty and 2 form which you previously had." •Death immediately hid his ferocity and put on 3 his youthful beauty which he previously had. •Abraham said to Death, "Why did you do this, that you killed all my male and female servants? Was it for the sake 4 of this that God sent you here today?" •And Death said, "No, my lord Abraham, 5 it is not as you say. Rather, I was sent here for[a] you." •Abraham said to Death, 6 "Then how did these die? Did not the Lord even say (that they should)?" •Death said, "Believe, most righteous Abraham, that it is itself a marvel that you too 7 were not carried off with them. But still I tell you the truth: •For had not the right

---

17 a. For the variation of "soul" and "spirit," cf. ApMos 13:6 (soul); 32:4 (spirit).

b. Gk. *kerastēs;* see Prov 23:32.

c. Gk. *basiliskos:* LSJM: *"kind of serpent, basilisk,* perh. *Egyptian cobra"*; Sophocles: "an imaginary reptile."

d. Each of these two pairs apparently counts as one.

e. Gk. *eis oligōrian thanatou,* "into indifference

of death." Perhaps the meaning is "entered the state of indifference produced by fear or certainty of death." The phrase apparently does not mean a "faint" (as Stone), though perhaps "faintness" (Box) is implied. Note 20:7–9 below, where, in this state, Abraham kisses Death's hand.

18 a. See ch. 16 n. g above.

hand of God been with you in that hour, you too would have had to depart from
8 this life." • The righteous Abraham said, "Now I know that I entered into the
9 depression of death, so that my spirit failed. • But I beg you, all-destroying Death,
since the servants died untimely, come, let us plead to the Lord our God that he
10 should heed us and raise those who died untimely through your ferocity." • And
Death said, "Amen, let it be so." Then Abraham arose and fell upon the face of
11 the earth and prayed, and Death with him, • and God sent a spirit of life into the
dead, and they were made alive again.[b] Then, therefore, the righteous Abraham
gave glory to God.

1 **19** And he went up into his room and lay down. And Death also came and stood
2 before him. • Abraham said to him, "Leave me, because I wish to rest; for my
3 spirit is beset with depression." • And Death said, "I shall not depart from you
4 until I take your soul." • And Abraham, with a harsh countenance and an angry
look, said to Death, "Who has commanded you to say these things?[a] You on your
own say these words, boasting; and I will by no means follow you until the
5 Commander-in-chief Michael comes to me; and I shall go with him. • But I will
say this to you: If you want me to follow you, teach me all your metamorphoses,
the seven fiery heads of the dragons, and what is the face of the precipice, and
what the sharp sword, and what the great turbulent river, and what the turbid,
6 fiercely storm-tossed sea. • Teach me too about the unendurable thunder and the
frightening lightning and what is the ill-smelling cup mixed (with) poisons. Teach
7 me concerning all (these)." • And Death said, "Hear, righteous Abraham, for
seven ages[b] I ravage the world and I lead everyone down into Hades—kings and
rulers, rich and poor, slaves and free I send into the depth of Hades. And on this
8 account I showed you the seven heads of the dragons. • And I showed you the face
of fire, since many will die burned by fire, and through the face of fire they see
9 death. • And I showed you the face of the precipice, since many men, coming down
from the heights of trees or frightening precipices, and passing out, die; and they
10 behold death in the shape of a frightening precipice. • And I showed you the face
of the sword, since many fall in wars by the sword, and they behold death in a
11 sword. • And I showed you the face of the great turbulent river, since many, being
carried off by the inundation[c] of many waters and swept away by great rivers, are
12 suffocated; and they die and see death untimely. • And I showed you the face of
the fierce, storm-tossed sea, since many, encountering a great wave at sea, are
13 shipwrecked and are (pulled) under the water and see the sea as death. • And I
showed you the unendurable thunder and the frightening lightning, since many
men, meeting in an hour of wrath unendurable thunder and frightening lightning
14 coming with a carrying off of men, become . . ., and thus they see death.[d] • I
showed you also venomous wild beasts—asps and cobras and leopards and lions
and lion cubs and bears and vipers—and in a word I showed you the face of every
wild beast, most righteous one, since many men are borne off by wild beasts,

---

b. Gk. *anazōopoieō*, a rare word and probably
Egyptian Jewish. See JosAsen 8:11; 15:4.

19 a. Cf. ch. 15 n. a above.
b. On the time limit of the world, see D. Winston, "The Iranian Component in the Bible, Apocrypha, and Qumran: A Review of the Evidence," *History of Religions* 5 (1966) 187.
c. Gk. *hypo embaseōs*.
d. As James notes, the passage is corrupt. Delcor (*Le Testament D'Abraham*, p. 170) comments, "Without changing the evidently corrupt text, the general idea seems to be the following: certain men who perish of violent death are victims of the divine wrath by reason of their sins and deserve a sudden punishment." Schmidt has considered more recent MS evidence and proposed the following for

19:13–15, which does not, however, solve all the
problems (see Schmidt, *Le Testament d'Abraham*,
vol. 1, p. 102; vol. 2, p. 122): "And I showed you
the unendurable thunder and the frightening lightning, since many men, at the hour of wrath of
dragons and asps, surprised by the coming of unendurable thunder and frightening lightning, are carried off; and thus they see death. I showed you also
venomous wild animals and asps and cobras and
leopards and lions and lion cubs and bears and in
a word I showed you the face of every wild animal,
most righteous Abraham, since many men are borne
off by wild animals; while others are snatched away
by lions; while others, being breathed on by asps,
and others by a viper, depart (life); while others
are killed by a venomous snake."

15 while others, being breathed on by venomous snakes—[dragons and asps and
16 horned serpents and cobras] and vipers—depart (life). • And I showed you also
mixed cups of noxious poisons, since many men are given poisons to drink by
other men, and they at once depart (life) unexpectedly.''

1 **20** Abraham said, "I beg you, is there also an unexpected death? Tell me."
2 Death said, "Truly, truly,[a] I tell you by the truth of God that there are seventy-two
deaths. And one is the just death which has (its appropriate) hour. And many men
3 go to death in one hour and are consigned to the grave. • Now behold, I have told
you everything that you have asked. Now I tell you, most righteous Abraham, set
aside every wish[b] and leave off questioning once and for all, and come, follow me
4 as the God and judge of all commanded me." • Abraham said to Death, "Leave
me yet a little while, that I may rest on my couch, for I feel very faint of heart.
5 For from the time when I beheld you with my eyes, my strength has failed; all
the limbs of my flesh seem to me to be like a lead weight, and my breath is very
6 labored.[c] Depart for a little; for I said, I cannot bear to see your form." • Isaac his
son came and fell upon his breast weeping. Then also his wife Sarah came and
7 embraced his feet, wailing bitterly. • Also all his male and female servants came
and encircled his couch, wailing greatly. And Abraham entered the depression of
8 death. • And Death said to Abraham, "Come, kiss my right hand, and may
9 cheerfulness and life and strength come to you." • For Death deceived Abraham.
And he kissed[d] his hand and immediately his soul cleaved to the hand of Death.
10 And immediately Michael the archangel stood beside him with multitudes of
angels, and they bore his precious soul in their hands in divinely woven linen.
11 And they tended the body of the righteous Abraham with divine ointments[e] and
perfumes until the third day after his death.[f] And they buried him in the promised
12 land at the oak of Mamre, • while the angels escorted[g] his precious soul[h] and
ascended into heaven singing the thrice-holy[i] hymn to God, the master of all, and
13 they set it (down) for the worship[j] of the God and Father. • And after great praise
in song and glorification had been offered to the Lord, and when Abraham had
worshiped, the undefiled voice of the God and Father came speaking thus:
14 "Take, then, my friend Abraham into Paradise, where there are the tents of my
righteous ones and (where) the mansions[k] of my holy ones, Isaac and Jacob, are
in his bosom,[l] where there is no toil, no grief, no moaning, but peace and exultation
15 and endless life." • [Let us too, my beloved brothers, imitate the hospitality of the
patriarch Abraham and let us attain to his virtuous behaviour, so that we may be
worthy of eternal life, glorifying the Father and the Son and the Holy Spirit: to
whom be the glory and the power forever. Amen.][m]

20 a. *Amēn, amēn.*

b. Cf. above, 9:4: "you have fulfilled my every
wish," but there were still further requests.

c. Gk. *to pneuma mou epi polu talanizetai:* The
usual meaning of the verb, in all periods, is "call
unhappy." As a seventh meaning Lampe gives
"vex, torture," citing this passage and one in
Chrysostom. The meaning appears to be otherwise
unattested. The passage should perhaps be translated "my spirit is exceedingly unhappy." The
Romanian has "my spirit is trembling within me."

d. The soul is taken by a kiss or greeted with
a kiss (in Gk., *aspazō*): TJob 52:8; ApPaul 14;
PetMos, *BHM*, vol. 1, p. 129; DeutR 11:10.

e. Angels anoint the body: ApMos 40:1

f. The third day: TJob 53:7; cf. Jn 11:6, 39;
4Bar 9:7–14. In the last case the soul returns in the
three-day period. Cf. further Winston, *History of
Religions* 5 (1966) 196 and n. 34.

g. Angels receive and escort the soul: TJob
47:11; 52:2, 5 ("creatures of God" and the like);

ApMos 33:2; PetMos, *BHM*, vol. 1, p. 129; DeutR
11:10 (in the last two, accompanying God himself);
ApPaul 14.

h. The soul is taken and the body buried: TJob
52:10f.; ApMos 32–42; Clement of Alexandria,
Strom 6:15 (apparently from the lost AsMos); by
implication in Ps-Philo, *LAB* 23:13; PetMos, *BHM*,
vol. 1, p. 129; DeutR 11:10; ApPaul 14. ApMos
41:1–3 and ApPaul 14, among others, definitely
state that at the resurrection body and soul will be
reunited, and this may be implied in TJob: See
4:9. See also TAb B7.16.

i. The *Trisagion,* based on Isa 6:3. Cf. also 1En
39:12; ApMos 40:5; bHull 91b.

j. Gk. *eis proskunēsin;* cf. ApMos 35:2, "on its
face."

k. Gk. *monai,* as in Jn 14:2.

l. Illogically, Abraham's bosom is already in
Paradise, as are his descendants. For Abraham's
bosom, see Lk 16:22f.

m. A Christian exhortation and doxology.

TESTAMENT OF ABRAHAM
Recension B

1 **1** It came to pass, when the days of Abraham's death drew near, the Lord said
2 to Michael, •"Arise and go[a] to Abraham my servant and say to him, 'You shall
3 depart from life, •because behold, the days of your temporal life are fulfilled,' so
that he may administer the affairs of his household before he dies."

1 **2** And Michael went and came to Abraham, and he found him sitting before his
oxen (used) for plowing. He was very old in appearance, and he had his son in
2 his arms.[a] •Then when Abraham saw the archangel Michael, he arose from the
3 ground and welcomed him, not knowing who he was, and said to him, •"God
4 save you! May you be well as you continue your journey!" •And Michael answered
5 him, "You are a benevolent man, good father." • And Abraham answered and
said to him, "Come, draw near to me, brother, and sit for a little while so that
6 I may command an animal to be brought, •in order that we may go to my house
and you may rest with me, because it is near evening; and you may rise early and
go wherever you wish, lest (now) an evil wild beast meet you and harm you."
7 Michael asked Abraham, saying, "Tell me your name before I enter your house,
8 lest I become burdensome to you." • And Abraham answered and said, "My
parents named me Abram, and the Lord renamed me Abraham, saying, 'Arise and
go from your house and from your family and come into a land which I shall show
9 you.'[b] •And when I left for the land which the Lord showed me, he said to me,
'Your name shall no longer be called Abram, but your name shall be Abraham.' "[c]
10 Michael answered and said to him, "Bear with me, my father, man who has been
taken thought of by God, because I am a stranger, and I heard about you when
you went apart forty stadia and took a calf and slaughtered it, entertaining angels   Gen 18:1-8
11 as guests in your house, so that they might rest." •While they were talking about
12 these things, they rose and went to the house. •Abraham called one of his servants
and said to him, "Go, bring me a beast (of burden) so that the stranger might sit
13 on it, because he is tired from walking." •And Michael said, "Do not trouble the
youth, but let us go in high spirits[d] until we reach your house, for I love your
company."

1,2 **3** And they rose and went. •And as they drew near to the city, about three
stadia away, they found a great tree, having three hundred branches, like a tamarisk.
3 And they heard a voice singing from its branches, "Holy (are you), because you
4 carried out the purpose concerning (the things for) which you were sent."[a] •And
Abraham heard the voice and hid the mystery in his heart, saying to himself,
5 "What, then, is the mystery that I have heard?" •As he came into the house,
Abraham said to his servants, "Arise and go out to the flock and bring three
lambs and slaughter (them) quickly and prepare (them), so that we may eat and
6 drink, because this day is (a day of) good cheer." •And the servants brought the

---

1 a. The verb for "go" is *poreuomai*, which is frequent in B but absent from A.

2 a. The last phrase does not appear in MS E.
b. In close agreement with Gen 12:1 LXX.
c. Virtually verbatim with Gen 17:5 LXX.
d. A: *apelthōmen . . . pezeuontes . . . meteōrizomenoi;* B: *apelthōmen meteōrizomenoi.* It is best to understand *meteōrizomenoi* as "being in high spirits," or some similar meaning (See Lampe and Sophocles), rather than as itself implying

walking ("lifting [our feet]"). Thus B makes no explicit mention of walking, and no reason for avoiding riding is given, at least in the text as printed by James. Several Gk. MSS, however, have *peripatēsōmen* for *apelthōmen*, thus solving the difficulty (so A C D E). Both the Slavonic and the Ar., which are generally closer to B than A, explicitly have the word "walk."

3 a. MS E: "Holy is the one who brings news."

lambs, and Abraham called his son Isaac and said to him, "Isaac, my child, arise and put water into the vessel, so that we may wash the feet of this stranger."
7,8 And he brought (it) as he was commanded. •And Abraham said, "I have an insight (into) what will come to pass, that in this bowl I shall not again wash the
9 feet of a man who is entertained as a guest with us." •When Isaac heard his father saying these things, he wept and said to him, "My father, what is this that you
10 say, 'It is my last time to wash a stranger's feet'?" •And when Abraham saw his son crying he also cried greatly. And Michael, seeing them crying, also cried. And Michael's tears fell into the vessel and became a precious stone.

1 **4** When Sarah heard their crying (for she was inside her house),[a] she came out
2 and said to Abraham, "My lord, why is it that you cry thus?" •And Abraham answered and said to her, "It is nothing evil. Go into your house[a] and do your own
3 work, lest we become burdensome to the man." •And Sarah departed, because
4 she was about to prepare supper. •And the sun was near setting. And Michael went outside the house, and he was taken up into the heavens to worship[b] before God;
5 for at the setting of the sun all angels worship God;[c] and the same Michael is the
6,7 first of the angels. •And all worshiped and left, each to his own place.[d] •But Michael answered before God and said, "Lord, command me to be questioned
8 before your holy glory." •And the Lord said to Michael, "Tell whatever you
9 wish." •The archangel answered and said, "Lord, you sent me to Abraham to say
10 to him, 'Depart from your body and leave the world; the Lord calls you.' •And I cannot bring myself, Lord, to be revealed to him,[e] because he is your friend and
11 a righteous man, who welcomes strangers. •But I beseech you, Lord, command
12 the mention of Abraham's death to enter into his heart, •and let me not tell it to him. For it is very curt to say, 'Leave the world,' and above all from one's own
13 body. •For from the beginning you made him to have mercy on the souls of all
14 men."[f] •Then the Lord said to Michael, "Arise and go to Abraham and stay with
15 him as a guest. •And whatever you see (him) eating, you also eat; and wherever
16 he sleeps, you also sleep there; •for I shall thrust the mention of Abraham's death into the heart of Issac his son in a dream."

1 **5** Then Michael left for Abraham's house in that evening, and he found them
2 preparing supper. And they ate and drank and made merry.[a] •And Abraham said to his son Isaac, "Arise, child, spread out the man's couch so that he may rest,
3 and place the lamp on the lampstand."[b] •And Isaac did as his father commanded.
4,5 And Isaac said to his father, "Father, I am also coming to sleep near you." •And Abraham answered him, "No, my child, lest we become burdensome to this man;
6 but go to your room and rest." •And Isaac, not wanting to disobey his father's command, went and rested in his room.

1 **6** And it came to pass, around the seventh hour of the night, Isaac woke up and went to the door of his father's house crying out and saying, "Father, open (the
2 door), so that I may enjoy (the sight of) you before they take you from me." •And Abraham arose and opened (the door), and Isaac entered and hung upon his father's
3 neck crying; and bewailing, he kissed him. •And Abraham cried with his son. And

---

4 a. MS E has "tent."

  b. Gk. *proskuneō;* see A3 n. b.

  c. The angels worship God at a set time: ApMos 7:2; 17:1; especially at sunset (ApPaul 7). Morning and evening prayers are standard in Judaism: mBer 1:1–4 (with no insistence on precise correspondence with the sun); probably implied in 1QS 10:10; Philo, *Vita cont* 27 (correspondence with sunset and sunrise).

  d. Cf. 2En A20:3f.

  e. MS E: "to reveal (the) message (*logos*) to him."

f. MS E: "for this message (*logos*) is very curt: 'Do not depart in the body.' Rather, you, Lord, from the beginning had mercy on our souls." Neither reading yields good sense: Note the "*our* souls" of MS E and "made *him* to have" of James's text.

5 a. For this sequence of verbs, see 3Ezra 9:54 LXX; Lk 12:19.

  b. MS E: "and leave a light (on) in the house." Note "tent" above, 4:1.

4 Michael saw them crying and he too cried. • And when Sarah heard the crying
5 from her bed chamber,[a] she cried out, saying, • "My lord Abraham, what is the
crying about? Did the stranger tell you about your nephew Lot,[b] that he has died?
6 Or has anything else happened to us?" •Michael answered and said to Sarah, "No,
Sarah, I did not bring news about Lot; rather, I learned about all your[c] benevolence,
7 that you surpass all who are on the earth, and God has remembered you."[d] •Then
Sarah said to Abraham, "How could you dare cry when the man of God has come
8 to you? • And how could your eyes, the fountains[e] of light, shed tears? Because
9 today is (a day of) rejoicing." •Then Abraham said to her, "Whence do you know
10 that he is a man of God?" •Sarah answered and said, "Because I declare and say
that this is one of the three men who stayed as our guests at the oak of Mamre,   Gen 18:1-8
11 when one of the servants went and brought a calf and you slaughtered (it). • And
you said to me, 'Rise, prepare, so that we may eat with these men in our house.' "
12,13 And Abraham answered and said, "You have perceived well, O wife; •for I too,
when I bathed his feet, knew in my heart that these are the feet that I bathed at
the oak of Mamre. And when I began to inquire about his journey, he said to me,   Gen 19:12f.
'I am going to protect (your) brother Lot from Sodom.' And then I knew the
mystery."

1 **7** Abraham said to Michael, "Tell me, man of God, and reveal to me why you
2 have come here."[a] •And Michael said, "Your son Isaac will disclose (it) to you."
3 And Abraham said to his son, "My beloved son, tell me what you saw in a dream
4 today and became alarmed. Tell me." •And Isaac answered his father, "I saw the
5 sun and the moon in my dream. •And there was a crown upon my head, and there
was an enormous man, shining exceedingly from heaven, as (the) light which is
6 called father of light.[b] • And he took the sun from my head, and then he left the
7 rays with me. •And I cried and said, 'I beseech you, my lord, do not take off the
8 glory of my head and the light of my house and all my glory.' •The sun and the
moon and the stars mourned, saying, 'Do not take off the glory of our power.'
9 And that radiant man answered and said to me, 'Do not cry because I took the
light of your house. For it has been taken up from labors into rest and from
10 lowliness into height; •they are taking it from straitness into spaciousness,[c] they
11 are taking it from darkness into light.' •I said to him, 'I beseech you, lord, take
12 also the rays with it.' •He said to me, 'There are twelve hours of the day, and
13 then I take all the rays.' •When the radiant man said these things, I saw the sun
14 of my house going up into heaven, but I saw that crown no more. •That sun was
15 like you, my father." •And Michael said to Abraham, "Your son Isaac has spoken
16 the truth; for you are (the sun), and you will be taken up into the heavens, •while
your body remains on the earth until seven thousand ages are fulfilled.[d] For then
17 all flesh will be raised.[e] •Now, therefore, Abraham, make a will (governing) the
things of your household and concerning your sons, for you have heard completely

---

6 a. MS E: "in her tent, and she arose and went
to the door of the room where Abraham was
asleep."

b. MS E: "brother."

c. Gk. *humōn*, plural, referring to both Abraham
and Sarah.

d. MS E: "'No, Sarah, (you) who minister to
the righteous, I did not bring news about Lot.'
And as Sarah heard Michael speaking, she knew
(by) his distinction of speech that he surpassed all
men who dwell up on the earth, because his voice
was glorious." Cf. A6:1.

e. Gk. *zeuma:* LSJM cites it only from the 5th-
cent. lexicographer Hesychius as a Phrygian equivalent of *pēgē*. *Zeuma* is not in Sophocles, and
Lampe cites only this passage. MS E reads "How
can your eyes shed tears, since the light of the *bēma*
has risen in our house?" Schmidt (*Le Testament
d'Abraham*, vol. 1, p. 84) explains *bēma* as a

transliteration of the Heb. *bîmah*, "an elevated
stand for public meetings" (Jastrow), and proposes
that Michael is thus identified as a reader at a
liturgical service.

7 a. MS E here has a further exchange: "Michael
answered and said, 'I am Michael.' And Abraham
said to him, 'Declare why you have come.' "

b. Or, "shining exceedingly from heaven as
light, called the father of light."

c. The nouns are cognate with the adjectives
"strait" and "spacious" used to describe the two
ways or gates in A11:2f.

d. MS E: "And Michael answered and said, 'In
truth it has happened truly. The sun, Isaac, is your
father. Abraham will be taken up into the heavens,
while his body . . . until 6,000 years are fulfilled.' " Cf. A19 n. b.

e. See A20 n. h.

18 the dispensation concerning you." •And Abraham answered and said to Michael, "I beseech you, lord, if I am to leave my body, I want to be taken up bodily, in order that I may see the things of creation which the Lord my God created in 19 heaven and on earth." •And Michael answered and said, "This is not my task, but I shall go and report to the Lord[f] about this, and if I am commanded I shall show you all these things."

1 **8** And Michael went up in the heavens and spoke before the Lord concerning 2 Abraham. •And the Lord answered Michael, "Go and take up Abraham in the body and show him everything, and whatever he says to you, do (it), as (you 3 would) for him who is my friend."[a] •Then Michael left and took Abraham up onto 4 a cloud in the body and bore him up to the river Oceanus.[b] •And Abraham looked 5 and saw two gates, one small and the other large. • And between the two gates there sat a man upon a throne of great glory. And a multitude of angels encircled 6 him. •And (sometimes) he was crying and again laughing, and the crying exceeded 7 his laughter sevenfold. •And Abraham said to Michael, "Who is this who is seated between the two gates with great glory, and sometimes he laughs but others he 8 cries, and the crying exceeds the laughter sevenfold?" • And Michael said to 9,10 Abraham, "Do you not know who he is?" • And he said, "No, lord." • And Michael said to Abraham, "Do you see these two gates, the small and large? 11,12 These are the (gates) which lead to life and to destruction,[c] •and this man who is 13 sitting between them, this is Adam, the first man whom God formed.[d] • And he placed him in this place to see every soul leaving (its) body, since everyone is 14 from him. •When, therefore, you see him crying, know that he has seen many 15 souls being led to destruction. •But when you see him laughing, he has seen a few 16 souls being led to life. •Do you see him, how the crying exceeds the laughter? Since he sees the greater part of the world being led through the broad (gate)[e] to destruction, therefore the crying exceeds the laughter sevenfold."

1 **9** And Abraham said, "Is one who is unable to enter through the strait gate unable 2 to enter into life?" •Then Abraham cried, saying, "Woe to me, what shall I do? 3 Because I am a man of broad body, and how shall I be able to enter into the strait 4 gate, into which a child of fifteen years[a] would not be able to enter?" •And Michael answered and said to Abraham, "Do not you fear, father, nor grieve; for you will 5 enter through it unhindered, as will all those who are like you."[b] •And as Abraham was standing and marveling, behold (there was) an angel of the Lord driving six 6 myriads of souls of sinners to destruction.[c] •And Abraham said to Michael, "Are 7 all these going to destruction?" • And Michael said to him, "Yes, but let us go and seek among these souls, (to see) if there is even one among them (which is) 8 righteous."[d] •And when they went, they found an angel holding in his hand one soul of a woman from among the six myriads, because he found (her) sins evenly balanced with all her works, and they were neither in distress nor at rest, but in 9,10 an intermediate place.[e] • But those (other) souls he took to destruction. • And Abraham said to Michael, "Lord, is this the angel who brings forth the souls from

f. MSS A C E: "my father."

8 a. MS E: "because he is my friend."
  b. See Introduction, n. 37.
  c. "Lead to life," "to destruction": see A11 n. b.
  d. Gk. *ho prōtos anthrōpos hon eplasen ho kyrios.* Cf. A11.9: *prōtoplastos.*
  e. From this point the adjectives become the same as in Mt 7:13f. and A11. At this point MS E reads "being led through the gate which leads to destruction," but MS E does have "strait" at the beginning of ch. 9.

9 a. MS E: "ten years."

b. MS E adds "but the majority of the world enter through the gate which takes (them) to destruction."
  c. MS E: ". . . driving about six myriads of souls, but holding one in his hand; and he took away the myriads of souls into the gate which leads to destruction."
  d. "if . . .": MS E reads "and if we find (one) worthy to be brought to life, let us bring it."
  e. MS E: "and Michael and Abraham went and sought and did not find (one) worthy of life, except only that one which the angel held in his hand; for he found (its) sins evenly balanced with its good works. And he did not leave it in distress nor at rest, but in an intermediate place."

11 the body, or not?'' •Michael answered and said, "This (i.e. the latter) is Death, and he leads them to the place of judgment, so that the judge may judge them.''

1 **10** And Abraham said, "My lord, I beseech you that you should conduct me to 2 the place of judgment so that I too may see how they are judged.'' •Then Michael 3 took Abraham onto a cloud, and he brought him to Paradise. •And when he reached the place where the judge was, the angel went and gave that soul to the judge. 4,5 The soul said, "Have mercy on me, lord.''[a] •And the judge said, "How shall I have mercy on you, since you did not have mercy on the daughter whom you bore, 6 the fruit of your womb? Why did you murder her?'' •And she answered, "No, lord, the murder did not come from me, but my daughter has herself lied against 7,8 me.'' •The judge commanded the one who writes the records to come. •And behold, (there came) cherubim bearing two books, and with them was a very 9 enormous man. And he had on his head three crowns, •and one crown was higher 10 than the other two crowns. The crowns are called the crowns of witness. •And the man had in his hand a golden pen. And the judge said to him, "Give proof 11 of the sin of this soul.'' •And that man opened one of the books which the cherubim had and sought out the sin of the woman's soul, and he found (it). 12 And the judge said, "O wretched soul, how can you say that you have not 13 committed murder? •Did you not, after your husband's death, go and commit 14 adultery with your daughter's husband and kill her?'' •And he charged her also 15 with her other sins, including whatever she had done from her childhood. •When the woman heard these things, she cried aloud, saying, "Woe is me, woe is me! Because I forgot all my sins which I committed in the world, but here they were 16 not forgotten.''[b] •Then they took her too and handed (her) over to the torturers.

1 **11** And Abraham said to Michael, "Lord, who is this judge? And who is the 2 other one who brings the charges of sins?'' •And Michael said to Abraham, "Do you see the judge? This is Abel, who first bore witness,[a] and God brought him 3 here to judge. •And the one who produces (the evidence) is the teacher of heaven 4 and earth and the scribe of righteousness, Enoch.[b] •For the Lord sent them here in order that they might record[c] the sins and the righteous deeds of each person.'' 5 And Abraham said, "And how can Enoch bear the weight of the souls, since 6 he has not seen death? Or how can he give the sentence of all the souls?'' •And Michael said, "If he were to give sentence concerning them, it would not be 7 accepted. But it is not Enoch's business to give sentence; •rather, the Lord is the 8 one who gives sentence, and it is this one's (Enoch's) task only to write. •For Enoch prayed to the Lord saying, 'Lord, I do not want to give the sentence of the 9 souls, lest I become oppressive to someone.' •And the Lord said to Enoch, 'I shall command you to write the sins of a soul that makes atonement, and it will enter 10 into life. •And if the soul has not made atonement and repented, you will find its sins (already) written, and it will be cast into punishment.' ''[d]

---

10 a. MS E: "Then when he reached the place where the judge was, he heard a soul crying, 'Have mercy on me, lord.' '' The soul is not identified with the one of 9:8.

b. Cf. Ab 2:1, where the point of knowing that all of one's deeds are written in a book is that then one will not fall into transgression. In Ab 2:1 and B10 the bookkeeping theme is not based on a theory of balancing of deeds, as it is in A12:18, but has the paraenetic purpose of assuring that transgressions are not forgotten. Thus the reference to "evenly balanced" deeds in B9:8 has no context. It appears to be a remnant of the story in A.

11 a. Gk. *martyrēsas:* possibly "the first martyr." b. Enoch as scribe: Jub 4:23; 1En 12:3f.; 15:1; 2En 23:1–4; 40:13; 53:2; 64:5; 68:2. See further

B. A. Pearson, SCS 6, p. 238, and nn.; J. T. Milik, *The Books of Enoch* (Oxford, 1976) pp. 103–06, 237, 262.

c. Gk. *apographōsin.* Note the plural (two angels record) in A12:12 (*apegraphonto*) and 13:1 (*hoi apographomenoi*). In B11:4 the plural logically includes Abel, but Abel is not in fact depicted as recording, but only judging; Enoch records. MS E avoids the difficulty: "and the Lord sent *him* (Enoch) here so that *he* might record . . ." Similarly D B F, all of which have a singular verb.

d. Apparently the meaning is that, to make Enoch's task less onerous, God commands him to record only the sins that do not count, since they had been atoned for; while if a person has not made atonement and is therefore to be condemned, Enoch himself does not record the sins but only has to

1 **12** And after Abraham saw the place of judgment, the cloud took him down to
2 the firmament below.[a] •And when Abraham looked down upon the earth, he saw
3 a man committing adultery with a married woman. •And Abraham turned and said
to Michael, "Do you see this sin? But, lord, send fire from heaven, that it may
4 consume them." •And immediately fire came down from heaven and consumed
5 them. •For the Lord (had) said to Michael, "Whatever Abraham asks you to do B8:2
6 for him, do." •And again Abraham looked up and saw other men slandering (their)
7,8 fellows, •and he said, "Let the earth open and swallow them up." •And while he
9 was speaking, the earth swallowed them up alive. •And again the cloud brought
him to another place. And Abraham saw some people leaving for a desert place
10 to commit murder. •And he said to Michael, "Do you see this sin? But let wild
11 beasts come out of the desert and rend them in two." •And in that very hour wild
12 beasts came out of the desert and devoured them. •Then the Lord God spoke to
Michael, saying, "Turn Abraham away to his house, and do not let him go round
13 all the creation which I made, because his heart is not moved for sinners, •but my
heart is moved for sinners, so that they may convert and live and repent of their
14 sins and be saved."[b] •And about the ninth hour Michael returned Abraham to his
15 house. •But Sarah, his wife, since she had not seen what had become of Abraham,
16 was consumed with grief and gave up her soul. •And after Abraham returned, he
found her dead, and he buried her.

1 **13** Now when the days of Abraham's death drew near, the Lord God said to
Michael, "Death will not dare draw near to take away the soul of my servant,
2 because he is my friend. •But you go and adorn Death with great youthful beauty
3 and send him thus to Abraham so that he may see him with his eyes. •And Michael
immediately, as he was commanded, adorned Death with great youthful beauty,
and sent him thus to Abraham so that he might see him. And he sat down near
4 Abraham. •When Abraham saw Death sitting near him, he was struck with great
5 fear. •And Death said to Abraham, "Greetings, holy soul. Hail, friend of the Lord
6 God. Hail, hospitable consolation of travelers." •And Abraham said, "Welcome,
servant of God Most High.[a] I beseech you, tell me who you are and come into the
house and partake of food and drink and take leave of me. For from the time when
7 I saw you sitting near me, my soul has been troubled. •For I am entirely unworthy
to be in close proximity with you, for you are a high spirit, while I am flesh and
8 blood, and therefore I cannot bear your glory. •For I see that your youthful beauty
9 is not of this world." •And Death said to Abraham, "I tell you, in all the creation
10 which God created, there is not to be found one like you. •For even God himself
11 has searched and has not found such a one on the entire earth."[b] •And Abraham
said to Death, "How do you dare to lie? Because I see that your youthful beauty
12 is not of this world." •And Death said to Abraham, "Do not think, Abraham,
13 that this youthful beauty is mine, or that I come thus to every man.[c] •No, but if
anyone is righteous as you are, I take crowns thus and go to him. But if he is a
sinner, I go in great decay; and from their sin I make a crown for my head, and
14 I trouble them with great fear, so that they may be dismayed."[c] •Then Abraham

look them up in the book, where they have (already) been written (he finds them written, *gegrammenas*), by whose agency we are not told. MS E is clearer: "If a soul has shown mercy, you will find its sins atoned for and it will enter into life. But if the soul has not shown mercy, you will find its sins written, and it will be cast into punishment."

12 a. MS E: "the cloud took him away to the firmament."
  b. MS E: ". . . lest he destroy all the creation which I made. His heart is not moved for them, since he did not make them. But I made them; therefore my heart is moved for them. Perhaps they

shall convert and repent of their sins and be saved."

13 a. For this exchange of greetings, cf. A2:3f. as well as the parallel in A16:9f. The exchange is not in MS E, supported by A D B F.
  b. MS E: ". . . like you. For he searched among the angels and archangels, and principalities and powers, as well as thrones; and (upon) all the earth, including four-footed animals and wild beasts of the earth and everything that is in the water, as far as heaven, and he did not find (one) like you." A similar list is in D.
  c. MS E omits here; see below.

15 said to him, "And whence comes this youthful beauty?" •And Death said, "There
16 is no other more full of decay than I." •Abraham said to him, "You are not, are
17 you, the one called Death?"[d] •He answered him and said, "I am the bitter name:
I am crying . . ."[e]

14 Abraham said to Death, "Show us your decay."[a] •And Death made his decay
1,2
3 manifest. And he had two heads: •The one had the face of a dragon, and through
4 it some die suddenly by asps; •and the other head was like a sword. On account
5 of it some die by the sword, as (they do) by bow and arrows. • On that day
6 Abraham's servants died because of the fear of Death. •When Abraham saw them
7 he prayed to the Lord, and he raised them. • Then God turned and drew out the
soul of Abraham as in a dream, and the Commander-in-chief Michael took it into
8 the heavens. • And Isaac buried his father near his mother Sarah, glorifying and
9 praising God. •For to him belong glory, honor, and worship, of the Father and of
the Son and of the Holy Spirit, now and always and forever and ever. AMEN.[b]

d. MS E: "Show me who you are."

e. MS E: " 'I am the most bitter name: I am crying; I am the calamity of all.' Abraham said to him, 'And who are you?' And Death said, 'I am Death, who brings the souls out of the body.' And Abraham said, 'Are you Death? Are you able to impel all to be cast out of the body?' Death said to Abraham, 'Do you think that this youthful beauty is mine? Or that I act (thus) with all? No, but if anyone is righteous, they take to him all righteousness and it becomes a crown on my head and I go to him in persuasiveness and his (own) righteousness. But if he is a sinner I go to him in great decay, but they also make all his sins a crown on my head in great fear. And I trouble him greatly.' " The original ending of the ch. may be reflected here. E is here supported in general by D, although there are variants. F has a continuation which is in partial agreement.

14 a. MS E inserts "and Death took (his) righteousness off of himself."

b. MS E: "and it came to pass, as Abraham turned, Death brought forth his soul as in a dream. And chariots of the Lord God came and took his soul into the heavens, blessing the friend of the Lord. They brought him into rest. And Isaac buried his father Abraham near his mother, glorifying the Most High God, to whom be glory forever and ever. Amen." C has a longer ending, but agrees with E in having "chariot of the Lord" for "the Commander-in-chief Michael." MS F has "the archangel Michael" take Abraham's soul. Thus this one appearance of "Commander-in-chief" may not be original in B.

TESTAMENT OF ISAAC

(Second Century A.D.)

A NEW TRANSLATION AND INTRODUCTION
BY W. F. STINESPRING

This document commemorates Isaac on a fixed day in the Coptic Church calendar. Sometimes a narrator speaks, sometimes Isaac himself. After the Trinitarian formula is stated, Isaac delivers a brief homily on the futility of the worldly life and the glorious, eternal rewards promised to the faithful. Then God sends the archangel Michael to Isaac to announce the approaching end of the patriarch's life. Isaac is willing to go but is concerned about Jacob. The angel assures him that all will be well with Jacob, from whom twelve tribes will come forth. Michael departs and Isaac informs Jacob of what is about to happen. Jacob is disturbed and wishes to accompany his father. Isaac explains that God's decrees cannot be changed, and tells Jacob of his great ancestry from Adam on, and of his great future as progenitor of the twelve tribes and ultimately of Jesus the Messiah, son of the Virgin Mary and incarnation of God.

At this point the narrator tells of the extreme asceticism of Isaac, such as his frequent fasting and praying night and day, also his abstention from meat and fruit and his refusal to sleep on a bed. A crowd gathers and Isaac delivers a lengthy homily on the strict obligations incumbent on all who are devout, and especially on all priests, among whom Isaac includes himself. After this an angel comes and takes Isaac for a preliminary visit to the next world. He is shown hell and some of the horrible tortures being inflicted on sinners, especially those who have died still in enmity with others. Soon he declares that he cannot endure the sight of any more horrors.

The angel takes him to heaven, where he sees his father Abraham and many saints. They lead him up to a curtain, behind which is the throne of God. God utters a few words of welcome to Isaac, but most of the conversation is between God and Abraham. God emphasizes that he is very compassionate and forgiving to all who earnestly try to live a good life. The conversation concluded, God orders Michael to bring a delegation of angels and saints, along with the chariot of the seraphim. With the cherubim and angels going ahead, they descend to bring Isaac back. Again Jacob is disturbed and needs to be reassured. Then the Lord takes Isaac's soul, white and pure as snow, to heaven in the holy chariot, with the cherubim and angels singing before it. The narrator ends by describing the delights of heaven, exhorting the readers to celebrate the special day of Isaac, and affirming the eternal nature of the Holy Trinity.

Texts

The present translation was based on the Arabic text, with some help from the Coptic and Ethiopic. The principal manuscripts are these:

Arabic
Paris, Bibl. Nat., MS no. 132, fols. 2ᵛ–24ʳ, dated A.D. 1269. The translation may have been made around the year 800.

Coptic (Bohairic)
Rome, Vatican Library, Coptic MS no. 61, fols. 163ᵛ–189ᵛ, dated A.D. 962.

Coptic (Sahidic)
New York, Pierpont Morgan Library, MS no. M 577, fols. 12ᵛ–25ᵛ, dated A.D. 894–895.
Ethiopic (Christian)
Paris, Bibl. Nat., MS no. 134 in the catalogue of Zotenberg.

Original language, date, and provenance

The Testament of Isaac is now extant only in the languages listed above, all from the area south of the Mediterranean. Unlike the Testament of Abraham, it is not extant in Greek or in the northern versions, Romanian and Slavic. The dependence on the Testament of Abraham, however, makes it possible that the Testament of Isaac was originally written in Greek, shortly after the Testament of Abraham and in the same milieu.

There are pronounced Christian elements in the Testament of Isaac as it now stands, and in its present form it has the function of emphasizing the date of the deaths of Abraham and Isaac as commemorated in the Coptic Church. Thus it would be possible to see the work as springing from the Coptic Christian Church. The Christianizing is not thoroughgoing, however, and it seems more likely that the original composition was a product of Egyptian Judaism.

Historical and theological importance

The Testament of Isaac maintains the universalism of the Testament of Abraham (see 2:9, "fathers to all the world"), and the admonitions concerning proper behavior remain quite general. (See, for example, 4:11–54.) It is also noteworthy that Jacob is called "the father of many nations" as well as of the twelve tribes (2:22), despite the wording of the Bible, which limits Jacob's progeny to the twelve tribes of Israel. Thus, assuming that the Testament of Isaac was originally Jewish, it represents very much the same values as are represented by the Testament of Abraham: Men should set their houses in order in preparation for death, they should live good moral lives, they should remember the judgment, but they should forget neither the mercy of God nor the need that they themselves be merciful.

BIBLIOGRAPHY

Charlesworth, *PMR*, pp. 123–25, 131–33.
Denis, *Introduction*, p. 34.

Box, G. H. *The Testament of Abraham*, with appendix on The Testaments of Isaac and Jacob by S. Gaselee. TED; London, 1927.
Delcor, M. *Le Testament d'Abraham: Introduction, traduction du texte grec et commentaire de la recension grecque longue, suivie de la traduction des Testaments d'Abraham, d'Isaac et de Jacob d'après les versions orientales.* SVTP 2; Leiden, 1973.
James, M. R. *The Testament of Abraham*, with appendix on The Testament of Isaac and Jacob by W. E. Barnes. T&S 2.2; Cambridge, 1892.
Kuhn, K. H. "An English Translation of the Sahidic Version of the Testament of Isaac," *JTS* n.s. 18 (1967) 325–36.
———. "The Sahidic Version of the Testament of Isaac," *JTS* n.s. 8 (1957) 225–39.

THE TESTAMENT OF ISAAC

1 **1** In the name of the Father, the Son, and the Holy Spirit, the One God.
2   We begin with the help of God and through his mediation to celebrate the death of the patriarch Isaac, son of the patriarch Abraham, and his ascension from his
3 body on this same day, which is the twenty-eighth of the month Misri. •May the blessing of his intercession be with us and protect us from the temptations of the enemy! Amen!
4   [Now the patriarch Isaac wrote his testament and addressed his words of instruction to Jacob his son and all those who were gathered together with him.]ᵃ
5   He said, "Hear, my brethren and my beloved ones, this speaker's instruction
6 and this curative medicine. •Because the way of God goes on forever, hear not only with chaste bodily ears, but also with the depth of the heart and with true faith without any doubt, as it is written, 'Behold, you have heard a firm word as to what a man should become. If he has heard it with a pure heart, God will give him compassion when he asks for something from him.'
7   "And it also is written, 'There is no profit for someone to ask God for what human beings solicit on earth.' And if God has given us mastery on the earth, then how much the advantage of the one who has been firm in the faith in the word of God, and has held fast without doubt and with an upright heart to the knowledge of the commandments of God and the stories of his saints; for he will be the inheritor of the kingdom of God.
8   "For behold, God is compassionate and merciful, the one who has received unto himself thieves and tax collectors in past times because of the sincerity of their faith that comes from God. And God, moreover, is with the ages to come."

1 **2** It came to pass, when the time drew near for our father Isaac, the father of fathers, to depart from this world and to go out from his body, that the Compassionate, the Merciful One sent to him the chief of the angels, Michael, the one TAb A1:4 whom he had sent to his father Abraham, on the morning of the twenty-eighth day B1:1 of the month Misri.
2   The angel said to him, "Peace be upon you, O chosen son, our father Isaac!"
3 Now it was customary every day for the holy angels to speak to him. So he
4 prostrated himself and saw that the angel resembled his father Abraham. •Then he opened his mouth, cried with a loud voice, and said with joy and exultation, "Behold, I have seen your face as if I had seen the face of the merciful Creator."
5   Then the angel said to him, "O my beloved Isaac, I have been sent to you from the presence of the living God to take you up to heaven to be with your father
6 Abraham and all the saints. •For your father Abraham is awaiting you; he himself
7 is about to come for you, but now he is resting. •There has been prepared for you
8 the throne beside your father Abraham; likewise for your beloved son Jacob. •And all of you shall be above every one else in the kingdom of heaven in the glory of
9 the Father and the Son and the Holy Spirit. •You shall be entrusted with this name for all future generations: The Patriarchs. Thus you shall be fathers to all the world, O faithful elder, our father Isaac."
10   Isaac answered, saying to the angel, "I am truly amazed concerning you. Are
11 you not my father Abraham?" •Then said the angel to him, "I am not your Father
12 Abraham, but I am the one who ministers to your father Abraham. •So now rejoice and be glad; for you will not be smitten (with disease)ᵃ and will not be taken (in
13 death) with pain but with joy. •You shall attain to blessings and repose forever and TAb B7:10

---

1 a. Supplied from the Sahidic Cop. version. [In the Cop. calendar the three patriarchs are commemorated on Sept. 4. J.H.C.] See also 8:1.

2 a. Words in parentheses are explanatory additions by the translator.

14 shall go forth from confinement into spaciousness. • Also you shall go away to rejoicing which has no end, and to light and bliss which have no limit, and to acclaim and delight without ceasing.

15 "And now, make your will and set your house in order; for you are about to TAb A1:4
16 go away to (final) rest. • Nevertheless, blessedness shall be upon the father who B1:3 begot you and upon your offspring which shall come after you!"

17 Now when our father Jacob heard them talking in this manner with one another,
18 he began to listen to them, but he did not speak. • Then our father Isaac said to the angel with patience and humility, "What shall I do now with regard to the
19 light of my eye, my beloved Jacob? • I fear concerning him on account of Esau. You, of course, know the whole story."

20 Then the angel said to him, "My beloved Isaac, all the peoples which are in the world, if they were gathered together in one place, would not be able to undo Gen 27 your blessing upon Jacob; because, at that time when you blessed him, he was blessed by the supreme God, also by the Son and the Holy Spirit, and by your
21 father Abraham; all of them responded, saying, 'Amen.' • The iron (sword?) will not frighten him, but he will be exceedingly strong and will gain sovereignty.
22 Then he will become the father of many nations, and twelve tribes will come forth Gen 28:10-22
23 from him." • Then Isaac said to the angel, "You have informed me and have
24 brought me good news. • But let Jacob not hear, for he will be sad and disturbed; for I have never pained his heart at all."

25 Then the angel of the Lord said, "O my beloved Isaac, all the righteous who go out from their bodies have blessedness, and they are blissful when they see
26 God, the Merciful, the Compassionate. • But woe, woe three times, to the sinner
27 when he has been born upon the earth, for he has many pains. • You shall teach your sons your ways and the commandments of your father—all of them which
28 he commanded you. • And do not hide these things from Jacob, that they may be a reminder to the generations of his offspring after him, so that the faithful may
29 observe them and by them attain to the life eternal, which is forever. • But I shall
30 take account of your concern. • Behold, I came to you with joy, speedily. The
31 peace which the Lord gave, I give to you. • And now I go quickly to the one who sent me."

1 **3** When the angel had said this, he rose from the bed of our father Isaac and
2 moved away from him. • Isaac kept looking at him and was amazed at what he had
3 heard and seen. • So he undertook to say, "I shall not see the light until you send for me."

4 While he was meditating on this, Jacob had come forward to the door of his
5 father's chamber. • The angel had already cast sleep upon him to prevent him from
6 hearing them. • So when he entered the resting place of his father, he said, "Father,
7 with whom were you speaking?" • Isaac his father said to him, "Now you must hear me, my son. Word has been sent to your venerable father that he shall be
8 taken from you, O my son Jacob." • Then Jacob embraced his father and wept, saying, "My strength has gone from me; will you make me an orphan, O my
9 father, so that this day I shall become wretched?" • Again he embraced our father Isaac and kissed him; both of them wept until they were worn and weary.

10 Then Jacob said, "O father, I will go away with you and I will not give you
11 up." • But Isaac said to him, "My boy, this is not for me to do, O my child and my beloved Jacob; but I thank God that you also have become a father and that
12 you will remain until you are summoned . . .ᵃ • As my father Abraham informed TAb A8:9 me, I am not able to set aside any part of the decree, which is valid for everyone;
13 thus it will come to pass, for what is written will not be frustrated. • But God knows, my son, that my heart is weary on account of you. Yet I am happy in my
14 going to the Lord. • So now that you have experienced growth in the Spirit, put away from you this weeping and lamenting.

---

3 a. There are some difficult words at this point, and the other versions do not help.

15 "Listen, my boy, that I may speak to you and give you understanding about the
first man, I mean our father Adam, the created one, whom God formed with his Gen 2:7
own hand; likewise our mother Eve; also Abel and Seth and our father Enoch
(Enosh?) and Mahalalel, the father of Methusaleh, and Lamech, the father of Jared,
and Enosh (Enoch?), the father of our father Noah and his sons, Shem, Ham, and
Japheth; and after them Phinehas and Kenan and Noah(?)[b] and Eber and Reu and
16 Terah and Nahor and my father Abraham and Lot the son of his brother. •All of Gen 5:24
these death took away except our father Enoch, the perfect one who ascended to
heaven.

7,18   "And after this there shall come forth twelve giants.[c] •Then will come Jesus the Mt 1:18-25
19 Messiah from your descendants out of a virgin named Mary.[d] •And God will Lk 1:34-38
become incarnate in him until the completion of a hundred years."

1,2 **4** Now Isaac used to fast every day, not breaking his fast until evening. •He would
offer up sacrifices for himself and for all people of his household, for the salvation
3 of their souls. •He would rise up for prayer in the middle of the night, and in the
4 daytime he would pray to God. He kept on doing this for many years. •He would
also fast the three forty-day periods, every time the forty-day period came around.[a]
5,6 And he would not eat meat or drink wine all his life long. •He also would not
enjoy the taste of fruit, nor would he sleep upon a bed, because he was devoted
to prayer every day and to supplication to God all his life.

7   So when the crowds heard that a man of God had appeared, they flocked to him
from all the districts and places to hear his instructions and life-giving recom-
8 mendations and to be assured that the spirit of God was speaking in him. •Then
the great ones who had flocked to him said, "What is this power which descended
upon you after the time when the brightness of your eyesight went from you, and
how have you had a reprieve to see now?"

9   Then the faithful old man smiled and said to them, "As to those who have
presented themselves, I will inform them that God healed me when he saw that
10 I had drawn near to the gate of death. •He awarded me this honor in my old age
that I might be a priest of the Lord."

11   Then someone (Jacob?) said to him, "Begin for me a discourse that I may be
12 consoled by it and hold fast to it." •So our father Isaac said to him, "If you speak
13 in anger, guard yourself from slander and beware of empty boasting. •See that you
14 do not converse alone (with a woman).[b] •Be careful that an evil word does not
15 come forth from your mouth. •Guard your body, that it may be pure, for it is the
16 temple of the Holy Spirit, which dwells within it. •Take care of the lesser functions
17 of your body, that it may be pure and sanctified. •See that you do not make sport
with your tongue lest an evil word go forth from your mouth.

8,19   "Beware of stretching out your hand to what you do not own. •Do not present
an offering when you are not ritually clean; bathe yourself in water when you
20 intend to approach the altar. •Do not mingle your thoughts with the thoughts of
21 the world, as you stand at the altar in the presence of God. •Make your offering
22 so that you may be a peacemaker between men. •As you are about to present your
offering to God, when you have moved forward to approach the altar, you shall
pray to God a hundred times without ceasing.

23   "At the beginning you shall voice this thanksgiving, as follows, 'O God, the
incomprehensible, who cannot be searched out, the possessor of power, the source
24 of purity, cleanse me by your mercy, a free gift from you to me. •For I am a
25 creature of flesh and blood, fleeing to you. •I know of my uncleanness, and surely
you will cleanse me, O Lord.

6,27   " 'For behold, my cause is in your hands and my recourse is to you. •I know

---

b. All the versions show confusions and contradictions in their lists of patriarchs at this point.
  c. Other versions say "tribes."
  d. Ar. "Maryam."

4 a. Apparently three times a year.
  b. The words "with a woman," necessary to
complete the sentence, are added from the Bohairic
Cop. and Eth. versions.

my sin, so cleanse me, O Lord, that I may enter into your presence with self-
28 respect. •Now my offenses are weighty; I have drawn near to the fire which burns.
29 Your mercy is upon all things, so that you can take away all my transgressions.
30,31 Pardon me, even me, the sinner. •And pardon all your creatures whom you have
fashioned, but who have not heard and learned of you.
32   " 'I am like all who are in your image. I have turned to the doing of what is
33 forbidden to me. •I have come to you and I am your servant and the sinful son
34 of your nation, but you are the very forgiving one. •Forgive me by the graciousness
that comes from you, and hear my entreaty that I may be worthy of standing at
35,36 your holy altar. •May this burnt offering be acceptable to you. •Do not turn me
37 back to my ignorance because of my sins. Receive me like the lost sheep. •May
the God who provided for our father Adam, and Abel and Noah, and our father
38 Abraham, be with you, O Jacob, and with me also. •Receive my offering from
me.'
39   "So if you have approached and have done this before your ascent to the altar,
40 then offer your sacrifice. •But you shall take care and be alert that you do not
41 grieve the spirit of the Lord. •For the work of the priesthood is not easy, since it
is incumbent upon every priest, from today until the completion of the last of the
generations and the end of the world, that he should not be filled by the drinking
of wine nor be satisfied by the eating of bread; and that he should not talk about
42 the concerns of the world nor listen to one who does talk about them. •But priests
must expend all of their efforts and their lives in prayer and watchfulness and
perseverance in piety, in order that each one may petition the Lord successfully.
43   "Moreover, every man on earth, whether wretched or fortunate, has incumbent
44 upon him the keeping of the proper commandments. •For men, after a short time,
45 will be removed from this world and its intense anxiety. •Then they will be engaged
46 in holy, angelic service by reason of purity. •They will be presented before the
47 Lord and his angels because of their pure offerings and their angelic service. •For
their earthly conduct will be reflected in heaven, and the angels will be their friends
48 because of their perfect faith and purity. •Great is their esteem before the Lord,
and there is no one either small or great in whom the Lord will not make
improvement; for the Lord wishes that each be without fault or offense.
49   "And now, continue to supplicate God with repentance for your past sins, and
50 do not commit more sin. •Accordingly, do not kill with the sword, do not kill with
the tongue, do not fornicate with your body, and do not remain angry until sunset.
51 Do not let yourself receive unjustified praise, and do not rejoice at the fall of your
52,53 enemies or of your brothers. •Do not blaspheme; beware of slander. •Do not look
54 at a woman with a lustful eye. •These things and what is like them you shall guard
against, in order that each one of you may be saved from the wrath which will be
manifested from heaven.' '

1 **5** When the throngs who were surrounding them heard this, they cried out with
one accord, saying, "Truly everything which this venerable man has said is worthy
2 of attention." •But he remained silent, pulled up his cloak, and covered his face.
3 The assemblage and the priest who was present, after a silence, said: "Let him
rest a little."
4,5   Then the angel of God came to him and took him to the heavens. •There he
6,7 beheld certain things in fear. •Many wild beasts(?) were within easy reach. •The
sides . . . (?) like the brothers so that they could not get sight of one another.[a]
8 Their faces were like the faces of camels and some were like the faces of dogs.
9 Others were like the faces of lions and hyenas and tigers; and some had only one
eye.
10   Isaac said, "I looked and, behold, they had agreed on a person and were hurrying

---

5 a. This sentence seems to be confused in all the
versions. The general idea seems to be that these
creatures were frightful in appearance.

11 him along. •And when they had made a sign to the lions, those who were walking
12 with him withdrew from him. •Then the lions turned upon him, tore him apart in
13 the middle, dismembered him, and chewed and swallowed him. •After this they
14 ejected him from their mouths and he returned to his original state. •And after the
15 lions the others came forward and did the same thing to him. •One after the other
   they would take him, and every one of them would chew him, swallow him, and
16 eject him, and he would return to his original state." •Then I said to the angel,
   "O my lord, what is the sin which this man has committed that he should have
   to endure a burden like this?"
17 The angel said to me, "It is because this man, whom you see, was in enmity
   with his neighbor for five hours, and he died without having been reconciled with
18 him. •So he was handed over to five of the tormentors that they might torment him
   a whole year for each of the five hours which he spent as the enemy of his friend."
19 Then the angel said to me, "O my beloved Isaac, see here the sixty myriads who
20 inflict torture for each hour that the man remains hostile to his neighbor. •He is
   brought here to these creatures who torture him, each one of them for an hour until
   a full year is completed if he had not been making peace and repenting of his sin
   before his removal and his separation from his body."
21 Then he brought me to a river of fire. I saw it throbbing, with its waves rising
22 to about thirty cubits; and its sound was like rolling thunder. •I looked upon many
23 souls being immersed in it to a depth of about nine cubits. •They were weeping
   and crying out with a loud voice and great groaning, those who were in that river.
24 And that river had wisdom in its fire: It would not harm the righteous, but only
25 the sinners by burning them. • It would burn every one of them because of the
   stench and repugnance of the odor surrounding the sinners.
26 Then I observed the deep river[b] whose smoke had come up before me, and I
   saw a group of people at the bottom of it, screaming, weeping, every one of them
27 lamenting. •The angel said to me, "Look at the bottom to observe those whom
   you see at the lowest depth. They are the ones who have committed the sin of
   Sodom; truly, they were due a drastic punishment."
28,29 Then I saw the overseer of punishment and he was all of him fire. •He would
   strike the myrmidons of hell (his helpers) and say to them, "Kill them that it may
30 be known that God exists forever." •Then the angel said to me, "Lift up your
31 eyes and look at the whole gamut of punishments." •But I said to the angel, "My
   sight cannot embrace them because of their great number; but I desire to understand
32 how long these people are to be in this torture." •He said to me, "Until the God
   of mercy becomes merciful and has mercy on them."

1,2 **6**.After this the angel took me to heaven and I saw Abraham. •So I prostrated
3 myself before him and he received me graciously, he and all the godly ones. •Then
4 they all came together and did me honor because of my father. •Then they took
5 me by the hand and led me to the curtain before the throne of the Father. •So I
   prostrated myself before him and worshiped him with my father and all the saints,
   while we uttered praises and cried aloud, saying, "Most holy, most holy, most TAb A20:12
   holy is the Lord Sabaoth! Heaven and earth are filled with your sanctified glory."
6 Then the Lord said to me from his holy height, "As to everyone who shall name
   his son after my beloved Isaac, my blessing shall rest upon him and be in his house
7 forever. •Excellent is your coming, O Abraham, faithful one; excellent is your
8 lineage, and excellent is the presence here of this blessed lineage. • So now,
   everything which you ask in the name of your beloved son Isaac you shall have
   today as a covenant forever."
9 Then my father Abraham answered and said, "Yours is the sovereignty, O Lord,
10 ruler of the universe." •The Lord from his holy height said to my father Abraham,

b. The Bohairic Cop. and Sahidic Cop. versions
have "abyss," a more appropriate term.

"Every man who shall call his son by the name of my beloved Isaac, or shall write his own testament, shall have a blessing which shall not come to an end, and my
11 blessing upon his house shall not cease. • Or if anyone will give a poor man something to eat on the day of the festival of my beloved Isaac then I will give him to you in my kingdom."
12 　　Then my father Abraham said, "O Father, God, ruler of the universe, even if he is not able to write his testament or his covenant, let your blessing and your
13 mercy enfold him, for you are the merciful one." • The Lord said to Abraham, "Let him feed the hungry one with bread and I will give him a place in my kingdom and he shall be present with you from the first moment of the millennial banquet."
14 The saving God also said to my father Abraham, "And if he is so poor that he does not find bread in his house, then let him spend a whole night commemorating my beloved Isaac without sleeping and I will bestow upon him a heritage in my kingdom."
15 　　My father Abraham said, "And if he is weak and cannot endure the vigil, then
16 may your mercy and compassion still enfold him." • So the Lord said to him, "Then let him offer a little incense in my name on the memorial day of my beloved
17 Isaac, your son. • And if it should be that he does not know how to read, then let
18 him go to hear the reading from one who can read it. • If he cannot do any of these things, then let him enter his house, lock the door behind him, and pray a hundred
19 prayers of repentance; then I will give him to you as a son in my kingdom. • But above and beyond all this, let him bring an offering on the memorial day of my
20 beloved Isaac. • And all those who shall do all that I have said shall be granted the
21 inheritance of the kingdom in my heaven. • And all who took pains to write their testaments and covenants and life stories, and showed mercy if only (by giving) a cup of cold water, and believed with all their hearts—with them shall be my　Mt 25:35
22 strength and my Holy Spirit for the prosperity of their affairs in the world. • There shall not be any trouble in their departure (from this world), I will grant them a lifetime in my kingdom, and they shall be present from the first moment of the
23 millennial banquet. • Peace be upon you, O my beloved ones, the saints!"
24 　　When he had concluded all this discourse, the heavenly beings began to cry out, saying, "Most holy, most holy, most holy is the Lord, Sabaoth! Heaven and earth　6:5
25 are filled with your sanctified glory." • The Father who controls everything answered from this holy place and said, "O Michael, my faithful servant, call in all the
26 angels and all the saints." • Then he mounted the chariot of the seraphim, while　TAb A20
27 the cherubim went before [with the angels. • And when they had come to the couch of our father Isaac, our father Isaac immediately beheld the face of our Lord, full
28 of joy toward him. • He cried out, "It is well that you have come, my Lord, with your great archangel, Michael. It is well that you have come, my Father, with all the saints."].[a]
29 　　When he has said this, Jacob was greatly disturbed and he clung to his father　TAb A5:9
30 and kissed him, weeping. • Then our father Isaac raised him up and made a sign　B6:2
31 to him, giving a hint with his eyes, meaning, "Be silent, my boy." • So Abraham said to the Lord, "O Lord, remember also my (grand)son Jacob."
32 　　Then the Lord said to him, "My power shall be with him, he shall glorify my name, he shall become master of the land of promise, and the enemy shall not hold
33 sway over him." • And our father Isaac said, "Jacob, my beloved son, keep my
34 injunction which I lay down today that you preserve my body. • Do not profane the image of God by how you treat it; for the image of man was made like the image of God; and God will treat you accordingly at the time when you meet him　Isa 44:6
35 and see him face to face. • He is the first and the last, as the prophets have said."　Rev 1:8

1 **7** When Isaac had said this, the Lord took his soul from his body and it was white　TAb B14:7
as snow; he took possession of it and carried it with him upon his holy chariot and　A20

---

6 a. This necessary section, missing in the Ar. is
supplied from the Sahidic Cop. version.

ascended with it to the heavens, while the cherubim were singing praises before
2 it, likewise his holy angels. •The Lord bestowed upon him the kingdom of heaven;
and everything which our father desired out of the abundance of blessings from
God he had, including the fulfillment of his covenant forever.

1 **8** Such was the decease of our father Abraham and our father Isaac, son of
Abraham, on the twenty-eighth day of the month of Misri, on this very day. This
2 day we have consecrated and designated. •And on the day when our father Abraham
offered the sacrifice to God, on the twenty-eighth day of the month of Amshir, the
heavens and the earth were filled with the sweet fragrance of his way of life before
the Lord.
3 And our father Isaac was like the silver which is burned, smelted, purified, and
refined in the fire; likewise everyone who shall come forth from our father Isaac,
4 the father of fathers. •On the day when Abraham, the father of fathers, offered him Gen 22
as a sacrifice to God, the perfume of his sacrifice ascended to the veil of the curtain
of the one who controls everything.
5 Blessed is everyone who manifests mercy on the memorial day of the father of
fathers, our father Abraham and our father Isaac, for each of them shall have a
dwelling in the kingdom of heaven, because our Lord has made with them his true Gen 17
6 covenant forever. • And he will keep it for them and for those who come after
them, saying to them, "Whatever person has manifested mercy in the name of my
beloved Isaac, behold I will give him to you in the kingdom of heaven and he shall
be present with them at the first moment of the millennial banquet to celebrate with
them in the everlasting light in the kingdom of our Master and our God and our
7 King and our Savior, Jesus the Messiah. •He is the one to whom are due the
glory, the dignity, the majesty, the dominion, the reverence, the honor, the praise,
and the adoration, along with the merciful Father and the Holy Spirit now and for
all time, and to all eternity and forever and ever, amen!"

1 **9** The obsequies of our father Isaac are finished. Thanks and praise to God,
always, forever, and eternally.

TESTAMENT OF JACOB

(Second to Third Century A.D.?)

A NEW TRANSLATION AND INTRODUCTION

BY W. F. STINESPRING

After the statement of the Trinitarian formula, the narrator begins a commemoration of Jacob on the same day set aside in the church calendar to honor Isaac. As in the case of Isaac, the Lord sends the archangel Michael to Jacob to announce his imminent demise. Jacob, accustomed to speaking with angels, replies that he is ready to die, now that he has been able to come to Egypt to see and enjoy his son Joseph once more (Gen 46:30).

After an interval, another angel, resembling Isaac, appears and somewhat frightens Jacob. Then the heavenly visitor identifies himself as Jacob's guardian angel, who has already saved him from Laban, Esau, and various dangers, and will continue to see that all will be well. The angel departs, with Jacob's confidence restored. Jacob then requires Joseph to swear that he will take his body back to the land of Canaan to be buried in the ancestral tomb (Gen 47:29–31). Next the narrator relates the story of the blessing of Ephraim and Manasseh (Gen 48), followed by a condensed version of Jacob's blessing on his twelve sons (Gen 49).

Then, like Isaac, Jacob is taken up for a preliminary tour of the next world, first to hell with all its horrors, afterward to heaven with all its bliss. He returns to earth and dies at the age of 147 years. The Lord and his angels come down and take his soul to heaven. Joseph orders his body embalmed in the Egyptian manner. Many days of mourning ensue (Gen 50:2f.). Then follows the great procession of Israelites and Egyptians to the land of Canaan to bury Jacob's body (Gen 50:4–14).

In conclusion, the narrator presents his own views and advice. He recommends reading the Torah, written by Moses (sic), and imitating the patriarchs in one's own life to avoid the tortures of hell. Much prayer and fasting are necessary, likewise alms freely given out of mercy and compassion. Such living will drive away demons. Avoid danger, depravity, and all sexual immorality, including homosexuality. Honor the patriarchs every year on their special day. Finally, all we weak sinners will have urgent need of intercessors in heaven on the day of judgment. We must plead for mercy before Jesus the Messiah, who is both judge and helper. Our best intercessors will be the Virgin Mary, "mistress of intercessions" and "mother of salvation," also the martyrs and saints and all who have pleased the Lord with pious deeds.

Texts

The present translation is based on the Arabic text, with some help from the Coptic and Ethiopic. The principal manuscripts are the same as those used for the Testament of Isaac, except that in the Sahidic Coptic version only the Testament of Isaac is extant.

THE TESTAMENT OF JACOB

1 **1** In the name of the Father, the Son, and the Holy Spirit, the one God.
2 We begin, with the help of God Most High and through his mediation, to write
the life story of our father, the patriarch Jacob, son of the patriarch Isaac, on the TIsaac 1:2; 8:1
3 twenty-eighth day of the month of Misri. •May the blessing of his prayer guard
us and protect us from the temptations of the obstinate enemy. Amen, amen, amen!
4 He said, "Come, listen, my beloved ones and my brethren who love the Lord,
5 to what has been received." •Now when the time of our father Jacob, father of
fathers, son of Isaac, son of Abraham, approached and drew near for him to steal
6 away from his body, this faithful one was advanced in years and distinction. •So TAb A1:4
the Lord sent to him Michael, the chief of the angels, who said to him, "O Israel, B1:1
my beloved, of noble lineage, write down your spoken legacy and your instruction TIsaac 2:1
for your household and give them a covenant; also concern yourself with the proper TAb A1:4
ordering of your household, for the time has drawn near for you to go to your B1:3
fathers to rejoice with them forever." TIsaac 2:15
7 So when our father Jacob, the faithful one, heard this from the angel, he answered TIsaac 2:3
and said, as was his custom every day to speak in this manner with the angels,
8 "Let the will of the Lord be done." •And God pronounced a blessing upon our
9 father Jacob. •Jacob had a secluded place which he would enter to offer his prayers
10 before the Lord in the night and in the day. •The angels would visit him and guard
him and strengthen him in all things.
11 God blessed him and multiplied his people in the land of Egypt at the time when Gen 46:1-7
12 he went down to the land of Egypt to meet his son Joseph. •His eyes had become
dull from weeping, but when he went down to Egypt he saw clearly when he
13 beheld his son. •So Jacob-Israel bowed with his face to the ground, then fell upon
the neck of his son Joseph and kissed him, while weeping and saying, "I can die
now, O my son, because I have seen your face once more in my lifetime; O my Gen 46:30
beloved son."

1 **2** Joseph continued to rule over all Egypt, while Jacob stayed in the land of Gen 46:34
Goshen for seventeen years and became very old, so that his life-span was
2,3 completed. •He continually kept all the commandments and feared the Lord. •His
eyes grew dim and his lifetime was so nearly finished that he could not see a single
person because of his long life and senility.
4 Then he lifted his eyes toward the light of Isaac,[a] but he was afraid and became
5 disturbed. •So the angel said to him, "Do not fear, O Jacob; I am the angel who
6 has been walking with you and guarding you from your infancy. •I announced that
7 you would receive the blessing of your father and of Rebecca, your mother. •I am
the one who is with you, O Israel, in all your acts and in everything which you
8 have witnessed. • I saved you from Laban[b] when he was endangering you and
9 pursuing you. •At that time I gave you all his possessions and blessed you, your
wives, your children, and your flocks.
10,11 "I am the one who saved you from the hand of Esau. •I am the one who
accompanied you to the land of Egypt, O Israel, and a very great people was given
12 to you. •Blessed is your father Abraham, for he has become the friend of God— TAb A1:6
may he (God) be exalted!—because of his generosity and love of strangers.
13 Blessed is your father Isaac who begot you, for he was a perfect sacrifice, TAb A1:1,2,5
acceptable to God.
14,15 "Blessed are you also, O Jacob, for you have seen God face to face. •You saw

2 a. An angel that resembled Isaac; cf. TIsaac 2.
b. The French translation in Delcor, *Le Testament d'Abraham*, p. 262, has "Satan" here. There seems to be no MS evidence for this reading. [The error appears to originate with Delcor's typist; "Satan" looks like and is more familiar than "Laban." J.H.C.]

the angel of God—may he be exalted!—and you saw the ladder standing firm on
16 the ground with its top in the heavens. •Then you beheld the Lord sitting at its top
17 with a power which no one could describe. •You spoke out and said, 'This is the
18 house of God and this is the gate of heaven.' •Blessed are you, for you have come
near to God and he is strong among mankind, so now do not be troubled, O chosen
one of God.

19,20   "Blessed are you, O Israel, and blessed is all your progeny. •For all of you will   TIsaac 2:9
be called 'the patriarchs' to the end of the age and of the epochs; you are the
21 people and the lineage of the servants of God. •Blessed be the nation which will
22 strive for your purity and will see your good works. •Blessed be the man who will   TIsaac 8:5
23 remember you on the day of your noble festival. •Blessed be the one who will
perform acts of mercy in honor of your several names, and will give someone a
cup of water to drink, or will come with an offering to the sanctuary, or will take   TIsaac 6:21
in strangers, or visit the sick and console their children, or will clothe a naked one
in honor of your several names.

24   "Such a one shall neither lack any of the good things of this world, nor life
25 everlasting in the world to come. •Moreover, whoever shall have caused to be
written the stories of your several lives and sufferings at his own expense, or shall   TIsaac 6:21
have written them by his own hand, or shall have read them soberly, or shall hear
them in faith, or shall remember your deeds—such persons will have their sins
forgiven and their trespasses pardoned, and they will go on account of you and
your progeny into the kingdom of heaven.

26   "And now rise up, Jacob, for you will be translated from hardship and pain of   TIsaac 2:13
heart to eternal rest, and you will enter into the repose which shall not pass away,
27 into mercy, eternal light, and spiritual joy. •So now make your statement to your
household, and peace be upon you, for I am about to go to him who sent me.''

1 **3** So when the angel had made this statement to our father Jacob, he ascended
2 from him into heaven, as Jacob bade him farewell. •Those who were around Jacob
3 heard him as he thanked God and glorified him with praise. •And all the members
of his household, great and small, gathered around him, weeping over him, deeply
4 grieving and saying, "You are going away and leaving us as orphans." •And they
kept on saying to him, "O our beloved father, what shall we do, for we are in a
5 strange land?" •So Jacob said to them, "Do not fear; God himself appeared to me
in Upper Mesopotamia[a] and said to me, 'I am the God of your fathers; do not fear,
for I am with you forever and with your descendants who will come after you.
6 This land in which you are I am about to give to you and to your descendants after   Gen 46:1-7
7,8 you forever. •And do not be afraid to go down to Egypt. •I will make for you a
9 great people and your descendants will increase and multiply forever. •Joseph will
put his hand on your eyes and your people will multiply in the land of Egypt.
10,11 Afterward they will come to this place and will be without care. •I will do good
to them for your sake, though for the time being they will be displaced from
here.' "

1,2 **4** After this, the time for Jacob-Israel to leave his body had arrived. • So he   Gen 47:27-31
summoned Joseph and said to him, "If indeed you have found grace, place your
blessed hand under my side and swear an oath before the Lord that you will place
3 my body in the tomb of my fathers." •Then Joseph said to him, "I will do exactly
4 what you command me, O beloved of God." •But he said to Joseph, "I want you
5 to swear to me." •So Joseph swore to Jacob, his father, to the effect that he would
carry his body to the tomb of his fathers, and Jacob accepted the oath of his son.
6,7   Afterward, this report reached Joseph: "Your father has become uneasy." •So
he took his two sons, Ephraim and Manasseh, and went before his father Jacob.
8 Joseph said to him, "These are my sons whom God has given me in the land of

---

3 a. The translator in Delcor, *Le Testament*   but the Ar. word for "island" is also the word for
d'Abraham, has rendered "l'île," "the island,"   "Upper Mesopotamia."

9,10 Egypt to come after me." •Israel said, "Bring them closer to me here." •For the
eyes of Israel had become dim from his advanced age so that he could not see.
11,12 So Joseph brought his sons closer and Jacob kissed them. •Then Joseph commanded
them, namely Ephraim and Manasseh, to bow down before Jacob to the ground.
13 Joseph took Manasseh and put him at Israel's right hand and Ephraim at his left
14 hand. •But Israel reversed his hands and let his right hand rest upon the head of Gen 48
15 Ephraim and his left hand upon the head of Manasseh. •He blessed them and gave
them back to their father and said, "May the God under whose authority my
fathers, Abraham and Isaac, served in reverence, the God who has strengthened
me from my youth up to the present time when the angel has saved me from all
16 my afflictions, may he bless these lads, Manasseh and Ephraim. •May my name
be upon them, also the names of my holy fathers, Abraham and Isaac."
17　　After this, Israel said to Joseph, "I shall die, and all of you will return to the
18 land of your fathers and God will be with you. •And you personally have received
a mighty favor, greater than that of your brothers, for I have taken this arrow with
my bow and my sword from the Amorites(?)."[a]

1 **5** Then Jacob sent for all his children and said to them, "Gather around me that
I may inform you of everything which will come upon you and what will overtake
2 each one of you in the last days." •So they gathered around Israel from the eldest
3 to the youngest of them. •Then Jacob-Israel spoke up and said to his sons, "Listen,
O sons of Jacob, listen to your father Israel, from Reuben my firstborn to Benjamin."
4 Then he told them what would come upon the twelve children, calling each one
of them and his tribe by name; and he blessed them with the celestial blessing.
5,6 After this they were silent for a short time in order that he might rest. •So the
heavens rejoiced that he could observe the places of repose.[a]
7　　And behold, there approached numerous tormentors differing in their aspects. TIsaac 5
8 They were prepared to torment the sinners, who are these: adulterers, male and
female; those lusting after males; the vicious who degrade the semen given by
God;[b] the astrologers and the sorcerers; the evildoers and the worshipers of idols
who hold onto abominations; and the slanderers who pass judgment(?) with two
9 tongues (deceitfully). • And as to all these sinners, their punishment is the fire
which will not be extinguished and the outer darkness where there is weeping and Mt 8:12; 22:13
gnashing of teeth.
10　　[Here there is a lacuna in the Arabic text. In the Bohairic, Jacob is again taken
11 up, this time to heaven, where all is light and joy. •He sees Abraham and Isaac
12 and is shown all the joys of the redeemed. •Jacob returns to earth, gives instructions
for his burial in the land of his fathers, and passes away at the age of 147 years.
13 The Lord comes down with the angels Michael and Gabriel to bear Jacob's soul TIsaac 6:26
14 to heaven. •Joseph orders his father's body to be embalmed in the Egyptian manner.
15 Forty days are spent in the embalming process, and eighty more days are spent
in mourning for the patriarch.]

1 **6** And when the days of their mourning were finished, Pharaoh was still weeping
2 over Jacob because of his regard for Joseph. •Then Joseph addressed the nobles
of Pharaoh and said to them, "Since I have found favor with you, will you speak
on my behalf to Pharaoh the king, and say to him that Jacob made me take an oath
that when he went out from his body I would bury his body in the tomb of my
3 fathers in the land of Canaan, in that very place?" •So Pharaoh said to Joseph, Gen 50:6
"Go in peace and bury your father in accordance with the oath which he required
4 of you. •And take with you chariots and horses, the best of my kingdom and from
my own household as you desire."
5　　So Joseph worshiped God in the presence of Pharaoh, went forth from him,

---

4 a. The end of this sentence is corrupt in the Ar.
text. This tentative translation relies partly upon the
Bohairic Cop. and Eth.

5 a. I.e. places where the dead go; he was taken
up to these places, as other versions say.
b. masturbators?

6 and set out to bury his father. •And there set out with him the slaves of Pharaoh,
the elders of Egypt, all the household of Joseph, and his brothers and all Israel.
7 They all went up with him into the chariots, and the entourage moved along like
8 a great army. •They descended into the land of Canaan to the riverbank across the
9 Jordan and they mourned for him in that place with very great grief indeed. •They
10 maintained that great grief for him for seven days. •So when the inhabitants of
Dan heard about the mourning in their land, they said, "This great mourning is
11 that of the Egyptians." •To this day [they call that place "the Mourning of the
Egyptians"].[a]
12 Then Israel was carried forward and was buried in the land of Canaan in the
13 second tomb. •This is the one which Abraham had bought with authorization for
14 burials from Ephron opposite Mamre. •After that Joseph returned to the land of
15 Egypt with his brothers and all the retinue of Pharaoh. •And Joseph lived after the
16 death of his father many years. •He continued to rule over Egypt, though Jacob
had died and was left behind with his own people.

1 **7** This is what we have transmitted: We have described the demise of and the
mourning for the father of fathers, Jacob-Israel, to the extent of our ability to do
this; also as it is written in the spiritual books of God and as we have found it in
the ancient treasury of knowledge of our fathers, the holy, pure apostles.
2 And if you wish to know the life history and get new knowledge of the father
3 of fathers, Jacob, then take a father who is attested in the Old Testament. •Moses
4 is the one who wrote it, the first of the prophets, the author of the Law. •Read
5 from it and enlighten your insights. •You will find this and more in it, written for
6 your sake. •You will find that God and his angels were their friends while they
were in their bodies, and that God kept on speaking to them many times in various
7 passages from the Book. • Also he says in many passages with regard to the
patriarch Jacob, the father of fathers, in the Book, thus, "My son, I will bless   Gen 35:11-15
8 your descendants like the stars of the heavens." •And our father Jacob would speak
to his son Joseph and say to him, "My God appeared to me in the land of Canaan
at Luz and blessed me and said to me, 'I will bless you and multiply you and make
9 you a mighty people. •They shall go out (to war?) like the other nations of this
earth and your descendants will increase forever.' "
10 This is what we have heard, O my brothers and my loved ones, from our fathers,   2:20
11 the patriarchs. •And it is incumbent upon us that we have zeal for their deeds, their
purity, their faith, their love of mankind, and their acceptance of strangers; in
order that we may lay claim to be their sons in the kingdom of heaven, so that they
will intercede for us before God that we may be saved from the torture of hell.
12,13 These are the ones whom the Arabs have designated as the holy fathers. •Jacob
instructed his sons with regard to punishment, and he would call them the sword
of the Lord, which is the river of fire, prepared with its waves to engulf the
14 evildoers and the impure. •These are the things the power of which the father of
fathers, Jacob, expounded and taught to all his sons that the wise ones might hear
15 and pursue righteousness in mutual love with mercy and compassion. •For mercy
16 saves people from penalties and mercy overcomes a multitude of wrongs. •Truly,
one who shows mercy to the poor, that one makes a loan to God.
17 So now, my beloved sons, do not slacken from prayer and fasting ever at any
18 time, and by the life of the religion you will drive away the demons. •O my dear
son, avoid the evil ways of the world, which are anger and depravity and all vicious
19,20 deeds. •And beware of injustice and blasphemy and abduction. •For the unjust will   1Co 6:9
not inherit the kingdom of God, nor will the adulterers, nor the accursed, nor those
who commit outrages and have sexual intercourse with males, nor the gluttons,
nor the worshipers of idols, nor those who utter imprecations, nor those who
pollute themselves outside of pure marriage; and others whom we have not
presented or even mentioned shall not come near the kingdom of God.

---

6 a. The sentence is completed from the Bohairic
Cop.

21 O my sons, honor the saints, for they are the ones who will intercede for you.

22 O my sons, be generous to strangers and you will be given exactly what was TAb A1:2
given to the great Abraham, the father of fathers, and to our father Isaac, his son.

23 O my sons, do for the poor what will increase compassion for them here and
now, so that God will give you the bread of life forever in the kingdom of God. JosAsen 8:5

24 For to the one who has given a poor person bread in this world God will give Jn 6

25 a portion from the tree of life. •Clothe the poor person who is naked on the earth,
so that God may clothe you with the apparel of glory in the kingdom of heaven,
and you will be the sons of our holy fathers, Abraham, Isaac, and Jacob in heaven

26 forever. •Be concerned with the reading of the word of God in his books here
below, and remember the saints who have written of their lives, their sufferings,

27 and their prostrations in prayer. •In the future, it shall not be prevented that they

28 should be inscribed in the book of life in the kingdom of heaven. •And you will
be counted among the saints, those who pleased God in their lifetime and will
rejoice with the angels in the land of eternal life.

1 **8** You shall honor the memory of our fathers, the patriarchs, at this time each TIsaac 1:2; 8:1

2 year and on this same day, which is the twenty-eighth of the month of Misri. •This
is what we have found written in the ancient documents of our fathers, the saints

3 who were pleasing to God. •Because of their intercession and their prayer, we
shall have all things, namely a share and a place in the kingdom of heaven which
belongs to our Lord and our God and our Master and our Savior, Jesus the Messiah.

4 He is the one whom we ask to forgive us for our mistakes and our errors and to

5 overlook our misdeeds. •May he be kind to us on the day of his judgment and let
us hear the voice filled with joy, kindness, and gladness, saying, "Come to me,
O blessed ones of my Father, inherit the kingdom which was yours from before
the creation of the world."

6 And may we be worthy to receive his divine secrets, which are the means to

7 the pardon of our sins. •May he help us toward the salvation of our souls, and may

8 he ward off from us the blows of the wicked enemy. •May he let us stand at his
right hand on the great and terrible day for the intercession of the mistress of
intercessions, the source of purity, generosity, and blessings, the mother of salvation;[a] and for the intercession of all the martyrs, saints, doers of pleasing deeds,
and everyone who has pleased the Lord with his pious deeds and his good will.

9 Amen, amen, amen. •And praise to God always, forever, eternally.

8 a. A reference to the Virgin Mary as an aid in
intercession for sinners.

TESTAMENT OF MOSES

(First Century A.D.)

A NEW TRANSLATION AND INTRODUCTION

BY J. PRIEST

The Testament of Moses is the farewell exhortation given by Moses to his chosen successor Joshua just prior to the leader's death and Israel's entrance into the promised land. Apart from a few responses of Joshua, which serve to facilitate the flow of Moses' speech, the format is a predictive delineation of the history of the people from their entrance into Canaan until the end of days.

In summary fashion, Moses outlines the conquest (2:1–2), the time of the judges and the united kingdom (2:3–4), and the period of the divided kingdoms (2:5–9). Chapter 3 speaks of the fall of Jerusalem (3:1–3) and the reunion of all Israel in the land of their exile (3:4–14). Next, Moses foretells the return from captivity (4:1–6) and the rebuilding of Jerusalem (4:7–9).

The return is, however, followed by a renewed apostasy (5:1–6; 7:1–9). Those responsible for this apostasy are usually considered to be the hellenizing priests of the Seleucid period (175–165 B.C.) and/or the priest-kings of the Hasmonean era (142–37 B.C.). The consequence of these evil deeds is the partial destruction of the Temple (6:9), and the torture, imprisonment, and death of the faithful (6:3–9; 8:1–5).

An episode that appears to be the culmination of this historical survey tells of the resolve of a Levite and his seven sons to die rather than betray their ancestral faith (9:1–7). There follows an eschatological hymn that portrays the destruction of the evil one at the hands of Israel's guardian angel (10:1–2), cataclysmic cosmic events (10:3–6), and the exaltation of Israel in the end of days (10:7–10).

Finally, there is a dialogue between Moses and Joshua in which the latter questions his own ability to lead the people and laments that Moses' death will encourage Israel's enemies to attack, once they believe that his presence will no longer protect the chosen people (11:1–12:1). Moses, however, assures Joshua that God is in complete control of all that is and will be (12:1–5). It is his will and mercy, not the merit of Moses, that have guarded the people up to now (12:6–7), and the same will suffice in the days of Joshua (12:8–9). The concluding verses exhort faithfulness to the commandments, promising good to those who fulfill them and evil to those who disregard them (12:10–11), and affirm that, in spite of all hazards, a nucleus of God's people will survive in accord with the covenant promises made long ago (12:12–13).

At this point, in the middle of a sentence, there is a break in the text and the remaining contents of the document are lost.

Text

The sole extant copy of our text is a Latin palimpsest discovered by A. M. Ceriani in the Ambrosian Library in Milan in 1861. It dates from the sixth century, but the style and orthography indicate that the original Latin text is about a century earlier. The preserved text is clearly incomplete with perhaps one third to one half being lost. There are gaps in those sections that do remain, and in many places the writing is scarcely legible.[1] Further, it is apparent that either the Latin translator or the copyist, or both, were careless in both spelling and grammar. Consequently, editors and translators have had to resort to many emendations and reconstructions.

Original language

It was apparent to the first editors of the text that the Latin was translated from Greek. A few Greek words appear as transliterations, certain syntactical constructions clearly reflect a Greek background, and some difficult passages may be clarified by reconstructing the Greek that underlies the Latin. Most of the first editors and translators assumed that the original language was indeed Greek. Further investigation, however, indicates that the Greek itself was, in all probability, a translation of a Semitic original. This view is almost universally accepted today, but there remains a question as to whether the original was Aramaic or Hebrew. Certainty is not possible, but the balance of probability leans toward Hebrew.[2] That the text is a translation of a translation further complicates the problem for modern translators as will be indicated in some of the notes.

Date

Widely differing estimates have been proposed for the date of the document, but these may be classified into three broad categories: (1) in the first half of the second century A.D., most likely in the period just following the war of A.D. 132–135; (2) during the period of the Maccabean revolt, i.e. 168–165 B.C.; and (3) in the first century A.D., before the fall of Jerusalem in A.D. 70 and most likely during the first three decades of that century. The first option has been most vigorously argued by S. Zeitlin,[3] but though many of his arguments deserve careful attention, they fail to carry conviction as a whole. The second option has most recently been proposed by J. Licht[4] and adopted especially by G. Nickelsburg.[5] The thrust of Licht's argument rests on his theological interpretation of the role of Taxo in chapter 9 and of the eschatological hymn in chapter 10. Nickelsburg accepts this position but develops more intricate arguments for the Maccabean dating. He bases his position on a form-critical analysis of the document as a whole and on the apparent description of the persecutions of Antiochus IV Epiphanes in chapter 8. He believes that the vividness of this description indicates that the persecution was contemporary with the author. However, chapter 6 contains a serious difficulty for a Maccabean dating as there is near universal agreement that Herod's reign and death are there referred to. This would mean that the text, in its present form, could not have been written before 4 B.C. Licht and Nickelsburg solve this problem by suggesting that chapter 6, and perhaps chapter 7, are interpolations into a document that had its origin in the Maccabean period.

The arguments for a date in the first century A.D., before A.D. 70, were stated in their fullest form by R. H. Charles.[6] His main points were that the date must be (1) before A.D. 70, since the Temple is still standing (1:17); (2) after 4 B.C., since Herod is already dead (4:6); (3) before A.D. 30, since it is stated that Herod will beget heirs who will reign for shorter periods than he (6:7), i.e. less than his reign of thirty-four years; and (4) after A.D. 7 since he supposed that the text implies that Archelaus has already been deposed.

---

[1] D. H. Wallace, in private correspondence, has indicated that all technological efforts to restore illegible portions of the text have thus far resulted in failure.

[2] See the discussions in E. M. Laperrousaz, *Le Testament de Moïse*, pp. 16–25; R. H. Charles, *The Assumption of Moses*, pp. xxxvi–xlv; R. H. Charles, *APOT*, vol. 2, p. 410; D. H. Wallace, "The Semitic Origin of the Assumption of Moses," *TZ* 11 (1955) 321–28.

[3] S. Zeitlin, "The Assumption of Moses and the Bar Kokhba Revolt," *JQR* 38 (1947/48) 1–45.

[4] J. Licht, "Taxo, or the Apocalyptic Doctrine of Vengeance," *JJS* 12 (1961) 95–103.

[5] G. Nickelsburg, *Resurrection, Immortality and Eternal Life in Inter-Testamental Judaism* (HTS 26; Cambridge, 1972) especially pp. 28–31, 43–45, 97; and "An Antiochan Date for the Testament of Moses," *Studies on the Testament of Moses*, pp. 33–37.

[6] Charles, *Assumption*, pp. lv–lviii; *APOT*, vol. 2, p. 411.

[7] Charles, *Assumption*, pp. 28–30; *APOT*, vol. 2, p. 420. Some scholars have modified this view and transpose only ch. 8. See H. H. Rowley, *The Relevance of Apocalyptic*, p. 107.

Just as the obvious Herodian references in chapter 6 posed a serious problem for a Maccabean date, so also the apparent chronological discrepancy in chapters 5 through 9 required Charles to propose a theory of dislocation of the text and a suggested rearrangement. Since he believed that in those chapters the author was describing historical events with chronological consistency, the references to Herod's reign in chapters 6 and 7 should follow chapters 8 and 9, which reflect the persecutions of Antiochus IV Epiphanes. Concluding that at some stage of transmission there was dislocation, he solved the problem by inserting chapters 8 and 9 between 5 and 6, thus restoring what he presumed to be the original order.[7]

Although this proposal has been widely accepted, it is cogent only if one assumes that contemporary canons of consistency must apply to an apocalyptic author. Rejection of Charles's theory on this point does not, however, affect his overall argument for a first-century A.D. date, while acceptance of the interpolation proposal is mandatory for a Maccabean dating. The possibility of interpolation is not to be dismissed arbitrarily. Indeed, it is probable that the text has a long and obscure literary history, which includes additions, interpolations, and other forms of editing. The fragmentary, often untrustworthy, nature of the Latin, itself one language removed from the Semitic original, precludes operating with the critical precision implicit in any specific theory of interpolation, dislocation, or rearrangement. Consequently, it is better to retain the first-century date of the document, with the recognition that some of the materials may have had a considerable prior history in either oral or written form.

Provenance and historical importance

The geographical locale of the Testament of Moses has elicited little discussion by commentators. A few have tentatively proposed a Western, probably Roman origin, but most assume a Palestinian locale. Though specific evidence is lacking, the latter proposal is probably correct.

The question of the community to which the author belonged has prompted a wide variety of answers. At one time or another almost every well-known Jewish religious group from the Sadducees to the Samaritans has been suggested.[8] Three suggestions seem to warrant serious consideration: (1) the rather amorphous group called the Hasidim, known to us to have been a party from Maccabean times at least; (2) a branch of the Pharisaic party; and (3) the Essenes. Two difficulties, neither insurmountable, appertain to the first suggestion. Information about the Hasidim is too general in nature to isolate specific features that might separate them ideologically; and it is generally agreed that from the first century B.C. onward the general Hasidic movement became focused in more clearly defined sectarian groups. The question of the date of the Testament of Moses, therefore, is significant in determining the group in which it originated. A Maccabean date would be appropriate for the general Hasidic movement while the first century A.D. date would require a more specific identification.

Charles presented the most forceful argument for a Pharisaic origin. He insisted that the author was a Pharisaic quietist who was resisting a growing nationalistic tendency within the party. Charles also noted the continuity between the outlook of the author and of the old Hasidic ideals. The majority of commentators since Charles have accepted his position.

A few early commentators suggested that the book came from Essene circles and the discovery of the Qumran and related materials resulted in fresh adherents to this opinion. There are, indeed, many parallels between the Qumran materials and the Testament of Moses. Some of these will be found in the notes. That no fragments of the work have been identified at Qumran is a serious, though by no means decisive, objection to the Essene theory. Some may subsequently be identified, and there is no reason to suppose that the entire corpus of Essene literature has been preserved. The Testament of Moses does appear to have closer affinities with the Essenes than with any other *known* group in the Judaism of the period.

There is increasing evidence, however, that the Judaism of this period was quite complex. It would appear unwise, therefore, to insist on the identification of every document with a

---

[8] For a convenient review, see Laperrousaz, *Testament*, pp. 88–95. Charles, *Assumption*, pp. li–liv, and *APOT*, vol. 2, p. 411, surveyed earlier scholarship but his review needs to be brought up to date.

specific group.[9] Our present information requires a measure of tentativeness. It seems preferable not to assign to the Testament of Moses either a Pharisaic or an Essene origin but to state simply that it reflects the general outlook of the later Hasidic movement with a stress on apocalyptic motifs. Whether this was an individual or sectarian view cannot be ascertained.[10]

Theological importance

E. Laperrousaz has rightly remarked that the theology of the Testament of Moses is not very original.[11] Fundamentally, the theology reflects apocalyptic determinism although the Deuteronomic view that evildoers will be punished and the righteous will be rewarded is also present (12:10–11). This somewhat paradoxical combination is not unknown in other works of the period.

The deterministic theme, however, is dominant. All that has happened in the past was determined by God and revealed to Moses (3:11–12; 12:4–5). Thus, the promises of Moses that God's eschatological intervention is at hand (10:1–12) and that his covenant promises will not fail (12:3–13, and see below) may be received with full assurance. This, of course, is a primary purpose of apocalyptic, to give hope to those who are oppressed and in despair. The Testament of Moses fully shares that purpose.

The central argument for the assertion of Israel's final hope lies in the author's conviction that the covenant promises of God are certain (cf. 1:8–9; 3:9; 4:2–6; 12:7–13). Moses asserts that just as the guidance in the wilderness was not due to his strength (12:7) nor the impending conquest due to the piety of the people (12:8), so the final deliverance would result solely from the action of God, predetermined by his covenant and oath (12:13).

It has been claimed that the statement in 1:12 "God has created the world on behalf of his people" is not found in any work prior to the first century B.C. though it is found often in subsequent writings.[12] Chronological priority may belong to our document, but whether the idea originated with the author of the Testament of Moses cannot be determined.

Similarly, 1:14 says, "But he did design and devise me, who (was) prepared from the beginning of the world, to be the mediator of his covenant." This has been cited as being original in speaking of Moses' pre-existence and in designating him as a mediator. It seems dubious that the text can bear the weight of claiming pre-existence for Moses as a *person*, though this is not impossible since such a claim *may* have been made for the Son of Man in 1 Enoch (see especially 48:2, 3, 6; 62:7) and 4 Ezra (especially 12:32; 13:26) and since some Alexandrian Jewish circles taught the pre-existence of all souls. It seems wiser simply to say that our author, consistent with his thorough determinism, stated that Moses' *role* had been decreed from the beginning of the world. Whether he believed that Moses himself was "precreated" is not clear.

Moses' decreed role is clearly that of mediator. It is true that in the Old Testament Moses is not called a mediator and that the word occurs only in Job 9:33, but many narratives portray him in that role and the designation is quite well known in other documents of the first century A.D. (e.g. Gal 3:18; Heb 8:6; 9:15; 12:21; Philo, *Vita Mos* 3:19). Again, chronological priority *may* reside with the Testament of Moses, but it is probably too much to claim originality. Both the ideas of pre-existence and the designation of Moses as a mediator were in the air at the time.

One passage, the story of Taxo and his seven sons (ch. 9) warrants a more detailed examination. Not here applicable is whether its significance belongs properly to the issue of theological importance, historical importance, or relation to apocryphal works; that issue

---

[9] Charles, *Assumption*, p. liv, and *APOT*, vol. 2, p. 411, felt required to subdivide the Pharisees and speak of the author as a "quietistic Pharisee." Laperrousaz, *Testament*, p. 95, argues for Essene origin but notes that the author was an Essene with particular qualities. The necessity of such qualifications damages attempts to make clear positive identifications.

[10] M. Smith, in *Palestinian Parties and Politics that Shaped the Old Testament* (New York, 1971) p. 157, suggests that the author of TMos founded a sect that declared all sacrifices of the second Temple impure (see 5:4–5). The evidence is somewhat tenuous.

[11] Laperrousaz, *Testament*, p. 80. For convenient summaries of the theology of TMos as a whole, see Laperrousaz *Testament*, pp. 80–87; Charles, *Assumption*, pp. lviii–lxi, and *APOT*, vol. 2, pp. 411–12.

[12] Other views, that the world was created for the righteous, e.g. 2Bar 14:19; 15:7; 21:24; 4Ezra 9:13; or for al mankind, e.g. 4Ezra 8:1, 44, are also common.

is problematical and results perhaps from an arbitrary division. Most scholars who have dealt with Taxo attempted to decipher the cryptic name and thus identify him historically. Their ingenuity is impressive but not very productive.[13] Focus on the function of Taxo rather than on historical identification is a more fruitful angle of approach.

C. J. Lattey suggested that Taxo be understood as the suffering Messiah whose appearance and death bring about the divine consummation.[14] The methods by which the name Taxo is made to refer to the Messiah are too oblique to convince many of the identification, but an understanding of Taxo as the one who precipitates the divine vengeance that inaugurates the end-time has recently gained considerable support.[15] It has been maintained that the death of Taxo and his sons was intended to provoke the divine vengeance and thus be the instrument provoking the onset of the eschatological age. The death of Taxo and his sons will "compel God to exercise His vengeance."[16]

Comparison of the story of Taxo and his sons with other accounts of martyrdom in contemporary documents, particularly 1, 2, and 4 Maccabees, raises questions about this conclusion. There the reasons for and the results of martyrdom are by no means consistent. In some cases the martyrs are innocent, in others they suffer for their own sins. Their deaths may be simply exemplary, they may lead to restoration of life, or they may serve as a vicarious expiation for the sinful community. It should be noted that even when expiation is mentioned, there is no eschatological dimension envisaged.[17]

It might, nevertheless, be argued that the role of a righteous sufferer as provoking divine vengeance is a unique teaching in the Testament of Moses. This is possible, but the text does not demand such an interpretation. It is more likely that the author has used a typical martyr story to introduce his pronouncement of the end of time. He has included in the story motifs, known to us elsewhere, of God's avenging innocent suffering and, perhaps, has hinted at the idea of vicarious propitiation, although this is not clear. That he has set forth a unique teaching that Taxo's innocent suffering is the act that provokes the divine vengeance that leads to the consummation of the end-time seems to require much more than the text will bear.

Taxo is better seen as a singular example of the extreme woes that will beset God's people in the last days than as one who plays a significant part in precipitating the advent of those days. That the Testament of Moses proclaims divine vengeance is not to be denied. That Taxo is the instrument of that divine vengeance remains unproved. For the author of the Testament of Moses, God alone is the worker of his predetermined will.

Relation to canonical books

The most obvious relationship between the Testament of Moses and the Hebrew canon is with Deuteronomy, especially chapters 31 to 34 of that book. The basic outline of the Testament of Moses follows the pattern of those chapters to such an extent that the Testament of Moses may be considered a virtual rewriting of them.[18] This is true not only with respect to general outline but also regarding specific allusions and theological perspective. Deuteronomy 31–34 is clearly the author's model, though he has recast his own work in light of the history of the people from the conquest to his own day and through the prism of his own apocalyptic outlook.

Influence by other canonical books is much more difficult to assess. Attention has been drawn to possible relationships between the Testament of Moses and Daniel. Most commentators conclude that the person in the Testament who prays for the people at 4:1 is Daniel and note the passage in Daniel 4:4–19. Further, parallels between the judgment scene in Daniel 12 and the hymn in Testament of Moses 10 have been cited. It is probable that the

---

[13] Convenient summaries of this interesting episode in the history of scholarship may be found in Rowley, *Relevance*, pp. 149–56; Zeitlin, *JQR* 38 (1947/48) 4–5.

[14] C. J. Lattey, "The Messianic Expectation in 'The Assumption of Moses,' " *CBQ* 4 (1942) 9–21.

[15] Licht, *JJS* 12 (1961) 95–103. Cf. n. 4 above.

[16] Licht, *JJS* 12 (1961) 98.

[17] For a more extensive treatment comparing the martyr stories, see J. Priest, *Perspectives in Religious Studies* 4 (1977) 99–103. The entire article, 92–111, elaborates a number of points alluded to in this introduction.

[18] Nickelsburg, *Resurrection*, p. 29. The use of Deut 31–34 is so extensive that marginal references to biblical parallels in the translation will note only those that contain direct verbal allusions.

identification of the prayer with Daniel is correct. This, however, would not necessarily mean that the author of the Testament of Moses was familiar with the book of Daniel but rather with certain Danielic traditions. There are enough differences between the judgment scenes in Daniel and the Testament of Moses to raise serious questions about the precise nature of their relationship.[19] Thus, though it is probable that the author of the Testament of Moses was acquainted with the book of Daniel, it is not possible to assert definite dependence on his part. Allusions, both verbal and in thought, to a number of Old Testament books do appear in the Testament and will be noted in the references to the following translation. However, the Testament of Moses does not seem to reflect direct influence by any work other than Deuteronomy. It may be noted that priestly interests occur prominently but hardly as a reflection of any definite text.

Some influence by the Testament of Moses on a number of New Testament passages has been suggested. Those most often cited are Jude 9, 12–13, 16; 2 Peter 2:13; Acts 7:36–43; and Matthew 24:19–21 (with parallels). Jude 9 refers to the story of the dispute between Michael and Satan for the body of Moses, an account that does not appear in our text. That the episode was contained in the lost ending of the Testament of Moses or in a cognate work, properly called the Assumption of Moses, is possible; but our present information does not warrant any positive conclusion. (The relation between a Testament of Moses and an Assumption of Moses will be discussed below.) Jude 12–13 utilizes nature metaphors reminiscent of Testament of Moses 10:5–6[20] and Jude 16 describes opponents in language similar to a number of passages in our document. In both instances, however, the contexts are quite different. Nevertheless, the strongest case for possible knowledge of the Testament of Moses by a New Testament writer is with the letter of Jude. The other proposals are not compelling. The possibility exists that some New Testament authors were familiar with the Testament of Moses, but it would be better to say that both the Testament of Moses and certain New Testament texts show familarity with common traditional material.[21]

Relation to apocryphal books

Evidence for literary relations among apocryphal books is difficult to assess. Two factors, primarily, contribute to this difficulty. First is the problem of relative dating. There is far from universal agreement regarding the date of most works, and even the relative dates suggested may vary widely. Second, unless there is a direct reference linking two works together, there is the possibility, even probability, that similar passages represent a similar development of Old Testament passages or common sources rather than direct dependence of one on the other. Many phrases and themes in the Testament of Moses do have parallels in other apocryphal works, but they should probably be considered as parallel statements emanating from a common milieu. Evidence of dependence or acquaintance cannot be demonstrated.

Since the view that the Testament of Moses is of Essene origin has been renewed,[22] its relationship with the Qumran materials should be mentioned. There are, indeed, many instances of verbal similarities, particularly with CD and 1QH.[23] Further, some of the polemic interests in the Qumran materials are also to be found in the Testament of Moses. But the overall theological perspective of the Testament of Moses differs so much at crucial junctures from the Qumran literature that it is difficult to see how it could be a product of the Qumran community, though it is not improbable that the author, given the date proposed here, could have been acquainted with the thought and perhaps some of the writings of that sect.

---

[19] Nickelsburg, *Resurrection*, p. 30.

[20] See the discussion by D. J. Rowton, "The Most Neglected Book in the New Testament" *NTS* 21 (1974/75) 558.

[21] For detailed discussions, see Charles, *Assumption*, pp. lxii–lxv, and *APOT*, vol. 2, pp. 412f.; Laperrousaz, *Testament*, pp. 50–76.

[22] E.g. by A. Dupont-Sommer, *The Essene Writings from Qumran* (Cleveland, 1967) p. 96, and the discussion in Laperrousaz, *Testament*, pp. 91–95.

[23] A number of similarities will be referred to in the nn. on the translation. One Qumran text, 1QDM, could be of considerable interest, but the extant fragments show no particular connections with TMos. The editors remark that "One may suppose that the composition ended with the death of Moses, and eventually his assumption" (p. 91). Of this there is no textual evidence. See D. Barthelemy and J. T. Milik, *Qumran Cave I* (Oxford, 1955) pp. 91–97, and plates xviii–xix.

Nevertheless, his own sectarian outlook did have its own peculiar development. And again, a common milieu may account for the apparent parallels.

Finally, apocryphal works associated with the name of Moses are mentioned frequently in early Jewish and Christian sources.[24] Precise identification is often difficult or impossible. Of particular interest, however, are those references that speak of both an Assumption of Moses and a Testament of Moses. Both are mentioned in some lists of noncanonical books,[25] and the former is specifically named in some early Greek and Latin writings.[26] Other writings, though not specifically naming a source, cite material that would be appropriate to a work describing the death and assumption of Moses.

Ceriani identified the present manuscript as the Assumption of Moses on the basis of a passage from the Acts of the Council of Nicea that appeared to cite 1:14, and perhaps parts of 1:6 and 1:9, as "having been written in the book of the Assumption of Moses." Later on, the same text spoke of the struggle between the archangel Michael and the devil, which is known from other early texts to be a part of the Assumption of Moses, and again cited its source as "book of the Assumption of Moses."[27] Since his initial identification, the book has regularly been called the Assumption of Moses.

Commentators on the manuscript discovered by Ceriani have regularly noted that the extant text nowhere mentions the assumption of Moses. Indeed all references to his impending death imply that it is to be a natural one (1:15; 3:3; 10:12, 14). The form of the present text is that of a farewell speech, or testament, which is a well-known genre in itself. Since the ancient lists recorded both an Assumption of Moses and a Testament of Moses, was Ceriani correct in identifying the manuscript as the Assumption or would it be more appropriate to infer that it is indeed the Testament?

There is no unambiguous answer to this question. Since the extant manuscript is clearly incomplete it may be that the lost section did go on to tell of Moses' death and assumption. The evidence from the Acts of the Council of Nicea can be interpreted in this way. Charles proposed that there were originally two separate works, a testament and an assumption account, which were joined together at an early period and that subsequently the whole was referred to as the Assumption of Moses.[28] This is an attractive suggestion but cannot be demonstrated. The matter remains open but since the only text we have is a farewell speech, a testament, most modern commentators prefer to refer to it as the Testament of Moses, and that is the practice followed in this work.

SELECT BIBLIOGRAPHY

Charlesworth, *PMR*, pp. 163–66.
Delling, *Bibliographie*, pp. 164f.
Denis, *Introduction*, pp. 128–41.

Charles, R. H. *The Assumption of Moses*. London, 1897. (This contains the unemended Lat. text, a proposed emended text, introduction, translation, and copious annotation.)
———. *The Apocrypha and Pseudepigrapha of the Old Testament*. Oxford, 1913. vol. 2, pp. 407–24. (This is an abbreviated version of the previous entry, with modest modifications of position.)

---

[24] See J. H. Charlesworth, *PMR*, pp. 159–66 and the literature cited there.

[25] A convenient collection of various lists, with a brief discussion, may be found in D. H. Russell, *The Method and Message of Jewish Apocalyptic* (Philadelphia, 1964) pp. 391–95.

[26] The citations and discussion may be found in Laperrousaz, *Testament*, pp. 29–62; Charles, *Assumption*, pp. xlv–l, 105–10; and *APOT*, vol 2, pp. 407–10; A. M. Denis, *Fragmenta pseudepigraphorum quae supersunt graeca*, pp. 63–67.

[27] Denis, *Fragmenta*, pp. 63–64.

[28] Charles, *Assumption*, pp. xlv–l, and *APOT*, vol. 2, p. 208.

Denis, A. M. *Fragmenta pseudepigraphorum quae supersunt graeca.* PVTG 3; Leiden, 1970; pp. 63–67. (This contains the actual Gk. citations which are directly related to TMos.)

Laperrousaz, E. M. *Le Testament de Moïse (généralement appelé 'Assomption de Moïse'): Traduction avec introduction et notes.* Semitica 19; Paris, 1970. (This is the most recent and most important full-scale treatment. The Introduction is superb and the translation eminently readable. The conclusions, in the main, follow Charles though the author proposes an Essene origin and reduces the number of emendations proposed by Charles.)

Lattey, C. J. "The Messianic Expectation in 'The Assumption of Moses,' " *CBQ* 4 (1942) 9–21. (Lattey attempts to identify Taxo as a suffering Messiah. While the result is not convincing, the evidence adduced warrants careful attention.)

Licht, J. "Taxo, or the Apocalyptic Doctrine of Vengeance," *JJS* 12 (1961) 95–103. (Licht stresses that it is the martyrdom of Taxo which brings about the divine vengeance and that this teaching is unique with TMos. Though that view is not accepted here, the evidence deserves serious attention. The article is also important for the influence it has had upon recent scholarship which argues for a Maccabean dating for TMos.)

Nickelsburg, G. (ed.). *Studies on the Testament of Moses.* SCS 4; Cambridge, 1973. (This is a valuable collection of working papers devoted to a number of aspects of the study of TMos.)

Priest, J. "Some Reflections on the Assumption of Moses," *Perspectives in Religious Studies* 4 (1977) 92–111. (This deals particularly with the function of Taxo and the eschatological hymn in ch. 10.)

Rowley, H. H. *The Relevance of Apocalyptic.* New York, 1963; pp. 106–10, 149–56. (This is a valuable review of different scholarly opinions about TMos.)

Wallace, D. H. "The Semitic Origin of the Assumption of Moses," *TZ* 11 (1955) 321–28. (This is a cautious and constructive survey of the evidence for a Semitic original.)

Zeitlin, S. "The Assumption of Moses and the Bar Kokhba Revolt," *JQR* 38 (1947/48) 1–45. (Zeitlin's citations of rabbinic materials and some of his conjectural translations are useful and stimulating.)

THE TESTAMENT OF MOSES

1 **1** [The first three lines of text are missing. There was probably some reference
to the year of Moses' life when he delivered the farewell speech to Joshua. Cf.
2 Deut 31:2; 34:7.] . . . ᵃ•which is twenty five hundred years after the creation of
3 the world, •but according to an oriental chronology [. . .] after the departure from
4 Phoenecia.ᵃ •When, after the exodus, which had been ledᵇ by Moses, the people
5 had gone up to Amman across the Jordan, •this is the prophecy which was made
by Moses in the book of Deuteronomy.

6 Mosesᶜ called to himself Joshua, the son of Nun, a man approved by the Lord, _{Deut 31:7}
7 that Joshua might become the ministerᵈ for the people in the tent of testimony
8 which contained all the holy objects, •and that he might lead the people into the
9 land which had been promised to their fathers,ᵉ •(the land) which he, inᶠ the tent, _{Deut 31:14f.}
had declared by covenant and oath that he would give them through the leadershipᵍ
10 of Joshua. •ʰThen Moses spoke to Joshua this word, "Go forward with all your _{Josh 1:7}
strength, that you may do everything which has been commanded in such a way
11 as will cause you no blame in the sight of God. •For this is what the Lord of the
12,13 world has decreed.ʰ •He created the world on behalf of his people, •but he did not
make this purpose of creation openly known from the beginning of the world so
that the nations might be found guilty, indeed that they might abjectly declare
themselves guilty by their own (mistaken) discussions (of creation's purpose).
14 "But he did design and devise me, who (was) prepared from the beginning of
15 the world, to be the mediator of his covenant. •Therefore, I shall speak plainly to
you. The years of my lifeⁱ have come to an end and, in the presence of the entire
16 community, I am going to sleep with my fathers.ʲ •But (you) take this writing so
that later you will remember how to preserve the books which I shall entrust to
17 you. • You shall arrange them, anoint them with cedar, and deposit them in
earthenware jars in the place which (God) has chosen from the beginning of the
18 creation of the world, •(a place) where his name may be called upon until the day
of recompense when the Lord will surely have regard for his people.ᵏ

1 **2** "[. . .]ᵃ (The people), under your leadership,ᵇ will enter into the land which
2 (God) firmly promisedᶜ to give to their fathers. •In that land,ᵈ you will bless them
and give to each of them their individual portions. Further, you shall firmly establish
a kingdom for them and, with discernment and justice, you shall appoint local

---

1 a. Ancient sources give various dates for Moses'
death. If the scheme used by TMos were known
it might help date the composition of the book, but
this is not the case. The reference to an oriental
chronology, probably another dating system known
to the author, is too broken to be reconstructed.

b. Lit. "given."

c. Lit. "who."

d. Lat. "successor." It has been suggested that
Gk. *diadochos* is underlying; LXX uses that word
for chief minister in 1Chr 18:17; 2Chr 26:11; 28:7;
and Sir 46:1. The usage is also found in Josephus,
Ant 15.10, and frequently in Philo.

e. Lit. "with respect to their tribes."

f. Lit. "and."

g. Lit. "by means of."

h. Lit. "Speaking to Joshua this word, and go
forth according to your strength so that you may
do all things which have been commanded without
blame. It is for this purpose the Lord of the world
speaks."

i. Lit. "the time of the years of my life."

j. The biblical account of Moses' death (Deut
34:5–8) states that no one witnessed the death.
Later Jewish tradition is divided on the matter.
Some writings assert that Joshua and Caleb were
present while others affirm that Moses did not die
at all.

k. Lit. "so that his name may be called upon
till the day of recompence (or repentance) with
regard to which the Lord will regard them in the
consummation of the end of days." This is a clear
attempt to render literally a Semitic original.

2 a. The lacuna, of four to seven letters, is often
restored with "and now" or "behold now."

b. Lit. "through you."

c. Lit. "he determined and promised." This is
another example of a literal rendering of a Semitic
original.

d. Lit. "in which."

3 magistrates in accordance with the will of the Lord. • Then, (some)[e] years after they shall have entered their land, they shall be ruled by leaders and princes for eighteen years. (But during a period) of nineteen years the ten tribes will separate themselves.[f]

4 "(During the first-mentioned time) the twelve[g] tribes will move the tent of testimony to the place where the God of heaven will build a place for his sanctuary.[h]
5 The two holy tribes will be settled there. • But the ten tribes will establish for
6 themselves their own kingdom with its own ordinances.[i] • (The two tribes will)
7 offer sacrifices in the chosen place for twenty years.[j] • Seven will strongly build the walls, and I will protect nine. (Four), however, will violate the covenant of
8 the Lord and defile the oath which the Lord made with them.[k] • They will offer their sons to foreign gods and they will set up idols in the Temple[l] that they may
9 worship them. •(Yes), even in the house of the Lord they will perpetrate idolatry[m] and carve images of all sorts of animals.

2Kgs 16:3; 21:6
Ezek 16:20;
20:26
Ps 106:34-39
Ezek 8:8-16

1 **3** "[. . .] in those days a king against them from the east and (his) cavalry will
2 overrun their land.[a] • And with fire he will burn their city[b] with the holy Temple
3 of the Lord and he will carry off all the holy vessels. • And he will exile all the people and will lead them to his own land, yea the two tribes he will take with him.

2Chr 36:7
Jer 27:18-22

4 "Then, considering[c] themselves like a lioness in a dusty plain, hungry and
5 parched, the two tribes will call upon the ten tribes, •and shall declare loudly, 'Just and holy is the Lord. For just as you sinned, likewise we, with our little ones,[d]
6 have now been led out with you.' •Then, hearing the reproachful words of the two
7 tribes, the ten tribes will lament • and will say, 'What shall we, with you, do,
8 brothers? Has not this tribulation come upon the whole house of Israel?'[e] •Then
9 all the tribes will lament, crying out to heaven and saying, • 'God of Abraham, God of Isaac, and God of Jacob, remember your covenant which you made with them, and the oath which you swore to them by yourself, that their seed would never fail from the land which you have given them.'

Gen 22:16-18
Ex 32:13
Heb 6:13-18

10 "Then, in that day, they will remember me, saying from tribe to tribe, even
11 each man to his neighbor, • 'Is this not that which was made known to us in prophecies by Moses, who suffered many things in Egypt and at the Red Sea and
12 in the wilderness for forty years •(when) he solemnly called heaven and earth as

Acts 7:36-41

---

e. Although the text reads only "years" there is a space and most commentators insert a specific number, the choices being five, six, or seven, depending on the length of time assumed for the conquest. See Josh 14:10 and Josephus, *Ant* 5.1.19.

f. References are to the fifteen judges, the three kings of the united monarchy, and the nineteen kings of the northern kingdom.

g. Text "two," but the historical reference is to a time when the tribes were still united. The error may be due to mention of the two holy tribes later in the vs., or it may be a sectarian rewriting of history, which limited the association of the ark to the two faithful tribes, although this is doubtful.

h. The Lat. *"fecit palam scenae suae et ferrum sancturii sui . . ."* is hardly translatable. The translation gives the general sense.

i. This vs. is parenthetical as it interrupts the story of the two southern tribes begun in the previous vs. and continued in the following.

j. A reference to the twenty monarchs of the southern kingdom.

k. There are three textual problems in this vs., though only the first is important for interpretation. The verb here translated "protect" indicates a positive attitude toward the second grouping of Judean monarchs, but translated "beset" or "besiege" it would connote a negative attitude. The final number "four" is not in the text but is supplied to bring the total to twenty as in the previous vs. Finally, the Lat. here translated "oath" is *finem* ("end," "aim," or "purpose"). "Oath" is used because of the close connection between "covenant and oath" elsewhere (1:9; 3:9; 11:17; 12:13).

l. Lit. "tent."

m. Lit. "will act wickedly."

3 a. The reference is probably to the invasion by Nebuchadnezzar. 1QpHab 3.6–14 offers an interesting parallel.

b. Lit. "colony," reflecting a date for the translation after A.D. 135, as Jerusalem was made a Roman colony at that time.

c. Lat. *ducent se*. Perhaps *docent* should be read, but *duco* can bear the meaning proposed in the translation.

d. In the text "with our little ones" is in the previous vs., but seems to belong here.

e. It has been suggested that the two tribes blame their present plight on the previous sins of the other ten, but the mention of the sinful acts of the last Judean kings (2:7–9) precludes this interpretation. The fact of mutual exile, in any event, restores the solidarity of the entire community.

witnesses against us that we should not transgress God's[f] commandments of which   Deut 4:26;
13 he had become the mediator for us? •These things which have come upon us since   30:19; 31:28
that time are according to his admonition declared to us at that time. And (those   Dan 9:13
words) have been confirmed even to our being led as captives in the land of the
14 East.' •And they will be as slaves for about seventy-seven years.[g]

1 **4** "Then one who is over them[a] will come upon the scene, and he will stretch   Dan 9:4-19
2 forth his hands, and bow his knees and pray for them, saying, •'Lord of all, king
on the lofty throne, you who rules the world, who has willed that this people be
for you a chosen people, yea, who has willed to be called their God according to
3 the covenant which you made with their fathers, •yet they, with their wives and
children, have gone as captives into a foreign land, surrounded by the gates of
4 strangers where there is great majesty.[b] •Have regard for them, and have compassion for them, O heavenly Lord.'
5   "Then God will remember them because of the covenant which he made with
6 their fathers and he will openly show his compassion. •And in those times he will   2Chr 36:22-23
inspire a king to have pity on them and send them home to their own land.[c]   Ezra 1:1-4
7 Then some parts of the tribes will arise and come to their appointed place, and   Neh 2:17;
8 they will strongly build its walls.[d] •Now, the two tribes will remain steadfast in   6:15-16
their former faith, sorrowful and sighing because they will not be able to offer   Ezra 6:6-12
9 sacrifices to the Lord of their fathers.[e] •But the ten tribes will grow and spread out
among the nations during the time of their captivity.[f]

1 **5** [a]"And when the times of exposure come near and punishment arises through
2 kings who (though) sharing their crimes yet punish them, •then they themselves
3 will be divided as to the truth. •Consequently the word was fulfilled that they will   Deut 31:16
avoid justice and approach iniquity; and they will pollute the house of their worship
with the customs of the nations; and they will play the harlot after foreign gods.[b]
4 For they will not follow the truth of God, but certain of them will pollute the high
altar by [four to six letters are lost] the offerings which they place before the Lord.
5 They are not (truly) priests (at all), but slaves, yea sons of slaves.[c] •For those who
are the leaders, their teachers, in those times will become admirers of avaricious   Isa 5:23
persons, accepting (polluted) offerings, and they will sell justice by accepting
6 bribes.[d] •Therefore, their city[e] and the full extent of their dwelling places[f] will be

---

f. Lit. "his."
g. According to Jer 25:11–12 and 29:10, the
exile was to last seventy years. Dan 9:21 interprets
this to mean seventy weeks of years. The background of the number here is unknown, but apocalyptic numerology often defies precise interpretation.

4 a. The "one over them" is usually interpreted
as Daniel. This is probable, though Ezra or an angel
(see Zech 1:12) have also been suggested.
b. Text *maiestas*, which is retained here. The
emendation to *vanitas* ("vanity") is often made.
c. Lit. "their own land and region."
d. Lit. "they will build a palisade, restoring the
place." This is another clear attempt to render a
Semitic original.
e. "Former" is more properly translated
"given" but this hardly changes the meaning. The
crucial issue is whether the author rejects all sacrifice in the second Temple or deplores the conditions in the second Temple as compared with the
First. That the situation in the second Temple was
deplored in works of the period is clear, cf. 1En
89:73; 2Bar 68:5–6; and many instances from Qum-

ran and in PssSol. The evidence in TMos does not
permit a definitive interpretation. That the second
Temple was considered inferior to the first is a
common theme in both biblical and extrabiblical
writings and that TMos asserts more than this is
not likely.
f. The Lat. does not make sense and the translation is an educated guess based on several emendations.
5 a. Ch. 5 probably refers to the Hasmonean period
(142–63 B.C.). This negative attitude toward the
Hasmoneans is also found at Qumran but this need
not mean that TMos and the Qumran literature
emanate from the same group. Though there are
many parallels, these should be attributed to a common situation rather than to a common source.
b. See PssSol 1:8; 2:2; 8:13, 16; etc.; and CD
4.16–18; 5.6–7; etc., for similar examples of sectarian controversy.
c. This charge was made against (John Hyrcanus), Josephus, *Ant* 13.10.5.
d. Lit. "atonement fees."
e. Lit. "colony."
f. Lit. "bounds of their habitation." This is
another clear Semitism.

filled with crimes and iniquities. For they will have in their midst judges who will act with impiety toward the Lord and will judge just as they please.ᵍ

1 **6** "Then powerful kings will rise over them, and they will be called priests of the
2 Most High God. They will perform great impietyᵃ in the Holy of Holies. •And a wanton king, who will not be of a priestly family, will follow them. He will be
3 a man rash and perverse, and he will judge them as they deserve. •He will shatter their leaders with the sword, and he will (exterminate them) in secret placesᵇ so
4 that no one will know where their bodies are.ᶜ •He will kill both old and young, showing mercy to none.ᵈ
5,6 "Then fear of him will be heapedᵉ upon them in their land, •and for thirty-four years he will impose judgments upon them as did the Egyptians, and he will punish
7 them. •And he will beget heirs who will reign after him for shorter periods of
8 time.ᶠ •After his death there will come into their land a powerful king of the West
9 who will subdue them; •and he will take away captives, and a part of their temple he will burn with fire. He will crucify some of them around their city.ᵍ

1,2 **7** "When this has taken place, the times will quickly come to an end. •[. . .]ᵃ
3 Then will rule destructive and godless men, who represent themselves as being
4 righteous, •but who will (in fact) arouse their inner wrath,ᵇ for they will be deceitful men, pleasing only themselves, false in every way imaginable, (such as) loving feasts at any hour of the day—devouring, gluttonous.
5 "[Seven lines of the text are either totally missing or are so broken as to permit
6 no translation.] •But really they consume the goods of the (poor), saying their acts
7 are according to justice, •(while in fact they are simply) exterminators,ᶜ deceitfully seeking to conceal themselves so that they will not be known as completely godless
8 because of their criminal deeds (committed) all the day long,ᵈ •saying, 'We shall have feasts, even luxurious winings and dinings. Indeed, we shall behave ourselves
9 as princes.' •They, with hand and mind, will touch impure things, yet their mouths
10 will speak enormous things, and they will even say, •'Do not touch me, lest you pollute me in the position I occupy . . .'ᵉ

1 **8** "And there will come upon them [. . .]ᵃ punishment and wrath such as has never happened to them from the creation till that time when he stirs up against

Dan 12:1
Mt 24:21
Ezra 7:12
Ezek 26:7
Dan 2:37

g. This vs. contains an obvious lengthy dittography. The translation represents a plausible reconstruction.

6 a. Lit. "making, they will make impiety." A Semitism.

b. The bulk of this ch. (6:2–7) almost certainly reflects the reign of Herod the Great (37–4 B.C.). Precise historical details need not be expected in an apocalyptic writing, but the reference to a reign of thirty-four years (vs. 6) is decisive. See Josephus, *Ant* 17.8.1.

c. The text of the second half of this vs. is confused. There is a dittography and the main verb has dropped out. The translation is an attempt to paraphrase accurately the difficult Lat. text.

d. Lit. "he will not spare" or "he will not refrain from injury."

e. The Lat. *aceruus* (*acervus*?) is often emended to *acerbus* ("bitter"). The sense of the passage, however, is clear.

f. The text is slightly broken in this vs.

g. Lit. "colony."

7 a. The rest of this vs. and the following are badly broken. Mention is made of "four hours" or "at the fourth hour" which will come, of the "nine tribes," something to do with "three,"

"seven," and "in the third part of two." Though many attempts have been made to restore the lacunae, this seems impossible. We have a stock apocalyptic introduction. The times have passed and the author is convinced that he is living in the last days. The details would, of course, be of philological, historical, and theological interest, but the lacunae are so extensive as to render reconstructions too tenuous to be of value.

b. Lit. "the wrath of their minds."

c. The text here is fragmentary.

d. Lit. "from morning till evening."

e. The whole of this ch. is an attack on the enemies of the author and his party. The identification of the enemies is not certain, although they are wealthy and apparently connected with the Temple. Similar attacks against an avaricious priesthood are found in the Qumran materials, e.g. CD 2.12–20; 6.12–17; 20.20–27; 1QpHab 8.8–13; 11.4–15; 12.1–10; and in the PssSol, especially psalms 1; 2; 4; and 8. One should be cautious in attempting to identify precisely as documents of this type tend to use stereotyped language for both praise and vilification.

8 a. Most of the first line is illegible. Many restore "second" in the illegible portion and then speculate about the "first" punishment. It appears doubtful

them a king of the kings of the earth who, having supreme authority, will crucify
2 those who confess their circumcision. •Even those who deny[b] it, he will torture
3 and hand them over to be led to prison in chains. •And their wives will be given
to the gods of the nations[c] and their young sons will be cut by physicians to bring
4 forward their foreskins.[d] •Still others among them will be punished by torture,
both by fire and sword, and they will be compelled to bear publicly (as burdens)
5 idols which are polluted just as those who revere them are polluted. •Likewise,
they will be compelled by their torturers to enter into their secret place, where they
will be compelled to blaspheme outrageously the word, and finally (to blaspheme)
both their laws and what they had placed upon their own altar.[d]

1 **9** "Then, even as he was speaking,[a] there will be a man from the tribe of Levi
2 whose name is Taxo. He, having seven sons, will speak earnestly to them, •'See
(my) sons, behold a second[b] punishment has befallen the people; cruel, impure,
3 going beyond all bounds of mercy—even exceeding the former one. •For which
nation or which province or which people, who have (all) done many crimes
4 against the Lord,[c] have suffered such evils as have covered us? •Now, therefore,
sons, heed me. If you investigate, you will surely know[d] that never did (our) fathers
5 nor their ancestors tempt God by transgressing his commandments.[e] •Yea, you
6 will surely know that this is our strength. Here is what we shall do. •We shall
fast for a three-day period and on the fourth day we shall go into a cave,[f] which
is in the open country. There let us die rather than transgress the commandments
7 of the Lord of Lords, the God of our fathers. •For if we do this, and do die, our
blood will be avenged before the Lord.'[g]

1 **10** "Then his kingdom will appear throughout his whole creation.
Then the devil will have an end.
Yea, sorrow will be led away with him.

---

that the precise historical setting of this ch. can be
discovered through any restoration. Similar allusions in other works are also inconclusive. For
example, CD 19.11 = 7.21 mentions a "first" or
"former" punishment (Heb. *pqdh*, which probably
lies behind the Lat. here), but this has been variously
interpreted as an allusion to the fall of Jerusalem
in 587 B.C., the Antiochan persecution, the capture
of Jerusalem by Pompey in 63 B.C., or to some
otherwise unknown historical event. It seems better
to assume that the author has put together many
past events that he believes are about to be replicated
in the end-time. See also the n. on 9:2 below.
  b. The verb translated "deny" has been
emended from *necantes* ("to kill or slay") to *ne-
gantes* as a parallel to *confitentes* ("confess"), but
another emendation would yield the parallelism
"conceal and reveal."
  c. The reading, if correct, probably refers to
sacred prostitution (cf. 2Mac 6:4). The text is often
emended to read "will be violently given to the
nations" (cf. 2Mac 5:24). The general sense is the
same as slavery might well involve prostitution.
  d. The text of these two vss. is very uncertain.
The coerced participation of Jews in pagan rites is
mentioned in 2Mac 6:7–9.

9 a. The text *illo dicente* ("even as he was speaking") is usually emended to *illo die* ("in that day"),
and this may well be correct. The translation
adopted here presupposes that ch. 9 is part of an
originally independent document and that *illo dicente* refers to someone not mentioned in the present
text.
  b. Lat. *altera*. "Another" is an alternative translation, but in the present form of TMos the typological use of the fall of Jerusalem as punishing
event (3:1–3) weighs in favor of the translation
adopted.
  c. Lat. *domum* ("house"). The translation assumes an emendation to *dominum*.
  d. Lit. "look and know."
  e. The assertion of sinlessness seems out of place
in the work and may support the view that the ch.
had an independent origin. Consistency, however,
is not a characteristic of apocalyptic writing.
  f. Refuge in caves was common in times of
persecution, e.g. 1Mac 1:53; 2:31; 2Mac 6:11; 10:6;
Josephus, *Ant* 12.6.2 and the caves at Qumran.
There is a story of a man who took refuge in a cave
with his wife and seven sons, slew all of them, and
committed suicide rather than submit to Herod (*Ant*
14.15.5).
  g. The function of Taxo's proposed martyrdom
was discussed in the Introduction.

2   Then will be filled the hands of the messenger,
           who is in the highest place appointed.
       Yea, he will at once avenge them of their enemies.[a]

3   For the Heavenly One will arise[b] from his kingly throne.   Micah 1:3
       Yea, he will go forth from his holy habitation[c]   Deut 26:15
           with indignation and wrath on behalf of his sons.   Isa 63:15
                                                          Jer 25:30

4   And the earth will tremble, even to its ends shall it be shaken.
       And the high mountains will be made low.
       Yea, they will be shaken, as enclosed valleys will they fall.

5   The sun will not give light.
       And in darkness the horns of the moon will flee.
       Yea, they will be broken in pieces.

       It will be turned wholly into blood.
       Yea, even the circle of the stars will be thrown into disarray.

6   And the sea all the way to the abyss will retire,
           to the sources of waters which fail.
       Yea, the rivers will vanish away.[d]

7   For God Most High will surge forth,
           the Eternal One alone.
       In full view will he come to work vengeance on the nations.
       Yea, all their idols will he destroy.

8   Then will you be happy, O Israel!
       And you will mount up above the necks and the wings of an eagle.
       Yea, all things will be fulfilled.[e]

9   And God will raise you to the heights.
       Yea, he will fix you firmly in the heaven of the stars,
           in the place of their habitations.[f]

10   And you will behold from on high.
       Yea, you will see your enemies on the earth.[g]

       And recognizing them, you will rejoice.
       And you will give thanks.
       Yea, you will confess your creator.

10 a. "Filling the hands" is a technical term for ordination to the priesthood. The messenger, usually identified as Michael, the guardian angel of Israel (see Dan 10:13, 21; 12:1; 1En 20:5; 1QM 9.15–16; 17.6–7), is here more a warrior than a priest. There is an interesting parallel in 11QMelch where Melchizedek, a heavenly priest, works vengeance against Belial. Some late Jewish sources identify Michael and Melchizedek, but there is no evidence for this identification at the time of TMos. "Yea" at the beginning of 10:2b assumes that a Lat. *qui* (Gk. *kai* or Semitic *Wālw*) has been lost in transmission.

b. There are three or four letters missing at the beginning of this line. "Will arise" is a suitable reconstruction.

c. See 1QS 10.2; 1QSb 4.25; 1QM 12.1f.; and 1QH 12.2.

d. The cosmic events described here are common in apocalyptic literature, though the exact formulations often differ. No attempt has been made to emend the text, as Charles did, to bring it into conformity with other documents as this seems to imply a uniformity not implicit in apocalyptic. Further, it does not seem appropriate to cite possible allusions from other writings as the language is too typical to assume verbal dependence.

e. The meaning of this vs. is not clear as it is susceptible of two quite different interpretations. The translation adopted assumes that the author is referring to Israel's exaltation (see the following vs.) being achieved by being borne aloft as by an eagle. Cf. Deut 32:11–13; Isa 40:31; 1En 96:2. However, the reference may be to the extermination of Israel's enemies, in which case the appropriate translation would be, "You will arise upon the

11,12   "But you, Joshua son of Nun, keep these words and this book, •for from my
13 death and burial[h] until his coming there will pass 250 times. •And this is the course
14 [three to five letters are lost] times[i] which come until they be completed. •However,
15 I shall be asleep with my fathers. •Therefore, you, Joshua son of Nun, be strong;
     for God has chosen you to be my successor[j] in the same covenant.''

1 **11** And when Joshua heard the words of Moses, so written in his testament, all
2 the things which he had said, he tore his garments and fell at Moses' feet. •And
3 Moses, though he wept with him, encouraged him, •and Joshua replied to him,
4 saying, •''Why do you console me,[a] master Moses, and in what way may I be
   consoled concerning that bitter message spoken, which has gone forth from your
   mouth, a message full of tears and sobbings? Because you are departing from this
5,6 people [five to seven letters are lost] •[b]What place will receive you •or where
7 will be the marker of your sepulcher? •Or who as a man will dare to move your
8 body from place to place?[b] •For all who die, there are appropriately[c] their sepulchers
   in the earth,[d] but your sepulcher is from the rising to the setting of the sun, and
   from the South to the limits of the North, the whole world is your sepulcher.
9,10   "Now, master, you are going away,[e] and who will sustain this people? •Or who
11 will have compassion on them, and will be for them a leader on (their) way?
11 Or who will pray for them,[f] not omitting a single day, so that I may lead them
12 into the land of their forefathers?[g] •How, therefore, can I be (guardian) of this
   people, as a father is to his only son, or as a mother[h] is to her virgin daughter
   (who) is being prepared to be given to a husband; a mother who is disquieted,
   guarding (the daughter's) body from the sun and (seeing to it) that (the daughter's)
13 feet are not without shoes when she runs upon the ground?[i] •[five to seven letters
   are lost] can I be responsible for food for them as they desire and drink according
14 to their will?[j] •[six to eight letters are lost] for there were 100,000[k] of them, but
15 they have, by your prayers, increased so much, master Moses. •And what wisdom
   and intelligence do I have, either to judge or give an opinion in the house [five
16 to seven letters are lost][l] •Moreover, when the kings of the Amorites hear (of your
   death), believing that there is no longer with us that sacred spirit, worthy of the

---

necks and wings of the eagle, and they will be brought to an end.'' One might see then an allusion to Josh 10:24 and 1QM 12.11; 19.3. The alternative is attractive, especially if the allusion is to the eagle of Rome.

f. Whether this is to be interpreted literally or metaphorically remains problematical. Of the many parallels usually cited, the most significant are Dan 12:3; 1En 104:2–7; 2Bar 51:5–12; and 1QM 17.7.

g. Lat. *in terram.* Charles's emendation to ''in Gehenna'' has been widely accepted and the conclusion drawn that TMos thus speaks of a totally extramundane salvation and damnation. The translation here assumes simply an imagistic contrast between the exaltation of Israel and the fall of its enemies. Another alternative is that *in terram* (Heb. *ba 'ares*) is used in the sense of the lower regions, which would be equivalent to Gehenna. Theology based on emendation and/or imagery is precarious.

h. The word translated ''burial'' has sometimes been rendered ''assumption'' and taken to be an interpolation attempting to relate TMos to an AsMos proper. This is unnecessary. See 11:5–6.

i. Lat. *horum* (''hours or moments'').

j. Lat. *successor.* See n. on 1:7.

11 a. Lat. *celo* (''to hide or conceal''). The translation follows the usual emendation to *solor* (''comfort, console'').

b. The text of vss. 5–7 is difficult and hardly legible in places. Many reconstructions have been proposed. Two attractive ones are: ''Who will dare to move your body, as if it were that of a mere man, from place to place?'' and ''Who will dare to move your body from within the earth from place to place?''

c. Lit. ''according to their times.''

d. Perhaps ''in their lands.''

e. Lat. *ab his.* The translation assumes the emendation to *abis.*

f. *LAB* 19:3 speaks of Moses' praying for the sins of the people at all times.

g. Lat. *araborum,* emended here to *atavorum.* Some emend to *Amorreorum* (''Amorites''). The meaning is the same, the reference is to the land of promise.

h. Lat. *dominam,* ''mistress of the house.''

i. The Lat. is virtually untranslatable and many emendations and transpositions have been proposed. The words in parentheses are intended to facilitate an understanding of the general sense of the passage. Joshua is comparing his new role to that of a father who has but one son or to that of a mother who seeks to shield her betrothed daughter from all harm.

j. Lit. ''can I, according to their will, be responsible to them for food and drink according to the will of their will.'' Something is clearly amiss here.

k. Most emend to ''600,000'' on the basis of numerous passages in Ex and Num.

l. ''Of the Lord'' is often restored in the lacuna.

Lord, manifold and incomprehensible, master of leaders,[m] faithful in all things, the divine prophet for the whole earth, the perfect teacher in the world, now
17 believing that they can storm us, they will say,[n] 'Let us go up against them. •If the enemies have, up till now, but a single time, acted impiously against their Lord, there is (now) no advocate for them who will bear messages to the Lord on their behalf in the way that Moses was the great messenger. He, in every hour both day and night, had his knees fixed to the earth, praying and looking steadfastly toward him who governs the whole earth with mercy and justice, reminding the
18 Lord of the ancestral covenant and the resolute oath.'[o] •Thus they will say, 'He is no longer with them. Therefore, let us go up and crush[p] them from the face of
19 the earth.' •What, then, will happen to these people, master Moses?''

1 **12** And when he had finished (speaking these) words, Joshua again fell at the feet
2 of Moses. •And Moses grasped his hand and raised him into the seat before him,
3 and responding to him, he said, •''Joshua, do not demean (yourself), but free
4 yourself from care and pay attention to my words. •God has created all the nations which are in the world (just as he created) us. And he has foreseen both them and us from the beginning of the creation of the world even to the end of the age. Indeed, nothing, to the least thing, has been overlooked by him. But, (rather), he
5 has seen all things and [a]he is the cause of all.[a] •[. . .][b] has seen beforehand all things which may come to be in the world, and, behold, they have come to pass
6 [twelve to eighteen letters are lost] •established me for them, and for their sins [eleven to seventeen letters are lost] and [four to seven letters are lost] on their
7 behalf.[c] •Yet (this is) not on account of either my strength or weakness,[d] (it is)
8 simply that his mercies and long-suffering have lighted on me. •Likewise, I say to you, Joshua, that it is not on account of the piety of this people that you will   Deut 31:3-8
9 drive out the nations.[e] •All of the supports of the canopy of heaven, created and
10 declared good by God, are indeed under the ring[f] of his right hand. •Therefore, those who truly fulfill[g] the commandments of God [h]will flourish and will finish[h]
11 the good way, •but those who sin by disregarding the commandments will deprive themselves of the good things[i] which were declared before. They, indeed, will be
12 punished by the nations with many tortures. •But it is not possible for the nations
13 to drive them out or extinguish them completely. •For God, who has foreseen all things in the world,[j] will go forth, and his covenant which was established, and by the oath which . . .'' [MS ends.]

---

m. Lit. "master of the word." This may well be correct. The translation here assumes that the Heb. consonants *dbr* were read by the Gk. translator as "word" but that the intention of the Heb. was "leader," a possible though less used rendering.

n. This vs. is a curious mixture of both dittography and omissions.

o. Lit. "and propitiating the Lord with an oath."

p. Lit. "throw them into disorder." The translation follows the usual emendation of *confundamus* to *contundamus*. It is not likely that the two verbs would connote any difference to an apocalyptic writer.

12 a. These words are conjectural. The verb in the clause must be emended and six to eight letters are illegible. The sense is clear; God is in control from beginning to end.

b. Traces of letters in this lacuna support the restoration of *dominus* ("the Lord").

c. The text is too broken to allow reconstruction. The sense of the vs. might be "It is the Lord who has established me as a mediator for them, that I might pray unceasingly for their sins and make intercession on their behalf."

d. The Semitic idiom underlying this would mean "not by me or in any way at all."

e. Cf. CD 8.14.

f. Lat., *nullo* ("by nothing"). The translation adopts an emendation to *anulo* ("ring").

g. Lit. "those who do and fulfill." Another literal rendering of a Semitic original.

h. Lit. "flourish and finish." The shift of tenses is not otherwise unknown in the text.

i. The grammar and syntax here are difficult. A literal rendering would be "to those who sin and neglect the commandments to be absent from the good."

j. Or "forever."

TESTAMENT OF SOLOMON

(First to Third Century A.D.)

A NEW TRANSLATION AND INTRODUCTION

BY D. C. DULING

The Testament of Solomon is a haggadic-type folktale about Solomon's building the Temple of Jerusalem combined with ancient lore about magic, astrology, angelology, demonology, and primitive medicine. According to the majority of manuscripts, the testament begins with the story of Solomon's favorite, a boy who inspires the artisans of the Temple, but whose soul is being sucked out of him by a pesky demon, Ornias. In response to Solomon's prayer to God for aid, the archangel Michael grants Solomon a magic seal ring by which he is able to call up the demons, to interrogate them as to their names, astrological locations, demonic activities (pains, diseases, immoral deeds), to compel them to reveal their thwarting angels, and to enlist their help with the construction of the Temple. Thus, Solomon learns that the pesky demon is named Ornias, is located in Aquarius, can undergo several transformations (strangler of those who are located under Aquarius; a man who craves bodies of effeminate boys; a heavenly, winged creature), and is thwarted by the archangel Ouriel. With Ouriel's help, Ornias is sentenced to cut stone in the stone quarry and, with the aid of the ring, to go and get Beelzeboul, the Prince of Demons (chs. 1–3). Beelzeboul is interrogated and promises to bring forth the unclean spirits bound. Beelzeboul shows Solomon Onoskelis, a cliff-dwelling satyra, who associates with men and travels by the full moon; she is commanded to spin hemp for construction ropes (ch. 4). Beelzeboul brings forth the impertinent Asmodeus, who is the Great Bear constellation, who spreads the wickedness of men, hatches plots against newlyweds, spreads madness about women through the stars, and commits murders; Solomon learns that Asmodeus is thwarted by the angel Raphael and smoke from a burning liver and gall of a fish (ch. 5). Solomon learns that Beelzeboul is a fallen angel who destroys by means of tyrants, causes demons to be worshiped, arouses desires in holy men, brings about jealousies and murders, and instigates wars. Beelzeboul prophesies about the Arabian wind demon Ephippas (chs. 22–24), tells that he is thwarted by the Almighty God and the oath "the Elo-i," and informs Solomon about heavenly things; he is commanded to cut marble (ch. 6). Solomon interrogates the wind demon Lix Tetrax, learns that he creates divisions among men, makes whirlwinds, starts fires, disrupts households, is the offspring of the Great One, has a star near the tip of the southern moon, and is thwarted by the archangel Azael; he is commanded to hurl stones up to the heights of the Temple for the workmen (ch. 7).

Solomon interrogates the seven heavenly bodies (Deception, Strife, Fate, Distress, Error, Power, The Worst), learns of their evil activities and their thwarting angels (respectively, Lamechiel, Baruchiel, Marmaroth, Balthioul, Ouriel, Asteraoth, [name unknown]), seals them with the ring, and commands them to dig the Temple foundation (ch. 8). Solomon interrogates the headless demon called Murder, who sees through his breasts, attacks the voices of infants, cuts off heads, attaches them to himself and consumes them through his neck, inflames limbs, inflicts feet, and produces festering sores; he is ordered to stay with Beelzeboul (ch. 9). Solomon interrogates the doglike demon, Scepter, who deceives those who follow his star and subdues the hearts of men through their throats; Scepter then helps Solomon to obtain an emerald stone for the Temple; Solomon learns that the demon is thwarted by the great Briathos (ch. 10). Solomon interrogates the Lion-Shaped Demon, who prolongs illness and rules a legion of demons; they are thwarted by Emmanouel, who will drive them over the cliff into the water; the legion is commanded to carry wood and the Lion-Shaped One is made to saw it with his claws and to fuel the perpetually burning kiln (ch. 11). Solomon interrogates the three-headed dragon spirit, Head of the Dragons, and learns that he blinds fetuses and makes them deaf and dumb, and causes men to fall down and grind their teeth; he is thwarted by the place marked "Place of the Skull" and the angel of the Wonderful Counselor on the cross; after revealing a treasure of gold in the Temple, he is sealed and ordered to make bricks for the Temple (ch. 12).

Solomon interrogates Obyzouth, the female demon with disheveled hair, who strangles newborn infants at birth, injures eyes, condemns mouths, destroys minds, and creates pain; learning that she is thwarted by the angel Raphael, or writing her name on a piece of papyrus when women give birth, Solomon binds her by the hair and hangs her in front of the Temple (ch. 13). Solomon interrogates the Winged Dragon, who copulates through the buttocks of women who have beautiful bodies and who suddenly sets on fire with his breath wood for constructing the Temple. Learning that the demon is thwarted by Bazazath, Solomon invokes the angel and condemns the demon to cut marble for constructing the Temple (ch. 14). Solomon interrogates Enepsigos, the female demon with two heads, learns that she hovers near the moon, can also take the form of Kronos or another form, and that she is thwarted by the angel Rathanael; Solomon prays to God, invokes Rathanael, seals Enepsigos with a triple-link chain, and after she prophesies the destruction of kingdom, Temple, and Jerusalem, the scattering of the demons, and the coming of the Son of God, Emmanouel, who is crucified on a cross and born of a virgin, Solomon explains that he wrote the testament so that the sons of Israel might know the powers and forms of the demons and their thwarting angels (ch. 15). Solomon interrogates Kunopegos, the cruel sea-horse demon who becomes a great wave that causes ships to capsize, drowns men, and causes seasickness; learning that he is thwarted by the angel Iameth, Kunopegos is sealed in a bowl and stored away in the Temple (ch. 16). Solomon interrogates a lecherous spirit born from a giant in the age of giants, a spirit who has the shadowy form of a man and gleaming eyes; at midnight in the tombs the demon slays men with a sword or possesses a man, causing him to gnaw his own flesh; learning that the demon will be thwarted by the Savior or his mark written on the forehead (the sign of the cross), Solomon locks up the demon (ch. 17). Solomon interrogates the thirty-six heavenly bodies who are divisions (decans) of the Zodiac; he learns their names, the mental, physical, and social illnesses they cause, their thwarting angels, and orders them to bear water and to go to the Temple (ch. 18).

Riches are given to Solomon by all the kings of the earth, including Sheeba, the Queen of the South, who is a witch (ch. 19). Solomon hears the conflict between an old man and his son; Ornias the demon prophesies that the son will die and Solomon compels him to explain how he knows God's plan for the future; Ornias tells that demons in the heavens overhear God's decisions and that falling stars are really demons who are exhausted because they have no way stations on which to rest; Ornias's prophecy is fulfilled (ch. 20). Sheeba, impressed with the new Temple, contributes ten thousand shekels (ch. 21).

A letter from Adarkes, king of Arabia, requests Solomon's help against the wind demon Ephippas, which kills man and beast; when the gigantic cornerstone of the Temple cannot be moved by the artisans or demons, Solomon dispatches his servant boy to Arabia, where the boy entraps the wind demon in a leather flask by the aid of the ring; the boy brings the demon to the Temple, where he is interrogated by Solomon, who learns that his thwarting angel is the one who will be born of a virgin and crucified by the Jews (ch. 22). Solomon learns that the wind demon has great powers and requests that he put the cornerstone in place; the demon agrees and states that, with the aid of the demon who lives in the Red Sea, he will lift up the pillar of air which is in the Red Sea and place it where Solomon wishes; the cornerstone is inserted in place by the wind demon, fulfilling the keystone prophecy (Ps 118:22; ch. 23). The Arabian demon Ephippas and the demon of the Red Sea bring back the pillar from the Red Sea and continue to hold it in the air to this very day (ch. 24). Solomon interrogates the demon from the Red Sea, learns that his name is Abezethibou, that he was the one whom Iannes and Iambres called to their aid against Moses in Egypt, that he hardened Pharaoh's heart and caused the pursuit of the sons of Israel to the Red Sea, where, with the company of the Egyptians, he was trapped when the waters receded; Solomon adjures him to continue holding up the pillar (ch. 25). Solomon falls madly in love with a beautiful Shummanite woman; to have her, he sacrifices five locusts to the foreign gods Raphan and Moloch, and takes her to his palace; the glory of God departs from Solomon after he builds temples to her idols; to those who hear he writes his testament (ch. 26).

Texts

The standard edition of the Greek text of the Testament of Solomon, introduced and edited by C. C. McCown, comments on fourteen Greek manuscripts.[1] Another Greek manuscript[2] and a fragment[3] are known. A description of seven manuscripts in order of importance, according to McCown, is as follows:[4]

1. D: Dionysius monastery, Mount Athos, No. 132, folios 367 (recto)–374 (verso), sixteenth century, entitled *peri tou Solomōntos* ("About Solomon"). The text of this manuscript was published in V. M. Istrin's *Griečeski spiski zabesania Solomona* ("Greek Manuscripts of the Testament of Solomon") (Odessa, 1898) and in *Lietopis istoriko-phil-ologetscheskago Obtchestva* VII (Byzantine Division IV; Odessa, 1899; pp. 49–98; contains also MSS I and Q). McCown collated the manuscript from photographs from which the title is missing; the pages are deleted by transverse lines; it is carefully written and well preserved. The manuscript is *not really the testament*, but a biography of Solomon characterized by a strong demonological interest. McCown believed that it was a revision of the story (*d*) which lay behind the testament and printed it separately.[5] It includes David's sin with Bathsheba (1:1–3); God's inability to stop David (1:4–6); Nathan's reproof of David (1:7–11); Solomon's birth, reign, power, and wisdom (1:12f.); the building of the Temple (2:1); Solomon's favorite servant (2:2); Solomon's prayer about the matter (2:3); Solomon's interrogation of the servant (2:3f.); Solomon's supplication for him (2:5); the granting of the magic ring (2:6f.); Solomon's gift of the ring to the servant (2:8f.); the capture of Ornias the demon (2:10–13); Solomon's interrogation of Ornias (3:1–4); treatment of the demons (3:5–9); dispute of father and son and Ornias's prophecy (4:1–18); the admiration of the Temple by the "Queen of the South" and others (5:1); the king of Arabia's letter to Solomon (6:1f.);

---

[1] C. C. McCown, ed., *The Testament of Solomon*, pp. 10–28 of the Introduction (p. numbers of the Introduction have no asterisk; those of the Gk. text and apparatus do), describes eleven texts in the order of their importance to him (MSS D, H, I, L, P, Q, S, T, U, V, W) and lists a twelfth from Mt. Athos (No. 3221), which he was not able to obtain and which apparently has never been studied. To these twelve MSS should be added two others which McCown discovered too late to be evaluated in their proper order. The first (MS N) is described and its variants listed separately as an appendix to the Introduction, pp. 112–23; it is included in the list of most important MSS here (see n. 9). The other (MS E) is described by McCown separately (pp. 123–26), but because it is not the full testament, it is printed separately (pp. 102–20*; the same is the case for MS D, pp. 88–97*). Apart from MSS D, E, and N, the MSS are collated and printed as an eclectic text with three recs.: A (MSS H I L), B (MSS P Q), and C (MSS S T U V W). Furthermore, parts of rec. C (TSol 1:1–5; 9:8–13:15) have such unique material that they are also printed separately (pp. 76–87*). All three recs. are distinguished in the opening VSS. where McCown favors rec. B over what he considered the best rec. overall, rec. A. [The introduction to TSol is longer than usual because of the complexity of the issues involved and the relative unfamiliarity of the document itself. —J.H.C.]

[2] Bibliothèque Nationale No. 2011, printed in a collection of Solomonic texts, A. Delatte, *Anecdota Atheniensia* 36 (1927) 211–27. This is an 18th-cent. MS, 17.4 × 11.5 CCS. It is not the full testament but a shortened form like MSS D and E. Briefly, its contents include a narrative of David's sin, Nathan's rebuke, and the birth and glories of Solomon; Solomon's favorite boy and the story of the boy; the gift of the ring through Michael; the capture of Ornias by the boy with the ring; Solomon's interrogation of Ornias; fetching of Beelzeboul by the boy and Ornias; interrogation of Beelzeboul, thwarted by Raphael; the story of the old man and his son interspersed with material about Ornias and Michael; Sheeba (Sibulla); the letter of the king of Arabia; fetching of Ephippas by the boy; interrogation of Ephippas; the cornerstone account; a parenthetical remark about Jesus; bringing of the pillar by the boy with the seal and Ephippas; Solomon's learning about the chief Satan, Chathrou Samael; the fetching of the demon and his corps by the boy and Ornias; observation of the demons at work on the Temple; interrogation of Chathrou Samael, thwarted by the Savior of the world, the Son and Word of God; rebuke of Samael, who is commanded to work on the Temple; account of the kings of the earth who are impressed by the Temple and Solomon's power; glories of the Temple; parenthetical remark about John of Damascus and the Church; parenthetical remark about Christ, the disciples, and the Temple; Jeremiah and the Temple; the destruction of the Temple by the Chaldeans; Christian conclusion and note about the boy, whose name is Chiram.

[3] K. Preisendanz, "Ein Wiener Papyrusfragment zum Testamentum Salomonis," *EOS* 48 (1956) 161–67. Note also J. H. Charlesworth's discovery of, and brief description of, a Syriac MS (see Bibliography).

[4] McCown, *Testament*, pp. 10–28; see n. 9 below on MS N.

[5] McCown, *Testament*, pp. 32–36.

Solomon's instructions to his servant on how to trap the Arabian wind demon Ephippas (6:3–5); the servant's entrapment of the demon and return of him to Solomon (6:6–8); Ephippas's placement of the keystone (6:9–11); Ephippas, Abezethibou, and the air pillar (6:12–14); Solomon and the demon prince, Samael (7:1–6); the glory and wisdom of Solomon (8:1–7).[6]

2. H: private library of the Earl of Leicester, Holkham Hall, Norfolk, England, No. 99. This sixty-eight-page manuscript from the fifteenth century, perhaps from Greece, measuring 16 × 21.5 centimeters per folio page, is entitled *diēgēsis peri tēs diathēkēs Solomōntos* . . . ("An Account Concerning the Testament of Solomon . . ."). It is clear, has many abbreviations, and places rubrics before the chief divisions of the story. Its title and the initial letters of lesser sections are in red. It omits 14:3–16:1 (cf. MS L). Except for 26:8–10, its text is usually abbreviated.

3. I: Bibliothèque Nationale, Paris, Supplément grec, No. 500. This manuscript is from the sixteenth century and measures 16 × 22 centimeters. The testament is found on folios 78–82. Its title begins *Solomōntos* . . . (["concerning] Solomon"), with *diathēkē t* ("Testament o[f]") carelessly written in the upper margin (see TSol 1:00, n. c). The manuscript is well preserved. It was published by Istrin (see MS D, above). The Testament of Solomon follows Ecclesiastes and Song of Songs in the codex. The copyist seems to have wearied of the many demons, for he broke off in the middle of a sentence in the middle of a column at 5:8.

4. L: Harleian MSS, British Museum, No. 5596. This fifteenth-century manuscript measures 23 × 34 centimeters and has a catalog description "*Geomantica, exorcismi, divinationes et huius modi*" ("Geomantics, exorcisms, divinations and things of this sort") with the addition "*quaedam Salominis*" ("certain things of Solomon"). It is well preserved. Folios 8 (recto) to 18 (recto) of manuscript 5596 contain the incomplete testament, omitting 14:3–16:1 (cf. MS H) and ending at 18:41. Other portions of the manuscript make up "MS T"[7] because they represent for McCown recension C rather than A in which manuscript H falls. The testament has been worked over by a medieval magician who included magical, astrological, and demonological lore. The largest section of the manuscript is the *Clavicula Salomonis*, probably the best-known medieval Solomonic document.[8] Titles to sections in the *Clavicula*, a large circular seal containing magical signs, and the numbers of "MS T^d" are painted with silver over red. Places that direct one to a magical remedy for disease are marked with a cross and a circle.

5. N: Library of the Greek Patriarchate, Jerusalem, Sancti Saba, No. 422. This is a fifteenth- or sixteenth-century manuscript measuring 11 × 15 centimeters. The beginning and end of the codex are missing. The testament begins on folio 49 and ends on folio 93, though its first page is missing, causing it to go unnoticed until McCown rediscovered it in 1920–21. Too late to be collated with the others, McCown described it and printed its variant readings separately as an appendix, pp. 112–23.[9] The manuscript often makes no sense, but it is virtually complete and McCown judged it closer to the original form of the testament than manuscript P (rec. B), to which it is most similar. It is the only other manuscript besides manuscript P to contain Testament of Solomon 14:3–16:1, the latter part of which incorporates the testament's most Christian comment (TSol 15:10–12) and a separate explanation as to why the testament was written (TSol 15:13–15; cf. 26:7f.). Yet, near the end of the testament, manuscript N supports manuscript H (rec. A) enough that McCown, who had come to have more confidence in recension B and to print it at that point, was willing to revise his judgment back in favor of recension A (cf. TSol 26:8, n. f). Finally, it should be noted that manuscript N equates each of the thirty-six decans in chapter 18 with ten days of the Coptic month. This equation relates manuscript N to Egypt.

---

[6] McCown, *Testament*, pp. 88–97.* The two other shorter versions of the testament are MS E, which McCown discovered too late to collate with MS D (McCown, *Testament*, pp. 123–26; 102–20*), and Delatte's Bibliothèque Nationale No. 2011 (summarized in n. 2 above).

[7] Three fragments from this MS are designated by McCown as T⁰, Tʳ, and T^d since they are separate fragments and belong to his rec. C. They make up his eighth "MS."

[8] See below, "Cultural importance."

[9] MS N is not included among McCown's eleven MSS in this order (see n. 1), but he writes that "It is certainly much nearer the original than P . . ." in most instances (McCown, *Testament*, p. 113). Therefore, I have placed MS N before MSS P and Q.

6. P: Bibliothèque Nationale, Paris, Anciens fonds grecs, No. 38 (Colbert 4895). This sixteenth-century manuscript has twenty-four folios and measures 15.5 × 20.5 centimeters. Its title begins *diathēkē Solomōntos* (for the full title, see TSol 1:00). The manuscript, which belonged to the library of M. le President de Mesmes (died 1596), is carefully written and worked over by an editor. It is cataloged as "no. 38 olim Colbert." Though known and occasionally cited by scholars in the seventeenth century, it was first printed by F. F. Fleck in *Wissenschaftliche Reise durch das südliche Deutschland, Italien, Sicilien und Frankreich 2/3, Anecdota maximam partem sacra* (Leipzig, 1837, pp. 113–40). This text of the testament became the standard work until Istrin (see above, MS D); but Istrin's work was in Russian and not easily accessible in the West. The Fleck text of manuscript P was reprinted by J. Fürst, *Der Orient* 5 (1844) and 7 (1846), with a German translation, and in *Literaturblatt* editions; but it was incomplete. It was also reprinted in the standard collection of early Christian writings in Greek (cf. J. P. Migne, *Patrologia graeca*, vol. 122 [Paris, 1864], cols. 1315–58). McCown wrote that "Fleck rather inaccurately copied the *editio princeps* from MS P, mistaking many letters, and so causing himself and those who have had to depend upon his edition much difficulty."[10] Yet, the only English translation to date is based on the Fleck edition (cf. F. C. Conybeare, *JQR* 11 [1898] 1–45). To facilitate comparison with Conybeare's translation of Fleck, the present translation attempts to follow, where possible, Conybeare's paragraph divisions and places his paragraph division numbers in parentheses in the margin. There is also an English paraphrase of the testament in L. Ginzberg's *The Legends of the Jews* (trans. H. Szold; 7 vols. [Philadelphia, 1913] vol. 4, pp. 150–54). F. A. Bornemann (*Zeitschrift für die historische Theologie* 14 [1844] 9–56) translated Fleck's edition into German.

7. Q: Andreas Convent, Mount Athos, No. 73. This represents folios 11–15 of the materials published by Istrin (see above, MS D), who bracketed many letters and omitted sections, indicating to McCown many lacunae. Testament of Solomon 3:1–20:9 is missing.

It is important to understand why these manuscripts are given in this particular order.[11] The first manuscript, D, is not the testament but, according to McCown, a revision of the story (*d*) which lay behind the testament. For that reason, it is not translated below; rather, the base text is McCown's eclectic text, which is an attempt to reconstruct the Testament of Solomon which lay behind recensions A (MSS HIL) and B (MSS PQ, to which note must be taken of N). Hence, manuscripts HIL, or recension A, come next, followed by NPQ, or recension B. McCown described five other manuscripts or parts thereof (MSS STUVW) which he called recension C. Mount Athos 3221 (not obtained) and manuscript E (McCown, pp. 123–26; 102–20*) account for the other two manuscripts.

Original language

In 1896, Moses Gaster, on the basis of what he considered to be a misunderstanding of a Hebrew term, argued that the testament (the Fleck edition of MS P) was a translation from the Hebrew.[12] McCown, skeptical of an argument based on a single instance from what he, in his day, knew to be a single manuscript among several, turned up two more possibilities,[13] one in an important passage of Egyptian origin.[14] However, though it is possible that the testament has Semitic language materials behind it, or its sources, these meager instances cannot support the hypothesis that it is a translation document. McCown's conclusion still stands: the native language of the writer of the Testament of Solomon *as a testament* was Koine Greek, the commonly spoken Greek of the hellenistic era, and thus of the New Testament.[15] It is no surprise that in most respects the language and style of the testament are similar to that of the Greek New Testament.[16]

---

[10] McCown, *Testament*, p. 28.

[11] See n. 1, and TSol, Title, n. a.

[12] See M. Gaster, "The Sword of Moses," *JRAS* (1896) 155, 170; reprinted in *Studies and Texts in Folklore, Magic, Medieval Romance, Hebrew Apocrypha, and Samaritan Archeology*, 3 vols. (New York 1928; repr. 1971) vol. 1, pp. 294, 309.

[13] McCown, *Testament*, pp. 42f.; TSol 2:4; 18:24–40.

[14] E.g. Rhyx (*-ruaḥ*, "Spirit"), TSol 18:24–40.

[15] McCown, *Testament*, p. 43, and scholars since him.

[16] Ibid., p. 40. With respect to recs. A and B, McCown suggests the grammar probably points to the period subsequent to the NT. Readers of the Gk. NT will find many terms of the NT on every page.

Date

The story of the Testament of Solomon purports to take place during the reign of Solomon in the tenth century B.C. Nonetheless, there is no doubt that it comes from much later times, not only because of its language, but because it presupposes events, some in the form of prophecies, which took place in the first century A.D., and because in general it assumes thought forms generally accepted as having arisen in hellenistic times.[17] Nonetheless, because explicit references to historical events, apart from the story line and prophecy, are lacking, opinions about its date have varied. In the preface to the testament in Migne's patrology (1864), F. F. Fleck argued that the writing (again, MS P) was a Byzantine work from the Middle Ages;[18] the Russian Istrin, who discovered manuscript D and first argued in 1898 that it was the basis for the testament, thought that the latter was written about A.D. 1200.[19] In 1844, the German F. A. Bornemann moved the date back to the early fourth century, because he believed that its demonology resembled Lactantius' "Institutiones,"[20] and in 1907 this view was echoed by C. H. Toy in the *Jewish Encyclopedia*.[21] Meanwhile, A. Harnack, though he would not fix a date, thought it might *not* be in the earliest period,[22] while E. Schürer left the date open.[23]

In 1898, F. C. Conybeare, in the preface to his English translation of the testament (MS P), noted that it was quoted as one of Solomon's authentic writings in the Greek *Dialogue of Timothy and Aquila*. The *Dialogue*, a Christian document from about A.D. 400, was thought by Conybeare to go back to an earlier dialogue from the middle of the second century.[24] During the course of the *Dialogue*, the Christian applies Psalm 2:7 ("You are my son, today I have become your father") to Jesus as Messiah. The Jew, however, says the passage refers to Solomon and adds 2 Samuel 7:14 ("I will be a father to him and he a son to me") as further proof. The Christian responds, with reference to 1 Kings 11:3–6, that the promise to David's son was conditional on Solomon's walking in the Lord's ways as David did; but Solomon did not keep God's commandments. He sacrificed locusts to idols. The dialogue continues:

> The Jew responded, "Not sacrificed [*esphaxen*, "split the throat"], but unwillingly crushed [*ethlasen*] in his hand. The Book of Kings does not encompass these things, but it is written in his Testament."
> The Christian said, "On this I take my stand with confidence, because this was not made clear by the hand of a historian, but out of the mouth of Solomon himself."[25]

This reference unambiguously refers to the Testament of Solomon (cf. TSol 26:5). Conybeare went on to propose that the testament was a Christian revision of a *Jewish* document, the original form of which might well have been "the very collection of incantations which, according to Josephus, was composed and bequeathed by Solomon,"[26] that is, in one form it goes back at least to the late first century A.D. Conybeare also suggested that certain *Christian* additions to this originally Jewish document sounded very "archaic" and "seem to belong to about 100 A.D.,"[27] that the section about the thirty-six heavenly bodies (TSol 18) shared a common demonology with the apostle Paul, and that its faith had an analogue in that of the Essenes, a Jewish sect described by Josephus (*Wars* 2.142).[28] K. Kohler

---

[17] See the discussion below.

[18] F. F. Fleck in Migne, *PG*, vol. 122, p. 1315.

[19] Istrin, *Grieĉeski spiski zabesania Solomona* (Odessa, 1898) pp. 18f.

[20] F. A. Bornemann, *Zeitschrift für die historische Theologie* 14 (Leipzig, 1844) Introduction.

[21] C. H. Toy, "Solomon, Testament of," *The Jewish Encyclopedia*, ed. I. Singer (New York, 1901–6) vol. 11, p. 449.

[22] A. Harnack, *Geschichte der altchristlichen Literatur bis Eusebius* (Leipzig, 1893) vol. 1, p. 858.

[23] E. Schürer, *Geschichte des jüdischen Volkes im Zeitalter Jesu Christi* (Leipzig, 1901–9) vol. 3, p. 419.

[24] F. C. Conybeare, "The Testament of Solomon," *JQR* 11 (1898) 14.

[25] F. C. Conybeare, ed., *The Dialogues of Athanasius and Zachaeus and of Timothy and Aquila. Anecdota Oxoniensia* (Classical Series, Part 8; Oxford, 1898) p. 70. C. C. McCown, "The Christian Tradition as to the Magical Wisdom of Solomon," *JPOS* 2 (1922) 15, states, "The writer of the *Dialogue* claims a greater trustworthiness for the *Testament* than for the Book of Kings."

[26] Conybeare, *JQR* 11 (1898) 12.

[27] Ibid.

[28] Ibid., p. 8.

accepted Conybeare's results in the *Jewish Encyclopedia* (1907),[29] and so did G. Salzberger in his extensive study of the whole Solomon legend in Semitic literature.[30]

In his ground-breaking critical edition of the testament (1922), McCown suggested that the latest possible date, on the basis of the *Dialogue of Timothy and Aquila*, was about A.D. 400. In some respects, he agreed with Conybeare, for he stated that if one removed the Christian and pagan elements, "the *Test* comes to be of assistance in reconstructing the thought world of the Palestinian Jew in the first century of our era . . ."[31] He even pointed to a number of ideas which he thought represented first-century Judaism.[32] Yet, in contrast to Conybeare, McCown stressed the view that the testament *as a testament* was a *Christian* work (i.e. not simply a Jewish work edited by a Christian) from the early third century A.D. Building on Istrin's hypothesis that manuscript D was closer to the original form of the document which *later* became the testament, McCown suggested that originally there existed a collection of first-century Jewish Midrashim, or interpretative stories, about Solomon and the demons. These came from Palestine, perhaps Galilee.[33] They formed a more connected story (the hypothetical *d*), a revision of which is preserved in manuscript D, which was transcribed by an educated Greek from Byzantine times.[34] From *d*, an early third-century Christian—his demonology is like that found in Origen's *Against Celsus*—removed the episodes about David's sin and Nathan's inability to warn David on account of the devil; he added demonologic, astrological, and magical material, concluding with Solomon's demise. This work our Christian author called a "testament"[35]; it is best represented by recension A (MSS HIL). Then, another Christian from the fourth or fifth century added especially demonologic, but also gnostic, cabalistic, and Christian elements;[36] these can be seen in recension B (MSS PQ, along with N, collated separately).[37] Recension B, which is better at the beginning and end of the testament, is to be compared with recension A to arrive at the autograph.[38] Finally, a Christian of the Middle Ages, perhaps in the twelfth or thirteenth century, added magical formulas, gnostic-sounding terms, and a number of medieval ideas to make recension C.[39] To McCown, it was

> inconceivable that any one should take the *Test* as found in Recs. A, B, or C, and, by eliminating all the magico-medical element and the "testament" motif, reduce it to the simple tale of Solomon's birth and greatness, his temple building with demons, which appears in MS D.[40]

In 1922, M. R. James found McCown's theory of the evolution of the testament "plausible, but not wholly convincing,"[41] and raised the question whether such a reduction to the simple tale might not have taken place, just as the author of the "Greek Legend of Isaiah" pruned the *Ascension of Isaiah*; nonetheless, James went on to accept McCown's early third-century dating of the testament itself, as have most other scholars since McCown, notably A.-M. Denis.[42] An exception to this trend, however, is the recognized authority on the magical papyri, K. Preisendanz, who suggested that the original was from the first or second century

---

[29] K. Kohler, "Demonology," *The Jewish Encyclopedia*, vol. 4, p. 578.

[30] G. Salzberger, *Die Salomosage in der semitischen Literatur* (Berlin, 1907) p. 10.

[31] McCown, *Testament*, p. 3.

[32] Ibid., pp. 59–62.

[33] Ibid., pp. 85, 108.

[34] Ibid., pp. 35, 86. The contents of *d*, he suggested, consisted of that which is common to MS D and the testament, e.g. essentially TSol 1–2, 20, 22–24.

[35] TSol 15:13–15 from a redactional critical perspective sounds like an ending; McCown, *Testament*, p. 83, suggests that it is "probably the work of the B redacteur," noting that the term "testament" occurs in TSol 15:14 and in 26:8, the latter reference being also probably a Christian addition.

[36] McCown, *Testament*, p. 89, argued that there was too much Christian material in the testament to be Jewish and that Josephus the Jew would not have referred to a Christian document. The argument is, of course, circular.

[37] Ibid., pp. 35, 82f.

[38] McCown modified his distrust of rec. A at the end of TSol in the light of his discovery of MS N; see above, "Texts" (N) and note 1; Textual Emendations; TSol 26:8, n. f.

[39] McCown, *Testament*, pp. 83f., 100, 108.

[40] Ibid., p. 32.

[41] M. R. James, "The Testament of Solomon (Review)," *JTS* 24 (1922) 468.

[42] A.-M. Denis, *Introduction*, p. 67. Denis and M. de Jonge ("The Greek Pseudepigrapha of the Old Testament," *NovT* 7 [1965] 322) judge the testament "too late to be included in our collection."

A.D.[43] Whether one follows McCown's early third-century dating or Preisendanz's earlier one, there is general agreement that much of the testament reflects first-century Judaism in Palestine.

Before concluding a discussion of the testament's date, one unexpected and interesting datum should be mentioned. In 1945, Coptic translations of fifty-one tractates, mostly gnostic, were discovered in southern Egypt in the vicinity of Nag Hammadi. Four of the tractates mention Solomon,[44] and one of them, "On the Origin of the World," mentions "the Book of Solomon." The context of this reference deals with "Death," begotten by the First Father of Chaos, Ialdabaoth, and set up over the sixth heaven. The passage continues:

> Then since Death was androgynous, he mixed with his nature and begot seven androgynous sons. These are the names of the males: Jealousy, Wrath, Weeping, Sighing, Mourning, Lamenting, Tearful Groaning. And these are the names of the females: Wrath, Grief, Lust, Sighing, Cursing, Bitterness, Quarrelsomeness. They had intercourse with one another, and each one begot seven so that they total forty-nine androgynous demons.
> Their names and their functions you will find in "the Book of Solomon."[45]

The identification of "the Book of Solomon" which gives the names and functions of the forty-nine demons has given rise to several hypotheses. J. Doresse originally offered two suggestions. The reference might have been to the "Epistle to Rehoboam," also called the "Hygromancie of Solomon" or "The Key to Hydromancy," perhaps composed in first-century B.C. Egypt.[46] This Solomonic book contains lists of the seven planets, of angels, and of demons which influence each of the twenty-four hours of each day of the week, followed by prayers to the planets and the angels, magical signs of each planet, and the plants of the zodiacal signs and planets. Doresse, however, thought it might be more likely that the reference was "to something in that vast collection entitled the *Testament of Solomon*, which enumerates a crowd of genies and mentions, for example, as rulers of this terrestrial world, Deception, Discord, Quarrelsomeness, Violent Agitation, Error, Violence, and Perversity."[47] Doresse appears to refer here to the seven "world rulers" (*stoicheia*) of the Testament of Solomon, chapter 8. Doresse's specific reference to the testament, chapter 8, has the complication that, if Giversen's retranslation of the male and female demons of the passage from Coptic into Greek is correct,[48] the only common name with the Testament, chapter 8, is *Eris*, "Strife," "Discord." Yet, the reference is to the forty-nine demons; though the testament does not have exactly forty-nine, it does have more than forty-nine,

[43] Preisendanz, "Salomo," (Pauly-Wissowa Supplement 8 [1956] col. 689, and *EOS* 48 [1956] 161–62) draws upon the classic study of W. Gundel, *Dekane und Dekansternbilder, Studien der Bibliothek Warburg* 19 (Hamburg, 1936), who discusses TSol at length (pp. 49–62), and suggests that ch. 18 was in use in pre-Christian Egypt. In his latter article (*EOS* 48 [1956] 161) Preisendanz states that the formulation of the Gk. text of the testament itself appears to go back to the 1st or 2nd cent. A.D. However, he uses as one of his arguments a reference to McCown, *Testament*, p. 40, where McCown does not date the testament itself. For McCown, presumably only the hypothetical *d* might have been that early. See esp. TSol 18:1, n. a.

[44] II, 5:*107*, 3 (On the Origin of the World); V, 5:*78*, 30, *79*, 3, 10 (The Apocalypse of Adam); VII, 2:*63*, 11 (The Second Treatise of the Great Seth); and IX, 3:*70*, 6, 27 (The Testimony of Truth). S. Giversen ("Solomon und die Dämonen," in *Essays on the Nag Hammadi Texts in Honor of Alexander Böhlig*, ed. M. Krause, pp. 16–21) discusses three of these codices (II, 5; V, 5; IX, 3) and attempts to show that Solomon's use of the demons to build Jerusalem makes him an enemy, thus reversing the usual Jewish and Arabic legends.

[45] H.-G. Bethge and O. W. Wintermute, trans., "On the Origin of the World (II, 5 and XIII, 2)," in *The Nag Hammadi Library in English*, ed. J. M. Robinson (New York, 1977) p. 167.

[46] J. Doresse, *The Secret Books of the Egyptian Gnostics*, trans. P. Mairet, revised and augmented by the author (London, 1960) p. 170. Doresse's first suggestion was taken up by A. Böhlig and P. Labib, *Die koptisch-gnostische Schrift ohne Titel aus Codex II von Nag Hammadi* (Deutsche Akademie der Wissenschaften zu Berlin Institut für Orientforschung; Berlin, 1962) p. 32. The text was first mentioned by R. Reitzenstein, *Poimandres. Studien zur griechisch-ägyptischen und frühchristlichen Literatur* (Leipzig, 1904) pp. 186f., in connection with the Solomon story in Josephus, *Ant* 8.2.5, TSol, and *Korē Kosmou*. The text of the Epistle to Rehoboam was edited by J. Heeg in *Catalogus codicum astrologorum Graecorum* VIII.2 (Brussels, 1911) pp. 139–65; cf. also A. M. J. Festugière, *La Révélation d'Hermès Trismégiste*, 4 vols. (Paris, 1949–54) vol. 1, pp. 339f.; E. R. Goodenough, *Jewish Symbols in the Greco-Roman World*, vol. 2, p. 233.

[47] Doresse, *Secret Books*, p. 171.

[48] Giversen, in Krause, *Essays*, p. 20, n. 1.

and some of them are commonly found in the Nag Hammadi texts as a whole.[49] Either the reference is to the testament in the general sense, or one must admit that precise identification is as yet impossible among the many Solomonic· magical works known to have existed.[50] If the former is so, we have evidence of the testament probably from late third-century Alexandria.

Author and provenance

There is nothing in the Testament of Solomon which would clearly identify its author. As the above discussion indicates, the author did not write in either Hebrew or Aramaic. If a Greek-speaking Jew originally wrote it, it was edited by a Christian; more recent scholarship, however, accepts the view that the author was a Greek-speaking Christian. This is reinforced by what appear to be the final stages of redaction (cf. TSol 11:6; 12:3; 15:10–15).

Equally difficult to establish is its provenance, for, like most hellenistic (-Jewish) magic, the testament has an international quality. Certain elements suggest Babylonia. The ascription of ailments and diseases to specific demons was deeply rooted there, and so was the wind demon, which causes a fever (TSol 22).[51] There are also connections with the Babylonian Talmud, for example, the demons assisting Solomon's temple building, or the lengthy treatment of the legend of Ashmedai (= Asmodeus).[52] Furthermore, the popular magic of the Aramaic Incantation Bowls from Babylonia, though from about A.D. 600, is in many respects like the magic of the testament, most notably in the importance of Solomon as a "Son of David" whose name is invoked to exorcise the demons.[53] Yet, some judge that the testament is both pre-talmudic in its demonology and earlier than the type of magic associated with the sixth-century bowls; thus, Babylonia is not usually suggested as the place of origin.[54]

A second possibility is Asia Minor. The Book of Acts stresses that Ephesus was an important center for the magical arts; whether accurate or not, the claim is made that magical books worth 50,000 pieces of silver were consumed in a book burning at Ephesus (Acts 19:11–20). Though somewhat meager, there are other indications of active magical activity in Asia Minor; for example, a whole magical apparatus has been discovered at Pergamum.[55] Among the scholars, McCown, followed by James, mildly and cautiously favored Ephesus or some part of Asia Minor, McCown because "no decisive objections appear."[56]

The third, and perhaps most obvious possibility, is Egypt, that melting pot of ancient magical lore. Ethiopia received its Jewish and Christian traditions via Egypt, and Ethiopia preserved magic, demonology, and legends about the Queen of Sheeba and Solomon's demise similar to those found in the testament.[57] The magic of the testament is very much

---

[49] For example, Error and Power (cf. TSol 8:5); one also finds in the Nag Hammadi texts Orneos, Michael, Gabriel, cherubim and seraphim, and various forms of Uriel (Ouriel). For an account of the fallen angels (cf. TSol 5:3; 6:2), see On the Origin of the World (II, 5:*123*). The widespread Jewish tradition that Solomon built Jerusalem (e.g. the Temple) with the aid of the demons is expressed in IX, 3:*70*.

[50] H.-G. Bethge, *"Vom Ursprung der Welt." Die fünfte Schrift aus Nag-Hammadi-Codex II neu herausgegeben und unter bevorzugter Auswertung anderer Nag-Hammadi-Texte erklärt* (diss., Berlin, 1975) p. 270. I am grateful to B. Layton for making Bethge's dissertation available to me. On Solomonic books, see nn. 82, 94, 110–12.

[51] The *ašakku marsu;* cf. McCown, *Testament*, p. 53.

[52] B. A. Pearson in his *The Coptic Gnostic Library. Nag Hammadi Codices IX and X* (Nag Hammadi Studies; Leiden, 1980), parts of which he has kindly supplied to me in advance, lists in his notes on *70*, 7–9 the Jewish haggadic texts which center on the view that Solomon built the Temple with the aid of demons: b. Giṭṭ 68ab; ExR 52.4; Midrash Canticles 1.1.5; NumR 11.3; PR 6.7; cf. b. Meg 11b; Pesikṭa de-Rab Kahana; Josephus, *Ant* 8.2.5; the Mandaean account of the building of the Temple in Lidzbarski, *Ginza*, pp. 28, 46. See also his "Jewish Haggadic Traditions in *The Testimony of Truth* from Nag Hammadi (CG IX, 3)," *Ex orbe religionum. Studia Geo Widengren*, vol. 1 (*Numen* Supp. 21; Leiden, 1972) p. 459. Other traditions related to TSol are mentioned by L. Ginsberg, *The Legends of the Jews*, 7 vols. (Philadelphia, 1913) vol. 4, pp. 292f., n. 56.

[53] McCown, *Testament*, pp. 65f.; D. Duling, "Solomon, Exorcism, and the Son of David," *HTR* 68 (1975) 245–47.

[54] The pre-talmudic view on demonology in TSol is expressed by K. Kohler ("Demonology," *The Jewish Encyclopedia*, vol. 4, p. 518) and echoed by McCown (*Testament*, pp. 30, 65).

[55] R. Wünsch, ed., *Antikes Zaubergerät aus Pergamon* (Jahrbuch des Kaiserlich Deutschen Archäologischen Instituts, 6th Ergänzungsheft; Berlin, 1905).

[56] McCown, *Testament*, p. 110; James, *JTS* 24 (1922) 468.

[57] McCown, *Testament*, pp. 71–73; E. A. W. Budge, *The Queen of Sheba and Her Only Son Menyelek* (London, 1922).

like the hellenistic magical papyri discovered in Egypt (which mention Solomon), and the account of the thirty-six heavenly bodies which attack various parts of the human body (TSol 18) is a variation of the thirty-six decans, or 10° divisions and deities of the 360° zodiac, known especially from Egypt. Presumably the papyrus fragments of the decan chapter of the testament came from Egypt.[58] Gnostic amulets frequently drew on the name of Solomon, and gnostic texts from Nag Hammadi refer to a "Book of Solomon" and the tradition of Solomon and the demons.[59] Finally, the earliest literary reference to the testament is likely from Egypt (*Dialogue of Timothy and Aquila*).[60] Conybeare thought that the testament was probably a favorite book among the Egyptian Ophians or some analogous gnostic sect, but McCown objected to Conybeare's gnostic interpretation of the Testament of Solomon, chapter 8, and believed that neither the testament's cosmology nor its dualism was gnostic enough to derive it from Egyptian gnosticism.[61]

A final possibility is Syria-Palestine. The Jews and Samaritans were known in the Greco-Roman world for magic, and the Solomonic magical tradition is well documented in Palestinian Judaism, as will be presently shown.[62] If Conybeare's suggestion that Josephus was referring to the testament seems a bit farfetched, it is also clear that McCown's primary reason for preferring Asia Minor over Palestine (Galilee)—the testament is "thoroughly Greek in its language and much of its material"[63]—would no longer be accepted by an increasing number of scholars who are convinced of the hellenization of Palestine.[64] Thus, the fourth possibility, Syria-Palestine, emerges as more of a live option than could have been possible in McCown's day.

In short, McCown's judgment that it is impossible to reach any certain conclusion about the testament's place of origin must be reaffirmed; but his view of the ascending order of probability—Galilee, Egypt, Asia Minor[65]—might just as likely be stated as Babylonia, Asia Minor, Egypt, Palestine.

Historical importance

The Testament of Solomon is the product of the growth of a legend about a famous biblical character combined with a variety of syncretistic beliefs about astrology, demonology, angelology, magic, and medicine. As the product of long tradition, it represents not only its own period of composition but the period of the Second Jewish Commonwealth and the rise of earliest Christianity. The testament is an important response to basic human problems: the presence of human frailty, sickness, and potential death. It therefore invites comparison with similar responses from the arena of ancient eastern Mediterranean civilizations, especially Persian, Babylonian, Egyptian, Greek, Jewish, Christian, and Islamic religions. Points of

---

[58] K. Preisendanz, *Papyri Graecae Magicae. Die griechischen Zauberpapyri*, 2nd ed. by A. Henrichs (Stuttgart, 1973, 1974), and McCown, *Testament*, pp. 66–68. McCown states, "The *Test* . . . differs from the magic papyri chiefly in that it is the work of a Christian using heathen materials rather than that of a heathen working on Jewish or Christian matter." The important papyrus fragment of TSol 18 was published by Preisendanz, *EOS* 48 (1956) 161–67.

[59] Gnostic amulets (invoking Solomon's name have been preserved: See McCown, *Testament*, p. 70, n. 1; Goodenough, *Jewish Symbols*; see Bibliography.

[60] Conybeare, *Dialogues*, p. xxxiv: "The title affixed to TA describes the debate as having taken place in Alexandria in the days of the Archbishop Cyril . . . But this title really no more than marks the time at which the work assumed its present form . . . it is a recension of some older dialogue . . ."

[61] Conybeare, *JQR* 11 (1898) 14; Origen, *Contra* 6.24–38, discusses a "Diagram of the Ophians," which Conybeare compared to the seven *stoicheia* of TSol 8; see W. Foerster, *"Ophites and Ophians,"* in *Gnosis*, trans. R. McL. Wilson (Oxford, 1972) vol. 1, pp. 84–89. McCown, *Testament*, p. 70, objects that they are not the gnostic seven but the Pleiades, or seven daughters of Atlas in Gk. myth; cf. Job 9:9; Amos 5:8; TSol 8:2, n. a.

[62] See the following discussion. For Jewish magic, see L. Blau, *Das altjüdische Zauberwesen* (Budapest, 1898; repr. Westmead, England, 1970); J. Golden, "The Magic of Magic and Superstition," *Aspects of Religious Propaganda in Judaism and Early Christianity*, ed. E. S. Fiorenza (Notre Dame, 1976) pp. 115–47, which includes a short discussion of the 3rd–4th cent. Jewish magical document, the *Sepher Ha-Razim*; M. Margalioth, *Sepher Ha-Razim. A Newly Recovered Book of Magic from the Talmudic Period* (Jerusalem, 1966 [Heb.]); Michael Morgan, *Sefer HaRazim* (SBL Texts and Translations; Chico, Calif., forthcoming). J. M. Hull, *Hellenistic Magic and the Synoptic Tradition* (SBT 28, N.S.; Naperville, Ill., 1974); M. Smith, *Jesus the Magician* (New York, 1978); see n. 82 below.

[63] McCown, *Testament*, p. 110.

[64] Goodenough, *Jewish Symbols*; M. Hengel, *Judaism and Hellenism*, trans. J. Bowden (Philadelphia, 1973) vol. 1, especially pp. 239–41; M. Smith, "Prologomena to a Discussion of Aretalogies, Divine Men, the Gospels, and Jesus," *JBL* 90 (1971) 174–99.

[65] McCown, *Testament*, p. 110.

comparison will be found in apocryphal and pseudepigraphic literature, talmudic legends, the Dead Sea Scrolls, Jewish and early Christian literary and non-literary magical and medical conceptions, hellenistic magical papyri, gnosticism, Greek myth, and astrology. It can also be seen in the context of the history of magic, medicine, and science.[66]

One of the historically important features of the testament is that it represents a popular hellenistic Jewish-Christian view of King Solomon, one of the key figures of the Jewish Scriptures, midway between the time he actually lived (10th cent. B.C.) and the period when many of the surviving texts about him stressed his character as the magician *par excellence* (15th–16th cent. A.D.). The view that Solomon was a magician goes back to ancient interpretations of 1 Kings 4:29–34 (5:9–14 in Heb.):[67]

> Yahweh gave Solomon immense wisdom and understanding, and a heart as vast as the sand on the seashore. The wisdom of Solomon surpassed the wisdom of all the sons of the East, and all the wisdom of Egypt. He was wiser than any other, wiser than Ethan the Ezrahite, wiser than Heman and Calcol and Darda, the cantors. He composed three thousand proverbs; and his songs numbered a thousand and five. He could talk about plants from the cedar in Lebanon to the hyssop growing on the wall; and he could talk of animals, and birds and reptiles and fish. Men from all nations came to hear Solomon's wisdom, and he received gifts from all the kings of the world, who heard of his wisdom.

This Old Testament tradition is expanded in the following way: Solomon's wisdom is increasingly seen to include magical knowledge, and his literary productivity grows to include magical incantations and magical books. The literary side to his productivity can already be observed in the Old Testament itself, for it is claimed that he authored Proverbs (Prov 1:1), Song of Songs (Song 1:1; cf. 1:5; 3:7, 9, 11; 8:11), Ecclesiastes (Eccl 1:1, 12, 16–18), and, if extended to the apocrypha, it is implied that he authored the Wisdom of Solomon (WisSol 8:10f.; 9:7f., 12). Other pseudepigraphic books include the Odes of Solomon, the Psalms of Solomon, and the work under consideration, the Testament of Solomon.

In the Wisdom of Solomon (WisSol 7:15–22), probably from second-century B.C. Egypt, it is claimed that Solomon knows astrology, "powers of roots," and "forces of spirits," in part an extension of his knowledge of plants in 1 Kings 5. Perhaps from about the same time and place came a Septuagint translator who changed 1,005 "songs" in 1 Kings 5:12 (4:32) to 5,000 "odes" (Gk. *ōdai*), and this may be the source of the later view that Solomon wrote "incantations" (Gk. *epōdai*; cf. Josephus, *Ant* 8.2.5). In any case, it is clear that Solomon's fame grew in Egypt at a very early period.

Meanwhile, though sometimes difficult to trace, the popular tradition was also growing in Palestine. Josephus wrote that the Essenes, usually thought to have written the Dead Sea Scrolls, did "research into medicinal roots and properties of stones for the healing of diseases" (*War·*2.8.6). It may be that Solomon was known among them as an exorcist of demons. Certainly, Abraham in the Genesis Apocryphon and probably Daniel in the Prayer of Nabonidus are viewed as types of exorcists. Recently, there has turned up a curious recension of Psalm 91, which was known among the Rabbis as an exorcistic psalm (y.Shab 6:8b: "song for the stricken"; b.Shebuʿoth 15b: "song referring to evil demons"; y.ʿErub 10:26c: "song for the demons"), which contains Solomon's name just before the term "demons" in column 1.[68] These Dead Sea Scrolls references are at least so early as the first century A.D.

From the late first or early second century A.D., in all probability, comes Pseudo-Philo's *Liber antiquitatum biblicarum* 60, originally a separate literary piece written in Hebrew, and probably from Palestine. It contains a psalm said to have been played by David on his harp to rebuke the demon that troubled Saul. At the end of the psalm there is a prophecy that some commentators think might refer to Solomon. D. Harrington translates the prophecy

---

[66] See L. Thorndike, *A History of Magic and Experimental Science*, 5 vols. (New York, 1923) especially vol. 1 and vol. 2.

[67] For much of what follows, see D. Duling, *HTR* 68 (1975) 235–49; McCown, *JPOS* 2 (1922) 1–24; Preisendanz, Pauly-Wissowa Supplement 8 (1956) passim.

[68] J. M. van der Ploeg, "Un Petit Rouleau de psaumes apocryphes (11QPsApᵃ)" in *Tradition und Glaube, Festgabe für K. G. Kuhn* (Göttingen, 1971) pp. 128–39; E. Lövestam, "Jésus Fils de David chez les Synoptiques," *ST* 28 (1974) 97–109.

"But let the new womb from which I was born rebuke you, from which after a time one born from my loins will rule over you."[69]

To these early Palestinian Jewish materials one might add The Apocalypse of Adam, a tractate discovered at Nag Hammadi, Egypt, in 1945. The document contains many Jewish, Iranian, and Mandaean ideas and many scholars believe it is non-Christian; in fact, A. Böhlig, G. MacRae, and C. Hedrick would locate it in a first- or second-century A.D. Syrian-Palestinian baptismal sect.[70] It is interesting in this regard to note that the Mandaean *Ginza* views Solomon as the ruler over the demons and the seven planetary Dēvs.[71] In any case the Apocalypse of Adam 7:1–48 lists thirteen false explanations for the origin of a redeemer figure called the *Photor*, or "Illuminator." Hedrick has attempted to trace the redactional history of this section in Palestinian-Jewish baptismal sects prior to its incorporation into its present context sometime prior to A.D. 150.[72] The fourth explanation for the origin of the *Photor* reads:

> The fourth kingdom says [of him]:
> "He came [from a virgin . . . Solomon] sought her, he and Phersalo and Sauel and his armies which had been sent out. *Solomon also sent his army of demons* to seek the virgin. And they did not find the one they sought, but the virgin who was given to them was the one they fetched. Solomon took her. The virgin conceived and gave birth to the child there.
> She nourished him on a border of the desert. When he had been nourished,
> He received glory and power from the seed from which he had been begotten.
> And thus he came to the water."[73] [ApAdam 7:13–16; Italics mine.]

Though the tradition of the virgin who bore Solomon a child is new, it is clear that the text knows of the legend of Solomon's control of an army of demons so prominent in other Jewish sources, and specifically in the testament. In short, it is possible that the Apocalypse of Adam should be added to early Jewish Palestinian source material about Solomon.

The tradition of Solomon as magician, which is only roughly represented in the above material, is clearly present in Josephus' *Antiquities* 8.2.5. This important passage reads:

> Now so great was the prudence and wisdom which God granted Solomon that he surpassed the ancients, and even the Egyptians, who are said to excel all men in understanding, were not only, when compared with him, a little inferior but proved to fall far short of the king in sagacity . . . He also composed a thousand and five books of odes and songs, and three thousand books of parables and similitudes, for he spoke a parable about every kind of tree from the hyssop to the cedar, and in like

[69] M. R. James, "Citharismus regis David contra demonium Saulis," *Apocrypha Anecdota*, (T&S 2.3; Cambridge, 1893) pp. 83–85; L. Cohn, "An Apocryphal Work Ascribed to Philo of Alexandria," *JQR* 10 (1898) 277–332; also L. H. Feldman, "Prologomenon," in M. R. James, *The Biblical Antiquities of Philo* (New York, 1917; repr. 1971) pp ix–clxix. [See Harrington's contribution on *LAB* herein. —J.H.C.]

[70] A. Böhlig, "Die Adamapocalypse aux Codex V von Nag Hammadi als Zeugnis jüdisch-iranischer Gnosis," *OrChr* 48 (1964) 44–49; G. MacRae, "The Coptic Gnostic Apocalypse of Adam," *Hey J* 6 (1965) 27–35; "The Apocalypse of Adam Reconsidered," *The Society of Biblical Literature One Hundred Eighth Annual Meeting: Book of Seminar Papers*, 2 vols. ed. L. C. McGaughy, ([Missoula, Mont.], 1972) vol. 2, p. 577; C. W. Hedrick, *The Apocalypse of Adam: A Literary and Source Analysis* (diss., Claremont Graduate School, 1977, pp. 266–68, kindly lent to me by Layton of Yale University; Hedrick has a history of research in ch. 1); see also K. Rudolph, "Gnosis und Gnostizismus, ein Forschungsbericht," *ThRu*, N.F. 34 (1969) 160–69; A. F. J. Klijn, *Seth in Gnostic Literature* (*NovT*Sup 46; Leiden, 1977) pp. 90f., n. 42. [Also see MacRae's contribution on ApAdam herein. —J.H.C.]

[71] M. Lidzbarski, *Ginza* (Göttingen, 1925), p. 28 (right): "190. Then King Solomon, the Son of David, is born and appears, and he becomes king of Judah and the powerful ruler over Jerusalem. The demons and the dēvs submit to him and walk according to his will until he glorifies himself and is ungrateful for the goodness of his Lord. Then the demons and the dēvs turn away from his speech and dominion is taken from him."

[72] Hedrick, *The Apocalypse of Adam*, pp. 161–268, suggests that the catalog was originally a collection of thirteen theological statements about the birth of some unknown individual which was then taken up as a baptismal liturgy in an initiation rite with thirteen stages paralleling the ascent of the *Photor* through the thirteen evil powers and cohorts of the creator god. Subsequently, it was adapted by an anti-water baptism community to illustrate thirteen false explanations of the *Photor's* origin. Finally, a redactor who combined a Jewish gnostic source (A) with a largely non-Jewish but certainly non-Christian gnostic source (B) incorporated the catalog into source (B). According to Hedrick, the document was "redacted prior to A.D. 150 during an early stage of the Sethian-Archontic tradition by a representative of a minority faction who argued for a spiritualized understanding of baptism and an ascetic life style" (pp. ii–iii). The redaction may have taken place in Palestine, possibly in the Transjordan (p. 266).

[73] G. MacRae's translation. [See his contribution on ApAdam herein. —J.H.C.]

manner about birds and all kinds of terrestrial creatures and those that swim and those that fly. There was no form of nature with which he was not acquainted or which he passed over without examining, but he studied them all philosophically and revealed the most complete knowledge of their several properties. And God granted him knowledge of the art used against demons for the benefit and healing of men. He also composed incantations by which illnesses are relieved, and left behind forms of exorcisms with which those possessed by demons drive them out, never to return. And this kind of cure is of very great power among us to this day, for I have seen a certain Eleazar, a countryman of mine, in the presence of Vespasian, his sons, tribunes and a number of other soldiers, free men possessed by demons, and this was the manner of the cure: he put to the nose of the possessed man a ring which had under its seal one of the roots prescribed by Solomon, and then, as the man smelled it, drew out the demon through his nostrils, and, when the man at once fell down, adjured the demon never to come back into him, speaking Solomon's name and reciting the incantations which he had composed. Then, wishing to convince the bystanders and prove to them that he had this power, Eleazar placed a cup or footbasin full of water a little way off and commanded the demon, as it went out of the man, to overturn it and make known to the spectators that he had left the man. And when this was done, the understanding and wisdom of Solomon were clearly revealed, on account of which we have been induced to speak of these things, in order that all men may know the greatness of his nature and how God favored him, and that no one under the sun may be ignorant of the king's surpassing virtue of every kind.[74]

In this passage, the allusions are clearly to 1 Kings 4:29–34 (5:9–14 in Heb.) again. The numbers 1,005 and 3,000 are those of the Hebrew text (not the Septuagint), but now Josephus refers to 1,005 *books* of odes (*ōdai*) *and* songs and 3,000 *books* of parables *and* similitudes, including those about all kinds of trees and creatures (the natural sources for magical incantations). Solomon is thus said to have composed "incantations" (*epōdai*, perhaps suggested by *ōdai*) and exorcistic formulas by which one can drive out the demons. In addition, the ring is introduced, though it is really the root under the seal of the ring by which Eleazar performs the exorcism. Finally, Solomon's wisdom and greatness are so acknowledged that speaking his name and reciting his incantations help bring about the exorcism. All of this is an "art" (*technē*) employed by the ancient physician or magician. Because of its military setting Preisendanz connected this event with Vespasian's campaign in Palestine during the Jewish wars with Rome (A.D. 66–70), and Conybeare suggested (rather implausibly) that the testament might be the very book of incantations about which Josephus wrote.[75]

The interpretation of 1 Kings 5:13 (4:33) occurs again in the Targum Sheni to Esther.

Solomon *ruled* over the wild beasts, *over* the birds of the heaven, and *over* the creeping beasts of the earth, as well as *over the devils, the spirits of the night*; and he understood the language of all these according as it is written, "and he talked with the trees."[76] [Italics mine.]

In this targum, Solomon's mastery over the demons includes the "demons of the night" (Heb. *lilîn*; cf. Isa 34:14, "night hag").

The reference to the "demons of the night" recalls the Aramaic Incantation Bowls, another example of Jewish magic.[77] These bowls are about the size of soup tureens. They are reported to have been found upside down, usually in houses, often in the four corners of the houses, but also in cemeteries. There are several theories about bowl praxis, the most likely being that they were meant to trap or overturn the demons in some way. Almost all contain Eastern Aramaic inscriptions in ink, most frequently written on the inside and in spiral fashion from

---

[74] Josephus, *Ant* 8.2.5 (LCL, trans. H. St. J. Thackery and R. Marcus, pp. 593–97).

[75] Preisendanz, Pauly-Wissowa Supplement 8 (1956) col. 667; Conybeare, *JQR* 11 (1898) 12.

[76] For the Heb., see Salzberger, *Salomosage*, pp. 93f.; the translation is from McCown, *JPOS* 2 (1922) 5.

[77] J. A. Montgomery, *Aramaic Incantation Texts from Nippur* (Philadelphia, 1913); cf. Duling, *HTR* 68 (1975) 245, n. 42 for Bibliography, to which should be added Charles D. Isbell, *Corpus of the Aramaic Incantation Bowls* (Missoula, Mont., 1975).

the inside out, and sometimes containing in the center a primitive drawing of a demon, often chained. The inscriptions are incantations in the category of "white magic," that is, they are meant to protect homes, families, and possessions from all sorts of witchcraft, diseases, and demons. At least eighteen bowls refer to "King Solomon, Son of David" and twelve or thirteen of them refer to his seal ring. A sample of this protective magic is as follows:

> The demon NṬY', ṬṬY QLY', BTY', Nuriel, Holy Rock. (2) Sealed and countersealed and fortified are Aḥât, the daughter of Immâ; Rabbî, Malkî and Dipshî, the sons of Aḥât; and Yanâi (3) the daughter of Aḥât, and Aḥât the daughter of Immâ, and Aṭyônâ the son of Qarqôi, and Qarqôi the daughter of Shîltâ, and Shîltâ the daughter of Immî (4)—they and their houses and their children and their property are sealed with the seal-ring of El Shaddai, blessed be He, *and with the seal ring of King (5) Solomon, the son of David, who worked spells on male demons and female liliths.* Sealed, countersealed and fortified against the male demon (6) and female lilith and spell and curse and incantation and knocking and evil eye and evil black-arts, against the black-arts of mother (7) and daughter, and against those of daughter-in-law and mother-in-law, and against those of the presumptuous woman, who darkens the eyes and blows away the soul (i.e. causes despair), and against the evil black-arts, that are wrought by (8) men, and against everything bad. In the name of the Lord. Lord, Hosts is His name, Amen, amen, selah. This charm is to thwart the demon Tîtînôs. Sealed are the bodies(?) of 'Š QL, the bodies(?) of 'Š QL MYLY MYLY 'TYGL'.[78] [Italics mine.]

The incantation bowls are relatively late and their demonology and magic are sometimes considered more developed than that in the testament; yet, there are similar incantations from an earlier period. An especially pertinent example is a Jewish incantation written in Hebrew on a small metal-foil amulet which was discovered in 1853 at the southern tip of the Sea of Galilee. Dated in the second or third century A.D., the thirty-two-line inscription is a piece of protective magic for an unborn infant, and it is very similar to an incantation on one of the bowls. It begins with the magician's magical equipment: "And now with the wand of Moses and the shining-plate of Aaron the high priest, and with *the seal of Solomon,* and with [the Shield] of David, and with the mitre of the chief priest have I pronounced(?) [the wo]rd . . ."[79] [Italics mine.]

Among the Rabbis, Solomon's wisdom was both exonerated as his greatest asset and deprecated as that which led to his downfall. The testament has obvious points in common with the rabbinic stories about Asmodeus (cf. Tob), who is called Ashmedai.[80] When Solomon requires the stone-cutting worm, the *shamîr* ("flint," "diamond"), to cut stones for the Temple—according to law they could not be cut with iron tools (cf. 1Kgs 6:7)—it was surmised that the archdemon Ashmedai alone knew of its location. On earthly visits to watch debates in houses of learning, Ashmedai was known to get a drink at a mountain well which he then capped daily with a large rock and which he always examined before reopening. To obtain the coveted *shamîr,* Solomon gave his chief man, Benaiah ben Jehoiadah, a chain engraved with the divine name, a ring engraved with the divine name, a bundle of wool, and a skin of wine, and dispatched him to the mountain well. Benaiah drilled a hole and drained off the water, and then, stuffing the hole with the bundle of wool, he filled the well with wine. When Ashmedai, descending from heaven, discovered the wine, he was suspicious; finally, however, he gave in to his thirst, became drowsy with the wine, and fell asleep. Benaiah then chained him about the neck, and when Ashmedai awoke and tried to get free, Benaiah stated that "the name of thy Lord is upon thee" (presumably, the demon was sealed

---

[78] C. H. Gordon, "Aramaic Magical Bowls in the Istanbul and Baghdad Museums," *ArOr* 6 (1934) 324–26 (Text B); Montgomery, *Aramaic Incantation Texts,* p. 170, contains an incantation in which the ring has on it "the Ineffable Name" (No. 11).

[79] J. A. Montgomery, "Some Early Amulets from Palestine," *JAOS* 31 (1911) 274. For other Solomonic amulets, see P. Perdrizet, *Sphragis Solomônos* ("Solomon's Seal"), *Revue des études grecques* 16 (1903) 42–61; Goodenough, *Jewish Symbols,* vol. 1, p. 68; vol. 2, pp. 226–38; vol. 7, pp. 198–200; vol. 9, pp. 1044–67.

[80] See Ginsberg, *Legends,* pp. 165–69; "Asmodeus, or Ashmedai," *The Jewish Encyclopedia,* vol. 2, pp. 217–20; M. Seligsohn and M. W. Mendelbaum, "Solomon," *The Jewish Encyclopedia,* vol. 11, pp. 448f. The key text is b. Giṭ 68ab. See also Strack-Billerbeck, *Kommentar,* vol. 4, Excursus 21; Salzberger, *Salomosage,* passim; McCown, *Testament,* pp. 62f.; McCown, *JPOS* 2 (1922) 5–8; discussion below and TSol 5, nn.

with the ring as well). After the completion of the Temple, the king told Ashmedai he did not understand how the demons' power could be so strong if their chieftain could be bound by a human. Ashmedai responded that if Solomon were to remove the chains and lend the magic ring to him, Ashmedai would prove his greatness. When Solomon agreed, Ashmedai hurled Solomon four hundred parasangs from Jerusalem, and then put himself forward as king. After much wandering, Solomon's lover, the Ammonite Naamah, recovered the magic ring from the belly of a fish, for Ashmedai had thrown it into the sea. Putting it on his finger, Solomon was immediately transported to Jerusalem, where he drove out Ashmedai and ascended the throne.

There are other rabbinic stories that can be compared to stories in the testament. Of Solomonic magical *books*, however, there was scarcely mention until about the twelfth century when Solomon once again appeared as the source of all wisdom. It may be that the Rabbis were referring to this lack when they said that Hezekiah "suppressed the book of recipes," for medieval commentators said that this book referred to a book which Solomon wrote.[81] In any case, it appears that such books were ignored or, more likely, discouraged. In this connection it may be recalled that the *Sepher Ha-Razim*, a Jewish magical work pieced together by M. Margalioth and perhaps coming from third- or fourth-century Palestine, noted that Solomon was *heir* to the Books of the Mysteries, and that these gave him power over all the spirits and demons.[82]

The earliest *Christian* tradition about the magical wisdom of Solomon, suggest some modern interpreters, is already implied in the New Testament.[83] They refer primarily to the cryptic passage which states "something greater than Solomon is here" (Matt 12:42), which is followed by the story of the return of the unclean spirit (Matt 12:43–45).[84] One is also led to raise the possibility with the Son of David pericope (Mark 12:35–37 and parallels) and the Markan theology as a whole, e.g. as a conception Mark opposed.[85] But if such connections are rejected, the first clear reference in the Christian literary tradition is found in Origen's commentary on Matthew 26:63 in which Origen states, "It is customary to adjure demons with adjurations written by Solomon. But they themselves who use these adjurations sometimes use books not properly constituted; indeed they even adjure demons with some books taken from Hebrew."[86] Possibly Origen was referring to the passage about Eleazar in Josephus, as do later Christian writers, but he might also have been thinking of the testament or the *Sepher Ha-Razim*.

It has been noted above that the Nag Hammadi texts mention "the Book of Solomon" and contain what is probably a Jewish-gnostic baptismal text from Palestine which refers to Solomon and his army of demons. There are also two Christian gnostic texts from Nag Hammadi which mention Solomon. The first, The Second Treatise of the Great Seth, which is a polemic against "orthodox" Christianity, contains a "laughingstock" passage which polemicizes against a series of Old Testament figures. The litany-like pattern is that an Old Testament figure (Adam; Abraham, Isaac, Jacob; David; Solomon; the twelve prophets; or Moses) is called a "laughingstock," followed by a reason related to the Hebdomad's (Jaldabaoth's) false claims about them to make himself stronger than the gnostics, concluded

---

[81] j. Ber 10a; Pes 56a; cf. McCown, *JPOS* 2 (1922) 6f. The medieval commentators are Maimonides and Rashi.

[82] M. Morgan, *Sefer HaRazim*, renders the Opening, 12f.: "And when he [Noah] came forth from the ark, he used (the book [of mystery given to Noah by the angel Raziel]) all the days of his life, and at the time of his death he handed it down [two manuscripts: to Shem, and Shem] to Abraham, and Abraham to Isaac, and Isaac to Jacob, and Jacob to Levi, and Levi to Kohath, and Kohath to Amram, and Amram to Moses, and Moses to Joshua, and Joshua to the elders, and the elders to the prophets, and the prophets to the sages, and thus generation by generation until Solomon the king arose. And the Books of the Mysteries were disclosed to him and he became very learned in books of understanding and so ruled over everything he desired, over all the spirits and demons that wander in the world, and from the wisdom of this book he imprisoned and released, and sent and brought in, and built and prospered." Cf. TSol 18:1, n. a. Also cf. I. Gruenwald, *Apocalyptic and Merkavah Mysticism* (Leiden, 1980) pp. 225–34.

[83] L. Fisher, "Can This Be the Son of David?" in *Jesus and the Historian*. Written in honor of Ernest Cadman Colwell, ed. F. T. Trotter (Philadelphia 1968) pp. 82–97; E. Lövestam, *ST* 28 (1974) 97–109 (originally published in Swedish in 1972); K. Berger, "Die königlichen Messiastraditionen des Neuen Testaments," *NTS* 20 (1973) 1–44; Duling, *HTR* 68 (1975) 235–52.

[84] See previous note and also Goodenough, *Jewish Symbols*, vol. 2, p. 226.

[85] Duling, *HTR* 68 (1975) 49–52.

[86] *In Mattheum comm. ser.* (tract. 33) 110, Migne, PG, vol. 13, col. 1757; McCown, *Testament*, p. 94; *JPOS* 2 (1922) 9.

by a refrain: "We are innocent before him, since we have not sinned."[87] The Solomon statement reads, "Solomon was a laughingstock, since he thought that he was Christ, having become vain through the Hebdomad, as if he had become stronger than I and my brothers. But we are innocent with respect to him."[88] One wonders whether Solomon's "strength" in thinking he had become Christ was related to stories of his miracle working.

Perhaps most interesting of the Nag Hammadi references to Solomon is that found in "The Testimony of Truth" (IX, 3), a Christian gnostic tractate which combines a homily with polemics against "orthodox" Christianity and other gnostic groups. A strongly ascetic (Encratite) document from perhaps the late second or late third century A.D., the tractate's Solomon section has a large lacuna which must be filled. Referring to hypocrites who say they renounce the world but do not, the passage continues as follows:

> They become wicked in their action, and some of them fall away [to the worship of] idols. [Others] have [demons] dwelling with them [as did] David the king. He is the one who laid the foundation of Jerusalem; and his son Solomon, whom he begat in [adultery], is the one who built Jerusalem by means of the demons, because he received [their powers]. When he [had finished building, he imprisoned] the demons [in the temple]. He [placed them] into seven [waterpots. They remained] a long [time in] the [waterpots], abandoned [there]. When the Romans [went] up to [Jerusalem] they discovered [the] waterpots, [and immediately] the [demons] ran out of the waterpots as those who escape from prison. And the waterpots [remained] pure (thereafter). [And] since those days [they dwell] with men who are [in] ignorance, and [they have remained upon] the earth.
>
> Who, then, is [David]? And who is Solomon? [And] what is the foundation? And what is the wall which surrounds Jerusalem? And who are the demons? And what are the waterpots? And who are the Romans? But these [are mysteries . . .][89]

B. A. Pearson connects this passage with Jewish haggadic traditions, referring to a "David-Solomon midrash," and thinks that the author "is probably quoting or adapting from a written source [or sources] . . ."[90] S. Giversen also makes the link with Solomon's rule over the demons, especially as it is found in other Nag Hammadi texts.[91] The connection with the testament is somewhat stronger if the lacuna at the end of the third sentence just quoted is restored to read "he received [power]" or "he received [wisdom]," thus reading, "Solomon . . . is the one who built Jerusalem by means of the demons, because he received power [or wisdom]."[92] In the testament the gifts of power and wisdom are from God; it is not the power of the demons ("their power"). Finally, there are instances in the testament when Solomon traps demons in vessels and places them in the Temple until they are freed, though the freeing occurs at the first destruction, not at the coming of "the Romans,"[93] and the tradition of seven waterpots is known elsewhere.[94]

---

[87] J. A. Gibbons, *A Commentary on "The Second Logos of the Great Seth,"* (Ph.D. diss., Yale University, 1972) p. 255. Gibbons makes no attempt to date or locate the tractate; cf. his views in *The Nag Hammadi Library*, p. 329.

[88] R. A. Bullard, trans., in *The Nag Hammadi Library*, p. 335.

[89] S. Giversen and B. A. Pearson, trans., "The Testimony of Truth (IX, 3)," in *The Nag Hammadi Library*, p. 415.

[90] B. A. Pearson, "Introduction" in his *Nag Hammadi Codices IX and X; cf.* n. 52 above for the texts of the haggadic tradition.

[91] Giversen, in Krause, *Essays.*

[92] This is the opinion of B. Layton. NHC IX 3:*70*, 9 will be restored in B. Pearson's *Nag Hammadi Codices IX and X*, thanks to a proposal from S. Emmel, so that the translation will contain "[power]" rather than "[their powers]."

[93] TSol 15:8–11; 16:7; cf. 17:5; 18:3, 41f.; 23:16; 25:8. Pearson, "Introduction," in *Nag Hammadi Codices IX and X* suggests "the Romans" means Pompey (cf. Josephus, *Ant* 14.72f.).

[94] The alchemist Zosimus of Panopolis, about A.D. 300 in Egypt, writes, "Among the Egyptians there is a book called *The Seven Heavens* attributed to Solomon, against the demons; but it is not true that it is by Solomon because these bottles were brought (from Jerusalem) long ago to our (Egyptian) priests. That is what the language used to denote them makes one suppose; for the term 'bottles of Solomon' is a Hebraic expression . . . After these writings had spread everywhere, being still incomplete, they were corrupted. It is he (sc. Solomon) that invented them (sc. the talismanic bottles), as I said above. But Solomon only wrote a single work concerning the seven bottles; and people composed commentaries at different epochs to explain the things that this work contained. Now in these commentaries there was some fraud; (but) all (of them), or almost all, are in agreement on the work of the bottles directed against the demons. These bottles acted (in the same way) as the prayer and the nine letters written by Solomon; the demons cannot resist them . . . The seven bottles in which Solomon shut up the demons were made of electrum. We must

From the time of Origen on, Solomon is found in Christian tradition even more than in Jewish tradition. Many writers praise his magical powers, and he is found in the popular tradition on amulets, talismans, and lintels. When, however, the Jews attribute messianic passages to Solomon that Christians believe Jesus fulfills, the Christian writers become critical of Solomon.[95]

Solomon's fame as a magician in Judaism and Christianity carried over into the magic of the larger hellenistic world, and at least one example must be cited. This is a reference in the Paris Magical Papyrus, probably from the third or fourth century A.D. but containing traditional material of a much older date. The text reads, "I adjure thee, every demonic spirit, say whatsoever thou art. For I adjure thee by the seal which Solomon laid upon the tongue of Jeremiah and he spoke."[96] Though the passage occurs in a larger context which is probably a Jewish liturgical exorcism and undoubtedly refers to Jeremiah's inability to speak (Jer 1:6), the precise tradition which relates Jeremiah to Solomon's seal has not yet been traced. Nonetheless, it would be generally recognized that the passage illustrates an example of the use of Jewish, specifically Solomonic, magic in the magic of the Greco-Roman world.

Islamic folklore developed the Solomonic tale in tremendously fertile and imaginative ways.[97] Solomon is the greatest of the world rulers, a true apostle of Allah, his messenger, and a prototype of Muḥammad. 1 Kings 4:33 (5:13 in Heb.) is recalled and so are rabbinic traditions such as the stone-cutting worm, the *samur* (*shamîr*). Solomon's fantastic powers to trap the jinn are recounted, and his ring is said to be engraved with "the most great name" of God. Solomon's seal is a charm, usually in the form of a pentagram or hexagram.

The major historical importance of the Testament of Solomon is that it provides a resource for understanding one type of common religious experience in hellenistic Jewish Christianity, an experience related to everyday problems of sickness and health, death and life. But it is also historically important as a means of seeing a high point in the development of the Solomonic legend. Finally, it is an important religious text to compare with other religious texts of the period.

Theological importance

The Testament of Solomon is a mixed collection of religious legends and beliefs, not a systematically constructed theology. Abstracted from such material is the following:

GOD

In the testament, God is the God of the Bible, but the accent falls heavily on his authority over the demons. He is the one and only God (TSol 26:3), the living God (TSol 1:13; 5:12), the "Lord God of Israel" (TSol 1:13) and the "Holy One of Israel" (TSol 4:12). His most frequent designation, "the God of heaven and earth" (TSol 1:8; 2:9; 3:6; 17:4; 18:41; 20:21),

---

believe, in this respect, the Jewish writings concerning the demons. The altered book which we possess, and which is entitled *The Seven Heavens*, contains, in summary, the following: [?] The angel ordered Solomon to make these bottles. (The book) adds (that) Solomon made the seven bottles, according to the number of the seven planets, in conformity to the divine prescriptions . . . The wise Solomon knows also how to evoke the demons; he gives a formula of conjuration, and he indicates the electrum, that is, the bottles of electrum, on the surface of which he inscribed this formula." This text comes from a 15th cent. Syr. MS of some of Zosimus's alchemical writings published in French by M. P. E. Berthelot, *Histoire des sciences: La Chimie au Moyen-âge* (Paris, 1893) vol. 2, pp. 264–66, and translated by W. Scott and A. S. Ferguson, *Hermetica IV: Testimonia* (Oxford, 1936) pp. 140f. Zosimus may also know of a document in which a certain Mambres spoke to Solomon instructing him about sacrifices to drive off, or make powerless, the demons; see Scott-Ferguson, *Hermetica IV*, pp. 111, 139f. if Reitzenstein (*Poimandres*, p. 214) is correct to suggest this is Jambres, "the Egyptian sorcerer," this could be another point of contact with TSol (TSol 25:4; cf. 2Tim 3:8f.). On Jannes and Jambres see TSol 25:4, n. a. [Also see the contribution herein on JanJam. —J.H.C.]

[95] McCown, *JPOS* 2 (1922) 14–16.

[96] Paris Papyrus 3,009 in Preisendanz, *Papyri Graecae Magicae*, IV, 3,039f.; C. K. Barrett, *The New Testament Background: Selected Documents* (New York, 1961) pp. 31–35; McCown, *Testament*, p. 64, n. 2; *JPOS* 2 (1922) 5 and n. 4; A. Dieterich, *Abraxas* (Leipzig, 1891) pp. 138–41; W. L. Knox, "Jewish Liturgical Exorcism," *HTR* 31 (1938) 191–203; in general, A. D. Nock, "Greek Magical Papyri," *Journal of Egyptian Archeology* 15 (1929) 219–35.

[97] Salzberger, *Salomosage;* M. Seligsohn and M. W. Mendelbaum, "Solomon," *The Jewish Encyclopedia*, vol. 11, pp. 444f.; "Sulaiman," *Shorter Encyclopedia of Islam*, ed. H. A. Gibb and J. H. Kramers (Ithaca, N.Y., 1953) pp. 549–51; McCown, *Testament*, pp. 78–82, 94.

implies that all of creation is under his rule, though nothing is said of creation itself. He is designated "the great God Most High" (TSol 11:6), indicating that his abode is in the heavens (cf. TSol 18:3); there he makes decisions about men (TSol 20:12). He is also called simply "God" (TSol 16:1; 25:9), the "Lord God" (TSol 1:7, 13; 5:12; 10:10), the "Lord God Almighty" (TSol 3:5), and the "Lord Sabaoth" (TSol 1:6f.; 5:9), all designations of power and authority. His rule also extends to the underworld, for initially he has "authority over all the spirits of the air, the earth, and (the regions) beneath the earth" (TSol 18:3). Solomon prays to him as one of unquestioned authority (TSol 1:5, 8; 15:1; 18:41). This God, whose power can bind demons with unbreakable bonds (TSol 5:11), gives Solomon power over the demons (TSol 1:00; 18:3), grants him a ring for such power through his archangel Michael (TSol 1:6), and instructs him on how to respond to their evil plots (TSol 7:4). Solomon's power, therefore, always is recognized as a gift for which Solomon continually gives God praise, glory, and thanks (viz. TSol 1:5). When Solomon's lust drives him to idolatry, God's spirit departs from him (TSol 26).

MAN

There is no developed conception of humanity in the testament, but it is clear that apart from Solomon, who has been graciously granted special powers, human beings, who are also "sons of Israel" in the story (TSol 15:14), are to be contrasted with the supernatural angels and demons as "sons of men" and "of earthly origin" (TSol 5:3). As such, they are constantly subjected to all those moral, spiritual, and physical catastrophes brought on by the demons. Even the most holy men and priests can be aroused to desire (TSol 6:4). The only protection against the demonic powers is knowledge of their names, their activities, and their thwarting angels, or magical-medical formulas and praxes, all of which comes from God through Solomon and is preserved in the testament itself (TSol 15:14; 26:8).

COSMOLOGY

The cosmos is tripartite, with the heavens above, the earth in the middle, and hell beneath the earth (TSol 18:3). It is God's world for he is "God of heaven and earth," and he dwells in the highest heaven (TSol 20:11–17). The heavens are also the abode of God's angels (TSol 5:9; 2:7), and the demons are actually "fallen angels." The earth is the realm of nature and the stage for human drama, though God can interrupt natural law. Both angels and demons appear there, and demons like to frequent the more desolate places (TSol 4:4, 6; 17:2). The Prince of Demons, Beelzeboul, is said to hold men bound in Tartarus, the underworld region in control of the demon Abezethibou (TSol 6:3; 23–25).

What is most characteristic of the testament's cosmology is the combination of astrology and demonology. Demons are said "to reside" (*keimai*) in a "star" or "constellation" (*astēr*), as well as in a sign of the zodiac (TSol 2:2). One demon travels (*hodeuō*) with the moon (TSol 4:9). The stars are usually viewed as demonic and seem to have a special destructive power over those humans who share the same constellation (TSol 2:2; 4:6). Indeed, Asmodeus is said to spread madness about women through the stars (TSol 5:8). There are two chapters which especially illustrate this notion, both dealing with the "world rulers" or "heavenly bodies" (*stoicheia*). In chapter 8 seven small stars, the "rulers of this world of darkness" (TSol 8:2), are described as seven "vices" (Deception, Strife, Fate, Distress, Error, Power, The Worst); each is responsible for certain religious, social, or political evils, and each (with the exception of the last) has a thwarting angel.[98] In chapter 18 the stars are the thirty-six "world rulers of the darkness of this age" (TSol 18:2), the first of whom is called "the first decan of the zodiac" (TSol 18:4). This refers to the thirty-six decans, or deities, each of whom rules over 10° of the 360° zodiac, a widespread astrological concept in the ancient world.[99] However, in the testament the decans are demons who cause mental and physical illnesses.

DEMONOLOGY

The Testament of Solomon shares with many ancient Jewish writings the belief (based

---

[98] See above, "Date"; TSol 8:2, n. a.
[99] See above, "Date"; TSol 18:2, n. a. Conybeare, *JQR* 11 (1898) 6–10; McCown, *Testament*, pp. 56–59.

on an interpretation of Gen 6:1–4) that the demons are fallen angels (TSol 6:2), or at least the offspring of fallen angels and human women (TSol 5:3). Sometimes in Jewish literature the offspring were thought to be giants and perhaps the testament reflects that view (TSol 17:1). One, a female demon, is said to be generated from "a voice of the echo of a black heaven, emitted in matter" (TSol 4:8); another demon is the "offspring of The Great One" (TSol 7:5). As the above summary of the contents of the testament shows, the demons are primarily spirits who take one or several forms or change forms (especially TSol 3:6; 15:5; 20:13). They can be perceived as gods if the names of their thwarting angels are unknown (TSol 5:5; cf. 14:2; 15:3). Their forms include heavenly bodies perceived as vices or persons, forces of nature such as fire or wind, mythical personages such as dragons, part animal and part human creatures such as satyrs, some of whom are female, others of whom are headless or two-headed. Beelzeboul, formerly the highest-ranking angel in heaven (TSol 6:2), is their ruler (TSol 3:6); he seems to rule over the earth as well (subject to God). Yet, though he is consulted by Kunopegos, Beelzeboul's role as Prince of the Demons is not highly developed. Beelzeboul's crony, Abezethibou, rules Tartarus, the underworld (TSol 6:3; 25). Beyond this, no complicated hierarchy of demons is developed. Almost all the demons are given names.

There are "spirits of the air, the earth, and beneath the earth" (TSol 22:1). Many of the demons are stars or are in some way associated with the stars. Demons, as mentioned, reside in constellations and, because they can fly up to heaven (TSol 2:3), they sometimes overhear God's plans for the life of men and know the future (TSol 20:14–17). They also frequent desolate places (TSol 4:4, 6) and haunt tombs (TSol 17:2). Their major function is the implementation of all kinds of wickedness, immorality, natural disaster, deformity, disease, and death. A strikingly Christian view is found in 15:10: "We (the demons) will lead astray all the inhabited world for a long time until the Son of God is stretched upon the cross."

ANGELOLOGY

Nothing is said of the precise origin or hierarchy of all the angels in the testament, but their major function is clear; each angel has one or more demons which he is able to render powerless or ineffective (*katargeō*: "I make powerless," "I destroy," rendered below as "I thwart"). To know the name of the appropriate "thwarting angel" for a particular demon and to call on him is to gain power over that particular demon and the evil he causes. If human beings do not know the names of the thwarting angels, the demons will be worshiped as gods (TSol 5:5). The angels are also God's emissaries (TSol 1:7).

Four of the seven archangels, Michael, Ouriel, Raphael, and Gabriel, are found in the testament.[100] Michael, Ouriel, and Raphael are the first three angels to be mentioned by name (TSol 1:6; 2:4; 5:9) and each of the four is said to have power over one of the first four of the thirty-six heavenly bodies (TSol 18:5–8). Specifically, Michael delivers the magic ring granted by God to Solomon and announces to him that he will have power over the demons (TSol 1:6f.); Michael also imprisons the first of the thirty-six heavenly bodies, Ruax, the headache demon (TSol 18:4f.). Ouriel is the first to be introduced as a thwarting angel, namely in connection with the demon Ornias (TSol 2:4); he also thwarts Error, one of the seven heavenly bodies (TSol 8:9), and imprisons Artosael, the third of the thirty-six heavenly bodies, who damages the eyes (TSol 18:7). Raphael thwarts Asmodeus (TSol 5:9) and the Medusa-like Obyzouth (TSol 13:6); he also imprisons Oropel, the fourth of the thirty-six heavenly bodies, who causes sore throat (TSol 18:8). Gabriel imprisons Barsafael, the second of the thirty-six heavenly bodies, who is also a headache demon (TSol 18:6).

There are many other thwarting angels in the testament, usually with Semitic-sounding names. One is called "The Almighty God," or "Patike" by the Hebrews, or "Emmanouel" by the Greeks (TSol 6:8).

DUALISM

The Testament of Solomon contains no absolute dualism. God responds to Solomon's prayer for help against the demons by granting him power over them. With the aid of the

---

[100] These four archangels are commonly found together in Judaism and Jewish magic; cf. S. Eitrem, *Papyri Osloenses: Fasc. 1. Magical Papyri* (Oslo, 1925) p. 111; Goodenough, *Jewish Symbols*, vol. 2, pp. 229, 232.

magical ring, the demons are subdued and their thwarting angels known. Overpowered, they are put to work constructing the Temple.

MAGIC, MEDICINE

The major interest of the author of the testament was medical. Chapter 18 sounds very much like an ancient family medical encyclopedia.[101] Here, the "heavenly bodies," most of whom cause physical and mental disease, are made to "retreat" (*anachōrō*) not only by reciting the magical formula, "Angel X, imprison Demon Y" (the first ten, the fifteenth, and the nineteenth demons), but also by certain exorcistic words, sometimes simply spoken, sometimes said in conjunction with "medical" rites, sometimes written, usually on various apotropaic materials, sometimes worn on the person, sometimes posted at various protective locations. For example, "The tenth said, 'I am called Metathiax. I cause pains in the kidneys. If I hear "Adonael, imprison Metathiax" I retreat immediately' " (TSol 18:14). "Rhyx Hapax, who unleashes insomnia, retreats if anyone writes '*Kok; phedismos*' and wears it from the temples" (TSol 18:32). "Rhyx Mianeth, who holds grudges against the body, demolishes houses, and causes flesh to rot, flees from a house if anyone writes '*Melto Ardad Anaath*' on the front entrance of the house" (TSol 18:40).

Similar ideas occur in the earlier parts of the testament. The Lion-Shaped Demon, in control of a legion of demons, is adjured by the suffering Emmanouel, who binds them and who drives them over a cliff, a passage which recalls the story in Mark 5:1–13 (TSol 11:1–7). In a slight alteration of the Tobit story, Asmodeus is thwarted by Raphael ("but also a liver and a gall of a fish smoking on coals of charcoal . . ."), and the fish is identified as a sheatfish (TSol 5:9f.). Also an apparently dangerous form of magic is revealed—Solomon rebukes Beelzeboul for revealing it—when Solomon is told how to support his household (TSol 6:10f.). In the following chapter Solomon stops the wind demon Lix Tetrax by spitting on the ground and sealing him with his magic ring (TSol 7:3).

ETHICS

The demons involve man in actions that are contrary to traditional biblical morality. Likewise, God is a good God and his angels stand ready to thwart the demons in man's behalf. Thus, insofar as mental, physical, and moral health is a good, and mental, physical, and moral sickness is an evil, there is a strong ethical flavor in the document.

AFTERLIFE

There is no view of the afterlife expressed. In 25:8, Solomon adjures Abezethibou to hold up the pillar of air "until the End," and in 26:8 (rec. B) Solomon writes his testament "in order that those who hear might pray about, and pay attention to, the last things and not to the first things, in order that they might finally find grace forever."

Relation to canonical books

The Testament of Solomon has numerous connections with both the Hebrew Scriptures and the New Testament. There is only one citation, the cornerstone, or keystone, prophecy from Psalm 118:22 (TSol 23:4). Other connections appear to be non-literary. With regard to the Hebrew Scriptures, the major associations are Solomon's building the Temple (1Kgs 6f.), Solomon's wisdom (1Kgs 4:29–34), the story of the Queen of Sheeba (1Kgs 10; TSol 19:1–3; 21:1–4), Solomon's many wives and downfall due to the worship of foreign gods (1Kgs 11; TSol 26), all of which are elaborated in Jewish and Arabic folklore, and the story of the Exodus (Ex 14; TSol 6:3f.; 22:7; 23:2; 24–25). One also finds mention of the divided kingdom (1Kgs 12; TSol 5:5; 15:8), the fall of the angels (Gen 6:1–4; TSol 5:3; 6:1–4), the prophecies of the Wonderful Counselor (Isa 9:6; TSol 12:3) and Emmanouel (Isa 7:14; TSol 6:8; 11:6; 15:11), and the cherubim and seraphim (1Kgs 7:48f.; TSol 18:34; cf. 21:2). As mentioned above, the archangels Michael (Dan 10:13; 12:1; TSol 1:6 [n. j]; 18:5) and Gabriel (Dan 8:16; 9:21; TSol 18:6) are found. Finally, as in the hellenistic magical papyri and gnostic literature, many Semitic-sounding names occur throughout the testament, though these do not necessarily point directly to the Scriptures.

[101] See TSol 18:2, n. a.

The testament is also related orally to the New Testament. Conybeare isolated a number of common phrases between the New Testament and manuscript P,[102] some of which are simply illustrations of a common environment. Yet, there are clear allusions to the story of the Gerasene demoniacs (Mark 5:1–13; TSol 11), and Beelzeboul occupies a major place in the documents (cf. Mk 3:22; Mt 10:25; 12:24; Lk 11:15; TSol 3; 4:2). The "virgin" (Mt 1:18–25; Lk 1:25–38) is implied once (TSol 15:10) and explicitly mentioned once (TSol 22:20). The implicit reference occurs in what is the clearest reference to Jesus which McCown thinks *might* be the work of the redactor of recension B,[103] though he prints it in his eclectic text:

> We will lead astray all the inhabited world for a long time until the Son of God is stretched upon the cross. For there has not yet arisen a king like him, one who thwarts all of us, whose mother shall not have sexual intercourse with a man. •Who holds such authority over the spirits except that one? The one whom the first devil shall seek to tempt, but shall not be able to overcome, the letters of whose name add up to six hundred forty-four—he is Emmanouel (TSol 15:10f.).

The virgin, the reference to the Son of God, the temptation of Jesus, Jesus' rule over the demons, the crucifixion, and the name Emmanouel are clear. Moreover, there is the curious reference to the number 644. This number is connected with the name Emmanouel in manuscript P of 6:8, which states in response to Solomon's question about a thwarting angel that the one who thwarts Beelzeboul is "the holy and precious name of the almighty God, the one called *by the Hebrews* by a row of numbers, of which the sum is 644, and among the Greeks it is Emmanouel." [Italics mine.] Now 11:6 speaks of a suffering Emmanouel as one who thwarts the Lion-Shaped One, and adds, "As he moves about he is conjured up by means of three letters." The three letters used for the number 644 in manuscript P of 6:8, however, are *Greek* letters (*chi, mu, delta*). Moreover, manuscript P of 11:6 adds, "The 'Great Among Men' who is to suffer many things whose name is the formula 644, who is Emmanouel . . ." It is never explicitly stated, but the *Greek* letters of Emmanouel's name also add up to 644 (TSol 6:8, n. i).

The crucifixion of Jesus by the Jews is mentioned again in 22:20, and in a difficult passage in 12:3 the three-headed dragon spirit states, "But there is a way by which I am thwarted, (namely,) by (the site) which is marked 'Place of the Skull,' for there an angel of the Wonderful Counselor foresaw that I would suffer, and he will dwell publically on the cross." An oath called "the Elo-i," recalling Jesus' words on the cross from Psalm 22:1 (Mk 15:34; Mt 27:46) occurs in 6:8 and the sign of the cross written on the forehead thwarts the lecherous spirit in 17:4.

Special notice should also be taken of the fact that in these references Jesus functions very much like a thwarting angel in the testament (TSol 6:8, n. h).

Finally, there are a number of general relationships such as demonology and the designation of Solomon as "Son of David" (TSol 1:7; 20:1) which have led some scholars to believe that the testament provides an excellent background for understanding many parts of the New Testament.

Relation to apocryphal and pseudepigraphic books

It is already clear that the testament shares much with the apocryphal and pseudepigraphic literature. The account of Asmodeus, who hatches plots against newlyweds and is thwarted by the angel Raphael and a smoking liver and gall of a fish (TSol 5:7–10), reflects the main narrative of Tobit, though in Tobit it is the smoking *heart* and liver of the fish that cause Asmodeus to flee the newlyweds' bedchamber, the gall being held in reserve to cure Tobit's blindness. McCown discovered what he thought was one phrase from the Wisdom of Solomon as well (WisSol 9:4; cf. TSol 3:5).[104] An important theme from the pseudepigraphic literature is the theme of the fall of the angels based on Genesis 6:1–4 (1En 6–7; 15f.; Jub 7:21–25; 10:5; TSol 6:2; 5:3). The fourth major archangel of the testament, Ouriel, is also frequently

---

[102] Conybeare, *JQR* 11 (1898) 5f.
[103] McCown, *Testament*, pp. 83, 89.
[104] McCown, *Testament*, p. 61.

found in the Pseudepigrapha (e.g. 4Ezra 5:20; 10:27; 1En 9:1; 10:1). In general, it may be said with McCown, "The angelology and demonology of the *Test* are practically those of the Apocrypha and Pseudepigrapha."[105] Such connections with the testament appear to have been brought about by oral traditions.

Cultural importance

Though the tradition of Solomon's magical wisdom was perpetuated in Judaism, Christianity, and Islam—witness the growth of Solomonic legends in the Talmud, Ethiopic Christianity, the Koran, and *Arabian Nights* as well as the plethora of amulets, talismans, lintels, and the pentagrams and hexagrams scratched on every type of magical material—the attestation of Solomonic magical *books* seems to have been avoided in official Judaism until the twelfth century. The Rabbis preserved the tradition that Hezekiah hid the "book of recipes." Hippolytus (c. A.D. 160–236) seems to have been the first Christian writer to mention the notion of the suppression of Solomon's books by Hezekiah, an idea continued in early Christian writers, perhaps in a lost account of Eusebius.[106] Clearly, in the early period, magical books by Solomon were considered suspect, partly because "official" Judaism and Christianity associated the practice of magic with paganism, and perhaps partly because the practice of magic in the Roman Empire was legally punishable by death.[107] Nonetheless, it was quite difficult to distinguish magic from medicine and in practice it flourished everywhere in the popular culture. Thus, alongside the beloved tales of Solomon's great wisdom and magical prowess, Solomonic magical books existed and some survived the sporadic book burnings. Theodoret (A.D. 385/393–458), for example, mentions in his interpretation of 1 Kings 4:33 the existence of Solomon's "medical books" and praises Solomon as the source of all medical knowledge.[108] The first clear reference to the testament, however, attacks Solomon's reputation by referring to his demise in 1 Kings 11:31–36. This is the *Dialogue of Timothy and Aquila* from about A.D. 400. Other Christian writers also attack Solomon's reputation, but usually only when claims for him come into conflict with claims about Jesus, as in the *Dialogue*. Where the conflict with Judaism was absent, Solomon's reputation as a healer of diseases seems, in the early period, to have been maintained.[109]

In the medieval period, probably about the twelfth century, and probably under Arabian influence, Solomon became known especially as a writer of scientific and magical books. M. Seligsohn mentions forty-nine of these books listed in Arabic and Hebrew literature,[110] and McCown adds that this list is by no means exhaustive.[111] Perhaps most famous of all these medieval works was the *Key of Solomon*, known in Greek, Hebrew, and Latin (*Clavicula Salomonis*), so named because like a key which unlocks a treasure, it was believed to unlock the mysteries of the magical arts.[112] By the fifteenth century, books of magical secrets were attributed to many major characters of the Jewish Scriptures, including Adam and Moses, and especially Solomon. To this company, Zoroaster, Hermes Trismegistus, Aristotle, Alexander the Great, Virgil, and Muḥammad were joined. Students of history of Western mysticism will recognize here a number of common features with the mystical Jewish cabala, which developed the myths of fallen angels found in Genesis 6:1–4 and

---

[105] Ibid., p. 59.

[106] Hippolytus, *Commentary on Canticles*, fragmentarily preserved; see McCown, *JPOS* 2 (1922) 11 and n. 3. Official Islam appears to have considered Solomonic books to be works of the devil; cf. Koran, Sura 2:95f.; McCown, *Testament*, pp. 98f., on Eusebius.

[107] Important texts are the Laws of the Twelve Tables (451–450 B.C.); Julius Paulus, *Sententiae* 5:21, 1–3; 5:23, 17, 19 (early 3rd cent. A.D.); Justinian, *Pandects* 48:8, 13f. R. Beckmann, *Zauberei und Recht in Roms Frühzeit* (Osnabrück, Germany, 1923); E. Tavenner, *Studies in Magic from Latin Literature* (New York, 1916) pp. 12–17; E. Massonneau, *Le Crime de magie dans la droit romaine* (Paris, 1933); R. MacMullen, *Enemies of the Roman Order* (Cambridge, 1966) pp. 124–27.

[108] Theodoret, *Quaestiones in III Reg.*, Qu. X, quoted from Migne, PG, vol. 80, p. 676AB in McCown, *Testament*, p. 95; *JPOS* 2 (1922) 10.

[109] McCown, *JPOS* 2 (1922) 14–16.

[110] M. Seligsohn, "Solomon—Apocryphal Works," *The Jewish Encyclopedia*, vol. 11, p. 447; Charlesworth, *PMR* (1976), 199–201.

[111] McCown, *Testament*, p. 100. See also the indices to *Catalogus Codicum Astrologorum Graecorum* IV, V, VI, VII, VIII under "Solomon."

[112] H. Gollancz, *Clavicula Salomonis. A Hebrew Manuscript* (Frankfurt, 1903); *Sepher Mephteah Shelomo* ("The Book of the Key of Solomon") (London, 1914) has facsimiles, texts, and translations.

1 Enoch 6–11. In much of this there is a movement away from the testament's focus on knowledge of the demons as a way of coping with evil toward the attempt to manipulate the demons for positive benefits. Similarly, partly due to Neoplatonic influence, there was an increasing tendency to arrange the demons in hierarchies of power.[113] Manuscript T[d] of recension C of the testament (dated by McCown to about the 12th or 13th cent.),[114] represents these technical works for the professional astrologer and magician by including in chapter 10 a list of fifty or fifty-one demons who are summoned for the purpose of gaining wealth, power, and happiness. Indeed, this manuscript is really a fragment of a longer manuscript containing a whole body of magical, astrological, and demonologic lore, most notably the *Key of Solomon*. Many of the other manuscripts, which are from the fifteenth or sixteenth century, also contain such lore, including many pentacles and Solomonic drawings.[115]

In conclusion, it should be stressed that the Testament of Solomon is an important document for understanding everyday religion in the early centuries of Christianity. On the one hand, there is the romantic story of Solomon. Solomon built the temple and, according to Scripture, "it was with stone prepared at the quarry; so that neither hammer nor ax nor any tool of iron was heard in the temple while it was being built" (1Kgs 6:7). He was a lover of women, which led to his demise. But he was also the wise king, whose knowledge included the magical properties of plants and animals. Most tantalizing is the account of his magical ring and its power over the demons.[116] The story provides a backdrop for all manner of important information about sickness, disease, natural tragedy, and death: who causes it (the demons), the world in which it exists (God's mysterious world with its stars and planets), and what to do about it (knowledge about angels, medicine, and magical incantation). As such, the testament is a sample of what R. Ellwood calls the "alternative" religious tradition in the West.[117] It arises out of the broader religious environment of which Christianity was a part rather than being a normative document of what orthodox Christianity was to become. If its thought, especially its demonology, helps clarify the type of literature that orthodoxy came to accept as normative, its basic thrust, limited in its Christology, found much in common with, and contributed to, a persistent mysticism, astrology, magic, and what has continued in the modern period as the occult.

TEXTUAL EMENDATIONS

Translator's Note: The text translated is the printed eclectic text of C. C. McCown, *The Testament of Solomon*, pp. 5–75*; it therefore adheres to his original preference for rec. B at both the beginning and the end. McCown's late discovery of manuscript N (noted above) caused him to make a few minor revisions and, most important, to shift his view of the conclusion back toward rec. A. These revisions are listed as "Emendationes in Textum" in McCown, *The Testament of Solomon*, pp. 121–22*. *I have placed his revised conclusion in n. f of TSol 26:8.* The following represents his list of minor changes:

1:9	"As fast as you can before he thinks of things which would stop you."
1:10	Read *phlegon* ("flaming") for *phlegomenon* ("flaming").
2:3	Add "when commanded by all the demons" after "of a lion."
2:8	Omit the difficult reading "and cast his fate," modifying to "their species on the (dry) land. There he also subjected."
5:13	Read "untying Asmodeus I lit a fire under him because."
6:5	Insert "the kind" after "whom you said is."
6:5	Read "He retorted, 'I will not bring him back to you.'"
6:8	Change "a" to "the" before "great name."
7:3	Change "the moving air" to "that moving air."

[113] E. M. Butler, *Ritual Magic* (Cambridge, 1949) ch. 1, has a good discussion of the medieval Solomonic cycle; ch. 2 is based on the "disciples of Solomon"; see pp. 29–44 for a discussion of Jewish elements in magic.

[114] McCown, *Testament*, p. 108.

[115] Ibid., pp. 13–15, 18–20, on Harleian MS no. 5596 in the British Museum.

[116] In speaking of the cornelian stone of the bishop's ring as a prophylactic against demons, Conybeare (*Myth, Magic, and Morals: A Study of Christian Origins* [London, 1909] p. 324) wrote, "The ring in itself has a magical use of the same kind, and one of the three great relics kissed by Christian pilgrims to Jerusalem in the fourth century was the ring with which King Solomon controlled the demons and forced them to help him build his temple."

[117] R. S. Ellwood, Jr., *Religious and Spiritual Groups in Modern America* (Englewood Cliffs, N.J., 1973) pp. 42–87.

8:4	Change "gods" to "goddesses" (with corresponding feminine forms following).
8:10	Read "And likewise" for "likewise."
8:11	After "but to me," read "in contrast, (it is) a desire for wisdom."
10:2	Read "I was extremely strong, even restraining the stars of heaven."
10:6	Read "and bring the demon here to me," reading "the demon" for "the ring."
10:9	Change "leek" to "small horn."
11:3	Read "I have another activity. I send forth the legions of demons subject to me, but when the sun is setting I am at the (various) places, together with all the demons who are legions under me . . ."
11:4	Read *Leontophrōn* for *Leontophoron* ("Lion-Shaped Demon").
11:7	Read *Leontophrona* for *Leontophron.*
12:2	Read "infants" for "children."
18:2	Read *hoi* (masculine) for *hai* (feminine).
18:23	Insert "Rhyx" before "Mardero."
18:28	Read "nail" for "a piece of wood."
25:2	Read "Abezebithou" for "Abezethibou."
26:7–8	See TSol 26:8, n. f.

BIBLIOGRAPHY

Charlesworth, *PMR*, pp. 197–202.
Delling, *Bibliographie*, pp. 177f.
Denis, *Introduction*, p. 67.

Conybeare, F. C. "The Testament of Solomon," *JQR* 11 (1898) 1–45. (Conybeare translated F. F. Fleck's text of the testament [McCown's MS P] and included an important introduction. It is the only other extant English translation. Most of Conybeare's paragraphing has been followed in the translation below, designated by numbers in parentheses in the margin.)

Delatte, A. "Testament de Salomon" in *Anecdota Atheniensia* 36 (1927) 211–27. (In a volume of Solomonic magical, astrological, alchemical, and divinitory literature, these pages print a highly modified version of the testament not included in McCown [Bibliothèque Nationale No. 2011]; there is one page of introduction included.)

Duling, D. C. "Solomon, Exorcism, and the Son of David," *HTR* 68 (1975) 235–52. (This article tracks the trajectory of the magical wisdom of Solomon primarily in Judaism and makes suggestions about its possible connection to the Gospels; the footnotes contain references to recent bibliography.)

Giversen, S. "Solomon und die Dämonen," *Essays on the Nag Hammadi Texts in Honor of Alexander Böhlig*, ed. M. Krause. NHS 3; Leiden, 1972; pp. 16–21. (Giversen discusses three of the four passages in the Nag Hammadi texts in which Solomon is mentioned [II, 5:*107*; V, 5:*78* and *79*; IX, 3:*70*] and concludes that the Jewish tradition of Solomon's control over the demons is represented, but criticized.)

Goodenough, E. R. *Jewish Symbols in the Greco-Roman World.* 13 vols.; Bollingen Series 37; New York, 1953–68; vol. 1, p. 68; vol. 2, pp. 226–38; vol. 7, pp. 198–200; vol. 9, pp. 1044–67. (Goodenough draws from other works and summarizes much of the amulet and talisman material about Solomon from ancient Judaism; the drawings are especially helpful.)

Gundel, W. *Dekane und Dekansternbilder.* Glückstadt, 1936. (Gundel's work on the decans is extremely important.)

James, M. R. "*The Testament of Solomon* (Review)," *JTS* 24 (1922) 467–68. (James summarizes McCown's results; although he is highly complimentary, he does not think McCown's evolution of the testament beginning with MS D is wholly convincing.)

McCown, C. C."The Christian Tradition as to the Magical Wisdom of Solomon," *JPOS* 2 (1922) 1–24. (After brief sections on the pre-Christian and the Semitic tradition, the article briefly sketches the literary and "living" Christian tradition of Solomon's wisdom.)

———. *The Testament of Solomon*. Leipzig, 1922. (This is the indispensable critical edition, containing an eclectic text and an apparatus along with MS D, the text of rec. C where it varies, the text of MS E, a conspectus of titles, grammatical and syntactical index, Greek indices, and an English index.)

Preisendanz, K. "Ein Wiener Papyrusfragment zum Testamentum Salomonis," *EOS* 48 (1956) 161–67. (Preisendanz, the noted authority on the magical papyri, publishes the most recent discovery of the Gk. testament, a papyrus of TSol 18:34–40 [Vindobonensis 330, designated G 330] which he discovered in 1955 in the Austrian National Library in Vienna. He believes that it is further evidence that ch. 18, if not the testament itself, was in use in Egypt; indeed, he speculates that the fragment could be a thousand years earlier than the other MS associated with Egypt, MS N from Jerusalem [Sancti Saba No. 422; 15th cent. A.D.]. It is the oldest fragment known.)

———. "Salomo." Pauly-Wissowa Supplement 8 (1956) cols. 660–704. (This lengthy article is an excellent summary of the Solomon tradition with an extensive bibliography.)

Salzberger, G. *Die Salomosage in der semitischen Literatur*. Berlin, 1907. (Salzberger's dissertation is an extensive study and is especially helpful for the Ar. legends.)

THE TESTAMENT OF SOLOMON[a]

The Greek title[c]

1:00
(1)[b]
Testament of Solomon, Son of David,[d] who reigned in Jerusalem, and subdued all the spirits of the air, of the earth, and under the earth; through (them) he also accomplished all the magnificent works of the Temple; (this tells) what their authorities are against men, and by what angels these demons are thwarted.[e]

Prologue: Solomon's praise[f]

1:0
Blessed are you, Lord God, who has given this authority to Solomon. Glory and power to you forever. Amen.[g]

1:5

5:13
Ps 72:18

Title and Prologue. a. The standard edition, C. C. McCown, *The Testament of Solomon,* is the basis for the translation. McCown presents, with the exception of the first three VSS., an eclectic text which attempts to reconstruct the original TSol behind recs. A (MSS H I L) and B (MSS P Q). Rec. C (MSS S T U V W), he judged, was descended from rec. B and carried little weight against rec. A; however, when C agreed with A against B, he argued that this agreement came closest to the original. In rec. A, he considered MS H to be the best MS and his rule was "When in doubt, follow H" (McCown, *Testament,* p. 38). There was an exception to this generalization: McCown thought rec. A to be secondary at the beginning, and here he relied more on rec. B (for the conclusion, see Introduction, MS N; TSol 26:8, n. f). Finally, McCown printed various combinations of MSS in the first three VSS. sometimes separating, sometimes combining recs. A and B, and sometimes printing MS L separately, but always printing MSS V W separately.

b. The numbers in parentheses in the margin correspond, where possible, to the paragraph numbers of F. C. Conybeare's translation of F. F. Fleck's edition of MS P (1837), considered by McCown to contain many errors. I have attempted to follow Conybeare's paragraph divisions in most cases, despite the differences in the underlying Gk. text. These numbers will facilitate comparison with the only other English translation of the text of TSol. Furthermore, I have occasionally put variants from MSS, especially P as found in McCown, in the nn. See F. C. Conybeare, "The Testament of Solomon," *JQR* 11 (1898) 1–45 for another translation. The subheadings in bold type are those of the translator.

c. This Gk. title, along with others, is printed separately by McCown, *Testament,* p. 99*. In accord with McCown's judgments about rec. A being secondary at the beginning, I have selected the rec. B (MSS P Q) text here. MS I of rec. A reads, "Solomon, Son of David, who reigned in Jerusalem; and concerning the demons whom he subdued, and what are the authorities against the demons to be granted to him by God, and by what angels the demons are thwarted, and the works of the Temple which he (so) magnificently accomplished," with the words "Testament o[f]" written by another hand and placed in the margin above. Perhaps the original Gk. implied "concerning," that is, "Concerning Solomon . . . and concerning the demons . . . ," and the scribe, seeing the genitive form (*Solomōntos*), interpreted it as a possessive genitive, or "*Testament* of Solomon . . ." as in rec. B. MS H of rec. A states simply, "An account about the Testament of Solomon, the coming of the demons, and the construction of the Temple." Rec. C (MSS V W), found in McCown, *Testament,* p. 99*, states, "Testament of the wisest Solomon with its parallel names which were guarded as mysteries by Hezekiah after David the king died." There is a lengthy tradition mentioned in the Talmud (Bet 10a; Pes 56a) and found in early Christian writers that Hezekiah suppressed Solomon's magical writings (cf. Introduction) and this tradition has influenced TSol C 13. See McCown, *Testament,* pp. 36, 98–100 and pp. 85–87*; also McCown, "The Christian Tradition as to the Magical Wisdom of Solomon," *JPOS* 2 (1922) 5–7, 9–14. See also TSol 26:8, n. f.

d. Solomon is called Son of David in Gk. titles of MSS P Q I; MS L and rec. C; Prologue 1:1; rec. C 12:1; 13:12; MS D 1:1; MS E 11:1; MS H 26:9; and in McCown, TSol 1:7; 20:1. He is called "son of the prophet David" in MS E 1:1; 2:1. The address "Son of David" could be a link between the magical tradition about Solomon and the activity of Jesus as exorcist and healer.

e. The Gk. verb *katargeō* is translated throughout TSol as "I thwart." It can mean "I make ineffective," "I make powerless," or "I abolish," "I wipe out," "I set aside." A usual demand of Solomon is that the demon identify the name of the thwarting angel. To know the angel who has power over a demon is to be able to ward off the demon and solve the trouble. The demon Asmodeus later indicates that if men do not know the names of demons, the latter will be worshiped as gods (TSol 5:5). The term *katargeō* is used to describe the annihilation of the "lawless one" at the coming of the Lord in 2Thes 2:8.

f. McCown combined rec. A (MSS H I; MS L is printed separately in *Testament,* p. 5* beginning with TSol 1:1) with rec. B (MSS P Q) in this Prologue; rec. C has a lengthy five-verse Prologue; see McCown, *Testament,* pp. 76*f.

g. The Prologue is apparently meant to be in the third person; TSol is told in the first person.

Ornias the demon tries to interfere with the boy who helps Solomon build the Temple[a]

1　**1** Once upon a time,[b] when the Temple of the city of Jerusalem was being built　1Kgs 6-7
2　and the artisans were working on it, • Ornias the demon[c] came as the sun was
(2)　setting and took half the wages and provisions of[d] the master workman's[e] little
boy.[f] Also, each day (the demon) was sucking[g] the thumb of (the boy's) right
hand. So the little boy, who was much loved by me, grew thin.

Solomon interrogates the boy[h]

3　　But I, Solomon, interrogated the boy one day and said to him, "Have I not
(3)　loved you more than all the other artisans working in the Temple of God, and have
I not been paying you double wages and provisions? Why then are you growing
thinner every day?"
4　　The boy said, "I beg you, King, listen to what is happening to me. After we
(4)　are dismissed from work on the Temple of God, when the sun has set and I am
resting, an evil spirit comes and makes off with half my pay and half my provisions.
Also he grabs my right hand and sucks my thumb. You can see that when my soul
is in distress, my body grows thinner every day."

1 a. TSol 1:1 begins with rec. B in McCown (MSS
P Q) mainly because it is in the first person. Note
that McCown's preferred rec. is printed first where
he prints more than one rec. in the main text. See
TSol 1:2, n. h.

b. A free translation of the biblical *kai idou*,
"and behold." MSS H I of rec. A begin, "Once
upon a time, when Jerusalem was being built and
the artisans were at work, a certain boy who had
tremendous enthusiasm for the construction of the
Temple was making the artisans more enthusiastic
for their work and all who heard about it were
rejoicing over the boy's enthusiasm. As a result he
was much loved by me, Solomon, and received
twice as much pay and provisions as all the other
artisans. So I, Solomon, was continually rejoicing
and happy, praising God for the construction of the
Temple." MS L of rec. A reads, "Solomon, Son
of David, wanting to rebuild and construct Zion,
commanded that.there be brought together artisans
from every region and district to work on the Temple
of God . . ." and continues in TSol 1:1 much like
the others; see below, TSol 1:2, n. h. After its
extensive Prologue (see above, n. f), rec. C (MSS
V W) is similar to A and B, but describes the boy
as "exceedingly strong and a master craftsman,
whom the king loved very much because he (the
boy) was wise and kind. So the king sent him food
from his table and was paying him double wages
by means of the meal." This identification of the
boy with the master craftsman (*architechnitēs*) is
one possible rendering of the meaning of TSol 1:2;
see below, n. f.

c. Rec. C (MSS V W) calls him the "pesky
demon named Ornias." Rec. A does not name him
until 1:10; see below, TSol 1:10, n. m.

d. Recs. A (MSS H I) and B (MSS P Q) merge
at this point; see McCown, *Testament*, p. 6, n. 3.
MS L of rec. A continues, "After being paid and
dismissed from work, the evil spirit would come
and [cry out. Then the reader spoke for the third
time of the one who was talking loudly over the
crowded room; then] take the finger of the boy's
right hand . . ." The puzzling words beginning

with "cry out" and ending with "room; then"
seem to be a comment about confusion in the scrip-
torium.

e. Gk. *tou prōtomaïstoros*, from *ho prōto-
maïstōr*, is conjectured as "master workman" in
Lampe, p. 1200; Conybeare (*JQR* 11 [1898] 15)
translates "chief deviser."

f. Gk. *to hēmisu tou misthou tou prōtomaïstoros
paidariou ontos kai ta hēmisu sitia*. This might be
read "half the wages of the master workman, being
a little boy, as well as half his provisions," in
which case it would agree with rec. C in identifying
the boy as a "master craftsman"; see above, n. b.

g. Gk. *buzanō*, "I suckle," is a cognate of *ta
buzia*, "the breasts," in TSol 18:35; cf. Lampe,
p. 306. The demon is capable of "sapping" the
boy's energy by sucking it out of the thumb; see
the boy's description in TSol 1:4.

h. McCown, *Testament*, p. 8*, now begins to
print all of rec. A (MSS H I L) with rec. B (MSS
P Q) with variant readings of words in the apparatus;
rec. C (MSS V W) reads, "Then one day King
Solomon stretched out his hands toward heaven and
said, 'God of gods and alone King of kings, reveal
to me the boy's complete torment for the sake of
your fearful and all-holy name.' Then a voice came,
saying, 'Speak as follows into the right ear of the
boy: "Daphōn, Magata, Palipoul." Then write
these words on a piece of parchment made from an
unborn animal. Commit it to fire and burn it up,
holding also in your hand the grass called ivy and
a healing stone; and at the fifth hour of the night,
question the boy, and he will tell you everything.'
When he had heard these things and performed
them to the letter, Solomon questioned the boy."
The parchment from "an unborn animal" (*agen-
netos chartes*) refers to fine quality velum from the
fetus of an animal; "a healing stone" (*lithos ia-
saphētēs*) may refer to a jasper; see Lampe, p. 662
(cf. 1En 18:7). Josephus reports that the Essenes
did "research into medicinal roots and the properties of stones for the healing of diseases" (*War*
2.8.6).

Through the archangel Michael the Lord God grants Solomon the magical ring which gives Solomon power over the demons

5
(5)
When I, Solomon, heard these things, I went into the Temple of God and, praising him day and night, begged with all my soul that the demon might be 5:13

6 delivered into my hands and that I might have authority over him. •Then it happened 18:1; 20:7 that while I was praying to the God of heaven and earth, there was granted me Dan 10:13,20f.; from the Lord Sabaoth[i] through the archangel Michael[j] a ring which had a seal Jub 1:29f. 1En 20:5f.;

7 engraved on precious stone.[k] •He said to me, "Solomon, Son of David,[l] take the 68:1f. gift which the Lord God, the highest Sabaoth, has sent to you; (with it) you shall 3Bar 11-15 imprison all the demons, both female and male, and with their help you shall build Rev 12:7 Jerusalem when you bear this seal of God." PssSol 17:23 Mk 10:47f.; 12:35 Mt 1:1,20; 9:27;

According to Solomon's instructions, the boy brings back the demon with the aid of the magical ring

12:23; 15:22; 20:20,31; 21:9,15

8
(6)
Now I became so joyful that I continually sang hymns of praise to the God of Heaven and earth and glorified him. The next day, I ordered the child to come to

9 me and I gave the seal to him. •Then I said to him, "At the moment the demon 1:11; 3:3 appears to you, fling this ring into his chest and say to him, 'Come! Solomon summons you!' and come running back to me as fast as you can before he says anything that would frighten you."

10 Now it happened that at his usual time the pesky demon Ornias[m] came like a 2:1
(7) flaming fire[n] to take the little boy's pay, as was his custom. •According to Solomon's 9:3; 20:6f.,11 LetAris 47

11 instructions to him, the little boy flung the ring into the chest of the demon and said to him, "Come! Solomon summons you!" and started to take off running to 1:9; 3:3

12 Solomon as fast as he could go. •But the demon screamed[o] and said to the little boy, "Why have you done this? Remove the ring and give it back to Solomon, and I shall give you all the silver and gold of the earth."

13
(8)
But the little boy replied, "As the Lord God of Israel lives, I will never withstand Judg 8:19 you if I do not deliver you to Solomon." Then the little boy went and spoke to Solomon, "King Solomon, I brought the demon to you just as you commanded

---

i. Gk. *ho Kyrios,* "the Lord," translates YHWH, the name of God, in the LXX; *sabaōth* is an indeclinable transliteration of the Heb. *ṣabah,* "army." The meaning is "Lord of the (heavenly) armies."

j. Heb. *Mikā'ēl,* "who is like (the Canaanite god) El." Michael in the Book of Daniel is called a "chief prince" or "prince" who assists the angel Gabriel against the "prince" of the kingdom of Persia; cf. Dan 10:13, 21; 12:1. In general, he is the protector of the Jewish people. In Jude 9, he is an "archangel" who contends with the devil about the body of Moses (who, according to Jewish tradition, was charged by the devil with being a murderer and therefore not worthy of burial); in Rev 12:7 he leads the angelic armies against the dragon, and his angels cause the latter to be expelled from heaven. See Eitrem, *Papyri Graecae Magicae* (Leipzig, 1928) p. 111.

k. On magical rings in general, see Eitrem, *Papyri Graecae Magicae,* p. 112. The connection of Solomon with a magical ring is first documented in Josephus, *Ant* 8.2.5. The MSS of TSol carry on

this seal tradition, e.g. it is a pentalpha (MSS P Q), a thirty-one-letter word written in the second and third of a series of concentric circles (MS L), an engraving with "O Lord our God" plus a group of Semitic-sounding names (MSS H L); the medieval MSS of Solomonic literature frequently contain primitive sketches of these seals. For bibliography, see Duling, *HTR* 68 (1975) 236, n. 7, and 244, n. 39.

l. On Son of David, see TSol 1:00, n. d.

m. For Ornias, see TSol 1:1, n. c; 2:1; 20:6f.; NHC VIII, 1:*127,* 22. *Chalepos,* "pesky," or "hard to bear," "hard to deal with," "troublesome," "difficult," "mischievous," "ill-tempered," describes the Gerasene demoniacs in Mt 8:28.

n. Demons occasionally appear as fire in hellenistic literature; see Lampe, p. 1208; Acts 7:30 states that an angel appeared to Moses on Mount Sinai "in a flame of fire in a bush."

o. The Gk. verb *kraugazō,* "I shout," describes the response of the exorcised demons who "shout" that Jesus is the Son of God in Lk 4:41.

me; observe how he is standing bound[p] in front of the gates outside, crying out[q] Mk 5:5; 9:39
with a great voice to give me all the silver and gold of the earth so that I would
not deliver him to you.''

Solomon interrogates the demon, learns his name and his activity, and by the power of the seal ring commands him to work on the Temple

1 **2** When I heard these things, I, Solomon, got up from my throne and saw the
(9) demon shuddering and trembling with fear. I said to him, "Who are you? What 1:10f.; 9:3; 20:6f.; 20:11
is your name?" The demon replied, "I am called Ornias."[a] LetAris 47

2 I said to him, "Tell me, in which sign of the zodiac[b] do you reside?" The
(10) demon replied, "In Aquarius;[c] I strangle those who reside in Aquarius because of 2En 21:6; 30:3f. SibOr 5:209,
3 their passion for women whose zodiacal sign is Virgo.[d] • Moreover, while in a 521,527
trance I undergo three transformations. Sometimes I am a man who craves the
bodies of effeminate boys and when I touch[e] them, they suffer great pain. Sometimes
I become a creature with wings (flying) up to the heavenly regions. Finally, I 1Pet 5:8
4 assume the appearance of a lion.[f] • In addition, I am descended from an archangel 2:7f.; 8:9; 18:7,27
of the power of God,[g] but I am thwarted[h] by Ouriel, the archangel."[i] 1En 9:1; 10:1f.; 20:1

5 When I, Solomon, heard the archangel's name mentioned, I honored and glorified
(11) the God of heaven and earth. After I sealed (the demon) with my seal, I ordered
him into the stone quarry to cut for the Temple stones which had been transported
6 by way of the Arabian Sea and dumped along the seashore.[j] • But being terrified
to touch iron,[k] he said to me, "I beg you, King Solomon, let me have a measure
7 of freedom, and I shall bring up all the demons." • Since he did not want to be 2:4; 8:9; 18:7, 27

---

p. "Binding" demons is a common theme in apocryphal and pseudepigraphic literature. The angel Raphael has the task of binding the demon Asmodeus (Tob 3:17; 8:3; cf. TSol 5; 13:6); Raphael was also commanded to bind Azazel "hand and feet, and cast him into the darkness" (1En 10:4; 6–13) where he would eventually be judged; the fallen angels (cf. Gen 6:1–4), described as "stars" and "beasts" (1En 90:23–24; Jub 5:6; Jude 6–7; cf. TSol 5:1; 6:2), are bound presumably by the angels Michael, Gabriel, Raphael, and Phanuel; the hosts of Azazel will be bound in the future (1En 54–56); and Beliar will be bound by the "new priest" (TLev 18:12). Also, demons are frequently bound, and portrayed as such in art, in the Aramaic Incantation Bowls. See TSol 5:12, n. p. Finally, note M. Eliade, "The 'God Who Binds' and the Symbolism of Knots," ch. 3 of *Images and Symbols*, trans. P. Mairet (New York, 1969), especially p. 94, n. 9, for literature.

q. The Gk. verb *krazō*, "I cry out," like *kraugazō* (n. o), is also used of demons in the NT; cf. the Gaderene demoniac (Mk 5:5) and the deaf and dumb spirit in the boy (Mk 9:26; cf. Lk 9:39).

2 a. See TSol 1:2, n. c.

b. 2En 21:6 states that the twelve signs of the zodiac are above the seventh heaven and that their heavenly homes are in the ninth heaven.

c. Gk. *ho Hydrochoos*, "the Waterpourer."

d. Gk. *he Parthenos*, "the Virgin," second largest constellation, the goddess of love or mother goddess in myth (or Justice among the Greeks).

e. Gk. *haptomenou*, from *haptomai*, "I touch," "I take hold of," sometimes with reference to sexual intercourse with a woman; cf. 1Cor 7:1. Gk. *thēlykos*, the adjective that goes with *paidion*, "child," "boy," normally means "feminine" or "effeminate." The reference appears to be either

to sexual intercourse with young girls or sexual activity with effeminate boys.

f. Cf. Origen, *Contra* 6.30; the devil is said to go about like a roaring lion in 1Pet 5:8.

g. Gk. *hē dynamis*, "(the) power," seems to refer to a personal, supernatural angel, or spirit, as it frequently does in Mediterranean religions; cf. Acts 8:10.

h. On the thwarting angel, see Title, n. e.

i. Seven archangels are named in 1En 20:1f. as Uriel ("over the world and over Tartarus"), Raphael ("over the spirits of men"), Raguel ("takes vengeance on the world of luminaries"), Michael ("set over the best part of mankind and over chaos"), Saraqael ("set over the spirits, who sin in the spirit"), Gabriel ("over Paradise and the serpents and the cherubim"), and Remiel ("over those who rise"); cf. 1En 9:1; 10:1. The four archangels that are prominent in TSol—Michael, Uriel, Raphael, and Gabriel—are well attested together in Judaism in general and magic in particular. Uriel is probably Suriel, mentioned in Origen, *Contra* 6.30, as "bull-like." In magical materials, he is lord of the second or third heaven. See TSol 18:7, n. k.

j. The Babylonian Talmud (b. Giṭṭ 68ab) tells the story that Solomon sought the coveted stone-cutting worm, the *shamîr*, to help build the Temple. After binding a male and a female demon, Solomon sent Benaiahu to get the *shamîr* from the Prince of Demons, Ashmedai; to bind him, Benaiahu was given, among other things, a chain and a ring, each engraved with the divine name. See Introduction.

k. Conybeare, *JQR* 11 (1898) 18, n. 1, recalls the tradition in folklore that the evil demons fear iron; cf. T. Hopfner, *Griechisch-ägyptischer Offenbarungszauber*, 2 vols. (Leipzig, 1921–24) vol. 1, § 596. See TSol 5:12, n. p.

subject to me, I prayed that the archangel Ouriel would come to help me. Immediately I saw the archangel Ouriel descending to me from heaven.

1En 9:1; 10:1;
20:1
4Ezra 6:48f.
1En 60:7
2Bar 29:4

The archangel Ouriel aids Solomon in overcoming Ornias

8
(12) The angel commanded sea monsters to arise out of the sea and he withered up their species and cast his fate to the ground.[1] In this same way he also subjected the great demon Ornias to cut stones and to bring to completion the construction 9 of the Temple which I, Solomon, was in the process of building. •Again, I glorified the God of heaven and earth and I commanded Ornias to come near according to his fate. Then I gave him the seal and said, "Go and bring here to me the Prince of Demons."[m]

6:1f.; 16:3
Mk 3:22
Mt 9:34; 10:25;
12:24
Lk 11:15
Jn 12:31; 14:30;
16:11

Ornias the demon brings Beelzeboul, the Prince of Demons, to Solomon with the help of the magical ring

(13) 1 **3** So Ornias took the ring and went to Beelzeboul,[a] and said to him, "Come! 2 Solomon summons you!" •But Beelzeboul said to him, "Tell me, who is the 3 Solomon of whom you speak?" •Then Ornias flung the ring into the chest of 4 Beelzeboul and replied, "Solomon the king summons you!" •Beelzeboul cried out like (one who is burned) from a great burning flame of fire, and when he had 5 gotten up, he followed (Ornias) under coercion and came to me. •When I saw the (14) Prince of Demons approaching, I glorified God and said, "Blessed are you, Lord God Almighty, who has granted to your servant Solomon wisdom, the attendant of your thrones,[b] and who has placed in subjection all the power of the demons."

Mk 3:22
Mt 10:25; 12:24
Lk 11:15
1:9,11

4:11; 8:11; 22:1;
24:3
1Kgs 4:29-34
(LXX)
Prov 1:1
Song 1:1
Eccl 1:1
WisSol 7:15-22;
8:10f.; 9:4
LAB 60

Solomon interrogates Beelzeboul

6
(15) Then I interrogated him and said, "Tell me, who are you?" The demon said, "I am Beelzeboul, the ruler of the demons." I demanded that without interruption he sit next to me and explain the manifestations of the demons. Then he promised to bring to me all the unclean spirits bound. Again, I glorified the God of heaven and earth, continually giving thanks to him.

Solomon interrogates Onoskelis and learns of her activity

(16) 1 **4** I now asked the demon if there were any female demons. When he replied that 2 there were, (I said that) I wanted to see (one). •Beelzeboul went off and showed me Onoskelis,[a] who had a very beautiful form. Her body was that of a woman

---

1. This sentence is not clear. Gk. *autōn tēn merida*, "their species," could mean "their part" or "their limb," that is, a member of the body. Gk. *autou tēn moiran*, "his fate," could also mean "his part," and either sense could refer to Ouriel, whose fate is mentioned in the next vs. On the other hand, Conybeare, *JQR* 11 (1898) 18, n. 2, suggests that the angels and demons both have "destinies" which determine their powers from all eternity, an idea found in the *Arabian Nights*. "His" is therefore left intentionally ambiguous. See "Textual Emendations" at the end of the Introduction. The sea monsters are named as Behemoth (the male) and Leviathan (the female) in 4Ezra 6:48–52; 1En 60:7.

m. MS Q omits TSol 3:1–20:9; D omits 3:1–18:42; 19; 25–26; and has its own closing.

3 a. Gk. *ho Beelzeboul* is a NT name for the Prince of Demons by whose authority Jesus was accused by the Pharisees of exorcising demons; cf. Mt 12:24; Lk 11:15; Mk 3:22. In Mt 10:25, Jesus is called Beelzeboul. The Heb. *baʿal-zebub* is probably a

contemptuous corruption of a Philistine god (2Kgs 1:2, 6), its obvious meaning being "lord of the flies." LXX MSS have Beelzeboul, perhaps referring to Ugaritic Aleyan Baal, "Baal Prince."

b. The Gk. phrase *tōn sōn thronōn paredron sophian* [or *sophōn*], "Wisdom, the attendant of your thrones," occurs in WisSol 9:4. It is the tradition of Solomon's wisdom which led to the belief in his power over the demons; cf. 1Kgs 4:29–34 (Heb 5:9–14).

4 a. The Gk. *hē onoskelis* means "she with the ass's legs." The term was used to describe Empusa, a hobgoblin able to assume various shapes. McCown, *Testament*, p. 67 (cf. p. 88), says she is probably the Gk. female demon, but her manner of birth is found also in Jewish sources (see below, n. d). In TSol she is a satyra, or female satyr. In Gk. myth, the satyr was a half-man, half-beast, a spirit that roamed the woods and hills. He was lustful and mischievous. On Gk. vases satyrs are portrayed as chasing nymphs or reveling at drinking

with a fair complexion, but her legs were those of a mule.[b]

3,4 When she came to me, I said to her, "Tell me who you are." •She responded,
(17) "My name is Onoskelis. I am a spirit which has been made into a body. I recline
in a den on the earth. I make my home in caves. However, I have a many-sided
5 character. •Sometimes I strangle men; sometimes I pervert them from their true
6 natures. Most of the time, my habitats are cliffs, caves, and ravines. •Frequently,
I also associate with men who think of me as a woman, especially with those
whose skin is honey-colored, for we are of the same constellation.[c] It is also true
that they worship my star secretly and openly. They do not know that they deceive
7 themselves and excite me to be an evildoer all the more. •For they want to obtain
gold by remembering (me), but I grant little to those who seriously worship me."

8 Next I asked her how she came into being. She said, "I was generated from an
(18) unexpected voice which is called a voice of the echo of a black heaven,[d] emitted
in matter."

9 I said to her, "By what heavenly body do you travel?" She replied, "By the
(19) full moon, because by the moon I pass over more things." •Then I said, "What
10 angel thwarts you?"[e] She responded, "One that is also in *you*, King!" •Now
11 because I thought these (remarks were meant) in ridicule, I commanded a soldier
to strike her. But she cried out in a loud voice and said, "I say to you, King, by
God's wisdom I have been entrusted to your power."

3:5; 8:11; 22:1;
24:3
1Kgs 4:29-34

Onoskelis compelled to spin hemp for the construction ropes

12 So I uttered the name of the Holy One of Israel[f] and commanded her to spin the
(20) hemp for the ropes used in the construction of the Temple of God. She was sealed
and bound in such a way that she was made powerless, so that she had to stand
day and night to spin the hemp.

1Jn 2:20

Solomon interrrogates Asmodeus and learns of his activity

1 **5** I commanded another demon be brought to me; and he (Beelzeboul) brought
(21) **2** me the evil demon Asmodeus,[a] bound. •I asked him, "Who are you?" He scowled
3 at me and said, "And who are *you*?" •I said to him, "You (dare to) answer (so
arrogantly) when you have been punished like this?" He continued to give forth
the same look and said to me, "How *should* I answer you? You are the son of a
man, but although I was born of a human mother, I (am the son) of an angel;[b] it
is impossible for one of heavenly origin (to speak) an arrogant word to one of

Tob 3:8,17
6:2
Gen 6:1-4
1En 6-8; 51:3;
69:4f.; 86:1f.;
106:13
2En 18:3
2Bar 56:11-13

---

parties with the god of wine, Dionysus. Usually, they have horses' ears and tails as well as goats' legs and hoofs. Origen (*Contra* 6.30) mentions the Seven Ruling Demons who were probably accepted by the Ophians and described by Celsus; the seventh is said to have the appearance of an ass. See TSol 8 and nn.; Conybeare, *JQR* 11 (1898) 12–14.

b. Gk. *ho hēmionos*, "half-ass."

c. Apparently Onoskelis is referring to the constellation Capricorn, the Goat, which is the tenth sign of the zodiac. The ancients identified Capricorn with the god Pan, the god of forests and fields. Pan had goats' horns and hoofs, was a musician who played the pipes, and was always falling in love with the nymphs. See TSol 4:1, n. a.

d. The meaning is uncertain. The term translated "black" (*ho molybdos*) means "lead." The MSS attempt various explanations. Conybeare (*JQR* 11 [1898] 19 [see n. 8]), conjectures "ordure" and suggests an analogy between *ho echos*, "echo," and the "Daughter Voice" (Heb. *bath kōl*) in Jewish literature, which refers to God's voice. Also see *LAB* 60. James (*The Biblical Antiquities of Philo* [New York, 1971; reprint] p. 233)

notes the Leyden Magical Papyrus quoted in A. Dieterich (*Abraxas: Studien zur Religionsgeschichte des spätern Altertums* [Leipzig, 1891] p. 17–19) which includes, "God laughed seven times, and when he laughed seven gods were born . . . He laughed the second time . . . and the earth heard the echo [*ēchous*] . . . and a god appeared"; p. 19 has *kai egennēthē ek tou ēchous megas theos* . . . or "a great god was begotten out of an echo."

e. Solomon's first question about a thwarting angel; see TSol Title, n. e.

f. Gk. *to onoma tou Hagiou Israēl*, "The Name of the Holy One of Israel," a circumlocution for Yahweh.

5 a. In Tob, Asmodeus is the evil demon who slays the seven husbands of Sarah before the marriages are consummated. TSol 5 has a number of contacts with the Tobit story; see especially TSol 5:9f.; Introduction on Rabbinic Ashmedai.

b. This comment is apparently based on the common Jewish interpretation of Gen 6:1–4 that the angels fell when they lusted after beautiful human women and produced children who were giants; see TSol 6:1f. and n. b.

4 earthly origin. •My constellation (is like an animal which) reclines in its den in heaven; some men call me the Great Bear, but others the Offspring of a Dragon.[c] Moreover, a smaller constellation accompanies my constellation, for the high 5 position and throne of my father is always in the sky.[d] •So do not ask me so many things, Solomon, for eventually your kingdom will be divided. This glory of yours is temporary. You have us to torture for a little while; then we shall disperse[e] among human beings again with the result that we shall be worshiped as gods because men do not know the names of the angels who rule over us."

6 When I, Solomon, heard this things, I bound him with greater care. Then I
(22) ordered him to be flogged with a rod and to defend himself by stating his name 7 and (reporting) his activity. •The demon stated, "I am the renowned Asmodeus; I cause the wickedness of men to spread[f] throughout the world. I am always hatching plots against newlyweds; I mar the beauty of virgins and cause their hearts to grow cold."[g]

8 I said to him, "Is this all that you do?" He spoke again: "I spread madness
(23) about women through the stars[h] and I have often committed a rash of murders."[i]

Asmodeus thwarted by the angel Raphael, as well as smoking liver and gall of a fish

9 Then I adjured him by the name of the Lord Sabaoth, "Asmodeus, fear God,
(24) and tell me by which angel you are thwarted." The demon said, "Raphael, the one who stands before God;[j] but also a liver and a gall of a fish smoking on coals 10 of charcoal drives me away."[k] •I asked him again, saying, "Do not hide anything from me, for I am Solomon, Son of David.[l] Tell me the name of the fish you fear." He replied, "It is called the sheatfish.[m] It is found in the rivers of Assyria and it is hatched only there; I am also found in those parts."

Marginal references:
15:8,12
1Kgs 12
26:7

Deut 32:17
Ps 106:37
Bar 4:7
1En 19:1

5:1
Tob 3:8,16f.
Tob 7:11f.

Tob 3:17; 5:4;
6:10f.; 9:5;
12:15
1En 9:1; 10:4;
20:3; 22:3,6;
40:9; 54:6;
68:2f.; 71:8f.
1:7; 20:1

Tob 6:2

---

c. Gk. *hamaxan*, from *hē hamaxa*, otherwise called *hē arktos*, the constellation "The Greater Bear." It is the third largest constellation, seven of its stars forming the Big Dipper. A *hamaxa* was the chassis of a wagon, or the four-wheeled wagon itself, and the Akkadians referred to "The Greater Bear" as "The Long Chariot." Gk. *drakontopoda*, from *ho drakontopais*, "offspring of a dragon," so Lampe, p. 386. Was the dragon the constellation Hydra?

d. Gk. *mikrotera astra*, "a smaller constellation," perhaps a reference to "The Smaller Bear," otherwise known as the Little Dipper. Does the reference to "my father" refer to Polaris at the tip of the handle of the Little Dipper?

e. Gk. *nomen echomen*, "we have pasture." The spreading out of sheep in a pasture was used figuratively for the diffusion of disease through the body like a cancer.

f. Gk. *oidainomai*, "I cause to swell," a medical term.

g. Gk. *alloioō*, "I change," "I alter," usually for the worse, thus "to grow cold." The references to newlyweds, virgins, and Asmodeus clearly allude to story of Tobit; cf. Tob 3:8; 3:16f.; 8:2f. and TSol 5:1, n. a.

h. Gk. *dia tōn astrōn*, "through the stars." K. Dieterich (*Untersuchungen zur Geschichte der griechischen Sprache von der hellenistischen Zeit bis zum 10.Jahrhundert nach Christus* [Byzantinisches Archiv als Ergänzung der Byzantinischen Zeitschrift, Heft 1; Leipzig, 1898] pp. 220, 230f.) suggested the verb *strōnō*, "I spread," was perhaps

an error for *oistrō*, "I sting [or "goad"] to madness" (like a gadfly). Perhaps the stars themselves are mad about women, that is, they are demons, so Lampe, p. 650. If so, the implication could be the fallen angels again; see TSol 5:3f.; 6:1f.; and n. b.

i. Gk. *eis trikumias kai heōs heptas ēphoneusa*, "I have committed murder for a group of three waves [e.g. a mighty wave or swell] and up to seven." MS I ends at this point; MSS V W omit TSol 5:6–8.

j. Raphael, according to a vision of Enoch in 1En 71, is one of the heavenly angels who accompanies the Head of Days. In 1En 40:9 he is set over all the diseases and all the wounds of mankind.

k. In Tob, Raphael instructs Tobit to remove the gall, heart, and liver of a fish taken from the Tigris River (see "rivers of Assyria" in the next vs.), promising that they will be useful for medication. In Media, Raphael tells Tobit that the smoking *heart* and liver before a man or woman who is attacked by a demon or evil spirit will result in the demon's fleeing forever; this method is then applied by Tobit against Asmodeus on Tobit's and Sarah's wedding night; see TSol 5, nn. a and g. Raphael then pursues the demon to Egypt, where he binds and fetters him (TSol 1:13, n. r). The gall is later used to cure Tobit's blindness. In TSol, the liver and gall are smoked.

l. TSol Title, n. d.

m. Gk. *ho, hē glanis*, "sheatfish," a large catfish, so LSJM, p. 350.

Asmodeus required to mold clay for the vessels of the Temple

11 (25) I said to him, "Is there not something else about you,[n] Asmodeus?" He said to me, "The power of God which binds me with unbreakable bonds by his seal knows that what I have related to you is true. I beg you, King Solomon, do not 11:6 Mk 5:13 condemn me to water."[o] •But I smiled and replied, "As the Lord, the God of my 2:6 fathers lives, you shall have irons to wear[p] and you shall mold clay for all the vessels of the Temple, eliminating the cost of the mold." Then I ordered ten water jars to be made available and (I commanded) him to be encircled[q] by them. Though he complained bitterly, the demon carried out the things which he had been 13 commanded. Asmodeus did this because he also had knowledge of the future. •So 1:0 I, Solomon, glorified God, who gave me this authority; then, taking the liver and 1:5 the gall of the fish, along with a branch of storax,[r] I lit a fire under Asmodeus because he was powerful, and his voice was thwarted, as well as a tooth full of venom.[s]

Solomon interrogates Beelzeboul again and learns of his activities

1 (26) **6** Then I summoned Beelzeboul to appear before me again. When he was seated, 2:9; 3:1f.; 3:6f.; I thought it appropriate to ask him, "Why are you alone Prince of the Demons?"[a] 10:3

2 He replied, "Because I am the only one left of the heavenly angels (who fell).[b] 5:3

3 I was the highest-ranking angel in heaven, the one called Beelzeboul. •There also Gen 6:1-4 accompanied me another ungodly (angel) whom God cut off and now, imprisoned 1En 6-11 here, he holds in his power the race of those bound by me in Tartarus.[c] He is being 1En 20:2 nurtured in the Red Sea;[d] when he is ready, he will come in triumph." Sib 4:186 12:4; 23-25

4 (27) I said to him, "What are your activities?" He replied, "I bring destruction by means of tyrants; I cause the demons to be worshiped alongside men; and I arouse

---

n. Gk. *ouden heteron para sou*, "nothing else about you?" The context suggests that Solomon wants to know the truth of what has already been said.

o. Demons often prefer desert regions; cf. Mk 1:12f.; Jesus condemns the Gerasene demoniacs to the swine, who then stampede down the cliff into the sea; cf. Mk 5:13.

p. Gk. *sidera echeis phoresai*, "you have iron to wear," is loosely translated. Ornias is said to fear iron in TSol 2:5 (cf. TSol 2:5, n. k). On binding, see TSol 1:13, n. f. In the Aramaic Incantation Bowls from 6th-cent. Babylon primitive art occasionally shows the demon wearing irons. An Aram. incantation bowl reads, "bound is the bewitching lilith who haunts the house of Zakoy, with a belt of iron on her *pate*; bound is the bewitching lilith with a peg of iron in her nose; bound is the bewitching lilith with *pinchers* of iron in her *mouth*; bound is the bewitching lilith who haunts the house of Zakoy with a chain of iron on her *neck*; bound is the bewitching lilith with fetters of iron on her hands; bound is the bewitching lilith with stocks of stone on her feet . . ." (See C. H. Gordon, "Two Magic Bowls in Teheran," *Orientalia* 20 [1951] 310.)

q. Gk. *perichonnusthai*. Gk. *perichonnumi* means "heap earth around" and in the passive voice "to be covered with." Perhaps the meaning is that the demon was drenched with the water in the jars.

r. Gk. *meta klasmatos styrakos leukou*. Gk. *ho styrax* means "the spike at the butt end of a spear shaft"; cf. Conybeare's translation of MS P as "spike of a reed" (p. 21). Gk. *hē styrax* means "the shrub or tree which yields the gum called storax." Storax is a fragrant balsam obtained from

the bark of an Asiatic tree (*Liquidambar orientalis*) of the witchhazel family that was used as incense, an ingredient of perfume, or a respiratory decongestant. The term can refer also to shrubs or trees of the storax family; these have clusters of drooping white flowers. McCown (*Testament*, p. 25) conjectures *lotou*, that is, *ho lōtus*, referring to plants and trees of the lotus family, or to fodder plants such as clover; see LSJM, p. 1070. The translation "storax" is suggestive because it can be used medicinally for the respiratory system and it is Asmodeus' *voice* that is thwarted.

s. Gk. *kai plērēs odous pikrias*, "and a full tooth of venom." MS L has *kai plērois hodou pikrias*, "and with (words) full of the way of malice." See "Textual Emendations."

6 a. TSol 3:1, n. a.

b. The widespread Jewish myth that the angels fell because they lusted after beautiful human women and produced children who were giants is based on Gen 6:1-4. A Gk. version that renders "sons of God" in this passage as "angels of God" is preserved in Philo *Gig*, Justin Martyr *Apol* 2:5, Eusebius, Augustine, and Ambrose. The myth is well illustrated by 1En 6-11, but is found in many Jewish and early Christian writings; see *APOT*, vol. 2, p. 191 for numerous references.

c. Tartarus, the murky world of darkness, or hell; the place in which the wicked are punished. See TSol 2:4, n. i.

d. This second demon refers to the one-winged demon Abezethibou, who lived in the first heaven, who was Moses' adversary in Egypt, and who was trapped in the Red Sea when the parted waters returned, so TSol 23-25.

desire in holy men and select priests. I bring about jealousies and murders in a country, and I instigate wars."[e]

5
(28) Then I said to him, "Bring to me the one you said is being nurtured in the Red Sea." He retorted, "I will bring no one back to you. But there will come a certain demon whose name is Ephippas[f] who will bind him and bring him up out of the 12:4; 22:1-24:5
6 abyss." •I responded, "Tell me why he is in the abyss of the Red Sea and what his name is." He, however, said, "Do not ask me; you are not able to learn that
7 from me. He will come to you because I, too, am with you." •So I said to him, 24:1f. "Tell me in which star you reside." "The one called by men the Evening Star,"[g] he said.

Beelzeboul thwarted by "the Almighty God"

8
(29) Then I said, "Tell me which angel thwarts you." "The Almighty God," he replied. "He is called by the Hebrews Patike,[h] the one who descends from the 11:6; 15:11 heights; he is (called) by the Greeks Emmanouel.[i] I am always afraid of him, and Isa 7:14; 8:8 Mt 1:23 trembling. If anyone adjures me with the oath (called) 'the Elo-i,'[j] a great name Ps 22:1 for his power, I disappear." Mk 15:34 Mt 27:46

Beelzeboul compelled to cut marble for the Temple

9
(30) Now when I, Solomon, heard these things, I commanded him to cut blocks of Theban marble.[k] As he was beginning to cut, all the demons cried out with a loud voice because (he was their) king, Beelzeboul.

Beelzeboul required to inform Solomon about heavenly things

10
(31) Nevertheless, I, Solomon, persisted in interrogating him, saying, "If you wish to obtain a release, inform me about heavenly things." Beelzeboul replied, "Listen, King, if you burn oil of myrrh, frankincense, and bulbs of the sea[l] along with spikenard and saffron, and light seven lamps during an earthquake,[m] you will strengthen (your) house. And if, being ritually clean, you light (them) at the crack 2Kgs 23:11 of dawn, just before the sun comes up, you will see the heavenly dragons and the Sir 72:5; 75:3f. SibOr 5:22
11 way they wriggle along and pull the chariot of the sun."[n] •When I, Solomon,
(32) heard these things, I rebuked him and said, "Be silent[o] and continue cutting marble just as I ordered you."

e. MS P reads, "I, Solomon, said to him, 'Beelzeboul, what is your activity?' And he said, 'I destroy kings; I ally myself with foreign tyrants. I impose my demons on men in order that they might believe in them and be destroyed. And I excite desire in the chosen servants of God, priests and faithful men, for wicked sins, evil heresies, and lawless deeds; they obey me and I lead them to destruction. I also inspire men with envy, murder, wars, sodomy, and other evil things. And I will destroy the world.' "

f. TSol 22–24. Ephippas is an Arabian wind demon who will eventually be trapped in Arabia by Solomon's boy servant; the demon then helps bring back the Red Sea demon, Abezethibou.

g. Gk. hesperia, hē, "the Western Star," or "the Evening Star," perhaps with reference to the planet Venus.

h. Conybeare (JQR 11 [1898] 11) notes that Jesus is called "the God of the Hebrews" in the Paris Magical Papyrus 3009. Is Patikē a corruption of ho patēr, "father"?

i. MS P states, "I said to him, 'Tell me by what

angel you are thwarted.' And he replied, 'By the holy and precious name of the almighty God, the one called by the Hebrews by a row of numbers, of which the sum is 644, and among the Greeks it is Emmanouēl [E = 5; m = 40; m = 40; a = 1; n = 50; o = 70; u = 400; ē = 8; l = 30]. And if one of the Romans adjure me by the great name of power, Eleēth, I disappear." See Introduction.

j. Aram. "my God"; cf. Ps 22:1 and Jesus' cry on the cross (Mk 15:34; Mt 27:46).

k. Presumably, Thebes in Egypt.

l. Conybeare (JQR 11 [1898] 22, n. 5) writes, "Perhaps the 'sea-bulbs' were balls of hair-like texture which the sea washes up on Mediterranean shores, e.g. in Tunisia."

m. Gk. en seismō, "in motion," perhaps swinging. Conybeare (JQR 11 [1898] 6) conjectures en eirmō, "in a row."

n. The view in classical myth was that the sun drove a chariot pulled by horses across the sky from sea to sea.

o. Gk. siōpēsai, "be silent." Jesus so rebukes the unclean spirit in Mk 1:25.

Solomon interrogates Lix Tetrax, the demon of the wind

1 **7** After I praised God, I, Solomon, requested the presence of another demon and
he appeared before me. He was bearing his face on the air high above and the
2 remaining part of his body was crawling along like a little snail. • Suddenly, he
broke through a large contingent of soldiers, raised up a blustering cloud of dust   Jub 2:2
from the earth, transported it upward, and hurled it against me many times (while   1En 60:12
I watched) in amazement. I exclaimed, "What do we have here?"[a] [But this
3 continued] for a long time.[b] • When I stood up, I spat on the ground at that spot
and I sealed (him) with the ring of God. As a result, the moving air stopped. Then
I asked him, saying, "Who are you?" After he had stirred up another cloud of
4 dust, he answered me, "What do you want, King Solomon?" • I answered him,
"Tell me what you are called; also, I want to interrogate you." Thus, I give thanks
to God who instructs me as to how to respond to their evil plots.
5   So the demon said to me, "I am called Lix Tetrax."[c] "What is your activity?"
(33) I queried. He responded, "I create divisions among men, I make whirlwinds, I   8:11
start fires, I set fields on fire, and I make households non-functional. Usually, I   Jub 2:2
4Mac 7:11
carry on my activity in the summertime. If I get the chance, I slither in under the
corners of houses during the night or day. I am the direct offspring of the Great
6 One."[d] • I asked him, "In which constellation do you reside?" He replied, "Toward
the very tip of the horn of the moon when it is found in the South—there is my
star. Therefore, I was assigned to draw out the fever which strikes for a day and
a half. As a result, many men, when they see (this), pray about the day-and-a-half
fever, (invoking) these three names, 'Baltala, Thallal, Melchal,' and I heal them."
7 Then I, Solomon, said to him, "But when you wish to do evil, who grants you
the power?" He replied, "The angel by whom also the day-and-a-half fever is
stopped."

The demon Lix Tetrax, thwarted by the archangel Azael, is compelled to help raise stones for the Temple workmen

Finally, I asked him, "By what name are you thwarted?" He responded, "The
8 name of the archangel Azael."[e] • Then I placed my seal on the demon and
commanded him to pick up stones and hurl them up to the heights of the Temple
for the workmen; compelled, the demon complied with his orders.

Solomon interrogates the seven heavenly bodies of this world of darkness, and learns of their activities and thwarting angels

1 **8** Again, I glorified God, who gave me this authority, and I commanded another   1En 18:13f.;
(34) demon to appear before me. There came seven spirits bound up together hand and   21:1f.
foot, fair of form and graceful. When I, Solomon, saw them, I was amazed and
2 asked them, "Who are you?" • They replied, "We are heavenly bodies,[a] rulers   15:5; 18:2,4
Gal 4:3,9

---

7 a. Gk. *tina echō erōtēsai*, "Whom do I have to
ask?"

b. Gk. *heōs epi polu*, "as long as much." The
meaning is uncertain.

c. Gk. *Lix Tetrax. Lix* is a magical term referring
to the earth, 803; *tetrax* refers to a four-seasoned
year; see Lampe, pp. 803, 1391. McCown (*Testament*, p. 67) followed by Preisendanz (Pauly-
Wissowa Sup. 8, col. 686) identifies Lix Tetrax as
an old Ephesian name which, in a tablet from
Crete, is connected with a wind. "Blast demons"
are found in the Aram. incantation texts; see
C. H. Gordon, *Orientalia* 10 (1941) 121.

d. Gk. *tou megalou*, "the great [name un-
known]." The reference is not clear; perhaps it
refers to Beelzeboul. The goddess Artemis, whose

worship centered in Ephesus, was called "the
Great" (cf. Acts 19:24, 27f., 34f.); she is mentioned in TSol 8:11; see TSol 8:11, n. m.

e. The name Azael, found in 2Ezra 9:14, is not
mentioned in the lists of the archangels in 1En
9–10; Azazel, mentioned in relation to the scapegoat
sent into the desert in Lev 16:8, 26, becomes an
archdemon in Jewish literature, perhaps because
demons were believed to dwell in the desert (cf.
Isa 31:21; 34:11f.; Tob 8:3; Mt 12:43; 1En 9:6;
10).

8 a. Gk. *esmen stoicheia*, "we are heavenly bodies." In antiquity the *stoicheia* are mentioned as
letters of the alphabet (TSol 17:4); the four basic
elements of the world, namely, earth, air, fire, and

3 of this world of darkness.''[b] •The first said, "I am Deception." The second said,
"I am Strife." The third said, "I am Fate." The fourth said, "I am Distress."
4 The fifth said, "I am Error." The sixth said, "I am Power." •The seventh said,
"I am The Worst. Our stars in heaven look small, but we are named like gods.
We change our position together and we live together, sometimes in Lydia,
sometimes in Olympus, sometimes on the great mountain."[c]

5
(35) Then I, Solomon, continued questioning them, beginning with the first. "Tell
me what you do." He responded, "I am Deception. I plot deception and I devise
the most evil heresies. But there is one who thwarts me, the angel Lamechiel."[d]

6
(36) The second said, "I am Strife. I cause strife by making available clubs, pellets,
and swords, my implements of war. But I have an angel who thwarts me,
Baruchiel."[e]

7
(37) Likewise, the third said, "I am called[f] Fate. I cause every man to fight in battle
rather than make peace honorably with those who are winning.[g] But why am I
talking so much? There is an angel who thwarts me, Marmaroth."[h]

8
(38) The fourth (, Distress,) said, "I cause men to lack moderation; I divide them
into factions; I keep them separated. Since Strife follows in my footsteps, I set
men against each other and do many other similar things to them. But why am I
talking so much? There is an angel who thwarts me, the great Balthioul."[i]

9
(40) The fifth said, "I am Error, King Solomon, and I am leading you into error,
and I led you into error when I made you kill your brothers.[j] I lead people into
error by hunting for graves and I teach them (how) to dig them up. I lead (men's)
minds to stray away from religion, and I do many other bad things. However,
there is the angel who thwarts me, Ouriel."[k]

10
(39) Likewise, the sixth said, "I am Power. I raise up tyrants, I depose kings, and
I grant power to all those who are enemies. There is an angel who thwarts me,
Asteraoth."[l]

11
(41) Similarly, the seventh said, "I am The Worst, and you, King, I shall harm
when I order (you to be bound) with the bonds of Artemis.[m] Because these things
affect you, you have desire like a beloved one, but to me (that is) a desire which

Margin references: Col 2:8,20; Eph 6:12; 18:28; 18:33; 2:4; 2:7f.; 18:7; 4Ezra 6:48f; 1En 9:1; 10:1f.; Acts 19:24, 27f.,34f.; SibOr 5:293

---

water (WisSol 7:17; 19:18; 4Mac 12:13; Josephus,
Ant 3.7.7; 2Pet 3:10f.); sometimes worshiped as
deities (Philo, Vita Cont 3); and heavenly bodies,
worthy of worship, often identified with the twelve
signs of the zodiac (perhaps Gal 4:3, 9; Col 2:8,
20). One should compare the "seven spirits of
deceit" in TReu 2f. and the "seven ruling demons"
in Origen, Contra 6.30. These are demonic
stars grouped by seven (cf. 1En 21:3), a sacred
number in ancient astrology (TReu 2; Mt 12:45;
Lk 8:2; 11:26; Rev 1:16, 20; 2:1; Origen, Contra
6.30). McCown (Testament, p. 70) states that these
seven are to be identified with the Pleiades, the
seven daughters of Atlas; originally they were stars,
though only six are visible. Cf. Job 9:9; Amos 5:8.
The stoicheia, who are the kosmokratores tou
skotous (n. b), are the thirty-six decans of the
zodiac in TSol 18; see TSol 18:2, 4, nn. d, f; cf.
also TSol 15:5. See "Textual Emendations" on
8:4.
b. Gk. kosmokratores tou skotous, "world rulers
of the darkness." In hellenistic religions, kosmokratores are gods or spirits who control parts of the
cosmos. The Rabbis adopted the term to apply to
evil spirits, specifically the angel of death. This
phrase is linked with the stoicheia here and in TSol
18:2 (n. a). See also Eph 6:12.
c. Lydia was in southwestern Asia Minor and
bordered Gk. colonies on its western border; Olympus, the highest mountain in northeastern Greece,
was believed to reach up to the heavens and to be
the abode of the gods; presumably "the great mountain" is a similar mythical mountain, or Olympus

is being viewed as a mysterious abode of the gods
above all mountains.
d. Lamechiel is not named among the archangels
of 1En 9, 10; on Lamech, see Gen 4:18–24.
e. Baruchiel is also not named among the
archangels of 1En; on "Baruch," meaning
"blessed," see Jer 51:59.
f. Gk. kykliskomai, "I encircle." Perhaps "I
am Fate. I encircle (soldiers) and cause
(them) . . ."; McCown (Testament, p. 33) conjectures kikléskomai, "I am called . . ."
g. Gk. periexousin, from periechō, "I surround," "I blockade," "I outflank."
h. Marmaroth; see TSol 18:28, n. z2, and Sepher
Ha-Razim 4:10.
i. Balthioul does not seem to be mentioned elsewhere in this period.
j. Gk. tous adelphous, "the brothers." MS P
reads ton adelphon sou, "your brother," probably
a reference to 1Kgs 2:25, Solomon's execution of
Adonijah. Note the reverse order of (39) and (40)
in MS P.
k. TSol 2:4, n. i; 18:7, n. k.
l. Asteraôth, perhaps a variation of a Canaanite
fertility goddess Ashtoreth (deliberately misvocal-
ized in Heb.). Solomon patronized her cult, 1Kgs
11:5.
m. Gk. kakōsō hote keleuthō Artimidos desmois,
"I shall harm when I -?- with the bonds of Artemis." Gk. keleuthō is not clear; Conybeare (JQR
11 [1898] 25, n. 5), following Fleck, conjectured
keleusō, "I (should) order." In Gk. myth Artemis
(a non-Gk. name) was usually a virgin huntress of

corresponds to myself (which is) wisdom.[n] For if anyone is wise, he will not follow in my steps.'"[o]   3:5; 4:11; 22:1; 24:3

12 (42) But I, Solomon, when I heard these things, sealed them with the ring of God and commanded them to dig the foundation of the Temple. It stretched out 250 cubits in length. So all the things which were commanded them were accomplished.   1Kgs 7:2

Solomon interrogates the headless demon called Murder and learns of his activity and what thwarts him

1 (43) 9 Again I asked that other demons visit me in succession and there was brought 2 to me a demon, a man (who had) all his limbs, but no head.[a] •I said to him, "Tell me who you are and what you are called." The demon replied, "I am called Murder; for I devour heads, wishing to get a head for myself, but I do not consume enough. I long for a head to do exactly what you do, King."

3 (44) When I heard these things, I stretched out my hand against his chest and put my seal on him. Then the demon jumped up, tore himself loose, and muttered, 4 saying, "Woe is me! How did I fall in with a traitor, Ornias? I do not see." • So I said to him, "How is it possible for you to see?" He replied, "Through my 5 breasts!" • When I, Solomon, heard the delight in his voice, I wished to learn more. So I asked him, "How is it possible for you to speak?" He responded, "My voice has taken over voices from many men; for I have closed up the heads of those among men who are called dumb. When infants are ten days old, and if one cries during the night, I become a spirit and I rush in and attack (the infant) 6 through his voice. •What is more, my visit to premature (infants) is harmful. My strength happens to reside in my hands, that is, like (that which takes place) at an executioner's block,[b] I grab hold of heads, cut (them) off, and attach (them) to myself; then, by the fire which is continually (burning) in me, I consume (them) through my neck. I am the one who inflames the limbs, inflicts the feet, and 7 produces festering sores.[c] •It is by a fiery flash of lightning that I am thwarted." (45,46)[c] I ordered him to stay with Beelzeboul until the time when a friend might arrive.[d]   1:1-3:4 20:6-18 LetAris 47   10:8

Solomon interrogates the doglike demon, Scepter

1 (47) 10 Then I ordered another demon to make his presence before me. He came before me in the form of a gigantic dog,[a] and he spoke to me in a loud voice,   SibOr 5:526

the wild and associated with the young of all living things, especially wildlife. She was therefore the goddess of birth and patroness of hunting. Sudden, violent deaths among women were said to come from her bow. Artemis of Ephesus, mentioned in Acts 19, was predominantly a mother goddess and patroness of fertility like Cybele or Ashtoreth; she was a many-breasted goddess housed in the Artemisium, one of the Seven Wonders of the Ancient World. See TSol 7:5, n. d.

    n. Text uncertain; see "Textual Emendations."
    o. Gk. *ouk epistrepsei ichnos pros me*, "a footstep will not return to me."

9 a. Eitrem (*Magical Papyri*, p. 48) notes that the "headless demon" is an old Egyptian conception with astrological associations, and is known as the demon who causes quartan fever. McCown (*Testament*, p. 67) identifies him with the headless demon of the magical papyri (Lond. P 46, 145ff.; *Gr. Pap. Br. Mus.* I, 69f.).
    b. Gk. *hōs epi xylou*, "as upon wood." "Executioner's block" is suggested in Lampe, p. 933.
    c. MS P (Conybeare, *JQR* 11, paragraph [45]) adds, "And when I, Solomon, heard these things, I said to him, 'Tell me how you discharge the fire. From what sources do you emit it?' The spirit

replied, 'From the rising sun. For here there has not yet been found that Elbourion as the one to whom one prays. And men light lights to him, and the seven demons call upon his name before men and he heals them.' " For *Anatolē*, "rising sun," see LXX Zech 3:8; 6:12 where it translates the messianic "Shoot (of David)"; Lk 1:78. MS P (Conybeare, *JQR* 11, paragraph [46]) continues, "But I said to him, 'Tell me his name.' He answered, 'I cannot tell you. For if I tell his name, I make myself incurable. But he is one who responds to his name.' When I, Solomon, heard these things, I said to him, 'Tell me, therefore, by what angel you are thwarted.' He replied, 'By the fiery flash of lightning.' " MSS V W read, "When I, Solomon, heard these things, I said, 'Tell me, therefore by what angel you are thwarted.' He replied, 'Through the fiery angel.' "
    d. Gk. *mechri kai toutou philos paragenētai*, perhaps "until the time when something pleasing might be present."

10 a. Origen (*Contra* 6.30) says that the sixth of the Seven Ruling Demons, according to Celsus, had the face of a dog, and in a diagram which he had obtained, the demon was called Erataoth; cf. TSol 18:1.

2 "Hail, O King Solomon!" •I was astounded and said to him, "Who are you, dog?" He said, "You suppose that I am a dog; but before your time, King, I was a man. I accomplished many unlawful deeds in the world and I was so extremely strong that I restrained the stars of heaven, and now I am preparing more evil 3 works. •Consequently, I deceive men who follow my star closely and I lead (them) into stupidity; I also subdue the hearts[b] of men through their throats and in this way I destroy (them)."

The demon Scepter helps Solomon obtain an emerald stone for the Temple and Solomon learns of Scepter's thwarting angel

4,5
(48)
I said to him, "What is your name?" He replied, "Scepter." •Then I said to him, "What is your activity and why do you seem to me to be so prosperous?" The demon said, "Turn over your manservant to me and I shall spirit him off to a place in the mountains where I shall show him an emerald stone shaken loose from its foundation. With it, you will adorn the Temple of God."

6
(49)
When I heard these things, I immediately ordered my household servant to accompany him and to take the ring bearing God's seal with him. I told him, "Go with him and whoever shows you the emerald stone, seal him with the ring, 7 observe the place in detail, and bring the ring back to me." •So when (the demon) went out and showed him the emerald stone, (the household servant) sealed him 8 with the ring of God, and brought the emerald stone back to me.[c] •I then decided 9:1-7 to have the two demons, the headless one and the dog, bound, and (to request that) the stone be carried about day and night like, as it were, a light for the working artisans.[d]

9
(50)
10
Next I extracted from that moving stone 200 shekels for the supports of the altar,[e] for the stone was shaped like a leek. •Then I, Solomon, when I had glorified the Lord God, locked up the treasure chest containing the stone[f] and commanded the demons to cut marble for the construction of the Temple. Also, I asked the dog in private, "By which angel are you thwarted?" He replied, "By the great Briathos."[g]

Solomon interrogates the Lion-Shaped Demon

1 **11** I commanded another demon to come before me. He came roaring like a
(51) stately lion and he took his place and questioned me by word: "King Solomon, 2 I have this particular form (and am) a spirit which can never be bound. •I am one who sneaks in and watches over all who are lying ill with a disease and I make 3 it impossible for man to recover from his taint.[a] •I have another activity. I involve the legions of demons subject to me for I am at the places (where they are) when the sun is setting.[b] The name for all demons which are under me is legion."[c]   Mk 5:9,15
                                                                                        Mt 26:53

---

b. Gk. *tas phrenas*, "the hearts," or "the minds," "the thoughts," refers to the midriff regions. The meaning is literal; the way to the midriff is through the throat.

c. An odd sequence since the *ring* was to be returned; see "Textual Emendations."

d. At vs. 8, MS P seems to read, "to bind the two, the headless demon, likewise the dog that was so gigantic, and the dog to keep the fiery spirit as lamps lighting the way through their opening for the artisans night and day."

e. Gk. *kai ēra egō ek tou metoikismou ekeinou tou lithou diakosious siklous en tois anaphoreusi tou thysiastēriou*, perhaps "Next I levied out of the crystals of that stone 200 shekels from among the bearers of the altar . . ." McCown (*Testament*, p. 39*) questions whether the text should not read "*eiar . . . etrechen . . . epi tou thysiasteriou*," that is,

"a prime part of that moving stone was moving quickly among those lifting up upon the altar."

f. Gk. *ton thēsauron tou lithou*, perhaps simply "treasure of the stone."

g. Briathos is not mentioned elsewhere in the Pseudepigrapha.

11 a. Gk. *tēn aitian*, "cause," "reason," "charge" (legal); the meaning here is also physical, hence "taint."

b. Gk. *dytikon*, "closing at sunset," from *dytikos*, "able to dive," "setting," "western." MS P has *dektikos*, "received," which Conybeare (*JQR* 11 [1898] 28) interprets as referring to the evil spirit's capability of being received into the habitation of the human body.

c. A clear reference to the Gerasene demoniacs, Mk 5:1–13; cf. TSol 11:6.

4 Then I asked him, "What is your name?" He replied, "The Lion-Shaped Demon,[d]
5 an Arab[e] by descent." •So I said to him, "How are you and your demons thwarted,
that is, who is your angel?" The demon said, "If I tell you his name, I place not
only myself in chains, but also the legion of demons under me."

6 So I said to him, "I adjure you by the name of the great God Most High: By
(52) what name are you and your demons thwarted?" The demon said, "By the name
of the one who at one time submitted to suffer many things (at the hands) of men, 6:8; 15:11
whose name is Emmanouel,[f] but now he has bound us and will come to torture Is 7:14; 8:8
us (by driving us) into the water at the cliff. As he moves about, he is conjured Mt 1:23
up by means of three letters."[g] 5:11
                                                                                  Mk 5:13

7 So I sentenced his legion to carry wood from the grove (of trees). Then I
(53) sentenced) the Lion-Shaped One to saw it up as kindling with his claws and to
throw it under the perpetually burning kiln.

Solomon interrogates the three-headed dragon spirit, Head of the Dragons, and learns that he is thwarted by the angel of the Wonderful Counselor who ascended at the "Place of the Skull"

1 **12** Now when I had worshiped the God of Israel I ordered another demon to Rev 12:1-17
(54) come forward. This time a three-headed dragon with an awful skin appeared before
2 me. •I asked him, "Who are you?" He said, "I am a three-pronged spirit, one
who overpowers by means of three deeds. In the wombs of women, I blind children.
I also turn their ears around backward and make them dumb and deaf. Finally, I
strike men against the body and I make (them) fall down, foam (at the mouth), Mk 9:18,20
3 and grind their teeth. •But there is a way by which I am thwarted (, namely,) by 15:10; 22:20
(the site) which is marked 'Place of the Skull',[a] for there an angel of the Wonderful Mk 15:22
Counselor[b] foresaw that I would suffer, and he will dwell publicly on the cross.[c] Mt 27:22
He is the one who will thwart me, being the one among (the angels) to whom I Jn 19:17
am subject.   Isa 9:6
                                                                                   11:10; 22:20

4 "But at the place at which he ascended, King Solomon, he will erect a dark 6:5; 22:1-24:5
(55) pillar formed on the air after Ephippas has brought gifts from the Red Sea, from
inside Arabia.[d] In the foundation of the Temple which you have begun to build,
King Solomon, there is hidden away much gold. Dig it up and confiscate it." So
I, Solomon, sent my servant and found (that it was) just as the demon told me.
After I sealed (him with) the ring, I praised God.

5 Next I said to him, "Tell me what you are called." The demon replied, "Head
(56) of the Dragons." So I ordered him to make bricks for the Temple of God.

Solomon interrogates Obyzouth, the female demon with disheveled hair, and learns of her activity

1 **13** Then I ordered another demon to appear before me. There came before me
(57) one who had the shape of a woman but she possessed as one of her traits the form

---

d. Gk. *Leontophoron*, "Lion-bearer." Origen
(*Contra* 6.30) says that the first of the Seven Ruling
Demons mentioned by Celsus was a goat shaped
like a lion, but that in the diagram he obtained, he
was called Michael the Lion-like.

e. *Araps*, perhaps a name?

f. Emmanouel, see TSol 6:8, n. i.

g. MS P reads, "The 'Great Among Men' who
is to suffer many things whose name is the formula
644, who is Emmanouel . . ."; see TSol 6:8,
n. i; Introduction.

12 a. Gk. *topou engkephalou*, "place within the
head," presumably a reference to "Place of the

Skull," or Golgotha (cf. Judg 9:53; 2Kgs 9:35).
The usual early Christian term in Gk. is *to kranion*;
the Vulgate has *calvaria*. This is a clear allusion
to the crucifixion of Jesus; cf. TSol 15:10; 22:20.

b. Gk. *angelos tēs megalēs boulēs*, "angel of
the Wonderful Counselor," apparently a reference
to Christ as the one who fulfilled Isa 9:6; see Lampe,
p. 302.

c. The references are a little confusing; if "angel
of the Wonderful Counselor" is not Christ, "I
would suffer" should be perhaps "he should suffer," referring to Christ.

d. The story of the Arabian demon Ephippas and
the demon of the Red Sea is found in TSol 22–24.

2 of one with disheveled hair.[a] •I said to her, "Who are you?" She replied, "And who are you? Or what need is there for you to inquire about the sort of deeds I do? But if you want to inquire, go to the royal chambers and, after you have washed your hands,[b] sit again on your throne and ask me and then you will learn, King, who I am."

3 When I had done this and had sat on my throne, I, Solomon, asked her and said,
(58) "Who are you?" She replied, "Obyzouth. I do not rest at night, but travel around all the world visiting women and, divining the hour (when they give birth), I search (for them) and strangle their newborn infants.[c] I do not go through a single night WisSol 12:3f. without success. You are not able to give me orders. I even make the rounds (and
4 go) into the remotest areas.[d] •Otherwise, my work is limited to killing newborn infants, injuring eyes, condemning mouths, destroying minds, and making bodies feel pain."

Obyzouth, thwarted by the angel Raphael and by writing her name on a piece of papyrus, is hung by her hair in front of the Temple

5 When I, Solomon, heard these things, I was amazed. I did not look at her shape,
(59)
6 for her body was darkness and her hair savage. •I, Solomon, said to her, "Tell Tob 3:17; 5:4; me, evil spirit, by what angel are you thwarted?" She said to me, "By the angel 6:10,14,18; 9:5; 12:15 Raphael; and when women give birth, write my name on a piece of papyrus and 1En 9:1; 10:4; 20:3; 22:3,6;
7 I shall flee from them to the other world." •When I heard these things I ordered 32:6; 40:9; 54:6; 68:2f.; 71:8f. her to be bound by the hair and to be hung up in front of the Temple in order that all those sons of Israel who pass through and see might glorify the God of Israel who has given me this authority.

Solomon interrogates the Winged Dragon and learns of his activities

1 **14** I again ordered another demon to appear before me; and there came to me one SibOr 5:522
(60) who was in the form of a wallowing dragon, having the limbs of a dragon and
2 wings on its back, but the face and feet of a man. •When I saw him, and became amazed, I said to him, "Who are you and from where have you come?"
(61) The spirit said to me, "This is the first time I have stood before you, King Solomon, a spirit made a god among men, but thwarted by the seal which was
3 given to you by God. •Well, I am the so-called Winged Dragon. I do not copulate with many women, but with only a few who have beautiful bodies, who possess
4 a name of Touxylou[a] of this star. •I rendezvous with them in the form of a winged spirit, copulating (with them) through their buttocks. One woman I attacked is bearing (a child) and that which is born from her becomes Eros.[b] Because it could
5 not be tolerated by men, that woman perished. This is my activity. •Suppose, then, that I alone am content while the rest of the demons troubled by you, being downcast, should speak the whole truth; they will cause the stack of wood about to be gathered by you for construction in the Temple to be consumed by fire."
6 As the demon was saying these things, suddenly the breath coming out of his
(62)

---

13 a. Disheveled hair was characteristic of the Gk. Medusa, guardian goddess of Aphrodite. In the primitive artwork of Aramaic Incantation Bowls the *lilith* is frequently pictured with disheveled hair, and is sometimes so described; see Montgomery (*Aramaic Incantation Texts* [Philadelphia, 1913] p. 190). For an obsidian Medusa on an amulet on a Jewish corpse, see Goodenough, *Jewish Symbols*, vol. 2, p. 236 (cf. n. 186).
  b. Apparently a magical cleansing rite.
  c. Gk. *ta brephē*, "fetuses" or "newborns." The sense may be that the appropriate moment (*hōra*, "hour") is just prior to birth.
  d. Gk. *ta dysēkē merē*, meaning uncertain. Per-

haps "hard-of-hearing parts" or (less likely) "the hard-of-hearing classes of people." MS H has *disēka*, "doubly soft," "gentle"; MS L has *dysika*, "western," and Conybeare (*JQR* 11 [1898] 30) took *ta dytika merē* (MS P) as "westering parts."

14 a. Conjectured for *tou xylou*, "of the wood," e.g. "who possess a name of the wood of this star."
  b. Gk. Erō[s], "the god of love." Erō is the name of a decan in the magical papyri; cf. H. G. Gundel, *Weltbild und Astrologie* (Munich, 1968), p. 22. Cf. also NHC II, 5:*109*, 2, 10, 14, 16, 20, 25:*111*, 9, 19.

mouth set the forest of Lebanon on fire and burned up all the wood which I was
7 going to put into the Temple of God. •Now I, Solomon, saw what the spirit had
done and I was amazed.
(63)   After I glorified God I asked the dragon-shaped demon, saying, "Tell me by
what angel you are thwarted." He replied, "By the great angel who is seated in
8 the second heaven, who is called in Hebrew Bazazath."ᶜ •When I, Solomon, heard
these things and invoked his angel, I condemned him to cut marble for construction
of the Temple of God.

Solomon interrogates Enepsigos, the female demon with two heads, learns of her activities and her thwarting angel, Rathanael

1 **15** Then I praised God and commanded another demon to come before me.
(64)   Again, there came before me a spirit who had the shape of a woman, but on
2 her shoulders were two separate heads with arms. •I asked her, "Tell me who you
.are." She answered, "I am Enepsigos,ᵃ but I am called by countless names."
3 Then I said to her, "By what angel are you thwarted?" She responded to me,
"What are you after? What do you want? I can change my appearance, first being
4 taken for a goddess, and then becoming one who has some other shape. • In this
regard, do not expect to know all things about me, but because you are here in
my presence, listen to this: I hover near the moon and because of this I assume
5 three forms. •At times, I am conjured up as Kronosᵇ by the wise men. At other   Amos 5:26
times, I descend around those who bring me down and appear in another form.   2En 30:3
The capacity of the heavenly bodyᶜ is invincible, incalculable, and impossible to   8:2; 18:2,4
thwart. At any rate, changing into three different forms, I also descend and become
6 like what you see. •I am thwarted by the angel Rathanael,ᵈ who takes his seat in
the third heaven. On account of this, therefore, I say to you, this Temple cannot
contain me."

The demon Enepsigos, sealed with a triple-link chain, prophesies

7   Accordingly, when I, Solomon, had prayed to my God and invoked the angel
65)   Rathanael about whom he spoke, I made use of the seal and sealed her down with
8 a triple-link chain;ᵉ and as I bound her down, I made use of the seal of God. •Then
the (evil) spirit prophesied to me, saying, "You are doing these things to us now,
King Solomon, but after a period of time your kingdom shall be divided. At still   5:5; 15:12
a later time this Temple shall be destroyed and all Jerusalem shall be demolished   1Kgs 12
by the king(s) of the Persians and Medes and Chaldeans. Also, the implements of   2Kgs 25:8-17
                                                                                    Dan 8:20; 9:1
9 this Temple which you are making shall serve other gods. • Along with these
(events), also all the vessels in which you have entrapped us shall be broken in
pieces by the hands of men. Then we shall come forth with much power and we
10 shall be scattered here and there throughout the world. •We will lead astray all the
inhabited world for a long time until the Son of God is stretched upon the cross.ᶠ   12:3; 22:20
For there has not yet arisen a king like him, one who thwarts all of us, whose

---

c. Bazazath, not mentioned elsewhere in the
Pseudepigrapha.

15 a. McCown (*Testament*, p. 67) says she is probably Hecate, the moon goddess with three forms.
For Hecate in Judaism, see Goodenough, *Jewish
Symbols*, vol. 2, p. 236.
  b. The god Kronos, "Time," was identified with
the Roman god Saturn, and was the son of Uranos
and Gai, the husband of Rhea, and the father of
Zeus. His "time" was the "golden age." In Gk.
astrology, Kronos is found as a name for one of
the seven planets; cf. H. G. Gundel, *Weltbild und
Astrologie*, p. 42.
  c. Gk. *stoicheiou*; see TSol 8:2, n. a; 18:2, 4,

nn. d, f.
  d. Rathanael, not mentioned elsewhere in the
Pseudepigrapha.
  e. In the Talmud, Solomon gives Benaiahu "a
chain on which was graven the divine Name and
a ring on which was graven the Name . . ." to bind
Ashmedai; cf. Introduction and nn. (especially
b.Giṭṭ 68ab); TSol 1:13, n. p on binding demons.
  f. A clear allusion to the crucifixion of Jesus; cf.
Mk 15:39; TSol 12:3; 22:20; Origen (*Contra* 1.60,
in which, at the birth of Jesus, "The demons lost
their strength and became weak; their sorcery was
confuted and their power overthrown"). Thus, the
magi came to Judea because they were not able to
perform their usual feats by charms or trickery.

11 mother shall not have sexual intercourse with a man. •Who holds such authority over the spirits except that one? The one whom the first devil shall seek to tempt, but shall not be able to overcome, the letters of whose name add up to six hundred 12 forty-four—he is Emmanouel.[g] •Because of this, King Solomon, your time is evil, your years are short, and your kingdom shall be given to your servant."[h]

6:8; 11:6
Isa 7:14; 8:8
Mt 1:23
5:5; 15:8
1Kgs 12

Solomon explains why he wrote the testament

13 When I, Solomon, heard these things, I glorified God. Though I was amazed (66) at the defense of the demons, I distrusted them and did not believe the things 14 which were said by them until they occurred. •But when they happened, then I understood, and at my death I wrote this testament to the sons of Israel and I gave (it) to them so that (they) might know the powers of the demons and their forms, 15 as well as the names of the angels by which they are thwarted. •When I had glorified the God of Israel, I commanded the spirit to be bound up with unbreakable bonds.

26:8

Solomon interrogates Kunopegos, the cruel sea-horse demon

1 **16** When I had praised God, I commanded another spirit to appear before me. (67) There came before me another demon who had the form of a horse in front and a fish in back. He said in a great voice, "King Solomon, I am a cruel spirit of the sea. I rise up and come on the open seas with the sea and I trip up the greater 2 number of men (who sail) on it. •I raise myself up like a wave and, being transformed, I come in against the ships, for this is my activity: to receive beneath the sea treasures and men. For I raise myself up, take men, and hurl them under the sea. So I am always lusting after (their) bodies, but until now I have been 3 casting (the treasures) out of the sea. •However, since Beelzeboul, the ruler of the spirits of the air and the earth and beneath the earth gives advice about the activities with respect to each one of us, I therefore came up out of the sea to have some consultation with him.

Jude 13

2:9; 3:1f.,6

4 "But I also have another reputation and activity: I change myself into waves, (68) come up from the sea, and show myself to men. They call me Kunopegos[a] because I change myself into a man. The name is true to me. Moreover, I cause a type of 5 seasickness when I pass into men. •So when I came for a consultation with the ruler Beelzeboul, he bound me up and delivered me into your hands. Now I am standing before you and, because of not having water for two or three days, my spirit is ceasing from speaking to you."

The demon Kunopegos, thwarted by the angel Iameth, is sealed in a bowl and stored away in the Temple of God

6 So I said to him, "Tell me by what angel you are thwarted." He replied, "By (69) Iameth."[b] •Then I ordered him to be cast into a broad, flat bowl, and ten receptacles 7 of seawater to be poured over (it). I fortified the top side all around with marble and I unfolded and spread asphalt, pitch, and hemp rope around over the mouth of the vessel. When I had sealed it with the ring, I ordered (it) to be stored away in the Temple of God.[c]

---

g. See TSol 6:8, n. i and TSol 11:6, nn. f, g.

h. Conybeare (*JQR* 11 [1898] 32, n. 6): "This prophecy corresponds roughly to the one which Lactantius (*DivInst* 4.18) quotes from an apocryphal *Book of Solomon.*" McCown (*Testament*, p. 104) is correct to doubt the reference.

16 a. Gk. *kunopēgos.* The term for "wave" is *to kuma*; *pēgazō* means "I flow abundantly," "I well up," frequently with reference to the source of water. MS P has *Kuno[s]paston.* Conybeare (*JQR*

11 [1898] 33, n. 4) attempts an explanation with references to Pliny (*Natural History*, 24.74) which might be translated: "Cynosbaton, otherwise called Cynospaston, or neurospaston; its leaf is similar to the footstep of a man. The plant is wild and has black berries in whose center is a string; therefore it is called 'nervefood' [*neurospastos*]." McCown (*Testament*, p. 67) identifies him with Poseidon.

b. Iameth, presumably a compound from Yah-, or *iaomai*, "I heal."

c. See the discussion in the Introduction.

Solomon interrogates a lecherous spirit and learns of his activity and that he will be thwarted by the Savior or by the Savior's mark on the forehead

1 **17** I ordered another spirit to appear before me. There came a spirit having the
(70) shadowy form of a man and gleaming eyes. I asked him, saying, "Who are you?"
He replied, "I am a lecherous[a] spirit of a giant man who died in a massacre in the
2 age of giants."[b] • So I said to him, "Tell me what you accomplish on earth and
where you make your dwelling."
(71) He replied, "My home is in inaccessible places. My activity is this: I seat myself
near dead men in the tombs and at midnight I assume the form of the dead; if I
3 seize anyone, I immediately kill him with the sword. • If I should not be able to
kill him, I cause him to be possessed by a demon and to gnaw his own flesh to
4 pieces and the saliva of his jowls to flow down." • So I said to him, "Fear the God
of heaven and earth and tell me by what angel you are thwarted." He replied,
"He who is about to return (as) Savior thwarts me. If his mark is written on (one's)
forehead, it thwarts me, and because I am afraid of it, I quickly turn and flee from
5 him. This is the sign of the cross." • When I heard these things, I, Solomon, locked
up the demon just like the other demons.

Gen 6:4
3Mac 2:4
Jdt 16:7
WisSol 14:6
1Bar 3:26
Jub 5:1; 7:22
1En 7:2,4; 9:9;
10:12; 15:8,11;
16:1
Tob 6:14

Lk 2:11
Acts 13:23
Phil 3:20
Rev 9:14;
13:16,17; 14:1

Solomon interrogates the thirty-six heavenly bodies and learns of their activities and what thwarts them

1 **18** Then I commanded another demon to appear before me. There came to me
(72) thirty-six heavenly bodies,[a] their heads like formless dogs.[b] But there were among
them (those who were) in the form of humans, or of bulls, or of dragons, with
2 faces like the birds, or the beasts, or the sphinx.[c] • When I, Solomon, saw these
beings, I asked them, saying, "Well, who are you?" All at once, with one voice,
they said, "We are thirty-six heavenly bodies, the world rulers[d] of the darkness
3 of this age. • But you, King, are not able to harm us or to lock us up; but since
God gave you authority over all the spirits of the air, the earth, and (the regions)
beneath the earth, we have also taken our place before you like the other spirits."
4 Then I, Solomon, summoned[e] the first spirit and said to him, "Who are you?"
(73)

8:2; 15:5
Gal 4:3,9
Col 2:8,20
Eph 6:12

---

17 a. Gk. *ocheikon*, uncertain; perhaps read *och-
eion*, used of stallions kept for breeding, e.g.
"lewd," or "lecherous." MS P has *ochikon*(?).

b. On the battle of the giants, cf. especially 1En
10:12; TSol 6:1, n. b.

18 a. Gk. *stoicheia*; cf. TSol 8:2, n. a; 15:5; 18:2.
TSol 18 is the most discussed passage in the testament; cf. the Introduction. Consult especially W.
Gundel, *Dekane und Dekansternbilder* (Glückstadt,
1936) pp. 1–21, 37–81; H. G. Gundel, *Weltbild
und Astrologie*, pp. 17–24. W. Gundel (p. 45) says
the archetype for TSol 18 is 1st cent. B.C. and (p.
49) notes that in TSol 18 the traditional names of
the decans are consciously distorted and relegated
from deities to secondary evil demons (cf. Origen,
Contra 8.58; TSol 18:4, n. f) and that new names
and beings are present which dominate the others.
Both authors give helpful charts of the names of
the decans and include TSol. The discussions of the
names of the decans will be based largely on Gundel.

b. Gk. *kunes*, perhaps "watchdogs," that is,
watchers of the gods; cf. TSol 10:1, n. a.

c. Lit. "human-shaped, bull-shaped, beast-
faced, dragon-shaped, Sphinx-faced, bird-faced."
Gk. *hē sphinx*, a "she-monster."

d. Gk. *stoicheia*; cf. TSol 8:2, n. a; 15:5; 18:1,
n. a; 18:4, n. f. Gk. *hoi kosmokratores tou skotous
tou aiōnos toutou*; cf. TSol 8:2, n. b.

e. MS P reads, "Then I, Solomon, invoked the
name of the Lord Sabaoth, and I asked each one
what his manner of life happened (to be) and I
commanded each of them to come forward and
tell about his activity. Then the first came and
said . . ."

5 He replied, "I am the first decan of the zodiac[f] (and) I am called Ruax.[g] •I cause heads of men to suffer pain and I cause their temples to throb. Should I hear only, 'Michael,[h] imprison Ruax,' I retreat immediately."

6 The second said, "I am called Barsafael. I cause men who reside in my time
(74) period to have pains on the sides of their heads. Should I hear, 'Gabriel,[i] imprison Barsafael,' I retreat immediately."

7 The third said, "I am called Artosael.[j] I do much damage to the eyes. Should
(75) I hear, 'Ouriel,[k] imprison Artosael,' I retreat immediately."

8 The fourth[l] said, "I am called Oropel.[m] I attack throats, (resulting in) sore throats and mucus. Should I hear, 'Raphael,[n] imprison Oropel,' I retreat immediately."

9 The fifth said, "I am called Kairoxanondalon.[o] I cause ears to have obstructions.
(76) If I should hear, 'Ourouel,[p] imprison Kairoxanondalon,' I retreat immediately."

10 The sixth said, "I am called Sphendonael.[q] I produce tumors of the parotid
(77) gland and tetanic recurvation.[r] If I hear, 'Sabael, imprison Sphendonael,' I retreat immediately."

11 The seventh said, "I am called Sphandor.[s] I weaken the strength of the shoulders
(78) and deaden the nerves of the hand, and I make limbs paralyzed. If I hear, 'Arael,[t] imprison Sphandor,' I retreat immediately."

12 The eighth said, "I am called Belbel. I pervert the hearts and minds of men
(79) [. . .] If I hear, 'Karael, imprison Belbel,' I retreat immediately."

13 The ninth said, "I am called Kourtael.[u] I send forth colics into the bowels. If
(80)

Marginal references:

1:6
Dan 10:13,20f.;
12:1

Dan 8:16; 9:21
Lk 1:19
ApMos 40:1
1En 9:1; 10:1;
20:7; 40:9; 54:6
2En 21:3,5; 24:1
2:4,7f.; 8:9;
18:27
1En 9:1; 10:1;
20:1
Tob 3:17; 5:4;
6:10f.; 9:5;
12:15
1En 9:1; 10:4;
20:3; 22:3f.;
32:6; 40:9; 54:6;
68:2f.; 71:8f.

---

f. This statement explains the *stoicheia* in TSol 18:1. The decans were thirty-six deities, each of whom ruled over 10° of the 360° zodiac. Cf. TSol 18:1, n. a. Origen (*Contra* 8.58) wrote that "among these demons, even down to the least ones, there exists some one or another to whom authority (*exousia*) has been given, may be learned by any one from what the Egyptians say, namely, that thirty-six demons, or ethereal gods of a kind, have distributed among themselves man's body, which is apportioned into a corresponding number of parts. Some say the number of these demons is much greater. One demon then is appointed to take care of one part and another of another. Of these demons they know the names in the local speech (i.e. Coptic), as, for example, Khnoumên, and Khnakoumen, and Knat, and Sikat, and Bion, and Eron, and Erebion, and Ramanor, and Reianoor, and the rest of the names used in their tongue. And, of course, by invoking these demons, they cure the sufferings of the several parts" (Conybeare, *JQR* 11 [1898] 7). Whereas Celsus stated that propitiation of these demons was necessary for health, Origen replied from Phil 2:10 that all are subject to Jesus and that Christians need only trust in the living God. For the *stoicheia* as the seven demonic stars, see TSol 8:2, n. a, where it is noted that Origen (*Contra* 6.30) also speaks of the Seven Ruling Demons.

g. Perhaps Rhyx; cf. TSol 18:24–35. The first decan is most important; the name may mean "the Lord" (Gundel, *Dekane*, pp. 50f.) and be related to *rex*, "ruler," "king," "prince." It corresponds to Sro, the ram, in Manilius' list of decans.

h. On Michael, cf. Introduction; TSol 1:6f. and n. q; NHC II, 1:17,30.

i. On Gabriel, cf. Introduction; NHC III, 2:52, 23;53,6;57,[7];64,26; VIII,1:57,9;58,22.

j. Gundel (*Dekane*, p. 50) suggests the root *artos*, "a loaf (of wheat bread)."

k. On Uriel, see G. Vermes, "The Archangel

Sariel," in *Christianity, Judaism and Other Greco-Roman Cults. Studies for Morton Smith at Sixty*, ed. J. Neusner (Studies in Judaism in Late Antiquity 12.3; (Leiden, 1975). Uriel is also common in gnostic texts; cf. NHC Index in *The Nag Hammadi Library in English* (Oroiael, Oriel, Oroiel, Ariael, Ouriel).

l. MS P has a lacuna at this point; thus Conybeare's paragraph numbers skip TSol 18:8; i.e. 18:7 is (75) and 18:9 is (76).

m. Perhaps the Egyptian god Horus, or (suggests Gundel [*Dekane*, p. 50]) "press" from *oros* in analogy with the twenty-third Egyptian decan Sesme.

n. On Raphael, cf. Introduction; TSol 5:9; 13:6.

o. Gundel (*Dekane*, p. 51) suggests the name is built up out of *kairoō*, "I fit the right point in time," *xainō*, "to comb (wool), to make it fit for spinning," and *dalos*, "torch," and could be analogous to the decan Lampadias, the "torch carrier."

p. Ourouel: a variation of Uriel? Cf. TSol 18:7, n. k above.

q. Gundel (*Dekane*, p. 50) suggests the root *sphendonē*, "a sling," or anything shaped like it, in this case the arrow of the protector, or the ax.

r. Conybeare (*JQR* 11 [1898] 35, n. 5): "The Greek medical terms which stand in the Greek text are found in Hippocrates, Galen, and Cael. Aurel." Gk. *opisthotonous*, "tetanic recurvation," is a disease in which the body draws back and stiffens.

s. Gundel (*Dekane*, p. 50) suggests that *doron* or *phandoron* could indicate "the Lightgiver," that is, Lampadias again; cf. TSol 18:9, n. o.

t. Another variation of Uriel? Cf. TSol 18:7, n. k; Gundel (*Dekane*, p. 61) suggests a variation of the decan Arou, e.g. Ouare.

u. Gundel (*Dekane*, p. 51) suggests the roots *kouros*, "youthful," or *kourizō*, "cut," and perhaps either a eunuch or a deity who cuts himself.

I should hear, 'Iaoth,[v] imprison Kourtael,' I retreat immediately.''

14
(81) The tenth said, ''I am called Metathiax.[w] I cause pains in the kidneys. If I hear, 'Adonael, imprison Metathiax,' I retreat immediately.''

15
(82) The eleventh said, ''I am called Katanikotael.[x] I unleash fights and feuds in homes. If anyone wishes to make peace, let him write on seven laurel leaves the names of those who thwart me: 'Angel, Eae, Ieo, Sabaoth,[y] imprison Katanikotael,' and when he has soaked the laurel leaves (in water), let him sprinkle his house with the water and I retreat immediately.''

16
(83) The twelfth said, ''I am called Saphthorael.[z] I put dissensions into the minds of men and I delight when I cause them to stumble. If anyone writes down these words, 'Iae, Ieo, sons of Sabaoth,'[a2] and wears them around his neck, I retreat immediately.''

17
(84) The thirteenth said, ''I am called Phobothel.[b2] I cause loosenings of the tendons. If I hear, 'Adonai,'[c2] I retreat immediately.''

18
(85) The fourteenth said, ''I am called Leroel.[d2] I bring on chill(s) and shivering and sore throat. If I hear, 'Iax, do not stand fast, do not be fervent, because Solomon is fairer than eleven fathers,'[e2] I retreat immediately.''

19
(86) The fifteenth said, ''I am called Soubelti. I unleash shivering and numbness. If I hear only, 'Rizoel, imprison Soubelti,' I retreat immediately.''

20
(87) The sixteenth said, ''I am called Katrax.[f2] I inflict incurable fevers on men. If anyone wants to regain health, let him pulverize coriander[g2] and rub it on his lips, saying, 'I adjure you by Zeus,[h2] retreat from the image of God,' and I retreat immediately.''

21
(88) The seventeenth said, ''I am called Ieropa.[i2] I sit on the stomach of a man and cause convulsions[j2] in the bath; and on the street I find the man and make (him) fall to the ground.[k2] Whoever says into the right ear of the afflicted for the third time, 'Iouda Zizabou,'[l2] you see, makes me retreat.''

---

v. Gundel (*Dekane*, pp. 60f.) notes that the angels called upon in TSol 18:9–14 have Jewish-sounding names found in gnostic texts and magical papyri, i.e. Iaoth; Adonael; Angel, Eae, Ieo, Sabaoth; Iae, Ieo, sons of Sabaoth; Adonai; and Iax. [See the contribution on PrJac contained herein. —J.H.C.]

w. Gundel (*Dekane*, p. 51) suggests Metathiax goes back to Thiax, a variant of Satyros, that is, Apollo.

x. Gundel (*Dekane*, p. 52) suggests (cautiously) the goddess Satis, or the decan-goddess Krebses.

y. In addition to gnostic materials and magical papyri, amulets contain such names, e.g. Goodenough, *Jewish Symbols*, p. 229: ''Iaō, Sabaō, Michaēl, Gabriēl, Ouriēl, Cheroubin, Serapi[n].'' This amulet also contains the cavalier, e.g. Solomon.

z. Gundel (*Dekane*, p. 52) thinks it likely that the name is built out of *sapha*, ''clearly,'' and *thoraios*, another name for Apollo, i.e. ''the one who is fit for the seed, the one who qualified for procreating.'' He relates him to the Egyptian New Year.

a2. In NHC II, 5:*106*, Sabaoth begets Death, who begets seven androgynous sons who beget forty-nine androgynous demons; in *107* the text states, ''Their names and their functions you will find in 'the Book of Solomon.' '' Cf. Introduction. Sabaoth occurs frequently in the Nag Hammadi texts.

b2. Gundel (*Dekane*, p. 52) suggests a personification of *phobos*, ''fear,'' who may be related to the old decan Knuphis, who is called to protect against evil powers.

c2. Adonai, ''my Lord,'' from the Heb. Bible, is common to gnosticism and magic; Gundel (*Dekane*, p. 60) thinks he is placed here to show his power over the gods of the Egyptian pantheon.

d2. Gundel (*Dekane*, p. 52) guesses the name might refer to a windbag, buffoon, gossip, or also to ornaments and jewelry.

e2. Gk. *hoti kallion esti Solomōn hendeka paterōn*, ''because Solomon is fairer than eleven fathers.'' Gk. *kallion*, ''fairer,'' could mean ''more powerful.'' Gk. *paterōn*, ''fathers,'' might refer to demons, so Lampe, p. 1051; cf. TSol 22:20, n. a (MS P). For the view that the eleven fathers are gnostic, see McCown (*Testament*, p. 82).

f2. Gundel (*Dekane*, p. 52) suggests this decan might mean either a peacock or a cat.

g2. Gk. *to koliandron*, ''coriander,'' either of two plants in the parsley family, one of whose aromatic seeds is used to flavor pastries. The magical use is found in Pliny, *Natural History* 20:20.

h2. The Gk. is *tou Dan*, which, according to Gundel (*Dekane*, pp. 58–59), could be a local name related to the seaport Dan on the Red Sea.

i2. Gundel (*Dekane*, p. 52) suggests one is reminded of Isis, Dike, and Musa.

j2. Reading *spasmous* (MS L) instead of *aspasmous*, ''embraces'' (MS H), see n. k2.

k2. Gk. *ptōmatizō*, ''I make to fall''; *hoi ptōmatizomenoi* in Gk. can refer to ''those who have the falling sickness,'' e.g. epilepsy.

l2. McCown (*Testament*, p. 71) says the words may have a gnostic origin.

22
(89) The eighteenth said, "I am called Modebel.[m2] I separate wife from husband. If anyone writes the names of the eight fathers[n2] and places them in the doorways,[o2] I retreat immediately."

23
(90) The nineteenth said, "I am called Mardero.[p2] I inflict incurable fevers; write my name in some such way in the house, and I retreat immediately."

24
(91) The twentieth said, "I am called Rhyx Nathotho.[q2] I locate myself in the knees of men. If anyone writes on a piece of papyrus, 'Phounebiel,'[r2] I retreat immediately."

25
(92) The twenty-first said, "I am called Rhyx Alath.[s2] I produce the croup in infants. If anyone writes, 'Rarideris,'[t2] and carries it,[u2] I retreat immediately."

26 The twenty-second said, "I am called Rhyx Audameoth.[v2] I inflict heart pain. If anyone writes, 'Raiouoth,'[w2] I retreat immediately."

27
(93) The twenty-third said, "I am called Rhyx Manthado. I cause the kidneys to suffer pain. If anyone writes, 'Iaoth, Ouriel,'[x2] I retreat immediately."

(right margin) 2:4,7f.; 8:9; 18:7 1En 9:1; 10:1f.;

28
(94) The twenty-fourth said, "I am called Rhyx Aktonme. I cause the ribs to suffer pain. If anyone writes on a piece of wood from a ship which has run aground,[y2] 'Marmaraoth of mist,'[z2] I retreat immediately."

(right margin) 20:1 8:7; 18:33

29
(95) The twenty-fifth said, "I am called Rhyx Anatreth.[a3] I send gas[b3] and burning up into the bowels. If I hear, 'Arara, Arare,'[c3] I retreat immediately."

30
(96) The twenty-sixth said, "I am called Rhyx, the Enautha.[d3] I make off with minds and alter hearts. If anyone writes, 'Kalazael,' I retreat immediately."

31
(97) The twenty-seventh said, "I am called Rhyx Axesbuth.[e3] I cause men to suffer from diarrhea[f3] and hemorrhoids. If anyone adjures me in pure wine and gives it to the one who is suffering, I retreat immediately."

---

m2. Gundel (*Dekane*, p. 52) says the term might refer to either "water lily" or "rug." A woman with a water lily is known from later decan literature.

n2. Gundel (*Dekane*, p. 58) associates the "eight fathers" with the Egyptian deities of the Ogdoas, the archetypal "Eight." As the original Father and Mother, they are the foundation of everything through their power.

o2. In white magic, protection of openings of dwellings where demons might enter is necessary; cf. W. K. Prentice, "Magical Formulae on Lintels of the Christian Period in Syria," *American Journal of Archeology* 10 (1906) 137–50; Montgomery, *Aramaic Incantation Texts*, pp. 40–45.

p2. Mardero, suggests Gundel (*Dekane*, p. 53) combined a rare word for "hand," *marē*, and *derō*, "to skin," "to flay," with reference to the hand of the virgin.

q2. On Rhyx, see TSol 18:4, n. g. Nathotho, according to Gundel (*Dekane*, p. 53) could be the moon-god Thoth, found in old Egyptian decan lists; it could also be a combination of *naos*, "temple," and *thōs*, "cow," "jackal."

r2. Gundel (*Dekane*, p. 59) suggests that Phounebiel is based on the deity Phtah-Nun, the father of Atum.

s2. Alath, says Gundel (*Dekane*, p. 53), might be a name for the wargod Mars, and would therefore be related to the Egyptian wargod Horus.

t2. Rarideris, writes Gundel (*Dekane*, p. 58), might reflect the Egyptian goddess Thueris, who appears as a hippopotamus or a pig among the decans.

u2. Gk. *bastazei*, "carries" (on one's person) or perhaps "touches" (the infant).

v2. Gundel (*Dekane*, p. 53) states that the Heb. author substituted a Syrian sun-god Aumos. MS P has a lacuna which skips TSol 18:26. There is no (92) margin.

w2. Gundel (*Dekane*, p. 58): it is from *rhēouō*, meaning "The One in the Sun Barque," i.e. Re.

x2. Cf. TSol 18:7, n. k.

y2. Gk. *astochēsantos*, "which has failed (to make harbor)"; Lampe, p. 247, suggests "which has been lost."

z2. Gk. *aeriou*, "of air," is possible. A. Audollent (*Defixionum Tabellae* [Frankfurt, 1904; repr. 1967] p. 328) suggests Marmaroth means "Lord of lords" (Aram. *mar* means "lord"). Gundel (*Dekane*, p. 59) suggests a derivation from *marmairō*, "to flash," "to sparkle," "to glisten," and *aoth*, or *Jaoth*, for Yahweh. This would then be "the glittering, shining God," recalling the Gk. names of the planets Phaethon and Phainon. Cf. TSol 8:7 in which Marmaroth (note spelling) thwarts Fate, who encourages war, leading Gundel to make the association with Mars. Cf. TSol 18:33.

a3. Gundel (*Dekane*, p. 53) suggests a connection of Anatreth with the sun-god Re (Ret, Rat, Srat) or with the Gk. word *anatrētos*, suggesting "boring through," since an old Egyptian decan is called "The One Who Bores Through."

b3. Gk. *zeseis*, "seethings," "effervescences," "boilings."

c3. Arara, Arare, is mentioned in the Gk. Magical Papyri (19a.48); Gundel (*Dekane*, p. 58) thinks it is a variation of the decan Aroi Aroi.

d3. Gundel (*Dekane*, p. 54) suggests Enautha contains either the goddess of the heaven, Nut, or the Gk. verb *enauō* with the meaning "to start a fire," having to do with ancient Gk. and Egyptian notions of fire.

e3. For Axesbuth, Gundel (*Dekane*, p. 54) proposes a derivation from *axetos*, "unpolished," "coarse," and *bythos*, "(the) deep," suggesting the Indic decan associated with a snake.

f3. Gk. *hypektikous*, meaning uncertain. Perhaps *hypaktikos*, "suffering from diarrhea," or *hyphektikos*, "consumptive," cf. Lampe, p. 1436.

32 The twenty-eighth said, "I am called Rhyx Hapax.[g3] I unleash insomnia. If
(98) anyone writes, 'Kok; Phedismos,' and wears it down from the temples, I retreat immediately."

33 The twenty-ninth said, "I am called Rhyx Anoster.[h3] I unleash hysteria and
(99) cause pains in the bladder. If anyone mashes up the seeds of laurel into pure oil   8:7; 18:28
and massages (the body with it), saying, 'I adjure you by Marmaraoth,'[i3] I retreat immediately."

34 The thirtieth said, "I am called Rhyx Physikoreth. I bring on long-term illnesses.
(100) If anyone puts salt into (olive) oil and massages his sickly (body with it) saying,   21:2
'Cherubim, seraphim,[j3] help (me),' I retreat immediately."   Ex 25:18-20
                                                                                     1Kgs 6:23-28

35 The thirty-first said, "I am called Rhyx Aleureth.[k3] (In the case of) swallowing   Ps 18
(101) fish bones, if anyone puts a bone from his fish into the breasts of the one who is   Isa 6:2f.
suffering, I retreat immediately."

36 The thirty-second said, "I am called Rhyx Ichthuon.[l3] I detach tendons. If I
(102) hear, 'Adonai,[m3] malthē,' I retreat immediately."

37 The thirty-third said, "I am called Rhyx Achoneōth.[n3] I cause sore throat and
(103) tonsillitis. If anyone writes on ivy leaves, 'Leikourgos,' heaping them up in a
pile,[o3] I retreat immediately."

38 The thirty-fourth said, "I am called Rhyx Autoth. I cause jealousies and squabbles
(104) between those who love each other. But the letters Alpha and Beta, written down,
thwart me."

39 The thirty-fifth said, "I am called Rhyx Phtheneoth.[p3] I cast the evil eye on
(105) every man. But the much-suffering eye,[q3] when inscribed, thwarts me."

40 The thirty-sixth said, "And I am called Rhyx Mianeth. I hold a grudge against
(106) the body; I demolish houses; I cause the flesh to rot. If anyone writes on the front
entrance of his house as follows, 'Melto Ardad Anaath,'[r3] I flee from that place."

41 When I, Solomon, heard these things, I glorified the God of heaven and earth
(107)
42 and I ordered them to bear water. •Then I prayed to God that the thirty-six demons
who continually plague humanity go to the Temple of God.[s3]

---

g3. Hapax, according to Gundel (*Dekane*, p. 54), might be associated with the Gk. word *hapax*, "one time," perhaps containing number symbolism; the variant Harpax refers to a decan with long, sharp teeth.

h3. Gundel (*Dekane*, p. 55) suggests Anoster could contain the word *nostos*, "a return home," and could refer to an evil demon who prevents one from returning home.

i3. On Marmaraoth, cf. TSol 18:28; TSol 8:7 (Marmaroth).

j3. For cherubim and seraphim on a protective amulet, see above, TSol 18:15, n. y; cf. also NHC II,5:*105*,19; VII, 2:*54*,34; IX, 1:*10*,4.

k3. Gundel (*Dekane*, p. 55) thinks, cautiously, that Aleureth could be related to *aleuron*, "wheat flour," and thus the Egyptian name for the wine press; it could also have to do with the decan of trouble and tribulation.

l3. Was Ichthuon suggested by *ichthuos*, "fish," in the previous vs. (TSol 18:35)?

m3. On Adonai, see TSol 18:17, n. c2.

n3. Gundel (*Dekane*, p. 55) attempts an explanation of Achoneōth in relation to the Egyptian decans Chont-har and Chont-chre (rams), modified by the Gk. Anchonion, suggestive of hangman or strangler, yielding a throat god or a strangler god; note that he causes sore throat and tonsillitis.

o3. Gk. *botrydon anachōris* is not clear. Gk. *botrydon* means "in clusters," or "like a bunch of grapes." Gk. *anachōris* is obscure; perhaps it was originally *anachōsis*, "raising an embankment."

p3. In Phtheneoth, Gundel (*Dekane*, p. 55) sees Phtha, the Egyptian god of the art of forging metals.

q3. On the "much suffering eye," usually thought to be a protection against the "evil eye," cf. C. Bonner, *Studies in Magical Amulets Chiefly Graeco-Egyptian* (Ann Arbor, 1950) pp. 96–100; Goodenough, *Jewish Symbols*, vol. 2, pp. 238–41. Both Solomon and the "seal of Solomon" are found on "much suffering eye" amulets; the "much suffering eye," if Bonner is correct in his interpretation, based partly on this vs., is found on the synagogue at Dura; cf. Goodenough, vol. 2, p. 238, and figs. 1065, 1066.

r3. Gundel (*Dekane*, p. 58) says Ar-ta, an Egyptian creator god, is hidden in Ardad; in Anaath is Neith, an Egyptian crocodile god.

s3. MS P reads at this point, "I condemned some of the demons to do the heavy work of the construction of the Temple of God. Some I locked up in prisons. Others I ordered to battle the fire in (the production of) gold and silver, and to sit down beside lead and cinerary urns, and for the rest of the demons to prepare places in which they ought to be locked up.

"And I, Solomon, had much quiet in all the earth, and spent my life in much peace, honored by all men and those under heaven. I built the whole Temple of God. My kingdom was prosperous and my army was with me. As for the rest, the city of Jerusalem was a repose, rejoicing and delighted. And all the kings of the earth came to me from the other side of the earth to see the Temple which I built for the Lord God. When they heard about the

Riches are given to Solomon by all the kings of the earth, including Sheeba, the Queen of the South, who was a witch

(108) **19** Then I, Solomon, was honored by all men under heaven, for I was building
2 the Temple of God and my kingdom was running well. •All the kings were coming
to me to observe the Temple of God that I was building, and they supplied me with 1Kgs 5; 10:1-10
gold and silver, and brought in bronze, iron, lead, and wood for the Temple 2Chr 9:1-10
furnishings.
3   Among them Sheeba, Queen of the South, who was a witch, came with much 21:1f.
(109) arrogance and bowed down before me.[a]   1Kgs 10:1-13
                                                                                  2Chr 9:1-12
                                                                                  Mt 12:42
                                                                                  Lk 11:31

Solomon hears the conflict between an old man and his son

(110) **20** Now it happened that one of the artisans, a dignified man, threw himself down 1:7
before me, saying, "King Solomon, Son of David, have mercy on me,[a] an elderly PssSol 17:23
2 man." I said to him, "Tell me, old man, what you want." •He replied, "I beg Mk 10:47f.;
you, King. I have a son, my only son, and every day he does terribly violent 12:23; 15:22;
things to me, striking me in the face and head and threatening to send me to a 20:20,31;
terrible death. Because he did this, I came forward (to request) a favor—that you 21:9,15
will avenge me."
(111) 3   When I heard these things I commanded his son to be brought before me. When
4 he came I said to him, "Do you admit to this?" •He replied, "I did not become
so filled with rage, King, that I struck my father with my hand. Be kind to me,
O King; for it is not right to pay attention to such a story and (to his) distress."
5 Therefore, when I, Solomon, heard the young man, I summoned the elderly man
to come and reconsider. But he did not want (to come) and said, "Let him be put
to death."

The demon Ornias prophesies that the son will die

6   Then, noticing that the demon Ornias was laughing, I became very angry that 1:12-3:4; 9:3;
he would laugh in my presence. Dismissing the young man, I ordered Ornias to 20:11
7 come out and I said to him, "Cursed one, did you laugh at me?" •He replied, LetAris 47
"I beg you, King; I did not laugh because of you, but because of the wretched
old man and the miserable young man, his son, because after three days he will
die. See, the old man has the intent of doing away with him in an evil manner."
(112) 8   I said, "Does he really have such an intent?" The demon said, "Yes, King."
9 Then I commanded the demon to go away and the old man and his son to come
10 back, and I ordered them to become friends.[b] •Then I said to the elderly man,
"In three days bring your son back to me." When they had prostrated themselves
before me, they departed.

---

wisdom which was given to me they bowed down before me in the Temple. [They brought] gold and silver and precious stones many and excellent, and bronze, and iron, and lead, and cedar logs. And they brought me types of wood that do not deteriorate for the furnishings of the Temple of God." This statement could have concluded one version of the TSol.

19 a. The introduction of the Queen of Sheeba at this point seems strange; moreover, her admiration for the Temple in TSol 21 is unrelated to the story of the old man. MS P appears to make the connection in TSol 21 by means of Solomon's wisdom, e.g. by including her amazement at the story. At this point in TSol 19, MS P adds, "bowed down

before me to the earth, and because she had heard of my wisdom, she glorified the God of Israel; in these things also she tested all of my wisdom by examination, so much did I instruct her according to the wisdom given to me. And all the sons of Israel glorified God." In TSol 21, MSS H P Q continue after the story of the old man, "Sheeba, the Queen of the South, saw all these things and marveled . . ."

20 a. Gk. *huios Daveid, eleēson me*, "Son of David, have mercy on me," recalls the cry of Barimaeus in Mk 10:47 and 28. See TSol Title, n. d.

b. MS Q, which has TSol 3:1–20:9 missing, resumes at this point.

Ornias is compelled to explain how he knows God's plan for the future

11
13) Then I ordered Ornias to be brought to me again and I said to him, "Tell me
12 how you know that the young man will die in three days." •He responded, "We
demons go up to the firmament of heaven, fly around among the stars, and hear
13 the decisions which issue from God concerning the lives of men.[c] •The rest of the
time we come and, being transformed, cause destruction, whether by domination,
or by fire, or by sword, or by chance."
14
14) I asked him, "Tell me, then, how you, being demons, are able to ascend into
15 heaven." •He replied, "Whatever things are accomplished in heaven (are accomplished) in the same way also on earth; for the principalities and authorities and
16 powers above fly around and are considered worthy of entering heaven. •But we
who are demons are exhausted from not having a way station from which to ascend
or on which to rest; so we fall down like leaves from the trees and the men who
17 are watching think that stars are falling from heaven. •That is not true, King; rather,
we fall because of our weakness and, since there is nothing on which to hold, we
are dropped like flashes of lightning to the earth. We burn cities down and set
fields on fire. But the stars of heaven have their foundations laid in the firmament."

Margin refs: 1:1-3:4; 9:3; 20:6 LetAris 47

The prophecy of Ornias the demon is fulfilled

18
115)
19 When I, Solomon, heard these things, I commanded the demon to be kept under
guard for five days. •After five days I summoned the old man but he did not want
to come. Then when he did come, I saw that he was depressed and mourning.
20 I said to him, "Where is your son, old man?" He replied, "I have become
21 childless, O King, and without hope I keep watch at the grave of my son." •Upon
hearing these things and knowing that the things which were spoken to me by the
demon were true, I glorified the God of heaven and earth.

Sheeba, the Queen of the South, tours the Temple

1
16) **21** Now when Sheeba, the Queen of the South, saw the Temple[a] I was building,
she thought it was marvelous and contributed ten thousand copper shekels.
2 She entered the inner part of the Temple and saw the altar, the cherubim
and seraphim overshadowing the mercy seat, the two hundred gems glittering from
the various ornaments of the lamps, and lamps also decorated with emeralds,
3 hyacinth,[b] and lapis lazuli. •She also saw the silver, bronze, and gold vessels and
the bases of the pillars entwined with bronze wrought in the pattern of a chain.
4 Finally, she saw the Bronze Sea, which was supported by thirty-six bulls. •And
all were busy working in the Temple [. . .][c] of pay amounting to one gold talent
apart from the demons.

Margin refs: 19:3 1Kgs 10:1-10 2Chr 9:1-10 Mt 12:42 Lk 11:31 18:34 1Kgs 7:48-50 1Kgs 7:23f. 2Chr 4:2 2Kgs 25:13 1Chr 18:8 Jer 52:17

A letter from Adarkes, king of Arabia, requesting Solomon's help against the wind demon

1
17) **22** The king of Arabia, Adarkes, sent a letter containing the following:
"King of Arabia, Adarkes, to King Solomon, greetings. I have heard about the
wisdom which has been granted to you and that, being a man from the Lord, there
has been given to you understanding about all the spirits of the air, the earth, and
2 beneath the earth. •There still exists a spirit in Arabia. Early in the morning a fresh
gust of wind blows until the third hour. Its terrible blast even kills man and beast
3 and no (counter-) blast is ever able to withstand the demon. •I beg you, therefore,

Margin refs: 3:5; 4:11; 8:11; 24:3 1Kgs 4:29-34 Prov 1:1 Song 1:1 Eccl 1:1 WisSol 7-9 LAB 60

c. For flying demons who know the future, see b.Hag 16a. Also, the *Aboth* of R. Nathan notes how demons change appearances; see McCown (*Testament*, pp. 62f.).

21 a. See TSol 19:3, n. a.

b. Gk. *hyakinthou tōn lithōn*, "hyacinth of stones," a violet-blue mineral resembling a sapphire.

c. A lacuna. Did the non-demonic workers get paid one talent?

since this spirit is like a wind, do something wise according to the wisdom which 7:2
has been given to you by the Lord your God and decide to send out a man who Jub 2:2
4 is able to bring it under control. •Then we shall belong to you, King Solomon, I 1En 60:12
and all my people and all my land; and all Arabia will be at peace if you carry out
5 this act of vengeance for us. •Consequently, we implore you, do not ignore our
prayer and do become our lord for all time. Farewell my lord, as ever.''

The immovable cornerstone

6 After I, Solomon, read this letter, I folded it, gave it to my servant, and said
(118)
7 to him, "After seven days, remind me of this letter." •So Jerusalem was being 23:2-4
built and the Temple was moving toward completion. Now there was a gigantic
cornerstone which I wished to place at the head of the corner to complete the Ps 118:22
8 Temple of God. •All the artisans and all the demons who were helping came to Isa 28:16
the same (location) to bring the stone and mount it at the end of the Temple, but Mk 12:10
they were not strong enough to budge it. Mt 21:42
　　　　　　　　　　　　　　　　　　　　　　　　　　　　　　　　Lk 20:17f.
　　　　　　　　　　　　　　　　　　　　　　　　　　　　　　　　Acts 4:11
　　　　　　　　　　　　　　　　　　　　　　　　　　　　　　　　1Pet 2:6-8

Solomon's servant boy entraps the Arabian wind demon in a leather flask with the aid of the ring

9 When seven days had passed and I remembered the letter of the king of Arabia,
(119)
I summoned my servant boy and said to him, "Load up your camel, take a leather
10 flask and this seal, •and go off to Arabia to the place where the spirit is blowing.
Then take hold of the wineskin and (place) the ring in front of the neck of the flask
11 (against the wind). •As the flask is being filled with air, you will discover that it
is the demon who is filling it up. Carefully, then, tie up the flask tightly and when
you have sealed (it) with the ring, load up the camel and come back here. Be off,
now, with blessings.''
12 Then the boy obeyed the orders and went to Arabia. Now the men from the
(120)
region doubted whether it was possible to bring the evil spirit under control.
13 Nonetheless, before dawn the house servant got up and confronted the spirit of the
wind. He put the flask on the ground and placed the ring on (its mouth). (The
14 demon) entered the flask and inflated it. •Yet the boy stood firm. He bound up the
mouth of the flask in the name of the Lord Sabaoth and the demon stayed inside
15 the flask. •To prove that the demon had been overcome, the boy remained three
days and, (when) the spirit did not blow any longer, the Arabs concluded that he
had really trapped the spirit.

The Arabian wind demon, named Ephippas, is brought to the Temple, where it is interrogated by Solomon and puts the immovable cornerstone in place

16 Then he loaded the flask on the camel. The Arabs sent the boy on his way with
(121)
gifts and honors, shouting praises to God, for they were left in peace. Then the
17 boy brought in the spirit and put it in the foremost part of the Temple. •The
following day I, Solomon, went into the Temple (for) I was very worried about
the cornerstone. (Suddenly,) the flask got up, walked for seven steps, and fell
18 down on its mouth before me. •I was amazed that (even though the demon was
entrapped in) the flask, he had the power to walk around, and I ordered him to get
19 up. Panting, the flask arose and stood up. •Then I asked him, saying, "Who are 6:5; 12:4; 24:1
you?" From inside the spirit said, "I am a demon called Ephippas (and I live) in
Arabia.''
20 I said to him, "By what angel are you thwarted?" He said, "By the one who 15:10
(122)
is going to be born from a virgin and be crucified by the Jews.''[a] Mt 1:18-25
　　　　　　　　　　　　　　　　　　　　　　　　　　　　　　　　Lk 1:26-38
　　　　　　　　　　　　　　　　　　　　　　　　　　　　　　　　11:10; 12:3

---

22 a. An explicit reference to the story of Jesus;
cf. TSol 12:3, n. b and 15:10, n. f. For TSol
22:19f., MS P (Q is similar) reads, "And I said to

him, 'Is this your name?' He answered, 'Yes; for
wherever I want, I alight and set fire and put to
death.' And I said to him, 'By what angel are you

1 **23** Then I said to him, "What can you do for me?" He responded, "I am able
to move mountains, to carry houses from one place to another, and to overthrow
2 kings." •I said to him, "If you have the power, lift this stone into the beginning 22:7
of the corner of the Temple." But he responded, "I will raise not only this stone,
King; but, with (the aid of) the demon who lives in the Red Sea, (I will) also (lift 6:3f.
up) the pillar of air (which is) in the Red Sea and you shall set it up where you Ex 13:21f.;
wish."[a]   14:19f.
                                                                            Neh 9:12,19
3   When he had said these things, he went in underneath the stone, lifted it up, Ps 99:7
(123) went up the flight of steps carrying the stone, and inserted it into the end of the 1Kgs 7:2f.
4 entrance of the Temple. • I, Solomon, being excited, exclaimed, "Truly the 22:7
Scripture which says, *It was the stone rejected by the builders that became the* Ps 118:22
keystone, has now been fulfilled," and so forth.[b]   Mk 12:10
                                                                            Mt 21:42
                                                                            Lk 20:17
                                                                            Acts 4:11
                                                                            1Pet 2:4,7

The demon Ephippas and the demon of the Red Sea bring back the pillar and lift it up in the air

1 **24** Again, I said to him, "Go, bring to me the one you said (would help lift up 6:3f.; 12:4;
(124) the) pillar (which is) in the Red Sea. So Ephippas went off and brought forth the 22:19
2 demon and both transported the pillar from Arabia. •However, having outwitted
(them) because these two demons could have upset the whole world with one tip
of the scales, I sealed (them) around on one side and the other, and said, "Keep
3 watch (on them) carefully." •Thus, they have remained holding up the pillar in
4 the air until this very day as a proof of the wisdom granted to me. •The enormous 3:5; 4:11; 8:11
pillar was suspended through the air, lifted up by the spirits, and thus from below 1Kgs 4:29-34
5 the spirits appeared just like air lifting (it) up. •When we looked intently, the lower
part of the pillar became somewhat oblique, and so it is to this day.[a]

Solomon interrogates the demon from the Red Sea (named Abezethibou), learns of his history and activity, and adjures him to hold up the pillar

1 **25** Then I interrogated the other spirit, the one who came up out of the sea with
(125) the pillar. "Who are you, what are you called, and what is your activity? For I
2 have heard many things about you." •But the demon said, "I, King Solomon, am
called Abezethibou; and once I sat in the first heaven whose name is Amelouth.
3 Therefore, I am a hostile, winged demon with one wing, plotting against every
wind under the heavens. I was present at the time when Moses appeared before
4 Pharaoh, king of Egypt, hardening his heart. •I am the one whom Jannes and JanJam
Jambres, those who opposed Moses in Egypt, called to their aid.[a] I am the adversary Ex 7-11
of Moses in (performing) wonders and signs."   Acts 7:36
                                                                            Ex 7:11-13
                                                                            2Tim 3:8

thwarted?' And he said, 'The sovereign God who
has authority over me even to be heard, who is
going to be born through a virgin and crucified by
the Jews on a cross, whom angels (and) archangels
worship. He is the one who thwarts me and saps
me of my great power which has been given to me
by my father the devil.''

23 a. The pillar is explained in TSol 24:3–5,7–9.
McCown (*Testament*, p. 46) suggests that the pillar
of cloud in the OT is transferred to the heavens
and he agrees with M. R. James that the pillar is
the Milky Way. See also TSol 24:5, n. a.
   b. Ps 118:22 is one of the most quoted testimonies in the NT and early Christian literature. It
is the only explicit NT testimony in TSol.

24 a. Conybeare (*JQR* 11 [1898] 44, n. 5): "This
legend of the heavy corner-stone and of the spirits
supporting a column in the Temple reappears in the
Georgian Acts of Nouna in the fourth century.

There it is a huge wooden column that is lifted by
spirit agency, when the king and workmen had
failed to move it into place. The spirits support it
in the air before letting it sink into its place."

25 a. Cf. 2 Tim 3:6–9. Jewish tradition named the
leaders of the Egyptian magicians of Ex 7:11–13
Jannes and Jambres (or "Mambres") and said they
were disciples (or sons) of Balaam (Num 22–24).
Apuleius, *Apologia* 90, lists Jannes with other magicians and sorcerers, including Moses. Zosimus
of Panopolis, c. A.D. 300, may know of a tradition
in which Jambres instructed Solomon about sacrifices to drive off, or make powerless, the demons
(see the contribution on JanJam herein). Jannes and
Jambres may be identical with the two angels who
teach men sorcery, Harut and Marut, in the Koran,
Sura 2.96. For further references, see *PMR*, pp.
133–34; L. L. Grabbe, "The Jannes/Jambres Tradition in Targum Pseudo-Jonathan and its Date,"
JBL 98 (1979) 393–401.

5
(126)
I therefore said to him, "How is it that you are found in the Red Sea?" He responded, "During the time of the Exodus of the sons of Israel, I gave Pharaoh Ex 14:8f. pangs of anxiety and hardened the heart of him, as well as of his subordinates.

6 I caused them to pursue closely after the sons of Israel, and Pharaoh followed with (me) and (so did) all the Egyptians. I was there at that time and we followed

7 together. We all approached the Red Sea. •Then it happened that at the time when Ex 14:21-23 the sons of Israel crossed over, the water turned back upon us and covered over the company of the Egyptians. I was (to be) found there. I, too, was engulfed by the water, and I remained in the sea, being held down there by the pillar until Ephippas arrived."[b]

8
(127)[b]
Next I, Solomon, adjured him to hold up the pillar until the End.

9
(128)
Then, under (the direction of) God, I adorned the Temple of God in total beauty. And I was rejoicing and praising God.

Solomon falls madly in love with a beautiful Shummanite woman and sacrifices to Jebusite gods to obtain her

1 **26** I now took countless wives from every land and kingdom. I also took a journey to the kingdom of the Jebusites and saw a woman in their kingdom, and

2 I fell madly in love with her and wanted her to be a wife in my harem. •So I said to their priests, "Give me this Shummanite[a] because I am madly in love with her." They replied, "If you love our daughter, fall down before our gods, the

3 great Raphan and Moloch,[b] and take her." •However, I did not want to worship (their gods), so I said to them, "I worship no foreign god."[c]

4
(129)[c]
But they threatened violence against the maiden, saying, "If you have the opportunity to go to the kingdom of Solomon, say to him, 'I will not go to bed with you unless you become like my people and take five locusts and sacrifice

5 them in the name of Raphan and Molech.' " •So because I loved the girl—she was in full bloom and I was out of my senses—I accepted as nothing the custom (of sacrificing) the blood of the locusts. I took them in my hands and sacrificed in the name of Raphan and Molech to idols, and I took the maiden to the palace of my kingdom.[d]

Margin references:
1Kgs 11:1-8
Gen 10:16
Josh 18:16,28
1Chr 11:4f.
2Sam 5:6f.
Song 6:3
1Kgs 2:13-46
Amos 5:26
Acts 7:43
Lev 18:21;
20:2-5
Jer 32:35; 49:1f.
Amos 1:15
1Kgs 11:7,33
2Kgs 23:10

---

b. Eitrem, *Magical Papyri*, p. 57, notes that the magicians were fascinated with the idea that God had dried up the Red Sea; MSS P Q continue, " 'But when Ephippas came, sent by you shut up in the vessel of a flask, you made me come up to you.' I, Solomon, heard these things and glorified God and adjured the demons not to disobey men, but to remain supporting the pillar. And both swore, saying, '(As) the Lord God lives, we will never let loose on this pillar until the end of the age. But on whatever day this stone should fall, then shall be the end of the age.' And I, Solomon, glorified God and adorned the Temple of the Lord with all beauty, and I was continually glad in spirit in my kingdom and there was peace in my days."

26 a. Perhaps the reference is to the beautiful Shunammite woman brought to David in his old age (1Kgs. 1:1–4, 15; 2:17–22). Her name was Abishag, and Solomon executed Adonijah for treason when he wanted her (1Kgs 2:13–25). McCown (*Testament*, p. 64) suggests its derivation from the "maid of Shulam" in Song 6:12; 7:1.

b. Raphan and Moloch are mentioned in Acts 7:43 in a quotation from Amos 5:26. Raphan is the LXX translation of Kaiwan, an astral deity. Moloch is the LXX translation of Sakkuth; it is said that Moloch was a deity to whom human sacrifice was made in the Valley of Hinnom (2Kgs 23:10; Jer 32:35; cf. Lev 18:21).

c. MS P (Q is similar) adds, " 'What is this proposal that you compel me to do so much?' But they said, 'That you should become like our fathers.' And when I answered that I would on no account worship foreign gods, they even told the maiden not to sleep with me until I was persuaded to sacrifice to the gods."

d. For TSol 26:5, MS P (Q is similar) *appears* to read, "Though I, hostile and embittered, was moved, the crafty one (shot) bolts of the maiden's love; I gave pause, but she brought me five grasshoppers, saying, 'Take these grasshoppers and crush them together in the name of the god Molech, and I shall go to bed with you.' This very thing I did."

The glory of God departs from Solomon and he writes this testament

6   So the spirit of God departed from me and from that day on my words became   1Kgs 11:1-8
as idle talk. She convinced me to build temples of idols.[e]

7   As a result I, wretched man that I am, carried out her advice and the glory of
(130) God completely departed from me; my spirit was darkened and I became a   5:5
8 laughingstock to the idols and demons. •For this reason I have written out this,
my testament, in order that those who hear might pray about, and pay attention   15:14
to, the last things and not to the first things, in order that they might finally find
grace forever. Amen.[f]

e. For TSol 26:6, MS P (cf. Q) reads, "And immediately the Spirit of God departed from me and I became weak as well as foolish in my words. From this also I was compelled by her to build a temple of idols to Baal and to Rapha and to Moloch and to the other idols."

f. McCown's late discovery of MS N, which is mainly rec. B but supports rec. A at the conclusion, caused him to base the conclusion on rec. A. See McCown, *Testament*, pp. 121–22*. My translation of his reconstructed conclusion, based on MSS H N: "(7) But I, wretched man that I am, built (them) because of my total love for her, and my kingdom was broken up and I cried aloud greatly, and my spirit was dispersed and ten tribes were taken into slavery with Jeroboam. Then I understood the things spoken to me by the demons, because they said to me, 'By our hands you are about to meet your end.' (8) And I wrote this, my testament, to the Jews and bequeathed it to them as a remembrance of my end. Let my testament be guarded for you as a great mystery against the unclean spirits so that you know the devices of the evil demons and the powers of the holy angels; because a great Lord Sabaoth, the God of Israel, prevails, and he made subject to me all the demons, by whom was given to me a seal of an eternal testament. (9) And I died in my kingdom and was added to my fathers in peace, and the Temple of the LORD God, to whom honor and worship are fitting for ever and ever, was completed. Amen." For other minor textual changes, see "Textual Emendations." MS H by itself continues TSo. 28:8–9a: "Therefore I have written these things which I have come upon among the sons of Israel about spirits and the spirit of unclean insults they offer in the Holy of Holies. (9) Accordingly, I Solomon, Son of David, son of Jesse, have written my testament and have sealed it with the ring of God." After the comment about Solomon's death and burial "in Jerusalem" (v. 9 of the reconstructed text), MS H continues vv. 9f.: "And the Temple of the LORD God, in which a river has its source under his throne, was completed, in which there stood ten thousand angels and a thousand archangels, and cherubim shouting and seraphim calling and saying, 'Holy, holy, holy, Lord Sabaôth,' and 'blessed are you forever and ever. Amen.' "

(10) "Glory to thee, my God and LORD, glory to thee with exceedingly well renowned God-bearer, and (with) the honored

Precursor, and all the saints, glory to thee."

MS D closes with sections on Solomon and the demon prince Samael, and the glory and wisdom of Solomon (D 7:1–8:7; McCown, *Testament*, pp. 96f.). McCown's rec. C (MSS S T U V W, V W being most extensive, McCown, *Testament*, pp. 76–87). Rec. C includes a conversation of Solomon with the spirit Paltiel Tzamal (McCown, *Testament*, pp. 84–87). MS V has a subscription noting that the testament was written down by a physician, John of Aro(?), after Solomon, Son of David, died. John gives the time as December 14, 1440.

TESTAMENT OF ADAM

(Second to Fifth Century A.D.)

A NEW TRANSLATION AND INTRODUCTION

BY S. E. ROBINSON

The Testament of Adam is divided into three sections known as the Horarium, or hours of the day and night, the Prophecy, and the Hierarchy. The first two sections are attributed to Adam, and Adam speaks in the first person; the third section is not attributed to any specific figure. In the first section, the Horarium, Adam speaks to his son Seth, listing the hours of the day and night and revealing to him which portion of the created world praises God at each hour. In the second section, the Prophecy, Adam reveals information to Seth about the creation and fall of man and foretells the Flood, the birth, passion, and death of Christ, and the final end of the world. At the end of this section, Seth adds that he has personally recorded the testament of his father, Adam, and that he buried it in the legendary Cave of Treasures. The third section, the Hierarchy, is a list of the nine different orders of heavenly beings (angels, archangels, powers, etc.) and a description of the function of each of the nine orders in the divine economy.

Texts

The Syriac Testament of Adam is found in three recensions, witnessed by eight manuscripts which date between the early ninth and late eighteenth centuries. Of these three recensions, recension 1 is the most original.[1] The most important manuscript for recension 1 is British Museum MS Add 14,624 (MS A, 9th cent.). This is the oldest and most important of all the Syriac manuscripts and serves as the base for the translation of the Horarium and Prophecy which follows. The second witness for recension 1 is Vatican Syriac MS 58 (MS B, late 16th cent.). In the translation that follows, lacunae in A have been restored according to B. The Hierarchy is found in only one Syriac manuscript, the best witness for recension 2, Vatican Syriac MS 164 (A.D. 1702). The translation of the Hierarchy is taken from this manuscript. Recension 3 is witnessed by four manuscripts, three of which contain only the Horarium. The fourth, Vatican Syriac MS 159 (A.D. 1632), contains both the Horarium and the Prophecy. One of the other witnesses to recension 3, British Museum MS Arund Or 53 (16th cent., referred to below as E), contains several important variants.

Original language

The Testament of Adam is extant in Syriac, Greek, Arabic, Karshuni, Ethiopic, Old Georgian, and Armenian. M. R. James was also of the opinion that a quotation in Latin by Nicetas of Remesiana was taken from the Testament of Adam, although this is uncertain.[2] Three languages have been proposed as the original of the Testament of Adam: Hebrew,

---

[1] See G. J. Reinink, "Das Problem des Ursprungs des Testamentes Adams," *OCA* 197 (1972) 391–95, especially n. 19; see also S. E. Robinson, *The Testament of Adam: An Examination of the Syriac and Greek Traditions*, pp. 46, 102–4. The author is indebted to J. H. Charlesworth for his invaluable aid in the preparation of both the dissertation and the present article.

[2] See M. R. James, "Notes on Apocrypha," *JTS* 7 (1906) 562f., and Robinson, *Testament of Adam*, pp. 13f.

Greek, and Syriac. The other languages in which the testament is extant are excluded from consideration by the relatively late dates of their development. The Karshuni and Ethiopic are dependent upon the Arabic, but the Arabic is dependent upon Syriac recension 3 and repeats its errors and expansions.[3]

The only evidence for a Hebrew original of the testament is the appearance in one of the Greek manuscripts of Hebrew names for each of the hours. M. R. James and others have suggested that these Hebrew names represent the last vestiges of the original Hebrew text. However, examination reveals that these names are not in fact Hebrew but rather Greek words written in Hebrew characters.[4]

F. Nau suggested that the Testament of Adam was originally written in Greek by Apollonius of Tyana. This is untenable for several reasons. First, the extremely large number of biblical allusions in the text make it unlikely that it was written by a pagan. Second, none of the Greek manuscripts is older than the fifteenth century, and all of them employ Byzantine vocabulary not attested before the tenth century A.D., by which time the Testament of Adam had already been circulating in Syriac for six hundred years. Third, the Greek version corresponds most closely with Syriac recension 3, the least reliable of the Syriac recensions.

There can be little doubt that the original language of the Testament of Adam is Syriac, since it has been convincingly shown that the Greek text is dependent upon the Syriac.[5] None of the variant readings in the Syriac text seem to be instances of alternate translations of the same Greek word, or of mistranslated Greek words, as we should expect if Greek were the original language, but are rather a result of the scribes having mistaken one Syriac word for another.[6] Further, there are several striking paronomasiae in the Prophecy section which are possible only in Syriac. The Hierarchy section is extant only in Syriac and quotes Zechariah 1:8 according to the Syriac Peshitta version of the Old Testament rather than the Septuagint version.[7] Finally, the Testament of Adam is known to have been circulating in Syriac by the late fourth century A.D., centuries before there is evidence of its existence in any other language.

Date

The three sections of the Testament of Adam were not written at the same time, but the final Christian redaction, in which the testament took on its present form, probably occurred in the middle or late third century A.D. This tentative date for the final redaction of the Testament of Adam is supported by several bits of evidence. First, the testament is familiar with the Christian traditions found in the New Testament and must therefore be dated after, say, A.D. 100. Second, part of the Prophecy section is quoted in the Syriac *Transitus Mariae*, which is dated in the late fourth century. Third, the Testament of Adam demonstrates a literary relationship at one point with the Coptic Apocalypse of Elijah, which is dated in the third century A.D. Ordinarily this might be due to copying at some later date, but here the Testament of Adam seems to preserve the passage (a description of the signs of the Messiah) in a more original form than does the Apocalypse of Elijah and should probably not be dated after that document.

Since the Jewish portions of the testament are likely older than the Christian additions, the Horarium and perhaps some of the Prophecy may date from considerably before the third century A.D. The final section, the Hierarchy, is an accretion which does not lend itself to a firm dating, although it may have been composed between the second and fifth centuries A.D.[8]

---

[3] See E. Bratke, "Handschriften Überlieferung und Bruchstücke der Arabisch-aethiopischen Petrusapokalypse," *ZWT* 1 (1893) 493; S. Grebaut, "Littérature éthiopienne Pseudo-Clémentine," *ROC* 6 (1911) 73; and Reinink, *OCA* 197 (1972) 391f.

[4] See A. Delatte, *Anecdota Atheniensia* (Liege, 1927) p. 446, and Robinson, *Testament of Adam*, especially pp. 111, 136f.

[5] E.g. by Reinink, *OCA* 197 (1972) 387–99.

[6] Robinson, *Testament of Adam*, p. 140.

[7] A quotation from Zech 1:8 is found in vs. 7 of the Hierarchy. See Robinson, *Testament of Adam*, p. 143.

[8] Robinson, *Testament of Adam*, pp. 148–53.

Provenance

The provenance of the Testament of Adam cannot presently be determined with precision beyond what is suggested by its original language, Syriac. While it was most likely written in Syria or Palestine, the precise location is unknown.

Historical importance

Historically, the Testament of Adam witnesses a pattern in its composition which is also found in some other documents among the Pseudepigrapha. An originally Jewish composition has been redacted (heavily in the Prophecy, lightly in the Horarium and Hierarchy) by a Christian.[9] The original work, or works if the sections are considered to have circulated separately, has been transformed from a Jewish Midrash on the creation story to a defense of the Church's claim that Jesus was the Messiah. The Testament of Adam thus reflects the high regard in which Jewish traditions were held by many Christians. It also reflects the willingness of some Christians to modify and expand those traditions in support of their own theological position.

Theological importance

In the Testament of Adam, God is represented primarily as the creator of the world and all that is in it. He receives praises at each hour of the day and night from some portion of his creation. There is no dualism; God is the creator of all, including both angels and devils, good and evil, and all things render him proper reverence. There is a definite order to creation and a proper time for every function. In this the document is reminiscent of Jewish wisdom literature.

In the Testament of Adam the cosmos is depicted in familiar Old Testament terms. However, the Flood is said to have been caused by the daughters of Cain, and the career of the world is to last for six thousand years after the Flood, or, presumably, for seven thousand years in all.

One striking theological feature of the Testament of Adam is that Adam is intended from the beginning to become a god; his deification is promised in no uncertain terms (3:2,4). The fall of man is seen as an unfortunate misstep, but the outcome is sure: Adam will become a god. The forbidden fruit is identified as the fig.

The most fully developed doctrine in the Testament of Adam is its angelology, although this is confined mainly to the latest section of the testament, the Hierarchy. While angels and demons are referred to in the Horarium, and both cherubim and seraphim are mentioned, the Hierarchy describes all nine orders of angels and specifies their functions. Angels, the lowest order, act as guardians for human beings. Archangels, the next order, direct the affairs of the rest of creation, human beings excluded. Archons control the weather. Authorities have jurisdiction over the heavenly lights: the sun, the moon, and the stars. The powers keep the demons from destroying the world in general and human beings in particular. Dominions have authority over political kingdoms and grant victory or administer defeat in battle. Angels called "thrones" guard the gate of the holy of holies and stand before the throne of the Lord. Cherubim carry the throne of the Lord and are the keepers of the divine seals. Seraphim serve the inner chamber of the Lord.

Relation to canonical books

Despite its extensive Christian additions, the Testament of Adam is a pseudepigraphon of the Old Testament. Both the Horarium and Prophecy dwell on the themes of creation and the story of Adam and Eve found in Genesis 1–3. It is likely that these two sections were originally Midrashic expansions of the account of the creation in Genesis.[10] Moreover, the Horarium demonstrates striking similarities to Psalm 148, which also deals with the

---

[9] Robinson, *Testament of Adam*, pp. 156–60.
[10] M. R. James, "Apocrypha," in *Encyclopedia Biblica* (New York, 1899) vol. 1, col. 253. See also Robinson, *Testament of Adam*, pp. 156–60.

themes of the creation. Other biblical allusions and quotations may be found at Testament of Adam 1:3 (Ps 148:7f.), 1:4 (Isa 6:1–6 and Ezek 3:13), 1:5 (Gen 1:7f.; Ps 148:4; and Ezek 1:24), 1:12 (Ps 104:4), 2:1f. (Ps 148:1f.), 2:10 (Gen 1:2), 4:7 (Zech 1:7–11).

Relation to apocryphal books

Beyond its dependence on the Old and New Testaments, the Testament of Adam manifests a clear literary relationship with several other books from the Apocrypha and Pseudepigrapha, and with rabbinic Judaism. Of particular significance are the parallels to the story of Adam and Eve found elsewhere in Jewish literature. The Testament of Adam has much in common with the Life of Adam and Eve (both the *Vita* and the ApMos), with the gnostic Apocalypse of Adam found at Nag Hammadi, and with the Armenian Death of Adam. Particularly, Adam's prediction of the Flood (3:5) is found also in Josephus' *Antiquities* 1.2.3 and in the Apocalypse of Adam 69:2–70:9. The death and burial of Adam (3:6) is found in the Apocalypse of Moses 33:1–40:2, *Vita Adae et Evae* 45:3–46:1, Jubilees 4:29, and in the Armenian Death of Adam. The sisters of Cain and Abel mentioned in the Testament of Adam are a commonplace in rabbinic writing (GenR 22.2, 7; PRE 21; Yeb 62a). The identification of the fig as the forbidden fruit from recension 2 (3:4a) is also found in the Apocalypse of Moses 20:4f. and Genesis Rabbah 15.

The Testament of Adam shares a common passage with the Coptic Apocalypse of Elijah (ApEl 3:5–11), although the passage in the testament appears to be more original (TAdam 3:1; see also recension 2). The passage is a description of the signs of the Messiah based on Jesus' miracles in the New Testament, but in the Apocalypse of Elijah it has been adapted to describe the deceits of the Antichrist.

The testament itself has influenced several later compositions, including the Syriac *Transitus Mariae* (late 4th cent.), and the Arabic Book of the Rolls (c. 8th–9th cent.). The angelology of the Hierarchy appears to have influenced the Book of the Bee by Solomon of Basra (13th cent.) and may also have influenced the Celestial Hierarchy of Pseudo-Dionysius the Areopagite (c. A.D. 500).

SELECT BIBLIOGRAPHY

Charlesworth, *PMR*, pp. 91f.
Denis, *Introduction*, pp. 7–14.

Frey, J. B. "Adam (Livres apocryphes sous son nom)," *DBSup*, vol. 1, cols. 117–25.
Gibson, M. D. *Apocrypha Arabica*. Studia Sinaitica 8; London, 1901; pp. 1–58.
James, M. R. *The Lost Apocrypha of the Old Testament*. New York, 1920; pp. xi–xiv, 1–4.
Kmosko, M. "Testamentum Adae," *Patrologia Syriaca*, ed. R. Graffin. Paris, 1907; vol. 2, pp. 1309–60.
Nau, F. "Apotelesmata Apollonii Tyanensis," *Patrologia Syriaca*, ed. R. Graffin. Paris, 1907; vol. 2, pp. 1363–85.
Reinink, G. J. "Das Problem des Ursprungs des Testamentes Adams," *OCA* 197 (1972) 387–99.
Renan, E. "Fragments du livre gnostique intitulé Apocalypse d'Adam, ou Pénitence d'Adam ou Testament d'Adam," *JA* 5.2 (1853) 427–71.
Robinson, S. E. *The Testament of Adam: An Examination of the Syriac and Greek Traditions*. SBLDS 52; Chico, Calif., 1982.

THE TESTAMENT OF OUR FATHER ADAM[a]

1 1 The first hour of the night is the praise of the demons; and at that hour they
2 do not injure or harm any human being. •The second hour is the praise of the
3 doves.[b] •The third hour is the praise of the fish and of fire and of all the lower   Ps 148:7f.
4 depths. •The fourth hour is the "holy, holy, holy" praise of the seraphim. And   Isa 6:2f.
so I used to hear, before I sinned, the sound of their wings in Paradise when the
seraphim would beat them to the sound of their triple praise. But after I transgressed
5 against the law, I no longer heard that sound. •The fifth hour is the praise of the   Gen 1:7f.
waters that are above heaven. And so I, together with the angels, used to hear the
sound of mighty waves,[c] a sign which would prompt them to lift a hymn of praise   Ezek 1:24
6 to the Creator. •The sixth hour is the construction of clouds and of the great fear   2Bar 29:7
7 which comes in the middle of the night. •The seventh hour is the viewing of their
powers while the waters are asleep. And at that hour the waters (can be) taken up
and the priest of God mixes them with consecrated oil and anoints those who are   Jas 5:14f.
afflicted and they rest.   ApMos 9:3
                            Vita 36:2
8 The eighth hour is the sprouting up of the grass of the earth while the dew
9,10 descends from heaven.[d] •The ninth hour is the praise of the cherubim. •The tenth   3Bar 10:10
hour is the praise of human beings, and the gate of heaven is opened through
which the prayers of all living things enter, and they worship and depart. And at
that hour whatever a man will ask of God is given to him when the seraphim and   3Bar 6:16
11 the roosters beat their wings. •The eleventh hour there is joy in all the earth when
12 the sun rises from Paradise and shines forth upon creation. •The twelfth hour is
the waiting for incense, and silence is imposed on all the ranks of fire and wind   Ps 104:4
until all the priests burn incense to his divinity. And at that time all the heavenly
powers are dismissed.
The End of the Hours of the Night.

1 2 The Hours of the Day[a]
2 The first hour of the day is the petition of the heavenly ones. •The second hour   Ps 148:1f.
3,4 is the prayer of the angels. •The third hour is the praise of the birds. •The fourth
5 hour is the praise of the beasts. •The fifth hour is the praise which is above
6 heaven. •The sixth hour is the praise of the cherubim who plead against the
7 iniquity of our human nature. •The seventh hour is the entry and exit from the   1En 40:6
presence of God, when the prayers of all living things enter, and they worship
and depart.
8,9 The eighth hour is the praise of fire and of the waters. •The ninth hour is the
10 entreaty of those angels who stand before the throne of majesty. •The tenth hour
is the visitation of the waters when the spirit descends and broods upon the waters   Gen 1:2
and upon the fountains. And if the spirit of the Lord did not descend and brood
upon the waters and upon the fountains, human beings would be injured, and
everyone the demons saw they would injure. And at that hour the waters (are)
taken up and the priest of God mixes them with consecrated oil and anoints those
11 who are afflicted and they are restored and healed. •The eleventh hour is the
12 exultation and joy of the righteous.[b] •The twelfth hour, the hour of the evening,
is the entreaty of human beings, for the gracious will of God, the Lord of all.

---

1 a. The translation offered below attempts to render the Syr. into idiomatic English. For a more literal rendering see S. E. Robinson, *The Testament of Adam: An Examination of the Syriac and Greek Traditions*, pp. 53–85.

b. Syr. recs. 2 and 3 read "of the fish."

c. E reads "wheels" for "wings." Cf. 3En 19:5f.

d. Roosters beat their wings and crow at the rising of the sun; apparently the seraphim behave similarly in the presence of God.

2 a. Rec. 2 omits the hours of the day and rec. 3 puts them before the hours of the night.

b. The Gk. reads "elect."

1 **3** (The Prophecy)[a]

Adam said to Seth, his son, "You have heard, my son, that God is going to come into the world after a long time, (he will be) conceived of a virgin and put on a body, be born like a human being, and grow up as a child. He will perform signs and wonders on the earth, will walk on the waves of the sea. He will rebuke the winds and they will be silenced. He will motion to the waves and they will stand still! He will open the eyes of the blind and cleanse the lepers. He will cause the deaf to hear, and the mute to speak. He will straighten the hunchbacked, strengthen the paralyzed, find the lost, drive out evil spirits, and cast out demons.

Vita 29:2-8
ApAdam 76:8

ApEl 3:5-11

2 "He spoke to me about this in Paradise after I picked some of the fruit in which death was hiding: 'Adam, Adam do not fear. You wanted to be a god; I will make you a god,[b] not right now, but after a space of many years. I am consigning you to death, and the maggot and the worm will eat your body.' • "And I answered and said to him, 'Why, my Lord?' And he said to me, 'Because you listened to the words of the serpent, you and your posterity will be food for the serpent. But after a short time there will be mercy on you because you were created in my image, and I will not leave you to waste away in Sheol. For your sake I will be born of the Virgin Mary. For your sake I will taste death and enter the house of the dead. For your sake I will make a new heaven, and I will be established over your posterity.

3

ApMos 13:26

4 " 'And after three days, while I am in the tomb, I will raise up the body I received from you. And I will set you at the right hand of my divinity, and I will make you a god just like you wanted. And I will receive favor from God, and I will restore to you and to your posterity that which is the justice of heaven.'[c]

5 • "You have heard, my son Seth,[d] that a Flood is coming and will wash the whole earth because of the daughters of Cain, your brother, who killed your brother Abel out of passion for your sister Lebuda,[e] since sins had been created through your mother, Eve. And after the Flood there will be six thousand years (left) to the form of the world, and then its end will come."

6 And I, Seth, wrote this testament. And my father died, and they buried him at the east of Paradise opposite the first city built on the earth, which was named (after) Enoch. And Adam was borne to his grave by the angels and powers of heaven because he had been created in the image of God. And the sun and the moon were darkened, and there was thick darkness for seven days. •And we sealed the testament and we put it in the cave of treasures[f] with the offerings Adam had taken out of Paradise, gold and myrrh and frankincense. And the sons of kings, the magi, will come and get them, and they will take them to the son of God, to Bethlehem of Judea, to the cave.[g]

Vita 45:2
Jub 4:29

ApMos 33-35
Vita 46:1

ApMos 29:5f.

The End of the Testament of Our Father Adam.

---

3 a. The widespread tradition of Adam's prophecy of future world history is also found in *Ant* 1.2.3; *ApAd* 64:2–6 and 85:19–31; *Vita* 25:1f.; and in the Armenian Death of Adam (M. Stone, "The Death of Adam—An Armenian Adam Book," *HTR* 59 [1966] 283–91).

b. The explicit promise of deification to Adam is unexpected but not without precedent. Cf. Jn 10:33–36.

c. Here rec. 2 adds, "And I, Seth, said to my father, Adam, 'What is the name of the fruit you ate?' And he said to me, 'The fig, my son, was the gate by which death entered into me and my posterity, and by it life shall come to me and my children when our Lord becomes a man through the virgin and puts on a holy body at the end of the ages.' "

d. The Syr. can be read "I heard in the begin-

ning" or "you have heard, my son Seth," although the word division and diacritical marks clearly intend the latter. In rec. 2 these indicate the former, in a clear example of a variant which could arise only in Syr.

e. See also GenR 22.7 and PRE 21; L. Ginzberg, *Legends of the Jews* (Philadelphia, 1928) vol. 1, pp. 180f.; vol. 5, pp. 138f.

f. See E. A. W. Budge, *The Book of the Cave of Treasures* (London, 1927) pp. 72f.

g. Here rec. 3 adds, "Your father David sang psalms to you before you came, only begotten God; for he sang to you about the gold of Ophir in his prophecy. And behold, the literal meaning of your psalm has stood firm. Behold gold and myrrh and frankincense heaped before you, little child. Gold for your royalty, frankincense for your divine substance, and myrrh for your burial."

1 **4** Also from the Testament of Our Father Adam[a]
The heavenly powers: what they are like and how each of their orders is occupied in the service and the plan of this world. Listen, my beloved,[b] as they are set in order one after another from the bottom, until we reach those who carry our Lord Jesus the Messiah and bear him up. The lowest order is the angels.[c] And the plan has been revealed to it by God concerning every human being whom they watch over, because one angel from this lowest order accompanies every single human being in the world for his protection. And this is its service.

2   The second order is the archangels. This is the service: directing everything in this creation according to the plan of God, whether powers or animals, birds, or creeping things, or fish, and to speak briefly and in short, whatever exists in this creation, besides human beings, they care for it and guide it.

3   The third order, which is the archons. This is its service: moving the air so that a cloud rises from the ends of the earth, according to the words of David the prophet, and rain falls upon the earth. And this (order) makes all the variations in the atmosphere, sometimes rain and sometimes snow and sometimes hail and sometimes dust and sometimes blood. And it varies them. These also belong to this (order): thunder and the fire of lightning.

4   The fourth order, which is authorities. This is its service: the administration of the lights, of the sun and the moon and the stars.

5   The fifth order, which is the powers. This is its service: they keep the demons from destroying the creation of God out of their jealousy toward human beings; for if the cursed nature of the demons were allowed to accomplish the lust of its will, in an hour and a moment they would overthrow the whole creation. But the divine power stops them, for a watch is set over them lest they succeed in achieving the lust of their will.

6   The sixth order, which is the dominions. This is its service: they rule over kingdoms, and in their hands are victory and defeat in battle. And this is shown (to be) so by (the example of) the Assyrian king. For when he went up against Jerusalem, an angel descended and ravaged the camp of the wicked, and one 7 hundred eighty-five thousand died in one moment. •And also the blessed Zechariah saw the angel in the form of a man riding on a red horse standing among the trees of the tabernacle, and following him (were others on) white and red horses with lances in their hands. And Judah the Maccabee also saw the angel riding on a red horse all decked out with gold trappings. When they saw him, the camp of Antiochus the wicked fled before him. And wherever there is victory or defeat, these bestow it at the prompting of the living God, who commands them in the hour of battle.

8   These other orders, thrones and seraphim and cherubim, stand before the majesty of our Lord Jesus the Messiah and serve the throne of his magnificence, glorifying him hourly with their "holy, holy, holy." The cherubim bear up and reverence his throne and keep the seals; the seraphim serve the inner chamber of our Lord; the thrones guard the gate of the holy of holies. This is truly the explanation of the services according to the plan of the angels in this world.

By the Power of Our Lord's Help the End of the Writing, the Testament of Our Father Adam.

Margin references: 2Kgs 19:35 / Isa 37:36 / Zech 1:7-11 / 2Mac 3:24-26

---

4 a. This section is found in only one Syr. MS.
b. The use of the plural here indicates that this is no longer Adam speaking to Seth.
c. Cf. Col 1:16; Eph 1:21; 2En 20:1; and TLevi

3:7f. Angelologies similar to that which follows are found in the Book of the Bee, ch. 5, in the hierarchy of Pseudo-Dionysius the Areopagite, in the opening lines of CavTr, and in VisIs.

THE
OLD TESTAMENT
PSEUDEPIGRAPHA

VOLUME 1
APOCALYPTIC LITERATURE AND TESTAMENTS

VOLUME 2
EXPANSIONS OF THE "OLD TESTAMENT" AND OTHER LEGENDS, WISDOM AND PHILOSOPHICAL LITERATURE, PRAYERS, PSALMS, AND ODES, FRAGMENTS OF LOST JUDEO-HELLENISTIC WORKS

Apocalypse of Abraham

Apocalypse of Adam

Testament of Adam

Life of Adam and Eve

Ahiqar

Letter of Aristeas

Aristeas the Exegete

Aristobulus

Artapanus

2 Baruch

3 Baruch

4 Baruch

Cleodemus Malchus

Apocalypse of Daniel

More Psalms of David

Demetrius
the Chronographer

Eldad and Modad

Apocalypse of Elijah

1 Enoch

2 Enoch